A colourful start

Places to stay

The main body of this guide is divided into 12 sections corresponding to England's tourist regions. Each regional section begins with a brief introduction and map, with details of major attractions and events. Cities, towns and villages with accommodation are then listed alphabetically.

Information pages

Key to symbols

Fold out the inside back cover and you'll find a key to every symbol used in the guide.

1

Welcome to the guide

» **This 'Where to Stay' guide** is designed to give you all the information you need to help you find accommodation in England in the right place, at the right price and with the facilities and services that are right for you.

» **Whatever your reason** for staying away from home — holiday, a shopping trip, visiting friends or relatives — you're sure to find in this guide accommodation that suits you best.

» **And to help** in your selection, most of the accommodation entries in this guide show their classifications and quality commendations awarded by the Tourist Board (see pages 4-5).

'Where to Stay' is a series of four guides, all available from your local bookshop. Whatever your accommodation needs, one of the guides will help you to find the best. Hotels & Guesthouses in England £6.95 Bed & Breakfast, Farmhouses, Inns & Hostels in England £5.95 Self-Catering Holiday Homes in England £4.95 Camping and Caravan Parks in Britain £4.95

» **A unique** and helpful feature of this 'Where to Stay' guide is that all the essential information you need is presented in a straightforward and easy-to-read style, along with a brief description of the establishment.

» **Symbols** are used only to give you all the very detailed — but perhaps necessary — information about additional services and facilities. But there's no need to flick back and forth between pages to find out what all the

symbols mean — just fold out the back cover and you can check them as you go.

·》 This guide also contains full-colour maps (towards the back), which not only pinpoint all those cities, towns and villages with accommodation listings, but are also useful as route maps. They show all major towns, motorways, main 'A' roads, airports, towns with BR InterCity stations, main ferry routes, and much, much more.

·》 Also at the back is a comprehensive town index to make it easy for you to check out what accommodation is available in a particular place.

·》 And there's more! Each of the 12 regional sections features an introduction and map to the region, suggests places to visit and gives details of major events through the year. Throughout the guide you'll also find thumbnail town descriptions to give you a quick picture of each place.

·》 To complete the 'Where to Stay' package you'll find the Information Pages (starting on page 549) full of useful advice on such things as booking, cancellation, accommodation for physically handicapped people, complaints, etc.

Crowns and

English Tourist Board
COMMENDED
FACILITIES

>> When you see the Crown or 'Listed' sign at a hotel, guesthouse, farmhouse, inn or B&B or in their advertising you can be confident that the establishment has been inspected and found to meet tourist board standards for facilities and services.

>> Over 16,000 places throughout England, Scotland and Wales now offer the reassurance of a national Crown classification – and the number grows daily.

>> **A brief guide to the Crown classifications appears below and you'll find a more detailed explanation of the National Crown Scheme on page 556.**

>> Whatever the classification, ranging from 'Listed' to Five Crown, every establishment is inspected each year to make sure that standards have been maintained.

>> More Crowns simply mean a wider range of facilities and services. A lower classification does not imply lower standards; although the range of facilities and services may be smaller, they may be provided to a high standard.

Listed
Clean and comfortable accommodation, although the range of facilities and services may be limited.

Accommodation with additional facilities, including washbasins in all bedrooms, a lounge area and use of a telephone.

A wider range of facilities and services, including morning tea/coffee and calls, bedside lights, colour TV in lounge or bedrooms, assistance with luggage.

At least one-third of the bedrooms with ensuite WC and bath or shower, plus easy chair and full-length mirror; shoe cleaning facilities and hairdryers available. Hot evening meals available.

At least three-quarters of the bedrooms with ensuite WC and bath or shower, plus colour TV, radio and telephone. 24-hour access, lounge service until midnight and last orders for evening meals 20.30hrs or later.

All bedrooms with ensuite WC, bath and shower. A wide range of facilities and services, including room service, all-night lounge service and laundry service. Restaurant open for breakfast, lunch and dinner.

commendations

·» To help you find accommodation that offers even higher standards than those required for a simple classification, the tourist boards have introduced three levels of quality commendation, using the terms **APPROVED, COMMENDED** and **HIGHLY COMMENDED.**

·» Establishments that apply for a quality commendation are subject to a more rigorous inspection, which takes into account such important aspects as warmth of welcome, atmosphere and efficiency of service as well as the quality of furnishings, fitments and equipment.

·» The new quality commendations apply to all the classification bands. A 'Listed' or One Crown B&B or guesthouse may be Highly Commended if its facilities and services, although limited in range, are provided to an exceptionally high quality standard. When granted, the quality commendation appears alongside the classification, as in this example:

👑 👑 👑 **COMMENDED**

·» The absence of a quality commendation does not imply low standards. All classified accommodation is required to maintain high standards of cleanliness and service. Some establishments may have applied for a quality commendation but have yet to be assessed.

·» **Establishments which have achieved Highly Commended status are listed on page 547.**

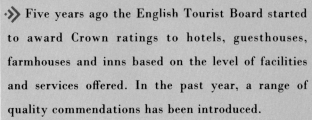

England

·》 It's 9 in the morning. You've had breakfast, packed your cases and are just checking out at reception. In the corner you spot the manager, in earnest discussion with someone clutching a clipboard. You catch the tail-end of the conversation: "Could we now look at the bedrooms, starting at the top?" "By all means," is the reply.

·》 You have just spotted a Tourist Board inspector in action!

·》 There are 45 Tourist Board inspectors, men and women, in England. They are professionals, carefully trained and supervised to do a good job for you and the accommodation industry.

·》 Five years ago the English Tourist Board started to award Crown ratings to hotels, guesthouses, farmhouses and inns based on the level of facilities and services offered. In the past year, a range of quality commendations has been introduced.

·》 This year, 1991, is the first full year that both Crown ratings (from 'Listed' up to 5 Crown) and quality commendations (Approved, Commended or Highly Commended) are appearing all over England — on premises, in advertising and in Tourist Board literature and guide books, including this 'Where to Stay' guide.

·》 The award of a Crown rating and, if appropriate, a quality commendation follows a voluntary application by the establishment to the Tourist Board. One of the Board's team of inspectors will visit the establishment to check the facilities and services available. Where a quality commendation is sought, the inspector, without revealing his identity, will stay overnight.

·》 The inspector judges the quality and presentation of the food at both dinner and breakfast, the appearance

inspects...

of the building, the tidiness of the grounds and the standard of decor of all the public rooms and areas.

» From arrival to departure, the inspector is also assessing such intangible aspects as warmth of welcome, efficiency of service, attitude and appearance of staff and general atmosphere and ambience.

» After paying the bill, the inspector reveals his identity to the management and tours the establishment, checking and assessing the quality standard of everything he sees.

» The inspector is now in a position to make an objective judgment of the establishment's facilities and services (for the Crown rating) and a quality judgment of the standard of those items (for the commendation). He discusses his findings with the manager and offers help and advice on standards.

» In a sense, the Tourist Board inspector is working as a 'professional guest' on your behalf, with the twin aims of raising standards and providing you with more and better information on which to base your choice of a place to stay.

» Whenever you see the Crown sign, often with a quality commendation, you'll know that the Tourist Board slogan "We've been there before you" really means what it says. And every place is inspected every year.

Photographs taken at Audleys Wood Thistle Hotel, Alton Road, Basingstoke, Hampshire. See page 468 for guide entry.

Finding a place to stay

⬦» With this 'Where to Stay' guide, finding accommodation in England to suit your mood and your pocket is easy — just follow the notes below and you'll get the best out of this guide.

How the guide is arranged

⬦» The main part of the guide (beginning on page 13) is divided into 12 sections which correspond to England's tourist regions (shown on the map on page 10).

⬦» Each regional section begins with a map and an introduction with details of major attractions and events for 1991.

⬦» The region's cities, towns and villages with their accommodation are then listed alphabetically.

⬦» Accompanying each place name is a map reference which refers to the colour maps towards the back of the guide.

⬦» These colour maps pinpoint all the places with accommodation listed in the guide.

⬦» A comprehensive town index at the end of the guide gives page numbers for all the places with accommodation.

Choosing accommodation

·》 If you already know the name of the city, town or village in which you want to stay, simply use the town index to find the number of the page which lists the accommodation there.

·》 If the place name is not in the index or you only know the general area in which you want to stay, look at the colour maps to find place names in the area and then refer to the town index for page numbers.

·》 The accommodation listings have been designed to help you select suitable establishments.

·》 Some of the information in the listings is represented by symbols. You will find a key to these on the fold-out flap inside the back cover.

POINTS TO NOTE

·》 Changes may have occurred since the guide went to press or may occur during 1991 — so please check any aspects which are important to you before you make a firm booking. ·》 We also advise you to read the Information Pages towards the back of the guide, particularly the section on cancellations. ·》 The enquiry coupons in the Information Pages section will help you when contacting individual establishments or advertisers in this guide.

England's tourist

·>> England is divided into 12 tourist regions, each of which has its own section in this guide. The regions are shown on the map and also listed opposite together with an index which identifies the region in which each county is located.

Northumbria

Cumbria

Yorkshire & Humberside

North West

East Midlands

Heart of England

East Anglia

Thames & Chilterns

London

South of England

South East England

West Country

·>> Colour maps showing all the places with accommodation listed in this guide and an index to the place names can be found towards the back.

regions

page:

County index

Your information centre

·》 Helping you to get the best out of a visit to an unfamiliar area or town is the job of the local Tourist Information Centre.

·》 There are over 800 such centres in Britain — and more than 560 of them are in England. The centres are staffed by people who are trained to provide advice and information that's friendly — and free!

·》 Here are just some of the services and information they can help you with:

Look out for these signs when you're travelling:

▶ Places to visit within a 50-mile radius — opening times, admission charges, etc. ▶ Places to stay and accommodation lists (in some cases, they'll make a reservation for you). ▶ What's on in the area — entertainment and events. ▶ Local facilities — places to eat, shop, play sport, etc. ▶ Comprehensive selection of brochures, maps and guides — some free, some for sale. ▶ Travel information. ▶ Free service for residents as well as out-of-town visitors. ▶ Opening hours usually 9am to 5pm, Mondays to Fridays; longer hours (including weekends) in summer.

Details of the locations of Tourist Information Centres are available from the English Tourist Board, Thames Tower, Black's Road, London W6 9EL, or from England's Regional Tourist Boards.

London

Which is the greatest city in the world? Surely London wins hands down when you consider its enormous variety of things to see and do.

›**»** Not just at the centre, although nobody can deny the magic of events like the Changing of the Guard, Promenade Concerts, Trooping the Colour, or places like Trafalgar Square, Westminster Abbey or Hyde Park. Venture out and you'll find that London

Tower Bridge was built in 1894. Much of the original machinery for raising and lowering the bridge is still in place, and the walkway has fine panoramic views.

is made up of many connected towns and villages, each with its own special attraction.

›**»** Following the Thames is an ideal way to experience this diversity. In the east there's the incredible Thames Barrier protecting the capital from flood. Greenwich contains a vast treasure of architecture, ships and museums — including the Old Royal Observatory, the Royal Naval College, the Cutty Sark, Gipsy Moth IV, and the National Maritime Museum with its newly refurbished Queen's House.

›**»** Cruise past the regenerated Docklands, the Tower of London, Tower Bridge, the Houses of Parliament and Big Ben. See the new Chelsea Harbour development and the University Boat Race course. Allow at least a day at Hampton Court Palace. Every mile packed with wonders, this whole voyage of discovery can be taken on boats offering lunch, supper, bars, commentaries — whatever your taste.

›**»** How to choose from the thousands of other sights and sounds of the world's greatest city? Put a pin in the map and you might find ▶

▶ Islington, north of the centre, with no less than seven theatres — including Sadler's Wells, the Little Angel marionette theatre, and the Kings Head pub offering the fringe and dinner (with drinks charged for in pre-decimal currency). Islington is typical of many London boroughs.

≫ And everywhere red buses, black taxis, silver tube trains, cheerful good humour — and as much culture, food, fun and sophistication as you'll find anywhere in the world. London — the magnet you just cannot resist!

Which part of London?

The majority of tourist accommodation is situated in Central London and is therefore very convenient for most of the city's attractions and night life.

However, there are many hotels in Outer London which provide other advantages, such as easier parking. We have divided London into two main areas — Central London and Outer London — as shown on colour maps 6 and 7 at the back of this guide.

These areas are further subdivided as shown below.

CENTRAL 1 *(see page 21)*
Covering West End, Piccadilly, Soho, Regent Street, Mayfair, Park Lane, Westminster, Victoria, Elephant and Castle, Whitehall.

CENTRAL 2 *(see page 24)*
Covering Knightsbridge, South Kensington, Chelsea, Earl's Court, Fulham.

CENTRAL 3 *(see page 26)*
Covering High Street Kensington, West Kensington, Holland Park, Notting Hill, Olympia, Hammersmith.

CENTRAL 4 *(see page 28)*
Covering Bayswater, Paddington, Maida Vale.

CENTRAL 5 *(see page 30)*
Covering King's Cross, St. Pancras, Euston, Bloomsbury, Kingsway, Marylebone, Regents Park, Leicester Square, Strand, Charing Cross, Fleet Street, Holborn, City.

EAST LONDON *(see page 32)*
Covering the London boroughs of Barking, Hackney, Havering, Newham, Redbridge, Tower Hamlets, Waltham Forest.

NORTH LONDON *(see page 33)*
Covering the London boroughs of Barnet, Brent, Camden, Enfield, Haringey, Harrow, Islington.

SOUTH EAST LONDON *(see page 36)*
Covering the London boroughs of Bexley, Bromley, Croydon, Greenwich, Lewisham, Southwark.

SOUTH WEST LONDON *(see page 38)*
Covering the London boroughs of Kingston upon Thames, Lambeth, Merton, Richmond upon Thames, Sutton, Wandsworth.

WEST LONDON *(see page 40)*
Covering the London boroughs of Ealing, Hammersmith, Hillingdon, Hounslow, also London Airport (Heathrow).

Where to go, what to see

Thames Barrier Visitors' Centre
Unity Way, Woolwich, London SE18 5NJ
☎ 081-854 1373
Two audio-visual exhibitions about the history of the construction of the barrier and why it is necessary to prevent flooding.

Cabinet War Rooms
Clive Steps, King Charles Street, London SW1A 2AQ
☎ 071-930 6961
A suite of 21 historic rooms, including Cabinet Room, transatlantic telephone room, map room and Prime Minister's room, operational 1939-1945.

Courtauld Institute Galleries
Somerset House, The Strand, London WC2
☎ 071-873 2526
Princes Gate Collection of Old Master paintings and drawings. Samuel Courtauld Collection of Impressionist and Post-Impressionist paintings.

Chessington World of Adventures
Leatherhead Road, Chessington, Surrey KT9 2NE
☎ Epsom (0372) 729560
A world of adventure, with exciting theme areas, rides, circus and the famous zoo. Rides include Dragon River in the Mystic East and Runaway Mine Train.

Freud Museum
20 Maresfield Gardens, Hampstead, London NW3 5SX
☎ 071-435 2002
Library and study of Sigmund Freud's London home. Includes Freud's antiquity collection, library and furniture. Exhibitions and videos.

Shakespeare Globe Museum
1 Bear Gardens, Bankside, London SE1 9EB
☎ 071-928 6342
Museum depicting Elizabethan theatre history 1550-1642 with models and replicas of the 'Globe' and 'Cockpit' playhouses.

Imperial War Museum
Lambeth Road, London SE1 6HZ
☎ 071-416 5000
Illustrates and records all aspects of World Wars I and II and other conflicts involving Britain and the Commonwealth since 1914. Blitz Experience, Operation Jericho.

Museum of the Moving Image
National Film Theatre, London SE1 8XT
☎ 071-928 3535
Museum charting developments in film and TV history with 'hands-on' exhibits and over 50 exhibition areas including a TV studio with cameras.

Royal Botanic Gardens
Kew, Richmond, Surrey TW9 3AB
☎ 081-940 1171
300 acres, formerly owned by the royal family, containing living collections of over 25,000 plant species and varieties. Glasshouses and museums.

Tower Bridge
London SE1 2UP
☎ 071-403 3761
Video film of raising of bridge, museum with original steam-powered engines and walkway with panoramic views of London. Gift shop.

Ragged School Museum
46-48 Copperfield Road, Bow, London E3 4RR
☎ 081-980 6405
Museum about the East End in canalside warehouses which once housed Barnardo's largest Ragged School. Displays include reconstructed Victorian classroom.

London Toy and Model Museum
21-23 Craven Hill, London W2 3EN
☎ 071-262 9450/7905
Extensive collection of commercially-made European toys and models dating from 1850, including trains, cars, planes, nursery toys.

Syon House and Park
Brentford, Middlesex TW8 8JG
☎ 081-560 0881/2/3
London home of the Duke of Northumberland. Interiors designed by Adam with gardens laid out by 'Capability' Brown. In Syon Park: London Butterfly Centre, Heritage Motor Museum, art centre and garden centre.

Bank of England Museum
Bartholomew Lane, London EC2
☎ 071-601 5545
Illustrates the history and role of this famous British financial institution since 1694, including an insight into its current functions. Displays include banknotes, gold, inter-active videos.

Design Museum
Butler's Wharf, Shad Thames, London SE1
☎ 071-403 6933
A study collection showing the development of design in mass production. Review of new products, graphics gallery and changing programme of exhibitions.

Florence Nightingale Museum
2 Lambeth Palace Road, London SE1 7EW
☎ 071-620 0374
History of Florence Nightingale told through films, audio-visual, period settings. Resource centre.

▶

▶ **Horniman Museum and Library**
London Road, Forest Hill,
London SE23 3PQ
☎ 081-699 1872/2339
Museum about the world we live in — our cultures, beliefs, crafts, products, and the natural environment. Musical instrument collection.

Rock Circus
London Pavilion, Piccadilly
Circus, London W1
☎ 071-437 7733
Brings to life the story of rock and pop from the 1950s to present day. Electronically controlled moving, speaking, singing figures, including the Beatles and Elvis Presley.

Make a date for...

London International Boat Show
Earl's Court Exhibition Centre,
Warwick Road, London SW5
3 — 13 January

Daily Mail Ideal Home Exhibition
Earl's Court Exhibition Centre,
Warwick Road, London SW5
14 March — 7 April

World Cup Marathon
Greenwich Park, London SE10,
to Westminster Bridge,
London SW1   *21 April*

Chelsea Flower Show
Royal Hospital, Chelsea,
London SW3   *21 — 24 May*
  (Members only 21 — 22 May)

**Trooping the Colour —
the Queen's Official Birthday
Parade**
Horse Guards Parade,
Whitehall, London SW1
15 June

Lawn Tennis Championships
All England Lawn Tennis and
Croquet Club, Wimbledon,
London SW19 *24 June — 7 July*

**BBC Henry Wood
Promenade Concerts**
Royal Albert Hall, Kensington
Gore, London SW7
19 July — 14 September

*BBC Henry Wood Promenade Concerts
19 July — 14 September*

**Motorfair —
the London Motor Show**
Earl's Court Exhibition Centre,
Warwick Road, London SW5
17 — 27 October

**Royal Smithfield Show
and Agricultural Machinery
Exhibition**
Earl's Court Exhibition Centre,
Warwick Road, London SW5
1 — 5 December

Find out more

Further information about
holidays and attractions in the
London region is available
from:
**London Tourist Board
and Convention Bureau,**
26 Grosvenor Gardens, London
SW1W 0DU.
☎ 071-730 3488.

Lawn Tennis Championships, Wimbledon — 24 June — 7 July

Tourist Information

Tourist and leisure information can be obtained from Tourist Information Centres throughout England. Details of centres and other information services in Greater London are listed below. The symbol ⋒ means that an accommodation booking service is provided. Centres marked with a ✳ are open during the summer months only.

Tourist Information Centres

Central London

Victoria Station, Forecourt, SW1 ⋒
Easter – October: daily 0800 – 2000. Reduced opening hours in winter.
The information centre on the station forecourt provides a London and Britain tourist information service, offers a hotel accommodation booking service, stocks free and saleable publications on Britain and London and sells theatre tickets, tourist tickets for bus and underground and tickets for sightseeing tours.

Liverpool Street Underground Station, EC2 ⋒
Monday – Saturday 0930 – 1830. Sunday 0830 – 1530.
The information centre at the main entrance from the station to the underground provides a London and Britain information service, offers a hotel accommodation booking service, stocks free and saleable publications on Britain and London and sells theatre tickets and tour and transport tickets.

British Travel Centre ⋒
12 Regent Street, Piccadilly Circus, SW1
☎ 071-730 3400
Monday – Friday 0900 – 1830.

Saturday 0900 – 1700. Sunday 1000 – 1600. Reduced opening hours in winter.
Information on travel, accommodation, events and entertainment in England, Scotland, Wales and Northern Ireland. Booking service for rail, air, coach and car travel, sightseeing tours, theatre tickets and accommodation. Bureau de change, bookshop and gift shop.

Bloomsbury Tourist Information Centre ⋒
35-36 Woburn Place, WC1H 0JR
☎ 071-580 4599
Daily 0730 – 1930.
Information on the London area, free literature on London and England, tickets for sightseeing tours and an accommodation booking service.

Clerkenwell Heritage Centre ⋒
35 St. John's Square, EC1M 4DN
☎ 071-250 1039
April – September: Monday – Friday 1000 – 1730. October – March: Monday – Friday 1000 – 1700.
This centre offers information on Clerkenwell and the London Borough of Islington and provides an accommodation booking service.

Selfridges ⋒
Oxford Street, W1 (Basement Services Arcade) and
Harrods ⋒
Knightsbridge, SW1 (Basement Banking Hall)
Open during normal store hours, these centres supply tourist information, leaflets, useful publications, tourist tickets for bus and underground and sightseeing tours and provide an accommodation booking service.

Tower of London ⋒ ✳
West Gate, HM Tower of London, EC3
April – October: daily 1000 – 1800.
This centre offers information, sells theatre and tourist tickets and publications on London and provides an accommodation booking service.

Greater London

Heathrow Terminals 1,2,3 Underground Station Concourse (Heathrow Airport) ⋒
Daily 0800 – 1830.
This centre provides tourist information on London and Britain, stocks free and saleable publications and offers a hotel accommodation booking service.

Croydon Tourist Information Centre
Katharine Street, Croydon, Surrey CR9 1ET
☎ 081-760 5630 (direct line) or 081-760 5400 ext. 2984/5
Monday 0930 – 1900.
Tuesday – Friday 0930 – 1800.
Saturday 0900 – 1700.

Greenwich Tourist Information Centre ⋒
46 Greenwich Church Street, SE10 9BL
☎ 081-858 6376
April – September: daily 1000 – 1800. October – March: daily 1000 – 1700.

Harrow Tourist Information Centre
Civic Centre, Station Road, Harrow, Middlesex HA1 2UH
☎ 081-424 1103.
Monday – Friday 0900 – 1700.

Hillingdon Tourist Information Centre
Central Library, High Street, Uxbridge, Middlesex
☎ Uxbridge (0895) 50706
Monday – Friday 0930 – 2000.
Saturday 0930 – 1700.

Kingston upon Thames Tourist Information Centre
Heritage Centre, Fairfield West, Kingston upon Thames, Surrey KT1 2PS
☎ 081-546 5386
Monday – Saturday 1000 – 1700.

Lewisham Tourist Information Centre
Lewisham Library, Lewisham High Street, SE13 6LG
☎ 081-690 8325
Saturday, Monday 0930 – ▶

▶ 1700. Tuesday, Thursday
0930 − 2000. Friday 0930 −
1300.

Redbridge Tourist
Information Centre

Town Hall, High Road, Ilford,
Essex IG1 1DD
☎ 081-478 3020
Monday − Friday 0830 − 1700.

Richmond Tourist
Information Centre 👝

Old Town Hall, Whittaker
Avenue, Richmond upon
Thames, Surrey
☎ 081-940 9125
Monday, Tuesday, Thursday,
Friday 1000 − 1800.
Wednesday 1000 − 2000.
Saturday 1000 − 1700.
Telephone for Sunday and
Bank Holiday opening hours.

Tower Hamlets Tourist
Information Centre

Mayfield House, Cambridge
Heath Road, E2 9LJ
☎ 081-980 4831 ext. 5313/5
Monday − Friday 0900 − 1700.

Twickenham Tourist
Information Centre

Civic Centre, York Street,
Twickenham, Middlesex
TW1 3BZ
☎ 081-891 1411
Monday − Friday 0900 − 1700.

Telephone
Information Service

A telephone information
service on Greater London is
provided from Monday to
Friday, 0900 − 1800, on
071-730 3488 (an automatic
queueing system is in
operation). A Riverboat
Information Service operates
on 071-730 4812.

Hotel
Accommodation
Service

The London Tourist Board
and Convention Bureau helps
visitors to find and book
accommodation at a wide
range of prices in hotels and
guesthouses, including budget
accommodation, within 20
miles of Central London.
Reservations are made with
hotels which are members of
LTB denoted in this guide with
the symbol **M** by their name.

Reservations can be made
by credit card holders via the

telephone accommodation
booking service on 071-824
8844. Simply give the
reservations clerk your card
details and room requirements
and a booking can be made for
up to six weeks in advance.
LTB takes an administrative
booking fee and a deposit
which is refunded at the
establishment reserved. The
service operates Monday −
Friday 0900 − 1800.

For bookings more than six
weeks in advance, please write
to the Accommodation
Services advance booking
department at LTB's head
office at 26 Grosvenor
Gardens, London SW1W 0DU
at least six weeks before you
intend to arrive. The Board
acts as an introductory agency
and will make a provisional
reservation on your behalf.
Unless the booking is
confirmed with the hotel direct
and a copy sent to LTB the
reservation will be cancelled.

Reservations on arrival are
handled at the Tourist
Information Centres operated
by LTB at Victoria Station
forecourt, Heathrow Terminals
1, 2, 3 Underground Station
Concourse, HM Tower of
London, Harrods and
Selfridges. Go to any of them
on the day when you need
accommodation. A
communication charge and a
refundable deposit are payable
when making a reservation.

Key to symbols

Information about many of the services
and facilities at establishments listed in
this guide is given in the form of
symbols. The key to these symbols is
inside the back cover flap. You may
find it helpful to keep the flap open
when referring to the entry listings.

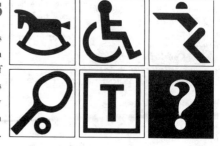

London index

» If you are looking for accommodation in a particular establishment in London and you know its name, this index will give you the page number of the full entry in the guide.

The signs of confidence

Look for signs like these when you're booking accommodation in a hotel, guesthouse, farmhouse, inn or B&B — they tell you that the establishment has been inspected by the Tourist Board and that it meets or exceeds minimum quality standards.

All you have to remember is that the classification (from Listed up to Five Crown) indicates the range of facilities and services while the commendation (Approved, Commended or Highly Commended) indicates the quality standard of the facilities and services.

The absence of a quality commendation from any entry in this 'Where to Stay' guide may be because the establishment had not been quality assessed at the time of going to press.

Places to stay

⊹》 Accommodation entries in this regional section are listed under 5 Central London areas and 5 Outer London areas — shown on colour maps 6 and 7 towards the end of the guide. If you want to look up a particular establishment, use the index to establishments (pages 19 − 20) to find the page number.

⊹》 The symbols at the end of each accommodation entry give information about services and facilities. A 'key' to these symbols is inside the back cover flap, which can be kept open for easy reference.

CENTRAL LONDON 1

Covering West End, Piccadilly, Soho, Regent Street, Mayfair, Park Lane, Westminster, Victoria, Elephant and Castle, Whitehall. See map 6.

Alexander House Hotel
Listed
32 Hugh St., London
SW1 1RT
☎ 071-834 5320
Bedrooms: 2 single, 3 double
& 2 twin, 2 family rooms.
Bathrooms: 2 public.
Bed & breakfast: £17-£22
single, £26-£30 double.

Apollo Hotel
Listed
64 Queensborough Ter.,
London W2 3SH
☎ 071-727 3066 & 071-229
5180
*Pleasant bed and breakfast,
comfortable sized rooms with
private facilities. Situated
opposite Kensington Gardens,
convenient for the new
Whiteleys shopping complex
and Oxford Street.*
Bedrooms: 4 single, 2 double
& 3 twin, 10 family rooms.
Bathrooms: 19 private.
Bed & breakfast: £25-£36
single, £36-£45 double.

Athenaeum Hotel M
116 Piccadilly, London
W1V 0BJ
☎ 071-499 3464 Telex 261589
Rank
*On Piccadilly overlooking Green
Park, well placed for the
fashionable shopping areas of
Knightsbridge and Bond Street.*

Bedrooms: 16 single,
22 double & 52 twin,
22 family rooms.
Bathrooms: 112 private.
Bed & breakfast: £168-£171
single, £189-£210 double.
Lunch available.
Evening meal 6pm (l.o.
10.30pm).
Credit: Access, Visa, C.Bl.,
Diners, Amex.

Bentinck House Hotel M
20 Bentinck St., London
W1M 5RL
☎ 071-935 9141 Fax 071-224
5903 Telex 912881
*Family-run bed and breakfast
hotel in the heart of London's
fashionable West End, close to
Bond Street underground and
Oxford Street.*
Bedrooms: 7 single, 3 double
& 3 twin, 4 family rooms.
Bathrooms: 9 private,
4 public.
Bed & breakfast: £30-£45
single, £48-£58 double.
Half board: £40-£55 daily,
£210-£315 weekly.
Credit: Access, Visa, C.Bl.,
Diners, Amex.

Blandford Hotel
COMMENDED
80 Chiltern St., London
W1M 1PS
☎ 071-486 3103 Telex 262594
*Centrally located hotel, close to
Baker Street underground
station and Madame Tussauds.
Harley Street and Oxford
Street within walking distance.*
Bedrooms: 9 single, 6 double
& 13 twin, 5 family rooms.

Bathrooms: 33 private.
Bed & breakfast: from £60
single, from £75 double.
Credit: Access, Visa, Diners,
Amex.

Caswell Hotel
Listed APPROVED
25 Gloucester St., London
SW1V 2DB
☎ 071-834 6345
*Pleasant, family-run hotel,
near Victoria coach and rail
stations, yet in a quiet location.*
Bedrooms: 1 single, 4 double
& 6 twin, 7 family rooms.
Bathrooms: 7 private, 5 public.
Bed & breakfast: £23-£33
single, £32-£63 double.

Chesham House Hotel M
64-66 Ebury St., London
SW1W 9QD
☎ 071-730 8513 Telex 912881
*Cheerful simplicity is the
hallmark of this hotel, which is
not far from Victoria.*
Bedrooms: 5 single, 7 double
& 8 twin, 3 family rooms.
Bathrooms: 6 public.
Bed & breakfast: £28 single,
£43 double.
Credit: Access, Visa, Diners,
Amex.

Chester House M
Listed APPROVED
134 Ebury St., London
SW1W 9QQ
☎ 071-730 3632 & 7646 &
071-824 8444
*Small, friendly bed and
breakfast close to Sloane
Square. Harrods a 10 minute
walk.*

Bedrooms: 3 single, 3 double
& 4 twin, 2 family rooms.
Bathrooms: 4 private,
2 public.
Bed & breakfast: £30-£43
single, £44-£49 double.
Credit: Access, Visa, C.Bl.,
Diners, Amex.

Clifton Ford Hotel
Welbeck St., London
W1M 8DN
☎ 071-486 6600 Telex 22569
*Centrally located in a quiet
Georgian street, offering
comfort and service.*
Bedrooms: 65 single, 81 double
& 65 twin, 4 family rooms.
Bathrooms: 215 private.
Bed & breakfast: £123.50-
£146.50 single, £155-£218.25
double.
Half board: £148.50-£171.50
daily.
Lunch available.
Evening meal 6pm (l.o. 11pm).
Parking for 20.
Credit: Access, Visa, Diners,
Amex.

Collin House M
104 Ebury St., London
SW1W 9QD
☎ 071-730 8031
*Convenient for Victoria rail,
underground and coach
stations. Ideal base for visiting
London and surrounding area.*
Bedrooms: 2 single, 4 double
& 3 twin, 4 family rooms.
Bathrooms: 8 private,
3 public.
Bed & breakfast: £30-£34
single, £40-£50 double.

CENTRAL LONDON 1

Continued

Corona Hotel
APPROVED
87-89 Belgrave Rd., Victoria,
London SW1V 2BQ
☎ 071-828 9279
Fax 071-931 8576
Bedrooms: 1 single, 11 double
& 14 twin, 8 family rooms.
Bathrooms: 18 private,
6 public; 2 private showers.
Bed & breakfast: £30-£40
single, £38-£52 double.
Credit: Access, Visa, Diners,
Amex.

Easton Hotel M
36-40 Belgrave Rd., London
SW1V 1RG
☎ 071-834 5938
*Bed and breakfast hotel close
to Victoria station with good
rail, underground and coach
connections.*
Bedrooms: 16 single,
17 double & 12 twin, 9 family
rooms.
Bathrooms: 11 private,
10 public.
Bed & breakfast: £26-£36
single, £35-£45 double.
Credit: Access, Visa, Amex.

Ebury Court Hotel M
26 Ebury St., London
SW1W 0LU
☎ 071-730 8147
*Charming country house hotel
in Belgravia with restaurant.
Family owned and run for 59
years. Victoria station close by.*
Bedrooms: 19 single,
12 double & 10 twin.
Bathrooms: 15 private,
10 public; 2 private showers.
Bed & breakfast: £50 single,
£75-£95 double.
Half board: £90-£110 daily,
£455-£770 weekly.
Lunch available.
Evening meal 7pm (l.o. 9pm).
Credit: Access, Visa.

Eccleston Chambers M
APPROVED
30 Eccleston Sq., London
SW1V 2NZ
☎ 071-828 7924
*In the heart of London, within
easy reach of West End and
Victoria coach station.*
Bedrooms: 1 single, 6 double
& 5 twin, 6 family rooms.
Bathrooms: 18 private.

Bed & breakfast: £42-£48
single, £50-£58 double.
Credit: Access, Visa.

Eccleston Hotel M
Eccleston Sq., London
SW1V 1PS
☎ 071-834 8042
Telex 8955775
Friendly
*Centrally located within
minutes of Victoria railway
and coach stations. Conference
and banqueting facilities
available.*
Bedrooms: 37 single,
21 double & 57 twin.
Bathrooms: 109 private,
6 public.
Bed & breakfast: £49-£58.50
single, £58.50-£65 double.
Half board: £40.75-£70 daily.
Lunch available.
Evening meal 6pm (l.o.
10pm).
Credit: Access, Visa, Diners,
Amex.

Edward House Hotel
5 St. George's Drive, London
SW1V 4DP
☎ 071-834 5207 & 071-828
8456
*Near the National Express
coach station, 2 minutes from
Victoria underground and
mainline station. All rooms
have full central heating, TV,
tea making facilities and direct
dial telephone.*
Bedrooms: 2 single, 6 double
& 3 twin, 9 family rooms.
Bathrooms: 4 private,
3 public; 10 private showers.
Bed & breakfast: £22-£28
single, £32-£40 double.
Credit: Access, Visa, Amex.

The Edward Lear Hotel M
30 Seymour St., London
W1H 5WD
☎ 071-402 5401
Fax 071-706 3766
*Family-run Georgian town
residence, with informal but
efficient atmosphere, in a
central location; 1 minute from
Oxford Street and Marble
Arch.*
Bedrooms: 14 single, 5 double
& 9 twin, 4 family rooms.
Bathrooms: 4 private,
7 public; 8 private showers.
Bed & breakfast: £37-£40
single, £50-£65 double.
Credit: Access, Visa.

Elizabeth Hotel M
37 Eccleston Sq., London
SW1V 1PB
☎ 071-828 6812
*Friendly, quiet hotel
overlooking lovely gardens of
stately residential square (circa
1835), close to Belgravia and
within 5 minutes' walk of
Victoria.*
Bedrooms: 11 single, 4 double
& 4 twin, 6 family rooms.
Bathrooms: 3 private,
6 public; 4 private showers.
Bed & breakfast: £30-£46
single, £46-£69 double.
*Display advertisement
appears on page 44.*

Georgian House Hotel M
87 Gloucester Pl., London
W1H 3PG
☎ 071-935 2211
Fax 071-486 7535
Telex 266079 GLAD G
*Small comfortable hotel
providing personal service.
Newly refurbished rooms with
private facilities.*
Bedrooms: 4 single, 6 double
& 5 twin, 4 family rooms.
Bathrooms: 15 private;
4 private showers.
Bed & breakfast: £40-£45
single, £55-£60 double.
Credit: Visa, Amex.

Glynne Court Hotel M
41 Great Cumberland Pl.,
Marble Arch, London
W1H 7GH
☎ 071-262 4344 & 071-724
2384 Fax: 071-724 2071
*Friendly hotel. Convenient for
shops and theatres, 3 minutes'
walk from Marble Arch, Hyde
Park and Oxford Street.*
Bedrooms: 3 single, 5 double
& 3 twin, 3 family rooms.
Bathrooms: 6 public.
Bed & breakfast: £25-£35
single, £40-£50 double.
Credit: Access, Visa, Diners,
Amex.

Hallam Hotel M
Listed
12 Hallam St., Portland Pl.,
London W1N 5LJ
☎ 071-580 1166
Fax 071-323 4527
*Quiet, family-run hotel in the
heart of London's West End.
Close to shops, theatres and
main tourist attractions.*

Bedrooms: 13 single, 10 twin.
Bathrooms: 23 private.
Bed & breakfast: £50-£55
single, £70-£77 double.
Credit: Access, Visa, Diners,
Amex.

The Hereford Hotel M
5-7 Prince's Sq., Bayswater,
London W2 4NP
☎ 071-792 2800
Fax 071-792 3488
*Newly refurbished Victorian-
style hotel, situated close to the
West End and all major
attractions.*
Bedrooms: 30 single, 9 double
& 27 twin, 2 family rooms.
Bathrooms: 68 private.
Bed & breakfast: £62-£65
single, £80-£85 double.
Lunch available.
Evening meal 7pm (l.o.
10pm).
Credit: Access, Visa, Diners,
Amex.

Hilton Mews at Park Lane M
Stanhope Row, Park Lane,
London W1Y 7HE
☎ 071-493 7222 Telex 24665
Hilton
*Good Mayfair location, just off
Park Lane. Near Oxford
Street and Knightsbridge.
Direct underground from Hyde
Park Corner to Heathrow.
Refurbished in 1988.*
Bedrooms: 12 single,
30 double & 30 twin.
Bathrooms: 72 private.
Bed & breakfast: from £50
single, from £100 double.
Lunch available.
Evening meal 6pm (l.o.
10pm).
Parking for 8.
Credit: Access, Visa, C.Bl.,
Diners, Amex.

Holiday Inn Mayfair
3 Berkeley St., London
W1X 6NE
☎ 071-493 8282 Fax 071-629
2827 Telex 24561
Holiday Inn
*Elegant hotel in the heart of
Mayfair. International cuisine
in Berkeley Room Restaurant.*
Bedrooms: 143 double &
43 twin.
Bathrooms: 186 private.
Bed & breakfast: from £140
single, from £170 double.
Lunch available.

Evening meal 6pm (l.o.
11pm).
Credit: Access, Visa, C.Bl.,
Diners, Amex.

Huttons Hotel M
[APPROVED]
55 Belgrave Rd., London
SW1V 2BB
☎ 071-834 3726
*5 minutes' walk from Victoria
and central London.*
Bedrooms: 5 single, 5 double
& 35 twin, 8 family rooms.
Bathrooms: 25 private,
10 public.
Bed & breakfast: £30-£36
single, £37-£42 double.
Credit: Access, Visa, C.Bl.,
Diners, Amex.

Hotel Intercontinental,
London M
[crowns]
1 Hamilton Pl., Hyde Park
Corner, London W1V 0QY
☎ 071-409 3131 Telex 25853
*In the heart of London, on
Hyde Park Corner, high
standard hotel close to
Piccadilly, West End shopping
and theatres.*
Bedrooms: 107 double &
256 twin, 127 family rooms.
Bathrooms: 490 private.
Bed & breakfast: from £180
single, from £205 double.
Half board: from £210 daily.
Lunch available.
Evening meal 7pm (l.o.
11pm).
Parking for 100.
Credit: Access, Visa, C.Bl.,
Diners, Amex.

The symbol **CR**
and the name of a
hotel group or
consortium after a
hotel address means
that bookings can
be made through a
central reservations
office. These are
listed on pages
559 & 560.

Lincoln House Hotel M
[Listed]
33 Gloucester Pl., London
W1H 3PD
☎ 071-935 6238
Fax 071-486 0166
Telex 21879 ATT : LNC
*Newly refurbished Georgian
hotel, offering budget
accommodation in the heart of
London's West End. Close to
theatres, nightlife and Oxford
Street shops.*
Bedrooms: 6 single, 5 double
& 5 twin, 3 family rooms.
Bathrooms: 18 private,
2 public.
Bed & breakfast: £32-£39
single, £45-£55 double.
Credit: Access, Visa, Amex.

London Hilton on Park
Lane M
[crowns] [HIGHLY COMMENDED]
22 Park Lane, London
W1A 2HH
☎ 071-493 8000 Telex 24873
LONHIT G
CR Hilton
*In the heart of Mayfair
overlooking Hyde Park, Green
Park and St James's Park.
Convenient for Knightsbridge
shops and theatreland. An
ETB "5 Gold Crown" award
hotel.*
Bedrooms: 38 single,
197 double & 121 twin,
92 family rooms.
Bathrooms: 448 private.
Bed & breakfast: from £105
single, from £150 double.
Lunch available.
Evening meal 7pm (l.o.
midnight).
Parking for 350.
Credit: Access, Visa, C.Bl.,
Diners, Amex.

Luna House Hotel M
[Listed]
47 Belgrave Rd., London
SW1V 2BB
☎ 071-834 5897
*Friendly, good value, bed and
breakfast hotel within easy
walking distance of Victoria
rail, underground and coach
stations. Opposite bus stop.*
Bedrooms: 2 single, 7 double
& 5 twin, 3 family rooms.
Bathrooms: 8 private,
2 public; 1 private shower.
Bed & breakfast: £17-£20
single, £30-£42 double.

Melita House Hotel M
[Listed]
35 Charlwood St., London
SW1V 2DU
☎ 071-828 0471 & 071-834
1387 Fax: 071-630 8905
*Family-run, budget bed and
breakfast establishment with
homely atmosphere. Near
Victoria station.*
Bedrooms: 3 single, 6 double
& 5 twin, 2 family rooms.
Bathrooms: 8 private,
2 public; 4 private showers.
Bed & breakfast: £22-£32
single, £34-£45 double.

Mostyn Hotel M
[crowns]
17-19 Bryanston St., London
W1H 0DE
☎ 071-935 2361 Telex 27656
*Recently renovated hotel close
to Marble Arch, Oxford Street,
Regent Street and the many
West End theatres.*
Bedrooms: 38 single,
43 double & 38 twin, 4 family
rooms.
Bathrooms: 123 private.
Bed & breakfast: £92-£108
single, £115-£135 double.
Lunch available.
Evening meal 6pm (l.o.
11.45pm).
Credit: Access, Visa, C.Bl.,
Diners, Amex.

Oxford Guest House
49 Upper Berkeley St.,
London W1H 7PF
☎ 071-723 5920
*A small, elegant house close to
Marble Arch and Hyde Park
giving easy access to public
transport.*
Bedrooms: 2 single, 3 double
& 3 twin, 2 family rooms.
Bathrooms: 4 public.
Bed & breakfast: £20-£28
single, £30-£38 double.

Prince Regent Hotel M
[APPROVED]
37 Nottingham Pl., London
W1M 3FF
☎ 071-487 5153 & 071-935
4276 Fax: 071-224 1582
*In the heart of London's West
End yet in a dignified quiet
position. Ideal for people
coming to Harley Street
hospitals and clinics. Near
Regents Park and Baker
Street underground stations.*
Bedrooms: 4 single, 3 double
& 4 twin, 9 family rooms.

Bathrooms: 17 private,
2 public.
Bed & breakfast: £30-£35
single, £45-£50 double.
Credit: Visa, Amex.

Richmond House Hotel
[Listed]
38b Charlwood St., Victoria,
London SW1V 2DX
☎ 071-834 4577
*Small, family-run bed and
breakfast guesthouse.*
Bedrooms: 2 single, 2 double
& 3 twin, 5 family rooms.
Bathrooms: 3 public.
Bed & breakfast: £20-£22
single, £34-£36 double.
Open February-November.

Royal Court Hotel M
[crowns]
Sloane Sq., London
SW1W 8EG
☎ 071-730 9191 Telex 296818
CR Queens Moat Houses
*Country house style hotel
featuring Twelve Sloane
Square Restaurant, "Courts"
Wine Bar and a traditional
English Tavern.*
Bedrooms: 19 single,
30 double & 41 twin,
12 family rooms.
Bathrooms: 102 private.
Bed & breakfast: from £120
single, from £145 double.
Half board: from £143.50
daily, from £1004.50 weekly.
Lunch available.
Evening meal 6pm (l.o.
10.30pm).
Parking for 5.
Credit: Access, Visa, Diners,
Amex.

Royal Horseguards
Thistle Hotel M
Whitehall Court, London
SW1A 2EJ
☎ 071-839 3400 Telex 917096
CR Thistle
*Overlooking the waterside
splendour of the Thames
opposite the Royal Festival
Hall. The hotel blends
traditional style and elegance
with the convenience of modern
facilities and provides an
excellent base to view London's
attractions.*
Bedrooms: 62 single,
103 double & 211 twin.
Bathrooms: 376 private.
Bed & breakfast: from
£101.95 single, from £116.90
double.
Lunch available.

Continued ▶

CENTRAL LONDON 1
Continued

Evening meal 6pm (l.o. 10.30pm).
Credit: Access, Visa, C.Bl., Diners, Amex.

Royal Westminster Thistle Hotel M
Buckingham Palace Rd., London SW1W 0QT
☎ 071-834 1821 Telex 916821
Thistle
An elegant, modern hotel offering high standards of air-conditioned accommodation. Ideally located for Buckingham Palace, Westminster and the shops and theatres of the West End.
Bedrooms: 8 single, 34 double & 64 twin, 28 family rooms.
Bathrooms: 134 private.
Bed & breakfast: from £114.25 single, from £148.50 double.
Lunch available.
Evening meal 6pm (l.o. 11.30pm).
Credit: Access, Visa, C.Bl., Diners, Amex.

Rubens Hotel M
39-41 Buckingham Palace Rd., London SW1W 0PS
☎ 071-834 6600 Telex 916577
Traditional hotel opposite the Royal Mews of Buckingham Palace.
Bedrooms: 33 single, 52 double & 95 twin, 11 family rooms.
Bathrooms: 191 private.
Bed & breakfast: £89.95-£99.95 single, £114.90-£124.90 double.
Half board: £105.45-£115.45 daily, £629.65-£699.65 weekly.
Lunch available.
Evening meal 6pm (l.o. 8pm).
Credit: Access, Visa, Diners, Amex.

The Selfridge Hotel M
Orchard St., London W1H 0JS
☎ 071-408 2080 Telex 22361
Thistle
One of London's most centrally placed hotels, close to the shopping areas of Bond Street and Oxford Street and within easy reach of the capital's famous nightlife. The hotel combines traditional comfort with the convenience of modern facilities.

Bedrooms: 36 single, 104 double & 154 twin, 4 family rooms.
Bathrooms: 298 private.
Bed & breakfast: from £133.25 single, from £163.50 double.
Lunch available.
Evening meal 6.30pm (l.o. 10.30pm).
Credit: Access, Visa, C.Bl., Diners, Amex.

Sidney Hotel
APPROVED
76 Belgrave Rd., London SW1V 4LU
☎ 071-834 2738 & 2860 & 071-828 8298
Friendly establishment, a few minutes' walk from Victoria rail and coach stations.
Bedrooms: 10 single, 11 double & 10 twin, 9 family rooms.
Bathrooms: 25 private, 3 public; 6 private showers.
Bed & breakfast: £30-£40 single, £38-£52 double.
Credit: Access, Visa, Diners, Amex.

Stakis St. Ermin's Hotel M
Caxton St., London SW1H 0QW
☎ 071-222 7888 Telex 917731
Stakis
An elegant Edwardian property. Traditional furnishings add charm in a relaxing atmosphere. The terraced facade hides an efficient, recently refurbished hotel. Adjacent to St. James's Park underground.
Bedrooms: 52 single, 92 double & 131 twin, 15 family rooms.
Bathrooms: 290 private.
Bed & breakfast: from £126 single, from £166 double.
Lunch available.
Evening meal 6pm (l.o. 9.30pm).
Parking for 22.
Credit: Access, Visa, C.Bl., Diners, Amex.

Windermere Hotel M
142-144 Warwick Way, Victoria, London SW1V 4JE
☎ 071-834 5163 & 5480
Fax 071-630 8931
Telex 94017182 WIREG

Well-maintained small hotel, nicely equipped bedrooms and pretty breakfast room. Hospitable proprietors create a welcoming atmosphere.
Bedrooms: 2 single, 11 double & 6 twin, 5 family rooms.
Bathrooms: 20 private, 2 public.
Bed & breakfast: £35-£42 single, £40-£60 double.
Half board: £43-£50 daily.
Evening meal 6pm (l.o. 9pm).
Credit: Access, Visa.

Wyndham Hotel
Listed
30 Wyndham St., London W1H 1DD
☎ 071-723 7204 & 9400
A small family-run bed and breakfast close to Baker Street and Marylebone stations. Well within walking distance of Oxford Street.
Bedrooms: 6 single, 2 double & 3 twin.
Bathrooms: 1 public; 10 private showers.
Bed & breakfast: £22-£24 single, £32-£34 double.

CENTRAL LONDON 2
Covering Knightsbridge, South Kensington, Chelsea, Earl's Court, Fulham. See map 6.

Abcone Hotel M
APPROVED
10 Ashburn Gdns., London, SW7 4DG
☎ 071-370 3383/4/5
Telex 926054 ABCONE G
Close to Gloucester Road underground and convenient for High Street Kensington, Knightsbridge, Olympia, Earl's Court, museums and Hyde Park.
Bedrooms: 6 single, 9 double & 8 twin, 12 family rooms.
Bathrooms: 27 private, 8 public.
Bed & breakfast: £35-£49 single, £59-£88 double.
Credit: Access, Visa, Diners, Amex.

Adelphi Hotel M
127-129 Cromwell Rd., London SW7 4DT
☎ 071-373 7177
Telex 8813164
Centrally situated within easy reach of Knightsbridge, museums, Royal Albert Hall, Earl's Court and Olympia.

Bedrooms: 10 single, 13 double & 18 twin, 11 family rooms.
Bathrooms: 52 private, 3 public.
Bed & breakfast: £50-£60 single, £65-£75 double.
Half board: £55-£65 daily.
Lunch available.
Credit: Access, Visa, C.Bl., Diners, Amex.

Alexander Hotel M
9 Sumner Pl., London SW7 3EE
☎ 071-581 1591 Telex 917133
Best Western
Small Victorian terrace hotel ideally located in South Kensington for easy access to Knightsbridge etc. Added attraction of small private conservatory.
Bedrooms: 5 single, 16 double & 15 twin, 1 family room.
Bathrooms: 37 private.
Bed & breakfast: £70 single, £90-£130 double.
Lunch available.
Credit: Access, Visa, Diners, Amex.

Ashburn Hotel M
111 Cromwell Rd., London SW7 4DR
☎ 071-370 3321 & 071-373 9286 Telex 9413687
ASHBRN G
Close to West End and with easy access to M4, M3, M25 and Piccadilly line underground direct to Heathrow.
Bedrooms: 16 single, 2 double & 17 twin, 4 family rooms.
Bathrooms: 34 private, 3 public; 5 private showers.
Bed & breakfast: £35-£47.50 single, £52.50-£70 double.
Credit: Access, Visa, Diners, Amex.

Barkston Hotel M
(symbols)
Barkston Gdns., London SW5 0EW
☎ 071-373 7851
Telex 8953154
Traditional, friendly hotel situated in garden square. Near underground and exhibition centre, within easy reach of Hyde Park, Knightsbridge and museums.
Bedrooms: 31 single, 12 double & 26 twin, 8 family rooms.
Bathrooms: 77 private.

Bed & breakfast: from £54 single, from £72 double.
Lunch available.
Evening meal 6.30pm (l.o. 9.30pm).
Credit: Access, Visa, C.Bl., Diners, Amex.

The Beaufort ⚑
😊😊😊😊
33 Beaufort Gdns., London SW3 1PP
☎ 071-584 5252 Telex 929200
Town house hotel close to Harrods. Warm, friendly atmosphere, complimentary bar and room service.
Bedrooms: 3 single, 13 double & 5 twin, 7 family rooms.
Bathrooms: 28 private.
Bed & breakfast: £160-£280 single, £175-£280 double.
Credit: Access, Visa, Diners, Amex.

Beaver Hotel ⚑
😊😊 APPROVED
57-59 Philbeach Gdns., London SW5 9ED
☎ 071-373 4553
In a quiet, tree-lined crescent of late Victorian terraced houses, close to Earl's Court Exhibition Centre and 10 minutes from the West End.
Bedrooms: 18 single, 7 double & 9 twin, 4 family rooms.
Bathrooms: 19 private, 9 public.
Bed & breakfast: £25-£42 single, £35-£52 double.
Parking for 23.
Credit: Access, Visa, Amex.

Blair House Hotel ⚑
😊😊😊 APPROVED
34 Draycott Pl., London SW3 2SA
☎ 071-581 2323/4/5
In a quiet elegant street close to Harrods and museums.
Bedrooms: 5 single, 2 double & 4 twin, 6 family rooms.
Bathrooms: 4 private, 5 public; 1 private shower.
Bed & breakfast: £35-£55 single, £50-£65 double.
Credit: Access, Visa, Diners, Amex.

Blakes Hotel
😊😊😊😊
33 Roland Gdns., London SW7 3PF
☎ 071-370 6701
Telex 8813500

In a quiet residential area close to Harrods, Chelsea and all amenities.
Bedrooms: 10 single, 24 double & 4 twin, 14 family rooms.
Bathrooms: 52 private.
Bed & breakfast: £121-£141 single, from £183.50 double.
Lunch available.
Evening meal 7.30pm (l.o. 11.30pm).
Credit: Access, Visa, Diners, Amex.

Brompton Hotel ⚑
😊😊 COMMENDED
30-32 Old Brompton Rd., London SW7 3DL
☎ 071-584 4517
Recently refurbished, close to South Kensington underground station.
Bedrooms: 2 single, 10 double & 2 twin, 2 family rooms.
Bathrooms: 16 private.
Bed & breakfast: £40-£46 single, £60-£69 double.
Credit: Access, Visa.
⚑ Display advertisement appears on page 44.

Concord Hotel ⚑
155-157 Cromwell Rd., London SW5 0TQ
☎ 071-370 4151
Centrally placed on direct line to Heathrow Airport. Comfortable rooms, friendly 24-hour service.
Bedrooms: 14 single, 9 double & 12 twin, 5 family rooms.
Bathrooms: 12 private, 6 public; 5 private showers.
Bed & breakfast: £28.50-£37 single, £42-£59.50 double.
Credit: Access, Visa, Amex.

Eden Plaza Hotel ⚑
68-69 Queens Gate, London SW7 5JJ
☎ 071-370 6111 Telex 916228
Ⓡ Consort
Centrally located, the hotel is within easy access of the airport, London's museums, exhibition centres and the West End. Within walking distance of Harrods, Knightsbridge, Hyde Park. Friendly modern hotel.
Bedrooms: 23 single, 17 double & 21 twin, 4 family rooms.
Bathrooms: 65 private.
Bed & breakfast: from £59 single, from £79 double.
Lunch available.

Evening meal 6.30pm (l.o. 10pm).
Credit: Access, Visa, C.Bl., Diners, Amex.

Enterprise Hotel ⚑
😊😊😊
15-25 Hogarth Rd., London SW5 0QJ
☎ 071-373 4502 Telex 298303
Ⓡ Minotels
Ideally located with connections by underground to the West End and Knightsbridge, and Kensington High Street shops nearby.
Bedrooms: 17 single, 11 double & 30 twin, 37 family rooms.
Bathrooms: 61 private, 22 public; 2 private showers.
Bed & breakfast: £44-£48 single, £60-£66 double.
Half board: £50-£54 daily, £280-£300 weekly.
Lunch available.
Evening meal 6pm (l.o. 10.30pm).
Credit: Access, Visa, Diners, Amex.

Fenja Hotel ⚑
😊😊😊
69 Cadogan Gdns., London SW3 2RB
☎ 071-589 7333
Fax 071-581 4958
Telex 934272
Ⓡ Prestige
An Edwardian town house, meticulously restored, overlooking Cadogan Gardens in Knightsbridge. Individually designed bedrooms, well appointed and furnished with antiques.
Bedrooms: 1 single, 3 double & 10 twin.
Bathrooms: 14 private.
Bed & breakfast: from £101 single, £139-£202 double.
Lunch available.
Evening meal 7pm (l.o. 8pm).
Credit: Access, Visa, Diners, Amex.

Five Sumner Place Hotel ⚑
😊😊😊 COMMENDED
5 Sumner Pl., South Kensington, London SW7 3EE
☎ 071-584 7586
Fax 071-823 9962
Victorian terrace hotel close to South Kensington station. Small rear garden with Victorian conservatory where breakfast is provided.

Bedrooms: 3 single, 6 double & 4 twin.
Bathrooms: 13 private.
Bed & breakfast: £55-£70 single, £70-£95 double.
Credit: Access, Visa, Amex.
⚑ Display advertisement appears on page 44.

The Gloucester ⚑
Harrington Gdns., London SW7 4LH
☎ 071-373 6030 Telex 917505
Ⓡ Rank
In a quiet location just 2 minutes' walk from Gloucester Road underground station, making Knightsbridge and the West End only minutes away.
Bedrooms: 15 single, 177 double & 312 twin, 31 family rooms.
Bathrooms: 535 private.
Bed & breakfast: £129.75-£152.50 single, £157.50-£193 double.
Lunch available.
Evening meal 6pm (l.o. 10.30pm).
Parking for 100.
Credit: Access, Visa, C.Bl., Diners, Amex.

Half Moon Hotel ⚑
Listed
10 Earl's Court Sq., London SW5 9DP
☎ 071-373 9956 & 2900
Telex 949631 DELTA G
In a central position 2 minutes' walk from the underground station and with easy access to the M4 and Heathrow Airport.
Bedrooms: 8 single, 10 double & 5 twin, 4 family rooms.
Bathrooms: 11 private, 5 public; 4 private showers.
Bed & breakfast: £19-£22 single, £28-£32 double.

Henley House Hotel ⚑
😊😊😊
30 Barkston Gdns., Earl's Court, London SW5 0EN
☎ 071-370 4111
Overlooking a beautiful garden square, within minutes of the West End, the hotel offers elegant accommodation in a friendly atmosphere.
Bedrooms: 5 single, 5 double & 7 twin, 3 family rooms.
Bathrooms: 9 private, 3 public; 6 private showers.
Bed & breakfast: £31-£40 single, £39-£53 double.
Credit: Access, Visa, Amex.

25

CENTRAL LONDON 2
Continued

John Howard Hotel M
♛♛♛♛
4 Queens Gate, London
SW7 5EH
☎ 071-581 3011
Telex 8813397 HHOTLS G
🇬🇧 Best Western
*Small well-appointed hotel
near Kensington Gardens.
Close to Knightsbridge and the
West End. Serviced
apartments also available.*
Bedrooms: 7 single, 23 double
& 9 twin, 1 family room.
Bathrooms: 40 private.
Bed & breakfast: £90-£135
single, £150-£185 double.
Half board: £102.50-£147.50
daily.
Lunch available.
Evening meal 6pm (l.o.
11pm).
Credit: Access, Visa, Diners,
Amex.
♨♿📞🅿️🍽️📺⚫🌐
🔼🅿️🛗♿🐕🥛DAP🚭
SP T

Leicester Court Hotel M
41 Queen's Gate Gdns.,
London SW7 5NB
☎ 071-584 0512/3/4
Telex 8813164
*Near museums, Knightsbridge,
Hyde Park and the Albert
Hall. Elegant dining room and
restful lounges.*
Bedrooms: 27 single,
19 double & 21 twin,
10 family rooms.
Bathrooms: 35 private,
11 public.
Bed & breakfast: £25-£45
single, £30-£60 double.
Half board: £30-£50 daily.
Lunch available.
Evening meal 6pm (l.o. 9pm).
Credit: Access, Visa, Diners,
Amex.
♨♿📞🅿️🍽️V🌐📺⚫🍽️
🔼🛗🥛DAP🚭SP🎱T

Manor Court Hotel M
33-35 Courtfield Gdns.,
London SW5 0PJ
☎ 071-373 8585 Telex 296236
*Georgian-style building in
garden square. Gloucester
Road and Earl's Court
underground stations nearby.*
Bedrooms: 10 single,
17 double & 28 twin,
20 family rooms.
Bathrooms: 55 private,
2 public; 1 private shower.
Bed & breakfast: £28-£40
single, £38-£50 double.
Credit: Access, Visa, Diners,
Amex.
♨♿📞🅿️🍽️🌐📺⚫🍽️
🐕🐈SP T

Manor Hotel M
23 Nevern Pl., London
SW5 9NR
☎ 071-370 6018 & 4164
Telex 949631 DELTA
*Centrally located and offering
a pleasant atmosphere.*
Bedrooms: 7 single, 11 double
& 4 twin, 5 family rooms.
Bathrooms: 5 private,
4 public; 9 private showers.
Bed & breakfast: £19-£22
single, £28-£32 double.
Parking for 5.
♨♿📞🅿️UL🌐📺⚫🍽️
🖥️DAP🚭SP T

Merlyn Court Hotel M
2 Barkston Gdns., London
SW5 0EN
☎ 071-370 1640
*Well-established, family-run
hotel in quiet Edwardian
square, close to Earl's Court
and Olympia, with direct
underground link to Heathrow,
the West End and most rail
stations.*
Bedrooms: 4 single, 4 double
& 4 twin, 5 family rooms.
Bathrooms: 6 public;
2 private showers.
Bed & breakfast: £20-£25
single, £30-£40 double.
Credit: Access, Visa.
♨♿📞UL🌐🅿️📺🍽️🖥️DAP
🥛SP

Norfolk Hotel M
♛♛♛♛
2-10 Harrington Rd., London
SW7 3ER
☎ 071-589 8191 Telex 268852
🇬🇧 Queens Moat Houses
*Improved facilities including
jacuzzi whirlpool baths, French
restaurant, traditional English
pub, wine bar, mini-gym, sauna
and sunbed.*
Bedrooms: 14 single,
18 double & 49 twin,
15 family rooms.
Bathrooms: 96 private.
Bed & breakfast: £44.50-£110
single, £89-£140 double.
Half board: £62-£97 daily.
Lunch available.
Evening meal 7pm (l.o.
10.30pm).
Credit: Access, Visa, C.Bl.,
Diners, Amex.
♨♿📞🅿️🏊🥛🍸V🌐📺
⚫🔼🛗🥛🍽️♨🥛DAP SP T

Oxford Hotel
24 Penywern Rd., London
SW5 9SU
☎ 071-370 1161 & 5162
*Family-run hotel comprising 3
terraced houses, centrally
situated with easy access to
underground and bus, shopping
and restaurant facilities.*

Bedrooms: 12 single,
15 double & 20 twin,
18 family rooms.
Bathrooms: 25 private,
3 public; 22 private showers.
Bed & breakfast: £20-£32
single, £28-£40 double.
♨♿📞🅿️UL CB🍽️⚫
🖥️T

Prince Hotel M
6 Sumner Pl., London
SW7 3EE
☎ 071-589 6488 Telex 917133
*Small, Victorian terrace hotel,
ideally located in South
Kensington for easy access to
Knightsbridge, Hyde Park etc.*
Bedrooms: 5 single, 7 double
& 8 twin.
Bathrooms: 12 private;
7 private showers.
Bed & breakfast: £30-£40
single, £45-£55 double.
Credit: Access, Visa, C.Bl.,
Diners, Amex.
♨📞🅿️🖥️UL V🍽️⚫
🔼🖥️T

Swallow International Hotel M
♛♛♛♛
Cromwell Rd., London
SW5 0TH
☎ 071-973 1000
Fax 071-244 8194
Telex 27260
🇬🇧 Swallow
*Bright modern hotel with
leisure complex, near the
museums, Earl's Court and
Olympia Exhibition Centres.
Within walking distance of
fashionable Knightsbridge and
Kensington's parks and
museums.*
Bedrooms: 78 single,
81 double & 210 twin,
48 family rooms.
Bathrooms: 417 private.
Bed & breakfast: £95-£102
single, £110-£117 double.
Lunch available.
Evening meal 6pm (l.o.
midnight).
Parking for 70.
Credit: Access, Visa, Diners,
Amex.
♨📞🅿️🖥️🥛V🍽️⚫
🔼🖥️🥛🍽️🏊🐈🥛SP T

Windsor House M
Listed
12 Penywern Rd., London
SW5 9ST
☎ 071-373 9087
*Budget-priced bed and
breakfast establishment in
Earl's Court. Easily reached
from airports and motorway.
The West End is minutes away
by underground.*
Bedrooms: 2 single, 5 double
& 3 twin, 5 family rooms.
Bathrooms: 1 private,
5 public; 5 private showers.

Bed & breakfast: £22-£28
single, £28-£38 double.
Parking for 10.
Credit: Access, Visa, C.Bl.,
Diners, Amex.
♨♿UL🅿️📺⚫🖥️🥛DAP
🚭SP

York House Hotel
Listed
28 Philbeach Gdns., London
SW5 9EA
☎ 071-373 7519 & 7579
*Bed and breakfast hotel,
conveniently located close to
the Earl's Court and Olympia
Exhibition Centres and the
West End.*
Bedrooms: 20 single,
12 double, 6 family rooms.
Bathrooms: 8 public.
Bed & breakfast: £21-£22
single, £33-£35 double.
Credit: Access, Visa.
♨♿🖥️🅿️📺🐈

CENTRAL LONDON 3
Covering High Street
Kensington, West
Kensington, Holland Park,
Notting Hill, Olympia,
Hammersmith. See map
6.

Hotel Apollo M
18-22 Lexham Gdns., London
W8 5JE
☎ 071-835 1133
Fax 071-370 4853
Telex 264189
*Modernised Victorian building
near museums, Albert Hall,
Hyde Park, antique shops and
markets, Olympia and Earls
Court Exhibition Centres.*
Bedrooms: 28 single, 3 double
& 24 twin, 4 family rooms.
Bathrooms: 50 private,
8 public.
Bed & breakfast: £30-£44
single, £50-£54 double.
Credit: Access, Visa, C.Bl.,
Diners, Amex.
♨♿🏊🥛🍽️🖥️🅿️🍽️⚫
🖥️🥛🍽️🐈🥛SP T

Hotel Atlas M
24-30 Lexham Gdns., London
W8 5JE
☎ 071-835 1155
Fax 071-370 4853
Telex 264189
*Modernised Victorian building
close to High Street
Kensington, Earl's Court and
Gloucester Road underground
stations. Airbus to Heathrow
nearby.*
Bedrooms: 35 single, 4 double
& 19 twin, 7 family rooms.
Bathrooms: 50 private,
6 public.

Bed & breakfast: £30-£44 single, £50-£54 double.
Credit: Access, Visa, C.Bl., Diners, Amex.

Avonmore Hotel M

66 Avonmore Rd., Kensington, London W14 8RS
☎ 071-603 3121 & 4296
Telex 945922 Gladex G(Att AV32)
Privately owned, with a friendly atmosphere. 3 minutes' walk from West Kensington underground station, Olympia Exhibition Centre and Earl's Court.
Bedrooms: 1 single, 2 double & 3 twin, 3 family rooms.
Bathrooms: 5 public.
Bed & breakfast: £33-£35 single, £44-£46 double.

B & B Flatlets M

72 Holland Park Ave., London W11 3QZ
☎ 071-229 9233
2 clean, friendly, family-run guesthouses offering budget accommodation. Full English breakfast served to rooms, all rooms have their own complete cooking facilities. Near public transport. Also at 64 Holland Road, London W14.
Bedrooms: 3 double, 2 family rooms.
Bathrooms: 1 private, 2 public.
Bed & breakfast: £20-£23 single, £27-£40 double.

The Gate Hotel M

Listed COMMENDED
6 Portobello Rd., London W11 3DG
☎ 071-221 2403
Bed and breakfast hotel near Notting Hill underground station in the famous Portobello Road. Close to all the antique shops.
Bedrooms: 2 single, 4 double, 2 family rooms.
Bathrooms: 3 private, 1 public; 2 private showers.
Bed & breakfast: £32-£35 single, £55-£60 double.
Credit: Visa.

Gillett Hotel

120 Shepherds Bush Rd., London W6 7PD
☎ 071-603 0784 & 2811

Family-run hotel close to Hammersmith and Shepherds Bush. Convenient for Olympia, Earl's Court and West End.
Bedrooms: 1 single, 1 double & 4 twin, 4 family rooms.
Bathrooms: 3 public.
Bed & breakfast: £23-£25 single, £27.60-£32.20 double.

Janus Hotel M

26 Hazlitt Rd., London W14 0JY
☎ 071-603 6915 & 3119
Homely hotel, quietly but centrally situated within easy reach of the West End. No parking restrictions.
Bedrooms: 7 single, 3 double & 6 twin, 2 family rooms.
Bathrooms: 2 public; 2 private showers.
Bed & breakfast: £18-£24 single, £24-£30 double.

Kensington Palace Thistle Hotel M

De Vere Gdns., London W8 5AF
☎ 071-937 8121 Telex 262422
CR Thistle
Offering modern hotel facilities close to the shopping areas of Knightsbridge and the West End. Overlooking Kensington Gardens.
Bedrooms: 67 single, 55 double & 149 twin, 27 family rooms.
Bathrooms: 298 private.
Bed & breakfast: from £98.95 single, from £122.90 double.
Lunch available.
Evening meal 6.30pm (l.o. 10.45pm).
Credit: Access, Visa, C.Bl., Diners, Amex.

Hotel Lexham M

32-38 Lexham Gdns., London W8 5JU
☎ 071-373 6471
Fax 071-244 7827
Telex 268141 METMAK/HOTLEX
Long-established, owner-run hotel, with a pleasant outlook over a garden square. Conveniently central and close to the museums.
Bedrooms: 21 single, 8 double & 23 twin, 12 family rooms.
Bathrooms: 40 private, 11 public.
Bed & breakfast: £32.50-£44.50 single, £41.50-£64.50 double.
Half board: £29-£40.50 daily, £191-£265 weekly.
Lunch available.

Evening meal 6.45pm (l.o. 8pm).
Credit: Access, Visa.

London Kensington Hilton M

179-199 Holland Park Ave., London W11 4UL
☎ 071-603 3355 Telex 919763 KENHIL
CR Hilton
Modern hotel with easy access to shops, exhibition centres and Heathrow Airport by Airbus A2 service.
Bedrooms: 193 single, 136 double & 277 twin.
Bathrooms: 606 private.
Bed & breakfast: £71.50-£102 single, £129-£180 double.
Half board: £97-£142 daily.
Lunch available.
Evening meal 5.30pm (l.o. 10.30pm).
Parking for 100.
Credit: Access, Visa, C.Bl., Diners, Amex.

London Tara Hotel M

COMMENDED
Scarsdale Pl., Wrights Lane, London W8 5SR
☎ 071-937 7211 Telex 918834
CR Best Western
A large modern hotel, convenient for the West End, the city and major motorways. Wide choice of bars and restaurants.
Bedrooms: 204 double & 627 twin.
Bathrooms: 831 private.
Bed & breakfast: £93.40-£123.40 single, £114.80-£146.80 double.
Lunch available.
Evening meal 5.30pm (l.o. 1.30am).
Parking for 90.
Credit: Access, Visa, C.Bl., Diners, Amex.

Medway Guest House

102 Hammersmith Grove, London W6 7HB
☎ 081-748 1581 & 081-741 7657
In a pleasant residential area only 200 yards from central Hammersmith, with good underground and bus connections.
Bedrooms: 5 single, 6 twin.

Bathrooms: 3 public.
Bed & breakfast: from £17 single, from £30 double.

Novotel London M

1 Shortlands, London W6 8DR
☎ 081-741 1555 Telex 934539
CR Novotel
A modern air-conditioned hotel for business and leisure, with quick connections to and from London's airports, the City and the West End.
Bedrooms: 40 double & 560 twin, 40 family rooms.
Bathrooms: 640 private.
Bed & breakfast: £77 single, £84 double.
Lunch available.
Evening meal 5pm (l.o. midnight).
Parking for 250.
Credit: Access, Visa, C.Bl., Diners, Amex.

Observatory House Hotel M

37 Hornton St., London W8 7NR
☎ 071-937 1577 & 6353
Telex 914972 OBSERV
Elegant hotel in an attractive residential and shopping area 10 minutes from central London. All modern facilities.
Bedrooms: 5 single, 9 double & 5 twin, 6 family rooms.
Bathrooms: 25 private, 1 public.
Bed & breakfast: £57.40-£62.90 single, £80.40-£87.90 double.
Credit: Access, Visa, Diners, Amex.

Pearl Hotel

Listed
40 West Cromwell Rd., Earl's Court, London SW5 9QL
☎ 071-373 9610 & 071-835 2007 Fax: 071-244 6835
Located near Earl's Court Tube Station. 15 minutes from West End.
Bedrooms: 13 single, 3 double & 2 twin, 2 family rooms.
Bathrooms: 2 private, 5 public; 12 private showers.
Bed & breakfast: £12-£13 single, £18-£20 double.
Credit: Access, Visa.

LONDON

CENTRAL LONDON 3
Continued

Royal Garden Hotel M
Kensington High St., London
W8 4PT
☎ 071-937 8000 Telex 263151
Rank
*This modern hotel overlooks
Hyde Park and Kensington
Gardens.*
Bedrooms: 99 single,
105 double & 165 twin,
21 family rooms.
Bathrooms: 390 private.
Bed & breakfast: £143.95-
£175.75 single, £185.90-
£206.50 double.
Lunch available.
Evening meal 5pm (l.o.
11.30pm).
Parking for 160.
Credit: Access, Visa, C.Bl.,
Diners, Amex.

Terry's Hotel M
28-34 Glenthorne Rd.,
Hammersmith, London
W6 0LS
☎ 081-748 6181
Fax 081-748 2195
*Friendly hotel offering value
for money, easy access to West
End and M4, M25.*
Bedrooms: 10 single, 4 double
& 17 twin, 18 family rooms.
Bathrooms: 41 private,
4 public.
Bed & breakfast: £45-£65
single, £55-£75 double.
Lunch available.
Evening meal 6pm (l.o. 9pm).
Credit: Access, Visa, Diners,
Amex.
Display advertisement
appears on page 46.

Hotel West Six
Listed APPROVED
99 Shepherds Bush Rd.,
Hammersmith, London W6
☎ 071-603 0948 Telex 916808
*Bed and breakfast
accommodation with en-suite
shower, WC and colour TV.*
Bedrooms: 4 single, 4 double
& 1 twin, 2 family rooms.
Bathrooms: 11 private.
Bed & breakfast: £23-£28
single, £38-£42 double.
Credit: Access, Visa, Amex.
Display advertisement
appears on page 46.

Windsor Guest House
43 Shepherds Bush Rd.,
London W6 7LU
☎ 071-603 2116

*Family-run establishment close
to Hammersmith Broadway
underground station.*
Bedrooms: 2 single, 2 twin,
2 family rooms.
Bathrooms: 1 public;
4 private showers.
Bed & breakfast: £15 single,
£30 double.

CENTRAL LONDON 4
Covering Bayswater,
Paddington, Maida Vale.
See map 6.

Abbey Court Hotel M
Listed
174 Sussex Gdns., London
W2 1TP
☎ 071-402 0704
*Central London hotel,
reasonable prices. Within
walking distance from
Lancaster Gate, Paddington
station and Hyde Park.*
Bedrooms: 1 single, 16 double
& 20 twin, 8 family rooms.
Bathrooms: 8 private,
3 public; 20 private showers.
Bed & breakfast: £22-£28
single, £28-£42 double.
Parking for 12.
Credit: Access, Visa, C.Bl.,
Diners, Amex.
Display advertisement
appears on page 42.

Allandale Hotel
3 Devonshire Ter., Lancaster
Gate, London W2 3DN
☎ 071-723 8311 & 7807
*Small family-run hotel, close to
West End and many of
London's attractions.*
Bedrooms: 1 single, 11 double
& 4 twin, 4 family rooms.
Bathrooms: 14 private,
1 public; 2 private showers.
Bed & breakfast: £30-£33
single, £35-£43 double.
Credit: Access, Visa, Diners.

Andrews House Hotel M
Listed
12 Westbourne St., Hyde
Park, London W2 2TZ
☎ 071-723 5365 & 4514
*Within walking distance of
Oxford Street and all tourist
attractions, 2 minutes from
Lancaster Gate and
Paddington underground
stations, also the air bus to
Heathrow.*
Bedrooms: 1 single, 6 double
& 4 twin, 6 family rooms.
Bathrooms: 1 private,
3 public; 9 private showers.

Bed & breakfast: £20-£25
single, £28-£35 double.
Credit: Access, Visa, Diners.

Balmoral House Hotel M
156 Sussex Gdns., London
W2 1UD
☎ 071-723 7445 & 4925
*A small family-run hotel well
located for business people and
holiday makers alike. Offering
friendly hospitality and good
traditional English breakfast.*
Bedrooms: 2 single, 4 double
& 5 twin, 6 family rooms.
Bathrooms: 1 private,
5 public; 2 private showers.
Bed & breakfast: £22-£25
single, £34-£36 double.
Parking for 2.

Barry House Hotel M
Listed APPROVED
12 Sussex Pl., London
W2 2TP
☎ 071-723 7340 & 071-723
0994 Fax: 071-723 9775
*Family-run bed and breakfast
hotel, 3 minutes walking
distance from Paddington
Station. Hyde Park, Marble
Arch and Oxford Street close
by.*
Bedrooms: 3 single, 1 double
& 6 twin, 7 family rooms.
Bathrooms: 13 private,
2 public.
Bed & breakfast: £26-£35
single, £40-£50 double.
Credit: Access, Visa, Amex.
Display advertisement
appears on page 44.

Beverley House Hotel M
142 Sussex Gdns., London
W2 1UB
☎ 071-723 3380
Fax 071-402 3292
*Opened in July 1990, a bed
and breakfast hotel with a high
standard at low prices. Close
to Paddington station, Hyde
Park and museums.*
Bedrooms: 6 single, 5 double
& 6 twin, 6 family rooms.
Bathrooms: 23 private.
Bed & breakfast: £32-£46
single, £34-£54 double.
Parking for 2.
Credit: Access, Visa, C.Bl.,
Diners, Amex.

The Blakemore Hotel M
30 Leinster Gdns., London
W2 3AU
☎ 071-262 4591 Telex 291634
LENTOW G

*Close to Queensway,
convenient for shopping in
West End and near Hyde Park
and Kensington Gardens.
Cocktail bar and banqueting
facilities available.*
Bedrooms: 59 single,
22 double & 66 twin,
23 family rooms.
Bathrooms: 170 private.
Bed & breakfast: max. £60
single, max. £70 double.
Evening meal 6pm.
Credit: Access, Visa, C.Bl.,
Diners, Amex.

Camelot Hotel M
COMMENDED
45-47 Norfolk Sq.,
Paddington, London W2 1RX
☎ 071-723 9118 & 071-262
1980 Telex 268312 WESCOM
G CENTRAL
*Beautifully restored town
house, now a bed and breakfast
hotel offering good-value,
charming and stylish
accommodation in central
London.*
Bedrooms: 13 single,
11 double & 12 twin, 8 family
rooms.
Bathrooms: 34 private,
1 public; 6 private showers.
Bed & breakfast: £35.50-£52
single, £68 double.
Credit: Access, Visa.

Coburg Hotel
129 Bayswater Rd., London
W2 4RJ
☎ 071-823 7020 Telex 268235
Best Western
*Newly refurbished Edwardian
hotel conveniently located
overlooking Kensington
Gardens, ideal for tourists and
business travellers.*
Bedrooms: 23 single,
39 double & 62 twin, 6 family
rooms.
Bathrooms: 130 private.
Bed & breakfast: £69.50
single, £94.50-£104.50 double.
Lunch available.
Credit: Access, Visa, C.Bl.,
Diners, Amex.

Duke of Leinster M
34 Queen's Gdns., London
W2 3AA
☎ 071-258 0079 & 1839
Telex 264266
*Listed building near Hyde
Park. Former residence of the
Duke of Leinster.*
Bedrooms: 2 single, 11 double
& 21 twin, 8 family rooms.
Bathrooms: 42 private.

Bed & breakfast: £35-£45
single, £50-£60 double.
Credit: Access, Visa, Diners,
Amex.

Garden Court Hotel M
COMMENDED

30-31 Kensington Gardens
Sq., London W2 4BG
☎ 071-727 8304 & 071-229
2553
*Small friendly hotel in a quiet
Victorian garden square in
central London. Convenient for
all transport.*
Bedrooms: 15 single, 6 double
& 10 twin, 6 family rooms.
Bathrooms: 12 private,
6 public.
Bed & breakfast: £25-£36
single, £36-£49 double.
Credit: Access, Visa.

Henry VIII Hotel M
♕♕♕

19 Leinster Gdns., London
W2 3AN
☎ 071-262 0117 Telex 261365
*Convenient for Queensway and
Bayswater underground
stations, with Hyde Park
nearby. Banqueting
accommodation for up to 100
persons.*
Bedrooms: 30 single, 8 double
& 62 twin, 7 family rooms.
Bathrooms: 107 private.
Bed & breakfast: max. £71.50
single, max. £88 double.
Lunch available.
Evening meal 6pm (l.o.
10pm).
Credit: Access, Visa, C.Bl.,
Diners, Amex.

Hyde Park
International M

52-56 Inverness Ter., London
W2 3LB
☎ 071-229 8841
Telex 8953210 HPI
*Close to Hyde Park, 1 minute's
walk from Queensway and
Bayswater underground
stations and shops and
restaurants in Queensway.*
Bedrooms: 6 single, 6 double
& 35 twin, 13 family rooms.
Bathrooms: 54 private,
3 public.
Bed & breakfast: £34-£38
single, £49.50-£66.50 double.
Parking for 4.
Credit: Access, Visa, Diners.

Kingsway Hotel M

27 Norfolk Sq., Hyde Park,
London W2 1RX
☎ 071-723 5569 & 7784
Fax 071-723 7317
Telex 885299
*In a quiet square, close to
Paddington underground and
Hyde Park. High standard
hotel, with lift and en-suite
facilities.*
Bedrooms: 10 single, 8 double
& 6 twin, 10 family rooms.
Bathrooms: 24 private,
3 public; 8 private showers.
Bed & breakfast: £25-£42
single, £38-£53 double.
Credit: Access, Visa, Amex.

Lancaster Court
Hotel M

202-204 Sussex Gdns., Hyde
Park, London W2 3UA
☎ 071-402 8438 & 6369
Fax 071-706 3794
Telex 21879 LANCO
*2 minutes from Lancaster
Gate, Paddington underground
and a stroll from Hyde Park. 1
minute from Heathrow Airbus
stop. Oxford Street and
theatres nearby. Friendly,
courteous service, meals can be
arranged for groups. Limited
free car parking.*
Bedrooms: 13 single, 6 double
& 7 twin, 16 family rooms.
Bathrooms: 20 private,
3 public; 22 private showers.
Bed & breakfast: £27-£34
single, £38-£51 double.
Half board: from £29 daily,
£203-£252 weekly.
Parking for 8.
Credit: Access, Visa, Diners,
Amex.

⚭ Display advertisement
appears on page 45.

Linden House Hotel M
Listed

4 Sussex Pl., London W2 2TP
☎ 071-723 9853 & 071-262
0804 Fax: 071-724 1454
*Regency-style building close to
Hyde Park, with a friendly
family atmosphere.*
Bedrooms: 4 single, 5 double
& 8 twin, 14 family rooms.
Bathrooms: 20 private,
4 public.
Bed & breakfast: £25-£40
single, £36-£52 double.

London House Hotel M

80 Kensington Gardens Sq.,
London W2 4DJ
☎ 071-727 0696 Telex 24923

*Friendly, comfortable budget
hotel, convenient for shops,
theatres and sightseeing.
Public transport within easy
reach.*
Bedrooms: 3 single, 13 double
& 11 twin, 19 family rooms.
Bathrooms: 7 public;
13 private showers.
Bed & breakfast: max. £35
single, max. £43 double.

Mornington Hotel M
♕♕♕

12 Lancaster Gate, London
W2 3LG
☎ 071-262 7361 Telex 24281
ⓑ Best Western
*Modernised hotel in a quiet
residential street opposite Hyde
Park.*
Bedrooms: 34 single, 9 double
& 23 twin, 2 family rooms.
Bathrooms: 68 private.
Bed & breakfast: from £71
single, £82-£92 double.
Credit: Access, Visa, C.Bl.,
Diners, Amex.

Nayland Hotel M
♕♕♕

132-134 Sussex Gdns.,
London W2 1UB
☎ 071-723 4615 Telex 268312
*Opened in July 1990 after
complete refurbishment. Close
to museums, Paddington
station and Oxford Street, bus
stop to Heathrow airport.*
Bedrooms: 11 single, 8 double
& 17 twin, 5 family rooms.
Bathrooms: 41 private.
Bed & breakfast: £34-£50
single, £38-£60 double.
Parking for 5.
Credit: Access, Visa, C.Bl.,
Diners, Amex.

Norfolk Plaza Hotel

29-33 Norfolk Sq., London,
W2 1RX
☎ 071-723 0792 Telex 266799
*Close to Paddington mainline
and underground stations.
Hyde Park and Oxford Street
shopping centres nearby.*
Bedrooms: 1 single, 5 double
& 61 twin, 20 family rooms.
Bathrooms: 87 private.
Bed & breakfast: £60-£70
single, £75-£85 double.
Half board: £85-£95 daily.
Lunch available.
Evening meal 7.30pm (l.o.
9pm).
Credit: Access, Visa, Diners,
Amex.

⚭ Display advertisement
appears on page 45.

Norfolk Towers Hotel M
♕♕♕ APPROVED

34 Norfolk Pl., London
W2 1QW
☎ 071-262 3123 Telex 268583
NORTOW
*Elegant hotel, completely
renovated and refurbished, with
cocktail bar, restaurant and
wine bar. Close to city centre
and West End.*
Bedrooms: 14 single,
22 double & 46 twin, 3 family
rooms.
Bathrooms: 85 private.
Bed & breakfast: max. £65
single, max. £75 double.
Lunch available.
Evening meal 6pm (l.o.
9.30pm).
Credit: Access, Visa, C.Bl.,
Diners, Amex.

Parkwood Hotel M
♕♕♕ COMMENDED

4 Stanhope Pl., London
W2 2HB
☎ 071-402 2241 Fax: 071-
402 1574
*Smart town house convenient
for Hyde Park and Oxford
Street. Comfortable bedrooms
and friendly atmosphere.*
Bedrooms: 4 single, 4 double
& 5 twin, 5 family rooms.
Bathrooms: 12 private,
2 public.
Bed & breakfast: £42.50-£59
single, £57.75-£69.75 double.
Credit: Access, Visa.

Pembridge Court
Hotel M
♕♕♕

34 Pembridge Gdns., London
W2 4DX
☎ 071-229 9977 Telex 298363
*Small privately-owned town
house hotel located in quiet
tree-lined gardens. Easy access
to West End shops and
theatres.*
Bedrooms: 10 single, 9 double
& 6 twin.
Bathrooms: 25 private.
Bed & breakfast: £65-£74
single, £80-£120 double.
Evening meal 6pm (l.o.
11.15pm).
Parking for 2.
Credit: Access, Visa, Diners,
Amex.

Phoenix Hotel M

1-8 Kensington Gardens Sq.,
Queensway, London W2 4BH
☎ 071-229 2494 Telex 298854
PHENIX G

Continued ▶

CENTRAL LONDON 4

Continued

Centrally located, close to many amenities, within walking distance of Hyde Park and Oxford Street.
Bedrooms: 42 single, 17 double & 52 twin, 14 family rooms.
Bathrooms: 125 private.
Bed & breakfast: £67-£76 single, £83-£94.50 double.
Half board: £79-£86 daily, £539-£602 weekly.
Lunch available.
Evening meal 5.30pm (l.o. 10.30pm).
Credit: Access, Visa, Diners, Amex.

Royal Lancaster Hotel M

Lancaster Ter., London W2 2TY
☎ 071-262 6737 Telex 24822
CR Rank
Modern hotel overlooking Hyde Park and close to Marble Arch and Oxford Street. 4 conference suites, largest seating 1,000. Restaurant, cafe and bar.
Bedrooms: 25 single, 148 double & 225 twin, 20 family rooms.
Bathrooms: 418 private.
Bed & breakfast: £148-£226 single, £176-£237 double.
Lunch available.
Evening meal 6pm (l.o. 10.45pm).
Parking for 130.
Credit: Access, Visa, C.Bl., Diners, Amex.

Royal Park Hotel M

2-5 Westbourne Ter., London W2 3UL
☎ 071-402 6187
Built in 1854, the hotel is modernised, comfortable and well placed for bus and underground to the West End.
Bedrooms: 8 single, 10 double & 35 twin, 8 family rooms.
Bathrooms: 61 private.
Bed & breakfast: max. £51 single, max. £65 double.
Parking for 12.
Credit: Access, Visa, Amex.

St. Charles Hotel

66 Queensborough Ter., London W2 3SH
☎ 071-221 0022

A well-appointed small hotel, 2 minutes' walk from Kensington Gardens and within easy reach of the West End.
Bedrooms: 5 single, 3 double & 5 twin, 3 family rooms.
Bathrooms: 4 private; 12 private showers.
Bed & breakfast: £22-£27 single, £34-£37 double.

Sass House Hotel M

Listed
10 & 11 Craven Ter., London W2 3QT
☎ 071-262 2325
Budget accommodation, convenient for central London, Hyde Park and the West End. Paddington and Lancaster Gate underground stations nearby.
Bedrooms: 4 single, 4 double & 4 twin, 6 family rooms.
Bathrooms: 3 public.
Bed & breakfast: £18-£26 single, £26-£34 double.
Parking for 4.
Credit: Access, Visa, Diners, Amex.

AD Display advertisement appears on page 42.

Hotel Slavia M

2 Pembridge Sq., London W2 4EW
☎ 071-727 1316 & 071-229 0803 Telex 917458 SLAVIA
Family-run modernised hotel in a quiet garden square, 150 yards from Bayswater Road. Portobello antique market nearby.
Bedrooms: 4 single, 6 double & 13 twin, 8 family rooms.
Bathrooms: 31 private.
Bed & breakfast: £26-£42 single, £30-£57 double.
Parking for 1.
Credit: Access, Visa, Diners, Amex.

Strutton Park Hotel M

Listed
45 Palace Ct., London W2 4LS
☎ 071-727 5074 & 071-229 6330 & 3098 Telex 896559 GECOMS G STRUTTON
Attractive Victorian building in quiet Bayswater area close to Hyde Park, museums and antique markets. Direct transport to most places including airport.
Bedrooms: 8 single, 7 double & 10 twin, 2 family rooms.
Bathrooms: 2 public; 24 private showers.

Bed & breakfast: £27.50-£32 single, £38.50-£45 double.
Credit: Access, Visa, Diners, Amex.

Victoria Garden Hotel M

100 Westbourne Ter., London W2 5QE
☎ 071-262 1161 Telex 892676 VICGDN G
On a quiet tree-lined Bayswater terrace. Hyde Park and Marble Arch are within easy walking distance.
Bedrooms: 5 single, 10 double & 34 twin, 22 family rooms.
Bathrooms: 71 private.
Bed & breakfast: max. £60 single, max. £70 double.
Parking for 4.
Credit: Access, Visa, C.Bl., Diners, Amex.

West Two Hotel M

22-23 Kensington Gardens Sq., London W2 4BG
☎ 071-229 6085 Telex 24923
In a quiet garden square, close to bustling Queensway and convenient for central London.
Bedrooms: 7 single, 6 twin, 17 family rooms.
Bathrooms: 7 public.
Bed & breakfast: max. £30 single, max. £38 double.

Westland Hotel

APPROVED
154 Bayswater Rd., London W2 4HP
☎ 071-229 9191
Telex 94016297 WEST G
Small, friendly hotel. Well located for West End shopping, touring or relaxing in a beautiful park. Your home from home.
Bedrooms: 6 single, 2 double & 25 twin, 8 family rooms.
Bathrooms: 30 private, 4 public.
Bed & breakfast: £50.60-£59.20 single, £61.60-£72.60 double.
Half board: £58-£68 daily.
Evening meal 6.30pm (l.o. 10.30pm).
Parking for 9.
Credit: Access, Visa, C.Bl., Diners, Amex.

The Westminster M

16 Leinster Sq., London W2 4PR
☎ 071-286 5294 Telex 24923

Convenient for major shopping centres and places of interest.
Bedrooms: 30 single, 12 double & 52 twin, 8 family rooms.
Bathrooms: 102 private.
Bed & breakfast: £71.50-£82.50 single, £88-£92.50 double.
Evening meal 6pm (l.o. 10pm).
Credit: Access, Visa, C.Bl., Diners, Amex.

Westpoint Hotel M

Listed
170-172 Sussex Gdns., London W2 1TP
☎ 071-402 0281
Inexpensive accommodation in central London. Close to Paddington and Lancaster Gate underground stations. Easy access to tourist attractions and Hyde Park.
Bedrooms: 5 single, 7 double & 8 twin, 5 family rooms.
Bathrooms: 19 private, 3 public.
Bed & breakfast: £20-£26 single, £26-£40 double.
Parking for 8.
Credit: Access, Visa, C.Bl., Diners, Amex.

AD Display advertisement appears on page 42.

CENTRAL LONDON 5

Covering King's Cross, St. Pancras, Euston, Bloomsbury, Kingsway, Marylebone, Regents Park, Leicester Square, The Strand, Charing Cross, Fleet Street, Holborn, City. See map 6.

Academy Hotel M

COMMENDED
17-21 Gower St., London WC1E 6HG
☎ 071-631 4115
Fax 071-636 3442
Telex 24364 ASTOR HG
Newly refurbished Georgian hotel in Bloomsbury. New restaurant and bar. Library, patio garden for afternoon tea.
Bedrooms: 8 single, 14 double & 7 twin, 2 family rooms.
Bathrooms: 22 private, 4 public.
Bed & breakfast: £45-£80 single, £70-£95 double.
Half board: £60-£95 daily, £250-£320 weekly.
Lunch available.
Evening meal 6pm (l.o. midnight).

Credit: Access, Visa, Diners, Amex.

Acorns Hotel
Listed

42 Tavistock Pl., London
WC1H 9RE
☎ 071-837 3077 & 2723
Grade II listed Victorian house, well-placed between West End and the city, ideal for business or pleasure. Minutes walk to Russell Square, Euston or Kings Cross. Value for money.
Bedrooms: 2 single, 6 double & 4 twin, 2 family rooms.
Bathrooms: 4 public.
Bed & breakfast: £18-£25 single, £28-£35 double.
Credit: Access, Visa, C.Bl., Diners, Amex.

Albany Hotel
Listed

34 Tavistock Pl., London
WC1H 9RE
☎ 071-837 9139 & 071-833 0459
Bedrooms: 3 single, 3 double & 4 twin, 1 family room.
Bathrooms: 4 public.
Bed & breakfast: £30-£32 single, £42-£44 double.
Lunch available.
Evening meal 6.30pm (l.o. 9.30pm).
Credit: Access, Visa, Diners, Amex.

Arran House Hotel M
Listed

77 Gower St., London
WC1E 6HJ
☎ 071-636 2186 & 071-637 1140
A small comfortable family-run bed and breakfast hotel in central London, convenient for theatres, shopping and public transport.
Bedrooms: 6 single, 4 double & 4 twin, 10 family rooms.
Bathrooms: 4 private, 7 public; 7 private showers.
Bed & breakfast: £25-£28 single, £38-£42 double.
Lunch available.
Evening meal 5.30pm (l.o. 7.30pm).
Credit: Access, Visa.

Bedford Hotel M

Southampton Row, London
WC1B 4HD
☎ 071-636 7822 Fax 071-837 4653 Telex 263951

Modern refurbished hotel in central London with attractive sun terrace and private garden. Direct link to Heathrow.
Bedrooms: 110 single, 10 double & 54 twin, 5 family rooms.
Bathrooms: 179 private.
Bed & breakfast: £50-£54 single, £63-£69 double.
Half board: £57.50-£61.50 daily, £345.50-£368 weekly.
Lunch available.
Evening meal 6pm (l.o. 10.45pm).
Parking for 50.
Credit: Access, Visa, C.Bl., Diners, Amex.

Bonnington Hotel M
COMMENDED

92 Southampton Row, London WC1B 4BH
☎ 071-242 2828 Telex 261591
Between the city and West End. Close to mainline stations and on the underground to Heathrow Airport.
Bedrooms: 109 single, 44 double & 45 twin, 17 family rooms.
Bathrooms: 215 private.
Bed & breakfast: £67-£76 single, £88-£100 double.
Half board: £65-£91 daily.
Lunch available.
Evening meal 6pm (l.o. 9.30pm).
Credit: Access, Visa, Diners, Amex.

Crescent Hotel M
Listed

49-50 Cartwright Gdns., London WC1H 9EL
☎ 071-387 1515
Family-run hotel in a quiet Georgian crescent, with private gardens and tennis courts. Comfortable and central. Colour TV lounge.
Bedrooms: 12 single, 5 double & 5 twin, 7 family rooms.
Bathrooms: 1 private, 6 public; 3 private showers.
Bed & breakfast: £26-£28 single, £40-£50 double.
Credit: Access, Visa.

Drury Lane Moat House

10 Drury Lane, London
WC2B 5RE
☎ 071-836 6666
Telex 8811395
Queens Moat Houses
Modern city centre hotel, convenient for the West End, City and theatres. Suitable for businessmen and tourists alike.

Bedrooms: 9 single, 67 double & 72 twin, 5 family rooms.
Bathrooms: 153 private.
Bed & breakfast: £118-£129 single, £157-£186 double.
Half board: £98.50-£113 daily.
Lunch available.
Evening meal 6pm (l.o. 11pm).
Parking for 20.
Credit: Access, Visa, C.Bl., Diners, Amex.

Euro Hotel
Listed

51-53 Cartwright Gdns., London WC1H 9EL
☎ 071-387 6789
Fax 071-383 5044
Centrally located hotel close to the West End and British Museum. Bright, spacious rooms with TV, tea/coffee facilities, video films etc.
Bedrooms: 8 single, 2 double & 11 twin, 15 family rooms.
Bathrooms: 12 public.
Bed & breakfast: £28-£31 single, £41-£44 double.
Credit: Access, Visa.

Display advertisement appears on page 45.

Gower House Hotel M
Listed

57 Gower St., London
WC1E 6HJ
☎ 071-636 4685
Friendly bed and breakfast hotel, close to Goodge Street underground station, and within easy walking distance of British Museum, shops, theatres, and restaurants.
Bedrooms: 4 single, 2 double & 6 twin, 4 family rooms.
Bathrooms: 3 private, 3 public.
Bed & breakfast: £23-£26 single, £34-£37 double.
Credit: Access, Visa.

Grays Hotel M

109 Guilford St., London
WC1
☎ 071-439 3732 & 071-833 2474 Telex 25335 SURIS G
Victorian town house, grade II listed building, restored to provide good accommodation. All rooms with hair-dryer, mini-bar, tea bar, trouser press, video, TV and direct dial telephone.
Bedrooms: 3 double & 5 twin.
Bathrooms: 8 private, 1 public.
Bed & breakfast: £55-£80 single, £65-£100 double.

Evening meal 6pm (l.o. 10pm).
Credit: Access, Visa, Diners, Amex.

Montague Park Hotel

Montague St., Bloomsbury, London WC1B 5BJ
☎ 071-637 1001 Telex 23307 MONTGU G
The hotel has recently undergone major refurbishment and re-opened in October 1990.
Bedrooms: 36 single, 53 double & 18 twin, 2 family rooms.
Bathrooms: 109 private.
Bed & breakfast: £90-£120 single, £120-£140 double.
Half board: £100-£130 daily, £700-£910 weekly.
Lunch available.
Evening meal 6pm (l.o. 10.30pm).
Credit: Access, Visa, Diners, Amex.

Pastoria Hotel M

3-6 St. Martin's St., Leicester Square, London WC2H 7HL
☎ 071-930 8641 Telex 25538
A small friendly hotel in central London between Leicester Square and Trafalgar Square. Ideal for businessmen and visitors alike. Prices do not include breakfast.
Bedrooms: 11 single, 15 double & 32 twin.
Bathrooms: 58 private.
Bed & breakfast: £81-£85 single, £99-£105 double.
Lunch available.
Credit: Access, Visa, Diners, Amex.

Royal Adelphi Hotel M
APPROVED

21 Villiers St., London
WC2N 6ND
☎ 071-930 8764 Telex 291829 RAH
Centrally located, near Embankment and Charing Cross underground. All rooms with colour TV, hair-dryers, tea/coffee facilities. Discount on group rates and English breakfast supplement.
Bedrooms: 28 single, 13 double & 12 twin, 2 family rooms.
Bathrooms: 18 private, 8 public.

Continued ▶

CENTRAL LONDON 5
Continued

Bed & breakfast: £30-£45 single, £45-£55 double.
Credit: Access, Visa, Diners, Amex.

Royal Trafalgar Thistle Hotel
Whitcomb St., London WC2H 7HG
☎ 071-930 4477 Telex 298564
Thistle
Off a quiet back street, this modern hotel is close to Trafalgar Square and the National Gallery.
Bedrooms: 36 single, 24 double & 48 twin.
Bathrooms: 108 private.
Bed & breakfast: from £95.95 single, from £116.90 double.
Lunch available.
Evening meal 5.30pm (l.o. 11.30pm).
Credit: Access, Visa, C.Bl., Diners, Amex.

St. Giles Hotel
Bedford Ave., London WC1B 3AS
☎ 071-636 8616 Telex 22683
Close to Oxford Street, and 2 minutes' walk to the British Museum. Parking available at extra cost.
Bedrooms: 234 single, 222 double & 132 twin, 12 family rooms.
Bathrooms: 600 private, 47 public.
Bed & breakfast: £53-£57 single, £85-£92 double.
Half board: £59-£63 daily.
Lunch available.
Evening meal 6pm (l.o. 10.30pm).
Parking for 150.
Credit: Access, Visa, Diners, Amex.

Somerset House Hotel
Listed
6 Dorset Sq., London NW1 6QA
☎ 071-723 0741
Spacious rooms with colour TV. Bridal suites available. Cooked breakfast. Located close to Baker Street station. All rooms with en-suite bathroom.
Bedrooms: 5 single, 10 double & 5 twin, 8 family rooms.
Bathrooms: 28 private, 1 public.

Bed & breakfast: £26.50-£36.50 single, £36.50-£49.50 double.
Evening meal 6pm (l.o. 10pm).
Credit: Access, Visa, Diners, Amex.

Thanet Hotel
Listed APPROVED
8 Bedford Pl., London WC1B 5JA
☎ 071-636 2869 & 071-580 3377
Comfortable, family-run hotel, with colour TV in all rooms. Full English breakfast.
Bedrooms: 2 single, 2 double & 4 twin, 4 family rooms.
Bathrooms: 4 private, 4 public.
Bed & breakfast: £30-£40 single, £42-£52 double.
Credit: Access, Visa.

The Tower Thistle Hotel
St. Katharine's Way, London E1 9LD
☎ 071-481 2575 Telex 885934
Thistle
Alongside the Tower and Tower Bridge, in a captivatingly historic setting. All the hotel's 808 rooms offer spectacular views of the Thames or St. Katharine's Docks.
Bedrooms: 101 single, 126 double & 531 twin, 50 family rooms.
Bathrooms: 808 private.
Bed & breakfast: from £107.95 single, from £129.90 double.
Lunch available.
Evening meal 3.30pm (l.o. midnight).
Parking for 136.
Credit: Access, Visa, C.Bl., Diners, Amex.

The White House
Regents Park, London NW1 3UP
☎ 071-387 1200 Telex 24111
Rank
Near Regents Park, the zoo and Madame Tussaud's. A few minutes from Euston Station and about 10 minutes' walk from Oxford Circus. There are 3 underground stations within walking distance.
Bedrooms: 64 single, 103 double & 307 twin, 93 family rooms.
Bathrooms: 567 private.

Bed & breakfast: £113-£130 single, £134-£155 double.
Lunch available.
Evening meal 6.30pm (l.o. 11.30pm).
Credit: Access, Visa, C.Bl., Diners, Amex.

EAST LONDON

Covering the boroughs of Barking, Hackney, Havering, Newham, Redbridge, Tower Hamlets, Waltham Forest. See map 7.

Balfour Hotel
31 Balfour Rd., Ilford, Essex IG1 4HP
☎ 081-514 3238
Small friendly hotel close to Ilford station, the M11 and M25. Colour TV in rooms.
Bedrooms: 2 single, 1 twin, 2 family rooms.
Bathrooms: 2 public.
Bed & breakfast: £22-£26 single, £30 double.
Parking for 3.

Gidea Park Hotel
115 Main Rd., Gidea Park, Romford, Essex RM2 5EL
☎ Romford (0708) 746676 & 746628 Fax (0708) 744044
A large Victorian house on the A118. Built in 1880, owned originally by Sir Henry Raphael.
Bedrooms: 11 single, 5 double & 1 twin, 1 family room.
Bathrooms: 18 private.
Bed & breakfast: £37-£50 single, £39-£60 double.
Half board: from £44 daily, from £300 weekly.
Evening meal 7pm (l.o. 10pm).
Parking for 17.
Credit: Access, Visa, Amex.

Grangewood Lodge Hotel
Listed
104 Clova Rd., Forest Gate, London E7 9AF
☎ 081-534 0637
Comfortable budget accommodation in a quiet road, pleasant garden. Easy access to central London, Docklands and M11. Special weekly rates.
Bedrooms: 10 single, 6 twin, 4 family rooms.
Bathrooms: 3 public; 1 private shower.

Bed & breakfast: £11-£15 single, £22-£28 double.
Credit: Access, Visa.

Grove Hill Hotel
38 Grove Hill, South Woodford, London E18 2JG
☎ 081-989 3344
Just off the A11/M11 and A406; convenient for underground station, cinemas, shops and restaurants. Lounge bar and lock-up garaging. Half minute walk from town centre, tube and trains.
Bedrooms: 8 single, 9 double & 2 twin, 2 family rooms.
Bathrooms: 12 private, 3 public.
Bed & breakfast: £27-£36 single, £43-£51 double.
Parking for 13.
Credit: Access, Visa, Amex.

Manor House Hotel
235 Romford Rd., Forest Gate, London E7 9HL
☎ 081-519 5432
Family-run hotel close to Central Line station at Stratford. Near city and Docklands, easy access to M11, M25 and North Circular road. Comfortable rooms and friendly service. For a nicer tomorrow be our guest tonight.
Bedrooms: 8 single, 4 double & 2 twin.
Bathrooms: 14 private.
Bed & breakfast: £27-£29 single, £36-£41 double.
Parking for 12.
Credit: Access, Visa, Amex.

Repton Private Hotel
18 Repton Dr., Gidea Park, Romford, Essex RM2 5LP
☎ Romford (0708) 45253
Small family-run hotel in quiet residential area. Central London easily accessible.
Bedrooms: 4 single, 2 double & 2 twin, 1 family room.
Bathrooms: 1 private, 2 public.
Bed & breakfast: from £20 single, from £32 double.

Sans Souci House
11 Chelmsford Rd., Leytonstone, London E11 1BT
☎ 081-539 1367
Fax 081-558 9189

Comfortable accommodation with all amenities, in a quiet road near Leytonstone underground station. 20 minutes from central London. Easy access to M11 and M25.
Bedrooms: 5 twin, 2 family rooms.
Bathrooms: 2 public.
Bed & breakfast: £13.80-£20.70 single, £23-£36.80 double.
Parking for 4.
[symbols]

Woodford Moat House
[symbols]
Oak Hill, Woodford Green, Essex IG8 9NY
☎ 081-505 4511 Telex 264428 WDFMHS
Ⓖ Queens Moat Houses
Set in a forest clearing at the entrance to the Essex countryside and just 10 miles from London's West End.
Bedrooms: 1 single, 44 double & 51 twin, 2 family rooms.
Bathrooms: 98 private.
Bed & breakfast: £78-£82 single, £90-£94 double.
Lunch available.
Evening meal 7pm (l.o. 10.15pm).
Parking for 150.
Credit: Access, Visa, Diners, Amex.
[symbols]

NORTH LONDON
Covering the boroughs of Barnet, Brent, Camden, Enfield, Haringey, Harrow, Islington. See map 7.

Brookland Guest House
220 Golders Green Rd., London NW11 9AT
☎ 081-455 6678
In a residential area, close to Brent Cross underground station, 20 minutes from the West End. Free parking.
Bedrooms: 4 single, 7 twin, 1 family room.
Bathrooms: 3 private, 2 public.
Bed & breakfast: £20-£22 single, £30-£32 double.
Parking for 6.
[symbols]

Brookside Hotel
[APPROVED]
32 Brook Ave., Wembley Pk., London HA9 8PH
☎ 081-904 0019 & 081-908 5336

20 minutes from central London, a stone's throw from Wembley stadium and conference centre.
Bedrooms: 4 single, 4 double & 1 twin, 2 family rooms.
Bathrooms: 3 private, 2 public.
Bed & breakfast: £20-£25 single, £35-£45 double.
Half board: £27-£30 daily, from £145 weekly.
Lunch available.
Evening meal 6pm (l.o. 7.30pm).
Parking for 6.
Credit: Access, Visa.
[symbols]

Buckland Hotel ⋒
[Listed]
6 Buckland Cres., Swiss Cottage, London NW3 5DX
☎ 071-722 5574 & 5317
Fax 071-722 5594
Victorian house built circa 1860, 4 minutes from underground and buses. Quiet residential area, fairly close to city centre.
Bedrooms: 4 single, 2 double & 6 twin, 3 family rooms.
Bathrooms: 11 private, 1 public; 1 private shower.
Bed & breakfast: £20-£30 single, £40-£46 double.
Credit: Access, Visa, Amex.
[symbols]

Cavendish Guest House
24 Cavendish Rd., London NW6 7XP
☎ 081-451 3249
In a quiet residential street, 5 minutes' walk from Kilburn underground station, 20 minutes travelling time to the West End.
Bedrooms: 4 single, 3 double & 1 twin.
Bathrooms: 3 public.
Bed & breakfast: max. £17 single, max. £28 double.
Half board: £100-£156 weekly.
[symbols]

Central Hotel ⋒
[Listed] [APPROVED]
35 Hoop Lane, Golders Green, London NW11 8BS
☎ 081-458 5636
Fax 081-455 4792
In a quiet residential area, 5 minutes' walk from Golders Green underground station.
Bedrooms: 9 single, 6 double & 16 twin, 4 family rooms.
Bathrooms: 17 private, 6 public.
Bed & breakfast: £35-£45 single, £45-£65 double.

Parking for 8.
Credit: Access, Visa, Diners, Amex.
[symbols]

Charles Bernard Hotel
[symbols]
5 Frognal, Hampstead, London NW3 6AL
☎ 071-794 0101 Telex 23560
Purpose built hotel (1971), approximately 4 miles from Oxford Circus, offering a happy, friendly atmosphere.
Bedrooms: 4 single, 9 double & 44 twin.
Bathrooms: 57 private.
Bed & breakfast: £52-£72 single, £63-£85 double.
Lunch available.
Evening meal 6.30pm (l.o. 9.30pm).
Parking for 18.
Credit: Access, Visa, C.Bl., Diners, Amex.
[symbols]

Chumleigh Lodge Hotel ⋒
[symbols]
226-228 Nether St., Finchley, London N3 1HU
☎ 081-346 1614 & 0059
Comfortable, clean and pleasant rooms, with colour TV, tea/coffee facilities. Easy access to M1, A1, North Circular, West End, Alexandra Palace and Wembley. Residential bar and full English breakfast.
Bedrooms: 7 single, 4 double & 3 twin, 4 family rooms.
Bathrooms: 3 private, 4 public; 2 private showers.
Bed & breakfast: £23-£40 single, £33-£40 double.
Parking for 6.
Credit: Access, Visa, Amex.
[symbols]

Clive Hotel at Hampstead ⋒
Primrose Hill Rd., Hampstead, London NW3 3NA
☎ 071-586 2233 Telex 22759
Ⓖ Hilton
Near Primrose Hill, the hotel offers a relaxed atmosphere. Popular restaurant and bar.
Bedrooms: 14 single, 10 double & 60 twin.
Bathrooms: 84 private.
Bed & breakfast: £38-£78 single, £76-£93 double.
Lunch available.
Evening meal 7pm (l.o. 10pm).
Parking for 12.

Credit: Access, Visa, Diners, Amex.
[symbols]

Crescent Lodge Hotel ⋒
[symbols] [COMMENDED]
58-60 Welldon Cres., Harrow, Middlesex HA1 1QR
☎ 081-863 5491 & 5163 & (0836) 779203 Fax: 081-427 5965
In a quiet residential area, 5 minutes' walk from Harrow on the Hill underground station. Homely atmosphere. 10 minutes to Wembley Conference Centre by train, 20 minutes to the West End.
Bedrooms: 6 single, 6 double & 7 twin, 2 family rooms.
Bathrooms: 7 private, 5 public.
Bed & breakfast: £30-£48 single, £50-£58 double.
Half board: £45-£63 daily, £300-£426 weekly.
Lunch available.
Evening meal 7pm (l.o. 8.30pm).
Parking for 7.
Credit: Access, Visa, Diners.
[symbols]

Croft Court Hotel ⋒
[symbols] [APPROVED]
44 Ravenscroft Ave., London NW11 8AY
☎ 081-458 3331
Fax 081-455 9175
Within 20 minutes of town centre and close to M1, M4, M25, Brent Cross shopping centre and Wembley complex. Good service and personal attention.
Bedrooms: 2 single, 3 double & 15 twin.
Bathrooms: 20 private.
Bed & breakfast: from £49 single, from £64 double.
Parking for 3.
Credit: Access, Visa, Amex.
[symbols]

Cumberland Hotel
[symbols]
St. John's Rd., Harrow, Middlesex HA1 2EF
☎ 081-863 4111 Fax 081-863 5668 Telex 917201
Popular hotel, close to Wembley, 25 minutes to West End and Heathrow.
Bedrooms: 37 single, 17 double & 22 twin, 5 family rooms.
Bathrooms: 81 private.
Bed & breakfast: £60-£65 single, £75-£79 double.
Lunch available.
Continued ▶

33

Evening meal 7pm (l.o. 9.30pm).
Parking for 65.
Credit: Access, Visa, Diners, Amex.

🏃 ♿ 📞 📺 🖕 ♨ 🖊 🎦 V 🖬
🛌 ● ▦ ♨ ✕ 🌀 SP T

Elm Hotel M
👑👑 COMMENDED
1-7 Elm Rd., Wembley, Middlesex HA9 7JA
☎ 081-902 1764
1200 yards from Wembley Stadium and conference centre. 150 yards from Wembley Central underground and mainline station.
Bedrooms: 9 single, 6 double & 9 twin, 6 family rooms.
Bathrooms: 17 private, 5 public.
Bed & breakfast: £30-£40 single, £40-£50 double.
Parking for 6.
🏃 ♿ 📞 📺 🖕 UL 🖊 V 🛌
● ▦ ♨ 🍴 🐕 ✕

Endsleigh House
Listed
18 Woodside Grove, Finchley, London N12 8QU
☎ 081-445 4877
Comfortable, well-furnished guesthouse in quiet residential area, 10 minutes from M1 and 30 minutes by underground from the West End.
Bedrooms: 1 single, 1 double & 3 twin, 1 family room.
Bathrooms: 2 public.
Bed & breakfast: £18 single, £32 double.
🏃5 ♿ 📺 🖕 UL 🛌 TV 🐕 ✕ 🌀

Eric Hotel
328 Green Lanes, London N4 1BX
☎ 081-800 6125
Opposite Manor House underground station on the Piccadilly Line. Free car park.
Bedrooms: 6 single, 24 double & 6 twin, 4 family rooms.
Bathrooms: 32 private, 2 public.
Bed & breakfast: £19-£34 single, £28-£48 double.
Half board: £29-£44 daily, £203-£308 weekly.
Evening meal 7pm (l.o. 10pm).
🏃 ♿ 📺 🖕 UL ● ▦ ♨ ✕ 🌀 SP

Five Kings Guest House M
👑
59 Anson Rd., Tufnell Park, London N7 0AR
☎ 071-607 3996 & 6466

A well-maintained friendly guesthouse offering personal service. Easily accessible from A1, underground and buses. 15 minutes from the West End.
Bedrooms: 7 single, 3 double & 3 twin, 3 family rooms.
Bathrooms: 3 public; 3 private showers.
Bed & breakfast: £14-£16 single, £24-£28 double.
Credit: Access, Visa, C.Bl., Diners, Amex.
🏃3 ♿ 📺 🖕 UL 🛌 TV ● ▦ ♨ ✕
🌀 SP

Forty
4 Forty Lane, Wembley, Middlesex HA9 9EB
☎ 081-904 5629 & 081-908 6694
Close to Wembley Stadium, Wembley Park underground, 15 minutes from West End. Attractive decor, TV, bath, WC. Bar and lounge. Car park.
Bedrooms: 1 single, 3 double & 2 twin, 2 family rooms.
Bathrooms: 3 public.
Bed & breakfast: £22-£28 single, £35-£48 double.
Parking for 8.
🏃 ♿ 📺 🖕 UL 🛌 TV ● ▦ ♨
🍴 ✕ 🌀 DAP 🌀 SP

Hazelcroft Guest House M
155 Golders Green Rd., Golders Green, London NW11 8BX
☎ 081-349 1357 & 081-458 4186
Friendly establishment on the main road near the station, convenient for all amenities. All rooms with colour TV.
Bedrooms: 5 single, 7 double & 3 twin, 1 family room.
Bathrooms: 6 private, 3 public; 3 private showers.
Bed & breakfast: £30-£38 single, £48-£55 double.
Parking for 12.
Credit: Access.
🏃 ♿ 📺 🖕 UL 🛌 TV 🐕
✕ T

Hazelwood House Hotel
865 Finchley Rd., Golders Green, London NW11 8LX
☎ 081-458 8884
Bright, sunny rooms and friendly atmosphere. Easy access to the West End and the city.
Bedrooms: 2 single, 1 double & 1 twin, 1 family room.
Bathrooms: 2 public.
Bed & breakfast: £22-£24 single, £34-£36 double.
Parking for 6.
🏃4 📺 🖕 🛌 TV ▦ ♨ 🌀 DAP
🌀 SP T

Hilltop 88
Listed
88 Wembley Hill Rd., Wembley, Middlesex HA9 8DZ
☎ 081-902 7540
Close to Wembley Stadium complex and underground stations.
Bedrooms: 3 single, 1 double, 1 family room.
Bathrooms: 1 public.
Bed & breakfast: £18-£25 single, £35-£38 double.
Parking for 3.
🏃 ♿ 📺 🖕 UL ▦ ♨ ✕

Hilton National Wembley M
👑👑👑👑
Empire Way, Wembley, Middlesex HA9 8DS
☎ 081-902 8839 Telex 24837
ⓒ Hilton
Adjacent to the Wembley complex, this is the headquarters hotel for the conference centre. Within easy reach of major motorways and 20 minutes on the underground from central London.
Bedrooms: 4 single, 82 double & 188 twin, 26 family rooms.
Bathrooms: 300 private.
Bed & breakfast: £93-£100 single, £125-£135 double.
Lunch available.
Evening meal 6.45pm (l.o. 10pm).
Parking for 300.
Credit: Access, Visa, Diners, Amex.
🏃 📞 📺 🖕 ♨ 🖊 V 🖬
● 🌀 ▦ ♨ 🍴 🐕 SP T

Hindes Hotel
👑👑
8 Hindes Rd., Harrow, Middlesex HA1 1SJ
☎ 081-427 7468
Homely owner-run bed and breakfast hotel near the M1. West End 15 minutes by underground. Convenient for Wembley Stadium complex.
Bedrooms: 3 single, 1 double & 7 twin, 2 family rooms.
Bathrooms: 1 private, 3 public.
Bed & breakfast: £28-£30 single, £38-£40 double.
Parking for 5.
Credit: Access, Visa.
🏃 ♿ 📺 🖕 UL 🖊 V 🛌
● ▦ ♨ 🍴 ✕

Holiday Inn Swiss Cottage
128 King Henry's Rd., Swiss Cottage, London NW3 3ST
☎ 071-722 7711 Telex 267396
ⓒ Holiday Inn

Just north of Regent's Park in elegant suburban surroundings, within minutes of the M1, M40 and M4.
Bedrooms: 138 double, 165 family rooms.
Bathrooms: 303 private.
Bed & breakfast: £119-£139 single, £142-£160 double.
Lunch available.
Evening meal 6.30pm (l.o. 10.30pm).
Parking for 132.
Credit: Access, Visa, C.Bl., Diners, Amex.
🏃 ♿ 📺 🖕 UL 🖊 ♨ 🖬
● 🌀 ▦ ♨ 🍴 🐕 🌀 🌀
🌀 ❄ 🌀 SP T

J and T Guest House
98 Park Ave., North, Willesden Green, London NW10 1JY
☎ 081-452 4085
Fax 081-450 2503
Small guesthouse in north west London close to underground. Easy access to Wembley Stadium Complex. 5 minutes from M1.
Bedrooms: 1 single, 1 twin, 1 family room.
Bathrooms: 1 private, 2 public.
Bed & breakfast: £12.50-£15 single, £27-£35 double.
Parking for 2.
🏃 ♿ 📺 🖕 UL ▦ ♨ ✕ 🌀

Kempsford House Hotel
👑👑
21-23 St. John's Rd., Harrow, Middlesex HA1 2EE
☎ 081-427 4983 & 0390
Comfortable, family-run hotel in central Harrow. Convenient for shops, the station and Heathrow Airport.
Bedrooms: 15 single, 7 double & 7 twin, 3 family rooms.
Bathrooms: 10 private, 4 public; 8 private showers.
Bed & breakfast: £29.90-£41.40 single, £41.40-£52.90 double.
Parking for 20.
Credit: Access, Visa.
🏃 ♿ 📺 📺 🖕 🖊 🛌 ● ▦ 🌀 SP
T

Mr and Mrs Kim's Private Guest House
Listed
85 Station Rd., Finchley, London N3 2SH
☎ 081-346 4413 & (0707) 56436
Close to Finchley Central underground and near shops. 15 minutes to central London, access to M1 and M25. German spoken.
Bedrooms: 2 single, 1 double & 1 twin.
Bathrooms: 1 public.

Bed & breakfast: £14-£16
single, £28-£32 double.
Parking for 2.
♿ ⌧ ▭ ⓊL ⌕ ☎ TV ▥ ☐ ⋈
☐ T

La Gaffe M
♛♛
107-111 Heath St.,
Hampstead, London
NW3 6SS
☎ 071-435 4941 & 8965
*On Hampstead Heath, 200
yards from the underground
and 12 minutes from the West
End.*
Bedrooms: 3 single, 6 double
& 4 twin.
Bathrooms: 9 private;
2 private showers.
Bed & breakfast: from £42.50
single, from £65 double.
Lunch available.
Evening meal 6.30pm (l.o.
11.30pm).
Credit: Access, Visa, Diners,
Amex.
♿ ☎ ⊡ ▭ CB ▤ ▤ ⌕ ▥
☐ ⊥ ⌂ ⋈ ⋒ T

The Langorf Hotel M
20 Frognal, Hampstead,
London NW3 6AG
☎ 081-794 4483
*3 minutes' walk from the
underground, elegant
Edwardian residence in
Hampstead boasts 32
attractive bedrooms with full
facilities.*
Bedrooms: 4 single, 20 double
& 8 twin.
Bathrooms: 32 private.
Bed & breakfast: from £49.50
single, from £63 double.
Lunch available.
Evening meal 7pm (l.o. 9pm).
Parking for 5.
Credit: Access, Visa, Diners,
Amex.
♿ ☎ ⌕ ⊡ ▭ ⌕ ⓊL ▤ ⌕
● ▤ ▥ ☐ ⋈ DAP SP ⋒ T

Lindal Hotel
♛♛ COMMENDED
2 Hindes Rd., Harrow,
Middlesex HA1 1SJ
☎ 081-863 3164
*Close to busy town centre with
extensive shopping facilities,
restaurants and cinemas. Easy
reach motorways, central
London and Wembley.*
Bedrooms: 10 single, 3 double
& 7 twin, 1 family room.
Bathrooms: 18 private,
1 public.
Bed & breakfast: £28-£43
single, £45-£53 double.
Evening meal 7pm (l.o.
8.45pm).
Parking for 20.
Credit: Access, Visa.
♿ ☎ ⌕ ⊡ ▭ ⌕ ▤ ⌕ ●
☐ ⊥ ☐ ⋈ ⋒ SP

Mansion House at
Grims Dyke M
♛♛♛♛ COMMENDED
Old Redding, Harrow Weald,
Middlesex HA3 6SH
☎ 081-954 4227
Telex 94014082 MHGD G
*Former residence of W. S.
Gilbert, set in 20 acres of
magnificent gardens and
woodland. A lovely Victorian
country house.*
Bedrooms: 16 double &
27 twin.
Bathrooms: 43 private.
Bed & breakfast: £44-£85
single, £88-£120 double.
Half board: £59-£103 daily,
£550-£589 weekly.
Lunch available.
Evening meal 7pm (l.o.
9.30pm).
Parking for 100.
Credit: Access, Visa, C.Bl.,
Diners, Amex.
♿ ⌧ ▭ ⌕ ⊡ ☐ ⋈ ▥ ☐
⌕ ⌕ ● ▥ ☐ ⊥ ⋃ ⊳ ✳
DAP ⋈ SP ⋒ T

Monksdene Hotel M
2-12 Northwick Park Rd.,
Harrow, Middlesex HA1 2NT
☎ 081-427 2899
Fax 081-863 2314
Telex 919171
*Quiet, comfortable hotel very
close to the centre of Harrow.
Within easy reach of
Heathrow, Wembley
Conference Centre and
Stadium and central London.*
Bedrooms: 17 single,
23 double & 34 twin, 16 family
rooms.
Bathrooms: 90 private.
Bed & breakfast: max. £58
single, max. £75 double.
Lunch available.
Evening meal 7pm (l.o.
9.45pm).
Parking for 65.
Credit: Access, Visa, Diners,
Amex.
♿ ☎ ⌕ ⊡ ▭ ⌕ ⊡ ▤ ▥
TV ● ▥ ☐ ⊥ ⋈ SP T

Moss Hall Hotel M
Listed
10-11 Moss Hall Cres.,
Finchley, London N12 8NY
☎ 081-445 6980
*A Grade II listed building,
comfortable bed and breakfast
hotel. Rooms with en-suite
facilities, colour TV. Close to
tube and buses, free parking.
Full English breakfast.*
Bedrooms: 3 single, 2 double
& 2 twin, 2 family rooms.
Bathrooms: 4 private,
2 public.

Bed & breakfast: £15-£25
single, £25-£40 double.
Parking for 3.
♿ ⌧ ⌕ ⌕ ⊡ ⌕ ⊡ ▤ ▥
☐ TV ▥ ☐ ⋈ ⋈ DAP ⌕ SP ⋒
T

Redland Hotel M
♛♛
418 Seven Sisters Rd.,
London N4 2LX
☎ 081-800 1826 & 9961
Telex 265218 SPRING G
*Next to Manor House
underground station offering
easy access to West End, City
and Heathrow Airport and
close to Alexandra Palace.*
Bedrooms: 8 single, 8 double,
8 family rooms.
Bathrooms: 6 public;
2 private showers.
Bed & breakfast: £30 single,
£39.50 double.
Parking for 12.
Credit: Access, Visa, Diners,
Amex.
♿ ☎ ⊥ ⌕ ⊡ ▤ ⓊL ⌕ TV
☐ ⊥ ⋈ T

Rosslyn House Hotel
♛♛♛
2 Rosslyn Hill, Hampstead,
London NW3 1PH
☎ 071-431 3873 & 3745
Fax 071-433 1775
*Small bed and breakfast hotel
with car parking facilities.*
Bedrooms: 1 single, 3 double
& 8 twin, 3 family rooms.
Bathrooms: 14 private,
2 public.
Bed & breakfast: £39-£49
single, £59-£75 double.
Half board: £48-£58 daily,
£300-£520 weekly.
Evening meal 7pm (l.o. 8pm).
Parking for 12.
Credit: Access, Visa.
♿ ☎ ⌕ ⊡ ▭ ⌕ ▤ ▤ ▥
⋈ DAP SP

Royal Chace Hotel
♛♛♛♛ COMMENDED
162 The Ridgeway, Enfield,
Middlesex EN2 3AR
☎ 081-366 6500 Telex 266628
*A pleasant hotel of character,
set in Green Belt, with access
to London and motorway.
Ideal for businessmen and
tourists.*
Bedrooms: 43 double &
47 twin, 3 family rooms.
Bathrooms: 93 private.
Bed & breakfast: max. £70
single, max. £90 double.
Lunch available.
Evening meal 6pm (l.o.
10pm).
Parking for 300.
Credit: Access, Visa, Diners,
Amex.
♿ ☎ ⌕ ⌕ ⊡ ▭ ⌕ ▤ ▥
☐ ● ▥ ☐ ⊥ ⌕ ✳ ⋈ DAP ⋈ SP
T

Royal Park Hotel
♛♛
350-356 Seven Sisters Rd.,
Finsbury Park, London
N4 2PQ
☎ 081-800 0528 Telex 295141
TXLINK-G
*Facing Finsbury Park with
free car park and garden.
Large public rooms, all
bedrooms with video films,
satellite TV, telephone,
tea/coffee facilities. 4-5
minutes' walk to underground,
city bus stop outside hotel. 24
hour reception, photocopier
available.*
Bedrooms: 10 single, 9 double
& 14 twin, 3 family rooms.
Bathrooms: 8 private,
8 public; 1 private shower.
Bed & breakfast: £30-£35
single, from £45 double.
Half board: £45-£50 daily.
Evening meal 6pm (l.o. 9pm).
Parking for 30.
Credit: Access, Visa, C.Bl.,
Diners, Amex.
♿ ☎ ⌕ ⊡ ▭ ⌕ ▤ ▥ ☐
● ▥ ☐ ⊥ ⌕ ✳ ⋈ DAP SP T

Seaford Lodge M
♛♛
2 Fellows Rd., Hampstead,
London NW3 3LP
☎ 071-722 5032
*Small family-run guest house
convenient for central London
and the City. This hotel has 2
bedrooms that have wheelchair
access and are equipped with
rails in the bathrooms etc.*
Bedrooms: 2 single, 5 double
& 7 twin, 1 family room.
Bathrooms: 15 private.
Bed & breakfast: £35-£46
single, £75-£90 double.
Parking for 6.
Credit: Access, Visa, Diners.
♿ ☎ ⌕ ⊡ ▭ ⌕ ▤ ▥
▭ ☐ ⊥ ☐ T

Spring Park Hotel M
♛♛♛
400 Seven Sisters Rd.,
London N4 2LX
☎ 081-800 6030
Fax 081-802 5652
Telex 265218 SPRING G
*Overlooking Finsbury Park,
next to Manor House
underground station for
Piccadilly line direct to the
West End and Heathrow
Airport.*
Bedrooms: 7 single, 21 double
& 13 twin.
Bathrooms: 19 private,
8 public.
Bed & breakfast: £45-£55
single, £55-£63 double.
Half board: from £54 daily.
Lunch available.
Evening meal 6pm (l.o.
10.45pm).

Continued ▶

35

NORTH LONDON
Continued

Parking for 50.
Credit: Access, Visa, C.Bl., Diners, Amex.

🐎 ♿ 📞 🅿 🖵 💷 🛉 ⬜ 📺 🌐 ⬛ 🎿 ♣ 🗝 SP 📋

Stage Coach Guest House
Listed

58 Brondesbury Rd., London NW6 6BS
☎ 071-624 0274
Small bed and breakfast establishment close to Queens Park underground station. Parking facilities available.
Bedrooms: 1 single, 2 double & 2 twin, 3 family rooms.
Bathrooms: 4 public.
Bed & breakfast: £20-£22 single, from £30 double.
Half board: £140-£150 weekly.
Parking for 3.

🐎 ▮ ♿ 🖵 UL CB 🌐 ⬛ ♣ 🐾

Swiss Cottage Hotel M
👑👑👑👑 **COMMENDED**

4 Adamson Rd., Swiss Cottage, London NW3 3HP
☎ 071-722 2281 Telex 297232
Privately-owned Victorian-style hotel. A la carte restaurant. 24 hour room service. Close to West End.
Bedrooms: 14 single, 24 double & 23 twin, 3 family rooms.
Bathrooms: 58 private, 3 public.
Bed & breakfast: £39-£85 single, £68-£115 double.
Half board: £54-£95 daily, £280-£325 weekly.
Lunch available.
Evening meal 6.30pm (l.o. 9pm).
Parking for 5.
Credit: Access, Visa, C.Bl., Diners, Amex.

🐎 ♿ 📞 🅿 🖵 💷 ⬜ 📺 🌐 ⬛ 🎿 ♣ 🗝 🐾 SP 📋

Tudor Lodge Hotel
50 Field End Rd., Eastcote, Pinner, Middlesex HA5 2QN
☎ 081-429 0585 & 081-866 6027
16th C hotel, with character and taste, offering all modern amenities. Convenient for London airports, motorways and many golf-courses. 25 minutes from town.
Bedrooms: 10 single, 9 double & 6 twin, 8 family rooms.
Bathrooms: 27 private, 5 public.

Bed & breakfast: £25-£62 single, £35-£72 double.
Parking for 40.
Credit: Access, Visa, Amex.

🐎 ♿ 📞 🅿 💷 🖵 🌐 📺 ⬛
🖵 ⬜ ♣ 🎿 ✈ 🗝 SP 🚰

West Lodge Park
👑👑👑👑👑 **COMMENDED**

Cockfosters Rd., Hadley Wood, Near Barnet, Hertfordshire EN4 0PY
☎ 081-440 8311 Telex 24734
White-painted Georgian country house set in 35 acres of grounds in rolling countryside.
Bedrooms: 20 single, 20 double & 10 twin.
Bathrooms: 50 private.
Bed & breakfast: £75-£82.50 single, £99.50 double.
Lunch available.
Evening meal 7pm (l.o. 9.30pm).
Parking for 100.
Credit: Access, Visa, Amex.

🐎 ▮ 📞 🅿 🖵 💷 🛉 ⬜
🌐 ⬛ 🎿 ♣ 🗝 ✈ SP
🚰 📋

White Lodge Hotel M
👑👑👑

1 Church Lane, Hornsey, London N8 7BU
☎ 081-348 9765
Small, friendly family hotel offering personal service. Extended and refurbished in 1989. Easy access to all transport.
Bedrooms: 8 single, 5 double & 3 twin, 2 family rooms.
Bathrooms: 6 private, 3 public.
Bed & breakfast: £20-£22 single, £30-£32 double.
Credit: Access, Visa.

🐎 ♿ 🅿 🖵 💷 UL CB 🌐 📺
🌐 ⬜ ⬛ ✈ 🗝

SOUTH EAST LONDON

Covering the boroughs of Bexley, Bromley, Croydon, Greenwich, Lewisham, Southwark. See map 7.

Alpine Hotel M
16-22 Moreton Rd., South Croydon, Surrey CR2 7DL
☎ 081-688 6116
Family-run hotel, half a mile from Croydon centre and rail stations. Convenient for Victoria, London Bridge and Charing Cross.
Bedrooms: 14 single, 5 double & 12 twin, 4 family rooms.
Bathrooms: 24 private, 4 public.
Bed & breakfast: £33-£42 single, £42-£48 double.

Half board: £41.50-£50.50 daily, £210-£336 weekly.
Lunch available.
Evening meal 7pm (l.o. 9.15pm).
Parking for 28.
Credit: Access, Visa, C.Bl., Diners, Amex.

🐎 ♿ 📞 🅿 🖵 💷 🛉 🖵 📺 🌐
🌐 ⬛ 🎿 ♣ 🗝 SP 📋

The Apollo Hotel
Listed

35-37 Morland Ave., East Croydon, Surrey CR0 6EA
☎ 081-656 8584 & 081-653 2830
Small family-run hotel within 10 minutes' walk of East Croydon station.
Bedrooms: 3 single, 3 double & 3 twin, 5 family rooms.
Bathrooms: 2 public; 10 private showers.
Bed & breakfast: £25-£30 single, £42-£48 double.
Half board: £31-£36 daily.
Evening meal 6.30pm (l.o. 8pm).
Parking for 16.

🐎 ♿ 🅿 🖵 💷 UL 🛉 V 🎿
🖵 ⬛ ♣

Bailey's
77 Belmont Hill, London SE13 5AX
☎ 081-852 7373
Extensively restored old house in good position near Greenwich. 15 minutes by train from central London and 5 minutes from station and local shops.
Bedrooms: 2 twin, 1 family room.
Bathrooms: 1 public.
Bed & breakfast: £12.50-£15 single, £25-£30 double.
Parking for 1.

🐎 ♿ 🅿 🖵 💷 UL 🛉 📺 🖵 ♣
DAP

Be My Guest M
79 Venner Rd., London SE26 5HU
☎ 081-659 5413 & 071-233 0201 Fax: 071-233 0742
The proprietor of this Victorian residence provides bed and breakfast or full board accommodation. Car and driver available on request. Convenient for central London.
Bedrooms: 1 double, 2 family rooms.
Bathrooms: 1 private, 2 public.
Bed & breakfast: £30-£40 single, £36-£45 double.
Half board: £27.50-£50 daily, £161-£350 weekly.
Evening meal (l.o. 10pm).
Parking for 1.

🐎 ♿ 📞 🖵 💷 UL 🛉 V 🖵
🐾 ♣ DAP

Briarley Hotel
👑👑👑

8 Outram Rd., Croydon, Surrey CR0 6XE
☎ 081-654 1000
Fax 081-656 6084
Victorian exterior with a modern 1990s interior, all private facilities. Caring atmosphere.
Bedrooms: 20 single, 8 double & 8 twin, 2 family rooms.
Bathrooms: 38 private.
Bed & breakfast: £55 single, £65 double.
Evening meal 6.30pm (l.o. 10pm).
Parking for 25.
Credit: Access, Visa, Diners, Amex.

🐎 ▮ 📞 🅿 🖵 🛉 V 🎿
🖵 📺 ⬜ ⬛ ♣ 🗝 SP 📋

Buxted Lodge
40 Parkhurst Rd., Bexley, Kent DA5 1AS
☎ Crayford (0322) 54010
Victorian lodge retaining many of the original features, with beautiful grounds. 30 minutes to central London by British Rail.
Bedrooms: 3 single, 3 double & 6 twin, 2 family rooms.
Bathrooms: 2 private, 4 public.
Bed & breakfast: £15-£20 single, £30-£45 double.
Half board: £20-£30 daily, £130-£200 weekly.
Evening meal 6.30pm (l.o. 8pm).
Parking for 14.

🐎 ▮14 ▮ 🅿 🖵 UL ⬜ ⬛
♣ ✈ 🗝

Central Hotel
👑👑👑 **APPROVED**

3-5 South Park Hill Rd., Croydon, Surrey CR2 7DY
☎ 081-688 0840
Fax 081-760 0861
Telex 9312102241 BHG
Small, friendly hotel situated in a quiet residential area. 15 minutes from Croydon town centre.
Bedrooms: 16 single, 4 double & 2 twin, 1 family room.
Bathrooms: 19 private, 1 public; 4 private showers.
Bed & breakfast: £50-£55 single, £60-£65 double.
Lunch available.
Evening meal 6.30pm (l.o. 8pm).
Parking for 30.
Credit: Access, Visa.

🐎 ♿ 🌐 ⬜ 📞 🖵 🛉 V 🖵
📺 🌐 ⬛ ♣ 🗝 SP 📋

Clarendon Hotel M
🌻🌻🌻 APPROVED
8-16 Montpelier Row,
Blackheath, London
SE3 0RW
☎ 081-318 4321 Telex 896367
CLADN G
*Facing the heath and 22
minutes by train from central
London. 10 minutes' walk from
Greenwich, 5 minutes' walk
from Greenwich Royal Park.*
Bedrooms: 47 single,
81 double & 82 twin, 5 family
rooms.
Bathrooms: 170 private,
18 public.
Bed & breakfast: £40.15-£44
single, £65.50-£74.25 double.
Half board: £52.65-£56.50
daily, £368.55-£395.50
weekly.
Lunch available.
Evening meal 6.30pm (l.o.
9.45pm).
Parking for 80.
Credit: Access, Visa, Diners,
Amex.
🌻🐾📞🖭💷🎐🏵💷🗑
🖭💷🎐🐾💷🛥❀🐾
SP 🏮 T

Clevedun Hotel
🌻🌻🌻
503 Footscray Rd., New
Eltham, London SE9 3UH
☎ 081-859 6215
*Close to New Eltham station.
20 minutes from London
Bridge. All rooms have TV and
tea and coffee making
facilities.*
Bedrooms: 2 single, 3 double
& 3 twin, 1 family room.
Bathrooms: 1 private,
3 public.
Bed & breakfast: max. £25
single, £33-£42 double.
Parking for 5.
Credit: Access, Visa.
🌻🐾🎐💷📖💷💷🖭
🎐🏵🐾

Dereen
14 St. Augustines Ave., South
Croydon, Surrey CR2 6BB
☎ 081-686 2075
Small, family guesthouse.
Bedrooms: 1 single, 2 double.
Bathrooms: 2 public.
Bed & breakfast: £13-£14
single, £26-£28 double.
🌻🐾🖭💷🖭📖💷🖭🐾
🐾

Diana Hotel
Listed
88 Thurlow Park Rd.,
London SE21 8HY
☎ 081-670 3250
*Small friendly hotel in a
pleasant suburb of Dulwich, 10
minutes from central London.*

Bedrooms: 2 single, 3 double
& 3 twin, 4 family rooms.
Bathrooms: 2 public;
2 private showers.
Bed & breakfast: £25-£40
single, £30-£40 double.
Evening meal 6pm (l.o.
7.30pm).
Parking for 3.
🌻🐾🖭💷📖💷🎐🏮 T

Driscoll House Hotel
172 New Kent Rd., London
SE1 4YT
☎ 071-703 4175
*Founded in 1913 and opened
by HRH the Princess Louise.
Encouraged and visited by
HM Queen Alexandra. It has
provided accommodation for
50,000 people from 174
countries.*
Bedrooms: 200 single.
Bathrooms: 60 public.
Half board: max. £25 daily,
max. £120 weekly.
Evening meal 5.30pm (l.o.
7pm).
Parking for 10.
🐾📖💷🎐💷📖💷🎐
🐾 DAP 🐾 SP

Glendevon House Hotel
🌻🌻🌻
80 Southborough Rd.,
Bickley, Kent BR1 2EN
☎ 081-467 2183
*Small hotel with private car
park. Convenient for central
London. Caters for tourists and
businessmen.*
Bedrooms: 5 single, 2 double
& 2 twin, 1 family room.
Bathrooms: 1 private,
1 public; 3 private showers.
Bed & breakfast: £18-£24
single, £30-£34 double.
Parking for 6.
Credit: Access, Visa.
🌻🐾🎐💷📖💷📖💷🎐

Haling Park Hotel
🌻🌻
3 Haling Park Rd., South
Croydon, Surrey CR2 6NG
☎ 081-686 6487
*Comfortable family hotel close
to central Croydon and Crystal
Palace. Easy access to
Gatwick Airport.*
Bedrooms: 3 single, 3 double
& 3 twin.
Bathrooms: 1 public.
Bed & breakfast: £12.50-£15
single, £28-£30 double.
Parking for 4.
🌻🐾📖💷🖭💷📖💷🎐
🐾 DAP 🐾 SP

The symbols are
explained on the
flap inside the
back cover.

Holiday Inn London -
Croydon
7 Altyre Rd., Croydon,
Surrey CR9 5AA
☎ 081-680 9200 Telex 8956268
HICROY-G
🆑 Holiday Inn
*An international hotel in the
centre of the business
community, adjacent to East
Croydon station and 18 miles
from Gatwick Airport.*
Bedrooms: 94 single,
80 double & 40 twin.
Bathrooms: 214 private.
Bed & breakfast: £103.50-
£110 single, £124-£132
double.
Lunch available.
Evening meal 6.30pm (l.o.
10.30pm).
Parking for 118.
Credit: Access, Visa, C.Bl.,
Diners, Amex.
🌻🐾📞📖💷🏵🔔💷🖂
🐾📖💷🎐🐾🛥🔔🐾🗑
🐾🏵🗑 SP T

Lonsdale Hotel
🌻🌻
158 Lower Addiscombe Rd.,
Croydon, Surrey CRO 6AG
☎ 081-654 2276
*A small family-run hotel, near
the centre of Croydon. Golf,
swimming, tennis nearby. 10
minutes from Crystal Palace.*
Bedrooms: 6 single, 2 double
& 1 twin, 3 family rooms.
Bathrooms: 2 private,
5 public.
Bed & breakfast: max. £32
single, max. £46 double.
Evening meal 6pm (l.o. 7pm).
Parking for 12.
Credit: Access, Visa.
🌻5📖💷🏵🔔🎐🖭💷🖭
🐾🐾🐾 SP

Markington Hotel
🌻🌻🌻
9 Haling Park Rd., South
Croydon, Surrey CR2 6NG
☎ 081-681 6494
Fax 081-688 6530
*Family-run Victorian property
fitted out to modern standards,
in a quiet road overlooking
woodland. Bus stop 100 yards.*
Bedrooms: 9 single, 8 double
& 4 twin, 1 family room.
Bathrooms: 20 private,
2 public.
Bed & breakfast: £30-£50
single, £48-£60 double.
Half board: £40-£60 daily.
Evening meal 6.30pm (l.o.
8.30pm).
Parking for 17.
Credit: Access, Visa, Amex.
🌻📞💷📖💷🏵🔔💷🖂🖭
🖭💷🎐🐾🛥🐾🐾 SP T

Meadow Croft Lodge M
🌻🌻
96-98 Southwood Rd., New
Eltham, London SE9 3QS
☎
*Between A2 and A20, near
New Eltham station with easy
access to London. Warm and
friendly atmosphere. TV in
rooms.*
Bedrooms: 4 single, 3 double
& 9 twin, 1 family room.
Bathrooms: 1 private,
4 public; 10 private showers.
Bed & breakfast: £20-£27
single, £35-£42 double.
Parking for 9.
Credit: Access, Visa.
🌻📖💷🎐💷💷🖭💷🎐
🐾

Norfolk House Hotel M
🌻🌻🌻
587 London Rd., Thornton
Heath, Croydon, Surrey
CR4 6AY
☎ 081-689 8989
Fax 081-689 0335
*Hotel with wide range of
facilities. Discounts for
weekend group bookings.*
Bedrooms: 35 single,
29 double & 47 twin, 3 family
rooms.
Bathrooms: 114 private.
Bed & breakfast: £24.50-£61
single, £39-£72 double.
Lunch available.
Evening meal 6.30pm (l.o.
10pm).
Parking for 80.
Credit: Access, Visa, Diners,
Amex.
🌻🐾📞💷📖💷🏵🔔💷
🗑💷🎐🐾🛥 DAP SP T

Norwood Lodge Hotel
🌻🌻
17-19 South Norwood Hill,
London SE25 6AA
☎ 081-653 3962
Fax 081-653 0332
*A small comfortable hotel with
a friendly atmosphere. All
rooms with en-suite facilities,
colour TV, trouser press, direct
dial telephone and tea/coffee
making facilities.*
Bedrooms: 6 single, 5 double
& 8 twin, 1 family room.
Bathrooms: 20 private,
1 public.
Bed & breakfast: £35-£55
single, £45-£65 double.
Half board: £30-£62 daily.
Lunch available.
Evening meal 6pm (l.o. 8pm).
Parking for 15.
Credit: Access, Visa, Diners,
Amex.
🌻🐾📞💷📖💷🏵🔔💷🖂🖭
🔔💷🎐🐾🛥🐾 DAP 🐾 SP

SOUTH EAST LONDON

Continued

Rodway Guest House
33 Rodway Rd., Bromley,
Kent BR1 3JP
☎ 081-460 4033
Quiet family-run guesthouse close to Bromley and convenient for London.
Bedrooms: 8 single, 4 double, 3 family rooms.
Bathrooms: 7 private, 3 public.
Bed & breakfast: £25-£30 single, £32-£40 double.
Parking for 8.

Rye Hotel
48 Sydenham Rd., Croydon,
Surrey CR0 2EF
☎ 081-680 1769
Friendly family-run bed and breakfast hotel in the centre of Croydon. Microwave, tea facilities and TV. Bus and train stations within 5 minutes.
Bedrooms: 2 single, 2 double & 7 twin, 4 family rooms.
Bathrooms: 7 private, 5 public.
Bed & breakfast: max. £30 single, from £38 double.
Half board: from £36 daily.
Parking for 15.

Selsdon Park Hotel M
☜ COMMENDED
Sanderstead, South Croydon,
Surrey CR2 8YA
☎ 081-657 8811 Telex 945003
Country house hotel, 10 minutes from the M25, 30 minutes from London and Gatwick. Set in 200 acres of parkland. Special weekend rates.
Bedrooms: 40 single, 50 double & 80 twin.
Bathrooms: 170 private.
Bed & breakfast: £117-£119 single, £130-£158 double.
Half board: £588-£1078 weekly.
Lunch available.
Evening meal 7.30pm (l.o. 9.15pm).
Parking for 265.
Credit: Access, Visa, Diners, Amex.

Shirwin House
Listed
33 Bargery Rd., Catford,
London SE6 2LJ
☎ 081-698 6381

Victorian semi in tree lined road. Comfortable rooms, warm, homely atmosphere. Good transport facilities to Central London.
Bedrooms: 2 double & 6 twin, 2 family rooms.
Bathrooms: 4 public; 2 private showers.
Bed & breakfast: £15-£18 single, £20-£26 double.
Half board: £18-£21 daily, £100-£105 weekly.
Evening meal 6.30pm (l.o. 8pm).
Parking for 1.

Stafford House
7 & 16 Stafford Rd., Sidcup,
Kent DA14 6PX
☎ 081-300 6655
Offering comfortable accommodation with no parking restrictions. Close to 2 railway stations, 30 minutes to Charing Cross.
Bedrooms: 2 single, 1 double & 4 twin, 1 family room.
Bathrooms: 3 public.
Bed & breakfast: £16-£20 single, £30-£35 double.
Parking for 1.

Mrs. J. Stock
Listed
51 Selcroft Rd., Purley,
Surrey CR8 1AJ
☎ 081-660 3054
Central London 20 minutes by train. Convenient for M25, M23 and Gatwick Airport.
Bedrooms: 2 twin.
Bathrooms: 1 public.
Bed & breakfast: £16-£22 single, £32-£44 double.
Open January-November.

Stonehall House Hotel
☜
37 Westcombe Park Rd.,
Blackheath, London
SE3 7RE
☎ 081-858 8706 & (0895) 51948
In a residential area bordering on historic Greenwich. 30 minutes' travelling time to central London.
Bedrooms: 6 single, 6 double & 3 twin, 12 family rooms.
Bathrooms: 4 private, 6 public.
Bed & breakfast: £21-£26 single, £32-£36 double.
Credit: Access, Visa.

Stowcroft Guest House
☜ COMMENDED
Stowcroft, off Lower Camden,
Chislehurst, Kent BR7 5JH
☎ 081-467 7406
Victorian house set in an acre of wooded grounds. Close to M25 and M20, easy access to London.
Bedrooms: 1 single, 1 double & 1 twin, 1 family room.
Bathrooms: 1 private, 1 public; 1 private shower.
Bed & breakfast: £24-£28 single, £37-£40 double.
Half board: £25.50-£31 daily, £153-£186 weekly.
Evening meal 7pm (l.o. 8pm).
Parking for 4.

Traditional Bed and Breakfast
34 Devonshire Dr.,
Greenwich, London SE10 8JZ
☎ 081-691 1918
Small Victorian guesthouse in historic Greenwich. Period decor, good breakfasts, 24-hour access to rooms on separate guest floor.
Bedrooms: 1 single, 1 double & 1 twin.
Bathrooms: 1 public.
Bed & breakfast: £18 single, £32-£36 double.

Wellesley Hotel, Wellesley Centre M
1 Lansdowne Rd., Croydon,
Surrey CR0 2BX
☎ 081-760 9885
Part of the Wellesley Centre with conference facilities, restaurant, leisure and sports complex.
Bedrooms: 10 single, 12 double & 18 twin, 2 family rooms.
Bathrooms: 42 private.
Bed & breakfast: from £49 single, from £59 double.
Half board: £39-£56.50 daily, £232.50-£329.50 weekly.
Lunch available.
Evening meal 5.15pm (l.o. 8pm).
Credit: Access, Visa, Amex.

The White House
Listed
242 Norwood Rd., West Norwood, London
SE27 9AW
☎ 081-670 3607
Listed Georgian house with forecourt parking, on main road. Buses and Southern Region trains to the city. Close to the Crystal Palace Sports Centre.

Bedrooms: 3 single, 1 family room.
Bathrooms: 1 private, 2 public.
Bed & breakfast: £8.50-£10.50 single, £18-£20 double.
Parking for 3.

Wood Vale Hotel
94 Wood Vale, Forest Hill,
London SE23 3ED
☎ 081-693 2438
Bedrooms: 2 single, 5 double & 3 family rooms.
Bathrooms: 1 private, 2 public.
Bed & breakfast: £18-£20 single, £36-£40 double.
Parking for 4.

SOUTH WEST LONDON

Covering the boroughs of Kingston upon Thames, Lambeth, Merton, Richmond, Sutton, Wandsworth. See map 7.

Arundel Hotel
Arundel Ter., London
SW13 9DP
☎ 081-748 8005
Quiet, family-run hotel close to the River Thames and near Kensington. Good, unrestricted parking. Special weekly rates available.
Bedrooms: 9 single, 8 double & 10 twin, 2 family rooms.
Bathrooms: 5 private, 4 public.
Bed & breakfast: from £22.95 single, from £42 double.

Bremic Guest House
☜ COMMENDED
10 Russell Rd., Twickenham,
Middlesex
☎ 081-892 9664
Small family-run guesthouse conveniently located 30 minutes from central London and 20 minutes from Heathrow.
Bedrooms: 3 single, 2 twin, 1 family room.
Bathrooms: 2 private, 1 public.
Bed & breakfast: £25-£30 single, £35-£45 double.
Parking for 5.

Bushy Park Lodge Hotel
Listed
6 Sandy Lane, Teddington,
Middlesex TW11 0DR
☎ 081-943 5428

Close to Kingston Bridge and Hampton Court. Purpose built for 1989: 6 bedrooms with en-suite bathrooms. No restaurant.
Bedrooms: 5 double & 1 twin.
Bathrooms: 6 private.
Bed & breakfast: £35-£45 single, £45-£60 double.
Parking for 8.
Credit: Access, Visa, Amex.

Cannizaro House M
West Side, Wimbledon Common, London SW19 4UF
☎ 081-879 1464
Telex 9413837
CB Thistle
A historic Georgian mansion, set in garden parkland on the edge of Wimbledon Common, offering elegance and tranquillity within easy reach of the capital.
Bedrooms: 29 double & 15 twin, 7 family rooms.
Bathrooms: 51 private.
Bed & breakfast: from £93 single, from £115 double.
Lunch available.
Evening meal 7.30pm (l.o. 10.30pm).
Parking for 60.
Credit: Access, Visa, C.Bl., Diners, Amex.

Charlton Hotel M
The Green, Hampton Court Rd., East Molesey, Surrey KT8 9BW
☎ 081-941 3781
Old world cottage style hotel with banqueting facilities, licensed restaurant and private members club. Close to Hampton Court Palace.
Bedrooms: 6 single, 3 double & 3 twin.
Bathrooms: 7 private, 1 public.
Bed & breakfast: £40-£48 single, £55-£62 double.
Half board: £54-£62 daily.
Lunch available.
Evening meal 7pm (l.o. 9.30pm).
Parking for 35.
Credit: Access, Visa, Diners, Amex.

Chase Lodge
10 Park Rd., Hampton Wick, Kingston upon Thames, Surrey KT1 4AS
☎ 081-943 1862

In conservation area and next to Hampton Court, Bushy Park and River Thames. 20 minutes from centre of London.
Bedrooms: 2 double & 2 twin, 1 family room.
Bathrooms: 3 private, 1 public.
Bed & breakfast: £22-£42 single, £42-£51 double.
Credit: Access, Visa, Amex.

Compton Guest House
Listed
65 Compton Rd., Wimbledon, London SW19 7QA
☎ 081-947 4488 & 081-879 3245
Family-run guesthouse of a high standard, in a pleasant and peaceful area, 5 minutes from Wimbledon station (British Rail and District line), offering quick and easy access to the West End and central London.
Bedrooms: 2 single, 1 double & 2 twin, 3 family rooms.
Bathrooms: 2 public.
Bed & breakfast: £30-£40 single, £40-£50 double.
Evening meal 7pm (l.o. 8pm).
Parking for 2.

Dene Hotel
39 Cheam Rd., Sutton, Surrey SM1 2AT
☎ 081-642 3170
Small family-run hotel in a pleasant garden setting, adjacent to Sutton town centre.
Bedrooms: 11 single, 3 double & 11 twin, 3 family rooms.
Bathrooms: 12 private, 4 public; 2 private showers.
Bed & breakfast: £20.70-£48.30 single, £41.40-£59.80 double.
Parking for 18.

The Dittons Hotel
47 Lovelace Rd., Long Ditton, Surrey KT6 6NA
☎ 081-399 7482
Small country house hotel with a large garden surrounded by trees. Convenient for Hampton Court, Wimbledon, Sandown Park and Richmond. 16 minutes to Waterloo by train.
Bedrooms: 4 single, 3 double & 3 twin, 1 family room.
Bathrooms: 3 public.
Bed & breakfast: £25-£28.75 single, £46 double.
Half board: £40-£50 daily, £150-£250 weekly.
Lunch available.

Evening meal 8pm (l.o. 10pm).
Parking for 8.
Credit: Amex.

Eaton Court Hotel
49 Eaton Rd., Sutton, Surrey SM2 5ED
☎ 081-643 6766
Near countryside, yet only 5 minutes from Sutton station and a 20 minute train journey from London. Ideal for business or pleasure.
Bedrooms: 8 single, 4 double & 7 twin, 2 family rooms.
Bathrooms: 9 private, 2 public.
Bed & breakfast: £31-£41 single, £42-£51 double.
Parking for 10.
Credit: Access, Visa, Amex.

Gloucester House Toplodge M
140 Cavendish Rd., London SW12 0DD
☎ 081-675 4167 & 081-673 6867 Fax: 081-673 1466
Modernised Victorian house of character with up-to-date facilities and direct bus routes to the West End. Offers a happy holiday in a family hotel.
Bedrooms: 2 single, 15 double.
Bathrooms: 17 private, 1 public.
Bed & breakfast: £20-£37 single, £30-£47 double.
Lunch available.
Evening meal 6pm (l.o. 11pm).
Parking for 7.
Credit: Access, Visa, Amex.

The Kew Hotel M
339 Sandycombe Rd., Richmond, Surrey TW9 3NA
☎ 081-948 2902 & 081-940 6114
In a pleasant residential area, two minutes' walk from Kew Gardens underground station and buses.
Bedrooms: 7 single, 6 double & 5 twin.
Bathrooms: 3 private, 4 public; 7 private showers.
Bed & breakfast: from £23 single, from £38 double.
Parking for 8.
Credit: Access, Visa, Amex.

Northside Bed and Breakfast
28 Streatham Common North, London SW16 3HP
☎ 081-761 0510 & 8986 & 081-769 9124
Large detached house offering bed and breakfast accommodation. Overlooking parkland.
Bedrooms: 4 single, 5 double, 3 family rooms.
Bathrooms: 3 private, 3 public; 1 private shower.
Bed & breakfast: £8-£12 single, £12-£15 double.
Half board: £12-£15 daily, £75-£125 weekly.
Parking for 4.

Richmond Park Hotel M
3 Petersham Rd., Richmond, Surrey TW10 6UH
☎ 081-948 4666 Telex 267594 LONSHL
Privately-owned hotel in the heart of Richmond. All rooms en-suite with direct dial telephone, colour TV, radio, tea and coffee making facilities.
Bedrooms: 9 single, 9 double & 6 twin, 3 family rooms.
Bathrooms: 27 private.
Bed & breakfast: max. £69 single, £75-£82 double.
Half board: £84-£89 daily.
Credit: Access, Visa, Diners, Amex.

Riverside Hotel
23 Petersham Rd., Richmond, Surrey TW10 6UH
☎ 081-940 1339
An elegant Victorian house overlooking the Thames, close to Richmond Bridge.
Bedrooms: 4 single, 4 double & 3 twin, 1 family room.
Bathrooms: 9 private, 2 public; 3 private showers.
Bed & breakfast: £37-£48 single, £53-£58 double.
Credit: Access, Visa.

Thatched House Hotel
COMMENDED
135 Cheam Rd., Sutton, Surrey SM1 2BN
☎ 081-642 3131
An old cottage-style detached thatched hotel. Completely modernised. A few minutes from Sutton station and 20 minutes from Central London.

Continued ▶

SOUTH WEST LONDON

Continued

Bedrooms: 8 single, 13 double & 8 twin.
Bathrooms: 18 private, 4 public; 1 private shower.
Bed & breakfast: £32.50-£47.50 single, £47.50-£62.50 double.
Half board: £43-£58 daily.
Evening meal 7pm (l.o. 8.45pm).
Parking for 20.
Credit: Access, Visa, C.Bl.

Warwick Guest House

321 Ewell Rd., Surbiton, Surrey KT6 7BX
☎ 081-399 2405 & 5837
A comfortable family-run guesthouse, close to Kingston town centre, Hampton Court and both the London airports. About 10 miles from London, with a fast train service to the West End. Ideal for tourists and business people.
Bedrooms: 1 single, 4 double & 2 twin, 2 family rooms.
Bathrooms: 1 private, 2 public; 3 private showers.
Bed & breakfast: £26-£32 single, £36-£42 double.
Half board: £23-£37 daily, £150-£225 weekly.
Evening meal 6.30pm (l.o. 4pm).
Parking for 8.
Credit: Access, Visa.

White Walls Guest House

12 Lingfield Ave., Kingston upon Thames, Surrey KT1 2TN
☎ 081-546 2719
Small friendly guesthouse convenient for London, Hampton Court, Windsor Castle, Heathrow and Gatwick Airports.
Bedrooms: 3 single, 2 twin, 3 family rooms.
Bathrooms: 3 private, 1 public; 2 private showers.
Bed & breakfast: from £31.05 single, from £41.40 double.
Parking for 4.

Wimbledon Hotel

78 Worple Rd., Wimbledon, London SW19 4HZ
☎ 081-946 9265 & 081-946 1581

Small hotel offering a high standard of service and friendly, courteous attention. Within easy reach of London, Hampton Court and Kingston.
Bedrooms: 3 single, 6 double & 7 twin, 5 family rooms.
Bathrooms: 5 private, 2 public; 6 private showers.
Bed & breakfast: £38-£42 single, £48-£54 double.
Parking for 9.
Credit: Access, Visa.

WEST LONDON

Covering the boroughs of Ealing, Hammersmith, Hillingdon, Hounslow, also London Airport (Heathrow). See map 7.

Acton Hill Guest House

311 Uxbridge Rd., London W3 9QU
☎ 081-992 2553
Small, friendly guesthouse, close to tube, buses, parks and shops. Rooms with TV, showers. 15 minutes from central London and Heathrow airport. Reasonable rates.
Bedrooms: 4 single, 2 double & 2 twin.
Bathrooms: 3 public; 4 private showers.
Bed & breakfast: £15-£20 single, £25-£30 double.
Parking for 3.

Acton Park Hotel

116 The Vale, Acton, London W3 7JT
☎ 081-743 9417
Fax 081-743 9417
Telex 919412
Just off the North Circular Road, between Heathrow and the West End, overlooking parkland. Ample parking.
Bedrooms: 7 single, 4 double & 8 twin, 2 family rooms.
Bathrooms: 21 private.
Bed & breakfast: from £46 single, from £56.35 double.
Lunch available.
Evening meal 6pm (l.o. 9.30pm).
Parking for 20.
Credit: Access, Visa, C.Bl., Diners, Amex.

Ashleigh

22 Lingwood Gdns., Osterley, Middlesex TW7 5LZ
☎ 081-568 3800

In quiet cul-de-sac, close to Osterley underground station and National Trust house and parkland. Convenient for Heathrow Airport.
Bedrooms: 1 double & 1 twin, 2 family rooms.
Bathrooms: 1 public.
Bed & breakfast: £16-£20 single, £24-£28 double.
Parking for 2.

The Cedars

59 Grange Rd., Ealing, London W5 5BU
☎ 081-579 1070
Privately run bed and breakfast close to Ealing Broadway underground station. Easy access to Heathrow Airport and central London.
Bedrooms: 1 single, 1 double & 1 twin, 2 family rooms.
Bathrooms: 5 private.
Bed & breakfast: £27 single, £38 double.
Parking for 7.

Chiswick Hotel

73 High Rd., London W4 2LS
☎ 081-994 1712 & 4033
Large Victorian house, carefully converted, retaining many original features and with a friendly personal atmosphere. Between Heathrow Airport and central London.
Bedrooms: 19 single, 5 double & 26 twin.
Bathrooms: 50 private, 2 public.
Bed & breakfast: £41-£45 single, £55-£59.50 double.
Half board: £37-£55 daily, £210-£300 weekly.
Evening meal 6pm (l.o. 8pm).
Parking for 15.
Credit: Access, Visa, Diners, Amex.

Grange Lodge

48-50 Grange Rd., Ealing, London W5 5BX
☎ 081-567 1049 Telex 269571
Quiet, comfortable hotel within a few hundred yards of the underground station. Midway between central London and Heathrow.
Bedrooms: 6 single, 1 double & 3 twin, 4 family rooms.
Bathrooms: 4 private, 2 public.

Bed & breakfast: £27-£33 single, £38-£44 double.
Parking for 10.

Gresham Hotel

Listed
10 Hanger Lane, Ealing, London W5 3HH
☎ 081-992 0801
Fax 081-993 7468
Conveniently located family-run bed and breakfast, ideal for London Airport and city centre. Colour TV with Sky movies, tea/coffee facilities in all rooms.
Bedrooms: 4 single, 2 double & 4 twin, 3 family rooms.
Bathrooms: 5 private, 3 public; 3 private showers.
Bed & breakfast: £26-£40 single, £42-£65 double.
Half board: £36-£55 daily.
Evening meal 6.20pm.
Parking for 10.
Credit: Access, Visa.

Kenton House Hotel

5 Hillcrest Rd., Ealing, London W5 2JL
☎ 081-997 8436
Telex 8812544
Family-run hotel with a quiet location opposite a park. Convenient for access to central London.
Bedrooms: 36 single, 3 double & 5 twin, 7 family rooms.
Bathrooms: 51 private.
Bed & breakfast: £53.75-£63.75 single, £61.75-£71.75 double.
Evening meal 6.30pm (l.o. 10pm).
Parking for 27.
Credit: Access, Visa, Diners, Amex.

The Lancers Hotel

34 Barrowgate Rd., London W4 4QY
☎ 081-994 5306 & 9985
Small family-run hotel close to Chiswick Park and Kew Gardens.
Bedrooms: 4 single, 9 twin, 2 family rooms.
Bathrooms: 9 private, 2 public.
Bed & breakfast: £25-£49 single, £44-£55 double.
Evening meal 6pm (l.o. 11pm).
Parking for 6.
Credit: Access, Visa.

Mrs H.E. Miles
37 Brewster Gdns., London
W10 6AQ
☎ 081-969 7024
Pleasant room in a family house, on the bus route to the West End. Close to shops and White City underground station on the Central line.
Bedrooms: 1 family room.
Bathrooms: 1 public.
Bed & breakfast: £7 single, £12-£14 double.
🛏 🛆 Ⅿ Ⅵ ⒸⒷ 🚭 ✕ 🖃

Royal Crimea Hotel Ⓜ
Listed
354 Uxbridge Rd., Acton,
London W3 9SL
☎ 081-992 3853 & 1068
2 minutes' walk from Ealing underground station, offering quick links to Heathrow and the West End.
Bedrooms: 4 single, 7 double & 4 twin.
Bathrooms: 9 private,
3 public.
Bed & breakfast: £23-£30 single, £35-£40 double.
Evening meal 6pm (l.o. 7pm).
Parking for 10.
🛏 🛆 🖃 🖾 ⒯⒱ ▥ 🚭 ✕ ⒹⒶⓅ
🐾 🆂🅿 🆃

St. Peters Hotel Ⓜ
😄😄
407-411 Goldhawk Rd.,
London W6 0SA
☎ 081-741 4239
Situated in West London and opposite an underground station, within easy reach of Heathrow or central London.

Bedrooms: 5 single, 3 double & 7 twin.
Bathrooms: 11 private, 1 public.
Bed & breakfast: £30-£35 single, £40-£48 double.
Credit: Access, Visa, Amex.
🛏 🖃 🖾 ⒯⒱ ▥ 🚭 ✕ 🆂🅿 🆃

Shalimar Hotel Ⓜ
😄😄😄
215-221 Staines Rd.,
Hounslow, Middlesex
TW3 3JJ
☎ 081-572 2816 & 081-577 7070
Family-run hotel. All rooms en-suite with TV, telephone, tea and coffee bar. Close to Heathrow, M4, M25, underground and shopping centre. Residents' bar, evening meals, attractive dining room and lounge.
Bedrooms: 4 single, 5 double & 6 twin, 13 family rooms.
Bathrooms: 18 private; 10 private showers.
Bed & breakfast: £32-£36 single, £42-£46 double.
Half board: £38-£42 daily.
Evening meal 7pm (l.o. 8.30pm).
Credit: Access, Visa, Diners, Amex.
🛏 🛆 📞 🖃 ⒴ ✂ 🚭 ⒯⒱ ◐
▥ 🛆 🕯 🌸 ✕ 🐾 🆂🅿
🆃

Swan Private Guest House
17 Thornton Ave., Chiswick, London W4 1QE
☎ 081-994 2870
Small guest house convenient for Heathrow Airport and central London.
Bedrooms: 6 single, 2 double & 2 twin.
Bathrooms: 1 private, 3 public.
Bed & breakfast: £18-£25 single, £45 double.
Half board: £26.50-£53.50 daily, £175-£374.50 weekly.
Evening meal 6pm (l.o. 9.30pm).
Parking for 4.
🛏 🛆 ⒸⒷ 🖃 ▥ ⓘ ⒱ 🚭 ⒯⒱
◐ ▥ 🛆 🍴 🌸 ✕ ⒹⒶⓅ 🐾 🆂🅿

Wellmeadow Guest House Ⓜ
😄😄
24 Wellmeadow Rd., London W7 2AL
☎ 081-567 7294
Fax 081-566 3468
Charming guesthouse offers high standard accommodation and a warm welcome. Close to tube, easy access to centre and Heathrow.
Bedrooms: 2 single, 2 double.
Bathrooms: 2 public.
Bed & breakfast: £27.50-£33 single, from £44 double.
🛏 📞 ⒸⒷ 🖃 ✂ ▥ ⓘ ⒱ 🚭
⒯⒱ ▥ 🛆 ✕ 🖃

White House
9 Woodville Gdns., Ealing, London W5 2LG
☎ 081-998 9208
Friendly guesthouse in a pleasant part of Ealing, close to public transport and convenient for Heathrow Airport. Large garden.
Bedrooms: 2 single, 8 twin, 2 family rooms.
Bathrooms: 3 public.
Bed & breakfast: from £22 single, from £32 double.
🛏 🛆 ▥ 🖃 ⒯⒱ ◐ ▥ ✕ 🖃

LONDON HEATHROW AIRPORT

Heathrow Sterling Hotel Ⓜ
Terminal 4, Heathrow Airport, Hounslow, Middlesex, TW6 3AF
☎ 081-759 7755 Telex 925094
Opened autumn 1990, connected by covered walkway to Terminal 4. Impressive atrium with 3 restaurants. Leisure club with pool.
Bedrooms: 236 double & 164 twin.
Bathrooms: 400 private.
Bed & breakfast: £110-£125 single, £125-£150 double.
Lunch available.
Evening meal 6pm (l.o. 11pm).
Parking for 250.
Credit: Access, Visa, C.Bl., Diners, Amex.
🛏 🛆 📞 ⒸⒷ 🖃 ✂ ⓘ ⒱ ✂
🖃 ◐ 🅸 ▥ 🛆 🕯 ⊕ 🐾 🆃
🆂🅿 🆃

Key to symbols

Information about many of the services and facilities at establishments listed in this guide is given in the form of symbols. The key to these symbols is inside the back cover flap. You may find it helpful to keep the flap open when referring to the entry listings.

THE HOTEL

Modern facilities in a traditional building. We are an established (20 years), small, clean, family run, bed and breakfast hotel with large rooms, and some very large rooms, all with en-suite facilities.

The hotel has been fully refurbished with considerable care to retain as many of the original features as possible. All bedrooms have full central heating, hot and cold water at all times, colour television and telephones. All the bedrooms having en-suite facilities, you have a choice of bath or shower. The bedrooms are luxuriously decorated with pink, grey and blue being the hotel colours. Special care has been taken to match the curtains, bed spreads, the decor and so forth. All fabric items have been made to measure by hand.

THE PROPERTY

23 Gloucester Place forms part of "one of the most extensive and intact sequence of Georgian terraced houses in London". It was built in the 1700's by Portman Estate, who own large parts of Marble Arch area. Originally used by single families with servants. It reflects the bygone days of the upstairs/downstairs television series. The most obvious feature of the time is the elegant iron lamp standards in front of the buildings. The whole building is listed — Grade two.

SERVICES

The hotel provides the usual facilities, but in addition, with the consent of the management, the use of the kitchen for making one's own tea, coffee and small snacks as well as the use of the microwave is permitted, the criteria is safety and cleanliness.

RATES

As we are well established we are pleased to state that we are extremely competitively priced. There are special discounts for the fourth floor.

CUSTOMERS

Almost 90% of our customers come to us because someone has recommended us. If you are a family, or a seasoned traveller, or require good value, then contact us.

DISADVANTAGE

We have no lift.

3 MINUTES TO OXFORD STREET

23 Gloucester Place,

Portman Square,

London W1H 3PB.

Tel: 071-935 0928
Fax: 071-487 4254

GROUPS WELCOMED

THE LOCATION

LESS THEN FIVE MINUTES WALK FROM:

TUBE STATIONS
Marble Arch, Baker Street and Bond Street.

SHOPPING
Oxford Street with shops like Marks & Spencer, Littlewoods, Selfridges and C&A.

FAMOUS HOTELS
Churchill, Portman, Cumberland and Selfridges.

TOURIST ATTRACTIONS
Madame Tussaud's, Planetarium, Hyde Park, Regents Park and Restaurants to suit every taste.

Use a coupon

When requesting further information from advertisers in this guide, you may find it helpful to use the advertisement enquiry coupons which can be found towards the end of the guide. These should be cut out and mailed direct to the companies in which you are interested. Do remember to include your name and address.

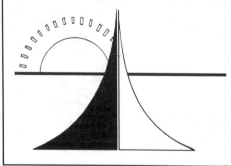

The signs of confidence

Look for signs like these when you're booking accommodation in a hotel, guesthouse, farmhouse, inn or B&B — they tell you that the establishment has been inspected by the Tourist Board and that it meets or exceeds minimum quality standards.

All you have to remember is that the classification (from Listed up to Five Crown) indicates the range of facilities and services while the commendation (Approved, Commended or Highly Commended) indicates the quality standard of the facilities and services.

The absence of a quality commendation from any entry in this 'Where to Stay' guide may be because the establishment had not been quality assessed at the time of going to press.

Check the maps

The place you wish to visit may not have accommodation entirely suited to your needs, but there could be somewhere ideal quite close by. Check the colour maps towards the end of this guide to identify nearby towns and villages with accommodation listed in the guide, and then use the town index to find page numbers.

Hector Breeze

Use a coupon

When enquiring about accommodation you may find it helpful to use the booking enquiry coupons which can be found towards the end of the guide. These should be cut out and mailed direct to the establishments in which you are interested. Do remember to include your name and address.

Cumbria

Mountains and lakes and streams, lush green meadows, waterfalls on rivers running down to a long, lonely coast.

» Crunchy blue snow-frosting in winter, flower carpets in spring, sun-hats and lake-splashed cotton in summer, crisp air and rich purple-russet in autumn. That's Cumbria and its Lake District. Each season outbursting the other.

» Before you come, prepare yourself for an explosion of the senses, not just from scenery but from food — Cumbria is a gastronome's delight! Tucked over hillsides are world-famous hotels and restaurants, just begging to indulge you with creations international and local.

» As you might expect in a mountainous region, there are still arts and crafts unaffected by the 20th century. You can visit a working Victorian woollen mill, see traditional furniture being handmade, watch pottery being thrown, lead crystal blown, and that's just a smidgen.

» Cumbria's heritage is everywhere. From castles like Carlisle, Brougham and Brough to crumbling priories, from Wordsworth's homes to houses more stately, from galleries with local views and priceless art to the Beatrix Potter Gallery, from indoor museums to the magnificent Hadrian's Wall — all this you can avoid only with great ingenuity.

» And then there are the towns. Like historic Carlisle among the forests and sheep-dotted hills of the Borders, and Alston on the wild North Pennine Moors, England's highest market town, complete with cobbled streets and

Hadrian's Wall is so famous and photographed that you might expect your first sight of it to disappoint. Not so: it surpasses expectation!

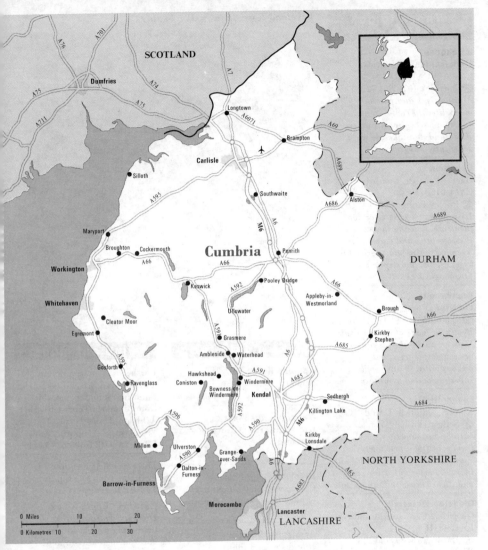

narrow-gauge railway. The port of Whitehaven was the home of Jonathan Swift, and way south are pretty Sedbergh in the Dales and Grange-over-Sands on Morecambe Bay.

»> **Please refer to the colour maps at the back of this guide for all places with accommodation listings.**

»> Include Lakeland haunts such as Kendal, Keswick and Windermere and you have something even Disney couldn't reproduce — the genuine article!

Where to go, what to see

Mirehouse
Underskiddaw, Keswick,
Cumbria CA12 4QE
☎ Keswick (076 87) 72287
*Manuscripts and portraits with
many literary connections.
Victorian schoolroom/nursery.
Woodland and lakeside walk,
adventure playgrounds.*

Dalemain
Dacre, Penrith, Cumbria
CA11 0HB
☎ Pooley Bridge (076 84) 80450
*Historic house with Georgian
furniture, housing the
Westmorland and Cumberland
Yeomanry Museum. Agricultural
bygones, adventure playground,
famous gardens.*

Brantwood
Coniston, Cumbria LA21 8AD
☎ Coniston (053 94) 41396
*Beautiful home of John Ruskin
housing works by Ruskin and
his contemporaries and
memorabilia. Nature walk,
superb lake and mountain views.*

Levens Hall
Kendal, Cumbria LA8 0PB
☎ Sedgwick (053 95) 60321
*Elizabethan mansion
incorporating a pele tower.
Famous topiary garden laid out
in 1692, steam collection, play
and picnic areas, plants for sale.*

Gleaston Watermill
Gleaston, Ulverston, Cumbria
LA12 0QH
☎ Bardsea (0229) 869244
*Water cornmill in working
order. Impressive wooden
machinery and waterwheel.
Farm equipment and tools
display, craft workshop.*

Kendal Museum
Station Road, Kendal,
Cumbria LA7 6BZ
☎ Kendal (0539) 721374
*Outstanding natural history
gallery with reconstructions of
Lake District habitats, World
Wildlife Gallery. Local history
in Westmorland Gallery.*

Lakeland Rose Show – 13–14 July

Make a date for...

Appleby Horse Fair
Appleby, Cumbria
6–12 June

Musgrave Rushbearing
Great Musgrave, Brough,
Cumbria
6 July

Lakeland Rose Show
Cark Showfield, Flookburgh,
Grange-over-Sands, Cumbria
13–14 July

Ambleside Sports
Rydal Park, Rydal,
Ambleside, Cumbria
1 August

Carlisle Great Fair
Carlisle, Cumbria
24 August–1 September

Egremont Crab Fair
Baybarrow, Egremont,
Cumbria
14 September

Find out more

Further information about
holidays and attractions in the
Cumbria region is available
from: **Cumbria Tourist Board,**
Ashleigh, Holly Road,
Windermere, Cumbria
LA23 2AQ. ☎ (096 62) 4444.

These publications are
available from the Cumbria
Tourist Board (post free):

*Cumbria English Lake
District Touring Map*
(including tourist information
and touring caravan and
camping parks) £1.95

*Places to Visit and Things
to Do in Cumbria English
Lake District* (over 200 ideas
for a great day out) 75p

Wordsworth's Lake District
(an illustrated guide and map)
25p

Places to stay

➤ Accommodation entries in this regional section are listed in alphabetical order of place name, and then in alphabetical order of establishment.

➤ The map references refer to the colour maps towards the end of the guide. The first figure is the map number; the letter and figure which follow indicate the grid reference on the map.

➤ The symbols at the end of each accommodation entry give information about services and facilities. A 'key' to these symbols is inside the back cover flap, which can be kept open for easy reference.

ALSTON

Cumbria
Map ref 5B2

Market town amongst the highest fells of the Pennines and close to the Pennine Way in an area of outstanding natural beauty.

High Fell Hotel M
COMMENDED

Alston, CA9 3BP
☎ (0434) 381597
Built in 1623 and situated off the road above Alston town on the A686. Fine open views across the South Tyne valley.
Bedrooms: 1 single, 4 double & 1 twin.
Bathrooms: 5 private, 2 public.
Bed & breakfast: £19.25-£27.50 single, £38.50-£55 double.
Half board: £30.25-£41.25 daily, £181.50-£247.50 weekly.
Evening meal 8pm (l.o. 8pm).
Parking for 20.
Credit: Access, Visa.

Hillcrest Hotel M

Townfoot, Alston, CA9 3RN
☎ (0434) 381251
Fine country house hotel in a magnificent setting, a warm welcome, relaxed atmosphere and fine food. A perfect break.
Bedrooms: 1 single, 4 double & 4 twin.
Bathrooms: 3 private, 4 public.
Bed & breakfast: £21-£30 single, £40-£55 double.

Lunch available.
Evening meal 7pm (l.o. 8.30pm).
Parking for 25.
Credit: Access, Visa.

Lovelady Shield Country House Hotel M
COMMENDED

Nenthead Rd., Alston, CA9 3LF
☎ (0434) 381203 Fax (0434) 381515
Attractive Georgian-style country house standing in its own grounds. Idyllic and peaceful situation in the scenic high Pennines.
Bedrooms: 2 single, 6 double & 4 twin.
Bathrooms: 12 private.
Bed & breakfast: £32 single, £29-£41 double.
Half board: £48-£59 daily, £306-£370 weekly.
Lunch available.
Evening meal 7.30pm (l.o. 8.30pm).
Parking for 25.
Open February-December.
Credit: Access, Visa, Diners, Amex.

Lowbyer Manor Hotel M
APPROVED

Alston, CA9 3JX
☎ Alston (0434) 381230

We advise you to confirm your booking in writing.

Traditional 17th C stone-built manor house in its own gardens and grounds, offering a quiet, warm and friendly atmosphere. Retaurant with traditional a la carte menu. Old world bar. Elegant drawing room.
Bedrooms: 1 single, 6 double & 4 twin.
Bathrooms: 11 private.
Bed & breakfast: £29 single, £50.50 double.
Half board: £38.05-£44.10 daily, £245-£265 weekly.
Lunch available.
Evening meal 7pm (l.o. 8.30pm).
Parking for 14.
Credit: Access, Visa, Diners, Amex.

Nent Hall Country House Hotel M
COMMENDED

Nenthall, Alston, CA9 3LQ
☎ (0434) 381584
Country house hotel of character and charm located 3 miles out of Alston on A689 Stanhope to Durham road.
Bedrooms: 8 double.
Bathrooms: 8 private.
Bed & breakfast: £25-£30 single, £40-£60 double.
Half board: £37-£45 daily, £200-£280 weekly.
Lunch available.
Evening meal 7pm (l.o. 9pm).
Parking for 24.
Credit: Access, Visa.

AMBLESIDE

Cumbria
Map ref 5A3

4m NW. Windermere
At the head of Lake Windermere and surrounded by fells. Good centre for touring, walking and sailing.

Birch House M

11 Birch St., Windermere, LA23 1EG
☎ (096 62) 5070
Small family-run guesthouse in quiet street, near to shops, restaurants and station.
Bedrooms: 4 double.
Bathrooms: 4 private.
Bed & breakfast: £10-£15 single, £17-£30 double.
Half board: £119-£210 weekly.

Borrans Park Hotel M

Borrans Rd., Ambleside, LA22 0EN
☎ (053 94) 33454
Recently converted Georgian house in a secluded position between the village and the lake. We offer candlelit dinners, four-posters and 120 fine wines.
Bedrooms: 1 single, 10 double & 3 twin.
Bathrooms: 13 private, 1 public.
Bed & breakfast: £26-£60 single, £52-£64 double.
Half board: £39-£45 daily, £260-£302 weekly.
Continued ▶

51

AMBLESIDE
Continued

Evening meal 7pm (l.o. 8pm).
Parking for 20.
Credit: Access, Visa.

Brantfeil Guest House M
Rothay Rd, Ambleside,
LA22 0BZ
☎ (053 94) 32239
A traditional Victorian house in the centre of Ambleside with views towards the fells.
Bedrooms: 1 single, 2 double & 2 twin, 1 family room.
Bathrooms: 2 private, 2 public.
Bed & breakfast: £11.50-£14.50 single, £23-£35 double.
Half board: £19.50-£25.50 daily, £125-£161 weekly.
Evening meal 7pm (l.o. 7.15pm).
Parking for 1.

Chapel House Hotel
Kirkstone Rd., Ambleside,
LA22 9DZ
☎ (053 94) 33143
In old Ambleside and converted from 16th C cottages. Overlooking the village and fells, our aim is to provide friendly service, food and wine in relaxed and comfortable surroundings.
Bedrooms: 2 single, 5 double & 2 twin, 1 family room.
Bathrooms: 4 private, 2 public.
Bed & breakfast: £48-£63 double.
Half board: £29.50-£31.50 daily, £154-£168 weekly.
Evening meal 7pm (l.o. 7pm).
Parking for 6.
Open March-December.

Cherry Garth Hotel M
Old Lake Rd., Ambleside,
LA22 0DH
☎ (053 94) 33128
Lakeland house in landscaped gardens, midway between the town and the head of Lake Windermere, with uninterrupted views. Attractive bedrooms.
Bedrooms: 8 double & 2 twin.
Bathrooms: 8 private, 1 public.
Bed & breakfast: £19-£32 single, £38-£64 double.
Half board: £29-£42 daily, £130-£220 weekly.

Evening meal 7pm (l.o. 9pm).
Parking for 10.
Credit: Access, Visa.

Compston House Hotel M
APPROVED
Compston Rd., Ambleside,
LA22 9DJ
☎ (053 94) 32305
Lakeland-stone hotel in Ambleside village, with lovely views of surrounding fells. All rooms en-suite with colour TV and teamakers.
Bedrooms: 6 double & 1 twin, 1 family room.
Bathrooms: 8 private.
Bed & breakfast: £29-£45 double.
Evening meal 7pm (l.o. 5pm).

Crow How Hotel M
Rydal Rd., Ambleside,
LA22 9PN
☎ (053 94) 32193
Victorian country house in a quiet location, with 2 acres of grounds. Only 1 mile from the centre of Ambleside.
Bedrooms: 6 double & 1 twin, 2 family rooms.
Bathrooms: 9 private.
Bed & breakfast: £20-£23 single, £48-£55 double.
Half board: £30-£37.50 daily, £189-£220 weekly.
Evening meal 7.30pm (l.o. 7.30pm).
Parking for 12.

The Dower House
Wray Castle, Ambleside,
LA22 0JA
☎ (053 94) 33211
The house overlooks Lake Windermere, 3 miles from Ambleside. Come through the main gates of Wray castle and up the drive.
Bedrooms: 2 double & 1 twin.
Bathrooms: 2 public.
Bed & breakfast: £17.50 single, £34-£35 double.
Half board: £25-£25.50 daily, £175-£178.50 weekly.
Evening meal 7pm (l.o. 7.30pm).
Parking for 14.

Elder Grove Hotel M
COMMENDED
Lake Rd., Ambleside,
LA22 0DB
☎ (053 94) 32504

Elegant Victorian family-run hotel. Central and with a unique Lakeland stone dining room, imaginative cooking, relaxing bar and pretty bedrooms.
Bedrooms: 2 single, 7 double & 2 twin, 1 family room.
Bathrooms: 12 private.
Half board: from £35.75 daily, £219-£235 weekly.
Evening meal 7.30pm (l.o. 7.30pm).
Parking for 14.
Open March-November.
Credit: Access, Visa.

Eltermere Country House Hotel M
COMMENDED
Elterwater, Ambleside,
LA22 9HY
☎ Langdale (096 67) 207
Friendly country house hotel. Personally run by the owners in a quiet rural setting in the heart of the Langdale Valley.
Bedrooms: 3 single, 8 double & 7 twin.
Bathrooms: 15 private, 3 public.
Bed & breakfast: £25-£28 single, £50-£56 double.
Half board: £35-£39.50 daily, £235-£248 weekly.
Evening meal 7pm (l.o. 8pm).
Parking for 20.

Eversly
Low Gale, Ambleside,
LA22 0BB
☎ (053 94) 33311
Family-run guesthouse above the noise, yet only a few minutes' walk from the town centre.
Bedrooms: 1 single, 2 double & 2 twin, 1 family room.
Bathrooms: 1 public.
Bed & breakfast: £12-£15 single, £24-£28 double.
Parking for 1.

Ferndale Hotel M
Lake Rd., Ambleside,
LA22 0DB
☎ (0966) 32207
Small friendly family-run hotel in the heart of the Lakes, offering comfortable accommodation and traditional English fare.
Bedrooms: 6 double & 1 twin, 1 family room.
Bathrooms: 7 private, 1 public.
Bed & breakfast: £13.50-£17.50 single, £27-£35 double.
Half board: £22-£26 daily, £147-£171.50 weekly.

Lunch available.
Evening meal 7pm.
Parking for 6.

Fisherbeck Farmhouse M
Old Lake Rd., Ambleside,
LA22 0DH
☎ (053 94) 32523
Off the main road, a few minutes' level walk from the centre of Ambleside. Not a working farm.
Bedrooms: 2 double & 1 twin.
Bathrooms: 1 public.
Bed & breakfast: £13-£15 single, £26-£30 double.
Parking for 3.
Open March-November.

Fisherbeck Hotel M
COMMENDED
Lake Rd., Ambleside,
LA22 0DH
☎ (053 94) 33215
Family-run hotel ideally situated for touring and all lakeland activities, overlooking Loughrigg Fell. Reputation for good food and comfort.
Bedrooms: 1 single, 14 double & 2 twin, 3 family rooms.
Bathrooms: 17 private, 2 public; 1 private shower.
Bed & breakfast: £26.50-£29.50 single, £45-£54 double.
Half board: £29-£39 daily, £195-£265 weekly.
Lunch available.
Evening meal 7pm (l.o. 7.30pm).
Parking for 20.
Credit: Access, Visa.

The Gables Hotel M
Compston Rd., Ambleside,
LA22 9DJ
☎ (053 94) 33272
In a quiet residential area overlooking the park, tennis courts, bowling green and Loughrigg Fell. Convenient for the shops, walking and water sport.
Bedrooms: 3 single, 6 double, 4 family rooms.
Bathrooms: 13 private.
Bed & breakfast: £17-£20 single, £35-£40 double.
Half board: £27-£30 daily, from £189 weekly.
Evening meal 7pm (l.o. 5pm).
Parking for 7.
Open January-November.

Ghyll Head Hotel ⋔
≝≝≝

Waterhead, Ambleside,
LA22 0HD
☎ (053 94) 32360
Family hotel in a good position overlooking Lake Windermere and well placed for touring the Lake District.
Bedrooms: 1 single, 3 double & 7 twin, 1 family room.
Bathrooms: 12 private.
Bed & breakfast: £23-£26 single, £46-£52 double.
Half board: £30-£35 daily, £210-£234 weekly.
Evening meal 6.30pm (l.o. 7.30pm).
Parking for 12.
⑃ ➡ 🖵 🛉 🌢 ▮ Ⓥ ᓚ 🎮 🖷
🚻 🏴 🐾 ❀ ⚲ SP

Grey Friar Lodge Country House Hotel ⋔
≝≝≝

Brathay, Ambleside,
LA22 9NE
☎ (053 94) 33158
Lovely, traditional Lakeland stone country house overlooking the River Brathay valley.
Bedrooms: 5 double & 2 twin, 1 family room.
Bathrooms: 8 private.
Half board: £29.50-£38 daily, £178-£238 weekly.
Evening meal 7pm (l.o. 7.30pm).
Parking for 12.
Open March-October.
⑃ 12 🖵 🕮 ▯ 🖵 🛉 ▮ Ⓥ ⚡
ᓚ 🖷 🏴 ❀ 🚻 🏴 SP

Hillsdale Hotel ⋔
≝≝ APPROVED

Church St., Ambleside,
LA22 0BT
☎ (053 94) 33174
Family-run hotel in centre of village. 10 minutes' walk from lake. Central for touring all lakes and near bowling green, tennis courts and putting green.
Bedrooms: 1 single, 6 double & 1 twin.
Bathrooms: 1 private, 1 public; 4 private showers.
Bed & breakfast: from £18 single, £30-£36 double.
⑃ ➡ 🖵 UL 🛉 ▮ Ⓥ ᓚ 🖷
ᓚ 🏴

The Horseshoe Hotel ⋔
≝≝≝

Rothay Rd., Ambleside,
LA22 0EE
☎ (053 94) 32000
Well-appointed hotel with magnificent mountain views. Healthy traditional and wholefood cuisine. Parking.

Bedrooms: 1 single, 6 double & 5 twin, 8 family rooms.
Bathrooms: 14 private, 2 public.
Bed & breakfast: £23-£27 single, £46-£58 double.
Half board: £30-£39 daily, £210-£270 weekly.
Evening meal 7.30pm (l.o. 8pm).
Parking for 20.
Credit: Access, Visa.
⑃ ➡ 🖵 🛉 ▮ Ⓥ ⚡ ᓚ 🖷
ᓚ 🏴 ⚲ SP ⊤

Kirkstone Foot Country House Hotel ⋔
≝≝≝ COMMENDED

Kirkstone Pass Rd.,
Ambleside, LA22 9EH
☎ (053 94) 32232
Secluded 17th C manor house in its own grounds, with adjoining self-contained apartments and cottages.
Bedrooms: 1 single, 9 double & 4 twin, 2 family rooms.
Bathrooms: 16 private.
Half board: £35-£47.50 daily, £253-£311.50 weekly.
Evening meal 8pm (l.o. 8.30pm).
Parking for 30.
Open February-December.
Credit: Access, Visa, Diners, Amex.
⑃ ➡ 🖵 🛉 🌢 ▮ Ⓥ ᓚ
🖷 ᓚ 🕮 ⚲ ➘ ❀ 🏴 🏴 ⚲ SP
⊤

Langdale Hotel ⋔
≝≝≝≝

Great Langdale, Nr.
Ambleside, LA22 9JB
☎ (096 67) 302 Telex 65188
En-suite hotel, winner of 1986 Civic Trust environmental award, in 35 acres of wooded grounds. Indoor country club, large pool, spa-bath, sports facilities, restaurants and bars. Minimum stay 2 nights.
Bedrooms: 38 double & 27 twin.
Bathrooms: 65 private.
Half board: from £59 daily.
Lunch available.
Evening meal 7pm (l.o. 10pm).
Parking for 120.
Credit: Access, Visa, Diners, Amex.
⑃ ➡ ➡ 📞 🕮 🖵 🛉 ▮ Ⓥ
ᓚ ⚫ 🖷 ᓚ 🛉 🌢 🕒 ➘ 🕮
⚲ ⊤ 🏴 ◔ 🕮 🏴 🌢 🏴 ⚲ 🔟
🏴 ⊤
⚫ Display advertisement appears on page 86.

Lattendale Hotel ⋔
≝≝≝

Compston Rd., Ambleside,
LA22 9DJ
☎ (053 94) 32368

Traditional Lakeland hotel, in the heart of Ambleside. A good base for many pursuits, offering interesting food and wines in a comfortable and relaxed atmosphere.
Bedrooms: 2 single, 2 double & 2 twin, 1 family room.
Bathrooms: 5 private, 1 public.
Bed & breakfast: £12-£13.50 single, £30-£34 double.
Half board: £21-£26.50 daily, £140-£170 weekly.
Evening meal 5.30pm (l.o. 7.30pm).
Open February-December.
Credit: Access, Visa.
⑃ ➡ 🖵 🛉 🌢 ▮ Ⓥ ᓚ 🖷 🖷
ᓚ 🏴 🏴 ⚲ SP

Laurel Villa Hotel ⋔
≝≝ COMMENDED

Lake Rd., Ambleside,
LA22 0DB
☎ (053 94) 33240 &
(053 94) 32744 (Guests)
Recently refurbished family-run Victorian house overlooking the fells. Within easy walking distance of the village and Lake Windermere.
Bedrooms: 2 single, 5 double & 2 twin.
Bathrooms: 9 private.
Bed & breakfast: £50 double.
Half board: £40 daily.
Evening meal 7pm (l.o. 5pm).
Parking for 14.
Open February-November.
Credit: Access, Visa.
⑃ ➡ 🖵 🛉 🌢 Ⓥ ⚡ 🖷 ᓚ
➘ 🏴 🏴 🏴 SP ⊤

Loughrigg Brow ⋔
≝≝

Ambleside, LA22 9SA
☎ (053 94) 3229
Telex 667047
A large country house beautifully positioned amongst some of the finest mountain scenery to be found in the British Isles.
Bedrooms: 6 single, 14 twin, 6 family rooms.
Bathrooms: 10 public.
Half board: £26.45-£28.45 daily, £185-£199 weekly.
Lunch available.
Evening meal 7pm.
Parking for 20.
⑃ 2 🌢 🖵 ▮ Ⓥ ᓚ 🖷 ᓚ 🛉
🔫 ❀ 🏴 🏴 🏴 ⚲ SP ⊤

Lyndhurst Hotel ⋔
≝≝

Wansfell Rd., Ambleside,
LA22 0EG
☎ (053 94) 32421
Attractive Victorian lakeland stone family-run hotel, with private car park. In quiet position. Friendly service, all amenities.
Bedrooms: 4 double & 2 twin, 1 family room.

Bathrooms: 7 private.
Bed & breakfast: £17.50-£19.50 single, £35-£44 double.
Half board: £25.50-£30.50 daily, £175-£205 weekly.
Evening meal 6.30pm (l.o. 8pm).
Parking for 8.
Open February-December.
⑃ 🖵 🛉 🌢 ▮ Ⓥ ᓚ 🖷
🖷 🏴 🏴 DAP ⚲ SP

Meadowbank
≝≝≝

Rydal Rd., Ambleside,
LA22 9BA
☎ (053 94) 32710
Overlooking open meadowland and Loughrigg Fell. Ideal for walking, lovely views from the garden.
Bedrooms: 1 single, 2 double & 2 twin, 2 family rooms.
Bathrooms: 3 private, 2 public.
Bed & breakfast: £29-£37 double.
Parking for 10.
Open March-November.
⑃ 🌢 🛉 UL Ⓥ ⚡ ᓚ 🖷 🖷 ᓚ
ᓚ 🏴 ❀ 🏴 🏴 🏴

Melrose Guest House
≝≝

Church St., Ambleside,
LA22 0BT
☎ (053 94) 32500
Typical stone terraced Victorian Lakeland house on four floors.
Bedrooms: 1 single, 1 twin, 4 family rooms.
Bathrooms: 3 private, 1 public.
Bed & breakfast: £11.50-£15 single, £23-£32 double.
⑃ 4 🖵 🛉 UL Ⓥ ᓚ 🖷 🖷 ᓚ
🏴 SP

Nanny Brow Country House Hotel ⋔
≝≝≝≝ COMMENDED

Clappersgate, Ambleside,
LA22 9NF
☎ (053 94) 32036
Country house in 5 acres of secluded gardens with magnificent views. Lying below Loughrigg Fell, 2 miles from Ambleside.
Bedrooms: 1 single, 10 double & 5 twin, 3 family rooms.
Bathrooms: 17 private, 1 public.
Bed & breakfast: £53-£88 single, £86-£156 double.
Half board: £50-£85 daily, £335-£565 weekly.
Evening meal 7.45pm (l.o. 7.45pm).
Parking for 22.
Open February-November.
Credit: Access, Visa, Amex.
⑃ ➡ 📞 🖵 🛉 🌢 ▮ Ⓥ ᓚ
🖷 ᓚ 🛉 🕒 ➘ ❀ 🏴 🏴 SP ⊤

CUMBRIA

AMBLESIDE
Continued

The Old Vicarage M
Vicarage Rd., Ambleside,
LA22 9DH
☎ (053 94) 33364
*Lakeland stone house
pleasantly situated in own
grounds in heart of village.
Lovely views. All en-suite. Own
car park.*
Bedrooms: 5 double & 2 twin,
2 family rooms.
Bathrooms: 9 private.
Bed & breakfast: from £38
double.
Parking for 11.

Queens Hotel M
Market Place, Ambleside,
LA22 9BU
☎ (053 94) 32206
Fax (053 94) 32721
*2 fully licensed bars and 1
restaurant. In the heart of the
Lakes and convenient for
walking, climbing and other
leisure activities.*
Bedrooms: 4 single, 15 double
& 2 twin, 3 family rooms.
Bathrooms: 24 private,
2 public.
Bed & breakfast: £25-£30
single, £20-£25 double.
Half board: £32-£37 daily.
Lunch available.
Evening meal 7pm (l.o.
10pm).
Parking for 10.
Credit: Access, Visa, Diners,
Amex.

Riverside Hotel M
Under Loughrigg, Nr.
Rothay Bridge, Ambleside,
LA22 9LJ
☎ (053 94) 32395
*Small country hotel in a
peaceful setting overlooking the
river; with extensive grounds
and direct access on to the
fells.*
Bedrooms: 6 double & 2 twin,
2 family rooms.
Bathrooms: 10 private.
Bed & breakfast: £25-£32
single, £48-£60 double.
Half board: £34-£38 daily,
£227.50-£240 weekly.
Evening meal 7pm (l.o. 8pm).
Parking for 20.
Open February-November.
Credit: Access, Visa.

Rothay Garth Hotel M
COMMENDED
Rothay Rd., Ambleside,
LA22 0EE
☎ (053 94) 32217
*Comfortable, warm, distinctive
hotel in central Lakeland.
Elegant Loughrigg restaurant
overlooks lovely gardens and
nearby mountains. Close to
village centre and Lake
Windermere. All-season
breaks.*
Bedrooms: 2 single, 8 double
& 3 twin, 3 family rooms.
Bathrooms: 14 private,
2 public.
Bed & breakfast: £23-£39
single, £46-£78 double.
Half board: £35-£52 daily,
£223-£317 weekly.
Lunch available.
Evening meal 7pm (l.o. 8pm).
Parking for 17.
Credit: Access, Visa, Diners,
Amex.

Rothay Manor Hotel M
COMMENDED
Rothay Bridge, Ambleside,
LA22 0EH
☎ (053 94) 33605
*Elegant Regency country house
hotel with a well-known
restaurant. Balcony rooms
overlook the garden. Family
suites. Disabled guests and
children welcome.*
Bedrooms: 2 single, 6 double
& 3 twin, 7 family rooms.
Bathrooms: 18 private.
Bed & breakfast: £63 single,
£88-£98 double.
Half board: £66-£71 daily,
£435-£466 weekly.
Lunch available.
Evening meal 8pm (l.o. 9pm).
Parking for 40.
Open February-December.
Credit: Access, Visa, Diners,
Amex.

The Rysdale Hotel M
Rothay Rd., Ambleside,
LA22 0EE
☎ (053 94) 32140
*Enjoy the friendly atmosphere
of our family-run hotel. Good
food and magnificent views of
the Lakeland fells. En-suite
and family rooms.*
Bedrooms: 1 single, 4 double
& 1 twin, 3 family rooms.
Bathrooms: 4 private,
2 public; 1 private shower.
Bed & breakfast: £15-£20
single, £30-£40 double.

Half board: £25-£29 daily,
£160-£190 weekly.
Evening meal 7pm (l.o. 5pm).
Parking for 2.
Open January-November.
Credit: Access, Visa.

The Salutation Hotel M
Lake Road, Ambleside,
LA22 9BX
☎ (053 94) 32244
Fax (053 94) 34157
*A 32-bedroomed hotel in the
centre of Ambleside. Recent
redevelopment under new
ownership.*
Bedrooms: 2 single, 20 double
& 6 twin, 4 family rooms.
Bathrooms: 32 private.
Bed & breakfast: £22-£31
single, £44-£62 double.
Half board: £33-£43 daily.
Lunch available.
Evening meal 7pm (l.o. 9pm).
Parking for 40.
Credit: Access, Visa.

Skelwith Bridge Hotel M
Ambleside, LA22 9NJ
☎ (053 94) 32115
*A traditional 17th C Lakeland
hotel set in the heart of the
Lakes at the gateway to the
Langdale Valley.*
Bedrooms: 4 single, 10 double
& 7 twin, 3 family rooms.
Bathrooms: 24 private.
Bed & breakfast: £20-£37
single, £38-£65 double.
Half board: £25-£47 daily,
£175-£300 weekly.
Evening meal 7pm (l.o. 9pm).
Parking for 60.
Credit: Access, Visa.

Thorneyfield Guest House M
APPROVED
Compston Rd., Ambleside,
LA22 9DJ
☎ (053 94) 32464
*Cosy family-run guesthouse in
the town centre with friendly
and helpful service. Close to
the park, miniature golf, tennis
and lake.*
Bedrooms: 1 single, 2 double
& 1 twin, 2 family rooms.
Bathrooms: 2 public.
Bed & breakfast: £13-£15
single, £28-£32 double.
Parking for 3.

Wanslea Guest House M
APPROVED
Lake Rd., Ambleside,
LA22 0DB
☎ (053 94) 33884
*Spacious, comfortable, family-
run Victorian guesthouse.
English cooking a speciality.
Superb views. Easy walk to
lake and village. Packed
lunches available.*
Bedrooms: 1 single, 3 double
& 1 twin, 3 family rooms.
Bathrooms: 2 private,
3 public.
Bed & breakfast: £15-£20
single, £30-£38 double.
Half board: £23-£28 daily,
£140-£155 weekly.
Evening meal 6.45pm (l.o.
6.45pm).

Wateredge Hotel M
COMMENDED
Waterhead Bay, Ambleside,
LA22 0EP
☎ (053 94) 32332
*Delightful location with
gardens extending to lake's
edge. Private jetty. Relaxed,
friendly atmosphere. Log fires.*
Bedrooms: 3 single, 11 double
& 8 twin, 1 family room.
Bathrooms: 23 private.
Bed & breakfast: £40.50-
£51.50 single, £68-£124
double.
Half board: £42-£70 daily,
£294-£420 weekly.
Lunch available.
Evening meal 7pm (l.o.
8.30pm).
Parking for 25.
Open February-December.
Credit: Access, Visa, Amex.
Display advertisement
appears on page 87.

Waterhead Hotel M
APPROVED
Ambleside, LA22 0ER
☎ (053 94) 32566
Telex 65273 WATERHEAD
Fax (053 94) 34275
*On the edge of Lake
Windermere, makes an ideal
central base for touring the
lovely English Lakes.*
Bedrooms: 3 single, 10 double
& 12 twin, 1 family room.
Bathrooms: 26 private.
Bed & breakfast: £32-£53
single, £64-£102 double.
Half board: £47-£56 daily,
£259-£378 weekly.
Lunch available.
Evening meal 7pm (l.o.
8.30pm).
Parking for 50.

54

Credit: Access, Visa, Diners, Amex.

♨ 🍴 📞 📺 🖥 🏧 🔊 Ⅴ ⬜ 📺 🅿 🍴 ⟳ ♪ ▶ ✳ ⚲ SP Ⓣ

APPLEBY-IN-WESTMORLAND
Cumbria
Map ref 5B3

Former county town of Westmorland, at the foot of the Pennines in the Eden Valley. The castle was rebuilt in the 17th C, except for its Norman keep and the ditches and ramparts. It now houses a Rare Breeds Survival Trust Centre. Good centre for walking and exploring the Eden Valley.
Tourist Information Centre ☎ *(07683) 51177*

Appleby Manor Country House Hotel M
😊😊😊😊 COMMENDED

Roman Rd., Appleby-in-Westmorland, CA16 6JD
☎ (076 83) 51571
Telex 94012971
Ⓑ Best Western
Country house hotel with fine timber features, in wooded grounds overlooking Appleby Castle. Panoramic views of the Pennines and the Lakeland Fells. Indoor leisure club.
Bedrooms: 11 double & 11 twin, 8 family rooms.
Bathrooms: 30 private.
Bed & breakfast: £42.50-£51 single, £65-£80 double.
Half board: £42-£60 daily, £270-£387 weekly.
Lunch available.
Evening meal 7pm (l.o. 9pm).
Parking for 48.
Credit: Access, Visa, Diners, Amex.

♨ 🍴 ♿ 📞 ® 🖥 📺 🔊 Ⅴ ✂ ⬜ 🏧 🍴 ⚙ 🎿 🅡 ⟳ ▶ ✳ ⚲ SP 🏤 Ⓣ

Bongate House M
😊😊😊 APPROVED

Appleby-in-Westmorland, CA16 6UE
☎ (076 83) 51245
Family-run Georgian guesthouse on the outskirts of a small market town. Large garden. Relaxed friendly atmosphere and good food.
Bedrooms: 1 single, 1 double & 2 twin, 4 family rooms.
Bathrooms: 5 private, 1 public.
Bed & breakfast: £13.50 single, £27-£32 double.

Half board: £19.50-£22 daily, £125-£140 weekly.
Evening meal 7pm (l.o. 6pm).
Parking for 10.

♨ 7 ⚙ 🖥 🍴 📺 🖥 🏧 🍴
⟳ 🅿 ✳ DAP SP 🏤

New Inn
Brampton, Appleby-in-Westmorland, CA16 6JS
☎ (076 83) 51231
A small family-run inn of character, circa 1730. In the Vale of Eden, midway between the dales and Lake District.
Bedrooms: 1 double & 1 twin, 1 family room.
Bathrooms: 2 public.
Bed & breakfast: £17.50-£20 single, £35 double.
Lunch available.
Evening meal 7pm (l.o. 9pm).
Parking for 30.

♨ 🖥 🏧 🖥 Ⅴ ⬜ 🏧 ⟳ ▶ ✂ 🏤 🏤

Royal Oak Inn M
😊😊😊 COMMENDED

Bongate, Appleby-in-Westmorland, CA16 6UN
☎ (076 83) 51463
Historic coaching inn with beamed ceilings and oak panelling. Offering traditional ales, malt whiskies, food, wine and a warm welcome.
Bedrooms: 2 single, 2 double & 3 twin.
Bathrooms: 4 private, 1 public.
Bed & breakfast: £23.50-£34 single, from £50 double.
Lunch available.
Evening meal 6.30pm (l.o. 9pm).
Parking for 9.
Credit: Access, Visa, Diners.

♨ 🖥 ⚙ 🖥 🏧 Ⅴ ⬜ 🏧 ⟳ 🍴 🏤 SP 🏤

The Tufton Arms Hotel
😊😊😊😊 COMMENDED

Market Sq., Appleby-in-Westmorland, CA16 6XA
☎ Appleby (076 83) 51593
Ⓑ Consort
Coaching and posting inn at the centre of this historic county town. Ideal for the beautiful Eden Valley, the Lakes, High Pennines, Yorkshire Dales and Hadrian's Wall.
Bedrooms: 5 single, 6 double & 6 twin, 2 family rooms.
Bathrooms: 17 private, 1 public.
Bed & breakfast: £30-£45 single, £45-£95 double.
Half board: £30-£55 daily, £210-£385 weekly.
Lunch available.
Evening meal 7pm (l.o. 9.30pm).
Parking for 35.

Credit: Access, Visa, Diners, Amex.

♨ 🍴 ⟳ 📞 🖥 ⚙ 🖥 Ⅴ ⬜ 🖥 Ⓣ

ASPATRIA
Cumbria
Map ref 5A2

8m NE. Maryport
Market town in agricultural surroundings on the A596 between Wigton and Maryport. Facilities for bowls and tennis at St. Mungo's park.

Field End M
Listed

Parsonby, Aspatria, CA5 2DE
☎ (069 73) 21720
Small guesthouse in a quiet village 1.5 miles from Lake District National Park. Home cooking. 6 miles from Cockermouth, just off B5301.
Bedrooms: 1 double & 1 twin, 1 family room.
Bathrooms: 1 public.
Bed & breakfast: from £26 double.
Half board: from £19.50 daily, from £136.50 weekly.
Evening meal 7pm.
Parking for 4.

♨ 6 ⬜ 🖥 🏧 📺 🖥 🏤

BAMPTON
Cumbria
Map ref 5B2

3m NW. Shap

Haweswater Hotel M
Lakeside Rd., Bampton, Nr. Penrith, CA10 2RP
☎ (093 13) 235
9 miles from exit 39 on M6 via Shap, Bampton. Most rooms have magnificent views of the lake. Tranquil isolation.
Bedrooms: 6 single, 5 double & 3 twin, 3 family rooms.
Bathrooms: 4 public; 2 private showers.
Bed & breakfast: £20-£23 single, £32-£40 double.
Half board: £27.95-£30.95 daily.
Lunch available.
Evening meal 7pm (l.o. 9pm).
Parking for 6.
Credit: Access, Visa, Diners, Amex.

♨ 12 ⚙ 🖥 🏧 Ⅴ ✂ 🏧 📺 🖥
🏧 🍴 ✳ DAP ⚲ SP 🏤

BARROW-IN-FURNESS
Cumbria
Map ref 5A3

Modern shipbuilding and industrial centre on a peninsula in Morecambe Bay. Ruins of 12th C Cistercian Furness Abbey. Sandy beaches and a nature reserve on Walney Island.
Tourist Information Centre ☎ *(0229) 870156*

Abbey House Hotel M
😊😊😊😊

Abbey Rd., Barrow-in-Furness, LA13 0PA
☎ Barrow (0229) 838282
Fax (0229) 820403
Friendly and inviting country house hotel, an excellent base for touring the Lakes.
Bedrooms: 3 single, 11 double & 5 twin, 8 family rooms.
Bathrooms: 27 private.
Bed & breakfast: £60.50-£65.50 single, £75.50-£85.50 double.
Half board: £77-£82 daily.
Evening meal 7pm (l.o. 10pm).
Parking for 60.
Credit: Access, Visa, Diners, Amex.

♨ 🍴 🏧 📞 🖥 ⚙ 🖥 Ⅴ
🏧 ● 🏧 🏧 🍴 ⚙ & ▶ ✳ SP 🏤 Ⓣ

Arlington House Hotel and Restaurant M
😊😊😊😊 COMMENDED

200/202 Abbey Rd., Barrow-in-Furness, LA14 5LD
☎ (0229) 831976
A relaxed hotel with an elegant restaurant. In the town, yet not far away from the Lakes and sea.
Bedrooms: 8 double.
Bathrooms: 8 private.
Bed & breakfast: £40-£47.50 single, £60-£75 double.
Half board: from £55 daily.
Evening meal 7.30pm (l.o. 9pm).
Parking for 32.
Credit: Access, Visa.

♨ 📞 🖥 ⚙ 🖥 Ⅴ ⬜ 🖥
🏧 🍴 🎿 ✳ ✂ 🏤

Chetwynde Hotel
😊😊😊

369 Abbey Rd., Barrow-in-Furness, LA13 9JS
☎ (0229) 811011
Quiet hotel with a residential restaurant. Near Furness Hospital and Furness Abbey. Pleasant beaches and beautiful countryside. Family rooms are available.

Continued ▶

55

CUMBRIA

BARROW-IN-FURNESS
Continued

Bedrooms: 3 single, 12 double & 4 twin, 1 family room.
Bathrooms: 20 private.
Bed & breakfast: £41.50-£66 single, £53-£79.50 double.
Lunch available.
Evening meal 7pm (l.o. 9pm).
Parking for 30.
Credit: Access, Visa, Amex.

East Mount Hotel
55, East Mount, Barrow-in-Furness, LA13 9AD
☎ (0229) 825242
Easy access to amenities, close to bus route. Some en-suite rooms available, TV, tea/coffee facilities in all rooms. Home cooking.
Bedrooms: 4 single, 3 double & 3 twin, 2 family rooms.
Bathrooms: 2 private, 2 public; 1 private shower.
Bed & breakfast: £15-£25 single, £26-£35 double.
Half board: £20-£30 daily.
Evening meal 6pm (l.o. 4pm).
Parking for 12.
Credit: Visa.

The Gables
197 Abbey Rd., Barrow-in-Furness, LA14 5JP
☎ (0229) 825497
Friendly family-run hotel, all bedrooms with TV and tea-making facilities. Restaurant and licensed bar.
Bedrooms: 7 single, 2 double & 5 twin.
Bathrooms: 2 public; 3 private showers.
Bed & breakfast: £12-£17 single, £28-£36 double.
Evening meal 7pm (l.o. 9pm).
Parking for 6.

Lisdoonie Private Hotel M
307 Abbey Rd., Barrow-in-Furness, LA14 5LF
☎ (0229) 827312
Small family owned hotel with extensive banqueting facilities.
Bedrooms: 3 single, 4 double & 4 twin, 1 family room.
Bathrooms: 12 private.
Bed & breakfast: £25-£40 single, £35-£50 double.
Half board: £32-£47 daily, £220-£299 weekly.

Evening meal 6pm (l.o. 8pm).
Parking for 40.
Credit: Access, Visa, Amex.

BASSENTHWAITE
Cumbria
Map ref 5A2
Village near the north end of Bassenthwaite Lake. The area is visited by many varieties of migrating birds.

Overwater Hall M
Bassenthwaite, Ireby Nr. Carlisle, CA15 1HH
☎ (059 681) 566
Peaceful and secluded 18th C country house with superb views, in 20 acres of woodland and gardens.
Bedrooms: 1 single, 6 double & 3 twin, 3 family rooms.
Bathrooms: 13 private.
Bed & breakfast: £31 single, £52 double.
Half board: £40-£45 daily, from £230 weekly.
Evening meal 7pm (l.o. 8.30pm).
Parking for 25.
Open February-December.
Credit: Access, Visa.

Ravenstone Hotel M
Bassenthwaite, Nr. Keswick, CA12 4QG
☎ (059 681) 240
Charming dower house offering comfort and relaxation in beautiful surroundings. Hospitable bar, full-size snooker table, games room. Personal service.
Bedrooms: 1 single, 9 double & 3 twin, 1 family room.
Bathrooms: 14 private, 1 public.
Bed & breakfast: £22-£24 single, £44-£48 double.
Half board: £28-£30 daily, £189-£203 weekly.
Evening meal 7pm (l.o. 7.30pm).
Parking for 20.
Open April-October.

Rigg's Cottage
Routenbeck, Bassenthwaite Lake, Cockermouth, CA13 9YN
☎ (059 681) 580
Small, very quiet and off the beaten track. 17th C oak-beamed building with inglenook fireplace, log fires and orchard and stream. We use fresh produce and home-made bread and jams.

Bedrooms: 1 double & 1 twin, 1 family room.
Bathrooms: 1 public.
Bed & breakfast: max. £19.50 double.
Half board: max. £25 daily.
Lunch available.
Evening meal 6.30pm (l.o. 6.30pm).
Parking for 3.
Open February-November.

BORROWDALE
Cumbria
Map ref 5A3
Lying south of Derwentwater in the heart of the Lake District, the valley is backed by towering fells and mountains. Good centre for walking and climbing.

Borrowdale Gates Country House Hotel & Restaurant M
Grange-in-Borrowdale, Keswick, CA12 5UQ
☎ (059 684) 204 & 606
Country house hotel central for walking, windsurfing and fishing. 4 bedrooms are especially fitted out for wheelchairs.
Bedrooms: 3 single, 10 double & 8 twin, 2 family rooms.
Bathrooms: 23 private, 1 public.
Bed & breakfast: £27.50-£40 single, £51-£75 double.
Half board: £39-£50 daily.
Lunch available.
Evening meal 7pm (l.o. 8.45pm).
Parking for 40.
Credit: Access, Visa.

Derwent House M
COMMENDED
Grange-in-Borrowdale, Borrowdale, CA12 5UY
☎ (076 87) 77658
Victorian, family-run guesthouse in the lovely Borrowdale Valley. All rooms enjoy beautiful views of surrounding fells.
Bedrooms: 5 double & 4 twin, 1 family room.
Bathrooms: 6 private, 1 public.
Bed & breakfast: £21-£26 single, £32-£42 double.
Half board: £25-£30 daily, £175-£210 weekly.
Evening meal 7pm (l.o. 7pm).

Parking for 10.
Open February-December.
Credit: Diners.

Hazel Bank Hotel M
COMMENDED
Rosthwaite, Borrowdale, Nr. Keswick, CA12 5XB
☎ (076 87) 77248
Victorian country house in 4 acres of parkland with views of the Lakeland mountains. Elegant lounge and bar with log fires.
Bedrooms: 1 single, 4 double & 4 twin.
Bathrooms: 8 private, 2 public.
Half board: £30-£32 daily, £195-£210 weekly.
Evening meal 7pm.
Parking for 12.
Open March-November.

Leathes Head Hotel M
Borrowdale, Keswick, CA12 5UY
☎ (059 684) 247
In the peaceful Borrowdale Valley and within easy reach of the surrounding fells and lakes.
Bedrooms: 2 single, 5 double & 4 twin.
Bathrooms: 9 private, 1 public.
Bed & breakfast: £23-£27.50 single, £40-£50 double.
Half board: £30.50-£45 daily, £210-£250 weekly.
Evening meal 7.30pm (l.o. 8.15pm).
Parking for 20.
Open January-November.
Credit: Access, Visa.

Royal Oak Hotel M
COMMENDED
Rosthwaite, Borrowdale, Nr. Keswick, CA12 5XB
☎ (076 87) 77214
Small family-run, traditional Lakeland hotel 6 miles south of Keswick. Cosy atmosphere, home cooking and friendly service.
Bedrooms: 2 single, 4 double & 2 twin, 4 family rooms.
Bathrooms: 8 private, 3 public.
Half board: £20-£31 daily, £144-£203 weekly.
Evening meal 7pm (l.o. 7pm).
Parking for 12.
Open January-November.
Credit: Access.

BOWLAND BRIDGE

Cumbria
Map ref 5A3

Hare & Hounds Inn M

Bowland Bridge, Grange-over-Sands, LA11 6NN
☎ Crosthwaite (044 88) 777 or 333
An inn with oak beams and log fires. In the beautiful Winster Valley, 5 miles from Lake Windermere.
Bedrooms: 13 double & 1 twin, 2 family rooms.
Bathrooms: 13 private, 1 public.
Bed & breakfast: £28-£38 single, £40-£50 double.
Half board: £30-£38 daily.
Lunch available.
Evening meal 7pm (l.o. 9pm).
Parking for 100.
Credit: Access, Visa.

BRAITHWAITE

Cumbria
Map ref 5A3

At the entry to Whinlatter Pass, the starting point for climbing Grisedale Pike.

Coledale Inn M
☸☸☸ COMMENDED
Braithwaite, Keswick, CA12 5TN
☎ (059 682) 272
Victorian country house hotel and Georgian inn in a peaceful hillside position away from traffic, with superb mountain views.
Bedrooms: 1 single, 2 double & 1 twin, 4 family rooms.
Bathrooms: 8 private.
Bed & breakfast: £16-£18 single, £36-£44 double.
Lunch available.
Evening meal 6.30pm (l.o. 9pm).
Parking for 15.
Credit: Access, Visa.

Ivy House Hotel M
☸☸☸ COMMENDED
Braithwaite, Keswick, CA12 5SY
☎ (059 682) 338
Oak-beamed house with log fires, in a small village among the fells. An elegant restaurant offers traditional English and French dishes. Restaurant is non-smoking.
Bedrooms: 8 double & 1 twin.
Bathrooms: 9 private.
Bed & breakfast: £58-£70 double.

Half board: £252-£294 weekly.
Evening meal 7pm (l.o. 7pm).
Parking for 8.
Open February-December.
Credit: Access, Visa, Diners, Amex.

BRAMPTON

Cumbria
Map ref 5B2

9m NE. Carlisle
Pleasant market town and a good centre from which to explore Hadrian's Wall. Lanercost Priory is 2 miles away.

Kirby Moor Country House Hotel M
☸☸☸ COMMENDED
Longtown Rd., Brampton, CA8 2AB
☎ (069 77) 3893
A detached Victorian house on the A6071 well back from the road with ample parking and extensive views. 6 miles from Hadrian's Wall. Set in 2.5 acres of grounds.
Bedrooms: 1 single, 3 double & 1 twin, 1 family room.
Bathrooms: 6 private, 1 public.
Bed & breakfast: from £25 single, from £32 double.
Half board: from £35 daily, from £160 weekly.
Lunch available.
Evening meal 7pm (l.o. 9.30pm).
Parking for 30.
Credit: Access, Visa.

White Lion Hotel M
☸☸
High Cross St., Brampton, CA8 1RP
☎ (069 77) 2338
Comfortable 17th C hotel in centre of market town with log fires and home cooking. Well positioned for Hadrian's Wall and Carlisle.
Bedrooms: 1 single, 5 double & 3 twin.
Bathrooms: 6 private, 1 public.
Bed & breakfast: £16.50-£22 single, £33-£40 double.
Lunch available.
Evening meal 6pm (l.o. 9pm).
Parking for 6.
Credit: Access, Visa.

BROUGHTON-IN-FURNESS

Cumbria
Map ref 5A3

Old market village whose historic charter is still proclaimed every year on the first day of August in the market square, when coins are distributed. Good centre for touring the Duddon Valley.

The Garner Guest House M
Church St., Broughton-in-Furness, LA20 6HJ
☎ (0229) 716462
Comfortable Victorian family house of character, with a sunny walled garden. On the outskirts of this old market town.
Bedrooms: 2 double & 1 twin.
Bathrooms: 1 private, 1 public.
Bed & breakfast: max. £16.50 single, £25-£28 double.
Half board: £21.25-£22.75 daily, £148.75-£159.25 weekly.
Evening meal 7pm.

BUTTERMERE

Cumbria
Map ref 5A3

Halfway between the north end of Buttermere Lake and Crummock Water, this village is an ideal centre for walking and climbing the nearby peaks.

Bridge Hotel Limited M
☸☸☸
Buttermere, Cockermouth, CA13 9UZ
☎ (059 685) 252
A typical Lakeland hotel with modern comforts and facilities, in an area of outstanding beauty which is superb walking country.
Bedrooms: 2 single, 12 double & 8 twin.
Bathrooms: 22 private.
Half board: £41-£46 daily, £266-£301 weekly.
Lunch available.
Evening meal 7pm (l.o. 8.30pm).
Parking for 30.

CALDBECK

Cumbria
Map ref 5A2

Quaint limestone village lying at the northern edge of the Lake District National Park. John Peel, the famous huntsman who is immortalised in song, is buried in the churchyard.

High Greenrigg House M
☸☸☸ APPROVED
Caldbeck, Wigton, CA7 8HD
☎ Caldbeck (069 98) 430
Converted 17th C farmhouse in the remote northern fells of the Lake District National Park. Home cooking and a warm welcome.
Bedrooms: 2 single, 3 double & 2 twin, 1 family room.
Bathrooms: 6 private, 1 public.
Bed & breakfast: £19.50-£24.50 single, £39 double.
Half board: £29.50-£34.50 daily, £177-£207 weekly.
Evening meal 7pm (l.o. 4pm).
Parking for 8.
Open March-October.

CARLISLE

Cumbria
Map ref 5A2

Near the border with Scotland, this cathedral city suffered years of strife through the centuries, often changing hands between England and Scotland. The red sandstone cathedral with its beautiful east window is the second smallest cathedral in England. The castle was founded in 1092 and later enlarged. The keep now houses a museum of the history of the Border Regiment.
Tourist Information Centre ☎ *(0228) 512444*

Avondale
3 St. Aidan's Road Carlisle
☎ (0228) 23012
ttractive Edwardian house, quiet situation close to city centre. All rooms with own bath, T.V. Private parking. M6 Junction 43.
Bedrooms: 1 double & 2 twin.
Bathrooms: 3 private, 1 public.
Bed & breakfast: £13-£15 single, £26-£30 double.

Continued ▶

Half board: £17.50-£19.50 daily, £116-£130 weekly. Evening meal 6.30pm (l.o. midday).
Parking for 3.
♿ ⃣ ♨ ✉ UL CB Ⓥ 🛏 TV ▦
🛆 ✂ ✗ ⌗ ⃝DAP SP

Broad Lea Guest House ⋔
👑👑
25 Broad St., Carlisle, CA1 2AG
☎ (0228) 24699
Within 10 minutes' walk of the city centre, railway and bus stations. A quiet residential area near the park, golf-course and river.
Bedrooms: 2 single, 1 double & 1 twin.
Bathrooms: 1 public; 4 private showers.
Bed & breakfast: £14-£14.50 single, £26-£27 double.
Half board: £18 daily, £126 weekly.
Lunch available.
Evening meal 6pm (l.o. 4pm).
Parking for 4.
Credit: Access, Visa, Amex.
Ⓡ ⃣ ♨ UL 🛡 Ⓥ 🛏 TV ▦
🛆 ⌗ ⃠ SP Ⓣ

Calreena Guest House ⋔
🅰APPROVED
123 Warwick Road, Carlisle, CA1 1JZ
☎ Carlisle (0228) 25020
Comfortable friendly guesthouse. Central heating. Home cooking. Colour TV and tea making facilities in all rooms. 2 minutes from city centre, railway and bus stations. 2 minutes from M6 junction 43.
Bedrooms: 1 single, 1 double & 1 twin, 1 family room.
Bathrooms: 2 public.
Bed & breakfast: £11 single, £22 double.
Half board: £15 daily.
Evening meal 5pm (l.o. 8pm).
♿ ⃣ ♨ UL 🛡 Ⓥ 🛏 TV 🛆
⌗ SP

Central Plaza Hotel ⋔
👑👑👑
Victoria Viaduct, Carlisle, CA3 8AL
☎ (0228) 20256 Fax (0228) 514657
Elegant, traditional hotel with comfortable accommodation. Ideal base for exploring Lakes, Borders and the many historic attractions of this area.

Bedrooms: 19 single, 36 double & 25 twin, 4 family rooms.
Bathrooms: 84 private.
Bed & breakfast: £55-£65 single, £66-£76 double.
Half board: £69.50-£79.50 daily, £276.50-£350 weekly.
Lunch available.
Evening meal 7pm (l.o. 9pm).
Parking for 25.
Credit: Access, Visa, Diners, Amex.
♿ ✆ ⃝ ⃣ ♨ 🛡 Ⓥ 🛏 TV
⬤ ⃞ ▦ 🛆 ⌗ DAP ⃠ SP 🎏
Ⓣ

Chatsworth Guesthouse ⋔
👑👑 APPROVED
22 Chatsworth St., Carlisle, CA1 1HF
☎ (0228) 24023
Listed Victorian town house, overlooking Chatsworth Gardens. Floral frontage mentioned in 1988 "Cumbria in Bloom" competition. Close to shops, restaurants, bus and train stations, castle and cathedral. M6 exit 43.
Bedrooms: 1 single, 3 twin, 2 family rooms.
Bathrooms: 1 private, 2 public.
Bed & breakfast: £12.50-£18 single, £22-£30 double.
Half board: £16-£21 daily, £100-£150 weekly.
Evening meal 5pm (l.o. 6.30pm).
Parking for 2.
♿ ⃣ ♨ UL 🛡 TV ▦ 🛆 ✝
❄ ✗ DAP SP

Cornerways ⋔
107 Warwick Rd., Carlisle, CA1 1EA
☎ (0228) 21733
5 minutes to rail and bus stations, city centre. M6 exit 43. Lounge, colour TV, central heating, payphone bedrooms, tea and coffee facilities. Private parking.
Bedrooms: 2 single, 1 double & 4 twin, 1 family room.
Bathrooms: 2 public.
Bed & breakfast: £10.50 single, £21 double.
Half board: £14 daily, £95 weekly.
Lunch available.
Parking for 6.
♿ ♨ ⃣ ♨ UL Ⓥ 🛏 TV
▦ 🛆 DAP ⃠ SP

County Hotel ⋔
4, Botchergate, Carlisle, CA1 1QS
☎ (0228) 31316 Fax (0228) 515456
Follow signs to railway station, 200 yards from the station turn right onto Botchergate. Built in 1853.

Bedrooms: 30 single, 31 double & 16 twin, 8 family rooms.
Bathrooms: 85 private.
Bed & breakfast: £32-£38 single, £39-£48 double.
Half board: £38-£42 daily.
Lunch available.
Evening meal 7pm (l.o. 10pm).
Parking for 120.
Credit: Access, Visa, Diners, Amex.
♿ ✆ ⃝ ⃣ ♨ 🛡 Ⓥ ⃠ 🛆
TV ⬤ ⃞ ▦ 🛆 ✝ 👫 DAP
SP 🎏

Crown Hotel ⋔
👑👑👑👑
Wetheral, Nr. Carlisle, CA4 8ES
☎ (0228) 61888 Telex 64175
In a country village, 2 miles from the M6. Originally an 18th C farmhouse; now a hotel providing conference and leisure facilities.
Bedrooms: 4 single, 27 double & 17 twin, 1 family room.
Bathrooms: 49 private.
Bed & breakfast: £83-£97 single, £100-£114 double.
Half board: £97-£111 daily.
Lunch available.
Evening meal 7pm (l.o. 9.30pm).
Parking for 60.
Credit: Access, Visa, Diners, Amex.
♿ 🛆 🏊 ⃠ ✆ ⃝ ⃣ ♨ Ⓥ
🏹 ☉ ⃞ ❄ ⃠ SP 🎏 Ⓣ

Cumbrian Hotel ⋔
👑👑👑👑 COMMENDED
Court Square, Carlisle, CA1 1QY
☎ (0228) 31951 Telex 64287
Ⓖ Best Western
This building dates from 1852, was used by Queen Victoria and overlooks the Crown Court and the old city.
Bedrooms: 26 single, 36 double & 30 twin, 4 family rooms.
Bathrooms: 96 private.
Bed & breakfast: from £72 single, from £87.50 double.
Lunch available.
Evening meal 7pm (l.o. 10pm).
Parking for 30.
Credit: Access, Visa, C.Bl., Diners, Amex.
♿ ⃣ ✆ ⃝ ⃣ 🛡 Ⓥ ⃠
🛏 ⬤ ⃞ ▦ 🛆 ✝ ✗ ⃠ SP
🎏 Ⓣ

Howard House ⋔
👑👑👑 COMMENDED
27 Howard Place, Carlisle, CA1 1HR
☎ (0228) 29159

Lawrence and Sandra invite you to their Victorian home. Four-poster, 2 rooms en-suite, all with colour TV and tea making. Quiet location, 2 minutes to city centre. Family historians welcome.
Bedrooms: 1 single, 1 double & 1 twin, 2 family rooms.
Bathrooms: 2 private, 2 public.
Bed & breakfast: £12-£13 single, £22-£30 double.
Half board: £16-£21 daily, £107-£120 weekly.
Evening meal 6pm (l.o. 10am).
♿ ⃣ ⃝ ⃣ ♨ UL 🛡 Ⓥ 🛆
TV ▦ 🛆 ▸ SP Ⓣ

Killoran Country House Hotel ⋔
The Green, Wetheral, Carlisle, CA4 8ET
☎ Wetheral (0228) 60200
Built in 1878 as a private residence, catering for both residential and business functions. Overlooking the River Eden. Exit 42 off M6, B6263 to Wetheral.
Bedrooms: 3 single, 4 double & 2 twin, 1 family room.
Bathrooms: 2 public; 6 private showers.
Bed & breakfast: £25-£27 single, £40-£45 double.
Half board: £36.95-£38.95 daily, £200-£259 weekly.
Lunch available.
Evening meal 6pm (l.o. 9.30pm).
Parking for 73.
Credit: Access, Visa.
♿ ⃣ ♨ 🛡 Ⓥ 🛏 TV ▦ 🛆
❄ ⌗ DAP SP 🎏

Kingstown House Hotel
246/248 Kingstown Rd., Carlisle, CA3 0DE
☎ (0228) 515292
Convenient touring base for Lakes, Scotland or over-night stops. Near to M6 junction 44. Licensed a la carte restaurant. Private car park.
Bedrooms: 1 single, 1 double & 2 twin, 2 family rooms.
Bathrooms: 2 public; 2 private showers.
Bed & breakfast: from £17 single, from £27 double.
Half board: from £22 daily, from £154 weekly.
Evening meal 7pm (l.o. 9pm).
Parking for 7.
Credit: Access, Visa.
♿ ⃣ ♨ 🛡 Ⓥ 🛏 TV ▦ 🛆
✝ ❄ ✗ ⌗ DAP SP

Riverston Guest House ⋔
68 St. James Rd., Denton Holme, Carlisle, CA2 5PD
☎ (0228) 20825

Large Victorian house on the west side of city in quiet residential area. Close to river Calden, park, bowling greens, shopping area.
Bedrooms: 2 single, 2 double & 1 twin, 1 family room.
Bathrooms: 2 public; 1 private shower.
Bed & breakfast: £12-£12.50 single, £24-£26 double.
Half board: £17-£17.50 daily, £100-£110 weekly.
Evening meal 6pm (l.o. 8pm).
Parking for 3.

Royal Hotel M
9 Lowther St., Carlisle, CA3 8ES
☎ (0228) 22103
Family-run hotel. All 24 bedrooms have colour TV; 11 have en-suite facilities. Breakfast, bar lunches and evening meals served.
Bedrooms: 9 single, 4 double & 8 twin, 3 family rooms.
Bathrooms: 11 private, 5 public.
Bed & breakfast: £17-£25 single, £25-£35 double.
Half board: £25 daily, £175 weekly.
Lunch available.
Evening meal 5.30pm (l.o. 6.30pm).
Credit: Access, Visa.

Swallow Hilltop Hotel M
London Rd., Carlisle, CA1 2PQ
☎ (0228) 29255 Telex 64292
Ⓡ Swallow
Modern comfortable hotel with leisure facilities, making a good touring base for the Border, Lakes, Roman Wall and the Solway Coast. Special cabaret weekends. Winner of English Tourist Board's "England Entertains" best promotion award.
Bedrooms: 2 single, 25 double & 56 twin, 10 family rooms.
Bathrooms: 93 private.
Bed & breakfast: from £65 single, from £80 double.
Half board: from £350 weekly.
Lunch available.
Evening meal 7pm (l.o. 10pm).
Parking for 351.
Credit: Access, Visa, Diners, Amex.

Wallfoot Hotel & Restaurant M
Park Broom, Carlisle, CA6 4QH
☎ (0228) 73696
Warm welcome and good food in family-run hotel. Located in beautiful countryside on route of Hadrian's Wall, yet only 3 minutes from exit 44 M6 (follow airport signs) and 10 minutes from Carlisle city centre. Ideal for Border break or overnight stop en-route for Scotland.
Bedrooms: 3 single, 2 double & 2 twin, 3 family rooms.
Bathrooms: 6 private, 2 public.
Bed & breakfast: £18-£28 single, £35-£56 double.
Half board: £28-£30 daily, £196-£210 weekly.
Lunch available.
Evening meal 6pm (l.o. 10pm).
Parking for 30.
Credit: Access, Visa.

White Lea Guest House
191 Warwick Rd., Carlisle, CA1 1LP
☎ (0228) 33139
Take the M6 junction 43, straight on to the Warwick road and into Carlisle. Located 10 minutes' walk from the city centre. Municipal golf-course, park and shops are close by.
Bedrooms: 2 single, 1 double & 1 twin, 1 family room.
Bathrooms: 2 public.
Bed & breakfast: £11.50-£14 single, £23-£27 double.
Half board: £16.50-£18 daily.
Evening meal 6pm.
Parking for 5.

Woodlands Hotel and Restaurant M
264/266, London Rd., Carlisle, CA1 2QS
☎ (0228) 45643 Fax (0228) 45643
Family-run hotel near centre of historic city of Carlisle on the A6, 2 miles from M6 junction 42.
Bedrooms: 4 single, 3 double & 7 twin, 1 family room.
Bathrooms: 5 private, 4 public.
Bed & breakfast: £25-£35 single, £42-£50 double.
Half board: £32.50-£36.50 daily, £192.50-£224 weekly.
Lunch available.
Evening meal (l.o. 9pm).

Parking for 20.
Credit: Access, Visa, Diners, Amex.

A picturesque conserved village based on a 12th C priory with a well-preserved church and gatehouse. Just over 3 miles north of Morecambe Bay and 8 miles from the south tip of Lake Windermere. A peaceful base for fell-walking, with historic houses and beautiful scenery.

Cavendish Arms Hotel
Cavendish St., Cartmel, Grange-over-Sands, LA11 6QA
☎ (044 854) 240
The oldest country inn in Cartmel with open fires and a cosy candlelit dining room, serving guaranteed Aberdeen Angus steaks.
Bedrooms: 3 double & 2 twin.
Bathrooms: 2 public.
Bed & breakfast: £17.50-£25 single, £35-£55 double.
Lunch available.
Evening meal 6pm (l.o. 9.30pm).
Parking for 20.
Credit: Access.

The Grammar Hotel M
⚜⚜ APPROVED
Cartmel, Grange-over-Sands, LA11 7SG
☎ (053 95) 36367
17th C country hotel in beautiful Vale of Cartmel. All rooms en-suite, with colour TV and tea making facilities. Peace and tranquillity guaranteed.
Bedrooms: 4 double & 4 twin, 2 family rooms.
Bathrooms: 10 private.
Bed & breakfast: £30-£36 single, £60-£64 double.
Half board: £39-£42 daily, £210-£240 weekly.
Lunch available.
Evening meal 6.30pm (l.o. 8.30pm).
Parking for 30.
Open March-December.
Credit: Access, Visa.

6 miles from the Georgian port of Whitehaven is Cleator, with easy access to the western fells.

The Ennerdale Country House Hotel M
Cleator, CA23 3DT
☎ (0946) 813907
16th C country house hotel set in 3 acres of gardens, on the A5086 Cockermouth to Egremont road. Easy access to the Solway Coast, Lakes and fells of the Lake District.
Bedrooms: 1 single, 2 double & 7 twin, 2 family rooms.
Bathrooms: 7 private, 2 public.
Bed & breakfast: £30-£45 single, £45-£70 double.
Lunch available.
Evening meal 9pm (l.o. 11pm).
Parking for 35.
Credit: Access, Visa.

Market town at the confluence of the Rivers Cocker and Derwent, and the birthplace of William Wordsworth, the Lakeland poet, in 1770. The house where he was born stands at one end of the town's broad, tree-lined main street and is now owned by the National Trust. Good base for motoring tours into the Lake District.
Tourist Information Centre ☎ *(0900) 822634*

The Grecian Villa's Hotel M
⚜⚜ COMMENDED
Crown Street, Cockermouth, CA13 OEH
☎ (0900) 827575 Fax (0900) 827772
13-bedroomed hotel providing all en-suite facilities and modern conveniences. Within easy walking distance of Wordsworth's house.
Bedrooms: 2 single, 7 double & 3 twin, 1 family room.
Bathrooms: 13 private.
Bed & breakfast: max. £45 single, max. £55 double.
Continued ▶

COCKERMOUTH
Continued

Half board: max. £60 daily, max. £375 weekly.
Lunch available.
Evening meal 7pm (l.o. 9.30pm).
Parking for 26.
Credit: Access, Visa.

Pheasant Inn M
Bassenthwaite Lake, Nr. Cockermouth, CA13 9YE
☎ (076 87) 76234
Peacefully situated just off the A66 at the northern end of Bassenthwaite Lake. A 16th C farmhouse with all the charm and character of that age.
Bedrooms: 4 single, 9 double & 7 twin.
Bathrooms: 20 private.
Bed & breakfast: £40 single, £70 double.
Half board: £58 daily, £350 weekly.
Lunch available.
Evening meal 7pm (l.o. 8.30pm).
Parking for 80.

The Rook M
9 Castlegate, Cockermouth, CA13 9EU
☎ (0900) 822441
Cosy and friendly 17th C guesthouse, which is an ideal base for touring the Lake District. Home cooking.
Bedrooms: 2 single, 1 double & 1 twin, 1 family room.
Bathrooms: 2 public.
Bed & breakfast: £11-£12 single, £22-£24 double.

Rose Cottage Guest House
COMMENDED
Lorton Rd., Cockermouth, CA13 9DX
☎ (0900) 822189
In a pleasant position, this guesthouse is within easy reach of the Lakes and the coast.
Bedrooms: 2 single, 4 double & 2 twin, 2 family rooms.
Bathrooms: 2 private, 3 public.
Bed & breakfast: £17.50-£20 single, £32-£35 double.
Half board: £26-£28.50 daily, £110-£126 weekly.
Evening meal 6.30pm (l.o. 4.30pm).
Parking for 10.

CONISTON
Cumbria
Map ref 5A3

Village lying at the north end of Coniston Water. To the north-west of the village run the Coniston Fells, dominated by Coniston Old Man. Fine centre for walkers. John Ruskin, the Victorian critic, is buried beneath a splendidly-carved cross in the churchyard.

Coniston Lodge Private Hotel M
HIGHLY COMMENDED
Sunny Brow, Coniston, LA21 8HH
☎ (053 94) 41201
A small family-run hotel offering accommodation and food to a high standard in beautiful surroundings. A non-smoking establishment.
Bedrooms: 3 double & 3 twin.
Bathrooms: 6 private.
Bed & breakfast: £24-£35 single, £48-£60.50 double.
Half board: £35.50-£43 daily.
Evening meal 7pm (l.o. 7.30pm).
Parking for 9.
Credit: Access, Visa.

Coniston Sun Hotel M
Coniston, LA21 8HQ
☎ (053 94) 41248
Country house hotel and 16th C inn, in spectacular mountain setting on the fringe of the village and at the foot of the Coniston Old Man.
Bedrooms: 1 single, 6 double & 3 twin.
Bathrooms: 10 private.
Bed & breakfast: £30-£35 single, £60-£70 double.
Half board: £91-£101 daily, £210-£333 weekly.
Lunch available.
Evening meal 8pm (l.o. 9.30pm).
Parking for 25.
Open February-December.
Credit: Access, Visa.

Crown Hotel M
Coniston, LA21 8EA
☎ (053 94) 41243
At the foot of Coniston Old Man, 10 minutes' walk to the lake where Donald Campbell attempted to break the world water speed record.
Bedrooms: 1 single, 2 double & 1 twin, 3 family rooms.

Bathrooms: 2 public.
Bed & breakfast: £18-£20 single, £30-£36 double.
Half board: £23-£30 daily, £150-£200 weekly.
Lunch available.
Evening meal 7pm (l.o. 9pm).
Parking for 30.
Credit: Access, Visa, Diners, Amex.

Old Rectory House Hotel M
Torver, Coniston, LA21 8AY
☎ (053 94) 41353
Converted rectory in rural setting 2 miles south of Coniston. Set in 3 acres of garden, close to lake shore.
Bedrooms: 4 double & 2 twin, 1 family room.
Bathrooms: 7 private.
Bed & breakfast: £50-£55 double.
Half board: £35-£37.50 daily, £227.50-£245 weekly.
Evening meal 7.30pm (l.o. 7.30pm).
Parking for 10.

Wheelgate Hotel M
COMMENDED
Little Arrow, Coniston, LA21 8AU
☎ (053 94) 41418
Well positioned and an ideal touring base, with pretty bedrooms and lovely views. Cosy bar, homecooking, selected wines and personal supervision.
Bedrooms: 5 double & 2 twin.
Bathrooms: 5 private, 2 public.
Bed & breakfast: £30-£45 double.
Half board: £27-£34.50 daily, £178.50-£225.75 weekly.
Evening meal 7.30pm (l.o. 7.30pm).
Parking for 8.
Open March-November.

The symbol **CR** and the name of a hotel group or consortium after a hotel address means that bookings can be made through a central reservations office. These are listed on pages 559 & 560.

CROOKLANDS
Cumbria
Map ref 5B3

6m SE. Kendal
A village set amid the rolling fields, hedges and hills of England's largest drumlin belt.

Crooklands Hotel M
Crooklands, Nr. Milnthorpe, LA7 7NW
☎ (044 87) 432
Telex 94017303
CR Best Western
Exposed beams and interesting features remain after the careful conversion of this farm and ale-house, which dates back 4 centuries. Close to Kirkby Lonsdale on the A65, 1.5 miles from the M6 junction 36. Ideal for touring the Lakes and dales.
Bedrooms: 7 double & 24 twin.
Bathrooms: 31 private.
Bed & breakfast: £60-£75 single, £75-£90 double.
Half board: £75-£90 daily.
Lunch available.
Evening meal 7pm (l.o. 9.30pm).
Parking for 120.
Credit: Access, Visa, Diners, Amex.

CROSTHWAITE
Cumbria
Map ref 5A3

Crosthwaite House M
COMMENDED
Crosthwaite, Nr. Kendal, LA8 8BP
☎ (044 88) 264
A mid-18th C building with unspoilt views of the Lyth and Winster valleys, 5 miles from Bowness and Kendal. Family atmosphere and home cooking.
Bedrooms: 1 single, 3 double & 2 twin.
Bathrooms: 6 private.
Bed & breakfast: £18-£20 single, £36-£40 double.
Half board: £28-£30 daily, £185-£200 weekly.
Evening meal 7pm (l.o. 7pm).
Parking for 10.
Open March-November.

Please check prices and other details at the time of booking.

DALTON-IN-FURNESS

Cumbria
Map ref 5A3

Old capital of the Furness district until the Dissolution. A restored 14th C pele tower stands in the market-place. Birth place of George Romney, the portrait-painter, in 1734.

Chequers Motel & Restaurant

10 Abbey Rd., Dalton-in-Furness, LA15 8LF
☎ (0229) 62124
Converted school building offering quality en-suite accommodation with all modern facilities. Fine home-cooked meals served every lunchtime and evening.
Bedrooms: 1 single, 6 double & 6 twin.
Bathrooms: 10 private, 1 public.
Bed & breakfast: £15-£35 single, £30-£50 double.
Lunch available.
Evening meal 6.30pm (l.o. 10pm).
Parking for 25.
Credit: Access, Visa.

EGREMONT

Cumbria
Map ref 5A3

Small town with the ruins of a Norman castle.
Tourist Information Centre ☎ (0946) 820693

Old Vicarage Guest House

Nr. Thornhill, Egremont, CA22 2NX
☎ Beckermet (094 684) 577
Imposing 19th C vicarage of character in attractive grounds. Within easy reach of sea and mountains.
Bedrooms: 2 twin, 1 family room.
Bathrooms: 2 public.
Bed & breakfast: £10-£11 single, £20-£22 double.
Parking for 6.

ESKDALE

Cumbria
Map ref 5A3

Several minor roads lead to the west end of this beautiful valley. The approach from the east is over the extremely steep Hardknott Pass. The Scafell peaks and Bow Fell lie to the north. A miniature railway links the Eskdale Valley with Ravenglass on the coast.

Bower House Inn M
APPROVED

Eskdale, CA19 1TD
☎ (094 03) 244
A 17th C inn, full of charm and character, in one of Lakeland's loveliest valleys. 22 rooms all en-suite. Superb food, real ales, conference facilities. Ideal for walking, touring or business.
Bedrooms: 3 single, 9 double & 7 twin, 3 family rooms.
Bathrooms: 22 private.
Bed & breakfast: £35-£40 single, £50-£60 double.
Half board: £40-£50 daily.
Lunch available.
Evening meal 7pm (l.o. 8.30pm).
Parking for 60.
Credit: Access, Visa.

Brook House Hotel and Restaurant. M
COMMENDED

Boot, Eskdale, CA19 1TG
☎ (094 03) 288
Small family-run hotel in the beautiful unspoilt valley of Eskdale. Magnificent views from all bedrooms. Home cooking.
Bedrooms: 1 double & 4 twin, 2 family rooms.
Bathrooms: 5 private, 2 public; 2 private showers.
Bed & breakfast: £18-£21 single, £36-£43 double.
Half board: £27.50-£31.50 daily, £114-£175 weekly.
Lunch available.
Evening meal 7pm (l.o. 8.30pm).
Parking for 15.
Credit: Access, Visa.

Forest How M

Eskdale, Holmrook, CA19 1TR
☎ (094 03) 201
Large country guesthouse. In the valley of Eskdale, set in own grounds.
Bedrooms: 1 single, 2 twin, 2 family rooms.
Bathrooms: 2 private, 2 public.
Bed & breakfast: £15.50-£18.50 single, £30-£37 double.
Half board: £23-£26 daily, £160-£180 weekly.
Evening meal 7pm (l.o. 5pm).
Parking for 12.

Stanley Ghyll House M

Boot, Holmrook, CA19 1TF
☎ (094 03) 327 Telex 667047
A centre for walking holidays in one of the valleys of Cumbria. Ideal for touring Scafell and Wasdale.
Bedrooms: 2 single, 9 twin, 14 family rooms.
Bathrooms: 11 public.
Half board: £23.50-£25 daily, £163-£177 weekly.
Lunch available.
Evening meal 7pm.
Parking for 20.
Open March-September.

GOSFORTH

Cumbria
Map ref 5A3

2m NE. Seascale
The famous Gosforth Cross bearing Christian and pagan symbols stands in the village churchyard.

Westlakes Hotel and Restaurant M

Gosforth, Seascale, CA20 1HP
☎ (094 05) 221
A traditional Georgian country house hotel set in 2.5 acres of well maintained grounds with views of Scafell and Wasdale.
Bedrooms: 2 double & 2 twin.
Bathrooms: 2 public.
Bed & breakfast: £22-£32 single, £33-£43 double.
Lunch available.
Evening meal 7pm (l.o. 9pm).
Parking for 20.
Credit: Access, Visa.

GRANGE-OVER-SANDS

Cumbria
Map ref 5A3

Sheltered seaside resort overlooking Morecambe Bay. Pleasant seafront walks and beautiful gardens. The bay attracts many species of wading birds. Large seawater swimming pool.

Clare House
COMMENDED

Park Rd., Grange-over-Sands, LA11 7HQ
☎ (053 95) 33026
A charming hotel with well-appointed bedrooms and pleasant lounges set in grounds with magnificent bay views.
Bedrooms: 3 single, 2 double & 11 twin, 1 family room.
Bathrooms: 16 private, 2 public.
Bed & breakfast: £23-£25 single, £46-£50 double.
Half board: £33-£37 daily, £190-£230 weekly.
Lunch available.
Evening meal 6.45pm.
Parking for 16.
Open April-October.

Craiglands Hotel M
APPROVED

Methven Terrace, Kents Bank Rd., Grange-over-Sands, LA11 7DP
☎ (053 95) 32348
Family-run hotel with traditional home cooking. Some rooms with sea view. Sun lounge and patios. Open all year round.
Bedrooms: 2 single, 2 double & 3 twin, 8 family rooms.
Bathrooms: 8 private, 2 public.
Bed & breakfast: £21.50-£29.50 single, £33-£39 double.
Half board: £29-£32 daily, £110-£180 weekly.
Evening meal 6.30pm (l.o. 5.30pm).
Parking for 7.
Credit: Access, Visa.

Elton Hotel M
COMMENDED

2/3 Windermere Rd., Grange-over-Sands, LA11 6EQ
☎ (053 95) 32838
Value-for-money hotel, close to shops, promenade and gardens. High standard accommodation and a restful atmosphere.
Continued ▶

Classifications and quality commendations were correct at the time of going to press but are subject to change. Please check at the time of booking.

GRANGE-OVER-SANDS

Continued

Bedrooms: 1 single, 4 double & 2 twin.
Bathrooms: 5 private; 2 private showers.
Bed & breakfast: £19-£21 single, £32-£36 double.
Half board: £24-£26 daily, £150.50-£171.50 weekly.
Evening meal 7.30pm (l.o. 4pm).

⌖6 ♨ ☐ ✿ ⓘ 📞 Ⓥ ⊭ 📺 🎱
△ ✗ ℡ OAP ⊠ SP

Graythwaite Manor Hotel ▲

Fernhill Rd., Grange-over-Sands, LA11 7JE
☎ (053 95) 32001 & (053 95) 33755
Attractive family-run country house hotel with extensive gardens and views. Well-equipped bedrooms, spacious lounges, fine cuisine and wine cellar.
Bedrooms: 5 single, 3 double & 12 twin, 2 family rooms.
Bathrooms: 20 private, 4 public.
Bed & breakfast: £35-£50 single, £60-£90 double.
Half board: £37-£52 daily, £241.50-£350 weekly.
Lunch available.
Evening meal 7pm (l.o. 8.30pm).
Parking for 35.
Credit: Access, Visa.

⌖ ♨ ℂ ☐ ✿ ⓘ Ⓥ ⊭
▥ ☎ 🍷 ♣ ✿ ✗ 🎱 SP
🎏

Holme Lea Guest House ▲
▥▥

90 Kentsford Rd., Kents Bank, Grange-over-Sands, LA11 7BB
☎ (053 95) 32545
Quiet position overlooking bay. Food plentiful, varied and home-made. Large lounge with colour TV and log fire. Bedrooms well furnished. Tea and coffee facilities, shaver points. Private car park. Packed lunches available. Full central heating.
Bedrooms: 2 single, 2 double & 1 twin, 2 family rooms.
Bathrooms: 2 public.
Bed & breakfast: £12 single, £24 double.
Half board: £17 daily, £110 weekly.
Evening meal 6.30pm (l.o. 5pm).
Parking for 8.
Open February-November.

⌖ ✿ UL ⓘ Ⓥ ⊭ 📺 🎱 △
🎏 OAP SP

Lyndene Guest House ▲

Kentsford Rd., Kents Bank, Grange-over-Sands, LA11 7BB
☎ (053 95) 33189
Homely guesthouse, personally supervised and providing home cooking. Pleasant garden, deck chairs and sea views. Early morning tea available.
Bedrooms: 1 single, 1 double, 4 family rooms.
Bathrooms: 2 public.
Bed & breakfast: £11-£12 single, £22-£24 double.
Half board: £14-£15 daily, £90-£100 weekly.
Evening meal 6pm (l.o. 4pm).
Parking for 3.

⌖ ♨ M UL ⓘ Ⓥ ⊭ 📺 △
🎏 OAP SP

Netherwood Hotel ▲
▥▥▥

Grange-over-Sands, LA11 6ET
☎ (053 95) 32552 & (044 84) 2230
Built in 1893 and a building of high architectural and historic interest.
Bedrooms: 5 single, 8 double & 6 twin, 4 family rooms.
Bathrooms: 17 private, 2 public.
Bed & breakfast: £32.75-£33.75 single, £65.50-£67.50 double.
Half board: £42-£43 daily, £292-£299 weekly.
Lunch available.
Evening meal 7pm (l.o. 8.30pm).
Parking for 100.

⌖ ℂ ℗ ☐ ✿ ⓘ Ⓥ ⊭ 📺
⬤ 🖂 ▥ △ 🍷 ✿ SP 🎏
◐ 🖂 ▥ △ 🍷 ✿ SP 🎏

Prospect House Hotel ▲
▥▥

Kents Bank Rd., Grange-over-Sands, LA11 7DJ
☎ (053 95) 32116
Our best advertisement is the many return visits we receive every year. Imaginative meals and a friendly welcome are guaranteed.
Bedrooms: 1 single, 4 double.
Bathrooms: 5 private.
Bed & breakfast: £19-£20.50 single, £31.50-£35 double.
Half board: £23.55-£25.30 daily, £155-£163 weekly.
Evening meal 6.45pm (l.o. 3.30pm).
Parking for 5.

⌖6 ℗ ☐ ✿ ⓘ Ⓥ ⊭ 📺
▥ △ 🎏 ⊠ SP

The symbols are explained on the flap inside the back cover.

Somerset House
▥▥

Kents Bank Rd., Grange-over-Sands, LA11 7EY
☎ (053 95) 32631
The house is well-furnished, providing holiday accommodation and facilities for the benefit of our guests plus 30 years' experience.
Bedrooms: 1 single, 2 double & 1 twin, 4 family rooms.
Bathrooms: 1 public; 4 private showers.
Bed & breakfast: £14-£17 single, £28-£32 double.
Half board: £20-£24 daily, £135-£142 weekly.
Evening meal 6.30pm (l.o. 5.30pm).

⌖ ☐ ✿ ⓘ Ⓥ ⊭ 📺 △
OAP SP

GRASMERE

Cumbria
Map ref 5A3

Described by William Wordsworth as 'the loveliest spot that man hath ever found', this village is in a beautiful setting by-passed by the main road and overlooked by Helm Crag. Wordsworth lived at Dove Cottage for 9 years and the cottage and museum are now open to the public. Grasmere gingerbread is made in the old school to a traditional village recipe. Good centre for touring and walking.

2 Ben Place ▲
▥▥ APPROVED

Grasmere, Ambleside, LA22 9RL
☎ (096 65) 581
In a very quiet area near the village, with a secluded garden and lovely views from all the rooms.
Bedrooms: 1 single, 1 twin, 1 family room.
Bathrooms: 3 private showers.
Bed & breakfast: £18-£20 single, £34-£38 double.
Half board: from £120 weekly.
Parking for 6.
Open January-October.

⌖ ✿ ℗ UL ⓘ Ⓥ ⊭ 📺
△ ✿ ✗ 🎏 ⊠ SP

Bramriggs Guesthouse
Grasmere, Nr. Ambleside, LA22 9RU
☎ (096 65) 360

Small residence with lovely views from all windows. Opposite Helm Crag, overlooking Grasmere valley and sited well back from the main Grasmere to Keswick road. Garden borders footpath to Helvellyn mountain. Non-smokers only please.
Bedrooms: 1 single, 1 twin, 2 family rooms.
Bathrooms: 1 public.
Bed & breakfast: £13-£14 single, £26-£28 double.
Half board: £90-£100 weekly.
Parking for 5.

⌖ M ✿ ⓘ Ⓥ 📺 🎱 ℡

Bridge House Hotel ▲
▥▥▥ COMMENDED

Stock Lane, Grasmere, LA22 9SN
☎ (096 65) 425
Family-run hotel close to the village centre, in 2 acres of garden. Relaxing atmosphere, home cooking and ample parking. Room available for special occasions such as honeymoon and anniversary.
Bedrooms: 2 single, 5 double & 5 twin.
Bathrooms: 10 private, 1 public.
Bed & breakfast: £23-£30 single, £46-£60 double.
Half board: £30-£38 daily, £200-£230 weekly.
Evening meal 7pm (l.o. 7.30pm).
Parking for 20.
Open March-November.
Credit: Access, Visa.

⌖3 ☐ ✿ ⓘ 📞 △ 🍷
✿ ✗ 🎏 SP

Chestnut Villa ▲
Keswick Rd., Grasmere, LA22 9RE
☎ (096 65) 218
On the A591 close to the village and surrounded by Lakeland fells making it good for fell walking and all the boating amenities.
Bedrooms: 2 single, 3 double, 2 family rooms.
Bathrooms: 1 public.
Bed & breakfast: £14-£15 single, £28-£30 double.
Parking for 10.

⌖ UL ⊭ 📺 ▥ △

Forest Side ▲
Grasmere, Ambleside, LA22 9RN
☎ (096 65) 250
Stands in nearly 40 acres of grounds close to the village of Grasmere in the very heart of the Lake District.
Bedrooms: 5 single, 15 twin, 9 family rooms.
Bathrooms: 16 public.

Half board: £27.85-£30.29
daily, £195-£212 weekly.
Evening meal 7pm.
Parking for 40.
⊠2 🛏 UL 🔒 V 🖵 ▦ ▲ ⚘
❄ 🐩 DAP ⚬ SP T

The Grasmere Hotel M
♛♛♛♛
Grasmere, LA22 9TA
☎ (096 65) 277
*In the midst of beautiful
mountain scenery with the
restaurant overlooking a large
garden, the river and
surrounding hills.*
Bedrooms: 1 single, 8 double
& 3 twin.
Bathrooms: 12 private,
1 public.
Bed & breakfast: £30-£40
single, £56-£80 double.
Half board: £33-£45 daily,
£210-£294 weekly.
Evening meal 7.30pm (l.o.
8pm).
Parking for 14.
Open February-December.
Credit: Access, Visa.
⊠6 🛏 ▦ ⚓ ⊙ 🖵 ⚬ 🔒 V
🖵 ▦ ⚓ ▲ 🍴 ❄ 🐿 DAP ⚬ SP
T

Harwood Hotel M
Red Lion Square, Grasmere,
LA22 9SP
☎ (096 65) 248
*Small family-run hotel in the
centre of Grasmere, offering
home cooking with personal
service. Ideal for walking,
climbing and touring.*
Bedrooms: 2 single, 6 double
& 2 twin, 1 family room.
Bathrooms: 2 private,
3 public.
Bed & breakfast: £20-£22
single, £40-£44 double.
Half board: £29.50-£31.50
daily, £190-£200 weekly.
Lunch available.
Evening meal 7pm (l.o.
7.30pm).
Parking for 10.
Open January-November.
⊠⚓ ⚬ 🔒 V 🖵 ▦ ⚓
🍴 ✗ 🐿 SP
🕐 Display advertisement
appears on page 86.

Lake View Guest
House M
♛♛♛ COMMENDED
Lake View Drive, Grasmere,
LA22 9TD
☎ (096 65) 384
*In private grounds and
overlooking the lake with
private access. Located in the
village but off the main road.*
Bedrooms: 2 single, 3 double
& 1 twin.
Bathrooms: 2 private,
1 public.
Bed & breakfast: from £18
single, from £36 double.

Half board: from £26.50
daily, from £177 weekly.
Evening meal 6.30pm (l.o.
midday).
Parking for 10.
Open March-November.
⊠12 ⚬ UL 🔒 V 🖵 ▦ ⚓
🖊 ❄ ✗ 🐿 SP

Lancrigg Vegetarian
Country House Hotel
Easedale, Grasmere,
LA22 9QN
☎ (096 65) 317
*Historic listed building in 27
acres, in peaceful Easedale, 10
minutes' walk from Grasmere
village. Good walking, views,
log fires and vegetarian
wholefood.*
Bedrooms: 2 single, 4 double
& 2 twin, 3 family rooms.
Bathrooms: 5 private,
2 public.
Half board: £30-£56.50 daily,
£195-£365 weekly.
Evening meal 7pm (l.o. 7pm).
Parking for 12.
⊠⚓ ▦ 🖵 ⚬ 🔒 V ✗ ⚓
▦ ⚓ 🍴 ❄ 🐿 ✗ DAP 🐿 SP
🐿

Moss Grove Hotel M
♛♛♛ APPROVED
Grasmere, Nr. Ambleside,
LA22 9SW
☎ (096 65) 251 Fax 09665
251
*Elegant Lakeland hotel,
centrally situated. Recently
refurbished. Four-poster
bedrooms with south-facing
balconies. Cosy bar. Sauna and
exercise area.*
Bedrooms: 2 single, 7 double
& 3 twin, 2 family rooms.
Bathrooms: 13 private,
2 public.
Bed & breakfast: £21.95-
£31.95 single, £50-£63.50
double.
Half board: £31.50-£41.50
daily, £220.50-£290.50
weekly.
Lunch available.
Evening meal 7.30pm (l.o.
8.30pm).
Parking for 16.
Open March-December.
Credit: Access, Visa.
⊠⚓ ⚓ 🔒 🖵 ⚬ 🔒 V 🖵
⚓ 🍴 ⚬ ✗ SP T

Oak Bank Hotel M
Broadgate, Grasmere,
LA22 9TA
☎ (096 65) 217 & 685
*Traditionally built 100 years
ago in Lakeland stone and now
modernised throughout.
Delicious cordon bleu cuisine,
good cellar - pamper yourself!*
Bedrooms: 1 single, 9 double
& 3 twin, 1 family room.
Bathrooms: 14 private.

Bed & breakfast: £24-£34
single, £48-£68 double.
Half board: £60-£80 daily,
£214-£245 weekly.
Evening meal 7pm (l.o. 8pm).
Parking for 14.
Open February-December.
Credit: Access, Visa.
⊠⚓ ▦ ⚓ ⊙ 🖵 ⚬ 🔒 V 🖵
T ▦ ⚓ 🍴 ❄ SP T

Red Lion M
♛♛♛♛
Grasmere, LA22 9SS
☎ (096 65) 456
CR Consort
*200-year-old coaching inn, in
the centre of Wordsworth
country.*
Bedrooms: 8 single, 11 double
& 12 twin, 5 family rooms.
Bathrooms: 36 private.
Bed & breakfast: £25-£33
single, £50-£66 double.
Half board: £36-£46 daily.
Lunch available.
Evening meal 7pm (l.o. 9pm).
Parking for 30.
Credit: Access, Visa, Diners,
Amex.
⊠⚓ ⚓ 🖵 ⚬ 🔒 V 🖵 ⊞
▦ ⚓ 🍴 🐿 SP T

Riversdale
♛♛ COMMENDED
White Bridge, Grasmere,
LA22 9RQ
☎ (096 65) 619
*Charming guesthouse
overlooking River Rothay with
fine fell views offering every
comfort: log fires, warm
hospitality, good food, private
parking.*
Bedrooms: 3 double & 1 twin.
Bathrooms: 2 private,
2 public.
Bed & breakfast: £32-£36
double.
Parking for 6.
Open February-November.
⊠13 ⚬ UL 🔒 V 🖵 ▦ ▦
⚓ ✗

Roundhill M
Easedale, Grasmere,
LA22 9QT
☎ Grasmere (096 65) 233
*Enjoy true Lakeland
atmosphere in our traditional
stone-built family house;
peacefully situated with
stunning, elevated views.
Vegetarian and English
breakfasts.*
Bedrooms: 1 double & 1 twin,
1 family room.
Bathrooms: 1 public.
Bed & breakfast: £14-£17
single, £27-£35 double.
Parking for 4.
⊠3 ⚓ UL 🔒 V ✗ ▦ ▦ ✗
▦ ▦ T

Wordsworth Hotel M
Grasmere, LA22 9SW
☎ (096 65) 592 Telex 65329
*A traditional style hotel with
amenities for both business and
leisure including the stylish
Prelude Restaurant, jacuzzi,
mini-gym, pool, sauna and
solarium.*
Bedrooms: 1 single, 17 double
& 15 twin, 4 family rooms.
Bathrooms: 37 private.
Bed & breakfast: £46.50-£50
single, £96-£112 double.
Half board: £66.50-£87.50
daily.
Lunch available.
Evening meal 7pm (l.o. 8pm).
Parking for 54.
Credit: Access, Visa, Diners,
Amex.
⊠⚓ ⚓ ⚓ ⚓ ⊙ 🖵 ⚬ 🔒 V
🖵 ▦ ⚓ ▦ 🖵 ⚓ 🍴 ⚬ ♿ 🐿 ⚓
🐿 ✗ ✗ 🐿 SP ▦ T

GRETNA
Cumbria
Map ref 5A2

Gretna, the first
settlement in Scotland, is
renowned for its many
'marriage booths' in
history, including a
blacksmith's shop. It still
has an air of romance
today.

The Gretna Chase
Hotel M
♛♛♛ COMMENDED
Gretna, Carlisle, CA6 5JB
☎ (0461) 37517
*Tastefully modernised
Victorian house set in 2.5 acres
of beautiful, award-winning
gardens. Full-colour brochure
available.*
Bedrooms: 2 single, 5 double
& 2 twin.
Bathrooms: 6 private;
3 private showers.
Bed & breakfast: £33-£50
single, £42-£80 double.
Lunch available.
Evening meal 5.30pm (l.o.
10pm).
Parking for 40.
Open February-December.
Credit: Access, Visa, Diners,
Amex.
⊠⚓ ⚓ ⚬ 🔒 V 🖵 ▦ ▲
🍴 ❄ ✗ ▦ T

Hunters Lodge Hotel
Gretna, Carlisle, CA6 5DL
☎ (0461) 38214
*In the heart of Gretna, "The
Gateway to Scotland", offering
a warm and friendly
atmosphere.*
Bedrooms: 1 single, 4 double
& 1 twin, 2 family rooms.
Continued ▶

GRETNA

Continued

Bathrooms: 4 private,
1 public.
Bed & breakfast: £20-£22
single, £30-£38 double.
Evening meal 7pm (l.o. 8pm).
Parking for 20.

GRIZEDALE

Cumbria
Map ref 5A3

Pepper House ♨

Satterthwaite, LA12 8LS
☎ Barrow (0229) 860206
*Peaceful position in Grizedale
forest park. 10 en-suite
bedrooms. English regional
food in farmhouse setting.
Groups welcome.*
Bedrooms: 9 double & 1 twin.
Bathrooms: 10 private.
Bed & breakfast: £17 single,
£34 double.
Half board: £25 daily, £119-
£169 weekly.
Evening meal 7pm (l.o.
10.30pm).
Parking for 14.

✪ Display advertisement
appears on page 87.

HAVERTHWAITE

Cumbria
Map ref 5A3

Set in the Levens Valley
south-west of Newby
Bridge. Headquarters of
the Lakeside and
Haverthwaite Railway
Company. Many craft
workshops.

Broad Oaks

Haverthwaite, Nr. Ulverston,
LA12 8AL
☎ Newby Bridge
(053 95) 31756
*An unusual modern building in
a woodland setting. Elevated
residents' lounge and dining
room giving views at tree-top
level.*
Bedrooms: 1 double & 1 twin.
Bathrooms: 2 private.
Bed & breakfast: £16-£20
single, £32-£40 double.
Half board: £25-£29 daily,
£150 weekly.
Evening meal 7pm.
Parking for 4.
Open March-November.

HAWKSHEAD

Cumbria
Map ref 5A3

Lying near Esthwaite
Water, this village has
great charm and
character. Its small
squares are linked by
flagged or cobbled alleys
and the main square is
dominated by the market
house or Shambles
where the butchers had
their stalls in days gone
by.

Belmount Guest House

Outgate, Hawkshead,
LA22 0NJ
☎ Hawkshead (096 66) 535
*Fine, family-run Georgian
house standing in 3 acres.
Superb views. Warm welcome.*
Bedrooms: 4 double & 1 twin,
5 family rooms.
Bathrooms: 3 public.
Bed & breakfast: £20-£25
single, £34-£39 double.

The Drunken Duck Inn ♨

COMMENDED

Barngates, Ambleside,
LA22 0NG
☎ (096 66) 347
*An old fashioned inn amidst
magnificent scenery, oak-
beamed bars, cosy log fires and
charming bedrooms. Good food
and beers.*
Bedrooms: 9 double & 1 twin.
Bathrooms: 10 private.
Bed & breakfast: £35-£45
single, £54-£72.50 double.
Half board: £44.50-£62.50
daily.
Lunch available.
Evening meal 6.30pm (l.o.
8.45pm).
Parking for 30.
Credit: Access, Visa.

Greenbank Country House Hotel ♨

COMMENDED

Hawkshead, Ambleside,
LA22 0NS
☎ (096 66) 497
*Well-appointed country house
hotel in the picturesque village
of Hawkshead. Central for all
activities. Good home cooking.*
Bedrooms: 3 single, 4 double
& 2 twin, 1 family room.
Bathrooms: 4 private,
2 public.
Bed & breakfast: £16-£17.50
single, £32-£35 double.

Half board: £24-£26.50 daily,
£150-£164 weekly.
Evening meal 4pm.
Parking for 12.

Highfield House Hotel ♨

COMMENDED

Hawkshead Hill, Nr.
Ambleside, LA22 0PN
☎ (096 66) 344
*A traditional Lakeland country
house with extensive views, in
2.5 acres of grounds. An ideal
centre for walking and touring.*
Bedrooms: 2 single, 5 double
& 3 twin, 1 family room.
Bathrooms: 8 private,
2 public.
Bed & breakfast: from £26.50
single, from £48 double.
Half board: from £36 daily,
from £235 weekly.
Lunch available.
Evening meal 7pm (l.o. 8pm).
Parking for 12.

Ivy House Hotel ♨

APPROVED

Main St., Hawkshead,
LA22 0NS
☎ (096 66) 204
*Attractive Georgian house and
Grade II listed building located
in the centre of village. Family-
run hotel providing good
English food in a friendly and
relaxed atmosphere.*
Bedrooms: 6 double & 3 twin,
2 family rooms.
Bathrooms: 6 private,
2 public.
Bed & breakfast: £17.25-
£21.75 single.
Half board: £22.25-£29.75
daily, £155.75-£187.25
weekly.
Evening meal 7pm (l.o. 4pm).
Parking for 15.
Open March-November.

Queens Head Hotel ♨

Hawkshead, LA22 0NS
☎ (096 66) 271
*Located between Lakes
Windermere and Coniston. The
home of Beatrix Potter,
Wordsworth's grammar school
and Ann Tyson's cottage.
Amenities include mountain
bikes and a bowling green.*
Bedrooms: 6 double & 2 twin,
2 family rooms.
Bathrooms: 6 private,
2 public.
Bed & breakfast: £23-£30
single, £39-£46 double.
Half board: £45-£61 daily.
Lunch available.

Evening meal 6.15pm (l.o.
9.30pm).
Credit: Access, Visa, Amex.

✪ Display advertisement
appears on page 87.

HELTON

Cumbria
Map ref 5B2

6m S. Penrith
'A place on the side of a
hill', Helton nestles in a
quiet, undisturbed corner
of the Lakes yet has easy
access to Penrith and
junction 40 of the M6.

Beckfoot Country House ♨

COMMENDED

Helton, Penrith, CA10 2QB
☎ Bampton (093 13) 241
*Beautiful country house in an
unspoilt corner of the National
Park. Exit 39 on the M6 from
the South and exit 40 from the
North.*
Bedrooms: 1 single, 3 double
& 2 twin, 1 family room.
Bathrooms: 7 private.
Bed & breakfast: £18-£22
single, £36-£44 double.
Half board: £27-£31 daily,
£175-£180 weekly.
Evening meal 7pm (l.o. 7pm).
Parking for 12.
Open April-November.

Holywell Country Guest House ♨

APPROVED

Helton, Nr. Penrith,
CA10 2QA
☎ Hackthorpe (093 12) 231
*Situated between Ullswater
and Haweswater, overlooking
Lowther Valley. An excellent
base for touring the Lakes.*
Bedrooms: 2 double & 2 twin.
Bathrooms: 2 private,
1 public.
Bed & breakfast: £14-£16
single, £28-£32 double.
Half board: £22.50-£24.50
daily, £152.50-£166.50
weekly.
Evening meal 7pm (l.o.
11am).
Parking for 6.
Open February-November.

**Map references
apply to the colour
maps towards the
end of this guide.**

HEVERSHAM

Cumbria
Map ref 5B3

6m SW. Kendal
This attractive village is set on a hill, and has a grammar school founded in 1613.

The Blue Bell at Heversham M
♛♛♛♛

Princes Way, Heversham, Milnthorpe, LA7 7EE
☎ Milnthorpe (053 95) 62018
Country hotel in a rural haven which makes it an ideal touring centre.
Bedrooms: 9 single, 10 double & 7 twin.
Bathrooms: 21 private, 3 public.
Bed & breakfast: £30-£40 single, £55 double.
Half board: £39-£49 daily.
Lunch available.
Evening meal 7pm (l.o. 9.15pm).
Parking for 100.
Credit: Access, Visa.
📖 ⊕ 🖵 🍴 ♿ ☕ 🚗 ♻ 📺 ▥
🚪 ⚓ ¶ ✗ 🐴 SP T

KENDAL

Cumbria
Map ref 5B3

The 'Auld Grey Town', so called because of its many grey limestone buildings, lies in the valley of the River Kent with a backcloth of limestone fells on 3 sides. Situated just outside the Lake District National Park, a good centre from which to tour the Lakes and surrounding countryside. The ruined Norman castle was the birthplace of Catherine Parr, Henry VIII's 6th wife.
Tourist Information Centre ☎ (0539) 725758

Beech House M

40 Greenside, Kendal, LA9 4LD
☎ (0539) 20385
Charming small hotel offering comfort and hospitality. 2 minutes' from town centre. Overlooking green. Ideal touring base. Traditional Lakeland fare. Mountain activity holidays arranged.
Bedrooms: 1 single, 2 double & 2 twin, 1 family room.
Bathrooms: 2 public.
Bed & breakfast: £13-£17 single, £26-£28 double.

Half board: £19-£24 daily, £120-£150 weekly.
Evening meal 6.30pm (l.o. 7pm).
Parking for 6.
🖵 🍴 ♿ ☕ 🚗 📺 ▥ ⚓ 🐴 ✗
OAP ♻ SP

Brantholme M

7 Sedbergh Rd., Kendal, LA9 6AD
☎ (0539) 722340
Family-run guesthouse in own grounds. All rooms with private facilities. Good meals from fresh local produce.
Bedrooms: 2 twin, 1 family room.
Bathrooms: 3 private.
Bed & breakfast: £18.50-£20 single, £26-£28 double.
Half board: £18.50-£25 daily, £120-£134 weekly.
Evening meal 6.30pm (l.o. 5.30pm).
Parking for 6.
Open March-October.
📖 ♿ ▯ ⊡ ☕ 📺 ▥ ❀ 🐴 OAP
SP ▥

Burrow Hall Country Guesthouse M
♛♛♛ COMMENDED

Plantation Bridge, Kendal, LA8 9JR
☎ Staveley (0539) 821711
Beautifully furnished, centrally heated, 17th C Lakeland House. Oak-beamed lounge plus TV lounge. All bedrooms have private facilities. Excellent cuisine. Ample parking.
Bedrooms: 1 double & 2 twin.
Bathrooms: 3 private.
Bed & breakfast: £35-£45 double.
Half board: £28.75-£33.75 daily, £189-£220.50 weekly.
Evening meal 8pm (l.o. 7pm).
Parking for 8.
® ♿ 🖵 📺 ▥ ⚓ ❀ 🐴 ▥
♻ SP

Gateway Hotel & Inn

Crook Rd., Plumgarth, Kendal, LA8 8LX
☎ (0539) 720605 & 724187
A Victorian house in its own grounds, with ornate ceilings and large picture windows. At the gateway to the Lakes with panoramic views, yet just off the main A591 road.
Bedrooms: 2 single, 3 double & 2 twin, 2 family rooms.
Bathrooms: 4 private, 2 public.
Bed & breakfast: £20-£30 single, £40-£58 double.
Lunch available.

Evening meal 7pm (l.o. 9.30pm).
Parking for 32.
Credit: Access, Visa.
📖 ⊕ 🖵 🍴 ♿ ⓘ ♻ ▥ ⚓ ¶
🚩 ❀ OAP

Headlands Hotel M
♛♛ COMMENDED

53 Milnthorpe Rd., Kendal, LA9 5QG
☎ (0539) 720424
Small family hotel, 10 minutes' walk from town centre. Central for touring the Lakes, Yorkshire Dales and the coast.
Bedrooms: 1 single, 1 double & 2 twin, 3 family rooms.
Bathrooms: 4 private, 1 public.
Bed & breakfast: £13-£25 single, £26-£36 double.
Half board: £22-£34 daily, £154-£238 weekly.
Evening meal 7pm (l.o. 5pm).
Parking for 8.
📖 🖵 🍴 ♿ ⓘ ▯ 📺 ▥ ⚓ ¶

Heaves Hotel M
♛♛

Nr. Kendal, LA8 8EF
☎ Sedgwick (053 95) 60269 & 60396
Georgian mansion in 10 acres, 4 miles from the M6 junction 36 and Kendal.
Bedrooms: 5 single, 4 double & 4 twin, 3 family rooms.
Bathrooms: 7 private, 3 public.
Bed & breakfast: £17-£20 single, £34-£40 double.
Half board: £25-£28 daily, £160-£180 weekly.
Lunch available.
Evening meal 7pm (l.o. 8pm).
Parking for 24.
Credit: Access, Visa, Diners, Amex.
▯ ☕ ⓘ ▯ ▥ ⚓ ⊕ 📺 ⚓ ¶ ♣
❀ SP ▥ T

Hillside Guest House
♛♛ COMMENDED

4 Beast Banks, Kendal, LA9 4JW
☎ (0539) 22836
Small guesthouse near the shops and town facilities and handy for the Lakes, Yorkshire Dales and Morecambe Bay.
Bedrooms: 2 single, 3 double & 1 twin.
Bathrooms: 4 private, 2 public.
Bed & breakfast: £13-£17 single, £26-£34 double.
Parking for 2.
📖 🖵 ☕ ▯ ▥ 📺 ▥ ⚓ 🐴

Holmfield

41 Kendal Green, Kendal, LA9 5PP
☎ (0539) 720790

Elegant Edwardian house, edge of town, large gardens, panoramic views, swimming pool. 3 pretty bedrooms, 2 guest bathrooms. Private parking. Non-smoking establishment.
Bedrooms: 2 double & 1 twin.
Bathrooms: 2 public.
Bed & breakfast: £25-£30 double.
Parking for 5.
🛇 ⊕ ☕ 🍴 ▯ ▥ ⅏ ⚓ 📺
▥ ⚓ ❀ 🐴 ▥

Lane Head House Country Hotel M
♛♛♛ COMMENDED

Helsington, Kendal, LA9 5RJ
☎ (0539) 731283
Country hotel of character enjoying magnificent panoramic views of surrounding fells. On the southern boundary of Kendal, half a mile off the A6 Milnthorpe road.
Bedrooms: 4 double & 3 twin.
Bathrooms: 7 private.
Bed & breakfast: £33-£38 single, £50-£58 double.
Half board: from £30 daily.
Evening meal 7pm (l.o. 5pm).
Parking for 10.
Credit: Access, Visa.
▥12 ♿ ♣ ® 🖵 ☕ ⓘ ▥
▥ ⚓ ¶ ❀ ✗ 🐴 ▥ OAP ♻ SP
▥ T

Rainbow Hotel

32 Highgate, Kendal, LA9 4SX
☎ (0539) 724178
Old town centre coaching house, opposite the town hall and market square. Open oak beams, dining room and residents' lounge.
Bedrooms: 1 single, 3 double & 2 twin, 1 family room.
Bathrooms: 7 private.
Bed & breakfast: £20-£34 single, £34-£50 double.
Lunch available.
Parking for 30.
Open January-October, December.
📖 ♿ ⓘ ▯ 📺 ⚓ ♣ ¶
✗ 🐴 OAP SP ▥ T
👁 Display advertisement appears on page 87.

Riverside Hotel & Restaurant M
♛♛♛♛ COMMENDED

Stramongate Bridge, Kendal, LA9 4BZ
☎ (0539) 724707

Continued ▶

CUMBRIA

KENDAL

Continued

A converted 17th C tannery fully modernised with 2 restaurants, conference and banqueting facilities for up to 200 persons.
Bedrooms: 37 double & 2 twin, 8 family rooms.
Bathrooms: 47 private.
Bed & breakfast: £50-£55 single, £66-£72 double.
Half board: £318.50-£350 weekly.
Lunch available.
Evening meal 6pm (l.o. 10pm).
Credit: Access, Visa, Diners, Amex.

Riversleigh

49 Milnthorpe Rd., Kendal, LA9 5QG
☎ (0539) 26392
Family-run guest house. Residents' lounge, colour TV, tea/coffee facilities in rooms. Private parking. 5 minutes from town centre.
Bedrooms: 1 single, 2 double.
Bathrooms: 1 public.
Bed & breakfast: £12-£14 single, £24-£28 double.
Parking for 6.

Sundial House

51 Milnthorpe Rd., Kendal, LA9 5QG
☎ (0539) 724468
Victorian house on raised terrace. Level walking distance to town centre. Family-run with accent on caring. Excellent fresh local food. Residents' lounge full of Lakeland information. Ideal holiday base.
Bedrooms: 1 single, 1 twin, 4 family rooms.
Bathrooms: 2 public.
Bed & breakfast: £13.50-£15.50 single, £25-£28.75 double.
Half board: £21.50-£25 daily, £145-£160 weekly.
Evening meal 6.30pm.
Parking for 10.

> **The symbols are explained on the flap inside the back cover.**

KESWICK

Cumbria
Map ref 5A3

Attractive town in a beautiful position beside Derwentwater and below the mountains of Skiddaw and Saddleback. A natural convergence of roads makes it a good base for touring. Motor-launches operate on Derwentwater and motor boats and rowing boats can be hired.
Tourist Information Centre ☎ (07687) 72645

Acorn House Hotel ⋒
COMMENDED
Ambleside Rd., Keswick, CA12 4DL
☎ (076 87) 72553
Detached Georgian house with spacious rooms, set in own garden. Quiet location close to town centre and 10 minutes from the Derwentwater.
Bedrooms: 5 double & 2 twin, 3 family rooms.
Bathrooms: 9 private, 1 public.
Bed & breakfast: £16-£20 single, £30-£40 double.
Evening meal 6.30pm (l.o. 4.30pm).
Parking for 10.
Credit: Access, Visa.

Allerdale House ⋒
COMMENDED
1 Eskin St., Keswick, CA12 4DH
☎ (076 87) 73891
Spacious Victorian guesthouse, convenient for the town centre and the lake, with well-equipped bedrooms and the comforts of home.
Bedrooms: 3 double & 1 twin, 2 family rooms.
Bathrooms: 6 private.
Bed & breakfast: £17.50 single, £35 double.
Half board: £25 daily, £175 weekly.
Evening meal 6.30pm (l.o. 6.45pm).
Parking for 6.
Open January-November.

Berkeley Guest House ⋒

The Heads, Keswick, CA12 5ER
☎ (076 87) 74222

On a quiet road overlooking the mini golf-course, with splendid views from each comfortable room. Close to the town centre and lake.
Bedrooms: 4 double & 1 twin.
Bathrooms: 1 public; 2 private showers.
Bed & breakfast: £25-£33 double.
Half board: £19-£23 daily, £126-£154 weekly.
Evening meal 6.30pm (l.o. 2pm).
Parking for 3.
Open February-December.

Bluestones
Listed
7, Southey St., Keswick, CA12 4EG
☎ (076 87) 74237
Warm, comfortable family guesthouse. Convenient for town centre and amenities. Lounge with TV and beverage making facilities. Open all year.
Bedrooms: 1 single, 1 double, 2 family rooms.
Bathrooms: 1 public.
Bed & breakfast: £11-£12 single, £22-£24 double.

Bonshaw Guest House ⋒
Listed
20 Eskin St., Keswick, CA12 4DG
☎ (076 87) 73084
Small, friendly, comfortable guesthouse, providing home cooking. Convenient for town centre and all amenities.
Bedrooms: 2 single, 2 double & 1 twin, 1 family room.
Bathrooms: 1 public.
Bed & breakfast: £11 single, £22 double.
Half board: £16 daily, £109 weekly.
Evening meal 6.30pm (l.o. 5pm).

Brienz Guesthouse
3, Greta Street, Keswick, CA12 4HS
☎ (076 87) 71049
Small, friendly guesthouse offering a high standard of comfort. Imaginative home cooking, choice of menu. Bedrooms with shower. Non-smoking.
Bedrooms: 1 double & 2 twin.
Bathrooms: 1 public; 2 private showers.
Bed & breakfast: £22-£25 double.

Half board: £17.50-£19 daily, £117-£128 weekly.
Evening meal 7pm (l.o. 8pm).

Brierholme Guest House ⋒

21 Bank St., Keswick, CA12 5JZ
☎ (076 87) 72938
Friendly guesthouse in town centre. Private parking. Close to park, spa, lake. Choice of en-suite or standard rooms with mountain views.
Bedrooms: 5 double, 1 family room.
Bathrooms: 5 private; 1 private shower.
Bed & breakfast: £27-£34 double.
Half board: £21-£24.50 daily.
Evening meal 6.30pm (l.o. 3pm).
Parking for 6.

Castle Inn Hotel ⋒

Bassenthwaite, Keswick, CA12 4RG
☎ (059 681) 401 Fax (059 681) 604
A quality hotel with extensive leisure and conference facilities in a rural location yet with easy access to major routes.
Bedrooms: 2 single, 12 double & 13 twin, 9 family rooms.
Bathrooms: 36 private.
Bed & breakfast: £39-£49 single, £64-£75 double.
Half board: £44-£49.50 daily.
Lunch available.
Evening meal 7pm (l.o. 9.30pm).
Parking for 200.
Credit: Access, Visa, Diners, Amex.

Century Guest House
17 Church St., Keswick, CA12 4DT
☎ (076 87) 72843
A 100-year-old manse converted to a high standard and family run.
Bedrooms: 2 single, 2 double & 1 twin, 2 family rooms.
Bathrooms: 1 public.
Bed & breakfast: from £12 single, from £24 double.
Evening meal 6pm (l.o. 7pm).

Charnwood M
⌂⌂⌂ COMMENDED
6 Eskin St., Keswick,
CA12 4DH
☎ (076 87) 74111
*Victorian house centrally
situated in quiet position but
near to town centre. Fine home
cooking, friendly service.
Spacious, comfortable rooms,
all facilities.*
Bedrooms: 1 single, 1 double,
4 family rooms.
Bathrooms: 3 private,
2 public; 2 private showers.
Bed & breakfast: £24-£32
double.
Half board: £18.50-£22.50
daily, £124-£152 weekly.
Evening meal 6.30pm (l.o.
4pm).
Parking for 1.
🐕🌙📞🖁👤 ⓥ ⊬ ⊟ ⌂
✗ 🏠 ⒸⒶⓅ ☜ ⓈⓅ 🏛

Chaucer House Hotel M
⌂⌂⌂ COMMENDED
Ambleside Rd., Keswick,
CA12 4DR
☎ (076 87) 72318/73223
*Quiet, informal, comfortable,
licensed family-run hotel
overlooking Skiddaw,
Grisedale and Derwentwater.
Fresh home-cooked food our
speciality.*
Bedrooms: 10 single,
12 double & 4 twin, 6 family
rooms.
Bathrooms: 23 private,
7 public; 3 private showers.
Bed & breakfast: £19-£25
single, £27.60-£48 double.
Half board: £22.80-£34 daily,
£143.80-£214 weekly.
Evening meal 7.30pm (l.o.
5.30pm).
Parking for 25.
Open March-October.
Credit: Access, Visa, Diners,
Amex.
🐕⑧🖁👤 ⓥ ⊬ ⊟ ⓉⓋ
◖🖳🝢♪🝠 ⒸⒶⓅ ⓈⓅ

Cherry Trees M
⌂⌂⌂ COMMENDED
16 Eskin St., Keswick,
CA12 4DQ
☎ (076 87) 71048
*Character Edwardian town
house. Antique furnishings,
home-cooking. Vegetarian food
available. Peace and quiet
paramount, warm welcome and
personal service assured. Non-
smokers only please.*
Bedrooms: 2 single, 2 double
& 1 twin, 1 family room.
Bathrooms: 2 private,
2 public.
Bed & breakfast: from £13
single, £26-£30 double.

Half board: £19.50-£21.50
daily, £127-£141 weekly.
Evening meal 7pm (l.o. 6pm).
Credit: Access, Visa.
🐕🝢📞◖🖳🝠👤 ⓥ ⊬ ⊟
🖳 🝠 ⒸⒶⓅ ⓈⓅ 🏛

Claremont House
⌂⌂ COMMENDED
Chestnut Hill, Keswick,
CA12 4LT
☎ (076 87) 72089
*Comfortable, homely
guesthouse with home-made
bread and fresh produce,
hikers' breakfast, choice of
starter for dinner, home-made
sweets, cream teas, and
barbecues in fine weather.*
Bedrooms: 1 single, 3 double
& 1 twin, 1 family room.
Bathrooms: 3 private,
1 public.
Bed & breakfast: £18.50-£22
single, £37-£42 double.
Half board: £31.50-£35.50
daily.
Evening meal 7pm (l.o. 4pm).
Parking for 6.
🐕⑧🖁👤 ⓥ ⊟ ⓉⓋ 🖳 ☼
☜ ⓈⓅ

Clarence House M
⌂⌂⌂ COMMENDED
14 Eskin St., Keswick,
CA12 4DQ
☎ (076 87) 73186
*Friendly, well-appointed
establishment offering home
cooking. 5 minutes' walk from
the seaside, parks and shops.
Non-smokers only please.*
Bedrooms: 2 single, 4 double
& 2 twin, 1 family room.
Bathrooms: 7 private,
1 public.
Bed & breakfast: £13.50-
£14.50 single, £32-£34 double.
Half board: £23-£24 daily,
£160-£165 weekly.
Evening meal 6.30pm (l.o.
3pm).
🐕🝢🖃🏵👤 ⓥ ⊬ ⊟ ⓉⓋ 🖳
ⒸⒶⓅ ☜ ⓈⓅ

Crow Park Hotel M
⌂⌂⌂
The Heads, Keswick,
CA12 5ER
☎ (076 87) 72208
*Quiet but central, between the
lake and the town centre.
Magnificent views all round of
the Lakeland fells.*
Bedrooms: 4 single, 14 double
& 7 twin, 1 family room.
Bathrooms: 26 private.
Bed & breakfast: £19-£24
single, £38-£48 double.
Half board: £27.50-£35 daily,
£192-£245 weekly.
Evening meal 6.45pm (l.o.
8pm).

Parking for 26.
Open January-November.
Credit: Access, Visa.
🐕🝢📞⑧🖁👤 ⓥ ⊬ ⊟
🖳 🝠 ⒸⒶⓅ ⓈⓅ

Cumbria Hotel M
⌂⌂ COMMENDED
1 Derwentwater Place,
Keswick, CA12 4DR
☎ (076 87) 73171
*Early Victorian house, close to
the centre of Keswick and
within easy walking distance of
the lake. Lovely views from
most bedrooms.*
Bedrooms: 3 single, 4 double,
2 family rooms.
Bathrooms: 4 private,
2 public.
Bed & breakfast: £14.50
single, £29-£34 double.
Half board: £22-£24.50 daily,
£140-£156 weekly.
Evening meal 6.45pm (l.o.
6.45pm).
Parking for 8.
Open February-October.
Credit: Access, Visa.
🐕⑧🏵👤 ⓥ ⊟ ⓉⓋ 🖳 🝠
✗ 🏠 ⓈⓅ

Dale Head Hall M
⌂⌂⌂⌂ COMMENDED
Thirlmere, Keswick,
CA12 4TN
☎ (076 87) 72478
*16th C former Lord Mayor's
country retreat. On the shores
of Thirlmere, halfway between
Keswick and Grasmere.
Unique peaceful setting. Non-
smoking establishment.*
Bedrooms: 6 double & 2 twin,
1 family room.
Bathrooms: 9 private.
Bed & breakfast: £70-£86
double.
Half board: £49.25-£56.25
daily, £315-£355 weekly.
Evening meal 7.30pm (l.o.
7pm).
Parking for 20.
Credit: Access, Visa.
🐕12🝡🖁📞⑧🏵👤 ⓥ
⊬ ⊟ 🝠♪🝠 ☼ ✗
🏠 ☜ 🏛 Ⓣ

Dalegarth House
Country Hotel M
⌂⌂⌂
Portinscale, Keswick,
CA12 5RQ
☎ (076 87) 72817
*Edwardian house 1 mile from
Keswick, with views of
Skiddaw and Derwentwater.
Licensed bar, 2 lounges and 5-
course evening meal. Non-
smokers only please.*
Bedrooms: 4 double & 2 twin.
Bathrooms: 6 private.
Bed & breakfast: £20-£22
single, £40-£44 double.
Half board: £29.50-£32 daily,
£190-£210 weekly.

Evening meal 7pm (l.o.
5.30pm).
Parking for 8.
Credit: Access, Visa.
🐕5⑧🝢👤 ⓥ ⊬ ⊟ ⓉⓋ
🖳 🝠 ☼ ✗ 🏠 🝡 ⓈⓅ

Daleview Hotel M
⌂⌂⌂ COMMENDED
Lake Rd., Keswick,
CA12 5DQ
☎ (076 87) 72666
*Small family-run hotel in an
excellent position for the lake,
town centre and miniature golf-
course. Views of surrounding
fells.*
Bedrooms: 2 single, 7 double
& 3 twin, 3 family rooms.
Bathrooms: 10 private,
1 public.
Bed & breakfast: £24-£26.50
single, £38-£51 double.
Half board: £29.50-£36 daily,
£104.50-£145 weekly.
Lunch available.
Evening meal 7pm (l.o. 9pm).
Parking for 17.
Open February-November.
Credit: Access, Visa.
🐕🝢🖁👤 ⊟ 🝠🖳🝠 🝡 ✗ ⓈⓅ

Derwentwater Hotel M
⌂⌂⌂⌂
Portinscale, Keswick,
CA12 5RE
☎ (076 87) 72538 Fax
(076 87) 71002 Telex 57515
CONSORT G. EXT 11.
Ⓖ Consort
*Well-positioned on the shore of
Lake Derwentwater in 16 acres
of grounds, offering
comfortable accommodation.*
Bedrooms: 6 single, 35 double
& 36 twin, 6 family rooms.
Bathrooms: 83 private.
Bed & breakfast: £45-£68
single, £77-£89 double.
Half board: £174-£350
weekly.
Lunch available.
Evening meal 7pm (l.o.
9.30pm).
Parking for 140.
Credit: Access, Visa, Diners,
Amex.
🐕🝡🝢📞⑧🖳🝢🏵👤 ⓥ
⊬ ⊟ 🝠🖳🝠 🝡🝠 🝡 Ⓤ
♪ ☼ 🝠 ⓈⓅ Ⓣ
🕮 Display advertisement
appears on page 85.

Dorchester Guest
House M
⌂⌂
17 Southey St., Keswick,
CA12 4EG
☎ (076 87) 73256
*A quiet and central guesthouse
near the parks and lake.
Family-run for 20 years,
offering home cooking. TV in
bedrooms. Private showers.*
Bedrooms: 1 single, 3 double
& 1 twin, 3 family rooms.
Continued ▶

KESWICK
Continued

Bathrooms: 1 public;
4 private showers.
Bed & breakfast: £10-£12
single, £20-£24 double.
Open March-November.

ॐ2 ▯ ▮ ☐ ☞ 🖵 Ⅲ 🗯 SP

Fell House
ॐॐ COMMENDED

28 Stanger St., Keswick,
CA12 5JU
☎ (076 87) 72669
*Spacious, centrally situated
Victorian house with
comfortable accommodation
and informal hospitality.
Mountain views. Colour TV in
all bedrooms (not metered).*
Bedrooms: 1 single, 3 double
& 1 twin, 1 family room.
Bathrooms: 2 private,
1 public.
Bed & breakfast: £11-£14.25
single, £22-£32.50 double.
Half board: £17-£22.75 daily,
£110-£138 weekly.
Evening meal 6.30pm (l.o.
10am).
Parking for 4.

ॐ ▯ ☐ ⓤ Ⅴ ☞ ☐ Ⅲ ▯
🗯 🐾 🖁 SP

Foye House ⋔
☐

23 Eskin St., Keswick,
CA12 4DQ
☎ (076 87) 73288
*Friendly comfortable well-
established guesthouse offering
good home cooking. Situated in
quiet residential area, 4
minutes' walk from town.*
Bedrooms: 3 single, 1 double
& 1 twin, 1 family room.
Bathrooms: 2 public.
Bed & breakfast: £12.75-
£13.75 single, £25.50-£27.50
double.
Half board: £20.45-£21.45
daily, £85.80-£140 weekly.
Evening meal 7pm (l.o. 4pm).

ॐ ▯ ☐ ☼ Ⅴ ✂ Ⅲ ▯ ☒
🗯 SP

Glaramara ⋔

Seatoller, Keswick,
CA12 5XQ
☎ Borrowdale (059 684) 222
Telex 667047
*Purpose-built holiday centre at
the foot of Honister Pass.*
Bedrooms: 19 single, 14 twin.
Bathrooms: 14 public.
Half board: £26.45-£28.45
daily, £185-£199 weekly.
Lunch available.
Evening meal 7pm.
Parking for 30.

ॐ2 ☐ ⓤ ▮ Ⅴ ✂ ☐ ☒
⫪ 🌂 ❋ 🗯 🖁 ☐ ᴅᴀᴘ 🐾 SP ☐

Glaramara Guest House
ॐॐ

9 Acorn St., Keswick,
CA12 4EA
☎ (076 87) 73216
*Comfortable family-run
guesthouse, home-cooked food.
4 minutes' easy walk of town
centre and lake. Rooms with
showers.*
Bedrooms: 1 single, 2 double
& 1 twin, 1 family room.
Bathrooms: 1 public;
2 private showers.
Bed & breakfast: £11-£11.50
single, £23-£24 double.
Half board: £16-£18 daily.
Evening meal 6.30pm (l.o.
4pm).
Parking for 1.

ॐ ☼ ▮ Ⅴ ☞ ☐ Ⅲ ▯

Glencoe Guesthouse

21 Helvellyn St., Keswick,
CA12 4EN
☎ (076 87) 71016
*Recently renovated Victorian
town house. Run by qualified
chef/cook with emphasis on
cleanliness and good food. A
family atmosphere with the
professional approach.*
Bedrooms: 3 double.
Bathrooms: 2 public.
Bed & breakfast: £11-£12.50
single, £20-£22 double.
Half board: £16.50-£19 daily,
£115-£125 weekly.
Lunch available.
Evening meal 6pm.
Open February-December.

ॐ ☐ ☼ ▮ Ⅴ ☞ ☐ Ⅲ
▯ 🗯 ᴅᴀᴘ SP

Glendale Guest House
ॐॐ

7 Eskin St., Keswick,
CA12 4DH
☎ (076 87) 73562
*A Victorian building in
excellent condition throughout.
A short walk from the town
centre and the lake.*
Bedrooms: 2 single, 1 double,
4 family rooms.
Bathrooms: 2 public.
Bed & breakfast: £13-£14
single, £26-£28 double.
Half board: £20-£21 daily,
from £140 weekly.
Evening meal 6.30pm (l.o.
4.30pm).

ॐ5 ☼ ▮ Ⅴ ✂ ☞ ☐ Ⅲ 🗯
🗯

Goodwin House ⋔

29 Southey St., Keswick,
CA12 4EE
☎ (076 87) 74634
*Warm, friendly, comfortable
guesthouse with home cooking.
In a quiet area, with easy
access to shops, Lakes and
fells. Own keys, open all year.*

Bedrooms: 1 single, 1 double
& 1 twin, 3 family rooms.
Bathrooms: 1 private,
3 public.
Bed & breakfast: from £12
single, from £24 double.
Half board: from £17.50
daily.
Evening meal 6.30pm.

ॐ ☐ ☼ ⓤ ▮ Ⅲ 🗯 SP 🖁

The Grange Country
House Hotel ⋔
ॐॐॐ COMMENDED

Manor Brow, Ambleside Rd.,
Keswick, CA12 4BA
☎ (076 87) 72500
*A building of charm, fully
restored and refurbished, with
many antiques. Quiet,
overlooking Keswick with
panoramic mountain views.
Log fires, freshly prepared
food, lovely bedrooms and good
company.*
Bedrooms: 7 double & 3 twin.
Bathrooms: 10 private,
1 public.
Bed & breakfast: £54-£64
double.
Half board: £34-£39 daily,
£229-£245 weekly.
Lunch available.
Evening meal 7pm (l.o.
8.30pm).
Parking for 13.
Open February-November.
Credit: Access, Visa.

ॐ5 🖤 ☎ ⓔ ☐ ▮ Ⅴ ✂
☞ Ⅲ ☒ ♨ ∪ ⫪ ❋ 🗯 🐾 SP
🖁 ☐

Greta View Guest
House ⋔

2 Greta St., Keswick,
CA12 4HS
☎ (076 87) 73102
*Appealing stone-built house
with uninterrupted views of
Skiddaw and Latrigg. Minutes
from the town centre.
Comfortable, well-furnished
accommodation with good
home cooking.*
Bedrooms: 3 double, 3 family
rooms.
Bathrooms: 3 private,
1 public.
Bed & breakfast: £35-£47
double.
Half board: £50-£65 daily.
Evening meal 6.30pm (l.o.
5pm).
Credit: Access, Visa, Diners,
Amex.

ॐ 🖤 ☐ ☼ ▮ Ⅴ ☞ ☐ Ⅲ
☒ 🐾 ☐

Greystones ⋔
ॐॐॐ COMMENDED

Ambleside Rd., Keswick,
CA12 4DP
☎ (076 87) 73108

*Friendly hotel with a fine
reputation and personal service.
Ideally located for town, lake
and fells.*
Bedrooms: 1 single, 6 double
& 2 twin.
Bathrooms: 8 private,
1 public; 1 private shower.
Bed & breakfast: £17.50
single, £30-£34 double.
Half board: £23.50-£25.50
daily, £152.50-£163 weekly.
Evening meal 6.30pm (l.o.
2pm).
Parking for 9.
Open February-November.

ॐ8 ⓔ ☼ ☐ ▮ Ⅴ ☞ Ⅲ ☒
⫪ ⯈ 🗯 🗯 SP 🖁 ☐

Hazeldene Hotel ⋔
ॐॐॐ

The Heads, Keswick,
CA12 5ER
☎ (076 87) 72106
*Beautiful and central with open
views over Derwentwater to
Borrowdale and the Newlands
Valley. Close to the town
centre and shops.*
Bedrooms: 5 single, 8 double
& 4 twin, 5 family rooms.
Bathrooms: 18 private,
3 public.
Bed & breakfast: £15.50-
£20.50 single, £31-£41 double.
Half board: £27-£32 daily,
£182.50-£219.50 weekly.
Evening meal 6.30pm (l.o.
4pm).
Parking for 18.
Open March-November.

ॐ 🖤 ☐ ☼ ▮ Ⅴ ☞ ☐ Ⅲ
☒ 🐾 🗯 SP

Hazelgrove ⋔
ॐॐ COMMENDED

4 Ratcliffe Place, Keswick,
CA12 4DZ
☎ (076 87) 73391
*A warm friendly guesthouse
with home cooking, convenient
for shops, parks and lake.
Under supervision of owner.*
Bedrooms: 1 single, 2 double
& 1 twin, 1 family room.
Bathrooms: 3 private,
1 public.
Bed & breakfast: £22-£24
double.
Half board: £17-£18 daily,
£112-£122 weekly.
Evening meal 6.30pm (l.o.
6.30pm).
Open March-October.

ॐ ⓔ ☐ ☼ ⓤ ▮ Ⅴ ☞ ☐
☒ ᴅᴀᴘ SP

Highfield Hotel ⋔
ॐॐॐ COMMENDED

The Heads, Keswick,
CA12 5ER
☎ (076 87) 72508

A small hotel near the town and the lakeside. Peaceful situation with superb views. Home-made bread.
Bedrooms: 5 single, 7 double & 4 twin, 3 family rooms.
Bathrooms: 15 private, 1 public.
Bed & breakfast: £15.50-£23 single, £38-£46 double.
Half board: £26-£33.50 daily, £182-£234.50 weekly.
Evening meal 7pm (l.o. 6pm).
Parking for 19.
Open April-October.
⌂ 5 ♻ ▮ Ⓥ ⌘ 📺 ▥ ♨ ♨

The Homestead ♏
♨♨
Braithwaite, Keswick,
CA12 5RY
☎ Braithwaite (059 682) 229
Midway between Bassenthwaite and Derwentwater, overlooking the Skiddaw mountain range and lovely countryside.
Bedrooms: 3 double, 3 family rooms.
Bathrooms: 2 public.
Bed & breakfast: £24-£25 double.
Half board: £18-£19.50 daily, £126-£136.50 weekly.
Evening meal 7pm (l.o. 4pm).
Parking for 16.
⌂ ⓑ ✿ Ⓤ ▮ ♨ 📺 ❄ ♒

Ladstock Country House Hotel ♏
♨♨♨ COMMENDED
Thornthwaite, Keswick,
CA12 5RZ
☎ Braithwaite (059 682) 210
18th C country house hotel 3 miles from Keswick, set in own grounds. Panoramic views. Rooms with four-poster beds. 3 day breaks. Weddings and conferences.
Bedrooms: 2 single, 13 double & 6 twin, 2 family rooms.
Bathrooms: 3 private, 2 public; 7 private showers.
Bed & breakfast: £28-£30 single, £36-£45 double.
Half board: £28-£55 daily, £190-£385 weekly.
Lunch available.
Evening meal 7pm (l.o. 9pm).
Parking for 60.
Open February-December.
Credit: Access, Visa.
⌂ ♨ ♒ ⌘ ♨ ▮ Ⓥ ⌘ 📺 ▥ ♨ ♒ ✿ ❄ [DAP] ♨ SP ♒ ♒ ⓣ

Latrigg Lodge Hotel ♏
♨♨♨ COMMENDED
Lake Rd., Keswick,
CA12 5DQ
☎ (076 87) 73545

In a quiet, traffic-free road only a few minutes' walk from the market square, the lake and beautiful fells.
Bedrooms: 6 double & 1 twin.
Bathrooms: 7 private, 1 public.
Bed & breakfast: £29-£32 single, £48-£54 double.
Half board: £37-£40 daily, £233-£252 weekly.
Lunch available.
Evening meal 6pm (l.o. 11pm).
Parking for 7.
Credit: Access, Visa.
⌂ ♨ ♒ ⌘ ⌂ ✿ ▮ Ⓥ ⌘ ▥ ♨ ♒ ⓣ ▶ ♨ ♒ SP ⓣ

Linnett Hill Hotel ♏
♨♨♨ COMMENDED
4 Penrith Rd., Keswick,
CA12 4HF
☎ (076 87) 73109
Charming 1812 hotel overlooking Skiddaw and Latrigg Hills. Opposite parks, gardens and river. Fresh home-cooked food, including a la carte menus with quality wines.
Bedrooms: 1 single, 6 double & 2 twin.
Bathrooms: 9 private.
Bed & breakfast: £20 single, £36 double.
Half board: £26.50-£30 daily, £178.50-£203 weekly.
Lunch available.
Evening meal 7pm (l.o. 6.30pm).
Parking for 12.
Credit: Access, Visa.
⌂ 5 ♨ ♒ ▮ ⌘ ▥ ♨ ♒ ♨ SP ▥ ⓣ

Littletown Farm ♏
Newlands, Keswick,
CA12 5TU
☎ Braithwaite (059 682) 353
150-acre mixed farm. In the beautiful, unspoilt Newlands Valley. En-suite bedrooms. Comfortable residents' lounge, dining room and cosy bar. Traditional 4-course dinner 6 nights a week.
Bedrooms: 1 single, 4 double & 2 twin, 2 family rooms.
Bathrooms: 5 private, 2 public.
Bed & breakfast: from £20 single, £36-£45 double.
Half board: £25-£28 daily, £160-£180 weekly.
Evening meal 7pm.
Parking for 10.
Open March-December.
⌂ ♨ ♒ ✿ ▮ Ⓥ ⌘ ▥ ♨ ♒ ❄ ♒ ♒ ♨

Lynwood Guest House ♏
♨♨♨
12 Ambleside Rd., Keswick,
CA12 4DL
☎ (076 87) 72081

Large Victorian guesthouse convenient for all amenities. Spacious comfortable bedrooms, choice en-suite or standard. Good home cooking. Licensed. Non-smokers only please.
Bedrooms: 1 single, 4 double & 2 twin, 2 family rooms.
Bathrooms: 5 private, 2 public.
Bed & breakfast: £13-£14 single, £26-£35 double.
Half board: £21.50-£25 daily, £145-£170 weekly.
Evening meal 6.30pm (l.o. 4.30pm).
Credit: Access, Visa.
⌂ 3 ♒ ♨ ▮ Ⓥ ✁ ⌘ ▥ ♨ ♒ ✿ ♒ ♒

Lyzzick Hall Hotel ♏
Underskiddaw, Nr. Keswick,
CA12 4PY
☎ (076 87) 72277
Peaceful country house hotel in its own grounds, with excellent views, good food and a friendly, relaxed atmosphere.
Bedrooms: 4 single, 7 double & 5 twin, 4 family rooms.
Bathrooms: 20 private, 1 public.
Bed & breakfast: £23.50-£26 single, £47-£52 double.
Half board: £33.50-£35 daily, £215-£230 weekly.
Lunch available.
Evening meal 7pm (l.o. 9.30pm).
Parking for 30.
Open January, March-December.
Credit: Access, Visa, Diners, Amex.
⌂ ♨ ♒ ⌂ ⌘ ✿ ▮ Ⓥ ⌘ ▥ ♨ ♒ ⓣ ❄ ❄ ❄ ♒ SP ♒

Monkstones
62 Blencathra St., Keswick
CA12 4HX
☎ (076 87) 74098
We pride ourselves on making guests feel as comfortable as possible. A friendly home-from-home.
Bedrooms: 1 single, 1 double & 1 twin, 2 family rooms.
Bathrooms: 2 public.
Bed & breakfast: £9.50 single, £19 double.
Half board: £14.50 daily, £101.50 weekly.
Evening meal 6pm (l.o. 7pm).
Parking for 3.
⌂ 5 ♒ ♨ ▮ Ⓥ ✁ ⌘ 📺 ⬆ ♨ ♒ ❄ ♒ [DAP] ♨ SP ⓣ

Powe House
Portinscale, Nr. Keswick,
CA12 5RW
☎ (076 87) 73611

Offers a high standard of comfort and accommodation. Private facilities available in most rooms. Residential licence.
Bedrooms: 1 single, 3 double & 1 twin, 1 family room.
Bathrooms: 3 private, 1 public.
Bed & breakfast: £14-£16 single, £34-£36 double.
Half board: £26-£28 daily, £176-£180 weekly.
Evening meal 7pm.
Parking for 8.
⌂ ♨ ♒ ▮ ⌘ 📺 ▥ ♨ ❄ ♨ ♒

Queen's Hotel ♏
♨♨♨
Main St., Keswick,
CA12 5JF
☎ (076 87) 73333
In the centre of Keswick, well placed for both the shops and countryside.
Bedrooms: 8 single, 8 double & 2 twin, 18 family rooms.
Bathrooms: 36 private.
Bed & breakfast: £26-£32.40 single, £42-£60 double.
Half board: £28-£35 daily.
Lunch available.
Evening meal 6.30pm (l.o. 8.30pm).
Parking for 16.
Credit: Access, Visa, Diners, Amex.
⌂ ♨ ♒ ⌂ ⌘ ✿ ▮ Ⓥ ⌘ ▥ ♨ ♒ ⓣ ❄ ❄ [DAP] ♨ SP ⓣ

Ravensworth Hotel ♏
♨♨♨
Station St., Keswick,
CA12 5HH
☎ (076 87) 72476
A pleasant, family-run licensed hotel where you can be at your ease, adjacent to Fitz Park and the town centre.
Bedrooms: 8 double.
Bathrooms: 8 private.
Bed & breakfast: £30-£36 double.
Half board: £23-£26 daily, £154-£180 weekly.
Evening meal 7pm (l.o. 7pm).
Parking for 5.
Open February-December.
Credit: Access, Visa.
⌂ ♒ ▮ Ⓥ ⌘ 📺 ▥ ♨ ♒ ❄ ♒ ♒ SP ⓣ

Red House Hotel ♏
♨♨♨
Keswick, CA12 4QA
☎ (076 87) 72211
Country house hotel in extensive wooded grounds with superb mountain views. Ideal for Lakeland holidays. Outstanding food. Dogs particularly welcome.
Bedrooms: 2 single, 7 double & 9 twin, 4 family rooms.
Continued ▶

69

Bathrooms: 20 private,
2 public.
Half board: £36-£42 daily,
£245-£275 weekly.
Lunch available.
Evening meal 7pm (l.o.
8.30pm).
Parking for 25.
Open March-December.
Credit: Access, Visa.

Rickerby Grange
☺☺☺ COMMENDED
Portinscale, Keswick,
CA12 5RH
☎ (076 87) 72344
*Detached country hotel in its
own gardens, in a quiet village
on the outskirts of Keswick.
Provides imaginative cooking,
a bar and 2 TV lounges.*
Bedrooms: 2 single, 8 double
& 1 twin, 3 family rooms.
Bathrooms: 11 private,
1 public; 1 private shower.
Bed & breakfast: £19.50-£23
single, £39-£46 double.
Half board: £29-£32.50 daily,
£193-£214 weekly.
Evening meal 7pm (l.o. 6pm).
Parking for 13.

Rooking House ♨
☺☺☺ COMMENDED
Portinscale, Keswick,
CA12 5RD
☎ (076 87) 72506
*A fine Edwardian house with
superb views of Lake
Derwentwater and hills.
Friendly atmosphere.*
Bedrooms: 2 double & 3 twin.
Bathrooms: 5 private.
Bed & breakfast: from £20
single, £35-£40 double.
Half board: £27.50-£30 daily,
£173.50-£190 weekly.
Evening meal 7.30pm (l.o.
6pm).
Parking for 6.
Open February-December.

Seven Oaks Guest House
☺☺
7 Acorn St., Keswick,
Cumbria. CA12 4EA
☎ (076 87) 72088
*Small terraced guesthouse in a
quiet, residential area within
easy walking distance of town
centre, parks and lake.
Comfortable rooms, cleanliness
guaranteed.*
Bedrooms: 1 single, 2 double
& 2 twin, 1 family room.

Bathrooms: 1 public;
5 private showers.
Bed & breakfast: £12-£12.50
single, £24-£25 double.
Half board: £17.50-£18 daily,
£122.50-£126 weekly.
Evening meal 6.30pm (l.o.
6.30pm).
Parking for 2.
Open February-November.

Skiddaw Grove Hotel ♨
☺☺☺
Vicarage Hill, Keswick,
CA12 5QB
☎ (076 87) 73324
*A comfortable family hotel,
well-appointed and close to all
the local amenities, with
magnificent views of Skiddaw.*
Bedrooms: 1 single, 6 double
& 2 twin, 1 family room.
Bathrooms: 9 private,
1 public.
Bed & breakfast: £14-£19
single, £28-£35 double.
Half board: £22-£25 daily,
£145-£166 weekly.
Evening meal 7pm (l.o. 5pm).
Parking for 13.

Skiddaw Hotel ♨
☺☺☺
Main St., Keswick,
CA12 5BN
☎ (076 87) 72071
Fax (076 87) 74850
*Family-owned and supervised
hotel in the town centre. Closes
only for the Christmas period.*
Bedrooms: 7 single, 14 double
& 11 twin, 8 family rooms.
Bathrooms: 40 private.
Bed & breakfast: £26.75-£30
single, £47.50-£53 double.
Lunch available.
Evening meal 6.30pm (l.o.
9pm).
Parking for 20.
Credit: Access, Visa, Amex.

Squirrel Lodge
43 Eskin St., Keswick,
CA12 4DG
☎ (076 87) 73091
*Candlelit 4-course dinners,
lounge. Colour TV, tea and
coffee facilities in all rooms.
Bargain breaks from November
to May. Non-smokers only
please.*
Bedrooms: 2 single, 3 double
& 1 twin.
Bathrooms: 2 public.
Bed & breakfast: £13.50-
£14.50 single, £26-£28 double.
Half board: £20-£21.50 daily,
£125-£128 weekly.

Evening meal 7pm (l.o.
4.30pm).
Parking for 2.
Open January-October,
December.
Credit: Access, Visa.

Stakis Lodore Swiss Hotel ♨
☺☺☺☺ HIGHLY COMMENDED
Keswick, CA12 5UX
☎ Borrowdale (059 684) 285
Telex 64305
ⒼⒷ Stakis
*The original part of the local
stone building dates back to
1660 and the main building is
19th C. Famous Lodore Falls
are within the grounds.*
Bedrooms: 9 single, 13 double
& 50 twin.
Bathrooms: 72 private,
1 public.
Bed & breakfast: max. £105
double.
Lunch available.
Evening meal 7.30pm (l.o.
9.30pm).
Parking for 143.
Open February-December.
Credit: Access, Visa, Diners,
Amex.

Strathmore Guest House ♨
☺☺ COMMENDED
8 St. Johns Terrace, Keswick,
CA12 4DP
☎ (076 87) 72584
*Warm, traditional stone-built
guesthouse at quiet end of town,
5 minutes to centre. Genuine
home cooking. "Heartbeat"
award for health options.*
Bedrooms: 1 single, 3 double
& 1 twin, 3 family rooms.
Bathrooms: 3 public.
Bed & breakfast: £13.50-
£14.50 single, £27-£29 double.
Half board: £20-£22 daily,
£128-£145 weekly.
Evening meal 6.30pm (l.o.
4pm).
Parking for 3.
Open February-November.

Swinside Lodge ♨
☺☺☺ HIGHLY COMMENDED
Newlands, Keswick,
CA12 5UE
☎ (076 87) 72948
*Well-appointed, secluded and
informal Victorian house
beneath Catbells. High
standard of food, service and
accommodation. Comfortable
and tranquil surroundings.*

Bedrooms: 4 double & 4 twin,
1 family room.
Bathrooms: 8 private,
3 public.
Half board: £36-£47.50 daily.
Evening meal 7.30pm (l.o.
8pm).
Parking for 14.
Open February-November.

Tarn Hows Guest House ♨
☺☺☺
5 Eskin St., Keswick,
CA12 4DH
☎ (076 87) 73217
*Long established and
comfortably appointed
guesthouse. Pleasantly situated
in quiet residential area. Close
to town centre and lakeside.
Private parking.*
Bedrooms: 1 single, 5 double
& 1 twin, 1 family room.
Bathrooms: 2 public;
2 private showers.
Bed & breakfast: max. £12.50
single, £24-£25 double.
Half board: £17.50-£18 daily,
£122.50-£126 weekly.
Evening meal 6.30pm (l.o.
4.30pm).
Parking for 6.

Thelmlea ♨
☺☺
Braithwaite, Nr. Keswick,
CA12 5TD
☎ (059 682) 305
*Country house set in 2 acres of
grounds, 2 miles from Keswick.
Between Derwentwater and
Bassenthwaite Lake, offering
relaxed atmosphere and
friendly personal service.*
Bedrooms: 4 family rooms.
Bathrooms: 2 private,
2 public.
Bed & breakfast: £26-£34
double.
Half board: £19-£24 daily.
Lunch available.
Evening meal 6.30pm (l.o.
7pm).
Parking for 9.

Wentworth Guest House ♨
☺☺
41 Eskin St., Keswick,
CA12 4DG
☎ (076 87) 73355
*Warm, friendly guesthouse,
quiet and close to the park. 5
minutes' walk from the town
centre. Comfortable lounge and
unrestricted parking.*
Bedrooms: 1 single, 1 double
& 2 twin.

Bathrooms: 1 public.
Bed & breakfast: £11.75-£12
single, £23.50-£24 double.
🔟 ☎ ⓊⓁ 🍴 ⛩ 📺 ⅏ 🏃
SP

KIRKBY LONSDALE

Cumbria
Map ref 5B3

Charming old town of
narrow streets and
Georgian buildings. The
Devil's Bridge over the
River Lune is probably
13th C.
*Tourist Information
Centre* ☎ *(05242) 71437*

Abbot Hall M

Kirkby Lonsdale, Via
Carnforth, Lancashire
LA6 2AB
☎ (052 42) 71406
*17th C farmhouse with old
world character, log fires, oak
beams, flag floors and large
double rooms, all with private
facilities.*
Bedrooms: 9 double.
Bathrooms: 9 private.
Bed & breakfast: £18 single,
£32-£34 double.
Half board: £24.50 daily,
£101-£154 weekly.
Evening meal 7pm (l.o. 6pm).
Parking for 7.
Open March-November.
🔟 ☎ ⛩ 🍴 ⓊⓁ 🍴 📺 🏃
📺 ⅏ 🏃

The Copper Kettle
Listed **APPROVED**

3 & 5 Market St., Kirkby
Lonsdale, Via Carnforth,
Lancashire, LA6 2AU
☎ (0468) 71714
*Part of an old manor house,
built in 1610, on the border
between the Yorkshire Dales
and the Lakes.*
Bedrooms: 1 double & 1 twin,
2 family rooms.
Bathrooms: 3 public.
Bed & breakfast: £16 single,
£25 double.
Half board: £22-£25 daily,
£154-£175 weekly.
Lunch available.
Evening meal 9pm (l.o. 9pm).
Credit: Access, Visa, Diners,
Amex.
🔟 ☎ ⛩ 🍴 Ⓥ ⅏ 🏃 🏃
🏃

Hipping Hall M

Cowan Bridge, Kirkby
Lonsdale, LA6 2JJ
☎ (052 42) 71187
*17th C country estate in 4-
acres of walled garden near
Kirkby Lonsdale. Ideal for the
Lakes and dales.*
Bedrooms: 5 double & 2 twin.

Bathrooms: 7 private.
Bed & breakfast: £46 single,
£58 double.
Half board: £44 daily, £265
weekly.
Evening meal 8pm (l.o.
8.30pm).
Parking for 13.
Open March-December.
Credit: Access, Visa.
🔟 12 ☎ 🍴 ⛩ 🍴 Ⓥ ⅏ 📺
🏃 ⛩ 🍴 ❋ 🏃 ⅏ Ⓣ

Pheasant Inn M
👑👑👑

Casterton, Kirkby Lonsdale,
Via Carnforth, Lancashire
LA6 2RX
☎ (052 42) 71230
*An old world country inn
specializing in good food and
service, an ideal location for
touring the lakes, dales and
coast.*
Bedrooms: 3 single, 6 double
& 3 twin, 1 family room.
Bathrooms: 13 private.
Bed & breakfast: max. £35
single, max. £55 double.
Half board: max. £38.50
daily, max. £269.50 weekly.
Lunch available.
Evening meal 7pm (l.o.
9.15pm).
Parking for 60.
Credit: Access, Visa.
🔟 ⛩ 🍴 🍷 ⓇⒹ 🍴 ⛩ Ⓥ
⅏ 🍴 📺 🍴 ⛩ 🍴 ❋
🏃 SP 🏃

Whoop Hall Inn M
👑👑👑 **COMMENDED**

Burrow with Burrow, Kirkby
Lonsdale, Carnforth,
Lancashire LA6 2HT
☎ (052 42) 71284
Fax (052 42) 72154
*15th C hostelry once a
coaching and drovers' inn, now
fully refurbished with all home
comforts.*
Bedrooms: 4 single, 5 double
& 5 twin, 2 family rooms.
Bathrooms: 16 private.
Bed & breakfast: £35-£40
single, £50-£65 double.
Half board: from £227.50
weekly.
Lunch available.
Evening meal 6pm (l.o.
10pm).
Parking for 120.
Credit: Access, Visa.
🔟 ⛩ 🍴 🍷 ⓇⒹ 🍴 ⛩ 🍴 Ⓥ
🍴 ⅏ ⛩ 🍴 ⛩ ⛩ ❋
ⒹⒶⒻ 🍴 SP 🏃

**The enquiry
coupons at the
back will help you
when contacting
proprietors.**

KIRKBY STEPHEN

Cumbria
Map ref 5B3

Old, picturesque market
town on the River Eden.
Good centre for exploring
the Eden Valley.
*Tourist Information
Centre* ☎ *(07683) 71199*

The Fat Lamb M
👑👑👑

Cross Bank, Ravenstonedale,
Kirkby Stephen, CA17 4LL
☎ Newbiggin-on-Lune
(058 73) 242
*Comfortable family-run
country inn offering traditional
warm welcome in beautiful
location. On A683, between
Sedbergh and Kirkby Stephen.*
Bedrooms: 7 double & 1 twin,
4 family rooms.
Bathrooms: 12 private.
Bed & breakfast: £27-£29.50
single, £42-£48 double.
Half board: £33.50-£36.50
daily, £205-£224 weekly.
Lunch available.
Evening meal 6.30pm (l.o.
9pm).
Parking for 30.
🔟 ⛩ ⛩ 🍴 Ⓥ ⅏ 📺 ⅏ 🏃
🍴 ⛩ ❋ 🏃 🏃 SP 🏃 Ⓣ

Ing Hill House
👑👑👑

Mallerstang, Kirkby Stephen,
CA17 4JT
☎ (076 83) 71153
*Delightful Georgian country
house in Mallerstang Valley
with glorious views. Peace,
quiet, open fires, home cooking
and a warm welcome.*
Bedrooms: 1 single, 2 double
& 1 twin.
Bathrooms: 3 private,
1 public.
Bed & breakfast: £20-£21
single, £36-£42 double.
Half board: £30.50-£33 daily,
£203-£224 weekly.
Evening meal 6.30pm (l.o.
8pm).
Parking for 5.
🔟 ⓇⒹ 🍴 ⛩ ⓊⓁ 🍴 ⅏ 🏃
❋ 🏃 ⒹⒶⒻ 🏃 SP

Kings Arms Hotel M
👑👑👑

Kirkby Stephen, CA17 4QN
☎ (076 83) 71378
*17th C former posting inn, in
the centre of the market town,
providing home-made food,
local game and fresh garden
produce.*
Bedrooms: 1 single, 3 double
& 4 twin, 1 family room.
Bathrooms: 3 private,
3 public.

Bed & breakfast: £24.50-£29
single, £40-£47.50 double.
Lunch available.
Evening meal 6.45pm (l.o.
9pm).
Parking for 12.
Credit: Access, Visa.
🔟 ⛩ 🍴 Ⓥ 🍴 📺 ⅏ 🍴 🍷
❋ ⒹⒶⒻ SP 🏃

The Town Head
House M
👑👑👑 **COMMENDED**

High St., Kirkby Stephen,
CA17 4SH
☎ (076 83) 71044
*Georgian/Victorian town house
with garden. Spacious en-suite
bedrooms with handsome
plasterwork, telephone and TV.
Four-posters available.
Restaurant. 16 miles from
junction 38 of the M6.*
Bedrooms: 1 single, 4 double
& 1 twin.
Bathrooms: 6 private.
Bed & breakfast: £31-£39
single, £50-£58 double.
Evening meal 7pm (l.o. 8pm).
Parking for 8.
🔟 11 ⛩ 🍷 ⓇⒹ 🍴 🍴 Ⓥ
🍴 🍴 ⅏ ⛩ ❋ 🏃 SP

LAKESIDE

Cumbria
Map ref 5A3

10m NE. Ulverston
There is a pier at
Lakeside for the lake
steamer service on
Windermere and steam
trains run from here along
the 3-mile track to
Haverthwaite during the
summer.

The Knoll Country
Guest House M
👑👑👑

Lakeside, Newby Bridge,
LA12 8AU
☎ Newby Bridge
(053 95) 31347
*Victorian detached residence in
quiet grounds backing on to
Grizedale forest. 3 minutes'
walk from the steamer pier and
lakeside.*
Bedrooms: 2 single, 3 double
& 1 twin, 3 family rooms.
Bathrooms: 6 private,
1 public.
Bed & breakfast: £13 single,
£31 double.
Half board: £22.50-£25 daily,
£155-£170 weekly.
Evening meal 7pm (l.o.
4.30pm).
Parking for 16.
Credit: Visa.
🔟 ⛩ 🍴 Ⓥ 🍴 📺 ⅏ 🍴 ❋
🍴 🏃 SP 🏃 Ⓣ

LANGDALE
Cumbria
Map ref 5A3

The 2 Langdale valleys (Great Langdale and Little Langdale) lie in the heart of beautiful mountain scenery. The craggy Langdale Pikes are almost 2500 ft high. An ideal walking and climbing area.

Britannia Inn ♠
♛♛♛

Elterwater, Nr. Ambleside, LA22 9HP
☎ Langdale (096 67) 210 & 382
A 400-year-old traditional Lake District inn on a village green in the beautiful Langdale Valley. A warm welcome to all. TV available in bedrooms.
Bedrooms: 7 double & 2 twin.
Bathrooms: 6 private, 2 public.
Bed & breakfast: £32-£40.50 single, £37-£51.50 double.
Half board: £32.50-£49.50 daily, £217-£336 weekly.
Lunch available.
Evening meal 7.30pm (l.o. 7.30pm).
Parking for 10.
Credit: Access, Visa.
➣ ⌨ ♡ 🛎 ⑪ 🖩 🎟 🖿 ⏍
🎏 Ⓣ

Three Shires Inn ♠
♛♛♛ COMMENDED

Little Langdale, Ambleside, LA22 9NZ
☎ (096 67) 215
On the eastern foot of the Wrynose Pass which goes on to Hard Knott and the Roman fort. A popular area for walkers and touring.
Bedrooms: 1 single, 4 double & 5 twin, 1 family room.
Bathrooms: 7 private, 2 public.
Bed & breakfast: £24-£29 single, £48-£58 double.
Half board: £30-£40 daily, £220-£260 weekly.
Lunch available.
Evening meal 7pm (l.o. 8pm).
Parking for 18.
Open February-November.
➣ ♡ 🛎 Ⓥ ⌴ 🎟 ⑪ 🖩 🖿
🗡 🎏 ⧄ SP

Half board prices shown are per person but in some cases may be based on double/twin occupancy.

LITTLE CLIFTON
Cumbria
Map ref 5A2

5m SW. Cockermouth
A very small village between Cockermouth and Workington, with an interesting 19th C church.

Crossbarrow Motel ♠
📺🖩

Little Clifton, Workington, CA14 1XS
☎ Workington (0900) 61443
Situated in a quiet corner of West Cumbria between the Lake District National Park and the sea with superb views of the Lakeland fells.
Bedrooms: 10 double & 16 twin, 1 family room.
Bathrooms: 27 private.
Bed & breakfast: £34 single, £52 double.
Half board: £35-£43 daily.
Lunch available.
Evening meal 7pm (l.o. 9.30pm).
Parking for 50.
Credit: Access, Visa, Amex.
➣ 🖾 ⌨ ⊙ ⌨ 🛎 Ⓥ ⌴
🖩 🖿 🎟 ⧄ SP

LOWESWATER
Cumbria
Map ref 5A3

This village lies between Loweswater, one of the smaller lakes of the Lake District, and Crummock Water. Several mountains lie beyond the village.

Grange Country House Hotel

Loweswater, Water-End, Cockermouth, CA13 0SU
☎ Lamplugh (0946) 861211
Peaceful 17th C manor house and modern annexe in an attractive garden overlooking the lake and fells, with log fires and colour TV. 2 four-poster suites are available.
Bedrooms: 4 double & 5 twin, 1 family room.
Bathrooms: 9 private, 3 public; 1 private shower.
Bed & breakfast: £23-£25 single, £46-£50 double.
Half board: £35-£37 daily, £225-£235 weekly.
Lunch available.
Evening meal 7pm (l.o. 8pm).
Parking for 32.
Open March-December.
➣ 🖾 ♡ ⊙ 🛎 Ⓥ ⌴ 🕾 🖩
🖿 🎟 ✳ 🎏 DAP SP 🎏

Scale Hill Hotel ♠
Loweswater, Nr. Cockermouth, CA13 9UX
☎ Lorton (090 085) 232
A 17th C coaching inn with modern comforts, nestling among the beautiful Buttermere and Loweswater Fells and the 3 lakes of the valley.
Bedrooms: 5 single, 5 double & 5 twin, 2 family rooms.
Bathrooms: 16 private, 1 public.
Half board: £39-£58 daily, £240-£360 weekly.
Evening meal 7.30pm (l.o. 7.45pm).
Parking for 25.
Open March-November.
➣ 🖾 🛎 ✂ ⌴ 🖩 🖿 🎟
♿ ✳ 🎏 SP 🎏

LUPTON
Cumbria
Map ref 5A3

Lupton Tower ♠
Lupton, Nr. Kirkby Lonsdale
☎ Crooklands (044 87) 400
Charming 18th C country house. Ideal location for dales and Lakes, beautiful views from all bedrooms, tastefully decorated throughout. Non-smoking establishment.
Bedrooms: 2 double & 2 twin, 2 family rooms.
Bathrooms: 4 private, 1 public.
Bed & breakfast: £18.50-£21 single, £29-£37 double.
Half board: £28-£32 daily, £176.40-£189 weekly.
Evening meal 8pm (l.o. 8pm).
Parking for 20.
➣ 🛎 Ⓥ ✂ ⌴ 🖿 🎟 ✳
🎏 ⬟ SP 🎏

MEALSGATE
Cumbria
Map ref 5A2

6m SW. Wigton
A scattered village between Cockermouth and Wigton, the birthplace of the 19th C philanthropist, George Moore.

Pink House Hotel
♛♛♛ COMMENDED

Mealsgate, Nr. Wigton, Carlisle, CA5 1JP
☎ Low Ireby (096 57) 229
A small Victorian country house hotel set amongst lovely trees and gardens. Beautifully appointed rooms and open fires. Warm, friendly atmosphere.

Bedrooms: 1 single, 2 double & 1 twin, 2 family rooms.
Bathrooms: 6 private.
Bed & breakfast: from £30 single, from £42 double.
Lunch available.
Evening meal 6.30pm (l.o. 8.45pm).
Parking for 20.
Credit: Access, Visa.
➣ ⌨ ⊙ ⌴ 🛎 Ⓥ ⌴ 🕾 🖩
🖿 🎟 🗡 ✳ 🎏 SP

MILNTHORPE
Cumbria
Map ref 5B3

Attractive limestone village with popular market. Near Levens Hall. Many lovely walks over nearby marshes.

Rigney Bank House ♠
♛♛

17 The Square, Milnthorpe, LA7 7QJ
☎ (053 95) 62236 Fax (053 95) 63487
Former 17th C inn on a picturesque village green in an unspoilt area. Ideal for touring and outdoor holiday activities.
Bedrooms: 1 single, 2 twin, 1 family room.
Bathrooms: 3 public.
Bed & breakfast: £12-£14 single, £23-£27 double.
Half board: £17-£19 daily, £107-£119 weekly.
Lunch available.
Evening meal 6.30pm (l.o. midday).
Parking for 4.
Credit: Access, Visa.
➣ ♡ ⓤ Ⓥ ⌴ 🕾 🖩 🖿 🖾
⟲ 🗡 🎏 DAP SP 🎏 Ⓣ

MUNGRISDALE
Cumbria
Map ref 5A2

The simple, white church in this hamlet has a 3-decker pulpit and box pews.

Near Howe Farm Hotel ♠
♛♛♛ COMMENDED

Mungrisdale, Penrith, CA11 0SH
☎ (059 683) 678
350-acre mixed farm. Farmhouse in quiet surroundings 1 mile from Mungrisdale, half a mile from the A66 and within easy reach of all the lakes.
Bedrooms: 3 double & 1 twin, 3 family rooms.
Bathrooms: 5 private, 1 public.

Bed & breakfast: £12.50-£15.50 single, £25-£31 double.
Half board: £20-£23 daily, £140-£161 weekly.
Evening meal 7pm (l.o. 5pm).
Parking for 12.
Open April-October.

NEWBY BRIDGE

Cumbria
Map ref 5A3

At the southern end of Windermere on the River Leven, this village has an unusual stone bridge with arches of unequal size. The Lakeside and Haverthwaite Railway has a stop here, and steamer cruises on Lake Windermere leave from Lakeside.

Landing Cottage M
🏵

Lakeside, Newby Bridge
Ulverston, LA12 8AS
☎ (053 95) 31719
19th C Lakeland-stone cottage, 100 yards from the shores of Lake Windermere, close to the steamer boat terminal and the Lakeside/Haverthwaite pleasure steam train.
Bedrooms: 3 double, 2 family rooms.
Bathrooms: 2 private, 2 public.
Bed & breakfast: £15-£19 single, £26-£30 double.
Half board: £21-£23 daily, £140-£150 weekly.
Evening meal 7pm (l.o. 4.30pm).
Parking for 6.

Swan Hotel M
🏵🏵🏵 COMMENDED

Newby Bridge, Nr. Ulverston,
LA12 8NB
☎ (053 95) 31681
Telex 65108 Fax (053 95) 31917
Inter
Privately-owned hotel enjoying a beautiful site at the foot of Lake Windermere. We offer facilities appreciated by both holiday and business visitors.
Bedrooms: 7 single, 13 double & 10 twin, 6 family rooms.
Bathrooms: 36 private.
Bed & breakfast: £46-£66 single, £74-£105 double.
Half board: £48-£65 daily, £336-£435 weekly.
Lunch available.
Evening meal 7pm (l.o. 9.30pm).
Parking for 106.

Credit: Access, Visa, Diners, Amex.

PENRITH

Cumbria
Map ref 5B2

This ancient and historic market town is the northern gateway to the Lake District. Penrith Castle was built as a defence against the Scots. Its ruins, open to the public, stand in the public park. High above the town is the famous Penrith Beacon.
Tourist Information Centre ☎ *(0768) 67466*

Agricultural Hotel
🏵🏵 APPROVED

Castlegate, Penrith,
CA11 7JE
☎ (0768) 62622
A superb Victorian building opposite Penrith Castle and park. 3 minutes from town centre. Close to railway station.
Bedrooms: 2 double & 2 twin.
Bathrooms: 1 public.
Bed & breakfast: £18-£20 single, £30 double.
Lunch available.
Evening meal 6pm (l.o. 9.30pm).
Parking for 28.

Brackenrigg Hotel

Watermillock, Penrith,
CA11 OLP
☎ Pooley Bridge
(076 84) 86206
18th C coaching inn overlooking Ullswater with 11 bedrooms, 3 self-catering cottages recently converted from old stables, 1 bar, games room and breakfast room/dining room. Open to non-residents.
Bedrooms: 6 double & 2 twin, 3 family rooms.
Bathrooms: 2 public.
Bed & breakfast: £14-£16.50 single, £25-£30 double.
Lunch available.
Evening meal 6.30pm (l.o. 9.30pm).
Parking for 30.
Open March-December.

George Hotel M
🏵🏵🏵

Penrith, CA11 7SU
☎ (0768) 62696 Fax (0768) 68223

A 300-year-old, famous coaching inn providing modern facilities, in the centre of Penrith. Privately owned and managed.
Bedrooms: 12 single, 10 double & 9 twin.
Bathrooms: 30 private, 1 public.
Bed & breakfast: £35-£40 single, £47.50-£60 double.
Half board: from £45.50 daily.
Lunch available.
Evening meal 7pm (l.o. 8.30pm).
Parking for 30.
Credit: Access, Visa.

The Grotto M
🏵🏵🏵 COMMENDED

Yanwath, Penrith, CA10 2LF
☎ (0768) 63288 Fax (0768) 63432
Large country house, dating from 1773, in beautiful, cultivated grounds. 2 miles south of Penrith, adjacent to Ullswater.
Bedrooms: 1 single, 1 double & 2 twin, 2 family rooms.
Bathrooms: 4 private, 1 public.
Bed & breakfast: £20 single, £40 double.
Half board: £32 daily, £200 weekly.
Evening meal 7.15pm.
Parking for 12.
Credit: Access.

Display advertisement appears on page 86.

Norcroft Guesthouse
🏵🏵🏵

Graham St., Penrith,
CA11 9LQ
☎ (0768) 62365
Spacious Victorian house with large comfortable rooms. In a quiet residential area near the town centre.
Bedrooms: 2 double & 4 twin, 2 family rooms.
Bathrooms: 5 private, 1 public.
Bed & breakfast: £13.50-£19.50 single, £27.50-£33 double.
Half board: £20-£27 daily, £140-£175 weekly.
Evening meal 7.30pm (l.o. 4.30pm).
Parking for 8.

We advise you to confirm your booking in writing.

The North Lakes Hotel M
🏵🏵🏵🏵🏵 COMMENDED

Ullswater Rd., Penrith,
CA11 8QT
☎ (0768) 68111 Telex 64257
Modern hotel in traditional hunting lodge style, where full use has been made of local stone and timber. Just off junction 40 on the M6.
Bedrooms: 38 double & 41 twin, 6 family rooms.
Bathrooms: 85 private.
Bed & breakfast: £84-£100 single, £108-£124 double.
Half board: £98-£114 daily.
Lunch available.
Evening meal 7pm (l.o. 9.45pm).
Parking for 150.
Credit: Access, Visa, Diners, Amex.

Nunnery House M

Staffield, Penrith, CA10 1EU
☎ Lazonby (076 883) 537
An 18th C house built on the site of a Benedictine nunnery and in its own grounds. Leave M6 at junction 41 to Lazonby-Kirkoswald and 2 miles on Armathwaite Road.
Bedrooms: 1 single, 2 double & 4 twin, 2 family rooms.
Bathrooms: 6 private, 3 public.
Bed & breakfast: £17-£21 single, £26-£38 double.
Half board: £25.50-£29.50 daily, £119-£147 weekly.
Lunch available.
Evening meal 7.30pm (l.o. 7.30pm).
Parking for 30.
Open March-December.

The Pategill Hotel

Carlton Rd., Penrith,
CA11 8JW
☎ (0768) 63153
Hotel with friendly service, 5 minutes from town centre. A la carte menu, children's menu, also lunches available. Parking area.
Bedrooms: 2 single, 1 twin, 8 family rooms.
Bathrooms: 2 public.
Bed & breakfast: £16.50-£18 single, £30-£36 double.
Half board: £20-£30 daily, £95-£105 weekly.
Lunch available.
Evening meal 6pm (l.o. 9pm).
Parking for 14.

PENRITH

Continued

Queens Head Hotel M
Tirril, Penrith, CA10 2JF
☎ (0768) 63219
17th C country inn 1.5 miles
from Ullswater and 2 miles
from the M6 junction 40.
Bedrooms: 1 single, 6 double,
1 family room.
Bathrooms: 2 private,
2 public.
Bed & breakfast: £15-£22
single, £25-£35 double.
Half board: £20.50-£25.50
daily.
Lunch available.
Evening meal 7pm (l.o.
10.30pm).
Parking for 36.

Woodland House Hotel M
Wordsworth St., Penrith,
CA11 7QY
☎ (0768) 64177
Elegant red sandstone house
with a library of books and
maps for walkers, nature lovers
and sightseers. Most bedrooms
en-suite. No smoking in hotel.
Bedrooms: 3 single, 2 double
& 2 twin, 1 family room.
Bathrooms: 6 private,
1 public.
Bed & breakfast: £15-£18
single, £28-£33 double.
Half board: £22-£25 daily,
£146-£166 weekly.
Evening meal 6.45pm (l.o.
5pm).
Parking for 13.

RAVENGLASS
Cumbria
Map ref 5A3

Coastal village on the
River Esk Estuary. The
Romans established a
supply base here, and a
well-preserved bath
house just south of the
village can be seen. A
miniature railway runs
from Ravenglass to Boot
in the Eskdale Valley.
Muncaster Castle, open
to the public, stands on a
wooded headland west of
the village.

Muncaster Country Guesthouse
Muncaster, Ravenglass,
CA18 1RD
☎ (0229) 717693

Licensed country guesthouse,
originally the village school,
conveniently situated opposite
Muncaster Castle gardens.
Friendly, cosy atmosphere.
Ideal for exploring western
Lakeland. Pleasant garden.
Ample parking. Outdoor
holidays and fell walking
organised.
Bedrooms: 1 single, 3 double
& 2 twin, 1 family room.
Bathrooms: 2 private,
3 public.
Bed & breakfast: £17-£20
single, £30-£38 double.
Half board: £26-£32 daily,
£210-£260 weekly.
Evening meal 6.30pm (l.o.
6.30pm).
Parking for 20.

Pennington Arms Hotel M
Main St., Ravenglass,
CA18 1SD
☎ (0229) 717222 & 717626
A family-run country inn in
lovely Ravenglass. Ideal for
touring the coast and valleys.
Bedrooms: 6 single, 11 double
& 6 twin, 5 family rooms.
Bathrooms: 13 private,
6 public.
Bed & breakfast: £15.50-£29
single, £26.50-£44 double.
Half board: £24.50-£38 daily,
£171.50-£266 weekly.
Lunch available.
Evening meal 6pm (l.o.
10pm).
Parking for 52.

Rosegarth M
Main St., Ravenglass,
CA18 1SQ
☎ (0229) 717275
In a rural seaside village with
views across the village green
to the Irish Sea.
Bedrooms: 3 double & 2 twin.
Bathrooms: 1 private,
2 public.
Bed & breakfast: from £12.50
single, from £25 double.
Parking for 3.

**Half board prices
shown are per
person but in some
cases may be based
on double/twin
occupancy.**

RAVENSTONEDALE
Cumbria
Map ref 5B3

Set below Ash Fell, this
village has a fine church
with an unusual interior
where sections of the
congregation sit facing
each other and there is a
3-decker pulpit.

The Black Swan Hotel M
COMMENDED
Ravenstonedale, Kirkby
Stephen, CA17 4NG
☎ Newbiggin-on-Lune
(058 73) 204
A delightful family-run hotel,
set amidst beautiful
countryside in a picturesque
village. Renowned for fine
food, comfort and hospitality.
Bedrooms: 1 single, 10 double
& 4 twin, 1 family room.
Bathrooms: 15 private,
1 public.
Bed & breakfast: £36 single,
£49-£52 double.
Half board: £32.50-£42.50
daily, £235-£250 weekly.
Lunch available.
Evening meal 7pm (l.o.
9.30pm).
Parking for 20.
Credit: Access, Visa, Amex.

RYDAL
Cumbria
Map ref 5A3

Hamlet at the east end of
Rydal Water, a small,
beautiful lake sheltered
by Rydal Fell. A good
centre for touring and
walking.

The Glen Rothay Hotel M
Rydal, Nr. Ambleside,
LA22 9LR
☎ Ambleside (053 94) 32524
A 17th C historic inn with
Wordsworth associations, in a
beautiful setting facing Rydal
Water.
Bedrooms: 3 single, 5 double
& 1 twin, 2 family rooms.
Bathrooms: 11 private,
1 public.
Bed & breakfast: £25-£30
single, £50-£80 double.
Half board: £35-£45 daily,
£231-£301 weekly.
Lunch available.

Evening meal 7.30pm (l.o.
8pm).
Parking for 40.
Credit: Access, Visa.

ST BEES
Cumbria
Map ref 5A3

Small coastal resort with
a good beach. The cliffs
at nearby St. Bees Head
are a sanctuary for
nesting sea birds. Home
of a public school which
was founded in the 16th
C.

Seacote Hotel M
APPROVED
Beach Rd., St. Bees,
CA27 0ES
☎ (0946) 822777
Overlooking St. Bees Beach
and St. Bees Head. Excellent
walking area, bird sanctuary,
golf-course. Conference and
function facilities for up to 250.
Ideal base for touring the
Lakes.
Bedrooms: 7 single, 12 double
& 11 twin, 2 family rooms.
Bathrooms: 32 private,
1 public.
Bed & breakfast: £25-£26
single, £38-£40 double.
Half board: £34-£36 daily,
£238-£252 weekly.
Lunch available.
Evening meal 6.30pm (l.o.
10pm).
Parking for 60.
Credit: Access, Visa, Amex.

SATTERTHWAITE
Cumbria
Map ref 5A3

4m S. Hawkshead
Secluded village set in the
heart of the Grizedale
Forest with visitors'
centre. Forest trails and
pretty waterfalls nearby.

Force Mill Farm M
Satterthwaite, Ulverston,
LA12 8LQ
☎ (022 984) 205 & 317
50-acre stock rearing farm.
Manor farmhouse maintaining
its traditional character and
located in a peaceful rural area
4 miles south of Hawkshead.
Bedrooms: 2 double & 2 twin.
Bathrooms: 4 private.
Bed & breakfast: from £17.50
single, from £35 double.

Half board: £24-£25 daily,
£155-£160 weekly.
Lunch available.
Evening meal 6pm (l.o.
7.30pm).
Parking for 8.
Credit: Access, Visa.
🛇8▣🖵♥ 🛄 V 🖭 ℡ ▥
🖰 🖵 🖾 SP

SAWREY

Cumbria
Map ref 5A3

Far Sawrey and Near
Sawrey lie near Esthwaite
Water. Both villages are
small but Near Sawrey is
famous for Hill Top Farm,
home of Beatrix Potter,
now owned by the
National Trust and open
to the public.

Ees Wyke Country House M
🕌🕌🕌

Nr. Sawrey, Ambleside,
LA22 0JZ
☎ Hawkshead (096 66) 393
*Charming Georgian country
house overlooking the peaceful
and beautiful Esthwaite Water.
Fine views of the lake,
mountains and fells.*
Bedrooms: 4 double & 2 twin.
Bathrooms: 6 private,
1 public.
Bed & breakfast: £46-£50
double.
Half board: £36-£40 daily.
Lunch available.
Evening meal 7pm (l.o. 7pm).
Parking for 11.
🛇8▣🖵 🛄 V 🖂 ▥
🖭▲🖰🖵 ♨ 🖾 🖾 SP 🖽
🇹

Sawrey Hotel M
🕌🕌🕌

Far Sawrey, Nr. Ambleside,
LA22 0LQ
☎ Windermere (096 62) 3425
*Country inn on the quieter side
of Windermere, 1 mile from the
car ferry on the B5285 to
Hawkshead. The bar is in the
old stables and has log fires.*
Bedrooms: 4 single, 6 double
& 4 twin, 3 family rooms.
Bathrooms: 13 private,
1 public.
Bed & breakfast: £17.50-
£21.50 single, £35-£43 double.
Half board: £25-£29.50 daily,
£160-£185 weekly.
Lunch available.
Evening meal 7pm (l.o.
8.45pm).
Parking for 30.
🛇🖧℡🖵 🛄 V 🖂 ▲🖟
🖰 ♨ 🖾 SP 🖽

Sawrey House Country Hotel M
🕌🕌🕌 APPROVED

Near Sawrey, Nr. Ambleside,
LA22 0LF
☎ Hawkshead (096 66) 387
*Near Sawrey (home of Beatrix
Potter). Warm friendly
atmosphere, comfortable
accommodation, good food,
magnificent views.*
Bedrooms: 2 single, 3 double
& 2 twin, 3 family rooms.
Bathrooms: 7 private,
2 public.
Bed & breakfast: from £18.75
single, £37.50-£43.50 double.
Half board: £28.50-£31.50
daily, £120-£145 weekly.
Evening meal 7pm (l.o.
midday).
Parking for 15.
Open March-October.
🛇▲♥ 🛄 V 🖂 ▥ ▲
🖟🖵 ♨ 🖾 SP

West Vale Country Guest House M
🕌🕌🕌

Far Sawrey, Nr. Hawkshead,
Ambleside, LA22 0LQ
☎ Windermere (096 62) 2817
*A warm welcome awaits you at
this peaceful family-run
guesthouse, with home cooking,
log fire and fine views.*
Bedrooms: 5 double & 1 twin,
2 family rooms.
Bathrooms: 7 private,
1 public.
Bed & breakfast: £15-£17
single, £30-£34 double.
Half board: £23-£25 daily,
£147-£161 weekly.
Lunch available.
Evening meal 7pm (l.o. 4pm).
Parking for 8.
🛇7♥ 🛄 V 🖂 ℡ ▥ ▲🖟
🖰 🖵 🖾

SEASCALE

Cumbria
Map ref 5A3

Small seaside resort with
good sands and a golf-
course.

Calder House Hotel
🕌🕌

The Banks, Seascale,
CA20 1QP
☎ (094 67) 28538
*Family-run private hotel,
overlooking beach, offering
bed, breakfast and evening
meal. Also golf weekend
breaks.*
Bedrooms: 8 single, 10 twin,
1 family room.
Bathrooms: 6 private,
6 public.

Bed & breakfast: £16-£18
single, £30-£34 double.
Half board: £21-£24 daily,
from £140 weekly.
Evening meal 7pm (l.o.
midday).
Parking for 15.
🛇▲℡🖂🖵♥ 🛄 V 🖾
🖂 ℡ ▥▲♨ 🖟 ♨ 🖾 🖽
🖾

The Cottage Guest House M
🕌🕌🕌

Black How, Seascale,
CA20 1LQ
☎ (094 67) 28416
*Family-run guesthouse with
private facilities. Near a sandy
beach and a golf-course and
ideally located for fell walking.*
Bedrooms: 2 single, 3 double
& 2 twin, 1 family room.
Bathrooms: 8 private.
Bed & breakfast: max. £20
single, max. £32 double.
Half board: max. £28 daily.
Evening meal 7pm (l.o. 9am).
Parking for 10.
🛇▲🖧🖂🖵♥ 🛄 🖂 ℡ ▥
▲ ♨ 🖾 🖽

SEDBERGH

Cumbria
Map ref 5B3

This busy market town
set below the Howgill
Fells is an excellent
centre for walkers. The
noted boys' school was
founded in 1525.

Dalesman Country Inn
🕌🕌🕌 COMMENDED

Main St., Sedbergh,
LA10 5BN
☎ (053 96) 21183
*On entering Sedbergh from the
M6, the Dalesman is the first
inn on the left. 17th C but
recently refurbished by local
craftsmen. 10% discount on
weekly bookings.*
Bedrooms: 1 double & 2 twin,
2 family rooms.
Bathrooms: 3 private,
1 public.
Bed & breakfast: £36-£40
double.
Lunch available.
Evening meal 6.30pm (l.o.
9.30pm).
Parking for 10.
🛇🖵🖂♥ 🛄 V 🖂 ▥▲🖰 U
🖟 🖾 SP 🇹

Farfield Country Guest House

Hawes Rd., Sedbergh,
LA10 5LP
☎ (053 96) 20537

*Secluded accommodation with
attractive country views and
traditional menus. Ideal for
birdwatching, walking or
touring Yorkshire Dales and
lakes. 1 mile east of Sedbergh
on A684. Ample parking.*
Bedrooms: 1 single, 3 double
& 2 twin, 1 family room.
Bathrooms: 2 public.
Bed & breakfast: £15.50-£17
single, £30-£34 double.
Half board: £23.50-£25 daily,
£158-£165 weekly.
Evening meal 6.30pm.
Parking for 20.
Open March-October.
🛇8🖂 🛄 🛄 V 🖂 ℡ ▲
🖟 ♨ 🖾 🖾 🖽

Oakdene Country Hotel M
🕌🕌🕌 COMMENDED

Garsdale Rd., Sedbergh,
LA10 5JN
☎ (053 96) 20280
*Unique, Victorian residence 1
mile from Sedbergh on the
A684 Hawes Road. Ideal
centre for touring the Lakes
and dales.*
Bedrooms: 1 single, 3 double
& 1 twin, 1 family room.
Bathrooms: 6 private.
Bed & breakfast: £27-£29
single, £22.50-£27 double.
Half board: £33-£37.50 daily,
£215.25-£243.60 weekly.
Evening meal 7pm (l.o.
9.15pm).
Parking for 20.
Open March-December.
Credit: Access, Visa.
🛇8🖵 🛄 V 🖂 ▲
🖟 ♨ 🖾 SP 🖽

SHAP

Cumbria
Map ref 5B3

Village lying nearly 1000 ft
above sea-level. Shap
Abbey, open to the public,
is hidden in a valley
nearby. Most of the ruins
date from the early 13th
C, but the tower is 16th C.

Kings Arms Hotel M

Main St., Shap, Penrith,
CA10 3NU
☎ (093 16) 277
*Comfortable friendly
accommodation on the fringe of
the Lake District near M6
junction 39. Directly on the
"Coast to Coast" walk.*
Bedrooms: 2 double & 2 twin,
2 family rooms.
Bathrooms: 2 public.
Bed & breakfast: max. £15
single, max. £30 double.
Lunch available.

Continued ▶

SHAP
Continued

Evening meal 7pm (l.o. 10pm).
Parking for 15.
Credit: Access.

Shap Wells Hotel M
♛♛♛

Shap, Nr. Penrith,
CA10 3QU
☎ (093 16) 628 & 744
A traditional hotel catering for many varied groups amid 30 acres of woodland and gardens.
Bedrooms: 10 single,
32 double & 41 twin, 7 family rooms.
Bathrooms: 86 private,
3 public.
Bed & breakfast: £32-£48 single, £48-£75 double.
Half board: £31-£50 daily,
£200-£250 weekly.
Lunch available.
Evening meal 7pm (l.o. 8.30pm).
Parking for 100.
Open February-December.
Credit: Access, Visa, Diners, Amex.

SILLOTH-ON-SOLWAY
Cumbria
Map ref 5A2

Small port and coastal resort on the Solway Firth with wide cobbled roads and an attractive green leading to the promenade and seashore.
Tourist Information Centre ☎ (06973) 31944

Skinburness Hotel M
♛♛♛

Silloth-on-Solway, CA5 4QY
☎ (069 73) 32332
A beautifully restored Victorian hotel on the Solway Firth. 1 mile north of Silloth, offering a high standard of comfort and fine cuisine.
Bedrooms: 4 single, 10 double & 11 twin.
Bathrooms: 25 private.
Bed & breakfast: £44-£59 single, £76-£86 double.
Half board: £285-£345 weekly.
Lunch available.
Evening meal 7pm (l.o. 9.30pm).
Parking for 85.

Credit: Access, Visa, Diners, Amex.

TEMPLE SOWERBY
Cumbria
Map ref 5B3

Pleasant village with a green, an old church and a 4-arch bridge. On the outskirts is Acorn Bank, a red sandstone house. Its walled rose and herb gardens are open to the public.

Kings Arms Hotel
♛♛

Temple Sowerby, Penrith,
CA10 1SB
☎ Kirkby Thore
(076 83) 61211
Hotel with public bars and catering for residents and non-residents. Bar meals and evening meals available (reservations only).
Bedrooms: 4 single, 4 double & 4 twin.
Bathrooms: 4 public;
4 private showers.
Bed & breakfast: from £22 single, £30-£34 double.
Half board: £25-£27 daily,
£175-£189 weekly.
Lunch available.
Evening meal 7pm (l.o. 9pm).
Parking for 12.

THORNTHWAITE
Cumbria
Map ref 5A3

3m NW. Keswick
Small village, west of Keswick, at the southern tip of Bassenthwaite Lake. Forest trails in Thornthwaite Forest.

Thwaite Howe Hotel M
♛♛♛ **APPROVED**

Thornthwaite, Keswick,
CA12 5SA
☎ Braithwaite (059 682) 281
Country house hotel in its own grounds with spectacular views of Skiddaw. Close to Bassenthwaite Lake.
Bedrooms: 4 double & 4 twin.
Bathrooms: 8 private.
Bed & breakfast: £23-£35 single, £46-£50 double.
Half board: £30-£42 daily,
£199.50-£269.50 weekly.
Evening meal 7pm (l.o. 7pm).
Parking for 12.
Open March-November.

ULLSWATER
Cumbria
Map ref 5A3

This beautiful lake, which is over 7 miles long, runs from Patterdale to Pooley Bridge. Lofty peaks ranging round the lake make an impressive background. A steamer service operates along the lake between Pooley Bridge and Glenridding in the summer.

Brantwood Country House Hotel M
♛♛♛

Stainton, Penrith, CA11 0EP
☎ (0768) 62748
Family-owned and run. Standing in secluded gardens, 1.5 miles from M6 junction 40 and 3 miles from Ullswater.
Bedrooms: 2 single, 6 double & 2 twin, 1 family room.
Bathrooms: 11 private,
1 public.
Bed & breakfast: £26-£30 single, £44-£55 double.
Half board: £35-£40 daily,
£175-£200 weekly.
Lunch available.
Evening meal 6.30pm (l.o. 9pm).
Parking for 40.
Credit: Access, Visa.

Cragside Cottage M
Listed

Thackthwaite, Ullswater,
Penrith, CA11 0ND
☎ Pooley Bridge
(076 84) 86385
Mountainside location, 3 miles north of Ullswater. All rooms have toilet, shower and washbasin, tea making facilities, TV. Reserved parking spaces. Meals served in room. Brochure available.
Bedrooms: 2 double, 3 family rooms.
Bathrooms: 5 private.
Bed & breakfast: £26.50 double.
Half board: £18 daily,
£121.36 weekly.
Evening meal 6.30pm (l.o. 4pm).
Parking for 5.
Open March-November.
Credit: Access, Visa.

> **The National Crown Scheme is explained in full on pages 556–558.**

Glenridding Hotel M

Glenridding, Penrith,
CA11 0PB
☎ Glenridding
(076 84) 82228 Fax (076 84) 82555
Best Western
Old established family hotel, adjacent to the lake and surrounded by mountains. We offer value breaks, log fires and traditional food.
Bedrooms: 9 single, 16 double & 15 twin, 5 family rooms.
Bathrooms: 45 private.
Bed & breakfast: from £41 single, from £65 double.
Half board: from £282 weekly.
Evening meal 7pm (l.o. 8.30pm).
Parking for 40.
Open February-December.
Credit: Access, Visa, Diners, Amex.

Knotts Mill Country Guest House M

Watermillock, Ullswater,
Penrith, CA11 0JN
☎ Pooley Bridge
(076 84) 86472 Fax (076 84) 86699
Rural location with superb views. Bedrooms well-fitted and a comfortable lounge. Good quality English fare. 10 minutes M6 junction 40.
Bedrooms: 3 double & 1 twin, 1 family room.
Bathrooms: 5 private.
Bed & breakfast: £20-£30 single, £30-£50 double.
Half board: from £25 daily.
Evening meal 7.30pm (l.o. 8pm).
Parking for 12.
Credit: Access, Visa.

Moss Crag

Glenridding, Penrith,
CA11 0PA
☎ Glenridding
(076 84) 82500
By Glenridding Beck, 200 yards from the lake, with views of Place Fell and Ullswater. Post office and general store nearby.
Bedrooms: 1 single, 4 double & 1 twin, 1 family room.
Bathrooms: 3 private,
1 public.
Bed & breakfast: £12.50-£13.50 single, £25-£35 double.
Half board: £23.50-£24.50 daily, £160-£195 weekly.

Evening meal 7.30pm (l.o. 7.30pm).
Parking for 4.
≿5⇩🕽Ⓤ🅻♿🅅⤢🍴🖿 ✗🛏ⒼⒶⓅ

Patterdale Hotel ♨
≋≋≋
Patterdale, Lake Ullswater, Nr. Penrith, CA11 0NN
☎ Glenridding (076 84) 82231
Family-run hotel, within the same family for 65 years. All rooms with private facilities, colour TV and telephone.
Bedrooms: 14 single, 16 double & 23 twin, 4 family rooms.
Bathrooms: 57 private, 10 public.
Bed & breakfast: £25-£27 single, £50-£54 double.
Half board: £35-£37 daily, £250-£280 weekly.
Lunch available.
Evening meal 7pm (l.o. 8pm).
Parking for 100.
Open March-November.
Credit: Access, Visa.
≿🖑📞🕽⇩🅻🅅⤢🆃🆅
🖿 ⤵❋

Swiss Chalet Inn ♨
≋≋≋ APPROVED
Pooley Bridge, Penrith, CA10 2NN
☎ (076 84) 86215
Authentic Swiss chalet, in a charming village, 5 minutes' walk from Lake Ullswater. Swiss and continental cuisine, served to the highest standards.
Bedrooms: 5 double & 1 twin, 2 family rooms.
Bathrooms: 8 private.
Bed & breakfast: £25-£30 single, £40-£48 double.
Lunch available.
Evening meal 6pm (l.o. 9.45pm).
Parking for 40.
Open February-December.
Credit: Access, Visa.
≿🛏📞🕽⇩🅻🖿 ⤵
🎯🛏🆃

Wreay Farm Guest House ♨
Listed COMMENDED
Watermillock, Ullswater, Cumbria. CA11 0LT
☎ (085 36) 296
Comfortable guesthouse in beautiful area, overlooking Lake Ullswater. Home cooking done by proprietor.
Bedrooms: 7 double, 3 family rooms.
Bathrooms: 5 private, 2 public.
Bed & breakfast: max. £18.97 single, max. £37.94 double.

Half board: max. £24.72 daily, max. £156.97 weekly.
Evening meal 7.30pm.
Parking for 12.
Open March-November.
≿🖑📞🕽🅻⤢🆃🍴
♿🛏

Market town lying between green fells and the sea. The lighthouse on the Hoad is a monument to Sir John Barrow, founder of the Royal Geographical Society.
Tourist Information Centre ☎ *(0229) 57120*

Clarence House Country Hotel and Restaurant
≋≋≋ COMMENDED
Skelgate, Dalton-in-Furness, LA15 8BQ
☎ (0229) 62508
Elegant, family-run, late Victorian country hotel and restaurant, set in 3 acres of beautiful grounds.
Bedrooms: 12 double & 2 twin.
Bathrooms: 14 private.
Bed & breakfast: £45-£55 single, £55-£65 double.
Lunch available.
Evening meal 6pm (l.o. 9.30pm).
Parking for 40.
Credit: Visa.
≿🖑📞🕽⇩🅻⤢
🍴🆃⦿🖿⤵🎯❋✗🛏
ⓈⓅ

Lonsdale House Hotel (Ulverston) Ltd. ♨
≋≋≋
Daltongate, Ulverston, LA12 7BD
☎ (0229) 52598
Located in beautiful walled garden. All rooms with bathroom, TV, video, tea/coffee facilities, trouser press and telephone.
Bedrooms: 8 single, 6 double & 5 twin, 1 family room.
Bathrooms: 20 private.
Bed & breakfast: £23-£37.95 single, £46-£57.95 double.
Lunch available.
Evening meal 7pm (l.o. 9pm).
Parking for 2.
Credit: Access, Visa, Diners, Amex.
≿🖑📞🕽⇩🅻🅅⤢
🆃🖿⤵🎯✗🛏ⓈⓅ🕭
🆃

Sefton House Hotel
34 Queen St., Ulverston, LA12 7AF
☎ (0229) 52190
A small privately owned Georgian house in the centre of a busy market town.
Bedrooms: 6 single, 4 double & 3 twin, 1 family room.
Bathrooms: 10 private, 2 public.
Bed & breakfast: £25.50-£38.50 single, £42-£55 double.
Half board: £35-£47 daily.
Lunch available.
Evening meal 7pm (l.o. 10.30pm).
Parking for 23.
Credit: Access, Visa.
≿📞🕽⇩🅻🅅⤢🆃🖿
⤵✗🛏ⓈⓅ

Trinity House Hotel
≋≋≋ COMMENDED
Prince's St., Ulverston, LA12 7NB
☎ (0229) 57639
Former Georgian rectory, licensed restaurant with local food and ensuite bedrooms.
Bedrooms: 4 double & 1 twin, 1 family room.
Bathrooms: 6 private.
Bed & breakfast: £27.50-£30 single, £45-£50 double.
Half board: £35-£45 daily, £220-£250 weekly.
Evening meal 7pm (l.o. 9pm).
Parking for 7.
Open February-December.
Credit: Access, Visa, Amex.
≿🖑📞🕽⇩🅻🅅⤢
⤵🎯♿🛏ⓈⓅ

Virginia House Hotel & Restaurant
Queen St., Ulverston, LA12 7AF
☎ (0229) 54844
An original Georgian town house dated 1785 which is a listed building. All bedrooms en-suite, with direct dial telephone and colour TV.
Bedrooms: 3 single, 2 double & 2 twin.
Bathrooms: 7 private.
Bed & breakfast: £30-£38 single, £40-£55 double.
Evening meal 7pm (l.o. 9.30pm).
Credit: Access, Visa, Diners, Amex.
≿📞🕽⇩🅻🅅⤢🖿
⤵🎯✗🛏ⓈⓅ🕭

In the valley lies Wastwater, the deepest English lake. A road leads along its north-west side as far as Wasdale Head, a starting point for ascending the majestic Scafell peaks and other mountains.

Low Wood Hall Hotel ♨
≋≋≋ COMMENDED
Nether Wasdale, Wasdale, CA20 1ET
☎ Wasdale (094 67) 26289
Gracious Victorian country house with fine views across Wasdale. Close to Scafell, Wastwater and sea. Bar, billiard room. Extensive dinner menu.
Bedrooms: 6 double & 7 twin.
Bathrooms: 13 private.
Bed & breakfast: £26-£30 single, from £44 double.
Half board: £30-£40 daily, £192.50-£245 weekly.
Evening meal 6.30pm (l.o. 8.45pm).
Parking for 24.
≿🖑⦿📞🕽⇩🅻🅅⤢🆃
🖿⤵🎯❋✗🛏ⓈⓅ🕭🆃

Wasdale Head Inn ♨
≋≋≋
Wasdale Head, Nr. Gosforth, CA20 1EX
☎ Wasdale (094 06) 229
Traditional mountain inn with modern facilities and secluded setting, at the head of one of Lakeland's remote and unspoilt valleys. Birth place of rock climbing in Great Britain.
Bedrooms: 2 single, 4 double & 2 twin, 2 family rooms.
Bathrooms: 13 private.
Bed & breakfast: from £42 single, from £80 double.
Half board: £40-£42 daily, £259-£273 weekly.
Lunch available.
Evening meal 7.30pm (l.o. 7.30pm).
Parking for 50.
Open March-November.
Credit: Access, Visa.
≿📞🕽⇩🅅⤢🖿⤵🎯❋
✗🛏🕭

Individual proprietors have supplied all details of accommodation. Although we do check for accuracy, we advise you to confirm prices and other information at the time of booking.

WHITEHAVEN

Cumbria
Map ref 5A3

Small port on the west
coast. The town was
developed in the 17th C
and many of the fine
buildings of that period
have been preserved.
*Tourist Information
Centre ☎ (0946) 695678*

Corkickle Guesthouse
1, Corkickle, Whitehaven,
CA28 8AA
☎ (0946) 692073
*Small homely guesthouse
offering a high standard of
comfort. Within easy walking
distance of town centre.*
Bedrooms: 3 single, 1 double
& 2 twin.
Bathrooms: 2 private,
1 public; 2 private showers.
Bed & breakfast: £17-£22
single, £32-£35 double.
Parking for 2.
🛇 🖵 🗢 Ⓤ 🛉 Ⓥ ⌿ TV ▥
🗢 🏠 ⌂

Howgate Hotel M
Howgate, Whitehaven,
CA28 6PL
☎ (0946) 66286
*Family owned and run hotel 2
miles from Whitehaven. Easy
access to Lake District and
West Cumbria.*
Bedrooms: 2 single, 3 double
& 1 twin.
Bathrooms: 6 private.
Bed & breakfast: from £35
single, £48 double.
Half board: from £37 daily,
from £259 weekly.
Lunch available.
Evening meal 7pm (l.o.
9.30pm).
Parking for 50.
Credit: Access, Visa.
🛇 📞 🖵 🗢 🛉 Ⓥ ⌿ ▥ 🗢
🍴

WIGTON

Cumbria
Map ref 5A2

Wigton has a centuries-
old market as well as
cattle and sheep
auctions. A popular horse
show is held annually in
October.

Wheyrigg Hall Hotel
Wigton, CA7 0DH
☎ Abbeytown (069 73) 61242
Fax (069 73) 61020
*Family-run hotel and
restaurant, 4 miles from
Wigton on B5302 Silloth Rd.*
Bedrooms: 2 single, 2 twin,
2 family rooms.

Bathrooms: 5 private;
1 private shower.
Bed & breakfast: max. £28
single, max. £42.50 double.
Half board: £35-£45 daily,
from £185 weekly.
Lunch available.
Evening meal midday (l.o.
9pm).
Parking for 50.
Credit: Access, Visa, Amex.
🛇 🖚 ⑩ 🖵 🗢 🛉 Ⓥ ▥ 📺
🗢 🍴 ✿ 🐾 🏠 SP

WINDERMERE

Cumbria
Map ref 5A3

This tourist centre was
once a tiny hamlet before
the introduction of the
railway in 1847. The town
adjoins Bowness which is
on the lakeside. It is an
inland water centre for
sailing and boating. A
scenic way of seeing the
lake is to take a trip on a
passenger steamer.
Windermere Steamboat
Museum has a fine
collection of old
steamboats.
*Tourist Information
Centre ☎ (09662) 6499*

Adam Place M
1 Park Avenue, Windermere,
LA23 2AR
☎ (096 62) 4600
*Small friendly guesthouse,
close to lake and all amenities.*
Bedrooms: 1 single, 2 double,
2 family rooms.
Bathrooms: 2 private,
1 public.
Bed & breakfast: £10-£17.50
single, £20-£35 double.
Parking for 5.
🛇 🗢 Ⓤ 🛉 Ⓥ ▥ 📺 ▥ 🐾
Ⓣ

Albert Hotel M
Queen's Square, Bowness-on-
Windermere, LA23 3BY
☎ (096 62) 3241
*This family-run village centre
inn offers you a warm welcome
either to stay or to enjoy our
restaurant and bars.*
Bedrooms: 4 double & 1 twin,
1 family room.
Bathrooms: 6 private.
Bed & breakfast: £43.50-
£49.50 double.
Half board: £20-£28.75 daily.
Lunch available.
Evening meal 6pm (l.o.
9.30pm).
Parking for 5.
Credit: Access, Visa, Diners,
Amex.
🛇 🖚 ⑩ 🖵 🗢 🛉 Ⓥ ▥ ▥
🗢 🍴 ▣ 🐾 SP Ⓣ

Almeria House M
⚜⚜
17 Broad St., Windermere,
LA23 2AB
☎ (096 62) 3026
*Homely accommodation with a
pleasant atmosphere, close to
all amenities.*
Bedrooms: 1 single, 3 double,
1 family room.
Bathrooms: 2 public.
Bed & breakfast: £10-£15
single, £20-£28 double.
Half board: £16-£20 daily,
£70-£98 weekly.
Evening meal 6pm (l.o. 4pm).
Open February-October.
🛇 🗢 🛉 Ⓥ ▥ TV ▥ 🐾
▥ OAP 🐾 SP

Applegarth Hotel M
⚜⚜⚜⚜
College Rd., Windermere,
LA23 2AE
☎ (096 62) 3206
*Elegant Victorian mansion
house with individually
designed bedrooms and four-
poster suites with lake and fell
views.*
Bedrooms: 4 single, 5 double
& 1 twin, 5 family rooms.
Bathrooms: 15 private.
Bed & breakfast: £25-£30
single, £30-£60 double.
Lunch available.
Evening meal 7pm (l.o. 8pm).
Parking for 26.
Open April-December.
Credit: Access, Visa, Amex.
🛇 🖚 📞 ⑩ 🖵 🗢 Ⓥ ▥ 📺
▥ 🗢 🍴 ✿ 🐾 SP ⌂

The Archway M
⚜⚜⚜ COMMENDED
13 College Rd., Windermere,
LA23 1BY
☎ (096 62) 5613
*Victorian stone-built
guesthouse, beautifully
furnished throughout. Antiques,
interesting paintings, fresh
flowers. Marvellous mountain
views, gourmet homecooking.*
Bedrooms: 1 single, 2 double
& 2 twin.
Bathrooms: 4 private,
1 public.
Bed & breakfast: £15-£22
single, £38-£44 double.
Half board: £28.50-£35.50
daily.
Evening meal 6.45pm (l.o.
4pm).
Parking for 3.
🛇 12 🖚 📞 ⑩ 🖵 🗢 Ⓥ ⌿
▥ ▥ 🗢 🐾 🏠 SP

Ashleigh M
⚜ APPROVED
11 College Rd., Windermere,
LA23 1BU
☎ (096 62) 2292

*Small, central, family-run
guesthouse with panoramic
views, offering home cooking.
Colour TV in all rooms. Non-
smokers only please.*
Bedrooms: 1 single, 2 double
& 2 twin.
Bathrooms: 2 public.
Bed & breakfast: £13-£17
single, £25-£30 double.
Half board: £18-£23 daily,
£120-£150 weekly.
Evening meal 7pm.
🛇 🗢 🛉 Ⓥ ⌿ ▥ 📺
▥ 🐾 🏠 SP

Belmont Manor
Hotel M
⚜⚜⚜⚜ COMMENDED
Windermere, LA23 1LN
☎ (0966) 33316
*A new hotel in 7 acres of
beautiful grounds. Whirlpools
in every bathroom. Emphasis
on food and service. 10%
discount on weekly bookings.*
Bedrooms: 10 double &
4 twin.
Bathrooms: 14 private.
Bed & breakfast: from £90
double.
Half board: from £46 daily.
Lunch available.
Evening meal 7.30pm.
▣ 📞 ⑩ 🖵 🗢 🛉 Ⓥ ⌿ ▥
⏻ ▥ 🗢 🍴 ✿ 🐾 OAP 🐾 🐾
Ⓣ

Belsfield Guest House
⚜⚜ COMMENDED
4 Belsfield Terrace, Kendal
Rd., Bowness-on-
Windermere, LA23 3EQ
☎ (096 62) 5823
*Family-run guesthouse in the
heart of Bowness, 1 minute's
walk from the lake front.*
Bedrooms: 2 single, 2 double
& 1 twin, 4 family rooms.
Bathrooms: 9 private.
Bed & breakfast: £20-£25
single, £37-£43 double.
🛇 🖚 🗢 Ⓤ 🛉 Ⓥ ▥ ▥ 🗢
🐾 🐾 OAP SP

Biskey Howe Villa Hotel
and Restaurant M
⚜⚜⚜
Craig Walk, Bowness-on-
Windermere, LA23 3AX
☎ (096 62) 3988/5396
*In a peaceful spot above Lake
Windermere, commanding
beautiful views of the lake and
surrounding mountains. Close
to Bowness Bay.*
Bedrooms: 6 double & 2 twin,
3 family rooms.
Bathrooms: 10 private,
1 public.
Bed & breakfast: £25-£30
single, £44-£50 double.
Half board: £34-£37 daily,
£216-£259 weekly.
Lunch available.

Evening meal 6.30pm (l.o. 8.30pm).
Parking for 11.
Credit: Access, Visa.

🐎 🦮 📞 💷 🖨 📶 💡 Ⓥ 📺 🖵
🎱 🏃 💥 🗙 🐾 📶 SP T

Blenheim Lodge M
👑👑 APPROVED

Brantfell Rd., Bowness-on-Windermere, Windermere, LA23 3AE
☎ (096 62) 3440
Beautiful Lakeland-stone house overlooking Lake Windermere. Set against National Trust land at the end of the Dalesway footpath.
Bedrooms: 3 single, 5 double & 2 twin.
Bathrooms: 8 private, 1 public.
Bed & breakfast: £16.50-£23 single, £37-£52 double.
Half board: £27.50-£36 daily, £189-£240 weekly.
Evening meal 7pm (l.o. 4pm).
Parking for 12.

🐎6 🦮 📶 💡 Ⓥ 🗙 ≯
📺 🏃 🎱 ♪ 🐾 🗙 🐾 🐾
SP 🏤 T

Bordriggs Country House Hotel M
👑👑👑👑👑

Longtail Hill, Bowness-on-Windermere, Windermere, LA23 3LD
☎ (096 62) 3567 Fax (096 62) 6949
Charming country house in beautiful gardens, with pool. Graciously appointed, elegant lounge, pretty bedrooms. Lake and golf-course nearby.
Bedrooms: 1 single, 6 double & 2 twin, 2 family rooms.
Bathrooms: 11 private.
Bed & breakfast: from £30 single, from £55 double.
Half board: from £40 daily, from £266 weekly.
Evening meal 7pm (l.o. 8.30pm).
Parking for 14.
Open February-November.

🐎10 🦮 📶 📞 💷 💡 Ⓥ
🖨 📶 🎱 🍽 🕹 🔆 ❄
🗙 🏃 SP T

Bowfell Cottage M
👑👑

Middle Entrance Drive, Storrs Park, Bowness-on-Windermere, LA23 3JY
☎ (096 62) 4835
Cottage in a delightful setting, about 1 mile south of Bowness, offering traditional Lakeland hospitality.
Bedrooms: 1 double & 1 twin, 1 family room.
Bathrooms: 1 public.
Bed & breakfast: £13-£14 single, £24-£26 double.

Braemount House M
👑👑 APPROVED

Sunny Bank Rd., Windermere, LA23 2EN
☎ (096 62) 5967
Elegant, well-equipped Victorian house. Quiet location but within walking distance of Bowness and Windermere villages.
Bedrooms: 2 double & 1 twin, 1 family room.
Bathrooms: 4 private.
Bed & breakfast: £28-£35 single, £39-£52 double.
Half board: £31-£37.50 daily, £206-£249 weekly.
Evening meal 7pm.
Parking for 4.
Open March-December.
Credit: Access, Visa, Diners, Amex.

🐎8 📞 💷 🖨 💡 Ⓥ 🗙 🖨
📶 🏃 🏤 🗙 SP T

Brooklands M
👑👑👑 COMMENDED

Ferry View, Windermere, LA23 3JB
☎ (096 62) 2344
Comfortable guesthouse on the outskirts of Bowness village, with fine lake and mountain views. Accent on food and hospitality.
Bedrooms: 1 single, 1 double & 1 twin, 3 family rooms.
Bathrooms: 3 private, 1 public.
Bed & breakfast: from £19 single, £34-£38 double.
Half board: £32-£34 daily, £210-£224 weekly.
Evening meal 5.30pm.
Parking for 6.

🐎 💡 Ⓥ 🖨 📺 📶 🏃 🖨 DAP
🏃 SP

The Burn How Garden House Hotel & Motel M
👑👑👑 COMMENDED

Back Belsfield Rd., Windermere, LA23 3HH
☎ (096 62) 6226
Unique combination of Victorian houses and private chalets in secluded gardens in the heart of a picturesque village. All facilities, fully serviced. Four-poster beds available.
Bedrooms: 2 single, 8 double & 8 twin, 8 family rooms.
Bathrooms: 26 private.
Bed & breakfast: £39-£43 single, £58-£66 double.
Half board: £38-£49 daily, £190-£290 weekly.

Lunch available.
Evening meal 7pm (l.o. 9.15pm).
Parking for 30.
Credit: Access, Visa, Amex.

🐎 🦮 📶 📞 💷 🖨 💡 Ⓥ
🔆 🖨 📶 🏃 🍽 🛁 🐾 ❄ 🗙
🏃 SP T

Cambridge House M
Listed

9 Oak St., Windermere, LA23 1AN
☎ (096 62) 3846
Friendly and comfortable, traditional Lakeland guesthouse, conveniently situated in village centre. An ideal base for exploring the Lakes.
Bedrooms: 5 double, 1 family room.
Bathrooms: 6 private.
Bed & breakfast: £29-£34 double.
Half board: £20-£25.50 daily, £137-£173.50 weekly.
Evening meal 6pm (l.o. 7pm).

🐎5 📶 🖨 💡 📶 🔆 📶 🗙 🖨

Cedar Manor Hotel M
👑👑👑 COMMENDED

Ambleside Rd., Windermere, LA23 1AX
☎ (096 62) 3192
Traditional Lakeland house with interesting architectural features. Elegantly furnished and in a country garden setting. Some rooms have lake views.
Bedrooms: 7 double & 3 twin, 2 family rooms.
Bathrooms: 12 private.
Bed & breakfast: £33.50-£40 single, £51-£64 double.
Half board: £34-£42 daily, £196-£252 weekly.
Evening meal 7.30pm (l.o. 8.30pm).
Parking for 20.
Credit: Access, Visa.

🐎 🦮 📶 📞 💷 🖨 💡 Ⓥ
🖨 📶 🛁 🕐 🕹 🔆 🗙 🐾 SP
🏤

Clifton Guest House M

28 Ellerthwaite Rd., Windermere, LA23 2AH
☎ (096 62) 4968
A small friendly guesthouse in a very quiet part of the village, about 4 minutes' walk from the shops and restaurants.
Bedrooms: 2 single, 3 double, 1 family room.
Bathrooms: 1 private, 1 public; 3 private showers.
Bed & breakfast: £13-£15 single, £24-£34 double.
Half board: £80-£105 weekly.
Parking for 4.

🐎 📶 💡 📶 🖨 📺 📶 🛁
🗙 🏃

Crag Brow Cottage Hotel M
👑👑👑 COMMENDED

Helm Rd., Bowness-on-Windermere, LA23 3BU
☎ Windermere (096 62) 4080
In heart of Bowness, 2 minutes to lake. High standard en-suite rooms, a la carte and table d'hote restaurant. Ample parking.
Bedrooms: 10 double, 1 family room.
Bathrooms: 11 private.
Bed & breakfast: from £37.50 single, £50-£70 double.
Half board: £40-£50 daily.
Lunch available.
Evening meal 6.30pm (l.o. 9.30pm).
Parking for 30.
Credit: Access, Visa.

🐎 🦮 📞 🖨 💷 💡 Ⓥ 🖨
📶 🛁 🍽 🐾 🗙 📶 SP T
✆ Display advertisement appears on page 577.

Cragwood Country House Hotel and Restaurant M

Windermere, LA23 1LQ
☎ (096 62) 88177
In 20 acres of gardens, meadows and private woodland with 450 yards of lake frontage.
Bedrooms: 1 single, 14 double & 5 twin, 3 family rooms.
Bathrooms: 23 private, 5 public.
Bed & breakfast: £40 single, £80 double.
Half board: £58 daily, £210 weekly.
Lunch available.
Evening meal 7pm (l.o. 8.30pm).
Parking for 60.
Credit: Access, Visa.

🐎 🦮 📞 💡 Ⓥ 🖨 📺 🖨
🍽 🕹 ❄ 📶 SP 🏤

Cranleigh Hotel M
👑👑👑 COMMENDED

Kendal Rd., Bowness-on-Windermere, LA23 3EW
☎ (096 62) 3293
Quiet and within a short walk of the village centre and Bowness Bay. Well placed for a touring holiday.
Bedrooms: 2 single, 9 double & 3 twin, 1 family room.
Bathrooms: 15 private.
Bed & breakfast: £31-£38 single, £42-£56 double.
Half board: £34-£40 daily, £200-£240 weekly.
Evening meal 7pm (l.o. 9pm).
Parking for 15.
Open March-November.
Credit: Access, Visa, Amex.

🐎5 📶 🖨 💡 🔆 🖨 📺 🖨
🛁 🍽 🗙 🏃 📶 SP T

WINDERMERE

Continued

Damson Dene Hotel ♨
♛♛♛
Lyth Valley, Nr. Bowness-on-Windermere, Kendal,
LA8 8JE
☎ Crosthwaite (044 88) 676
Fax (044 88) 227
Friendly family-run country hotel, indoor pool, jacuzzi, sauna, squash court. Candlelit dinners, log fires, all rooms en-suite.
Bedrooms: 3 single, 23 double & 5 twin, 3 family rooms.
Bathrooms: 34 private,
2 public.
Bed & breakfast: from £44 single, from £77 double.
Half board: from £54.75 daily.
Lunch available.
Evening meal 5pm (l.o. 9pm).
Parking for 80.
Credit: Access, Visa.

Dene Crest ♨
13 Woodland Rd.,
Windermere, LA23 2AE
☎ (096 62) 4979
Small and friendly guesthouse which has been modernised throughout, offering home cooking and a choice on all menus.
Bedrooms: 3 double & 1 twin, 1 family room.
Bathrooms: 1 public.
Bed & breakfast: £10-£15 single, £20-£30 double.
Half board: £16-£22 daily, £105-£145 weekly.
Evening meal 6.30pm (l.o. 4pm).

Denehurst ♨
♛♛ APPROVED
Queens Drive, Windermere,
LA23 3EL
☎ (096 62) 4710
We specialise in breakfast, English and continental. Eat and sleep well in our cosy period home near Windermere, Bowness and the lake.
Bedrooms: 3 double & 1 twin, 2 family rooms.
Bathrooms: 4 private,
1 public.
Bed & breakfast: £26-£32 double.
Open January-October.

Eastbourne Hotel ♨
♛♛♛
Biskey Howe Rd., Bowness-on-Windermere, LA23 2JR
☎ (096 62) 3525
A family-run small hotel offering private facilities and a friendly welcome. Located in a quiet position close to Lake Windermere and an ideal central touring base.
Bedrooms: 2 single, 2 double, 4 family rooms.
Bathrooms: 4 private,
1 public; 1 private shower.
Bed & breakfast: £13.50-£18.50 single, £27-£39 double.
Half board: £23-£29 daily, £150-£190 weekly.
Evening meal 6.30pm (l.o. 6.30pm).
Parking for 3.
Credit: Access, Visa.

Elim Bank Hotel ♨
♛♛♛
Lake Rd., Bowness-Windermere, LA23 2JJ
☎ (096 62) 4810
Outstanding Victorian slate-built house, close to all amenities. Noted for its friendly atmosphere, comfort and breakfasts.
Bedrooms: 1 single, 5 double, 3 family rooms.
Bathrooms: 6 private,
1 public.
Bed & breakfast: £16-£22 single, £32-£40 double.
Half board: £22-£32 daily, £150-£200 weekly.
Lunch available.
Evening meal 6.30pm (l.o. 9.30pm).
Parking for 8.
Credit: Access, Visa.

Elim House ♨
♛♛♛
Biskey Howe Rd., Bowness-on-Windermere, LA23 2JP
☎ (096 62) 2021
Family-run, warm, friendly with lake and shops close by. Offers good breakfast, en-suite rooms, TV, tea/coffee facilities in all rooms. Private car park.
Bedrooms: 6 double, 2 family rooms.
Bathrooms: 4 private,
1 public.
Bed & breakfast: £28-£40 double.
Parking for 8.

Ellerthwaite Lodge ♨
New Rd., Windermere,
LA23 2LA
☎ (096 62) 5115

All rooms with private facilities, colour TV, telephone, hair-dryer, tea/coffee facilities. Private car park and residential licence. Discounts for stays over 2 nights.
Bedrooms: 3 single, 4 double & 5 twin, 3 family rooms.
Bathrooms: 15 private.
Bed & breakfast: £15-£30 single, £36-£70 double.
Half board: £28-£40 daily.
Lunch available.
Evening meal 7pm (l.o. 8.30pm).
Parking for 20.
Open March-November.
Credit: Access, Visa.

Fairfield Country House Hotel ♨
♛♛♛
Brantfell Rd., Bowness-Windermere, LA23 3AE
☎ (096 62) 6565 & 6566
Small, friendly 200-year-old country house with half an acre of peaceful secluded gardens. 2 minutes' walk from Lake Windermere and village.
Bedrooms: 1 single, 3 double & 1 twin, 3 family rooms.
Bathrooms: 7 private,
1 public.
Bed & breakfast: £33-£35 single, £46-£50 double.
Lunch available.
Parking for 14.
Credit: Access, Visa.

Fir Trees ♨
♛♛♛
Lake Rd., Windermere,
LA23 2EQ
☎ (096 62) 2272
An elegant, small bed and breakfast hotel within easy walking distance of Windermere and Bowness-on-Windermere.
Bedrooms: 5 double & 1 twin, 1 family room.
Bathrooms: 7 private.
Bed & breakfast: £22.50-£26.50 single, £35-£43 double.
Parking for 8.
Credit: Access, Visa, Amex.

Four Seasons Leisure Hotel
Storrs Park, Bowness-on-Windermere, LA23 3LQ
☎ (096 62) 3022
Country house accommodation with in-house leisure facilities. 300 yards from lake in three quarter acre garden. Special interest breaks available in winter, autumn and spring.

Bedrooms: 2 single, 2 double & 2 twin, 1 family rooms.
Bathrooms: 8 private.
Bed & breakfast: £20-£28 single, £39-£55 double.
Half board: £31-£39 daily, £196-£260 weekly.
Evening meal 7.15pm (l.o. 5.50pm).
Parking for 12.
Open February-December.
Credit: Access, Visa.

⊕ Display advertisement appears on page 86.

Gilpin Lodge Country House Hotel & Restaurant ♨
♛♛♛♛ HIGHLY COMMENDED
Crook Rd., Windermere,
LA23 3NE
☎ (096 62) 2295
2 miles from Windermere in 17 acres of wooded moorland. Tranquillity, comfort, friendliness and delicious 5-course dinners!
Bedrooms: 9 double.
Bathrooms: 9 private.
Bed & breakfast: £40-£60 single, £60-£90 double.
Half board: £35-£75 daily, £210-£368 weekly.
Lunch available.
Evening meal 7.30pm (l.o. 9pm).
Parking for 25.
Credit: Access, Visa, Diners, Amex.

Glencree Hotel ♨
♛♛♛
Lake Rd., Windermere,
LA23 2EQ
☎ (096 62) 5822
A delightful, elegantly furnished and decorated house. Lovely woodland outlook. Convenient location, warm hospitality.
Bedrooms: 4 double & 1 twin.
Bathrooms: 5 private.
Bed & breakfast: £40-£55 double.
Half board: £37.50-£45 daily.
Evening meal 7pm.
Parking for 9.
Open February-November.
Credit: Access, Visa.

Greenriggs Guest House ♨
♛♛
8 Upper Oak St.,
Windermere, LA23 2LB
☎ (096 62) 2265

Friendly, comfortable guesthouse in quiet cul-de-sac. Convenient for all services. Home cooking. Optional evening meal, snacks, packed lunches. Brochure available.
Bedrooms: 2 single, 3 double & 1 twin, 1 family room.
Bathrooms: 4 private, 1 public; 1 private shower.
Bed & breakfast: £11.50-£13 single, £27-£33 double.
Half board: £18.50-£23.50 daily, £123-£158 weekly.
Evening meal 6.30pm (l.o. midday).
Parking for 4.

Hawksmoor ⋈
COMMENDED
Lake Rd., Windermere, LA23 2EQ
☎ (096 62) 2110
Ivy-covered house with a large garden to the side and woodlands to the rear.
Bedrooms: 7 double, 3 family rooms.
Bathrooms: 10 private.
Bed & breakfast: £21-£25 single, £34-£50 double.
Half board: £27-£35 daily, £175-£210 weekly.
Evening meal 6.30pm (l.o. 5.30pm).
Parking for 12.
Open February-November.

Heatherbank Guest House ⋈
COMMENDED
13 Birch St., Windermere, LA23 1EG
☎ (096 62) 6503
Family-run Victorian guesthouse, quiet and comfortable. Convenient for local amenities and beauty spots. Ideal for sightseers and walkers alike. Residential licensed bar.
Bedrooms: 2 double & 1 twin, 2 family rooms.
Bathrooms: 5 private.
Bed & breakfast: £26-£36 double.
Half board: £19-£24 daily, £125-£155 weekly.
Evening meal 7pm (l.o. 11am).
Parking for 4.
Credit: Access, Visa.

Hideaway Hotel ⋈
APPROVED
Phoenix Way, Windermere, LA23 1DB
☎ (096 62) 3070

A friendly and small hotel away from the main road, with a pleasant garden, a Swiss-trained chef, log fires and well-equipped, comfortable bedrooms.
Bedrooms: 3 single, 6 double & 4 twin, 2 family rooms.
Bathrooms: 15 private.
Bed & breakfast: £26-£40 single, £52-£80 double.
Half board: £31-£45 daily.
Evening meal 7.30pm (l.o. 7.30pm).
Parking for 15.

🆔 Display advertisement appears on page 579.

Hilton House Hotel ⋈
New Rd., Windermere, LA23 2EE
☎ (096 62) 3934
Large Lakeland residence in a woodland setting. Colour TV in all rooms. Golf, riding, boating nearby. Non-smoking room available.
Bedrooms: 1 single, 4 double, 1 family room.
Bathrooms: 4 private, 1 public.
Bed & breakfast: £23-£25 single, £34-£38 double.
Parking for 14.
Open March-October.

Holbeck Ghyll Country House Hotel ⋈
Holbeck Lane, Windermere, LA23 1LU
☎ Ambleside (053 94) 32375
Magnificent 19th C country house overlooking Lake Windermere. Set in own peaceful grounds. Spacious lounges, log fires.
Bedrooms: 10 double & 3 twin, 1 family room.
Bathrooms: 14 private.
Half board: £45-£60 daily.
Evening meal 7pm (l.o. 9pm).
Parking for 22.
Open February-December.
Credit: Access, Visa.

Holly Lodge ⋈
APPROVED
6 College Rd., Windermere, LA23 1BX
☎ (096 62) 3873
Traditional Lakeland stone guesthouse, built in 1854. In a quiet area off the main road, close to the village centre, buses, railway station and all amenities.

Bedrooms: 1 single, 3 double & 4 twin, 3 family rooms.
Bathrooms: 3 public.
Bed & breakfast: from £14 single, from £28 double.
Half board: from £22 daily, from £154 weekly.
Evening meal 7pm.
Parking for 7.

Holly Park House ⋈
1 Park Rd., Windermere, LA23 2AW
☎ (096 62) 2107
Handsome stone-built Victorian guesthouse with spacious rooms. Quiet area, convenient for village shops and coach/rail services.
Bedrooms: 6 double.
Bathrooms: 6 private.
Bed & breakfast: £22-£25 single, £28-£35 double.
Parking for 3.
Open March-October.

Hollythwaite Guest House ⋈
Listed
Holly Rd., Windermere, LA23 2AF
☎ (096 62) 2219
Family-run guesthouse in a quiet, central position. Within walking distance of rail and bus terminus. 1 mile from the lake.
Bedrooms: 2 single, 2 double & 2 twin, 1 family room.
Bathrooms: 2 public.
Bed & breakfast: £11-£11.50 single, £22-£23 double.
Half board: £17.50-£18 daily, from £115 weekly.
Evening meal 6.30pm (l.o. 3.30pm).
Open March-November.

Kirkwood Guest House ⋈
Prince's Rd., Windermere, LA23 2DD
☎ (096 62) 3907
Traditional Lakeland-stone house on a quiet corner, between Windermere and Bowness. Convenient for all Lakeland activities and amenities.
Bedrooms: 1 double & 1 twin, 5 family rooms.
Bathrooms: 4 private, 1 public.
Bed & breakfast: £25-£36 double.

Half board: £170-£245 weekly.
Parking for 1.

Knoll Hotel ⋈
Lake Rd., Windermere, LA23 2JF
☎ (096 62) 3756
In quiet grounds, with magnificent views overlooking Lake Windermere and the mountains. Free use of Parklands leisure club.
Bedrooms: 4 single, 3 double & 1 twin, 4 family rooms.
Bathrooms: 9 private, 1 public.
Bed & breakfast: from £27 single.
Half board: from £39.50 daily.
Evening meal 7pm (l.o. 7.30pm).
Parking for 15.
Open March-October.
Credit: Access, Visa.

Lakeside Hotel on Windermere ⋈
Newby Bridge, LA12 8AT
☎ (053 95) 31207
Telex 65149
Traditional Victorian hotel by steamer jetty and Lakeside-to-Haverthwaite steam train. Boat launching and moorings available. The summer terrace and refurbished rooms, restaurant and lounges have magnificent views over the lake. A new conservatory has just been built.
Bedrooms: 3 single, 15 double & 60 twin, 2 family rooms.
Bathrooms: 80 private.
Bed & breakfast: £60-£75 single, £90-£120 double.
Half board: £79.50-£94.50 daily, max. £590 weekly.
Lunch available.
Evening meal 6pm (l.o. 9.30pm).
Parking for 100.
Credit: Access, Visa, Diners, Amex.

Langdale Chase Hotel ⋈
Windermere, LA23 1LW
☎ Ambleside (053 94) 32201
Country house hotel in landscaped gardens on the edge of Lake Windermere.
Continued ▶

WINDERMERE
Continued

Bedrooms: 7 single, 13 double & 10 twin, 2 family rooms.
Bathrooms: 31 private, 2 public.
Bed & breakfast: £40-£50 single, £90-£100 double.
Half board: £60-£70 daily.
Lunch available.
Evening meal 7pm (l.o. 8.45pm).
Parking for 50.
Credit: Access, Visa, Diners, Amex.

Langdale View Guest House **M**

114 Craig Walk, Off Helm Rd., Bowness-on-Windermere, LA23 3AX
☎ (096 62) 4076
Traditional, Lakeland guesthouse with home cooking. En-suite rooms and mountain views. Minutes from the lake. We collect you from the station.
Bedrooms: 1 single, 2 double & 1 twin, 1 family room.
Bathrooms: 5 private.
Bed & breakfast: £16.50 single, £30-£32 double.
Half board: £22.75-£23.75 daily, £158-£165 weekly.
Evening meal 6pm (l.o. 4pm).
Parking for 8.

Laurieston Guesthouse **M**
Listed

40 Oak St., Windermere, LA23 1EN
☎ (096 62) 4253
Traditional stone-built house, offering home comforts with fine cuisine in a friendly atmosphere. Renowned for evening meals.
Bedrooms: 3 double & 1 twin, 1 family room.
Bathrooms: 2 private, 1 public.
Bed & breakfast: from £16 single, £24-£36 double.
Half board: £20-£26 daily, £130-£175 weekly.
Evening meal 7pm (l.o. 8pm).

Linthwaite Hotel **M**
COMMENDED

Crook Rd., Windermere, LA23 3JA
☎ (096 62) 3688 & (096 62) 2321

Peaceful location in 14 acres of gardens, 1 mile south of village with panoramic views over the lake.
Bedrooms: 11 double & 4 twin.
Bathrooms: 15 private.
Bed & breakfast: from £35 single, £70-£100 double.
Half board: £45-£55 daily, £300-£360 weekly.
Evening meal 7pm (l.o. 8pm).
Parking for 25.
Credit: Access, Visa.

Lonsdale Hotel **M**

Lake Rd., Bowness-on-Windermere, LA23 2JJ
☎ (096 62) 3348
In Bowness on the main road from Windermere. Within easy walking distance of the shops, buses and lake shore.
Bedrooms: 2 double, 7 family rooms.
Bathrooms: 9 private.
Bed & breakfast: £18-£24 single, £36-£48 double.
Parking for 10.
Open February-October.
Credit: Access, Visa.

Loreto **M**

Queens Drive, Windermere, LA23 2EL
☎ (096 62) 6374
Small friendly guesthouse, offering that little extra in food and comfort. 5 minutes' walk from Bowness and Lake Windermere.
Bedrooms: 1 single, 2 double & 1 twin, 1 family room.
Bathrooms: 1 public.
Bed & breakfast: £14-£16 single, £28-£32 double.
Half board: £20-£22 daily, £130-£140 weekly.
Evening meal 5pm (l.o. midday).

Low Spring Wood Hotel **M**

Thornbarrow Rd., Windermere, LA23 2DF
☎ (096 62) 6383
In an acre of landscaped garden with magnificent scenery and lake views, midway between Bowness and Windermere. Close to all amenities.
Bedrooms: 1 single, 4 double & 1 twin, 1 family room.
Bathrooms: 7 private.
Bed & breakfast: £18-£24 single, £36-£48 double.

Half board: £28-£36 daily, £196-£252 weekly.
Evening meal 7.30pm (l.o. 8pm).
Parking for 12.
Open March-December.

Low Wood Hotel **M**

Windermere, LA23 1LP
☎ Ambleside (053 94) 33338
Telex 65273 Fax (053 94) 34072
Almost a mile of lake frontage. Boat launching, water ski tuition and superb lake and mountain views. Also leisure centre, indoor heated swimming pool, bubble beds, sauna room, health and beauty centre, gymnasium, conference centre for 300, syndicate rooms, video and computer link-up.
Bedrooms: 5 single, 45 double & 47 twin, 2 family rooms.
Bathrooms: 99 private, 2 public.
Bed & breakfast: £54-£85 single, £108-£150 double.
Half board: £56-£95 daily, £364-£570 weekly.
Lunch available.
Evening meal 6.30pm (l.o. 10pm).
Parking for 200.
Credit: Access, Visa, Diners, Amex.

Meadfoot **M**

New Rd., Windermere, LA23 2LA
☎ (096 62) 2610
Modern detached house on the edge of the village of Windermere. It has a beautiful garden for guests to enjoy.
Bedrooms: 1 single, 5 double & 2 twin, 1 family room.
Bathrooms: 4 private, 1 public; 1 private shower.
Bed & breakfast: £14-£16 single, £28-£35 double.
Parking for 9.
Open February-November.

Mylne Bridge House **M**
COMMENDED

Brookside, Lake Rd., Windermere, LA23 2BX
☎ (096 62) 3314
Large private hotel. Cosy and friendly atmosphere. Family-run. Quiet yet central location.
Bedrooms: 2 single, 6 double & 2 twin.

Bathrooms: 7 private, 1 public.
Bed & breakfast: £15.50-£17.50 single, £27-£31 double.
Parking for 12.
Open March-November.

Oakleigh Guesthouse **M**
Listed

Lake Rd., Windermere, LA23 2JA
☎ (096 62) 4857
Family-run guesthouse on main lake road. Between Bowness and Windermere. Within easy walking distance of the lake. Non-smoking establishment.
Bedrooms: 4 double, 1 family room.
Bathrooms: 1 public.
Bed & breakfast: £18-£28 single, £26-£30 double.
Half board: £22-£24 daily, £154-£168 weekly.
Evening meal 7pm (l.o. 7pm).
Parking for 5.
Credit: Access, Visa.

Oldfield House **M**
COMMENDED

Oldfield Rd., Windermere, LA23 2BY
☎ (096 62) 88445
Traditionally built Lakeland residence with a friendly, informal atmosphere and in quiet, central location. Drying room, swimming and leisure facilities available.
Bedrooms: 2 single, 3 double & 1 twin, 1 family room.
Bathrooms: 4 private, 2 public.
Bed & breakfast: £13-£18.50 single, £26-£35 double.
Parking for 7.
Credit: Access, Visa.

Osborne Guest House

3 High St., Windermere, LA23 1AF
☎ (096 62) 6452
Traditional Lakeland house, central for all transport, tours and walks. Clean, comfortable accommodation. Full breakfast and a homely reputation.
Bedrooms: 1 double, 2 family rooms.
Bathrooms: 2 private, 1 public.
Bed & breakfast: £25-£30 double.
Half board: £154-£196 weekly.

The Poplars ₼
♛♛

Lake Rd., Windermere,
LA23 2EQ
☎ (096 62) 2325 & 6690
*Small family-run guesthouse on
the main lake road offering
every home comfort. A limited
number of non-residents
catered for - advanced booking
essential for evening meal.*
Bedrooms: 1 single, 3 double
& 2 twin, 1 family room.
Bathrooms: 3 private,
2 public.
Bed & breakfast: £15.50-£19
single, £31-£38 double.
Half board: £24.50-£28 daily,
£168-£192.50 weekly.
Evening meal 6.30pm (l.o.
7pm).
Parking for 7.

Quarry Garth Country House and Restaurant ₼
♛♛♛

Troutbeck Bridge,
Windermere, LA23 1LF
☎ (096 62) 3761/88282
*A Lakeland country house
hotel set in 8 acres of beautiful
gardens. Rich oak panelling
and log fires. Light lunches
and traditional dinners
available.*
Bedrooms: 1 single, 4 double
& 3 twin, 2 family rooms.
Bathrooms: 10 private.
Bed & breakfast: £30-£50
single, £50-£80 double.
Half board: £35-£60 daily,
£225-£350 weekly.
Lunch available.
Evening meal 7pm (l.o. 9pm).
Parking for 50.
Credit: Access, Visa, C.Bl.,
Diners, Amex.

Ravensworth Hotel ₼
♛♛♛

Ambleside Rd., Windermere,
LA23 1BA
☎ (096 62) 3747
*Close to the village centre, lake
and fells. Providing English and
Continental cooking. Variety of
accommodation available.*
Bedrooms: 2 single, 9 double
& 2 twin, 1 family room.
Bathrooms: 14 private.
Bed & breakfast: £26.50-£30
single, £48-£60 double.
Half board: £38.50-£42.50
daily, £210-£235 weekly.
Evening meal 7pm (l.o. 8pm).
Parking for 16.
Credit: Access, Visa.

Rosemount Private Hotel ₼
♛♛ COMMENDED

Lake Rd., Windermere,
LA23 2EQ
☎ (096 62) 3739
*Small, family-run hotel. Well
appointed, tastefully decorated
and furnished. Just a short
stroll from Lake Windermere
and Bowness.*
Bedrooms: 2 single, 5 double
& 1 twin.
Bathrooms: 8 private.
Bed & breakfast: £16.50-£22
single, £33-£44 double.
Parking for 8.
Credit: Access, Visa.

Royal Hotel ₼
♛♛♛♛ APPROVED

Queens Square, Bowness-on-
Windermere, LA23 3DB
☎ (096 62) 3045 & 5267
Telex 65464 ROYAL
Fax (096 62) 2498
*One of Lakeland's oldest
hotels, offering modern
amenities and only 100 yards
from the lake. Most rooms
have lake and mountain views.*
Bedrooms: 6 single, 11 double
& 7 twin, 5 family rooms.
Bathrooms: 29 private.
Bed & breakfast: £28-£36
single, £54-£72 double.
Half board: £37-£45 daily,
£227.50-£294 weekly.
Lunch available.
Evening meal 6pm (l.o.
10pm).
Parking for 21.
Credit: Access, Visa, Diners,
Amex.

St. John's Lodge ₼

Lake Rd., Windermere,
LA23 2EQ
☎ (096 62) 3078
*A small private hotel midway
between Windermere and the
lake, managed by the
chef/proprietor and convenient
for all amenities and services.*
Bedrooms: 10 double &
2 twin, 2 family rooms.
Bathrooms: 14 private.
Bed & breakfast: £16.50-£20
single, £33-£38 double.
Half board: £25-£28 daily,
£115-£180 weekly.
Evening meal 7pm (l.o. 6pm).
Parking for 11.

South View ₼

Cross St., Windermere,
LA23 1AE
☎ (096 62) 2951
*Small Georgian hotel in a quiet
position, central for attractions
and transport. Accent on good
food and friendliness. Indoor
swimming pool.*
Bedrooms: 1 single, 4 double
& 2 twin.
Bathrooms: 5 private,
2 public.
Bed & breakfast: £17-£23
single, £34-£46 double.
Half board: £26-£32 daily,
£150-£210 weekly.
Evening meal 6.30pm (l.o.
4pm).
Parking for 5.

Sunny-Bec ₼

Thornbarrow Rd.,
Windermere, LA23 2EN
☎ (096 62) 2103
*Spacious, detached Lakeland
guesthouse, a short walk from
the lake and shops. Quiet, with
a friendly atmosphere. Gardens
with stream.*
Bedrooms: 1 single, 1 double
& 1 twin, 1 family room.
Bathrooms: 1 public.
Bed & breakfast: £12-£13
single, £25-£30 double.
Half board: £19.50-£22 daily,
£130-£150 weekly.
Evening meal 6pm.
Parking for 5.

Thornbank Private Hotel ₼
♛♛ APPROVED

4 Thornbarrow Rd.,
Windermere, LA23 2EW
☎ (096 62) 3724
*A small family-run hotel
offering comfortable
accommodation and home-
cooked English food.
Convenient for shops and lake.*
Bedrooms: 1 single, 7 double
& 1 twin, 1 family room.
Bathrooms: 3 private,
2 public.
Bed & breakfast: £14.50-£17
single, £24-£33 double.
Half board: £20-£24.50 daily,
£129.50-£157.50 weekly.
Evening meal 6.45pm (l.o.
4pm).
Parking for 11.
Open February-December.
Credit: Access, Visa.

Villa Lodge ₼

Cross St., Windermere,
LA23 1AE
☎ (096 62) 3318
*A comfortable establishment in
a quiet cul-de-sac overlooking
Windermere village close to
shops, bus and railway
stations. Private parking.*
Bedrooms: 5 double & 2 twin,
1 family room.
Bathrooms: 2 private,
2 public.
Bed & breakfast: £11-£15
single, £22-£30 double.
Evening meal 6pm (l.o. 4pm).
Parking for 8.

Westbourne Hotel ₼
♛♛♛ COMMENDED

Biskey Howe Rd., Bowness-
on-Windermere, LA23 2JR
☎ (096 62) 3625
*In a peaceful area of Bowness
within a short walk of the lake
and shops.*
Bedrooms: 1 single, 3 double
& 1 twin, 2 family rooms.
Bathrooms: 7 private.
Bed & breakfast: £39-£50
double.
Half board: £28.50-£30 daily,
from £192 weekly.
Evening meal 6.30pm.
Parking for 10.
Credit: Access, Visa.

Westlake ₼

Lake Rd., Windermere,
LA23 2EQ
☎ (096 62) 3020
*Family-run, private hotel
between Windermere and
Bowness. All rooms en-suite,
with colour TV and tea-making
facilities. Brochure available.*
Bedrooms: 5 double & 1 twin,
2 family rooms.
Bathrooms: 8 private.
Bed & breakfast: £34-£42
double.
Half board: £27-£31 daily,
from £185 weekly.
Evening meal 6.30pm.
Parking for 8.

Wild Boar Hotel ₼
♛♛♛♛ COMMENDED

Crook, Nr. Windermere,
LA23 3NF
☎ (096 62) 5225 Telex 65464
Fax (096 62) 2498
*A former 17th C inn, renowned
for its food. Amidst the Gilpin
Valley, on the B5284, 3 miles
from the lake.*

Continued ▶

Please mention this guide when making a booking.

WINDERMERE
Continued

Bedrooms: 1 single, 16 double & 17 twin, 2 family rooms.
Bathrooms: 36 private.
Bed & breakfast: £40-£50 single, £80-£100 double.
Half board: £58.50-£68.50 daily, £287-£378 weekly.
Lunch available.
Evening meal 7pm (l.o. 8.45pm).
Parking for 80.
Credit: Access, Visa, Diners, Amex.

The Willowsmere Hotel ⋀
👑👑

Ambleside Rd., Windermere, LA23 1ES
☎ (096 62) 3575
Offers a comfortable and friendly atmosphere. Run by the fifth generation of local hoteliers. Fine food using fresh local produce.
Bedrooms: 2 single, 4 double & 1 twin, 7 family rooms.
Bathrooms: 14 private.
Bed & breakfast: from £23.50 single, from £47 double.
Half board: £37.50-£40 daily, £222-£243 weekly.
Lunch available.
Evening meal 7pm (l.o. 7pm).
Parking for 30.
Open March-November.
Credit: Access, Visa, Diners, Amex.

Winbrook House ⋀
👑👑 **COMMENDED**

30 Ellerthwaite Rd., Windermere, LA23 2AH
☎ (096 62) 4932
Modern guesthouse with a friendly atmosphere, offering English cooking. Access to rooms at all times. Private parking.
Bedrooms: 1 single, 4 double & 1 twin.
Bathrooms: 3 private; 3 private showers.
Bed & breakfast: £12-£18 single, £23.50-£33.50 double.
Half board: £77-£112 weekly.
Lunch available.
Parking for 7.
Open March-December.

Yorkshire House ⋀
👑👑 **APPROVED**

1 Upper Oak St., Windermere, LA23 2LB
☎ (096 62) 4689
Situated in secluded cul-de-sac close to town centre. Bright rooms, plentiful home-cooked food served in a warm, friendly atmosphere. Licensed.
Bedrooms: 2 double, 3 family rooms.
Bathrooms: 2 public.
Bed & breakfast: £12-£14 single, £24-£28 double.
Half board: £19-£21 daily, £126-£140 weekly.
Evening meal 6.30pm (l.o. 11am).
Parking for 5.

WORKINGTON
Cumbria
Map ref 5A2

A deep-water port on the Solway Firth. There are the ruins of the 14th C Workington Hall, where Mary Queen of Scots stayed in 1568.

Morven Guest House ⋀
Siddick Road, Siddick, Workington, CA14 1LE
☎ (0900) 602118 & 602002
Detached house north-west of Workington. Ideal base for touring the Lake District and West Cumbria. Large car park.
Bedrooms: 2 single, 1 double & 2 twin, 1 family room.
Bathrooms: 5 private, 1 public.
Bed & breakfast: £15-£22 single, £26-£38 double.
Lunch available.
Evening meal 6pm (l.o. 4pm).
Parking for 18.

The Viaduct Hotel
Falcon St., Workington, CA14 2XD
☎ (0900) 603733 & 61359
Fax (0900) 68837
Ideal for rail and road connections. Suitable for weddings, conferences and long stay holidays.
Bedrooms: 10 single, 5 double & 5 twin, 2 family rooms.
Bathrooms: 20 private, 4 public; 2 private showers.
Bed & breakfast: £18-£40 single, £30-£50 double.
Half board: £25-£46 daily, £146-£273 weekly.
Lunch available.
Evening meal 6.30pm (l.o. 9.30pm).
Parking for 20.
Credit: Access, Visa, Amex.

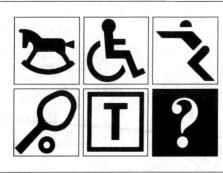

Key to symbols

Information about many of the services and facilities at establishments listed in this guide is given in the form of symbols. The key to these symbols is inside the back cover flap. You may find it helpful to keep the flap open when referring to the entry listings.

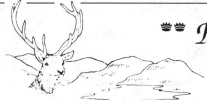

Northumbria
Once a powerful kingdom in its own right, Northumbria still demands awe and admiration from today's common traveller.

The first view of Bamburgh Castle takes the breath away — turrets piled upon turrets surmounting a cliff of natural stone.

>» A place of magic and legend, later the cradle of British Christianity, you can sense in the very air memories of centuries past. It's more than just history.

>» More is also the word for its scenery, which ranges from wild and open to the gently mellow. Northwards will find you in the spectacular Northumberland National Park with its beckoning Cheviot Hills and forbidding Hadrian's Wall. To the west are the wild heights and grassy dales of the North Pennines Area of Outstanding Natural Beauty.

>» A little south and you're offered Roseberry Topping — a delicious but stark treat, being a summit on the magnificent Cleveland Hills. And to the east, some of the country's most romantic coastline, dotted with islands, castles, bays and sandy beaches, with holiday resorts to suit all lifestyles.

>» As befits a region dripping with history, there are museums everywhere; to coal and lead-mining, railways and aircraft, seafaring and fishing, the Roman army and early Christianity, steam and beam engines, bagpipes and more. There are historic houses and castles, gardens and galleries, local arts and crafts. There's the great Durham Cathedral looking over its wooded gorge, and there are perfect churches everywhere.

>» Why not walk the Cleveland or Pennine Ways? Or fish sportingly in rivers, or watersport on Europe's largest man-made lake? Or shop in the

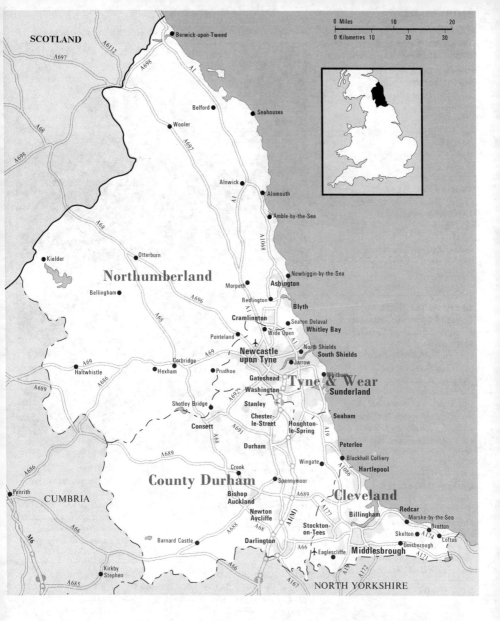

vast MetroCentre or at a weekly market? Or watch football or ice hockey? Northumbria is a whole jigsaw of things to see and do.

·≫ Add to all this the open-handed, open-hearted welcome first made famous by the Geordie, and you have the holiday experience of a lifetime!

≫ **Please refer to the colour maps at the back of this guide for all places with accommodation listings.**

Where to go, what to see

Captain Cook Birthplace Museum
Stewart Park, Marton, Middlesbrough, Cleveland TS7 8AS
☎ Middlesbrough (0642) 311211
Early life and voyages of Captain Cook.

Preston Hall Museum
Yarm Road, Stockton-on-Tees, Cleveland TS18 8RH
☎ Stockton-on-Tees (0642) 781184
Social history museum with period street and rooms, working craftsmen, arms, armour and transport.

Beamish: The North of England Open Air Museum
Beamish, Stanley, Co. Durham DH9 0RG
☎ Stanley (0207) 231811
A living museum vividly showing Northern life around the turn of the century. Four completely reconstructed main areas — the town; the colliery village, including drift mine; the railway station; the working farm. European Museum of the Year 1987.

Durham Cathedral
Durham, Co. Durham
☎ 091-386 2367
Durham Cathedral and precincts are probably the finest example of a Norman church in England. Tombs of St. Cuthbert and the Venerable Bede.

Raby Castle
Staindrop, Darlington, Co. Durham DL2 3AH
☎ Staindrop (0833) 60202
Medieval castle in 200-acre park, with 600-year-old kitchen, carriage collection, walled gardens.

Bowes Museum
Barnard Castle, Co. Durham DL12 8NP
☎ Staindrop (0833) 690606

The west front of Durham Cathedral, with the Castle to the left.

Fine and decorative art collections of 15th and 19th C. Paintings, furniture, ceramics and textiles from Britain and Western Europe.

Alnwick Castle
Alnwick, Northumberland NE66 1NQ
☎ Alnwick (0665) 510777
Home of the Percy family, the Dukes of Northumberland. Magnificent border fortress dating back to the 11th C. Main restoration done by Salvin in 19th C.

Housesteads Roman Fort
Bardon Mill, Northumberland
☎ Haltwhistle (0434) 344363
5-acre fort, taking in part of Roman Wall. Best preserved of the Roman forts.

Vindolanda Trust
Haltwhistle, Northumberland NE47 7JN
☎ Haltwhistle (0434) 344277
Visitors may wander through the excavations of the Roman fort to the superb museum set in ornamental gardens.

Cragside House and Country Park
Cragside, Rothbury, Morpeth, Northumberland NE65 7PX
☎ Rothbury (0669) 20333
House built 1864 for first Lord Armstrong, Tyneside industrialist. The power circuit in the grounds illustrates the world's first hydro-electric scheme used to light the house.

Morpeth Chantry Bagpipe Museum
The Chantry, Bridge Street, Morpeth, Northumberland NE61 1PJ

☎ Morpeth (0670) 519466

One of the most extensive collections of its kind in the world. Northumbrian small pipes, Scottish and Irish pipes, Border half-longs and many foreign bagpipes. Visitors can hear the music associated with each display through personal headphones.

Lindisfarne Castle
Holy Island, Northumberland

☎ Berwick-upon-Tweed (0289) 89244

Built about 1550. Sir Edwin Lutyens' inspired restoration (1903) provided a comfortable home within the castle.

MetroCentre
Gateshead, Tyne & Wear NE13 7LU

☎ 091-493 2046

Largest shopping and leisure complex in Western Europe. Free parking for 7,000 cars. Glass-roofed malls with superb decor, arts & crafts and antique centres, most major retailers. Mediterranean village and indoor theme park. Extensive catering facilities.

Morpeth Northumbrian Gathering
Various venues, Morpeth, Northumberland   *5 – 7 April**

Fish Quay Festival
North Shields, Tyne & Wear   *25 – 27 May**

Cookson Country Festival
Various venues, South Shields, Tyne & Wear   *22 June – 26 August*

Alnwick Medieval Fair
Various venues, Alnwick, Northumberland   *30 June – 7 July*

Durham Miners' Gala
Durham, Co. Durham   *13 July**

Billingham International Folklore Festival
Various venues, Billingham, Cleveland   *10 – 17 August*

Saltburn Victorian Celebrations
Various venues, Saltburn, Cleveland   *11 – 18 August**

Sunderland Illuminations
Roker and Seaburn, Sunderland, Tyne & Wear   *23 August – 5 November*

Allendale Baal Fire Festival
Market Place, Allendale, Northumberland   *31 December*

* Provisional dates only

Further information about holidays and attractions in the Northumbria region is available from:
Northumbria Tourist Board, Aykley Heads, Durham DH1 5UX.
☎ 091-384 6905.

The following publications are available free from the Northumbria Tourist Board:

Northumbria Holiday Guide 1991

Bed & Breakfast map

Short Breaks map

Self-Catering map

Attractions and Gardens map

Also available are (prices include postage and packing):

Northumbria Touring map and guide £4.30

Video of Northumbria (VHS 30 mins) £10.99

From Seahouses you can book trips to the Farne Islands in one of the colourful boats at the quayside.

Places to stay

≫ Accommodation entries in this regional section are listed in alphabetical order of place name, and then in alphabetical order of establishment.

≫ The map references refer to the colour maps towards the end of the guide. The first figure is the map number; the letter and figure which follow indicate the grid reference on the map.

≫ The symbols at the end of each accommodation entry give information about services and facilities. A 'key' to these symbols is inside the back cover flap, which can be kept open for easy reference.

ALLENDALE
Northumberland
Map ref 5B2

10m SW. Hexham
Attractive small town set amongst moors, 10 miles south-west of Hexham and claimed to be the geographical centre of Britain. Surrounded by unspoilt walking country, with many well-signposted walks along the East and West Allen Rivers. On New Year's Eve the Allendale Fire is a spectacular traditional event.

Heatherlea Hotel M
😊😊 APPROVED
Allendale, Hexham,
NE47 9BJ
☎ (0434) 683236
Family-run hotel, noted for home cooking and baking. Facilities include snooker and table tennis. The garden has a putting green, bowls, swings and sun lounge.
Bedrooms: 4 single, 5 double & 5 twin, 3 family rooms.
Bathrooms: 8 private,
3 public.
Bed & breakfast: £15.50-£22 single.
Half board: £20-£27 daily,
£115-£135 weekly.
Lunch available.
Evening meal 7pm (l.o. 8pm).
Parking for 10.
Open May-October,
December.
🐾🍴 📺 🛏 📺 🖥 🎎 🌳 ⬤ 🕐 ❄ 🔥
✿ 🐕 🚗 ⬇ SP

ALNMOUTH
Northumberland
Map ref 5C1

4m SE. Alnwick
Quiet village with pleasant old buildings, at the mouth of the River Aln where extensive dunes and sands stretch along Almouth Bay. 18th C granaries, some converted to dwellings, still stand.

Blue Dolphins M
😊😊😊
Riverside Road, Alnmouth,
Alnwick, NE66 2RS
☎ (0665) 830893
Beautifully situated, well-furnished Edwardian house with uninterrupted views over mouth of River Aln and North Sea. All rooms en-suite.
Bedrooms: 4 double & 1 twin.
Bathrooms: 5 private.
Bed & breakfast: £17-£20 single, £34.40-£40 double.
Parking for 5.
🐾🍴 📺 🖥 UL 📺 🛏 🖥 🎎
✿ 🐕 SP

> **Classifications and quality commendations were correct at the time of going to press but are subject to change. Please check at the time of booking.**

ALNWICK
Northumberland
Map ref 5C1

17m N. Morpeth
Ancient and historic market town, entered through the Hotspur Tower, an original gate in the town walls. The medieval castle, the second biggest in England and still the seat of the Dukes of Northumberland, was restored from ruin in the 18th C. The castle has 7 acres of grounds landscaped by Capability Brown and its Italianate interiors contrast with the powerful exterior. Fishing enthusiasts will enjoy the House of Hardy Museum.
Tourist Information Centre ☎ (0665) 510665

Bondgate House Hotel M
😊😊😊 APPROVED
20 Bondgate Without,
Alnwick, NE66 1PN
☎ (0665) 602025 Fax (0665) 602554
A small family-run hotel near the medieval town gateway and interesting local shops. Well placed for touring.
Bedrooms: 3 double & 2 twin,
3 family rooms.
Bathrooms: 3 private,
2 public.
Bed & breakfast: £26-£30 double.
Half board: £22-£24 daily,
£135-£149 weekly.

Evening meal 6.30pm (l.o. 4.30pm).
Parking for 8.
🐾🍴 📺 🍴 ⬤ V 🛏 🖥 🎎 ⬤ 🕐
🐕 SP 🔥

Glendower Guest House
23 Argyle Street, Alnmouth,
NE66 2SB
☎ (0665) 830262
Near the river and sea, with rail and bus links.
Chef/proprietor. Warm welcome assured.
Bedrooms: 2 single, 1 twin,
1 family room.
Bathrooms: 2 public.
Bed & breakfast: £15-£20 single, £30-£40 double.
Half board: £22-£30 daily,
£154-£210 weekly.
Evening meal 6.20pm (l.o. 8pm).
Credit: Access, Visa.
🐾✿ 📺 🍴 ⬤ V 🛏 📺 🖥
🎎 🐕 🚗 🐾 ⬇ SP

Hotspur Hotel M
😊😊😊
Bondgate Without, Alnwick,
NE66 1PR
☎ (0665) 510101 Fax (0665) 605033
Originally a coaching inn, we offer old-style friendly hospitality with up-to-date standards of comfort and Northumbrian food.
Bedrooms: 4 single, 8 double & 14 twin, 1 family room.
Bathrooms: 21 private,
3 public.
Bed & breakfast: £25-£30 single, £45-£50 double.
Half board: £34-£36 daily,
£200-£250 weekly.
Lunch available.

Evening meal 7pm (l.o. 9pm).
Parking for 20.
Credit: Access, Visa.

Marine House Private Hotel M

1 Marine Road, Alnmouth,
Alnwick, NE66 2RW
☎ (0665) 830349
This converted granary is 200 years old and overlooks the golf links and the sea. We have a cocktail bar and offer home cooking.
Bedrooms: 3 double & 4 twin, 3 family rooms.
Bathrooms: 10 private, 1 public.
Bed & breakfast: £36-£46 double.
Half board: £29-£33 daily, £200-£228 weekly.
Evening meal 7pm.
Parking for 12.

The Oaks Hotel M
COMMENDED
South Road, Alnwick, NE66 2PN
☎ (0665) 510014
A stone-built building (part circa 1800) comprising recently refurbished cocktail bar, dining room and bedrooms.
Bedrooms: 1 single, 8 double & 3 twin, 1 family room.
Bathrooms: 13 private.
Bed & breakfast: from £37.50 single, from £60 double.
Lunch available.
Evening meal 7pm (l.o. 9pm).
Parking for 25.
Credit: Access, Visa, Diners, Amex.

> **Half board prices shown are per person but in some cases may be based on double/twin occupancy.**

> **Individual proprietors have supplied all details of accommodation. Although we do check for accuracy, we advise you to confirm prices and other information at the time of booking.**

AMBLE-BY-THE-SEA
Northumberland
Map ref 5C1

Small fishing town at the mouth of the River Coquet, with fine, quiet, sandy beaches to north and south. The harbour and estuary are popular for sailing and bird-watching. Coquet Island lies 1 mile offshore. A new marina opened in 1987.

The Granary Hotel M

Links Road, Amble, Morpeth, NE65 0SD
☎ (0665) 710872 Fax (0665) 710681
Converted old granary with all en-suite rooms and panoramic sea views. Well established restaurant with food and wine.
Bedrooms: 2 single, 2 double & 8 twin, 1 family room.
Bathrooms: 13 private.
Bed & breakfast: £32.95-£35 single, £48-£65 double.
Half board: £35-£40 daily, £245-£280 weekly.
Lunch available.
Evening meal 7pm (l.o. 10pm).
Parking for 200.
Credit: Access, Visa, Amex.

Harbour Guest House M
24 Leazes St., Amble, Morpeth, NE65 0AA
☎ Alnwick (0665) 710381
Family-run guest house by Amble harbour with views of the River Coquet. Fishing parties by arrangement.
Bedrooms: 2 single, 1 double & 2 twin, 2 family rooms.
Bathrooms: 1 public.
Bed & breakfast: from £12 single, from £23 double.
Half board: from £16 daily, from £100 weekly.
Evening meal 6pm (l.o. 6pm).
Parking for 7.

BAMBURGH
Northumberland
Map ref 5C1

Village with a spectacular red sandstone castle standing 150 ft above the sea. On the village green the magnificent Norman church stands opposite a museum containing mementos of the heroine Grace Darling.

Lord Crewe Arms Hotel M

Front Street, Bamburgh, NE69 7BL
☎ (066 84) 243 & 393
Cosy village hotel offering modern comfort and old world charm, with oak beams and open fires, featuring a restaurant and buttery. Near Bamburgh Castle.
Bedrooms: 1 single, 10 double & 13 twin, 1 family room.
Bathrooms: 20 private, 3 public.
Bed & breakfast: £30-£33 single, £52-£56 double.
Half board: £42-£46 daily, £235-£260 weekly.
Lunch available.
Evening meal 7pm (l.o. 9pm).
Parking for 34.
Open March-October.
Credit: Access, Visa.

Mizen Head Hotel M

Lucker Road, Bamburgh, NE69 7BS
☎ (066 84) 254
A privately-owned, family-run hotel in its own grounds, with accent on food and service. Convenient for beaches, castle and golf.
Bedrooms: 3 single, 6 double & 4 twin, 3 family rooms.
Bathrooms: 3 private, 4 public.
Bed & breakfast: £16-£25 single, £26-£44 double.
Half board: £22.75-£37.75 daily, £147-£197 weekly.
Lunch available.
Evening meal 6.30pm (l.o. 8.30pm).
Parking for 35.
Credit: Access, Visa.

BARDON MILL
Northumberland
Map ref 5B2

Small hamlet midway between Haydon Bridge and Haltwhistle, within easy walking distance of Vindolanda, an excavated Roman settlement, and near the best stretches of Hadrian's Wall.

Vallum Lodge Hotel M
COMMENDED
Military Road, Twice Brewed, Bardon Mill, Hexham, NE47 7AN
☎ (0434) 344248
Small, quiet, comfortable hotel on the B6318, in the Northumberland National Park. Close to the most spectacular part of Hadrian's Wall and the Pennine Way. Good choice of freshly cooked food.
Bedrooms: 1 single, 2 double & 4 twin.
Bathrooms: 1 private, 2 public.
Bed & breakfast: £16-£19 single, £30-£34 double.
Half board: £26-£29 daily, £168-£175 weekly.
Lunch available.
Evening meal 7pm (l.o. 8.30pm).
Parking for 25.
Open February-November.

BARNARD CASTLE
Co. Durham
Map ref 5B3

High over the Tees, a thriving market town with a busy market square. Bernard Baliol's 12th C castle (now ruins) stands nearby. The Bowes Museum, housed in a grand 19th C French chateau, holds fine paintings and furniture. Nearby are the magnificent Raby Castle, Boose Castle, Rokeby Hall and Egglestone Abbey.
Tourist Information Centre ☎ *(0833) 690909*

The Coach House
Whorlton, Barnard Castle, DL12 8XQ
☎ (0833) 27237
Secluded modernised stables in small village. 3 miles east of Barnard Castle on banks of River Tees.
Bedrooms: 1 double & 1 twin.
Continued ▶

BARNARD CASTLE
Continued

Bathrooms: 1 public.
Bed & breakfast: from £25 double.
Parking for 2.
Open April-October.

[symbols]

Morritt Arms Hotel M
Greta Bridge, Barnard Castle, DL12 9SE
☎ Teesdale (0833) 27232/27392 Fax (0833) 27570
Fine Georgian building in own grounds. Associated with Charles Dickens. Open log fires.
Bedrooms: 3 single, 9 double & 8 twin, 3 family rooms.
Bathrooms: 16 private, 4 public.
Bed & breakfast: max. £42 single, max. £65 double.
Lunch available.
Evening meal 7.30pm (l.o. 8.45pm).
Parking for 103.
Credit: Access, Visa, Diners, Amex.

[symbols]

Rose & Crown Hotel M
Romaldkirk, Barnard Castle, DL12 9EB
☎ Teesdale (0833) 50213
A 17th C stone-built coaching inn with log fires and offering traditional comfort. Overlooking the green in Teesdale's most attractive village.
Bedrooms: 1 single, 4 double & 5 twin, 1 family room.
Bathrooms: 11 private.
Bed & breakfast: from £44 single, from £55 double.
Lunch available.
Evening meal 7.30pm (l.o. 9.30pm).
Parking for 60.
Credit: Access, Visa.

[symbols]

The symbol **CR** and the name of a hotel group or consortium after a hotel address means that bookings can be made through a central reservations office. These are listed on pages 559 & 560.

BELFORD
Northumberland
Map ref 5B1

Small market town on the old coaching road, close to the coast, the Scottish border and the north-east flank of the Cheviots. Built mostly in stone and very peaceful now that the A1 has by-passed the town, Belford makes an ideal centre for excursions to the moors and to the beautiful unspoilt coastline around Holy Island.
Tourist Information Centre ☎ (0668) 213888

Blue Bell Hotel M
[symbols]
Market Place, Belford, NE70 7NE
☎ (0668) 213543 Telex 53168
CR Consort
Beautiful old hotel building covered in virginia creeper only 1 mile from the A1, with extensive gardens. A perfect centre for touring the lovely Northumbrian coastline.
Bedrooms: 1 single, 6 double & 7 twin, 1 family room.
Bathrooms: 15 private.
Bed & breakfast: £35-£45 single, £60-£80 double.
Lunch available.
Evening meal 7.15pm (l.o. 8.45pm).
Parking for 12.
Credit: Access, Visa, Diners, Amex.

[symbols]

BELLINGHAM
Northumberland
Map ref 5B2

Set in the beautiful valley of the North Tyne, small border town close to the Kielder Forest, Kielder Water and lonely moorland below the Cheviots. The church, which stands close to the river and to St. Cuthbert's Well, has an ancient stone wagon roof fortified in the 18th C with buttresses.
Tourist Information Centre ☎ (0434) 220616

The Cheviot M
[symbols]
Bellingham, Hexham, NE48 2AU
☎ (0434) 220216

In the town centre, this old country inn features traditional open fireplaces in the lounge and bar, and a large selection of whiskies.
Bedrooms: 1 single, 2 double & 3 twin.
Bathrooms: 6 private.
Bed & breakfast: £20.35-£21.27 single, £40.70-£42.54 double.
Half board: £31.90-£33.35 daily, £207.90-£217.35 weekly.
Lunch available.
Evening meal 7pm (l.o. 9.30pm).
Parking for 10.
Credit: Access, Visa.

[symbols]

Display advertisement appears on page 109.

Lyndale Guest House M
[symbols]
Bellingham, Hexham, NE48 2AW
☎ (0434) 220361
Attractive dormer bungalow in pleasant village amid moors. Close to the river and ideal for touring Roman Wall and Kielder Water.
Bedrooms: 1 single, 2 double & 1 twin.
Bathrooms: 2 public.
Bed & breakfast: £13-£16 single, £26-£30 double.
Half board: £21-£24 daily, £142-£163 weekly.
Evening meal 6pm (l.o. 2pm).
Parking for 6.

[symbols]

BERWICK-UPON-TWEED
Northumberland
Map ref 5B1

Guarding the mouth of the Tweed, England's northernmost town with the best 16th C city walls in Europe. The handsome Guildhall and barracks date from the 18th C. The church, unusually, was completed by the Puritans. 3 bridges cross to Tweedmouth, the oldest built in 1634. The Barracks hold the regimental museum, town museum and part of the Burrell Art Collection.
Tourist Information Centre ☎ (0289) 330733

Harberton Guest House
181 Main Street, Spittal, Berwick-upon-Tweed, TD15 1RP
☎ (0289) 308813

Attractive stone-built house, overlooking sandy beach. Magnificent views. Home cooking to suit all. Newly refurbished. Licensed. Fire certificate.
Bedrooms: 1 single, 3 double & 1 twin.
Bathrooms: 3 private, 1 public.
Bed & breakfast: £15-£16.50 single, £30-£40 double.
Half board: £23.50-£28.50 daily, £154.50-£190 weekly.
Lunch available.
Evening meal 6pm (l.o. 8pm).
Parking for 6.

[symbols]

Meadow Hill Guest House M
[symbols] COMMENDED
Duns Road, Berwick-upon-Tweed, TD15 1UB
☎ (0289) 306325
Attractive 150-year-old house with panoramic views of the River Tweed and Cheviot hills.
Bedrooms: 4 family rooms.
Bathrooms: 1 private, 2 public.
Bed & breakfast: £13.50-£20 single, £27-£40 double.
Half board: £20-£27 daily.
Evening meal 7.30pm (l.o. 9am).
Parking for 10.

[symbols]

Ness Gate Hotel M
1 Palace Street East, Berwick-upon-Tweed, TD15 1HT
☎ (0289) 307123
A family-run hotel in an early 19th C listed building, close to the old town walls and the sea. Convenient for the shops, cinema and theatre.
Bedrooms: 6 single, 7 double & 4 twin, 4 family rooms.
Bathrooms: 7 private, 4 public; 4 private showers.
Bed & breakfast: £15-£21.50 single, £30-£43 double.
Half board: £21-£28 daily, £126-£168 weekly.
Lunch available.
Evening meal 6.15pm (l.o. 7.30pm).
Credit: Access, Visa, Diners.

[symbols]

The Old Vicarage Guest House M
[symbols] COMMENDED
24, Church Road, Tweedmouth, Berwick-upon-Tweed, TD15 2AN
☎ (0289) 306909

Spacious, detached 19th C vicarage, recently refurbished to a high standard. 10 minutes' walk from town centre and beautiful beaches.
Bedrooms: 1 single, 2 double & 2 twin, 3 family rooms.
Bathrooms: 4 private,
1 public.
Bed & breakfast: £10-£13 single, £22-£36 double.
⌂ ♨ 🛏 🖤 ☺ ♿ 🍴 ⬛
🅿 SP

Turret House Hotel M
👑👑👑👑 COMMENDED
Etal Road, Tweedmouth,
Berwick-upon-Tweed,
TD15 2EG
☎ (0289) 330808 Fax
(0289) 330467
Ⓒ Inter
Privately owned and run, the hotel is quietly set in 2 acres of grounds very near the town centre.
Bedrooms: 2 single, 7 double & 3 twin, 1 family room.
Bathrooms: 13 private.
Bed & breakfast: £42.50-£46.50 single, £57-£63 double.
Lunch available.
Evening meal 7.30pm (l.o. 9pm).
Parking for 100.
Credit: Access, Visa, Diners, Amex.
⌂ ♨ 📞 🖤 ☺ ♿ 🍴 🅅 🛏
⬛ 🖤 🍴 ♿ ► ☼ 🌂 🚂
🅣

BILLINGHAM
Cleveland
Map ref 5C3

A Teesside boom-town of the early 20th C, originally a 10th C settlement, with echoes of the 'Anglo-Saxon' in its church. The town centre has an ambitious modern complex providing shopping, culture, entertainment and sporting facilities. The town holds an annual international folk festival.

Billingham Arms Hotel M
👑👑👑👑
The Causeway, Billingham,
TS23 2HD
☎ Stockton (0642) 553661
Telex 587746
In the town square, this modern hotel is perfectly placed for both station and airport, and touring Captain Cook country.
Bedrooms: 16 single, 41 double & 3 twin, 9 family rooms.

Bathrooms: 69 private,
5 public.
Bed & breakfast: £21.50-£50 single, £43-£65 double.
Half board: £26.50-£60 daily.
Lunch available.
Evening meal 6pm (l.o. 11pm).
Parking for 200.
Credit: Access, Visa, C.Bl., Diners, Amex.
⌂ ♨ 🖤 ☺ ♿ 🍴 🖤 🅅 ✂
🛏 🖤 🌐 ► ⬛ ⬛ ♨ 🍴 ♿ ♣
SP 🅣

BISHOP AUCKLAND
Co. Durham
Map ref 5C2

Busy market town on the bank of the Wear. The Palace, a castellated Norman manor house altered in the 18th C, stands in beautiful gardens. Open to the public and entered from the market square by a handsome 18th C gatehouse, the park is a peaceful retreat of trees and streams.

The Gables M
👑👑👑
10 South View, Middlestone
Moor, Spennymoor,
DL16 7DF
☎ (0388) 817544
A spacious Victorian detached house in quiet residential area. 7 miles from Durham city centre between Bishop Auckland and Spennymoor.
Bedrooms: 2 double & 4 twin.
Bathrooms: 2 private,
2 public.
Bed & breakfast: £13-£14 single, £20-£22 double.
Half board: £19-£20 daily, £120-£135 weekly.
Evening meal 6.45pm (l.o. 7pm).
Parking for 7.
♨5 ♨ 🖤 ☺ ♿ 🅅 ✂ 🛏 ⬛
⬛ 🚂 SP

BURNOPFIELD
Co. Durham
Map ref 5C2

6m SW. Gateshead

Burnbrae Country House M
👑👑👑 COMMENDED
Leazes Villas, Burnopfield,
Co. Durham NE16 6HN
☎ (0207) 70432
Georgian house in small Durham village. MetroCentre and Beamish Museum 10 minutes away. Non-smokers only please.

Bedrooms: 2 single, 3 double & 1 twin, 1 family room.
Bathrooms: 5 private,
1 public.
Bed & breakfast: £25-£40 single, £42-£60 double.
Half board: £31-£41 daily, £210-£294 weekly.
Evening meal 6.30pm.
Parking for 7.
Credit: Access, Visa.
♨ ♨ 🖤 ☺ 🖤 🅅 ⬛ 🅅
🛏 🖤 ⬛ ⬛ Ⓤ ► ☼ 🌂 🚂
SP

CHESTER-LE-STREET
Co. Durham
Map ref 5C2

Originally a Roman military site, town with modern commerce and light industry on the River Wear. The ancient church replaced a wooden sanctuary which sheltered the remains of St. Cuthbert for 113 years. The Anker's house beside the church is now a museum.

Lambton Arms Hotel
👑👑
Front Street, Chester-le-Street, DH3 3BJ
☎ 091-388 3265
A convenient hotel for both business and tourist attractions including Beamish Open Air Museum. Only half a mile from the A1M.
Bedrooms: 1 single,
11 double.
Bathrooms: 3 private,
3 public.
Bed & breakfast: from £35 single, from £48 double.
Half board: £42.50-£55.50 daily.
Lunch available.
Evening meal 7pm (l.o. 9pm).
Parking for 40.
Credit: Access, Visa.
♨ 🖤 ☺ 🅅 🛏 ⬛ 🍴 🚂
SP

The Lambton Worm
👑👑
North Road, Chester-le-Street, DH3 4AJ
☎ 091-388 3386
Traditional small hotel just off the A1M, close to Durham, Washington and Newcastle. Our 2 bars offer a good range of reasonably-priced bar meals.
Bedrooms: 4 single, 6 double & 3 twin.
Bathrooms: 1 private,
2 public.

Bed & breakfast: £20-£25 single, £30-£35 double.
Lunch available.
Evening meal 7.30pm (l.o. 10pm).
Parking for 45.
Credit: Visa.
⬛ ♨ 🖤 🛏 ⬛ 🌂 🚂

Lumley Castle Hotel M
👑👑👑
Chester-le-Street, DH3 4NX
☎ 091-389 1111 Telex 537433
14th C castle surrounded by the River Wear, in 7 acres of parkland. 7 miles from Durham, 13 miles from Newcastle. Easily accessible from the A1M motorway.
Bedrooms: 13 single,
35 double & 14 twin, 3 family rooms.
Bathrooms: 65 private.
Bed & breakfast: £57.50-£97 single, £90-£110 double.
Half board: £76-£145 daily, £375-£725 weekly.
Lunch available.
Evening meal 6.30pm (l.o. 9.45pm).
Parking for 200.
Credit: Access, Visa, Diners, Amex.
♨ ♨ 📞 🖤 ☺ ♿ 🍴 🅅
✂ 🛏 🌐 ⬛ ⬛ 🍴 ♿ ♨ ♣
► ☼ 🌂 OAP ⬛ SP 🚂 🅣

CONSETT
Co. Durham
Map ref 5B2

Former steel town on the edge of rolling moors. Modern development includes the shopping centre and a handsome Roman Catholic church, designed by a local architect. To the west, the Derwent Reservoir provides water sports and pleasant walks.

Bee Cottage Farm M
Listed APPROVED
Castleside, Consett,
DH8 9HW
☎ (0207) 508224
46-acre livestock farm. 1.5 miles west of the A68, between Castleside and Tow Law. Unspoilt views. Ideally located for Beamish Museum and Durham.
Bedrooms: 1 single, 5 double & 5 twin, 3 family rooms.
Bathrooms: 1 private,
5 public.
Bed & breakfast: £14-£20 single, £28-£40 double.
Half board: £22.50-£28.50 daily, £147.50-£199.50 weekly.
Lunch available.

Continued ►

95

CONSETT
Continued

Evening meal 5pm (l.o. 9.30pm).
Parking for 26.
🛏 🗼 ♨ 🛁 🅿 Ⅴ ✗ ⛽ ℡
▥ ♨ 🍴 ∪ ⚲

Castlenook Guest House M
♨♨
18/20 Front Street,
Castleside, Consett,
DH8 9AR
☎ (0207) 506634
On the A68 within easy reach of Durham City, Hadrian's Wall, Beamish Museum and MetroCentre. Excellent village amenities.
Bedrooms: 1 double & 2 twin.
Bathrooms: 3 private.
Bed & breakfast: £12.50-£18 single, £25 double.
Evening meal 5pm (l.o. 7pm).
Parking for 5.
Credit: Access, Visa.
🛏 ♨ Ⓤ 🛁 Ⅴ ⛽ ℡ ▥ ♨
❄ ✗ ⛽ 🌺

CORBRIDGE
Northumberland
Map ref 5B2

Small town on the River Tyne. Close to by are extensive remains of the Roman military town Corstopitum, with a museum housing important discoveries from excavations. The town itself is attractive with shady trees, a 17th C bridge and interesting old buildings, notably a 14th C fortified vicarage and a pele tower house about 200 years older.

Angel Inn M
♨♨ APPROVED
Main Street, Corbridge,
NE45 5LA
☎ (0434) 632119
Old coaching inn in the centre of Corbridge providing an excellent base for touring the Roman Wall area and Northumberland.
Bedrooms: 3 double & 2 twin.
Bathrooms: 5 private.
Bed & breakfast: from £30 single, from £46 double.
Half board: £37.50-£53.50 daily.
Lunch available.
Evening meal 7pm (l.o. 9pm).
Parking for 20.
Credit: Access, Visa, Diners, Amex.
🛏 🖵 🌺 🛁 Ⅴ ⛽ ℡ ▥ 🍴
🌺 SP 🌺

Clive House M
♛♛♛♛
Appletree Lane, Corbridge,
NE45 5DN
☎ (0434) 632617
Old village school (1840) converted to dwelling house; tasteful decor throughout, exposed beams, gallery, and a log fire in breakfast room. Good eating places nearby.
Bedrooms: 2 double & 1 twin.
Bathrooms: 3 private.
Bed & breakfast: £26-£28 single, £33-£38 double.
Parking for 3.
Credit: Access, Visa.
🛏12 ♨ ℡ ▥ 🖵 🌺 🛁 Ⅴ
⛽ ♨ ▥ 🛁 ✗ 🌺 SP 🌺

Fellcroft M
♛
Station Road, Corbridge,
NE45 5AY
☎ (0434) 632384
Stone-built Edwardian house with full private facilities and colour TV in all bedrooms. Quiet road, half a mile south of Corbridge market square. Excellent choice of eating places nearby.
Bedrooms: 2 twin.
Bathrooms: 2 private.
Bed & breakfast: £15-£17 single, £26-£28 double.
Open April-October.
🛏10 ⊙ 🖵 🌺 Ⓤ ⛽ ▥
🛁 ∪ ✗ 🌺

Lion of Corbridge Hotel M
♛♛♛♛ COMMENDED
Bridge End, Corbridge,
NE45 5AX
☎ (0434) 632504
Family-run hotel on the bank of the River Tyne with emphasis on comfort and good food. 1 room on the ground floor especially equipped for the disabled. Special 2-3 day breaks available (cost room, breakfast and dinner £125.00 to £175.00 respectively).
Bedrooms: 1 single, 5 double & 8 twin.
Bathrooms: 14 private.
Bed & breakfast: £45 single, £58 double.
Lunch available.
Evening meal 6.30pm (l.o. 9.30pm).
Parking for 60.
Credit: Access, Visa, Diners, Amex.
🛏 🗼 🌺 ℡ ⊙ 🖵 🌺 🛁 Ⅴ
⛽ ▥ 🛁 🍴 ♿ ❄ ✗ 🌺 🌺
SP

Wheatsheaf Hotel M
♛♛♛♛ COMMENDED
St. Helens Street, Corbridge,
NE45 5HE
☎ (0434) 632020
Traditional country village inn, friendly and comfortable, offering home-cooking, live music. All rooms with TV and en-suite facilities. Large car park.
Bedrooms: 1 single, 2 double & 1 twin, 2 family rooms.
Bathrooms: 6 private.
Bed & breakfast: £26-£40 single, £36-£46 double.
Half board: £32-£50 daily.
Lunch available.
Evening meal 7pm (l.o. 9.30pm).
Parking for 40.
Credit: Access, Visa, Amex.
🛏 🗼 ℡ 🌺 🛁 Ⅴ ⛽
▥ 🛁 🍴 ❄ ✗ 🌺 OAP 🌺 ℡

CROOK
Co. Durham
Map ref 5C2

5m NW. Bishop Auckland
Pleasant market town sometimes referred to as 'the gateway to Weardale'. The town's shopping centre surrounds a large, open green, attractively laid out with lawns and flowerbeds around the Devil's Stone, a relic from the Ice Age.

Greenhead Country House Hotel M
♨♨♨
Fir Tree, Crook, DL15 8BL
☎ Bishop Auckland
(0388) 763143
Newly established enterprise with well-appointed en-suite bedrooms. Overlooks secluded fields and wooded area. Lounge with sandstone arches, log fire and oak beams.
Bedrooms: 1 single, 4 double & 1 twin.
Bathrooms: 6 private, 1 public.
Bed & breakfast: £27-£27.50 single, £38 double.
Half board: £189-£192 weekly.
Evening meal 6pm (l.o. 5pm).
Parking for 15.
Credit: Access, Visa.
🛏13 🗼 🌺 ⊙ 🖵 🌺 🛁 ♨
Ⅴ ▥ 🛁 🍴 ∪ ✗ ❄ ✗ 🌺
SP 🌺 ℡
✪ Display advertisement appears on page 109.

Helme Park Hall Country House Hotel M
♨♨♨ COMMENDED
Fir Tree, Crook, DL13 4NW
☎ Bishop Auckland
(0388) 730970
Comfortable with open fires. Warm and welcoming atmosphere. Fully refurbished, 10 en-suite rooms, lounge, reading room, bar and restaurant using some home grown produce. 5-acre grounds, spectacular views over the dales. A haven of peace and tranquillity.
Bedrooms: 1 single, 6 double & 1 twin, 2 family rooms.
Bathrooms: 10 private.
Bed & breakfast: £44 single, £59.50-£79 double.
Half board: £54 daily, £375-£450 weekly.
Lunch available.
Evening meal 7pm (l.o. 10.30pm).
Parking for 70.
Credit: Access, Visa, Amex.
🛏 🗼 ℡ ⊙ 🖵 🌺 🛁 Ⅴ ⛽
℡ ▥ 🛁 🍴 ❄ ✗ 🌺 🌺 🌺
🌺
✪ Display advertisement appears on page 110.

CROOKHAM
Northumberland
Map ref 5B1

3.5m S. Cornhill-on-Tweed
Pretty hamlet taking its name from the winding course of the River Till which flows in the shape of a shepherd's crook. 3 castles - Etal, Duddo and Ford - can be seen, and nearby the restored Heatherslaw Mill is of great interest.

The Coach House M
♨♨♨
Crookham, Cornhill-on-Tweed, TD12 4TD
☎ (089 082) 293
Spacious rooms, arranged round a courtyard, in rolling country near the Scottish Border. Home-cooked, quality fresh food. We have rooms specially equipped for our disabled guests.
Bedrooms: 2 single, 2 double & 5 twin.
Bathrooms: 7 private, 2 public.
Bed & breakfast: £19-£26 single, £38-£52 double.
Half board: £30.50-£37.50 daily, £213.50-£262.50 weekly.

Map references apply to the colour maps towards the end of this guide.

Evening meal 7.30pm (l.o. 7.30pm).
Parking for 12.
Open March-October.
ॐ 🖐 ♥ V ⊨ TV ▥ ◢ ₺
♠ ❀ ⋈ ⊞

DARLINGTON

Co. Durham
Map ref 5C3

Industrial town on the River Skerne, home of the earliest passenger railway which first ran to Stockton in 1825. Now the home of a railway museum. Originally a prosperous market town occupying the site of an Anglo-Saxon settlement, it still holds an open market in the square.
Tourist Information Centre ☎ *(0325) 382698*

Grange Hotel

South End, Coniscliffe Road, Darlington, DL3 7HZ
☎ (0325) 464555
Imposing stately mansion built 1804, once the home of Joseph Pease, first Quaker MP and promoter of early railways.
Bedrooms: 2 single, 2 double & 6 twin, 1 family room.
Bathrooms: 11 private, 1 public.
Bed & breakfast: from £32 single, from £42 double.
Evening meal 5pm (l.o. 6pm).
Parking for 50.
ॐ ⊞ ➷ ♥ 🛱 V ⅍ ⊨ TV
▥ ◢ ▼ ❀ SP ⊞ T

Walworth Castle Hotel ⋈

♛♛♛
Walworth, Darlington, DL2 1LY
☎ (0325) 485470 Fax (0325) 462257
A 12th C castle in 18 acres of lawns and woods, privately owned, offering comfort and food at modest prices. 3 miles west of Darlington off the A68.
Bedrooms: 4 single, 25 double & 3 twin, 4 family rooms.
Bathrooms: 36 private, 2 public.
Bed & breakfast: £30-£45 single, £55-£75 double.
Half board: £35-£65 daily, £170-£380 weekly.
Lunch available.
Evening meal 6.30pm (l.o. 10pm).
Parking for 250.
Credit: Access, Visa, Diners, Amex.
ॐ 🖐 ➷ ➷ ⊞ 🛱 ♥ 🛱 V
⊨ TV ● ▥ ◢ ▼ ✓ ❀ DAP
⅍ SP ⊞ T

DURHAM CITY

Co. Durham
Map ref 5C2

Ancient city with its Norman castle and cathedral set on a bluff high over the Wear. A market and university town and regional centre, spreading beyond the market-place on both banks of the river. July Miners' Gala is a celebrated Durham tradition.
Tourist Information Centre ☎ *091-384 3720*

Bay Horse Inn ⋈

♛♛♛
Brandon Village, Durham City, DH7 8ST.
☎ 091-378 0498
3 miles from Durham city centre. Stone-built chalets all with shower, toilet, TV, tea and coffee facilities and telephone. Ample car parking.
Bedrooms: 4 twin.
Bathrooms: 4 private.
Bed & breakfast: £24 single, £32 double.
Lunch available.
Evening meal 7pm (l.o. 10pm).
Parking for 15.
Credit: Access.
ॐ 🖐 ➷ 🛱 ⊞ ♥ V ⅍ ⊨
▥ ◢ ₺ ♠ ▶ ❀ ⊞
✿ Display advertisement appears on page 109.

Castle View Guest House ⋈

4 Crossgate, Durham City, DH1 4PS
☎ 091-386 8852
A 250-year-old, listed building in the heart of the old city with woodland and riverside walks, and a magnificent view of the cathedral and castle.
Bedrooms: 1 single, 2 double & 2 twin, 1 family room.
Bathrooms: 3 private, 1 public; 1 private shower.
Bed & breakfast: £15-£30 single, £30-£40 double.
ॐ 🖐 UL ⊞ V ⅍ ⊨ TV ▥
⋈ ⊞ ⊞

Country View Guest House ⋈

Listed
40 Claypath, Durham City, DH1 1QS
☎ 091-386 1436
Family-run guesthouse in city centre with splendid views over open countryside. 5 minutes' walk from city castle and cathedral, close to A1.
Bedrooms: 1 single, 3 double & 2 twin, 5 family rooms.

Bathrooms: 4 private, 3 public.
Bed & breakfast: £15-£20 single, £26-£35 double.
Half board: £19-£26 daily.
Evening meal 6pm.
ॐ 🖐 ⊞ ❑ ⊨ ♥ UL ⅍ V ⊨
TV ▥ ◢ ⋈ DAP SP ⊞

Crossways Hotel ⋈

♛♛♛♛
Dunelm Road, Thornley, Durham City, DH6 3HT
☎ Wellfield (0429) 821248
Fax (0429) 820034
Well-appointed private hotel, all rooms en-suite, satellite TV, solarium, 3 bars, ballroom and an a la carte restaurant. Entertainment certain nights. Durham Cathedral 6 miles.
Bedrooms: 5 single, 5 double & 9 twin.
Bathrooms: 19 private.
Bed & breakfast: £38.50-£42.50 single, £49.50-£60 double.
Half board: £27.50-£70 daily, £190-£490 weekly.
Lunch available.
Evening meal 7pm (l.o. 9.45pm).
Parking for 100.
Credit: Access, Visa, Diners, Amex.
ॐ 🖐 ➷ ⊞ ❑ ♥ 🛱 V ⅍
⊨ TV ● ▥ ◢ ▼ ₺ ♠ ❀
⅍ SP T

Drumforke

⊞
25 Crossgate Peth, Durham City, DH1 4PZ
☎ 091-384 2966
Near the city centre and providing a useful base for touring the beautiful dales of Weardale and Teesdale.
Bedrooms: 2 twin, 1 family room.
Bathrooms: 1 public.
Bed & breakfast: from £12.50 single, from £25 double.
Parking for 4.
ॐ 1 UL ⊨ TV ▥ ◢ ⋈

Duke of Wellington

Darlington Road, Nevilles Cross, Durham City, DH1 3QN
☎ 091-384 2735
Pleasant and popular pub/restaurant on A167 offering vegetarian and flambe dishes, together with cask ale. Accommodation in annexe.
Bedrooms: 12 single, 2 double & 3 twin.
Bathrooms: 4 public.
Bed & breakfast: £14-£19 single, £28-£34 double.
Half board: £18-£35 daily.

Lunch available.
Evening meal 6pm (l.o. 11pm).
Parking for 50.
ॐ 🖐 ➷ ⅍ 1 V ⊨ TV ▥

The Gables Hotel ⋈

Haswell Plough, Durham City, DH6 2EW
☎ 091-526 2982
Small family-run hotel 6 miles east of Durham City on the B1283. Traditional after-dinner entertainment. Horsedrawn wagon tours of rural Durham.
Bedrooms: 2 double & 2 twin, 1 family room.
Bathrooms: 2 public.
Bed & breakfast: £20-£25 single, £32-£45 double.
Half board: £30-£35 daily.
Lunch available.
Evening meal 7pm (l.o. 10pm).
Parking for 30.
ॐ 🖐 ➷ ⅍ 1 V ▥ ▶ ⋈ ⋈
SP

The Garth Lodge

West Sherburn, Durham City, DH1 2TD
☎ 091-386 3394
Comfortably furnished new bungalow adjacent to the caravan park, just off the A1M on the A690.
Bedrooms: 2 single, 4 double & 2 twin.
Bathrooms: 2 private, 2 public; 2 private showers.
Bed & breakfast: £12.50-£15 single, £25-£30 double.
Evening meal 6pm (l.o. 7pm).
Parking for 6.
ॐ 🖐 ❑ ⊨ UL V ▥ ◢ ⋈
DAP

The Georgian Town House ⋈

10 Crossgate, Durham City, DH1 4PS
☎ 091-386 8070
Georgian town house overlooking the cathedral and castle. 2 minutes' walk from city centre and close to riverside walks.
Bedrooms: 1 double & 3 twin, 2 family rooms.
Bathrooms: 6 private.
Bed & breakfast: £25-£35 single, £35-£40 double.
ॐ ⅍ ⊞ ❑ ⅍ ♥ ⊨ TV
▥ ◢ ▼ ⋈ ⋈ DAP ⊞

Queens Head Hotel

2-6 Sherburn Road, Gilesgate Moor, Durham City, DH1 2JR
☎ 091-386 5649
Under a mile from the city centre in a main road position.
Bedrooms: 1 single, 3 double & 3 twin, 2 family rooms.
Continued ▶

DURHAM CITY
Continued

Bathrooms: 2 private,
2 public.
Bed & breakfast: £14 single,
£24-£26 double.
Lunch available.
Parking for 12.
🛇 ⚓ 🕮 🖩 ⚅ ❄ ✻ 🛏 🚗

Ramside Hall Hotel M
Carrville, Durham City,
DH1 1TD
☎ 091-386 5282 Telex 537681
*82 attractive en-suite
bedrooms, 3 eating areas,
entertainment nightly. Set in
240 acres of farm and
parkland, 3 miles from
Durham.*
Bedrooms: 2 single, 32 double
& 48 twin.
Bathrooms: 82 private.
Bed & breakfast: £68-£75
single, £82-£92 double.
Lunch available.
Evening meal 7pm (l.o.
10.30pm).
Parking for 500.
Credit: Access, Visa, Diners,
Amex.
🛇 ⚓ 🕮 📞 ⓔ 🖵 ⚅ 🎁 🛇 V
✂ 🛏 ⬤ 🎇 🖩 ⚓ 🏓 👤 ❄
SP 🚗 T

St. Aidan's College M
Listed
Windmill Hill, Durham City,
DH1 3LJ
☎ 091-374 3269
*A comfortable, modern college
designed by the late Sir Basil
Spence, in beautiful landscaped
gardens overlooking the
cathedral. Free tennis and
croquet.*
Bedrooms: 213 single,
52 twin.
Bathrooms: 2 private,
48 public.
Bed & breakfast: £13-£14
single, £26-£28 double.
Half board: £20-£21 daily,
£126-£130 weekly.
Lunch available.
Evening meal 6.30pm (l.o.
7pm).
Parking for 50.
Open January, March-April,
July-September.
🛇 ⚓ 🎁 V 🛏 📺 🖩 ⚓ 🏓
🏓 👤 ➤ ❄ ✻ 🚗

Half board prices
shown are per
person but in some
cases may be based
on double/twin
occupancy.

EAGLESCLIFFE
Cleveland
Map ref 5C3

Railway suburb of
Stockton-on-Tees on the
road to Yarm. Preston
Hall Park has a zoo,
riverside walks, fishing
and picnicking places.

Sunnyside Hotel
580-582 Yarm Road,
Eaglescliffe, Stockton-on-
Tees, TS16 0DF
☎ (0642) 780075
*A friendly family hotel, ideal
for touring Cleveland and
North Yorkshire, with easy
access to all main roads, the
station and airport.*
Bedrooms: 15 single, 6 double
& 2 twin, 3 family rooms.
Bathrooms: 16 private,
2 public.
Bed & breakfast: £18-£25
single, £31-£41 double.
Evening meal 6.45pm (l.o.
4pm).
Parking for 22.
🛇 ⓔ 🖵 ⚅ 🎁 🛛 🛏 📺 🖩 ⚓
DAP

EBCHESTER
Co. Durham
Map ref 5B2

Old village standing on
the 4-acre Roman fort
Vindomara near to the
place where the Roman
road Dere Street crossed
the River Derwent.

The Raven Hotel M
👑👑👑👑 **COMMENDED**
Broomhill, Ebchester,
DH8 6RY
☎ (0207) 560367/560082 Fax
(0207) 560262
*Stone-built, traditionally
decorated hotel with views of
Derwent Valley from
conservatory and all rooms.
Situated on B6309 Ebchester
to Leadgate road, only 15
minutes either way to the
Gateshead MetroCentre on
A694 or historic Durham City
on A691.*
Bedrooms: 3 single, 1 double
& 17 twin, 7 family rooms.
Bathrooms: 28 private.
Bed & breakfast: £42-£51
single, £56-£67.50 double.
Half board: £52-£65 daily,
£350 weekly.
Lunch available.
Evening meal 7pm (l.o. 9pm).

Parking for 100.
Credit: Access, Visa.
🛇 ⚓ 🕮 📞 ⓔ 🖵 ⚅ 🎁 🛛 V
⬤ 🖩 ⚓ 🎇 🛇 ❄ ➤ ✻ ✻
⚅ SP
⚡ Display advertisement
appears on page 110.

FALSTONE
Northumberland
Map ref 5B2

Remote village on the
edge of Kielder Forest
where it spreads beneath
the heathery slopes of the
south-west Cheviots
along the valley of the
North Tyne. Just 1 mile
west lies Kielder Water, a
vast man-made lake
which adds boating and
fishing to forest
recreations.

The Pheasant Inn, (by
Kielder Water) M
👑👑 **APPROVED**
Stannersburn, Falstone,
Hexham, NE48 1DD
☎ (0434) 240382
*Historic inn with beamed
ceilings and open fires. Home
cooking. Fishing, riding and all
water sports nearby. Close to
Kielder Water, Hadrian's Wall
and the Scottish borders.*
Bedrooms: 5 single, 2 double
& 3 twin, 1 family room.
Bathrooms: 2 private,
2 public.
Bed & breakfast: £17-£20
single, £32-£40 double.
Half board: £26-£30 daily.
Lunch available.
Evening meal 7pm (l.o. 9pm).
Parking for 30.
🛇 ⚓ 🎁 🛛 V 🛏 🖩 ⚓ 🏓
🛏 SP 🚗

GAINFORD
Co. Durham
Map ref 5C3

Interesting and beautiful
village hidden from the
main road beside the
River Tees. Darlington
merchants built the
Georgian and Regency
residences facing the
large, sloping green,
where curving High Row
with its walled back
gardens has a charming
mixture of fine houses
and humbler cottages.

Headlam Hall Hotel M
👑👑👑👑 **COMMENDED**
Headlam, Nr. Gainford,
Darlington, DL2 3HA
☎ (0325) 730238

---

*Charming old country house in
own secluded farmland and
beautiful gardens. Residential
and catering facilities for
holidays, business
accommodation, conferences
and weddings.*
Bedrooms: 12 double &
6 twin, 2 family rooms.
Bathrooms: 20 private.
Bed & breakfast: £42-£57
single, £54-£69 double.
Half board: from £54 daily.
Lunch available.
Evening meal 7.30pm (l.o.
10pm).
Parking for 60.
Credit: Access, Visa, Amex.
🛇 ⚓ 📞 ⓔ 🖵 ⚅ 🎁 🛛 V ✂
🛏 🖩 ⚓ 🎇 🛇 🏓 🛒 👤 🏓
✒ ❄ SP 🚗 T

GATESHEAD
Tyne & Wear
Map ref 5C2

Facing Newcastle across
the Tyne, a busy
industrial centre which
grew rapidly early this
century. Now it is a town
of glass, steel and
concrete buildings with an
ancient church almost
entirely rebuilt after the
devastating fire of 1854.
Home of Europe's largest
indoor shopping and
leisure complex, the
MetroCentre.
*Tourist Information
Centre* ☎ 091-477 3478
or 460 6345

Ravensworth Arms M
👑👑👑👑 **COMMENDED**
Lamesley, Gateshead,
NE11 0EQ
☎ 091-487 6023
Fax 091-482 1454
*Set in rural surroundings,
excellent base for visiting
the Beamish Museum,
MetroCentre, Newcastle and
Durham.*
Bedrooms: 13 double &
6 twin.
Bathrooms: 19 private.
Bed & breakfast: £42.50-
£52.50 single, £52.50-£62.50
double.
Half board: £50-£60 daily.
Lunch available.
Evening meal 7pm (l.o.
9.30pm).
Parking for 100.
Credit: Access, Visa, Diners,
Amex.
🛇 ⚓ 📞 ⓔ 🖵 ⚅ 🎁 🛛 V 🛏
🖩 ⚓ 🎇 ❄ 🛇 🚗

Shaftesbury House M
245 Prince Consort Road,
Gateshead, NE8 4DT
☎ 091-478 2544
*Family business close to
Gateshead Leisure Centre,
MetroCentre, Sports Stadium,
Eldon Square, beaches, famous
Quayside Sunday Market.
A6127 route.*
Bedrooms: 2 single, 2 double
& 4 twin, 2 family rooms.
Bathrooms: 2 private,
3 public.
Bed & breakfast: £38-£50
single, £39-£55 double.
Half board: £48-£63 daily,
£203-£262.50 weekly.
Evening meal 5pm (l.o.
6.30pm).
Parking for 8.

Swallow Hotel M
High West Street,
Gateshead, NE8 1PE
☎ 091-477 1105 Telex 53534
CR Swallow
*A modern hotel 1 mile from
Newcastle city centre just
south of the River Tyne.
Leisure complex incorporating
pool, sauna, solarium and mini-
gym. Well placed for visiting
the MetroCentre.*
Bedrooms: 28 single,
37 double & 31 twin, 7 family
rooms.
Bathrooms: 103 private.
Bed & breakfast: £65-£105
single, £75-£120 double.
Half board: from £80 daily.
Lunch available.
Evening meal 6.30pm (l.o.
10pm).
Parking for 140.
Credit: Access, Visa, Diners,
Amex.

The symbol **CR**
and the name of a
hotel group or
consortium after a
hotel address means
that bookings can
be made through a
central reservations
office. These are
listed on pages
559 & 560.

GUISBOROUGH
Cleveland
Map ref 5C3

Busy market town below
the northern edge of the
North York Moors. The
skeletal remains of its
Augustinian priory rise
from the grounds of
Guisborough Hall. The
town is within easy reach
of Teesside, the moors
and the fascinating
coastline between
Saltburn and Whitby.
*Tourist Information
Centre* ☎ *(0287) 633801*

Fox Inn
10 Bow Street, Guisborough,
TS14 6BP
☎ (0287) 32958
*An old inn in the centre of this
attractive market town, ideal
for touring both the North
Yorkshire Moors and Durham
Dales.*
Bedrooms: 2 single, 2 double
& 3 twin.
Bathrooms: 2 public.
Bed & breakfast: from £15
single, from £28 double.
Half board: from £22.50
daily.
Lunch available.
Evening meal 7pm (l.o.
9.30pm).
Parking for 15.
Credit: Access, Visa, Amex.

HALTWHISTLE
Northumberland
Map ref 5B2

Small market town with a
tree-shaded Early English
church. Around Hadrian's
Wall, situated just north of
it, are numerous Roman
sites; further south along
the river stands
Featherstone Castle, a
medieval pele tower with
a Jacobean mansion built
on.
*Tourist Information
Centre* ☎ *(0434) 322002*

Ashcroft M
🏆 COMMENDED
Haltwhistle, NE49 0DA
☎ (0434) 320213
*Large, stone-built, early 19th C
residence, south facing, with
mature terraced gardens. Well
placed for exploring the
Roman Wall and
Northumberland.*
Bedrooms: 2 double & 1 twin,
3 family rooms.
Bathrooms: 3 public.

Bed & breakfast: from £15
single, £24-£28 double.
Half board: from £144
weekly.
Evening meal 6pm (l.o. 6pm).
Parking for 14.

HAMSTERLEY FOREST
Co. Durham

*See Barnard Castle,
Bishop Auckland, Crook,
Wolsingham.*

HARTLEPOOL
Cleveland
Map ref 5C2

Major industrial port north
of Tees Bay. Occupying
an ancient site, the
town's buildings are
predominantly modern.
Local history can be
followed in the Gray
Museum and Art Gallery
and there is a good
maritime museum.
*Tourist Information
Centre* ☎ *(0429) 266522
ext 375*

The Dalton Lodge M
Dalton Piercy, Hartlepool,
TS27 3HN
☎ (0429) 267142
*Set in pleasant rural
surroundings on the main A19
trunk road. Between Peterlee
and Billingham.*
Bedrooms: 8 double & 3 twin,
1 family room.
Bathrooms: 12 private.
Bed & breakfast: from £38.50
single, from £48 double.
Half board: £46-£55.50 daily.
Lunch available.
Evening meal 7pm (l.o.
9.30pm).
Parking for 250.
Credit: Access, Visa.

Grand Hotel M
Swainson Street, Hartlepool,
TS24 8AA
☎ (0429) 266345
CR Consort
*Traditional 19th C city centre
hotel close to modern enclosed
shopping centre. Extensively
refurbished and an excellent
base for visiting North Yorks
Moors and Durham Cathedral.*
Bedrooms: 22 single, 9 double
& 17 twin.
Bathrooms: 40 private,
7 public.

Bed & breakfast: £25-£51.50
single, £45-£72.50 double.
Lunch available.
Evening meal 7.30pm (l.o.
10pm).
Parking for 5.
Credit: Access, Visa, C.Bl.,
Diners, Amex.

Melbourne Hotel M
🏆🏆🏆 APPROVED
16 Stockton Road,
Hartlepool, TS25 1RL
☎ (0429) 262828
*Small friendly family-owned
hotel close to town centre, with
imaginative home cooking.
Private weddings. Private car
park.*
Bedrooms: 1 single, 3 double
& 3 twin, 2 family rooms.
Bathrooms: 3 private,
1 public; 2 private showers.
Bed & breakfast: £18.65-
£29.50 single, £32.95-£43.50
double.
Half board: £26.65-£37.50
daily, £172-£243 weekly.
Evening meal 6pm (l.o.
6.30pm).
Parking for 12.

Milton Guest House
77 Milton Road, Hartlepool,
TS26 8DS
☎ (0429) 270811
*A town centre guest house,
close to main shopping precinct
and entertainment.*
Bedrooms: 1 single, 3 double.
Bathrooms: 2 public.
Bed & breakfast: £12 single,
£24 double.
Half board: £16 daily, £112
weekly.
Lunch available.
Evening meal 6pm (l.o. 9pm).

Ryedale Moor Hotel M
3 Beaconsfield Street,
Hartlepool, TS24 ONX
☎ (0429) 264224
*Family-run hotel with sea
views. Licensed bar, all rooms
en-suite, fishing and golf
facilities.*
Bedrooms: 3 single, 9 twin.
Bathrooms: 12 private,
1 public.
Bed & breakfast: £35-£39
single, £44-£60 double.
Half board: £40-£60 daily,
£210-£480 weekly.
Lunch available.
Continued ▶

HARTLEPOOL
Continued

Evening meal 6pm (l.o. 8pm).
Parking for 6.
Credit: Access, Visa, Amex.

🖧 📞 🕎 🗗 🏇 🛈 🚾 🛏 📺
🌀 🕮 ◿ 🍴 🎿 ⛶ 🆂🅿 🏠

Staincliffe Hotel
The Cliff, Seaton Carew,
Hartlepool, TS25 1AB
☎ Hartlepool (0429) 264301
*A popular hotel on the seafront
at Seaton Carew, close to local
golf-course. Wedding
receptions are a speciality.
Leisure complex opens 1991
with swimming pool, spa,
squash, gym, aerobics, health
and beauty salon, creche, and
cafe area.*
Bedrooms: 7 single, 7 double
& 7 twin, 2 family rooms.
Bathrooms: 16 private,
2 public.
Bed & breakfast: £28.50-£31
single, £35.50-£43 double.
Half board: £36-£58.50 daily.
Lunch available.
Evening meal 7pm (l.o. 9pm).
Parking for 35.
Credit: Access, Visa, Diners,
Amex.

🖧 📞 🕎 🗗 🏇 🛈 🚾 ◑ 🌀
🍴 🎯 🎿 🆂🅿

HAYDON BRIDGE
Northumberland
Map ref 5B2

Small town on the banks
of the South Tyne with an
ancient church, built of
stone from sites along the
Roman Wall just north.
Ideally situated for
exploring Hadrian's Wall
and the Border country.

Anchor Hotel ♨
👑👑👑
John Martin Street, Haydon
Bridge, Hexham, NE47 6AB
☎ (0434) 684277
*Riverside inn, in a village close
to the Roman Wall. Ideal
centre for touring the North
Pennines and Northumberland
National Park.*
Bedrooms: 1 single, 5 double
& 4 twin, 2 family rooms.
Bathrooms: 10 private,
1 public.
Bed & breakfast: £29-£35
single, £39-£45 double.
Half board: £159-£178
weekly.
Lunch available.
Evening meal 7pm (l.o.
8.30pm).
Parking for 20.

Credit: Access, Visa, Diners,
Amex.

🖧 📞 🕎 🗗 🏇 🛈 🚾 🛏 📺
🌀 🕮 ◿ 🍴 🎿 ⛶ 🆂🅿 🏠

HEXHAM
Northumberland
Map ref 5B2

Old coaching and market
town near Hadrian's Wall.
Lively social and
commercial centre for the
fertile Tyne Valley. Since
pre-Norman times a
weekly market has been
held in the centre with its
market-place and abbey
park, and the richly-
furnished 12th C abbey
church has a superb
Anglo-Saxon crypt. There
is a racecourse at High
Yarridge.
*Tourist Information
Centre* ☎ *(0434) 605255*

Beaumont Hotel ♨
👑👑👑 COMMENDED
Beaumont Street, Hexham,
NE46 3LT
☎ (0434) 602331
*Attractive refurbished hotel
overlooking the lovely park and
abbey. 2 comfortable bars and
an a la carte restaurant.
Lunch/dinner, morning coffee
and afternoon teas served
daily. Lift to all floors.*
Bedrooms: 6 single, 10 double
& 6 twin, 1 family room.
Bathrooms: 23 private.
Bed & breakfast: from £42
single, from £66 double.
Lunch available.
Evening meal 7pm (l.o.
9.45pm).
Credit: Access, Visa, Diners,
Amex.

🖧 🖀 📞 🕎 🗗 🏇 🛈 🚾 ✁
🛏 ◑ 🖲 🕮 ◿ 🍴 🎿 🆂🅿 🏠

County Hotel ♨
👑👑👑 COMMENDED
Priestpopple, Hexham,
NE46 1PS
☎ (0434) 602030
*A warm and comfortable hotel
in the town centre. Ideal for
touring the Roman Wall and
border country, Kielder Water
and Forest.*
Bedrooms: 2 single, 4 double
& 3 twin.
Bathrooms: 9 private,
1 public.
Bed & breakfast: £38 single,
£50 double.
Lunch available.
Evening meal 7pm (l.o.
9.30pm).
Parking for 2.
Credit: Access, Visa, Amex.

🖧 📞 🕎 🗗 🏇 🛈 🚾 🛏 ◑
🕮 ◿ 🍴 🆂🅿 🏠

High Reins
Leazes Lane, Hexham,
NE46 3AT
☎ (0434) 603590
*Large detached, stone-built
house in quiet residential area.
Close to open countryside and
golf-course.*
Bedrooms: 1 single, 2 double
& 1 twin.
Bathrooms: 4 private.
Bed & breakfast: £17-£23
single, £33-£40 double.
Evening meal 6.30pm (l.o.
7pm).
Parking for 10.

🖧 🖧 🗗 🏇 ⅏ 🛈 🚾 🛏 📺
🕮 ◿ 🍴 🎯 🎿 ✳ 🎿 🆘 🏠
🆂🅿

Low Barns
Wall, Hexham, NE46 4DR
☎ (0434) 606680
*300-acre mixed farm.
Delightful, converted award
winning old farm buildings and
farm cottages. Full facilities,
most rooms en-suite. Many
pleasant riverside walks, midway between Acomb and
Hadrian's Wall on A6079.*
Bedrooms: 3 single, 1 double
& 2 twin, 1 family room.
Bathrooms: 4 private,
3 public.
Bed & breakfast: £15-£25
single, £25-£60 double.
Evening meal 6pm (l.o. 8pm).
Parking for 20.

🖧 🎿 ⅏ 🛈 🚾 🛏 📺 🕮 🍷
✳ 🎿 🦮 🆂🅿 🏠

Mariners Cottage Hotel
Fallowfield Dene Road,
Acomb, Hexham, NE46 4RP
☎ Hexham (0434) 603666
*Hotel in a country setting with
splendid views over Tynedale.
3 miles from the market town
of Hexham and near the
Roman Wall.*
Bedrooms: 2 single, 1 double
& 2 twin, 1 family room.
Bathrooms: 2 private,
2 public.
Bed & breakfast: £15-£20
single, £26-£36 double.
Lunch available.
Evening meal 7.30pm (l.o.
9pm).
Parking for 60.

🖧 🗗 🏇 🛈 🕮 🍴 🎿

Royal Hotel ♨
👑👑👑
22-26 Priestpopple, Hexham,
NE46 1PQ
☎ (0434) 602270 Telex 57515
ATTN.115
Ⓡ Consort
*Former coaching inn offering
modern comfort in traditional
surroundings. A la carte
restaurant and cocktail bar.
Private car park.*

Bedrooms: 5 single, 7 double
& 9 twin, 3 family rooms.
Bathrooms: 24 private.
Bed & breakfast: £37-£40
single, £57 double.
Half board: £37.50-£50 daily,
£260-£315 weekly.
Lunch available.
Evening meal 7pm (l.o.
9.30pm).
Parking for 20.
Credit: Access, Visa, Diners,
Amex.

🖧 📞 🕎 🗗 🏇 🛈 🚾 🛏 📺
🕮 ◿ 🍴 ⛶ 🆂🅿 🏠 🏠

Westbrooke Hotel ♨
👑👑 COMMENDED
Allendale Road, Hexham,
NE46 2DE
☎ (0434) 603818
*Family-run Victorian hotel in a
quiet residential area of the
attractive market town of
Hexham.*
Bedrooms: 5 single, 4 double
& 1 twin, 1 family room.
Bathrooms: 2 private,
2 public; 4 private showers.
Bed & breakfast: from £17
single, from £30 double.
Half board: from £25 daily,
from £110 weekly.
Lunch available.
Evening meal 6pm (l.o. 9pm).
Parking for 3.
Credit: Access, Visa.

🖧 🗗 🏇 🛈 🚾 🛏 📺 ◿ 🍴
🎯 🆂🅿 🏠

KIELDER FOREST
Northumberland

See Bellingham, Falstone.

LANCHESTER
Co. Durham
Map ref 5C2

Village set at the edge of
the north-east Pennines,
close to the site of a
Roman fort. Set up to
guard the route from York
to Hadrian's Wall, the fort
was destroyed in the 18th
C through use as building
material.

Kings Head Hotel
Station Road, Lanchester,
DH7 0EX
☎ (0207) 520054
*In the centre of an attractive
small town near Durham City.
Suitable for both tourist and
business traveller.*
Bedrooms: 1 single, 1 double
& 3 twin.
Bathrooms: 2 public.
Bed & breakfast: from £16.50
single, from £27.50 double.
Half board: from £24 daily.
Lunch available.

Evening meal 7.15pm (l.o.
9.15pm).
Parking for 150.
Credit: Access, Visa, Diners,
Amex.
⑁◻♨🛈📺🎱🏧

LANGLEY-ON-TYNE

Northumberland
Map ref 5B2

Small hamlet by a tiny
lake, set in beautiful
countryside south of
Haydon Bridge and the
River South Tyne. The
road from Haydon Bridge
to Langley winds through
woodland and past the
Derwentwater Memorial
and Langley Castle.

Langley Castle ♨
👑👑👑👑 COMMENDED
Langley-on-Tyne, Hexham,
NE47 5LU
☎ Haydon Bridge
(0434) 688888
*14th C castle restored to a
magnificent and comfortable
hotel. 2 miles south west of
Haydon Bridge, 30 minutes
from Newcastle and 40 minutes
from Newcastle Airport. A69-
A686.*
Bedrooms: 6 double & 2 twin.
Bathrooms: 8 private.
Bed & breakfast: £48-£85
single, £65-£98 double.
Half board: £60-£115 daily.
Lunch available.
Evening meal 7.30pm (l.o.
9pm).
Parking for 100.
Credit: Access, Visa, Diners,
Amex.
⑁🍷🐾📷◻🛈📺🖩🏧
🍽🍴🏧✿🔌 SP 🏧 T

LONGFRAMLINGTON

Northumberland
Map ref 5B1

Pleasant village with an
interesting church of the
Transitional style. On Hall
Hill are the remains of a
camp with triple
entrenchment.

Anglers Arms Inn
Weldon Bridge, Morpeth,
NE65 8AX
☎ (0665) 570655
*Attractive 18th C former
coaching inn by the lovely
River Coquet, just off the A697
north of Morpeth.*
Bedrooms: 1 single, 3 double.
Bathrooms: 3 private,
1 public.
Bed & breakfast: £39-£49
single, £49-£69 double.

Lunch available.
Evening meal 7pm (l.o.
10pm).
Parking for 50.
Credit: Access, Visa, Diners,
Amex.
⑁🍴🍷📷◻♨🛈 V 🖩🎱
🍴♪✿🏧🏨

Embleton Hall ♨
👑👑👑👑 COMMENDED
Longframlington, Morpeth,
NE65 8DT
☎ (0665) 570247/570206
*Family-run country house hotel
set in 5 acres of woodland and
landscaped gardens,
specialising in home cooking
using own produce.*
Bedrooms: 2 single, 5 double
& 2 twin, 1 family room.
Bathrooms: 10 private.
Bed & breakfast: £42 single,
£55 double.
Half board: £44.50 daily,
£287.50 weekly.
Lunch available.
Evening meal 7pm (l.o.
9.30pm).
Parking for 43.
Credit: Access, Visa, Diners,
Amex.
⑁🍷📷◻♨🛈 V 🎱
🔌🖩🍴🍴🔍🚶🔌✿ DAP
🕸 SP 🏧

MIDDLESBROUGH

Cleveland
Map ref 5C3

Boom-town of the mid
19th C, today's Teesside
industrial and conference
town has a modern
shopping complex and
predominantly modern
buildings. An engineering
miracle of the early 20th
C is the Transporter
Bridge which replaced an
old ferry.
Middlesbrough's ancient
history is told in the
Dorman Museum near
Albert Park. The Captain
Cook Birthplace Museum
in Stewart Park traces the
explorer's exciting life.
*Tourist Information
Centre ☎ (0642) 243425
or 245432*

Ashley Guest House
22/26 Park Road North,
Middlesbrough, TS1 3LF
☎ (0642) 224658
*Within walking distance of the
main commercial and shopping
areas of Middlesbrough. Close
to the art gallery overlooking
Albert Park.*
Bedrooms: 6 single, 3 double
& 3 twin, 4 family rooms.
Bathrooms: 4 public.

Bed & breakfast: £11.50-£20
single.
Parking for 4.
⑁🐾◻♨🖩🎱◻📺🖩🎱
🍴🏧

Highfield Hotel ♨
358, Marton Road,
Middlesbrough, TS4 2PA
☎ (0642) 817638
*Large former family house,
built in early 1900s, set in its
own gardens. Conveniently
placed for the shopping centre.*
Bedrooms: 4 single, 11 double
& 8 twin.
Bathrooms: 23 private.
Bed & breakfast: £41-£47.50
single, from £54 double.
Lunch available.
Evening meal 6pm (l.o.
10.30pm).
Parking for 104.
Credit: Access, Visa, Diners,
Amex.
⑁🍴🍷📷◻♨🛈 V ✂
🍴📺🎱🖩🎱🍴🏧 SP

Norman Conquest ♨
👑👑 APPROVED
Flatts Lane, Normanby,
Middlesbrough, TS6 0NP
☎ (0642) 454000
*An estate hotel at the foot of
the Eston Hills.*
Bedrooms: 4 single, 2 double
& 2 twin.
Bathrooms: 8 private.
Bed & breakfast: from £21.50
single, from £33 double.
Lunch available.
Evening meal 7.30pm (l.o.
9.30pm).
Parking for 60.
⑁◻♨🛈 V 🖩🎱🍴🏧

Southern Cross Hotel
Dixons Bank, Marton,
Middlesbrough, TS7 8NX
☎ (0642) 317539
*Near Captain Cook's museum,
on the south side of the city.*
Bedrooms: 4 single, 1 double
& 1 twin.
Bathrooms: 2 public.
Bed & breakfast: from £12.50
single, from £20 double.
Half board: from £20 daily.
Lunch available.
Evening meal 7pm (l.o.
10pm).
Parking for 200.
Credit: Access, Visa.
⑁♨🛈 V 🍴📺🖩🎱🍴
🔌🏧 SP

**Half board prices
shown are per
person but in some
cases may be based
on double/twin
occupancy.**

MIDDLETON-IN-
TEESDALE

Co. Durham
Map ref 5B3

Small stone town of
hillside terraces
overlooking the river,
developed by the London
Lead Company in the
18th C. There is a
handsome Victorian
fountain and the company
headquarters is now a
shooting lodge. 5 miles
up-river is the spectacular
70-ft waterfall, High
Force.

Bluebell House
Market Place, Middleton-in-
Teesdale, Barnard Castle,
DL12 0QG
☎ Teesdale (0833) 40584
*Quiet, comfortable rooms at
the rear of the house, all with
private shower and wc, some
rooms on ground floor. At
centre of attractive Dales
village.*
Bedrooms: 2 double & 1 twin.
Bathrooms: 3 private.
Bed & breakfast: £24-£26
double.
Parking for 3.
⑁5🐾♨🛈 V ✂🍴🖩🚶
🏧🏨

Brunswick House ♨
👑👑
55 Market Place, Middleton-
in-Teesdale, DL12 0QH
☎ (0833) 40393
*18th C listed stone-built
guesthouse retaining much
character and many original
features. Comfort, friendly
service and home cooking are
assured.*
Bedrooms: 2 double & 1 twin,
1 family room.
Bathrooms: 2 private,
1 public.
Bed & breakfast: £25-£30
double.
Half board: £20.45-£22.95
daily, £125-£140 weekly.
Lunch available.
Evening meal 7.30pm (l.o.
7.30).
Parking for 4.
⑁🐾📷◻♨🛈 V 🍴🖩
🍴🚶🏧 DAP SP 🏧

Teesdale Hotel ♨
👑👑👑 APPROVED
Middleton-in-Teesdale,
Barnard Castle, DL12 0QG
☎ Teesdale (0833) 40264
Continued ▶

MIDDLETON-IN-TEESDALE

Continued

Tastefully modernised family-run 18th C coaching inn serving home cooking and fine wines. All rooms can have telephone, radio and TV. Also 4 holiday cottages.
Bedrooms: 2 single, 7 double & 3 twin, 1 family room.
Bathrooms: 10 private, 1 public.
Bed & breakfast: from £30 single, from £55 double.
Half board: from £45.95 daily.
Lunch available.
Evening meal 7.30pm (l.o. 8.30pm).
Parking for 24.
Credit: Access, Visa.

MORPETH

Northumberland
Map ref 5C2

Market town on the River Wansbeck. Vanbrugh's Town Hall was rebuilt in 1870 and there are other interesting Victorian buildings. There are charming gardens and parks, among them Carlisle Park which lies close to the ancient remains of Morpeth Castle. The 14th C parish church contains some fine medieval glass. The chantry building houses the Northumbrian Craft Centre and the bagpipe museum.
Tourist Information Centre ☎ (0670) 511323

Waterford Lodge M
✿✿ APPROVED

Castle Square, Morpeth, NE61 1YD
☎ Morpeth (0670) 512004
On the site of an early 19th C coaching inn, Waterford Lodge has a recently completed conservatory and beer garden.
Bedrooms: 1 single, 3 double & 3 twin, 3 family rooms.
Bathrooms: 5 private, 2 public.
Bed & breakfast: from £35 single, from £65 double.
Lunch available.
Evening meal 6pm (l.o. 9.30pm).
Parking for 14.
Credit: Access, Visa, Diners, Amex.

NEWCASTLE UPON TYNE

Tyne & Wear
Map ref 5C2

Commercial and cultural centre of the North East, with a large indoor shopping centre, Quayside market, museums and theatres which offer an annual 6 week season by the Royal Shakespeare Company. The Norman castle keep and the town's medieval alleys are near the river with its 6 bridges, old Guildhall and timbered merchants' houses.
Tourist Information Centre ☎ 091-261 0691 ext 231

Adelphi Hotel

63 Fern Avenue, Jesmond, Newcastle upon Tyne, NE2 2QU
☎ 091-281 3109
Large Victorian house in a quiet residential area close to the city centre.
Bedrooms: 1 single, 1 double & 1 twin.
Bathrooms: 1 public.
Bed & breakfast: £19.50-£26 single, £35-£45 double.
Evening meal 6pm (l.o. 9.30pm).
Parking for 3.
Credit: Access, Visa, Diners, Amex.

Bewick Lodge
Listed

93 Bewick Road, Gateshead, NE8 1RR
☎ 091-477 3401
Situated in a mixed commercial/residential area. Close to all amenities. With ample parking in front road.
Bedrooms: 4 single, 5 twin.
Bathrooms: 2 public; 4 private showers.
Bed & breakfast: from £18 single, from £30 double.
Half board: from £20 daily, from £130 weekly.
Evening meal 5pm (l.o. 6.30pm).

The County Hotel M

Neville Street, Newcastle upon Tyne, NE99 1AH
☎ 091-232 2471 Telex 537873
Recently restored 19th C hotel opposite the station, retaining wood-panelled restaurant and original decorative ceilings. Close to the city centre and shopping areas. 8 miles from Newcastle Airport.
Bedrooms: 54 single, 24 double & 36 twin, 1 family room.
Bathrooms: 115 private.
Bed & breakfast: from £72.75 single, from £90.50 double.
Lunch available.
Evening meal 6.30pm (l.o. 9.45pm).
Parking for 25.
Credit: Access, Visa, C.Bl., Diners, Amex.

Dene Hotel M
✿✿

40-42 Grosvenor Road, Jesmond, Newcastle upon Tyne, NE2 2RP
☎ 091-281 1502
In a quiet residential area close to beautiful Jesmond Dene with its small children's zoo. Within easy reach of the city centre.
Bedrooms: 10 single, 4 twin, 3 family rooms.
Bathrooms: 3 public; 14 private showers.
Bed & breakfast: £17.50-£25 single, £31-£39.50 double.
Half board: £22.50-£30.50 daily.
Lunch available.
Evening meal 5.30pm (l.o. 6pm).
Parking for 9.
Credit: Access, Visa, Diners.

Grosvenor Hotel M
✿✿✿ APPROVED

24-28 Grosvenor Road, Jesmond, Newcastle upon Tyne, NE2 2RR
☎ 091-281 0543
Fax 091-281 9217
Friendly hotel in quiet residential suburb, offering a wide range of facilities. Close to city centre.
Bedrooms: 19 single, 11 double & 13 twin, 1 family room.
Bathrooms: 30 private, 5 public.
Bed & breakfast: £15-£40 single, £30-£50 double.
Half board: £23-£43 daily, £105-£300 weekly.
Lunch available.
Evening meal 6.30pm (l.o. 8.30pm).

Parking for 30.
Credit: Access, Visa, Diners, Amex.

Grove Hotel M
✿✿✿

134 Brighton Grove, Newcastle upon Tyne, NE4 5NT
☎ 091-273 8248
Fax 091-272 5609
In a residential area, central and convenient. All modern facilities, intimate bar, lounge, licensed restaurant and pool room.
Bedrooms: 13 single, 6 double & 6 twin, 2 family rooms.
Bathrooms: 15 private, 4 public.
Bed & breakfast: £22-£34 single, from £38 double.
Lunch available.
Evening meal 6pm (l.o. 8.30pm).
Parking for 20.
Credit: Access, Visa.

Hansen Hotel

131 Sandyford Road, Jesmond, Newcastle upon Tyne, NE2 1QR
☎ 091-281 0289 & 091-266 2202
Brick-built house with a small garden, on the edge of the city centre, close to Jesmond Metro Station.
Bedrooms: 8 single, 3 double.
Bathrooms: 4 public.
Bed & breakfast: £14-£18 single, £24-£30 double.

Holiday Inn Newcastle M
✿✿✿✿✿

Great North Road, Seaton Burn, Newcastle upon Tyne, NE13 6BP
☎ 091-236 5432 Telex 53271
☎ Holiday Inn
Low 2-storey building in rural setting close to Northumbrian countryside and Newcastle Airport, with easy access to the city centre.
Bedrooms: 78 double, 72 family rooms.
Bathrooms: 150 private.
Bed & breakfast: £49.50-£91.45 single, £74-£102.90 double.
Half board: £52.50-£66.95 daily, from £425.30 weekly.
Lunch available.
Evening meal 7pm (l.o. 10.30pm).
Parking for 250.

Credit: Access, Visa, C.Bl., Diners, Amex.

🛏 ⦿ 📞 🖥 🛋 🍴 ⚕ 🎱 🎣 ✆ 🅿
🕐 ❀ 🎿 SP T

Imperial Swallow Hotel M
≋≋≋≋ COMMENDED

Jesmond Road, Newcastle upon Tyne, NE2 1PR
☎ 091-281 5511 Telex 537972
CR Swallow
Modern hotel 10 minutes' walk from the city centre, near Jesmond Metro station, with leisure facilities and popular bars with a friendly atmosphere. Leisure club.
Bedrooms: 56 single,
26 double & 40 twin, 7 family rooms.
Bathrooms: 127 private.
Bed & breakfast: max. £75 single, max. £85 double.
Lunch available.
Evening meal 7pm (l.o. 10pm).
Parking for 140.
Credit: Access, Visa, C.Bl., Diners, Amex.
🛏 🖥 📞 ⦿ 🖥 ⚕ 🅥 🖊
🛋 ⦿ 🎱 🖥 🛋 🍴 ✆ 🅿
SP T

New Kent Hotel M
≋≋≋ COMMENDED

Osborne Road, Jesmond, Newcastle upon Tyne, NE2 2TB
☎ 091-281 1083
Family-run hotel in a quiet suburban area, with accent on food and warm personal service. Congenial atmosphere. Established 20 years ago.
Bedrooms: 16 single, 6 double & 6 twin, 4 family rooms.
Bathrooms: 32 private.
Bed & breakfast: £38.50-£65.50 single, £61.50-£76.50 double.
Half board: £48.50-£75.50 daily.
Evening meal 6pm (l.o. 10pm).
Parking for 15.
Credit: Access, Visa, C.Bl., Diners, Amex.
🛏 📞 ⦿ 🖥 🖊 ⚕ 🅥 🖊 ⦿
🖥 🛋 🎣 🅿 OAP 🎿 SP T

Newcastle Moat House Hotel M
≋≋≋ COMMENDED

Coast Road, Wallsend, Newcastle upon Tyne, NE28 9NH
☎ 091-262 8989 Telex 53853
CR Queens Moat Houses
A modern hotel 7 miles from Newcastle on the A1 just north of the Tyne Tunnel. Changes Leisure Club now open.

Bedrooms: 71 single,
42 double & 29 twin, 8 family rooms.
Bathrooms: 150 private.
Bed & breakfast: £65-£70 single, £75-£80 double.
Half board: £40-£78 daily.
Lunch available.
Evening meal 6.30pm (l.o. 9.45pm).
Parking for 300.
Credit: Access, Visa, C.Bl., Diners, Amex.
🛏 📞 ⦿ 🖥 ⚕ 🅥 🖊 🖊
⦿ 🛋 🖥 🛋 🍴 ✆ 🅿 OAP
SP T

Novotel Newcastle M

Ponteland Road, Kenton, Newcastle upon Tyne, NE3 3HZ
☎ 091-214 0303
CR Novotel
Situated north west of city, adjacent to western by-pass. With restaurant, bar, indoor leisure and extensive conference/banqueting facilities.
Bedrooms: 126 double.
Bathrooms: 126 private.
Bed & breakfast: £66-£72 single, £78-£84 double.
Lunch available.
Evening meal 6pm (l.o. midnight).
Credit: Access, Visa, Diners, Amex.
🛏 📞 ⦿ 🖥 🖊 🅥 🖊 🖊 🖥
🛋 🍴 🎣 ✆ 🅿

Osborne Hotel M
≋≋≋

Osborne Road, Jesmond, Newcastle upon Tyne, NE2 2AE
☎ 091-281 3385
Well-appointed owner-managed hotel, with emphasis on cleanliness and food. All amenities in bedrooms to ensure comfort.
Bedrooms: 20 single, 2 double & 3 twin, 1 family room.
Bathrooms: 10 private, 4 public.
Bed & breakfast: £20-£38 single, £40-£58 double.
Evening meal 5pm (l.o. 8.30pm).
Parking for 6.
Credit: Access, Visa.
🛏 🖥 📞 ⦿ 🖥 🖊 ⚕ 🅥 🖊
TV 🖥 🛋 🍴 SP T

The Rise, Newcastle Airport M

Main Road, Woolsington, Newcastle upon Tyne, NE13 8BN
☎ 091-286 4963

An attractive, detached house standing in 1 acre of beautiful gardens. In a rural setting within half a mile of Newcastle Airport on the A696 to Scotland.
Bedrooms: 2 single, 3 twin.
Bathrooms: 2 private, 1 public.
Bed & breakfast: £20-£30 single, £30-£40 double.
Parking for 8.
🛏 🖥 ⦿ 🖥 🖊 UL 🖊 TV 🖥 🍴
🛋 ❀ 🎣 🅿

Ryton Park Country House Hotel M
≋≋≋ COMMENDED

Holburn Lane, Ryton, NE40 3PF
☎ 091-413 3535
Hotel in a quiet area, with easy access to many leisure activities including golf. Close to MetroCentre and Beamish Museum.
Bedrooms: 8 single, 9 double & 2 twin, 1 family room.
Bathrooms: 20 private.
Bed & breakfast: £33-£48 single, £48-£69 double.
Half board: £44-£64 daily.
Lunch available.
Evening meal 7pm (l.o. 9.30pm).
Parking for 23.
Credit: Access, Visa.
🛏 📞 ⦿ 🖥 🖊 ⚕ 🅥 TV ⦿
🖥 🛋 🍴 🎣 OAP 🎿 SP T

Springfield Hotel M
≋≋≋≋

Durham Road, Gateshead, NE9 5BT
☎ 091-477 4121 Telex 538197
CR Embassy
Extensively renovated hotel providing 60 bedrooms with modern facilities and the Carving Room Restaurant. On the main route to Newcastle city centre.
Bedrooms: 24 single,
15 double & 19 twin, 2 family rooms.
Bathrooms: 60 private.
Bed & breakfast: £25-£80 single, £70-£95 double.
Half board: £70-£90 daily, £339.50-£490 weekly.
Lunch available.
Evening meal 6.30pm (l.o. 9.30pm).
Parking for 100.
Credit: Access, Visa, C.Bl., Diners, Amex.
🛏 🖥 📞 ⦿ 🖥 🖊 ⚕ 🅥 🖊
🖊 ⦿ 🖥 🛋 🍴 🎣 SP T

Swallow Gosforth Park Hotel M

High Gosforth Park, Newcastle upon Tyne, NE3 5HN
☎ 091-236 4111 Telex 53655
CR Swallow
In wooded parkland near the city centre and airport, the hotel offers a high standard of facilities. Leisure centre includes swimming pool, squash, tennis, gym, sauna, solarium, golf and "trim trail".
Bedrooms: 178 single,
76 double & 86 twin, 5 family rooms.
Bathrooms: 178 private.
Bed & breakfast: £40-£98 single, £80-£118 double.
Lunch available.
Evening meal 6pm (l.o. 10.30pm).
Parking for 300.
Credit: Access, Visa, C.Bl., Diners, Amex.
🛏 🖥 📞 ⦿ 🖥 🖊 🅥 🖊
🖊 TV ⦿ 🖥 🛋 🍴 ⚕ 🎱
🖥 🎣 🎱 🖊 ❀ OAP 🎿 SP T

West Parade Hotel

West Parade, Newcastle upon Tyne, NE4 7LB
☎ 091-273 3034
Purpose-built hotel in its own grounds half a mile from the Central Station and the Redheugh Bridge ring road.
Bedrooms: 25 single, 6 double & 31 twin, 3 family rooms.
Bathrooms: 30 private, 4 public.
Bed & breakfast: £20-£28 single, £32-£38 double.
Lunch available.
Evening meal 6pm (l.o. 9.30pm).
Parking for 56.
Credit: Access, Visa, Diners, Amex.
🛏 🖥 📞 ⦿ ⚕ 🅥 🖊 TV ⦿
🖥 🛋 🍴 🎱 🎣 SP

Whites Hotel M
≋≋ APPROVED

38-42 Osborne Road, Jesmond, Newcastle upon Tyne, NE2 2AL
☎ 091-281 5126
Well-furnished comfortable hotel run by resident owners. Suburban but convenient for the city centre, near the Metro and bus services.
Bedrooms: 11 single,
18 double & 8 twin, 2 family rooms.
Bathrooms: 24 private, 4 public; 6 private showers.
Bed & breakfast: £28-£37 single, £38-£47 double.
Half board: £25.95-£31.45 daily, £196-£259 weekly.
Lunch available.
Continued ▶

The National Crown Scheme is explained in full on pages 556 − 558.

NEWCASTLE UPON TYNE

Continued

Evening meal 6pm (l.o. 9.30pm).
Parking for 30.
Credit: Access, Visa, Diners, Amex.

NORTH SHIELDS

Tyne & Wear
Map ref 5C2

Alexandra Villa

10 Heaton Park View,
Heaton, Newcastle upon
Tyne, NE6 5AH
☎ 091-265 9371
*A large Victorian house
originally built for the Sheriff
of Newcastle. Set in gardens
with delightful views. Newly
decorated in Victorian style.*
Bedrooms: 2 twin.
Bathrooms: 1 public.
Bed & breakfast: £17 single,
£28 double.
Evening meal 6pm (l.o.
midday).
Parking for 2.

OTTERBURN

Northumberland
Map ref 5B1

Small village set at the
meeting of the River Rede
with Otter Burn, the site
of the Battle of Otterburn
in 1388. A peaceful
tradition continues in the
sale of Otterburn tweeds
in this beautiful region,
which is ideal for
exploring the Border
country and the Cheviots.

The Butterchurn ⋔
APPROVED

Main Street, Otterburn,
NE19 1TP
☎ (0830) 20585
*In the centre of the village on
the River Rede. Central for
Roman Wall and forts. Within
easy reach of Northumberland
coast. Fishing permits
available.*
Bedrooms: 2 double & 1 twin,
2 family rooms.
Bathrooms: 5 private.
Bed & breakfast: £15-£18
single, £26-£30 double.
Half board: £19-£21 daily,
£133-£147 weekly.
Lunch available.

Evening meal 7pm (l.o.
8.30pm).
Parking for 10.

Redesdale Arms Hotel ⋔
👑👑👑

Rochester, Otterburn,
Newcastle upon Tyne, Tyne
& Wear NE19 1TA
☎ (0830) 20668
*Family-run old coaching inn
with log fires. Central for
Hadrian's Wall and the
Kielder Forest.*
Bedrooms: 3 single, 5 double
& 3 twin, 1 family room.
Bathrooms: 4 private,
2 public; 1 private shower.
Bed & breakfast: £17-£25
single, £34-£47 double.
Lunch available.
Evening meal 7pm (l.o.
10pm).
Parking for 34.
Credit: Access, Visa, Diners.

PETERLEE

Co. Durham
Map ref 5C2

*Tourist Information
Centre* ☎ *091-586 4450*

Peterlee Lodge Hotel

Bede Way, Peterlee,
SR8 1BU
☎ 091-586 2161
*This hotel is in the centre of
Peterlee overlooking Castle
Eden Dene. We have
conference suites available.*
Bedrooms: 19 single, 2 double
& 6 twin.
Bathrooms: 27 private.
Bed & breakfast: £29.50
single, £40-£60 double.
Lunch available.
Evening meal 7pm (l.o.
9.30pm).
Parking for 50.
Credit: Access, Visa, C.Bl.,
Diners, Amex.

> **Map references
> apply to the colour
> maps towards the
> end of this guide.**

> **We advise you to
> confirm your
> booking in writing.**

REDCAR

Cleveland
Map ref 5C3

Lively holiday resort near
Teesside with broad
sandy beaches, a fine
racecourse, a large
indoor funfair at Coatham
and other seaside
amusements. Britain's
oldest existing lifeboat
can be seen at the
Zetland Museum.
*Tourist Information
Centre* ☎ *(0642) 471921*

Clarendon Hotel ⋔
👑👑

High St., Redcar, TS10 3DU
☎ (0642) 484879
*Small seaside hotel with
modern facilities, between
Redcar Racecourse and the
beach.*
Bedrooms: 4 single, 3 double
& 2 twin, 1 family room.
Bathrooms: 10 private.
Bed & breakfast: £19-£25
single, £29-£39 double.
Half board: £26.50-£32.50
daily.
Lunch available.
Evening meal 7pm (l.o.
10pm).
Credit: Access, Visa, Amex.

Falcon Hotel ⋔
👑👑

13 Station Road, Redcar,
TS10 1AH
☎ (0642) 484300
*Small licensed hotel in centre
of town providing home
cooking and a warm welcome.
Within easy reach of the
Cleveland Hills and
surrounding countryside.*
Bedrooms: 4 single, 3 twin,
4 family rooms.
Bathrooms: 3 private,
3 public.
Bed & breakfast: £13-£14
single, £23-£25 double.
Half board: £17-£19 daily,
£119-£133 weekly.
Evening meal 5pm (l.o. 7pm).

Park Hotel ⋔
👑👑👑 **COMMENDED**

Granville Terrace, Redcar,
TS10 3AR
☎ (0642) 490888
*The hotel is a small family-run
business catering to both eat
and reside in comfortable
surroundings.*
Bedrooms: 3 single, 13 double
& 9 twin.
Bathrooms: 25 private.

Bed & breakfast: £30-£50
single, £45-£60 double.
Half board: £29-£58.50 daily,
£202-£399.50 weekly.
Lunch available.
Evening meal 7pm (l.o.
9.30pm).
Parking for 40.
Credit: Access, Visa, Diners,
Amex.

Swan Hotel
👑👑👑👑

High Street, Redcar,
TS10 3DE
☎ (0642) 477301 Fax (0642)
477301
*Friendly and popular modern
town centre hotel. Situated on
High Street and close to shops.
Value for money.*
Bedrooms: 13 single, 4 double
& 17 twin.
Bathrooms: 18 private,
3 public.
Bed & breakfast: £19-£29
single, £30-£39 double.
Half board: £35-£50 daily.
Lunch available.
Evening meal 6.45pm (l.o.
9pm).
Parking for 15.
Credit: Access, Visa, Diners,
Amex.

Waterside House ⋔
👑 **APPROVED**

35 Newcomen Terrace,
Redcar, TS10 1DB
☎ (0642) 481062
*Large terraced property
overlooking the sea. Close to
town centre and leisure centre.
Warm friendly atmosphere
with true Yorkshire hospitality.*
Bedrooms: 2 single, 4 family
rooms.
Bathrooms: 2 public.
Bed & breakfast: £11.50-£13
single, £21-£23 double.
Half board: £15.50-£17 daily,
£108.50-£119 weekly.
Evening meal 5pm (l.o. 7pm).

> **The symbols are
> explained on the
> flap inside the
> back cover.**

> **Please check prices
> and other details at
> the time of booking.**

RIDING MILL

Northumberland
Map ref 5B2

A small village on the
south bank of the River
Tyne, near historic
Corbridge and the
Thomas Bewick Musuem.

Morningside Guest House
COMMENDED
Riding Mill, NE44 6HL
☎ (0434) 682350
*Old stone-built blacksmith's
house in a quiet country
setting, close to Hadrian's
Wall and the beautiful River
Tyne.*
Bedrooms: 1 single, 1 double
& 2 twin, 1 family room.
Bathrooms: 1 private,
1 public.
Bed & breakfast: £16 single,
£28-£34 double.
Half board: £20-£25 daily,
£108-£130 weekly.
Evening meal 6pm (l.o.
7.30pm).
Parking for 5.

ROTHBURY

Northumberland
Map ref 5B1

Old market town on the
River Coquet near the
Simonside Hills. With its
leafy, sloping main street,
attractive green and
lovely views of river and
hills it makes an ideal
centre for walking and
fishing and for exploring all
this beautiful area from
the coast to the Cheviots.
Cragside House and
Gardens (National Trust)
are open to the public.

Orchard Guest House M
High Street, Rothbury,
Morpeth, NE65 7TL
☎ (0669) 20684
*Charming guesthouse in the
middle of a lovely village, an
ideal centre for visiting all
Northumbria's attractions.
Comfortable surroundings.*
Bedrooms: 3 double & 2 twin,
1 family room.
Bathrooms: 4 private,
4 public.
Bed & breakfast: £16-£18
single, £32-£36 double.
Half board: £26-£28 daily,
£175-£189 weekly.
Evening meal 7pm (l.o. 7pm).
Open March-December.

SALTBURN-BY-SEA

Cleveland
Map ref 5C3

Set on fine cliffs just
north of the Cleveland
Hills, a gracious Victorian
resort with later
developments and wide,
firm sands. Further north
lies Teesside and a
fascinating high coastline
stretches south-eastward
to Whitby. A handsome
Jacobean mansion at
Marske can be reached
along the sands.
*Tourist Information
Centre* ☎ *(0287) 622422*

Rushpool Hall Hotel M
Saltburn Lane, Saltburn-by-
Sea, TS12 1HD
☎ Guisborough
(0287) 624111 & 624982
Fax (0287) 624111
*You can be assured of a warm
welcome and an old fashioned
atmosphere in our Victorian
country house set in 90 acres of
woodland.*
Bedrooms: 1 single, 13 double
& 2 twin, 4 family rooms.
Bathrooms: 20 private.
Bed & breakfast: £30-£65
single, £60-£85 double.
Lunch available.
Evening meal 7pm (l.o.
9.30pm).
Parking for 150.
Credit: Access, Visa, Diners,
Amex.

Westerlands Guest House
27 East Parade, Skelton,
Saltburn-by-Sea, TS12 2BJ
☎ Guisborough (0287) 50690
*On the Cleveland Way with
beautiful views of both sea and
country. Ideal touring base for
North Yorkshire Moors and
Yorkshire's top resorts. Private
parking and good home
cooking. Overnight stays
welcome.*
Bedrooms: 3 single, 3 double.
Bathrooms: 3 public.
Bed & breakfast: £11 single,
£22 double.
Half board: £16 daily, £100
weekly.
Evening meal 7pm (l.o. 7pm).
Parking for 5.

SEAHOUSES

Northumberland
Map ref 5C1

Small modern resort
developed around a 19th
C herring port. Just
offshore, and reached by
boat from here, are the
rocky Farne Islands
(National Trust) where
there is an important bird
reserve. The bird
observatory occupies a
medieval pele tower.

Bamburgh Castle Hotel M
Seahouses, NE68 7SQ
☎ (0665) 720283 Fax
(0665) 720283
*In its own grounds, overlooking
the harbour, with magnificent
views of the Farne Islands,
Bamburgh Castle and Holy
Island.*
Bedrooms: 3 single, 10 double
& 7 twin, 2 family rooms.
Bathrooms: 22 private.
Bed & breakfast: £26-£29
single, £50-£55 double.
Half board: £35-£37.50 daily,
£215-£235 weekly.
Lunch available.
Evening meal 7pm (l.o. 9pm).
Parking for 40.

Beach House Hotel M
COMMENDED
Sea Front, Seahouses,
NE68 7SR
☎ (0665) 720337
*Quiet, comfortable and
friendly, family-run hotel
overlooking the Farne Islands,
specialising in imaginative
home cooking and baking.*
Bedrooms: 2 single, 4 double
& 6 twin, 2 family rooms.
Bathrooms: 14 private,
2 public.
Bed & breakfast: £24-£32.50
single, £48-£59 double.
Half board: £38-£40 daily,
£220-£248 weekly.
Evening meal 6.30pm (l.o.
7.30pm).
Parking for 16.
Open March-November.
Credit: Access, Visa.

Links Hotel
8 King Street, Seahouses,
NE68 7XP
☎ (0665) 720062

*All rooms with colour TV and
tea making facilities. Lounge,
bar and dining room. 2 minutes
from harbour.*
Bedrooms: 3 double & 3 twin,
3 family rooms.
Bathrooms: 4 private,
2 public.
Bed & breakfast: £44-£55
double.
Lunch available.
Evening meal 7pm (l.o. 7pm).
Parking for 16.
Credit: Access, Visa.

The Lodge M
APPROVED
146 Main Street, North
Sunderland, Seahouses,
NE68 7UA
☎ (0665) 720158
*Small hotel with licence, in the
quiet part of Seahouses.
Restaurant, bar meals served
daily.*
Bedrooms: 4 double, 1 family
room.
Bathrooms: 5 private.
Bed & breakfast: from £17.50
single, from £35 double.
Lunch available.
Evening meal 6.30pm (l.o.
10pm).
Parking for 6.
Credit: Access, Visa.

Olde Ship Hotel M
APPROVED
Seahouses, NE68 7RD
☎ (0665) 720200
*Hotel with a long-established
reputation for food and drink
in comfortably relaxing old-
fashioned surroundings.*
Bedrooms: 2 single, 5 double
& 5 twin, 2 family rooms.
Bathrooms: 14 private,
2 public.
Bed & breakfast: £25.50-
£26.50 single, £51-£53 double.
Half board: £36.50-£37.50
daily, £220-£240 weekly.
Lunch available.
Evening meal 7pm (l.o.
8.30pm).
Parking for 12.
Open March-October.

Railston House M
COMMENDED
133 Main Street, North
Sunderland, Seahouses,
NE68 7TS
☎ (0665) 720912
*Country house in a fine
Georgian residence with
elegant rooms, log fires and sea
views beyond walled gardens.*

Continued ▶

SEAHOUSES
Continued

Bedrooms: 2 double & 2 twin.
Bathrooms: 2 private,
1 public.
Bed & breakfast: £17-£19
double.
Lunch available.
Evening meal 6.30pm (l.o.
8pm).
Parking for 2.

The St. Aidan Hotel and Restaurant M

Seafront, Seahouses,
NE68 7SR
☎ (0665) 720355
*On the seafront, overlooking
the Farne Islands. The food is
prepared and presented by the
internationally trained
chef/proprietor.*
Bedrooms: 1 single, 2 double
& 5 twin, 2 family rooms.
Bathrooms: 6 private,
1 public; 1 private shower.
Bed & breakfast: £15-£30
single, £30-£49 double.
Half board: £33-£36.50 daily.
Evening meal 6.30pm (l.o.
8.30pm).
Parking for 15.
Open February-November.
Credit: Access, Visa, Diners.

SEDGEFIELD
Co. Durham
Map ref 5C2

Ancient market town, a
centre for hunting and
steeplechasing, with a
racecourse nearby.
Handsome 18th C
buildings include the town
council's former Georgian
mansion and the rectory.
The church with its
magnificent spire has
17th C wood-carvings by
a local craftsman. Nearby
is Hardwick Hall country
park.

Crosshill Hotel & Restaurant M
APPROVED

1 The Square, Sedgefield,
Stockton-on-Tees, Cleveland
TS21 2AB
☎ (0740) 20153 & 21206
*In a conservation area
overlooking the village green
and the 13th C church, in the
heart of historic County
Durham.*

Bedrooms: 1 single, 5 double,
2 family rooms.
Bathrooms: 8 private.
Bed & breakfast: £40-£45
single, £50-£60 double.
Half board: £47-£61 daily,
£380-£427 weekly.
Lunch available.
Evening meal 7.30pm (l.o.
10.30pm).
Parking for 7.
Credit: Access, Visa, Amex.

SOUTH SHIELDS
Tyne & Wear
Map ref 5C2

At the mouth of the Tyne,
shipbuilding and industrial
centre developed around
a 19th C coalport and
occupying the site of an
important Roman fort and
granary port. The
seafront has sands,
gardens and parks. The
town's museum has
mementoes of the earliest
self-righting lifeboat, built
here in 1789.
*Tourist Information
Centre ☎ 091-454 6612*

Cleopatra Guest House

67 Beach Road, South
Shields, NE33 2QT
☎ 091-427 1900
*Late Victorian building on 4
floors with original character.
Only 5 minutes' walk to city
centre and beach.*
Bedrooms: 2 single, 1 double
& 5 twin, 1 family room.
Bathrooms: 3 private.
Bed & breakfast: £12-£15
single, £20-£25 double.
Half board: £15-£18 daily,
£95-£116 weekly.
Evening meal 5pm (l.o. 9pm).
Parking for 1.

New Crown Hotel M
APPROVED

Mowbray Road, South
Shields, NE33 3NG
☎ 091-455 3472
*On the seafront with lovely
views of the harbour and
beaches. Ideal for both
business and tourists.*
Bedrooms: 2 single, 6 double
& 2 twin, 1 family room.
Bathrooms: 7 private,
2 public.
Bed & breakfast: £26-£29
single, £45-£49 double.
Half board. £33.50-£36.50
daily.
Lunch available.
Evening meal 7pm (l.o. 9pm).

Parking for 40.
Credit: Access, Visa, Diners,
Amex.

Sea Hotel M

Sea Road, South Shields,
NE33 2LD
☎ 091-427 0999 Telex 53533
*On the seafront in the heart of
Catherine Cookson country.
Popular restaurant offering
French and English cooking.*
Bedrooms: 18 single, 6 double
& 6 twin, 3 family rooms.
Bathrooms: 33 private.
Bed & breakfast: from £49.80
single, from £60.80 double.
Half board: from £57.80
daily.
Lunch available.
Evening meal 7pm (l.o.
9.30pm).
Parking for 65.
Credit: Access, Visa, Diners,
Amex.

SPENNYMOOR
Co. Durham
Map ref 5C2

Booming coal and iron
town from the 18th C until
early in the present
century when traditional
industry gave way to
lighter manufacturing and
trading estates were built.
On the moors south of
the town there are fine
views of the Wear Valley.

Idsley House M
Listed **APPROVED**

4 Green Lane, Spennymoor,
DL16 6HD
☎ Bishop Auckland
(0388) 814237
*Long established guesthouse on
A167/A688. Ideal for Durham
City. Tea/coffee and colour TV
in bedrooms. Ample parking on
premises.*
Bedrooms: 1 single, 3 twin,
1 family room.
Bathrooms: 1 public.
Bed & breakfast: from £12.50
single, from £25 double.
Evening meal 6pm (l.o. 8pm).
Parking for 8.

The enquiry
coupons at the
back will help you
when contacting
proprietors.

STANLEY
Co. Durham
Map ref 5C2

Small town on the site of
a Roman cattle camp. At
the Beamish North of
England Open Air
Museum numerous set-
pieces and displays
recreate industrial and
social conditions
prevalent in the
area's past.

Harperley Hotel

Harperley, Stanley,
DH9 9TY
☎ Stanley (0207) 234011
*Converted granary on the
outskirts of Stanley, in the
country park area close to the
old water mill. Fishing and
shooting can be arranged.*
Bedrooms: 3 single, 2 double.
Bathrooms: 5 private.
Bed & breakfast: max. £27.50
single, max. £39.50 double.
Half board: £34.50-£40 daily,
£150-£200 weekly.
Lunch available.
Evening meal 7.30pm (l.o.
10pm).
Parking for 200.
Credit: Access, Visa.

STOCKTON-ON-TEES
Cleveland
Map ref 5C3

Industrial complex on
Teesside, first developed
in the 19th C around the
ancient market town with
its broad main street and
stately 18th C Town Hall.
The street has been the
site of a regular market
since 1310. Green
Dragon Yard has a
Georgian theatre and old
inn among other heritage
buildings.
*Tourist Information
Centre ☎ (0642) 615080*

Parkmore Hotel M

636 Yarm Road, Eaglescliffe,
Stockton-on-Tees, TS16 0DH
☎ (0642) 786815 Telex 58298
GB Best Western
*Warm, friendly hotel with
leisure club opposite golf-course
near Yarm. Ideal for visiting
North Yorkshire Moors, the
Dales, Durham and York.*
Bedrooms: 18 single,
18 double & 16 twin, 3 family
rooms.
Bathrooms: 55 private.

Bed & breakfast: £46-£58 single, £60-£70 double.
Lunch available.
Evening meal 6.45pm (l.o. 9.30pm).
Parking for 100.
Credit: Access, Visa, Diners, Amex.

SUNDERLAND

Tyne & Wear
Map ref 5C2

Ancient coal and shipbuilding port on Wearside, with important glassworks since the 17th C. Today's industrial complex dates from the 19th C; modern building includes the Civic Centre. North across the Wear, Monkwearmouth has a historic church with an Anglo-Saxon tower and a grand Victorian railway station preserved as a museum. Nearby are the twin resorts of Roker and Seaburn.
Tourist Information Centre ☎ 091-565 0960 or 565 0990

Bed & Breakfast Stop M
Listed APPROVED
183 Newcastle Road, Fulwell, Sunderland, SR5 1NR
☎ 091-548 2291
Tudor-style semi-detached house on the A1018 Newcastle to Sunderland road, 5 minutes to the railway station and 10 minutes to the seafront. All bedrooms with own TV.
Bedrooms: 1 single, 1 twin, 1 family room.
Bathrooms: 1 public.
Bed & breakfast: £12-£13 single, £22-£24 double.
Half board: £16-£17 daily, £105-£112 weekly.
Evening meal 6pm (l.o. midday).
Parking for 2.

Felicitations M
94 Ewesley Road, High Barnes, Sunderland, SR4 7RJ
☎ 091-522 0960 & 091-528 9062
Private guesthouse and china-painting workshop. Hand-painted products on display. Near main bus route, polytechnic, Empire Theatre and Crowtree Leisure Centre.
Bedrooms: 1 single, 1 double, 1 family room.
Bathrooms: 1 public.

Bed & breakfast: £12-£16 single, £20-£28 double.
Half board: £19-£21 daily, £114-£133 weekly.
Evening meal 6pm (l.o. 6.30pm).
Parking for 1.
Open April-October.

Friendly Hotel M
Abingdon Way, Junction A1/A19 Boldon, NE35 9PE
☎ 091-519 1999
CR Friendly
Purpose built 82-bedroom hotel and leisure centre with conference facilities for 220 and several smaller meeting rooms. Opened June 1990.
Bedrooms: 43 double & 27 twin, 12 family rooms.
Bathrooms: 82 private.
Bed & breakfast: £52-£62.50 single, £68.50-£73 double.
Half board: £45.75-£74 daily.
Lunch available.
Evening meal 7pm (l.o. 9.45pm).
Credit: Access, Visa, Diners, Amex.

Roker Hotel M
Roker Terrace, Roker, Sunderland, SR6 0PH
☎ 091-567 1786
Hotel taking its name from popular nearby seaside resort. Situated almost on the beach, within easy reach of the town centre.
Bedrooms: 20 single, 8 double & 9 twin, 8 family rooms.
Bathrooms: 45 private.
Bed & breakfast: £42.50-£48.50 single, from £54.50 double.
Lunch available.
Evening meal 6pm (l.o. 10.30pm).
Parking for 200.
Credit: Access, Visa, Diners, Amex.

Washington Moat House M
Stone Cellar Road, High Usworth, District 12, Washington, NE37 1PH
☎ 091-417 2626 Telex 537143
CR Queens Moat Houses
Fine modern hotel. Leisure facilities include gymnasium, solarium, snooker club and golf-course. An ideal all-year touring centre.

Bedrooms: 50 double & 47 twin, 9 family rooms.
Bathrooms: 106 private.
Bed & breakfast: £42-£72.50 single, £70-£90 double.
Half board: from £45 daily.
Lunch available.
Evening meal 7pm (l.o. 10pm).
Parking for 200.
Credit: Access, Visa, Diners, Amex.

TYNEMOUTH

Tyne & Wear
Map ref 5C2

At the mouth of the Tyne, old Tyneside resort adjoining North Shields with its fish quay and market. The pier is overlooked by the gaunt ruins of a Benedictine priory and a castle. Splendid sands, amusement centre and park.

Hope House M
47 Percy Gardens, Tynemouth, NE30 4HH
☎ 091-257 1989
Double-fronted Victorian house with superb coastal views from most rooms. Period furnishing with large bedrooms.
Bedrooms: 2 double & 1 twin.
Bathrooms: 3 private, 1 public.
Bed & breakfast: £30-£38.50 single, £34-£45 double.
Half board: £27-£32.50 daily, £189-£227.50 weekly.
Lunch available.
Evening meal 6pm (l.o. 9pm).
Parking for 5.
Credit: Amex.

> **Individual proprietors have supplied all details of accommodation. Although we do check for accuracy, we advise you to confirm prices and other information at the time of booking.**

WARKWORTH

Northumberland
Map ref 5C1

A pretty village overlooked by its medieval castle. A 14th C fortified bridge across the wooded Coquet gives a superb view of 18th C terraces climbing to the castle. Fishing on the river, sandy beaches on the coast. Upstream is a curious 14th C Hermitage and in the market square is the Norman church of St. Lawrence.

Sun Hotel M
6 Castle Terrace, Warkworth, Morpeth, NE65 0UP
☎ Alnwick (0665) 711259
Accommodation opposite Warkworth Castle. With views of estuary and surrounding countryside.
Bedrooms: 1 single, 5 double & 6 twin, 2 family rooms.
Bathrooms: 14 private.
Bed & breakfast: £42 single, £60-£70 double.
Half board: from £55 daily, from £239 weekly.
Lunch available.
Evening meal 7pm (l.o. 9.30pm).
Parking for 60.
Credit: Access, Visa.

WHITLEY BAY

Tyne & Wear
Map ref 5C2

Seaside resort just north of Tyneside. A wide variety of diversions include a large golf-course, amusement parks and an ice-rink. The town is edged with wide sands which stretch northward toward a more rugged coastline.
Tourist Information Centre ☎ 091-252 4494

Argyll Hotel and Guest House
21 South Parade, Whitley Bay, NE26 2RE
☎ 091-251 3096
Large, corner terraced house situated in the commercial sector of Whitley Bay. All rooms have TV, tea and coffee facilities. On-site car parking.
Continued ▶

WHITLEY BAY
Continued

Bedrooms: 3 single, 1 double
& 1 twin, 2 family rooms.
Bathrooms: 2 public.
Bed & breakfast: £14 single,
£28 double.
Half board: £19 daily, £133
weekly.
Evening meal 4pm (l.o. 9pm).
Parking for 6.

Barbaraellas Hotel
69 Percy Road, Whitley Bay,
NE26 2AY
☎ 091-251 5110
*Situated off main promenade,
close to all amenities.*
Bedrooms: 1 single, 1 double
& 2 twin, 1 family room.
Bathrooms: 1 public.
Bed & breakfast: £11.50-£15
single, £23-£25 double.
Half board: £27.50-£29.50
daily, £165-£177 weekly.
Lunch available.
Evening meal 5.30pm (l.o.
7pm).

Marlborough Hotel M
20-21 East Parade, The
Promenade, Whitley Bay,
NE26 1AP
☎ 091-251 3628
*Traditional seaside hotel in the
centre of the promenade with
fine sea views.*
Bedrooms: 6 single, 2 double
& 3 twin, 3 family rooms.
Bathrooms: 7 private,
2 public; 2 private showers.
Bed & breakfast: £18-£24
single, £36-£38 double.
Half board: £24.95-£25.95
daily, £110-£150 weekly.
Evening meal 6pm (l.o.
6.30pm).
Parking for 10.
Credit: Access, Visa, Diners.

Melrose Guest House
45 Esplanade, Whitley Bay,
NE26 2AR
☎ 091-251 4037
*A small guesthouse offering
home cooking and warm
friendly atmosphere. 2 minutes'
walk from the sea, shops and
metro station.*
Bedrooms: 1 single, 2 twin,
1 family room.
Bathrooms: 1 public.
Bed & breakfast: £11.50-
£12.50 single, £23-£25 double.
Half board: £15.50-£16.50
daily, £80.50-£108.50 weekly.

Evening meal 5pm (l.o. 6pm).
Parking for 4.

Seacrest Hotel M
APPROVED
North Parade, Whitley Bay,
NE26 1PA
☎ 091-253 0140
*Adjoining the promenade, close
to the Metro and places of
entertainment. Within easy
travelling distance of historic
monuments, castles and ruins.
Excellent shopping in
Newcastle and the largest
shopping centre in Europe,
Gateshead MetroCentre.*
Bedrooms: 12 single,
6 double, 6 family rooms.
Bathrooms: 8 private,
3 public; 7 private showers.
Bed & breakfast: £24.75-
£57.50 single, £41.40-£48.30
double.
Half board: £33.95-£66.70
daily.
Lunch available.
Evening meal 6pm (l.o. 8pm).
Parking for 6.
Credit: Access, Visa, Diners,
Amex.

White-Surf Guest House
8 South Parade, Whitley Bay,
NE26 2RG
☎ 091-253 0103
*A family-run guesthouse at the
gateway to Northumbria.
Central for all amenities, 2
minutes from beach and Metro
transport.*
Bedrooms: 3 single, 1 double
& 3 twin, 2 family rooms.
Bathrooms: 2 public.
Bed & breakfast: £12.50-
£14.50 single, £25-£29 double.
Half board: £18.50-£20.50
daily, £125.50-£140.50
weekly.
Evening meal 6pm (l.o.
5.30pm).
Parking for 9.

Windsor Hotel M
35-45 South Parade, Whitley
Bay, NE25 8UT
☎ 091-252 3317 Telex 537388
*A private hotel close to the
seafront and amusement park.
An ice rink, roller rink and
excellent leisure pool are
nearby.*
Bedrooms: 21 single,
12 double & 11 twin, 9 family
rooms.
Bathrooms: 36 private,
6 public; 9 private showers.
Bed & breakfast: £25-£40

single, £44-£60 double.
Half board: £32-£36 daily.
Evening meal 6pm (l.o.
9.30pm).
Parking for 22.
Credit: Access, Visa, Diners,
Amex.

York House Hotel M
APPROVED
30 Park Parade, Whitley Bay,
NE26 1DX
☎ 091-252 8313
*Established over 20 years. All
rooms en-suite with TV/radio,
tea/coffee facilities. Menu
choice for both breakfast and
dinner. Direct dial telephone.*
Bedrooms: 1 single, 3 double
& 2 twin, 2 family rooms.
Bathrooms: 7 private;
1 private shower.
Bed & breakfast: from £18
single, from £31 double.
Half board: from £22 daily,
from £147 weekly.
Evening meal 7pm (l.o.
7.30pm).
Parking for 2.
Credit: Access, Visa.

WOLSINGHAM
Co. Durham
Map ref 5B2

Gateway to the moors of
Upper Weardale, small
town set at the
confluence of the Wear
and Waskerley Beck. The
moors abound in old
lead-workings and
quarries; on Waskerley
Beck, Tunstall Reservoir
is the haunt of bird-
watchers. Well-placed for
exploring the fells and
dales.

Bay Horse Hotel
Upper Town, Wolsingham,
DL13 3EX
☎ Weardale (0388) 527220
*A traditional English pub with
2 bars, real ale and
comprehensive menu. There is
a pool table and dartboard.*
Bedrooms: 1 single, 4 double
& 2 twin.
Bathrooms: 4 private,
1 public.
Bed & breakfast: £15-£20
single, £25-£35 double.
Half board: £25-£30 daily,
£140-£280 weekly.
Lunch available.
Evening meal 7pm (l.o.
10pm).
Parking for 20.
Credit: Access, Visa.

WOOLER
Northumberland
Map ref 5B1

Old grey-stone town,
market-place for foresters
and hill farmers, set at the
edge of the north-east
Cheviots. This makes a
good base for excursions
to Northumberland's
loveliest coastline, or for
angling and walking in the
Border lands.

Loreto Guest House M
1 Ryecroft Way, Wooler,
NE71 6BW
☎ (0668) 81350
*Family-run early Georgian
house with spacious grounds, in
the lovely Cheviot village of
Wooler. Central for touring
and walking and close to
coastline.*
Bedrooms: 1 single, 2 double
& 2 twin, 2 family rooms.
Bathrooms: 4 private,
2 public.
Bed & breakfast: £13-£13.50
single, £27-£29 double.
Evening meal 6.30pm (l.o.
7pm).
Parking for 12.

Classifications
and quality
commendations
were correct at the
time of going to
press but are
subject to change.
Please check at the
time of booking.

108

Situated in the quaint village of Brandon, only 3 miles from the historical city of Durham. The stone built accommodation comprises four twin bedded rooms each with private facilities of shower, washbasin and toilet. The double glazed, centrally heated rooms are attractively furnished with duvets, colour TV, tea and coffee making facilities, reading lights above each bed and telephones. There is ample parking and full English breakfasts are served in the Inn.

**The Bay Horse Inn, Brandon Village,
County Durham DH7 8ST. Telephone: (091) 378 0498**

The Cheviot Hotel
**Bellingham, Northumberland NE48 2AU
☎(0434) 220216**

A 300 years old coaching inn set in a beautiful rural area of Northumberland. A centre for touring Northumberland, the Scottish borders and the Roman walls and remains. Bellingham is at the gateway to the Northumberland National Park and Kielder Water.
The Cheviot Hotel provides centrally heated comfort with private bathrooms. The cuisine and bars are excellent with a full a la carte menu which includes a speciality of nine game items. The Cheviot Hotel and Game Kitchen Restaurant.

The Greenhead Country House Hotel
Firtree, Crook, Co. Durham. DL15 8BL. ☎ 0388 763143
One of the most prestigious new developments created for touring the Prince Bishops Countryside. Located at the foot of Weardale this new hotel has complete en-suite accommodation located some 15 miles from Durham City, 15 miles from Beamish, 20 miles from Kilhope Lead Mining Centre. Lovely rural location. Fully licensed. B & B booking rates: **£40** double **twin room en-suite**
£30 single room en-suite
Evening meals available on request.
Contact Paul & Anne Birbeck

Use a coupon

When requesting further information from advertisers in this guide, you may find it helpful to use the advertisement enquiry coupons which can be found towards the end of the guide. These should be cut out and mailed direct to the companies in which you are interested. Do remember to include your name and address.

Follow the sign

It leads to over 560 Tourist Information Centres throughout England offering friendly help with accommodation and holiday ideas as well as suggestions of places to visit and things to do.

In your home town there may be a centre which can help you before you set out. Details of the locations of Tourist Information Centres are available from the English Tourist Board, Thames Tower, Black's Road, London W6 9EL, or from England's Regional Tourist Boards.

Hector Breeze

Check the maps

The place you wish to visit may not have accommodation entirely suited to your needs, but there could be somewhere ideal quite close by. Check the colour maps towards the end of this guide to identify nearby towns and villages with accommodation listed in the guide, and then use the town index to find page numbers.

Use a coupon

When enquiring about accommodation you may find it helpful to use the booking enquiry coupons which can be found towards the end of the guide. These should be cut out and mailed direct to the establishments in which you are interested. Do remember to include your name and address.

North West

Standing proudly between the mountains of Wales and the English Lakes is the North West, a region of moors and forests, hills and valleys, and a wild and lonely coastline with spectacular sea-reflected sunsets.

» Before you visit, look at the map. You'll see an area criss-crossed with motorways — probably the best road connections in Britain — making it easy to get into and around. Then there are fast rail links, Manchester's international airport, and even lazy canals for those with the notion to abandon getting there in favour of almost stopping there.

» Here, contrasts of mood and style rival any in England. It is where much of the nation's wealth was created during the Industrial Revolution, producing a cluster of self-confident Victorian towns. The Roman legacy still lives in places like Chester, Lancaster, Liverpool, Manchester and Ribchester, while the Tudors embellished Cheshire in particular with an explosion of black-and-white architecture.

» The last 100 years have seen families flocking to resorts like the glittering, non-stop Blackpool with its seven miles of illuminations, or to seaside of a quieter nature, even fishing villages. Just one of the organised breaks on offer is a Soccer Weekend with Liverpool FC and Everton FC which includes a Big Match — heady stuff for boys of all ages.

» Just as you are never far from coast or country, heritage is everywhere. There are museums celebrating the illustrious past of ships and canals, silks and cottons, Beatles and mining, salt and glass, and more — there's even one sited in the Manchester sewers.

>> Whether you shop in cosmopolitan Manchester, take the
ferry across the Mersey, listen to the Hallé, walk the
Sandstone Trail, whoop at the Grand National, play golf at a
Royal course or just snooze on some warm and salty beach —
there's never a dull moment in the North West!

>> Please refer to
the colour maps at
the back of this
guide for all places
with accommodation
listings.

Where to go, what to see

Bridgemere Garden World
Bridgemere, Nantwich, Cheshire CW5 7QB
☎ Bridgemere (093 65) 381/2
One of the largest garden centres in England with 2 acres of display gardens, tropical and indoor plants. Large collection of heathers, alpines and herbs, garden shop, Egon Ronay recommended coffee shop.

Dunham Massey Hall
Altrincham, Greater Manchester WA14 4SJ
☎ 061-941 1025
200-acre formal park with fallow deer. Historic house with outstanding collections of 18th C furniture, silver and portraits.

Lewis Textile Museum
3 Exchange Street, Blackburn, Lancashire BB1 7AH
☎ Blackburn (0254) 667130
Working examples of Hargreaves Spinning Jenny, Kays Flying Shuttle, Cromptons Mule, spinning wheel and hand loom. Art Gallery.

Sandcastle
Promenade, Blackpool, Lancashire FY4 1BB
☎ Blackpool (0253) 43602
Leisure pool, wave pool, giant slides, amusements, live entertainment, snooker, pool, nightclub, children's playland.

The Wildfowl Trust
Martin Mere, Burscough, Nr. Ormskirk, Lancashire L40 0TA
☎ Burscough (0704) 895181
Superb natural setting for 1,600 ducks, geese, swans and flamingos from all over the world. Acres of wild marshland are home to many wild birds each winter.

Look out for flamingos at The Wildfowl Trust

The Magical Kingdom of Camelot
Park Hall Road, Charnock Richard, Chorley, Lancashire PR7 5LP
☎ Chorley (0257) 453044
Family theme park with over 80 rides and attractions.

Tatton Park
Knutsford, Cheshire WA16 6QN
☎ Knutsford (0565) 54822
Georgian mansion with 60-acre garden and 1,000-acre deer park. Medieval Old Hall, 1930s farm, shop, restaurant.

Lancaster Maritime Museum
Customs House, St. George's Quay, Lancaster, Lancashire LA1 1RB
☎ Lancaster (0524) 64637
Building of 1764, former Custom House with displays illustrating 18th C trade with West Indies and the fishing communities of Morecambe Bay.

Albert Dock
Liverpool, Merseyside L3 4AA
☎ 051-709 9199
Britain's largest Grade I listed historic building. Restored four-sided dock, including shops, wine bars, entertainment, marina and Maritime Museum.

Fletcher Moss Museum
Wilmslow Road, Didsbury, Manchester, Greater Manchester M20 8AU
☎ 061-236 5244
History of Manchester, old maps and views. Furniture, glass, clocks, paintings.

Frontierland
Marine Road, Morecambe, Lancashire LA4 4DG
☎ Morecambe (0524) 410024
Over 30 thrill rides, including Texas Tornado and Stampede Roller Coaster, in Wild West theme park.

Knowsley Safari Park
Prescot, Merseyside L34 4AN
☎ 051-430 9009
Five-mile drive through game reserves, set in 400 acres of parkland containing lions, tigers, elephants, rhinos, etc. Picnic areas and children's amusement park.

Wigan Pier
Wallgate, Wigan, Greater Manchester WN3 4EU
☎ Wigan (0942) 323666
Heritage Centre, The Way We Were 1900, world's largest steam engine, schools centre, water buses, picnic areas.

Boat Museum
Dock Yard Road, Ellesmere Port, Cheshire L65 4EF
☎ 051-355 5017
Over 50 historic craft — largest floating collection in the world. Craft workshops. Exhibitions in restored warehouses, 19th C steam engines.

Castlefield Urban Heritage Park
330 Deansgate, Manchester, Greater Manchester M3 4FN
☎ 061-832 4244

Explore the space gallery at Castlefield Urban Heritage Park, Manchester

Britain's first urban heritage park. Includes Greater Manchester Museum of Science and Industry, Roman Fort Gate, Canals, Air and Space Gallery, Information Centre, GMEX Exhibition Centre.

Granada Studios Tour
Granada Television Ltd, Quay Street, Manchester, Greater Manchester M60 9EA
☎ 061-832 9090
Entertaining insight into television and films, including the Coronation Street set, Baker Street and the House of Commons.

Gulliver's World
Warrington, Cheshire WA5 5YZ
☎ Warrington (0925) 444888
Theme park for the family, based on the Gulliver fairy tale.

Chester Zoo
Upton-by-Chester, Cheshire CH2 1LH
☎ Chester (0244) 380280
Britain's largest zoological gardens outside London.

Blackpool Pleasure Beach
South Shore, Blackpool, Lancashire FY4 1EZ
☎ Blackpool (0253) 41033

Large amusement park with big thrill rides, Space Invader, Big Dipper, Revolution, etc.

Jodrell Bank Science Centre
Lower Withington, Nr. Holmes Chapel, Macclesfield, Cheshire SK11 9DL
☎ Holmes Chapel (0477) 71339
Exhibition of modern astronomy, planetarium, gardens and arboretum.

Make a date for...

Boaters Gathering and Craft Fair
Boat Museum, Ellesmere Port, Cheshire   29 March – 1 April

**Horse racing –
Grand National Meeting**
Aintree Racecourse, Aintree, Liverpool, Merseyside
                                                                      4 – 6 April

Mersey River Festival
River Mersey, Liverpool, Merseyside   7 – 30 June

Royal Lancashire Show
Astley Park, Chorley, Lancashire   26 – 28 July

Southport Flower Show
Victoria Park, Southport, Merseyside   22 – 24 August

Morecambe Illuminations
Promenade, Morecambe, Lancashire   7 – 31 August

Blackpool Illuminations
Promenade, Blackpool, Lancashire
                                         30 August – 5 November

Grand Christmas Craft Fair
Boat Museum, Ellesmere Port, Cheshire   23 – 24 November

Find out more

Further information about holidays and attractions in the North West region is available from: **North West Tourist Board,** The Last Drop Village, Bromley Cross, Bolton, Lancashire BL7 9PZ. ☎ (0204) 591511.

These publications are available free from the North West Tourist Board:

England's North West Holiday Guide

Discover England's North West (map)

Conference brochure

Overseas brochure

Party Visits

Bed & Breakfast map

115

Places to stay

⟫ Accommodation entries in this regional section are listed in alphabetical order of place name, and then in alphabetical order of establishment.

⟫ The map references refer to the colour maps towards the end of the guide. The first figure is the map number; the letter and figure which follow indicate the grid reference on the map.

⟫ The symbols at the end of each accommodation entry give information about services and facilities. A 'key' to these symbols is inside the back cover flap, which can be kept open for easy reference.

ACCRINGTON

Lancashire
Map ref 4A1

5m E. Blackburn
Victorian town noted for its red bricks which were extensively used in public buildings throughout Britain. Famous for textiles and general engineering. The Haworth Art Gallery contains collections of Early English watercolours and Tiffany glass.

Dunkenhalgh Hotel M

Blackburn Road, Clayton-le-Moors, Accrington, BB5 5JP
☎ (0254) 398021 Telex 63282
Ⓖ Character
Gothic-fronted mansion house with Georgian interior, set in 17 acres of parkland, at exit 7 of the M65. Many fine public rooms and conference facilities for up to 400. Sauna and indoor heated swimming pool.
Bedrooms: 6 single, 21 double & 19 twin, 10 family rooms.
Bathrooms: 56 private.
Bed & breakfast: £44-£70 single, £69-£84 double.
Lunch available.
Evening meal 7pm (l.o. 9.45pm).
Parking for 250.
Credit: Access, Visa, Diners, Amex.

ALDERLEY EDGE

Cheshire
Map ref 4B2

5m S. Manchester Airport
Residential town taking its name from the hill which rises to a height of 600 ft from the Cheshire Plain. The Edge is a well-known beauty spot with superb views. Many historic buildings including Chorley Old Hall (the oldest surviving manor house in Cheshire).

The Alderley Edge Hotel M

Macclesfield Road, Alderley Edge, SK9 7JB
☎ (0625) 583033
Converted country mansion built originally for one of the Manchester cotton barons. Close to the Edge beauty spot and near to the village of Alderley, Jodrell Bank and Gawsworth Hall.
Bedrooms: 21 twin, 11 family rooms.
Bathrooms: 32 private.
Bed & breakfast: £35-£86.95 single, £66-£112.90 double.
Half board: £50.95-£74.40 daily.
Lunch available.
Evening meal 7pm (l.o. 10.30pm).
Parking for 70.
Credit: Access, Visa, Diners, Amex.

ALTRINCHAM

Gtr. Manchester
Map ref 4A2

8m SW. Manchester
On the edge of the Cheshire Plain, close to Manchester. Once a thriving textile town, Altrincham is now mainly residential. Good centre for local beauty spots including 18th C Dunham Massey Hall (National Trust) with its deer park.
Tourist Information Centre ☎ 061-941 7337

Beech Mount Hotel M
APPROVED
46 Barrington Road, Altrincham, WA14 1HN
☎ 061-928 4523
Family-run hotel with restaurant, within easy reach of Manchester Airport and city centre. Convenient for public transport and shopping centre.
Bedrooms: 15 single, 7 double & 11 twin, 3 family rooms.
Bathrooms: 29 private, 2 public; 6 private showers.
Bed & breakfast: £27.60-£29.90 single, max. £48.30 double.
Half board: from £30 daily.
Evening meal 6.30pm (l.o. 8.30pm).
Parking for 32.
Credit: Access, Visa.

We advise you to confirm your booking in writing.

Bowdon Hotel M
COMMENDED
Langham Road, Bowdon, Altrincham, WA14 2HT
☎ 061-928 7121 & 8825
Telex 668208
Victorian house incorporating modern extension and facilities. Set in rural suburbs at the gateway to the lovely Cheshire countryside.
Bedrooms: 26 single, 11 double & 43 twin, 2 family rooms.
Bathrooms: 82 private.
Bed & breakfast: £30-£58 single, £46-£70 double.
Half board: £42-£70 daily, £350 weekly.
Lunch available.
Evening meal 7pm (l.o. 10pm).
Parking for 170.
Credit: Access, Visa, Diners, Amex.

Cresta Court Hotel M
Church Street, Altrincham, Cheshire WA14 4DP
☎ 061-927 7272 Telex 667242
Ⓖ Best Western
Privately owned town centre hotel, opened in 1973 and designed to provide all modern facilities. Easy access to M56, M6, M62, M63. 10 minutes to Manchester International Airport. Car parking for 300 cars.
Bedrooms: 45 single, 81 double & 8 twin, 5 family rooms.
Bathrooms: 139 private.
Bed & breakfast: £30-£54 single, £38.50-£65 double.

Evening meal 6pm (l.o. 11pm).
Parking for 300.
Credit: Access, Visa, Diners, Amex.

♿ 🍸 ⌨ 📺 ✧ 🛈 Ⅴ 🔌 ●
🖬 🗓 🍴 🕭 SP 🆃

ASHTON-UNDER-LYNE

Gtr. Manchester
Map ref 4B1

6m E. Manchester
Now part of the borough of Tameside, this old market town lies on the north bank of the River Tame. The Assheton family, who owned the manor of Ashton from the 14th C, are portrayed in the stained glass windows of St. Michael's Church.

Lynwood Hotel
⌨

3 Richmond Street, Ashton-under-Lyne, OL6 7TX
☎ 061-330 5358
Small, comfortable, family-run hotel in quiet position. Convenient for shops, theatre, cinema, station and buses. Direct bus service to Manchester.
Bedrooms: 1 single, 1 double & 2 twin.
Bathrooms: 1 private, 1 public; 1 private shower.
Bed & breakfast: from £19 single, £34-£40 double.
Parking for 4.

♿ 🍸 ⌨ 📺 Ⅷ 🛈 🔌 📺 🖬
🍴 🗓 🕭 SP

Welbeck House Hotel
🏆🏆🏆 COMMENDED

324 Katherine Street, Ashton-Under-Lyne, OL6 7BD
☎ 061-344 0751
Small exclusive hotel offering personal service and run entirely by the owners.
Bedrooms: 6 single, 2 family rooms.
Bathrooms: 8 private.
Bed & breakfast: £38-£42 single, £48-£52 double.
Half board: £40-£50 daily.
Evening meal 4pm (l.o. 8pm).
Parking for 20.
Credit: Access, Visa, Diners, Amex.

♿ 🍸 ⌨ 🕭 🛈 📺 ●
🖬 🍴 🗓 DAP ♝ SP

York House Hotel M
🏆🏆🏆 COMMENDED

York Place, Off Richmond Street, Ashton-under-Lyne, OL6 7TT
☎ 061-330 5899

Recently refurbished hotel with restaurant. Emphasis on food and fine wines. Garden, function room. Ideal base for touring the north of England.
Bedrooms: 8 single, 19 double & 5 twin, 2 family rooms.
Bathrooms: 34 private.
Bed & breakfast: £45-£52 single, from £62 double.
Lunch available.
Evening meal 7pm (l.o. 9.30pm).
Parking for 36.
Credit: Access, Visa, C.Bl., Diners, Amex.

♿ 🍸 ⌨ 🕭 ⌨ 📺 ✧ 🛈 Ⅴ
🔌 ● 🖬 🍴 🗓 ❄ SP 🆃

BEBINGTON

Merseyside
Map ref 4A2

3m S. Birkenhead
Town on the Wirral Peninsula, the mainstay of which is the Unilever complex of chemical, soap, detergent and food companies. Port Sunlight model village, built for Unilever employees, houses a fine collection of paintings and sculpture in the Lady Lever Art Gallery.

The Bebington Hotel M
24 Town Lane, Bebington, Wirral, L63 5JG
☎ 051-645 0608
A well-appointed private hotel, ideally located for tourists or business people visiting Merseyside, Liverpool, Chester and Wales.
Bedrooms: 4 single, 3 double & 1 twin, 3 family rooms.
Bathrooms: 11 private, 2 public.
Bed & breakfast: £19.50-£28.50 single, £35-£39 double.
Half board: £25-£36 daily.
Evening meal 7pm (l.o. 9pm).
Parking for 20.

♿ 🍸 ⌨ 🕭 🛈 Ⅴ 📺 📺
● 🖬 🍴 🗓 ❄ DAP ♝ SP 🆃

Individual proprietors have supplied all details of accommodation. Although we do check for accuracy, we advise you to confirm prices and other information at the time of booking.

BEESTON

Cheshire
Map ref 4A2

11m SE. Chester
Hamlet below the Peckforton Hills which rise from the Cheshire Plain to 740 ft. Medieval Beeston Castle (English Heritage) overlies a prehistoric hill fort.

Wild Boar Hotel M
🏆🏆🏆🏆 COMMENDED

Tarporley Road, Beeston, Nr. Tarporley, CW6 9NW
☎ Bunbury (0829) 260309
Telex 61455
ⓒⓡ Character
18th C black and white building of character, in typical style of Cheshire. 13 miles from Chester, this 37-bedroomed hotel is ideally located for exploring the Cheshire countryside.
Bedrooms: 22 double & 3 twin, 12 family rooms.
Bathrooms: 37 private.
Lunch available.
Evening meal 7pm (l.o. 9.45pm).
Parking for 100.
Credit: Access, Visa, C.Bl., Diners, Amex.

♿ 🍸 ⌨ 🕭 ⌨ 🛈 Ⅴ 🔌
📺 ● 🖬 🍴 🗓 ▶ ❄ ♝ SP
🏔 🆃

BIRKENHEAD

Merseyside
Map ref 4A2

Shipbuilding, docks and later the Mersey Tunnel turned Birkenhead into a busy town. Good Victorian architecture in Hamilton Square and Town Hall. Williamson Art Gallery contains English watercolours, pottery and porcelain.
Tourist Information Centre ☎ 051-647 6780

Ashgrove M
14 Ashville Road, Claughton, Birkenhead, L43 8SA
☎ 051-653 3794
Friendly, family-run establishment overlooking Birkenhead Park. 10 minutes' walk to train and 2 stops to Liverpool station. Excellent shopping facilities nearby, numerous sports facilities. Resident folk singer (owner).
Bedrooms: 2 single, 2 double & 3 twin, 1 family room.

Bathrooms: 2 private, 3 public.
Bed & breakfast: £12-£16 single, £22-£32 double.
Half board: £16-£20 daily, £105-£126 weekly.
Lunch available.
Evening meal 6pm (l.o. 4pm).
Parking for 10.

♿ 🍸 ⌨ 🕭 ⌨ Ⅷ 🛈 Ⅴ 🔌
📺 🖬 🍴 🕭 ❄ 🏔 DAP
SP 🏔

Central Hotel
🏆🏆🏆🏆

Clifton Crescent, Birkenhead, L41 2QH
☎ 051-647 6347
Town centre hotel, close to railway station and Liverpool tunnel entrance.
Bedrooms: 14 single, 11 double & 10 twin, 2 family rooms.
Bathrooms: 30 private, 2 public.
Bed & breakfast: £31.75-£39.75 single, £47.75-£60.95 double.
Half board: £39.60-£47.60 daily, £222.25-£251.20 weekly.
Lunch available.
Evening meal 6.30pm (l.o. 9pm).
Credit: Access, Visa, Diners, Amex.

♿ 🍸 ⌨ 📺 ✧ 🛈 Ⅴ 🔌 ●
🖬 🍴 🗓 🏔 SP 🆃

Lincluden Lodge Hotel
114 Storeton Road, Prenton, Birkenhead, Wirral, L42 8NA
☎ 051-608 3732
For discerning guests looking for a warm welcome and value for money. Convenient for Chester, Liverpool, the Lakes and North Wales. 1 mile along the B5151 from the M53 junction 4.
Bedrooms: 6 single, 6 double & 7 twin, 1 family room.
Bathrooms: 5 private, 3 public.
Bed & breakfast: £18-£26 single, £30-£36 double.
Half board: £25-£32 daily, £150-£175 weekly.
Lunch available.
Evening meal 6pm (l.o. 7.50pm).
Parking for 18.

♿ 🍸 ⌨ 🛈 Ⅴ 🔌 📺 🖬
🍴 🗓 DAP ♝ SP 🏔 🆃

Shrewsbury Guest House
🏆🏆🏆

31 Shrewsbury Road, Oxton, Birkenhead, L43 2JF
☎ 051-652 4029

Continued ▶

BIRKENHEAD

Continued

Friendly guesthouse offering good home cooking. Colour TV in all rooms. Free tea and coffee facilities always available. Relaxed atmosphere.
Bedrooms: 3 double & 5 twin.
Bathrooms: 5 private,
1 public; 1 private shower.
Bed & breakfast: £15-£17.50 single, £22-£26 double.
Half board: £18-£22.50 daily.
Evening meal 5pm (l.o. 8pm).
Parking for 10.

Yew Tree Hotel

58 Rock Lane West, Rock Ferry, Birkenhead, L42 4PA
☎ 051-645 4112
Warm, comfortable accommodation in friendly, elegant, Georgian house, all rooms with TV and Sky satellite TV. Quiet situation, convenient for motorways, Birkenhead tunnel, public transport, Irish and Manx ferries.
Bedrooms: 8 single, 1 double & 4 twin, 1 family room.
Bathrooms: 5 private,
3 public; 2 private showers.
Bed & breakfast: £19.50-£28 single, £35-£45 double.
Half board: £22-£36.50 daily, £105-£174 weekly.
Evening meal 7pm (l.o. 8pm).
Parking for 20.
Credit: Access, Visa.

BLACKBURN

Lancashire
Map ref 4A1

Once a thriving cotton town. Models of the old machinery may be seen in Lewis Textile Museum. Relics of the Roman occupation in Blackburn Museum. 19th C cathedral, Victorian landscaped Corporation Park.
Tourist Information Centre ☎ (0254) 53277 or 55201 ext 214

Millstone Hotel ♨

Church Lane, Mellor, Nr. Blackburn, BB2 7JR
☎ Mellor (0254) 813333
Telex 635309

A beautiful old village inn with all the facilities of a modern hotel, in one of the loveliest villages of the Ribble Valley. Traditional hospitality. Gourmet restaurant and friendly bar offering good bar meals.
Bedrooms: 8 single, 8 double & 2 twin, 1 family room.
Bathrooms: 19 private.
Bed & breakfast: £57-£66 single, from £80 double.
Half board: from £71 daily.
Lunch available.
Evening meal 7pm (l.o. 9.45pm).
Parking for 45.
Credit: Access, Visa, Diners, Amex.

Northcote Manor Hotel ♨

COMMENDED
Northcote Road, Old Langho, Nr. Blackburn, BB6 8BE
☎ (0254) 240555
Fax (0254) 246568
Pleasant country house hotel in true English style. Warm and friendly atmosphere in an ideal location for business and pleasure.
Bedrooms: 4 double & 2 twin.
Bathrooms: 6 private.
Bed & breakfast: £57-£67 single, £67-£77 double.
Half board: £77-£87 daily.
Lunch available.
Evening meal 7pm (l.o. 9.30pm).
Parking for 50.
Credit: Access, Visa, Diners, Amex.

BLACKPOOL

Lancashire
Map ref 4A1

Largest fun resort in the North with every entertainment including amusement parks, piers, tram-rides along the promenade, sandy beaches and the famous Tower. Among its annual events are the 'Milk Race', the Veteran Car Run and the spectacular autumn illuminations.
Tourist Information Centre ☎ (0253) 21623 or 21891 or (weekdays only) 25212

Adelphi Private Hotel ♨

44 King Edward Avenue, Blackpool, FY2 9TA
☎ (0253) 52932

Family-owned and run hotel, off North Promenade, close to Gynn Gardens and North Shore Golf Club.
Bedrooms: 5 single, 1 double, 3 family rooms.
Bathrooms: 5 private, 1 public.
Bed & breakfast: £13-£15 single, £26-£30 double.
Half board: £15-£17 daily, £101.50-£115.50 weekly.
Evening meal 5pm (l.o. 5pm).

Alberts Ramsden Arms Hotel ♨

Listed
204 Talbot Road, Blackpool, FY1 3AZ
☎ (0253) 23215
Traditional inn adjacent to station, theatre, town centre, beach. Offers real ale, real people and real atmosphere.
Bedrooms: 3 twin.
Bathrooms: 2 public.
Bed & breakfast: £15 single, £23 double.
Parking for 10.

Alderley Hotel ♨

APPROVED
581 South Promenade, Blackpool, FY4 1NG
☎ (0253) 42173
Family-run promenade hotel with emphasis on food and service. Convenient for all Blackpool's attractions.
Bedrooms: 6 double, 4 family rooms.
Bathrooms: 10 private.
Bed & breakfast: £30-£35 single, £45-£55 double.
Half board: £25-£30 daily.
Lunch available.
Evening meal 6pm (l.o. 6pm).
Parking for 8.
Credit: Access, Visa.

Ash Lodge

131 Hornby Road, Blackpool, FY1 4JG
☎ (0253) 27637
Small, private licensed hotel with a warm friendly welcome and good home cooking. Centrally located with ample car parking.
Bedrooms: 7 double & 2 twin, 3 family rooms.
Bathrooms: 5 private, 3 public.
Bed & breakfast: £11.50-£13 single, £23-£26 double.
Half board: £15-£18 daily, £98-£119 weekly.

Evening meal 5pm (l.o. 6.30pm).
Parking for 15.

Ashbeian Guest House

49 High Street, Blackpool N.S., FY1 2BN
☎ (0253) 26301
Convenient for lights, beach, central Blackpool and railway, yet in a quiet location. Choice of menu, good public parking.
Bedrooms: 3 double, 3 family rooms.
Bathrooms: 1 public.
Bed & breakfast: £9-£16 single, £17-£32 double.
Half board: £12-£19 daily, £70-£125 weekly.
Evening meal 5pm (l.o. 7pm).

The Hotel Bambi ♨

27 Bright Street, Blackpool S.S., FY4 1BS
☎ (0253) 43756
Friendly, family-run guesthouse with good facilities.
Bedrooms: 1 single, 3 double, 1 family room.
Bathrooms: 5 private.
Bed & breakfast: £12-£12.50 single, £24-£25 double.
Half board: £15.50-£16 daily, £108.50-£112 weekly.
Evening meal 5pm.
Parking for 2.
Credit: Access, Amex.

Baricia

40-42 Egerton Road, Blackpool C., FY1 2NW
☎ (0253) 23130
7 bedrooms with en-suite facilities, 5 bedrooms with washbasins and toilets. Separate tables and bar lounge, TV lounge. Home cooking.
Bedrooms: 3 single, 6 double & 3 twin.
Bathrooms: 7 private, 1 public.
Bed & breakfast: £12-£19 single, £24-£38 double.
Half board: £15-£22 daily, £105-£119 weekly.
Evening meal 5pm.
Open March-November.

Baron Hotel ♨

APPROVED
296 North Promenade, Blackpool, FY1 2EY
☎ (0253) 22729

Small, friendly hotel offering good food and personal service. Prominent position on the promenade, within easy reach of all amenities. All rooms en-suite.
Bedrooms: 8 double & 3 twin, 11 family rooms.
Bathrooms: 22 private.
Bed & breakfast: £20-£24 single, £36-£40 double.
Half board: £20-£22 daily, £119-£140 weekly.
Evening meal 5pm.
Parking for 12.

Bedford Hotel
298-300 North Promenade, Blackpool, FY1 2EY
☎ (0253) 23475
A well-managed family-run hotel on the seafront with indoor swimming pool and large comfortable bedrooms. Choice of menu available for all meals.
Bedrooms: 18 double & 6 twin, 18 family rooms.
Bathrooms: 42 private.
Bed & breakfast: £20-£40 single, £36-£72 double.
Half board: £20-£40 daily, £140-£240 weekly.
Lunch available.
Evening meal 6pm (l.o. 6.30pm).
Parking for 24.
Credit: Access, Visa.

Belmont Private Hotel M
Listed
9 Napier Avenue, Blackpool S.S., FY4 1PA
☎ (0253) 42383
Comfortable, family-run, relaxing hotel with friendly atmosphere. All bedrooms tastefully furnished. Well-stocked bar, personal and caring service. Close to promenade, Pleasure Beach and Sandcastle.
Bedrooms: 4 single, 3 double & 1 twin, 1 family room.
Bathrooms: 1 public.
Bed & breakfast: £12-£15 single, £24-£30 double.
Half board: £14-£17 daily, £70-£95 weekly.
Evening meal 5pm.
Parking for 4.

Berwyn Hotel
COMMENDED
1 Finchley Road, Gynn Square, Blackpool, FY1 2LP
☎ (0253) 52896

20-bedroom residential licensed hotel overlooking the lovely Gynn Gardens. Chef de cuisine. Our standards are high and our aim is to please.
Bedrooms: 1 single, 10 double & 3 twin, 3 family rooms.
Bathrooms: 3 private, 3 public.
Bed & breakfast: £18-£22 single, £36-£44 double.
Half board: £21-£25 daily, £140-£150 weekly.
Evening meal 6pm (l.o. 6pm).
Parking for 3.

Beverley Hotel
27 Bank Street, Blackpool, FY1 1RN
☎ (0253) 24972
30-bedroomed, licensed hotel adjacent to promenade and close to North Pier, railway station, shops and theatre. Tea-making facilities in all rooms. Car park. Coaches welcome.
Bedrooms: 4 single, 20 double & 3 twin, 3 family rooms.
Bathrooms: 5 public.
Bed & breakfast: £10-£14 single, £20-£28 double.
Half board: £12-£17 daily, £84-£119 weekly.
Evening meal 5pm (l.o. 6pm).

Boston Hotel M
34 Queens Promenade, Blackpool, FY2 9RN
☎ (0253) 51451
Family-owned and managed hotel overlooking the cliffs, offering a choice of menu at all meals.
Bedrooms: 5 single, 21 double & 12 twin, 20 family rooms.
Bathrooms: 54 private, 2 public.
Bed & breakfast: £23.50-£29 single.
Half board: £29.50-£35 daily, £149-£196 weekly.
Lunch available.
Evening meal 6pm (l.o. 8pm).
Parking for 25.
Credit: Access, Visa, Amex.

The Brentwood Guest House
Listed APPROVED
18 Crystal Road, Blackpool, FY1 6BS
☎ (0253) 44462
Friendly, family-run guesthouse, very close to promenade and all amenities. We pride ourselves on cleanliness and good food.

Bedrooms: 2 single, 4 double, 4 family rooms.
Bathrooms: 2 public.
Bed & breakfast: £10-£15 single, £20-£30 double.
Half board: £13-£18 daily, £90-£126 weekly.
Evening meal 5pm (l.o. 5.30pm).
Open February-December.

Burlington Hotel
106 Burlington Road, Blackpool, FY4 1JR
☎ (0253) 44458
Small family-run hotel with home cooking, fully licensed with late bar, adjacent to pleasure beach and Sandcastle Leisure Centre. Ample parking.
Bedrooms: 3 double & 1 twin, 3 family rooms.
Bathrooms: 7 private.
Bed & breakfast: £11-£13.50 single.
Half board: £14.50-£17.50 daily, £89-£109.50 weekly.
Evening meal 5pm.

Carlee Guest House
115 Park Road, Blackpool C., FY1 4ET
☎ (0253) 28409
Small, guesthouse with friendly atmosphere. All of our guests leave as friends.
Bedrooms: 1 single, 4 double, 1 family room.
Bathrooms: 6 private.
Bed & breakfast: £15-£17 single, £26-£30 double.
Half board: £119-£133 weekly.
Evening meal 5.15pm (l.o. 5.30pm).
Parking for 5.

Ceba Hotel
COMMENDED
327 South Promenade, Blackpool, FY1 6BN
☎ (0253) 46489
Centrally situated on the promenade between the south and central piers, overlooking the Irish Sea.
Bedrooms: 12 double & 2 twin, 6 family rooms.
Bathrooms: 14 private, 3 public.
Bed & breakfast: £36-£50 double.
Evening meal 6pm (l.o. 8pm).
Parking for 6.
Open April-November.
Credit: Access, Visa.

Claremont House Hotel M
Listed COMMENDED
14 Gynn Avenue, Blackpool N.S., FY1 2LD
☎ (0253) 51783
Licensed private hotel. Home cooking. Close to town centre and theatres, situated on quiet North Shore. Family owned and managed. En-suite rooms available.
Bedrooms: 2 single, 3 double & 2 twin, 3 family rooms.
Bathrooms: 1 private, 2 public; 1 private shower.
Bed & breakfast: £12-£25 single, £24-£50 double.
Half board: £16-£25 daily, £75-£135 weekly.
Evening meal 5pm (l.o. 5.30pm).

Cliff Head M
APPROVED
174 Queens Promenade, Bispham, Blackpool, FY2 9JN
☎ (0253) 591086
Family-run hotel excellent corner position on the promenade. Overlooking the sea and with views to Cumbrian mountains.
Bedrooms: 1 single, 3 double & 2 twin, 1 family room.
Bathrooms: 7 private.
Bed & breakfast: £12.65-£17.25 single, £25.30-£34.50 double.
Half board: £16.70-£23 daily, £97.75-£125 weekly.
Evening meal 5pm (l.o. 7pm).
Parking for 4.

Cliffs Hotel M
Queens Promenade, Blackpool, FY2 9SG
☎ (0253) 52388 Fax (0253) 50039 Telex 67191 CLIFFS
Impressive 1930's style building. Seafront hotel with sauna, swimming pool and squash court. Entertainment nightly June-October.
Bedrooms: 1 single, 77 double & 70 twin, 13 family rooms.
Bathrooms: 161 private.
Bed & breakfast: £26.50-£50 single, £53-£82 double.
Half board: £36-£54 daily, £175-£250 weekly.
Lunch available.
Evening meal 6.30pm (l.o. 9pm).
Parking for 70.
Credit: Access, Visa, Amex.

BLACKPOOL
Continued

Collingwood Hotel ⋒
👑👑👑

8-10 Holmfield Road,
Blackpool N.S., FY2 9SL
☎ (0253) 52929
In a select area just off Queens Promenade and Gynn Gardens. Good reputation for service, home cooking, cleanliness and value for money. All rooms en-suite.
Bedrooms: 2 single, 9 double & 2 twin, 4 family rooms.
Bathrooms: 17 private.
Bed & breakfast: £14.95-£16.10 single, £29.90-£32.20 double.
Half board: £17.25-£19 daily, £95-£133 weekly.
Lunch available.
Evening meal 5pm.
Parking for 13.
Credit: Access, Visa.

Colris Hotel ⋒
👑👑👑

209 Central Promenade,
Blackpool, FY1 5DL
☎ (0253) 25461
Redesigned and newly appointed, giving the comfort of a continental hotel. Minutes from the town centre and shows.
Bedrooms: 2 single, 13 double & 11 twin, 4 family rooms.
Bathrooms: 30 private.
Bed & breakfast: £20-£25 single, £36-£42 double.
Half board: £25-£30 daily, £154-£175 weekly.
Lunch available.
Evening meal 5pm (l.o. 6pm).
Open March-October, December.

Dorchester Hotel

28 Queens Promenade,
Blackpool N.S., FY2 9RN
☎ (0253) 52508
Ideal seafront location on prestigious North Shore. Close to Tower, entertainment, shops, golf-course, Derby pool, children's boating and fun pool. Very spacious public areas for parties and functions.
Bedrooms: 16 double & 2 twin, 14 family rooms.
Bathrooms: 24 private, 5 public.
Bed & breakfast: £15-£30 single, £30-£60 double.
Half board: £17.50-£32.50 daily, £122.50-£160 weekly.
Lunch available.

Evening meal 6pm (l.o. 5pm).
Parking for 6.
Credit: Access, Visa.

Durban Guest House
Listed

32 Hesketh Avenue,
Bispham, Blackpool,
FY2 9JX
☎ (0253) 52844
Home-from-home. Small, family guesthouse, only 2 minutes to promenade and trams, adjacent to promenade and cliffs, overlooking fine sandy beaches.
Bedrooms: 4 double & 1 twin, 2 family rooms.
Bathrooms: 2 public.
Half board: £12.50-£15 daily.
Evening meal 5pm (l.o. 6pm).

Elgin Hotel ⋒

40-42 Queens Promenade,
Blackpool, FY2 9RW
☎ (0253) 51433
Friendly, family-run hotel offering good entertainment, fun, fine food. High standard of service in beautiful surroundings.
Bedrooms: 1 single, 9 double & 15 twin, 17 family rooms.
Bathrooms: 34 private, 2 public; 3 private showers.
Bed & breakfast: £18.50-£66.80 single, £28-£74 double.
Half board: £18.90-£41.50 daily, £125.30-£202.30 weekly.
Evening meal 5.45pm (l.o. 5.45pm).
Parking for 8.

Fern Royd Hotel

35 Holmfield Road,
Blackpool N.S., FY2 9TE
☎ (0253) 51066
Friendly family-run hotel adjacent to Queens Promenade. Good home cooking. Fresh produce used. Personal attention all times. Whirl-spa bath available.
Bedrooms: 1 single, 8 double & 2 twin, 2 family rooms.
Bathrooms: 4 private, 2 public.
Bed & breakfast: £11.50-£14 single.
Half board: £14.50-£17 daily, £100-£119 weekly.
Evening meal 5pm (l.o. 5.30pm).
Parking for 6.

Mains Hall Country House Hotel ⋒

Mains Lane, (A585), Poulton-le-Fylde, FY6 7LE
☎ (0253) 885130
16th C manor house steeped in history on the banks of the River Wyre, close to Blackpool and the Lake District.
Bedrooms: 4 double & 4 twin, 1 family room.
Bathrooms: 9 private.
Bed & breakfast: £35-£50 single, £55-£90 double.
Half board: £50-£65 daily, £350-£455 weekly.
Evening meal 7pm (l.o. 9pm).
Parking for 62.
Credit: Access, Visa.

Manor Private Hotel ⋒
👑👑👑

32 Queens Promenade,
Blackpool, FY2 9RN
☎ (0253) 51446
A friendly, family-run hotel, with accent on food and service.
Bedrooms: 2 single, 15 double & 9 twin, 3 family rooms.
Bathrooms: 27 private, 1 public.
Bed & breakfast: £36.38 double.
Half board: £19.80-£21.40 daily, £130.54-£133.75 weekly.
Lunch available.
Evening meal 5pm (l.o. 6pm).
Parking for 10.

Manor Royd Hotel
👑

96-98 Albert Road, Blackpool C., FY1 4PR
☎ (0253) 23175 & 26437
Central hotel, close to Winter Gardens, Tower, promenade and all holiday and shopping amenities.
Bedrooms: 22 double & 1 twin, 10 family rooms.
Bathrooms: 26 private, 2 public.
Bed & breakfast: £20-£34 single, £28-£46 double.
Half board: £18-£28 daily, £90-£150 weekly.
Evening meal 5pm (l.o. 5.30pm).
Parking for 9.

Motel Mimosa ⋒
👑👑👑 **APPROVED**

24A Lonsdale Road,
Blackpool C., FY1 6EE
☎ (0253) 41906

Purpose built apartotel, personally supervised by resident owners. Adjacent to new car parking centre. Central yet in quiet location. Evening meal by arrangement. All rooms en-suite, central heating, car park.
Bedrooms: 12 double & 3 twin.
Bathrooms: 15 private.
Bed & breakfast: £15-£30 single, £30-£40 double.
Half board: £20-£30 daily, £110-£220 weekly.
Parking for 13.
Credit: Visa.

New Emerald Hotel ⋒

6-10 Regent Road, Blackpool, FY1 4LY
☎ (0253) 26075
Family-run hotel in town centre. Close to Winter Gardens, Stanley Park and North Station.
Bedrooms: 3 single, 12 double & 7 twin, 2 family rooms.
Bathrooms: 8 private, 5 public.
Bed & breakfast: £11.50-£15.50 single, £23-£31 double.
Half board: £14.50-£17.50 daily, £100-£120 weekly.
Evening meal 5pm (l.o. 4pm).
Parking for 5.

Newlyn Rex Hotel
👑👑👑

56-58 Central Drive,
Blackpool, FY1 5QB
☎ (0253) 25444
Located centrally for promenade, theatres, clubs, discos and shopping centre. Opposite car park for 800 cars.
Bedrooms: 6 single, 18 double & 3 twin, 7 family rooms.
Bathrooms: 16 private, 3 public.
Bed & breakfast: £17 single, £30-£34 double.
Half board: £18.50-£20.50 daily, £129.50-£143.50 weekly.
Evening meal 5pm.
Parking for 3.

The Ocean Hotel ⋒
👑👑👑

180-182 North Promenade,
Blackpool, FY1 1RJ
☎ (0253) 25958 & 23808
Family-run hotel close to the town centre and North Pier, with views of the Irish Sea.
Bedrooms: 2 single, 9 double & 6 twin, 6 family rooms.
Bathrooms: 23 private.

Bed & breakfast: £15-£25 single, £30-£50 double.
Half board: £19-£29 daily, £120-£150 weekly.
Evening meal 5.30pm (l.o. 6.30pm).
Parking for 16.

Parthian Guest House
35 Milbourne Street, Blackpool, FY1 3EU
☎ (0253) 25687
Family-run guesthouse close to town centre, Tower, entertainments, bus and rail depots. Offering clean, comfortable accommodation. Late keys provided.
Bedrooms: 3 double, 2 family rooms.
Bathrooms: 1 public.
Bed & breakfast: £10 single, £20 double.
Half board: £13 daily, £84 weekly.
Evening meal 5pm (l.o. 2.30pm).

Richmond House
270 Central Drive, Blackpool, FY1 5JB
☎ (0253) 48100
Small, friendly, licensed establishment close to town centre, promenade and leisure facilities.
Bedrooms: 1 single, 2 double & 1 twin, 4 family rooms.
Bathrooms: 2 private, 2 public.
Bed & breakfast: £9-£15 single, £18-£30 double.
Half board: £11.50-£18 daily, £80.50-£126 weekly.
Evening meal 5.30pm (l.o. 3pm).
Parking for 2.

Rock Dene Guest House
50 St. Chads Road, Blackpool, FY1 6BP
☎ (0253) 45810
Excellent home cooking on premises. Clean comfortable rooms, clients' individual needs catered for. Close to promenade and entertainments.
Bedrooms: 2 single, 6 double, 3 family rooms.
Bathrooms: 5 private, 2 public; 1 private shower.
Bed & breakfast: £10-£17 single, £20-£34 double.
Half board: £12-£20 daily, £65-£120 weekly.
Evening meal 5pm.
Parking for 2.

Roseheath Private Hotel ₥
110 Palatine Road, Blackpool, FY1 4HG
☎ (0253) 27613
Licensed private hotel in central Blackpool. Separate dining room, sun lounge, bar lounge and games room. Full central heating, hydro spa bath. Bedrooms fitted with satellite colour television and piped video.
Bedrooms: 2 double, 7 family rooms.
Bathrooms: 2 public.
Bed & breakfast: £12.65-£18.40 single, £25.30-£36.80 double.
Half board: £16.10-£21.85 daily, £69-£111.15 weekly.
Evening meal 5pm (l.o. 5pm).

Royal York Hotel
👑👑👑
242 North Promenade, Blackpool, FY1 1RZ
☎ (0253) 752424
All rooms en-suite with colour TV, tea making facilities, telephone. Choice of menu, entertainment nightly. Lift to all floors.
Bedrooms: 6 single, 15 double & 24 twin, 25 family rooms.
Bathrooms: 70 private.
Bed & breakfast: £19.50-£27.50 single, £39-£45 double.
Half board: £23.50-£30.50 daily, £164.50-£210.50 weekly.
Evening meal 6pm (l.o. 7pm).
Parking for 25.
Credit: Access, Visa.

Ruskin Hotel ₥
👑👑👑
55-61 Albert Road, Blackpool, FY1 4PW
☎ (0253) 24063 Fax (0253) 23571
Completely refurbished town centre hotel. Comfortable with good standards of service and cuisine. Conveniently located for all the shops, theatres and shows.
Bedrooms: 7 single, 30 double & 28 twin, 15 family rooms.
Bathrooms: 80 private.
Bed & breakfast: £30-£35 single, £50-£60 double.
Half board: £34-£39 daily, £210-£245 weekly.
Lunch available.
Evening meal 6pm (l.o. 8pm).

Parking for 16.
Credit: Access, Visa.

Sal-Mar Guest House
Listed APPROVED
138 Albert Road, Blackpool, FY1 4PL
☎ (0253) 23183
Small, central hotel, convenient for all Blackpool has to offer the visitor.
Bedrooms: 3 single, 2 double, 2 family rooms.
Bathrooms: 1 public.
Bed & breakfast: £11.50-£12.50 single, £22-£24 double.
Half board: £12.50-£13.50 daily, £84-£91 weekly.
Lunch available.
Evening meal 5pm (l.o. 6pm).
Parking for 4.

Shellard Hotel ₥
👑👑👑 COMMENDED
18-20 Dean Street, Blackpool S.S., FY1 4AU
☎ (0253) 42679
The hotel is tastefully decorated and furnished, providing comprehensive facilities for visitors, business delegates, disabled and elderly. Fully licensed. Car parking facilities.
Bedrooms: 2 single, 7 double & 7 twin, 4 family rooms.
Bathrooms: 20 private.
Bed & breakfast: £24-£26 single, £48-£52 double.
Half board: £29-£31 daily, £142-£171 weekly.
Evening meal 6pm (l.o. 7.30pm).
Parking for 17.
Credit: Access, Visa.

Sherwood Private Hotel ₥
👑👑👑
414 North Promenade, Blackpool, FY1 2LB
☎ (0253) 51898
A friendly hotel, occupying one of the finest positions on the promenade overlooking the sea. Our aim is to provide that extra personal touch with quality, at prices you can afford.
Bedrooms: 3 single, 14 double & 3 twin, 11 family rooms.
Bathrooms: 20 private, 2 public.
Bed & breakfast: £15.50-£17 single, £31-£34 double.

Half board: £19.50-£21.50 daily, £122.50-£136.50 weekly.
Lunch available.
Evening meal 5pm (l.o. 10pm).
Parking for 3.
Credit: Access, Visa.

Sunray Hotel ₥
👑👑👑 COMMENDED
42 Knowle Avenue, Blackpool, FY2 9TQ
☎ (0253) 51937
All-round service and care at modest prices, especially in low season.
Bedrooms: 3 single, 2 double & 2 twin, 2 family rooms.
Bathrooms: 9 private, 1 public.
Bed & breakfast: £20-£25 single, £40-£50 double.
Half board: £28-£35 daily, £180-£230 weekly.
Evening meal 5pm (l.o. 3pm).
Parking for 6.
Open January-November.

Tara Hotel ₥
👑👑👑 APPROVED
318-324 North Promenade, Blackpool, FY1 2JG
☎ (0253) 24460 Telex 677334
Promenade hotel with 62 bedrooms, all en-suite with private facilities. 3 bars, 2 restaurants, sun lounge and night spot, licensed until 2 am.
Bedrooms: 31 double & 31 twin.
Bathrooms: 62 private.
Bed & breakfast: £26-£32 single, £52-£150 double.
Half board: £26-£36 daily, £140-£252 weekly.
Evening meal 7pm (l.o. 9.30pm).
Parking for 30.
Credit: Access, Visa, Diners, Amex.

Warwick Hotel ₥
👑👑👑
603-609 New South Promenade, Blackpool, FY4 1NG
☎ (0253) 42192 Telex 677334
Ⓡ Best Western
Modern, seafront hotel with heated swimming pool, 2 bars, solarium and comfortable lounges.
Bedrooms: 9 single, 12 double & 4 twin, 27 family rooms.
Bathrooms: 52 private.

Continued ▶

BLACKPOOL
Continued

Bed & breakfast: £30.50-£38.50 single, £51.50-£65.50 double.
Half board: £34.25-£42 daily, £227.75-£279.25 weekly.
Lunch available.
Evening meal 7pm (l.o. 9pm).
Parking for 50.
Credit: Access, Visa, Diners, Amex.

⛷ ▓ ◫ ▤ ♿ 🅿 ⓘ Ⓥ ◄ ◉
▦ ⚓ 🏋 🐕 ⁽ᴰᴬᴾ⁾ ⚲ SP T

Wilton Hotel
22 Alexandra Road,
Blackpool, FY1 6BU
☎ (0253) 46673
Ideal family hotel close to all amenities. 50 yards from beach. Cabarets and entertainment.
Bedrooms: 10 double, 8 family rooms.
Bathrooms: 11 private, 2 public.
Bed & breakfast: from £24 double.
Half board: from £28.75 daily, from £88.50 weekly.
Evening meal 5pm (l.o. 4pm).
Parking for 15.

⛷ ▤ ♿ ⓘ Ⓥ ◄ ◉ ⚓ ▲ ✿
✱ ⁽ᴰᴬᴾ⁾ ⚲ SP T

The Windsor Hotel
♔♔♔
21 King Edward Avenue,
Blackpool, FY2 9UH
☎ (0253) 53735
A small select hotel with beautifully furnished public rooms, offering home cooking from quality produce. Polite efficient service.
Bedrooms: 2 single, 4 double & 2 twin.
Bathrooms: 5 private, 1 public.
Bed & breakfast: £14-£16 single, £28-£32 double.
Half board: £32-£38 daily.
Evening meal 5pm.
Parking for 2.

▤ ♿ ⓘ Ⓥ ◄ ⓉⓋ ▦ ✱ ▨
⁽ᴰᴬᴾ⁾ ⚲ SP T

Woodleigh Private Hotel M
Listed
32 King Edward Avenue,
Blackpool, FY2 9TA
☎ (0253) 593624
Small, friendly hotel, 2 minutes to Queens Promenade. Tea-making facilities in all rooms. Full central heating. En-suite rooms available.
Bedrooms: 2 single, 5 double & 1 twin, 2 family rooms.
Bathrooms: 6 private, 1 public.

Bed & breakfast: £11-£14 single, £22-£28 double.
Half board: £14.50-£18.50 daily, £87.50-£110 weekly.
Evening meal 5pm.
Open April-November.

⛷ ▤ ♿ ⓤⓛ ⓘ ◄ ⓉⓋ ▦ ✱
▦ ⁽ᴰᴬᴾ⁾ SP

BOLTON
Gtr. Manchester
Map ref 4A1

Once a prosperous cotton town with Civil War connections. Attractions include Hall i' th' Wood, Smithill's Hall, Central Museum, Art Gallery and Octagon Theatre.
Tourist Information Centre ☎ (0204) 22311 ext 1025/1026/1029 or 384174

Egerton House Hotel M
♔♔♔♔ **COMMENDED**
Blackburn Road, Egerton,
Bolton, BL7 9PL
☎ (0204) 57171 Fax (0204) 593030 Telex 635322
ⓒⓡ Character
Dating back to the 17th C, this small country house hotel, set in 4.5 acres of landscaped gardens, offers the elegance of years gone by enhanced with 20th C facilities.
Bedrooms: 7 single, 17 double & 1 twin, 7 family rooms.
Bathrooms: 32 private.
Bed & breakfast: £50-£67 single, £65-£83 double.
Lunch available.
Evening meal 7pm (l.o. 9.30pm).
Parking for 150.
Credit: Access, Visa, Diners, Amex.

⛷ ✆ ▤ ♿ ⓘ Ⓥ ◄ ◉
▦ ⚓ 🏋 🐾 ✿ SP T

Last Drop Village Hotel M
♔♔♔
Hospital Road, Bromley Cross, Bolton, BL7 9PZ
☎ (0204) 591131
Telex 635322
ⓒⓡ Character
A collection of 18th C farm buildings transformed into a "living village", with 2 restaurants, tea shop, leisure club and hotel.
Bedrooms: 25 double & 35 twin, 23 family rooms.
Bathrooms: 83 private.
Bed & breakfast: £50-£70 single, £65-£85 double.
Lunch available.
Evening meal 7pm (l.o. 10.30pm).
Parking for 400.

Credit: Access, Visa, Diners, Amex.

⛷ ▓ ◫ ✆ ▤ ♿ ⓘ Ⓥ
▦ ◉ Ⓤ ▦ ⚓ 🏋 ⚲ ☒ ✱ ♿
▶ ✿ ⚲ SP ▦ T

Morden Grange
15 Chadwick Street, Haulgh,
Bolton, BL2 1JN
☎ (0204) 22000
Attractive double fronted detached residence with several stained glass windows and antique pine staircase. Situated 5 minutes' walking distance from the town centre.
Bedrooms: 1 single, 1 double & 1 twin, 4 family rooms.
Bathrooms: 1 public.
Bed & breakfast: from £12 single, from £22 double.
Half board: £15-£16 daily, £95-£102 weekly.
Evening meal 6pm.

⛷ ▤ ♿ ⓤⓛ ⓘ Ⓥ ◄ ⓉⓋ ▦
⚓ ✱

BRAMHALL
Gtr. Manchester
Map ref 4B2

Tourist Information Centre ☎ (061) 440 8400

Bramhall Moat House M
♔♔♔♔♔
Bramhall Lane South,
Bramhall, Stockport,
Cheshire SK7 2EB
☎ 061-439 8116 Fax 061-440 8071 Telex 668464
ⓒⓡ Queens Moat Houses
Modern purpose-built hotel in residential area, between Peak District National Park and Manchester city centre.
Bedrooms: 1 single, 11 double & 51 twin, 2 family rooms.
Bathrooms: 65 private.
Bed & breakfast: £40-£77.50 single, £55-£95 double.
Half board: £52.95-£90.45 daily, max. £520.65 weekly.
Lunch available.
Evening meal 7pm (l.o. 9.45pm).
Parking for 130.
Credit: Access, Visa, Diners, Amex.

⛷ ▓ ✆ ▤ ♿ ⓘ Ⓥ ◄
◉ ⚲ ▦ ⚓ 🏋 ♿ ⚙ ✱ SP
T

BROMBOROUGH
Merseyside
Map ref 4A2

Residential town in beautiful Wirral countryside, yet within easy reach of Birkenhead, Liverpool and Chester.

Cromwell Hotel M
♔♔♔♔ **COMMENDED**
High Street, Bromborough,
Wirral, L62 7HZ
☎ 051-334 2917 Fax 051-346 1175 Telex 628225
ⓒⓡ Lansbury
A new hotel, convenient for the bustling city of Liverpool and the countryside of north Wales.
Bedrooms: 3 single, 7 double & 18 twin, 3 family rooms.
Bathrooms: 31 private.
Bed & breakfast: £22-£64 single, £44-£78 double.
Half board: from £33 daily.
Lunch available.
Evening meal 7pm (l.o. 10pm).
Parking for 102.
Credit: Access, Visa, Diners, Amex.

⛷ ▓ ✆ ◫ ▤ ♿ ⓘ Ⓥ
⚲ ◄ ◉ ⚓ 🏋 SP T

Dresden Hotel
♔♔♔
866 New Chester Road,
Bromborough, L62 7HF
☎ 051-334 1331 & 1353
Owned and managed by a Swiss family on continental lines and with the Swiss tradition of personal service.
Bedrooms: 4 single, 1 double & 1 twin.
Bathrooms: 2 private, 1 public.
Bed & breakfast: from £22.50 single, £30.80-£39.50 double.
Half board: from £30 daily, from £200 weekly.
Lunch available.
Evening meal 7pm (l.o. 9pm).
Parking for 20.

⛷ ◉ ♿ ⓘ Ⓥ ◄ ⓉⓋ ▦ ⚓
🏋 ✱ ▦

Individual proprietors have supplied all details of accommodation. Although we do check for accuracy, we advise you to confirm prices and other information at the time of booking.

BURNLEY

Lancashire
Map ref 4B1

Once the largest cotton-weaving centre in the world but now dominated by engineering. 14th C Towneley Hall has fine period rooms and the entrance hall houses an art gallery and museum. The Kay-Shuttleworth collection of lace and embroidery can be seen at Gawthorpe Hall (National Trust).
Tourist Information Centre ☎ (0282) 30055

Alexander Hotel
👑👑👑 COMMENDED

2 Tarleton Avenue, Todmorden Road, Burnley, BB11 3ET
☎ (0282) 22684
Family-run hotel with accent on personal service. Near the town centre, in quiet residential area.
Bedrooms: 8 single, 4 double & 4 twin, 1 family room.
Bathrooms: 13 private, 1 public; 1 private shower.
Bed & breakfast: £20-£33 single, £44 double.
Half board: £25-£42 daily.
Evening meal 6.15pm (l.o. 9pm).
Parking for 16.
Credit: Access, Visa.

Higher Trapp Country House Hotel M
👑👑👑 COMMENDED

Trapp Lane, Simonstone, Nr. Burnley, BB12 7QW
☎ (0282) 72781
Country house hotel with terraced gardens set in 4.5 acres. Take the M65 junction 8 turn-off, follow the A6068 Clitheroe road, turn left at second set of lights, first right, 1.5 miles on left.
Bedrooms: 4 single, 9 double & 3 twin.
Bathrooms: 16 private.
Bed & breakfast: £30-£45 single, £45-£55 double.
Lunch available.
Evening meal 7pm (l.o. 10pm).
Parking for 70.
Credit: Access, Visa.

Keirby Hotel M
👑👑👑👑

Keirby Walk, Burnley, BB11 2DH
☎ (0282) 27611 Telex 63119
Friendly
Modern town centre hotel with banqueting and conference facilities for 300.
Bedrooms: 38 single, 4 double & 4 twin, 3 family rooms.
Bathrooms: 49 private.
Bed & breakfast: £49-£58 single, £58.50-£66 double.
Half board: £40.75-£70 daily.
Lunch available.
Evening meal 7pm (l.o. 10pm).
Parking for 64.
Credit: Access, Visa, C.Bl., Diners, Amex.

Oaks Hotel M
👑👑👑👑

Colne Road, Reedley, Pendle, Burnley, BB10 2LF
☎ (0282) 414141
Telex 635309 The Oak G
Offering sophisticated bedroom amenities and leisure and conference facilities. Indoor pool, jacuzzi, gym, sauna and solarium.
Bedrooms: 12 single, 35 double & 5 twin, 6 family rooms.
Bathrooms: 58 private.
Bed & breakfast: £75-£85 single, £90-£100 double.
Half board: £89-£99 daily.
Lunch available.
Evening meal 7pm (l.o. 9.45pm).
Parking for 150.
Credit: Access, Visa, Diners, Amex.

Ormerod Private Hotel
121-123 Ormerod Road, Burnley, BB11 3QW
☎ (0282) 23255
Small bed and breakfast hotel in quiet, pleasant surroundings, facing local parks. Recently refurbished, all en-suite facilities. 5 minutes from town centre.
Bedrooms: 3 single, 3 double & 3 twin, 1 family room.
Bathrooms: 10 private.
Bed & breakfast: £16-£22 single, £30-£33 double.
Parking for 7.

BURY

Gtr. Manchester
Map ref 4B1

Birthplace of Sir Robert Peel, Prime Minister and founder of police force, commemorated by statue in market-place. Transport Museum contains items connected with steam railways.

The Bolholt Hotel & Restaurant M
👑👑👑

off Walshaw Road, Bury, BL8 1PS
☎ 061-764 5239 & 3888
Large family-run hotel and conference centre in a historic and picturesque setting. Home-cooked fresh food our speciality.
Bedrooms: 11 single, 26 double & 8 twin, 2 family rooms.
Bathrooms: 41 private, 3 public.
Bed & breakfast: £38-£47 single, max. £59 double.
Half board: £39.50-£58 daily.
Lunch available.
Evening meal 7pm (l.o. 9pm).
Parking for 150.
Credit: Access, Visa, Diners, Amex.

Normandie Hotel M
👑👑👑👑 COMMENDED

Elbut Lane, Birtle, Bury, BL9 6UT
☎ 061-764 3869 Telex 635091
A modern comfortable hotel, noted locally for the preparation and presentation of traditional French cooking.
Bedrooms: 7 single, 10 double & 7 twin.
Bathrooms: 24 private.
Bed & breakfast: £55-£65 single, £69-£79 double.
Lunch available.
Evening meal 7pm (l.o. 9.30pm).
Parking for 60.
Credit: Access, Visa, Diners, Amex.

The Old Mill Hotel & Restaurant M
👑👑👑👑👑 COMMENDED

Springwood, Ramsbottom, Nr. Bury, BL0 9DS
☎ (0706) 822991 Fax (0706) 822991
Converted old mill with old world appearance but 36 very modern bedrooms. Standing in its own grounds, close to city and country life. Full leisure centre, swimming pool, sauna, whirlpool, solarium and gymnasium.
Bedrooms: 12 single, 12 double & 12 twin.
Bathrooms: 36 private.
Bed & breakfast: £26.50-£39.50 single, £39-£54 double.
Half board: £38.50-£51.50 daily.
Lunch available.
Evening meal 6.30pm (l.o. 10.30pm).
Parking for 100.
Credit: Access, Visa, Diners, Amex.

CARNFORTH

Lancashire
Map ref 5B3

Permanent home of the 'Flying Scotsman' in Steamtown Railway Museum. Nearby are Borwick Hall, an Elizabethan manor house, and Leighton House which has good paintings and early furniture and is open to the public.

New Capernwray Farm
👑👑👑 COMMENDED

Capernwray, Nr. Carnforth, LA6 1AD
☎ (0524) 734284
Built 1697 with exposed beams and stone walls. Situated in peaceful valley with fine views. Convenient for M6. Reputation for warmth, comfort and good food.
Bedrooms: 1 double & 2 twin.
Bathrooms: 3 private.
Bed & breakfast: £34.50-£36.50 single, £49-£53 double.
Half board: from £51 daily.
Evening meal 7.30pm.
Parking for 4.

The Pine Lake Hotel M
👑👑👑👑

Pine Lake Resort, Carnforth, LA6 1JZ
☎ (0524) 736191 Telex 65459
Set amidst the 110 acres of Pine Lake Resort. Short distance from the M6 junction 35.
Bedrooms: 7 double & 13 twin, 3 family rooms.
Bathrooms: 23 private.
Continued ▶

The National Crown Scheme is explained in full on pages 556 – 558.

CARNFORTH
Continued

Bed & breakfast: £35-£46.50 single, £50-£55 double.
Half board: £37.50-£47.50 daily, £215-£450 weekly.
Lunch available.
Evening meal 6pm (l.o. 9.30pm).
Parking for 75.
Credit: Access, Visa, Diners, Amex.

Royal Station Hotel ⚑
APPROVED
Market Street, Carnforth, LA5 9BT
☎ (0524) 733636
Refurbished, comfortable, friendly hotel in centre of this historic market town surrounded by the beautiful countryside of Lonsdale. English Lakes 20 minutes, 1 mile junction 35 M6. English, French, Italian cooking.
Bedrooms: 1 single, 7 double & 3 twin, 1 family room.
Bathrooms: 12 private, 4 public.
Bed & breakfast: £24.50 single, £42 double.
Lunch available.
Evening meal 6pm (l.o. 8.30pm).
Parking for 18.
Credit: Access, Visa, Diners, Amex.

CHESTER
Cheshire
Map ref 4A2

Interesting Roman and medieval walled city rich in architectural and archaeological treasures. Fine timber-framed and plaster buildings. Shopping in the Rows (galleried arcades reached by steps from the street). Grosvenor Museum (Roman remains), 14th C cathedral, castle and zoo.
Tourist Information Centre ☎ (0244) 324324 or 351609

Abbots Well Hotel and Leisure Club ⚑
Whitchurch Road, Christleton, Chester, CH3 5QL
☎ (0244) 332121 Telex 61561

Embassy
Located 1.5 miles from Chester with extensive gardens adjoining open Green Belt. Modern comfortable bedrooms, pleasant atmosphere and popular bar. Leisure facilities.
Bedrooms: 26 single, 15 double & 85 twin, 1 family room.
Bathrooms: 127 private.
Bed & breakfast: £26-£29 single, £80-£92 double.
Half board: £36-£39 daily.
Lunch available.
Evening meal 7pm (l.o. 10pm).
Parking for 250.
Credit: Access, Visa, Diners, Amex.

Aplas Guest House ⚑
Listed APPROVED
106 Brook Street, Chester, CH1 3DU
☎ (0244) 312401
Family-run guesthouse offering a warm and friendly service. 5 minutes from city centre, 2 minutes from railway station.
Bedrooms: 1 single, 3 double & 2 twin, 1 family room.
Bathrooms: 5 private, 1 public.
Bed & breakfast: max. £15 single, £20-£25 double.

Cavendish Hotel ⚑
42-44 Hough Green, Chester, CH4 8JQ
☎ (0244) 675100
Fax (0244) 679942
Beautifully restored Victorian hotel set in landscaped gardens. 1 mile from city centre on main A549 coast road to north Wales.
Bedrooms: 2 single, 6 double & 8 twin, 4 family rooms.
Bathrooms: 16 private, 3 public.
Bed & breakfast: £25-£39.50 single, £39.50-£49.50 double.
Half board: min. £29 daily.
Lunch available.
Evening meal 7pm (l.o. 9pm).
Parking for 32.
Credit: Access, Visa, Diners, Amex.

Chester Grosvenor ⚑
HIGHLY COMMENDED
Eastgate Street, Chester, CH1 1LT
☎ (0244) 324024 Fax (0244) 313246 Telex 61240
Prestige

Owned by and named after one of England's oldest aristocratic families. The hotel completed a £12 million refurbishment in spring 1988. An ETB "5 Gold Crown" award hotel.
Bedrooms: 87 double.
Bathrooms: 87 private.
Bed & breakfast: from £115 single, from £175 double.
Lunch available.
Evening meal 6pm (l.o. 11pm).
Parking for 600.
Credit: Access, Visa, C.Bl., Diners, Amex.

Chestermill Euro Hotel ⚑
Milton Street, Chester, CH1 3NF
☎ (0244) 350035
Fax (0244) 45635
Old character Victorian cornmill conversion, offering the best of modern hotel facilities. City centre, free car park, cathedral and shops 5 minutes' walk. Restaurant, bar. 2 conference rooms. Please ask about our health club.
Bedrooms: 10 double & 28 twin, 14 family rooms.
Bathrooms: 52 private.
Bed & breakfast: £52-£62 single, £52-£70 double.
Half board: from £252 weekly.
Lunch available.
Evening meal 7pm (l.o. 10pm).
Parking for 80.
Credit: Access, Visa, Diners, Amex.

City Walls Hotel & Restaurant ⚑
City Walls Road, 14 Stanley Place, Chester, CH1 2LU
☎ (0244) 313416
A charming Georgian hotel situated on the old city walls, overlooking Chester racecourse. Noted for accommodation, food and service.
Bedrooms: 4 single, 6 double & 2 twin, 4 family rooms.
Bathrooms: 16 private.
Bed & breakfast: from £35 single, from £50 double.
Half board: from £37 daily, from £222 weekly.
Lunch available.

Evening meal 7pm (l.o. 8.30pm).
Parking for 3.
Credit: Access, Visa.

Crabwall Manor Hotel and Restaurant ⚑
HIGHLY COMMENDED
Parkgate Road, Mollington, Chester, CH1 6NE
☎ Great Mollington
(0244) 851666 Telex 61220 CRAWAL
Country house hotel set in 11 acres of formal gardens and parkland, 2 miles north of Chester. Reputation for high standards and quality of service and food. Indoor heated pool, sauna, squash courts (completion in Spring 1991), snooker room completed.
Bedrooms: 2 double & 46 twin.
Bathrooms: 48 private.
Bed & breakfast: £80-£142.50 single, £120-£160 double.
Lunch available.
Evening meal 7pm (l.o. 9.45pm).
Parking for 120.
Credit: Access, Visa, Diners, Amex.

Curzon Hotel ⚑
54 Hough Green, Chester, CH4 8JQ
☎ (0244) 678581
Queens Moat Houses
Large Victorian house set well back in its own grounds. Close to golf, River Dee, racecourse, leisure centre and all amenities.
Bedrooms: 6 single, 7 double & 1 twin, 2 family rooms.
Bathrooms: 16 private.
Bed & breakfast: £38-£40 single, £48-£50 double.
Half board: £80-£85 daily.
Evening meal 7pm (l.o. 9.30pm).
Parking for 18.
Credit: Access, Visa, Diners, Amex.

Half board prices shown are per person but in some cases may be based on double/twin occupancy.

Dene Hotel M
🏆🏆🏆🏆 APPROVED

Hoole Road, Chester,
CH2 3ND
☎ (0244) 321165 Fax (0244)
350277
*Family-owned hotel
conveniently situated on A56
approach to city centre.
Adjacent to Alexandra Park.*
Bedrooms: 11 single,
21 double & 13 twin, 4 family
rooms.
Bathrooms: 47 private,
2 public.
Bed & breakfast: £35-£37
single, £46-£48 double.
Evening meal 7pm (l.o.
8.30pm).
Parking for 50.
Credit: Access, Visa.

Derry Raghan Guest House M
Listed APPROVED

54 Hoole Road, Chester,
CH2 3NL
☎ (0244) 318740
*Friendly, spacious Victorian
guesthouse 1 mile from historic
city centre, 2 miles from
Chester Zoo. Close to
motorway network M56 and
M53.*
Bedrooms: 1 single, 2 double
& 1 twin.
Bathrooms: 2 private,
1 public.
Bed & breakfast: £13-£15
single, £24-£26 double.
Parking for 6.

Edwards House Hotel M
🏆🏆🏆

61-63 Hoole Road, Chester,
CH2 3NJ
☎ (0244) 318055
*Early Victorian hotel with well
proportioned bedrooms, all en-
suite and fitted to a high
standard.*
Bedrooms: 4 double, 4 family
rooms.
Bathrooms: 8 private.
Bed & breakfast: £25-£26
single, £34-£35 double.
Half board: £28-£28.50 daily,
£190-£193.25 weekly.
Evening meal 6.30pm (l.o.
7.30pm).
Parking for 8.
Credit: Access, Visa.

Frogg Manor Hotel & Restaurant M
🏆🏆🏆🏆 COMMENDED

Fullers Moor, Nantwich
Road, Broxton, Chester,
CH3 9JH
☎ Broxton (082 925) 629
*Grade II listed period house of
Georgian origins, located
between Nantwich and
Wrexham on the A534.*
Bedrooms: 6 double.
Bathrooms: 6 private,
1 public.
Bed & breakfast: £44.70-
£72.75 single, £46.50-£85.50
double.
Half board: £64.70-£92.75
daily.
Lunch available.
Evening meal 7pm (l.o.
10pm).
Parking for 30.
Credit: Access, Visa, C.Bl.,
Diners, Amex.

Gables Guest House M
Listed APPROVED

5 Vicarage Road, Off Hoole
Road, Chester, CH2 3HZ
☎ (0244) 323969
*Guesthouse in quiet road 1 mile
from city centre. Park and
tennis courts nearby. Easy
access to motorways.*
Bedrooms: 2 double & 2 twin,
3 family rooms.
Bathrooms: 2 public.
Bed & breakfast: £13-£18
single, £26-£28 double.
Parking for 7.

Glann Hotel M
🏆🏆 APPROVED

2 Stone Place, Hoole,
Chester, CH2 3NR
☎ (0244) 344800
*Friendly relaxed atmosphere,
family owned in a quiet
location. Comfortable lounge
with bar and large private car
park. Good food.*
Bedrooms: 2 single, 3 double
& 2 twin.
Bathrooms: 5 private,
1 public.
Bed & breakfast: £16-£18
single, £30-£40 double.
Half board: £24-£26 daily.
Evening meal 6.30pm (l.o.
8pm).
Parking for 15.
Credit: Access, Visa.

Green Bough Hotel M
🏆🏆🏆

60 Hoole Road, Chester,
CH2 3NL
☎ (0244) 326241
*A comfortable, family-run hotel
with friendly, relaxed
atmosphere. Tastefully
decorated with many antique
furnishings. Restaurant
renowned for good English
cooking.*
Bedrooms: 11 double &
2 twin, 5 family rooms.
Bathrooms: 16 private,
1 public.
Bed & breakfast: £34.50-£38
single, £43-£47 double.
Half board: £30.45-£33.50
daily, £196-£215.60 weekly.
Lunch available.
Evening meal 7pm (l.o. 8pm).
Parking for 21.
Credit: Access, Visa.

Hoole Hall Hotel
Warrington Road, Hoole
Village, Chester, CH1 3PD
☎ (0244) 350011 Fax (0244)
320251 Telex 61292
*Set in 5 acres of parkland, 1
mile from Chester, half mile
from terminal junction M53.
High quality modern amenities
complement the historic
aspects.*
Bedrooms: 57 double &
42 twin.
Bathrooms: 99 private.
Bed & breakfast: from £74.50
single, from £89 double.
Lunch available.
Evening meal 7pm (l.o.
10pm).
Parking for 200.
Credit: Access, Visa, Amex.

Latymer House M
🏆🏆

82 Hough Green, Chester,
CH4 8JW
☎ (0244) 675074
*Charming, comfortable house
set in its own gardens. All
bedrooms en-suite. Residential
licence. Large car park.
Emphasis on cooking to guests'
tastes.*
Bedrooms: 3 single, 3 double
& 4 twin, 1 family room.
Bathrooms: 11 private,
1 public.
Bed & breakfast: £20.50-£25
single, £33-£37 double.
Half board: £25-£33.50 daily,
£175-£234.50 weekly.
Evening meal 7pm (l.o. 5pm).
Parking for 20.

Malvern Guest House
21 Victoria Road, Chester,
CH2 2AX
☎ (0244) 380865
*Victorian terraced town house
comprising 2 storeys, within 8
minutes' walk of the cathedral
and adjacent to a leisure
centre.*
Bedrooms: 1 single, 1 double
& 2 twin, 2 family rooms.
Bathrooms: 2 public.
Bed & breakfast: £10-£12
single, £20-£24 double.
Half board: £14-£16 daily,
£87.50-£99.50 weekly.
Evening meal 6pm (l.o. 5pm).

Ormonde Guest House
126 Brook Street, Chester,
CH1 3DU
☎ (0244) 328816
*This 18th C Tudor style
building was frequented by a
former Duke of Westminster
whose horse was named
Ormonde, hence the name. 2
minutes from the railway
station.*
Bedrooms: 2 single, 3 double
& 5 twin, 2 family rooms.
Bathrooms: 8 private,
1 public.
Bed & breakfast: £12-£15
single, £23-£25 double.

Plantation Quality Inn M
🏆🏆🏆🏆

Liverpool Road, Chester,
CH2 1AG
☎ (0244) 374100 Telex 61263
*Elegantly converted Georgian
mansion house, only 5 minutes'
walk from the city centre.
Squash and swimming
available 100 yards away.
Dancing available until 2.00am
Tuesday to Friday, with dinner
dances held each Saturday
evening. Free parking for 150
vehicles.*
Bedrooms: 22 single,
16 double & 34 twin, 6 family
rooms.
Bathrooms: 78 private.
Bed & breakfast: £52.50-£76
single, £69.50-£101 double.
Lunch available.
Evening meal 7pm (l.o.
10.30pm).
Parking for 150.
Credit: Access, Visa, C.Bl.,
Diners, Amex.

**Map references apply to the colour maps
towards the end of this guide.**

CHESTER
Continued

Hotel Romano ♨
♛♛♛
51 Lower Bridge Street,
Chester, CH1 1RS
☎ (0244) 320841
*17th C listed building
decorated in Romano/Italian
style. Languages spoken:
English, Italian, Spanish and
French. Children and group
bookings welcome.*
Bedrooms: 2 single, 8 double
& 5 twin, 3 family rooms.
Bathrooms: 16 private,
1 public; 2 private showers.
Bed & breakfast: £40-£60
single, £60-£80 double.
Half board: £48-£68 daily.
Lunch available.
Evening meal 6pm (l.o.
11.30pm).
Parking for 24.
Credit: Access, Visa, Diners,
Amex.

Rowton Hall Hotel ♨
Rowton Lane, Whitchurch
Road, Rowton, Chester,
CH3 6AD
☎ (0244) 335262 Telex 61172
ⓒ Consort
*Country house hotel set in 8
acres of garden, 2 miles from
Chester. Restaurant and bar
open to non-residents. Heated
indoor swimming pool.*
Bedrooms: 1 single, 24 double
& 14 twin, 3 family rooms.
Bathrooms: 42 private.
Bed & breakfast: £70-£80
single, £86-£96 double.
Lunch available.
Evening meal 7pm (l.o.
9.30pm).
Parking for 206.
Credit: Access, Visa, Diners,
Amex.

Vicarage Lodge Guest House
♛♛♛
11 Vicarage Road, Hoole,
Chester CH2 3HZ
☎ 0244-319533
*Large, Victorian house, off
Hoole Road. 1 mile from city
centre. Large car park.*
Bedrooms: 1 double & 3 twin.
Bathrooms: 1 private,
1 public; 1 private shower.
Bed & breakfast: £14-£20
single, £24-£27 double.

Half board: £20-£26 daily,
£77-£132 weekly.
Evening meal 7pm.
Parking for 7.

Westminster Hotel ♨
♛♛♛
City Road, Chester,
CH1 3AF
☎ (0244) 317341
*This hotel and the Belgrave
Hotel are two friendly hotels
adjacent to the railway station.
Entertainment most evenings.*
Bedrooms: 13 single,
11 double & 35 twin,
10 family rooms.
Bathrooms: 69 private.
Bed & breakfast: £33-£41
single, £49-£58 double.
Half board: £32-£42 daily,
£189-£231 weekly.
Lunch available.
Evening meal 6.30pm (l.o.
9pm).
Credit: Access, Visa.

Weston Hotel ♨
♛♛♛ APPROVED
82 Hoole Road, Chester,
CH2 3NT
☎ (0244) 326735
*The hotel is situated on a tree-
lined avenue, less than 1 mile
from the centre of historic
Chester, convenient for
M53/M56 and M6.*
Bedrooms: 1 single, 2 double
& 3 twin, 2 family rooms.
Bathrooms: 5 private,
1 public.
Bed & breakfast: £23-£30
single, £35-£40 double.
Evening meal 7pm (l.o. 8pm).
Parking for 30.
Credit: Access, Visa.

CHIPPING
Lancashire
Map ref 4A1

Gibbon Bridge Country House & Restaurant ♨
Moss Lane, Chipping, Nr.
Preston, PR3 2TQ
☎ (0995) 61456 Fax (0995)
61277
*Delightful country house in the
heart of the Ribble Valley.
Privately owned and run
accommodation with health
and gym facilities, beauty
salon, tennis court, helipad and
conference facilities.*
Bedrooms: 1 single, 3 double
& 5 twin, 22 family rooms.
Bathrooms: 31 private.

Bed & breakfast: £50-£100
single, £60-£110 double.
Half board: £50-£115 daily.
Lunch available.
Evening meal 7pm (l.o. 8pm).
Parking for 150.
Credit: Access, Visa.

CHORLEY
Lancashire
Map ref 4A1

*10m NW. Bolton
Despite its cotton-
weaving background,
Chorley has a busy
market town atmosphere.
Jacobean Astley Hall, set
in extensive parkland, has
fine furniture and long
gallery with shovel-board
table.*

Hartwood Hall Hotel ♨
Preston Road, Chorley,
PR6 7AX
☎ (025 72) 69966
Fax (025 72) 41678
*A delightful hotel close to M61
and M6 motorways, within
easy reach of the coast and
Lake District.*
Bedrooms: 7 single, 9 double
& 4 twin, 2 family rooms.
Bathrooms: 18 private,
1 public; 4 private showers.
Bed & breakfast: £35-£50
single, £45-£60 double.
Lunch available.
Evening meal 7pm (l.o. 9pm).
Parking for 150.
Credit: Access, Visa, Diners,
Amex.

Roseneath Guest House ♨
♛♛
Preston Road, Charnock
Richard, Nr. Chorley,
PR7 5HH
☎ Coppull (0257) 791772
*Country guesthouse with large
gardens. All rooms en-suite
with colour TV and tea/coffee
facilities. Ample parking.
Situated on A49 between
Preston and Wigan, near
Charnock Richard service
area.*
Bedrooms: 1 single, 5 double
& 3 twin, 1 family room.
Bathrooms: 9 private,
1 public.
Bed & breakfast: £20-£22
single, £34-£36 double.
Parking for 23.

CLAYTON-LE-MOORS
Lancashire
Map ref 4A1

Small industrial town, 5
miles north-east of
Blackburn.

Sparth House Hotel & Restaurant ♨
♛♛♛ COMMENDED
Whalley Road, Clayton-le-
Moors, Accrington, BB5 5RP
☎ (0254) 872263
*Delightful, attractively
furnished listed building set in
its own large gardens, with
antique showroom attached.*
Bedrooms: 1 single, 9 double
& 4 twin.
Bathrooms: 14 private.
Bed & breakfast: £32-£50
single, £42-£75 double.
Lunch available.
Evening meal 8pm.
Parking for 53.
Credit: Access, Visa.

CLITHEROE
Lancashire
Map ref 4A1

*10m NE. Blackburn
Intriguing town with the
castle, set in lovely
gardens, as its chief
attraction. The castle and
keep house a museum
with special features
including an exhibition
relating to the Salthill
Geology Trail. The
Edisford Recreation Area
with pitch and putt, picnic
area and Ribblesdale
Pool, and the unique Civic
Hall cinema are further
attractions. Country
market on Tuesdays and
Saturdays.
Tourist Information
Centre ☎ (0200) 25566*

Calf's Head Hotel ♨
♛♛♛
Worston, Clitheroe,
BB7 1QA
☎ Clitheroe (0200) 41218
*Nestling at the foot of Pendle
Hill, relaxing hotel and
restaurant offering discerning
guests speciality dishes or
traditional fare. Restaurant
open daily for lunch and
dinner.*
Bedrooms: 3 double & 2 twin,
1 family room.
Bathrooms: 6 private,
1 public.

Bed & breakfast: £35-£40
single, £47-£55 double.
Lunch available.
Evening meal 7pm (l.o.
9.30pm).
Parking for 100.
Credit: Access, Visa, Diners,
Amex.

Manor House Cottage
28 Bridge Road, Chatburn,
Nr. Clitheroe, BB7 4AW
☎ (0200) 40111
*Cosy 17th C cottage full of
charm and character. Close to
A59 in centre of pretty Ribble
Valley village.*
Bedrooms: 1 single, 2 double
& 1 twin.
Bathrooms: 2 public.
Bed & breakfast: £13.50-£15
single, £27-£30 double.
Half board: £20-£21.50 daily.
Evening meal 6pm.
Parking for 4.
Credit: Visa.

Spread Eagle Hotel M
Sawley, Clitheroe, BB7 4NH
☎ (0200) 41202 & 41406
*Delightful old coaching inn on
banks of River Ribble, offering
modern accommodation in old
converted adjoining barn.
Luncheons and dinners served
daily.*
Bedrooms: 2 single, 6 twin,
2 family rooms.
Bathrooms: 10 private.
Bed & breakfast: £38-£52
single, £58-£62 double.
Lunch available.
Evening meal 7pm (l.o. 9pm).
Parking for 80.
Credit: Access, Visa, Diners,
Amex.

COWAN BRIDGE
Lancashire
Map ref 5B3

2m S. Kirkby Lonsdale

**Cobwebs Country House
and Restaurant** M
COMMENDED
Leck, Cowan Bridge, Kirkby
Lonsdale, Cumbria LA6 2HZ
☎ (052 42) 72141
*Victorian residence of
character. Log fires, creative
cooking, extensive wine list.
Located 2 miles east of Kirkby
Lonsdale on the A65. Dining
conservatory.*
Bedrooms: 3 double & 2 twin.

Bathrooms: 5 private.
Bed & breakfast: max. £30
single, max. £50 double.
Half board: max. £42.50
daily, max. £267 weekly.
Lunch available.
Evening meal 7.30pm (l.o.
8pm).
Parking for 20.
Open March-December.
Credit: Access, Visa.

CREWE
Cheshire
Map ref 4A2

Famous for its railway
junction. The railway
reached Crewe in 1837
when the Warrington to
Birmingham line passed
through, transforming this
small market town into
the first great railway
town.
*Tourist Information
Centre ☎ (0270) 583191
ext 691*

Crewe Arms Hotel M
Nantwich Road, Crewe,
CW1 1DW
☎ (0270) 213204
Ⓒ Embassy
*Victorian hotel 1 mile from
Crewe's town centre.
Comfortable bedrooms,
restaurant and popular bars.
Excellent road and rail links,
an ideal stopping place for
travellers.*
Bedrooms: 12 single,
16 double & 25 twin.
Bathrooms: 53 private.
Bed & breakfast: £50-£60
single, £65-£80 double.
Half board: from £62 daily,
from £344 weekly.
Lunch available.
Evening meal 7pm (l.o.
9.30pm).
Parking for 150.
Credit: Access, Visa, Diners,
Amex.

**Classifications
and quality
commendations
were correct at the
time of going to
press but are
subject to change.
Please check at the
time of booking.**

FORTON
Lancashire
Map ref 4A1

4m N. Garstang
Small, picturesque village
in the north-east of the
borough surrounded by
beautiful countryside.
*Tourist Information
Centre ☎ (0524) 792181*

Rank Motor Lodge M
Forton Services, M6 between
exits 32 & 33, Forton, Nr.
Lancaster, LA2 9DV
☎ (0524) 792227
*41 modern bedrooms, well
located for tourists and
business travellers to Lancaster
and the Lake District. Self-
service restaurant open 24
hours.*
Bedrooms: 2 double &
18 twin, 21 family rooms.
Bathrooms: 41 private.
Bed & breakfast: from £27.50
single, from £34.50 double.
Lunch available.
Evening meal 5pm (l.o.
10pm).
Parking for 50.
Credit: Access, Visa, Diners,
Amex.

FRODSHAM
Cheshire
Map ref 4A2

3m S. Runcorn
Spacious, tree-lined main
street flanked by 17th,
18th and 19th C buildings.
Near Delamere Forest
and Sandstone Trail.

Forest Hills Hotel M
COMMENDED
Belle Monte Road, Overton
Hill, Frodsham, WA6 6HH
☎ Runcorn (0928) 35255
Fax (0928) 35517
*Modern hotel with leisure
complex, situated on top of
Overton Hill with panoramic
views over the Mersey and
Weaver Valley.*
Bedrooms: 24 double &
30 twin, 4 family rooms.
Bathrooms: 58 private.
Bed & breakfast: £35-£65
single, £50-£80 double.
Half board: £35-£55 daily,
£245-£385 weekly.
Lunch available.
Evening meal 7pm (l.o.
9.45pm).
Parking for 250.

Credit: Access, Visa, Diners,
Amex.
● Display advertisement
appears on page 577.

Old Hall Hotel M
Main Street, Frodsham,
WA6 7AB
☎ (0928) 32052 & 31452
Telex 629794
*15th C town centre hotel
beautifully and sympathetically
modernised under the direction
of the resident owners.*
Bedrooms: 8 single, 12 double
& 2 twin, 1 family room.
Bathrooms: 23 private.
Bed & breakfast: £40-£55
single, £50-£65 double.
Lunch available.
Evening meal 7pm (l.o.
10pm).
Parking for 30.
Credit: Access, Visa, Diners,
Amex.

GARSTANG
Lancashire
Map ref 4A1

10m N. Preston
Garstang is in the east of
the borough and is a
picturesque country
market town. Regarded
as the gateway to the
fells, it stands on the
Lancaster Canal and is
popular as a cruising
centre. Close by are the
remains of Greenhalgh
Castle and the Bleasdale
Circle.

Crofters Hotel M
A6, Cabus, Garstang,
PR3 1PH
☎ (099 52) 4128
Ⓒ Consort
*A family owned and managed
hotel with all modern facilities,
situated midway between
Preston and Lancaster.*
Bedrooms: 1 single, 4 double
& 14 twin, 1 family room.
Bathrooms: 20 private.
Bed & breakfast: from £39.50
single, from £44.50 double.
Lunch available.
Evening meal 7pm (l.o.
10pm).
Parking for 200.
Credit: Access, Visa, Diners,
Amex.

GARSTANG

Continued

The Pickerings Country House Hotel & Restaurant M
♛♛♛

Garstang Road, Catterall, Nr. Garstang, PR3 0HA
☎ (0995) 602133
A delightful country house set in floodlit gardens, offering food for both traditional and more adventurous tastes.
Bedrooms: 2 single, 9 double & 2 twin, 1 family room.
Bathrooms: 14 private.
Bed & breakfast: £34-£50 single, £58-£90 double.
Lunch available.
Evening meal 7pm (l.o. 10pm).
Parking for 40.
Credit: Access, Visa, Diners.

HELSBY

Cheshire
Map ref 4A2

8m NE. Chester
Residential village with its own industries. Helsby Hill rises to 460 ft with fine views over the Helsby Estuary. Attractive hilly countryside to the south.

Highlands Private Hotel
♛♛♛

Alvanley Road, Helsby, WA6 9PT
☎ (092 82) 2664
The hotel, set in its own grounds on the wooded slopes of Helsby Hill, provides a peaceful and relaxing atmosphere.
Bedrooms: 6 single, 2 double & 1 twin.
Bathrooms: 5 private, 1 public.
Bed & breakfast: £24-£30 single, £50-£55 double.
Half board: £33-£35.50 daily.
Evening meal 6.30pm (l.o. 6.15pm).
Parking for 10.
Credit: Access.

The enquiry coupons at the back will help you when contacting proprietors.

HOLMES CHAPEL

Cheshire
Map ref 4A2

4m E. Middlewich
Large village with some interesting 18th C buildings and St. Luke's Church encased in brick hiding the 15th C original.

Holly Lodge Hotel
♛♛♛

70 London Road, Holmes Chapel, CW4 7AS
☎ (0477) 37033 Fax (0477) 35823
Charming Victorian country hotel, professionally managed and family-owned. Friendly and efficient service. Close to M6.
Bedrooms: 6 single, 15 double & 10 twin, 2 family rooms.
Bathrooms: 33 private.
Bed & breakfast: £27-£51 single, £43-£62 double.
Half board: £38.30-£62.30 daily, £300 weekly.
Lunch available.
Evening meal 7.30pm (l.o. 10pm).
Parking for 90.
Credit: Access, Visa, Diners, Amex.

HOYLAKE

Merseyside
Map ref 4A2

7m W. Birkenhead
Once a major port, this residential resort has good beaches, a 4-mile promenade and, nearby, the Royal Liverpool Golf Club. Variety of bird life on small offshore Hillbre Islands.

Kings Gap Court Hotel
♛♛

Valentia Road, Hoylake, Wirral, L47 2AN
☎ 051-632 2073
Old established family hotel close to seafront and many championship golf-courses. Ideal centre for Wales, Chester and Liverpool.
Bedrooms: 4 single, 22 twin, 1 family room.
Bathrooms: 17 private, 5 public.
Bed & breakfast: £22-£27 single, £30-£35 double.
Half board: £23.50-£27 daily, £125-£152 weekly.
Lunch available.

Evening meal 6.30pm (l.o. 7.30pm).
Parking for 89.

KNUTSFORD

Cheshire
Map ref 4A2

6m W. Wilmslow
Derives its name from Canute, King of the Danes, said to have forded the local stream. Ancient and colourful May Day celebrations. Nearby is the Georgian mansion of Tatton Park.
Tourist Information Centre ☎ (0565) 2611

The Cottons Hotel M
♛♛♛♛

Manchester Road, Knutsford, WA16 0SU
☎ (0565) 50333 Telex 669931
Hotel in the style of New Orleans, with restaurant offering traditional Creole dishes. Located in the heart of the Cheshire countryside, yet only minutes from Manchester Airport and the M6. 20 minutes from Chester.
Bedrooms: 29 double & 49 twin, 8 family rooms.
Bathrooms: 86 private.
Bed & breakfast: £94-£104 single, £110-£118 double.
Half board: £108-£118 daily.
Lunch available.
Evening meal 7pm (l.o. 10pm).
Parking for 200.
Credit: Access, Visa, Diners, Amex.

Dixon Arms Hotel M
♛♛♛

Knutsford Road, Chelford, Nr. Macclesfield, SK11 9AZ
☎ (0625) 861313
Originally a coaching house, on the A537 halfway between Knutsford and Macclesfield. Close to many places of interest.
Bedrooms: 2 single, 2 double & 5 twin, 2 family rooms.
Bathrooms: 11 private.
Bed & breakfast: £28-£42 single, £38-£52 double.
Lunch available.
Evening meal 6pm (l.o. 10pm).
Parking for 100.
Credit: Access, Visa, C.Bl., Diners, Amex.

Longview Hotel M
♛♛♛♛ COMMENDED

Manchester Road, Knutsford, WA16 0LX
☎ (0565) 2119 Fax (0565) 52402 Telex 61556
Period Victorian hotel with many antiques and a relaxed comfortable atmosphere, overlooking town common. Fine food. Close to exit 19 M6 and airport.
Bedrooms: 6 single, 8 double & 7 twin, 2 family rooms.
Bathrooms: 23 private.
Bed & breakfast: £30-£44 single, £45-£55 double.
Evening meal 7pm (l.o. 8.30pm).
Parking for 17.

Pickmere House
Listed

Park Lane, Pickmere, Nr. Knutsford, WA16 0JX
☎ (0565) 893433
Spacious rooms, most en-suite, in Georgian farmhouse, with extensive views over farmland. Rural location, 2.5 miles from M6 junction 19. Evening meal on request. Non-smokers only please.
Bedrooms: 3 single, 1 double & 2 twin, 3 family rooms.
Bathrooms: 5 private, 2 public.
Bed & breakfast: £15.50-£25.50 single, £28-£35 double.
Parking for 12.

Royal George Hotel M
♛♛♛

King Street, Knutsford, WA16 6EE
☎ (0565) 4151
In the historic town of Knutsford, close to the M6 and 5 miles south of Manchester. Built in the 14th C, one of the oldest hostelries in Cheshire. "Royal" because of Princess Victoria's visit. Mrs Gaskell wrote "Cranford" here.
Bedrooms: 13 single, 9 double & 5 twin, 4 family rooms.
Bathrooms: 31 private.
Bed & breakfast: £59-£65 single, max. £73 double.
Lunch available.
Evening meal 6pm (l.o. 10.30pm).
Parking for 47.
Credit: Access, Visa, Diners, Amex.

The Swan ♨
Chester Road, Bucklow Hill,
Nr. Knutsford, WA16 6RD
☎ (0565) 830295 Fax (0565)
830614 Telex 666911
🆑 De Vere
*In the beautiful Cheshire
countryside lies the uniquely
historic Swan. A blend of
history and modernity.*
Bedrooms: 21 single,
23 double & 15 twin,
11 family rooms.
Bathrooms: 70 private.
Bed & breakfast: £30-£70
single, £60-£80 double.
Lunch available.
Evening meal 7pm (l.o.
10pm).
Parking for 200.
Credit: Access, Visa, Diners,
Amex.
🕹 🖐 🚗 ☎ 🖵 🌣 🎅 📺 Ⓥ
🛏 ◉ 🏛 ♨ 🍴 🕹 ☀ 🅿 SP 📞
Ⓣ

Toft Hotel ♨
Toft Road, Knutsford,
WA16 9EH
☎ (0565) 3470 & 4443
Telex 667441
*A delightful Cheshire cottage-
style farmhouse. Tastefully
converted into a hotel and
restaurant. Close to M6, three-
quarters of mile south of
Knutsford on the A50. Non-
smokers only please.*
Bedrooms: 2 single, 8 double
& 2 twin.
Bathrooms: 12 private,
1 public.
Bed & breakfast: £19.50-£35
single, £31-£50 double.
Half board: £21.50-£31 daily.
Evening meal 7.30pm (l.o.
9pm).
Parking for 30.
Credit: Access, Visa.
🕹 10 🌣 Ⓥ ❌ 🛏 📺 💷 💻
🎅 🐾 🎅 SP 📞

**Individual
proprietors have
supplied all details
of accommodation.
Although we do
check for accuracy,
we advise you to
confirm prices and
other information
at the time of
booking.**

**Half board prices shown are per person
but in some cases may be based on
double/twin occupancy.**

Lancashire
Map ref 4A1

Interesting old county
town on the River Lune
with history dating back
to Roman times. Norman
castle, St. Mary's Church,
Customs House, Town
Hall (Regimental Museum
and Lancaster Museum),
Ashton Memorial are
among many places of
note. Good centre for
touring the Lake District.
*Tourist Information
Centre ☎ (0524) 32878*

Clarendon Hotel ♨
🏵🏵🏵 APPROVED
76 Marine Road West,
Morecambe, LA4 4EP
☎ (0524) 410180
*On the promenade and close to
entertainment. Panoramic
views of the Lakeland hills.*
Bedrooms: 5 single, 6 double
& 17 twin, 3 family rooms.
Bathrooms: 28 private,
4 public; 2 private showers.
Bed & breakfast: £28 single,
£39 double.
Half board: from £35.50
daily, from £180 weekly.
Lunch available.
Evening meal 7pm (l.o. 9pm).
Parking for 2.
Credit: Access, Visa, Diners,
Amex.
🕹 ☎ 🖵 🌣 🎅 Ⓥ 🛏 📺
◉ 🏆 🏛 💷 🍴 🕹 🐾 🍷 ☀ ◻ SP
Ⓣ

The Old Mill House ♨
🏵🏵 COMMENDED
Waggon Road, Lower
Dolphinholme, Nr. Lancaster,
LA2 9AX
☎ Forton (0524) 791855
*17th C mill house with
extensive landscaped gardens
on River Wyre. Private
woodland and ponds, adjacent
Forest of Bowland. 5 minutes
from junction 33 of M6.*
Bedrooms: 2 double & 1 twin.
Bathrooms: 2 public;
1 private shower.
Bed & breakfast: £19-£21
single, £28-£31 double.
Half board: £24.50-£30 daily,
£145-£190 weekly.
Evening meal 7pm (l.o.
midday).
Parking for 5.
🕹 🛏 ☎ 🌣 🎅 Ⓥ 🛏 📺 🏛
💷 ♄ 🎿 ☀ 🐾 SP 📞

Lancashire
Map ref 4A1

This parish can trace its
history back to Saxon
times when in 798 AD a
battle was fought at
Billangohoh from which
the names of Billington
and Langho were derived.
A flourishing community
of mainly cattle farms,
near both the River
Ribble and the River
Calder.

Mytton Fold Farm Hotel ♨
🏵🏵🏵 COMMENDED
Whalley Road, Langho, Nr.
Blackburn, BB6 8AB
☎ Blackburn (0254) 240662
Fax (0254) 248119
*10 miles from the M6 exit 31.
Peacefully secluded, yet only
300 yards from the A59. Ideal
centre for walking, fishing and
golf.*
Bedrooms: 13 double &
14 twin.
Bathrooms: 27 private.
Bed & breakfast: £29-£47
single, £46-£68 double.
Half board: £31-£55 daily,
£217-£385 weekly.
Lunch available.
Evening meal 6.30pm (l.o.
9.30pm).
Parking for 100.
Credit: Access, Visa.
🕹 6 🖐 🛏 ☎ 🖵 🌣 🎅 Ⓥ
🛏 🏛 💷 🍴 🕹 ☀ 🎅 SP 📞

Gtr. Manchester
Map ref 4B1

3m NE. Rochdale
Industrial town near
Hollingworth Lake and
the Pennine Way.
Rakewood viaduct and
country park.

Dearnley Cottage Hotel
🏵🏵🏵 COMMENDED
New Road, Littleborough,
Nr. Rochdale, OL15 8PL
☎ (0706) 79670
*Old world hotel, near country
park, moorland walks, sailing,
fishing, golfing and Pennine
Way.*
Bedrooms: 1 single, 7 double
& 2 twin.
Bathrooms: 10 private.
Bed & breakfast: £25-£32
single, £37-£47 double.
Half board: £30-£41 daily.
Lunch available.

Evening meal 6.30pm (l.o.
9.45pm).
Parking for 50.
Credit: Access, Visa.
🕹 🖐 🛏 ☎ 🖵 🌣 🎅 📺 Ⓥ ❌
🛏 ◉ 🏛 💷 SP

Merseyside
Map ref 4A2

Shipping and the sugar
and slave trades
transformed Liverpool
into a major port in the
18th C. Landmarks
include 2 cathedrals
(Anglican and Roman
Catholic), Town Hall,
Walker Art Gallery,
Merseyside Maritime
Museum. Excellent
shopping centre,
entertainment and sports
facilities (Aintree
Racecourse). Speke Hall
(National Trust).
*Tourist Information
Centre ☎ 051-709 3631
or 708 8854*

Aachen Hotel ♨
89-91 Mount Pleasant,
Liverpool, L3 5TB
☎ 051-709 3477 & 1126
*Listed building in conservation
area. Close to city centre,
theatres, shops, cinemas, rail
and bus stations and numerous
restaurants. Albert Dock and
Maritime Museum close by.*
Bedrooms: 2 single, 4 double
& 5 twin, 6 family rooms.
Bathrooms: 3 private,
3 public; 3 private showers.
Bed & breakfast: £17-£24
single, £30-£40 double.
Half board: £22.75-£44 daily,
£119-£208.25 weekly.
Evening meal 6.30pm (l.o.
8.30pm).
Parking for 2.
Credit: Access, Visa, Diners,
Amex.
🕹 🖐 🛏 ☎ 🖵 🌣 🎅 Ⓥ 🛏
📺 ◉ 🏛 💷 🎅 ◻ SP 📞 Ⓣ

Abbotsford
Listed
7 Adelaide Road, Crosby,
Seaforth, Liverpool, L21 1AR
☎ 051-928 6568
*Large Victorian house with
character. Pleasant garden.
Play facilities for children. TV,
tea and coffee facilities in
bedrooms. Close to Crosby
Marina and beach. Reduced
rates for children.*
Bedrooms: 1 single, 2 family
rooms.
Bathrooms: 2 public.
Continued ▶

LIVERPOOL
Continued

Bed & breakfast: max. £13.50 single, max. £26 double.
Parking for 4.
Open April-October.
⟋ ⟋ ⟋ ⟋ ⟋ ⟋ ⟋ ⟋ ⟋
⟋ ⟋

Alicia Hotel ⋔
3 Aigburth Drive, Inside Sefton Park, Liverpool, L17 3AA
☎ 051-727 4411 Telex 627657
Hotel in tranquil parkland setting but only a short distance from city centre. Ideal base for business or local tourist attractions. Only 5 minutes from Liverpool Airport. Courtesy transport available.
Bedrooms: 8 single, 20 double & 9 twin, 6 family rooms.
Bathrooms: 37 private, 1 public.
Bed & breakfast: £39.95-£55 single, £51.95-£68 double.
Lunch available.
Evening meal 6.30pm (l.o. 8.15pm).
Parking for 100.
Credit: Access, Visa, C.Bl., Diners, Amex.

Antrim Hotel ⋔
APPROVED
73 Mount Pleasant, Liverpool, L3 5TB
☎ 051-709 5239 & 9212
Fax 051-709 7169
Friendly, family-run city centre hotel, convenient for shops, railway and bus stations, Albert Dock, and 20 minutes from the airport.
Bedrooms: 6 single, 4 double & 8 twin, 2 family rooms.
Bathrooms: 7 private, 1 public; 9 private showers.
Bed & breakfast: £20-£30 single, £32-£42 double.
Half board: £28-£38 daily, £196-£266 weekly.
Evening meal 6pm (l.o. 8pm).
Parking for 2.
Credit: Access, Visa, Diners, Amex.

Aplin House Hotel ⋔
35 Clarendon Road, Garston, Liverpool, L19 6PJ
☎ 051-477 5047
Detached Victorian residence facing park. Airport 2 miles. City centre 10 minutes by frequent trains. Roadside parking.

Bedrooms: 3 twin, 2 family rooms.
Bathrooms: 1 public; 1 private shower.
Bed & breakfast: £19.80-£21 single, £30.50-£32.50 double.
Half board: £25-£28.60 daily, £175-£185 weekly.
Evening meal 6.30pm (l.o. 9am).

Blundellsands Hotel
APPROVED
The Serpentine, Blundellsands, Crosby, Liverpool, L23 6TN
☎ 051-924 6515 Fax 051-931 5364 Telex 626270
Ⓖ Lansbury
Magnificent red brick building in a quiet suburb of Crosby.
Bedrooms: 20 single, 9 double & 6 twin, 6 family rooms.
Bathrooms: 41 private.
Bed & breakfast: £22-£63 single, £44-£76 double.
Half board: from £34 daily.
Lunch available.
Evening meal 7pm (l.o. 9pm).
Parking for 250.
Credit: Access, Visa, Diners, Amex.

Bradford Hotel
Tithebarne Street, Liverpool, L2 2EW
☎ 051-236 8782
City centre hotel, ideal for shops, nightlife, business district and all tourist attractions. Close to mainline railway and ferry terminals.
Bedrooms: 16 single, 10 double & 16 twin, 2 family rooms.
Bathrooms: 32 private, 8 public; 1 private shower.
Bed & breakfast: £20-£45 single, £30-£55 double.
Half board: £27-£52 daily.
Lunch available.
Evening meal 7pm (l.o. 9.30pm).
Parking for 28.
Credit: Access, Visa, Diners, Amex.

Feathers Hotel ⋔
119-125 Mount Pleasant, Liverpool, L3 5TF
☎ 051-709 9655 Telex 627657
Large privately-owned hotel, in Mount Pleasant, the city's most historic area. Easy access to rail stations, bus and ferry terminals. Courtesy transport available.
Bedrooms: 39 single, 21 double & 16 twin, 4 family rooms.

Bathrooms: 22 private, 10 public; 18 private showers.
Bed & breakfast: £25-£44 single, £37-£65 double.
Lunch available.
Evening meal 6pm (l.o. 9.30pm).
Parking for 50.
Credit: Access, Visa, C.Bl., Diners, Amex.

Hardman House Hotel
15-33 Hardman Street, Liverpool, L1 9AS
☎ 051-708 8303
Hotel with restaurant, coffee shop, bars and ballroom. Central to all amenities including Albert Dock and Beatle Cavern.
Bedrooms: 5 single, 2 double & 9 twin, 1 family room.
Bathrooms: 1 private, 8 public.
Bed & breakfast: from £14 single, from £28 double.
Half board: from £20 daily, from £125 weekly.
Lunch available.
Evening meal 5pm (l.o. 11.50pm).
Parking for 10.
Credit: Access, Visa.

Park Hotel ⋔
Dunningsbridge Road, Netherton, L30 3SU
☎ 051-525 7555 Telex 629772
Ⓖ De Vere
Convenient for Liverpool centre, and with easy access to motorway systems. Municipal golf-course and Aintree Race Course half a mile.
Bedrooms: 35 single, 13 double & 12 twin.
Bathrooms: 60 private.
Bed & breakfast: £50-£55 single, £60-£70 double.
Half board: from £60 daily, from £420 weekly.
Lunch available.
Evening meal 6.30pm (l.o. 9.30pm).
Parking for 253.
Credit: Access, Visa, Diners, Amex.

Solna Hotel ⋔
4 Croxteth Drive, Liverpool, L17 3AD
☎ 051-733 1943
In quiet position overlooking Sefton Park. Close to motorways, city centre, docks and airport. Ideal base for business meetings and conferences. Courtesy transport available.

Bedrooms: 4 single, 12 double & 3 twin.
Bathrooms: 19 private.
Bed & breakfast: £39.95-£55 single, £51.95-£68 double.
Lunch available.
Evening meal 6pm (l.o. 9.30pm).
Parking for 50.
Credit: Access, Visa, Diners, Amex.

Ullet Lodge ⋔
Listed
77 Ullet Road, Liverpool, L17 2AA
☎ 051-733 1680
3 storey Victorian family home overlooking Sefton Park. Convenient for city centre, airport and M62. Spacious, comfortable rooms.
Bedrooms: 2 double & 2 twin, 4 family rooms.
Bathrooms: 2 public.
Bed & breakfast: £13-£15 single, £21-£26 double.
Parking for 3.

LONGRIDGE
Lancashire
Map ref 4A1

Comprises the parishes of Alston and Dilworth and serves as the shopping and social centre for the surrounding farming districts.

Brickhouse Hotel & Restaurant ⋔
COMMENDED
Chipping, Nr. Preston, PR3 2QH
☎ (0995) 61316
18th C former farmhouse with spectacular views from intimate restaurant, providing home-cooked food in this tastefully modernised hotel.
Bedrooms: 2 double & 2 twin, 1 family room.
Bathrooms: 5 private.
Bed & breakfast: £33 single, £45.50 double.
Half board: £47-£54 daily, £320-£360 weekly.
Lunch available.
Evening meal 6pm (l.o. 9.30pm).
Parking for 100.
Credit: Access, Visa.

Lancashire
Map ref 4A1

12m W. Preston
Pleasant resort famous
for its championship golf-
courses, notably the
Royal Lytham and St.
Annes. Fine sands and
attractive gardens. Some
half-timbered buildings
and an old windmill
recently restored.
*Tourist Information
Centre ☎ (0253) 721222
or 725610*

Chadwick Hotel M
⚋⚋⚋ APPROVED

South Promenade, Lytham
St. Annes, FY8 1NP
☎ (0253) 720061
*Modern family-run hotel and
leisure complex. Accent on
food, comfort and personal
service.*
Bedrooms: 10 single,
10 double & 30 twin,
20 family rooms.
Bathrooms: 70 private.
Bed & breakfast: £29.50-£34
single, £39.50-£45 double.
Half board: £31.50-£35 daily,
£205.80-£245 weekly.
Lunch available.
Evening meal 7pm (l.o.
8.30pm).
Parking for 40.
Credit: Access, Visa, Diners,
Amex.
⏣ ⚐ 🛏 ♨ 🖥 ⚑ 🍴 ⚙ 📺 🛎 🅥
🍷 Display advertisement
appears on page 143.

Clifton Arms Hotel M
⚋⚋⚋

West Beach, Lytham St.
Annes, FY8 5QJ
☎ (0253) 739898 Fax (0253)
730657 Telex 677463
⊕ Lansbury
*In the lovely old town of
Lytham, overlooking the
famous Green and the River
Ribble.*
Bedrooms: 12 single,
13 double & 10 twin, 6 family
rooms.
Bathrooms: 41 private.
Bed & breakfast: £37-£80
single, £74-£94 double.
Half board: from £48 daily.
Lunch available.
Evening meal 7pm (l.o.
10pm).
Parking for 40.
Credit: Access, Visa, Diners,
Amex.
⏣ ⚐ 🛏 ♨ 🖥 📺 🛎 🍷 🅥 ⚑ 🍴 ⚙
📺

Cullerne Hotel M
⚋⚋

55 Lightburne Avenue,
Lytham St. Annes, FY8 1JE
☎ (0253) 721753
*Located just off the
promenade, offering
comfortable accommodation
with colour TV in all rooms.*
Bedrooms: 1 single, 1 double
& 1 twin, 2 family rooms.
Bathrooms: 1 public.
Bed & breakfast: £12 single,
£24 double.
Half board: £16 daily, £102
weekly.
Evening meal 5.30pm.
Parking for 4.
⏣ ⚐ ♨ 📺 ⚑ 📺 🏧 ✕ 🚫

Dalmeny Hotel M
⚋⚋⚋ APPROVED

19-27 South Promenade,
Lytham St.Annes, FY8 1LX
☎ (0253) 712236
Fax (0253) 724447
*Room-only rate on application.
Choose any of the 4
restaurants or use the small
kitchen in the suites specially
designed for families with
babies and small children.*
Bedrooms: 14 double,
79 family rooms.
Bathrooms: 93 private,
1 public.
Bed & breakfast: £29.75-
£54.75 single, £41.50-£67.50
double.
Half board: £59-£95 daily,
£175-£637 weekly.
Lunch available.
Evening meal 5pm (l.o.
10.30pm).
Parking for 95.
Credit: Access, Visa.
⏣ ⚐ ♨ 🖥 ⚐ 🛏 🅥 ⚑
📺 ⚙ 🛎 🍴 🛎 ⚙ 🍴 🛏
🚫 ⚑ 🕈 ♻ ⚑ 🏧 🚫 📺

Lindum Hotel M
⚋⚋⚋ APPROVED

63-67 South Promenade,
Lytham St. Annes, FY8 1LZ
☎ (0253) 721534 & 722516
*Family-run, seafront hotel with
good reputation for cooking
and comfortable
accommodation. Close to fine
shops and championship golf
courses.*
Bedrooms: 3 single, 37 double
& 9 twin, 31 family rooms.
Bathrooms: 80 private,
5 public.
Bed & breakfast: £25-£30
single, £38-£40 double.
Half board: £26-£28 daily,
£182-£196 weekly.
Evening meal 6pm (l.o. 7pm).

Parking for 25.
Credit: Access, Visa, Amex.
⏣ ⚐ ♨ 🖥 ⚑ 🛏 🅥 ⚑ 📺
SP
🍷 Display advertisement
appears on page 143.

Cheshire
Map ref 4B2

Former silk-
manufacturing town with
cobbled streets and
picturesque cottages
overlooking Bollin Valley.
West Park Museum and
Art Gallery and
Gawsworth Hall are
places of interest.
*Tourist Information
Centre ☎ (0625) 21955
ext 114/115*

Chadwick House M
⚋⚋⚋ COMMENDED

55 Beech Lane, Macclesfield,
SK10 2DS
☎ (0625) 615558
*Tastefully refurbished large
town house, close to town
centre and stations. Licensed
bar and restaurant for
residents.*
Bedrooms: 3 single, 7 double
& 2 twin.
Bathrooms: 6 private,
2 public.
Bed & breakfast: £20.50-£40
single, £40-£70 double.
Parking for 10.
⚐ ♨ ⚐ ♨ 🅥 ⚑ 📺 🛏
🍴 ✕ 🚫

Crofton Hotel
⚋⚋⚋

22 Crompton Road,
Macclesfield, SK11 8DS
☎ (0625) 34113
*All rooms beautifully appointed
with en-suite bath or shower
and WC, tea and coffee
equipment and TV. Lounge
bar, restaurant and laundry
facilities.*
Bedrooms: 2 single, 1 double
& 3 twin, 2 family rooms.
Bathrooms: 8 private.
Bed & breakfast: £38-£43
single, £59-£65 double.
Lunch available.
Evening meal 6.30pm (l.o.
9pm).
Parking for 8.
Credit: Access, Visa.
⏣ ⚐ ⚐ ♨ 🅥 🅥 ⚑ 🛏
🍴 ✕ 🏧 🏠 📺

Moorhayes House Hotel M
⚋⚋

27 Manchester Road,
Tytherington, Macclesfield,
SK10 2JJ
☎ (0625) 33228
*Modern, comfortable house in
secluded position half a mile
from town centre. 5 minutes
from Peak District National
Park, 20 minutes from
Manchester Airport.*
Bedrooms: 2 single, 5 double
& 2 twin.
Bathrooms: 5 private,
2 public.
Bed & breakfast: £26-£38
single, £46.50-£50 double.
Parking for 10.
⏣ ⚐ ⚐ ♨ ⯑ 📺 ✕ 🚫

Park Villa Hotel M
⚋⚋⚋ COMMENDED

Park Lane, Macclesfield,
SK11 8AE
☎ (0625) 511428
Fax (0625) 514637
*Small privately-run hotel,
lovingly restored to preserve a
gracious Victorian atmosphere.
Easily accessible via
Manchester International
Airport, InterCity and
motorway network.*
Bedrooms: 2 single, 1 double
& 2 twin, 2 family rooms.
Bathrooms: 7 private,
1 public.
Bed & breakfast: £35-£50
single, £53-£72 double.
Half board: £45-£60 daily.
Lunch available.
Evening meal 6.30pm (l.o.
9pm).
Parking for 16.
Credit: Access, Visa, Diners,
Amex.
⏣ ⚐ ⚐ ♨ ⚐ ♨ 🅥 ⚑
📺 ⚙ 🛎 🍴 🍴 🛏 🚫
SP

Cheshire
Map ref 4A2

Red Lion Tudor Cottage Hotel

1 Old Hall Street, Malpas,
SY14 8NE
☎ Whitchurch (0948) 860368
*Old coaching inn in the centre
of Malpas, with old oak
panelling and Jacobean-style
staircase. Originally built
around 14th C but modified
through time. Tudor cottage
dating from late 16th C, fully
modernised without loss of
character.*
Bedrooms: 3 single, 4 double
& 2 twin, 1 family room.
Continued ▶

131

MALPAS
Continued

Bathrooms: 10 private.
Bed & breakfast: £19.95-£25
single, £39.90-£50 double.
Half board: £28.45-£33.40
daily.
Lunch available.
Evening meal 7.30pm (l.o.
9pm).
Parking for 30.

MANCHESTER

Gtr. Manchester
Map ref 4B1

The industrial capital of
the North, second only to
London as a commercial,
financial, banking and
newspaper centre.
Victorian architecture,
many churches,
museums, art galleries,
libraries, 15th C cathedral
and Belle Vue Zoo. New
shopping centre at
Piccadilly.
*Tourist Information
Centre* ☎ 061-234 3157
or 3158

Albany Guest House ⚑
21 Albany Road, Chorlton-
cum-Hardy, Manchester,
M21 1AY
☎ 061-881 6774
*Recently renovated Victorian
guesthouse, convenient for city
centre, airport and leisure
activities. Family-run with
warm atmosphere.*
Bedrooms: 7 single, 6 double
& 6 twin, 3 family rooms.
Bathrooms: 6 private,
5 public; 10 private showers.
Bed & breakfast: £15-£25
single, £30-£35 double.
Parking for 8.

Ashdene Hotel ⚑
👑👑👑
48 Wellington Road, Eccles,
Manchester, M30 9QW
☎ 061-789 4762 Fax 061-787
8394
*Centrally located in the Eccles
area, just off exit 2 of the
M602. 4.5 miles from
Manchester city centre. Ideal
for business; convenient for
Manchester Airport.*
Bedrooms: 3 single, 1 double
& 2 twin, 1 family room.
Bathrooms: 7 private.
Bed & breakfast: £37.50-
£41.50 single, £52-£57 double.
Half board: £44.50-£46.50
daily, £223-£243 weekly.
Lunch available.

Evening meal 7pm (l.o. 9pm).
Parking for 6.
Credit: Access, Visa.

Baron Hotel ⚑
👑👑
116 Palatine Road, West
Didsbury, Manchester,
M20 9ZA
☎ 061-434 3688
*A newly opened hotel, all
rooms with en-suite facilities. 3
miles from Manchester Airport
and city centre. Half a mile
from the motorway network.*
Bedrooms: 10 single, 5 twin,
1 family room.
Bathrooms: 16 private.
Bed & breakfast: £20-£25
single, £30-£38 double.
Evening meal 7pm (l.o.
8.30pm).
Parking for 25.
Credit: Access, Visa, Diners.

Copthorne Hotel ⚑
👑👑👑👑 COMMENDED
Clipper Quay, Salford Quays,
Manchester, M5 3DL
☎ 061-873 7321 Telex 669090
COPMAN G
*Waterfront location, close to
city centre. Local attractions
include Old Trafford, Granada
TV studio tours, G-Mex
Centre and China Town.*
Bedrooms: 111 double &
55 twin.
Bathrooms: 166 private.
Bed & breakfast: £75-£85
single, £85-£95 double.
Half board: £60-£75 daily.
Lunch available.
Evening meal 7pm (l.o.
10.45pm).
Parking for 103.
Credit: Access, Visa, Diners,
Amex.

Crescent Gate Hotel ⚑
👑👑👑 COMMENDED
Park Crescent, Victoria Park,
Manchester, M14 5RE
☎ 061-224 0672
Fax 061-257 2822
*2 miles from city centre, in
quiet residential crescent,
convenient for airport. One of
Manchester's popular
independent hotels.*
Bedrooms: 21 single, 2 double
& 2 twin, 1 family room.
Bathrooms: 16 private,
2 public.
Bed & breakfast: £21-£30
single, £45 double.
Half board: £33-£38 daily.
Lunch available.

Evening meal 7pm (l.o. 8pm).
Parking for 18.
Credit: Access, Visa, Diners,
Amex.

🌐 Display advertisement
appears on page 143.

The Dominion ⚑
👑👑
48-50 Whitworth Street,
Manchester, M1 6JQ
☎ 061-953 1280
*3 buildings refurbished to
highest standard providing city
centre accommodation suites,
include fitted kitchen, lounge,
bathroom, 1-2 bedrooms. Ideal
for tourists.*
Bedrooms: 8 single, 15 double
& 2 twin, 20 family rooms.
Bathrooms: 45 private.
Bed & breakfast: £35-£55
single, £50-£65 double.
Evening meal 6pm (l.o.
10pm).
Credit: Access, Visa, C.Bl.,
Diners, Amex.

Ebor Hotel ⚑
👑👑
402 Wilbraham Road,
Chorlton-cum-Hardy,
Manchester, M21 1UH
☎ 061-881 4855 & 1911
*Hotel offering comfortable
accommodation and friendly
service, within easy reach of
airport, Manchester city centre
and motorway network.*
Bedrooms: 6 single, 3 double
& 4 twin, 3 family rooms.
Bathrooms: 1 private,
3 public; 3 private showers.
Bed & breakfast: £20-£26
single, £31-£36 double.
Half board: £27.50-£33.50
daily, £126-£163 weekly.
Evening meal 6.30pm (l.o.
5pm).
Parking for 20.

🌐 Display advertisement
appears on page 143.

Elm Grange Hotel ⚑
👑👑👑
559-561 Wilmslow Road,
Withington, Manchester,
M20 9GJ
☎ 061-445 3336
*On main bus routes and near
city centre and airport.
Cleanliness, service, value for
money. Warm welcome
assured.*
Bedrooms: 17 single, 4 double
& 11 twin.
Bathrooms: 15 private,
3 public.
Bed & breakfast: £21.85-
£33.92 single, £37.95-£47.72
double.

Half board: £26.95-£39.92
daily, £161.70-£239.52
weekly.
Evening meal 6pm (l.o. 8pm).
Parking for 41.
Credit: Access, Visa.

Gardens Hotel ⚑
👑👑👑👑 COMMENDED
55 Piccadilly, Manchester,
M1 2AP
☎ 061-236 5155
*Situated in the heart of the
city, overlooking Piccadilly
Gardens. This 97-bedroomed
hotel is furnished to modern
standards.*
Bedrooms: 12 single,
42 double & 43 twin.
Bathrooms: 97 private.
Bed & breakfast: £67.50-£99
single, £85-£114.50 double.
Lunch available.
Evening meal 6.30pm (l.o.
10pm).
Credit: Access, Visa, Diners,
Amex.

Granada Hotel ⚑
👑👑👑
404 Wilmslow Road,
Withington, Manchester,
M20 9BM
☎ 061-445 5908
Fax 061 445 4902
*Comfortable hotel close to
Manchester city centre and
airport. En-suite rooms, colour
TV, telephone, hair-dryer.
Lounge, bar and restaurant.
Parking.*
Bedrooms: 3 single, 2 double
& 3 twin, 2 family rooms.
Bathrooms: 10 private.
Bed & breakfast: £25-£35
single, £35-£45 double.
Evening meal 6pm (l.o.
11.30pm).
Parking for 20.
Credit: Access, Visa, Diners,
Amex.

Imperial Hotel ⚑
👑👑
157 Hathersage Road,
Manchester, M13 0HY
☎ 061-225 6500
*A recently modernised and
refurbished hotel. 1.25 miles
from city centre, in the vicinity
of university and teaching
hospitals.*
Bedrooms: 13 single, 5 double
& 9 twin.
Bathrooms: 21 private,
3 public.
Bed & breakfast: £24-£30
single, from £38 double.

Evening meal 6.30pm (l.o.
8.30pm).
Parking for 30.
Credit: Access, Visa, Diners,
Amex.

Hotel Montana M
59 Palatine Road, West
Didsbury, Manchester,
M20 9LJ
☎ 061-445 6427
Small family hotel with
pleasant atmosphere. English
and continental food.
Bedrooms: 4 single, 9 double
& 20 twin, 1 family room.
Bathrooms: 17 private,
3 public.
Bed & breakfast: £17.25-
£25.30 single, £30-£34.50
double.
Half board: £22-£32 daily,
£120-£161 weekly.
Evening meal 6pm (l.o. 8pm).
Parking for 22.
Credit: Access, Diners.

Parkside Guest House
58 Cromwell Road, Stretford,
Manchester, M32 8QJ
☎ 061-865 2860
Clean, friendly service in a
quiet residential area,
convenient for Old Trafford
football and cricket ground,
city centre M65 exit 7.
Children over 7 welcome.
Family rooms by arrangement.
Bedrooms: 5 single, 2 double
& 3 twin, 2 family rooms.
Bathrooms: 3 private,
1 public.
Bed & breakfast: £14.50-
£16.50 single, £27-£29 double.
Parking for 3.

Hotel Piccadilly M
P.O. Box 107, Piccadilly,
Manchester, M60 1QR
☎ 061-236 8414 Telex 668765
ⓒⓡ Embassy
Situated in the heart of
Manchester, minutes away
from the shopping areas, the
hotel has every facility,
including a health and leisure
club.
Bedrooms: 150 single,
61 double & 60 twin.
Bathrooms: 271 private.
Bed & breakfast: £36.50-£105
single, £73-£130 double.
Lunch available.
Evening meal 6.30pm (l.o.
10pm).
Parking for 280.

The Portland Thistle Hotel M
Portland Street, Piccadilly
Gardens, Manchester,
M1 6DP
☎ 061-228 3400 Fax 061-228
6347 Telex 669157
ⓒⓡ Thistle
Traditional style hotel
combining old world charm
with full modern facilities
including a recently completed
leisure centre. Overlooks
Piccadilly Gardens in the heart
of the city's commercial and
shopping area.
Bedrooms: 107 single,
75 double & 11 twin,
12 family rooms.
Bathrooms: 205 private.
Bed & breakfast: from £87.50
single, from £112 double.
Lunch available.
Evening meal 6pm (l.o.
10pm).
Credit: Access, Visa, C.Bl.,
Diners, Amex.

The Royals Hotel M
APPROVED
Altrincham Road,
Wythenshawe, Manchester,
M22 4BJ
☎ 061-998 9011
ⓒⓡ Consort
Large mock Tudor inn beside
M56, near to M63 and 2 miles
from Manchester Airport.
Sharston/Altrincham exit.
Bedrooms: 10 single, 9 double
& 11 twin, 4 family rooms.
Bathrooms: 34 private.
Bed & breakfast: from £41.40
single, from £59.80 double.
Lunch available.
Evening meal 7pm (l.o.
9.45pm).
Parking for 100.
Credit: Access, Visa, Diners,
Amex.

Willow Bank Hotel M
COMMENDED
340 Wilmslow Road,
Fallowfield, Manchester,
M14 6AF
☎ 061-224 0461 Fax 061-257
2561 Telex 668222

International restaurant. Easy
access to Manchester Airport,
the M6, M56, M62 and M63,
city centre, and conference and
exhibition sites. Weekend rates
available.
Bedrooms: 64 single,
27 double & 29 twin, 2 family
rooms.
Bathrooms: 122 private.
Bed & breakfast: £47-£55
single, £68-£73 double.
Half board: £43-£64 daily.
Lunch available.
Evening meal 7pm (l.o.
10.15pm).
Parking for 110.
Credit: Access, Visa, Diners,
Amex.

Wilmslow Hotel
356 Wilmslow Road,
Fallowfield, Manchester,
M14 6AB
☎ 061-225 3030
Fax 061-257 2854
Comfortable hotel close to city
centre, shops and nightlife. On
direct bus route for Manchester
Airport.
Bedrooms: 16 single,
17 double & 9 twin, 10 family
rooms.
Bathrooms: 24 private,
5 public; 9 private showers.
Bed & breakfast: £19-£31.75
single, £29-£38.20 double.
Half board: from £25 daily,
£175-£264 weekly.
Evening meal 6.30pm (l.o.
9pm).
Parking for 35.
Credit: Access, Visa, Amex.

MANCHESTER AIRPORT
Map ref 4B2

See also Alderley Edge,
Altrincham, Bramhall,
Manchester, Sale,
Salford, Stockport,
Stretford, Wilmslow.

Wilmslow Moat House M
Altrincham Road, Wilmslow,
Cheshire SK9 4LR
☎ (0625) 529201
Telex 666401
ⓒⓡ Queens Moat Houses
Tyrolean-style hotel near
Manchester Airport and
Wilmslow on the fringe of
Styal Country Park. All rooms
en-suite together with Country
Club offering jacuzzi, saunas,
gymnasium, steamroom, squash
courts, sunbeds and snooker
room. Special weekend rates.

Bedrooms: 13 single,
76 double & 36 twin.
Bathrooms: 125 private.
Bed & breakfast: £38-£72
single, £50-£83 double.
Lunch available.
Evening meal 7pm (l.o.
10pm).
Parking for 400.
Credit: Access, Visa, Diners,
Amex.

MORECAMBE
Lancashire
Map ref 5A3

3m NW. Lancaster
Famous for its shrimps,
Morecambe is a
traditional resort on a
wide bay with spacious
beaches, entertainments
and seafront
illuminations. Marineland
oceanarium with
performing dolphins, and
Morecambe Leisure
Centre. Carnforth Railway
Museum nearby.
Tourist Information
Centre ☎ (0524) 414110

Craigwell Hotel M
APPROVED
372 Marine Road East,
Morecambe, LA4 5AH
☎ (0524) 410095 & 418399
Licensed, seafront hotel with
lovely views, overlooking
Morecambe Bay. Choice of
menu, including vegetarian.
Bedrooms: 6 single, 5 double
& 2 twin, 2 family rooms.
Bathrooms: 15 private.
Bed & breakfast: £18-£22
single, £36-£44 double.
Half board: £25-£30 daily,
£164-£194 weekly.
Evening meal 6pm.
Parking for 4.
Credit: Access, Visa.

Farringford Hotel
405 Marine Road East,
Morecambe, LA4 5AR
☎ (0524) 832321
Fax (0524) 417829
Seaside holiday hotel on
central promenade, overlooking
Morecambe Bay. 27 rooms,
lift, ample parking, licensed
bar, choice of menu all rooms
en-suite, colour TV, radios and
tea making facilities.
Bedrooms: 3 single, 8 double
& 12 twin, 4 family rooms.
Bathrooms: 27 private.
Continued ▶

MORECAMBE
Continued

Bed & breakfast: £20-£30 single, £38-£50 double.
Half board: £25-£38 daily, £140-£175 weekly.
Lunch available.
Evening meal 6pm (l.o. 7pm).
Parking for 16.
Credit: Access, Visa.

Harwood House
1 Chatsworth Road , Morecambe, LA4 4JF
☎ (0524) 412845
Family-run private hotel, near to sea, shops, coach operators, (for day trips) and all other amenities. No parking restrictions.
Bedrooms: 4 single, 4 double & 1 twin, 5 family rooms.
Bathrooms: 2 public.
Bed & breakfast: £10.50-£11.50 single, £21-£23 double.
Half board: £13-£14 daily, £87-£94 weekly.
Lunch available.
Evening meal 5.30pm (l.o. 3pm).
Parking for 1.
Credit: Access, Visa.

Midland Hotel M
APPROVED
Marine Road, Morecambe, LA4 4BZ
☎ (0524) 417180
Unique bayside setting, art deco design by premier art deco archiitect, Oliver Hill. Opened July 1933. Centre of town facilities.
Bedrooms: 13 single, 9 double & 21 twin, 4 family rooms.
Bathrooms: 47 private.
Bed & breakfast: £49-£65 single.
Lunch available.
Evening meal 7pm (l.o. 9.30pm).
Parking for 80.
Credit: Access, Visa, Diners, Amex.

Uppington Licensed Private Hotel M
15 Thornton Road, Morecambe, LA4 5PD
☎ (0524) 410887
Small, friendly hotel, adjacent to promenade. Pleasant and relaxed atmosphere. Children and pets welcome. En-suite rooms available.

Bedrooms: 2 single, 6 double & 1 twin, 4 family rooms.
Bathrooms: 4 private, 2 public.
Bed & breakfast: £9.50-£11.50 single, £19-£23 double.
Half board: £13-£16 daily, £75-£90 weekly.
Evening meal 6pm (l.o. 4pm).
Parking for 6.
Open April-October.

Hotel Warwick
394 Marine Road East, Morecambe, LA4 5AN
☎ (0524) 418151
Small, fully modernised and redecorated to high standard. Lakeland views from many rooms.
Bedrooms: 5 single, 3 double & 11 twin, 4 family rooms.
Bathrooms: 11 private, 3 public.
Bed & breakfast: £16.50-£22.50 single, £33-£41 double.
Half board: £24.50-£30.50 daily, £150-£164 weekly.
Lunch available.
Evening meal 6pm (l.o. 7pm).
Credit: Access, Visa.

Westleigh Hotel M
9 Marine Road, Morecambe, LA3 1BS
☎ (0524) 418352
Comfortable family-run hotel on the promenade, overlooking gardens, Morecambe Bay and Lakeland hills. Close to all tourist amenities. Stair lift. Colour TVs in all bedrooms.
Bedrooms: 1 single, 3 double & 6 twin, 2 family rooms.
Bathrooms: 9 private, 1 public.
Bed & breakfast: £10-£13 single, £20-£26 double.
Half board: £14-£17 daily, £85-£95 weekly.
Evening meal 5pm (l.o. 6pm).
Credit: Access, Visa.

NANTWICH
Cheshire
Map ref 4A2

Pleasant old market town on the River Weaver made prosperous in Roman times by salt springs. Fire destroyed the town in 1583 and many fine buildings were rebuilt in Elizabethan style. Churche's Mansion (open to the public) survived the fire. Surrounding agricultural area produces Cheshire cheese.
Tourist Information Centre ☎ (0270) 623914

Alvaston Hall Hotel M
Middlewich Road, Nantwich, CW5 6PD
☎ (0270) 624341 Telex 36311
CR Character
18th C country house set in 14 acres of grounds. Silver Cloud restaurant. Facilities include full leisure complex, golf driving range.
Bedrooms: 26 single, 36 double & 22 twin, 5 family rooms.
Bathrooms: 89 private.
Bed & breakfast: £40-£70 single, £55-£88 double.
Lunch available.
Evening meal 7pm (l.o. 10pm).
Parking for 200.
Credit: Access, Visa, Diners, Amex.

Crown Hotel M
COMMENDED
24 High Street, Nantwich, CW2 7BN
☎ Crewe (0270) 625283
In the heart of Nantwich, one of the oldest, most interesting buildings in this charming Cheshire town. Half-timbered black and white, built in 1583 after the Great Fire.
Bedrooms: 3 single, 5 double & 10 twin.
Bathrooms: 18 private.
Bed & breakfast: £38-£43 single, £40-£55 double.
Half board: £50-£55 daily.
Lunch available.
Evening meal 5pm (l.o. 11pm).
Parking for 30.
Credit: Access, Visa, Diners, Amex.

Lamb Hotel M
Hospital Street, Nantwich, CW5 5RH
☎ (0270) 625286
200-year-old coaching inn with restaurant, in the centre of historic Nantwich. We have a popular lounge bar and offer a wide selection of cold and hot food, 7 days a week.
Bedrooms: 4 single, 3 double & 7 twin, 2 family rooms.
Bathrooms: 13 private, 2 public.
Bed & breakfast: £22-£33 single, £38-£50 double.
Lunch available.
Evening meal 7pm (l.o. 9.30pm).
Parking for 35.
Credit: Access, Visa.

Rookery Hall M
HIGHLY COMMENDED
Worleston, Nr. Nantwich, CW5 6DQ
☎ (0270) 626866 Fax (0270) 626027 Telex 367169 Photel G Rookhall
Set in nearly 200 acres of wooded parkland, 1 mile outside Nantwich, just off the A51 to Chester. Grade II listed Georgian house with accent on food and comfort.
Bedrooms: 2 single, 2 double & 7 twin.
Bathrooms: 11 private.
Bed & breakfast: £122.50 single, £200-£320 double.
Lunch available.
Evening meal 7pm (l.o. 9.15pm).
Parking for 52.
Credit: Access, Visa, Diners, Amex.

NELSON

Lancashire
Map ref 4B1

4m N. Burnley
The name of this textile town was taken from the 'Nelson Inn', called after the famous admiral and around which the town grew in 19th C. Bronze Age and Roman artefacts have been found in the area.
Tourist Information Centre ☎ (0282) 692890 or 67731 ext 283

Wintersfield Hotel ▲
▲▲
230-236 Manchester Road, Nelson, BB9 7DE
☎ (0282) 65379
Modern family-run hotel, clean and friendly, adjacent to exit 12 of the M65. Easy access to many local beauty spots and places of interest.
Bedrooms: 7 single, 3 double & 7 twin, 2 family rooms.
Bathrooms: 3 public.
Bed & breakfast: £13-£13.50 single, £24-£25 double.
Evening meal 6.15pm.
Parking for 16.

NESTON

Cheshire
Map ref 4A2

Elm Grove House Hotel ▲
▲▲▲
44 Parkgate Road, Neston, South Wirral Merseyside L64 6QG
☎ 051-336 3021
Situated within 300 yards of Neston centre. Family-run, offering a high standard of personal service in elegant surroundings.
Bedrooms: 1 single, 1 double & 3 twin, 2 family rooms.
Bathrooms: 7 private.
Bed & breakfast: £22-£31 single, £44-£55 double.
Half board: £30-£39 daily, £210-£246 weekly.
Evening meal 7pm (l.o. 9.30pm).
Parking for 16.

NEWTON-LE-WILLOWS

Merseyside
Map ref 4A2

5m E. St. Helens
Small industrial town with some 17th C cottages and Elizabethan farmhouses.

Kirkfield Hotel ▲
▲▲ APPROVED
4 Church Street, Newton-le-Willows, WA12 9SU
☎ (092 52) 28196
Family hotel with bar and function facilities. Easy access to M6 and M62, close to Haydock Park racecourse.
Bedrooms: 6 single, 5 double & 4 twin, 1 family room.
Bathrooms: 13 private, 1 public.
Bed & breakfast: £23.50-£32 single, £36-£46 double.
Lunch available.
Evening meal 7pm (l.o. 8.30pm).
Parking for 50.
Credit: Access, Visa.

NORTHWICH

Cheshire
Map ref 4A2

An important salt-producing town since Roman times, Northwich has been replanned with a modern shopping centre and a number of black and white buildings. Unique Anderton boat-lift on northern outskirts of town.

Blue Cap Hotel ▲
520 Chester Road, Sandiway, Northwich, CW8 2DN
☎ (0606) 883006
Picturesque 18th C inn. Legend has it that the master of the pack tied lead weights around Blue Cap's neck, so that the others could keep up with this celebrated foxhound.
Bedrooms: 5 single, 4 double & 3 twin.
Bathrooms: 12 private.
Bed & breakfast: £42-£45 single, from £53 double.
Lunch available.
Evening meal 7pm (l.o. 9.30pm).
Parking for 200.
Credit: Access, Visa, Diners, Amex.

Friendly Floatel ▲
London Road, Northwich, CW9 5HD
☎ (0606) 44443
The first "hotel on water", constructed at the meeting point of the Weaver and Dane rivers.
Bedrooms: 21 single, 21 double & 16 twin, 2 family rooms.
Bathrooms: 60 private.
Bed & breakfast: £49-£58 single, £58-£66 double.
Half board: max. £70 daily.
Lunch available.
Evening meal 6.30pm (l.o. 10pm).
Parking for 60.
Credit: Access, Visa, C.Bl., Diners, Amex.

Springfield Guest House ▲
▲▲
Chester Road, Oakmere, Northwich, CW8 2HB
☎ Sandiway (0606) 882538
Family guesthouse erected in 1863. On A556 close to Delamere Forest, midway between Chester and M6 motorway junction 19. Manchester Airport 25 minutes' drive.
Bedrooms: 4 single, 1 double & 1 twin, 1 family room.
Bathrooms: 2 private, 1 public.
Bed & breakfast: £20 single, £35 double.
Half board: from £24 daily.
Evening meal 6pm (l.o. 8pm).
Parking for 10.

OLDHAM

Gtr. Manchester
Map ref 4B1

Large important textile town, boosted in 19th C by Arkwright's spinning-frame and Watt's steam engine. Outstanding watercolours in Art Gallery and impressive neo-classical Town Hall.
Tourist Information Centre ☎ 061-678 4654

Avant Hotel ▲
▲▲▲▲ COMMENDED
Windsor Road, Manchester Street, Oldham, OL8 4AS
☎ 061-627 5500
Telex 668264 AVANTI G

Located just 5 miles from Manchester city centre and 4 miles from the M62 connecting east and west.
Bedrooms: 3 single, 30 double & 66 twin, 4 family rooms.
Bathrooms: 103 private.
Bed & breakfast: from £56 single, from £62 double.
Half board: from £68.50 daily, from £326.10 weekly.
Lunch available.
Evening meal 7pm (l.o. 10pm).
Parking for 152.
Credit: Access, Visa, Diners, Amex.

The Old Bell Inn and Hotel
▲▲▲▲ APPROVED
1 Huddersfield Road, Delph, Nr. Oldham, OL3 5EG
☎ (0457) 876597 & 870130
Friendly family-run old coaching inn, maintained to highest standards, half an hour from Manchester city centre, yet close to moorlands.
Bedrooms: 2 single, 7 double & 1 twin.
Bathrooms: 10 private.
Bed & breakfast: £38.50-£45.50 single, £43.50-£54.50 double.
Lunch available.
Evening meal 7.30pm (l.o. 9.30pm).
Parking for 25.
Credit: Access, Visa.

Periquito Hotel ▲
▲▲▲▲ COMMENDED
Manchester Street, Oldham, OL8 1UZ
☎ 061-624 0555
130 bedrooms fitted to a high modern standard. Easy access to main rail routes, motorway systems and Manchester Airport.
Bedrooms: 14 single, 61 double & 55 twin.
Bathrooms: 130 private.
Bed & breakfast: £54.50-£61 single, £60-£67 double.
Lunch available.
Evening meal 7pm (l.o. 10.30pm).
Parking for 300.
Credit: Access, Visa, Diners, Amex.

Map references apply to the colour maps towards the end of this guide.

The symbols are explained on the flap inside the back cover.

PARKGATE

Cheshire
Map ref 4A2

1m NW. Neston
Once a busy port on the Dee Estuary, Parkgate was the scene of Handel's departure for the great performance of 'Messiah' in Dublin in 1741. The George Inn where he stayed is now Mostyn House School.

Parkgate Hotel M
😕😕😕

Boathouse Lane, Parkgate, L64 6RD
☎ 051-336 5001 Fax 051-336 8504 Telex 629469 Pagdte G
🅒 Lansbury
Rural Wirral hotel, just 20 minutes' drive from Chester, with an immaculately landscaped garden and illuminated fountain.
Bedrooms: 1 single, 6 double & 16 twin, 4 family rooms.
Bathrooms: 27 private.
Bed & breakfast: £22-£63 single, £44-£76 double.
Half board: from £33 daily.
Lunch available.
Evening meal 7pm (l.o. 10.30pm).
Parking for 125.
Credit: Access, Visa, Diners, Amex.
🔣

PRESTON

Lancashire
Map ref 4A1

Scene of decisive Royalist defeat by Cromwell in the Civil War and later of riots in the Industrial Revolution. Local history exhibited in Harris Museum.
Tourist Information Centre ☎ *(0772) 53731*

Barton Grange Hotel M
Garstang Road, Barton, Nr. Preston, PR3 5AA
☎ Broughton (0772) 862551
Fax (0772) 861267
Telex 67392
🅒 Best Western
Family-owned hotel, set in 5 acres of garden centre. Ideal for conferences, meetings, or just to relax.
Bedrooms: 7 single, 34 double & 19 twin, 6 family rooms.
Bathrooms: 66 private.
Bed & breakfast: £41-£61 single, £48-£75 double.
Half board: £52.50-£74.50 daily.

Lunch available.
Evening meal 7pm (l.o. 10pm).
Parking for 250.
Credit: Access, Visa, Diners, Amex.
🔣

Brook House Guest House M
😕😕 COMMENDED

544 Blackpool Road, Ashton, Preston, PR2 1HY
☎ (0772) 728684
Detached property 10 minutes from town centre and on bus route. TV lounge, car park, en-suite rooms and tea/coffee facilities. Non-smoking establishment.
Bedrooms: 2 single, 1 double & 1 twin.
Bathrooms: 2 private, 1 public.
Bed & breakfast: £15-£25 single.
Half board: £23-£33 daily, £161-£231 weekly.
Evening meal 6pm (l.o. 6pm).
Parking for 6.
🔣

Brook House Hotel M
😕😕😕

662 Preston Road, Clayton-le-Woods, Nr. Chorley, PR6 7EH
☎ (0772) 36403
Set in half an acre and personally supervised by the resident owners, this licensed hotel offers the businessman and tourist comfortable rooms with a high standard of facilities, at sensible prices.
Bedrooms: 3 single, 5 double & 3 twin, 2 family rooms.
Bathrooms: 8 private, 2 public.
Bed & breakfast: £20-£28 single, £32-£40 double.
Evening meal 7pm (l.o. 8.30pm).
Parking for 15.
Credit: Access, Visa.
🔣

Byron Hotel M
😕😕 APPROVED

25-35 Grimshaw Street, Preston, PR1 3DD
☎ (0772) 556310
Fax (0772) 562008
Family-run hotel catering mainly for contract workers and business people, located in the town centre. Train station 8 minutes, bus station 4 minutes by foot.
Bedrooms: 21 single, 7 double & 11 twin, 1 family room.

Bathrooms: 13 private, 5 public.
Bed & breakfast: £14.50-£25 single, £26-£38 double.
Half board: £21-£31 daily, £101.50-£147 weekly.
Evening meal 5pm (l.o. 6.30pm).
Parking for 14.
Credit: Access, Visa.
🔣

Claremont Hotel
😕😕 APPROVED

516 Blackpool Road, Ashton, Preston, PR2 1HY
☎ (0772) 729738
Fax (0772) 726274
Large Victorian house in own grounds. Homely atmosphere and friendly service.
Bedrooms: 9 single, 3 double & 3 twin, 1 family room.
Bathrooms: 10 private, 3 public.
Bed & breakfast: £30-£35 single, £40-£48 double.
Half board: £28-£43 daily.
Evening meal 7pm (l.o. 8.30pm).
Parking for 25.
Credit: Access, Visa.
🔣

Dean Court Hotel M
😕😕😕 COMMENDED

Brownedge Lane, Bamber Bridge, Preston, PR5 6TB
☎ (0772) 35114
Family-run licensed hotel and restaurant specialising in fresh, traditional English dishes and Lancashire hospitality. New stables bar for bar meals. Four-poster bedrooms, bridal suites.
Bedrooms: 1 single, 6 double & 2 twin.
Bathrooms: 9 private, 1 public.
Bed & breakfast: £25-£45 single, £37-£70 double.
Lunch available.
Evening meal 6.30pm (l.o. 9.30pm).
Parking for 40.
Credit: Access, Visa.
🔣

Olde Duncombe House M
😕😕😕 COMMENDED

Garstang Road, Bilsborrow, Nr. Preston, PR3 0RE
☎ (0995) 40336
In the beautiful Ribble Valley next to the Lancaster canal, convenient for canal boat enthusiasts. 4 miles north of the M6 junction 32.
Bedrooms: 1 single, 5 double & 2 twin, 2 family rooms.

Bathrooms: 10 private.
Bed & breakfast: £25-£35 single, £32.50-£39.50 double.
Lunch available.
Evening meal 6pm (l.o. 8.30pm).
Parking for 12.
Credit: Access, Visa.
🔣

Railway Hotel M
Listed

11 Butler Street, Preston, PR1 8BN
☎ (0772) 53951
Bed and breakfast hotel offering budget accommodation.
Bedrooms: 2 single, 2 double & 2 twin, 1 family room.
Bathrooms: 2 public.
Bed & breakfast: £12-£15 single, £23-£26 double.
Lunch available.
🔣

Tickled Trout Hotel M
😕😕😕😕 COMMENDED

Preston New Road, Samlesbury, Preston, PR5 0UJ
☎ (0772) 877671
Telex 677625
🅒 Character
Magnificent views from all bedrooms of this hotel situated on the banks of the River Ribble. Located at exit 31 of the M6, halfway between London and Glasgow.
Bedrooms: 1 single, 12 double & 5 twin, 54 family rooms.
Bathrooms: 72 private.
Bed & breakfast: £47-£66 single, £60-£79 double.
Lunch available.
Evening meal 7pm (l.o. 10pm).
Parking for 170.
Credit: Access, Visa, Diners, Amex.
🔣

Tulketh Hotel M
😕😕😕 COMMENDED

209 Tulketh Road, Ashton, Preston, PR2 1ES
☎ (0772) 728096 & 726250
A hotel of fine quality and personal service, in a quiet residential area. A la carte menu. 5 minutes from town centre, 10 minutes from the M6 motorway.
Bedrooms: 5 single, 2 double & 5 twin.
Bathrooms: 11 private, 1 public.
Bed & breakfast: £27-£36 single, £38-£46 double.

Evening meal 6.30pm (l.o. 7.30pm).
Parking for 12.
Credit: Access, Visa.

🛇 🖈 📞 🖭 📺 🕯 Ⓥ 🖾
📺 🎵 🍴 🗙 SP 🅟 🆃

Vineyard Hotel & Restaurant M
Cinnamon Hill, Chorley Road, Walton-le-Dale, Preston, PR5 4JN
☎ (0772) 54646 & (0772) 58967
Ⓒ Consort
A cosmopolitan-style hotel, convenient for motorways, with restaurant and bar. Emphasis on service.
Bedrooms: 4 double & 9 twin, 1 family room.
Bathrooms: 14 private.
Bed & breakfast: £40-£55 single, £52-£71 double.
Half board: £65-£85 daily.
Lunch available.
Evening meal 7pm (l.o. 10pm).
Parking for 150.
Credit: Access, Visa, Diners, Amex.

🛇 📞 🖭 📺 🕯 Ⓥ 🖾 ●
🎵 🍴 GAP 🍷 SP

2m SW. Bury
Radcliffe has a local history museum containing exhibits about the district from prehistoric times and the remains of Radcliffe Tower.

Hawthorn Hotel M
♨♨
139-143 Stand Lane, Radcliffe, M26 9JR
☎ 061-723 2706
Comfortable family hotel convenient for M62 junction 17, motorway network and close to Bury, Bolton and Manchester. Offers home cooking and car parking facilities.
Bedrooms: 6 single, 2 double & 4 twin, 1 family room.
Bathrooms: 5 private, 2 public; 3 private showers.
Bed & breakfast: £19.55-£29.90 single, £36.80-£41.40 double.
Half board: £26.45-£37.95 daily, from £132.25 weekly.
Evening meal 6pm (l.o. 7pm).
Parking for 9.

🛇 🖈 📺 🕯 Ⓥ 🖾 📺 🎵
🍴

See Clitheroe, Langho, Slaidburn, Whalley.

Old Pennine mill town made prosperous by wool and later cotton-spinning, famous for the Co-operative Movement started in 1844 by a group of Rochdale working men. Birthplace of John Bright (Corn Law opponent) and more recently Gracie Fields. Roman and Bronze Age antiquities in museum.
Tourist Information Centre ☎ (0706) 356592

Midway Hotel
Manchester Road, Castleton, Nr. Rochdale, OL11 2XX
☎ (0706) 32881
Comfortable bedrooms with colour TV, radio and telephone and tea/coffee. Wine bar, and steakhouse. Large car park.
Bedrooms: 16 single, 5 double & 6 twin.
Bathrooms: 20 private, 3 public.
Bed & breakfast: £38-£50 single, £49.50-£60 double.
Half board: from £48.50 daily.
Lunch available.
Evening meal 6pm (l.o. 11pm).
Parking for 100.
Credit: Access, Visa, Amex.

🛇 🖈 📞 🖭 🕯 Ⓥ 🖾
● 🎵 🍴 🗙 SP 🆃

Norton Grange Hotel M
♨♨♨♨ COMMENDED
Manchester Road, Castleton, Rochdale, OL11 2XZ
☎ (0706) 30788 Fax (0706) 49313
Ⓒ Character
19th C character hotel located just 5 minutes' drive from the M62 exit 20 and 15 minutes' drive from Manchester. Facilities include 50 newly refurbished bedrooms, the Pickwick Bar and an a la carte restaurant serving international cuisine.
Bedrooms: 6 single, 13 double & 4 twin, 27 family rooms.
Bathrooms: 50 private.
Bed & breakfast: £35-£68 single, £57-£80 double.
Lunch available.
Evening meal 7pm (l.o. 10pm).
Parking for 120.

Credit: Access, Visa, C.Bl., Diners, Amex.

🛇 🖈 📞 🖭 📺 🕯 Ⓥ 🖾
● 🎵 🍴 🍷 🦮 🆁 ▶
❋ SP 🅟 🆃

Sykeside Country House Hotel M
♨♨♨♨ COMMENDED
Rawtenstall Road End, Haslingden, Rossendale, BB4 6QE
☎ (0706) 831163
Fax (0706) 830090
Listed country house hotel offering traditional English cooking. Personal service from the owners. Easy motorway access.
Bedrooms: 4 single, 3 double & 3 twin.
Bathrooms: 10 private.
Bed & breakfast: £45-£70 single, £55-£80 double.
Evening meal 7pm (l.o. 9pm).
Parking for 25.
Credit: Access, Visa, Diners, Amex.

🛇 🖈 🍴 📞 🖭 📺 🕯 Ⓥ
🖾 📺 🎵 🍷 🦮 🆁 ❋ 🍴
SP 🅟

6m E. Oldham

Bobbin House Hotel M
♨♨♨♨ COMMENDED
The Square, High Street, Uppermill, Saddleworth, OL3 6BD
☎ (0457) 870800
Small hotel and tea rooms in the centre of Uppermill.
Bedrooms: 2 double & 2 twin, 2 family rooms.
Bathrooms: 6 private.
Bed & breakfast: £38.50 single, £42.50-£50 double.
Lunch available.
Evening meal 6pm (l.o. 8.30pm).
Parking for 8.
Credit: Access, Visa, Amex.

🛇 🖈 📞 🖭 📺 🕯 Ⓥ 🖾
🎵 🍴 SP

Half board prices shown are per person but in some cases may be based on double/twin occupancy.

St. Helens has a world-wide reputation for its glass industry and exhibits of English and continental ware are on show at Pilkington Glass Museum. Town is also famous for Rainhill Trials (Stephenson's 'Rocket') and as the birthplace of Sir Thomas Beecham.

Haydock Thistle Hotel M
Penny Lane, Haydock, St. Helens, WA11 9SG
☎ (0942) 272000
Ⓒ Thistle
High standard country house hotel set in 11 acres of landscaped gardens, adjacent to the world famous racecourse.
Bedrooms: 2 single, 84 double & 40 twin, 13 family rooms.
Bathrooms: 139 private.
Bed & breakfast: from £72.75 single, from £95.50 double.
Lunch available.
Evening meal 7pm (l.o. 11pm).
Parking for 180.
Credit: Access, Visa, C.Bl., Diners, Amex.

🛇 🖈 📞 🖭 📺 🕯 Ⓥ 🚫
🖾 ● 📺 🎵 🍴 🦽 🆁 ❋
🍷 SP 🆃

Residential district of Manchester which developed as a result of the opening in 1849 of the railway between Altrincham and Manchester.

Belforte House Hotel
7-9 Broad Road, Sale, M33 2AE
☎ 061-973 8779
Tastefully refurbished hotel, facing Sale Leisure Complex. Convenient for motorway links, bus, road and rail routes into Manchester city centre.
Bedrooms: 14 single, 7 twin.
Bathrooms: 17 private; 4 private showers.
Bed & breakfast: from £30 single, from £45 double.
Half board: from £39.50 daily.
Lunch available.

Continued ▶

SALE
Continued

Evening meal 6.30pm (l.o. 8.30pm).
Parking for 21.
Credit: Access, Visa.

⌖ 🚗 ♨ ☎ ✕ SP T
🏠 ♨ ♈ ✕ SP T

Brookland's Lodge Guest House M
Listed APPROVED

208 Marsland Road, Sale, Cheshire, M33 3NE
☎ 061-973 3283
Delightful black and white Victorian house of unusual design, with attractive gardens. Close to railway station and the M63 junction 8.
Bedrooms: 5 single, 1 double, 3 family rooms.
Bathrooms: 1 private, 2 public.
Bed & breakfast: £16-£25 single, £30-£40 double.
Half board: from £24 daily, from £102 weekly.
Evening meal 6pm (l.o. 9am).
Parking for 6.

⌖ 🚗 ® ♨ ⬒ Ⓤ ⬚ ♨ 🍴 ✕ 🏠

Cornerstones M
230 Washway Road, Sale, M33 4RA
☎ 061-962 6909
Elegantly refurbished, offering every comfort and service. Ideally situated on the A56 only minutes from city and airport. Fun-friendly atmosphere in attractive surroundings. A good value treat.
Bedrooms: 1 single, 2 double & 2 twin, 4 family rooms.
Bathrooms: 3 private, 1 public; 3 private showers.
Bed & breakfast: from £20 single, £32-£35 double.
Half board: £38-£41 daily, £140-£220 weekly.
Parking for 9.

⌖ ® ♨ ⬒ ♨ ⬚ Ⓤ V ♨ ☎
🏠 ♨ 🍴 ☺ ✦ ✕ 🏠

Individual proprietors have supplied all details of accommodation. Although we do check for accuracy, we advise you to confirm prices and other information at the time of booking.

SALFORD
Gtr. Manchester
Map ref 4B1

Industrial city close to Manchester with Roman Catholic cathedral and university. Lowry often painted Salford's industrial architecture and much of his work is in the local art gallery.
Tourist Information Centre ☎ 061-745 8773

Beaucliffe Hotel M
♨♨

254 Eccles Old Road, Salford, M6 8ES
☎ 061-789 5092
Recently modernised, family-run hotel with friendly bar and restaurant. Easy access to centre of Manchester, airport and motorway network.
Bedrooms: 10 single, 2 double & 8 twin, 1 family room.
Bathrooms: 17 private, 1 public.
Bed & breakfast: £27-£34 single, £40-£47 double.
Half board: £36-£47 daily, £240-£295 weekly.
Lunch available.
Evening meal 6.45pm (l.o. 8.45pm).
Parking for 32.
Credit: Access, Visa, Diners, Amex.

⌖ 6 🚗 ® ♨ ⬚ ♨ V ♨ ☎
🏠 ♨ 🍴 ✕ 🏠 SP T

Inn of Good Hope M
♨♨♨ APPROVED

226 Eccles Old Road, Salford, M6 8AG
☎ 061-707 6178
The inn is located close to the major motorways and is only 10 minutes from Manchester city centre.
Bedrooms: 2 single, 2 double & 4 twin.
Bathrooms: 8 private.
Bed & breakfast: £41.50-£46 single, max. £53 double.
Lunch available.
Evening meal 7pm (l.o. 9.30pm).
Parking for 50.
Credit: Access, Visa, Diners, Amex.

⌖ ♨ ⬚ ♨ ⬒ V ♨ ⬚ 🍴
✕ 🏠 SP

White Lodge Private Hotel
♨♨

87-89 Great Cheetham Street West, Broughton, Salford, M7 9JA.
☎ 061-792 3047
Small, family-run hotel, close to city centre amenities.

Bedrooms: 3 single, 3 double & 3 twin.
Bathrooms: 2 public.
Bed & breakfast: from £17 single, from £30 double.
Parking for 6.

⌖ 2 V ♨ ☎ 🏠 ♨ ✕ 🏠

SANDBACH
Cheshire
Map ref 4A2

5m NE. Crewe
Small industrial town, originally important for salt production. Contains narrow, winding streets, timbered houses and a cobbled market-place. Town square has 2 Anglo-Saxon crosses placed there 1300 years ago to commemorate the conversion to Christianity of the son of the King of Mercia.
Tourist Information Centre ☎ (0270) 760460 or 761879

Chimney House Hotel M
♨♨♨

Congleton Road, Sandbach, CW11 0ST
☎ Crewe (0270) 764141 Fax (0270) 768916 Telex 367323
Ⓖ Lansbury
Set in 7.5 acres, 500 yards from the M6 exit 17. Convenient for interrupting your journey north or south, or for your business appointment in the north west.
Bedrooms: 18 single, 22 double & 8 twin, 2 family rooms.
Bathrooms: 50 private.
Bed & breakfast: £24-£74 single, £48-£87 double.
Half board: from £35 daily.
Lunch available.
Evening meal 7pm (l.o. 10pm).
Parking for 110.
Credit: Access, Visa, Diners, Amex.

⌖ 🚗 ♨ ® ♨ ⬚ ♨ V ♨
♨ ● 🏠 ♨ 🍴 ♿ ☺ ✕
⬚ SP T

Poplar Mount Guest House M
♨♨ COMMENDED

2 Station Road, Elworth, Sandbach, CW11 9JG
☎ (0270) 761268
Family-run guesthouse, convenient for M6, railway station and Manchester Airport.
Bedrooms: 2 single, 1 double & 1 twin, 1 family room.
Bathrooms: 2 private, 1 public.
Bed & breakfast: £13.50-£22.50 single, £27-£32 double.

Half board: £19.50-£28.50 daily, from £87.50 weekly.
Lunch available.
Evening meal 6.30pm (l.o. 8pm).
Parking for 6.

⌖ Ⓤ ⬒ ♨ ☎ 🏠 ♨ ♨ 🏠 DAP

Saxon Cross Hotel M
♨♨♨ COMMENDED

M6 Exit 17, Sandbach, CW11 9SE
☎ Crewe (0270) 763281
Telex 367169
Adjacent to the M6 exit 17, in a quiet rural setting 1 mile from Sandbach.
Bedrooms: 10 single, 10 double & 18 twin, 14 family rooms.
Bathrooms: 52 private.
Bed & breakfast: £33-£54 single, £45-£68 double.
Half board: £46.50-£67.50 daily.
Lunch available.
Evening meal 7pm (l.o. 10pm).
Parking for 200.
Credit: Access, Visa, Diners, Amex.

⌖ 🚗 ♨ ® ♨ ⬚ ♨ V ♨
● 🏠 ♨ 🍴 ♿ ☺ SP T

SLAIDBURN
Lancashire
Map ref 4A1

7m N. Clitheroe
Picturesque grey-stone village set in moorland region of the Forest of Bowland, with 13th C church, old grammar school, village green and war memorial.

Gold Hill Country House Hotel M
♨♨ APPROVED

Woodhouse Lane, Slaidburn, Clitheroe, BB7 3AH
☎ (020 06) 202
Family-run 16th C country house with log fires, minstrels' gallery and accent on cooking. Set in 150 acres with breath-taking views and sporting rights. 1 mile from Slaidburn. Liquor licence applied for.
Bedrooms: 1 double & 2 twin, 1 family room.
Bathrooms: 4 private, 1 public.
Bed & breakfast: max. £15 single, max. £30 double.
Half board: max. £36.50 daily, max. £150 weekly.
Lunch available.
Evening meal 7pm.
Parking for 20.
Credit: Access, Visa.

⌖ 🚗 ♨ ⬒ Ⓤ ⬒ ♨ V ♨ ☎
🏠 ♨ Ⓤ ✦ ☺ 🏠 DAP ♨ SP
🏠

SOUTHPORT

Merseyside
Map ref 4A1

Pleasant resort noted for its gardens, long sandy beach and many golf-courses, particularly Royal Birkdale. Southport Flower Show is an annual event. Lord Street is a tree-lined boulevard with fine shops. Atkinson Art Gallery and Steamport Transport Museum are attractions.
Tourist Information Centre ☎ *(0704) 533333*

Allendale Hotel M
21 Avondale Road,
Southport, PR9 0EP
☎ (0704) 530032
Small friendly, private hotel, between Lord Street and the promenade. Home-cooked food. Value for money.
Bedrooms: 1 single, 2 double & 1 twin, 2 family rooms.
Bathrooms: 1 public.
Bed & breakfast: from £12 single, from £23 double.
Half board: from £16.50 daily.
Evening meal 6pm (l.o. 3pm).
Parking for 6.
🛇🖪5🖪🕏🛏🚪TV🎦IIII🖪💷OAP SP

Ambassador Private Hotel
😃😃😃
13 Bath Street, Southport,
PR9 0DP
☎ (0704) 530459 & 543998
Delightful guesthouse centrally situated, 200 yards from promenade and conference centre. All rooms en-suite, TV, beverages.
Bedrooms: 1 single, 2 double & 3 twin, 2 family rooms.
Bathrooms: 8 private,
2 public.
Bed & breakfast: £23-£26 single, £40 double.
Half board: £28 daily, £160 weekly.
Lunch available.
Evening meal 6pm (l.o. 6.30pm).
Parking for 6.
Credit: Access, Visa.
🛇4🖪🕏®🖵🛏🖪🛏TV🖪IIII
🖪🖪🚪OAP🖪

Balmoral Lodge M
😃😃😃😃 COMMENDED
41 Queens Road, Southport,
PR9 9EX
☎ (0704) 544298 & 530751
Fax (0704) 501224

High standard accommodation, close to town centre. All rooms en-suite, with attractive garden wing balcony rooms available. Free sauna. Bargain breaks.
Bedrooms: 4 single, 3 double & 7 twin, 1 family room.
Bathrooms: 15 private,
2 public.
Bed & breakfast: £25-£35 single, £50-£60 double.
Half board: £36-£41 daily, £215-£250 weekly.
Lunch available.
Evening meal 6.30pm (l.o. 8.30pm).
Parking for 10.
Credit: Access, Visa.
🛇2🖪🕏®🛏🖪🖵🕏🛏🖪
TV🎦IIII🖪🖼❋🛦🗡🖪SP

Carlton House Hotel
43 Bath Street, Southport,
PR9 0DP
☎ (0704) 542290
Friendly, family-run private hotel, centrally situated between the famous Lord Street shopping boulevard and promenade. Convenient for theatre, conference centre, cinemas and 6 golf-courses.
Bedrooms: 3 single, 4 double & 2 twin, 4 family rooms.
Bathrooms: 5 private,
2 public.
Bed & breakfast: £13-£16.50 single, £26-£33 double.
Half board: £17-£20.50 daily, £78-£123 weekly.
Evening meal 6pm (l.o. 7pm).
Parking for 6.
🛇🖪🛏🖵🛏UL🗎🖪V🛏TV
IIII🖪🖪OAP🗡

Dukes Folly Hotel M
11 Duke Street, Southport,
PR8 1LS
☎ (0704) 533355
Ideally situated at the Birkdale end of Lord Street, all rooms en-suite. A la carte restaurant and conservatory. Opposite indoor shopping centre and winter garden.
Bedrooms: 8 single, 2 double & 8 twin, 1 family room.
Bathrooms: 19 private,
1 public.
Bed & breakfast: £28.50-£36.50 single, £44-£48 double.
Half board: £39-£47 daily, £195-£225 weekly.
Evening meal 6pm (l.o. 10pm).
Parking for 12.
Credit: Access, Visa, Amex.
🛇🖪🖪🛏®🖵🕏🖪V
🗡🛏TV🎦IIII🖪🖪🗡🖪SP🖪

Gables Private Hotel
😃😃😃
110 Leyland Road,
Southport, PR9 0JG
☎ (0704) 535554

Small private hotel, quietly situated near North Promenade, within a few minutes' walk of main amenities.
Bedrooms: 1 single, 4 double & 4 twin.
Bathrooms: 8 private,
1 public.
Bed & breakfast: £36-£40 double.
Half board: £25-£28 daily, £158-£170 weekly.
Evening meal 5.45pm (l.o. 6.15pm).
Parking for 10.
Open April-October.
🖪🖪🖵🕏🖪🛏TV🎦IIII🖪🖼
🗡🛏OAP

Leicester Hotel
😃😃
24 Leicester Street,
Southport, PR9 0EZ
☎ (0704) 530049
Family run hotel with personal attention, clean and comfortable, close to all amenities. Car park. Licensed bar.
Bedrooms: 2 single, 4 double & 2 twin, 1 family room.
Bathrooms: 1 private,
2 public.
Bed & breakfast: £13-£16 single, £24-£28 double.
Half board: £18-£21 daily.
Evening meal 6pm.
Parking for 6.
Credit: Access, Visa.
🛇🖪🕏🖵🖪V🖼TV🎦IIII🖪🗡
OAP SP

Lockerbie House Hotel M
😃😃😃
11 Trafalgar Road, Birkdale,
Southport, PR8 2EA
☎ (0704) 565298
Large detached hotel, comfortably furnished, in a quiet location close to Royal Birkdale and Hillside Golf Clubs. Full-size snooker table available.
Bedrooms: 4 single, 2 double & 6 twin, 2 family rooms.
Bathrooms: 14 private.
Bed & breakfast: from £25 single, from £46 double.
Half board: from £33.50 daily, from £180 weekly.
Evening meal 7pm (l.o. 8pm).
Parking for 16.
Credit: Access, Visa, Diners, Amex.
🛇🖪🖵🕏🖪V🛏TV🎦IIII
🖪🗡🖪OAP SP

Metropole Hotel M
😃😃😃
3 Portland Street, Southport,
PR8 1LL
☎ (0704) 536836

Family hotel with resident proprietors. Centrally located with 6 golf-courses nearby. Full-size snooker table. Full licence.
Bedrooms: 14 single, 3 double & 5 twin, 3 family rooms.
Bathrooms: 18 private,
4 public.
Bed & breakfast: £22-£30 single, £39.60-£53.50 double.
Half board: £31-£39 daily, £200-£250 weekly.
Lunch available.
Evening meal 7pm (l.o. 8.30pm).
Parking for 12.
Credit: Access, Visa, Amex.
🛇🖪®🖵🕏🖪V🛏TV
IIII🖪🖪🕏🗡🖪SP

Radley Hotel M
😃😃😃 COMMENDED
26 The Promenade,
Southport, PR8 1QU
☎ (0704) 530310
On the promenade in the heart of Southport, this friendly old hotel offers food and accommodation of a high standard. Bar snacks served at lunch time.
Bedrooms: 1 single, 7 double & 3 twin, 1 family room.
Bathrooms: 6 private,
3 public.
Bed & breakfast: £17-£22 single, £32-£40 double.
Half board: £22-£29 daily, £125-£145 weekly.
Evening meal 6pm (l.o. 7pm).
Parking for 8.
Credit: Access, Visa.
🛇🖪🖵🕏🖪V🛏TV🎦IIII
🖪🗡🗡OAP🖪SP🖪

Rosedale Hotel M
😃😃😃 APPROVED
11 Talbot Street, Southport,
PR8 1HP
☎ (0704) 530604
Well-established, family-run, private hotel. Centrally situated with licensed bar and reading room. All bedrooms with tea and coffee making facilities, some en-suite.
Bedrooms: 3 single, 3 double & 1 twin, 3 family rooms.
Bathrooms: 5 private,
1 public.
Bed & breakfast: £14-£18 single, £28-£36 double.
Half board: £20-£24 daily, £110-£140 weekly.
Evening meal 6pm (l.o. 4pm).
Parking for 10.
🛇🖪🖵🕏🗎V🛏IIII🖪🗡
OAP🖪SP🖪

Please mention this guide when making a booking.

SOUTHPORT
Continued

Scarisbrick Hotel M
👑👑👑👑 COMMENDED
239 Lord Street, Southport,
PR8 1NZ
☎ (0704) 542300 Telex 67107
Cb Consort
*Prominent town centre hotel
with modern interior, clad in
Victorian style. Family owned
and managed. Several bars
and function suites.*
Bedrooms: 8 single, 21 double
& 24 twin, 5 family rooms.
Bathrooms: 58 private,
1 public.
Bed & breakfast: £52-£65
single, £65-£105 double.
Half board: £233-£303
weekly.
Lunch available.
Evening meal 7pm (l.o.
9.30pm).
Parking for 40.
Credit: Access, Visa, Diners,
Amex.
🛇 🖾 📞 🖵 🖵 🌡 ⓘ Ⅴ 🛏
🖬 ⊞ 🖬 📠 🍷 ⚓ ⚷ ⊠ ❊ 🛠
🏛 T

Sidbrook Hotel M
👑👑
14 Talbot Street, Southport,
PR8 1HP
☎ (0704) 530608 & 531491
*Detached Victorian house in
quiet street, yet centrally
located. Sauna, sunbed, pool
table and free in-room Sky
satellite TV. Secluded garden.*
Bedrooms: 2 single, 2 double
& 4 twin, 2 family rooms.
Bathrooms: 6 private,
1 public.
Bed & breakfast: £15-£18
single, £30-£36 double.
Half board: £21-£24 daily,
£95-£145 weekly.
Evening meal 6pm (l.o.
6.30pm).
Parking for 10.
Credit: Access, Visa, Amex.
🛇 🖾 📞 🖵 🖵 🌡 ⓘ Ⅴ 🛏 ⊞
📠 ⚷ ⚓ 🖬 🖬 ⓐ ⊠ ⓢ

Stutelea Hotel, and Leisure Club M
👑👑👑👑 COMMENDED
Alexandra Road, Southport,
PR9 0NB
☎ (0704) 544220
*Charming, licensed hotel, in
pleasant gardens with heated
indoor swimming pool, sauna,
jacuzzi, gymnasium, solarium
and games room. Convenient
for promenade, marina, golf-
courses and shopping centre.
Also 9 self-catering
apartments.*
Bedrooms: 1 single, 11 double
& 8 twin, 7 family rooms.

Bathrooms: 27 private,
4 public.
Bed & breakfast: from £40
single, from £60 double.
Half board: from £40 daily,
from £220 weekly.
Lunch available.
Evening meal 6.30pm (l.o.
8pm).
Parking for 16.
Credit: Access, Visa, Diners,
Amex.
🛇 🖾 📞 🖵 🖵 🌡 ⓘ Ⅴ 🛏
🖬 ⊞ 📠 🍷 ⚷ ⚓ ⓢ ⚷ ❊ 🛠
🏛 T

Talbot Hotel M
👑👑👑
23-25 Portland Street,
Southport, PR8 1LR
☎ (0704) 533975 & 530126
*Detached, medium-sized
family-run hotel, in a central,
quiet position near main
shopping areas, entertainments
and services.*
Bedrooms: 2 single, 5 double
& 15 twin, 2 family rooms.
Bathrooms: 18 private,
2 public.
Bed & breakfast: £27.50-
£37.50 single, £44-£50 double.
Half board: £33-£48 daily,
£180-£248 weekly.
Lunch available.
Evening meal 6pm (l.o. 8pm).
Parking for 30.
Open January-November.
Credit: Access, Visa, Amex.
🛇 🖾 📞 🖵 🖵 🌡 ⓘ Ⅴ 🛏
TV 📠 🍷 ⚓ ⚷ OAP ⚷ ⓢ

STOCKPORT
Gtr. Manchester
Map ref 4B2

This former market town
on the River Mersey, built
by Cheshire gentry,
became an important
cotton-spinning and
railway centre. Town has
an impressive railway
viaduct and a shopping
precinct covering the
Mersey, and an ancient
grammar school. Lyme
Hall and Vernon Park
Museum nearby.
*Tourist Information
Centre* ☎ 061-474 3320

Ascot House Hotel
👑👑
195 Wellington Road North,
Heaton Norris, Stockport,
SK4 2PB
☎ 061-432 2380 Telex 666514
Tortec G
*Convenient for Manchester
Airport, city centre and the
Peak District. 2 minutes from
the M63.*
Bedrooms: 6 single, 7 double
& 5 twin.

Bathrooms: 12 private,
3 public; 4 private showers.
Bed & breakfast: £15-£35
single, £30-£45 double.
Evening meal 5.30pm (l.o.
7.15pm).
Parking for 21.
Credit: Access, Visa, Amex.
🛇 🖾 🖾 ⓒ 🖵 🖵 🌡 🖵 TV
📠 ⚓ ⚷ ⚓ ⚷ 🛠 ⓢ T

Brackley House Hotel M
👑👑 COMMENDED
292 Wellington Road North,
Heaton Chapel, Stockport,
SK4 2QS
☎ 061-432 1684
*Family-owned hotel with en-
suite facilities, on main
Manchester to Stockport bus
and rail routes. 12 minutes to
airport, 5 minutes to station.*
Bedrooms: 4 single, 2 double,
1 family room.
Bathrooms: 5 private,
1 public.
Bed & breakfast: £17.25-
£20.70 single, £36-£41.40
double.
Half board: £26.70-£30 daily.
Evening meal 6.30pm (l.o.
6.30pm).
Parking for 10.
🛇 🖾 🖾 🖵 🖵 🌡 🖵 TV 🖬 📠
🛠 🖬 ⓢ

Durham Villa Hotel M
👑👑 APPROVED
261 Wellington Road North,
Heaton Chapel, Stockport,
SK4 5BS
☎ 061-431 8194
*Victorian family home now
converted into small family
guest house/hotel. Situated on
main A6 trunk road. 1 mile to
Stockport town centre and then
on to the famous Peak District.*
Bedrooms: 4 single, 1 twin,
2 family rooms.
Bathrooms: 2 public.
Bed & breakfast: from £15
single, from £28 double.
Parking for 8.
Credit: Access, Visa, C.Bl.,
Diners, Amex.
🛇 🌡 UL Ⅴ 🛠 🖵 TV ● 🖬
📠 🛠 🖬

Ravenoak Hotel
Ravenoak Road, Cheadle
Hulme, Cheadle, Cheshire
SK8 7EQ
☎ 061-485 3376/1095
*Only 9 miles from Manchester
city centre, 4 miles from
Stockport, 3 miles from
Manchester Airport,
(Ringway), a gateway to the
world. Also well placed for
travellers wishing to join the
M6, M62, M63 and M56
motorways.*
Bedrooms: 30 single, 1 double
& 6 twin, 1 family room.

Bathrooms: 20 private,
4 public; 3 private showers.
Bed & breakfast: £35.50-
£40.50 single, £46.50-£57
double.
Evening meal 6.30pm (l.o.
8.45pm).
Parking for 62.
Credit: Access, Visa, Diners,
Amex.
🛇 🖾 📞 ⓒ 🌡 ⓘ Ⅴ 🛏 TV
🖬 📠 🍷 ⚓ ⚷

STRETFORD
Gtr. Manchester
Map ref 4B2

Famous as home of
Manchester United
Football Club and
Lancashire County
Cricket Club at Old
Trafford, Stretford
developed with the
opening of the
Manchester Ship Canal in
1894.

Greatstone Hotel
845 Chester Road, Stretford,
M32 0RN
☎ 061-865 1640
*Family-run hotel a few miles
from Manchester city centre.
Most rooms have tea and
coffee making facilities. Close
to Old Trafford and
Manchester United Football
Club and Sports Centre.*
Bedrooms: 12 single, 5 double
& 10 twin, 2 family rooms.
Bathrooms: 7 private,
3 public; 10 private showers.
Bed & breakfast: £20-£22
single, £36-£42 double.
Lunch available.
Evening meal 6pm (l.o. 9pm).
Parking for 74.
Credit: Access.
🛇 🖾 🖾 🖵 ⓘ Ⅴ 🛏 TV ●
🖬 🍷 ⚓

THORNTON
Lancashire
Map ref 4A1

The Victorian House M
👑👑👑👑 COMMENDED
Trunnah Road, Thornton,
Cleveleys, FY5 4HF
☎ (0253) 860619
*Victorian house set in 1 acre of
gardens. Has authentic
Victorian decor but with a
restaurant providing French
cuisine. Open for lunch
Tuesday to Saturday served in
our conservatory.*
Bedrooms: 3 double.
Bathrooms: 3 private.
Bed & breakfast: max. £37.50
single, £55-£65 double.
Half board: max. £43 daily.

Evening meal 7pm (l.o. 9.30pm).
Parking for 20.
Credit: Access, Visa.

WALLASEY
Merseyside
Map ref 4A2

Resort and residential area on the north east corner of the Wirral peninsula overlooking the Mersey Estuary and linked to Liverpool by a short ferry crossing. Pleasant seafront promenade from Wallasey to New Brighton with sandy beach continuing to Hoylake.

Wellington House Private Hotel M
65 Wellington Road, New Brighton, Wallasey, L45 2NE
☎ 051-639 6594
Family-run business, convenient for train station and bus routes. Snack meals available until 11.30 p.m.
Bedrooms: 6 double & 3 twin, 2 family rooms.
Bathrooms: 4 private, 3 public.
Bed & breakfast: £12-£18 single, £22-£31 double.
Half board: £16.95-£22.95 daily.
Evening meal 6.30pm (l.o. 8pm).
Parking for 14.

WARRINGTON
Cheshire
Map ref 4A2

16m SW. Manchester
Has prehistoric and Roman origins. Once the 'beer capital of Britain' because so much beer was brewed here. Developed in the 18th and 19th C as a commercial and industrial town. Municipal Museum and Art Gallery contain local history.
Tourist Information Centre ☎ (0925) 36501

Fir Grove Hotel M
COMMENDED
Knutsford Old Road, Warrington, WA4 2LD
☎ (0925) 67471 Fax (0925) 601092 Telex 628117

Situated in residential area, on A50 2 miles from exit 20 of M6.
Bedrooms: 20 single, 10 double & 10 twin.
Bathrooms: 40 private.
Bed & breakfast: £50-£60 single, £60-£70 double.
Half board: £60-£70 daily.
Lunch available.
Evening meal 7pm (l.o. 9.45pm).
Parking for 100.
Credit: Access, Visa, Diners, Amex.

Garden Court Holiday Inn M
1 Woolston Grange Avenue, Woolston, Warrington, WA1 4PX
☎ Padgate (0925) 831158
Fax (0925) 838859
Holiday Inn
Reduced service brand hotel, offering bedrooms at value for money price. Price is per room, regardless of the number of occupants.
Bedrooms: 86 double, 14 family rooms.
Bathrooms: 100 private.
Bed & breakfast: £38-£61 single, £44-£67 double.
Half board: £33-£44 daily, £300 weekly.
Evening meal 6.30pm (l.o. 9.45pm).
Parking for 100.
Credit: Access, Visa, C.Bl., Diners, Amex.

Haydock Lodge Hotel
60b High Street, Golborne, Nr. Warrington, WA3 3BH
☎ (0942) 715516
Small, friendly hotel close to M6 juction 23 off A580, halfway between Manchester and Liverpool.
Bedrooms: 3 single, 2 double & 8 twin, 2 family rooms.
Bathrooms: 3 private, 4 public; 2 showers.
Bed & breakfast: £14.90-£17.90 single, £23-£26.90 double.
Half board: £19.65-£24.65 daily.
Evening meal 6.30pm (l.o. 7.30pm).
Parking for 16.

The symbols are explained on the flap inside the back cover.

Kenilworth Hotel M
2 Victoria Road, A50 Knutsford Road, Grappenhall, Warrington, WA4 2EN
☎ (0925) 62323
Large Victorian detached residence on corner site adjacent to the A50 Warrington South.
Bedrooms: 10 single, 3 double & 3 twin, 1 family room.
Bathrooms: 17 private, 1 public.
Bed & breakfast: £18-£30 single, £30-£40 double.
Parking for 18.
Credit: Access, Visa, Diners.

Tyrol House Hotel M
Folly Lane, Bewsey, Warrington, WA5 5LZ
☎ (0925) 30106
Family-run hotel 2 miles from the M62 and M6. Convenient for both Liverpool and Manchester airports.
Bedrooms: 17 single, 2 double & 5 twin, 1 family room.
Bathrooms: 25 private.
Bed & breakfast: £22-£36 single, £38-£48 double.
Lunch available.
Evening meal 7pm (l.o. 9pm).
Parking for 100.
Credit: Access, Visa, Amex.

WEST KIRBY
Merseyside
Map ref 4A2

Riders Hay Guest House
189 Greasby Road, Greasby, Wirral, L49 2PE
☎ 051-677 0682
Small, comfortable, family-run guesthouse offering a high standard of cleanliness. Good food and furnishings throughout. Evening meal Monday-Thursday. Non-smokers only please.
Bedrooms: 2 single, 2 twin.
Bathrooms: 2 public.
Bed & breakfast: from £16 single, from £30 double.
Half board: from £22 daily.
Evening meal 6pm (l.o. 6.30pm).
Parking for 6.

WHALLEY
Lancashire
Map ref 4A1

Interesting village on the River Calder containing the ruins of Whalley Abbey founded by Cistercian monks in 1300. Noteworthy buildings are 13th C St. Mary's Church, the old grammar school and the cottage where Harrison Ainsworth wrote 'The Lancashire Witches'.

Easterly Farm M
Listed HIGHLY COMMENDED
Whalley, Nr. Blackburn, BB6 9DS
☎ (025 482) 2210
Attractively converted stone-built barn with lovely views from all windows. Offering a high standard of accommodation.
Bedrooms: 1 double & 1 twin.
Bathrooms: 2 private.
Bed & breakfast: £18 single, £25-£28 double.
Parking for 6.

WIGAN
Gtr. Manchester
Map ref 4A1

Although a major industrial town, Wigan is an ancient settlement which received a royal charter in 1246. Famous for its pier distinguished in Orwell's 'Road to Wigan Pier'. The pier has now been developed as a major tourist attraction and reinstated to its former working condition.
Tourist Information Centre ☎ (0942) 825677

Bel-Air Hotel M
236 Wigan Lane, Wigan, WN1 2NU
☎ (0942) 41410 Telex 67428
Comfortable family-run hotel in leafy suburb. On A49, 3 miles from junction 27, 1 mile from Wigan town centre.
Bedrooms: 4 single, 3 double & 3 twin, 2 family rooms.
Bathrooms: 11 private, 2 public.
Bed & breakfast: £33-£36 single, £43-£46 double.
Half board: £40-£46 daily.
Lunch available.
Evening meal 6pm (l.o. 9.30pm).
Parking for 10.
Credit: Access, Visa.

WIGAN
Continued

Bellingham Hotel M
♛♛♛
149 Wigan Lane, Wigan,
WN1 2NB
☎ (0942) 43893
*Former Victorian terrace
house, fully reconstructed in
1990, and situated close to
town centre on A49 road near
to Haigh Park.*
Bedrooms: 9 single, 9 double
& 10 twin, 2 family rooms.
Bathrooms: 30 private.
Bed & breakfast: £35-£50
single, £50-£70 double.
Half board: £35-£45 daily.
Lunch available.
Evening meal 7pm (l.o.
9.45pm).
Parking for 40.
Credit: Access, Visa, Amex.

Kilhey Court Hotel M
♛♛♛♛
Chorley Road, Worthington,
Wigan, WN1 2XN
☎ Standish (0257) 472100
Fax (0257) 422401
Telex 67460
*Country house hotel with
superb indoor leisure club set in
10 acres of gardens, fringed by
Worthington lakes and nature
reserve.*
Bedrooms: 28 double &
26 twin.
Bathrooms: 54 private.
Bed & breakfast: £35-£80
single, £45-£85 double.
Half board: £50-£95 daily,
£350-£500 weekly.
Lunch available.
Evening meal 7pm (l.o.
9.45pm).
Parking for 210.
Credit: Access, Visa, Diners,
Amex.

Prescott's Farm Restaurant and Country Motel M
COMMENDED
Lees Lane, Dalton, Nr.
Wigan, WN8 7RB
☎ Parbold (025 76) 4137
*Ideally located in 2 acres of
peaceful gardens and orchards.
7 minutes from exit 27 of M6.*
Bedrooms: 2 single, 2 double
& 1 twin.
Bathrooms: 5 private.
Bed & breakfast: £45 single,
£58 double.
Lunch available.

Evening meal 6.30pm (l.o.
10pm).
Parking for 25.
Credit: Access, Visa.

WILMSLOW
Cheshire
Map ref 4B2

This residential suburb of
Manchester is on the
River Bollin and bordered
on 3 sides by open
country.

Dean Bank House M
Adlington Road, Wilmslow,
SK9 2BT
☎ (0625) 524268
*Easily accessible from M6,
M56, M63 and Manchester
Airport. Family-run Victorian
farmhouse with converted,
modern ground-floor annexe.
Set in lawned gardens and
surrounded by fields. 2 miles
from centre of Wilmslow. Ideal
base for many interesting
outings.*
Bedrooms: 2 single, 6 double
& 5 twin, 4 family rooms.
Bathrooms: 12 private,
1 public.
Bed & breakfast: from £16
single, £36-£45 double.
Evening meal 6.30pm (l.o.
2pm).
Parking for 18.
Credit: Access, Visa.

Laburnum Cottage M
Listed COMMENDED
Knutsford Road, Mobberley,
Nr. Knutsford, WA16 7PU
☎ (0565) 872464
*A small country house set
amidst Cheshire countryside on
B5085 close to Tatton Park, 4
miles from Manchester Airport,
4 miles from Wilmslow, 1.5
miles from M6 exit 19 and 2
miles from M56. Pretty garden
and log fires. Non-smokers
only please.*
Bedrooms: 2 single, 1 double
& 2 twin.
Bathrooms: 4 private,
1 public.
Bed & breakfast: £18-£23
single, £30-£38 double.
Parking for 6.
Open January-November.

Lisieux M
COMMENDED
199 Wilmslow Road,
Handforth, Wilmslow,
SK9 3JX
☎ (0625) 522113

*Homely with spacious gardens,
offering a high standard of
accommodation. Manchester
airport 3 miles. English
breakfast available at whatever
time required by guests. Ample
parking.*
Bedrooms: 1 single, 1 double
& 1 twin.
Bathrooms: 2 private,
1 public.
Bed & breakfast: £25 single,
£35 double.
Half board: £33.50 daily,
£234.50 weekly.
Evening meal 6pm (l.o.
7.30pm).
Parking for 5.

Milverton House Hotel M
♛♛
Wilmslow Road, Alderley
Edge, SK9 7QL
☎ (0625) 583615 & 585555
*Well-appointed Victorian villa
on main road with open
country views. Home cooking.*
Bedrooms: 4 single, 5 double
& 3 twin, 2 family rooms.
Bathrooms: 5 private,
4 public; 5 private showers.
Bed & breakfast: £35-£45
single, £45-£60 double.
Half board: from £45 daily,
from £180 weekly.
Evening meal 6.30pm.
Parking for 16.
Credit: Access, Visa.

Moss House Guest House M
Moss Lane, Styal, Wilmslow,
SK9 4LG
☎ 061-499 1721
*Pleasant guesthouse with
homely atmosphere, set in its
own grounds. Free courtesy
service to the airport and
parking facilities for your car
while you are on holiday.*
Bedrooms: 1 single, 3 double
& 2 twin.
Bathrooms: 2 public.
Bed & breakfast: from £16
single, from £24 double.
Parking for 100.

WINCLE
Cheshire
Map ref 4B2

5m SE. Macclesfield
The sign on the Ship Inn
at this remote hamlet high
up in the Peak District
depicts the 'Nimrod', the
vessel in which the local
Sir Philip Brocklehurst
accompanied Shackleton
to the Antarctic.

Fourways Diner Motel
♛♛♛ **APPROVED**
Cleulow Cross, Wincle, Nr.
Macclesfield, SK11 0QL
☎ (0260) 227228
*Small family-run motel and
licensed restaurant with
panoramic views, in the Peak
District National Park
overlooking Dane Valley and
Roaches.*
Bedrooms: 5 double & 2 twin,
3 family rooms.
Bathrooms: 10 private.
Bed & breakfast: £25-£50
single, £35-£40 double.
Evening meal 5.50pm (l.o.
8pm).
Parking for 40.
Credit: Access, Visa.

WIRRAL
*See Bebington,
Birkenhead,
Bromborough, Hoylake,
Neston, Parkgate,
Wallasey, West Kirby.*

**Classifications and quality commendations
were correct at the time of going to press
but are subject to change. Please check at
the time of booking.**

**The National Crown Scheme is explained
in full on pages 556 – 558.**

May — Dene Private Hotel
(LICENSED)

10 Dean Street, South Shore, Blackpool FY4 1AU

A well recommended friendly family Hotel, in a Sun-Trap Area, close to the Prom South Pier Sandcastle & Pleasure Beach.

★ Good Food ★ Full Central Heating ★ Open All Year ★ Car Park

Bed & Breakfast: £10-£13 (single)   £20-£26 (double)
Half Board: £12.50-£17.50 daily   £80-£105 weekly
Discounts for OAPs and children

Write or Phone for Brochure. (0253) 43464

Needham's Farm

**Uplands Road, Werneth Low, Gee Cross,
Nr Hyde, Cheshire SK14 3AQ.
Tel: 061-368 4610   Fax: 061-367 9106**

APPROVED   RAC Acclaimed

Needhams is a small working farm, dating back to the 16th century. Offering 6 bedrooms, 3 en-suite. All rooms have telephone, radio, colour TV and tea/coffee makers. Delicious meals are served with a hint of a Scottish flavour. Horse riding and golf courses are nearby. The farm is situated just outside the boundary of the Peak National Park, nestling between Werneth Low Country Park and Etherow Valley.
**£15 single, £16 en-suite single.
£30 double, £32 en-suite double.**

The Pheasant

COMMENDED

Higher Burwardsley,
Tattenhall, Cheshire
Telephone: (0829) 70434

The Pheasant is a three hundred year old Inn, nestling on the top of the Peckforton Hills just 10 miles from Chester. All bedrooms have central heating, colour TV, radio/alarm and en suite facilities plus panoramic views over the Cheshire plain. Bistro and bar snack menu available 7 days. Fully licensed. Large car park. An ideal centre for touring Cheshire. Under personal management.

Use a coupon

When requesting further information from advertisers in this guide, you may find it helpful to use the advertisement enquiry coupons which can be found towards the end of the guide. These should be cut out and mailed direct to the companies in which you are interested. Do remember to include your name and address.

The signs of confidence

Look for signs like these when you're booking accommodation in a hotel, guesthouse, farmhouse, inn or B&B — they tell you that the establishment has been inspected by the Tourist Board and that it meets or exceeds minimum quality standards.

All you have to remember is that the classification (from Listed up to Five Crown) indicates the range of facilities and services while the commendation (Approved, Commended or Highly Commended) indicates the quality standard of the facilities and services.

The absence of a quality commendation from any entry in this 'Where to Stay' guide may be because the establishment had not been quality assessed at the time of going to press.

Check the maps

The place you wish to visit may not have accommodation entirely suited to your needs, but there could be somewhere ideal quite close by. Check the colour maps towards the end of this guide to identify nearby towns and villages with accommodation listed in the guide, and then use the town index to find page numbers.

🍀 Enjoy the countryside and respect its life and work 🍀 Guard against all risk of fire 🍀 Fasten all gates 🍀 Keep your dogs under close control 🍀 Keep to public paths across farmland 🍀 Use gates and stiles to cross fences, hedges and walls 🍀 Leave livestock, crops and machinery alone 🍀 Take your litter home 🍀 Help to keep all water clean 🍀 Protect wildlife, plants and trees 🍀 Take special care on country roads 🍀 Make no unnecessary noise

Yorkshire & Humberside

A breath of fresh air under a big and breezy sky — that's the Yorkshire and Humberside region.

》 From the western swath of the Dales, Peaks and Pennines, across the Vale of York and Broad Acres to the Moors, Wolds and east coast — everywhere you'll enjoy an unrivalled variety of scenery and things to do. Variety is one of the region's great assets, so whatever your taste, this is the place to be.

》 A kaleidoscope of towns and cities beckons you — like flower-bedecked Harrogate, bustling Leeds and cosmopolitan Bradford; like ancient Barnsley, seafaring Hull and the fishing port of Grimsby. Is shopping your bag? It can be elegant in places such as York, and modern in huge undercover centres like Sheffield's Meadowhall. Everywhere arts and crafts are bought in studios and workshops, bargains sought in markets and factory shops.

》 The region has every kind of seaside. The broad sweep of Robin Hood's Bay and its steep streets matches the different charm of Scarborough's twin beaches, while traditional holidays are for the taking in Whitby, Cleethorpes, Bridlington and Filey. Nowhere is birdwatching more exciting than at mighty Flamborough Head or more tranquil than from the small fishing villages dotted among the coves and cliffs.

》 You could climb a limestone crag, maybe, or walk a lush green dale

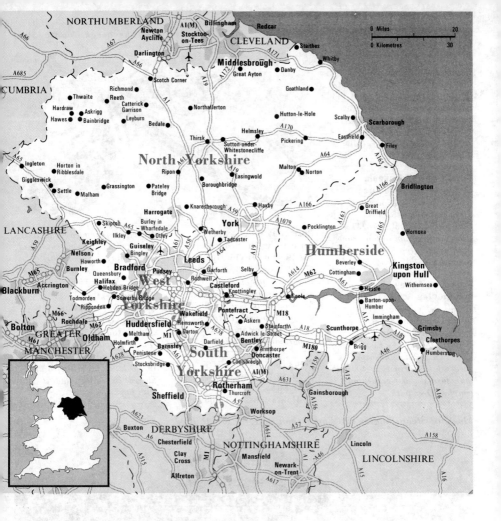

or cycle around stunning television locations. Not for you? Then glide, ride, swim, or pothole; visit historic houses and gardens or browse through museums celebrating everything from Roman artefacts to television. There are Beverley and York Minsters to marvel at, waterfalls to wonder at, the world's longest single-span suspension bridge to gaze at, white-knuckle rides to lose your tummy at... always meeting the friendliest people everywhere.

>> Yorkshire and Humberside is waiting for you. What are you waiting for?

·>> **Please refer to the colour maps at the back of this guide for all places with accommodation listings.**

Where to go, what to see

Try your hand at fly fishing at Thrybergh Country Park

Castle Howard
Malton, N. Yorkshire YO6 7BZ
☎ Coneysthorpe (065 384) 333
Set in 1,000 acres of magnificent parkland with nature walks, scenic lake and stunning rose gardens. Important furniture and works of art.

Cusworth Hall Museum of South Yorkshire Life
Cusworth Lane, Doncaster, S. Yorkshire DN5 7TU
☎ Doncaster (0302) 782342
Georgian mansion in landscaped park, containing Museum of South Yorkshire Life.

Fountains Abbey and Studley Royal
Ripon, N. Yorkshire HG4 3DZ
☎ Sawley (076 586) 333
Largest monastic ruin in Britain, founded by Cistercian monks in 1132. Landscaped garden laid out in 1720-40, with lake, formal water-garden and temples. Deer park.

Normanby Hall
Normanby, Nr. Scunthorpe, Humberside DN15 9HU
☎ Scunthorpe (0724) 720215
Regency mansion by Sir Robert Smirke, architect of British Museum. Furnished and decorated in period, with displays of costume. 350 acres of parkland, deer park.

Piece Hall
Halifax, W. Yorkshire HX1 1RE
☎ Halifax (0422) 358087
Historic colonnaded Cloth Hall, surrounding open-air courtyard and comprising shops, art gallery and museum.

Skipton Castle
Skipton, N. Yorkshire BD23 1AQ
☎ Skipton (0756) 792442
One of the most complete and well-preserved medieval castles in England. Fully roofed and floored. Beautiful Conduit Court with famous yew.

Masham Steam Engine and Fair Organ Rally – 20 – 21 July

Thrybergh Country Park
Doncaster Road, Rotherham,
S. Yorkshire S65 4NU
☎ Rotherham (0709) 850353
*63-acre country park with lake.
Fly fishing, sailing, wind-
surfing, canoeing. Craft for hire.
Picnic areas.*

Hull and East Riding Museum
High Street, Hull, Humberside
☎ Hull (0482) 222737
*Humberside archaeology, Iron
Age Hasholme boat and chariot
burials, Romano-British mosaics.*

Make a date for...

**Bicentennial Celebrations
1791-1991**
Yorkshire Mining Museum,
Caphouse Colliery, Overton,
Wakefield, West Yorkshire
2 January – 31 December

Jorvik Viking Festival
Various venues, York, North
Yorkshire
2 – 23 February

**Harrogate International
Youth Music Festival**
Various venues, Harrogate,
North Yorkshire
27 March – 3 April

Beverley Folk Festival
Various venues, Beverley,
Humberside
14 – 16 June

Great Yorkshire Show
Great Yorkshire Showground,
Harrogate, North Yorkshire
9 – 11 July

World Student Games
Sheffield, South Yorkshire
14 – 25 July

**Masham Steam Engine
and Fair Organ Rally**
Low Burton Hall, Masham,
North Yorkshire
20 – 21 July

Great Autumn Flower Show
Exhibition Centre, Ripon Road,
Harrogate, North Yorkshire
13 – 14 September

Find out more

Further information about
holidays and attractions in the
Yorkshire & Humberside
region is available from:
**Yorkshire & Humberside
Tourist Board,** 312 Tadcaster
Road, York, North Yorkshire
YO2 2HF. ☎ (0904) 707961.

Please contact the board for
details of publications available.

Follow the sign

It leads to over 560 Tourist Information Centres throughout
England offering friendly help with accommodation and holiday
ideas as well as suggestions of places to visit and things to do.

In your home town there may be a centre which can help
you before you set out. Details of the locations of Tourist
Information Centres are available from the English Tourist
Board, Thames Tower, Black's Road, London W6 9EL, or from
England's Regional Tourist Boards.

Places to stay

»> Accommodation entries in this regional section are listed in alphabetical order of place name, and then in alphabetical order of establishment.

»> The map references refer to the colour maps towards the end of the guide. The first figure is the map number; the letter and figure which follow indicate the grid reference on the map.

»> The symbols at the end of each accommodation entry give information about services and facilities. A 'key' to these symbols is inside the back cover flap, which can be kept open for easy reference.

ACASTER MALBIS
N. Yorkshire
Map ref 4C1

5m S. York

Manor Country Guest House ⋒
Acaster Malbis, York, YO2 1UL
☎ York (0904) 706723
Peacefully modernised 18th C house in 6 acres of landscaped woodland gardens by the River Ouse. 4 and a half miles from York centre.
Bedrooms: 4 single, 2 double & 4 twin, 2 family rooms.
Bathrooms: 5 private, 2 public.
Bed & breakfast: £13-£18 single, £30-£36 double.
Half board: £21.50-£24.50 daily, £145.50-£165.50 weekly.
Evening meal 6pm (l.o. 6.30pm).
Parking for 16.

Classifications and quality commendations were correct at the time of going to press but are subject to change. Please check at the time of booking.

APPLETON-LE-MOORS
N. Yorkshire
Map ref 5C3

5m NW. Pickering
Small village on the edge of the North York Moors, with spired Victorian church.

Dweldapilton Hall Hotel ⋒
Appleton-le-Moors, York, YO6 6TF
☎ Lastingham (075 15) 227
Telex 57468
A mellowed, early Victorian villa with fine Italian plasterwork. Enhanced by mature specimen trees in a pleasant 2-acre setting.
Bedrooms: 1 single, 5 double & 6 twin.
Bathrooms: 12 private.
Bed & breakfast: £38-£40 single, £76-£80 double.
Half board: £55.50-£57 daily, £325-£340 weekly.
Lunch available.
Evening meal 7pm (l.o. 8pm).
Parking for 20.
Credit: Access, Visa, Amex.

Map references apply to the colour maps towards the end of this guide.

ARNCLIFFE
N. Yorkshire
Map ref 5B3

On the River Skirfare in Littondale, Arncliffe is an attractive Dales village with a green and 17th C stone cottages and houses.

Amerdale House Hotel ⋒
Arncliffe, (Littondale), Skipton, BD23 5QE
☎ (075 677) 250
Country house hotel with beautiful open views of Littondale. Offering comfortable, elegant accommodation, with emphasis on food and friendly, caring hospitality.
Bedrooms: 6 double & 4 twin, 2 family rooms.
Bathrooms: 12 private, 1 public.
Half board: £46-£49 daily.
Evening meal 7pm (l.o. 8.30pm).
Parking for 20.
Open March-November.
Credit: Access, Visa.

Littondale Country House Hotel ⋒
🏠🏠🏠 COMMENDED
Litton, Skipton, BD23 5QE
☎ Arncliffe (075 677) 293
Tastefully furnished country house hotel with magnificent views.
Bedrooms: 3 double & 2 twin, 1 family room.
Bathrooms: 6 private.

Bed & breakfast: £37-£44 double.
Half board: £29.45-£32.95 daily.
Evening meal 7pm (l.o. 8pm).
Parking for 6.

ARRATHORNE
N. Yorkshire
Map ref 5C3

5m NW. Bedale

Elmfield House ⋒
🏠🏠🏠 APPROVED
Arrathorne, Bedale, DL8 1NE
☎ Bedale (0677) 50558
Country house in its own grounds with open views of the countryside. Special emphasis on standards and home cooking. Solarium.
Bedrooms: 4 double & 3 twin, 2 family rooms.
Bathrooms: 9 private, 1 public.
Bed & breakfast: £20-£22 single, £32-£36 double.
Half board: £24.50-£28.50 daily, £164-£178 weekly.
Evening meal 6pm.
Parking for 10.

The symbols are explained on the flap inside the back cover.

ASKRIGG

N. Yorkshire
Map ref 5B3

4m NW. Aysgarth
The name of this Dales village means 'ash tree ridge'. It is centred on a steep main street of high, narrow 3-storey houses and thrived on cotton and later wool in 18th C. A TV location for James Herriot series. Once famous for its clock making.

Kings Arms Hotel & Restaurant ⚲
APPROVED
Market Place, Askrigg, Wensleydale, DL8 3HQ
☎ (0969) 50258
Minotels
Old coaching inn of great character, featured in the Drovers Arms in BBC's James Herriot series, in the heart of the Yorkshire Dales National Park.
Bedrooms: 7 double & 2 twin, 1 family room.
Bathrooms: 10 private.
Bed & breakfast: £28-£37.50 single, £50-£60 double.
Half board: £37.50-£45 daily, £250-£275 weekly.
Lunch available.
Evening meal 6.30pm (l.o. 8.45pm).
Parking for 7.
Credit: Access, Visa.

Winville Hotel & Restaurant ⚲
COMMENDED
Askrigg, Leyburn, DL8 3HG
☎ Wensleydale (0969) 50515
19th C country house hotel with stunning views of the dales. In Herriot country and featured in "All Creatures Great and Small".
Bedrooms: 6 double & 3 twin, 2 family rooms.
Bathrooms: 11 private.
Bed & breakfast: £38-£42 double.
Half board: £34-£38 daily.
Lunch available.
Evening meal 7pm (l.o. 9pm).
Parking for 22.
Credit: Access, Visa, Diners, Amex.

AYSGARTH

N. Yorkshire
Map ref 5B3

Famous for its beautiful Falls - a series of 3 cascades extending for half a mile on the River Ure in Wensleydale. There is a coach and carriage museum with a crafts centre at Old Yore Mill and a National Park Centre.

Stow House ⚲
Aysgarth, Leyburn, DL8 3SR
☎ Wensleydale (0969) 663635
Imposing Victorian country house with panoramic views, on the A684 near Aysgarth Falls. An excellent location for holidays in the Yorkshire Dales National Park.
Bedrooms: 4 double & 3 twin, 1 family room.
Bathrooms: 8 private.
Bed & breakfast: £48-£58 double.
Half board: £36-£41 daily.
Evening meal 7pm (l.o. 8pm).
Parking for 11.
Credit: Access.

Wheatsheaf Hotel ⚲
COMMENDED
Carperby, Leyburn, DL8 4DF
☎ Wensleydale (0969) 663216
Delightful Dales country hotel offering every facility, and made famous when the real life James Herriot spent his honeymoon here.
Bedrooms: 1 single, 5 double & 2 twin.
Bathrooms: 8 private.
Bed & breakfast: £24 single, £45-£55 double.
Half board: £65-£75 daily.
Lunch available.
Evening meal 7.30pm (l.o. 10pm).
Parking for 25.
Credit: Visa, Diners, Amex.
🔁 Display advertisement appears on page 205.

BAINBRIDGE

N. Yorkshire
Map ref 5B3

This Wensleydale grey-stone village, with fine views of the River Bain, reputedly England's shortest river, was once a Roman settlement, some of it still visible. Boating and water-skiing on nearby Semerwater. Ancient foresters' custom of hornblowing still continues.

Riverdale House Country Hotel ⚲
APPROVED
Bainbridge, Leyburn, DL8 3EW
☎ Wensleydale (0969) 50311
Tastefully-appointed, comfortable house, with special emphasis on food. In the centre of a lovely village in Upper Wensleydale, the area used for the filming of the James Herriot stories.
Bedrooms: 8 double & 6 twin, 2 family rooms.
Bathrooms: 12 private, 3 public.
Bed & breakfast: from £24.50 single, from £46 double.
Half board: from £36 daily.
Evening meal 7.30pm.
Parking for 4.
Open March-November.

Rose & Crown Hotel ⚲
Bainbridge, Wensleydale, DL8 3EE
☎ Wensleydale (0969) 50225
Comfort, specialist cooking and a warm welcome are hallmarks of this 15th C coaching inn. Overlooking the beautiful greens of one of Herriot's favourite dales' villages. Fishing available.
Bedrooms: 9 double & 2 twin, 1 family room.
Bathrooms: 12 private, 1 public.
Bed & breakfast: from £33 single, from £58 double.
Half board: £40-£44 daily, £280-£308 weekly.
Lunch available.
Evening meal 7pm (l.o. 9.30pm).
Parking for 60.
Credit: Access, Visa.

BARTON-UPON-HUMBER

Humberside
Map ref 4C1

Eminent river port on the Humber before Hull became important, now a rambling riverside town with some attractive buildings and narrow, winding streets. Magnificent views of Humber Bridge.

Southgarth ⚲
2 Caistor Rd., Barton-upon-Humber, S. Humberside DN18 5AH
☎ (0652) 32833
Original gatekeeper's lodge at the entrance to Baysgarth Park and Museum. Tennis, swimming, bowls and a putting green are available in the park. 2 minutes' walk from the town centre and 1 mile from the Humber Bridge. Close to the motorway.
Bedrooms: 3 twin.
Bathrooms: 2 public; 2 private showers.
Bed & breakfast: £14-£16 single, £24-£26 double.
Parking for 7.

Westfield Lakes Hotel
Far Ings Rd., Barton-upon-Humber, S. Humberside DN18 5RG
☎ (0652) 32313
In an area of natural beauty, by the River Humber and a nature conservation park. 17 acres of private fishing lakes fully stocked for coarse fishing.
Bedrooms: 5 single, 2 double & 8 twin.
Bathrooms: 2 public; 6 private showers.
Bed & breakfast: from £25 single, from £33 double.
Lunch available.
Evening meal 6.30pm (l.o. 9.45pm).
Parking for 60.
Credit: Access.

Half board prices shown are per person but in some cases may be based on double/twin occupancy.

The enquiry coupons at the back will help you when contacting proprietors.

BEDALE

N. Yorkshire
Map ref 5C3

Ancient church of St. Gregory and Georgian Bedale Hall occupy commanding positions over this market town situated in good hunting country. The Hall, which contains interesting architectural features including great ballroom and flying-type staircase, now houses a library and museum.
Tourist Information Centre ☎ *(0677) 24604*

Motel Leeming ⋔
▱▱

A1/A684 Intersection, Great North Rd., Bedale, DL8 1DT
☎ (0677) 22122 & 23611
Modern motor hotel beside the A1, on the junction of the main route into the dales. A central location for touring North Yorkshire.
Bedrooms: 10 single, 15 double & 12 twin, 3 family rooms.
Bathrooms: 40 private.
Bed & breakfast: £27.50-£37.50 single, £39.50-£49.50 double.
Half board: £28.50-£33.50 daily, £175-£225 weekly.
Lunch available.
Evening meal 5pm (l.o. 9.45pm).
Parking for 107.
Credit: Access, Visa, Diners, Amex.
▱▱▱▱▱▱▱▱▱▱
▱▱▱▱▱▱▱▱

BEVERLEY

Humberside
Map ref 4C1

Beverley's most famous landmark is its beautiful medieval Minster with Percy family tomb. Many attractive squares and streets, notably Wednesday and Saturday Market, North Bar Gateway and the Museum of Army Transport, Flemingate. Famous racecourse.
Tourist Information Centre ☎ *(0482) 867430 or 867813*

Eastgate Guest House ⋔
▱▱

7 Eastgate, Beverley, N. Humberside HU17 0DR
☎ Hull (0482) 868464

Family-run Victorian guesthouse, established and run by the same proprietor for 23 years. Close to the town centre, Minster, Army Transport Museum and railway station.
Bedrooms: 5 single, 5 double & 4 twin, 4 family rooms.
Bathrooms: 5 private, 3 public.
Bed & breakfast: £15-£27 single, £24-£37 double.
▱▱▱▱▱▱▱▱▱

Lairgate Hotel

30 Lairgate, Beverley, N. Humberside HU17 8EP
☎ Hull (0482) 882141
Privately-owned and run hotel in a building of considerable character. Relaxed, happy atmosphere.
Bedrooms: 10 single, 9 double & 3 twin, 2 family rooms.
Bathrooms: 18 private, 3 public; 1 private shower.
Bed & breakfast: £25-£45 single, £40-£70 double.
Half board: £32.50-£52.50 daily, £210-£350 weekly.
Lunch available.
Evening meal 7pm (l.o. 9.30pm).
Parking for 20.
Credit: Access, Visa.
▱▱▱▱▱▱▱▱▱
▱▱▱▱▱▱▱

Tickton Grange Hotel & Restaurant ⋔
▱▱▱▱

Tickton Grange, Tickton, Beverley, N. Humberside HU17 9SH
☎ Hornsea (0964) 543666
Telex 527254
Family-run Georgian country house set in rose gardens, 2 miles from historic Beverley. Country house cooking.
Bedrooms: 3 single, 10 double & 2 twin, 1 family room.
Bathrooms: 16 private.
Bed & breakfast: £35-£63 single, £50-£78 double.
Lunch available.
Evening meal 7pm (l.o. 9.30pm).
Parking for 65.
Credit: Access, Visa, Diners, Amex.
▱▱▱▱▱▱▱▱▱
▱▱▱▱▱▱▱▱▱

We advise you to confirm your booking in writing.

Please check prices and other details at the time of booking.

BINGLEY

W. Yorkshire
Map ref 4B1

Bingley Five-Rise is an impressive group of locks on the Leeds and Liverpool Canal. Town claims to have first bred the Airedale terrier originally used for otter hunting. Among fine Georgian houses is Myrtle Grove where John Wesley stayed. East Riddlesden Hall, a 17th C manor house, is nearby.

The Croft Hotel & Restaurant ⋔
▱▱▱ COMMENDED

Otley Rd., High Eldwick, Bingley, BD16 3BE
☎ Bradford (0274) 567789
17th C farmhouse on the edge of Ilkley Moor with panoramic views of the Aire Valley. Drawing room with a double open fire and an intimate restaurant with open fire and beamed ceiling. Furnishings, paintings and antiques help create an elegant old world ambience.
Bedrooms: 1 single, 1 double & 3 twin.
Bathrooms: 5 private.
Bed & breakfast: £35 single, £47.50-£50 double.
Half board: £46-£52.50 daily, £312-£367.50 weekly.
Lunch available.
Evening meal 7.30pm (l.o. 9.30pm).
Parking for 20.
Open February-December.
Credit: Access.
▱▱▱▱▱▱▱▱
▱▱▱▱▱▱

BOLTON ABBEY

N. Yorkshire
Map ref 4B1

This hamlet is best known for its priory situated near a bend in the River Wharfe. It was founded in 1151 by Alicia de Romilly and before that was site of Anglo-Saxon manor. Popular with painters, amongst them Landseer.

Devonshire Arms Country House Hotel ⋔
▱▱▱▱ HIGHLY COMMENDED

Bolton Abbey, Skipton, BD23 6AJ
☎ (075 671) 441 Telex 51218
Ⓖ Best Western

Traditional country house hotel in the Yorkshire Dales. Open log fires in handsome lounges furnished with antiques from the Duke and Duchess of Devonshire's home, Chatsworth. International cuisine with local game in season.
Bedrooms: 21 double & 19 twin.
Bathrooms: 40 private.
Bed & breakfast: from £75 single, max. £110 double.
Lunch available.
Evening meal 7pm (l.o. 9.45pm).
Parking for 150.
Credit: Access, Visa, C.Bl., Diners, Amex.
▱▱▱▱▱▱▱▱▱
▱▱▱▱▱▱▱▱
▱▱▱▱

BOROUGHBRIDGE

N. Yorkshire
Map ref 5C3

On the River Ure, Boroughbridge was once an important coaching centre with 22 inns and in the 18th C a port for Knaresborough's linens. It has fine old houses, many trees, a cobbled square with market cross, also fishing and boating. Nearby stand 3 megaliths known as the Devil's Arrows.

Crown Hotel ⋔
▱▱▱ COMMENDED

Horsefair, Boroughbridge, York, Y05 9LB
☎ (0423) 322328 Telex 57906
Fully-modernised 12th C coaching inn, 1 mile from the A1 and halfway between Edinburgh and London.
Bedrooms: 13 single, 14 double & 13 twin, 2 family rooms.
Bathrooms: 42 private.
Bed & breakfast: £36-£42 single, £55-£82.50 double.
Lunch available.
Evening meal 7pm (l.o. 9.30pm).
Parking for 45.
Credit: Access, Visa, Diners, Amex.
▱▱▱▱▱▱▱▱▱
▱▱▱▱▱▱▱▱▱
▱▱▱

Map references apply to the colour maps towards the end of this guide.

BOSTON SPA

W. Yorkshire
Map ref 4B1

Largest of a cluster of villages on the lower Wharfe built of limestone from Tadcaster quarries. Saline waters were discovered in 1774 and the town developed as a spa with fine Georgian houses until superseded by Harrogate.

Royal Hotel
COMMENDED

182 High St., Boston Spa, Wetherby, LS23 7AY
☎ Wetherby (0937) 842142
Originally a coaching inn dating back to 1771, now a comfortable family hotel with a friendly atmosphere.
Bedrooms: 4 single, 7 double & 2 twin.
Bathrooms: 13 private.
Bed & breakfast: £38-£42 single, max. £50 double.
Lunch available.
Evening meal 7pm (l.o. 10.30pm).
Parking for 65.
Credit: Access, Visa, Diners, Amex.

BRADFORD

W. Yorkshire
Map ref 4B1

City founded on wool, with fine Victorian and modern buildings. Attractions include the cathedral, city hall, Cartwright Hall, Lister Park, Moorside Mills Industrial Museum and National Museum of Photography and Television.
Tourist Information Centre ☎ (0274) 753678

Balmoral Hotel M
8 Blenheim Mount, Manningham La., Bradford, BD8 7NE
☎ (0274) 491310
Family-run establishment providing a home-from-home service. Of special interest to steam railway enthusiasts. Lunch is available on request.
Bedrooms: 5 single, 6 double & 3 twin, 3 family rooms.
Bathrooms: 15 private, 2 public.
Bed & breakfast: £13.80-£21.85 single, £30-£37.95 double.

Half board: £19.30-£26.35 daily.
Evening meal 6pm (l.o. 9pm).
Parking for 10.

Easby Hotel
2 Easby Rd., Morley St., Bradford, BD7 1QX
☎ (0274) 724498
Guesthouse with all the comforts of home, close to the university and the city centre. Sun bed.
Bedrooms: 3 single, 12 double.
Bathrooms: 4 private, 3 public.
Bed & breakfast: from £17.50 single, from £29 double.
Parking for 10.

Farcliffe Guest House M
1 Farcliffe Terrace, Bradford, BD8 8QE
☎ (0274) 547813
Large, sandstone house on the corner of a terrace with an attractive garden and fish pond. Lounge, TV room and dining room. Close to Listers Mill, Cartwright Hall and Listers Park.
Bedrooms: 2 single, 2 twin, 2 family rooms.
Bathrooms: 3 public.
Bed & breakfast: £12-£14 single, £22-£24 double.
Parking for 4.

Five Flags Hotel
COMMENDED

Manywell Heights, Cullingworth, Bradford, BD13 5EA
☎ Bradford (0274) 834188 & 834594
26-bedroomed hotel with a la carte restaurant seating 80 and bistro seating 70, public bar, function suite accommodating 230 with adjoining bar. Large car park.
Bedrooms: 6 double & 9 twin, 11 family rooms.
Bathrooms: 26 private.
Bed & breakfast: £47-£58 single, £63-£78 double.
Half board: from £54 daily.
Lunch available.
Evening meal 7.30pm (l.o. 10.30pm).
Parking for 150.
Credit: Access, Visa, Diners, Amex.

Northgate Hotel
COMMENDED

22 North Park Rd., Heaton, Bradford, BD9 4NT
☎ (0274) 490678 Fax (0274) 544028
Old private house recently converted in to a 10-bedroomed hotel with a further 25 to follow.
Bedrooms: 2 single, 3 double & 3 twin, 2 family rooms.
Bathrooms: 10 private.
Bed & breakfast: £32-£45 single, £50-£65 double.
Parking for 30.
Credit: Access.

Novotel Bradford M
Adjacent M606, Merrydale Rd., Bradford, BD4 6SA
☎ (0274) 683683
Telex 517312
Novotel
10 minutes' drive from Bradford city and 2 minutes from the M62 with easy access to the Leeds/Bradford Airport.
Bedrooms: 132 family rooms.
Bathrooms: 132 private.
Bed & breakfast: £20-£62 single, £40-£69 double.
Lunch available.
Evening meal 6pm (l.o. midnight).
Parking for 120.
Credit: Access, Visa, Diners, Amex.

Park Drive Hotel M
COMMENDED

12 Park Drive, Heaton, Bradford, BD9 4DR
☎ (0274) 480194
Beautifully appointed, small, licensed hotel quietly set amongst mature trees in a select residential area. Parking in grounds.
Bedrooms: 5 single, 2 double & 4 twin.
Bathrooms: 11 private.
Bed & breakfast: £35-£43 single, £45-£53 double.
Half board: £33-£37 daily.
Evening meal 7pm (l.o. 8pm).
Parking for 9.
Credit: Access, Visa, Amex.

Park Hotel M
6 Oak Avenue, Manningham, Bradford, BD8 7AQ
☎ (0274) 546262

Large, family-run hotel recently completely refurbished. 1 mile from the city centre, just off the A650 with easy access to motorways and the airport. Large gardens, lounges and 3 bars. All bedrooms en-suite.
Bedrooms: 11 single, 6 twin, 3 family rooms.
Bathrooms: 20 private.
Bed & breakfast: £20-£30 single, £40-£56 double.
Half board: £25-£35 daily, £157.50-£220.50 weekly.
Lunch available.
Evening meal 5pm (l.o. 9pm).
Parking for 20.
⊛ Display advertisement appears on page 203.

Regency Hotel M
2-3 Blenheim Mount, Manningham La., Bradford, BD8 7NE
☎ (0274) 498099
Family-run, comfortable, commercial hotel with private bar and home-cooked meals. TV in all rooms and early morning tea/coffee included.
Bedrooms: 12 single, 2 double & 6 twin, 1 family room.
Bathrooms: 3 private, 8 public; 3 private showers.
Bed & breakfast: £18-£24 single, £32-£38 double.
Evening meal 6.30pm (l.o. 8.30pm).
Parking for 12.
Credit: Access, Visa, Diners, Amex.

Stakis Norfolk Gardens Hotel M

Hall Ings, Bradford, BD1 5SH
☎ (0274) 734734
Telex 517573
Stakis
In the city centre, adjacent to train and coach terminals, with easy access to the airport and motorways. Special weekend breaks available.
Bedrooms: 56 double & 70 twin.
Bathrooms: 126 private.
Bed & breakfast: £88-£98 single, from £119 double.
Lunch available.
Evening meal 7pm (l.o. 10pm).
Credit: Access, Visa, Diners, Amex.

The National Crown Scheme is explained in full on pages 556 – 558.

BRANDESBURTON

Humberside
Map ref 4D1

6m W. Hornsea

Burton Lodge Hotel **M**
🏰🏰🏰 **COMMENDED**
Brandesburton, Driffield,
N. Humberside YO25 8RU
☎ Hornsea (0964) 542847
New country hotel situated on a 9 hole parkland golf course, 7 miles from Beverley on the A165.
Bedrooms: 1 single, 1 double & 4 twin.
Bathrooms: 5 private;
1 private shower.
Bed & breakfast: £28-£35 single, £50-£60 double.
Half board: £37.50-£45 daily, £230-£250 weekly.
Evening meal 7pm (l.o. 9pm).
Parking for 13.
Credit: Access, Visa.
🛥 🕿 📺 🛋 🔌 🖤 📺 ▥ 🛏 📍 ✳ 🐾 SP

BRIDLINGTON

Humberside
Map ref 5D3

Lively seaside resort with long sandy beaches, Leisureworld and busy harbour with fishing trips in cobles. Priory church of St. Mary whose Bayle Gate is now a museum. Mementoes of flying pioneer, Amy Johnson, in Sewerby Hall. Harbour Museum and Aquarium.
Tourist Information Centre ☎ (0262) 673474 or 679626 or 606383

Alnwick Guest House
🏰🏰
42 West St., Bridlington,
N. Humberside YO15 3DT
☎ (0262) 677662
Quiet, comfortable family-run guesthouse offering friendly atmosphere and personal service. Convenient for Spa Theatre, harbour and south shore.
Bedrooms: 2 single, 2 double, 1 family room.
Bathrooms: 1 public;
3 private showers.
Bed & breakfast: max. £9 single, max. £18 double.
Half board: max. £12.50 daily, max. £87.50 weekly.
Evening meal 5.30pm.
🛥 🕏 📺 📶 🔶 🛋 📺 ▥ 🛏 🐾 SP

Bay Ridge Hotel **M**
🏰🏰🏰 **COMMENDED**
11-13 Summerfield Rd.,
Bridlington, N. Humberside
YO15 3LF
☎ (0262) 673425
Friendly, comfortable and caring hotel near the South Beach and Spa Complex. Good value for money.
Bedrooms: 2 single, 6 double & 2 twin, 4 family rooms.
Bathrooms: 12 private,
1 public; 2 private showers.
Bed & breakfast: £15-£15.30 single, £30-£33 double.
Half board: £17.50-£18.50 daily, £112-£120 weekly.
Lunch available.
Evening meal 5.45pm (l.o. 6.15pm).
Parking for 7.
Credit: Visa.
🛥 🕐 📶 🔌 🖤 🖐 🔶 SP ▥

Flaneburg Hotel **M**
🏰🏰🏰
North Marine Rd.,
Flamborough, Bridlington,
N. Humberside YO15 1LF
☎ Bridlington (0262) 850284
Family-owned, purpose-built hotel in a heritage coastal fishing village. An ornithologist's, geologist's and rambler's paradise. Minimum 2 day stay, in spring and autumn 10% reduction on room and breakfast tariff.
Bedrooms: 4 single, 6 double & 2 twin, 2 family rooms.
Bathrooms: 8 private,
2 public.
Bed & breakfast: £18-£22 single, £32-£38 double.
Half board: £25-£29 daily, £148-£158 weekly.
Evening meal 7pm (l.o. 10pm).
Parking for 20.
Open March-December.
🛥 🕐 🔌 🔶 📺 🛋 🛏 📍 ✳ 🐾 SP

Glen Alan Hotel
🏰
21 Flamborough Rd.,
Bridlington, N. Humberside
YO15 2HU
☎ (0262) 674650
Licensed family-run hotel offering fine freshly cooked meals and Yorkshire hospitality. Close to Leisure World, beach and town centre.
Bedrooms: 3 single, 6 double & 1 twin, 2 family rooms.
Bathrooms: 2 private,
3 public.
Bed & breakfast: £12-£13 single, £24-£26 double.

Half board: £16.50-£17.50 daily, £100-£115 weekly.
Evening meal 5.30pm (l.o. 5.30pm).
Open April-October.
🛥 🔶 🔌 📺 ▥ 🖐 🛏 DAP

Manor Court Hotel & Restaurant **M**
🏰🏰 **APPROVED**
53 Main St., Carnaby,
Bridlington, N. Humberside
YO16 4UJ
☎ Bridlington (0262) 606468
Fax (0262) 400217
Family-run hotel, 3 miles from Bridlington, incorporating the Wishing Well inn, popular for bar meals.
Bedrooms: 1 single, 3 double & 1 twin, 2 family rooms.
Bathrooms: 7 private.
Bed & breakfast: £38 single, £52 double.
Lunch available.
Evening meal 7pm (l.o. 10pm).
Parking for 60.
Credit: Access, Visa, Amex.
🛥 🕐 📶 🔌 🖤 📺 ▥ 🛏 📍 ✳ 🐾 SP

Mount Hotel **M**
🏰🏰 **APPROVED**
2 Roundhay Rd., Bridlington,
N. Humberside YO15 3JY
☎ (0262) 672306
Small, family hotel only 100 metres from the seafront. Under the personal supervision of the resident proprietors.
Bedrooms: 3 single, 4 double & 1 twin, 2 family rooms.
Bathrooms: 4 private,
3 public.
Bed & breakfast: £14-£15.50 single, £28-£31 double.
Half board: £18-£19.50 daily, £105-£120 weekly.
Lunch available.
Evening meal 6pm (l.o. 6pm).
Parking for 9.
Open February-December.
Credit: Access, Visa.
🛥 🕔 🔌 🖤 🔶 📺 ▥ 🛏 DAP 🐾

Northcote Inn & Hotel **M**
🏰🏰🏰
8 Trinity Rd., Bridlington,
N. Humberside YO15 2EY
☎ (0262) 675764 & 678888
Close to the sea, parks and shops. En-suite bedrooms with colour TV, some four-poster beds. Fully licensed bar. Car park.
Bedrooms: 3 single, 5 double & 2 twin, 2 family rooms.
Bathrooms: 12 private,
1 public.
Bed & breakfast: £16-£17 single, £28-£30 double.

Half board: £16-£17 daily, £98-£105 weekly.
Lunch available.
Evening meal 5.30pm.
Credit: Access, Visa.
🛥 4 🔌 🖤 🔶 📺 ▥ 🛏 📍 🐾 🖤 DAP 🐾 SP T

Park View Licensed Family Hotel **M**
🏰🏰
9-11 Tennyson Avenue,
Bridlington, N. Humberside
YO15 2EU
☎ (0262) 672140
Small, family-run hotel 250 yards from the beach and close to all amenities including the new indoor centre, Leisure World.
Bedrooms: 5 single, 4 double & 4 twin, 4 family rooms.
Bathrooms: 4 public.
Bed & breakfast: £10-£12 single, £20-£24 double.
Half board: £13-£16 daily.
Evening meal 5pm (l.o. 5pm).
Open April-October.
🛥 🔶 🛋 📺 ▥ 🛏 📍 DAP

Popinjays Guest House **M**
🏰🏰
58 Wellington Rd.,
Bridlington, N. Humberside
YO15 2AZ
☎ (0262) 606409
Small and friendly family guesthouse in a quiet area of town, a few minutes' walk from the centre and all amenities - coach and rail stations, bowling greens and tennis courts.
Bedrooms: 3 double & 1 twin, 2 family rooms.
Bathrooms: 2 public.
Bed & breakfast: £10 single, £20 double.
Half board: £14 daily, £91 weekly.
Evening meal 5.30pm (l.o. 6pm).
🛥 🔌 UL 🔶 V ▥ 📺 ▥ 🛏 🖐 DAP 🐾 SP

St. Aubyn's Hotel
🏰
111-113 Cardigan Rd.,
Bridlington, N. Humberside
YO15 3LP
☎ (0262) 673002
In a quiet residential area, 5 minutes' walk to the beach. Close to golf-course and bowling green.
Bedrooms: 4 single, 6 double, 8 family rooms.
Bathrooms: 18 private.
Bed & breakfast: £12-£14.75 single, £24-£29.50 double.
Half board: £15.75-£19.50 daily, £94.50-£117 weekly.

Evening meal 5.30pm (l.o. 2pm).
Parking for 10.
ﾖ ﾑ ﾛ ﾍ ﾟ 🖫 V ﾞ 🅣 ﾚ ﾖ ﾎ ﾝ ﾚ ﾞ OAP ﾚ SP T

Spa Hotel M
South Marine Drive,
Bridlington, N. Humberside
YO15 3JJ
☎ (0262) 674225
Seafront hotel near to the harbour, golf and entertainments. Choice of English cooking. Colour TV available in bedrooms on request.
Bedrooms: 7 single, 9 double & 9 twin, 9 family rooms.
Bathrooms: 14 private,
5 public.
Bed & breakfast: £19-£25 single, £38-£50 double.
Half board: £26-£34 daily,
£160-£190 weekly.
Lunch available.
Evening meal 6pm (l.o. 7pm).
Parking for 5.
Open March-October,
December.
Credit: Access, Visa.
ﾖ ﾛ ﾟ 🖫 V ﾞ 🅣 ﾞ ﾎ ﾝ
ﾂ ﾟ OAP ﾚ SP T

Sunnyside Guest House
18 Horsforth Avenue,
Bridlington, N. Humberside
YO15 3DF
☎ (0262) 672210
2 chair lifts available for disabled guests on both floors. Pets welcome.
Bedrooms: 2 double & 1 twin,
2 family rooms.
Bathrooms: 2 public.
Bed & breakfast: £10-£11 single, £20-£22 double.
Half board: £13-£15 daily,
from £85 weekly.
ﾖ ﾝ UL 🖫 V ﾞ 🅣 U ﾝ
OAP SP

The Tennyson
🏰🏰🏰 APPROVED
19 Tennyson Avenue,
Bridlington, N. Humberside
YO15 2EY
☎ (0262) 604382
Hotel offers varied cuisine in attractive surroundings, close to sea and Leisureworld. Special diets catered for. Free newspapers.
Bedrooms: 3 double & 2 twin,
1 family room.
Bathrooms: 6 private.
Bed & breakfast: £16-£20 single, £25-£26 double.
Half board: £16.50-£24 daily,
£100-£146 weekly.
Evening meal 6pm (l.o. 8.30pm).
Parking for 3.
ﾖ ﾍ ﾛ ﾛ ﾟ 🖫 V ﾞ ﾞ
🅣 ﾎ ﾂ ﾝ ﾚ

N. Yorkshire
Map ref 5C3

3m E. Richmond

The Tudor Hotel
🏰🏰🏰
Gatherley Rd., Brompton-on-Swale, Richmond, DL10 7JF
☎ Richmond (0748) 818021
Tudor-style building with lots of character, beautifully restored and refurbished, retaining a high vaulted ceiling and elegant fireplaces.
Bedrooms: 1 single, 2 double & 2 twin, 1 family room.
Bathrooms: 6 private.
Bed & breakfast: £20-£25 single, £30-£40 double.
Half board: £25-£38 daily,
£115-£250 weekly.
Lunch available.
Evening meal 7pm (l.o. 9.30pm).
Parking for 50.
Credit: Access, Visa.
ﾖ ﾛ ﾛ ﾟ 🖫 V ﾚ ﾎ ﾂ
ﾝ OAP ﾚ SP ﾝ

N. Yorkshire
Map ref 5B3

Charming Wensleydale street village over a mile long.

The Grayford M
🏰🏰
Carperby, Leyburn,
DL8 4DW
☎ Wensleydale (0969) 663517
Private hotel with a licensed restaurant open to non-residents. Small parties catered for. In heart of Herriot country.
Bedrooms: 3 double, 1 family room.
Bathrooms: 2 public.
Bed & breakfast: £33-£35 double.
Evening meal 7pm (l.o. 9pm).
Parking for 12.
Credit: Access, Visa.
ﾖ ﾛ ﾛ ﾟ 🖫 ﾞ 🅣 ﾚ ❋
ﾝ

Map references
apply to the colour
maps towards the
end of this guide.

N. Yorkshire
Map ref 5C3

A military camp since Roman times, known then as Cataractonium, Catterick used to be a major coaching stop on Great North Road. Crowds once gathered to watch cock-fighting where nowadays they come to Catterick Bridge for horse-racing.

Rose Cottage Guest House, Tea Room & Shop M
🏰🏰 APPROVED
26 High St., Catterick Village, Richmond,
DL10 7LJ
☎ Richmond (0748) 811164
Family-run period stone cottage of character. Close to A1, between London and Edinburgh, and convenient for the Yorkshire Dales and the moors.
Bedrooms: 1 double & 2 twin.
Bathrooms: 3 private.
Bed & breakfast: £15.50 single, £31-£37 double.
Half board: £22.50-£24.50 daily, £98.50-£116.60 weekly.
Lunch available.
Evening meal 7.30pm (l.o. 8.30pm).
Parking for 3.
ﾖ ﾛ ﾛ UL 🖫 V ﾚ ﾚ ﾞ 🅣
ﾎ ﾂ ❋ ﾝ SP

N. Yorkshire
Map ref 5B3

Neat village of grey-stone houses and whitewashed cottages; a pot-holing centre. Upstream are Ingleborough Cave and Gaping Gill with its huge underground chamber. National Park Centre.

Arbutus House M
🏰🏰
Riverside, Clapham,
Lancaster, Lancashire
LA2 8DS
☎ (046 85) 240 &
(052 42) 51240
Family-run guesthouse offering home cooking and a friendly atmosphere. Ideal for touring, walking and relaxing.
Bedrooms: 2 double & 2 twin,
1 family room.
Bathrooms: 2 private,
1 public.
Bed & breakfast: £17.50-£19 single, £30-£34.50 double.

Half board: £22-£24.50 daily,
£131.50-£148 weekly.
Evening meal 6.30pm (l.o. midday).
Parking for 6.
Open February-November.
ﾖ ﾛ UL 🖫 V ﾞ 🅣 ﾝ ﾝ
ﾝ

New Inn Hotel M
Clapham, Lancaster,
Lancashire LA2 8HH
☎ (046 85) 203 & (052 42)
51203 Fax (046 85) 496
18th C coaching inn in a picturesque Yorkshire Dales village 6 miles north-west of Settle, in dramatic river, waterfall and fell country.
Bedrooms: 9 double & 2 twin,
2 family rooms.
Bathrooms: 13 private.
Bed & breakfast: from £23 single, from £42 double.
Half board: from £37 daily,
from £240 weekly.
Lunch available.
Evening meal 7pm (l.o. 9.30pm).
Parking for 50.
Credit: Access, Visa, Amex.
ﾖ ﾛ ﾛ ﾟ 🖫 V ﾞ 🅣 ﾚ
ﾂ ﾟ U ﾝ ﾝ SP ﾝ

W. Yorkshire
Map ref 4B1

Prospect Hall Hotel M
🏰🏰🏰 APPROVED
Prospect Rd., Cleckheaton,
BD19 3HD
☎ Bradford (0274) 873022
Telex 517429 PHH
Hall, converted to provide a well-appointed hotel, close to the M62, Bronte country, the dales and Peak District.
Bedrooms: 7 single, 13 double & 3 twin.
Bathrooms: 23 private.
Bed & breakfast: £38-£42 single, from £52 double.
Half board: £50-£55 daily.
Lunch available.
Evening meal 7pm (l.o. 9.30pm).
Parking for 50.
Credit: Access, Visa, Diners, Amex.
ﾖ ﾍ ﾟ ﾛ ﾛ ﾟ 🖫 V ﾟ
🅣 ﾎ ﾂ ﾝ

The symbols are
explained on the
flap inside the
back cover.

YORKSHIRE & HUMBERSIDE

CRAYKE

N. Yorkshire
Map ref 5C3

Pretty hillside village once belonging to the Bishopric of Durham, hence the name of the village inn, the 'Durham Ox'.

Crayke Castle M
Crayke, York, YO6 4TA
☎ Easingwold (0347) 22285
Fax (0347) 22942
An atmosphere of peace amid 20th C comforts is offered by this 15th C castle. Magnificent views over the Vale of York.
Bedrooms: 1 single, 2 double & 1 twin.
Bathrooms: 3 private, 2 public.
Bed & breakfast: from £45 single, £80 double.
Half board: from £58.50 daily.
Evening meal 8pm (l.o. 9.30pm).
Parking for 10.
Credit: Access, Visa.

DEWSBURY

W. Yorkshire
Map ref 4B1

Although this town is most famous for its woollen products, its history stretches back to Saxon times. Robin Hood is reputed to have died and been buried in the Cistercian convent in Kirklees Park.

Heath Cottage Hotel & Restaurant
COMMENDED
Wakefield Rd., Dewsbury, WF12 8ET
☎ (0924) 465399 Fax (0924) 459405
An impressive Victorian house in well-kept gardens. On the A638, 2.5 miles from M1 junction 40.
Bedrooms: 9 single, 8 double & 1 twin, 2 family rooms.
Bathrooms: 20 private, 1 public.
Bed & breakfast: from £47 single, from £60 double.
Half board: from £57 daily, from £399 weekly.
Lunch available.

Evening meal 6.30pm (l.o. 9.30pm).
Parking for 40.

DONCASTER

S. Yorkshire
Map ref 4C1

Ancient Roman town famous for its railway works, heavy industries, butterscotch and racecourse (St. Leger), also centre of agricultural area. Attractions include 18th C Mansion House, Cusworth Hall Museum, Doncaster Museum of Roman and Saxon relics, St. George's Church, The Dome and Doncaster Leisure Park.
Tourist Information Centre ☎ (0302) 734309

Almel Hotel M
APPROVED
20-24 Christchurch Rd., Doncaster, DN1 2QL
☎ (0302) 365230
Licensed hotel in the town centre, close to the racecourse. Coach parties welcome.
Bedrooms: 2 single, 1 double & 11 twin, 8 family rooms.
Bathrooms: 1 private, 6 public.
Bed & breakfast: £18-£22 single, min. £32 double.
Half board: £22-£26 daily.
Lunch available.
Evening meal 5pm (l.o. 8pm).
Parking for 8.
Credit: Access, Visa.

Ashlea Hotel M
81 Thorne Rd., Doncaster, DN1 2ES
☎ (0302) 363374
100-year-old detached house with 7 bedrooms and a converted annexe with 5 bedrooms.On the main road, close to the town centre and market.
Bedrooms: 4 single, 3 double & 1 twin, 4 family rooms.
Bathrooms: 10 private, 1 public; 2 private showers.
Bed & breakfast: £20-£22 single, £35-£37 double.
Parking for 10.

C & A Bed & Breakfast M
Listed
25 Windsor Rd., Town Moor, Doncaster, DN2 5BS
☎ (0302) 327006
Beautiful old house 10 minutes from the town centre and racecourse. Evening meals by arrangement.
Bedrooms: 1 single, 1 double & 2 twin.
Bathrooms: 1 private, 2 public.
Bed & breakfast: £10.50-£12.50 single, £21-£25 double.
Half board: £14.50-£16.50 daily, £70-£84 weekly.
Evening meal 6.20pm.
Parking for 2.

Mount Pleasant Hotel M
COMMENDED
Great North Rd., Rossington, Doncaster, DN11 0HP
☎ Doncaster (0302) 868219 & 868696 Fax (0302) 865130
Local eating house specialising in accommodation for business executives, conferences, small business meetings and parties for all occasions. In Pilgrim Father country, and a good touring base for the whole area.
Bedrooms: 21 single, 11 double & 5 twin.
Bathrooms: 33 private, 1 public.
Bed & breakfast: £22-£25 single, £49.50-£54.50 double.
Half board: £32-£37.50 daily.
Lunch available.
Evening meal 7pm (l.o. 9.30pm).
Parking for 107.
Credit: Access, Visa.

Regent Hotel M
Regent Square, Doncaster, DN1 2DS
☎ (0302) 364180 & 364336
Telex 54480
A home-from-home to all our visitors. Bar, restaurant and function facilities to suit every occasion.
Bedrooms: 10 single, 11 double & 11 twin, 2 family rooms.
Bathrooms: 34 private.
Bed & breakfast: £35-£47.50 single, £45-£57.50 double.
Half board: £44.50-£57 daily.
Lunch available.
Evening meal 6pm (l.o. 10pm).
Parking for 26.

Credit: Access, Visa, Diners, Amex.

DRIFFIELD

Humberside
Map ref 4C1

Lively market town on edge of Wolds with fine Early English church, All Saints. Popular with anglers for its trout streams which flow into the River Hull. Its 18th C canal is lined with barges and houseboats.

Wold House Country Hotel M
Wold Rd., Nafferton, Driffield, N. Humberside YO25 0LD
☎ Driffield (0377) 44242
Family-owned and managed private hotel with home cooking, log fires and personal attention. Panoramic views, close to York and the coast.
Bedrooms: 2 single, 1 double & 5 twin, 4 family rooms.
Bathrooms: 8 private, 1 public.
Bed & breakfast: £30-£36 single, £40-£52 double.
Half board: £32.50-£38.50 daily, £190-£225 weekly.
Lunch available.
Evening meal 7.30pm (l.o. 8.45pm).
Parking for 40.
Credit: Access, Visa.

EASINGWOLD

N. Yorkshire
Map ref 5C3

Market town of charm and character with a cobbled square and many fine Georgian buildings.

Old Farmhouse Country Hotel & Restaurant M
COMMENDED
Raskelf, York, YO6 3LF
☎ Easingwold (0347) 21971
Former farmhouse converted to a comfortable country hotel, offering home cooking, log fires and a warm welcome. In Herriot country, 3 miles from Easingwold and 15 miles from York.
Bedrooms: 6 double & 2 twin, 2 family rooms.
Bathrooms: 10 private.

We advise you to confirm your booking in writing.

Half board: £28-£37 daily,
£196-£238 weekly.
Evening meal 7pm (l.o.
8.30pm).
Parking for 12.
Open February-December.
🛇 📼 📠 V 🛏 TV 🎞 ♿ 🍴
SP T

Station Hotel M
😊😊😊 APPROVED
Knott La., Easingwold,
York, YO6 3NT
☎ (0347) 22635
*Small hotel, refurbished to
reflect the Victorian age. All
rooms en-suite with colour TV,
tea/coffee facilities.*
Bedrooms: 3 double & 2 twin,
2 family rooms.
Bathrooms: 7 private,
1 public.
Bed & breakfast: £24-£26
single, £44-£48 double.
Half board: £27-£34 daily.
Lunch available.
Evening meal 7.30pm (l.o.
9.30pm).
Parking for 11.
Credit: Visa.
🛇 📤 🍴 ✿ V 🛏 🎞 🍴 ♨
▶ 🐾 DAP SP 🖩

EBBERSTON
N. Yorkshire
Map ref 5D3

6m E. Pickering
Picturesque village with a
Norman church and hall,
overlooking the Vale of
Pickering.

Foxholm Hotel M
😊😊😊 APPROVED
Ebberston, Scarborough,
YO13 9NJ
☎ Scarborough (0723) 85550
*Small, family-run country hotel
in a peaceful, rural setting
within easy reach of the moors,
dales, sea and York.*
Bedrooms: 2 single, 2 double
& 4 twin, 1 family room.
Bathrooms: 6 private,
3 public; 2 private showers.
Bed & breakfast: £18-£22
single, £36-£40 double.
Half board: £26-£29 daily,
£184-£198 weekly.
Evening meal 7.30pm (l.o.
7pm).
Parking for 14.
Open March-October,
December.
🛇 📤 🍴 ✿ V 🛏 TV 🎞
♨ 🐾 🐾 SP

FILEY
N. Yorkshire
Map ref 5D3

Resort with elegant
Regency buildings along
the front and 6 miles of
sandy beaches bounded
by natural breakwater,
Filey Brigg. Starting point
of the Cleveland Way.

Carr-Naze Private Hotel
😊😊 COMMENDED
70 Muston Rd., Filey,
YO14 0AL
☎ Scarborough
(0723) 513525
*Small hotel with pleasant
gardens 10 minutes' walk from
the sea and town. Run by
family providing a friendly
atmosphere and home-cooked
food. Car park.*
Bedrooms: 1 single, 2 double
& 2 twin, 1 family room.
Bathrooms: 1 public;
1 private shower.
Bed & breakfast: £14-£15
single, £28-£30 double.
Half board: £19-£20 daily,
£130-£140 weekly.
Evening meal 6pm (l.o. 6pm).
Parking for 8.
🛇 🍴 V 🛏 TV 🎞 ♿ 🍴 ✿

Downcliffe Hotel M
😊😊😊
The Beach, Filey, YO14 9LA
☎ Scarborough
(0723) 513310
*Licensed, detached, seafront
hotel with magnificent views
over Filey Bay. Rooms en-
suite, also TV and tea making
facilities. Car park.*
Bedrooms: 4 single, 1 double
& 2 twin, 9 family rooms.
Bathrooms: 6 private,
3 public.
Bed & breakfast: £17-£19.50
single, £34-£39 double.
Half board: £21.50-£23.50
daily, £150.50-£164.50
weekly.
Evening meal 6pm.
Parking for 10.
Open April-November.
🛇 📤 🍴 ✿ V 🛏 TV 🎞 ♿
🍴 🐾 DAP SP 🖩

The Forge Guest House M
😊😊😊
23 Rutland St., Filey,
YO14 9JA
☎ Scarborough
(0723) 512379
*Victorian town house, 2
minutes' walk from the sea and
town centre. Family-run,
offering traditional Yorkshire
home cooking.*

Bedrooms: 3 double & 1 twin,
1 family room.
Bathrooms: 3 private,
1 public.
Bed & breakfast: £13 single,
£24-£28 double.
Half board: £17-£19 daily,
£109-£126 weekly.
Evening meal 5pm (l.o. 6pm).
🛇 📤 🍴 UL 🍴 🛏 🎞 ♿ 🍴
DAP 🐾 SP

Seafield Hotel M
😊😊😊
9-11 Rutland St., Filey,
YO14 9JA
☎ Scarborough
(0723) 513715
*Small, friendly and
comfortable hotel in the centre
of Filey, close to the beach and
all amenities. Open at New
Year.*
Bedrooms: 1 single, 4 double
& 1 twin, 7 family rooms.
Bathrooms: 9 private,
2 public.
Bed & breakfast: £15-£16.50
single, £30-£38 double.
Evening meal 6pm (l.o. 4pm).
Parking for 7.
🛇 📤 🍴 ✿ V 🛏 TV 🎞
♿ 🍴 🐾 🐾 DAP 🐾 SP 🎞

GARGRAVE
N. Yorkshire
Map ref 4B1

Unspoilt Dales village in
the Aire gap, where the
River Aire meanders by
the roadside. Interesting
church and the most
northerly section of the
Leeds and Liverpool
Canal.

Kirk Syke Hotel M
😊😊😊 APPROVED
19 High St., Gargrave,
Skipton, BD23 3RA
☎ Skipton (0756) 749356
*Small family-run hotel in the
heart of the Yorkshire Dales.
Regret, no animals accepted.*
Bedrooms: 1 single, 5 double
& 5 twin, 1 family room.
Bathrooms: 9 private,
1 public.
Bed & breakfast: £24 single,
£36 double.
Half board: £27-£33 daily,
£180-£220 weekly.
Evening meal 7pm (l.o.
10am).
Parking for 10.
🐾 🍴 ✿ TV 🐾 🐾

GIGGLESWICK
N. Yorkshire
Map ref 5B3

Picturesque Pennine
village of period stone
cottages with ancient
market cross, stocks and
tithe barn. Parish church
is dedicated to St. Alkeda,
an Anglo-Saxon saint
martyred by the Danes,
and has a lychgate,
market cross, Roman and
Bronze Age relics and a
ebbing and flowing well.
During restoration work
the tomb of a 15th C
knight with his horse was
discovered.

Black Horse Hotel M
😊😊
Church St., Giggleswick,
Settle, BD24 OBJ
☎ (072 92) 2506
*A secluded, friendly hotel,
within easy reach of the
Yorkshire Dales and the Lake
District. Bar meals.*
Bedrooms: 1 double & 1 twin,
1 family room.
Bathrooms: 3 private.
Bed & breakfast: max. £34
double.
Half board: £22-£26.50 daily.
Lunch available.
Evening meal (l.o. 9pm).
Parking for 20.
Credit: Access, Diners.
🛇 ✿ 🍴 ✂ 🛏 TV 🎞 🐾 🐾
🖩

Mount View M
😊😊😊
Belle Hill, Giggleswick,
Settle, BD24 0BA
☎ Settle (072 92) 2953
*Attractive accommodation in
the Yorkshire Dales. All rooms
en-suite with TV and tea/coffee
making facilities. Homely
atmosphere.*
Bedrooms: 2 double, 1 family
room.
Bathrooms: 3 private.
Bed & breakfast: £27-£30
double.
Parking for 3.
🛇 ① 📤 ✿ UL 🍴 🛏 TV 🎞
🐾 🐾

Please check prices
and other details at
the time of booking.

Half board prices shown are per person
but in some cases may be based on
double/twin occupancy.

GOATHLAND

N. Yorkshire
Map ref 5D3

Spacious village has several large greens grazed by sheep and is an ideal centre for walking North York Moors. Nearby are several waterfalls, among them Mallyan Spout. Plough Monday celebrations held in January.

Barnet House Guest House

[APPROVED]

Goathland, Whitby, YO22 5NG
☎ Whitby (0947) 86201
Stone-built house standing in its own grounds outside the village with fine views of the surrounding moorland.
Bedrooms: 3 double & 3 twin, 1 family room.
Bathrooms: 2 public.
Bed & breakfast: £24-£28 double.
Half board: £18.25-£21 daily.
Evening meal 6.30pm (l.o. 6.30pm).
Parking for 7.
Open March-November.

Fairhaven Country House Hotel M

The Common, Goathland, Whitby, YO22 5AN
☎ Whitby (0947) 86361
Edwardian country house in the centre of Goathland village, superb moorland setting, offering personal attention and relaxed atmosphere. Log fires.
Bedrooms: 1 single, 5 double & 5 twin, 1 family room.
Bathrooms: 4 private, 3 public.
Bed & breakfast: £15-£19 single, £30-£38 double.
Half board: £25-£28 daily, £150-£165 weekly.
Evening meal 7pm (l.o. 5pm).
Parking for 10.

Heatherdene Hotel M

Goathland, Whitby, YO22 5AN
☎ Whitby (0947) 86334
Small, family-run comfortable country hotel, with panoramic views. Ideally situated for exploring the North Yorkshire moors and coast.

Bedrooms: 1 single, 1 double & 1 twin, 3 family rooms.
Bathrooms: 4 private, 1 public.
Bed & breakfast: from £16 single, £32 double.
Half board: £25-£29 daily.
Evening meal 6.30pm (l.o. 1.30pm).
Parking for 12.
Open April-October.

Inn on the Moor M

[COMMENDED]

Goathland, Whitby, YO22 5LZ
☎ Whitby (0947) 86296
Country house hotel overlooking the Yorkshire Moors. A warm welcome, pleasant service, English food, fresh air and peace. All rooms have colour TV, 5 with four-poster beds, a family suite with 2 singles and a double bedroom.
Bedrooms: 15 double & 11 twin, 1 family room.
Bathrooms: 27 private, 2 public.
Bed & breakfast: £16-£32.50 single, £32-£65 double.
Half board: £28-£45 daily, £196-£280 weekly.
Lunch available.
Evening meal 7pm (l.o. 8.30pm).
Parking for 30.
Credit: Access, Visa.

Mallyan Spout Hotel M

[COMMENDED]

Goathland, Whitby, YO22 5LZ
☎ Whitby (0947) 86206
Comfortable hotel with welcoming log fires and good dining facilities. North Yorkshire Moors, an ideal centre for walking.
Bedrooms: 1 single, 12 double & 8 twin, 3 family rooms.
Bathrooms: 24 private.
Bed & breakfast: £40-£60 single, £60-£100 double.
Half board: £60-£80 daily.
Lunch available.
Evening meal 7pm (l.o. 9pm).
Parking for 100.
Credit: Access, Visa, Diners, Amex.

Whitfield House Hotel M

Darnholm, Goathland, Whitby, YO22 5LA
☎ Whitby (0947) 86215

Former 17th C farmhouse in quiet backwater, friendly atmosphere. Residential licence. All rooms en-suite with TV, radio tea/coffee making facilities.
Bedrooms: 2 single, 5 double & 1 twin, 1 family room.
Bathrooms: 8 private, 1 public.
Bed & breakfast: £19.50 single, £39 double.
Half board: £28.50 daily, £190 weekly.
Evening meal 7pm (l.o. 6.30pm).
Parking for 10.
Open February-November.

GRANTLEY

N. Yorkshire
Map ref 5C3

St. George's Court M

[Listed] [APPROVED]

Old Home Farm, Grantley, Ripon, HG4 3EU
☎ Sawley (076 586) 618
Beautifully situated accommodation in converted farm buildings around courtyard. Hoping to develop three quarter of an acre pond with the help of the British Trust for Conservation Volunteers to encourage natural wildlife and fauna.
Bedrooms: 4 twin, 1 family room.
Bathrooms: 5 private.
Bed & breakfast: £30-£35 double.
Parking for 12.

GRASSINGTON

N. Yorkshire
Map ref 5B3

Tourists visit this former lead-mining village to see its 'smiddy', antique and craft shops and Upper Wharfedale Museum of Country Trades. Popular with fishermen and walkers. Numerous prehistoric sites. Grassington Feast in October.

Ashfield House Hotel

Grassington, Skipton, BD23 5AE
☎ (0756) 752584
Quiet and secluded 17th C hotel near the village square. Open fires and creative home cooking using only fresh foods.
Bedrooms: 5 double & 2 twin.
Bathrooms: 5 private, 1 public.

Bed & breakfast: £40-£47 double.
Half board: £30-£33.25 daily, £180-£205 weekly.
Evening meal 7pm (l.o. 7pm).
Parking for 7.
Open February-December.

Grassfields Country House Hotel M

[COMMENDED]

Wath Rd., Pateley Bridge, Harrogate, HG3 5HL
☎ Harrogate (0423) 711412
Handsome Georgian building in over 2 acres of lawns and trees, within level walking distance of Pateley Bridge.
Bedrooms: 1 single, 2 double & 4 twin, 2 family rooms.
Bathrooms: 9 private, 1 public.
Bed & breakfast: £22-£24 single, £40-£42 double.
Half board: £29-£30 daily, £189-£196 weekly.
Evening meal 7pm (l.o. 6.45pm).
Parking for 15.
Open March-October.

Greenways Guest House M

Wharfeside Avenue, Threshfield, Skipton, BD23 5BS
☎ Skipton (0756) 752598
Overlooking a most spectacular reach of the River Wharfe. An excellent centre for touring the dales by foot, car or cycle and ideal for a relaxing holiday.
Bedrooms: 1 single, 4 twin.
Bathrooms: 2 public.
Bed & breakfast: £16.50-£20 single, £33 double.
Half board: £25.50-£29 daily, £160-£181 weekly.
Evening meal 7.30pm (l.o. 7.30pm).
Parking for 8.
Open April-October.

Lodge Guest House M

[APPROVED]

8 Wood Lane, Grassington, Skipton, BD23 5LU
☎ (0756) 752518
In a quiet location yet only 100 yards from the square. Ideal walking or touring base, near Harrogate and York. Children and dogs welcome. Full central heating.
Bedrooms: 3 double & 4 twin, 1 family room.
Bathrooms: 1 private, 2 public.

Bed & breakfast: £19 single, £28-£36 double.
Half board: £22-£26 daily, £145-£175 weekly.
Evening meal 7pm (l.o. 4.15pm).
Parking for 7.
Open March-December.

New Laithe House M

Wood Lane, Grassington, Skipton, BD23 5LU
☎ (0756) 752764
Large detached house, converted from a barn, on the edge of the village. Magnificent views of the River Wharfe.
Bedrooms: 3 double & 2 twin, 2 family rooms.
Bathrooms: 3 private, 1 public; 2 private showers.
Bed & breakfast: £30-£36 double.
Parking for 8.

Townhead Guest House M
COMMENDED

1 Low La., Grassington, Skipton, BD23 5AU
☎ (0756) 752811
Small, modern guesthouse in the heart of beautiful countryside.
Bedrooms: 3 double & 1 twin, 1 family room.
Bathrooms: 3 private, 1 public.
Bed & breakfast: £26-£32 double.
Half board: £21-£24 daily, £147-£168 weekly.
Evening meal 6.30pm (l.o. 5pm).
Parking for 5.

Bay Horse Inn M
COMMENDED

York Rd., Green Hammerton, York, YO5 8BN
☎ Boroughbridge
(0423) 330338 & (0423) 331113
Village inn 10 miles from York and Harrogate on the A59 and 3 miles off the A1.
Bedrooms: 1 single, 3 double & 5 twin, 1 family room.
Bathrooms: 10 private.
Bed & breakfast: £25-£30 single, £35-£40 double.
Lunch available.

Evening meal 7pm (l.o. 10pm).
Parking for 40.
Credit: Access, Visa, Diners.

Skipbridge Farm
Green Hammerton, York, YO5 8EZ
☎ Boroughbridge (0423) 331015
12.5-acre sheep/poultry/goat farm. Spacious Regency farmhouse of character, with traditional range in dining room, and old pine furniture and log fires in the public rooms. Old world farm atmosphere in miniature with plenty of animals and space for children to play.
Bedrooms: 2 double, 3 family rooms.
Bathrooms: 3 private, 1 public.
Bed & breakfast: £15-£25 single, £22-£35 double.
Half board: £154-£245 weekly.
Evening meal 6pm (l.o. 7pm).
Parking for 12.

Founded 1000 years ago by a Danish fisherman named Grim, Grimsby is today a major fishing port and docks. It has modern shopping precincts and Welholme Galleries Fishing and Maritime Museum.
Tourist Information Centre ☎ (0472) 240410

Millfields M
COMMENDED

53 Bargate, Grimsby, S. Humberside DN34 5AD
☎ (0472) 356068 Fax (0472) 250286
Built in 1879, Millfields is an exclusive residential hotel and leisure club, close to the centre of Grimsby and surrounded by its own grounds.
Bedrooms: 4 double & 6 twin.
Bathrooms: 10 private.
Bed & breakfast: £45-£50 single, £60-£70 double.
Lunch available.
Evening meal 6.30pm (l.o. 9pm).
Parking for 50.
Credit: Access, Visa, Amex.

6m W. Reeth
Taking its name from the Viking chieftain 'Gunner', the village has a humpbacked bridge known as 'Ivelet Bridge' spanning the river which is said to be haunted by a headless dog.

Rogan's Country House
Satron, Gunnerside, Richmond, DL11 6JW
☎ Richmond (0748) 86414
Delightful country house built in 1812, at the foot of Rogan's Seat, a 2000-ft-high peak overlooking the River Swale, in the heart of the Yorkshire Dales National Park. On the B6270 midway between Gunnerside and Muker.
Bedrooms: 1 double & 1 twin, 1 family room.
Bathrooms: 3 private.
Bed & breakfast: from £16.50 single, £33-£35 double.
Half board: max. £27 daily.
Parking for 6.
Open February-November.

Founded on the cloth trade, and famous for its building society, textiles, carpets and toffee. Most notable landmark is Piece Hall where wool merchants traded, now restored to house shops, museums and art gallery. National Museum of the Working Horse.
Tourist Information Centre ☎ (0422) 386725

Glenmore M

19 Savile Park, Halifax, HX1 3EA
☎ (0422) 341500
Victorian house in a pleasant residential area on the edge of a leafy park, 1 mile from the town centre. All rooms en-suite. Brochure available.
Bedrooms: 2 double & 1 twin.
Bathrooms: 3 private.
Bed & breakfast: £25 single, £35 double.
Half board: £25-£32.50 daily, £175-£220 weekly.
Parking for 6.

The Hobbit M
COMMENDED

Hob La., Sowerby Bridge, HX6 3QL
☎ Halifax (0422) 832202 Fax (0422) 835381
Country inn nestling on the hillside above Sowerby Bridge, with panoramic views over the Calder Valley.
Bedrooms: 4 single, 8 double & 11 twin.
Bathrooms: 23 private.
Bed & breakfast: £25-£52 single, £38-£66 double.
Lunch available.
Evening meal 5pm (l.o. 11pm).
Parking for 100.
Credit: Access, Visa, Amex.

Holdsworth House M
COMMENDED

Holdsworth, Holmfield, Halifax, HX2 9TG
☎ (0422) 240024 Telex 51574 Fax (0422) 245174
Converted country house, renovated and lovingly restored. Dining room is 350 years old. Emphasis on service and carefully prepared food. Civic Trust award for bedroom extension (1985).
Bedrooms: 20 single, 18 double & 2 twin.
Bathrooms: 40 private.
Bed & breakfast: £65-£80 single, £80-£95 double.
Half board: £90-£120 daily.
Lunch available.
Evening meal 7pm (l.o. 10pm).
Parking for 61.
Credit: Access, Visa, C.Bl., Diners, Amex.

Norland House M
Listed APPROVED

695 Great Horton Rd., Bradford, BD7 4DU
☎ (0274) 571698
Family-run guesthouse in a detached Victorian residence, in quiet, pleasant surroundings 1.5 miles from Bradford city centre.
Bedrooms: 3 single, 1 double & 3 twin, 1 family room.
Bathrooms: 1 public.
Bed & breakfast: £17.20-£17.75 single, £32.10-£33.35 double.
Half board: £23.52-£24.25 daily, £120.40-£124.25 weekly.
Evening meal 6.30pm (l.o. 5pm).
Parking for 11.

HALIFAX
Continued

Tower House Hotel M
Master La., (off Upper Washer La.,) King Cross, Halifax, HX2 7DX
☎ (0422) 362481 Fax (0422) 320875
Family-run hotel. All bedrooms en-suite, colour TV and tea making facilities, good restaurant and bar snacks. Ample, safe parking.
Bedrooms: 5 single, 6 double & 2 twin, 3 family rooms.
Bathrooms: 16 private.
Bed & breakfast: £30-£46 single, £41-£52 double.
Half board: £42-£58 daily.
Lunch available.
Evening meal 7pm (l.o. 10pm).
Parking for 60.
Credit: Access, Visa, Amex.

Victoria Hotel M
APPROVED
31-35 Horton St., Halifax, HX1 1QE
☎ (0422) 351209 & 358392
Close to tourist attractions, town centre, rail and motorway links. 23 bedrooms most en-suite, restaurant and bars. Weekend entertainment with music and dancing.
Bedrooms: 4 single, 6 double & 7 twin, 6 family rooms.
Bathrooms: 12 private, 3 public; 11 private showers.
Bed & breakfast: £15-£30 single, £30-£46 double.
Half board: £21-£37.50 daily, £147-£262.50 weekly.
Lunch available.
Evening meal 5pm (l.o. 8pm).
Credit: Access, Visa, Amex.

The symbol **CR** and the name of a hotel group or consortium after a hotel address means that bookings can be made through a central reservations office. These are listed on pages **559 & 560.**

HARROGATE
N. Yorkshire
Map ref 4B1

A major conference, exhibition and shopping centre, renowned for its spa heritage and award winning floral displays. Beautiful Victorian architecture complemented by spacious parks and gardens. Famous for antiques, toffee, fine shopping and excellent tea shops, also its Royal Pump Rooms and Baths. Nearby is Ripley Castle.
Tourist Information Centre ☎ (0423) 525666

Abingdon
14 Spring Mount, Harrogate, HG1 2NX
☎ (0423) 525010
A short walk to conference and other amenities makes this a convenient and comfortable base for business and holiday visitors.
Bedrooms: 2 single, 1 double & 1 twin.
Bathrooms: 1 public; 3 private showers.
Bed & breakfast: £20 single, max. £35 double.
Half board: £21.50-£24 daily.
Parking for 2.

Acacia Lodge
21 Ripon Rd., Harrogate, HG1 2JL
☎ (0423) 560752
Attractive, old stone house with a warm, homely atmosphere. In a pleasant area with gardens and good private parking facilities. Conference centre and town amenities quarter of a mile.
Bedrooms: 1 single, 1 double & 2 twin, 1 family room.
Bathrooms: 4 private, 1 public.
Bed & breakfast: max. £20 single, max. £38 double.
Parking for 6.

Alamah M
COMMENDED
88 Kings Rd., Harrogate, HG1 5JX
☎ (0423) 502187
Good base for touring the Yorkshire Dales. Close to the Valley Gardens, swimming pool, theatre and shops. 100 metres from the conference centre. Garages/parking.

Bedrooms: 2 single, 2 double & 1 twin, 1 family room.
Bathrooms: 2 private, 1 public; 2 private showers.
Bed & breakfast: £15-£18 single, £28-£38 double.
Half board: £23-£26 daily.
Evening meal 6.30pm (l.o. 4.30pm).
Parking for 8.

Alexa House Hotel and Stable Cottages M
26 Ripon Rd., Harrogate, HG1 2JJ
☎ (0423) 501988
Small hotel, built for Baron de Ferrier in 1830. Maintaining the old and gracious traditions of personal service and true Yorkshire hospitality.
Bedrooms: 3 single, 3 double & 6 twin, 1 family room.
Bathrooms: 11 private, 1 public; 1 private shower.
Bed & breakfast: £18-£21 single, from £42 double.
Parking for 12.
Credit: Access, Visa.

Alexander Guesthouse
88 Franklin Rd., Harrogate, HG1 5EN
☎ (0423) 503348
Friendly family-run elegant Victorian guesthouse, ideal for conference centre and Harrogate town. Good touring centre for dales.
Bedrooms: 1 single, 1 twin, 2 family rooms.
Bathrooms: 2 public; 1 private shower.
Bed & breakfast: £14-£16 single, £28-£32 double.
Parking for 3.

Ascot House Hotel M
53 Kings Rd., Harrogate, HG1 5HJ
☎ (0423) 531005 Fax (0423) 503523
CR Minotels
An impressive Victorian house near Harrogate's conference and town centres, offering comfort and a warm welcome. Car park.
Bedrooms: 15 single, 5 double & 4 twin, 1 family room.
Bathrooms: 13 private, 1 public; 12 private showers.
Bed & breakfast: £35-£49 single, £47.50-£75 double.
Half board: £32.75-£47.95 daily, £196.50 weekly.

Evening meal 7pm (l.o. 9pm).
Parking for 14.
Credit: Access, Visa, Diners, Amex.

Ashley House Hotel M
COMMENDED
36-40 Franklin Rd., Harrogate, HG1 5EE
☎ (0423) 507474 & 560858
Charming and friendly 17-bedroom hotel in quiet tree-lined avenue. Minutes from town centre. Colour TV, tea/coffee, telephone, radio alarm in all rooms. Cosy old world bar and 2 lounges. Beautifully decorated throughout.
Bedrooms: 5 single, 6 double & 4 twin, 2 family rooms.
Bathrooms: 11 private, 2 public.
Bed & breakfast: £18.75-£25 single, £32-£46 double.
Half board: £28.50-£30 daily, from £180 weekly.
Evening meal 6.15pm (l.o. 6.30pm).
Parking for 7.
Credit: Access, Visa.

Ashwood House M
COMMENDED
7 Spring Grove, Harrogate, HG1 2HS
☎ (0423) 560081
Edwardian, double-fronted guesthouse in a quiet cul-de-sac. 5 minutes from the town centre and local amenities. Four-poster bedroom available.
Bedrooms: 2 single, 4 double & 3 twin, 2 family rooms.
Bathrooms: 9 private, 1 public.
Bed & breakfast: £18-£25 single, £34-£42 double.
Parking for 5.

Aygarth Guest House M
11 Harlow Moor Drive, Harrogate, HG2 0JX
☎ (0423) 568705
Older-type, Yorkshire stone house overlooking the famous and beautiful Valley Gardens. 5 minutes' stroll to the town centre and conference halls.
Bedrooms: 2 single, 1 double & 2 twin, 2 family rooms.
Bathrooms: 3 public.
Bed & breakfast: £15-£16 single, £30-£32 double.

Half board: £46-£48 daily, from £322 weekly.
Evening meal 5.30pm (l.o. 5pm).

The Belfry
Listed
27 Belmont Rd., Harrogate, HG2 0LR
☎ (0423) 522783
Friendly, family guesthouse within easy walking distance of the town centre and all tourist amenities. A wide choice of cooked breakfast is offered.
Bedrooms: 2 single, 1 double & 1 twin.
Bathrooms: 1 public.
Bed & breakfast: £12.50 single, £25 double.

Berronton Hotel
25
30 Ripon Rd., Harrogate, HG1 2JJ
☎ (0423) 569582
Detached, Victorian house on the A61, a short walk to the town and conference centre. Close to 4 golf-courses and other leisure amenities.
Bedrooms: 4 single, 1 double & 6 twin, 1 family room.
Bathrooms: 3 private, 3 public.
Bed & breakfast: £16-£18 single, £30-£36 double.
Parking for 8.

Caesars Hotel M
COMMENDED
51 Valley Drive, Harrogate, HG2 0JH
☎ (0423) 565818
Victorian family home overlooks delightful Valley Gardens. Comfortable base for touring Yorkshire Dales and Bronte country. Local produce a regular feature of the popular restaurant. Families with young children especially welcome.
Bedrooms: 2 single, 1 double & 3 twin, 3 family rooms.
Bathrooms: 9 private.
Bed & breakfast: from £42.50 single, from £60 double.
Half board: from £44.50 daily, from £280 weekly.
Evening meal 7.30pm (l.o. 8.30pm).
Credit: Access, Visa.

Cavendish Hotel M
COMMENDED
3 Valley Drive, Harrogate, HG2 0JJ
☎ (0423) 509637
Overlooking the beautiful Valley Gardens at the town end of Valley Drive. Recently refurbished, all rooms en-suite. Lunches and dinners available.
Bedrooms: 2 single, 5 double & 3 twin.
Bathrooms: 10 private.
Bed & breakfast: £25-£35 single, £40-£60 double.
Half board: £35-£45 daily.
Evening meal 6.30pm (l.o. 8pm).
Credit: Access, Visa, Diners, Amex.

Craigleigh Guest House
Listed
6 West Grove Rd., Harrogate, HG1 2AD
☎ (0423) 564064
Large Victorian house of distinct character providing comfortable accommodation and emphasis on home cooking. Close to the town centre with easy access to the dales.
Bedrooms: 2 single, 2 double & 2 twin, 1 family room.
Bathrooms: 2 public.
Bed & breakfast: £13-£16 single, £26-£32 double.
Parking for 2.

Croft Hotel M
25 25 25
42-46 Franklin Rd., Harrogate, HG1 5EE
☎ (0423) 563326
Friendly, family-run hotel in a quiet, tree-lined avenue close to shopping centre and conference centre.
Bedrooms: 2 single, 5 double & 5 twin, 1 family room.
Bathrooms: 12 private, 1 public.
Bed & breakfast: £25-£30 single, £40-£48 double.
Half board: £28-£32 daily, £196-£224 weekly.
Lunch available.
Evening meal 7pm (l.o. 9.30pm).
Parking for 10.
Credit: Access, Visa.

Dales Hotel M
APPROVED
101 Valley Drive, Harrogate, HG2 0JP
☎ (0423) 507248

Overlooking the beautiful Valley Gardens, tennis courts and children's play area. A few minutes' walk to the town centre and conference halls.
Bedrooms: 2 single, 2 double & 2 twin, 2 family rooms.
Bathrooms: 3 private, 1 public; 3 private showers.
Bed & breakfast: £18-£19 single, £34-£40 double.
Half board: £25.50-£28.50 daily.
Evening meal 6pm (l.o. 5.30pm).
Parking for 8.

Daryl House Hotel M
25
42 Dragon Parade, Harrogate, HG1 5DA
☎ (0423) 502775
Small hotel offering a wide range of amenities and personal, friendly service from the proprietor. Close to the town centre, stations and exhibition hall. Evening meal by arrangement only.
Bedrooms: 2 single, 2 twin, 2 family rooms.
Bathrooms: 2 public.
Bed & breakfast: £12-£13 single, £24-£26 double.
Half board: £18-£19 daily, £100-£110 weekly.

Delaine Hotel M
COMMENDED
17 Ripon Rd., Harrogate, HG2 1JL
☎ (0423) 567974
Small, friendly hotel close to conference facilities. Most rooms en-suite, colour TV, welcome tray. Ideal for business or holiday guests.
Bedrooms: 3 single, 3 double & 3 twin, 2 family rooms.
Bathrooms: 7 private, 2 public.
Bed & breakfast: max. £25 single, £40-£50 double.
Half board: £28.95-£33.95 daily.
Evening meal 6.30pm (l.o. 7pm).
Parking for 8.
Credit: Access, Visa.

Elizabethan Guest House M
25 25
70 Franklin Rd., Harrogate, HG1 5EN
☎ (0423) 506767
Spacious guesthouse, offering friendly service from the proprietor. Close to town centre and conference complex.

Bedrooms: 2 single, 1 twin, 2 family rooms.
Bathrooms: 2 public.
Bed & breakfast: £13-£14 single, £26-£28 double.
Half board: £19.50-£20.50 daily, £136.50-£143.50 weekly.
Evening meal 6pm (l.o. 8pm).
Parking for 2.

Eton House M
25
3 Eton Terrace, Knaresborough Rd., Harrogate, HG2 7SU
☎ (0423) 886850
Homely guesthouse with spacious, comfortable rooms. On the main A59, on the edge of parkland close to the town.
Bedrooms: 1 single, 2 double & 1 twin, 3 family rooms.
Bathrooms: 3 public.
Bed & breakfast: £13 single, £26-£30 double.
Parking for 10.

Franklin Lodge M
Listed
6 Franklin Rd., Harrogate, HG1 5EE
☎ (0423) 563599
Within 150 yards of the Harrogate International Centre and town centre. We offer standards of service and facilities usually associated with larger establishments.
Bedrooms: 3 single, 2 twin, 2 family rooms.
Bathrooms: 2 private, 1 public; 3 private showers.
Bed & breakfast: £13.50-£14.50 single, £27-£29 double.
Half board: £21-£22 daily, £126-£132 weekly.
Evening meal 6pm (l.o. 7.30pm).

Gables Hotel M
25 25
2 West Grove Rd., Harrogate, HG1 2AD
☎ (0423) 505625
Small owner-run hotel close to the town centre. A la carte menu, choice of bath or shower, colour TV and electric trouser press in all rooms. Guide dogs are accepted.
Bedrooms: 4 single, 1 double & 2 twin, 2 family rooms.
Bathrooms: 8 private; 1 private shower.
Bed & breakfast: £21.50-£25 single, £43-£50 double.
Half board: £29.50-£35 daily, £200-£245 weekly.

Continued ▶

HARROGATE
Continued

Evening meal 7.30pm (l.o. 8.30pm).
Parking for 9.
Credit: Access, Visa.

Garden House Hotel M
COMMENDED
14 Harlow Moor Drive, Harrogate, HG2 0JX
☎ (0423) 503059
Small, family-run, Victorian hotel overlooking the Valley Gardens, in a quiet location with unrestricted parking. Home cooking using fresh produce only.
Bedrooms: 3 single, 1 double & 3 twin.
Bathrooms: 5 private; 2 private showers.
Bed & breakfast: £18-£20 single, £36-£40 double.
Half board: £27-£29 daily, £171-£183 weekly.
Evening meal 7pm (l.o. midday).

Gillmore Hotel M
98 Kings Rd., Harrogate, HG1 5HH
☎ (0423) 503699 & 507122
Private hotel offering homely accommodation, run by the same family for 21 years. Just a few minutes' walk from the conference centre.
Bedrooms: 3 single, 4 double & 8 twin, 8 family rooms.
Bathrooms: 5 private, 5 public.
Bed & breakfast: £17.50-£20 single, £33-£36 double.
Half board: £24-£26 daily, from £105 weekly.
Evening meal 6pm (l.o. 7pm).
Parking for 25.

Glenayr Hotel M
19 Franklin Mount, Harrogate, HG1 5EJ
☎ (0423) 504259
Quietly situated, spacious Victorian house within 5 minutes' walk of all amenities. Home cooking and a comfortable, relaxing atmosphere.
Bedrooms: 2 single, 2 double & 3 twin.
Bathrooms: 5 private, 1 public.
Bed & breakfast: £17.50-£19.50 single, £40-£45 double.
Half board: £27-£32 daily, £175-£210 weekly.

Evening meal 6.30pm (l.o. 4pm).
Parking for 4.

Grants Hotel & Chimney Pots Restaurant M
Swan Rd., Harrogate, HG1 2SS
☎ (0423) 560666 Fax (0423) 502550
Small yet professionally run, family-owned hotel. Quiet location close to town centre, Valley Gardens and conference centre.
Bedrooms: 13 single, 9 double & 13 twin, 2 family rooms.
Bathrooms: 37 private.
Bed & breakfast: £37.50-£75 single, £42.50-£85 double.
Half board: £51.45-£88.95 daily, £360.15-£622.25 weekly.
Lunch available.
Evening meal 7pm (l.o. 9.30pm).
Parking for 19.
Credit: Access, Visa, Diners, Amex.

Green Park Hotel M
APPROVED
Valley Drive, Harrogate, HG2 0JT
☎ (0423) 504681 & 521921
Telex 57515 ATT. 31
Consort
Peaceful, privately-owned hotel, 5 minutes' walk from the town centre and opposite the lovely Valley Gardens. Lift and conference room. Snack lunches only.
Bedrooms: 14 single, 5 double & 22 twin, 2 family rooms.
Bathrooms: 43 private.
Bed & breakfast: £45 single, £63 double.
Half board: £42.25-£55.75 daily, £273.70-£358.75 weekly.
Lunch available.
Evening meal 7pm (l.o. 8.30pm).
Parking for 10.
Credit: Access, Visa, Diners, Amex.

Lamont House M
COMMENDED
12 St. Mary's Walk, Harrogate, HG2 0LW
☎ (0423) 567143

Built at the turn of this century in a peaceful location, yet close to the Valley Gardens, shops and the new conference centre.
Bedrooms: 2 single, 3 double & 1 twin, 3 family rooms.
Bathrooms: 2 private, 2 public.
Bed & breakfast: £16-£30 single, £30-£45 double.
Evening meal 6pm (l.o. 6pm).

Langham Hotel M
21-27 Valley Drive, Harrogate, HG2 0JL
☎ (0423) 502179
Beautiful, family owned hotel in the heart of Harrogate overlooking the Valley Gardens. Fine restaurant.
Bedrooms: 16 single, 19 double & 13 twin, 2 family rooms.
Bathrooms: 50 private.
Bed & breakfast: £34-£58 single, £60-£78 double.
Half board: £37.50-£73 daily, £210-£265 weekly.
Lunch available.
Evening meal 7pm (l.o. 10pm).
Credit: Access, Visa, Diners, Amex.

Lynton House M
APPROVED
42 Studley Rd., Harrogate, HG1 5JU
☎ (0423) 504715
In a central, quiet tree-lined avenue, 100 yards from the exhibition halls and swimming pool, and close to the Valley Gardens. Personal supervision. Own keys. Non-smokers only please.
Bedrooms: 2 single, 2 double & 1 twin.
Bathrooms: 1 public.
Bed & breakfast: £14 double.

Madeira House M
COMMENDED
117 Franklin Rd., Harrogate, HG1 5EN
☎ (0423) 505752
Victorian villa with friendly, family atmosphere set in a tree-lined avenue. 5 minutes' walk from conference centre, 10 minutes from town.
Bedrooms: 2 single, 1 double & 1 twin.
Bathrooms: 4 private.
Bed & breakfast: £16.50-£17.50 single, £31-£32 double.
Half board: £38-£40 daily, £150-£175 weekly.

Evening meal 7pm (l.o. 8.30pm).
Parking for 2.

Park Gate Hotel M
61-63 Valley Drive, Harrogate, HG2 0JW
☎ (0423) 567010
Overlooking the Valley Gardens and 10 minutes' walk from the conference centre and town. Comfortable hotel with emphasis on personal service and food.
Bedrooms: 4 single, 4 double & 5 twin, 3 family rooms.
Bathrooms: 12 private, 2 public.
Bed & breakfast: £18-£19 single, £38-£40 double.
Half board: £25-£26 daily, £170-£175 weekly.
Evening meal 6pm (l.o. 8pm).
Parking for 3.

Roan
90 Kings Rd., Harrogate, HG1 5JX
☎ (0423) 503087
In a central position, 3 minutes from the conference centre, the Valley Gardens, town, bus and rail stations. Ideal for touring the Dales. Home cooking.
Bedrooms: 3 single, 2 double & 1 twin, 1 family room.
Bathrooms: 3 private, 1 public.
Bed & breakfast: from £15 single, from £28 double.
Half board: from £22.50 daily.
Evening meal 6.15pm (l.o. 4.30pm).

Scotia House Hotel M
66 Kings Rd., Harrogate, HG1 5JR
☎ (0423) 504361
Immediately opposite the conference centre and close to the town centre, Valley Gardens and all amenities. An ideal base for exploring Yorkshire.
Bedrooms: 5 single, 3 double & 5 twin, 1 family room.
Bathrooms: 11 private, 2 public; 1 private shower.
Bed & breakfast: £22-£25 single, £44-£50 double.
Half board: £32-£35 daily, £200-£220 weekly.

Evening meal 6pm (l.o. 8pm).
Parking for 8.
Credit: Access, Visa.

☇7 ⚀ 🛎 📞 ☑ ❖ ☎ 🐘 V ☐
TV ▤ ♻ 🍽 OAP SP T

Shannon Court Hotel M
☺☺☺ COMMENDED

65 Dragon Avenue,
Harrogate, HG1 5DS
☎ (0423) 509858
*Charming Victorian house
retaining many original
features, offering modern
facilities and a warm friendly
atmosphere.*
Bedrooms: 2 single, 2 double
& 1 twin, 2 family rooms.
Bathrooms: 7 private.
Bed & breakfast: £18-£22.50
single, £36-£45 double.
Half board: £25-£33 daily,
£175-£200 weekly.
Evening meal 7pm (l.o.
midday).
Parking for 3.

☺ ♻ ❖ ☎ V ☐ TV ▤
♻ 🍽 SP

Spring Lodge Guest House M
☺☺

22 Spring Mount, Harrogate,
HG1 2HX
☎ (0423) 506036
*In a cul-de-sac, a few minutes'
walk from the town centre,
bus/railway stations, Royal
Hall, conference centre,
gardens, theatres and
swimming pool.*
Bedrooms: 1 single, 2 double
& 1 twin, 2 family rooms.
Bathrooms: 1 private,
1 public; 2 private showers.
Bed & breakfast: £16-£20
single, £32-£40 double.
Evening meal 5pm (l.o. 3pm).
Parking for 4.

☺ ⚀ ❖ ☎ V ☐ TV ▤ ♻
🕱

Stoney Lea Guest House M
☺☺ COMMENDED

13 Spring Grove, Harrogate,
HG1 2HS
☎ (0423) 501524
*Small guesthouse in a quiet
cul-de-sac. Centrally located
within walking distance of all
the town's tourist and business
facilities.*
Bedrooms: 2 single, 1 double
& 3 twin.
Bathrooms: 6 private.
Bed & breakfast: £19-£25
single, from £38 double.
Parking for 3.

☺5 ♻ ☎ ☑ ▤ ♻ TV ▤ ♻
🕱 🕱

Studley Hotel M
Swan Rd., Harrogate,
HG1 2SE
☎ (0423) 560425 Telex 57506
*Small hotel with an intimate
French restaurant and genuine
charcoal grill. Near the Valley
Gardens and within easy reach
of the shopping centre. All
bedrooms have trouser press,
hair-dryer, colour TV, Sky
satellite TV and tea making
facilities.*
Bedrooms: 16 single,
10 double & 10 twin.
Bathrooms: 36 private.
Bed & breakfast: £60-£70
single, £70-£95 double.
Lunch available.
Evening meal 7.30pm (l.o.
10pm).
Parking for 14.
Credit: Access, Visa, Diners,
Amex.

☺8 ☑ ☎ ▤ ❖ ♻ V ☐ TV
◉ ♻ ▤ ♻ 🕱 ♻ 🍽 SP
👀 Display advertisement
appears on page 204.

Valley Hotel M
APPROVED

93-95 Valley Drive,
Harrogate, HG2 0JP
☎ (0423) 504868 Fax (0423)
531940
*Hotel overlooking the Valley
Gardens, offering a warm
welcome to both tourists and
business people. Licensed
restaurant.*
Bedrooms: 2 double & 5 twin,
6 family rooms.
Bathrooms: 13 private.
Bed & breakfast: £30-£45
single, £40-£55 double.
Half board: £38.50-£53.50
daily.
Lunch available.
Evening meal 6pm (l.o.
9.30pm).
Parking for 4.
Credit: Access, Visa.

☺ ☑ ☎ ▤ ❖ ♻ V ☐ TV
♻ ▤ ♻ 🕱 ♻ SP

West Park Hotel M
19 West Park, Harrogate,
HG1 1BL
☎ (0423) 524471 Fax (0423)
524471
*We are able to provide both
conference facilities and family
rooms, combined with a
friendly but professional
atmosphere.*
Bedrooms: 2 single, 3 double
& 12 twin.
Bathrooms: 16 private,
2 public.
Bed & breakfast: £20-£42
single, £20-£49 double.
Half board: £180-£240
weekly.
Lunch available.

Evening meal 6pm (l.o.
11pm).
Parking for 12.
Credit: Access, Visa, Diners,
Amex.

☺ ☑ ☎ ▤ ❖ ♻ 🐘 V ❚
♻ TV ◉ ▤ ♻ 🕱 ♻ ✓ SP
🕱

Wharfedale House
☺☺

28 Harlow Moor Drive,
Harrogate, HG2 0JY
☎ (0423) 522233
*Overlooking beautiful gardens,
woodlands and leisure park.
Peaceful, comfortable house
with a warm welcome. Offering
traditional vegetarian or
special diets.*
Bedrooms: 3 single, 1 double
& 2 twin, 2 family rooms.
Bathrooms: 8 private.
Bed & breakfast: £24 single,
£44 double.
Half board: £30.50-£32.50
daily, £191.50-£203.50
weekly.
Lunch available.
Evening meal 6.30pm (l.o.
2pm).
Parking for 3.

☺ ☑ ⚀ ☎ ▤ ❖ V ☐ ▤
♻ 🕱 OAP ✓ SP

Youngs Hotel M
☺☺☺☺ APPROVED

15 York Rd., (Off Swan Rd.),
Harrogate, HG1 2QL
☎ (0423) 567336 & 521231
*Family-run hotel with large
attractive gardens in a quiet
residential area, within walking
distance of the town.*
Bedrooms: 5 single, 5 double
& 4 twin, 2 family rooms.
Bathrooms: 16 private,
1 public.
Bed & breakfast: £30-£40
single, £45-£60 double.
Half board: £33-£40 daily,
from £200 weekly.
Evening meal 7pm (l.o. 7pm).
Parking for 19.
Credit: Access, Visa.

☺ ☎ ☑ ⚀ ▤ ❖ ☑ V ☐
▤ ♻ 🕱 ♻ OAP SP

Individual
proprietors have
supplied all details
of accommodation.
Although we do
check for accuracy,
we advise you to
confirm prices and
other information
at the time of
booking.

The capital of Upper
Wensleydale on the
famous Pennine Way,
renowned for great
cheeses. Popular with
walkers. Dales National
Park Information Centre
and Folk Museum.
Nearby is spectacular
Hardraw Force Waterfall.
*Tourist Information
Centre* ☎ *(0969) 667450*

Herriots Hotel & Restaurant M
☺☺

Main St., Hawes, DL8 3QU
☎ (0969) 667536
*Friendly hotel and restaurant
offering an extensive selection
of food and wines. Situated in
the centre of Hawes, ideal for
touring the dales.*
Bedrooms: 3 double & 2 twin,
1 family room.
Bathrooms: 6 private.
Bed & breakfast: £27.50-
£28.50 single, £38-£42 double.
Lunch available.
Evening meal 7pm (l.o.
10pm).
Open February-October.
Credit: Access, Visa.

☺ ♻ ▤ ❖ ☑ V ▤ ♻ 🕱 ♻ 🕱
♻ SP

Highfield Guest House M
☺☺

Spring Bank, Hawes,
DL8 3NW
☎ (0969) 667395
*Imposing house with panoramic
views from all the windows,
oak panelled staircase and
light airy rooms. Terraced
gardens with well kept lawns.
Private road for parking.
Licensed.*
Bedrooms: 4 double & 1 twin.
Bathrooms: 1 private,
1 public.
Bed & breakfast: £24-£30
double.
Half board: £19-£22 daily.
Evening meal 6.30pm.
Parking for 7.
Open February-November.

☺7 ❖ ☑ ▤ TV ▤ ❂ 🕱

Rookhurst Georgian Country Hotel M
☺☺

West End, Gayle, Hawes,
DL8 3RT
☎ (0969) 667454

Continued ▶

HAWES
Continued

Personal service and a varied menu with home-made specialities using fresh food. Peace and quiet in unique period surroundings. Antique furnishings and bridal suite.
Bedrooms: 4 double & 1 twin.
Bathrooms: 5 private.
Bed & breakfast: from £28 single, £68-£92 double.
Half board: £46-£53 daily.
Evening meal 7.30pm (l.o. 6.30pm).
Parking for 10.
Open February-December.

Simonstone Hall ᴍ
COMMENDED
Hawes, DL8 3LY
☎ Wensleydale (0969) 667255 Fax (0969) 667741
Family-run 18th C country house hotel in a glorious Wensleydale setting with panoramic views. Tawny Owl bar and extensive cellar. Dogs welcome.
Bedrooms: 6 double & 3 twin, 1 family room.
Bathrooms: 10 private.
Bed & breakfast: £90-£115 double.
Half board: £55-£67.50 daily.
Lunch available.
Evening meal 7pm (l.o. 8.30pm).
Parking for 22.
Credit: Access, Visa, Diners, Amex.

Stone House Hotel ᴍ
COMMENDED
Sedbusk, Hawes, DL8 3PT
☎ (0969) 667571
Fine old country house hotel in a beautiful old English garden with panoramic views of Upper Wensleydale.
Bedrooms: 2 single, 8 double & 3 twin, 2 family rooms.
Bathrooms: 14 private, 1 public.
Bed & breakfast: £25-£35 single, £40-£60 double.
Half board: £33-£43 daily.
Evening meal 7pm (l.o. 8pm).
Parking for 15.
Credit: Access, Visa.

White Hart Inn ᴍ
Main St., Hawes, DL8 3QL
☎ Wensleydale (0969) 667259

Small country inn with a friendly welcome, offering home-cooked meals using local produce. An ideal centre for exploring the Yorkshire Dales.
Bedrooms: 1 single, 4 double & 2 twin.
Bathrooms: 2 public.
Bed & breakfast: from £15 single, from £26 double.
Lunch available.
Evening meal 7pm (l.o. 8.30pm).
Parking for 7.
Open February-November.

HAWORTH
W. Yorkshire
Map ref 4B1

This small Pennine town is famous as home of the Bronte family. The parsonage is now a Bronte Museum where furniture and possessions of the family are displayed. Moors and Bronte waterfalls nearby and steam trains on the Keighley and Worth Valley Railway pass through the town.
Tourist Information Centre ☎ *(0535) 42329 or 45864*

Bridge House Private Hotel ᴍ
Bridgehouse Lane, Haworth, Keighley, BD22 8PA
☎ (0535) 42372
Small family-run licensed hotel built as mill owner's Georgian house. In the famous tourist village of Haworth, home of the Bronte sisters close to the Keighley and Worth Valley Railway. Bar snacks available.
Bedrooms: 1 single, 1 double & 3 twin.
Bathrooms: 3 private, 1 public.
Bed & breakfast: £13-£16 single, £32-£34 double.
Parking for 12.

Ferncliffe
Hebden Rd., Haworth, Keighley, BD22 8RS
☎ (0535) 43405
Well-appointed, private hotel with panoramic views overlooking Haworth and the Worth Valley Steam Railway.
Bedrooms: 2 single, 2 double & 1 twin, 1 family room.
Bathrooms: 6 private.
Bed & breakfast: £19-£26 single, £38-£42 double.

Half board: £27.50-£33.50 daily.
Lunch available.
Evening meal 7pm (l.o. 9pm).
Parking for 12.
Credit: Visa.

Haworth Old Hall Hotel
Sun St., Haworth, Keighley, BD22 8BP
☎ (0535) 42709
16th C stone-built free house, restaurant and hotel, open 365 days a year. Traditional hand-pulled beers.
Bedrooms: 2 double, 2 family rooms.
Bathrooms: 4 private, 1 public.
Bed & breakfast: £17-£24 single, £35-£45 double.
Lunch available.
Evening meal 7pm (l.o. 10pm).
Parking for 60.
Credit: Access, Visa, Diners, Amex.

Moorfield Guest House ᴍ
80 West La., Haworth, Keighley, BD22 8EN
☎ (0535) 43689
Victorian house between the moors and village, with superb views over Bronte land. Garden terrace overlooks the cricket field.
Bedrooms: 1 single, 2 double & 2 twin, 1 family room.
Bathrooms: 5 private, 1 public.
Bed & breakfast: £15-£18 single, £28-£30 double.
Half board: £35-£40 daily, £245-£280 weekly.
Evening meal 7.15pm (l.o. 4.30pm).
Parking for 6.
Credit: Access, Visa.

Old White Lion Hotel ᴍ
APPROVED
Haworth, Keighley, BD22 8DU
☎ (0535) 42313
Family-run hotel with a candlelit restaurant. Close to the museum, parsonage and steam railway. Special weekend breaks available.
Bedrooms: 3 single, 6 double & 2 twin, 3 family rooms.
Bathrooms: 14 private.
Bed & breakfast: from £30 single, from £44 double.
Lunch available.
Evening meal 7pm (l.o. 10pm).

Parking for 10.
Credit: Access, Visa, Diners, Amex.

The Rydings Country Hotel ᴍ
COMMENDED
Bridgehouse La., Haworth, Keighley, BD22 8QE
☎ (0535) 45206 & 46933 Fax (0535) 46997
Elegant Edwardian house extended and totally refurbished during 1989. 13 new bedrooms, new conservatory and extended restaurant finished in 1990.
Bedrooms: 3 single, 16 double & 2 twin, 2 family rooms.
Bathrooms: 23 private.
Bed & breakfast: £26-£35 single, £36-£45 double.
Half board: £26-£45 daily, £182-£315 weekly.
Lunch available.
Evening meal 7pm (l.o. 10pm).
Parking for 26.
Credit: Access, Visa, Diners, Amex.

HEBDEN BRIDGE
W. Yorkshire
Map ref 4B1

Originally small town on packhorse route, Hebden Bridge grew into booming mill town in 18th C with rows of 'up-and-down' houses of several storeys built against hillsides. Ancient 'pace-egg play' custom held on Good Friday.
Tourist Information Centre ☎ *(0422) 843831*

Carlton Hotel ᴍ
Albert St., Hebden Bridge, HX7 8ES
☎ (0422) 844400
Consort
In the centre of Hebden Bridge, close to the shops and railway station. 18 en-suite bedrooms with every modern facility.
Bedrooms: 6 single, 4 double & 8 twin.
Bathrooms: 18 private.
Bed & breakfast: £47-£53 single, £67-£75 double.
Half board: from £40 daily.
Lunch available.

Evening meal 7.30pm (l.o. 9.30pm).
Credit: Access, Visa, Amex.
🛇 📞 ☐ 🌣 🛉 Ⅵ 🔄 🖭
🎛 ⚓ 🍴 🕹 💥 🚌 🕮 SP

Hebden Lodge Hotel M
❦❦❦❦ APPROVED
New Rd., Hebden Bridge, HX7 8AD
☎ (0422) 845272
Small family-run hotel offering a high standard of decor and facilities, with cuisine by chef/proprietor.
Bedrooms: 3 single, 6 double & 3 twin, 1 family room.
Bathrooms: 13 private.
Bed & breakfast: £25-£30 single, £50-£60 double.
Half board: £37-£42 daily.
Lunch available.
Evening meal 7pm (l.o. 9pm).
Credit: Access, Visa, Amex.
🛇 📞 ▦ 📞 ☐ 🌣 🛉 ⚓ 🍴 🕹 ☞ SP 🕮

Redacre Mill M
❦❦❦ COMMENDED
Redacre, Mytholmroyd, Hebden Bridge, HX7 5DQ
☎ Halifax (0422) 885563
Small country hotel featured on "Wish You Were Here". Peaceful canal side location, convenient for Bronte country, South Pennines and the Yorkshire Dales.
Bedrooms: 3 double & 2 twin.
Bathrooms: 5 private, 1 public.
Bed & breakfast: £30-£35 single, £40-£45 double.
Half board: £28.50-£38.50 daily, £180-£240 weekly.
Evening meal 6pm (l.o. 8pm).
Parking for 8.
Open February-November.
🛇 ☐ 🌣 🛉 Ⅵ 🔄 🕮 ⚓ ❄
💥 🚌 SP 🏠

HELMSLEY
N. Yorkshire
Map ref 5C3

Pretty town on the River Rye at the entrance to Ryedale and the North York Moors, with large cobbled square and remains of 12th C castle, several inns, notably the 16th C 'Black Swan', and All Saints' Church.

Beaconsfield Guest House
❦❦
Bondgate, Helmsley, York, YO6 5BW
☎ (0439) 71346

Large country house adjacent to market square. Comfortable, elegantly furnished rooms with TV, tea/coffee making facilities. Ideal for moors, York and coast.
Bedrooms: 1 single, 4 double & 2 twin.
Bathrooms: 2 public.
Bed & breakfast: from £23 single, from £38 double.
Parking for 8.
☐ 🌣 ▥ 🛉 Ⅵ 🔄 💥 🚌
DAP SP

Crown Hotel M
❦❦❦ COMMENDED
Market Place, Helmsley, York, YO6 5BJ
☎ (0439) 70297
16th C inn with a Jacobean dining room offering traditional country cooking using fresh local produce whenever possible. Most rooms en-suite, all with colour TV and direct dial telephones. Special breaks October to May. Dogs welcome.
Bedrooms: 5 single, 4 double & 4 twin, 1 family room.
Bathrooms: 12 private, 1 public.
Bed & breakfast: £24-£26 single, £48-£52 double.
Half board: £35-£37 daily, £226-£240 weekly.
Lunch available.
Evening meal 7.15pm (l.o. 8pm).
Parking for 15.
Credit: Access, Visa.
🛇 ▦ ▥ 📞 🕮 ☐ 🌣 🛉 Ⅵ 🔄
🔄 TV 🕮 🍴 ☞ ☺ ❄ 🚌 🕮
SP 🏠 🕮

Feversham Arms Hotel M
❦❦❦ COMMENDED
1 High St., Helmsley, York, YO6 5AG
☎ (0439) 70766
CB Best Western
Warm, elegant, family-run, historic inn in the North Yorkshire Moors National Park. Wide variety of food and wines. 5 four-poster rooms, 6 ground floor rooms have hair-dryer, trouser press and safe.
Bedrooms: 1 single, 7 double & 7 twin, 1 family room.
Bathrooms: 18 private.
Bed & breakfast: £45-£55 single, £70-£80 double.
Lunch available.
Evening meal 7pm (l.o. 9pm).
Parking for 30.
Credit: Access, Visa, Diners, Amex.
🛇 ▦ ▥ 📞 🕮 ☐ 🌣 🛉 Ⅵ
🔄 🕮 ⚓ 🍴 🕹 🎾 ☺ ☞ ❄
DAP SP 🏠 🕮

Lockton House Farm M
Bilsdale West, Helmsley, YO6 5NE
☎ Bilsdale (043 96) 303
400-acre mixed farm. Part of the house is a 16th C cruck house with oak beams, 7 miles out of Helmsley on the B1257 Teesside road. Ideal walking and touring area.
Bedrooms: 1 single, 1 double, 1 family room.
Bathrooms: 1 public.
Bed & breakfast: £10 single, £20 double.
Evening meal 6pm (l.o. 6pm).
Parking for 6.
Open March-October.
🛇 ▦ 🌣 ▥ 🛉 Ⅵ 🔄 TV 🕮 ⚓
💥 🏠

Pheasant Hotel M
❦❦❦❦
Harome, York, YO6 5JG
☎ Helmsley (0439) 71241
In a quiet rural village, with a terrace and gardens overlooking the village pond. Oak-beamed bar in a former blacksmith's shop, English food and log fires. Children over 12 years are welcome.
Bedrooms: 5 double & 6 twin, 1 family room.
Bathrooms: 12 private.
Bed & breakfast: £20-£32 single, £40-£64 double.
Half board: £37-£50 daily, £259-£350 weekly.
Lunch available.
Evening meal 7.30pm (l.o. 8pm).
Parking for 20.
Open March-December.
▦ 📞 🕮 ☐ 🌣 🛉 Ⅵ 🔄 🔄
🕮 ⚓ 🍴 🕹 ☞ 🎾 💥 SP 🕮

HESSLE
Humberside
Map ref 4C1

Hesslewood Hall Hotel M
❦❦❦❦
Ferriby Rd., Hessle, N. Humberside HU13 0JB
☎ Hull (0482) 641990 Fax (0482) 640990
English country mansion in 20 acres of private grounds. Magnificent views of the Humber and Humber Bridge. 6 minutes' drive from the city centre.
Bedrooms: 3 single, 14 double, 3 family rooms.
Bathrooms: 20 private.
Bed & breakfast: £34-£60.95 single, £58.50-£90.90 double.
Half board: £39.80-£60.95 daily, £265-£366 weekly.
Lunch available.
Evening meal 7.30pm (l.o. 10.30pm).

Parking for 300.
Credit: Access, Visa.
🛇 ▦ 📞 🕮 ☐ 🌣 🛉 Ⅵ 🔄
TV ⚓ ▥ ⚓ 🍴 🕹 🎾 ☺ ❄ SP
🏠 🕮

HOLMFIRTH
W. Yorkshire
Map ref 4B1

5m S. Huddersfield
This village has become famous as the location for the filming of the TV series 'Last of the Summer Wine'. It has a postcard museum and is on the edge of the Peak District National Park.
Tourist Information Centre ☎ *(0484) 684992 or 687603*

Old Bridge Hotel M
❦❦❦
Norridge Bottom, Holmfirth, Huddersfield, HD7 1DA
☎ Huddersfield (0484) 681212 Fax (0484) 687978
Well-appointed hotel in the heart of the "Summer Wine" country. Pub food and a restaurant providing attentive service.
Bedrooms: 7 single, 11 double & 2 twin.
Bathrooms: 20 private.
Bed & breakfast: £35-£45 single, £50-£60 double.
Half board: £40-£60 daily, £280-£400 weekly.
Lunch available.
Evening meal 7pm (l.o. 9.30pm).
Parking for 25.
Credit: Access, Visa, Amex.
🛇 📞 ☐ 🌣 🛉 Ⅵ 🔄 ◐
🕮 ⚓ 🍴 ☞ SP 🏠

HOOTON ROBERTS
S. Yorkshire
Map ref 4C2

4m NE. Rotherham

Earl of Strafford
❦❦❦❦❦ COMMENDED
Doncaster Rd., Hooton Roberts, Rotherham, S65 4PF
☎ Rotherham (0709) 852737 Fax (0709) 851903
Former dower house for Lady Strafford converted into an hotel with a 42-seater restaurant, function room and 2 public bars.
Bedrooms: 4 single, 14 double & 6 twin, 3 family rooms.
Bathrooms: 27 private.
Bed & breakfast: £50-£65 single, £55-£70 double.
Continued ▶

HOOTON ROBERTS

Continued

Half board: from £61 daily, from £407 weekly.
Lunch available.
Evening meal 7pm (l.o. 9.30pm).
Parking for 60.
Credit: Access, Visa, Diners, Amex.

HORNSEA

Humberside
Map ref 4D1

Small holiday town situated on strip of land between beach bordering North Sea and Hornsea Mere, a large natural freshwater lake. Some sailing and fishing permitted on protected nature reserve. Hornsea Pottery attracts many visitors.

Sandhurst Guest House

3 Victoria Avenue, Hornsea, N. Humberside HU18 1NH
☎ (0964) 534653
Guesthouse with sea views 30 yards from the beach, close to all amenities. Light snacks and basket meals are available. Residents' TV lounge.
Bedrooms: 2 twin, 1 family room.
Bathrooms: 1 public.
Bed & breakfast: £12-£14 single, £24-£28 double.
Evening meal 6pm (l.o. 7pm).
Parking for 1.

HORTON-IN-RIBBLESDALE

N. Yorkshire
Map ref 5B3

5m N. Settle
On the River Ribble and an ideal centre for pot-holing. The Pennine Way runs eastward over Pen-y-ghent, one of the famous 'Three Peaks'.
Tourist Information Centre ☎ (07296) 333

Crown Hotel M
APPROVED

Horton-in-Ribblesdale, Settle, BD24 0HF
☎ (072 96) 209

Small family-run country inn offering a warm welcome and friendly hospitality, in the heart of the dales.
Bedrooms: 3 single, 3 double, 4 family rooms.
Bathrooms: 1 private, 2 public; 6 private showers.
Bed & breakfast: £15.75-£21.50 single, £31.50-£43 double.
Half board: £23.90-£29.65 daily, £164.35-£183.40 weekly.
Lunch available.
Evening meal 6.30pm (l.o. 7pm).
Parking for 15.
Credit: Diners.

Wagis Guest House M

Townend Cottage, Horton-in-Ribblesdale, Settle, BD24 0EX
☎ (072 96) 320
Farm and barn (dated 1735) conversion in a beautiful limestone area close to the Three Peaks, Pennine Way, Settle/Carlisle Railway and Yorkshire Dales National Park.
Bedrooms: 1 double & 1 twin, 1 family room.
Bathrooms: 3 public.
Bed & breakfast: £12-£14 single, £24-£28 double.
Evening meal 6.30pm (l.o. 6.30pm).
Parking for 6.

HOWDEN

Humberside
Map ref 4C1

Small town near the River Ouse, dominated by partly-ruined medieval church of St. Peter's which has ancient origins but was rebuilt with a range of architectural styles over the centuries.

Wellington Hotel (Howden) M

Bridgegate, Howden, Goole, N. Humberside DN14 7JG
☎ (0430) 430258 Fax (0430) 432139
16th C coaching inn with modern facilities in historic market town. Popular restaurant, bars and beer garden. Ideal for business or pleasure.
Bedrooms: 3 single, 2 double & 3 twin, 1 family room.
Bathrooms: 9 private.

Bed & breakfast: £24-£28 single, £35-£40 double.
Lunch available.
Evening meal 6pm (l.o. 9.30pm).
Parking for 60.
Credit: Access, Visa.

⊕ Display advertisement appears on page 205.

HUDDERSFIELD

W. Yorkshire
Map ref 4B1

Founded on wool and cloth, has a famous choral society. Town centre redeveloped, but several good Victorian buildings remain, including railway station, St. Peter's Church, Tolson Memorial Museum, art gallery and nearby Colne Valley Museum. Castle Hill overlooks the town.
Tourist Information Centre ☎ (0484) 430808

Ashdene Guest House

15 Park Drive, Huddersfield, HD1 4EB
☎ (0484) 26089
Homely atmosphere and pleasant views overlooking Greenhead Park. Within walking distance of Huddersfield town centre.
Bedrooms: 2 single, 3 double & 2 twin.
Bathrooms: 1 public.
Bed & breakfast: £12 single, £22 double.
Parking for 6.

Briar Court Hotel M

Halifax Rd., Birchencliffe, Huddersfield, HD3 3NT
☎ (0484) 519902
Telex 518260 Fax (0484) 431812
Yorkshire stone-built hotel with bar, lounges and a dining room, adjoining an Italian restaurant. 2 minutes from the M62 juntion 24. Guide dogs are accepted.
Bedrooms: 2 single, 41 double & 2 twin, 3 family rooms.
Bathrooms: 48 private.
Bed & breakfast: £35-£60 single, £45-£75 double.
Lunch available.
Evening meal 6pm (l.o. 11pm).
Parking for 140.
Credit: Access, Visa.

Castle Hill Hotel M

Lumb La., Almondbury, Huddersfield, HD4 6TA
☎ (0484) 435445 Fax (0484) 431963
Traditional friendly pub hotel, prominently standing on ancient monument located next to Victoria Tower, high above Huddersfield, with incomparable panoramic views.
Bedrooms: 3 single, 4 double, 2 family rooms.
Bathrooms: 9 private.
Bed & breakfast: £26.50-£42 single, £37.50-£53 double.
Half board: £26-£49 daily, £200-£269 weekly.
Lunch available.
Evening meal 6pm (l.o. 9.30pm).
Parking for 130.
Credit: Access, Visa.

Huddersfield Hotel & Rosemary Lane Bistro M
APPROVED

33-47 Kirkgate, Huddersfield, HD1 1QT
☎ (0484) 512111 Telex 51575 HUDHOT G
Conference facilities, night club, jacuzzi, sauna, solarium and 4 public bars. 150 car spaces within 150 metres.
Bedrooms: 20 single, 10 double & 7 twin, 3 family rooms.
Bathrooms: 40 private.
Bed & breakfast: £18.50-£39 single, £32.50-£55 double.
Evening meal 6pm (l.o. midnight).
Parking for 30.
Credit: Access, Visa, C.Bl., Diners, Amex.

HULL

See Kingston-upon-Hull.

Classifications and quality commendations were correct at the time of going to press but are subject to change. Please check at the time of booking.

HUNMANBY

N. Yorkshire
Map ref 5D3

3m SW. Filey
The name of this village is
believed to signify 'House
of Dog Maw', a place
where dogs were kept for
hunting the wolves of the
Wold country. The parish
church dates from 1080,
the base and shaft of the
medieval cross still
survive; a hospital was
once run here for
travellers who had been
attacked by beasts.

Wrangham House M
♛♛♛
Stonegate, Hunmanby, Filey,
YO14 0NS
☎ Scarborough
(0723) 891333
*Delightful Georgian house in
its own grounds, in the centre
of this popular village 3 miles
from Filey. Comfortable,
traditional hospitality and
accommodation in an informal,
relaxing atmosphere. Ample
parking.*
Bedrooms: 2 single, 7 double
& 4 twin.
Bathrooms: 13 private.
Bed & breakfast: £28-£30
single, £56-£60 double.
Half board: £38.50-£44.50
daily, £238-£276.50 weekly.
Lunch available.
Evening meal 6.30pm (l.o.
8.30pm).
Parking for 26.
Credit: Access, Visa, Diners,
Amex.

HUTTON-LE-HOLE

N. Yorkshire
Map ref 5C3

2m N. Kirkbymoorside
Listed in Domesday
Book, this pretty village of
red-tiled stone cottages
situated around Hutton
Beck became a refuge for
persecuted Quakers in
17th C. Ryedale Folk
Museum.

Barn Hotel and Tea
Room M
♛♛ COMMENDED
Hutton-le-Hole, York,
YO6 6UA
☎ Lastingham (075 15) 311

*Stone walls and an inner
courtyard are part of the
character of this extended
barn. Centrally situated in
delightful Hutton-le-Hole.*
Bedrooms: 2 single, 4 double
& 2 twin.
Bathrooms: 3 private,
2 public.
Bed & breakfast: from £16
single, £32-£40 double.
Half board: £26-£30 daily,
£170-£195 weekly.
Lunch available.
Evening meal 7.30pm (l.o.
8pm).
Parking for 15.
Open March-December.
Credit: Access, Visa.

ILKLEY

W. Yorkshire
Map ref 4B1

This moorland spa town,
famous for its ballad, is a
lively tourist centre with
many hotels and shops.
16th C manor house, now
a museum, displays local
prehistoric and Roman
relics. Popular walk leads
up Heber's Ghyll to Ilkley
Moor, with the mysterious
Swastika Stone and
White Wells, 18th C
plunge baths.
*Tourist Information
Centre* ☎ (0943) 602319

Cow and Calf Hotel M
♛♛♛
Moor Top, Ilkley, LS29 8BT
☎ (0943) 607335
*Hotel of charm and character
on Ilkley Moor, commanding
unrivalled views of the
Yorkshire Dales. Bargain
breaks available.*
Bedrooms: 2 single, 9 double
& 5 twin, 1 family room.
Bathrooms: 17 private.
Bed & breakfast: £50-£65
single, £60-£75 double.
Half board: £37.50-£55 daily,
£262.50-£385 weekly.
Lunch available.
Evening meal 7.15pm (l.o.
9.30pm).
Parking for 102.
Credit: Access, Visa, C.Bl.,
Diners, Amex.

Crescent Hotel M
♛♛♛
Brook St., Ilkley, LS29 8DG
☎ (0943) 600012 & 600062
*Fully modernised hotel with
family rooms and self-catering
suites. In a central position in
town. Convenient for the dales.*

Bedrooms: 1 single, 4 double
& 12 twin, 3 family rooms.
Bathrooms: 20 private.
Bed & breakfast: £40-£45
single, £48-£58 double.
Half board: £34-£39 daily.
Lunch available.
Evening meal 6.30pm (l.o.
8.45pm).
Parking for 25.
Credit: Access, Visa, Amex.

Grove Hotel M
♛♛♛ APPROVED
The Grove, Ilkley, LS29 9PA
☎ (0943) 600298
*Small friendly, private hotel
offering well-appointed
accommodation. Convenient for
Ilkley town centre, shops and
gardens.*
Bedrooms: 1 single, 3 double
& 2 twin.
Bathrooms: 6 private,
1 public.
Bed & breakfast: £33-£36
single, £46-£48 double.
Half board: £39-£46 daily,
£273-£322 weekly.
Lunch available.
Evening meal 7pm (l.o.
8.30pm).
Parking for 5.
Credit: Access, Visa.

Moorview Guest
House M
♛♛♛ APPROVED
104 Skipton Rd., Ilkley,
LS29 9HE
☎ (0943) 600156
*Fully refurbished and
redecorated Victorian villa on
the River Wharfe, providing
small hotel accommodation.
Ideal for touring the dales and
Bronte country.*
Bedrooms: 3 single, 3 double
& 2 twin, 5 family rooms.
Bathrooms: 7 private,
2 public.
Bed & breakfast: £26-£36
single, £36-£46 double.
Evening meal 6.30pm (l.o.
6.30pm).
Parking for 14.

Rombald's Hotel &
Restaurant M
♛♛♛♛
West View, Wells Rd.,
Ilkley, LS29 9JG
☎ (0943) 603201 & 816586
Telex 51593 ROMTEL G
*Elegant Georgian restoration
on the edge of Ilkley Moor,
600 yards from the town
centre. Restaurant.*

Bedrooms: 4 single, 5 double
& 2 twin, 5 family rooms.
Bathrooms: 16 private.
Bed & breakfast: £55-£75
single, £78-£95 double.
Half board: £60-£72 daily,
£345-£380 weekly.
Lunch available.
Evening meal 7pm (l.o.
9.30pm).
Parking for 22.
Credit: Access, Visa, Diners,
Amex.

INGLETON

N. Yorkshire
Map ref 5B3

Ingleton is a thriving
tourist centre for fell-
walkers, climbers and
pot-holers. Popular walks
up beautiful Twiss Valley
to Ingleborough Summit,
Whernside, White Scar
Caves and waterfalls.

Bridge End Guest
House M
♛♛
Mill Lane, Ingleton,
Carnforth, Lancashire
LA6 3EP
☎ (052 42) 41413
*Former mill house retaining
many Georgian features.
Vegetarians welcome. In a
pleasant location adjacent to
the entrance to the waterfalls
in the Yorkshire Dales
National Park. Within easy
reach of the Lake District.*
Bedrooms: 1 single, 1 double,
1 family room.
Bathrooms: 1 private,
1 public.
Bed & breakfast: £15-£19
single, £24-£30 double.
Half board: £21-£25 daily,
£135-£170 weekly.
Lunch available.
Evening meal 6.30pm (l.o.
9am).
Parking for 10.

Langber Country Guest
House
♛♛
Ingleton, Carnforth,
Lancashire LA6 3DT
☎ Ingleton (052 42) 41587
*Detached country house with
large gardens and panoramic
views. Ideal for family
holidays. Good touring centre
for the Lake District,
Yorkshire Dales and coast.*
Bedrooms: 1 single, 2 double
& 2 twin, 2 family rooms.
Continued ▶

INGLETON
Continued

Bathrooms: 3 private,
2 public.
Bed & breakfast: £11.75-
£14.75 single, £23-£28 double.
Half board: £15.75-£19 daily,
£105-£119 weekly.
Evening meal 6.30pm (l.o.
5pm).
Parking for 6.

Moorgarth Hall Country House Hotel ♨
☗ ☗ ☗ COMMENDED

New Rd., Ingleton,
Carnforth, Lancashire
LA6 3HL
☎ (052 42) 41946
*Delightful Victorian country
house in wooded grounds.
Family-run. All rooms en-suite
with colour TV and central
heating. Ideal for lakes and
dales.*
Bedrooms: 1 single, 2 double
& 5 twin.
Bathrooms: 8 private.
Bed & breakfast: £24.50-
£26.50 single, £45-£49 double.
Half board: £34-£36 daily,
£208-£240 weekly.
Evening meal 7.30pm (l.o.
8.30pm).
Parking for 12.
Open February-December.
Credit: Access, Visa.

Pines Country House Hotel ♨
Ingleton, Carnforth,
Lancashire LA6 3HN
☎ (052 42) 41252
*Panoramic views. Ideal base
for walking and touring the
Yorkshire Dales, Lake District
and West Coast.*
Bedrooms: 4 double & 1 twin.
Bathrooms: 4 private,
1 public.
Bed & breakfast: £20-£22
single, £32-£36 double.
Half board: £26.50-£28.50
daily, £112-£126 weekly.
Evening meal 7.30pm (l.o.
8pm).
Parking for 14.

Springfield Private Hotel ♨
☗ ☗ ☗

Main St., Ingleton,
Carnforth, Lancashire
LA6 3HJ
☎ (052 42) 41280

*Detached Victorian villa in its
own small grounds with a
fountain and conservatory.*
Bedrooms: 1 single, 1 double
& 1 twin, 3 family rooms.
Bathrooms: 4 private,
2 public.
Bed & breakfast: £14-£16
single, £28-£32 double.
Half board: £21.50-£23.50
daily, £135-£150 weekly.
Evening meal 6.30pm (l.o.
5pm).
Parking for 12.
Open January-October.

KEIGHLEY
W. Yorkshire
Map ref 4B1

Pleasant Victorian town
where Charlotte Bronte
used to shop. Cliffe
Castle is an art gallery
and museum with large
collection of Victorian
bygones. 17th C East
Riddlesden Hall (National
Trust) has fine medieval
tithe barn. Trips on
Keighley and Worth
Valley Railway.

Airedale Guest House
☗
70-72 Devonshire St.,
Keighley, BD21 2BL
☎ (0535) 607597
*Family-run guesthouse near
the town centre, Haworth, the
Worth Valley Steam Railway
and canal boat centres. An
ideal tourist area.*
Bedrooms: 6 single, 2 twin,
5 family rooms.
Bathrooms: 2 public;
3 private showers.
Bed & breakfast: £12-£14
single, £24-£28 double.
Parking for 10.
Credit: Access, Visa.

Dalesgate Hotel ♨
☗ ☗ ☗
406 Skipton Rd., Utley,
Keighley, BD20 6HP
☎ Keighley (0535) 664930
*Charming, family-run hotel
near the town. Ideal tourist
area for the dales, Haworth,
York and the steam railways.*
Bedrooms: 9 single, 9 double
& 2 twin, 1 family room.
Bathrooms: 21 private.
Bed & breakfast: £24.50-
£32.50 single, £38-£44 double.
Half board: £29.50-£47.50
daily.

Evening meal 7pm (l.o.
11pm).
Parking for 22.
Credit: Access, Visa, Diners,
Amex.

KETTLEWELL
N. Yorkshire
Map ref 5B3

Set in the spectacular
scenery of the Yorkshire
Dales National Park in
Wharfedale, this former
market town is a
convenient stopping
place for climbers and
walkers. Dramatic rock
formation of Kilnsey Crag
is 3 miles south.

Langcliffe House
☗ ☗ ☗
Kettlewell, Skipton,
BD23 5RJ
☎ (075 676) 243
*Detached guesthouse in the
heart of the Yorkshire Dales
with peaceful surroundings and
magnificent scenery. Ideal for
touring and walking in the
National Park. Home cooking.*
Bedrooms: 1 single, 2 double
& 2 twin, 2 family rooms.
Bathrooms: 7 private.
Bed & breakfast: £23-£26
single, £40-£43 double.
Half board: £30-£32 daily,
£180-£190 weekly.
Evening meal 7pm (l.o. 7pm).
Parking for 7.
Open February-December.
Credit: Access, Visa.

**Individual
proprietors have
supplied all details
of accommodation.
Although we do
check for accuracy,
we advise you to
confirm prices and
other information
at the time of
booking.**

**The enquiry
coupons at the
back will help you
when contacting
proprietors.**

KINGSTON-UPON-HULL
Humberside
Map ref 4D1

Busy seaport with a
modern city centre and
excellent shopping
facilities. Deep-sea
fishing base at junction of
the Rivers Hull and
Humber, founded by
Cistercian monks in 12th
C. Maritime traditions in
the town, docks and the
museum, and the home of
William Wilberforce, the
slavery abolitionist,
whose house is now a
museum. The world's
longest single-span
suspension bridge
crosses the Humber 5
miles west.
*Tourist Information
Centre* ☎ (0482) 223344
or 223559 or 702118

Earlsmere Hotel
☗ ☗
76-78 Sunnybank, Off Spring
Bank West, Kingston-upon-
Hull, N. Humberside
HU3 1LQ
☎ (0482) 41977 Fax (0482)
214121 Telex 592729 FASTA
*Small family-run hotel in a
quiet area overlooking the
private grounds of Hymers
College. Private suites
available.*
Bedrooms: 11 single, 4 family
rooms.
Bathrooms: 7 private,
2 public.
Bed & breakfast: £18.40-
£26.45 single, £40.25-£46
double.
Half board: £27-£35 daily,
£185-£240 weekly.
Evening meal 6pm (l.o. 5pm).

Hollies Hotel ♨
☗ ☗
96 Park Avenue, Kingston-
upon-Hull, N. Humberside
HU5 3ET
☎ (0482) 41487
*Family-run hotel in a quiet
area, with licensed bar and
private lock-up car park.*
Bedrooms: 8 single, 1 double
& 1 twin, 1 family room.
Bathrooms: 2 private,
3 public.
Bed & breakfast: from £18.40
single, from £30 double.
Half board: from £24.40
daily.

Evening meal 6.30pm (l.o. 4pm).
Parking for 8.

Kingstown Hotel M
Hull Rd., Hedon, Kingston-upon-Hull, N. Humberside HU12 9DJ
☎ (0482) 890461 Fax (0482) 890713
New, family-run hotel with high standard of comfort, cleanliness, service and value. Adjacent to continental ferry terminal.
Bedrooms: 10 single, 4 double & 20 twin.
Bathrooms: 34 private.
Bed & breakfast: £56.95-£71.95 single, £73.90-£88.90 double.
Half board: £47.90-£55.40 daily, £335.30-£387.80 weekly.
Lunch available.
Evening meal 7pm (l.o. 10pm).
Parking for 74.
Credit: Access, Visa.

The Mayfair M
333-335 Beverley Rd., Kingston-upon-Hull, N. Humberside HU5 1LD
☎ (0482) 42402 & 441196
Clean and comfortable family-run establishment providing home-cooked food. Restaurant and residential licence, ideal for weddings and small functions.
Bedrooms: 8 single, 4 double & 4 twin, 4 family rooms.
Bathrooms: 4 public.
Bed & breakfast: £11-£12 single, £23 double.
Half board: £14-£16 daily, £98-£112 weekly.
Evening meal 6pm (l.o. 11pm).
Parking for 12.

Paragon Hotel M
Paragon St., Kingston-upon-Hull, N. Humberside HU1 3PJ
☎ (0482) 26462 Telex 592431
Modern city centre hotel with conference and banqueting facilities for up to 240. Convenient for all public transport.
Bedrooms: 28 single, 30 double & 66 twin, 1 family room.
Bathrooms: 125 private.
Bed & breakfast: £47-£67.50 single, £69-£84 double.
Lunch available.

Evening meal 7pm (l.o. 9.45pm).
Credit: Access, Visa, Diners, Amex.

Parkwood Hotel M
113 Princes Avenue, Kingston-upon-Hull, N. Humberside HU5 3JL
☎ (0482) 445610
Regency building in a tree-lined residential area close to the town centre. Run by the proprietor, providing a warm, friendly, relaxed atmosphere.
Bedrooms: 4 single, 3 double & 1 twin, 1 family room.
Bathrooms: 6 private, 2 public.
Bed & breakfast: £21-£29 single, £38-£42 double.
Half board: £31-£39 daily, £150-£207 weekly.
Evening meal 6.50pm (l.o. 9.30pm).
Parking for 5.
Credit: Access, Visa.

Pearson Park Hotel M
Pearson Park, Kingston-upon-Hull, N. Humberside HU5 2TQ
☎ (0482) 43043
In a delightful park with bowling greens and a lake. Swimming pool nearby. 1 mile from the city centre. Bar with open fire.
Bedrooms: 14 single, 11 double & 8 twin, 2 family rooms.
Bathrooms: 29 private, 1 public; 4 private showers.
Bed & breakfast: £30-£42 single, max. £52 double.
Half board: £39-£51 daily.
Lunch available.
Evening meal 6.30pm (l.o. 9pm).
Parking for 30.
Credit: Access, Visa, Diners, Amex.

Royal Hotel M
Ferensway, Kingston-upon-Hull, N. Humberside HU1 3UF
☎ (0482) 25087 Telex 592450
⊕ Friendly
Large Victorian city centre hotel with direct access to coach and railway stations. Extensive conference facilities.
Bedrooms: 61 single, 31 double & 25 twin, 5 family rooms.

Bathrooms: 122 private.
Bed & breakfast: £49-£58.50 single, £58.50-£66 double.
Half board: £40.75-£70 daily.
Lunch available.
Evening meal 7pm (l.o. 10pm).
Parking for 50.
Credit: Access, Visa, Diners, Amex.

N. Yorkshire
Map ref 5C3

Attractive market town with remains of Norman castle. Good centre for exploring moors. Nearby are wild daffodils of Farndale.

George & Dragon Hotel M
Market Place, Kirkbymoorside, York, YO6 6AA
☎ (0751) 31637
13th C inn of character at the foot of the Yorkshire Moors. Extensively modernised bedrooms, all with colour TV.
Bedrooms: 3 single, 14 double & 5 twin, 2 family rooms.
Bathrooms: 22 private, 1 public.
Bed & breakfast: from £30 single, from £55 double.
Half board: from £40 daily, from £250 weekly.
Lunch available.
Evening meal 7pm (l.o. 9.30pm).
Parking for 20.
Credit: Access, Visa.

Lion Inn
Blakey Ridge, Kirkbymoorside, York, YO6 6LQ
☎ Lastingham (075 15) 320
13th C free house in the centre of the North York moors, with breathtaking views.
Bedrooms: 7 double & 1 twin, 1 family room.
Bathrooms: 4 private, 1 public; 2 private showers.
Bed & breakfast: £16.50 single, £35-£48 double.
Half board: £21-£32 daily.
Lunch available.
Evening meal (l.o. 10.30pm).
Parking for 100.

White Horse Hotel
5 Market Place, Kirkbymoorside, York, YO6 6AB
☎ (0751) 31296
A small, friendly and comfortable market town hotel offering good accommodation and ale.
Bedrooms: 3 double.
Bathrooms: 1 public.
Bed & breakfast: £29 double.
Parking for 3.
Open April-October.

N. Yorkshire
Map ref 4B1

Picturesque market town on the River Nidd, famous for its 11th C castle ruins, overlooking town and river gorge. Attractions include oldest chemist's shop in country, prophetess Mother Shipton's cave, Dropping Well and Court House Museum. Boating on river.

Ebor Mount M
18 York Road, Knaresborough, HG5 0AA
☎ Harrogate (0423) 863315
250-year-old coaching house with comfortable, refurbished, en-suite rooms. Ideal touring centre.
Bedrooms: 1 single, 3 double & 2 twin, 2 family rooms.
Bathrooms: 8 private, 1 public.
Bed & breakfast: £16.50-£20 single, £30-£42 double.
Evening meal 7pm (l.o. midday).
Parking for 10.
Credit: Access, Visa.

Newton House Hotel M
York Place, Knaresborough, HG5 0AD
☎ Harrogate (0423) 863539
Beautifully converted Georgian town house of special historic interest, 2 minutes' walk from the market square, castle and river.
Bedrooms: 1 single, 7 double & 4 twin.
Bathrooms: 12 private.
Bed & breakfast: £25-£32.50 single, £40-£50 double.
Half board: from £40 daily.
Continued ▶

KNARESBOROUGH

Continued

Parking for 9.
Credit: Access, Visa, Diners, Amex.

🛏 🖒 ♨ ✆ ⊡ ➡ Ⅴ ⊨
⊡ ▥ ▬ ⓐ ⍏ ♻ ✕ DAP ☖
SP ⊞

Toronto House M
👑👑

19 Briggate, Knaresborough, HG5 8BQ
☎ Harrogate (0423) 865919
Grade II listed period guesthouse in the centre of the historic market town, adjacent to the Wellington Inn.
Bedrooms: 1 single, 3 double & 1 twin.
Bathrooms: 1 public.
Bed & breakfast: from £16 single, from £30 double.
Half board: £22-£23 daily, £154-£161 weekly.
Parking for 3.

🛏 ⊡ ➡ ⓐ 🁢 ♻ Ⅴ ⊨ ⊡ ▥
▬ ✕ ⊞ DAP SP

The Villa Hotel
Listed COMMENDED

Kirkgate, Knaresborough, HG5 8BZ
☎ Harrogate (0423) 865370
Small family-run hotel, with panoramic views over the River Nidd, viaduct and castle in conservation area. Central for touring.
Bedrooms: 1 single, 2 double & 2 twin, 1 family room.
Bathrooms: 4 private, 1 public.
Bed & breakfast: £12-£16.50 single, £36-£40 double.

🛏 🖒 ⊡ ➡ ♻ Ⅴ ⊨ ⊡ ▥
▬ ✕ 🏠

Yorkshire Lass M
👑👑👑 **APPROVED**

High Bridge, Harrogate Rd., Knaresborough, HG5 8DA
☎ Harrogate (0423) 862962
Detached inn on main Harrogate/York road, overlooking River Nidd. Real ales, wines, large selection of whiskies. Specialising in traditional Yorkshire dishes.
Bedrooms: 1 single, 3 double & 2 twin.
Bathrooms: 6 private.
Bed & breakfast: £25-£30 single, £40-£45 double.
Half board: £29-£32 daily, £175-£200 weekly.
Lunch available.
Evening meal 5pm (l.o. 10pm).
Parking for 34.
Credit: Access, Visa, Amex.

🛏 ✆ ⊡ ➡ ⓐ 🁢 ♻ ▥ ▬
⍏ ▶ ✕ 🏠 ♻ SP ⊡

LEAVENING

N. Yorkshire
Map ref 5C3

5m S. Malton

The Jolly Farmers
👑

Main St., Leavening, Malton, YO17 9SA
☎ Burythorpe (065 385) 276
Pleasant country inn in beautiful countryside close to the historic city of York and the North Yorkshire Moors National Park.
Bedrooms: 2 twin.
Bathrooms: 1 public.
Bed & breakfast: £34-£50 double.
Half board: £28-£35 daily, £180-£230 weekly.
Lunch available.
Evening meal 7pm (l.o. 9.30pm).
Parking for 24.

🁢 ⊡ ➡ ♻ ⓐ Ⅴ ▥ ▬ ✕
🏠 DAP SP

LEEDS

W. Yorkshire
Map ref 4B1

Large city with excellent modern shopping centre and much splendid Victorian architecture. Notable buildings include the Town Hall with its 225-ft clock tower, Civic Hall built of white Portland stone, Mechanics Institute and the oval-shaped Corn Exchange. Museums and galleries including Temple Newsam House (the Hampton Court of the North). Home of Opera North and a new playhouse.
Tourist Information Centre ☎ (0532) 462454 or 462455

Aintree Hotel M
👑👑

38 Cardigan Rd., Headingley, Leeds, LS6 3AG
☎ (0532) 758290
Small semi-detached family hotel on a tree-lined road, overlooking Headingley Cricket Ground. Close to the Arndale Shopping Centre. Evening meal by arrangement only.
Bedrooms: 5 single, 1 double & 1 twin, 1 family room.
Bathrooms: 3 private, 2 public.

Bed & breakfast: £18-£20 single, £28-£30 double.
Half board: £26-£28 daily.
Parking for 11.

🛏 ⊡ ➡ ♻ ⊡ ⊡ ▥ ▬ ✕

The Airedale
64 Ridge Ter., Headingley, Leeds, LS6 2DA
☎ (0532) 757229
Small, pleasant, family-run hotel in a quiet, elevated position. Convenient for the city centre, cricket ground and university.
Bedrooms: 4 single, 1 twin.
Bathrooms: 1 public.
Bed & breakfast: £15 single, £27 double.
Half board: £19.50 daily, from £107 weekly.
Evening meal 6pm (l.o. 2pm).
Parking for 2.
Credit: Access.

🛏 🁢 🖾 ♻ UL ⊨ ⊡ ▥ ▬ ✕
⊡

Aragon Hotel M
👑👑

250 Stainbeck La., Leeds, LS7 2PS
☎ (0532) 759306 & 757166
Converted late Victorian house in quiet, wooded surroundings, 2 miles from the city centre. Tea/coffee making facilities in all bedrooms.
Bedrooms: 4 single, 6 double & 3 twin, 1 family room.
Bathrooms: 9 private, 2 public.
Bed & breakfast: £23.40-£33.92 single, £35.30-£44.27 double.
Evening meal 7pm (l.o. 6pm).
Parking for 25.
Credit: Access, Visa, Diners, Amex.

🛏 ⊡ ➡ ♻ ⓐ ⊨ ▥ ▬ ⓐ ⍏ ✿
✕ ⊡

Avalon Guest House M
132 Woodsley Rd., Leeds, LS2
☎ (0532) 432545 & 432848
Victorian building close to the university, with bus stop at the gate for service into town. Some rooms have private facilities. Large car park.
Bedrooms: 3 single, 2 double & 5 twin, 1 family room.
Bathrooms: 3 private, 3 public.
Bed & breakfast: from £15 single, from £28 double.
Parking for 10.

🛏 🖒 ⊡ ➡ UL ♻ ▥ ▬ ⓐ ✕
⊞

Boundary Hotel M
42 Cardigan Rd., Headingley, Leeds, LS6 3AG
☎ (0532) 757700 & 751523

Small, family-run hotel overlooking the famous Headingley Cricket Ground. Specialising in home cooked food and a friendly welcome. Good local facilities and 2 miles from the city centre.
Bedrooms: 5 single, 4 double & 1 twin, 3 family rooms.
Bathrooms: 1 private, 2 public.
Bed & breakfast: £20 single, £30-£45 double.
Evening meal 6.30pm (l.o. 9.30pm).
Parking for 13.

🛏 ⊡ ➡ 🁢 Ⅴ ⊨ ⊡ ◉ ▥
ⓐ ✕

Broomhurst Hotel M
👑👑 **COMMENDED**

Chapel La., Headingley, Leeds, LS6 3BW
☎ (0532) 786836
Small, comfortable, owner-run hotel in a quiet, pleasantly wooded conservation area, 1.5 miles from the city centre. Convenient for the Yorkshire County Cricket Ground and the university.
Bedrooms: 5 single, 2 double & 3 twin, 1 family room.
Bathrooms: 2 private, 2 public; 1 private shower.
Bed & breakfast: £17.50-£27 single, £27-£35.50 double.
Evening meal 6pm (l.o. 9am).
Parking for 5.

🛏 🖾 ⊡ ➡ ♻ ⊨ ⊡ ▥ ▬ ⓐ ✕
⊞ SP

Cardigan Private Hotel M
Listed APPROVED

36 Cardigan Rd., Headingley, Leeds, LS6 3AG
☎ (0532) 784301
Family-run hotel next to Headingley Cricket/Rugby League Ground and near to public transport and shopping facilities, 2 miles from the city centre. Evening meals available Monday to Thursday only.
Bedrooms: 4 single, 4 double & 2 twin, 1 family room.
Bathrooms: 4 private, 2 public.
Bed & breakfast: £19-£30 single, £28.50-£40 double.
Half board: £21.50-£37 daily.
Evening meal 6pm (l.o. 9am).
Parking for 9.

🛏 ⊡ ➡ ♻ 🁢 Ⅴ ⊨ ⊡ ▥
⊞

Cliff Lawn Hotel
👑👑

44-45 Cliff Rd., Headingley, Leeds, LS6 2ET
☎ (0532) 785442

Large Victorian mansion set in well kept grounds and in a quiet location. Approximately 1 mile from Leeds city centre.
Bedrooms: 11 single, 8 double & 5 twin.
Bathrooms: 5 private, 5 public.
Bed & breakfast: £25-£34.50 single, £36.50-£46 double.
Half board: £28-£56 daily.
Evening meal 6pm (l.o. 8pm).
Parking for 20.
Credit: Access.

Cresta
381 Street Lane, Moortown, Leeds, LS17 6SE
☎ (0532) 661706
Small private hotel providing a friendly, personal service. Pleasant north Leeds suburb with easy access to Harrogate, York and the North Yorkshire countryside.
Bedrooms: 4 single, 2 twin, 2 family rooms.
Bathrooms: 2 public.
Bed & breakfast: from £14 single, from £24 double.
Parking for 6.

Eagle Tavern M
Listed
North St., Leeds, LS7 1AF
☎ (0532) 457146
Traditional pub in a commercial district of Leeds. Offering friendly service at reasonable prices. Close to the city centre. Colour TV in all rooms.
Bedrooms: 1 single, 6 twin, 2 family rooms.
Bathrooms: 2 public.
Bed & breakfast: £16.50-£18.50 single, £32-£36 double.
Parking for 8.

Glenn's Restaurant
281-283 Dewsbury Rd., Leeds, LS11 5HN
☎ (0532) 705187 & 719398
Guest house, restaurant and licensed bar close to the M1, M62. From Leeds city centre take A653 for 2 miles.
Bedrooms: 8 single, 2 double.
Bathrooms: 2 public.
Bed & breakfast: £15 single, £25 double.
Half board: £20 daily, £80-£105 weekly.
Lunch available.
Evening meal 5.30pm (l.o. 11.50pm).
Parking for 6.
Credit: Access, Visa.

Harewood Arms Hotel M
COMMENDED
Harrogate Rd., Harewood, Leeds, LS17 9LH
☎ (0532) 886566
Stone-built hotel and restaurant of character with a rural aspect, 8 miles from Harrogate and Leeds. Opposite Harewood House and close to all amenities, including golf and racing.
Bedrooms: 3 single, 9 double & 12 twin.
Bathrooms: 24 private.
Bed & breakfast: £42-£56 single, £55-£70.50 double.
Lunch available.
Evening meal 7pm (l.o. 10pm).
Parking for 60.
Credit: Access, Visa, Diners, Amex.

Hilton National Leeds Garforth M
Wakefield Rd., Garforth, Leeds, LS25 1LH
☎ Leeds (0532) 866556
Telex 556324
Ⓗ Hilton
Features Dukes Piano Bar and Restaurant. Leisure centre with pool, gym and sauna.
Bedrooms: 44 single, 19 double & 54 twin, 26 family rooms.
Bathrooms: 143 private.
Bed & breakfast: £82-£95 single, £114-£130 double.
Half board: £100-£115 daily.
Lunch available.
Evening meal 7pm (l.o. 10pm).
Parking for 300.
Credit: Access, Visa, C.Bl., Diners, Amex.

Holiday Inn Crowne Plaza Leeds M
Wellington St., Leeds, LS1 4DL
☎ (0532) 442200
Ⓗ Holiday Inn
City centre hotel, 125 executive bedrooms with suites, Lady Executive and study rooms.
Bedrooms: 125 double.
Bathrooms: 125 private.
Bed & breakfast: £110-£140 double.
Lunch available.
Evening meal 7pm (l.o. 10.30pm).

Parking for 120.
Credit: Access, Visa, C.Bl., Diners, Amex.

Manxdene Private Hotel M
154 Woodsley Rd., Leeds, LS2 9LZ
☎ (0532) 432586
Large, Victorian, terraced, family-run hotel adjacent to the university and half a mile from the city centre. Unlimited street parking. Close to bus services.
Bedrooms: 6 single, 1 double & 2 twin, 3 family rooms.
Bathrooms: 3 public.
Bed & breakfast: £18-£20 single, £28-£30 double.
Half board: £26-£28 daily.
Evening meal 6.15pm (l.o. 6.15pm).

Old Vicarage Guest House M
COMMENDED
Bruntcliffe Rd., Morley, Leeds, LS27 0JZ
☎ Leeds (0532) 532174
Within minutes of motorways, providing a Yorkshire welcome with home comforts in an authentic Victorian setting. Weekend rates available.
Bedrooms: 10 single, 3 double & 2 twin.
Bathrooms: 15 private.
Bed & breakfast: from £40 single, from £50 double.
Half board: from £48 daily, from £336 weekly.
Evening meal 6pm (l.o. 7pm).
Parking for 15.
Credit: Access, Visa.

Pinewood Private Hotel M
78 Potternewton La., Leeds, LS7 3LW
☎ (0532) 622561 & 628485
Friendly hotel with resident proprietors and emphasis on cleanliness.
Bedrooms: 4 single, 2 double & 2 twin, 2 family rooms.
Bathrooms: 6 private, 1 public; 3 private showers.
Bed & breakfast: £25-£31 single, £37.50-£46 double.
Evening meal 6.30pm (l.o. 10am).

St. Michael's Tower Hotel M
5 St. Michael's Villas, Cardigan Rd., Headingley, Leeds, LS6 3AF
☎ (0532) 755557
Licensed, private hotel with easy access to Leeds city centre (2 miles) and close to both the university and Yorkshire Cricket Ground.
Bedrooms: 3 single, 3 double & 2 twin, 4 family rooms.
Bathrooms: 2 private, 3 public.
Bed & breakfast: £15-£25 single, £23-£30 double.
Parking for 12.

Stakis Windmill Hotel M
Ring Rd., Seacroft, Leeds, LS14 5QP
☎ (0532) 732323 Telex 55452
Ⓒ Stakis
Ideal for both business and holiday makers. On the main Leeds to York road with easy access to the airport and motorways.
Bedrooms: 22 single, 18 double & 60 twin.
Bathrooms: 100 private.
Bed & breakfast: £83-£93 single, £106-£116 double.
Lunch available.
Evening meal 7pm (l.o. 10pm).
Parking for 120.
Credit: Access, Visa, Diners, Amex.

LEEDS/BRADFORD AIRPORT

See Bingley, Bradford, Leeds, Otley, Pool.

LEEMING BAR

N. Yorkshire
Map ref 5C3

Just off the A1 between dales and moors.

White Rose Hotel M
Leeming Bar, Northallerton, DL7 9AY
☎ Bedale (0677) 22707 & 24941 & (0677) 23235 Fax (0677) 28133

Continued ▶

Please mention this guide when making a booking.

LEEMING BAR
Continued

Family-run, private hotel and restaurant in a village half a mile from the A1 motorway. Access to the Yorkshire Dales and coastal resorts.
Bedrooms: 9 single, 1 double & 7 twin, 1 family room.
Bathrooms: 18 private, 1 public.
Bed & breakfast: from £25 single, from £40 double.
Half board: from £34.50 daily.
Lunch available.
Evening meal 7.30pm (l.o. 9pm).
Parking for 40.
Credit: Access, Visa, Diners, Amex.

LEYBURN
N. Yorkshire
Map ref 5B3

Attractive dales market town where Mary Queen of Scots was reputedly captured after her escape from Bolton Castle. Fine views over Wensleydale from nearby.
Tourist Information Centre ☎ (0969) 23069 or 22773

Eastfield Lodge Private Hotel M

St. Matthews Terrace, Leyburn, DL8 5EL
☎ Wensleydale (0969) 23196
Family-run, private hotel providing home cooking and large comfortable rooms, with views over Wensleydale. Central for touring the dales and excellent for walking.
Bedrooms: 4 double & 1 twin, 3 family rooms.
Bathrooms: 3 public.
Bed & breakfast: £15-£18 single, £24-£30 double.
Evening meal 6.30pm (l.o. 9.30pm).
Parking for 10.
Credit: Access, Visa.

Golden Lion Hotel & Licensed Restaurant M

Market Place, Leyburn, DL8 5AS
☎ Wensleydale (0969) 22161
Small family-run hotel in the market place of a busy dales' town. A good base for touring the surrounding countryside.

Bedrooms: 2 single, 5 double & 3 twin, 4 family rooms.
Bathrooms: 11 private, 2 public.
Bed & breakfast: £20-£25 single, £40-£52 double.
Half board: £30-£35 daily, £19-£225 weekly.
Lunch available.
Evening meal 7pm (l.o. 9pm).
Parking for 12.
Credit: Access, Visa, Diners.

Grove Hotel M
APPROVED

8 Grove Square, Leyburn, DL8 5AE
☎ Wensleydale (0969) 22569
Recently renovated listed building with a wealth of panelling and beams, in the oldest of Leyburn's 3 squares.
Bedrooms: 1 single, 3 double & 2 twin, 3 family rooms.
Bathrooms: 6 private, 1 public.
Bed & breakfast: £16-£17.50 single, £27-£35 double.
Lunch available.
Evening meal 5pm (l.o. 9.30pm).
Parking for 10.
Credit: Access, Visa.

Park Gate House

Constable Burton, Leyburn, DL8 5RG
☎ Bedale (0677) 50466
250-year-old family-run house of character.
Bedrooms: 1 single, 1 double & 1 twin, 1 family room.
Bathrooms: 1 public.
Bed & breakfast: £12-£13.50 single, £24-£29 double.
Half board: £19.50-£22 daily, £125-£140 weekly.
Evening meal 7pm.
Parking for 5.

Priory Guest House M

The Priory, Middleham, Leyburn, DL8 4QG
☎ Wensleydale (0969) 23279
Georgian house with many historic features, adjacent to Middleham Castle. Central heating and tea-making facilities. An ideal centre for touring the dales.
Bedrooms: 1 single, 3 double & 2 twin, 2 family rooms.
Bathrooms: 4 private, 2 public.
Bed & breakfast: £13-£14 single, £26-£32 double.

Half board: £20-£23 daily, £127-£145 weekly.
Evening meal 6.30pm (l.o. 7pm).
Parking for 9.
Open March-November.

Secret Garden House M

Grove Square, Leyburn, DL8 5HE
☎ Wensleydale (0969) 23589
Georgian house with a secluded walled garden, in the middle of a busy market town in the heart of James Herriot country.
Bedrooms: 1 single, 2 double & 2 twin, 2 family rooms.
Bathrooms: 5 private, 1 public.
Bed & breakfast: £17.50-£20.50 single, £35-£41 double.
Half board: £29-£32 daily, £200-£220 weekly.
Evening meal 7.30pm (l.o. 8.30pm).
Parking for 10.
Credit: Access.

Sunnyholme
8 St. Mary's Mount, Leyburn, DL8 5JB
☎ Wensleydale (0969) 23352
Well-situated family guesthouse.
Bedrooms: 1 double & 1 twin, 1 family room.
Bathrooms: 1 public.
Bed & breakfast: £22-£24 double.
Half board: £16 daily, £107 weekly.
Evening meal 6.30pm.
Parking for 2.

White Swan Hotel
Market Place, Middleham, Leyburn, DL8 4PE
☎ Wensleydale (0969) 22093
Country inn near the castle, offering comfort and friendly service. Home-cooked food. In the heart of the Yorkshire Dales, an ideal base for touring.
Bedrooms: 2 double & 2 twin, 2 family rooms.
Bathrooms: 3 private, 2 public.
Bed & breakfast: £14-£20 single, £26-£36 double.
Half board: £17.50-£22.50 daily, £110-£135 weekly.
Lunch available.
Evening meal 6.30pm (l.o. 8.30pm).
Parking for 6.

LIVERSEDGE
W. Yorkshire
Map ref 4B1

3m NW. Dewsbury

Healds Hall Hotel M

Leeds Rd., Liversedge, WF15 6JA
☎ Liversedge (0924) 409112
Family-run hotel built in the 18th C and set in large gardens.
Bedrooms: 4 single, 17 double, 5 family rooms.
Bathrooms: 26 private.
Bed & breakfast: £35-£45 single, £45-£65 double.
Half board: £40-£50 daily, £280-£350 weekly.
Lunch available.
Evening meal 7pm (l.o. 9pm).
Parking for 49.
Credit: Access, Visa.

LONG PRESTON
N. Yorkshire
Map ref 4B1

Village surrounded by limestone country and overlooking Ribblesdale.

Maypole Inn M
APPROVED

Maypole Green, Main St., Long Preston, Skipton, BD23 4PH
☎ (072 94) 219
17th C inn, with open fires, on the village green. Easy access to many attractive walks in the surrounding dales.
Bedrooms: 1 single, 3 double & 1 twin, 1 family room.
Bathrooms: 2 public.
Bed & breakfast: £17 single, £29 double.
Half board: from £21 daily.
Lunch available.
Evening meal 6.30pm (l.o. 9pm).
Parking for 25.
Credit: Access, Visa.

Plough Inn M

Wigglesworth, Skipton, BD23 4RJ
☎ Long Preston (072 94) 243
Once an inn and working farm which was part of a large country estate, now converted to provide high standard accommodation in a rural setting.
Bedrooms: 6 double & 4 twin, 1 family room.
Bathrooms: 11 private.

Bed & breakfast: £29-£31 single, £42-£46 double. **Half board**: £29.50-£35.75 daily, £195-£215 weekly. Lunch available. Evening meal 7pm (l.o. 10.30pm). Parking for 50. Credit: Access, Visa, Diners.

LOW ROW

N. Yorkshire
Map ref 5B3

4m W. Reeth
Swaledale village full of character with grey-stone houses. There is a village custom where children attending chapel who are able to recite psalms are given a Bible.

Gables Country Guest House **M**

Low Row, Richmond, DL11 6NH
☎ Richmond (0748) 86429
Peaceful location in the heart of Swaledale, 15 miles from Richmond. Spacious rooms, some en-suite. Home cooking and a friendly welcome.
Bedrooms: 1 double & 1 twin, 3 family rooms.
Bathrooms: 2 private, 1 public.
Bed & breakfast: from £23.50 single, £41-£47 double.
Half board: £31-£34 daily.
Evening meal 7pm (l.o. 5pm).
Parking for 6.
Open April-October.

LUDDENDEN FOOT

W. Yorkshire
Map ref 4B1

In the Calder Valley. Branwell Bronte was put in charge of the station here in 1840.

Collyers Hotel

Burnley Rd., Luddenden Foot, Halifax, HX2 6AH
☎ Halifax (0422) 882624
Small personal hotel, with elegant restaurant, lounge bar and individually styled bedrooms.
Bedrooms: 2 single, 2 double & 2 twin.
Bathrooms: 4 private, 1 public.
Bed & breakfast: from £21 single, from £49 double.
Half board: from £35 daily.
Lunch available.

Evening meal 7pm (l.o. 9.30pm).
Parking for 15.
Credit: Access, Visa.

MALHAM

N. Yorkshire
Map ref 5B3

11m NW. Skipton
Hamlet of stone cottages amid magnificent rugged limestone scenery in the Yorkshire Dales National Park. Malham Cove is a curving, sheer white cliff 240 ft high. Malham Tarn, one of Yorkshire's few natural lakes, belongs to the National Trust. National Park Centre.

Beck Hall Guest House

Malham, Skipton, BD23 4DJ
☎ Airton (072 93) 332
Family-run guesthouse set in a spacious riverside garden. Homely atmosphere, four-poster beds, log fires and home cooking.
Bedrooms: 1 single, 4 double & 3 twin, 3 family rooms.
Bathrooms: 7 private, 3 public.
Bed & breakfast: £15-£20 single, £26-£31 double.
Half board: £19-£21.50 daily.
Lunch available.
Evening meal 7pm (l.o. 8pm).
Parking for 30.
Open January-November.

Eastwood House **M**
Listed

Malham, Skipton, BD23 4DA
☎ Airton (072 93) 409
Bed and breakfast guesthouse in the centre of the village. Heaters in every bedroom, on the landings and in the dining room.
Bedrooms: 1 single, 2 double & 1 twin, 1 family room.
Bathrooms: 2 public.
Bed & breakfast: £12.50-£17.50 single, £25 double.
Parking for 3.
Open January-November.

Half board prices shown are per person but in some cases may be based on double/twin occupancy.

MALTON

N. Yorkshire
Map ref 5D3

A thriving farming town on the River Derwent with large livestock market. Famous for race horse training. The local museum has Roman remains and many World War II relics from the 'Eden' prisoner of war camp on site in the town. Castle Howard within easy reach.

Norton Manor Hotel **M**
APPROVED

Welham Rd., Norton, Malton, YO17 9DS
☎ (0653) 692027 & 695333
Charming country house hotel, minutes from the centre of town, yet in the quiet suburbs of Malton.
Bedrooms: 3 single, 5 double & 4 twin, 2 family rooms.
Bathrooms: 14 private.
Bed & breakfast: £30-£32.50 single, £40-£55 double.
Half board: £32.50-£37.50 daily, £455-£525 weekly.
Lunch available.
Evening meal 7pm (l.o. 9.30pm).
Parking for 44.
Credit: Access, Visa, Amex.

Oakdene Country House Hotel **M**
COMMENDED

29 Middlecave Rd., Malton, YO17 ONE
☎ (0653) 693363
Elegant Victorian residence in its own grounds, in a select residential area of this beautiful market town in the heart of Ryedale. Home-grown vegetables in season and traditional home cooking.
Bedrooms: 4 double & 2 twin.
Bathrooms: 6 private.
Bed & breakfast: £19.50-£27.50 double.
Evening meal 7pm (l.o. 7.30pm).
Parking for 6.

Wentworth Arms Hotel **M**

Town St., Old Malton, Malton, YO17 OHD
☎ (0653) 692618

Former coaching inn, built early 1700s and run by the same family for 100 years. 20 miles from York. An excellent base for touring the Yorkshire Dales, North York Moors and the East Coast.
Bedrooms: 2 single, 3 double & 2 twin.
Bathrooms: 2 public.
Bed & breakfast: from £18 single, £36-£40 double.
Lunch available.
Evening meal 6pm (l.o. 8.45pm).
Parking for 30.
Credit: Visa.

MARKET WEIGHTON

Humberside
Map ref 4C1

Small town on the western side of the Yorkshire Wolds. A tablet in the parish church records the death of William Bradley in 1820 at which time he was 7ft 9in tall and weighed 27 stone!

Londesborough Arms Hotel **M**

44 High St., Market Weighton, York, N. Yorkshire YO4 3AH
☎ (0430) 872219 & 872214
Fine 3-storey Georgian hotel, fully restored to its original beauty. Contains Giant Bradley's chair - tallest ever British man.
Bedrooms: 3 double & 12 twin, 1 family room.
Bathrooms: 16 private, 2 public.
Bed & breakfast: £45-£50 single, £75-£120 double.
Lunch available.
Evening meal 7pm (l.o. 10pm).
Parking for 51.
Credit: Access, Visa, Diners, Amex.

Individual proprietors have supplied all details of accommodation. Although we do check for accuracy, we advise you to confirm prices and other information at the time of booking.

MIDDLEHAM

N. Yorkshire
Map ref 5C3

Town famous for racehorse training, with cobbled squares and houses of local stone. Norman castle, once principal residence of Warwick the Kingmaker and later Richard III. Ruins of Jervaulx Abbey nearby.

Miller's House Hotel M
COMMENDED

Market Place, Middleham, Leyburn, DL8 4NR
☎ Wensleydale (0969) 22630
Elegant Georgian country house in peaceful village of Middleham, heart of Herriot's Yorkshire Dales. Charming en-suite rooms and four-poster, colour TV, telephones, tea/coffee facilities. 20 minutes from A1.
Bedrooms: 1 single, 3 double & 3 twin.
Bathrooms: 7 private.
Bed & breakfast: £32-£35 single, £64-£70 double.
Half board: £47-£50 daily, £294-£315 weekly.
Lunch available.
Evening meal 7.30pm (l.o. 9pm).
Parking for 8.
Open February-December.
Credit: Access, Visa.

Richard III Hotel

Market Place, Middleham, Leyburn, DL8 4NP
☎ Wensleydale (0969) 23240
Tastefully refurbished old hostelry providing a good base for visiting places of interest in the Dales and surrounding areas.
Bedrooms: 4 double & 2 twin.
Bathrooms: 6 private.
Bed & breakfast: from £23.50 single, £37-£50 double.
Half board: £23-£31 daily, £161-£200 weekly.
Lunch available.
Evening meal 6pm (l.o. 9pm).
Parking for 50.
Credit: Access, Visa.

MIRFIELD

W. Yorkshire
Map ref 4B1

Just off the M62 between Dewsbury and Huddersfield.

Flowerpot Motel
3 Granny La., Mirfield, WF14 8LA
☎ (0924) 493398
Imaginatively converted 18th C cottages with colour TV and refreshments in every bedroom. Central heating throughout and a cosy restaurant. Good centre for business or pleasure. Exit 40 of the M1 and exit 25 of the M62.
Bedrooms: 3 double & 4 twin, 1 family room.
Bathrooms: 2 private, 4 public.
Bed & breakfast: £27-£35 single, £37-£45 double.
Half board: £33.95-£43.95 daily, £237.65-£307.65 weekly.
Evening meal 6.30pm (l.o. 7.30pm).
Parking for 5.
Credit: Access, Visa, Amex.

MURTON

N. Yorkshire
Map ref 4C1

3m E. York

Dray Lodge Hotel M
COMMENDED

Moor La., Murton, York, YO1 3UH
☎ York (0904) 489591 Fax (0904) 488587
19th C horse carriage works, converted to a country hotel. On the east side of York, 3 miles from city centre.
Bedrooms: 2 single, 5 double & 2 twin, 1 family room.
Bathrooms: 10 private, 2 public.
Bed & breakfast: £26.45-£29.10 single, £41.40-£45.54 double.
Evening meal 6.30pm (l.o. 8pm).
Parking for 12.
Credit: Access, Visa.

NEWBIGGIN

N. Yorkshire
Map ref 5B3

2m S. Aysgarth
Village in Bishopdale with footpaths to the summit of Noughtberry Hill and Buckden Pike.

Bishop Garth M
COMMENDED

Newbiggin (Bishopdale), Leyburn, DL8 3TD
☎ Wensleydale (0969) 663429
Comfortably-furnished, modernised, old stone cottage of the traditional dales' type, off the B6160. On a 6-acre smallholding in a peaceful village. Home-cooked food. Packed lunches on request. En-suite available. No small children please.
Bedrooms: 1 single, 2 double & 1 twin.
Bathrooms: 1 private, 1 public.
Bed & breakfast: £13-£17 single, £26-£34 double.
Half board: £21-£25 daily, £135-£165 weekly.
Evening meal 7pm.
Parking for 6.

NORTH DALTON

Humberside
Map ref 4C1

6m SW. Great Driffield
Pretty village in the Yorkshire Wolds, midway between Pocklington and Driffield.

Old School
North Dalton, Driffield, N. Humberside YO25 9UX
☎ Middleton-on-the-Wolds (037 781) 618
Former old school house, still retaining its original architectural character and charm. Adjoining the former school, which is now used by Mrs. Carter as a soft furnishing workroom, showroom and tearoom, tea garden. The dining room is set out in one of the former classrooms and contains railway and other memorabilia items. 3 rooms have hot and cold water.
Bedrooms: 1 single, 1 double & 2 twin.
Bathrooms: 2 public.
Bed & breakfast: from £15 single, from £30 double.
Half board: from £22.50 daily, from £135 weekly.

Lunch available.
Evening meal 5.30pm (l.o. 9pm).
Parking for 2.

NORTHALLERTON

N. Yorkshire
Map ref 5C3

Formerly a staging post on coaching route to the North and later a railway town. Today a lively market town and administrative capital of North Yorkshire. Parish church of All Saints dates from 1200.

Alverton Guest House

26 South Parade, Northallerton, DL7 8SG
☎ (0609) 776207
Family-run guesthouse convenient for county town facilities and ideal for touring the dales, moors and coastal areas.
Bedrooms: 2 single, 1 double & 1 twin, 1 family room.
Bathrooms: 3 private, 1 public.
Bed & breakfast: £14.50-£16 single, £29-£32 double.
Half board: £21.50-£23 daily, £145-£160 weekly.
Evening meal 7pm (l.o. 7pm).
Parking for 5.

Porch House M
APPROVED

68 High St., Northallerton, DL7 8EG
☎ (0609) 779831
Small family house, 16th and 18th C Grade II and III listed, associated with Charles I. Parish church nearby.
Bedrooms: 1 double & 4 twin.
Bathrooms: 5 private.
Bed & breakfast: £27.50-£30.50 single, £39.50-£43.50 double.
Half board: £29.60-£41.50 daily, £192.40-£269.75 weekly.
Evening meal 7pm (l.o. 7pm).
Parking for 5.
Credit: Access, Visa.

Sundial Hotel M
COMMENDED

Darlington Rd., Northallerton, DL6 2XF
☎ (0609) 780525
Fax (0609) 780491

Newly-built, elegantly-appointed hotel for businessmen and tourists alike. Fireside cocktail lounge and restaurant, conference facilities for up to 100. Facilities for the disabled.
Bedrooms: 3 double & 25 twin.
Bathrooms: 28 private.
Bed & breakfast: from £55 single, from £66 double.
Half board: from £315 weekly.
Lunch available.
Evening meal 6.30pm (l.o. 9.30pm).
Parking for 100.
Credit: Access, Visa, Diners, Amex.

Windsor Guest House
56 South Parade, Northallerton, DL7 8SL
☎ (0609) 774100
Victorian house in a tree-lined road near to the town centre, main-line railway station, County Hall and Records Office. Open except for 24 December to 2 January.
Bedrooms: 3 twin, 3 family rooms.
Bathrooms: 2 public.
Bed & breakfast: £17 single, £27 double.
Half board: £23.75 daily.
Evening meal 6pm.

2m SW. Keighley
This village lies on the route of the Worth Valley Railway which was the location of the film 'The Railway Children', and is only 1 mile north of Haworth.

Railway Cottage
59 Station Rd., Oakworth, Keighley, BD22 0DZ
☎ Haworth (0535) 42693
Small guesthouse adjacent to Oakworth station on the Keighley and Worth Valley Railway. Ground floor accommodation suitable for disabled visitors.
Bedrooms: 2 single, 3 double.
Bathrooms: 5 private.
Bed & breakfast: £12-£18 single, £22-£34 double.
Parking for 5.

4m S. Helmsley
Village on the hillside overlooking the valley which separates the Howardian and Hambleton Hills. In the Domesday Book as 'Oswaldeschurcha' meaning the church of Oswald.

Thirklewood House
Oswaldkirk, York, YO6 5YB
☎ Ampleforth (043 93) 229
Large country house in 2 acres of gardens on the B1257 between Helmsley and Malton. All rooms have central heating and tea/coffee making facilites. Friendly atmosphere.
Bedrooms: 2 double & 1 twin, 1 family room.
Bathrooms: 1 private, 3 public.
Bed & breakfast: £24-£30 double.
Parking for 6.

Market and manufacturing town in Lower Wharfedale, the birthplace of Thomas Chippendale. Has a Maypole, several old inns, rebuilt medieval bridge and a local history museum. All Saints Church dates from Norman times.
Tourist Information Centre ☎ (0943) 465151

Riverdale Guest House
Listed **APPROVED**
1 Riverdale Rd., Otley, LS21 1AS
☎ (0943) 461387
Victorian, stone-built house in a quiet location near the River Wharfe and close to the town centre. Coal fires and home cooking.
Bedrooms: 2 double & 2 twin, 1 family room.
Bathrooms: 1 public.
Bed & breakfast: from £20 single, from £32 double.
Half board: from £27.50 daily.
Evening meal 6.30pm.

4m W. Huddersfield

Old Golf House Hotel M
New Hey Rd., Outlane, Huddersfield, HD3 3YP
☎ Elland (0422) 379311 & 372694 Telex 51324
CR Lansbury
A stone-built hotel set in 3 acres of gardens adjacent to the M62 with 50 bedrooms and conference facilites.
Bedrooms: 4 single, 30 double & 13 twin, 4 family rooms.
Bathrooms: 50 private.
Bed & breakfast: £22-£65 single, £44-£77 double.
Half board: £33-£78 daily.
Lunch available.
Evening meal 7pm (l.o. 10pm).
Parking for 70.
Credit: Access, Visa, Diners, Amex.

Small market town at centre of Upper Nidderdale. Flax and linen industries once flourished in this remote and beautiful setting.

Middlesmoor Crown Hotel M
Middlesmoor, Pateley Bridge, Harrogate, HG3 5ST
☎ Harrogate (0423) 755296 & 755204
Family-run hotel at the head of Nidderdale with panoramic views, 8 miles from Pateley Bridge. Restaurant and bar meals.
Bedrooms: 1 single, 2 double & 2 twin, 2 family rooms.
Bathrooms: 1 private, 2 public.
Bed & breakfast: £20-£21 single, £31-£33 double.
Lunch available.
Evening meal 7pm (l.o. 9pm).
Parking for 20.
Credit: Access, Visa.

Talbot Hotel M
COMMENDED
High St., Pateley Bridge, Harrogate, HG3 5AL
☎ Harrogate (0423) 711597

Small hotel in the centre of Pateley Bridge, in beautiful Nidderdale, ideal for touring the dales. Family owned and run.
Bedrooms: 1 single, 5 double & 1 twin, 1 family room.
Bathrooms: 6 private, 1 public.
Bed & breakfast: £18-£20 single, £27-£34 double.
Half board: £23-£26.50 daily, £161-£185.50 weekly.
Evening meal 7pm (l.o. 6pm).
Parking for 9.
Open February-October.
AD Display advertisement appears on page 204.

Yorke Arms Hotel M
Ramsgill, Harrogate, HG3 5RL
☎ Harrogate (0423) 75243
18th C. hostelry on village green. In the heart of unspoilt Nidderdale at the head of Gouthwaite Reservoir Nature Reserve.
Bedrooms: 3 single, 3 double & 5 twin, 2 family rooms.
Bathrooms: 13 private.
Bed & breakfast: £45-£50 single, £65-£75 double.
Half board: £47-£60 daily.
Lunch available.
Evening meal 7.30pm (l.o. 9pm).
Parking for 50.
Credit: Access, Visa.
AD Display advertisement appears on page 205.

Market town and tourist centre on edge of North York Moors. Parish church has complete set of 15th C wall paintings depicting lives of saints. Part of 12th C castle still stands. Beck Isle Museum. The North York Moors Railway begins here.

Beansheaf Restaurant Hotel M
COMMENDED
Malton Rd., Kirby Misperton, Malton, YO17 0UE
☎ (065 386) 614 & 488
Continued ▶

175

PICKERING

Continued

Modern hotel with wine bar and coffee shop surrounded by fields and near Flamingo Zoo. Pickering 2 miles, York 20 minutes, central for Scarborough and Whitby.
Bedrooms: 7 single, 7 double & 4 twin, 2 family rooms.
Bathrooms: 20 private, 1 public.
Bed & breakfast: £22.50-£24.50 single, £36-£40 double.
Half board: £27-£29.50 daily.
Lunch available.
Evening meal 7pm (l.o. 9.30pm).
Parking for 50.
Credit: Access, Visa.

Burgate House Hotel & Restaurant M

17 Burgate, Pickering, YO18 7AU
☎ (0751) 73463
A Georgian residence with parts dating from the 16th C. 100 yards from Pickering Castle.
Bedrooms: 4 double & 1 twin, 1 family room.
Bathrooms: 2 private, 2 public; 2 private showers.
Bed & breakfast: £20-£32 single, £30-£55 double.
Half board: £30-£42 daily, £180-£241 weekly.
Lunch available.
Evening meal 7pm (l.o. 9pm).
Parking for 8.
Credit: Access, Visa.

Cottage Leas Country Hotel M
COMMENDED

Nova, Middleton, Pickering, Y018 8PN
☎ Pickering (0751) 72129
Secluded and peaceful 18th C country hotel, with fine restaurant, comfortable rooms, gardens, tennis court. Resident proprietors.
Bedrooms: 9 double & 1 twin, 2 family rooms.
Bathrooms: 12 private.
Bed & breakfast: £30.50-£35.50 single, £61-£72 double.
Half board: £42.50-£47 daily, £255-£300 weekly.
Lunch available.
Evening meal 7pm (l.o. 9.30pm).

Parking for 35.
Credit: Access, Visa.

Crossways Hotel M

134 Eastgate, Pickering, YO18 7DW
☎ (0751) 72804
Hotel with a restaurant, bar, comfortable surroundings, car park and private, walled garden.
Bedrooms: 2 single, 3 double & 2 twin, 3 family rooms.
Bathrooms: 7 private, 2 public.
Bed & breakfast: £20-£25 single, £46-£55 double.
Half board: £28-£35 daily.
Lunch available.
Evening meal 7pm (l.o. 9pm).
Parking for 24.
Credit: Access, Visa.

Forest & Vale Hotel M

Malton Rd., Pickering, YO18 7DL
☎ (0751) 72722 Telex 57515
CONSRT G
Consort
Georgian manor house offering every comfort, good food and relaxing ambience. Central for sea, moors and many interesting attractions.
Bedrooms: 2 single, 9 double & 3 twin, 3 family rooms.
Bathrooms: 17 private, 3 public.
Bed & breakfast: £38-£58 single, £58-£82 double.
Lunch available.
Evening meal 7pm (l.o. 9.30pm).
Parking for 75.
Credit: Access, Visa, Diners, Amex.

Lodge Country House Hotel M

Middleton Rd., Pickering, YO18 8NQ
☎ (0751) 72976
Peaceful Victorian lodge set in 3 acres of lawns and terraces. Tastefully furbished throughout. Elegant restaurant and delightful bar.
Bedrooms: 1 single, 4 double & 2 twin, 2 family rooms.
Bathrooms: 9 private.
Bed & breakfast: £23-£30 single, £46-£60 double.
Half board: £33-£40 daily, £225-£275 weekly.

Lunch available.
Evening meal 6.30pm (l.o. 9pm).
Parking for 14.
Credit: Access, Visa, Amex.

Oldmanse Guest House

Middleton Rd., Pickering, YO18 8AL
☎ (0751) 76484
Edwardian house with large en-suite rooms, in an acre of garden. Short walk to the steam railway and town centre. Choice of menu.
Bedrooms: 2 double & 1 twin, 2 family rooms.
Bathrooms: 5 private.
Bed & breakfast: £31-£35 double.
Half board: £23-£24.50 daily, £153.50-£157 weekly.
Evening meal 6.30pm (l.o. 7pm).
Parking for 5.
Open March-October.

PICKHILL

N. Yorkshire
Map ref 5C3

5m SE. Leeming

Nags Head Country Inn M

Pickhill, Thirsk, YO7 4JG
☎ Thirsk (0845) 567570
Retaining the character of an old country inn and restaurant, whilst offering the facilities of a modern hotel. Fresh produce cooked to order with real ale and extensive wine list. Family-run and owned. Only 1.5 miles from the A1.
Bedrooms: 3 single, 8 double & 4 twin.
Bathrooms: 15 private.
Bed & breakfast: from £27 single, from £40 double.
Lunch available.
Evening meal 7pm (l.o. 9.30pm).
Parking for 50.
Credit: Access, Visa.

POCKLINGTON

Humberside
Map ref 4C1

Homely market town at the foot of the Yorkshire Wolds. Burnby Hall on outskirts has gardens with finest collection of water lilies in Europe. Penny Arcadia with fine exhibition of amusement machines located in former Ritz cinema.

Star Inn M
COMMENDED

North Dalton, Driffield, N. Humberside YO25 9UX
☎ Middleton-on-the-Wolds (037 781) 688 & 7791
18th C former coaching inn, beside the pond in a beautiful village nestling in the Yorkshire Wolds.
Bedrooms: 5 double & 2 twin.
Bathrooms: 7 private.
Bed & breakfast: from £37.50 single, from £49 double.
Lunch available.
Evening meal 7pm (l.o. 10pm).
Parking for 30.
Credit: Access, Visa.

Yorkway Hotel M
APPROVED

South Moor, Hull Rd., Pocklington, York, N. Yorkshire YO4 2NX
☎ (0759) 303071
Farmhouse converted into a hotel and restaurant with chalet accommodation and ample parking. Situated halfway between Beverley and York on the A1079.
Bedrooms: 2 single, 3 double & 5 twin.
Bathrooms: 9 private, 2 public.
Bed & breakfast: £34-£40 single, £48-£56 double.
Lunch available.
Evening meal 6.30pm (l.o. 9pm).
Parking for 24.
Credit: Access, Visa.

Classifications and quality commendations were correct at the time of going to press but are subject to change. Please check at the time of booking.

The National Crown Scheme is explained in full on pages 556 – 558.

PONTEFRACT

W. Yorkshire
Map ref 4C1

Close to the A1, this town has a long history, being one of the oldest boroughs in the country. Famous for its castle and locally-processed liquorice, used for sweets and medicines. Also well-known for its racecourse.

Kings Croft Hotel
Wakefield Rd., Pontefract, WF8 4HA
☎ (0977) 703419
Georgian building on the outskirts of the town, in a quiet parkland area. Ample parking facilities.
Bedrooms: 10 single, 2 double & 7 twin.
Bathrooms: 4 private, 2 public.
Bed & breakfast: £30 single, £38-£50 double.
Half board: £36 daily, £240 weekly.
Lunch available.
Evening meal 6.30pm (l.o. 10.30pm).
Parking for 200.
Credit: Access, Visa, Amex.

Parkside Inne M
Park Rd., Pontefract, WF8 4QD
☎ (0977) 709911
Directly opposite Pontefract racecourse, 400 yards from junction 32 of the M62. 15 rooms are on the ground floor.
Bedrooms: 8 single, 2 double & 14 twin, 3 family rooms.
Bathrooms: 27 private.
Bed & breakfast: £29.50-£48.60 single, £37.60-£64.08 double.
Lunch available.
Evening meal 7pm (l.o. 9.45pm).
Parking for 200.
Credit: Access, Visa, Diners, Amex.

Red Lion Hotel
Market Place, Pontefract, WF8 1AX
☎ (0977) 702039
17th C former coaching inn, now a warm and friendly, family-run hotel. Containing public bars, lively fun bar with a disco and a DJ, a pool table, videos and darts. Open until 2 at weekends.

Bedrooms: 3 single, 4 double & 5 twin.
Bathrooms: 3 public.
Bed & breakfast: from £13.50 single, from £25 double.
Half board: from £15.95 daily.
Evening meal 7pm (l.o. 8.30pm).
Parking for 10.

POOL

W. Yorkshire
Map ref 4B1

3m E. Otley

Pool Court Restaurant M
Pool Bank, Pool (Wharfedale), Otley, LS21 1EH
☎ Leeds (0532) 842288 Fax (0532) 843115
A fine Georgian mansion approximately 9 miles from Harrogate, Leeds and Bradford. High standards of food and accommodation.
Bedrooms: 1 single, 3 double & 2 twin.
Bathrooms: 6 private.
Bed & breakfast: £70-£95 single, £85-£120 double.
Evening meal 7pm (l.o. 9.30pm).
Parking for 65.
Credit: Access, Visa, Diners, Amex.

Rawson Garth
Pool Bank Farm, Pool (Wharfedale), Otley, LS21 1EU
☎ Leeds (0532) 843221
6-acre pig/sheep farm. Attractively-converted coach house with modern facilities and open country views in Emmerdale Farm area. 5 minutes from the airport and well placed for Leeds, Otley, Bradford and Harrogate. Non-smokers only please.
Bedrooms: 1 double & 1 twin.
Bathrooms: 1 public.
Bed & breakfast: from £18 single, from £25 double.
Parking for 10.

> **Half board prices shown are per person but in some cases may be based on double/twin occupancy.**

RAVENSCAR

N. Yorkshire
Map ref 5D3

Splendidly-positioned small coastal resort with magnificent views over Robin Hood's Bay. Its Old Peak is the end of the famous Lyke Wake Walk or 'corpse way'.

Crag Hill M
Ravenhall Rd., Ravenscar, Scarborough, YO13 0NA
☎ Scarborough (0723) 870925
Magnificent coastal views. Golf and pony trekking are accessible locally. TV in all rooms. Please send for brochure.
Bedrooms: 3 double & 2 twin.
Bathrooms: 3 private, 1 public.
Bed & breakfast: £26-£30 double.
Half board: £20.50-£22.50 daily, £143.50-£157.50 weekly.
Evening meal 6.30pm.
Parking for 9.
Open April-October.

REDMIRE

N. Yorkshire
Map ref 5B3

Peaceful and little-known dales village at east end of Wensleydale. Pale stone cottages scattered around a large green with ancient oak tree and pinfold where stray animals were penned.

Elm House M
Elm House Estate, Redmire, Leyburn, DL8 4EW
☎ Wensleydale (0969) 22313
Stone-built, 17th C manor house, fully modernised to provide every comfort. In a peaceful garden setting, overlooking beautiful Wensleydale. Personal service by resident owners.
Bedrooms: 1 double & 1 twin, 1 family room.
Bathrooms: 3 private.
Bed & breakfast: £32-£38 double.
Half board: £26-£29 daily, £182-£203 weekly.
Evening meal 7pm.
Parking for 10.

REETH

N. Yorkshire
Map ref 5B3

Once a market town and lead-mining centre, Reeth today serves holiday-makers in Swaledale with its folk museum and 18th C shops and inns lining the green at High Row.

Buck Hotel M
COMMENDED
Reeth, Richmond, DL11 6SW
☎ Richmond (0748) 84210
In the heart of Swaledale and within the Yorkshire Dales National Park. Excellent fishing in the River Swale, good walking area.
Bedrooms: 1 single, 4 double & 4 twin, 1 family room.
Bathrooms: 10 private, 1 public.
Bed & breakfast: max. £30 single, max. £44 double.
Half board: max. £200 weekly.
Lunch available.
Evening meal 6.30pm (l.o. 9.30pm).
Credit: Access, Visa, Diners, Amex.

RICHMOND

N. Yorkshire
Map ref 5C3

Pleasant market town on edge of Swaledale with 11th C castle and Georgian and Victorian buildings surrounding large, cobbled market-place. Green Howards' Museum is in the former Holy Trinity Church. Attractions include the Georgian Theatre, Richmondshire Museum and Easby Abbey.
Tourist Information Centre ☎ (0748) 850252

Black Lion Hotel M
APPROVED
12 Finkle St., Richmond, DL10 4QB
☎ (0748) 3121
Old coaching inn with 3 bars, bar meals, wine cellar and restaurant.
Bedrooms: 4 single, 7 double & 3 twin, 1 family room.
Bathrooms: 5 public.
Bed & breakfast: from £18 single, from £32 double.
Lunch available.

Continued ▶

RICHMOND

Continued

Evening meal 6.30pm (l.o. 9.30pm).
Parking for 12.
⌂ ▥ 🖵 ⌚ ♨ ⋔ ▥ 🗝 TV ▦
🖼 🍴 ⚲ SP ♨

Frenchgate Hotel ⋔
🏅🏅🏅
59-61 Frenchgate, Richmond,
DL10 7AE
☎ (0748) 2087 & 3596
Once a Georgian gentleman's residence, now a quiet family-run hotel providing comfort, emphasis on food and personal attention from the owners.
Bedrooms: 3 single, 4 double & 6 twin.
Bathrooms: 7 private, 3 public.
Bed & breakfast: £24-£32 single, £44-£50.50 double.
Half board: £32-£42 daily.
Evening meal 7pm (l.o. 8.30pm).
Parking for 6.
Open February-December.
Credit: Access, Visa, Diners, Amex.
⌂7 ▥ ☎ ❻ 🖵 ⌚ ♨ ⋔ ▥
▦ 🖼 ▶ 🍴 🐾 SP ♨ 🍴

King's Head Hotel ⋔
Market Place, Richmond,
DL10 4HS
☎ (0748) 850220 Telex 53168
🆑 Consort
Recently refurbished to a high standard, this historic building overlooks the cobbled market-place and Richmond Castle. Ideal for touring Herriot country and the Yorkshire Dales.
Bedrooms: 7 single, 13 double & 9 twin.
Bathrooms: 29 private.
Bed & breakfast: £45-£50 single, £65-£80 double.
Lunch available.
Evening meal 7pm (l.o. 9.30pm).
Parking for 25.
Credit: Access, Visa, Diners, Amex.
⌂ ▥ ☎ ❻ 🖵 ⌚ ♨ ⋔ ▥ ⅍
🖵 🖼 ▦ 🖼 🍴 DAP ⚲ SP ▦
🍴

47 Maison Dieu
Richmond, DL10 7AU
☎ (0748) 5982
Large stone-built family house with pleasant aspect and gardens. Excellent views of the castle and falls and Richmond old town. On main road to Richmond from Brompton-on-Swale.
Bedrooms: 1 single, 1 twin, 1 family room.

Bathrooms: 1 public.
Bed & breakfast: £11-£12 single, £22-£24 double.
Parking for 5.
⌂ ⌚ ♨ ▥ 🖵 ▥ ▦ 🍴

Pottergate Guest House ⋔
🏅🏅 APPROVED
4 Pottergate, Richmond,
DL10 4AB
☎ (0748) 3826
Small, family-run guesthouse 2 minutes' stroll from the town centre. Emphasis on comfort and value for money.
Bedrooms: 2 double & 1 twin, 2 family rooms.
Bathrooms: 2 public.
Bed & breakfast: £15-£16 single, £24-£26 double.
Half board: £160-£175 weekly.
Parking for 5.
⌂ 🖵 ⌚ ♨ ▥ ⅍ ▥ TV ▦
🖼 ⊙ ▦ DAP SP

Ridgeway Guest House ⋔
🏅🏅 APPROVED
47 Darlington Rd.,
Richmond, DL10 7BG
☎ (0748) 3801
Charming detached 1920's house with private parking. Convenient A1 and town. Comfortable rooms, imaginative home cooking and personal services. Pets welcome. Non-smokers only please.
Bedrooms: 4 double & 2 twin.
Bathrooms: 3 private, 2 public.
Bed & breakfast: £25-£33 double.
Half board: £20.50-£24.50 daily, £136-£163 weekly.
Parking for 6.
⌂ ▥ ⌚ ♨ ▥ ▥ ⅍ 🖵 TV
▦ 🖼 ❋ 🍴

West End Guest House ⋔
🏅🏅🏅
45 Reeth Rd., Richmond,
DL10 4EX
☎ (0748) 4783
Peaceful 19th C house within a large garden, close to town and river. Home cooking a speciality. Ample parking. Dogs welcome.
Bedrooms: 1 single, 2 double & 1 twin, 1 family room.
Bathrooms: 3 private, 2 public.
Bed & breakfast: from £15 single, from £28 double.
Half board: from £21 daily.
Evening meal 7pm (l.o. 5pm).
Parking for 9.
⌂ ▣ 🖵 ⌚ ♨ ▥ ⅍ 🖵 ▦
🖼 ❋ 🍴

Windsor House ⋔
9 Castle Hill, Richmond,
DL10 4QP
☎ (0748) 3285
Family-run guesthouse with all home-cooking. 2 minutes' walk from the bus service. Central for the dales and coast.
Bedrooms: 1 single, 2 double & 1 twin, 4 family rooms.
Bathrooms: 2 public.
Bed & breakfast: £12-£13 single, £24-£26 double.
Evening meal 6pm (l.o. 7.30pm).
⌂ 🖵 ⌚ ♨ ▥ ▥ ▦ 🖼 🍴
▦

RIPLEY
N. Yorkshire
Map ref 4B1

Moorfield Guest House
Listed
Moorfield House, Bishop Thornton, Harrogate,
HG3 3LE
☎ Sawley (076 586) 680 & Ripon (0765) 620680
Warm welcome with home comforts and home cooking. Ideally situated for touring the beautiful dales with Harrogate 9 miles away.
Bedrooms: 1 double & 1 twin, 1 family room.
Bathrooms: 1 public.
Half board: max. £17 daily.
Evening meal 6.30pm.
Parking for 4.
Open April-October.
⌂9 ▥ TV ▦ 🍴

RIPON
N. Yorkshire
Map ref 5C3

Small, ancient city with impressive cathedral containing Saxon crypt which houses church treasures from all over Yorkshire. 'Setting the Watch' tradition kept nightly by horn-blower in Market Square. Fountains Abbey nearby.

Crescent Lodge ⋔
🏅🏅
42-42a North St., Ripon,
HG4 1EN
☎ (0765) 2331
Reputedly the former Archbishop of York's town residence. Early Georgian house within easy walking distance of the city centre. Ample street parking. Special rates for children.
Bedrooms: 1 single, 4 double & 1 twin, 4 family rooms.
Bathrooms: 2 private, 3 public.

Bed & breakfast: £14 single, £24-£34 double.
Half board: £168-£224 weekly.
⌂ 🖵 ⌚ ♨ 🍴 TV ▦ 🖼 🍴
▦ SP ▦

Nordale Private Hotel ⋔
🏅🏅 APPROVED
1 & 2 North Parade, North Rd., Ripon, HG4 1ES
☎ (0765) 3557
Long-established business in Victorian residence close to the town centre. Under new ownership, with accent on standards. Excellent centre for touring North Yorkshire.
Bedrooms: 2 single, 3 double & 3 twin, 2 family rooms.
Bathrooms: 5 private, 2 public.
Bed & breakfast: £15 single, £28-£40 double.
Half board: £22-£28 daily.
Parking for 12.
⌂6 ▥ 🖵 ⌚ ▥ ▥ TV ▦ 🖼
🍴 🐾 DAP SP

ROBIN HOOD'S BAY
N. Yorkshire
Map ref 5D3

Picturesque village of red-roofed cottages with main street running from clifftop down ravine to seashore. Scene of much smuggling and shipwrecks in 18th C. Robin Hood reputed to have escaped to continent by boat from here.

Meadowfield ⋔
Mount Pleasant North, Robin Hood's Bay, Whitby, YO22 4RE
☎ Whitby (0947) 880564
Comfortable, family-run Victorian house. Well-presented accommodation offering a choice of traditional English, vegetarian or vegan food.
Bedrooms: 1 single, 1 double & 1 twin, 1 family room.
Bathrooms: 1 public.
Bed & breakfast: £14-£16 single, £23-£27 double.
Half board: £17-£19.50 daily, £119-£136.50 weekly.
Evening meal 5.30pm (l.o. 4pm).
⌂ ▥ ⌚ ♨ ▥ ▥ ⅍ 🖵 TV ▦
🍴 ▦ DAP ⚲

Please mention this guide when making a booking.

ROSEDALE ABBEY

N. Yorkshire
Map ref 5C3

Sturdy hamlet built around Cistercian nunnery in the reign of Henry II, in the middle of Rosedale, largest of the moorland valleys.

Blacksmiths Arms Hotel ▲
ᴗᴗᴗ COMMENDED

Hartoft End, Rosedale Abbey, Pickering, YO18 8EN
☎ Lastingham (075 15) 331
Family-owned and managed country hotel in a beautiful forest and moorland setting. Tastefully decorated restaurant with special emphasis on traditional English food and good wine.
Bedrooms: 10 double & 4 twin.
Bathrooms: 14 private.
Bed & breakfast: £45 single, £70-£76 double.
Half board: £48-£53 daily, £260-£310 weekly.
Lunch available.
Evening meal 7pm (l.o. 9.30pm).
Parking for 150.
Credit: Access, Visa, Diners.
💆 📞 🖥 🛏 🧴 🕯 Ⓥ 🍴 📺 🎱 ↯ 🛏 🍴 Ů 😊 ✗ 🐾 ⚡ SP 🐎

Milburn Arms Hotel ▲
ᴗᴗᴗᴗ COMMENDED

Rosedale Abbey, Pickering, YO18 8RA
☎ Lastingham (075 15) 312
Historic inn in a picturesque conservation area village, central to the national park and 15 miles from the Yorkshire Heritage Coast.
Bedrooms: 9 double & 2 twin.
Bathrooms: 11 private.
Bed & breakfast: £30-£50 single, £50-£70 double.
Half board: £38-£45 daily.
Lunch available.
Evening meal 7pm (l.o. 9.30pm).
Parking for 30.
Credit: Access, Visa.
💆 📞 🖥 📞 🖥 🛏 🧴 🕯 Ⓥ 🍴 📺 🎱 ↯ 🛏 🍴 Ů 😊 🐾 📖 DAP ⚡ SP 🐎

White Horse Farm Hotel ▲
ᴗᴗᴗ

Rosedale Abbey, Pickering, YO18 8SE
☎ Lastingham (075 15) 239
ⒼⓇ Minotels

Charming Georgian country inn. Magnificent views over Rosedale. Ideal base for a walking or touring holiday.
Bedrooms: 11 double & 3 twin, 1 family room.
Bathrooms: 15 private, 1 public.
Bed & breakfast: £32-£40 single, £54-£60 double.
Half board: £39.25-£44.25 daily, £38.25-£41 weekly.
Lunch available.
Evening meal 7pm (l.o. 8.45pm).
Parking for 50.
Credit: Access, Visa, Diners, Amex.
💆 🖥 📞 😊 🕯 🛏 Ⓥ 🍴 📺 ↯ Ů 🍴 😊 🐾 🐎 🐕 SP 📺

ROTHERHAM

S. Yorkshire
Map ref 4B2

In the Don Valley, Rotherham became an important industrial town in 19th C with discovery of coal and development of iron and steel industry by Joshua Walker who built Clifton House, now the town's museum. Magnificent 15th C All Saints Church is town's showpiece.
Tourist Information Centre ☎ (0709) 823611

Consort Hotel, Banqueting & Conference Suite ▲
ᴗᴗᴗ COMMENDED

Brampton Rd., Thurcroft, Rotherham, S66 9JA
☎ Rotherham (0709) 530022
Fax (0709) 531529
On the junction of the M1 and M18, access exits 1 on the M18 and 31 and 33 on the M1.
Bedrooms: 10 double & 8 twin.
Bathrooms: 18 private.
Bed & breakfast: £30-£65 single, £46-£75 double.
Half board: £43-£77 daily, £470 weekly.
Lunch available.
Evening meal 6.30pm (l.o. 9pm).
Parking for 96.
Credit: Access, Visa, Amex.
💆 📞 🖥 📞 🖥 🛏 🧴 🕯 Ⓥ ✂ 🍴 😊 🛏 🍴 ✗ 📺

Elton Hotel ▲
ᴗᴗᴗ COMMENDED

Main St., Bramley, Rotherham, S66 0SF
☎ (0709) 545681

200-year-old, stone-built, extended farmhouse with emphasis on cooking. Half a mile from junction 1 of M18, 2 miles from M1.
Bedrooms: 7 single, 5 double & 3 twin.
Bathrooms: 5 private, 3 public; 2 private showers.
Bed & breakfast: £20-£46 single, £40-£58 double.
Half board: £33.95-£59.95 daily, £367.65 weekly.
Lunch available.
Evening meal 7pm (l.o. 9.30pm).
Parking for 26.
Credit: Access, Visa, Amex.
💆 📞 📞 🖥 🧴 🕯 Ⓥ 🍴 ● 🛏 🍴 😊 DAP SP 🐎 📺

Regis Hotel
ᴗᴗ

1 Hall Rd., Moorgate, Rotherham, S60 2BP
☎ (0709) 376666 & 382564
Large stone-built hotel in its own grounds with a private car park. 2 minutes to Rotherham centre and 4 minutes to the M1 exit 33.
Bedrooms: 2 single, 2 double & 7 twin.
Bathrooms: 4 private, 2 public.
Bed & breakfast: £21-£30 single, £32-£40 double.
Parking for 10.
Credit: Access, Visa, Diners, Amex.
💆 📞 🖥 😊 🕯 Ⓥ 📺 🎱 🍴 SP

Rotherham Moat House
ᴗᴗᴗᴗ

Moorgate Rd., Rotherham, S60 2BG
☎ (0709) 364902 Fax (0709) 368960 Telex 547810
ⒼⒹ Queens Moat Houses
Modern hotel with conference facilities, a restaurant and theme bar. In a residential area, close to the M1 motorway.
Bedrooms: 40 single, 14 double & 27 twin.
Bathrooms: 81 private.
Bed & breakfast: £26-£62 single, £34-£72 double.
Lunch available.
Evening meal 7.30pm (l.o. 9.45pm).
Parking for 122.
Credit: Access, Visa, Diners, Amex.
💆 📞 🖥 📞 📞 🖥 🛏 🧴 🕯 Ⓥ ✂ 🍴 📺 ● 🎱 🍴 🛏 🍴 😊 SP 📺

RUFFORTH

N. Yorkshire
Map ref 4C1

Village west of York. There is a small airfield, and it is also the home of the York Gliding Centre.

Rosedale Guest House ▲
Listed COMMENDED

Wetherby Rd., Rufforth, York, YO2 3QB
☎ (090 483) 297
Small, family-run guesthouse with a homely atmosphere and all facilities, in a delightful, unspoilt village 4 miles from York.
Bedrooms: 1 single, 2 double & 1 twin, 1 family room.
Bathrooms: 2 public; 1 private shower.
Bed & breakfast: £12.50-£13 single, £22-£26 double.
Parking for 5.
💆 🐾 🖥 Ⓥ ⛛ UL 🕯 Ⓥ 🍴 📺 🎱 🛏 🍴 😊 DAP ⚡ SP

RUNSWICK BAY

N. Yorkshire
Map ref 5D3

Cliffemount Hotel ▲
ᴗᴗᴗ APPROVED

Runswick Bay, Saltburn-by-the-Sea, Cleveland TS13 5HU
☎ Whitby (0947) 840103
Relaxing hotel on the clifftop with panoramic views of Runswick Bay. 9 miles north of Whitby.
Bedrooms: 4 double & 1 twin, 1 family room.
Bathrooms: 4 private, 2 public.
Bed & breakfast: £15-£30 single, £34-£44 double.
Half board: £25-£45 daily.
Lunch available.
Evening meal 7pm (l.o. 9.30pm).
Parking for 30.
💆 📞 😊 🕯 Ⓥ 🍴 🛏 😊 ✗ 🐎 SP

The enquiry coupons at the back will help you when contacting proprietors.

Half board prices shown are per person but in some cases may be based on double/twin occupancy.

SCARBOROUGH

N. Yorkshire
Map ref 5D3

Large, popular east coast seaside resort, formerly a spa town. Beautiful gardens and splendid sandy beaches in North and South Bays. Castle ruins date from 1100, fine Georgian and Victorian houses in old town. September angling, theatres, cricket festivals and seasonal entertainment.
Tourist Information Centre ☎ (0723) 373333

Ainsley Hotel ⋀
👑👑👑

4 Rutland Terrace, Queens Parade, Scarborough, YO11 1HX
☎ (0723) 364832
Superb views overlooking the North Bay. Colour TV, radio clock/alarms and central heating. Home cooking. Licensed.
Bedrooms: 2 single, 7 double & 1 twin, 2 family rooms.
Bathrooms: 4 private, 3 public.
Bed & breakfast: £13.50-£14.50 single, £27-£29 double.
Half board: £18.50-£19 daily, £129-£133 weekly.
Evening meal 5pm (l.o. 2pm).
Parking for 2.
📺 Ⓔ 🅟 🍴 📺 🛏 📖 ⚓ 🍷 🐾 🆓 ⊞

Alver Hotel ⋀

8 Blenheim Terrace, Scarborough, YO12 7HF
☎ (0723) 373256
In an unrivalled position overlooking the North Bay and within easy walking distance of most amenities.
Bedrooms: 5 double & 3 twin, 5 family rooms.
Bathrooms: 3 public.
Bed & breakfast: £14.50-£16 single, £29-£32 double.
Half board: £18.50-£20 daily, £119-£433 weekly.
Evening meal 5pm.
Open April-October.
📺 🅟 🛏 📺 🛏 📖 ⚓ 🍴 🐾 🆓

Ambassador Hotel ⋀
👑👑👑👑

Esplanade, Scarborough, YO11 2AY
☎ (0723) 362841

Please mention this guide when making a booking.

Warm, hospitable, privately-owned hotel on the esplanade overlooking the harbour, South Bay and spa and opposite the Italian Gardens. Bar snacks available Monday to Saturday and lunch on Sunday.
Bedrooms: 10 single, 18 double & 12 twin, 5 family rooms.
Bathrooms: 33 private, 1 public; 12 private showers.
Bed & breakfast: £26.50-£31 single, £52-£62 double.
Half board: £29-£34.50 daily, £200-£240 weekly.
Evening meal 6.30pm (l.o. 7.30pm).
Open March-November.
📺 🅟 📞 📖 🅟 🛏 📺 ● 🅟 ⊞
🎿 🍴 🍽 🛏 🐾 🆓 🆃

Amber Lodge Guest House ⋀
👑👑

17 Trinity Rd., South Cliff, Scarborough, YO11 2TD
☎ (0723) 369088
Elegant Victorian guesthouse with private car park. En-suite rooms. Vegetarian food available. Close to South Bay and Spa.
Bedrooms: 2 single, 2 double & 1 twin, 2 family rooms.
Bathrooms: 4 private, 2 public.
Bed & breakfast: £12-£13 single, £24-£30 double.
Half board: £16.50-£19.50 daily, £115-£136 weekly.
Parking for 6.
Open April-October.
📺 🅟 🛏 🆄🅻 🛏 📖 🛏 📺 🛏 ⚓
🍽 🛏 🐾 🆓

Argo Hotel

134 North Marine Rd., Scarborough, YO12 7HZ
☎ (0723) 375745
Small, family hotel close to all amenities. Licensed. Colour TV and tea/coffee facilities in all rooms. Open all year. Central heating.
Bedrooms: 2 single, 3 double & 1 twin, 3 family rooms.
Bathrooms: 2 public.
Bed & breakfast: £11-£13 single, £22-£26 double.
Half board: £14-£16 daily.
Evening meal 5.30pm (l.o. 5.30pm).
📺 🛏 🅟 📖 🛏 📺 📺 ⚓
🅟 🐾 🆓

Arran Licensed Hotel
👑👑

114 North Marine Rd., Scarborough, YO12 7JA
☎ (0723) 364692

Small, family-run, private licensed hotel with views of the sea and cricket ground. Central for all amenities with car parking nearby by arrangement.
Bedrooms: 2 single, 1 double, 5 family rooms.
Bathrooms: 2 public.
Bed & breakfast: max. £24 double.
Half board: max. £15 daily, £87-£97 weekly.
Evening meal 5.30pm (l.o. 5.30pm).
Open March-December.
📺 🅟 🛏 🆅 🛏 📺 ● 📖 ⚓
🍴 🍽 🅟 🐾 🆓

Avoncroft Hotel ⋀

5, 6 & 7 Crown Terrace, South Cliff, Scarborough, YO11 2BL
☎ (0723) 372737
Listed Georgian terrace overlooking Crown Gardens. Close to spa and sports facilities. Convenient for town centre and all entertainments.
Bedrooms: 7 single, 10 double & 5 twin, 12 family rooms.
Bathrooms: 20 private, 5 public.
Bed & breakfast: £16-£18 single, £32-£36 double.
Half board: £20.50-£22.50 daily, £133.25-£146.25 weekly.
Lunch available.
Evening meal 5.30pm (l.o. 6.15pm).
📺 🅟 🛏 🅟 🛏 🆅 🛏 📺 📖
⚓ 🍴 🍷 🅟 🐾 🆓 🅟 🆃

Boundary Hotel ⋀
Listed

124-126 North Marine Rd., Scarborough, YO12 7HZ
☎ (0723) 376737
Comfortable family-run hotel on the north side of Scarborough. Overlooking cricket ground, close to town centre and all amenities.
Bedrooms: 2 single, 2 double, 7 family rooms.
Bathrooms: 11 private, 1 public.
Bed & breakfast: £15-£16.50 single, £30-£33 double.
Half board: £19-£21 daily, £133-£147 weekly.
Evening meal 6pm (l.o. 6pm).
📺 1 🛏 📞 📺 🛏 🅟 🆅 ✂
🛏 📺 📖 🍴 🅟 🐾 🆓

Central Guest House

6 & 7 Bell Vue Parade, Scarborough, YO11 1SU
☎ (0723) 372810
Close to the rail and bus stations, small family guesthouse offering home cooking. Tea making facilities, TV lounge and games room.

Bedrooms: 1 single, 4 double & 1 twin, 5 family rooms.
Bathrooms: 2 public.
Bed & breakfast: £9-£10 single, £18-£20 double.
Half board: £12.50-£13 daily.
Evening meal 5pm (l.o. 3pm).
📺 Ⓔ 🅟 🆄 🆅 🛏 📺 ⚓ 🍷
🅟 🅟

Central Hotel & Restaurant ⋀
👑👑👑 **APPROVED**

1-3 The Crescent, Scarborough, YO11 2PW
☎ (0723) 365766
Property of historic interest in a beautiful Georgian crescent. Central for all amenities, shops, sea and spa. Car park. Restaurant and wine bar with bar menu. Family owned and managed.
Bedrooms: 9 single, 13 double & 14 twin, 3 family rooms.
Bathrooms: 21 private, 5 public.
Bed & breakfast: £26.75-£31 single, £47-£55.50 double.
Half board: £34.75-£39 daily, £208-£235 weekly.
Lunch available.
Evening meal 6pm (l.o. 9.30pm).
Parking for 15.
Credit: Access, Visa, Diners, Amex.
📺 📞 Ⓔ 🅟 🛏 🅟 🆅 🛏 🅟
📖 ⚓ 🍴 🅟 🐾 🆓 🅟 🆃

Crawford Private Hotel ⋀
👑👑👑

8-9 Crown Terrace, Scarborough, YO11 2BL
☎ (0723) 361494
Under personal supervision of the proprietors. Convenient for all town and South Cliff facilities.
Bedrooms: 4 single, 5 double & 8 twin, 4 family rooms.
Bathrooms: 19 private, 2 public.
Bed & breakfast: £18.50-£20 single, £18.50-£20 double.
Half board: £21.50-£26.50 daily, £143.50-£175 weekly.
Evening meal 6pm (l.o. 6.30pm).
Open March-October.
📺 1 🏠 🅟 🛏 🆅 🛏 🅟 🛏
⚓ 🍴 🅟 🆓 🅟

Cumberland Carlton Hotel ⋀

Belmont Rd., South Cliff, Scarborough, YO11 2AB
☎ (0723) 361826
On the beautiful South Cliff. All rooms have private bathrooms. Dancing and entertainment each night from May to October.

Bedrooms: 25 single, 35 double & 55 twin, 10 family rooms.
Bathrooms: 125 private.
Bed & breakfast: £15-£21 single, £30-£40 double.
Half board: £19-£25 daily, £105-£147 weekly.
Evening meal 6.30pm (l.o. 7pm).
Parking for 8.
Open March-December.
Credit: Access, Visa.

Durley Dene

5 Victoria Park Avenue, Scarborough, YO12 7TR
☎ (0723) 364573
Small family-run private hotel, close to Peasholm Park and all North Bay amenities.
Bedrooms: 3 single, 2 double, 4 family rooms.
Bathrooms: 1 public.
Bed & breakfast: £12-£13 single, £22-£24 double.
Half board: £14-£15 daily, £98-£105 weekly.
Evening meal 5.30pm (l.o. 5.30pm).
Open April-October.

East Ayton Lodge Country Hotel & Restaurant M

Moor Lane, East Ayton, Scarborough, YO13 9EW
☎ (0723) 864227
Fax (0723) 862680
Country hotel and restaurant in a beautiful 3-acre setting by the River Derwent, in the National Park only 3 miles from Scarborough.
Bedrooms: 8 double & 5 twin, 4 family rooms.
Bathrooms: 17 private.
Bed & breakfast: £30-£45 single, £40-£70 double.
Half board: £35-£50 daily, £200-£300 weekly.
Lunch available.
Evening meal 6pm (l.o. 10pm).
Parking for 60.
Credit: Access, Visa, Diners, Amex.

El-Wedy Private Hotel M

Listed
128 Columbus Ravine, Scarborough, YO12 7QZ
☎ (0723) 362800
A modern and comfortable private hotel. Ideal for beach, swimming pools, parks, Kinderland Cricket ground, bowling, golf course and other amenities.

Bedrooms: 2 single, 6 double & 2 twin, 7 family rooms.
Bathrooms: 2 private, 3 public.
Bed & breakfast: £12.50-£13.50 single, £25-£27 double.
Half board: £16.50-£17.50 daily, £115.50-£122.50 weekly.
Evening meal 5.30pm (l.o. 5.30pm).
Parking for 7.
Open January-November.

Hotel Ellenby

Listed
95-97 Queens Parade, Scarborough, YO12 7HY
☎ (0723) 372916
Family-run hotel overlooking Scarborough North Bay and close to the cricket ground, town centre and main children's entertainments. Home cooked food.
Bedrooms: 5 single, 7 double & 2 twin, 3 family rooms.
Bathrooms: 5 private, 2 public.
Bed & breakfast: £14 single, £28 double.
Half board: £17.50 daily, £120 weekly.
Evening meal 5pm (l.o. 4pm).
Parking for 8.

Esplanade Hotel M

Belmont Rd., Scarborough, YO11 2AA
☎ (0723) 360382
Welcoming period-style hotel in well appointed position on Scarborough's South Cliff. Close to beach, spa and town centre. Landau restaurant, parlour bar and roof terrace.
Bedrooms: 18 single, 17 double & 28 twin, 10 family rooms.
Bathrooms: 73 private, 7 public.
Bed & breakfast: £33-£40 single, £61-£67.50 double.
Half board: £239-£246.50 weekly.
Lunch available.
Evening meal 6.30pm (l.o. 8.30pm).
Parking for 24.
Credit: Access, Visa, Diners, Amex.

Excelsior Private Hotel M

1 Marlborough St., Scarborough, YO12 7HG
☎ (0723) 360716

Centrally situated on corner of North Bay seafront, personal service. Fresh produce, home-made bread, soups and sweets. No smoking in lounge and dining room.
Bedrooms: 3 single, 2 double & 1 twin, 3 family rooms.
Bathrooms: 2 public.
Bed & breakfast: £11-£13 single, £22-£26 double.
Half board: £13-£16 daily, £75-£95 weekly.
Evening meal 5.30pm.
Open April-October.

Flower in Hand Hotel M

Burr Bank, Scarborough, YO11 1PN
☎ (0723) 371471
Delightful old house with wide sea views overlooking South Bay and beach. Warm welcome, vegetarians and vegans specially catered for.
Bedrooms: 1 single, 3 double, 4 family rooms.
Bathrooms: 3 private, 2 public.
Bed & breakfast: £18-£21 single, £30-£36 double.
Half board: £23.50-£26.50 daily, £160-£180 weekly.
Evening meal 5.30pm (l.o. midday).
Credit: Access, Visa.

Gordon Hotel

24 Ryndleside, Scarborough, YO12 6AD
☎ (0723) 362177
By the side of Peasholm Park, the North Bay, Waterslash World and the new children's Kinderland. Offering English fare and efficient, courteous service. Tea and coffee facilities in all rooms. Some family and double en-suite rooms.
Bedrooms: 4 single, 5 double & 1 twin, 3 family rooms.
Bathrooms: 6 private, 3 public; 1 private shower.
Bed & breakfast: £12-£14 single, £24-£28 double.
Half board: £16.50-£20 daily, £115.50-£140 weekly.
Evening meal 5.30pm (l.o. 4pm).
Parking for 10.
Open April-October.

Green Gables Private Hotel M

Listed
West Bank, Scarborough, YO12 4DX
☎ (0723) 361005
Originally a late Victorian hydropathic establishment, now a family-owned hotel particularly suited to family holidays. Children very welcome.
Bedrooms: 5 twin, 20 family rooms.
Bathrooms: 12 private, 6 public.
Bed & breakfast: £11.80-£14.30 single, £23.60-£28.60 double.
Half board: £16.75-£19.25 daily, £117.25-£134.75 weekly.
Evening meal 6pm (l.o. 6pm).
Parking for 26.
Open April-October.

Greno Seafront Hotel M

Listed
25 Blenheim Terrace, Scarborough, YO12 7HD
☎ (0723) 375705
Overlooking the North Bay and close to all amenities. Licensed with live entertainment. TV, tea/coffee facilities in all rooms. Reductions for children.
Bedrooms: 1 single, 6 double & 2 twin, 8 family rooms.
Bathrooms: 4 private, 3 public.
Bed & breakfast: £14.50-£19 single, £29-£38 double.
Half board: £18.50-£23 daily, £129.50-£161 weekly.
Evening meal 5.30pm (l.o. 5.30pm).
Parking for 6.
Open March-October, December.

Harcourt Hotel M

45 Esplanade, Scarborough, YO11 2AY
☎ (0723) 373930
Comfortable hotel overlooking the South Bay, opposite the Rose Gardens and close to the Spa complex and cliff lift.
Bedrooms: 3 single, 6 double & 6 twin, 2 family rooms.
Bathrooms: 17 private, 1 public.
Bed & breakfast: £18-£20 single, £34-£38 double.
Continued ▶

We advise you to confirm your booking in writing.

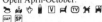

SCARBOROUGH

Continued

Half board: £19.50-£21.50 daily, £136.50-£150.50 weekly.
Evening meal 6pm (l.o. 6pm).
Open April-October.

Holmelea Guest House M

Listed

8 Belle Vue Parade, Scarborough, YO11 1SU
☎ (0723) 360139
Family-run guesthouse. Rooms centrally heated with divans, duvets, tea/coffee making, colour TV with satellite/video link, radio alarms and razor points.
Bedrooms: 2 single, 3 double, 1 family room.
Bathrooms: 1 public.
Bed & breakfast: £10 single, £20 double.
Half board: £13 daily, £87 weekly.
Evening meal 5.30pm.

Invergarry M

4 St. Martin's Square, South Cliff, Scarborough, YO11 2DQ
☎ (0723) 372013
Quiet, family-run guesthouse in a pleasant square, within 2 minutes' walk of the seafront and South Cliff Gardens.
Bedrooms: 3 single, 6 double & 1 twin.
Bathrooms: 2 public.
Bed & breakfast: £10-£10.50 single, £20-£21 double.
Half board: £13-£13.50 daily, £91-£94.50 weekly.
Evening meal 5.30pm.
Open January-October.

Ivyholme Hotel M

30 West St., Scarborough, YO11 2QP
☎ (0723) 360649
2 storey, detached building with adequate parking, close to the esplanade and main bus route. Personal attention from the owners. Some bedrooms have TV.
Bedrooms: 1 single, 5 double & 2 twin.
Bathrooms: 3 private, 1 public; 1 private shower.
Bed & breakfast: £13-£16 single, £25-£29 double.
Half board: £18-£21 daily, £108-£147 weekly.
Evening meal 6pm (l.o. 8pm).

Manor Heath Hotel M

67 Northstead Manor Drive, Scarborough, YO12 6AF
☎ (0723) 365720
Detached hotel with pleasant gardens and a private car park, overlooking Peasholm Park and the sea. Close to all North Bay attractions.
Bedrooms: 3 single, 8 double & 1 twin, 4 family rooms.
Bathrooms: 11 private, 2 public.
Bed & breakfast: £14-£18 single, £28-£36 double.
Half board: £18-£22 daily, £120-£154 weekly.
Evening meal 6pm.
Parking for 12.

Melbourne M

APPROVED

57 Moorland Rd., Scarborough, YO12 7RD
☎ (0723) 371172
Small, comfortable, family-run guesthouse close to all North Bay amenities and the town centre.
Bedrooms: 2 single, 1 twin, 2 family rooms.
Bathrooms: 1 public.
Bed & breakfast: £10.50-£11.50 single, £24-£31 double.
Half board: £14-£15 daily, £91-£108 weekly.
Evening meal 6pm (l.o. 1pm).

Moseley Lodge Private Hotel

26 Avenue Victoria, South Cliff, Scarborough, YO11 2QT
☎ (0723) 360564
Elegant Victorian villa close to town, esplanande, spa, Italian Gardens and amenities. Residential licence. All diets catered for.
Bedrooms: 1 single, 5 double & 3 twin.
Bathrooms: 2 private, 2 public.
Bed & breakfast: from £16 single, £32-£50 double.
Half board: £19.50-£25 daily.
Lunch available.
Evening meal 6pm (l.o. 6pm).

Mount House Hotel M

33 Trinity Rd., South Cliff, Scarborough, YO11 2TD
☎ (0723) 362967

Traditional, family hotel with home cooking, central heating and a free car park. Tea/coffee making in all rooms, hair-dryer and laundry facilities available. Bar open to guests and friends.
Bedrooms: 4 single, 3 double & 1 twin, 2 family rooms.
Bathrooms: 4 private, 2 public.
Half board: £130-£150 weekly.
Evening meal 6pm.
Parking for 6.
Open April-October.

Mountview Private Hotel M

Listed

32 West St., South Cliff, Scarborough, YO11 2QP
☎ (0723) 372501
Well-appointed private hotel on the beautiful South Cliff. Personal attention and a friendly atmosphere. Easy parking. Open all year.
Bedrooms: 2 single, 4 double & 3 twin, 1 family room.
Bathrooms: 7 private, 1 public.
Bed & breakfast: £11.50-£12.50 single, £24-£31 double.
Evening meal 6pm (l.o. 6pm).

Northcote M

114 Columbus Ravine, Scarborough, YO12 7QZ
☎ (0723) 367758
Modern, semi-detached private hotel with bedrooms on 2 floors only. Special offers available for senior citizens. Most rooms en-suite and all with colour TV. Non-smokers only please.
Bedrooms: 1 single, 3 double & 2 twin, 2 family rooms.
Bathrooms: 7 private, 1 public.
Bed & breakfast: £12.50-£15 single, £25-£30 double.
Half board: £17.50-£20 daily, £100-£125 weekly.
Evening meal 5.30pm.
Parking for 5.
Open April-October.

Number One

1 Trafalgar Sq., Scarborough, YO12 7PZ
☎ (0723) 367831
Comfortable guesthouse where cleanliness and varied food are assured. Overlooking the cricket ground and convenient for all amenities. Satellite TV. Tea/coffee facilities in all rooms.

Bedrooms: 5 double, 4 family rooms.
Bathrooms: 1 public.
Bed & breakfast: from £11 single.
Half board: from £14 daily, from £90 weekly.
Evening meal 5.30pm (l.o. 5.30pm).
Credit: Access, Visa.

Palm Court Hotel M

COMMENDED

St. Nicholas Cliff, Scarborough, YO11 2ES
☎ (0723) 368161
Fax (0723) 371547
Telex 527579
Centrally situated yet only minutes from the beach. Ideal for conferences, seminars and private functions. Private car park available.
Bedrooms: 14 single, 15 double & 10 twin, 11 family rooms.
Bathrooms: 50 private, 3 public.
Bed & breakfast: £38-£43 single, £60-£65 double.
Half board: £41-£54 daily, £263-£298 weekly.
Lunch available.
Evening meal 7pm (l.o. 9pm).
Parking for 6.
Credit: Access, Visa, Diners, Amex.

Parade Hotel M

Listed

29 Esplanade, South Cliff, Scarborough, YO11 2AQ
☎ (0723) 361285
Victorian terraced hotel maintaining traditional elegance with modern facilities. Overlooking the sea and 50 yards from the spa lift. Emphasis on preparation of fresh food.
Bedrooms: 5 single, 8 double & 1 twin, 3 family rooms.
Bathrooms: 16 private, 1 public.
Bed & breakfast: £20.50-£22 single, £41-£44 double.
Half board: £28-£29.50 daily, £168-£178.50 weekly.
Evening meal 6pm (l.o. 6.30pm).

Parmelia Hotel M

COMMENDED

17 West St., Southcliff, Scarborough, YO11 2QN
☎ (0723) 361914

Spacious, licensed hotel with emphasis on comfort, quality and home cooking. On the South Cliff near the Esplanade Gardens, the cliff lift to the spa and the beach.
Bedrooms: 2 single, 4 double & 6 twin, 3 family rooms.
Bathrooms: 10 private, 2 public; 1 private shower.
Bed & breakfast: £15-£17.50 single, £30-£35 double.
Half board £18-£20.50 daily.
Evening meal 6pm (l.o. 5pm).
Open April-October.

Premier Hotel M
66 Esplanade, Scarborough, YO11 2UZ
☎ (0723) 361484 & 373926
On the South Cliff offering unsurpassed sea views, among beautiful gardens and pleasant walks.
Bedrooms: 6 single, 5 double & 5 twin, 3 family rooms.
Bathrooms: 19 private.
Bed & breakfast: from £30 single, from £50 double.
Half board: from £32 daily, from £210 weekly.
Evening meal 6pm (l.o. 6pm).
Parking for 7.
Open March-November.

Raincliffe Hotel
21 Valley Rd., Scarborough, YO11 2LY
☎ (0723) 373541
Newly refurbished, period style hotel set in mature gardens. Close to town centre, beach, spa and entertainments. Free street parking.
Bedrooms: 2 single, 7 double & 3 twin, 1 family room.
Bathrooms: 9 private, 2 public.
Bed & breakfast: £13.50-£15.50 single, £27-£31 double.
Half board: £18-£20 daily, £119-£133 weekly.
Evening meal 5.30pm (l.o. 6pm).
Open April-October.
Credit: Access, Visa.

Red Lea Hotel M
COMMENDED
Prince of Wales Terrace, Scarborough, YO11 2AJ
☎ (0723) 362431
Traditional hotel with sea views, close to the Spa centre. Restaurant, bar, lounges, lift and colour TVs. Solarium and indoor heated swimming pool.

Bedrooms: 19 single, 12 double & 37 twin.
Bathrooms: 68 private.
Bed & breakfast: £26-£27 single, £52-£54 double.
Half board: £36-£51 daily, £240-£255 weekly.
Lunch available.
Evening meal 6.30pm (l.o. 8pm).
Credit: Access, Visa.

Riga Hotel M
APPROVED
10 Crown Crescent, Scarborough, YO11 2BJ
☎ (0723) 363994
Family-run, licensed hotel on the South Cliff, overlooking the Crown Gardens. Choice of menu. Children under 3 free.
Bedrooms: 2 single, 4 double & 2 twin, 4 family rooms.
Bathrooms: 1 private, 3 public.
Bed & breakfast: £10.50-£12.50 single, £21-£25 double.
Half board: £15.50-£17.50 daily, £108.50-£122.50 weekly.
Evening meal 6pm (l.o. 3.30pm).
Credit: Access, Visa.

Rivelyn Hotel M
1-4 Crown Crescent, South Cliff, Scarborough, YO11 2BJ
☎ (0723) 361248
Family-run hotel in a quiet and attractive area close to the Spa, gardens, golf and town.
Bedrooms: 10 single, 16 double & 21 twin, 8 family rooms.
Bathrooms: 55 private, 1 public.
Bed & breakfast: £17-£20 single, £32-£38 double.
Half board: £19-£23 daily, £125-£153 weekly.
Evening meal 6pm.
Parking for 22.
Open April-October, December.

Riviera Hotel M
St. Nicholas Cliff, Scarborough, YO11 2ES
☎ (0723) 372277
Ideal central location within yards of beach, spa, town centre and theatres. All bedrooms with full facilities for maximum comfort.

Bedrooms: 5 single, 6 double & 2 twin, 7 family rooms.
Bathrooms: 20 private.
Bed & breakfast: £23-£30 single, £46-£60 double.
Half board: £33-£40 daily, £220-£255 weekly.
Evening meal 6pm (l.o. 7pm).
Credit: Access, Visa.

Rockingham Hotel M
APPROVED
Blands Cliff, Scarborough, YO11 1NR
☎ (0723) 351423
Hotel within easy reach of the Futurist Theatre, the spa, the beach and harbour, shopping facilities and all other amenities.
Bedrooms: 4 single, 7 double & 3 twin, 2 family rooms.
Bathrooms: 4 private, 2 public.
Bed & breakfast: £15-£18 single, £30-£36 double.
Half board: £20-£23 daily, £129.50-£150.50 weekly.
Lunch available.
Evening meal 6pm (l.o. 9pm).
Credit: Access, Visa.

Ryndle Court Private Hotel
47 Northstead Manor Drive, Scarborough, YO12 6AF
☎ (0723) 375188
Imposing detached hotel with bedrooms on 2 floors, in quiet surroundings overlooking Peasholm Park. Close to all amenities. Lunch available on request. TV and hair-dryer in all bedrooms.
Bedrooms: 2 single, 4 double & 4 twin, 5 family rooms.
Bathrooms: 8 private, 2 public.
Bed & breakfast: £16-£20 single, £30-£40 double.
Half board: £18-£23 daily, £125-£161 weekly.
Evening meal 5.30pm (l.o. 5pm).
Parking for 10.

Stewart Hotel M
St. Nicholas Cliff, Scarborough, YO11 2ES
☎ (0723) 361095
In an ideal position with sea views overlooking the South Bay and close to the beach and shopping centre.
Bedrooms: 2 single, 4 double & 2 twin, 9 family rooms.
Bathrooms: 6 private, 2 public.

Bed & breakfast: £15-£20 single, £30-£40 double.
Half board: £23-£28 daily, £90-£125 weekly.
Evening meal 5.30pm (l.o. 6.30pm).
Credit: Access, Visa.

Suncrest Hotel M
31 Trinity Rd., Scarborough, YO11 2TD
☎ (0723) 362512
Private hotel in a quiet location within easy reach of the spa, South Cliff and all amenities.
Bedrooms: 4 single, 3 double, 4 family rooms.
Bathrooms: 4 private, 3 public.
Bed & breakfast: £12.50-£15 single, £25-£30 double.
Half board: £17.50-£20 daily, £120-£140 weekly.
Evening meal 6pm (l.o. 6.30pm).
Parking for 6.
Credit: Access, Visa.

Weston Hotel M
APPROVED
33-34 Esplanade, Scarborough, YO11 2AR
☎ (0723) 373423
36-bedroomed hotel commanding a superb position on the Esplanade with magnificent views. Only yards away from the Spa Conference Centre, beaches and shops.
Bedrooms: 9 single, 8 double & 13 twin, 6 family rooms.
Bathrooms: 24 private, 4 public.
Bed & breakfast: £17-£30 single, £34-£58 double.
Half board: £20-£33 daily, £144-£220 weekly.
Evening meal 6pm.
Credit: Access, Visa.

Wharncliffe Hotel M
Listed
26 Blenheim Terrace, Scarborough, YO12 7HD
☎ (0723) 374635
Overlooking beautiful North Bay, large family hotel with a homely atmosphere, friendly service, emphasis on food and entertainment. Close to all amenities.
Bedrooms: 1 single, 10 double, 3 family rooms.
Bathrooms: 4 private, 2 public.
Bed & breakfast: £14-£19 single, £28-£38 double.

Continued ▶

SCARBOROUGH
Continued

Half board: £18-£23 daily,
£126-£161 weekly.
Evening meal 5.30pm (l.o.
5.30pm).

Wrea Head Country Hotel M
COMMENDED
Barmoor La., Wrea Head,
Scalby, Scarborough,
YO13 0PB
☎ Scarborough
(0723) 378211
*Victorian country house hotel
in 14 acres of woodland and
parkland on the edge of the
North Yorkshire Moors
National Park. Lunch provided
if required.*
Bedrooms: 4 single, 4 double
& 10 twin, 3 family rooms.
Bathrooms: 21 private.
Bed & breakfast: £45-£65
single, £90-£130 double.
Half board: £52.50-£72.50
daily, £315-£435 weekly.
Lunch available.
Evening meal 7pm (l.o.
9.15pm).
Parking for 101.
Credit: Access, Visa, Amex.

SCOTCH CORNER
N. Yorkshire
Map ref 5C3

Famous milestone at the
junction of the A1 and
A66 near Richmond.

Hunters End M
Morris Grange, Scotch
Corner, Richmond,
DL10 6PA
☎ Richmond (0748) 2895
*Detached country house in a
quiet location. Ideal touring
base for the dales, lakes and
historic North. Half a mile
south of Scotch Corner off A1.*
Bedrooms: 1 double & 1 twin,
1 family room.
Bathrooms: 2 public.
Bed & breakfast: £16-£18
single, £24-£28 double.
Half board: £22-£30 daily,
£138-£192 weekly.
Evening meal 6pm (l.o.
7.30pm).
Parking for 7.

Rank Motor Lodge M
Middleton Tyas La., Scotch
Corner (A1/A66), Richmond,
DL10 6PQ
☎ Darlington (0325) 377177
*Lodge with 50 modern bedrooms.
Ideally located for tourist,
leisure and business travellers to
the Pennines, Tyneside,
Teesside and the dales.*
Bedrooms: 18 double &
20 twin, 12 family rooms.
Bathrooms: 50 private.
Bed & breakfast: from £27.50
single, from £34.50 double.
Lunch available.
Evening meal 5pm (l.o. 9pm).
Parking for 50.
Credit: Access, Visa, Diners,
Amex.

Scotch Corner Hotel M
COMMENDED
Scotch Corner, Richmond,
DL10 6NR
☎ Richmond (0748) 850900
Telex 587447
*On the A1 midway between
London and Glasgow, offering
a welcoming, comfortable
atmosphere for the tourist or
business man covering the
North of England. 3 suites.*
Bedrooms: 16 single,
21 double & 48 twin, 6 family
rooms.
Bathrooms: 90 private.
Bed & breakfast: from £65
single, from £81.50 double.
Lunch available.
Evening meal 7pm (l.o.
10pm).
Parking for 208.
Credit: Access, Visa, Diners,
Amex.

Vintage Hotel M
COMMENDED
Scotch Corner, Richmond,
DL10 6NP
☎ Richmond (0748) 4424 &
2961
*Extremely convenient for a
meal or overnight stay, or a
good base for touring the
Yorkshire Dales. Richmond is
only 3 miles away.*
Bedrooms: 3 single, 3 double
& 2 twin.
Bathrooms: 5 private,
1 public.
Bed & breakfast: £25-£34.50
single, £39.50-£47.50 double.
Half board: £30-£47.50 daily,
£200-£300 weekly.
Lunch available.
Evening meal 6.30pm (l.o.
9.30pm).
Parking for 50.
Credit: Access, Visa.

SCUNTHORPE
Humberside
Map ref 4C1

Consisted of 5 small
villages until 1860 when
extensive ironstone beds
were discovered. Today a
densely populated
industrial centre with
some interesting modern
buildings. Nearby
Normanby Hall contains
fine furniture.
*Tourist Information
Centre* ☎ *(0724) 860161*

Bridge House Hotel M
Station Rd., Scunthorpe,
S. Humberside DN15 6PY
☎ (0724) 847590 Fax (0724)
861708
*Ideally situated within easy
reach of the town centre and
local amenities.*
Bedrooms: 2 single, 9 double
& 8 twin, 1 family room.
Bathrooms: 20 private.
Bed & breakfast: £38.75-
£52.50 single.
Lunch available.
Evening meal 7pm (l.o.
9.45pm).
Parking for 50.
Credit: Access, Visa.

Briggate Lodge Hotel M
COMMENDED
Ermine St., Broughton,
Brigg, S. Humberside
DN20 0NQ
☎ Brigg (0652) 650770 Fax
(0652) 650495
*Built 1988 in 5 acres of mature
woodland. Located 200 yards
from the M180 junction 4, on
the crossroads of the A18 and
A15. 20 miles from Lincoln, 10
miles from the Humber Bridge
and Humberside Airport. 5 18-
hole golf-courses within 6
miles. Most rooms overlook the
Ancholme Valley.*
Bedrooms: 8 double &
13 twin.
Bathrooms: 21 private.
Bed & breakfast: £49-£52
single, £62-£72 double.
Half board: from £62 daily.
Lunch available.
Evening meal 7pm (l.o.
10pm).
Parking for 125.
Credit: Access, Visa.

The Downs Guest House
Listed APPROVED
33 Deyne Avenue,
Scunthorpe, S. Humberside
DN15 7PZ
☎ (0724) 850710

*Homely, family-run
guesthouse.*
Bedrooms: 2 single, 2 double
& 2 twin, 1 family room.
Bathrooms: 2 public.
Bed & breakfast: from £12
single, from £24 double.
Evening meal 6pm.
Parking for 4.

SELBY
N. Yorkshire
Map ref 4C1

Small market town with
toll bridge on the River
Ouse, believed to have
been birthplace of Henry
I, with a magnificent
abbey containing much
fine Norman and Early
English architecture.
*Tourist Information
Centre* ☎ *(0757) 703263*

Brook Street Guest House
20 Brook St., Selby,
YO8 0AR
☎ (0757) 708208
*Clean and comfortable
guesthouse run on a friendly,
personal basis to ensure an
enjoyable stay, close to the
town centre. Fire certificate.*
Bedrooms: 1 single, 3 twin,
1 family room.
Bathrooms: 1 public.
Bed & breakfast: £12-£15
single, £22-£24 double.
Evening meal 5pm (l.o. 8pm).
Parking for 3.

Chestnut Forge
COMMENDED
Dam Lane, Thorpe
Willoughby, Selby, YO8 9LU
☎ Selby (0757) 707018
*12th C garthing and dovecote
converted into a homely hotel
with bedrooms around the
courtyard. Within easy reach
of York, Selby and Beverley
Minsters.*
Bedrooms: 2 double & 1 twin.
Bathrooms: 3 private.
Bed & breakfast: £34-£39
single, £45-£52 double.
Half board: £42-£47 daily,
£230-£294 weekly.
Lunch available.
Evening meal 6pm (l.o. 8pm).
Parking for 12.
Credit: Access, Visa.

Compton Court Hotel M

Rythergate, Cawood, Selby,
YO8 0TP
☎ (075 786) 315 & 316
*Family-run Georgian hotel
providing home cooking and a
varied menu. In a quiet rural
village with easy access to
York, Selby and Harrogate.*
Bedrooms: 3 single, 2 double
& 3 twin.
Bathrooms: 7 private,
2 public.
Bed & breakfast: £30 single,
£42 double.
Half board: £38 daily, from
£230 weekly.
Evening meal 7.30pm (l.o.
8.30pm).
Parking for 9.
Credit: Access, Visa, Diners.

Londesborough Arms Hotel M
COMMENDED

Market Place, Selby,
YO8 0NS
☎ (0757) 707355
*Former Georgian coaching inn,
next to the 11th C Selby
Abbey. Ideally located for
visiting the historic city of
York.*
Bedrooms: 12 single,
10 double & 4 twin, 1 family
room.
Bathrooms: 23 private,
1 public.
Bed & breakfast: £40-£49
single, £52-£54 double.
Lunch available.
Evening meal 7pm (l.o.
9.30pm).
Parking for 24.
Credit: Access, Visa, Diners,
Amex.

Park View Hotel & Licensed Restaurant M
APPROVED

20 Main St., Riccall, York,
YO4 6PX
☎ (075 784) 458
*Attractive country house hotel
and a la carte restaurant. 4
miles from Selby and 9 miles
from York, off the A19.*
Bedrooms: 5 double & 1 twin,
1 family room.
Bathrooms: 7 private.
Bed & breakfast: £32-£35
single, £38-£44 double.
Half board: £170-£189
weekly.
Lunch available.

Evening meal 7pm (l.o.
9.30pm).
Parking for 20.
Credit: Access, Visa.

SETTLE
N. Yorkshire
Map ref 5B3

Town of narrow streets
and Georgian houses in
an area of great
limestone hills and crags.
Panoramic view from
Castleberg Crag which
stands 300 ft above town.

Falcon Manor Hotel M
APPROVED

Skipton Rd., Settle,
BD24 9BD
☎ (072 92) 3814 Fax (072 92)
2087
CR Consort
*Family-owned country house
hotel in the dales market town
of Settle. Ideal for walking,
motoring and the Settle to
Carlisle Railway.*
Bedrooms: 12 double &
5 twin, 3 family rooms.
Bathrooms: 20 private.
Bed & breakfast: £45-£60
single, £60-£88 double.
Half board: from £52 daily,
£287-£367 weekly.
Lunch available.
Evening meal 7pm (l.o.
10pm).
Parking for 80.
Credit: Access, Visa, Diners.

Liverpool House M

Chapel Square, Settle,
BD24 9HR
☎ (072 92) 2247
*18th C house standing in a
quiet, yet central part of this
Yorkshire Dales' market town.
Close to all amenities. Home
cooking.*
Bedrooms: 2 single, 3 double
& 2 twin.
Bathrooms: 2 public.
Bed & breakfast: £15-£18
single, £30-£36 double.
Half board: £26-£29 daily,
£182-£203 weekly.
Lunch available.
Evening meal 7pm.
Open February-December.
Parking for 8.

Oast Guest House M

5 Pen-Y-Ghent View, Settle,
BD24 9JJ
☎ (072 92) 2989

*Small, comfortable guesthouse.
Relaxed friendly atmosphere.
Ideally situated for Yorkshire
dales and Settle/Carlisle
railway. Out of season
discount.*
Bedrooms: 1 double & 3 twin,
1 family room.
Bathrooms: 2 private,
1 public; 3 private showers.
Bed & breakfast: £28-£35
double.
Half board: £22-£25 daily,
£147-£166 weekly.
Evening meal 6pm (l.o. 5pm).
Parking for 4.

Whitefriars M

Church St., Settle, BD24 9JD
☎ (072 92) 3753
*Comfortable family-run guest
house set in spacious gardens
in centre of Settle. Central for
exploring Yorkshire Dales,
Settle/Carlisle Railway. Non-
smokers only please.*
Bedrooms: 1 single, 3 double
& 2 twin, 3 family rooms.
Bathrooms: 3 private,
2 public.
Bed & breakfast: £13.50-£15
single, £27-£35 double.
Half board: £20.50-£24.50
daily, £136.30-£162.90
weekly.
Evening meal 6.30pm (l.o.
8.30pm).
Parking for 9.

Yorkshire Rose Guest House M
APPROVED

Duke St., Settle, BD24 9AJ
☎ (072 92) 2032
*Spacious Georgian house with
a large, walled "secret" garden
and a friendly homely
atmosphere. Within 5 minutes
of the beautiful market town of
Settle. Home cooking, en-suite
available.*
Bedrooms: 1 single, 1 double
& 1 twin, 2 family rooms.
Bathrooms: 1 private,
1 public.
Bed & breakfast: £14-£16
single, £28-£34 double.
Half board: £22.50-£34.50
daily.
Lunch available.
Evening meal 6.30pm (l.o.
7.30pm).
Parking for 5.

> **Please check prices
> and other details at
> the time of booking.**

SHEFFIELD
S. Yorkshire
Map ref 4B2

Local iron ore and coal
gave Sheffield its
prosperous steel and
cutlery industries. The
modern city centre retains
many interesting buildings
- cathedral, Cutlers' Hall,
Crucible Theatre, Graves
and Mappin Art Galleries
- and has an excellent
shopping centre.
*Tourist Information
Centre* ☎ (0742) 734671
or 734672

Beauchief Hotel M

161 Abbeydale Road South,
Sheffield, S7 2QW
☎ (0742) 620500 & 350197
Telex 54164
CR Lansbury
*Recently built hotel, well
placed for the city of Sheffield
and the beautiful Peak
District.*
Bedrooms: 28 double &
13 twin.
Bathrooms: 41 private.
Bed & breakfast: £31-£74
single, £62-£86 double.
Half board: £42-£88 daily.
Lunch available.
Evening meal 7pm (l.o.
10pm).
Parking for 200.
Credit: Access, Visa, Diners,
Amex.

Charnwood Hotel M
COMMENDED

10 Sharrow La., Sheffield,
S11 8AA
☎ (0742) 589411
*Charming Georgian residence
extended to form a well-
appointed country house hotel
within the heart of the city.*
Bedrooms: 9 single, 5 double
& 7 twin.
Bathrooms: 21 private.
Bed & breakfast: £65-£75
single, £80-£90 double.
Lunch available.
Evening meal 7pm (l.o.
10pm).
Parking for 22.
Credit: Access, Visa, Diners,
Amex.

Critchleys M

6 Causeway Head Rd., Dore,
Sheffield, S17 3DT
☎ Sheffield (0742) 364328
Continued ▶

SHEFFIELD
Continued

Modern property, well-furnished and appointed with good-sized rooms. Near the Peak District National Park, city centre and all facilities.
Bedrooms: 1 single, 2 double.
Bathrooms: 1 private,
2 public.
Bed & breakfast: from £14 single, from £28 double.
Parking for 4.

Etruria House Hotel
APPROVED
91 Crookes Rd., Broomhill, Sheffield, S10 5BD
☎ (0742) 662241 & 670853
Family-run hotel in elegant Victorian house, close to all amenities and city centre. Ideal base for Peak District.
Bedrooms: 5 single, 3 double & 2 twin, 1 family room.
Bathrooms: 7 private,
2 public.
Bed & breakfast: £22-£27 single, £35-£40 double.
Half board: £24.50-£33.50 daily.
Evening meal 6.30pm (l.o. midday).
Parking for 13.
Credit: Access, Visa.

Ivory House Hotel M
34 Wostenholm Rd., Sheffield, S7 1LJ
☎ (0742) 551853
Within easy reach of both the city centre and countryside. Personal service from the family management. Tea and coffee facilities in all rooms.
Bedrooms: 2 single, 2 twin, 2 family rooms.
Bathrooms: 2 public.
Bed & breakfast: £16-£20 single, £30-£36 double.
Evening meal 6pm (l.o. 7pm).
Parking for 4.

Lindum Hotel M
Listed
91 Montgomery Rd., Nether Edge, Sheffield, S7 1LP
☎ (0742) 552356
On a quiet, tree-lined boulevard 1 mile from the city centre, on the route to Derbyshire and the Peak District.
Bedrooms: 6 single, 1 double & 5 twin.
Bathrooms: 1 private,
2 public.
Bed & breakfast: £15.50-£25 single, £31-£38 double.
Lunch available.

Evening meal 6pm (l.o. 7.30pm).
Parking for 4.

Moorgate
Edale Rd., Hope, Sheffield, S30 2RF
☎ Hope Valley (0433) 21219
Telex 667047
Purpose-built for the Countrywide Holidays Association. In the heart of the Peak District.
Bedrooms: 7 single, 23 twin, 1 family room.
Bathrooms: 14 public.
Half board: £26.45-£28.45 daily, £185-£199 weekly.
Lunch available.
Evening meal 7pm.
Parking for 35.

Peace Guest House M
92 Brocco Bank, Sheffield, S11 8RS
☎ (0742) 685110 & 670760
Small, family-run guesthouse established in 1981, providing pleasant surroundings. Adjacent to Endcliffe Park. Convenient for travelling into or out of Sheffield.
Bedrooms: 3 single, 1 double & 1 twin, 1 family room.
Bathrooms: 2 public.
Bed & breakfast: £13-£15 single, £27-£28.50 double.
Half board: £77-£85 weekly.
Lunch available.
Evening meal 6.30pm (l.o. 9.30pm).
Parking for 7.

Rutland Hotel M
Glossop Rd., Sheffield, S10 2PY
☎ (0742) 664411 Fax (0742) 670348 Telex 547500
Fully modernised old hotel, 5 minutes from the city centre and open countryside. Ideal as a touring centre or conference venue.
Bedrooms: 50 single, 16 double & 15 twin, 9 family rooms.
Bathrooms: 87 private, 3 public.
Bed & breakfast: £38-£56 single, £58-£62 double.
Half board: £35-£66 daily.
Lunch available.
Evening meal 6.30pm (l.o. 9.30pm).
Parking for 80.
Credit: Access, Visa, Diners, Amex.

Sharrow View Hotel M
Sharrow View, Nether Edge, Sheffield, S7 1ND
☎ (0742) 551542 & 557854
Small private hotel in quiet residential area near city centre and Derbyshire. Friendly service, good food, parking and bar service. Non-smokers only please.
Bedrooms: 14 single, 4 double & 1 twin, 2 family rooms.
Bathrooms: 4 public.
Bed & breakfast: £21.45-£23.60 single, £32.45-£35.70 double.
Half board: £29.40-£31.55 daily, £150.15-£165.20 weekly.
Lunch available.
Evening meal 7pm (l.o. 8.30pm).
Parking for 25.
Open January-July, September-December.

Sheffield Moat House Hotel
♛♛♛
Chesterfield Road South, Sheffield, S8 8BW
☎ (0742) 375376 Fax (0742) 378140 Telex 547890
Queens Moat Houses
Ideal for the business traveller or as a base for a touring holiday in the Peak District.
Bedrooms: 3 single, 21 double & 56 twin, 15 family rooms.
Bathrooms: 95 private.
Bed & breakfast: £78-£80 single, £99-£100 double.
Lunch available.
Evening meal 7pm (l.o. 10pm).
Parking for 260.
Credit: Access, Visa, Diners, Amex.

Staindrop Lodge Hotel & Restaurant M
♛♛♛
Lane End, Chapeltown, Sheffield, S30 4UH
☎ (0742) 846727 Fax (0742) 846783
Country-type, recently refurbished hotel with special emphasis on standards and cuisine. 1 mile from the M1 junction 35.
Bedrooms: 1 single, 8 double & 3 twin, 1 family room.
Bathrooms: 13 private.
Bed & breakfast: £45-£62 single, £45-£80 double.
Half board: £40-£83 daily.
Lunch available.
Evening meal 7pm (l.o. 9.30pm).

Parking for 56.
Credit: Access, Visa, Diners, Amex.

Stratford Hotel
234 Broomhall St., Sheffield, S3 7SQ
☎ (0742) 729777
Friendly service, homely atmosphere. Off Ecclesall Road, near the city centre.
Bedrooms: 6 single, 2 double & 2 twin.
Bathrooms: 2 public.
Bed & breakfast: £12-£15 single, £24-£30 double.
Half board: £16-£19 daily, £80-£100 weekly.
Evening meal 4pm.
Parking for 12.

SHELLEY
W. Yorkshire
Map ref 4B1

5m SE. Huddersfield

Three Acres Inn & Restaurant
♛
Roydhouse, Shelley, Huddersfield, HD8 8LR
☎ Huddersfield (0484) 602606
An attractive country inn, convenient for all Yorkshire's major conurbations and motorway networks. Restaurant, traditional beers.
Bedrooms: 8 single, 7 double & 1 twin, 3 family rooms.
Bathrooms: 18 private, 1 public.
Bed & breakfast: from £45 single, from £55 double.
Lunch available.
Evening meal 7pm (l.o. 9.30pm).
Parking for 100.
Credit: Access, Visa, Amex.

SHIPTON-BY-BENINGBROUGH
N. Yorkshire
Map ref 4C1

5m NW. York
Village on the A19 north of York. Beningbrough Hall (National Trust) nearby.

Redworth House M
♛♛ APPROVED
Main St., Shipton-by-Beningbrough, York, YO6 1AA
☎ York (0904) 470694

Family-run guesthouse 5 miles north of York on the A19, close to the Yorkshire Dales. Ground floor rooms available with all facilities.
Bedrooms: 2 double, 2 family rooms.
Bathrooms: 4 private.
Bed & breakfast: £30-£40 double.
Parking for 11.

SKIPTON

N. Yorkshire
Map ref 4B1

Pleasant market town with farming community atmosphere, at gateway to Dales with a Palladian Town Hall, parish church and fully roofed Castle at the top of High Street.
Tourist Information Centre ☎ *(0756) 792809*

Airedale View ᴍ
APPROVED
26 Belle Vue Terrace, Skipton, BD23 1RU
☎ (0756) 791195
Small, family-run establishment with a reputation for a warm welcome.
Bedrooms: 1 single, 1 twin, 2 family rooms.
Bathrooms: 2 public.
Bed & breakfast: £13 single, £25 double.
Half board: £20 daily, £140 weekly.
Lunch available.
Evening meal 5.30pm (l.o. 8.30pm).
Parking for 2.

Craven House ᴍ
APPROVED
56 Keighley Rd., Skipton, BD23 2NB
☎ (0756) 794657
Well-appointed Victorian house in an ideal position for touring Yorkshire. All rooms with TV, hot and cold water, tea/coffee facilities, some en-suite.
Bedrooms: 1 single, 4 double & 2 twin.
Bathrooms: 3 private, 1 public; 2 private showers.
Bed & breakfast: from £15 single, £28-£34 double.

Highfield Hotel ᴍ
58 Keighley Rd., Skipton, BD23 2NB
☎ (0756) 793182 & 798834

Friendly, family-run hotel noted for home cooking. Most rooms en-suite. 5 minutes from bus and rail stations.
Bedrooms: 4 single, 5 double & 2 twin.
Bathrooms: 8 private, 1 public.
Bed & breakfast: £17-£18 single, £34-£36 double.
Half board: £26-£27 daily.
Evening meal 7pm (l.o. 5.30pm).
Open February-December.
Credit: Visa.

Oats Restaurant Hotel
HIGHLY COMMENDED
Chapel Hill, Skipton, BD23 1NL
☎ (0756) 798118
Fax (0756) 792369
In a unique dales' location. Personal attention, exclusive bedrooms and a gourmet restaurant.
Bedrooms: 1 single, 1 double & 3 twin.
Bathrooms: 5 private.
Bed & breakfast: £46 single, £56 double.
Lunch available.
Evening meal 7pm (l.o. 9.30pm).
Parking for 20.
Credit: Access, Visa, Amex.

Randells Hotel, Conference & Leisure Centre ᴍ
Keighley Rd., Snaygill, Skipton, BD23 2TA
☎ (0756) 700100 & 700112 & (0756) 700107 Fax (0756) 518321
Newly-built, independent, 61-bedroomed hotel on the edge of Skipton, gateway to the dales. Individually designed rooms and suites, 2 restaurants and conference facilities for 2 to 400 persons. Leisure centre.
Bedrooms: 33 double & 20 twin, 8 family rooms.
Bathrooms: 61 private.
Bed & breakfast: from £65 single, from £85 double.
Lunch available.
Parking for 150.
Credit: Access, Visa, Amex.

SLEIGHTS

N. Yorkshire
Map ref 5D3

4m SW. Whitby
Village close to Whitby at the bottom of Blue Bank and on the broad, deep point of the River Esk.

Netherby ᴍ
APPROVED
90 Coach Rd., Sleights, Whitby, YO22 5EQ
☎ Whitby (0947) 810211
Well-situated Victorian villa with 2 acres of garden overlooking the Esk Valley. Family-run, home cooking using local and home-grown produce.
Bedrooms: 1 single, 3 double & 2 twin, 1 family room.
Bathrooms: 7 private, 1 public.
Bed & breakfast: £18-£24 single, £30-£40 double.
Half board: £27-£34 daily, £180-£238 weekly.
Lunch available.
Evening meal 7.30pm (l.o. 9.30pm).
Parking for 11.
Credit: Access, Visa.

SOUTH MILFORD

N. Yorkshire
Map ref 4C1

Small village, close to the A1 and just north of Monk Fryston.

Cocked Hat Motel ᴍ
York Rd., South Milford, Leeds, W. Yorkshire LS25 5DP
☎ (0977) 683945
Free-house motel with 3 bars - one for bar food, one a cocktail bar and one a functions bar. Also a 140-seater dining room.
Bedrooms: 8 double & 60 twin, 1 family room.
Bathrooms: 67 private, 1 public.
Bed & breakfast: £25-£45 single, £30-£55 double.
Lunch available.
Evening meal 7pm (l.o. 10.30pm).
Parking for 120.
Credit: Access, Visa, Diners.

STANBURY

W. Yorkshire
Map ref 4B1

1m W. Haworth
Hamlet close to Haworth, the home of the Bronte family.

Old Silent Inn ᴍ
APPROVED
Hob La., Stanbury, Keighley, BD22 0HW
☎ Haworth (0535) 42503
Built over 200 years ago, formerly known as the Eagle. Close to High Withens and featured in the book by Halliwell Sutcliffe, "Ricroft of Withens". Bonnie Prince Charlie took refuge here and forbade locals to speak of his name, hence its new name.
Bedrooms: 3 single, 5 double & 1 twin.
Bathrooms: 9 private.
Bed & breakfast: £20-£25 single, £40 double.
Lunch available.
Evening meal 7pm (l.o. 10pm).
Parking for 50.
Credit: Access, Visa, Amex.

STARBOTTON

N. Yorkshire
Map ref 4B1

2m N. Kettlewell
Quiet, picturesque village midway between Kettlewell and Buckden in Wharfedale. Many buildings belong to the 17th C and several have dated lintels.

Hilltop Country Guest House ᴍ
COMMENDED
Starbotton, Skipton, BD23 5HY
☎ Kettlewell (075 676) 321
17th C house with beckside gardens overlooking an unspoilt dales' village. Spacious and comfortable bedrooms with splendid views. Local and international dishes with sensibly-priced wines. Log fires and a welcoming bar.
Bedrooms: 2 double & 2 twin, 1 family room.
Bathrooms: 5 private, 1 public.
Half board: £33-£37 daily, £205-£225 weekly.
Continued ▶

Classifications and quality commendations were correct at the time of going to press but are subject to change. Please check at the time of booking.

STARBOTTON

Continued

Evening meal 7pm (l.o. 6pm).
Parking for 7.
Open March-November.
ち ⌂ ℠ ℉ 🛆 V ⊨ ▥
✿ ✈ 🞐 ▥

STILLINGFLEET

N. Yorkshire
Map ref 4C1

8m S. York

Gamekeepers Lodge Guest House & Tearooms ₼
Cawood Rd., Stillingfleet,
York, YO5 6HR
☎ Escrick (090 487) 212
*Old house with oak beams and
curios. Charming tearoom
location.*
Bedrooms: 2 double & 1 twin,
1 family room.
Bathrooms: 2 private,
1 public.
Bed & breakfast: £15-£25
single, £25-£40 double.
Half board: £150-£180
weekly.
Lunch available.
Parking for 10.
ち ⌂ ♥ ℉ 🛆 V ◑ ▥ ⌘ 🞐
SP

STOKESLEY

N. Yorkshire
Map ref 5C3

Handsome market town
midway between the
North Yorkshire Moors
and the Cleveland border.
Famous for its annual
show in September.

Wainstones Hotel ₼
👑👑👑 COMMENDED
High St., Great Broughton,
Middlesbrough, Cleveland
TS9 7EW
☎ Wainstones (0642) 712268
Fax (0642) 711560
*Stone-built hotel with a unique
restaurant and alcoves for
private parties and a large
character bar.*
Bedrooms: 2 single, 4 double
& 10 twin.
Bathrooms: 16 private.
Bed & breakfast: £35-£40
single, £45-£50 double.
Half board: £45-£50 daily,
£275-£300 weekly.
Lunch available.
Evening meal 7pm (l.o.
9.45pm).
Parking for 48.
Credit: Access, Visa.
ち ⌂ ⌘ ℠ ◑ ⏰ ♥ ℉ V
⊨ ▥ 🛆 ♈ ✿ ✈ 🞐 SP T

SUTTON UPON DERWENT

Humberside
Map ref 4C1

Through the village
meadows and cornfields
the River Derwent winds
towards the Ouse. The
attractive church stands
among trees; there is an
interesting village hall and
a nearby 2-arched
stonebridge carrying the
road to Elvington.

Old Rectory Hotel
👑👑👑
Sutton upon Derwent, York,
N. Yorkshire YO4 5BN
☎ Elvington (090 485) 548
*Georgian house of character,
furnished to a high standard.
In a pleasant village 7 miles
from York.*
Bedrooms: 1 single, 2 double
& 2 twin, 1 family room.
Bathrooms: 2 private,
1 public; 4 private showers.
Bed & breakfast: £27-£37
single, £40-£44 double.
Evening meal 6pm (l.o. 8pm).
Parking for 20.
Credit: Access.
ち ⏰ ♥ ℉ V ⊨ ▥ 🛆 ♈
✿ SP 🞐

TADCASTER

N. Yorkshire
Map ref 4C1

9m SW. York
Known for its breweries
which have been
established here since
18th C. Wharfe Bridge
has 7 arches. Above it
stands the 'virgin viaduct'
built for the railway which
never arrived.

Shann House Hotel
👑👑 APPROVED
47 Kirkgate, Tadcaster,
LS24 9AQ
☎ (0937) 833931
*Protected historic building,
tastefully restored in the
traditional manner. In peaceful
seclusion, in the centre of the
town and only minutes away
from the A1.*
Bedrooms: 2 single, 5 twin,
1 family room.
Bathrooms: 8 private.
Bed & breakfast: from £18.50
single, from £28 double.
Evening meal 5.30pm (l.o.
7pm).
Parking for 12.
Credit: Access, Visa.
ち ⌂ ⏰ ♥ V ⊨ ▥ 🛆 ♈
🞐

THIRSK

N. Yorkshire
Map ref 5C3

Thriving market town with
cobbled square
surrounded by old shops
and inns and also with a
local museum. St. Mary's
Church is probably the
best example of
Perpendicular work in
Yorkshire.

Doxford House ₼
👑👑 APPROVED
Front St., Sowerby, Thirsk,
YO7 1JP
☎ (0845) 523238
*Handsome, Georgian house
with attractive gardens and
paddock with animals,
overlooking the greens of
Sowerby.*
Bedrooms: 1 double & 1 twin,
2 family rooms.
Bathrooms: 4 private.
Bed & breakfast: £12-£17
single, £24-£26 double.
Half board: £18-£20 daily,
£122-£134 weekly.
Evening meal 6.30pm.
Parking for 4.
ち ⏰ ♥ ⓤⓛ ⊨ TV ▥ 🛆 ♿
♈ ✿ 🞐 🞐

Fourways Guest House
👑👑
Town End, Thirsk, YO7 1PY
☎ (0845) 522601
*Guesthouse close to the town
centre, 2 minutes' walk from
the surgery of the famous vet
and author James Herriot.
Centrally located for touring
the North Yorkshire Moors
and the Yorkshire Dales.*
Bedrooms: 1 single, 2 double
& 3 twin.
Bathrooms: 3 private,
1 public.
Bed & breakfast: £11.50-
£13.50 single, £23-£27 double.
Half board: £16.50-£18.50
daily, £115.50-£129.50
weekly.
Evening meal 6.30pm (l.o.
7.30pm).
Parking for 9.
ち ⏰ ♥ ⓤⓛ ▥ 🛆 🞐 SP

Golden Fleece ₼
👑👑
Market Place, Thirsk,
YO7 1LL
☎ (0845) 523108
*17th C coaching inn in the
town's cobbled market place.
200 yards away from James
Herriot's surgery.*
Bedrooms: 8 single, 10 double
& 4 twin.
Bathrooms: 6 private,
5 public.

Bed & breakfast: £30-£45
single, £60-£90 double.
Half board: £30-£45 daily.
Lunch available.
Evening meal 7pm (l.o. 9pm).
Parking for 50.
Credit: Access, Visa, C.Bl.,
Diners, Amex.
ち ⌂ ℉ ⏰ ◑ ♥ ℠ ℉ V ✂
⊨ ▥ 🛆 ♈ ⏰ 🞐 ♽ SP
T

Old Red House ₼
👑👑 APPROVED
Station Rd., Thirsk,
YO7 4LT
☎ (0845) 524383
*2-storey Georgian building with
a bar lounge and open fire.*
Bedrooms: 6 double & 6 twin.
Bathrooms: 12 private.
Bed & breakfast: £16-£20
single, £26-£30 double.
Half board: £21-£30 daily,
£115-£130 weekly.
Lunch available.
Evening meal 7pm (l.o.
9.30pm).
Parking for 30.
Credit: Visa, Diners, Amex.
ち ⌂ ℠ ⏰ ♥ ℉ V ▥ 🛆
♈ 🞐 ⌂ SP ♽

Sheppard's Hotel & Restaurant ₼
👑👑 COMMENDED
Church Farm, Sowerby,
Thirsk, YO7 1JF
☎ Thirsk (0845) 523655
*17th C building on the village
green. Carefully developed,
giving every comfort whilst
maintaining its rural
atmosphere. An ideal centre for
touring Herriot's Yorkshire.*
Bedrooms: 1 single, 6 double
& 3 twin, 2 family rooms.
Bathrooms: 10 private,
1 public.
Bed & breakfast: £35-£45
single, £45-£55 double.
Lunch available.
Evening meal 7pm (l.o.
9.30pm).
Parking for 35.
Credit: Access, Visa.
⌂ ℠ ◑ ⏰ ♥ ℉ V ✂ ⊨
▥ 🛆 ♈ ✿ SP 🞐

Shires Court Hotel ₼
👑👑 COMMENDED
Knayton, Thirsk, YO7 4BS
☎ Thirsk (0845) 537210
*Clean and comfortable
accommodation amidst peace
and tranquillity, beneath the
Hambleton Hills.*
Bedrooms: 2 single, 13 family
rooms.
Bathrooms: 15 private.
Bed & breakfast: £27-£30
single, £44-£50 double.
Half board: £31-£39 daily,
£147-£199.50 weekly.

Evening meal 7pm (l.o. 8.30pm).
Parking for 20.
Open March-October.

THORNTON DALE

N. Yorkshire
Map ref 5D3

Picturesque village with Thorntondale Beck, traversed by tiny stone footbridges at the edge of pretty cottage gardens.

Bridgefoot Guest House M

Thornton Dale, Pickering, YO18 7RR
☎ Pickering (0751) 74749
17th C house of character, near a trout beck in beautiful village of Thornton Le Dale. Emphasis on comfort. All bedrooms have electric blankets.
Bedrooms: 1 single, 2 double & 3 twin, 2 family rooms.
Bathrooms: 5 private, 2 public.
Bed & breakfast: £12.50-£14.50 single, £24-£28 double.
Evening meal 6.30pm (l.o. 6pm).
Parking for 6.
Open April-October.

Easthill M

Thornton Dale, Pickering, YO18 7LP
☎ Pickering (0751) 74561
Large, detached, friendly, family house with magnificent views and private woodland. Located in a picturesque village on the edge of the North Yorkshire Moors.
Bedrooms: 2 single, 2 double & 1 twin, 3 family rooms.
Bathrooms: 8 private, 1 public.
Bed & breakfast: £18 single, £31-£35 double.
Half board: £22.50-£24.50 daily, £150.50-£164.50 weekly.
Evening meal 6.30pm (l.o. 6.30pm).
Parking for 10.

The symbols are explained on the flap inside the back cover.

THORNTON WATLASS

N. Yorkshire
Map ref 5C3

3m SW. Bedale

The Buck Inn M
APPROVED

Thornton Watlass, Ripon, HG4 4AH
☎ Bedale (0677) 22461
Friendly village inn overlooking the delightful cricket green in a small village, 3 miles from Bedale on the Masham Road, and close to the A1. In James Herriot country. Ideal for walking.
Bedrooms: 2 single, 2 twin, 1 family room.
Bathrooms: 5 private.
Bed & breakfast: from £22 single, from £42 double.
Lunch available.
Evening meal 7pm (l.o. 9.30pm).
Parking for 40.
Credit: Access, Visa.

THWAITE

N. Yorkshire
Map ref 5B3

10m N. Hawes
Quiet village, ideal for walking the almost untrodden fells of Great Shunner, Kisdon, High Seat, Rogan's Seat and Lovely Seat. Magnificent scenery.

Kearton Guest House M

Thwaite, Richmond, DL11 6DR
☎ Richmond (0748) 86277
In the charming village of Thwaite in Swaledale, within easy reach of York, the Lake District, Herriot country and the Yorkshire Dales.
Bedrooms: 1 single, 4 double, 8 family rooms.
Bathrooms: 4 public; 3 private showers.
Bed & breakfast: from £15 single, from £30 double.
Half board: max. £21 daily, max. £136.50 weekly.
Lunch available.
Evening meal 6.30pm.
Parking for 20.
Open March-December.

TODMORDEN

W. Yorkshire
Map ref 4B1

8m NE. Rochdale
In beautiful scenery on the edge of the Pennines at junction of 3 sweeping valleys. Until 1888 the county boundary between Yorkshire and Lancashire cut this old cotton town in half, running through the middle of the Town Hall.
Tourist Information Centre ☎ *(0706) 818181*

The Queen Hotel M

Rise La., Todmorden, Lancashire OL14 7AA
☎ (0706) 812961
Built in the 1840s of Yorkshire stone. Located opposite the railway station and 1 minute's walk from the town centre. 2 function/dining rooms.
Bedrooms: 2 double & 4 twin, 1 family room.
Bathrooms: 3 private, 2 public; 1 private shower.
Bed & breakfast: £18-£25 single, £35-£46 double.
Lunch available.
Evening meal 7pm (l.o. 10pm).
Parking for 12.
Credit: Access, Visa.

TODWICK

S. Yorkshire
Map ref 4B2

South Yorkshire village near the M1.

Red Lion Hotel M

Worksop Rd., Todwick, Sheffield, S31 ODJ
☎ Worksop (0909) 771654 & 773704 Telex 54120
Lansbury
Recently built hotel close to the M1, ideal for visiting Sherwood Forest or shopping in the popular city of Sheffield.
Bedrooms: 10 double & 19 twin.
Bathrooms: 29 private.
Bed & breakfast: £28-£70 single, £56-£82 double.
Half board: £39-£84 daily.
Lunch available.
Evening meal 7pm (l.o. 10pm).
Parking for 90.
Credit: Access, Visa, Diners, Amex.

WAKEFIELD

W. Yorkshire
Map ref 4B1

Wool trade important here for 700 years from Norman Conquest, now its economy based on North Yorkshire coalfield. Cathedral church of All Saints has 247-ft spire. Old Bridge, a 9-arched structure, has fine medieval chantry chapels of St. Mary's. Fine Georgian architecture and good shopping centre (The Ridings), Yorkshire Mining Museum nearby.
Tourist Information Centre ☎ *(0924) 295000/1*

Bank House Hotel M

11 Bank St., Wakefield, WF1 1EH
☎ (0924) 368248
Small licensed city centre hotel with emphasis on quality of service.
Bedrooms: 1 single, 4 double, 1 family room.
Bathrooms: 1 private, 2 public; 2 private showers.
Bed & breakfast: £16.50-£27 single, £27-£33 double.
Half board: £17.50-£31.30 daily, £115.50-£189 weekly.
Lunch available.
Evening meal 4pm (l.o. 9pm).
Parking for 2.
Credit: Access, Visa.

Cedar Court Hotel M

Denby Dale Rd., Calder Grove, Wakefield, WF4 3QZ
☎ (0924) 276310
Telex 557647
International hotel, designed and built to high specifications. Close to the M1 and M62 motorways halfway between London and Scotland. Suitable for business people, conferences, private functions and holidaymakers.
Bedrooms: 119 double & 23 twin, 9 family rooms.
Bathrooms: 151 private.
Bed & breakfast: £60-£95 single, £70-£110 double.
Lunch available.
Evening meal 6.30pm (l.o. 11pm).
Parking for 240.
Credit: Access, Visa, Diners, Amex.

Continued ▶

189

WAKEFIELD

Continued

East View Guest House
Listed

2-3 Longcauseway, Off
Eastmoor Rd., Wakefield,
WF1 3SE
☎ (0924) 373312
*Family-run guesthouse in a
quiet area off the main road.
Everyone is made welcome.*
Bedrooms: 3 single, 3 double
& 4 twin, 4 family rooms.
Bathrooms: 3 public.
Bed & breakfast: £12-£15
single, £25-£28 double.
Parking for 14.
⛄ Ⓜ ⇄ 📞 ⮕ 📺 V ⅋ ⇥
📺 ☎ Ü ⚏ SP Ⓣ

Parklands Hotel ⋒
143 Horbury Rd., Wakefield,
WF2 8TY
☎ (0924) 377407
*Family-run hotel with emphasis
on service. On the A642
overlooking Wakefield Park, 2
minutes from the city centre.
Direct dial telephones.*
Bedrooms: 8 single, 4 double
& 3 twin, 1 family room.
Bathrooms: 10 private,
1 public; 3 private showers.
Bed & breakfast: £32.50-£36
single, £42-£50 double.
Evening meal 6.45pm (l.o.
6pm).
Parking for 20.
Credit: Access, Visa.
⛄ 📞 ⮕ 📺 ◊ ⮕ V ⇥ 📺
📺 ☎ ⏴ ⮕ ♿ SP ⚏ Ⓣ

The Poplars ⋒
⚘ ⚘
Bradford Rd., Wrenthorpe,
Wakefield, WF2 0QL
☎ (0924) 375682
*Tastefully restored, 200-year-
old house with open beams.
Country location close to
Wakefield (A650), M1 exit 41
and M62 exit 29.*
Bedrooms: 4 twin.
Bathrooms: 4 private.
Bed & breakfast: max. £25
single, max. £30 double.
Parking for 6.
Credit: Access.
⛄ ⮕ UL ⮕ ⇥ 📺 📺 ⮕
Ü ⚏ ⮕ ⚏ ⚏

Saville Guest House
78 Saville St., Wakefield,
WF1 3LN
☎ (0924) 374761
*A quiet and spacious
establishment close to the city
and all facilities. All rooms
with TV and tea-making.
Private car parking.*
Bedrooms: 2 single, 2 double
& 4 twin, 1 family room.
Bathrooms: 3 private,
3 public.

Bed & breakfast: £16-£24
single, £32-£36 double.
Evening meal 6pm (l.o.
midday).
Parking for 8.
⛄ ⇄ ◊ UL ⮕ V ⅋ ⇥ 📺
📺 ⮕ ⚏ SP

Waterton Park Hotel ⋒
⚘ ⚘ ⚘ ⚘ **COMMENDED**

Walton Hall, Walton,
Wakefield, WF2 6PW
☎ Wakefield (0924) 257911
Fax (0924) 240082
*On a picturesque island
surrounded by a 28 acre lake
with access via an 18th C
bridge. The hall was re-built in
1767 and restored in 1974 and
1987 to provide well-equipped
bedrooms. Excellent leisure
facilities, indoor swimming
pool.*
Bedrooms: 4 single, 15 double
& 10 twin, 2 family rooms.
Bathrooms: 31 private.
Bed & breakfast: £62-£68
single, £70-£90 double.
Half board: £75.75-£87.25
daily.
Lunch available.
Evening meal 7pm (l.o.
9.30pm).
Parking for 100.
Credit: Access, Visa, Diners,
Amex.
⛄ ⇄ ⮕ 📞 ⮕ ⮕ ⮕ V
⇥ 📺 ⮕ ⮕ ⮕ ⚏ ⮕ ⮕
⚏ ⮕ ⚏ SP ⚏ Ⓣ

WEST WITTON

N. Yorkshire
Map ref 5B3

Popular Wensleydale
village, where the burning
of 'Owd Barle', effigy of
an 18th C pig rustler, is
held in August.

The Old Star
⚘ ⚘
West Witton, Leyburn,
DL8 4LU
☎ Wensleydale (0969) 22949
*17th C stone-built former
coaching inn, in a farming
community, with uninterrupted
views of Wensleydale. Home
cooking and a friendly
atmosphere.*
Bedrooms: 3 double & 1 twin,
2 family rooms.
Bathrooms: 4 private,
1 public.
Bed & breakfast: £11.50-£14
single, £23-£28 double.
Half board: £19-£21.50 daily,
£119-£136.50 weekly.
Evening meal 6.30pm (l.o.
7.30pm).
Parking for 20.
⛄ ⇄ ◊ ⮕ V ⮕ 📺 📺 ⮕
⮕ ⮕ ⚏ ⮕ SP ⚏

Wensleydale Heifer ⋒
⚘ ⚘ ⚘ **COMMENDED**

Main St., West Witton,
Wensleydale, DL8 4LS
☎ Wensleydale (0969) 22322
Fax (0969) 24183 Telex 57515
Attn. 80
🅒🅡 Consort
*A 17th C inn in the heart of
James Herriot's Yorkshire
Dales. Exposed beams and log
fires in winter.*
Bedrooms: 12 double &
6 twin, 1 family room.
Bathrooms: 19 private.
Bed & breakfast: £45 single,
£60-£80 double.
Half board: £47.50-£57.50
daily, £299-£379 weekly.
Lunch available.
Evening meal 7pm (l.o.
9.30pm).
Parking for 20.
Credit: Access, Visa, Diners,
Amex.
⛄ ⇄ ◊ 📞 ⮕ ⮕ ◊ ⮕ V
⇥ 📺 ⮕ ⮕ ⮕ ⮕ SP ⚏
Ⓣ
✪ Display advertisement
appears on page 205.

WETHERBY

W. Yorkshire
Map ref 4B1

Prosperous market town
on the River Wharfe
noted for horse-racing.
*Tourist Information
Centre* ☎ *(0937) 62706*

The Grange ⋒
⚘ ⚘
Harewood Rd., Collingham,
Wetherby, LS22 5BL
☎ Collingham Bridge
(0937) 72752
*Stone-built (1892), comfortably
furnished, decorated and
appointed. Pleasant, secluded
gardens, bordered by a stream.
Close to the village centre with
inns and squash courts nearby.*
Bedrooms: 1 double & 2 twin.
Bathrooms: 3 private.
Bed & breakfast: £22-£27
single, £35-£43 double.
Parking for 10.
⛄ ⇥ ⮕ ◊ UL V 📺 📺 ⮕ ⚏
⮕ ⮕ SP

Prospect House ⋒
Listed

8 Caxton St., Wetherby,
LS22 4RU
☎ (0937) 62428
*Established for over 28 years,
with easy access for Harrogate,
York, the dales and James
Herriot country. Colour TV.
Pets welcome*
Bedrooms: 1 single, 2 double
& 2 twin, 1 family room.

Bathrooms: 1 public.
Bed & breakfast: £13-£13.50
single, £26-£27 double.
Parking for 6.
⛄ ⮕ UL ⮕ V ⮕ 📺 📺 ⮕

Wood Hall Hotel ⋒
⚘ ⚘ ⚘ ⚘ ⚘

Trip Lane, Linton,
Wetherby, LS22 4JA
☎ Wetherby (0937) 67271
Fax (0937) 64353
*Georgian mansion with
extensive grounds, converted
into a country house hotel. In
an officially designated area of
outstanding natural beauty.*
Bedrooms: 5 double &
17 twin.
Bathrooms: 22 private.
Bed & breakfast: £85-£105
single, £95-£115 double.
Lunch available.
Evening meal 7.30pm (l.o.
10pm).
Parking for 50.
Credit: Access, Visa, Diners,
Amex.
⛄ ⇄ ⮕ 📞 ⮕ ⮕ V ⇥
⮕ 📺 ⮕ ⮕ ⮕ ⮕ ⮕ ⮕
⅋ ❄ ⮕ ⚏ SP ⚏ Ⓣ

WHARRAM LE STREET

N. Yorkshire
Map ref 5D3

6m SE. Malton

Red House
Wharram le Street, Malton,
YO17 9TL
☎ North Grimston
(094 46) 455
*Large country house with
spacious rooms and a beautiful
garden of character. Take A64
from York to Malton, then
B1248 Beverley road to
Wharram. Grass tennis court.*
Bedrooms: 1 single, 2 double
& 1 twin.
Bathrooms: 4 private.
Half board: £32-£34 daily.
Lunch available.
Evening meal 7pm.
Parking for 8.
Open February-November.
⛄ ⮕ ◊ ⮕ V ⮕ 📺 ⮕ ⮕
⮕ ❄ ⚏ SP

**Classifications
and quality
commendations
were correct at the
time of going to
press but are
subject to change.
Please check at the
time of booking.**

WHITBY

N. Yorkshire
Map ref 5D3

Quaint holiday town with narrow streets and steep alleys at the mouth of the River Esk. Captain James Cook, the famous navigator, lived in Grape Lane. 199 steps lead to St. Mary's Church and St. Hilda's Abbey overlooking harbour. Connections with Dracula, who is reputed to have landed here, are traced at the "Dracula Experience". Sandy beach.
Tourist Information Centre ☎ *(0947) 602674*

Abbey House M
East Cliff, Whitby,
YO22 4JT
☎ (0947) 600557
Extensively modernised house with magnificent views over the harbour and sea.
Bedrooms: 6 single, 19 twin, 6 family rooms.
Bathrooms: 11 public.
Half board: £26.45-£28.45 daily, £185-£199 weekly.
Lunch available.
Evening meal 7pm.
Parking for 25.
Open March-December.
🛇 2 🕭 Ⓤ ⌷ ⅋ 📖 ⌷ 🔔 ♣
✿ ✗ ⌷ ⓢ SP 🏠 Ⓣ

Arundel House Hotel & Restaurant
Bagdale, Whitby, YO21 1QJ
☎ (0947) 603645
Georgian manor house with attractive restaurant, within easy reach of the town centre. Car parking available.
Bedrooms: 2 single, 3 double & 2 twin, 2 family rooms.
Bathrooms: 3 private, 1 public; 2 private showers.
Bed & breakfast: £20-£28 single, £30-£38 double.
Evening meal 7pm (l.o. 9pm).
Parking for 6.
Credit: Access, Visa.
🛇 ⌷ 🕭 ⓥ ⅋ ⌷ 📖 🔔 🔪
⚲ SP 🏠

Bungalow Hotel M
Sandsend, Whitby,
YO21 3TG
☎ Whitby (0947) 83272
Overlooking Mulgrave Wood and close to a 2 mile stretch of sandy beach, 1 mile from Whitby. Restaurant.
Bedrooms: 6 single, 6 double & 5 twin, 6 family rooms.
Bathrooms: 10 private, 2 public.

Bed & breakfast: £19-£22 single, £38-£44 double.
Half board: £27-£30 daily.
Evening meal 6.30pm (l.o. 7.45pm).
Parking for 50.
Open April-October.
🛇 ⌷ ⓥ ⅋ ⌷ 📖 ⌷ 🔔 ☓ ♣
▶ ✿ OAP SP

Corra Lynn Private Hotel M
🕮🕮🕮
28 Crescent Avenue, Whitby,
YO21 3EW
☎ (0947) 602214
All rooms have private facilities, colour TV and hospitality tray. Private parking. Convenient for coast, country and local amenities. Warm welcome assured.
Bedrooms: 1 single, 1 double & 1 twin, 3 family rooms.
Bathrooms: 6 private.
Bed & breakfast: £17.50-£19.50 single, £35-£39 double.
Half board: £28.50-£30.50 daily, £196-£210 weekly.
Evening meal 6pm (l.o. 3pm).
Parking for 4.
Open March-November.
🛇 ⌷ ⅋ 🕭 ⌷ 🔔 ⓣ 📖 🔔 🔪
SP

Dunsley Hall M
🕮🕮🕮 COMMENDED
Dunsley, Whitby, YO21 3TL
☎ (0947) 83437
Peaceful, elegant country hall in 4 acres of secluded grounds within North York Moors National Park. Relaxing and friendly atmosphere. Oak-panelling, carved billiard room with stained-glass windows. Indoor heated swimming pool, fitness room, tennis, croquet and putting green.
Bedrooms: 4 double & 1 twin.
Bathrooms: 5 private.
Bed & breakfast: £35-£50 single, £54-£66 double.
Half board: £41-£44 daily.
Evening meal 7.30pm (l.o. 6pm).
Parking for 10.
Credit: Access, Visa.
🛇 🍴 🐎 🕭 ⌷ ⅋ 🕭 🔪 ⅋
📖 🔔 ♣ 🐾 🏌 ▶ ✿ SP Ⓣ

Esklet Guest House M
🕮🕮
22 Crescent Avenue, West Cliff, Whitby, YO21 3ED
☎ (0947) 605663
Edwardian guesthouse with a comfortable lounge and colour TV. Home-cooked food served in a pleasant dining room.
Bedrooms: 1 single, 2 double & 1 twin, 2 family rooms.
Bathrooms: 2 public.
Bed & breakfast: £10-£12.50 single, £20-£25 double.

Half board: £16-£18.50 daily, from £65 weekly.
Evening meal 6pm (l.o. 4pm).
Parking for 1.
🛇 ⅋ Ⓤ 🕭 ⓥ ⅋ ⌷ 📖
🔔 🏠

Falcon Guest House
29 Falcon Terrace, Whitby,
YO21 1EH
☎ (0947) 603507
Quiet area, 7 minutes' walk from harbour and town centre. Good street parking. Full breakfast, catering for all diets. Lounge available.
Bedrooms: 1 double & 1 twin, 1 family room.
Bathrooms: 1 public.
Bed & breakfast: £10 single, £20 double.
🛇 🍴 Ⓤ 🕭 ⓥ ⅋ ✗ ♣

Haven Crest Hotel M
🕮🕮🕮
137 Upgang Lane, Whitby,
YO21 3JW
☎ (0947) 602726
Small, family-run, licensed hotel with home cooking. On the outskirts of the town overlooking the golf-course and close to the beach. Full English breakfast and early morning tea. Home-baked bread.
Bedrooms: 1 single, 4 double & 2 twin.
Bathrooms: 3 private, 1 public.
Bed & breakfast: £11-£12 single, £22-£30 double.
Evening meal 6.30pm.
Parking for 7.
Open March-November.
🛇 🕭 🕭 ⓥ ⅋ ⓣ 📖 🔔 🔔
OAP

Larpool Hall Country Hotel and Restaurant M
🕮🕮🕮🕮 COMMENDED
Larpool La., Whitby,
YO22 4ND
☎ (0947) 602737
One of the miniature stately homes of England, built in 1796, set in 10 acres overlooking the Esk Valley. 1 mile from town centre.
Bedrooms: 2 single, 5 double & 4 twin, 3 family rooms.
Bathrooms: 14 private.
Bed & breakfast: £28.50-£35 single, £50-£70 double.
Lunch available.
Evening meal 7pm (l.o. 9pm).
Parking for 20.
Credit: Access, Visa.
🛇 🍴 📞 🕭 ⌷ 🕭 🕭 ⓥ 🔪
⅋ ⓣ 📖 🔔 🔔 ♣ 🐾 Ⓤ ✿ ✗
OAP SP 🏠

Old Hall Hotel
High St., Ruswarp, Whitby,
YO21 1NH
☎ Whitby (0947) 602801

Elegant Jacobean hall with its own grounds, in a village setting. Built 1603, of exceptional historic, architectural and artistic interest. Offering charm, comfort and personal attention.
Bedrooms: 4 single, 9 double & 5 twin, 4 family rooms.
Bathrooms: 7 private, 3 public.
Bed & breakfast: £17-£20 single, £34-£40 double.
Evening meal 6.30pm (l.o. 6pm).
Parking for 20.
Open April-October.
🛇 3 🕭 🕭 🕭 ⓥ ⅋ ⓣ 📖 🔔 ♣
✿ ✗ 🏠 SP 🏠 Ⓣ

Riviera Hotel
🕮🕮 COMMENDED
4 Crescent Terrace, West Cliff, Whitby, YO21 3EL
☎ (0947) 602533
Family-run hotel overlooking the sea and only a few minutes' walk from the harbour and all amenities.
Bedrooms: 2 single, 4 double & 2 twin, 5 family rooms.
Bathrooms: 10 private, 2 public.
Bed & breakfast: £20-£21 single, £38-£40 double.
Half board: £26-£29 daily.
Evening meal 6pm.
Open March-October.
🛇 2 ⌷ 🕭 🕭 ⓥ ⅋ ⓣ 🔔 ♣

Sandbeck Hotel M
🕮🕮
2 Crescent Terrace, West Cliff, Whitby, YO21 3EL
☎ (0947) 604012
Located on the seafront with seaviews.
Bedrooms: 11 double & 3 twin, 2 family rooms.
Bathrooms: 16 private.
Bed & breakfast: £25-£45 single, £35-£48 double.
Open March-October.
Credit: Access, Visa, Amex.
🛇 5 🕭 🐎 ⌷ ⌷ 🕭 🕭 ⓥ ⅋
ⓣ 📖 🔔 🏠
🏩 Display advertisement appears on page 204.

Saxonville Hotel M
🕮🕮🕮 COMMENDED
Ladysmith Avenue, Whitby,
YO21 3HX
☎ (0947) 602631
Family-owned hotel, in operation since 1946, proud of its cuisine and friendly atmosphere.
Bedrooms: 2 single, 11 double & 7 twin, 4 family rooms.
Bathrooms: 24 private.
Bed & breakfast: from £27.50 single, from £55 double.
Half board: from £37.50 daily, from £262.50 weekly.

Continued ▶

WHITBY

Continued

Lunch available.
Evening meal 7pm (l.o. 8.30pm).
Parking for 20.
Open May-October.
Credit: Access, Visa, Amex.
[symbols]

Seacliffe Hotel
APPROVED

12 North Promenade, West Cliff, Whitby, YO21 3JX
☎ (0947) 603139
Small, friendly hotel with a restaurant offering an a la carte menu. In a prime position on the seafront.
Bedrooms: 13 double & 2 twin, 4 family rooms.
Bathrooms: 19 private, 1 public.
Bed & breakfast: £37.50-£42.50 single, £47-£49 double.
Evening meal 6pm (l.o. 9pm).
Parking for 8.
Credit: Access, Visa, Diners, Amex.
[symbols]

Seaview ⋔

5 East Crescent, Whitby, YO21 3HD
☎ (0947) 604462
Family-run guesthouse with emphasis on standards of cleanliness. Beautiful views of the sea; unrestricted parking nearby.
Bedrooms: 1 single, 1 double & 3 twin, 2 family rooms.
Bathrooms: 2 public.
Bed & breakfast: £13.50-£14.50 single, £25-£27 double.
Parking for 2.
[symbols]

Stakesby Manor ⋔
COMMENDED

High Stakesby, Whitby, YO21 1HL
☎ (0947) 602773 & 602140
Georgian house dating back to 1710, in its own grounds, on the outskirts of Whitby in the National Park. Facing south with views of the North Yorkshire Moors.
Bedrooms: 6 double & 2 twin.
Bathrooms: 8 private.
Bed & breakfast: max. £34.50 single, £49.50-£52 double.
Half board: £30.50-£34 daily, £213.50-£238 weekly.
Lunch available.
Evening meal 7pm (l.o. 9.30pm).

Parking for 30.
Credit: Access, Visa.
[symbols]

Wentworth House ⋔

27 Hudson St., West Cliff, Whitby, YO21 3EP
☎ (0947) 602433
Spacious Victorian house offering comfortable accommodation. Traditional food, also specialising in wholefood vegetarian meals. Close to beach, harbour and town.
Bedrooms: 4 single, 1 twin, 3 family rooms.
Bathrooms: 2 public.
Bed & breakfast: £12-£15 single, £24-£30 double.
Half board: £17-£20 daily, from £109 weekly.
Lunch available.
Evening meal 6pm.
[symbols]

Wheeldale Hotel

11 North Promanade, Whitby, YO21 3JX
☎ (0947) 602365
Detached, private hotel overlooking the sea. Private car park, colour TV and bar lounge. All double rooms are en-suite.
Bedrooms: 2 single, 6 double & 1 twin, 1 family room.
Bathrooms: 8 private, 1 public.
Bed & breakfast: £19 single, £38-£40 double.
Half board: £26-£27 daily, £126-£182 weekly.
Evening meal 6pm (l.o. 6pm).
Parking for 9.
Open February-November.
[symbols]

York House Private Hotel
COMMENDED

High Hawsker, Whitby, YO22 4LW
☎ Whitby (0947) 880314
Small hotel with parking, in peaceful location, 3 miles from Whitby. En-suite rooms, all with courtesy tray and TV. Non-smoking. Sorry no pets.
Bedrooms: 1 double & 3 twin.
Bathrooms: 4 private, 2 public.
Half board: £31-£33 daily, £210-£224 weekly.
Evening meal 7.30pm (l.o. 7.30pm).
Parking for 10.
Open March-November.
[symbols]

WHITWELL-ON-THE-HILL

N. Yorkshire
Map ref 5C3

5m SW. Malton
Pretty village on the Howardian Hills with magnificent views overlooking the Vale of York and the lands of Castle Howard Estate. The houses, set about with parkland, line the approach to the Hall.

Whitwell Hall Country House Hotel ⋔

Whitwell-on-the-Hill, York, YO6 7JJ
☎ (065 381) 551 Fax (065 381) 554 Telex 57697 YORVEX G
Genuine country house hotel with a galleried hall, in 18 acres of gardens and woodlands overlooking York. Good sized indoor swimming pool.
Bedrooms: 4 single, 11 double & 8 twin.
Bathrooms: 23 private, 1 public.
Bed & breakfast: £49-£53 single, £64-£104 double.
Half board: £45-£55 daily.
Lunch available.
Evening meal 7.30pm (l.o. 8.30pm).
Parking for 56.
Credit: Access, Visa, Amex.
[symbols]

WILLERBY

Humberside
Map ref 4C1

5m NW. Hull
A suburb of Hull lying east of the Wolds and north of the Humber.

Grange Park Hotel ⋔

Main St., Willerby, Kingston-upon-Hull, N. Humberside HU10 6EA
☎ Hull (0482) 656488 Fax (0482) 655848 Telex 592773
Ⓒ Best Western
In its own 12 acres of grounds, very close to the centre of Hull.
Bedrooms: 4 single, 42 double & 59 twin, 4 family rooms.
Bathrooms: 109 private.
Bed & breakfast: £57-£88 single, £77-£98 double.
Half board: £79-£110 daily.
Lunch available.
Evening meal 6.30pm (l.o. 10.30pm).

Parking for 600.
Credit: Access, Visa, C.Bl., Diners, Amex.
[symbols]
☎ Display advertisement appears on page 578.

Willerby Manor Hotel ⋔

Well Lane, Willerby, Hull, N. Humberside HU10 6ER
☎ Hull (0482) 652616
Telex 592629
In 3 acres of well-manicured gardens, with a restaurant serving modern French cuisine.
Bedrooms: 4 single, 24 double & 10 twin.
Bathrooms: 38 private.
Bed & breakfast: £39.40-£60.40 single, £57.80-£88.90 double.
Lunch available.
Evening meal 6.45pm (l.o. 9.30pm).
Parking for 200.
Credit: Access, Visa, Amex.
[symbols]

YORK

N. Yorkshire
Map ref 4C1

Roman walled city nearly 2000 years old containing many well-preserved medieval buildings (The Shambles, Stonegate). Its Minster has over 100 stained glass windows spanning 800 years. Castle Museum contains city's history and there is the National Railway Museum, Railway Show and famous racecourse. Many attractions including Wax Museum, Jorvik Viking Centre and York Dungeon.
Tourist Information Centre ☎ (0904) 621756 or 643700 or 620557

Abacus Guest House ⋔

5 Wenlock Terrace, Fulford Rd., York, YO1 4DU
☎ (0904) 632301
Friendly, informal guesthouse, half a mile from the city walls and three quarters of a mile from the town centre, opposite the police headquarters.
Bedrooms: 1 single, 2 double & 1 twin, 4 family rooms.
Bathrooms: 1 private, 2 public.
Bed & breakfast: £12-£15 single, £24-£30 double.

Half board: £17-£20 daily, £84-£105 weekly.
Lunch available.
Evening meal 6pm (l.o. 4pm).
🛇 🖵 ♥ UL ♿ V ⊟ TV 📶
📠 🍽 DAP ♒ SP T

Abbey Guest House ⋈
14 Earlsborough Terrace, Marygate, York, YO3 7BQ
☎ (0904) 627782
Small family-run guesthouse on the banks of the River Ouse, 450 yards from the city centre.
Bedrooms: 2 single, 3 double & 1 twin, 1 family room.
Bathrooms: 2 public.
Bed & breakfast: £14.50-£17.50 single, £27-£32 double.
Half board: £21.50-£40 daily.
Evening meal 6.30pm (l.o. 1pm).
Parking for 7.
Credit: Access, Visa.
🛇 🖵 ♥ UL ♿ TV 📶 📠
🍽 🐾 SP

Abbots Mews Hotel ⋈
🏰🏰🏰 APPROVED
6 Marygate La., Bootham, York, YO3 7DE
☎ (0904) 634866 & 622395
Telex 57777
Converted Victorian coachmen's cottages, quietly located in a mews, with easy access to the city centre.
Bedrooms: 1 single, 23 double & 18 twin, 8 family rooms.
Bathrooms: 50 private.
Bed & breakfast: £35-£40 single, £60-£70 double.
Half board: £42-£47 daily.
Lunch available.
Evening meal 7pm (l.o. 9.30pm).
Parking for 30.
Credit: Access, Visa, Diners, Amex.
🛇 ♿ 📞 🖵 ♥ V ⊟
📶 📠 🍽 ✕ ♒ SP 📮 T

Aberford House Hotel ⋈
🏰🏰
35-36 East Mount Rd., York, YO2 2BD
☎ (0904) 622694
Centrally situated and privately-owned small hotel. Colour TV in all bedrooms and a cellar bar. Brochure on request.
Bedrooms: 2 single, 6 double & 4 twin, 1 family room.
Bathrooms: 2 private, 3 public; 4 private showers.
Bed & breakfast: £18-£20 single, £35-£45 double.
Evening meal 7pm.
Parking for 7.
Credit: Access, Visa, Amex.
🛇 ♿ 🖵 ♥ ♿ V ⊟ 📶
📠 ✕ DAP SP T

Acer House Hotel ⋈
🏰🏰🏰
52 Scarcroft Hill, The Mount, York, YO2 1DE
☎ (0904) 653839
Victorian hotel in a quiet residential area adjoining the Knavesmire and racecourse. Half a mile from the city centre.
Bedrooms: 2 double & 2 twin, 2 family rooms.
Bathrooms: 4 private, 1 public.
Bed & breakfast: £25-£35 single, £40-£50 double.
Half board: £27.50-£32.50 daily, £190-£216 weekly.
Lunch available.
Evening meal 6pm (l.o. 8pm).
Parking for 4.
Credit: Access, Visa, Amex.
🛇 ♿ 📞 ♥ ♿ V ⊟ ✕
TV 📶 📠 ♿ DAP ♒ SP 📮
⑳ Display advertisement appears on page 203.

Acorn Guest House ⋈
🏰🏰 APPROVED
1 Southlands Rd., York, YO2 1NP
☎ (0904) 620081
Late 19th C Victorian town house, close to the town centre and most attractions. Full fire certificate.
Bedrooms: 1 single, 2 double & 1 twin, 2 family rooms.
Bathrooms: 2 private, 1 public.
Bed & breakfast: £11-£14 single, £20-£26 double.
Half board: £16-£19 daily, £63-£84 weekly.
Lunch available.
Evening meal 6pm (l.o. 10am).
🛇 🖵 ♥ UL ♿ V ⊟ 📶
📠 DAP ♒ SP T

Aldwark Manor ⋈
🏰🏰🏰
Aldwark, Alne, York, YO6 2NF
☎ Tollerton (034 73) 8146
19th C manor house in extensive parkland with its own 9-hole golf-course.
Bedrooms: 1 single, 7 double & 6 twin, 2 family rooms.
Bathrooms: 16 private.
Bed & breakfast: from £72 single, £99.50-£132 double.
Lunch available.
Evening meal 7pm (l.o. 9.30pm).
Parking for 100.
Credit: Access, Visa, Diners, Amex.
🛇 ♿ 📞 🖵 ♥ ♿ V ✕
⊟ ⚫ 📶 📠 🍽 ♪ ⚑ ✓ ✽
DAP ♒ SP 📮 T

Alexander's Hotel ⋈
🏰🏰🏰
18 Boroughbridge Rd., York, YO2 5RU
☎ (0904) 795334
Family-run hotel 1.5 miles from the city centre. Private car park. Speciality vegetarian food available.
Bedrooms: 1 single, 5 double & 4 twin, 4 family rooms.
Bathrooms: 14 private.
Bed & breakfast: £25-£35 single, £38-£48 double.
Half board: £27.50-£35 daily, £180-£250 weekly.
Lunch available.
Evening meal 6.30pm (l.o. 8.30pm).
Parking for 12.
Credit: Access, Visa, Diners, Amex.
🛇 ♿ 📞 🖵 ♥ ♿ V ✕
⊟ 📶 📠 🍽 ♿ DAP ♒ SP T

Alhambra Court Hotel ⋈
🏰🏰🏰 APPROVED
31 St Mary's, Bootham, York, YO3 7DD
☎ (0904) 628474
Early Georgian town house in a quiet cul-de-sac near to the city centre. Family-run hotel with bar, restaurant, open to non-residents. Lift and parking.
Bedrooms: 3 single, 9 double & 10 twin, 3 family rooms.
Bathrooms: 25 private.
Bed & breakfast: £27.50-£33 single, £45-£52 double.
Half board: £33-£36.50 daily.
Evening meal 6pm (l.o. 9pm).
Parking for 20.
Credit: Access, Visa.
🛇 ♿ 🏨 📞 ⚫ 🖵 ♥ ♿ V
⊟ TV ⚑ 📶 📠 DAP ♒ SP 📮
T

Ambleside Guest House
62 Bootham Crescent, Bootham, York, YO3 7AH
☎ (0904) 637165
Warm, friendly service, with access to rooms at all times. Only minutes from the city centre.
Bedrooms: 3 double & 2 twin, 1 family room.
Bathrooms: 4 private, 2 public.
Bed & breakfast: £24-£36 double.
🛇 ⑩ 🖵 ♥ UL V ⊟ TV 📶
✕ DAP

Annjoa House ⋈
🏰🏰 COMMENDED
34 Millfield Rd., Scarcroft Rd., York, YO2 1NQ
☎ (0904) 653731

Quiet family-run hotel, close to the city centre and racecourse. Offering a friendly atmosphere and home cooking.
Bedrooms: 3 single, 5 double & 2 twin, 2 family rooms.
Bathrooms: 6 private, 2 public.
Bed & breakfast: £11-£16 single, £22-£32 double.
Half board: £18-£23 daily, £126-£161 weekly.
Evening meal 6.30pm (l.o. midday).
🛇 🖵 ♥ ♿ V ⊟ TV 📶 📠
✕ SP

Arndale Hotel ⋈
🏰🏰🏰 COMMENDED
290 Tadcaster Rd., York, YO2 2ET
☎ (0904) 702424
Welcoming, traditionally furnished Victorian gentleman's residence. Most rooms have four-poster or half-tester beds. Whirlpool baths. Overlooking racecourse and close to city centre.
Bedrooms: 6 double & 2 twin, 1 family room.
Bathrooms: 9 private.
Bed & breakfast: £39-£57 double.
Half board: £24.50-£41 daily.
Evening meal 6.30pm (l.o. midday).
Parking for 15.
🛇 ⑧ ♿ 🏨 ⚫ 🖵 ♥ ⊟ 📶
✽ ✕ SP 📮 T

Ashbourne House Hotel ⋈
🏰🏰
139 Fulford Road, York, YO1 4HG
☎ (0904) 639912
Charming, comfortable family owned and run licensed private hotel. On main route into York from the South. Walking distance to city centre.
Bedrooms: 3 double & 3 twin.
Bathrooms: 2 private, 1 public.
Bed & breakfast: £30-£40 double.
Half board: £20-£25 daily, £120-£150 weekly.
Parking for 7.
Credit: Access, Visa.
🛇 🖵 ♥ ♿ V ⊟ TV 📶 📠
🍽 ✕ ♿ DAP ♒ SP

Ashcroft Hotel ⋈
🏰🏰🏰 APPROVED
294 Bishopthorpe Rd., York, YO2 1LH
☎ (0904) 659286
© Minotels
Continued ▶

YORK
Continued

Former Victorian mansion in 2.5 acres of wooded grounds overlooking the River Ouse, only 1 mile from the city centre. All bedrooms have colour TV, radio, mini-bar, telephone, coffee and tea making facilities, hair-dryer and trouser press.
Bedrooms: 1 single, 6 double & 5 twin, 3 family rooms.
Bathrooms: 15 private.
Bed & breakfast: from £32 single, from £55 double.
Half board: from £37 daily, from £217 weekly.
Lunch available.
Evening meal 6.30pm (l.o. 7.30pm).
Parking for 40.
Credit: Access, Visa, Diners, Amex.

Ashwood Place

19 Nunthorpe Avenue, Off Scarcroft Rd., York, YO2 1PF
☎ (0904) 623412
Small, comfortable and friendly guesthouse close to the city centre and station. Families welcome, very reasonable rates.
Bedrooms: 2 single, 2 double & 1 twin, 1 family room.
Bathrooms: 2 public; 1 private shower.
Bed & breakfast: £12.50-£15 single, £25-£40 double.
Evening meal 6pm (l.o. 6pm).

Astoria Hotel

6 Grosvenor Terrace, Bootham, York, YO3 7AG
☎ (0904) 659558
Licensed hotel near the Minster. Some bathrooms are en-suite including the ground floor rooms. Parties and groups catered for. Dogs welcome.
Bedrooms: 4 single, 5 double & 4 twin, 10 family rooms.
Bathrooms: 8 private, 6 public; 3 private showers.
Bed & breakfast: £16-£20 single, £32-£40 double.
Evening meal 6.30pm.
Parking for 15.
Credit: Visa.

Avimore House Hotel

78 Stockton La., York, YO3 0BS
☎ (0904) 425556

Edwardian house, now a family-run hotel in a pleasant residential area on the east side of the city.
Bedrooms: 2 single, 1 double & 2 twin, 1 family room.
Bathrooms: 6 private.
Bed & breakfast: £17-£22 single, £30-£38 double.
Half board: £24-£30 daily.
Lunch available.
Evening meal 6pm (l.o. midday).
Parking for 6.

Barbican Hotel
APPROVED

20 Barbican Rd., York, YO1 5AA
☎ (0904) 627617
Small, friendly family-run Victorian residence of charm and character overlooking Medieval bar walls. 7 minutes' walk to tourist attractions.
Bedrooms: 4 double & 2 twin, 1 family room.
Bathrooms: 7 private, 1 public.
Bed & breakfast: £32-£44 double.
Half board: £24.50-£30.50 daily, £171.50-£213.50 weekly.
Evening meal 6.30pm.
Parking for 7.
Credit: Access, Visa.

Bedford Hotel

108/110 Bootham, York, YO3 7DG
☎ (0904) 624412
Small family-run hotel, 5 minutes' walk along historic Bootham to the famous Minster and city centre.
Bedrooms: 2 single, 7 double & 2 twin, 3 family rooms.
Bathrooms: 14 private.
Bed & breakfast: £24-£32 single, £34-£44 double.
Half board: £25-£40 daily, £175-£280 weekly.
Evening meal 6.30pm (l.o. midday).
Parking for 14.
Credit: Access, Visa.

Beechwood Close Hotel
APPROVED

19 Shipton Rd., Clifton, York, YO3 6RE
☎ (0904) 658378 Fax (0904) 647124
Minotels

Spacious, detached, family-run house set among trees, located on the A19, 1 mile north of the city centre. Restaurant, bar, lounge, car park and a 9-hole putting green.
Bedrooms: 3 single, 4 double & 2 twin, 5 family rooms.
Bathrooms: 14 private.
Bed & breakfast: £31.50-£35 single, £54-£60 double.
Half board: £35.75-£44.25 daily, £243.25-£302.25 weekly.
Lunch available.
Evening meal 7pm (l.o. 9pm).
Parking for 36.
Credit: Access, Visa, Diners, Amex.

The Bentley

25 Grosvenor Terrace, Bootham, York, YO3 7AG
☎ (0904) 644313
Fine house in Victorian terrace, with views of the minster. Close to city centre. Friendly service, care and comfort guaranteed.
Bedrooms: 3 double, 3 family rooms.
Bathrooms: 2 private, 2 public.
Bed & breakfast: £28-£40 double.
Half board: £20.50-£26.50 daily.
Evening meal 6pm (l.o. 4pm).
Open February-November.

Blakeney Hotel

180 Stockton La., York, YO3 0ES
☎ (0904) 422786
Quietly situated in a delightful area of York, the Blakeney offers a hospitable welcome. Only 5 minutes' drive to city.
Bedrooms: 3 single, 9 double & 4 twin, 2 family rooms.
Bathrooms: 6 private, 3 public.
Bed & breakfast: £18-£22 single, £26-£44 double.
Half board: £28-£32 daily, £190-£220 weekly.
Evening meal 6pm (l.o. 7pm).
Parking for 15.
Credit: Access, Visa.

Blue Bridge Hotel

Fishergate, York, YO1 4AP
☎ (0904) 621193
Friendly, private hotel, reputation for food, relaxed atmosphere and a warm welcome. Short riverside walks to city. Private car parks.

Bedrooms: 2 single, 6 double & 3 twin, 5 family rooms.
Bathrooms: 14 private, 1 public.
Bed & breakfast: £38-£45 single, £48-£56 double.
Evening meal 6.30pm (l.o. 9.30pm).
Parking for 20.
Credit: Access, Visa.

Bootham Bar Hotel
Listed

4 High Petergate, York, YO1 2EH
☎ (0904) 658516
The hotel garden is bordered by the city walls. 150 yards from York Minster. Luggage lift.
Bedrooms: 4 double & 3 twin, 2 family rooms.
Bathrooms: 9 private.
Bed & breakfast: £40-£58 double.
Lunch available.
Credit: Access, Visa.

⑩ Display advertisement appears on page 202.

Bootham Park Hotel
COMMENDED

9 Grosvenor Terrace, Bootham, York, YO3 7AG
☎ (0904) 644262
An elegant Victorian house 5 minutes' walk from York Minster and other tourist attractions. En-suite rooms, with hair-dryer and alarm clock.
Bedrooms: 2 double & 2 twin, 2 family rooms.
Bathrooms: 6 private, 1 public.
Bed & breakfast: £32-£38 double.
Half board: £24-£27 daily, £168-£189 weekly.
Evening meal 6.30pm (l.o. 8pm).
Parking for 6.
Credit: Access, Visa.

Bowen House

4 Gladstone St., Huntington Rd., York YO3 7RF
☎ (0904) 636881
Newly refurbished, late Victorian, family-run guesthouse 5 minutes' walk from the city centre. Private parking. No-smoking throughout.
Bedrooms: 1 single, 2 double & 1 twin, 1 family room.
Bathrooms: 2 private, 1 public; 1 private shower.

Bed & breakfast: from £16 single, £27-£38 double.
Parking for 4.

🕙 ♿ 🖵 ⬜ Ⓤ 🛅 📺 ✂ 🏢
🛏 🛪 🎀 DAP SP 🏮 T

Briar Lea Guest House M
👑👑

8 Longfield Terrace, Bootham, York, YO3 6HD
☎ (0904) 635061
Victorian house, 5 minutes' walk from the city centre and railway station.
Bedrooms: 1 single, 2 double & 1 twin, 1 family room.
Bathrooms: 2 public.
Bed & breakfast: £12-£15 single, £23-£33 double.
Parking for 1.

🕙 5 🖵 🖤 Ⓤ 🛅 ⬜ 📺 🏢
🛏 ♿ 🛪 🎀 DAP SP

Byron House Hotel M
👑👑👑 APPROVED

7 Driffield Terrace, The Mount, York, YO2 2DD
☎ (0904) 632525 Fax (0904) 613174
Friendly, personal service in a pleasant atmosphere surrounded by period elegance and charm. Emphasis on food and wines.
Bedrooms: 3 single, 3 double, 4 family rooms.
Bathrooms: 7 private, 1 public.
Bed & breakfast: £26-£39 single, £58-£68 double.
Half board: £41-£54 daily, £260-£324 weekly.
Evening meal 7pm (l.o. 8pm).
Parking for 7.
Credit: Access, Visa, Diners, Amex.

🕙 🛐 ♿ Ⓒ 🖵 🖤 🛅 ⬜ 📺
⬜ 🛏 ♿ 🛪 🎀 DAP SP T

Carlton House Hotel
👑👑

134 The Mount, York, YO2 2AS
☎ (0904) 622265
Family-run hotel, a short walk from the city centre, railway station and racecourse.
Bedrooms: 1 single, 7 double & 3 twin, 4 family rooms.
Bathrooms: 3 private, 3 public; 2 private showers.
Bed & breakfast: £16-£17 single, £30-£36 double.
Parking for 7.

🕙 🖤 Ⓒ 🖵 🎀 ⬜ 🛏 🛪 🏮

Cavalier Private Hotel M
👑👑

39 Monkgate, York, YO3 7PB
☎ (0904) 636615

Small family-run hotel close to the city centre, only yards from the ancient Bar Walls and many of York's famous historical landmarks.
Bedrooms: 2 single, 4 double, 4 family rooms.
Bathrooms: 7 private, 3 public.
Bed & breakfast: £13-£14 single, £30-£32 double.
Half board: £23.50-£24.50 daily.
Evening meal 6pm (l.o. 3.30pm).

🕙 🖵 🖤 ♿ 🛅 ⬜ 📺 ⬜ 🏢
♿ 🛪 🎀 🏮

Chantry Hotel M
👑👑

130 The Mount, York, YO2 2AS
☎ (0904) 659150
Elegant Georgian listed residence, built in 1830, tastefully restored. Near the station and Micklegate Bar, an ancient entrance to the old city.
Bedrooms: 2 single, 3 double & 1 twin, 2 family rooms.
Bathrooms: 4 private, 1 public; 2 private showers.
Bed & breakfast: £22.50-£28.50 single, £40-£54 double.
Half board: £30-£38.50 daily, £200-£260 weekly.
Evening meal 6.30pm (l.o. 8.30pm).
Parking for 2.
Credit: Access, Visa.

🕙 2 Ⓒ 🖵 🖤 🛅 ⬜ 📺
⬜ 🛪 🎀 SP 🏮

City Guest House M
👑👑

68 Monkgate, York, YO3 7PF
☎ (0904) 622483
Cosy guesthouse 3 minutes from York Minster. En-suite rooms and car parking. Non-smokers only please.
Bedrooms: 1 single, 1 double & 1 twin, 3 family rooms.
Bathrooms: 3 private; 3 private showers.
Bed & breakfast: £18-£22 single, £30-£40 double.
Parking for 5.

🕙 2 🖵 🖤 Ⓤ 🛅 ✂ 🎀 📺 ⬜
🛏 🛪 SP

Clarence Gardens Hotel & Squash Courts M
👑👑👑

Haxby Rd., York, YO3 7JS
☎ (0904) 624252
Comfortable accommodation with emphasis on service. Use of squash courts free of charge to residents. 10 minutes' walk to the city centre.
Bedrooms: 4 double & 7 twin, 1 family room.
Bathrooms: 12 private.
Bed & breakfast: £28-£33 single, £39-£46 double.

Evening meal 5.30pm (l.o. 7pm).
Parking for 60.
Credit: Access, Visa, Amex.

🕙 🖵 🖤 ⬜ 🎀 📺 🌑 ⬜ 🛏
🛪 🛪 🎀

Clifton Bridge Hotel M
👑👑👑

Water End, Clifton, York, YO3 6LL
☎ (0904) 610510
On the north side of the city between the A19 and A59. Adjacent to a delightful riverside walk into the city centre and opposite a very pleasant park.
Bedrooms: 2 double & 9 twin, 1 family room.
Bathrooms: 12 private.
Bed & breakfast: £28-£38 single, £48-£56 double.
Half board: £33.75-£37.75 daily.
Lunch available.
Evening meal 6.30pm (l.o. 7.45pm).
Parking for 14.
Credit: Access, Visa.

🕙 🛐 Ⓒ Ⓒ 🖵 🖤 🛅 ⬜ 📺
⬜ 🛏 🛠 ♿ DAP SP T

Clifton Guest House M
👑👑👑 APPROVED

127 Clifton, York, YO3 6BL
☎ (0904) 634031
Small family-run guesthouse with bedrooms on the ground and first floors. Less than a mile from York Minster.
Bedrooms: 1 single, 1 double & 2 twin, 3 family rooms.
Bathrooms: 3 private, 3 public.
Bed & breakfast: £13-£15 single, £26-£32 double.
Half board: £22-£25 daily, £154-£175 weekly.
Evening meal 6pm (l.o. 9am).
Parking for 6.

🕙 🛐 🖵 🖤 Ⓤ 🛅 ⬜ 📺 ⬜
🛪 🎀 SP

Clifton View Guest House M
👑👑

118 Clifton, York, YO3 6BQ
☎ (0904) 625047
Family-run guesthouse with private parking, 15 minutes' walk from the city centre. All rooms have colour TV.
Bedrooms: 4 double & 2 twin, 4 family rooms.
Bathrooms: 2 public; 8 private showers.
Bed & breakfast: £22-£28 double.
Half board: £16.50-£19.50 daily.
Evening meal 6pm (l.o. 10.30am).
Parking for 6.

🕙 🛐 🖵 🖤 Ⓤ 🛅 ⬜ 📺 ⬜ 🛏
DAP SP

Collingwood Hotel M
👑👑👑

163 Holgate Rd., York, YO2 4DF
☎ (0904) 783333
Georgian building with adequate parking within its own grounds. Dining room, lounge and lounge bar.
Bedrooms: 4 double & 3 twin, 3 family rooms.
Bathrooms: 10 private, 1 public.
Bed & breakfast: £28-£36 single, from £36 double.
Half board: from £25 daily, from £175 weekly.
Evening meal 6pm (l.o. 6.30pm).
Parking for 11.
Credit: Access, Visa, Diners, Amex.

🕙 Ⓒ 🖵 🖤 🛅 ⬜ 📺 ⬜ 🛏
🛪 DAP SP 🏮

Copper's Lodge M
👑👑

15 Alma Terrace, Fulford Rd., York, YO1 4DQ
☎ (0904) 639871
Family-run guesthouse offering personal service. In a quiet location with a river walk close by and only 5 minutes' walk to the city centre.
Bedrooms: 1 single, 1 double & 1 twin, 4 family rooms.
Bathrooms: 3 public.
Bed & breakfast: £12-£15 single, from £24 double.
Half board: £17-£19 daily.
Evening meal 6pm (l.o. 6pm).
Parking for 7.

🕙 🖵 🖤 🛅 ⬜ 🛏 🛪 DAP SP T

Cottage Hotel M
👑👑👑👑 APPROVED

1 Clifton Green, York, YO3 6LH
☎ (0904) 643711
Family-run hotel within 15 minutes' walking distance of the city centre, overlooking the beautiful Clifton Green.
Bedrooms: 2 single, 10 double & 5 twin, 3 family rooms.
Bathrooms: 20 private.
Bed & breakfast: £35-£45 single, £55-£65 double.
Half board: £74-£84 daily.
Evening meal 7pm (l.o. 9pm).
Parking for 18.
Credit: Access, Visa, Diners, Amex.

🕙 🛐 Ⓒ Ⓒ 🖵 🖤 Ⓥ 🎀 ⬜
⬜ 🛪 SP

Crescent Guest House
👑👑👑 APPROVED

77 Bootham, York, YO3 7DQ
☎ (0904) 623216

Continued ▶

YORK
Continued

Yorkshire family-run establishment close to the city centre and an ideal base for visiting the surrounding countryside and coast. Interesting Georgian, part-beamed building.
Bedrooms: 1 single, 4 double, 5 family rooms.
Bathrooms: 6 private, 2 public.
Bed & breakfast: £14.50-£17.50 single, £27-£40 double.
Half board: £22.50-£28.50 daily, £157.50-£199.50 weekly.
Evening meal 6pm (l.o. 10am).
Parking for 4.
Credit: Access, Visa, Diners, Amex.

Curzon Lodge and Stable Cottages ♨
COMMENDED
23 Tadcaster Rd., Dringhouses, York, YO2 2QG
☎ (0904) 703157
Delightful 17th C listed house and converted stables in grounds overlooking racecourse. All en-suite, colour TV, tea/coffee facilities. Some four poster and period brass beds. Many antiques. Large enclosed car park. Ideally situated.
Bedrooms: 1 single, 4 double & 3 twin, 2 family rooms.
Bathrooms: 10 private.
Bed & breakfast: £27-£32 single, £42-£48 double.
Parking for 16.

Disraeli's Hotel ♨
140 Acomb Rd., York, YO2 4HA
☎ (0904) 781181
In beautiful grounds and ideal for both the business person and tourist.
Bedrooms: 2 single, 5 double & 2 twin, 4 family rooms.
Bathrooms: 13 private.
Bed & breakfast: £35-£47 single, £62-£70 double.
Half board: £40-£57 daily.
Evening meal 7pm (l.o. 9.30pm).
Parking for 35.
Credit: Access, Visa, Amex.

Duke of Connaught ♨
Copmanthorpe Grange, Copmanthorpe, York, YO2 3TN
☎ Appleton Roebuck (090 484) 318
Former famous Hackney Stud farm retaining the character of the original tack room and farm buildings. Set in woods and farmland 4 miles from York.
Bedrooms: 1 single, 4 double & 2 twin, 3 family rooms.
Bathrooms: 10 private.
Bed & breakfast: £25-£27 single, £40-£45 double.
Half board: £29-£31.50 daily, £200-£220 weekly.
Evening meal 6pm (l.o. 7.30pm).
Parking for 50.

Elliotts ♨
APPROVED
Sycamore Place, Bootham Terrace, York, YO3 7DW
☎ (0904) 623333
Small, privately-run hotel with extensive restaurant facilities and emphasis on comfort and hospitality.
Bedrooms: 2 single, 9 double & 4 twin, 3 family rooms.
Bathrooms: 18 private.
Bed & breakfast: max. £25 single, £40-£50 double.
Half board: £30.50-£35.50 daily.
Lunch available.
Evening meal 6.30pm (l.o. 9.30pm).
Parking for 17.
Credit: Access, Visa, Diners, Amex.

Elmbank Hotel ♨
The Mount, York, YO2 2DD
☎ (0904) 610653 Telex 57476 Fax (0904) 627139
A building of historic interest. 10 minutes' walk from the city walls, close to the racecourse and Knavesmire.
Bedrooms: 6 single, 11 double & 25 twin, 6 family rooms.
Bathrooms: 48 private.
Bed & breakfast: £50-£60 single, £81-£95 double.
Half board: £40.50-£45 daily.
Lunch available.
Evening meal 6.30pm (l.o. 9.30pm).
Parking for 25.
Credit: Access, Visa, Diners, Amex.

Fairfax House, University of York ♨
99 Heslington Rd., York, YO1 5BJ
☎ (0904) 656593
Student residence in quiet, spacious grounds within walking distance of the city centre. Colour TV and car park. Reduced rates for children under 12.
Bedrooms: 85 single.
Bathrooms: 14 public.
Bed & breakfast: £10-£15 single.
Parking for 40.
Open July-September.

Hotel Fairmount ♨
APPROVED
230 Tadcaster Rd., Mount Vale, York, YO2 2ES
☎ (0904) 638298 Telex 557720 APO/G
Large, tastefully furnished, Victorian villa dated 1881, with open views over the racecourse and within walking distance of medieval York. All rooms have a colour TV, mini-bar, tea making facilities and hair-dryer. Reduced weekly rates available.
Bedrooms: 2 single, 4 double & 1 twin, 3 family rooms.
Bathrooms: 10 private.
Bed & breakfast: £30-£35 single, £50-£56 double.
Half board: £40-£45 daily, £252-£290 weekly.
Lunch available.
Evening meal 7pm (l.o. 9pm).
Parking for 10.
Credit: Access, Visa.

Farthings Hotel ♨
APPROVED
5 Nunthorpe Avenue, York, YO2 1PF
☎ (0904) 653545
Lovingly renovated Victorian residence with a friendly, informal atmosphere. In a quiet cul-de-sac approximately 10 minutes' walk from the city centre.
Bedrooms: 4 double & 1 twin, 2 family rooms.
Bathrooms: 3 private, 2 public.
Bed & breakfast: £26-£32 double.
Open March-November.

Four Seasons Hotel ♨
7 St. Peter's Grove, Clifton, York, YO3 6AQ
☎ (0904) 622621

Licensed Victorian house in a cul-de-sac, with own car park. English breakfast. Only 5 minutes' walk from the Minster.
Bedrooms: 2 double & 1 twin, 2 family rooms.
Bathrooms: 1 private, 1 public; 2 private showers.
Bed & breakfast: £29-£39 double.
Parking for 7.

Fourposter Lodge ♨
68-70 Heslington Rd., York, YO1 5AU
☎ (0904) 651170
Victorian villa lovingly restored and furnished, and 10 minutes' walk from historic York and all its fascinations.
Bedrooms: 1 single, 6 double & 1 twin, 2 family rooms.
Bathrooms: 7 private, 1 public; 1 private shower.
Bed & breakfast: £20-£24 single, £33-£50 double.
Half board: £25-£35 daily, £168-£238 weekly.
Evening meal 6.30pm (l.o. 11pm).
Parking for 7.
Credit: Visa.

Gleneagles Lodge Guest House
27 Nunthorpe Avenue, York, YO2 1PF
☎ (0904) 637000
In a cul-de-sac close to the station, city centre and museums. Within easy walking distance of the racecourse.
Bedrooms: 2 double & 2 twin, 2 family rooms.
Bathrooms: 2 public.
Bed & breakfast: £12-£15 single, £24-£27 double.
Parking for 2.

Grange Hotel ♨
HIGHLY COMMENDED
Clifton, York, YO3 6AA
☎ (0904) 644744 Telex 57210 Fax (0904) 612453
Classical, Regency town house hotel with all bedrooms individually decorated with antiques and English chintz. Within easy walking distance of the Minster.
Bedrooms: 3 single, 9 double & 17 twin.
Bathrooms: 29 private.
Bed & breakfast: £82-£88 single, £98-£123 double.
Half board: £118-£143 daily.
Lunch available.

Evening meal 6.30pm (l.o. 11pm).
Parking for 26.
Credit: Access, Visa, Diners, Amex.

Grange Lodge ⚑

Listed

52 Bootham Crescent, Bootham, York, YO3 7AH
☎ (0904) 621137
Attractive, tastefully furnished Victorian town house with a friendly atmosphere. Special emphasis is given to food, cleanliness and hospitality. Basic and en-suite rooms available. Evening meal by arrangement.
Bedrooms: 1 single, 3 double & 1 twin, 4 family rooms.
Bathrooms: 4 private, 1 public.
Bed & breakfast: £11.50-£13.50 single, £23 double.
Half board: £18-£23.50 daily, from £126 weekly.
Evening meal 6pm.

Greenside

124 Clifton, York, YO3 6BQ
☎ (0904) 623631
Owner-run guesthouse, fronting Clifton Green, ideally situated for all York's attractions. Offers many facilities and a homely atmosphere.
Bedrooms: 1 single, 3 double & 2 twin, 2 family rooms.
Bathrooms: 4 private, 1 public.
Bed & breakfast: from £13 single, from £24 double.
Half board: from £19.50 daily.
Evening meal 6pm (l.o. 6pm).
Parking for 6.

The Hazelwood ⚑

☺☺ APPROVED

24/25 Portland St., Gillygate, York, YO3 7EH
☎ (0904) 626548 Fax (0904) 628032
Care and comfort in a quiet city centre location off Gillygate. Close to all of York's major attractions and many restaurants.
Bedrooms: 2 single, 8 double & 5 twin.
Bathrooms: 11 private, 3 public.
Bed & breakfast: £16.20-£18 single, £28.35-£44 double.
Parking for 9.
Credit: Access, Visa.

Hedley House ⚑

☺☺ APPROVED

3-4 Bootham Terrace, York, YO3 7DH
☎ (0904) 637404
Family-run guesthouse close to the city centre. 1 ground floor bedroom. All rooms en-suite. Home-cooking, special diets catered for.
Bedrooms: 2 single, 5 double & 5 twin, 3 family rooms.
Bathrooms: 15 private.
Bed & breakfast: £20-£30 single, £36-£46 double.
Half board: £27-£32 daily.
Lunch available.
Evening meal 6.30pm (l.o. 6.30pm).
Parking for 12.
Credit: Access, Visa.

Heworth Court Hotel ⚑

☺☺☺☺ APPROVED

76-78 Heworth Green, York, YO3 7TQ
☎ (0904) 425156 Telex 57571 Fax (0904) 415290
On the A1036 east side of York. Privately-owned, family-run hotel with emphasis on food and service.
Bedrooms: 3 single, 10 double & 6 twin, 6 family rooms.
Bathrooms: 25 private.
Bed & breakfast: £36-£39.50 single, £50-£75 double.
Half board: £40.50-£44.50 daily, £238-£262.50 weekly.
Lunch available.
Evening meal 6.30pm (l.o. 9.30pm).
Parking for 25.
Credit: Access, Visa, Diners, Amex.

Heworth Guest House ⚑

126 East Parade, Heworth, York, YO3 7YG
☎ (0904) 426384
We welcome you to our family-run hotel in a quiet conservation area, with easy parking, 15 minutes' walk from the city centre. Excitingly different menus are our speciality, vegetarian and vegan dishes are always available.
Bedrooms: 3 single, 1 double & 2 twin, 1 family room.
Bathrooms: 2 public.
Bed & breakfast: £11.50-£14.50 single, £23-£29 double.

Please mention this guide when making a booking.

Evening meal 6pm (l.o. 3pm).
Parking for 2.
Credit: Access, Visa.

Hilbra Court Hotel ⚑

169 York Rd., Haxby, York, YO3 8HB
☎ York (0904) 768335
Owner-run hotel with emphasis on providing a friendly service and varied food. Near the Haxby ring-road junction, convenient for York city centre, Norther Business Parks and North York Moors.
Bedrooms: 7 single, 3 double & 2 twin.
Bathrooms: 4 private, 1 public; 8 private showers.
Bed & breakfast: £30-£34 single, £40-£44 double.
Lunch available.
Evening meal 7pm (l.o. 9.45pm).
Parking for 42.
Credit: Access, Visa, Diners, Amex.

Hillcrest Guest House ⚑

☺

110 Bishopthorpe Rd., York, YO2 1JX
☎ (0904) 653160
2 elegant Victorian terraced houses converted into a guesthouse, close to the city centre, racecourse and station. Emphasis on offering personal attention and value for money.
Bedrooms: 3 single, 4 double & 1 twin, 4 family rooms.
Bathrooms: 3 public; 1 private shower.
Bed & breakfast: from £13 single, from £26 double.
Half board: from £18.50 daily.
Evening meal 6pm.
Parking for 8.

Hobbits Hotel ⚑

☺☺ APPROVED

9 St. Peter's Grove, York, YO3 6AQ
☎ (0904) 624538
Edwardian-style small hotel in a quiet cul-de-sac, within easy walking distance of the city centre.
Bedrooms: 1 single, 2 twin, 2 family rooms.
Bathrooms: 5 private.
Bed & breakfast: £20 single, £35-£40 double.
Parking for 5.
Credit: Visa.

Holgate Bridge Hotel ⚑

☺☺☺

106-108 Holgate Rd., York, YO2 4BB
☎ (0904) 635971 & 647288
Early Victorian town houses, converted into a small friendly, family-run hotel. On the A59, within easy walking distance of the city centre. Own car park and restaurant.
Bedrooms: 2 single, 7 double & 1 twin, 4 family rooms.
Bathrooms: 11 private, 1 public.
Bed & breakfast: £18-£36 single, £35-£48 double.
Lunch available.
Evening meal 6.30pm (l.o. 9pm).
Parking for 11.
Credit: Access, Visa.

Holgate Hill Hotel ⚑

☺☺☺☺ APPROVED

124 Holgate Rd., York, YO2 4BB
☎ (0904) 653786
Family hotel where home cooking is a speciality. Close to the city centre, points of historic interest and the racecourse.
Bedrooms: 6 single, 15 double & 7 twin, 5 family rooms.
Bathrooms: 33 private, 2 public.
Bed & breakfast: from £28 single, from £46 double.
Half board: from £32.50 daily.
Lunch available.
Evening meal 7pm (l.o. 8.30pm).
Parking for 14.
Credit: Access, Visa, Diners, Amex.

The Hollies ⚑

☺☺ APPROVED

141 Fulford Rd., York, YO1 4HG
☎ (0904) 634279
Comfortable family-run guesthouse with easy access to city centre. Tea/coffee facilities, colour TV in all rooms, some en-suite. Car parking. Evening meal in low season by arrangement.
Bedrooms: 1 single, 2 double & 2 family rooms.
Bathrooms: 2 private, 1 public.
Bed & breakfast: £17-£25 single, £25-£40 double.
Parking for 5.

Holly Lodge M
🌳🌳🌳

206 Fulford Rd., York,
YO1 4DD
☎ (0904) 646005
*Listed Georgian building on
the A19, convenient for both
the north and south and within
walking distance of the city
centre. Quiet rooms and
private car park.*
Bedrooms: 2 double & 2 twin,
1 family room.
Bathrooms: 4 private,
1 public.
Bed & breakfast: from £25
single, £34-£40 double.
Half board: from £25 daily,
from £175 weekly.
Evening meal 6.30pm (l.o.
4pm).
Parking for 5.
Open January-October.
Credit: Access, Visa.

Holmwood House Hotel M
🌳🌳🌳 COMMENDED

112-114 Holgate Rd.,
YO2 4BB
☎ (0904) 626183
*Listed Victorian townhouse, 10
minutes from city walls,
redecorated and furnished with
antiques. Offers elegant
comfort in 10 attractive en-
suite rooms.*
Bedrooms: 6 double & 3 twin,
1 family room.
Bathrooms: 10 private.
Bed & breakfast: £35-£38
single, £45-£48 double.
Parking for 10.
Credit: Access, Visa.

Hudson's Hotel M
🌳🌳🌳

60 Bootham, York, YO3 7BZ
☎ (0904) 621267 Telex 57715
RE HUDSONS
*Within easy walking distance
of the city, minster and Jorvik
Viking Centre. Victorian-style
restaurant and bar.*
Bedrooms: 1 single, 13 double
& 11 twin, 3 family rooms.
Bathrooms: 28 private.
Bed & breakfast: £38-£45
single, £65-£72 double.
Half board: £49-£56 daily.
Lunch available.
Evening meal 6.30pm (l.o.
9.30pm).
Parking for 34.

Credit: Access, Visa, Diners,
Amex.

Jorvik Hotel M
🌳🌳🌳 APPROVED

Marygate, Bootham, York,
YO3 7BH
☎ (0904) 653511
*Small well-appointed family
hotel overlooking the gates of
Saint Mary's Abbey and the
Museum Gardens. Close to the
River Ouse.*
Bedrooms: 1 single, 11 double
& 8 twin, 2 family rooms.
Bathrooms: 21 private.
Bed & breakfast: £19-£25
single, £38-£42 double.
Half board: £27.50-£34.50
daily.
Evening meal 6.30pm (l.o.
8pm).
Parking for 6.
Credit: Access, Visa.

Keys House M
Listed COMMENDED

137 Fulford Rd., York,
YO1 4HG
☎ (0904) 658488
*Comfortable Edwardian house
providing spacious bedrooms
with showers and WCs. Own
key provided. Reductions for 3
or more nights.*
Bedrooms: 2 double & 2 twin,
1 family room.
Bathrooms: 5 private.
Bed & breakfast: £25.20-£30
double.
Parking for 5.

Kilima Hotel M
🌳🌳🌳

129 Holgate Rd., York,
YO2 4DE
☎ (0904) 625787 Telex 57928
CR Inter
*Extensively refurbished, 19th C
building with a fine restaurant
serving a la carte and table d'
hote.*
Bedrooms: 3 single, 6 double
& 5 twin, 1 family room.
Bathrooms: 15 private.
Bed & breakfast: £38-£42
single, £56-£60 double.
Half board: £38-£48 daily,
£239-£300 weekly.
Lunch available.
Evening meal 6.30pm (l.o.
9.30pm).
Parking for 20.
Credit: Access, Visa, Diners,
Amex.

Knavesmire Manor Hotel M
🌳🌳🌳

302 Tadcaster Rd., York,
YO2 2HE
☎ (0904) 702941 Fax (0904)
430313
*Built in 1833, this magnificent
house stands elevated,
commanding uninterrupted
views across the Knavesmire
and parkland site of York's
famous racecourse. Leisure and
health spa.*
Bedrooms: 3 single, 10 double
& 6 twin, 3 family rooms.
Bathrooms: 18 private,
1 public; 1 private shower.
Bed & breakfast: £25-£49.50
single, £43-£65 double.
Half board: £32.50-£45 daily,
£225-£300 weekly.
Evening meal 7pm (l.o.
10pm).
Parking for 27.
Credit: Access, Visa, Diners,
Amex.

Lady Anne Middleton's Hotel M
🌳🌳🌳 APPROVED

Skeldergate, York, YO1 1DS
☎ (0904) 632257 & 630456 &
(0904) 611570 Fax (0904)
613043
*Historic buildings in English
gardens in the centre of York,
near the river. Jacuzzi and
sauna.*
Bedrooms: 2 single, 18 double
& 28 twin, 2 family rooms.
Bathrooms: 50 private.
Bed & breakfast: £48 single,
£60 double.
Half board: £32.50-£42 daily,
£227.50-£294 weekly.
Evening meal 6pm (l.o. 9pm).
Parking for 50.
Credit: Access, Visa, Amex.

Linden Lodge M
🌳🌳

6 Nunthorpe Avenue,
Scarcroft Rd., York,
YO2 1PF
☎ (0904) 620107
*Victorian town house in a quiet
cul-de-sac 10 minutes' walk
from racecourse, rail station
and city centre.*
Bedrooms: 1 single, 7 double
& 2 twin, 2 family rooms.
Bathrooms: 2 private,
3 public.

Bed & breakfast: £16-£18
single, £14-£25 double.
Open January-November.
Credit: Visa.

Martin's Guest House M
Listed

5 Longfield Terrace,
Bootham, York, YO3 7DJ
☎ (0904) 634551
*Small, family-run guesthouse
with well-appointed bedrooms
and emphasis on standards.
Evening meal served on
request. 5 minutes' walk from
city centre and 10 minutes
from railway station.*
Bedrooms: 1 single, 2 double
& 1 twin, 1 family room.
Bathrooms: 1 public.
Bed & breakfast: £12-£13.50
single, £24-£27 double.
Half board: £20-£21.50 daily.
Evening meal 6pm.
Parking for 1.
Open January-November.

Middlethorpe Hall M
🌳🌳🌳🌳

Bishopthorpe Rd.,
Middlethorpe, York,
YO2 1QB
☎ (0904) 641241 & 620176
Telex 57802
CR Prestige
*A handsomely appointed and
beautifully furnished Queen
Anne country house with a fine
kitchen and carefully chosen
wine list. In 27 acres of green
gardens bordering the
racecourse, 1.5 miles from the
centre of York.*
Bedrooms: 5 single, 12 double
& 12 twin, 1 family room.
Bathrooms: 30 private.
Bed & breakfast: from £88
single, £139-£152 double.
Half board: £80-£152 daily.
Lunch available.
Evening meal 7.30pm (l.o.
9.45pm).
Parking for 70.
Credit: Access, Visa, Diners,
Amex.

Midway House Hotel
🌳🌳🌳 APPROVED

145 Fulford Rd., York,
YO1 4HG
☎ (0904) 659272
*A modernised Victorian villa
offering spacious and
comfortable bedrooms, lounge
and grounds. Near city centre
and university.*

Bedrooms: 8 double & 2 twin, 2 family rooms.
Bathrooms: 11 private, 1 public.
Bed & breakfast: £20-£40 single, £34-£46 double.
Half board: £26-£32 daily, £175-£220 weekly.
Evening meal 6pm (l.o. 8pm).
Parking for 14.
Credit: Access, Visa.

Minster View Guest House

2 Grosvenor Terrace, Bootham, York, YO3 7AG
☎ (0904) 655034
Restored Victorian residence with parkland views of the cathedral, 5 minutes' walk from the city centre. Family-run with emphasis on food.
Bedrooms: 2 single, 1 double, 6 family rooms.
Bathrooms: 4 private, 2 public.
Bed & breakfast: from £15 single, £30-£36 double.
Half board: £25-£28 daily, £175-£196 weekly.
Evening meal 6.30pm (l.o. midday).
Parking for 6.

Newington Hotel ⋒

147-157 Mount Vale, York, YO2 2DJ
☎ (0904) 625173 & 623090
Telex 65430 BURNS G
Hotel in a fine Georgian terrace, next to a large open area, within walking distance of the city centre. Large car park, solarium.
Bedrooms: 4 single, 15 double & 18 twin, 3 family rooms.
Bathrooms: 40 private, 3 public.
Bed & breakfast: £25-£38 single, £48-£58 double.
Half board: £33-£36 daily, £231-£245 weekly.
Lunch available.
Evening meal 6pm (l.o. 9.15pm).
Parking for 32.
Credit: Access, Visa, Diners, Amex.

Novotel York ⋒

Fishergate, York, YO1 4AD
☎ (0904) 611660 Telex 57556
Fax (0904) 610925
ⓒ Novotel

Newly-built hotel on the riverside with terrace and indoor pool, 5 minutes' walk from the city centre. Special packages available for children sharing parents' room.
Bedrooms: 124 family rooms.
Bathrooms: 124 private.
Half board: £45-£50 daily.
Lunch available.
Evening meal 6pm (l.o. 11.50pm).
Parking for 150.
Credit: Access, Visa, Diners, Amex.

4 Nunthorpe Drive

Bishopthorpe Rd., York, YO2 1DY
☎ (0904) 653171
Semi-detached house with a large lounge and a garden and patio. 10 minutes from the city centre.
Bedrooms: 1 single, 2 double.
Bathrooms: 1 private, 1 public.
Bed & breakfast: from £11 single, £24-£26 double.
Half board: from £11 daily.
Parking for 3.

The Old Vic Hotel

2 Wenlock Terrace, York, YO1 4DU
☎ (0904) 637888
Family-run guesthouse retaining many original features from the Victorian era. All our guests who arrive leave as friends.
Bedrooms: 2 single, 4 double & 1 twin, 3 family rooms.
Bathrooms: 3 private, 3 public.
Bed & breakfast: £13-£15 single, £26-£40 double.
Evening meal 6pm.
Parking for 3.

Orchard Court Hotel ⋒

4 St. Peter's Grove, Bootham, York, YO3 6AQ
☎ (0904) 653964
Small, Victorian hotel in a quiet location within easy walking distance of all places of interest.
Bedrooms: 3 single, 4 double & 2 twin, 2 family rooms.
Bathrooms: 8 private, 1 public.
Bed & breakfast: £19-£29 single, £40-£56 double.
Half board: £30-£40 daily.
Lunch available.

Evening meal 6pm (l.o. 8pm).
Parking for 10.
Credit: Access, Visa.

Pauleda House Hotel ⋒

123 Clifton, York, YO3 6BL
☎ (0904) 634745
Family-run hotel with well-decorated, spacious rooms. Less than 1 mile from the city centre on the A19 north. Managed by the owners.
Bedrooms: 1 single, 5 double & 2 twin.
Bathrooms: 8 private.
Bed & breakfast: £35-£45 double.
Half board: £25-£32 daily.
Evening meal 6.30pm (l.o. midday).
Parking for 8.
Credit: Access, Visa, Diners, Amex.

Priory Hotel ⋒

126-128 Fulford Rd., York, YO1 4BE
☎ (0904) 625280
A family hotel in a residential area with an adjacent riverside walk to the city centre.
Bedrooms: 1 single, 9 double & 6 twin, 4 family rooms.
Bathrooms: 20 private.
Bed & breakfast: £20-£25 single, £40-£50 double.
Evening meal 6.30pm (l.o. 9.30pm).
Parking for 24.
Credit: Access, Visa, Diners, Amex.

Regency House ⋒

7 South Parade, Blossom St., York, YO2 2BA
☎ (0904) 633053
A fine example of Georgian architecture set on a private cobbled road, 5 minutes' walk from the station and 3 minutes from the Bar Walls.
Bedrooms: 1 single, 3 double & 2 twin, 1 family room.
Bathrooms: 2 private, 2 public; 2 private showers.
Bed & breakfast: £13-£15 single, £27-£33 double.
Parking for 3.
Open January-November.

Riverside Walk Hotel ⋒
APPROVED

9 Earlsborough Terrace, Marygate, York, YO3 7BQ
☎ (0904) 620769 & 646249

Family-run hotel, a 450-yard riverside walk from the city centre. Close to all amenities and the railway station.
Bedrooms: 2 single, 4 double & 2 twin, 2 family rooms.
Bathrooms: 10 private.
Bed & breakfast: £20-£26 single, £36-£44 double.
Half board: £26-£32 daily.
Lunch available.
Evening meal 7pm (l.o. 1pm).
Parking for 14.
Credit: Access, Visa.

Royal York Hotel ⋒

Station Rd., York, YO2 2AA
☎ (0904) 653681
Telex 57912 Fax (0904) 623503
A grand Victorian building with all the comforts of a modern hotel. All major attractions within short walking distance.
Bedrooms: 20 single, 100 double, 5 family rooms.
Bathrooms: 113 private, 6 public.
Bed & breakfast: £70-£90 single, £95-£190 double.
Half board: £50-£65 daily.
Lunch available.
Evening meal 6.30pm (l.o. 9.45pm).
Parking for 100.
Credit: Access, Visa, C.Bl., Diners, Amex.

Russells Hotel ⋒

Monkbar Court, Monkbar, York, YO3 7PF
☎ (0904) 638086
32 attractive bedrooms, situated only 200 yards from the minster and all tourist attractions. Jacuzzi and four-poster rooms available.
Bedrooms: 26 double & 6 twin.
Bathrooms: 32 private.
Bed & breakfast: £39.50-£49.50 single, £69.50-£79.50 double.
Lunch available.
Evening meal (l.o. 10pm).
Parking for 30.
Credit: Access, Visa, C.Bl., Diners, Amex.

St. Georges House Hotel ⋒

6 St. George's Place, Tadcaster Rd., York, YO2 2DR
☎ (0904) 625056
Continued ▶

YORKSHIRE & HUMBERSIDE

Small family-run hotel in a quiet cul-de-sac near the racecourse and convenient for the city centre. Good car parking facilities.
Bedrooms: 1 single, 4 double & 4 twin, 3 family rooms.
Bathrooms: 7 private, 1 public; 1 private shower.
Bed & breakfast: £16-£20 single, £30-£38 double.
Half board: £22-£26 daily, £140-£175 weekly.
Evening meal 6pm.
Parking for 9.
Open February-December.
Credit: Access, Visa.

Savages Hotel M
👑👑👑👑 APPROVED
15 St. Peter's Grove, Clifton, York, YO3 6AQ
☎ (0904) 610818 Fax (0904) 627729
Detached house and garden in a quiet cul-de-sac close to the city centre and historic attractions. Solarium and mini-gymnasium.
Bedrooms: 3 single, 6 double & 7 twin, 2 family rooms.
Bathrooms: 18 private.
Bed & breakfast: £32-£36 single, £52-£64 double.
Half board: £36.50-£47.50 daily, £255-£332.50 weekly.
Lunch available.
Evening meal 6pm (l.o. 9pm).
Parking for 14.
Credit: Access, Visa, Diners, Amex.

Scarcroft Hotel M
👑👑 COMMENDED
61 Wentworth Rd., York, YO2 1DG
☎ (0904) 633386
Small family-run traditional Tudor-style licensed hotel. Overlooking Knavesmire, racecourse and 10 minutes' walk from city centre. Ample parking.
Bedrooms: 2 single, 3 double, 2 family rooms.
Bathrooms: 7 private.
Bed & breakfast: £20-£24 single, £40-£45 double.
Evening meal 6.30pm (l.o. 9pm).
Credit: Access, Visa.

Sheppard Hotel M
👑👑👑
63 The Mount, York, YO2 2AX
☎ (0904) 620500 Telex 57950
Privately owned, offering good food and service. Close to railway station and York's amenities.
Bedrooms: 3 single, 10 double & 5 twin, 3 family rooms.
Bathrooms: 16 private; 4 private showers.
Bed & breakfast: £28-£38 single, £42-£54 double.
Half board: £35-£45 daily, £210-£293 weekly.
Lunch available.
Evening meal 7pm (l.o. 9.30pm).
Parking for 16.
Credit: Access, Visa.

Shoulder of Mutton
64 Heworth Green, York, YO3 7TQ
☎ (0904) 424793
Victorian house built in 1898, with beautiful carved ceilings, award winning garden. Comfortable with a family atmosphere.
Bedrooms: 4 single, 2 double & 1 twin, 1 family room.
Bathrooms: 2 public.
Bed & breakfast: max. £14 single, max. £28 double.
Lunch available.
Parking for 60.
Credit: Access, Visa.

Skeldergate House Hotel M
👑👑👑
56 Skeldergate, York, YO1 1DS
☎ (0904) 635521
Central Georgian town house, originally built by the internationally known John Carr (former Lord Mayor of York) and recently restored by the resident owners.
Bedrooms: 2 single, 3 double & 1 twin, 2 family rooms.
Bathrooms: 8 private.
Bed & breakfast: £23-£48 single, £48-£50 double.
Half board: £33.50-£58.50 daily.
Evening meal 6pm (l.o. 7pm).
Parking for 6.
Credit: Access, Visa.

Staymor Guest House M
👑👑
2 Southlands Rd., York, YO2 1NP
☎ (0904) 626935

Hospitality, comfort and food at its best in a traditional guesthouse, quietly situated just 10 minutes' walk from the city centre. Fire certificate.
Bedrooms: 1 single, 1 double & 1 twin, 3 family rooms.
Bathrooms: 4 private, 1 public.
Bed & breakfast: £12-£14 single, £23-£31 double.
Half board: £18-£22.50 daily.
Evening meal 6pm (l.o. 9.30am).

Swallow Chase Hotel M
👑👑👑👑👑
Tadcaster Rd., Dringhouses, York, YO2 2QQ
☎ (0904) 701000 Telex 57582
CR Swallow
Set on the edge of York's beautiful racecourse on the Knavesmire. A traditional hotel with the extensive range of facilities of a Swallow Leisure Club, attractive bedrooms and a restaurant overlooking the hotel grounds.
Bedrooms: 8 single, 37 double & 61 twin, 10 family rooms.
Bathrooms: 116 private.
Bed & breakfast: from £72 single, from £92 double.
Lunch available.
Evening meal 7pm (l.o. 10pm).
Parking for 200.
Credit: Access, Visa, Diners, Amex.

Sycamore Hotel
Listed APPROVED
19 Sycamore Place, Bootham, York, YO3 7DW
☎ (0904) 624712
Family-owned and run hotel in a quiet cul-de-sac. Close to the river, city centre, Minster and museums.
Bedrooms: 5 double, 1 family room.
Bathrooms: 3 private, 1 public.
Bed & breakfast: £26-£34 double.
Parking for 3.

Tower Guest House
👑👑👑
2 Feversham Crescent, Wigginton Rd., York, YO3 7HQ
☎ (0904) 655571/635924
Within easy walking distance of York Minster and the city centre. All en-suite, colour satellite TV and car park.
Bedrooms: 1 double & 1 twin, 4 family rooms.

Bathrooms: 6 private.
Bed & breakfast: £30-£38 double.
Parking for 6.
Open February-December.
Credit: Access, Visa.

Tree Tops
Listed
21 St. Mary's, Bootham, York, YO3 7DD
☎ (0904) 658053
Elegant Victorian guesthouse, 5 minutes from the Minster, river and city centre.
Bathrooms on all floors.
Bedrooms: 1 single, 3 double & 2 twin, 1 family room.
Bathrooms: 3 public.
Bed & breakfast: £15-£17.50 single, £25-£34 double.
Parking for 5.

Victoria Villa
Listed
72 Heslington Rd., York, YO1 5AU
☎ (0904) 631647
Victorian town house, close to city centre, offering clean and friendly accommodation and a good full English breakfast.
Bedrooms: 1 single, 2 double & 1 twin, 2 family rooms.
Bathrooms: 2 public.
Bed & breakfast: £12-£15 single, £20-£24 double.
Parking for 2.

Viking Hotel M
👑👑👑👑
North St., York, YO1 1JF
☎ (0904) 659822 Telex 57937
CR Queens Moat Houses
188-bedroomed hotel beautifully situated on the riverside, within the old stone walls of York.
Bedrooms: 5 single, 45 double & 128 twin, 10 family rooms.
Bathrooms: 188 private.
Bed & breakfast: £68-£78 single, £89-£99 double.
Half board: £50-£65 daily.
Lunch available.
Evening meal 7pm (l.o. 10pm).
Parking for 78.
Credit: Access, Visa, C.Bl., Diners, Amex.

> **We advise you to confirm your booking in writing.**

Westpark M
5 Acomb Rd., York,
YO2 4EP
☎ (0904) 798449
*Georgian house, built 1804, in
one fifth of an acre of walled
gardens, within walking
distance of city centre.*
Bedrooms: 2 single, 3 double,
2 family rooms.
Bathrooms: 3 private,
2 public.
Bed & breakfast: £14-£18
single, £24-£36 double.
Parking for 4.

🛏 ♨ ☐ ♦ Ⓤ 🅹 ▥ ▲ 🐾
⒟ 🕊 SP 🛏

**Wold View House
Hotel M**
173-175 Haxby Rd., York,
YO3 7JL
☎ (0904) 632061
*Family-run hotel with a
restaurant and full licence. All
rooms en-suite. Ample parking.
Close to all places of interest.*
Bedrooms: 1 single, 5 double
& 2 twin, 2 family rooms.
Bathrooms: 10 private.
Bed & breakfast: £17.50-
£18.50 single, £35-£37 double.
Half board: £26.25-£27.25
daily, £115.50-£122.50
weekly.

Lunch available.
Evening meal 6pm (l.o. 6pm).
Parking for 4.

🛏 Ⓡ ☐ ♦ 🅹 Ⓥ 🅯 TV ▥
▲ 🕊 🐾 ⒟ 🕊 SP Ⓣ

York Pavilion Hotel M
🏵🏵🏵🏵 COMMENDED
45 Main St., Fulford, York,
YO1 4PJ
☎ (0904) 622099
*Georgian country house 1.5
miles from the city centre. 21
bedrooms of individual
character, en-suite with all
facilities. Private car park.*
Bedrooms: 1 single, 9 double
& 11 twin.
Bathrooms: 21 private.
Bed & breakfast: from £63.50
single, from £83 double.
Lunch available.
Evening meal 6.30pm (l.o.
9.30pm).
Parking for 45.
Credit: Access, Visa, Diners,
Amex.

🛏 ♨ ℄ Ⓡ ☐ ♦ 🅹 Ⓥ 🅯
▥ ▲ 🕊 ♿ ᛈ ❄ 🐾 ⒟ 🕊
SP 🛏

Key to symbols

Information about many of the services
and facilities at establishments listed in
this guide is given in the form of
symbols. The key to these symbols is
inside the back cover flap. You may
find it helpful to keep the flap open
when referring to the entry listings.

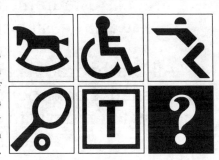

Hector Breeze

Check the maps

The place you wish to visit may not
have accommodation entirely suited
to your needs, but there could be
somewhere ideal quite close by. Check
the colour maps towards the end of
this guide to identify nearby towns
and villages with accommodation
listed in the guide, and then use the
town index to find page numbers.

The Acer

**52 Scarcroft Hill, The Mount, York
YO2 1DE. ☎(0904) 653839/628046
Fax: (0904) 640421**

♛♛♛ RAC   AA   LES ROUTIERS

Highly Recommended small private hotel
where the customer is most important.
Fully refurbished to the highest standard of
comfort & decor.

AMBASSADOR
HOTEL · YORK

123-125, The Mount, York YO2 2DA. ☎ (0904) 641316.

Built in 1842, the Ambassador is an elegant Georgian haven
of peace, ten easy minutes walk from York city centre.

Set in over 1.5 acres of mature gardens, the twenty
beautifully appointed bedrooms all have en suite facilities,
colour television, radio, direct dial telephones and hospitality
trays.

The Washington restaurant offers deliciously creative Table
d'hote or A La Carte lunches and dinners.

Refreshments are served in the gracious and relaxing lounge
which boasts an open marble fireplace.

We can also offer ample free car parking within the hotel
grounds.

We very much look forward to affording you 'York's
Warmest Welcome'.

Bradley Court Hotel

**7-9 Filey Road, Scarborough, YO11 2SE
Tel: (0723) 360476 Fax: (0723) 376661.**

AA & RAC ★★   ETB ♛♛♛ COMMENDED

40 bedrooms all en-suite, tea/coffee making facilities, lift.
Large private car park, colour TV, baby listening.

The Park Hotel

**6 Oak Avenue, Manningham, Bradford BD8 7AQ
☎(0274) 546262**

20 en-suite bedrooms, each room has
colour TV, and tea making facilities.
Large function room ideal for: Exhibitions –
Conferences – Wedding Parties – Receptions.
Ample parking space – set in beautiful
gardens.

Rudstone Walk Farm

South Cave, Brough, E. Yorkshire HU15 2AH.
☎ (0430) 422230

Highly Commended by Les Routier

Stay with us in our luxurious architect designed cottages (ETB 4 Key up to Highly Commended) or our beautiful 400 year old farmhouse (ETB Listed Commended), mentioned in the Domesday Book. Unrivalled views over Vale of York. Excellent location for York, Beverley coast and Moors. Licenced for drinks. Farmhouse cooking.
Brochure from Mrs Pauline Greenwood.

Sandbeck Hotel

ETB 👑👑   RAC Acclaimed   We accept Visa Access E/C Amex

Central location – overlooking the sea within easy walking distance for the beach, harbour, gardens and shops. All rooms with bath and shower or shower en-suite. Colour TV and tea/coffee making facilities.
Elegant cocktail bar, comfortable lounge and spacious dining room/restaurant. Discounts for 4 or more nights. Open weekends only November to Easter. Fully open Easter to the end of October. All major credit cards accepted. Proprietor: J R Todd.
West Cliff, Whitby, N. Yorkshire YO21 2CL.   ☎ (0947) 604012/602699.

The Studley Hotel

Swan Road, Harrogate HG1 2SE.
Tel: (0423) 560425 Fax: (0423) 530967 Telex: 57506 STUDLY G.

AA ★★★

"The Studley" is one of the most attractively situated hotels in Harrogate.
Adjacent to the beautiful valley gardens and within easy walking distance of the town centre and conference facilities.
The hotel has 36 bedrooms with en-suite bathrooms and all rooms have direct dial telephone, colour TV, tea and coffee making facilities, hair dryer and trouser press.
There are 2 small executive suites and a small private room for use as a meeting/dining room for up to 16 people.
The French Restaurant, established since 1975, has built up a reputation for good food and friendly service. A feature of the restaurant is the genuine Charcoal Grill, on which certain dishes are cooked, from the extensive menu.

The Talbot Hotel

High Street, Pateley Bridge, Harrogate
This small family run Hotel is perfectly situated for exploring the Dales.
Excellent home cooking & personal attention of Donald & Sheila Jones.
Most bedrooms with bathroom ensuite/Tea making facilities/Residential licence/Residents lounge with Colour TV. 👑👑
Bed & Breakfast from £14.00   COMMENDED
Bargain weekend breaks £45.00 FEB/MAR/APRIL/OCT   *A warm welcome awaits*   **Tel: 0423 711597**

Heart of England

The Heart of England seems the ideal place to base yourself for a national tour — but its beauty and variety are such that you're not likely to get very far!

The 3-spired Lichfield Cathedral

⟫ Stretching from the blue hills of the Welsh border to the dramatic outcrops of the Peak District and down to the gentler Cotswolds in the south, it contains much of England's most celebrated scenery.

⟫ At the hub — of everything — is Birmingham, cosmopolitan and great, full of entertainment, sophistication and friendliness. North, towards the Peak District National Park, you can visit many factories of the Potteries, as well as the world-famous Alton Towers, ornate Lichfield Cathedral, Cannock Chase, and much more. Lovely Shropshire to the west boasts historic Ironbridge and fine old towns, plus the dreamy River Severn keeping company along the way with the Severn Valley Steam Railway.

⟫ South-west and you're in the wonderful world of black and white towns and villages. Here, the Malvern Hills shimmer blue, the River Wye wanders through its romantic valley past the Royal Forest of Dean, and Worcester vies with Hereford for the title of best, loveliest, whatever-you-will — but only you can decide.

⟫ Then there are the cherished Cotswolds with hamlets of harvest-coloured stone, lovely Roman Gloucester and elegant Regency Cheltenham Spa. The famous homeland of the Bard of Avon to the east includes Coventry with its inspiring cathedral, and the old castles of Kenilworth

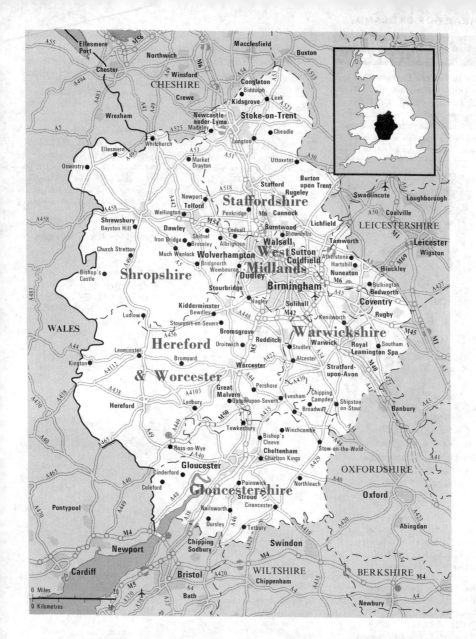

and Warwick to complement Stratford itself.

>> Far more than scenery excels here in the big Heart of England. Offering everything from museums to hang-gliding, plus that famous big-hearted welcome, there's absolutely no reason to holiday anywhere else!

>> Please refer to the colour maps at the back of this guide for all places with accommodation listings.

Where to go, what to see

Alton Towers Leisure Park
Alton, Staffordshire ST10 4DB
☎ Oakamoor (0538) 702200
*Europe's premier leisure park
with more than 100 attractions,
set in the magnificent former
estate of the Earls of Shrewsbury.*

Birmingham Botanical Gardens
Westbourne Road, Edgbaston,
Birmingham, West Midlands
B15 3TR
☎ 021-454 1860
*15 acres of ornamental gardens
and glasshouses. Tropical
plants of botanical interest,
aviaries with exotic birds.
Children's play area.*

The Patrick Collection
180 Lifford Lane, Birmingham,
West Midlands B30 3NT
☎ 021-459 9111
*Three exhibition halls covering
cars from 1904 to 1990 in
period settings. Terraced garden
with water features.*

Charlecote Park
Charlecote, Wellesbourne,
Warwickshire CV35 9ER
☎ Stratford-upon-Avon (0789)
840277

*Home of Lucy family since
1247, present house built 1550.
Park, landscaped by 'Capability'
Brown, supports herd of red and
fallow deer. Tudor gatehouse.*

Dean Heritage Centre
Camp Mill, Soudley, Cinderford,
Gloucestershire GL14 7UG
☎ Dean (0594) 22170
*Museum displays housed in old
flour mill. Water wheel, beam
engine, Forest of Dean history,
smallholding. Nature trails.*

Black Country Museum
Tipton Road, Dudley, West
Midlands DY1 4SQ
☎ 021-557 9643
*Open-air museum on 26-acre
site, with many rescued buildings
including shops, chapel and
chainmaker's house. Canal,
coalmine and electric tramway.*

Stuart Crystal
Redhouse Glassworks,
Wordsley, Stourbridge, West
Midlands DY8 4AA
☎ Stourbridge (0384) 71161
*Factory tours showing all aspects
of the production of world-
famous Stuart Crystal from
glassblowing and annealing to
the final process of cutting and
decorating. Redhouse Cone and
museum, factory shop.*

Nature in Art
Wallsworth Hall, Twigworth,
Gloucestershire GL2 9PA
☎ Gloucester (0452) 731422
*Nature brought to life in
masterpieces of wildlife art, in
all media and from any period.
Nature garden and pond, gallery
shop, coffee shop, play area and
Kids' Corner.*

Ironbridge Gorge Museum
Ironbridge, Nr. Telford,
Shropshire TF8 7AW
☎ Ironbridge (095 245) 3522
*World's first cast-iron bridge,
Museum of the River, Coalport
China, Jack Geld Tile Museum,
Coalbrookdale Museum, Blists
Hill Open-Air Museum, Rosehill
House.*

Lichfield Cathedral
Lichfield, Staffordshire
WS13 7LD
☎ Lichfield (0543) 250300

Alton Towers — Europe's premier leisure park

The only English cathedral with three spires. The exterior is a fine example of Early English and Decorated styles. Especially noteworthy are the Flemish glass windows.

Packwood House
Packwood, Nr. Hockley Heath, West Midlands B94 6AT
☎ Lapworth (056 43) 2024
Mainly built about 1560, timber-framed house with a wealth of tapestries and furniture. Gardens include Carolean formal garden and notable yew garden.

Batsford Arboretum
Batsford, Moreton-in-Marsh, Gloucestershire GL56 9QF
☎ Moreton-in-Marsh (0608) 50722
50-acre arboretum containing one of the largest private collections of rare trees in the country, most spectacular in spring and autumn. Garden centre and nursery.

Aerospace Museum
RAF Cosford, Shifnal, West Midlands TF11 8UP
☎ Albrighton (090 722) 4872/4112
One of the largest collections of aircraft, rockets, missiles and aero engines in Europe. Display includes British, American, Japanese and German warplanes.

Watch pots being thrown at the Jinney Ring Craft Centre

National Waterways Museum
Llanthony Warehouse, Gloucester Docks, Gloucestershire GL1 2EH
☎ Gloucester (0452) 307009
Three floors of dockside warehouse with lively displays telling the story of Britain's canals. Outside craft area with demonstration. Shop.

West Midlands Safari and Leisure Park
Spring Grove, Bewdley, Worcestershire DY12 1LF
☎ Bewdley (0299) 402114
Set in 195 acres of countryside, animal reserves, pets corner. Leisure area with pirate ship, amusement rides, train, canoes, pedal boats. Sealion show.

Royal Worcester Ltd
Severn Street, Worcester, Worcestershire
☎ Worcester (0905) 23221
The largest and most comprehensive collection of Worcester Porcelain in the world, covering the period from start of manufacture in 1751 to present day.

Warwick Castle
Warwick, Warwickshire CV34 4QU
☎ Warwick (0926) 495421
State rooms, armoury, dungeon, torture chamber, clock tower and barbican, towers, in 60 acres of grounds.

Jinney Ring Craft Centre
Hanbury, Bromsgrove, Worcestershire B60 4BU
☎ Hanbury (052 784) 272
Old farm buildings converted to craft centre. Craftsmen can be seen working on woodcarving, pottery, jewellery, stained glass, leather, fashion design, crystal glass. Wildlife artist. Shop and gallery.

Royal Shakespeare Company
Stratford-upon-Avon, Warwickshire
☎ Stratford-upon-Avon (0789) 296655
The RSC has three theatres in Stratford-upon-Avon: the Royal Shakespeare Theatre, Swan Theatre and the Other Place.

Make a date for...

Horse racing – Cheltenham Gold Cup Meeting
Cheltenham Racecourse, Prestbury, Cheltenham, Gloucestershire
12 – 14 March

Malvern Festival and Fringe
Various venues, Malvern, Hereford & Worcester
19 May – 1 June

Shrewsbury International Music Festival
Various venues, Shrewsbury, Shropshire
26 June – 3 July

Royal International Agricultural Show
National Agricultural Centre, Stoneleigh, Kenilworth, Warwickshire
1 – 4 July

Lichfield Festival and Fringe
Various venues, Lichfield, Staffordshire
5 – 14 July

Birmingham International Jazz Festival
Various venues, Birmingham, West Midlands
5 – 14 July

Cheltenham International Festival of Music
Various venues, Cheltenham, Gloucestershire
6 – 21 July

Town and Country Festival
National Agricultural Centre, Stoneleigh, Kenilworth, Warwickshire
24 – 26 August

Find out more

Further information about holidays and attractions in the Heart of England region is available from:
Heart of England Tourist Board, Woodside, Larkhill, Worcester WR5 2EQ. ☎ (0905) 763436.

These publications are available free from the Heart of England Tourist Board:
Bed & Breakfast Touring Map
Shakespeare's Country, Cotswolds and Heart of England

Short Breaks Guides, including:
The Cotswolds
Peak and Potteries
The Marches (where England and Wales meet)

Area accommodation guides (Shropshire, Hereford & Worcester, Staffordshire, The Black Country and Birmingham, Gloucestershire and Warwickshire)

Events List

Fact Sheets

Also available are:
Places to Visit in the Heart of England £1.95
Heart of England map £1.95

Follow the sign

It leads to over 560 Tourist Information Centres throughout England offering friendly help with accommodation and holiday ideas as well as suggestions of places to visit and things to do.

In your home town there may be a centre which can help you before you set out. Details of the locations of Tourist Information Centres are available from the English Tourist Board, Thames Tower, Black's Road, London W6 9EL, or from England's Regional Tourist Boards.

Places to stay

>> Accommodation entries in this regional section are listed in alphabetical order of place name, and then in alphabetical order of establishment.

>> The map references refer to the colour maps towards the end of the guide. The first figure is the map number; the letter and figure which follow indicate the grid reference on the map.

>> The symbols at the end of each accommodation entry give information about services and facilities. A 'key' to these symbols is inside the back cover flap, which can be kept open for easy reference.

ABBERLEY

Hereford & Worcester
Map ref 4A3

5m SW. Stourport-on-Severn
Village with some interesting buildings which include a pre-Reformation rectory and a Gothic clock tower with 20 bells. At Great Witley nearby is a magnificent 18th C church with rich plasterwork, paintings and carving and the ruined gardens of Witley Court.

The Elms Hotel M
☺☺☺☺☺ COMMENDED
Abberley, Worcester, Worcestershire WR6 6AT
☎ Great Witley
(0299) 896666 Telex 337105
CR Queens Moat Houses
Queen Anne country house set in 10 acres of parkland and gardens. Croquet, putting and tennis court. Open log fires, four-poster bed. Central for touring the Cotswolds, Wales and the Heart of England.
Bedrooms: 2 single, 14 double & 9 twin.
Bathrooms: 25 private.
Bed & breakfast: from £80 single, £95-£105 double.
Lunch available.
Evening meal 7.30pm (l.o. 9.30pm).
Parking for 62.
Credit: Access, Visa, Diners, Amex.

ACOCKS GREEN

W. Midlands
Map ref 4B3

4m SE. Birmingham

The Garden Croft
☺☺☺
2 Sherbourne Drive, Acocks Green, Birmingham
☎ 021-706 5557
Attractive small English country garden hotel. All modern amenities with stylish comfort, offering a high standard of food and service.
Bedrooms: 4 twin.
Bathrooms: 2 private, 2 public.
Bed & breakfast: £21-£34.80 single, £41.80-£46 double.
Half board: £28-£44.80 daily.
Lunch available.
Evening meal 8pm (l.o. 9pm).
Parking for 8.

> Half board prices shown are per person but in some cases may be based on double/twin occupancy.

> The symbols are explained on the flap inside the back cover.

ALCESTER

Warwickshire
Map ref 2B1

7m W. Stratford-upon-Avon
Town has Roman origins and many old buildings around the High Street. It is close to Ragley Hall, the 18th C Palladian mansion with its magnificent baroque Great Hall.

Icknield House M
☺☺
54 Birmingham Rd., Alcester, B49 5EG
☎ (0789) 763287 & 763681
Comfortable, well-furnished Victorian house of character, on the main A435. Close to Warwick and the Cotswolds. 10 minutes from Stratford-upon-Avon. Excellent touring centre.
Bedrooms: 2 single, 2 double & 2 twin.
Bathrooms: 2 public; 3 private showers.
Bed & breakfast: £16-£18 single, £29.50-£32 double.
Half board: £21.50-£26.50 daily, £148.75-£171.50 weekly.
Evening meal 6.30pm (l.o. 7.30pm).
Parking for 8.

ALREWAS

Staffordshire
Map ref 4B3

5m NE. Lichfield
Delightful village of black and white cottages, past which the willow-fringed Trent runs. The Trent and Mersey Canal enhances the scene and Fradley Junction, 1 mile away, is one of the most charming inland waterway locations in the country.

George and Dragon/Claymar Hotel M
☺☺☺☺ APPROVED
Main St., Alrewas, Burton upon Trent, DE13 7AE
☎ Burton upon Trent
(0283) 790202 &
(0283) 791281 Fax
(0283) 791465
Homely inn and Rafters Restaurant in Claymar Hotel. Bar food also available. Sunday lunches available in Rafters.
Bedrooms: 6 single, 3 double & 4 twin, 5 family rooms.
Bathrooms: 18 private.
Bed & breakfast: £34 single, £44 double.
Lunch available.
Evening meal 7.30pm (l.o. 10pm).
Parking for 50.
Credit: Access, Visa.

> Map references apply to the colour maps towards the end of this guide.

ALTON

Staffordshire
Map ref 4B2

4m E. Cheadle
Alton Castle, an impressive 19th C building now a school, dominates the village which is set in spectacular scenery. Nearby is Alton Towers, a romantic 19th C ruin with innumerable tourist attractions in its 800 acres of magnificent gardens.

The Admiral Jervis Inn and Restaurant M
🛏🛏🛏

Mill Rd., Oakamoor, Stoke-on-Trent, ST10 3AG
☎ (0538) 702187
Old riverside restaurant and inn with chef/proprietor. Peaceful and picturesque setting. 2 miles from Alton Towers and 9 miles from the Potteries.
Bedrooms: 1 double & 1 twin, 4 family rooms.
Bathrooms: 6 private.
Bed & breakfast: from £25 single, from £39 double.
Evening meal 7.30pm (l.o. 9.30pm).
Parking for 10.
Credit: Access, Visa, Amex.
🛇 🖳 🖵 🌢 🗄 Ⓥ 🛏 🛆
🍴 🛠 🏠 🏤

Bridge House Hotel M
🛏🛏 COMMENDED

Station Road, Alton, Stoke-on-Trent, ST10 4BX
☎ Oakamoor (0538) 702338
17th C cottage-style accommodation nestled in Churnet Valley, half a mile from Alton Towers. High standards of cuisine, a la carte and children's menu.
Bedrooms: 4 double.
Bathrooms: 1 private, 2 public; 2 private showers.
Bed & breakfast: £25-£30 single, £30-£45 double.
Lunch available.
Evening meal 7pm (l.o. 10pm).
Parking for 30.
Credit: Access, Visa.
🛇 🖳 🖵 🗄 Ⓥ 🖳 🛏 📺 🛆
🛆 🍴 🖳 Ⓤ 🎵 📍 ✳ 🛠
🏠 DAP 🐾 SP 🏤

Bulls Head Inn M
🛏🛏 APPROVED

High St., Alton, Stoke-on-Trent, ST10 4AQ
☎ Oakamoor (0538) 702307

In the village of Alton close to Alton Towers. An 18th C inn with real ale and home cooking.
Bedrooms: 3 double & 1 twin, 2 family rooms.
Bathrooms: 3 private, 1 public; 3 private showers.
Bed & breakfast: £30-£40 single, £35-£50 double.
Lunch available.
Evening meal 7pm (l.o. 10pm).
Parking for 10.
Credit: Access, Visa.
🛇 🖳 🖵 🌢 🗄 Ⓥ 🛏 🛆
🛠 🏠 🏤

Wild Duck Inn
Listed

New Rd., Alton, Stoke-on-Trent, ST10 4AF
☎ Oakamoor (0538) 702218
A large country inn, within view of Alton Towers Leisure Park. Comfortable bedrooms and a pleasant restaurant and bar.
Bedrooms: 7 family rooms.
Bathrooms: 1 private, 1 public.
Bed & breakfast: £25-£64 double.
Evening meal 7pm (l.o. 9pm).
Parking for 50.
Open March-November.
Credit: Access, Visa.
🛇 🖵 🌢 🖳 📺 🛆 🐾 🛠 🖳
🏤

ALVECHURCH

Hereford & Worcester
Map ref 4B3

3m N. Redditch
Close to industrial Redditch, Alvechurch has grown rapidly from village to town in recent years, but retains much of its old world charm. A centre for canal boat hire.

Westmead Hotel & Restaurant M
🛏🛏🛏🛏🛏

Redditch Rd., Hopwood, Alvechurch, Birmingham, W Midlands B48 7AL
☎ 021-445 1202 Telex 335956 Fax 021-445 6163
Ⓖ Lansbury
The hotel is situated off Junction 2 of the M42. Recently opened and within easy reach of Birmingham, Redditch and the National Exhibition Centre.
Bedrooms: 4 single, 18 double & 38 twin.
Bathrooms: 60 private.
Bed & breakfast: £22-£74 single, £44-£87 double.
Half board: from £33 daily.
Lunch available.

Evening meal 7pm (l.o. 10pm).
Parking for 250.
Credit: Access, Visa, Diners, Amex.
🛇 🖳 🖵 🌢 ☎ Ⓞ 🖵 🗄 🛆 Ⓥ
⌦ 🖵 📺 ⓝ 📶 🛆 🍴 🛠 🐾
SP Ⓣ

AMPNEY CRUCIS

Gloucestershire
Map ref 2B1

3m E. Cirencester
This is one of the 4 Ampney villages and is situated in pleasant countryside. Its church has Saxon features. The very attractive gardens at nearby Barnsley House are open Monday to Friday 10am - 6pm and offer plants for sale.

Crown of Crucis
🛏🛏🛏🛏

Ampney Crucis, Cirencester, GL7 5RS
☎ Cirencester (0285) 851806 Fax (0285) 851 735
Privately owned Cotswold hotel, 2.5 miles east of Cirencester on A417. 16th C building with bar and restaurant. 26 new en-suite bedrooms.
Bedrooms: 8 double & 16 twin, 2 family rooms.
Bathrooms: 26 private.
Bed & breakfast: £22-£45 single, £44-£58 double.
Half board: £32.50-£55.50 daily.
Lunch available.
Evening meal 6pm (l.o. 10pm).
Parking for 80.
Credit: Access, Visa, Amex.
🛇 🖳 🖵 🌢 🗄 Ⓥ 🛏 🛆
🛆 🍴 SP

The symbol Ⓒ and the name of a hotel group or consortium after a hotel address means that bookings can be made through a central reservations office. These are listed on pages **559 & 560.**

ARLINGHAM

Gloucestershire
Map ref 2B1

9m NW. Stroud
A small, quiet village in a horseshoe bend of the River Severn. The parish church contains medieval glass and interesting sculptures. Berkeley Castle and the Wildfowl Trust at Slimbridge are nearby and there is easy access from the M5 and A38.

Horseshoe View M
Listed

Overton La., Arlingham, Gloucester, GL2 7JJ
☎ Gloucester (0452) 740293
Ideally situated for touring. Close to the Forest of Dean, Wildfowl Trust and the M5, with many other places of interest nearby.
Bedrooms: 1 single, 2 double & 1 twin.
Bathrooms: 1 private, 1 public.
Bed & breakfast: £10 single, £20 double.
Evening meal 6.30pm (l.o. 8pm).
Parking for 5.
🛇 5 🎿 UL 🛏 📺 🛠 🏠 DAP SP

ATHERSTONE

Warwickshire
Map ref 4B3

Pleasant market town with some 18th C houses and interesting old inns. Every Shrove Tuesday a game of football is played in the streets, a tradition which dates from the 13th C. Twycross Zoo is nearby with an extensive collection of reptiles and butterflies.

Chapel House Guest House and Restaurant M

Friars Gate, Market Sq., Atherstone, CV9 1EY
☎ (0827) 718949
Fine example of an 18th C gentleman's house, with Victorian additions, on the borders of Warwickshire, Leicestershire and Staffordshire. Now a small hotel with modern comforts but preserving original elegance and style.
Bedrooms: 6 single, 3 double & 4 twin.
Bathrooms: 11 private, 2 public; 2 private showers.

Bed & breakfast: £35-£45 single, £49.50-£55 double.
Half board: £45-£55.50 daily.
Evening meal 7.30pm (l.o. 8.30pm).
Credit: Access, Visa, Diners.
🛏10 ✆ 🖿 🗖 🛐 Ⅴ 🛏 �📺
🖿 🛉 ✳ 🗙 🖼 🎠

BALSALL COMMON

W. Midlands
Map ref 4B3

6m NW. Kenilworth
Close to Kenilworth and within easy reach of Coventry.

Haigs Hotel ⋒
😊😊 COMMENDED
Kenilworth Rd., Balsall Common, Nr. Coventry, CV7 7EL
☎ Berkswell (0676) 32142
Family-run hotel within easy reach of Kenilworth, Warwick and the Warwickshire countryside, yet only 5 minutes from Birmingham Airport and the M6.
Bedrooms: 10 single, 4 twin.
Bathrooms: 11 private, 1 public; 3 private showers.
Bed & breakfast: £24-£45 single, £39-£56 double.
Evening meal 7.30pm (l.o. 9pm).
Parking for 25.
Credit: Access, Visa, Diners, Amex.
🛏7 🖎 ✆ 🗖 🛐 Ⅴ 🛏 �📺 🖿
🖿 🛉 ✳ 🖼 SP T

BALTERLEY

Staffordshire
Map ref 4A2

2m W. Audley
Hamlet on the Staffordshire/Cheshire border with an interesting modern church and a black and white Tudor hall.

Balterley Hall Farm ⋒
😊😊
Balterley, Crewe, Cheshire CW2 5QG
☎ Crewe (0270) 820206
240-acre arable farm. A 17th C farmhouse offering a warm and friendly welcome. Set in peaceful surroundings near the Potteries. 3.5 miles from the M6.
Bedrooms: 1 single, 1 twin, 1 family room.
Bathrooms: 1 private, 1 public.
Bed & breakfast: £12-£18 single, £24-£30 double.
Half board: £18-£24 daily.

Evening meal 6pm (l.o. 7.30pm).
Parking for 10.
🖎 🗖 🛐 UL 🛐 Ⅴ 🛏 �📺 🖊
🖿 ✳ 🖼 🎠

BERKELEY

Gloucestershire
Map ref 2B1

Town dominated by the castle where Edward II was murdered. Dating from Norman times, it is still the home of the Berkeley family and is open to the public. Slimbridge Wildfowl Trust is nearby.

Green Acres Farm Guest House ⋒
Breadstone, Berkeley, GL13 9HF
☎ Dursley (0453) 810348
45-acre horse breeding and beef farm. Rural position, in beautiful Berkeley Vale. Tastefully furnished, warm welcome. Excellent touring centre for Cotswolds, Wales, Bath and Bristol.
Bedrooms: 2 single, 1 double & 1 twin.
Bathrooms: 4 private.
Bed & breakfast: £13.50-£17.50 single, £31-£35 double.
Parking for 6.
Open January-November.
🛏10 🖎 UL 🛐 🛐 �📺 🖊 🖿
🖿 ∪ ✳ 🗙 🖼 OAP

BERKSWELL

W. Midlands
Map ref 4B3

6m W. Coventry
Pretty village with an unusual set of 5-holed stocks on the green. It has some fine houses, cottages, a 16th C inn and a windmill open to the public every Sunday from May until the end of September (2.30 - 5.30). The Norman church is one of the finest in the area.

Nailcote Hall Hotel and Restaurant ⋒
😊😊😊
Nailcote Lane, Berkswell, Coventry, CV7 7DE
☎ Coventry (0203) 466174
Fax (0203) 470720
A historic country house hotel and restaurant. Ideally located for Heart of England visitors. Situated along the B4101 Knowle to Coventry road.
Bedrooms: 1 single, 6 double & 13 twin.

Bathrooms: 20 private.
Bed & breakfast: £85-£105 single, £105-£135 double.
Lunch available.
Evening meal 7pm (l.o. 9.30pm).
Parking for 50.
Credit: Access, Visa, Diners, Amex.
🛏 🖎 🖽 ✆ 🖎 🗖 🛐 🛐 Ⅴ
🖊 ⊙ 🖽 🖿 🛉 ⚷ ∪ ▶ ✳
🐾 SP 🖼 T

BEWDLEY

Hereford & Worcester
Map ref 4A3

Attractive hillside town above the River Severn and approached by a bridge designed by Telford. The town has many elegant buildings and an interesting museum. It is the southern terminus of the Severn Valley Steam Railway.
Tourist Information Centre ☎ (0299) 404740

Alton Guest House & Tea Rooms
😊😊 APPROVED
Alton House, Long Bank, Bewdley, Worcestershire DY12 2UL
☎ Rock (0299) 266733
Be our guest, bed and breakfast to full board. Tea rooms open 7 days a week. On the A456, 2.5 miles west of Bewdley, adjacent to Wyre Forest.
Bedrooms: 1 single, 1 twin.
Bathrooms: 1 public.
Bed & breakfast: from £16.50 single, from £30 double.
Half board: from £23.45 daily, from £140 weekly.
Lunch available.
Evening meal 7pm (l.o. 8pm).
Parking for 12.
Credit: Access, Visa.
🛏 🖎 🗖 ✆ UL 🛐 Ⅴ 🖊 🛏
⊙ 🖽 🖿 🛉 ∪ ▶ 🗙 🖼 SP

BIBURY

Gloucestershire
Map ref 2B1

Village on the River Coln with stone houses and the famous 17th C Arlington Row, former weavers' cottages. Arlington Mill is now a folk museum with a trout farm nearby which is open to the public.

Bibury Court Hotel ⋒
😊😊😊 APPROVED
Bibury, Cirencester, GL7 5NT
☎ (028 574) 337 Fax (028 574) 660
Jacobean manor house in 6 acres of grounds by River Coln. Family-run with informal country house atmosphere.
Bedrooms: 2 single, 10 double & 4 twin, 1 family room.
Bathrooms: 16 private, 1 public.
Bed & breakfast: £40-£50 single, £60-£66 double.
Lunch available.
Evening meal 7.30pm (l.o. 9.30pm).
Parking for 100.
Credit: Access, Visa.
🛏 🖎 ✆ 🗖 🛐 Ⅴ 🛏 �📺 🖊
🖿 🛉 ⚶ ✳ 🖼 SP 🖼 T

BIDDULPH

Staffordshire
Map ref 4B2

Village set in the heart of moorlands and high hills in the north-west corner of Staffordshire near the Cheshire border. The River Trent has its source near here. In the parish church are some Crusader monuments, and the remains of Biddulph Old Hall stand as a memorial to civil strife between King Charles and Parliament.

Badger Hill Guest House ⋒
😊😊
Rock End, Knypersley, Biddulph, Stoke-on-Trent, ST8 7NR
☎ (0782) 519203
5.5-acre goat farm. Picturesque country guesthouse and smallholding in unique rural setting, 1.5 miles off A527, east of Biddulph in Staffordshire Moorlands.
Bedrooms: 1 single, 1 double & 1 twin, 1 family room.
Continued ▶

Individual proprietors have supplied all details of accommodation. Although we do check for accuracy, we advise you to confirm prices and other information at the time of booking.

BIDDULPH

Continued

Bathrooms: 2 private,
1 public.
Bed & breakfast: £14-£17.50
single, £28-£35 double.
Evening meal 6pm (l.o.
8.30pm).
Parking for 5.

BIDFORD-ON-AVON

Warwickshire
Map ref 2B1

Attractive village with an
ancient 8-arched bridge
and a main street with
some interesting 15th C
houses.

Broom Hall Inn M
APPROVED
Broom, Alcester, B50 4HE
☎ (0789) 773757
*Family-owned country inn with
carvery restaurant and
extensive range of bar meals.
Close to Stratford-upon-Avon
and Cotswolds.*
Bedrooms: 4 single, 4 double
& 4 twin.
Bathrooms: 12 private.
Bed & breakfast: from £35
single, from £50 double.
Half board: from £30 daily.
Lunch available.
Evening meal 7pm (l.o.
10pm).
Parking for 80.
Credit: Access, Visa, Diners,
Amex.

Fosbroke Country
House Hotel M

4 High St., Bidford-on-Avon,
Alcester, B50 4BU
☎ (0789) 772327
*Listed Georgian country house
in beautiful garden in a historic
riverside village, 6 miles from
Stratford and Evesham. Ideal
touring centre. Private parking.*
Bedrooms: 1 single, 3 double
& 1 twin.
Bathrooms: 5 private.
Bed & breakfast: £17.50-£20
single, £35-£42 double.
Half board: £23.50-£25.50
daily, £150-£245 weekly.
Evening meal 6.30pm (l.o.
7.30pm).
Parking for 7.

BIRDLIP

Gloucestershire
Map ref 2B1

7m SE. Gloucester
Hamlet at the top of a
very steep descent down
to the Gloucester Vale
and close to the Crickley
Hill Country Park.

Kingshead House
APPROVED
Birdlip, Gloucester, GL4 8JH
☎ Gloucester (0452) 862299
*Traditional Cotswold-stone
former coaching inn, now
comfortable accommodation
with an elegant restaurant
offering a high standard of
cooking by the proprietor.*
Bedrooms: 1 double.
Bathrooms: 1 private.
Bed & breakfast: max. £48
double.
Half board: max. £46.50
daily.
Lunch available.
Evening meal 7.30pm (l.o.
10pm).
Parking for 12.
Credit: Access, Visa, Diners,
Amex.

Royal George Hotel M
COMMENDED
Birdlip, Gloucester, GL4 8JH
☎ (0452) 862506
Telex 437238 Fax (0452)
862277
CR Lansbury
*At the top of Birdlip Hill, this
hotel was opened in September
1986.*
Bedrooms: 2 single, 7 double
& 23 twin, 4 family rooms.
Bathrooms: 36 private.
Bed & breakfast: £30-£67
single, £60-£80 double.
Half board: from £41 daily.
Lunch available.
Evening meal 7pm (l.o.
10pm).
Parking for 90.
Credit: Access, Visa, Diners,
Amex.

**Half board prices
shown are per
person but in some
cases may be based
on double/twin
occupancy.**

BIRMINGHAM

W. Midlands
Map ref 4B3

Britain's second city, with
many attractions
including the City Art
Gallery, Barber Institute
of Fine Arts, 17th C Aston
Hall, a science museum, 2
cathedrals and the 10-
acre Botanical Gardens. It
is well placed for
exploring Shakespeare
country.
*Tourist Information
Centre ☎ 021-780 4321
or 643 2514*

Asquith House Hotel
19 Portland Rd., Edgbaston,
Birmingham, BI6 9HN
☎ 021-454 5282 & 6699
*Listed building of 1854, now a
licensed private hotel. All
rooms en-suite with colour TV,
telephone, tea and coffee
making facilities.*
Bedrooms: 2 single, 7 double,
1 family room.
Bathrooms: 10 private,
2 public.
Bed & breakfast: £48.70-£55
single, max. £65.78 double.
Half board: £66.70-£73 daily.
Evening meal 7.30pm.
Parking for 10.
Credit: Access, Amex.

Astoria Hotel
311 Hagley Rd., Edgbaston,
Birmingham, BI6 9LQ
☎ 021-454 0795 Fax 021-456
3537
*A small traditional hotel with
interesting decor.*
Bedrooms: 8 single, 7 double
& 4 twin, 5 family rooms.
Bathrooms: 24 private.
Bed & breakfast: max. £34
single, max. £45 double.
Lunch available.
Evening meal 7pm (l.o.
9.30pm).
Parking for 25.
Credit: Access, Visa, Amex.

Awentsbury Hotel M

21 Serpentine Rd., Selly
Park, Birmingham, B29 7HU
☎ 021-472 1258 & 021-472
7634 Telex 333482 Fax 021-
428 1527
*Victorian country house set in
its own large garden. Close to
buses, trains, Birmingham
University, BBC Pebble Mill,
Queen Elizabeth Hospital,
Selly Oak Hospital. Only 2
miles from the city centre.*

Bedrooms: 6 single, 2 double
& 6 twin, 2 family rooms.
Bathrooms: 5 private,
2 public; 6 private showers.
Bed & breakfast: £20-£29
single, £34-£40 double.
Half board: £27-£36 daily,
£171-£227 weekly.
Evening meal 7pm (l.o.
7.30pm).
Parking for 12.

Beech House Hotel

21 Gravelly Hill North,
Erdington, Birmingham,
B23 6BT
☎ 021-373 0620
*Edwardian Tudor-style house
set well back from the road
behind beautiful large beech
trees.*
Bedrooms: 4 single, 3 twin,
2 family rooms.
Bathrooms: 3 private,
1 public.
Bed & breakfast: £25.30-
£32.20 single, £39.10-£46
double.
Half board: £36.80-£43.70
daily, £257.60-£305.90
weekly.
Evening meal 6pm (l.o. 7pm).
Parking for 10.
Credit: Access, Visa.

Copthorne Hotel M
COMMENDED
Paradise Circus, Birmingham,
B3 3HJ
☎ 021-200 2727 Telex 339026
*Built to international
standards, with restaurant,
bars, leisure club and
conference facilities.*
Bedrooms: 3 single,
148 double & 49 twin,
11 family rooms.
Bathrooms: 211 private.
Bed & breakfast: £88-£97
single, £95-£110 double.
Half board: £65-£75 daily.
Lunch available.
Evening meal 6pm (l.o.
8.30pm).
Parking for 40.
Credit: Access, Visa, C.Bl.,
Diners, Amex.

Gables Residential Club
& Hotel
43 Oxford Rd., Moseley,
Birmingham, B13 9ER
☎ 021-449 1146

A club restaurant offering accommodation, bar and restaurant facilities. 2 miles from city centre and 1 mile from golf course.
Bedrooms: 10 single, 7 double, 2 family rooms.
Bathrooms: 19 private.
Bed & breakfast: £21.50-£27.50 single, £30.50-£37.50 double.
Half board: £29.50-£40 daily.
Lunch available.
Evening meal 7.15pm (l.o. 10.45pm).
Parking for 30.
Credit: Access, Visa, C.Bl., Diners, Amex.

Great Barr Hotel and Conference Centre M
Pear Tree Dr., Newton Rd., Great Barr, Birmingham, B43 6HS
☎ 021-357 1141 Telex 336406
Fax 021-357 7557
Situated in a quiet suburb, 5 miles from Birmingham centre. Perfect for the busy executive or for exploring the Heart of England.
Bedrooms: 98 single, 12 double & 4 twin.
Bathrooms: 114 private.
Bed & breakfast: £61-£65 single, £71-£75 double.
Half board: £74-£79 daily.
Lunch available.
Evening meal 7pm (l.o. 12.45pm).
Parking for 250.
Credit: Access, Visa, Diners, Amex.

Greenway House Hotel
978 Warwick Rd., Acocks Green, Birmingham, B27 6QG
☎ 021-706 1361
A small comfortable, privately-run hotel, close to the city centre, airport and National Exhibition Centre. Traditional English cooking, personal service and friendly atmosphere.
Bedrooms: 5 single, 2 double & 1 twin.
Bathrooms: 2 private, 1 public.
Bed & breakfast: £18.50-£19.50 single, £26-£30 double.
Half board: £22-£26 daily.
Lunch available.
Evening meal 6.30pm (l.o. 7.30pm).
Parking for 4.

Hagley Court Hotel M
229 Hagley Rd., Edgbaston, Birmingham, B16 9RP
☎ 021-454 6514 Fax 021-456 2722
A private hotel and restaurant, all rooms en-suite with TV, telephone. Rates include English breakfast and VAT. 1.5 miles from city centre.
Bedrooms: 9 single, 16 double & 3 twin.
Bathrooms: 28 private.
Bed & breakfast: £27-£44 single, £34-£53 double.
Evening meal 6pm (l.o. 10pm).
Parking for 27.
Credit: Access, Visa, Diners, Amex.

Heath Lodge Hotel M
Coleshill Rd., Marston Green, Birmingham, B37 7HT
☎ 021-779 2218
Small privately-owned hotel offering warm and friendly hospitality at a reasonable price. 1.5 miles from the M6 junction 4 and 1 mile from the National Exhibition Centre.
Bedrooms: 5 single, 2 double & 5 twin.
Bathrooms: 6 private, 1 public.
Bed & breakfast: £26-£35 single, £37-£48 double.
Half board: £25-£35 daily.
Lunch available.
Evening meal 6.30pm (l.o. 8.30pm).
Parking for 24.
Credit: Access, Visa.

Holiday Inn M
Holliday St., Central Square, Birmingham, B1 1HH
☎ 021-631 2000 Telex 337272
Holiday Inn
City centre hotel. Tropical indoor pool, a la carte restaurant and 2 bars.
Bedrooms: 90 double, 205 family rooms.
Bathrooms: 295 private.
Bed & breakfast: from £87 single, from £98 double.
Half board: from £111 daily, from £700 weekly.
Lunch available.
Evening meal 7pm (l.o. 11pm).
Parking for 500.
Credit: Access, Visa, C.Bl., Diners, Amex.

Lyndhurst Hotel M
135 Kingsbury Rd., Erdington, Birmingham, B24 8QT
☎ 021-373 5695
Within half a mile of M6 junction 6 and within easy reach of the city and National Exhibition Centre. Comfortable bedrooms, spacious restaurant. Personal service in a quiet friendly atmosphere.
Bedrooms: 9 single, 1 double, 3 family rooms.
Bathrooms: 5 private, 3 public; 2 private showers.
Bed & breakfast: £26-£32.50 single, £39-£44 double.
Half board: £36-£42.50 daily.
Evening meal 6pm (l.o. 8pm).
Parking for 12.
Credit: Access, Visa, Diners, Amex.

Madeira Hotel M
85 Bunbury Rd., Northfield, Birmingham, B31 2ET
☎ 021-475 1352
Modernised hotel and restaurant, 5 miles south of Birmingham centre and within easy reach of the motorway network.
Bedrooms: 3 single, 3 double & 4 twin.
Bathrooms: 2 public; 5 private showers.
Bed & breakfast: £19.95-£35 single, £34.50-£45 double.
Half board: £30-£46 daily, £210-£320 weekly.
Evening meal 6pm (l.o. 7.30pm).
Parking for 18.
Credit: Access, Visa.

Meadow Court Hotel
397 Hagley Rd., Edgbaston, Birmingham, B17 8BL
☎ 021-429 2377 & 021-420 3437 Fax 021-434 3140
Privately owned hotel recently refurbished throughout. All rooms en-suite. 5 minutes city/convention centre, 20 minutes National Exhibition Centre.
Bedrooms: 2 single, 5 double & 5 twin.
Bathrooms: 12 private.
Bed & breakfast: £43.70-£46 single, £58 double.
Half board: £54.45-£56.75 daily.
Lunch available.
Evening meal 6pm (l.o. 8.30pm).

Parking for 18.
Credit: Access, Visa, Diners, Amex.

New Cobden Hotel M
166-174 Hagley Rd., Edgbaston, Birmingham, B16 9NZ
☎ 021-454 6621 Telex 333851
Friendly
Set in its own beautiful gardens, 2 miles west of the city centre and New Street Station, on the A456.
Bedrooms: 108 single, 31 double & 96 twin, 8 family rooms.
Bathrooms: 214 private, 18 public.
Bed & breakfast: £49-£58.50 single, £58.50-£66 double.
Half board: £40.75-£70 daily.
Lunch available.
Evening meal 7pm (l.o. 10pm).
Parking for 160.
Credit: Access, Visa, Diners, Amex.

Norfolk Hotel M
257-267 Hagley Rd., Edgbaston, Birmingham, B16 9NA
☎ 021-454 8071 Telex 339715
Friendly
Set in its own gardens, 2 miles west of the city centre and New Street Station, on the A456. Ample free parking.
Bedrooms: 105 single, 12 double & 54 twin, 8 family rooms.
Bathrooms: 88 private, 33 public.
Bed & breakfast: from £49 single, from £58.50 double.
Half board: from £40.75 daily.
Lunch available.
Evening meal 6pm (l.o. 10pm).
Parking for 103.
Credit: Access, Visa, Diners, Amex.

Norton Place Hotel M
180 Lifford Lane, Kings Norton, Birmingham, B30 3NT
☎ 021-433 5656 Fax 021-433 3048

Continued ▶

Set in the walled gardens of the Patrick Collection grounds. Each room has been individually designed to a high standard all are on the ground floor. Residents will enjoy the use of the already renowned gourmet Lombard Room restaurant. Easy to find - travel to junction 3 of the M42 and follow the signs for the Patrick Collection in Kings Norton.
Bedrooms: 10 double.
Bathrooms: 10 private.
Bed & breakfast: £135-£255 single, £170-£270 double.
Half board: £155-£275 daily.
Lunch available.
Evening meal 7pm (l.o. 9.45pm).
Parking for 300.
Credit: Access, Visa, Diners, Amex.

Old Farm Hotel and Peaches Restaurant

108 Linden Rd., Bournville, Birmingham, B30 1LA
☎ 021-458 3146 & 021-458 5108
A private hotel in the unique district of Bournville, 5 miles from the city centre.
Bedrooms: 10 single, 3 double & 1 twin.
Bathrooms: 4 private, 3 public; 8 private showers.
Bed & breakfast: £27-£36.50 single, £40-£47.50 double.
Evening meal 7pm (l.o. 10pm).
Parking for 15.
Credit: Access, Visa, Diners, Amex.

Rollason Wood Hotel

130 Wood End Rd., Erdington, Birmingham, B24 8BJ
☎ 021-373 1230
Friendly family-run hotel, 1 mile from M6 exit 6. Ideal for National Exhibition Centre. Bar, a la carte restaurant.
Bedrooms: 18 single, 5 double & 9 twin, 3 family rooms.
Bathrooms: 12 private, 5 public; 1 private shower.
Bed & breakfast: £15.70-£32 single, £26.50-£46 double.
Evening meal 6pm (l.o. 9pm).

Parking for 43.
Credit: Access, Visa, Diners, Amex.

Royal Angus Thistle Hotel M

St. Chad's Queensway, Birmingham, B4 6HY
☎ 021-236 4211 Telex 336889
Thistle
City centre hotel with 120-seater restaurant, cocktail bar and lounge. Meetings and functions for 2 to 200 persons.
Bedrooms: 36 single, 59 double & 38 twin, 2 family rooms.
Bathrooms: 135 private.
Bed & breakfast: from £79.75 single, from £97.50 double.
Lunch available.
Evening meal 6.30pm (l.o. 10pm).
Parking for 600.
Credit: Access, Visa, C.Bl., Diners, Amex.

Strathallan Thistle Hotel M

Hagley Rd., Edgbaston, Birmingham, B16 9RY
☎ 021-455 9777 Telex 336680
Thistle
Modern hotel near the city centre, recently refurbished, with a French brasserie and restaurant.
Bedrooms: 119 single, 16 double & 27 twin, 5 family rooms.
Bathrooms: 167 private.
Bed & breakfast: from £79.75 single, from £97.50 double.
Lunch available.
Evening meal 6.30pm (l.o. 10pm).
Parking for 250.
Credit: Access, Visa, C.Bl., Diners, Amex.

Swiss Cottage Hotel

475 Gillott Rd., Edgbaston, Birmingham B16 9LJ
☎ 021-454 0371
Privately run hotel giving personal service and English and continental food. Situated 1 mile from the city centre.
Bedrooms: 8 single, 1 double & 2 twin, 1 family room.
Bathrooms: 3 public.
Bed & breakfast: £15-£17 single, £28-£30 double.

Half board: £20-£21 daily.
Evening meal 6pm (l.o. 7pm).
Parking for 14.

Villanova Hotel

2 Grove Hill Rd., Handsworth Wood, Birmingham, B21 9PA
☎ 021-523 7787 & 021-551 1139
Our tastes are simple and we insist on the best. We promise you a thoroughly enjoyable stay.
Bedrooms: 7 single, 3 double & 5 twin, 2 family rooms.
Bathrooms: 1 private, 4 public; 5 private showers.
Bed & breakfast: £25-£35 single, £40-£50 double.
Half board: £38-£50 daily, £250-£300 weekly.
Lunch available.
Evening meal 6pm (l.o. 9pm).
Parking for 20.

Western House Hotel and Annexe M

14-16 Yardley Rd., Acocks Green, Birmingham, B27 6ED
☎ 021-706 0009
Friendly guesthouse convenient for National Exhibition Centre, airport, city and Warwickshire countryside. Rail, bus and motorway links nearby. New car hire service available.
Bedrooms: 2 single, 2 double & 8 twin, 6 family rooms.
Bathrooms: 2 private, 6 public; 1 private shower.
Bed & breakfast: £17-£20 single, £30-£40 double.
Half board: from £22 daily, £50-£200 weekly.
Parking for 22.
Credit: Access, Visa.

Westley Arms Hotel

Westley Rd., Acocks Green, Birmingham, West Midlands B27 7UJ
☎ 021-706 4312
An attractive cream 2-storey building set in its own grounds in a suburb of Birmingham. Near the National Exhibition Centre.
Bedrooms: 8 single, 7 double & 21 twin, 1 family room.
Bathrooms: 37 private.
Bed & breakfast: £54.50-£79.50 single, £64.50-£79.50 double.
Lunch available.

Evening meal 7pm (l.o. 10pm).
Parking for 100.
Credit: Access, Visa.

Willow Tree Hotel M

759 Chester Rd., Erdington, Birmingham, B24 0BY
☎ 021-373 6388
Convenient for city centre, National Exhibition Centre, airport, motorway network, shops, petrol stations, car hire, taxis and trains. Large mature garden.
Bedrooms: 3 single, 2 twin, 2 family rooms.
Bathrooms: 5 private, 1 public.
Bed & breakfast: £18-£31 single, £34.85-£44.85 double.
Lunch available.
Evening meal 5pm (l.o. 8pm).
Parking for 8.
Credit: Access, Visa.

Woodlands Hotel M

379-381 Hagley Rd., Edgbaston, Birmingham, B17 8DL
☎ 021-429 3935 & 021-420 2341
Family-run hotel with easy access to Birmingham University, city centre and M5 and M6. Licensed - optional evening meal.
Bedrooms: 3 single, 7 double & 6 twin, 1 family room.
Bathrooms: 3 public; 6 private showers.
Bed & breakfast: £20-£30 single, £34-£38 double.
Half board: £29.50-£39.50 daily, £206.50-£276.50 weekly.
Evening meal 6pm (l.o. 8pm).
Parking for 25.
Credit: Access, Visa, Diners, Amex.

Woodville House

39 Portland Rd., Edgbaston, Birmingham, B16 9HN
☎ 021-454 0274
Bed and breakfast with some en-suite rooms, 1 mile from city centre. Offering high standard accommodation with colour TV, tea/coffee facilities in all rooms.
Bedrooms: 4 single, 4 twin, 2 family rooms.
Bathrooms: 6 private, 3 public.

Bed & breakfast: max. £16.50 single, £30-£35 double.
Parking for 10.

ॐ ♨ ❑ ↻ Ⓤ ⅃ ◑ Ⅲ ♙
☂ ❅ ☿ ✠ SP

BIRMINGHAM AIRPORT

See Acocks Green, Balsall Common, Berkswell, Birmingham, Coleshill, Coventry, Hampton-in-Arden, Knowle, Meriden, Solihull.

BISHOP'S CASTLE

Shropshire
Map ref 4A3

A 12th C Planned Town with a castle site at the top of the hill and a church at the bottom of the main street. Many interesting buildings with original timber frames hidden behind present day houses. On the Welsh border close to the Clun Forest in quiet, unspoilt countryside. An excellent centre for exploring Offa's Dyke and the Shropshire countryside.

The Boars Head M
😊😊😊

Church St., Bishop's Castle, SY9 5AE
☎ (0588) 638521
Old world inn, with en-suite accommodation in original stables. Comfortable dining area serves wide choice from bar snacks to a la carte meals.
Bedrooms: 1 single, 2 twin, 1 family room.
Bathrooms: 4 private.
Bed & breakfast: £18-£24 single, £30-£38 double.
Lunch available.
Evening meal 7pm (l.o. 9pm).
Parking for 20.

ॐ ♨ ❑ ↻ ✠ Ⅲ ♙ ☙ ✠
₰

Individual proprietors have supplied all details of accommodation. Although we do check for accuracy, we advise you to confirm prices and other information at the time of booking.

BLAKENEY

Gloucestershire
Map ref 2B1

4m NE. Lydney
Village near the Forest of Dean and the Severn Estuary in wooded hills. It is close to Lydney where the Norchard Steam Centre has full size railway engines, a museum and steam days.

Lower Viney Country Guesthouse M
😊😊😊 COMMENDED

Viney Hill, Blakeney, GL15 4LT
☎ Dean (0594) 516000
Detached period farmhouse set in delightful gardens of approximately half an acre. Lovely rural setting with extensive views of surrounding countryside.
Bedrooms: 1 single, 3 double & 3 twin.
Bathrooms: 7 private.
Bed & breakfast: £15-£20 single, £30-£40 double.
Half board: £22.50-£32 daily.
Evening meal 7pm (l.o. 5pm).
Parking for 7.
Credit: Access, Visa.

ॐ ✿ Ⓤ ♨ Ⅰ ♙ ᵺ Ⅲ ♙
↻ ❅ ✠ ✠ SP

BLEDINGTON

Gloucestershire
Map ref 2B1

4m SE. Stow-on-the-Wold
Village close to the Oxfordshire border with a pleasant green and a beautiful church.

Kings Head Inn & Restaurant M
😊😊😊 COMMENDED

The Green, Bledington, Kingham, Oxford, Oxfordshire OX7 6HD
☎ Kingham (060 871) 365
15th C inn located in the heart of the Cotswolds, facing the village green. Main building has 2 bars, one with inglenook fireplace.
Bedrooms: 5 double & 1 twin.
Bathrooms: 6 private, 6 public.
Bed & breakfast: £28-£30 single, from £49 double.
Lunch available.
Evening meal 7pm (l.o. 10.15pm).
Parking for 60.

ॐ ↻ Ⓑ ❑ ♨ Ⅰ Ⅴ ⅃ ᵺ
Ⅳ Ⅲ ♙ ✠ ✠ ☿ ✠ ♙ GAP
SP Ⓣ

BOURTON-ON-THE-WATER

Gloucestershire
Map ref 2B1

The River Windrush flows through this famous Cotswold village which has a green, and cottages and houses of Cotswold stone. Its many attractions include a model village, Birdland and a Motor Museum.

Chester House Hotel & Motel M
😊😊😊

Victoria St., Bourton-on-the-Water, Cheltenham, GL54 2BU
☎ Cotswold (0451) 20286
Fax (0451) 20471
Ⓜ Minotels
Ideal centre for touring the Cotswolds. Colour TV in all bedrooms.
Bedrooms: 1 single, 6 double & 9 twin, 7 family rooms.
Bathrooms: 23 private, 1 public.
Bed & breakfast: £35-£38 single, £54-£66 double.
Half board: £41.95-£47.95 daily, £264.30-£307.10 weekly.
Lunch available.
Evening meal 7pm (l.o. 9.30pm).
Parking for 22.
Open February-December.
Credit: Access, Visa, C.Bl., Diners, Amex.

ॐ ♨ ❑ ↻ Ⅰ Ⅴ ᵺ
Ⅲ ♙ Ⅰ ✠ SP Ⓣ
⊕ Display advertisement appears on page 265.

Coombe House M
😊😊😊 COMMENDED

Rissington Rd., Bourton-on-the-Water, Cheltenham, GL54 2DL
☎ Cotswold (0451) 21966
Small, comfortable, owner-run hotel. All en-suite facilities. Pleasant garden and ample parking, traditional cooking.
Bedrooms: 5 double & 2 twin.
Bathrooms: 7 private.
Bed & breakfast: £26-£30 single, £42-£46 double.
Half board: £31-£35 daily, £207-£235 weekly.
Evening meal 7.15pm.
Parking for 10.
Open March-October.

ॐ ♨ Ⓑ ❑ ♨ Ⅰ Ⅴ ᵺ
♙ ❅ ✠ ✠ ♙ SP

Finden Lodge Hotel, Whiteshoots Hill M
😊😊😊

Cirencester Rd., Bourton-on-the-Water, Cheltenham, GL54 2LE
☎ Cotswold (0451) 20387
Private fully-licensed hotel with restaurant and bar open to non-residents.
Bedrooms: 11 double, 1 family room.
Bathrooms: 12 private.
Bed & breakfast: £30-£40 single, £50-£65 double.
Half board: £35-£42 daily, £240-£295 weekly.
Lunch available.
Evening meal 5pm (l.o. 9.30pm).
Parking for 30.
Credit: Access, Visa.

ॐ ❑ ↻ ❑ ♨ Ⅰ Ⅴ ⅃
ᵺ Ⅳ Ⅲ ♙ Ⅰ ↻ ⌣ ❅ ✠
GAP ♙ ♙
⊕ Display advertisement appears on page 265.

The Old Bakery

Sherbourne St., Bourton-on-the-Water, Cheltenham, GL54 2BY
☎ (0451) 21227
Character Cotswold old bakery, with exposed beams, 3 double rooms, each having its own bathroom. Can be 2 family rooms.
Bedrooms: 3 double.
Bathrooms: 3 private.
Bed & breakfast: £30-£35 single, £35-£40 double.
Half board: £27-£35 daily, £175-£195 weekly.
Lunch available.
Evening meal 6pm (l.o. 3pm).

ॐ 6 ❑ ♨ ❑ Ⅰ ⅃ Ⅲ ♙
↻ ✠ ♙ GAP SP

Old New Inn M
😊😊😊 APPROVED

Bourton-on-the-Water, Cheltenham, GL54 2AF
☎ Cotswold (0451) 20467
Run by the same family for over 50 years. Traditional cooking and service. Log fires in winter. Large gardens. Ideal centre for touring.
Bedrooms: 8 single, 8 double & 5 twin, 1 family room.
Bathrooms: 8 private, 3 public; 1 private shower.
Bed & breakfast: £24-£30 single, £48-£60 double.
Half board: £37.50-£43.50 daily, £286-£300 weekly.
Lunch available.
Evening meal 7.30pm (l.o. 8.30pm).
Parking for 32.
Credit: Access, Visa.

ॐ ♨ ♨ Ⅰ Ⅴ ᵺ Ⅳ Ⅲ ♙
❅ ♙ SP ₰

BREDWARDINE

Hereford & Worcester
Map ref 2A1

Peaceful village on the
River Wye, crossed by an
18th C brick bridge in an
attractive rural setting. An
excellent base for walking
and fishing close to the
Welsh border.

Bredwardine Hall Guest House M
😃😃😃 **COMMENDED**
Bredwardine, Hereford,
Herefordshire HR3 6DB
☎ Moccas (098 17) 596
*19th C house, personally run,
in its own mature gardens in
the beautiful Wye Valley.*
Bedrooms: 3 double & 2 twin.
Bathrooms: 5 private.
Bed & breakfast: £26-£28
single, £40-£44 double.
Half board: £29-£31 daily,
£198-£212 weekly.
Evening meal 7.30pm (l.o.
7pm).
Parking for 7.
Open March-October.

BRIDGNORTH

Shropshire
Map ref 4A3

Interesting red sandstone
town in 2 parts - High and
Low - linked by a cliff
railway. It has much of
interest including a ruined
Norman keep, half-
timbered 16th C houses,
Midland Motor Museum
and Severn Valley
Railway.
*Tourist Information
Centre* ☎ *(07462) 3358*

The Croft Hotel M
😃😃😃
St. Mary's St., Bridgnorth,
WV16 4DW
☎ (0746) 762416 &
(0746) 767155
*Listed building with a wealth
of oak beams in an old street.
Family-run and an ideal centre
for exploring the delightful
Shropshire countryside.*
Bedrooms: 2 single, 5 double
& 3 twin, 2 family rooms.
Bathrooms: 10 private,
1 public.
Bed & breakfast: £20-£39
single, £43-£47 double.
Half board: £31.50-£34.50
daily.
Lunch available.

Evening meal 6pm (l.o.
8.30pm).
Credit: Access, Visa, Amex.

Cross Lane House Hotel
😃😃😃 **COMMENDED**
Astley Abbotts, Bridgnorth,
WV16 4SJ
☎ (0746) 764 887
*Georgian farmhouse of great
charm and character. Family
owned and run and set in 2
acres of garden.*
Bedrooms: 2 single, 4 double
& 2 twin.
Bathrooms: 8 private.
Bed & breakfast: £47-£52
single, £55-£60 double.
Half board: £40-£72 daily,
£288-£305 weekly.
Lunch available.
Evening meal 7.30pm (l.o.
9.30pm).
Parking for 11.
Credit: Access, Visa.

Falcon Hotel
😃😃 **APPROVED**
St. John's St., Low Town,
Bridgnorth, WV15 6AG
☎ (0746) 763134 Fax (0746)
765401
*Fully-licensed residential 17th
C coaching inn and restaurant.
Situated in rural market town,
bordering River Severn.
Wedding receptions and
conferences catered for.*
Bedrooms: 7 single, 5 double,
3 family rooms.
Bathrooms: 14 private,
1 public; 1 private shower.
Bed & breakfast: £27.50-£38
single, £45-£48 double.
Lunch available.
Evening meal 7pm (l.o.
9.30pm).
Parking for 200.
Credit: Access, Visa, Amex.

Old Vicarage Hotel M
😃😃😃 **HIGHLY COMMENDED**
Worfield, Bridgnorth,
WV15 5JZ
☎ Worfield (074 64) 497
Telex 35438 G Telcom
*Country house hotel in a quiet
peaceful location, ideal for
business or pleasure, close to
Ironbridge Gorge and Severn
Valley Railway.*
Bedrooms: 1 single, 9 double.
Bathrooms: 10 private.
Bed & breakfast: £60-£70
single, £74 50-£82.50 double.
Half board: £54.75-£77.50
daily, £297.50-£350 weekly.
Lunch available.

Evening meal 7.30pm (l.o.
9.30pm).
Parking for 30.
Credit: Access, Visa, Diners,
Amex.

Parlors Hall Hotel M
😃😃😃 **COMMENDED**
Mill St., Low Town,
Bridgnorth, WV15 5AL
☎ (0746) 761931 Fax (0746)
767058
*15th C residence of the Parlor
family, built in 1419, with fine
carved wood fireplaces and
18th C panelled lounge.*
Bedrooms: 6 single, 8 double
& 1 twin, 1 family room.
Bathrooms: 12 private,
1 public.
Bed & breakfast: £42 single,
£50 double.
Lunch available.
Evening meal 7pm (l.o.
10pm).
Parking for 26.
Credit: Access, Visa.

Severn Arms Hotel M
😃😃😃 **COMMENDED**
Underhill St., Bridgnorth,
WV16 4BB
☎ (0746) 764616
*Listed building overlooking the
River Severn, within walking
distance of Severn Valley
Railway. Close to the famous
Ironbridge Gorge Museums.*
Bedrooms: 2 single, 1 double
& 3 twin, 3 family rooms.
Bathrooms: 5 private,
2 public.
Bed & breakfast: £21-£32
single, £34-£41 double.
Half board: £25.50-£29 daily.
Evening meal 6.30pm (l.o.
8pm).
Credit: Access, Visa.

Whitburn Grange Hotel and Restaurant M
😃😃
35 Salop St., Bridgnorth,
WV16 5BH
☎ (0746) 766786 & 2188/9
*Recently renovated building,
300 yards from main High
Street, half a mile from river,
1 mile from golf-course.*
Bedrooms: 6 single, 3 double
& 4 twin, 2 family rooms.
Bathrooms: 5 private,
3 public.
Bed & breakfast: £23-£33
single, £39-£46 double.
Half board: £32-£42 daily,
£171-£252 weekly.
Lunch available.

Evening meal 7pm (l.o.
9.30pm).
Parking for 12.
Credit: Access, Visa, Amex.

BROADWAY

Hereford & Worcester
Map ref 2B1

Beautiful Cotswold village
called the 'Show village of
England', with 16th C
stone houses and
cottages. Near the village
is Broadway Tower with
magnificent views over 12
counties and a country
park with nature trails and
adventure playground.

Collin House Hotel & Restaurant M
😃😃😃 **COMMENDED**
Collin La., Broadway,
Worcestershire WR12 7PB
☎ (0386) 858354 & 852544
*16th C family-run, secluded
Cotswold hotel, with traditional
atmosphere and furnishings.
Four-poster bedrooms,
inglenook fireplaces, fine
gardens and views.*
Bedrooms: 1 single, 2 double
& 4 twin.
Bathrooms: 6 private;
1 private shower.
Bed & breakfast: from £37.50
single, £69-£79 double.
Half board: £49-£54 daily.
Lunch available.
Evening meal 7pm (l.o. 9pm).
Parking for 30.
Credit: Access, Visa.

Dormy House M
😃😃😃😃
Willersey Hill, Broadway,
Worcestershire WR12 7LF
☎ (0386) 852711
Telex 338275 Fax (0386)
85836
*Converted 17th C farmhouse,
combining traditional charm
with modern facilities,
surrounded by golf-course. Log
fires in winter.*
Bedrooms: 7 single, 40 double
& 2 twin.
Bathrooms: 49 private.
Bed & breakfast: £54-£70
single, £108-£125 double.
Half board: £80-£96 daily.
Lunch available.
Evening meal 7pm (l.o.
9.30pm).
Parking for 90.
Credit: Access, Visa, Diners,
Amex.

Eastbank ⚈

Station Drive, Broadway,
Worcestershire WR12 7DF
☎ (0386) 852659
*Home cooking and friendly
atmosphere. Very quiet
location about half a mile from
the village. Free brochure
available.*
Bedrooms: 2 double & 2 twin,
2 family rooms.
Bathrooms: 6 private.
Bed & breakfast: £20-£25
single, £30-£38 double.
Evening meal 7pm (l.o.
10am).
Parking for 6.

Leasow House ⚈
COMMENDED

Laverton Meadow,
Broadway, Worcestershire
WR12 7NA
☎ Stanton (038 673) 526
*17th C Cotswold stone
farmhouse tranquilly set in
open countryside close to
Broadway village.*
Bedrooms: 2 double & 2 twin,
3 family rooms.
Bathrooms: 7 private.
Bed & breakfast: £36-£50
double.
Parking for 14.
Credit: Access, Visa, Amex.

The Old Rectory ⚈
HIGHLY COMMENDED

Church St., Willersey,
Broadway, Worcestershire
WR12 7PN
☎ (0386) 853729
*A combination of the standards
of a good hotel with the
warmth of a private home.*
Bedrooms: 4 double & 2 twin.
Bathrooms: 6 private.
Bed & breakfast: £49-£85
single, £59-£95 double.
Parking for 10.
Credit: Access, Visa.

Olive Branch Guest House ⚈

78 High St., Broadway,
Worcestershire WR12 7AJ
☎ (0386) 853440
*Old house with modern
amenities close to centre of
village. Traditional English
breakfast served.*

Bedrooms: 2 single, 1 double
& 4 twin, 2 family rooms.
Bathrooms: 5 private,
2 public.
Bed & breakfast: £15-£17
single, £30-£34 double.
Half board: £23-£25 daily.
Parking for 8.

Pathlow House ⚈
Listed

82 High St., Broadway,
Worcestershire WR12 7AJ
☎ (0386) 853444
*Comfortable period house,
central for village amenities.*
Bedrooms: 3 double & 2 twin.
Bathrooms: 4 private.
Bed & breakfast: £30-£34
double.
Parking for 6.

Small Talk Lodge ⚈

Keil Close, High Street,
Broadway, Worcestershire
WR12 7DP
☎ (0386) 858953
*First-floor accommodation in
traditional Cotswold lodge.
Quiet location in mews,
adjacent to Lygon Arms Hotel
and in village centre.*
Bedrooms: 4 double & 3 twin,
1 family room.
Bathrooms: 4 private,
2 public.
Bed & breakfast: £25-£40
single, £30-£50 double.
Evening meal 7pm (l.o.
8.30pm).
Credit: Access, Visa.

Southwold House ⚈

Station Rd., Broadway,
Worcestershire WR12 7DE
☎ (0386) 853681
*Warm welcome, friendly
service and traditional cooking
at this large Edwardian house,
only 4 minutes from village
centre. Reductions for 3 or
more nights.*
Bedrooms: 1 single, 4 double
& 3 twin.
Bathrooms: 3 private,
2 public; 1 private shower.
Bed & breakfast: from £16
single, £32-£36 double.
Half board: £26-£28 daily,
£166-£180 weekly.
Evening meal 7pm (l.o. 2pm).
Parking for 8.
Credit: Access, Visa.

White Acres ⚈
COMMENDED

Station Rd., Broadway,
Worcestershire WR12 7DE
☎ (0386) 852320
*All rooms have private
showers, WCs, teasmades, and
remote control colour TV. A
separate guests' lounge is
available. 4-course English
breakfast served. Ideal centre
for tourist areas.*
Bedrooms: 4 double & 2 twin.
Bathrooms: 6 private.
Bed & breakfast: £36-£38
double.
Parking for 6.
Open March-October.

Windrush House ⚈
Listed **COMMENDED**

Station Rd., Broadway,
Worcestershire WR12 7DE
☎ (0386) 853577
*Edwardian guesthouse on the
A44, half a mile from the
village centre, offering personal
service. Evening meals with
choice of menu. 3 day break at
Christmas.*
Bedrooms: 3 double & 1 twin.
Bathrooms: 4 private.
Bed & breakfast: £36 double.
Half board: £29 daily, £173
weekly.
Lunch available.
Evening meal 7pm.
Parking for 5.

BROMSGROVE

Hereford & Worcester
Map ref 4B3

This market town in the
Lickey Hills has an
interesting 14th C church
with fine tombs and a
Carillon tower. The
Avoncroft Museum of
Buildings is nearby where
many old buildings have
been re-assembled,
having been saved from
destruction.
*Tourist Information
Centre ☎ (0527) 31809*

Bromsgrove Country Hotel ⚈
COMMENDED

249 Worcester Rd., Stoke
Heath, Bromsgrove,
Worcestershire B61 7JA
☎ (0527) 35522
*A quiet elegant Victorian
residence with modern
amenities, suitable for business
or pleasure. Close to the
M6/M42/M5 junctions and
historic countryside.*

Bedrooms: 1 single, 4 double
& 2 twin, 3 family rooms.
Bathrooms: 9 private,
1 public.
Bed & breakfast: £30-£35
single, £39-£46 double.
Half board: £39-£44 daily.
Evening meal 7.30pm (l.o.
2pm).
Parking for 20.
Credit: Access, Visa.

Country Court Hotel ⚈

Birmingham Rd.,
Bromsgrove, Worcestershire
B61 0JB
☎ 021-447 7888 & 021-447
7979 Telex 336976 Fax 021-
447 7273
ⓒ Stakis
*Attractive 2-storey hotel built
around a central landscaped
courtyard, with purpose built
conference centre and leisure
club.*
Bedrooms: 104 double &
27 twin, 10 family rooms.
Bathrooms: 141 private.
Bed & breakfast: from £80
single, from £96 double.
Lunch available.
Evening meal 7pm (l.o.
10pm).
Parking for 100.
Credit: Access, Visa, C.Bl.,
Diners, Amex.

Grafton Manor Restaurant

Grafton Lane, Bromsgrove,
Worcestershire B61 7HA
☎ (0527) 579007 Fax (0527)
575221
*Once the home of the Earls of
Shrewsbury; a magnificent
Elizabethan manor house, now
run as a small, stylish hotel.*
Bedrooms: 1 single, 4 double
& 2 twin, 2 family rooms.
Bathrooms: 9 private.
Bed & breakfast: £80-£105
single, £99-£110 double.
Evening meal 7.30pm (l.o.
9pm).
Parking for 50.
Credit: Access, Visa, Diners,
Amex.

Marlgrove Motel ⚈

408 Birmingham Rd.,
Marlbrook, Bromsgrove,
Worcestershire B61 0HP
☎ (0527) 72889

Continued ▶

BROMSGROVE

Continued

Chalet type rooms, with central building housing full restaurant. Evening meal and dancing. Licensed bars. 1 mile from junction 4, M5, a third of a mile from junction 1, M42.
Bedrooms: 7 single, 12 twin.
Bathrooms: 19 private.
Bed & breakfast: £23-£35 single, £34-£45 double.
Half board: £31.95-£43.95 daily, £223.65-£307.65 weekly.
Lunch available.
Evening meal 7.30pm (l.o. 10pm).
Parking for 100.
Credit: Access, Visa, Diners, Amex.

Victoria Guest House
31 Victoria Rd., Bromsgrove, Worcestershire B61 0DW
☎ (0527) 75777
Homely, family-run guesthouse near Bromsgrove town centre, M5 and M42. Convenient for the National Exhibition Centre and touring the Cotswolds and Midlands. Interest holidays and courses.
Bedrooms: 3 single, 1 family room.
Bathrooms: 1 public.
Bed & breakfast: £13.50-£19.50 single, £24 double.
Half board: £17.50-£23.50 daily, £118.50-£160.50 weekly.
Evening meal 6pm (l.o. 5pm).
Parking for 3.

BUCKLAND

Gloucestershire
Map ref 2B1

1m S. Broadway
Village with a church full of interesting features including a 15th C glass east window. The rectory, also 15th C, is one of the oldest in England. Nearby is Snowshill Manor, owned by the National Trust.

Buckland Manor ⋈
♛♛♛♛ HIGHLY COMMENDED
Buckland, Broadway, Worcestershire WR12 7LY
☎ Broadway (0386) 852626

13th C Cotswold manor in 10 acres, in idyllic secluded valley. Log fires, central heating. Tennis, riding, and complete tranquillity. Closed for three and a half weeks from mid January.
Bedrooms: 6 double & 5 twin.
Bathrooms: 11 private.
Bed & breakfast: £125-£200 single, £135-£210 double.
Lunch available.
Evening meal 7.30pm (l.o. 8.45pm).
Parking for 30.
Credit: Access, Visa.

BURTON UPON TRENT

Staffordshire
Map ref 4B3

An important brewing town with the Bass Museum of Brewing, where the Bass Shire horses are stabled. There are 3 bridges with views over the river and some interesting public buildings including the 18th C St. Modwen's Church.
Tourist Information Centre ☎ (0283) 45454

Craythorne Farm Hotel
Craythorne Rd., Stretton, Burton upon Trent, DE13 0AZ
☎ (0283) 31648
Modernised farmhouse, all rooms to a high standard, off A38 between Stretton and Rolleston. Own golf course and driving range adjacent.
Bedrooms: 4 twin.
Bathrooms: 4 private.
Bed & breakfast: £35-£40 single, £45 double.
Lunch available.
Parking for 10.
Credit: Access, Visa.

The Delter Hotel
♛♛
5 Derby Rd., Burton upon Trent, DE14 1RU
☎ (0283) 35115
Conveniently situated hotel aiming to please with hospitality and the comfort of en-suite bedrooms, private dining room and licensed bar.
Bedrooms: 1 single, 1 double & 2 twin, 1 family room.
Bathrooms: 5 private.
Bed & breakfast: from £28 single, from £38 double.

Evening meal 6pm (l.o. 11pm).
Parking for 8.
Credit: Access, Visa.

Edgecote Hotel ⋈
♛♛♛
179 Ashby Rd., Burton upon Trent, DE15 0LB
☎ (0283) 68966
Family-run Victorian hotel with friendly atmosphere. 5 minutes from town centre. Attractive intimate restaurant. Small parties/functions catered for.
Bedrooms: 6 single, 2 double & 2 twin, 2 family rooms.
Bathrooms: 1 private, 3 public.
Bed & breakfast: £17-£32 single, £28-£42 double.
Half board: £21-£39 daily.
Evening meal 7pm (l.o. 8.15pm).
Parking for 10.
Credit: Access, Visa.

Stanhope Hotel
Ashby Rd East, Bretby, Burton upon Trent, DE15 0PU
☎ (0283) 217954
Telex 347185 Fax (0283) 226199
Ⓒ Lansbury
On the A50 between Burton and Leicester, with good restaurant and banqueting facilites.
Bedrooms: 3 single, 15 double & 9 twin.
Bathrooms: 27 private.
Bed & breakfast: £28-£62 single, £56-£74 double.
Half board: £39-£76 daily.
Lunch available.
Evening meal 7pm (l.o. 10pm).
Parking for 240.
Credit: Access, Visa, Diners, Amex.

The Station Hotel
Listed
Borough Rd., Burton upon Trent DE14 2DA
☎ (0283) 64955
Small, friendly, family hotel situated next to the railway station in the brewing capital of England. Landlord is an Ansells Master of Ales and a member of the Guild of Master Cellarmen.
Bedrooms: 1 double & 3 twin, 2 family rooms.
Bathrooms: 3 private, 1 public.

Bed & breakfast: £17.50-£20 single, £33-£38 double.
Lunch available.
Evening meal 7pm (l.o. 10pm).
Parking for 108.

CANNOCK

Staffordshire
Map ref 4B3

Industrial town with Cannock Chase to the north, a former hunting forest now heath and woodlands with picnic areas and forest trails. It is ideal for walking and riding.
Tourist Information Centre ☎ (0543) 466453

Roman Way Hotel ⋈
♛♛♛
Watling St., Hatherton, Cannock, WS11 1SH
☎ (054 35) 72121
Fax (054 35) 2749
Modern hotel conveniently situated 1 mile from M6. Ideal for tourists and business executives.
Bedrooms: 2 double & 18 twin, 4 family rooms.
Bathrooms: 24 private.
Bed & breakfast: from £52 single, from £67 double.
Lunch available.
Evening meal 7pm (l.o. 10pm).
Parking for 200.
Credit: Access, Visa, Amex.

CHEADLE

Staffordshire
Map ref 4B2

Market town dominated by the 19th C Roman Catholic Church with its 200-ft spire. To the east of the town lie 300 acres of Hawksmoor Nature Reserve with many different birds and trees. Alton Towers is nearby.

High Gables
♛♛ COMMENDED
Totmonslow, Draycott Rd., Tean, Stoke-on-Trent, ST10 4JJ
☎ (0538) 722638
Small country residence with all the comforts of home.
Bedrooms: 2 double & 1 twin, 1 family room.
Bathrooms: 1 public.

Bed & breakfast: £15-£18
single, £25-£28 double.
Parking for 8.
Open February-October.
🛇 📺 📺 ⅲ 💪 ✕ 🛏
🦯 SP

The Manor

Watt Pl., Cheadle, Stoke-on-
Trent ST10 1NZ
☎ (0538) 753450
*Georgian house, a former
rectory, built in 1758.*
Bedrooms: 1 double & 1 twin,
12 family rooms.
Bathrooms: 10 private,
1 public.
Bed & breakfast: from £24
single, from £30 double.
Lunch available.
Evening meal 6pm (l.o. 8pm).
Parking for 25.
🛇 🖳 🖵 📺 ⅲ 💪 ❀
🦯

Park Lodge Guest House M
😋😋 COMMENDED

1 Tean Rd., Cheadle, Stoke-
on-Trent, ST10 1LG
☎ Cheadle (0538) 753562
*A family run guest house
offering a warm welcome.
Alton Towers 10 minutes'
drive, Potteries and indoor
waterworld 20 minutes away,
close to Peak District.*
Bedrooms: 2 double & 1 twin,
3 family rooms.
Bathrooms: 3 private,
1 public.
Bed & breakfast: £15-£20
single, £25-£30 double.
Parking for 7.
🛇 🖳 🖵 UL ⅰ 🖾 📺 ⅲ
❀ DAP

Wheatsheaf Hotel
😋😋😋

High St., Cheadle, Stoke-on-
Trent, ST10 1AR
☎ (0538) 752797
*Within 20 miles of Peaks,
Potteries, Festival Park, pony
trekking, fell walking, Alton
Towers and Uttoxeter racing.
Coaching inn of character,
lively atmosphere,
entertainment, functions,
quality restaurant and new
premium rooms.*
Bedrooms: 3 double & 3 twin,
4 family rooms.
Bathrooms: 4 private,
3 public; 1 private shower.
Bed & breakfast: £23-£37
single, £32-£55 double.
Lunch available.

**The symbols are
explained on the
flap inside the
back cover.**

Evening meal 6pm (l.o.
9.30pm).
Parking for 50.
Credit: Access, Visa, Amex.
🛇 🖳 🛇 📞 🖵 🛇 ⅰ 📺
✕ 🖾 💪 🍴 DAP 🦯 SP 🦯

Woodhouse Farm Guest House M
😋

Lockwood Rd., Cheadle,
Stoke-on-Trent, ST10 4QU
☎ (0538) 754250
*Old barns, renovated and
modernised, situated in the
peace and quiet of the Churnet
Valley, 4 miles from Alton
Towers, and close to the Peak
District and the Potteries.*
Bedrooms: 7 double & 3 twin,
4 family rooms.
Bathrooms: 9 private,
2 public.
Bed & breakfast: £15-£19
single, £26-£32 double.
Half board: £20.50-£26.50
daily.
Lunch available.
Evening meal 6.30pm.
Parking for 20.
Credit: Access, Visa.
🛇 🖳 ⅰ 🖾 📺 ⅲ 💪 ❀
✕ DAP 🦯 SP 🦯

Gloucestershire
Map ref 2B1

Cheltenham was
developed as a spa town
in the 18th C and has
some beautiful Regency
architecture, in particular
the Pittville Pump Room.
It holds international
music and literature
festivals and is also
famous for its race
meetings and cricket.
*Tourist Information
Centre* ☎ *(0242) 522878*

The Abbey Hotel M
😋😋😋

16 Bath Parade, Cheltenham,
GL53 7HN
☎ (0242) 516053
Telex LANSDO G 437369
Fax (0242) 227765
*Recently completely
refurbished with most rooms
en-suite. 14 bedrooms
providing comfortable, clean
accommodation with all
facilities.*
Bedrooms: 6 single, 3 double
& 3 twin, 2 family rooms.
Bathrooms: 7 private,
1 public; 4 private showers.
Bed & breakfast: £15-£22
single, £36-£40 double.
Half board: £24-£31 daily,
£90-£130 weekly.

Evening meal 6.30pm (l.o.
7.30pm).
Credit: Access, Visa.
ⅲ 💪 ❀ 🖾 🖵 🛇 ⅰ 🖾
✕ 🦯 SP

Afortie Hotel M
😋😋

London Rd., Charlton Kings,
Cheltenham, GL52 6UU
☎ (0242) 231061
*Situated on the edge of town in
an area of outstanding natural
beauty, offering private car
parking, warm hospitality and
quality accommodation at
sensible prices.*
Bedrooms: 6 single, 3 double
& 3 twin, 2 family rooms.
Bathrooms: 14 private.
Bed & breakfast: £40-£70
single, £70-£85 double.
Half board: £45-£70 daily.
Evening meal 7pm (l.o. 9pm).
Parking for 26.
Credit: Access, Visa.
🛇 🖳 📞 🖾 🖵 🛇 ⅰ 📺 🖾
ⅲ 💪 🍴 ❀ 🖾 🦯 SP 🦯 T

Allards Hotel M
😋😋

Shurdington Rd.,
Shurdington, Cheltenham,
GL51 5XA
☎ (0242) 862498
*On the A46, surrounded by
hills and fields. All rooms have
modern facilities, providing
comfort and convenience.*
Bedrooms: 1 single, 5 double
& 5 twin, 2 family rooms.
Bathrooms: 13 private,
1 public.
Bed & breakfast: £20-£21
single, £40-£42 double.
Half board: £50-£52 daily.
Evening meal 6.30pm (l.o.
7.30pm).
Parking for 17.
Credit: Access, Visa.
🛇 🖳 📞 🖵 ❀ UL 🖾 ⅲ 💪
🍴 ❀ ✕ SP 🦯 T

Beaumont House Hotel M
😋😋 COMMENDED

56 Shurdington Rd.,
Cheltenham, GL53 0JE
☎ (0242) 245986
*A gracious, detached, Victorian
listed building set in pleasant
gardens. On the A46, minutes
from town centre, with ample
private parking on premises.*
Bedrooms: 5 single, 5 double
& 5 twin, 3 family rooms.
Bathrooms: 14 private,
1 public; 3 private showers.
Bed & breakfast: £16-£32
single, £39-£50 double.
Half board: £25.50-£34 daily,
£175-£280 weekly.
Lunch available.

Evening meal 7pm (l.o. 2pm).
Parking for 21.
Credit: Access, Visa.
🛇 🖳 🖵 🛇 📺 🛇 ✕ 🦯 🖾
ⅲ 💪 🍴 🛇 ❀ DAP 🦯 SP 🦯

Beechworth Lawn Hotel M
😋😋😋 COMMENDED

133 Hales Rd., Cheltenham,
GL52 6ST
☎ (0242) 522583
*Carefully modernised and well-
appointed, detached Victorian
hotel, set in conifer and shrub
gardens. Convenient for
shopping centre and
racecourse.*
Bedrooms: 2 single, 1 double
& 2 twin, 2 family rooms.
Bathrooms: 4 private,
1 public.
Bed & breakfast: £17-£24
single, £32-£40 double.
Half board: £24-£31 daily.
Evening meal 6pm (l.o. 2pm).
Parking for 12.
🛇 🖵 🛇 UL ⅰ 🖾 📺 ⅲ 💪
🦯

Bentons M
Listed

71 Bath Rd., Cheltenham,
GL53 7LH
☎ (0242) 517417
*Guesthouse supplying bed and
breakfast.*
Bedrooms: 2 single, 1 double
& 3 twin, 1 family room.
Bathrooms: 1 public.
Bed & breakfast: £13-£15
single, £26-£30 double.
🖳 🛇 🛇 UL ✕ 🦯

Bowler Hat Hotel
😋😋

130 London Rd.,
Cheltenham, GL52 6HN
☎ (0242) 523614
*Small Regency hotel 10
minutes' walk from
Cheltenham town centre.
Family and commercial
accommodation at reasonable
rates.*
Bedrooms: 2 single, 2 double
& 1 twin, 1 family room.
Bathrooms: 1 private,
1 public; 2 private showers.
Bed & breakfast: £18-£23
single, £30-£40 double.
Parking for 8.
🛇 10 🖵 🛇 🖾 ⅲ 💪 ✕ 🦯 🦯

Broomhill
😋😋

218 London Rd., Charlton
Kings, Cheltenham,
GL52 6HW
☎ (0242) 513086
*An imposing house
conveniently situated on the
Cotswold side of the town and
close to all amenities.*
Continued ▶

221

CHELTENHAM
Continued

Bedrooms: 1 single, 1 double & 1 twin.
Bathrooms: 1 private, 2 public.
Bed & breakfast: £15-£17.50 single, £30-£35 double.
Evening meal 6.30pm (l.o. 7.30pm).
Parking for 8.

Carlton Hotel M
APPROVED
Parabola Rd., Cheltenham, GL50 3AQ
☎ (0242) 514453 Telex 43310
The hotel is quietly and conveniently placed in Regency Cheltenham, an ideal base for the town, Cotswolds and surroundings.
Bedrooms: 20 single, 10 double & 38 twin.
Bathrooms: 68 private.
Bed & breakfast: £50-£55 single, £72 double.
Half board: £61.50-£66.50 daily, £280.50 weekly.
Lunch available.
Evening meal 7pm (l.o. 9.30pm).
Parking for 35.
Credit: Access, Visa, Diners, Amex.

Central Hotel M
7-9 Portland St., Cheltenham, GL52 2NZ
☎ (0242) 582172 & 524789
Family-run hotel close to town centre, shops, coach station, racecourse, cinema and theatre. Fully-licensed bar and restaurant.
Bedrooms: 3 single, 5 double & 7 twin, 2 family rooms.
Bathrooms: 8 private, 2 public; 2 private showers.
Bed & breakfast: £20-£29 single, £37-£46 double.
Half board: £29-£38 daily.
Lunch available.
Evening meal 6pm (l.o. 9pm).
Parking for 5.
Credit: Access, Visa, Diners, Amex.

The Cheltenham Park Hotel M
Cirencester Rd., Charlton Kings, Cheltenham, GL53 8EA
☎ (0242) 222021
Telex 437364 G

Beautifully renovated country house hotel, situated on the Cirencester Road in Charlton Kings, adjacent to the Lillybrok Golf Course. 2.5 miles from the centre of Cheltenham Spa.
Bedrooms: 22 single, 60 double & 60 twin.
Bathrooms: 142 private.
Bed & breakfast: from £70 single, £94-£140 double.
Lunch available.
Evening meal 7.30pm (l.o. 9.45pm).
Parking for 150.
Credit: Access, Visa, Diners, Amex.
⊕ *Display advertisement appears on page 265.*

Crossways Guest House, Oriel Place
APPROVED
57 Bath Rd., Cheltenham, GL53 7LH
☎ (0242) 527683
A fine Regency building, right in the heart of Cheltenham. A friendly and informal atmosphere with emphasis on quality food and service.
Bedrooms: 1 single, 2 double & 2 twin, 1 family room.
Bathrooms: 3 private, 1 public.
Bed & breakfast: £16-£25 single, £30-£40 double.

Golden Valley Thistle Hotel M
Gloucester Rd., Cheltenham, GL51 0TS
☎ (0242) 232 691
Telex 43410
CR Thistle
In a quiet rural setting minutes from the centre of Cheltenham, the hotel is ideal for business or pleasure. Extensive modern facilities include a new fully-equipped leisure centre.
Bedrooms: 32 double & 65 twin.
Bathrooms: 97 private.
Bed & breakfast: from £76.75 single, from £93.50 double.
Lunch available.
Evening meal 7.30pm (l.o. 10pm).
Parking for 280.
Credit: Access, Visa, C.Bl., Diners, Amex.

Grovelands M
APPROVED
12 Montpellier Grove, Cheltenham, GL50 2XB
☎ (0242) 525311 & 231462
Small family guesthouse in the centre of town has spacious bedrooms, all with TV, radio and telephone.
Bedrooms: 1 double & 3 twin, 2 family rooms.
Bathrooms: 2 public.
Bed & breakfast: £15-£16 single, £30-£32 double.
Parking for 6.

Hallery House M
48 Shurdington Rd., Cheltenham, GL53 0JE
☎ (0242) 578450
Beautiful Grade II listed house, offering a warm and friendly atmosphere and varied food. Colour and satellite TV all rooms. Close to town centre.
Bedrooms: 7 single, 4 double & 4 twin, 1 family room.
Bathrooms: 10 private, 1 public.
Bed & breakfast: £16-£30 single, £30-£60 double.
Half board: £26-£40 daily, £175-£275 weekly.
Lunch available.
Evening meal 7pm (l.o. 6.30pm).
Parking for 23.
Credit: Access, Visa.

Hanover House M
65 St George's Rd.; Cheltenham, GL50 3DU
☎ (0242) 529867
Well-appointed and spacious accommodation in elegant, listed Victorian Cotswold stone house. Close to theatre, town hall, gardens and shopping facilities.
Bedrooms: 2 single, 2 double & 1 twin, 1 family room.
Bathrooms: 2 private, 2 public.
Bed & breakfast: £15.50-£31 single, £33-£45 double.
Half board: £24-£32 daily.
Evening meal 6.30pm (l.o. 9am).
Parking for 4.

Hollington House Hotel M
115 Hales Road., Cheltenham, GL52 6ST
☎ (0242) 519718
Detached Victorian house with ample parking, 1 mile from centre. 9 en-suite bedrooms, colour TV, in-room beverages. Breakfast and dinner with menu choices. A warm welcome is assured.
Bedrooms: 2 single, 1 double & 4 twin, 2 family rooms.
Bathrooms: 9 private.
Bed & breakfast: £28-£35 single, £38-£47 double.
Half board: £25-£30 daily, £193-£207 weekly.
Evening meal 7pm (l.o. 7.30pm).
Parking for 12.
Credit: Access, Visa, Amex.
⊕ *Display advertisement appears on page 266.*

Hughenden
Listed
Western Rd., Cheltenham, GL50 3RJ
☎ (0242) 524409
Large Victorian semi-detached house with homely atmosphere.
Bedrooms: 4 single, 1 twin.
Bathrooms: 2 public.
Bed & breakfast: £12-£13 single, £24-£26 double.
Parking for 4.

Ivy Dene Guest House M
APPROVED
145 Hewlett Rd., Cheltenham, GL52 6TS
☎ (0242) 521726 & 521776
Ideal base for exploring Cotswolds. A charming corner house in its own grounds, situated in a residential area. Within walking distance of the town.
Bedrooms: 2 single, 2 double & 2 twin, 3 family rooms.
Bathrooms: 3 public.
Bed & breakfast: £12.50-£15 single, £25-£30 double.
Parking for 8.

Lonsdale House M
Montpellier Drive, Cheltenham, GL50 1TX
☎ (0242) 232379
Regency house situated 5 minutes' walk from the Town Hall, promenade, shopping centre, parks and theatre. Easy access to all main routes.

Bedrooms: 5 single, 1 double
& 2 twin, 3 family rooms.
Bathrooms: 4 public.
Bed & breakfast: £15-£17
single, £30-£34 double.
Parking for 6.

Micklinton Hotel
奫
12 Montpellier Dr.,
Cheltenham, GL50 1TX
☎ (0242) 520000
*Family-run, semi-detached,
Victorian private hotel. 5
minutes' walk away from
theatres, the town hall and the
tourist information office.*
Bedrooms: 1 single, 1 double
& 2 twin, 2 family rooms.
Bathrooms: 2 public;
2 private showers.
Bed & breakfast: £14-£17
single, £28-£34 double.
Half board: £21-£24 daily.
Evening meal 6.30pm (l.o.
7pm).
Parking for 6.

Milton House M
奫奫奫
12 Royal Pde., Bayshill Rd.,
Cheltenham, GL50 3AY
☎ (0242) 582601 & 573631
*Set among tree-lined Regency
avenues, only 4 minutes' stroll
from the promenade. Spacious
en-suite rooms, generous
wholesome breakfasts with a
quiet relaxing atmosphere.*
Bedrooms: 4 single, 1 double
& 1 twin, 3 family rooms.
Bathrooms: 9 private.
Bed & breakfast: £28.75-£35
single, £40-£48 double.
Evening meal 7.30pm (l.o.
9pm).
Parking for 5.
Credit: Access, Visa, Amex.

Stretton Lodge M
奫奫奫
Western Rd., Cheltenham,
GL50 3RN
☎ (0242) 528724 & 570771
*Carefully restored, early
Victorian house with warm and
comfortable relaxing
atmosphere. Spacious well-
appointed rooms. Quiet central
location. Brochure available.*
Bedrooms: 1 single, 3 double
& 3 twin, 2 family rooms.
Bathrooms: 9 private.
Bed & breakfast: £25-£40
single, £45-£55 double.
Half board: £36-£52 daily,
£220-£320 weekly.

Evening meal 6.30pm.
Parking for 5.
Credit: Access, Visa, Amex.

Willoughby Hotel M
APPROVED
1 Suffolk Sq., Cheltenham,
GL50 2DR
☎ (0242) 522798
*Large Regency house of
architectural interest. Double
glazed throughout. Situated in
quiet square overlooking
garden and bowling green.*
Bedrooms: 3 single, 3 double
& 3 twin, 1 family room.
Bathrooms: 5 private,
2 public.
Bed & breakfast: £23-£30
single, £42-£50 double.
Half board: £32.50-£39.50
daily.
Evening meal 6.30pm (l.o.
4pm).
Parking for 10.

**Wishmoor Guest
House** M
COMMENDED
147 Hales Rd., Cheltenham,
GL52 6TD
☎ (0242) 238504
*Friendly family guesthouse
with parking off the road, 1
mile from the town centre and
convenient for the countryside.*
Bedrooms: 3 single, 2 double
& 2 twin, 2 family rooms.
Bathrooms: 4 private,
3 public.
Bed & breakfast: £15-£25
single, £30-£45 double.
Half board: £23.50-£33.50
daily, £105-£175 weekly.
Evening meal 6pm (l.o.
midday).
Parking for 8.

Wyastone Hotel M
奫奫奫
Parabola Rd., Cheltenham,
GL50 3BG
☎ (0242) 245549/516654 Fax
(0242) 522659
*Victorian building in well-
favoured Montpellier district,
which has beautiful gardens
and excellent shops.*
Bedrooms: 5 single, 3 double
& 5 twin, 1 family room.
Bathrooms: 14 private.
Bed & breakfast: £48-£53
single, £68-£85 double.
Half board: £39-£64.95 daily,
£275-£454 weekly.
Lunch available.
Evening meal 5pm (l.o. 9pm).

Parking for 20.
Credit: Access, Visa, Diners,
Amex.

CHIPPING
CAMPDEN

Gloucestershire
Map ref 2B1

Outstanding Cotswold
wool town with many old
stone gabled houses, a
splendid church and 17th
C almshouses. There is a
collection of historic
sports cars and nearby
are Kiftsgate Court
Gardens and Hidcote
Manor Gardens (National
Trust).

Charingworth Manor M
奫奫奫奫
Charingworth, Chipping
Campden, GL55 6NS
☎ Paxford (038 678) 555
Telex 333444 CHARMAG
*An attractive 14th C country
house in rural Cotswold setting,
overlooking its own 50 acres.
Exceptional restaurant and
extensive wine list.*
Bedrooms: 14 double &
8 twin, 3 family rooms.
Bathrooms: 25 private.
Bed & breakfast: £80-£105
single, £95-£195 double.
Half board: from £72 daily.
Lunch available.
Evening meal 7pm (l.o.
10.30pm).
Parking for 30.
Credit: Access, Visa, Diners,
Amex.

**Cotswold House Hotel
and Restaurant** M
奫奫奫奫 HIGHLY COMMENDED
The Square, Chipping
Campden, GL55 6AN
☎ Evesham (0386) 840330
Fax (0386) 840310
*Comfort, elegance, good food
and friendly, personal service -
all to be found at our recently
refurbished historic country
town house hotel.*
Bedrooms: 3 single, 7 double
& 5 twin.
Bathrooms: 15 private.
Bed & breakfast: £48-£59
single, £81-£109 double.
Half board: £70.50-£81.20
daily.
Lunch available.
Evening meal 7.15pm (l.o.
9.30pm).
Parking for 14.

Credit: Access, Visa, Diners,
Amex.

Kings Arms Hotel M
High St., Chipping
Campden, GL55 4AW
☎ Evesham (0386) 840256
*Delightful Georgian facade
hides a wealth of open
inglenook fires and lounges.
Range of traditional and
modern dishes. Famous for
food and hospitality. Recently
refurbished.*
Bedrooms: 4 single, 20 double
& 8 twin, 2 family rooms.
Bathrooms: 34 private,
4 public.
Bed & breakfast: from £30
single, £50-£70 double.
Lunch available.
Evening meal 6pm (l.o.
10.30pm).
Parking for 20.
Credit: Access, Visa, Amex.

The Malt House M
奫奫奫 COMMENDED
Broad Campden, Chipping
Campden, GL55 6UU
☎ Evesham (0386) 840295
*A historic house of 16th C
origin, with traditional English
garden.*
Bedrooms: 1 single, 1 double
& 2 twin.
Bathrooms: 3 private,
1 public.
Bed & breakfast: £20-£22
single, £66-£90 double.
Evening meal 7.30pm.
Parking for 5.
Credit: Access, Visa.

Three Ways Hotel M
奫奫奫
Chapel La., Mickleton,
Chipping Campden,
GL55 6SB
☎ (0386) 438429/438231
Telex 337242, Fax (0386)
438858
Inter
*Family-run country village
hotel famous for its Pudding
Club. Convenient for Stratford-
upon-Avon and the Cotswolds.*
Bedrooms: 3 single, 14 double
& 19 twin, 4 family rooms.
Bathrooms: 40 private.
Bed & breakfast: £39-£49
single, £62-£72 double.
Half board: from £46 daily,
from £322 weekly.
Lunch available.
Evening meal 7pm (l.o. 9pm).
Continued ▶

CHIPPING CAMPDEN

Continued

Parking for 40.
Credit: Access, Visa, Diners, Amex.

CHURCH STRETTON

Shropshire
Map ref 4A3

Church Stretton lies under the eastern slope of the Longmynd surrounded by hills. It is ideal for walkers, with marvellous views, golf and gliding. The town has a small puppet theatre and Wenlock Edge is not far away.

Belvedere Guest House M

Burway Rd., Church Stretton, SY6 6DP
☎ (0694) 722232
Quiet detached house set in its own grounds, convenient for Church Stretton town centre and Longmynd Hills. Adequate parking.
Bedrooms: 3 single, 3 double & 2 twin, 4 family rooms.
Bathrooms: 6 private, 3 public.
Bed & breakfast: £15.50-£17 single, £31-£34 double.
Half board: £23-£24.50 daily, £144.90-£154.35 weekly.
Evening meal 7pm (l.o. 6pm).
Parking for 8.

Jinlye

Castle Hill, All Stretton, Church Stretton, SY6 6JP
☎ (0694) 723243
15-acre sheep and horses farm. Set in a lovely elevated position with magnificent views and large garden. Log fires in winter and very peaceful.
Bedrooms: 2 double & 1 twin.
Bathrooms: 1 private, 2 public.
Bed & breakfast: £15 single, £30 double.
Half board: £25 daily, £164 weekly.
Evening meal 7pm (l.o. 9pm).
Parking for 9.

Longmynd Hotel M

Cunnery Rd., Church Stretton, SY6 6AG
☎ (0694) 722244
Family-run country hotel commanding panoramic views of the south Shropshire highlands. Situated in an area of outstanding natural beauty. Self-catering lodges available.
Bedrooms: 5 single, 25 double & 18 twin, 6 family rooms.
Bathrooms: 50 private, 4 public.
Bed & breakfast: from £35 single, from £60 double.
Half board: £40.50-£45.50 daily, £190-£225 weekly.
Lunch available.
Evening meal 7pm (l.o. 9.30pm).
Parking for 150.
Credit: Access, Visa, Diners, Amex.

Mynd House Hotel M APPROVED

Little Stretton, Church Stretton, SY6 6RB
☎ (0694) 722212 Fax (0694) 724180
Small Edwardian house hotel and restaurant. 2 suites available. Dine a la carte or table d'hote.
Bedrooms: 1 single, 3 double & 3 twin, 2 family rooms.
Bathrooms: 9 private.
Bed & breakfast: £28-£32 single, £42-£65 double.
Half board: £32-£45 daily, £224-£315 weekly.
Lunch available.
Evening meal 7.30pm (l.o. 9.15pm).
Parking for 16.
Open February-December.
Credit: Access, Visa.

Paddock Lodge Luxury Guest House M

Shrewsbury Rd., All Stretton, Church Stretton, SY6 6HG
☎ (0694) 723702
Peacefully situated in south Shropshire hill country, which provides superb riding and walking. Local produce used extensively, including home-grown vegetables.
Bedrooms: 1 double & 1 twin, 1 family room.
Bathrooms: 3 private, 1 public.
Bed & breakfast: £32-£34 double.
Half board: from £26 daily.

Evening meal 7pm (l.o. 7.30pm).
Parking for 15.

CIRENCESTER

Gloucestershire
Map ref 2B1

'Capital of the Cotswolds', Cirencester was Britain's second most important Roman town with many finds housed in the Corinium Museum. It has a very fine Perpendicular church and old houses around the market place. Cirencester Park is open to the public with polo in summer.
Tourist Information Centre ☎ (0285) 654180

Corinium Court Hotel & Restaurant

12 Gloucester St., Cirencester, GL7 2DG
☎ (0285) 659711 Fax (0285) 659711
Former wool merchant's house with old beams, open fire and attractive walled garden.
Bedrooms: 1 single, 10 double & 4 twin, 1 family room.
Bathrooms: 16 private.
Bed & breakfast: £45-£50 single, £48-£65 double.
Half board: £35-£50 daily, £245-£350 weekly.
Lunch available.
Evening meal 7.30pm (l.o. 9.30pm).
Parking for 40.
Credit: Access, Visa, Amex.

2 Cove House M

Ashton Keynes, Cirencester, Wiltshire SN6 6NS
☎ (0285) 861221
Original part of historic Cotswold 17th C manor house, set in a beautiful garden. Well placed for visiting Bath, Oxford and the Cotswold countryside. At White Hart, Ashton Keynes turn east. Entrance 100 yards on left.
Bedrooms: 1 double & 2 twin, 1 family room.
Bathrooms: 3 private, 2 public.
Bed & breakfast: £17-£29 single, £32-£40 double.
Half board: £29-£41 daily, £168-£273 weekly.
Evening meal 7pm (l.o. 8pm).
Parking for 7.
Open January-November.

King's Head Hotel M APPROVED

Market Pl., Cirencester, GL7 2NR
☎ (0285) 653322 Telex 43470 Fax (0285) 655103
Best Western
Formerly a historic coaching inn, the hotel now combines old world charm with modern comfort. In 1642 the first blood of the Civil War was shed outside.
Bedrooms: 18 single, 22 double & 26 twin, 4 family rooms.
Bathrooms: 70 private.
Bed & breakfast: £45-£56 single, £65-£74 double.
Half board: £36-£45 daily, £216-£234 weekly.
Lunch available.
Evening meal 7pm (l.o. 9pm).
Parking for 20.
Credit: Access, Visa, C.Bl., Diners, Amex.

Raydon House Hotel and Restaurant M

3 The Avenue, Cirencester, GL7 1EH
☎ (0285) 653485 & (0285) 650625
19th C Victorian detached residence in a tree-lined avenue close to the centre of the town.
Bedrooms: 4 single, 8 double & 2 twin, 1 family room.
Bathrooms: 14 private, 1 public; 1 private shower.
Bed & breakfast: £30-£44 single, £40-£55 double.
Half board: £40-£55 daily, £260-£385 weekly.
Evening meal 7pm (l.o. 8.30pm).
Parking for 5.
Credit: Access, Visa, Amex.

Warwick Cottage Guest House M APPROVED

75 Victoria Rd., Cirencester, GL7 1ES
☎ (0285) 656279
Attractive Victorian townhouse, 5 minutes from the town centre. Good base for touring the Cotswolds. Family rooms available as doubles or twins.
Bedrooms: 1 double & 1 twin, 2 family rooms.
Bathrooms: 1 public; 2 private showers.
Bed & breakfast: £17.50-£20 single, £24-£30 double.

Half board: £18.50-£23 daily,
£113.50-£149 weekly.
Evening meal 6.30pm.
Parking for 4.

Wimborne House M
⚜⚜⚜
91 Victoria Rd., Cirencester,
GL7 1ES
☎ (0285) 653890
*Cotswold-stone house, built in
1886, with a warm and friendly
atmosphere and spacious
rooms. Non-smokers only
please.*
Bedrooms: 4 double & 1 twin.
Bathrooms: 5 private.
Bed & breakfast: £20-£25
single, £25-£30 double.
Half board: £175-£200
weekly.
Evening meal 6.30pm (l.o.
5.30pm).
Parking for 6.

CLEEVE HILL
Gloucestershire
Map ref 2B1

*4m NE. Cheltenham
Settlement with wonderful
all round views above
Cheltenham on the road
to Winchcombe and
Broadway.*

Rising Sun Hotel M
⚜⚜⚜
Cleeve Hill, Cheltenham,
GL52 3PX
☎ Cheltenham (0242) 676281
Fax (0242) 673069
ⓒⓡ Lansbury
*Spectacular hilltop location
with panoramic Cotswolds
views, close to racecourse and
golf-course. Ideal for exploring
the Cotswolds.*
Bedrooms: 3 single, 15 double
& 6 twin.
Bathrooms: 24 private.
Bed & breakfast: £30-£63
single, £60-£76 double.
Half board: from £42 daily.
Lunch available.
Evening meal 7pm (l.o.
10.30pm).
Parking for 70.
Credit: Access, Visa, Diners,
Amex.

CLEOBURY
MORTIMER
Shropshire
Map ref 4A3

*Village with attractive
timbered and Georgian
houses and a church with
a wooden spire. It is
close to the Clee Hills
with marvellous views
and Clee Hill Garden with
over 400 birds and
animals.*

The Redfern Hotel M
⚜⚜⚜
Cleobury Mortimer,
Kidderminster,
Worcestershire DY14 8AA
☎ Cleobury Mortimer
(0299) 270395 Telex 335176.
Fax (0299) 271011
ⓒⓡ Minotels
*18th C stone-built hotel in old
market town. Attractive
bathrooms and 4-poster
available.*
Bedrooms: 5 double & 5 twin,
1 family room.
Bathrooms: 11 private.
Bed & breakfast: £35-£49
single, £50.50-£68 double.
Half board: £32-£40 daily,
£215-£300 weekly.
Lunch available.
Evening meal 7.30pm (l.o.
10pm).
Parking for 20.
Credit: Access, Visa, Diners,
Amex.

CODSALL
Staffordshire
Map ref 4B3

*Expanding residential
village a few miles from
Wolverhampton.*

Moors Farm and
Country Restaurant M
⚜⚜⚜
Chillington La., Codsall,
Wolverhampton, WV8 1QF
☎ (090 74) 2330
*100-acre mixed farm. 200-
year-old farmhouse, 1 mile
from pretty village. All home
produce used. Many local
walks and places of interest.*
Bedrooms: 1 double & 2 twin,
3 family rooms.
Bathrooms: 2 private,
2 public.
Bed & breakfast: £21-£26
single, £34-£42 double.
Half board: £25-£34 daily.
Lunch available.

Evening meal 6.30pm (l.o.
7pm).
Parking for 20.

COLEFORD
Gloucestershire
Map ref 2A1

*Small town in the Forest
of Dean with the ancient
iron mines at Clearwell
Caves nearby, where
mining equipment and
geological samples are
displayed. There are
several forest trails in the
area.*
*Tourist Information
Centre ☎ (0594) 36307*

Forest House Hotel M
⚜⚜⚜
Cinder Hill, Coleford
GL16 8HQ
☎ Dean (0594) 32424
*Gracious listed building with
spacious, well-furnished rooms,
2 minutes' walk from town
centre.*
Bedrooms: 2 single, 3 double
& 2 twin.
Bathrooms: 1 private,
2 public.
Bed & breakfast: £14-£15
single, £28-£37 double.
Half board: £22.50-£27 daily.
Evening meal 7pm (l.o.
8.30pm).
Parking for 10.

The Lambsquay House
Hotel M
⚜⚜⚜
Royal Forest of Dean,
Coleford, GL16 8QB
☎ Dean (0594) 33127
*Georgian country house in the
Royal Forest of Dean,
surrounded by garden and
fields. Well-equipped,
comfortable accommodation.
Varied food and wine.*
Bedrooms: 1 single, 5 double
& 2 twin, 1 family room.
Bathrooms: 9 private.
Bed & breakfast: £25-£45
single, £39-£60 double.
Half board: £27-£35 daily,
£189-£245 weekly.
Evening meal 7pm (l.o.
8.30pm).
Parking for 30.
Credit: Access, Visa, Diners.

Poolway House Hotel &
Restaurant M
⚜⚜⚜⚜
Gloucester Rd., Coleford,
GL16 8BN
☎ Dean (0594) 33937
*Situated in an area of
outstanding natural beauty, set
between the River Severn and
the scenic grace of the River
Wye. Enjoy a relaxing break
in our cosy oak beamed manor.
Good food and a warm
welcome assured.*
Bedrooms: 3 double & 3 twin,
1 family room.
Bathrooms: 7 private.
Bed & breakfast: £20-£33
single, £40-£44 double.
Half board: from £25.50
daily, from £178.50 weekly.
Lunch available.
Evening meal 6pm (l.o.
9.30pm).
Parking for 15.
Credit: Visa.

COLESHILL
Warwickshire
Map ref 4B3

*9m E. Birmingham
Close to Birmingham's
many attractions
including the 17th C
Aston Hall with its
plasterwork and
furnishings, the Railway
Museum and Sarehole
Mill, an 18th C water-
powered mill restored to
working order.*

Coleshill Hotel
⚜⚜⚜ COMMENDED
152 High St., Coleshill,
Birmingham, W. Midlands
B46 3BG
☎ (0675) 465527
Telex 333868 Fax (0675)
464013
ⓒⓡ Lansbury
*In traditional coaching inn
style with restaurant, cellar
bar, lounge bar and
function/conference facilities.*
Bedrooms: 2 single, 11 double
& 10 twin.
Bathrooms: 23 private.
Bed & breakfast: £25-£62
single, £50-£74 double.
Half board: £36-£76 daily.
Lunch available.
Evening meal 7pm (l.o.
10pm).
Parking for 48.
Credit: Access, Visa, Diners,
Amex.

We advise you to
confirm your
booking in writing.

Please mention this
guide when making
a booking.

225

COTSWOLDS

See Ampney Crucis, Arlingham, Berkeley, Bibury, Birdlip, Blakeney, Bledington, Bourton-on-the-Water, Broadway, Cheltenham, Chipping Campden, Cirencester, Cleeve Hill, Coleford, Fairford, Fossebridge, Gloucester, Huntley, Lechlade, Minchinhampton, Moreton-in-Marsh, Nailsworth, Newnham, North Nibley, Northleach, Nympsfield, Painswick, Slimbridge, Stonehouse, Stow-on-the-Wold, Stroud, Tetbury, Tewkesbury, Whitminster, Winchcombe, Withington.

COVENTRY

W. Midlands
Map ref 4B3

Modern city with a long history. It has many places of interest including the post-war and ruined medieval cathedrals, art gallery and museums, some 16th C almshouses, St. Mary's Guildhall, Lunt Roman fort and the Belgrade Theatre.
Tourist Information Centre ☎ *(0203) 832311*

Ansty Hall ♏
Ansty, Coventry, CV7 9HZ
☎ Shilton (0203) 612222
Red brick country house hotel built in 1678 nestling in 8 acres of formal and informal gardens. Just outside Coventry in Ansty village.
Bedrooms: 15 double & 15 twin.
Bathrooms: 30 private.
Bed & breakfast: £74.50 single, £99-£107 double.
Lunch available.
Evening meal 7pm (l.o. 9.45pm).
Parking for 50.
Credit: Access, Visa, Diners, Amex.

Arlon Guest House
25 St. Patricks Rd., Coventry, CV1 2LP
☎ (0203) 225942
Detached comfortable accommodation in a homely and friendly atmosphere. Close to railway station and central for all other amenities. Near

National Exhibition Centre and National Agricultural Centre.
Bedrooms: 1 single, 2 twin, 1 family room.
Bathrooms: 2 private, 1 public.
Bed & breakfast: from £14 single, from £26 double.
Parking for 5.

Ashleigh House
Listed
17 Park Rd., Coventry, CV1 2LH
☎ (0203) 223804
Newly renovated guesthouse only 100 yards from the railway station. All city amenities within 5 minutes' walk.
Bedrooms: 6 twin, 4 family rooms.
Bathrooms: 3 public.
Bed & breakfast: £15-£18 single, £26-£28 double.
Evening meal 5pm (l.o. 7pm).
Parking for 12.
Credit: Access, Amex.

Avalon Guest House ♏
Listed
28 Friars Rd., Coventry, CV1 2LW
☎ (0203) 251839
Well-appointed guesthouse 3 minutes' walk from the city centre and rail station. All rooms have colour TV, tea/coffee facilities and full central heating.
Bedrooms: 3 single, 2 twin, 3 family rooms.
Bathrooms: 5 private, 1 public; 1 private shower.
Bed & breakfast: £15-£18 single, £30-£36 double.
Parking for 6.

Beechwood Hotel ♏
Sandpits Lane, Keresley, Coventry, CV6 2FR
☎ (0203) 338662
Family-run hotel set in its own grounds and adjacent to the National Exhibition Centre. Centrally situated for touring historic central England.
Bedrooms: 16 single, 6 double & 2 twin.
Bathrooms: 24 private.
Bed & breakfast: from £39.50 single, £52-£54 double.
Lunch available.
Evening meal 7pm (l.o. 9.50pm).

Parking for 60.
Credit: Access, Visa, Diners, Amex.

Brooklands Grange Hotel and Restaurant ♏
COMMENDED
Holyhead Rd., Coventry, CV5 8HX
☎ (0203) 601601 Fax (0203) 601277
Originally a Jacobean farmhouse now a prestigious 30 bedroomed privately owned hotel with restaurant. Ideally situated for touring the historic attractions in the county of Warwickshire.
Bedrooms: 4 single, 17 double & 8 twin, 1 family room.
Bathrooms: 30 private.
Bed & breakfast: £75-£78 single, £88-£92 double.
Lunch available.
Evening meal 7pm (l.o. 10pm).
Parking for 54.
Credit: Access, Visa, Amex.

Churchill Hotel
Walsgrave Rd., Ball Hill, Coventry, CV2 4EB
☎ (0203) 447459
Telex 333388 Fax (0203) 550112
Family establishment offering relaxed atmosphere 5 minutes from Coventry's historic buildings and modern shops. Near major motorways and the National Exhibition Centre.
Bedrooms: 4 double & 8 twin.
Bathrooms: 12 private showers.
Bed & breakfast: £32.50-£34.50 single, £39.50-£42 double.
Half board: £30.25-£42.50 daily.
Lunch available.
Evening meal 6.30pm (l.o. 10pm).
Parking for 21.
Credit: Access, Visa, Amex.

Coombe Fields Guest House
Listed
496 Binley Rd., Coventry, CV3 2DQ
☎ (0203) 451030
Small friendly guesthouse on southern outskirts of city, on main bus route.
Bedrooms: 3 single, 1 double & 1 twin.
Bathrooms: 1 public.

Bed & breakfast: £14-£15 single.
Evening meal 6pm.
Parking for 6.

Fairlight Guest House
14 Regent St., off Queen's Rd., Coventry, CV1 3EP
☎ (0203) 224215
3-storey, double-fronted Victorian house, half a mile from the city centre and cathedral, quarter of a mile from the station.
Bedrooms: 6 single, 1 double & 3 twin, 1 family room.
Bathrooms: 1 private, 3 public.
Bed & breakfast: £13-£15 single, £26-£32 double.
Parking for 6.

Hearsall Lodge Hotel ♏
1 Broad La., Coventry, CV5 7AA
☎ (0203) 674543
Family-run hotel, all bedrooms with TV, showers and tea/coffee making facilities. Ample parking with easy access to A45 and M6 plus local amenities. Direct dial telephone.
Bedrooms: 6 single, 6 double & 5 twin, 1 family room.
Bathrooms: 1 private, 4 public; 14 private showers.
Bed & breakfast: £28-£37.50 single, £42-£47.50 double.
Half board: £35-£44.50 daily.
Evening meal 6.30pm (l.o. 7.30pm).
Parking for 19.

Hotel Leofric
Broadgate, Coventry, CV1 1LZ
☎ (0203) 221371
Telex 311193
Hotel with restaurant, coffee shop and 3 bars. Near Coventry Cathedral, Kenilworth and Warwick Castle.
Bedrooms: 40 single, 10 double & 36 twin, 5 family rooms.
Bathrooms: 91 private, 1 public.
Bed & breakfast: from £65 single, from £84.50 double.
Lunch available.
Evening meal 7pm (l.o. 9.45pm).
Credit: Access, Visa, Diners, Amex.

Merrick Lodge Hotel M
COMMENDED
80-82 St. Nicholas St.,
Coventry, CV1 4BP
☎ (0203) 553940 Fax (0203) 550112
Former manor house, 5 minutes' walk from city centre. Fully licensed, table d'hote and a la carte restaurant, 3 bars. Private parties catered for.
Bedrooms: 3 single, 9 double & 10 twin, 4 family rooms.
Bathrooms: 26 private.
Bed & breakfast: £36-£42.50 single, £52.50 double.
Half board: £36.25-£52.50 daily, £253.75-£367.50 weekly.
Lunch available.
Evening meal 6.30pm (l.o. 11pm).
Parking for 60.
Credit: Access, Visa, Amex.

Northanger House M
35 Westminster Rd.,
Coventry, CV1 3GB
☎ (0203) 226780
Friendly home 5 minutes from the city centre. Close to railway and bus stations. Convenient for all amenities.
Bedrooms: 2 single, 2 double & 3 twin, 2 family rooms.
Bathrooms: 3 public.
Bed & breakfast: £15-£16 single, £26-£28 double.
Parking for 1.

Novotel M
Wilsons La., Longford,
Coventry, CV6 6HL
☎ (0203) 365000 Telex 31545
Novotel
Coventry and the Novotel, a venue for business, holiday weekends or as a relaxing stop-over between journeys.
Bedrooms: 100 family rooms.
Bathrooms: 100 private.
Bed & breakfast: £35-£62 single, £47-£72 double.
Lunch available.
Evening meal 6pm (l.o. 11.59pm).
Parking for 150.
Credit: Access, Visa, C.Bl., Diners, Amex.

The Old Mill Hotel M
COMMENDED
Mill Hill, Baginton, Coventry,
CV8 2BS
☎ (0203) 303588
Hotel retaining many interesting features preserved from its working days as a mill. The hotel's 5 acres of gardens run down to the banks of the River Sowe.
Bedrooms: 11 double & 4 twin, 5 family rooms.
Bathrooms: 20 private.
Bed & breakfast: from £58 single, from £71 double.
Lunch available.
Evening meal 7pm (l.o. 9.30pm).
Parking for 200.
Credit: Access, Visa, Diners, Amex.

Victoria Guest House
39 St. Patrick's Rd.,
Coventry, CV1 2LP
☎ (0203) 221378
Small bed and breakfast establishment in centre of town, offering friendly service. Convenient for station, cathedral and city centre shopping. On-street parking.
Bedrooms: 2 single, 1 double & 1 twin, 1 family room.
Bathrooms: 2 public.
Bed & breakfast: £14-£16 single, £26-£30 double.

3m W. Evesham
Pretty village of mainly black and white cottages overlooking the River Avon.

Cedars Guest House
Evesham Rd., Cropthorne,
Pershore, Worcestershire
WR10 3JU
☎ Evesham (0386) 860219
Country house with friendly atmosphere, between Evesham and Pershore on A44.
Tea/coffee facilities and TV in all bedrooms. TV lounge, bar and separate dining room.
Bedrooms: 1 single, 1 double & 2 twin, 1 family room.
Bathrooms: 1 private, 2 public.
Bed & breakfast: £12-£12.50 single, £30.50-£38 double.
Parking for 5.

Old town with natural brine springs, developed as a spa town at the beginning of the 19th C. It has some interesting churches, in particular the Church of the Sacred Heart with splendid mosaics. There are several fine parks and a Heritage Centre.

Richmond Guest House M
3 Ombersley St. West,
Droitwich, Worcestershire
WR9 8HZ
☎ (0905) 775722
Victorian-built guesthouse in the town centre, 5 minutes from railway station and bus route. English breakfast.
Bedrooms: 6 single, 1 double & 4 twin, 3 family rooms.
Bathrooms: 2 public.
Bed & breakfast: £13-£15 single, £23-£25 double.
Parking for 12.

A 13th C castle dominates this iron-producing town and in its wooded grounds is Dudley Zoo, which can be reached by chair lift. The Black Country Museum depicts the history of the town and there are trips into the Canal Tunnel.
Tourist Information Centre ☎ *(0384) 50333*

Station Hotel M
Castle Hill, Dudley,
DY1 4RA
☎ (0384) 253418
Telex 335464 Fax (0384) 457503
Recently refurbished and situated within easy reach of the town centre, Dudley Zoo, castle and Black Country Museum. Easy access from the M5.
Bedrooms: 14 single, 10 double & 7 twin, 7 family rooms.
Bathrooms: 38 private.
Bed & breakfast: from £50.50 single, from £63.50 double.
Lunch available.

Evening meal 7pm (l.o. 10pm).
Parking for 75.
Credit: Access, Visa, Amex.

Ward Arms M
Birmingham Rd., Dudley,
DY1 4RN
☎ (0384) 458070
Telex 335464 Fax (0384) 457502
Easy access to M5/M6. Full a la carte and carvery restaurant. Luncheons all week (Saturdays excluded). Totally refurbished hotel.
Bedrooms: 24 double & 24 twin.
Bathrooms: 48 private.
Bed & breakfast: from £55 single, from £69.50 double.
Lunch available.
Evening meal 7pm (l.o. 10pm).
Parking for 150.
Credit: Access, Visa, Amex.

Kingfisher Hotel M
Newport St., Hay-on-Wye,
Hereford, Herefordshire
HR3 5BE
☎ Hay-on-Wye
(0497) 820448
Small, comfortable hotel, near Hay-on-Wye, recently modernised and refurnished to a high standard, with many interesting features.
Bedrooms: 1 single, 3 double & 2 twin, 2 family rooms.
Bathrooms: 2 private, 2 public; 1 private shower.
Bed & breakfast: £16-£22 single, £28-£40 double.
Half board: £24-£30 daily.
Lunch available.
Evening meal 7pm (l.o. 9pm).
Parking for 6.
Credit: Access, Visa.

Half board prices shown are per person but in some cases may be based on double/twin occupancy.

The National Crown Scheme is explained in full on pages 556 – 558.

ELLESMERE

Shropshire
Map ref 4A2

Small market town with old streets and houses and situated close to 9 lakes. The largest, The Mere, has many recreational facilities and some of the other meres have sailing and fishing.

The Mount M
COMMENDED
St John's Hill, Ellesmere, SY12 0EY
☎ (0691) 622466
A few guests at a time are invited to stay in a professional couples' listed Georgian house in Ellesmere's conservation area. Bed and breakfast. Non-smoking.
Bedrooms: 1 double & 1 twin.
Bathrooms: 2 private.
Bed & breakfast: £18.50-£20 single, £32-£35 double.
Parking for 4.

EVESHAM

Hereford & Worcester
Map ref 2B1

Evesham is a market town in the centre of a fruit-growing area. There are pleasant walks along the River Avon and many old houses and inns. A fine 16th C bell tower stands between 2 churches.
Tourist Information Centre ☎ (0386) 6944

Evesham Hotel M
COMMENDED
Cooper's La., off Waterside, Evesham, Worcestershire WR11 6DA
☎ (0386) 765566
Telex 339342 Fax (0386) 765443
Family-run Tudor mansion in 2.5-acre garden, offering unusual food and wine and all modern facilities. Ideal touring centre. New indoor pool.
Bedrooms: 6 single, 22 double & 11 twin, 1 family room.
Bathrooms: 40 private.
Bed & breakfast: £52-£58 single, £70-£76 double.
Lunch available.
Evening meal 7pm (l.o. 9.30pm).

Parking for 45.
Credit: Access, Visa, Diners, Amex.

The Mill at Harvington M
Anchor Lane, Harvington, Evesham, Worcestershire WR11 5NR
☎ (0386) 870688
Peaceful, riverside hotel tastefully converted from beautiful house and mill. In acres of gardens, quarter of a mile from Evesham to Stratford road.
Bedrooms: 12 double & 3 twin.
Bathrooms: 15 private.
Bed & breakfast: £52-£58 single, £75-£85 double.
Half board: £66-£70 daily.
Lunch available.
Evening meal 7pm (l.o. 8.45pm).
Parking for 25.
Credit: Access, Visa.

Nightingale Hotel M
COMMENDED
Bishampton, Pershore, Worcestershire WR10 2NH
☎ (038 682) 521 & (038 682) 384
200-acre beef and arable farm. Near Evesham and within easy reach of Stratford, Cotswolds and Malvern. Golfing, riding and sports centre close by. A friendly atmosphere awaits you.
Bedrooms: 1 single, 1 double & 1 twin, 1 family room.
Bathrooms: 4 private.
Bed & breakfast: £30 single, £40 double.
Half board: £45 daily.
Evening meal 7.30pm (l.o. 9pm).
Parking for 24.
Credit: Access, Visa.

Park View Hotel M
APPROVED
Waterside, Evesham, Worcestershire WR11 6BS
☎ (0386) 442639
Riverside hotel offering personal attention. Traditional English breakfast included, evening meal available. Base for touring Cotswolds and Shakespeare country
Bedrooms: 13 single, 3 double & 11 twin, 2 family rooms.
Bathrooms: 6 public.

Bed & breakfast: £16.50-£19 single, £30-£34 double.
Half board: £24-£27 daily.
Lunch available.
Evening meal 6pm (l.o. 7pm).
Parking for 50.
Credit: Access, Visa.

Riverside Hotel M
COMMENDED
The Parks, Offenham Rd., Evesham, Worcestershire WR11 5JP
☎ (0386) 446200 Fax (0386) 40021
A small country house hotel offering panoramic views across the Avon.
Bedrooms: 3 double & 4 twin.
Bathrooms: 7 private.
Bed & breakfast: £50-£55 single, £65-£85 double.
Half board: £65-£70 daily, £455-£490 weekly.
Lunch available.
Evening meal 7.30pm (l.o. 9pm).
Parking for 45.
Credit: Access, Visa.

The Waterside Hotel M
56 Waterside, Evesham, Worcestershire WR11 6JZ
☎ (0386) 442420
Independent hotel with relaxed happy atmosphere. Bedrooms refurbished in peach and pink theme. New restaurant with open fire, oak beams. Riverside gardens.
Bedrooms: 8 double & 1 twin, 4 family rooms.
Bathrooms: 10 private, 1 public.
Bed & breakfast: £23.60-£43.80 single, £39.40-£54.70 double.
Half board: £28.20-£52.30 daily.
Lunch available.
Evening meal 6.30pm (l.o. 9.30pm).
Parking for 30.
Credit: Access, Visa, Amex.

> **Classifications and quality commendations were correct at the time of going to press but are subject to change. Please check at the time of booking.**

FAIRFORD

Gloucestershire
Map ref 2B1

Small town with a 15th C wool church famous for its complete 15th C stained glass windows, interesting carvings and original wall paintings. It is an excellent touring centre and the Cotswolds Wildlife Park is nearby.

Hyperion House Hotel M
London St., Fairford, GL7 4AH
☎ Cirencester (0285) 712 349
Consort
Privately run Cotswold hotel in central location, convenient for Stratford, Oxford and Bath. Close to upper reaches of the Thames.
Bedrooms: 4 single, 11 double & 7 twin, 4 family rooms.
Bathrooms: 26 private.
Bed & breakfast: £70-£80 single, £80-£90 double.
Half board: £100-£120 daily.
Lunch available.
Evening meal 7pm (l.o. 9.30pm).
Parking for 35.
Credit: Access, Visa, Diners, Amex.

FOSSEBRIDGE

Gloucestershire
Map ref 2B1

3m S. Northleach Hamlet on the Roman road from Northleach to Cirencester where it crosses the River Coln, and the meeting place of 3 parishes.

Fossebridge Inn M
Fossebridge, Nr. Northleach, Cheltenham, GL54 3JS
☎ Cirencester (0285) 720 721
Attractively decorated, traditional Cotswold inn offering modern facilities and an informal atmosphere. Delightful gardens and lake with an abundance of wildlife.
Bedrooms: 11 double & 3 twin.
Bathrooms: 14 private, 1 public.
Bed & breakfast: £40-£50 single, £55-£70 double.
Half board: £45-£80 daily.
Lunch available.
Evening meal 7pm (l.o. 9.30pm).

Parking for 50.
Credit: Access, Visa, C.Bl.,
Diners, Amex.

GLOUCESTER

Gloucestershire
Map ref 2B1

A Roman city and inland
port on the Severn, its
cathedral is one of the
most beautiful in Britain.
Gloucester's many
attractions include
museums, old buildings
and inns and the house of
Beatrix Potter's 'Tailor of
Gloucester'.
*Tourist Information
Centre* ☎ *(0452) 421188*

Chosen Lodge

41A Albemarle Rd.,
Churchdown, Gloucester,
GL3 2HE
☎ (0452) 713159
*Newly built lodge with en-suite
bedrooms. Situated mid-way
between Cheltenham and
Gloucester, close to Cotswolds.
Non-smokers only please.*
Bedrooms: 2 double & 1 twin.
Bathrooms: 2 private,
1 public.
Bed & breakfast: £26-£32
single, £36-£44 double.
Evening meal 6pm.
Parking for 3.

Denmark Road Hotel

36 Denmark Road
Gloucester, GL1 3JQ
☎ (0452) 303808
*Small family hotel close to city
centre.*
Bedrooms: 8 single, 2 double,
1 family room.
Bathrooms: 4 private,
2 public.
Bed & breakfast: £17.25-£23
single, £29.90-£36.80 double.
Half board: £23-£28.75 daily,
£138-£172.50 weekly.
Evening meal 6pm (l.o.
7.30pm).
Parking for 17.

Hatton Court M

Upton Hill, Upton St.
Leonards, Gloucester,
GL4 8DE
☎ (0452) 617412
Telex 437334 HATCRT G

*17th C Cotswold stone country
house set in 7 acres gardens
and 30 acres pastures, 600 feet
above Gloucester, with
panoramic views of Severn
Valley and Malvern Hills.*
Bedrooms: 24 double &
22 twin.
Bathrooms: 46 private.
Bed & breakfast: £73-£90
single, £97-£121 double.
Half board: £80-£92.50 daily,
from £378 weekly.
Lunch available.
Evening meal 7.30pm (l.o.
10pm).
Parking for 70.
Credit: Access, Visa, Diners,
Amex.

The Limes

Stroud Rd., Brookthorpe,
Gloucester, GL4 0UQ
☎ Painswick (0452) 812645
*A charming Georgian 3-storey
house on the A4173 between
Gloucester and Stroud, set in
the Cotswold Escarpment.*
Bedrooms: 4 single, 2 double
& 2 twin, 1 family room.
Bathrooms: 3 private,
3 public.
Bed & breakfast: £17-£20
single, £30-£35 double.
Half board: £23-£27 daily.
Lunch available.
Evening meal 6pm (l.o. 8pm).
Parking for 10.
Credit: Access, Visa.

Lulworth

12 Midlands Rd., Gloucester,
GL1 4UF
☎ (0452) 21881
Half a mile from city centre.
Bedrooms: 2 single, 2 double
& 2 twin, 2 family rooms.
Bathrooms: 2 private,
3 public.
Bed & breakfast: £13-£16
single, £26-£32 double.
Parking for 12.

New County Hotel M

Southgate St., Gloucester,
GL1 2DU
☎ (0452) 307000 Fax (0452)
500487

> **Map references
> apply to the colour
> maps towards the
> end of this guide.**

*Convenient for Gloucester's
good shopping centre. New
pub/wine bar serving real ales
and home-made traditional
country food.*
Bedrooms: 12 single,
11 double & 5 twin, 3 family
rooms.
Bathrooms: 31 private.
Bed & breakfast: £40-£46.75
single, £45-£56.50 double.
Half board: £55-£65 daily.
Lunch available.
Evening meal 7pm (l.o.
9.15pm).
Credit: Access, Visa, Diners,
Amex.

Nicki's Hotel & Taverna

105-107 Westgate St.,
Gloucester, GL1 2PG
☎ (0452) 301359
*Restaurant with full a la carte
menu, English and Greek food.
Refurbished in 1989. Near city
centre, cathedral and docks.*
Bedrooms: 3 single, 3 double
& 4 twin, 4 family rooms.
Bathrooms: 13 private,
2 public; 1 private shower.
Bed & breakfast: £23-£25
single, £35-£40 double.
Half board: £30-£35 daily,
£175-£185 weekly.
Lunch available.
Evening meal 5pm (l.o.
11pm).
Credit: Visa, Amex.

The Retreat M

116 Bristol Rd., Quedgeley,
Gloucester, GL2 6NA
☎ (0452) 728296
*Large double-fronted detached
house.*
Bedrooms: 1 single, 1 double
& 6 twin, 3 family rooms.
Bathrooms: 1 private,
6 public; 3 private showers.
Bed & breakfast: £15-£20
single, £25-£30 double.
Parking for 10.

Rotherfield House Hotel M

5 Horton Rd., Gloucester,
GL1 3PX
☎ (0452) 410500
*Quiet side road location, 1 mile
from city centre. Family
business. Choice of freshly-
cooked dishes.*
Bedrooms: 5 single, 1 double
& 2 twin, 2 family rooms.
Bathrooms: 8 private,
2 public.

Bed & breakfast: £16.95-
£25.95 single, max. £35.95
double.
Half board: £24.45-£33.35
daily, £162.60-£223.08
weekly.
Evening meal 6.45pm (l.o.
7.15pm).
Parking for 9.
Credit: Access, Visa, Diners,
Amex.

Twigworth Lodge Hotel & Restaurant M

Tewkesbury Rd., Twigworth,
Gloucester, GL2 9PG
☎ (0452) 730266 Fax (0452)
730099
*Grade II listed building, well-
known for good food, bar
snacks and friendly
atmosphere.*
Bedrooms: 2 single, 19 double
& 6 twin, 1 family room.
Bathrooms: 27 private,
1 public.
Bed & breakfast: £22-£45
single, £40-£70 double.
Half board: from £31 daily.
Lunch available.
Evening meal 7pm (l.o.
9.30pm).
Parking for 40.
Credit: Access, Visa, Diners,
Amex.

GREAT WITLEY

Hereford & Worcester
Map ref 2B1

Hundred House Hotel M
COMMENDED

Great Witley, Worcester,
Worcestershire WR6 6HS
☎ (0299) 896888 Fax (0299)
896588
*Family owned country hotel.
Situated on A443 Worcester to
Tenbury road. Only 40 minutes
from National Exhibition
Centre, yet close to the Welsh
border.*
Bedrooms: 2 single, 6 double
& 9 twin, 2 family rooms.
Bathrooms: 19 private.
Bed & breakfast: from £40
single, from £55 double.
Lunch available.
Evening meal 7pm (l.o.
9.45pm).
Parking for 120.
Credit: Access, Visa.

HEART OF ENGLAND

GRINDON

Staffordshire
Map ref 4B2

7m E. Leek
Isolated village standing high up in moorland country above the deep-set valley of the River Hamps, much of which is owned by the National Trust. The church with its distinctive spire is sometimes called the 'Cathedral of the Moors'.

Porch Farmhouse
♛♛♛

Grindon, Leek, ST13 7TP
☎ Onecote (053 88) 545
Award winning 400-year-old Peak District farmhouse ideally situated overlooking the beautiful Manifold Valley. Peaceful surroundings, wonderful walks and scenery.
Bedrooms: 2 double & 1 twin.
Bathrooms: 3 private.
Bed & breakfast: £34-£38 double.
Half board: £28.50-£31 daily.
Evening meal 7pm (l.o. 8pm).
Parking for 3.
🛏🕭💷⛽🆄🅻 ⬚ 🆅 📺
〰 ⛴ 🍽 ᴼᴬᴾ SP

HAMPTON-IN-ARDEN

W. Midlands
Map ref 4B3

The Hollies
Kenilworth Rd., Hampton-in-Arden, Solihull, B92 0LW
☎ Hampton-in-Arden (067 55) 2941 & Hampton-in-Arden (067 55) 2681
On the A452, ideally located for many major attractions of the Midlands, including the National Agricultural Centre at Kenilworth, Warwick Castle and Stratford-upon-Avon. Only 5 minutes to National Motorcycle Museum and the National Exhibition Centre.
Bedrooms: 1 single, 1 double & 5 twin.
Bathrooms: 4 private, 1 public.
Bed & breakfast: £15-£20 single, £35-£40 double.
Parking for 10.
🛏🕭⛽🆄🅻 ⬚ 🆅 🇷 📺
〰 ⛴ 🍽 ❄
⚙ Display advertisement appears on page 266.

HENLEY-IN-ARDEN

Warwickshire
Map ref 2B1

Old market town which in Tudor times stood in the Forest of Arden. It has many ancient inns, a 15th C Guildhall and parish church. Coughton Court with its Gunpowder Plot connections is nearby.

Ardencote Manor Hotel and Country Club M
♛♛♛

Lye Green Rd., Claverdon, Warwick, CV35 8LS
☎ (092 684) 3111 Fax 0926 842646
Set in secluded gardens and parkland, between Warwick and Henley-in-Arden with easy access to the National Exhibition Centre, National Agricultural Centre and Stratford-upon-Avon.
Bedrooms: 10 single, 69 twin.
Bathrooms: 79 private.
Bed & breakfast: £65-£70 single, £75-£85 double.
Half board: £95-£100 daily.
Lunch available.
Evening meal 7.30pm (l.o. 9.30pm).
Parking for 250.
Credit: Access, Visa, Diners, Amex.
🛏🕭💷🅻 ⬚ 🆅 🇷
🔵〰 ⛴ 🍽 ⚑ 🥂 🏹 ♪
🕛 ▶ ❄ 🅂🄿 🎬 🅣

Avonlodge Hotel
♛♛♛

Bearley Crossroads, Birmingham Rd., Wootton Wawen, B95 6DR
☎ Stratford-upon-Avon (0789) 731111
Quiet hotel, serving home cooked food, located on the main Birmingham road (A34).
Bedrooms: 11 single, 9 double & 5 twin, 4 family rooms.
Bathrooms: 29 private.
Bed & breakfast: £35-£40 single, £40-£70 double.
Half board: £45-£50 daily.
Lunch available.
Evening meal 6.30pm (l.o. 10pm).
Parking for 48.
Credit: Access, Visa.
🛏🕭⛽🅻 🕭 ⬚ 🆅 ⚲
🇷 📺 🔵 ⚑ 🍽 🅂🄿 🅣

HEREFORD

Hereford & Worcester
Map ref 2A1

Agricultural county town, its cathedral containing much Norman work and a large chained library. The city's varied attractions include the Bulmer Railway Centre and several museums including a cider museum.
Tourist Information Centre ☎ *(0432) 268430*

The Ancient Camp Inn M
👑👑 COMMENDED

Ruckhall, Eaton Bishop, Hereford, Herefordshire HR2 9QX
☎ Golden Valley (0981) 250449
This inn is on the site of an Iron Age fort dating from the 4th-5th C BC. Spectacular views of the River Wye. Restaurant and bar food a speciality.
Bedrooms: 3 double & 1 twin.
Bathrooms: 4 private.
Bed & breakfast: £30-£40 single, £42.50-£52.50 double.
Lunch available.
Evening meal 7pm (l.o. 9.30pm).
Parking for 45.
Credit: Access, Visa.
🛏7 🕭💷⛽ ⬚ 🆅 🇷 📺〰
⚑ ♪ ❄ 🏹 🎬 🅣

Belmont Lodge Hotel and Golf Club
Belmont House, Ruckhall Rd., Hereford, Herefordshire HR2 9SA
☎ (0432) 352666
Comfortable hotel situated off the A465 Abergavenny road, 2 miles from Hereford city centre.
Bedrooms: 4 double & 26 twin.
Bathrooms: 30 private.
Bed & breakfast: £50-£55 single.
Lunch available.
Evening meal 7pm (l.o. 9.45pm).
Parking for 120.
Credit: Access, Visa, Diners, Amex.
🛏🕭🕭💷⛽ ⬚ 🆅 🇷
📺 🔵 ⚑ 🍽 🥂 ♪ ▶
❄ 🏹 🅂🄿 🎬

Castle Pool Hotel M
👑👑👑👑 APPROVED

Castle St., Hereford, Herefordshire HR1 2NR
☎ (0432) 356321

Castle Pool garden is part of the old castle moat. Located minutes from the cathedral, river and sports facilities.
Bedrooms: 9 single, 8 double & 8 twin, 2 family rooms.
Bathrooms: 27 private.
Bed & breakfast: from £44 single, from £60 double.
Half board: £45-£59 daily, £280-£385 weekly.
Lunch available.
Evening meal 7.30pm (l.o. 9.30pm).
Parking for 14.
Credit: Access, Visa, Diners, Amex.
🛏🕭🕭🕭💷⛽ ⬚ 🆅
🇷 📺〰 ⚑ 🍽 🥂 🅂🄿 🎬 🅣

Cedar Tree Guest House M
🏠

123 Whitecross Rd., Whitecross Hereford, Herefordshire HR4 0LS
☎ (0432) 267235
Situated on touring route, approximately 1 mile from Hereford, this Georgian family guesthouse has private parking.
Bedrooms: 1 twin, 3 family rooms.
Bathrooms: 1 public.
Bed & breakfast: £14-£16 single, £24-£26 double.
Parking for 10.
🛏🕭⛽🆄🅻 🇷 📺〰
⚑ 🏹 ❄

Chesley House M
👑👑 COMMENDED

9 Southbank Rd., Hereford, Herefordshire, HR1 2TJ
☎ (0432) 274800
A comfortable, family-run detached Victorian guesthouse, in a quiet part of the city near the centre, bus and train stations. Spacious gardens.
Bedrooms: 1 single, 1 double & 1 twin, 1 family room.
Bathrooms: 1 public; 2 private showers.
Bed & breakfast: £14.50-£18.50 single, £28-£36 double.
Half board: £22-£26 daily, £147-£175 weekly.
Lunch available.
Evening meal 6pm (l.o. 1pm).
Parking for 6.
🛏🕭⛽🆄🅻 ⬚ 🆅 🇷 📺〰
⚑ ❄ 🏹 ᴼᴬᴾ 🔑 🅂🄿

Collins House Hotel and Restaurant M
👑👑👑👑 COMMENDED

19 St Owens St., Hereford, Herefordshire HR1 2JB
☎ (0432) 272416
Unique Georgian city hotel. Elegant dining room, with cuisine and service to the highest standard.
Bedrooms: 3 double & 1 twin.

Half board prices shown are per person but in some cases may be based on double/twin occupancy.

Bathrooms: 4 private.
Bed & breakfast: from £65 single, from £90 double.
Half board: from £70 daily, from £490 weekly.
Lunch available.
Evening meal 7pm (l.o. 9.30pm).
Credit: Access, Visa, Diners, Amex.

Dormington Court Country House Hotel & Restaurant M

Dormington, Hereford, Herefordshire HR1 4DA
☎ (0432) 850370
A small 17th C Georgian country house, now a family-run hotel, set in delightful countryside.
Bedrooms: 3 double & 3 twin.
Bathrooms: 6 private.
Bed & breakfast: £24-£35 single, £44-£64 double.
Lunch available.
Evening meal 7pm (l.o. 8.45pm).
Parking for 20.
Credit: Access, Visa.

Ferncroft Hotel M

Ledbury Rd., Hereford, Herefordshire HR1 2TB
☎ (0432) 265538
Family hotel set in its own grounds with ample parking. Colour TV in all bedrooms, some of which are en-suite. Licensed dining room.
Bedrooms: 4 single, 3 double & 2 twin, 2 family rooms.
Bathrooms: 6 private, 2 public.
Bed & breakfast: £20-£25 single, £36-£42 double.
Half board: £30-£35 daily.
Evening meal 6.30pm (l.o. 7pm).
Parking for 8.
Credit: Access, Visa.

Graftonbury Hotel

Grafton Lane, Hereford, Herefordshire HR2 8BN
☎ (0432) 356411
Hotel in pleasant surroundings with own garden. 2 miles from historic city centre on A49 Ross road.
Bedrooms: 5 single, 12 double & 13 twin, 1 family room.
Bathrooms: 26 private, 2 public.
Bed & breakfast: £25-£40 single, £56-£70 double.
Lunch available.
Evening meal 7pm (l.o. 9pm).

Parking for 100.
Credit: Access, Visa, Diners, Amex.

Hereford Moat House M

Belmont Rd., Hereford, Herefordshire HR2 7BP
☎ (0432) 354301
Ⓒ Queens Moat Houses
Recently built hotel combining good food and efficient service with a quiet, relaxing atmosphere. Ideal centre for touring.
Bedrooms: 17 double & 43 twin.
Bathrooms: 60 private.
Bed & breakfast: £50-£63 single, £60-£75 double.
Half board: £45-£75 daily.
Lunch available.
Evening meal 7pm (l.o. 9.45pm).
Parking for 150.
Credit: Access, Visa, Diners, Amex.

Hopbine Hotel M

The Hopbine, Roman Rd., Hereford, Herefordshire HR1 1LE
☎ (0432) 268722
Licensed guesthouse with extensive grounds and car parks. All rooms with colour TV, tea/coffee facilities. 1 mile from town centre, racecourse, golf and leisure centre.
Bedrooms: 3 single, 4 double & 2 twin, 1 family room.
Bathrooms: 2 private, 4 public.
Bed & breakfast: £17-£21 single, £29-£34 double.
Half board: £25.50-£29.50 daily, £170-£194 weekly.
Evening meal 7pm (l.o. 5pm).
Parking for 16.

Longworth Hall M

Lugwardine, Hereford, Herefordshire HR1 4DF
☎ (0432) 850223
Elegant Georgian mansion with lovely views over the Wye Valley. Within easy reach of Cheltenham and cathedral cities of Hereford, Worcester and Gloucester.
Bedrooms: 3 double & 6 twin, 1 family room.
Bathrooms: 10 private.

Bed & breakfast: £44.85-£49.85 single, £74.75-£86.25 double.
Half board: £50.70-£62.80 daily, £215.75-£278.30 weekly.
Lunch available.
Evening meal 7.30pm (l.o. 9.45pm).
Parking for 50.
Credit: Access, Visa, Diners, Amex.

Merton Hotel M
COMMENDED

Commercial Rd., Hereford, Herefordshire HR1 2BD
☎ (0432) 265925 Fax (0432) 354983
Of Georgian origin, this charming hotel has been modernised to provide comfortable, well-appointed accommodation with elegant "Governor's" restaurant.
Bedrooms: 8 single, 7 double & 3 twin, 1 family room.
Bathrooms: 19 private.
Bed & breakfast: from £41.50 single, £64-£70 double.
Half board: £52-£61.50 daily, £307-£366 weekly.
Lunch available.
Evening meal 6.30pm (l.o. 9.30pm).
Parking for 6.
Credit: Access, Visa, Diners, Amex.

Munstone House Country Hotel M

Munstone, Hereford, Herefordshire HR1 3AH
☎ (0432) 267122
Spacious country house set in over 2 acres with splendid views of surrounding countryside and only 2 miles from Hereford city centre.
Bedrooms: 2 single, 3 double & 1 twin, 1 family room.
Bathrooms: 5 private, 1 public.
Bed & breakfast: £21-£26 single, £45-£48 double.
Half board: £46.95-£54 daily, £250-£330 weekly.
Lunch available.
Evening meal 7pm (l.o. 9.15pm).
Parking for 30.

The New Priory Hotel M

Stretton Sugwas, Hereford, Herefordshire HR4 7AR
☎ (0432) 760264

Hotel in pleasant peaceful surroundings, 2 miles from the centre of Hereford, with real ale and real atmosphere.
Bedrooms: 2 single, 3 double & 2 twin, 1 family room.
Bathrooms: 6 private, 1 public.
Bed & breakfast: £20-£30 single, £30-£45 double.
Half board: £25-£35 daily.
Lunch available.
Evening meal 7pm (l.o. 9.45pm).
Parking for 60.
Credit: Access, Visa.

The Old Tudor Guest House

33 Breinton Rd., Hereford, Herefordshire HR4 0JU
☎ (0432) 272765
Attractive mock Tudor house near to city centre and river. Generous breakfast, pleasant bedrooms (with showers), overlooking secluded gardens. All rooms named after Tudor characters.
Bedrooms: 1 single, 3 twin, 1 family room.
Bathrooms: 2 public; 2 private showers.
Bed & breakfast: £16-£17.50 single, £30-£34 double.
Half board: £24-£25 daily, £105-£119 weekly.
Evening meal 6pm (l.o. 7pm).
Parking for 6.

Somerville Hotel M
COMMENDED

Bodenham Rd., Hereford, Herefordshire HR1 2TS
☎ (0432) 273991
A quiet family-run hotel convenient for the city centre, bus and railway stations. Licensed restaurant, ample free parking, children welcome.
Bedrooms: 4 single, 4 double & 2 twin, 2 family rooms.
Bathrooms: 6 private, 3 public.
Bed & breakfast: £21-£27 single, £38-£45 double.
Half board: £28.25-£32 daily, £177-£190 weekly.
Lunch available.
Evening meal 7pm (l.o. 8pm).
Parking for 12.
Credit: Access, Visa.

HIMLEY

Staffordshire
Map ref 4B3

5m S. Wolverhampton
Village to the south of
Dudley whose Himley Hall
Park is open to the public.
The grounds of the Hall
were landscaped by
Capability Brown and
there are pools with trout
and coarse fishing
facilities. Dudley Show is
held here in August.

Himley House Hotel M
♨♨♨

Himley, Dudley,
W. Midlands, DY3 4LD
☎ Wombourne
(0902) 892468
*Fine Georgian style building,
dating from the late 17th C
and retaining a wealth of
period features. Set in beautiful
grounds. 15 minutes from
Birmingham.*
Bedrooms: 6 single, 8 double
& 8 twin, 2 family rooms.
Bathrooms: 24 private.
Bed & breakfast: from £50
single, from £69 double.
Lunch available.
Evening meal 6pm (l.o.
10.30pm).
Parking for 120.
Credit: Access, Visa, Diners,
Amex.
🛇 🛏 📞 🖵 🕯 🖭 V ⌷ 🖃
● 🎞 🛆 ⮝ ᴧ 🛠 ✕ SP ⌑

HOCKLEY HEATH

W. Midlands
Map ref 4B3

Village near the National
Trust property of
Packwood House with its
well-known yew garden
and Kenilworth.

Nuthurst Grange
Country House Hotel &
Restaurant M
♨♨♨♨ COMMENDED

Nuthurst Grange La.,
Hockley Heath, Solihull,
B94 5NL
☎ Lapworth (056 43) 3972
Telex 333485 NUT GR
Fax (056 43) 3919
*Completely secluded in 7.5
acres of landscaped woods and
gardens, with spectacular rural
views from all bedrooms.*
Bedrooms: 5 double & 3 twin.
Bathrooms: 8 private.
Bed & breakfast: from £85
single, £99-£125 double.
Lunch available.
Evening meal 7pm (l.o.
9.30pm).
Parking for 46.

Credit: Access, Visa, Diners,
Amex.
🛇 🛏 📞 📞 🖭 🖵 🕯 V 🖃
🎞 🛆 ⮝ ⮝ 🔆 ᴧ ✕ SP
⊤

HUNTLEY

Gloucestershire
Map ref 2B1

Birdwood Villa Farm M
Listed

Main Rd., Birdwood,
Huntley, Gloucester,
GL19 3EQ
☎ (045 275) 451
*18-acre arable farm. Friendly
atmosphere providing hearty
breakfast, tea/coffee facilities
in bedrooms. On A40 with easy
access to Forest of Dean and
Cotswolds.*
Bedrooms: 2 double & 1 twin.
Bathrooms: 1 public.
Bed & breakfast: £11-£14
single, £22-£28 double.
Parking for 10.
🛇 🛠 ᴧ 🖵 V ⌷ 🖭 🎞
⮝ 🔆 🖃 ⌑ SP

IRONBRIDGE

Shropshire
Map ref 4A3

Small town on the Severn
where the Industrial
Revolution began. It has
the world's first iron
bridge built in 1774. The
Ironbridge Gorge
Museum contains several
industrial sites and
museums spread over 2
miles and is exceptionally
interesting.
*Tourist Information
Centre ☎ (095245) 2166*

Bridge House M
♨♨ COMMENDED

Buildwas, Telford, TF8 7BN
☎ Ironbridge (095 245) 2105
*Half-timbered country
residence on the banks of the
River Severn, immediately
opposite Buildwas Abbey. On
the B3480, 2 miles from
Ironbridge. Many interesting
features and friendly
atmosphere.*
Bedrooms: 2 double & 1 twin,
1 family room.
Bathrooms: 1 private,
2 public; 1 private shower.
Bed & breakfast: £16-£17
single, £42-£44 double.
Parking for 12.
🛇 🛏 ᴧ 🖵 🕯 🖭 🎞 🛆
🔆 ✕ 🖃 ⌑ SP 🏛

Broseley Guest House M
♨♨♨

The Square, Broseley,
TF12 5EW
☎ Telford (0952) 882043
*Well-appointed spacious
accommodation in the centre of
Broseley. All rooms with TV,
tea and coffee facilities. Most
rooms en-suite.*
Bedrooms: 3 single, 2 double
& 3 twin.
Bathrooms: 4 private,
2 public; 4 private showers.
Bed & breakfast: £18-£22
single, £34-£40 double.
Evening meal 7pm (l.o.
8.30pm).
Credit: Access, Visa.
🛇 🛏 🖵 🕯 🕯 ⌷ 🖃 🖭
🎞 🛆 🖃

Cradle Meadow M
♨♨♨

Prince St., Madeley, Telford,
TF7 4EB
☎ (0952) 587753
*Cradle Meadow is situated on
the marked tourist route for
Ironbridge museums, 15
minutes' walk to Blists Hill.*
Bedrooms: 5 twin, 2 family
rooms.
Bathrooms: 7 private.
Bed & breakfast: £20 single,
£32 double.
Half board: £26 daily, £170
weekly.
Lunch available.
Evening meal 5pm (l.o.
6.45pm).
Parking for 6.
Credit: Access, Visa.
🛇 🛏 📞 🖵 🕯 🖭 🕯 🖃
🎞 ✕ SP

Hundred House Hotel M
♨♨♨♨ COMMENDED

Bridgnorth Rd., A442.,
Norton, Shifnal, TF11 9EE
☎ (095 271) 353 Fax
(095 271) 355
*Character, charm and a warm
atmosphere in family-run
country inn. Patchwork theme
bedrooms with antique
furniture and all facilities. On
the A442 at Norton between
Bridgnorth.*
Bedrooms: 1 single, 2 double
& 1 twin, 5 family rooms.
Bathrooms: 9 private.
Bed & breakfast: £55-£59
single, £65-£75 double.
Half board: £42.50-£47.50
daily.
Lunch available.
Evening meal 6pm (l.o.
10pm).
Parking for 30.
Credit: Access, Visa, Amex.
🛇 🛏 📞 🖵 🕯 🕯 🖭 🎞
🛆 ⮝ 🔆 🔆 🖃 🏛 SP 🏛
⊤

Madeley Court Hotel M
♨♨♨♨ COMMENDED

Telford, TF7 5DW
☎ (0952) 680068 Fax (0952)
684275
*Country house style hotel
converted from 16th C manor
house in the heart of Telford
and the Ironbridge Gorge.*
Bedrooms: 7 single, 8 double
& 1 twin.
Bathrooms: 16 private.
Bed & breakfast: £75-£95
single, £95-£120 double.
Lunch available.
Evening meal 7pm (l.o.
10.30pm).
Parking for 121.
Credit: Access, Visa, Diners,
Amex.
🛇 🛏 📞 🖵 🕯 🕯 V ⌷
🖃 🎞 🛆 ⮝ ᴧ 🔆 ✕ ⌑
🏛 SP 🏛 ⊤

KENILWORTH

Warwickshire
Map ref 4B3

The main feature of the
town is the ruined 12th C
castle. It has many royal
associations but was
damaged by Cromwell. A
good base for visiting
Coventry, Leamington
Spa and Warwick.
*Tourist Information
Centre ☎ (0926) 52595*

Abbey Guest House M
♨♨♨

41 Station Road, Kenilworth,
CV8 1JD
☎ (0926) 512707
*Beautiful Victorian house full
of charm and character.
Tastefully presented, cosy
bedrooms, all with colour TV.*
Bedrooms: 1 single, 2 double
& 3 twin, 1 family room.
Bathrooms: 2 private,
1 public; 1 private shower.
Bed & breakfast: £16-£19
single, £28-£34 double.
Evening meal 7pm (l.o. 2pm).
Parking for 3.
🛇 🖵 🕯 V 🖃 🖭 🎞 🛆
✕ 🖃

Castle Laurels Hotel M
♨♨♨ COMMENDED

22 Castle Rd., Kenilworth,
CV8 1NG
☎ (0926) 56179
*Large Victorian house situated
in old part of of Kenilworth,
overlooking castle and close to
Abbey Fields, swimming pool
and restaurants.*
Bedrooms: 3 single, 5 double
& 3 twin, 1 family room.

Bathrooms: 12 private.
Bed & breakfast: £24-£28 single, £39-£45 double.
Half board: £27.95-£36 daily.
Evening meal 7pm (l.o. 7pm).
Parking for 14.

Clarendon House Hotel/Castle Tavern Restaurant M
☺☺☺☺ APPROVED

Old High St., Kenilworth, CV8 1LZ
☎ (0926) 57668 Telex 311240 Hotel G
Unique and historic inn dating from 1430 and still supported by the old oak tree around which the former "Castle Tavern" was built. Own 16th C well. Antique brass, copper, silver, china and maps.
Bedrooms: 15 single, 9 double & 5 twin, 1 family room.
Bathrooms: 30 private.
Bed & breakfast: £50-£55 single, £75-£80 double.
Half board: £61.50-£66.50 daily.
Lunch available.
Evening meal 7pm (l.o. 9.30pm).
Parking for 34.
Credit: Access, Visa.

Enderley Guest House M
☺☺ APPROVED

20 Queens Rd., Kenilworth, CV8 1JQ
☎ (0926) 55388
Family-run guesthouse, quietly situated near town centre and convenient for Warwick, Stratford-upon-Avon, Stoneleigh, Warwick University and the National Exhibition Centre.
Bedrooms: 1 single, 1 double & 2 twin, 1 family room.
Bathrooms: 5 private.
Bed & breakfast: £23 single, £35 double.
Parking for 2.

Ferndale Guest House M
☺☺

45 Priory Rd., Kenilworth, CV8 1LL
☎ (0926) 53214
Delightfully modernised Victorian house in a tree-lined avenue. Attractive bedrooms with colour TV. Ideal for National Exhibition Centre and the National Agricultural Centre at Stoneleigh.
Bedrooms: 2 single, 3 double & 2 twin, 2 family rooms.

Bathrooms: 6 private, 1 public; 2 private showers.
Bed & breakfast: £28-£32 single, £28-£32 double.
Half board: £20.50-£23.50 daily.
Evening meal 6.30pm (l.o. 7.30pm).
Parking for 8.

Hollyhurst Guest House M
☺☺

47 Priory Rd., Kenilworth, CV8 1LL
☎ (0926) 53882
Comfortable family-run guesthouse ideally situated for easy access to National Exhibition Centre, Royal Showground and tourist areas of Stratford-upon-Avon, Warwick and Coventry.
Bedrooms: 2 single, 1 double & 3 twin, 2 family rooms.
Bathrooms: 3 private, 2 public.
Bed & breakfast: £14-£18 single, £27-£33 double.
Half board: £17.50-£26.50 daily, £90-£120 weekly.
Lunch available.
Evening meal 6.45pm (l.o. 9.30pm).
Parking for 9.

Honiley Court Hotel M
Honiley, Kenilworth, CV8 1NP
☎ (0926) 484234
Telex 311306 Fax (0926) 484474
🄶🄱 Lansbury
Set in its own grounds and tastefully furnished with a fully equipped children's play area and full a la carte restaurant.
Bedrooms: 1 single, 7 double & 53 twin.
Bathrooms: 61 private.
Bed & breakfast: £30-£68 single, £60-£80 double.
Half board: from £42 daily.
Lunch available.
Evening meal 7pm (l.o. 10pm).
Parking for 110.
Credit: Access, Visa, Diners, Amex.

Hereford & Worcester
Map ref 4B3

The town is the centre for carpet manufacturing. It has a medieval church with good monuments and a statue of Sir Rowland Hill, a native of the town and founder of the penny post. West Midlands Safari Park is nearby.

Brockencote Hall M
☺☺☺☺ HIGHLY COMMENDED

Chaddesley Corbett, Kidderminster, Worcestershire DY10 4PY
☎ (0562) 777876
Telex 333431 Brokal
Country house hotel set in 70 acres of parkland, offering traditional French cooking in an elegant and relaxed atmosphere.
Bedrooms: 7 double & 2 twin.
Bathrooms: 9 private.
Bed & breakfast: from £57 single, £85-£108 double.
Lunch available.
Evening meal 7.30pm (l.o. 9.30pm).
Parking for 50.
Credit: Access, Visa, Diners, Amex.

Cedars Hotel M
☺☺

Mason Road, Kidderminster, Worcestershire DY11 6AL
☎ (0562) 745869
Telex 334994
🄶🄱 Minotels
A charming conversion of a Georgian building close to the River Severn, Severn Valley Railway and Worcestershire countryside. 15 minutes from the M5.
Bedrooms: 1 single, 7 double & 7 twin, 5 family rooms.
Bathrooms: 20 private.
Bed & breakfast: £42.50-£47.50 single, £52-£56.50 double.
Half board: £54.50-£60 daily.
Parking for 21.
Credit: Access, Visa, Diners, Amex.

The Granary Hotel and Restaurant M
☺☺☺☺ COMMENDED

Shenstone, Kidderminster, Worcestershire DY10 4BS
☎ Chaddesley Corbett (056 283) 535 & (056 283) 251
Family-owned restaurant and hotel renowned for food. Quiet rural location off A450 near Kidderminster. Close to motorways and railway stations.
Bedrooms: 5 double & 13 twin.
Bathrooms: 18 private.
Bed & breakfast: £35.50-£48.85 single, £40-£53.50 double.
Half board: £54.95-£69.50 daily, £419-£450 weekly.
Lunch available.
Evening meal 6.30pm (l.o. 9.30pm).
Parking for 60.
Credit: Access, Visa, C.Bl., Diners, Amex.

Hereford & Worcester
Map ref 2A1

Village on the Welsh border, with Offa's Dyke close by. The Hergest Croft Gardens are well-known for their beautiful displays of azaleas and rhododendrons during May and June.

Burton Hotel M
☺☺☺☺

Mill St., Kington, Herefordshire HR5 3BQ
☎ (0544) 230323
Attractively modernised, authentic coaching inn, in centre of small market town near Welsh border and Offa's Dyke footpath.
Bedrooms: 2 single, 4 double & 5 twin, 4 family rooms.
Bathrooms: 15 private.
Bed & breakfast: from £36.50 single, from £48 double.
Half board: £36.50-£49 daily, £227.50-£311.50 weekly.
Lunch available.
Evening meal 7.30pm (l.o. 9.30pm).
Parking for 47.
Credit: Access, Visa, Diners, Amex.

KINGTON
Continued

Penrhos Court Hotel and Restaurant M
Kington, Leominster, Herefordshire HR5 2LH
☎ Kington (0544) 230720
Medieval timber framed building on the border of Herefordshire and Wales. 6 acres of gardens.
Bedrooms: 12 double & 7 twin.
Bathrooms: 19 private.
Bed & breakfast: £100-£130 double.
Lunch available.
Evening meal 7.30pm (l.o. 9.30pm).
Parking for 102.
Credit: Access, Visa, C.Bl., Diners, Amex.

KNOWLE
W. Midlands
Map ref 4B3

Knowle lies on the outskirts of Solihull and although there is much modern building, the centre still has some old buildings, including the medieval Chester House, which is now a library. Kenilworth Castle and Packwood House (National Trust) are nearby.

Ivy House
Warwick Rd., Heronfield, Knowle, Solihull, B93 0EB
☎ (0564) 770247
Set in 6 acres of its own land overlooking fields. Approximately 5 miles from the National Exhibition Centre and airport.
Bedrooms: 4 single, 2 double & 2 twin.
Bathrooms: 8 private.
Bed & breakfast: £22-£25 single, £30-£36 double.
Parking for 20.

> **Half board prices shown are per person but in some cases may be based on double/twin occupancy.**

LAPWORTH
Warwickshire
Map ref 4B3

The village church is over 800 years old, though its Norman nave has been added to in 3 different styles. Among the furnishings are an Elizabethan altar table and choir stalls made from the old rood screen.

Lapworth Lodge M
Bushwood Lane, Lapworth, Solihull, W. Midlands B94 5PJ
☎ (0564) 783038
Large comfortable 18th C house with spacious rooms, all with extensive views over peaceful countryside. Convenient for National Exhibition Centre, Stratford, Warwick and the Cotswolds.
Bedrooms: 2 double & 1 twin, 2 family rooms.
Bathrooms: 5 private.
Bed & breakfast: £30-£40 single, £40-£46 double.
Parking for 20.
Credit: Access, Visa.

LEAMINGTON SPA
Warwickshire
Map ref 4B3

18th C spa town with many fine Georgian and Regency houses. Tea can be taken in the 19th C Pump Room. The attractive Jephson Gardens are laid out alongside the river and there is a museum and art gallery.
Tourist Information Centre ☎ *(0926) 311470*

Adams Hotel
22 Avenue Rd., Leamington Spa, CV31 3PQ
☎ (0926) 450742 & 422758
Fax (0926) 313110
17th C listed hotel, with modern, en-suite bedrooms, standing back from the road in a typical Regency setting.
Bedrooms: 5 single, 4 double & 4 twin, 1 family room.
Bathrooms: 9 private, 1 public; 2 private showers.
Bed & breakfast: £32-£48 single, £48-£52 double.
Half board: £46-£50 daily.
Evening meal 6pm (l.o. 8pm).

Parking for 10.
Credit: Access, Visa, Diners, Amex.

Ashbourne Hotel M
28 Kenilworth Rd., Leamington Spa, CV32 6JE
☎ (0926) 833498
Family-run establishment, built 1860, offering modern facilities. Conveniently situated for touring and business in the Midland area.
Bedrooms: 7 single, 5 double & 3 twin.
Bathrooms: 14 private; 1 private shower.
Bed & breakfast: £29-£38 single, £38-£52 double.
Half board: £38.50-£47.50 daily, £305.50 weekly.
Lunch available.
Evening meal 7pm (l.o. 9pm).
Parking for 16.
Credit: Access, Visa, Diners, Amex.

Beech Lodge Hotel M
28 Warwick New Rd., Leamington Spa, CV32 5JJ
☎ (0926) 422227
An elegant Regency building with a spacious lounge, dining room and residents' bar. All bedrooms with colour TV, radio, telephone and tea/coffee making facilities.
Bedrooms: 7 single, 4 double & 1 twin.
Bathrooms: 9 private, 2 public; 1 private shower.
Bed & breakfast: £28-£36 single, £48-£55 double.
Half board: £31-£49 daily, £252-£343 weekly.
Lunch available.
Evening meal 7pm (l.o. 9pm).
Parking for 14.
Credit: Access, Visa, Amex.

Blackdown Hotel and Licensed Restaurant M
Sandy La., Leamington Spa, CV32 6RD
☎ (0926) 424761 & 421998
Fax (0926) 421998
Jacobean-style house built of local stone about 1873, standing in 9 acres of landscaped gardens. Convenient for National Exhibition Centre and National Agricultural Centre.
Bedrooms: 1 single, 2 double & 8 twin.
Bathrooms: 11 private.

Bed & breakfast: max. £65 single, max. £77 double.
Half board: max. £81 daily, max. £511 weekly.
Lunch available.
Evening meal 7.30pm (l.o. 10pm).
Parking for 200.
Credit: Access, Visa, Diners, Amex.

Buckland Lodge Hotel M
35 Avenue Rd., Leamington Spa, CV31 3PG
☎ (0926) 423843
Central for rail and bus depots, shops, parks and the town's beautiful gardens.
Bedrooms: 3 single, 2 double & 3 twin, 2 family rooms.
Bathrooms: 6 private, 2 public.
Bed & breakfast: £18-£21 single, £30-£42 double.
Half board: £25-£36 daily, £175-£252 weekly.
Evening meal 6.30pm (l.o. 2.30pm).
Parking for 12.
Credit: Access, Visa, Diners, Amex.

Flowerdale House Hotel M
58 Warwick New Rd., Leamington Spa, CV32 6AA
☎ (0926) 426002
A tastefully modernised Victorian house with conservatory, overlooking a small garden. All bedrooms with private facilities and colour TV. Reduced rates for more than 1 night.
Bedrooms: 1 single, 2 double & 3 twin.
Bathrooms: 6 private.
Bed & breakfast: £19-£23 single, £32-£37 double.
Evening meal 7pm (l.o. 9pm).
Parking for 6.
Credit: Access, Visa.

Garden Court Holiday Inn M
Olympus Avenue, Tachbrook Park, Leamington Spa, CV31 6RJ
☎ (0926) 881313 & 425522
Fax (0926) 881322
CH Holiday Inn

In a country setting, offering a high standard of bedroom accommodation together with a comfortable and relaxed atmosphere, and beautiful views of Warwick Castle.
Bedrooms: 86 double & 12 twin, 2 family rooms.
Bathrooms: 100 private.
Bed & breakfast: £48.90-£59.90 double.
Lunch available.
Evening meal 6.30pm (l.o. 10pm).
Parking for 108.
Credit: Access, Visa, C.Bl., Diners, Amex.

Regent Hotel ⋒
😃😃😃 APPROVED

The Parade, Leamington Spa, CV32 4AX
☎ (0926) 427231
Telex 311715
⓰ Best Western
Elegant Regency hotel, featured in the Guinness Book of Records as the world's largest hotel in 1819. Old fashioned service proliferates. We clean shoes.
Bedrooms: 24 single, 14 double & 36 twin, 6 family rooms.
Bathrooms: 80 private.
Bed & breakfast: £55-£72 single, £75-£90 double.
Half board: from £47.50 daily.
Lunch available.
Evening meal 6.45pm (l.o. 10.45pm).
Parking for 100.
Credit: Access, Visa, Diners, Amex.

Trendway Guest House ⋒
😃😃 APPROVED

45 Avenue Rd., Leamington Spa, CV31 3PF
☎ (0926) 316644
3-storey Victorian house with 6 letting bedrooms, just off the town centre and 5 minutes from railway station.
Bedrooms: 5 twin, 1 family room.
Bathrooms: 2 private, 2 public; 1 private shower.
Bed & breakfast: £18-£25 single, £25-£30 double.
Half board: £18.50-£21.50 daily, £129.50-£150.50 weekly.
Evening meal 6pm (l.o. 7pm).
Parking for 8.

Tuscany Hotel
😃😃😃

34 Warwick Place, Leamington Spa, CV32 5DE
☎ Leamington Spa
(0926) 332233 Fax (0926) 332232
Listed Regency house restored as a no smoking hotel. 8 en-suite rooms, comprehensive business facilities, good restaurant and friendly service.
Bedrooms: 5 double & 3 twin.
Bathrooms: 8 private.
Bed & breakfast: from £39 single, max. £85 double.
Lunch available.
Evening meal 7pm (l.o. 9.30pm).
Parking for 8.
Credit: Access, Visa, Diners, Amex.

⓴ Display advertisement appears on page 266.

⓴ Display advertisement appears on page 266.

LECHLADE
Gloucestershire
Map ref 2B1

Attractive village on the River Thames and a popular spot for boating. It has a number of fine Georgian houses and a 15th C church. Nearby is Kelmscott Manor, with its William Morris furnishings, and 18th C Buscot House (National Trust).

The Bell Hotel
😃😃

Market Place, Faringdon, Oxfordshire SN7 7HP
☎ (0367) 240534 Fax (0367) 241824
A 16th C posting house. The original character and structure have been maintained, although many improvements have been made. Ideal for exploring the beauty of the Vale of White Horse and the Cotswolds.
Bedrooms: 3 single, 4 double & 2 twin, 2 family rooms.
Bathrooms: 7 private, 1 public.
Bed & breakfast: £27.50-£32.50 single, £40-£45 double.
Half board: max. £40 daily, max. £260 weekly.
Evening meal 7.30pm (l.o. 9.30pm).
Parking for 25.
Credit: Access, Visa, Amex.

⓴ Display advertisement appears on page 329.

⓴ Display advertisement appears on page 329.

LEDBURY
Hereford & Worcester
Map ref 2B1

The town has cobbled streets and many black and white timbered houses, including the 17th C market house and old inns. Nearby is Eastnor Castle with an interesting collection of tapestries and armour. *Tourist Information Centre ☎ (0531) 2461 or (Summer Saturdays only) 5680*

The Barn House ⋒
😃😃 COMMENDED

New St., Ledbury, Herefordshire HR8 2DX
☎ (0531) 2825
House of great character in the centre of the old market town of Ledbury, close to the Malverns.
Bedrooms: 2 double & 1 twin.
Bathrooms: 1 public; 1 private shower.
Bed & breakfast: £33-£43 double.
Parking for 4.
Open March-December.

Feathers Hotel ⋒
😃😃😃

High St., Ledbury, Herefordshire HR8 1DS
☎ (0531) 2600 & 5266 Fax (0531) 2001
Traditional Elizabethan coaching inn, situated in the centre of a small market town nestling under the Malvern Hills.
Bedrooms: 5 double & 5 twin, 1 family room.
Bathrooms: 11 private.
Bed & breakfast: £49.50-£55 single, £69.50-£75 double.
Half board: £80-£89.50 daily.
Lunch available.
Evening meal 6.30pm (l.o. 9.30pm).
Parking for 40.
Credit: Access, Visa, Diners, Amex.

The Royal Oak Hotel ⋒
😃😃😃

The Southend, Ledbury, Herefordshire HR8 2EY
☎ (0531) 2110 Fax (0531) 4761
Family-owned historic coaching inn/hotel (15th C) with spacious bedrooms. Free house, bar meals and restaurant (14th C). Children welcome.

Bedrooms: 2 single, 2 double & 4 twin, 2 family rooms.
Bathrooms: 7 private, 1 public.
Bed & breakfast: £19.50-£32.50 single, £32.50-£45.50 double.
Lunch available.
Evening meal 6.45pm (l.o. 9pm).
Parking for 28.
Credit: Access, Visa, Diners, Amex.

Verzons Hotel ⋒
😃😃😃

Hereford Rd., Trumpet, Ledbury, Herefordshire, HR8 2PZ
☎ Trumpet (053 183) 381
Large 18th C farmhouse set in 4 acres of grounds with magnificent views to the Malvern Hills. Bar meals lunchtime and evening and a la carte/table d'hote restaurant.
Bedrooms: 2 single, 2 double & 3 twin, 2 family rooms.
Bathrooms: 7 private, 2 public.
Bed & breakfast: £33-£43 single, £55-£65 double.
Half board: £35-£40 daily, £260-£280 weekly.
Lunch available.
Evening meal 7pm (l.o. 9pm).
Parking for 50.
Credit: Access, Visa, Amex.

Ye Olde Talbot Hotel ⋒
😃😃 APPROVED

New Street, Ledbury, Herefordshire HR8 2DX
☎ (0531) 2963
Formerly an old coaching house, a Grade II listed, timber-framed inn built circa 1596.
Bedrooms: 2 double & 3 twin, 2 family rooms.
Bathrooms: 3 private, 2 public.
Bed & breakfast: £32-£39 single, £42-£49 double.
Lunch available.
Evening meal 7pm (l.o. 9pm).
Parking for 5.
Credit: Access, Visa, Diners.

The enquiry coupons at the back will help you when contacting proprietors.

LEEK

Staffordshire
Map ref 4B2

Old silk and textile town, with some interesting buildings and a number of inns dating from the 17th C. Its art gallery has displays of embroidery. Brindley Mill, designed by James Brindley, has been restored as a museum.
Tourist Information Centre ☎ (0538) 381000

Bank End Farm Motel ♠
[COMMENDED]
Old Leek Rd., Longsdon, Stoke-on-Trent, ST9 9QJ
☎ Leek (0538) 383638
62-acre mixed farm. Pleasant motel in converted dairy and old stone barn, on a quiet lane close to Leek and Peak Park.
Bedrooms: 1 single, 2 double & 2 twin, 3 family rooms.
Bathrooms: 7 private, 1 public.
Bed & breakfast: £20-£22.50 single, £33-£36 double.
Half board: £28-£30 daily.
Evening meal 6.30pm.
Parking for 10.

The Jester at Leek ♠
[APPROVED]
81 Mill St., Leek, ST13 8EU
☎ (0538) 383997
Family-owned, 200-year-old inn with old world atmosphere.
Bedrooms: 2 single, 4 double & 6 twin, 2 family rooms.
Bathrooms: 10 private, 1 public; 4 private showers.
Bed & breakfast: £27.50-£29.50 single, £39.50-£42.50 double.
Lunch available.
Evening meal 7pm (l.o. 9.30pm).
Parking for 80.
Credit: Visa.

Hotel Rudyard ♠
[APPROVED]
Rudyard, Leek, ST13 8RN
☎ (053 833) 208 Fax (053 833) 249
Approximately 200 years old, by the side of Rudyard Lake.
Bedrooms: 7 single, 8 double & 2 twin, 2 family rooms.
Bathrooms: 19 private.
Bed & breakfast: from £27.50 single, from £44 double.
Lunch available.
Evening meal 7pm (l.o. 9.30pm).

Parking for 200.
Credit: Access, Visa.

Three Horseshoes Inn ♠
[APPROVED]
Blackshaw Moor, Leek, ST13 8TW
☎ Blackshaw (053 834) 296
Beneath the Roaches in the Staffordshire moorlands. An ideal centre for pleasure or business and for visiting Alton Towers.
Bedrooms: 1 single, 3 double & 1 twin, 1 family room.
Bathrooms: 6 private, 2 public.
Bed & breakfast: max. £33 single, max. £36 double.
Lunch available.
Evening meal 7pm (l.o. 9.30pm).
Parking for 100.
Credit: Access, Visa, Diners, Amex.

LEINTWARDINE

Hereford & Worcester
Map ref 4A3

7m W. Ludlow
Attractive border village where the Rivers Teme and Clun meet. It has some black and white cottages, old inns and an impressive church. It is near Hopton Castle and the beautiful scenery around Clun.

Lower House ♠
Adforton, Leintwardine, Craven Arms, Shropshire SY7 0NF
☎ Wigmore (056 886) 223
Well-furnished 16th C former farmhouse with exposed beams. Open fires and feature inglenook in dining room. Home-grown produce.
Bedrooms: 2 double & 2 twin.
Bathrooms: 2 private, 1 public.
Bed & breakfast: £16-£22.50 single, £32-£45 double.
Half board: £23-£29.50 daily, £150-£190 weekly.
Evening meal 7pm (l.o. 7.30pm).
Parking for 10.
Open March-October.

LEOMINSTER

Hereford & Worcester
Map ref 2A1

The town owed its prosperity to wool and has many interesting buildings, notably the timber-framed Grange Court, a former town hall. The impressive Norman priory church has 3 naves and a ducking stool. Berrington Hall (National Trust) is nearby.
Tourist Information Centre ☎ (0568) 611100

Copper Hall ♠
[COMMENDED]
South St., Leominster, Herefordshire HR6 8JN
☎ (0568) 611622
Comfortable 17th C house with spacious garden. English cooking and homely atmosphere. Convenient touring centre for Wales, Wye Valley and the Malverns.
Bedrooms: 1 double & 1 twin, 1 family room.
Bathrooms: 1 public.
Bed & breakfast: £30-£40 double.
Half board: £25-£30 daily, £150-£180 weekly.
Evening meal 6pm (l.o. 6pm).
Parking for 6.

Royal Oak Hotel ♠
Minotels
South St., Leominster, Herefordshire HR6 8JA
☎ (0568) 2610
A Georgian coaching hotel since 1723, providing home cooking, real ales and log fires in winter. Located in the town itself.
Bedrooms: 2 single, 9 double & 5 twin, 2 family rooms.
Bathrooms: 18 private.
Bed & breakfast: £25.50-£28.50 single, £38-£42 double.
Lunch available.
Evening meal 6.30pm (l.o. 9.30pm).
Parking for 24.
Credit: Access, Visa, Diners, Amex.

Withenfield Private Hotel ♠
[HIGHLY COMMENDED]
South Street, Leominster, Herefordshire HR6 8JN
☎ (0568) 2011

Elegantly furnished Georgian house with conservatory overlooking garden, conveniently situated for Leominster centre. All modern facilities. Fluent French, Spanish and some German spoken.
Bedrooms: 1 single, 2 double & 1 twin.
Bathrooms: 4 private.
Bed & breakfast: £39-£45 single, £56-£62 double.
Half board: £41.75-£44.75 daily, £263-£282 weekly.
Lunch available.
Evening meal 6.30pm.
Parking for 5.
Credit: Access, Visa.

LICHFIELD

Staffordshire
Map ref 4B3

Lichfield is Dr. Samuel Johnson's birthplace and commemorates him with a museum and statue. The 13th C cathedral has 3 spires and the west front is full of statues. There is a regimental museum and Heritage Centre.
Tourist Information Centre ☎ (0543) 252109

Angel Croft Hotel/Westgate House ♠
Beacon St., Lichfield, WS13 7AA
☎ Lichfield (0543) 258737
Fax (0543) 415605
Georgian town house with family atmosphere opposite the cathedral. Set in 3 acres of gardens.
Bedrooms: 1 single, 5 double & 12 twin, 2 family rooms.
Bathrooms: 18 private, 1 public.
Bed & breakfast: £30-£60 single, £40-£70 double.
Evening meal 7pm (l.o. 9pm).
Parking for 60.
Credit: Access, Visa, Diners.

George Hotel ♠
Bird St., Lichfield, WS13 6PR
☎ (0543) 414822
Embassy
In the heart of the Midlands, an attractive venue for both business people and tourists.
Bedrooms: 20 single, 5 double & 10 twin, 3 family rooms.

Bathrooms: 38 private.
Bed & breakfast: £21-£66
single, £42-£80 double.
Half board: £24.50-£34 daily,
£178.50-£462 weekly.
Lunch available.
Evening meal 7pm (l.o.
9.30pm).
Parking for 64.
Credit: Access, Visa, C.Bl.,
Diners, Amex.

Little Barrow Hotel M
😄😄😄😄 COMMENDED
Beacon St., Lichfield,
WS13 7AR
☎ (0543) 414500
*Modern hotel offering old
world charm, situated near to
Lichfield's famous cathedral
and Dr. Johnson's house.*
Bedrooms: 8 double &
16 twin.
Bathrooms: 24 private.
Bed & breakfast: max. £55
single, max. £65 double.
Half board: max. £65.50
daily.
Lunch available.
Evening meal 7pm (l.o.
9.30pm).
Parking for 70.
Credit: Access, Visa, Diners,
Amex.

LLANYMYNECH
Shropshire
Map ref 4A3

Right on the Welsh
border with views over
Shropshire plains from
the summit of
Llanymynech Hill, where
the Romans built
earthworks to defend
their copper mines. The
village church was built in
the Norman style in 1845
and Offa's Dyke can be
found nearby.

Lion Hotel M
Llanymynech, Powys,
SY22 6EJ
☎ (0691) 830234
*Fully-licensed hotel and
restaurant on the A483
between Oswestry and
Welshpool. Half in England
and half in Wales.*
Bedrooms: 4 single, 3 double
& 4 twin, 1 family room.
Bathrooms: 4 private,
3 public.
Bed & breakfast: £15-£16.50
single.
Evening meal 6pm.
Parking for 50.

LUDLOW
Shropshire
Map ref 4A3

Outstandingly interesting
border town with a
magnificent castle high
above the River Teme, 2
half-timbered old inns and
an impressive 15th C
church. The Reader's
House should also be
seen with its 3-storey
Jacobean porch.

Cecil Guest House M
😄😄
Sheet Rd., Ludlow, SY8 1LR
☎ (0584) 872442
*Quietly located modern guest
house under personal
supervision in historic Ludlow.*
Bedrooms: 3 single, 1 double
& 5 twin, 1 family room.
Bathrooms: 2 private,
2 public.
Bed & breakfast: £15.50
single, £31-£36 double.
Half board: £24-£26.50 daily,
£156-£170 weekly.
Evening meal 7pm (l.o. 9am).
Parking for 11.
Credit: Access, Visa.

Cliffe Hotel M
😄😄😄
Dinham, Ludlow, SY8 2JE
☎ (0584) 872063
*Hotel facing Ludlow Castle
next to the River Teme, with a
panoramic view of the
Shropshire countryside.*
Bedrooms: 3 single, 2 double
& 4 twin, 1 family room.
Bathrooms: 7 private,
1 public.
Bed & breakfast: £22.50-£29
single, £44-£50 double.
Half board: £32-£35 daily.
Lunch available.
Evening meal 7pm (l.o.
9.30pm).
Parking for 50.
Credit: Access, Visa.

Dinham Weir Hotel and Restaurant M
😄😄😄😄 COMMENDED
Dinham Bridge, Ludlow,
SY8 1EH
☎ (0584) 874431
*Beautifully situated on the
banks of River Teme. All
bedrooms with riverside views.
Intimate candelit restaurant.*
Bedrooms: 4 double & 2 twin.
Bathrooms: 6 private.
Bed & breakfast: £35-£40
single, £50-£55 double.
Half board: £36-£40 daily,
£225-£250 weekly.
Lunch available.

Evening meal 7pm (l.o.
8.30pm).
Parking for 8.
Credit: Access, Visa, Diners,
Amex.

The Feathers at Ludlow M
😄😄😄😄
Bull Ring, Ludlow, SY8 1AA
☎ (0584) 875261 Telex 35637
Fax (0584) 876030
*Historic inn with Jacobean
interior and exterior, sited
within the medieval walls of
historic Ludlow in "England as
it used to be".*
Bedrooms: 11 single,
14 double & 12 twin, 3 family
rooms.
Bathrooms: 40 private.
Bed & breakfast: £60-£75
single, £90-£110 double.
Half board: £60-£70 daily.
Lunch available.
Evening meal 7pm (l.o. 9pm).
Parking for 40.
Credit: Access, Visa, C.Bl.,
Diners, Amex.

28 Lower Broad St. M
😄😄😄
Ludlow, SY8 1PQ
☎ (0584) 876996
*Half-timbered town house,
centrally situated below the
Broad Gate, close to Ludford
Bridge and River Teme. En-
suite bedrooms.*
Bedrooms: 1 double & 1 twin.
Bathrooms: 2 private.
Bed & breakfast: £22-£25
single, £38-£44 double.
Half board: £26-£30 daily.
Evening meal 7.50pm (l.o.
8.50pm).

Overton Grange Hotel M
😄😄😄😄 COMMENDED
Ludlow, SY8 4AD
☎ (0584) 873500
*A country house hotel in its
own grounds, with commanding
views over the Shropshire
countryside.*
Bedrooms: 2 single, 8 double
& 4 twin, 2 family rooms.
Bathrooms: 12 private,
3 public.
Bed & breakfast: £35-£60
single, £66-£90 double.
Half board: £42-£70 daily,
£210-£400 weekly.
Lunch available.
Evening meal 7pm (l.o.
9.30pm).

Parking for 80.
Credit: Access, Visa, Diners,
Amex.

LYDNEY
Gloucestershire
Map ref 2B1

Small town in the Forest
of Dean close to the River
Severn where Roman
remains have been found.
It has a steam centre with
engines, coaches and
wagons.

Feathers Hotel M
High St., Lydney, GL15 5DN
☎ Dean (0594) 842862 &
(0594) 842815
*Catering for commercial and
holiday visitors, convenient for
Severn Bridge, Forest of Dean
and Wye Valley. Bedrooms
recently refurbished.*
Bedrooms: 6 single, 3 double
& 3 twin, 2 family rooms.
Bathrooms: 14 private.
Bed & breakfast: £35.50-
£39.50 single, £47.50-£49.50
double.
Half board: £30-£55 daily,
£200-£300 weekly.
Lunch available.
Evening meal 7pm (l.o. 9pm).
Parking for 50.
Credit: Access, Visa, Amex.

MALVERN
Hereford & Worcester
Map ref 2B1

Spa town in Victorian
times, its water is today
bottled and sold
worldwide. 6 resorts, set
on the slopes of the Hills,
form part of Malvern.
Great Malvern Priory has
splendid 15th C windows.
It is an excellent walking
centre with fine views
from the Worcestershire
Beacon.
*Tourist Information
Centre* ☎ (0684) 892289

Colwall Park Hotel M
😄😄😄😄 COMMENDED
Colwall, Malvern,
Worcestershire WR13 6QG
☎ Colwall (0684) 40206
Telex 335626
*Family-run hotel with new
bedrooms. English menus.
Quiet gardens leading to
Malvern Hills. Ideal for
walking, touring and exploring.*
Continued ▶

MALVERN
Continued

Bedrooms: 4 single, 8 double
& 6 twin, 2 family rooms.
Bathrooms: 20 private.
Bed & breakfast: £46.50-
£52.50 single, £65-£75 double.
Half board: £62-£68.50 daily,
£265-£297.50 weekly.
Lunch available.
Evening meal 7.30pm (l.o.
9pm).
Parking for 40.
Credit: Access, Visa, Amex.

Cottage in the Wood Hotel M
COMMENDED
Holywell Rd., Malvern Wells,
Malvern, Worcestershire
WR14 4LG
☎ (0684) 573487 Fax (0684)
560662
Consort
*Country house in 7 acres high
on the Malvern Hills, with
stunning 30-mile views. All
bedrooms en-suite.*
Bedrooms: 2 single, 14 double
& 4 twin.
Bathrooms: 20 private,
1 public.
Bed & breakfast: £55 single,
£72-£105 double.
Half board: £69-£95 daily,
£241.50-£332.50 weekly.
Lunch available.
Evening meal 7pm (l.o.
8.30pm).
Parking for 40.
Credit: Access, Visa.

Essington Hotel M
COMMENDED
Holywell Rd., Malvern
Wells, Malvern,
Worcestershire WR14 4LQ
☎ (0684) 561177
*Country house hotel in terraced
gardens on the side of the
Malvern Hills, offering superb
views, walks and touring.*
Bedrooms: 2 single, 4 double
& 3 twin, 1 family room.
Bathrooms: 10 private.
Bed & breakfast: from £27
single, from £50 double.
Half board: from £39.50
daily, from £195 weekly.
Evening meal 7pm (l.o.
8.15pm).
Parking for 30.
Credit: Access, Visa.

Foley Arms Hotel & Restaurant M
Worcester Rd., Malvern,
Worcestershire WR14 4QS
☎ (0684) 573397
Telex 437287
Best Western
*Regency coaching inn with the
comfort and atmosphere of a
country house hotel. Ideal for
touring the Cotswolds and
Wales. Panoramic views and
lovely walks.*
Bedrooms: 6 single, 13 double
& 6 twin, 2 family rooms.
Bathrooms: 26 private.
Bed & breakfast: £55-£60
single, £72-£90 double.
Half board: £40-£50 daily.
Lunch available.
Evening meal 7pm (l.o.
9.30pm).
Parking for 50.
Credit: Access, Visa, Diners,
Amex.

Harcourt Cottage M
252 West Malvern Rd., West
Malvern, Malvern,
Worcestershire WR14 4DQ
☎ (0684) 574561
*Nestling on the west side of the
Malvern Hills, well placed for
walking holidays or as a base
for touring. English and
French cooking.*
Bedrooms: 1 double & 1 twin,
1 family room.
Bathrooms: 1 public;
2 private showers.
Bed & breakfast: £12-£17
single, £24-£26 double.
Half board: £18.50-£23.50
daily, £116.50-£148 weekly.
Evening meal 6.45pm (l.o.
6pm).
Parking for 3.

Holdfast Cottage Hotel M
Marlbank Rd., Welland,
Malvern, Worcestershire
WR13 6NA
☎ Hanley Swan
(0684) 310288
*Small oak-beamed country
house set in 2 acres of gardens
amid orchard and farmland at
the foot of the Malvern Hills.*
Bedrooms: 1 single, 5 double
& 2 twin.
Bathrooms: 8 private,
1 public.
Bed & breakfast: £36-£54
single, £66-£72 double.
Half board: £48-£52 daily,
max. £275 weekly.

Evening meal 7.30pm (l.o.
9.30pm).
Parking for 20.
Credit: Access.

Malvern Hills Hotel M
British Camp, Wynd's Point,
Malvern, Worcestershire
WR13 6DW
☎ Colwall (0684) 40237 &
40191 Fax (0684) 40327
*Set in the midst of the
beautiful Malvern Hills. Ideal
for walking and touring.
Friendly and efficient staff.*
Bedrooms: 2 single, 8 double
& 6 twin.
Bathrooms: 15 private,
1 public.
Bed & breakfast: £36-£40
single, £55 double.
Half board: from £52 daily.
Lunch available.
Evening meal 7pm (l.o.
9.30pm).
Parking for 30.
Credit: Access, Visa.

Mellbreak
APPROVED
177 Wells Rd., Malvern
Wells, Malvern,
Worcestershire WR14 4HE
☎ (0684) 561287
*Listed building with large
garden and fine views. Near
the Three Counties
Showground. Comfort and
convenience. Informal, homely
atmosphere.*
Bedrooms: 1 single, 1 double
& 1 twin, 1 family room.
Bathrooms: 1 public;
3 private showers.
Bed & breakfast: £14 single,
£28 double.
Half board: £22.50 daily,
£149 weekly.
Evening meal 6pm.
Parking for 4.

Mount Pleasant Hotel M
Belle Vue Ter., Malvern,
Worcestershire WR14 4PZ
☎ (0684) 561837
*Georgian building with
orangery, in 1.5 acres of
garden with beautiful views.
Close to theatre and shops with
direct access to Malvern Hills.*
Bedrooms: 3 single, 6 double
& 5 twin, 1 family room.
Bathrooms: 14 private,
1 public.

Bed & breakfast: £37.50-£47
single, £47.50-£63 double.
Half board: £225-£305
weekly.
Lunch available.
Evening meal 7pm (l.o.
9.30pm).
Parking for 20.
Credit: Access, Visa, Diners,
Amex.

The Nupend M
Cradley, Malvern,
Worcestershire WR13 5NP
☎ Ridgeway Cross
(0886) 880881
*Elegant Georgian farmhouse
set in grounds of 2 acres and
enjoying glorious views of
Malvern Hills. Ideal for
walkers, bird-watchers,
painters or as a touring base.
Peacefully situated off A4103.
French/German spoken. Non-
smokers only please.*
Bedrooms: 1 double & 3 twin.
Bathrooms: 4 private.
Bed & breakfast: £26-£34
single, £36-£44 double.
Evening meal 6pm (l.o.
7.30pm).
Parking for 10.

Priory Holme M
APPROVED
18 Avenue Rd., Malvern,
Worcestershire WR14 3AR
☎ (0684) 568455
*Elegantly furnished large
Victorian house in a tree-lined
avenue. Well situated for all
local amenities.*
Bedrooms: 1 single, 1 double
& 1 twin, 1 family room.
Bathrooms: 1 private,
2 public.
Bed & breakfast: £16-£20
single, £28-£36 double.
Half board: £21-£28 daily,
£147-£175 weekly.
Evening meal 7pm (l.o. 8pm).
Parking for 5.

Priory Park Hotel M
COMMENDED
4 Avenue Rd., Malvern,
Worcestershire WR14 3AG
☎ (068 45) 65194
*Family home on the fringe of
Great Malvern's Priory Park,
close to the town centre yet
beautiful and quiet. Theatre
and leisure activities all close
by. German and French
spoken.*
Bedrooms: 2 double & 1 twin,
3 family rooms.
Bathrooms: 6 private.

Bed & breakfast: £38-£58 single, £48-£68 double.
Half board: £40-£60 daily, £250-£350 weekly.
Lunch available.
Evening meal 6pm (l.o. 10pm).
Parking for 9.
Credit: Access.

Royal Malvern Hotel ⚥
🖤🖤 COMMENDED
Graham Rd., Malvern, Worcestershire WR14 2HN
☎ (0684) 563411 Fax (0684) 560514
CR Minotels
Small hotel in the centre of Malvern close to the Winter Gardens, with all amenities. Run by the proprietors.
Bedrooms: 1 single, 8 double & 5 twin.
Bathrooms: 12 private, 1 public.
Bed & breakfast: £38-£50 single, £50-£60 double.
Lunch available.
Evening meal 6.15pm (l.o. 9pm).
Parking for 9.
Credit: Access, Visa, Diners, Amex.

Sidney House ⚥
🖤🖤🖤 COMMENDED
40 Worcester Rd., Malvern, Worcestershire WR14 4AA
☎ (0684) 574994
Small, attractive Georgian hotel with personal and friendly service. Magnificent views over the Worcestershire countryside. Close to town centre and hills.
Bedrooms: 1 single, 3 double & 2 twin, 2 family rooms.
Bathrooms: 4 private, 1 public; 1 private shower.
Bed & breakfast: £17-£35 single, £36-£46 double.
Half board: £32-£50 daily.
Evening meal 7pm (l.o. 3pm).
Parking for 10.
Credit: Access, Visa, Amex.

Spa Guest House ⚥
16 Manby Rd., Malvern, Worcestershire WR14 3BB
☎ (068 45) 61178
Pleasant Victorian house with hill views. Very convenient for the shopping facilities of Malvern and 2 minutes from the station.
Bedrooms: 1 single, 2 double & 1 twin, 1 family room.

Bathrooms: 2 public.
Bed & breakfast: £15-£18 single, £30-£32 double.
Evening meal 6.30pm (l.o. 8pm).
Parking for 10.

Studley House ⚥
Listed APPROVED
260 Wells Road, Malvern Wells, Malvern, Worcestershire WR14 4HD
☎ (0684) 573339
Comfortable Victorian house with superb views, set in spacious garden on slopes of Malvern Hills. Home cooking.
Bedrooms: 1 single, 2 double & 1 twin.
Bathrooms: 1 private, 2 public.
Bed & breakfast: from £14 single, from £23 double.
Evening meal 7pm (l.o. 8.15pm).

Walmer Lodge Hotel ⚥
🖤🖤🖤
49 Abbey Rd., Malvern, Worcestershire WR14 3HH
☎ (0684) 574139
Friendly, family-run hotel in quiet location, convenient for town centre. Special terms for short breaks and extended stays.
Bedrooms: 4 double & 3 twin, 1 family room.
Bathrooms: 8 private.
Bed & breakfast: from £24.50 single, from £42.50 double.
Evening meal 7pm (l.o. 8.30pm).
Parking for 6.
Credit: Access, Visa.

MARKET DRAYTON
Shropshire
Map ref 4A2

Old market town with black and white buildings and 17th C houses. Hodnet Hall is in the vicinity with its beautiful landscaped gardens covering 60 acres.

Corbet Arms ⚥
🖤🖤🖤 APPROVED
High St., Market Drayton, TF9 1PY
☎ (0630) 2037
Telex 94070685 CORB.G.
Town centre position with ample car parking and own bowling green. Golfing and fishing by arrangement with local clubs.

Bedrooms: 3 single, 3 double & 4 twin, 2 family rooms.
Bathrooms: 10 private, 1 public.
Bed & breakfast: £32-£35 single, £48-£54 double.
Lunch available.
Evening meal 7pm (l.o. 9pm).
Parking for 62.
Credit: Access, Visa, Diners, Amex.

Rosehill Manor ⚥
🖤🖤🖤 APPROVED
Tern Hill, Market Drayton, TF9 2JF
☎ Tern Hill (063 083) 532
Country house in 1.5 acres with chef/proprietor. Log fires in winter. Convenient for Ironbridge, the Potteries and Wales.
Bedrooms: 3 single, 2 double, 1 family room.
Bathrooms: 4 private, 2 public.
Bed & breakfast: £22-£40 single, £33-£52 double.
Half board: £35-£55 daily, £136-£320 weekly.
Lunch available.
Evening meal 6.30pm (l.o. 9pm).
Parking for 20.
Credit: Access, Visa.

MERIDEN
W. Midlands
Map ref 4B3

Village halfway between Coventry and Birmingham. Said to be the centre of England, marked by a cross on the green.

The Forest of Arden Hotel, Golf & Country Club ⚥
Maxstoke Lane, Meriden, Coventry, CV7 7HR
☎ (0676) 22335 Telex 312604
Off A45, 3 miles from M6 and the M42, new hotel, golf and country club development, set in 400 acres of wooded parkland.
Bedrooms: 77 double & 76 twin.
Bathrooms: 153 private.
Bed & breakfast: from £98 single, from £116 double.
Lunch available.
Evening meal 7pm (l.o. 10pm).
Parking for 300.

Credit: Access, Visa, Diners, Amex.

Innellan House ⚥
Eaves Green Lane, Meriden, Coventry, CV7 7JL
☎ (0676) 22548 & (0676) 23005
Detached country house surrounded by 18 acres of meadowland. Approximately one mile from Meriden village, good touring centre, convenient for the railway, airport and the National Exhibition Centre. Non-smokers only please.
Bedrooms: 1 double & 2 twin.
Bathrooms: 2 private.
Bed & breakfast: £18-£20 single, £30-£33 double.
Parking for 11.

Woodlands Farm House ⚥
Back La., Meriden, Coventry, CV7 7LD
☎ (0676) 22317
12-acre farm. Oak-beamed, comfortable farmhouse in old Warwickshire countryside. Ideal for touring Kenilworth, Warwick and Stratford-upon-Avon. Central for theatre, concert and sports facilities. Access to major road network, airport, rail and the National Exhibition Centre.
Bedrooms: 1 double & 2 twin.
Bathrooms: 2 private, 1 public.
Bed & breakfast: £18-£20 single, £30-£35 double.
Parking for 10.

> The symbol **CR** and the name of a hotel group or consortium after a hotel address means that bookings can be made through a central reservations office. These are listed on pages 559 & 560.

MINCHINHAMPTON

Gloucestershire
Map ref 2B1

4m SE. Stroud
A stone-built town, with
many 17th/18th C
buildings, owing its
existence to the wool and
cloth trades. A 17th C
pillared market house
may be found in the town
square, near which is the
Norman and 14th C
church.

The Ragged Cot Inn M

Hyde, Chalford, Stroud,
GL6 8PE
☎ Brimscombe (0453)
884643 & 731333
*Half a mile from Gatcombe
Park and adjacent to 600 acres
of National Trust commonland.
Cheltenham 15 miles, Bath 20
miles and Stroud 5 miles.*
Bedrooms: 2 double & 8 twin.
Bathrooms: 10 private.
Bed & breakfast: from £45
single, £62.50-£75 double.
Lunch available.
Evening meal 7pm (l.o.
9.30pm).
Parking for 55.
Credit: Access, Visa, Amex.

MORETON-IN-MARSH

Gloucestershire
Map ref 2B1

Attractive town of
Cotswold stone with 17th
C houses, an ideal base
for touring the Cotswolds.
Some of the local
attractions include
Batsford Park Arboretum,
the Jacobean Chastleton
House and Sezincote
Garden.

Manor House Hotel M
COMMENDED

High St., Moreton-in-Marsh,
GL56 0LJ
☎ (0608) 50501 Telex 837151
*16th C privately-owned manor
house with original features.
Some four-poster beds, indoor
pool and walled garden. All-
weather tennis court.*
Bedrooms: 5 single, 17 double
& 12 twin.
Bathrooms: 34 private.
Bed & breakfast: £55-£65
single, £63-£79.50 double.

Half board: £49.50-£56 daily.
Lunch available.
Evening meal 7.15pm (l.o.
9.30pm).
Parking for 30.
Credit: Access, Visa, Diners,
Amex.

Moreton House M
APPROVED

Moreton-in-Marsh,
GL56 0LQ
☎ (0608) 50747
*Family-run guesthouse
providing full English breakfast
and optional evening meal. Tea
shop, open 6 days a week,
lounge bar with restaurant.
Ideal for touring the
Cotswolds. Children and dogs
welcome.*
Bedrooms: 3 single, 6 double
& 3 twin.
Bathrooms: 5 private,
2 public.
Bed & breakfast: £18.50-£22
single, £34-£44 double.
Lunch available.
Evening meal 6pm (l.o.
8.30pm).
Parking for 5.
Credit: Access, Visa.

MUCH BIRCH

Hereford & Worcester
Map ref 2A1

6m S. Hereford
Village on the road
between Ross-on-Wye
and Hereford, with
splendid views towards
the Black Mountains.

Pilgrim Hotel M
COMMENDED

Hereford, Herefordshire
HR2 8HJ
☎ Golden Valley
(0981) 540742 Telex 35332,
Attn Pilgrim Hotel
Inter
*Country house hotel combining
modern facilities with old
world charm. Popular with
country lovers and golfers. Set
in 4 acres of grounds.*
Bedrooms: 1 single, 9 double
& 10 twin.
Bathrooms: 20 private.
Bed & breakfast: £46-£54
single, £58-£68 double.
Half board: £50-£70 daily,
£247-£325 weekly.
Lunch available.
Evening meal 7pm (l.o.
10pm).
Parking for 40.

Credit: Access, Visa, Diners,
Amex.

MUCH WENLOCK

Shropshire
Map ref 4A3

Small town close to
Wenlock Edge in beautiful
scenery and full of
interest. In particular
there are the remains of
an 11th C priory with fine
carving and the black and
white 16th C Guildhall.

Gaskell Arms Hotel M

Much Wenlock, TF13 6HF
☎ Telford (0952) 727212
*17th C coaching inn built of
stone and brick, with beamed
ceilings. Family-run free house.
Own private car park.*
Bedrooms: 1 single, 6 double
& 3 twin, 1 family room.
Bathrooms: 3 private,
2 public.
Bed & breakfast: £25-£30
single, £38-£50 double.
Half board: £30-£45 daily,
£157.50-£189 weekly.
Lunch available.
Evening meal 7pm (l.o.
10pm).
Parking for 30.
Credit: Access, Visa.

Raven Hotel M

Barrow St., Much Wenlock,
TF13 6EN
☎ (0952) 727251
17th C coaching inn.
Bedrooms: 2 single, 3 double
& 1 twin, 3 family rooms.
Bathrooms: 9 private.
Bed & breakfast: from £30
single, from £40 double.
Lunch available.
Evening meal 7pm (l.o.
10pm).
Parking for 40.
Credit: Visa, Amex.

Wheatland Fox Hotel M
COMMENDED

High St., Much Wenlock,
TF13 6AD
☎ (0952) 727292
*Charming, small, privately-
owned hotel. Grade II listed
building in main street of
ancient town. Convenient for
Ironbridge, Wenlock Edge and
the Longmynd.*
Bedrooms: 5 double & 2 twin.
Bathrooms: 7 private.

Bed & breakfast: £40-£50
single, £55-£65 double.
Half board: £55-£65 daily.
Lunch available.
Evening meal 7.30pm (l.o.
9.30pm).
Parking for 20.
Open February-December.
Credit: Access, Visa, Amex.

NAILSWORTH

Gloucestershire
Map ref 2B1

Ancient wool town with
several elegant Jacobean
and Georgian houses,
surrounded by wooded
hillsides with fine views.

Apple Orchard House M

Orchard Close, Springhill,
Nailsworth, Stroud,
GL6 0LX
☎ (0453) 832503
*Large house in secluded
garden with lovely views.
Mostly spacious, well-furnished
en-suite private rooms.
Interesting south Cotswold
touring centre.*
Bedrooms: 1 double & 1 twin,
1 family room.
Bathrooms: 2 private,
1 public.
Bed & breakfast: £16-£17
single, £26-£28 double.
Half board: £20-£21 daily,
£140-£147 weekly.
Evening meal 6pm (l.o.
10am).
Parking for 3.

NEWCASTLE-UNDER-LYME

Staffordshire
Map ref 4B2

Industrial town whose
museum and art gallery
give evidence of its past.
The Guildhall was built in
the 18th C and there is
the modern university of
Keele.
*Tourist Information
Centre* ☎ *(0782) 618125*

Borough Arms Hotel M

King St., Newcastle-under-
Lyme, ST5 1HX
☎ Stoke-on-Trent
(0782) 629421 Fax (0782)
712388

*Former coaching inn close to
town centre with easy access to
all pottery towns. Lounge bar
and a la carte restaurant.*
Bedrooms: 27 single, 6 double
& 12 twin.
Bathrooms: 45 private.
Bed & breakfast: £33-£43
single, £48-£57 double.
Lunch available.
Evening meal 7pm (l.o.
10pm).
Parking for 45.
Credit: Access, Visa, Diners,
Amex.

Clayton Farmhouse M

The Green, Clayton,
Newcastle-under-Lyme,
ST5 4AA
☎ (0782) 620401
*Comfortable, modernised
farmhouse in country setting.
1.5 miles from the town centre
and half a mile from the M6
junction 15.*
Bedrooms: 2 double & 2 twin,
1 family room.
Bathrooms: 3 private,
1 public.
Bed & breakfast: £21.50-£24
single, £32-£36 double.
Half board: £22-£24 daily.
Evening meal 6pm (l.o.
midday).
Parking for 12.

The Deansfield M

98 Lancaster Rd., Newcastle-
under-Lyme, ST5 1DS
☎ (0782) 619040
Telex 669581
*Elegant small hotel, quietly
situated, convenient to town
centre and M6. A la carte
restaurant open to non-
residents.*
Bedrooms: 6 single, 2 double
& 1 twin, 2 family rooms.
Bathrooms: 11 private,
1 public.
Bed & breakfast: £27.50
single, £35 double.
Lunch available.
Evening meal 7pm (l.o.
9.30pm).
Parking for 36.
Credit: Access, Visa, Diners,
Amex.

Durlston Guest House M
Listed

Kimberley Rd., Newcastle-
under-Lyme, ST5 9EG
☎ (0782) 611708

*Small family-run guesthouse on
A34. Convenient for M6
junction 15/16, the Potteries,
the Peak District and Alton
Towers.*
Bedrooms: 3 single, 1 double
& 1 twin, 2 family rooms.
Bathrooms: 2 public.
Bed & breakfast: max. £16
single, max. £30 double.
Parking for 10.

The Gables M
Listed

570-572 Etruria Rd.,
Newcastle-under-Lyme,
ST5 0SU
☎ (0782) 619748
*Gracious Edwardian hotel with
extensive grounds. On the A53
with easy access to the M6.
Adjacent to the New Victoria
Theatre. Well placed for
visitors to Stoke-on-Trent's
pottery factories and Alton
Towers.*
Bedrooms: 5 double & 2 twin,
6 family rooms.
Bathrooms: 3 public;
10 private showers.
Bed & breakfast: £15-£20
single, £25-£30 double.
Half board: £23.50-£28.50
daily.
Evening meal 6pm (l.o. 9pm).
Parking for 18.

Haydon House Hotel M

Haydon St., Basford, Stoke-
on-Trent, ST4 6JD
☎ (0782) 711311 Telex 36600
HAYHO
*Country house in the city. Fine
food and service. Executive
accommodation including
suites. A landmark in
Staffordshire.*
Bedrooms: 10 single, 3 double
& 10 twin, 10 family rooms.
Bathrooms: 33 private,
1 public.
Bed & breakfast: £48-£75
single, £64-£110 double.
Half board: from £45 daily.
Lunch available.
Evening meal 6.30pm (l.o.
10pm).
Parking for 50.
Credit: Access, Visa, Diners,
Amex.

Thomas Forshaw Hotel M

Liverpool Rd., Cross Heath,
Newcastle-under-Lyme,
ST5 9DX
☎ (0782) 717000 Telex 36681
Consort
*Modern hotel with all facilities,
located on A34 between
junctions 15 and 16 on the M6.*
Bedrooms: 29 double &
42 twin, 3 family rooms.
Bathrooms: 74 private.
Bed & breakfast: £42-£53
single, £54-£65 double.
Half board: £64.50-£75.50
daily.
Lunch available.
Evening meal 7pm (l.o.
9.45pm).
Parking for 125.
Credit: Access, Visa, C.Bl.,
Diners, Amex.

NEWNHAM-ON-SEVERN
Gloucestershire
Map ref 2B1

Small town on the Severn
Estuary near the Forest
of Dean. It has some 18th
C houses and fine views
of the Severn.

Victoria Hotel M

Newnham-on-Severn,
GL14 1AD
☎ Dean (0594) 516221
Minotels
*An early 17th C coaching inn
in attractive village and 12
miles from Gloucester on A48.*
Bedrooms: 1 single, 6 double
& 2 twin.
Bathrooms: 9 private.
Bed & breakfast: £32-£38
single, £50-£68 double.
Half board: £37.50-£44.50
daily.
Lunch available.
Evening meal 6.30pm (l.o.
9pm).
Parking for 40.
Credit: Access, Visa, Diners,
Amex.

NEWPORT
Shropshire
Map ref 4A3

Small market town on the
Shropshire Union Canal
has a wide High Street
and a church with some
interesting monuments.
Newport is close to
Aqualate Mere which is
the largest lake in
Staffordshire.
*Tourist Information
Centre* ☎ *(0952) 814109*

Bridge Inn
APPROVED

Chetwynd End, Newport,
TF10 7JB
☎ (0952) 811785
*Small, family-run
establishment, serving a wide
range of home-cooked food.
Parts of the building date from
1664.*
Bedrooms: 2 single, 1 double
& 2 twin.
Bathrooms: 2 private,
1 public.
Bed & breakfast: £15-£17
single, £30-£38 double.
Lunch available.
Evening meal 7pm (l.o.
10pm).
Parking for 40.
Credit: Access, Visa, C.Bl.,
Diners, Amex.

Norwood House Hotel and Restaurant M

Pave La., Newport,
TF10 9LQ
☎ (0952) 825896
*Hotel of character with
inglenook fireplace and log
fires. Just off the A41
Whitchurch to Wolverhampton
road.*
Bedrooms: 1 single, 3 double
& 2 twin.
Bathrooms: 6 private.
Bed & breakfast: £28.50-£30
single, £39-£42 double.
Lunch available.
Evening meal 7pm (l.o.
10.30pm).
Parking for 26.
Credit: Access, Visa, Amex.

Royal Victoria Hotel M

St. Mary's St., Newport,
TF10 7AB
☎ (0952) 820331
Telex 335464
*Old established town centre
inn, visited by Princess Victoria
in 1832.*
Continued ▶

**Classifications and quality commendations
were correct at the time of going to press
but are subject to change. Please check at
the time of booking.**

NEWPORT
Continued

Bedrooms: 11 single, 8 double & 4 twin, 1 family room.
Bathrooms: 24 private.
Bed & breakfast: from £45.50 single, from £62 double.
Lunch available.
Evening meal 6pm (l.o. 10pm).
Parking for 100.
Credit: Access, Visa, Amex.

NORTH NIBLEY
Gloucestershire
Map ref 2B1

2m SW. Dursley
Pleasant little village near Dursley dominated by the Tyndale Monument, a tapering stone tower erected in 1966 in memory of the translator of the New Testament.

Burrows Court Hotel M
APPROVED

Nibley Green, North Nibley, Dursley, GL11 6AZ
☎ Dursley (0453) 546230
Converted stone-built weaving mill with many exposed beams, commanding beautiful views of Cotswolds escarpment. Peaceful and homely atmosphere.
Bedrooms: 1 single, 7 double & 2 twin.
Bathrooms: 10 private.
Bed & breakfast: £27-£34 single, £35-£47 double.
Half board: £29-£37 daily, £189-£220 weekly.
Evening meal 7pm (l.o. 9pm).
Parking for 10.
Credit: Access, Visa.

Half board prices shown are per person but in some cases may be based on double/twin occupancy.

The enquiry coupons at the back will help you when contacting proprietors.

NORTHLEACH
Gloucestershire
Map ref 2B1

Village famous for its beautiful 15th C wool church with its lovely porch and interesting interior. There are also some fine houses including 16th C almshouses, a 17th C manor house and a collection of agricultural instruments in the former prison.

Cotteswold House M
Listed COMMENDED

Market Pl., Northleach, Cheltenham, GL54 3EG
☎ Cotswold (0451) 60493
A traditional Cotswold stone house with many interesting architectural features and modernised to a high standard. Ideal base from which to tour, or rest.
Bedrooms: 1 double & 2 twin, 1 family room.
Bathrooms: 3 public.
Bed & breakfast: £15-£17 single, £28-£30 double.

NUNEATON
Warwickshire
Map ref 4B3

Busy town with an art gallery and museum which has a permanent exhibition of the work of George Eliot. The library also has an interesting collection of material. Arbury Hall, a fine example of Gothic architecture, is nearby.
Tourist Information Centre ☎ (0203) 384027

Abbey Grange Hotel
100 Manor Court Rd., Nuneaton, CV11 5HQ
☎ (0203) 385535
Friendly hotel with good food and hospitality. Discounts for weekend groups. Ideal for the National Exhibition Centre, 15 minutes away, or anywhere in the Midlands.
Bedrooms: 5 single, 2 double & 5 twin.
Bathrooms: 6 private, 2 public; 2 private showers.
Bed & breakfast: £19.50-£25.50 single, £30-£37 double.

Evening meal 6.30pm (l.o. 9.30pm).
Parking for 30.
Credit: Access, Visa, Diners, Amex.

Drachenfels Hotel M
25 Attleborough Rd., Nuneaton, CV11 4HZ
☎ (0203) 383030
Built in early 20th C by a German nobleman along the lines of a German castle. Ample bathroom, shower, toilet facilities, some en-suite. Colour TV in all bedrooms. Cocktail bar. Overlooks playing fields.
Bedrooms: 2 single, 2 double & 3 twin, 1 family room.
Bathrooms: 2 private, 3 public.
Bed & breakfast: £18.50-£22 single, £27-£32 double.
Lunch available.
Evening meal 6pm (l.o. 9.30pm).
Parking for 8.
Credit: Access, Visa.

Triple 'A' Lodge Guest House
Listed

94-96 Coleshill Rd., Chapel End, Nuneaton, CU10 0PH
☎ Coventry (0203) 394515
Family-run guesthouse on the outskirts of Nuneaton, in the pleasant village of Chapel End. Newly refurbished to a high standard. Colour TV all rooms. Evening meals available.
Bedrooms: 3 double & 3 twin.
Bathrooms: 2 public.
Bed & breakfast: £15-£18 single, £24-£30 double.
Evening meal 6pm (l.o. 9.30pm).
Parking for 12.
Credit: Access, Visa, Diners, Amex.

Individual proprietors have supplied all details of accommodation. Although we do check for accuracy, we advise you to confirm prices and other information at the time of booking.

NYMPSFIELD
Gloucestershire
Map ref 2B1

3m W. Nailsworth
Pretty village high up in the Cotswolds, with a simple mid-Victorian church and a prehistoric long barrow nearby.

Rose and Crown Inn M
Listed

Nympsfield, Stonehouse, GL10 3TU
☎ Dursley (0453) 860240
300-year-old inn in extremely quiet Cotswold village, close to Cotswold Way and Nympsfield Gliding Club. Easy access to M4/M5.
Bedrooms: 1 double, 3 family rooms.
Bathrooms: 1 private, 1 public.
Bed & breakfast: £19.50-£21 single, £28 double.
Half board: £24-£30 daily, £140-£165 weekly.
Lunch available.
Evening meal 6.30pm (l.o. 10pm).
Parking for 30.
Credit: Access, Visa.

OMBERSLEY
Hereford & Worcester
Map ref 2B1

4m W. Droitwich
A particularly fine village full of black and white houses including the 17th C Dower House and some old inns. The church contains the original box pews.

The Crown and Sandys Arms M
APPROVED

Ombersley, Droitwich, Worcestershire WR9 0EW
☎ Worcester (0905) 620252
A free house with comfortable bedrooms, draught beers and open fires. Home-cooked meals available lunch and evenings, 7 days a week.
Bedrooms: 1 single, 5 double & 1 twin.
Bathrooms: 5 private, 1 public.
Bed & breakfast: £16-£25 single, £32-£40 double.
Lunch available.
Evening meal 6pm (l.o. 10pm).
Parking for 100.
Credit: Access, Visa.

ONNELEY

Staffordshire
Map ref 4A2

6m SW. Newcastle-under-Lyme

The Wheatsheaf Inn at Onneley ♠
♛♛♛

Bar Hill Rd., Onneley,
CW3 9QF
☎ Stoke-on-Trent
(0782) 751581 Fax (0782) 751499
18th C country inn with bars, restaurant, conference and functions facilities. On the A525, 3 miles from Bridgemere and Keele University, 7 miles from Newcastle-under-Lyme.
Bedrooms: 4 double & 1 twin.
Bathrooms: 5 private.
Bed & breakfast: £37-£42 single, £42-£52 double.
Half board: £49.95-£54.95 daily, £327 weekly.
Lunch available.
Evening meal 6pm (l.o. 10pm).
Parking for 150.
Credit: Access, Visa.

OSWESTRY

Shropshire
Map ref 4A3

Town close to the Welsh border, the scene of many battles. To the north are the remains of a large Iron Age hill fort. An excellent centre for exploring Shropshire and Offa's Dyke.
Tourist Information Centre ☎ (0691) 662488 or 654411

Bear Hotel ♠
♛♛

Salop Rd., Oswestry,
SY11 2NR
☎ (0691) 652093
A family-run hotel in the town centre, offering a warm welcome and good home cooking for healthy appetites. Some en-suite rooms.
Bedrooms: 3 single, 4 double & 2 twin, 1 family room.
Bathrooms: 5 private, 1 public.
Bed & breakfast: £17.50-£28 single, £27.50-£37 double.
Lunch available.
Evening meal 7pm (l.o. 10pm).
Parking for 25.
Credit: Access, Visa, Amex.

Pen-y-Dyffryn Hall Hotel ♠
♛♛♛

Rhyd-y-Croesau, Oswestry,
SY10 7DT
☎ (0691) 653700
Charming stone-built Georgian rectory in 5 acres of grounds in Shropshire/Welsh border hill country. Fully licensed, extensive a la carte menu. Quiet and relaxed atmosphere. Shrewsbury 20 minutes.
Bedrooms: 1 single, 3 double & 3 twin, 1 family room.
Bathrooms: 8 private.
Bed & breakfast: £30-£34 single, £40-£54 double.
Half board: £30-£37 daily, £190-£225 weekly.
Lunch available.
Evening meal 7pm (l.o. 9pm).
Parking for 38.
Credit: Access, Visa.

The Wynnstay ♠
♛♛♛♛ COMMENDED

Church St., Oswestry,
SY11 2SZ
☎ Oswestry (0691) 655261
Fax (0691) 661845
Attractively refurbished Georgian country house hotel in town centre, with crown bowling green and walled gardens. Close to Chester and Shrewsbury.
Bedrooms: 2 single, 11 double & 11 twin, 2 family rooms.
Bathrooms: 26 private.
Bed & breakfast: £45.50-£90 single, £58.50-£115 double.
Half board: £41-£97 daily, £311-£549 weekly.
Lunch available.
Evening meal 7pm (l.o. 11.30pm).
Parking for 70.
Credit: Access, Visa, C.Bl., Diners, Amex.

> **Map references apply to the colour maps towards the end of this guide.**

> **The symbols are explained on the flap inside the back cover.**

OXHILL

Warwickshire
Map ref 2C1

6m SE. Stratford-upon-Avon
Village in the Vale of Red Horse not far from the battlefield of Edgehill. Its church retains much that is Norman.

Nolands Farm and Country Restaurant ♠
♛♛♛

Oxhill, Warwick, CV35 0RJ
☎ Kineton (0926) 640309
300-acre arable farm. In a tranquil valley surrounded by fields. All rooms in converted barn annexe. Peaceful and quiet, overlooking old stable yard. Stocked lake, woods, walks and wildlife. Elegant four-poster bedrooms. Licensed restaurant with fresh country produce.
Bedrooms: 5 double & 1 twin, 3 family rooms.
Bathrooms: 9 private, 1 public.
Bed & breakfast: from £20 single, £24-£36 double.
Lunch available.
Evening meal 6.30pm (l.o. 6.30pm).
Parking for 11.
Credit: Access.

PAINSWICK

Gloucestershire
Map ref 2B1

Picturesque wool town with inns and houses dating from the 14th C. Painswick House is a Palladian mansion with Chinese wallpaper. The churchyard is famous for its yew trees.
Tourist Information Centre ☎ (0452) 812569

Falcon Hotel
Painswick, Stroud, GL6 6UN
☎ (0452) 812189
Small family owned hotel, built in 1553, in a very pretty village in the heart of the Cotswolds.
Bedrooms: 5 double & 5 twin.
Bathrooms: 10 private, 2 public.
Bed & breakfast: from £34.50 single, from £49.50 double.
Half board: £37.25-£47 daily.
Lunch available.
Evening meal 7pm (l.o. 10pm).

Parking for 50.
Credit: Access, Visa, Diners, Amex.

PERSHORE

Hereford & Worcester
Map ref 2B1

Attractive Georgian town on the River Avon close to the Vale of Evesham, with fine houses and old inns. The remains of the beautiful Pershore Abbey form the parish church.
Tourist Information Centre ☎ (0386) 554711

Fern House ♠
♛♛♛

42 Bridge St., Pershore,
Worcestershire WR10 1AT
☎ (0386) 555807
Listed Georgian town house, situated between the old bridge and abbey, central to all amenities. Non-smokers only please.
Bedrooms: 2 double & 1 twin.
Bathrooms: 1 public.
Bed & breakfast: £12.50-£16 single, £25-£28 double.
Half board: £18.50-£22 daily.
Lunch available.
Evening meal 6pm (l.o. 4pm).
Parking for 1.
Open April-October.

REDDITCH

Hereford & Worcester
Map ref 4B3

Town has remains of a Cistercian Abbey which have been excavated to reveal the Abbey's history. Forge Mill is close by with a restored water wheel and Wynyates Craft Centre.
Tourist Information Centre ☎ (0527) 60806

Abbey Park Golf and Country Club ♠
Dagnell End Rd., Redditch,
Worcestershire B98 7BD
☎ (0527) 584140 &
(0527) 63918 Fax (0527) 65872
Golf, country club and hotel open to the public.
Bedrooms: 16 twin, 16 family rooms.
Bathrooms: 32 private.
Bed & breakfast: £35-£48.50 single, £40-£57 double.

Continued ▶

REDDITCH
Continued

Half board: £45.45-£58.95 daily, £318.15-£412.65 weekly.
Lunch available.
Evening meal 7pm (l.o. 10pm).
Parking for 250.
Credit: Access, Visa, Diners, Amex.

Hotel Montville ✿✿
101 Mount Pleasant, Redditch, Worcestershire B97 4JE
☎ (0527) 44411 & 44341
Refurbished hotel convenient for the town centre, with a friendly, family atmosphere.
Bedrooms: 6 single, 1 double & 2 twin, 2 family rooms.
Bathrooms: 8 private; 3 private showers.
Bed & breakfast: £36-£44 single, £55-£66 double.
Half board: £41.50-£59 daily.
Lunch available.
Evening meal 6.30pm (l.o. 9pm).
Parking for 18.
Credit: Access, Visa.

Southcrest Hotel M
Pool Bank, Southcrest, Redditch, Worcestershire B97 4JG
☎ (0527) 541511
Telex 338455
Country house hotel with French restaurant, set in 26 acres of landscaped gardens and woods.
Bedrooms: 10 single, 21 double & 27 twin.
Bathrooms: 58 private.
Bed & breakfast: £60-£77 single, £70-£87 double.
Half board: £72-£90 daily.
Lunch available.
Evening meal 7pm (l.o. 9.15pm).
Parking for 100.
Credit: Access, Visa, Diners, Amex.

ROCESTER
Staffordshire
Map ref 4B2

Hollybank Guesthouse
Hollington Rd., Rocester, Uttoxeter, ST14 5HX
☎ (0889) 590695

Large Victorian house, in spacious grounds, with bar and TV lounge. Take B5030 to Rocester. Continue on this road until you see signs for Hollybank Guesthouse.
Bedrooms: 4 single, 3 twin, 2 family rooms.
Bathrooms: 1 private, 3 public.
Bed & breakfast: £14-£14.50 single, £28-£29 double.
Half board: £21.50-£22 daily, £109.20-£131.10 weekly.
Lunch available.
Evening meal 6.30pm (l.o. midday).
Parking for 12.

ROLLESTON-ON-DOVE
Staffordshire
Map ref 4B3

3m NW. Burton upon Trent
Village close to Repton and Sudbury Hall, a National Trust property with a Museum of Childhood. The village church has a Saxon crypt.

The Brookhouse Inn M
✿✿✿ COMMENDED
Brookside, Rolleston-on-Dove, Burton upon Trent, DE13 9AA
☎ Burton upon Trent (0283) 814188
Individually designed bedrooms with antique furniture and bathrooms en-suite. Intimate romantic restaurant. Also has a relaxing conservatory.
Bedrooms: 8 single, 10 double & 1 twin.
Bathrooms: 19 private.
Bed & breakfast: £54-£59 single, £69-£75 double.
Lunch available.
Evening meal 7.30pm (l.o. 10pm).
Parking for 40.
Credit: Access, Visa, Diners, Amex.

> **Half board prices shown are per person but in some cases may be based on double/twin occupancy.**

ROSS-ON-WYE
Hereford & Worcester
Map ref 2A1

Attractive market town set above the River Wye with a 17th C market hall. There are lovely views from the Prospect.
Tourist Information Centre ☎ (0989) 62768

The Arches Country House M
✿✿ APPROVED
Walford Rd., Ross-on-Wye, Herefordshire HR9 5TP
☎ (0989) 63348
Family-run Georgian style hotel set in half an acre of lawns, 10 minutes' walk from the town centre. All bedrooms are individually decorated and have views of the lawned garden. Warm and friendly atmosphere with personal service.
Bedrooms: 1 single, 2 double & 1 twin, 2 family rooms.
Bathrooms: 1 private, 2 public.
Bed & breakfast: £16-£18.50 single, £29-£40 double.
Evening meal 7pm (l.o. 5pm).
Parking for 8.

Bridge House Hotel M
✿✿✿ COMMENDED
Wilton, Ross-on-Wye, Herefordshire HR9 6AA
☎ (0989) 62655
Small riverside hotel with panoramic views from the gardens and pride in its comfort and cuisine. All rooms en-suite. Break terms available.
Bedrooms: 4 double & 3 twin.
Bathrooms: 7 private, 1 public.
Bed & breakfast: £29-£31 single, £48-£50 double.
Half board: £33.50-£35.50 daily, £200-£220 weekly.
Evening meal 7pm (l.o. 9pm).
Parking for 12.
Credit: Access, Visa.

Brockhampton Court Hotel M
✿✿✿
Brockhampton, Hereford, Herefordshire HR1 4TQ
☎ How Caple (098 986) 239
Country mansion with panelled interior in 6 acres of gardens and lawns.
Bedrooms: 4 single, 9 double & 7 twin, 6 family rooms.
Bathrooms: 26 private.

Bed & breakfast: £20-£25 single, £50-£60 double.
Half board: £30-£40 daily, £200-£300 weekly.
Lunch available.
Evening meal 7pm (l.o. 8.15pm).
Parking for 100.

Chase Hotel M
✿✿✿
Gloucester Rd., Ross-on-Wye, Herefordshire HR5 5LH
☎ (0989) 763161 Telex 35658
Fax (0989) 768330
Ⓒ Consort
Georgian country house set in 11 acres of lovely grounds with 2 small lakes. Short walk to town's market place. Ideal touring centre.
Bedrooms: 4 single, 22 double & 12 twin, 2 family rooms.
Bathrooms: 40 private.
Bed & breakfast: max. £65 single, max. £93 double.
Lunch available.
Evening meal 7pm (l.o. 9.45pm).
Parking for 200.
Credit: Access, Visa, Diners, Amex.

Chasedale Hotel M
✿✿✿
Walford Rd., Ross-on-Wye, Herefordshire HR9 5PQ
☎ (0989) 62423 & 65801
Family-run country house hotel half a mile from Ross-on-Wye town centre, set in an English rose garden.
Bedrooms: 3 single, 4 double & 1 twin, 3 family rooms.
Bathrooms: 9 private, 1 public.
Bed & breakfast: £29-£31 single, £46-£50 double.
Half board: £31.50-£40 daily, £204-£250 weekly.
Lunch available.
Evening meal 7pm (l.o. 9pm).
Parking for 25.
Credit: Access, Visa, Diners.

Edde Cross House M
✿✿ COMMENDED
Edde Cross St., Ross-on-Wye, Herefordshire HR9 7BZ
☎ (0989) 65088
Georgian town house overlooking river, close to town centre. Bedrooms decorated and furnished to a high standard, with colour TV, and tea/coffee facilities. Some en-suite rooms. Non-smokers only please.

Bedrooms: 1 single, 3 double
& 1 twin.
Bathrooms: 2 private,
1 public.
Bed & breakfast: £16-£17
single, £32-£40 double.
Evening meal 7pm (l.o. 5pm).
Open February-November.
➽10 ▯ 🍴 🅤 Ⓥ Ⅴ 🍴 📠 🎀
🛋 🛏 🗡 📠 ▯

Glewstone Court Hotel M
♛♛♛♛ COMMENDED
Glewstone, Ross-on-Wye,
Herefordshire HR9 6AW
☎ Llangarron (098 984) 367
*Elegant, listed, Georgian
country house set in 4 acres of
gardens overlooking the Wye
Valley. Emphasis on informal
comfort and hospitality coupled
with good food and fine wine.*
Bedrooms: 2 double & 2 twin,
2 family rooms.
Bathrooms: 6 private,
2 public.
Bed & breakfast: £43-£51
single, £64-£75 double.
Half board: £49-£60 daily,
£359-£429 weekly.
Lunch available.
Evening meal 7pm (l.o.
10pm).
Parking for 20.
Credit: Access, Visa, Amex.
➽ 🍴 ▯ 🍴 🅤 ☎ 📺
▥ 🛋 🗡 🎀 📠 ▯ 🕎 🏧 ▯

Orles Barn Hotel & Restaurant M
♛♛♛ COMMENDED
Wilton, Ross-on-Wye,
Herefordshire HR9 6AE
☎ (0989) 62155
*Country house hotel set in 1.5
acres of gardens, with south-
facing rooms. Home cooking
by proprietors using fresh local
produce.*
Bedrooms: 1 single, 5 double
& 2 twin, 1 family room.
Bathrooms: 9 private.
Bed & breakfast: £30-£45
single, £50-£70 double.
Half board: £39-£54 daily,
£195-£230 weekly.
Lunch available.
Evening meal 7pm (l.o.
9.30pm).
Parking for 20.
Credit: Access, Visa, Diners,
Amex.
➽ 🍴 ▯ 🍴 ▯ 🅤 Ⓥ 🍴 ▥ 🛋
🗡 🛏 🎀 🏧 📠 ▯

Pencraig Court Hotel M
♛♛♛
Pencraig, Ross-on-Wye,
Herefordshire HR9 6HR
☎ (098 984) 306

*Georgian country house hotel,
privately owned, providing both
English and French cooking.
Large attractive garden
overlooking the River Wye.*
Bedrooms: 2 single, 4 double
& 4 twin, 1 family room.
Bathrooms: 11 private.
Bed & breakfast: £22-£35
single.
Half board: £33-£46 daily.
Evening meal 7pm (l.o.
9.30pm).
Parking for 20.
Open March-December.
Credit: Access, Visa, Diners,
Amex.
➽ 🍴 ▯ ▯ 🅤 ▯ Ⓥ 🍴 ▥ 🗡 ☀
🛏 📠 ▯

Pengethley Manor
♛♛♛♛
Nr. Ross-on-Wye,
Herefordshire HR9 6LL
☎ Harewood End
(098 987) 211 Telex 35332
HSA G (ATTN PH)
Ⓑ Best Western
*Elegant Georgian country
house in superb gardens with
magnificent views over
Herefordshire countryside.
Restaurant has list of over 200
wines.*
Bedrooms: 2 single, 10 double
& 7 twin, 3 family rooms.
Bathrooms: 22 private.
Bed & breakfast: £60-£110
single, £100-£150 double.
Half board: £60-£85 daily,
£399-£550 weekly.
Lunch available.
Evening meal 6.45pm (l.o.
9.30pm).
Parking for 72.
Credit: Access, Visa, Diners,
Amex.
➽ 🍴 ▯ 🍴 Ⓛ 🍴 ☎ 🍴 Ⓥ
🍴 ▥ 🛋 🗡 🗡 ⚅ ✇ Ὂ 🎀 ▯
☀ ⚆ 📠 ▯

Sunnymount Hotel M
♛♛♛ COMMENDED
Ryefield Rd., Ross-on-Wye,
Herefordshire HR9 5LU
☎ (0989) 63880
*Warm, comfortable hotel in
quiet location on edge of town,
offering French and English
cooking with home-grown and
local produce freshly cooked
for each meal.*
Bedrooms: 2 single, 3 double
& 4 twin.
Bathrooms: 4 private,
1 public.
Bed & breakfast: £16-£29
single, £33-£44 double.
Half board: £26.50-£39.50
daily, £110-£195 weekly.
Evening meal 7pm (l.o.
5.30pm).
Parking for 7.
Credit: Access, Visa.
➽ 🍴 ▯ Ⓥ 🍴 📺 ▥ 🛋 🗡
📠 ▯ ▯

Wharton Lodge Country House Hotel M
♛♛♛♛
Weston-under-Penyard, Ross-
on-Wye, Herefordshire
HR9 7JX
☎ Lea (098 981) 795 Fax
(098 981) 700
*An elegant Georgian home with
nine attractive en-suite
bedrooms. Situated in 15 acres
of parkland with beautiful
terraces and walled gardens.*
Bedrooms: 6 double & 3 twin.
Bathrooms: 9 private.
Bed & breakfast: £85-£120
single, £95-£130 double.
Half board: £72.50-£90 daily.
Lunch available.
Evening meal 7pm (l.o.
9.30pm).
Parking for 31.
Credit: Access, Visa, Amex.
➽ 🍴 🍴 📺 ▯ 🍴 Ⓥ 🍴 ▥ 🛋
🗡 ✇ ☀ 🛏 🎀 📠 ▯

Wilton Court Hotel M
Wilton, Ross-on-Wye,
Herefordshire HR9 6AQ
☎ (0989) 62569
*16th C hotel on the banks of
the Wye set in own delightful
gardens. Restaurant and bar
meals available.*
Bedrooms: 1 single, 5 double
& 1 twin, 1 family room.
Bathrooms: 6 private,
1 public.
Bed & breakfast: £32-£55
single, £50-£60 double.
Half board: £200-£250
weekly.
Lunch available.
Evening meal 7pm (l.o.
9.30pm).
Parking for 25.
Credit: Access, Visa.
➽12 📺 ▯ 🍴 ▯ Ⓥ 🍴 ▥
🛋 🗡 🗡 ☀ 📠 🎀 📠 ▯

Ye Hostelrie Hotel
Goodrich, Ross-on-Wye,
Herefordshire HR9 6HX
☎ Symonds Yat
(0600) 890241
*Listed building of pseudo-
Gothic architecture, in a
peaceful village near the
renowned Goodrich Castle,
overlooking the River Wye.
The original building dates
from the 17th C.*
Bedrooms: 1 single, 3 double
& 3 twin, 1 family room.
Bathrooms: 4 private,
2 public.
Bed & breakfast: £20-£24
single, £36 double.
Half board: £30-£28 daily.
Evening meal 7.30pm (l.o.
9pm).
Parking for 31.
➽ 🍴 ▯ Ⓥ 🍴 📺 ▥ 🛋 🗡
🗡 ☀ 🎀 📠 ▯

RUGBY
Warwickshire
Map ref 4C3

Town famous for its
public school which gave
its name to Rugby Union
football and which
featured in 'Tom Brown's
Schooldays'.
*Tourist Information
Centre ☎ (0788) 71813 or
535348*

Avondale Guest House M
♛♛ APPROVED
16 Elsee Rd., Rugby,
CV21 3BA
☎ (0788) 578639
*Victorian town residence close
to Rugby School, convenient
for Warwick Castle, Coventry
Cathedral, Leamington Spa,
National Exhibition Centre
and Birmingham.*
Bedrooms: 3 twin, 1 family
room.
Bathrooms: 1 private,
2 public; 1 private shower.
Bed & breakfast: max. £30
double.
Evening meal 6pm (l.o. 3pm).
Parking for 8.
➽ 🍴 Ⓛ ▯ 🍴 📺 ▥ 🛋 🗡
🎀

Brownsover Hall Hotel M
Brownsover Lane, Rugby,
CV21 1HU
☎ (0788) 546 100
Telex 31658 BHHG-G
Ⓡ Character
*Dating back to the 18th C and
originally designed by Sir
Gilbert Scott, the hotel is set in
7 acres of parkland, just
minutes away from exit 1 of
the M6. Table d'hote and a la
carte menus, lounge bar and
conference facilities.*
Bedrooms: 9 single, 15 double
& 5 twin, 2 family rooms.
Bathrooms: 31 private.
Bed & breakfast: £35-£79
single, £45-£92 double.
Lunch available.
Evening meal 7.30pm (l.o.
9.30pm).
Parking for 120.
Credit: Access, Visa, Diners,
Amex.
➽ 🍴 ▯ ☎ 📺 ▯ 🍴 Ⓥ ⚆
🍴 ▥ 🗡 🗡 🗡 ▯ 🛏
☀ ⚆ 📠 🎀 ☎ ▯

The Golden Lion Inn of Easenhall M
♛♛♛
Easenhall, Rugby, CV23 0JA
☎ (0788) 832265
Continued ▶

RUGBY

Continued

Individually styled bedrooms all en-suite, in a traditional 16th C building in beautiful village surrounding. 5 minutes from M6 junction 1. Double room with whirlpool bath.
Bedrooms: 1 single, 1 double & 1 twin.
Bathrooms: 3 private.
Bed & breakfast: £39.50-£44 single, £49.50-£54 double.
Lunch available.
Evening meal 7pm (l.o. 10pm).
Parking for 60.
Credit: Access, Visa, C.Bl., Diners, Amex.

Hillmorton Manor Hotel M

78 High St., Hillmorton, Rugby, CV21 4EE
☎ (0788) 565533 & 72403
Hotel in pleasant area of town with a la carte restaurant.
Bedrooms: 5 single, 3 double & 2 twin, 1 family room.
Bathrooms: 11 private.
Bed & breakfast: £35-£45 single, £45-£58 double.
Lunch available.
Evening meal 7pm (l.o. 10pm).
Parking for 45.
Credit: Access, Visa, Amex.

Mound Hotel of Rugby M

17-21 Lawford Rd., Rugby, CV21 2EB
☎ (0788) 543486
A welcoming and comfortable private hotel near Rugby School. An excellent base for touring places of interest in the Heart of England.
Bedrooms: 2 single, 7 double & 4 twin, 4 family rooms.
Bathrooms: 6 private, 2 public.
Bed & breakfast: £16.96-£24.72 single, £28.46-£36.05 double.
Evening meal 6.30pm (l.o. 3pm).
Parking for 17.
Credit: Access.

ST BRIAVELS

Gloucestershire
Map ref 2A1

Village set above the Wye Valley in the Forest of Dean with remains of a 13th C castle. Tintern, with its magnificent abbey ruins, is nearby.

Cinderhill House M
Listed

St. Briavels, Lydney, GL15 6RH
☎ Dean (0594) 530393
Lovely country house commanding a magnificent position high over the River Wye, on the edge of a historic village. Parties of up to 12 can be accommodated.
Bedrooms: 1 double & 3 twin, 1 family room.
Bathrooms: 5 private.
Bed & breakfast: £19.50-£25 single, £25-£30 double.
Half board: £32-£35 daily, £224-£245 weekly.
Evening meal 6.30pm (l.o. 9pm).
Parking for 6.

SHIFNAL

Shropshire
Map ref 4A3

Small market town, once an important staging centre for coaches on the Holyhead road. Where industrialism has not prevailed, the predominating architectural impression is Georgian, though some timber-framed houses survived the Great Fire of 1591. Within easy reach of the Ironbridge Gorge Museum.

Park House Hotel M
APPROVED

Park St., Shifnal, TF11 9BA
☎ Telford (0952) 460128
Telex 35438
CR Character
Magnificent character hotel converted from 2 17th C country houses. Located just a few minutes' drive from exit 4 of the M54. 40 minutes from Birmingham. Leisure facilities.
Bedrooms: 5 single, 29 double & 18 twin, 2 family rooms.
Bathrooms: 54 private.
Bed & breakfast: £52-£79 single, £75-£92 double.
Lunch available.
Evening meal 6.30pm (l.o. 10.30pm).

Parking for 150.
Credit: Access, Visa, Diners, Amex.

SHREWSBURY

Shropshire
Map ref 4A3

Beautiful historic town on the River Severn retaining many fine, old timber-framed houses. Its attractions include Rowley's Museum with Roman finds, remains of a castle, Clive House Museum, St. Chad's 18th C round church and rowing on the river.
Tourist Information Centre ☎ *(0743) 50761 or 50762*

Albright Hussey Hotel and Restaurant M
HIGHLY COMMENDED

Ellesmere Rd., Broad Oak, Shrewsbury, SY4 3AF
☎ Bomere Heath
(0939) 290571 & 290523
Historic 16th C Shropshire manor, with moat, pretty gardens and assorted wildlife including mandarin ducks and black swans. 2 miles from Shrewsbury town centre.
Bedrooms: 4 double & 2 twin.
Bathrooms: 6 private.
Bed & breakfast: £45-£75 single, £60-£95 double.
Half board: £60-£100 daily, £350-£600 weekly.
Lunch available.
Evening meal 7pm (l.o. 10pm).
Parking for 60.
Credit: Access, Visa, C.Bl., Diners, Amex.

Albrighton Hall Hotel M

Albrighton, Shrewsbury, SY4 3AG
☎ Bomere Heath
(0939) 291000 Telex 35726
ALBHAL G
CR Character
Just 2 miles from Shrewsbury town centre, set in 15 acres of landscaped gardens with ornamental lake. Full leisure facilities. 39 bedrooms, many four-posters.
Bedrooms: 9 single, 20 double & 6 twin, 4 family rooms.
Bathrooms: 39 private.
Bed & breakfast: £55-£70 single, £70-£88 double.
Lunch available.

Evening meal 7pm (l.o. 10pm).
Parking for 300.
Credit: Access, Visa, Diners, Amex.

The Bancroft M
Listed

17 Coton Cres., Shrewsbury, SY1 2NY
☎ (0743) 231746
Bed and breakfast accommodation close to Shrewsbury centre and railway station. All rooms have TV, tea/coffee making facilities and wash basin.
Bedrooms: 1 single, 1 twin, 1 family room.
Bathrooms: 1 public.
Bed & breakfast: from £14 single, from £25 double.
Half board: from £18.50 daily.
Evening meal 6.30pm.
Parking for 3.

College Hill Guest House M

11 College Hill, Shrewsbury, SY1 1LZ
☎ (0743) 65744
Town centre 16th C oak-beamed listed building in town centre. All rooms have colour TV, tea and coffee making facilities. Most rooms en-suite.
Bedrooms: 1 single, 4 twin, 1 family room.
Bathrooms: 3 private, 1 public; 1 private shower.
Bed & breakfast: £14-£18 single, £25-£36 double.

Hawkstone Park Hotel M

Weston-under-Redcastle, Shrewsbury, SY4 5UY
☎ Lee Brockhurst
(093 924) 611 Telex 35793
Fax (093 924) 311
CR Best Western
Busy golfing country hotel in 300-acre Shropshire estate with famous antiquities. 2 18-hole golf-courses. Sandy Lyle learned his game here. Non-residents welcome. Restaurants, bars and extensive conference/banqueting facilities. Golf professional shop with buggies for hire. 14 miles north of Shrewsbury, off A49 Whitchurch road.

Bedrooms: 5 single, 2 double
& 48 twin, 4 family rooms.
Bathrooms: 59 private.
Bed & breakfast: £60-£75
single, £88-£100 double.
Half board: £75-£115 daily.
Lunch available.
Evening meal 7.30pm (l.o.
9.45pm).
Parking for 300.
Credit: Access, Visa, Diners,
Amex.

Lion and Pheasant Hotel M

49-50 Wyle Cop, Shrewsbury,
SY1 1XJ
☎ (0743) 236288 Fax (0743)
3740
⬤R Consort
*Ancient inn of character with
many exposed beams and
original fireplaces. Bars and
restaurant open to non-
residents.*
Bedrooms: 5 single, 3 double
& 11 twin, 1 family room.
Bathrooms: 12 private,
2 public.
Bed & breakfast: £27.50-
£38.50 single, £44-£55 double.
Half board: £37.50-£48.50
daily.
Lunch available.
Evening meal 7pm (l.o.
9.30pm).
Parking for 15.
Credit: Access, Visa, Diners,
Amex.

Radbrook Hall Hotel M

Radbrook Rd., Shrewsbury,
SY3 9BQ
☎ (0743) 236676
*Country house with a colourful
history, set in 5 acres of
grounds just outside
Shrewsbury, with squash
courts, games room, sunbed,
jacuzzi and sauna. Just off A5
on A488 to Bishops Castle.*
Bedrooms: 3 single, 14 double
& 8 twin, 3 family rooms.
Bathrooms: 28 private.
Bed & breakfast: £48-£56
single, from £62 double.
Lunch available.
Evening meal 6pm (l.o.
10.30pm).
Parking for 250.
Credit: Access, Visa, Diners,
Amex.

Restawhile M

36 Coton Crescent, Coton
Hill, Shrewsbury, SY1 2NZ
☎ (0743) 240969
*10 minutes' walk to town
centre, railway station, and bus
station.*
Bedrooms: 1 single, 1 double
& 2 twin.
Bathrooms: 4 private.
Bed & breakfast: £15-£16
single, £30-£32 double.
Half board: £20 daily, £105-
£112 weekly.
Lunch available.
Evening meal 5.30pm (l.o.
8pm).

Rowton Castle M

Shrewsbury, SY5 9EP
☎ (0743) 884044 Fax (0743)
884949
*Rowton Castle has been
tastefully converted into a
hotel, set in 20 acres yet only
10 minutes from historic
Shrewsbury.*
Bedrooms: 2 single,
17 double.
Bathrooms: 19 private.
Bed & breakfast: £55-£60
single, £65-£75 double.
Half board: £75-£80 daily,
from £550 weekly.
Lunch available.
Evening meal 7pm (l.o.
10.30pm).
Parking for 120.
Credit: Access, Visa, Amex.

Sydney House Hotel M
COMMENDED

Coton Cres., Coton Hill,
Shrewsbury, SY1 2LJ
☎ (0743) 54681
*Edwardian town house with
period features, 10 minutes'
walk from town centre and
railway station. All rooms with
direct dial telephones, colour
TV and hot drink facilities,
some en-suite. Car parking for
7.*
Bedrooms: 2 single, 2 double
& 2 twin, 1 family room.
Bathrooms: 3 private,
2 public.
Bed & breakfast: £24.50-£37
single, £36-£48 double.
Half board: £27-£46 daily,
£169-£289 weekly.
Evening meal 7pm (l.o. 9pm).
Parking for 8.
Credit: Access, Visa.

Tudor House

2 Fish St., Shrewsbury,
SY1 1UR
☎ (0743) 51735
*Centrally situated in a quiet
medieval street. A listed Tudor
building (circa 1450) with a
wealth of oak beams. Licensed.*
Bedrooms: 2 double & 2 twin.
Bathrooms: 2 private,
2 public; 1 private shower.
Bed & breakfast: £22-£28
single, £30-£36 double.
Half board: £200-£236
weekly.
Evening meal 6pm.

The White House

Hanwood, Shrewsbury,
SY5 8LP
☎ (0743) 860414
*16th C half-timbered black and
white hotel, small and friendly,
in a quiet village. Fresh food,
wine and good company.*
Bedrooms: 1 single, 4 double
& 1 twin.
Bathrooms: 2 private,
1 public.
Bed & breakfast: £19.70
single, £39.40-£50.40 double.
Half board: £31.90-£37.40
daily, £180.60-£219.10
weekly.
Evening meal 7pm (l.o. 8pm).
Parking for 15.

SLIMBRIDGE

Gloucestershire
Map ref 2B1

The Wildfowl Trust was
founded by Sir Peter
Scott and has the world's
largest collection of
wildfowl. Of special
interest are the wild
swans and the geese
which wander around the
grounds.

Tudor Arms Lodge

Shepherds Patch, Slimbridge,
Gloucester, GL2 7BP
☎ Dursley (0453) 890306
*Newly built lodge adjoining an
18th C freehouse, alongside
Gloucester Sharpness Canal.
Renowned Slimbridge
Wildfowl Trust only 800 yards
away.*
Bedrooms: 2 double & 8 twin,
2 family rooms.
Bathrooms: 12 private.
Bed & breakfast: £39-£42
single, £49-£52 double.

Evening meal 7pm (l.o.
10pm).
Parking for 70.
Credit: Access, Visa.

SOLIHULL

W. Midlands
Map ref 4B3

On the outskirts of
Birmingham. Some Tudor
houses and a 13th C
church remain amongst
the new public buildings
and shopping centre. The
16th C Malvern Hall is
now a school and the
15th C Chester House at
Knowle is now a library.
*Tourist Information
Centre* ☎ *021-704 6130*

Arden Hotel and Leisure Club M

Coventry Rd., Bickenhill,
Birmingham, B92 0EH
☎ Hampton-in-Arden
(067 55) 32216 Telex 334913
Arden G
*Adjacent to the National
Exhibition Centre, railway
station, and M42, and close to
Birmingham Airport. Privately
owned and managed. Guests
have full use of leisure
facilities.*
Bedrooms: 4 single, 12 double
& 59 twin, 1 family room.
Bathrooms: 76 private.
Bed & breakfast: £64-£74
single, £80-£85 double.
Half board: £74-£84 daily.
Lunch available.
Evening meal 6pm (l.o.
10pm).
Parking for 150.
Credit: Access, Visa, Diners,
Amex.

The Bridgewater Hotel and Restaurant M

2110 Warwick Rd., Knowle,
Solihull, B93 0EE
☎ (0564) 771177
*Canal-side hotel set in 5 acres
of rural England. Situated on
the A41, 1 mile south of
Knowle and 9 miles from
Warwick.*
Bedrooms: 4 single, 15 double
& 1 twin.
Bathrooms: 20 private.
Bed & breakfast: £45-£75
single, £50-£85 double.
Half board: £60-£90 daily.
Lunch available.
Evening meal 7pm (l.o.
10pm).

Continued ▶

Parking for 40.
Credit: Access, Visa, Diners, Amex.

Cedarwood House M

347 Lyndon Road, Solihull, B92 7QT
☎ 021-743 5844 Fax 021-733 3053
Private guesthouse, all bedrooms elegantly furnished, en-suite bathrooms. Within 2 miles of the National Exhibition Centre, airport, station and Solihull centre.
Bedrooms: 3 single, 1 double & 1 twin.
Bathrooms: 5 private.
Bed & breakfast: £30-£40 single, £40-£50 double.
Parking for 6.

Ennerdale Hotel

990 Warwick Rd., Acocks Green, Birmingham, B27 6QB
☎ 021-707 8778
A happy, friendly hotel with a variety of amenities including a full size snooker table.
Bedrooms: 4 single, 2 double & 6 twin, 2 family rooms.
Bathrooms: 12 private, 2 public; 1 private shower.
Bed & breakfast: £25 single, £35 double.
Evening meal 6pm (l.o. 9pm).
Parking for 24.

Regency Hotel M

Stratford Rd., Shirley, Solihull, Birmingham, B90 4EB
☎ 021-745 6119 Telex 334400 Fax 021-733 3801
Regency period building, situated in a wooded green belt, close to Birmingham, National Exhibition Centre, M42 and M6. Swimming and leisure facilities.
Bedrooms: 9 single, 10 double & 22 twin, 16 family rooms.
Bathrooms: 57 private.
Bed & breakfast: from £74.50 single, from £89 double.
Lunch available.
Evening meal 7pm (l.o. 9.45pm).
Parking for 288.
Credit: Access, Visa, Amex.

Silica Country Guest House

Bakers Lane, Knowle, Solihull, B93 0DZ
☎ Knowle (0564) 773712
Guesthouse with exposed beams and located alongside the canal. 2 miles south of Knowle, Solihull, a quarter of a mile off the A4141, 15 minutes from the National Exhibition Centre.
Bedrooms: 2 single, 1 double & 1 twin.
Bathrooms: 2 private, 2 public.
Bed & breakfast: £17-£20 single, £34-£40 double.
Evening meal 6pm.
Parking for 8.

The town has a long history and some half-timbered buildings still remain, notably the 16th C High House. There are several museums in the town and Shugborough Hall and the famous angler Izaak Walton's cottage, now a museum, are nearby.
Tourist Information Centre ☎ *(0785) 40204*

Abbey Hotel M

65-68 Lichfield Rd., Stafford, ST17 4LW
☎ (0785) 58531
Friendly, comfortable hotel within walking distance of town. Good road and rail links.
Bedrooms: 12 single, 4 double & 3 twin, 1 family room.
Bathrooms: 11 private, 3 public.
Bed & breakfast: £18.50-£30 single, £32-£46 double.
Lunch available.
Evening meal 7pm (l.o. 8.30pm).
Parking for 20.
Credit: Access, Visa.

Fairfield Guest House M

70 Lichfield Rd., Stafford, ST17 4LW
☎ (0785) 52854
All rooms have colour TV with video and sky movies, hot and cold water, radio alarm, tea and coffee making facilities.
Bedrooms: 4 single, 3 double & 1 twin, 1 family room.

Bathrooms: 2 public; 2 private showers.
Bed & breakfast: £12-£16 single, £20-£22 double.
Half board: £14-£20 daily, £84-£120 weekly.
Evening meal 6.30pm (l.o. 5.30pm).
Parking for 9.

Garth Hotel M

Moss Pit, Stafford, ST17 9JR
☎ (0785) 56124 Telex 36479 Fax (0785) 55152
Set in its own grounds, 1 mile from M6 Junction 13. Recently modernised and an ideal centre for touring the area.
Bedrooms: 36 double & 24 twin.
Bathrooms: 60 private.
Bed & breakfast: from £51 single, from £67.50 double.
Lunch available.
Evening meal 7pm (l.o. 10pm).
Parking for 175.
Credit: Access, Visa, Amex.

Swan Hotel M

Greengate St., Stafford, ST16 2JA
☎ (0785) 58142
Handsome 400-year-old former coaching inn in a central position, retaining many of its original oak beams, with a hidden priest hole and Jacobean-style reception area. Some of the oak panelling was once in Stafford Castle.
Bedrooms: 12 single, 11 double & 4 twin, 5 family rooms.
Bathrooms: 32 private.
Bed & breakfast: £43-£47.50 single, from £61 double.
Lunch available.
Evening meal 6pm (l.o. 10pm).
Parking for 50.
Credit: Access, Visa, Diners, Amex.

Vine Hotel M

Salter St., Stafford, ST16 2JU
☎ (0785) 51071 & 44112 Telex 36479
Situated in a quiet part of town centre, possibly the oldest hostelry in Stafford.
Bedrooms: 11 single, 12 double & 3 twin, 1 family room.
Bathrooms: 27 private.

Bed & breakfast: from £42.50 single, from £59 double.
Lunch available.
Evening meal 7pm (l.o. 10pm).
Parking for 30.
Credit: Access, Visa, Amex.

Famous for its pottery. Factories of several famous makers, including Josiah Wedgwood, can be visited. The City Museum has one of the finest pottery and porcelain collections in the world.
Tourist Information Centre ☎ *(0782) 411222 or 404810 or 202173*

Clovelly Guest House M
Listed

92 Uttoxeter Road, Blythe Bridge, Stoke-on-Trent, ST11 9JG
☎ (0782) 398958
A large Victorian house out of the town, with a quarter of an acre garden. Within easy reach of the countryside, Alton Towers and the Potteries.
Bedrooms: 2 single, 2 double & 1 twin, 1 family room.
Bathrooms: 3 public.
Bed & breakfast: £15-£17 single, £30-£34 double.
Parking for 7.

The Corrie Guest House M

13 Newton St., Basford, Stoke-on-Trent, ST4 6JN
☎ (0782) 614838
Owner-run guesthouse in quiet residential area, close to public transport and local amenities. Within walking distance of the New Victoria Theatre and midway between Hanley and Newcastle-under-Lyme.
Bedrooms: 3 single, 1 double & 2 twin, 1 family room.
Bathrooms: 1 private, 3 public.
Bed & breakfast: £16.50-£21 single, £29.50-£35 double.
Half board: £22-£26 daily.
Evening meal 6pm (l.o. 4.30pm).
Parking for 6.

The Crown Hotel ♨
❀❀❀❀

Times Sq., Longton, Stoke-
on-Trent, ST3 1HD
☎ Stoke-on-Trent
(0782) 599343
*Completely refurbished town
centre hotel, with easy access
to neighbouring pottery towns.
Carvery and a la carte
restaurant. 2 bars.*
Bedrooms: 21 single,
12 double & 7 twin.
Bathrooms: 40 private.
Bed & breakfast: £31-£39.50
single, £45-£51 double.
Lunch available.
Evening meal 7pm (l.o.
10pm).
Parking for 45.
Credit: Access, Visa, Diners,
Amex.
⌖ ☌ ☐ ⚲ ☖ V ◉ ▥ ▱
☂ ✕ SP T

Flower Pot Hotel

46 Snow Hill, Shelton, Stoke-
on-Trent, ST1 4LY
☎ (0782) 286417 & 214484
*Homely hotel with easy access
to M6, central for pottery firms
and within easy reach of Alton
Towers. Half a mile from rail
and bus stations.*
Bedrooms: 3 single, 5 double,
4 family rooms.
Bathrooms: 2 public.
Bed & breakfast: £16-£20
single, £30-£40 double.
Half board: £21-£25 daily.
Evening meal 6pm (l.o. 8pm).
Parking for 6.
⌖ ☌ ☐ ⚲ ▤ ▮ V ☖ ◉
▥ ▱ ☂

Northwood Hotel
Listed

146 Keelings Rd.,
Northwood, Hanley, Stoke-
on-Trent, ST1 6QA
☎ (0782) 279729 & 271203
*Near Hanley town centre, next
to Northwood sports stadium,
conveniently situated for all
leisure and business locations
in Potteries area.*
Bedrooms: 2 single, 1 double
& 3 twin, 1 family room.
Bathrooms: 1 private,
1 public; 2 private showers.
Bed & breakfast: £17-£19
single, £32-£40 double.
Half board: £21-£24 daily,
£126-£138 weekly.
Evening meal 6.30pm (l.o.
7.30pm).
Parking for 9.
⌖3 ☐ ⚲ ▤ ☖ ◉ ▥ ▱ ✕

Peacock Hay Guest House ♨

Peacock Hay Farm, Talke,
Stoke-on-Trent, ST7 1UN
☎ Stoke-on-Trent
(0782) 773511

---

*Refurbished farmhouse in open
countryside with fine views, 3
miles from M6. Good access to
the Potteries.*
Bedrooms: 3 single, 3 double
& 4 twin, 2 family rooms.
Bathrooms: 3 private,
2 public.
Bed & breakfast: £16-£20
single, £32-£40 double.
Parking for 20.
⌖ ⚲ ☖ UL ▤ ☖ ▥ ▱
☂ ✳ OAP SP

Stakis Grand Hotel ♨
❀❀❀❀❀ COMMENDED

Trinity St., Hanley, Stoke-on-
Trent, ST1 5NB
☎ (0782) 202361
Telex 367264
🅱 Stakis
*In the centre of Hanley, the
commercial hub of the city of
Stoke-on-Trent. Late Victorian
building, recently renovated
and refurbished. Facilities for
conference and social
occasions. Indoor swimming
pool and leisure club.*
Bedrooms: 30 single,
61 double & 30 twin, 7 family
rooms.
Bathrooms: 128 private.
Bed & breakfast: £85-£95
single, from £106 double.
Lunch available.
Evening meal 6.30pm (l.o.
10pm).
Parking for 130.
Credit: Access, Visa, Diners,
Amex.
⌖ ☌ ☐ ⚲ ▮ V ✕ ☖
▥ ▱ ☂ ▲ ⚙ 🕭 ✕
OAP ✎ SP T

White Gables Hotel ♨
❀❀

Trentham Rd., Blurton,
Stoke-on-Trent, ST3 3DT
☎ (0782) 324882
*Elegant, peaceful country
house style hotel in own
grounds. Beautifully
maintained with good facilities
for discerning businessman and
families alike. Owner run. 1
mile from Wedgwood, 10 miles
from Alton Towers.*
Bedrooms: 1 single, 2 double
& 3 twin, 1 family room.
Bathrooms: 3 private,
2 public.
Bed & breakfast: £25-£40
single, £36-£52 double.
Half board: from £30.25
daily.
Evening meal 5pm (l.o. 7pm).
Parking for 11.
Credit: Access, Visa.
⌖ ▲ ☐ ☌ ☖ UL ▮ V ✕
▤ ☖ ▥ ▱ ☂ ▲ ● ♪ ∪ ✳
🕭 ▱ T

Woodcroft ♨

119 Leek Rd., Stockton
Brook, Stoke-on-Trent,
ST9 9NJ
☎ (0782) 502067
*Victorian house situated on the
A53, with a pleasant country
outlook. Easy access to the
Potteries and Leek Moorlands.*
Bedrooms: 1 single, 1 twin,
1 family room.
Bathrooms: 1 public.
Bed & breakfast: £10-£15
single, £20 double.
Parking for 3.
⌖ ▲ ⚲ UL ▤ ☖ ▥ ▲ ✕

STONE

Staffordshire
Map ref 4B2

Town on the River Trent
which has the remains of
a 12th C Augustinian
priory. It is surrounded by
pleasant countryside.
Trentham Gardens with
500 acres of parklands
and recreational facilities
is within easy reach.

The Hayes ♨
❀❀

Hayes Bank, Stone,
ST15 8SY
☎ (0785) 814589
*Elegant Regency mansion in
elevated position overlooking
beech woods and stream.
Spacious rooms furnished in
period mode. All rooms with
washbasins and tea making
facilities.*
Bedrooms: 2 single, 3 double
& 3 twin, 3 family rooms.
Bathrooms: 1 private,
3 public.
Bed & breakfast: £17.50-£22
single, £32.50-£40 double.
Evening meal 6pm (l.o.
7.30pm).
Parking for 10.
⌖ ▲ ⚲ ☐ ▮ V ▤ ☖ ▥
▲ ☂ ✳ ❋ OAP SP 🕭 T

Stone House Hotel ♨
❀❀❀❀ COMMENDED

Stone, ST15 0BQ
☎ (0785) 815531 Fax (0785)
814764
🅱 Lansbury
*This elegant building, set in its
own delightful grounds, offers
modern comfort and facilties.*
Bedrooms: 18 single,
19 double & 8 twin, 3 family
rooms.
Bathrooms: 48 private.
Bed & breakfast: £24-£74
single, £48-£87 double.
Half board: from £35 daily.
Lunch available.
Evening meal 7pm (l.o.
10pm).

Parking for 100.
Credit: Access, Visa, C.Bl.,
Diners, Amex.
⌖ ▲ ☐ ☌ ☐ ⚲ ▮ V
✕ ▤ ☖ ● ▥ ▲ ☂ ♪ ⚙
▱ ♪ ✕ ✎ ✳ SP T

STONEHOUSE

Gloucestershire
Map ref 2B1

Village in the Stroud
Valley with an Elizabethan
Court, later restored and
altered by Lutyens.

The Grey Cottage ♨
❀❀❀ COMMENDED

Bath Rd., Leonard Stanley,
Stonehouse, GL10 3LU
☎ Stonehouse (0453) 822515
*1807 Cotswold cottage
featuring tessellated tiling,
stonework and open log fires.
Charming garden with
distinctive Wellingtonia.
Family hospitality. Fresh
seasonal cooking, no
microwaved food.*
Bedrooms: 1 double & 2 twin.
Bathrooms: 2 private,
1 public.
Bed & breakfast: from £20
single, from £40 double.
Half board: from £35 daily.
Evening meal 7pm (l.o.
7.30pm).
Parking for 5.
⌖10 ☌ ☐ ⚲ UL ▮ V
✕ ▤ ☖ ▥ ▲ ✳ ✕ ▱ 🕭

STOURBRIDGE

W. Midlands
Map ref 4B3

Town on the River Stour,
famous for its
glassworks. Several of
the factories can be
visited and glassware
purchased at the factory
shops.

The Limes Hotel ♨
❀❀

260 Hagley Rd., Pedmore,
Stourbridge, DY9 0RW
☎ Hagley (0562) 882689
*Private hotel based on a
Victorian house run by the
owners and in half an acre of
grounds.*
Bedrooms: 9 single, 1 double
& 3 twin, 2 family rooms.
Bathrooms: 5 private,
2 public.
Bed & breakfast: £24.50-
£27.50 single, £69-£75 double.
Half board: £31-£34 daily,
£197.50-£218.50 weekly.
Continued ▶

STOURBRIDGE
Continued

Evening meal 6pm (l.o. 7.30pm).
Parking for 12.
Credit: Access, Visa.

Talbot Hotel ⚕

High St., Stourbridge, DY8 1DW
☎ (0384) 394350
Telex 335464 Fax (0384) 371318
Very old coaching inn situated in the centre of Stourbridge - home of English crystal.
Bedrooms: 7 single, 7 double & 9 twin, 2 family rooms.
Bathrooms: 25 private.
Bed & breakfast: from £52 single, from £67.50 double.
Lunch available.
Evening meal 7pm (l.o. 9.30pm).
Parking for 25.
Credit: Access, Visa, Amex.

STOURPORT-ON-SEVERN

Hereford & Worcester Map ref 4B3

Town standing at the confluence of the Rivers Stour and Severn and on the Staffordshire and Worcestershire Canal which was built in the 18th C and is now a popular place for pleasure boats. Some fine Georgian houses remain.

Lenchford Hotel ⚕

Shrawley, Worcester
Worcestershire WR6 6TB
☎ Worcester (0905) 620229
Late Georgian house with modern additions and amenities in beautiful countryside on the right bank of the Severn. On B4196 Worcester to Stourport road.
Bedrooms: 4 single, 7 double & 4 twin, 1 family room.
Bathrooms: 15 private, 1 public.
Bed & breakfast: £42.50-£45.50 single, £55.50-£60.50 double.
Half board: £50-£70 daily, from £350 weekly.
Lunch available.

Evening meal 7pm (l.o. 9.30pm).
Parking for 75.
Credit: Access, Visa, Diners, Amex.

Stourport Moat House ⚕

35 Hartlebury Rd., Stourport-on-Severn, Worcestershire DY13 9LT
☎ (0299) 827733
Telex 333676 Fax (029 93) 78520
CB Queens Moat Houses
Set in 23.5 acres, the hotel has 2 squash courts, tennis courts, golf range, snooker room, sauna and swimming pool.
Bedrooms: 1 single, 23 double & 41 twin, 3 family rooms.
Bathrooms: 68 private.
Bed & breakfast: £60-£65 single, £70-£75 double.
Half board: £70-£75 daily, £320-£355 weekly.
Lunch available.
Evening meal 7pm (l.o. 10pm).
Parking for 400.
Credit: Access, Visa, Diners, Amex.

STOW-ON-THE-WOLD

Gloucestershire Map ref 2B1

Attractive Cotswold wool town with a large market-place and some fine houses, especially the old grammar school. There is an interesting church dating from Norman times. Stow-on-the-Wold is surrounded by lovely countryside and Cotswold villages.
Tourist Information Centre ☎ *(0451) 31082*

Auld Stocks Hotel ⚕

The Square, Stow-on-the-Wold, Cheltenham, GL54 1AF
☎ Cotswold (0451) 30666
17th C hotel refurbished to combine modern-day comforts with original charm and character. Facing quiet village green on which original stocks still stand. Exposed stone walls, oak timbers and roaring log fires.
Bedrooms: 1 single, 13 double & 2 twin, 1 family room.
Bathrooms: 17 private.

Bed & breakfast: £25-£30 single, £50-£60 double.
Half board: £30-£38.95 daily, £216-£250 weekly.
Lunch available.
Evening meal 7pm (l.o. 9.30pm).
Parking for 16.
Credit: Access, Visa, Diners, Amex.

Fosse Manor Hotel ⚕
COMMENDED

Fosseway, Stow-on-the-Wold, Cheltenham, GL54 1JX
☎ Cotswold (0451) 30354
Manor house in own grounds. Golf, riding and hunting nearby and surrounded by beauty spots.
Bedrooms: 3 single, 9 double & 6 twin, 3 family rooms.
Bathrooms: 20 private, 3 public.
Bed & breakfast: £38-£68 single, £68-£100 double.
Lunch available.
Evening meal 7.30pm (l.o. 9.30pm).
Parking for 55.
Credit: Access, Visa, Diners, Amex.

Grapevine Hotel ⚕
COMMENDED

Sheep St., Stow-on-the-Wold, Cheltenham, GL54 1AU
☎ Cotswold (0451) 30344
Telex 43423 EXPORT G, Fax (0451) 32278
CB Best Western
Exceptional small hotel in antique centre of Cotswolds. Accent on food and hospitality. Lovely furnishings complement the romantic, vine-clad conservatory restaurant.
Bedrooms: 1 single, 9 double & 4 twin, 3 family rooms.
Bathrooms: 17 private.
Bed & breakfast: £57-£72 single, £78-£106 double.
Half board: £38.50-£86 daily, £269.50-£602 weekly.
Lunch available.
Evening meal 7pm (l.o. 9.30pm).
Parking for 17.
Credit: Access, Visa, Diners, Amex.

Stow Lodge Hotel ⚕
COMMENDED

The Square, Stow-on-the-Wold, Cheltenham, GL54 1AB
☎ Cotswold (0451) 30485

In own grounds overlooking the market square of a famous Cotswold town. Log fires in lounge and bar.
Bedrooms: 1 single, 12 double & 9 twin.
Bathrooms: 20 private, 1 public.
Bed & breakfast: £33-£43 single, £47-£67 double.
Evening meal 7pm (l.o. 9pm).
Parking for 30.
Credit: Diners, Amex.

White Hart Hotel ⚕

The Square, Stow-on-the-Wold, Cheltenham, GL54 1AF
☎ Cotswold (0451) 30674
16th C coaching inn in town square.
Bedrooms: 3 double & 1 twin, 3 family rooms.
Bathrooms: 3 private, 2 public.
Bed & breakfast: £26-£33 single, £35.50-£59.50 double.
Half board: £29.50-£40.50 daily, £87-£158.50 weekly.
Lunch available.
Evening meal 6pm (l.o. 10pm).
Parking for 12.
Credit: Access, Visa, Diners.

Wyck Hill House ⚕
HIGHLY COMMENDED

Burford Rd., Stow-on-the-Wold, GL54 1HY
☎ (0451) 31936
Telex WYKHIL G 43611
Country manor house hotel, set in 100 acres of its own grounds, in the heart of the Cotswolds. It lies 2 miles south of Stow-on-the-Wold on the A424 Stow/Burford road.
Bedrooms: 19 double & 14 twin, 2 family rooms.
Bathrooms: 33 private.
Bed & breakfast: from £75 single, £90-£165 double.
Half board: £67.50-£87.50 daily.
Lunch available.
Evening meal 7.30pm (l.o. 9.30pm).
Parking for 100.
Credit: Access, Visa, C.Bl., Diners, Amex.

The National Crown Scheme is explained in full on pages 556 – 558.

STRATFORD-UPON-AVON

Warwickshire
Map ref 2B1

Famous as Shakespeare's home town, Stratford's many attractions include his birthplace, New Place where he died, the Royal Shakespeare Theatre and Gallery, 'The World of Shakespeare' audio-visual theatre, Hall's Croft (his daughter's house) and Holy Trinity Church where he was buried. *Tourist Information Centre* ☎ *(0789) 293127 or 67522*

Aberfoyle Guest House
3 Evesham Place, Stratford-upon-Avon, CV37 6HT
☎ (0789) 295703
Guesthouse is within 5 minutes' walk of town centre. Guests are free to come and go as they choose.
Bedrooms: 1 double & 1 twin.
Bathrooms: 1 private, 1 public.
Bed & breakfast: £27-£32 double.
Parking for 3.
🐃7🛏♿👶 ⓤ 🅿 Ⓥ ⅢⅢ

Ambleside Guest House ♨
❤❤
41 Grove Rd., Stratford-upon-Avon, CV37 6PB
☎ (0789) 297239/295670
Small friendly guesthouse close to town centre. Green park opposite. Local proprietors, established 1961. Large on-site car park.
Bedrooms: 1 single, 1 double & 1 twin, 3 family rooms.
Bathrooms: 2 private, 1 public; 1 private shower.
Bed & breakfast: £14-£16 single, £28-£38 double.
Parking for 21.
Credit: Access, Visa.
🐃🛏💷👶 ⓤ Ⓥ 🅿 ⓣⅤ ⅢⅢ ♨ SP

Avon View Hotel ♨
❤❤ APPROVED
121 Shipston Rd., Stratford-upon-Avon, CV37 7LW
☎ (0789) 297542
Small family-run hotel within easy walking distance of the town, offering a warm welcome.
Bedrooms: 2 single, 5 double & 1 twin, 1 family room.
Bathrooms: 9 private.
Bed & breakfast: £28-£32 single, £43-£50 double.
Evening meal 5pm (l.o. 4pm).

Parking for 16.
Credit: Access, Visa, Diners, Amex.
🐃♿💷🛏👶 🗐 ✂ 🅿 ⓣⅤ
ⅢⅢ 🛏 🍴 🗙 🐾 ⟨ SP 🅃

Barbette ♨
❤❤
165 Evesham Rd., Stratford-upon-Avon, CV37 9BP
☎ (0789) 297822
Approximately 10 minutes' walk from the town centre, with access all day and ample parking. Guests have use of the garden.
Bedrooms: 2 single, 1 double, 1 family room.
Bathrooms: 1 public; 2 private showers.
Bed & breakfast: £14-£18 single, £24-£30 double.
Parking for 5.
🐃10♿🛏👶 ⓤ 🅿 ⓣⅤ ⅢⅢ

Billesley Manor Hotel & Restaurant ♨
❤❤❤❤
Alcester, Nr. Stratford-upon-Avon, B49 6NF
☎ (0789) 400888
Telex 312599
🅖🅡 Queens Moat Houses
Elizabethan manor set in 11 acres of gardens, 4 miles from Stratford-upon-Avon on the A422. Fine oak-panelled restaurant.
Bedrooms: 1 single, 15 double & 20 twin, 5 family rooms.
Bathrooms: 41 private, 2 public.
Bed & breakfast: £95-£105 single, £117-£130 double.
Lunch available.
Evening meal 7.30pm (l.o. 9.30pm).
Parking for 100.
Credit: Access, Visa, Diners, Amex.
🐃♿💷🛏👶 🗐 Ⓥ 🛏
🌑 ⅢⅢ 🛏 🍴 🗐 🐾 ▶ ✿
🗙 🅿 🐾 SP 🅡 🅃

Bradbourne Guest House ♨
❤❤
44 Shipston Rd., Stratford-upon-Avon, CV37 7LP
☎ (0789) 204178
Detached Tudor-style property, 8 minutes' walk from the town and theatre. All rooms recently refurbished, ground floor bedrooms available.
Bedrooms: 1 single, 2 double & 2 twin, 1 family room.
Bathrooms: 2 private, 2 public; 2 private showers.
Bed & breakfast: £12-£18 single, £22-£38 double.
Parking for 8.
🐃2♿🛏👶 🅿 ⓤ Ⓥ 🅿 ⅢⅢ
🅿 SP

Bridge House ♨
❤
190 Alcester Road, Stratford-upon-Avon, CV37 9DR
☎ (0789) 67723
Detached house, 1 mile from Stratford-upon-Avon town centre, and easy walk from Anne Hathaway's cottage. Colour TV all rooms. Tea/coffee facilities.
Bedrooms: 2 double & 1 twin.
Bathrooms: 2 public; 1 private shower.
Bed & breakfast: £26-£28.50 double.
Evening meal 7pm (l.o. 7pm).
Parking for 6.
🐃♿💷🛏 ⓤ Ⅲ ⅢⅢ 🅿 🅿

Bronhill Guest House ♨
Listed APPROVED
260 Alcester Rd., Stratford-upon-Avon, CV37 9JQ
☎ (0789) 299169
Detached family house in elevated position, 1 mile from Stratford-upon-Avon.
Bedrooms: 1 single, 2 double.
Bathrooms: 2 public; 1 private shower.
Bed & breakfast: £12.50-£15 single, £20-£22 double.
Parking for 5.
Open April-October.
🐃5🌑 🗐🛏💷 ⓤ ✂ ⅢⅢ 🅿

Brook Lodge ♨
❤❤ COMMENDED
192 Alcester Rd., Stratford-upon-Avon, CV37 9DR
☎ (0789) 295988
Large detached guesthouse, well-appointed and family-run with a friendly atmosphere. Ample car park.
Bedrooms: 4 double & 1 twin, 2 family rooms.
Bathrooms: 5 private, 1 public; 2 private showers.
Bed & breakfast: £18-£24 single, £30-£36 double.
Half board £185-£220 weekly.
Parking for 13.
Credit: Access, Visa.
🐃🗐🛏💷👶 🅿 ⓣⅤ ⅢⅢ
🅿 SP 🅃

Carlton Guest House ♨
❤❤ COMMENDED
22 Evesham Pl., Stratford-upon-Avon, CV37 6HT
☎ (0789) 293548
Tasteful decor, elegantly furnished, combining Victorian origins with modern facilities. A peaceful home, happily shared with guests.
Bedrooms: 2 single, 2 double & 1 twin, 1 family room.

Bathrooms: 1 private, 2 public.
Bed & breakfast: £16-£19 single, £32-£44 double.
🐃🅿 ⓤ Ⓥ 🅿 ⅢⅢ 🛏 🗙
🅿

Charlecote Pheasant Country Hotel ♨
❤❤❤❤
Charlecote, Warwick, CV35 9EW
☎ (0789) 470333 Telex 31688
Fax (0789) 842761
🅖🅡 Queens Moat Houses
18th C farmhouse converted into a comfortable hotel, opposite Charlecote Park. Set in beautiful Warwickshire countryside, 4 miles from Stratford-upon-Avon.
Bedrooms: 5 single, 48 double & 5 twin, 2 family rooms.
Bathrooms: 60 private.
Bed & breakfast: £65-£74 single, £80-£90 double.
Half board: £41.50-£52.25 daily, £290.50-£365.75 weekly.
Lunch available.
Evening meal 7pm (l.o. 10pm).
Parking for 130.
Credit: Access, Visa, C.Bl., Diners, Amex.
🐃♿🗐💷 🅿 🛏 👶 Ⓥ
🐾 🌑 ⅢⅢ 🛏 🍴 🐾 🅃 ♿ 🐾 🗐
🐾 🅿 ✿ SP 🅃
⚑ Display advertisement appears on page 264.

Clomendy Guest House ♨
❤❤
157 Evesham Rd., Stratford-upon-Avon, CV37 9BP
☎ (0789) 66957
Small, detached, mock Tudor family-run guesthouse, convenient for town centre, Anne Hathaway's cottage and theatres.
Bedrooms: 1 single, 1 double & 1 twin.
Bathrooms: 1 public; 1 private shower.
Bed & breakfast: £11-£15 single, £22-£30 double.
Parking for 4.
🐃🅿 👶 ⓤ ✂ ⓣⅤ ⅢⅢ 🅿 ✿
🗙 🅿 🅿 SP 🅃

The Coach House Hotel ♨
❤❤
17 Warwick Rd., Stratford-upon-Avon, CV37 6YW
☎ (0789) 204109 & 299468
A Regency-style family-run private hotel within 6 minutes' walk of town centre. Adjacent to sports centre and golf-courses.
Bedrooms: 3 single, 11 double & 6 twin, 3 family rooms.
Continued ▶

STRATFORD-UPON-AVON

Continued

Bathrooms: 18 private,
2 public.
Bed & breakfast: £19-£35
single, £35-£79 double.
Half board: £27.50-£55.50
daily.
Lunch available.
Evening meal 5.30pm (l.o.
10.30pm).
Parking for 32.
Credit: Access, Visa.

Compton House M
Listed
22 Shipston Rd., Stratford-
upon-Avon, CV37 7LP
☎ (0789) 205646
*Small family guesthouse,
extending a warm and homely
welcome to all our guests. 5
minutes' walk from the theatre
and town centre.*
Bedrooms: 1 single, 1 double,
3 family rooms.
Bathrooms: 1 public.
Bed & breakfast: max. £17
single, max. £28.50 double.
Parking for 6.

Courtland Hotel M
APPROVED
12 Guild St., Stratford-upon-
Avon, CV37 7LW
☎ (0789) 292401
*Elegant Georgian house in
town centre at rear of
Shakespeare's Birthplace.
Antique furniture. 3-4 minutes
from theatre, close to coach
terminal.*
Bedrooms: 1 single, 4 double
& 1 twin, 1 family room.
Bathrooms: 2 private,
2 public.
Bed & breakfast: £14-£15
single, £27-£40 double.
Parking for 3.

Craig Cleeve House M
67-69 Shipston Rd.,
Stratford-upon-Avon,
CV37 7LW
☎ (0789) 296573
*Small family guesthouse close
to the town centre and theatre.*
Bedrooms: 2 single, 6 double
& 4 twin, 3 family rooms.
Bathrooms: 9 private,
4 public.
Bed & breakfast: £17.50-£31
single, £37-£45 double.

Evening meal 6pm (l.o. 6pm).
Parking for 15.
Credit: Access, Visa.

The Croft M
Listed APPROVED
49 Shipston Rd., Stratford-
upon-Avon, CV37 7LN
☎ (0789) 293419
*Small family-run hotel, 5
minutes from all amenities.
Garden, car parking, guests'
lounge, tea and coffee facilities
and colour TVs.*
Bedrooms: 1 single, 3 double
& 2 twin, 3 family rooms.
Bathrooms: 3 private,
1 public; 3 private showers.
Bed & breakfast: £16-£27
single, £25-£43 double.
Half board: £20.50-£29.50
daily, £136.50-£199.50
weekly.
Evening meal 6pm.
Parking for 4.
Credit: Access, Visa.

Dukes Hotel M
COMMENDED
Payton St., Stratford-upon-
Avon, CV37 6UA
☎ (0789) 297921 & 269300
Telex 31430 Fax (0789)
414700
*A quiet garden setting,
alongside the Stratford canal
and within 2 minutes' walk of
the town centre and
Shakespeare's birthplace.
Large private car park.*
Bedrooms: 4 single, 10 double
& 8 twin.
Bathrooms: 22 private.
Bed & breakfast: from £45
single, £65-£95 double.
Lunch available.
Evening meal 6pm (l.o.
9.30pm).
Parking for 30.
Credit: Access, Visa, Diners,
Amex.

Dylan Guesthouse M
Listed
10 Evesham Place, Stratford-
upon-Avon, CV37 6HT
☎ (0789) 204819
*Located in the town, 5 minutes'
walk from the shops and the
Royal Shakespeare Theatre.*
Bedrooms: 1 single, 2 double
& 2 twin.
Bathrooms: 5 private.
Bed & breakfast: £12-£16
single, £26-£36 double.

Half board: £20-£26 daily,
£140-£182 weekly.
Evening meal 6pm (l.o. 7pm).
Parking for 3.

East Bank House M
19 Warwick Rd., Stratford-
upon-Avon, CV37 6YW
☎ (0789) 292758
*Fine Victorian house set in
well-tended grounds, with
interesting architecture. 300
yards from the town centre.*
Bedrooms: 1 single, 6 double
& 4 twin.
Bathrooms: 6 private.
Bed & breakfast: £18.50-£35
single, £30-£48 double.
Parking for 5.
Credit: Access, Visa.

Eastnor House Hotel M
COMMENDED
Shipston Rd., Stratford-upon-
Avon, CV37 7LN
☎ (0789) 268115
*Quiet comfortable private
hotel, oak panelled and
tastefully furnished. Spacious
bedrooms with private
bathrooms. Centrally located,
River Avon 125 metres, theatre
300 metres.*
Bedrooms: 3 double & 2 twin,
4 family rooms.
Bathrooms: 9 private.
Bed & breakfast: £42-£51
double.
Parking for 9.
Credit: Access, Visa, Amex.

Ettington Park Hotel M
HIGHLY COMMENDED
Alderminster, Stratford-upon-
Avon, CV37 8BS
☎ (0789) 740740
Telex 311825 Fax (0789)
87472
*Set in 40 acres of parkland, 5
miles from Stratford-upon-
Avon, offering a combination of
country house comfort and
modern leisure facilities.*
Bedrooms: 20 double &
15 twin, 13 family rooms.
Bathrooms: 48 private.
Bed & breakfast: £95-£185
single, £125-£185 double.
Half board: £125-£215 daily,
£612.50-£1032.50 weekly.
Lunch available.
Evening meal 7pm (l.o.
9.30pm).
Parking for 120.
Credit: Access, Visa, Diners,
Amex.

Eversley Bears' Guest House M
37 Grove Rd., Stratford-
upon-Avon, CV37 6PB
☎ (0789) 292334
*Family-run guesthouse close to
town centre, with a collection
of teddy bears, some of which
are on display.*
Bedrooms: 2 single, 1 double
& 1 twin, 2 family rooms.
Bathrooms: 3 public;
2 private showers.
Bed & breakfast: £15-£17
single, £30-£34 double.
Parking for 3.

Glenavon Guest House
6 Chestnut Walk, Old Town,
Stratford-upon-Avon,
CV37 6HG
☎ (0789) 292588
*Centrally situated guest house,
3 minutes from town centre
and Royal Shakespeare
Theatre.*
Bedrooms: 1 single, 4 double
& 5 twin, 1 family room.
Bathrooms: 3 public.
Bed & breakfast: £13-£15
single, £26-£30 double.

Grosvenor House Hotel M
Warwick Rd., Stratford-
upon-Avon, CV37 6YT
☎ (0789) 269213
Telex 311699
Best Western
*Friendly hotel with restaurant
overlooking gardens. Many
refurbished bedrooms, 5
minutes' walk from town centre
and theatre. Ample free
parking.*
Bedrooms: 14 single,
13 double & 22 twin, 2 family
rooms.
Bathrooms: 51 private.
Bed & breakfast: £45-£55
single, £66-£95 double.
Lunch available.
Evening meal 6pm (l.o.
8.45pm).
Parking for 50.
Credit: Access, Visa, Diners,
Amex.

Hardwick House M
1 Avenue Rd., Stratford-
upon-Avon, CV37 6UY
☎ (0789) 204307
*Family-run Victorian
guesthouse in a quiet area, a
short walking distance from
town, theatre, swimming pool
and other amenities.*

Bedrooms: 2 single, 6 double
& 4 twin, 2 family rooms.
Bathrooms: 7 private,
4 public.
Bed & breakfast: £15.50-
£18.50 single, £31-£25.50
double.
Parking for 12.
Credit: Access, Visa, Amex.

Houndshill House M

Banbury Rd., Ettington,
Stratford-upon-Avon,
CV37 7NS
☎ (0789) 740267
*Large, family-run country
house with restaurant. 4 miles
from Stratford-upon-Avon.
Informal and friendly
atmosphere.*
Bedrooms: 2 single, 3 double
& 2 twin, 1 family room.
Bathrooms: 8 private.
Bed & breakfast: from £25
single, from £40 double.
Lunch available.
Evening meal 7pm (l.o.
10pm).
Parking for 50.
Credit: Access, Visa.

King's Lodge M
COMMENDED

Long Marston, Stratford-
upon-Avon, CV37 8RL
☎ (0789) 720705
*Historic country house set in
4.5 acres of garden and
parkland. Within easy reach of
Stratford-upon-Avon and the
Cotswolds, and near the
National Exhibition Centre,
Birmingham.*
Bedrooms: 2 double & 1 twin.
Bathrooms: 1 private,
2 public.
Bed & breakfast: £16.50
single, £32-£44 double.
Half board: £25-£30.50 daily,
£155-£195 weekly.
Evening meal 7pm.
Parking for 11.
Open February-November.

Melita Private Hotel M
COMMENDED

37 Shipston Rd., Stratford-
upon-Avon, CV37 7LN
☎ (0789) 292432
*Small family hotel, close to
theatre and Shakespearean
attractions. Convenient for
touring the Cotswolds,
National Exhibition Centre
and National Agricultural
Centre. Lounge bar.*

Bedrooms: 3 single, 3 double
& 3 twin, 3 family rooms.
Bathrooms: 12 private.
Bed & breakfast: £27-£38
single, £45-£52 double.
Parking for 12.
Credit: Access, Visa.

Moat House International M

Bridgefoot, Stratford-upon-
Avon, CV37 6YR
☎ (0789) 414411
Telex 311127
Queens Moat Houses
*A modern hotel standing in its
own gardens by the River
Avon. Close to the town centre
and Royal Shakespeare
Theatre.*
Bedrooms: 76 double &
173 twin.
Bathrooms: 249 private.
Bed & breakfast: from £75
single, from £99 double.
Half board: from £52.50
daily, from £367.50 weekly.
Lunch available.
Evening meal 6pm (l.o.
11.30pm).
Parking for 350.
Credit: Access, Visa, Diners,
Amex.

Moonraker House M
COMMENDED

40 Alcester Rd., Stratford-
upon-Avon, CV37 9DB
☎ (0789) 299346 &
(0789) 67115
*Family-run, near town centre.
Beautifully co-ordinated decor
throughout. Some rooms with
four-poster beds and garden
terrace available for non-
smokers.*
Bedrooms: 15 double &
3 twin, 2 family rooms.
Bathrooms: 20 private.
Bed & breakfast: £25-£30
single, £32-£50 double.
Half board: £31-£40 daily,
£217-£270 weekly.
Evening meal 5.30pm (l.o.
7pm).
Parking for 20.

Nando's M

18-19 Evesham Pl., Stratford-
upon-Avon, CV37 6HT
☎ (0789) 204907

*Convenient for the theatre,
town centre and Shakespeare
properties. Full English
breakfast. Always a warm
welcome.*
Bedrooms: 5 single, 5 double
& 6 twin, 5 family rooms.
Bathrooms: 7 private,
5 public.
Bed & breakfast: £14.50-
£16.50 single, £22-£28 double.
Half board: £18-£20 daily.
Lunch available.
Evening meal 6pm.
Parking for 8.
Credit: Access, Visa.

Oxstalls Farm

Warwick Rd., Stratford-
upon-Avon, CV37 0NS
☎ (0789) 205277
*60-acre stud farm. Beautifully
situated overlooking the
Welcome Hills and golf-course.
1 mile from Stratford-upon-
Avon.*
Bedrooms: 1 single, 11 double
& 4 twin, 4 family rooms.
Bathrooms: 9 private,
4 public; 3 private showers.
Bed & breakfast: £13-£20
single, £26-£40 double.
Parking for 20.

Parkfield M
APPROVED

3 Broad Walk, Stratford-
upon-Avon, CV37 6HS
☎ (0789) 293313
*Delightful Victorian house.
Quiet location, 5 minutes' walk
from theatre and town. En-
suite available. Colour TV, tea
and coffee facilities and
parking.*
Bedrooms: 1 single, 2 double
& 2 twin, 2 family rooms.
Bathrooms: 4 private,
1 public.
Bed & breakfast: £14-£18
single, £28-£40 double.
Parking for 9.
Credit: Access, Visa.

Peartree Cottage M
COMMENDED

7 Church Rd., Wilmcote,
Stratford-upon-Avon,
CV37 9UX
☎ Stratford-upon-Avon
(0789) 205889
*Elizabethan house, furnished
with antiques, set in beautiful
garden overlooking Mary
Arden's house. Pub and
restaurant within walking
distance.*

Bedrooms: 2 double & 2 twin,
1 family room.
Bathrooms: 5 private.
Bed & breakfast: £20-£24
single, £32-£36 double.
Parking for 6.

Penryn House Hotel M
Listed

126 Alcester Rd., Stratford-
upon-Avon, CV37 9DP
☎ (0789) 293718
*On the A422, 5 minutes from
the centre of Stratford and
Ann Hathaway's cottage.
Ample parking space.*
Bedrooms: 2 single, 2 double
& 1 twin, 3 family rooms.
Bathrooms: 5 private,
1 public.
Bed & breakfast: £14-£30
single, £30-£45 double.
Parking for 9.
Credit: Access, Visa.

Ravenhurst M
APPROVED

2 Broad Walk, Stratford-
upon-Avon, CV37 6HS
☎ (0789) 292515
*Quietly situated a few minutes'
walk from the town centre and
places of historic interest.
Comfortable home, with
substantial breakfast provided.*
Bedrooms: 3 double & 2 twin,
2 family rooms.
Bathrooms: 3 private,
2 public.
Bed & breakfast: £28-£40
double.
Half board: £190-£270
weekly.
Credit: Access, Visa, Diners,
Amex.

Sequoia House M

51-53 Shipston Rd.,
Stratford-upon-Avon,
CV37 7LN
☎ (0789) 268852 & 294940 &
204805 Fax (0789) 414559
*Charmingly-appointed private
hotel with large car park and
delightful garden walk to the
theatre, riverside gardens and
Shakespeare properties.*
Bedrooms: 2 single, 7 double
& 6 twin, 6 family rooms.
Bathrooms: 15 private,
5 public; 2 private showers.
Bed & breakfast: £27.50-£45
single, £33-£59 double.
Lunch available.
Evening meal 6pm (l.o. 4pm).
Parking for 33.
Credit: Access, Visa, Diners,
Amex.

Stratford House Hotel M
☺☺☺☺ COMMENDED

Sheep St., Stratford-upon-Avon, CV37 6EF
☎ (0789) 68288 Fax (0789) 295580
Privately-owned hotel, with fine restaurant, 100 yards from The Royal Shakespeare Theatre. Theatre booking service.
Bedrooms: 1 single, 4 double & 4 twin, 1 family room.
Bathrooms: 10 private.
Bed & breakfast: £50-£65 single, £54-£80 double.
Lunch available.
Evening meal 5.45pm (l.o. 9.30pm).
Credit: Access, Visa, Diners, Amex.

Stratheden Hotel M
☺☺ COMMENDED

5 Chapel St., Stratford-upon-Avon, CV37 6EP
☎ (0789) 297119
Built in 1673 and located in one of the most historical parts of Stratford-upon-Avon. 2 miles' walk from the theatre and town centre.
Bedrooms: 1 single, 5 double & 3 twin, 1 family room.
Bathrooms: 7 private, 1 public.
Bed & breakfast: £15-£35 single, £30-£48 double.
Parking for 5.
Credit: Access.

Stretton House M
☺

38 Grove Rd., Stratford-upon-Avon, CV37 6PB
☎ (0789) 68647
Victorian town house overlooking lovely fir gardens. Convenient for theatre and town centre.
Bedrooms: 1 single, 2 double & 2 twin, 2 family rooms.
Bathrooms: 2 public; 3 private showers.
Bed & breakfast: £14-£24 single, £24-£38 double.
Half board: £20.50-£25.50 daily.
Evening meal 5pm (l.o. 4pm).
Parking for 3.

Swan House Hotel M
☺☺ APPROVED

The Green, Wilmcote, Stratford-upon-Avon, CV37 9XJ
☎ Stratford-upon-Avon (0789) 67030
Friendly hotel, part 18th C inn, 100 yards from Mary Arden's house. Ideal for exploring Shakespeare country, 3 miles from Stratford. Varied menu.
Bedrooms: 1 single, 5 double & 4 twin, 2 family rooms.
Bathrooms: 12 private.
Bed & breakfast: £32-£35 single, £52-£56 double.
Lunch available.
Evening meal 7.30pm (l.o. 9.30pm).
Parking for 35.
Credit: Access, Visa, Amex.

Twelfth Night M
☺☺☺

Evesham Place, Stratford-upon-Avon, CV37 6HT
☎ (0789) 414595
Gracious, centrally-located Victorian villa, formerly owned by The Royal Shakespeare Theatre for 21 years for accommodating actors. Tastefully refurbished for your comfort. Non-smokers only please.
Bedrooms: 1 single, 2 double & 3 twin, 1 family room.
Bathrooms: 5 private, 1 public; 1 private shower.
Bed & breakfast: £17-£30 single, £32-£46 double.
Parking for 5.

Welcombe Hotel and Golf Course M
☺☺☺☺ COMMENDED

Warwick Rd., Stratford-upon-Avon, CV37 0NR
☎ (0789) 295252 Telex 31347
Jacobean-style mansion house hotel, set in 157 acres, with conference facilities, restaurants, 18-hole golf-course, tennis courts and croquet.
Bedrooms: 2 single, 36 double & 38 twin.
Bathrooms: 76 private.
Bed & breakfast: £85-£100 single, £120-£135 double.
Lunch available.
Evening meal 7pm (l.o. 9.30pm).
Parking for 120.
Credit: Access, Visa, Diners, Amex.

Windmill Park Hotel and Country Club M
☺☺☺☺

Warwick Road, Stratford-upon-Avon, CV37 0PY
☎ (0789) 731173
A warm welcome awaits you at this newly constructed hotel situated 3 miles outside of Stratford in the heart of Shakespeare's country.
Bedrooms: 38 double & 62 twin.
Bathrooms: 100 private.
Bed & breakfast: from £65 single, from £78 double.
Lunch available.
Evening meal 6.30pm (l.o. 10pm).
Parking for 220.
Credit: Access, Visa, Diners, Amex.

STROUD

Gloucestershire
Map ref 2B1

This old town has been producing broadcloth for centuries.
Tourist Information Centre ☎ (04536) 5768 or 4252

The Amberley Inn M
☺☺☺

Amberley, Stroud, GL5 5AF
☎ Amberley (045 387) 2565
Telex 94012242 AMBERLEY
ⓒ Best Western
Cotswolds stone country inn on Minchinhampton Common, with panoramic views of Woodchester Valley.
Bedrooms: 3 single, 5 double & 5 twin, 1 family room.
Bathrooms: 14 private.
Bed & breakfast: £52-£60 single, £64-£72 double.
Half board: £46-£72 daily, £315-£497 weekly.
Lunch available.
Evening meal 7.30pm (l.o. 9.30pm).
Parking for 20.
Credit: Access, Visa, Amex.

Ashleigh House M
☺☺☺

Bussage, Stroud, GL6 8AZ
☎ Brimscombe (0453) 883944
Ideal Cotswold touring centre in beautiful village setting, providing cleanliness and comfort. All rooms en-suite.
Bedrooms: 3 double & 3 twin, 3 family rooms.

Bathrooms: 9 private.
Bed & breakfast: from £31.90 single, from £46.50 double.
Half board: £34.10-£42.80 daily, £153-£191 weekly.
Evening meal 6.30pm (l.o. 7pm).
Parking for 10.
Open April-October.

Bell Hotel M
☺☺☺ APPROVED

Wallbridge, Stroud, GL5 3JA
☎ (0453) 763556
Newly refurbished and extended. All bedrooms with TV and telephone. 2 have jacuzzis. 1 bridal suite. 2 minutes' walk from railway station and centre.
Bedrooms: 1 single, 4 double & 5 twin, 2 family rooms.
Bathrooms: 10 private, 1 public.
Bed & breakfast: £30-£60 single, £45-£80 double.
Half board: from £40 daily, from £265 weekly.
Lunch available.
Evening meal 7pm (l.o. 9.30pm).
Parking for 12.
Credit: Access, Visa, Diners.

Imperial Hotel M
☺☺☺ COMMENDED

Station Rd., Stroud, GL5 3AP
☎ (045 376) 4077
Covered in ivy and over 150-years-old, the hotel was originally a coaching and railway inn. Recently refurbished to a high standard.
Bedrooms: 3 single, 8 double & 12 twin, 2 family rooms.
Bathrooms: 25 private.
Bed & breakfast: £42-£46 single, from £58 double.
Lunch available.
Evening meal 6pm (l.o. 10.30pm).
Parking for 15.
Credit: Access, Visa, Diners, Amex.

London Hotel and Restaurant M
☺☺☺ COMMENDED

30-31 London Rd., Stroud, GL5 2AJ
☎ (0453) 759992
Attractive ivy clad, Georgian town centre hotel. Conveniently situated for touring the Cotswolds. Extensive menu available in candlelit restaurant.

Bedrooms: 2 single, 5 double & 3 twin.
Bathrooms: 8 private, 2 public.
Bed & breakfast: £25-£45 single, £39-£59 double.
Half board: £32-£42 daily.
Lunch available.
Evening meal 7pm (l.o. 9.30pm).
Parking for 10.
Credit: Access, Visa, Diners.

Old Vicarage Guest House ▲
COMMENDED
167 Slad Rd., Stroud
GL5 1RD
☎ (0453) 752315
Overlooking the beautiful Slad Valley, half a mile from Stroud. Offering comfort, good food and personal service. All rooms en-suite.
Bedrooms: 2 double, 1 family room.
Bathrooms: 3 private.
Bed & breakfast: £20-£24 single, £26-£31 double.
Half board: £19.70-£32.50 daily, £134.05-£155 weekly.
Evening meal 7.30pm (l.o. 9.30pm).
Parking for 7.
Open February-December.

SUTTON COLDFIELD
W. Midlands
Map ref 4B3

Old market town now part of the conurbation of Birmingham. The 2400-acre Sutton Park has facilities for golf, fishing and riding, with walks around the woodlands and lakes.

The Berni Royal Hotel ▲
High St., Sutton Coldfield, B72 1UD
☎ 021-355 8222
Located right in the heart of this busy Midlands town, this hotel is an attractive Georgian building which has undergone sympathetic refurbishment.
Bedrooms: 3 single, 9 double & 7 twin, 3 family rooms.
Bathrooms: 22 private.
Bed & breakfast: £48-£53.50 single, from £64 double.
Lunch available.
Evening meal 6pm (l.o. 10pm).

Parking for 80.
Credit: Access, Visa, Diners, Amex.

Lady Windsor Hotel ▲
APPROVED
17 Anchorage Rd., Sutton Coldfield, B74 2PJ
☎ 021-354 5181 & 6868 & 021-355 5552
Small family-run hotel close to Wyndley Leisure Centre with all sporting facilities, and to 2800-acre Sutton Park with boating and golf. Close to railway station and town centre.
Bedrooms: 10 single, 5 double & 7 twin.
Bathrooms: 22 private.
Bed & breakfast: £33-£65 single, £59-£68 double.
Half board: £44-£75 daily, £290-£400 weekly.
Lunch available.
Evening meal 6.30pm (l.o. 10pm).
Parking for 32.
Credit: Access, Visa, Amex.

Manor Guest House ▲
3 Manor Rd., Sutton Coldfield, B73 6EJ
☎ 021-354 6259
Centrally situated in Sutton Coldfield town and close to Sutton Court Hotel, with indoor heated pool and sports complex nearby.
Bedrooms: 1 double & 1 twin, 2 family rooms.
Bathrooms: 1 private, 2 public.
Bed & breakfast: £15-£17.50 single, £30-£35 double.
Lunch available.
Parking for 8.

New Hall ▲
Walmley Rd., Sutton Coldfield, B76 8QX
☎ 021-378 2442 Telex 333580
Thistle
Set in 25 acres of attractive grounds, this is the oldest inhabited moated manor house in England. It offers well-appointed accommodation, modern facilities, gourmet cuisine and a chance to explore the beautiful countryside.
Bedrooms: 4 single, 36 double & 18 twin, 6 family rooms.
Bathrooms: 64 private.
Bed & breakfast: from £87 single, from £111 double.

Lunch available.
Evening meal 7.30pm (l.o. 10pm).
Parking for 100.
Credit: Access, Visa, C.Bl., Diners, Amex.

Sutton Court Hotel & Court Yard Restaurant ▲
APPROVED
60-66 Lichfield Rd., Sutton Coldfield, B74 2NA
☎ 021-355 6071 Telex 334175
SUTTON G
Consort
Half a mile walking distance from the town centre, the Sutton Court Hotel retains its Victorian elegance combined with the best of modern facilities and old fashioned hospitality.
Bedrooms: 17 single, 20 double & 26 twin, 1 family room.
Bathrooms: 64 private.
Bed & breakfast: £35-£75 single, £45-£98 double.
Half board: £37.50-£90 daily, £369-£510 weekly.
Lunch available.
Evening meal 7pm (l.o. 10pm).
Parking for 80.
Credit: Access, Visa, Diners, Amex.

SWINSCOE
Staffordshire
Map ref 4B2

4m NW. Ashbourne Hamlet close to Alton Towers.

Dog & Partridge Inn ▲
Swinscoe, Ashbourne, Derbyshire DE6 2HS
☎ Ashbourne (0335) 43183
A 17th C inn close to the Peak District, Ashbourne and Alton Towers.
Bedrooms: 6 double & 2 twin, 14 family rooms.
Bathrooms: 22 private.
Bed & breakfast: £42-£45 single, £45-£55 double.
Half board: £29-£35 daily, £175-£225 weekly.
Lunch available.
Evening meal 5.30pm (l.o. 10.30pm).
Parking for 82.
Credit: Access, Visa, Amex.

SWYNNERTON
Staffordshire
Map ref 4B2

Village with thatched cottages, a 17th C inn and an interesting Norman church.

Home Farm Hotel
Listed
Swynnerton, Stone, ST15 0RA
☎ (078 135) 241
Traditional, rural, small family-run hotel which welcomes children and senior citizens. Special rates on request. Near Alton Towers.
Bedrooms: 3 single, 2 double & 1 twin, 2 family rooms.
Bathrooms: 3 private, 2 public.
Bed & breakfast: £10-£15 single, £20-£26 double.
Half board: £70-£100 weekly.
Evening meal 7pm (l.o. 8pm).
Parking for 33.
Credit: Access, Visa.

SYMONDS YAT EAST
Hereford & Worcester
Map ref 2A1

Well-known beauty spot where the River Wye loops back on itself in a narrow gorge. It is close to the ruins of Goodrich Castle, the Forest of Dean and the Welsh border.

Forest View Hotel ▲
COMMENDED
Symonds Yat East, Ross-on-Wye, Herefordshire HR9 6JL
☎ Symonds Yat (0600) 890210
Set deep in the Wye Valley, a small family hotel on the banks of the River Wye.
Bedrooms: 5 double & 2 twin.
Bathrooms: 7 private.
Half board: £38 daily, £216 weekly.
Evening meal 7.30pm (l.o. 7.30pm).
Parking for 10.
Open February-November.

Royal Hotel ▲
Symonds Yat East, Herefordshire HR9 6JL
☎ Symonds Yat (0600) 890238

Continued ▶

SYMONDS YAT EAST

Continued

Quiet country house in Alpine type setting, next to the River Wye. Ideal touring location. Only 6 miles from Ross-on-Wye and Monmouth.
Bedrooms: 2 single, 14 double & 4 twin.
Bathrooms: 20 private, 1 public.
Bed & breakfast: £29.50-£37.50 single.
Half board: £34.50-£44.50 daily.
Lunch available.
Evening meal 7pm (l.o. 9.30pm).
Parking for 80.
Open February-December.
Credit: Access, Visa, Amex.

SYMONDS YAT WEST

Hereford & Worcester Map ref 2A1

Jubilee Maze and Exhibition was created here in 1977 to commemorate Queen Elizabeth II's Jubilee. The area of Symonds Yat is a world-renowned beauty spot.

Riversdale Lodge Hotel
COMMENDED

Symonds Yat West, Ross-on-Wye, Herefordshire HR9 6BL
☎ Symonds Yat (0600) 890445
Early 20th C country house with commanding views across the rapids. In 2 acres, a perfect retreat for a vacation.
Bedrooms: 5 double.
Bathrooms: 5 private.
Bed & breakfast: £19-£22 single, £38-£44 double.
Half board: £29.50-£32.50 daily, £206.50-£220.50 weekly.
Evening meal 6.30pm (l.o. 1pm).
Parking for 11.

Walnut Tree Cottage Hotel M

Symonds Yat West, Ross-on-Wye, Herefordshire HR9 6BN
☎ Symonds Yat (0600) 890828

Charming 18th C cottage with panoramic views of the Wye Valley and river. Full English breakfast, traditional food.
Bedrooms: 1 single, 4 double & 1 twin.
Bathrooms: 3 private; 3 private showers.
Bed & breakfast: £18-£19 single, £36-£40 double.
Half board: £28-£30 daily, £196-£210 weekly.
Evening meal 7pm (l.o. 6pm).
Parking for 10.

Woodlea Hotel M

Symonds Yat West, Ross-on-Wye, Herefordshire HR9 6BL
☎ Symonds Yat (0600) 890206
Family-run Victorian country house hotel in a quiet position amid glorious scenery. Imaginative home cooking and friendly service.
Bedrooms: 2 single, 3 double & 2 twin, 2 family rooms.
Bathrooms: 6 private, 2 public.
Bed & breakfast: from £19.75 single, from £39.50 double.
Half board: from £29 daily, from £179 weekly.
Evening meal 7pm (l.o. 7.30pm).
Parking for 9.
Open March-December.
Credit: Access, Visa.

Ye Olde Ferrie Inne M
APPROVED

Symonds Yat West, Ross-on-Wye, Herefordshire HR9 6BL
☎ Symonds Yat (0600) 890232
Attractive 15th C inn on banks of the River Wye. Ideally situated for country holiday pursuits. Renowned riverside steak restaurant.
Bedrooms: 4 double & 4 twin, 1 family room.
Bathrooms: 6 private, 1 public.
Bed & breakfast: £19-£24 single, £33-£43 double.
Half board: £24-£29 daily.
Lunch available.
Evening meal 7pm (l.o. 9.45pm).
Parking for 60.
Credit: Access, Visa, Diners.

TAMWORTH

Staffordshire Map ref 4B3

Town with a Norman castle which has a Tudor banqueting hall and a museum with coins minted at Tamworth in Saxon times when it was an important royal town. The church has a magnificent tower.
Tourist Information Centre ☎ (0827) 311222

Castle Hotel
Ladybank, Tamworth, B79 7NB
☎ (0827) 57181
Ⓒ Character
Dating back to the 17th C, this 34-bedroomed hotel is situated in the shadow of Tamworth Castle in the historic area of Ladybank. Facilities include real ale pub and sophisticated nightclub.
Bedrooms: 5 single, 18 double & 11 twin.
Bathrooms: 34 private.
Bed & breakfast: £37-£57 single, £54-£73 double.
Lunch available.
Evening meal 7pm (l.o. 10pm).
Credit: Access, Visa, Diners, Amex.

The Gungate Hotel M
62 Upper Gungate, Tamworth, B79 8AA
☎ (0827) 63120 Fax (0827) 61035
Restored Victorian building with carved panelling and fire surround in dining room and period furniture throughout.
Bedrooms: 5 single, 1 double & 2 twin.
Bathrooms: 3 private, 1 public; 2 private showers.
Bed & breakfast: £28.75-£34.50 single, £46-£51.75 double.
Half board: £40-£45 daily, £175-£210 weekly.
Lunch available.
Evening meal 7pm (l.o. 9.30pm).
Parking for 12.
Credit: Access, Visa, Diners, Amex.

TELFORD

Shropshire Map ref 4A3

New Town named after Thomas Telford the famous engineer who designed many of the country's canals, bridges and viaducts. It is close to Ironbridge with its monuments and museums to the Industrial Revolution, including restored 18th C buildings.
Tourist Information Centre ☎ (0952) 291370

Arleston Inn Hotel
COMMENDED

Arleston Lane, Nr Lawley, Wellington, Telford TF1 2LA
☎ Telford (0952) 501881
Tudor-style building with many exposed beamed ceilings. M54, 5 minutes from junction 6. A la carte and bar menus.
Bedrooms: 12 single, 1 double & 3 twin.
Bathrooms: 16 private.
Bed & breakfast: £32-£34 single, £43-£45 double.
Half board: £35-£45 daily.
Lunch available.
Evening meal 7pm (l.o. 10pm).
Parking for 40.
Credit: Access, Visa.

Buckatree Hall Hotel M

The Wrekin, Wellington, Telford, TF6 5AL
☎ (0952) 641821 Telex 35701 BCKTRE Fax (0952) 47540
Ⓒ Best Western
Set in woodlands on the slopes of the Wrekin Hill. Most rooms overlook either the lake or hotel gardens. Videos in rooms and video library in reception. Close to exit 7 of the M54.
Bedrooms: 3 single, 14 double & 20 twin.
Bathrooms: 37 private.
Bed & breakfast: £59-£65 single, £69-£75 double.
Half board: £78.50-£84.50 daily.
Lunch available.
Evening meal 7.30pm (l.o. 10pm).
Parking for 120.
Credit: Access, Visa, Diners, Amex.

Please check prices and other details at the time of booking.

The Granville Hotel ⋀

Wrockwardine Wood,
Telford, TF2 7AB
☎ (0952) 618563
*A former hostelry dating from
1734 with beamed dining room.
Provides comfortable
accommodation with all
modern facilities, run by the
resident proprietors.*
Bedrooms: 2 single, 6 double
& 3 twin, 1 family room.
Bathrooms: 12 private.
Bed & breakfast: £38-£42
single, £45-£49 double.
Half board: £32-£34.50 daily,
£195 weekly.
Lunch available.
Evening meal 7pm (l.o. 9pm).
Parking for 30.
Credit: Access, Visa, Amex.
🔾 🐾 📞 🖵 🎱 📶 🗻 🚪 🛏 ▦
🍴 🐾 SP

The Oaks Hotel ⋀
👑👑

Redhill, St. Georges, Telford,
TF2 9NZ
☎ (0952) 620126
*Family-owned hotel, 2.5 miles
from Telford town centre.
Restaurant, public bar. En-
suite bedrooms with telephone,
colour TV, tea/coffee facilities.*
Bedrooms: 3 twin, 2 family
rooms.
Bathrooms: 5 private.
Bed & breakfast: £35-£42
single, £42-£50 double.
Half board: £45-£60 daily,
£315-£420 weekly.
Lunch available.
Evening meal 7pm (l.o.
9.30pm).
Parking for 36.
Credit: Access, Visa.
🔾 🖵 🎱 📶 🗻 🚪 ▦ 🐾 ❋
🗙 🏠

Old Bell of Shifnal

Church St., Shifnal,
TF11 9AA
☎ Telford (0952) 460475
*17th C inn with renowned
restaurant in small town near
Ironbridge Gorge.*
Bedrooms: 2 single, 4 double
& 2 twin.
Bathrooms: 8 private.
Bed & breakfast: £30-£40
single, £45-£55 double.
Lunch available.
Evening meal 7pm (l.o.
9.30pm).
Parking for 20.
Credit: Access, Visa, Diners,
Amex.
🔾 📞 🖵 🎱 📶 🗻 📶 🚪 ▦
🗻 🏠 🏡

Old Rectory
👑👑

Stirchley Village, Telford,
TF3 1DY
☎ (0952) 596308

*Large, comfortable guesthouse
dating from 1734. Set in an
acre of secluded gardens, on
edge of town park. Convenient
for town centre and Ironbridge
museums.*
Bedrooms: 2 single, 1 twin,
1 family room.
Bathrooms: 2 public.
Bed & breakfast: max. £13.50
single, max. £24 double.
Half board: max. £18.50
daily, max. £129.50 weekly.
Evening meal 6pm (l.o.
10.30pm).
Parking for 6.
🔾 🎱 🖵 🎱 🗻 📶 🗻 📶 🐾 🏠 🏡
📺 ▦ 🗻 🍴 🚶 ♿ ❋ 🏠 🏡

Station Inn ⋀
Listed

Station Rd., Horsehay,
Telford, TF4 2NJ
☎ (0952) 503006
*We serve a range of meals in a
traditional English pub
atmosphere. Small function
room, available for private
parties. No smoking in dining
area.*
Bedrooms: 1 double & 1 twin.
Bathrooms: 1 public.
Bed & breakfast: from £17.50
single, from £28 double.
Lunch available.
Evening meal 7pm (l.o.
10pm).
Parking for 48.
Credit: Access, Visa.
🔾 🎱 🎱 🎱 🎱 🗻 📶 🗻 🚶 ▦
🗻 🍴 🗙 🏠

Swan Hotel ⋀
👑

Watling St., Wellington,
Telford, TF1 2NH
☎ (0952) 223781
*Small family-run hotel with 50
seater carvery restaurant, run
by proprietor.*
Bedrooms: 3 single, 2 double
& 3 twin, 4 family rooms.
Bathrooms: 3 public.
Bed & breakfast: £25-£30
single, £32-£37 double.
Lunch available.
Evening meal 6pm (l.o.
11pm).
Parking for 100.
Credit: Access, Visa, Diners,
Amex.
🔾 🎱 🖵 🎱 🗻 📶 🗻 📶 ▦
🗻 🍴 ➤ ❋ 📺

Telford Hotel Golf &
Country Club ⋀
👑👑👑👑 **COMMENDED**

Great Hay, Sutton Hill,
Telford, TF7 4DT
☎ (0952) 585642 Telex 35481
ⓒⓡ Queens Moat Houses
*Hotel, conference centre and
sporting complex with 18-hole
golf-course, overlooking
Ironbridge Gorge.*

Bedrooms: 3 double &
54 twin, 2 family rooms.
Bathrooms: 59 private,
2 public.
Bed & breakfast: max. £67.50
single, max. £77.50 double.
Half board: max. £79.50
daily.
Lunch available.
Evening meal 7.30pm (l.o.
10pm).
Parking for 200.
Credit: Access, Visa, Diners,
Amex.
🔾 🐾 📞 🖵 🎱 🗻 📶 V 🗻
▦ 🗻 🍴 🎱 🗻 📶 🗻 🏠 ➤ ✓
❋ 🐾 SP 📺

Telford Moat House ⋀
👑👑👑👑

Forgegate, Telford Centre,
Telford, TF3 4NA
☎ (0952) 291291 Telex 35588
ⓒⓡ Queens Moat Houses
*Modern hotel close to many
historic sights such as
Ironbridge, Coalport and Much
Wenlock. M54 junction 5.*
Bedrooms: 54 double &
86 twin, 8 family rooms.
Bathrooms: 148 private.
Bed & breakfast: £68-£72
single, £80-£85 double.
Lunch available.
Evening meal 7pm (l.o.
10pm).
Parking for 350.
Credit: Access, Visa, Diners,
Amex.
🔾 🐾 📞 🖵 🎱 🗻 📶 V 🗻
● 🎱 ▦ 🗻 🍴 🎱 🗻 📶 🗻
➤ SP 📺

Valley Hotel
👑👑👑

Ironbridge, Telford,
TF8 7DW
☎ (095 245) 2247 & 3280
*A Georgian listed building
situated in World Heritage
Site of Ironbridge. Recently
refurbished to high standards.*
Bedrooms: 8 single,
24 double, 2 family rooms.
Bathrooms: 34 private.
Bed & breakfast: £36-£50
single, £45-£55 double.
Half board: £68-£78 daily,
£376-£440 weekly.
Lunch available.
Evening meal 7pm (l.o.
10pm).
Parking for 100.
Credit: Access, Visa.
🔾 🐾 📞 🖵 🎱 🗻 📶 V 🗻
● 🎱 ▦ 🗻 🍴 ❋ 🗙 SP 🏠
⓪ Display advertisement
appears on page 264.

White House Hotel ⋀
👑👑

Wellington Rd., Donnington,
Muxton, Telford, TF2 8NG
☎ (0952) 604276

*Country house hotel set in 1
acre of lawns and gardens
close to Britain's National
Recreation Centre and
Ironbridge.*
Bedrooms: 10 single, 6 double
& 6 twin, 5 family rooms.
Bathrooms: 20 private,
2 public.
Bed & breakfast: £43.50-
£48.50 single, £54.50-£60
double.
Lunch available.
Evening meal 7pm (l.o.
10pm).
Parking for 100.
Credit: Access, Visa, Amex.
🔾 🐾 🐾 📞 🖵 🎱 🗻 📶 V
🗻 📺 🎱 🗻 ❋ SP

TENBURY WELLS

Hereford & Worcester
Map ref 4A3

Small market town on the
Teme possessing many
fine black and white
buildings. In 1839 mineral
springs were found here
and there were hopes of
a spa centre developing.
The waters never became
fashionable and today
only the old Pump Room
remains, a curious iron
structure which has a
wistful attraction. Nearby
Burford House Gardens
contain many rare plants
and trees.

Cadmore Lodge Country
Hotel
👑👑👑

Berrington Green, Tenbury
Wells, Worcestershire
WR15 8TQ
☎ (0584) 810044
*Family-run lakeside hotel and
licensed restaurant. Private
golf, trout fishing, nature
reserve and Domesday mill on
50 acre estate.*
Bedrooms: 1 single, 2 double
& 1 twin.
Bathrooms: 2 private,
1 public.
Bed & breakfast: £18-£20
single, £45-£60 double.
Half board: £30-£50 daily,
£189-£315 weekly.
Lunch available.
Evening meal 7.30pm (l.o.
9pm).
Parking for 50.
Credit: Access, Visa.
🔾 🖵 🎱 🗻 📶 V 🚶 🗻 📺 ●
▦ 🎱 🗻 🍴 ♿ ➤ ✓ ❋
🗙 🐾 SP 🏡

**We advise you to
confirm your
booking in writing.**

HEART OF ENGLAND

TETBURY

Gloucestershire
Map ref 2B2

Small market town with 18th C houses and an attractive 17th C Town Hall. It is a good touring centre with many places of interest nearby including Badminton House and Westonbirt Arboretum.

Hare and Hounds Hotel M

Westonbirt, Tetbury, GL8 8QL
☎ Westonbirt (066 688) 233
Telex 94012242
GR Best Western
A family-run, Cotswold-stone hotel in 10 acres of garden and woodland.
Bedrooms: 4 single, 12 double & 12 twin, 2 family rooms.
Bathrooms: 30 private.
Bed & breakfast: £52-£60 single, £70-£80 double.
Half board: £357-£462 weekly.
Lunch available.
Evening meal 7.30pm (l.o. 9pm).
Parking for 89.
Credit: Access, Visa, Amex.

Hunters Hall Inn M

Kingscote, Tetbury, GL8 8XZ
☎ Dursley (0453) 860393
16th C coaching inn with open fireplaces and beamed ceilings with separate restaurant and large gardens. Situated on the A4135 between Tetbury and Dursley.
Bedrooms: 5 double & 6 twin, 1 family room.
Bathrooms: 12 private.
Bed & breakfast: £47-£52 single, £57-£62 double.
Half board: £32-£38 daily.
Lunch available.
Evening meal 7pm (l.o. 9.45pm).
Parking for 100.
Credit: Access, Visa, Diners, Amex.

Snooty Fox Hotel M

Market Place, Tetbury, GL8 8DD
☎ (0666) 502 436
Telex 437334 ATT Snooty Fox

16th C inn in centre of market town with a combination of modern facilities and traditional charm.
Bedrooms: 1 single, 7 double & 2 twin, 2 family rooms.
Bathrooms: 12 private.
Bed & breakfast: £73-£90 single, £97-£121 double.
Half board: £80-£92.50 daily, from £378 weekly.
Lunch available.
Evening meal 7.30pm (l.o. 10pm).
Credit: Access, Visa, Diners, Amex.

Tavern House M
COMMENDED

Willesley, Tetbury, GL8 8QU
☎ (066 688) 444 & 254
A Grade II listed Cotswold stone house (formerly a staging post) on the A433 Bath road, 1 mile from the Arboretum and 4 miles from Tetbury.
Bedrooms: 2 double & 2 twin.
Bathrooms: 4 private.
Bed & breakfast: £39-£65 double.
Parking for 4.
Credit: Access, Visa.

TEWKESBURY

Gloucestershire
Map ref 2B1

Tewkesbury's outstanding possession is its magnificent church, built as an abbey with a great Norman tower and beautiful 14th C interior. The town stands at the confluence of the Severn and Avon and has many old houses, inns and several museums.

Bell Hotel M

52 Church St., Tewkesbury, GL20 5SA
☎ (0684) 293293 Telex 43535
GR Best Western
A historic black and white Tudor hotel full of charm and character and run on a highly personalised basis. Log fires when chilly.
Bedrooms: 8 single, 11 double & 6 twin.
Bathrooms: 25 private.
Bed & breakfast: £53-£60 single, £66-£75 double.
Half board: £260-£320 weekly.
Lunch available.
Evening meal 6.30pm (l.o. 9.30pm).

Parking for 50.
Credit: Access, Visa, Diners, Amex.

Corse Lawn House Hotel M
COMMENDED

Corse Lawn, Gloucester, GL19 4LZ
☎ Tirley (045 278) 479
Telex 437348
Queen Anne period country house hotel with highly acclaimed restaurant. 5 miles south-west of Tewkesbury on B4211.
Bedrooms: 2 single, 12 double & 5 twin.
Bathrooms: 19 private.
Bed & breakfast: £60-£65 single, £67.50-£85 double.
Half board: £82.50-£87.50 daily.
Lunch available.
Evening meal 7pm (l.o. 10pm).
Parking for 50.
Credit: Access, Visa, Diners, Amex.

Jessop House Hotel

65 Church St., Tewkesbury, GL20 5RZ
☎ (0684) 292017
Georgian house facing the abbey and medieval cottages, peacefully overlooking "Tewkesbury's Ham".
Bedrooms: 3 double & 5 twin.
Bathrooms: 8 private.
Bed & breakfast: from £46 single, from £57 double.
Evening meal 7.30pm (l.o. 8.30pm).
Parking for 4.
Credit: Access, Visa.

Upper Court M
COMMENDED

Kemerton, Tewkesbury, GL20 7HY
☎ Overbury (038 689) 351
Small family-run Georgian country house hotel with four-poster beds, antiques, beautiful grounds and personal service.
Bedrooms: 2 double & 1 twin.
Bathrooms: 3 private, 1 public.
Bed & breakfast: £45 single, £70 double.
Parking for 10.
Credit: Access, Visa, Amex.

Wren's Nest M

Stow Rd., Teddington Hands, Tewkesbury, GL20 8NF
☎ Overbury (038 689) 382
Country house in beautiful surroundings. All rooms have private entrance. Teashop serving cream teas and home-made cakes. Licensed restaurant and residents' bar now open. Dinner by arrangement.
Bedrooms: 3 double & 2 twin.
Bathrooms: 5 private.
Bed & breakfast: £25-£30 single, £35-£45 double.
Half board: £30-£40 daily, £150-£200 weekly.
Lunch available.
Evening meal 6pm (l.o. 10pm).
Parking for 40.
Credit: Access, Visa, Amex.

TUTBURY

Staffordshire
Map ref 4B3

Small town on the River Dove with an attractive High Street, old houses and the remains of a castle where Mary Queen of Scots was imprisoned.

Ye Olde Dog & Partridge Hotel M

High St., Tutbury, Burton upon Trent, DE13 9LS
☎ Burton upon Trent (0283) 813030 Telex 347220
Fax (0283) 813178
Coaching inn with wealth of beams and a French restaurant. Carvery with grand piano played in the evenings. Beautiful gardens.
Bedrooms: 2 single, 7 double & 7 twin, 1 family room.
Bathrooms: 17 private.
Bed & breakfast: £54-£59 single, £66-£75 double.
Lunch available.
Evening meal 6.30pm (l.o. 9.45pm).
Parking for 100.
Credit: Access, Visa, Amex.

> The enquiry coupons at the back will help you when contacting proprietors.

Hereford & Worcester
Map ref 2A1

6m SW. Bromyard
Village close to Hereford
with its many attractions
including the cathedral
and the cider museum.

The Steppes ⋒
♔♔♔

Ullingswick, Hereford,
Herefordshire HR1 3JG
☎ Hereford (0432) 820424 &
(0432) 820424
*17th C listed building with oak
beams, log fires and inglenook
fireplaces. Cordon bleu cuisine.
Intimate atmosphere.*
Bedrooms: 3 double & 2 twin.
Bathrooms: 5 private,
1 public.
Half board: £35-£44 daily,
£245-£300 weekly.
Evening meal 7.30pm.
Parking for 8.
♿ 📞 ▢ ♻ î V ✂ ⛨
▥ ♨ ▲ ☂ ❋ ♨ ⊠ SP ⊞

Hereford & Worcester
Map ref 2B1

Attractive country town
on the banks of the
Severn and a good river
cruising centre. It has
many pleasant old
houses and inns.

Pool House Riverside
Country House Hotel ⋒
♔♔♔ COMMENDED

Hanley Rd., Upton-upon-
Severn, Worcester,
Worcestershire WR8 0PA
☎ (068 46) 2151
*Fine Queen Anne country
house in large picturesque
garden running down to the
River Severn. Quiet,
comfortable accommodation.*
Bedrooms: 3 double & 4 twin,
2 family rooms.
Bathrooms: 6 private,
1 public.
Bed & breakfast: £19-£33
single, £32-£52 double.
Half board: £29-£62 daily.
Evening meal 6.30pm.
Parking for 20.
Open February-November.
Credit: Access, Visa.
♿ ♨ V ⛨ ☎ TV ▲ ♨ ♩
❋ ✻ ♨ SP ⊞

White Lion Hotel ⋒
♔♔♔♔ COMMENDED

Upton-upon-Severn,
Worcester, Worcestershire
WR8 OHJ
☎ (068 46) 2551
*Former 16th C coaching inn
with Georgian facade, in the
historic town of Upton-upon-
Severn. Tudor dining room
with full a la carte menu.*
Bedrooms: 2 single, 4 double
& 4 twin.
Bathrooms: 10 private,
2 public.
Bed & breakfast: from £46
single, from £62 double.
Half board: from £37.50
daily, from £262.50 weekly.
Lunch available.
Evening meal 7pm (l.o.
9.30pm).
Parking for 21.
Credit: Access, Visa, Diners,
Amex.
♿ ♨ 📞 ▢ ♻ î V ◫
▥ ▲ ☂ SP ♨ ⊞

Staffordshire
Map ref 4B2

Small market town which
is famous for its
racecourse. There are
half-timbered buildings
round the Market Square.

Bank House Hotel ⋒
♔♔♔♔ APPROVED

Church St., Uttoxeter,
ST14 8AG
☎ Uttoxeter (0889) 566922
Telex 0889 567565
*Listed Georgian town house
with 16 bedrooms, restaurant,
lounge bar and conference
facilities.*
Bedrooms: 5 single, 9 double
& 1 twin, 1 family room.
Bathrooms: 16 private.
Bed & breakfast: £45-£48
single, £60-£70 double.
Lunch available.
Evening meal 7pm (l.o.
10pm).
Parking for 16.
Credit: Access, Visa, Diners,
Amex.
♿ ♨ 📞 ▢ ♻ î V ◫
▥ ▲ ☂ ♨ SP ⊞

**Please check prices
and other details at
the time of booking.**

**Half board prices shown are per person
but in some cases may be based on
double/twin occupancy.**

W. Midlands
Map ref 4B3

Industrial town with a
magnificent collection of
pictures and antiquities in
its museum and art
gallery. It has a fine
arboretum with lakes and
walks and illuminations
each September.

County Hotel
Birmingham Rd., Walsall,
WS1 2NG
☎ (0922) 32323 Fax (0922)
648763
*All rooms en-suite with remote
control TV, tea and coffee
making facilities. Free 24 hour
satellite channels.*
Bedrooms: 27 single,
10 double & 7 twin, 2 family
rooms.
Bathrooms: 46 private,
5 public.
Bed & breakfast: £45-£55
single, £55-£65 double.
Half board: £55-£60 daily.
Lunch available.
Evening meal 6.30pm (l.o.
9.45pm).
Parking for 35.
Credit: Access, Visa, Diners,
Amex.
♿ ♨ ▢ ♻ î ♨ ◑ ◫
▲ ☂ SP ⊞

Fairlawns Hotel and
Restaurant ⋒
♔♔♔♔

Little Aston Rd., Aldridge,
Walsall, WS9 0NU
☎ Aldridge (0922) 55122
Telex 339873
Ⓡ Consort
*Modern hotel in its own
grounds, in a quiet, rural
location, 20 minutes from
Birmingham and 30 minutes
from the National Exhibition
Centre.*
Bedrooms: 6 single, 19 double
& 5 twin, 6 family rooms.
Bathrooms: 36 private.
Bed & breakfast: £42.50-
£69.50 single, £65-£85 double.
Lunch available.
Evening meal 7pm (l.o.
10pm).
Parking for 82.
Credit: Access, Visa, Diners,
Amex.
♿ ♨ 📞 ▢ ♻ î V ✂
▥ ◑ ▥ ▲ ☂ ☼ ⌨ SP ⊞

Friendly Hotel ⋒
♔♔♔♔

Junction 10, M6,
20 Wolverhampton Rd.
West, Bentley, Walsall,
WS2 0BS
☎ (0922) 724444 Telex 334854
Ⓡ Friendly

*Hotel offering wide range of
conference facilities for up to
200 persons. Carvery and a la
carte menus. Own leisure
complex. Direct access to M6
from the hotel's location at
junction 10.*
Bedrooms: 7 double &
89 twin, 24 family rooms.
Bathrooms: 120 private.
Bed & breakfast: £52-£62
single, £68.50-£73 double.
Half board: £45.75-£74 daily.
Lunch available.
Evening meal 7pm (l.o.
10pm).
Parking for 135.
Credit: Access, Visa, Diners,
Amex.
♿ ♨ ♨ 📞 ▢ ♻ î V
✂ ▥ ◑ ▥ ▲ ☂ ♨ ♨ ♨
⌨ ♨ SP ⊞

Warwickshire
Map ref 2B1

Warwick is outstanding
for its castle rising above
the River Avon and for
the 15th C Beauchamp
Chapel attached to St.
Mary's Church. The
medieval Lord
Leycester's Hospital
almshouses and several
museums are amongst
the other attractions.
*Tourist Information
Centre* ☎ *(0926) 492212*

Austin House ⋒
♔♔

96 Emscote Rd., Warwick,
CV34 5QJ
☎ (0926) 493583
*Black and white Edwardian
house situated half a mile from
Warwick Castle, 1 mile from
Royal Leamington Spa and 6
miles from Stratford-upon-
Avon.*
Bedrooms: 1 single, 1 double
& 3 twin, 2 family rooms.
Bathrooms: 5 private,
1 public.
Bed & breakfast: £13.50-
£16.50 single, £27-£33 double.
Half board: £19.50-£22.50
daily, £136.50-£157.50
weekly.
Evening meal 6pm (l.o.
7.30pm).
Parking for 8.
♿ ♨ ▢ ♻ UL î ▥ TV ⛨
▲ ⌨ SP

Chesterfield ⋒
♔ APPROVED

84 Emscote Rd., Warwick,
CV34 5QJ
☎ (0926) 492396 Fax (0926)
494059

Continued ▶

WARWICK

Continued

Family-run guesthouse with pleasant decor throughout and colour TV in all rooms. Most rooms have private showers and king-size beds.
Bedrooms: 2 single, 2 double & 1 twin, 3 family rooms.
Bathrooms: 1 public; 5 private showers.
Bed & breakfast: £14-£22 single, £24-£30 double.
Evening meal 7pm (l.o. 6.30pm).
Parking for 10.
Credit: Access, Visa, Amex.
🛏 Ⓑ 🖵 🛆 Ⓥ ▥ 🛆 DAP SP

The Croft ⋔
ⓦ COMMENDED
Haseley Knob, Warwick, CV35 7NL
☎ Haseley Knob (0926) 484447
4-acre smallholding with friendly family atmosphere in picturesque rural setting. On A4177 between Balsall Common and Warwick, convenient for the National Exhibition Centre, National Agricultural Centre, Stratford and Coventry. 15 minutes from Birmingham Airport.
Bedrooms: 1 double & 1 twin, 1 family room.
Bathrooms: 1 private, 2 public.
Bed & breakfast: £13-£18 single, £26-£33 double.
Half board: £20-£25 daily, £120-£150 weekly.
Evening meal 6pm (l.o. 8pm).
Parking for 11.
🛏 🔥 ☎ Ⓑ 🖵 ⓤ 🛢 Ⓥ
✂ TV ▥ 🛆 ✿ 🎇 🛆

Hilton National Warwick ⋔
ⓦⓦⓦⓦ APPROVED
A46, Stratford Rd., Warwick, CV34 6RE
☎ (0926) 499555
Telex 312468
Ⓖⓑ Hilton
Well-situated for business or pleasure and offering modern facilities. Set in own grounds with a large car park.
Bedrooms: 18 single, 75 double & 78 twin, 10 family rooms.
Bathrooms: 181 private.
Bed & breakfast: £47-£120 single, £90-£135 double.
Half board: £63-£136 daily.
Lunch available.
Evening meal 7pm (l.o. 10pm).
Parking for 220.

Credit: Access, Visa, Diners, Amex.
🛏 ☎ Ⓑ 🖵 🛢 ⓘ Ⓥ 🛢 🛆
Ⓞ 🅴 ▥ 🛆 🎇 🛆 Ⓡ 🎇 ☀ DAP
🛆 SP T

Lord Leycester ⋔
ⓦⓦⓦ
17 Jury Street, Warwick, CV34 4EJ
☎ (0926) 491481 Telex 41363
Ⓖⓑ Calotels
Georgian hotel situated opposite Warwick Castle, 8 miles from Stratford, 2 miles from Leamington Spa.
Bedrooms: 14 single, 12 double & 23 twin, 4 family rooms.
Bathrooms: 53 private.
Bed & breakfast: £42-£47 single, £59-£65 double.
Lunch available.
Evening meal 7pm (l.o. 8.30pm).
Parking for 50.
Credit: Access, Visa, Diners, Amex.
🛏 🔥 ☎ Ⓑ 🖵 🛢 ⓘ Ⓥ 🛢
Ⓞ 🅴 ▥ 🛆 🛢 🎇 🛆 🎇 T

Northleigh House ⋔
ⓦⓦⓦ COMMENDED
Five Ways Rd., Hatton, Warwick, CV35 7HZ
☎ Warwick (0926) 484203
Comfortable, peaceful country house where the elegant rooms all have en-suite bathrooms and colour TV.
Bedrooms: 2 single, 3 double & 1 twin.
Bathrooms: 6 private.
Bed & breakfast: £26-£32 single, £40-£44 double.
Parking for 6.
🛏 Ⓑ 🖵 🛆 ⓤ Ⓥ 🛢 🛆
TV ▥ 🛆 ✿ 🎇

The Old Fourpenny Shop Hotel ⋔
ⓦⓦⓦ COMMENDED
27-29 Crompton St., Warwick, CV34 6HJ
☎ (0926) 491360
Recently refurbished, offering real ale and real food. Very close to Warwick Castle, race and golf courses and town centre.
Bedrooms: 2 single, 3 double & 2 twin.
Bathrooms: 7 private.
Bed & breakfast: £27.50-£30 single, £45-£50 double.
Half board: £30-£40 daily.
Lunch available.
Evening meal 7pm (l.o. 10pm).
Parking for 7.
Open February-December.
Credit: Access, Visa.
Ⓑ 🖵 🛆 ⓘ Ⓥ ✂ ▥ 🛆 🛢
▶ ☀ 🎇 🎇 SP 🎇 T

Old Rectory
Stratford Rd., Sherbourne, Warwick, CV35 8AB
☎ Barford (0926) 624562
Georgian country house with beams and inglenook fireplaces, furnished with antiques. Well-appointed bedrooms, many with brass beds, en-suite facilities and colour TV. Hearty breakfast. Situated half a mile from M40 junction 15.
Bedrooms: 5 double & 1 twin, 2 family rooms.
Bathrooms: 7 private, 1 public.
Bed & breakfast: £18-£28 single, £34-£40 double.
Parking for 10.
🛏 🔥 🖵 🛆 Ⓥ 🛢 TV ▥ 🛆
🛆 ☀ 🎇 SP 🎇

Pageant Lodge ⋔
Listed COMMENDED
2 Castle Lane, Warwick, CV34 4BU
☎ (0926) 491244
Situated next to the castle entrance and the famous Dolls Museum. The property dates from 1482.
Bedrooms: 1 single, 2 double.
Bathrooms: 1 private, 1 public.
Bed & breakfast: £12-£17 single, £24-£34 double.
Parking for 2.
🛏 🖵 🛆 ⓤ Ⓥ Ⓞ ▥ 🛆 🎇
🎇

Penderrick Hotel ⋔
ⓦⓦⓦ
36 Coten End, Warwick, CV34 4NP
☎ (0926) 499399
Early Victorian family-run hotel near castle, convenient for National Agricultural Centre, National Exhibition Centre, Stratford, Cotswolds. Tea-making facilities, TV, telephone, comfortable en-suite bedrooms. Residents' bar.
Bedrooms: 2 single, 1 double & 2 twin, 2 family rooms.
Bathrooms: 4 private, 1 public; 2 private showers.
Bed & breakfast: £25-£29.50 single, £44-£49 double.
Half board: £27.50-£30 daily, £173.25-£189 weekly.
Evening meal 7pm (l.o. 7pm).
Parking for 9.
Credit: Access, Visa, Diners, Amex.
🛏 ☎ Ⓑ 🛆 ⓘ Ⓥ 🛢 TV ▥
🛆 🎇 SP 🎇 T

Tudor House Hotel ⋔
ⓦⓦⓦ
90-92 West St., Warwick, CV34 6AW
☎ (0926) 495447 Fax (0926) 492 948

An inn of character dating from 1472 with a wealth of beams and one of the few buildings to survive the great fire of Warwick in 1694. Opposite Warwick Castle and close to Warwick race course.
Bedrooms: 3 single, 5 double & 2 twin, 1 family room.
Bathrooms: 6 private, 1 public; 2 private showers.
Bed & breakfast: £25-£55 single, £50-£65 double.
Half board: £35-£65 daily.
Lunch available.
Evening meal 6pm (l.o. 11pm).
Parking for 6.
Credit: Access, Visa, Diners, Amex.
🛏 🖵 ☎ Ⓑ 🖵 🛆 ⓘ Ⓥ ▥
🛆 🎇 🎇 🎇 T

Woodside ⋔
ⓦⓦ
Langley Rd., Claverdon, Warwick, CV35 8PJ
☎ (092 684) 2446
Quiet, warm and comfortable, in acres of English garden and woodland. Near Warwick, Shakespeare country and National Exhibition Centre. Excellent touring centre.
Bedrooms: 2 twin, 1 family room.
Bathrooms: 2 public.
Bed & breakfast: £14-£20 single, £28-£34 double.
Half board: £26.50-£32.50 daily, £95-£135 weekly.
Evening meal 7pm (l.o. 2pm).
Parking for 13.
🛏 🔥 Ⓑ ⓤ ⓘ Ⓥ TV ▥ 🛆
🛢 🛆 ✿ 🎇 🛆 SP

WATERHOUSES

Staffordshire
Map ref 4B2

8m SE. Leek
Village in the valley of the River Hamps, once the terminus of the Leek and Manifold Light Railway, 8 miles of which is now a macadamised walkers' path.

Croft House Farm Guest House ⋔
ⓦⓦ
Waterfall, Waterhouses, Stoke-on-Trent, ST10 3HZ
☎ (0538) 308553
17th C farmhouse in Waterfall, between Ashbourne and Leek, surrounded by beautiful countryside. Offers warm, friendly hospitality and home cooking. Reduction for children.
Bedrooms: 2 double & 2 twin, 2 family rooms.
Bathrooms: 3 public.

Bed & breakfast: from £17 single, from £31 double.
Half board: from £27 daily.
Lunch available.
Evening meal 7pm (l.o. 8pm).
Parking for 15.

Old Beams Restaurant with Rooms M

Leek Rd., Waterhouses, ST10 3HW
☎ (0538) 308254
Attractive 18th C house with log fires and an abundance of flowers. Good cuisine prepared by chef/patron Nigel Wallis. Beautiful bedrooms.
Bedrooms: 6 double.
Bathrooms: 6 private.
Bed & breakfast: £50-£70 single, £70-£85 double.
Lunch available.
Evening meal 7pm (l.o. 10pm).
Parking for 22.
Credit: Access, Visa, Diners, Amex.

WELLESBOURNE

Warwickshire
Map ref 2B1

Picturesque village with several noteworthy inns. The River Dene, which divides the place in two, once separated Wellesbourne Hastings from Wellesbourne Mountford, but now both parts are regarded as one village.

Chadley House M

Loxley Road, Wellesbourne, Warwick, CV35 9JL
☎ Stratford-upon-Avon (0789) 840994
Georgian farmhouse set in 6.5 acres, with small restaurant. En-suite facilities in all rooms. Close to Stratford and Cotswolds.
Bedrooms: 1 single, 4 double & 4 twin.
Bathrooms: 9 private.
Bed & breakfast: £28-£40 single, £46-£56 double.
Half board: £225-£280 weekly.
Evening meal 7pm (l.o. 10pm).
Parking for 23.
Credit: Access, Visa, Amex.

WEM

Shropshire
Map ref 4A3

Small town connected with Judge Jeffreys who lived in Lowe Hall. Well-known for its ales.

Soulton Hall M

Wem, Shrewsbury, SY4 5RS
☎ (0939) 32786
560-acre mixed farm. Tudor manor house with moated Domesday site in grounds, offering relaxing holiday. Private riverside and woodland walks.
Bedrooms: 1 double & 2 twin.
Bathrooms: 3 private, 1 public.
Bed & breakfast: £21-£31.50 single, £41.80-£50.60 double.
Half board: £35-£39.50 daily, £220-£249 weekly.
Evening meal 7pm (l.o. 8.30pm).
Parking for 6.

The Woodlands Country House Hotel M

Ellesmere Rd., Wolverley, Wem, Shrewsbury, SY4 5NQ
☎ (0939) 33268
Friendly, family-owned country house hotel. Grounds of 5 acres. Ample parking. In lovely rural Shropshire, near Ellesmere, Chester and north Wales.
Bedrooms: 2 single, 16 double, 1 family room.
Bathrooms: 17 private, 2 public.
Bed & breakfast: £25 single, £40 double.
Half board: £31-£40 daily.
Lunch available.
Evening meal 7pm (l.o. 9pm).
Parking for 70.
Credit: Access, Visa.

Classifications and quality commendations were correct at the time of going to press but are subject to change. Please check at the time of booking.

WEOBLEY

Hereford & Worcester
Map ref 2A1

One of the most beautiful Herefordshire villages and full of attractive black and white timber-framed houses. It is dominated by the church which has a fine spire.

Unicorn House Hotel and Restaurant M

High St., Weobley, Hereford, Herefordshire HR4 8SL
☎ (0544) 318230
Black and white building in picturesque black and white village between Hereford and Leominster.
Bedrooms: 2 single, 3 double, 1 family room.
Bathrooms: 4 private, 1 public; 2 private showers.
Bed & breakfast: £18 single, £40 double.
Half board: £28 daily, £195.65 weekly.
Lunch available.
Evening meal 7pm (l.o. 10pm).
Parking for 5.
Credit: Access, Visa, C.Bl., Diners, Amex.
✿ Display advertisement appears on page 266.

WHITCHURCH

Hereford & Worcester
Map ref 2A1

Village close to the River Wye and Symonds Yat, well placed for visiting the Forest of Dean and the ruins of Goodrich Castle.

Crown Hotel M

Whitchurch, Ross-on-Wye, Herefordshire HR9 6DB
☎ Symonds Yat (0600) 890234
Tudor beamed bedrooms, some with 4-poster beds and TV. All rooms en-suite. Log fires.
Bedrooms: 3 double, 2 family rooms.
Bathrooms: 5 private, 1 public.
Bed & breakfast: £25-£30 single, £40-£45 double.
Half board: £22-£30 daily, £150-£170 weekly.
Lunch available.
Evening meal 7pm (l.o. 9.30pm).

Parking for 40.
Credit: Access, Visa, Diners, Amex.

WHITMINSTER

Gloucestershire
Map ref 2B1

9m S. Gloucester
Village close to the Wildfowl Trust at Slimbridge with the world's largest collection of wildfowl.

Whitminster Hotel

Whitminster, Gloucester, GL2 7NY
☎ (0452) 740234
Old coaching inn, recently refurbished, in ideal position for visiting local beauty spots, easy to reach from M5. Family-run, experienced staff.
Bedrooms: 4 single, 3 double & 1 twin, 2 family rooms.
Bathrooms: 10 private.
Bed & breakfast: max. £33 single, max. £43 double.
Lunch available.
Evening meal 7pm (l.o. 10.15pm).
Parking for 80.
Credit: Access, Visa.

WINCHCOMBE

Gloucestershire
Map ref 2B1

Ancient town with a folk museum and railway museum. To the south lies Sudeley Castle with its fine collection of paintings and toys and an Elizabethan garden.

Postlip House
COMMENDED

Winchcombe, Cheltenham, GL54 5AH
☎ (0242) 602390
Cotswold manor house set in 7 acres of wooded grounds and gardens with beautiful views. Tastefully furnished rooms.
Bedrooms: 2 twin.
Bathrooms: 2 private.
Bed & breakfast: £30-£32 single, £38.50-£40 double.
Half board: £36-£40 daily, £235 weekly.
Parking for 30.

WITHINGTON

Gloucestershire
Map ref 2B1

8m SE. Cheltenham
Village near Chedworth
Roman Villa which is one
of the best preserved in
England.

Halewell Close ⚑
👑👑👑 COMMENDED

Withington, Cheltenham,
GL54 4BN
☎ (024 289) 238
*Monastic, 15th C building with
hammer beam roof and gallery,
oak panelled dining room and
log fires in winter.*
Bedrooms: 4 double & 2 twin.
Bathrooms: 6 private.
Bed & breakfast: £45-£50
single, £70-£80 double.
Half board: £50-£65 daily.
Evening meal 8pm (l.o. 8pm).
Parking for 6.
Credit: Access, Visa.
🛇 ⚿ ⊡ ⌨ ⚙ ⅟ ⚐ ▥
🖴 🍽 ⚷ ↻ ∪ ✿ ☼ 🅿 ⚑
🎪

WOLVERHAMPTON

W. Midlands
Map ref 4B3

Modern industrial town
with a long history, a fine
parish church and an
excellent art gallery.
There are several places
of interest in the vicinity
including Moseley Old
Hall and Wightwick Manor
with its William Morris
influence.
*Tourist Information
Centre ☎ (0902) 312051*

Connaught Hotel ⚑
👑👑👑👑

Tettenhall Rd.,
Wolverhampton, WV1 4SW
☎ (0902) 24433 Telex 338490
CHAMCON WOLVES
*A friendly independently
owned hotel, beautifully
refurbished with a fine
restaurant and health and
beauty centre. Half a mile to
the town centre and easy
access to the motorways.*
Bedrooms: 44 single,
15 double & 21 twin.
Bathrooms: 80 private,
1 public.
Bed & breakfast: £49.50-£55
single, £57.50-£75 double.
Half board: £59.75-£72.50
daily, £386.25-£507.50
weekly.
Lunch available.
Evening meal 7pm (l.o.
9.45pm).

Parking for 100.
Credit: Access, Visa, Diners,
Amex.
🛇 🖴 ⊡ ⌨ ⚙ ⅟ ⚐ V ⚐ ◗
⊞ 🍽 ⚷ 🖴 🍽 ⚷ 🌣 ⚬ 🅿 ⊤

Featherstone Farm ⚑
Listed

New Rd., Featherstone,
Wolverhampton,
WV10 7NW
☎ (0902) 725371
*5-acre horse farm. 17th C
farmhouse with listed
barn/stables completely
refurbished. Open fires. Near
M6 and M54, and close to
Weston Hall.*
Bedrooms: 3 single, 3 double
& 2 twin, 1 family room.
Bathrooms: 2 private,
1 public.·
Bed & breakfast: £20-£35
single, £35-£55 double.
Half board: £28.50-£45 daily.
Lunch available.
Evening meal 6pm (l.o.
7.30pm).
Parking for 20.
🛇 🖴 ⊡ ⌨ V⚐ ⚙ ⚐ ▥
🖴 🍽 ✿ 🎪

Fox Hotel ⚑
👑👑👑

School St., Wolverhampton,
WV3 0NR
☎ (0902) 21680 &
(0902) 21719
*Town centre, free parking,
nearby shopping. All rooms en-
suite, satellite TV, direct dial
telephones. Bar and restaurant.*
Bedrooms: 27 single, 3 double
& 3 twin.
Bathrooms: 33 private.
Bed & breakfast: £24.50-
£34.50 single, £34.50-£44.50
double.
Lunch available.
Evening meal 7pm (l.o. 9pm).
Parking for 20.
Credit: Access, Visa, Diners,
Amex.
🛇 ⚿ ⊡ ⌨ ⚙ ⅟ ⚐ V ⚐ ◗
▥ 🖴 🍽 ✕ ⚬ 🅿 ⊤

Glenville Hotel ⚑
👑👑

282 Penn Rd., (A449),
Wolverhampton, WV4 4AD
☎ (0902) 334649 Fax (0902)
340148
*Family-run hotel, 1 mile from
town centre on main A449.
Large car park. Standard and
en-suite rooms.*
Bedrooms: 8 single, 15 double
& 13 twin, 3 family rooms.
Bathrooms: 23 public;
2 private showers.
Bed & breakfast: £16-£30
single, £30-£40 double.
Half board: £22-£36 daily.
Evening meal 6.30pm.
Parking for 30.
🛇 🖴 ⊡ ⌨ ⚐ 🖴 ⚐ ▥ 🖴 🍽
🖴 ✿ ✕ ⚬ ⚬ ⚬

Rank Motor Lodge ⚑

Hilton Park Services,
M6 Motorway, Between exits
10a & 11, Wolverhampton,
West Midlands WV11 2DR
☎ (0922) 414100 Fax (0922)
418762
*64 modern bedrooms, close to
all the Midland tourist and
business destinations. Self-
service restaurant open 24
hours.*
Bedrooms: 6 double &
36 twin, 22 family rooms.
Bathrooms: 64 private.
Bed & breakfast: from £27.50
single, from £34.50 double.
Lunch available.
Evening meal (l.o. 10pm).
Parking for 60.
Credit: Access, Visa, Diners,
Amex.
🛇 🖴 ⊡ ⌨ ⚙ V ⅟ ⚐ ◗ ▥
🖴 ⚬ ⊤

Wulfrun Hotel

37 Pipers Row,
Wolverhampton, WV1 3BJ
☎ (0902) 24017
*Small homely hotel in the town
centre, near railway, bus and
coach stations.*
Bedrooms: 3 single, 5 double
& 5 twin, 1 family room.
Bathrooms: 3 public.
Bed & breakfast: from £21
single, from £32 double.
Half board: £25-£30 daily,
from £126 weekly.
Lunch available.
Evening meal 4pm (l.o.
11.30pm).
Credit: Access, Visa.
🛇 ⚿ ⊡ ⌨ ⚙ ⚐ ▥ ⚐ ◗ ▥
🖴 ✕

York Hotel ⚑
👑👑

138-140 Tettenhall Rd.,
Wolverhampton, WV6 0BQ
☎ (0902) 754743 & 758211
*A small privately owned hotel
near to the town and
countryside. Cosy restaurant
and lounge bar, with extensive
menu. New restaurant
extension with cocktail bar.*
Bedrooms: 5 single, 2 double
& 7 twin, 2 family rooms.
Bathrooms: 16 private.
Bed & breakfast: £30-£48
single, £40-£60 double.
Half board: £40-£60 daily,
£200-£280 weekly.
Lunch available.
Evening meal 7pm (l.o.
10pm).
Parking for 40.
Credit: Access, Visa, Diners,
Amex.
🛇 🖴 ⚿ ⊡ ⌨ ⚙ ⅟ ⚐ ▥
▥ ◗ ▥ 🖴 🍽 🅿

WORCESTER

Hereford & Worcester
Map ref 2B1

Lovely city which is
dominated by its Norman
and Early English
cathedral, King John's
burial place. The city has
many old buildings
including the 15th C
Commandery and the
18th C Guildhall. There
are several museums and
the Royal Worcester
porcelain factory.
*Tourist Information
Centre ☎ (0905) 723471
ext 201 or 202 or 204*

Abbeydore Guest House
🏠 APPROVED

34 Barbourne Rd.,
Worcester, Worcestershire
WR1 1HU
☎ (0905) 26731
*Family-run guesthouse within
walking distance of the city
centre, shops, cathedral,
racecourse and sports facilities.*
Bedrooms: 2 single, 1 double
& 1 twin, 3 family rooms.
Bathrooms: 2 public.
Bed & breakfast: £12-£16
single, £24-£28 double.
Credit: Access, Visa.
🛇 ⊡ ⌨ ⚙ ⚐ ⅟ ⚐ V ⚐ ▥
🖴 ✕ 🅿

Croft Guest House ⚑
👑👑

Bransford, Worcester
Worcestershire WR6 5JD
☎ Leigh Sinton (0886) 32227
*16th/18th C house in beautiful
country, with view to Malvern
Hills. Family-run, with
comfortable surroundings and
family jacuzzi. 10 minutes
from M5 on A4103.*
Bedrooms: 3 double & 1 twin,
1 family room.
Bathrooms: 2 private,
2 public.
Bed & breakfast: £15-£22
single, £30-£44 double.
Half board: £21-£28 daily,
£125-£180 weekly.
Evening meal 7pm (l.o. 7pm).
Parking for 8.
🛇 ⚙ ⚐ ⅟ ⚐ V ⚐ ▥ ◗ ▥ 🖴 ⚬
✿ ✕ 🅿 🎪

Fownes Hotel ⚑
👑👑👑👑👑 COMMENDED

City Walls Rd., Worcester,
Worcestershire WR1 2AP
☎ (0905) 613151
Telex 335021 FOWNES
*Located in city centre near the
cathedral, river and
commandery. Also close to
shopping centre, cricket ground
and racecourse.*

Bedrooms: 13 single,
15 double & 30 twin, 3 family
rooms.
Bathrooms: 61 private.
Bed & breakfast: £85-£95
single, £108-£170 double.
Lunch available.
Evening meal 7.30pm (l.o.
10pm).
Parking for 94.
Credit: Access, Visa, Diners,
Amex.

Loch Ryan Hotel M
119 Sidbury, Worcester,
Worcestershire WR5 2DH
☎ (0905) 351143
*Historic hotel very close to the
cathedral, Royal Worcester
Porcelain Factory and
Commandery. Attractive
terraced garden.*
Bedrooms: 6 single, 3 double
& 3 twin, 1 family room.
Bathrooms: 3 private,
2 public.
Bed & breakfast: £25-£35
single, £42-£60 double.
Lunch available.
Evening meal 6pm (l.o. 8pm).

The Maximillian Hotel M
COMMENDED
Cromwell St., Shrub Hill,
Worcester, Worcestershire,
WR4 9EF
☎ (0905) 23867 &
(0905) 21694
*Georgian hotel situated just
outside city centre, with ample
car parking and easy access to
Shrub Hill railway station and
M5 junction 7.*
Bedrooms: 6 single, 4 double
& 5 twin, 2 family rooms.
Bathrooms: 13 private,
1 public.
Bed & breakfast: £19.50-
£32.55 single, £42.50 double.
Half board: £41-£49 daily,
£196-£277.25 weekly.
Lunch available.
Evening meal 7pm (l.o.
10pm).
Parking for 15.
Credit: Access, Visa.

Shrubbery Guest House M
38 Barbourne Rd.,
Worcester, Worcestershire
WR1 1HU
☎ (0905) 24871

*Large Victorian house within
15 minutes' walking distance of
Worcester Cathedral, city
centre and Royal Worcester
Factory.*
Bedrooms: 3 double & 2 twin,
1 family room.
Bathrooms: 2 private,
2 public; 2 private showers.
Bed & breakfast: from £13
single, from £26 double.

Star Hotel M
Foregate St., Worcester,
Worcestershire WR1 1DX
☎ (0905) 24308 Telex 335075
Fax (0905) 23440
*Historic town centre hotel,
dating back to 1588, with large
car park and easy access to
station and local tourist
attractions.*
Bedrooms: 17 single,
12 double & 15 twin, 2 family
rooms.
Bathrooms: 46 private.
Bed & breakfast: from £55
single, from £67.50 double.
Lunch available.
Evening meal 7pm (l.o.
10pm).
Parking for 55.
Credit: Access, Visa, Amex.

Wyatt Guest House M
40 Barbourne Rd.,
Worcester, Worcestershire
WR1 1HU
☎ (0905) 26311
*A small, family-run guest
house close to city centre,
parks, river and racecourse.*
Bedrooms: 1 single, 1 double
& 2 twin, 4 family rooms.
Bathrooms: 4 private,
1 public; 1 private shower.
Bed & breakfast: £15-£16
single, £24-£28 double.
Evening meal 6pm (l.o. 7pm).
Credit: Access, Visa.

Ye Olde Talbot Hotel M
Friar St., Worcester,
Worcestershire WR1 2NA
☎ (0905) 23573 Telex 333315
Fax (0905) 612760
Ⓖ Lansbury
*Originally an old courtroom,
located close to the town centre
and the cathedral, to which it
once belonged. Recently
renovated.*
Bedrooms: 10 single,
15 double & 4 twin.
Bathrooms: 29 private.

Bed & breakfast: £24-£63
single, £48-£76 double.
Half board: from £35 daily.
Lunch available.
Evening meal 7pm (l.o.
10.30pm).
Parking for 8.
Credit: Access, Visa, C.Bl.,
Diners, Amex.

WRINEHILL
Staffordshire
Map ref 4A2

*6m NW. Newcastle-
under-Lyme*

The Hand and Trumpet Inn
Main Rd., Wrinehill, Crewe,
Cheshire CW3 9BJ
☎ (0270) 820048 &
(0270) 820087
*A comfortable rural inn,
convenient for Crewe and the
Potteries, offering
accommodation, grill room and
full a la carte restaurant.*
Bedrooms: 3 twin.
Bathrooms: 3 private.
Bed & breakfast: from £28
single, from £40 double.
Lunch available.
Evening meal 7pm (l.o.
10pm).
Parking for 20.
Credit: Access, Visa.

WYE VALLEY

*See Hereford, Much
Birch, Ross-on-Wye, St.
Briavels, Symonds Yat
East, Symonds Yat West,
Whitchurch.*

**Classifications
and quality
commendations
were correct at the
time of going to
press but are
subject to change.
Please check at the
time of booking.**

**Individual proprietors have supplied all
details of accommodation. Although we
do check for accuracy, we advise you to
confirm prices and other information at
the time of booking.**

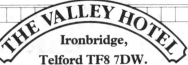

Barons Court Hotel

A461 Lichfield to Walsall Road, Walsall Wood WS9 9AH.
Tel: (0543) 452020   Fax: (0543) 361276.

👑👑👑👑 Best Western.

100 elegant bedrooms graded Executive, Superior, Baroness and Standard.
Barons Restaurant and Milady's Carvery. Leisure Club. 5 conference rooms.
15 minutes – M6/M5/M69/A5.
30 minutes – ICC/Birmingham City Centre.
45 Minutes – NEC/Birmingham Int. Airport.
We look forward to welcoming you to Barons Court Hotel – A fine English hotel.

The Cheltenham Park Hotel

Cirencester Road, Charlton Kings, Cheltenham
GL53 8EA. Tel (0242) 222021 Telex: 437364 G.

👑👑👑👑

Beautifully renovated country house hotel, situated on the Cirencester Road in Charlton Kings, adjacent to the Lillybrok Golf Course. 2.5 miles from the centre of Cheltenham Spa.
Bedrooms: 22 single, 136 double & twin.
Bathrooms: 158 private.
Bed & Breakfast: £74-£86 single, £100-£115 double.
Half board: £62.50-£70 daily, £437.50-£490 weekly.
Lunch available. Evening meal 7.00 pm (l.o. 9.45 pm).
Parking for 350. Credit: Access, Visa, Diners, Amex.

CHESTER HOUSE HOTEL & MOTEL

Bourton-on-the-Water, Gloucestershire, GL54 2BU
Telephone: Cotswold (0451) 20286
Proprietors: Mr & Mrs Julian Davies

We Offer:
- **High standards for all our guests**
- **Attractive guest rooms**
- **En suite bathrooms**
- **Motel style units available**
- **Direct dial telephones**
- **Colour TV and tea making facilities**
- **Four poster bedrooms available**

English Tourist Board

Finden Lodge Hotel

Cirencester Road, Bourton-on-the-Water,
Gloucestershire GL54 2LE ☎ (0451) 20387

👑👑👑👑 AA ★★ RAC ★★ (with merits)

Run by the Finden-Smart family and situated just outside Bourton-on-the-Water, the Finden Lodge Hotel has impressive countryside views and is ideally located for touring the Cotswolds. Fully licensed, with a quality restaurant, the home-from-home atmosphere invites you to relax and enjoy your break. 4 Crown, 2 Star (with merits) RAC and AA classification indicates the minimum service expected.

Follow the sign

It leads to over 560 Tourist Information Centres throughout England offering friendly help with accommodation and holiday ideas as well as suggestions of places to visit and things to do.

In your home town there may be a centre which can help you before you set out. Details of the locations of Tourist Information Centres are available from the English Tourist Board, Thames Tower, Black's Road, London W6 9EL, or from England's Regional Tourist Boards.

Use a coupon

When requesting further information from advertisers in this guide, you may find it helpful to use the advertisement enquiry coupons which can be found towards the end of the guide. These should be cut out and mailed direct to the companies in which you are interested. Do remember to include your name and address.

♣ Enjoy the countryside and respect its life and work ♣ Guard against all risk of fire ♣ Fasten all gates ♣ Keep your dogs under close control ♣ Keep to public paths across farmland ♣ Use gates and stiles to cross fences, hedges and walls ♣ Leave livestock, crops and machinery alone ♣ Take your litter home ♣ Help to keep all water clean ♣ Protect wildlife, plants and trees ♣ Take special care on country roads ♣ Make no unnecessary noise

FOLLOW THE COUNTRY CODE

East Midlands

They are called the Shires of Middle England, to reflect both history and geography.

Join the world's greatest medieval adventure at 'The Tales of Robin Hood' in Nottingham

» Everywhere are reminders of kings and queens and knights and ladies, their castles and grand houses and gardens. Everywhere you will see wonderful countryside, made better by its enormous variety.

» Travelling the region's four magnificent corners takes you first to the Peak District National Park; then Lincolnshire's Areas of Outstanding Natural Beauty in the Wolds; followed by the flat, moody Fens; and finally Northamptonshire's 'Cotswold Country' — while in the middle are Robin Hood's Sherwood Forest, and Rutland with its vast lake and rolling hills. Add the miles of safe empty beaches in the sunny east and you have a still-undiscovered holiday region, simply packed with things to do.

» Take the towns and cities. Nottingham is an elegant shopping centre, Lincoln a historic jewel with a magnificent hilltop cathedral and castle, Buxton is one of England's highest towns. Skegness and the whole coast offer family fun, as do inland resorts like Matlock Bath. Bustling Northampton is a good touring centre for the County of Spires and Squires, while visits to the clustered stone towns of Oakham, Uppingham and Oundle, with their famous schools, are well rewarded.

» For the energetic there are theme parks like Ilkeston's rootin' tootin' American Adventure with its white-knuckle rides, motor racing at Silverstone and Cadwell Park, championship golf at Woodhall Spa, climbing in the Peaks, walking along the many footpaths. Then there are museums and windmills, trams and steam trains, canals and rivers,

farm parks and nature reserves, caves and even a cable car. Always remember, too, the big welcome and those empty roads in the east, both of which take you back 40 years.

·») And 40 years on you may well look back to 1991 and remember the first of your 40 annual holidays in the wonderful Shires of Middle England!

·») **Please refer to the colour maps at the back of this guide for all places with accommodation listings.**

Where to go, what to see

Penguins at Skegness Natureland Marine Zoo & Seal Sanctuary

Chatsworth
Bakewell, Derbyshire DE4 1PP
☎ Baslow (0246) 582204
Built between 1687 and 1707.
Gardens laid out by 'Capability'
Brown. Collection of pictures,
books, drawings and furniture.

Lincoln Cathedral
Lincoln, Lincolnshire
☎ Lincoln (0522) 544544
Magnificent triple-towered
cathedral on hilltop site, with
Norman west front, Angel Choir
(1280), Wren library (1674).
Coffee shop.

Skegness Natureland Marine Zoo and Seal Sanctuary
North Parade, The
Promenade, Skegness,
Lincolnshire PE25 1DB
☎ Skegness (0754) 4345
Seal sanctuary and hospital,
penguins, aquarium, crocodiles,
snakes, terrapins, scorpions,
butterfly house.

The Tales of Robin Hood
30-38 Maid Marian Way,
Nottingham, Nottinghamshire
NG1 6GF
☎ Nottingham (0602) 414414/
483284
Join the world's greatest medieval
adventure and hide out in the
Sheriff's eerie cave. Ride
through the magical Greenwood
and play the Silver Arrow game.

Wirksworth Heritage Centre
Crown Yard, Market Place,
Wirksworth, Derbyshire
DE4 4ET
☎ Wirksworth (0629) 825225
Interpretative displays of town's
past, present and future. Café
and working smithy. Crown
Yard also holds a silversmith's
workshop and cabinet maker's
workshop.

Sherwood Forest Visitor Centre and Country Park
Edwinstowe, Mansfield,
Nottinghamshire NG21 9HN
☎ Mansfield (0623) 823202

450 acres of ancient Sherwood
Forest containing the Major
Oak. Robin Hood exhibition,
slide shows, films, talks, shop.

Belvoir Castle
Belvoir, Nr. Grantham,
Lincolnshire NG32 1PD
☎ Grantham (0476) 870262
Seat of the Dukes of Rutland
since Henry VIII's time,
rebuilt in 1816. Notable
pictures, state rooms and
museum of 17th/21st Lancers.

The Lace Hall
High Pavement, Nottingham,
Nottinghamshire NG1 1HN
☎ Nottingham (0602) 484221
The Story of Nottingham Lace
exhibition, including audio-
visual presentation, with lace
shops and coffee shop, in fine
converted chapel.

The Canal Museum
Stoke Bruerne, Towcester,
Northamptonshire NN12 7SE
☎ Roade (0604) 862229
Traditional decorated items,
model boat horse, cabin replica,
boat engines, photographs
illustrating the history of
Britain's canals and waterways.

Great Central Railway
Great Central Road,
Loughborough, Leicestershire
LE11 1RW
☎ Loughborough (0509) 230726
Steam railway operating
through over five miles of
attractive countryside. Museum
and depot. Station buffet and
dining car.

Farmworld
Stoughton Farm Park, Gartree
Road, Oadby, Leicester,
Leicestershire LE2 2FB
☎ Leicester (0533) 710355
Modern milking parlour, rare
breeds, working forge, pottery,
Edwardian ale house, museum,
exhibits and displays, woodland
walks, lake, garden centre, gift
shop, refreshments.

Althorp House
Althorp, Northampton,
Northamptonshire NN7 4HG
☎ Northampton (0604)
769368
Home of Earl and Countess
Spencer, built by Sir John
Spencer in 1508, altered by
Henry Holland in 1790, with
fine pictures, porcelain and
furniture. Tea room.

Rockingham Castle
Rockingham, Market
Harborough, Leicestershire
LE16 8TH
☎ Rockingham (0536) 770240
Elizabethan house within walls
of Norman castle. Fine
pictures. Extensive views and
gardens with roses and ancient
yew hedge.

Boston Guildhall Museum
South Street, Boston,
Lincolnshire PE21 6HT
☎ Boston (0205) 365954
15th C building with cells where
early Pilgrim Fathers were
imprisoned in 1607. Pictures,
local history collections, regular
special exhibitions.

Discover the history of Britain's canals and waterways at the Canal Museum, Stoke Bruerne

Make a date for...

Spalding Flower Festival and Parade
Spalding, Lincolnshire
4 − 6 May

Medieval Jousting Tournaments
Belvoir Castle, Belvoir, Leicestershire
26 − 27 May, 25 − 26 August

Stamford Shakespeare Company Season
Rutland Theatre, Tolethorpe Hall, Little Casterton, Stamford, Lincolnshire
14 June − 24 August

Buxton International Festival
Various venues, Buxton, Derbyshire
*20 July − 10 August**

Bakewell Show
The Showground, Coombe Road, Bakewell, Derbyshire
7 − 8 August

Nottingham Goose Fair
Forest Recreation Ground, Nottingham, Nottinghamshire
3 − 5 October

World Conker Championship
Village Green, Ashton, Nr. Oundle, Northamptonshire
13 October

Lincoln Christmas Market
Bailgate and Castle Square, Lincoln, Lincolnshire
12 − 15 December

* *Provisional dates only*

Find out more

Further information about holidays and attractions in the Shires of Middle England is available from:
East Midlands Tourist Board,
Exchequergate, Lincoln
LN2 1PZ.
☎ (0522) 531521.

These publications are available from the East Midlands Tourist Board (prices include post and packing):

Your Guide to the Shires of Middle England (places to visit) £1

Shires of Middle England Leisure Map £2.50

Peak District Holidays 95p

Robin Hood Holiday Country 95p

The Village Green of England 95p

Lincolnshire's Coast, Wolds and Fens 95p

Also available is an *Events List* (free, but large stamped and addressed envelope would be appreciated)

Places to stay

•》 Accommodation entries in this regional section are listed in alphabetical order of place name, and then in alphabetical order of establishment.

•》 The map references refer to the colour maps towards the end of the guide. The first figure is the map number; the letter and figure which follow indicate the grid reference on the map.

•》 The symbols at the end of each accommodation entry give information about services and facilities. A 'key' to these symbols is inside the back cover flap, which can be kept open for easy reference.

ALDWARK

Derbyshire
Map ref 4B2

5m SW. Matlock

Tithe Farm M
COMMENDED
Grange Mill, Aldwark, Via Derby, DE4 4HX
☎ Carsington (062 985) 263
Peacefully situated, within 10 miles of Matlock, Bakewell, Ashbourne, the dales and historic houses. Fresh produce and home baking are a speciality.
Bedrooms: 3 twin.
Bathrooms: 1 public.
Bed & breakfast: £26 double.
Half board: £21 daily, £126 weekly.
Evening meal 7pm (l.o. 6pm).
Parking for 6.
Open April-October.

Individual proprietors have supplied all details of accommodation. Although we do check for accuracy, we advise you to confirm prices and other information at the time of booking.

ASHBOURNE

Derbyshire
Map ref 4B2

Market town on the edge of the Peak District National Park and an excellent centre for walking. Its impressive church with 212-ft spire stands in an untouched old street. Ashbourne is well-known for gingerbread and its Shrovetide football match.
Tourist Information Centre ☎ (0335) 43666

Bentley Brook M
COMMENDED
Fenny Bentley, Nr. Ashbourne, DE6 1LF
☎ Thorpe Cloud (033 529) 278
A traditional owner-operated country inn in the Peak District National Park, close to Dovedale, Alton Towers and Chatsworth.
Bedrooms: 1 single, 4 double & 2 twin, 1 family room.
Bathrooms: 4 private, 2 public.
Bed & breakfast: £30-£35 single, £45-£50 double.
Half board: £41.50-£46.50 daily, £175-£190 weekly.
Lunch available.
Evening meal 7pm (l.o. 9.30pm).
Parking for 60.
Credit: Access, Visa.
Display advertisement appears on page 300.

Compton Guest House M
27-31 Compton, Ashbourne, DE6 1BX
☎ (0335) 43100
Centrally placed in the historic market town of Ashbourne, an ideal base for walking or touring the Peak District.
Bedrooms: 3 double & 2 twin, 1 family room.
Bathrooms: 1 private, 1 public.
Bed & breakfast: £15-£17 single, £26-£30 double.
Half board: £19-£23 daily.
Lunch available.
Evening meal 6.30pm (l.o. 6pm).
Parking for 1.

Stone Cottage M
Listed COMMENDED
Green Lane, Clifton, Ashbourne, DE6 2BL
☎ Ashbourne (0335) 43377
Charming 19th C cottage in the Derbyshire Dales. All bedrooms have colour TV and tea making facilities. Near Dovedale, Chatsworth, Haddon Hall and Alton Towers.
Bedrooms: 1 double, 2 family rooms.
Bathrooms: 1 private, 1 public.
Bed & breakfast: £18-£24 single, £27-£36 double.
Half board: £20.50-£25 daily, £140-£170 weekly.
Evening meal 6pm (l.o. 7.30pm).
Parking for 4.

White Lion Hotel
Buxton Hill, Ashbourne, DE6 1EX
☎ (0335) 46158
A family-run hotel with a comfortable atmosphere, and traditional English food and ales.
Bedrooms: 4 double & 2 twin, 1 family room.
Bathrooms: 4 private, 1 public; 1 private shower.
Bed & breakfast: £18-£25 single, £34-£38 double.
Lunch available.
Evening meal 7pm (l.o. 10pm).
Parking for 8.
Credit: Access, Visa.

ASHBY-DE-LA-ZOUCH

Leicestershire
Map ref 4B3

Lovely market town with late 15th C church, impressive ruined 15th C castle, an interesting small museum and a wide, sloping main street with Georgian buildings. Twycross Zoo is nearby.
Tourist Information Centre ☎ (0530) 411767

The Cedars
APPROVED
60 Burton Road, Ashby-de-la-Zouch, LE6 5LN
☎ (0530) 412017
A substantial Victorian house with a pleasant garden and large rooms, within walking distance of the town centre, castle, pubs and restaurants.

Bedrooms: 4 single, 2 double & 3 twin, 1 family room.
Bathrooms: 5 private, 2 public.
Bed & breakfast: £12-£15 single, £24-£30 double.
Parking for 12.
ᗱ ᵶ 🕭 ⑩ Ⅴ ᵺ ⑪ ▥ ⌂
& ⨝

ASHFORD-IN-THE-WATER
Derbyshire
Map ref 4B2

2m NW. Bakewell
Limestone village in attractive surroundings of the Peak District approached by 3 bridges over the River Wye. There is an annual well-dressing ceremony and the village was well-known in the 18th C for its black marble quarries.

The Ashford Hotel and Restaurant
ᨌᨌᨌ COMMENDED
Church Street, Ashford-in-the-Water, Near Bakewell, DE4 1QB
☎ Bakewell (0629) 812725
A traditional and friendly country hotel where you will receive personal attention throughout your stay. There are open fires and a wealth of oak beams. An ideal location to relax.
Bedrooms: 1 single, 5 double & 1 twin.
Bathrooms: 7 private.
Bed & breakfast: £45-£55 single, £65-£75 double.
Lunch available.
Evening meal 7pm (l.o. 9.30pm).
Parking for 45.
Credit: Access, Visa.
ᗱ ᵶ ℂ ⑩ ᗑ ᵹ ᵺ Ⅴ ᵺ
▥ ᵲ ᵺ ᵹ ⨝ ᵬ SP ⨝

Riverside Country House Hotel ⋒
ᨌᨌᨌᨌ COMMENDED
Fennel Street, Ashford-in-the-Water, Bakewell, DE4 1QF
☎ Bakewell (0629) 814275
This 17th C manor house has its own river frontage and an acre of garden which supplies home produce. Inside is a panelled bar, antiques, four-poster beds and an inglenook fireplace with log fires.
Bedrooms: 5 double & 2 twin.
Bathrooms: 7 private.
Bed & breakfast: £65-£68 single, £76-£85 double.
Lunch available.
Evening meal 7pm (l.o. 9.30pm).

Parking for 25.
Credit: Access, Visa, Amex.
ᗱ ᵶ ℂ ⑩ ᗑ ᵹ ᵺ Ⅴ ᵻ
ᵺ ⑪ ⦿ ▥ ᵲ ᵺ ⨝ ᵺ ᵹ ⨝
ᵬ SP ⨝

BAKEWELL
Derbyshire
Map ref 4B2

Pleasant market town, famous for its pudding. It is set in beautiful countryside on the River Wye and is an excellent centre for exploring the Derbyshire Dales, the Peak District National Park, Chatsworth and Haddon Hall.
Tourist Information Centre ☎ *(0629) 813227*

Croft Country House Hotel ⋒
ᨌᨌᨌ COMMENDED
Main Street, Great Longstone, Bakewell, DE4 1TF
☎ Great Longstone (062 987) 278
An interesting English country house in 4 acres in this beautiful Peak Park village. Freshly-cooked food with traditional hospitality.
Bedrooms: 1 single, 7 double & 1 twin.
Bathrooms: 7 private, 2 public.
Bed & breakfast: £44-£48 single, £55-£71 double.
Half board: £43-£52 daily, £234-£256 weekly.
Evening meal 7.30pm (l.o. 8.30pm).
Parking for 20.
Open March-December.
Credit: Access, Visa.
ᗱ ⑩ ᵹ ᵹ Ⅴ ᵺ ⑪ ⊞
▥ ᵲ ᵺ ᵹ ⋃ ᵹ ⨝ ⨝ SP
⨝

Merlin House
ᨌᨌ
Ashford Lane, Monsal Head, Bakewell, DE4 1NL
☎ Great Longstone (062 987) 475
A small private hotel set in its own attractive garden amid outstanding scenery, in the heart of the Peak District National Park. Close to Bakewell, Chatsworth and Haddon Hall.
Bedrooms: 1 single, 4 double & 1 twin.
Bathrooms: 6 private.
Bed & breakfast: £21 single, £38-£42 double.

Evening meal 7.15pm (l.o. midday).
Parking for 6.
Open March-October.
ᵹ ᵹ ᵺ ⑪ ▥ ᵹ ⨝ ⨝

Milford House Hotel ⋒
ᨌᨌᨌ
Mill Street, Bakewell, DE4 1DA
☎ (0629) 812130
Once owned by Robert Cross, the water engineer for the 4 Arkwright cotton mills, the house retains much of his work on it.
Bedrooms: 2 single, 5 double & 5 twin.
Bathrooms: 12 private, 1 public.
Bed & breakfast: £28.75-£34 single, £52-£65 double.
Half board: £40-£48 daily, £260-£300 weekly.
Lunch available.
Evening meal 7pm (l.o. 7.30pm).
Parking for 24.
Open March-November.
ᗱ 10 ⑩ ᵹ ᵻ Ⅴ ᵺ ᵺ ⌂
ᵹ ⨝ ⨝ ⨝

Rutland Arms Hotel ⋒
ᨌᨌᨌ
The Square, Bakewell, DE4 1BT
☎ (0629) 812812
Telex 377077 MINEX G
This is the hotel in which the famous Bakewell Pudding was accidentally created and Jane Austen is alleged to have stayed.
Bedrooms: 9 single, 9 double & 17 twin, 1 family room.
Bathrooms: 36 private.
Bed & breakfast: £42-£51 single, £59-£69 double.
Half board: £45-£55 daily, £285-£330 weekly.
Lunch available.
Evening meal 7pm (l.o. 9.30pm).
Parking for 37.
Credit: Access, Visa, Diners, Amex.
ᗱ ᵶ ℂ ⑩ ᗑ ᵹ ᵻ Ⅴ ᵺ
▥ ᵲ ᵺ ᵹ ⨝ ᵬ SP ⨝ ⊤
⑮ Display advertisement appears on page 300.

Classifications and quality commendations were correct at the time of going to press but are subject to change. Please check at the time of booking.

BAMFORD
Derbyshire
Map ref 4B2

12m NE. Buxton
Village in the Peak District near the Upper Derwent Reservoirs of Ladybower, Derwent and Howden. An excellent centre for walking.

The Snake Pass Inn
Ashopton Woodlands, Bamford, Via Sheffield, S30 2BJ
☎ Hope Valley (0433) 51480
An 18th C coaching house set in the beautiful Ashopton Woodlands of the Peak District. All bedrooms en-suite. Satellite TV.
Bedrooms: 2 double & 4 twin, 1 family room.
Bathrooms: 7 private.
Bed & breakfast: £27-£30 single, £45-£50 double.
Half board: £33-£36 daily, £230-£252 weekly.
Lunch available.
Evening meal 6pm (l.o. 9pm).
Parking for 35.
Credit: Access, Visa.
ᗱ ᵶ ⑩ ᗑ ᵹ ᵻ Ⅴ ᵺ ᵺ ▥
ᵲ ᵹ ⨝ ᵬ SP ⨝

BASLOW
Derbyshire
Map ref 4B2

Small village on the River Derwent with a stone-built toll-house and a packhorse bridge. Chatsworth, home of the Duke of Devonshire, is nearby.

Cavendish Hotel ⋒
ᨌᨌᨌᨌ
Baslow, DE4 1SP
☎ (0246) 582311
Fax (0246) 582312
Telex 547150 CAVTEL G
Set on Chatsworth Estate in the heart of the Peak District National Park, this famous 18th C fishing inn - formerly the Peacock - has been extensively renovated.
Bedrooms: 11 double & 12 twin, 1 family room.
Bathrooms: 24 private.
Bed & breakfast: £65-£75 single, £85-£100 double.
Lunch available.
Evening meal 7pm (l.o. 11pm).
Parking for 40.
Credit: Access, Visa, Diners, Amex.
ᗱ ᵺ ᵶ ℂ ⑩ ᗑ ᵹ ᵻ Ⅴ
ᵻ ᵺ ⦿ ▥ ᵲ ᵺ ᵹ ᵹ ⨝
ᵬ SP ⊤

BEESTON

Nottinghamshire
Map ref 4C2

Brackley House Hotel M
♛♛♛

31 Elm Avenue, Beeston,
Nottingham, NG9 1BU
☎ (0602) 251787 & 256739
*The hotel incorporates
Hildegard's German
Restaurant and Wine Bar, in a
Victorian setting with antique
furniture and sales of antique
jewellery in foyer. Evening
meals are not served on
Sunday.*
Bedrooms: 4 single, 3 double
& 7 twin, 1 family room.
Bathrooms: 3 private,
1 public; 7 private showers.
Bed & breakfast: £30-£40
single, £50-£60 double.
Half board: £42.50-£52.50
daily.
Evening meal 6pm (l.o.
8.30pm).
Parking for 15.
Credit: Access, Visa, Amex.
ঌ6 ℄ ◻ ᠍ ⓥ ◿ ⁊ ⅏ ⍐ ▾
◹ ☀ ✕ ⊻ ⊁ ▥ ⌑

BELTON

Leicestershire
Map ref 4C3

6m W. Loughborough

The George Hotel
♛♛♛

Market Place, Belton,
Loughborough, LE12 9UH
☎ Coalville (0530) 222426
*An 18th C coaching inn with
an a la carte restaurant and
real ales. Easy access to
Ashby, Loughborough,
Donington Race Track, East
Midlands Airport and the M1.*
Bedrooms: 4 single, 4 double
& 9 twin, 3 family rooms.
Bathrooms: 13 private,
1 public; 1 private shower.
Bed & breakfast: £22.95-
£34.95 single, £39.90-£49
double.
Half board: £27.95-£50 daily.
Lunch available.
Evening meal 7pm (l.o.
11pm).
Parking for 25.
Credit: Access, Visa, Diners,
Amex.
ঌ♒ ℄ ◻ ⌗ ᠍ ⓥ ◿
⍐ ▾ ⟍ ⊕ ⌑

**The symbols are
explained on the
flap inside the
back cover.**

BELTON

Lincolnshire
Map ref 3A1

3m NE. Grantham

Belton Woods Hotel and Country Club M

Belton, Near Grantham,
NG32 2LN
☎ Grantham (0476) 590924
*New development of 96
bedrooms, and suites, 2
restaurants, luxury leisure club,
2 golf courses, driving range,
tennis courts and fishing. Due
to open on 1st March 1991.*
Bedrooms: 32 double &
64 twin, 4 family rooms.
Bathrooms: 100 private.
Bed & breakfast: £80 single,
£115 double.
Evening meal 6.30pm (l.o.
9.30pm).
Parking for 366.
Credit: Access, Visa, C.Bl.,
Diners, Amex.
ঌ ♒ ⬀ ◻ ⌗ ᠍ ⓥ ◿
● ▥ ⍐ ⌗ ☭ ☎ ↻ ⊍ ⌁
☀ ᗇ ⬥ ▥ ⊺
⑳ Display advertisement
appears on page 576.

BLYTH

Nottinghamshire
Map ref 4C2

Village on the old Great
North Road. A busy
staging post in Georgian
times with many
examples of Georgian
Gothic architecture. The
remains of a Norman
Benedictine priory survive
as the parish church.

The Charnwood M

Sheffield Road, Blyth, Near
Worksop, S81 8HF
☎ Worksop (0909) 591610
*On the A634 Sheffield road
between the village of Blyth
and Oldcotes, standing in 3
acres of landscaped gardens
with a natural wildlife pond.*
Bedrooms: 3 single, 11 double
& 6 twin.
Bathrooms: 20 private.
Bed & breakfast: £40-£60
single, £50-£70 double.
Half board: £53.50-£73.50
daily.
Lunch available.
Evening meal 7pm (l.o.
9.45pm).
Parking for 75.
Credit: Access, Visa, Diners,
Amex.
ঌ♒ ⬀ ℄ ◻ ⌗ ⬀ ᠍ ⓥ ◿
⍐ ▾ ⍐ ☀ ✕ ⊁ ▥ ⊺

BOSTON

Lincolnshire
Map ref 3A1

Historic town famous for
its church tower, the
Boston Stump, 272 ft
high. Still a busy port, the
town is full of interest and
has links with Boston
Massachusetts through
the Pilgrim Fathers. The
cells where they were
imprisoned can be seen
in the medieval Guildhall.
*Tourist Information
Centre* ☎ (0205) 356656

Park Lea Guest House

85 Norfolk Street, Boston,
PE21 6PE
☎ (0205) 356309
*In a conservation area
overlooking the central park
within easy walking distance of
the town centre and close to
places of historical interest,
particularly to US tourists.
Coarse fishing available
nearby.*
Bedrooms: 1 double & 3 twin,
1 family room.
Bathrooms: 2 public.
Bed & breakfast: max. £12.50
single, max. £25 double.
Evening meal 6pm (l.o. 4pm).
Parking for 6.
ঌ♒ ♒ ⬀ ⅏ ᠍ ⓥ ◿ ⅏
⌓ ✕ ▥

BOURNE

Lincolnshire
Map ref 3A1

Market town with remains
of a Norman abbey
incorporated into the
parish church. The
birthplace of Lord
Burghley.

Angel Hotel M
♛♛♛

Market Place, Bourne,
PE10 9AE
☎ (0778) 422346
*This 16th C coaching inn in the
heart of a market town was
once the offices of the Collector
of Taxes. Good centre for golf,
fishing, wildlife and flower
gardens.*
Bedrooms: 4 single, 5 double
& 4 twin, 1 family room.
Bathrooms: 14 private.
Bed & breakfast: £18-£32
single, £36-£50 double.
Lunch available.
Evening meal 7pm (l.o.
9.30pm).
Credit: Access, Visa, Amex.
ঌ ⌗ ℄ ◻ ◻ ⬀ ᠍ ⓥ ⅏
⅏ ⍐ ✕ ⬥ ▥ ⊕ ⊺

BUXTON

Derbyshire
Map ref 4B2

The highest market town
in England and one of the
oldest spas, with an
elegant Crescent,
Micrarium, Poole's
Cavern, Opera House and
attractive Pavilion
Gardens. An excellent
centre for exploring the
Peak District.
*Tourist Information
Centre* ☎ (0298) 25106

Alison Park Hotel M
♛♛♛

3 Temple Road, Buxton,
SK17 9BA
☎ (0298) 22473
*Owner managed hotel set in its
own grounds near all
amenities. Facilities for
disabled, en-suite bedrooms,
TV, telephones.*
Bedrooms: 7 single, 4 double
& 8 twin, 2 family rooms.
Bathrooms: 11 private,
3 public.
Bed & breakfast: £21-£23
single, £42-£46 double.
Half board: £31-£38 daily.
Lunch available.
Evening meal 6.45pm (l.o.
8pm).
Parking for 20.
Credit: Access, Visa.
ঌ♒ ⬀ ℄ ⬀ ⅏ ᠍ ⓥ ◿ ⅏ ⬦
▥ ⅏ ⍐ ⬥ ᠍ ⓥ ◿ ▥

Brunswick Guest House M
♛♛ APPROVED

31 St. John's Road, Buxton,
SK17 6XG
☎ (0298) 71727
*We overlook the Serpentine
Gardens and the River Wye.
We are 2 minutes from the
Opera House, Pavilion
Gardens and a swimming pool.
Ideal base for walking in the
Peak District.*
Bedrooms: 1 double & 1 twin,
1 family room.
Bathrooms: 2 private,
1 public; 1 private shower.
Bed & breakfast: £18 single,
£30-£36 double.
Half board: £23 daily, £200-
£226 weekly.
Parking for 5.
ঌ♒ ℄ ⬀ ⅏ ᠍ ⓥ ◿ ⍐
⅏ ☀ ✕ ⬥ ⊺ ▥

Buckingham Hotel M
♛♛♛♛ COMMENDED

1 Burlington Road, Buxton,
SK17 9AS
☎ (0298) 70481
⟲ Consort

A long-established, owner-managed, traditional hotel on a broad, tree-lined avenue overlooking the Pavilion Gardens.
Bedrooms: 4 single, 10 double & 13 twin, 3 family rooms.
Bathrooms: 30 private.
Bed & breakfast: from £48 single, from £65 double.
Half board: from £62 daily, from £275 weekly.
Lunch available.
Evening meal 7.30pm (l.o. 9.30pm).
Parking for 20.
Credit: Access, Visa, Diners, Amex.

Buxton View ⚊

74 Corbar Road, Buxton, SK17 6RJ
☎ (0298) 79222
Guesthouse built from local stone, offers a friendly and relaxed atmosphere. In a quiet area with a commanding view over the town and surrounding hills, only a few minutes' walk from the town's amenities.
Bedrooms: 1 single, 1 double & 2 twin, 1 family room.
Bathrooms: 5 private.
Bed & breakfast: £18-£20 single, £30-£32 double.
Half board: £24-£29 daily, £150-£180 weekly.
Evening meal 7pm (l.o. 8pm).
Parking for 7.
Open March-November.

Coningsby ⚊ COMMENDED

6 Macclesfield Road, Buxton, SK17 9AH
☎ (0298) 26735
A comfortable detached Victorian house of character in a pleasant area, close to the Pavilion Gardens and the many other attractions of this splendid spa resort. Non-smokers only please.
Bedrooms: 2 double & 1 twin.
Bathrooms: 3 private.
Bed & breakfast: £30-£36 double.
Half board: £24.50-£28.50 daily.
Evening meal 6pm (l.o. 4pm).
Parking for 6.

The Grosvenor House Hotel ⚊

1 Broad Walk, Buxton, SK17 6JE
☎ (0298) 72439

Family-run hotel with attractively refurbished rooms, overlooking the opera house and Pavilion Gardens. Quiet, friendly and relaxed atmosphere.
Bedrooms: 5 double & 1 twin, 2 family rooms.
Bathrooms: 8 private.
Bed & breakfast: £35-£45 single, £50-£70 double.
Half board: £37.50-£57.50 daily, £225-£345 weekly.
Lunch available.
Evening meal 7.30pm (l.o. 8.30pm).
Parking for 4.
Credit: Access, Visa.

Hawthorn Farm Guest House ⚊

Fairfield Road, Buxton, SK17 7ED
☎ (0298) 23230
A 400-year-old ex-farmhouse which has been in the family for 10 generations. Full English breakfast.
Bedrooms: 3 single, 4 double & 3 twin, 2 family rooms.
Bathrooms: 2 public.
Bed & breakfast: £14-£15 single, £28-£30 double.
Parking for 15.
Open April-October.

Lakenham Guest House ⚊

11 Burlington Road, Buxton, SK17 9AL
☎ (0298) 79209
Elegant Victorian house in own grounds overlooking Pavilion Gardens. Furnished in Victorian manner and offering personal service in a friendly relaxed atmosphere.
Bedrooms: 2 double & 2 twin, 2 family rooms.
Bathrooms: 5 private, 1 public.
Bed & breakfast: from £20.70 single, from £32.20 double.
Half board: from £25.10 daily, from £155.20 weekly.
Evening meal 6pm (l.o. midday).
Parking for 6.
Credit: Access.

Lee Wood Hotel ⚊

The Park, Buxton, SK17 6TQ
☎ (0298) 23002 Telex 669848 LEWOOD
🅡 Best Western

A Georgian building facing due south in its own grounds which, although fully modernised, retains its original charm.
Bedrooms: 8 single, 16 double & 11 twin, 2 family rooms.
Bathrooms: 37 private.
Bed & breakfast: £52-£60 single, £64-£72 double.
Half board: from £44 daily.
Lunch available.
Evening meal 7.15pm (l.o. 9.30pm).
Parking for 50.
Credit: Access, Visa, Diners, Amex.

Netherdale Guest House ⚊ COMMENDED

16 Green Lane, Buxton, SK17 9DP
☎ (0298) 23896
A guest house in a quiet, central residential area offering mostly en-suite facilities and ground floor accommodation.
Bedrooms: 2 single, 5 double & 2 twin, 2 family rooms.
Bathrooms: 8 private, 1 public; 1 private shower.
Bed & breakfast: £15-£16 single, £35-£36 double.
Half board: £24-£27 daily.
Evening meal 6pm (l.o. 6pm).
Parking for 14.

Old Hall Hotel ⚊ COMMENDED

The Square, Buxton, SK17 6BD
☎ (0298) 22841
This historic hotel, restaurant and wine bar is run by the proprietors and offers warm and friendly service. Located opposite the restored Opera House and 23 acres of parkland.
Bedrooms: 9 single, 17 double & 12 twin.
Bathrooms: 32 private, 2 public.
Bed & breakfast: £25-£45 single, £38-£60 double.
Half board: £48-£75 daily.
Lunch available.
Evening meal 6pm (l.o. 11pm).
Parking for 10.
Credit: Access, Visa, Amex.

> **Please mention this guide when making a booking.**

Portland Hotel and Park Restaurant ⚊

32 St. John's Road, Buxton, SK17 6XQ
☎ (0298) 71493/72453
A comfortable, family-run, Peak District hotel, with new conservatory restaurant. Opposite Buxton's Pavilion Gardens and swimming pool.
Bedrooms: 3 single, 11 double & 11 twin.
Bathrooms: 25 private.
Bed & breakfast: £50-£60 double.
Half board: £42-£45 daily.
Lunch available.
Evening meal 6.45pm (l.o. 9pm).
Parking for 17.
Credit: Access, Visa.

Quarnford Lodge ⚊

Quarnford, Buxton, SK17 0TL
☎ Buxton (0298) 25565
Country house of character, with restaurant, 4 miles from Buxton, 8 miles from Leek on A53. In the Peak District National Park, with lovely views.
Bedrooms: 1 single, 3 double & 2 twin.
Bathrooms: 2 private, 2 public.
Bed & breakfast: £40-£48 double.
Half board: £34-£37 daily.
Lunch available.
Evening meal 7pm (l.o. 9pm).
Parking for 18.
Credit: Access, Visa.

Rock Guest House ⚊

1 Rock Terrace, Buxton, SK17 6HN
☎ (0298) 79724
Centrally located in higher Buxton. Pavilion Gardens, the opera house and shopping are all nearby. The Peak District National Park is 10 minutes' drive away.
Bedrooms: 3 single, 1 double & 2 twin, 1 family room.
Bathrooms: 3 public.
Bed & breakfast: £12 single, £24 double.
Half board: from £17.50 daily, from £122.50 weekly.
Evening meal 6pm (l.o. 4pm).

BUXTON
Continued

Sevenways Guest House M
♛♛
1 College Road, Buxton,
SK17 9DZ
☎ (0298) 24293
Grade II listed, family-run, close to all amenities. All rooms en-suite. Car park. Children welcome. Non-smokers only please.
Bedrooms: 1 twin, 4 family rooms.
Bathrooms: 5 private.
Bed & breakfast: £22.50-£27.50 single, £35-£40 double.
Parking for 8.
Credit: Access, Visa.
⌂⊞⌂⌂☎⊎✂⊟⊠▦✕▦▦

Westminster Hotel M
21 Broad Walk, Buxton,
SK17 6JR
☎ (0298) 23929
A private family hotel overlooking the Pavilion Gardens and close to the town, shops and opera house. Personal service and a varied menu. An ideal base for exploring the Peak District.
Bedrooms: 5 double & 5 twin, 2 family rooms.
Bathrooms: 12 private.
Bed & breakfast: from £22 single, from £36 double.
Half board: from £25.50 daily, from £160 weekly.
Evening meal 6.30pm (l.o. 3pm).
Parking for 14.
Open February-December.
Credit: Access, Visa, Amex.
⌂⊞⌂⌂☎🅟⊡⊠⊟▦▦⌂▼✕▦▦⌂

CASTLE BYTHAM
Lincolnshire
Map ref 3A1

8m N. Stamford
Attractive village with castle earthworks dating from Saxon times and a parish church, churchyard and several houses of interest. It also has a duck pond and stream.

Bank House
♛♛ HIGHLY COMMENDED
Cumberland Gardens, Castle Bytham, Near Grantham,
NG3 4SQ
☎ Stamford (0780) 410523

High standard accommodation in a modern private house. Restful garden with panoramic views, on the edge of historic conservation village. 3 miles off the A1, north of Stamford. Evening meals by arrangement.
Bedrooms: 2 twin.
Bathrooms: 2 private.
Bed & breakfast: £20-£25 single, £40-£50 double.
Half board: £27.50-£35 daily. Evening meal 7pm (l.o. 8pm).
Parking for 4.
⌂⊞⌶☎⊡▼⊟📺▦⌂∪🅟✿✕▦

CASTLE DONINGTON
Leicestershire
Map ref 4C3

A Norman castle once stood here. The world's largest collection of single-seater racing cars is displayed at Donington Park alongside the racing circuit, and an Aeropark Visitor Centre can be seen at nearby East Midlands International Airport.

Delven Hotel M
♛
12 Delven Lane, Castle Donington, Derby DE7 2LJ
☎ Derby (0332) 810153/850507
A small, family-run hotel, 1 mile from Donington Race Track and 2 miles from East Midlands Airport.
Bedrooms: 2 double & 4 twin, 1 family room.
Bathrooms: 3 public; 3 private showers.
Bed & breakfast: £15-£16.50 single, £28-£35 double.
Half board: £19-£25 daily, £133-£175 weekly.
Evening meal 5pm (l.o. 9pm).
Parking for 5.
Credit: Access, Visa.
⌂⊞⌂⌶▼⊟⊙▦▦⊟

Donington Manor Hotel
♛♛♛♛ COMMENDED
High Street, Castle Donington, Derby, DE7 2PP
☎ Derby (0332) 810253
Telex 934999
This 18th C coaching inn with modern bedroom extensions has French and English menus, is 2 miles from the M1 junction 24 and is close to Donington Park motor circuit and East Midlands Airport.
Bedrooms: 17 single, 10 double & 7 twin, 3 family rooms.

Bathrooms: 35 private; 2 private showers.
Bed & breakfast: £40-£60 single, £50-£70 double.
Half board: from £49 daily.
Lunch available.
Evening meal 7pm (l.o. 9.30pm).
Parking for 60.
Credit: Access, Visa, Diners, Amex.
⌂⊞⌂☎⊡⊠⊎🅟⊟▦📺⊙🍴✕▦▦⊟

The Donington Thistle Hotel M
East Midlands International Airport, Castle Donington, Derby DE7 2SH
☎ Derby (0332) 850700
Telex 377632
℗ Thistle
A modern hotel in pleasant rural surroundings, adjacent to East Midlands International Airport and easily accessible from the motorway network. Leisure centre includes indoor swimming pool, sauna and gym.
Bedrooms: 50 double & 56 twin, 4 family rooms.
Bathrooms: 110 private.
Bed & breakfast: from £75.75 single, from £100.50 double.
Lunch available.
Evening meal 7pm (l.o. 10.15pm).
Parking for 180.
Credit: Access, Visa, C.Bl., Diners, Amex.
⌂⊞⌂⊡⊠⊎🅟⊟▼✂⊟⊙▦⌂🍴♿🛏∪✿🆂🅿⊟

The Lady in Grey
♛♛♛
Wilne Lane, Shardlow, Derbyshire DE7 2HA
☎ Derby (0332) 792331
A delightful 100-year-old mansion in quiet surroundings just off the A6. Convenient for the East Midlands Airport and junction 24 of the M1.
Bedrooms: 3 single, 5 double & 1 twin.
Bathrooms: 9 private.
Bed & breakfast: £30-£37.50 single, £45-£47.50 double.
Lunch available.
Evening meal 7pm (l.o. 10pm).
Parking for 40.
Credit: Access, Visa, Diners, Amex.
⌂⊞⌂⊡⌂⊎🅟⊟▼⊟▦⌂✿✕▦▦🆂⊟

Morton House Hotel M
♛♛
78 Bondgate, Castle Donington, Derby DE7 2NR
☎ Derby (0332) 812415

A family-run private hotel with a comfortable atmosphere and a lounge bar, only 1.5 miles from both the M1, junction 24, and from the East Midlands Airport. Satellite TV available.
Bedrooms: 1 single, 2 double & 4 twin, 3 family rooms.
Bathrooms: 2 private, 2 public.
Bed & breakfast: £17-£21 single, £27-£32 double.
Half board: £22-£27 daily, from £130 weekly.
Evening meal 7pm (l.o. 8.30pm).
Parking for 10.
Credit: Access, Visa, Diners, Amex.
⌂⊟⊎🅟▼⊟▦⌂▦⊟

Park Farmhouse Hotel M
♛♛♛
Melbourne Road, Isley Walton, Castle Donington, Derby DE7 2RN
☎ Derby (0332) 862409
40-acre mixed farm. A half-timbered farmhouse dating back to the 1760s, in its own grounds. Old world charm, log fires, spacious rooms and a warm, friendly atmosphere.
Bedrooms: 1 single, 2 double & 3 twin, 3 family rooms.
Bathrooms: 6 private, 2 public.
Bed & breakfast: £29-£42 single, £39-£49 double.
Half board: £37-£50 daily, from £180 weekly.
Evening meal 6pm (l.o. 8pm).
Parking for 15.
Credit: Access, Visa, Diners, Amex.
⌂⊞⌂⊡⌂⊎🅟▼⊟▦⌂✿🆂▦⊟

Priest House Hotel M
♛♛♛
Kings Mills, Castle Donington, Derby, DE7 2RR
☎ Derby (0332) 810649
Telex 341995
℗ Inter
Former watermill in beautiful private woodland on River Trent. Real ales, 60 types of whisky, four-posters, log fires, peace and tranquillity.
Bedrooms: 2 single, 13 double & 17 twin, 2 family rooms.
Bathrooms: 34 private.
Bed & breakfast: £48-£60 single, £58-£80 double.
Lunch available.
Evening meal 7pm (l.o. 9.30pm).
Parking for 150.
Credit: Access, Visa, Diners, Amex.
⌂⊞⌂⌂☎⊡⊠⊎🅟▼✂⊟▦⌂🍴♿🏌✿🆂▦⊟

CASTLETON

Derbyshire
Map ref 4B2

5m W. Hathersage
Large village in a spectacular setting with a ruined Norman castle and 4 great show caverns, where the Blue John stone and lead were mined. One cavern offers a mile-long underground boat journey.

Kelsey's Swiss House M
🏶🏶🏶 COMMENDED

How Lane, Castleton, Via Sheffield, S. Yorkshire S30 2WJ
☎ Hope Valley (0433) 21098
Small, family-run hotel completely refurbished in 1990. All rooms en-suite with colour TV, tea/coffee facilities. Parking. Popular licensed restaurant. Hospitality assured.
Bedrooms: 1 single, 6 double & 2 twin, 1 family room.
Bathrooms: 10 private.
Bed & breakfast: £30-£33 double.
Half board: £25.50-£28.50 daily, £161-£183 weekly.
Evening meal 6.30pm (l.o. 8.30pm).
Parking for 15.
🛏🖂🖵💺🛈 Ⓥ ⇥ 🍽 ☎ 🍴
Ü ✕ 🏧 🏮 SP

Ye Olde Cheshire Cheese Inn
How Lane, Castleton, Via Sheffield, S. Yorkshire S30 2WJ
☎ Hope Valley (0433) 20330
A 17th C inn providing home-cooked food, set in the heart of the Peak District.
Bedrooms: 1 single, 3 double & 2 twin.
Bathrooms: 6 private.
Bed & breakfast: £22-£25 single, £37-£45 double.
Lunch available.
Evening meal 6pm (l.o. 10.50pm).
Parking for 100.
Credit: Access, Visa.
🛏🖵💺🛈 Ⓥ 🖩 🍴 🍷
Ü ✕ 🏧 🏮

Ye Olde Nags Head M
🏶🏶🏶 COMMENDED

Castleton, Via Sheffield, S. Yorkshire, S30 2WH
☎ Hope Valley (0433) 20248
An old world hotel in the beautiful countryside of the Peak District National Park, near the famous caverns and ancient Peveril Castle.
Bedrooms: 6 double & 2 twin.
Bathrooms: 8 private.

Bed & breakfast: £39.50-£62 single, £43-£78 double.
Lunch available.
Evening meal 7pm (l.o. 10pm).
Parking for 16.
Credit: Access, Visa, Diners, Amex.
🛏🖂💺🖵🗘 💺🛈 Ⓥ ⇥
🖩 🍴 Ü ✕ 🏮

CHAPEL ST. LEONARDS

Lincolnshire
Map ref 4D2

The Beachcomber Hotel M
Seabank Road, Chapel St. Leonards, Skegness, PE24 5QU
☎ Skegness (0754) 73818
Family-run seafront hotel offering quality home cooking, en-suite rooms, licensed bar, TV and tea/coffee facilities. Quiet village location.
Bedrooms: 1 single, 1 double & 2 twin, 2 family rooms.
Bathrooms: 4 private, 1 public.
Bed & breakfast: £14 single, £28 double.
Half board: £20 daily, £98-£125 weekly.
Evening meal 5.30pm (l.o. 6.30pm).
Parking for 20.
🛏🖂🖵🗘 💺 ⇥ 🖩
✕ 🏧 OAF 🔏 SP

CHESTERFIELD

Derbyshire
Map ref 4B2

Famous for the twisted spire of its parish church, Chesterfield has some fine modern buildings and excellent shopping facilities, including a large, traditional open-air market. Hardwick Hall and Bolsover Castle are nearby.
Tourist Information Centre ☎ (0246) 207777

Abbey Dale Hotel M
🏶🏶🏶🏶 COMMENDED

1 Cobden Road, Chesterfield, S40 4TD
☎ (0246) 277849
This hotel is run by resident proprietors. It is in a quiet location a few minutes' walk from the town centre.
Bedrooms: 5 single, 2 double & 3 twin, 1 family room.
Bathrooms: 9 private, 1 public.
Bed & breakfast: £23-£37 single, £42 double.

Half board: £31-£47 daily, £205-£233 weekly.
Evening meal 6.30pm (l.o. 8pm).
Parking for 12.
Credit: Access, Visa, Amex.
🛏🖂💺🖵🗘 💺🛈 Ⓥ ⇥
🖩 🍴 🛈 ✕ SP

Chesterfield Hotel M
Malkin Street, Chesterfield, S41 7UA
☎ (0246) 271141
Telex 547492 CHCH
Ⓖ Best Western
Centrally located hotel with a friendly, comfortable atmosphere close to historic buildings, museums and theatre. Ideal family base for touring Peak District National Park and Sherwood Forest. Full leisure facilities including large pool.
Bedrooms: 16 single, 34 double & 22 twin, 1 family room.
Bathrooms: 73 private.
Bed & breakfast: £34-£57 single, £54-£70 double.
Half board: from £34 daily.
Lunch available.
Evening meal 7pm (l.o. 10pm).
Parking for 160.
Credit: Access, Visa, Amex.
🛏🖵💺🖂🗘 💺🛈 Ⓥ ⇥ 📺
🔵 🖩 🍴 🗘 🐟 🔏
SP Ⓣ

The Gables Hotel
85-87 Newbold Road, Newbold, Chesterfield, S41 7PU
☎ (0246) 278695
A comfortable, family-run hotel with home-cooked food. Well placed for the town centre, local amenities and Derbyshire's Peak District.
Bedrooms: 9 single, 3 double & 2 twin, 2 family rooms.
Bathrooms: 5 private, 2 public.
Bed & breakfast: £19-£22.50 single, £34-£42 double.
Half board: £25.50-£28.50 daily, £153-£174.50 weekly.
Evening meal 5.30pm (l.o. 7.30pm).
Parking for 5.
🛏🖂🖵🗘 💺🛈 Ⓥ ⇥ 📺 🔵
🖩 🍴 ✷ SP 🏮

Sarnia House
62 Brockwell Lane, Chesterfield, S40 4EE
☎ (0246) 279391
A small, private guesthouse with guests' own garden and patio. Convenient for the town centre. Within a short drive of the Derbyshire countryside.
Bedrooms: 2 double & 1 twin.
Bathrooms: 2 private, 1 public.

Bed & breakfast: £12.50-£14.50 single, £25-£27 double.
Half board: £18.45-£20.45 daily, £125-£132 weekly.
Evening meal 6.30pm (l.o. 7pm).
Parking for 2.
Credit: Access, Visa.
🛏🖵💺 ⓊⓁ 🛈 Ⓥ ⇥ 🖩
⇥

Waterloo Hotel and Restaurant
Locko Road, Lower Pilsley, Chesterfield, S45 8DN
☎ (0246) 851011/851328
A family-run hotel 5 minutes from M1, within 20 minutes of Peak District, Chatsworth and many other attractions.
Bedrooms: 3 single, 3 double & 1 twin, 2 family rooms.
Bathrooms: 6 private, 1 public; 2 private showers.
Bed & breakfast: £15-£28 single, £30-£35 double.
Lunch available.
Evening meal 7pm (l.o. 10pm).
Parking for 50.
Credit: Access, Visa.
🛏💺🖵🗘 Ⓥ 🖩 🍴
✕ OAF SP

COALVILLE

Leicestershire
Map ref 4C3

Tourist Information Centre ☎ (0530) 35951 or 35952

Hermitage Park Hotel
Whitwick Road, Coalville, LE6 3FA
☎ (0530) 814814
A new, purpose built hotel with a health centre, bars and a restaurant contained in a 150 foot long glazed atrium.
Bedrooms: 20 double & 4 twin.
Bathrooms: 24 private.
Bed & breakfast: £35-£65 single, £40-£75 double.
Lunch available.
Evening meal 6pm (l.o. 10pm).
Parking for 48.
Credit: Access, Visa, Amex.
🛏🖂💺🖵🗘 💺🛈 Ⓥ ⅄
⇥ 🖩 🍴 🍷 🗘 🔏 SP

Half board prices shown are per person but in some cases may be based on double/twin occupancy.

CORBY

Northamptonshire
Map ref 3A1

New Town with modern shopping, sports and recreational facilities. On the outskirts is the 100-acre East Carlton Park with rural craft workshops. Rockingham Castle and the partly-roofed Kirby Hall with 17th C gardens are nearby.
Tourist Information Centre ☎ (0536) 402551 or 402552 (Saturdays)

Macallan
18-20 Lundy Avenue, Corby, NN18 8BU
☎ (0356) 61848
Close to the town centre, bus and rail stations. Easy access to the A1, M1 and M6.
Bedrooms: 2 single, 2 twin.
Bathrooms: 2 public.
Bed & breakfast: £12.50-£15 single, £24-£30 double.
Parking for 6.
🖵 ♢ ⓤ 🅻 ⓘ ✂ 🚪 🖃 ⓣⓥ 🛏 ⓜ 🕱

DAVENTRY

Northamptonshire
Map ref 2C1

Ancient market town with an Iron Age camp on Borough Hill, from which 7 counties can be seen. The town still retains some Georgian buildings and 2 old inns and there is a country park with a reservoir nearby.
Tourist Information Centre ☎ (0327) 300277

The Penguin Hotel M
👑👑👑👑👑
London Road, Daventry, NN11 4EN
☎ (0327) 77333 Telex 312228
Modern hotel recently refurbished with pleasant restaurant, bar and extensive conference facilities. 6 miles West of the M1 in a market town.
Bedrooms: 48 single, 68 double & 28 twin, 4 family rooms.
Bathrooms: 148 private.
Bed & breakfast: £65-£70 single, £85-£90 double.
Lunch available.
Evening meal 7pm (l.o. 9.30pm).
Parking for 120.

Credit: Access, Visa, Diners, Amex.
🖰 ☎ ⓑ 🖵 ♢ ⓘ ⓥ ✂ 🚪 ● 🅸 🛏 🖃 ⓣ 🕱 ⚓ 🅡 🔌 SP ⓣ

Staverton Park Hotel and Golf Complex M
Staverton, Near Daventry, NN11 6JT
☎ Daventry (0327) 705911
A modern, comfortable hotel in a 150-acre golf-course in rural Northamptonshire. Convenient for the M1, junctions 16 and 18. 1 mile west of Daventry on the A425.
Bedrooms: 5 double & 42 twin, 5 family rooms.
Bathrooms: 52 private.
Bed & breakfast: from £65 single, from £90 double.
Half board: from £80 daily.
Lunch available.
Evening meal 6pm (l.o. 9.30pm).
Parking for 100.
Credit: Access, Visa, Amex.
🖰 🚲 ☎ ⓑ 🖵 ♢ ⓘ ⓥ ✂ 🖃 ⓣⓥ 🖃 🛏 🖃 🅡 🔌 SP ⓣ

Windsor Lodge Hotel M
👑👑 APPROVED
5 New Street, Daventry, NN11 4BT
☎ (0327) 76533
A town centre hotel close to the market square and within easy reach of free parking. We offer comfortable accommodation and good food.
Bedrooms: 1 single, 2 double & 2 twin, 2 family rooms.
Bathrooms: 1 private, 1 public; 3 private showers.
Bed & breakfast: £27-£32 single, £38-£45 double.
Lunch available.
Evening meal 7.30pm (l.o. 9.30pm).
Credit: Access, Visa.
🖰 🖵 ♢ ⓘ ⓥ 🚪 ⓣⓥ 🖃 🛏 🖃 🔌 SP 🅜

Classifications and quality commendations were correct at the time of going to press but are subject to change. Please check at the time of booking.

We advise you to confirm your booking in writing.

DERBY

Derbyshire
Map ref 4B2

Modern industrial city but with ancient origins. There is a wide range of facilities including several museums (notably Royal Crown Derby), a theatre, a concert hall, the cathedral with fine ironwork and Bess of Hardwick's tomb, and Elvaston Castle Country Park.
Tourist Information Centre ☎ (0332) 290664

Ascot Hotel
724 Osmaston Road, Derby, DE2 8GT
☎ (0332) 41916
1.5 miles from Derby town centre on the main A514 Melbourne road.
Bedrooms: 15 single, 3 double & 2 twin, 1 family room.
Bathrooms: 1 private, 4 public; 3 private showers.
Bed & breakfast: £12-£16 single, £20-£35 double.
Half board: £16-£21 daily.
Evening meal 6pm (l.o. 9.30pm).
Parking for 12.
Credit: Access, Visa.
🖰 🚲 ⓑ 🖃 ⓣⓥ 🖃 🛏 ⓣ

Aston Court Hotel
👑👑👑👑 COMMENDED
Midland Road, Derby, DE1 2SL
☎ (0332) 42716
Formerly the Duke of Devonshire's town house, the hotel is opposite Derby's new railway station, 10 minutes' walk from the city centre. East Midlands Airport 20 minutes drive; 40 minutes to the National Exhibition Centre.
Bedrooms: 13 single, 25 double & 14 twin, 3 family rooms.
Bathrooms: 55 private.
Bed & breakfast: £49-£55 single, £60-£68 double.
Half board: from £38.50 daily.
Lunch available.
Evening meal 7pm (l.o. 9.45pm).
Parking for 36.
Credit: Access, Visa, C.Bl., Diners, Amex.
🖰 🚲 ☎ ⓑ 🖵 ♢ ⓘ ⓥ 🚪 ⓣⓥ ● 🖃 🛏 🖃 ⓣ 🔌 SP 🅜

Braemar Guest House M
1061 London Road, Alvaston, Derby, DE2 8PZ.
☎ (0332) 572522

Family-run guesthouse near the city centre, Donington Park, M1, airport, Alton Towers, BMX track and Moor Ways sports centre.
Bedrooms: 8 single, 2 double & 2 twin, 4 family rooms.
Bathrooms: 1 private, 5 public; 5 private showers.
Bed & breakfast: £15-£16 single, £28-£30 double.
Evening meal 6.30pm (l.o. 5.30pm).
Parking for 10.
🖰 🚲 ♢ ⓤ 🅻 ⓘ ⓥ ✂ 🖃 ⓣⓥ 🖃 🛏 🖃 🅡 🅳🅰🅿 🔌

Breadsall Priory Hotel, Golf & Country Club M
👑👑👑👑👑
Moor Road, Morley, Nr. Derby, DE7 6DL
☎ (0332) 832235
This secluded English manor house is surrounded by its own 18-hole golf-course and is only 3 miles north of Derby, close to the M1 and A38.
Bedrooms: 2 single, 71 twin, 1 family room.
Bathrooms: 74 private.
Bed & breakfast: £75-£85 single, £90-£95 double.
Half board: £90-£100 daily.
Lunch available.
Evening meal 7pm (l.o. 9.45pm).
Parking for 300.
Credit: Access, Visa, Diners, Amex.
🖰 🚲 🍴 ☎ ⓑ 🖵 ♢ ⓘ ⓥ 🚪 ⓣⓥ 🖃 🛏 🖃 🅡 ⚓ 🔌 SP 🅜 ⓣ 🏸 ⚔ 🅡 🌣 🔌 SP 🅜 ⓣ

Clarendon Hotel M
👑👑👑
Midland Road, Derby, DE1 2SL
☎ (0332) 365235
Situated within 100 yards of the railway station with easy access to the M1 and East Midlands Airport. Raffles restaurant and lounge bar. Weekend rates available.
Bedrooms: 32 single, 8 double & 8 twin, 1 family room.
Bathrooms: 19 private, 7 public.
Bed & breakfast: £21.50-£37.50 single, £33.50-£49.50 double.
Half board: £31-£47 daily.
Lunch available.
Evening meal 7pm (l.o. 9.45pm).
Parking for 80.
Credit: Access, Visa, Diners, Amex.
🖰 ♢ ⓑ ⓘ ⓥ 🚪 ⓣⓥ ● 🖃 🛏 🍴 🔌 SP ⓣ

Dalby House Hotel
👑👑

100 Radbourne Street, (Off
Windmill Hill Lane), Derby,
DE3 3BU
☎ (0332) 42353
*A large, detached, Georgian-
style house in a very quiet
residential area. Convenient for
both the town centre and
countryside.*
Bedrooms: 4 single, 1 double
& 2 twin, 2 family rooms.
Bathrooms: 2 public.
Bed & breakfast: £17-£18
single, £30-£33 double.
Half board: £24-£25 daily.
Evening meal 6.30pm (l.o.
6pm).
Parking for 11.

Gables Hotel M
👑👑👑

119 London Road, Derby,
DE1 2QR
☎ (0332) 40633
*A city centre hotel providing a
good choice of food and
facilities for short-stay business
and holiday people.*
Bedrooms: 21 single,
40 double & 38 twin, 2 family
rooms.
Bathrooms: 101 private.
Bed & breakfast: £33-£58
single, £46-£67 double.
Lunch available.
Evening meal 6pm (l.o.
9.45pm).
Parking for 90.
Credit: Access, Visa, Amex.

Georgian House Hotel
32-34 Ashbourne Road,
Derby, DE3 3AD
☎ (0332) 49806
*This listed building is in a
conservation area half a mile
north of the city centre and
Assembly Rooms.*
Bedrooms: 10 single, 3 double
& 3 twin, 5 family rooms.
Bathrooms: 14 private,
2 public.
Bed & breakfast: £19.50-£35
single, £32-£42 double.
Half board: £30.25-£45.75
daily.
Lunch available.
Evening meal 6.30pm (l.o.
9.30pm).
Parking for 20.

> Map references
> apply to the colour
> maps towards the
> end of this guide.

International Hotel & Restaurant M
👑👑👑👑 COMMENDED

Burton Road (A5250), Derby,
DE6 6AD
☎ (0332) 369321
Telex 377759
*A privately-owned modern
hotel with a continental
atmosphere, close to the city
centre.*
Bedrooms: 11 single,
32 double & 4 twin, 4 family
rooms.
Bathrooms: 51 private.
Bed & breakfast: £20-£70
single, £30-£75 double.
Lunch available.
Evening meal 7.30pm (l.o.
10.30pm).
Parking for 70.
Credit: Access, Visa, Diners,
Amex.

Midland Hotel M
👑👑👑👑

Midland Road, Derby,
DE1 2SQ
☎ (0332) 45894 Telex 378373
*Built beside the station in 1841
as the world's first railway
hotel. It has a private, tree-
lined garden, has been recently
refurbished, and has easy
access to the M1 and East
Midlands Airport.*
Bedrooms: 37 single, 8 double
& 15 twin.
Bathrooms: 48 private,
3 public.
Bed & breakfast: £57.50-£74
single, £69.50-£86 double.
Half board: £69-£85.50 daily.
Lunch available.
Evening meal 7pm (l.o.
10pm).
Parking for 80.
Credit: Access, Visa, Diners,
Amex.

Ockbrook House
Listed

Flood Street, Ockbrook,
Derby, DE7 3RF
☎ Derby (0332) 662208
*A large Georgian country
house with an adjoining cottage
in delightful mature gardens.
Evening meals can be provided
by arrangement.*
Bedrooms: 2 double & 1 twin.
Bathrooms: 2 private.
Bed & breakfast: £20-£25
single, £30-£35 double.
Parking for 4.

Pennine Hotel
👑👑👑

Macklin Street, Derby,
DE1 1LF
☎ (0332) 41741
🄲🄳 De Vere
*A modern city centre hotel
within easy reach of the
Midlands and tourist
attractions such as Chatsworth,
Peak District and Alton
Towers.*
Bedrooms: 44 single,
18 double & 38 twin.
Bathrooms: 100 private.
Bed & breakfast: £44-£66
single, £70-£80 double.
Half board: £32.50-£80 daily.
Lunch available.
Evening meal 7pm (l.o.
9.45pm).
Parking for 30.
Credit: Access, Visa, Diners,
Amex.

Rangemoor Hotel
👑

67 Macklin Street, Derby,
DE1 1LF
☎ (0332) 47252
*Family-run city centre hotel
within walking distance of all
amenities and with a large
lock-up car park.*
Bedrooms: 12 single, 5 double
& 4 twin, 3 family rooms.
Bathrooms: 6 public.
Bed & breakfast: £21-£23
single, £30-£34 double.
Parking for 28.

Rollz Hotel
👑👑 APPROVED

684-688 Osmaston Road,
Derby, DE2 8GT
☎ (0332) 41026
*A friendly, family-run hotel
with a comfortable atmosphere,
5 minutes from the city centre
and close to a park and sports
complex.*
Bedrooms: 6 single, 1 double
& 6 twin, 1 family room.
Bathrooms: 3 public.
Bed & breakfast: from £18.40
single, from £36.80 double.
Half board: from £24.72
daily, from £173.04 weekly.
Lunch available.
Evening meal 6.30pm (l.o.
9pm).
Parking for 10.

> The symbols are
> explained on the
> flap inside the
> back cover.

DISEWORTH
Leicestershire
Map ref 4C3

6m NW. Loughborough

Little Chimneys Guest House
👑

19 The Green, Diseworth,
Derby DE7 2QN
☎ Derby (0332) 812458
*A modern building in the
pleasant village of Diseworth
close to the M1, East
Midlands Airport and
Donington race track.*
Bedrooms: 4 twin, 1 family
room.
Bathrooms: 5 private.
Bed & breakfast: max. £18.50
single, £28.50 double.
Parking for 7.
Credit: Access, Visa.

DRAKEHOLES
Nottinghamshire
Map ref 4C2

1m NW. Wiseton

The Griff Inn
Drakeholes, Near Bawtry,
Doncaster, South Yorkshire
DN10 5DF
☎ Retford (0777) 817206
*A 200-year-old country inn
lying between Bawtry and
Gainsborough, serving food 7
days a week. There is also a
craft shop.*
Bedrooms: 1 double & 2 twin.
Bathrooms: 3 private.
Bed & breakfast: max. £35
single, max. £50 double.
Lunch available.
Evening meal 7pm (l.o.
10pm).
Parking for 80.
Credit: Access, Visa.

DRONFIELD
Derbyshire
Map ref 4B2

Charnwood Hotel
23 Cecil Road, Dronfield,
Via Sheffield, S. Yorkshire
S18 6GW
☎ (0246) 413217
*This hotel has a friendly
atmosphere and is in a quiet
area, off the main road. Easy
access to both the Peak
District and Sheffield.*
Bedrooms: 3 single, 1 double
& 1 twin, 2 family rooms.
Bathrooms: 1 public.
Continued ▶

DRONFIELD
Continued

Bed & breakfast: £14.50-£19.50 single, £29-£35 double.
Half board: £19.50-£24.50 daily, from £136.50 weekly.
Evening meal 6pm (l.o. 7pm).
Parking for 5.
Credit: Access, Visa.
�''🕭🛇 ⅋ 🅥 🛏 📺 ⅲ ➔ 🗙 🎿

EDALE
Derbyshire
Map ref 4B2

Rambler Inn
😊😊
Edale, Sheffield, S. Yorkshire
S30 2ZA
☎ Hope Valley (0433) 70268
A small, stone-built hotel in its own grounds in Edale village at the start of the Pennine Way. Walkers are very welcome.
Bedrooms: 2 double & 3 twin, 3 family rooms.
Bathrooms: 3 public.
Bed & breakfast: £17-£22 single, £30-£37 double.
Half board: £23-£30 daily, £161-£210 weekly.
Lunch available.
Evening meal 6.30pm (l.o. 9pm).
Parking for 20.
Credit: Access, Visa, Amex.
🚱🗆🛇 ⅋ 🅥 🗙 🛏 ⅲ 🍴 🍷 ❄ 🅂🅿

Stonecroft Hotel
Grindsbrook, Edale, Via Sheffield S30 2ZA
☎ Hope Valley (0433) 70262
A small, family-run hotel with lovely views. Specialists in walking holidays and vegetarian meals. Coffee, lunches and cream teas are available in season at the weekends. No smoking in the bedrooms or dining room.
Bedrooms: 2 double & 1 twin.
Bathrooms: 2 public.
Bed & breakfast: £15-£17 single, £30-£32 double.
Half board: £25-£27 daily, £175-£189 weekly.
Evening meal 7.30pm (l.o. 8pm).
Parking for 5.
🚱🗆🛇 ⅋ 🅥 🗙 🛏 📺 ⅲ 🍴 ∪ 🗙 🎿 🛇

EMPINGHAM
Leicestershire
Map ref 3A1

White Horse ⋔
😊😊😊
Main Street, Empingham, Oakham, LE15 8PR
☎ (078 086) 221 & 521

In the heart of Rutland by the side of Europe's largest man-made lake, this low stone building with its traditional slate roof was once the village court-house. The stables are now 8 bedrooms en-suite, retaining the stable structure.
Bedrooms: 1 single, 3 double & 5 twin, 3 family rooms.
Bathrooms: 8 private, 2 public.
Bed & breakfast: £21.50-£32.50 single, £29.50-£55 double.
Half board: £27-£45 daily, £189.95-£220 weekly.
Lunch available.
Evening meal 7.15pm (l.o. 9.45pm).
Parking for 30.
Credit: Access, Visa, C.Bl., Diners, Amex.
🚱 ⅏ 🛇 🛇 ⅋ 🅥 ⅲ 🛏 🍴 ∪ 🍷 🗙 🅿 🎿

FARTHINGSTONE
Northamptonshire
Map ref 2C1

5m SE. Daventry

Barn Court
Farthingstone, Towcester, NN12 8HE
☎ Preston Capes (032 736) 580
This stone village house has beautiful views to the rear and many walks and historic houses within easy reach. A golf and squash club and a pub serving food are close by. Close to Silverstone and Tadcaster race tracks.
Bedrooms: 1 single, 1 double & 2 twin, 1 family room.
Bathrooms: 2 public.
Bed & breakfast: £18.50 single, £35 double.
Parking for 4.
🚱🎿🛇 ⅏ 📺 ⅲ ∪ 🏴 🗙 🎿

FINEDON
Northamptonshire
Map ref 3A2

Large ironstone village with interesting Victorian houses and cottages and an ironstone 14th C church. The inn claims to be the oldest in England.

Tudor Gate Hotel ⋔
35 High Street, Finedon, Near Wellingborough, NN9 5JN
☎ Wellingborough (0933) 680408

Converted from a 16th C farmhouse with 3 four-poster beds, conference facilities and a good range of restaurant facilities. Close to the new A1/M1 link.
Bedrooms: 4 single, 11 double & 1 twin.
Bathrooms: 16 private.
Bed & breakfast: £48-£65 single, £57-£75 double.
Half board: £68-£86 daily.
Lunch available.
Evening meal 7pm (l.o. 9.45pm).
Parking for 25.
Credit: Access, Visa, Diners, Amex.
🚱 ⅏ 🛇 🛇 ⅋ 🅥 🎿 ⅲ 🍴 ∪ 🏴 🗙 🅿 🎿

FLORE
Northamptonshire
Map ref 2C1

Heyford Manor Hotel ⋔
😊😊😊😊
High Street, Flore, NN7 4LP
☎ Weedon (0327) 349022
Telex 312437
ⓒⓡ Lansbury
A recently opened modern hotel in a rural setting, only 1 mile from junction 16 of the M1.
Bedrooms: 25 double & 29 twin.
Bathrooms: 54 private.
Bed & breakfast: £28-£76 single, £56-£88 double.
Half board: £39-£90 daily.
Lunch available.
Evening meal 6.30pm (l.o. 9.30pm).
Parking for 100.
Credit: Access, Visa, Diners, Amex.
🚱 ⅏ 🛇 🗆 ⅲ ⅋ 🅥 🗙 🎿 🛏 🍴 🛇 🐾 🏴 🗙 🅂🅿 🅃

GAINSBOROUGH
Lincolnshire
Map ref 4C2

White Hart Hotel ⋔
😊😊😊
Lord Street, Gainsborough, DN21 2DU
☎ (0427) 612018
Originally a 17th C coaching inn, this family-run hotel is in the centre of a market town and offers a secure, undercover car park.
Bedrooms: 3 single, 2 double & 7 twin, 1 family room.
Bathrooms: 13 private.
Bed & breakfast: £27.50-£30 single, £40-£55 double.
Half board: £36-£70 daily, from £150 weekly.
Lunch available.

Evening meal 7pm (l.o. 9.45pm).
Parking for 23.
Credit: Access, Visa.
🚱🎿🛇🛇🗆⅋🅥ⅲ🍴📺 ⅲ🛏🍴🅿🛇🅂🅿🎿

GLASTON
Leicestershire
Map ref 3A1

2m NE. Uppingham

The Monckton Arms Hotel
😊😊😊
Glaston, Near Uppingham, LE15 9BP
☎ (0572) 822326
16th C inn on the A47 offering 10 high standard en-suite rooms, food, cosy bars and a friendly atmosphere.
Bedrooms: 1 single, 5 double & 4 twin.
Bathrooms: 10 private.
Bed & breakfast: from £45 single, from £50 double.
Lunch available.
Evening meal 6.30pm (l.o. 10pm).
Parking for 30.
Credit: Access, Visa, Amex.
🚱🎿🛇🛇🗆⅋🅥ⅲ 🛏 🗙 🎿 🅿 🅂🅿 🅃

GLOSSOP
Derbyshire
Map ref 4B2

Town in dramatic moorland surroundings with views over the High Peak. The settlement can be traced back to Roman times but expanded during the Industrial Revolution.
Tourist Information Centre ☎ (0457) 855920

Wind in the Willows Hotel ⋔
😊😊😊😊 COMMENDED
Derbyshire Level, off Sheffield Road, (A57), Glossop, SK13 9PT
☎ (0457) 868001
Friendly country house hotel with open fires, offering home cooking, peace and relaxation. Views over the magnificent Peak District National Park. Adjacent to golf-course in excellent walking country.
Bedrooms: 5 double & 2 twin, 1 family room.
Bathrooms: 8 private.
Bed & breakfast: £52-£70 single, £63-£90 double.
Half board: from £50 daily.

Evening meal 7.30pm (l.o. 4pm).
Parking for 12.
Credit: Access, Visa, Amex.
⛄7🅿♿📞🔟🛗♿📺🍽🔻
🏢▦♨️🍴▶️✳️🎿🏮🏵🔺🕕

GRANTHAM

Lincolnshire
Map ref 3A1

On the road from London to York, Grantham has several old inns and its splendid parish church has a fine spire and chained library. Sir Isaac Newton was educated here and his statue stands in front of the museum which includes displays on Newton and other famous local people.
Tourist Information Centre ☎ (0476) 66444

Kings Hotel
😋😋😋😋

North Parade, Grantham, NG31 8AU
☎ (0476) 590800
A Georgian-style hotel serving dinner from table d'hote and a la carte menus, luncheon bar meals, and featuring a new buttery open from 7.30 am until 11.00 pm. Conference and function facilities for up to 100 are also offered.
Bedrooms: 2 single, 7 double & 14 twin.
Bathrooms: 21 private, 2 public.
Bed & breakfast: £27.50-£40 single, £55 double.
Half board: from £49.25 daily.
Lunch available.
Evening meal 7pm (l.o. 11pm).
Parking for 50.
Credit: Access, Visa, Diners, Amex.
⛄♿📞🔟🛗♿📺🍽🔻
●🏢▦♨️🍴♿♨️♿🔟🔺

Lanchester Guest House M
😋😋

84 Harrowby Road, Grantham, NG31 9DS
☎ (0476) 74169
Well established, the Lanchester is run professionally to high standards but retains its warm and friendly atmosphere. All rooms can be let as singles. Light suppers can be served until 9.00 pm.
Bedrooms: 2 twin, 1 family room.
Bathrooms: 1 private, 1 public.

Bed & breakfast: £14-£22.50 single, £26-£35 double.
Half board: £21-£29.50 daily.
Evening meal 6pm (l.o. midday).
Parking for 3.
⛄🔟🛗🔟📺🔻🎿🔺📺
●🏢▦♨️🎿🔳

GRINDLEFORD

Derbyshire
Map ref 4B2

Good centre for walking, at the eastern end of the Hope Valley. Longshaw Estate is nearby with 1500 acres of moorland and woodland.

Maynard Arms Hotel M
😋😋😋😋

Main Road, Grindleford, Via Sheffield, S. Yorkshire S30 1HP
☎ Hope Valley (0433) 30321
An established hotel with a relaxed, friendly atmosphere and working proprietors. Picturesque gardens with lovely views of Hope Valley and Peak Park. There is excellent walking nearby.
Bedrooms: 1 single, 5 double & 7 twin.
Bathrooms: 11 private; 2 private showers.
Bed & breakfast: £53-£55 single, £64-£69 double.
Lunch available.
Evening meal 7pm (l.o. 9.30pm).
Parking for 80.
Credit: Access, Visa, Diners, Amex.
⛄🔟♿📞🔟🛗♿🔟📺
🏢▦♨️🍴🕐♨️🎿🏮🔳

HARRINGWORTH

Northamptonshire
Map ref 3A1

6m NE. Corby
Village with a medieval cross, a 12th C church, an inn and old manor house. The 82 arches of the 19th C Welland railway viaduct dominate the valley, which forms the Northamptonshire/ Leicestershire border.

The White Swan M
😋😋😋

Seaton Road, Harringworth, Near Corby, NN17 3AF
☎ Morcott (057 287) 543
15th C freehouse coaching inn offering en-suite accommodation, including a self-contained cottage, in a delightful village. Home-cooked food and real ales.

Bedrooms: 1 single, 4 double & 1 twin, 1 family room.
Bathrooms: 7 private.
Bed & breakfast: from £35 single, from £50 double.
Lunch available.
Evening meal 7pm (l.o. 10pm).
Parking for 15.
Credit: Access, Visa.
⛄🔟🏢📞🔟🛗📺🔟♿
🍴🎿🏮🏵

HARTINGTON

Derbyshire
Map ref 4B2

Village with a large market-place set in fine surroundings near the River Dove, well-known for its fishing and Izaak Walton, author of 'The Compleat Angler'.

Manifold Valley Hotel M
😋😋 APPROVED

Hulme End, Hartington, Buxton, SK17 0EX
☎ Hartington (029 884) 537
Interesting country freehouse beside the River Manifold, in superb walking/fishing/touring countryside, at the start of the beautiful Manifold Valley trail. Real ale, English and French food, bar snacks.
Bedrooms: 1 single, 3 double & 1 twin.
Bathrooms: 5 private.
Bed & breakfast: £40-£50 double.
Lunch available.
Evening meal 7.30pm (l.o. 9pm).
Parking for 20.
Credit: Access, Visa.
⛄🔟🛗♿🔟📺🔻📺🔟
▦♨️🎿🏮🔳

Minton House Hotel M
😋😋😋

Market Place, Hartington, Buxton, SK17 0AL
☎ (0298) 84368/84253
A small private hotel in a pretty village in the heart of the Peak District, offering a wide range of bar lunches and an extensive menu of English home cooking.
Bedrooms: 2 double & 2 twin, 2 family rooms.
Bathrooms: 4 private, 3 public.
Bed & breakfast: £20-£26 single, £35-£45 double.
Half board: £30-£34 daily, £190-£220 weekly.
Lunch available.
Evening meal 5pm (l.o. 9.30pm).

Parking for 8.
Credit: Access, Visa, Amex.
⛄🔟🏢📞🔟♿🔟📺🎿🔻
📺▦♨️🍴🕐♨️🎿🏮🔳
🔲🏵

HATHERSAGE

Derbyshire
Map ref 4B2

Hillside village in the Peak District, dominated by the church with many good brasses and monuments to the Eyre family which provide a link with Charlotte Bronte. Little John, friend of Robin Hood, is said to be buried here.

George Hotel M
😋😋😋

Main Road, Hathersage, S30 1BB
☎ Hope Valley (0433) 50436
Telex 547196
Ⓡ Lansbury
A 16th C coaching inn located at the focal point of the Hope Valley. Easy access to the Derbyshire Peak District.
Bedrooms: 10 double & 5 twin, 3 family rooms.
Bathrooms: 18 private.
Bed & breakfast: from £64 single, from £76 double.
Half board: £47-£78 daily.
Lunch available.
Evening meal 7pm (l.o. 10pm).
Parking for 50.
Credit: Access, Visa, Diners, Amex.
⛄🔟♿📞🔟♿🔟📺🔻
🔻🏢▦♨️🍴▶️🎿🏮🔳
🏵🔟

HAYFIELD

Derbyshire
Map ref 4B2

9m N. Buxton
Village set in spectacular scenery at the highest point of the Peak District with the best approach to the Kinder Scout plateau via the Kinder Downfall. An excellent centre for walking. 3 reservoirs close by.

Sportsman Inn

Kinder Road, Hayfield, Stockport, Cheshire SK12 5LE
☎ New Mills (0663) 42118
Easy access to Stockport, Manchester motorway and Airport. Friendly atmosphere with Thwaites beers, bar food and restaurant menus available.

Continued ▶

HAYFIELD
Continued

Bedrooms: 3 double & 3 twin,
1 family room.
Bathrooms: 5 private,
1 public; 2 private showers.
Bed & breakfast: £24.50-
£29.50 single, £39-£49 double.
Evening meal 7pm (l.o. 9pm).
Parking for 20.
Credit: Access, Visa.
🛇🖙♦️®️🖵♥ 🛉 Ⓥ 🖾 🛋
🔔 ⒹⒶⓅ ⚲ SP

HEMINGTON
Leicestershire
Map ref 4C3

7m NW. Loughborough

Hemington Court Hotel
23 Main Street, Hemington,
Derby, Derbyshire
☎ Derby (0332) 811859
*42-bedroomed hotel set in the
heart of rural England, yet
within 2 miles of M1 junction
24, and 3 miles from East
Midlands Airport.*
Bedrooms: 8 single, 20 double
& 11 twin, 3 family rooms.
Bathrooms: 38 private,
4 public.
Bed & breakfast: £25-£38
single, £38-£54 double.
Half board: £45-£61 daily.
Lunch available.
Evening meal 6pm (l.o.
10pm).
Parking for 100.
Credit: Access, Visa, Amex.
🛇🖙♦️®️🖵♥ 🛉 Ⓥ ⚡
🖾 ⒯Ⓥ 🖾 🛋 🍴 ♨ ⚙️ SP

HINCKLEY
Leicestershire
Map ref 4B3

The town has an
excellent leisure centre.
Bosworth Battlefield, with
its Visitor Centre and
Battle Trail, is 5 miles
away.
*Tourist Information
Centre* ☎ *(0455) 230852
or 635106*

Ambion Court
🏵🏵🏵
The Green, Dadlington,
Nuneaton, Warwickshire
CV13 6JB
☎ Hinckley (0455) 212292
*Charming, modernised
farmhouse hotel overlooking
tranquil village green, 2 miles
north of Hinckley.
Conveniently located for M1,
M6, M69, National Exhibition
Centre and Birmingham
Airport.*

Bedrooms: 1 single, 3 double
& 3 twin.
Bathrooms: 7 private.
Bed & breakfast: £30-£45
single, £40-£60 double.
Half board: £42-£57 daily,
£250-£350 weekly.
Evening meal 7pm (l.o.
8.30pm).
Parking for 8.
Credit: Access, Visa.
🛇5♦️ ♥ ®️🖵♥ 🛉 Ⓥ ⚡
ⓉⓋ 🖾 🛋 🍴 🖾 ⒹⒶⓅ SP Ⓣ

Highcross House ⋒
Highcross, A5, Hinckley
LE17 5AT
☎ Hinckley (0455) 220840
*Set in historic Roman setting, a
high standard of hospitality
awaits visitors. Renowned for
cuisine and homely comfort.*
Bedrooms: 2 double & 2 twin,
1 family room.
Bathrooms: 2 private,
1 public.
Bed & breakfast: £25-£45
single, £50-£90 double.
Half board: £35-£60 daily,
£170-£300 weekly.
Lunch available.
Evening meal (l.o. 10pm).
Parking for 10.
🛇🖙♦️ 🖵♥ ⓊⓁ 🛉 Ⓥ ⚡ ⚡
ⓉⓋ ⦿ 🖾 🛋 🍴 🖾 ♨ 🖾 ⒹⒶⓅ
⚲ 🖾

Hollycroft Private Hotel
24 Hollycroft, Hinckley,
LE10 0HG
☎ (0455) 637356
*Spacious, tastefully decorated,
detached residence near to the
town centre and opposite a
park.*
Bedrooms: 2 double & 3 twin.
Bathrooms: 5 private,
1 public.
Bed & breakfast: £17.50
single, £28 double.
Half board: £18.50-£22 daily.
Evening meal 6pm (l.o.
6.30pm).
Parking for 6.
🛇🖙♦️🖵♥ ⓊⓁ 🛉 Ⓥ ⚡ ⓉⓋ
🖾 🛋 🍴 ♨

Kings Hotel & Restaurant
🏵🏵🏵
13-19 Mount Road, Hinckley,
LE10 1AD
☎ Hinckley (0455) 637193
*Hotel with lawns and gardens
to the front and rear, in the
centre of town yet in a quiet,
residential area.*
Bedrooms: 4 single, 3 double.
Bathrooms: 7 private.
Bed & breakfast: £49.50-
£59.50 single, £59.50-£69.50
double.
Half board: £59.50-£69.50
daily, £300-£400 weekly.
Lunch available.

Evening meal 7pm (l.o.
10pm).
Parking for 23.
Credit: Access, Visa, Diners,
Amex.
🛇🖙♥ ®️🖵♥ 🛉 Ⓥ 🖾 ⚡ ◉
🖾 🛋 🍴 🖻 ➤ ✈ 🖾 🖾 SP
Ⓣ

Woodside Farm
🏵🏵🏵 **COMMENDED**
Ashby Road, Stapleton,
LE9 8JE
☎ Market Bosworth
(0455) 291929
*16-acre horse/arable farm.
Situated close to the Battle of
Bosworth site and Kirkby
Mallory race track. 3 miles to
North Hinckley on A447.*
Bedrooms: 1 single, 2 double
& 2 twin, 2 family rooms.
Bathrooms: 2 private,
2 public; 2 private showers.
Bed & breakfast: from £13.50
single, from £26 double.
Half board: max. £17.50
daily, from £80 weekly.
Lunch available.
Evening meal 6pm (l.o. 9pm).
Parking for 17.
🛇🖵♥ 🛉 Ⓥ 🖾 ⚡ ⓉⓋ 🖾 🛋
🍴 Ⓤ ➤ ❄ ✈ 🖾 🖾 ⒹⒶⓅ ⚲ SP
Ⓣ

HOLBEACH
Lincolnshire
Map ref 3A1

Small town, mentioned in
the Domesday Book, has
a splendid 14th C church
with a fine tower and
spire. The surrounding
villages also have
interesting churches, and
the area is well-known for
its bulbfields.

The Mansion House
🏵🏵🏵
45 High Street, Holbeach,
Spalding, PE12 7DY
☎ (0406) 23533
*Set in the heart of a
Lincolnshire fen town. 5 miles
east of Spalding, the famous
bulb growing area.*
Bedrooms: 1 double & 3 twin.
Bathrooms: 4 private.
Bed & breakfast: £15-£30
single, £20-£40 double.
Half board: from £28 daily,
from £100 weekly.
Lunch available.
Evening meal 7pm (l.o.
11pm).
Parking for 6.
Credit: Access, Visa, Diners,
Amex.
🛇®️🖵♥ 🛉 Ⓥ 🖾 🍴 ✈
🖾 ⚲ 🖽

KEGWORTH
Leicestershire
Map ref 4C3

Village on the River Soar
close to East Midlands
Airport and Donington
Park racing circuit. It has
a 14th C church with a
fine nave and chantry
roof. The nearby
churches of Staunton
Harold, Melbourne and
Breedon-on-the-Hill are of
exceptional interest.

Yew Lodge Hotel ⋒
🏵🏵🏵🏵 **COMMENDED**
33 Packington Hill,
Kegworth, Derby DE7 2DF
☎ (0509) 672518
Telex 341995 Ref 211
*Privately-owned hotel with
restaurant offering English and
continental cooking. 1 minute
from the M1, exit 24. 5
minutes from East Midlands
Airport.*
Bedrooms: 29 single, 9 double
& 16 twin.
Bathrooms: 54 private.
Bed & breakfast: £53-£66
single, £71-£84 double.
Half board: £63-£76 daily.
Lunch available.
Evening meal 6.30pm (l.o.
10pm).
Parking for 120.
Credit: Access, Visa, Diners,
Amex.
🛇🖙♥ ®️🖵♥ 🛉 Ⓥ 🖾 ⚡ ◉
⚡ 🖾 🛋 🍴 ♨ ❄ SP

KERSALL
Nottinghamshire
Map ref 4C2

5m SE. Ollerton

Hill Farm Guest House
🏵🏵 **COMMENDED**
Kersall, Newark, NG22 0BJ
☎ Caunton (063 686) 274
*A 17th C farm cottage with
splendid views over the
countryside, a beamed dining
room and a comfortable lounge
with an open log fire.
Southwell Minster, Newark
and the Sherwood Forest
Visitor Centre are all nearby.*
Bedrooms: 1 double & 1 twin.
Bathrooms: 1 private,
1 public.
Bed & breakfast: £15 single,
£25-£28 double.
Parking for 6.
Open May-September.
🛇2®️🖵♥ ⓊⓁ 🛉 Ⓥ 🖾 ⚡
🖾 🛋 ❄ ✈ 🖾 🖽

KETTERING

Northamptonshire
Map ref 3A2

Ancient industrial town
based on shoe-making.
Wicksteed Park to the
south has many
children's amusements.
The splendid 17th C ducal
mansion of Boughton
House is to the north.
*Tourist Information
Centre* ☎ *(0536) 410266
or 410333 ext 212*

Cransley Hall
Church Lane, Cransley,
Kettering, NN14 1PX
☎ (0536) 790259
*A Queen Anne mansion in its
own grounds, 3 miles south
west of Kettering.*
Bedrooms: 1 single, 2 double
& 2 twin.
Bathrooms: 5 private,
2 public.
Bed & breakfast: max. £22
single, max. £36 double.
Evening meal 6pm (l.o.
11am).
Parking for 9.
☎ ☐ ♥ ⒰ 🛉 Ⓥ ☒ ⓉⓋ ▴
🛉 ♠ ♫ ✻ 🐴 🏧

Pennels Guest House
175 Beatrice Road,
Kettering, NN16 9QR
☎ (0536) 81940
*Homely guesthouse in quiet
area for a relaxing holiday.
Also ideal for the business
person staying long or short
term.*
Bedrooms: 2 single, 1 double
& 3 twin.
Bathrooms: 1 private,
3 public.
Bed & breakfast: £14.50-£15
single, £29-£30 double.
Half board: £21 daily,
£101.50-£105 weekly.
Lunch available.
Evening meal 6pm (l.o. 5pm).
Parking for 4.
☎ ☐ ♥ ⒰ 🛉 Ⓥ ☒ ⓉⓋ ▥
▴ ♿ 🏧

Periquito Hotel Ⓜ
👑👑👑 COMMENDED
Market Square, Kettering,
NN16 0AJ
☎ (0536) 520732
*An Edwardian hotel in the
town centre ideal for business
traveller and tourist.
Specialising in conferences and
receptions.*
Bedrooms: 16 single,
15 double & 6 twin, 2 family
rooms.
Bathrooms: 38 private,
1 public.
Bed & breakfast: £54.50-£61
single, £60-£67 double.

Lunch available.
Evening meal 7pm (l.o.
10.30pm).
Parking for 59.
Credit: Access, Visa, Diners,
Amex.
☎ ☚ ☏ ⒭ ☐ ♥ 🛉 Ⓥ ☒
◑ ▥ ▴ 🛉 ♫ ⒼⒶⓅ ✻ SP 🏧
Ⓣ

KIRK IRETON

Derbyshire
Map ref 4B2

*3m SW. Wirksworth
Stone-built village within
easy reach of Dovedale
and Matlock.*

Barley Mow Inn
Kirk Ireton, Derby, DE4 4JP
☎ Ashbourne (0335) 70306
*17th C village inn in a stone,
hilltop village equidistant from
Matlock, Ashbourne and
Belper. En-suite rooms, with
all facilities.*
Bedrooms: 3 double & 2 twin.
Bathrooms: 4 private,
1 public.
Bed & breakfast: max. £18
single, max. £32 double.
Half board: max. £20 daily.
Evening meal 7.30pm (l.o.
7.30pm).
☎ ☐ ♥ Ⓥ ☒ ▥ ▴ 🐴 🏧

KIRK LANGLEY

Derbyshire
Map ref 4B2

5m NW. Derby

Meynell Arms Hotel Ⓜ
👑👑👑
Ashbourne Road, Kirk
Langley, DE6 4NF
☎ (033 124) 515
Ⓖ Minotels
*A family establishment,
offering a selection of bar food
for the business traveller or
tourist.*
Bedrooms: 3 single, 4 double
& 1 twin, 2 family rooms.
Bathrooms: 7 private,
1 public.
Bed & breakfast: £24-£34
single, £38-£50 double.
Lunch available.
Evening meal 6.30pm (l.o.
9.30pm).
Parking for 100.
Credit: Access, Visa.
☎ ☚ ☏ ⒭ ☐ ♥ 🛉 Ⓥ ▥
▥ ▴ 🛉 ✻ 🐴 SP 🏧 Ⓣ

**The National Crown
Scheme is explained
in full on pages
556 – 558.**

KIRKBY-IN-
ASHFIELD

Nottinghamshire
Map ref 4C2

Mining town surrounded
by man-made grassy hills.
The family home of Lord
Byron, Newstead Abbey,
is close by. It is set in
over 300 acres of
parkland and contains
many of Byron's
possessions.

Kirkby House Hotel &
Restaurant
Kirkby House Drive,
Kirkby-in-Ashfield,
Nottingham, NG17 8LA
☎ Mansfield (0623) 752373
*A Victorian country house in a
suburban conservation area.
Where possible the character of
the house has been retained.*
Bedrooms: 1 single, 2 double
& 2 twin, 3 family rooms.
Bathrooms: 5 private,
1 public.
Bed & breakfast: £23-£40
single, £36-£100 double.
Half board: £22-£60 daily,
£161-£280 weekly.
Lunch available.
Evening meal 7pm (l.o.
11pm).
Parking for 50.
Credit: Access, Visa.
☎ ☐ ♥ 🛉 Ⓥ ☒ ▥ ⓉⓋ
▥ ▴ 🛉 ✻ ⒼⒶⓅ Ⓣ

KNIPTON

Leicestershire
Map ref 4C2

*7m SW. Grantham
Leicestershire Wolds
village close to Belvoir
Castle, where medieval
jousting tournaments and
other special events add
to the attractions in
summer.*

Red House Inn
👑👑
Knipton, Grantham,
Lincolnshire NG32 1RH
☎ Grantham (0476) 870352
*In the beautiful Vale of
Belvoir, within 1 mile of the
castle, this listed building was
a hunting lodge for
approximately 200 years.*
Bedrooms: 2 single, 2 double
& 2 twin, 2 family rooms.
Bathrooms: 3 private,
2 public.
Bed & breakfast: £18-£28
single, £30-£40 double.
Half board: £22-£40 daily.
Lunch available.

Evening meal 7pm (l.o.
9.30pm).
Parking for 60.
Credit: Access, Visa.
☎ ☐ ♥ 🛉 Ⓥ ⓉⓋ ▥ ▴ 🛉
✻ 🐴 ♿ SP 🏧

LANEHAM

Nottinghamshire
Map ref 4C2

8m SE. Retford

Old Cottage Restaurant
Main Street, Laneham,
Retford, DN22 0NA
☎ Dunham-on-Trent
(077 785) 555
*A family-run country
restaurant with comfortable
accommodation, convenient for
Lincoln, Newark and
Sherwood Forest. Riding and
fishing are available nearby.*
Bedrooms: 1 single, 1 double
& 1 twin, 1 family room.
Bathrooms: 3 private,
1 public.
Bed & breakfast: £18-£20
single, £27-£30 double.
Lunch available.
Evening meal 7pm (l.o.
7.30pm).
Parking for 18.
Credit: Access, Visa.
☎5 ☐ ♥ 🛉 Ⓥ ▥ ▴ 🛉 ∪
✻ 🐴 SP 🏧

LEADENHAM

Lincolnshire
Map ref 3A1

*9m E. Newark
Village on the Lincoln
Edge, noted for its fine
church spire.*

George Hotel Ⓜ
High Street, Leadenham,
Lincoln, LN5 0PN
☎ Loveden (0400) 72251
*A 17th C coaching inn where
we pride ourselves on our
international menu and our
collection of over 500 whiskies
from all over the world.*
Bedrooms: 2 single, 2 double
& 3 twin.
Bathrooms: 2 private,
2 public.
Bed & breakfast: £18-£25
single, £25-£35 double.
Lunch available.
Evening meal 7pm (l.o.
9.45pm).
Parking for 150.
Credit: Access, Visa, Amex.
☎ ☚ ☐ ♥ 🛉 Ⓥ ⓉⓋ ▥ 🛉
🐴 🏧 Ⓣ

LEICESTER

Leicestershire
Map ref 4C3

Modern industrial city with a wide variety of attractions including Roman remains, ancient churches, Georgian houses and a Victorian clock tower. There are pedestrianised shopping precincts, an excellent market, several museums, theatres, concert hall and sports and leisure centres.
Tourist Information Centre ☎ (0533) 511300 or 526086

Alexandra Hotel
342 London Road,
Stoneygate, Leicester,
LE2 2PJ
☎ (0533) 703056
An established family-run hotel situated on the A6, 1.5 miles from the city centre, in a select residential area. All family rooms can be let as doubles or twins. All rooms are en-suite with colour TV, telephone and refreshment facilities.
Bedrooms: 4 single, 4 double & 6 twin.
Bathrooms: 13 private; 1 private shower.
Bed & breakfast: £28-£32 single, £40-£46 double.
Half board: from £36.50 daily.
Evening meal 6.30pm (l.o. 8pm).
Parking for 14.
Credit: Access, Visa.

Belmont Hotel ⚕
De Montfort Street,
Leicester, LE1 7GR
☎ (0533) 544773 Telex 34619
Ⓡ Best Western
This family-owned hotel is in a peaceful Victorian conservation area convenient for the city centre.
Bedrooms: 23 single, 16 double & 16 twin, 3 family rooms.
Bathrooms: 58 private.
Bed & breakfast: £65-£75 single, £75-£85 double.
Lunch available.
Evening meal 7pm (l.o. 10pm).
Parking for 50.
Credit: Access, Visa, Diners, Amex.

Charnwood Hotel ⚕
APPROVED
48 Leicester Road,
Narborough, Leicester,
LE9 5DF
☎ (0533) 862218
A quiet family hotel in 1.5 acres of gardens, catering for business people and tourists.
Bedrooms: 11 single, 6 double & 3 twin.
Bathrooms: 20 private.
Bed & breakfast: £25-£50 single, £30-£60 double.
Lunch available.
Evening meal 7pm (l.o. 9.30pm).
Parking for 40.
Credit: Access, Visa, Amex.

Country Court Hotel
Junction 21 Approach,
Braunstone, Leicester,
LE3 2WQ
☎ Leicester (0533) 630066
Attractive 2-storey hotel built around a central landscaped courtyard. Purpose built conference and leisure club.
Bedrooms: 88 single, 4 double & 39 twin, 10 family rooms.
Bathrooms: 141 private.
Bed & breakfast: from £80 single, from £96 double.
Lunch available.
Evening meal 7pm (l.o. 10pm).
Parking for 160.
Credit: Access, Visa, Diners, Amex.

Craigleigh Hotel
17-19 Westleigh Road,
Leicester, LE3 0HH
☎ (0533) 546875
A small family-run hotel 1 mile from the city centre, with easy access to the M1 and M69. Close to sporting venues.
Bedrooms: 4 single, 2 double & 5 twin.
Bathrooms: 2 public.
Bed & breakfast: £19-£22 single, £33-£35 double.
Half board: £27.50-£30.50 daily.
Evening meal 6.30pm (l.o. 4pm).

Fosse Park Hotel
APPROVED
189/191 Hinckley Road,
Westcotes, Leicester,
LE3 0TF
☎ (0533) 622767

Friendly, licensed hotel with en-suite facilities, colour TV and clock/radio. Approximately 1 mile from M1. Reduced rates for contract workers.
Bedrooms: 1 double & 4 twin, 2 family rooms.
Bathrooms: 6 private, 1 public.
Bed & breakfast: £16-£18 single, £28-£25 double.
Half board: £20-£25 daily, £140-£175 weekly.
Lunch available.

Gables Hotel ⚕
368 London Road, Leicester,
LE2 2PN
☎ (0533) 706969
A comfortable hotel, offering a traditional atmosphere with modern facilities and a high standard of cooking and service.
Bedrooms: 2 single, 3 double & 4 twin, 1 family room.
Bathrooms: 10 private.
Bed & breakfast: £33-£35 single, £50-£56 double.
Half board: £41-£43 daily.
Evening meal 6.30pm (l.o. 8.30pm).
Parking for 9.
Credit: Access, Visa.

Holiday Inn Hotel ⚕
St. Nicholas Circle,
Leicester, LE1 5LX
☎ (0533) 531161
Telex 341281
Ⓡ Holiday Inn
Leicester's Holiday Inn offers the Hayloft Restaurant, with a wide selection of dishes, and the Careys, both of which have comfortable, rural decor.
Bedrooms: 46 single, 34 double & 108 twin.
Bathrooms: 188 private.
Bed & breakfast: £84-£99.50 single, £87-£103 double.
Half board: from £65.75 daily, from £385 weekly.
Lunch available.
Evening meal 7pm (l.o. 10.15pm).
Parking for 260.
Credit: Access, Visa, C.Bl., Diners, Amex.

Leicestershire Moat House ⚕
Wigston Road, Oadby,
Leicester, LE2 5QE
☎ (0533) 719441
Ⓡ Queens Moat Houses

This modern hotel prides itself on its accommodation, service, food, wine and conference facilities. 3 miles from the city centre and 5 miles from the M1, it is an excellent base for Leicester.
Bedrooms: 8 single, 16 double & 30 twin, 3 family rooms.
Bathrooms: 57 private.
Bed & breakfast: £28-£66 single, £42-£82 double.
Half board: £30-£77.50 daily.
Lunch available.
Evening meal 7pm (l.o. 9.45pm).
Parking for 160.
Credit: Access, Visa, Diners, Amex.

Park Hotel
125 London Road, Leicester,
LE2 0QT
☎ (0533) 554329
A comfortable, friendly hotel under personal supervision. Convenient for the railway station, university, De Montfort Hall and the city centre.
Bedrooms: 8 single, 5 double & 4 twin, 4 family rooms.
Bathrooms: 1 private, 3 public; 5 private showers.
Bed & breakfast: £20-£30 single, £28-£38 double.
Half board: from £27.50 daily.
Parking for 4.
Credit: Access, Visa.

Park International ⚕
Humberstone Road,
Leicester, LE5 3AT
☎ (0533) 620471
Telex 341460
A city centre hotel, adjacent to the exhibition centre, with banqueting accommodation for up to 500.
Bedrooms: 122 single, 45 double & 39 twin, 3 family rooms.
Bathrooms: 209 private.
Bed & breakfast: £32.95-£74.45 single, £49.90-£90.90 double.
Lunch available.
Evening meal 6.30pm (l.o. 9.30pm).
Parking for 25.
Credit: Access, Visa, C.Bl., Diners, Amex.

Spindle Lodge Hotel
APPROVED
2 West Walk, Leicester,
LE1 7NA
☎ (0533) 551380

This Victorian house has a friendly atmosphere and is within easy walking distance of the city centre, the university, the station, and the civic and entertainment centres.
Bedrooms: 5 single, 3 double & 3 twin, 2 family rooms.
Bathrooms: 3 private, 4 public.
Bed & breakfast: £20-£28 single, £36-£44 double.
Half board: £27.50-£38.50 daily.
Evening meal 6.30pm (l.o. midday).
Parking for 7.

The Stage Hotel ▲

299 Leicester Road, Wigston Fields, Leicester, LE8 1JW
☎ (0533) 886161
Establishment offers professional conference facilities for delegates, business meetings or seminars, and wedding receptions. Up to 200 persons can be seated for meals. Ample parking is available.
Bedrooms: 10 double & 28 twin.
Bathrooms: 38 private.
Bed & breakfast: £42-£52 single, £52-£62 double.
Half board: £50.95-£60.95 daily.
Lunch available.
Evening meal 7pm (l.o. 10pm).
Parking for 192.
Credit: Access, Visa, C.Bl., Diners, Amex.

Time Out Hotel & Leisure

15 Enderby Road, Blaby, Leicester, LE8 3GD
☎ (0533) 778746 & 771154
Newly opened family-run hotel with extensive leisure facilities - please see the symbols - plus snooker. Frequently changed table d'hote menu offers fresh local produce whenever possible and food is available in both the restaurant and bars.
Bedrooms: 5 single, 14 double & 5 twin.
Bathrooms: 24 private.
Bed & breakfast: £48-£58.50 single, £65 double.
Lunch available.
Evening meal 7pm (l.o. 10pm).
Parking for 70.

Credit: Access, Visa, Diners, Amex.

Waltham House ▲

500 Narborough Road, Leicester, LE3 2FU
☎ (0533) 891129
Victorian detached house.
Bedrooms: 1 single, 2 twin.
Bathrooms: 1 public.
Bed & breakfast: £15-£16 single, £24-£26 double.
Half board: £22-£23 daily, £154-£161 weekly.
Evening meal 6pm.
Parking for 4.

LINCOLN

Lincolnshire
Map ref 4C2

Ancient city dominated by the magnificent 11th C cathedral with its triple towers. A Roman gateway is still used and there are medieval houses lining narrow, cobbled streets. Other attractions include the Norman castle, several museums and the Usher Gallery.
Tourist Information Centre ☎ (0522) 529828 or 512971

Alder Hotel ▲

2 Hamilton Road, St. Catherine's, Lincoln, LN5 8ED
☎ (0522) 528243
A small family-run Victorian hotel with modern amenities and a comfortable atmosphere, just over 1 mile to the south of the city centre.
Bedrooms: 1 single, 1 double & 4 twin, 2 family rooms.
Bathrooms: 2 public; 3 private showers.
Bed & breakfast: £13-£15.65 single, £23.50-£26 double.
Parking for 8.
Credit: Access, Visa.

Barbican Hotel ▲

St. Mary's Street, Lincoln, LN5 7EQ
☎ (0522) 543811

Victorian hotel with sympathetically refurbished bedrooms, licensed bars and restaurant. Central position for all transport services and the shopping precinct. Bargain breaks available throughout the year.
Bedrooms: 8 single, 6 double & 3 twin, 2 family rooms.
Bathrooms: 14 private, 2 public; 2 private showers.
Bed & breakfast: £29-£34 single, £41.50-£46 double.
Lunch available.
Evening meal 7pm (l.o. 9.30pm).
Credit: Access, Visa, Diners, Amex.

Brierley House Hotel ▲

54 South Park, Lincoln, LN5 8ER
☎ (0522) 526945
A Victorian family-run hotel adjacent to the south common with its municipal golf-course.
Bedrooms: 4 single, 2 double & 5 twin.
Bathrooms: 6 private, 2 public.
Bed & breakfast: £16-£18 single, £28-£32 double.
Half board: £22.50-£24.50 daily.
Evening meal 7pm.

D'Isney Place Hotel ▲

Eastgate, Lincoln, LN2 4AA
☎ (0522) 538881
A small family-run hotel near the cathedral, with individually styled bedrooms and an emphasis on comfort and privacy.
Bedrooms: 2 single, 10 double & 4 twin, 2 family rooms.
Bathrooms: 18 private.
Bed & breakfast: £38-£51 single, £59-£68 double.
Parking for 12.
Credit: Access, Visa, Diners, Amex.

Eardleys Hotel

21 Cross O'Cliff Hill, Lincoln LN5 8PN
☎ (0522) 523050
A small comfortable Edwardian style hotel, with a licensed bar and restaurant and a homely atmosphere. Located opposite a recreational park.
Bedrooms: 1 single, 2 double & 1 twin, 1 family room.
Bathrooms: 1 public; 2 private showers.

Bed & breakfast: from £19 single, £35-£40 double.
Half board: £25.50-£45.50 daily, £126-£245 weekly.
Lunch available.
Evening meal 7pm (l.o. 10pm).
Parking for 12.

Fittock Cottage ▲

Silver Street, Branston, Lincoln, LN4 1LR
☎ (0522) 791444
Comfortable stone cottage retaining old world charm, in a delightful country village only 4 miles from Lincoln. Parking.
Bedrooms: 1 single, 1 double & 1 twin.
Bathrooms: 1 public; 1 private shower.
Bed & breakfast: from £14.50 single, from £29 double.
Half board: from £24 daily, from £161 weekly.
Evening meal 7pm (l.o. 9pm).
Parking for 3.

Grand Hotel ▲

⚜⚜⚜⚜ APPROVED
St. Mary's Street, Lincoln, LN5 7EP
☎ (0522) 524211 Telex 56401 GRANDH G
A modernised city centre hotel, near the transport terminals and shops. Breakaway weekends are available all year round.
Bedrooms: 18 single, 13 double & 13 twin, 3 family rooms.
Bathrooms: 47 private.
Bed & breakfast: £39-£40 single, £49-£51 double.
Lunch available.
Evening meal 7pm (l.o. 9pm).
Parking for 30.
Credit: Access, Visa, Diners, Amex.

Hillcrest Hotel ▲

⚜⚜⚜⚜ COMMENDED
15 Lindum Terrace, Lincoln, LN2 5RT
☎ (0522) 510182
A Victorian rectory overlooking gardens and the arboretum. A peaceful location within 5 minutes' walk of the cathedral and the city centre.
Bedrooms: 6 single, 5 double & 2 twin, 4 family rooms.
Bathrooms: 17 private.
Bed & breakfast: £36.50 single, £49.50 double.
Lunch available.
Continued ▶

LINCOLN

Continued

Evening meal 7pm (l.o. 9pm).
Parking for 7.
Credit: Access, Visa.

👪 🖋 🔌 🖵 🛇 🟇 🛡 Ⓥ 🛏
🎞 ♨ 🍴 SP T

Loudor Hotel

37 Newark Road, North
Hykeham, Lincoln, LN6 8RB
☎ (0522) 680333
*Small family-run hotel, 3.5
miles south of the city centre
on the Lincoln to Newark road.
A friendly and comfortable
atmosphere, and a warm
welcome from the resident
proprietors.*
Bedrooms: 4 single, 3 double
& 2 twin, 1 family room.
Bathrooms: 10 private.
Bed & breakfast: £28-£32
single, £40-£42 double.
Lunch available.
Evening meal 7.30pm (l.o.
9pm).
Parking for 14.
Credit: Access, Visa, Diners,
Amex.

👪 🖋 🗣 ⓒ 🖵 🛇 🛡 Ⓥ 🛏
🎞 ♨ 🍴 🦮 🐾 SP

Mayfield Guest House

😀 APPROVED

213 Yarborough Road,
Lincoln, LN1 3NQ
☎ (0522) 533732
*Small homely guesthouse with
views of the Trent Valley, a
short walk from the cathedral.
Private enclosed car park.*
Bedrooms: 1 single, 1 double
& 1 twin, 2 family rooms.
Bathrooms: 3 private,
1 public.
Bed & breakfast: £13-£15
single, £25 double.
Parking for 4.

👪 ⓒ 🖵 🛇 🛡 Ⓥ 🗲 🛏
🖵 🎞 ♨ 🐾 🚶 T

Moor Lodge Hotel ₥

😀😀😀😀 COMMENDED

Branston, Nr. Lincoln,
LN4 1HU
☎ (0522) 791366 Telex 56396
EPS LTD
*This owner-managed hotel is in
the attractive village of
Branston, 3 miles south-east of
historic Lincoln on the B1188.*
Bedrooms: 4 single, 4 double
& 13 twin, 4 family rooms.
Bathrooms: 25 private.
Bed & breakfast: £57.20-
£64.90 single, £74.80-£85.80
double.
Half board: £50-£80.20 daily,
£292.60-£338.80 weekly.
Lunch available.
Evening meal 7pm (l.o.
9.15pm).

Parking for 150.
Credit: Access, Visa, Diners,
Amex.

👪 🖋 🗣 🖵 🛇 🛡 Ⓥ 🛏 📺
🎞 ♨ 🍴 🛆 ⒹⒶⓅ 🦮 SP T

Portland Guest House ₥

49-55 Portland Street,
Lincoln, LN5 7JZ
☎ (0522) 521098
*A city centre guesthouse,
convenient for transport
facilities.*
Bedrooms: 5 single, 3 double
& 3 twin, 1 family room.
Bathrooms: 3 public;
1 private shower.
Bed & breakfast: £12.50-£15
single, £22.70-£25 double.
Parking for 12.

👪 🖋 🖵 🛡 🗲 🛏 📺 🎞 ♨
🔴 🚶 T

Tennyson Hotel ₥

😀😀😀 APPROVED

7 South Park Avenue,
Lincoln, LN5 8EN
☎ (0522) 521624/513684
*Hotel with a comfortable
atmosphere, overlooking the
South Park, 1 mile from the
city centre. Personally
supervised. Wide choice of
food.*
Bedrooms: 2 single, 3 double
& 2 twin, 1 family room.
Bathrooms: 8 private.
Bed & breakfast: £25-£27
single, £40 double.
Half board: £35-£37 daily.
Lunch available.
Evening meal 6.30pm (l.o.
8pm).
Parking for 8.
Credit: Access, Visa, Amex.

👪 🖋 ⓒ 🖵 🛇 🛡 Ⓥ 🛏 📺
🎞 ♨ 🚶 ⒹⒶⓅ SP T

Washingborough Hall
Country House Hotel ₥

😀😀😀😀 COMMENDED

Church Hill,
Washingborough, Nr.
Lincoln, LN4 1BE
☎ (0522) 790340
Ⓖ Minotels
*A stone-built, former manor
house in grounds of 3 acres, in
a pleasant village 2.5 miles
from the historic cathedral city
of Lincoln.*
Bedrooms: 2 single, 5 double
& 5 twin.
Bathrooms: 12 private,
1 public.
Bed & breakfast: £42-£50
single, £59-£70 double.
Half board: £230-£260
weekly.
Evening meal 7pm (l.o. 9pm).
Parking for 50.
Credit: Access, Visa, Diners,
Amex.

👪 🖋 🗣 ⓒ 🖵 🛇 🛡 Ⓥ 🗲
🛏 🎞 ♨ 🍴 🐟 🐾 🚶 🦮 SP
🔴 T

LOUGHBOROUGH

Leicestershire
Map ref 4C3

*Industrial town famous
for its bell foundry and
47-bell Carillon Tower.
The Great Central
Railway operates steam
railway rides of over 7
miles through the
attractive scenery of
Charnwood Forest.
Tourist Information
Centre ☎ (0509) 230131*

Bridgeway Guest House

Listed

19a Bridge Street,
Loughborough, LE11 1NQ
☎ (0509) 266678
*A large Victorian, semi-
detached house close to the
town centre and bus station.*
Bedrooms: 1 single, 1 double
& 2 twin, 1 family room.
Bathrooms: 1 public.
Bed & breakfast: from £11
single, from £21 double.
Half board: from £15 daily,
from £90 weekly.
Evening meal 6pm (l.o. 8pm).
Parking for 5.

👪6 🖋 🖵 🛇 🛡 🆄 🛡 Ⓥ
🛏 📺 🎞 🛆 🔾 🧵 🚶 ⒹⒶⓅ 🦮
SP

De Montfort Hotel

😀😀 APPROVED

88 Leicester Road,
Loughborough, LE11 2AQ
☎ (0509) 216061
*Comfortable, family-run hotel
within easy walking distance of
the town centre, opposite a
park.*
Bedrooms: 1 single, 1 double
& 6 twin, 1 family room.
Bathrooms: 3 public.
Bed & breakfast: £17.50
single, £30 double.
Half board: £21-£23.50 daily,
£129-£146.50 weekly.
Evening meal 6pm (l.o. 4pm).
Credit: Access, Visa.

👪 🖵 🛇 🛡 🛏 📺 🎞 ♨ SP

Forest Rise Hotel

😀😀 COMMENDED

55 Forest Road,
Loughborough, LE11 3NW
☎ (0509) 215407
*A friendly family-run hotel,
fully modernised, on the
Charnwood Forest side of
town, with its own garden.
Weddings and parties catered
for.*
Bedrooms: 9 single, 8 double
& 2 twin, 4 family rooms.
Bathrooms: 15 private;
8 private showers.
Bed & breakfast: £28-£34
single, £44-£49 double.

Evening meal 6.30pm (l.o.
5.50pm).
Parking for 25.
Credit: Access, Visa.

👪 🖋 🎞 🛆 🍴 🐾 SP 🛡 Ⓥ 🛏
📺 🎞 ♨ 🍴 🐾 SP

The Hunting Lodge
Hotel

😀😀 COMMENDED

South Street, Barrow upon
Soar, LE12 8LZ
☎ Loughborough
(0509) 412337
*Set in a quiet, rural location.
A la carte restaurant and
choice of real ales. All rooms
have en-suite facilities.*
Bedrooms: 3 double & 1 twin,
2 family rooms.
Bathrooms: 6 private.
Bed & breakfast: £25-£35
single, £30-£50 double.
Lunch available.
Evening meal 6.30pm (l.o.
9.30pm).
Parking for 52.
Credit: Access, Visa, C.Bl.

👪 🖋 🗣 ⓒ 🖵 🛇 🛡 Ⓥ 🎞
♨ 🍴 🐾 ⒹⒶⓅ 🦮 SP

The Mountsorrel Hotel

Listed

217 Loughborough Road,
Mountsorrel, Loughborough,
LE12 7AR
☎ Quorn (0509) 412627 &
416105
*A small friendly, family-run
hotel in secluded grounds, off
the main A6 midway between
Leicester and Loughborough.
Bradgate Park and
Charnwood Forest are nearby.*
Bedrooms: 5 single, 2 double
& 1 twin, 1 family room.
Bathrooms: 1 public;
1 private shower.
Bed & breakfast: £22.50-
£25.50 single, £29-£32 double.
Half board: £31-£34 daily,
£155-£175 weekly.
Evening meal 6.30pm (l.o.
8pm).
Parking for 10.
Credit: Access, Visa.

👪 🖵 🛇 🛡 Ⓥ 📺 🎞 🚶

Peachnook ₥

154 Ashby Road,
Loughborough, LE11 3AG
☎ (0509) 264390
*Small friendly guest house
built around 1890. Near to all
amenities. Open all year.*
Bedrooms: 1 single, 3 twin.
Bathrooms: 1 public.
Bed & breakfast: £10-£15
single, from £20 double.
Half board: £70-£105 weekly.

👪5 🖀 🖋 🖵 🛇 🛡 ♨ 🛆
🔴

The Poplars ₥
Listed

Watling Street, Mountsorrel,
Loughborough, LE12 7BD
☎ Leicester (0533) 302102
A Victorian house with a
wooded secluded garden, on a
hill overlooking the Soar
Valley.
Bedrooms: 5 single, 1 double
& 1 twin.
Bathrooms: 3 public.
Bed & breakfast: from £12.50
single, from £23 double.
Parking for 15.
⌖ ⊠ ⊕ ⊙ ʊ ᴸ ▯ ⽧ ⌀ ⊞
▥ ⏍ ❋ ⋉ ▨ ▩ ᴰᴬᴾ

LYDDINGTON

Leicestershire
Map ref 3A1

2m SE. Uppingham

Marquess of Exeter Hotel ₥
❀❀❀

52 Main Street, Lyddington,
Nr. Uppingham, LE15 9LR
☎ Uppingham (0572) 822477
16th C coaching inn with low
beams and an inglenook
fireplace, between Corby and
Uppingham off the A6003.
Bedrooms: 10 double &
7 twin.
Bathrooms: 16 private;
1 private shower.
Bed & breakfast: £42-£55
single, £52-£70 double.
Lunch available.
Evening meal 7.30pm (l.o.
9.45pm).
Parking for 60.
Credit: Access, Visa, Diners,
Amex.
⌖ ⽧ ⌀ ⊙ ⊡ ⽧ ▯ ⽧ ⊞
▨ ⏍ ⌀ ⋉ ▨ ▩ ꜱᴘ ⽧

MANSFIELD

Nottinghamshire
Map ref 4C2

Ancient town, now an
industrial and shopping
centre, with a popular
market, in the heart of
Robin Hood country.
There is an impressive
19th C railway viaduct, 2
interesting churches, an
18th C Moot Hall and a
museum and art gallery.

Appleby Guest House ₥
❀❀

Chesterfield Road, Pleasley,
Mansfield, NG19 7PF
☎ Mansfield (0623) 810508
Large old house in 2 acres of
grounds, on the A617, 3 miles
from the M1 junction 29.

Bedrooms: 2 single, 1 double
& 2 twin.
Bathrooms: 2 public.
Bed & breakfast: £16 single,
£28 double.
Parking for 12.
⌖ ⽧ ʊ ▯ ⽧ ⌀ ⊞ ▥ ▨
❋ ⋉ ▨

Carr Bank Manor ₥
❀❀❀❀ **COMMENDED**

Windmill Lane, Mansfield,
NG18 2AL
☎ (0623) 22644
Picturesque 18th C manor
house set in landscaped
parkland. All rooms en-suite.
Price includes English
breakfast. Large car park.
Bedrooms: 5 double & 5 twin.
Bathrooms: 10 private.
Bed & breakfast: £25-£46
single, £40-£60 double.

Dalestorth Guest House ₥
Listed **APPROVED**

Skegby Lane, Skegby,
Sutton-in-Ashfield,
NG17 3DH
☎ Mansfield (0623) 551110
18th C ancestral house, on
Sutton-in-Ashfield bypass.
Central for Nottinghamshire
and Derbyshire attractions.
Equipped to high standard.
Fresh linen daily.
Bedrooms: 8 single, 3 double
& 1 twin.
Bathrooms: 7 public.
Bed & breakfast: £20-£25
single, £36-£45 double.
Half board: £25-£30 daily,
£119-£210 weekly.
Evening meal 6.30pm (l.o.
5.30pm).
Parking for 12.
⌖ ⊠ ⌀ ʊ ▯ ⽧ ⌀ ⊞ ▥ ▨
❋ ⋉ ▨ ▩

Nags Head

Low Street, Sutton-in-
Ashfield, NG17 1DH
☎ Mansfield (0623) 554605
A town centre
hotel/pub/restaurant serving
traditional pub lunches each
day and Sunday lunch.
Bedrooms: 4 single, 4 twin,
1 family room.
Bathrooms: 3 public.
Bed & breakfast: £11.50-£15
single, £22-£28 double.
Half board: £15-£25 daily,
£75-£100 weekly.
Evening meal 7pm (l.o. 9pm).
Parking for 6.
⌖ ⊕ ▯ ⽧ ▯ ⽧ ▯ ⌀ ⽧ ▩
⋉ ▨

MARKET HARBOROUGH

Leicestershire
Map ref 4C3

There have been markets
here since the early 13th
C, and the town was also
an important coaching
centre, with several
ancient hostelries. The
early 17th C grammar
school was once the
butter market.
Tourist Information
Centre ☎ *(0858) 462649*
or 462699

Dingley Lodge ₥
Harborough Road, Dingley,
Market Harborough,
LE16 8PJ
☎ Dingley (085 885) 365
An elegant, spacious country
house in its own grounds,
recently restored, commanding
extensive views. Home cooking,
comfortably furnished and en-
suite facilities.
Bedrooms: 1 single, 3 double
& 2 twin, 1 family room.
Bathrooms: 7 private.
Bed & breakfast: £19-£25
single, £32-£35 double.
Half board: £26.50-£32.50
daily, £166.50-£202.50
weekly.
Evening meal 7pm.
Parking for 15.
⌖ ▯ ⽧ ▯ ▯ ⽧ ⌀ ⊞ ▥ ▨
❋ ▨

MARKFIELD

Leicestershire
Map ref 4C3

8m NW. Leicester

Field Head Hotel
❀❀❀❀ **COMMENDED**

Markfield Lane, Markfield,
LE6 0RS
☎ (0530) 245454 Fax (0530)
243740 Telex 342296
⊕ᴿ Lansbury
A new hotel on the A50, 1 mile
from junction 22 off the M1.
Originally an old farmhouse,
the hotel has been built in local
stone.
Bedrooms: 10 double &
16 twin, 2 family rooms.
Bathrooms: 28 private.
Bed & breakfast: £28-£70
single, £56-£82 double.
Half board: £39-£84 daily.
Lunch available.
Evening meal 7pm (l.o.
10pm).
Parking for 70.

Credit: Access, Visa, Diners,
Amex.
⌖ ▯ ⊡ ⽧ ⌀ ⊡ ⽧ ▯ ▯ ⊠
⌖ ⽧ ⊙ ▥ ▯ ⌀ ⽧ ▷ ⋉
▨ ꜱᴘ ▩ ⊞

MATLOCK

Derbyshire
Map ref 4B2

The town lies beside the
narrow valley of the River
Derwent surrounded by
steep wooded hills. Good
centre for exploring
Derbyshire's best
scenery.

Coach House ₥
⊠

Lea, Near Matlock,
DE4 5GJ
☎ Dethick (0629) 534346
Converted farm buildings with
restaurant and bar. TV, tea
and coffee facilities, heated
towel rails in all rooms and en-
suite.
Bedrooms: 1 double & 2 twin.
Bathrooms: 1 private,
1 public.
Bed & breakfast: £13.50-£20
single, £27-£40 double.
Half board: £20-£26.50 daily,
£126-£252 weekly.
Lunch available.
Evening meal 7pm (l.o.
10pm).
Parking for 25.
Credit: Access.
⌖ ⽧ ▯ ⽧ ⽧ ⌀ ⊞ ⏍ ⌀ ⊙ ▩
ᴰᴬᴾ ⽧ ꜱᴘ ⊞

Derwent House ₥
❀❀

Knowleston Place, Matlock,
DE4 3BU
☎ (0629) 584681
We are next to a park and the
River Derwent, a few minutes'
walk from the town centre.
Bedrooms: 2 single, 1 double
& 1 twin, 1 family room.
Bathrooms: 1 private,
1 public.
Bed & breakfast: £13 single,
£26-£30 double.
Parking for 2.
⌖ 1 ⊡ ⽧ ʊ ▯ ⽧ ⌀ ⊞ ▥
⋉ ▩

Jackson Tor House ₥
❀❀

76 Jackson Road, Matlock,
DE4 3JQ
☎ (0629) 582348
We are a family hotel
overlooking Matlock. Ideal for
touring the National Park, the
many historic houses and the
picturesque countryside.
Bedrooms: 10 single, 4 double
& 8 twin, 3 family rooms.
Continued ▶

The enquiry coupons at the back will
help you when contacting proprietors.

MATLOCK
Continued

Bathrooms: 7 public;
1 private shower.
Bed & breakfast: £16-£18
single, £30-£35 double.
Half board: £22-£26 daily.
Evening meal 6pm (l.o. 5pm).
Parking for 25.
ら ⓒ ⌷ ⋔ ⌷ ▦ ※ ⋇
⌷⌷ ⌷

Lane End House
Green Lane, Tansley, Near
Matlock, DE4 5FJ
☎ Matlock (0629) 583981
*250-year-old farmhouse,
alongside the village green and
overlooking Riber Castle.
Offering comfortable
accommodation, adventurous
and interesting home-cooked
food.*
Bedrooms: 2 single, 2 double.
Bathrooms: 3 private,
1 public.
Bed & breakfast: £22.50-
£29.50 single, £39.50-£42.50
double.
Half board: £33-£40 daily,
£210-£250 weekly.
Evening meal 7.30pm (l.o.
7pm).
Parking for 6.
Open March-October.
ら10 ※ ⓒ ⌷ ♡ ⓊⓁ ▋ ⋇
⌷⌷ ▦ ⌷ ⌷ ※ ⌷

Parkfield Guest House M
🏅🏅🏅
115 Lime Tree Road,
Matlock, DE4 3DU
☎ (0629) 57221
*This house is built of
Derbyshire stone and overlooks
the surrounding hills. All
bedrooms are fully en-suite.*
Bedrooms: 1 double & 2 twin,
1 family room.
Bathrooms: 4 private,
1 public.
Bed & breakfast: £25-£28
single, £45-£48 double.
Half board: £31.50-£33.50
daily, £205-£220 weekly.
Parking for 12.
ら ⌷ ⓒ ⌷ ♡ ⓊⓁ ▋ ⌷ ⌷
⊙ ▦ ⌷ ⌷ ⋔ ⌷ ⌷ ⌷ ⌷

The Red House Hotel
🏅🏅🏅
Old Road, Darley Dale, Near
Matlock, DE4 2ER
☎ Matlock (0629) 734854
*Attractive country house
situated on the edge of the
beautiful Peak District
National Park. Delightful
gardens and panoramic views.*
Bedrooms: 1 single, 5 double
& 2 twin, 1 family room.
Bathrooms: 9 private.

Bed & breakfast: £40-£45
single, £55-£65 double.
Half board: £42-£47.50 daily,
£260-£294 weekly.
Lunch available.
Evening meal 7.30pm (l.o.
9pm).
Parking for 20.
Credit: Access, Visa, Diners,
Amex.
ら ⌷ ⌷ ⌷ ⓒ ⌷ ♡ ▋ ⌷
⌷ ⌷ ⌷ ⌷ ♡ ※ ⌷ ⌷
⌷

Riber Hall M
🏅🏅🏅🏅
Matlock, DE4 5JU
☎ (0629) 582795
*An Elizabethan hotel in
peaceful Derbyshire
countryside with beautiful
walks. Features a collection of
antique four-poster beds in
intimate surroundings, and
whirlpool baths.*
Bedrooms: 11 double.
Bathrooms: 11 private,
1 public.
Bed & breakfast: £58-£75
single, £78-£120 double.
Lunch available.
Evening meal 7pm (l.o.
9.30pm).
Parking for 50.
Credit: Access, Visa, C.Bl.,
Diners, Amex.
ら10 ⌷ ⌷ ⌷ ⓒ ⌷ ▋
⌷ ⌷ ▦ ⌷ ⌷ ♡ ※ ⋔ ⌷
⌷ ⌷ ⌷

Robertswood M
🏅🏅🏅 COMMENDED
Farley Hill, Matlock,
DE4 3LL
☎ (0629) 55642
*Spacious Victorian residence
on the edge of Matlock, with
panoramic views. Near
Chatsworth. Friendly, warm
welcome.*
Bedrooms: 4 double & 3 twin.
Bathrooms: 7 private,
1 public.
Bed & breakfast: £24-£29
single, £44-£49 double.
Half board: £34-£39 daily,
£203-£273 weekly.
Evening meal 7pm (l.o.
midday).
Parking for 8.
Credit: Access, Visa.
ら12 ⌷ ⓒ ⌷ ♡ ⌷ ⌷ ⌷
⌷ ▦ ⌷ ⌷ ※ ⌷ ⌷ ⌷

Sheriff Lodge Hotel
51 Dimple Road, Matlock,
DE4 3JX
☎ (0629) 582973
*Small family-run establishment
with a comfortable and homely
atmosphere. We pride
ourselves on our varied and
reasonably priced cuisine.*
Bedrooms: 2 single, 7 double
& 3 twin, 1 family room.

Bathrooms: 11 private;
2 private showers.
Bed & breakfast: £25-£35
single, £45-£55 double.
Lunch available.
Evening meal 6pm (l.o.
10pm).
Parking for 20.
Credit: Access, Visa.
ら ⌷ ⓒ ⌷ ⌷ ▋ ⌷ ⌷ ⌷
⌷ ⌷ ⌷ ※ ※ ⌷ ⌷ ⌷ ⌷

Sycamore Guest House M
🏅🏅
76 High Street, Town Head,
Bonsall, Nr. Matlock,
DE4 2AA
☎ Wirksworth (0629) 823903
*A small family guest house on
the edge of the Peak District
National Park, central to most
of Derbyshire's beauty spots
and ideal for walking or
touring holidays.*
Bedrooms: 1 single, 3 double
& 2 twin, 1 family room.
Bathrooms: 3 public.
Bed & breakfast: £16.50-£17
single, £29-£34 double.
Half board: £22.50-£25 daily,
£150-£160 weekly.
Evening meal 6.30pm (l.o.
7.30pm).
Parking for 6.
ら ♡ ⌷ ⌷ ⌷ ⌷ ⌷ ▦
⌷ ⌷

Thornleigh
🏅🏅
11 Lime Grove Walk,
Matlock, DE4 3FD
☎ (0629) 57626
*Small guesthouse with private
parking, convenient for bus and
rail stations, shops. Non-
smokers only please.*
Bedrooms: 1 single, 1 double,
1 family room.
Bathrooms: 1 public.
Bed & breakfast: £12 single,
£24 double.
Half board: £15-£17 daily,
£110 weekly.
Parking for 3.
Open April-October.
ら4 ⌷ ♡ ⓊⓁ ▋ ⌷ ⌷ ⌷
⌷ ⋔ ⌷

Winstaff Guest House M
🏅🏅 COMMENDED
Derwent Avenue, (Off Old
English Road), Matlock,
DE4 3LX
☎ (0629) 582593
*In a pleasant, quiet and private
cul-de-sac with a garden
backing on to the River
Derwent. Central for many
tourist attractions.*
Bedrooms: 4 double & 2 twin,
1 family room.
Bathrooms: 2 private,
2 public.

Bed & breakfast: £18-£22
single, £32-£38 double.
Half board: £27-£31 daily,
from £102 weekly.
Evening meal 6.30pm (l.o.
midday).
Parking for 6.
ら ♡ ⓊⓁ ▋ ⌷ ⋇ ⌷ ⌷ ▦
♩ ※ ⌷ ⌷ ⌷ ⌷

MATLOCK BATH
Derbyshire
Map ref 4B2

19th C spa town with
many attractions
including several caverns
to visit, a lead mining
museum and a family fun
park. There are
marvellous views over the
surrounding countryside
from the Heights of
Abraham, to which a
cable car gives easy
access.
*Tourist Information
Centre ☎ (0629) 55082*

Sunnybank Guest House M
COMMENDED
Clifton Road, Matlock Bath,
DE4 3PW
☎ Matlock (0629) 584621
*A comfortable and spacious
Victorian house with views over
peaceful surroundings, offering
a high standard of
accommodation. Near to
Chatsworth and the Derbyshire
Dales.*
Bedrooms: 1 single, 2 double
& 3 twin.
Bathrooms: 3 private,
1 public.
Bed & breakfast: £18-£23
single, £34.20-£42 double.
Half board: £26.60-£30.50
daily, £168-£192 weekly.
Evening meal 7pm (l.o.
10am).
Credit: Access, Visa.
ら12 ♡ ⌷ ⌷ ⌷ ▦ ⌷ ※
⌷ ⌷ ⌷ ⌷

Temple Hotel M
🏅🏅🏅 COMMENDED
Temple Walk, Matlock Bath,
DE4 3PG
☎ Matlock (0629) 583911
*The hotel nestles comfortably
amid "Little Switzerland"
scenery of picturesque Matlock
Bath, overlooking the Vale of
the River Derwent from a
steep, wooded hillside. All
bedrooms en-suite with colour
TV.*
Bedrooms: 1 single, 7 double
& 3 twin, 3 family rooms.
Bathrooms: 14 private.
Bed & breakfast: £41-£48
single, £54 double.
Half board: £50-£57 daily.

Lunch available.
Evening meal 6.30pm (l.o. 10pm).
Parking for 32.
Credit: Access, Visa, Diners, Amex.

MELTON MOWBRAY
Leicestershire
Map ref 4C3

Close to the attractive Vale of Belvoir and famous for its pork pies and Stilton cheese which are the subjects of special displays in the museum. It has a beautiful church with a tower 100 ft high.
Tourist Information Centre ☎ *(0664) 69946*

Amberley
4 Church Lane, Asfordby, Melton Mowbray, LE14 3RU
☎ (0664) 812314
Modern, ranch-style bungalow with 1 acre of lawns, floodlit gardens and river frontage with fishing. 3 miles west of Melton, tucked away behind a church.
Bedrooms: 1 single, 1 double & 1 twin.
Bathrooms: 1 public.
Bed & breakfast: £11-£13 single, £22-£26 double.
Parking for 6.

George Hotel
High Street, Melton Mowbray, LE13 0TR
☎ (0664) 62112
Best Western
Restaurant with a la carte and table d'hote menus. All modern facilities in bedrooms.
Bedrooms: 5 single, 10 double & 5 twin.
Bathrooms: 20 private.
Bed & breakfast: from £55 single, from £65 double.
Lunch available.
Evening meal 7pm (l.o. 9.30pm).
Parking for 16.
Credit: Access, Visa, Diners, Amex.

Sysonby Knoll Hotel
COMMENDED
Asfordby Road, Melton Mowbray, LE13 0HP
☎ (0664) 63563

A family owned and run hotel, in its own grounds, offering a cosy bar and restaurant serving home-cooked food. Overlooks gardens and a river.
Bedrooms: 6 single, 11 double & 7 twin, 3 family rooms.
Bathrooms: 21 private, 2 public.
Bed & breakfast: £26-£36 single, £36-£46 double.
Lunch available.
Evening meal 7pm (l.o. 9pm).
Parking for 30.
Credit: Access, Visa.

MONSAL HEAD
Derbyshire
Map ref 4B2

3m NW. Bakewell

Castle Cliffe Private Hotel
Monsal Head, Bakewell, DE4 1NL
☎ Great Longstone (062 987) 258
A stone house with views of Monsal Dale and its viaduct. Follow signs to Monsal Dale from Ashford on the A6.
Bedrooms: 3 double & 4 twin, 2 family rooms.
Bathrooms: 2 private, 2 public; 7 private showers.
Bed & breakfast: £33-£36 double.
Half board: £25-£26.50 daily, £157.50-£167.50 weekly.
Lunch available.
Evening meal 7pm (l.o. 6pm).
Parking for 15.
Credit: Access, Visa.

Cliffe House
Monsal Head, Bakewell, DE4 1NL
☎ Great Longstone (062 987) 376
This country house, decorated with care, has splendid views of Monsal Dale and is an ideal base for exploring the Peak District. Traditional home cooking.
Bedrooms: 8 double, 2 family rooms.
Bathrooms: 8 private, 1 public.
Bed & breakfast: £34-£38 double.
Half board: £25-£27 daily.

Evening meal 7.30pm (l.o. 10am).
Parking for 12.
Credit: Access, Visa.

Monsal Head Hotel
Monsal Head, Bakewell, DE4 1NL
☎ Great Longstone (062 987) 250
An ideal centre for a holiday or weekend break in the centre of the Peak District National Park. All bedrooms enjoy excellent views of the countryside, some with a conservatory/balcony directly overlooking the Monsal Dale.
Bedrooms: 6 double & 1 twin, 1 family room.
Bathrooms: 6 private, 2 public.
Bed & breakfast: £40-£60 double.
Half board: £60-£80 daily, £380-£500 weekly.
Lunch available.
Evening meal 7pm (l.o. 9.30pm).
Parking for 12.
Credit: Access, Visa.

NEW MILLS
Derbyshire
Map ref 4B2

8m NW. Buxton

Sycamore Inn
Sycamore Road, Birchvale, Via Stockport, Cheshire SK12 5AB
☎ New Mills (0663) 42715 or 47568
Free house on the banks of the River Sett, serving home-made food and traditional beers.
Bedrooms: 2 single, 2 double & 2 twin, 1 family room.
Bathrooms: 7 private.
Bed & breakfast: £25-£30 single, £30-£45 double.
Lunch available.
Evening meal 6.30pm (l.o. 10.30pm).
Parking for 50.
Credit: Access, Visa.

Half board prices shown are per person but in some cases may be based on double/twin occupancy.

NEWARK
Nottinghamshire
Map ref 4C2

The town has many fine old houses and ancient inns near the large, cobbled market-place. Substantial ruins of the 12th C castle, where King John died, dominate the riverside walk and there are several interesting museums. Sherwood Forest is nearby.
Tourist Information Centre ☎ *(0636) 78962*

The Appleton Hotel
73 Appletongate, Newark, NG24 1LN
☎ (0636) 71616
A homely, family-run hotel, 300 yards from the main railway station. Lunches and evening meals available by prior arrangement.
Bedrooms: 3 single, 2 double, 1 family room.
Bathrooms: 6 private.
Bed & breakfast: £26-£32 single, from £42 double.
Lunch available.
Evening meal 7pm (l.o. 7.30pm).
Parking for 6.
Credit: Access, Visa, C.Bl.

Beechlea Guest House
2 London Road, New Balderton, Newark, NG24 3AJ
☎ (0636) 72480
A traditional house set in its own grounds, with easy access to the A1.
Bedrooms: 2 single, 3 double & 1 twin, 2 family rooms.
Bathrooms: 2 private, 2 public.
Bed & breakfast: £12.50-£15.50 single, £25-£31 double.
Parking for 8.

Chapel House
Chapel Lane, Coddington, Newark, NG24 2PW
☎ (0636) 706785
Comfortable family home, originally a chapel built in 1865. Evening meals are available by arrangement only.
Bedrooms: 1 single, 1 double & 1 twin.
Bathrooms: 1 private, 1 public.
Bed & breakfast: £15-£27.50 single, £30-£40 double.

Continued ▶

NEWARK
Continued

Half board: £20-£35 daily, £120-£200 weekly.
Parking for 3.
⌖ ⚒ ⓊⓁ ⚐ Ⅴ ⊨ TV ⊞ ➡ ❖ ⌘ ⌧

The Grange Hotel
⚜⚜⚜ **COMMENDED**
73 London Road, Newark, NG24 1RZ
☎ (0636) 703399
An attractive red brick Victorian property in a quiet residential area, only a short walk from the historic town centre.
Bedrooms: 2 single, 4 double & 2 twin, 1 family room.
Bathrooms: 9 private.
Bed & breakfast: £40-£50 single, £50-£65 double.
Half board: £48.45-£65.05 daily.
Lunch available.
Evening meal 7pm (l.o. 9pm).
Parking for 9.
Credit: Access, Visa.
⌖ ☏ ⊡ ⌘ ⚐ ⓘ Ⅴ ⊨ ⊞
➡ ⌦ ⌧ ⌘ SP

South Parade Hotel ⋀
⚜⚜⚜
117 Balderton Gate, Newark, NG24 1RY
☎ (0636) 703008
Privately-owned hotel in ideal quiet location. Close to castle, river and market-place. 5 minutes' walk from town centre.
Bedrooms: 6 single, 5 double & 3 twin, 2 family rooms.
Bathrooms: 8 private, 2 public; 1 private shower.
Bed & breakfast: £31-£36.50 single, £42.50-£49.50 double.
Lunch available.
Evening meal 7pm (l.o. 8.30pm).
Parking for 12.
Credit: Access, Visa.
⌖ ⚒ ☏ ⌦ ⚐ ⓘ Ⅴ ⊨ ◐
⊞ ➡ ⌦ SP ⌘ T

The Willow Tree Inn ⋀
Front Street, Barnby-in-the-Willows, Newark, NG24 2SA
☎ (0636) 626613
A heavily beamed inn in a conservation village surrounded by historical places. Close to the Trent and Witham Fisheries, and Newark, off the A17 and A1.
Bedrooms: 2 single, 1 double & 1 twin.
Bathrooms: 1 public.

Bed & breakfast: from £15 single, from £25 double.
Lunch available.
Parking for 100.
⌖ ☏ ⊡ ⌦ ⚐ Ⅴ ⊞ ➡ ⌦
⌧ ⌘ ⌦ ⌦ SP ⌘

NORTHAMPTON
Northamptonshire
Map ref 2C1

A bustling town and a shoe manufacturing centre, with excellent shopping facilities, several museums and parks, a theatre and a concert hall. Several old churches include 1 of only 4 round churches in Britain.
Tourist Information Centre ☎ (0604) 22677

Aarandale Regent Hotel & Guest House ⋀
⚜⚜
6-8 Royal Terrace, Barrack Road, Northampton, NN1 3RF
☎ (0604) 31096
Small and cosy, family-run hotel/guesthouse situated within easy walking distance of town centre, bus and train stations. Evening meals by arrangement only.
Bedrooms: 4 single, 6 double & 6 twin, 4 family rooms.
Bathrooms: 5 public.
Bed & breakfast: £18-£22 single, £31-£36 double.
Parking for 14.
⌖ ⚒ ⌦ ⚐ ⓘ Ⅴ ⊨ TV ⊞
➡ ⌦ T

Birchfields ⋀
Listed **APPROVED**
17 Hester Street, Northampton, NN2 6AP
☎ (0604) 28199
A small friendly guesthouse off the M1 exit 15.
Bedrooms: 1 single, 2 double & 3 twin.
Bathrooms: 2 public.
Bed & breakfast: £13 single, £26 double.
⌖ 2 ⌦ ⌦ ⚐ ⓊⓁ Ⅴ ⊞ ⌦ ⌘ ⌦
⌦

10 Church View
Wootton, Northampton, NN4 0LJ
☎ (0604) 761626
A quiet, friendly family-run guest house close the the M1. Ideal for Collingtree Golf Course and Turners Musical Merry-go-round. Lunches and evening meals are served by prior arrangement.
Bedrooms: 1 single, 1 double & 1 twin.
Bathrooms: 2 public.

Bed & breakfast: £12.50-£15 single, £26-£30 double.
Half board: £19-£21.50 daily, £133-£150.50 weekly.
Parking for 6.
⌖ 12 ⚒ ⌦ ⚐ ⓊⓁ ⓘ ⊨ TV
⊞ ➡ ⌦ ⌦

The Coach House ⋀
⚜⚜⚜
8-10 East Park Parade, Northampton, NN1 4LA
☎ (0604) 250981
Friendly hotel 1 mile north of the town centre, overlooking a park. Convenient for shops and industrial areas.
Bedrooms: 9 single, 13 double & 5 twin, 3 family rooms.
Bathrooms: 21 private, 2 public; 7 private showers.
Bed & breakfast: £25-£50 single, £50-£70 double.
Lunch available.
Evening meal 7pm (l.o. 9.30pm).
Parking for 14.
Credit: Access, Visa, Diners, Amex.
⌖ ⚒ ☏ ⊡ ⌦ ⚐ ⓘ ⊨
➡ TV ◐ ⊞ ➡ ⌦ ⌦ SP

Fish Inn
11 Fish Street, Northampton, NN1 2AA
☎ (0604) 234040
This Victorian inn, named after the street in which it is situated, has been recently refurbished and is a convivial, popular meeting place. Explore the town and 5 country parks nearby.
Bedrooms: 5 single, 5 double & 2 twin.
Bathrooms: 2 private, 2 public; 8 private showers.
Bed & breakfast: £32-£42 single, £46.50-£53 double.
Lunch available.
Evening meal 7.30pm (l.o. 10pm).
Parking for 3.
Credit: Access, Visa, Diners, Amex.
⌖ ☏ ⌦ ⚐ ⓘ Ⅴ ⊞ ➡ ⌦
⌦ SP ⌘

Four Seasons Hotel
⚜⚜ **COMMENDED**
16 East Park Parade, Kettering Road, Northampton, NN1 4LE
☎ (0604) 20810
A private hotel close to Northampton town centre, providing a warm and friendly atmosphere.
Bedrooms: 13 single, 3 double & 8 twin, 6 family rooms.
Bathrooms: 1 private; 29 private showers.
Bed & breakfast: £23-£30 single, £35-£42 double.
Half board: £27.50-£40 daily, £190-£270 weekly.

Lunch available.
Evening meal 5pm (l.o. 10pm).
Parking for 12.
Credit: Access, Visa.
⌖ ⚒ ☏ ⌦ ⚐ Ⅴ ⊨ TV ●
⊞ ➡ T ⌦ ⌦ SP
⚐ Display advertisement appears on page 300.

Langham Hotel
4-5 Langham Place, Barrack Road, Northampton, NN4 6AA
☎ (0604) 39917
A family-run well established hotel, 10 minutes from the town centre and overlooking the racecourse. On the main road to Leicester. A warm welcome is assured.
Bedrooms: 7 single, 7 double & 6 twin, 5 family rooms.
Bathrooms: 25 private, 2 public.
Bed & breakfast: £42-£44 single, £55-£58 double.
Half board: £54-£58 daily.
Evening meal 5.30pm (l.o. 8pm).
Parking for 24.
Credit: Access, Visa, Diners, Amex.
⌖ ⚒ ☏ ⌦ ⚐ ⓘ Ⅴ ⌦ ⊨
⊞ ➡ ⌦ ⌦ SP

Northampton Moat House ⋀
⚜⚜⚜⚜⚜ **COMMENDED**
Silver Street, Northampton, NN1 2TA
☎ (0604) 22441 Telex 311142
⊕ Queens Moat Houses
A modern town-centre hotel decorated to an executive standard. Banqueting facilities for 5 to 500 persons.
Bedrooms: 15 single, 47 double & 76 twin, 4 family rooms.
Bathrooms: 142 private.
Bed & breakfast: from £71 single, from £87 double.
Half board: from £47 daily.
Lunch available.
Evening meal 5pm (l.o. 10.30pm).
Parking for 250.
Credit: Access, Visa, Diners, Amex.
⌖ ☏ ⊡ ⌦ ⚐ ⓘ Ⅴ ⌦ ⊨
● ⛾ ⊞ ➡ T ⌦ ∪ SP T

Plough Hotel
Bridge Street, Northampton, NN1 1PF
☎ (0604) 38401
A recently refurbished, impressive Victorian building restored to old fashioned charm of bygone ages. In the centre of Northampton.
Bedrooms: 15 single, 4 double & 7 twin, 1 family room.
Bathrooms: 19 private, 3 public.

Bed & breakfast: £41-£44 single, £53-£56 double.
Half board: £49-£52 daily, £316-£335 weekly.
Lunch available.
Evening meal 7pm (l.o. 10pm).
Parking for 100.
Credit: Access, Visa, Diners, Amex.

Poplars Hotel
COMMENDED

Cross Street, Moulton, Nr. Northampton, NN3 1RZ
☎ (0604) 643983
Personal attention is given at this small country hotel in the heart of Northamptonshire. Within easy reach of many tourist attractions.
Bedrooms: 12 single, 4 double & 1 twin, 4 family rooms.
Bathrooms: 15 private, 2 public.
Bed & breakfast: £15-£30 single, £40-£50 double.
Half board: £25-£40 daily.
Evening meal 6.30pm (l.o. 6.30pm).
Parking for 21.
Credit: Access, Visa.

Swallow Hotel M
COMMENDED

Eagle Drive, Northampton, NN4 0HW
☎ (0604) 768700 Telex 31562
CR Swallow
A new hotel incorporating a leisure centre, in a rural setting overlooking a lake and golf-course. Easy access to the motorway.
Bedrooms: 50 single, 16 double & 44 twin, 12 family rooms.
Bathrooms: 122 private.
Bed & breakfast: max. £75 single, from £95 double.
Lunch available.
Evening meal 7pm (l.o. 10.30pm).
Parking for 166.
Credit: Access, Visa, Diners, Amex.

Wistmans Wood

5 Orchard Way, Cogenhoe, Northampton, NN7 1LZ
☎ (0604) 891538
A small country guest house within easy reach of motorways and country beauty spots, offering a warm and friendly welcome.
Bedrooms: 1 single, 2 double & 2 twin.
Bathrooms: 2 public.

Bed & breakfast: from £12.50 single, from £25 double.
Half board: from £17.50 daily, from £120 weekly.
Evening meal 6pm (l.o. 8pm).
Parking for 4.

NORTON
Nottinghamshire
Map ref 4C2

5m S. Worksop

Norton Grange Farm
Listed

Norton Cuckney, Near Mansfield, NG20 9LP
☎ Mansfield (0623) 842666
172-acre mixed farm. A Georgian stone farmhouse in the heart of the Welbeck Estate, a part of the world-famous Sherwood Forest.
Bedrooms: 1 double & 1 twin, 1 family room.
Bathrooms: 1 public.
Bed & breakfast: from £12 single, from £24 double.
Parking for 5.

NOTTINGHAM
Nottinghamshire
Map ref 4C2

Modern city with a wide range of industries including lace. Its castle is now a museum and art gallery with a statue of Robin Hood outside. Many attractions include "The Tales of Robin Hood", with 'flight to Sherwood' experience; the Lace Hall in a converted church; excellent shopping facilities, theatres, museums, Wollaton Hall and the National Water Sports Centre.
Tourist Information Centre ☎ (0602) 470661 or 823558

Cambridge Hotel M
APPROVED

63-65 Loughborough Road, West Bridgford, Nottingham, NG2 7LA
☎ (0602) 811036/815927
Friendly atmosphere, close to the city centre, cricket ground, water sports centre and university. Licensed bar and snooker room. All rooms with complimentary video and satellite TV.
Bedrooms: 12 single, 4 double & 4 twin.
Bathrooms: 11 private, 4 public; 3 private showers.

Bed & breakfast: £32-£46 single, £56-£60 double.
Half board: from £38 daily, from £190 weekly.
Evening meal 6pm (l.o. 9.30pm).
Parking for 30.
Credit: Access, Visa, Diners, Amex.

Clifton Hotel
APPROVED

126 Nottingham Road, Long Eaton, Nottingham, NG10 2BZ
☎ Long Eaton (0602) 734277
Friendly, family-run hotel close to M1, exit 25. 10 minutes from Donington Racecourse, East Midlands Airport, Derby and Nottingham.
Bedrooms: 4 single, 2 double & 2 twin, 2 family rooms.
Bathrooms: 2 private, 2 public.
Bed & breakfast: £18-£27 single, £28-£33 double.
Half board: £24-£31 daily.
Evening meal 6.30pm (l.o. 5.30pm).
Parking for 25.

The Croft Hotel M
Listed **APPROVED**

6-8 North Road, West Bridgford, Nottingham, NG2 7NH
☎ (0602) 812744
A small, private hotel in a quiet residential area. Close to Trent Bridge, water sports centre and 1.5 miles from city centre.
Bedrooms: 8 single, 4 double & 2 twin, 2 family rooms.
Bathrooms: 5 public.
Bed & breakfast: from £17 single, from £28 double.
Evening meal 6pm (l.o. 8pm).
Parking for 12.

Hotel Des Clos

Old Lenton Lane, Nottingham, NG7 2SA
☎ (0602) 866566
Converted Victorian farm buildings in a Green Belt area on the banks of the River Trent, but close to the city centre.
Bedrooms: 1 single, 6 double & 2 twin.
Bathrooms: 9 private.
Bed & breakfast: £54.50-£86.50 single, £64-£93 double.
Half board: £69.45-£105.45 daily.
Lunch available.

Evening meal 7pm (l.o. 9.30pm).
Parking for 24.
Credit: Access, Visa, Amex.

Europa Hotel M

20-22 Derby Road, Long Eaton, Nottingham, NG10 1LW
☎ Long Eaton (0602) 728481
Telex 377494
On the A6005 midway between Nottingham and Derby, 1.5 miles from the M1 junction 25 and the A52, and 6 miles from East Midlands Airport.
Bedrooms: 8 single, 3 double & 7 twin, 1 family room.
Bathrooms: 13 private, 1 public; 6 private showers.
Bed & breakfast: £32-£40 single, £42-£50 double.
Lunch available.
Evening meal 6.30pm (l.o. 8.30pm).
Parking for 20.
Credit: Access, Visa, Diners, Amex.

Garden Court Holiday Inn

Castle Marina Park, Nottingham, NG7 1GX
☎ (0602) 500600
CR Holiday Inn
Situated on the edge of town. Easily accessible from M1 junction 24. 100 bedrooms, all en-suite, bistro-style bar and restaurant.
Bedrooms: 86 double & 14 twin.
Bathrooms: 100 private.
Bed & breakfast: £56-£60 single, £62-£66 double.
Half board: £72-£75 daily, £500-£600 weekly.
Lunch available.
Evening meal 6.30pm (l.o. 10pm).
Parking for 120.
Credit: Access, Visa, C.Bl., Diners, Amex.

George Hotel M

George Street, Nottingham, NG1 3BP
☎ (0602) 475641
Telex 378150
CR Friendly
A city centre hotel with an atmosphere of charm and character. Although the hotel has been extensively modernised, its historic links with the past have been carefully retained.

Continued ▶

NOTTINGHAM
Continued

Bedrooms: 23 single, 20 double & 26 twin, 1 family room.
Bathrooms: 70 private.
Bed & breakfast: £49-£58.50 single, £58.50-£66 double.
Half board: £40.75-£70 daily.
Lunch available.
Evening meal 7pm (l.o. 9.15pm).
Credit: Access, Visa, Diners, Amex.
⟐ 🖭 ⚓ © ◻ ✿ î 🆅 ✂
🗗 🖵 ● 🔄 ▥ ☎ î ⚓ 🆂🅿 🎬
🆃

Grantham Hotel
⬭
24-26 Radcliffe Road, West Bridgford, Nottingham, NG2 5FW
☎ (0602) 811373
A family-run hotel offering modern accommodation in a comfortable atmosphere. Convenient for the centre of Nottingham, Trent Bridge and the National Water Sports Centre.
Bedrooms: 17 single, 2 double & 5 twin.
Bathrooms: 3 public.
Bed & breakfast: £18-£20 single, £27-£32 double.
Parking for 8.
Credit: Access, Visa.
⟐3 ◻ 🆄🅻 î 🆅 ⚓ 🖭 ▥ ☎
🆃

Greenwood Lodge
⬭⬭⬭
Third Avenue, Sherwood Rise, Nottingham, NG7 6JH
☎ (0602) 621206
1 mile from city centre. All rooms en-suite with tea and coffee facilities, trouser press, TV, telephone. Car park.
Bedrooms: 1 double & 2 twin.
Bathrooms: 3 private.
Bed & breakfast: £23-£27.50 single, £33-£37.50 double.
Parking for 5.
Credit: Access, Visa.
⟐5 © ◻ ✿ 🆄🅻 🆅 ⚓ ▥
☎ 🖵 🆂🅿

The Milford Hotel ⋒
⬭⬭ APPROVED
Pavilion Road, West Bridgford, Nottingham, NG2 5FG
☎ (0602) 811464
A family-run hotel. Close to the River Trent, county cricket ground, Water Sports Centre and the city centre.
Bedrooms: 6 single, 2 double & 5 twin, 1 family room.
Bathrooms: 4 public.
Bed & breakfast: £16-£18 single, £30-£34 double.

Half board: £20-£22 daily, £133-£147 weekly.
Evening meal 6pm (l.o. 7pm).
Parking for 14.
Credit: Access, Visa, Diners, Amex.
⟐ ◻ ✿ î 🆅 ⚓ 🖭 ▥ ⚓
☼ 🖵 🆃

Nottingham Moat House ⋒
⬭⬭⬭ COMMENDED
Mansfield Road, Nottingham, NG5 2BT
☎ (0602) 602621
Telex 377429
ⓒⓡ Queens Moat Houses
A modern hotel with 3 restaurants, 3 bars, direct-dial telephones and tea and coffee facilities, offering heavily reduced weekend rates.
Bedrooms: 109 single, 42 double & 18 twin, 3 family rooms.
Bathrooms: 172 private.
Bed & breakfast: £24-£65 single, £48-£86.50 double.
Half board: £34.85-£75.85 daily.
Lunch available.
Evening meal 6pm (l.o. 10.30pm).
Parking for 800.
Credit: Access, Visa, Diners, Amex.
⟐ ⚓ © ◻ ✿ î 🆅 ✂ ⚓
● 🔄 ▥ ☎ î ⚓ 🆂🅿 🆃

P & J Hotel
⬭⬭ APPROVED
277 Derby Road, Lenton, Nottingham, NG7 2DP
☎ (0602) 783998
Red brick, 3-storey building on a main road with a car park at the rear. Located half a mile from the city centre and close to the Queen Medical Hospital and University. Direct access to M1 junction 25.
Bedrooms: 3 single, 7 double & 7 twin, 2 family rooms.
Bathrooms: 6 private, 6 public; 2 private showers.
Bed & breakfast: £22-£32 single, £37-£45 double.
Evening meal 6pm (l.o. 8pm).
Parking for 10.
Credit: Access, Visa, Amex.
⟐ ◻ ✿ 🆄🅻 🆅 ⚓ 🖭 ▥
⚓ î ⚓ 🖵 🆂🅿

Royal Moat House International ⋒
Wollaton Street, Nottingham, NG1 5RH
☎ (0602) 414444 Telex 37101
ⓒⓡ Queens Moat Houses
Modern city hotel with 201 bedrooms and 14 conference rooms.
Bedrooms: 125 single, 44 double & 32 twin.
Bathrooms: 201 private.

Bed & breakfast: £28.60-£64.90 single, £54.90-£82.50 double.
Half board: from £45.10 daily.
Lunch available.
Evening meal 6pm (l.o. 11pm).
Parking for 700.
Credit: Access, Visa, C.Bl., Diners, Amex.
⟐ ⚓ © ◻ ✿ î 🆅 ✂ ⚓
● 🔄 ▥ ☎ î ⚓ ⚓ 🖵 🗡
⚓ 🆂🅿 🆃

St. Andrews Private Hotel ⋒
⬭⬭ APPROVED
310 Queens Road, Beeston, Nottingham, NG9 1JA
☎ (0602) 254902
A friendly, family-run guest house with easy access to Nottingham city centre, the university, M1 and East Midlands Airport. Convenient for Sherwood Forest and Derbyshire.
Bedrooms: 4 single, 1 double & 3 twin, 2 family rooms.
Bathrooms: 1 private, 4 public.
Bed & breakfast: £17-£26 single, £26-£35 double.
Half board: £23.50-£32.50 daily, £164.50-£227.50 weekly.
Evening meal 5.45pm (l.o. 7.30pm).
Parking for 6.
⟐ ✿ 🆄🅻 î 🆅 ⚓ 🖭 ▥ ⚓
🗡 ⚓

Springers Guest House
86 Musters Road, West Bridgford, Nottingham, NG2 7PS
☎ (0602) 815054
A friendly, family-run guesthouse close to the city centre and all amenities.
Bedrooms: 6 single, 2 twin, 1 family room.
Bathrooms: 2 public.
Bed & breakfast: £14.50-£15 single, £26-£28 double.
Parking for 5.
⟐ ✿ 🆄🅻 ⚓ 🖭 ▥ ⚓ 🗡 ⚓

Stakis Victoria Hotel ⋒
⬭⬭⬭⬭
Milton Street, Nottingham, NG1 3PZ
☎ (0602) 419561 Telex 37401
ⓒⓡ Stakis
Centrally situated within easy walking distance of the Theatre Royal, Nottingham's many nightlife activities, shopping centres and the castle.
Bedrooms: 45 single, 81 double & 40 twin.
Bathrooms: 166 private.
Bed & breakfast: max. £80 single, max. £98 double.
Lunch available.

Evening meal 7pm (l.o. 9.45pm).
Parking for 18.
Credit: Access, Visa, Diners, Amex.
⟐ ⚓ © ◻ ✿ î 🆅 ✂
⚓ 🖭 ● 🔄 ▥ ☎ î ⚓ 🖵 🗤
⚓ 🆂🅿 🆃

Strathdon Thistle Hotel
Derby Road, Nottingham, NG1 5FT
☎ (0602) 418501
Telex 377185
ⓒⓡ Thistle
A modern hotel offering a wide choice of food and a friendly atmosphere. Placed between the 2 theatres and within walking distance of the castle, shopping areas and business centre.
Bedrooms: 44 single, 6 double & 13 twin, 6 family rooms.
Bathrooms: 69 private.
Bed & breakfast: from £63.75 single, £87.50-£88.50 double.
Lunch available.
Evening meal 7pm (l.o. 10.30pm).
Parking for 10.
Credit: Access, Visa, C.Bl., Diners, Amex.
⟐ ⚓ © ◻ ✿ î 🆅 ✂ ⚓
● 🔄 ▥ ☎ î ⚓ 🆂🅿 🆃

Swans Hotel and Restaurant
84-90 Radcliffe Road, West Bridgford, Nottingham, NG2 5HH
☎ (0602) 814042
A privately-owned hotel offering a wide range of facilities for the discerning traveller.
Bedrooms: 11 single, 12 double & 4 twin, 4 family rooms.
Bathrooms: 31 private.
Bed & breakfast: £25-£70 single, £40-£75 double.
Half board: £32.50-£105 daily.
Lunch available.
Evening meal 7pm (l.o. 10pm).
Parking for 30.
Credit: Access, Visa, Diners, Amex.
⟐ ⚓ ⚓ © ◻ ✿ î 🆅 ✂ ⚓
🖭 ● 🔄 ▥ ☎ î ⚓ 🗡 ⚓
⚓ 🆂🅿 🆃

Waltons Hotel ⋒
⬭⬭⬭⬭
North Lodge, North Road, The Park, Nottingham, NG7 1AG
☎ (0602) 475215

> **Please mention this guide when making a booking.**

A hotel with a country house atmosphere and individually designed bedrooms near the city centre, within walking distance of the castle. There is an intimate dining room offering fresh food and a selection of wines.
Bedrooms: 5 single, 9 double & 3 twin.
Bathrooms: 17 private.
Bed & breakfast: £47-£60 single, £60-£80 double.
Half board: £62-£75 daily.
Lunch available.
Evening meal 7.30pm (l.o. 10.30pm).
Parking for 12.
Credit: Access, Visa, Amex.

OAKHAM

Leicestershire
Map ref 4C3

Pleasant former county town of Rutland has a fine 12th C Great Hall, part of its castle, housing a historic collection of horseshoes. An octagonal Butter Cross stands in the market-place and Rutland County Museum, Rutland Farm Park and Rutland Water are other attractions.
Tourist Information Centre ☎ (0572) 724329

Barnsdale Country Club ♨
Stamford Road, Near Oakham, LE15 8AB
☎ (0572) 757901
Set in 60 acres overlooking Rutland Water, offering extensive leisure and sporting facilities and a gourmet restaurant. Self catering lodges are also available.
Bedrooms: 14 single, 35 double & 8 twin, 2 family rooms.
Bathrooms: 53 private, 3 public.
Bed & breakfast: from £72 single, from £105 double.
Lunch available.
Evening meal 7pm (l.o. 9.45pm).
Parking for 170.
Credit: Access, Visa, C.Bl., Diners, Amex.

We advise you to confirm your booking in writing.

Boultons Country House Hotel ♨
4 Catmos Street, Oakham, LE15 6HW
☎ (0572) 722844
A 16th C former hunting lodge, quiet, friendly and recently refurbished. Modern comforts in traditional surroundings, close to many attractions.
Bedrooms: 7 single, 13 double & 3 twin, 2 family rooms.
Bathrooms: 25 private.
Bed & breakfast: from £50 single, from £60 double.
Half board: from £43.50 daily.
Lunch available.
Evening meal 7pm (l.o. 9.30pm).
Parking for 15.
Credit: Access, Visa, Diners, Amex.

Madhatters
Listed COMMENDED
35 Main Street, Cottesmore, Oakham, LE15 7DH
☎ Oakham (0572) 812550
A character, 300-year-old, thatched cottage 4 miles from the A1. Hairdressing, beauty and natural therapies and a tea room are available.
Bedrooms: 1 twin, 1 family room.
Bathrooms: 1 public.
Bed & breakfast: £18.50-£22.50 single, £30-£40 double.
Half board: £25-£30 daily, £120-£160 weekly.
Lunch available.
Evening meal 6pm (l.o. 9pm).
Parking for 2.

Normanton Park Hotel ♨
Normanton Park, South Shore, Rutland Water, LE15 8RP
☎ Stamford (0780) 720315
A family-run 16-bedroomed conversion of a Georgian coach house. Restaurant and coffee lounge open all year. Unique position on the south shore of Rutland Water. 6 miles from Oakham.
Bedrooms: 1 single, 5 double & 5 twin, 5 family rooms.
Bathrooms: 14 private, 1 public.
Bed & breakfast: £40-£46 single, £61-£70 double.
Lunch available.
Evening meal 7.30pm (l.o. 9.45pm).

Parking for 100.
Credit: Access, Visa, C.Bl., Diners, Amex.

The Whipper-in Hotel ♨
Market Place, Oakham, LE15 6DT
☎ (0572) 756971
A 17th C coaching inn filled with antiques and fresh flowers, in the original market place of Rutland's county town.
Bedrooms: 8 single, 10 double & 6 twin.
Bathrooms: 24 private.
Bed & breakfast: from £68 single, from £80 double.
Half board: from £82.50 daily.
Lunch available.
Evening meal 7.30pm (l.o. 9.30pm).
Credit: Access, Visa, Diners, Amex.

OUNDLE

Northamptonshire
Map ref 3A1

Historic town situated on the River Nene with narrow alleys and courtyards and many stone buildings, including a fine church and historic inns.
Tourist Information Centre ☎ (0832) 274333

Castle Farm Guest House ♨
Castle Farm, Fotheringhay, Peterborough, Cambridgeshire PE8 5HZ
☎ Cotterstock (083 26) 200
850-acre mixed farm. An early 19th C stone farmhouse in beautiful surroundings, with lawns running down to the River Nene and adjoining the Fotheringhay Castle site. 2 rooms can be adapted to family arrangement. Packed lunches by arrangement.
Bedrooms: 4 twin, 2 family rooms.
Bathrooms: 5 private, 1 public.
Bed & breakfast: £18-£25 single, £28-£37 double.
Half board: £22-£25 daily, £154-£175 weekly.
Evening meal 7pm.
Parking for 12.

PEAK DISTRICT

See Aldwark, Ashbourne, Ashford-in-the-Water, Bakewell, Bamford, Baslow, Buxton, Castleton, Edale, Glossop, Grindleford, Hartington, Hathersage, Hayfield, Monsal Head, New Mills, Pilsley, Rowarth, Rowsley.

PILSLEY

Derbyshire
Map ref 4B2

Shoulder of Mutton Hotel ♨
Hardstoft, Pilsley, Chesterfield, S45 8AF
☎ Chesterfield (0246) 850276
Hotel with a la carte restaurant and brasserie style restaurant. Conference and banqueting facilities for up to 500.
Bedrooms: 2 double & 1 twin.
Bathrooms: 3 private.
Bed & breakfast: from £35 single, from £45 double.
Half board: from £40 daily, from £250 weekly.
Lunch available.
Evening meal 7.30pm (l.o. 10pm).
Parking for 100.
Credit: Access, Visa, Diners, Amex.

QUORN

Leicestershire
Map ref 4C3

*3m SE. Loughborough
The Great Central Railway, a preserved steam railway, runs through attractively wooded countryside at the edge of village.*

Quorn Grange Restaurant
Quorn Grange, Wood Lane, Quorn, Loughborough, LE12 8DB
☎ (0509) 412167
Old country house on the edge of Bradgate Park, set in its own gardens.
Bedrooms: 2 single, 5 double & 8 twin, 2 family rooms.
Bathrooms: 17 private.
Bed & breakfast: £30-£60 single, £60-£90 double.
Half board: £45-£90 daily, £395-£505 weekly.
Lunch available.
Evening meal 7pm (l.o. 10pm).

Continued ▶

QUORN

Continued

Parking for 101.
Credit: Access, Visa, C.Bl.,
Diners, Amex.

RADCLIFFE-ON-TRENT

Nottinghamshire
Map ref 4C2

5m E. Nottingham

Yew Trees Hotel

16 Shelford Road, Radcliffe-on-Trent, Nottingham,
NG12 2AG
☎ (0602) 333818
In a village location, close to the shops and to rail and bus services to Nottingham. Also conveniently placed for the National Water Sports Centre.
Bedrooms: 6 single, 1 twin,
1 family room.
Bathrooms: 3 private,
1 public.
Bed & breakfast: £15-£19
single, £27.50-£32.50 double.
Half board: £22-£26 daily,
£94-£127 weekly.
Evening meal 6.30pm (l.o.
4pm).
Parking for 6.

RAGNALL

Nottinghamshire
Map ref 4C2

13m N. Newark-on-Trent

Ragnall House

APPROVED
Ragnall, Newark,
NG22 0UR
☎ Dunham-on-Trent
(077 785) 575 or (0777)
228575
A large listed Georgian family house with a late Victorian extension, in three quarters of an acre of grounds. Close to the River Trent in rolling countryside. There are good pubs and restaurants nearby.
Bedrooms: 1 single, 1 double
& 1 twin, 1 family room.
Bathrooms: 1 private,
1 public; 2 private showers.
Bed & breakfast: £11-£12
single, £22-£24 double.
Parking for 8.

RETFORD

Nottinghamshire
Map ref 4C2

Market town on the River Idle with a pleasant market square and Georgian houses. The surrounding villages were the homes and meeting places of the early Pilgrim Fathers.
Tourist Information Centre ☎ *(0777) 860780*

Elms Hotel

London Road, Retford,
DN22 7DX
☎ (0777) 708957
A 19th C house with extensive gardens. All bedrooms en-suite with TV, radio, telephone, tea and coffee facilities. A la carte dining.
Bedrooms: 1 single, 4 double
& 3 twin, 1 family room.
Bathrooms: 9 private.
Bed & breakfast: £30-£35
single, £40-£45 double.
Half board: from £38 daily,
from £283 weekly.
Lunch available.
Evening meal 7pm (l.o.
10pm).
Parking for 120.
Credit: Access, Visa, Diners,
Amex.

West Retford Hotel M

24 North Road, Retford,
DN22 7XG
☎ (0777) 706333 Telex 56143
18th C country house located in extensive grounds. Recently refurbished and developed, the hotel now offers 63 bedrooms, an a la carte restaurant and 3 bars. Ideal base for touring Sherwood Forest and the Dukeries.
Bedrooms: 8 double &
22 twin, 33 family rooms.
Bathrooms: 63 private.
Bed & breakfast: £37-£66
single, £53-£78 double.
Lunch available.
Evening meal 7pm (l.o.
10pm).
Parking for 100.
Credit: Access, Visa, Diners,
Amex.

Ye Olde Bell M

Barnby Moor, Retford,
DN22 8QS
☎ Retford (0777) 705121

A 17th C coaching inn in beautiful countryside close to A1 and Sherwood Forest. All modern amenities and good restaurant.
Bedrooms: 19 single,
22 double & 14 twin.
Bathrooms: 55 private.
Bed & breakfast: £60-£75
single, £75-£90 double.
Lunch available.
Evening meal 7pm (l.o.
9.45pm).
Parking for 250.
Credit: Access, Visa, Diners,
Amex.

RIPLEY

Derbyshire
Map ref 4B2

10m N. Derby

Hammersmith House Hotel M

Hammersmith, Ripley,
DE5 3RA
☎ (0773) 742574/745462
Large countryside house, convenient for the Peak District National Park and many stately homes, with good leisure facilities nearby.
Bedrooms: 2 single, 5 double
& 3 twin, 2 family rooms.
Bathrooms: 10 private,
1 public.
Bed & breakfast: £30 single,
£40 double.
Half board: £37.50 daily,
£230 weekly.
Evening meal 7pm (l.o. 8pm).
Parking for 40.
Credit: Access, Visa.

ROWARTH

Derbyshire
Map ref 4B2

2m NE. New Mills

Little Mill Inn M

Rowarth, Stockport,
SK12 5EB
☎ (0663) 743178
Delightful old country inn nestling in the foothills of Derbyshire, with a stream running through beautiful gardens. Separate restaurant, en-suite accommodation.
Bedrooms: 2 double & 1 twin.
Bathrooms: 3 private.
Bed & breakfast: £17.50-£20
single, £32-£35 double.
Half board: £29-£32 daily,
£140-£182 weekly.
Lunch available.

Evening meal 6pm (l.o.
10pm).
Parking for 100.
Credit: Access, Visa, Amex.

ROWSLEY

Derbyshire
Map ref 4B2

4m SE. Bakewell
Village at the meeting point of the Rivers Wye and Derwent, and on the edge of the Haddon and Chatsworth estates. 19th C water-powered flour mill, working and open to visitors, with craft workshops.

East Lodge M

COMMENDED
Rowsley, Matlock, DE4 2EF
☎ (0629) 734474
A small, tastefully furnished country house hotel in 10 acres of grounds, close to Chatsworth House and Haddon Hall.
Bedrooms: 1 single, 4 double
& 4 twin.
Bathrooms: 9 private.
Bed & breakfast: £37-£50
single, £60-£80 double.
Half board: £42-£65 daily,
£290-£420 weekly.
Evening meal 7.30pm (l.o.
8.30pm).
Credit: Access, Visa.

Peacock Hotel M

Rowsley, Matlock, DE4 2EB
☎ Matlock (0629) 733518
Embassy
Formerly the Dower House to Haddon Hall, the hotel is furnished with antiques from that era.
Bedrooms: 3 single, 7 double
& 7 twin, 3 family rooms.
Bathrooms: 15 private,
2 public.
Bed & breakfast: £44-£83
single, £64-£91 double.
Half board: £67-£96 daily,
£277-£385 weekly.
Lunch available.
Evening meal 7pm (l.o. 9pm).
Parking for 50.
Credit: Access, Visa, C.Bl.,
Diners, Amex.

> **Please check prices and other details at the time of booking.**

SHERWOOD FOREST

See Kersall, Laneham, Mansfield, Ragnall, Retford, Tuxford, Worksop.
Tourist Information Centre ☎ (0623) 824545 or 824490

SKEGNESS

Lincolnshire
Map ref 4D2

Famous seaside resort with 6 miles of sandy beaches and bracing air. Its attractions include swimming pools, bowling greens, gardens, Natureland Marine Zoo, golf-courses and a wide range of entertainment at the Embassy Centre. To the south lies Gibraltar Point, a large nature reserve.
Tourist Information Centre ☎ (0754) 4821

Amalfi Hotel
102 Drummond Road, Skegness, PE25 3EH
☎ (0754) 5236
Attractive Edwardian hotel close to promenade and town centre. Professionally run by ex-restaurateur, where well-presented food and friendliness are important.
Bedrooms: 1 single, 5 double & 2 twin, 5 family rooms.
Bathrooms: 2 public.
Bed & breakfast: £12-£15.50 single, £24-£29 double.
Half board: £17-£25 daily, £90-£140 weekly.
Evening meal 5.30pm (l.o. 6pm).
Parking for 8.
Credit: Access, Visa.
⏚ 👹 🛉 ▯ 🖃 📺 🎔 ➰ 🍵
✖ ⅅ⅋ℙ ⊗ ℙ

Fairways
1 Cavendish Road, Skegness, PE25 2QU
☎ (0754) 67556
A small, licensed, friendly guest house, a few minutes' walk from the sea front and local amenities.
Bedrooms: 1 single, 2 double & 1 twin, 2 family rooms.
Bathrooms: 2 public.
Bed & breakfast: £9-£10 single, £18-£20 double.
Half board: £12.50-£13.50 daily, £65-£78 weekly.
Evening meal 5.30pm (l.o. 5.30pm).
Parking for 5.
⏚ 👹 ▯ 🖃 📺 🎔 ➰ ⅅ⅋ℙ
⊗ ℙ

Grosvenor House Hotel M
🐝🐝
North Parade, Skegness, PE25 2TE
☎ (0754) 3376
The hotel is midway along the seafront, near the bathing pool, bowling greens, sun castle, and the Embassy Conference Centre.
Bedrooms: 13 single, 11 double & 6 twin, 9 family rooms.
Bathrooms: 14 private, 6 public.
Bed & breakfast: £18-£22.75 single, £36-£45.50 double.
Half board: £25.30-£30 daily, £163.45-£196.35 weekly.
Lunch available.
Evening meal 6.30pm (l.o. 7.30pm).
Parking for 6.
Open April-October.
Credit: Access, Visa, Diners, Amex.
⏚ 👹 🛉 ▯ 🖃 📺 ➰ ⊡ ➰
🍵 ⅅ⅋ℙ ℙ ⊤

Knighton Lodge Hotel
9 Trafalgar Avenue, Skegness, PE25 3EU
☎ (0754) 4354
The hotel has an indoor swimming pool and all bedrooms are en-suite. The beach is 25 yards away and the town centre is 10 minutes' walk away.
Bedrooms: 1 single, 3 double & 2 twin, 3 family rooms.
Bathrooms: 9 private.
Bed & breakfast: £16.50-£25 single, £33-£50 double.
Parking for 4.
Credit: Access, Visa, Diners, Amex.
⏚ 👹 🖃 ▯ 🖃 ✂ 🖃 ➰
➰ ● 🔲 🖃 ⅅ⅋ℙ ℙ

Merrydale Guest House M
🐝🐝
13 Glentworth Crescent, Skegness, PE25 2TG
☎ (0754) 66485
A family-run guesthouse with a warm, friendly atmosphere and home cooking. In a quiet yet central position.
Bedrooms: 1 single, 6 double & 2 twin, 2 family rooms.
Bathrooms: 3 public; 3 private showers.
Bed & breakfast: £8-£10 single, £16-£20 double.
Half board: £10-£12.50 daily, £60-£78 weekly.
Evening meal 5.30pm.
Parking for 4.
Open January, March-December.
⏚ 👹 👹 ▯ 🖃 🖃 ➰
🔲 🖃 ⅅ⅋ℙ ⊗ ℙ

New Links Hotel
🐝🐝
Drummond Road, Skegness, PE25 3BT
☎ (0754) 3605
2-storey Tudor-style brick building with neat gardens, a large lawn and central for the beach, golf and Gibraltar Point Nature Reserve.
Bedrooms: 8 single, 6 double & 1 twin, 1 family room.
Bathrooms: 8 private, 2 public.
Bed & breakfast: £21.50-£23.50 single, £39-£43 double.
Half board: £30-£34 daily, £180-£204 weekly.
Lunch available.
Evening meal 7pm (l.o. 9pm).
Parking for 40.
Credit: Access, Visa.
⏚ 👹 ▯ 🖃 ➰ 🛉 ▯ 🖃 📺
🔲 🖃 🍵 ✂ ⅅ⅋ℙ ⊗ ℙ

Saxby Hotel M
🐝🐝 **COMMENDED**
12 Saxby Avenue, Skegness, PE25 3LG
☎ (0754) 3905
A family-run hotel on a corner in a quiet residential area of Skegness. 300 yards from sea-front.
Bedrooms: 2 single, 8 double & 1 twin, 3 family rooms.
Bathrooms: 4 private, 2 public.
Bed & breakfast: £13.50-£14.50 single, £26.50-£28.50 double.
Half board: £19.50-£20.50 daily, £94.50-£144 weekly.
Evening meal 6pm (l.o. 6pm).
Parking for 10.
Open March-December.
⏚ 👹 🛉 ▯ 🖃 📺 🔲 🖃 ➰ ➰

SLEAFORD

Lincolnshire
Map ref 3A1

Market town whose parish church has one of the oldest stone spires in England and particularly fine tracery round the windows.
Tourist Information Centre ☎ (0529) 414294

The Lincolnshire Oak Hotel M
🐝🐝🐝🐝 **COMMENDED**
East Road, Sleaford, NG34 7EQ
☎ (0529) 413807
Comfortable hotel, privately run with restaurant, function and conference facilities for up to 140 people. Just off the A17.

Bedrooms: 5 single, 7 double & 2 twin.
Bathrooms: 14 private.
Bed & breakfast: £42-£46 single, £60-£66 double.
Half board: £54-£60 daily, £340-£378 weekly.
Evening meal 7pm (l.o. 9pm).
Parking for 50.
Credit: Access, Visa, Amex.
⏚ 👹 ● ▯ 🖃 🛉 ▯ 🖃 📺
➰ 🍵 ✂ ✖ ⊗ ℙ 🖃

The Mallards Hotel M
🐝🐝🐝
6-8 Eastgate, Sleaford, NG34 7DJ
☎ (0529) 303062
Grade II listed hotel in the centre of town offers a good restaurant, fine wines and comfortable, relaxing rooms.
Bedrooms: 3 single, 6 double & 4 twin.
Bathrooms: 9 private, 4 public.
Bed & breakfast: £28-£35 single, £38-£46 double.
Half board: £40-£47 daily.
Lunch available.
Evening meal 7pm (l.o. 9pm).
Parking for 7.
Credit: Access, Visa.
⏚ 👹 ➰ ▯ 🖃 🛉 ▯ 🖃 🔲
🖃 🖃 🖃

The Tally Ho Inn M
Aswarby, Nr. Sleaford, NG34 8SA
☎ Culverthorpe (052 95) 205
This 200-year-old inn, carefully converted from stables, offers en-suite bedrooms, real ale, a small restaurant and log fires in winter.
Bedrooms: 2 double & 4 twin.
Bathrooms: 6 private.
Bed & breakfast: £26-£28 single, £38-£42 double.
Half board: £35-£40 daily, £210-£310 weekly.
Lunch available.
Evening meal 7pm (l.o. 9.45pm).
Parking for 50.
⏚ 👹 ▯ 🖃 🛉 ▯ 🖃 🔲 🖃
✂ 🖃

Individual proprietors have supplied all details of accommodation. Although we do check for accuracy, we advise you to confirm prices and other information at the time of booking.

295

SOUTHWELL

Nottinghamshire
Map ref 4C2

Town dominated by the Norman minster which has some beautiful 13th C stone carvings in the Chapter House. Charles I spent his last night of freedom in one of the inns. The original Bramley apple tree can still be seen.

Old Forge
♨♨♨

2 Burbage Lane, Southwell, NG25 0ER
☎ (0636) 812809
A carefully restored old forge with an attractive garden, peacefully located in a small minster town. A few minutes' walk from shops and restaurants. Private parking facilities and 10% reduction on longer stays.
Bedrooms: 3 double & 2 twin, 1 public.
Bed & breakfast: £30-£32 single, £42-£45 double.
Parking for 7.
Credit: Access, Visa.
♨♨♨♨♨♨♨♨♨♨♨

Old National School Hotel
♨♨♨ APPROVED

Nottingham Road, Southwell, NG25 0LG
☎ (0636) 814360
Tastefully converted to give a high standard of comfort and attractively furnished beamed bedrooms, four-posters and twin bedded. All rooms en-suite.
Bedrooms: 2 double & 4 twin, 1 family room.
Bathrooms: 7 private.
Bed & breakfast: max. £22 single, max. £33 double.
Half board: £125-£175 weekly.
Parking for 6.
Credit: Access, Visa.
♨♨♨♨♨♨♨♨♨♨♨♨

Half board prices shown are per person but in some cases may be based on double/twin occupancy.

SPALDING

Lincolnshire
Map ref 3A1

This Fenland town is famous for its bulbfields which attract visitors from all over the world. A spectacular Flower Parade takes place at the beginning of May each year and the tulips at Springfields show gardens are followed by displays of roses and bedding plants in summer. Interesting local museum.
Tourist Information Centre ☎ (0775) 725468

Cley Hall Hotel ♨
♨♨♨♨ COMMENDED

22 High Street, Spalding, PE11 1TX
☎ (0775) 725157
Georgian hotel has river frontage with mature gardens, and a period restaurant, bars and bistro with varied and changing menus. 500 metres from the town centre.
Bedrooms: 4 single, 3 double & 4 twin.
Bathrooms: 11 private.
Bed & breakfast: £25-£47 single, £36-£54 double.
Half board: £34.25-£56.25 daily.
Lunch available.
Evening meal 7pm (l.o. 9.30pm).
Parking for 20.
Credit: Access, Visa, Diners, Amex.
♨♨♨♨♨♨♨♨♨♨♨

Red Lion Hotel ♨

Market Place, Spalding, PE11 1SU
☎ (0775) 722869
Town centre free house offers a warm welcome, good food, real ales, relaxed atmosphere and value for money.
Bedrooms: 2 single, 1 double & 7 twin.
Bathrooms: 4 private, 3 public.
Bed & breakfast: £30-£40 single, £45-£55 double.
Lunch available.
Evening meal 7pm (l.o. 10pm).
Credit: Access, Visa, Diners, Amex.
♨♨♨♨♨♨♨♨♨♨♨

Stables Motel ♨
♨♨♨♨

Cowbit Road, Spalding, PE11 2RJ
☎ (0775) 767290

Converted from farm buildings, the motel complements the 17th C farmhouse. Three quarters of a mile from the centre of Spalding on the A1073 Peterborough road. Most units are on the ground floor with their own porches and all are equipped with refrigerators and colour TV.
Bedrooms: 4 single, 4 double & 2 twin.
Bathrooms: 10 private.
Bed & breakfast: £25-£45 single, £45-£70 double.
Half board: £55-£75 daily.
Lunch available.
Evening meal 7.30pm (l.o. 9.30pm).
Parking for 50.
Credit: Access, Visa, Diners, Amex.
♨♨♨♨♨♨♨♨♨♨♨♨♨♨♨♨♨♨

SPILSBY

Lincolnshire
Map ref 4D2

Market town in attractive countryside on the edge of the Lincolnshire Wolds and the Fens. Birthplace of explorer Sir John Franklin and has associations with the poet Tennyson, born in nearby Somersby. It has a medieval market cross.

Shades Hotel ♨

Church Street, Spilsby, PE23 5JT
☎ (0790) 52200
A small, family-run hotel close to the Lincolnshire Wolds.
Bedrooms: 2 single, 1 double & 1 twin.
Bathrooms: 1 public.
Bed & breakfast: £11-£12 single, £22-£24 double.
Half board: £16-£17 daily.
Lunch available.
Evening meal 5pm (l.o. 6.30pm).
Parking for 50.
♨♨♨♨♨♨♨♨♨

Classifications and quality commendations were correct at the time of going to press but are subject to change. Please check at the time of booking.

STAMFORD

Lincolnshire
Map ref 3A1

Exceptionally beautiful and historic town with many houses of architectural interest, several notable churches and other public buildings all in the local stone. Burghley House, built by William Cecil, is a magnificent Tudor mansion on the edge of the town.
Tourist Information Centre ☎ (0780) 55611

Candlesticks Hotel & Restaurant ♨
Listed APPROVED

1 Church Lane, Stamford, PE9 2JU
☎ (0780) 64033
Hotel with a pleasant atmosphere and all the comfort we can provide. Our restaurant has a fixed price menu and serves English, French and Portuguese food.
Bedrooms: 2 single, 3 double & 3 twin.
Bathrooms: 3 private; 5 private showers.
Bed & breakfast: from £25 single, from £35 double.
Lunch available.
Evening meal 7pm (l.o. 9.45pm).
Parking for 4.
Credit: Access, Visa.
♨♨♨♨♨♨♨♨♨♨♨♨♨

SUDBURY

Derbyshire
Map ref 4B2

5m E. Uttoxeter
Attractive village with red brick cottages and a 17th C inn. The National Trust's Sudbury Hall, which was built in the reign of Charles II, has beautiful carving by Grinling Gibbons and a magnificent staircase and plasterwork. The servants' wing contains the Museum of Childhood.

Boars Head

Lichfield Rd., Draycott-in-the-Clay, Sudbury, DE6 5GX
☎ Burton upon Trent (0283) 820344
17th C inn and restaurant with beamed interior, now a new hotel with reception and residents' lounge.

Bedrooms: 3 single, 15 double & 10 twin.
Bathrooms: 28 private.
Bed & breakfast: £29.50-£49.50 single, £42.50-£60 double.
Half board: £32.50-£52.50 daily.
Lunch available.
Evening meal 7pm (l.o. 10pm).
Parking for 80.
Credit: Access, Visa, Diners, Amex.

THRAPSTON

Northamptonshire
Map ref 3A2

8m SW. Oundle

The 16th C. Woolpack Hotel M

6 Kettering Road, Islip, Nr. Thrapston, NN14 3JU
☎ Thrapston (080 12) 2578
Overlooking the River Nene, this 16th C inn is in a quiet village.
Bedrooms: 1 double & 12 twin.
Bathrooms: 13 private.
Bed & breakfast: from £36 single, from £48 double.
Lunch available.
Evening meal 6.30pm (l.o. 9.15pm).
Parking for 50.
Credit: Access, Visa.

TOWCESTER

Northamptonshire
Map ref 2C1

Town built on the site of a Roman settlement. It has some interesting old buildings, including an inn featured in one of Dickens' novels. The racecourse lies alongside the A5 Watling Street.

Plum Park

Paulerspury, Towcester
☎ (032 733) 727
12-acre farm. Off the A5, 1.5 miles south of Towcester, near Paulerspury. Approach up a tree lined drive with mature gardens and a sun patio around the pool.
Bedrooms: 2 double & 6 twin.
Bathrooms: 8 private.
Bed & breakfast: £15-£32 single, £30-£45 double.

Half board: £22-£39 daily, £95-£185 weekly.
Lunch available.
Evening meal 6pm (l.o. 10.50pm).
Parking for 8.
Credit: Visa, Amex.

TUXFORD

Nottinghamshire
Map ref 4C2

12m N. Newark
Small town on the old Great North Road, convenient for exploring nearby Sherwood Forest and the Dukeries.

Mr. & Mrs. Frow
Listed APPROVED

Blenheim House, Newcastle Street, Tuxford, Newark, NG22 0LR
☎ (0777) 870677
A family guesthouse with a comfortable atmosphere, 5 minutes' walk from the shops and pubs. A cup of tea is provided on arrival! Hot and cold water in all rooms.
Bedrooms: 1 double, 1 family room.
Bathrooms: 2 public.
Bed & breakfast: £9 single, £18 double.
Half board: £63 weekly.
Parking for 3.

Newcastle Arms Hotel

Market Place, Tuxford, Newark, NG22 0LA
☎ (0777) 870208
An 18th C coaching inn in a village near Sherwood Forest, with good access to both the A1 and M1.
Bedrooms: 2 single, 4 double & 4 twin, 1 family room.
Bathrooms: 11 private.
Bed & breakfast: £42-£47 single, £52-£57 double.
Lunch available.
Evening meal 7pm (l.o. 9.30pm).
Parking for 52.
Credit: Access, Visa, Diners, Amex.

UPPINGHAM

Leicestershire
Map ref 4C3

Quiet market town dominated by its famous public school which was founded in 1584. It has many stone houses and is surrounded by attractive countryside.

Crown Hotel M

High Street East, Uppingham, Oakham, LE15 9PY
☎ (0572) 822302
A 17th C listed building near Rutland Water. Trout and coarse fishing are available nearby.
Bedrooms: 2 single, 3 double & 1 twin, 1 family room.
Bathrooms: 7 private.
Bed & breakfast: £30 single, £40 double.
Lunch available.
Evening meal 7pm (l.o. 9pm).
Parking for 20.
Credit: Access, Visa.

Rutland House

61 High Street East, Uppingham, Oakham, LE15 3PY
☎ (0572) 822497
Centrally located in ancient Uppingham, our small family-run hotel has bedrooms individually designed to complement its Victorian architecture. Our aim is to offer stylish accommodation and value for money.
Bedrooms: 2 single, 1 double & 1 twin, 1 family room.
Bathrooms: 5 private.
Bed & breakfast: from £25 single, from £35 double.
Parking for 3.

WEEDON

Northamptonshire
Map ref 2C1

Crossroads Hotel M
COMMENDED

High Street, Weedon, Northampton, NN7 4PX
☎ (0327) 40354 Telex 312311
Ⓒ Best Western

A privately-owned hotel at the junction of the A5 and A45, 3 miles from the M1 junction 16. Full conference and dining facilities in character surroundings. Facilities include 2 rooms for the physically handicapped.
Bedrooms: 5 single, 18 double & 20 twin, 5 family rooms.
Bathrooms: 48 private.
Bed & breakfast: £60-£70 single, £70-£85 double.
Lunch available.
Evening meal 6pm (l.o. 10pm).
Parking for 100.
Credit: Access, Visa, Diners, Amex.

Globe Hotel M
COMMENDED

High Street, Weedon, Northampton, NN7 4QD
☎ (0327) 40336
17th C countryside inn with a Royal Charter. Old world atmosphere and free house hospitality with English cooking.
Bedrooms: 3 single, 5 double & 5 twin, 2 family rooms.
Bathrooms: 15 private.
Bed & breakfast: £33-£40 single, £39.50-£55 double.
Half board: from £35 daily.
Lunch available.
Evening meal 11am (l.o. 10pm).
Parking for 40.
Credit: Access, Visa, Diners, Amex.

WELLINGBOROUGH

Northamptonshire
Map ref 3A2

Manufacturing town, mentioned in the Domesday Book, with some old buildings and inns, in one of which Cromwell stayed on his way to Naseby. It has attractive gardens in the centre of the town and 2 interesting churches. *Tourist Information Centre* ☎ (0933) 228101

Columbia Hotel

19 Northampton Road, Wellingborough, NN8 3HG
☎ (0933) 229333
Family-run hotel offering a friendly and personal service, half a mile from centre of thriving market town.
Bedrooms: 7 single, 14 double & 7 twin, 1 family room.

Continued ▶

The National Crown Scheme is explained in full on pages 556 − 558.

WELLINGBOROUGH

Continued

Bathrooms: 29 private.
Bed & breakfast: £28-£43
single, £40-£54 double.
Lunch available.
Evening meal 6.30pm (l.o.
9.30pm).
Parking for 18.
Credit: Access, Visa, Amex.

High View Hotel

156 Midland Road,
Wellingborough, NN8 1NG
☎ (0933) 78733/278733
Attractive Victorian building
with a pleasant garden, in a
quiet area, near the town centre,
station, and trading estates.
Bedrooms: 6 single, 4 double
& 6 twin, 1 family room.
Bathrooms: 14 private,
1 public.
Bed & breakfast: £20-£44
single, £30-£50 double.
Lunch available.
Evening meal 6.30pm (l.o.
8.30pm).
Parking for 9.
Credit: Access, Visa, Diners,
Amex.

Hind Hotel M

Sheep Street,
Wellingborough, NN8 1BY
☎ (0933) 222827
Queens Moat Houses
A market-town-centre
Cromwellian hotel offering
traditional English and
continental cuisine. Ideal for
Althorp, Wicksteed Park,
Silverstone, Nene Valley
Steam Railway and Stoke
Bruerne Waterways Museum.
Bedrooms: 11 single,
12 double & 10 twin, 1 family
room.
Bathrooms: 34 private.
Bed & breakfast: £55-£62
single, £70-£82 double.
Half board: £65.95-£72.95
daily.
Lunch available.
Evening meal 7.30pm (l.o.
9.30pm).
Parking for 16.
Credit: Access, Visa, C.Bl.,
Diners, Amex.

Oak House Private Hotel M

9 Broad Green,
Wellingborough, NN8 4LE
☎ (0933) 71133

A small, homely hotel with a
comfortable atmosphere, on the
edge of the town centre,
featuring double-glazing and
an enclosed car park.
Bedrooms: 3 single, 3 double
& 4 twin.
Bathrooms: 9 private;
1 private shower.
Bed & breakfast: £28-£30
single, £38-£40 double.
Half board: £26.50-£37.50
daily, £185.50-£262.50
weekly.
Evening meal 6.15pm (l.o.
midday).
Parking for 9.
Credit: Access, Visa.

WEST HADDON

Northamptonshire
Map ref 4C3

7m NE. Daventry

Pytchley Hotel M
COMMENDED

High Street, West Haddon,
Northampton, NN6 7AP
☎ (078 887) 426 & 209
A 200-year-old Georgian
building in the centre of a
small village surrounded by
lovely countryside. Close to
many large towns, Althorp
House and places of interest.
Bedrooms: 4 single, 3 double
& 7 twin, 3 family rooms.
Bathrooms: 17 private.
Bed & breakfast: £45-£48
single, £56-£60 double.
Lunch available.
Evening meal 7pm (l.o.
10.30pm).
Parking for 60.
Credit: Access, Visa, Diners,
Amex.

WIRKSWORTH

Derbyshire
Map ref 4B2

Small town which was
once the centre of the
lead-mining industry in
Derbyshire. It has many
old buildings of interest,
including the church of St.
Mary, narrow streets and
alleys, a Heritage Centre
and the National Stone
Centre. There is a well-
dressing ceremony in
May.

Henmore Grange M
APPROVED

Hopton, Near Wirksworth,
Derby, DE4 4DF
☎ (062 985) 420

An old farmhouse, built about
1700 in mellow old stone. In
1986 Henmore Grange was
awarded a certificate of merit
in the British Tourist
Authority's "Come to Britain"
promotion. Attractive garden,
planted to attract butterflies.
Bedrooms: 1 single, 3 double
& 2 twin, 4 family rooms.
Bathrooms: 8 private,
1 public.
Bed & breakfast: £30 single,
£55 double.
Half board: £37.50-£40 daily,
£210-£280 weekly.
Evening meal 6.30pm (l.o.
8.30pm).
Parking for 12.

WOODHALL SPA

Lincolnshire
Map ref 4D2

Attractive town which was
formerly a spa. It has
excellent sporting
facilities with a
championship golf-course
and is surrounded by pine
woods.

Claremont Guest House
APPROVED

9-11 Witham Road,
Woodhall Spa, LN10 6RW
☎ (0526) 52000
Family-run guesthouse within
easy reach of the town's
sporting and leisure facilities.
We offer personal service and a
friendly atmosphere. Evening
meal by request.
Bedrooms: 2 single, 1 double
& 4 twin, 1 family room.
Bathrooms: 2 public.
Bed & breakfast: from £16
single, from £27 double.
Lunch available.
Parking for 5.

Oglee Guest House M
APPROVED

16 Stanhope Avenue,
Woodhall Spa, LN10 6SP
☎ (0526) 53512
Privately-run guesthouse in a
tree-lined avenue in this pretty,
wooded town.
Bedrooms: 1 double & 2 twin,
2 family rooms.
Bathrooms: 2 private,
2 public.
Bed & breakfast: £19-£21
single, £30-£34 double.
Half board: £25-£27 daily,
£165-£185 weekly.

Evening meal 8pm.
Parking for 6.
Credit: Access, Visa.

Petwood Hotel M

Stixwould Road, Woodhall
Spa, LN10 6QF
☎ (0526) 52411
A unique country house in 30
acres of mature woodland.
Half-a-mile from the village.
Bedrooms: 4 single, 29 double
& 9 twin, 4 family rooms.
Bathrooms: 46 private.
Bed & breakfast: £67-£77
single, £77-£97 double.
Lunch available.
Evening meal 7pm (l.o.
9.30pm).
Parking for 70.
Credit: Access, Visa, Diners,
Amex.

WOOTTON

Northamptonshire
Map ref 2C1

The Queen Eleanor Hotel M

London Road, Wootton,
Northampton, NN4 0JJ
☎ (0604) 762468
A popular hotel which takes its
name from a cross erected by
Edward I in loving memory of
Queen Eleanor. Open plan bar
and restaurant. Large garden,
patio and children's play area.
1 mile off junction 15 of the
M1, on the Northampton ring
road.
Bedrooms: 4 double &
11 twin, 4 family rooms.
Bathrooms: 19 private.
Bed & breakfast: from £53
single, from £60.50 double.
Lunch available.
Evening meal 7pm (l.o.
10pm).
Parking for 120.
Credit: Access, Visa, Diners,
Amex.

Half board prices
shown are per
person but in some
cases may be based
on double/twin
occupancy.

WORKSOP

Nottinghamshire
Map ref 4C2

Market town close to the Dukeries, where a number of Ducal families had their estates, some of which, like Clumber Park, may be visited. The upper room of the 14th C gatehouse of the priory housed the country's first elementary school in 1628.
Tourist Information Centre ☎ *(0909) 501148*

Carlton Road Guest House ⋀

67 Carlton Road, Worksop, S80 1PP
☎ (0909) 483084
A family guest house run by the resident owners. Close to railway station, town centre and M1/A1 trunk roads.
Bedrooms: 2 single, 1 double & 1 twin, 1 family room.
Bathrooms: 1 private, 2 public.
Bed & breakfast: £13-£15.50 single, £26-£31 double.
ᵇ2 ◻ ❖ ⓤ Ⓥ ⅏ ▴ ♯

Sherwood Guest House ♛♛

57 Carlton Road, Worksop, S80 1PP
☎ (0909) 474209 & 478214
Recently modernised and converted, the Sherwood is in Robin Hood country, 100 yards from Worksop station and close to the town centre.
Bedrooms: 1 single, 5 twin, 1 family room.
Bathrooms: 2 private, 2 public.
Bed & breakfast: £13-£16 single, £26-£32 double.
ᵇ ⬥ ⓑ ◻ ❖ ⓤ ⓘ Ⓥ ♯
ⓣⓥ ⅏ ▴ ⅃ ♯ ⒹⒶⓅ

Key to symbols

Information about many of the services and facilities at establishments listed in this guide is given in the form of symbols. The key to these symbols is inside the back cover flap. You may find it helpful to keep the flap open when referring to the entry listings.

Check the maps

The place you wish to visit may not have accommodation entirely suited to your needs, but there could be somewhere ideal quite close by. Check the colour maps towards the end of this guide to identify nearby towns and villages with accommodation listed in the guide, and then use the town index to find page numbers.

Hector Breeze

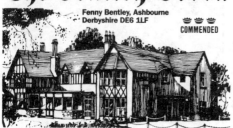

Use a coupon

When requesting further information from advertisers in this guide, you may find it helpful to use the advertisement enquiry coupons which can be found towards the end of the guide. These should be cut out and mailed direct to the companies in which you are interested. Do remember to include your name and address.

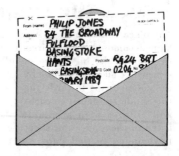

The signs of confidence

Look for signs like these when you're booking accommodation in a hotel, guesthouse, farmhouse, inn or B&B — they tell you that the establishment has been inspected by the Tourist Board and that it meets or exceeds minimum quality standards.

All you have to remember is that the classification (from Listed up to Five Crown) indicates the range of facilities and services while the commendation (Approved, Commended or Highly Commended) indicates the quality standard of the facilities and services.

The absence of a quality commendation from any entry in this 'Where to Stay' guide may be because the establishment had not been quality assessed at the time of going to press.

♣ Enjoy the countryside and respect its life and work ♣ Guard against all risk of fire ♣ Fasten all gates ♣ Keep your dogs under close control ♣ Keep to public paths across farmland ♣ Use gates and stiles to cross fences, hedges and walls ♣ Leave livestock, crops and machinery alone ♣ Take your litter home ♣ Help to keep all water clean ♣ Protect wildlife, plants and trees ♣ Take special care on country roads ♣ Make no unnecessary noise

Follow the sign

It leads to over 560 Tourist Information Centres throughout England offering friendly help with accommodation and holiday ideas as well as suggestions of places to visit and things to do. In your home town there may be a centre which can help you before you set out. Details of the locations of Tourist Information Centres are available from the English Tourist Board, Thames Tower, Black's Road, London W6 9EL, or from England's Regional Tourist Boards.

Thames & Chilterns

London's Country — that's the byline for the region forming a north-westerly arc around the capital and including some of England's best-loved beauty spots, all in attractive, typically English countryside.

»From horse-racing country in the west, the wide Berkshire Downs run inward to leafy Goring Gap where the Thames cuts through. Here, the glorious, beech-clad Chilterns begin their curve north-east towards the breezy vistas of the Dunstable Downs. Further out the touring slopes of Oxfordshire's Cotswolds beckon, with perfect villages and manors of honey-coloured stone — romantic enough for any honeymoon.

» In between is rich agricultural land, from the lanes of well-wooded Hertfordshire and Buckinghamshire to the fertile valley of Bedfordshire's Great Ouse; from the Thames near its source, on towards London and the sea, passing exquisite riverside towns and villages on the way.

» Everywhere, the gentle beauty of these prosperous Home Counties will lead you to well-patronised country pubs with adventurous food, a profusion of teashops and restaurants, and myriad places to stay from sumptuous country manors to charming town-centre bed and breakfasts.

» The towns and cities are particularly special. St Albans has famous Roman remains, medieval buildings and a lovely hilltop cathedral with a

The Sheldonian Theatre in Oxford, seen here in 1847, is the principal assembly room of the university

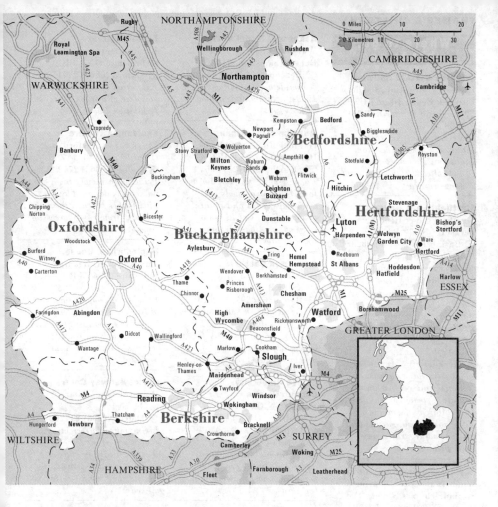

spectacularly long nave. Oxford, city of dreaming spires, is simply not to be missed; it would take days to see everything. Windsor, with its Royal castle and other attractions, is an unforgettable experience — like so many towns and villages waiting to be explored.

»» Please refer to the colour maps at the back of this guide for all places with accommodation listings.

»» The region is much more than history and beauty. Awaiting you are safari parks and zoos, stately homes and gardens, museums and waxworks, floating cruisers and steam railways, galleries and glass studios. If you live in London, it's 100 great days out. If you live elsewhere — the Thames and Chilterns are the perfect place for a holiday!

Where to go, what to see

Leighton Buzzard Railway
Page's Park Station, Leighton Buzzard, Bedfordshire LU7 8TN
☎ Leighton Buzzard (0525) 373888
Preserved industrial railway, with steam locomotives from India and French Cameroons. Diesel collection, three miles of 2' gauge railway.

Stratfield Saye House
Stratfield Saye, Reading, Berkshire RG7 2BT
☎ Basingstoke (0256) 882881
House built in 1630, now displays many personal possessions of the Iron Duke, including funeral hearse. Gardens.

Wellington Country Park
Riseley, Reading, Berkshire RG7 1SP
☎ Heckfield (0734) 326444
500-acre country park with National Dairy Museum, miniature steam railway, crazy golf, children's farm and playground, wind-surfing and boating, nature trails, deer park, fishing.

Royalty and Empire Exhibition
Windsor and Eton Central Station, Thames Street, Windsor, Berkshire SL4 1PJ
☎ Windsor (0753) 857837
Restored GWR station built in 1897 for Queen Victoria's Diamond Jubilee. Exhibition includes theatre show '60 Glorious Years' with animated figures of the period.

Courage Shire Horse Centre
Cherry Garden Lane, Maidenhead Thicket, Maidenhead, Berkshire SL6 3QD
☎ Littlewick Green (062 882) 4848
Home of Courage prize-winning shire horses. Display of harness and brasses, farrier's workshop, small animal/bird area, play area, tea room.

Bekonscot Model Village
Warwick Road, Beaconsfield, Buckinghamshire HP9 2PL
☎ Beaconsfield (0494) 672919
A complete model village of the 1930s, with an outdoor model railway.

Museum of St. Albans
Hatfield Road, St. Albans, Hertfordshire AL1 3RR
☎ St. Albans (0727) 56679
Purpose-built museum dating from 1898. Craft tools and workshops, local and natural history, displays telling the story of St. Albans from Roman times to present.

Broughton Castle
Banbury, Oxfordshire OX15 5EB
☎ Banbury (0295) 262624
Medieval moated house built in 1300 and enlarged in 1554. Home of the same family for 600 years. Fine plaster ceilings, fireplaces, panelling, furniture.

Oxford University Botanic Garden
Rose Lane, Oxford, Oxfordshire OX1 4AX
☎ Oxford (0865) 276920
Collection of over 8,000 species of plants in gardens and greenhouses, plus herbaceous borders, rock and bog gardens.

Bodleian Library
Broad Street, Oxford, Oxfordshire OX1 3BG
☎ Oxford (0865) 277170
Exhibition of early books and manuscript works in the Exhibition Room.

Sheldonian Theatre
Broad Street, Oxford, Oxfordshire OX1 3AZ
☎ Oxford (0865) 277299
Principal assembly room of university, designed by Sir Christopher Wren. Fine views over city from easily accessible cupola.

Mapledurham House
Mapledurham, Reading, Berkshire RG4 7TR
☎ Reading (0734) 723350
Elizabethan mansion on banks of River Thames. Interesting collection of paintings, family portraits, oak staircase, moulded ceilings, 15th C operational watermill.

Didcot Railway Centre
Didcot, Oxfordshire OX11 7NJ
☎ Didcot (0235) 817200
Living museum recreating the golden age of the Great Western Railway. Steam locomotives and trains, engine shed, small relics museum.

The Courage Shire Horse Centre is the home of prize-winning horses owned by the Courage brewery

The Didcot Railway Centre recreates the golden age of steam

Royal Windsor Horse Show
Home Park, Windsor,
Berkshire   *8 – 12 May*

Golf – Dunhill British Masters
Woburn Golf and Country
Club, Bow Brickhill, Milton
Keynes, Buckinghamshire
30 May – 2 June

Horse racing – Royal Ascot
Ascot Racecourse, Ascot,
Berkshire   *18 – 21 June*

Henley Royal Regatta
Henley-on-Thames,
Oxfordshire   *3 – 7 July*

British Rose Festival
Gardens of the Rose, Chiswell
Green, St Albans, Hertfordshire
6 – 7 July

**Blenheim CCI International
Horse Trials**
Blenheim Palace, Woodstock,
Oxfordshire   *19 – 22 September*

Find out more

Further information about
holidays and attractions in the
Thames & Chilterns region is
available from: **Thames &
Chilterns Tourist Board,** The
Mount House, Church Green,
Witney, Oxfordshire OX8 6DZ.
☎ (0993) 778800.

Ashmolean Museum
Beaumont Street, Oxford,
Oxfordshire OX1 2PH
☎ Oxford (0865) 278000
*Some of the greatest art and
archaeological treasures in the
country.*

Windsor Safari Park
Winkfield Road, Windsor,
Berkshire SL4 4AY
☎ Windsor (0753) 830886
*African theme park; African
Queen river boat ride, Seaworld,
parrot show, animal reserves.*

**Knebworth House,
Gardens and Park**
Knebworth, Stevenage,
Hertfordshire SG3 6PY
☎ Stevenage (0438) 812661
*Tudor manor house refashioned
in 19th C by Bulwer Lytton. Fine
collection of manuscripts and
portraits, Jacobean banquet hall,
adventure playground, gift shop.*

The Oxford Story
6 Broad Street, Oxford,
Oxfordshire OX1 3AJ
☎ Oxford (0865) 728822
*Heritage centre depicting eight
centuries of university history
in sights, sounds, personalities
and smells. Visitors are
transported in moving desks.*

These publications are
available free from the Thames
& Chilterns Tourist Board:
A Cottage in the Country
(Self-Catering Holidays)
*River Thames Holidays
Brochure*
*Historic Houses in the
Thames & Chilterns*
Oxfordshire: Places to Visit
Also available are:
*Where to Go in the Thames
& Chilterns* £2.50
*Thames & Chilterns Official
Tourist Map* £2.40
Welcome to Oxford 50p
Welcome to Henley 20p
*Churches of the Thames &
Chilterns* 30p

Places to stay

·» Accommodation entries in this regional section are listed in alphabetical order of place name, and then in alphabetical order of establishment.

·» The map references refer to the colour maps towards the end of the guide. The first figure is the map number; the letter and figure which follow indicate the grid reference on the map.

·» The symbols at the end of each accommodation entry give information about services and facilities. A 'key' to these symbols is inside the back cover flap, which can be kept open for easy reference.

ABINGDON
Oxfordshire
Map ref 2C1

6m S. Oxford
Attractive former county town on River Thames with many interesting buildings, including 17th C County Hall, now a museum, in the market-place and the remains of an abbey.
Tourist Information Centre ☎ *(0235) 522711*

Abingdon Lodge Hotel ⋔
♨♨♨♨
Marcham Rd., Abingdon, OX14 1TZ
☎ (0235) 553456
Telex 837750
⊕ Consort
Modern hotel with restaurant and 7 function rooms. Situated on the A34/A415 junction into Abingdon, 5 miles from Oxford.
Bedrooms: 32 double & 31 twin.
Bathrooms: 63 private.
Bed & breakfast: £40-£72 single, £48-£77 double.
Half board: £38-£83 daily, £250-£432 weekly.
Lunch available.
Evening meal 7pm (l.o. 10pm).
Parking for 85.
Credit: Access, Visa, Diners, Amex.
♿ ♨ ☎ ⊞ ♫ ✓ ⅋ Ⅴ ⌿
◑ ▥ ⟡ ♨ ⌶ ✕ ⑆ ᴾ Ⓣ

Chez Joel Hotel & Restaurant ⋔
17A Bridge St., Abingdon, OX4 3HN
☎ (0235) 521788
15th C listed building located in town centre. 2 minutes from River Thames and leisure centre. All rooms beautifully decorated 15th C style with en-suite and TV.
Bedrooms: 2 single, 2 twin, 1 family room.
Bathrooms: 2 private, 1 public; 2 private showers.
Bed & breakfast: £20-£25 single, £40-£50 double.
Lunch available.
Evening meal 6pm (l.o. 9pm).
Credit: Access, Visa, Diners, Amex.
♿ ⌷ ⟡ ♨ Ⅴ ▥ ⌶ ✕ ⑆
Ⓣ

Crown and Thistle Hotel ⋔
♨♨♨ COMMENDED
Bridge St., Abingdon, OX14 3HS
☎ (0235) 522556
Lovely old coaching inn, which is a listed building, with an attractive cobbled courtyard. Dating from around 1605, its name signifies the union of England and Scotland by James I. Close to the town centre and River Thames.
Bedrooms: 5 single, 9 double & 4 twin, 3 family rooms.
Bathrooms: 21 private.
Bed & breakfast: £43-£54 single, £70-£75 double.
Lunch available.
Evening meal 6pm (l.o. 10.30pm).

Parking for 36.
Credit: Access, Visa, Diners, Amex.
♿ ♨ ☎ ⊞ ⌷ ⟡ ♨ Ⅴ ⅋
◑ ▥ ▱ ♨ ⌶ ✕ ⑆ ᴾ ⑆

Knowl Hotel
52 Stert St., Abingdon
☎ (0235) 554661
Recently refurbished guesthouse retaining many historical features. Centrally situated near town centre. Plenty of parking nearby.
Bedrooms: 3 single, 6 double & 8 twin, 1 family room.
Bathrooms: 14 private, 3 public.
Bed & breakfast: £25-£42 single, £37-£50 double.
Half board: £32-£58 daily.
Evening meal 5pm (l.o. 7.30pm).
Parking for 5.
Credit: Visa.
♿ ♨ ⌷ ⟡ ♨ ⌷ ▥ ▱
⌶ ⒢ ⅋ ⑆

Thame Lane House ⋔
⊞
1 Thame Lane, Culham, Abingdon, OX14 3DS
☎ (0235) 524177
Large, comfortable house set in wooded gardens. Off the A415 by the European School, Culham. French cuisine in evenings.
Bedrooms: 3 single, 1 twin, 1 family room.
Bathrooms: 1 private, 2 public.
Bed & breakfast: £20-£35 single, £34-£45 double.

Half board: £30-£48 daily.
Evening meal 7pm (l.o. 8.30pm).
Parking for 7.
♿3 ⌷ ⟡ ♨ Ⅴ ▥ ▱ ✕ ⑆

ASCOT
Berkshire
Map ref 2C2

Small country town famous for its racecourse which was founded by Queen Anne. The race meeting each June is attended by the Royal Family.

Brockenhurst Hotel ⋔
Brockenhurst Rd., South Ascot, SL5 9HA
☎ (0990) 21912 Fax 081-591 8559
Old Edwardian house, situated near shops and station.
Bedrooms: 7 double, 3 family rooms.
Bathrooms: 10 private.
Bed & breakfast: £55-£69 single, £65-£85 double.
Lunch available.
Evening meal 6pm (l.o. 10pm).
Parking for 14.
Credit: Access, Visa, C.Bl., Amex.
♿ ♨ ☎ ⊞ ⌷ ⟡ ♨ Ⅴ ⅋
⑆ ▥ ▱ ⌶ ❄ ✕ ⑆

Deepfold Farm
London Rd., Bracknell, RG12 6QR
☎ (0344) 428367 & (0990) 20257

Map references apply to the colour maps towards the end of this guide.

5-acre horses farm. *Early 19th C coach house/farmhouse on the A329. A few minutes from Ascot, Bracknell and Windsor.*
Bedrooms: 1 double & 1 twin, 1 family room.
Bathrooms: 1 public.
Bed & breakfast: £15-£22 single, £30-£40 double.
Parking for 10.

The Royal Berkshire Hotel M

London Rd., Sunninghill, Ascot, SL5 0PP
☎ Ascot (0990) 23322
Telex 847280
Hilton
Queen Anne country mansion set in 15 acres of mature parkland.
Bedrooms: 15 single, 50 double & 17 twin.
Bathrooms: 82 private.
Bed & breakfast: £60-£130 single, £120-£365 double.
Half board: £82.50-£150 daily.
Lunch available.
Evening meal 7.30pm (l.o. 10pm).
Parking for 150.
Credit: Access, Visa, Diners, Amex.

ASTON CLINTON

Buckinghamshire
Map ref 2C1

Village far-spread on the escarpment of the Downs, with many Jacobean thatched cottages and an inn which has been receiving travellers since John Hampden's days. 14th C church with its original chancel and fine arch still stands today.

The Bell Inn M

Aston Clinton, HP22 5HP
☎ Aylesbury (0296) 630252
Telex 83252 BELINN G
15th C English coaching inn, many original features remaining. Extensive gardens and croquet lawn. Conference suites, wine shop and renowned restaurant.
Bedrooms: 3 double & 10 twin, 8 family rooms.
Bathrooms: 21 private.
Bed & breakfast: £86-£95 single, £100-£125 double.
Lunch available.
Evening meal 7.30pm (l.o. 10pm).

Parking for 200.
Credit: Access, Visa.

West Lodge Hotel M

45 London Rd., Aston Clinton, HP22 5HL
☎ Aylesbury (0296) 630331 & 630362
Elegant Victorian hotel offering comfortable accommodation and surrounded by beautiful estate and countryside. Situated on the A41 with London 50 minutes away.
Bedrooms: 2 single, 3 double & 2 twin.
Bathrooms: 7 private.
Bed & breakfast: £30-£44 single, £52-£58 double.
Half board: £38-£52 daily, £266-£365 weekly.
Evening meal 7pm (l.o. 8pm).
Parking for 11.
Credit: Access, Visa, Amex.

AYLESBURY

Buckinghamshire
Map ref 2C1

Historic county town in the Vale of Aylesbury. The cobbled market square has a Victorian clock tower and the 15th C King's Head Inn (National Trust). Interesting county museum and 13th C parish church. Twice-weekly livestock market.
Tourist Information Centre ☎ (0296) 382308

Belmore Hotel

COMMENDED
Risboro Rd., Stoke Mandeville, Nr. Aylesbury, HP22 5UT
☎ (0296) 612022
Telex 837520 ADTRAV G
A caring hotel surrounded by its own gardens and fields. Swimming pool. Easy ground floor access to all rooms. 40 cover restaurant, country cooking.
Bedrooms: 2 single, 4 double & 9 twin.
Bathrooms: 15 private.
Bed & breakfast: £38.20-£48.20 single, £52.40-£62.40 double.
Half board: £50.20-£60.20 daily.
Lunch available.
Evening meal 7pm (l.o. 9pm).

Parking for 32.
Credit: Access, Visa, Diners, Amex.

Hartwell House M

Oxford Rd., Aylesbury, HP17 8NL
☎ (0296) 747444
Telex 837108
2 miles from Aylesbury on A418 toward Oxford, Hartwell House is one of the most historic houses of Buckinghamshire.
Bedrooms: 5 single, 13 double & 14 twin.
Bathrooms: 32 private.
Bed & breakfast: £83-£95 single, £127-£185 double.
Lunch available.
Evening meal 7.30pm (l.o. 9.45pm).
Parking for 70.
Credit: Access, Visa, Diners, Amex.

BAMPTON

Oxfordshire
Map ref 2C1

5m SW. Witney
Small market town, well known for its Spring Bank Holiday Monday Fete with Morris Dance Festival.

Romany Inn M

Listed
Bridge St., Bampton, OX8 2HA
☎ Bampton Castle (0993) 850237
A listed building dating from the 17th C. Lounge bar with separate dining room. Log fires in winter.
Bedrooms: 2 double & 1 twin.
Bathrooms: 1 public.
Bed & breakfast: £15-£18 single, £23-£30 double.
Lunch available.
Evening meal 6.30pm (l.o. 10pm).
Parking for 3.

Talbot Hotel

APPROVED
Market Square, Bampton, OX8 2HA
☎ Bampton Castle (0993) 850326
Traditional 12th C village hotel in the heart of Bampton-in-the-Bush, 5 miles south of Witney and 12 miles west of Oxford. Weekend breaks available, details on request.

Bedrooms: 1 single, 1 double & 4 twin, 1 family room.
Bathrooms: 5 private, 1 public.
Bed & breakfast: £28-£32 single, £46-£56 double.
Half board: £186-£214 weekly.
Lunch available.
Evening meal 6pm (l.o. 10pm).
Credit: Access, Visa.

BANBURY

Oxfordshire
Map ref 2C1

22m N. Oxford
Famous for its cattle market, cakes and Nursery Rhyme Cross. Founded in Saxon times, it has some fine houses and interesting old inns. A good centre for touring Warwickshire and the Cotswolds.
Tourist Information Centre ☎ (0295) 259855

Belmont Guest House

34 Crouch St., Banbury, OX16 9PR
☎ (0295) 262308
Family-run guesthouse approximately 200 yards from Banbury Cross. Away from the main road.
Bedrooms: 2 single, 1 double & 2 twin, 3 family rooms.
Bathrooms: 3 private, 1 public.
Bed & breakfast: £18-£25 single, £25-£35 double.
Parking for 6.
Credit: Access, Visa.

Calthorpe Lodge Guest House

4 Calthorpe Rd., Banbury, OX16 8HS
☎ (0295) 252325
Family-run period house near town centre.
Bedrooms: 2 single, 2 double & 1 twin.
Bathrooms: 5 private.
Bed & breakfast: £25-£35 single, £35-£45 double.
Evening meal 6.30pm (l.o. 8pm).
Parking for 6.

Kelvedon Guest House

11 Broughton Rd., Banbury, OX16 9QB
☎ (0295) 263028

Continued ▶

BANBURY
Continued

Friendly, comfortable guesthouse, a few minutes from Banbury Cross.
Bedrooms: 2 twin, 2 family rooms.
Bathrooms: 1 private, 2 public.
Bed & breakfast: £16-£20 single, £26-£30 double.
Parking for 3.
⟁ ⌷ ♥ ⅏ ⊁ ⊡ ⅏ ⋈

Prospect House Guest House ♨
👑👑👑
70 Oxford Rd., Banbury, OX16 9AN
☎ (0295) 268749
Detached house with lovely grounds. Situated in the most convenient area of town.
Bedrooms: 2 single, 5 double & 2 twin.
Bathrooms: 9 private, 1 public.
Bed & breakfast: £25-£32 single, £35-£45 double.
Half board: £26-£40 daily.
Parking for 10.
Credit: Access, Visa, Amex.
⟁ ⅏ ⓑ ⌷ ⌷ ⅏ ⊡ ⅏
⟁ ❃ ⋈ ⋈ ⋈ SP

Thatched House Hotel ♨
👑👑👑 APPROVED
Sulgrave, Banbury, OX17 2SE
☎ (029 576) 232 & 262
A well-preserved 17th C thatched building in a cottage garden, directly opposite Sulgrave Manor, the ancestral home of George Washington.
Bedrooms: 3 single, 2 double & 2 twin.
Bathrooms: 5 private, 1 public.
Bed & breakfast: £27-£35 single, from £60 double.
Lunch available.
Evening meal 7.30pm (l.o. 9.30pm).
Parking for 14.
Credit: Access, Visa, Diners, Amex.
⟁ ⌷ ♥ ⅏ �V ⊁ ⅏ ⟁ ⅏
▶ ❃ ⋈ ⋈ SP ⋈

Wroxton House Hotel ♨
👑👑👑
Wroxton St. Mary, Nr. Banbury, OX15 6QB
☎ (0295) 730482 Telex 83409
Picturesque thatched hotel in lovely village 3 miles from Banbury. Candlelit restaurant specialising in fish and game dishes according to season. Luxury and four-poster rooms available.

Bedrooms: 6 single, 14 double & 12 twin.
Bathrooms: 32 private, 1 public.
Bed & breakfast: £55-£75 single, £65-£110 double.
Half board: £45-£49 daily.
Lunch available.
Evening meal 7.30pm (l.o. 9.30pm).
Parking for 50.
Credit: Access, Visa, C.Bl., Diners, Amex.
⟁ ⅏ ⊡ ⌷ ♥ ⅏ ⅏ �V
⟁ ⊡ ● ⅏ ⟁ ⅏ ❃ ❄ ⅏
SP ⋈ ⊡

BEDFORD
Bedfordshire
Map ref 2D1

Busy county town with interesting buildings and churches near the River Ouse which has pleasant riverside walks. Many associations with John Bunyan including Bunyan Meeting House, museum and statue. The Bedford Museum and Cecil Higgins Art Gallery are of interest.
Tourist Information Centre ☎ *(0234) 215226*

Barns Hotel & Restaurant ♨
Cardington Rd., Bedford, MK44 3SA
☎ (0234) 270044
Telex 827748 Fax (0234) 273102
⊛ Lansbury
A new hotel developed from a 17th C manor house and adjacent to the Great Ouse river.
Bedrooms: 19 double & 28 twin, 2 family rooms.
Bathrooms: 49 private.
Bed & breakfast: from £31 single, £62-£82 double.
Half board: £42-£84 daily.
Lunch available.
Evening meal 7pm (l.o. 10pm).
Parking for 120.
Credit: Access, Visa, Diners, Amex.
⟁ ⅏ ⊡ ⟁ ⓑ ⌷ ♥ ⅏
❄ ⅏ ● ⅏ ⟁ ⅏ ♨ ⛄ ❃
❄ SP ⋈ ⊡

Clarendon House Hotel
25-27 Ampthill Rd., Bedford, MK42 9JP
☎ (0234) 266054
Converted from an Edwardian house. On the A6 south of Bedford with good access to M1, A1, Woburn Abbey and Bedford.
Bedrooms: 10 single, 2 double & 5 twin.

Bathrooms: 13 private, 2 public; 3 private showers.
Bed & breakfast: £19.50-£29.50 single, £35.50-£41 double.
Half board: from £26.75 daily.
Evening meal 7pm (l.o. 8pm).
Parking for 16.
Credit: Access, Visa, Diners, Amex.
⟁ ⅏ ⌷ ♥ ⅏ ⅏ ⅏ ⅏
⟁ ⋈

No. 1 The Grange
👑👑👑 COMMENDED
Sunderland Hill, Ravensden, MK44 2SH
☎ Bedford (0234) 771771
Spacious family-run accommodation set in elegant rural surroundings.
Bedrooms: 1 single, 1 double & 1 twin.
Bathrooms: 1 private, 2 public.
Bed & breakfast: from £17 single, from £30 double.
Half board: £26.50-£28.50 daily.
Evening meal 6.30pm (l.o. midday).
Parking for 10.
⟁3 ⌷ ♥ ⅏ ⅏ ⅏ ⊁ ⊡
⟁ ❃ ⋈ ⋈ ⋈

The Queens Head Hotel ♨
👑👑 COMMENDED
2 Rushden Rd., Milton Ernest, Bedford, MK44 1RV
☎ (0234) 272822
Telex 94014159 FMCL G (Ref QH)
Restored country inn on the A6, 5 miles north of Bedford. Bars and restaurant open to non-residents.
Bedrooms: 1 single, 7 double & 5 twin.
Bathrooms: 13 private.
Bed & breakfast: from £48 single, from £60 double.
Lunch available.
Evening meal 7pm (l.o. 10pm).
Parking for 21.
Credit: Access, Visa, Amex.
⟁ ⅏ ⟁ ⓑ ⌷ ♥ ⅏ ⅏ ⅏
⊁ ⅏ ⅏ ⟁ ⊁ ⛄ ⋈ SP ⋈

Woodlands Manor ♨
👑👑👑👑 COMMENDED
Green Lane, Clapham, Bedford, MK41 6EP
☎ (0234) 63281 Fax (0234) 272390 Telex 825007
A Victorian manor house, managed by proprietor, set in 4 acres of gardens. 2 miles north of Bedford town centre.
Bedrooms: 22 double & 2 twin, 1 family room.
Bathrooms: 25 private.

Bed & breakfast: £55-£90 single, £68-£90 double.
Lunch available.
Evening meal 7.30pm (l.o. 9.45pm).
Parking for 150.
Credit: Access, Visa, Amex.
⟁7 ⅏ ⓑ ⌷ ⅏ �V ⅏ ● ⅏
⟁ ⊁ ❃ ⋈ ⅏ SP ⅏ ⊡

BERKHAMSTED
Hertfordshire
Map ref 2D1

Hilltop town on Grand Union Canal surrounded by pleasant countryside and a 1200-acre common. It has remains of an important castle with earthworks and moat. Birthplace of William Cowper, the poet.
Tourist Information Centre ☎ *(0442) 864545*

Pennyfarthing House ♨
👑👑👑👑 COMMENDED
296-298 High St., Berkhamsted, HP4 1AJ
☎ (0442) 872828
Attractive new hotel located behind established English restaurant.
Bedrooms: 10 double & 2 twin.
Bathrooms: 12 private.
Bed & breakfast: £45-£75 single, £55-£80 double.
Lunch available.
Evening meal 7pm.
Parking for 30.
Credit: Access, Visa, Diners, Amex.
⟁ ⅏ ⟁ ⓑ ⌷ ♥ ⅏ ⅏ ⅏
⅏ ⟁ ⊁ ⛄ ⋈ ⅏ SP ⋈

BICESTER
Oxfordshire
Map ref 2C1

Market town with large army depot and well-known hunting centre with hunt established in the late 18th C. The ancient parish church displays work of many periods. Nearby is the Jacobean mansion of Rousham House with gardens landscaped by William Kent.

Littlebury Hotel
Kings End, Bicester, OX6 7DR
☎ (0869) 252595
Comfortable, family-run hotel. Completely modernised.
Bedrooms: 8 single, 8 double & 8 twin, 12 family rooms.
Bathrooms: 33 private, 3 public; 1 private shower.

Bed & breakfast: £32-£44.50 single, £57 double.
Half board: £32-£45 daily.
Lunch available.
Evening meal 7pm (l.o. 10pm).
Parking for 52.
Credit: Access, Visa.

Bedfordshire
Map ref 2D1

Busy centre for market gardening set on the River Ivel spanned by a 14th C bridge. Some interesting old buildings in the market-place. Nearby are the Shuttleworth collection of historic aeroplanes and Jordan's Mill.

Stratton House Hotel M
APPROVED
London Rd., Biggleswade, SG18 8EO
☎ (0767) 312442 & 314540 & (0767) 312631
Completely refurbished hotel in centre of the town. Continental and English cooking.
Bedrooms: 14 single, 4 double & 12 twin, 5 family rooms.
Bathrooms: 29 private, 2 public; 1 private shower.
Bed & breakfast: £30-£42 single, £46-£54 double.
Lunch available.
Evening meal 6pm (l.o. 10pm).
Parking for 40.
Credit: Access, Visa, Diners.

BOREHAMWOOD

Hertfordshire
Map ref 2D1

A busy town beside the A1 Great North Road.
Tourist Information Centre ☎ 081-207 2277

Hartwood
36 Gables Avenue, Borehamwood, WD6 4SP
☎ 081-207 6891
Detached family house.
Bedrooms: 1 single, 1 double.
Bathrooms: 1 private, 1 public.
Bed & breakfast: £13-£15 single, £30-£35 double.
Evening meal 7pm.

BRACKNELL

Berkshire
Map ref 2C2

Designated a New Town in 1949, the town has ancient origins. Set in heathlands, it is an excellent centre for golf and walking. South Hill Park, an 18th C mansion, houses an art centre.
Tourist Information Centre ☎ (0344) 423149

Hilton National Bracknell M
Bagshot Road, Bracknell, RG12 3QJ
☎ (0344) 424801
Telex 848058
Hilton
Well-situated in a thriving part of Berkshire, with comfortable facilities.
Bedrooms: 25 single, 71 double & 51 twin.
Bathrooms: 147 private.
Bed & breakfast: £70-£119.50 double.
Lunch available.
Evening meal 7pm (l.o. 9.45pm).
Parking for 250.
Credit: Access, Visa, Diners, Amex.

BURFORD

Oxfordshire
Map ref 2B1

One of the most beautiful Cotswold wool towns with Georgian and Tudor houses, many antique shops and a picturesque High Street sloping to the River Windrush.
Tourist Information Centre ☎ (099382) 3558

The Bird in Hand M
Whiteoak Green, Hailey, Nr. Witney, OX8 5XP
☎ (099 386) 8321 Fax (0993) 86702
Recently restored inn, with attractive cottage style bedrooms and surrounding a quiet courtyard. Home-cooked food, real ales and open fires.
Bedrooms: 10 double & 4 twin, 2 family rooms.
Bathrooms: 16 private.
Bed & breakfast: from £39.50 single, £49.50-£55.50 double.
Half board: £40-£50 daily, £280-£350 weekly.
Lunch available.
Evening meal 7pm (l.o. 10pm).

Parking for 100.
Credit: Access, Visa, Diners, Amex.

Elm Farm House M
COMMENDED
Meadow Lane, Fulbrook, Burford, OX8 4BW
☎ (099 382) 3611/2
Cotswold-stone house with walled garden, in quiet village.
Bedrooms: 1 single, 2 double & 4 twin.
Bathrooms: 3 private, 1 public.
Bed & breakfast: £26-£30 single, £35-£50 double.
Half board: £31.50-£44 daily, £217-£301 weekly.
Evening meal 7.30pm (l.o. 7.30pm).
Parking for 10.
Open February-December.
Credit: Access, Visa, Amex.

The Highway Hotel M
APPROVED
High St., Burford, OX8 4RG
☎ (099 382) 2136
Telex 838736 Hussey
Family-run, beamed medieval Cotswold hotel offering comfortable modern amenities. A wide variety of fresh local produce is served lunchtime and evenings.
Bedrooms: 8 double & 1 twin, 1 family room.
Bathrooms: 8 private, 1 public.
Bed & breakfast: £27-£35 single, £35-£40 double.
Lunch available.
Evening meal 7.30pm (l.o. 9pm).
Credit: Access, Visa, Diners, Amex.

Hillborough Hotel M
COMMENDED
The Green, Milton-under-Wychwood, OX7 6JH
☎ Shipton-under-Wychwood (0993) 830501
Victorian country house facing village green. Open fires. Friendly bar. Restaurant open to non-residents. Leafy conservatory coffee lounge. Pretty gardens.
Bedrooms: 3 double & 2 twin, 1 family room.
Bathrooms: 6 private.
Bed & breakfast: max. £39 single, max. £49 double.
Half board: max. £38.50 daily, max. £224 weekly.
Lunch available.

Evening meal 7pm (l.o. 9.30pm).
Parking for 15.
Open February-December.
Credit: Access, Visa, Amex.

The Maytime Inn M
Listed COMMENDED
Asthall, OX8 4HW
☎ Burford (099 382) 2068
Century-old stone building with restaurant, on eastern edge of the Cotswolds.
Bedrooms: 2 double & 4 twin.
Bathrooms: 6 private.
Bed & breakfast: from £35 single, from £48 double.
Half board: from £36.50 daily.
Lunch available.
Evening meal 7pm (l.o. 10pm).
Parking for 100.
Credit: Access, Visa, Amex.

CHALFONT ST. PETER

Buckinghamshire
Map ref 2D2

The Greyhound Inn
High Street, Chalfont St. Peter, SL9 9RA
☎ Gerrards Cross (0753) 883404
14th C beamed coaching inn with intimate atmosphere, log fires, carvery, bar and 50-seat restaurant. Gardens on river. On the A413 Amersham/London road at Greyhound roundabout.
Bedrooms: 4 single, 3 double & 2 twin, 1 family room.
Bathrooms: 2 public.
Bed & breakfast: from £39 single, from £49 double.
Lunch available.
Evening meal 7pm (l.o. 10pm).
Parking for 125.
Credit: Access, Visa, Diners, Amex.

Classifications and quality commendations were correct at the time of going to press but are subject to change. Please check at the time of booking.

CHENIES

Hertfordshire
Map ref 2D1

Picturesque village built by the Russell family with attractive estate houses around a green. Chenies Manor is open to visitors in the summer.

Bedford Arms Thistle Hotel M
💷💷💷

Chenies, Rickmansworth, WD3 6EQ
☎ Chorleywood
(092 78) 3301 Telex 893939
Ⓒ Thistle
A delightful Elizabethan style country hotel in a small historic village.
Bedrooms: 3 single, 3 double & 4 twin.
Bathrooms: 10 private.
Bed & breakfast: from £75.90 single, from £95.80 double.
Lunch available.
Evening meal 7.30pm (l.o. 10pm).
Parking for 120.
Credit: Access, Visa, C.Bl., Diners, Amex.

CHINNOR

Oxfordshire
Map ref 2C1

4m SE. Thame

Plough and Harrow M
💷💷💷💷 APPROVED

Sydenham, Chinnor, OX9 4LD
☎ Kingston Blount
(0844) 51367
Traditional beer house providing a full a la carte menu, table d'hote and bar food.
Bedrooms: 2 single, 2 double & 3 twin.
Bathrooms: 7 private.
Bed & breakfast: £25-£50 single, £40-£65 double.
Half board: £35-£70 daily, £200-£350 weekly.
Lunch available.
Evening meal 7pm (l.o. 10pm).
Parking for 40.
Credit: Access, Visa, Diners, Amex.

CHIPPING NORTON

Oxfordshire
Map ref 2C1

Old market town set high in the Cotswolds and an ideal touring centre. The wide market-place contains many 16th C and 17th C stone houses and the Town Hall and Tudor Guildhall.

Southcombe Guest House
💷💷

Southcombe, Chipping Norton, OX7 5JF
☎ (0608) 643068
A well-decorated pebbledash guesthouse set in 3.5 acres, at the junction of the A44/A34, 2 miles south of Chipping Norton.
Bedrooms: 1 single, 2 double & 2 twin, 1 family room.
Bathrooms: 2 private, 2 public.
Bed & breakfast: £16-£21 single, £30-£36 double.
Half board: £22-£25 daily, £147-£168 weekly.
Lunch available.
Evening meal 7pm (l.o. 6pm).
Parking for 10.

CHISLEHAMPTON

Oxfordshire
Map ref 2C1

Village close to Oxford near the site of the famous Civil War battle of Chalgrove Field. An obelisk marks the site.

The Coach and Horses M
💷💷 COMMENDED

Stadhampton Rd., Chislehampton, OX9 7UX
☎ Stadhampton
(0865) 890255
Picturesque 16th C. listed coaching inn with beamed restaurant. Rooms with views of the countryside surround a landscaped and cobbled courtyard. One room has been thoughtfully designed for disabled guests.
Bedrooms: 5 double & 4 twin.
Bathrooms: 9 private.
Bed & breakfast: £33-£49 single, £46-£64 double.
Half board: £45-£61 daily, £247-£348 weekly.
Lunch available.
Evening meal 7pm (l.o. 10pm).

Parking for 30.
Credit: Access, Visa, Diners, Amex.

CHURCHILL

Oxfordshire
Map ref 2C1

The Forge House M
💷💷

Churchill, Nr. Chipping Norton, OX7 6NJ
☎ Kingham (0608) 658713
All bedrooms en-suite and one with jacuzzi. Well placed for touring the beautiful Cotswolds and for visiting Blenheim Palace and villages of historic interest.
Bedrooms: 3 double & 1 twin, 1 family room.
Bathrooms: 5 private.
Bed & breakfast: £20-£45 single, £40-£50 double.
Parking for 6.

CLANFIELD

Oxfordshire
Map ref 2C1

Pretty brookside village. Nearby lies the moated Friars Court, on the site of which once stood a building of the Knights Hospitallers.

Plough Hotel & Restaurant M
💷💷💷 COMMENDED

Clanfield, Oxford, OX8 2RB
☎ (036 781) 222 & 494
Telex 437334 attention Plough
Elizabethan manor, dating from 1560, in the heart of the Cotswolds.
Bedrooms: 6 double.
Bathrooms: 6 private.
Bed & breakfast: £73-£90 single, £88-£121 double.
Half board: £89.50-£94 daily, £378-£448 weekly.
Lunch available.
Evening meal 7.30pm (l.o. 10pm).
Parking for 40.
Credit: Access, Visa, Diners, Amex.

CLIFTON HAMPDEN

Oxfordshire
Map ref 2C2

3m SE. Abingdon
Picturesque village on the River Thames with attractive timber-framed cottages. The thatched riverside inn 'The Barley Mow', featured in 'Three Men in a Boat', faces the village from across the river. Fine views of village from parish church.

The Barley Mow Hotel M
💷💷

Clifton Hampden, Abingdon, OX14 3EH
☎ (086 730) 7847
Jerome K. Jerome described this pretty inn's distinctive 13th C black and white timbering and its charm in "Three Men in a Boat". It is tucked away on the backwaters of the River Thames.
Bedrooms: 2 single, 2 double.
Bathrooms: 1 private, 2 public.
Bed & breakfast: £34.50-£41.50 single, from £54 double.
Lunch available.
Evening meal 7.30pm (l.o. 9.30pm).
Parking for 250.
Credit: Access, Visa, Diners, Amex.

CROWTHORNE

Berkshire
Map ref 2C2

Village which has grown up around Wellington and Broadmoor Hospital. The Devil's Highway Roman road passes through the village and 2 Roman milestones can still be seen.

Dial House Private Hotel M
💷💷💷💷

62 Dukes Ride, Crowthorne, RG11 6DL
☎ (0344) 776941 Fax (0344) 777191
Small family-run hotel offering English and German cooking and refreshment. Fully-licensed. Close to Windsor, Bracknell, Ascot, Wokingham, Sandhurst and Camberley.
Bedrooms: 6 single, 5 double & 2 twin, 3 family rooms.
Bathrooms: 14 private, 1 public.

We advise you to confirm your booking in writing.

Please check prices and other details at the time of booking.

Bed & breakfast: £32-£69 single, £55-£76 double. **Half board**: £45-£82 daily, £405-£532 weekly. Lunch available. Evening meal 7.30pm (l.o. 7.30pm). Parking for 20. Credit: Access, Visa.

🔒 📞 🅱 🖥 🛏 ⚜ 📺 🏧 🍴 ❄ ✈ SP

DATCHET

Berkshire
Map ref 2D2

Boating and angling remain the town's chief attractions, with Black Potts being a favourite haunt of anglers. Datchet Mead is associated with a misadventure of Falstaff in the 'Merry Wives of Windsor'.

The Manor Hotel M
😊😊😊

The Green, Datchet, SL3 9EA
☎ Slough (0753) 43442
Telex 41363
🆑 Calotels
Tranquil village hotel, 1 mile downstream from Windsor. Within easy reach of Heathrow Airport.
Bedrooms: 7 single, 12 double & 11 twin.
Bathrooms: 30 private.
Bed & breakfast: £59-£65 single, £79-£87 double.
Lunch available.
Evening meal 7.30pm (l.o. 10pm).
Parking for 20.
Credit: Access, Visa, Diners, Amex.

🔒 📞 🅱 🖥 🛏 ⚜ 📺 🏧 ☀ 🍴 ❄ SP 🎱 T

DEDDINGTON

Oxfordshire
Map ref 2C1

Attractive former market town with a large market square and many fine old buildings.

Holcombe Hotel & Restaurant M
😊😊😊😊 COMMENDED

High St., Deddington, OX5 4SL
☎ (0869) 38274
🆑 Best Western
300-year-old hotel in scenic Cotswold village on A423 between Oxford and Banbury. Ideal for touring Stratford, Oxford, Blenheim and the Cotswolds.

Bedrooms: 2 single, 8 double & 4 twin, 1 family room.
Bathrooms: 15 private.
Bed & breakfast: £54-£65 single, £66-£76 double.
Half board: £40-£48 daily, £280-£315 weekly.
Lunch available.
Evening meal 7pm (l.o. 10.30pm).
Parking for 60.
Credit: Access, Visa, Amex.

🔒 📞 🅱 🖥 🛏 ⚜ 📺 🍴 ☀ ✿ 🏧 🕯 🌴 🎱 SP 🎱 T

DUNSTABLE

Bedfordshire
Map ref 2D1

Modern town with remains of a 12th C Augustinian priory in the parish church. The Dunstable Downs are famous for gliding and in the parkland of Whipsnade Zoo on the edge of the Downs many animals roam freely.
Tourist Information Centre ☎ (0582) 471012

Bellows Mill
Bellows Mill, Eaton Bray, Dunstable, LU6 1QZ
☎ (0525) 220548/220205
Delightful old water mill in converted stables. Tennis court, fly fishing, games room. All rooms en-suite with TV and telephone.
Bedrooms: 4 double & 1 twin, 1 family room.
Bathrooms: 6 private.
Bed & breakfast: £40-£45 single, from £42.55 double.
Half board: £50-£55 daily, £250-£275 weekly.
Lunch available.
Evening meal 7pm (l.o. 10pm).
Parking for 12.
Credit: Access, Visa.

🔒 🅱 📞 🖥 ⚜ 🛏 📺 ⚜ 🍴 🚗 🕯 ❄ ✈ 🎱 🎱

The Highwayman Hotel M
😊😊😊

London Road, Dunstable, LU6 3DX
☎ (0582) 601122
Telex 94014159 REF:HM
Hotel on A5, Luton Airport 8 miles away. Close to Woburn Abbey and Whipsnade Zoo.
Bedrooms: 23 single, 3 double & 11 twin.
Bathrooms: 37 private.
Bed & breakfast: from £42 single, from £55 double.
Lunch available.
Evening meal 7pm (l.o. 9pm).

Parking for 50.
Credit: Access, Visa, Diners, Amex.

🔒 🅱 📞 🖥 🛏 ⚜ 🍴 ❄ SP T

ELSTREE

Hertfordshire
Map ref 2D1

Edgwarebury Hotel M
😊😊😊😊 COMMENDED

Barnet Lane, Elstree, WD6 3RE
☎ 081-953 8227
Telex 918707
🆑 Lansbury
Large country house hotel set in 10 acres of landscaped gardens.
Bedrooms: 20 single, 17 double & 13 twin.
Bathrooms: 50 private.
Bed & breakfast: £33-£88 single, £66-£101 double.
Half board: £44-£116 daily.
Lunch available.
Evening meal 7pm (l.o. 10pm).
Parking for 120.
Credit: Access, Visa, Diners, Amex.

🔒 🅱 🌀 📞 🖥 🛏 ⚜ 🍴 ❄ 🕯 🍴 🎱 ✈ 🌴 SP 🎱 T

FARINGDON

Oxfordshire
Map ref 2B2

Ancient stone-built market town in the Vale of the White Horse. The 17th C market hall stands on pillars and the 13th C church has some fine monuments. A great monastic tithe barn is nearby at Great Coxwell.
Tourist Information Centre ☎ (0367) 242191

The Crown Hotel M
Market Place, Faringdon, SN7 7HU
☎ (0367) 22744
12-bedrooms (8 en-suite) with TV and tea-making facilities. Good buttery and bar food. Conference and banqueting services available.
Bedrooms: 2 single, 4 double & 5 twin, 1 family room.
Bathrooms: 8 private, 1 public.
Bed & breakfast: £31-£42.75 single, £38-£49 double.
Half board: £26.50-£30.50 daily.
Lunch available.

Evening meal 6pm (l.o. 10pm).
Parking for 20.
Credit: Access, Visa.

🔒 🌀 📞 🖥 🛏 ⚜ 🍴 🎱 📺 ✈ 🏧
🍴 SP 🎱

Faringdon Hotel M
😊😊😊

Market Place, Faringdon, SN7 7HL
☎ (0367) 20536
Comfortable and completely refurbished hotel situated in the market square.
Bedrooms: 6 single, 11 double & 2 twin, 3 family rooms.
Bathrooms: 22 private.
Bed & breakfast: £38 single, £48 double.
Half board: £50-£58 daily.
Evening meal 7pm (l.o. 9.30pm).
Parking for 5.
Credit: Access, Visa, Diners, Amex.

🔒 🌀 🅱 📞 🖥 🛏 ⚜ 🍴 ✈ 🎱 🍴 🎱 T

Portwell Guest House M
😊😊😊 APPROVED

Market Place, Faringdon, SN7 7HU
☎ (0367) 240197
In the centre of the market-place of this country market town. Within easy reach of the Cotswolds.
Bedrooms: 1 single, 2 double & 2 twin, 2 family rooms.
Bathrooms: 7 private.
Bed & breakfast: from £25 single, £32-£33 double.
Half board: from £32 daily.
Lunch available.
Evening meal 7pm (l.o. 8pm).
Parking for 3.

🔒 🅱 🖥 ⚜ ✈ 📺 🎱
🎱 SP 🎱

GERRARDS CROSS

Buckinghamshire
Map ref 2D2

On the London Road, Gerrards Cross is distinguished by its wide gorse and beech tree common.

Bull Hotel M
Oxford Rd., Gerrards Cross, SL9 7PA
☎ (0753) 885995
Telex 847747
🆑 De Vere
17th C coaching house steeped in history with gardens, specialist cuisine and extensive wine list.
Bedrooms: 13 single, 45 double & 35 twin, 2 family rooms.
Bathrooms: 95 private.
Continued ▶

GERRARDS CROSS

Continued

Bed & breakfast: £70-£94 single, £80-£175 double. Lunch available. Evening meal 7.30pm (l.o. 9.30pm). Parking for 166. Credit: Access, Visa, Diners, Amex.

ら 耄 甬 ℄ ⊙ ⌁ ♺ 📷 V ⊟ ● 📋 🎏 ᛊ ♨ T ᚅ ✲ ✕ 🅖 SP 🏮 T

Ethorpe Hotel ⋔
👑👑

Packhorse Rd., Gerrards Cross, SL9 8HY
☎ (0753) 882039
In its own pretty, landscaped gardens, a splendid building close to this delightful Buckinghamshire town.
Bedrooms: 4 single, 17 double & 4 twin, 4 family rooms.
Bathrooms: 29 private.
Bed & breakfast: £69-£77.50 single, from £84 double.
Lunch available.
Evening meal 6pm (l.o. 10.30pm).
Parking for 80.
Credit: Access, Visa, Diners, Amex.

ら 耄 甬 ℄ ⊙ ⌁ ♺ 📷 V ✂ ● 🎏 ᛊ ♨ T ᚅ ✲ ✕ 🏮 SP

GORING ON THAMES

Oxfordshire
Map ref 2C2

Riverside town on the Oxfordshire/Berkshire border, linked by an attractive bridge to Streatley with views to the Goring Gap.

Miller of Mansfield
👑👑

High St., Goring-on-Thames, RG8 9AW
☎ (0491) 872829 Fax (0491) 874200
Ivy-covered inn with Tudor style exterior. Interior has original beams, open fires and comfortable bedrooms.
Bedrooms: 3 single, 4 double & 3 twin.
Bathrooms: 4 private, 2 public.
Bed & breakfast: £27-£40 single, £42-£55 double.
Lunch available.
Evening meal 7pm (l.o. 10pm).
Parking for 10.
Credit: Access, Visa.

ら ⊙ 🖵 ♺ 📷 V 🏮 ᚄ SP 🏮

HARPENDEN

Hertfordshire
Map ref 2D1

Delightful country town with many scenic walks through surrounding woods and fields. Harpenden train station provides a fast service into London.

The Laurels Guest House

22 Leyton Road, Harpenden, AL5 2HU
☎ (0582) 712226
Modernised guesthouse overlooking the common in picturesque town. Close to shops and amenities. 20 minutes to London.
Bedrooms: 3 single, 2 double & 2 twin, 3 family rooms.
Bathrooms: 2 public.
Bed & breakfast: £21-£22 single, £33-£34 double.
Parking for 3.

ら 🖵 ♺ ⓤ 📷 📺 ᚄ ✕ 🏮

Milton Hotel ⋔
🖵

25 Milton Rd., Harpenden, AL5 5LA
☎ (0582) 762914
Family-run hotel in residential area close to mainline station, junction 9/10, M1 and M25. Large car park.
Bedrooms: 5 single, 2 double & 1 twin.
Bathrooms: 3 private, 2 public.
Bed & breakfast: £20-£25 single, £32-£35 double.
Evening meal 6.30pm (l.o. 8pm).
Parking for 9.

ら 📷 V ᚄ 📺 🖵 ᚅ ✲ ✕ 🏮

HATFIELD

Hertfordshire
Map ref 2D1

The old town is dominated by the great Jacobean Hatfield House, built for Robert Cecil and still in the Cecil family. It has many interesting exhibits and extensive gardens open to the public.

Comet Hotel ⋔
👑👑👑 COMMENDED

301 St. Albans Road West, Hatfield, AL10 9RH
☎ (0707) 265411
🄲🄱 Embassy

A hotel in the style of the 1930s, combining traditional comfort and service with modern design. Ideally located for London and Hertfordshire countryside.
Bedrooms: 19 single, 20 double & 15 twin, 3 family rooms.
Bathrooms: 54 private, 1 public.
Bed & breakfast: £36-£72 single, £56-£94 double.
Half board: £31.50-£80 daily.
Lunch available.
Evening meal 6.30pm (l.o. 9.55pm).
Parking for 150.
Credit: Access, Visa, Diners, Amex.

ら 耄 ℄ ⊙ 🖵 ♺ 📷 V ● 🎏 ᚄ ♨ 🕭 ᚅ ✲ 🅖 SP 🏮 T

Hazel Grove Hotel ⋔

Roehyde Way, Hatfield, AL10 9AF
☎ (0707) 275701 (6 lines)
Telex 916580
Modern hotel with restaurant, bars and conference facilities. Close to A1, M25, and M1 intersections. High standard rooms and honeymoon suite. Gymnasium.
Bedrooms: 48 double & 14 twin, 14 family rooms.
Bathrooms: 76 private.
Bed & breakfast: £60-£90 single, £70-£100 double.
Lunch available.
Evening meal 7pm (l.o. 9.30pm).
Parking for 92.
Credit: Access, Visa, Diners, Amex.

ら 耄 ℄ ⊙ 🖵 ♺ 📷 V ✂ ᚄ ● 🎏 ᚄ ♨ 🕭 ᚅ ✕ 🐾 SP

HEMEL HEMPSTEAD

Hertfordshire
Map ref 2D1

Pleasant market town greatly expanded since the 1950s but with older origins. The High Street has pretty cottages and 18th C houses and the Norman parish church has a fine 14th C timber spire. The Grand Union Canal runs nearby.
Tourist Information Centre ☎ (0442) 64451

Southville Private Hotel

9 Charles St., Hemel Hempstead, HP1 1JH
☎ (0442) 51387
Small, family-run hotel in a quiet residential road. Within walking distance of town centre, bus and railway station. Car park.

Bedrooms: 10 single, 2 double & 6 twin, 1 family room.
Bathrooms: 6 public.
Bed & breakfast: £18.50-£26 single, £33-£39 double.
Parking for 9.

ら 耄 🖵 ♺ ⓤ ᚄ 📷 📺 🏮 SP

HENLEY-ON-THAMES

Oxfordshire
Map ref 2C2

The famous Thames Regatta is held in this prosperous and attractive town at the beginning of July each year. The town has many Georgian buildings and old coaching inns and the parish church has some fine monuments.
Tourist Information Centre ☎ (0491) 578034

Phyllis Court Club ⋔

Marlow Rd., Henley-on-Thames, RG9 2HT
☎ (0491) 574366
Telex 849041 Sharet G. Ref. 346
A private members' club with bedrooms available to non-members by prior booking. Jacket and tie after 7.30 p.m.
Bedrooms: 2 single, 2 double & 6 twin.
Bathrooms: 10 private.
Bed & breakfast: £60-£75 single, £85-£95 double.
Lunch available.
Evening meal 7.30pm (l.o. 9pm).
Parking for 100.
Credit: Access, Visa, Diners, Amex.

ら ℄ 🖵 ♺ 📷 V ᚄ 📺 🖵 ᚄ ♨ ✕ 🐾 🏮

Regency House Hotel ⋔
👑👑👑

4 River Terrace, Henley-on-Thames, RG9 1BG
☎ (0491) 571133
An elegant riverside hotel overlooking Henley Bridge and the Regatta course beyond. Well-appointed comfortable rooms with pleasant river views.
Bedrooms: 1 single, 3 double & 1 twin.
Bathrooms: 5 private.
Bed & breakfast: from £46 single, £58-£73 double.
Credit: Access, Visa, Amex.

ら 12 ℄ ⊙ 🖵 ♺ 📷 V 🎏 🕭 ✕ 🐾 SP

Please mention this guide when making a booking.

HERTFORD

Hertfordshire
Map ref 2D1

Old county town with attractive cottages and houses and fine public buildings. The remains of the ancient castle, childhood home of Elizabeth I, now form the Council offices and the grounds are open to the public.
Tourist Information Centre ☎ (0992) 584322

Hall House **M**
😊😊😊 HIGHLY COMMENDED
Broad Oak End, (Off Bramfield Rd.), Hertford, SG14 2JA
☎ (0992) 582807
Tranquil, 15th C country house, rebuilt in woodland setting on the edge of Hertford town. Non-smokers preferred.
Bedrooms: 3 double.
Bathrooms: 3 private, 1 public.
Bed & breakfast: £40 single, £55 double.
Half board: £43.50-£56 daily, £304.50-£392 weekly.
Evening meal 6pm (l.o. 8.30pm).
Parking for 7.
Credit: Access, Visa.
⊕ ⌗ ♦ ▥ ⌿ ♉ 📺 ▦ ♨
⟨ ✻ ⊁ ♫ ♬

HIGH WYCOMBE

Buckinghamshire
Map ref 2C2

Famous for furniture-making, historic examples of which feature in the museum. The 18th C Guildhall and the octagonal market house were designed by the Adam brothers. West Wycombe Park and Hughenden Manor (National Trust) are nearby.
Tourist Information Centre ☎ (0494) 421892

The Alexandra Hotel
Queen Alexandra Rd., High Wycombe, HP11 2JX
☎ (0494) 463494
Telex 837442 BEEKS G
New town centre hotel. Tastefully furnished bedrooms with an emphasis on quality. Conference facilities available too. Easy access to several major motorways and tourist towns such as Windsor and Oxford.

Bedrooms: 2 single, 23 double & 2 twin, 1 family room.
Bathrooms: 28 private.
Bed & breakfast: £66-£72 single, £78-£84 double.
Lunch available.
Evening meal 7pm (l.o. 8.30pm).
Parking for 30.
Credit: Access, Visa, Amex.
⟨ ♨ ⌂ ⊕ ⌗ ♦ ▥ ⌿ ▦ ♨ ⊁ ✻ SP

Belmont Guest House
9 & 11 Priory Avenue, High Wycombe, HP13 6SQ
☎ (0494) 27046
Victorian-style guesthouse within easy walking distance of the town and public transport. Centrally located for Oxfordshire, Berkshire and Buckinghamshire.
Bedrooms: 8 single, 1 double & 10 twin, 1 family room.
Bathrooms: 3 private, 3 public; 1 private shower.
Bed & breakfast: £20-£40 single, £33-£45 double.
Half board: £23-£47 daily.
Evening meal 6pm (l.o. 9pm).
Parking for 20.
Credit: Access, Visa, Diners, Amex.
⟨ ♨ ⌗ ♦ ▤ ⌿ ▦ ♨ ⊁ SP

The Chiltern
😊😊😊
181-183 West Wycombe Rd., High Wycombe, HP12 3AF
☎ (0494) 452597/436678 & (0494) 36678
Close to West Wycombe Caves and Country House. Halfway between Oxford and London. Home-cooked food and traditional beers.
Bedrooms: 7 single, 1 double & 6 twin, 2 family rooms.
Bathrooms: 8 private, 3 public.
Bed & breakfast: £27-£32 single, £39-£43 double.
Half board: £32-£42 daily, £190-£225 weekly.
Lunch available.
Evening meal 6.30pm (l.o. 8pm).
Parking for 16.
Credit: Access, Visa.
⟨ ♨ ⌂ ⊕ ⌗ ♦ ▥ ⌿ ♉ 📺 ▦ ♨ ⊁ ✻

Half board prices shown are per person but in some cases may be based on double/twin occupancy.

HITCHIN

Hertfordshire
Map ref 2D1

Once a flourishing wool town. Full of interest, with many fine old buildings centred around the market square. These include the 17th C almshouses, old inns and the Victorian Corn Exchange.
Tourist Information Centre ☎ (0462) 434738

The Blakemore Thistle Hotel **M**
Little Wymondley, Nr. Hitchin, SG4 7JJ
☎ Stevenage (0438) 355821
Telex 825479
⊕ Thistle
A secluded Georgian-style hotel set in 6 acres of garden. French cuisine. Swimming pool and sauna available. Luton Airport 8 miles.
Bedrooms: 6 single, 60 double & 14 twin, 2 family rooms.
Bathrooms: 82 private.
Bed & breakfast: from £71.75 single, from £90.50 double.
Lunch available.
Evening meal 7pm (l.o. 9.30pm).
Parking for 200.
Credit: Access, Visa, C.Bl., Diners, Amex.
⟨ ♨ ⌂ ⊕ ⌗ ♦ ▥ ⌿ ♉ ⊁ ✻ SP T

Highbury Lodge Hotel
😊😊
Highbury Rd., Hitchin, SG4 9RW
☎ (0462) 432983
Small family-run hotel in residential area overlooking parkland.
Bedrooms: 4 single, 1 double & 3 twin, 1 family room.
Bathrooms: 4 private, 2 public.
Bed & breakfast: £25-£30 single, £40-£43 double.
Parking for 10.
Credit: Access, Visa.
⟨ ⌗ ♦ ▥ ⌿ ♉ 📺 ▦ ♨ ⊁ ♫

The Lord Lister Hotel **M**
😊😊😊
Park St., Hitchin, SG4 9AH
☎ (0462) 432712 & 459451
Early Victorian, originally a Quaker school attended by Lord Lister. Close to town centre and all amenities.
Bedrooms: 7 single, 8 double & 6 twin, 1 family room.
Bathrooms: 10 private, 1 public; 9 private showers.

Bed & breakfast: £38-£47 single, £50-£57 double.
Half board: £48-£77 daily, £336-£539 weekly.
Evening meal 7pm (l.o. 9pm).
Credit: Access, Visa, Diners, Amex.
⟨ ♨ ⌗ ⊕ ⌗ ♦ ♉ ⌿ ♨ 📺 ▦ ♨ ⊁ ⟨ OAP ♫ SP ▦

The Red Lion and Lodge Hotel **M**
Listed COMMENDED
Kings Walden Rd., Great Offley, Nr. Hitchin, SG5 3DZ
☎ (0462) 76281 & 76792
16th C inn, set in Hertfordshire countryside, only 5 minutes' drive from Hitchin and Luton. A friendly and informal atmosphere.
Bedrooms: 3 double & 2 twin.
Bathrooms: 5 private.
Bed & breakfast: £35-£50 single, £40-£60 double.
Evening meal 7pm (l.o. 9.30pm).
Parking for 10.
Credit: Access, Visa, Diners, Amex.
⟨ ♨ ⌂ ⊕ ⌗ ♦ CB ▥ ◐ ▦ ♨ ✻ ⊁ ♫ ♬ OAP SP ▦

Redcoats Farmhouse Hotel **M**
😊😊😊 COMMENDED
Redcoats Green, Nr. Hitchin, SG4 7JR
☎ Stevenage (0438) 729500
Telex 83343 Ref: RFH
A 15th C farmhouse in open countryside offering secluded comfort and fresh food. Luton Airport is 20 minutes away.
Bedrooms: 1 single, 9 double & 2 twin, 2 family rooms.
Bathrooms: 11 private, 1 public.
Bed & breakfast: £38-£68 single, £45-£90 double.
Lunch available.
Evening meal 7pm (l.o. 9.30pm).
Parking for 35.
Credit: Access, Visa, Diners, Amex.
⟨ ♨ ⌂ ⌗ ♦ ▥ ♉ 📺 ▦ ♨ ⊁ ✻ ♫ SP ▦ T

Classifications and quality commendations were correct at the time of going to press but are subject to change. Please check at the time of booking.

HUNGERFORD
Berkshire
Map ref 2C2

Attractive town on the Avon Canal and the River Kennet, famous for its fishing. It has a wide High Street and many antique shops. Nearby is the Tudor manor of Littlecote with its large Roman mosaic.

The Bear Hotel M
⚜⚜⚜⚜
Charnham St., Hungerford, RG17 0EL
☎ (0488) 682512 Fax (0488) 684357
🆑 Resort
13th C coaching inn, traditionally furnished with timber beams and open fires. 3 miles from junction 14 on the M4, ideally situated for the Cotswolds, Berkshire Downs and Newbury Races.
Bedrooms: 3 single, 17 double & 18 twin, 3 family rooms.
Bathrooms: 41 private.
Bed & breakfast: £71.50-£81.50 single, £88-£98 double.
Lunch available.
Evening meal 7.30pm (l.o. 9.30pm).
Parking for 60.
Credit: Access, Visa, Diners, Amex.

Marshgate Cottage M
⚜⚜⚜⚜
Marsh Lane, Hungerford, RG17 0QX
☎ (0488) 682307
Family-run hotel ranges around south-facing walled courtyard, linked to 350-year-old thatched cottage. Overlooks marshland, trout streams and canal. Lovely walks, bird-watching. Important antiques centre. 1 hour from Heathrow. French, German and Scandinavian spoken.
Bedrooms: 1 single, 2 double & 4 twin, 2 family rooms.
Bathrooms: 7 private, 2 public.
Bed & breakfast: £23.50-£33 single, £33-£45.50 double.
Evening meal 7pm (l.o. 9pm).
Parking for 9.
Open February-December.
Credit: Access, Visa.

IVER HEATH
Buckinghamshire
Map ref 2D2

The nearby, attractive village of Iver has many houses of 16th and 17th C origin.

The Bridgettine Guest House & Conference Centre
Fulmer Common Rd., Iver Heath, SL0 0NR
☎ Fulmer (0753) 662073 & 662645
Basic accommodation run by members of a religious order.
Bedrooms: 11 single, 4 double & 3 twin, 4 family rooms.
Bathrooms: 7 public.
Bed & breakfast: from £16 single, from £32 double.
Half board: from £20 daily.
Lunch available.
Evening meal 6.45pm (l.o. 2pm).
Parking for 15.

KINGHAM
Oxfordshire
Map ref 2B1

Small village set in beautiful scenery near the River Evenlode and the woodlands of Wychwood. Popular with ornithologists for the variety of rare birds which can be seen here.

Conygree Gate Country House Hotel M
⚜⚜ COMMENDED
Church St., Kingham, OX7 6YA
☎ (060 871) 389
Old farmhouse tastefully modernised, located in a quiet village in the Cotswolds. Guests collected from station, 1 mile away. Most rooms with en-suite facilities.
Bedrooms: 1 single, 2 double & 3 twin, 2 family rooms.
Bathrooms: 6 private, 2 public.
Bed & breakfast: from £22 single, from £42 double.
Half board: from £31 daily, from £217 weekly.
Evening meal 7pm (l.o. 5pm).
Parking for 10.
Open February-December.
Credit: Access, Visa, Amex.

LEIGHTON BUZZARD
Bedfordshire
Map ref 2C1

Large market town with many buildings of interest including a fine 15th C market cross, the 17th C Holly Lodge and a number of old inns. The Grand Union Canal is nearby and in Page's Park is a narrow gauge railway.

Swan Hotel M
⚜⚜⚜⚜ COMMENDED
High St., Leighton Buzzard, LU7 7EA
☎ (0525) 372148 Fax (0525) 370444 Telex 825562 CHACOM-SWAN
Family-run, Georgian coaching inn. Comfortable bedrooms and welcoming atmosphere. Serving local fish, game and vegetarian dishes.
Bedrooms: 22 single, 11 double & 4 twin, 1 family room.
Bathrooms: 38 private.
Bed & breakfast: £72-£85 single, £85-£110 double.
Lunch available.
Evening meal 7pm (l.o. 9.30pm).
Parking for 12.
Credit: Access, Visa, Diners, Amex.

LUTON
Bedfordshire
Map ref 2D1

Bedfordshire's largest town with its own airport, several industries and an excellent shopping centre. The town's history is depicted in the museum and art gallery in Wardown Park. Luton Hoo has a magnificent collection of treasures.
Tourist Information Centre ☎ (0582) 401579 (Luton Airport (0582) 405100)

Ambassador Hotel
31 Lansdowne Road, Luton, LU8 1EE
☎ (0582) 31411
Privately owned hotel in quiet residential area. Close to town centre, airport, motorway, coach and train services.
Bedrooms: 9 single, 2 double & 3 twin.
Bathrooms: 14 private.

Bed & breakfast: £51.75 single, £66.70 double.
Evening meal 7pm (l.o. 8.45pm).
Parking for 20.
Credit: Access, Visa.

Applemoore
54 St. Ethelbert Avenue, Luton, LU3 1QJ
☎ (0582) 33359
Family-run guesthouse, convenient for Luton Airport. Free parking on premises whilst away.
Bedrooms: 1 twin, 1 family room.
Bathrooms: 1 public.
Bed & breakfast: £15-£17 single, £28-£32 double.
Half board: from £17 daily.
Evening meal 6pm (l.o. 9pm).
Parking for 4.

Centtral Hotel
⚜⚜⚜ COMMENDED
100 Park St., Luton, LU1 3EY
☎ (0582) 421371 Fax (0582) 411427 Telex 825562 CHACEN-G
Located in the town, near the M1 junctions 10 and 11 and the airport. Well-decorated, ideal for businessmen and tourists.
Bedrooms: 9 single, 7 double, 1 family room.
Bathrooms: 17 private.
Bed & breakfast: from £42 single, from £56 double.
Half board: from £52 daily.
Lunch available.
Evening meal 6pm (l.o. 11.30pm).
Credit: Access, Visa, Diners, Amex.

Pines Hotel M
☎
10 Marsh Rd., Leagrave, Luton, LU3 2NH
☎ (0582) 575552
Comfortable Tudor-style hotel set in pleasant grounds. Recently refurbished with restaurant and licensed bar. Easy access to Luton Airport.
Bedrooms: 4 single, 4 double & 9 twin, 3 family rooms.
Bathrooms: 6 public.
Bed & breakfast: £30-£40 single, £40-£50 double.
Half board: £35-£50 daily, £145-£350 weekly.
Lunch available.
Evening meal 7pm (l.o. 9pm).

Parking for 20.
Credit: Access, Visa, Diners,
Amex.
🐾 ♿ 📶 🛏 ⚓ V 🛏 📺 ●
📶 ⚓ 📍 ✗ SP

The Red Lion Hotel ⚊
🏵🏵🏵🏵

Castle St., Luton, LU1 3AA
☎ (0582) 413881
Telex 826856 Fax (0582)
23864
CR Lansbury
*Town centre hotel, convenient
for shopping facilities and local
tourist attractions. 1 mile from
Luton Airport.*
Bedrooms: 9 single, 14 double
& 13 twin, 2 family rooms.
Bathrooms: 38 private.
Bed & breakfast: from £70
single, from £82 double.
Half board: from £84 daily.
Lunch available.
Evening meal 7pm (l.o.
10.30pm).
Parking for 48.
Credit: Access, Visa, Diners,
Amex.
🐾 ♿ 📶 📞 📍 🛏 💠 🛏 🏆 📍
✂ 🛏 ● 📶 ⚓ 📍 🏆 ⚓ 🏧 ✗ SP

Strathmore Thistle
Hotel ⚊

Arndale Centre, Luton,
LU1 2TR
☎ (0582) 34199 Telex 825763
CR Thistle
*A comfortable modern hotel,
recently refurbished, with an
interesting themed restaurant
and bar. Conveniently located
1.5 miles from Luton Airport.*
Bedrooms: 33 single,
41 double & 73 twin, 3 family
rooms.
Bathrooms: 150 private.
Bed & breakfast: from £77.75
single, from £99.50 double.
Lunch available.
Evening meal 6pm (l.o.
11pm).
Parking for 44.
Credit: Access, Visa, C.Bl.,
Diners, Amex.
🐾 📞 📶 🛏 💠 🛏 V 🛏 ✂ 🛏
● 📍 📶 ⚓ 📍 🏆 ⚓ ✗ SP 📺

**The symbol CR
and the name of a
hotel group or
consortium after a
hotel address means
that bookings can
be made through a
central reservations
office. These are
listed on pages
559 & 560.**

Berkshire
Map ref 2C2

Attractive town on the
River Thames which is
crossed by an elegant
18th C bridge and by
Brunel's well-known
railway bridge. It is a
popular place for boating
with delightful riverside
walks. The Courage Shire
Horse Centre is nearby.
*Tourist Information
Centre* ☎ *(0628) 781110*

Clifton Guest House

21 Crauford Rise,
Maidenhead, SL6 7LR
☎ (0628) 23572
*Fully-licensed, family-run hotel
near town centre. Convenient
for Heathrow, Windsor Castle
and the M4, M40 and M25
motorways.*
Bedrooms: 3 single, 2 double
& 5 twin, 2 family rooms.
Bathrooms: 5 private,
4 public.
Bed & breakfast: £24-£27
single, £36-£44 double.
Evening meal 6pm (l.o.
9.30pm).
Parking for 10.
Credit: Access, Visa.
🐾 ♿ 📶 💠 V 🛏 📺 📶 ⚓
✿ 🐾 ✗ SP

Elva Lodge Hotel
🏵🏵

Castle Hill, Maidenhead,
SL6 4AD
☎ (0628) 22948 & 34883 Fax
(0628) 34885
*Located in central
Maidenhead, close to the M4
and 20 minutes from Heathrow
Airport.*
Bedrooms: 12 single, 8 double
& 5 twin, 5 family rooms.
Bathrooms: 6 private,
11 public; 9 private showers.
Bed & breakfast: £38-£60
single, £50-£65 double.
Half board: £50-£75 daily,
£315-£472.50 weekly.
Lunch available.
Evening meal 6pm (l.o.
10.30pm).
Parking for 31.
Credit: Access, Visa, Diners,
Amex.
🐾 ♿ 📶 💠 🏆 V 🛏 📺
📶 ⚓ 📍 🏆 ✗ SP

Fredrick's Hotel &
Restaurant ⚊

Shoppenhangers Rd.,
Maidenhead, SL6 2PZ
☎ (0628) 35934 & 24737
Telex 849966

---

*Conveniently situated in the
beautiful Thames Valley, close
to the centre of Maidenhead
and the M4. The hotel offers
comfort, good food in its
renowned restaurant, and
personal service.*
Bedrooms: 10 single,
13 double & 13 twin, 1 family
room.
Bathrooms: 37 private.
Bed & breakfast: £98.50-£110
single, £135-£145 double.
Lunch available.
Evening meal 7.15pm (l.o.
9.45pm).
Parking for 90.
Credit: Access, Visa, Diners,
Amex.
🐾 ♿ 📞 📶 🛏 💠 V 🛏 ●
📶 ⚓ 📍 🏆 ✿ ✗ 🐾

Kingswood Hotel ⚊
🏵🏵🏵🏵 COMMENDED

Boyn Hill Avenue,
Maidenhead, SL6 4EN
☎ (0628) 33598 Telex 847330
KINGS Fax (0628) 25516
*Converted Victorian house in
town centre, yet very quiet and
convenient for Heathrow,
Windsor Castle, Ascot Races
and Henley Regatta.*
Bedrooms: 4 single, 9 double
& 1 twin, 1 family room.
Bathrooms: 15 private.
Bed & breakfast: £50-£60
single, £70-£90 double.
Half board: from £70 daily.
Lunch available.
Evening meal 7pm (l.o.
9.45pm).
Parking for 18.
Credit: Access, Visa, Diners,
Amex.
🐾 ♿ 📶 📞 📍 🛏 💠 🏆 V
📺 ● 📶 ⚓ 📍 🏆 ⚓ 📍 🐾 OAP
🐾 SP 🏧

Monkey Island Hotel ⚊

Bray-on-Thames,
Maidenhead, SL6 2EE
☎ (0628) 23400 Telex 346589
Fax (0628) 784732
*Beautiful island in the Thames
Valley, approached by
footbridge. Close to Windsor,
Ascot, Henley and Oxford. 26
miles from London and 12
miles from Heathrow Airport.*
Bedrooms: 2 single,
23 double & 2 family rooms.
Bathrooms: 27 private.
Bed & breakfast: £65-£120
single, £85-£140 double.
Half board: £50-£70 daily.
Lunch available.
Evening meal 7pm (l.o.
9.30pm).
Parking for 100.
Credit: Access, Visa, Diners,
Amex.
🐾 ♿ 📞 📶 🛏 💠 🏆 V 🛏
● 📶 ⚓ 📍 🏆 🎵 📍 ✿ ✗ SP
🏧 📺

Old Court Hotel

Bath Rd., Taplow,
Maidenhead, SL6 0AH
☎ (0628) 71248 & 21440
*Late Victorian with original
mosaic, privately owned and
managed, providing a homely,
comfortable and friendly
atmosphere.*
Bedrooms: 11 single, 4 double
& 4 twin, 5 family rooms.
Bathrooms: 2 private,
5 public; 1 private shower.
Bed & breakfast: £31-£45
single, £41-£52 double.
Half board: £39-£55 daily.
Evening meal 7pm (l.o. 9pm).
Parking for 40.
🐾 ♿ 📶 💠 🛏 📺 📶
⚓ ✿ SP 🏧

Thamesbrook Guest
House

🏵🏵 COMMENDED

18 Ray Park Avenue,
Maidenhead, SL6 8DS
☎ (0628) 783855
*In a quiet location near river,
Boulters Lock and town centre.
Spacious, well-decorated
rooms. Pubs and restaurants
nearby.*
Bedrooms: 1 double & 2 twin,
1 family room.
Bathrooms: 1 private,
2 public.
Bed & breakfast: £20-£25
single, £32-£36 double.
Parking for 6.
🐾 📶 💠 UL 🛏 📺 📶 ⚓ ✗
📍 SP

Thicket Meadows North

Listed

Newlands Drive,
Maidenhead, SL6 4LL
☎ (0628) 29744
*Edwardian manor house in
lovely setting near "Thicket".
Owners are tennis professionals
and can include lessons for an
additional fee.*
Bedrooms: 1 double.
Bathrooms: 1 private,
1 public.
Bed & breakfast: from £15
single, from £35 double.
Half board: from £35 daily.
Parking for 6.
♿ 📶 💠 V ✂ 📺 📶 ⚓
📍 ✿ ✗ 🐾 🏧

**Half board prices
shown are per
person but in some
cases may be based
on double/twin
occupancy.**

315

MARLOW

Buckinghamshire
Map ref 2C2

Attractive Georgian town on the River Thames, famous for its 19th C suspension bridge. The High Street contains many old houses and there are connections with writers including Shelley and the poet T.S. Eliot.

The Country House M

Bisham, Marlow, SL7 1RP
☎ (0628) 890606 Fax (0628) 890983
Edwardian house in tranquil grounds. 300-yard level walk from Marlow Bridge and the High Street.
Bedrooms: 3 single, 3 double & 1 twin, 1 family room.
Bathrooms: 8 private.
Bed & breakfast: from £55 single, from £75 double.
Parking for 10.
Credit: Access, Visa, Amex.

Holly Tree House

COMMENDED
Burford Close, Marlow Bottom, SL7 3NF
☎ (0628) 891110
Large, modern detached house on three-quarter acre plot within Green Belt land. Quiet yet convenient location. All rooms full en-suite.
Bedrooms: 1 single, 2 double & 1 twin.
Bathrooms: 4 private.
Bed & breakfast: £45 single, £55-£59 double.
Parking for 8.
Credit: Access, Visa, Amex.

Individual proprietors have supplied all details of accommodation. Although we do check for accuracy, we advise you to confirm prices and other information at the time of booking.

MIDDLETON STONEY

Oxfordshire
Map ref 2C1

The great house in the park was for nearly 2 centuries the home of the Earls of Jersey. A splendid avenue of oaks, elms, beeches and cedars leads to a clerestoried church built by a supporter of King Stephen.

Jersey Arms Inn M

COMMENDED
Middleton Stoney, OX6 8SE
☎ (086 989) 234
Old inn with all the home comforts, in centre of village, on main A43 Oxford to Northampton road.
Bedrooms: 8 double & 8 twin.
Bathrooms: 16 private.
Bed & breakfast: £55-£70 single, £69-£90 double.
Lunch available.
Evening meal 7.30pm (l.o. 9.30pm).
Parking for 50.
Credit: Access, Visa, Diners, Amex.

MILTON COMMON

Oxfordshire
Map ref 2C1

9m E. Oxford

Belfry Hotel M

Milton Common, Oxford, OX9 2JW
☎ Great Milton (0844) 279381 Telex 837968
Inter
Tudor-style country hotel, privately owned. Well placed for touring. Indoor leisure complex with swimming pool, sauna, solarium, mini gym.
Bedrooms: 11 single, 36 double & 30 twin.
Bathrooms: 77 private.
Bed & breakfast: £65-£75 single, £72.50-£87.50 double.
Lunch available.
Evening meal 7.30pm (l.o. 9.30pm).
Parking for 200.
Credit: Access, Visa, Amex.

Display advertisement appears on page 576.

MILTON KEYNES

Buckinghamshire
Map ref 2C1

Designated a New Town in 1967, Milton Keynes offers a wide range of housing and is abundantly planted with trees. It has excellent shopping facilities and 3 centres for leisure and sporting activities. The Open University is based here.
Tourist Information Centre ☎ (0908) 691995

Broughton Hotel M

Broughton Village, nr Milton Keynes MK10 9AA
☎ (0908) 667726
On the outskirts of Milton Keynes, conveniently located for the M1.
Bedrooms: 4 double & 24 twin, 2 family rooms.
Bathrooms: 30 private.
Bed & breakfast: from £55 single, from £70 double.
Half board: from £45 daily.
Lunch available.
Evening meal 6pm (l.o. 9.45pm).
Parking for 58.
Credit: Access, Visa, Amex.

Friendly Hotel M

Monks Way, Two Mile Ash, Milton Keynes, MK8 8LY
☎ (0908) 561666
Telex 826152
Friendly
New hotel close to the centre of town and recreational areas.
Bedrooms: 15 double & 30 twin, 5 family rooms.
Bathrooms: 50 private.
Bed & breakfast: £52-£62 single, £68-£73 double.
Half board: £45.75-£74 daily.
Lunch available.
Evening meal 7pm (l.o. 10pm).
Parking for 76.
Credit: Access, Visa, Diners, Amex.

Kingfishers

9 Rylstone Close, Heelands, Milton Keynes, MK13 7QT
☎ (0908) 310231
Large private home set in quarter of an acre of grounds, near to centre of Milton Keynes.
Bedrooms: 1 single, 1 double & 1 twin.

Bathrooms: 2 private, 1 public.
Bed & breakfast: £20-£30 single, £35-£40 double.
Parking for 6.

Linford Lodge

Great Linford, Wood Lane, Milton Keynes, MK14 5AZ
☎ (0908) 605879
Telex 826932 Lin Lodge
17th C farmhouse converted into restaurant with accommodation and riding stables in peaceful surroundings. Only 3 miles from central Milton Keynes. Indoor swimming pool.
Bedrooms: 4 single, 4 double & 1 twin.
Bathrooms: 6 private.
Bed & breakfast: £39.50-£48 single, £48-£65 double.
Half board: £58-£68 daily.
Lunch available.
Evening meal 7pm (l.o. 10pm).
Parking for 40.
Credit: Access, Visa, Diners, Amex.

The Wayfarer Hotel M

Brickhill St., Willen Lake, Milton Keynes MK15 0DS
☎ (0908) 675222
Fax (0908) 674679
A purpose-built hotel with bar and restaurant. On the banks of Willen Lake, a popular water sports centre.
Bedrooms: 11 single, 20 double & 10 twin.
Bathrooms: 41 private.
Bed & breakfast: from £59.50 single, from £69.50 double.
Half board: from £79.50 daily, from £356.50 weekly.
Lunch available.
Evening meal 6.30pm (l.o. 10pm).
Parking for 50.
Credit: Access, Visa, Diners, Amex.

Woughton House Hotel M

Woughton-on-the-Green, Milton Keynes, MK6 3LR
☎ (0908) 661919
Telex 825264
Victorian hotel situated in 5 acres of grounds. 5 minutes to Milton Keynes City and shopping centre.
Bedrooms: 20 single, 29 double & 1 twin, 2 family rooms.

Bathrooms: 52 private,
2 public.
Bed & breakfast: £40-£80
single, £50-£140 double.
Half board: £56.95-£96.95
daily, £398.65-£678.65
weekly.
Lunch available.
Evening meal 7pm (l.o.
9.45pm).
Parking for 70.
Credit: Access, Visa, Diners,
Amex.

MINSTER LOVELL

Oxfordshire
Map ref 2C1

Picturesque village on the
River Windrush with
thatched cottages and
19th C houses. Minster
Lovell Hall, built in the
15th C by the Lovell
family, is the subject of
several legends and now
stands in ruins in a
beautiful riverside setting.

Minster Lovell Mill Hotel M
Minster Lovell, OX8 5RN
☎ Witney (0993) 74441
*A high quality hotel in a
beautiful riverside country
setting with good service and
cuisine. Completely renovated
during summer 1990.*
Bedrooms: 21 single, 5 double
& 12 twin.
Bathrooms: 38 private,
1 public.
Bed & breakfast: £89-£105
double.
Half board: £44.50-£81 daily.
Lunch available.
Evening meal 7pm (l.o. 8pm).
Parking for 20.
Credit: Access, Visa, Amex.

The Old Swan M
Minster Lovell, Nr. Witney,
OX8 5RN
☎ Witney (0993) 775614
*600-year-old inn with history
linked to Minster Lovell ruins
and Richard III. Delightful
Cotswold village. Completely
refurbished during summer
1990.*
Bedrooms: 2 single, 4 double
& 4 twin.
Bathrooms: 10 private.
Bed & breakfast: £89-£105
double.
Half board: £44.50-£81 daily.
Lunch available.

Evening meal 7.30pm (l.o.
9.30pm).
Parking for 50.
Credit: Access, Visa, Amex.

NEWBURY

Berkshire
Map ref 2C2

Ancient town surrounded
by the Downs and on the
Kennet and Avon Canal. It
has many buildings of
interest, including the
17th C Cloth Hall, which
is now a museum. The
famous racecourse is
nearby.
*Tourist Information
Centre* ☎ *(0635) 30267*

The Bell at Boxford
Lambourn Rd., Newbury,
RG16 8DD
☎ Boxford (048 838) 721
Fax: (048 838) 749
*Traditional inn with real ales,
food and extensive wine list. 4
miles from Newbury on the
Lambourn road. A la carte
restaurant.*
Bedrooms: 1 single, 8 double
& 1 twin.
Bathrooms: 10 private.
Bed & breakfast: £25-£60
single, £45-£75 double.
Half board: £30-£80 daily.
Lunch available.
Evening meal 7pm (l.o.
10pm).
Parking for 55.
Credit: Access, Visa, Diners,
Amex.

Enborne Grange Hotel M
Enborne St., Wash Common,
Newbury, RG14 6RP
☎ (0635) 40046
*Delightful rural setting
overlooking South Downs.
Within easy reach of Newbury
and major tourist attractions in
the South.*
Bedrooms: 5 single, 18 double
& 2 twin, 1 family room.
Bathrooms: 26 private,
1 public.
Bed & breakfast: £45-£60
single, £60-£70 double.
Half board: £43-£63 daily,
from £290 weekly.
Lunch available.
Evening meal 7.30pm (l.o.
9.30pm).
Parking for 80.
Credit: Access, Visa, Amex.

Hilton National Hotel M
Pinchington Lane, Newbury,
RG14 7HL
☎ (0635) 529000
Telex 848247
⑭ Hilton
*New hotel, situated just off the
A34, offering traditional
standards of service. Hotel
features Stubbs restaurant and
piano bar.*
Bedrooms: 66 double &
37 twin, 17 family rooms.
Bathrooms: 120 private.
Bed & breakfast: £40-£91
single, £80-£120 double.
Half board: £55-£111 daily.
Lunch available.
Evening meal 7pm (l.o.
11pm).
Parking for 120.
Credit: Access, Visa, Diners,
Amex.

Millwaters Hotel M
COMMENDED
London Road, Newbury,
RG13 2BY
☎ (0635) 528838 Telex 83343
ABTELX G ATTN
MILLWATERS
⑭ Consort
*Georgian country house with
resident proprietors. Listed
building in 8 acres of mature
gardens, through which the
rivers Kennet and Lambourn
flow.*
Bedrooms: 12 double &
5 twin.
Bathrooms: 17 private.
Bed & breakfast: from £75
single, from £95 double.
Half board: from £90 daily.
Lunch available.
Evening meal 7.30pm (l.o.
9.30pm).
Parking for 50.
Credit: Access, Visa, Diners,
Amex.

Nalderhill House
Wickham Heath, Stockcross,
Newbury, RG16 8EU
☎ (0635) 41783 & 37231
*Large Victorian country house
with exceptional views over
surrounding countryside.
Landscaped gardens and
grounds in peaceful setting. 4
miles to Newbury town centre.*
Bedrooms: 1 single, 4 double
& 4 twin, 2 family rooms.
Bathrooms: 6 private,
2 public; 2 private showers.
Bed & breakfast: £25-£35
single, £35-£45 double.

Half board: £30-£45 daily,
£190-£300 weekly.
Evening meal 7pm (l.o. 7pm).
Parking for 20.
Credit: Visa, Amex.

Regency Park Hotel M
COMMENDED
Bowling Green Rd.,
Thatcham, Nr. Newbury,
RG13 3RP
☎ Newbury (0635) 71555
Telex 847844 REGPRK
*Comfortable hotel that blends
architecturally with the former
family home constructed earlier
this century.*
Bedrooms: 20 single,
15 double & 15 twin.
Bathrooms: 50 private.
Bed & breakfast: £75-£90
single, £90-£100 double.
Half board: £100-£150 daily.
Lunch available.
Evening meal 6.30pm (l.o.
10.30pm).
Parking for 100.
Credit: Access, Visa, Diners,
Amex.

Stakis Newbury Hotel M
Oxford Road, Newbury,
RG16 8XY
☎ (0635) 247010
⑭ Stakis
*Modern hotel located off
junction 13 of M4. Leisure
club, restaurant, bar,
courtyard. Children's
programme weekends.*
Bedrooms: 63 double &
47 twin, 2 family rooms.
Bathrooms: 112 private.
Bed & breakfast: £85-£95
single, £104-£114 double.
Lunch available.
Evening meal 6.30pm (l.o.
10pm).
Parking for 150.
Credit: Access, Visa, Diners,
Amex.

The White Hart Inn
Hamstead Marshall,
Newbury, RG15 0HW
☎ Kintbury (0488) 58201
*Traditional rural inn with oak
beams, log fire and good food.
Comfortable accommodation in
barn conversion.*
Bedrooms: 2 single, 2 twin,
2 family rooms.
Bathrooms: 6 private.
Bed & breakfast: £40-£50
single, £50-£60 double.
Lunch available.

Continued ▶

317

Evening meal 7pm (l.o. 10pm).
Parking for 35.
Credit: Access, Visa, Diners, Amex.

NEWPORT PAGNELL

Buckinghamshire
Map ref 2C1

Busy town situated on 2 rivers with some Georgian as well as modern buildings.

The Coach House Hotel

London Rd., Moulsoe, Newport Pagnell, MK16 0JA
☎ (0908) 613688
Telex 333868 Fax (0908) 617335
Ⓛ Lansbury
New hotel built around a listed Georgian property, off junction 14 of the M1. Ideally situated, close to Milton Keynes.
Bedrooms: 24 double & 25 twin.
Bathrooms: 49 private.
Bed & breakfast: £31-£78 single, £62-£92 double.
Half board: £42-£93 daily.
Lunch available.
Evening meal 7pm (l.o. 10pm).
Parking for 162.
Credit: Access, Visa, Diners, Amex.

Swan Revived Hotel M

High St., Newport Pagnell, Milton Keynes, MK16 8AR
☎ (0908) 610565 Fax (0908) 210995 Telex 826801
Famous coaching inn, where guests can enjoy every modern comfort. Perfect stopping place for those travelling north or south, or for exploring.
Bedrooms: 20 single, 16 double & 3 twin, 2 family rooms.
Bathrooms: 41 private.
Bed & breakfast: £25-£54 single, £38-£58 double.
Half board: £35-£64 daily, £300 weekly.
Lunch available.
Evening meal 7.15pm (l.o. 10pm).
Parking for 18.

Credit: Access, Visa, Diners, Amex.

OLD WINDSOR

Berkshire
Map ref 2D2

2m SE. Windsor

Union Inn M

17 Crimp Hill, Old Windsor, SL4 2QY
☎ (0753) 861955 Fax (0753) 831378
Free-house hotel with 50-seat restaurant.
Bedrooms: 4 single, 8 double.
Bathrooms: 12 private.
Bed & breakfast: £45.50-£49.50 single, £57.50-£62.50 double.
Lunch available.
Evening meal 7pm (l.o. 10pm).
Parking for 32.
Credit: Access, Visa, Amex.

OLNEY

Buckinghamshire
Map ref 2C1

The White House Guest House

10 High Street South, Olney, MK46 4AA
☎ Bedford (0234) 711478
Country town guesthouse with family atmosphere Providing clean, warm, comfortable accommodation. Within easy reach of Bedford, Milton Keynes and Northampton.
Bedrooms: 2 single, 3 double & 4 twin, 1 family room.
Bathrooms: 1 public;
3 private showers.
Bed & breakfast: £22-£24 single, £35-£37 double.
Half board: £29-£31 daily, £174-£186 weekly.
Evening meal 6pm (l.o. 4pm).
Parking for 4.

**Half board prices
shown are per
person but in some
cases may be based
on double/twin
occupancy.**

OXFORD

Oxfordshire
Map ref 2C1

Beautiful university town with many ancient colleges, some dating from the 13th C, and numerous buildings of historic and architectural interest. The Ashmolean Museum has outstanding collections. There are lovely gardens and meadows with punting on the Cherwell.
Tourist Information Centre ☎ (0865) 726871

Acorn Guest House

260 Iffley Rd., Oxford, OX4 1SE
☎ (0865) 247998
Comfortable, friendly, convenient for all local amenities and close to the river.
Bedrooms: 2 single, 1 twin, 3 family rooms.
Bathrooms: 2 public.
Bed & breakfast: £15-£20 single, £28-£36 double.
Parking for 5.

Bath Place Hotel and Restaurant

4 & 5 Bath Place, Holywell St., Oxford, OX1 3SU
☎ (0865) 791812 Fax (0865) 790760 & 791834
Restored city centre hotel and restaurant, tucked between Oxford's Universities.
Bedrooms: 6 double & 2 twin.
Bathrooms: 8 private.
Bed & breakfast: £55-£70 single, £80-£95 double.
Lunch available.
Evening meal 7.15pm (l.o. 9.45pm).
Parking for 6.
Credit: Access, Visa, Diners, Amex.

Becket House

Listed

5 Becket St., Nr. Station, Oxford, OX1 1PP
☎ (0865) 724675
Friendly guesthouse convenient for rail and bus station, city centre and colleges.
Bedrooms: 4 single, 1 double & 3 twin, 1 family room.
Bathrooms: 3 public.

Bed & breakfast: £15-£17 single, £29-£34 double.
Credit: Access, Visa.

Bowood House Hotel M

238 Oxford Rd., Kidlington, Oxford, OX5 1EB
☎ Oxford (0865) 842288
Completely modernised family-run hotel close to shops. On the A423, 4.5 miles from Oxford city centre. Frequent bus service to Oxford.
Bedrooms: 7 single, 8 double & 4 twin, 3 family rooms.
Bathrooms: 20 private, 2 public.
Bed & breakfast: £35-£50 single, £65 double.
Half board: £47-£62 daily.
Evening meal 6.30pm (l.o. 8.30pm).
Parking for 27.
Credit: Access, Visa.

Bravalla Guest House M

242 Iffley Rd., Oxford, OX4 1SE
☎ (0865) 241326 & 250511
A small family-run guesthouse within half a mile of Magdalen College with its famous deer park. 1 mile from city centre.
Bedrooms: 2 double & 1 twin, 2 family rooms.
Bathrooms: 4 private, 2 public; 1 private shower.
Bed & breakfast: £20-£35 single, £30-£42 double.
Parking for 4.
Credit: Access, Visa.

Bronte Guest House M

282 Iffley Rd., Oxford, OX4 4AA
☎ (0865) 244594
Close to Iffley village and church, 1 mile from city centre. Bus stop outside, but easy walking distance along river towpath to city centre.
Bedrooms: 2 double & 2 twin, 1 family room.
Bathrooms: 1 private, 1 public.
Bed & breakfast: £26-£36 double.
Parking for 6.

Casa Villa M

COMMENDED

388 Banbury Rd., Oxford, OX2 7PW
☎ (0865) 512642

*Detached guesthouse in north
Oxford with spacious garden.
Friendly and pleasant service
provided. Close to all
amenities.*
Bedrooms: 2 single, 5 double
& 1 twin, 2 family rooms.
Bathrooms: 6 private,
2 public.
Bed & breakfast: £25-£30
single, £40-£45 double.
Half board: £30-£35 daily,
£245-£280 weekly.
Lunch available.
Evening meal 6.30pm (l.o.
9.30pm).
Parking for 6.
Credit: Visa, Amex.
⌖ ♨ ☎ 🖵 ♿ ♨ 🖵 📷 ♨ Ⓥ ⋈
🖵 🎦 ⌐ ❋ ⌖ SP

Combermere House
Listed
11 Polstead Rd., Oxford,
OX2 6TW
☎ (0865) 56971
*Victorian house in a quiet tree-
lined road.*
Bedrooms: 5 single, 2 twin,
2 family rooms.
Bathrooms: 9 private.
Bed & breakfast: £17-£25
single, £30-£38 double.
Parking for 3.
Credit: Access, Visa.
⌖ ♨ 🖵 🎦 Ⓤ ▮ Ⓥ ⌿ 🖵
⌐ 🎦 ☓ Ⓣ

Conifer Lodge ♨
♨♨
159 Eynsham Rd., Botley,
Oxford, OX2 9NE
☎ (0865) 862280
*House on the outskirts of
Oxford city, overlooking
farmland and offering a warm,
friendly welcome.*
Bedrooms: 1 single, 2 double
& 2 twin, 1 family room.
Bathrooms: 4 private,
1 public.
Bed & breakfast: £14-£20
single, £26-£40 double.
Half board: £20-£30 daily,
£130-£200 weekly.
Parking for 8.
⌖ 🎦 Ⓤ ▮ 🖵 📷 🖵 ⌐ ❋ ☓
🎦

Cotswold House
♨♨ COMMENDED
363 Banbury Rd., Oxford,
OX2 7PL
☎ (0865) 310558
*Well-situated elegant property
offering a high standard of
furnishings and facilities in
each of its 6 rooms.*
Bedrooms: 1 single, 2 double
& 2 twin, 1 family room.
Bathrooms: 6 private.

Bed & breakfast: £24-£27
single, £42-£50 double.
Parking for 5.
⌖6 ♨ 🖵 ♨ Ⓤ Ⓥ ⌐ 📷 📷
⌐ ☓

Courtfield Private Hotel
367 Iffley Road, Oxford,
OX4 4DP
☎ (0865) 242991
*Large individually designed
house in tree-lined road.
Modern, spacious bedrooms,
most en-suite. Ample parking.*
Bedrooms: 4 double & 1 twin,
1 family room.
Bathrooms: 4 private,
1 public.
Bed & breakfast: £24-£28
single, £36-£42 double.
Parking for 7.
Credit: Access, Visa.
⌖3 ♨ 🖵 Ⓤ Ⓥ ⌿ 🖵 📷 📷
⌐ ▶ ☓ 🎦 DAP SP

Falcon Guest House
♨♨
88-90 Abingdon Rd., Oxford,
OX1 4PX
☎ (0865) 722995
*Victorian building with modern
facilities, overlooks Queens
College playing fields. 10
minute walk to colleges and
city centre.*
Bedrooms: 2 single, 3 double
& 1 twin, 5 family rooms.
Bathrooms: 3 public;
4 private showers.
Bed & breakfast: £15 single,
£28-£40 double.
Parking for 8.
⌖ ♨ 🖵 ♨ Ⓤ 🖵 📷 📷 ⌐
☓

Foxcombe Lodge Hotel
Fox Lane, Boars Hill,
Oxford, OX1 5DP
☎ (0865) 730746 Fax (0865)
730628 Telex 837744
*Family-run hotel in tranquil
surroundings giving good
quality service. 3 miles from
Oxford and Abingdon.*
Bedrooms: 7 single, 7 double
& 3 twin, 3 family rooms.
Bathrooms: 20 private.
Bed & breakfast: £50-£75
single, £55-£90 double.
Lunch available.
Evening meal 7pm (l.o.
9.30pm).
Parking for 23.
Credit: Access, Visa, Diners,
Amex.
⌖ ♨ 🎦 ☎ ☎ 🖵 ♨ ▮ Ⓥ
🖵 📷 ⌐ ♐ ❋ ❋ SP Ⓣ

Gables
♨♨ COMMENDED
6 Cumnor Hill, Oxford,
OX2 9HA
☎ (0865) 862153

*Modern house, 2 miles from
city centre, but with a country
atmosphere. Direct route from
railway station. Within easy
reach of beautiful Cotswolds.*
Bedrooms: 2 double & 2 twin,
1 family room.
Bathrooms: 4 private,
2 public.
Bed & breakfast: £16-£18
single, £32-£36 double.
Parking for 10.
⌖ ♨ ☎ 🖵 ♨ Ⓤ 🖵 📷 📷 ⌐
🎦

Green Gables
♨ ♨ APPROVED
326 Abingdon Rd., Oxford,
OX1 4TE
☎ (0865) 725870
*Large house with gabled
exterior, 1.25 miles from
Oxford city centre. On A414,
secluded by trees.*
Bedrooms: 2 single, 2 double
& 1 twin, 1 family room.
Bathrooms: 3 private,
1 public.
Bed & breakfast: £16-£30
single, £28-£40 double.
Parking for 6.
Credit: Visa.
⌖ ♨ 🖵 ♨ Ⓤ 📷 📷 ⌐ ♿
☓ 🎦 🎦

Greenviews ♨
♨♨
95 Sunningwell Rd., Oxford,
OX1 4SY
☎ (0865) 249603
*Enjoying country views, located
beside a lake and bowling
green. Within walking distance
of the centre of Oxford.
Homely atmosphere.*
Bedrooms: 4 single, 1 double
& 2 twin.
Bathrooms: 1 private,
3 public.
Bed & breakfast: max. £15
single, £30-£36 double.
Parking for 4.
⌖ ♨ 🖵 ♨ Ⓤ Ⓥ 🖵 📷 📷
⌐ ♿ ☓ 🎦

Highfield West ♨
♨♨♨
188 Cumnor Hill, Oxford,
OX2 9PJ
☎ (0865) 863007
*Comfortable home in quiet
residential location. Good
access to city centre and ring
road. Large outdoor pool,
heated in summer.*
Bedrooms: 2 single, 1 double
& 1 twin, 1 family room.
Bathrooms: 3 private,
1 public.
Bed & breakfast: £17-£21
single, £37-£42 double.
Parking for 6.
⌖ 🖵 ♨ Ⓤ ▮ Ⓥ 🖵 📷 ⌐
❋ ☓ SP

Isis Guest House
♨♨
45-53 Iffley Rd., Oxford,
OX4 1ED
☎ (0865) 248894 & 242466
*Modernised, Victorian, city
centre guesthouse within
walking distance of colleges
and shops. Easy access to ring
road.*
Bedrooms: 9 single, 5 double
& 21 twin, 2 family rooms.
Bathrooms: 14 private,
7 public.
Bed & breakfast: £18-£20
single, £36-£40 double.
Parking for 17.
Open July-September.
Credit: Access, Visa.
⌖ ♨ 🖵 ♨ Ⓤ 🖵 📷 ⌐ DAP

Mount Pleasant
♨♨♨♨ APPROVED
76 London Rd., Headington,
Oxford, OX3 9AJ
☎ (0865) 62749
*A small, family-run hotel
offering full facilities. Situated
on the A40 and convenient for
Oxford, shopping, hospitals
and colleges.*
Bedrooms: 2 double & 5 twin,
1 family room.
Bathrooms: 8 private.
Bed & breakfast: £35-£50
single, £50-£65 double.
Half board: £37.50-£42.50
daily, £227.50-£280 weekly.
Lunch available.
Evening meal 6pm (l.o.
9.30pm).
Parking for 6.
Credit: Access, Visa, Diners,
Amex.
⌖ ☎ 🖵 🖵 ♨ ▮ Ⓥ ⌿ 🖵
📷 ⌐ ☓ ⊗

Mulberry Guest House
♨♨
265 London Rd.,
Headington, Oxford,
OX3 9EH
☎ (0865) 67114
*Good base for touring the
Cotswolds. Bus stops outside
for Oxford colleges, London,
Heathrow and Gatwick.*
Bedrooms: 1 single, 1 double
& 2 twin, 1 family room.
Bathrooms: 2 public.
Bed & breakfast: £18-£27
single, £28-£34 double.
Parking for 3.
⌖ 🖵 ♨ Ⓤ ♨ 🖵 📷 ☓ 🎦
⊗ SP

Norham Guest House
Listed
16 Norham Rd., Oxford,
OX2 6SF
☎ (0865) 515352

Continued ▶

OXFORD
Continued

Victorian house in conservation area. 500 yards from university parks and walking distance from city centre.
Bedrooms: 2 single, 1 double & 3 twin, 2 family rooms.
Bathrooms: 2 public.
Bed & breakfast: from £18 single, from £36 double.
Parking for 4.

The Old Black Horse Hotel M

102 St. Clements, Oxford, OX4 1AR
☎ (0865) 244691
Former coaching inn with private car park close to Magdalen Bridge, short walk to colleges, riverside walks and city centre.
Bedrooms: 1 single, 3 double & 2 twin, 2 family rooms.
Bathrooms: 8 private, 1 public.
Bed & breakfast: £46.50-£59.50 single, from £70.50 double.
Lunch available.
Evening meal 7pm (l.o. 9.45pm).
Parking for 25.
Credit: Access, Visa.

Parklands Hotel M

100 Banbury Rd., Oxford, OX2 6JU
☎ (0865) 54374 Telex 83201 BIZCOM G Ref P/H
Large Victorian residence in residential area with large walled garden.
Bedrooms: 8 single, 7 double, 3 family rooms.
Bathrooms: 12 private, 3 public.
Bed & breakfast: £30.50-£47 single, £42-£75 double.
Half board: £38-£65 daily.
Lunch available.
Evening meal 6.30pm (l.o. 8.30pm).
Parking for 12.
Credit: Access, Visa, Diners.

Pickwicks Guest House M
COMMENDED

17 London Rd., Headington, Oxford, OX3 7SP
☎ (0865) 750487 & 69413
Fax (0865) 742208

Large, detached, red brick, Edwardian-style house, recently completely renovated to cater for comfort of guests on holiday or business.
Bedrooms: 2 single, 5 double & 3 twin, 3 family rooms.
Bathrooms: 10 private, 2 public.
Bed & breakfast: £18-£28 single, £36-£45 double.
Parking for 18.
Credit: Access, Visa.

Pine Castle Hotel M
COMMENDED

290 Iffley Rd., Oxford, OX4 1AE
☎ (0865) 241497/727230
Friendly guesthouse close to the city and River Thames.
Bedrooms: 1 single, 1 double & 1 twin, 2 family rooms.
Bathrooms: 1 public; 1 private shower.
Bed & breakfast: £35-£40 double.
Evening meal 6pm (l.o. 6pm).
Parking for 4.

The Priory Hotel M
Church Way, Iffley, Oxford, OX4 4DZ
☎ (0865) 749988 Fax (0865) 748525
A country house hotel set in 3 acres of landscaped gardens, within the city of Oxford.
Bedrooms: 9 double & 6 twin.
Bathrooms: 15 private.
Bed & breakfast: £45-£75 single, £55-£90 double.
Half board: £47.50-£65 daily, £332.50-£455 weekly.
Lunch available.
Evening meal 7pm (l.o. 8.30pm).
Parking for 75.
Credit: Access, Visa, Amex.

Red Mullions Guest House

23 London Rd., Headington, Oxford, OX3 7RE
☎ (0865) 64727
Large detached house on London Road, close to shops, hospitals and ring road. Bus stops outside for city centre and London.
Bedrooms: 1 single, 7 double & 1 twin, 3 family rooms.
Bathrooms: 12 private.
Bed & breakfast: £24-£28 single, £38-£45 double.
Parking for 9.

River Hotel M

17 Botley Rd., Oxford, OX2 0AA
☎ (0865) 243475 Fax (0865) 724306
Dine overlooking the Thames, in this riverside hotel. Residents' bar. Within walking distance of city and colleges. Ample parking. Ideal for business and tourist travellers.
Bedrooms: 14 single, 6 double & 1 twin, 3 family rooms.
Bathrooms: 17 private, 2 public; 2 private showers.
Bed & breakfast: £33-£45 single, £50-£55 double.
Half board: £35-£55 daily.
Evening meal 6.30pm (l.o. 8pm).
Parking for 25.
Credit: Access, Visa.

Roundabout House

415 Banbury Rd., Oxford
☎ (0865) 513045
1920 architect designed detached property in half an acre garden. On main route for city centre and local attractions.
Bedrooms: 1 double & 1 twin.
Bathrooms: 2 private, 1 public.
Bed & breakfast: £30-£40 double.
Parking for 2.

Tilbury Lodge Private Hotel

5 Tilbury Lane, Eynsham Rd., Botley, Oxford, OX2 9NB
☎ (0865) 862138
Situated in a quiet country lane, just 2 miles west of the city centre. Ideal base for touring the Cotswolds and Shakespeare country.
Bedrooms: 2 single, 2 double & 3 twin, 2 family rooms.
Bathrooms: 8 private.
Bed & breakfast: £27-£30 single, £45-£60 double.
Parking for 9.
Credit: Access, Visa.

Walton Guest House
Listed

169 Walton St., Oxford, OX1 2HD
☎ (0865) 52137
Within walking distance of city centre, bus and railway station

and university area. Colour TV and tea/coffee facilities in all rooms.
Bedrooms: 1 single, 2 double & 3 twin, 1 family room.
Bathrooms: 2 public.
Bed & breakfast: from £14 single, from £28 double.

The Westgate Hotel

1 Botley Rd., Nr. Station, Oxford, OX2 0AA
☎ (0865) 726721
Close to rail and bus stations, 10 minutes' walk from city centre and colleges.
Bedrooms: 4 single, 5 double & 2 twin, 1 family room.
Bathrooms: 2 private, 3 public; 6 private showers.
Bed & breakfast: £23-£34 single, £35-£46 double.
Evening meal 6.30pm (l.o. 8pm).
Parking for 12.
Credit: Access, Visa.

The White House M
Listed COMMENDED

315 Iffley Rd., Oxford, OX4 4AG
☎ (0865) 244524
A warm and friendly home to share for visitors to Oxford and surrounding areas.
Bedrooms: 3 double & 3 twin, 2 family rooms.
Bathrooms: 2 public.
Bed & breakfast: £32-£38 double.
Evening meal 6pm (l.o. 8pm).
Parking for 7.

PANGBOURNE
Berkshire
Map ref 2C2

A pretty stretch of river where the Pang joins the Thames with views of the lock, weir and toll bridge. Once the home of Kenneth Grahame, author of 'Wind in the Willows'.

The Copper Inn M

Church Rd., Pangbourne-on-Thames, RG8 7AR
☎ (0734) 842244 Fax (0734) 845542
Resort
Elegantly restored Georgian coaching inn with beautiful, secluded garden. Emphasis on warm welcome.
Bedrooms: 2 single, 13 double & 6 twin, 1 family room.

Bathrooms: 22 private.
Bed & breakfast: £71.50-£81.50 single, £88-£98 double.
Lunch available.
Evening meal 7.30pm (l.o. 9.30pm).
Parking for 25.
Credit: Access, Visa, Diners, Amex.

George Hotel ♠
☸☸☸ COMMENDED

The Square, Pangbourne, Nr. Reading, RG8 7AJ
☎ (0734) 842237
Established in 1295 AD. All the cellars have been filled in because they are said to be haunted.
Bedrooms: 9 single, 8 double.
Bathrooms: 8 private; 9 private showers.
Bed & breakfast: £30-£50 single, £50-£55 double.
Half board: £44.75-£64.75 daily.
Lunch available.
Evening meal 7pm (l.o. 10pm).
Parking for 20.
Credit: Access, Visa, Diners, Amex.

PRINCES RISBOROUGH

Buckinghamshire
Map ref 2C1

Old market town with many 16th C cottages, houses and a brick Market House at its centre.

Bernard Arms Hotel
☸

Risborough Road, Great Kimble, Nr. Aylesbury, HP17 0XS
☎ Princes Risborough (084 44) 6172/6173
A small, friendly hotel, located in the Chilterns and near to the Ridgeway Path, between Princes Risborough and Aylesbury (A4010).
Bedrooms: 2 single, 3 double & 2 twin.
Bathrooms: 1 public; 7 private showers.
Bed & breakfast: £30-£35 single, £40-£48 double.
Half board: £32-£42 daily, £220-£290 weekly.
Lunch available.

Evening meal 7pm (l.o. 10pm).
Parking for 40.
Credit: Access, Visa.

PUCKERIDGE

Hertfordshire
Map ref 2D1

Vintage Corner Hotel ♠
☸☸ COMMENDED

Old Cambridge Rd., Puckeridge, SG11 1SA
☎ Ware (0920) 822722
Quiet modern hotel in picturesque village of Puckeridge, between junction A10 and A120. Garden restaurant.
Bedrooms: 5 single, 24 double & 19 twin.
Bathrooms: 48 private.
Bed & breakfast: £49.50-£72.50 single, £59.50-£82.50 double.
Lunch available.
Evening meal 7pm (l.o. 9.15pm).
Parking for 80.
Credit: Access, Visa, Diners, Amex.

READING

Berkshire
Map ref 2C2

Busy, modern county town with large shopping centre and many leisure and recreation facilities. There are several interesting museums and the Duke of Wellington's Stratfield Saye is nearby.
Tourist Information Centre ☎ *(0734) 566226*

Abbey House Private Hotel ♠
☸☸

118 Connaught Rd., Reading, RG3 2UF
☎ (0734) 590549
Telex 94081617 ABBEY G
Warm, friendly hotel run by the proprietors. Close to town centre.
Bedrooms: 10 single, 4 double & 6 twin.
Bathrooms: 5 private, 3 public; 1 private shower.
Bed & breakfast: £28-£42 single, £47.50-£54 double.
Half board: £37.50-£51.50 daily.
Evening meal 7pm (l.o. 8.30pm).
Parking for 14.
Credit: Access, Visa, Amex.

Aeron Private Hotel ♠
☸☸

191 Kentwood Hill, Tilehurst, Reading, RG3 6JE
☎ (0734) 424119 & 427654
Fax (0734) 451953
Small family-run hotel in residential area, catering for business people and holidaymakers.
Bedrooms: 13 single, 4 double & 5 twin, 2 family rooms.
Bathrooms: 6 private, 6 public; 2 private showers.
Bed & breakfast: £28.50-£46 single, £46-£60.50 double.
Evening meal 6.30pm (l.o. 8.15pm).
Parking for 24.
Credit: Access, Visa.

Caversham Hotel ♠
Caversham Bridge, Richfield Avenue, Caversham, Reading, RG1 8BD
☎ (0734) 391818
Telex 846933
CR Queens Moat Houses
New hotel on the banks of the River Thames overlooking Caversham Bridge. 5 minutes from train station. Easy access to M4.
Bedrooms: 1 single, 50 double & 49 twin, 8 family rooms.
Bathrooms: 108 private.
Bed & breakfast: £40-£103.50 single, £80-£119 double.
Half board: £58-£121.95 daily.
Lunch available.
Evening meal 7.30pm (l.o. 10pm).
Parking for 175.
Credit: Access, Visa, C.Bl., Diners, Amex.

George Hotel ♠
☸☸☸ APPROVED

King St., Reading, RG1 2HE
☎ (0734) 573445
A former coaching inn, on the London to Bath run, dating from the 15th C. Pretty cobbled courtyard, well-appointed bedrooms and 2 delightful restaurants.
Bedrooms: 18 single, 13 double & 35 twin, 2 family rooms.
Bathrooms: 68 private.
Bed & breakfast: £59-£65 single, from £70 double.
Lunch available.
Evening meal 7pm (l.o. 10.30pm).
Credit: Access, Visa, Diners, Amex.

The Mill House Hotel ♠
☸☸☸☸ COMMENDED

Old Basingstoke Rd., Swallowfield, Nr. Reading, RG7 1PY
☎ Reading (0734) 883124
Telex 847423 COC RG G REF M;10
Georgian mansion set in 2 acres of countryside and on the banks of the River Lodden. 10 minutes from Reading town centre, 45 minutes from Heathrow Airport.
Bedrooms: 5 single, 3 double, 2 family rooms.
Bathrooms: 10 private.
Bed & breakfast: £40-£75 single, £60-£110 double.
Half board: £75-£150 daily.
Lunch available.
Evening meal 7.30pm (l.o. 10pm).
Parking for 30.
Credit: Access, Visa, Diners, Amex.

Ramada Hotel ♠
☸☸☸☸

Oxford Rd., Reading, RG1 7RH
☎ (0734) 586222
Telex 847785
Hotel in town centre next to shopping area. Within walking distance of the rail station and River Thames.
Bedrooms: 62 single, 11 double & 127 twin.
Bathrooms: 200 private.
Bed & breakfast: £45-£100 single, £60-£120 double.
Lunch available.
Evening meal 6pm (l.o. 11.30pm).
Parking for 75.
Credit: Access, Visa, C.Bl., Diners, Amex.

The Thames House Hotel
☸☸

18-19 Thameside, Brigham Rd., Reading, RG1 8DR
☎ (0734) 507951
A Victorian property on the banks of the River Thames, but in proximity to town centre. Some rooms have balconies and overlook the river.
Bedrooms: 4 single, 2 double & 3 twin, 1 family room.
Bathrooms: 2 private, 2 public; 4 private showers.
Bed & breakfast: £25-£27 single, £34-£38 double.
Continued ▶

READING
Continued

Evening meal 7pm (l.o. 9pm).
Parking for 16.
Credit: Access, Visa.
♿ ☎ ⑧ ❑ ❤ ⌴ TV ⅢⅢ ▪
✿ ✠ 🏖 ◫ DAP ⚲ SP

Upcross Hotel M
😀😀😀😀

68 Berkeley Avenue,
Reading, RG1 6HY
☎ (0734) 590796
Fax (0734) 576517
Telex 849021 FRAN G
Small, personally-run country house hotel. 5 minutes to town centre, railway station, M4 junctions 11 and 12. 35 minutes to Heathrow Airport.
Bedrooms: 13 single, 4 double & 8 twin, 1 family room.
Bathrooms: 20 private, 4 public; 6 private showers.
Bed & breakfast: £48-£59.50 single, £70 double.
Lunch available.
Evening meal 7pm (l.o. 9.45pm).
Parking for 40.
Credit: Access, Visa, Amex.
♿ ♨ ☎ ⑧ ❑ ❤ ✿ ❗ ▪ V ◫
ⅢⅢ ▪ 🍴 🏖 ▶ ✿ ▪ DAP SP ▦

Warren Dene Guest House
1017 Oxford Rd., Tilehurst,
Reading, RG3 6TL
☎ (0734) 422556
Spacious, comfortable, family-run guesthouse with scenic views over Mapledurham Estate. All bedrooms have colour TV and welcome tray, some are fully en-suite. Family rooms available. Car park.
Bedrooms: 1 single, 1 double & 2 twin, 2 family rooms.
Bathrooms: 3 private, 2 public.
Bed & breakfast: £22-£36 single, £36-£44 double.
Parking for 6.
♿ ❑ ❤ ⌴ ✇ TV ⅢⅢ ▪ ✿
✠ ▦

The Willows Hotel M
😀😀

Bath Rd., Padworth, Nr.
Reading, RG7 5HT
☎ Woolhampton
(0734) 713282 Fax (0734) 712081
Easy access to M4 junction 12. Central to "Silicon Valley". Heathrow Airport 40 minutes, Oxford 30 minutes, Reading 15 minutes.
Bedrooms: 4 single, 8 double & 10 twin, 2 family rooms.
Bathrooms: 24 private.
Bed & breakfast: £28-£52.50 single, £46-£69 double.

Half board: £40-£64 daily, max. £379 weekly.
Lunch available.
Evening meal 7pm (l.o. 9.45pm).
Parking for 80.
Credit: Access, Visa, Diners, Amex.
♿ ♨ ☎ ⑧ ❑ ❤ ❗ ▪ V ◫
ⅢⅢ ▪ 🍴 ♨ ❤ ▶ ▪ DAP ⚲
SP T

RICKMANSWORTH
Hertfordshire
Map ref 2D2

Old town, where 3 rivers meet, now mainly residential. The High Street is full of interesting buildings, including the home of William Penn. Moor Park Mansion, a fine 18th C house, is now a golf club house.
Tourist Information Centre ☎ (0923) 776611 ext 205

Chorheron
Long Lane, Heronsgate,
Rickmansworth, WD3 5DE
☎ Chorleywood
(092 78) 2899
Country house in secluded position, half a mile from junction 17 on M25 and 25 miles from London. Moor Park golf club nearby. Missendon Abbey 9 miles away.
Bedrooms: 2 single, 1 double & 1 twin.
Bathrooms: 2 public.
Bed & breakfast: £18-£35 single.
Parking for 8.
♿ 10 ⌴ ✂ ⅢⅢ ✿ ✠ ▦

ROYSTON
Hertfordshire
Map ref 2D1

Old town lying at the crossing of the Roman road Ermine Street and the Icknield Way. It has many interesting old houses and inns.

The Old Bull Inn
😀😀 COMMENDED
56 High St., Royston,
SG8 9AW
☎ (0763) 242003 Fax (0763) 241273
Traditional town centre coaching inn. Conference and banqueting facilities.
Bedrooms: 8 single, 1 double & 1 twin, 1 family room.
Bathrooms: 11 private.
Bed & breakfast: from £45 single, from £55 double.

Lunch available.
Evening meal 7pm (l.o. 9.30pm).
Parking for 30.
Credit: Access, Visa, Amex.
♿ ♨ ☎ ❑ ❤ ❗ V ▪
ⅢⅢ ▪ 🍴 ✿ ▦ SP ▦

Sheen Mill
Station Rd., Melbourn,
Royston, SG8 6DH
☎ (0763) 261393
Restored 17th C watermill, set in idyllic surroundings, overlooking the mill pond.
Bedrooms: 4 single, 1 double & 3 twin.
Bathrooms: 8 private.
Bed & breakfast: from £40 single, £60-£75 double.
Lunch available.
Evening meal 7.30pm (l.o. 9.50pm).
Parking for 50.
Credit: Access, Visa, Diners, Amex.
♿ ☎ ⑧ ❑ ❗ V ▪ ⅢⅢ ▪ 🍴
✠ ▦ ▦

ST ALBANS
Hertfordshire
Map ref 2D1

As Verulamium this was one of the largest towns in Roman Britain and its remains can be seen in the museum. The Norman cathedral was built from Roman materials to commemorate Alban, the first British Christian martyr. The fortified clock tower is 1 of only 2 in Britain.
Tourist Information Centre ☎. (0727) 64511

The Apples Hotel M
😀😀😀😀 APPROVED
133 London Rd., St. Albans,
AL1 1TA
☎ (0727) 44111
Family-run hotel in beautiful gardens within easy reach of city centre, station and major motorways. Heated swimming pool. Parking. New disabled facilities for 1991.
Bedrooms: 1 single, 6 double & 2 twin.
Bathrooms: 9 private.
Bed & breakfast: £42-£48 single, £57-£65 double.
Half board: £38-£45 daily.
Evening meal 7.30pm (l.o. 9pm).
Parking for 10.
Credit: Access, Visa, Diners.
♿ ♨ ☎ ❑ ❤ V ▪ ⅢⅢ
▪ 🍴 ♨ ❤ ✿ ✠ ▦ ⚲

Ardmore House
😀😀
54 Lemsford Rd., St. Albans,
AL1 3PP
☎ (0727) 59313 & 61411
Large detached Edwardian house with garden, in conservation area. Close to Clarence Park, and within 5 minutes of city centre and railway station. Excellent base for visitors to London.
Bedrooms: 4 single, 2 double & 7 twin, 2 family rooms.
Bathrooms: 9 private, 2 public; 3 private showers.
Bed & breakfast: £28.75-£43.70 single, £39.10-£48.30 double.
Parking for 24.
♿ ♨ ❑ ❤ ⌴ ▪ ⅢⅢ ▪ ▪ ♿
✿ ▦

Grays Guest House
282 Hatfield Rd., St Albans
☎ (0727) 56535
Clean, comfortable Edwardian house. Personal friendly service. Easy acccess to London, A1, M25 and M1. Large car park.
Bedrooms: 5 single, 4 twin, 1 family room.
Bathrooms: 3 private, 2 public; 2 private showers.
Bed & breakfast: £20-£25 single, £32-£35 double.
Parking for 11.
♿2 ❤ ❑ ⌴ ⅢⅢ ▪ ✠ ▦

Hertfordshire Moat House M
😀😀😀😀 APPROVED
London Rd., Flamstead,
Markyate, St. Albans,
AL3 8HH
☎ Dunstable (0582) 840840
Telex 83343 HMH
🅒 Queens Moat Houses
Modern motor hotel on A5, 1 mile from junction 9 M1 motorway. 9 minutes from Luton Airport and 4 miles from Luton town centre.
Bedrooms: 30 double & 65 twin.
Bathrooms: 95 private.
Bed & breakfast: £85-£95 single, £95-£105 double.
Lunch available.
Evening meal 7pm (l.o. 10pm).
Parking for 200.
Credit: Access, Visa, Diners, Amex.
♿ ♨ ☎ ⑧ ❑ ❤ ❗ ▪ TV ◗
ⅢⅢ ▪ 🍴 ♨ ❤ ▶ DAP ⚲ SP T

Lake Holidays Hotel M
😀😀😀😀 COMMENDED
234 London Rd., St. Albans,
AL1 1JQ
☎ (0727) 40904 Telex 266020
CORAL P.G.

A family hotel, half a mile from the centre of the historic Roman city of Verulamium.
Bedrooms: 19 single, 5 double & 16 twin, 2 family rooms.
Bathrooms: 42 private.
Bed & breakfast: £53.90-£61.60 single, £73-£88.50 double.
Lunch available.
Evening meal 7pm (l.o. 9.30pm).
Parking for 70.
Credit: Access, Visa, Diners, Amex.

Melford House Hotel

24 Woodstock Road North, St. Albans, AL1 4QQ
☎ (0727) 53642
Attractive house, tastefully furnished. Residential area within easy walking distance of station and town centre.
Bedrooms: 5 single, 2 double & 3 twin, 2 family rooms.
Bathrooms: 4 private, 4 public.
Bed & breakfast: £24.15-£43 single, £36.80-£50 double.
Parking for 12.

Newpark House Hotel M

North Orbital Rd., Nr. London Colney Roundabout, St. Albans, AL1 1EG
☎ Bowmansgreen (0727) 824839 Fax (0727) 26700
On A414 trunk road eastbound to A1(M). Pebble-dash, 3-storey house, small landscaped garden with patio and fish pond.
Bedrooms: 10 single, 4 twin.
Bathrooms: 5 public.
Bed & breakfast: £21-£25 single, £42-£50 double.
Parking for 30.
Credit: Access, Visa.

The Noke Thistle Hotel M

Watford Rd., St. Albans, AL2 3DS
☎ (0727) 54252 Telex 893834
CR Thistle
Recently refurbished country house style hotel in its own grounds, close to the M1, M10 and M25. New executive wing.
Bedrooms: 50 double & 54 twin, 7 family rooms.
Bathrooms: 111 private.

Bed & breakfast: from £82.75 single, from £100.50 double.
Lunch available.
Evening meal 7pm (l.o. 10pm).
Parking for 150.
Credit: Access, Visa, C.Bl., Diners, Amex.

St. Michael's Manor Hotel M
COMMENDED

Fishpool Street, St. Albans, AL3 4RY
☎ (0727) 64444 Telex 917647 STMM
16th C manor house in centre of Roman Verulamium.
Bedrooms: 11 single, 7 double & 8 twin.
Bathrooms: 26 private.
Bed & breakfast: £50-£80 single, £70-£98 double.
Half board: £55-£74 daily.
Lunch available.
Evening meal 7pm (l.o. 9.30pm).
Parking for 70.
Credit: Access, Visa, Diners, Amex.

Bedfordshire
Map ref 2D1

Small town on the River Ivel on the site of a Roman settlement. Sandy is mentioned in Domesday.

Rose & Crown Hotel M
APPROVED

Market Square, Potton, Sandy, SG19 2NP
☎ Potton (0767) 260221 & 260409
Old Georgian coaching inn of architectural interest, situated in small market town. 1 mile from John O'Gaunt Golf Club.
Bedrooms: 4 single, 4 double & 4 twin, 3 family rooms.
Bathrooms: 10 private, 2 public; 2 private showers.
Bed & breakfast: £23-£35 single, £37-£50 double.
Lunch available.
Evening meal 6.30pm (l.o. 8pm).
Parking for 60.
Credit: Access, Visa.

Please mention this guide when making a booking.

Hertfordshire
Map ref 2D1

The Manor of Groves

High Wych, Sawbridgeworth, CM21 0LA
☎ Bishops Stortford (0279) 600777
A country manor hotel, set within its own 18 hole golf-course and country club.
Bedrooms: 31 twin, 1 family room.
Bathrooms: 32 private.
Bed & breakfast: £65-£120 single, £75-£135 double.
Lunch available.
Evening meal 7pm (l.o. 9.30pm).
Parking for 156.
Credit: Access, Visa, Diners, Amex.

Bedfordshire
Map ref 2D1

The Old George Hotel

High St., Silsoe, MK45 4EP
☎ (0525) 60218
A traditional inn with a large restaurant open to the general public.
Bedrooms: 3 single, 2 double & 1 twin, 1 family room.
Bathrooms: 2 public.
Bed & breakfast: from £23 single, from £36 double.
Half board: from £30 daily.
Lunch available.
Evening meal 7pm (l.o. 9.30pm).
Parking for 50.
Credit: Access, Visa, Amex.

Berkshire
Map ref 2D2

A busy town with a large trading estate, Slough is an excellent centre for recreation with many open spaces. The ancient village of Upton, now part of Slough, has an interesting Norman church and Cliveden House is nearby.

Colnbrook Lodge Guest House

Bath Rd., Colnbrook, Slough, SL3 0NZ
☎ (0753) 685958

Small family-run guesthouse 10 minutes from London Heathrow Airport. Easy access by bus to Windsor and London.
Bedrooms: 4 single, 1 double & 3 twin.
Bathrooms: 2 private, 2 public.
Bed & breakfast: £25-£35 single, £30-£45 double.
Parking for 10.
Credit: Access, Visa.

Highways Guest House M

95 London Rd., Langley, Slough, SL3 7RS
☎ (0753) 24715 & 23022
Comfortable accommodation set in half an acre of pleasant garden. Located on A4, convenient for London, Heathrow Airport and Windsor.
Bedrooms: 2 single, 2 double & 4 twin, 2 family rooms.
Bathrooms: 2 public.
Bed & breakfast: £22.50-£25 single, £35-£37.50 double.
Parking for 15.

Holiday Inn - Slough/Windsor M

Ditton Rd., Langley, Slough, SL3 8PT
☎ (0753) 44244 Telex 848646
CR Holiday Inn
Close to M4 and M25, with easy access to London and Heathrow Airport. Well-appointed bedrooms, restaurant, leisure club.
Bedrooms: 170 double, 132 family rooms.
Bathrooms: 302 private.
Bed & breakfast: £108-£140 single, £139-£180 double.
Half board: £126-£158 daily.
Lunch available.
Evening meal 7pm (l.o. 11pm).
Parking for 420.
Credit: Access, Visa, C.Bl., Diners, Amex.

Sussex Lodge Guest House M

91 Sussex Place, Slough, SL1 1NN
☎ (0753) 825674 & 825673 Fax (0753) 682511
Continued ▶

SLOUGH

Continued

15-bedroomed guest house located on main A4 route and a 5 minute walk from the town centre. Heathrow airport is 5 miles away.
Bedrooms: 7 single, 3 double & 4 twin, 1 family room.
Bathrooms: 7 private, 3 public.
Bed & breakfast: £28.75-£39.10 single, £40.25-£50.60 double.
Half board: from £33.75 daily.
Evening meal 6.30pm (l.o. 9.30pm).
Parking for 27.
Credit: Access, Visa.

STANDLAKE

Oxfordshire
Map ref 2C1

13th C church with an octagonal tower and spire standing beside the Windrush. The interior of the church is rich in woodwork.

The Old Rectory M

Church End, Standlake, Nr. Witney, OX8 7SG
☎ (0865) 300559
Delightful house of historic interest standing in grounds of 5 acres, on the banks of the River Windrush.
Bedrooms: 2 double & 1 twin.
Bathrooms: 3 private.
Bed & breakfast: £24.50-£40 single, £36-£66.50 double.
Evening meal 7.30pm.
Parking for 30.
Open February-November.

STEVENAGE

Hertfordshire
Map ref 2D1

New Town with many well-planned modern buildings, a museum and leisure centre. Much of the old town still remains with old houses, cottages and inns. Nearby is the great house and park of Knebworth.
Tourist Information Centre ☎ (0438) 369441

Gate Hotel

1 Gates Way, Stevenage, SG1 3LJ
☎ (0438) 314126 Telex 825566

Set in Old Stevenage in centre of town close to shops, rail and bus station, yet in very quiet and scenic surroundings.
Bedrooms: 5 single, 20 double & 18 twin, 2 family rooms.
Bathrooms: 45 private.
Bed & breakfast: £32-£54 single, £48-£64 double.
Lunch available.
Evening meal 7pm (l.o. 10.30pm).
Parking for 35.
Credit: Access, Visa, C.Bl., Diners, Amex.

Novotel M

Knebworth Park, Stevenage, SG1 2AX
☎ (0438) 742299
Telex 826132
Novotel
Ideally located in the centre of Hertfordshire at the entrance to Knebworth Park and House.
Bedrooms: 101 double.
Bathrooms: 101 private.
Bed & breakfast: £64-£67 single, £79-£82 double.
Lunch available.
Evening meal 6pm.
Parking for 120.
Credit: Access, Visa, Diners, Amex.

STREATLEY

Berkshire
Map ref 2C2

Pretty village on the River Thames, linked to Goring by an attractive bridge. It has Georgian houses and cottages and beautiful views over the countryside and the Goring Gap.

The Swan Diplomat M
COMMENDED

Streatley-on-Thames, RG8 9HR
☎ Goring on Thames (0491) 873737 Telex 848259
Beautifully situated on the banks of the River Thames, 1 hour's drive from Oxford, Windsor and London Heathrow.
Bedrooms: 9 single, 25 double & 11 twin, 1 family room.
Bathrooms: 46 private.
Bed & breakfast: £81-£97 single, £113-£125 double.
Half board: £101-£127 daily.
Lunch available.
Evening meal 7.30pm (l.o. 9.30pm).

Parking for 145.
Credit: Access, Visa, Diners, Amex.

SUNNINGDALE

Berkshire
Map ref 2D2

6m SW. Staines

Everest Lodge Guest House

74 Clarence Road, Windsor, SL4 5AU
☎ Slough (0753) 865633
Large semi-detached house near town centre and leisure centre. 5 minutes' walk to Windsor Castle and 15 minutes from Heathrow.
Bedrooms: 1 single, 2 double, 1 family room.
Bathrooms: 1 private, 1 public.
Bed & breakfast: £15-£20 single, £30-£35 double.
Parking for 2.

TAPLOW

Buckinghamshire
Map ref 2C2

Cliveden M
COMMENDED

Taplow, SL6 0JF
☎ (0628) 668561
Telex 846562
Prestige
One of Britain's few hotels that is also a stately home. Extensive sport and leisure facilities on the 376 acre estate.
Bedrooms: 3 single, 11 double & 17 twin.
Bathrooms: 31 private.
Bed & breakfast: from £150 single, from £185 double.
Lunch available.
Evening meal 7.30pm (l.o. 9.30pm).
Parking for 20.
Credit: Access, Visa, Diners.

> The symbols are explained on the flap inside the back cover.

TEMPSFORD

Bedfordshire
Map ref 2D1

The Anchor Hotel M

Great North Rd., Tempsford, Sandy, SG19 2AS
☎ (0767) 40233
Inn built in 1831 as a country mansion. Bounded by the River Ouse, with its own moorings and coarse fishing from hotel's river bank. 11 acres of grounds and a garden play area for children.
Bedrooms: 2 single, 7 double & 1 twin.
Bathrooms: 8 private, 1 public.
Bed & breakfast: £38-£45 single, from £56 double.
Lunch available.
Evening meal 6.30pm (l.o. 10pm).
Parking for 150.
Credit: Access, Visa, Diners, Amex.

THAME

Oxfordshire
Map ref 2C1

Historic market town on the River Thame. The wide, unspoilt High Street has many styles of architecture with medieval timber-framed cottages, Georgian houses and some famous inns.
Tourist Information Centre ☎ (084421) 2834

Peacock Hotel M
COMMENDED

Henton, Nr. Chinnor
☎ Kingston Blount (0844) 53519 Fax (0844) 53891
Charming thatched country hotel providing lounge bars, and a la carte restaurant. Four-poster beds and executive suite available.
Bedrooms: 9 single, 8 double & 2 twin.
Bathrooms: 19 private.
Bed & breakfast: £45-£55 single, £55-£85 double.
Half board: £60-£70 daily.
Lunch available.
Evening meal 6pm (l.o. 10.30pm).
Parking for 60.
Credit: Access, Visa, Amex.

> **Map references apply to the colour maps towards the end of this guide.**

The Spread Eagle Hotel M

👑👑👑👑

Cornmarket, Thame,
OX9 2BW
☎ (084 421) 3661
Telex 83343
Converted 17th C coaching inn in centre of small country market town. Fothergills restaurant featuring a choice of menus. Banqueting and conference facilities. Good base for touring the Thames Valley.
Bedrooms: 5 single, 14 double & 2 twin, 1 family room.
Bathrooms: 22 private.
Bed & breakfast: £65.95-£72.55 single, £76.95-£82.55 double.
Half board: £81.80-£88.45 daily, £572.60-£619.15 weekly.
Lunch available.
Evening meal 7pm (l.o. 10pm).
Parking for 80.
Credit: Access, Visa, Diners, Amex.

📇 ♿ 🅿 🛏 📺 🍴 ⛱ ● 🍺 ♦ ✕ 🐾 SP 🎠 Ⓣ

TRING

Hertfordshire
Map ref 2C1

Pleasant town near lovely countryside and woods. Tring has a fine church with a large 14th C tower. Tring Park houses the Rothschild Zoological Collection, now part of the Natural History Museum. The Tring Reservoirs National Nature Reserve is nearby.

The Pendley Manor Hotel M

👑👑👑👑 COMMENDED

Cow Lane, Tring, HP23 5QY
☎ (0442) 891891 Fax (0442) 890687
Set in 30 acres of woodland, this country house has undergone a major refurbishment to a high standard.
Bedrooms: 4 single, 62 double & 2 twin, 2 family rooms.
Bathrooms: 70 private.
Bed & breakfast: from £100 single, from £125 double.
Half board: from £125 daily, £875 weekly.
Lunch available.
Evening meal 7.30pm (l.o. 9.30pm).

Parking for 100.
Credit: Access, Visa, Diners, Amex.

📇 ♿ 🅿 🛏 📺 📶 🍴 ⛱ ● 🍺 🐾 🎠 Ⓣ ❄ 🎠 Ⓣ

The Rose & Crown M

👑👑👑 COMMENDED

High St., Tring, HP23 5AH
☎ (044 282) 4071
Telex 826538 Fax (0442) 890735
Ⓒ Lansbury
An attractive 28 bedroom Tudor-style hotel in the centre of a market town.
Bedrooms: 7 single, 15 double & 5 twin, 1 family room.
Bathrooms: 28 private.
Bed & breakfast: £33-£70 single, £66-£82 double.
Half board: £44-£83 daily.
Lunch available.
Evening meal 7pm (l.o. 10pm).
Parking for 70.
Credit: Access, Visa, Diners, Amex.

✕ ● 📺 📇 🍴 🐾 🎠 Ⓣ

The Royal Hotel M

👑👑👑

Tring, HP23 5QR
☎ (044 282) 7616 & 8588 Fax (0442) 890383
On the famous Ridgeway Path, close to the pretty village of Aldbury.
Bedrooms: 2 single, 8 double & 7 twin, 3 family rooms.
Bathrooms: 15 private, 1 public.
Bed & breakfast: £30-£54 single, £40-£64 double.
Lunch available.
Evening meal 7.30pm (l.o. 9pm).
Parking for 50.
Credit: Access, Visa, Diners, Amex.

📇 ♿ 🚪 ♿ 📺 🅿 ⛱ 🍴 🍴 SAP 🐾 SP 🎠

TUBNEY

Oxfordshire
Map ref 2C1

4m W. Abingdon

Tubney Warren House Hotel M

👑👑👑👑 COMMENDED

Oxford/Faringdon Rd.,
Tubney, Abingdon,
OX13 5QJ
☎ Frilford Heath
(0865) 390221 Fax (0865) 390210
Georgian country house set in 4 acres of secluded grounds. Traditional Aga cooking. Individual bedrooms tastefully furnished.

Bedrooms: 1 single, 1 double & 3 twin, 1 family room.
Bathrooms: 6 private.
Bed & breakfast: £58.50-£75 single, £77-£95 double.
Lunch available.
Evening meal 6.30pm (l.o. 9.30pm).
Parking for 8.
Credit: Access, Visa.

📇 8 ♿ ● 📺 🅿 ⛱ 📺 🍴 🍴 📇 🍴 ▶ ❄ ✕ 🎠 SP 🎠

WADDESDON

Buckinghamshire
Map ref 2C1

The first point-to-point steeplechase in England was run in 1835 from Waddesdon Windmill to a field just below Aylesbury Church, and is vividly described in Fowler's "Echoes of Old Country Life". The present manor house was built by Baron Ferdinand de Rothschild at the end of the 19th C in the style of a French chateau.

The Five Arrows

👑👑👑

High St., Waddesdon,
HP18 0JE
☎ Aylesbury (0296) 651727
Attractive hotel in pretty village setting not far from Waddesdon Manor. Good halfway house between London and the Cotswolds.
Bedrooms: 2 single, 2 double & 3 twin.
Bathrooms: 7 private.
Bed & breakfast: from £37.50 single, from £50 double.
Half board: £37.50-£60 daily.
Lunch available.
Evening meal 7.15pm (l.o. 9.30pm).
Parking for 15.
Credit: Access, Visa, Diners, Amex.

📇 ● 📺 ⛱ 🍴 📺 📶 📇 🍴 ❄ ✕ 🎠 SP 🎠

The symbol Ⓒ and the name of a hotel group or consortium after a hotel address means that bookings can be made through a central reservations office. These are listed on pages 559 & 560.

WALLINGFORD

Oxfordshire
Map ref 2C2

Site of an ancient ford over the River Thames, now crossed by a 900-ft-long bridge. The town has many timber-framed and Georgian buildings, Gainsborough portraits in the 17th C Town Hall and a few remains of a Norman Castle.
Tourist Information Centre ☎ (0491) 35351 ext 3810

The Shillingford Bridge Hotel M

👑👑👑👑

Shillingford, Wallingford,
OX10 8LZ
☎ Warborough
(086 732) 8567 Telex 837763
Situated on one of the reaches of the River Thames, with a quarter-mile stretch of river frontage. 11 miles from Oxford and Henley-on-Thames.
Bedrooms: 16 single, 17 double & 2 twin, 2 family rooms.
Bathrooms: 37 private.
Bed & breakfast: £55-£70 single, £75-£100 double.
Lunch available.
Evening meal 7.30pm (l.o. 10pm).
Parking for 120.
Credit: Access, Visa, Diners, Amex.

📇 ♿ 🚪 ♿ ● 📺 🅿 ⛱ 🍴 📺 🍴 🐾 ♦ 🎠 ✕ 🎠 Ⓣ

WANTAGE

Oxfordshire
Map ref 2C2

Market town in the Vale of the White Horse where King Alfred was born. His statue stands in the town square.

The Bear Hotel M

Market Place, Wantage,
OX12 8AB
☎ (023 57) 66366
Telex 41363
Ⓒ Calotels
16th C coaching inn with lots of character, in historic market town.
Bedrooms: 9 single, 10 double & 18 twin, 1 family room.
Bathrooms: 38 private.
Bed & breakfast: £46-£54 single, £72-£80 double.
Lunch available.

Continued ▶

WANTAGE
Continued

Evening meal 7pm (l.o. 9.30pm).
Credit: Access, Visa, Diners, Amex.

WARE
Hertfordshire
Map ref 2D1

Interesting riverside town with picturesque summer-houses lining the towpath of the River Lea. The town has many timber-framed and Georgian houses and the famous Great Bed of Ware is now in the Victoria and Albert Museum.

Briggens House Hotel M

Stanstead Rd., Stanstead Abbotts, Nr. Ware, SG12 8LD
☎ Roydon (027 979) 2416
Telex 817906
℀ Queens Moat Houses
A country house hotel, set in 80 acres of beautiful parkland, with own golf-course, tennis and swimming.
Bedrooms: 15 single, 35 double & 4 twin.
Bathrooms: 54 private.
Bed & breakfast: from £85.50 single, £108.50-£126 double.
Half board: from £107 daily.
Lunch available.
Evening meal 7.30pm (l.o. 10pm).
Parking for 100.
Credit: Access, Visa, Diners, Amex.

Feathers Inn M

Wadesmill, Nr. Ware, SG12 0TN
☎ (0920) 462606
Redbrick, ivy-clad building in old world style, with interior to match. Originally a 16th C coaching inn.
Bedrooms: 9 single, 5 double & 8 twin.
Bathrooms: 15 private, 3 public.
Bed & breakfast: £44.50-£48.50 single, £55.50-£59.50 double.
Lunch available.
Evening meal 7pm (l.o. 10.30pm).

Parking for 100.
Credit: Access, Visa, Diners, Amex.

Hanbury Manor
Thundridge, nr Ware, SG12 0SD
☎ Ware (0920) 487722
25 miles north of London, the hotel offers 10 conference rooms, extensive leisure facilities and cooking under the guidance of Albert Roux. Baby sitting and listening service available on request.
Bedrooms: 1 single, 33 double & 49 twin, 15 family rooms.
Bathrooms: 98 private.
Bed & breakfast: from £130 single, £155-£300 double.
Lunch available.
Evening meal 6.30pm (l.o. 10.30pm).
Parking for 200.
Credit: Access, Visa, Diners, Amex.

WATERPERRY
Oxfordshire
Map ref 2C1

7m E. Oxford
Location of the well-known Waterperry Horticultural Centre, open to visitors for most of the year.

Manor Farm
Waterperry, OX9 1LB
☎ Ickford (084 47) 263
140-acre mixed farm. 17th C manor farm in peaceful village location. Guests may walk beside or fish in the nearby River Thames.
Bedrooms: 2 double & 1 twin.
Bathrooms: 2 public.
Bed & breakfast: £13.50-£15.50 single, £25-£31 double.
Half board: £22.50-£24.50 daily, £147-£168 weekly.
Evening meal 6.30pm (l.o. 9pm).
Parking for 4.

WATFORD
Hertfordshire
Map ref 2D1

Large town with many industries but with some old buildings, particularly around St. Mary's Church which contains some fine monuments. The grounds of Cassiobury Park, once the home of the Earls of Essex, form a public park and golf-course.

Dean Park Hotel M
30/40 St. Albans Rd., Watford, WD1 1RN
☎ (0923) 229212
Telex 8813610
℀ Queens Moat Houses
Modern town centre hotel close to Heathrow Airport, M1 and M25 giving easy access to London and local tourist attractions. Discount weekend rates available.
Bedrooms: 40 single, 20 double & 30 twin.
Bathrooms: 90 private.
Bed & breakfast: £30-£83 single, £40-£83 double.
Half board: £40-£80 daily.
Lunch available.
Evening meal 6pm (l.o. 11pm).
Parking for 20.
Credit: Access, Visa, Diners, Amex.

Hilton National Watford M
Elton Way, Watford, WD2 8HA
☎ (0923) 35881 Telex 923422
℀ Hilton
Comfortable hotel just off the M1, 30 minutes from London and 10 minutes from the M25. Leisure centre.
Bedrooms: 103 double & 90 twin, 3 family rooms.
Bathrooms: 196 private.
Bed & breakfast: £83.50-£120 single, £107-£150 double.
Half board: £100-£150 daily, £585-£875 weekly.
Lunch available.
Evening meal 6.30pm (l.o. 10pm).
Parking for 350.
Credit: Access, Visa, Diners, Amex.

Spiders Web Hotel M
Watford by-Pass (A41), Watford, WD2 8HQ
☎ Bushey 081-950 6211
Telex 935213
℀ Consort
Close to junction 5 M1 and M25 and 30 minutes to London. Bedrooms have free 24 hour in-house movie facility, hair-dryer and trouser press. Free leisure facilities including gym.
Bedrooms: 7 single, 45 double & 108 twin, 10 family rooms.
Bathrooms: 170 private.
Bed & breakfast: £80-£85 single, £95-£100 double.
Lunch available.
Evening meal 7pm (l.o. 9.30pm).
Parking for 500.
Credit: Access, Visa, C.Bl., Diners, Amex.

WATLINGTON
Oxfordshire
Map ref 2C2

Interesting former market town on the Icknield Way with narrow streets and many old half-timbered houses. The gabled Town Hall was built in the 17th C and the church of St. Leonard has a painting by a pupil of Carracci.

The Well House Restaurant and Hotel M
34-40 High St., Watlington, OX9 5PY
☎ (049 161) 3333 Fax (049 161) 2025
Integrated period house and cottage plus 15th C restaurant in the High Street of small historic country town. 30 minutes from Heathrow.
Bedrooms: 1 single, 4 double & 4 twin.
Bathrooms: 9 private.
Bed & breakfast: £35-£45 single, £50-£65 double.
Half board: £41-£50 daily, £246-£300 weekly.
Lunch available.
Evening meal 7.30pm (l.o. 9.30pm).
Parking for 15.
Credit: Access, Visa, Diners, Amex.

Half board prices shown are per person but in some cases may be based on double/twin occupancy.

The enquiry coupons at the back will help you when contacting proprietors.

WINDSOR

Berkshire
Map ref 2D2

Town dominated by the spectacular castle and home of the Royal Family for over 900 years. Parts are open to the public. There are many attractions including the Great Park, Eton, Windsor Safari Park and trips on the river.
Tourist Information Centre ☎ *(0753) 852010*

Alma House
Listed
56 Alma Rd., Windsor,
SL4 3HA
☎ (0753) 862983 & 855620
An elegant Victorian house within 5 minutes' walk of Windsor Castle, town centre, river and parks. Heathrow Airport 11 miles.
Bedrooms: 1 single, 2 double, 1 family room.
Bathrooms: 1 public; 2 private showers.
Bed & breakfast: £15-£17 single, £30-£35 double.
Parking for 3.
🛏 🖵 🕭 ⓤ 🖩 🛋

The Beeches
19 The Avenue, Datchet,
SL3 9DQ
☎ Slough (0753) 580722
Charming Victorian house with well-appointed spacious rooms. All facilities, close to River Thames, Windsor and convenient for Heathrow and motorway systems.
Bedrooms: 1 single, 1 double & 2 twin, 1 family room.
Bathrooms: 3 private, 1 public; 1 private shower.
Bed & breakfast: £22.50-£27.50 single, £35-£39.50 double.
Parking for 7.
Credit: Visa.
🛏 🖿 ⓓ 🕭 ⓤ Ⓥ 🖩 🛋 ✗ 🛋

Clarence Hotel
👑👑
9 Clarence Rd., Windsor,
SL4 5AE
☎ (0753) 864436
Recently refurbished hotel run by the owner. Close to shopping centre, Windsor Castle and Eton College.
Bedrooms: 2 single, 3 double & 10 twin, 6 family rooms.
Bathrooms: 19 private, 1 public; 2 private showers.
Bed & breakfast: £26-£28 single, £45-£47 double.

Parking for 2.
Credit: Access, Visa, Diners, Amex.
🛏 🖧 🖵 🖩 ⓣⓥ 🖩 🛋 🍽 🅿 🆂🅿 ⓣ

Dorset Private Hotel
👑👑 COMMENDED
4 Dorset Rd., Windsor,
SL4 3BA
☎ (0753) 852669
A gracious Victorian residence in the heart of Royal Windsor, within walking distance of Windsor Castle, River Thames and Eton College.
Bedrooms: 5 twin.
Bathrooms: 5 private.
Bed & breakfast: £45-£55 single, £55-£65 double.
Parking for 7.
Credit: Access, Visa, Diners, Amex.
🛏🖤5 🖧 ⓓ 🖵 🕭 🛋 🖩 🛋 🍽 ✗ 🛋 🆂🅿

Eton Guest House
Listed
122-123 Eton High St., Eton,
Windsor, SL4 6AN
☎ (0753) 861033
Located in the middle of Eton High Street, 5 minutes' walk from Windsor Castle, Eton College and the River Thames.
Bedrooms: 4 single, 5 double & 6 twin, 3 family rooms.
Bathrooms: 4 private, 3 public; 1 private shower.
Bed & breakfast: £20-£30 single, £30-£35 double.
Parking for 12.
🛏 🖵 🖧 🛍 🕭 🖤 🛋 ⓣⓥ 🖩 🛋 🍽 ✗ 🛋 🛋

Fairlight Lodge Royal Windsor Hotel
👑👑👑 COMMENDED
41 Frances Rd., Windsor,
SL4 3AQ
☎ (0753) 861207
Comfortable Victorian property, once the mayoral residence, quietly situated, but close to River Thames, castle and town centre.
Bedrooms: 2 single, 2 double & 2 twin, 4 family rooms.
Bathrooms: 10 private.
Bed & breakfast: £30-£35 single, £47-£55 double.
Half board: £35-£40 daily, £240-£260 weekly.
Evening meal 7.30pm (l.o. 9.30pm).
Parking for 10.
Credit: Access, Visa.
🛏 🖿 🖵 🖧 Ⓥ ⓣⓥ 🖩 🛋 🍽 🛋 🛋

Melrose House
👑👑 COMMENDED
53 Frances Rd., Windsor,
SL4 3AQ
☎ (0753) 865328

Elegant Victorian detached residence, in the heart of Windsor. 5 minutes' walk from the castle.
Bedrooms: 4 double & 3 twin, 2 family rooms.
Bathrooms: 9 private.
Bed & breakfast: £28-£32 single, £38-£45 double.
Parking for 9.
🛏 🖧 🖵 🖧 ⓤ 🖧 🕭 ⓣⓥ ● 🖩 🛋 🛋 🛋

Whitegates
👑 APPROVED
132 Clarence Rd., Windsor,
SL4 5AT
☎ (0753) 830902
Modern, well-equipped, comfortable bed and breakfast accommodation located close to the Windsor relief road.
Bedrooms: 1 single, 2 double & 1 twin, 2 family rooms.
Bathrooms: 1 public; 2 private showers.
Bed & breakfast: £16-£19 single, £32-£38 double.
Parking for 10.
🛏 🖧 🖧 ⓤ 🛋 ⓣⓥ 🖩 🛋 ⓣ

Ye Harte and Garter Hotel ♨
👑👑👑👑
High St., Windsor, SL4 1LR
☎ (0753) 863426
Situated directly opposite Windsor Castle and a short walk from the river and shops. A period building of character. Beautiful ballroom for functions.
Bedrooms: 16 single, 16 double & 10 twin, 8 family rooms.
Bathrooms: 43 private, 2 public.
Bed & breakfast: £52-£68 single, £70-£85 double.
Lunch available.
Evening meal 6pm (l.o. 10.30pm).
Credit: Access, Visa, Amex.
🛏 🖤 ⓓ 🖵 🖧 🛍 Ⓥ 🖧 🛋 ● 🖪 🖩 🛋 🍽 🛋 ✗ 🆂🅿 🛋

> **Individual proprietors have supplied all details of accommodation. Although we do check for accuracy, we advise you to confirm prices and other information at the time of booking.**

WITNEY

Oxfordshire
Map ref 2C1

Town famous for its blanket-making and mentioned in the Domesday Book. The market-place contains the Butter Cross, a medieval meeting place, and there is a green with merchants' houses.
Tourist Information Centre ☎ *(0993) 775802*

Greystones Lodge Hotel
👑👑 COMMENDED
34 Tower Hill, Witney,
OX8 5ES
☎ (0993) 771898
Quiet, comfortable private hotel set in three quarters of an acre of pleasant garden. Conveniently located for visiting Oxford and the Cotswolds.
Bedrooms: 4 single, 3 double & 4 twin, 1 family room.
Bathrooms: 1 private, 1 public; 10 private showers.
Bed & breakfast: £18.50-£21.25 single, £35.50-£39.90 double.
Evening meal 7pm (l.o. 7.30pm).
Parking for 20.
Credit: Visa, Diners, Amex.
🛏 🖧 🖵 🖧 ⓥ 🛋 ⓣⓥ 🖩 🖢 ❄ 🛋

The Witney Lodge Hotel ♨
👑👑👑
Ducklington Lane, Witney,
OX8 7TJ
☎ (0993) 779777 Telex 83459
New hotel built in traditional Cotswold style, with conference facilities for up to 130 persons. Located on the A40 outside Witney.
Bedrooms: 16 double & 14 twin, 4 family rooms.
Bathrooms: 34 private.
Bed & breakfast: £27-£65 single, £48-£79 double.
Half board: £42-£78 daily, £281-£391 weekly.
Lunch available.
Evening meal 7pm (l.o. 10pm).
Parking for 160.
Credit: Access, Visa, C.Bl., Diners, Amex.
🛏 🖧 🖵 🖧 🖵 🛍 Ⓥ 🖧 🛋 ● 🖩 🛋 🛋 🍽 🛋 ✗ 🛋 🆂🅿 ⓣ

> **We advise you to confirm your booking in writing.**

WOBURN

Bedfordshire
Map ref 2D1

Attractive village with thatched cottages, Victorian almshouses and an impressive inn. Woburn Abbey, an 18th C mansion set in 3000 acres of parkland, is a major tourist attraction with a splendid art collection.

The Bell Inn M

21 Bedford St., Woburn, MK17 9QD
☎ (0525) 290280 Fax (0525) 290017
A family owned part Georgian part 17th C hotel. Full a la carte or bar food menus. 4 miles from M1.
Bedrooms: 13 single, 8 double & 2 twin, 2 family rooms.
Bathrooms: 25 private.
Bed & breakfast: £38-£60 single, £65-£74 double.
Lunch available.
Evening meal 7pm (l.o. 9.30pm).
Parking for 36.
Credit: Access, Visa, Diners, Amex.

WOKINGHAM

Berkshire
Map ref 2C2

Pleasant town which grew up around the silk trade and has some half-timbered and Georgian houses.

Cantley House M
COMMENDED

Milton Rd., Wokingham, RG11 5QG
☎ (0734) 789912 Fax (0734) 774294
Traditional Victorian house built 1880. Owned by Marquis of Ormonde. In rural location, 5 minutes from M4 junction 10.
Bedrooms: 14 single, 11 double & 3 twin, 1 family room.
Bathrooms: 29 private.
Bed & breakfast: £40-£62 single, £50-£72 double.
Half board: £37-£80 daily, £316-£600 weekly.
Lunch available.
Evening meal 7.30pm (l.o. 10pm).
Parking for 70.

Credit: Access, Visa, Diners, Amex.

Stakis St. Annes Manor Hotel M

London Rd., Wokingham, RG11 1ST
☎ (0734) 772550
Telex 847342
CD Stakis
Extended country manor house in 25 acres of parkland. 2 minutes from the M4, 10 minutes from the M3. Conference and banqueting facilities.
Bedrooms: 6 single, 30 double & 64 twin, 30 family rooms.
Bathrooms: 130 private.
Bed & breakfast: max. £105 single, max. £130 double.
Evening meal 7pm (l.o. 9.45pm).
Parking for 100.
Credit: Access, Visa, C.Bl., Diners, Amex.

WOLVERTON

Buckinghamshire
Map ref 2C1

6m NW. Bletchley

Roman Room Ristorante Italiano Hotel

42 Church St., Wolverton, Milton Keynes, MK12 5JN
☎ (0908) 318020 & (0908) 568793 after 6pm
Italian and continental restaurant, also English cooking. Weekly rates available. Parking.
Bedrooms: 1 single, 1 double & 6 twin, 1 family room.
Bathrooms: 5 private, 1 public.
Bed & breakfast: £23-£30 single, £37.50-£47.50 double.
Half board: £28.95-£35.45 daily.
Lunch available.
Evening meal 7pm (l.o. 10.30pm).
Parking for 10.
Credit: Access, Visa, Diners, Amex.

The enquiry coupons at the back will help you when contacting proprietors.

WOODSTOCK

Oxfordshire
Map ref 2C1

Small country town clustered around the park gates of Blenheim Palace, the superb 18th C home of the Duke of Marlborough. The town has well-known inns and an interesting museum. Sir Winston Churchill was born and buried nearby.

Feathers Hotel M

Market St., Woodstock, OX7 1SX
☎ (0993) 812291 Telex 83147 VIAORG
A small hotel filled with antiques and chintzes, with restaurant and a typical English bar.
Bedrooms: 1 single, 6 double & 8 twin.
Bathrooms: 15 private.
Bed & breakfast: from £75 single, £90-£125 double.
Lunch available.
Evening meal 7.30pm (l.o. 9.30pm).
Parking for 12.
Credit: Access, Visa, Diners, Amex.

Kings Head Inn

Chapel Hill, Wootton, Nr. Woodstock, OX7 1DX
☎ Woodstock (0993) 811340
Step back in time in this 16th C village inn, in the centre of Wootton. Close to Blenheim Palace.
Bedrooms: 2 double & 1 twin, 1 family room.
Bathrooms: 1 private, 1 public.
Bed & breakfast: £30-£35 single, £46-£56 double.
Half board: £221-£252 weekly.
Lunch available.
Evening meal 6.30pm (l.o. 10pm).
Parking for 10.
Credit: Access, Visa.

Punch Bowl Inn M
Listed

12 Oxford St., Woodstock, OX7 1TR
☎ (0993) 811218
Family-run pub in the centre of Woodstock. Close to Blenheim Palace main entrance. A good touring centre for Oxford and the Cotswolds.
Bedrooms: 3 single, 4 double & 1 twin, 2 family rooms.

Bathrooms: 3 private, 2 public.
Bed & breakfast: £25-£30 single, £35-£40 double.
Lunch available.
Evening meal 6.30pm (l.o. 9.30pm).
Parking for 20.
Credit: Access, Visa.

Classifications and quality commendations were correct at the time of going to press but are subject to change. Please check at the time of booking.

The National Crown Scheme is explained in full on pages 556 – 558.

Use a coupon

When requesting further information from
advertisers in this guide, you may find it helpful
to use the advertisement enquiry coupons which
can be found towards the end of the guide. These
should be cut out and mailed direct to the
companies in which you are interested. Do
remember to include your name and address.

East Anglia

Think of East Anglia, and maybe the first thing to come to mind is the long, sunny, sandy coastline.

›**»** From south-facing Southend it runs north past England's most easterly point at Lowestoft, and continues round to the cliffs of west-facing Hunstanton. En route are places as diverse as Clacton and Aldeburgh, Southwold and Great Yarmouth, Cromer and Wells-next-the-Sea. Endless summer days beckon on endless beaches — three have been awarded the coveted Blue Flag for excellence — but East Anglia is much more than the coast.

›**»** More, even, than the rivers and lakes of the Norfolk Broads, meandering past picturesque villages and home to wildlife and cabin cruisers of every species. More, too, than the fens and forests, however haunting, however beautiful. As East Anglia was long ago England's most populous area, the cradle of many institutions, turn any corner nowadays and you're likely to find something of historical significance.

›**»** Galleries abound, there are museums to everything, and for lovers of historic houses and gardens, Audley End, Ickworth, Sandringham and Wimpole Hall are just some of the most spectacular. Roman Colchester, once England's capital, is also its oldest recorded town; the Magna Carta was conceived in 1214 in Bury St. Edmunds; Cambridge remains as perfect as ever. Norwich has 33 medieval churches, two cathedrals and a castle. Ipswich has fine churches, too, and is well worth a visit. Almost every town and village rewards investigation.

The Norfolk Broads are alive with boating activity.

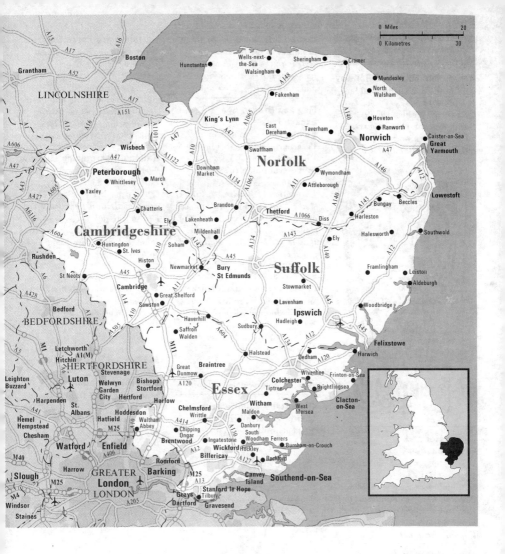

》 Windmills, nature reserves, cross-country walks and watersports are always close and there are amusement parks like Yarmouth's Pleasure Beach, one of the ten most visited tourist attractions in the country, and the spectacular Pleasurewood Hills at Lowestoft.

》 It all means that whether you're a buff or a sport, single or multiple, lazy or frenetic — you'll find a perfect holiday here, East in Eden!

》 **Please refer to the colour maps at the back of this guide for all places with accommodation listings.**

Where to go, what to see

Audley End Miniature Railway
Audley End, Saffron Walden, Essex CB11 4JG
☎ Saffron Walden (0799) 22354
Steam and diesel locomotives in 10.5 gauge, running through attractive woodland for 1.5 miles.

Colchester and Essex Museum
Colchester Castle, Colchester, Essex CO1 1TJ
☎ Colchester (0206) 712931/2
Norman keep on foundations of Roman temple. Archaeological material includes much on Roman Colchester.

Imperial War Museum
Duxford Airfield, Duxford, Cambridgeshire CB2 4QR
☎ Cambridge (0223) 833963/835000
Largest collection of military and civil aircraft in Britain, in historical surroundings of Battle of Britain fighter station. Artillery, vehicles, exhibitions, Concorde 101, adventure playground.

Ely Cathedral
The College, Ely, Cambridgeshire CB7 4DN
☎ Ely (0353) 667735
The 'Ship of the Fens', Ely Cathedral is one of the finest examples of the Romanesque style with the Octagon as one of its best features. Brass rubbing and stained glass museum.

Flag Fen Bronze Age Excavations
Fourth Drove, Fengate, Peterborough, Cambridgeshire PE1 5UR
☎ Peterborough (0733) 313414
Excavation of Bronze Age timber 'Lake Village'. Visitors can see and handle 3,000-year-old timber. Site includes an intact Roman road. Visitor centre and gift shop.

Easton Farm Park
Easton, Nr. Wickham Market, Woodbridge, Suffolk IP13 0EQ
☎ Wickham Market (0728) 746475
Victorian farm setting for over 40 species of farm animals, including rare breeds. Modern milking unit, Victorian dairy, working Suffolk horses. Trail.

Kilverstone Wildlife Park
Thetford, Norfolk IP24 2RL
☎ Thetford (0842) 5369/66606
Falabella miniature horses, animals from South America. Café, shop, garden centre, play area, miniature railway, amusements.

Norfolk Shire Horse Centre
West Runton Stables, West Runton, Cromer, Norfolk NR27 9QH
☎ West Runton (026 375) 339
Shire horses working and on display. Breeds of mountain and moorland ponies. Horse-drawn machinery and wagons.

National Horseracing Museum
99 High Street, Newmarket, Suffolk CB8 8JL
☎ Newmarket (0638) 667333
Story of Britain's greatest sport told in fine paintings, bronzes and memorabilia of personalities connected with the sport. Five galleries, coffee shop.

Never Never Land
Western Esplanade, Southend-on-Sea, Essex
☎ Southend-on-Sea (0702) 460618
Children's fantasy park of 2.5 acres. Animated fairytale themes and familiar children's characters.

Mountfitchet Castle
Stansted Mountfitchet, Essex CM24 8SP
☎ Bishops Stortford (0279) 813237
Reconstruction of a Norman motte-and-bailey castle and village of Domesday period. Grand Hall, church, prison, siege tower, weapons.

Imperial War Museum, Duxford Airfield

See the story of Britain's greatest sport at the National Horseracing Museum, Newmarket

Vala Olafsdottur

Pleasurewood Hills American Theme Park

Corton Road, Lowestoft, Suffolk NR32 5DZ

☎ Lowestoft (0502) 513626

Tempest chair lift, railway, pirate ship, fort, Aladdin's Cave, parrot shows, roller coaster, waveswinger, haunted castle.

The Thursford Collection

Thursford, Fakenham, Norfolk NR21 0AS

☎ Thursford (0328) 878477

Showman's locomotives, engines and organs. Midsummer musical evenings every Tuesday from end June-end September. Christmas shows.

The Otter Trust

Earsham, Nr. Bungay, Suffolk NR35 2AF

☎ Bungay (0986) 3470

A conservation organisation devoted to the breeding of the British otter and the return of these animals, after the relevant research work, to a suitable habitat. Lakes, waterfowl, deer.

Make a date for...

Mildenhall Air Fete

RAF Mildenhall, Mildenhall, Suffolk   *25 – 26 May**

Suffolk Show

Suffolk Showground, Ipswich, Suffolk   *29 – 30 May*

Aldeburgh Festival of Music and the Arts

Snape Maltings Concert Hall, Aldeburgh, Suffolk
7 – 23 June

Royal Norfolk Show

The Showground, Dereham Road, Norwich, Norfolk
26 – 27 June

Cambridge Festival

Various venues, Cambridge, Cambridgeshire   *13 – 28 July*

East of England Agricultural Show

East of England Showground, Peterborough, Cambridgeshire
16 – 18 July

Cambridge Folk Festival

Cherry Hinton Hall, Cambridge, Cambridgeshire
26 – 28 July

Norfolk and Norwich Festival

Various venues, Norwich, Norfolk   *9 – 20 October*

* Provisional dates only

Find out more

Further information about holidays and attractions in the East Anglia region is available from: **East Anglia Tourist Board**, Toppesfield Hall, Hadleigh, Suffolk IP7 5DN. ☎ (0473) 822922.

These publications are available free from the East Anglia Tourist Board:

Bed & Breakfast Touring Map for the East of England

Norfolk Coast and Countryside Holidays (accommodation guide)

Courtesy Breaks in Norwich and Norfolk Countryside

East Anglia Holidays

Also available are:

East Anglia Guide £2.45 (inc post and packing)

East Anglia Leisure Map £2.75 (inc post and packing)

Gardens to Visit in East Anglia 60p

Places to stay

•**》**Accommodation entries in this regional section are listed in alphabetical order of place name, and then in alphabetical order of establishment.

•**》**The map references refer to the colour maps towards the end of the guide. The first figure is the map number; the letter and figure which follow indicate the grid reference on the map.

•**》**The symbols at the end of each accommodation entry give information about services and facilities. A 'key' to these symbols is inside the back cover flap, which can be kept open for easy reference.

ACLE

Norfolk
Map ref 3C1

8m W. Great Yarmouth
Market town has church with 11th C round tower and font dating from 1410.

East Norwich Inn

👑👑👑

Old Rd., Acle, NR13 3QN
☎ Great Yarmouth
(0493) 751112
Family-run inn. 10 miles from Great Yarmouth/Norwich off A47. Set in heart of Broadlands National Park.
Bedrooms: 6 double & 4 twin, 2 family rooms.
Bathrooms: 12 private.
Bed & breakfast: £15.50-£21 single, £26-£32 double.
Half board: £18.50-£28 daily, £145-£180 weekly.
Lunch available.
Evening meal 7pm (l.o. 9pm).
Parking for 40.
Credit: Access, Visa.
🕭 🖒 ➡ 💱 🌡 Ⓥ 🖃 ▥ ▱
🍽 ➳ 🐾 ⊙ⅆⅉⅇ SP

ALCONBURY

Cambridgeshire
Map ref 3A2

4m NW. Huntingdon

Alconbury House Hotel M

👑👑👑

Alconbury Weston,
Huntingdon, PE17 5JG
☎ (0480) 890807
Fax (0480) 891259

A friendly hotel which is ideally located for exploring numerous historic and interesting locations.
Bedrooms: 14 single, 4 double & 7 twin, 1 family room.
Bathrooms: 26 private.
Bed & breakfast: £25-£49.50 single, £40-£60.50 double.
Half board: £30-£60.50 daily.
Lunch available.
Evening meal 7pm (l.o. 9.30pm).
Parking for 60.
Credit: Access, Visa, Diners, Amex.
🕭 🖒 ➡ ⊙ⅆⅉⅇ ➡ 💱 🌡 Ⓥ ✕
🖃 ▥ ➡ 🍽 ⊙ ➳ 🌂 🔆 OAP
🐾 SP ⒯

ALDEBURGH

Suffolk
Map ref 3C2

6m SE. Saxmundham
A prosperous port in the 16th C, now famous for the Aldeburgh Music Festival held annually in June. The 16th C Moot Hall, now a museum, is a timber-framed building once used as an open market.

Uplands Hotel M

👑👑👑

Victoria Rd., Aldeburgh,
IP15 5DX
☎ (0728) 452420 &
(0728) 452156
Country house hotel with an emphasis on comfort, courtesy and cleanliness. Restaurant overlooks the gardens.

Bedrooms: 3 single, 5 double & 10 twin, 2 family rooms.
Bathrooms: 17 private,
1 public.
Bed & breakfast: £25-£3⅃ single, from £55 double.
Half board: from £38 daily.
Evening meal 7pm (l.o. 8.30pm).
Parking for 20.
Credit: Access, Visa, Diners, Amex.
🕭 🖒 ➡ 💱 🌡 Ⓥ 🖃 TV
▥ 🍽 ➳ 🐾 🔆 SP 🐟

Wentworth Hotel M

👑👑👑 COMMENDED

Wentworth Rd., Aldeburgh,
IP15 5BB
☎ (072 885) 2312 & 3357
ⒸⓇ Consort
Privately owned and run country house hotel facing the sea. Two lounges, cosy bar and log fires. This hotel was awarded a Hotel with Restaurant Commendation by the British Tourist Authority.
Bedrooms: 7 single, 10 double & 14 twin.
Bathrooms: 28 private,
2 public.
Bed & breakfast: £25-£39 single, from £55 double.
Half board: from £38 daily.
Lunch available.
Evening meal 7pm (l.o. 9pm).
Parking for 16.
Credit: Access, Visa, Diners, Amex.
🕭 🖒 ➡ ⊙ⅆⅉⅇ ➡ 🌡 Ⓥ 🖃 ▥
🍽 🐾 🐟 SP ⒯

White Lion Hotel M

👑👑👑

Market Cross Place,
Aldeburgh, IP15 5BJ
☎ (0728) 452720
Telex 94017152
Imposing hotel standing directly on the seafront. Totally unspoilt fishing town of great charm, famous for classical music concerts.
Bedrooms: 2 single, 21 double & 14 twin, 1 family room.
Bathrooms: 38 private.
Bed & breakfast: £50-£60 single, £65-£90 double.
Lunch available.
Evening meal 7pm (l.o. 9pm).
Parking for 15.
Credit: Access, Visa, Diners, Amex.
🕭 🖒 ➡ ⊙ⅆⅉⅇ ➡ 🌡 Ⓥ ✕
🖃 ● 🌡 ▥ ➡ 🍽 ➳ 🐾 SP
🐟 ⒯

ATTLEBOROUGH

Norfolk
Map ref 3B1

Market town, mostly destroyed in 1559 by fire, now a cider-making centre. Church with fine Norman tower.

Earles M

👑👑👑

Stow Bedon House, Stow Bedon, Attleborough,
NR17 1BX
☎ Caston (095 383) 284

Half board prices shown are per person but in some cases may be based on double/twin occupancy.

Country house hotel with certain country club facilities free to guests. Secluded situation in Breckland. Just off the B1075 Thetford to Watton road.
Bedrooms: 1 single, 5 double & 1 twin.
Bathrooms: 6 private, 1 public.
Bed & breakfast: £30-£45 single, £50-£80 double.
Lunch available.
Evening meal 7pm (l.o. 9.30pm).
Parking for 25.
Open February-December.
Credit: Access, Visa.

Sherbourne Country House Hotel M
😋😋😋

Norwich Rd., Attleborough, NR17 2JX
☎ (0953) 454363
17th C country house in mature grounds, furnished in period style yet with modern comforts, offering home cooking. Convenient for many places of interest.
Bedrooms: 2 single, 4 double & 2 twin, 1 family room.
Bathrooms: 7 private, 1 public; 1 private shower.
Bed & breakfast: £20-£37.50 single, £40-£75 double.
Half board: £32-£49.50 daily, £196-£315 weekly.
Lunch available.
Evening meal 6.30pm (l.o. 8.30pm).
Parking for 50.
Credit: Access, Visa, Amex.

BACTON-ON-SEA
Norfolk
Map ref 3C1

5m NE. North Walsham

Seacroft Guest House
😋😋

Beach Rd., Bacton-on-Sea, Norwich, NR12 0HS
☎ Walcott (0692) 650302
Off B1159 via Seacroft caravan park. Large Victorian house close to shops and beach. Home cooking and personal supervision.
Bedrooms: 1 single, 3 double & 2 twin, 2 family rooms.
Bathrooms: 2 private, 3 public.
Bed & breakfast: £12.50-£16 single, £25-£32 double.
Half board: £20-£23.50 daily, £128.50-£161.50 weekly.

Evening meal 6pm (l.o. 8pm).
Parking for 15.
Open March-November.
Credit: Access, Visa.

BARDWELL
Suffolk
Map ref 3B2

2m N. Ixworth
Home of Bardwell Windmill, producing fine quality stoneground flours for sale. Traction engine in attendance and mill occasionally worked by steam.

Six Bells Inn M
😋😋😋 APPROVED
The Green, Bardwell, IP31 1AW
☎ Stanton (0359) 50820
16th C coaching inn off Bury/Diss road. Character restaurants. Stylish, quiet, ground floor en-suite accommodation in a converted barn.
Bedrooms: 3 single, 2 double & 3 twin.
Bathrooms: 8 private.
Bed & breakfast: £27.50-£40 single, £42.50-£50 double.
Lunch available.
Evening meal 7pm (l.o. 10pm).
Parking for 50.
Credit: Access, Visa.

BARNHAM BROOM
Norfolk
Map ref 3B1

4m N. Wymondham

Barnham Broom Hotel Conference & Leisure Centre M
😋😋😋
Barnham Broom, Norwich, NR9 4DD
☎ (060 545) 393 Telex 975711
⊕ Best Western
In 120 acres of beautiful countryside, with a relaxed and friendly atmosphere. Excellent sport facilities.
Bedrooms: 1 single, 7 double & 38 twin, 6 family rooms.
Bathrooms: 52 private.
Bed & breakfast: £55-£65 single, £70-£80 double.
Half board: £67-£78 daily, £320-£340 weekly.
Lunch available.
Evening meal 7.30pm (l.o. 9.30pm).
Parking for 200.

Credit: Access, Visa, Diners, Amex.

BASILDON
Essex
Map ref 3B3

One of the New Towns planned after World War II. It overlooks the estuary of the River Thames and is set in undulating countryside. The main feature is the town square with a traffic-free pedestrian concourse.

The Chichester Hotel
😋😋😋 COMMENDED
Old London Rd., Rawreth, Wickford, SS11 8UE
☎ (0268) 560555
A picturesque family-run hotel with restaurant, dinner-dance restaurant and functions complex. Surrounded by farmland in the Basildon, Chelmsford, Southend triangle.
Bedrooms: 17 single, 9 double & 8 twin.
Bathrooms: 34 private.
Bed & breakfast: £52-£62 single, £62-£72 double.
Half board: £64.50-£74.50 daily, £470-£470 weekly.
Lunch available.
Evening meal 7pm (l.o. 9.30pm).
Parking for 41.
Credit: Access, Visa, Diners, Amex.

BECCLES
Suffolk
Map ref 3C1

8m W. Lowestoft
Fire destroyed the town in the 16th C and it was rebuilt in Georgian red brick. The River Waveney, on which the town stands, is popular with boating enthusiasts and has an annual regatta. Home of Beccles and District Museum and the William Clowes Printing Museum.

The Swan
Loddon Rd., Gillingham, Beccles, NR34 0LD
☎ (0502) 712055
Modern motel offering chalet-type accommodation in 5 acres of grounds. Close to Norfolk Broads and historic town of Beccles.

Bedrooms: 2 single, 10 double & 1 twin, 4 family rooms.
Bathrooms: 17 private.
Bed & breakfast: £26-£30 single, £36-£40 double.
Lunch available.
Evening meal 6pm (l.o. 10.30pm).
Parking for 50.
Credit: Access, Visa.

BILDESTON
Suffolk
Map ref 3B2

6m NW. Hadleigh

The Crown Hotel
104 High St., Bildeston, IP7 7EB
☎ (0449) 740510
15th C building, originally a wool merchant's house, with a wealth of beams and fireplaces. Bars, restaurants, four-poster bed.
Bedrooms: 1 single, 9 double & 5 twin.
Bathrooms: 11 private, 2 public; 1 private shower.
Bed & breakfast: £22-£30 single, £30-£55 double.
Lunch available.
Evening meal 7pm (l.o. 9.30pm).
Parking for 30.
Credit: Access, Visa.

BIRCHANGER
Essex
Map ref 2D1

2m NE. Bishop's Stortford
Lying east of River Stort, the village is strung out along a winding road running up a hillside. Much restored small church with Norman nave and 2 12th C doorways.

The Cottage
😋😋😋
71 Birchanger Lane, Birchanger, Bishop's Stortford, Hertfordshire CM23 5QF
☎ Bishop's Stortford (0279) 812349
17th C house with panelled rooms and inglenook fireplaces. Quiet rural setting yet close to Stansted Airport and M11 junction 8.
Bedrooms: 2 single, 3 double & 4 twin, 1 family room.
Bathrooms: 8 private, 1 public.

Continued ▶

BIRCHANGER

Continued

Bed & breakfast: from £30 single, from £40 double.
Half board: from £39 daily.
Evening meal 6.30pm (l.o. 9am).
Parking for 9.

⌖ 🏃 ➡ 🛏 ▥ Ⅴ ⅄ ➡ ▦
🛋 ❈ 🗶 SP 🕭

BLAKENEY

Norfolk
Map ref 3B1

5m NW. Holt
Picturesque village on the north coast of Norfolk and a former port and fishing village. The 15th C red bricked Guildhall stands on a brick-vaulted undercroft. Marshy creeks extend towards Blakeney Point (National Trust) and are a paradise for naturalists, with trips to the reserve and to see the seals from Blakeney Quay.

Blakeney Hotel ⋀

😊😊😊😊
Quayside, Blakeney, Nr. Holt, NR25 7NE
☎ Cley (0263) 740797
Overlooking the harbour and National Trust saltings. Many features, including bird-watching and cycling. Minimum stay 2 nights.
Bedrooms: 8 single, 18 double & 21 twin, 4 family rooms.
Bathrooms: 51 private.
Bed & breakfast: £39-£53 single, £78-£118 double.
Half board: £44-£69 daily, £296-£386 weekly.
Lunch available.
Evening meal 7pm (l.o. 9.30pm).
Parking for 100.
Credit: Access, Visa, Diners, Amex.

⌖ 🏃 ➡ ❤ ⓡ ➡ ❖ ▥ Ⅴ
➡ ▦ 🛋 ✝ ᐃ 𝄢 ◆ 🔲
◡ 🧵 ▶ ❈ 🗶 SP Ⓣ

Flintstones Guest House ⋀

😊 COMMENDED
Wiveton, Holt, NR25 7TL
☎ Cley (0263) 740337
Attractive guesthouse in picturesque rural surroundings near village green. 1 mile from Cley and Blakeney with good sailing and bird-watching. Non-smokers only please.
Bedrooms: 2 double, 3 family rooms.
Bathrooms: 2 private, 1 public.

Bed & breakfast: £22-£28 double.
Half board: £18-£20.50 daily, £154-£196 weekly.
Evening meal 7pm (l.o. 5pm).
Parking for 5.

⌖ 🏃 ➡ ❤ ▣ 𝄞 ▥ Ⅴ ⅄ ➡
▦ 🛋 🗶 SP

BRAINTREE

Essex
Map ref 3B2

11m NE. Chelmsford
On the old Roman road from St. Albans to Colchester. The Heritage Centre in the Town Hall describes Braintree's former international importance in wool, silk and engineering, the Working Silk Museum houses England's last hand loom silk weaving mill. St. Michael's parish church includes some Roman bricks and Braintree market was first chartered in 1199. 6 miles to the north-east is Gosfield Hall, a Tudor courtyard house.

The Old House ⋀

😊😊
11 Bradford St., Braintree, CM7 6AS
☎ (0376) 550457
16th C timber-framed house with a Jacobean panelled bar and dining room. Large inglenook giving a warm, homely atmosphere.
Bedrooms: 1 single, 2 double & 1 twin, 1 family room.
Bathrooms: 2 private, 1 public.
Bed & breakfast: £17.25-£26.45 single, £32.20-£40.25 double.
Half board: £24.15-£33.35 daily, £164.22-£228.62 weekly.
Evening meal 5pm (l.o. 8pm).
Parking for 7.

⌖ 🏃 ▣ ➡ 🛏 ⅄ ➡ 🛋
❈ 🗶 🕭 OAP SP 🕭

The White Hart ⋀

😊😊😊😊
Bocking End, Braintree, CM7 6AB
☎ (0376) 21401 Telex 988835
Ⓖ Lansbury
35-bedroom town centre hotel, created around an original 15th C coaching inn.
Bedrooms: 7 single, 8 double & 16 twin, 4 family rooms.
Bathrooms: 35 private.
Bed & breakfast: £22-£60 single, £44-£72 double.
Half board: £33-£72 daily.
Lunch available.

Evening meal 6pm (l.o. 10.30pm).
Parking for 51.
Credit: Access, Visa, Diners, Amex.

⌖ 🏃 ❤ ▣ ➡ 𝄞 🛡 ▥ ⅄
➡ ◆ ▦ 🛋 ✝ 𝄢 SP 🕭 Ⓣ

BRANDON

Suffolk
Map ref 3B2

6m NW. Thetford
Set on the edge of Thetford Forest in an area known as Breckland where the old stone 5-arched bridge links Suffolk with Norfolk. 3 miles north-east is Grime's Graves, the largest prehistoric flint mine in Europe. 1 mile north are the ruins of Weeting Castle, a 12th C fortified manor house in a moated rectangular enclosure. 2 miles north-east is Santon Downham which has a 2 mile walk through forest plantations.

Brandon Park Lodge

Brandon Country Park, Brandon, IP27 0SU
☎ Thetford (0842) 812400
Set in 2600 acres of country park. Follow signs to country park.
Bedrooms: 21 double & 8 twin, 3 family rooms.
Bathrooms: 32 private, 1 public.
Bed & breakfast: £58-£68 single, £72-£84 double.
Half board: £70.50-£80.50 daily, £493.50-£563.50 weekly.
Lunch available.
Evening meal 7pm (l.o. 9pm).
Credit: Access, Visa, Diners, Amex.

⌖ 🏃 ❤ ➡ 𝄞 ▥ ➡ ◆ ▦
🛋 ✝ 𝄢 ♪ ◡ ▶ 🗶 🕭

BRENTWOOD

Essex
Map ref 2D2

11m SW. Chelmsford
The town grew up in the late 12th C and then developed as a staging post, being strategically placed close to the London to Chelmsford road. Deer roam by the lakes in the 428 acre park at South Weald, part of Brentwood's attractive Green Belt. Cater Museum is 5 miles to the east.

Brentwood Moat House ⋀

😊😊😊😊 COMMENDED
London Rd., Brentwood, CM14 4NR
☎ (0277) 225252
Telex 995182
Ⓖ Queens Moat Houses
Original Tudor building dating back to 1512. Hunting lodge owned by Catherine of Aragon.
Bedrooms: 16 double & 17 twin, 5 family rooms.
Bathrooms: 38 private.
Bed & breakfast: £83-£87 single, £85-£98 double.
Lunch available.
Evening meal 7.15pm (l.o. 10.15pm).
Parking for 120.
Credit: Access, Visa, Diners, Amex.

⌖ 🏃 ❤ ➡ 🛋 🛏 ▥ ➡
◆ ▦ 🛋 ✝ ❖ ❈ 🗶 SP 🕭

BRIGHTLINGSEA

Essex
Map ref 3B3

Anchor Hotel

Waterside, Brightlingsea, CO7 0AX
☎ (020 630) 2035
Most bedrooms have sea views. Observation room at the top of the building with an all round view.
Bedrooms: 1 single, 3 double & 4 twin.
Bathrooms: 1 private, 2 public; 1 private shower.
Bed & breakfast: £15 single, £30-£42 double.
Half board: £21-£28 daily, £94-£122 weekly.
Lunch available.
Evening meal (l.o. 9.30pm).
Parking for 2.
Credit: Access, Visa.

⌖ 𝄜 ➡ 🛏 ▥ 🛋 🗶 🐾

The symbol Ⓖ and the name of a hotel group or consortium after a hotel address means that bookings can be made through a central reservations office. These are listed on pages **559 & 560.**

BUNGAY

Suffolk
Map ref 3C1

14m SE. Wymondham
Market town and yachting
centre on the River
Waveney with the
remains of a great 12th C
castle. In the market-
place stands the Butter
Cross, rebuilt in 1689
after being largely
destroyed by fire. The
town's major industries
since the 18th C have
been printing and leather
working. Nearby at
Earsham is the Otter
Trust.

Dove Restaurant
Wortwell, Nr. Harleston,
Norfolk IP20 0EN
☎ (098 686) 315
*A former railway hotel, now
established restaurant offering
accommodation. On the
Norfolk/Suffolk border. Good
centre for the Waveney Valley.*
Bedrooms: 2 double & 1 twin.
Bathrooms: 2 private,
1 public.
Bed & breakfast: £15-£17.50
single, £28-£32 double.
Half board: £22.50-£25 daily.
Lunch available.
Evening meal 7pm (l.o.
9.30pm).
Parking for 15.
Credit: Access, Visa.
🅱 ⊁ 🅸 Ⓥ ⊁ ⓉⓋ ⓜ ⧉ 🍽
Ⓤ ▶ ⁂ 🐎

BUNWELL

Norfolk
Map ref 3B1

5m SE. Attleborough

Bunwell Manor Hotel M
👑👑👑
Bunwell St., Bunwell, Nr.
Norwich, NR16 1QU
☎ (095 389) 8304
*Tudor country manor house in
its own grounds. Comfortable
rooms, friendly service and
interesting menus. Situated in
Bunwell Street, 12 miles south
of Norwich.*
Bedrooms: 1 single, 6 double
& 2 twin, 1 family room.
Bathrooms: 10 private.
Bed & breakfast: £40-£44
single, £55-£60 double.
Half board: £49.50-£53.50
daily, £315 weekly.
Lunch available.

Evening meal 7pm (l.o.
9.30pm).
Parking for 25.
Credit: Access, Visa.
🅱 🅴 ⓒ Ⓠ ⚘ 🅸 Ⓥ ⧉ 🍽
⧉ 🍴 ⁂ 🐎 ⚲ SP 🏥 Ⓣ

BURNHAM-ON-CROUCH

Essex
Map ref 3B3

9m SE. Maldon
Popular yachting and
boatbuilding centre with 5
yacht clubs. The town lies
on the north bank of the
Crouch, 6 miles from the
sea. The High Street
contains a mixture of
Georgian and Victorian
architecture.

Ye Olde White Harte
👑👑👑
The Quay, Burnham-on-
Crouch, CM0 8AS
☎ Maldon (0621) 782106
*20th C and 17th C building
overlooking Crouch Estuary
and Essex Marshes.
Comfortably appointed, with
old world atmosphere in both
bars and restaurant.*
Bedrooms: 3 double & 6 twin,
2 family rooms.
Bathrooms: 11 private,
1 public.
Bed & breakfast: £18.15-£31
single, £31.90-£50 double.
Half board: £26-£39 daily.
Lunch available.
Evening meal 7.30pm (l.o.
9pm).
Parking for 15.
🅱 ⓒ Ⓠ 🅸 Ⓥ ⧉ ⓉⓋ ⧉ 🍴
🏥

BURY ST. EDMUNDS

Suffolk
Map ref 3B2

Ancient market and
cathedral town which
takes its name from the
martyred Saxon King, St.
Edmund. Bury St.
Edmunds has many fine
buildings including the
Athenaeum and Moyses
Hall, reputed to be the
oldest Norman house in
the county.
*Tourist Information
Centre ☎ (0284) 764667*

Angel Hotel M
👑👑👑👑
Angel Hill, Bury St.
Edmunds, IP33 1LT
☎ (0284) 753926
Telex 81630(ANGEL)

*Attractive Georgian hotel. 2
restaurants, ballroom,
individually decorated
bedrooms. Four-posters and
suites available.*
Bedrooms: 14 single,
11 double & 10 twin, 5 family
rooms.
Bathrooms: 40 private.
Bed & breakfast: £70-£80
single, £90-£115 double.
Lunch available.
Evening meal 7pm (l.o.
9.30pm).
Parking for 38.
Credit: Access, Visa, Diners,
Amex.
🅱 🅴 ⓒ 🅴 Ⓠ 🅸 Ⓥ ⊁ ⧉
⦿ 🍽 ⧉ 🍴 ⚘ SP 🏥 Ⓣ

Bradfield House
Restaurant and Hotel
👑👑👑 COMMENDED
Bradfield Combust, Bury St.
Edmunds, IP30 0LR
☎ Sicklesmere (028 486) 301
& 8196
*Timber framed 17th C house
overlooking village green set in
2 acres of own its grounds with
Victorian kitchen garden.
Lunch available on Sundays. 4
miles south of Bury on the
A134.*
Bedrooms: 1 single, 2 double
& 1 twin.
Bathrooms: 4 private.
Bed & breakfast: £35-£45
single, £45-£60 double.
Half board: £35-£57 daily,
£245-£287.50 weekly.
Evening meal 7pm (l.o.
9.30pm).
Parking for 14.
Credit: Access, Visa.
🅱 ⓒ Ⓠ ⚘ 🅸 Ⓥ ⧉ 🍽
⧉ 🍴 ⁂ 🐎 🏥 SP 🏥

Butterfly Hotel M
👑👑👑
A45 Bury East Exit, Moreton
Hall, Bury St. Edmunds,
IP32 7BW
☎ (0284) 760884
Telex 818360
*Modern building with rustic
style and decor, around open
central courtyard. Special
weekend rates available.*
Bedrooms: 23 single,
15 double & 12 twin.
Bathrooms: 50 private.
Bed & breakfast: £57-£60
single, £62-£65 double.
Half board: £41-£72 daily.
Lunch available.
Evening meal 7pm (l.o.
10pm).
Parking for 70.
Credit: Access, Visa, Diners,
Amex.
🅱 🅴 ⓒ 🅴 Ⓠ ⚘ 🅸 Ⓥ ⊁
⧉ ⦿ 🍽 ⧉ 🍴 🐎 🏥 SP Ⓣ

The Chantry Hotel
8 Sparhawk St., Bury St.
Edmunds, IP33 1RY
☎ (0284) 767427
*Georgian hotel in town centre,
near the Abbey Gardens,
cathedral and Theatre Royal.*
Bedrooms: 4 single, 6 double
& 5 twin, 2 family rooms.
Bathrooms: 17 private,
1 public.
Bed & breakfast: £36-£42
single, £48.50-£58.50 double.
Evening meal 7.30pm (l.o.
6.45pm).
Parking for 16.
Credit: Access, Visa.
🅱 🅴 ⓒ 🅴 ⚘ 🅸 🍽
⧉ 🏥 SP 🏥 Ⓣ

Dunston Guest
House/Hotel M
👑👑👑
8 Springfield Rd., Bury St.
Edmunds, IP33 3AN
☎ (0284) 767981
*Attractive Victorian
guesthouse/hotel providing high
standard accommodation,
quietly situated half a mile
from town centre. Licensed
with sun lounge, garden and
car park. Groups welcome.*
Bedrooms: 4 single, 3 double
& 4 twin, 4 family rooms.
Bathrooms: 9 private,
4 public.
Bed & breakfast: £16-£25
single, £28-£36 double.
Half board: £26-£35 daily,
£182-£245 weekly.
Evening meal 6pm.
Parking for 12.
🅱 🅴 ⓒ Ⓠ 🅸 Ⓥ ⧉ ⓉⓋ
🍽 ⧉ 🐎 ⁂ 🐕 ⊁

Grange Hotel M
👑👑👑 APPROVED
Barton Rd., Thurston, Bury
St. Edmunds, IP31 3PQ
☎ Pakenham (0359) 31260
*Family-owned country house
hotel with chef/proprietor.*
Bedrooms: 2 single, 7 double
& 5 twin, 1 family room.
Bathrooms: 11 private,
2 public; 2 private showers.
Bed & breakfast: £26-£45
single, £38-£58 double.
Lunch available.
Evening meal 7pm (l.o.
9.30pm).
Parking for 80.
Credit: Access, Visa.
🅱 ⓒ Ⓠ ⚘ 🅸 Ⓥ ⧉ 🍽 ⧉
🍴 ⁂ 🐎 🏥 SP

Hamilton House
👑👑
4 Nelson Rd., Bury St.
Edmunds, IP33 3AG
☎ (0284) 702201
Continued ▶

BURY ST. EDMUNDS
Continued

Refurbished Victorian house in quiet cul-de-sac, 3 minutes' walk from town centre. Guests' lounge and breakfast room. Non-smokers preferred please. Long-stay public car park adjacent.
Bedrooms: 2 single, 1 double, 1 family room.
Bathrooms: 2 private, 1 public.
Bed & breakfast: £15-£17 single, £32-£36 double.
⌕ ▯ ♦ ⒰ ▮ ✓ ⌐ ▥
▰ ✕ ⌂

Hamling House Hotel M
☖☖☖ APPROVED
Bull Rd., Pakenham, Bury St. Edmunds, IP31 2LW
☎ (0359) 30934
Delightfully appointed Alpine-style country house hotel in picturesque conservation village of Pakenham, near historic Bury St. Edmunds. Tranquil gardens.
Bedrooms: 1 single, 2 double & 3 twin, 1 family room.
Bathrooms: 7 private.
Bed & breakfast: £40 single, £50-£60 double.
Half board: £31.50-£54 daily, £220.50-£378 weekly.
Lunch available.
Evening meal 7pm (l.o. 8.30pm).
Parking for 10.
Credit: Access, Visa, Diners, Amex.
⌕ ▰ ⌐ ⓛ ▯ ⒰ ♦ ▮ ⓥ
⌐ ⒯ ▥ ▰ ⓣ ✳ SP ⓣ

High Green House M
☖☖
Nowton, Bury St. Edmunds, IP29 2LZ
☎ Sicklesmere (028 486) 293
Modernised Tudor house with a garden and ample parking, views of the surrounding countryside and home produce.
Bedrooms: 2 single, 1 double & 2 twin, 1 family room.
Bathrooms: 4 private.
Bed & breakfast: £15-£16 single, £30-£82 double.
Half board: £23-£24 daily, £150-£160 weekly.
Evening meal 7.30pm (l.o. 8pm).
Parking for 6.
⌕ ▰ ▱ ⒰ ⒰ ⒰ ▮ ⓥ ⌐ ⒯
▥ ▰ ⌂ ✳ ✕ ⒟ ⊠ SP ⌂

Map references apply to the colour maps towards the end of this guide.

Kingshotts Restaurant and Hotel
☖☖☖☖ COMMENDED
12 Angel Hill, Bury St. Edmunds, IP33 1UZ
☎ (0284) 704088
Located in a row of 19th C buildings in the centre of Bury St Edmunds. Noted for its cuisine and friendly service.
Bedrooms: 1 single, 7 double.
Bathrooms: 8 private.
Bed & breakfast: £50-£65 single, £65-£75 double.
Lunch available.
Evening meal 7pm (l.o. 9pm).
Parking for 3.
Credit: Access, Visa.
⌕ ▱ ⌐ ▮ ⓥ ⌐ ▥ ⓣ ✕
SP ⌂

Priory Hotel and Restaurant M
☖☖☖
Fornham Rd., Tollgate, Bury St. Edmunds, IP32 6EH
☎ (0284) 766181
Telex 8950511
⑮ Best Western
Well-known local establishment noted for high standards and cuisine. Set in 2 acres of landscaped gardens yet only minutes from the town.
Bedrooms: 4 single, 20 double & 5 twin, 1 family room.
Bathrooms: 30 private.
Bed & breakfast: £60-£65 single, £70-£75 double.
Half board: £75-£85 daily, £375 weekly.
Lunch available.
Evening meal 7pm (l.o. 9.30pm).
Parking for 62.
Credit: Access, Visa, Diners, Amex.
⌕ ▰ ▱ ⌐ ▯ ⒰ ▮ ⓥ ⌐
▥ ▰ ⓣ & ♉ ✳ ⒟ SP ⌂
ⓣ

The Olde White Hart
35 Southgate St., Bury St. Edmunds, IP33 2AZ
☎ (0284) 755547
Tudor Grade II listed building with original beams and chimneys. Ideally located for exploring East Anglia. Close to town centre and local amenities.
Bedrooms: 4 single, 3 double & 2 twin, 2 family rooms.
Bathrooms: 11 private, 1 public.
Bed & breakfast: £38-£42 single, £48-£54 double.
Parking for 7.
Credit: Access, Visa, Amex.
⌕ ▰ ⌐ ▯ ⒰ ⓥ ⌐ ▥
▰ & ✕ ▥ ⌂

CAMBRIDGE
Cambridgeshire
Map ref 2D1

A most important and beautiful city on the River Cam with 31 colleges forming one of the oldest universities in the world. Numerous museums, good shopping centre, restaurants, theatres, cinema and fine bookshops.
Tourist Information Centre ☎ (0223) 322640

All Seasons Guest House
Listed
219-221 Chesterton Rd., Cambridge, CB4 1AN
☎ (0223) 353386
Detached Georgian house with large rear garden, within walking distance of the city centre.
Bedrooms: 3 single, 1 double & 2 twin, 3 family rooms.
Bathrooms: 3 public.
Bed & breakfast: £12.50-£13 single, £25-£36 double.
Half board: £17-£18 daily, £114-£121 weekly.
Evening meal 6pm (l.o. 2pm).
Parking for 4.
⌕ ▰ ▯ ⒰ ▮ ⓥ ▥ ▰ ✕
⒟

Antwerp Guest House
☖☖
36 Brookfields, Mill Rd., Cambridge, CB1 3NW
☎ (0223) 247690
On A1134 ring road between Addenbrookes Hospital and Cambridge Airport. Near the city's amenities, and bus and railway stations. Pleasant gardens.
Bedrooms: 2 double & 5 twin, 1 family room.
Bathrooms: 2 private, 2 public.
Bed & breakfast: £22-£27 single, £28-£35 double.
Half board: £20-£24 daily, £140-£168 weekly.
Lunch available.
Evening meal 6.30pm (l.o. 4pm).
Parking for 8.
⌕2 ▰ ▯ ⒰ ▮ ⓥ ▥ ▥
▰ ⓣ ✕ ⊠ SP

Arundel House Hotel M
☖☖☖ APPROVED
53 Chesterton Rd., Cambridge, CB4 3AN
☎ (0223) 67701
Friendly, privately-owned 19th C terraced hotel. Beautiful location overlooking the River Cam, near the city centre and colleges.
Bedrooms: 33 single, 23 double & 25 twin, 7 family rooms.
Bathrooms: 79 private, 8 public.
Bed & breakfast: £26.50-£47 single, £39.50-£65 double.
Lunch available.
Evening meal 6.30pm (l.o. 9.30pm).
Parking for 70.
Credit: Access, Visa, Diners, Amex.
⌕ ▰ ⌐ ▯ ⒰ ▮ ⓥ ✓
⌐ ● ▥ ▰ ⓣ ✕ SP

Ashley Hotel M
☖☖
74 Chesterton Rd., Cambridge, CB4 1ER
☎ (0223) 350059
Well appointed small hotel with modern facilities. Nearby Arundel House Hotel's facilities available to Ashley residents (under same ownership).
Bedrooms: 2 single, 3 double & 4 twin, 1 family room.
Bathrooms: 8 private, 1 public.
Bed & breakfast: £23 single, £41 double.
Parking for 16.
Credit: Access, Visa.
⌕ ▰ ▯ ⒰ ⒰ ▮ ⓥ
⌐ ● ▥ ▰ ✕ SP

Ashtrees Guest House
Listed APPROVED
128 Perne Rd., Cambridge, CB1 3RR
☎ (0223) 411233
Comfort and an enjoyable stay is our priority. Individually decorated rooms to a high standard. Home cooking. Parking facilities.
Bedrooms: 1 single, 2 double & 2 twin, 1 family room.
Bathrooms: 1 private, 2 public.
Bed & breakfast: £16-£17 single, £28-£33 double.
Half board: £20-£23 daily.
Evening meal 5pm (l.o. 8pm).
Parking for 5.
⌕ ▰ ▯ ⒰ ▮ ⓥ ✓ ⌐
ⓣ ● ▥ ▰ ✕

The symbols are explained on the flap inside the back cover.

Assisi Guest House

193 Cherry Hinton Rd.,
Cambridge, CB1 4BX
☎ (0223) 412900
Warm welcoming family-run guest house ideally situated for city. All modern facilities including private shower, toilet and TV.
Bedrooms: 6 single, 2 double, 2 family rooms.
Bathrooms: 7 private, 1 public.
Bed & breakfast: £16-£24 single, £32-£40 double.
Parking for 12.
Credit: Access, Visa, Amex.

Bon Accord House M

COMMENDED

20 St. Margarets Square,
Cambridge, CB1 4AP
☎ (0223) 246568 & 411188
Quietly but conveniently situated, south of the fascinating historic centre of Cambridge. Non-smokers only please.
Bedrooms: 7 single, 3 double & 1 twin, 1 family room.
Bathrooms: 1 private, 3 public.
Bed & breakfast: £18-£26 single, £30-£38 double.
Parking for 14.
Credit: Access, Visa.

Cambridgeshire Moat House M

COMMENDED

Bar Hill, Cambridge,
CB3 8EU
☎ Crafts Hill (0954) 780555
Telex 817141
Queens Moat Houses
Purpose built hotel with extensive conference, banqueting and leisure facilities, only 1 hour from London.
Bedrooms: 8 double & 92 twin.
Bathrooms: 100 private.
Bed & breakfast: from £70 single, from £87 double.
Evening meal 7pm (l.o. 10pm).
Parking for 200.
Credit: Access, Visa, C.Bl., Diners, Amex.

The National Crown Scheme is explained in full on pages 556 – 558.

Centennial Hotel M

63-71 Hills Rd., Cambridge,
CB2 1PG
☎ (0223) 314652
Telex 817019
Modernised family-run hotel opposite the botanical gardens. Central, near entertainment and colleges. Fully licensed bar and restaurant, parking.
Bedrooms: 7 single, 20 double & 12 twin, 2 family rooms.
Bathrooms: 41 private, 1 public.
Bed & breakfast: £47-£50 single, £60-£70 double.
Half board: £55.50-£60.50 daily, £388.50-£425.50 weekly.
Lunch available.
Evening meal 6.30pm (l.o. 9.30pm).
Parking for 32.
Credit: Access, Visa, Diners, Amex.

Dresden Villa Guest House

34 Cherry Hinton Rd.,
Cambridge, CB1 4AA
☎ (0223) 247539
Friendly family guesthouse near the railway station, within easy reach of the city centre. Free tea and coffee. TV in all rooms.
Bedrooms: 2 single, 3 double & 2 twin, 2 family rooms.
Bathrooms: 4 private, 2 public; 1 private shower.
Bed & breakfast: £18-£21 single, £32-£34 double.
Half board: £26-£29 daily, £182-£203 weekly.
Evening meal 7pm (l.o. 8pm).
Parking for 8.

Dykelands Guest House

157 Mowbray Rd.,
Cambridge, CB1 4SP
☎ (0223) 244300
Detached guesthouse offering modern accommodation. On south side of city centre, on a direct bus route.
Bedrooms: 1 single, 2 double & 2 twin, 3 family rooms.
Bathrooms: 3 private, 1 public; 2 private showers.
Bed & breakfast: £18.50-£22.50 single, £32-£36 double.
Half board: £23-£29.50 daily.
Evening meal 6pm (l.o. 7.30pm).
Parking for 7.

Garden House Hotel M

Granta Place, off Mill Lane,
Cambridge, CB2 1RT
☎ (0223) 63421 Telex 81463
Modern hotel in riverside gardens close to the city centre, shops, principal colleges, and museums.
Bedrooms: 28 double & 83 twin, 7 family rooms.
Bathrooms: 118 private.
Bed & breakfast: from £73 single, from £99 double.
Half board: from £91.50 daily, from £524.50 weekly.
Lunch available.
Evening meal 7pm (l.o. 9.30pm).
Parking for 180.
Credit: Access, Visa, Diners, Amex.

Hamilton Lodge Hotel

156 Chesterton Rd.,
Cambridge, CB4 1DA
☎ (0223) 65664
Recently refurbished private hotel less than 1 mile from city centre.
Bedrooms: 5 single, 4 double & 4 twin, 3 family rooms.
Bathrooms: 10 private, 1 public.
Bed & breakfast: £18-£25 single, £25-£40 double.
Half board: £28-£35 daily.
Evening meal 7pm (l.o. 9pm).
Parking for 12.

⊕ Display advertisement appears on page 363.

Kirkwood House

Listed COMMENDED

172 Chesterton Rd.,
Cambridge, CB4 1DA
☎ (0223) 313874
Edwardian family house which is maintained to a high standard. Close to river and city centre.
Bedrooms: 1 single, 2 double & 2 twin.
Bathrooms: 2 public.
Bed & breakfast: £16-£18 single, £30-£35 double.
Parking for 4.
Open February-December.

L'Aquila Guest House

12 Rock Rd., Off Cherry Hinton Rd., Cambridge,
CB1 4UF
☎ (0223) 245432

A comfortable family-run guesthouse. Convenient for the station and about 20 minutes' walk from the city centre. All rooms with private facilities.
Bedrooms: 1 double & 1 twin, 1 family room.
Bathrooms: 3 private.
Bed & breakfast: £30-£32 double.
Parking for 2.

Lensfield Hotel M

53 Lensfield Rd., Cambridge,
CB2 1EN
☎ (0223) 355017
Telex 818183
A family-run central hotel with ample parking.
Bedrooms: 7 single, 8 double & 7 twin, 2 family rooms.
Bathrooms: 17 private, 3 public; 5 private showers.
Bed & breakfast: £30-£40 single, £48-£52 double.
Half board: £35-£45 daily.
Evening meal 6.30pm (l.o. 9.30pm).
Parking for 6.
Credit: Access, Visa, Diners, Amex.

Number Eleven

Listed COMMENDED

11 Glisson Rd., Cambridge,
CB1 2HA
☎ (0223) 461142
Fine 14C university town house, close to the colleges and city centre. High standard accommodation at bed and breakfast prices.
Bedrooms: 4 double, 1 family room.
Bathrooms: 3 private, 1 public.
Bed & breakfast: £32-£35 single, £36-£40 double.

Quy Mill Hotel M

Newmarket Rd., Stow cum Quy, Cambridge, CB5 9AG
☎ (022 385) 3383
A friendly country house that has preserved its unique heritage and affords all modern facilities. 3 miles from Cambridge.
Bedrooms: 3 single, 14 double & 7 twin, 2 family rooms.
Bathrooms: 22 private, 4 public; 1 private shower.
Bed & breakfast: £69-£77 double.
Evening meal 7.30pm (l.o. 9pm).

Continued ▶

CAMBRIDGE
Continued

Parking for 50.
Credit: Access, Visa, Diners.

Regent Hotel

41 Regent St., Cambridge,
CB2 1AB
☎ (0223) 351470
Small family-run hotel offering personal service, in a convenient, central location.
Bedrooms: 6 single, 7 double & 4 twin, 2 family rooms.
Bathrooms: 15 private, 2 public; 1 private shower.
Bed & breakfast: £29-£45 single, £42.50-£58 double.
Parking for 2.
Credit: Access, Visa, Diners, Amex.

Rosswill Guest House
APPROVED

17-19 Chesterton Rd.,
Cambridge, CB4 3AL
☎ (0223) 67871
Overlooking Jesus Green and River Cam; within 10 minutes' walk of King's College and city centre.
Bedrooms: 4 single, 3 double & 3 twin, 3 family rooms.
Bathrooms: 4 private, 2 public; 1 private shower.
Bed & breakfast: £17-£19 single, £30-£37.50 double.
Parking for 11.

Six Steps Guest House
Listed

93 Tenison Rd., Cambridge,
CB1 2DJ
☎ (0223) 353968
Within 4 minutes' walking distance of the railway station, and half a mile from the city centre.
Bedrooms: 11 single, 3 double & 2 twin, 3 family rooms.
Bathrooms: 1 private, 1 public; 5 private showers.
Bed & breakfast: £18-£23 single, £32-£36 double.
Parking for 12.

University Arms Hotel M

Regent St., Cambridge,
CB2 1AD
☎ (0223) 351241
Telex 817311

De Vere
Quietly situated near city centre, this spacious, traditional hotel offers modern facilities.
Bedrooms: 32 single, 25 double & 53 twin, 7 family rooms.
Bathrooms: 117 private.
Bed & breakfast: from £70 single, from £90 double.
Lunch available.
Evening meal 7pm (l.o. 9.45pm).
Parking for 70.
Credit: Access, Visa, C.Bl., Diners, Amex.

CAMPSEA ASH
Suffolk
Map ref 3C2

2m E. Wickham Market

The Old Rectory M

Campsea Ash, Woodbridge,
IP13 0PU
☎ Wickham Market
(0728) 746524
Large, family country house in mature grounds offering comfortable accommodation with food and wine under the owner's supervision.
Bedrooms: 1 single, 3 double & 3 twin.
Bathrooms: 7 private.
Bed & breakfast: from £27 single, £43-£45 double.
Half board: £33.50-£39 daily.
Evening meal 7.50pm (l.o. 9.30pm).
Parking for 20.
Credit: Access, Visa, Diners, Amex.

CAWSTON
Norfolk
Map ref 3B1

4m SW. Aylsham
Village with one of the finest churches in the country. St. Agnes, built in the Perpendicular style, was much patronised by Michael de la Pole, Earl of Suffolk (1414), and has a magnificent hammer-beam roof and numerous carved angels.

Grey Gables Country House Hotel M

Norwich Rd., Cawston, Nr.
Norwich, NR10 4EY
☎ (0603) 871259

Former rectory in pleasant, rural setting, 10 miles from Norwich, coast and broads. Wine cellar, emphasis on food. Comfortably furnished with many antiques.
Bedrooms: 2 single, 3 double & 1 twin, 1 family room.
Bathrooms: 5 private, 1 public.
Bed & breakfast: £30-£42 single, £40-£52 double.
Half board: £27-£40 daily, £178-£203 weekly.
Evening meal 7pm (l.o. 9pm).
Parking for 15.
Credit: Access, Visa.

CHATTERIS
Cambridgeshire
Map ref 3A2

7m S. March

Cross Keys M
APPROVED

16 Market Hill, Chatteris,
PE16 6BA
☎ (035 43) 3036 & 2644
Elizabethan coaching inn built around 1540, Grade II listed. A la carte menu, bar meals available. Friendly atmosphere, oak-beamed lounge with open log fires.
Bedrooms: 1 double & 5 twin, 1 family room.
Bathrooms: 5 private, 1 public.
Bed & breakfast: £19.50-£32.50 single, £29.50-£42.50 double.
Lunch available.
Evening meal 7pm (l.o. 10pm).
Parking for 10.
Credit: Access, Visa, Diners, Amex.

North Bank House

84 High St., Chatteris,
PE16 6NM
☎ (035 43) 5782
200 year old Georgian house. 10 miles from Ely on main A142. Closed Christmas.
Bedrooms: 1 single, 2 twin, 1 family room.
Bathrooms: 1 public.
Bed & breakfast: £14-£16 single, £28 double.
Half board: £19 daily.
Evening meal (l.o. 10pm).
Parking for 8.

CHEDISTON
Suffolk
Map ref 3C2

3m W. Halesworth

Saskiavill M

Chediston, Halesworth,
IP19 0AR
☎ (0986) 873067
Travelling west from Halesworth on the B1123, turn right after 2 miles at the signpost for Chediston Green. After crossing the hump-backed bridge over the stream, we are the fourth property on the left.
Bedrooms: 2 double & 2 twin, 1 family room.
Bathrooms: 2 private, 2 public.
Bed & breakfast: £12-£14 single, £24-£28 double.
Half board: £15-£14 daily, £98-£112 weekly.
Evening meal 6.30pm.
Parking for 8.

CHELMSFORD
Essex
Map ref 3B3

The county town of Essex, originally a Roman settlement, Caesaromagus, thought to have been destroyed by Boudicca. Situated in the heart of heavily cultivated farmland and with an important livestock market. Growth of the town's industry can be traced in the excellent museum in Oaklands Park. 15th C parish church has been Chelmsford Cathedral since 1914.
Tourist Information Centre ☎ (0245) 283400

Beechcroft Private Hotel

211 New London Rd.,
Chelmsford, CM2 0AJ
☎ (0245) 352462
A central hotel offering clean and comfortable accommodation with friendly service. Under family ownership and management.
Bedrooms: 12 single, 3 double & 3 twin, 2 family rooms.
Bathrooms: 8 private, 5 public.

Bed & breakfast: £24.85-£32 single, £39.50-£51.50 double.
Parking for 15.
Credit: Access, Visa.

Boswell House Hotel
₩₩₩
118 Springfield Rd.,
Chelmsford, CM2 6LF
☎ (0245) 287587
Victorian town house in central location, offering high-standard accommodation in friendly, informal surroundings. Homely atmosphere and home cooking.
Bedrooms: 5 single, 6 double, 2 family rooms.
Bathrooms: 13 private.
Bed & breakfast: £32-£38 single, £45-£51 double.
Half board: £40-£46 daily, £210-£320 weekly.
Lunch available.
Evening meal 7pm (l.o. 8.30pm).
Parking for 15.
Credit: Access, Visa, Diners, Amex.

The Chelmer Hotel
2-4 Hamlet Rd., Chelmsford, CM2 0EU
☎ (0245) 353360 & 261751
Friendly and homely atmosphere, with home cooking.
Bedrooms: 2 single, 2 double & 5 twin, 2 family rooms.
Bathrooms: 2 public.
Bed & breakfast: £16.50-£18 single, £30-£32 double.
Half board: £21.50-£23 daily, £150.50-£161 weekly.
Evening meal 6.30pm (l.o. 6.30pm).
Parking for 2.

Miami Motel ₩
₩₩₩₩
Princes Rd., Chelmsford, CM2 9AJ
☎ (0245) 264848 & 269603
Telex 995430
Family-run hotel, 1 mile from town centre.
Bedrooms: 28 single, 14 double & 8 twin.
Bathrooms: 50 private.
Bed & breakfast: £35-£60 single, £47-£75 double.
Half board: from £44 daily, from £275 weekly.
Lunch available.
Evening meal 6.30pm (l.o. 10pm).
Parking for 80.
Credit: Access, Visa, Diners, Amex.

South Lodge Hotel ₩
₩₩₩₩
196 New London Rd.,
Chelmsford, CM2 0AR
☎ (0245) 264564 Telex 99452
Pleasantly situated hotel with garden. Convenient for A12 to East Coast or London. Close to town centre and cricket ground.
Bedrooms: 21 single, 17 double, 3 family rooms.
Bathrooms: 41 private.
Bed & breakfast: £45-£60 single, £55-£75 double.
Half board: £55-£80 daily.
Lunch available.
Evening meal 6.30pm (l.o. 9.30pm).
Parking for 45.
Credit: Access, Visa, Diners, Amex.

CLACTON-ON-SEA
Essex
Map ref 3B3

Developed in the 1870s into a popular holiday resort with pier, pavilion, funfair, theatres and traditional amusements. The Martello Towers on the seafront were built like many others in the early 19th C to defend Britain against Napoleon.
Tourist Information Centre ☎ (0255) 423400

Chelsea House Christian Hotel ₩
₩₩
Collingwood Rd., Marine Parade West, Clacton-on-Sea, CO15 1UL
☎ (0255) 424018
This Christian hotel specialises in friendliness, fellowship and food. Many rooms have a sea view. Indoor swimming pool and spa pool.
Bedrooms: 10 single, 9 double & 9 twin, 3 family rooms.
Bathrooms: 16 private, 5 public.
Bed & breakfast: £17.50-£21.50 single, £35-£43 double.
Half board: £23.50-£31.25 daily, £129.65-£195.30 weekly.
Lunch available.
Evening meal 6pm (l.o. 7pm).
Parking for 8.
Open February-December.
Credit: Access, Visa.

Chudleigh Hotel
₩₩₩
Agate Rd., Marine Parade West, Clacton-on-Sea, CO15 1RA
☎ (0255) 425407
Licensed private hotel with resident proprietors, offering forecourt parking, only 200 metres from the central seafront gardens, near to the pier and main shops. Closed Christmas and the New Year.
Bedrooms: 3 single, 6 double & 1 twin, 2 family rooms.
Bathrooms: 9 private, 2 public.
Bed & breakfast: £20-£25 single, £38-£47 double.
Half board: £32.50-£35 daily, £170-£180 weekly.
Evening meal 6.15pm (l.o. 6.45pm).
Parking for 6.
Credit: Access, Visa, Amex.

CLARE
Suffolk
Map ref 3B2

7m NW. Sudbury
Attractive village with many of the houses displaying pargetting work and the site of a castle first mentioned in 1090. Clare Country Park occupies the site of the castle bailey and old railway station. Ancient House Museum in the 15th C priest's house contains local bygones.

Bell Hotel ₩
₩₩₩₩ COMMENDED
Market Hill, Clare, CO10 8NN
☎ (0787) 277741
Ⓡ Minotels
16th C posting house with beamed restaurant and wine bar. Within easy reach of ports. 60 miles from London.
Bedrooms: 2 single, 16 double & 3 twin, 2 family rooms.
Bathrooms: 20 private, 1 public.
Bed & breakfast: £32.50-£43.50 single, £55-£85 double.
Half board: £41.50-£56.50 daily.
Lunch available.
Evening meal 7pm (l.o. 9.30pm).
Parking for 16.
Credit: Access, Visa, Diners, Amex.

Seafarer Hotel
₩₩₩ COMMENDED
Nethergate St., Clare, CO10 8NP
☎ Sudbury (0787) 277449
Country hotel centrally situated in large village. 1 minute to country castle park, river walk, market place and shops.
Bedrooms: 1 single, 2 double & 2 twin.
Bathrooms: 3 private, 1 public.
Bed & breakfast: £31.95-£42.95 single, £43.95-£54.95 double.
Lunch available.
Evening meal 7pm (l.o. 10pm).
Parking for 8.
Credit: Access, Visa, Diners, Amex.

COLCHESTER
Essex
Map ref 3B2

Britain's oldest recorded town standing on the River Colne and famous for its oysters. Numerous historic buildings, ancient remains and museums. Plenty of parks and gardens, extensive shopping centre, theatre and zoo.
Tourist Information Centre ☎ (0206) 712920

King's Ford Park Hotel ₩
₩₩₩₩
Layer Rd., Colchester, CO2 0HS
☎ (0206) 34301
Telex 987562 G
Privately-owned 18th C manor house in 18 acres. Offering peace and tranquillity, yet within 2 miles of the town centre.
Bedrooms: 1 single, 8 double & 3 twin, 1 family room.
Bathrooms: 13 private, 1 public.
Bed & breakfast: £59-£63 single, £75-£80 double.
Half board: £71-£75 daily.
Lunch available.
Evening meal 7pm (l.o. 9.30pm).
Parking for 100.
Credit: Access, Visa, Diners, Amex.

COLCHESTER
Continued

King's Vineyard
👑👑

Fossetts Lane, Fordham,
Colchester, CO6 3NY
☎ (0206) 240 377
*3.5-acre arable, sheep farm.
Modern, centrally-heated
farmhouse in peaceful, quiet
countryside. Breakfast served
in beautiful conservatory. Ideal
centre for relaxing, walking
and exploring beautiful
countryside. Within easy reach
of Cambridge, Harwich,
Felixstowe and London.*
Bedrooms: 2 double & 1 twin.
Bathrooms: 2 public.
Bed & breakfast: £14-£16
single, £26-£28 double.
Evening meal 6pm.
Parking for 6.

Peveril Hotel ₥
👑

51 North Hill, Colchester,
CO1 1PY
☎ (0206) 574001
*Friendly, family-run hotel with
fine restaurant and bar. All
rooms have colour TV, alarm
clock, tea and coffee facilities.*
Bedrooms: 6 single, 5 double
& 4 twin, 2 family rooms.
Bathrooms: 3 public.
Bed & breakfast: £22-£25
single, £32-£38 double.
Half board: £27-£40 daily,
£189-£280 weekly.
Lunch available.
Evening meal 7pm (l.o.
10pm).
Parking for 4.
Credit: Access, Visa.

Scheregate Hotel ₥
👑

36 Osborne St., Colchester,
CO2 7DB
☎ (0206) 573034
*Interesting 15th C building,
centrally situated, providing
accommodation at moderate
prices.*
Bedrooms: 14 single, 11 twin,
1 family room.
Bathrooms: 1 private,
4 public.
Bed & breakfast: £14.50-
£15.50 single, £26-£40 double.
Half board: £78-£120 weekly.
Parking for 30.

Wellesley Court Private Hotel
Listed APPROVED

15 Wellesley Rd., Colchester,
CO3 3HE
☎ (0206) 766880
*Family-run hotel in a quiet cul-
de-sac. All rooms have colour
TV, tea and coffee making
facilities. Parking. 5 minutes'
walk to town centre.*
Bedrooms: 1 double & 9 twin,
3 family rooms.
Bathrooms: 3 private,
3 public.
Bed & breakfast: from £20
single, from £32 double.
Parking for 16.
Credit: Access, Visa.

Wivenhoe Park ₥
👑👑👑

Colchester, CO4 3SQ
☎ (0206) 863666
*Georgian mansion in 200 acres
of parkland on the outskirts of
Colchester.*
Bedrooms: 46 single, 9 double
& 13 twin.
Bathrooms: 40 private,
5 public.
Bed & breakfast: £28-£52.60
single, £59.90-£69.30 double.
Half board: £43.40-£68 daily.
Lunch available.
Evening meal 7pm (l.o. 9pm).
Parking for 80.
Credit: Access, Visa.

COLTISHALL
Norfolk
Map ref 3C1

*8m NE. Norwich
On the River Bure, with
an RAF station nearby.
The village is attractive
with many pleasant 18th
C brick houses.*

The Norfolk Mead Hotel ₥
👑👑👑

The Mead, Coltishall,
Norwich, NR12 7DN
☎ Norwich (0603) 737531
*Beautiful Georgian country
house set in 12 acres. Long
river frontage with private
moorings and slipway. Fishing
lake and outdoor swimming
pool.*
Bedrooms: 8 double, 2 family
rooms.
Bathrooms: 10 private.
Bed & breakfast: £45-£55
single, £60-£75 double.
Half board: £40-£65 daily,
£265-£365 weekly.
Evening meal 7pm (l.o. 9pm).

Parking for 50.
Credit: Access, Visa, Diners,
Amex.

CROMER
Norfolk
Map ref 3B1

*Once a small fishing
village and now famous
for its fishing boats that
still work off the beach
and offer freshly caught
crabs. A delightful resort
with excellent bathing on
sandy beaches fringed by
cliffs. The narrow streets
of old Cromer encircle the
church of SS. Peter and
Paul which has a splendid
tower. The town boasts a
fine pier, theatre, museum
and a lifeboat station.*

Abbeville
Cabbell Rd., Cromer,
NR27 9HU
☎ (0263) 514467
Telex 667047
*Cromer is well known for its
clean, sandy beaches and fresh
sea air. An ideal centre for the
family.*
Bedrooms: 9 single, 12 twin,
12 family rooms.
Bathrooms: 9 public.
Half board: £23.50-£25 daily,
£163-£177 weekly.
Lunch available.
Evening meal 7pm.
Open April-October.

Anglia Court Hotel ₥
👑👑

Seafront, 5 Runton Rd.,
Cromer, NR27 9AR
☎ (0263) 512443 &
(0263) 512273
*Seafront position with sea
views and close to all
amenities. Some bedrooms
have TV. Cromer crabs on
restaurant menu when in
season.*
Bedrooms: 8 single, 8 double
& 8 twin, 5 family rooms.
Bathrooms: 15 private,
5 public.
Bed & breakfast: from £23.50
single, from £47 double.
Half board: from £35 daily,
from £223 weekly.
Lunch available.
Evening meal 7pm (l.o.
8.45pm).
Parking for 22.
Credit: Access, Visa, Diners,
Amex.

The Bath House
👑👑👑

The Promenade, Cromer,
NR27 9HE
☎ (0263) 514260
*Enjoy a stay at this fine old
Regency inn, situated right on
the promenade only paces from
the beach.*
Bedrooms: 1 single, 3 double
& 3 twin.
Bathrooms: 7 private.
Bed & breakfast: £23-£25.50
single, £43-£46 double.
Half board: £28-£29.50 daily,
£175-£185.50 weekly.
Lunch available.
Evening meal 6.30pm (l.o.
9pm).
Parking for 7.
Open March-December.
Credit: Access, Visa.

Church Barn Restaurant and Hotel
👑👑👑 COMMENDED

Church St., Northrepps, Nr.
Cromer, NR27 0LG
☎ Overstrand (026 378) 691
*Traditionally built of Norfolk
flint and dated 1854. In the
tranquil village of Northrepps,
2 miles from Cromer off A140.*
Bedrooms: 1 single, 3 double,
1 family room.
Bathrooms: 5 private.
Bed & breakfast: £28.75
single, £57.50 double.
Half board: £40.75 daily,
£170-£240 weekly.
Evening meal 7pm (l.o. 9pm).
Parking for 8.
Credit: Access, Visa.

Cliftonville Hotel ₥
👑👑

Runton Rd., Cromer,
NR27 9AS
☎ (0263) 512543
*Victorian hotel on the West
Cliff facing the sea and
gardens. Partially central
heated. Ideal for touring
historic north Norfolk and
Norfolk Broads.*
Bedrooms: 13 single,
12 double & 15 twin, 4 family
rooms.
Bathrooms: 21 private,
7 public; 1 private shower.
Bed & breakfast: £22.50-
£36.50 single, £43-£61 double.
Half board: £34-£48 daily,
£215.50-£316.25 weekly.
Lunch available.
Evening meal 7.15pm (l.o.
9pm).
Parking for 22.

Credit: Access, Visa, Diners,
Amex.

Hotel De Paris
Jetty Cliff, Cromer,
Nr27 9HG
☎ (0263) 513141
*Large hotel of historic and
architectural interest situated
overlooking pier and close to
shops.*
Bedrooms: 14 single,
16 double & 23 twin, 4 family
rooms.
Bathrooms: 45 private,
4 public.
Bed & breakfast: £15.50-
£27.50 single, £27-£51 double.
Half board: £22-£35 daily,
£115-£200 weekly.
Lunch available.
Evening meal 7pm (l.o.
7.30pm).
Parking for 12.
Open February-November.

CROSTWICK
Norfolk
Map ref 3C1

5m NE. Norwich

Old Rectory
North Walsham Rd.,
Crostwick, Norwich,
NR12 7BG
☎ (0603) 738513
*Old Victorian rectory set
among 2.5 acres of mature
trees. Well placed for the
broads and Norwich. Homely
accommodation.*
Bedrooms: 3 double &
10 twin.
Bathrooms: 13 private.
Bed & breakfast: £23-£25.30
single, £34.50-£36.80 double.
Half board: £29.90-£32.20
daily, £200-£215 weekly.
Evening meal 6.30pm (l.o.
1pm).
Parking for 15.

> **Half board prices
> shown are per
> person but in some
> cases may be based
> on double/twin
> occupancy.**

DEDHAM
Essex
Map ref 3B2

6m NE. Colchester
A former wool town.
Dedham Vale is an area
of outstanding natural
beauty and there is a
countryside centre in the
village. This is John
Constable country and Sir
Alfred Munnings lived at
Castle House which is
open to the public.

Maison Talbooth and Le Talbooth Restaurant M
Stratford Rd., Dedham,
Colchester, CO7 6HN
☎ Colchester (0206) 322367
Telex 987083 LETALB G
*A country house hotel
overlooking the beautiful Vale
of Dedham. Half a mile away
is an internationally renowned
restaurant on the banks of the
River Stour.*
Bedrooms: 8 double & 2 twin.
Bathrooms: 10 private.
Bed & breakfast: £80-£105
single, £100-£135 double.
Lunch available.
Evening meal 7pm (l.o. 9pm).
Parking for 20.
Credit: Access, Visa.

DEREHAM
Norfolk
Map ref 3B1

16m W. Norwich
East Dereham is famous
for its associations with
the poet William Cowper
and also Bishop Bonner,
chaplain to Cardinal
Wolsey. His home is now
an archaeological
museum. Round the
charming market-place
are many notable
buildings.

The King's Head Hotel M
Norwich St., East Dereham,
NR19 1AD
☎ (0362) 693842
*A modernised 17th C hotel
within easy reach of Norwich,
the coastal resorts and Norfolk
Broads.*
Bedrooms: 8 single, 4 double
& 2 twin, 1 family room.
Bathrooms: 12 private,
2 public.
Bed & breakfast: £32-£35
single, £45-£48 double.
Lunch available.

Evening meal 7pm (l.o.
9.30pm).
Parking for 22.
Credit: Access, Visa, Diners,
Amex.

Lynn Hill Guest House
APPROVED
Lynn Hill, Yaxham Rd.,
Dereham, NR19 1HA
☎ East Dereham
(0362) 696142
*Modern establishment situated
on approach road to East
Dereham, 400 yards from the
town centre, 300 yards from
the by-pass exit.*
Bedrooms: 2 single, 1 double
& 4 twin, 1 family room.
Bathrooms: 3 private,
2 public.
Bed & breakfast: £15-£20
single, £27-£36 double.
Half board: £22-£27 daily,
£140-£160 weekly.
Evening meal 6pm (l.o. 8pm).
Parking for 8.

DISS
Norfolk
Map ref 3B2

19m SW. Norwich
An old market town built
around 3 sides of the
Mere, a placid water of 6
acres and beside the
village green. Although
modernised, some
interesting Tudor,
Georgian and Victorian
buildings around the
market-place remain. St
Mary's Church has a fine
knapped flint chancel.

Highfields Lodge
Listed COMMENDED
Thorpe Abbotts, Diss,
IP21 4JA
☎ Hoxne (037 975) 691 &
444
*Situated in a delightful quiet
Norfolk hamlet half a mile off
A143 between Harleston and
Scole.*
Bedrooms: 1 single, 2 double
& 3 twin, 1 family room.
Bathrooms: 4 private,
2 public.
Bed & breakfast: £20-£25
single, £40-£50 double.
Half board: £28-£35 daily.
Evening meal 5pm (l.o. 7pm).
Parking for 10.

DOWNHAM MARKET
Norfolk
Map ref 3B1

10m S. King's Lynn
Market town above the
surrounding Fens on the
River Ouse. Oxburgh Hall
(National Trust) is 8 miles
east, a magnificent 15th C
moated dwelling owned
by one family, the
Bedingfields, for almost
500 years.

Castle Hotel M
High St., Downham Market,
PE38 9HF
☎ (0366) 384311
Telex 817787
*17th C coaching inn in centre
of town. Restaurant, bar,
lounge, conference rooms and
function room (max. 80
persons). Four poster room
with jacuzzi. Vegetarian menu
in restaurant.*
Bedrooms: 1 single, 5 double
& 5 twin.
Bathrooms: 9 private,
1 public.
Bed & breakfast: £27.50-£33
single, £35-£42 double.
Half board: £24-£27.50 daily,
£140-£164.50 weekly.
Lunch available.
Evening meal 5.30pm (l.o.
10pm).
Parking for 27.
Credit: Access, Visa, Diners,
Amex.

The Crown Hotel M
Bridge St., Downham
Market, PE38 9DH
☎ (0366) 382322
*17th C coaching inn under the
personal supervision of the
owners, offering English
cooking and real ale. Ample
car parking.*
Bedrooms: 1 single, 5 double
& 4 twin.
Bathrooms: 7 private,
2 public.
Bed & breakfast: £24-£32
single, £34-£42 double.
Lunch available.
Evening meal 6pm (l.o.
10pm).
Parking for 30.
Credit: Access, Visa, Diners,
Amex.

> **Please mention this
> guide when making
> a booking.**

ELY

Cambridgeshire
Map ref 3A2

14m NE. Cambridge
Until the 17th C when the
Fens were drained, Ely
was an island. The
cathedral, completed in
1189, dominates the
surrounding area. One
particular feature is the
central octagonal tower
with a fan-vaulted timber
roof and wooden lantern.
Also has a local history
museum and stained
glass museum.
*Tourist Information
Centre ☎ (0353) 662062*

Castle Lodge Hotel
50 New Barns Rd., Ely,
CB7 4PW
☎ (0353) 662276
*Family-run hotel, minutes'
walk from city centre and
cathedral. Friendly
atmosphere. Home cooking by
the proprietor.*
Bedrooms: 3 single, 4 double
& 4 twin, 1 family room.
Bathrooms: 3 private,
3 public.
Bed & breakfast: £17.50-£20
single, £35-£45 double.
Half board: £25-£27.50 daily,
£157.50-£173.50 weekly.
Lunch available.
Evening meal 7.30pm (l.o.
9pm).
Parking for 8.
Credit: Access, Visa.
⏚ ⌷ ▯ ♿ ▮ Ⓥ ⊟ ◉ ▦ ♨ ☎
SP

Lamb Hotel ♨
👑👑👑👑
2 Lynn Rd., Ely, CB7 4EJ
☎ (0353) 663574
Ⓒ Queens Moat Houses
*In the shadow of Ely
Cathedral, this hotel has been
used by travellers since the
16th C.*
Bedrooms: 9 single, 4 double
& 13 twin, 6 family rooms.
Bathrooms: 32 private.
Bed & breakfast: £52-£55
single, £68-£75 double.
Half board: £35-£37.50 daily.
Lunch available.
Evening meal 7pm (l.o.
10pm).
Parking for 24.
Credit: Access, Visa, Diners,
Amex.
⏚ ⌷ 📞 ▯ ♿ ▮ Ⓥ ▦
◉ ▦ ♨ ☎ ▶ ✓ OAP 🐾 SP
🎣 Ⓣ

Nyton Hotel ♨
👑👑👑 APPROVED
7 Barton Rd., Ely, CB7 4HZ
☎ (0353) 662459

*In a quiet, residential area
overlooking Fenland
countryside and adjoining golf-
course. Close to city centre and
cathedral.*
Bedrooms: 4 single, 4 double
& 3 twin, 2 family rooms.
Bathrooms: 13 private.
Bed & breakfast: £30-£35
single, £40-£45 double.
Half board: £32-£47 daily,
£210-£315 weekly.
Lunch available.
Evening meal 6.30pm (l.o.
9pm).
Parking for 25.
Credit: Access, Visa, Diners,
Amex.
⏚ ⌷ ▯ ♿ ▮ ▦ ▦ ♨
& ⛛ ▶ ✿ ✕

EPPING

Essex
Map ref 2D1

Epping retains its identity
as a small market town
despite its nearness to
London. Epping Forest
covers 2000 acres and at
Chingford Queen
Elizabeth I's Hunting
Lodge houses a display
on the forest's history
and wildlife.

Parsonage Farm House
👑👑
Abridge Rd., Theydon Bois,
Epping, CM16 7NN
☎ (037 881) 4242
*6-acre livery stables. 15th C
farmhouse with old English
gardens and livery yard. Exit
26 of M25 about 2 miles. 30
minutes from London by
underground.*
Bedrooms: 1 single, 1 double
& 3 twin, 1 family room.
Bathrooms: 2 private,
2 public.
Bed & breakfast: £25-£35
single, £35-£45 double.
Parking for 10.
⏚ ⛛ ♿ ✓ ⊟ ▦ ♨ ✿ ✕
🎣

Uplands ♨
Listed
181a Lindsey St., Epping,
CM16 6RF
☎ (0378) 73733
*Private house with rural views.
Close to M25, M11 for
Stansted Airport and Central
Line underground for London.
Pay phone available.*
Bedrooms: 2 single, 1 twin,
1 family room.
Bathrooms: 2 public.
Bed & breakfast: from £15
single, from £32 double.
Parking for 6.
⏚ ✗ ♿ ▯ ♿ ⓒⒷ ▦ ✕ 🎣

FELIXSTOWE

Suffolk
Map ref 3C2

11m SE. Ipswich
Seaside resort that
developed at the end of
the 19th C. Lying in a
gently curving bay with a
2-mile-long beach and
backed by a wide
promenade of lawns and
floral gardens. Ferry links
to the continent.
*Tourist Information
Centre ☎ (0394) 276770*

Fludyer Arms Hotel ♨
Listed
Undercliff Rd. East,
Felixstowe, IP11 7LU
☎ (0394) 283279
*Small family-run hotel on
beach road, with restaurant
and bar meals. Sea views from
all rooms. The hotel has 2 bars
and specialises in home-cooked
food.*
Bedrooms: 2 single, 2 double
& 3 twin, 2 family rooms.
Bathrooms: 4 private,
2 public.
Bed & breakfast: £20-£30
single, £32-£40 double.
Lunch available.
Evening meal 7pm (l.o. 9pm).
Parking for 14.
Credit: Access, Visa.
⏚ ⌷ ⛛ ▯ Ⓥ ✓ ⊟ ▦ ♨
🎣 ✕

Marlborough Hotel ♨
👑👑👑👑
Sea Front, Felixstowe,
IP11 8BJ
☎ (0394) 285621
Telex 987047 ANMAR G
*Recently modernised seafront
hotel offering comfort and
attentive service to the
holidaymaker and business
person.*
Bedrooms: 5 single, 20 double
& 21 twin, 1 family room.
Bathrooms: 47 private.
Bed & breakfast: £42.45-£52
single, £55-£65.50 double.
Half board: £38.45-£43.75
daily, £245-£280 weekly.
Lunch available.
Evening meal 7pm (l.o.
9.45pm).
Parking for 20.
Credit: Access, Visa, Diners,
Amex.
⏚ ♿ 📞 ▯ ⌷ ♿ ▮ Ⓥ ⊟
ⓉⓋ ◉ ▦ ▦ ♨ 🎣 ▶ OAP 🐾
SP Ⓣ

The Norfolk Hotel
1 & 3 Holland Rd.,
Felixstowe, IP11 8BA
☎ (0394) 283160

*Small family-owned hotel, 25
yards from the seafront.
Catering mainly for the over
50's.*
Bedrooms: 5 single, 3 double
& 3 twin, 1 family room.
Bathrooms: 2 public.
Bed & breakfast: £15-£16.50
single, £30-£33 double.
Half board: £22-£24 daily,
£110-£126 weekly.
Evening meal 6.30pm.
Open March-December.
⏚ ♿ ⛛ ▯ ▮ Ⓥ ⊟ ▦ ✕ 🎣
OAP 🐾 SP

Ranevale Guest House
Listed
96 Ranelagh Rd., Felixstowe,
IP11 7HU
☎ (0394) 270001
*Attractive detached Victorian
house close to town and
convenient for railway station
and ferry terminal. Close to
sea and A45.*
Bedrooms: 2 single, 1 twin,
2 family rooms.
Bathrooms: 2 public.
Bed & breakfast: £13-£15
single, £26-£30 double.
Parking for 8.
⏚ ♿ ⌷ ♿ ▮ ✗ ▦ ♨ SP

FRINTON-ON-SEA

Essex
Map ref 3C2

5m NE. Clacton-on-Sea
Sedate town that
developed as a resort at
the end of the 19th C and
still retains an air of
Victorian gentility. Fine
sandy beaches, good
fishing and golf.

Maplin Hotel ♨
👑👑👑
The Esplanade, Frinton-on-
Sea, CO13 9EL
☎ (0255) 673832
*Overlooking the famous
greensward and sea, a small
family hotel in a bow-
windowed building.*
Bedrooms: 2 single, 7 twin,
2 family rooms.
Bathrooms: 9 private,
1 public.
Bed & breakfast: from £35
single, £70-£82 double.
Half board: from £46.75
daily.
Lunch available.
Evening meal 7pm (l.o. 9pm).
Parking for 12.
Open February-December.
Credit: Access, Visa, Diners,
Amex.
📞 ▯ ▯ ⛛ ▮ Ⓥ ⊟ ⓉⓋ ▦
▦ ⚲ 🎣

Uplands Guest House
41 Hadleigh Rd., Frinton-on-Sea, CO13 9HQ
☎ (0255) 674889
Relax in a friendly atmosphere, with home cooking and personal service. En-suite facilites available, hot and cold water in all rooms, centrally heated. Lounge with colour TV and residents' bar. 3 minutes to sea, shops and Crescent Gardens. Ample car parking. Regret no children under 6 years.
Bedrooms: 3 single, 3 double & 1 twin, 1 family room.
Bathrooms: 4 private, 2 public.
Bed & breakfast: £17.50-£23 single, £35-£46 double.
Half board: £27.10-£32.60 daily, £110-£197.50 weekly.
Evening meal 6.30pm (l.o. 2.30pm).
Parking for 6.
Open February-December.
🌣6 🛉 🗒 ⊤⊽ 🏢 ✗ 🐴

GARBOLDISHAM
Norfolk
Map ref 3B2

7m W. Diss

Ingleneuk Lodge M
👑👑👑 APPROVED
Hopton Rd., Garboldisham, Diss, IP22 2RQ
☎ (095 381) 541
Modern bungalow in quiet wooded countryside. South facing patio and riverside walk. Central for touring. On B1111, 1 mile south of village.
Bedrooms: 3 single, 4 double & 2 twin, 2 family rooms.
Bathrooms: 10 private, 1 public.
Bed & breakfast: £18-£26 single, £29.50-£39.50 double.
Half board: £25.75-£30.75 daily, £166-£199 weekly.
Evening meal 6.30pm (l.o. 1pm).
Parking for 20.
Credit: Access, Visa.
🌣 🖐 📞 🗒 ⊽ ✂ 🖐 🏢
🖐 ♈ 🕹 ◡ ♪ 🌣 🐴 SP 🐴

GISLINGHAM
Suffolk
Map ref 3B2

The Old Guildhall M
👑👑👑
Mill St., Gislingham, Nr. Eye, IP23 8JT
☎ Mellis (037 983) 361

15th C Guildhall in attractive grounds, retaining many historic features. Tranquil Suffolk village within 5 miles of Diss.
Bedrooms: 1 double & 2 twin.
Bathrooms: 3 private.
Bed & breakfast: max. £37.50 single, max. £45 double.
Half board: £46-£53.50 daily, £130-£140 weekly.
Evening meal 7pm (l.o. 9pm).
Parking for 5.
Open February-December.
🌣 📞 🗒 🕯 🛉 🖐 🏢 ◀
🌣 🐴 🐴 SP 🐴

GISSING
Norfolk
Map ref 3B2

4m NE. Diss

The Old Rectory
👑👑
Gissing, Diss, IP22 3XB
☎ Tivetshall (037 977) 575
Elegant Victorian house in 3 acres, peaceful, comfortable, tastefully decorated and furnished. Every effort made to ensure a memorable stay.
Bedrooms: 1 double & 1 twin, 1 family room.
Bathrooms: 3 private.
Bed & breakfast: £30-£32 single, £40-£44 double.
Half board: £34-£36 daily.
Evening meal 7.45pm (l.o. 7.45pm).
Parking for 6.
🌣 📞 🗒 🖐 UL 🛉 ⊽ ✂ 🖐
⊤⊽ 🏢 ◀ 🖐 🌣 🐴 SP 🐴

GORLESTON-ON-SEA
Norfolk
Map ref 3C1

A well-frequented seaside resort separated from Great Yarmouth by the River Yare. The long, sandy beach is backed by cliffs and there is a pavilion and a swimming pool. Fishing and sailing are popular.

Jennis Lodge
63 Avondale Rd., Gorleston-on-Sea, Great Yarmouth, NR31 6DJ
☎ (0493) 662840
Family-run hotel, with tea making and TV in all rooms. 200 yards from beach. Home-cooked food. Children welcome.
Bedrooms: 2 single, 5 double, 4 family rooms.
Bathrooms: 2 public.
Bed & breakfast: £12-£16 single, £24-£32 double.

Half board: £17-£21 daily, £95-£115 weekly.
Evening meal 6pm (l.o. 6.30pm).
🌣 ⊙ 🗒 🕯 🛉 ⊽ 🖐 ⊤⊽
🐴 🐴 SP

Pier Hotel M
👑👑👑 APPROVED
Harbours Mouth, Gorleston-on-Sea, Great Yarmouth, NR31 6PL
☎ (0493) 662631
Hotel situated by the beach, ideal for either families or businessmen and well known for local fish dishes.
Bedrooms: 10 single, 7 double & 2 twin, 1 family room.
Bathrooms: 20 private.
Bed & breakfast: £35-£45 single, £60-£65 double.
Half board: £45.50-£55.50 daily, £270-£300 weekly.
Lunch available.
Evening meal 6.30pm (l.o. 9.30pm).
Parking for 20.
Credit: Access, Visa, Amex.
🌣 📞 🗒 🖐 ⊽ 🖐 ◉ 🏢
◀ ♈ ◡ ♪ ▶ 🖐 🐴 SP

Squirrel's Nest
👑👑
71 Avondale Rd., Gorleston-on-Sea, Great Yarmouth, NR31 6DJ
☎ (0493) 662746
Friendly family hotel. Sea views from most rooms, 1 minute to sea and all amenities. From A12 straight on, leaving Texaco garage on left, past Station Hotel, next right, second left, end of the road.
Bedrooms: 1 single, 5 double & 2 twin, 1 family room.
Bathrooms: 9 private, 1 public.
Bed & breakfast: £15-£25 single, £30-£50 double.
Half board: £26-£32 daily, £160-£195 weekly.
Lunch available.
Evening meal 5.30pm (l.o. 9.30pm).
Parking for 5.
Credit: Access, Visa, Amex.
🌣 🖐 📞 🗒 🛉 ⊽ 🖐
⊤⊽ 🏢 ◀ 🖐 ♈ ◡ ♪ ▶ 🐴 SP
▶

White Lodge
Listed
5 Park Rd., Gorleston-on-Sea, Great Yarmouth, NR31 6EJ
☎ Great Yarmouth (0493) 661651
Family-run hotel giving friendly service. Adjacent to cliffs, bowling greens, tennis courts.

Bedrooms: 2 double, 6 family rooms.
Bathrooms: 2 public.
Bed & breakfast: £26-£30 double.
Evening meal 5.30pm (l.o. 5.30pm).
Parking for 2.
Open April-October.
🌣 🖐 UL 🛉 🖐 ⊤⊽ 🏢 ✗ 🐴

GRAYS
Essex
Map ref 3B3

Stifford Moat House
High Rd., North Stifford, Nr. Grays, RM16 1UE
☎ Grays Thurrock (0375) 390909 Telex 995126
🆑 Queens Moat Houses
An authentic Georgian house, set in 6 acres of gardens and featuring a Regency restaurant overlooking croquet lawns.
Bedrooms: 20 single, 12 double & 32 twin.
Bathrooms: 64 private.
Bed & breakfast: £42-£68 single, £58-£95 double.
Lunch available.
Evening meal 7pm (l.o. 9.40pm).
Parking for 80.
Credit: Access, Visa, Diners, Amex.
🌣 🖐 📞 ⊙ 🗒 🛉 ⊽ ◉
🏢 ◀ ♈ 🕹 ◡ 🌣 🖐 SP ⊤

GREAT BIRCHAM
Norfolk
Map ref 3B1

3m S. Docking

The King's Head Hotel M
👑👑
Great Bircham, King's Lynn, PE31 6RJ
☎ Syderstone (048 523) 265
Family-run country hotel with 3 bars, restaurant and beer garden. Near Sandringham estate and the coast.
Bedrooms: 2 double & 3 twin.
Bathrooms: 5 private.
Bed & breakfast: £38-£43 single, £48-£53 double.
Lunch available.
Evening meal 7pm (l.o. 10pm).
Parking for 80.
Credit: Access, Visa, Amex.
🌣 📞 🗒 🛉 🖐 ⊤⊽ 🏢 ◀ ♈
🌣 🐴 SP 🐴
🅐 Display advertisement appears on page 363.

Please check prices and other details at the time of booking.

GREAT DUNMOW

Essex
Map ref 3B2

9m E. Bishop's Stortford
On the main Roman road from Bishop's Stortford to Braintree. The artist Sir George Beaumont, co-founder of the National Gallery, lived here. Doctor's Pond, near the square, was where the first lifeboat was tested in 1785. Home of the Dunmow Flitch trials held every 4 years on Whit Monday.
Tourist Information Centre ☎ *(0371) 4533*

Winston's Hotel
3-5 North St., Great Dunmow, CM6 1AZ
☎ (0371) 872576 & (0371) 872274
Owner-run hotel with a relaxed atmosphere for the travelling executive. Situated in the town centre, 4 miles from new Stansted Airport terminal.
Bedrooms: 9 single, 1 double & 1 twin.
Bathrooms: 11 private.
Bed & breakfast: £40-£50 single, £60-£65 double.
Parking for 9.
Credit: Access, Visa.
⌕ 🗂 ♻ ⇱ �📺 ▥ 🅿 🗲 ♨
👜 SP ⊞

GREAT RYBURGH

Norfolk
Map ref 3B1

3m SE. Fakenham

The Boar Inn ♨
Listed APPROVED
Great Ryburgh, Nr. Fakenham, NR21 0DX
☎ (032 878) 212
Village inn opposite Saxon church. Beamed dining room and bar with inglenook. Log fire in winter.
Bedrooms: 1 single, 1 double & 2 twin.
Bathrooms: 1 public.
Bed & breakfast: £22-£24 single, £34-£37 double.
Lunch available.
Evening meal 7pm (l.o. 9.30pm).
Parking for 20.
Credit: Access, Visa.
♨ 🗂 ♻ ♿ V ▥ 👜 🅿

The symbols are explained on the flap inside the back cover.

GREAT YARMOUTH

Norfolk
Map ref 3C1

One of Britain's major seaside resorts with 5 miles of seafront and every possible amenity including an award winning leisure complex offering a huge variety of all-weather sports and entertainment facilities. Busy harbour and fishing centre. Interesting area around the quay with a number of museums. Maritime museum on seafront, Sea Life Centre opened in summer 1990.
Tourist Information Centre ☎ *(0493) 846345 or (accommodation) 846344*

Burlington Hotel ♨
♔♔♔
North Drive, Great Yarmouth, NR30 1EG
☎ (0493) 844568
Views of the sea and sandy beach. Facilities include a pool, solarium, sauna and car park.
Bedrooms: 2 single, 4 double & 12 twin, 10 family rooms.
Bathrooms: 26 private, 1 public.
Bed & breakfast: £25-£50 single, £38-£60 double.
Half board: £28-£40 daily, £130-£220 weekly.
Lunch available.
Evening meal 6pm (l.o. 8pm).
Parking for 40.
Open February-December.
Credit: Access, Visa.
♨ ⌕ ⌨ ♻ ♿ ♨ V 🗲 ⇱
📺 🌣 👜 🏌 ♿ 🍴 ⊞ 🅱 ⇱
SP T

Charron House
Listed
151 Nelson Rd., Central, Great Yarmouth, NR30 2HZ
☎ (0493) 843177
Friendly, licensed guest house offering personal service, home cooking and warm welcome. Central for all amenities and entertainments.
Bedrooms: 1 single, 4 double & 1 twin, 3 family rooms.
Bathrooms: 6 private, 1 public.
Bed & breakfast: £14-£16 single, £28-£32 double.
Half board: £19.50-£21.50 daily, £90-£130 weekly.
Evening meal 5.15pm (l.o. 5.15pm).
♨ ⌣ ♻ ♿ V ⇱ 📺 ▥ 👜
🅳 SP

Kingsley House Hotel
68 King St., Great Yarmouth, NR30 2PP
☎ (0493) 850948

Concorde Private Hotel
84 North Denes Rd., Great Yarmouth, NR30 4LW
☎ (0493) 843709
Family-run private hotel in popular area. Clean and comfortable, friendly atmosphere. Licensed bar. Near beach and entertainment. Home-cooked food.
Bedrooms: 6 double & 3 twin, 5 family rooms.
Bathrooms: 1 private, 3 public; 2 private showers.
Bed & breakfast: £12-£15 single, £24-£30 double.
Half board: £15-£18 daily, £74-£97 weekly.
Evening meal 5.30pm (l.o. 3pm).
Parking for 6.
Open April-September.
♻4 🗂 ♻ ♿ V 🗲 ⇱ 📺 ▥
👜 🏌 ♿ 🅳 SP

Elmfield Private Hotel
38 Wellesley Rd., Great Yarmouth, NR30 1EU
☎ (0493) 859827
All bedrooms have televisions and tea making facilities. Most rooms are en-suite. Car parking. Close to all amentities and seafront.
Bedrooms: 7 double, 3 family rooms.
Bathrooms: 7 private.
Bed & breakfast: £16-£20 double.
Half board: £20-£25 daily, £105-£140 weekly.
Evening meal 5.30pm (l.o. 5.30pm).
Parking for 6.
Open April-October.
♻ 🗂 ♻ ⇱ 📺 ▥ 👜 🏌 ♨
▥ 🅳 SP

Hazelhurst Hotel
♔♔♔♔
7-9 Norfolk Square, Great Yarmouth, NR30 1EE
☎ (0493) 844431
Just north of Britannia pier overlooking Norfolk Square. Choice of menu. Own car park. Open all year.
Bedrooms: 8 single, 19 double & 5 twin, 4 family rooms.
Bathrooms: 28 private, 3 public.
Bed & breakfast: £23.50-£40 single, £40-£65 double.
Lunch available.
Evening meal 6pm (l.o. 9.30pm).
Parking for 30.
Credit: Access, Visa, Amex.
♻ ⌕ ⌨ 🗂 ♻ ♿ V ⇱ 📺
◑ ▥ 👜 🏌 🌣 ✕ ♨ SP T

Character hotel in central position.
Character hotel in central position. All bedrooms en-suite with colour TV and refreshments. Spacious dining room. Licensed lounge, unrestricted parking.
Bedrooms: 4 double & 2 twin, 1 family room.
Bathrooms: 7 private.
Bed & breakfast: £12 single, £24 double.
Half board: £16 daily, £110 weekly.
Evening meal 6pm (l.o. 7pm).
♻ 🗂 ♻ ♿ V 🗲 ⇱ 📺
👜 🏌 ✕ ♨ 🅳

Sienna Lodge Hotel
17-18 Camperdown, Great Yarmouth, NR30 3JB
☎ (0493) 843361
Attractive Regency corner house within 100 yards of seafront. All rooms en-suite with colour TV, tea/coffee facilities. Full central heating. Every comfort assured. Licensed bar lounge.
Bedrooms: 2 single, 5 double, 7 family rooms.
Bathrooms: 14 private.
Bed & breakfast: £19-£23 single, £38-£46 double.
Half board: £25-£30 daily, £126-£152 weekly.
Lunch available.
Evening meal 5.30pm (l.o. 7.30pm).
Open April-October.
♻ ♿ 🗂 ♻ ♿ V ⇱ 📺 ▥
👜 🏌 🅳 ♨ SP ⊞

Spindrift Private Hotel ♨
♔♔♔
36 Wellesley Rd., Great Yarmouth, NR30 1EU
☎ (0493) 858674
Attractively situated small private hotel, excellent sea views. Close to all amenities. Beach, coach station and car park at rear.
Bedrooms: 2 single, 3 double & 1 twin, 2 family rooms.
Bathrooms: 4 private, 1 public.
Bed & breakfast: £16-£21 single, £28-£38 double.
Half board: £20-£24 daily, £105-£120 weekly.
Evening meal 5.15pm (l.o. 1pm).
♻3 🗂 ♻ 📺 ▥ 👜 ✕ ♨ 🅳

Hotel Victoria
Kings Rd., Great Yarmouth, NR30 3JW
☎ (0493) 843872
Family-run hotel, standing in its own grounds. 50 yards from the seafront in a quiet locality, but close to all amenities.
Bedrooms: 1 single, 19 double & 4 twin, 20 family rooms.

Bathrooms: 25 private,
4 public.
Bed & breakfast: £18-£21.50
single, £36-£40 double.
Half board: £28-£31.50 daily,
£115-£161 weekly.
Evening meal 5pm (l.o. 6pm).
Parking for 26.
Open March-November.

Windyshore Hotel

29 North Drive, Great
Yarmouth, NR30 4EW
☎ (0493) 844145
*A small detached hotel
standing in its own grounds
with front and side sea-views,
with a large free car park.*
Bedrooms: 2 single, 15 double
& 2 twin, 6 family rooms.
Bathrooms: 23 private,
1 public.
Bed & breakfast: £21.25-£25
single, £40-£48 double.
Half board: £25-£30 daily,
£168-£175 weekly.
Evening meal 6pm (l.o.
6.30pm).
Parking for 25.
Open April-October.

HADLEIGH

Suffolk
Map ref 3B2

*8m W. Ipswich
Former wool town, lying
on a tributary of the River
Stour. The church of St.
Mary stands among a
remarkable cluster of
medieval buildings.
Tourist Information
Centre ☎ (0473) 822922*

Edgehill Hotel M
COMMENDED

2 High St., Hadleigh,
IP7 5AP
☎ (0473) 822458
*Small privately owned hotel
with comfortable
accommodation. Ideal for
touring Constable country and
the east coast.*
Bedrooms: 2 single, 3 double
& 2 twin, 2 family rooms.
Bathrooms: 8 private,
1 public; 1 private shower.
Bed & breakfast: £22-£49.50
single, £33-£66 double.
Half board: £31-£60.50 daily,
£186-£363 weekly.
Lunch available.
Evening meal 7pm (l.o. 8pm).
Parking for 14.

Gables Hotel M
COMMENDED

Angel St., Hadleigh, IP7 5EY
☎ (0473) 827169
*A 15th C timbered hall
residence in historic market
town, recently converted to
private hotel offering all
modern amenities.*
Bedrooms: 1 single, 2 double
& 1 twin.
Bathrooms: 2 private,
2 public.
Bed & breakfast: £20-£36
single, £34-£56 double.
Half board: £38-£54 daily,
£246-£342 weekly.
Evening meal 7pm (l.o. 2pm).
Parking for 6.

HALSTEAD

Essex
Map ref 3B2

6m NE. Braintree

The Dog Inn

37 Hedingham Rd., Halstead,
CO9 2DB
☎ (0787) 477774
*Traditional inn with timbered
bar and open fires. A free
house serving traditional ales
and home-cooked meals.
Situated on A604.*
Bedrooms: 1 double & 1 twin,
1 family room.
Bathrooms: 1 public.
Bed & breakfast: £20 single,
£35 double.
Half board: £25 daily.
Lunch available.
Evening meal 7pm (l.o.
10pm).
Parking for 12.

HAPPISBURGH

Norfolk
Map ref 3C1

*6m E. North Walsham
This coastal village,
pronounced
'Hazeborough', has a red
and white striped
lighthouse built in 1791
that has helped save
many lives. The church
tower of St. Mary's is
over 100 ft high.*

Lighthouse Farm Hotel
and Restaurant

Whempstead St., Happisburgh,
NR12 0QD
☎ Walcott (0692) 650474

*Small hotel, restaurant and
freehouse situated on the coast
road between Great Yarmouth
and Cromer. Quarter of a mile
from the beach.*
Bedrooms: 1 single, 2 double,
2 family rooms.
Bathrooms: 2 public.
Bed & breakfast: £15-£17
single, £25-£30 double.
Lunch available.
Evening meal 8pm (l.o.
10pm).
Parking for 15.
Credit: Access, Visa.

HARLOW

Essex
Map ref 2D1

Although one of the New
Towns, it was planned so
that it could develop
alongside the existing old
town. It has a museum of
local history and a Nature
Reserve with nature trails
and study centre.

Churchgate Manor
Hotel M

Churchgate St., Old Harlow,
Harlow, CM17 0JT
☎ (0279) 20246 Telex 818289
CR Best Western
*Spacious hotel in secluded
grounds with large indoor
leisure complex and swimming
pool. Close to M11, M25 and
Stansted Airport. 16th C
restaurant and bars. Extensive
conference facilities available
for up to 200 persons. Special
value weekend breaks
available.*
Bedrooms: 22 single,
24 double & 24 twin,
15 family rooms.
Bathrooms: 85 private.
Bed & breakfast: £55-£85
single, £65-£95 double.
Lunch available.
Evening meal 7pm (l.o.
9.45pm).
Parking for 120.
Credit: Access, Visa, Diners,
Amex.

Harlow Moat House M

Southern Way, Harlow,
CM18 7BA
☎ (0279) 22441 Telex 81658
CR Queens Moat Houses
*Modern 120-bedroomed hotel
with comprehensive conference
facilities. Ideally located for
business people, travellers and
tourists.*

Bedrooms: 30 double &
90 twin.
Bathrooms: 120 private.
Bed & breakfast: £40-£80
single, £55-£90 double.
Lunch available.
Evening meal 7pm (l.o.
10pm).
Parking for 180.
Credit: Access, Visa, Diners,
Amex.

HARWICH

Essex
Map ref 3C2

*16m E. Colchester
A port where the Rivers
Orwell and Stour
converge and enter the
North Sea. The old town
still has a medieval
atmosphere with its
narrow streets. To the
south is the seaside
resort of Dovercourt with
long sandy beaches.
Tourist Information
Centre ☎ (0255) 506139*

The Captain Fryatt
Hotel and Restaurant

65 Garland Rd., Parkeston,
Harwich, CO12 4PA
☎ (0255) 503535
*Victorian building, convenient
for continental shipping routes
to Europe and Scandinavia.*
Bedrooms: 2 single, 1 double
& 3 twin, 2 family rooms.
Bed & breakfast: from £15
single, from £30 double.
Half board: £17.50-£25 daily,
from £95 weekly.
Lunch available.
Evening meal 6pm (l.o.
9.30pm).
Parking for 7.

Cliff Hotel M

Marine Parade, Dovercourt,
Harwich, CO12 3RE
☎ (0255) 503345 & 507373
Telex 987372
*Family-run hotel overlooking
the sea. A jacuzzi is installed.*
Bedrooms: 4 single, 8 double
& 12 twin, 5 family rooms.
Bathrooms: 28 private,
2 public; 1 private shower.
Bed & breakfast: from £40
single, from £50 double.
Lunch available.
Evening meal 6.30pm (l.o.
8.45pm).
Parking for 60.
Credit: Access, Visa, C.Bl.,
Diners, Amex.

HARWICH
Continued

The Pier at Harwich M
⛉⛉

The Quay, Harwich,
CO12 3HH
☎ (0255) 241212
*Victorian building, situated on
the quayside in old Harwich,
overlooking the twin estuaries
of the Stour and Orwell rivers.*
Bedrooms: 6 double.
Bathrooms: 6 private.
Bed & breakfast: £40-£55
single, £55-£65 double.
Lunch available.
Evening meal 6pm (l.o.
9.30pm).
Parking for 10.
Credit: Access, Visa.

HATFIELD HEATH
Essex
Map ref 2D1

Down Hall Country
House Hotel M
⛉⛉⛉⛉

Hatfield Heath, Bishop's
Stortford, Hertfordshire
CM22 7AS
☎ (0279) 731441 Telex 81609
DOWNHL G
*Victorian country mansion set
in 22 acres of grounds.
Extensively renovated and
restored. Leisure facilities in
grounds.*
Bedrooms: 16 single,
62 double & 25 twin.
Bathrooms: 103 private.
Bed & breakfast: £80.50-£97
single, £104.50-£121 double.
Half board: £60-£70 daily.
Lunch available.
Evening meal 7pm (l.o.
9.30pm).
Parking for 250.
Credit: Access, Visa, Diners,
Amex.

HETHERSETT
Norfolk
Map ref 3B1

5m SW. Norwich

Park Farm Hotel M
⛉⛉⛉⛉ COMMENDED

Hethersett, Norwich,
NR9 3DL
☎ Norwich (0603) 810264
*A family-run hotel in idyllic
countryside south of Norwich,
off the A11.*

Bedrooms: 1 single, 25 double
& 7 twin, 4 family rooms.
Bathrooms: 37 private,
1 public.
Bed & breakfast: £52-£88
single, £65-£105 double.
Half board: from £41 daily.
Lunch available.
Evening meal 7pm (l.o. 9pm).
Parking for 81.
Credit: Access, Visa, C.Bl.,
Diners, Amex.

HEVINGHAM
Norfolk
Map ref 3B1

Marsham Arms Hotel M
⛉⛉⛉

Holt Rd., Hevingham,
Norwich, NR10 5NP
☎ (060 548) 268
*Old established free house and
restaurant with 8 new self-
contained study bedrooms. 5
miles from Norwich airport on
the B1149.*
Bedrooms: 1 double & 7 twin.
Bathrooms: 8 private.
Bed & breakfast: £30-£40
single, £42-£52 double.
Lunch available.
Evening meal 6pm (l.o.
10pm).
Parking for 100.
Credit: Access, Visa, Amex.

HOLT
Norfolk
Map ref 3B1

10m W. Cromer
Much of the town centre
was destroyed by fire in
1708 but has since been
restored. The famous
Gresham's School
founded by Sir Thomas
Gresham is sited here.

Lawns Hotel M
⛉⛉⛉ COMMENDED

Station Rd., Holt, NR25 6BS
☎ (0263) 713390
*Elegant Georgian hotel with
charming rooms. Family-run to
a high standard. Emphasis on
fine cuisine and hospitality.
Short stroll from the town.*
Bedrooms: 2 single, 5 double
& 2 twin, 2 family rooms.
Bathrooms: 9 private,
1 public.
Bed & breakfast: from £30
single, £50-£55 double.
Half board: £40-£50 daily,
£250-£275 weekly.

Lunch available.
Evening meal 7pm (l.o.
8.30pm).
Parking for 12.
Credit: Access, Visa, Amex.

HORSFORD
Norfolk
Map ref 3B1

5m NW. Norwich

Becklands
105 Holt Rd., Horsford,
Norwich, NR10 3AB
☎ (0603) 898582 & 898020
*Quietly located modern house
overlooking open countryside. 5
miles north of Norwich.
Central for the Broads and
coastal areas.*
Bedrooms: 7 single, 1 double
& 2 twin.
Bathrooms: 4 public.
Bed & breakfast: from £14
single, from £28 double.
Parking for 20.

HUNDON
Suffolk
Map ref 3B2

5m NE. Haverhill

The Plough Inn
Listed

Hundon, Sudbury,
CO10 8DT
☎ (044 086) 789
*Traditionally-styled country
inn with elevated situation,
cosy, beamed interior. Friendly
atmosphere and large gardens.
1.5 miles from Hundon village
on Kedington road, from south
best approached via Kedington
(off A143).*
Bedrooms: 1 double & 3 twin,
1 family room.
Bathrooms: 5 private.
Bed & breakfast: £32.50-
£42.50 single, £40-£54 double.
Lunch available.
Evening meal 7pm (l.o.
9.30pm).
Parking for 50.
Credit: Access, Visa.

HUNSTANTON
Norfolk
Map ref 3B1

14m NE. King's Lynn
Seaside resort which
faces the Wash. The
shingle and sand beach is
backed by striped cliffs
and many unusual fossils
can be found here. The
town, sometimes known
as Hunstanton St.
Edmund, is predominantly
Victorian. Sea Life Centre
on the southern
promenade and Oasis
family leisure centre with
indoor and outdoor pools.
*Tourist Information
Centre* ☎ (0485) 532610

Claremont Guest House
⛉⛉⛉ COMMENDED

35 Greevegate, Hunstanton,
PE36 6AF
☎ (048 53) 33171
*Spacious, comfortable family-
run guest house. Close to
beach, shops and gardens.
Wholesome food. Sea views.*
Bedrooms: 1 single, 3 double
& 2 twin, 1 family room.
Bathrooms: 7 private.
Bed & breakfast: £16-£20
single, £32-£40 double.
Half board: £23-£28 daily,
£156-£178 weekly.
Evening meal 6.30pm.
Parking for 3.
Credit: Visa.

Le Strange Arms
Hotel M
⛉⛉⛉

Golf Course Rd., Old
Hunstanton, Hunstanton,
PE36 6JJ
☎ (048 53) 34411
Telex 817403 LESTRA-G
ⒸⓇ Consort
*Fine country house by the sea.
Large grounds with own
private beach and lovely views
over the sea and coastline.*
Bedrooms: 2 single, 8 double
& 11 twin, 6 family rooms.
Bathrooms: 27 private.
Bed & breakfast: from £57.50
single, from £85 double.
Lunch available.
Evening meal 7pm (l.o. 9pm).
Parking for 100.
Credit: Access, Visa, Diners,
Amex.

**Half board prices shown are per person
but in some cases may be based on
double/twin occupancy.**

Linksway Hotel

Golf Course Rd., Old
Hunstanton, Hunstanton,
PE36 6JE
☎ (0485) 532209
*Well-appointed hotel in a quiet
location, overlooking golf-
course. Indoor heated
swimming pool and spa,
residents' lounge/bar.*
Bedrooms: 1 single, 3 double
& 9 twin, 2 family rooms.
Bathrooms: 15 private.
Bed & breakfast: £30 single,
£60 double.
Lunch available.
Evening meal 7pm (l.o. 3pm).
Parking for 20.
♨ ♿ 🄿 ♻ ♻ Ⓥ ⌀ 📺
🖵 ▣ 🔼 ❄ 🏇 ⚓ SP Ⓣ

Sutton House Hotel

24 Northgate, Hunstanton,
PE36 6AP
☎ (048 53) 2552
*Edwardian house close to the
town centre, beaches and all
local amenities. Specialising in
home cooking and old
fashioned hospitality.*
Bedrooms: 1 single, 1 double
& 2 twin, 3 family rooms.
Bathrooms: 5 private,
1 public.
Bed & breakfast: £17-£25
single, £34-£50 double.
Half board: £26-£34 daily,
£180-£235 weekly.
Lunch available.
Evening meal 6pm (l.o.
7.30pm).
Parking for 5.
Open February-December.
Credit: Access, Visa.
♨ ♿ 🖵 ♻ ⌀ Ⓥ ⌀ 📺 🖵 ▣
🏇 ⚓ SP

Wash & Tope Hotel

♚♚
Le Strange Terrace,
Hunstanton, PE36 5AJ
☎ (048 53) 2250
*A small family-run hotel facing
the sea. 2 bars open to non-
residents. A la carte
restaurant. Ideal for golfing
and birdwatching.*
Bedrooms: 1 single, 3 double
& 4 twin, 2 family rooms.
Bathrooms: 6 private,
2 public.
Bed & breakfast: £15-£20
single, £28-£45 double.
Lunch available.
Evening meal 7pm (l.o.
10pm).
Parking for 19.
Credit: Access, Visa, Amex.
♨ ♿ 🖵 ♻ ⌀ Ⓥ ▣ 🔼 ⚓

**Please mention this
guide when making
a booking.**

Cambridgeshire
Map ref 3A2

*15m NW. Cambridge
Attractive, interesting
town which abounds in
associations with the
Cromwell family. The
town is connected to
Godmanchester by a
beautiful 14th C bridge
over the great River
Ouse.
Tourist Information
Centre* ☎ *(0480) 425831*

Brecklyn Guest House

9 Euston St., Huntington,
PE18 6QR
☎ (0480) 455564
*Homely accommodation near
town centre, Cromwell's birth
place and other historic
buildings. Fishing, bowls, river
cruising, cathedrals at
Peterborough, Ely. 1 hour from
London. 3 rooms with hot and
cold water.*
Bedrooms: 2 single, 1 twin,
1 family room.
Bathrooms: 1 public.
Bed & breakfast: from £13
single, from £26 double.
♨ 5 ♻ Ⓤ ⌀ 📺 🖵 ⚓ 🔼 🏇

Sandwich Villas Guest House

Listed
16 George St., Huntington,
PE18 6BD
☎ (0480) 458484
*Comfortable, well-appointed
Victorian building with
spacious rooms. Close to all
local amenities.*
Bedrooms: 1 single, 1 double
& 1 twin, 1 family room.
Bathrooms: 1 private,
1 public.
Bed & breakfast: £16-£25
single, £30-£34 double.
Half board: £21-£30 daily,
£147-£210 weekly.
Evening meal 6pm (l.o.
midday).
Parking for 5.
♨ ♿ 🖵 ♻ Ⓤ 🔼 📺 🖵 ⚓
🏇 🄿 ▣

**Classifications
and quality
commendations
were correct at the
time of going to
press but are
subject to change.
Please check at the
time of booking.**

Suffolk
Map ref 3B2

Interesting county town
and major port on the
River Orwell. Birthplace
of Cardinal Wolsey.
Christchurch Mansion set
in a fine park contains a
good collection of
furniture and pictures,
with works by
Gainsborough, Constable
and Munnings.
*Tourist Information
Centre* ☎ *(0473) 258070*

Anglesea Hotel ♨

♚♚ APPROVED
10 Oban St., Ipswich,
IP1 3PH
☎ (0473) 255630
*Victorian house, now tastefully
refurbished as a small hotel in
quiet conservation area. Within
easy walking distance of town
centre. Evening meal by
arrangement.*
Bedrooms: 1 single, 3 twin,
3 family rooms.
Bathrooms: 7 private.
Bed & breakfast: £35-£38
single, £48-£50 double.
Half board: £42-£50 daily,
£225-£245 weekly.
Evening meal 6.30pm (l.o.
9pm).
Parking for 9.
Credit: Access, Visa, Amex.
🖵 ♻ ⌀ Ⓥ 🔼 🖵 ⚓ 🏇 ▣

Carlton Hotel ♨

♚♚
Berners St., Ipswich,
IP1 3LN
☎ (0473) 254955 & 211145
*Town centre hotel with a
friendly atmosphere, home
cooking and personal service.*
Bedrooms: 8 single, 6 double
& 5 twin, 1 family room.
Bathrooms: 16 private,
4 public.
Bed & breakfast: from £35
single, from £45 double.
Half board: from £43 daily.
Evening meal 6pm (l.o. 9pm).
Parking for 14.
Credit: Access, Visa, Amex.
♨ ♿ ♻ ♻ 🖵 ⌀ Ⓥ ✂ 🔼
📺 🖵 ⚓ ⚙ GAP SP Ⓣ
Ⓐ *Display advertisement
appears on page 363.*

Chequers Hotel

Listed
7-9 Ancaster Rd., Ipswich,
IP2 9AG
☎ (0473) 602385
*Family-run hotel, close to
Ipswich station. Ample
parking. Colour TV all rooms,
some private facilities
available. Licensed.*

Bedrooms: 7 single, 3 double
& 4 twin, 3 family rooms.
Bathrooms: 3 public;
2 private showers.
Bed & breakfast: £16-£28
single, £28-£45 double.
Half board: £21-£33 daily,
£145-£230 weekly.
Evening meal 7pm (l.o. 8pm).
Parking for 20.
♨ 🖵 ⌀ Ⓥ 🔼 🖵 ⚓ 🄿 🏇

Ipswich Moat House ♨

♚♚♚♚
London Rd., Copdock,
Ipswich, IP8 3JD
☎ Copdock (047 386) 444
Telex 987207
Ⓒ Queens Moat Houses
*Modern hotel, 3 miles south of
Ipswich, just off the A12,
offering conference and
banqueting facilities.*
Bedrooms: 1 single, 16 double
& 2 twin, 55 family rooms.
Bathrooms: 74 private.
Bed & breakfast: £70-£80
single, £80-£95 double.
Lunch available.
Evening meal 6.30pm (l.o.
9.30pm).
Parking for 400.
Credit: Access, Visa, Diners,
Amex.
♨ ♿ ♿ ♻ 🄿 🖵 ♻ ⌀ Ⓥ
⊙ 🖵 ⚓ 🄿 ♻ ♻ Ⓤ 🄿 ❄
♻ SP Ⓣ

The Marlborough at Ipswich

♚♚♚♚ COMMENDED
Henley Rd., Ipswich, IP1 3SP
☎ (0473) 257677
*Quietly situated hotel opposite
Christchurch Park and
Mansion. Victorian restaurant
overlooking floodlit gardens.
All rooms, including a suite
and several with balconies, are
individually decorated.*
Bedrooms: 6 single, 6 double
& 8 twin, 2 family rooms.
Bathrooms: 22 private.
Bed & breakfast: £63-£77
single, £85-£95 double.
Lunch available.
Evening meal 7.30pm (l.o.
7.30pm).
Parking for 60.
Credit: Access, Visa, C.Bl.,
Diners, Amex.
♨ ♿ ♿ ♻ ♻ ⌀ Ⓥ 🔼
⊙ 🖵 ⚓ 🄿 ♻ 🄿 SP Ⓣ

Novotel ♨

♚♚♚♚
Greyfriars Rd., Ipswich,
IP1 1UP
☎ (0473) 232400
Telex 987684
Ⓒ Novotel

Continued ▶

IPSWICH
Continued

Town centre situation, access from A12/A45. 2 minutes from mainline station. All bedrooms have king-size bed and couch, radio, TV. Conference facilities. Restaurant, bar. Free parking for 45 cars. Weekend breaks.
Bedrooms: 95 double, 6 family rooms.
Bathrooms: 101 private.
Bed & breakfast: £56-£66 single, £56-£72 double.
Lunch available.
Evening meal 6pm (l.o. 11.30pm).
Parking for 45.
Credit: Access, Visa, Diners, Amex.

Orwell Meadows ♠
APPROVED
Priory Lane, Nacton, Ipswich, IP10 0JS
☎ (0473) 726666
Large modern lodge set in a 30 acre leisure park. Ideally located off A45 for Ipswich, Felixstowe and Woodbridge.
Bedrooms: 1 twin, 1 family room.
Bathrooms: 1 public.
Bed & breakfast: max. £20 single, max. £35 double.
Parking for 8.

Queenscliffe House Hotel
Queenscliffe Rd., Ipswich, IP2 9AS
☎ (0473) 690293
Elegant Victorian house close to the station and town centre, in quiet wooded area, not on main road. 5 minutes from the A12 and A45.
Bedrooms: 4 single, 1 double & 3 twin, 2 family rooms.
Bathrooms: 8 private, 3 public; 1 private shower.
Bed & breakfast: £31-£35 single, max. £49 double.
Half board: max. £43.50 daily, £234-£258 weekly.
Evening meal 7pm (l.o. 8pm).
Parking for 12.
Credit: Access, Visa.

The Waverley Hotel
19 Willoughby Rd., Ipswich, IP2 8AW
☎ (0473) 601239

Friendly family-run licensed hotel. 100 yards from station, close to town centre. All rooms have TV and tea-making facilities. Evening meals available.
Bedrooms: 1 single, 2 double & 2 twin, 1 family room.
Bathrooms: 1 private, 1 public; 3 private showers.
Bed & breakfast: £22.50-£28 single, £34.50-£36 double.
Half board: £29-£34.50 daily.
Evening meal 7pm (l.o. 8pm).
Parking for 5.
Credit: Access, Visa.

KING'S LYNN
Norfolk
Map ref 3B1

Combines the attractions of a busy town, port and agricultural centre. Many outstanding buildings. The Guildhall and Town Hall are both built of flint in a striking chequer design. The Customs House was built in 1683.
Tourist Information Centre ☎ (0553) 763044

The Beeches
APPROVED
2 Guanock Terrace, King's Lynn, PE30 5QT
☎ (0553) 766577
Detached Victorian house, all rooms with TV, tea/coffee facilities and most en-suite. Full English breakfast and cooked evening meal.
Bedrooms: 1 single, 1 double & 4 twin, 3 family rooms.
Bathrooms: 4 private, 2 public.
Bed & breakfast: £17-£22 single, £24-£32 double.
Half board: £22-£26 daily, £125-£200 weekly.
Evening meal 6.30pm (l.o. 7.30pm).
Parking for 3.

Butterfly Hotel ♠
A10-147 Roundabout, Hardwick Narrows, King's Lynn, PE30 4NB
☎ (0553) 771707
Telex 818313
Modern building with rustic style and decor, around open central courtyard. Special weekend rates available.
Bedrooms: 25 single, 15 double & 10 twin.
Bathrooms: 50 private.
Bed & breakfast: £57-£60 single, £62-£65 double.

Half board: £41-£72 daily.
Lunch available.
Evening meal 7pm (l.o. 10pm).
Parking for 70.
Credit: Access, Visa, Diners, Amex.

Congham Hall Country House Hotel ♠
COMMENDED
Grimston, King's Lynn, PE32 1AH
☎ Hillington (0485) 600250
Telex 81508 CHOTEL
A Georgian manor house in 40 acres, with a restaurant serving English dishes. From King's Lynn on the A149 on to the A148 Fakenham road for 100 yards. Turn right to Grimston. The hotel is 2.5 miles further on, on the left hand side.
Bedrooms: 1 single, 4 double & 6 twin.
Bathrooms: 11 private, 1 public.
Bed & breakfast: £70-£110 single, £95-£165 double.
Lunch available.
Evening meal 7.30pm (l.o. 9.30pm).
Parking for 50.
Credit: Access, Visa, Diners, Amex.

Globe Hotel ♠
Tuesday Market Place, King's Lynn, PE30 1EZ
☎ (0553) 772617
The original Globe existed around 1645, although it was probably built long before. The adjacent Tuesday Market Place was once a venue for public hangings. Centrally located, near the River Ouse.
Bedrooms: 11 single, 10 double & 17 twin, 2 family rooms.
Bathrooms: 40 private.
Bed & breakfast: £42.50-£50.50 single, from £59.50 double.
Evening meal 6pm (l.o. 10.30pm).
Parking for 23.
Credit: Access, Visa, Diners, Amex.

Havana Guest House
117 Gaywood Rd., King's Lynn, PE30 2PU
☎ (0553) 772331

Charming Victorian family-run guesthouse. All rooms centrally heated with colour TV, washbasin and tea/coffee facilities. Ample private parking.
Bedrooms: 1 single, 2 double & 2 twin, 1 family room.
Bathrooms: 1 private, 1 public.
Bed & breakfast: £15 single, £24-£30 double.
Parking for 8.

Knights Hill Hotel ♠
Knights Hill Village, South Wootton, King's Lynn, PE30 3HQ
☎ (0553) 675566
Telex 818118 Knight G
Ⓖ Best Western
Sympathetically restored farm offering a choice of accommodation styles, 2 restaurants, a country pub and an extensive health club.
Bedrooms: 5 single, 40 double & 13 twin.
Bathrooms: 58 private.
Bed & breakfast: £61-£75 single, £78-£90 double.
Half board: from £59 daily, from £295 weekly.
Lunch available.
Evening meal 6pm (l.o. 10pm).
Parking for 300.
Credit: Access, Visa, Diners, Amex.

Maranatha Guest House ♠
115 Gaywood Rd., Gaywood, King's Lynn, PE30 2PU
☎ (0553) 774596
Large carrstone and brick licensed residence with gardens front and rear. 10 minutes' walk from the town centre. Direct road to Sandringham and the coast.
Bedrooms: 2 single, 2 double & 2 twin.
Bathrooms: 1 private, 2 public.
Bed & breakfast: from £12 single, from £20 double.
Half board: from £16 daily, from £112 weekly.
Evening meal 6pm (l.o. 6pm).
Parking for 6.

Stuart House Hotel ♠
Goodwins Rd., King's Lynn, PE30 5QX
☎ (0553) 772169 & 774788

Warm welcome and friendly atmosphere, coupled with home-cooked fresh food and convivial company in the cocktail bar, awaits your arrival for a relaxing stay.
Bedrooms: 5 single, 7 double & 7 twin, 2 family rooms.
Bathrooms: 17 private, 2 public; 1 private shower.
Bed & breakfast: £27.50-£40 single, £40-£55 double.
Half board: £36-£48.50 daily, £186.50-£238 weekly.
Evening meal 7pm (l.o. 8.30pm).
Parking for 26.
Credit: Access, Visa.
⛟ ♨ ☎ ⓑ ▢ ♥ ⓘ Ⓥ ⌁
Ⓣ ▦ ⬛ ⓢⓟ

The Tudor Rose ♨
👑👑👑👑

St. Nicholas St., Off Tuesday Market Place, King's Lynn, PE30 1LR
☎ (0553) 762824
Owner-run, friendly, historic town centre hotel. 15th C beamed restaurant offering local fish, seafood, steaks and game. Real ale bars.
Bedrooms: 5 single, 7 double & 2 twin.
Bathrooms: 11 private, 1 public.
Bed & breakfast: £19.95-£35 single, £45 double.
Half board: £27.50-£38.50 daily, £190-£270 weekly.
Lunch available.
Evening meal 6.30pm (l.o. 8.30pm).
Credit: Access, Visa, Diners, Amex.
♨ ☎ ⓑ ▢ ♥ ⓘ Ⓥ ⌁ ▦
⬛ ⓣ ☀ 🐾 ⓢⓟ ⓕ Ⓣ

LAVENHAM
Suffolk
Map ref 3B2

6m NE. Sudbury
A former prosperous wool town of timber-framed buildings with the cathedral-like church and its tall tower. The market-place is 13th C and the Guildhall now houses a museum.

Angel Inn
Market Place, Lavenham, CO10 9QZ
☎ (0787) 247388
Family run 15th C inn overlooking famous Guildhall. All rooms en-suite. Freshly-cooked local food and real ales.
Bedrooms: 3 double & 3 twin, 1 family room.
Bathrooms: 7 private.

Bed & breakfast: £30-£35 single, £50-£65 double.
Half board: £40-£45 daily, £200-£300 weekly.
Lunch available.
Evening meal 7pm (l.o. 10pm).
Parking for 5.
Credit: Access, Visa, C.Bl.
⛟ ♨ ▢ ♥ ⓘ Ⓥ ⌁ Ⓣ ▦
⬛ ⓣ ⛊ ☀ 🐾 ⓓⓐⓟ ⓢⓟ ⓕ

The Great House Restaurant and Hotel ♨
Listed

Market Place, Lavenham, CO10 9QZ
☎ Sudbury (0787) 247431
A famous and historic house with covered outside courtyard, dating from the 15th C. Quietly and ideally located, full of warmth and oak furniture for a relaxing stay. French gourmet cuisine.
Bedrooms: 4 family rooms.
Bathrooms: 4 private.
Bed & breakfast: £50-£60 single, £68-£90 double.
Half board: from £46.95 daily.
Lunch available.
Evening meal 7pm (l.o. 10.30pm).
Parking for 10.
Open February-December.
Credit: Access, Visa, Amex.
⛟ ☎ ⓑ ▢ ♥ ⓘ Ⓥ ⌁ Ⓣ
▦ ⬛ ⓣ ☀ 🐾 ⓢⓟ ⓕ Ⓣ

LEISTON
Suffolk
Map ref 3C2

4m E. Saxmundham
Busy industrial town near the coast. The abbey sited here in 1363 was for hundreds of years used as a farm until it was restored in 1918.

White Horse Hotel ♨
👑👑👑

Station Rd., Leiston, IP16 4HD
☎ (0728) 830694
18th C Georgian hotel with a relaxed and informal atmosphere, only 2 miles from the sea, in the heart of bird-watching country.
Bedrooms: 4 single, 5 double & 3 twin, 1 family room.
Bathrooms: 9 private, 3 public.
Bed & breakfast: £29.50-£33.50 single, £45-£52 double.
Lunch available.
Evening meal 7.30pm (l.o. 10pm).
Parking for 16.
Credit: Access, Visa.
⛟ ☎ ▢ ♥ ⓘ Ⓥ ⛊ ⌁ ▦
⬛ ⓣ ☀ 🐾 ⓓⓐⓟ ⓢ ⓢⓟ Ⓣ

LETHERINGSETT
Norfolk
Map ref 3B1

1m W. Holt
Glavenside Guest House ♨
Listed

Letheringsett, Holt, NR25 7AR
☎ Holt (0263) 713181
River Glaven flows through the grounds to the sea at Blakeney, 5 miles away. Rock and water gardens. Boating. Good base for many places of interest.
Bedrooms: 1 single, 3 double, 2 family rooms.
Bathrooms: 4 public.
Bed & breakfast: £13-£17 single, £26-£34 double.
Parking for 8.
⛟ 🐾 ⓤⓛ ⓒⓑ ⌁ ⌁ ▦ ⬛ ⓣ
◡ ♪ ☀ 🐾 ⓕ

LITTLE BARNEY
Norfolk
Map ref 3B1

The Old Brick Kilns ♨
👑👑👑 COMMENDED

Little Barney, Fakenham, NR21 ONL
☎ Thursford (0328) 878305
Converted cottages in rural setting. Turn right off 148 Fakenham/Holt road. 200 yards right to Barney, left into Little Barney, house at end of lane.
Bedrooms: 1 single, 1 double & 1 twin.
Bathrooms: 3 private.
Bed & breakfast: £17-£20 single, £34-£40 double.
Half board: £28-£31 daily, £184-£203 weekly.
Evening meal 6pm (l.o. 10am).
Parking for 8.
⛟ ▢ ♥ ⓘ Ⓥ ⌁ Ⓣ ▦
⬛ ⓣ ☀ 🐾 🐾 ▦

LODDON
Norfolk
Map ref 3C1

6m NW. Beccles
Small town on the River Chet. Round the square are some good buildings and the large church of Holy Trinity has many interesting contents. Close by is the 18th C Loddon House.

Stubbs House ♨
👑👑👑

Stubbs Green, Loddon, Norwich, NR14 6EA
☎ (0508) 20231

200-acre arable farm. Georgian farmhouse is now a pleasantly run hotel with personal service and within easy reach of East Anglia's major tourist attractions.
Bedrooms: 3 double & 5 twin, 1 family room.
Bathrooms: 3 private, 3 public.
Bed & breakfast: £18-£22 single, £36-£44 double.
Half board: £27.50-£31.50 daily, £150-£175 weekly.
Evening meal 6.30pm.
Parking for 20.
Open March-November.
Ⓥ ⌁ Ⓣ ▦ ☀ 🐾 ⓢⓟ

LONG MELFORD
Suffolk
Map ref 3B2

3m N. Sudbury
One of Suffolk's loveliest villages, remarkable for the length of its main street. Holy Trinity Church is considered to be the finest village church in England. The National Trust own the Elizabethan Melford Hall and nearby Kentwell Hall is also open to the public.

Black Lion Hotel ♨
👑👑👑

The Green, Long Melford, Sudbury, CO10 9DN
☎ (0787) 312356
A restored 17th C coaching inn overlooking the village green.
Bedrooms: 1 single, 6 double & 2 twin, 1 family room.
Bathrooms: 10 private.
Bed & breakfast: £45-£55 single, £60-£80 double.
Half board: £50-£65 daily, £300-£400 weekly.
Lunch available.
Evening meal 7pm (l.o. 9.30pm).
Parking for 8.
Credit: Access, Visa.
⛟ ☀ ☎ ⓑ ▢ ♥ ⓘ Ⓥ ⌁
▦ ⬛ ⓣ 🐾 ▦

Crown Inn Hotel ♨
👑👑👑

Hall Street, Long Melford, Sudbury, CO10 9JL
☎ Sudbury (0787) 77666
Family-run hotel in an historic village. Traditional English food, a range of bar snacks and 5 real ales available. Log fires in the winter.
Bedrooms: 1 single, 6 double & 4 twin.
Bathrooms: 11 private.
Bed & breakfast: max. £35 single, max. £45 double.
Lunch available.

Continued ▶

LONG MELFORD

Continued

Evening meal 7pm (l.o. 9.30pm).
Parking for 6.
Credit: Access, Visa, Diners, Amex.

➤ 🍴 ♠ Ⓒ Ⓥ ♨ Ⓙ Ⓥ
✉ 📷 ☕ 🍽 ♿ Ⓕ ✳ Ⓡ ♏
SP 🏠

LOWESTOFT

Suffolk
Map ref 3C1

Seaside town with wide sandy beaches. Important fishing port with picturesque fishing quarter and also the site of the first recorded lighthouse in England. Home of the famous Lowestoft porcelain and birthplace of Benjamin Britten. Several museums with a maritime flavour.
Tourist Information Centre ☎ *(0502) 523000*

Aarland House
36 Lyndhurst Rd., Lowestoft, NR32 4PD
☎ (0502) 585148
Large Victorian house. Limited number of bedrooms with hot and cold water and tea facilities in all. Carefree and relaxed with home-from-home atmosphere.
Bedrooms: 1 double & 1 twin, 3 family rooms.
Bathrooms: 3 public.
Bed & breakfast: £13.50-£18 single, £26-£35 double.

➤ Ⓒ Ⓥ ♨ Ⓙ Ⓤ ✂ Ⓕ Ⓥ Ⓣ ⌹
☕ ✳ ♿ DAP SP 🏠

Amity Guest House 𝖠
♟♟♟
396 London Rd. South, Lowestoft, NR33 0BQ
☎ (0502) 572586
Comfortable, friendly, family-run guesthouse, with home cooking. Close to beaches and park.
Bedrooms: 3 single, 3 double, 6 family rooms.
Bathrooms: 6 private, 3 public.
Bed & breakfast: from £16.50 single, from £30 double.
Half board: from £23.25 daily, from £130 weekly.
Evening meal 6pm (l.o. 1pm).
Parking for 6.
Credit: Access, Visa.

➤ 🍴 Ⓥ ♨ Ⓙ Ⓥ Ⓕ Ⓥ ⌹
☕ ♨

The Fair Havens Christian Guest House
♟♟
8 Wellington Esplanade, Lowestoft, NR33 0QQ
☎ (0502) 574927
Christian guesthouse offering warm fellowship and uninterrupted sea views. All home comforts. Full board on Sundays.
Bedrooms: 1 single, 1 twin, 3 family rooms.
Bathrooms: 2 public.
Bed & breakfast: £14 single, £28 double.
Half board: £18.50 daily, £115 weekly.
Evening meal 6pm (l.o. 8pm).
Parking for 4.

➤ 🍴 Ⓤ UL Ⓙ Ⓥ Ⓕ Ⓣ ⌹
✳ Ⓡ SP

Fairways Guest House 𝖠
♟♟♟ APPROVED
398 London Rd. South, Lowestoft, NR33 0BQ
☎ (0502) 572659
Spacious, well furnished and comfortable guest house with personal service. Easy access to Suffolk Heritage Coast.
Bedrooms: 2 single, 1 twin, 4 family rooms.
Bathrooms: 3 private, 2 public.
Bed & breakfast: £14-£20 single.
Half board: £19.50-£25.50 daily.
Lunch available.
Evening meal 6pm (l.o. 7.50pm).
Parking for 4.
Credit: Access, Visa.

➤ Ⓥ Ⓡ DAP ♿ SP

Foxlea House 𝖠
♟♟
298 London Rd. South, Lowestoft, NR33 0BG
☎ (0502) 569753
Owner-run, friendly guesthouse, boasting high standards of accommodation, service and food. Close to beach and shops.
Bedrooms: 2 single, 3 double & 1 twin.
Bathrooms: 2 private, 1 public.
Bed & breakfast: £14-£20 single, £28-£45 double.
Half board: £21-£26 daily, £145-£175 weekly.
Evening meal 6pm (l.o. 6.15pm).

➤ Ⓒ Ⓥ ♨ Ⓙ Ⓥ Ⓕ ⌹
✳ Ⓡ ♿ DAP ♿ SP Ⓣ

Rockville House 𝖠
♟♟♟
6 Pakefield Rd., Lowestoft, NR33 0HS
☎ (0502) 581011
Quietly situated in south Lowestoft near Suffolk Heritage Coast. Private beach hut. All bedrooms have colour TV. Lounge with open fire.
Bedrooms: 3 single, 3 double & 1 twin, 1 family room.
Bathrooms: 3 private, 2 public.
Bed & breakfast: £16.50-£29.50 single, £28.50-£38.50 double.
Half board: £22.25-£37.50 daily, £134.25-£233.50 weekly.
Evening meal 6pm (l.o. 1pm).
Credit: Access, Visa.

➤ Ⓒ Ⓥ ♨ Ⓙ Ⓥ Ⓕ Ⓥ ⌹
✳ DAP ♿ SP Ⓣ

MANNINGTREE

Essex
Map ref 3B2

8m NE. Colchester
On the estuary of the River Stour. The village has many interesting Georgian and Victorian buildings and the Strand attracts swans in great numbers.

The Crown, Trinity House
♟♟
High St., Manningtree, CO11 1AH
☎ (0206) 392620
Small riverside inn and guesthouse adjacent to Constable country, historic Colchester and Harwich for the continent. Excellent views over Stour Estuary and Suffolk countryside.
Bedrooms: 1 single, 1 double & 1 twin, 3 family rooms.
Bathrooms: 2 public; 1 private shower.
Bed & breakfast: £18-£20 single, £36-£40 double.
Half board: £24-£32 daily, £150-£200 weekly.
Lunch available.
Evening meal 6pm (l.o. 8.30pm).
Parking for 13.
Credit: Access, Visa.

➤ 🍴 Ⓥ ♨ Ⓙ Ⓥ Ⓕ Ⓥ ⌹
Ⓡ

The enquiry coupons at the back will help you when contacting proprietors.

MAXEY

Cambridgeshire
Map ref 3A1

7m NW. Peterborough

Abbey House
♟♟
West End Rd., Maxey, Nr. Peterborough, PE6 9EJ
☎ Market Deeping (0778) 344642
Close to historic Stamford. Ideal for touring the Eastern Shires with their abundance of abbeys, cathedrals, stately homes and attractive villages. Evening meal by arrangement.
Bedrooms: 2 single, 3 double & 3 twin.
Bathrooms: 5 private, 1 public.
Bed & breakfast: £16-£21.50 single, £28-£38 double.
Parking for 12.

➤6 Ⓒ Ⓥ ♨ UL Ⓙ Ⓕ Ⓣ ⌹
♪ ✳ ✳ Ⓡ 🏠

MILDENHALL

Suffolk
Map ref 3B2

8m NE. Newmarket
Town that has grown considerably in size in the last 20 years but still manages to retain a pleasant small country town centre. The church of St. Mary and St. Andrew is the largest in Suffolk and over the porch is the Pervis Chamber, which was also used as a schoolroom in the Middle Ages. Mildenhall and District museum deals with local history, particularly RAF Mildenhall and the Mildenhall Treasure.

Bell Hotel
♟♟♟
High St., Mildenhall, IP28 7EA
☎ (0638) 717272
Telex 94011647
A former 17th C coaching inn in a busy market town. Friendly atmosphere.
Bedrooms: 6 single, 4 double & 8 twin, 3 family rooms.
Bathrooms: 16 private, 2 public.
Bed & breakfast: £27.50-£48 single, £44-£60 double.
Half board: £38-£58 daily.
Lunch available.
Evening meal 7pm (l.o. 9pm).
Parking for 25.
Credit: Access, Visa, Diners, Amex.

➤ ♠ Ⓒ Ⓥ ♨ Ⓙ Ⓥ Ⓕ ①
⌹ ☕ 🍴 ♻ ♿ SP 🏠 Ⓣ

Riverside Hotel M

Mill St., Mildenhall,
IP28 7DP
☎ (0638) 717274
Best Western
Grade II Regency-style manor house in picturesque riverside setting. Newly refurbished to a high standard. Bridge weekends.
Bedrooms: 4 single, 8 double & 4 twin, 3 family rooms.
Bathrooms: 15 private, 2 public.
Bed & breakfast: £40-£44 single, £56-£70 double.
Lunch available.
Evening meal 6.30pm (l.o. 9pm).
Parking for 50.
Credit: Access, Visa, Diners, Amex.

Smoke House Inn M

Beck Row, Mildenhall,
IP28 8DH
☎ (0638) 713223
Listed Tudor/Georgian manor house with inglenook fireplaces and comfortable, well-equipped rooms. 2 bars, licensed restaurant, barbecue in season. Conference centre.
Bedrooms: 110 twin.
Bathrooms: 110 private.
Bed & breakfast: £55-£60 single, £75-£80 double.
Half board: £65-£70 daily, £360-£400 weekly.
Lunch available.
Evening meal 6pm (l.o. 10pm).
Parking for 200.
Credit: Access, Visa, Amex.

MORSTON

Norfolk
Map ref 3B1

1m W. Blakeney

Morston Hall

COMMENDED
Morston, Holt, NR25 7AA
☎ Cley (0263) 741041
A 17th C country house hotel with delightful gardens, 2 miles from Blakeney. Fine restaurant, fully licensed. Attractive bedrooms. Peaceful.
Bedrooms: 1 double & 2 twin.
Bathrooms: 3 private.
Bed & breakfast: £30-£40 single, £70-£85 double.
Half board: £50-£57 daily, £280-£325 weekly.
Lunch available.

Evening meal 7.30pm (l.o. 9pm).
Parking for 10.
Credit: Access, Visa, Amex.
Display advertisement appears on page 363.

MUNDESLEY-ON-SEA

Norfolk
Map ref 3C1

4m NE. North Walsham
Small seaside resort with a superb sandy beach and excellent bathing. Nearby is a smock-mill still with cap and sails.

Manor Hotel

Coast Rd., Mundesley-on-Sea, NR11 8BG
☎ (0263) 720309
Family-run Victorian hotel with a friendly atmosphere, on the north Norfolk coast.
Bedrooms: 4 single, 12 double & 12 twin, 2 family rooms.
Bathrooms: 25 private, 2 public.
Half board: £130-£170 weekly.
Lunch available.
Evening meal 7pm (l.o. 8.50pm).
Parking for 40.

NEWMARKET

Suffolk
Map ref 3B2

Centre of the English horse-racing world and the headquarters of the Jockey Club and National Stud. Racecourse and horse sales. The National Horse Racing Museum traces the history and development of the Sport of Kings.

Bedford Lodge Hotel M

Bury Rd., Newmarket, CB8 7BX
☎ (0638) 663175
Telex 975711
Best Western
Georgian hunting lodge in secluded gardens. 18 bedrooms with private bath or shower, restaurant and homely lounge bar.
Bedrooms: 11 double & 7 twin.
Bathrooms: 18 private.
Bed & breakfast: £50-£65 single, £65-£85 double.
Lunch available.

Evening meal 7pm (l.o. 9.30pm).
Parking for 65.
Credit: Access, Visa, Diners, Amex.

The Bell Inn

Bury Rd., Kennett, Newmarket, CB8 7PP
☎ (0638) 750286
15th C black-white beamed coaching inn. Accommodation in the pub and at adjoining Claremont Cottage. All rooms en-suite with TV. Evening meals.
Bedrooms: 1 single, 4 double, 2 family rooms.
Bathrooms: 7 private.
Bed & breakfast: from £21.50 single, from £27.50 double.
Lunch available.
Evening meal 6.30pm (l.o. 10pm).
Parking for 8.
Credit: Access, Visa.

Live and Let Live Guest House M

76 High St., Stetchworth, Newmarket, CB8 9TJ
☎ (063 876) 8153
Converted 18th C public house, in quiet village, close to famous Newmarket racecourse, extremely homely and welcoming accommodation. Double rooms can be converted to family rooms if required.
Bedrooms: 3 single, 2 double & 1 twin, 1 family room.
Bathrooms: 2 private, 1 public.
Bed & breakfast: £16-£24 single, £30-£37 double.
Half board: £23-£31 daily, £144-£192 weekly.
Parking for 5.

Newmarket Moat House M

Moulton Rd., Newmarket, CB8 8DY
☎ (0638) 667171
Queens Moat Houses
Hotel of high standards in a quiet central position. Ideal location for touring, horseracing, and local countryside.
Bedrooms: 18 single, 20 double & 7 twin, 2 family rooms.
Bathrooms: 47 private.
Bed & breakfast: £60-£66 single, £80-£90 double.

Lunch available.
Evening meal 7pm (l.o. 9.45pm).
Parking for 60.
Credit: Access, Visa, Diners, Amex.

NORFOLK BROADS

See Acle, Beccles, Coltishall, Crostwick, Gorleston-on-Sea, Great Yarmouth, Loddon, Lowestoft, North Walsham, Norwich, Oulton Broad, Rollesby.

NORTH WALSHAM

Norfolk
Map ref 3C1

14m N. Norwich
Weekly market has been held here for 700 years. 1 mile south of town is a cross commemorating the Peasants' Revolt of 1381. Nelson attended the local Paston Grammar School, founded in 1606 and still flourishing.

Beechwood Hotel M

COMMENDED
20 Cromer Rd., North Walsham, NR28 0HD
☎ (0692) 403231
In its own gardens with many roses, shrubs, large trees, extensive lawns and numerous rhododendrons.
Bedrooms: 1 single, 2 double & 3 twin, 5 family rooms.
Bathrooms: 7 private, 2 public.
Bed & breakfast: £19-£22 single, £38-£44 double.
Half board: £28-£31 daily, £135-£200 weekly.
Evening meal 7pm (l.o. 7.30pm).
Parking for 11.

Felmingham Hall M

Felmingham, North Walsham, NR28 0LP
☎ Swanton Abbot
(069 269) 631
16th C Elizabethan manor house in very rural and secluded setting. 1.5 miles south of Felmingham Village and between the market towns of Aylsham and North Walsham.
Bedrooms: 24 double & 32 twin, 1 family room.
Bathrooms: 57 private.

Continued ▶

NORTH WALSHAM
Continued

Bed & breakfast: £38.50-£48 single, £77-£95 double.
Half board: £53.50-£70 daily, £346.50-£441 weekly.
Lunch available.
Evening meal 7.30pm (l.o. 10pm).
Parking for 100.
Credit: Access, Visa, Amex.

NORWICH
Norfolk
Map ref 3C1

Beautiful cathedral city and county town on the River Wensum with many fine museums and medieval churches. Norman castle, Guildhall and interesting medieval streets. Good shopping centre and market.
Tourist Information Centre ☎ *(0603) 666071 or (after hours) 761082*

The Almond Tree Hotel and Restaurant M

441 Dereham Rd., Costessey, Norwich, NR5 0SG
☎ (0603) 748798 & 749114
On the main A47 Dereham Road at Costessey, the hotel is easily located. Convenient for the commercial and industrial estates and the picturesque county towns and villages of East Anglia.
Bedrooms: 1 double & 5 twin.
Bathrooms: 6 private.
Bed & breakfast: from £37 single, from £51 double.
Half board: from £50.95 daily.
Lunch available.
Evening meal 7pm (l.o. 9.45pm).
Parking for 22.
Credit: Access, Visa.

Norwich Ambassador Hotel, Norwich Airport M

Norwich Airport, Cromer Rd., Norwich, NR6 6JA
☎ (0603) 410544
Newly built hotel in quiet location 5 minutes from city centre, modern facilities including leisure area and landscaped gardens.
Bedrooms: 4 single, 80 double & 20 twin, 4 family rooms.

Bathrooms: 108 private.
Bed & breakfast: £45-£60 single, £60-£72.50 double.
Half board: £39-£45 daily.
Lunch available.
Evening meal 7pm (l.o. 10.30pm).
Parking for 320.
Credit: Access, Visa, C.Bl., Diners, Amex.

Beeches Hotel M
APPROVED
4-6 Earlham Rd., Norwich, NR2 3DB
☎ (0603) 621167
Welcoming hotel, set in large, wooded gardens. Tastefully restored to form an oasis in the historic heart of Norwich.
Bedrooms: 14 single, 10 double & 3 twin, 3 family rooms.
Bathrooms: 17 private, 2 public.
Bed & breakfast: £26-£40 single, £55-£65 double.
Half board: £34-£48 daily, £229-£327 weekly.
Evening meal 6pm (l.o. 7pm).
Parking for 30.
Credit: Access, Visa.

Hotel Belmonte and Belmonte Restaurant
60-62 Prince of Wales Rd., Norwich, NR1 1LT
☎ (0603) 622533
Accommodation with 100 seater restaurant and bar. Live music Friday and Saturday with nightclub open Thursday, Friday and Saturday nights.
Bedrooms: 3 single, 4 double & 2 twin.
Bathrooms: 9 private.
Bed & breakfast: £30-£35 single, £45-£50 double.
Lunch available.
Evening meal 7pm (l.o. 11pm).
Credit: Access, Visa, Amex.

Butterfield Hotel M
4 Stracey Rd., Norwich, NR1 1EZ
☎ (0603) 624041
Family hotel with friendly atmosphere. Close to city, railway and coach stations. Fully-licensed, bar and lounge. Rooms with private facilities and colour TV.
Bedrooms: 4 single, 3 double & 3 twin, 2 family rooms.

Bathrooms: 4 private, 2 public.
Bed & breakfast: £13-£15 single, £26-£30 double.
Half board: £19-£21 daily, £84-£98 weekly.
Evening meal 6pm (l.o. 7pm).

Conifers Hotel M
162 Dereham Rd., Norwich, NR2 3AH
☎ (0603) 628737
Yorkstone-clad Victorian house close to city centre and local amenities.
Bedrooms: 4 single, 1 double & 2 twin, 1 family room.
Bathrooms: 1 private, 3 public.
Bed & breakfast: £14.50-£16 single, £29-£32 double.
Parking for 4.

The Corner House
62 Earlham Rd., Norwich, NR2 3DF
☎ (0603) 627928
Large victorian house with friendly atmosphere, 10 minutes from city centre. Car parking. TV, coffee/tea facilities in all bedrooms, plus residents' lounge area.
Bedrooms: 3 double.
Bathrooms: 2 public; 1 private shower.
Bed & breakfast: £16-£20 single, £26-£30 double.
Parking for 4.

Crofters Hotel M
2 Earlham Rd., Norwich, NR2 3DA
☎ (0603) 613287 & 620169
Commercial and family hotel in own secluded grounds. Central location near main business and shopping area.
Bedrooms: 2 single, 4 double & 4 twin, 5 family rooms.
Bathrooms: 10 private, 1 public.
Bed & breakfast: £20-£28 single, £32-£40 double.
Half board: £23-£35 daily, £140-£224 weekly.
Evening meal 6pm (l.o. 7pm).
Parking for 30.

Cumberland Hotel M
212-216 Thorpe Rd., Norwich, NR1 1TJ
☎ (0603) 34550 & 34560

Close to city centre in elevated position with ample private parking. Family-run hotel offering personal and friendly service.
Bedrooms: 12 single, 9 double & 4 twin, 5 family rooms.
Bathrooms: 17 private, 3 public.
Bed & breakfast: £27-£36 single, £35-£43 double.
Half board: from £23 daily, £160-£190 weekly.
Lunch available.
Evening meal 6.30pm (l.o. 9.30pm).
Parking for 63.
Credit: Access, Visa, Amex.

Edmar Lodge
APPROVED
64 Earlham Rd., Norwich, NR2 3DF
☎ (0603) 615599
Comfortable accommodation with all facilities. English breakfast. 10 minutes' walk from city centre, car park, keys provided.
Bedrooms: 2 single, 1 double & 1 twin, 1 family room.
Bathrooms: 2 private, 1 public; 1 private shower.
Bed & breakfast: £15-£17 single, £25-£35 double.
Parking for 6.

Elm Farm Chalet Hotel M
APPROVED
St. Faiths, Norwich, NR10 3HH
☎ Norwich (0603) 898366
Accommodation in chalets and farmhouse, in rural surroundings 4 miles north of Norwich. Easily accessible for touring Norfolk and Suffolk.
Bedrooms: 8 single, 8 double & 8 twin, 1 family room.
Bathrooms: 23 private, 2 public.
Bed & breakfast: £25-£33 single, £42.35-£49.50 double.
Half board: £35-£43 daily, £238-£294 weekly.
Lunch available.
Evening meal 6.30pm (l.o. 8pm).
Parking for 20.
Credit: Access, Visa, Amex.

Friendly Hotel M
2 Barnard Rd., Bowthorpe, Norwich, NR5 9JB
☎ (0603) 741161
Telex 975557

354

A new hotel on the A47, 4 miles west of Norwich city centre. Function facilities for 4 to 260 people.
Bedrooms: 33 double & 33 twin, 14 family rooms.
Bathrooms: 80 private.
Bed & breakfast: £52-£62.50 single, £68.50-£73 double.
Half board: £45.75-£74 daily.
Lunch available.
Evening meal 6.30pm (l.o. 10pm).
Parking for 100.
Credit: Access, Visa, Diners, Amex.

Fuchsias Guest House

Listed **APPROVED**

139 Earlham Rd., Norwich, NR2 3RG
☎ (0603) 51410
A friendly family-run Victorian guest house, convenient for city centre and university. On good bus routes.
Bedrooms: 1 single, 2 double & 1 twin, 2 family rooms.
Bathrooms: 1 public.
Bed & breakfast: £14-£17 single, £28-£35 double.

The Georgian House Hotel M

APPROVED

32-34 Unthank Rd., Norwich, NR2 2RB
☎ (0603) 615655
Hotel comprises 2 old, connected Georgian houses, with an a la carte menu and a bar. 5 minutes' walk from the city centre.
Bedrooms: 6 single, 12 double & 7 twin, 2 family rooms.
Bathrooms: 27 private.
Bed & breakfast: £36.50 single, £53 double.
Half board: £32-£42 daily, £195-£262 weekly.
Evening meal 6.30pm (l.o. 7.30pm).
Parking for 40.
Credit: Access, Visa, Diners, Amex.

Georgian Hotel and Leisure Club

Listed **APPROVED**

Salhouse Rd., Rackheath, Norwich NR13 6LA
☎ (0603) 721092 Fax (0603) 765689
Leisure centre providing en-suite accommodation, food, bar, squash, snooker, swimming, gymnasium, solarium and sauna. Country setting within easy reach of the city centre.

Bedrooms: 1 single, 7 double & 3 twin, 1 family room.
Bathrooms: 12 private, 4 public.
Bed & breakfast: £25.50-£27.50 single, £32-£38 double.
Half board: £31-£36 daily, £160-£210 weekly.
Lunch available.
Evening meal 6pm (l.o. 9pm).
Parking for 74.
Credit: Access, Visa.

Linden House M

557 Earlham Rd., Norwich, NR4 7HW
☎ (0603) 51303
Lovely house, all new facilities, ample parking and attractive gardens. 5 minutes' walk from university. Frequent mini-bus from house to city centre and university.
Bedrooms: 1 double & 1 twin, 1 family room.
Bathrooms: 3 private.
Bed & breakfast: from £25 single, from £38 double.
Half board: £27-£33 daily, £128-£186 weekly.
Parking for 9.
Credit: Access, Visa.

Marlborough Hotel

22 Stracey Rd., Norwich, NR1 1EZ
☎ (0603) 628005
Small family-run hotel near shopping centre and station. 15 minutes from city centre. Full central heating, licensed bar. All bedrooms have colour TV, tea and coffee making facilities. Double and family rooms have en-suites. Car park available.
Bedrooms: 3 single, 3 double & 2 twin, 2 family rooms.
Bathrooms: 6 private, 1 public.
Bed & breakfast: £15-£25 single, £33-£43 double.
Half board: £22-£31 daily, £154-£217 weekly.
Lunch available.
Evening meal 5.30pm (l.o. 4.30pm).
Parking for 8.

Hotel Nelson M

COMMENDED

Prince of Wales Rd., Norwich, NR1 1DX
☎ (0603) 760260
Telex 975203
CR Best Western

Modern, purpose-built hotel on the riverside close to the railway station and city centre. Easy access to the broads and coast.
Bedrooms: 26 single, 45 double & 50 twin.
Bathrooms: 121 private.
Bed & breakfast: £68.50-£72.50 single, £78.50-£82.50 double.
Lunch available.
Evening meal 6.45pm (l.o. 9.45pm).
Parking for 128.
Credit: Access, Visa, Diners, Amex.

Hotel Norwich M

COMMENDED

121-131 Boundary Rd., Norwich, NR3 2BA
☎ (0603) 787260
Telex 975337
CR Best Western
Modern, purpose-built hotel on the ring road, providing easy access to the airport, railway station, city centre, broads and coast.
Bedrooms: 17 single, 18 double & 50 twin, 17 family rooms.
Bathrooms: 102 private.
Bed & breakfast: from £57 single, £67-£70 double.
Half board: from £35 daily.
Lunch available.
Evening meal 7pm (l.o. 10pm).
Parking for 221.
Credit: Access, Visa, Diners, Amex.

Norwich Sport Village M

COMMENDED

Drayton High Rd., Hellesdon, Norwich, NR6 5DU
☎ (0603) 788898
Telex 975550
Situated on outer Norwich Ring Road on the A1067. Providing sports facilities, including tennis, squash, badminton, snooker, health centre, sauna, gymnasium, spa pool. On a pay and play basis. No membership.
Bedrooms: 54 twin, 2 family rooms.
Bathrooms: 56 private.
Bed & breakfast: £35-£55 single, £54-£84 double.
Evening meal 7pm (l.o. 9.30pm).
Parking for 1200.
Credit: Access, Visa, Diners, Amex.

The Old Rectory

COMMENDED

103 Yarmouth Rd., Norwich, NR7 0HF
☎ (0603) 39357
Fine Georgian family residence, offering tranquil setting overlooking the Yare Valley.
Bedrooms: 3 double & 2 twin.
Bathrooms: 5 private.
Bed & breakfast: £47.20-£51.70 single, £69.10-£78.10 double.
Lunch available.
Evening meal 6pm (l.o. 10pm).
Parking for 12.
Credit: Access, Visa, Amex.

Riverside Hotel

11-12 Riverside Rd., Norwich, NR1 1SQ
☎ (0603) 623978
Overlooking River Wensum, 2 minutes from main station, 5 minutes from cathedral and city centre. Warm welcome assured. Dutch, German and Italian spoken.
Bedrooms: 6 single, 6 double & 2 twin, 2 family rooms.
Bathrooms: 4 private, 3 public.
Bed & breakfast: £22.50-£30 single, £35-£45 double.
Parking for 7.
Credit: Access, Visa, Amex.

Shambles Guest House

55 Caernarvon Rd., Norwich, NR2 3HZ
☎ (0603) 610704
Large 19th C house. Use of garden. 5 minutes from city centre, just off Earlham road. Evening meal available on request.
Bedrooms: 3 single, 2 double & 1 twin, 2 family rooms.
Bathrooms: 1 private, 3 public; 1 private shower.
Bed & breakfast: £12-£15 single, £24-£30 double.
Half board: £17-£22 daily, £110-£125 weekly.
Evening meal 5pm (l.o. 7pm).
Parking for 2.

Station Hotel M

5-7 Riverside Rd., Norwich, NR1 1SQ
☎ (0603) 622556 & 611064
Continued ▶

EAST ANGLIA

NORWICH
Continued

Candlelit restaurant, fresh food and friendly staff. Facing the yacht station, 1 minute from railway station, 5 minutes from city centre and shops. Closed Christmas week.
Bedrooms: 6 single, 7 double & 7 twin.
Bathrooms: 13 private, 2 public.
Bed & breakfast: £24-£40 single, £40-£45 double.
Lunch available.
Evening meal 6pm (l.o. 9.30pm).
Parking for 12.
Credit: Access, Visa.

Wedgewood House ♨

42 St. Stephens Rd., Norwich, NR1 3RE
☎ (0603) 625730
Friendly accommodation. Close to coach station. Walking distance to shops and places of interest.
Bedrooms: 2 single, 4 double & 3 twin, 2 family rooms.
Bathrooms: 8 private, 1 public.
Bed & breakfast: £15-£16.50 single, £30-£36 double.
Half board: from £22.50 daily.
Evening meal 6.30pm (l.o. 7.30pm).
Parking for 7.
Credit: Access, Visa.

OULTON BROAD
Suffolk
Map ref 3C1

2m NW. Lowestoft
Oulton Broad is the most southerly of the Broads and is the centre of a very busy boating industry.

Parkhill Hotel

Parkhill, Oulton, Nr. Lowestoft, NR32 5DQ
☎ Lowestoft (0502) 730322
Telex 975391
Peaceful wooded grounds with gardens and lawns. The hotel offers a friendly and homely atmosphere.
Bedrooms: 8 single, 10 double.
Bathrooms: 18 private.
Bed & breakfast: £25-£48 single, £35-£58 double.
Half board: £30-£68 daily, £300-£400 weekly.
Lunch available.

Evening meal 7pm (l.o. 9.30pm).
Parking for 152.
Credit: Access, Visa, Amex.

PETERBOROUGH
Cambridgeshire
Map ref 3A1

Prosperous and rapidly expanding cathedral city on the edge of the Fens on the River Nene. Catherine of Aragon is buried in the cathedral. City Museum and Art Gallery. Ferry Meadows Country Park has numerous leisure facilities.
Tourist Information Centre ☎ (0733) 317336

Aaron Park Hotel and Lancaster House

109 & 112 Park Rd., Peterborough, PE1 2TR
☎ (0733) 64849
Family owned and run, just 5 minutes' walk from the Queensgate shopping centre.
Bedrooms: 9 single, 3 double & 3 twin, 2 family rooms.
Bathrooms: 4 private, 3 public; 4 private showers.
Bed & breakfast: £23-£40 single, £38-£52 double.
Half board: £29-£46 daily.
Evening meal 6.30pm (l.o. 7pm).
Parking for 15.
Credit: Access, Visa.

The Bell Inn

Great North Rd., Stilton, Peterborough, PE7 3RA
☎ (0733) 241066
Old coaching inn, restored to include a hotel, conference and banqueting facilities. Off A1, just south of Norman Cross roundabout.
Bedrooms: 2 single, 14 double & 2 twin, 1 family room.
Bathrooms: 19 private.
Bed & breakfast: £55-£60 single, £70-£75 double.
Lunch available.
Evening meal 7pm (l.o. 9.30pm).
Parking for 30.
Credit: Access, Visa, Amex.

Butterfly Hotel ♨

Thorpe Meadows, Off Longthorpe Parkway, Peterborough, PE3 6GA
☎ (0733) 64240 Telex 818360

Situated by water's edge at Thorpe Meadows, this modern hotel maintains all the traditional values of design and comfort. Whether travelling for business or pleasure you will find at the Butterfly a "home from home". Special weekend rates available.
Bedrooms: 33 single, 18 double & 15 twin, 4 family rooms.
Bathrooms: 70 private.
Bed & breakfast: £57-£60 single, £62-£65 double.
Lunch available.
Evening meal 7pm (l.o. 10pm).
Parking for 80.
Credit: Access, Visa, Diners, Amex.

Chesterton Priory
♨♨♨ COMMENDED

Chesterton, Peterborough, PE7 3UB
☎ (0733) 230085
Fine Victorian country house in 2 acres of secluded grounds. Close to the A1, East of England Showground and Peterborough Business Park.
Bedrooms: 1 single, 3 double & 2 twin.
Bathrooms: 6 private.
Bed & breakfast: £35-£45 single, £50-£70 double.
Half board: £45-£60 daily, £275-£350 weekly.
Evening meal 6pm (l.o. 9pm).
Parking for 20.

Dalwhinnie Lodge Hotel
♨♨ APPROVED

31-35 Burghley Rd., Peterborough, PE1 2QA
☎ (0733) 65968
Licensed family-run hotel with home cooking. 5 minutes from city centre, bus and train station. High standard maintained and a warm welcome always guaranteed.
Bedrooms: 7 single, 5 double & 5 twin.
Bathrooms: 2 private, 3 public; 4 private showers.
Bed & breakfast: £19.50-£22.50 single.
Evening meal 6pm (l.o. 6.30pm).
Parking for 15.
Credit: Visa.

The Lodge Hotel

130 Lincoln Rd., Peterborough, PE1 2NR
☎ (0733) 341489

Friendly licensed hotel and restaurant offering good facilities. Within easy walking distance of city centre, bus and railway stations.
Bedrooms: 5 single, 3 double & 2 twin, 1 family room.
Bathrooms: 9 private, 1 public.
Bed & breakfast: £43-£48 single, £54-£60 double.
Lunch available.
Evening meal 6pm (l.o. 9.30pm).
Parking for 9.
Credit: Access, Visa.

Peterborough Moat House ♨

Thorpe Wood, Peterborough, PE3 6SG
☎ (0733) 260000 Telex 32708
Queens Moat Houses
Modern hotel 1.5 miles from the city and adjacent to a golf-course. Features large banqueting facilities, a restaurant, bars and bar snacks.
Bedrooms: 29 double & 92 twin, 4 family rooms.
Bathrooms: 125 private.
Bed & breakfast: £50-£75 single, £60-£90 double.
Half board: £65-£81 daily.
Lunch available.
Evening meal 7pm (l.o. 10pm).
Parking for 220.
Credit: Access, Visa, Diners, Amex.

Swallow Hotel ♨

Lynch Wood, Peterborough Business Park, Peterborough, PE2 0GB
☎ (0733) 371111 Telex 32422
Swallow G
Swallow
This new hotel is within a minute of A1/A605 junction on the edge of Nene Country Park. In picturesque village of Alwalton. Large leisure complex.
Bedrooms: 2 single, 116 double & 38 twin, 7 family rooms.
Bathrooms: 163 private.
Bed & breakfast: max. £74 single, max. £92 double.
Half board: max. £88 daily.
Lunch available.
Evening meal (l.o. 10.30pm).
Parking for 250.

Credit: Access, Visa, Diners, Amex.

[symbols]

ROLLESBY

Norfolk
Map ref 3C1

7m NW. Great Yarmouth
Rollesby Broad forms
part of the Ormesby
Broad complex and fine
views can be seen from
the road which runs
through the middle.

The Old Court House M
COMMENDED
Court Rd., Rollesby, Great
Yarmouth, NR29 5HG
☎ Fleggburgh (0493) 369665
*Small family-run hotel set in a
peaceful rural location near the
Broads. 7 bedrooms, most en-
suite. Private bar and
swimming pool. Bicycles for
hire, tennis and fishing nearby.
Home cooking.*
Bedrooms: 2 double & 1 twin,
4 family rooms.
Bathrooms: 5 private,
2 public.
Bed & breakfast: £32-£37
double.
Half board: £23-£25.50 daily,
£145-£160 weekly.
Evening meal 6.30pm (l.o.
6.30pm).
Parking for 20.
Open February-November.

[symbols]

SAFFRON WALDEN

Essex
Map ref 2D1

12m N. Bishop's Stortford
Takes its name from the
saffron crocus once
grown around the town.
The church of St. Mary is
most impressive with
large, superb carvings,
magnificent roofs and
brasses. A town maze
can be seen on the
common. 2 miles south-
west is Audley End, a
magnificent Jacobean
mansion owned by
English Heritage.
*Tourist Information
Centre* ☎ *(0799) 24282*

Queens Head Inn
Littlebury, Saffron Walden,
CB11 4TD
☎ (0799) 22251

*Friendly, family-run free house
and hotel close to Audley End.
All rooms en-suite. Recently
refurbished. TV in all rooms.
Lunch available.*
Bedrooms: 2 single, 2 double
& 1 twin, 1 family room.
Bathrooms: 6 private.
Bed & breakfast: £39 single,
£49 double.
Half board: £34.50-£54.50
daily, £105-£265 weekly.
Lunch available.
Evening meal 7pm (l.o. 9pm).
Parking for 30.
Credit: Access, Visa.

[symbols]

ST IVES

Cambridgeshire
Map ref 3A2

5m E. Huntingdon
Picturesque market town
with a narrow 6-arched
bridge spanning the River
Ouse on which stands a
bridge chapel. There are
numerous Georgian and
Victorian buildings and
the Norris Museum has a
good local collection.

The Dolphin Hotel M
Bridgefoot, London Rd., St.
Ives, PE17 4EP
☎ (0480) 66966
*Hotel featuring carvery and
extensive a la carte menu.
Attractive riverside location
near to town centre.*
Bedrooms: 4 double &
16 twin, 2 family rooms.
Bathrooms: 22 private.
Bed & breakfast: £48-£53
single, £58-£63 double.
Half board: £59-£65 daily.
Lunch available.
Evening meal 7pm (l.o.
10pm).
Parking for 100.
Credit: Access, Visa, Diners,
Amex.

[symbols]

St. Ives Motel M
London Rd., St. Ives,
PE17 4EX
☎ (0480) 63857
*Modern, comfortable
accommodation with its own
garden, 1 mile from town.
Completely refurbished in
1989. Restaurant meals and
bar snacks served every day.
Friendly, personal service.*
Bedrooms: 5 double & 9 twin,
2 family rooms.
Bathrooms: 16 private.

Bed & breakfast: from £42
single, from £55 double.
Lunch available.
Evening meal 7.15pm (l.o.
9.30pm).
Parking for 80.
Credit: Access, Visa, Diners,
Amex.

[symbols]

Slepe Hall Hotel M
Ramsey Rd., St. Ives,
PE17 4RB
☎ (0480) 63122
*Former Victorian girls' school
converted in 1966. Now a
Grade II listed building, 5
minutes' walk from the Great
River Ouse and town centre.*
Bedrooms: 2 single, 7 double
& 6 twin, 1 family room.
Bathrooms: 16 private.
Bed & breakfast: from £57
single, from £70 double.
Half board: from £69 daily.
Lunch available.
Evening meal 7pm (l.o.
9.45pm).
Parking for 70.
Credit: Access, Visa, Diners,
Amex.

[symbols]

ST NEOTS

Cambridgeshire
Map ref 2D1

8m SW. Huntingdon
Pleasant market town on
the River Ouse with a
large square which grew
up around a 10th C
priory. There are many
interesting buildings and
St. Mary's is one of the
largest medieval
churches in the county.

Old Falcon Hotel
Market Square, St. Neots,
PE19 2AW
☎ Huntingdon (0480) 72749
*Old coaching inn situated in
town centre. Bar and
restaurant open to non-
residents, conference and
banqueting facilities available.*
Bedrooms: 6 single, 1 double
& 1 twin.
Bathrooms: 7 private,
1 public.
Bed & breakfast: from £36
single, from £46 double.
Lunch available.
Evening meal 7pm (l.o.
9.30pm).
Credit: Access, Visa, Diners,
Amex.

[symbols]

SCOLE

Norfolk
Map ref 3B2

2m E. Diss

Scole Inn M
Scole, Diss, IP21 4DR
☎ Diss (0379) 740481
Telex 975392 STORK G
*17th C Grade 1 listed coaching
inn with modern facilities and
comforts, retaining old
character. Situated on main
Ipswich to Norwich road.*
Bedrooms: 18 double &
3 twin, 2 family rooms.
Bathrooms: 23 private,
2 public.
Bed & breakfast: £45-£55
single, £64-£75 double.
Lunch available.
Evening meal 7pm (l.o.
9.45pm).
Parking for 100.
Credit: Access, Visa, Diners,
Amex.

[symbols]

SHERINGHAM

Norfolk
Map ref 3B1

Holiday resort with
Victorian and Edwardian
hotels and a sand and
shingle beach where the
fishing boats are hauled
up. The North Norfolk
Railway operates from
Sheringham Station
during the summer. Other
attractions include,
museums, theatre and
Splash Fun Pool.

The Bay Leaf Guest House
Listed COMMENDED
10 St. Peters Rd.,
Sheringham, NR26 8QY
☎ (0263) 823779
*Charming Victorian licensed
guesthouse, open all year.
Conveniently situated in the
town. Near golf-course and
woodlands; adjacent to steam
railway. 5 minutes from sea.*
Bedrooms: 1 double & 2 twin,
2 family rooms.
Bathrooms: 2 public.
Bed & breakfast: £12-£15
single, £24-£30 double.
Half board: £18-£21.50 daily,
£102-£114 weekly.
Evening meal 6.30pm (l.o.
6.30pm).
Parking for 4.

[symbols]

SHERINGHAM

Continued

The Beacon Hotel ⚑
🏰🏰🏰
1 Nelson Rd., Sheringham,
NR26 8BT
☎ (0263) 822019
*A small, quiet, peaceful hotel
by the sea, with accent on
cleanliness, comfort and
English food.*
Bedrooms: 2 single, 3 double
& 2 twin
Bathrooms: 3 private,
2 public.
Half board: £25-£26 daily,
£150-£165 weekly.
Evening meal 7pm (l.o. 7pm).
Parking for 6.
Open May-September.
Credit: Access, Visa.
🖐 🛏 📺 ▥ ♨ ✕ 🖾

SHIPDHAM

Norfolk
Map ref 3B1

4m SW. East Dereham

Shipdham Place ⚑
🏰🏰🏰
Church Close, Shipdham,
Nr. Thetford, IP25 7LX
☎ Dereham (0362) 820303
*Former Norfolk rectory serving
carefully prepared, 3-course set
dinners. Extensive wine list.
Located halfway between
Dereham and Watton. Special
rates for 2 nights or more.*
Bedrooms: 6 double & 2 twin.
Bathrooms: 7 private,
1 public.
Bed & breakfast: £35-£70
single, £44-£85 double.
Half board: £41-£61 daily,
£278-£540 weekly.
Lunch available.
Evening meal 7.45pm (l.o.
9.30pm).
Parking for 25.
Credit: Access, Visa.
🖐 ⌨ ↳ ▥ ☎ 🛏 📺 ▥ ♨
☕ 🅿 ❀ ⚶ 🆂🅿 🔳

**Individual
proprietors have
supplied all details
of accommodation.
Although we do
check for accuracy,
we advise you to
confirm prices and
other information
at the time of
booking.**

SOUTHEND-ON-SEA

Essex
Map ref 3B3

On the Thames Estuary
and the nearest seaside
resort to London. Famous
for its pier and unique
pier trains. Other
attractions include Peter
Pan's Playground, a
marine activity centre for
watersports, excellent
fishing facilities, indoor
swimming pools, indoor
rollerskating and ten pin
bowling. Numerous parks
and gardens including the
beautiful woodland and
nature reserves at
Belfairs with sports
facilities, riding school
and trotting track.
*Tourist Information
Centre ☎ (0702) 355122
or 355120*

Balmoral Hotel
🏰🏰🏰
34-36 Valkyrie Rd.,
Southend-on-Sea, SS0 8BU
☎ (0702) 342947
*Family-run hotel 500 yards
from the sea front and
Westcliff station. Close to the
centre of Southend and A13.*
Bedrooms: 11 single, 7 double
& 4 twin.
Bathrooms: 22 private.
Bed & breakfast: £35-£38
single, £48-£55 double.
Half board: £43.50-£65.50
daily, £275-£300 weekly.
Lunch available.
Evening meal 6.30pm (l.o.
8.30pm).
Parking for 18.
Credit: Access, Visa.
🖐 ↳ ☎ 🛏 ♨ ▮ ▥ 📺
▥ ♨ ☕ 🆂🅿

Cliffview Guesthouse
Listed
8 Clifftown Parade,
Southend-on-Sea, SS1 1DP
☎ 0702 (331 645)
*Within a conservation area, 5
minutes' walk from seafront,
town centre and main railway
lines.*
Bedrooms: 6 single, 5 double
& 3 twin, 3 family rooms.
Bathrooms: 2 public;
3 private showers.
Bed & breakfast: £18-£20
single, £30-£45 double.
Parking for 6.
Credit: Access, Visa.
🖐 ♨ ☎ 🛏 ♨ 🆄🅻 ▥ ♨ ☐
🔳

Malvern Lodge Guest House
Listed
29 Seaforth Rd., Southend-on-Sea, SS0 8HX
☎ (0702) 345692
*Small guesthouse under direct
supervision of proprietors.
Opposite station and near
seafront.*
Bedrooms: 4 single, 2 double
& 2 twin, 1 family room.
Bathrooms: 3 public.
Bed & breakfast: £11-£12
single, £22-£24 double.
Parking for 4.
🖐 ♨ ☐ ♨ ▮ ✕ 📺 ▥ ♨
✕ 🖾 🅾🅰🅿

Tower Hotel
🏰🏰🏰 APPROVED
146 Alexandra Rd.,
Southend-on-Sea, SS1 1HE
☎ (0702) 348635
*Newly restored Victorian hotel
in conservation area. Close to
sea, gardens, cliffs, pavilion,
shopping centre and railways
(London 45 minutes).*
Bedrooms: 14 single,
12 double & 3 twin, 3 family
rooms.
Bathrooms: 30 private,
3 public.
Bed & breakfast: £33-£39.50
single, £43-£52.90 double.
Half board: £40.50-£47 daily,
£255.15-£296.10 weekly.
Lunch available.
Evening meal 6pm (l.o.
9.30pm).
🖐 ♨ ↳ ☐ 🛏 ♨ ▮ ▥ ♨
📺 ◑ ▥ ♨ ☐ ♨ 🅾🅰🅿 ⚶ 🆂🅿 🔳
🆃

West Park Hotel
🏰🏰 APPROVED
11 Park Rd., Westcliff-on-
Sea, Southend-on-Sea,
SS0 7PQ
☎ (0702) 330729 & 334252
Warm and friendly hotel.
Bedrooms: 9 single, 10 double
& 1 twin.
Bathrooms: 16 private,
1 public; 4 private showers.
Bed & breakfast: £29-£31
single, £40-£50 double.
Half board: £29-£35 daily.
Evening meal 6pm (l.o. 7pm).
Parking for 16.
Credit: Access, Visa.
🖐 ♨ ↳ ☐ 🛏 ♨ ▮ ▥ 🛏
📺 ▥ ♨ ☐ ♨ 🅿

SOUTHWOLD

Suffolk
Map ref 3C2

8m E. Halesworth
Pleasant and attractive
seaside town with a
triangular market square
and spacious greens
around which stand flint,
brick and colour-washed
cottages. The parish
church of St. Edmund is
one of the greatest
churches in Suffolk.

Dunburgh Guest House
28 North Parade, Southwold,
IP18 6LT
☎ (0502) 723253
*Elegant Victorian house
overlooking the sea. All
bedrooms have sea views.
Comfortable and relaxed
atmosphere. Home cooking.*
Bedrooms: 2 double & 1 twin.
Bathrooms: 1 private,
2 public.
Bed & breakfast: £18-£20
single, £35-£37 double.
Half board: £25-£26 daily.
Evening meal 7pm (l.o. 7pm).
🖐 ☐ ♨ 🆄🅻 ▮ ▥ ♨ 📺
🔳

Peer Gynt House
28 Field Stile Rd., Southwold
☎ (0502) 723588
*Near beach and town centre.
Try our Danish cold table, one
of our specialities. Pets
welcome. Open all year.*
Bedrooms: 1 single, 1 double
& 1 twin.
Bathrooms: 1 public.
Bed & breakfast: £20-£25
single, £30 double.
Half board: £25-£40 daily,
£210-£280 weekly.
Lunch available.
Evening meal 6pm (l.o. 9pm).
🖐 ♨ ☐ 🛏 ♨ 🆄🅻 ▮ ▥ ✕
♨ 📺 ▥ ♨ 🖾

STANSTED AIRPORT

Stansted Harlequin Hotel ⚑
🏰🏰🏰 APPROVED
Round Coppice Rd., Stansted
Airport, Stansted, Essex
CM24 8SE
☎ (0279) 680800
Telex 818840
*Brand new hotel, the first at
the airport, with good facilities
including extensive leisure club,
and transport to terminal.*
Bedrooms: 100 double &
149 twin.
Bathrooms: 249 private.
Bed & breakfast: £59.50-£65
single, £69.50-£76.50 double.

**The enquiry coupons at the back will
help you when contacting proprietors.**

Half board: £72-£79 daily,
£360-£396 weekly.
Lunch available.
Evening meal 6.30pm (l.o.
11.59pm).
Parking for 250.
Credit: Access, Visa, Diners,
Amex.

STOKE HOLY CROSS

Norfolk
Map ref 3C1

4m S. Norwich

Salamanca Farm M

Stoke Holy Cross, Nr.
Norwich, NR14 8QJ
☎ Framingham Earl
(050 86) 2322
*175-acre mixed/dairy farm.
Victorian house offering full
English breakfast. Beautiful
undulating country, 4 miles
from Norwich.*
Bedrooms: 3 double & 1 twin.
Bathrooms: 1 private,
2 public.
Bed & breakfast: from £15
single, from £26 double.
Parking for 8.

STOKE-BY-NAYLAND

Suffolk
Map ref 3B2

5m SW. Hadleigh
Picturesque village with a
fine group of half-
timbered cottages near
the church of St. Mary,
the tower of which was
one of Constable's
favourite subjects. In
School Street are the
Guildhall and the
Maltings, both 16th C
timber-framed buildings.

The Angel Inn M
😃😃😃 COMMENDED
Polstead Rd., Stoke-by-
Nayland, Colchester, Essex
CO6 4SA
☎ Nayland (0206) 263245 &
(0206) 263246
*A beautifully restored
freehouse and restaurant in the
historic village of Stoke-by-
Nayland, in the heart of
Constable country.*
Bedrooms: 1 single, 4 double
& 1 twin.
Bathrooms: 6 private.
Bed & breakfast: £35 single,
£45 double.

Lunch available.
Evening meal 7pm (l.o. 9pm).
Parking for 25.
Credit: Access, Visa, Diners,
Amex.

STOWMARKET

Suffolk
Map ref 3B2

11m NW. Ipswich
Small market town where
routes converge. There is
an open-air museum of
rural life at the Museum
of East Anglian Life.
*Tourist Information
Centre ☎ (0449) 676800*

Cedars Hotel M

Needham Rd., Stowmarket,
IP14 2AJ
☎ (0449) 612668
*Family-run hotel, ideal for
those wishing to tour the many
attractive parts of Suffolk.
Ample parking.*
Bedrooms: 8 single, 11 double
& 3 twin, 2 family rooms.
Bathrooms: 24 private.
Bed & breakfast: from £37.50
single, from £50 double.
Lunch available.
Evening meal 7pm (l.o. 9pm).
Parking for 60.
Credit: Access, Visa, Amex.

Gipping Heights Hotel
😃😃😃 COMMENDED
Creeting Rd., Stowmarket,
IP14 5BT
☎ (0449) 675264
*Enjoys extensive views across
Gipping Valley. half a mile
from town and station, quarter
of a mile from the A45.
Peaceful, tastefully furnished
and managed by resident
proprietors.*
Bedrooms: 1 single, 2 double
& 1 twin.
Bathrooms: 4 private.
Bed & breakfast: £20-£30
single, £38-£42 double.
Half board: £29.50-£39.50
daily, £207.50-£246.50
weekly.
Evening meal 7pm (l.o. 9pm).
Parking for 7.
Credit: Access, Visa.

**The symbols are
explained on the
flap inside the
back cover.**

SUDBURY

Suffolk
Map ref 3B2

3m NW. Colchester
Former important cloth
and market town on the
River Stour. Birthplace of
Thomas Gainsborough
whose home is now an
art gallery and museum.
The Corn Exchange is an
excellent example of early
Victorian civic building.

Ingrams Well House
Ingrams Well Rd., Sudbury,
CO10 6XJ
☎ (0787) 73571
*Elegant country house
overlooking park. Convenient
for Constable country, Suffolk
villages and Cambridge. High
standard accommodation in
peaceful surroundings.*
Bedrooms: 2 double & 2 twin.
Bathrooms: 4 private.
Bed & breakfast: £36-£44
double.
Half board: £27-£34 daily,
£150-£180 weekly.
Evening meal 7pm (l.o. 8pm).
Parking for 11.
Open March-October.

Mill Hotel
Walnut Tree Lane, Sudbury,
CO10 6BD
☎ (0787) 75544 Telex 987623
Consort
*A converted water mill which
sits on the banks of the River
Stour in picturesque Sudbury.*
Bedrooms: 13 single,
19 double & 20 twin, 2 family
rooms.
Bathrooms: 54 private.
Bed & breakfast: £25-£50
single, £34-£68 double.
Lunch available.
Evening meal 7.30pm (l.o.
9.15pm).
Parking for 60.
Credit: Access, Visa, Diners,
Amex.

Old Bull and Trivets

Church St., Ballingdon,
Sudbury, CO10 6BL
☎ (0787) 74120
*16th C guesthouse and
restaurant of character and
charm. Within 10 minutes'
walk of town centre. Ideal
centre for touring.*
Bedrooms: 1 single, 3 double
& 1 twin, 4 family rooms.
Bathrooms: 6 private;
3 private showers.
Bed & breakfast: £21-£30
single, £32-£42 double.

Half board: £26-£48 daily.
Evening meal 7.30pm (l.o.
9pm).
Parking for 20.
Credit: Access, Visa, Diners,
Amex.

SWAFFHAM

Norfolk
Map ref 3B1

14m SE. King's Lynn
Busy market town with a
triangular market-place, a
domed rotunda built in
1783 and a number of
Georgian houses. The
15th C church possesses
a large library of ancient
books.

Corfield House M
😃😃😃 COMMENDED
Sporle, Swaffham, PE32 2EA
☎ Swaffham (0760) 23636
*Country guesthouse with
comfortable, well-fitted rooms,
1 on ground floor. Personal
service. Peaceful surroundings.
Well placed for touring north
Norfolk.*
Bedrooms: 1 single, 2 double
& 2 twin.
Bathrooms: 5 private.
Bed & breakfast: £17 single,
£30-£34 double.
Half board: £24.50-£26.50
daily, £155-£170 weekly.
Evening meal 7.30pm (l.o.
6pm).
Parking for 5.
Open April-December.
Credit: Access, Visa.

THAXTED

Essex
Map ref 3B2

6m SE. Saffron Walden
Small town rich in
outstanding buildings and
dominated by its hilltop
medieval church. The
magnificent Guildhall was
built by the Cutlers' Guild
in the late 14th C. A
windmill built in 1804 has
been restored and
houses a rural museum.

The Swan Hotel
😃😃😃😃 COMMENDED
Bullring, Thaxted, CM6 2DL
☎ (0371) 830321
Telex 817477

Continued ▶

THAXTED
Continued

A high standard inn, offering 2 restaurants, lovely village bar and attractive en-suite accommodation, some with jacuzzi. Weekend rates available.
Bedrooms: 5 single, 8 double & 7 twin, 2 family rooms.
Bathrooms: 21 private.
Bed & breakfast: from £65 single, from £70 double.
Lunch available.
Evening meal 6.30pm (l.o. 10pm).
Parking for 33.
Credit: Access, Visa, Diners, Amex.

THETFORD
Norfolk
Map ref 3B2

12m N. Bury St. Edmunds
Small, medieval market town with numerous reminders of its long history: the ruins of the 12th C priory, Iron Age earthworks at Castle Hill and a Norman castle mound. Timber-framed Ancient House is now a museum.
Tourist Information Centre ☎ (0842) 752599

The Historical Thomas Paine Hotel ♨

White Hart St., Thetford, IP24 1AA
☎ (0842) 755631 Telex 58298
Attention T.P.H.
Best Western
Historic Georgian hotel and restaurant, on the Norfolk/Suffolk border. An ideal touring base.
Bedrooms: 4 single, 7 double & 3 twin.
Bathrooms: 13 private; 1 private shower.
Bed & breakfast: £40-£45 single, £52-£58 double.
Lunch available.
Evening meal 7pm (l.o. 9.30pm).
Parking for 30.
Credit: Access, Visa, Diners, Amex.

THURSFORD
Norfolk
Map ref 3B1

5m NE. Fakenham
Noted for its collection of steam locomotives, mechanical musical organs and fairground engines.

Holly Lodge

1 The Street, Thursford Green, Thursford, NR21 OAS
☎ (0328) 878465
Part 18th C house in secluded gardens in quiet village. Turn left off A148 Fakenham/Cromer road at Crawfish. House situated 250 yards after Thursford museum on left.
Bedrooms: 1 single, 2 double & 2 twin, 1 family room.
Bathrooms: 4 private, 1 public.
Bed & breakfast: £16-£18 single, £32-£36 double.
Half board: from £24 daily.
Parking for 8.
Open February-December.

TITCHWELL
Norfolk
Map ref 3B1

5m E. Hunstanton
Titchwell Manor Hotel
COMMENDED
Titchwell, King's Lynn, PE31 8BB
☎ Brancaster (0485) 210221
Family-run hotel overlooking bird reserve and beach. Near Sandringham, Holkham Hall and 2 championship golf-courses. Specialities - seafood including oysters.
Bedrooms: 3 double & 2 twin, 4 family rooms.
Bathrooms: 9 private.
Bed & breakfast: £30-£38 single, £60-£80 double.
Half board: £34-£50 daily.
Lunch available.
Evening meal 7pm (l.o. 9.30pm).
Parking for 50.
Credit: Access, Visa, Diners, Amex.

WATERBEACH
Cambridgeshire
Map ref 3A2

5m NE. Cambridge
Denny Abbey has 12th C remains of a church of the Knights Templar.

Bridge Hotel (Motel) ♨

Clayhythe, Nr. Waterbeach, Cambridge, CB5 9HZ
☎ Cambridge (0223) 860252
Riverside hotel with motel rooms, 4 miles north of Cambridge. Situated between A45 and A10 on Waterbeach to Fen Ditton road.
Bedrooms: 10 single, 14 double & 4 twin, 1 family room.
Bathrooms: 29 private.
Bed & breakfast: £30-£35 single, £44-£50 double.
Half board: £36.50-£40 daily.
Lunch available.
Evening meal 7pm (l.o. 9pm).
Parking for 75.
Credit: Access, Visa, Diners, Amex.

WATTON
Norfolk
Map ref 3B1

8m SE. Swaffham

Clarence House Hotel ♨

78 High St., Watton, Thetford, IP25 6AH
☎ (0953) 884252 & 884484
Situated in the centre of Watton, a late Victorian gentleman's house restored to its original comfort and elegance.
Bedrooms: 2 double & 3 twin, 1 family room.
Bathrooms: 6 private, 1 public.
Bed & breakfast: £38-£42 single, £50-£55 double.
Half board: £51.25-£55.25 daily, £231-£245 weekly.
Lunch available.
Evening meal 7.30pm (l.o. 9pm).
Parking for 7.
Credit: Access, Visa, Diners, Amex.

Hare and Barrel ♨

80 Brandon Rd., Watton, Nr. Thetford, IP25 6LB
☎ (0953) 882752

Georgian house and outbuilding converted into a pub-restaurant and motel units off the road. Central to the whole of Norfolk. Close to golf-courses at Thetford, Swaffham, Dereham and Watton. Family rooms available on request.
Bedrooms: 2 double & 14 twin, 2 family rooms.
Bathrooms: 18 private.
Bed & breakfast: £21.50 single, £33.50 double.
Half board: from £35 daily.
Lunch available.
Evening meal 7pm (l.o. 9.50pm).
Parking for 40.
Credit: Access, Visa, Diners, Amex.

WELLS-NEXT-THE-SEA
Norfolk
Map ref 3B1

9m N. Fakenham
Seaside resort and small port on the north coast. The Buttlands is a large tree-lined green surrounded by Georgian houses and from here narrow streets lead to the quay.

The Cobblers Guest House

Standard Rd., Wells-next-the-Sea, NR23 1JU
☎ Fakenham (0328) 710155
8-bedroomed guesthouse in delightful, quiet setting. All bedrooms with TV and tea/coffee facilities. Ample car park.
Bedrooms: 2 single, 4 double & 1 twin, 1 family room.
Bathrooms: 1 private, 3 public.
Bed & breakfast: £15.50-£16.50 single, £29-£31 double.
Half board: £22-£23 daily.
Evening meal 6.30pm (l.o. 7pm).
Parking for 8.

Crown Hotel ♨

The Buttlands, Wells-next-the-Sea, NR23 1EX
☎ Fakenham (0328) 710209
Minotels
Famous old coaching inn set amongst Norfolk's finest coastal scenery.
Bedrooms: 1 single, 6 double & 4 twin, 4 family rooms.
Bathrooms: 8 private, 2 public.

Please check prices and other details at the time of booking.

360

Bed & breakfast: £38-£45 single, £48-£55 double.
Lunch available.
Evening meal 7.30pm (l.o. 9.30pm).
Parking for 10.
Credit: Access, Visa, Diners, Amex.

Scarborough House
APPROVED
Clubbs Lane, Wells-next-the-Sea, NR23 1DP
☎ Fakenham (0328) 710309
Spacious licensed Victorian manse with private parking. 3 lounges, family rooms, function room, garden and bar patio. Children and dogs welcome.
Bedrooms: 2 double & 2 twin, 2 family rooms.
Bathrooms: 2 private, 2 public.
Bed & breakfast: £23-£26 single, £36-£42 double.
Half board: £28.95-£36.95 daily, £192-£251 weekly.
Evening meal 7pm (l.o. 8pm).
Parking for 10.
Open April-October.
Credit: Access, Visa.

The Well House
Standard Rd., Wells-next-the-Sea, NR23 1JY
☎ Fakenham (0328) 710443
16th C manor house and gentleman's residence with old world charm, now a small family-run guesthouse overlooking salt marshes. Adjacent to quay, 1 mile from the sea, ideal for surfing. All rooms have en-suite facilities.
Bedrooms: 2 double & 1 twin, 1 family room.
Bathrooms: 4 private.
Bed & breakfast: £30-£34 double.
Parking for 4.

WEST RUNTON
Norfolk
Map ref 3B1

2m W. Cromer

Dormy House Hotel M
Cromer Rd., West Runton, NR27 9QA
☎ (026 375) 537

Family hotel in its own grounds, overlooking sea and golf-course. Bar lounge, table d'hote and a la carte menus. All rooms en-suite with colour TV, telephone, hair-dryer, trouser press, tea/coffee. Car park.
Bedrooms: 3 double & 11 twin, 2 family rooms.
Bathrooms: 16 private, 1 public.
Bed & breakfast: £38-£40 single, £52-£56 double.
Half board: £33-£38 daily, £224-£256 weekly.
Evening meal 7pm (l.o. 9pm).
Parking for 25.
Credit: Access, Visa, Amex.

WESTLETON
Suffolk
Map ref 3C2

3m E. Yoxford
Has a number of fine buildings including the gabled Elizabethan Moot House and the Crown Inn. The unusual thatched church holds an annual wild flower festival. The large green is bordered by an avenue of limes and a large duckpond.

The Crown at Westleton
Westleton, Nr. Saxmundham, IP17 3AD
☎ (072 873) 273 & 239 & 777
Traditional inn in the centre of village. Opposite thatched church and close to village green and duck pond. Less than 2 miles from Minsmere and the coast at Dunwich.
Bedrooms: 2 single, 14 double & 1 twin, 2 family rooms.
Bathrooms: 19 private.
Bed & breakfast: £37.50-£47.50 single, £56.50-£77.50 double.
Half board: max. £51.25 daily, £173.25-£358.75 weekly.
Lunch available.
Evening meal 7pm (l.o. 9.30pm).
Parking for 24.
Credit: Access, Visa, Diners, Amex.

WETHERDEN
Suffolk
Map ref 3B2

3m NW. Stowmarket

The Old Rectory
Wetherden, Stowmarket
☎ Elmswell (0359) 40144
Comfortable well-furnished Georgian house in 12 acres overlooking village. Situated off the A45 between Stowmarket and Bury St. Edmunds.
Bedrooms: 1 double & 2 twin.
Bathrooms: 2 private, 2 public.
Bed & breakfast: £20-£25 single, £35-£40 double.
Parking for 10.
Open March-November.

WITHAM
Essex
Map ref 3B3

9m NE. Chelmsford
Delightful town whose history goes back to the time of King Alfred. The High Street contains 16th C houses and the Spread Eagle, a famous Essex inn. The 14th C church is near the site of an ancient defensive mound.

Rivenhall Resort Hotel
Rivenhall End, Witham, CM9 3BH
☎ (0376) 516969 Telex 99414
Resort
Purpose-built single storey hotel situated on the A12 between Colchester and Chelmsford, close to the port of Maldon.
Bedrooms: 12 single, 29 double & 11 twin, 3 family rooms.
Bathrooms: 55 private.
Bed & breakfast: from £51.50 single, from £68 double.
Lunch available.
Evening meal 7pm (l.o. 9.30pm).
Parking for 150.
Credit: Access, Visa, Diners, Amex.

WIX
Essex
Map ref 3B2

5m SE. Manningtree

New Farm House M
Spinnell's Lane, Wix, Manningtree, CO11 2UJ
☎ (0255) 870365
50-acre arable farm. Modern comfortable farmhouse in large garden, 10 minutes' drive to Harwich port and convenient for Constable country. From Wix village crossroads, take Bradfield Road, turn right at top of hill; first house on the left.
Bedrooms: 3 single, 2 double & 2 twin, 5 family rooms.
Bathrooms: 7 private, 2 public.
Bed & breakfast: £15.50-£18.50 single, £29-£35 double.
Half board: £23-£26 daily, £142.70-£161.55 weekly.
Evening meal 6.30pm (l.o. 5.30pm).
Parking for 12.
Credit: Access, Visa.

WOODBRIDGE
Suffolk
Map ref 3C2

8m E. Ipswich
Once a busy seaport, the town is now a sailing centre on the River Deben. There are many buildings of architectural merit including the Bell and Angel Inns. The 18th C Tide Mill is now restored and open to the public.

Grove Guest House
39 Grove Rd., Woodbridge, IP12 4LG
☎ (039 43) 2202
Comfortable guest-house, recently extended, offering a warm and friendly service. On the Woodbridge by-pass, close to heritage coast.
Bedrooms: 2 single, 3 double & 3 twin, 1 family room.
Bathrooms: 6 private, 1 public.
Bed & breakfast: from £16 single, from £32 double.
Half board: from £22.50 daily.
Lunch available.
Evening meal 7pm (l.o. 9pm).
Parking for 9.

We advise you to confirm your booking in writing.

Half board prices shown are per person but in some cases may be based on double/twin occupancy.

WROXHAM

Norfolk
Map ref 3C1

7m NE. Norwich
Yachting centre on the River Bure which houses the headquarters of the Norfolk Broads Yacht Club. The church of St. Mary has a famous doorway and the manor house nearby dates back to 1623.

King's Head **M**
🏅🏅🏅

Station Rd., Wroxham, NR12 8UR
☎ (0603) 782429
Located in the town centre, with waterfront rooms and carvery restaurants.
Bedrooms: 4 double, 2 family rooms.
Bathrooms: 6 private.
Bed & breakfast: £36.50-£41.50 single, from £48.50 double.
Lunch available.
Evening meal 7.30pm (l.o. 9.30pm).

Parking for 50.
Credit: Access, Visa, Diners, Amex.
🛇 📞 🖵 🌣 ♬ Ⓥ ▥ 🖪 ✗ SP

Hotel Wroxham **M**
🏅🏅🏅

Wroxham, NR12 8AJ
☎ (0603) 782061
Modern, friendly hotel, privately owned, in a riverside setting next to Wroxham bridge. Busy shopping centre. In the heart of the Norfolk Broads, 8 miles from Norwich.
Bedrooms: 1 single, 10 double & 5 twin, 2 family rooms.
Bathrooms: 14 private, 1 public.
Bed & breakfast: £28-£42 single, £42-£59 double.
Half board: £37-£51.50 daily, £185-£250 weekly.
Lunch available.
Evening meal 7pm (l.o. 9.30pm).
Parking for 60.
Credit: Access, Visa, Diners, Amex.
🛇 📞 🖵 🌣 ♬ Ⓥ ∠ ⅂
Ⓣ🅥 ● ▥ 🖪 ⃓ ✔ 🌣 SP

WYMONDHAM

Norfolk
Map ref 3B1

9m SW. Norwich
Busy market town with a charming octagonal market cross. In 1615 a great fire destroyed most of its buildings but the Green Dragon Inn, now one of the oldest in the country, survived.

Abbey Hotel **M**
🏅🏅🏅

10 Church St., Wymondham, NR18 0PH
☎ (0953) 602148
Telex 975711
In a quiet street and noted for good value and home cooking. Central for touring Norfolk. Extensive sports and leisure facilities available at the nearby Barnham Broom Hotel, conference and leisure centre.
Bedrooms: 3 single, 12 double & 10 twin, 1 family room.
Bathrooms: 26 private.
Bed & breakfast: £40-£45 single, £55-£60 double.
Half board: £51.50-£57 daily.

Lunch available.
Evening meal 7.30pm (l.o. 9.30pm).
Parking for 3.
Credit: Access, Visa, Diners, Amex.
🛇 ♿ ⅂ ● 🖵 🌣 ♬ Ⓥ ⅂
● ⅌ ▥ 🖪 ⃓ ✔ ▷ 🌣 ✗ SP ⌗
Ⓣ

Sinclair Hotel **M**
🏅🏅🏅 APPROVED

28 Market St., Wymondham, NR18 0BB
☎ (0953) 606721
On the A11, in a market town with historic buildings, close to the famous Wymondham Abbey. 9 miles from the city of Norwich.
Bedrooms: 6 single, 5 double & 8 twin, 1 family room.
Bathrooms: 20 private.
Bed & breakfast: £39-£43 single, £49-£54 double.
Half board: £48.50-£55 daily.
Lunch available.
Evening meal 7pm (l.o. 9.30pm).
Parking for 8.
Credit: Access, Visa, Amex.
🛇 ♿ ⅂ 📞 🖵 🌣 ♬ Ⓥ ∠
⅂ ● ▥ 🖪 ⃓ 🖪 ▷ ✿ ✗
⃓ 🌣 SP

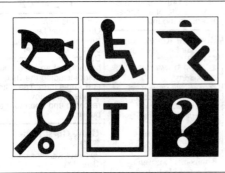

Key to symbols

Information about many of the services and facilities at establishments listed in this guide is given in the form of symbols. The key to these symbols is inside the back cover flap. You may find it helpful to keep the flap open when referring to the entry listings.

Check the maps

The place you wish to visit may not have accommodation entirely suited to your needs, but there could be somewhere ideal quite close by. Check the colour maps towards the end of this guide to identify nearby towns and villages with accommodation listed in the guide, and then use the town index to find page numbers.

Hector Breeze

IPSWICH

THE CARLTON HOTEL has 20 comfortable bedrooms (4 on ground floor) — most have private bathrooms. All have direct dial telephones, colour TV, tea and coffee making facilities. The hotel is licensed, with ample car parking and situated in the town centre. Personal attention is our speciality. We are pleased to accept Access, Visa and American Express.

Carlton Hotel, Berners Street, Ipswich, Suffolk IP1 3LN.
☎ (0473) 254955/211145

ETB 👑👑

Hamilton Hotel

156 Chesterton Road, Cambridge, Cambridgeshire.
Tel: Cambridge (0223) 65664 – reservations & enquiries
Fax: (0223) 314866

Member of Cambridge Hotels & Guest House Association. AA Listed.

Hamilton Hotel is situated approximately one mile from the city centre and is close to the River Cam. There are 15 comfortable bedrooms. All rooms have tea/coffee making facilities, colour TV, telephone, most with en-suite facilities. Our tariff includes a variety of breakfasts including the full traditional English. Our licensed bar offers a wide selection of snacks and bar meals.

King's Head Hotel

Gt. Bircham, King's Lynn, Norfolk PE31 6RJ
Tel: Syderstone (048 523) 265
(On B1153)   👑👑

Country hotel and restaurant, situated close to Sandringham, King's Lynn and the coast.
   Five en suite bedrooms, tea/coffee making facilities and colour TV.
   Wine and Dine in the lodge restaurant, food especially prepared by the proprietor. English and Continental cuisine. Fresh Norfolk seafood and produce, a la carte available lunchtime and evening, traditional Sunday lunch.

Morston Hall

Morston, Holt, Norfolk NR25 7AA.
Tel: Cley (0263) 741041. Fax: (0263) 741034.
👑👑👑👑 COMMENDED

A lovely 17th Century Country House Hotel with 3 large bedrooms, all with bathrooms, overlooking beautiful gardens. All rooms with TV and telephones.
Fully licensed, with a small restaurant open to non-residents, offering an individual menu, changed daily with emphasis on local seafoods. Jill Heaton, the co-owner is a cordon bleu chef.
Furnished to a very high standard, the hotel offers comfort and a peaceful atmosphere. A real country retreat.

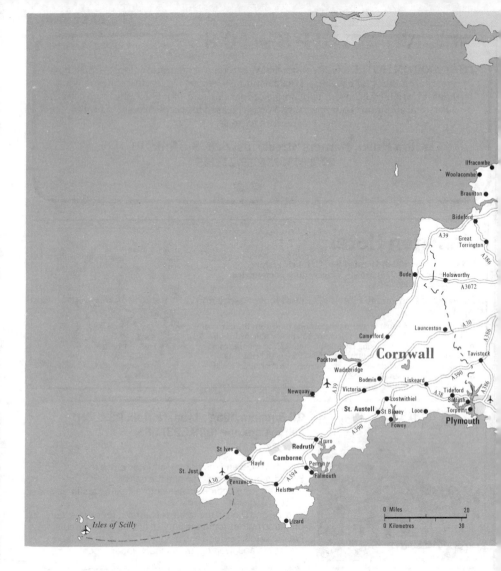

West Country
From Avon and the southern Cotswolds, from Wiltshire near the source of the mighty Thames, England's western peninsula thrusts towards the Isles of Scilly at its tip, some 28 miles into the Atlantic past Land's End.

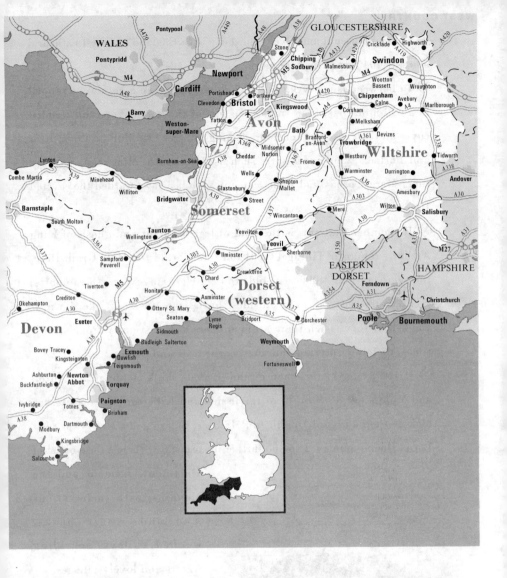

Here, spring flowers bloom by Christmas and Tresco has tropical gardens...

》 Please refer to the colour maps at the back of this guide for all places with accommodation listings.

》 Back in Avon, at Bath, 250,000 gallons of naturally hot water still rise daily into the reconstructed Roman baths, surrounded by Georgian architectural splendour. At Bristol there are museums and the works of Brunel to see, and in Wiltshire there's Swindon's ▶

► railway museum and lovely Salisbury with England's highest cathedral spire at 404 feet. Plus lots more.

》 In between is everything you could ever want in a holiday, wrapped in a 650-mile coastline. Among the surf of the north shore and wooded coves and inlets of the south are fishing villages like Mullion Cove, Beer and Porlock Weir and resorts such as Weymouth, Minehead, Weston-super-Mare, Torbay and Bude — many with beaches awarded the coveted Blue Flag.

》 Remember that this is the land of legend, giant and ghost, of King Arthur's romantic Tintagel Castle, of Camelot, of the Holy Grail. Here, too, you can find 4,000-year-old stone circles, massive earth ramparts, great figures cut in chalk hillsides, burial mounds from the dawn of English history. Then there are reminders of Christianity from earliest times, including myriad churches, cathedrals and abbeys.

》 If you prefer historic houses and gardens think of Longleat, Wilton and Montacute, or Stourhead, Trelissick and Killerton. Take a literary look at the haunts of Daphne du Maurier, Coleridge or Hardy, or visit Lorna Doone country. Look no further for scenery — there's the wonder of

Dartmoor, Exmoor and the Mendips, with their various moorland, granite peaks, wooded valleys, sparkling waters and lovely villages.

》 From theme parks to pony treks, from boats to balloons, from family fun to solitude ...the West Country has everything. It's a different world!

The thatched cottage where Thomas Hardy was born is tucked away in the tiny hamlet of Higher Bockhampton.

Where to go, what to see

The Exploratory Hands-on Science Centre

Bristol Old Station, Clock Tower Yard, Temple Gate, Bristol, Avon BS1 6QU
☎ Bristol (0272) 252008
Exhibition covering lights, lenses, lasers, bubbles, bridges, illusions, gyroscopes and much more.

Roman Baths Museum

Pump Room, Abbey Church Yard, Bath, Avon
☎ Bath (0225) 461111 Ext. 2785
Roman Baths and Temple Precinct; hot springs and Roman monuments. Jewellery, coins.

Dyrham Park

Dyrham, Nr. Bath, Avon SN14 8ER
☎ Abson (027 582) 2501
Mansion built between 1691 and 1702 for William Blathwayt. A herd of deer has roamed the park since Saxon times.

Cotehele

St. Dominick, Saltash, Cornwall PL12 6TA
☎ Liskeard (0579) 50434
Medieval house of grey granite. Watermill restored to working condition. Quay on River Tamar with small shipping museum. Sailing barge 'Shamrock'.

Flambards Triple Theme Park

Culdrose Manor, Helston, Cornwall TR13 0GA
☎ Helston (0326) 574549
Recently extended award-winning authentic life-size Victorian village with fully-stocked shops, carriages and fashions. 'Britain in the Blitz' recreation of a life-size wartime street. Historic aircraft. Cornwall's Exploratorium featuring 'hot rocks' energy project. Gardens.

St. Michael's Mount

Marazion, Cornwall TR17 0HT
☎ Penzance (0736) 710507
Originally the site of a Benedictine chapel, castle on its rock dates from the 14th C. Fine views towards Land's End and the Lizard.

Land's End

Sennen, Cornwall TR19 7AA
☎ Sennen (0736) 871501
Spectacular cliffs with breathtaking vistas. Superb multi-sensory Last Labyrinth show, and many other attractions and exhibitions.

Dobwalls Family Adventure Park

Dobwalls, Nr. Liskeard, Cornwall PL14 6HD
☎ Liskeard (0579) 20325
Two miles of scenically very dramatic miniature railway based on the American railroad scene. 'Mr Thorburn's Edwardian Countryside' — a unique exhibition of cameos and paintings depicting the life and times of famous natural history artist. Children's Adventureland.

The Big Sheep

Abbotsham Barton, Bideford, Devon EX39 5AP
☎ Bideford (0237) 472366
ETB award-winning attraction. Sheep dairy, sheep shearing, Craft centre where visitors can try spinning and weaving. Nature trail and adventure play area.

Lundy Island

Bristol Channel, Devon EX39 2LY
☎ Woolacombe (0271) 870870
Beautiful offshore island in the Bristol Channel. Ideal for birdwatching, climbing, diving and walking. Accommodation available in self-catering cottages.

▶

The Big Sheep, Abbotsham Barton, Bideford

Abbotsbury Swannery – a unique nesting colony of mute swans

▶ **Buckfast Abbey**
Buckfastleigh, Devon
TQ11 0EE
☎ Buckfastleigh (0364) 42882
*Living Benedictine monastery
built on medieval foundations,
world famous for works of art in
the church, the modern stained
glass, tonic wine and bee-
keeping.*

English Riviera Centre
Chestnut Avenue, Torquay,
Devon TQ2 5LZ
☎ Torquay (0803) 299992
*Leisure area with flume wave
pool, soda bar. Health club with
whirlpool, sauna, sunbeds,
multi-gym, steam bath. Squash
courts, video game machines.*

Model Village
Hampton Avenue,
Babbacombe, Torquay, Devon
TQ1 3LA
☎ Torquay (0803) 328669
*Hundreds of models and figures
laid out in four acres of beautiful
gardens to represent the English
countryside with modern town,
villages and rural areas.*

Plymouth Dome
Plymouth, Devon PL1 2NZ
☎ Plymouth (0752) 600608
New visitor centre on Plymouth

*Hoe with an interpretation of
the history of Plymouth and its
people from Stone Age
beginnings to satellite technology.*

The Devon Guild of Craftsmen
Riverside Mill, Bovey Tracey,
Devon TQ13 9AF
☎ Bovey Tracey (0626) 832223
*Old granite mill on the River
Bovey. Continuous series of
quality exhibitions by West
Country craftsmen throughout
the year.*

The Miniature Pony Centre
Wormhill Farm, North Bovey,
Nr. Moretonhampstead, Devon
TQ13 8RG
☎ Chagford (0647) 432400
*Traditional stable yard with
miniature ponies, covered barns
and yards with other miniature
animals. Paddocks with
stallions, mares and foals.
Lakes, children's assault course
and playground.*

**The Royal Horticultural
Society's Garden**
Rosemoor, Torrington, Devon
EX38 7EG
☎ Torrington (0805) 24067
*Trees, shrubs, roses, alpines and
arboretum. Nursery of rare plants.*

The Dinosaur Museum
Icen Way, Dorchester, Dorset
DT1 1EW
☎ Dorchester (0305) 269880
*The only museum in Britain
devoted exclusively to dinosaurs.
Fossils, full-size models,
computerised, mechanical and
electronic displays. Video
gallery.*

Abbotsbury Swannery
New Barn Road, Abbotsbury,
Dorset DT3 4JE
☎ Abbotsbury (0305) 871684
*Unique nesting colony of mute
swans. Eight miles of wetland of
international importance,
information centre.*

Brewers' Quay
Trinity House, 15 Trinity
Street, Weymouth, Dorset
DT4 8TP
☎ Weymouth (0305) 761111
*Former brewery now housing the
Timewalk, depicting 600 years
of Weymouth's history. Brewer's
Tale exhibition and Shopping
Village with restaurants.*

Glastonbury Abbey
The Abbey Gatehouse,
Glastonbury, Somerset
BA6 9EL
☎ Glastonbury (0458) 32267

Ruins of 12th-13th C abbey.
Unique Abbot's kitchen, fish
pond. Museum with superb
model of the 1539 abbey.

Wookey Hole Caves and Mill
Wookey Hole, Wells, Somerset
BA5 1BB
☎ Wells (0749) 72243
The most spectacular caves in
Britain. Working Victorian
paper mill. 'Fairground by
Night' exhibition. Madame
Tussaud's Cabinet of
Curiosities. Penny Pier
Arcade.

Combe Sydenham
Monksilver, Nr. Taunton,
Somerset TA4 4JG
☎ Stogumber (0984) 56284
Elizabethan hall with newly
restored west wing, gardens, deer
park, waymarked woodland
walks, trout ponds. Tearoom.

Cricket St. Thomas Wildlife Park
Cricket St. Thomas, Chard,
Somerset TA20 4DD
☎ Winsham (0460) 30755
Wildlife park, heavy horse
centre, playground, woodland
railway. Location for BBC TV
series 'To the Manor Born'.
Restaurant.

Avebury Stone Circles
Avebury, Nr. Marlborough,
Wiltshire SN8 1RF
☎ Avebury (067 23) 250
One of the most important
megalithic ceremonial
monuments in Europe. 28.5
acre site with stone circles
enclosed by a bank and ditch
with avenue of stones.

Fleet Air Arm Museum
Royal Naval Air Station,
Yeovilton, Somerset BA22 8HT
☎ Ilchester (0935) 840565
Over 50 historic aircraft, plus
displays and equipment,
including Concorde 002
prototype, Falklands Campaign
Exhibition, Kamikaze
exhibition, RNAS 1914-1918
and the Wrens.

Bowood House and Gardens
Calne, Wiltshire SN11 0LZ
☎ Calne (0249) 812102
18th C house by Robert Adam.
Paintings, watercolours,
Victoriana, Indiana and
porcelain. Landscaped park
with lake, terraces, waterfall,
grottos. Adventure playground,
gift shop, garden centre.

Wilton House
Wilton, Nr. Salisbury,
Wiltshire SP2 0BJ
☎ Salisbury (0722) 743115
Superb architecture and 17th C
state rooms by Inigo Jones.
World famous art and statuary
collection. Palladian bridge.

Stourhead House and Garden
Stourton, Nr. Mere, Wiltshire
BA12 6QH
☎ Bourton (0747) 840348
Gardens with temples and
grottos around the lake. Famous
for its trees and shrubs. Elegant
18th C house, furniture by
Chippendale the Younger.

Stonehenge
Nr. Amesbury, Wiltshire
SP4 7DE
☎ Amesbury (0980) 623108
World-famous prehistoric
monument built as ceremonial
centre. Started 5,000 years ago
and remodelled several times in
the following 1,500 years.

Salisbury and South Wiltshire Museum
The King's House, 65 The Close,
Salisbury, Wiltshire SP1 2EN
☎ Salisbury (0722) 332151
Unique Stonehenge collection.
Archaeology, Pitt-Rivers Wessex
collections, ceramics, local
history, prints and drawings.
New costume gallery.

Lions of Longleat Safari Park
Warminster, Wiltshire
BA12 7NJ
☎ Warminster (0985) 844266
Safari park, boat trips on lake
to see wild animals, pets' corner
with bird show. The only white
tigers in Britain.

Make a date for...

Cornwall Gardens Festival
Various gardens, Cornwall
1 April – 31 May

Badminton Horse Trials
Badminton, Avon   *2 – 5 May*

Bath International Festival
Various venues, Bath, Avon
24 May – 9 June

Royal Bath and West of England Show
Royal Bath and West
Showground, Shepton Mallet,
Somerset   *29 May – 1 June*

Three Spires Festival of the Arts
Truro Cathedral, High Cross,
Truro, Cornwall
21 June – 6 July

Sidmouth International Festival of Folk Arts
Various venues, Sidmouth,
Devon   *2 – 9 August*

Salisbury Festival
Various venues, Salisbury,
Wiltshire   *7 – 21 September*

Bridgwater Guy Fawkes Carnival
Town Centre, Bridgwater,
Somerset   *7 November*

Find out more

Further information about
holidays and attractions in the
West Country is available from:
West Country Tourist Board,
Trinity Court, Southernhay
East, Exeter, Devon EX1 1QS.
☎ (0392) 76351.

These publications are
available free from the West
Country Tourist Board:
West Country Holidays '91
Bed and Breakfast Touring Map '91
West Country Holiday Parks '91

Also available are:
Places to Visit £1.95
Where to Stay in the West Country 1991 £2.50

Places to stay

❯❯ Accommodation entries in this regional section are listed in alphabetical order of place name, and then in alphabetical order of establishment.

❯❯ The map references refer to the colour maps towards the end of the guide. The first figure is the map number; the letter and figure which follow indicate the grid reference on the map.

❯❯ The symbols at the end of each accommodation entry give information about services and facilities. A 'key' to these symbols is inside the back cover flap, which can be kept open for easy reference.

ABBOTSBURY

Dorset
Map ref 2A3

8m NW. Weymouth
Beautiful village near
Chesil Beach, with a long
main street of mellow
stone and thatched
cottages and the ruins of
a Benedictine monastery.
High above the village on
a hill is a prominent 15th
C chapel. Abbotsbury's
famous swannery and
sub-tropical gardens lie
just outside the village.

The Ilchester Arms
9 Market St., Abbotsbury,
DT3 4JR
☎ (0305) 871243
*9 miles from Weymouth,
Bridport and Dorchester. Set
in a small village. 5 minutes'
walk from the beach, St.
Catherine's chapel, Abbotsbury
Swanery, sub-tropical gardens.*
Bedrooms: 6 double & 3 twin,
1 family room.
Bathrooms: 10 private,
2 public.
Bed & breakfast: £40-£45
single, from £55 double.
Half board: from £210
weekly.
Lunch available.
Evening meal 7pm (l.o. 9pm).
Parking for 40.
Credit: Access, Visa.
🛏 ≛ ╰ 🖃 ✿ 🛡 Ⅴ ▥ ▨
🍴 ᕫ 🐾 SP ⍾

**Half board prices shown are per person
but in some cases may be based on
double/twin occupancy.**

AMESBURY

Wiltshire
Map ref 2B2

7m N. Salisbury
Standing on the banks of
the River Avon, this is the
nearest town to
Stonehenge on Salisbury
Plain. The area is rich in
prehistoric sites.
*Tourist Information
Centre ☎ (0980) 622833*

George Hotel
High St., Amesbury,
SP4 7ET
☎ (0980) 622108
*A traditional town centre hotel
offering food and
accommodation suiting
commercial and tourist
clientele. A stone's throw from
Stonehenge!*
Bedrooms: 14 single, 9 double
& 5 twin, 3 family rooms.
Bathrooms: 10 private,
6 public; 1 private shower.
Bed & breakfast: £20-£35
single, £35-£55 double.
Half board: £30-£45 daily,
£200-£275 weekly.
Lunch available.
Evening meal 7pm (l.o.
9.30pm).
Parking for 84.
Credit: Access, Visa, Diners,
Amex.
🛏 ⑤ 🛡 Ⅴ ᕫ 🍴 ▯ SP ⍾

ASHBURTON

Devon
Map ref 1C2

Formerly a thriving wool
centre and important as
one of Dartmoor's 4
stannary towns. Today's
busy market town retains
many period buildings
and an atmosphere of
medieval times. Ancient
tradition is maintained in
the annual ale-tasting and
bread-weighing
ceremony. Good centre
for exploring Dartmoor or
the South Devon coast.

**Holne Chase Hotel &
Restaurant ⋀**
⚜⚜⚜⚜ COMMENDED
Tavistock Rd., Ashburton,
TQ13 7NS
☎ Poundsgate (036 43) 471
Fax (036 43) 453
🆔 Inter
*In one of the most romantic
situations possible, Holne
Chase offers that traditional
hospitality which is part of
Britain's heritage.*
Bedrooms: 1 single, 5 double
& 8 twin.
Bathrooms: 14 private,
2 public.
Bed & breakfast: £55-£67.50
single, £76-£110 double.
Lunch available.
Evening meal 7.15pm (l.o.
9.30pm).
Parking for 30.
Credit: Access, Visa, Diners,
Amex.
🛏 ≛ ╰ ⑤ 🖃 ✿ 🛡 Ⅴ
ᕫ ▥ ▨ 🍴 ᕫ 🗡 ❄ ▨ ⍾ ᴰᴬᶠ
🐾 SP ⍾ 🅣

The Old Coffee House
Listed
27-29 West St., Ashburton,
TQ13 7DT
☎ (0364) 52539
*Charming 16th C listed
property on fringe of
Dartmoor. Licensed restaurant
with good guest facilities. Cosy
lounge. A non-smoking
establishment.*
Bedrooms: 1 double & 2 twin.
Bathrooms: 2 public.
Bed & breakfast: £13.50-£15
single, £23-£25 double.
Half board: £18.50-£19.50
daily, £120-£128 weekly.
Lunch available.
Evening meal 5.50pm (l.o.
7pm).
🛏 🖃 ✿ 🛡 Ⅴ ⋎ ᕫ 🕤 ▥
▨ 🍴 ⍾ ᴰᴬᶠ SP ⍾

AXMINSTER

Devon
Map ref 1D2

This tree-shaded market
town on the banks of the
River Axe was one of
Devon's earliest West
Saxon settlements, but is
better known for its
carpet making. Based on
Turkish methods, the
industry began in 1755,
declined in the 1830s and
was revived in 1937.

Lea Hill Hotel ⋀
⚜⚜⚜⚜ COMMENDED
Membury, Axminster,
EX13 7AQ
☎ Stockland (040 488) 388 &
(040 488) 604

14th C thatched farmhouse in tranquil setting with unparalleled views. Beautiful accommodation, friendly attentive service. Log fires.
Bedrooms: 7 double & 4 twin, 3 family rooms.
Bathrooms: 14 private, 2 public.
Bed & breakfast: £64-£92 double.
Half board: £47.50-£61.50 daily.
Lunch available.
Evening meal 7pm (l.o. 9.30pm).
Parking for 50.
Open March-December.
Credit: Access, Visa.

BADMINTON

Avon
Map ref 2B2

5m E. Chipping Sodbury
Small village close to Badminton House, a 17th to 18th C Palladian mansion which has been the seat of the Dukes of Beaufort for centuries. The 3-day Badminton Horse Trials are held in the Great Park every May.

Bodkin House Hotel
COMMENDED

A46, Bath to Stroud Rd., Badminton, GL9 1AF
☎ Didmarton (045 423) 310 & 422
Charming old Cotswold coaching inn with well-appointed rooms. Restaurant and freehouse.
Bedrooms: 6 double & 1 twin, 1 family room.
Bathrooms: 8 private.
Bed & breakfast: £30-£45 single, £55-£75 double.
Half board: £45-£60 daily, £280-£380 weekly.
Lunch available.
Evening meal 7pm (l.o. 10pm).
Parking for 35.
Credit: Access, Visa, Diners, Amex.

Petty France Hotel M
COMMENDED

A46, Dunkirk, Badminton, GL9 1AF
☎ Didmarton (045 423) 361
Informal country house atmosphere on the edge of the Cotswolds, good walking, many sights to visit, convenient Bath, Bristol.

Bedrooms: 2 single, 12 double & 5 twin, 1 family room.
Bathrooms: 20 private.
Bed & breakfast: £49-£85 single, £75-£105 double.
Half board: £49-£75 daily.
Lunch available.
Evening meal 7.30pm (l.o. 10pm).
Parking for 51.
Credit: Access, Visa, Diners, Amex.

BAMPTON

Devon
Map ref 1D1

6m N. Tiverton
Riverside market town, famous for its fair each October.

Bridge House Hotel
APPROVED

24 Luke St., Bampton, Tiverton, EX16 9NF
☎ (0398) 31298
Approximately 250 years old, built of local stone. Specialising in sporting breaks. Fly fishing, riding and clay pigeon shooting. Weekend and midweek breaks.
Bedrooms: 2 single, 2 double & 1 twin, 2 family rooms.
Bathrooms: 4 private, 1 public.
Bed & breakfast: £16-£20 single, £30-£35 double.
Lunch available.
Evening meal 6pm (l.o. 10pm).
Credit: Access, Visa.

Courtyard Hotel & Restaurant M

19, Fore St., Bampton, Tiverton, EX16 9ND
☎ (0398) 31536
Comfortable, small hotel and restaurant on the edge of Exmoor. Within easy reach of both coasts.
Bedrooms: 1 single, 3 double & 1 twin, 1 family room.
Bathrooms: 3 private, 1 public.
Bed & breakfast: £12-£14 single, £26 double.
Half board: £15-£20 daily.
Lunch available.
Evening meal 7pm (l.o. 9.30pm).
Parking for 40.
Credit: Access, Visa, Diners, Amex.

The Swan

Bampton, Tiverton, EX16 9NG
☎ (0398) 31257
Family-run 15th C hotel, offering extensive wine list and hospitality second to none. Right on the edge of Exmoor.
Bedrooms: 1 single, 3 double & 1 twin, 1 family room.
Bathrooms: 2 private, 1 public.
Bed & breakfast: £14-£18 single, £28-£36 double.
Half board: £20-£24 daily, £135-£160 weekly.
Evening meal 6pm (l.o. 10pm).
Credit: Access, Visa, Diners.

BARNSTAPLE

Devon
Map ref 1C1

At the head of the Taw Estuary, once a ship-building and textile town, now an important agricultural centre with attractive areas of period building, a modern civic centre and riverside leisure centre. Attractions include Queen Anne's Walk, a charming colonnaded arcade, Pannier Market and Cattle Market, open on Fridays, and the Athenaeum which houses a library.
Tourist Information Centre ☎ (0271) 47177

Barnstaple Motel M

Braunton Rd., Barnstaple, EX31 1LE
☎ (0271) 76221
Conveniently situated on the A361, a third of a mile from the town centre. We cater for both business and pleasure.
Bedrooms: 22 double & 31 twin, 4 family rooms.
Bathrooms: 57 private, 2 public.
Bed & breakfast: £40-£45 single, £55-£60 double.
Half board: £50-£55 daily, £255-£275 weekly.
Lunch available.
Evening meal 7pm (l.o. 10pm).
Parking for 210.
Credit: Access, Visa, Diners.

Downrew House Hotel M

Bishop's Tawton, Barnstaple, EX32 0DY
☎ Barnstaple (0271) 42497 & 46673 Fax (0271) 23947
Queen Anne country house in glorious setting. Own golf, heated pool, tennis, croquet. Ideal for coast and countryside.
Bedrooms: 4 double & 6 twin, 2 family rooms.
Bathrooms: 12 private.
Half board: £63.17-£84 daily.
Lunch available.
Evening meal 7pm (l.o. 9.30pm).
Credit: Access, Visa.

Highbury Guest House

Highbury Rd., Newport, Barnstaple, EX32 9BY
☎ (0271) 43502
1 mile from Barnstaple on bus route C 783, half a mile from North Devon link road. Open all year.
Bedrooms: 3 single, 3 double & 1 twin, 3 family rooms.
Bathrooms: 1 private, 3 public.
Bed & breakfast: £12.50-£13.50 single, £25-£26 double.
Half board: £19.50-£20 daily, £130-£135 weekly.
Evening meal 6.30pm (l.o. 6.30pm).
Parking for 11.

The Park Hotel M

Taw Vale, Barnstaple, EX32 9AD
☎ (0271) 72166 Telex 42551
EXONIA G REF BREND 6
Brend
Overlooking Rock Park, yet close to town centre, the hotel has recently undergone a complete refurbishment.
Bedrooms: 6 single, 18 double & 18 twin.
Bathrooms: 42 private.
Bed & breakfast: £44-£49 single, £66-£75 double.
Half board: £44-£60 daily, £240-£350 weekly.
Lunch available.
Evening meal 7pm (l.o. 9.30pm).
Parking for 80.
Credit: Access, Visa, Diners, Amex.

BARNSTAPLE

Continued

Royal & Fortescue Hotel M

Boutport St., Barnstaple, EX31 1HG
☎ (0271) 42289 Telex 42551
EXONIA G REF BREND 7
Ⓒ Brend
Traditional market town hotel centrally located, yet close to beaches and moor.
Bedrooms: 10 single, 23 double & 23 twin, 5 family rooms.
Bathrooms: 33 private, 7 public.
Bed & breakfast: £30-£39 single, £50-£60 double.
Half board: £35-£45 daily, £210-£315 weekly.
Lunch available.
Evening meal 7pm (l.o. 9.30pm).
Parking for 31.
Credit: Access, Visa, Diners, Amex.
➚ ♿ ☎ ⬛ �♢ ⓘ Ⓥ ⬟ ⓣⓥ ● ⬛ ⬛ ⌷ ♟ ₤ ♿ ⬟ SP ⬛ Ⓣ

Yeo Dale Hotel M
♛♛

Pilton Bridge, Barnstaple, EX31 1PG
☎ (0271) 42954
Family-run hotel located minutes from town centre. Ideal touring base for north Devon.
Bedrooms: 3 single, 1 double & 3 twin, 3 family rooms.
Bathrooms: 2 public.
Bed & breakfast: £14.50-£17 single, £28-£34 double.
Half board: £20.50-£23 daily, £143.50-£161 weekly.
Evening meal 7pm (l.o. 7pm).
Credit: Access, Visa.
➚ ☎ ⬛ ♢ ⌷ Ⓥ ⬟ ⓣⓥ ⬛ ⌷ SP ⬛ Ⓣ

Classifications and quality commendations were correct at the time of going to press but are subject to change. Please check at the time of booking.

The National Crown Scheme is explained in full on pages 556 – 558.

BATH

Avon
Map ref 2B2

Georgian spa city encircled by hills beside the River Avon. Important Roman site with impressive reconstructed baths, uncovered in 19th C. Bath Abbey built over Norman abbey on site of monastery where first king of England was crowned (AD 973). Fine architecture in mellow local stone. Pump Room, art gallery and other museums.
Tourist Information Centre ☎ (0225) 462831

Agra Holme Guest House

Gloucester Rd., Lower Swainswick, Bath, BA1 7BH
☎ (0225) 330370
Attractive guesthouse situated only 5 minutes from central Bath, occupying a commanding position with panoramic views of the city.
Bedrooms: 1 single, 2 double & 2 twin, 2 family rooms.
Bathrooms: 1 private, 2 public; 1 private shower.
Bed & breakfast: £15-£18 single, £30 double.
Parking for 10.
➚ ♿ ⌷ ♢ ⓊⓁ ⬛ ⌷ SP

Arden Hotel M
♛♛ COMMENDED

73 Great Pulteney St., Bath, BA2 4DL
☎ (0225) 466601
Small personal family-run hotel, situated in Bath's famous Great Pulteney Street. Elegantly restored and refurbished (1990) to offer the quietness and restfulness of a Georgian town house.
Bedrooms: 1 single, 3 double & 3 twin, 3 family rooms.
Bathrooms: 10 private.
Bed & breakfast: £45-£55 single, £55-£75 double.
Parking for 3.
Credit: Access, Visa.
➚ ♿ ⌷ ♢ ⓣⓥ ⬛ ⌷ ⬟ ⬛ SP ⬛ Ⓣ
Ⓐⓑ Display advertisement appears on page 456.

Armstrong House

41 Crescent Gardens, Upper Bristol Rd., Bath, BA1 2NB
☎ (0225) 442211
Victorian house in central Bath, only a short level walk to all attractions. Enjoy our spacious comfort and caring service.
Bedrooms: 2 double, 1 family room.

Bathrooms: 3 private.
Bed & breakfast: £35-£45 double.
Parking for 4.
➚ ♿6 ⌷ ♢ ⓊⓁ Ⓥ ⬟ ⬛ ⬛ ♟ ⬛
SP Ⓣ

Ashley Villa Hotel M
♛♛

26 Newbridge Rd., Bath, BA1 3JZ
☎ (0225) 421683
Comfortably furnished hotel with relaxing informal atmosphere, within easy reach of city centre. All rooms en-suite. Swimming pool. Car park.
Bedrooms: 2 single, 7 double & 2 twin, 3 family rooms.
Bathrooms: 14 private.
Bed & breakfast: £35-£40 single, £45-£60 double.
Parking for 10.
Credit: Access, Visa.
➚ ♿ ☎ ⬛ ♢ ⓘ ⌷ ⓣⓥ ⬛
⌷ ♟ ⥾ SP Ⓣ

Astor House
♛

14 Oldfield Rd., Bath, BA2 3ND
☎ (0225) 429134
Lovely Victorian house with comfortable, spacious rooms and large secluded garden. Peaceful, elegant atmosphere.
Bedrooms: 3 double & 4 twin.
Bathrooms: 2 public.
Bed & breakfast: £28-£30 double.
Parking for 4.
Open April-October.
➚ ♿7 ♢ ⓊⓁ Ⓥ ⬟ ⓣⓥ ⬛ ⌷
✤ ✿ ⬛ ⬛

Audley House
♛♛♛ HIGHLY COMMENDED

Park Gdns., Bath, BA1 2XP
☎ (0225) 333110
Fine listed residence in a secluded acre of lawns and mature trees, close to the city centre. Non-smokers only please.
Bedrooms: 2 double & 1 twin.
Bathrooms: 3 private.
Bed & breakfast: £40 single, £55 double.
Half board: max. £56 daily.
Evening meal 7.30pm (l.o. 8pm).
Parking for 7.
Credit: Access, Visa.
➚ ☎ ⬛ ♢ ⓊⓁ ⓘ Ⓥ ⬟ ⌷
⬛ ⌷ ✤ ✿ ⬛ ⬛ Ⓣ

Avon Hotel M

9 Bathwick St., Bath, BA2 6NX
☎ (0225) 446176/422226
Fax (0225) 447452

Situated on ring road A4/A36, 850 yards from Roman Baths and close to restaurants, parks and shops. Large car park.
Bedrooms: 4 single, 6 double & 7 twin, 3 family rooms.
Bathrooms: 17 private, 1 public.
Bed & breakfast: £25-£39 single, £34-£58 double.
Parking for 20.
Credit: Access, Visa, Diners, Amex.
➚ ♿ ☎ ⬛ ⌷ ♢ Ⓥ ⬟ ⌷
● ⬛ ⌷ ♟ DAP SP ⬛
Ⓐⓑ Display advertisement appears on page 455.

Avondale Riverside Guest House M

Avondale, Bathford, Bath, BA1 7RB
☎ (0225) 859847
Rambling Georgian/Victorian mansion in garden, riverside setting. Boating available. Easy parking. All rooms have good views. Lovely riverside gardens.
Bedrooms: 1 single, 10 double, 2 family rooms.
Bathrooms: 10 private, 2 public.
Bed & breakfast: from £20 single, from £35 double.
Parking for 30.
Credit: Access, Visa, Amex.
➚ ♢ ⓘ Ⓥ ⬟ ⓣⓥ ⬛ ⌷ ⌵
✿ DAP SP ⬛ Ⓣ

Bailbrook Lodge Hotel M
♛♛ COMMENDED

35/37 London Road West, Bath, BA1 7HZ
☎ (0225) 859090
Georgian house with splendid views overlooking the Avon Valley, near M4 and on the outskirts of Bath.
Bedrooms: 8 double & 5 twin.
Bathrooms: 13 private.
Bed & breakfast: £40-£55 single, £45-£60 double.
Lunch available.
Evening meal 7pm (l.o. 9pm).
Parking for 20.
Credit: Access, Visa.
➚ ♿ ⬛ ⌷ ♢ ⓘ Ⓥ ⬟ ⌷
ⓣⓥ ⬛ ⌷ ♟ ₤ ✤ ⥾ SP ⬛
Ⓐⓑ Display advertisement appears on page 456.

Bath Lodge Hotel & Restaurant M
♛♛♛ COMMENDED

Norton St. Philip, Bath, BA3 6NH
☎ Limpley Stoke
(0225) 723737 Fax
(0225) 723198

Small castle with four-poster beds and private balconies, overlooking natural waterfalled stream and gardens with adjacent forestry beyond. On the A36 south of Bath.
Bedrooms: 3 double, 1 family room.
Bathrooms: 4 private.
Bed & breakfast: £65-£85 single, £80-£100 double.
Lunch available.
Evening meal 7pm (l.o. 10pm).
Parking for 20.
Credit: Access, Visa, Amex.

The Bath Tasburgh ♨
⚜⚜⚜
Warminster Rd.,
Bathampton, Bath, BA2 6SH
☎ (0225) 425096/463842
Spacious, elegant Victorian house/hotel. 1 mile from city centre, set in 7 acres of gardens with beautiful views and canal frontage. En-suite rooms, ample parking.
Bedrooms: 1 single, 5 double & 3 twin, 4 family rooms.
Bathrooms: 10 private,
1 public.
Bed & breakfast: £30-£40 single, £40-£56 double.
Parking for 15.
Credit: Access, Visa, Diners, Amex.

Berni Royal Hotel
Manvers St., Bath, BA1 1JP
☎ (0225) 463134
Georgian in appearance, an attractive Victorian building in a central position, close to all services.
Bedrooms: 6 single, 13 double & 7 twin, 4 family rooms.
Bathrooms: 30 private.
Bed & breakfast: £54.50-£63.50 single, from £70 double.
Lunch available.
Evening meal 6pm (l.o. 10.30pm).
Credit: Access, Visa, Diners, Amex.

Blairgowrie Guest House ♨
⚜⚜
55 Wellsway, Bath, BA2 4RT
☎ (0225) 332266
Attractively decorated bedrooms with TV, refreshment facilities and extensive breakfast menu. 12 minute walk to Bath Abbey using original Fosseway.
Bedrooms: 1 twin, 1 family room.

Bathrooms: 2 private.
Bed & breakfast: £20-£30 single, £35-£45 double.

Brocks Guest House
⚜⚜
32 Brock Street, Bath,
BA1 2LN
☎ (0225) 338374
Elegant Georgian house between the Circus and the Royal Crescent. Offering care and personal attention.
Bedrooms: 2 single, 2 double & 2 twin, 2 family rooms.
Bathrooms: 4 private,
2 public; 1 private showers.
Bed & breakfast: £17.50-£18.50 single, £36-£48 double.

Brompton House Hotel ♨
⚜⚜ COMMENDED
St. John's Rd., Bathwick,
Bath, BA2 6PT
☎ (0225) 420972/448423
Elegant Georgian rectory in beautiful secluded gardens. 5 minutes' level walk to city centre. Car park.
Bedrooms: 2 single, 7 double & 2 twin, 1 family room.
Bathrooms: 12 private.
Bed & breakfast: £30-£35 single, £50-£55 double.
Parking for 12.
Credit: Access, Visa.

⊕ Display advertisement appears on page 456.

Carfax Hotel ♨
⚜⚜⚜⚜
Great Pulteney St., Bath,
BA2 4BS
☎ (0225) 462089 Fax (0225) 443 257
In a famous Georgian street, surrounded by beautiful Bath hills. The rear of Carfax overlooks Henrietta Park. A well maintained, listed building.
Bedrooms: 13 single, 8 double & 15 twin, 3 family rooms.
Bathrooms: 35 private,
2 public.
Bed & breakfast: £24-£42 single, £40-£60 double.
Half board: £27.50-£37.50 daily, £173.50-£236.25 weekly.
Evening meal 6.30pm (l.o. 7.50pm).
Parking for 17.
Credit: Access, Visa, Amex.

Circus Mansions
36 Brock St., Bath, BA1 2LJ
☎ (0225) 336462
Georgian house with original entrance hall and staircase, 2 double bedrooms with private bath/WC. Central heating in rooms. Located in the Circus.
Bedrooms: 1 single, 2 double & 1 twin, 1 family room.
Bathrooms: 5 private.
Bed & breakfast: max. £30 single, max. £42 double.

Cliffe Hotel ♨
⚜⚜⚜
Limpley Stoke, Bath,
BA3 6HY
☎ (0225) 723226
Telex 445731
Ⓒ Best Western
Country house hotel complete with elegant "Coterie Restaurant" overlooking spectacular views of Avon Valley. Outdoor heated pool.
Bedrooms: 4 double & 4 twin, 3 family rooms.
Bathrooms: 11 private.
Bed & breakfast: £65-£85 single, £75-£100 double.
Half board: £58-£63 daily, £370-£395 weekly.
Lunch available.
Evening meal 6.45pm (l.o. 9.30pm).
Parking for 30.
Credit: Access, Visa, Diners, Amex.

Dorian House
One Upper Oldfield Park,
Bath, BA2 3JX
☎ (0225) 426336
Gracious Victorian house on southern slopes of Bath overlooking the city. Free parking and only 10 minutes' walk to the centre.
Bedrooms: 1 single, 2 double & 2 twin, 2 family rooms.
Bathrooms: 7 private.
Bed & breakfast: £28-£38 single, £42-£54 double.
Parking for 9.
Credit: Access, Visa, Diners.

Dukes Hotel ♨
⚜⚜⚜
Great Pulteney St., Bath,
BA2 4DN
☎ (0225) 463512 Telex 449227
Elegantly refurbished Georgian town hotel. Centrally located. Full restaurant and bar. Personal service and welcome from resident proprietor and staff.

Bedrooms: 5 single, 9 double & 4 twin, 4 family rooms.
Bathrooms: 20 private,
1 public.
Bed & breakfast: £50-£65 single, £60-£95 double.
Lunch available.
Evening meal 6.45pm (l.o. 8.30pm).
Credit: Access, Visa, Amex.

Edgar Hotel
⚜⚜ APPROVED
64 Gt. Pulteney St., Bath,
BA2 4DN
☎ (0225) 420619
Small private hotel, proprietor-run, in Great Pulteney Street which leads to centre of Bath. Roman remains (approximately 600 yards).
Bedrooms: 2 single, 9 double & 4 twin, 1 family room.
Bathrooms: 16 private.
Bed & breakfast: £25-£30 single, £35-£50 double.

⊕ Display advertisement appears on page 457.

Forres Guest House
⚜⚜
172 Newbridge Rd., Lower Weston, Bath, BA1 3LE
☎ (0225) 427698
Edwardian family guesthouse with friendly, informative hosts, who are ex-teachers and love Bath. River Avon and Cotswold Way close by. Traditional and vegetarian breakfasts. Colour TV in all rooms.
Bedrooms: 2 double & 2 twin, 1 family room.
Bathrooms: 5 private,
1 public.
Bed & breakfast: £18 single, £26-£35 double.
Parking for 5.
Open April-October.

Gainsborough Hotel ♨
⚜⚜
Weston La., Bath, BA1 4AB
☎ (0225) 311380
Small country house hotel in quiet, secluded garden near Victoria Park. The abbey and Roman baths are 1.25 miles away.
Bedrooms: 2 single, 8 double & 4 twin, 2 family rooms.
Bathrooms: 16 private.
Bed & breakfast: £25-£35 single, £55-£68 double.
Half board: £35-£45 daily.

Continued ▶

BATH
Continued

Evening meal 7pm (l.o. 8.30pm).
Parking for 18.
Credit: Access, Visa, Amex.

Green Lane House M

1 Green La., Hinton Charterhouse, Bath, BA3 6BL
☎ (0225) 723631
Fully renovated, attractive stone house built in 1725, family-run and comfortably furnished. Quiet village in beautiful countryside, convenient for Bath, Bristol and Cotswolds.
Bedrooms: 2 double & 2 twin.
Bathrooms: 2 private, 1 public.
Bed & breakfast: £23-£39 single, £34-£52 double.
Half board: £32.50-£49.50 daily.
Evening meal 7.30pm (l.o. 10.30am).
Parking for 4.
Open February-November.
Credit: Access, Visa.

Haute Combe

176 Newbridge Rd., Bath, BA1 3LE
☎ (0225) 420061
Elegant family-run Victorian guesthouse with car park. Close to park and ride scheme, minutes from the attractions, yet far from the crowds.
Bedrooms: 1 single, 5 double, 2 family rooms.
Bathrooms: 5 private, 1 public; 1 private shower.
Bed & breakfast: £18-£28 single, £28-£44 double.
Half board: £28-£38 daily.
Evening meal 8pm (l.o. 6pm).
Parking for 8.
Credit: Access, Visa.

Horseshoe House M
COMMENDED

51 Sydney Buildings, Bath, BA2 6DB
☎ (0225) 466354
Georgian house taking only 5 guests enabling personal service and the atmosphere of living at home. 10 minutes' walk abbey/city centre.
Bedrooms: 1 single, 1 double & 1 twin.
Bathrooms: 1 private, 1 public.

Bed & breakfast: £24-£49 single, £48-£56 double.
Half board: £40.50-£44.50 daily, £262.50-£290.50 weekly.
Lunch available.
Evening meal 6pm (l.o. 8pm).

Jay Court

122 Walcot St., Bath, BA1 5BG
☎ (0225) 448838
Hotel apartments in central Bath, attractively furnished, serviced daily, cleaned, beds made, washing-up undertaken. Entrance hall, 2 double bedrooms, living/dining room, bathroom and kitchen. Prices quoted are per apartment accommodating up to 4, and do not include breakfast/evening meal. Colour brochure available.
Bedrooms: 6 double.
Bathrooms: 6 private.
Bed & breakfast: from £69 single.
Half board: from £396 weekly.
Credit: Access, Visa, Amex.

Kennard Hotel M
APPROVED

11 Henrietta St., Bath, BA2 6LL
☎ (0225) 310472 & (0225) 330159
Converted Georgian house in quiet street. A few minutes' level walk to city centre, abbey, Roman Baths, Pump Rooms and Henrietta Park.
Bedrooms: 2 single, 6 double & 3 twin, 1 family room.
Bathrooms: 9 private, 2 public.
Bed & breakfast: £25-£30 single, £35-£50 double.
Credit: Access, Visa.

Laura Place Hotel M
COMMENDED

3 Laura Pl., Great Pulteney St., Bath, BA2 4BH
☎ (0225) 463815
18th C town house, centrally located in Georgian square. 2 minutes from Roman Baths, Pump Rooms and abbey.
Bedrooms: 2 single, 3 double & 5 twin.
Bathrooms: 6 private, 2 public.
Bed & breakfast: £20-£40 single, £44-£70 double.
Parking for 10.
Open March-December.
Credit: Access, Visa, Amex.

Leighton House M
COMMENDED

139 Wells Rd., Bath, BA2 3AL
☎ (0225) 314769
An elegant and spacious Victorian guesthouse set in gardens of one third of an acre. 10 minutes' walk from city centre. Evening meals available by arrangement.
Bedrooms: 3 double & 2 twin, 2 family rooms.
Bathrooms: 7 private.
Bed & breakfast: £48-£55 double.
Parking for 7.
Credit: Access, Visa.

Limpley Stoke Hotel M

Lower Limpley Stoke, Bath, BA3 6HZ
☎ (0225) 723333. Fax (0225) 722406 Telex 57515
CR Consort
Delightfully situated in the noted valley of the River Avon. Bordered by the counties of Somerset, Wiltshire and Avon. 4 miles south of Bath on A36/B3108.
Bedrooms: 12 double & 33 twin, 10 family rooms.
Bathrooms: 55 private.
Bed & breakfast: from £54.50 single, from £68.50 double.
Half board: from £48.50 daily, from £295 weekly.
Evening meal 7pm (l.o. 8.30pm).
Parking for 60.
Credit: Access, Visa, Diners, Amex.

Millers Hotel M

69 Great Pulteney St., Bath, BA2 4DL
☎ (0225) 465798
Centrally situated in Bath and close to all attractions and amenities. Some bedrooms have colour TV.
Bedrooms: 4 single, 3 double & 4 twin, 3 family rooms.
Bathrooms: 5 private, 3 public.
Bed & breakfast: £24-£36 single, £36-£50 double.
Lunch available.

Monmouth Place Hotel M

Monmouth Pl., Upper Bristol Rd., Bath, BA1 2AU
☎ (0225) 429378
Convenient for shopping and sightseeing. Parking available

and courtesy car service. Small friendly hotel, 5 minutes' walk to city centre.
Bedrooms: 7 single, 2 double & 1 twin, 2 family rooms.
Bathrooms: 5 private, 3 public.
Bed & breakfast: £18-£24 single.
Parking for 8.
Credit: Access, Visa, Diners, Amex.

North Parade Hotel M
APPROVED

10, North Parade, Bath, BA2 4AL
☎ (0225) 463384
Georgian building in the city centre overlooking Parade Gardens. Run by resident family to ensure personal service.
Bedrooms: 9 single, 5 double & 4 twin.
Bathrooms: 12 private, 2 public.
Bed & breakfast: £24-£40 single, £52-£80 double.
Half board: £32.25-£50 daily, £204.75-£260 weekly.
Evening meal 6.30pm (l.o. 9pm).
Credit: Access, Visa, Diners, Amex.

Oakleigh House M

19 Upper Oldfield Pk., Bath, BA2 3JX
☎ (0225) 315698
Your comfort is assured at this tastefully modernised Victorian home, quietly situated only 10 minutes from the city centre.
Bedrooms: 3 double & 1 twin.
Bathrooms: 4 private.
Bed & breakfast: £30-£45 single, £40-£50 double.
Parking for 4.
Credit: Access, Visa.

Old Mill Hotel & Restaurant M
APPROVED

Tollbridge Rd., Bath, BA1 7DE
☎ Bath (0225) 858476
Situated on banks of River Avon, only 2 miles from Bath centre. New revolving water wheel restaurant. Rooms offer unique breathtaking riverside views.
Bedrooms: 1 single, 6 double & 6 twin, 2 family rooms.
Bathrooms: 15 private.
Bed & breakfast: £35-£38 single, £48-£58 double.

Half board: £35-£40 daily, £200-£250 weekly.
Lunch available.
Evening meal 7.30pm (l.o. 9.30pm).
Parking for 36.
Credit: Access, Visa, Diners, Amex.

⬛ Display advertisement appears on page 459.

The Old School House M
≝≝≝ COMMENDED
Church St., Bathford, Bath, BA1 7RR
☎ Bath (0225) 859593
Pretty Victorian schoolhouse of Bath stone in peaceful conservation area. Views and fine walks overlooking Avon valley. 3 miles to Bath centre. All rooms have full private facilities. Dinners, licensed. Non-smoking.
Bedrooms: 3 double & 3 twin.
Bathrooms: 6 private.
Bed & breakfast: £35 single, £48-£52 double.
Half board: £40-£51 daily, £246-£308 weekly.
Evening meal 7pm (l.o. 9pm).
Parking for 6.
Credit: Access, Visa.

Oldfields M
≝≝ COMMENDED
102 Wells Rd., Bath, BA2 3AL
☎ (0225) 317984
Large detached Victorian house decorated in harmony with the age of the house. 10 minutes' walk to Roman Baths.
Bedrooms: 7 double & 7 twin.
Bathrooms: 8 private, 2 public.
Bed & breakfast: £36-£48 double.
Parking for 10.
Credit: Access, Visa.

The Oxford Hotel
Listed
5 Oxford Row, Lansdown Rd., Bath, BA1 2QN
☎ (0225) 314039
18th C double fronted building, centrally situated minutes from Royal Crescent & Assembly Rooms. Rooms with TV, free tea/coffee facilities.
Bedrooms: 3 single, 4 double & 1 twin, 2 family rooms.

Bathrooms: 2 private, 2 public; 3 private showers.
Bed & breakfast: £18-£21 single, £34-£38 double.

Priory Hotel & Restaurant M
≝≝≝≝ HIGHLY COMMENDED
Weston Rd., Bath, BA1 2XT
☎ (0225) 331922 Fax (0225) 44612
Country house style hotel in a quiet suburb of Bath. Renowned restaurant, 21 beautifully appointed rooms and glorious garden.
Bedrooms: 3 single, 6 double & 12 twin.
Bathrooms: 21 private.
Bed & breakfast: from £85 single, from £135 double.
Lunch available.
Evening meal 7.15pm (l.o. 9.30pm).
Parking for 26.
Credit: Access, Visa, Diners, Amex.

Royal Crescent Hotel M
16 Royal Cres., Bath, BA1 2LS
☎ (0225) 319090
Telex 444251
⬛ Queens Moat Houses
This Georgian, Grade I listed building is at the centre of one of Europe's greatest architectural masterpieces and comprises the 2 central houses.
Bedrooms: 3 single, 21 double & 10 twin, 10 family rooms.
Bathrooms: 44 private.
Bed & breakfast: £99-£120 single, £130-£200 double.
Half board: £100-£135 daily.
Lunch available.
Evening meal 7pm (l.o. 9.30pm).
Parking for 16.
Credit: Access, Visa, Diners, Amex.

Siena Hotel M
≝≝
25 Pulteney Rd., Bath, BA2 4EZ
☎ (0225) 425495
Situated a few minutes' level walking distance from the city centre, overlooking Bath Abbey and the county cricket ground.
Bedrooms: 2 single, 4 double & 2 twin, 2 family rooms.
Bathrooms: 10 private.
Bed & breakfast: £20-£25 single, £34-£42 double.
Half board: £23-£27.50 daily, £150-£180 weekly.

Evening meal 6pm (l.o. 8pm).
Parking for 12.
Credit: Access, Visa.

Underhill Lodge
Warminster Rd., Bathampton, Bath, BA2 6XQ
☎ (0225) 464992
Distinctive, secluded, licensed property with delightful valley views. Offering high standard accommodation. 1.5 miles from Bath along A36 Warminster road.
Bedrooms: 1 single, 2 double & 1 twin.
Bathrooms: 4 private.
Bed & breakfast: £40-£42 single, £50-£55 double.
Evening meal 7.30pm (l.o. 7.30pm).
Parking for 10.
Credit: Access, Visa.

Villa Magdala Hotel
≝≝
Henrietta Rd., Bath, BA2 6LX
☎ (0225) 466329
Quietly situated villa, overlooking Henrietta Park. Close to the city centre and Roman Baths. All rooms en-suite. Car parking.
Bedrooms: 11 double & 4 twin, 2 family rooms.
Bathrooms: 17 private.
Bed & breakfast: £38-£40 single, £52-£75 double.
Parking for 15.
Credit: Access, Visa.

Wellsway Guest House
≝≝
51 Wellsway, Bath, BA2 4RS
☎ (0225) 423434
Comfortable, clean, warm small guesthouse on bus route. Close to local shops, only a few minutes' walk from city centre.
Bedrooms: 1 double & 2 twin, 1 family room.
Bathrooms: 1 public.
Bed & breakfast: £20-£32 double.
Parking for 3.

Wentworth House Hotel M
≝≝ COMMENDED
106 Bloomfield Rd., Bath, BA2 2AP
☎ (0225) 339193

Fine Victorian house in three-quarters of an acre of secluded grounds with swimming pool, large car park, lawns and gardens. In a quiet residential area.
Bedrooms: 3 single, 9 double & 6 twin, 2 family rooms.
Bathrooms: 13 private, 3 public.
Bed & breakfast: £21-£30 single, £35-£45 double.
Evening meal 7pm (l.o. 6.30pm).
Parking for 20.
Credit: Access, Visa.

BEAMINSTER
Dorset
Map ref 2A3

Old country town of mellow local stone set amid hills and rural vales. Mainly Georgian buildings; attractive almshouses date from 1603. The 17th C church with its ornate, pinnacled tower was extensively restored inside by the Victorians. Parnham, a Tudor manor house, lies 1 mile south.

Bridge House Hotel M
≝≝≝ APPROVED
Prout Bridge, Beaminster, DT8 3AY
☎ (0308) 862200
Attractive 13th C building with beautiful, walled garden. Rooms have all modern facilities. Restaurant serves fresh, local produce cooked to order.
Bedrooms: 1 single, 5 double & 2 twin, 1 family room.
Bathrooms: 9 private.
Bed & breakfast: £35.50-£42.50 single, £55-£65 double.
Half board: £44-£49 daily, £262-£291 weekly.
Lunch available.
Evening meal 7pm (l.o. 9pm).
Parking for 22.
Credit: Access, Visa.

Jenny Wrens
≝≝
1 Hogshill St., Beaminster, DT8 3AE
☎ (0308) 862814
17th C tea shop and bed and breakfast accommodation with full English breakfast.
Bedrooms: 2 double & 1 twin.
Bathrooms: 2 private, 1 public.

Continued ▶

BEAMINSTER

Continued

Bed & breakfast: £15-£18
single, £30-£36 double.
Parking for 1.

🛇12 🖭 📺 ❖ Ⓤ 🛉 🎮 📺
▥ ♨ 🎮 SP

BEER

Devon
Map ref 1D2

Formerly noted for lace-
making and smuggling,
this picturesque fishing
village lies close to some
of Devon's most striking
cliff scenery at Beer
Head. Good smugglers'
caves. Quarries to west
of village were worked in
Roman times.

Durham House Hotel
👑👑

Fore St., Beer, EX12 3JL
☎ Seaton (0297) 20449
*Small family hotel offering
comfort and traditional English
food. 3 minutes from sea, in
small Devon fishing village.*
Bedrooms: 3 single, 3 double
& 2 twin, 3 family rooms.
Bathrooms: 2 private,
2 public.
Bed & breakfast: £12.50-£15
single, £25-£30 double.
Half board: £19.50-£22 daily.
Evening meal 7pm (l.o. 7pm).
Credit: Access, Visa.

🛇 🎮 🛉 Ⓥ 🎮 📺 ▥ ♨
🍴 ⒹⒶⒻ SP

Garlands

Stovar Long La., Beer,
Seaton, EX12 3EA
☎ Seaton (0297) 20958
*An Edwardian character house
in an acre of grounds with
panoramic views of sea and
country.*
Bedrooms: 3 double & 1 twin,
2 family rooms.
Bathrooms: 4 private,
1 public.
Bed & breakfast: £14-£17.50
single, £28-£35 double.
Half board: £21.50-£25 daily,
£140-£160 weekly.
Lunch available.
Evening meal 6.30pm (l.o.
midday).
Parking for 12.

🛇 ❖ Ⓥ 🎮 📺 ▥ 🍴 ❖ ♨
SP 📺

Swallows Eaves 🏰
👑👑👑 COMMENDED

Colyford, Colyton, EX13 6QJ
☎ Colyton (0297) 53184

---

*Comfortable accommodation in
attractive gabled property.
Village setting between
Sidmouth and Lyme Regis.
Large natural garden.
Interesting menu using fresh
local produce.*
Bedrooms: 3 double & 3 twin.
Bathrooms: 6 private.
Bed & breakfast: £23.50-£25
single, £47-£50 double.
Half board: £25-£39 daily,
£210-£238 weekly.
Lunch available.
Evening meal 7pm (l.o. 8pm).
Parking for 10.

🛇8 ♨ 🖭 🎮 ❖ 🛉 Ⓥ 🎮 ▥
♨ 🍴 ❖ ⦿ 🎮 ▥ ♨ SP 📺

BERRYNARBOR

Devon
Map ref 1C1

Small village set in a
wooded valley, close to
Exmoor and to the wild
North Devon coast.

Langleigh House
👑👑 APPROVED

The Village, Berrynarbor,
Ilfracombe, EX34 9SG
☎ Combe Martin
(0271) 883410
*Friendly family-run guesthouse
providing all home-cooked
food, in the beautiful North
Devon village of Berrynarbor.*
Bedrooms: 1 single, 3 double
& 1 twin, 1 family room.
Bathrooms: 4 private,
1 public.
Bed & breakfast: £12.50-£14
single, £25-£28 double.
Half board: £18.50-£30 daily,
£120-£130 weekly.
Evening meal 6.30pm (l.o.
3pm).
Parking for 8.

🛇 🎮 Ⓤ 🛉 Ⓥ 🎮 📺 ▥ ♨
❖ ▥

Sandy Cove Hotel 🏰

Berrynarbor, Ilfracombe,
EX34 9SR
☎ Combe Martin
(0271) 882243
*In many acres of own grounds
incorporating garden, cliffs,
own beach and woods.
Overlooks Combe Martin Bay,
the beaches, sea and Exmoor.
Outdoor pool, sauna, sunbed,
gym equipment and whirlpool.*
Bedrooms: 2 single, 16 double
& 6 twin, 10 family rooms.
Bathrooms: 34 private.
Bed & breakfast: £35.50
single, £71 double.
Half board: £53.13 daily,
£305 weekly.
Lunch available.

Evening meal 7pm (l.o.
9.30pm).
Parking for 70.

🛇 ♨ 🖭 📞 🖭 🎮 ❖ 🛉 Ⓥ
▥ 📺 ▥ ♨ 🍴 ❖ ♨ ❖ 🍴
❖ ⦿ SP 📺

BIDEFORD

Devon
Map ref 1C1

Once the home port of Sir
Richard Grenville, this
handsome town with its
17th C merchants'
houses flourished as a
shipbuilding and cloth
town, later dealing in
Newfoundland cod and
American tobacco. The
mile-long quay is still
busy with light shipping
as well as pleasure craft.
The bridge of 24 arches
was built about 1460.
Charles Kingsley stayed
here while writing
Westward Ho!

The Mount Hotel 🏰
👑👑👑 APPROVED

North Down Rd., Bideford,
EX39 3LP
☎ (0237) 473748
*Small, family-run hotel over
200 years old, with character
and charm. Peaceful garden.
Few minutes' walk to town
centre and quay. Ideal base for
touring north Devon.*
Bedrooms: 2 single, 4 double
& 1 twin, 1 family room.
Bathrooms: 5 private,
1 public.
Bed & breakfast: £18.50-£23
single, £32-£39 double.
Half board: £25.50-£31 daily,
£154-£210 weekly.
Evening meal 6.30pm (l.o.
5.50pm).
Parking for 4.
Credit: Access, Visa.

🛇5 ❖ 🛉 Ⓥ ✂ 🎮 📺 ▥ ♨
🍴 ❖ ▥ ⒹⒶⒻ SP ▥

Riversford Hotel 🏰
👑👑👑 APPROVED

Limers La., Bideford,
EX39 2RG
☎ (023 72) 474239/470381
Ⓒ🅡 Inter
*Peace and tranquillity in
gardens beside the River
Torridge. Candlelit restaurant,
English cooking. Close to
sandy beaches and well placed
for touring. Take the A386
from Bideford to Northam for
a mile, turn right into Limmers
Lane.*
Bedrooms: 2 single, 7 double
& 5 twin, 2 family rooms.
Bathrooms: 14 private,
2 public.

Bed & breakfast: £42-£47
single, £64-£74 double.
Half board: £48.80-£53.80
daily, £220-£310 weekly.
Lunch available.
Evening meal 7pm (l.o. 9pm).
Parking for 22.
Credit: Access, Visa, Diners,
Amex.

🛇 ❖ 📞 🖭 🎮 ❖ 🛉 Ⓥ 🎮
📺 ⦿ ▥ ♨ 🍴 Ⓤ ❖ 🍴 ❖
❖ SP 📺

Royal Hotel 🏰

Barnstaple St., Bideford,
EX39 4AE
☎ (0237) 472005 Telex 42551
EXONIA G (REF BREND
8)
Ⓒ🅡 Brend
*Recently refurbished, this
historic hotel overlooks the
Bideford Bridge.*
Bedrooms: 5 single, 10 double
& 14 twin, 4 family rooms.
Bathrooms: 32 private,
6 public.
Bed & breakfast: £44-£50
single, £66-£77 double.
Half board: £44-£60 daily,
£265-£375 weekly.
Lunch available.
Evening meal 7pm (l.o. 9pm).
Parking for 34.
Credit: Access, Visa, Diners,
Amex.

🛇 ❖ 📞 🖭 🎮 ❖ 🛉 Ⓥ 🎮
⦿ ▥ ♨ 🍴 🛉 ❖ ❖ SP ▥
📺

Sunset Hotel 🏰

Landcross, Bideford,
EX39 5JA
☎ (023 72) 472962
*Small elegant hotel well-
situated overlooking Devon
beauty spot. High standard of
comfort and cleanliness with
en-suite rooms and home-made
food. Non-smokers only please.*
Bedrooms: 1 single, 2 double
& 1 twin, 2 family rooms.
Bathrooms: 5 private,
1 public.
Bed & breakfast: £16-£19
double.
Half board: £25-£26.50 daily,
£154-£162.50 weekly.
Evening meal 7pm (l.o. 7pm).
Parking for 10.
Open February-November.

🛇 ❖ 🛉 Ⓥ ✂ 🎮 📺 ▥ ♨
🍴 ❖ ⒹⒶⒻ SP

Yeoldon House Hotel &
Restaurant 🏰
👑👑👑

Durrant La., Northam,
Bideford, EX39 2RL
☎ (0237) 474400
Ⓒ🅡 Best Western

Victorian country house, now a small comfortable hotel. English and continental cooking and an interesting wine list. Hospitable owners and friendly staff.
Bedrooms: 4 double & 4 twin, 2 family rooms.
Bathrooms: 10 private, 1 public.
Bed & breakfast: £38.50-£40.50 single, £62.50-£65.50 double.
Half board: £49.75-£52.25 daily, £231-£243 weekly.
Lunch available.
Evening meal 7pm (l.o. 9pm).
Parking for 20.
Credit: Access, Visa, C.Bl., Diners, Amex.

Display advertisement appears on page 460.

BIGBURY-ON-SEA
Devon
Map ref 1C3

Small resort on Bigbury Bay at the mouth of the River Avon. Wide sands, rugged cliffs. Burgh Island can be reached on foot at low tide.

Henley Hotel
APPROVED
Folly Hill, Bigbury-on-Sea, Kingsbridge, TQ7 4AR
☎ (0548) 810240
Small comfortable hotel on the edge of the sea. Spectacular views from most rooms. Rural coastal village. Non-smokers only please.
Bedrooms: 3 single, 2 double & 2 twin, 1 family room.
Bathrooms: 6 private, 1 public.
Bed & breakfast: £18.50-£22.50 single, £39-£45 double.
Half board: £31-£34 daily, £189.75-£214.50 weekly.
Lunch available.
Evening meal 7pm (l.o. 8pm).
Parking for 10.
Credit: Access, Visa.

Half board prices shown are per person but in some cases may be based on double/twin occupancy.

BODMIN
Cornwall
Map ref 1B2

County town south-west of Bodmin Moor with a ruined Augustinian priory and beautiful church, containing the casket said to have held relics of St. Petroc, to whom the church is dedicated, Prior Vyvyan's tomb of local slate and a fine Norman font. Interesting buildings include Tudor Guildhall, classic Assize Courts and Victorian County Gaol. Nearby are Lanhydrock House and Pencarrow House.

Tredethy Country Hotel
Helland Bridge, Bodmin, PL30 4QS
☎ St. Mabyn (020 884) 262/364/325
Gracious living with spacious rooms, log fires in winter and absolute peace and quiet in beautiful surroundings. From Bodmin take the Launceston road, then the Helland turn off. Through Helland down to Helland Bridge. Tredethy is up the hill over the bridge.
Bedrooms: 1 single, 7 double & 3 twin.
Bathrooms: 11 private.
Bed & breakfast: £26-£34 single, £44-£72 double.
Half board: £30-£44 daily, £160-£280 weekly.
Evening meal 7pm (l.o. 8.30pm).
Parking for 30.
Credit: Access, Visa.

Wilbury Guest House
Fletchers Bridge, Bodmin, PL30 4AN
☎ (0208) 74001
Large new modern house, close to moors, sea, woods. Ideal for walking holidays. Home cooking a speciality. Home from home. Bodmin 1 mile.
Bedrooms: 1 double & 2 twin.
Bathrooms: 1 public.
Bed & breakfast: max. £10 single, max. £20 double.
Half board: max. £18 daily, max. £126 weekly.
Evening meal 6pm.
Parking for 10.

BOSCASTLE
Cornwall
Map ref 1B2

Small, unspoilt village in Valency Valley, steeply built at meeting of 2 rivers. Active as a port until onset of railway era and tourism, its dramatic natural harbour affords rare shelter on this wild coast. Attractions include spectacular blow-hole, Celtic field strips, part-Norman church. 2 miles east, St. Juliot Church was restored by Thomas Hardy (1872).

Bottreaux House Hotel
COMMENDED
Boscastle, PL35 0BG
☎ (084 05) 231
Character Georgian house overlooking unspoilt National Trust harbour village and enjoying superb panoramic views of sea, cliffs and countryside.
Bedrooms: 5 double & 2 twin.
Bathrooms: 7 private.
Bed & breakfast: from £28.50 single, £48-£52 double.
Half board: £34-£38.50 daily, £220-£230 weekly.
Evening meal 7.30pm (l.o. 9.30pm).
Parking for 10.
Open February-November.
Credit: Access, Visa.

Forrabury House
Forrabury Common, Boscastle, PL35 0DJ
☎ (084 05) 469
The former rectory to Forabury Church. Offers bed and breakfast, full board or half board accommodation. Various diets catered for on request.
Bedrooms: 2 double & 1 twin, 1 family room.
Bathrooms: 1 public; 4 private showers.
Bed & breakfast: £11.50-£12 single, £23-£24 double.
Half board: £18.50-£19 daily.
Lunch available.
Evening meal 6.30pm (l.o. 10am).
Parking for 5.

Lower Meadows House
Penally Hill, Boscastle Harbour, Boscastle, PL35 0HF
☎ (084 05) 570

Private licensed hotel, in peaceful rural setting with direct access to large public car park and adjoining gardens. Menu personally prepared by chef/proprietors.
Bedrooms: 1 single, 2 double & 1 twin, 1 family room.
Bathrooms: 3 public.
Bed & breakfast: £10.50-£15.50 single, £21-£31 double.
Half board: £18-£23 daily, £120-£155 weekly.
Lunch available.
Evening meal 7pm (l.o. 8pm).
Credit: Access, Visa.

Melbourne House
COMMENDED
New Rd., Boscastle, PL35 0DH
☎ (084 05) 650
Elegant Victorian house in National Trust area above Boscastle Harbour and village. Situated in area of outstanding natural beauty.
Bedrooms: 1 single, 3 double & 2 twin.
Bathrooms: 2 private, 2 public.
Bed & breakfast: £12-£14 single, £24-£32 double.
Half board: £19-£23 daily, £119-£144.90 weekly.
Evening meal 7.30pm (l.o. 6pm).
Parking for 8.
Credit: Access, Visa.

The Old Coach House
Tintagel Rd., Boscastle, PL35 0AS
☎ (084 05) 398
Relax in beautiful 300-year-old former coach-house. All en-suite with colour TV. Licensed. Friendly and helpful service.
Bedrooms: 1 single, 2 double & 2 twin, 1 family room.
Bathrooms: 6 private.
Bed & breakfast: £13-£20 single, £26-£40 double.
Half board: £22-£29 daily, £140-£183 weekly.
Lunch available.
Evening meal 7pm (l.o. 6pm).
Parking for 6.
Open March-November.
Credit: Access, Visa, Amex.

Tolcarne Hotel
APPROVED
Tintagel Rd., Boscastle, PL35 0AS
☎ (084 05) 654
Continued ▶

377

BOSCASTLE
Continued

Attractive house of character in own grounds with lovely views. Ample parking. Traditional cooking and a warm welcome.
Bedrooms: 1 single, 3 double & 4 twin, 1 family room.
Bathrooms: 6 private, 2 public.
Bed & breakfast: £16-£19.25 single, £24-£34.50 double.
Half board: £18.50-£23.75 daily, £129-£155 weekly.
Evening meal 7pm (l.o. 5.30pm).
Parking for 15.
Open April-October.
Credit: Access, Visa.
⌂ ❄ ♦ ⓘ 🔻 Ⅴ ꒰ ⓣⅴ ꜔ ▬
♨ ꜀ ❄ ꜱ꜀

Wellington Hotel ▲
🏵🏵🏵 COMMENDED
The Harbour, Boscastle,
PL35 0AQ
☎ (084 05) 202
Fax (084 05) 621
Historic listed 16th C coaching inn by Elizabethan harbour and National Trust walks. Georgian restaurant with Anglo-French cuisine. Free house, real ales and buffet. Open fire and beams.
Bedrooms: 8 single, 11 double & 2 twin.
Bathrooms: 16 private, 2 public.
Bed & breakfast: £17-£29 single, £48-£54 double.
Half board: £29-£42 daily, £180-£243 weekly.
Lunch available.
Evening meal 7pm (l.o. 9.30pm).
Parking for 20.
Open February-November.
Credit: Access, Visa, Diners, Amex.
⌂ 10 ꒰ ꜀ ⓑ 🔻 ❄ ⓘ Ⅴ
�꜀ ꒰ ⓣⅴ ꜔ ▬ ♨ ♦ ꒱ ♨
ꝑ ❄ ꜱ꜀ ꜰ ⓣ
⚙ Display advertisement appears on page 460.

BOVEY TRACEY
Devon
Map ref 1D2

Standing by the river just east of Dartmoor National Park, this old town has good moorland views. Its church, with a 14th C tower, holds one of Devon's finest medieval rood screens.

Dolphin Hotel
Station Rd., Bovey Tracey, TQ13 9AL
☎ (0626) 832413
Formerly a coaching house, has recently been completely refurbished and now offers a high standard of accommodation.
Bedrooms: 1 single, 3 double & 4 twin.
Bathrooms: 8 private.
Bed & breakfast: £30-£35 single, £50-£55 double.
Lunch available.
Evening meal 6.30pm (l.o. 9.30pm).
Parking for 50.
Credit: Access, Visa.
⌂ ꜀ ⓑ 🔻 ❄ ꜱ Ⅴ ꜔ ▬
♨ ꜀ ꝑ ꜰ ꜰ

Moorland Hotel ▲
🏵🏵🏵🏵 APPROVED
Haytor, Newton Abbot, TQ13 9XT
☎ (036 46) 407
Set in delightful grounds below Haytor Rock. Superb views of open moorland and coast from all rooms and self-catering apartments.
Bedrooms: 2 single, 9 double & 9 twin, 2 family rooms.
Bathrooms: 22 private.
Bed & breakfast: from £28 single, from £56 double.
Half board: from £40 daily, from £260 weekly.
Lunch available.
Evening meal 7.30pm (l.o. 9.30pm).
Parking for 50.
⌂ ꜀ ꜀ ⓑ 🔻 ❄ ꜱ ⓘ Ⅴ ꜔
♨ ▬ ♨ ꜰ ꜀ ❄ ꜱ ꜱ꜀ ꜰ
ⓣ

BRADFORD-ON-AVON
Wiltshire
Map ref 2B2

Huddled steeply beside the river, the old stone buildings of this former cloth-weaving town reflect continuing prosperity from the Middle Ages. There is a tiny Anglo-Saxon church, part of a monastery sacked by Danes. The part-14th C bridge carries a medieval chapel, later used as a gaol. Nearby are Westwood Manor, Great Chalfield Manor and one of England's largest tithe barns at Barton Farm.
Tourist Information Centre ☎ (02216) 5797

Bradford Old Windmill ▲
4 Masons La., Bradford-on-Avon, BA15 1QN
☎ (0225) 866842
Circular tower of converted windmill standing high above the Cotswold-stone town of Bradford-on-Avon. Peaceful situation close to Bath. Non-smokers only please.
Bedrooms: 1 single, 1 double & 1 twin, 1 family room.
Bathrooms: 3 private, 1 public.
Bed & breakfast: £24-£30 single, £40-£60 double.
Half board: £35-£45 daily.
Evening meal 8pm (l.o. 10am).
Parking for 4.
⌂ 6 ⓑ 🔻 ❄ ⓤ ⓘ Ⅴ ꜔ ▬
▬ ♨ ❄ ꜀ ꜱ ꜱ꜀ ꜰ

Leigh Park Hotel ▲
🏵🏵🏵🏵
Bradford-on-Avon, BA15 2RA
☎ (022 16) 4885 Telex 56396
Set in 4 acres, the Leigh Park Hotel is quiet and relaxing with personal attention from the owners. Facilities include a snooker room.
Bedrooms: 4 single, 8 double & 5 twin, 3 family rooms.
Bathrooms: 20 private, 1 public.
Bed & breakfast: £62-£82 single, £68-£98 double.
Half board: £70-£90 daily.
Lunch available.
Evening meal 7pm (l.o. 8.30pm).
Parking for 62.

Credit: Access, Visa, Diners, Amex.
⌂ ⌂ ꜀ ꜀ ⓑ 🔻 ❄ ⓘ Ⅴ
꜀ ⓣⅴ ꜔ ▬ ♨ ꜱ ꜀ ❄ ꜀ ꝑ ❄
⛎ ꜰ

Priory Steps ▲
🏵🏵🏵 COMMENDED
Newtown, Bradford-on-Avon, BA15 1NQ
☎ (022 16) 2230
17th C house in delightful location, with fine views over the Avon Valley. Comfortable and well-appointed accommodation.
Bedrooms: 3 double & 2 twin.
Bathrooms: 5 private.
Bed & breakfast: £34-£38 single, £48-£54 double.
Half board: £37-£41 daily.
Evening meal 7.30pm.
Parking for 7.
Credit: Access, Visa.
⌂ ꜀ ⓑ 🔻 ❄ ⓘ Ⅴ ꜔ ▬ ♨
꜀ ❄ ꜀ ꜱ ꜰ ⓣ

Widbrook Grange ▲
🏵🏵 COMMENDED
Trowbridge Rd., Bradford-on-Avon, BA15 1UH
☎ (022 16) 4750 & 3173
19th C Bath stone house with own grounds, in open countryside on the outskirts of Bradford-on-Avon. Riding and pony trekking nearby.
Bedrooms: 1 single, 5 double & 4 twin, 2 family rooms.
Bathrooms: 11 private, 1 public.
Bed & breakfast: £40-£49 single, £50-£70 double.
Parking for 55.
Credit: Access, Visa, Amex.
⌂ ꜀ ꜀ ꜀ ⓑ 🔻 ❄ Ⅴ ꜔
꜔ ▬ ♨ ꜀ ❄ ꜀ ꝑ ❄ ꜱ ꜰ
ⓣ

BRANSCOMBE
Devon
Map ref 1D2

5m E. Sidmouth
Scattered village of unusual character. Houses of cob and thatch are sited irregularly on the steep wooded slopes of a combe, which widens towards the sea. Much of Branscombe Estate is National Trust property.

The Bulstone ▲
🏵🏵🏵 COMMENDED
Higher Bulstone, Branscombe, Seaton, EX12 3BL
☎ (029 780) 446
Small friendly, family-run establishment offering personal service. Catering especially for those with young children.

Individual proprietors have supplied all details of accommodation. Although we do check for accuracy, we advise you to confirm prices and other information at the time of booking.

Please mention this guide when making a booking.

Bedrooms: 2 double,
10 family rooms.
Bathrooms: 6 private,
3 public.
Bed & breakfast: £32-£49
double.
Evening meal 7.45pm (l.o.
7.30pm).
Parking for 30.
Open February-November.

Portselda M
Listed
Branscombe, Seaton,
EX12 3DJ
☎ (029 780) 213
*Small guesthouse in village of
outstanding beauty, specialising
in fresh seafood, with a homely
atmosphere. Deep sea fishing
and golf available.*
Bedrooms: 1 double & 1 twin.
Bathrooms: 1 public.
Bed & breakfast: £12.50
single, £25 double.
Half board: £26 daily, £99.50
weekly.
Evening meal 7pm (l.o. 7pm).
Parking for 2.

Three Horseshoes M
Branscombe, Seaton,
EX12 3BR
☎ (029 780) 251
*Family-run inn with beams,
brasses, log fires. Short
distance from several seaside
resorts. Beautiful countryside
with excellent walks.*
Bedrooms: 2 single, 7 double
& 2 twin, 1 family room.
Bathrooms: 5 private,
2 public.
Bed & breakfast: £15-£18
single, £30-£36 double.
Half board: £20.50-£23.50
daily.
Evening meal 6pm (l.o.
10pm).
Parking for 102.
Credit: Access, Visa, Diners,
Amex.

The symbol **CR**
and the name of a
hotel group or
consortium after a
hotel address means
that bookings can
be made through a
central reservations
office. These are
listed on pages
559 & 560.

BRENT KNOLL
Somerset
Map ref 1D1

*2m NE. Burnham-on-Sea
Village sheltering beneath
the south-west slopes of
Brent Knoll, at the summit
of which is an Iron Age
fort (National Trust).
There are wide views
over levels toward the
sea. Among notable
features is the church is a
series of fine carvings on
3 medieval bench ends.
Easy access to the M5
between Bristol and
Exeter and to seaside
places on the
Somerset/Avon coast.*

Battleborough Grange Hotel M
COMMENDED
Bristol Rd., Brent Knoll,
TA9 4HJ
☎ (0278) 760208
*Comfortable hotel set in its
own grounds, on the A38, 1
mile from the M5 junction 22.
A la carte restaurant.*
Bedrooms: 1 single, 10 double
& 6 twin, 1 family room.
Bathrooms: 14 private,
1 public.
Bed & breakfast: £26-£46
single, £38-£60 double.
Half board: £38.50-£66 daily.
Lunch available.
Evening meal 7pm (l.o.
9.30pm).
Parking for 50.
Credit: Access, Visa, Diners,
Amex.

Shrub Farm Country House Hotel M
Burton Row, Brent Knoll,
Highbridge, TA9 4BX
☎ (0278) 760479
*Warm and friendly 500-year-
old farmhouse nestling in 3.5
acres of own grounds. All
rooms en-suite and attractively
decorated. Restaurant offers
table d'hote, a la carte, cream
teas, bar snacks and Sunday
lunches. Close to M5, exit 22.*
Bedrooms: 1 single, 6 double
& 2 twin, 1 family room.
Bathrooms: 10 private.
Bed & breakfast: £35-£45
single, £45-£55 double.
Half board: £31-£40 daily,
£175-£185 weekly.
Lunch available.
Evening meal 7pm (l.o.
9.30pm).

Parking for 20.
Credit: Access, Visa.

BRIDGWATER
Somerset
Map ref 1D1

Originally major medieval
port on the River Parrett,
now small industrial town
with mostly 19th C or
modern architecture.
Georgian Castle Street
leads to West Quay and
site of 13th C castle
razed to the ground by
Cromwell. Birthplace of
Cromwellian admiral
Robert Blake is now a
museum. Arts centre and
theatre, lido.

Appletree Inn
Keenthorne, Nether Stowey,
Bridgwater, TA5 1HZ
☎ (0278) 733238
*Small family hotel easily
located on the main A39
surrounded by rolling
Quantock Hills. Large car
park and gardens. Well known
restaurant.*
Bedrooms: 3 single, 5 double
& 4 twin, 3 family rooms.
Bathrooms: 15 private.
Bed & breakfast: £28-£35
single, from £40 double.
Lunch available.
Evening meal 6.30pm (l.o.
10pm).
Parking for 60.
Credit: Access, Visa, Amex.

Friarn Court Hotel M
37 St. Mary St., Bridgwater
☎ (0278) 452859 Fax (0278)
452988
*Fine restaurant. Cosy bar.
Ideal base for business or
pleasure. Interesting weekend
breaks. Send for our brochure.*
Bedrooms: 1 single, 4 double
& 7 twin.
Bathrooms: 10 private,
1 public.
Bed & breakfast: £44.50-
£59.50 single, £54.50-£69.50
double.
Lunch available.
Evening meal 7.30pm (l.o.
9.30pm).
Parking for 14.
Credit: Access, Visa, Diners,
Amex.

Walnut Tree Inn M
COMMENDED
North Petherton, Bridgwater,
TA6 6QA
☎ (0278) 662255
CR Best Western
*An 18th C coaching inn on
A38, 1 mile from M5 exit 24.
A welcome stopover for
businessmen and tourists.*
Bedrooms: 2 single, 17 double
& 7 twin, 2 family rooms.
Bathrooms: 28 private.
Bed & breakfast: £44-£50
single, £62-£72 double.
Lunch available.
Evening meal 7pm (l.o.
10pm).
Parking for 74.
Credit: Access, Visa, Diners,
Amex.

BRIDPORT
Dorset
Map ref 2A3

Market town and chief
producer of nets and
ropes just inland of
dramatic Dorset coast.
Ropes once made for
hangman's noose as well
as for shipping and
fishing boats. Old, broad
streets built for drying
and twisting, long back
gardens for rope-walks.
Grand arcaded Town Hall
and Georgian buildings,
traditional inns. Local
history museum has
Roman relics. Charles II
stopped here on his flight
to France.
*Tourist Information
Centre* ☎ *(0308) 24901*

Bridge House Hotel
115 East St., Bridport,
DT6 3LB
☎ (0308) 23371
*Converted 18th C school house
in the market town of Bridport,
near the River Asker. Ideal for
touring Dorset countryside.*
Bedrooms: 3 single, 2 double
& 2 twin, 3 family rooms.
Bathrooms: 10 private.
Bed & breakfast: £24-£27
single, £42-£46 double.
Half board: £30-£37 daily,
£180-£210 weekly.
Evening meal 7.30pm (l.o.
9pm).
Parking for 14.
Credit: Access, Visa.

BRIDPORT

Continued

Bridport Arms Hotel ⚏
▦▦ APPROVED
West Bay, Bridport,
DT6 4EN
☎ (0308) 22994
*16th C thatched hotel on
beach. Restaurant specialising
in local sea food.*
Bedrooms: 3 single, 4 double
& 3 twin, 3 family rooms.
Bathrooms: 6 private,
3 public.
Bed & breakfast: £19.50-
£27.50 single, £35-£55 double.
Half board: £27-£35 daily,
£185-£245 weekly.
Lunch available.
Evening meal 7pm (l.o. 9pm).
Parking for 14.
Credit: Access, Visa.

Britmead House Hotel ⚏
▦▦▦ COMMENDED
154 West Bay Rd., Bridport,
DT6 4EG
☎ (0308) 22941
*Elegant detached, tastefully
decorated house, renowned for
hospitality, comfort and meals.
10 minutes' walk to harbour
and beaches.*
Bedrooms: 4 double & 2 twin,
1 family room.
Bathrooms: 5 private,
1 public.
Bed & breakfast: £19-£26
single, £29-£40 double.
Half board: £23.75-£30 daily,
£159.25-£196 weekly.
Evening meal 7pm (l.o. 5pm).
Parking for 7.
Credit: Access, Visa, C.Bl.,
Diners, Amex.

Common Knapp House
Coast Rd., Burton Bradstock,
Bridport, DT6 4RJ
☎ (0308) 897428
*Quiet guesthouse with
extensive sea and country
views. Access to beach.
Optional evening meal using
produce from own garden.*
Bedrooms: 2 single, 5 double
& 5 twin, 1 family room.
Bathrooms: 10 private,
1 public.
Bed & breakfast: £20-£24
single, £40-£48 double.
Half board: £30-£32 daily,
£200-£210 weekly.
Evening meal 6.30pm (l.o.
4pm).
Parking for 21.
Open February-November.

Greyhound Hotel ⚏
▦▦ APPROVED
2 East St., Bridport,
DT6 3LF
☎ (0308) 22944
*Family-run freehouse hotel
offering informal carefree base
in town centre, 1.25 miles from
picturesque countryside and
sea front.*
Bedrooms: 5 single, 5 double
& 2 twin, 4 family rooms.
Bathrooms: 5 private,
4 public.
Bed & breakfast: £17.50-
£29.50 single, £32-£45 double.
Half board: £26-£39.50 daily.
Lunch available.
Evening meal 7pm (l.o. 9pm).
Parking for 10.
Credit: Access, Visa.

Haddon House Hotel ⚏
▦▦▦▦
West Bay, Bridport,
DT6 4EL
☎ (0308) 23626 &
(0308) 25323
*Country house hotel, situated
300 yards from picturesque
harbour and coast, renowned
for cooking. Well situated for
touring Dorset, Devon and
Somerset.*
Bedrooms: 2 single, 6 double
& 3 twin, 2 family rooms.
Bathrooms: 13 private.
Bed & breakfast: £37.50-
£42.50 single, £45-£55 double.
Lunch available.
Evening meal 7pm (l.o.
8.30pm).
Parking for 44.
Credit: Access, Visa, Diners,
Amex.

Roundham House Hotel ⚏
▦▦▦▦
Roundham Gardens, West
Bay Rd., Bridport, DT6 4BD
☎ Bridport, (0308) 22753 /
25779 Telex 417182 ENEL G
ATN ROUNDHAM
*Attractive stone house in
elevated position, within own
secluded 1-acre gardens, giving
superb sea and country views.*
Bedrooms: 1 single, 3 double
& 2 twin, 2 family rooms.
Bathrooms: 8 private.
Bed & breakfast: £27.50-£35
single, £42-£55 double.
Half board: £24.95-£42.50
daily, £205-£235 weekly.
Lunch available.
Evening meal 7.30pm (l.o.
8.30pm).
Parking for 15.

Open February-November.
Credit: Access, Visa, Diners,
Amex.

BRISTOL

Avon
Map ref 2A2

Important since Saxon
times, today a university
town and major port. City
grew around medieval
river docks, now the
Floating Harbour, then
busy with fish, trade, sea
warfare and exploration
(Cabot sailed for
Newfoundland 1497).
Merchant Venturers
founded here 1552. Fine
old churches and
cathedral; Georgian
theatre and Exchange;
wide views of Avon
Gorge from Brunel's
Clifton Bridge.
*Tourist Information
Centre ☎ (0272) 260767*

Alandale Hotel
▦▦
Tyndalls Park Rd., Bristol,
BS8 1PG
☎ (0272) 735407
*Formerly a Victorian
gentleman's residence, now an
elegant, warm and comfortable
hotel with personal service.
Close to city centre.*
Bedrooms: 8 single, 5 double
& 3 twin, 1 family room.
Bathrooms: 17 private.
Bed & breakfast: £30-£35
single, £40-£45 double.
Parking for 10.

Alcove Guest House
508/510 Fishponds Rd.,
Bristol, BS16 3DT
☎ (0272) 653886 & 652436
*Clean and comfortable
accommodation with personal
service. Noted for its food.*
Bedrooms: 1 single, 2 double
& 3 twin, 3 family rooms.
Bathrooms: 2 private,
4 public.
Bed & breakfast: £17-£25
single, £30-£35 double.
Evening meal 6.15pm (l.o.
3pm).
Parking for 9.

Arches Hotel
▦
132 Cotham Brow, Cotham,
Bristol, BS6 6AE
☎ (0272) 247398

Open February-November.
Credit: Access, Visa, Diners,
Amex.

*Small friendly, private hotel
close to central stations and
100 yards from main A38.
Option of traditional or
vegetarian breakfast.*
Bedrooms: 5 single, 4 double,
2 family rooms.
Bathrooms: 2 public.
Bed & breakfast: £18-£18.50
single, £32-£32.75 double.

The Aztec Hotel ⚏
Aztec West Business Park,
Almondsbury, Bristol,
BS12 4TS
☎ (0454) 201090
Telex 444454
*A hotel particularly suited to
business and conference market
with restaurant and leisure
facilities.*
Bedrooms: 77 double,
13 family rooms.
Bathrooms: 90 private.
Bed & breakfast: from £112
single, from £126 double.
Half board: from £126 daily.
Lunch available.
Evening meal 7.15pm (l.o.
9.45pm).
Parking for 200.
Credit: Access, Visa, Diners,
Amex.

Basca Guest House
▦
19 Broadway Rd.,
Bishopston, Bristol, BS7 8ES
☎ (0272) 422182
*Elegant Victorian home
restored to high standard.
Quiet residential area adjacent
A38. 15 minutes' walk from
centre. Friendly atmosphere.
Home cooking.*
Bedrooms: 1 single, 3 twin.
Bathrooms: 1 public.
Bed & breakfast: £15-£17
single, £28-£32 double.
Half board: £22-£24 daily.
Evening meal 6.30pm (l.o.
8pm).
Parking for 4.

600 Bath Road
▦
Kensington Hill, Brislington,
Bristol, BS4 3LE
☎ (0272) 779030
*Small family-run, comfortable
guesthouse 2 miles from the
city centre.*
Bedrooms: 2 single, 1 double,
1 family room.
Bathrooms: 1 public.
Bed & breakfast: £11-£15
single, £24-£28 double.

Bristol Moat House Hotel
Victoria St., Bristol,
BS1 6HY
☎ (0272) 255010
High standard hotel with 132 well-appointed bedrooms. Spires restaurant offers international cuisine.
Bedrooms: 3 single, 38 double & 84 twin, 7 family rooms.
Bathrooms: 132 private.
Bed & breakfast: from £95 single, from £105 double.
Half board: from £115 daily. Lunch available.
Evening meal 7pm (l.o. 10pm).
Parking for 120.
Credit: Access, Visa, Diners, Amex.

Camden Hotel
129 Coronation Rd.,
Southville, Bristol, BS3 1RE
☎ (0272) 231062
Small friendly hotel, only few minutes from city centre. Close to theatres, exhibition centre, museums and Bristol dockland.
Bedrooms: 4 single, 1 double & 1 twin, 4 family rooms.
Bathrooms: 5 public.
Bed & breakfast: from £15 single, from £29 double.
Half board: from £19 daily.
Evening meal 6pm (l.o. 7pm).
Parking for 2.

Clifton Hotel ⋒
St. Paul's Rd., Clifton,
Bristol, BS8 1LX
☎ (0272) 736882
Telex 449075
Located in an attractive and convenient area. Adventurous food and pleasant atmosphere in Racks Wine Bar and Restaurant. Shops and attractions nearby.
Bedrooms: 26 single, 11 double & 22 twin, 4 family rooms.
Bathrooms: 44 private, 6 public; 1 private shower.
Bed & breakfast: £28-£45 single, £45-£65 double.
Lunch available.
Evening meal 6.30pm (l.o. 10pm).
Parking for 12.
Credit: Access, Visa, Diners, Amex.

Courtlands Hotel
1 Redland Court Rd.,
Redland, Bristol, BS6 7EE
☎ (0272) 424432
A family-run hotel, north of the city centre, overlooking Redland Grove and offering quiet discreet service.
Bedrooms: 9 single, 3 double & 6 twin, 2 family rooms.
Bathrooms: 10 private, 4 public.
Bed & breakfast: £24-£32 single, £40-£50 double.
Half board: £26-£38 daily, £163.80-£239.40 weekly.
Lunch available.
Evening meal 5pm (l.o. 7pm).
Parking for 12.
Credit: Access, Visa.

Downlands Guest House
33 Henleaze Gdns.,
Henleaze, Bristol, BS9 4HH
☎ (0272) 621639
Comfortable Victorian house, in a pleasant tree-lined road bordering Durham Downs. On bus route and 2 miles from city centre.
Bedrooms: 3 single, 3 double & 3 twin, 1 family room.
Bathrooms: 1 private, 2 public.
Bed & breakfast: £20-£25 single, £35-£38 double.

Hilton International Bristol ⋒
Redcliffe Way, Bristol,
BS1 6NJ
☎ (0272) 260041
Telex 449240
ⓒⓡ Hilton
City centre hotel, recently refurbished. New Galleria Bar and Kiln Restaurant. Located very near Temple Meads railway station.
Bedrooms: 7 single, 98 double & 96 twin.
Bathrooms: 201 private.
Bed & breakfast: £84-£104 single, £100-£120 double.
Lunch available.
Evening meal 7pm (l.o. 10.30pm).
Parking for 150.
Credit: Access, Visa, Diners, Amex.

Holiday Inn Bristol ⋒
2 Lower Castle Rd., Old Market, Bristol, BS1 3AD
☎ (0272) 294281
Telex 449720
ⓒⓡ Holiday Inn
Modern hotel in pleasant city centre location. Close to main shops and easily accessible via M32, M4 and M5.
Bedrooms: 143 double, 141 family rooms.
Bathrooms: 284 private.
Bed & breakfast: £99-£114 single, £118-£133 double.
Half board: £117-£133 daily.
Lunch available.
Evening meal 7pm (l.o. 11pm).
Parking for 350.
Credit: Access, Visa, C.Bl., Diners, Amex.

Lyndhurst Hotel
10 St.Pauls Rd., Clifton, Bristol, BS8 1LT
☎ (0272) 737997
Quiet, commercial hotel convenient for city centre. Full English breakfast. All rooms with colour TV, radio, hot and cold water and tea making.
Bedrooms: 8 single, 7 double, 2 family rooms.
Bathrooms: 3 public.
Bed & breakfast: from £25 single, from £40 double.
Parking for 14.
Credit: Visa.

Oakdene Hotel
APPROVED
45 Oakfield Rd., Clifton, Bristol, BS8 2BA
☎ (0272) 735900
A small commercial hotel close to the university, zoo, restaurants, theatres and suspension bridge.
Bedrooms: 4 single, 6 double & 4 twin.
Bathrooms: 7 private, 3 public.
Bed & breakfast: £23-£29 single, £34-£40 double.
Evening meal 6pm (l.o. 7.30pm).
Parking for 8.

Rank Motor Lodge ⋒
Aust Services, M4 Motorway, Bristol, BS12 3BH
☎ Pilning (045 45) 3313
51 new bedrooms overlooking the Severn Bridge and estuary for tourists and business travellers. Self-service restaurant open 24 hours.
Bedrooms: 2 double & 28 twin, 21 family rooms.
Bathrooms: 51 private.
Bed & breakfast: from £27.50 single, from £34.50 double.
Lunch available.
Evening meal 5pm.

Parking for 100.
Credit: Access, Visa, Diners, Amex.

Rockleaze House
Listed
91 Gloucester Rd. North, Filton, Bristol, BS12 7PT
☎ (0272) 692536
A Victorian house situated between the M4/M5 interchange and Bristol Centre. Equally appealing to business person and tourist.
Bedrooms: 4 single, 1 double & 1 twin, 1 family room.
Bathrooms: 2 public.
Bed & breakfast: £16 single, £27-£29 double.
Parking for 4.

Sunderland Guest House
4 Sunderland Pl., Clifton, Bristol, BS8 1NA
☎ (0272) 737249
Small friendly guesthouse, well situated for Bristol centre or Clifton village.
Bedrooms: 4 single, 3 double & 2 twin, 1 family room.
Bathrooms: 4 private, 2 public; 2 private showers.
Bed & breakfast: £20-£22.50 single, £34-£36 double.
Parking for 3.

Toad Lodge
Listed
12 Cotham Park, Cotham, Bristol, BS6 6BU
☎ (0272) 247080
Large Georgian residence within half a mile of city centre. Offers all amenities, comfort, attractive decor and individual service.
Bedrooms: 1 single, 5 twin, 1 family room.
Bathrooms: 2 public.
Bed & breakfast: £14.50 single, £27.50 double.
Parking for 7.

Unicorn Hotel ⋒
Prince St., Bristol, BS1 4QF
☎ (0272) 230333 Telex 44315
ⓒⓡ Rank
Modern hotel overlooking quay and close to city centre. Special weekend rates. Restaurant, lounge bar and waterfront tavern.
Bedrooms: 127 single, 27 double & 38 twin, 2 family rooms.
Bathrooms: 194 private.

Continued ▶

BRISTOL

Continued

Bed & breakfast: £54.50-£72.95 single, £86-£90.90 double.
Lunch available.
Evening meal 6.30pm (l.o. 10pm).
Parking for 400.
Credit: Access, Visa, C.Bl., Diners, Amex.

Washington Hotel **M**
11-15 St. Paul's Rd., Bristol, BS8 1LX
☎ (0272) 733980
Telex 449075
Newly converted rooms, close to the shopping centre, suspension bridge and zoo.
Bedrooms: 16 single, 8 double & 14 twin, 5 family rooms.
Bathrooms: 29 private, 5 public.
Bed & breakfast: £28-£45 single, £45-£60 double.
Parking for 20.
Credit: Access, Visa, Diners, Amex.

Westbury Park Hotel
37 Westbury Rd., Bristol, BS9 3AU
☎ (0272) 620465
Small friendly hotel on edge of Bristol Durham Downs. Within easy distance of city and main commuter routes.
Bedrooms: 2 single, 3 double & 3 twin, 1 family room.
Bathrooms: 5 private, 1 public.
Bed & breakfast: £28-£38 single, £38-£48 double.
Half board: £40-£50 daily, £280-£350 weekly.
Lunch available.
Evening meal 7pm (l.o. 8.30pm).
Parking for 5.
Credit: Access, Visa.

Individual proprietors have supplied all details of accommodation. Although we do check for accuracy, we advise you to confirm prices and other information at the time of booking.

BRIXHAM

Devon
Map ref 1D2

Famous for its trawling fleet in the 19th C, a steeply-built fishing port overlooking the harbour and fish market. A statue of William of Orange recalls his landing here before deposing James II. There is an aquarium and museum. Good cliff views and walks.
Tourist Information Centre ☎ (08045) 2861

Cottage Hotel
Mount Pleasant Rd., Brixham, TQ5 9SD
☎ (080 45) 2123
Delightful 18th C family-run hotel with beamed ceilings and sea views. 2 minutes from town centre and harbour.
Bedrooms: 1 single, 4 double & 2 twin.
Bathrooms: 2 public; 4 private showers.
Bed & breakfast: £12-£17 single, £24-£34 double.
Half board: £20-£25 daily, £140-£175 weekly.
Evening meal 6.30pm (l.o. 4pm).
Parking for 6.

Harbour Side Guest House
Listed
65 Berry Head Rd., Brixham, TQ5 9AA
☎ (080 45) 58899
Overlooking the outer harbour and marina, opposite the lifeboat station. Close to Breakwater Beach. Within walking distance of town.
Bedrooms: 1 single, 1 double & 1 twin, 2 family rooms.
Bathrooms: 1 private, 1 public.
Bed & breakfast: £13.50-£15 single, £24-£30 double.
Half board: £20-£22 daily, £115-£130 weekly.
Evening meal 6pm (l.o. 8pm).

Richmond House Hotel
APPROVED
Higher Manor Rd., Brixham, TQ5 8HA
☎ (0803) 882391
Detached Victorian house with "Laura Ashley" interior, sun trap garden and adjacent car park. En-suite available. Convenient for shops and harbour, yet quiet location. First left after Golden Lion.

Bedrooms: 1 single, 1 double & 1 twin, 5 family rooms.
Bathrooms: 2 private, 3 public.
Bed & breakfast: from £15 single, from £26 double.
Parking for 5.
Open February-November.
Credit: Access, Visa.

BUCKFAST

Devon
Map ref 1C2

Situated on the south-east edge of Dartmoor, this village is visited for its handsome 20th C abbey which occupies the site of a Cistercian monastery. The main part was built from 1906-32 by untrained Benedictine monks, one member only having served a short apprenticeship as a stonemason. The chapel which was added in the 1960s is particularly fine.

Furzeleigh Mill Country Hotel **M**
Dartbridge, Buckfast, TQ11 0JP
☎ Buckfastleigh (0364) 43476
Former 16th C mill in own grounds within Dartmoor National Park. Excellent touring centre for coast and moor. Bargain breaks, moderate charges.
Bedrooms: 3 single, 7 double & 4 twin, 1 family room.
Bathrooms: 11 private, 2 public.
Bed & breakfast: £18.75-£23.25 single, £31.50-£40.75 double.
Half board: £24-£30.33 daily, £147.25-£183.50 weekly.
Lunch available.
Evening meal 6.45pm (l.o. 8pm).
Parking for 32.
Credit: Access, Visa.

BUCKFASTLEIGH

Devon
Map ref 1C2

Small manufacturing and market town just south of Buckfast Abbey on the fringe of Dartmoor. Return trips can be taken by steam train on a reopened line along the beautiful Dart Valley.

Royal Oak House **M**
APPROVED
59 Jordan St., Buckfastleigh, TQ11 0AX
☎ (0364) 43611
Small family-run guesthouse on the edge of Dartmoor, with spacious rooms and good breakfast menu.
Bedrooms: 1 double & 1 twin, 3 family rooms.
Bathrooms: 2 private, 2 public.
Bed & breakfast: £15-£21 single, £24-£30 double.
Open March-October.

Woodholme Guest House
113, Plymouth Rd., Buckfastleigh, TQ11 0DB
☎ (0364) 43350
Comfortable Victorian house situated close to Dartmoor. A warm welcome awaits all guests and a choice of a 4-course breakfast.
Bedrooms: 1 double & 1 twin, 1 family room.
Bathrooms: 1 private, 1 public.
Bed & breakfast: £13-£18 single, £26.50-£36 double.
Half board: £19.50-£24.50 daily, £126-£150 weekly.
Evening meal 6.30pm (l.o. 5pm).
Parking for 1.

The National Crown Scheme is explained in full on pages 556–558.

Classifications and quality commendations were correct at the time of going to press but are subject to change. Please check at the time of booking.

BUCKLAND MONACHORUM

Devon
Map ref 1C2

4m S. Tavistock
Village just north of Buckland Abbey, home of Sir Francis Drake. Founded by Cistercians, the building is of unique interest through its conversion into a country home by Sir Richard Grenville. Much of the interior and the nearby medieval tithe barn now serve as a museum of Drake and Grenville mementoes, including Drake's drum. Beautiful gardens.

Uppaton House ♨
APPROVED

Buckland Monachorum, Yelverton, PL20 7LL
☎ (0822) 853226
19th C house set in 2.5 acres of gardens on the edge of Dartmoor. Good views. Excellent base for touring.
Bedrooms: 2 single, 2 double & 2 twin, 2 family rooms.
Bathrooms: 2 public.
Bed & breakfast: from £12 single, from £24 double.
Half board: from £18.50 daily, from £126 weekly.
Evening meal 6pm (l.o. 8pm).
Parking for 10.

BUDE

Cornwall
Map ref 1C2

Sandy resort on dramatic Atlantic coast. High cliffs give spectacular sea and inland views. Georgian cottages beside canal basin, otherwise 19th and 20th C development. Golf-course, cricket pitch, folly, surfing, coarse-fishing and boating. Mother-town Stratton was base of Royalist Sir Bevil Grenville and birthplace of his famous retainer, the 'Cornish Giant', Anthony Payne. *Tourist Information Centre* ☎ (0288) 354240

Bude Haven Hotel
COMMENDED

Flexbury Ave., Bude, EX23 8NS
☎ (0288) 352305

Edwardian, family hotel with comfortable, relaxing atmosphere and friendly service, in a quiet, residential area. Convenient for beach, town, and golf-course.
Bedrooms: 1 single, 6 double & 4 twin, 2 family rooms.
Bathrooms: 13 private.
Bed & breakfast: £17-£18 single, £34-£36 double.
Half board: £23-£25 daily, £147-£161 weekly.
Evening meal 6.30pm (l.o. 7.30pm).
Parking for 8.
Credit: Access, Visa.

Burn Court Hotel
Burn View, Bude, EX23 8DB
☎ (0288) 2872
Situated at edge of town overlooking golf-course with easy access to beach. Centrally positioned for all amenities.
Bedrooms: 12 single, 10 double & 11 twin.
Bathrooms: 22 private, 3 public.
Bed & breakfast: £18-£22 single, £35-£44 double.
Half board: £26-£30 daily, £168-£195 weekly.
Lunch available.
Evening meal 7pm (l.o. 8pm).
Parking for 10.
Credit: Visa.

Camelot Hotel
APPROVED

Downs View, Bude, EX23 8RE
☎ (0288) 352361
A comfortable family-run hotel situated close to the famous Crooklets Beach and overlooking a championship golf-course.
Bedrooms: 2 single, 5 double & 11 twin, 3 family rooms.
Bathrooms: 21 private.
Bed & breakfast: £20-£22 single, £40-£44 double.
Half board: £30-£33 daily, £195-£210 weekly.
Lunch available.
Evening meal 7pm (l.o. 8.30pm).
Parking for 18.
Credit: Access, Visa.

Cliff Hotel ♨
COMMENDED

Crooklets Beach, Bude, EX23 8NG
☎ (0288) 353110

Indoor pool and spa, solarium, putting green and tennis court. In 5 acres of land, near National Trust cliffs and 200 yards from the beach. Chef/proprietor.
Bedrooms: 2 single, 3 double & 1 twin, 9 family rooms.
Bathrooms: 15 private.
Bed & breakfast: £16-£19 single, £32-£36 double.
Half board: £23-£27 daily, £130-£175 weekly.
Lunch available.
Evening meal 6.30pm (l.o. 7.30pm).
Parking for 15.
Open April-October.

Dorset House Licensed Hotel
Killerton Rd., Bude, EX23 8EN
☎ (0288) 352665
Building of charm and character quietly set in its own gardens only a few minutes' walk from town centre and beaches.
Bedrooms: 1 single, 2 double & 1 twin, 2 family rooms.
Bathrooms: 1 private, 2 public.
Bed & breakfast: £16-£20 single, £32-£40 double.
Half board: £20-£24 daily, £102-£134 weekly.
Evening meal 6.30pm (l.o. 6.30pm).
Parking for 6.
Credit: Access, Visa.

Edgcumbe Hotel ♨
19 Summerleaze Cres., Bude, EX23 8HJ
☎ (0288) 353846
Homely and friendly hotel where comfort and hospitality are assured. Beautiful views over sea and harbour.
Bedrooms: 3 single, 2 double & 4 twin, 6 family rooms.
Bathrooms: 8 private, 2 public; 1 private shower.
Bed & breakfast: £13.50-£16 single, £27-£32 double.
Half board: £20.50-£23 daily, £122.50-£146.85 weekly.
Lunch available.
Evening meal 6.30pm (l.o. 7.30pm).
Parking for 7.
Credit: Access, Visa.

Florida Hotel ♨
Summerleaze Cres., Bude, EX23 8HJ
☎ (0288) 352451

Superb location overlooking beach, downs and town. 5 choice menu, buffet Saturdays. Colour TV, radio, tea and coffee facilities in all rooms.
Bedrooms: 2 single, 10 double & 3 twin, 4 family rooms.
Bathrooms: 12 private, 3 public; 2 private showers.
Bed & breakfast: £15.40-£18 single, £30.80-£36 double.
Half board: £24.75-£26.40 daily, £162-£176 weekly.
Lunch available.
Evening meal 6.30pm (l.o. 6pm).
Parking for 10.
Open April-October.
Credit: Access, Visa.

Grosvenor Hotel
Summerleaze Cres., Bude, EX23 8HH
☎ (0288) 352062
Family hotel with views of beach and river. English and international food served, golfing holidays arranged. Children and dogs welcome.
Bedrooms: 1 single, 2 double & 4 twin, 6 family rooms.
Bathrooms: 11 private, 1 public.
Bed & breakfast: £17.75-£21.25 single, £33.50-£41 double.
Half board: £28.75-£32.75 daily, £167.50-£170 weekly.
Lunch available.
Evening meal 7pm (l.o. 8.30pm).
Parking for 5.
Open April-November.

Maer Lodge Hotel ♨
APPROVED

Maer Down, Crooklets Beach, Bude, EX23 8NG
☎ (0288) 353306
Semi-rural setting in its own grounds overlooking the seaward end of the golf-course near to Crooklets surfing beach.
Bedrooms: 4 single, 8 double & 4 twin, 3 family rooms.
Bathrooms: 15 private, 2 public.
Bed & breakfast: £16.50-£24 single, £33-£48 double.
Half board: £22.50-£30 daily, £157.50-£192.50 weekly.
Lunch available.
Evening meal 6.45pm (l.o. 7.30pm).
Parking for 20.
Open March-October.
Credit: Access, Visa, Diners, Amex.

BUDE

Continued

Meva-Gwin Hotel ♨
♚♚♚
Upton, Bude, EX23 0LY
☎ (0288) 352347
*On Marine Drive between
Bude and Widemouth Bay.
Coastal and rural views from
all rooms, friendly atmosphere,
traditional English cooking.*
Bedrooms: 2 single, 4 double
& 1 twin, 5 family rooms.
Bathrooms: 11 private,
1 public.
Bed & breakfast: £13-£18
single, £30-£36 double.
Half board: £20.50-£25.50
daily, £116-£150 weekly.
Lunch available.
Evening meal 6.30pm (l.o.
6.30pm).
Parking for 44.
Open April-October.
🖥 ⓑ ◻ ♥ 🅘 ☎ 📺 ▥ ❄
✕ SP

Hotel Penarvor
♚♚♚
Crooklets Beach, Bude,
EX23 8NE
☎ (0288) 352036
*Family-run hotel, 50 yards
from surf beach with
panoramic views of coast and
countryside. 200 yards from
golf-course.*
Bedrooms: 1 single, 9 double
& 6 twin.
Bathrooms: 16 private.
Bed & breakfast: £22-£25
single, £44-£50 double.
Half board: £30-£36 daily,
£180-£200 weekly.
Lunch available.
Evening meal 6.30pm (l.o.
8.30pm).
Parking for 20.
Credit: Access, Visa.
🖥 ♨ \ ⓑ ◻ ♥ 🅘 🅥 ☷
▥ 🍴 🐾 ∪ ▶ ❄ DAP SP T

St. Margarets Hotel ♨
Killerton Rd., Bude,
EX23 8EN
☎ (0288) 2252
*10-bedroomed hotel set in own
gardens, but within minutes of
town centre. Convenient for
holiday or business.*
Bedrooms: 1 single, 4 double
& 3 twin, 2 family rooms.
Bathrooms: 10 private.
Bed & breakfast: £23-£30
single, £46-£56 double.
Half board: £30-£37 daily,
£150-£200 weekly.
Lunch available.
Evening meal 7.30pm (l.o.
8.30pm).
Parking for 4.
Credit: Access, Visa.
🖥 🍴 \ ⓑ ◻ ♥ 🅘 🅥 ⊟
📺 ▥ ▱ 🍴 🐾 ❄ ⟋

BURBAGE

Wiltshire
Map ref 2B2

*4m E. Pewsey
Village close to
Savernake Forest,
famous as a habitat for
deer. Close by are the
remains of Wolf Hall
mansion, where a great
banquet in honour of
Jane Seymour took place
in 1536.*

The Old Vicarage ♨
♚♚♚ COMMENDED
Burbage, Marlborough,
SN8 3AG
☎ (0672) 810495
*Victorian country house in 2-
acre garden, offering peace,
comfort and varied food.
Within easy reach of Bath,
Salisbury, Oxford and
Windsor.*
Bedrooms: 1 single, 1 double
& 1 twin.
Bathrooms: 3 private.
Bed & breakfast: from £30
single, from £50 double.
Half board: £47-£52 daily.
Lunch available.
Evening meal 8pm (l.o. 6pm).
Parking for 10.
Open February-December.
Credit: Access, Visa.
\ ⓑ ◻ ♥ ⓤ 🅘 🅥 ⟋ ▱
📺 ▥ ▱ 🍴 ∪ ▶ ❄ ✕ ▥
T

BURNHAM-ON-SEA

Somerset
Map ref 1D1

Small resort with
extensive sands near the
National Nature Reserve
on Bridgwater Bay. The
resort grew in place of an
intended spa to be
funded from lighthouse
tolls. The lighthouse is
now one of the town's
attractions, as is the 15th
C church whose white
marble altar, made by
Grinling Gibbons to Inigo
Jones' design, was
salvaged from James II's
Whitehall Chapel.
*Tourist Information
Centre ☎ (0278) 787852*

Lulworth Guest House
7 Berrow Rd., Burnham-on-
Sea, TA8 2ET
☎ (0278) 784015
*Victorian house on main road
next to heated public swimming
pool. Tennis courts, putting
green and local gardens
opposite. Close to seafront and
beach. Ample parking.*

Bedrooms: 3 double, 2 family
rooms.
Bathrooms: 2 public.
Bed & breakfast: £14-£15
single, £28-£30 double.
Half board: £21-£22 daily,
£140-£150 weekly.
Evening meal 6pm (l.o. 8pm).
Parking for 6.
Credit: Access, Visa.
🖥 ⓑ ◻ ♥ 🅘 🅥 ☷ 📺 ▥
▱ ✕

The Queen's Hotel
♚♚♚
Pier St., Burnham-on-Sea,
TA8 1BT
☎ (0278) 783045
*Delightfully situated on the
seafront, with its own adjoining
car park. Built in 1850 and
now completely renovated to a
high standard, offering friendly
personal service. Comfortable
en-suite rooms with tea/coffee
facilities. Colour TV in all
rooms.*
Bedrooms: 2 single, 12 double
& 3 twin, 2 family rooms.
Bathrooms: 11 private,
4 public.
Bed & breakfast: £30-£35
single, £48-£60 double.
Lunch available.
Evening meal 6.15pm (l.o.
9.30pm).
Parking for 20.
Credit: Access, Visa.
🖥 ◻ ♥ 🅘 🅥 ▱ ▱ 🍴 ▥
T

Royal Clarence Hotel ♨
♚♚♚♚
31 The Esplanade, Burnham-
on-Sea, TA8 1BQ
☎ (0278) 783138
Ⓒ Minotels
*Seafront coaching inn,
providing comfortable
accommodation and
specialising in traditional ales.
Good base for touring
Somerset.*
Bedrooms: 3 single, 6 double
& 6 twin, 2 family rooms.
Bathrooms: 14 private;
3 private showers.
Bed & breakfast: from £25
single, from £40 double.
Half board: from £34 daily,
from £172 weekly.
Lunch available.
Evening meal 7pm (l.o.
8.30pm).
Parking for 20.
🖥 \ ⓑ ◻ ♥ 🅘 🅥 ▱ 📺
▥ ▱ 🍴 🐾 T

BURROWBRIDGE

Somerset
Map ref 1D1

4m NW. Langport

Old Bakery
Burrowbridge, Bridgwater,
TA7 0RB
☎ (082 369) 234
*Guesthouse, licensed restaurant
and tea rooms. A361 Taunton
to Glastonbury road, next to
Burrowbridge Mump (National
Trust site).*
Bedrooms: 1 single, 3 double
& 2 twin.
Bathrooms: 1 private,
1 public.
Bed & breakfast: £13.50-
£14.50 single, £27-£33 double.
Lunch available.
Evening meal 6pm (l.o. 9pm).
Parking for 7.
Credit: Access, Visa.
🖥 🅘 🅥 ▱ 📺 ▥ ✕ ▥

CALNE

Wiltshire
Map ref 2B2

Prosperity from wool in
the 15th C endowed this
ancient market town with
a fine church in the
Perpendicular style. To
the east are chalk
downlands and at
Oldbury Castle, an Iron
Age fort, a 17th C white
horse is carved into the
hillside.

Chilvester Hill House
♚♚♚ COMMENDED
Calne, SN11 0LP
☎ (0249) 813981 & 815785
Fax (0249) 814217
*Professional family accepting
guests in their spacious
Victorian house. Weekly rates
on application.*
Bedrooms: 1 double & 2 twin.
Bathrooms: 3 private,
1 public.
Bed & breakfast: £40-£50
single, £60-£75 double.
Half board: £48-£72 daily.
Evening meal 8pm (l.o.
10am).
Parking for 6.
Credit: Access, Visa, Diners,
Amex.
🖥12 ⓑ ◻ ♥ 🅘 🅥 ▱ 📺
▥ ▱ 🍴 ∪ ▶ ❄ ✕ ▥

**Classifications and quality commendations
were correct at the time of going to press
but are subject to change. Please check at
the time of booking.**

Lansdowne Strand Hotel and Restaurant. M

The Strand, Calne,
SN11 0JR
☎ (0249) 812488
Telex 444453
16th C coaching inn noted for cuisine and high standard of accommodation. Retains all original features.
Bedrooms: 3 single, 13 double & 9 twin, 1 family room.
Bathrooms: 26 private.
Bed & breakfast: £44 single, £52 double.
Half board: £61.50 daily, £350 weekly.
Lunch available.
Evening meal 7pm (l.o. 9.45pm).
Parking for 20.
Credit: Access, Visa, Diners, Amex.

CAMBORNE
Cornwall
Map ref 1B3

19th C mining town of granite terraces. Legacies of the tin and copper mining boom remain in light industries and the country's only school of metalliferous mining, internationally-known. Nearby Dolcoath mine, now closed, was once the world's deepest mine. A statue commemorates the mining engineer Richard Trethivick, inventor of the first passenger-carrying steam engine, born here in 1771.

Seaview Farm Guesthouse

Troon, Camborne
☎ (0209) 831260
Situated 1 mile past village of Troon near Camborne. Ideal base for north and south coast and all Cornwall's resorts.
Bedrooms: 1 double & 3 twin, 3 family rooms.
Bathrooms: 3 public.
Half board: £15.50-£18 daily, £102-£117 weekly.
Evening meal 6.30pm (l.o. 7pm).
Parking for 8.
Open January-November.

CARBIS BAY
Cornwall
Map ref 1B3

Overlooking St. Ives Bay and with fine beaches.

Endsleigh Guest House
Listed APPROVED

St. Ives Rd., Carbis Bay, St. Ives, TR26 2SF
☎ Penzance (0736) 795777
Family-run guesthouse with large dining room and 2 lounges. Near buses, beaches and golf-course, 1 mile from St. Ives town.
Bedrooms: 1 single, 5 double & 1 twin, 3 family rooms.
Bathrooms: 2 public.
Bed & breakfast: £9-£10.50 single, £18-£21 double.
Half board: £12-£13.50 daily, £80-£92 weekly.
Evening meal 6.30pm (l.o. 4pm).
Parking for 10.

Hotel Rotorua

Trencrom La., Carbis Bay, St. Ives, TR26 2TD
☎ Penzance (0736) 795419
Modern private hotel in quiet wooded lane near many sporting activities and beaches.
Bedrooms: 1 single, 1 double & 1 twin, 10 family rooms.
Bathrooms: 13 private, 1 public.
Bed & breakfast: £14-£19 single, £28-£38 double.
Half board: £20-£25 daily, £140-£175 weekly.
Lunch available.
Evening meal 7pm (l.o. 5.30pm).
Parking for 10.

CARLYON BAY
Cornwall
Map ref 1B3

Residential and retirement suburb near St. Austell, with fine cliff top golf-course.

Carlyon Bay Hotel M

Carlyon Bay, St. Austell, PL25 3RD
☎ Par (072 681) 2304
Telex 42551 EXONIA G BREND 3
CB Brend
High standard accommodation, complemented by extensive leisure facilites, including an 18-hole golf-course.
Bedrooms: 17 single, 11 double & 45 twin.

Bathrooms: 73 private, 2 public.
Bed & breakfast: £55-£69 single, £105-£155 double.
Half board: £60-£80 daily, £330-£580 weekly.
Lunch available.
Evening meal 7.30pm (l.o. 9pm).
Parking for 100.
Credit: Access, Visa, Diners, Amex.

CASTLE COMBE
Wiltshire
Map ref 2B2

One of England's prettiest villages, in a steep woodland valley by a brook. The handsome Perpendicular church recalls the village's prosperous times as a cloth-weaving centre. No trace remains of the original castle, but the 13th C effigy of its founder Walter de Dunstanville lies in the church.

Manor House M
HIGHLY COMMENDED

Castle Combe, Chippenham, SN14 7HR
☎ (0249) 782206 Fax (0249) 782159 Telex 449931
Country house dating from 14th C. Exquisite setting in one of England's prettiest villages in the southern Cotswolds. 12 miles from Bath.
Bedrooms: 35 double & 1 twin.
Bathrooms: 36 private.
Bed & breakfast: £105-£275 double.
Lunch available.
Evening meal 7.30pm (l.o. 9pm).
Parking for 100.
Credit: Access, Visa, Diners, Amex.

CHAGFORD
Devon
Map ref 1C2

Handsome stone houses, some from the Middle Ages, grace this former stannary town on northern Dartmoor. Since the last century it has been a popular centre for walking expeditions and for tours of the antiquities on the rugged moor. There is a splendid 15th C granite church, said to be haunted by the poet Godolphin.

Easton Court Hotel M

Easton Cross, Chagford, TQ13 8JL
☎ (0647) 433469
Small, quiet, 15th C hotel on the edge of Dartmoor, "Brideshead Revisited" written in the library.
Bedrooms: 1 single, 4 double & 2 twin, 1 family room.
Bathrooms: 8 private.
Bed & breakfast: £70-£74 double.
Half board: £50-£55 daily, £325-£350 weekly.
Evening meal 7.30pm (l.o. 8.30pm).
Parking for 16.
Credit: Access, Visa, Diners, Amex.

Mill End Hotel M

Sandypark, Chagford, Newton Abbot, TQ13 8JN
☎ (0647) 432282
Family-owned, situated in the Dartmoor National Park, on the banks of the River Teign. 3 miles from Whiddon Down on A382.
Bedrooms: 2 single, 5 double & 8 twin, 2 family rooms.
Bathrooms: 15 private.
Bed & breakfast: £32-£50 single, £53-£65 double.
Half board: £50-£65 daily, £378-£420 weekly.
Lunch available.
Evening meal 7.30pm (l.o. 9pm).
Parking for 21.
Credit: Access, Visa, Diners, Amex.

> The symbols are explained on the flap inside the back cover.

> **Half board prices shown are per person but in some cases may be based on double/twin occupancy.**

CHARD

Somerset
Map ref 1D2

Market town in hilly countryside. The wide main street has some handsome buildings, among them the Guildhall, court house and almshouses. Modern light industry and dairy produce have replaced 19th C lace making which came at decline of cloth trade after 600 years.

Ammonite Lodge
43 High St., Chard, TA20 1QL
☎ (0460) 63839/64727
Fax (0460) 61571
Small and friendly, provides comfortable accommodation with a tea/coffee room open all day. All rooms with remote control colour TV, most en-suite. Garden with a fish pond.
Bedrooms: 1 single, 4 double & 1 twin.
Bathrooms: 5 private, 2 public.
Bed & breakfast: £20-£25 single, £25-£35 double.
Parking for 5.
🖥 🖥 UL 🖥 V 🖥 🖥 📺 🖥 🖥 ⚓
▶ ✕ 🖥 🖥

Bath House Restaurant and Hotel
Listed APPROVED
Bath House, Holyroodstreet, Chard
☎ (046 06) 4106
Restaurant and hotel, 10 bedrooms all en-suite with telephone, radio, TV and tea making facilities.
Bedrooms: 4 single, 1 double & 5 twin.
Bathrooms: 10 private.
Bed & breakfast: £34-£39 single, £45-£54 double.
Lunch available.
Evening meal 7pm (l.o. 9.30pm).
Parking for 5.
Credit: Access, Visa, Diners, Amex.
🖥 🖥 ℗ 🖥 🖥 👤 V 🖥 ◖
🖥 ⚓ 🏆 ▶ ✕ 🖥 🖥

Half board prices shown are per person but in some cases may be based on double/twin occupancy.

CHARMOUTH

Dorset
Map ref 1D2

Set back from the fossil-rich cliffs, a small coastal town where Charles II came to the Queen's Armes when seeking escape to France. Just south at low tide, the sandy beach rewards fossil-hunters; at Black Ven in 1811 a fossilised ichthyosaurus (now in London's Natural History Museum) was found.

Hensleigh M
🏵🏵🏵
Lower Sea La., Charmouth, Bridport, DT6 6LW
☎ (0297) 60830
Comfortable, well-equipped, family-run hotel. Friendly atmosphere. Home cooking using local produce. Quiet position, 300 metres from sea and coastal walks.
Bedrooms: 2 single, 2 double & 2 twin, 4 family rooms.
Bathrooms: 10 private.
Bed & breakfast: £17-£20 single, £34-£40 double.
Half board: £25-£28 daily, £161-£182 weekly.
Lunch available.
Evening meal 6.45pm (l.o. 7.30pm).
Parking for 15.
Open February-November.
🖥 🖥 🖥 🖥 👤 V 🖥 🖥 🖥
SP

Newlands House
🏵🏵🏵
Stonebarrow La., Charmouth, DT6 6RA
☎ (0297) 60212
Former 16th C farmhouse of character extended and modernised to provide modern facilities. Set in 1.5 acres of garden, orchard and woodland. Situated on edge of National Trust Land. Non-smokers' bedrooms.
Bedrooms: 3 single, 4 double & 3 twin, 2 family rooms.
Bathrooms: 11 private, 1 public.
Bed & breakfast: £17.50-£20.50 single, £35-£41 double.
Half board: £171.60-£188 weekly.
Evening meal 7pm (l.o. midday).
Parking for 15.
Open March-October.
🖥6 🖥 ◖ 👤 V 👤 🖥 📺 🖥
⚓ ❋ 🖥 SP

Queen's Armes Hotel M
🏵🏵🏵 COMMENDED
The Street, Charmouth, Bridport, DT6 6QF
☎ (0297) 60339
Reputed to be the sixth oldest inn in England and where King Charles II stayed. Old oak beams, walls with original stone fireplaces, medieval paintings.
Bedrooms: 3 single, 5 double & 3 twin.
Bathrooms: 10 private.
Bed & breakfast: £24-£27 single, £48-£54 double.
Half board: £34-£37 daily, £221-£241 weekly.
Lunch available.
Evening meal 9pm (l.o. 10.50pm).
Parking for 15.
Open February-October.
Credit: Access, Visa.
🖥5 🖥 🖥 🖥 👤 V 👤 🖥 📺
🖥 🖥 ❋ 🖥 SP 🖥

Thatch Lodge M
🏵🏵🏵
The Street, Charmouth, DT6 6PQ
☎ (0297) 60407
Charming 16th C cottage with bar and interesting continental and English cooking.
Bedrooms: 4 double & 2 twin, 1 family room.
Bathrooms: 6 private, 1 public.
Bed & breakfast: £16-£19 single, £32-£38 double.
Half board: £24-£29 daily, £168-£203 weekly.
Evening meal 7pm (l.o. 8pm).
Parking for 15.
Credit: Access, Visa.
🖥4 🖥 🖥 🖥 👤 V 🖥 🖥 ⚓
❋ 🖥 DAP 🖥 SP 🖥 🖥

The White House M
🏵🏵🏵🏵 COMMENDED
2 Hillside, The Street, Charmouth, DT6 6PJ
☎ (0297) 60411
Listed Georgian house with many original period features including Georgian windows, bow doors and furnished in keeping with the period.
Bedrooms: 1 single, 4 double & 2 twin.
Bathrooms: 6 private; 1 private shower.
Bed & breakfast: £46-£48.50 single, £72-£77 double.
Half board: £52.50-£55 daily, £287-£301 weekly.
Lunch available.
Evening meal 7pm (l.o. 9.15pm).

Parking for 15.
Open March-November.
Credit: Access, Visa.
🖥14 🖥 🖥 ℗ 🖥 🖥 👤 V
🖥 🖥 U ▶ 🖥 🖥 SP 🖥 🖥

CHEDDAR

Somerset
Map ref 1D1

Large village at foot of Mendips just south of the spectacular Cheddar Gorge. Close by are Roman and Saxon sites and famous show caves. Traditional Cheddar cheese is still made here.

Gordons Hotel
🏵🏵🏵
Cliff St., Cheddar, BS27 3PT
☎ (0934) 742497
Once a farmhouse, now a comfortable hotel with considerable charm and character. Heated outdoor swimming pool. Steak house restaurant.
Bedrooms: 2 single, 8 double & 1 twin, 2 family rooms.
Bathrooms: 5 private, 2 public; 3 private showers.
Bed & breakfast: £16-£27.50 single, £32-£40 double.
Half board: £140-£175 weekly.
Lunch available.
Evening meal 6pm (l.o. 9pm).
Parking for 10.
Open February-December.
Credit: Access, Visa, Diners.
🖥 🖥 🖥 👤 V 🖥 📺 🖥
⚓ 🏆 U 🖥 ❋ SP

Market Cross Hotel
🏵🏵🏵
The Cross, Church St., Cheddar, BS27 3RA
☎ (0934) 742264
Privately-owned listed Regency hotel, 5 minutes' walk from the famous Cheddar Gorge, caves and Mendip Hills. Wells, Glastonbury, Bristol and Bath are within easy reach.
Bedrooms: 1 single, 2 double & 1 twin, 2 family rooms.
Bathrooms: 2 private, 1 public.
Bed & breakfast: £16-£17 single, £29-£38 double.
Half board: £23-£29 daily.
Evening meal 7pm (l.o. 8pm).
Parking for 8.
Credit: Access.
🖥 🖥 🖥 👤 V 👤 🖥 📺 🖥 ⚓
U ✕ 🖥 DAP SP 🖥

Tor Farm M
Listed
Nyland, Cheddar, BS27 3UP
☎ (0934) 743710 &
(0934) 742549

33-acre mixed farm. On A371 between Cheddar and Draycott, take the road signposted Nyland. Quiet and peaceful on Somerset Levels. Private fishing. Ideally situated for visiting Cheddar, Bath, Wookey Hole, Glastonbury, Wells and coast.
Bedrooms: 1 single, 5 double & 1 twin, 1 family room.
Bathrooms: 3 private, 3 public; 2 private showers.
Bed & breakfast: from £15 single, from £20 double.
Half board: from £17 daily, from £108 weekly.
Evening meal 6pm (l.o. 9am).
Parking for 10.

CHEDINGTON
Dorset
Map ref 2A3

4m SE. Crewkerne
Small village ideally situated for touring this historic area.

Chedington Court M
Chedington, Beaminster, DT8 3HY
☎ Corscombe (093 589) 265
Fax (093 589) 442
Small Jacobean style manor house set in 10 acres of gardens on Dorset hillside with panoramic views and a relaxing ambience. Special terms available for 2 nights or more.
Bedrooms: 5 double & 5 twin.
Bathrooms: 10 private.
Bed & breakfast: £45.50-£65.50 single, £71-£111 double.
Half board: £60-£80 daily, £385-£560 weekly.
Evening meal 7pm (l.o. 9pm).
Parking for 21.
Credit: Access, Visa, C.Bl., Amex.

CHELWOOD
Avon
Map ref 2A2

4m S. Keynsham

Chelwood House Hotel M
COMMENDED
Chelwood, BS18 4NH
☎ Compton Dando
(0761) 490730 Telex 44830
Accent G.

Small hotel with delightful conservatory-type dining room. Area of outstanding beauty, all rooms enjoy glorious views. Sunday lunches only.
Bedrooms: 2 single, 6 double & 2 twin.
Bathrooms: 10 private.
Bed & breakfast: £55-£59 single, £72-£95 double.
Evening meal 7pm (l.o. 9pm).
Parking for 14.
Credit: Access, Visa, Diners, Amex.

CHEW STOKE
Avon
Map ref 2A3

Attractive village in the Mendip Hills with an interesting Tudor rectory and the remains of a Roman villa. To the south is the Chew Valley reservoir with its extensive leisure facilities.

Orchard House
COMMENDED
Bristol Rd., Chew Stoke, Bristol, BS18 8UB
☎ Chew Magna
(0272) 333143
Comfortable accommodation in a carefully modernised Georgian house. Home cooking using local produce.
Bedrooms: 1 single, 1 double & 2 twin, 1 family room.
Bathrooms: 1 private, 3 public.
Bed & breakfast: from £14 single, from £28 double.
Half board: from £21 daily.
Evening meal 6.30pm (l.o. 10am).
Parking for 9.

CHICKLADE
Wiltshire
Map ref 2B2

8m NE. Shaftesbury

The Old Rectory Guest House
Chicklade, Hindon, Salisbury, SP3 5SU
☎ Hindon (074 789) 226
A 17th C country guesthouse ideal as a Wessex touring centre, set in beautiful natural gardens.
Bedrooms: 1 double & 1 twin, 1 family room.
Bathrooms: 2 public.

Bed & breakfast: max. £12.50 single, max. £25 double.
Half board: max. £17.50 daily, max. £100 weekly.
Evening meal 6.50pm (l.o. 7.50pm).
Parking for 10.

CHILLINGTON
Devon
Map ref 1C3

4m E. Kingsbridge

White House Hotel M
COMMENDED
Chillington, Kingsbridge, TQ7 2JX
☎ (0548) 580580
Georgian country house, between Salcombe and Dartmouth, 2 miles from the sea at Torcross. Sandy beaches, sailing, golf and cliff walks all within easy reach.
Bedrooms: 4 double & 3 twin, 1 family room.
Bathrooms: 6 private, 1 public.
Bed & breakfast: £40.40-£59 double.
Half board: £29.70-£39 daily, £166.25-£234.50 weekly.
Lunch available.
Evening meal 7pm (l.o. 8.05pm).
Parking for 8.
Open April-October.

CHIPPENHAM
Wiltshire
Map ref 2B2

12m NE. Bath
Ancient market town with modern industry, retaining a large cattle market and some half-timbered houses. Notable early buildings include the medieval Town Hall and the gabled 15th C Yelde Hall, now a local history museum, which has a wooden turret. On the outskirts Hardenhuish has a charming hilltop church by the Georgian architect John Wood of Bath.
Tourist Information Centre ☎ (0249) 657733

Sign of the Angel
Lacock, Chippenham, SN15 2LA
☎ (024 973) 230 & 671
14th C woollen merchant's house situated in the National Trust village of Lacock.

Bedrooms: 6 double & 3 twin.
Bathrooms: 9 private, 1 public.
Bed & breakfast: from £65 single, from £90 double.
Lunch available.
Evening meal 7.30pm (l.o. 8pm).
Parking for 6.
Credit: Access, Visa, Amex.

CHOLDERTON
Wiltshire
Map ref 2B2

5m E. Amesbury

Cholderton Country Hotel M
Parkhouse Corner, Cholderton, Salisbury, SP4 0EG
☎ (0980) 64484
Set in 5 acres of beautiful countryside within easy reach of Salisbury, Stonehenge, Winchester, Thruxton races, and the West Country. At junction A303/4338.
Bedrooms: 4 single, 4 double & 4 twin, 2 family rooms.
Bathrooms: 14 private.
Bed & breakfast: £34-£36 single, £44-£46 double.
Half board: £42-£48 daily.
Evening meal 7pm (l.o. 8.30pm).
Parking for 30.
Credit: Access, Visa, Diners, Amex.

Park House Guest House & Motel M
Cholderton, Salisbury, SP4 0EG
☎ (0980) 64265
17th C former coaching inn built of brick and flint with slate roof. 5 miles east of Stonehenge, 10 miles north of Salisbury and 9 miles west of Andover.
Bedrooms: 5 single, 9 double & 7 twin, 2 family rooms.
Bathrooms: 10 private, 3 public.
Bed & breakfast: £15.50-£26 single, £31-£36 double.
Half board: £19-£23 daily.
Evening meal 7pm (l.o. 8.30pm).
Parking for 30.
Display advertisement appears on page 459.

CHULMLEIGH

Devon
Map ref 1C2

8m S. South Molton
Small, hilly town above
the Little Dart River, long
since by-passed by the
main road. The large 15th
C church is noted for its
splendid rood screen and
38 carved wooden angels
on the roof.

Fox and Hounds, Eggesford House Hotel ♒

Eggesford, Chulmleigh,
EX18 7JZ
☎ Chulmleigh (0769) 80345
*Country hotel offering peace
and tranquillity. Set in some
30 acres of woodland. All
rooms en-suite.*
Bedrooms: 2 single, 7 double
& 11 twin, 1 family room.
Bathrooms: 21 private,
2 public.
Bed & breakfast: £27.50
single, £55 double.
Half board: £37.50 daily,
£225 weekly.
Lunch available.
Evening meal 7pm (l.o. 6pm).
Parking for 102.
Credit: Access, Visa.
🔔 🕹 ♨ ♥ ✿ 🛎 Ⓥ ☎ 🎨
🍴 🍷 ♨ ☕ 🎿 ▶ ❄ ◗ ✎
SP ⊞

CHURCHILL

Avon
Map ref 1D1

8m S. Clevedon
Village of stone houses,
just off the A38,
dominated by Churchill
Court, seat of some of
the ancestors of the first
Duke of Marlborough and
Sir Winston Churchill.

Winstons Hotel
≋≋≋
Bristol Road, Churchill,
Bristol, BS19 5NL
☎ (0934) 852348
*Attractive, privately owned
hotel offering warm welcome,
on edge of Mendips,
conveniently situated on A380
5 miles from Bristol Airport.*
Bedrooms: 6 single, 6 double
& 2 twin, 1 family room.
Bathrooms: 11 private,
1 public.
Bed & breakfast: £41-£47.50
single, £57.50-£67.50 double.
Lunch available.
Evening meal 7pm (l.o.
9.45pm).

Parking for 50.
Credit: Access, Visa, Diners,
Amex.
🔔 🕹 📞 🖥 🖵 ♥ 🛎 Ⓥ ☎
🞏 🍴 ♿ ✿ 🎨

CHURCHSTANTON

Somerset
Map ref 1D1

5m SE. Wellington

Strawbridges Farm Guest House
Strawbridges Farm,
Churchstanton, Taunton,
TA3 7PD
☎ (0823) 60591
*Non-working farm in idyllic
Blackdown hills. 6 miles
Taunton and M5. Tasteful,
homely atmosphere, ideal base
for touring.*
Bedrooms: 1 single, 2 double
& 2 twin.
Bathrooms: 1 private,
2 public.
Bed & breakfast: £11.50-£13
single, £30-£40 double.
Half board: £19.50-£28 daily,
£129-£189 weekly.
Parking for 8.
🔔 🖵 ♥ UL 🛎 ☎ 🎨 🛎 ✿
🞏 🎨 DAP SP ⊞

COLYTON

Devon
Map ref 1D2

Surrounded by fertile
farmland, this small
riverside town was an
early Saxon settlement.
Medieval prosperity from
the wool trade built the
grand church tower with
its octagonal lantern and
the church's fine west
window.

Old Bakehouse Hotel
Lower Church St., Colyton,
EX13 6ND
☎ (0297) 52518
*Former 17th C bakehouse, set
on the edge of this lovely old
town in glorious countryside,
only 2 miles from sea.*
Bedrooms: 3 single, 5 double
& 2 twin.
Bathrooms: 9 private,
2 public.
Bed & breakfast: £22-£23
single, £44-£46 double.
Half board: £32-£34 daily,
£200-£204 weekly.
Lunch available.
Evening meal 7pm (l.o.
9.30pm).
Parking for 10.
Credit: Visa.
🔔 🕹 📺 🖵 ♥ 🛎 Ⓥ ☎ 🎨
🛎 ☕ 🎨 ◗ SP

COMBE MARTIN

Devon
Map ref 1C1

Seaside village spreading
along its valley to a rocky
beach. Silver was mined
here in the Middle Ages,
market gardening yields
today's produce. An
unusual sight is the Pack
of Cards pub, while the
church with its gargoyles
is noted for panel
paintings on the 15th C
rood screen.

Almaza ♒
≋≋≋ APPROVED
3 The Woodlands, Combe
Martin, EX34 0AT
☎ (027 188) 3431
*Close to beach, own car park,
very comfortable rooms, en-
suite available. Menu to satisfy
all, licensed bar.*
Bedrooms: 3 double & 1 twin,
2 family rooms.
Bathrooms: 1 private,
2 public.
Bed & breakfast: £12.50-
£14.50 single, £25-£29.50
double.
Half board: £17-£18.50 daily,
£102-£111 weekly.
Evening meal 6.30pm (l.o.
4pm).
Parking for 6.
🔔 ♥ 🛎 Ⓥ ☎ 📺 🎨 🛎 🍴
🞏 🎨 ◗ SP

Channel Vista ♒
≋≋≋ COMMENDED
Woodlands, Combe Martin,
EX34 0AT
☎ (027 188) 3514
*Charming, Edwardian period
house, 150 yards from
picturesque cove. All rooms en-
suite, tea/coffee facilities.
Warm welcome, Devon fare.*
Bedrooms: 3 double & 1 twin,
3 family rooms.
Bathrooms: 7 private.
Bed & breakfast: £16-£18
single, £32-£36 double.
Half board: £22-£24 daily,
£114-£143 weekly.
Evening meal 6.30pm (l.o.
3pm).
Parking for 11.
Open March-October.
Credit: Access, Visa.
🔔 5 ♥ 🛎 Ⓥ ☎ 📺 🎨 🛎 🍴
🞏 DAP ◗ SP

Saffron House Hotel ♒
≋≋≋
King St., Combe Martin,
EX34 0BX
☎ (0271) 883521

*17th C hotel set in own
grounds close to beaches and
Exmoor. Well-appointed en-
suite rooms. Heated pool.
Children and pets very
welcome. Ideal touring centre.*
Bedrooms: 4 double & 1 twin,
5 family rooms.
Bathrooms: 5 private,
2 public; 3 private showers.
Bed & breakfast: £13-£15
single, £26-£30 double.
Half board: £20-£22 daily,
£119-£139 weekly.
Evening meal 6.30pm.
Parking for 10.
Credit: Access, Visa.
🔔 🕹 🛎 Ⓥ ☎ 📺 🎨 🛎 ✿
🎿 ◗ SP ⊞ T

White Gates Motel
≋≋≋
Woodlands, Combe Martin,
EX34 0AT
☎ (0271) 883511
*Fine views of Combe Martin
Bay and surrounding
countryside. All rooms en-suite,
some with balconies. Indoor
heated swimming pool.*
Bedrooms: 8 double & 6 twin,
4 family rooms.
Bathrooms: 18 private.
Bed & breakfast: £21-£24
single, £42-£48 double.
Half board: £25-£35 daily,
£175-£210 weekly.
Lunch available.
Evening meal 7pm (l.o.
9.30pm).
Parking for 60.
Credit: Access, Visa, Diners,
Amex.
🔔 🕹 📺 🖵 ♥ 🛎 Ⓥ ✂ ☎
📺 ◗ ✿ 🎨 🛎 🍴 ❄ ✿ 🎨 ✎
SP

CONSTANTINE BAY

Cornwall
Map ref 1B3

3m W. Padstow
Wide sands backed with
tall dunes looking toward
lighthouse on Trevose
Head. Beautiful sand-
dune golf-course has the
ruined chapel of St.
Constantine whose font
can be seen in St. Merryn
Church just inland.

Treglos Hotel ♒
Constantine Bay, Padstow,
PL28 8JH
☎ Padstow (0841) 520727
Telex 45795 WSTTLX G
TGS
🆑 Consort
*Overlooking sea and golf-
course. Offers varied
English/French food and
hospitality in quiet country
surroundings. Under personal
supervision of owners.*

Bedrooms: 8 single, 3 double & 29 twin, 4 family rooms.
Bathrooms: 44 private, 1 public.
Bed & breakfast: £39.50-£56.50 single, £74-£109 double.
Half board: £45-£62.50 daily, £245-£365 weekly.
Lunch available.
Evening meal 7.45pm (l.o. 9.30pm).
Parking for 60.
Open March-November.
Credit: Access.

[symbols]

CORSHAM
Wiltshire
Map ref 2B2

Growing town with old centre showing Flemish influence, legacy of former prosperity from weaving. The church, restored last century, retains Norman features. The Elizabethan Corsham Court, with additions by Capability Brown, has fine furniture and an outstanding collection of paintings.

Methuen Arms Hotel M
[symbols]
High St, Corsham, SN13 0HB
(0249) 714867 Fax (0249) 712004
14th C origins, charming stone-walled restaurant, 2 bars, skittle alley. Conveniently placed for Bath, Stonehenge and the Cotswolds.
Bedrooms: 6 single, 11 double & 7 twin, 1 family room.
Bathrooms: 24 private, 1 public; 1 private shower.
Bed & breakfast: £37-£42 single, £53-£58 double.
Half board: £42.85-£68 daily, from £243 weekly.
Lunch available.
Evening meal 7pm (l.o. 10pm).
Parking for 106.
Credit: Access, Visa.
[symbols]

Rudloe Park Hotel M
[symbols] COMMENDED
Leafy La., Corsham, SN13 0PA
Bath (0225) 810555
Fax (0225) 811412
An old country house set in 4 acres of lawns and gardens, with beautiful views down the valley to Bath. No smoking in the restaurant.

Bedrooms: 8 double & 2 twin, 1 family room.
Bathrooms: 11 private.
Bed & breakfast: £55-£60 single, £80-£90 double.
Half board: £55-£60 daily, £375-£410 weekly.
Lunch available.
Evening meal 7pm (l.o. 10pm).
Parking for 70.
Credit: Access, Visa, C.Bl., Diners, Amex.
[symbols]

COUNTISBURY
Devon
Map ref 1C1

2m E. Lynton
Small village in Exmoor National Park and close to the sea. 1 mile south is Watersmeet (National Trust).

The Exmoor Sandpiper M
[symbols]
Countisbury, Lynton, EX35 6NE
(059 87) 263
Beamed character inn/hotel, part 13th C, amidst thousands of acres of rolling Exmoor hills. A few hundred yards from Countisbury sea cliffs.
Bedrooms: 12 double & 2 twin, 2 family rooms.
Bathrooms: 16 private.
Bed & breakfast: £35.50 single, £71 double.
Half board: £53.13 daily, £305 weekly.
Lunch available.
Evening meal 7pm (l.o. 9.30pm).
Parking for 50.
[symbols]

CRACKINGTON HAVEN
Cornwall
Map ref 1C2

5m NE. Boscastle
Tiny village on the North Cornwall coast, with a small sandy beach and surf bathing. The highest cliffs in Cornwall lie to the south.

Crackington Manor M
[symbols] APPROVED
Crackington Haven, EX23 0JG
St. Gennys
(084 03) 397/536
Bedrooms: 3 double & 1 twin, 3 family rooms.
Bathrooms: 7 private.
Bed & breakfast: £13.50-£21.50 single, £27-£43 double.

Country house in a quiet cove, 100 yards from sea. Swimming pool, sauna, gymnasium and games room available. Children welcome.
Bedrooms: 2 single, 7 double & 4 twin, 2 family rooms.
Bathrooms: 12 private, 2 public; 1 private shower.
Bed & breakfast: £22-£25 single, £44-£50 double.
Half board: £32-£35 daily.
Lunch available.
Evening meal 8pm (l.o. 9pm).
Parking for 25.
Credit: Access, Visa.
[symbols]

CRANTOCK
Cornwall
Map ref 1B2

2m SW. Newquay
Pretty village of thatched cottages and seaside bungalows. Village stocks, once used against smugglers, are in the churchyard and the pub has a smugglers' hideout.

Crantock Bay Hotel M
Crantock, Newquay, TR8 5SE
(0637) 830229
CR Minotels
Long established family hotel on headland, with grounds leading directly on to beach. National Trust land nearby. Wonderful walking country.
Bedrooms: 9 single, 9 double & 18 twin.
Bathrooms: 36 private, 1 public.
Half board: £30.75-£42.75 daily.
Lunch available.
Evening meal 7pm (l.o. 8.30pm).
Parking for 36.
Open March-November.
Credit: Access, Visa, Diners, Amex.
[symbols]

Goose Rock Hotel
[symbols]
West Pentire, Crantock, TR8 5SE
(0637) 830755
Small intimate hotel surrounded by National Trust land overlooking Crantock Bay. Nearest hotel to Porth Joke beach and Vugga Cove.
Bedrooms: 3 double & 1 twin, 3 family rooms.
Bathrooms: 7 private.
Bed & breakfast: £13.50-£21.50 single, £27-£43 double.

Half board: £19.50-£27.50 daily, £130-£185 weekly.
Evening meal 7.30pm.
Parking for 20.
Open February-November.
[symbols]

CREDITON
Devon
Map ref 1D2

Ancient town in fertile valley, once prosperous from wool, now active in cider-making. Said to be the birthplace of St. Boniface. The 13th C Chapter House, the church governors' meeting place, holds a collection of armour from the Civil War.

Coombe House Country Hotel M
Coleford, Crediton, EX17 5BY
Copplestone (0363) 84487
Country hotel in beautiful, relaxed setting. Ideal for touring. Heated pool, tennis court. 5 acres of ground.
Bedrooms: 1 single, 4 double & 4 twin, 1 family room.
Bathrooms: 7 private, 2 public.
Bed & breakfast: £25-£30 single, £45-£55 double.
Half board: £35.50-£40 daily, £210-£270 weekly.
Lunch available.
Evening meal 7.30pm (l.o. 9.30pm).
Parking for 90.
Credit: Access, Visa, Amex.
[symbols]

The symbol CR and the name of a hotel group or consortium after a hotel address means that bookings can be made through a central reservations office. These are listed on pages 559 & 560.

Map references apply to the colour maps towards the end of this guide.

CREWKERNE

Somerset
Map ref 1D2

This charming little market town on the Dorset border nestles in undulating farmland and orchards in a conservation area. Built of local sandstone with Roman and Saxon origins. Dominated by the magnificent St. Bartholomew's Church dating from the 15th C. All set amidst peaceful countryside, thatched cottages, stately homes and romantic legends. St. Bartholomew's Fair is held in September.

Broadview ⚑
🏆🏆🏆 COMMENDED

43 East St., Crewkerne, TA18 7AG
☎ (0460) 73424
Secluded colonial-style bungalow, traditionally furnished with relaxing atmosphere, in an acre of landscaped grounds, featuring a water garden. Lovely views and comfortable individually furnished en-suite rooms. Home cooking.
Bedrooms: 1 double & 2 twin.
Bathrooms: 3 private.
Bed & breakfast: £14.50-£22.50 single, max. £29 double.
Half board: max. £23 daily, max. £161 weekly.
Evening meal 6.30pm (l.o. midday).
Parking for 6.

CROYDE

Devon
Map ref 1C1

7m SW. Ilfracombe
Pretty village with thatched cottages near Croyde Bay. To the south stretch Saunton Sands and their dunelands Braunton Burrows with interesting flowers and plants, nature reserve and golf-course. Cliff walks and bird-watching at Baggy Point, west of the village.

Croyde Bay House Hotel
🏆🏆 COMMENDED

Moor Lane, Croyde, Braunton, EX33 1PA
☎ (0271) 890270

Unique position overlooking bay, with the highest tides reaching the hotel's garden wall. All rooms with beautiful views, en-suite, tea making facilities.
Bedrooms: 3 double & 2 twin, 2 family rooms.
Bathrooms: 7 private, 1 public.
Bed & breakfast: £27-£43 single, £54-£70 double.
Half board: £40-£45 daily, £232-£260 weekly.
Evening meal 7.15pm (l.o. 8pm).
Open March-November.
Credit: Access, Visa.

Moorsands House Hotel
🏆🏆🏆

Moor Lane, Croyde Bay, Braunton, EX33 1NP
☎ (0271) 890781
Hotel with sea views, 5 minutes from beach. All rooms with en-suite shower and WC, TV and tea-making facilities. Varied menu, wine list, bar.
Bedrooms: 4 double & 1 twin, 3 family rooms.
Bathrooms: 8 private.
Bed & breakfast: £18-£20 single, £32-£36 double.
Half board: £23.50-£27.50 daily, £150.50-£178.50 weekly.
Evening meal 7pm (l.o. 6pm).
Parking for 8.
Open March-October.
Credit: Access, Visa.

The Whiteleaf at Croyde ⚑
🏆🏆🏆 COMMENDED

Hobbs Hill, Croyde, Braunton, EX33 1PN
☎ (0271) 890266
Experienced owners offer high standard of accommodation, in comfortable 30's home near sandy beach and old world village.
Bedrooms: 3 double & 1 twin, 1 family room.
Bathrooms: 5 private.
Bed & breakfast: £27-£29 single, £44-£48 double.
Half board: £37-£45 daily, £235-£290 weekly.
Evening meal 7.30pm (l.o. 8.30pm).
Parking for 8.
Credit: Access, Visa.

CULLOMPTON

Devon
Map ref 1D2

Market town on former coaching routes, with pleasant tree-shaded cobbled pavements and some handsome 17th C houses. Earlier prosperity from the wool industry is reflected in the grandness of the church with its fan-vaulted aisle built by a wool-stapler in 1526.

Rullands
Rull La., Cullompton, EX15 1NQ
☎ (0884) 33356
14th C country house amid beautiful Devon countryside. Within easy reach of all country pursuits, the M5 and the historic town of Tiverton.
Bedrooms: 1 single, 3 double.
Bathrooms: 3 private.
Bed & breakfast: from £15 single, £37-£39 double.
Half board: £31-£36 daily, £200-£250 weekly.
Lunch available.
Evening meal 7.15pm (l.o. 9pm).
Parking for 20.
Credit: Access, Visa.

DARTMOOR

See Ashburton, Bovey Tracey, Buckfast, Buckfastleigh, Buckland Monachorum, Chagford, Haytor, Horrabridge, Lydford, Moretonhampstead, Okehampton, Two Bridges, Widecombe-in-the-Moor, Yelverton.

Individual proprietors have supplied all details of accommodation. Although we do check for accuracy, we advise you to confirm prices and other information at the time of booking.

The symbols are explained on the flap inside the back cover.

DARTMOUTH

Devon
Map ref 1D3

Ancient port, now a resort, on wooded slopes above natural harbour at mouth of the Dart. Has fine period buildings, notably town houses near Quay and Butterwalk of 1635. The church is richly-furnished and the harbour castle ruin recalls earlier importance when Crusader fleets assembled here. Royal Naval College, grandly built in 1905, dominates from hill. Carnival, June; Regatta, August.
Tourist Information Centre ☎ (0803) 834224

The Captains House
🏆🏆 COMMENDED

18 Clarence St., Dartmouth, TQ6 9NW
☎ (0803) 832133
18th C listed house. Tasteful decor and personal service. Close to town and shops. Special diets on request.
Bedrooms: 3 double & 2 twin.
Bathrooms: 5 private.
Bed & breakfast: £20-£26 single, £28-£40 double.

George & Dragon
Mayors Ave., Dartmouth, TQ6 9NG
☎ (0803) 832325
Family-run friendly inn on level ground in town centre. Newly refurbished in 1990. Home-cooked specialities. Real ales, own keys.
Bedrooms: 2 double, 1 family room.
Bathrooms: 1 public.
Bed & breakfast: £30-£45 double.
Lunch available.
Evening meal 6.30pm (l.o. 10pm).
Parking for 6.

Royal Castle Hotel ⚑
🏆🏆🏆 COMMENDED

11 The Quay, Dartmouth, TQ6 9PS
☎ (0803) 833033 Fax (0803) 835445
Historic 17th C quayside coaching inn with resident proprietors, offering traditional style food and service. Open fires, comfortable bedrooms.
Bedrooms: 4 single, 10 double & 7 twin, 4 family rooms.
Bathrooms: 25 private.

Bed & breakfast: £35-£44 single, £64-£90 double.
Half board: £49-£59 daily, £300-£370 weekly.
Lunch available.
Evening meal 6.45pm (l.o. 9.45pm).
Parking for 3.
Credit: Access, Visa.

⌣ 🏠 📞 ⊙ 🖵 ♥ 🛈 Ⅴ 🛏
● 🖿 ☎ 🏍 🖊 ⇘ ⛛ SP 🎗 T

Stanborough Hundred Hotel

♨♨

Halwell, Totnes, TQ9 7JG
☎ East Allington
(054 852) 236
Country house hotel with 2 acres of landscaped garden dating from early 1800. Exceptional views of Dartmoor. Halwell is 5 miles south-west of Totnes.
Bedrooms: 2 double & 2 twin, 2 family rooms.
Bathrooms: 4 private, 1 public.
Bed & breakfast: £18.50-£25 single, £37-£42 double.
Half board: £29-£31.50 daily, £155-£172 weekly.
Evening meal 7.30pm (l.o. 6pm).
Parking for 10.
Open April-October.

⌣ ♨ ♥ 🛈 Ⅴ 🖵 📺 🖿 ⊿
🖊 & ⚘ ✕ 🎗 SP T

Stoke Lodge Hotel M

Cinders La., Stoke Fleming, Dartmouth, TQ6 0RA
☎ (0803) 770523
Country house hotel near the sea with lovely views. All rooms en-suite, heated indoor and outdoor swimming pools and leisure facilities.
Bedrooms: 3 single, 8 double & 8 twin, 5 family rooms.
Bathrooms: 24 private.
Bed & breakfast: £33-£40 single, £55-£66 double.
Half board: £35-£42 daily, £238-£287 weekly.
Lunch available.
Evening meal 7pm (l.o. 9pm).
Parking for 50.

⌣ 🏠 📞 ⊙ 🖵 ♥ 🛈 Ⅴ
🖵 🖿 🖿 ⊿ 🖊 🎗 🔔 ⛛ 🎗 ♂
⚘ 🖊 ⇘ SP 🎗

Sunnybanks Guest House

♨♨♨ APPROVED

1 Vicarage Hill, Dartmouth, TQ6 9EN
☎ (080 43) 2766
Detached property, south facing, with pleasant outlook over the bowling green. Situated on the level with the town.
Bedrooms: 1 single, 6 double & 2 twin, 1 family room.

Bathrooms: 4 private, 1 public; 5 private showers.
Bed & breakfast: £15-£20 single, £30-£40 double.
Half board: £23-£28 daily, £155-£185 weekly.
Evening meal 6pm (l.o. 9pm).
Parking for 3.

⌣ 🏠 🏍 ⊙ 🖵 ♥ 🛈 Ⅴ 🛏
📺 🖿 ⊿

Victoria Hotel M

Victoria Rd., Dartmouth, TQ6 9RX
☎ Dartmouth (0803) 832572
A small friendly town hotel with licensed bars. Open to non-residents. Five en-suite bedrooms. Rooms have own TV and tea making facilities.
Bedrooms: 2 single, 5 double & 2 twin, 2 family rooms.
Bathrooms: 5 private, 2 public.
Bed & breakfast: £16.50-£25 single, £33-£50 double.
Half board: £25-£34 daily, £175-£240 weekly.
Lunch available.
Evening meal 7pm (l.o. 9.30pm).
Credit: Access, Visa.

⌣ 🖵 ♥ 🛈 Ⅴ 🖿 ⊿ SP

Small resort, developed in Regency and Victorian periods beside Dawlish Water which runs down from the Haldon Hills. Town centre has ornamental riverside gardens with black swans. One of British Rail's most scenic stretches was built by Brunel alongside jagged red cliffs between the sands and the town.
Tourist Information Centre ☎ (0626) 863589

Brockington House M

♨♨♨ COMMENDED

139 Exeter Rd., Dawlish, EX7 0AN
☎ (0626) 863588
Licensed guesthouse on coast road (A379). 5 minutes' walk from sea. Town centre approximately three quarters of a mile away.
Bedrooms: 1 single, 7 double & 1 twin.
Bathrooms: 5 private, 1 public.
Bed & breakfast: £14.50-£16.50 single, £29-£39 double.
Half board: £23-£28 daily, £151-£237.50 weekly.

Evening meal 7pm (l.o. 5pm).
Parking for 10.
Credit: Access.

⌣ 🏠 ♥ Ⅴ 🖵 📺 🖿 ⊿ 🖊
DAP SP

Langstone Cliff Hotel M

♨♨♨♨ COMMENDED

Dawlish Warren, Dawlish, EX7 0NA
☎ (0626) 865155 Fax (0626) 867166
Ⓒ Consort
Family-owned hotel set in 19 acres of grounds, overlooking the sea. Extensive leisure and conference facilities.
Bedrooms: 10 single, 10 double & 10 twin, 34 family rooms.
Bathrooms: 64 private, 3 public.
Bed & breakfast: £40-£50 single, £70-£80 double.
Half board: £43-£53 daily.
Lunch available.
Evening meal 7pm (l.o. 9pm).
Parking for 200.
Credit: Access, Visa, Diners, Amex.

⌣ 🏠 📞 ⊙ 🖵 ♥ 🛈 Ⅴ 🛏
📺 ● 🖿 🖿 ⊿ 🖊 & ⇘ 🎗
⚘ ♂ ⚘ DAP ⇘ SP T

Radfords Country Hotel M

♨♨♨ COMMENDED

Lower Dawlish Water, Dawlish EX7 0QN
☎ Dawlish (0626) 863322
Highly residential family hotel near the sea. Service, entertainment and safety standards for children of all ages.
Bedrooms: 37 family rooms.
Bathrooms: 37 private.
Bed & breakfast: £17.50-£25 single, £35-£50 double.
Half board: £27.50-£42 daily, £180-£270 weekly.
Evening meal 6pm (l.o. 7pm).
Parking for 52.
Open March-November.

⌣ & ♥ 🛈 Ⅴ ✕ 🖵 📺 🖿
⊿ 🖊 🎗 ⛛ ⚘ 🖊 SP 🎗

The symbol Ⓒ and the name of a hotel group or consortium after a hotel address means that bookings can be made through a central reservations office. These are listed on pages 559 & 560.

Standing on the Kennet and Avon Canal, old market town near the Vale of Pewsey. Rebuilt Norman castle, good 18th C buildings and old inns. All 3 churches are of interest, notably St. John's with 12th C work and Norman tower. Museum of Wiltshire's archaeology and natural history reflects wealth of prehistoric sites on Salisbury Plain and at other locations nearby.
Tourist Information Centre ☎ (0380) 729408

Bear Hotel M

♨♨♨♨

Market Pl., Devizes, SN10 1DH
☎ (0380) 722444
Established before 1599. Overlooking attractive market square and within easy reach of Bath, Swindon, Salisbury, stately homes and gardens.
Bedrooms: 7 single, 10 double & 6 twin, 2 family rooms.
Bathrooms: 25 private, 1 public.
Bed & breakfast: from £45 single, from £60 double.
Lunch available.
Evening meal 7pm (l.o. 10pm).
Credit: Access, Visa.

⌣ 🏠 📞 ⊙ 🖵 ♥ 🛈 Ⅴ ✗
🖵 📺 🖿 ⊿ 🖊 ♂ SP 🎗 T

The Castle Hotel M

♨♨♨

New Park St., Devizes, SN10 1DS
☎ (0380) 729300 Fax (0380) 729155
Well-appointed accommodation in family-run environment. A la carte restaurant and popular bar. All rooms en-suite.
Bedrooms: 6 single, 5 double & 7 twin, 1 family room.
Bathrooms: 19 private.
Bed & breakfast: from £38 single, from £51 double.
Lunch available.
Evening meal 6.30pm (l.o. 10pm).
Parking for 4.
Credit: Access, Visa, Diners, Amex.

⌣ 📞 ⊙ 🖵 ♥ 🛈 Ⅴ ✗ 🖵
🖿 ⊿ 🖊 SP 🎗 T

Craven House

Station Rd., Devizes, SN10 1BZ
☎ (0380) 723514

Continued ▶

DEVIZES

Continued

Victorian town house, 1 minute from town centre and market-place. Easy walking distance for shops and restaurants.
Bedrooms: 1 double & 1 twin, 1 family room.
Bathrooms: 2 public.
Bed & breakfast: £14-£16 single, £24-£28 double.
Half board: £21-£24 daily, £84-£98 weekly.
Evening meal 6pm (l.o. 7.30pm).

Glenholme Guest House
APPROVED
77 Nursteed Rd., Devizes, SN10 3AJ
☎ (0380) 723187
Comfortable family home. Both bedrooms with own TV and tea making facilities. Special diets prepared by arrangement.
Bedrooms: 1 twin, 1 family room.
Bathrooms: 1 public.
Bed & breakfast: £16-£17 single, £26-£28 double.
Half board: £22-£24 daily.
Evening meal 5pm.
Parking for 2.

Pinecroft
Listed APPROVED
Potterne Rd., Devizes, SN10 5DA
☎ (0380) 721433
Comfortable Georgian family house with spacious rooms and exquisite garden. Only 3 minutes' walk from town centre.
Bedrooms: 2 double & 2 twin, 1 family room.
Bathrooms: 4 private, 1 public.
Bed & breakfast: £15-£22 single, £30-£34 double.
Parking for 6.
Credit: Access, Visa, Amex.

Rathlin
COMMENDED
Wick Lane, Devizes, SN10 5DP
☎ (0380) 721999
Elegant period charm, all rooms en-suite and individually furnished. Quiet location close to town centre. Tranquil gardens. Ample parking.
Bedrooms: 1 single, 1 double & 2 twin.
Bathrooms: 4 private, 1 public.

Bed & breakfast: £20 single, £34 double.
Parking for 5.

DORCHESTER

Dorset
Map ref 2B3

Busy medieval county town (cloth and ale-producing centre) destroyed by fires in 17th and 18th C. Cromwellian stronghold and scene of Judge Jeffrey's Bloody Assize (his High Street lodging is now a restaurant) after Monmouth Rebellion of 1685. Tolpuddle Martyrs were tried in Shire Hall. Museum has Roman and earlier exhibits and Hardy relics.
Tourist Information Centre ☎ (0305) 267992

Hadley Lodge
APPROVED
Main Rd., Winterbourne Abbas, Dorchester, DT2 9LW
☎ Martinstown (030 589) 558
Large modernised country house, providing comfortable accommodation, 5 miles west of Dorchester. Convenient for touring west Dorset. Home-cooked food.
Bedrooms: 1 double & 2 twin, 2 family rooms.
Bathrooms: 2 private, 1 public.
Bed & breakfast: £13-£16 single, £32-£36 double.
Half board: £23-£25 daily, £161-£175 weekly.
Evening meal 7pm (l.o. 7pm).
Parking for 6.
Open April-October.

Westwood House
COMMENDED
29 High West St., Dorchester, DT1 1UP
☎ (0305) 268018
Delightful Georgian listed town house. Tastefully furnished with all facilities. Ideal for overnight stay or as a base for touring Hardy's Wessex.
Bedrooms: 1 single, 3 double & 3 twin.
Bathrooms: 5 private, 1 public.
Bed & breakfast: £22-£36 single, £38-£48 double.
Credit: Access, Visa.

DULVERTON

Somerset
Map ref 1D1

Set among woods and hills of south-west Exmoor, a busy riverside town with a 13th C church. The Rivers Barle and Exe are rich in salmon and trout. The Exmoor National Park Headquarters at Dulverton Information Centre are open throughout the year.

Carnarvon Arms Hotel M
Brushford, Dulverton, TA22 9AE
☎ (0398) 23302 Fax (0398) 24022
Privately-owned country hotel overlooking the picturesque Barle Valley, on the edge of Exmoor National Park. Closed most of February.
Bedrooms: 6 single, 4 double & 14 twin, 2 family rooms.
Bathrooms: 22 private, 1 public.
Half board: £46-£50 daily, £280-£420 weekly.
Lunch available.
Evening meal 7.30pm (l.o. 9.30pm).
Parking for 100.
Credit: Access, Visa.

Exton House Hotel M
COMMENDED
Exton, Dulverton, TA22 9JT
☎ Winsford (064 385) 365
Former rectory in a delightful rural setting on the side of the Exe valley. Turn off A396 at Bridgetown and we are half a mile on right.
Bedrooms: 1 single, 2 double & 2 twin, 1 family room.
Bathrooms: 4 private, 1 public.
Half board: £24-£35 daily, from £154 weekly.
Evening meal 7.30pm (l.o. 2pm).
Parking for 6.
Credit: Access, Visa.

The enquiry coupons at the back will help you when contacting proprietors.

DUNSTER

Somerset
Map ref 1D1

Ancient town with views of Exmoor and the Quantocks whose historic hilltop castle has been continuously occupied since it was begun in 1070. Medieval prosperity from cloth built the octagonal Yarn Market, late 16th C, and the church with its broad wagon roof. A riverside mill, packhorse bridge and 18th C hilltop folly occupy other interesting corners in the town.

Bilbrook Lawns Hotel M
Bilbrook, Minehead, TA24 6HE
☎ Washford (0984) 40331
Detached Georgian country house hotel set in extensive lawned gardens bordered by a stream.
Bedrooms: 4 double & 3 twin.
Bathrooms: 4 private, 1 public.
Bed & breakfast: £19.50-£22.50 single, £30-£40 double.
Half board: £24.50-£29.50 daily, £137.50-£165 weekly.
Lunch available.
Evening meal 7.30pm (l.o. 7.30pm).
Parking for 8.
Open March-October, December.

Dollons House
COMMENDED
10 Church St., Dunster, Minehead, TA24 6SH
☎ (0643) 821880
Delightful listed building in centre of medieval village, nestling beneath the castle. Comfortable en-suite rooms, beautifully decorated. Non-smokers only please.
Bedrooms: 2 double & 1 twin.
Bathrooms: 3 private.
Bed & breakfast: £40-£45 double.
Half board: £28-£30 daily, £180.50-£185 weekly.
Open March-October.
Credit: Access, Visa, Amex.

Dunster Castle Hotel
APPROVED
5 High St., Dunster, TA24 6SG
☎ (0643) 821445 Fax (0643) 821558

Old style country hotel with large private car park, set in an historic village. Good base for walks and tours of Exmoor.
Bedrooms: 2 single, 5 double & 2 twin, 1 family room.
Bathrooms: 6 private, 2 public; 1 private shower.
Bed & breakfast: £60-£75 double.
Half board: £40-£47.50 daily.
Lunch available.
Evening meal 7pm (l.o. 9.30pm).
Parking for 30.
Credit: Access, Visa, Diners, Amex.

Exmoor House Hotel M
😋😋😋 COMMENDED
West St., Dunster, TA24 6SN
☎ (0643) 821268
Near Dunster Castle, Exmoor, Brendons, Quantocks and coast. Farm fresh food, interesting wines, lounges and restaurant. Home comforts. A non-smoking establishment.
Bedrooms: 3 double & 3 twin.
Bathrooms: 6 private.
Bed & breakfast: £29.50-£31.50 single, £44-£48 double.
Half board: £36-£38 daily, £210-£231 weekly.
Evening meal 7.30pm (l.o. 7pm).
Open February-November.
Credit: Access, Visa, Diners, Amex.

Yarn Market Hotel M
😋😋😋
25 High St., Dunster, TA24 8SL
☎ (0643) 821425
Central and accessible hotel in quaint English village, an ideal location from which to explore the Exmoor National Park.
Bedrooms: 1 single, 1 double & 1 twin, 1 family room.
Bathrooms: 4 private.
Bed & breakfast: £17.50-£25 single, £35-£50 double.
Half board: £23.50-£31 daily.
Lunch available.
Evening meal 4pm (l.o. 8pm).
Parking for 6.
Credit: Visa, Amex.

The National Crown Scheme is explained in full on pages 556 – 558.

Wiltshire
Map ref 2B2

5m NW. Ludgershall
Small village in fine open country, with a Gothic revival church of considerable beauty. Ideal for exploring Salisbury Plain and the Vale of Pewsey.

The Crown Hotel
Everleigh, Marlborough, SN8 3EY
☎ Collingbourne Ducis (026 485) 223
Family run country hotel between Salisbury and Marlborough, 6 miles from Stonehenge. Rural and quiet. Fresh vegetables, local game and friendly atmosphere. Trout fishing.
Bedrooms: 1 single, 2 double & 3 twin, 2 family rooms.
Bathrooms: 3 private, 2 public.
Bed & breakfast: £32-£40 single, £54-£70 double.
Half board: £224-£280 weekly.
Evening meal 7pm (l.o. 10pm).
Parking for 56.
Credit: Access, Visa, Amex.

Dorset
Map ref 2A3

Set in hilly country at source of the River Frome, a small village with a sophisticated, bow-fronted High Street of raised pavements. The church has an unusual spire.

The Acorn Inn Hotel M
28 Fore St., Evershot, Dorchester, DT2 0JW
☎ (0935) 83228
Hardy's historic 16th C village inn with beamed bars, log fires and candlelit restaurant. 1.5 miles off A37 Yeovil to Dorchester road.
Bedrooms: 5 double & 1 twin, 2 family rooms.
Bathrooms: 8 private, 1 public.
Bed & breakfast: £25 single, £44-£80 double.
Half board: £34.50-£49.50 daily, £157-£210 weekly.
Evening meal 6.30pm (l.o. 7.45pm).

Parking for 40.
Credit: Access, Visa.

Rectory House M
😋😋😋 COMMENDED
Fore St., Evershot, DT2 0JW
☎ (093 583) 273
Lovely 18th C rectory in picturesque village of Evershot.
Bedrooms: 4 double & 2 twin.
Bathrooms: 6 private.
Bed & breakfast: £25-£50 single, £46-£50 double.
Half board: £33.50-£35.50 daily, £189-£192 weekly.
Evening meal 6.30pm (l.o. 7.30pm).
Parking for 8.

Somerset
Map ref 1D1

2m NW. Bampton

The Anchor Inn and Hotel M
😋😋😋 COMMENDED
Exebridge, Dulverton, TA22 9AZ
☎ (0398) 23433
Charming residential country inn on the River Exe, with its own fishing. Stableblock restaurant overlooking river. Ideal base for exploring Exmoor.
Bedrooms: 2 double & 2 twin, 2 family rooms.
Bathrooms: 6 private.
Bed & breakfast: from £40 single, £54-£60 double.
Half board: £40-£43 daily, £215-£225 weekly.
Lunch available.
Evening meal 7pm (l.o. 9pm).
Parking for 100.
Credit: Access.
⓭ Display advertisement appears on page 456.

Classifications and quality commendations were correct at the time of going to press but are subject to change. Please check at the time of booking.

Devon
Map ref 1D2

University city rebuilt after the 1940s around its venerable cathedral. Suffered Danish raids under Anglo-Saxons but repulsed William I until 1068. Attractions include early Norman towers preserved in 13th C cathedral with fine west front; notable waterfront buildings; Maritime Museum; Guildhall; Cathedral library; Rougemont House Museum of Costume and Lace; Royal Albert Memorial Museum; Northcott Theatre.
Tourist Information Centre ☎ *(0392) 265297*

Barton Cross Hotel M
😋😋😋😋 COMMENDED
Huxham, Stoke Canon, Exeter, EX5 4EJ
☎ (0392) 841245 Telex 42603
A harmonious blend of 17th C charm and 20th C comfort. Half a mile off the A396 Tiverton to Exeter road.
Bedrooms: 2 single, 3 double & 2 twin.
Bathrooms: 7 private.
Bed & breakfast: £37-£67 single, £58-£80 double.
Half board: £45.50-£89 daily, from £300 weekly.
Lunch available.
Evening meal 7pm (l.o. 9.30pm).
Parking for 24.
Credit: Access, Visa, C.Bl., Diners, Amex.

Clock Tower Guest House M
16 New North Rd., Exeter, EX4 4HF
☎ (0392) 52493
Homely accommodation in the city centre for all tourists. Coach and railway stations within 10 minutes' walk. All modern facilities. Solarium.
Bedrooms: 1 single, 5 double & 3 twin, 2 family rooms.
Bathrooms: 3 private, 3 public.
Bed & breakfast: £11-£14.50 single, £18-£25 double.
Credit: Access, Visa, Diners, Amex.

393

EXETER
Continued

Countess Wear Lodge M
398 Topsham Rd., Exeter,
EX2 6HE
☎ Topsham (039 287) 5441
Telex 42551 EXMOAT
Ⓒ Queens Moat Houses
*Modern hotel close to the city
centre and the M5 junction 30.
Well-placed for touring the
West Country.*
Bedrooms: 10 single,
10 double & 23 twin, 1 family
room.
Bathrooms: 44 private.
Bed & breakfast: £33-£55
single, £54-£66 double.
Half board: £33-£36 daily,
£221-£242 weekly.
Lunch available.
Evening meal 7pm (l.o.
9.45pm).
Parking for 120.
Credit: Access, Visa, Diners,
Amex.
🅿 ♨ ↺ ⑱ ➡ ⇄ 🏮 Ⓥ ✂
⊭ ⓞ ◫ ➡ ⓣ ⚹ ♪ ▶ ⁂
Ⓓ ⚲ SP Ⓣ

Devon Motel M
Exeter-by-Pass, Matford,
Exeter, EX2 8XU
☎ (0392) 59268 Telex 42551
EXONIAG (REF BREND 5)
Ⓒ Brend
*Set in beautiful countryside,
yet offering easy accessibility
to the M5 and the centre of
Exeter.*
Bedrooms: 5 single, 16 double
& 17 twin, 3 family rooms.
Bathrooms: 41 private,
1 public.
Bed & breakfast: £44-£50
single, £55-£66 double.
Half board: £40-£60 daily,
£250-£340 weekly.
Lunch available.
Evening meal 7pm (l.o.
9.30pm).
Parking for 250.
Credit: Access, Visa, Diners,
Amex.
🅿 ♨ ↺ ⑱ ➡ ⇄ 🏮 Ⓥ ◉
◫ ➡ ⓣ ⚹ ⁂ ⚲ SP ⓕ Ⓣ

Ebford House Hotel M
😃😃😃😃 COMMENDED
Exmouth Rd., Ebford, Exeter,
EX3 0QH
☎ (0392) 877658
Ⓒ Minotels
*Beautifully restored Georgian
country house set in lovely
gardens, fine views. A warm
welcome assured. Leisure area.*
Bedrooms: 4 single, 10 double
& 4 twin.
Bathrooms: 18 private.
Bed & breakfast: £45-£52
single, £60-£73 double.
Half board: £52-£65 daily.

Lunch available.
Evening meal 6.30pm (l.o.
9.30pm).
Parking for 35.
Credit: Access, Visa, Amex.
🅿 ♨ ⑱ ↺ ⑱ ➡ ⇄ 🏮 Ⓥ
✂ ⊭ ◫ ➡ ⓣ ⚹ ✹ ✕ ⊭
SP ⓕ

Fairwinds Hotel M
😃😃😃😃 COMMENDED
Kennford, Exeter, EX6 7UD
☎ (0392) 832911
*Unique little hotel in beautiful
rural surroundings. High
standard of cleanliness and
service with a varied menu.
Non-smoking restaurant and
bar.*
Bedrooms: 2 single, 5 double
& 1 twin.
Bathrooms: 6 private;
2 private showers.
Bed & breakfast: £20-£38
single, £40-£46 double.
Half board: £28-£35 daily,
£160-£190 weekly.
Evening meal 7pm (l.o.
8.30pm).
Parking for 9.
Credit: Access, Visa.
🅿 ↺ ⑱ ➡ ⇄ 🏮 Ⓥ ✂ ⊭
◫ ➡ ✕ ⊭ Ⓓ SP

Globe Hotel
Fore St., Topsham, Exeter,
EX3 0HR
☎ (0392) 873471
*Family-run old coaching inn in
the centre of the old part of
Topsham.*
Bedrooms: 6 double & 8 twin.
Bathrooms: 14 private.
Bed & breakfast: from £30
single, £40-£50 double.
Lunch available.
Evening meal 7pm (l.o.
9.30pm).
Parking for 14.
Credit: Access, Visa, Amex.
🅿 ♨ ↺ ⑱ ➡ ⇄ 🏮 Ⓥ
◫ ➡ ⓣ ✕ ⓕ

Great Western Hotel M
😃😃😃
Station Approach, St.
David's, Exeter, EX4 4NU
☎ (0392) 74039
*Hotel has easy access to
railway station. Bar restaurant,
lounge, conference room and
car park.*
Bedrooms: 23 single, 7 double
& 9 twin, 1 family room.
Bathrooms: 28 private,
5 public.
Bed & breakfast: £25-£35
single, £36-£50 double.
Half board: £34-£44 daily,
£230-£300 weekly.
Lunch available.
Evening meal 7pm (l.o.
9.30pm).

Parking for 30.
Credit: Access, Visa, Diners,
Amex.
🅿 ♨ ↺ ⑱ ➡ ⇄ 🏮 Ⓥ ⊭ Ⓣⓥ
◫ ➡ ⓣ Ⓓ SP

The Lord Haldon Hotel M
Dunchideock, Exeter,
EX6 7YF
☎ (0392) 832483 Telex 42603
CHAMCO G.
*Family-run, historic former
mansion within own grounds,
offering panoramic views. 5
miles south-west of Exeter and
well placed for Dartmoor and
coast.*
Bedrooms: 2 single, 10 double
& 4 twin, 3 family rooms.
Bathrooms: 19 private,
1 public.
Bed & breakfast: £25-£32
single, £39-£49 double.
Half board: £34.50-£41.50
daily, £185-£220 weekly.
Lunch available.
Evening meal 7pm (l.o.
10pm).
Parking for 80.
Credit: Access, Visa.
🅿 ⑱ ↺ ⑱ ➡ ⇄ 🏮 Ⓥ ⊭
Ⓣⓥ ◉ ◫ ➡ ⓣ ↺ ⚹ ⊭ SP
ⓕ Ⓣ

St. Andrews Hotel M
😃😃😃
28 Alphington Rd., Exeter,
EX2 8HN
☎ (0392) 76784
*Established family-run
Victorian house with modern
hotel amenities. Relaxed
atmosphere and a warm
welcome.*
Bedrooms: 4 single, 8 double
& 3 twin, 2 family rooms.
Bathrooms: 17 private,
2 public.
Bed & breakfast: £35-£44
single, £54-£63 double.
Evening meal 7pm (l.o.
8.15pm).
Parking for 20.
Credit: Access, Visa, Amex.
🅿 ♨ ↺ ⑱ ➡ ⇄ 🏮 Ⓥ ⊭
◫ ➡ ⚹ ⊭

EXMOOR

*See Combe Martin,
Countisbury, Dulverton,
Dunster, Exebridge,
Lynmouth, Lynton,
Porlock, Simonsbath,
Wheddon Cross, Woody
Bay.*

**Map references
apply to the colour
maps towards the
end of this guide.**

EXMOUTH
Devon
Map ref 1D2

Developed as a seaside
resort in George III's
reign, set against the
woods of the Exe Estuary
and red cliffs of Orcombe
Point. Extensive sands,
small harbour, chapel and
almshouses, a model
railway and A la Ronde, a
16-sided house.

Aliston House M
😃😃😃 APPROVED
58 Salterton Rd., Exmouth,
EX8 2EW
☎ (0395) 274119
*Comfortably-appointed hotel
with restaurant, licensed bar,
attractive garden and ample
car parking facilities.*
Bedrooms: 1 single, 5 double
& 6 twin, 2 family rooms.
Bathrooms: 8 private,
2 public.
Bed & breakfast: £20-£22
single, £38-£40 double.
Half board: £27-£29 daily,
£180-£190 weekly.
Lunch available.
Evening meal 7pm (l.o.
8.30pm).
Parking for 16.
🅿 ♨ ⑱ ➡ ⇄ 🏮 Ⓥ ⊭ Ⓣⓥ
◫ ➡ ⓣ ↺ ⚹ Ⓓ ⚲ SP Ⓣ

Balcombe House Hotel M
😃😃😃
Stevenstone Rd., Exmouth,
EX8 2EP
☎ (0395) 266349
*Comfortable, quiet, small but
spacious hotel set in half an
acre walled garden. Personal
attention with wide choice of
menus. Ample parking.*
Bedrooms: 1 single, 4 double
& 5 twin, 2 family rooms.
Bathrooms: 12 private.
Bed & breakfast: £22-£25.50
single, £44-£51 double.
Half board: £32-£33.50 daily,
£197-£207 weekly.
Lunch available.
Evening meal 7pm (l.o. 6pm).
Parking for 15.
Open April-October.
🅿 10 ♨ ⑱ ➡ ⇄ 🏮 ✂ ⊭
◫ ➡ ↺ ⚹ ✕ ⊭ SP

Blenheim Guest House
39 Morton Rd., Exmouth,
EX8 1BA
☎ (0395) 264230
*Comfortable licensed
guesthouse, 100 yards from
beach, 500 yards to town and
services. All bedrooms with
colour TV and tea making.
Closed 24th-26th December.
Brochure on request.*

Bedrooms: 3 double & 1 twin,
2 family rooms.
Bathrooms: 1 public.
Bed & breakfast: £11-£12
single, £22-£24 double.
Half board: £15-£16 daily,
£94-£99 weekly.
Evening meal 6pm (l.o.
4.45pm).
Parking for 1.
Credit: Access, Visa.

The Kerans Hotel M
😃😃😃 COMMENDED
Esplanade, Exmouth,
EX8 1DS
☎ (0395) 275275
*Seaview rooms with mini-bar,
direct dial telephone, colour
TV, tea making and en-suite
facilities. Easy access by road
or rail.*
Bedrooms: 2 single, 3 double
& 1 twin, 1 family room.
Bathrooms: 6 private,
1 public.
Bed & breakfast: £21-£28
single, £42-£52 double.
Half board: £27-£36 daily,
£135-£170 weekly.
Evening meal 6.30pm (l.o.
midday).
Parking for 5.
Credit: Access, Visa.

Pendennis Guest House
😃😃
84 St. Andrews Rd.,
Exmouth, EX8 1AS
☎ (0395) 271458
*A large comfortable family
guesthouse. TV and bar
lounges, come and go as you
please and only 200 yards from
the beach.*
Bedrooms: 2 single, 2 double,
3 family rooms.
Bathrooms: 2 public.
Bed & breakfast: £10.50-
£13.50 single, £21-£27 double.
Half board: £15.25-£18.25
daily.
Evening meal 6.30pm (l.o.
3pm).
Parking for 3.
Open January-November.

Redcliff Court Hotel
4 Cyprus Rd., Exmouth,
EX8 2DZ
☎ (0395) 263363
*Small established hotel in quiet
setting with large garden near
sea and town centre.*
Bedrooms: 4 single, 3 double
& 1 twin, 4 family room.
Bathrooms: 4 private,
2 public.
Bed & breakfast: £17-£21
single, £34-£42 double.

Half board: £25-£29 daily,
£160-£190 weekly.
Evening meal 6.30pm (l.o.
7pm).
Parking for 8.

Royal Beacon Hotel M
😃😃😃😃
The Beacon, Exmouth,
EX8 2AF
☎ (0395) 264886 & 265269
Fax (0395) 268890
Ⓒ Best Western
*South facing with magnificent
sea views, 200 yards from town
centre and beach. Various diets
catered for by arrangement.*
Bedrooms: 6 single, 10 double
& 12 twin, 2 family rooms.
Bathrooms: 30 private,
4 public.
Bed & breakfast: £39-£42.35
single, £67.30-£80 double.
Half board: £52.50-£54.85
daily.
Lunch available.
Evening meal 6.30pm (l.o.
11.30pm).
Parking for 30.
Credit: Access, Visa, C.Bl.,
Diners, Amex.

Avon
Map ref 2B2

4m NE. Thornbury

Green Farm Guest House
A38, Falfield, Wotton under
Edge, Gloucs GL12 8DL
☎ (0454) 260319
*16th C stone farmhouse
tastefully converted into a
comfortable guesthouse.
Convenient for M4 and M5.
Surrounded by 100 acres of
farmland. Candlelit suppers
and log fires.*
Bedrooms: 1 single, 4 double
& 2 twin, 1 family room.
Bathrooms: 1 private,
1 public.
Bed & breakfast: £15-£25
single, £24-£35 double.
Half board: £24-£29 daily.
Evening meal 6.30pm (l.o.
9pm).
Parking for 12.

The Park Hotel
😃😃😃 APPROVED
Falfield, Wotton Under
Edge, Gloucs. GL12 8DR
☎ (0454) 260550

*A country house with a large
garden situated just off A38, 1
mile south of junction 14 on
M5.*
Bedrooms: 3 single, 4 double,
3 family rooms.
Bathrooms: 7 private,
2 public.
Bed & breakfast: £40-£45
single, £50-£55 double.
Lunch available.
Evening meal 7pm (l.o.
10pm).
Parking for 100.
Credit: Access, Visa, Diners,
Amex.

Cornwall
Map ref 1B3

Busy port and fishing
harbour, popular resort
on the balmy Cornish
Riviera. Henry VIII's
Pendennis Castle faces
St. Mawes Castle across
the broad natural harbour
and yacht basin Carrick
Roads, which receives 7
rivers.
*Tourist Information
Centre* ☎ (0326) 312300

Hotel Anacapri M
😃😃😃
Gyllyngvase Rd., Sea Front,
Falmouth, TR11 4DJ
☎ (0326) 311454
*Attractive hotel in a beautiful
spot overlooking Falmouth
Bay, offering pretty bedrooms,
comfort, personal service and
panoramic views. Bar.*
Bedrooms: 1 single, 6 double
& 7 twin, 2 family rooms.
Bathrooms: 16 private.
Bed & breakfast: £26.45
single, £46 double.
Half board: £28.75-£32.20
daily, £201.25-£225.40
weekly.
Evening meal 6.30pm (l.o.
7.30pm).
Parking for 16.
Credit: Access, Visa, Diners,
Amex.

Bosanneth
😃😃😃
1 Stracey Rd., Falmouth,
TR11 4DW
☎ (0326) 314649
*Situated 80 yards from beach
in quiet, residential area
overlooking Falmouth Bay, yet
within walking distance of all
amenities.*
Bedrooms: 2 single, 2 double
& 2 twin, 2 family rooms.

Bathrooms: 6 private,
1 public.
Bed & breakfast: £14-£16
single, £28-£32 double.
Evening meal 6pm (i.o.
6.45pm).
Parking for 6.

Bradgate Guest House
😃😃
4 Florence Pl., Falmouth,
TR11 3NJ
☎ (0326) 314108
*Small family guesthouse within
easy reach of beaches and town
facilities. Home comforts
provided.*
Bedrooms: 2 single, 2 double
& 1 twin, 2 family rooms.
Bathrooms: 2 public.
Bed & breakfast: £13.50-
£14.50 single, £27-£29 double.
Half board: £20-£21 daily,
£126-£132.30 weekly.
Evening meal 6.30pm (l.o.
4pm).
Parking for 5.
Open March-December.

Broadmead Hotel M
😃😃😃 COMMENDED
Kimberley Park Rd.,
Falmouth, TR11 2DD
☎ (0326) 315704
*Small hotel, tastefully
decorated and furnished, with
traditional English cooking.
Overlooking Kimberley Park,
near the centre of Falmouth.
Private car park.*
Bedrooms: 3 single, 6 double
& 3 twin.
Bathrooms: 10 private,
1 public; 1 private shower.
Bed & breakfast: £18-£22
single, £42-£48 double.
Half board: £28.50-£32.50
daily, £171-£195 weekly.
Lunch available.
Evening meal 7pm (l.o. 8pm).
Parking for 8.
Credit: Access, Visa.

Croft Hotel M
😃😃😃 COMMENDED
4-6 Gyllyngvase Hill,
Falmouth, TR11 4DN
☎ (0326) 312814
*All rooms en-suite, colour TV,
telephone and tea/coffee
facilities. Indoor pool 86F.*
Bedrooms: 4 single, 7 double
& 4 twin, 10 family rooms.
Bathrooms: 25 private.
Bed & breakfast: £23-£25
single, £46-£50 double.

Continued ▶

FALMOUTH
Continued

Half board: £29-£33 daily, £145-£205 weekly.
Lunch available.
Evening meal 6.30pm (l.o. 7.15pm).
Parking for 30.
Open January-November.
Credit: Access, Visa.

Falmouth Hotel M
Castle Beach, Falmouth, TR11 4NZ
☎ (0326) 312671 Telex 45262 Falbay
Modernised Victorian building in 5 acres of prize-winning gardens, overlooking the sea. Open all year.
Bedrooms: 16 single, 10 double & 42 twin, 5 family rooms.
Bathrooms: 73 private.
Bed & breakfast: £44-£61 single, £77-£102 double.
Half board: £50.50-£68 daily, £303-£364 weekly.
Lunch available.
Evening meal 7pm (l.o. 10pm).
Parking for 120.
Credit: Access, Visa, Diners, Amex.

Good Winds Guest House M
13 Stratton Ter., Falmouth, TR11 2SY
☎ (0326) 313200
Large detached Georgian house in spacious gardens close to the water. Lovely sea views. Located between the new marina and town.
Bedrooms: 1 single, 3 double & 2 twin, 5 family rooms.
Bathrooms: 8 private, 2 public.
Bed & breakfast: £14.75-£18.25 single, £26-£33 double.
Evening meal 6pm (l.o. 6pm).
Parking for 11.
Open April-October.

Green Lawns Hotel M
Western Ter., Falmouth, TR11 4QJ
☎ (0326) 312734 Telex 45169
Privately-run hotel specialising in comfort and cuisine. Leisure complex attached.
Bedrooms: 5 single, 16 double & 11 twin, 8 family rooms.
Bathrooms: 40 private, 3 public.

Bed & breakfast: £42.55-£60.20 single, £58.64-£89.70 double.
Half board: £44.32-£75.20 daily, £278.30-£368 weekly.
Lunch available.
Evening meal 6.45pm (l.o. 10pm).
Parking for 60.
Credit: Access, Visa, C.Bl., Diners, Amex.

Display advertisement appears on page 578.

Greenbank Hotel M
Harbourside, Falmouth, TR11 2SR
☎ (0326) 312440 Telex 45240
Privately-owned, historic hotel with panoramic views across one of the world's finest harbours. Uninterrupted views of yachting and shipping.
Bedrooms: 8 single, 11 double & 22 twin, 1 family room.
Bathrooms: 42 private, 1 public.
Bed & breakfast: £30-£65 single, £80-£115 double.
Half board: £51-£75 daily, £325-£430 weekly.
Lunch available.
Evening meal 7pm (l.o. 10pm).
Parking for 70.
Credit: Access, Visa, Diners, Amex.

Grove Hotel
Grove Pl., Falmouth, TR11 4AU
☎ (0326) 319577
Owner-managed, homely harbourside hotel. Level walk to coaches, railway, town and quays. Public car and dinghy parks opposite.
Bedrooms: 2 single, 5 double & 5 twin, 3 family rooms.
Bathrooms: 8 private, 3 public.
Bed & breakfast: £17.50-£19.50 single, £35-£39 double.
Half board: £25-£27 daily, from £150.50 weekly.
Evening meal 7pm (l.o. 10pm).
Open February-November.
Credit: Access, Visa.

Gyllyngvase House Hotel
Gyllyngvase Rd., Falmouth, TR11 4DJ
☎ (0326) 312956

---

2 minutes from Gyllyngvase beach near the town centre. Delightful house well decorated and furnished. Large sun lounge, terraced garden.
Bedrooms: 3 single, 7 double & 3 twin, 2 family rooms.
Bathrooms: 12 private, 2 public.
Bed & breakfast: from £16 single, from £36 double.
Half board: from £22.50 daily, from £160 weekly.
Evening meal 6.30pm (l.o. 7.30pm).
Parking for 16.
Open March-November.

Madeira Hotel
Sea Front, Falmouth, TR11 4NY
☎ (0326) 313531
Well-situated with views over Falmouth Bay. Entertainment most evenings.
Bedrooms: 6 single, 16 double & 19 twin, 6 family rooms.
Bathrooms: 49 private.
Bed & breakfast: £20-£29 single, £36-£54 double.
Half board: £27-£36 daily, £145-£225 weekly.
Lunch available.
Evening meal 7pm (l.o. 7.30pm).
Parking for 20.
Open March-November.
Credit: Access, Visa.

Park Grove Hotel M
Kimberley Park Rd., Falmouth, TR11 2DD
☎ (0326) 313276
A small hotel, centrally located, overlooking the beautiful Kimberley Park land. Supervised by resident proprietors.
Bedrooms: 3 single, 5 double & 5 twin, 4 family rooms.
Bathrooms: 15 private, 1 public.
Bed & breakfast: £21-£22 single, £42-£44 double.
Half board: £24-£28 daily, £155-£175 weekly.
Evening meal 6.30pm (l.o. 7pm).
Parking for 20.
Open March-October.
Credit: Access, Visa.

Display advertisement appears on page 459.

Penmere Manor Hotel M
Mongleath Rd., Falmouth, TR11 4PN
☎ (0326) 211411 Telex 45608 PMHTL
Best Western
Georgian country house with modern extensions overlooking Falmouth Bay. Leisure facilities include indoor and outdoor pools, jacuzzi, spa, sauna, solarium, snooker, games tables, croquet, chess, table tennis and darts. Well-appointed bedrooms. Closed at Christmas only.
Bedrooms: 8 single, 8 double & 7 twin, 16 family rooms.
Bathrooms: 39 private.
Bed & breakfast: £45-£50 single, £68-£97 double.
Half board: £51-£67 daily, £292-£430 weekly.
Lunch available.
Evening meal 7pm (l.o. 9pm).
Parking for 50.
Credit: Access, Visa, Diners, Amex.

Raffles
Fenwick Rd., Falmouth
☎ (0326) 313012
Beautiful Georgian house built 1780, facing south in 1.5 acres of grounds. Once the home of the late author Howard Spring. Peaceful and tranquil, yet only 200 yards from beach.
Bedrooms: 2 double & 1 twin.
Bathrooms: 3 private, 1 public.
Bed & breakfast: £17.50 single, £35 double.
Parking for 7.
Open April-October.

Royal Duchy Hotel M
Cliff Rd., Falmouth, TR11 4NX
☎ (0326) 313042
Brend
Falmouth's first and foremost hotel situated overlooking the bay. High standard accommodation with extensive leisure facilities.
Bedrooms: 7 single, 15 double & 19 twin, 9 family rooms.
Bathrooms: 50 private, 2 public.
Bed & breakfast: £44-£50 single, £77-£125 double.
Half board: £46-£70 daily, £250-£450 weekly.
Lunch available.
Evening meal 7pm (l.o. 9pm).
Parking for 62.

Credit: Access, Visa, Diners, Amex.

🐄 🕭 ╰ 🖭 ▯ ♥ ▮ ▯ ⊟
🖭 ● 🖫 🏧 ▲ ¶ 🔥 😊 🎈
🖫 ▶ ❄ ☇ SP T

St. Michaels of Falmouth M

⬥⬥⬥⬥ COMMENDED

Seafront, Gyllyngvase Beach, Falmouth, TR11 4NB
☎ (0326) 312707 Fax (0326) 319147 Telex 45540
🎯 Consort
"Hotel for all Seasons", in prizewinning gardens, adjoining the beach. Heated indoor swimming pool, sauna and jacuzzi. Magnificent sea views.
Bedrooms: 15 single, 20 double & 25 twin, 15 family rooms.
Bathrooms: 75 private.
Bed & breakfast: £49-£56 single, £89-£100.50 double.
Half board: £245-£410 weekly.
Lunch available.
Evening meal 7pm (l.o. 10pm).
Parking for 100.
Credit: Access, Visa, Diners, Amex.

🐄 🕭 ╰ 🖭 ▯ ♥ ▮ ▯ ¥
🏧 🖭 ● 🖫 🏧 ¶ 😊 🔥 ⊼ 🎋
🔑 ▶ ❄ DAP ☇ SP T

San Remo

⬥⬥⬥

7 Gyllyngvase Hill, Falmouth, TR11 4DN
☎ (0326) 312076
Small hotel 60 yards from Gyllyngvase Beach with views of bay and coastline. Easy walking distance to town and harbour.
Bedrooms: 1 single, 6 double & 2 twin, 1 family room.
Bathrooms: 8 private, 1 public.
Bed & breakfast: £16-£18.50 single, £32-£37 double.
Half board: £19.50-£23 daily, £116-£148 weekly.
Evening meal 6.30pm (l.o. 7pm).
Parking for 10.
Open April-October.

🐄5 🕭 🖭 ♥ UL ▯ ⊟ ▲ ✗
🎋

Tresillian House Hotel M

⬥⬥⬥

3 Stracey Rd., Falmouth, TR11 4DW
☎ (0326) 312425 / 311139
A family-run hotel in a quiet area, close to safe beaches, town and harbours. Traditional cuisine.
Bedrooms: 1 single, 4 double & 3 twin, 4 family rooms.
Bathrooms: 12 private.

Bed & breakfast: £18-£20 single, £36-£40 double.
Half board: £21.50-£24.20 daily, £136.50-£157.50 weekly.
Lunch available.
Evening meal 6.30pm (l.o. 7.30pm).
Parking for 8.
Open March-October.

🐄 🕭 ╰ 🖭 ♥ ▮ ▯ ¥ ⊟
🖭 ▲ ✗ 🎋 SP T

Westcott Hotel

Gyllyngvase Hill, Gyllyngvase Beach, Falmouth, TR11 4DN
☎ (0326) 311309
Charming hotel standing in own grounds only yards from safe sandy beach. Most rooms have sea views. Centrally heated.
Bedrooms: 2 single, 3 double & 2 twin, 4 family rooms.
Bathrooms: 9 private, 1 public.
Bed & breakfast: £13-£17 single, £26-£34 double.
Half board: £18-£23 daily, £114-£149 weekly.
Evening meal 6.30pm (l.o. 6.30pm).
Parking for 10.
Open January-October.

🐄 🕭 ♥ 🖭 ▯ ♥ ▮ ▯ ⊟ TV 🖭 ✗
🎋 SP T

4m NW. Radstock

The Streets Hotel

⬥⬥⬥ COMMENDED

The Street, Farmborough, Bath, BA3 1AR
☎ Timsbury (0761) 71452
Telex 44830 SHF ACCENT G
In picturesque village of Farmborough, 7 miles from Bath and 10 miles from Bristol, off the A39.
Bedrooms: 5 double & 3 twin.
Bathrooms: 8 private.
Bed & breakfast: £39-£44 single, £46-£53 double.
Half board: £51.50-£57.90 daily.
Evening meal 7.30pm (l.o. 8.50pm).
Parking for 8.
Credit: Access, Visa, Amex.

🐄5 🕭 ╰ 🖭 🖭 ♥ ▮ ⊟ TV
🖭 ▲ ⤵ 🕛 ❄ ✗ 🎋 SP 🎴

2m W. Midsomer Norton

Country Ways M

⬥⬥⬥

Marsh La., Farrington Gurney, BS18 5TT
☎ Temple Cloud (0761) 52449
Country hotel situated on edge of Mendips, halfway between Bath and Wells. Surrounded by fields and woodland.
Bedrooms: 1 single, 4 double & 1 twin.
Bathrooms: 6 private.
Bed & breakfast: £45-£49.50 single, £55-£60 double.
Half board: £37.50-£58 daily.
Lunch available.
Evening meal 7pm (l.o. 8.45pm).
Parking for 10.
Credit: Access, Visa, Diners.

🐄 🕭 ╰ 🖭 ♥ ▮ ▯ ⊟ 🖭
▲ ❄ ✗ 🎋 SP T

2m NE. Ottery St. Mary

Greyhound Inn

Fenny Bridges, Honiton, EX14 0BJ
☎ Honiton (0404) 850380
17th C thatched, cottage-style inn, heavily beamed. Former coaching inn retaining original charming character, now offering every modern amenity.
Bedrooms: 9 double & 1 twin.
Bathrooms: 10 private.
Bed & breakfast: from £36.50 single, from £49.50 double.
Lunch available.
Evening meal 7pm (l.o. 10pm).
Parking for 60.
Credit: Access, Visa, Diners, Amex.

🐄 🕭 ╰ 🖭 ♥ ¥ 🖭 ▲ ❄
✗ 🎋 SP 🖭

> **Please mention this guide when making a booking.**

7m SW. Launceston

The Casamoor

Five Lanes, Launceston, PL15 7RX
☎ Pipers Pool (0566) 86255
Guest house with licensed restaurant for resident and non-resident, meals, snacks and cream teas served throughout the day with a la carte menu in the evening. 8.5 miles south of Launceston and 12.5 miles north of Bodmin on the A30.
Bedrooms: 1 double & 3 twin, 2 family rooms.
Bathrooms: 2 public.
Bed & breakfast: £15-£20 single, £30-£38 double.
Lunch available.
Evening meal 6.30pm (l.o. 10pm).
Parking for 10.
Credit: Access, Visa.

🐄 🖭 ▯ ▮ ▯ 🖭 ✗ 🎋

7m NE. Shaftesbury

Beckford Arms M

⬥⬥⬥

Fonthill Gifford, Tisbury, SP3 6PX
☎ Tisbury (0747) 870385
Fax (0747) 51496
Tastefully refurbished, comfortable 18th C inn, between Tisbury and Hindon in area of outstanding beauty. 2 miles A303, convenient for Salisbury.
Bedrooms: 2 single, 4 double & 1 twin.
Bathrooms: 5 private; 2 private showers.
Bed & breakfast: £27.50-£29.50 single, £45-£49.50 double.
Half board: £32.50-£37.50 daily, £182.50-£207.50 weekly.
Evening meal 7pm (l.o. 10pm).
Parking for 42.
Credit: Access, Visa.

🐄 🖪 🖭 ╰ ♥ ▮ ▯ 🖭 ▲
¶ 🕛 ❄ ☇ SP 🎴

> **Classifications and quality commendations were correct at the time of going to press but are subject to change. Please check at the time of booking.**

> **The symbols are explained on the flap inside the back cover.**

FORD
Wiltshire
Map ref 2B2

5m W. Chippenham

White Hart Inn ▲
☆☆☆ APPROVED
Ford, Chippenham,
SN14 8RP
☎ Castle Combe
(0249) 782213
Ancient coaching inn by hump-back bridge and trout stream.
Bedrooms: 10 double &
1 twin.
Bathrooms: 11 private.
Bed & breakfast: max. £38.50
single, max. £53 double.
Half board: max. £256
weekly.
Lunch available.
Evening meal 7.30pm (l.o.
9.30pm).
Parking for 80.
Credit: Access, Visa.
🛇 ♿ �'🎗 ⑩ 🛏 ✪ 🖺 Ⅴ 🍴
▥ 🖦 🍲 🌣 ⚡ 🎿 🏐 SP

FOWEY
Cornwall
Map ref 1C3

Set on steep slopes at
the mouth of the Fowey
River, important clayport
and fishing town. Ruined
forts guarding the shore
recall days of 'Fowey
Gallants' who ruled local
seas. The handsome,
lofty church rises above
the town and nearby
Place House, rebuilt in
the 19th C, was refuge for
15th C townsfolk in
French raids. Ferries to
Polruan and Bodinnick;
Regatta, August.
*Tourist Information
Centre ☎ (0726) 833616*

Carnethic House Hotel ▲
☆☆☆ COMMENDED
Lambs Barn, Fowey,
PL23 1HQ
☎ (0726) 833336
*Regency house in 1.5 acres
mature gardens. Heated pool.
Home cooking with local fish a
speciality. Informal
atmosphere.*
Bedrooms: 1 single, 4 double
& 1 twin, 2 family rooms.
Bathrooms: 5 private,
2 public; 2 private showers.
Bed & breakfast: £25-£30
single, £50-£50 double.
Half board: £27-£35 daily,
£200-£225 weekly.
Lunch available.
Evening meal 7.30pm (l.o.
8.30pm).

Parking for 20.
Open February-November.
Credit: Access, Visa, Diners,
Amex.
🛇 ♿ ⑩ 🛏 ✪ ✿ Ⅴ 🍴 🍴
▥ 🖦 🍲 🎗 🔍 ♿ ▶ ✪ 🌣
🏐 DAP SP 🏓 ⑪ 🇹

Cormorant Hotel
Golant, Fowey, PL23 1LL
☎ (0726) 833426
*Small, attractive, family-run
hotel with panoramic views of
the Fowey estuary. Noted for
its hospitality and food. Indoor
heated swimming pool with
removable roof giving the best
of both worlds.*
Bedrooms: 4 double & 7 twin.
Bathrooms: 11 private.
Bed & breakfast: £45-£53
single, £66-£78 double.
Half board: £45-£50 daily.
Lunch available.
Evening meal 7pm (l.o.
8.30pm).
Parking for 15.
Credit: Access, Visa.
🛇 ♿ ⑩ 🛏 ✪ 🖺 Ⅴ 🍴
▥ 🖦 🍲 🏐 🌣 🏐 🏓 SP

Fowey Hall ▲
4 Hanson Dr., Fowey,
PL23 1ET
☎ (072 683) 833104/832321
*A magnificent country house
standing in lovely grounds and
overlooking the River Fowey
and estuary.*
Bedrooms: 11 single, 24 twin,
5 family rooms.
Bathrooms: 18 public.
Half board: £27.85-£30 daily,
£195-£212 weekly.
Lunch available.
Evening meal 7pm.
Parking for 60.
Open March-October.
🛇 ✿ 🔒 🖺 Ⅴ 🍴 ⑪ ▥ 🖦
🔍 🌣 🎿 🏐 🏓 🇹

Fowey Hotel
Esplanade, Fowey, PL23 1HX
☎ (072 683) 2551 Fax
(0726) 832125
*Superb views over the Fowey
estuary can be enjoyed from
the sun terrace and public
rooms of this hotel.*
Bedrooms: 7 single, 11 double
& 9 twin, 3 family rooms.
Bathrooms: 26 private,
4 public.
Bed & breakfast: £33.75-
£37.50 single, £62.55-£69.50
double.
Half board: £41.85-£46.50
daily, £263.70-£293 weekly.
Lunch available.
Evening meal 7pm (l.o. 9pm).
Parking for 24.
Credit: Access, Visa, Diners,
Amex.
🛇 🔒 ⑩ 🛏 ✿ 🖺 Ⅴ 🍴 ⑪
▥ ▦ 🖦 🍲 🎗 🔍 🌣 DAP 🏐 SP
🏓 🇹 .

Marina Hotel ▲
☆☆☆
Esplanade, Fowey,
PL23 1HY
☎ (0726) 833315
*Privately-run, comfortably
appointed Georgian hotel of
character with balcony rooms,
in quiet situation. Own
moorings, waterside garden
and restaurant.*
Bedrooms: 6 double & 5 twin.
Bathrooms: 11 private.
Bed & breakfast: £46-£68
double.
Half board: £37-£49 daily,
£230-£300 weekly.
Lunch available.
Evening meal 7pm (l.o.
8.30pm).
Open March-October.
Credit: Access, Visa, Diners,
Amex.
🛇 ♿ 🔒 ⑩ 🛏 ✪ 🖺 Ⅴ 🍴
⑪ ◐ ▥ 🖦 ▶ 🏐 SP 🏓

The Old Ferry Inn ▲
Bodinnick-By-Fowey,
PL23 1LX
☎ Polruan (0726) 870237
*Comfortably furnished and
with harbour views from lounge
and most bedrooms. Sailing
and cliff walks nearby. Food
includes local fish.*
Bedrooms: 4 double & 7 twin,
1 family room.
Bathrooms: 7 private,
3 public.
Bed & breakfast: £27.50-£35
single, £55-£70 double.
Half board: £45.50-£53 daily,
£280-£325 weekly.
Lunch available.
Evening meal 7.30pm (l.o.
8.15pm).
Parking for 14.
Open March-October.
Credit: Visa.
🛇 🎗 ✪ Ⅴ 🍴 ⑪ ▥ 🏐 🏓
🇹

Old Quay House Hotel
Fore St., Fowey, PL23 1AQ
☎ (0726) 833302
*Family-run hotel on water's
edge with private quay and
mooring. Specialises in home
cooking.*
Bedrooms: 2 single, 7 double
& 3 twin, 1 family room.
Bathrooms: 9 private,
1 public; 2 private showers.
Bed & breakfast: £19.50-£22
single, £36-£44 double.
Half board: £29-£33 daily,
£192.50-£220.50 weekly.
Lunch available.
Evening meal 7pm (l.o.
8.30pm).
Credit: Access, Visa.
🛇 ♿ 🖺 ✿ Ⅴ 🍴 ⑪ SP
🏓

The Wheelhouse
60 Esplanade, Fowey,
PL23 1JA
☎ (0726) 832452
*Delightful Victorian licensed
guesthouse. Sea and harbour
views, family-run, home
cooking.*
Bedrooms: 1 single, 3 double
& 2 twin, 1 family room.
Bathrooms: 2 public.
Bed & breakfast: £10-£15
single, £24-£30 double.
Half board: £20-£23 daily,
£120-£145 weekly.
Evening meal 7.30pm (l.o.
midday).
Open March-October.
⑩ ✿ 🖺 Ⅴ 🍴 ▥ 🎿 🏓

FROME
Somerset
Map ref 2B2

Old market town with
modern light industry, its
medieval centre watered
by the River Frome.
Above Cheap Street with
its flagstones and
watercourse is the church
showing work of varying
periods. Interesting
buildings include 18th C
wool merchants' houses.
Local history museum.

Abergele Guest House
☆☆
2 Fromefield, Frome,
BA11 2HA
☎ (0373) 63998
*Comfortable Georgian guest
house close to town centre,
which has good shopping
facilities and restaurants.*
Bedrooms: 1 single, 1 double
& 1 twin, 1 family room.
Bathrooms: 1 public.
Bed & breakfast: from £12
single, from £24 double.
Half board: from £18 daily.
Evening meal 6pm (l.o. 7pm).
Parking for 7.
🛇 ✿ 🔒 🖺 Ⅴ 🍴 ⑪ ▥
🖦 🏐 DAP 🏓

Fourwinds Guest House
19 Bath Rd., Frome,
BA11 2HJ
☎ (0373) 62618
*Chalet bungalow with some
bedrooms on ground floor. TV,
and tea making facilities.
Licensed.*
Bedrooms: 2 single, 2 double
& 1 twin, 2 family rooms.
Bathrooms: 3 private,
1 public.
Bed & breakfast: £18-£22
single, £32-£40 double.

Half board: max. £27 daily, from £180 weekly.
Evening meal 6pm (l.o. 7pm).
Parking for 10.

George Hotel M
Market Place, Frome, BA11 1AF
☎ (0373) 62584 Fax (0373) 51945
Friendly atmosphere in family-run hotel. All rooms recently re-furbished whilst still in keeping with the character of the hotel.
Bedrooms: 8 single, 2 double & 7 twin, 3 family rooms.
Bathrooms: 20 private.
Bed & breakfast: £42.50-£48.50 single, £54.50-£60.50 double.
Half board: £37.65-£40.75 daily, £202.95-£250 weekly.
Lunch available.
Evening meal 7pm (l.o. 10pm).
Parking for 18.
Credit: Access, Visa, Diners, Amex.

Mendip Lodge Hotel M
COMMENDED
Bath Rd., Frome, BA11 2HP
☎ (0373) 63223 Telex 44832
Set in 3.5 acres overlooking Mendip Hills, near Bath, Wells and Longleat.
Bedrooms: 6 single, 10 double & 12 twin, 12 family rooms.
Bathrooms: 40 private.
Bed & breakfast: £51-£56 single, £68-£75 double.
Lunch available.
Evening meal 7pm (l.o. 9.30pm).
Parking for 70.
Credit: Access, Visa, Diners, Amex.

> **Individual proprietors have supplied all details of accommodation. Although we do check for accuracy, we advise you to confirm prices and other information at the time of booking.**

Old market town associated with Joseph of Arimathea and the birth of English Christianity. Built around its once-glorious 7th C abbey, whose medieval remains are said to be the site of King Arthur's burial, it prospered from wool until the 19th C. Glastonbury Tor with its ancient tower gives panoramic views over flat country rich in remains of Celtic lake communities.

Berewall Farm Country Guest House
Cinnamon La., Glastonbury, BA6 8LL
☎ (0458) 31451
32-acre grazing farm. Comfortable farmhouse offering a homely welcome to all. Ponies are available for riding.
Bedrooms: 2 single, 2 double & 2 twin, 3 family rooms.
Bathrooms: 9 private.
Bed & breakfast: £37-£40 double.
Lunch available.
Evening meal 6.30pm (l.o. 10pm).
Parking for 12.
Credit: Access, Visa.

Number Three Restaurant and Hotel M
COMMENDED
3 Magdalene St., Glastonbury, BA6 9EW
☎ (0458) 32129
An elegant listed Georgian house. Its beautiful garden, floodlit at night, adjoins the abbey ruins.
Bedrooms: 3 double & 2 twin, 1 family room.
Bathrooms: 6 private.
Bed & breakfast: £45 single, £60-£70 double.
Half board: £54-£64 daily.
Evening meal 7pm (l.o. 9.30pm).
Parking for 8.
Open February-December.
Credit: Visa, Amex.

6m SW. St. Austell

Perran House M
Fore St., Grampound, Truro, TR2 4RS
☎ St. Austell (0726) 882066
Family-run guest house situated between St. Austell and Truro. Central for touring, with personal service.
Bedrooms: 1 single, 3 double & 1 twin.
Bathrooms: 3 private, 1 public.
Bed & breakfast: £11.50-£13.50 single, £23-£33 double.
Parking for 6.
Credit: Access, Visa.

5m W. Street

Greylake Motel & Licensed Restaurant M
Greinton, Bridgwater, TA7 9BP
☎ Ashcott (0458) 210383
Delightful 16th C motel with beams and inglenooks, offering 20th C facilities. On the A361, an ideal touring centre for Somerset.
Bedrooms: 3 single, 3 double & 2 twin.
Bathrooms: 5 private, 1 public.
Bed & breakfast: from £17.50 single, from £38.50 double.
Half board: from £24.75 daily, from £173.25 weekly.
Lunch available.
Evening meal 7pm (l.o. 9pm).
Parking for 24.
Credit: Access, Visa, Diners, Amex.

> **Classifications and quality commendations were correct at the time of going to press but are subject to change. Please check at the time of booking.**

Steep roadside village with late Georgian houses built when tin mining flourished here. One of the ancient entries into Cornwall, the 14th C 'New Bridge' still spans the Tamar.

Hingston House Country Hotel M
COMMENDED
St. Anns Chapel, Gunnislake, PL18 9HB
☎ Tavistock (0822) 832468
Beautiful country house overlooking Tamar Valley. Cotehele House and St. Mellion golf course nearby. Central for exploring Devon and Cornwall.
Bedrooms: 1 single, 6 double & 2 twin, 1 family room.
Bathrooms: 8 private, 1 public.
Bed & breakfast: £22.50-£28.50 single, £38.50-£47.50 double.
Half board: £30.75-£40 daily, £189.50-£273 weekly.
Lunch available.
Evening meal 7.30pm (l.o. 8.30pm).
Parking for 10.
Credit: Access, Visa.

5m S. Yeovil

Halstock Mill
Halstock, Yeovil, BA22 9SJ
☎ Corscombe (0935) 891278
Secluded, friendly 17th C mill in peaceful countryside. Food prepared with local and own produce.
Bedrooms: 1 single, 4 double.
Bathrooms: 5 private.
Bed & breakfast: from £22 single, from £40 double.
Half board: from £34 daily, from £248 weekly.
Evening meal 7pm (l.o. 8.30pm).
Parking for 9.
Open January-November.
Credit: Access, Visa.

HARBERTON

Devon
Map ref 1D2

2m SW. Totnes
Small village between southern Dartmoor and the Dart Estuary, noted for its grand 3-aisled church. The stone pulpit and rood screen are fine examples of late medieval carving.

Ford Farm Guest House M

Harberton, Totnes, TQ9 7SJ
☎ Totnes (0803) 863539
Friendly, comfortable, warm village house with secluded garden. Guests' lounge and parking. Village pub 3 minute walk for excellent suppers.
Bedrooms: 1 single, 1 double & 1 twin.
Bathrooms: 1 private, 1 public.
Bed & breakfast: £16-£19 single, £31-£37 double.
Parking for 6.

HARBERTONFORD

Devon
Map ref 1D2

2m S. Totnes

The Old Mill Country House Hotel & Restaurant M

COMMENDED
Harbertonford, Totnes, TQ9 7SW
☎ (080 423) 349
One of the most elegant places in Devon in 6 acres of garden. Peaceful, secluded and tranquil with a high standard of cuisine and service.
Bedrooms: 1 single, 5 double & 2 twin.
Bathrooms: 8 private.
Bed & breakfast: £30-£40 single, £38-£58 double.
Lunch available.
Evening meal 7pm (l.o. 9.30pm).
Parking for 50.
Credit: Access, Visa.

The symbols are explained on the flap inside the back cover.

HARTLAND

Devon
Map ref 1C1

4m W. Clovelly
Hamlet on high, wild country near Hartland Point. Just west, the parish church tower makes a magnificent landmark; the light, unrestored interior holds one of Devon's finest rood screens. There are spectacular cliffs around Hartland Point and the lighthouse.

Hartland Quay Hotel

Hartland, Bideford, EX39 6DU
☎ (0237) 441218
Small family-run hotel. Overlooking the Atlantic rugged coastline. Coastal walks. Important geological area.
Bedrooms: 2 single, 6 double & 6 twin, 2 family rooms.
Bathrooms: 8 private, 3 public.
Bed & breakfast: £14.50-£16 single, £29-£32 double.
Half board: £21.50-£23 daily, £125-£140 weekly.
Lunch available.
Evening meal 7pm (l.o. 9pm).
Parking for 100.
Open March-October.
Credit: Access, Visa.

HATCH BEAUCHAMP

Somerset
Map ref 1D1

5m SE. Taunton
Village with wooded slopes in the heart of rural Somerset. Hatch Court, a fine Bath stone Palladian mansion, is close by.

Farthings Country House Hotel

COMMENDED
Hatch Beauchamp, TA3 6SG
☎ (0823) 480664
Elegant Georgian house in lovely gardens, tastefully decorated and furnished. Friendly personal service in a comfortable and relaxed atmosphere.
Bedrooms: 1 single, 3 double & 2 twin.
Bathrooms: 6 private.
Bed & breakfast: £65-£95 single, £90-£115 double.
Lunch available.

Evening meal 7.30pm (l.o. 9pm).
Parking for 27.
Credit: Access, Visa.

HATHERLEIGH

Devon
Map ref 1C2

7m NW. Okehampton
Set in pastoral countryside, small town with thatched cottages and a cattle market. There are trout and salmon streams close by.

Pressland Country House

Hatherleigh, Nr Okehampton, EX20 3LW
☎ Okehampton (0837) 810347
Impressive Victorian mansion amongst 3 acres of secluded gardens with panoramic views across farmlands to Dartmoor. A warm, friendly, informal atmosphere i.e. "The guests' home in the country".
Bedrooms: 2 double & 1 twin, 1 family room.
Bathrooms: 4 private.
Bed & breakfast: £25-£30 single, £45-£50 double.
Half board: from £40 daily, from £250 weekly.
Lunch available.
Evening meal 7.30pm.
Parking for 20.
Open February-December.
Credit: Access, Visa.

HAYLE

Cornwall
Map ref 1B3

Former mining town with modern light industry on the Hayle Estuary. Most buildings are Georgian or early Victorian, with some Regency houses along the canal.

Hillside Hotel M

1 Grist La., Angarrack, Hayle, TR27 5HZ
☎ (0736) 752180
Large country house with walled garden, in rural village 1.5 miles from St. Ives Bay. Central for touring west Cornwall.
Bedrooms: 2 single, 3 double & 2 twin, 3 family rooms.
Bathrooms: 5 private, 2 public.

Bed & breakfast: £21-£26.50 single, £36.50-£43.50 double.
Half board: £29-£35 daily, £138-£199 weekly.
Lunch available.
Evening meal 7pm (l.o. 7.30pm).
Parking for 10.
Credit: Access, Visa.

HAYTOR

Devon
Map ref 1D2

5m N. Ashburton
Rugged moorland with dramatic craggy rock formation on the eastern edge of Dartmoor National Park. Granite from local quarries was used for the British Museum, the National Gallery and London Bridge. Near the village of Haytor Vale is a nature reserve with many species of trees and birds.

The Bel Alp House Country Hotel M

HIGHLY COMMENDED
Haytor, Nr. Bovey Tracey, Newton Abbot, TQ13 9XX
☎ (0364) 661217 Fax (0364) 661292
A small elegant country house hotel on the edge of Dartmoor in one of the most spectacular settings in the West Country. Comfort and personal service.
Bedrooms: 3 double & 6 twin.
Bathrooms: 9 private.
Bed & breakfast: £66-£78 single, £108-£132 double.
Half board: £84-£111 daily, £567-£651 weekly.
Lunch available.
Evening meal 7.30pm (l.o. 8.30pm).
Parking for 20.
Open February-November.
Credit: Access, Visa.

Classifications and quality commendations were correct at the time of going to press but are subject to change. Please check at the time of booking.

HELSTON

Cornwall
Map ref 1B3

Handsome town with steep, curving main street and narrow alleys. In medieval times it was a major port and one of Cornwall's 4 stannary towns. Most buildings date from Regency and Victorian periods, with 19th C Town Hall and classically-styled church. The famous May dance, the Furry, is thought to have pre-Christian origins. A museum of local history occupies the old Butter Market.

Gwealdues Hotel
👑👑👑

Falmouth Rd., Helston, TR13 8JX
☎ (0326) 572808 & (0326) 573331
Fully licensed modern hotel. En-suite rooms. Central heating. Bar meals and a la carte restaurant available. Swimming pool. Large banqueting room.
Bedrooms: 1 single, 5 double & 3 twin, 3 family rooms.
Bathrooms: 9 private, 2 public.
Bed & breakfast: £25-£30 single, £30-£40 double.
Lunch available.
Evening meal 7.30pm (l.o. 10pm).
Parking for 60.
Credit: Access, Visa.

Nansloe Manor Country Hotel

Meneage Rd., Helston, TR13 0SB
☎ (0326) 574691
Formerly a small manor house, more recently converted to a comfortable hotel. Set in own 4.5 acre grounds on the south side of Helston. Well situated for touring, golf and beaches.
Bedrooms: 5 double & 2 twin, 1 private shower.
Bathrooms: 6 private; 1 private shower.
Bed & breakfast: £28-£37 single, £50-£82 double.
Lunch available.
Evening meal 7pm (l.o. 9.30pm).
Parking for 40.
Credit: Access, Visa.

Parc-an-Ithan
👑👑 APPROVED

Sithney, Helston, TR13 0RN
☎ Helston (0326) 572565
Quiet, country residence 1 mile west of Helston and 200 yards off main A394 Helston to Penzance road. Central for visiting Lizard and Land's End Peninsulas. All diets catered for by prior arrangement.
Bedrooms: 1 double & 1 twin, 2 family rooms.
Bathrooms: 2 private, 1 public; 1 private shower.
Bed & breakfast: £9.50-£13.50 single, £19-£27 double.
Half board: £14.50-£26 daily, £101.50-£182 weekly.
Evening meal 5.30pm (l.o. 6.30pm).
Parking for 12.
Credit: Access, Visa.

HOLFORD

Somerset
Map ref 1D1

7m W. Bridgwater
Sheltered in a wooded combe on the edge of the Quantocks, small village near Alfoxden House where William Wordsworth and his sister Dorothy lived late in the 1790s. At Nether Stowey Samuel Coleridge occupied a cottage during the same period. Nearby Quantock Forest has nature trails.

Combe House Hotel M
👑👑👑 COMMENDED

Holford, Bridgwater, TA5 1RZ
☎ (027 874) 382
17th C country hotel in beautiful Butterfly Combe in the heart of the Quantock Hills. Traditional hospitality in rural peace and quiet.
Bedrooms: 6 single, 6 double & 8 twin.
Bathrooms: 15 private, 3 public.
Bed & breakfast: £30-£39 single, £60-£80 double.
Half board: £36-£48 daily, £199.50-£287 weekly.
Lunch available.
Evening meal 7.30pm (l.o. 8.30pm).
Parking for 20.
Open February-November.
Credit: Access, Visa, Amex.

HOLSWORTHY

Devon
Map ref 1C2

Busy rural town and centre of a large farming community. Market day attracts many visitors.

Coles Mill Guest House

Holsworthy, EX22 6LX
☎ (0409) 253313
Tastefully converted old watermill situated in picturesque valley on outskirts of old market town. Coarse fishing lake available.
Bedrooms: 1 single, 1 double & 3 twin.
Bathrooms: 5 private.
Bed & breakfast: £15-£16.50 single, £25-£29 double.
Half board: £20-£23.50 daily, £138-£150.10 weekly.
Evening meal 7pm (l.o. 5pm).
Parking for 20.
Open April-October.

Court Barn Country House Hotel M
👑👑👑👑 COMMENDED

Clawton, EX22 6PS
☎ North Tamerton (040 927) 219
Charming manor house set in 5 acres of beautiful gardens. Originally 15th C called Court Baron. Later partly rebuilt in 1853. Elegant rooms, intimate bar, lounges, restaurant, new dining room.
Bedrooms: 1 single, 3 double & 2 twin, 2 family rooms.
Bathrooms: 8 private, 1 public.
Bed & breakfast: £28-£32 single, £56-£62 double.
Half board: £42-£46 daily, £235-£265 weekly.
Lunch available.
Evening meal 8pm (l.o. 9.30pm).
Parking for 17.
Credit: Access, Visa, Diners, Amex.

Lyne Akres

Dunsland Cross, Holsworthy, EX22 7YH
☎ Beaworthy (0409) 221517
Converted railway station. The first archery leisure centre in UK with indoor and outdoor ranges. Catering and self-catering accommodation.
Bedrooms: 1 single, 2 twin.
Bathrooms: 1 public.
Bed & breakfast: £16 single, £32 double.

Half board: £25 daily, £175 weekly.
Lunch available.
Evening meal 6.30pm (l.o. 8pm).
Parking for 12.

HONITON

Devon
Map ref 1D2

Old coaching town in undulating farmland. Formerly famous for lace-making, it is now an antiques trade centre and market town. Small museum.

The Belfry Country Hotel M
👑👑👑👑 COMMENDED

Yarcombe, Nr Honiton, EX14 9BD
☎ Upottery (0404) 86234
Attractively converted old school building. Family-run hotel with friendly atmosphere, set in beautiful countryside and within easy reach of coast.
Bedrooms: 3 double & 2 twin, 1 family room.
Bathrooms: 6 private.
Bed & breakfast: £38 single, £58 double.
Half board: £43-£63 daily, £238 weekly.
Lunch available.
Evening meal 7.30pm (l.o. 9pm).
Parking for 10.
Credit: Access, Visa, Diners, Amex.

Honiton Motel M
👑👑👑 APPROVED

Turks Head La., Exeter Rd., Honiton, EX14 8PQ
☎ (0404) 43440 / 45400
Ideal midway point from Cornwall to the north for a 1 night stop or touring base. Friendly atmosphere.
Bedrooms: 4 double & 9 twin, 2 family rooms.
Bathrooms: 15 private.
Bed & breakfast: £22-£26 single, £39-£45 double.
Half board: from £31 daily, from £196 weekly.
Lunch available.
Evening meal 7pm (l.o. 9pm).
Parking for 150.
Credit: Access, Visa.

HOPE COVE

Devon
Map ref 1C3

4m W. Salcombe
Sheltered by the 400-ft headland of Bolt Tail, Hope Cove lies close to a small resort with thatched cottages, Inner Hope. Between Bolt Tail and Bolt Head lie 6 miles of beautiful National Trust cliffs.

Sand Pebbles Hotel
Hope Cove, Kingsbridge, TQ7 3HF
☎ Kingsbridge (0548) 561673
Set in the picturesque fishing village and surrounded by National Trust walks. Renowned for cuisine. Family-run for nearly 2 decades.
Bedrooms: 7 double & 3 twin.
Bathrooms: 10 private, 1 public.
Bed & breakfast: £20-£36 single, £40-£72 double.
Half board: £30-£45 daily.
Evening meal 7pm (l.o. 7.45pm).
Parking for 12.
Open March-October.

HORRABRIDGE

Devon
Map ref 1C2

4m SE. Tavistock
Beside the River Walkham at the south-west edge of Dartmoor.

Overcombe Hotel M
APPROVED
Horrabridge, Yelverton, PL20 7RN
☎ Yelverton (0822) 853501
Situated west Dartmoor, between Plymouth and Tavistock. Ideal for walking and touring. Friendly comfortable hotel offering personal service.
Bedrooms: 1 single, 5 double & 3 twin, 2 family rooms.
Bathrooms: 9 private, 2 public.
Bed & breakfast: £19-£24 single, £35-£40 double.
Half board: £29-£34.50 daily, £174-£207 weekly.
Lunch available.
Evening meal 7.30pm (l.o. 7.15pm).
Parking for 12.
Credit: Access, Visa, Diners, Amex.

ILFRACOMBE

Devon
Map ref 1C1

Seaside resort of Victorian grandeur set on hillside between cliffs with sandy coves. Earlier a small port and fishing town. On a rock at the mouth of the harbour stands an 18th C lighthouse, built over a medieval chapel. There are fine formal gardens and 2 working mills, restored and open to the public. Museum, donkey rides. Chambercombe Manor, interesting and charming old house, nearby.
Tourist Information Centre ☎ *(0271) 863001*

Capstone Hotel & Restaurant
St. James Pl., Ilfracombe, EX34 9BJ
☎ (0271) 863540
Family-run hotel with restaurant on ground floor. Close to harbour and all amenities. Local seafood a speciality.
Bedrooms: 1 single, 7 double & 1 twin, 3 family rooms.
Bathrooms: 12 private, 2 public.
Bed & breakfast: £15.75-£18.50 single, £30-£36 double.
Half board: £20-£25 daily, £130-£160 weekly.
Lunch available.
Evening meal 6pm (l.o. 10pm).
Open April-October.
Credit: Access, Visa, Amex.

Earlsdale Hotel M
51 St. Brannocks Rd., Ilfracombe, EX34 8EQ
☎ (0271) 862496
Friendly, homely atmosphere. A few minutes' walk to town, Bicclescombe Park and seafront.
Bedrooms: 1 single, 5 double & 1 twin, 4 family rooms.
Bathrooms: 5 private, 3 public.
Bed & breakfast: £10-£12.50 single, £20-£25 double.
Half board: £15-£17.50 daily, £105-£110 weekly.
Evening meal 6.30pm (l.o. 6.30pm).
Parking for 10.

Elmfield Hotel
Torrs Pk., Ilfracombe, EX34 8AZ
☎ (0271) 863377
In quiet position close to town, with 1 acre of gardens. Adjacent to the famous Torrs Walks.
Bedrooms: 1 single, 11 double & 2 twin.
Bathrooms: 13 private, 1 public.
Bed & breakfast: £28 single, £56 double.
Half board: £32 daily, £185 weekly.
Lunch available.
Evening meal 7pm (l.o. 7.30pm).
Parking for 15.
Open March-October.
Credit: Access, Visa.

The Ilfracombe Carlton Hotel M
COMMENDED
Runnacleave Rd., Ilfracombe, EX34 8AR
☎ (0271) 862446 Fax (0271) 8625379
CR Consort
Comfortable, friendly hotel with bars, dancing, buttery and 24-hour service. Central location adjacent to beach and seafront.
Bedrooms: 5 single, 20 double & 20 twin, 5 family rooms.
Bathrooms: 39 private, 7 public.
Bed & breakfast: £20-£25 single, £40-£50 double.
Half board: £32-£35 daily, £150-£195 weekly.
Lunch available.
Evening meal 7pm (l.o. 8.30pm).
Parking for 25.
Open March-November, December-January.
Credit: Access, Visa, Amex.

The Torrs Hotel M
APPROVED
Torrs Pk., Ilfracombe, EX34 8AY
☎ (0271) 862334
Victorian mansion with fine views, beside the Torrs Coastal Walk (National Trust). Close to the seafront and town centre.
Bedrooms: 1 single, 5 double & 3 twin, 5 family rooms.
Bathrooms: 14 private, 2 public.
Bed & breakfast: £18-£19.50 single, £36-£39 double.

Half board: £23-£25.50 daily, £161-£178.50 weekly.
Evening meal 6.30pm (l.o. 7.30pm).
Parking for 14.
Open March-October.
Credit: Access, Visa, Diners, Amex.

Trafalgar Hotel
Larkstone Ter., Ilfracombe, EX34 9NU
☎ (0271) 862145
Elegant Victorian hotel overlooking the harbour and close to all amenities, including golf-course and town.
Bedrooms: 2 single, 12 double & 5 twin, 5 family rooms.
Bathrooms: 22 private, 2 public; 2 private showers.
Bed & breakfast: from £27.50 single, £45-£52 double.
Half board: £29-£37.50 daily, £175-£195 weekly.
Lunch available.
Evening meal 7pm (l.o. 11pm).
Parking for 6.
Credit: Access, Visa, Diners, Amex.

Trimstone Manor Hotel M
Trimstone, Ilfracombe, EX34 8NR
☎ (0271) 862841
English country manor in 54 acres. Indoor leisure centre and complete outdoor activities. Situated 2 miles from Woolacombe sands.
Bedrooms: 1 single, 7 double & 5 twin, 5 family rooms.
Bathrooms: 15 private, 1 public; 3 private showers.
Half board: £22-£27 daily, £120-£160 weekly.
Lunch available.
Evening meal 7pm (l.o. 8.30pm).
Parking for 52.

Two Ways
APPROVED
39 St. Brannocks Road, Ilfracombe, EX34 8EP
☎ (0271) 864017
Victorian house near Bicclescombe Park offering old fashioned service with modern comforts including electric blankets. 4 course dinners. Licensed bar.

Bedrooms: 1 single, 2 double & 2 twin, 2 family rooms.
Bathrooms: 3 private, 2 public.
Bed & breakfast: from £10 single, from £20 double.
Half board: from £16 daily, from £105 weekly.
Evening meal 7pm (l.o. 7pm).
Parking for 7.

Westwell Hall Hotel
APPROVED
Torrs Pk., Ilfracombe, EX34 8AZ
☎ (0271) 862792
Elegant early Victorian house set in 2 acres of mature gardens, adjacent to National Trust walks. Overlooking the sea and town in quiet location.
Bedrooms: 2 single, 4 double & 3 twin, 2 family rooms.
Bathrooms: 11 private.
Bed & breakfast: £18-£20 single, £36-£40 double.
Half board: £23-£30 daily, £154-£175 weekly.
Evening meal 7pm (l.o. 8pm).
Parking for 12.
Credit: Access, Visa.

Wildercombe House Hotel
St. Brannocks Rd., Ilfracombe, EX34 8EP
☎ (0271) 862240
An impressive Regency building set in its own grounds overlooking Ilfracombe and the sea beyond. Activity holidays a speciality.
Bedrooms: 5 double & 3 twin, 3 family rooms.
Bathrooms: 11 private, 1 public.
Bed & breakfast: £17.50-£19.50 single, £35-£39 double.
Half board: £23-£27 daily, £160-£185 weekly.
Lunch available.
Evening meal 6pm (l.o. 8pm).
Parking for 15.
Credit: Access, Visa, Amex.

> Classifications and quality commendations were correct at the time of going to press but are subject to change. Please check at the time of booking.

ILMINSTER
Somerset
Map ref 1D2

Former wool town with modern industry, set in undulating, pastoral country. Fine market square of mellow ham stone and Elizabethan school house. The 15th C church has a handsome tower and a lofty, light interior with some notable brass memorials. Just north is an arts centre with theatre and art gallery.

Bay House
Bay Hill, Ilminster, TA19 0AT
☎ (0460) 52120
Family-run country guesthouse overlooking rural market town. Large gardens with magnificent views of the Blackdown Hills.
Bedrooms: 1 single, 2 double & 3 twin, 2 family rooms.
Bathrooms: 2 public.
Bed & breakfast: £16-£18 single, £27-£30 double.
Half board: £21-£25.50 daily, £125-£150 weekly.
Evening meal 6pm (l.o. 7pm).
Parking for 10.

Shrubbery Hotel M
APPROVED
Ilminster, TA19 9AR
☎ (0460) 52108 Fax (0460) 53660
Consort
Victorian gentleman's residence, converted into modernised country house hotel, built of local ham stone with terraced lawns. Ideal touring centre.
Bedrooms: 1 single, 3 double & 5 twin, 3 family rooms.
Bathrooms: 12 private.
Bed & breakfast: £35-£50 single, £70-£100 double.
Half board: £40-£58 daily, from £245 weekly.
Lunch available.
Evening meal 7.30pm (l.o. 9.30pm).
Parking for 100.
Credit: Access, Visa, C.Bl., Diners, Amex.

INSTOW
Devon
Map ref 1C1

Popular sailing centre on the Torridge Estuary, between Bideford and Barnstaple. Tapeley Park House, standing in Italian gardens, has fine 18th C plasterwork ceilings and collections of china and furniture.

Anchorage Hotel
The Quay, Instow, Bideford, EX39 4HX
☎ (0271) 860655/860475
Beautifully situated on Instow quay overlooking water. Quiet location but near many outstanding places of interest. Specialists in golfing holidays.
Bedrooms: 7 double & 8 twin, 2 family rooms.
Bathrooms: 14 private, 2 public.
Bed & breakfast: £16-£27 single, £30-£44 double.
Half board: £25-£32 daily, £150-£195 weekly.
Evening meal 7pm (l.o. 8.30pm).
Parking for 18.
Open February-December.
Credit: Access, Visa.

ISLES OF SCILLY
Cornwall
Map ref 1A3

Tiny, rocky islands grouped around main island of St. Mary's. Fish and spring flowers marketed; fields have tall windbreaks of pittisporum and escallonia set against vivid blue seas and silver sands. Tresco's tropical gardens have a collection of ships' figureheads. Hugh Town on St. Mary's, with its busy harbour, is the only town. Romantic history of shipwrecks, kelping and smuggling.
Tourist Information Centre ☎ *(0720) 22536*

Carnwethers Country House
Pelistry Bay, St. Mary's, Isles of Scilly, TR21 0NX
☎ Scillonia (0720) 22415

Family-run hotel in peaceful gardens close to secluded beaches, coastal walks and nature trails. Library and videos on marine and Scillonian subjects. Outdoor heated pool and croquet lawn.
Bedrooms: 1 single, 3 double & 3 twin, 2 family rooms.
Bathrooms: 8 private, 2 public; 1 private shower.
Half board: £27-£39 daily.
Evening meal 6.30pm (l.o. 6.30pm).
Parking for 3.
Open April-October.

Chafford
Bryher, Isles of Scilly, TR23 0PR
☎ (0720) 22241
New, small family-run guesthouse built in a cottage style, 100 yards from sandy beach. Overlooking Tresco.
Bedrooms: 2 double & 1 twin.
Bathrooms: 1 private, 1 public.
Bed & breakfast: £14.50 single, £29 double.
Half board: £39-£44 daily, £273-£308 weekly.
Lunch available.
Evening meal 6.30pm (l.o. 6.30pm).

Covean Cottage
Listed
St. Agnes, Isles of Scilly, TR22 0PL
☎ Scillonia (0720) 22620
Small cosy cottage guesthouse with sea views. Friendly atmosphere and personal attention assured. Ideal get away from it all holiday.
Bedrooms: 2 double & 1 twin.
Bathrooms: 2 private, 1 public.
Half board: £24.15-£28.75 daily, £169-£201.25 weekly.
Lunch available.
Evening meal 6pm (l.o. 7pm).
Open January-November.
Credit: Visa.

Harbourside Hotel
The Quay, St. Mary's, Isles of Scilly, TR21 0JZ
☎ (0720) 22352
A new small hotel situated right on St. Mary's Quay. Every room has a view of the sea.
Bedrooms: 4 double & 5 twin, 3 family rooms.
Bathrooms: 12 private.

Continued ▶

> The enquiry coupons at the back will help you when contacting proprietors.

ISLES OF SCILLY
Continued

Bed & breakfast: £45-£75 double.
Half board: £37.50-£47.50 daily, £262.50-£332.50 weekly.
Evening meal 6.30pm (l.o. 9pm).

Hell Bay Hotel ⋀
🏵🏵🏵 COMMENDED
Bryher, Isles of Scilly, TR23 0PR
☎ Scillonia (0720) 22947
Fax (0720) 23004
Only hotel on beautiful still unspoilt peaceful island. All rooms en-suite and have private lounge and TV. Safe sandy beaches, coastal walks, boat trips and fishing expeditions. Windsurfing.
Bedrooms: 5 double & 5 twin, 4 family rooms.
Bathrooms: 14 private.
Half board: £42-£58 daily, £259-£392 weekly.
Lunch available.
Evening meal 7.15pm (l.o. 8.45pm).
Open March-October.
Credit: Access, Visa.

Star Castle Hotel ⋀
🏵🏵🏵 COMMENDED
The Garrison, St. Mary's, Isles of Scilly, TR21 0JA
☎ Scillonia (0720) 22317
An Elizabethan castle in 4.5 acres of tropical gardens. Tennis, indoor heated pool, garden apartments and castle rooms. Family rooms.
Bedrooms: 2 single, 5 double & 12 twin, 5 family rooms.
Bathrooms: 24 private.
Bed & breakfast: £35-£40 single, £55-£60 double.
Half board: £40-£60 daily, £280-£385 weekly.
Evening meal 6.45pm (l.o. 8pm).
Open March-October.

Tremellyn Guest House
🏵🏵
St. Mary's, Isles of Scilly, TR21 0NA
☎ Scillonia (0720) 22656
A friendly holiday home for 14 people. Small, informal but professionally run by the owners.
Bedrooms: 2 single, 3 double & 3 twin.

Bathrooms: 2 private, 2 public.
Bed & breakfast: £19-£24.75 single, £38-£49.50 double.
Half board: £27.80-£33.30 daily, £194.60-£233.10 weekly.
Evening meal 6.30pm (l.o. 7pm).
Parking for 5.
Open March-November.

KEYNSHAM
Avon
Map ref 2B2

Busy town on the River Avon between Bath and Bristol.

Grasmere Court Hotel
🏵🏵
22-24 Bath Rd., Keynsham, Bristol, BS18 1SN
☎ Bristol (0272) 862662
Well-appointed hotel with high standard of decor and accommodation. Private facilities. Situated on A4 between Bath and Bristol.
Bedrooms: 7 single, 6 double & 3 twin, 2 family rooms.
Bathrooms: 15 private, 1 public.
Bed & breakfast: £30-£40 single, £40-£48 double.
Evening meal 6.30pm (l.o. 7.30pm).
Parking for 18.
Credit: Access, Visa.

KINGSBRIDGE
Devon
Map ref 1C3

Formerly important as a port, now a market town overlooking head of beautiful, wooded estuary winding deep into rural countryside. Summer art exhibitions; William Cookworthy Museum.
Tourist Information Centre ☎ (0548) 853195

Ashleigh House
🏵🏵 COMMENDED
Ashleigh Rd., Kingsbridge, TQ7 1HB
☎ (0548) 852893
Spacious accommodation, furnished to high standard, overlooking countryside but near to town and quay. Sun and TV lounges and choice of menu.
Bedrooms: 1 single, 4 double & 2 twin, 1 family room.

Bathrooms: 3 private, 2 public.
Bed & breakfast: £12.50-£14 single, £25-£28 double.
Half board: £18.50-£21 daily, £123-£139.65 weekly.
Evening meal 6.45pm (l.o. 4pm).
Parking for 6.
Open April-October.
Credit: Access, Visa.

Buckland-Tout-Saints Hotel ⋀
Kingsbridge, TQ7 2DS
☎ (0548) 853055 Fax (0548) 856261
ℂⅮ Prestige
Elegance with simplicity is the principle on which we operate. Individually decorated bedrooms, comfortable lounges with fresh flowers and pot-pourri. A peaceful oasis 2.5 miles north-east of Kingsbridge off A381.
Bedrooms: 1 single, 7 double & 4 twin.
Bathrooms: 12 private.
Bed & breakfast: £87.50-£97.50 single, £110-£145 double.
Half board: £75-£92.50 daily.
Lunch available.
Evening meal 7.30pm (l.o. 9.30pm).
Parking for 22.
Open February-December.
Credit: Access, Visa, C.Bl., Diners, Amex.

Fern Lodge
🏵🏵
Hope Cove, Kingsbridge, TQ7 3HF
☎ Kingsbridge (0548) 561326
Varied food and comfortable accommodation. All rooms en-suite with sea or country views. Lounge with TV.
Bedrooms: 2 single, 3 double & 1 twin, 2 family rooms.
Bathrooms: 8 private.
Bed & breakfast: max. £16 single, from £32 double.
Half board: max. £23.75 daily, max. £159.75 weekly.
Evening meal 7pm (l.o. 5pm).
Parking for 8.
Open April-October.

Greystone Hotel
🏵🏵🏵
Hope Cove, Kingsbridge, TQ7 3HH
☎ Kingsbridge (0548) 561233

Peaceful family hotel with spectacular views over Hope Cove and Bigbury Bay. Close to safe sandy beaches and wonderful cliff walks.
Bedrooms: 6 double & 3 twin.
Bathrooms: 8 private, 1 public.
Bed & breakfast: £17.50 single, £35 double.
Half board: £27.50 daily, £162.50-£175 weekly.
Evening meal 7.30pm (l.o. 9.30pm).
Parking for 20.
Credit: Access, Visa.

Kings Arms Hotel ⋀
🏵🏵
Fore St., Kingsbridge, TQ7 1AB
☎ (0548) 852071
17th C coaching inn famous for its collection of four-poster beds, part of the history of Kingsbridge.
Bedrooms: 2 single, 8 double & 1 twin.
Bathrooms: 11 private.
Bed & breakfast: £27.50-£30 single, £50-£55 double.
Half board: £35-£40 daily, £215-£230 weekly.
Lunch available.
Evening meal 7pm (l.o. 9pm).
Parking for 30.
Credit: Access, Visa.

Oddicombe House Hotel
Chillington, Kingsbridge, TQ7 2JD
☎ Frogmore (0548) 531234
Hotel and restaurant set in lovely grounds, with beautiful views over the hills. Imaginative, freshly prepared food.
Bedrooms: 3 single, 2 double & 3 twin, 2 family rooms.
Bathrooms: 6 private, 2 public.
Bed & breakfast: £22-£31 single, £44-£54 double.
Half board: £33-£42 daily, £200-£250 weekly.
Lunch available.
Evening meal 7pm (l.o. 8.15pm).
Parking for 15.
Open April-October.

KINGSKERSWELL
Devon
Map ref 1D2

The Barn Owl Inn ⋀
🏵🏵 COMMENDED
Aller Mills, Kingskerswell, Newton Abbot, TQ12 5AN
☎ (0803) 872130/872968

16th C farmhouse inn offering a high standard of accommodation, all rooms en-suite with colour TV, tea making and telephone. 3 bars, log fires, a la carte restaurant.
Bedrooms: 1 single, 5 double.
Bathrooms: 6 private.
Bed & breakfast: max. £45 single, £60-£75 double.
Evening meal 7pm (l.o. 9.30pm).
Parking for 60.

KNOWSTONE

Devon
Map ref 1D1

7m E. South Molton

Knowstone Court Country House Hotel & Restaurant M

COMMENDED
Knowstone, South Molton, EX36 4RW
☎ Anstey Mills (039 84) 457 & 511
Elegant Victorian rectory situated on the edge of small Devonshire village of thatched cottages and 13th C church.
Bedrooms: 1 single, 5 double & 2 twin.
Bathrooms: 7 private, 1 public.
Bed & breakfast: £40-£45 single, £60-£80 double.
Half board: £48-£58 daily, £280-£310 weekly.
Evening meal 7pm (l.o. 9pm).
Parking for 14.
Credit: Access, Visa.

LANDS END

Cornwall
Map ref 1A3

Sennen Cove Hotel M

Marias La., Sennen Cove, Penzance, TR19 7BZ
☎ (0736) 871275
Hotel overlooking Sennen Cove and Cape Cornwall. Magnificent views of sea from all rooms. Situated on cliff side.
Bedrooms: 1 single, 5 double & 3 twin, 1 family room.
Bathrooms: 3 private, 3 public.
Bed & breakfast: £16-£18 single, £32-£36 double.
Half board: £24-£26 daily, £98-£130 weekly.
Evening meal 7pm (l.o. 7.30pm).

Parking for 10.
Open January-November.
Credit: Access, Visa.

LAUNCESTON

Cornwall
Map ref 1C2

Medieval 'Gateway to Cornwall', county town until 1838, founded by the Normans under their hilltop castle near the original monastic settlement. Today's hilly market town, overlooked by its castle ruin, has a handsome square with Georgian houses and an elaborately-carved granite church.
Tourist Information Centre ☎ (0566) 772321

Country Friends Restaurant

St Leonards House, Polson, Launceston, PL15 9QR
☎ (0566) 774479
400-year-old Devon longhouse with stone fireplaces, exposed beams and wood burners. Cordon Bleu cuisine. Riding holidays available. Ideal touring area.
Bedrooms: 2 twin, 2 family rooms.
Bathrooms: 1 public; 3 private showers.
Bed & breakfast: £16-£17 single, £30-£32 double.
Half board: £26-£28 daily.
Evening meal 7.30pm (l.o. 9.30pm).
Open January, January-December.
Credit: Access, Visa.

Glencoe Villa

APPROVED
13 Race Hill, Launceston, PL15 9BB
☎ (0566) 7713012
Large 3-storey, hilltop Victorian type house with superb views across Tamar Valley. 4 minutes from town centre.
Bedrooms: 2 single, 2 double & 1 twin, 3 family rooms.
Bathrooms: 3 private, 2 public.
Bed & breakfast: £14-£18 single, £26-£30 double.
Evening meal 7pm (l.o. 9.30pm).
Parking for 6.
Credit: Access, Visa.

Lifton Cottage Hotel

Lifton, Devon PL16 0DR
☎ (0566) 84439
Gothic style house run by resident family. Now a listed building.
Bedrooms: 4 single, 4 double & 3 twin, 2 family rooms.
Bathrooms: 9 private, 2 public; 1 private shower.
Bed & breakfast: £20-£25 single, max. £45 double.
Half board: £29-£33 daily, £160-£205 weekly.
Lunch available.
Evening meal 7pm (l.o. 9pm).
Parking for 25.
Credit: Access, Visa, Diners, Amex.

LEWDOWN

Devon
Map ref 1C2

Small village on the very edge of Dartmoor. Lydford Castle is 4 miles to the east.

Stowford House Hotel M

APPROVED
Stowford, Lewdown, Okehampton, EX20 4BZ
☎ Lewdown (056 683) 415
Small family-run hotel offering warm welcome, quiet and tranquil surroundings complemented by the food which is our forte.
Bedrooms: 1 single, 2 double & 2 twin, 1 family room.
Bathrooms: 4 private, 1 public.
Bed & breakfast: £17-£25 single, £34-£39 double.
Half board: £25.50-£30 daily, £160-£185 weekly.
Evening meal 7pm (l.o. 9pm).
Parking for 8.

LIFTON

Devon
Map ref 1C2

Village in Lyd Valley, noted for salmon and trout fishing.

Thatched Cottage Restaurant & Hotel

COMMENDED
Sprytown, Lifton, PL16 0AY
☎ (0566) 84224

16th C thatched cottage with 4 well-appointed units, set in 2.5 acres of gardens. Licensed restaurant; 100 yards from A30 trunk road.
Bedrooms: 1 double & 1 twin, 2 family rooms.
Bathrooms: 4 private.
Bed & breakfast: £55 double.
Lunch available.
Evening meal 7.30pm (l.o. 9.30pm).
Parking for 10.
Credit: Access, Visa, Amex.

LISKEARD

Cornwall
Map ref 1C2

Former stannary town with a livestock market and light industry, situated at the head of a valley running to the Riviera coast. Handsome Georgian and Victorian residences and a fine Victorian Guildhall reflect the prosperity of the mining boom. The large church has an early 20th C tower and a Norman font.

Country Castle Hall M

APPROVED
Liskeard, PL14 4EB
☎ (0579) 42694
100 years old, with French-style tower, standing in 2.5 acres overlooking the Looe Valley and 1 mile from Liskeard centre.
Bedrooms: 4 single, 3 double & 3 twin, 1 family room.
Bathrooms: 10 private, 1 public.
Bed & breakfast: from £36 single, £50-£59 double.
Half board: £37.50-£42.50 daily.
Lunch available.
Evening meal 7pm (l.o. 8.30pm).
Parking for 50.
Open January-October, December.
Credit: Access, Visa.

Elnor Guest House

1 Russell St., Liskeard, PL14 4BP
☎ (0579) 42472
Home-from-home with friendly family atmosphere in 100-year-old town house between the station and market town.
Bedrooms: 2 single, 2 double & 1 twin, 1 family room.

Continued ▶

LISKEARD
Continued

Bathrooms: 1 private,
2 public.
Bed & breakfast: £13.50-
£16.50 single, £27-£33 double.
Half board: £21.50-£24.50
daily, £143.50-£164.50
weekly.
Evening meal 6pm (l.o. 6pm).
Parking for 6.

THE LIZARD
Cornwall
Map ref 1B3

Ending in England's most
southerly point, a treeless
peninsula with rugged,
many-coloured cliffs and
deep shaded valleys
facing the Helford River.
Kynance Cove famous for
serpentine cliffs, lovely
sands.

Housel Bay Hotel M
COMMENDED
Housel Cove, The Lizard,
Helston, TR12 7PG
☎ (0326) 290417
*Clifftop position near
England's most southerly point
overlooking the Atlantic
Ocean. Safe sandy beach,
coastal walks and breathtaking
views.*
Bedrooms: 4 single, 12 double
& 7 twin.
Bathrooms: 23 private.
Bed & breakfast: £20-£40
single, £40-£72 double.
Half board: £32-£53 daily,
£201-£311 weekly.
Lunch available.
Evening meal 7.30pm (l.o.
9pm).
Parking for 34.
Open February-December.
Credit: Access, Visa, Amex.

⊕ Display advertisement
appears on page 458.

Kynance Bay House
Hotel M
COMMENDED
Off Penmenner Rd, The
Lizard, TR12 7NR
☎ (0326) 290498
*Victorian country house of
character enjoying spectacular,
panoramic coastal views.
Accent on food, wine,
hospitality and comfort. Dogs
welcome.*
Bedrooms: 2 single, 5 double
& 2 twin.

Bathrooms: 7 private,
1 public; 1 private shower.
Bed & breakfast: £15-£22
single, £30-£44 double.
Half board: £24-£31 daily,
£168-£192.50 weekly.
Lunch available.
Evening meal 7.30pm (l.o.
8.30pm).
Parking for 15.
Open February-December.
Credit: Access, Visa, C.Bl.,
Diners, Amex.

Mounts Bay House
Hotel M
APPROVED
Penmenner Rd., The Lizard,
Helston, TR12 7NP
☎ (0326) 290305 / 290393
*Quiet position in own grounds
with lovely view of beautiful
Kynance Cove. Cosy bar.
Tempting choice of menu.*
Bedrooms: 1 single, 4 double
& 1 twin, 1 family room.
Bathrooms: 2 private,
1 public; 5 private showers.
Bed & breakfast: £16-£21
single, £32-£42 double.
Half board: £25-£30 daily,
£155-£198 weekly.
Evening meal 7.30pm (l.o.
6.30pm).
Parking for 10.
Open January-October.
Credit: Access, Visa.

Polbrean Hotel M
Sea Front, The Lizard,
Helston, Cornwall.
TR12 7NT
☎ (0326) 290418 & 290450
*England's most southerly hotel
with superb sea views. Food
ranges from bar snacks to a la
carte restaurant. Fully
licensed.*
Bedrooms: 2 single, 4 double
& 1 twin, 4 family rooms.
Bathrooms: 5 private,
3 public.
Bed & breakfast: £14-£30
single, £36-£60 double.
Half board: £25-£42 daily,
£165-£260 weekly.
Lunch available.
Evening meal 7pm (l.o. 9pm).
Parking for 53.
Credit: Access, Visa.

LODDISWELL
Devon
Map ref 1C3

3m NW. Kingsbridge

Woolston House M
COMMENDED
Loddiswell, Kingsbridge,
TQ7 4OU
☎ Kingsbridge (0548) 550341
*28-acre mixed farm. Elegant
restful home and 3 self-
contained flats, for holidays
and breaks. Craft/nature
rooms and nursery play area.
Cholesterol-reduced traditional
home cooking. Non-smokers
only please.*
Bedrooms: 1 double & 2 twin,
4 family rooms.
Bathrooms: 7 private,
1 public.
Half board: £33-£44 daily,
£210-£295 weekly.
Lunch available.
Evening meal 6pm (l.o.
10am).
Parking for 16.

LONG SUTTON
Somerset
Map ref 2A3

The Devonshire Arms
Hotel
COMMENDED
Long Sutton, Langport,
TA10 9LP
☎ (0458) 241271
*Built as a hunting lodge by the
Duke of Devonshire in 1787.*
Bedrooms: 3 double & 2 twin,
2 family rooms.
Bathrooms: 6 private,
1 public; 1 private shower.
Bed & breakfast: £24.50-
£28.50 single, £35-£45 double.
Half board: £34.50-£44.50
daily, £115-£135 weekly.
Lunch available.
Evening meal 7pm (l.o.
11pm).
Parking for 20.
Credit: Access, Visa.

LOOE
Cornwall
Map ref 1C2

Small resort developed
around former fishing and
smuggling ports
occupying the deep
estuary of the East and
West Looe Rivers.
Narrow winding streets,
with old inns; museums,
aquarium and art gallery
are housed in interesting
old buildings. West Looe
has a medieval seamen's
chapel restored with
timbers from a captured
Spanish ship. Shark
fishing centre, boat trips;
busy harbour.

Allhays Country House
Hotel M
COMMENDED
Talland Bay, Looe, PL13 2JB
☎ Polperro (0503) 72434
*Family-owned hotel in
extensive gardens overlooking
sea. Fresh fish, local and
homegrown products served in
our garden room restaurant.*
Bedrooms: 1 single, 3 double
& 3 twin, 1 family room.
Bathrooms: 4 private,
1 public; 3 private showers.
Bed & breakfast: £20-£22
single, £44-£66 double.
Half board: £31-£44 daily,
£192-£293 weekly.
Evening meal 7pm (l.o. 9pm).
Parking for 14.
Credit: Access, Visa.

Coombe Farm M
Widegates, Looe, PL13 1QN
☎ Widegates (050 34) 223
*10-acre smallholding.
Delightful country house with
superb views to sea. Log fires,
candlelit dining, croquet,
snooker and table tennis.*
Bedrooms: 1 single, 2 double
& 1 twin, 4 family rooms.
Bathrooms: 1 private,
2 public.
Bed & breakfast: £14.50-
£18.50 single, £29-£37 double.
Half board: £25-£29 daily,
£160-£186 weekly.
Evening meal 7pm (l.o. 7pm).
Parking for 12.
Open March-October.

Deganwy Hotel
Station Rd., East Looe,
PL13 1HL
☎ (050 36) 2984

**Individual proprietors have supplied all
details of accommodation. Although we
do check for accuracy, we advise you to
confirm prices and other information at
the time of booking.**

Small family hotel facing Looe River, within 5 minutes' walk of the town and beach.
Bedrooms: 2 single, 4 double & 1 twin, 3 family rooms.
Bathrooms: 2 private, 2 public.
Bed & breakfast: £10-£14 single, £20-£28 double.
Half board: £16.50-£20.50 daily, £115.50-£143.50 weekly.
Evening meal 6.30pm (l.o. 10am).

Fieldhead Hotel M
COMMENDED
Portuan Rd., Hannafore, West Looe, PL13 2DR
☎ (050 36) 2689
Turn-of-the-century-house set in lovely gardens in residential area, with panoramic views of the sea and bay.
Bedrooms: 2 single, 7 double & 3 twin, 2 family rooms.
Bathrooms: 12 private; 2 private showers.
Bed & breakfast: £30-£40 single, £44-£62 double.
Half board: £33-£40 daily, £199-£250 weekly.
Lunch available.
Evening meal 6.30pm (l.o. 8.30pm).
Parking for 15.
Open February-November.
Credit: Access, Visa, Amex.

The Panorama Hotel M
Hannafore Rd., Looe, PL13 2DE
☎ (050 36) 2123
Family hotel, varied food, friendly atmosphere. Magnificent setting overlooking miles of beautiful coastline.
Bedrooms: 1 single, 5 double & 2 twin, 3 family rooms.
Bathrooms: 7 private, 1 public.
Bed & breakfast: £18-£26.50 single, £36-£53 double.
Half board: £26-£34.50 daily, £156-£215 weekly.
Evening meal 6.30pm (l.o. 10pm).
Parking for 8.
Open March-October.
Credit: Access, Visa.

Pixies Holt M
Shutta, Looe, PL13 1JD
☎ (050 36) 2726

Small, friendly and comfortable. 1.5 acres of grounds with views over river and countryside. A few minutes' walk to picturesque Looe and beaches.
Bedrooms: 1 single, 3 double & 1 twin, 2 family rooms.
Bathrooms: 3 private, 1 public.
Bed & breakfast: £11-£20 single, £22-£40 double.
Evening meal 7pm (l.o. 6.30pm).
Parking for 8.
Open March-October.
Credit: Access, Visa, Amex.

Sundown
34 Goonwartha Rd., The Downs, West Looe, PL13 2PJ
☎ (050 36) 3359
Modern bed and breakfast accommodation within easy reach of town and overlooking woodland. Public footpath to cliffs and downs.
Bedrooms: 2 double & 2 twin, 1 family room.
Bathrooms: 2 public.
Bed & breakfast: £13.50-£14.50 single, £27-£29 double.
Parking for 2.
Credit: Access, Visa.

Westcliffe Guest Houses M
1 & 2 West Rd., West Looe, PL13 2EE
☎ (050 36) 2927
2 Victorian houses with panoramic views over harbour and out to sea. Modernised with en-suite rooms, central heating and double glazing. Bar.
Bedrooms: 2 single, 7 double & 3 twin, 6 family rooms.
Bathrooms: 13 private, 2 public.
Bed & breakfast: £10.50-£13 single, £21-£30 double.
Half board: £15-£17.50 daily, £98-£130 weekly.
Evening meal 6pm (l.o. 8am).
Open March-October.

Half board prices shown are per person but in some cases may be based on double/twin occupancy.

Tourist Information Centre ☎ (0208) 872207

Restormel Lodge Hotel M
19 Castle Hill, Lostwithiel, PL22 0DD
☎ Bodmin (0208) 872223
Set in the beautiful Fowey Valley. Warm, spacious well-equipped bedrooms. Imaginative menus and friendly, efficient service.
Bedrooms: 2 single, 15 double & 12 twin, 3 family rooms.
Bathrooms: 32 private.
Bed & breakfast: £34-£37 single, £49-£55 double.
Half board: £42-£46 daily, £60-£70 weekly.
Lunch available.
Evening meal 7pm (l.o. 9.30pm).
Parking for 45.
Credit: Access, Visa, Diners, Amex.

Former important tin mining town, a small village on edge of West Dartmoor. Remains of Norman castle where all falling foul of tinners' notorious 'Lydford Law' were incarcerated. Bridge crosses River Lyd where it rushes through a mile-long gorge of boulders and trees over pools, rocks and waterfall.

Lydford House Hotel M
Lydford, Okehampton, EX20 4AU
☎ (082 282) 347
⊕ Minotels
Family-run country house hotel, peacefully set in own grounds on edge of Dartmoor. Superb touring centre. Own riding stables.
Bedrooms: 3 single, 5 double & 3 twin, 2 family rooms.
Bathrooms: 11 private, 2 public.
Bed & breakfast: max. £26 single, max. £52 double.
Half board: max. £37 daily, £215-£229 weekly.
Lunch available.
Evening meal 7pm (l.o. 8pm).
Parking for 30.

Credit: Access, Visa, Diners, Amex.

Moor View Hotel and Restaurant M
Vale Down, Lydford, Okehampton, EX20 4BB
☎ (082 282) 220
Victorian country house hotel and restaurant set in over 1.5 acres of land. Large rooms with lovely views over the moors.
Bedrooms: 1 double, 3 family rooms.
Bathrooms: 4 private.
Bed & breakfast: from £19 single, from £32 double.
Half board: £24-£27 daily, £155-£176 weekly.
Lunch available.
Evening meal 7pm (l.o. 9pm).
Parking for 15.
Credit: Access, Visa.

Pretty, historic fishing town and resort set against the fossil-rich cliffs of Lyme Bay. In medieval times it was an important port and cloth centre. The Cobb, a massive stone breakwater, shelters the ancient harbour which is still lively with boats.
Tourist Information Centre ☎ (02974) 2138

Hotel Buena Vista M
Pound St., Lyme Regis, DT7 3HZ
☎ (029 74) 2494
⊕ Inter
Regency house with a country house atmosphere in an unrivalled position overlooking the bay. Close to the town and beaches.
Bedrooms: 4 single, 9 double & 5 twin, 1 family room.
Bathrooms: 19 private, 2 public.
Bed & breakfast: £30-£34 single, £52-£78 double.
Half board: £34-£47 daily, £180-£282 weekly.
Evening meal 7pm (l.o. 8pm).
Parking for 20.
Credit: Access, Visa, Diners, Amex.

Devon Hotel ⚑
Lyme Rd., Uplyme, Lyme
Regis, DT7 3TQ
☎ (029 74) 3231 Telex 42513
SHARET G
Ⓒ Best Western
*Country house set in
landscaped gardens, 1 mile
from sea and Cobb harbour.
Ideal centre for touring.*
Bedrooms: 2 single, 7 double
& 9 twin, 3 family rooms.
Bathrooms: 21 private.
Bed & breakfast: £33-£35
single, £66-£70 double.
Half board: £42-£44 daily,
£273-£287 weekly.
Lunch available.
Evening meal 7pm (l.o.
8.30pm).
Parking for 30.
Open March-November.
Credit: Access, Visa, Diners,
Amex.

Ilex Cottage Guest House
View Rd., Lyme Regis,
DT7 3AA
☎ (029 74) 2891
*Delightful old established
guesthouse, quietly situated a
short distance from sea.
Tastefully furnished. Old
fashioned courtesy.*
Bedrooms: 1 single, 3 double
& 1 twin, 2 family rooms.
Bathrooms: 2 public.
Bed & breakfast: £24-£30
double.
Half board: £18-£22 daily,
£112-£130 weekly.
Evening meal 6.30pm (l.o.
5pm).
Parking for 6.
Open April-September.

Kent House Hotel ⚑
Silver St., Lyme Regis,
DT7 3HT
☎ (029 74) 2020
*Family-run licensed hotel
where home cooking is a
speciality. Welcomes children.
Spring and autumn bargain
breaks. Vegetarian food. En-
suite rooms.*
Bedrooms: 2 double & 1 twin,
4 family rooms.
Bathrooms: 7 private,
1 public.
Bed & breakfast: £18.50-£28
single, £37-£48 double.

Half board: £29.50-£39 daily,
£170-£240 weekly.
Evening meal 7pm (l.o.
6.30pm).
Parking for 8.
Open March-October.

Orchard Country Hotel
Rousdon, Lyme Regis,
DT7 3XW
☎ (029 74) 2972
*Modern hotel, in own grounds
on the Devon/Dorset coastal
border. Under same
management for 7 years.*
Bedrooms: 1 single, 5 double
& 6 twin.
Bathrooms: 12 private.
Bed & breakfast: £27-£34
single, £50-£59 double.
Half board: £33-£40 daily,
£195-£215 weekly.
Evening meal 7.30pm (l.o.
8.15pm).
Parking for 20.
Open April-October.
Credit: Access, Visa.

St. Michaels Hotel ⚑
APPROVED
Pound St., Lyme Regis,
DT7 3HZ
☎ (029 74) 2503
*An elegant Georgian house
with views of Lyme Bay.*
Bedrooms: 2 single, 5 double
& 5 twin, 1 family room.
Bathrooms: 13 private.
Bed & breakfast: £25-£30.50
single, £50-£61 double.
Half board: £32.50-£37.50
daily.
Evening meal 6.30pm (l.o.
7.30pm).
Parking for 13.
Credit: Access, Visa.

White House
COMMENDED
47 Silver St., Lyme Regis,
DT7 3HR
☎ (029 74) 3420
*Fine views of Dorset coastline
from rear of this 18th C
guesthouse. A short walk from
beach, gardens and shops.*
Bedrooms: 5 double & 2 twin.
Bathrooms: 7 private.
Bed & breakfast: £31-£34
double.
Parking for 6.
Open April-October.

*4m NE. Burnham-on-Sea.
Attractive village south of
the narrow River Axe
Estuary. The local church
carries a notable tower
and both the manor
house and the village
cross date from the early
19th C.*

Batch Farm Country Hotel ⚑
Batch La., Lympsham,
Weston-super-Mare, Avon
BS24 0EX
☎ (0934) 750371
*Rural, peaceful and secluded,
set in its own grounds, with
panoramic views from all
rooms. Ample parking. Short
distance from M5. Open all
year except for Christmas.*
Bedrooms: 3 double & 2 twin,
3 family rooms.
Bathrooms: 8 private.
Bed & breakfast: £28-£31
single, £46-£48 double.
Half board: £33-£36 daily,
£185-£210 weekly.
Lunch available.
Evening meal 7pm (l.o.
8.30pm).
Parking for 50.
Credit: Access, Visa, Diners,
Amex.

*Resort set beneath lofty,
bracken-covered cliffs
and pinewood gorges
where 2 rivers meet,
cascade and flow
between boulders to the
town. Lynton, set on cliffs
above, can be reached by
water-operated cliff
railway from the Victorian
Esplanade. Valley of the
Rocks, to the west, gives
dramatic walks; eastward
from Countisbury are
wide views of Exmoor
and the bay.*

Bath Hotel ⚑
APPROVED
Lynmouth, EX35 6EL
☎ Lynton (0598) 52238
*A friendly, family-run hotel by
picturesque Lynmouth
Harbour. Ideal centre for
exploring Exmoor National
Park.*

Bedrooms: 1 single, 10 double
& 11 twin, 2 family rooms.
Bathrooms: 24 private.
Bed & breakfast: £21.50-£25
single, £43-£65 double.
Half board: £27-£40 daily,
£189-£275 weekly.
Lunch available.
Evening meal 7pm (l.o.
8.30pm).
Parking for 17.
Open March-October.
Credit: Access, Visa, Diners,
Amex.

East Lyn House
17 Watersmeet Rd.,
Lynmouth, EX35 6EP
☎ Lynton (0598) 52540
*Victorian property set on the
banks of the East Lyn River. 3
minutes' walk from the
picturesque harbour and
bustling village.*
Bedrooms: 6 double & 2 twin.
Bathrooms: 5 private;
3 private showers.
Bed & breakfast: £38-£40
double.
Half board: £29-£30 daily,
£180-£195 weekly.
Evening meal 6.30pm (l.o.
8.30pm).
Parking for 12.
Credit: Access, Visa.

Orchard House Hotel
12 Watersmeet Rd.,
Lynmouth, EX35 6EP
☎ Lynton (0598) 53247
*In a central location 3 minutes
from the harbour, with
panoramic views. Large car
park opposite.*
Bedrooms: 1 single, 4 double
& 2 twin, 1 family room.
Bathrooms: 1 public;
3 private showers.
Bed & breakfast: £14-£16.50
single, £28-£33 double.
Half board: £22.50-£25 daily.
Evening meal 7pm (l.o. 7pm).
Open April-October.

The Tors Hotel
COMMENDED
Lynmouth, EX35 6NA
☎ Lynton (0598) 53236
*Unrivalled position 200 feet
above sea level, with splendid
views over Lynmouth and the
sea.*
Bedrooms: 15 double &
15 twin, 5 family rooms.
Bathrooms: 33 private,
1 public.

Bed & breakfast: £32.50-£59 single, £54-£75 double.
Half board: £40-£49 daily, £231-£283.50 weekly.
Lunch available.
Evening meal 7pm (l.o. 8.45pm).
Parking for 40.
Open March-January.
Credit: Access, Visa, Diners, Amex.

Waterloo House Hotel M

Lydiate La., Lynton,
EX35 6AJ
☎ (0598) 53391
Charming Georgian property, one of the original lodging houses of Lynton. Situated in the centre close to all amenities.
Bedrooms: 2 single, 4 double & 2 twin, 2 family rooms.
Bathrooms: 8 private, 1 public.
Bed & breakfast: £16-£24 single, £32-£48 double.
Half board: £27-£35 daily, £165-£215 weekly.
Evening meal 7.30pm (l.o. 7.45pm).
Parking for 3.
Open March-December.

LYNTON

Devon
Map ref 1C1

Hilltop resort on Exmoor coast linked to its seaside twin, Lynmouth, by a water-operated cliff railway which descends from the town hall. Spectacular surroundings of moorland cliffs with steep chasms of conifer and rocks through which rivers cascade.

Alford House Hotel M

Alford Ter., Lynton,
EX35 6AT
☎ (0598) 52359
Beautifully situated, small hotel with coastal views. All rooms en-suite. Varied food and wine. Some four-poster beds.
Bedrooms: 6 double & 1 twin.
Bathrooms: 7 private, 1 public.
Bed & breakfast: £20-£23 single, £32-£40 double.
Half board: £22-£26 daily, £140-£165 weekly.
Evening meal 7pm (l.o. 5pm).
Credit: Access, Visa.

Gordon House Hotel M
COMMENDED

31 Lee Rd., Lynton,
EX35 6BS
☎ (0598) 53203
Attractive Victorian gentleman's residence sympathetically restored. Charming hotel with warm friendly atmosphere.
Bedrooms: 5 double & 1 twin, 1 family room.
Bathrooms: 7 private, 1 public.
Bed & breakfast: £18-£21 single, £36-£42 double.
Half board: £26-£29 daily, £172-£193 weekly.
Evening meal 7pm (l.o. 7.30pm).
Parking for 7.
Open March-November.

Ingleside Hotel M
APPROVED

Lynton, EX35 6HW
☎ (0598) 52223
Family-run hotel with high standards. Elevated position overlooking village. Ideal centre for exploring Exmoor.
Bedrooms: 4 double & 1 twin, 2 family rooms.
Bathrooms: 7 private.
Bed & breakfast: £21-£25 single, £38-£44 double.
Half board: £31-£37 daily, £210-£252 weekly.
Evening meal 7pm (l.o. 6pm).
Parking for 10.
Open March-October.
Credit: Access, Visa.

North Cliff Hotel M

Northwalk, Lynton,
EX35 6HJ
☎ (0598) 52357
Family-run hotel of character with secluded grounds. All rooms overlook Lynmouth Bay and Watersmeet Valley. Ample parking on forecourt.
Bedrooms: 2 single, 9 double & 2 twin, 2 family rooms.
Bathrooms: 12 private, 8 public.
Bed & breakfast: £17-£22 single, £31-£44 double.
Half board: £25.50-£30 daily, £160-£185 weekly.
Lunch available.
Evening meal 7pm (l.o. 8pm).
Parking for 15.
Open February-November.

Rockvale Hotel

Lee Road, Lynton,
EX35 6HW
☎ (0598) 52279/53343
Centrally, yet quietly located hotel with extensive views. Offering pretty en-suite rooms, choice of menu and large level car park.
Bedrooms: 1 single, 4 double & 1 twin, 2 family rooms.
Bathrooms: 6 private, 2 public.
Bed & breakfast: £17.50-£19.50 single, £35-£39 double.
Half board: £27-£30 daily, £180-£200 weekly.
Lunch available.
Evening meal 7pm (l.o. 7pm).
Parking for 10.
Open February-October.
Credit: Access, Visa.

The Rookery
APPROVED

Sinai Hill, Lynton,
EX35 6AR
☎ (0598) 52235
Victorian house with fine views. Wales and the Brecons on a clear day. 500 feet above sea level. Ideal centre for touring.
Bedrooms: 5 double & 1 twin, 2 family rooms.
Bathrooms: 3 private, 2 public; 1 private shower.
Bed & breakfast: £14-£16 single, £28-£32 double.
Half board: £21.50-£23 daily, £145-£160 weekly.
Evening meal 6.30pm.
Parking for 9.
Open March-October.

St. Vincent Licensed Guest House

Castle Hill, Lynton,
EX35 6AJ
☎ (0598) 52244
Charming, detached period guesthouse beside Exmoor museum in centre of Lynton. Residents' lounge with colour TV, bar and a small cottage tea garden.
Bedrooms: 1 single, 1 double & 2 twin, 2 family rooms.
Bathrooms: 2 private, 1 public.
Bed & breakfast: £11.50-£15 single, £23-£30 double.

Half board: £18.50-£22.50 daily, £125-£152 weekly.
Evening meal 6.30pm (l.o. 4pm).
Parking for 4.
Open April-October.

Sandrock Hotel M
COMMENDED

Longmead, Lynton,
EX35 6DH
☎ (0598) 53307
Comfortable family-run hotel, quietly situated near local beauty spots. Bowls green and tennis courts.
Bedrooms: 2 single, 4 double & 3 twin.
Bathrooms: 7 private, 1 public.
Bed & breakfast: £17-£21 single, £34-£46 double.
Half board: £27.50-£35 daily, £177-£223 weekly.
Evening meal 7pm (l.o. 8pm).
Parking for 9.
Open February-November.
Credit: Access, Visa, Amex.

Seawood Hotel
COMMENDED

North Walk Dr., Lynton,
EX35 6HJ
☎ (0598) 52272
Family-run country house hotel nestling on wooded cliffs overlooking Lynmouth Bay and headland. Varied menu and friendly service.
Bedrooms: 2 single, 7 double & 2 twin, 1 family room.
Bathrooms: 12 private, 2 public.
Bed & breakfast: £22-£26 single, £44-£48 double.
Half board: £30-£35 daily, £175-£200 weekly.
Evening meal 7pm (l.o. 7pm).
Parking for 14.
Open March-November.

Sylvia House Hotel M

Lydiate Lane, Lynton,
EX16 6HE
☎ (0598) 52391
A delightful Georgian hotel in the very heart of England's romantic little Switzerland. Offering hospitality of a bygone age and elegance at moderate terms.
Bedrooms: 2 single, 5 double & 1 twin.
Bathrooms: 6 private, 1 public.
Bed & breakfast: £12-£16.50 single, £32-£34 double.

Continued ▶

The National Crown Scheme is explained in full on pages 556 – 558.

LYNTON

Continued

Half board: £21-£26.50 daily, £140-£165 weekly.
Evening meal 7pm (l.o. 10am).
🔟📺⬛🅿️♿ℹ️ V ⚥ 🔇 📺 🎞️ ▲ 🍴 DAP ⚒️ SP

MAIDEN NEWTON

Dorset
Map ref 2A3

Maiden Newton House M
Maiden Newton, Dorchester, DT2 0AA
☎ (0300) 20336
Jacobean-style riverside manor house set in 21 acres. Well-appointed and furnished with antiques.
Bedrooms: 4 double & 2 twin.
Bathrooms: 6 private.
Bed & breakfast: £45-£88 single, £90-£135 double.
Half board: £65-£90 daily.
Evening meal 8pm (l.o. 8pm).
Parking for 12.
Open February-December.
Credit: Access, Visa.
⬛♿⬛ℹ️ V ▥ 🎞️ ▲ 🍴 ☀️ ⚒️ SP 🏕️ T

MALMESBURY

Wiltshire
Map ref 2B2

Overlooking the River Avon, an old town dominated by its great church, once a Benedictine abbey. The surviving Norman nave and porch are noted for fine sculptures, 12th C arches and musicians' gallery.
Tourist Information Centre ☎ (0666) 823748

Crudwell Court Hotel M
🎖️🎖️🎖️🎖️ COMMENDED
Crudwell, Malmesbury, SN16 9ET
☎ (066 67) 355 & 7194/5
17th C vicarage, comfortably furnished, with heated swimming pool and 3 acres of grounds. Panelled restaurant open to non-residents.
Bedrooms: 1 single, 14 double.
Bathrooms: 15 private.
Bed & breakfast: £40-£65 single, £77-£99 double.
Lunch available.
Evening meal 7pm (l.o. 9.30pm).

Parking for 16.
Credit: Access, Visa, Diners, Amex.
♿➡️⬛🅿️♿ℹ️ V ▥ 🎞️ ▲ 🍴 ⚒️ ► ☀️ ⚒️ SP 🏕️

Knoll House Hotel
🎖️🎖️🎖️ APPROVED
Swindon Road, Malmesbury, SN16 9LU
☎ (0666) 823114 Fax (0666) 823897
Recently refurbished, this country house stands in its own grounds outside England's oldest borough. Friendly service in fine surroundings.
Bedrooms: 9 single, 9 double & 3 twin, 1 family room.
Bathrooms: 22 private.
Bed & breakfast: £45-£50 single, £52-£67 double.
Half board: £57.50-£62.50 daily, £295-£320 weekly.
Evening meal 7pm (l.o. 9.15pm).
Parking for 50.
Credit: Access, Visa, Amex.
♿➡️⬛♿ℹ️ V 🎞️ ▲ 🍴 ☀️ ⚒️ DAP ⚒️ SP T

Mayfield House Hotel M
🎖️🎖️🎖️
Crudwell, Malmesbury, SN16 9EW
☎ (066 67) 409 & 7198
In own grounds with walled garden. Convenient for many stately homes, Cotswolds and spa towns of Bath and Cheltenham.
Bedrooms: 4 single, 8 double & 7 twin, 1 family room.
Bathrooms: 20 private.
Bed & breakfast: £40-£43 single, £53-£56 double.
Half board: £230-£275 weekly.
Evening meal 7pm (l.o. 9.30pm).
Parking for 50.
Credit: Access, Visa, Amex.
♿➡️⬛♿ℹ️ V ▥ 🎞️ ▲ 🍴 ☀️ SP T

Whatley Manor M
🎖️🎖️🎖️
Easton Grey, Malmesbury, SN16 0RB
☎ (0666) 822888
Telex 449380 WHOTEL
Cotswold manor house in extensive grounds, between Bath and the Cotswolds.
Bedrooms: 13 double & 13 twin, 3 family rooms.
Bathrooms: 29 private.
Bed & breakfast: £69-£79 single, £99-£115 double.
Lunch available.
Evening meal 7.30pm (l.o. 9pm).
Parking for 60.

Credit: Access, Visa, Diners, Amex.
♿➡️⬛🅿️♿⬛ V ▥ 🔇 ● ⬛ ▲ 🍴 🎿 ♣️ 🔥 ⚥ ℘ 🌸 ⚒️ SP 🏕️ T

MARAZION

Cornwall
Map ref 1B3

Old town sloping to Mount's Bay with views of St. Michael's Mount and a causeway to the island revealed at low tide. In medieval times it catered for pilgrims. The Mount is crowned by a 15th C castle built around the former Benedictine monastery of 1044.

Chymorvah Tolgarrick Hotel M
🎖️🎖️🎖️ COMMENDED
Marazion, TR17 0DQ
☎ Penzance (0736) 710497
Family-run hotel and tea garden overlooking St. Michael's Mount and Mount's Bay. Spacious grounds with own access to beach.
Bedrooms: 1 single, 5 double & 1 twin, 2 family rooms.
Bathrooms: 9 private, 1 public.
Bed & breakfast: £15-£18 single, £30-£42 double.
Half board: £22-£28.50 daily, £145-£191 weekly.
Lunch available.
Evening meal 6.30pm (l.o. 2.50pm).
Parking for 9.
Credit: Access, Visa.
♿➡️⬛♿⬛🅿️♿ UL ℹ️ V ▥ 🎞️ ▲ ♣️ ⚥ ☀️ DAP SP 🏕️

🆔 Display advertisement appears on page 457.

Old Eastcliffe House M
Eastcliffe La., Marazion, TR17 0AZ
☎ (0736) 710298
Attractive Georgian residence, ideally situated overlooking own gardens and St. Michael's Mount. Offers a high standard of accommodation at affordable prices. Antique brass beds, good breakfasts.
Bedrooms: 3 double & 2 twin, 1 family room.
Bathrooms: 2 private, 2 public.
Bed & breakfast: £30-£42 double.
Parking for 9.
Open April-October.
♿➡️ UL ♿⚥ ▥ 📺 🎞️ ▲ ☀️ 🗡️ ⚒️ DAP SP 🏕️

MARLBOROUGH

Wiltshire
Map ref 2B2

Important market town, in a river valley cutting through chalk downlands. The broad main street, with colonnaded shops on one side, shows a medley of building styles, mainly from the Georgian period. Lanes wind away on either side and a church stands at each end.

Kingsbury Court
37 Kingsbury St., Marlborough, SN8 1JA
☎ (0672) 514656
Attractive Georgian town house, close to town centre and all amenities, with own car park.
Bedrooms: 3 double & 1 twin, 2 family rooms.
Bathrooms: 6 private.
Bed & breakfast: £20-£25 single, £30-£35 double.
Half board: £30-£35 daily.
Parking for 6.
♿⬛🅿️ UL 🎞️ ▲ 🗡️

MELKSHAM

Wiltshire
Map ref 2B2

Small industrial town standing on the banks of the River Avon. Old weavers' cottages and Regency houses are grouped around the attractive church which has traces of Norman work. The 18th C Round House, once used for dyeing fleeces, is now a craft centre.
Tourist Information Centre ☎ (0225) 707424

Beechfield House M
Beanacre, Melksham, SN12 7PU
☎ (0225) 703700
Built 1878 of mellow Bath stone in ornate architectural style of Victorian era. Set in 8 acres of gardens. Sympathically restored into a fine small country house.
Bedrooms: 7 double & 17 twin.
Bathrooms: 24 private.
Bed & breakfast: £79-£89.50 single, £103-£115 double.
Lunch available.
Evening meal 7pm (l.o. 9.45pm).
Parking for 30.

Credit: Access, Visa, Diners, Amex.

🛇 👶 🏡 ⌕ 🕭 🛆 🖤 ▯ Ⅴ ✂
🖵 ▥ 🍽 ⟨ 🖉 ✿ 🛥 🖄 SP
🅶 🅃

Conigre Farm Hotel and Restaurant M

♛♛♛

Semington Rd., Melksham,
SN12 6BZ
☎ (0225) 702229
*Beautiful ivy-clad 17th C
farmhouse, personally run by
owners. New stables block
conversion, 'Mr Bumbles'
restaurant, with old English
cooking.*
Bedrooms: 4 single, 4 double
& 1 twin.
Bathrooms: 6 private,
1 public.
Bed & breakfast: £27-£34
single, £44-£48 double.
Half board: £37-£44 daily.
Lunch available.
Evening meal 7pm (l.o.
10.30pm).
Parking for 20.
Credit: Access, Visa.

🛇 👶 🏡 ⌕ 🕭 🖤 ▯ Ⅴ
🖵 ◉ ▥ 🍽 🖉 🖄 ✿ 🛥
SP 🅶

The Kings Arms Hotel M

♛♛♛ APPROVED

Market Pl., Melksham,
SN12 6EX
☎ Bath (0225) 707272 Fax
(0225) 702085
*Combines old world
atmosphere with modern
amenities and is an ideal centre
for touring historic Wiltshire.*
Bedrooms: 6 single, 2 double
& 6 twin.
Bathrooms: 10 private,
2 public.
Bed & breakfast: £27-£37
single, £48 double.
Half board: £33.50-£46.50
daily.
Lunch available.
Evening meal 7pm (l.o. 9pm).
Parking for 45.
Credit: Access, Visa, Diners,
Amex.

🛇 ⌕ 🕭 🛆 🖤 ▯ Ⅴ 🖵 ▥
🍽 🖉 DAP ✿ SP 🅶 🅃

Longhope Guest House

♛♛

9 Beanacre Rd., Melksham,
SN12 8AG
☎ (0225) 706737
*Situated in its own grounds on
the A350 Melksham -
Chippenham road. Half a mile
from Melksham town centre,
10 miles from M4 junction 17.*
Bedrooms: 2 single, 1 double
& 3 twin, 2 family rooms.
Bathrooms: 6 private,
1 public; 1 private shower.

Bed & breakfast: max. £17.50
single, max. £33 double.
Half board: max. £24 daily,
max. £142 weekly.
Evening meal 6.30pm (l.o.
7pm).
Parking for 12.

🛇 👶 🖵 🖤 UL Ⅴ 🖍 TV ▥
🛆 🖄

MERE

Wiltshire
Map ref 2B2

Small town with a grand
Perpendicular church
surrounded by Georgian
houses, with old inns and
a 15th C chantry house.
On the chalk downs
overlooking the town is
an Iron Age fort.
*Tourist Information
Centre ☎ (0747) 860341*

The Beeches

Chetcombe Rd., Mere,
BA12 6AU
☎ (0747) 860687
*Comfortable old toll house with
interesting carved stairway and
gallery. Standing in a beautiful
garden at entrance to an early
English village.*
Bedrooms: 1 double & 1 twin,
1 family room.
Bathrooms: 1 public;
2 private showers.
Bed & breakfast: £16-£17
single, £26-£34 double.
Half board: £24-£26 daily,
£135-£159 weekly.
Evening meal 6pm (l.o.
10pm).
Parking for 6.

🛇 🖤 UL ▯ Ⅴ 🖍 TV ▥ ∪ ✿
🖄 SP 🅶

Chetcombe House Hotel

♛♛♛ COMMENDED

Chetcombe Rd., Mere,
BA12 6AZ
☎ (0747) 860219
*Country house hotel set in 1
acre of mature gardens, close
to Stourhead gardens. Ideal
touring centre. Home-cooked
local produce a speciality.*
Bedrooms: 1 single, 2 double
& 2 twin.
Bathrooms: 5 private.
Bed & breakfast: £25-£27
single, £43-£46 double.
Half board: £34.75-£36.75
daily, £218.25-£225 weekly.
Lunch available.
Evening meal 7pm (l.o.
5.30pm).
Parking for 10.
Credit: Access, Visa.

🛇 🖵 🖤 ▯ Ⅴ 🖍 ▥ 🛆 ✿
🖄 SP 🅃

MEVAGISSEY

Cornwall
Map ref 1B3

Small fishing town, a
favourite with
holidaymakers. Earlier
prosperity came from
pilchard fisheries, boat-
building and smuggling.
By the harbour are fish
cellars, some converted,
and a local history
museum is housed in an
old boat-building shed on
the north quay. Handsome
Methodist chapel; shark
fishing, sailing.

Cawtes Cottage

37 Cliff St., Mevagissey,
PL26 6QJ
☎ (0726) 842396
*Guesthouse with some seaviews
and much character, near the
harbour in this picturesque old
fishing village. Lunch and
evening meals provided by
arrangement.*
Bedrooms: 3 double & 1 twin,
1 family room.
Bathrooms: 1 private,
1 public.
Bed & breakfast: £10-£12
single, £20-£24 double.
Half board: £16-£18 daily,
£108-£122 weekly.
Lunch available.
Evening meal 6.30pm (l.o.
3.30pm).

🛇 👶 🖵 🖤 UL ▯ Ⅴ 🖍 TV
▥ 🛆 🖄 DAP 🛥 SP 🅶

Harbour Lights Hotel M

Polkirt Hill, Mevagissey, St.
Austell, PL26 6UR
☎ (0726) 843249
*Clifftop position overlooking
Mevagissey harbour with sea
views from all bedrooms and
public rooms. Ideal touring
centre.*
Bedrooms: 2 single, 3 double
& 2 twin.
Bathrooms: 5 private,
1 public.
Bed & breakfast: £19-£21
single, £41-£43 double.
Lunch available.
Evening meal 6.30pm (l.o.
8pm).
Parking for 60.

⌕ 🖵 🖤 ▯ 🛆 Ⅴ 🖍 ▥
🛆 🍽 ✿ 🖄 🖄

Mevagissey House M

♛♛♛ COMMENDED

Vicarage Hiⁿ, Mevagissey,
PL26 6SZ
☎ (0726) 842427

---

*Georgian country house in a
woodland setting on a hillside,
set in 4 acres. Elegant,
spacious rooms, many facilities,
licensed bar, home cooking.*
Bedrooms: 3 double & 1 twin,
2 family rooms.
Bathrooms: 4 private,
1 public.
Bed & breakfast: £20-£25
single, £32-£42 double.
Half board: £27-£32 daily,
£175-£213 weekly.
Evening meal 7.30pm (l.o.
5pm).
Parking for 12.
Open March-October.
Credit: Access, Visa.

🛇7 🕭 🖵 🖤 ▯ Ⅴ 🖍 ▥ 🛆
✿ 🖄 🖄 SP 🅶 🅃

Seapoint House Hotel M

Battery Ter., Mevagissey,
PL26 6QS
☎ (0726) 842684
*Family-run hotel with beautiful
views overlooking the bay and
harbour. All bedrooms with en-
suite facilities, colour TV and
hot drinks.*
Bedrooms: 1 single, 6 double
& 1 twin, 2 family rooms.
Bathrooms: 10 private,
1 public.
Bed & breakfast: £22-£26
single, £44-£52 double.
Half board: £30-£34 daily,
£180-£200 weekly.
Evening meal 7pm (l.o. 7pm).
Parking for 10.
Credit: Access, Visa.

🛇 👶 🖵 🖤 ▯ Ⅴ ✂ 🖍 TV
◉ ▥ 🛆 🍽 🖉 🕭 ✿ 🖄 DAP 🖄
SP

Sharks Fin Hotel

♛♛

The Quay, Mevagissey,
PL26 6QU
☎ (072 684) 3241
*Old historic building situated
on the quay, tastefully
converted into a hotel.*
Bedrooms: 2 single, 5 double
& 1 twin, 3 family rooms.
Bathrooms: 4 private,
2 public; 7 private showers.
Bed & breakfast: £13.50-£17
single, £27-£45 double.
Lunch available.
Evening meal 5.45pm (l.o.
9.45pm).
Open February-November.
Credit: Access, Visa, Diners,
Amex.

🛇 🖵 🖵 🖤 ▯ Ⅴ 🖍 ▥ 🛆
🍽 🖄 🖄

Steep House M

♛♛

Portmellon Cove,
Mevagissey, St. Austell,
PL26 2PH
☎ (0726) 843732 Telex 45526
YOULDEN

Continued ▶

MEVAGISSEY
Continued

Bedrooms have tea/coffee facilities, colour TV, full central heating, some en-suite. Offers home cooking, private parking, outdoor pool and winter breaks. Breathtaking views.
Bedrooms: 6 double & 1 twin.
Bathrooms: 1 private, 2 public; 1 private shower.
Bed & breakfast: £23-£36 double.
Half board: £19.50-£26 daily.
Lunch available.
Evening meal 7pm (l.o. 7pm).
Parking for 10.

Treleaven Farm Guest House M
Mevagissey, St. Austell, PL26 6RZ
☎ (0726) 842413
200-acre mixed farm. Quiet position overlooking Mevagissey, only a few minutes' walk from the harbour.
Bedrooms: 4 double & 1 twin, 1 family room.
Bathrooms: 6 private, 1 public.
Bed & breakfast: £32-£44 double.
Half board: £145-£220 weekly.
Evening meal 6.30pm (l.o. 8pm).
Parking for 10.
Credit: Access, Visa.

Tremarne Hotel M
APPROVED
Polkirt, Mevagissey, St. Austell, PL26 6UY
☎ (0726) 842213
Situated in a quiet secluded area with views of sea and country. Within easy reach of Mevagissey harbour and Portmellon bathing beach.
Bedrooms: 8 double & 4 twin, 2 family rooms.
Bathrooms: 14 private, 1 public.
Bed & breakfast: £22-£22.50 single, £37-£44 double.
Half board: £26-£32 daily, £175-£196 weekly.
Evening meal 7pm (l.o. 8pm).
Parking for 14.
Open March-November.
Credit: Access, Visa.

Trevalsa Court Hotel M
Polstreath Hill, Mevagissey, St. Austell, PL26 6TH
☎ (0726) 842468
Clifftop position with superb sea views and access to beach in peaceful surroundings. Ideal for touring. Ample car parking. Accent on fresh food, vegetarian/special diets. Ground floor room ideal for disabled persons.
Bedrooms: 1 single, 4 double & 3 twin, 2 family rooms.
Bathrooms: 10 private.
Bed & breakfast: £20-£23 single, £19-£24 double.
Half board: £29-£35 daily, £196-£238 weekly.
Lunch available.
Evening meal 6.30pm (l.o. 9pm).
Parking for 40.
Credit: Access, Visa, Diners, Amex.

MILTON DAMEREL
Devon
Map ref 1C2

5m NE. Holsworthy
Tiny village beside the Rivers Waldon and Torridge, within easy reach of the charming market town of Great Torrington.

Woodford Bridge Hotel M
Milton Damerel, Holsworthy, EX22 7LL
☎ (040 926) 481 Fax (040 926) 328
Pretty, thatched coaching inn retaining many original features. A la carte and carvery restaurants. Indoor pool and sports facilities. On A388 between Holsworthy and Bideford.
Bedrooms: 1 single, 9 double & 2 twin.
Bathrooms: 12 private.
Bed & breakfast: £41-£50 single, £68-£80 double.
Half board: £52.50-£60 daily, £313-£360 weekly.
Lunch available.
Evening meal 7pm (l.o. 9pm).
Parking for 100.
Credit: Access, Visa, Diners, Amex.

Please check prices and other details at the time of booking.

MINEHEAD
Somerset
Map ref 1D1

Victorian resort with spreading sands developed around old, steeply-built fishing port on the coast below Exmoor. Former fishermen's cottages stand beside the 17th C harbour; cobbled streets of thatched cottages climb the hill in steps to the church. Boat trips, steam railway. Hobby Horse festival on 1 May.
Tourist Information Centre ☎ (0643) 702624

Kildare Lodge M
COMMENDED
Townsend Rd., Minehead, TA24 5RQ
☎ (0643) 702009 & (0643) 706516
An Edward Lutyens designed grade II listed building. Elegant a la carte, licensed bar. Comfortable en-suite accommodation. Open all year.
Bedrooms: 2 single, 4 double & 2 twin, 4 family rooms.
Bathrooms: 12 private.
Bed & breakfast: £19.50-£24.50 single, £32.50-£49.50 double.
Half board: £38.50-£42.50 daily, £195-£225 weekly.
Lunch available.
Evening meal 6.30pm (l.o. 9.30pm).
Parking for 38.
Credit: Access, Visa, Diners, Amex.

Marston Lodge Hotel M
COMMENDED
St. Michaels Rd., North Hill, Minehead, TA24 5JP
☎ (0643) 702510
In lovely gardens with excellent sea and moorland views. Offering value for money, comfort and good accommodation.
Bedrooms: 2 single, 5 double & 2 twin, 3 family rooms.
Bathrooms: 12 private.
Bed & breakfast: £16-£20 single, £32-£40 double.
Half board: £23-£28 daily, £158-£180 weekly.
Lunch available.
Evening meal 7pm (l.o. 7.30pm).
Parking for 7.
Open February-December.
Credit: Access, Visa.

Mayfair Hotel and Annexe
25 The Avenue, Minehead, TA24 5AZ
☎ (0643) 702719/702052
Dutch/English family-run, conveniently situated on level, 3 minutes shops and sea. Good home cooking. Decorated to high standard.
Bedrooms: 4 single, 7 double & 10 twin, 4 family rooms.
Bathrooms: 25 private.
Bed & breakfast: £19-£22 single, £40-£45 double.
Half board: £27-£28 daily, £140-£150 weekly.
Lunch available.
Evening meal 6.30pm (l.o. 9.30pm).
Parking for 22.
Credit: Access, Visa.

Mentone Hotel M
APPROVED
The Parks, Minehead, TA24 8BS
☎ (0643) 705229
Quiet, comfortable and near shops. All rooms have radio, TV, tea/coffee; most have private facilities.
Bedrooms: 2 single, 4 double & 3 twin.
Bathrooms: 7 private, 1 public.
Bed & breakfast: £15-£19 single, £30-£38 double.
Half board: £20-£24 daily, £115-£145 weekly.
Evening meal 6.45pm (l.o. 6.45pm).
Parking for 9.
Open April-October.

Northfield Hotel M
Northfield Rd., Minehead, TA24 5PU
☎ (0643) 705155 Telex 42513
Best Western
Set amidst 2 acres of beautiful gardens with views over hills and sea. High standard of hospitality and service. Indoor heated pool, gym and steam bath.
Bedrooms: 2 single, 7 double & 9 twin, 6 family rooms.
Bathrooms: 24 private.
Bed & breakfast: from £39 single, from £68 double.
Half board: from £46 daily, from £295 weekly.
Lunch available.
Evening meal 7pm (l.o. 8.15pm).
Parking for 44.

Credit: Access, Visa, Diners, Amex.

MODBURY

Devon
Map ref 1C3

Attractive South Hams town set in rolling countryside, whose Perpendicular church has a rare Devon spire.

Trebles Cottage Hotel

Kingston, Kingsbridge, TQ7 4PT
☎ Bigbury-on-Sea
(0548) 810268
Attractive 1801 cottage in large secluded grounds on village edge. High standard of food and comfort. Homely atmosphere.
Bedrooms: 3 double & 2 twin.
Bathrooms: 5 private.
Bed & breakfast: £33-£35 single, £44-£50 double.
Half board: £225-£250 weekly.
Lunch available.
Evening meal 7.15pm (l.o. 6pm).
Parking for 10.
Credit: Visa.

MONTACUTE

Somerset
Map ref 2A3

Picturesque estate village named after its 'steep hill' and noted for its splendid Elizabethan mansion of Ham stone. By the village church stands the gatehouse of a Cluniac priory, built with stone from the hilltop castle. An 18th C folly now crowns the hill, where the Holy Cross of Waltham Abbey was found.

Kings Arms Inn ♙
COMMENDED
Montacute, TA15 6UU
☎ Martock (0935) 822513
Picturesque 16th C hamstone inn situated in unspoilt Somerset village. Ideal touring location for West Country. Under personal supervision of proprietors.
Bedrooms: 8 double & 3 twin.
Bathrooms: 11 private.
Bed & breakfast: £42-£55 single, £58-£72 double.

Half board: £215-£330 weekly.
Lunch available.
Evening meal 7.30pm (l.o. 10pm).
Parking for 20.
Credit: Access, Visa, Amex.

MORETON-HAMPSTEAD

Devon
Map ref 1C2

Small market town with a row of 17th C almshouses standing on the Exeter road. Surrounding moorland is scattered with ancient farmhouses, prehistoric sites.

Cookshayes Country Guest House ♙
COMMENDED
33 Court St., Moretonhampstead, TQ13 8LG
☎ (0647) 40374
Guesthouse with antiques in 1-acre of attractive gardens on edge of Dartmoor. Accent on food and comfort.
Bedrooms: 1 single, 4 double & 2 twin, 1 family room.
Bathrooms: 6 private, 2 public.
Bed & breakfast: £18 single, £31-£39 double.
Half board: £26-£30 daily, £175-£192.50 weekly.
Evening meal 7pm (l.o. 5pm).
Parking for 15.
Open March-October.
Credit: Access, Visa.

Gate House
North Bovey, Newton Abbot, TQ13 8RB
☎ (0647) 40479
15th C thatched house in a beautiful Dartmoor village. Offering peace, seclusion and comfort. Traditional or vegetarian cooking. Closed at Christmas.
Bedrooms: 2 double & 1 twin.
Bathrooms: 3 private.
Bed & breakfast: £40 double.
Half board: £30 daily, £210 weekly.
Evening meal 7.30pm.
Parking for 4.

Three Crowns Hotel ♙
High St., Chagford, TQ13 8AJ
☎ (064 73) 3444

13th C hotel of character situated in picturesque village within Dartmoor National Park. Centrally heated with period furnishings including 2 four-poster beds. Function room.
Bedrooms: 4 single, 8 double & 6 twin, 2 family rooms.
Bathrooms: 8 private, 3 public.
Bed & breakfast: £22.50-£30 single, £45-£60 double.
Half board: £37-£40 daily, £185-£210 weekly.
Lunch available.
Evening meal 7pm (l.o. 9.30pm).
Parking for 21.
Credit: Access, Visa, C.Bl.

White Hart Hotel ♙

The Square, Moretonhampstead, TQ13 8NF
☎ (0647) 40406
Ⓒ Minotels
20-roomed historic inn in centre of moorland town. Antiques, log fires, rural bar. A la carte restaurant and bar meals.
Bedrooms: 1 single, 9 double & 6 twin, 4 family rooms.
Bathrooms: 20 private, 1 public.
Bed & breakfast: £33-£35 single, £53-£57 double.
Lunch available.
Evening meal 6pm (l.o. 8.30pm).
Parking for 12.
Credit: Access, Visa, Diners, Amex.

MORTEHOE

Devon
Map ref 1C1

Old coastal village with small, basically Norman church. Wild cliffs, inland combes; sand and surf at Woolacombe.

The Cleeve House ♙
COMMENDED
Mortehoe, Woolacombe, EX34 7ED
☎ Woolacombe
(0271) 870719
Newly refurbished Victorian house set in its own grounds, in the old world village of Mortehoe.
Bedrooms: 4 double & 2 twin.
Bathrooms: 4 private, 1 public.
Bed & breakfast: max. £19 single, £28-£36 double.

Half board: £184-£240 weekly.
Parking for 9.
Open March-November.

Gull Rock
Mortehoe, Woolacombe, EX34 7EA
☎ Woolacombe
(0271) 870534
Attractive Edwardian house quietly set amidst National Trust land with spectacular views, scenic walks, sandy beaches and secluded coves.
Bedrooms: 1 single, 2 double & 1 twin, 2 family rooms.
Bathrooms: 6 private, 1 public.
Bed & breakfast: £16.50-£17.50 single, £33-£35 double.
Half board: £19-£20 daily, £125-£130 weekly.
Evening meal 7pm (l.o. 7pm).
Parking for 7.

Sunnycliffe Hotel ♙

Mortehoe, Woolacombe, EX34 7EB
☎ Woolacombe
(0271) 870597
Small, select hotel beautifully situated above sandy cove overlooking beach. Traditional English food cooked by qualified chef/proprietor. Sorry no children or pets.
Bedrooms: 6 double & 2 twin.
Bathrooms: 8 private, 2 public.
Bed & breakfast: £22-£26 single, £38-£48 double.
Half board: £33-£37 daily, £176-£218 weekly.
Evening meal 7pm (l.o. 7pm).
Parking for 11.
Open February-November.

> **Individual proprietors have supplied all details of accommodation. Although we do check for accuracy, we advise you to confirm prices and other information at the time of booking.**

413

MOUSEHOLE

Cornwall
Map ref 1A3

2m S. Penzance
Old fishing port completely rebuilt after destruction in the 16th C by Spanish raiders. Twisting lanes and granite cottages with luxuriant gardens rise steeply from the harbour; just south is a private bird sanctuary.

Carn Du Hotel
♛♛♛
Raginnis Hill, Mousehole, Penzance, TR19 6SS
☎ Penzance (0736) 731233
An elegant Victorian house in an elevated position above Mousehole. Cosy lounge, delightful cocktail bar and licensed restaurant specialising in seafood and local vegetables. Terraced gardens.
Bedrooms: 1 single, 3 double & 3 twin.
Bathrooms: 7 private.
Bed & breakfast: £25-£30 single, £40-£50 double.
Half board: £32.50-£37.50 daily, £213.50-£245 weekly.
Lunch available.
Evening meal 7pm (l.o. 8.30pm).
Parking for 12.
Open January, March-December.
Credit: Access, Visa, Amex.
🛏 ⊕ ♿ 🅿 🛁 V 🖥 TV 🎛 ⚓
🎿 🐾 SP

Lobster Pot ♨
Mousehole, Penzance, TR19 6QX
☎ Penzance (0736) 731251
Perched on the harbour's edge in Mousehole, this unique hotel and restaurant offers a standard of comfort and cuisine out of the ordinary.
Bedrooms: 3 single, 12 double & 6 twin, 5 family rooms.
Bathrooms: 23 private, 1 public.
Bed & breakfast: £22-£35 single, £46-£77 double.
Half board: £31-£48.85 daily, £200-£342 weekly.
Lunch available.
Evening meal 7.30pm (l.o. 9.45pm).
Open January, March-December.
Credit: Access, Visa, Amex.
🛏 ♿ ☎ ⊕ 🅿 ♨ 🍴 V 🖥
🎛 ⚓ 🐕 🐾 SP 🌷
🅰 Display advertisement appears on page 459.

Tavis Vor Hotel
The Parade, Mousehole, Penzance, TR19 6PR
☎ Penzance (0736) 731306
One of the closest properties to the sea from the Lizard to Land's End. Panoramic views and private access to sea.
Bedrooms: 1 single, 4 double & 1 twin, 1 family room.
Bathrooms: 3 private, 1 public.
Bed & breakfast: £18.60-£19.50 single, £41.20-£43.20 double.
Half board: £28.10-£29.30 daily, £196.70-£205.10 weekly.
Lunch available.
Evening meal 7pm (l.o. 5pm).
Parking for 7.
Credit: Visa.
🛏 5 ♿ 🅿 🛁 TV 🎛 🌷 🐾

MULLION

Cornwall
Map ref 1B3

Small holiday village with a golf-course, set back from the coast. The church has a serpentine tower of 1500, carved roof and beautiful medieval bench-ends. Beyond Mullion Cove, with its tiny harbour, wild untouched cliffs stretch south-eastward toward Lizard Point.

Marconi Private Hotel ♨
♛♛♛ **APPROVED**
Cove Rd., Mullion, TR12 7DH
☎ (0326) 240483
Victorian house in unspoilt seaside village. TV and tea making in all rooms. Bar and car park. Cliff walks, golf-course, fishing etc.
Bedrooms: 1 single, 4 double, 2 family rooms.
Bathrooms: 3 private, 2 public.
Bed & breakfast: from £13.50 single, £27-£38 double.
Half board: £22-£26 daily.
Lunch available.
Evening meal 6.30pm (l.o. 8.30pm).
Parking for 10.
🛏 ♿ ⚓ 🅿 ⊕ 🛁 V 🖥 🍴 🎛 ⚓ 🍴 🐾 SP

Mullion Cove Hotel ♨
♛♛♛ **APPROVED**
Mullion Cove, Mullion, TR12 7EP
☎ (0326) 240328
A beautiful late Victorian hotel overlooking Mullion Cove and harbour. A warm and friendly atmosphere.

Bedrooms: 9 single, 13 double & 9 twin, 4 family rooms.
Bathrooms: 21 private, 6 public.
Bed & breakfast: £22-£33 single, £44-£66 double.
Half board: £35-£46 daily, £243-£299 weekly.
Lunch available.
Evening meal 7pm (l.o. 8.30pm).
Parking for 50.
Open March-November.
Credit: Access, Visa, Diners.
🛏 ♿ ☎ 🅿 🛁 V 🖥 TV ⚓
🍴 ⊕ 🐾 🍴 ♿ 🅿 🌷 🐕 🅳🅰🅿
🎿 SP 🐾

Tregaddra Farm ♨
♛♛ **COMMENDED**
Cury, Helston, TR12 7BB
☎ Mullion (0326) 240235
120-acre beef and arable farm. Early 18th C farmhouse with good views of sea, coast and countryside. Home produce used.
Bedrooms: 1 single, 2 double, 2 family rooms.
Bathrooms: 4 private, 1 public.
Bed & breakfast: from £15 single, from £30 double.
Half board: from £20 daily, from £140 weekly.
Evening meal 6.30pm (l.o. 10am).
Parking for 8.
🛏 ♿ 🖥 🛁 TV ⚓ 🍴 🌷 🐕 🐾
SP

NETHER STOWEY

Somerset
Map ref 1D1

6m W. Bridgwater
Winding village below east slopes of Quantocks with attractive old cottages of varying periods. A Victorian clock tower stands at its centre, where a village road climbs the hill beside a small stream.

Meadow House
Sea La., Kilve, Bridgwater, TA5 1EG
☎ Holford (027 874) 546
Comfortable, spacious, family-run hotel in peaceful country setting close to sea and hills.
Bedrooms: 5 double & 3 twin.
Bathrooms: 8 private.
Bed & breakfast: £43-£57 single, £74-£84 double.
Half board: £50-£60 daily, £315-£378 weekly.
Evening meal 8pm (l.o. 8pm).
Parking for 12.
Credit: Access, Visa, Amex.
🛏 ♿ ⚓ ⊕ 🅿 ⚓ 🖥 🛁 🍴
⚓ 🍴 ⚓ ⊕ 🌷 🐕 SP 🐾

NEWLYN

Cornwall
Map ref 1A3

1m S. Penzance
Cornwall's main fishing port, with a busy harbour and solid grey houses. By the harbour is the handsome building of the deep-sea fishermen's mission. The Passmore Edwards Gallery (known as the Newlyn Art Gallery), which exhibits local work, was built for the 19th C artists' colony which later moved to St. Ives.

Panorama Private Hotel
♛♛♛
Chywoone Hill, Newlyn, Penzance, TR18 5AR
☎ (0736) 68498
Panoramic views of Mount's Bay from nearly all rooms. Modern house and amenities. Friendly atmosphere and personal attention.
Bedrooms: 2 single, 5 double & 1 twin.
Bathrooms: 4 private, 1 public.
Bed & breakfast: £16-£19 single, £32-£38 double.
Half board: £25-£28 daily, £166-£186 weekly.
Evening meal 7pm (l.o. 4pm).
Parking for 12.
Credit: Access, Visa, Diners, Amex.
🛏 3 ♿ ⊕ 🅿 ⊕ 🛁 🖥 ●
🎛 ⚓ 🍴 🅿 🌷 🐕 🐾 SP

NEWQUAY

Cornwall
Map ref 1B2

Popular resort spread over dramatic cliffs around its old fishing port. Many beaches with abundant sands, caves and rock pools; excellent surf. Pilots' gigs are still raced from the harbour and on the headland stands the Huer's House of whitewashed stone, surviving from pilchard-fishing days.
Tourist Information Centre ☎ (0637) 871345

Aloha Guest House
♛♛
124 Henver Rd., Newquay, TR7 3EQ
☎ (0637) 878366

Friendly, comfortable family-run guesthouse with home cooking. Well situated for beaches, touring Cornwall and Newquay nightlife.
Bedrooms: 3 single, 2 double, 4 family rooms.
Bathrooms: 2 public; 4 private showers.
Bed & breakfast: £12-£16 single, £24-£32 double.
Half board: £15-£23 daily, £93-£130 weekly.
Evening meal 6.30pm (l.o. 10am).
Parking for 14.
Open February-December.
Credit: Access, Visa.

Bay Hotel M

Esplanade Rd., Newquay, TR7 1PT
☎ (0637) 872988
Fully-licensed hotel offering regular dancing and cabaret.
Bedrooms: 17 single, 25 double & 45 twin, 9 family rooms.
Bathrooms: 96 private.
Bed & breakfast: £21-£22 single, £42-£44 double.
Half board: £29-£30 daily, £160-£200 weekly.
Lunch available.
Evening meal 6.30pm (l.o. 8.30pm).
Parking for 65.
Open March-October, December.
Credit: Access, Visa.

Beach Hotel

Watergate Bay, Newquay
☎ (0637) 860238
Family hotel, 3 miles from Newquay and 100 yards from attractive Watergate beach. Entertainment, licensed bar and swimming pool.
Bedrooms: 4 single, 13 double & 5 twin, 21 family rooms.
Bathrooms: 36 private, 2 public.
Bed & breakfast: £17-£30 single, £34-£60 double.
Half board: £25-£38 daily, £100-£250 weekly.
Lunch available.
Evening meal 7pm (l.o. 8pm).
Parking for 36.
Open April-September.

Bedruthan Steps Hotel

Mawgan Porth, Newquay, TR8 4BU
☎ St. Mawgan (0637) 860555

Everything for a perfect family holiday in Cornwall, offering a high standard of facilities. 6 miles from Newquay.
Bedrooms: 6 single, 11 double & 6 twin, 53 family rooms.
Bathrooms: 76 private.
Half board: £18-£44 daily, £126-£308 weekly.
Lunch available.
Evening meal 7.30pm (l.o. 8.45pm).
Parking for 80.
Open March-November.
Credit: Access, Visa.

Charlton House Hotel M

6 Hilgrove Rd., Newquay, TR7 2QY
☎ (0637) 873392
Family hotel close to beaches and within easy walking distance of zoo, leisure gardens and shops. Tea and coffee facilities, TV in all rooms. Heated outdoor swimming pool.
Bedrooms: 3 single, 13 double & 8 twin, 4 family rooms.
Bathrooms: 15 private, 3 public.
Bed & breakfast: £12-£17.50 single, £24-£35 double.
Half board: £14.50-£22 daily, £99-£149 weekly.
Evening meal 6.30pm (l.o. 7pm).
Parking for 15.
Open April-October.
Credit: Access, Visa.

Coranne Guest House

25 Hilgrove Rd., Newquay, TR7 2QZ
☎ (0637) 873864
Bungalow guest house standing in its own grounds. Close to all amenities.
Bedrooms: 1 single, 2 double & 1 twin, 3 family rooms.
Bathrooms: 4 private, 1 public.
Bed & breakfast: £15-£17.50 single, £30-£35 double.
Half board: £21-£24 daily, £116-£134 weekly.
Evening meal 6.15pm.
Parking for 10.

Corisande Manor Hotel M

Riverside Ave., Pentire, Newquay, TR7 1PL
☎ (0637) 872042

South facing with 3 acres of peaceful grounds. Private foreshore, rowing boats and solarium. Same ownership since 1968.
Bedrooms: 5 single, 8 double & 3 twin, 3 family rooms.
Bathrooms: 16 private, 7 public.
Bed & breakfast: £15-£23.50 single, £30-£47 double.
Half board: £20-£28.50 daily, £120-£165 weekly.
Lunch available.
Evening meal 7pm (l.o. 7.30pm).
Parking for 19.
Open May-October.
Credit: Access, Visa.

The Croft

37 Mount Wise, Newquay, TR7 2BL
☎ (0637) 875088
Friendly atmosphere with resident proprietors. Only 4 minutes from town centre and beaches.
Bedrooms: 2 single, 4 double, 3 family rooms.
Bathrooms: 2 public.
Bed & breakfast: £11-£14 single, £22-£28 double.
Half board: £15-£19 daily, £100-£130 weekly.
Evening meal 6pm (l.o. 2pm).
Parking for 6.
Open March-November.

Eliot-Cavendish Hotel

Edgecumbe Ave., Newquay, TR7 2NH
☎ (0637) 878177/8
Large family hotel situated close to beaches. Heated outdoor pool, sauna and solarium.
Bedrooms: 6 single, 33 double & 23 twin, 13 family rooms.
Bathrooms: 75 private.
Bed & breakfast: £30-£50 double.
Half board: £22-£32 daily, £100-£195 weekly.
Lunch available.
Evening meal 7pm (l.o. 7.30pm).
Parking for 35.
Open March-November.
Credit: Access, Visa.

Euro Hotel M

APPROVED

9 Esplanade Rd., Pentire, Newquay, TR7 1PS
☎ (0637) 873333

Overlooking Fistral Bay with heated swimming pool. car park, games room, sauna and spa bath. All rooms with telephone and colour TV.
Bedrooms: 7 single, 22 double & 10 twin, 39 family rooms.
Bathrooms: 76 private, 2 public.
Bed & breakfast: £25-£49 single.
Lunch available.
Evening meal 7pm (l.o. 8.30pm).
Parking for 32.
Credit: Access, Visa.

Glendeveor Hotel

25-27 Mount Wise, Newquay, TR7 2BQ
☎ (0637) 872726
Family-run detached, centrally heated hotel with sea views and friendly atmosphere. Close to all amenities. Licensed, coach parties welcome.
Bedrooms: 3 single, 12 double & 3 twin, 7 family rooms.
Bathrooms: 13 private, 6 public.
Half board: £130-£179 weekly.
Evening meal 6.30pm (l.o. 7.30pm).
Parking for 31.
Credit: Access, Visa.

Hotel Palma Nova

21 Pentire Cres., Newquay, TR7 1PU
☎ (0637) 872979
A place for all the family to enjoy. Supervised by the resident proprietors. Solarium, sauna available. TV in all bedrooms.
Bedrooms: 3 single, 18 double & 5 twin, 11 family rooms.
Bathrooms: 36 private, 1 public.
Half board: £109-£184 weekly.
Evening meal 6.30pm (l.o. 6.30pm).
Parking for 35.
Open April-October.

Penruddock Hotel

58 Tower Rd., Newquay, TR7 1LU
☎ (0637) 876677

Continued ▶

A small family hotel situated opposite golf club and Fistral beach close to town and all amenities.
Bedrooms: 6 double & 1 twin, 5 family rooms.
Bathrooms: 1 private, 1 public; 11 private showers.
Bed & breakfast: £10-£18.50 single.
Half board: £12.50-£22.50 daily, £78-£132 weekly.
Evening meal 6pm.
Parking for 8.

Philema Hotel M

1 Esplanade Rd., Pentire, Newquay, TR7 1PY
☎ (0637) 872571
Recently refurbished family home with friendly, informal atmosphere overlooking Fistral Beach and golf-course. New leisure complex and apartments also available.
Bedrooms: 4 single, 8 double & 4 twin, 15 family rooms.
Bathrooms: 26 private, 4 public.
Bed & breakfast: £19.50-£23 single, £39-£46 double.
Half board: £24.50-£28 daily, £120-£190 weekly.
Evening meal 6.30pm (l.o. 7.30pm).
Parking for 31.
Open February-October.
Credit: Access, Visa.

Porth Enodoc Hotel M

APPROVED
4 Esplanade Rd., Pentire, Newquay, TR7 1PY
☎ (0637) 872372
In its own grounds overlooking Fistral Beach, set away from the town but within walking distance of the shopping centre.
Bedrooms: 2 single, 7 double & 3 twin, 3 family rooms.
Bathrooms: 15 private, 1 public.
Bed & breakfast: £15.50-£18 single, £31-£36 double.
Half board: £22-£24.50 daily, £106-£146 weekly.
Evening meal 6.45pm (l.o. 5.30pm).
Parking for 15.
Open March-October.

Porth Veor Manor M

Porth Way, Newquay, TR7 3LW
☎ (0637) 873274
19th C country manor house set in 2 acres, overlooking beach with magnificent sea views and private path to beach. 9-hole putting green and tennis court.
Bedrooms: 1 single, 9 double & 3 twin, 3 family rooms.
Bathrooms: 16 private, 1 public.
Bed & breakfast: £18.85-£31 single, £37.70-£66 double.
Half board: £22.85-£35 daily, £160-£217.25 weekly.
Lunch available.
Evening meal 6.30pm (l.o. 8pm).
Parking for 40.
Open January-October, December.
Credit: Access, Visa.

Quies Hotel M

APPROVED
84 Mount Wise, Newquay, TR7 2BS
☎ (0637) 872924
Family-run hotel in the centre of Newquay, with good sea views from most of the bedrooms and the dining room.
Bedrooms: 1 single, 5 double & 1 twin, 3 family rooms.
Bathrooms: 7 private, 2 public.
Bed & breakfast: £14-£22 single, £28-£44 double.
Half board: £19-£27 daily, £115-£163 weekly.
Lunch available.
Evening meal 6.30pm (l.o. 7.30pm).
Parking for 12.
Open March-December.
Credit: Access, Visa.

Sandown Guest House

19 Trenance Rd., Newquay, TR7 2LT
☎ (0637) 874742
Well-situated licensed guesthouse, clean, comfortable accommodation. All amenities within easy reach.
Bedrooms: 2 single, 1 double & 3 twin, 3 family rooms.
Bathrooms: 2 public; 2 private showers.
Bed & breakfast: £14-£16 single, £28-£32 double.
Half board: £17.50-£19.50 daily, £89-£109 weekly.
Evening meal 6pm (l.o. 6.30pm).
Open March-October.

Seavista Hotel

Mawgan Porth Newquay TR8 4AL
☎ Newquay (0637) 860276
A family-run hotel which puts the comfort of the guests foremost. Glorious sea and country views from most rooms.
Bedrooms: 2 single, 6 double & 1 twin, 1 family room.
Bathrooms: 1 public; 8 private showers.
Bed & breakfast: £10.50-£15 single, £21-£30 double.
Half board: £17.50-£22.50 daily.
Lunch available.
Evening meal 6.30pm (l.o. 7pm).
Parking for 10.

Tir Chonaill Lodge Hotel

106 Mount Wise, Newquay, TR7 1QP
☎ (0637) 876492
Licensed hotel offering a high standard of cooking and comfort. Close to town and beaches. Open all year. Free child accommodation in early or late season.
Bedrooms: 1 single, 9 double & 2 twin, 8 family rooms.
Bathrooms: 19 private, 1 public.
Bed & breakfast: from £14.75 single, £27-£34 double.
Half board: £95-£135 weekly.
Evening meal 6pm (l.o. 5pm).
Parking for 21.

Trebarwith Hotel

Island Estate, Newquay, TR7 1BZ
☎ (0637) 872288
Right on the sea edge with 350 feet of private sea frontage in a central position away from traffic noise.
Bedrooms: 3 single, 17 double & 16 twin, 6 family rooms.
Bathrooms: 42 private, 2 public.
Half board: £21-£40 daily, £145-£275 weekly.
Lunch available.
Evening meal 7.15pm (l.o. 8.30pm).
Parking for 35.
Open March-October.
Credit: Access, Visa.

Tregarn Hotel M

Pentire Cres., Newquay, TR7 1PX
☎ (0637) 874292
Family hotel with facilities for all weathers. Entertainment most nights.
Bedrooms: 6 single, 13 double & 7 twin, 16 family rooms.
Bathrooms: 34 private, 5 public.
Bed & breakfast: £14-£28 single, £28-£56 double.
Half board: £19-£33 daily, £129-£220 weekly.
Lunch available.
Evening meal 6.30pm (l.o. 7.30pm).
Parking for 50.
Open March-November.
Credit: Access, Visa.

Hotel Trevalsa

Whipsiderry, Porth, Newquay, TR7 3LX
☎ (0637) 873336
Modern, licensed hotel above beautiful Whipsiderry beach. Panoramic views of Newquay's coastline. Golf, fishing, wind-surfing, surfing, coastal and countryside walks.
Bedrooms: 3 single, 11 double & 3 twin, 5 family rooms.
Bathrooms: 18 private, 2 public; 2 private showers.
Bed & breakfast: £18-£28 single.
Half board: £20-£32 daily, £125-£199 weekly.
Evening meal 7pm (l.o. 7pm).
Parking for 20.
Open March-October.
Credit: Access, Visa.

Trevelgue Hotel

Porth, Newquay, TR8 2HR
☎ (0637) 872864
Purpose-built holiday hotel overlooking the ocean and surrounded by countryside. It has a comprehensive entertainment programme.
Bedrooms: 6 double & 12 twin, 52 family rooms.
Bathrooms: 70 private.
Bed & breakfast: £28-£40 single, £56-£80 double.
Half board: £33-£48 daily, £196-£280 weekly.
Evening meal 7.30pm (l.o. 9pm).
Parking for 75.
Open April-October.
Credit: Access, Visa.

Wheal Treasure Hotel
72 Edgcumbe Ave.,
Newquay, TR7 2NN
☎ (0637) 874136
*Lovely old house set in own
gardens adjacent to Trenance
Valley Gardens, bowling green,
tennis courts and zoo.*
Bedrooms: 1 single, 6 double
& 1 twin, 4 family rooms.
Bathrooms: 11 private,
2 public; 1 private shower.
Bed & breakfast: £16-£19
single, £32-£38 double.
Half board: £19-£22 daily,
£125-£150 weekly.
Evening meal 6.30pm (l.o.
5.30pm).
Parking for 10.
Open May-October.
🛇4 🖧 ♥ 🛉 ✕ 🖃 📺 ⠿ 🐾
🖾

Whipsiderry Hotel M
Trevelgue Rd., Porth,
Newquay, TR7 3LY
☎ (0637) 874777
*Set in own grounds overlooking
Porth Beach and Newquay
Bay.*
Bedrooms: 2 single, 11 double
& 2 twin, 5 family rooms.
Bathrooms: 20 private,
2 public.
Half board: £22-£37 daily,
£130-£190 weekly.
Evening meal 6.30pm (l.o.
8pm).
Parking for 30.
Open April-October.
🛇 🖧 ⓑ 🖵 ♥ 🛉 Ⓥ 🖃 📺
⠿ 🖾 🗶 🛉 ❋ SP

Windward Hotel
♨
Alexandra Rd., Porth,
Newquay, TR7 3NB
☎ (0637) 873185
*Newly extended hotel on
coastal road to Padstow,
overlooking Porth Bay. 1.5
miles north of Newquay.*
Bedrooms: 1 single, 10 double
& 1 twin, 2 family rooms.
Bathrooms: 14 private.
Bed & breakfast: £17-£23
single, £34-£46 double.
Half board: £22-£28 daily,
£124.25-£185 weekly.
Evening meal 6.30pm (l.o.
6.30pm).
Parking for 14.
🛇 🖧 🖵 ♥ 🛉 Ⓥ 🖃 📺 ⠿
🖾 🗶 🖾 🛝 SP

**Half board prices
shown are per
person but in some
cases may be based
on double/twin
occupancy.**

Devon
Map ref 1D2

Lively market town at the
head of the Teign
Estuary, a centre for the
clay mining district of
Dartmoor. A former
railway town, it is well-
placed for moorland or
seaside excursions.
Interesting old houses
nearby include Bradley
Manor dating from the
15th C and Forde House,
visited by Charles I and
William of Orange.
*Tourist Information
Centre ☎ (0626) 67494*

Hazelwood House
♨♨♨ APPROVED
33a Torquay Rd., Newton
Abbot, TQ12 2LW
☎ Newton Abbot
(0626) 66130
*Attractive, turn of the century
building in quiet residential
location, 5 minutes' walk from
town centre, rail and coach
stations. Own garden.*
Bedrooms: 1 single, 3 double
& 3 twin.
Bathrooms: 5 private,
2 public.
Bed & breakfast: £27.50-£33
single, £37.50-£44 double.
Half board: £35.75-£41 daily.
Lunch available.
Evening meal 7pm (l.o. 8pm).
Parking for 6.
Credit: Access, Visa.
🛇 🖧 📞 ⓑ 🖵 ♥ 🛉 Ⓥ ⠿

Passage House Hotel M
♨♨♨♨ COMMENDED
Hackney La., Kingsteignton,
Newton Abbot, TQ12 3QH
☎ (0626) 55515 Fax
(0626) 63336
*This modern hotel offers a high
standard of comfort and
service. Leave A380 for the
A381 and follow the racecourse
signs.*
Bedrooms: 10 single,
10 double & 10 twin, 9 family
rooms.
Bathrooms: 39 private.
Bed & breakfast: £63-£74
single, £97-£107 double.
Half board: from £76 daily.
Lunch available.
Evening meal 7pm (l.o.
9.30pm).
Parking for 200.
Credit: Access, Visa, Diners,
Amex.
🛇 🖧 📞 ⓑ 🖵 ♥ Ⓥ
❋ ⓣ 🗇 🖴 🛉 🛝 ▶
❋ 🛝 SP T

Devon
Map ref 1C2

6m NE. Okehampton

Kayden House Hotel
♨♨♨
High St., North Tawton,
EX20 2HF
☎ (0837) 82242
*Kayden House offers a
comfortable, homely
atmosphere, with lots of
country pursuits to enjoy.*
Bedrooms: 2 single, 2 double
& 2 twin, 1 family room.
Bathrooms: 5 private,
2 public.
Bed & breakfast: £18-£19.50
single, £28.50-£33 double.
Half board: £29-£30 daily,
£182-£204 weekly.
Lunch available.
Evening meal 7pm (l.o.
9.30pm).
Credit: Access, Visa.
🛇 🖵 ♥ 🛉 Ⓥ 🖃 📺 ⠿ 🖴
Ⓤ ▶ 🖾

Devon
Map ref 1D1

3m W. Bampton

Higher Western
Restaurant
Oakford, Tiverton, EX16 9JE
☎ Anstey Mills (039 84) 210
*Old world residential
restaurant, with accent on food
at realistic prices using fresh
local produce. Good touring
base.*
Bedrooms: 2 double & 1 twin.
Bathrooms: 3 private,
1 public.
Bed & breakfast: £12.50-£13
single, £25-£26 double.
Half board: £22.50-£23 daily,
£157.50-£161 weekly.
Lunch available.
Evening meal 7pm (l.o.
10pm).
Parking for 15.
Credit: Access, Visa.
🛇 🛉 Ⓥ 🖃 ⠿ 🖴 ❋ 🖾 SP

**Classifications
and quality
commendations
were correct at the
time of going to
press but are
subject to change.
Please check at the
time of booking.**

Devon
Map ref 1C2

Busy market town near
the high tors of Northern
Dartmoor. The Victorian
church, with William
Morris windows and a
15th C tower, stands on
the site of a Saxon
church.

Poltimore Guest House
♨♨♨ APPROVED
South Zeal, Okehampton,
EX20 2PD
☎ Okehampton
(0837) 840209
*Thatched country house on the
edge of Dartmoor with
panoramic views of Exmoor.*
Bedrooms: 2 single, 3 double
& 2 twin.
Bathrooms: 4 private,
1 public.
Bed & breakfast: £14-£19
single, £28-£38 double.
Half board: £23-£28 daily,
£141-£169 weekly.
Evening meal 7pm (l.o. 5pm).
Parking for 10.
♥ 🛉 Ⓥ 🖃 📺 ⠿ ❋ 🖾 🛝
SP T

Devon
Map ref 1D2

Former wool town with
modern light industry set
in countryside on the
River Otter. The
Cromwellian commander,
Fairfax, made his
headquarters here briefly
during the Civil War. The
interesting church is built
to cathedral plan, dating
from the 14th C. Rolling
of tar barrels custom on
Bonfire Night.

Fluxton Farm Hotel M
♨♨
Ottery St. Mary, EX11 1RJ
☎ (0404) 812818
*Spacious hotel in former
farmhouse with comfortable
bedrooms and sitting rooms.
Local fresh home-cooked food
served in candlelit dining room.
Log fires in season. Trout
fishing in the River Otter.*
Bedrooms: 3 single, 3 double
& 4 twin, 2 family rooms.
Bathrooms: 10 private,
1 public.
Bed & breakfast: £19.50-
£22.50 single, £39-£45 double.
Half board: £25-£29 daily,
£160-£190 weekly.
Continued ▶

OTTERY ST. MARY

Continued

Evening meal 6.50pm (l.o. 6pm).
Parking for 20.
🛇5 ⌷ ⊘ ♥ Ⅴ ⅍ ⊟ ⅏ ⅏ ▦
❄ ⋈ ⅍ ⒮⒫ ⅏

Stafford Hotel
5 Cornhill, Ottery St. Mary,
EX11 1DW
☎ (0404) 812025
Licensed, family-run and giving personal service in a relaxed and homely atmosphere.
Bedrooms: 1 single, 3 double & 3 twin, 1 family room.
Bathrooms: 8 private.
Bed & breakfast: £32.50-£36.50 single, £49-£54.50 double.
Half board: £39-£43.50 daily, £242-£269.50 weekly.
Lunch available.
Evening meal 6pm (l.o. 10.30pm).
Credit: Access, Visa, Amex.
🛇 ⌷ ⅊ Ⅴ ⊟ ⅏ ▦ ⅏ ⏾
⒟⒜⒫ ⅍ ⒮⒫ ⅏

PADSTOW

Cornwall
Map ref 1B2

Old town encircling its harbour on the Camel Estuary. The fine 15th C church overlooking the town has notable bench-ends and a carved font. There are fine houses such as the 15th C Abbey House on North Quay and Raleigh's Court House on South Quay. Tall cliffs and golden sands along the coast and ferry to Rock. Famous 'Obby 'Oss Festival on May Day.

The Cross House
Church St., Padstow,
PL28 8BG
☎ (0841) 532391
Peaceful Grade II Listed building in old part of Padstow, 300 yards from harbour. Small restaurant and pretty garden overlooking estuary.
Bedrooms: 1 single, 4 double & 1 twin, 1 family room.
Bathrooms: 2 private, 2 public.
Bed & breakfast: £15-£20 single, £40-£50 double.
Lunch available.
Evening meal 6pm.
🛇 ⌷ ⅊ ⊟ ⅏ ▦ ⅏ ⏾
⒟⒜⒫ ⅍ ⒮⒫ ⅏

The Dower House Private Hotel ⋒
⚜⚜⚜ COMMENDED
Fentonluna La., Padstow,
PL28 8BA
☎ (0841) 532317
Listed 19th C dower house, with views over Padstow, estuary and bird gardens. Few minutes from harbour.
Bedrooms: 1 single, 2 double & 2 twin, 3 family rooms.
Bathrooms: 5 private, 1 public.
Bed & breakfast: £20.50-£26.50 single, £31-£46 double.
Half board: £25.50-£33 daily, £161-£213.50 weekly.
Evening meal 7pm (l.o. 6.30pm).
Parking for 9.
Open March-December.
🛇 ⅊ ⊘ Ⅴ ⊟ ⅏ ▦ ⅏ ⅏
⏾ ⋈ ⅍ ⒮⒫ ⅏

Green Waves Hotel
⚜⚜⚜
Trevone, Padstow,
PL28 8RD
☎ Padstow (0841) 520114
Long established, small, family-run hotel in quiet cul-de-sac. Set in well-kept garden facing south to the sea. All rooms have colour TV. Half-size snooker table.
Bedrooms: 2 single, 9 double & 6 twin, 3 family rooms.
Bathrooms: 15 private, 4 public.
Bed & breakfast: £15-£19 single, £30-£38 double.
Half board: £21-£25 daily, £120-£150 weekly.
Evening meal 7pm (l.o. 7pm).
Parking for 17.
Open April-September.
🛇4 ⅊ ⌷ ⊘ ⊟ ⅏ ⅏ ⅏ ⋈ ⅏

Molesworth Manor
Little Petherick, Wadebridge,
PL27 7QT
☎ Rumford (0841) 540292
Elegant accommodation providing individual service in relaxed atmosphere. Most rooms furnished with antique furniture and retain many original features.
Bedrooms: 2 single, 6 double & 1 twin, 1 family room.
Bathrooms: 10 private.
Bed & breakfast: £12.50-£15 single, £28-£50 double.
Half board: £20-£37.50 daily, £119-£223.25 weekly.
Evening meal 7.20pm.
Parking for 15.
🛇4 ⅊ Ⅴ ⅍ ⊟ ⅏ ▦ ⏾ ⏾
⏾ ❄ ⋈ ⅍ ⅍ ⅏

St. Petroc's House Hotel
4 New St, Padstow,
PL28 8EA
☎ (0841) 532700
5th oldest building in Padstow. Renovated traditionally. Very friendly and situated centrally. English cooking.
Bedrooms: 2 single, 3 double & 3 twin, 3 family rooms.
Bathrooms: 8 private, 1 public.
Bed & breakfast: £25-£35 single, £40-£70 double.
Half board: £30-£45 daily, £189-£259 weekly.
Evening meal 6.30pm (l.o. 10pm).
Open March-December.
Credit: Access, Visa.
🛇 ⅊ ⌷ ⅊ ⊘ Ⅴ ⊟ ⅏
⏾ ⋈ ⅍ ⒮⒫ ⅏

Trevorrick Farm ⋒
Listed COMMENDED
St. Issey, Wadebridge,
PL27 7QH
☎ Rumford (0841) 540574
11-acre mixed farm. Delightful, comfortable farmhouse where quality and service come first. Located 1 mile from Padstow, overlooking Little Petherick Creek and the Camel Estuary.
Bedrooms: 2 double & 1 twin.
Bathrooms: 2 public.
Bed & breakfast: £14 single, £28 double.
Lunch available.
Parking for 9.
🛇 ⅊ ⅊ ⊟ ⅏ ▦ ⏾ ● ⅏ ⅏
⅊ ⅊ ❄ ⋈ ⊟ ⅍ ⒮⒫ ⅏

Woodlands Country House Hotel
⚜⚜⚜ APPROVED
Treator, Padstow, PL28 8RU
☎ (0841) 532426
Delightful country house in rural setting near beaches and golf-course, offering picturesque walks, modern amenities and choice of cuisine.
Bedrooms: 5 double & 1 twin, 3 family rooms.
Bathrooms: 9 private.
Bed & breakfast: £21.50-£23.50 single, £39-£43 double.
Half board: £27.50-£29.50 daily, £180-£195 weekly.
Evening meal 6.30pm (l.o. 5pm).
Parking for 15.
🛇 ⅊ ⊘ ⅊ Ⅴ ⊟ ⅏ ▦ ⅏
⅊ ⏾ ⅊ ❄ ⋈ ⅏ ⒟⒜⒫ ⅍ ⒮⒫ ⅏

PAIGNTON

Devon
Map ref 1D2

Lively seaside resort with a pretty harbour on Torbay. Bronze Age and Saxon sites are occupied by the 15th C church, which has a Norman door and font. The beautiful Chantry Chapel was built by local landowners, the Kirkhams, whose medieval family home is open to the public. *Tourist Information Centre ☎ (0803) 558383*

Bay Cottage Guest House
Listed APPROVED
4 Beach Rd., Paignton,
TQ4 6AY
☎ (0803) 525729
Delightful guesthouse, clean and comfortable, close to sea front. Home cooking. Torbay in Bloom award winners, 86, 87, 88, and 89.
Bedrooms: 3 single, 5 double & 1 twin, 1 family room.
Bathrooms: 2 private, 3 public.
Bed & breakfast: £10-£14 single, £20-£28 double.
Half board: £14-£17.50 daily, £75-£115 weekly.
Evening meal 6pm (l.o. 4pm).
🛇 ⅊ ⌷ ⊘ ⅊ Ⅴ ⅍ ⊟ ⏾
▦ ⅏ ⅊ ⏾ ⒟⒜⒫ ⅍ ⒮⒫

Channel View Private Hotel ⋒
8 Marine Pde., Paignton,
TQ3 2NU
☎ (0803) 522432
Situated on the water's edge with magnificent views over Torbay.
Bedrooms: 7 double & 2 twin, 3 family rooms.
Bathrooms: 12 private.
Bed & breakfast: £15-£25 single, £30-£50 double.
Half board: £20-£30 daily, £75-£195 weekly.
Lunch available.
Evening meal 6pm (l.o. 6pm).
Parking for 12.
Credit: Access.
🛇 ⅊ ⌷ ⊘ ⅊ ⊟ ⏾ ▦ ⅏
⅊ ⋈ ⅍ ⒮⒫ ⓣ

Cranmere Hotel ⋒
16, Youngs Pk. Rd.,
Goodrington, Paignton,
TQ4 6BU
☎ (0803) 557491
Licensed hotel overlooking park, 220 yards from beach. Close to Aqua Park and leisure centre. Renowned for cleanliness and cooking. Colour TV and tea facilities.

The symbols are explained on the flap inside the back cover.

Bedrooms: 3 single, 2 double, 6 family rooms.
Bathrooms: 3 public.
Bed & breakfast: £8-£16 single, £16-£32 double.
Half board: £13-£18 daily, £90-£124 weekly.
Evening meal 6pm.
Parking for 8.
Open May-September.

Danethorpe Hotel
APPROVED
23 St. Andrews Rd., Roundham, Paignton, TQ4 6HA
☎ (0803) 551251
Small, detached licensed hotel, close to all amenities. All rooms with colour TV, tea/coffee facilities, hair-dryer and clock radio. Car park.
Bedrooms: 2 single, 4 double & 2 twin, 2 family rooms.
Bathrooms: 4 private, 2 public.
Bed & breakfast: £14.50-£16.50 single, £29-£33 double.
Evening meal 6pm (l.o. 5.30pm).
Parking for 9.
Credit: Access, Visa.

Haldon Hotel
6 Beach Rd., Paignton, TQ4 6AY
☎ (0803) 551120
Small family-run licensed hotel with home cooking. Approximately 75 yards level walk to beach and all amenities.
Bedrooms: 2 single, 5 double & 2 twin, 1 family room.
Bathrooms: 1 public.
Bed & breakfast: £11-£15 single, £22-£30 double.
Half board: £14.50-£18.50 daily, £92-£109 weekly.
Lunch available.
Evening meal 6pm (l.o. 6pm).

Homestead
27 Kings Rd., Paignton, TQ3 2AN
☎ (0803) 551135
Small, homely guesthouse close to the beaches and town. Home-cooked food and friendly atmosphere.
Bedrooms: 1 single, 2 double & 1 twin, 2 family rooms.
Bathrooms: 1 public.
Bed & breakfast: £8.50-£9.50 single, £17-£19 double.
Half board: £12.50-£13.50 daily, £87.50-£94.50 weekly.
Evening meal 6pm (l.o. 4pm).

Marine Hotel
Seafront Paignton, TQ4 6AP
☎ (0803) 559778
Situated in the heart of Paignton on the level and right on the seafront, with panoramic views from all the public rooms and most bedrooms.
Bedrooms: 7 single, 3 double & 12 twin, 8 family rooms.
Bathrooms: 7 private, 4 public.
Bed & breakfast: £14-£18 single, £28-£36 double.
Half board: £17-£23 daily, £115-£145 weekly.
Lunch available.
Evening meal 6pm (l.o. 6pm).
Parking for 20.
Credit: Access, Visa.

Newholme Guest House
Listed
119 Torquay Rd., Paignton, TQ3 2SF
☎ (0803) 558289
Conveniently situated near beach, park, shops and all amenities. Open all year including Christmas (special rates).
Bedrooms: 2 double, 3 family rooms.
Bathrooms: 1 public.
Bed & breakfast: £10-£12.50 single, £20-£25 double.
Half board: £12.50-£15 daily, £75-£95 weekly.
Evening meal 6pm (l.o. 4pm).

Palm Beach Hotel M
49 Dartmouth Rd., Paignton, TQ4 5AE
☎ (0803) 558638
Small friendly hotel offering comfortable accommodation. Short level walk from town and beaches.
Bedrooms: 1 single, 5 double & 1 twin, 2 family rooms.
Bathrooms: 2 private, 1 public.
Bed & breakfast: £13.50-£15.50 single, £27-£31 double.
Half board: £20-£22 daily, £130-£149 weekly.
Evening meal 6pm (l.o. 9pm).
Parking for 6.
Credit: Access, Visa.

Palm Trees Guest House
3 Warefield Rd., Paignton, TQ3 2BH
☎ (0803) 559636

Family-run, with comfortable accommodation and relaxed atmosphere. Close to the beach. Showers available and tea-making facilities. Open all year.
Bedrooms: 1 single, 3 double & 1 twin, 4 family rooms.
Bathrooms: 1 public; 4 private showers.
Bed & breakfast: £8-£13 single, £16-£26 double.
Half board: £13-£18 daily, £80-£120 weekly.
Evening meal 6.30pm.
Parking for 6.

Preston Sands Hotel M
10/12 Marine Pde., Sea Front, Preston, Paignton, TQ3 2NU
☎ (0803) 558718
Hotel is situated 15 yards from the water's edge. All bedrooms are en-suite with radio, TV, tea making facilities. Parking.
Bedrooms: 1 single, 17 double & 8 twin.
Bathrooms: 24 private, 3 public.
Bed & breakfast: £18-£30 single, £32-£44 double.
Half board: £24-£29 daily, £125-£195 weekly.
Lunch available.
Evening meal 6pm (l.o. 7pm).
Parking for 24.

Redcliffe Hotel
Marine Dr., Paignton, TQ3 2NL
☎ (0803) 526397
Fax (0803) 528030
A choice location in 4 acres of grounds directly adjoining the beach. Games room and an outdoor swimming pool.
Bedrooms: 16 single, 18 double & 25 twin, 4 family rooms.
Bathrooms: 63 private, 3 public.
Bed & breakfast: £32-£40 single, £64-£80 double.
Half board: £38-£50 daily, £240-£336 weekly.
Evening meal 7pm (l.o. 8.30pm).
Parking for 100.
Credit: Access, Visa.

Hotel Retreat
43 Marine Dr., Paignton, TQ3 2NS
☎ (0803) 550596

Small private hotel in own grounds. On the level opposite sandy Preston beach. Suitable for all ages.
Bedrooms: 1 single, 7 double & 2 twin, 3 family rooms.
Bathrooms: 5 private, 3 public; 1 private shower.
Bed & breakfast: £16-£20 single, £32-£40 double.
Half board: £22-£30 daily, £132-£180 weekly.
Evening meal 6.45pm (l.o. 6pm).
Parking for 14.
Open April-October.
Credit: Access, Visa.

Roscrea Hotel M
2 Alta Vista Rd., Paignton, TQ4 6BZ
☎ (0803) 558706
Quiet, sunny position near the harbour and 2 beaches. Beautiful views of Torbay. All bedrooms en-suite.
Bedrooms: 1 single, 9 double & 3 twin, 4 family rooms.
Bathrooms: 17 private.
Bed & breakfast: £18-£25 single, £36-£50 double.
Half board: £22-£29 daily, £145-£180 weekly.
Evening meal 6.15pm.
Parking for 17.
Open March-October, December.
Credit: Access, Visa.

Rosslyn Hotel
Listed **COMMENDED**
16 Colin Rd., Paignton, TQ3 2NR
☎ (0803) 525578
Small family hotel 100 yards from the beach. Old world lounge bar, dance floor, party night. Bar snacks available. Video television.
Bedrooms: 1 single, 4 double, 5 family rooms.
Bathrooms: 4 private, 2 public.
Half board: £102-£145 weekly.
Evening meal 6pm (l.o. 6pm).
Parking for 8.

Sea Park Hotel M
15 Garfield Rd., Paignton, TQ4 6AX
☎ (0803) 556071
Quiet location overlooking Victoria Park. 150 yards from beach and very near shopping areas. Easy walking distance for coach and railway stations.

Continued ▶

PAIGNTON

Continued

Bedrooms: 1 single, 6 double
& 2 twin, 9 family rooms.
Bathrooms: 8 private,
4 public.
Bed & breakfast: £14-£20
single, £28-£40 double.
Half board: £18-£24 daily,
£120-£145 weekly.
Evening meal 6pm (l.o.
10am).
Parking for 14.
Credit: Access, Visa.

Seaford Hotel ♠
♨♨♨♨
2-4 Stafford Rd., Paignton,
TQ4 6EU
☎ (0803) 557341
*Family hotel with resident
proprietor. Level position close
to all amenities. Quiet cul-de-
sac siding onto cricket ground.*
Bedrooms: 2 single, 7 double
& 10 twin, 3 family rooms.
Bathrooms: 20 private.
Bed & breakfast: £25 single,
£45 double.
Half board: £35.50 daily,
£150-£200 weekly.
Evening meal 6.30pm (l.o.
8.30pm).
Parking for 10.
Credit: Access, Visa.

Silversea Guest House
♒
14 Norman Rd., Paignton,
TQ3 2BE
☎ (0803) 556331
*Small friendly guesthouse in a
level position, adjacent to
seafront, and short walk to
town, rail and bus stations.*
Bedrooms: 1 single, 1 double
& 1 twin, 2 family rooms.
Bathrooms: 2 public.
Bed & breakfast: £8.50-£12
single, £17-£24 double.
Half board: £13-£16.50 daily,
£70-£99 weekly.
Evening meal 6pm (l.o.
midday).
Open April-October.

South Sands Hotel
12 Alta Vista Rd.,
Goodrington, Paignton,
TQ4 6BZ
☎ (0803) 557231
*Friendly family hotel, licensed
and offering warm hospitality.
Wonderful location adjacent
beaches. Easy walk to town
and all amenities.*
Bedrooms: 2 single, 3 double,
14 family rooms.

Bathrooms: 18 private,
1 public.
Bed & breakfast: £18-£22
single, £36-£44 double.
Half board: £23-£27 daily,
£140-£160 weekly.
Evening meal 6pm (l.o. 7pm).
Parking for 17.
Credit: Access, Visa.

Southlawn Guest House ♠
68 Upper Manor Rd.,
Preston, Paignton, TQ3 2TJ
☎ (0803) 551305
*Licensed bungalow-style
guesthouse convenient for
beaches and other attactions.
Situated in quiet residential
area. Sauna, sunbed, TV and
tea making facilities.*
Bedrooms: 3 single, 4 double
& 1 twin, 2 family rooms.
Bathrooms: 2 public;
3 private showers.
Bed & breakfast: £9-£15
single, £18-£30 double.
Half board: £14-£18 daily,
£98-£126 weekly.
Evening meal 6pm (l.o.
midday).
Parking for 8.

Summerhill Hotel ♠
♨♨♨
Braeside Rd., Goodrington
Sands, Paignton, TQ4 6BX
☎ (0803) 558101
*Comfortable hotel with
spacious suntrap gardens.
Adjacent to sandy beach and
park. Close to harbour, leisure
centre and water theme park.*
Bedrooms: 3 single, 9 double
& 8 twin, 5 family rooms.
Bathrooms: 24 private,
1 public.
Bed & breakfast: £17-£24.50
single, £32-£45 double.
Half board: £21-£27 daily,
£139-£169 weekly.
Lunch available.
Evening meal 6.30pm (l.o.
6pm).
Parking for 25.
Open March-October.

Sunhill Hotel ♠
♨♨♨♨
Alta Vista Rd., Goodrington
Sands, Paignton, TQ4 6DA
☎ (0803) 557532 Fax (0803)
663850
*With access on to Goodrington
beach this quiet, spacious
comfortable hotel enjoys
spectacular views over Torbay.*

Bedrooms: 5 single, 17 double
& 6 twin, 1 family room.
Bathrooms: 29 private.
Bed & breakfast: £24-£30
single, £48-£66 double.
Half board: £33-£42 daily,
£198-£252 weekly.
Lunch available.
Evening meal 6.30pm (l.o.
7.30pm).
Parking for 30.
Credit: Access, Visa.

Torbay Holiday Motel ♠
♨♨♨♨
Totnes Rd., Paignton,
TQ4 7PP
☎ (0803) 558226
*On the A385 in peaceful
countryside, close to all
amenities of Torbay. Ideal
base for touring Devon.*
Bedrooms: 8 double & 8 twin,
2 family rooms.
Bathrooms: 18 private.
Bed & breakfast: £23-£26
single, £36-£42 double.
Half board: £23-£26 daily,
£161-£182 weekly.
Lunch available.
Evening meal 6pm (l.o.
10pm).
Parking for 100.
Credit: Access, Visa.

Wynncroft Hotel ♠
♨♨♨
2 Elmsleigh Pk., Paignton,
TQ4 5AT
☎ (0803) 525728
*A centrally situated hotel in
ideal level situation, where
comfort, friendliness and food
still matter.*
Bedrooms: 6 double & 2 twin,
3 family rooms.
Bathrooms: 8 private,
2 public; 3 private showers.
Bed & breakfast: £23-£25
single, £36-£40 double.
Half board: £22-£24 daily,
£135-£155 weekly.
Lunch available.
Evening meal 6pm (l.o. 7pm).
Parking for 8.
Open January-November.
Credit: Access, Visa.

PAR

Cornwall
Map ref 1B3

*Scattered coastal village
and clayport. Lovely hills
and woods surround the
coast here, notably the
beautiful Luxulyan Valley
a little way inland.*

Joesyleyr
45 Trenovissick Rd., St
Blazey Gate, Par PL24 2DY
☎ (072 681) 5692
*Small detached guest house in
rural setting, 3 miles east of St
Austell, three-quarters of a
mile from the coast.*
Bedrooms: 1 single, 1 double
& 1 twin.
Bathrooms: 1 public.
Bed & breakfast: £9.50-
£12.50 single, £19-£25 double.
Half board: £14.50-£17.50
daily, £98-£119 weekly.
Lunch available.
Evening meal 6pm (l.o. 7pm).

PARKHAM

Devon
Map ref 1C1

5m SW. Bideford

The Old Rectory
Parkham, Bideford,
EX39 5PL
☎ Horns Cross (023 75) 443
*Personally run, charming
country house. Peace and
tranquillity. Tastefully
furnished bedrooms, mostly en-
suite. Imaginative cuisine,
organically grown produce.*
Bedrooms: 3 double.
Bathrooms: 3 private.
Bed & breakfast: £31-£40
single, £52-£58 double.
Half board: £42.50-£45.50
daily, £279.30-£298.20
weekly.
Evening meal 7.30pm (l.o.
7pm).
Parking for 10.

**Individual proprietors have supplied all
details of accommodation. Although we
do check for accuracy, we advise you to
confirm prices and other information at
the time of booking.**

PENZANCE

Cornwall
Map ref 1B3

Granite-built resort and fishing port on Mount's Bay, with mainly Victorian promenade and some fine Regency terraces. Former prosperity came from tin trade, pilchard fishing and smuggling. Grand Georgian-style church by harbour. Georgian Egyptian building at head of Chapel Street and the municipal Morrab Gardens.
Tourist Information Centre ☎ (0736) 62207

Alexandra Hotel M
♛♛♛ APPROVED
Alexandra Ter., Seafront, Penzance, TR18 4NX
☎ (0736) 62644 & 66333
Telex 934999 TX LINKA
Family-run licensed hotel on seafront with friendly relaxed atmosphere. Large car park, superb sea-views. Open all year.
Bedrooms: 4 single, 10 double & 6 twin, 12 family rooms.
Bathrooms: 30 private, 1 public.
Bed & breakfast: £19-£25 single, £38-£50 double.
Half board: £28-£34 daily, £165.50-£215 weekly.
Lunch available.
Evening meal 7pm (l.o. 7.45pm).
Parking for 21.
Credit: Access, Visa, Amex.
⚹♿&⬟◻⎈✆ 🅿 V ⊨ TV
▥▭🍴⚲ SP 🌁 T

Ashton Family Guest House
14 Mennaye Rd., Penzance, TR18 4NG
☎ (0736) 62546
Friendly family guesthouse. All rooms have hot and cold water, colour TV and tea making facilities. Children and pets welcome.
Bedrooms: 1 single, 1 double & 2 twin, 2 family rooms.
Bathrooms: 1 public; 2 private showers.
Bed & breakfast: from £11 single, £22-£24 double.
Half board: from £16 daily, £100-£119 weekly.
Evening meal 5pm (l.o. 6.30pm).
⚹◻⎈ UL 🅿 ⊨ TV ▥ 🌁
DAP ⚲ SP

Beachfield Hotel
The Promenade, Penzance, TR18 4NW
☎ (0736) 62067
Elegant, newly refurbished hotel by the sea, facing south with panoramic views of Mount's Bay. Close to all amenities.
Bedrooms: 6 single, 7 double & 7 twin.
Bathrooms: 20 private.
Bed & breakfast: £35-£50 single, £90-£120 double.
Half board: £55-£70 daily.
Lunch available.
Evening meal 7pm (l.o. 9.30pm).
Credit: Access, Visa.
⚹✆ 🅿◻⎈ ✆ 🅿 V ⊨ TV
◉ ▥ ▭🍴⚲ SP

Cliff Hotel
1 Penrose Ter., Penzance, TR18 2HQ
☎ (0736) 68888/63524
Telex 94082662 CLIFF H
Superb panoramic views. Conveniently situated for rail, heliport and coaches. Run by the same family for over 60 years.
Bedrooms: 7 single, 6 double & 4 twin, 2 family rooms.
Bathrooms: 4 private, 3 public; 1 private shower.
Bed & breakfast: £19-£26 single, £38-£48 double.
Half board: £31-£38 daily, £217-£266 weekly.
Evening meal 6.30pm (l.o. 7pm).
Parking for 11.
Credit: Access, Visa, C.Bl., Diners, Amex.
⚹♿⎈ ✆ V ⊨ TV ▭ SP 🌁
T

Estoril Hotel M
♛♛♛ APPROVED
46 Morrab Rd., Penzance, TR18 4EX
☎ (0736) 62468 & 67471
A Victorian house carefully modernised to give comfortable accommodation together with personal service.
Bedrooms: 1 single, 4 double & 4 twin, 1 family room.
Bathrooms: 10 private.
Bed & breakfast: £22-£23 single, £44-£46 double.
Half board: £28-£33 daily, £190-£224 weekly.
Lunch available.
Evening meal 6.45pm (l.o. 7.30pm).
Parking for 4.
Open February-November.
Credit: Access, Visa.
⚹♿⎈ ✆ ◻⎈ ✆ V ⊨
◉ ▥ ▭🍴✂ 🌁 SP T

Glencree Guesthouse M
♛♛
19 Penare Rd., Penzance, TR18 3AJ
☎ (0736) 64775
Homely accommodation with personal service. All rooms have colour TV, free tea and coffee facilities. En-suite rooms available. Children welcome.
Bedrooms: 1 single, 2 double & 1 twin, 2 family rooms.
Bathrooms: 2 private, 2 public.
Bed & breakfast: £12-£14 single, £24-£28 double.
Half board: £18-£20 daily, £77-£90 weekly.
Lunch available.
Evening meal 6pm (l.o. 6.30pm).
⚹♿◻⎈ UL ✆ V ⊨ ▥
▭ 🌁 ⚲ SP

Glencree Private Hotel
2 Mennaye Rd., Penzance, TR13 4NG
☎ (0736) 62026
Established since 1946, close to promenade, tennis courts, bowling green, amusement arcade and bus tours.
Bedrooms: 1 single, 3 double & 1 twin, 2 family rooms.
Bathrooms: 2 private, 2 public.
Bed & breakfast: £8-£12 single, £16-£24 double.
Half board: £13-£17 daily, £56-£84 weekly.
Evening meal 6pm (l.o. 4pm).
Parking for 1.
Credit: Amex.
⚹ M ◻⎈ ✆ V ⊨ TV
▭ 🌁 DAP ⚲ SP

Kenegie Manor
Gulval, Penzance, TR20 8YN
☎ (0736) 69174
Historic 16th C Tudor manor house. Carvery restaurant and leisure centre with heated pool.
Bedrooms: 8 double & 3 twin, 12 family rooms.
Bathrooms: 23 private.
Bed & breakfast: £25-£29 single, £50-£58 double.
Half board: £36-£40 daily, £200-£258.50 weekly.
Evening meal 6.30pm (l.o. 9.30pm).
Parking for 60.
Credit: Access, Visa.
⚹ ✆ ◻⎈ ✆ V ⊨ TV ▥
▭ 🍴✂ ▦ 🎣 ♟ ✿ ❄ 🎱
SP 🌁

Ocean Breezes Guest House M
1 St. Marys Ter., Penzance, TR18 4DZ
☎ (0736) 64112

Small centrally situated guesthouse with views of Newlyn. Close to all amenities, town centre and Morrab Gardens. Private car park attached.
Bedrooms: 1 single, 1 double, 1 family room.
Bathrooms: 1 public.
Bed & breakfast: £10.50-£11.50 single, £20-£22 double.
Half board: £16-£16.50 daily, £112-£114 weekly.
Lunch available.
Evening meal 6.30pm (l.o. 8pm).
Parking for 4.
⎈ ◻⎈ UL ✆ V ✂ ⊨ TV
▥ ▭🍴🔔♨☼ ▦ DAP
SP

Penmorvah Hotel M
Alexandra Rd., Penzance, TR18 4LZ
☎ (0736) 63711 & (0736) 60100
350 yards from promenade, tree lined avenue. Easy reach of town centre, ideal location for touring.
Bedrooms: 2 single, 2 double & 2 twin, 4 family rooms.
Bathrooms: 10 private.
Bed & breakfast: £15-£22 single, £30-£44 double.
Half board: £22-£30 daily, £145-£195 weekly.
Evening meal 6.30pm (l.o. 6pm).
Credit: Access, Visa, Amex.
⚹♿✆ ◻⎈ ✆ V ⊨
▥ ▭ DAP 🌁 SP T

The Queens Hotel
♛♛♛♛
The Promenade, Penzance, TR18 4HG
☎ (0736) 62371
Victorian hotel with superb views across Mount's Bay. Strollers brasserie, bar, restaurant, exciting atmosphere.
Bedrooms: 15 single, 20 double & 27 twin, 9 family rooms.
Bathrooms: 71 private.
Bed & breakfast: £30-£35 single, £67-£78 double.
Half board: £37.50-£56 daily, £154-£203 weekly.
Evening meal 7pm (l.o. 8.45pm).
Parking for 100.
Credit: Access, Visa, C.Bl., Diners, Amex.
⚹ ✆ ◻⎈ ✆ ◉ ⊞ ▥ ▭
🍴♿&⚲ 🌁 SP T

Please mention this guide when making a booking.

PENZANCE

Continued

Sea & Horses Hotel M
🏆🏆🏆 APPROVED

Alexandra Ter., Sea Front,
Penzance, TR18 4NX
☎ (0736) 61961
*Hotel in quiet terrace
overlooking seafront, with
uninterrupted views over
Mount's Bay. Accent on
cleanliness, friendliness and
food.*
Bedrooms: 2 single, 2 double
& 3 twin, 4 family rooms.
Bathrooms: 8 private;
3 private showers.
Bed & breakfast: £17-£19.50
single, £34-£40 double.
Half board: £26-£28.50 daily,
£110-£130 weekly.
Evening meal 7pm (l.o. 6pm).
Parking for 12.
Credit: Access, Visa.

Tarbert Hotel M
🏆🏆🏆

11 Clarence St., Penzance,
TR18 2NU
☎ (0736) 63758
Ⓒ Minotels
*Georgian listed building,
featuring exposed granite walls
and open fires. In conservation
area near town centre, parks
and promenade.*
Bedrooms: 2 single, 6 double
& 4 twin.
Bathrooms: 12 private,
1 public.
Bed & breakfast: £22.50-
£25.50 single, £39-£51 double.
Half board: £30-£36 daily,
£180-£216 weekly.
Evening meal 7pm (l.o. 8pm).
Parking for 5.
Open January-November.
Credit: Access, Visa, Diners,
Amex.

Union Hotel M

Chapel St., Penzance,
TR18 4AE
☎ (0736) 62319
*16th C hotel, reputedly the
oldest in Penzance. Privately
run. Historic dining room and
theatre. Intimate restaurant
and 2 interesting bars.*
Bedrooms: 2 single, 8 double
& 14 twin, 4 family rooms.
Bathrooms: 21 private,
5 public.
Bed & breakfast: £15.95-
£24.95 single, £31-£43.95
double.
Half board: £23.95-£32.95
daily, £150-£200 weekly.
Lunch available.

Evening meal 6pm (l.o.
8.30pm).
Parking for 20.
Credit: Access, Visa, Diners,
Amex.

Warwick House Hotel M
🏆🏆 APPROVED

17 Regent Ter., Penzance,
TR18 4DW
☎ (0736) 63881
*Family-run hotel near the sea,
station and heliport. Tastefully
decorated rooms, most with sea
views. Some rooms with
showers.*
Bedrooms: 1 single, 2 double
& 3 twin, 1 family room.
Bathrooms: 1 public;
3 private showers.
Bed & breakfast: £15-£17
single, £30-£34 double.
Half board: £22-£24 daily,
£98-£161 weekly.
Evening meal 6.30pm (l.o.
6.30pm).
Parking for 10.
Open February-October.

PERRANPORTH

Cornwall
Map ref 1B2

Small seaside resort
developed around a
former mining village.
Today's attractions
include exciting surf,
rocks, caves and
extensive sand dunes.

Atlantic House Hotel

Cliff Rd., Perranporth,
TR6 0DR
☎ (0872) 572259
*Licensed family hotel, sun
lounge and bedrooms with
beach views, en-suite rooms.
Relaxing friendly atmosphere.*
Bedrooms: 1 single, 4 double
& 2 twin, 4 family rooms.
Bathrooms: 2 public.
Bed & breakfast: £13-£16
double.
Half board: £112-£133
weekly.
Evening meal 6pm (l.o. 6pm).
Open March-October.

Beach Dunes Hotel
🏆🏆🏆 APPROVED

Ramoth Way, Perranporth,
TR6 0BY
☎ (0872) 572263 Fax
(0872) 573824

*Situated in dunes overlooking
Perran Beach and adjoining
golf-course. Access to beach.*
Bedrooms: 2 single, 5 double
& 1 twin, 2 family rooms.
Bathrooms: 6 private,
1 public.
Bed & breakfast: £20.50-
£25.50 single, £41-£51 double.
Half board: £28.50-£35 daily,
£180-£225 weekly.
Evening meal 6.30pm (l.o.
7.30pm).
Parking for 15.
Open March-October.
Credit: Access, Visa, Amex.

Bolenna Court Hotel
🏆🏆

Perrancoombe Rd.,
Perranporth, TR6 0HT
☎ Truro (0872) 572751
*Family hotel, fronted by tennis
club and playing fields. 5
minutes from beach, shops,
boating lake, putting. Golf club
near by.*
Bedrooms: 3 double & 2 twin,
3 family rooms.
Bathrooms: 6 private,
1 public; 1 private shower.
Bed & breakfast: £14-£15
single, £28-£32 double.
Half board: £18.50-£20.50
daily, £129.50-£143.50
weekly.
Lunch available.
Evening meal 6.30pm (l.o.
9.30pm).
Parking for 20.

Cellar Cove Hotel

Droskyn Way, Perranporth,
TR6 0DS
☎ Truro (0872) 572110
*Friendly hotel with superb
views and own grounds
situated above a 3 mile beach.
Family atmosphere, barbecues
weekly. All children under 5
free.*
Bedrooms: 2 single, 4 double
& 1 twin, 7 family rooms.
Bathrooms: 4 private,
4 public.
Bed & breakfast: £14-£16.50
single, £28-£33 double.
Half board: £130-£150
weekly.
Lunch available.
Evening meal 6.30pm.
Parking for 20.
Credit: Access, Visa.

Droskyn Castle M

Perranporth, TR6 0DS
☎ (0872) 3989

*In a superb clifftop position,
enjoying one of the best views
in Cornwall. The castle has
many single rooms, most of
which face the sea.*
Bedrooms: 16 single, 11 twin,
10 family rooms.
Bathrooms: 12 public.
Half board: £26.50-£28.50
daily, £185-£199 weekly.
Evening meal 7pm.
Parking for 2.
Open May-September.

Sunnyside Guest House
🏆🏆

7 Sunnyside, Perranporth,
TR6 0HN
☎ (0872) 572088
*Licensed guesthouse in
approximately one third of an
acre of garden. About 800
yards from the beach and the
shops. TV lounge, pool table.
Most rooms en-suite.*
Bedrooms: 1 single, 2 double
& 1 twin, 4 family rooms.
Bathrooms: 4 private,
2 public.
Bed & breakfast: £12-£13.50
single, £24-£27 double.
Half board: £15-£16.50 daily,
£105-£115.50 weekly.
Evening meal 6.30pm (l.o.
7pm).
Parking for 8.

The Villa Margarita Country Hotel
🏆🏆

Bolingey, Perranporth,
TR6 0AS
☎ Truro (0872) 572063
*Elegantly furnished colonial
villa in beautiful countryside.
All bedrooms have tea and
coffee making facilities. This
establishment is licensed.*
Bedrooms: 1 single, 3 double
& 2 twin, 1 family room.
Bathrooms: 5 private,
1 public; 2 private showers.
Bed & breakfast: £17-£18.50
single, £34-£37 double.
Half board: £28-£29.50 daily,
£176-£185 weekly.
Evening meal 7pm (l.o. 5pm).
Parking for 8.

PIDDLETRENTHIDE

Dorset
Map ref 2B3

Old Bakehouse Hotel & Restaurant M
🏆🏆

Piddletrenthide, Dorchester,
DT2 7QR
☎ (030 04) 305

Country hotel in Hardy's Wessex. All bedrooms en-suite, colour TV. Swimming pool. Restaurant.
Bedrooms: 2 single, 6 double & 2 twin.
Bathrooms: 10 private.
Bed & breakfast: £25 single, £44-£50 double.
Half board: £34.50-£37.50 daily, £230-£255 weekly.
Lunch available.
Evening meal 7pm (l.o. 9pm).
Parking for 16.
Open February-December.
Credit: Access, Visa.

The Poachers Inn M
COMMENDED
Piddletrenthide, Dorchester, DT2 7QX
☎ (030 04) 358
16th C inn in beautiful Piddle Valley with riverside garden. Swimming pool. All rooms en-suite, colour TV. Tea-making facilities. Telephone. Brochure available.
Bedrooms: 1 single, 5 double & 2 twin, 3 family rooms.
Bathrooms: 11 private.
Bed & breakfast: £36 double.
Half board: £27 daily.
Lunch available.
Evening meal 6pm (l.o. 10pm).
Parking for 30.

PLYMOUTH
Devon
Map ref 1C2

Devon's largest city, major port and naval base, shopping and tourist centre. Rebuilt after bombing of the 1940s behind old harbour area, the Barbican. Old merchants' houses, Prysten House in Barbican and ambitious architecture in modern centre, with aquarium, museum and art gallery, The Dome - a new heritage centre on the Hoe. Superb coastal views over Plymouth Sound from the Hoe.
Tourist Information Centre ☎ *(0752) 264849*

Alexander Hotel
Greenbank Road, Plymouth, PL4 8NL
☎ (0752) 663247/225536

Friendly family-run hotel with well-furnished, spacious rooms, 5 with private showers. Ideal central for business and holidays.
Bedrooms: 2 single, 1 double & 2 twin, 2 family rooms.
Bathrooms: 1 public; 5 private showers.
Bed & breakfast: £11-£15 single, £22-£30 double.
Half board: £17-£21 daily, £115-£140 weekly.
Lunch available.
Evening meal 6pm (l.o. 8pm).
Parking for 8.
Credit: Access, Visa.

Avalon Guest House
167 Citadel Rd., Plymouth PL1 2HU
☎ (0752) 668127
Small family-run guesthouse on Plymouth Hoe, close to cross channel ferries, Barbican and city centre.
Bedrooms: 1 single, 2 double & 1 twin, 2 family rooms.
Bathrooms: 1 public; 2 private showers.
Bed & breakfast: from £13.80 single, £22.50-£27.60 double.
Half board: £13.80 daily, £90-£179.21 weekly.

Barley Guest House
26 Lipson Rd, Lipson, Plymouth, PL4 8PW
☎ (0752) 663466
Victorian guesthouse hotel offering spacious accommodation, including an elegant dining room. Now under new management.
Bedrooms: 1 single, 1 double & 1 twin, 1 family room.
Bathrooms: 2 public.
Bed & breakfast: £11.50-£12.50 single, £23-£25 double.
Half board: from £18 daily, from £125 weekly.
Evening meal 6pm (l.o. 7pm).
Parking for 3.

Boringdon Hall Hotel M
Colebrook, Plympton, Plymouth, PL7 4DP
☎ (0752) 344455
A Grade 1 Tudor mansion hotel. Offering four-poster accommodation, Admirals carvery, gallery restaurant, bars and leisure facilities. Set in 12 acres of landscaped grounds.
Bedrooms: 18 double & 15 twin.
Bathrooms: 33 private.
Bed & breakfast: £65.50-£67.50 single, £86-£110 double.

Half board: £73-£92.50 daily, £455-£647.50 weekly.
Lunch available.
Evening meal 7pm (l.o. 10pm).
Parking for 250.
Credit: Access, Visa, Diners, Amex.

Bowling Green Hotel M
9-10 Osborne Pl., Lockyer St., The Hoe Plymouth, PL1 2PU
☎ (0752) 667485
Rebuilt Victorian property with views of Dartmoor. Overlooking Sir Francis Drake's bowling green on beautiful Plymouth Hoe.
Bedrooms: 1 single, 6 double & 2 twin, 3 family rooms.
Bathrooms: 6 private; 6 private showers.
Bed & breakfast: £20-£27 single, £28-£38 double.
Parking for 4.
Credit: Access, Visa.

Caraneal Hotel
14 Pier St., West Hoe, Plymouth, PL1 3BS
☎ (0752) 663589 / 261931
Family-run licensed hotel overlooking children's park. Near to seafront and city centre. All rooms fully en-suite.
Bedrooms: 1 single, 7 double & 1 twin, 1 family room.
Bathrooms: 10 private.
Bed & breakfast: £27-£32 single, max. £46 double.
Evening meal 7pm (l.o. 8pm).
Parking for 3.
Credit: Access, Visa.

Churston Hotel
1 Apsley Rd., Plymouth, PL4 6PJ
☎ (0752) 664850
Small family-run hotel in residential area with unrestricted parking. Convenient for railway station, city centre and Central Park. Arrive guests - depart friends.
Bedrooms: 4 single, 3 twin, 1 family room.
Bathrooms: 2 public.
Bed & breakfast: £12.50-£15 single, £23-£30 double.
Half board: £19.50-£22 daily.
Evening meal 6pm (l.o. 6pm).
Parking for 3.

The Copthorne Plymouth M
COMMENDED
The Armada Centre, Armada Way, Plymouth, PL1 1AR
☎ (0752) 224161 Telex 45756
In the heart of the south-west, a hotel with unique room conversion ideal for executives and families. Exciting menus in imaginative surroundings. 2 minutes from the Hoe.
Bedrooms: 74 double & 61 twin.
Bathrooms: 135 private.
Bed & breakfast: £75-£85 single, £85-£95 double.
Half board: £60-£75 daily.
Lunch available.
Evening meal 5.30pm (l.o. 10.30pm).
Parking for 136.
Credit: Access, Visa, C.Bl., Diners, Amex.

Drake Hotel
1 & 2 Windsor Villas, Lockyer St., Plymouth, PL1 2QD
☎ (0752) 229730
In the attractive Hoe area, close to the city centre. Managed by the resident owners.
Bedrooms: 13 single, 14 double & 6 twin, 3 family rooms.
Bathrooms: 25 private, 4 public; 6 private showers.
Bed & breakfast: £23-£35 single, £36-£43 double.
Half board: £26-£43 daily, £170-£260 weekly.
Lunch available.
Evening meal 6.30pm (l.o. 9pm).
Parking for 25.
Credit: Access, Visa, Diners, Amex.

Fourways
29 Beaumont Rd, Plymouth
☎ (0752) 669738
Family-run guesthouse, conveniently situated for the city and surrounding countryside. Clean and comfortable accommodation. Licensed.
Bedrooms: 1 single, 2 double & 3 twin.
Bathrooms: 1 private, 2 public.
Bed & breakfast: £12-£14 single, £24-£28 double.

Continued ▶

PLYMOUTH

Continued

Half board: £19.50-£21.50 daily, £136.50-£150.50 weekly.
Evening meal 5.30pm (l.o. 6pm).
Parking for 4.

Furzehill Hotel

41-43 Furzehill Rd., Mutley Plain, Plymouth, PL4 7JZ
☎ (0752) 662625
Small family hotel on bus route to city centre, coach and railway station. Close to city shopping centre, the Hoe, Barbican, theatre, restaurants and other amenities.
Bedrooms: 2 single, 4 double & 2 twin, 2 family rooms.
Bathrooms: 2 public; 5 private showers.
Bed & breakfast: £12.50-£15.50 single, £25-£30 double.
Half board: from £19.25 daily, from £121 weekly.
Evening meal 6pm (l.o. 8pm).
Parking for 3.
Credit: Access, Visa.

Grand Hotel

COMMENDED
Elliott St., The Hoe, Plymouth, PL1 2PT
☎ (0752) 661195 & (0952) 600653 Telex 45359
Built in 1879 the hotel retains many of its original architectural details and combines sea views with quiet Victorian elegance. Weekend breaks available on a bed and breakfast basis, with or without dinner.
Bedrooms: 35 double & 38 twin, 4 family rooms.
Bathrooms: 77 private.
Bed & breakfast: £55-£75 single, £65-£85 double.
Evening meal 7pm (l.o. 10pm).
Parking for 70.
Credit: Access, Visa, C.Bl., Diners, Amex.
Display advertisement appears on page 458.

Lamplighter Hotel

103 Citadel Rd., The Hoe, Plymouth, PL1 2RN
☎ (0752) 663855
Small friendly hotel on Plymouth Hoe, 5 minutes' walk from the city centre.
Bedrooms: 6 double & 2 twin, 1 family room.
Bathrooms: 9 private.
Bed & breakfast: £20-£23 single, £30-£35 double.
Parking for 4.
Credit: Access, Visa.

Langdon Court Hotel & Restaurant

Down Thomas, Plymouth, PL9 0DY
☎ (0752) 862358
Elizabethan manor house in 7 acres of garden and woodland, yet only 6 miles from Plymouth city centre.
Bedrooms: 4 single, 5 double & 6 twin, 1 family room.
Bathrooms: 16 private.
Bed & breakfast: £26.50-£42 single, £50-£62 double.
Lunch available.
Evening meal 7.30pm (l.o. 9pm).
Parking for 100.
Credit: Access, Visa, Diners, Amex.

Loma Loma

Listed APPROVED
227 Citadel Rd., The Hoe, Plymouth, PL1 2NG
☎ (0752) 661859
Close to historic Barbican, Hoe, bus station and ferry terminal. Only 5 minutes' walk to main shopping centre. Supervised by the proprietors.
Bedrooms: 1 single, 2 double & 2 twin, 1 family room.
Bathrooms: 1 public; 4 private showers.
Bed & breakfast: £13-£14 single, £24 double.
Open April-October.

Olivers Hotel and Restaurant

COMMENDED
33 Sutherland Rd., Mutley, Plymouth, PL4 6BN
☎ (0752) 663923
Hotel and restaurant situated in a quiet residential area. En-suite rooms include trouser press, hair-dryer and telephone.
Bedrooms: 2 single, 2 double & 1 twin, 1 family room.
Bathrooms: 4 private, 1 public.
Bed & breakfast: £18-£25 single, £38-£45 double.
Evening meal 6pm (l.o. 9am).
Parking for 3.
Credit: Access, Visa, C.Bl., Diners, Amex.

Phantele Guest House

176 Devonport Rd., Stoke, Plymouth, PL1 5RD
☎ (0752) 561506
A small family-run guesthouse about 2 miles from city centre. Convenient base for touring. Close to continental and Torpoint ferries.
Bedrooms: 2 single, 2 twin, 2 family rooms.
Bathrooms: 2 private, 2 public.
Bed & breakfast: £10.50-£15.50 single, £20-£26 double.
Half board: £15.50-£20.50 daily, £94.50-£114 weekly.
Evening meal 6pm (l.o. 2pm).

Plymouth Moat House

Armada Way, Plymouth, PL1 2HJ
☎ (0752) 662866 Telex 45637
Fax (0752) 673812
CR Queens Moat Houses
Situated on historic Plymouth Hoe in the heart of the city. A short walk from the shopping centre and the Barbican.
Bedrooms: 42 single, 42 double & 65 twin, 65 family rooms.
Bathrooms: 214 private.
Bed & breakfast: £40-£80 single, £50-£95 double.
Lunch available.
Evening meal 7pm (l.o. 10.30pm).
Parking for 175.
Credit: Access, Visa, Diners, Amex.

Rosaland Hotel

APPROVED
32 Houndiscombe Rd., Plymouth, PL4 6HQ
☎ (0752) 664749
Fully-modernised and refurbished by new owners. Close to shops and station. Within walking distance of Hoe and Barbican.
Bedrooms: 3 single, 2 double & 1 twin, 2 family rooms.
Bathrooms: 2 public; 5 private showers.
Bed & breakfast: £15 single, £30 double.
Half board: £22 daily, £154 weekly.
Evening meal 6pm (l.o. 6pm).
Parking for 3.
Credit: Access, Visa.

St. Lawrence of St. James Guest House

16 St. James Place West, The Hoe, Plymouth P11 3AT
☎ (0752) 671901
Family-run guesthouse in a quiet location but a short walk from Barbican, city centre and bus station. Close to the Hoe and ferry port. Open all year. Pay phone and satellite TV.
Bedrooms: 1 single, 2 double & 2 twin, 1 family room.
Bathrooms: 2 public; 2 private showers.
Bed & breakfast: £15-£17 single, £26-£30 double.
Half board: £22-£22.50 daily, £154-£157.50 weekly.
Evening meal 6pm (l.o. 7.30pm).

Squires Guest House

7 St. James Place East, The Hoe, Plymouth, PL1 3AS
☎ (0752) 261459
A charming Victorian house converted to a high standard with modern facilities, within easy walking distance of the Hoe, city centre, Barbican and bus station.
Bedrooms: 2 single, 2 double & 1 twin, 3 family rooms.
Bathrooms: 1 private, 1 public; 5 private showers.
Bed & breakfast: £14-£16 single, £26-£28 double.
Half board: £90-£105 weekly.
Parking for 4.

Transatlantic Hotel

15 Garden Cres., West Hoe, Plymouth, PL1 3DA
☎ (0752) 223845
Friendly hotel situated on the Hoe close to all amenities. Fully licensed and serving plenty of home-cooked food.
Bedrooms: 2 single, 1 double & 4 twin, 1 family room.
Bathrooms: 5 private, 1 public.
Bed & breakfast: £9-£12 single, £18-£24 double.
Half board: £18-£24 daily, £91-£125 weekly.
Lunch available.
Evening meal 6pm (l.o. 7.45pm).
Credit: Visa.

White House Hotel

12 Athenaeum St., The Hoe, Plymouth, PL1 2RH
☎ (0752) 662356
Near to city centre, theatre, The Hoe and sea. Full en-suite facilities available.

Bedrooms: 5 double & 2 twin,
1 family room.
Bathrooms: 1 private,
2 public.
Bed & breakfast: £15-£20
single, £25-£30 double.

Cornwall
Map ref 1C2

6m W. Torpoint

The Old Mill House

Polbathic, Torpoint,
PL11 3HA
☎ St Germans (0503) 30596
*A 250-year-old mill
overlooking the river Lynher,
fully licensed and close to
many popular attractions.*
Bedrooms: 2 single, 3 double
& 1 twin, 2 family rooms.
Bathrooms: 2 public.
Bed & breakfast: £10-£12
single, £20-£24 double.
Half board: £16-£22 daily,
£100-£130 weekly.
Lunch available.
Evening meal 6pm (l.o. 7pm).
Parking for 13.

Cornwall
Map ref 1C3

Picturesque fishing village
clinging to steep valley
slopes above its harbour.
A river splashes past
cottages and narrow
lanes twist between. The
harbour mouth, guarded
by jagged rocks, is closed
by heavy timbers during
storms.

Claremont Hotel M

Polperro, PL13 2RG
☎ (0503) 72441
*Family-run hotel in historic
fishing village. Continental
atmosphere and French cuisine
for a relaxing holiday.*
Bedrooms: 1 single, 5 double
& 2 twin, 2 family rooms.
Bathrooms: 9 private,
1 public.
Bed & breakfast: £17-£23
single, £28-£45 double.
Half board: £25-£34 daily,
£165-£190 weekly.
Lunch available.
Evening meal 7.30pm (l.o.
8.30pm).
Parking for 16.
Credit: Access, Visa.

Crumplehorn Inn, Mill and Restaurant

Polperro, Looe, PL13 2RJ
☎ (0503) 72348
*16th C watermill and coaching
house converted to comfortable
bed and breakfast and self-
catering accommodation. Local
ales. Fresh fish and seafood
restaurant.*
Bedrooms: 2 single, 11 double
& 3 twin, 9 family rooms.
Bathrooms: 25 private.
Bed & breakfast: £21-£25
single, £34-£48 double.
Half board: £32-£40 daily,
£181-£273 weekly.
Lunch available.
Evening meal 6.30pm (l.o.
10pm).
Parking for 30.

Cornwall
Map ref 1B2

Small resort on Padstow
Bay and the widening
Camel Estuary, with
excellent sands and
bathing. Pentire Head
(National Trust), a notable
viewpoint, lies to the
north.

Seascape Hotel M

Polzeath, PL27 6SX
☎ Trebetherick
(0208) 863638
*Catering exclusively for adults,
renowned for food and a high
degree of comfort with
magnificent sea views.*
Bedrooms: 1 single, 11 double
& 3 twin.
Bathrooms: 11 private.
Bed & breakfast: £20 single,
£40-£44 double.
Half board: £30-£33 daily,
£182-£206 weekly.
Evening meal 7pm (l.o. 6pm).
Parking for 18.
Open March-October,
December.
Credit: Access, Visa.

**Half board prices
shown are per
person but in some
cases may be based
on double/twin
occupancy.**

Somerset
Map ref 1D1

Village set between steep
Exmoor hills and the sea
at the head of beautiful
Porlock Vale. The narrow
street shows a medley of
building styles. South
westward is Porlock Weir
with its old houses and
tiny harbour and further
along the wooded shingle
shore at Culbone is
England's smallest
medieval church.

Anchor & Ship Hotel M

APPROVED

Porlock Harbour, Exmoor,
Minehead, TA24 8PB
☎ (0643) 862636
*Attractive, comfortable hotel,
10 yards from the waters' edge
of small, picturesque harbour
amid Exmoor's magnificent
scenery and coastline.*
Bedrooms: 2 single, 9 double
& 12 twin, 3 family rooms.
Bathrooms: 20 private,
5 public.
Bed & breakfast: £30-£49
single, £55-£99 double.
Half board: £44-£63 daily,
£269-£392 weekly.
Lunch available.
Evening meal 7.30pm (l.o.
9.15pm).
Parking for 38.
Open February-December.
Credit: Access, Visa, C.Bl.

Doverhay Place M

Porlock, Minehead,
TA24 8EX
☎ (0643) 862398
Telex 667040
*Comfortable country house on
the outskirts of Porlock village,
with large attractive gardens.*
Bedrooms: 8 single, 12 twin,
8 family rooms.
Bathrooms: 8 public.
Half board: £26.45-£28.45
daily, £185-£199 weekly.
Lunch available.
Evening meal 7pm.
Parking for 30.

The Lorna Doone Hotel M

High St., Porlock, TA24 8PS
☎ (0643) 862404
*Personally run by owner and
wife. Comfortable rooms and a
wide choice of home-cooked
meals. Situated within Exmoor
National Park.*

Bedrooms: 1 single, 7 double
& 2 twin.
Bathrooms: 7 private,
2 public.
Bed & breakfast: £16.50-£18
single, £33-£36 double.
Lunch available.
Evening meal 7pm (l.o.
9.15pm).
Parking for 8.
Credit: Access, Visa.

Myrtle Cottage M

High St., Porlock, TA24 8PU
☎ (0643) 862978
*Charming 16th C thatched
cottage situated in picturesque
village centre, overlooking
Porlock Bay. Ideal base for
walking and exploring
Exmoor.*
Bedrooms: 1 single, 1 double
& 1 twin, 1 family room.
Bathrooms: 1 public.
Bed & breakfast: £12.50
single, £27-£29 double.
Half board: £22-£24 daily,
£149-£163 weekly.
Evening meal 7.30pm (l.o.
7.30pm).
Parking for 4.
Open March-December.

The Oaks Hotel M

COMMENDED

Porlock, TA24 8ES
☎ (0643) 862265
*Edwardian gentleman's
residence. Commanding
spectacular views of coast,
countryside and village.
Specialising in fresh local
produce with traditional
English and French style
cooking. Open log fires
throughout the year.*
Bedrooms: 1 single, 6 double
& 3 twin, 2 family rooms.
Bathrooms: 12 private.
Bed & breakfast: from £36.50
single, from £58 double.
Half board: max. £42.50
daily, from £275 weekly.
Evening meal 7pm (l.o.
8.30pm).
Parking for 12.
Credit: Amex.

Porlock Vale House and Riding Centre

Porlock Weir, Minehead.
TA24 8NY
☎ (0643) 862338
*Edwardian country house, set
in 24 beautiful acres with moor
and sea views. Riding facilities.
Sailing from Porlock Weir.
En-suite accommodation.*

Continued ▶

PORLOCK
Continued

Bedrooms: 5 double & 5 twin, 3 family rooms.
Bathrooms: 9 private, 2 public.
Bed & breakfast: £40-£50 double.
Half board: £32-£40 daily, £160-£180 weekly.
Evening meal 6.30pm (l.o. 8.30pm).
Parking for 12.
Credit: Access, Visa.

Sea Point
Upway, Porlock, TA24 8QE
☎ (0643) 862289
Spacious Edwardian house overlooking Porlock Bay. Beautiful moorland and sea views. Traditional and vegetarian food. Organised walking holidays available.
Bedrooms: 1 double & 1 twin, 2 family rooms.
Bathrooms: 4 private.
Bed & breakfast: £15 single, £30 double.
Half board: £23 daily, £146 weekly.
Evening meal 6.30pm.
Parking for 4.

PORT GAVERNE
Cornwall
Map ref 1B2

5m N. Wadebridge
Small village sheltering in a narrow inlet on the dramatic North Cornish coast. In the 19th C the shingle beach was a loading site for slate from the nearby Delabole Quarry.

Headlands Hotel M
Port Gaverne, Port Isaac, PL29 3SH
☎ Bodmin (0208) 880260
On clifftop overlooking Port Gaverne Cove, with breathtaking sea views. Comfortable bedrooms. Renowned for cuisine and hospitality.
Bedrooms: 5 double & 5 twin, 1 family room.
Bathrooms: 11 private.
Bed & breakfast: £26-£33 single, £52-£66 double.
Half board: £33-£44 daily, £220-£264 weekly.
Lunch available.
Evening meal 7pm (l.o. 10pm).
Parking for 35.

Credit: Access, Visa, Diners, Amex.

Port Gaverne Hotel M
Port Gaverne, Port Isaac, PL29 3SQ
☎ Bodmin (0208) 880244
Fax (0208) 880151
17th C Cornish coastal inn, gently and comfortably restored. Located in a sheltered cove in an area of unusual natural beauty.
Bedrooms: 2 single, 10 double & 3 twin, 4 family rooms.
Bathrooms: 19 private.
Bed & breakfast: £32-£41 single, £64-£82 double.
Half board: £45.50-£95.50 daily, £280-£322 weekly.
Lunch available.
Evening meal 7pm (l.o. 9.30pm).
Parking for 22.
Open February-December.
Credit: Access, Visa, Diners, Amex.

PORT ISAAC
Cornwall
Map ref 1B2

Old fishing port of whitewashed cottages, twisting stairways and narrow alleys. A stream splashes down through the centre to the harbour. Nearby stands a 19th C folly, Doyden Castle, with a magnificent view of the coast.

The Castle Rock Hotel M
APPROVED
4 New Rd, Port Isaac, PL29 3SB
☎ Bodmin (0208) 880300
Ideally situated overlooking the Atlantic and Port Isaac Bay. High standards of comfort and cuisine.
Bedrooms: 3 single, 8 double & 5 twin, 3 family rooms.
Bathrooms: 16 private, 1 public.
Bed & breakfast: £22-£28 single, £44-£56 double.
Half board: £33-£38 daily, £215-£245 weekly.
Lunch available.
Evening meal 7pm (l.o. 8.30pm).

Parking for 20.
Open March-December.
Credit: Access, Visa.

⊕ Display advertisement appears on page 457.

Fairholme
COMMENDED
30 Trewetha La., Port Isaac, PL29 3RW
☎ (0208) 880397
Homely guesthouse in higher part of quaint fishing village. Personal attention and home cooking.
Bedrooms: 3 double & 1 twin, 2 family rooms.
Bathrooms: 1 private, 2 public; 1 private shower.
Bed & breakfast: £12-£17.50 single, £24-£32 double.
Half board: £19.50-£22.50 daily, £133-£164 weekly.
Evening meal 6.30pm (l.o. 10.30am).
Parking for 8.
Open April-October.
Credit: Access, Visa.

Old School Hotel M
Fore St, Port Isaac, PL29 3RB
☎ (0208) 880721
Converted Victorian school, clifftop situation overlooking historic fishing village. Surrounded by National Trust property on North Cornwall Heritage Coast. 2 half-tester beds.
Bedrooms: 5 double & 4 twin, 4 family rooms.
Bathrooms: 13 private, 1 public.
Bed & breakfast: £16-£32 single, £32-£64 double.
Half board: £26-£52 daily, £182-£364 weekly.
Lunch available.
Evening meal 6.30pm (l.o. 9.30pm).
Parking for 28.
Credit: Access, Visa.

PORTESHAM
Dorset
Map ref 2B3

Small village at the foot of a hill near the fascinating coastline of Chesil Bank and the East and West Fleets.

Millmead Country Hotel
APPROVED
Portesham, Weymouth, DT3 4HE
☎ Abbotsbury (0305) 871432

Country house with its own grounds, in a beautiful village near the sea. Informal, friendly atmosphere with home cooking and own produce. Non-smokers only please.
Bedrooms: 2 single, 3 double & 3 twin.
Bathrooms: 5 private, 1 public; 3 private showers.
Bed & breakfast: from £19.50 single, £39-£55.50 double.
Half board: £31.25-£39.50 daily, £203.50-£257.50 weekly.
Lunch available.
Evening meal 7pm (l.o. 8pm).
Parking for 16.
Credit: Access, Visa.

PORTLAND
Dorset
Map ref 2B3

Joined by a narrow isthmus to the coast, a stony promontory sloping from the lofty landward side to a lighthouse on Portland Bill at its southern tip. Villages are built of the white limestone for which the 'isle' is famous.

Alexandria Hotel
71 Wakeham, Portland, DT5 1HW
☎ (0305) 822270
A well-equipped private hotel with comfortable bedrooms and a la carte restaurant. Satellite TV.
Bedrooms: 6 single, 4 double & 4 twin, 2 family rooms.
Bathrooms: 4 private, 3 public; 4 private showers.
Bed & breakfast: £17-£22 single, £29-£37 double.
Half board: £24-£35 daily, £160-£235 weekly.
Evening meal 6pm (l.o. 6pm).
Parking for 18.

The Old Higher Lighthouse
Portland Bill, DT5 2JT
☎ (0305) 822300
Lovingly restored privately owned lighthouse. Steeped in history and famous names. Peaceful and friendly atmosphere combined with breathtaking panoramic views.
Bedrooms: 1 single, 1 double & 2 twin, 1 family room.
Bathrooms: 2 public.
Bed & breakfast: £30-£34 double.

Evening meal 5pm (l.o. 10am).
Parking for 10.

Portland Heights Hotel
Yeates Corner, Portland, DT5 2EN
☎ (0305) 821361
Ⓖ Best Western
Modern hotel situated on the summit of of Portland, enjoying spectacular panoramic sea views.
Bedrooms: 1 single, 21 double & 40 twin, 4 family rooms.
Bathrooms: 66 private.
Bed & breakfast: £49-£64 single, £64-£78 double.
Half board: £40-£48 daily.
Lunch available.
Evening meal 7pm (l.o. 9.30pm).
Parking for 250.
Credit: Access, Visa, Diners, Amex.

PORTLOE
Cornwall
Map ref 1B3

6m SW. Mevagissey
Old fishing village and small resort where majestic cliffs rise from Veryan Bay. Unspoilt National Trust coast stretches south-westward to Nare Head.

Lugger Hotel M
Portloe, Truro, TR2 5RD
☎ Truro (0872) 501322
Fax (0872) 501691
Ⓖ Inter
17th C smugglers' inn, at the water's edge in a quiet, picturesque cove, where fishing boats moor alongside.
Bedrooms: 3 single, 8 double & 8 twin.
Bathrooms: 19 private.
Half board: £44-£49 daily.
Lunch available.
Evening meal 7pm (l.o. 9pm).
Parking for 27.
Open March-November.
Credit: Access, Visa, Diners, Amex.

PORTSCATHO
Cornwall
Map ref 1B3

Coastal village spreading along low cliffs of Gerrans Bay on the eastern side of the Roseland Peninsula. Seaside buildings show a variety of styles from late Georgian houses to small, interestingly-designed modern blocks.

Gerrans Bay Hotel M
COMMENDED
Gerrans, Portscatho, Truro, TR2 5ED
☎ (087 258) 338
Set in superb countryside, near sandy beaches. Home-cooked food and personal service. Complimentary golf and bowls. Adequate parking facilities.
Bedrooms: 2 single, 5 double & 5 twin, 2 family rooms.
Bathrooms: 12 private; 2 private showers.
Bed & breakfast: £23.50-£25.50 single.
Half board: £34.50-£37 daily, £210-£227 weekly.
Lunch available.
Evening meal 7.30pm (l.o. 8pm).
Parking for 16.
Open April-October, December.
Credit: Access, Visa, Amex.

Roseland House Hotel M
Rosevine, Portscatho, Truro, TR2 5EW
☎ (0872) 58644
Centrally-heated bedrooms with magnificent sea views over the bay. Path to secluded, private beach with coastal walks. Peaceful and quiet.
Bedrooms: 2 single, 9 double & 5 twin, 2 family rooms.
Bathrooms: 18 private.
Half board: £28-£35 daily, £196-£217 weekly.
Evening meal 7.30pm (l.o. 8pm).
Parking for 20.

PURTON
Wiltshire
Map ref 2B1

5m NW. Swindon

The Live and Let Live
Upper Pavenhill, Purton, Swindon, SN5 9DQ
☎ (0793) 770627
Converted stable, West of Swindon, north of M4 (J16) & Wootton Bassett. At Londis shop turn into Pavenhill. Proceed for 1/2 a mile to only right turning - Upper Pavenhill. House is 200 yards on left. Non-smokers preferred.
Bedrooms: 1 twin, 1 family room.
Bathrooms: 1 public.
Bed & breakfast: max. £16 single, max. £30 double.
Parking for 3.

RADSTOCK
Avon
Map ref 2B2

Thriving small town ideally situated for touring the Mendip Hills.

The Bell Hotel
Market Pl., Radstock, Bath, BA3 3AE
☎ (0761) 36218 & 33378
Family-run ensuring personal attention, professional chef. Large, comfortable rooms. Close to Bath, Downside Abbey, Cheddar Gorge and Wookey Hole Caves.
Bedrooms: 2 double & 1 twin, 2 family rooms.
Bathrooms: 5 private.
Bed & breakfast: from £25.88 single, from £34.50 double.
Half board: from £32 daily.
Lunch available.
Evening meal 7pm (l.o. 10pm).
Parking for 40.
Credit: Access, Visa.

RANGEWORTHY
Avon
Map ref 2A2

Rangeworthy Court Hotel M
APPROVED
Wotton Rd., Rangeworthy, Bristol, BS17 5ND
☎ (045 422) 347

17th C country manor house with relaxing, peaceful atmosphere and popular restaurant. Less than 20 minutes from the M4, M5 and Bristol.
Bedrooms: 4 single, 8 double & 2 twin.
Bathrooms: 14 private.
Bed & breakfast: £44-£52 single, £58-£66 double.
Half board: £35-£39 daily, £245-£273 weekly.
Lunch available.
Evening meal 7pm (l.o. 9pm).
Parking for 60.
Credit: Access, Visa, Diners, Amex.

REDLYNCH
Wiltshire
Map ref 2B3

Yew Tree Cottage
Grove Lane, Redlynch, Salisbury, SP5 2NR
☎ (0725) 21730
Attractive converted Victorian cottage set in large garden and paddock in the pretty new forest village of Redlynch. Near Salisbury.
Bedrooms: 1 single, 1 double & 1 twin.
Bathrooms: 1 public.
Bed & breakfast: £14 single, £28 double.
Parking for 6.

REDRUTH
Cornwall
Map ref 1B3

Originally West Cornwall's major mining centre, now a light-industrial town with handsome granite public buildings of the early 19th C.

Crossroads Motel
COMMENDED
Scorrier, Redruth, TR16 5BP
☎ St. Day (0209) 820551
Fax (0209) 820392
Lies 50 yards off the main A30 trunk road (Scorrier Exit) and is centrally situated for west Cornwall.
Bedrooms: 4 single, 10 double & 20 twin, 2 family rooms.
Bathrooms: 36 private.
Bed & breakfast: £37.50-£46 single, £40-£54 double.
Half board: £47.50-£56 daily, £120-£190 weekly.
Lunch available.

Continued ▶

Classifications and quality commendations were correct at the time of going to press but are subject to change. Please check at the time of booking.

REDRUTH

Continued

Evening meal 7pm (l.o.
9.30pm).
Parking for 140.
Credit: Access, Visa, Diners,
Amex.

ROCK

Cornwall
Map ref 1B2

6m NW. Wadebridge
Small resort and boating
centre beside the
abundant sands of the
Camel Estuary. A fine
golf-course stretches
northward along the
shore to Brea Hill,
thought to be the site of a
Roman settlement.
Passenger ferry service
from Padstow.

Pentire Rocks Hotel

New Polzeath, PL27 6US
☎ Trebetherick
(0208) 862213 & 862259
*Near Polzeath, ideal for
surfing, walking, golfing or
lazing by our outdoor heated
swimming pool. 16 bedrooms,
mostly en-suite with satellite
colour TV and direct dial
telephones.*
Bedrooms: 2 single, 10 double
& 2 twin, 2 family rooms.
Bathrooms: 15 private,
3 public.
Bed & breakfast: £30 single,
£60 double.
Half board: £40 daily, from
£240 weekly.
Evening meal 7pm (l.o.
9.30pm).
Parking for 30.
Open February-December.
Credit: Access, Visa.

Roskarnon House Hotel ♨

Rock, Wadebridge,
PL27 6LD
☎ Trebetherick
(020 886) 2785
*Edwardian house in an acre of
lawned gardens, facing south
and overlooking Camel
Estuary. 20 yards from the
beach and 50 yards from the
golf-course.*
Bedrooms: 2 single, 7 double
& 5 twin, 1 family room.
Bathrooms: 6 private,
4 public; 3 private showers.
Bed & breakfast: £16-£25
single, £30-£45 double.

Half board: £22-£30 daily,
£160-£210 weekly.
Lunch available.
Evening meal 7pm (l.o.
9.30pm).
Parking for 12.
Open March-October.

Silvermead

Rock, Wadebridge,
PL27 6LB
☎ Bodmin (0208) 862425
*Off main road affording superb
estuary views. Sailing club and
windsurfing. 150 yards from 36
hole golf course adjoining back
garden.*
Bedrooms: 1 single, 2 double
& 2 twin, 2 family rooms.
Bathrooms: 4 private,
1 public.
Bed & breakfast: £15-£27
single, £25-£34 double.
Half board: £19-£30 daily,
£130-£160 weekly.
Evening meal 6pm (l.o. 8pm).
Parking for 8.

RUANHIGHLANES

Cornwall
Map ref 1B3

11m SE. Truro
Village at the northern
end of the Roseland
Peninsula.

The Hundred House Hotel ♨

Ruan Highlanes, Nr. Truro,
TR2 5JR
☎ (0872) 501336
*Charming country hotel near
St. Mawes and Fal Estuary.
10 attractive en-suite
bedrooms. Log fires and home
cooking.*
Bedrooms: 2 single, 4 double
& 4 twin.
Bathrooms: 10 private.
Bed & breakfast: £26.50-£30
single, £53-£60 double.
Half board: £35-£40 daily,
£192.50-£260 weekly.
Evening meal 7.30pm (l.o.
5pm).
Parking for 15.
Open March-November.
Credit: Access, Visa.

> ### The enquiry
> ### coupons at the
> ### back will help you
> ### when contacting
> ### proprietors.

ST AGNES

Cornwall
Map ref 1B3

Small town in a once-rich
mining area on the north
coast. Miners' terraced
cottages and granite
houses slope to the
church. Some interesting
old mine workings
remain, but the chief
attraction must be the
magnificent coastal
scenery and superb
walks. St. Agnes Beacon
(National Trust) offers
one of Cornwall's most
extensive views.

The Beach Hotel

Porthtowan, Truro, TR4 8AE
☎ (0209) 890228
*Peaceful, informal hotel where
gardens adjoin beach and the
licensed restaurant overlooking
the sea offers gourmet cuisine
and fine wines.*
Bedrooms: 1 single, 5 double
& 3 twin, 5 family rooms.
Bathrooms: 7 private,
4 public; 3 private showers.
Bed & breakfast: £14.50-
£18.50 single, £29-£37 double.
Half board: £22.50-£52 daily,
£98-£180 weekly.
Evening meal 7pm (l.o. 8pm).
Parking for 16.
Open February-December.
Credit: Access, Visa, Diners,
Amex.

Driftwood Spars Hotel

Trevaunance Cove, St.
Agnes, TR5 0RT
☎ (087 255) 2428
*Delightful old inn with
enormous beams, stone walls
and log fires. Most bedrooms
have wonderful sea views. A la
carte restaurant. Parking.*
Bedrooms: 4 single, 5 double
& 1 twin, 1 family room.
Bathrooms: 5 private,
1 public; 3 private showers.
Bed & breakfast: from £19
single, from £38 double.
Half board: from £30 daily,
from £192 weekly.
Lunch available.
Evening meal 7pm (l.o.
11pm).
Parking for 100.
Credit: Access, Visa, Diners.

The Glen Hotel

Quay Rd., Saint Agnes,
TR5 0QS
☎ (0872) 552590

*Small family hotel set in three-
quarters of an acre of tiered
gardens. At the bottom of the
famous Stippy Stappy.*
Bedrooms: 1 single, 4 double
& 1 twin.
Bathrooms: 1 private,
2 public.
Bed & breakfast: £15-£20
single, £30-£40 double.
Half board: £21-£26 daily.
Evening meal 6.30pm.
Parking for 10.

Penkerris ♨

Penwinnick Rd., St. Agnes,
TR5 0PA
☎ (087 255) 2262
*Enchanting Edwardian
residence in own grounds, just
inside St. Agnes on B3277
road. Large lawn for
relaxation. Walking distance
from magnificent cliffs and
beach.*
Bedrooms: 1 single, 4 double
& 1 twin, 1 family room.
Bathrooms: 2 private,
3 public.
Bed & breakfast: £15-£22.50
single, £20-£35 double.
Half board: £16.50-£25 daily,
£109-£150 weekly.
Lunch available.
Evening meal 6.30pm (l.o.
10am).
Parking for 8.

Rose-in-Vale Country House Hotel ♨ COMMENDED

Mithian, St. Agnes, TR5 0QD
☎ St. Agnes (087 255) 2202
*Georgian country house of
character, with extensive
grounds, set in own secluded
wooded valley. Peaceful,
relaxed atmosphere. Four-
poster master bedroom. Special
breaks available.*
Bedrooms: 2 single, 8 double
& 4 twin, 3 family rooms.
Bathrooms: 17 private.
Bed & breakfast: £24.95
single, £49.90 double.
Half board: £29.95 daily,
£187.15-£209.65 weekly.
Lunch available.
Evening meal 7pm (l.o. 8pm).
Parking for 40.
Open March-October.
Credit: Access, Visa.

Rosevean Hotel
≋≋≋

32 Rosemundy Rd., St.
Agnes, TR5 0UD
☎ (087 255) 2277
*Detached 9-bedroomed,
licensed hotel. Ample parking.
800 yards to beach. Private
facilities in most rooms.
September to late May, 3 days
minimum, Dinner, Bed and
Breakfast £23 per person.*
Bedrooms: 1 single, 4 double
& 2 twin, 2 family rooms.
Bathrooms: 6 private,
1 public; 2 private showers.
Bed & breakfast: £20 single,
£40 double.
Half board: £26 daily, £178-
£206 weekly.
Evening meal 6.30pm (l.o.
7pm).
Parking for 18.
🕭 🗲 📞 🖵 🛢 🗍 Ⓥ 🗄 🎞 🛆
🍴 ❄ 🛏 SP

Tregarthen Country Cottage Hotel ♨
≋≋≋ COMMENDED

Mount Hawke, Truro,
TR4 8BW
☎ Porthtowan (0209) 890399
*Small, tastefully furnished
hotel in pleasant rural
surroundings. 6 lovely
bedrooms with private
facilities. 2 miles from the
North Cornish coast.*
Bedrooms: 6 double & 3 twin.
Bathrooms: 9 private.
Bed & breakfast: £20 single,
£40 double.
Half board: £30 daily, £170
weekly.
Evening meal 6.30pm (l.o.
7.30pm).
Parking for 12.
🕭 🛢 🗍 Ⓥ 🗄 🎞 🎟 🛆 🍴 ☊
❋ 🗡 🛏 🍷 SP

ST AUSTELL

Cornwall
Map ref 1B3

Cornwall's china-clay
town, on a slope between
the clay district's spoil-
cones and the clay ports
and bathing beaches on
St. Austell Bay. The
traffic-free centre has a
fine church of Pentewan
stone and an Italianate
Town and Market Hall,
still a busy market-place.

Boscundle Manor ♨
≋≋≋≋ HIGHLY COMMENDED

Tregrehan, St. Austell,
PL25 3RL
☎ Par (072 681) 3557

*Lovely 18th C house in
secluded grounds, furnished
with many antiques and run
like a private country house. 2
miles north-east of St. Austell.*
Bedrooms: 2 single, 6 double
& 3 twin.
Bathrooms: 11 private.
Bed & breakfast: £52.50
single, £80-£95 double.
Half board: £60-£72.50 daily,
£360-£435 weekly.
Evening meal 7.30pm (l.o.
8.30pm).
Parking for 15.
Open April-October.
Credit: Access, Visa.
🕭 🗲 📞 🛢 🗍 Ⓥ 🗄 🎞 🛆
🍴 ❋ 🛏 🎟 🖵

Clifden Hotel & Restaurant ♨
≋≋ APPROVED

36-39 Aylmer Sq., St. Austell,
PL25 5LJ
☎ (0726) 73691
*Family-run hotel in the centre
of town overlooking the
shopping precinct.*
Bedrooms: 10 single, 3 double
& 2 twin.
Bathrooms: 7 private,
2 public; 7 private showers.
Bed & breakfast: £24-£30
single, £48-£58 double.
Half board: from £30 daily.
Lunch available.
Evening meal 6pm (l.o. 9pm).
Credit: Access, Visa, Diners,
Amex.
🕭 🗲 📞 🛢 🖵 🍷 🛢 Ⓥ 🗄 🎞
🎞 🛆 🍴 🖵

Cliff Head Hotel ♨
≋≋≋≋

Sea Road, Carlyon Bay, St.
Austell, PL25 3RB
☎ Par (072 681) 2345
*Family-run hotel, set in own
grounds. Licensed bar, heated
pool and ample parking space.
Central for touring Cornwall.*
Bedrooms: 4 single, 21 double
& 22 twin, 6 family rooms.
Bathrooms: 49 private,
3 public.
Bed & breakfast: £33.72-
£37.03 single, £64.80 double.
Half board: £43.75-£47.61
daily, £215.40-£229.70
weekly.
Lunch available.
Evening meal 7.30pm (l.o.
9pm).
Parking for 84.
Credit: Access, Visa, Diners,
Amex.
🕭 🖴 🗄 📞 🛢 🖵 🍷 Ⓥ
🗄 🎞 ◑ 🎞 🛆 🍴 🗡 ⮕
❋ 🖵 SP 🖵

Pen-Star Guest House
≋≋

20 Cromwell Rd., St. Austell,
PL25 4PS
☎ (0726) 61367
*Guest accommodation offers
homely and friendly
atmosphere, lounge with colour
TV and licensed premises. 6
bedrooms and fire certificate.*
Bedrooms: 2 single, 4 family
rooms.
Bathrooms: 2 public.
Bed & breakfast: £15-£16
single, £30-£32 double.
Half board: £23-£24 daily,
£105-£112 weekly.
Evening meal 6pm (l.o.
10am).
Parking for 8.
Open January-November.
Credit: Access, Visa.
🕭 🖴 🗍 🍷 Ⓥ 🗄 🎞 🎞 🛆
🗄 DAP SP

Porth Avallen Hotel
Sea Rd., Carlyon Bay, St.
Austell, PL25 3SG
☎ Par (072 681) 2802
Fax (0726) 817097
*A country house hotel, quiet,
friendly and well-appointed.
Overlooking bay and many
local amenities.*
Bedrooms: 5 single, 9 double
& 5 twin, 4 family rooms.
Bathrooms: 23 private.
Bed & breakfast: £40.50-
£46.50 single, £65-£75 double.
Half board: £41-£55 daily,
£300-£360 weekly.
Evening meal 7pm (l.o.
8.30pm).
Parking for 50.
Credit: Access, Visa, Diners,
Amex.
🕭 🗲 📞 🛢 🍷 🛢 Ⓥ 🗄
🎞 ◑ 🎞 🛆 🍴 🗡 ⮕ SP 🖵

Selwood House Hotel ♨
≋≋ APPROVED

60 Alexandra Rd., St.
Austell, PL25 4QN
☎ (0726) 65707
*Detached, family-run hotel,
centrally situated for holiday
and business, in the beautiful
St. Austell Bay.*
Bedrooms: 3 single, 4 double
& 2 twin, 2 family rooms.
Bathrooms: 11 private.
Bed & breakfast: £27.50-
£31.50 single, £54-£58 double.
Half board: £36-£40.50 daily,
£249-£280 weekly.
Evening meal 6.30pm (l.o.
7pm).
Parking for 13.
Credit: Access, Visa, Diners,
Amex.
🕭 🖴 🛢 🖵 🍷 Ⓥ 🗄 🎞 🎞
🛆 🍴 ❋

White Hart Hotel ♨
≋≋≋

Church St., St. Austell,
PL25 4AT
☎ (0726) 72100
*Built in the late 16th C,
became the chief coaching inn
in the 18th C. Now a family-
run hotel.*
Bedrooms: 2 single, 13 double
& 2 twin, 1 family room.
Bathrooms: 18 private.
Bed & breakfast: £35-£45
single, £52-£60 double.
Half board: £45-£55 daily,
£165-£300 weekly.
Lunch available.
Evening meal 5pm (l.o.
8.30pm).
Credit: Access, Visa, Diners,
Amex.
🕭 🗲 📞 🍷 🛢 Ⓥ 🎞 🛆 🍴
⮕ ❋ SP 🖵
✪ Display advertisement
appears on page 460.

Winchmore
72 Alexandra Rd., St.
Austell, PL25 4QN
☎ (0726) 74585
*Homely family-run guesthouse
close to recreation centre, rail
and bus stations. Only 1.5
miles from picturesque
Charlestown harbour.*
Bedrooms: 1 single, 2 double
& 1 twin, 2 family rooms.
Bathrooms: 1 public.
Bed & breakfast: £10-£11
single, £20-£22 double.
Half board: £14-£15 daily,
£94.50-£101.50 weekly.
Evening meal 5.45pm (l.o.
5pm).
Parking for 4.
🕭 🖵 🍷 ⓊⓁ 🛢 🗄 🎞 🎞 🛆
DAP SP

ST IVES

Cornwall
Map ref 1B3

Old fishing port, artists'
colony and holiday town
with good surfing beach.
Fishermen's cottages,
granite fish cellars, a
sandy harbour and
magnificent headlands
typify a charm that has
survived since the 19th C
pilchard boom.
*Tourist Information
Centre* ☎ *(0736) 796297*

Anchorage
≋≋ APPROVED

5 Bunkers Hill, St. Ives,
TR26 1LJ
☎ Penzance (0736) 797135
*18th C fisherman's cottage
guest house with exceptional
decor. Short walk to beach.
Full of old world charm.*

Continued ▶

429

ST IVES
Continued

Bedrooms: 1 single, 3 double & 1 twin, 1 family room.
Bathrooms: 3 private, 1 public; 1 private shower.
Bed & breakfast: £12-£14 single, £24-£30 double.
🛇4 🕭 🖵 🖔 ᵁᴸ Ⓥ 🗎 ▥ ◛
🗙 ⚲ 🎣

Barnoon End Guest House
Listed
Barn-a-Woon, St. Ives, TR26 1JD
☎ Penzance (0736) 795754
Spacious house with panoramic views. Showers, colour TV and tea/coffee making. Licensed bar. 2 minutes from beach and harbour.
Bedrooms: 2 single, 1 double & 2 twin, 4 family rooms.
Bathrooms: 2 public; 5 private showers.
Bed & breakfast: £10-£13 single, £20-£28 double.
Half board: £15-£18 daily, £105-£126 weekly.
Evening meal 6.30pm (l.o. 7.30pm).
🛇 🖔 🛏 Ⓥ 🗎 ▥ Ⓣⓥ ◉ ▥
◛ ⓣ Ʊ 🏳 ᴰᴬᴾ ⚲ ˢᴾ 🎣

Blue Hayes Guest House
😋😋
Trelyon Ave., St. Ives, TR26 2AD
☎ Penzance (0736) 797129
Comfortable detached guesthouse with panoramic sea views over St. Ives Bay and a quiet, colourful garden. Warm and friendly atmosphere.
Bedrooms: 2 single, 5 double, 2 family rooms.
Bathrooms: 5 private, 2 public.
Bed & breakfast: £21-£25 single, £42-£50 double.
Half board: £30-£33.50 daily, £160-£200 weekly.
Evening meal 6.30pm.
Parking for 10.
Open March-October.
Credit: Access, Visa.
🛇5 🖵 🖔 Ⓥ 🗎 ▥ ◛ Ʊ 🏳
☀ 🎣

Blue Mist
😋😋😋 **APPROVED**
6 The Warren, St. Ives, TR26 2EA
☎ Penzance (0736) 795209
Comfortable establishment, most rooms with sea views and fully on suite. Only 1 minute from beach, town and parking.
Bedrooms: 2 single, 5 double & 1 twin, 1 family room.
Bathrooms: 8 private, 1 public.

Bed & breakfast: £15.40-£18.09 single, £30.80-£36.18 double.
Half board: £19.72-£24.06 daily, £138.04-£168.42 weekly.
Evening meal 6pm (l.o. 5.30pm).
Parking for 4.
Open March-November.
Credit: Access, Visa.
🛇4 📞 🖵 🖔 ᵁᴸ 🛏 Ⓥ 🗎 ▥
◛ ⚲ ᴰᴬᴾ

Chy-An-Drea Hotel M
The Terrace, St. Ives, TR26 2BP
☎ Penzance (0736) 795076
🄲🄳 Consort
Cornish granite building overlooking Porthminster Beach and close to the town. Own fitness room.
Bedrooms: 7 single, 12 double & 12 twin, 2 family rooms.
Bathrooms: 33 private, 1 public.
Bed & breakfast: £27-£36 single, £54-£72 double.
Half board: £40-£49.50 daily, £220-£300 weekly.
Lunch available.
Evening meal 7.15pm (l.o. 8.30pm).
Parking for 25.
Open March-October.
Credit: Access, Visa, Diners, Amex.
🛇5 🖔 📞 🖵 🖔 🛏 Ⓥ 🗎
▥ ◛ ⓣ ˢᴾ Ⓣ

Garrack Hotel M
😋😋😋 **COMMENDED**
Higher Ayr, St. Ives, TR26 3AA
☎ Penzance (0736) 796199
Fax (0736) 798955
Family-managed hotel with superb sea views. Quiet location. Ample free parking. Heated indoor pool, sauna, solarium. Open all year.
Bedrooms: 6 single, 7 double & 5 twin, 3 family rooms.
Bathrooms: 15 private, 5 public.
Bed & breakfast: £26-£43 single, £52-£86 double.
Half board: £38-£56 daily, £237-£355 weekly.
Lunch available.
Evening meal 7pm (l.o. 8.30pm).
Parking for 30.
Credit: Access, Visa, Diners, Amex.
🛇 🖔 📞 🖵 🖔 Ⓥ 🗎 Ⓣⓥ
▥ ◛ 🍺 🖾 🏳 ☀ ⚲ ⚲ ˢᴾ
Ⓣ

Hollies Hotel M
😋😋
4 Talland Rd., St. Ives, TR26 2DF
☎ Penzance (0736) 796605

Family hotel close to Porthminster beach, bus, railway station and town centre. Central heating and en-suite rooms. Open all year.
Bedrooms: 4 double & 1 twin, 4 family rooms.
Bathrooms: 9 private.
Bed & breakfast: £16-£21 single, £32-£42 double.
Half board: £23-£28 daily, £130-£175 weekly.
Evening meal 6pm (l.o. 6.30pm).
Parking for 12.
🛇 🖔 🖵 🖔 🛏 🗎 Ⓣⓥ ▥ ◛
⚲ ˢᴾ

Longships Hotel M
😋😋😋 **APPROVED**
Talland Rd., St. Ives, TR26 2DF
☎ Penzance (0736) 798180
Overlooking St. Ives Bay, minutes by foot from town centre and beaches. In-house entertainment. Special weekend breaks.
Bedrooms: 3 single, 8 double & 4 twin, 9 family rooms.
Bathrooms: 24 private.
Bed & breakfast: £14.50-£20 single, £29-£40 double.
Half board: £20.50-£26 daily, £129-£187 weekly.
Lunch available.
Evening meal 6pm (l.o. 7pm).
Parking for 18.
Credit: Access, Visa.
🛇 🖔 🖾 🖵 🖵 🛏 Ⓥ 🗎
Ⓣⓥ ▥ ◛ ⓣ 🏳 ☀ ᴰᴬᴾ ˢᴾ

Lyonesse Hotel
Talland Rd., St. Ives, TR26 2DF
☎ Penzance (0736) 796315
One of the original hotels in St Ives, now tastefully converted to provide modern facilities and retaining old world charm. Ideal location for touring, walking and sports.
Bedrooms: 8 double & 2 twin, 5 family rooms.
Bathrooms: 15 private, 1 public.
Bed & breakfast: £18-£25 single, £36-£50 double.
Evening meal 6.30pm (l.o. 6.30pm).
Parking for 10.
Open March-October.

The Nook Hotel
😋😋
St. Ives, TR26 1EQ
☎ Penzance (0736) 795913
Family hotel in secluded gardens, near cliff path, beaches and harbour. Children's play area and car park. Traditional home cooking.

Bedrooms: 3 single, 5 double & 2 twin, 3 family rooms.
Bathrooms: 6 private, 4 public.
Bed & breakfast: £13-£20 single, £26-£40 double.
Half board: £19-£26 daily, £125-£175 weekly.
Evening meal 6.30pm (l.o. 7pm).
Parking for 15.
Open April-October.
🛇 🖔 🛏 Ⓥ 🗎 Ⓣⓥ ▥ ◛ 🖾
🍺 ☀ 🗙 ⚲ ˢᴾ Ⓣ

Old Vicarage Hotel
😋😋😋 **COMMENDED**
Parc-an-Creet, St. Ives, TR26 2ET
☎ Penzance (0736) 796124
Well converted Victorian rectory with great character and charm in wooded grounds off the B3306. Just over half a mile from town centre and beaches.
Bedrooms: 2 single, 3 double, 3 family rooms.
Bathrooms: 4 private, 3 public; 2 private showers.
Bed & breakfast: £29-£36 double.
Evening meal 6.45pm (l.o. 6.45pm).
Parking for 15.
Open March-October.
Credit: Access, Visa.
🛇 🖔 🛏 🗎 Ⓣⓥ ▥ ◛ Ʊ ☀
🖾 🎣

Panorama Guest House
Listed
1 Barnoon Ter., St. Ives, TR26 1JE
☎ Penzance (0736) 795951
Close to the town centre, with a magnificent view of harbour, bay and the island from every window.
Bedrooms: 2 double, 3 family rooms.
Bathrooms: 1 public; 1 private shower.
Bed & breakfast: £24-£25 double.
Open April-October.
🛇5 🖔 ᵁᴸ 🗎 Ⓣⓥ ▥ 🗙 🎣

Pondarosa Guest House
😋😋 **COMMENDED**
10 Porthminster Ter., St. Ives, TR26 2DQ
☎ Penzance (0736) 795875
Charming Victorian house with well-appointed, comfortable accommodation in quiet location yet convenient for town and beaches. Interesting garden and conservatory.
Bedrooms: 1 single, 3 double & 1 twin, 4 family rooms.
Bathrooms: 2 private, 2 public; 2 private showers.
Bed & breakfast: £12-£13 single, £26-£32 double.

Half board: £19-£23 daily, £130-£155 weekly. Lunch available. Evening meal 6.30pm (l.o. 6.30pm). Parking for 10.

Porthminster Hotel M

1 The Terrace., St. Ives, TR26 2BN
☎ Penzance (0736) 795221
Best Western
Established family hotel overlooking Porthminster Beach, with magnificent views of bay from most bedrooms and public rooms.
Bedrooms: 5 single, 18 double & 18 twin, 9 family rooms.
Bathrooms: 50 private.
Bed & breakfast: £35-£45 single, £70-£90 double.
Half board: £45-£54 daily, £90-£108 weekly.
Lunch available.
Evening meal 7.15pm (l.o. 8.30pm).
Parking for 38.
Credit: Access, Visa, C.Bl., Diners, Amex.

Primavera Private Hotel

14 Draycott Ter., St. Ives, TR26 2EF
☎ Penzance (0736) 795595
Small friendly hotel overlooking Porthminster Beach, with warm, personal and efficient service. Carefully prepared food and special dietary needs catered for.
Bedrooms: 2 single, 3 family rooms.
Bathrooms: 1 public; 2 private showers.
Bed & breakfast: £12-£16 single, £24-£32 double.
Lunch available.
Open June-September.

Roboro House

17 Ayr Ter., St. Ives, TR26 1EN
☎ Penzance (0736) 796231
Large double-fronted property in quiet residential area of St. Ives close to beach and town. Some bedrooms have sea views.
Bedrooms: 3 double & 1 twin, 3 family rooms.
Bathrooms: 2 public.
Bed & breakfast: £10-£12 single, £26-£28 double.
Half board: £16.50-£18.50 daily, £115.50-£129.50 weekly.

Lunch available.
Evening meal 6.30pm (l.o. 7pm).

Sandsifter Hotel M
APPROVED

1 Godrevy Beach, St Ives Bay, Godrevy, Hayle, TR27 5ED
☎ (0736) 753314
Peaceful, comfortable hotel in over 2 acres of private garden, 1 mile to nearest house, 250 yards to beach. Chef/proprietor, a la carte menu. Sorry no children or dogs.
Bedrooms: 2 single, 3 double & 1 twin, 1 family room.
Bathrooms: 7 private.
Bed & breakfast: £20-£24 single, £36-£46 double.
Half board: £25-£30 daily, £165-£198 weekly.
Lunch available.
Evening meal 6.30pm (l.o. 9pm).
Parking for 80.
Credit: Visa.

Skidden House Hotel and Restaurant
COMMENDED

Skidden Hill, St. Ives, TR26 2DU
☎ Penzance (0736) 796899
Small, 16th C hotel adjacent to beach and harbour, in the centre of St Ives. Renowned for comfort, cuisine and fine wines.
Bedrooms: 1 single, 5 double & 1 twin.
Bathrooms: 5 private, 1 public.
Bed & breakfast: £29.50-£35 single, £59-£70 double.
Half board: £37-£45 daily, £259-£294 weekly.
Lunch available.
Evening meal 7pm (l.o. 9.50pm).
Parking for 7.
Open January-November.
Credit: Access, Visa.

Classifications and quality commendations were correct at the time of going to press but are subject to change. Please check at the time of booking.

ST JUST-IN-PENWITH

Cornwall
Map ref 1A3

4m N. Land's End
Coastal parish of craggy moorland scattered with engine houses and chimney stacks of disused mines. The old mining town of St. Just has handsome 19th C granite buildings. North of the town are the dramatic ruined tin mines at Botallack and, at Boscaswell, the Geevor Tin Mine Museum.

Kenython

St. Just-in-Penwith, Penzance, TR19 7PT
☎ (0736) 788607
A comfortable guesthouse, family-run, off the beaten track. A warm welcome and home cooking await you.
Bedrooms: 1 single, 1 double & 1 twin, 1 family room.
Bathrooms: 2 private, 1 public.
Bed & breakfast: £13-£14 single, £26-£28 double.
Half board: £21-£22 daily, £143-£150 weekly.
Evening meal 7pm (l.o. 10am).
Parking for 6.
Open April-October.

ST MAWES

Cornwall
Map ref 1B3

Small resort and yachting centre in a pretty estuary setting on the Roseland Peninsula. Enclosed by fields and woods of the Percuil River, it is said to be the warmest winter resort in Britain.

The Idle Rocks Hotel M

Tredenham Rd., St. Mawes, Truro, TR2 5AN
☎ (0326) 270771
Hotel at the water's edge overlooking yachting harbour, well known for locally-caught fish. Tranquillity and relaxed atmosphere.
Bedrooms: 2 single, 10 double & 2 twin, 5 family rooms.
Bathrooms: 19 private, 1 public.
Bed & breakfast: £25-£46 single, £50-£92 double.

Half board: £31-£60 daily, £195-£378 weekly.
Lunch available.
Evening meal 7.15pm (l.o. 9.15pm).
Credit: Access, Visa, Diners, Amex.

ST MAWGAN

Cornwall
Map ref 1B2

Pretty village on wooded slopes in the Vale of Lanherne. At its centre, an old stone bridge is overlooked by the church with its lofty buttressed tower. Among the ancient stone crosses in the churchyard is a 15th C lantern cross with carved figures.

Dalswinton Country House Hotel

St. Mawgan, Newquay, TR8 4EZ
☎ (0637) 860385
Small licensed hotel with log fires, in lovely rural setting with scenic views down wooded valley to sea.
Bedrooms: 3 double & 2 twin, 4 family rooms.
Bathrooms: 9 private.
Bed & breakfast: £12-£18 single, £24-£36 double.
Half board: £20.50-£26.50 daily, £135-£175 weekly.
Lunch available.
Evening meal 6.30pm (l.o. 7.30pm).
Parking for 14.
Credit: Access, Visa.

ST WENN

Cornwall
Map ref 1B2

4m E. St. Columb Major

Wenn Manor Hotel M
APPROVED

St. Wenn, Bodmin, PL30 5PS
☎ St.Austell (0726) 890240
Set in 4 acres, licensed, with an outdoor heated pool. 3 miles off A30 and A39.
Bedrooms: 1 single, 3 double & 2 twin, 1 family room.
Bathrooms: 6 private, 1 public.
Bed & breakfast: £19-£23 single, £38-£46 double.
Half board: £25-£28 daily, £175-£196 weekly.

Continued ▶

ST WENN

Continued

Lunch available.
Evening meal 6.45pm (l.o. 7.30pm).
Parking for 20.
Open March-November.
Credit: Access, Visa.

ᵍ ◻ ♥ ▮ Ⓥ ◅ ⒯ ⅷ ▪
Ⳁ ⌂ ❋ ⋈ ⨯ ⚏ ⍌ ⊞

SALCOMBE

Devon
Map ref 1C3

Sheltered yachting resort of whitewashed houses and narrow streets in a balmy setting on the Kingsbridge Estuary. Palm, myrtle and other Mediterranean plants flourish. There are sandy bays and creeks for boating.

Grafton Towers Hotel ⋈
ᵍᵍᵍ

Salcombe, TQ8 8LQ
☎ (054 884) 2882
Comfortable country house hotel commanding spectacular coastal views. Elegant dining room, local seafood and produce, homebaked pies and clotted cream.
Bedrooms: 7 double & 6 twin.
Bathrooms: 12 private, 1 public.
Half board: £34-£42 daily.
Evening meal 7.30pm (l.o. 8pm).
Parking for 12.
Open April-October.
Credit: Access, Visa.

ᵍ ◙ ◻ ♥ ▮ Ⓥ ◅ ▪ ❋
⚏ ⊞ ⒯

Knowle Hotel ⋈
ᵍᵍᵍ

Onslow Rd., Salcombe,
TQ8 8HY
☎ (054 884) 2846
Spacious Regency house set in wooded gardens overlooking estuary, with log fires. Central heating, colour TV and tea/coffee facilities.
Bedrooms: 3 single, 3 double & 6 twin, 3 family rooms.
Bathrooms: 8 private, 4 public.
Bed & breakfast: £23-£32.20 single, £46-£64.40 double.
Half board: £34.50-£43.70 daily, £227.70-£281.75 weekly.
Lunch available.
Evening meal 7pm (l.o. 7.45pm).

Parking for 40.
Open March-October.
Credit: Access, Visa.

ᵍ ⬦ ◻ ♥ ▮ Ⓥ ◅ ⒯
▪ ⌂ ♠ ❋ ⚏ ⊞

Sunnycliff Hotel
ᵍᵍᵍ

Cliff Rd., Salcombe,
TQ8 8JX
☎ (054 884) 2207
Informal family hotel on water's edge. Superb sea views from all rooms. Own moorings and landing stage. English fare.
Bedrooms: 3 single, 7 double & 4 twin, 5 family rooms.
Bathrooms: 9 private, 4 public; 2 private showers.
Bed & breakfast: £23-£27.50 single, £46-£55 double.
Half board: £31-£40 daily, £200-£250 weekly.
Lunch available.
Evening meal 7.30pm (l.o. 8pm).
Parking for 18.
Credit: Access, Visa.

ᵍ ▮ Ⓥ ◅ ⒯ ▪ Ⳁ ⌇ ❋
⊞

Torre View Hotel
ᵍᵍᵍ APPROVED

Devon Rd., Salcombe,
TQ8 8HJ
☎ (054 884) 2633
Large detached residence commanding extensive views of the estuary and sea.
Bedrooms: 5 double & 1 twin, 2 family rooms.
Bathrooms: 8 private.
Bed & breakfast: £23-£29 single, £39-£46 double.
Half board: £27-£31 daily, £179-£199 weekly.
Evening meal 7pm (l.o. 6pm).
Parking for 5.
Open February-October.
Credit: Access, Visa.

ᵍ ♥ ▮ ◅ ⒯ ▪ ∪ ⌇
⍌ ⊞

Woodgrange Hotel
ᵍᵍᵍ

Devon Rd., Salcombe,
TQ8 8HJ
☎ (054 884) 2439/2006
Ⓒ Minotels
A small Victorian hotel overlooking the beautiful Salcombe estuary, set in its own south facing grounds.
Bedrooms: 1 single, 5 double & 3 twin, 1 family room.
Bathrooms: 10 private.
Bed & breakfast: £21-£24 single, £42-£48 double.
Half board: £32-£35 daily, £196-£210 weekly.
Evening meal 7pm (l.o. 7.30pm).
Parking for 12.

Open April-October.
Credit: Access, Visa, Diners, Amex.

ᵍ ⌇ ◙ ◻ ♥ ▮ Ⓥ ◅ ⅷ
▪ ⚑ ⍌ ⊞

SALISBURY

Wiltshire
Map ref 2B3

Beautiful city and ancient regional capital set amid water meadows on its medieval plain. Buildings of all periods are dominated by the stately cathedral whose spire is the tallest in England. Built between 1220 and 1258, the cathedral is one of the purest examples of Early English architecture.
Tourist Information Centre ☎ *(0722) 334956*

Byways House ⋈
ᵍᵍᵍ

31 Fowlers Rd., Salisbury,
SP1 2QP
☎ (0722) 328364
Fax (0722) 322146
Attractive family-run Victorian house with cathedral view, in quiet area of city centre. Car park. Bedrooms en-suite with colour TV. Traditional English breakfast and evening meal.
Bedrooms: 4 single, 4 double & 7 twin, 5 family rooms.
Bathrooms: 13 private, 2 public.
Bed & breakfast: £17-£25 single, £30-£40 double.
Half board: £22.50-£25 daily, £150-£175 weekly.
Evening meal 6pm (l.o. 7pm).
Parking for 16.
Credit: Access, Visa.

ᵍ ♥ ▮ ◙ ◻ ♥ ⅷ ▮ Ⓥ
⍌ ◅ ⅷ ▪ ⌂ ❋ Ⓖ
⍌ ⊞

The Coach and Horses
39 Winchester St., Salisbury,
SP1 1HG
☎ (0722) 336254
Fax (0722) 414319
Salisbury's oldest coaching inn, recently refurbished and now offering comfort and varied cuisine. Only non-smoking accommodation available.
Bedrooms: 2 double.
Bathrooms: 2 private.
Bed & breakfast: £38.50-£41.50 single, £49.50-£52.50 double.
Lunch available.
Evening meal 5pm (l.o. 10pm).
Credit: Access, Visa.

ᵍ ◙ ◻ ♥ ▮ Ⓥ ⍌ ◅ ⅷ
▪ ⋈ ⍌ ⊞

County Hotel
ᵍᵍᵍ COMMENDED

Bridge St., Salisbury,
SP1 2ND
☎ (0722) 20229
Over 100 years old, built of mellow Salisbury stone, a Victorian listed building with its own ghost. Overlooking the river and close to the shops.
Bedrooms: 3 single, 15 double & 10 twin, 3 family rooms.
Bathrooms: 31 private.
Bed & breakfast: £53-£62.50 single, from £70 double.
Lunch available.
Evening meal 6pm (l.o. 10pm).
Parking for 31.
Credit: Access, Visa, C.Bl., Diners, Amex.

ᵍ ⌇ ◙ ◻ ♥ ▮ Ⓥ ⍌ ◅
◙ ⅷ ▪ ⌂ ⌇ ⋈ ⍌ ⊞

Glen Lyn Guest House
ᵍᵍ

6 Bellamy La., Milford Hill,
Salisbury, SP1 2SP
☎ (0722) 27880
Large Victorian house in quiet cul-de-sac near city centre. Easy parking.
Bedrooms: 1 single, 3 double & 2 twin, 1 family room.
Bathrooms: 4 private, 1 public.
Bed & breakfast: £15-£17 single, £28-£34 double.
Parking for 6.

ᵍ 12 ◻ ♥ ⅷ ⍌ ◅ ⅷ ▪
⋈ ⍌ ⒯

Holmhurst Guest House
ᵍᵍ

Downton Rd., Salisbury,
SP2 8AR
☎ (0722) 323164
Pleasant town house, a short walk from Salisbury Cathedral. Riverside and country walks. Easy access to coastal resorts.
Bedrooms: 1 single, 3 double & 3 twin, 1 family room.
Bathrooms: 5 private, 1 public.
Bed & breakfast: £15-£22 single, £26-£32 double.
Parking for 8.
Open April-October.

ᵍ 5 ⬦ ▮ Ⓥ ⍌ ◅ ⒯ ▪
⋈

Leena's Guest House
ᵍᵍ

50 Castle Rd., Salisbury,
SP1 3RL
☎ (0722) 335419
Attractive Edwardian house, close to riverside walks and park, friendly atmosphere. Modern facilities include en-suite and ground-floor rooms.

Bedrooms: 1 single, 2 double & 2 twin, 1 family room.
Bathrooms: 3 private, 1 public; 1 private shower.
Bed & breakfast: from £16 single, £26-£34 double.
Parking for 7.

Malvern
🏠🏠 **COMMENDED**
31 Hulse Rd., Salisbury, SP1 3LU
☎ (0722) 27995
Small guesthouse, situated in a quiet cul-de-sac backing on to the River Avon. 5 minutes' walk to town. Non-smokers only please.
Bedrooms: 1 double & 2 twin.
Bathrooms: 1 private, 1 public.
Bed & breakfast: £26-£32 double.
Parking for 3.

Meadow Cottage
103 Church Rd., Laverstock, Salisbury, SP1 1RB
☎ (0722) 338696
Modern, centrally heated, comfortable detached house with sun-room conservatory and lovely views from all windows. Walking distance from Salisbury.
Bedrooms: 1 single, 1 twin.
Bathrooms: 1 public.
Bed & breakfast: £11 single, £24 double.
Parking for 2.

Old Bell Inn M
🏠🏠
2 Saint Ann St., Salisbury, SP1 2DN
☎ (0722) 27958
Delightful period inn with restaurant, in the shadow of the soaring spire of Salisbury Cathedral.
Bedrooms: 5 double & 2 twin.
Bathrooms: 7 private.
Bed & breakfast: £50-£55 single, £50-£55 double.
Evening meal 7pm (l.o. 9.30pm).
Parking for 11.
Credit: Access, Visa, Diners, Amex.

Rose & Crown Hotel M
Harnham Rd., Salisbury, SP2 8JF
☎ (0722) 327908 Telex 47224 ROSCRN G
ⓒⓡ Queens Moat Houses
13th C inn on the banks of the River Avon, in the shadow of Salisbury Cathedral. 3 rooms are suitable for disabled guests.

Bedrooms: 7 double & 12 twin, 9 family rooms.
Bathrooms: 28 private.
Bed & breakfast: £70.50-£80.50 single, £88.50-£95 double.
Lunch available.
Evening meal 7pm (l.o. 9.30pm).
Parking for 50.
Credit: Access, Visa, C.Bl., Diners, Amex.

Stratford Lodge
4 Park La., Castle Rd., Salisbury, SP1 3NP
☎ (0722) 325177
Victorian detached residence in quiet road. Attractively furnished with antiques. Imaginative, varied cooking using local and home-grown produce.
Bedrooms: 1 single, 3 double & 3 twin, 2 family rooms.
Bathrooms: 9 private.
Bed & breakfast: £25-£35 single, £40-£50 double.
Half board: £32-£47 daily.
Evening meal 6.30pm (l.o. midday).
Parking for 12.

The Trafalgar Hotel
33 Milford St., Salisbury, SP1 2AP
☎ (0722) 338686
Fax (0722) 414496
ⓒⓡ Resort
Charming 14th C hotel offering good facilities and cuisine at an acceptable price.
Bedrooms: 4 single, 7 double & 5 twin.
Bathrooms: 16 private.
Bed & breakfast: £40-£50 single, £58-£70 double.
Lunch available.
Evening meal 7pm (l.o. 9.30pm).
Credit: Access, Visa, Diners, Amex.

Victoria Lodge Guest House M
🏠🏠 **APPROVED**
61 Castle Rd., Salisbury, SP1 3RH
☎ (0722) 20586 Fax (0722) 414507
Warm, comfortable guesthouse set away from main street, within easy walking distance of city centre.
Bedrooms: 2 single, 6 double & 5 twin, 2 family rooms.
Bathrooms: 14 private, 2 public.

Bed & breakfast: £20-£30 single, £30-£45 double.
Evening meal 6pm (l.o. 9pm).
Parking for 30.

SALISBURY PLAIN
See Amesbury, Chicklade, Cholderton, Everleigh, Salisbury, Warminster, Winterbourne Stoke.

SAUNTON
Devon
Map ref 1C1

Houses situated on a minor road at the end of Braunton Burrows, part of which is a nature reserve, important to botanists and ornithologists. Nearby is a fine golf-course and a 3 mile beach, Saunton Sands.

Preston House Hotel M
🏠🏠🏠 **APPROVED**
Saunton, Braunton, EX33 1LG
☎ Croyde (0271) 890472
Edwardian country house hotel, beautifully furnished, with sea view. Lovingly prepared country-fresh food.
Bedrooms: 1 single, 5 double & 6 twin.
Bathrooms: 12 private, 1 public.
Bed & breakfast: £27.50-£43 single, £55-£65 double.
Lunch available.
Evening meal 7.30pm (l.o. 8.30pm).
Parking for 12.
Open March-December.
Credit: Access, Visa.

Saunton Sands Hotel M
Saunton, Braunton, EX33 1LG
☎ Croyde (0271) 890212
Telex 42551 EXONIA G
REF BREND 1
ⓒⓡ Brend
Directly overlooks 5 miles of golden sands and is surrounded by unspoilt countryside. Offering a wealth of sports and leisure facilities.
Bedrooms: 19 single, 10 double & 22 twin, 39 family rooms.
Bathrooms: 90 private, 5 public.
Bed & breakfast: £56-£66 single, £105-£140 double.

Half board: £60-£77 daily, £240-£540 weekly.
Lunch available.
Evening meal 7.30pm (l.o. 9.30pm).
Parking for 208.
Credit: Access, Visa, Diners, Amex.

SEATON
Devon
Map ref 1D2

Small resort lying near the mouth of the River Axe. A mile-long beach extends to the dramatic cliffs of Beer Head. Annual arts and drama festival.
Tourist Information Centre ☎ (0297) 21660 or 21689

Beach End Guest House M
🏠🏠 **COMMENDED**
8 Trevelyan Rd., Seaton, EX12 2NL
☎ (0297) 23388
Nearest guesthouse to beach. All rooms have sea views. English cooking our speciality. Morning tea/evening beverages inclusive. Ample car parking.
Bedrooms: 1 single, 3 double & 1 twin, 1 family room.
Bathrooms: 2 public.
Bed & breakfast: £13-£13.50 single, £26-£27 double.
Half board: £22-£22.50 daily, £144-£147.50 weekly.
Evening meal 7pm (l.o. 3pm).
Parking for 8.
Open February-October.

SENNEN
Cornwall
Map ref 1A3

The last village before Land's End. Magnificent beach at Sennen Cove.

The Old Manor Hotel
🏠🏠 **APPROVED**
Sennen, Lands End, TR19 7AD
☎ (0736) 871280
On A30, 1 mile from Land's End, very easy to find, near superb beach. Built of hand-dressed granite for the squire.
Bedrooms: 4 double & 1 twin, 3 family rooms.
Bathrooms: 4 private, 2 public; 1 private shower.
Bed & breakfast: £28-£40 double.

Continued ▶

433

SENNEN
Continued

Half board: £21-£27 daily, £118-£160 weekly.
Lunch available.
Evening meal 6.30pm (l.o. 7.30pm).
Parking for 52.
Credit: Access, Visa.

⌂ ♨ ⌕ ▢ ✿ ‖ Ⅴ ⊨ ⓣ
▦ ⌂ ☽ ✕ ♨ ♨

The Old Success Inn ▲
♨♨♨
Sennen Cove, Land's End, Penzance, TR19 7DG
☎ Penzance (0736) 871232
This refurbished inn nestles in one of Cornwall's most beautiful bays, within yards of the superb Whitesands Beach.
Bedrooms: 1 single, 8 double & 2 twin.
Bathrooms: 9 private, 1 public.
Bed & breakfast: £20-£30 single, £40-£60 double.
Lunch available.
Evening meal 7pm (l.o. 9pm).
Parking for 20.
Credit: Visa.

⌂ ♨ ▢ ✿ ‖ ⊨ ⓣ ▦ ⍭
✕ ⋈ SP Ⓣ

SHALDON
Devon
Map ref 1D2

Pretty resort facing Teignmouth from the south bank of the Teign Estuary. Regency houses harmonise with others of later periods; there are old cottages and narrow lanes. On the Ness, a sandstone promontory nearby, a tunnel built in the 19th C leads to a beach revealed at low tide.

Glenside Hotel ▲
♨♨♨ **COMMENDED**
Ringmore Rd., Shaldon, TQ14 0EP
☎ (0626) 872448
Grade II listed building in conservation area overlooking the Teign Estuary. Family-run hotel with home cooking. Easy walking. Car park.
Bedrooms: 2 single, 5 double & 3 twin.
Bathrooms: 7 private, 1 public.
Bed & breakfast: £16-£19.65 single, £32-£40 double.
Half board: £25-£30 daily, £150-£188 weekly.
Evening meal 6.30pm (l.o. 6.30pm).

Parking for 10.
Open January-October, December.

⌂ ♨ ⌂ ✿ ‖ Ⅴ ⊨ ▦ ⌂ ⍭
SP

SHEEPWASH
Devon
Map ref 1C2

4m NW. Hatherleigh Hilltop village deep in rural Devon overlooking the salmon-rich Torridge. Thatched, colour-washed cottages, farmhouses and an inn are centred around the village square.

Half Moon Inn ▲
Sheepwash, Beaworthy, EX21 5NE
☎ Black Torrington (040 923) 376
Owned by the Inniss family for 30 years. The hotel contains all the charm and warmth of a village inn, with the facilities to ensure the comfort and enjoyment of our guests.
Bedrooms: 2 single, 4 double & 7 twin, 2 family rooms.
Bathrooms: 13 private, 2 public.
Bed & breakfast: £25-£28 single, £48-£56 double.
Half board: £38-£43 daily, £250-£275 weekly.
Lunch available.
Evening meal 8pm (l.o. 8.30pm).
Parking for 26.
Open February-December.
Credit: Access, Visa.

⌂ ♨ ⌂ ⊙ ▢ ✿ ‖ Ⅴ ⊨
▦ ⌂ ‖ ⍏ ♩ ♨ ⋈ SP

SHEPTON MALLET
Somerset
Map ref 2A2

Important, stone-built market town beneath the south-west slopes of the Mendips. Thriving rural industries include glove and shoe making, dairying and cider making; the remains of a medieval 'shambles' in the square date from the town's prosperity as a wool centre.

Bowlish House
Coombe Lane, Shepton Mallet, BA4 5JD
☎ (0749) 342022
Restaurant with accommodation in a listed Georgian house, on the Wells road outside Shepton Mallet.

Bedrooms: 3 double & 1 twin, 1 family room.
Bathrooms: 5 private.
Bed & breakfast: from £46 double.
Half board: from £41.50 daily.
Evening meal 7pm (l.o. 9.30pm).
Parking for 10.
Credit: Access, Visa.

⌂ ⊙ ▢ ✿ ‖ Ⅴ ⊨ ▦ ⌂
‖ ☽ ♨ ⋈ ♨

Pecking Mill Inn and Hotel
♨♨♨
A371, Evercreech, Shepton Mallet, BA4 6PG
☎ (0749) 830336/830006
16th C farmhouse with oak beamed restaurant and open log fire. Old world atmosphere with all modern amenities.
Bedrooms: 1 single, 5 double.
Bathrooms: 6 private.
Bed & breakfast: £29.50 single, £40 double.
Lunch available.
Evening meal 7pm (l.o. 10pm).
Parking for 23.
Credit: Access, Visa, Diners, Amex.

⌂ ♨ ⌂ ⊙ ▢ ✿ ‖ Ⅴ ⊨
▦ ⌂ ‖ ♨ ♨ ♨

SHERBORNE
Dorset
Map ref 2B3

Historic town of Ham stone with busy industries and an ancient centre. In Anglo-Saxon times it was a cathedral city and until the Dissolution there was a monastery here.
Tourist Information Centre ☎ (0935) 815341

Antelope Hotel
Greenhill, Sherborne, DT9 4EP
☎ Sherborne (0935) 812077
A delightful 18th C hotel, recently restored, in the centre of historic Sherborne. Convenient for touring the West Country.
Bedrooms: 4 single, 10 double & 4 twin, 1 family room.
Bathrooms: 19 private.
Bed & breakfast: £37-£39 single, £49-£59 double.
Half board: £47-£49 daily, £329-£343 weekly.
Lunch available.
Evening meal 6pm (l.o. 11.30pm).
Parking for 35.

Credit: Access, Visa, C.Bl., Diners, Amex.

⌂ ♨ ⌂ ☽ ⊙ ▢ ✿ ‖ Ⅴ
✗ ⊨ ● ▦ ⌂ ♩ ⚹ DAP SP
♨ Ⓣ

Britannia Inn
♨
Westbury, Sherborne, DT9 3EH
☎ (093 581) 3300
Originally the Lord Digby School for Girls, built in 1743, now a listed building.
Bedrooms: 1 single, 1 double & 3 twin, 2 family rooms.
Bathrooms: 1 private, 3 public.
Bed & breakfast: from £17 single, £32-£36 double.
Evening meal 7pm (l.o. 9pm).
Parking for 13.

⌂ ▢ ‖ Ⅴ ▦ ♩ ♨ ♨

Eastbury Hotel ▲
Long St., Sherborne, DT9 3BY
☎ (0935) 813131 Telex 46644
Gracious Georgian town house hotel with attractive walled garden, near town centre. Private car park.
Bedrooms: 6 single, 5 double & 4 twin.
Bathrooms: 15 private.
Bed & breakfast: from £55 single, from £75 double.
Lunch available.
Evening meal 7pm (l.o. 10pm).
Parking for 27.
Credit: Access, Visa.

⌂ ♨ ⌂ ☽ ⊙ ▢ ✿ ‖ Ⅴ ⊨
▦ ⌂ ♩ ☽ ♩ ⚹ ❋ ✕ ⋈ SP
♨ Ⓣ

The Medlycott
♨♨♨ **COMMENDED**
Sherborne Rd., Milborne Port, Sherborne, DT9 5AT
☎ (0963) 250229
Originally a Victorian vicarage. Comfortable coach house accommodation in spacious gardens. On the A30. Ask about our chauffeur-driven tours from your home. Jazz weekends.
Bedrooms: 1 single, 2 double & 1 twin.
Bathrooms: 4 private.
Bed & breakfast: £25-£30 single, £44-£55 double.
Half board: £32.50-£42 daily, £200 weekly.
Lunch available.
Evening meal 7pm (l.o. 9pm).
Parking for 40.
Credit: Access, Visa.

⌂ ♨9 ♨ ☽ ⊙ ▢ ‖ Ⅴ ✗
▦ ⌂ ♩ ☽ ♩ ⚹ ♨ DAP SP
♨ Ⓣ

SHIPHAM

Somerset
Map ref 1D1

3m N. Cheddar
Peaceful village on the
slopes of the Mendip
Hills, once a centre for
calamine mining.

Daneswood House Hotel

😁😁😁😁 COMMENDED
Chuck Hill, Shipham,
Winscombe, Avon BS25 1RD
☎ (093 484) 3145 Fax
(093 484) 3824
*Country house hotel situated
deep in the Mendip Hills in
quiet elevated woodland
setting. Emphasis on fine wines
and food.*
Bedrooms: 9 double & 3 twin.
Bathrooms: 12 private.
Bed & breakfast: £45-£65
single, £62.50-£89.50 double.
Half board: from £45 daily.
Lunch available.
Evening meal 7pm (l.o.
9.30pm).
Parking for 30.
Credit: Access, Visa, Diners,
Amex.
🛇 🛁 📞 ® 🖵 🎇 📺 🛏 ●
🃏 🖃 🌣 🏲 🆎 SP

Penscot Farm House Hotel ⋒

😁😁😁 APPROVED
Shipham, Winscombe,
BS25 1TW
☎ Winscombe
(093 484) 2659
🆑 Minotels
*Cosy old world atmosphere
with log fires in winter, oak
beams and English style food.
Situated in Mendip foothills
with lovely views and walks.*
Bedrooms: 3 single, 6 double
& 5 twin, 3 family rooms.
Bathrooms: 12 private,
3 public.
Bed & breakfast: £23.75-
£27.50 single, £37.50-£45
double.
Half board: £27-£30.50 daily,
£166.50-£197 weekly.
Lunch available.
Evening meal 7pm (l.o. 9pm).
Parking for 40.
Open January-November.
Credit: Access, Visa, C.Bl.,
Diners, Amex.
🛇 🛁 🎇 📞 ® 🛇 🛏 📺 ✂
🃏 📺 ● 🎇 🛁 🍽 🛡 🕛 🌣 SP
🆎 🅃

**The enquiry
coupons at the
back will help you
when contacting
proprietors.**

SIDBURY

Devon
Map ref 1D2

3m N. Sidmouth
Small, rural village set in
the deep valley of the
River Sid. Thatched or
slate-roofed cottages are
gathered around the
Norman church which has
an Anglo-Saxon crypt.
The countryside with its
old farmhouses is
beautiful and the coast
lies 3 miles to the south.

Orchardside Hotel and Restaurant

Cotford Rd., Sidbury,
Sidmouth, EX10 0SQ
☎ (039 57) 351
*Lovely small country hotel and
restaurant, set in 1 acre of
garden and surrounded by
outstanding countryside on
A375 Honiton to Sidmouth
road. Large car park.*
Bedrooms: 2 double & 2 twin,
1 family room.
Bathrooms: 3 private,
1 public.
Bed & breakfast: £16-£20
single, £30-£36 double.
Half board: £25-£28 daily,
£150-£165 weekly.
Lunch available.
Evening meal 6.30pm (l.o.
8.30pm).
Parking for 20.
Credit: Access, Visa.
🛇2 🛁 🖵 🛇 🛡 📺 🎇 🛁 🕯
🌣 🏲 🆎 🖃 🅰 SP

SIDMOUTH

Devon
Map ref 1D2

13m E. Exeter
Charming resort set amid
lofty red cliffs where the
River Sid meets the sea.
The wealth of ornate
Regency and Victorian
villas recalls the time
when this was one of the
south coast's most
exclusive resorts.
Museum; August
International Festival of
Folk Arts.

Belmont Hotel ⋒

The Esplanade, Sidmouth,
EX10 8RX
☎ (0395) 512555
🆑 Brend
*Traditionally one of
Sidmouth's finest seafront
hotels. Leisure facilities are
available at adjacent hotel, The
Victoria.*
Bedrooms: 9 single, 20 double
& 19 twin, 6 family rooms.
Bathrooms: 54 private.

Bed & breakfast: £60-£66
single, £90-£130 double.
Half board: £55-£75 daily,
£225-£480 weekly.
Lunch available.
Evening meal 7pm (l.o. 9pm).
Parking for 50.
Credit: Access, Visa, Diners,
Amex.
🛇 🛁 📞 ® 🖵 🛇 🛡 📺 🛁
● 🖃 📺 🍽 🛡 🛏 🌣 🏲 🆎
🅰 SP 🅃

Byes Links Hotel

Sid Rd., Sidmouth,
EX10 9AA
☎ (0395) 3129 & 3171
*A modern detached hotel
family owned and run, set in
over an acre of grounds.
Heated swimming pool
(outdoor April - November).*
Bedrooms: 2 single, 8 double
& 8 twin, 3 family rooms.
Bathrooms: 21 private,
1 public.
Bed & breakfast: £24-£30
single.
Half board: £32-£39.50 daily,
£225-£260 weekly.
Lunch available.
Evening meal 6.45pm (l.o.
9pm).
Parking for 40.
Open March-November.
🛇 🛁 🎇 ® 🖵 🛇 🛡 📺 🛁
📺 ● 🖃 🛁 🕯 🌣 🏲 🆎
SP

Devoran Hotel

😁😁😁 COMMENDED
Esplanade, Sidmouth,
EX10 8AU
☎ (0395) 513151
*Family-owned hotel
overlooking beach, very close to
town centre and amenities.
Relaxed, happy atmosphere,
with home-cooked food.*
Bedrooms: 4 single, 8 double
& 6 twin, 5 family rooms.
Bathrooms: 21 private,
3 public; 2 private showers.
Half board: £28-£40 daily,
£166-£220 weekly.
Evening meal 6.45pm (l.o.
7.30pm).
Parking for 6.
Open March-November.
🛇 🖵 🎇 🛡 📺 🛁 📺 ● 🖃
🖃 🛁 🏲 🆎 SP

Fortfield Hotel ⋒

😁😁😁😁
Station Rd., Sidmouth,
EX10 8NU
☎ (0395) 512403
*Country house style hotel
overlooking sea, with solarium
and leisure centre. Privately-
owned and family managed.
Elegant decor and friendly
atmosphere.*
Bedrooms: 6 single, 10 double
& 30 twin, 6 family rooms.

Bathrooms: 52 private,
3 public.
Bed & breakfast: £30-£50
single, £60-£100 double.
Half board: £35-£55 daily,
£245-£385 weekly.
Lunch available.
Evening meal 7pm (l.o.
8.30pm).
Parking for 60.
Credit: Access, Visa, Amex.
🛇 🛁 📞 ® 🖵 🛇 🛡 📺 ✂
🃏 📺 ● 🖃 🛁 🍽 🛡 🕯 🎇
🃏 🖃 🏲 🌣 🆎 🛇 SP 🆎 🅃

Groveside Guest House ⋒

😁😁 APPROVED
Vicarage Rd., Sidmouth,
EX10 8UQ
☎ (0395) 513406
*Family-run detached
guesthouse, comfortably
furnished and close to all
amenities.*
Bedrooms: 1 single, 4 double
& 2 twin, 1 family room.
Bathrooms: 3 private,
2 public.
Bed & breakfast: from £12.65
single, from £25.30 double.
Half board: from £19.55
daily, from £133.40 weekly.
Evening meal 6pm (l.o.
4.30pm).
Parking for 7.
Open April-October.
🛇3 🛇 🖃 🅺 🃏 📺 🆎 🎇

Mount Pleasant Hotel

😁😁😁
Salcombe Rd., Sidmouth,
EX10 8JA
☎ (0395) 514694
Fax (0395) 514694
*Early Georgian residence in a
quiet situation, close to all
amenities, with a pleasant
outlook and large garden. All
rooms en-suite, ample car
parking.*
Bedrooms: 2 single, 6 double
& 6 twin, 2 family rooms.
Bathrooms: 5 private;
11 private showers.
Bed & breakfast: £24-£27
single, £48-£50 double.
Half board: £33-£37 daily,
£200-£240 weekly.
Lunch available.
Evening meal 7pm (l.o. 8pm).
Parking for 21.
Open April-October.
🛇10 🛁 🅺 ® 🖵 🛇 🛡 ✂
🃏 🖃 🛁 🍽 🌣 🆎 SP 🆎

Hotel Riviera ⋒

😁😁😁
The Esplanade, Sidmouth,
EX10 8AY
☎ (0395) 515201 Telex 42551
Exonia G. Riviera
Continued ▶

SIDMOUTH
Continued

An attractive hotel offering old fashioned hospitality with modern amenities, superbly situated at the centre of the Esplanade overlooking Lyme Bay.
Bedrooms: 13 single, 6 double & 15 twin.
Bathrooms: 29 private, 3 public.
Bed & breakfast: £41-£57 single, £82-£114 double.
Half board: £47-£63 daily, £329-£441 weekly.
Lunch available.
Evening meal 7pm (l.o. 9pm).
Parking for 21.
Credit: Access, Visa, Diners, Amex.

Royal Glen Hotel

Glen Rd., Sidmouth, EX10 8RW
☎ (0395) 513221/578124/5
In its own grounds 1 minute from the seafront, this hotel was once the residence of Queen Victoria. All public rooms have sea views.
Bedrooms: 9 single, 4 double & 17 twin, 4 family rooms.
Bathrooms: 32 private, 2 public.
Bed & breakfast: £20.89-£38.08 single, £62-£94 double.
Half board: £24.70-£49.85 daily, £173.40-£349.40 weekly.
Lunch available.
Evening meal 7pm (l.o. 8pm).
Parking for 24.
Credit: Access, Visa, Amex.

Salcombe Hill House Hotel M

Beatlands Rd., Sidmouth, EX10 8JQ
☎ (0395) 514697 514398
Set in lovely grounds, quiet, yet close to all Sidmouth's amenities. Outdoor heated swimming pool. Ample parking. Mini-breaks available.
Bedrooms: 7 single, 6 double & 14 twin, 5 family rooms.
Bathrooms: 29 private, 3 public.
Half board: £31-£45.90 daily.
Lunch available.
Evening meal 7.15pm (l.o. 8.30pm).
Parking for 40.

Open March-October.
Credit: Access, Visa, Diners.

Sidholme

Elysian Fields, Sidmouth, EX10 8UJ
☎ (0395) 513633 & (0395) 515104
Christian-based holiday and conference centre set in 10 acres of grounds and situated in Sidmouth, a floral town of Europe.
Bedrooms: 30 single, 14 double & 23 twin, 9 family rooms.
Bathrooms: 11 private, 13 public.
Bed & breakfast: £20-£32.50 single, £40-£65 double.
Half board: £25-£35 daily, £140-£230 weekly.
Lunch available.
Evening meal 6.45pm (l.o. 6.45pm).
Parking for 77.

Sidmount Hotel M

Station Rd., Sidmouth, EX10 8XJ
☎ (0395) 513432
Imposing Georgian property, built 1825, on an elevated site with views from Salcombe Hill to Peak Hill and the sea.
Bedrooms: 6 double & 7 twin, 2 family rooms.
Bathrooms: 15 private.
Bed & breakfast: £20.60-£32 single, £41.20-£64 double.
Half board: £23.40-£33 daily, £142.50-£201 weekly.
Lunch available.
Evening meal 6.30pm (l.o. 7pm).
Parking for 17.
Open March-November.

Victoria Hotel M

The Esplanade, Sidmouth, EX10 8RY
☎ (0395) 512651 Telex 42551 EXONIAG (REF BREND 2)
Ⓑ Brend
Set in its own grounds, on Sidmouth's famous Regency seafront.
Bedrooms: 16 single, 15 double & 12 twin, 18 family rooms.
Bathrooms: 61 private.
Bed & breakfast: £60-£70 single, £99-£150 double.

Half board: £60-£85 daily, £285-£550 weekly.
Lunch available.
Evening meal 7.30pm (l.o. 9.30pm).
Parking for 64.
Credit: Access, Visa, Diners, Amex.

Westcliff Hotel M

Manor Rd., Sidmouth, EX10 8RU
☎ (0395) 513252
Fax (0395) 578203
Family-run hotel set in 2 acres of lovely grounds overlooking the sea. Outdoor heated pool and games room. International menu.
Bedrooms: 8 single, 7 double & 25 twin.
Bathrooms: 40 private.
Half board: £42.08-£65.80 daily, £267.75-£418.76 weekly.
Lunch available.
Evening meal 7.30pm (l.o. 8.30pm).
Parking for 50.
Open March-November.
Credit: Access, Visa.

SIMONSBATH

Somerset
Map ref 1C1

7m SE. Lynton
Village beside the beautiful River Barle, deep in Exmoor. From the Middle Ages until the 19th C this was stag-hunting country.

Emmetts Grange Farm Guest House M
🏆 COMMENDED

Simonsbath, Minehead, TA24 7LD
☎ Exford (064 383) 282
1200-acre hill stock farm. Attractive country house in a lovely, quiet position 2.5 miles out of Simonsbath on the South Molton road. Specialises in country cooking.
Bedrooms: 1 single, 1 double & 2 twin.
Bathrooms: 2 private, 1 public.
Bed & breakfast: £16.50-£19 single, £33-£38 double.
Half board: £27.50-£30 daily, £170-£185 weekly.

Evening meal 8pm (l.o. 6pm).
Parking for 6.
Open March-October.

SOMERTON

Somerset
Map ref 2A3

Old market town, important in Saxon times, situated at a gap in the hills south-east of Sedgemoor. Attractive red-roofed stone houses surround the 17th C octagonal market cross and among other handsome buildings are the Town Hall and almshouses of about the same period.

Church Farm Guest House

School La., Compton Dundon, Somerton, TA11 6PE
☎ (0458) 72927
Picturesque thatched cottage set amidst beautiful countryside with most accommodation in attractively converted barn. Easy reach of major routes, historic towns and coasts.
Bedrooms: 2 single, 1 double & 1 twin, 2 family rooms.
Bathrooms: 6 private.
Bed & breakfast: max. £17.50 single, max. £31 double.
Evening meal 7pm (l.o. 5pm).
Parking for 6.

The Unicorn at Somerton M

West St., Somerton, TA11 7PR
☎ (0458) 72101
Traditional English inn, serving home-cooked food, real ales, in comfortable atmospheric surroundings. Personal attention by the owners.
Bedrooms: 3 double & 3 twin.
Bathrooms: 3 private, 2 public.
Bed & breakfast: £22-£30 single, £32-£36 double.
Lunch available.
Evening meal 7pm (l.o. 10pm).
Parking for 45.
Credit: Access, Visa, Diners, Amex.

Map references apply to the colour maps towards the end of this guide.

SOUTH MOLTON

Devon
Map ref 1C1

Busy market town at the mouth of the Yeo Valley near southern Exmoor. Wool, mining and coaching brought prosperity between the Middle Ages and the 19th C and the fine square with Georgian buildings, a Guildhall and Assembly Rooms reflects this former affluence.

Marsh Hall Country House Hotel M

South Molton, EX36 3HQ
☎ (076 95) 2666
Elegant country house nestling in the foothills of Exmoor, overlooking the Mole River Valley, with lovely terrace, lawns and gardens.
Bedrooms: 1 single, 4 double & 2 twin.
Bathrooms: 7 private.
Bed & breakfast: £28-£35 single, £56-£70 double.
Half board: £37-£46 daily, £259-£280 weekly.
Evening meal 7.15pm (l.o. 8.45pm).
Parking for 15.
Credit: Access, Visa.

Park House Country Hotel M

COMMENDED
Station Rd, South Molton, EX36 3ED
☎ (076 95) 2610
Tranquil 18th C manor house with lovely 3 acre gardens. Elegant and spacious with a unique ambience. Antiques, cordon bleu cuisine, 70 wines. 15 minutes' walk to market town.
Bedrooms: 4 double & 4 twin.
Bathrooms: 8 private.
Bed & breakfast: £36-£40 single, £60-£68 double.
Half board: £44-£54 daily, £280-£350 weekly.
Lunch available.
Evening meal 7.30pm (l.o. 6pm).
Parking for 18.
Credit: Access, Visa.

STARCROSS

Devon
Map ref 1D2

Small village on the western shore of the Exe Estuary, with a harbour and 19th C seaside villas. Powderham Castle and Park, just north, make a pleasant excursion and a pedestrian ferry crosses the water to Exmouth.

The Croft Guest House M

Listed
Cockwood Bridge, Starcross, EX6 8QY
☎ (0626) 890282
Set in secluded gardens overlooking tranquil Cockwood harbour and River Exe estuary. Situated on A379 between Exeter and Dawlish.
Bedrooms: 1 single, 2 double & 2 twin, 2 family rooms.
Bathrooms: 2 public.
Bed & breakfast: £15-£16 single, £25-£30 double.
Parking for 7.
Open January-November.

STOKE FLEMING

Devon
Map ref 1D3

2m SW. Dartmouth

Endsleigh Hotel

Listed COMMENDED
Stoke Fleming, Dartmouth, TQ6 0NR
☎ (0803) 770381
Comfortable family-run hotel in picturesque South Hams, offering carefully prepared meals. Ideal base for touring and local beaches.
Bedrooms: 4 double & 1 twin, 2 family rooms.
Bathrooms: 2 private, 4 public.
Bed & breakfast: £16.50-£17.50 single, £33-£35 double.
Half board: £25-£26 daily, £168-£175 weekly.
Lunch available.
Evening meal 7pm (l.o. 7.30pm).
Parking for 20.

STOKE GABRIEL

Devon
Map ref 1D2

Fishing village on a sheltered creek near the head of the Dart Estuary. Old houses and cobble stones enhance views of water and boats; there is an old water-mill and a spreading yew tree more than 1000 years old leans in the churchyard.

Gabriel Court Hotel M

Stoke Gabriel, Totnes, TQ9 6SF
☎ (080 428) 206/207/267
Country house hotel, quiet and comfortable. Family-run. Ideal base for touring the many beauty spots of Devon.
Bedrooms: 3 single, 5 double & 12 twin.
Bathrooms: 20 private, 1 public.
Bed & breakfast: £40-£50 single, £66-£80 double.
Half board: £53-£60 daily, from £350 weekly.
Evening meal 7.30pm (l.o. 8.30pm).
Parking for 22.
Credit: Access, Visa, Diners, Amex.

The Red Slipper

Stoke Gabriel, TQ9 6RU
☎ (080 428) 315
English home-cooked food with well-appointed accommodation in a beautiful village on the River Dart.
Bedrooms: 1 double & 1 twin, 1 family room.
Bathrooms: 2 private; 1 private shower.
Bed & breakfast: £33-£35.20 double.
Half board: £29.75-£30.75 daily.
Lunch available.
Evening meal 7.30pm (l.o. 8.30pm).
Parking for 6.
Open April-October.

STOKENHAM

Devon
Map ref 1C3

Woodland View Guest House M

APPROVED
Kiln Lane, Stokenham, Kingsbridge, TQ7 2SQ
☎ (0548) 580542
Modern guesthouse in attractive village, ideally situated for beaches and coastal walking. Home cooking, choice of menu. Brochure send SAE.
Bedrooms: 2 double & 2 twin, 2 family rooms.
Bathrooms: 2 public.
Bed & breakfast: £11-£13.50 single, £22-£27 double.
Half board: £18.25-£21.25 daily, £120-£130 weekly.
Evening meal 6.30pm (l.o. 6.30pm).
Parking for 8.
Open March-October.

SWINDON

Wiltshire
Map ref 2B2

Wiltshire's industrial and commercial centre, an important railway town in the 19th C, situated just north of the Marlborough Downs. The original market town occupies the slopes of Swindon Hill and the railway village created in the mid-19th C has been preserved. Railway museum, art gallery and theatre.
Tourist Information Centre ☎ (0793) 530328

Holiday Inn Swindon M

Pipers Way, Swindon, SN3 1SH
☎ (0793) 512121 Fax (0793) 513114 Telex 445789
Holiday Inn
158 bedrooms including executive suites with king size beds, and double beds as standard in twins and singles. Indoor pool, squash and tennis courts.
Bedrooms: 98 single, 45 double & 12 twin, 3 family rooms.
Bathrooms: 158 private.
Bed & breakfast: £60-£88.95 single, £74-£106 double.
Lunch available.
Evening meal 6.30pm (l.o. 10.15pm).
Parking for 180.

Continued ▶

Half board prices shown are per person but in some cases may be based on double/twin occupancy.

The enquiry coupons at the back will help you when contacting proprietors.

437

SWINDON
Continued

Credit: Access, Visa, C.Bl., Diners, Amex.

🕭 📞 🖥 🛏 ♻ 👁 📺 ✕ 🛏
🅿 📶 🆃

Marsh Farm Hotel M
👑👑👑👑 COMMENDED

Coped Hall, Wootton Bassett, Swindon, SN4 8ER
☎ (0793) 848044
Fax (0793) 851528
Situated 2 miles from junction 16 M4. 28-bedroomed hotel with full conference and reception facilities.
Bedrooms: 6 single, 19 double & 3 twin.
Bathrooms: 28 private.
Bed & breakfast: £65 single, £80-£85 double.
Half board: £55-£60 daily.
Lunch available.
Evening meal 7pm (l.o. 9pm).
Parking for 100.
Credit: Access, Visa, Amex.

🕭 👁 📺 📞 ♻ 🛏 👁 ✕
🛏 🖥 🛏 ♨ ✕ 📶 🆃

Moormead Farm Hotel M
👑👑👑

Moormead Rd., Wroughton, Swindon, SN4 9BY
☎ (0793) 814744
Fax (0793) 814119
Privately-owned hotel, recently refurbished throughout to a high standard. Full a la carte menu.
Bedrooms: 6 single, 2 double & 26 twin.
Bathrooms: 34 private.
Bed & breakfast: £33-£59.75 single, £55-£81.50 double.
Half board: £47-£74 daily.
Lunch available.
Evening meal 7pm (l.o. 9.30pm).
Parking for 60.
Credit: Access, Visa, Amex.

🕭 📞 🖥 👁 ♻ 🛏 👁 ✕ 🛏
📺 🖥 🛏 ♨ ✕ ✕ 📶 🆃

Relian Guest House
👑👑

153 County Rd., Swindon, SN1 2EB
☎ (0793) 521416
Quiet house adjacent to Swindon Town Football Club and near town centre. Close to bus and rail stations. Free car parking.
Bedrooms: 4 single, 1 double & 2 twin, 1 family room.
Bathrooms: 2 public; 4 private showers.

Bed & breakfast: from £18 single.
Parking for 7.
🛏2 🖥 ♻ 🆄 🛏 🛏 📺 🖥 ✕ 🛏

Waite Meads House Private Hotel
👑👑👑

2 High St., Purton, Swindon, SN5 9AA
☎ (0793) 771972
5 minutes from junction 16 M4, on the edge of the Cotswolds.
Bedrooms: 5 single, 4 double & 6 twin.
Bathrooms: 15 private.
Bed & breakfast: £25-£40 single, £40-£55 double.
Evening meal 6.30pm (l.o. 7.30pm).
Parking for 12.
Credit: Access, Visa.

🛏 🖥 🛏 👁 ♻ 🛏 📺 🖥
🛏 ✕ 🖥 DAP 📶

TALLAND BAY
Cornwall
Map ref 1C3

Small, rocky bay sheltered by bracken-covered cliffs between Polperro and Looe. The old church with its carved bench-ends is set into a hillside, high over the sea.

Talland Bay Hotel M
👑👑👑

Talland Bay, Looe, PL13 2JB
☎ Polperro (0503) 72667
CR Inter
16th C Cornish country house with antique furniture, mentioned in the Domesday Book. Rural situation with 2 acres of gardens overlooking bay. Seafood specialities and fine wines.
Bedrooms: 4 single, 4 double & 11 twin, 3 family rooms.
Bathrooms: 22 private.
Half board: £38-£75 daily, from £266 weekly.
Lunch available.
Evening meal 7pm (l.o. 9pm).
Parking for 20.
Open February-December.
Credit: Access, Visa, Diners, Amex.

🛏 🖥 🛏 📞 👁 🖥 👁 🖥
📺 🖥 🛏 ✕ ♻ 🖥 ✕ ♨ ✕
📶 🛏 🆃

The National Crown Scheme is explained in full on pages 556 – 558.

TAUNTON
Somerset
Map ref 1D1

County town, well-known for its public schools, sheltered by gentle hill-ranges on the River Tone. Medieval prosperity from wool has continued in marketing and manufacturing and the town retains many fine period buildings.
Tourist Information Centre ☎ (0823) 274785

Brookfield Guest House M

16 Wellington Rd., Taunton, TA1 4EQ
☎ (0823) 272786
Family-run hotel providing personal service. Special diets by arrangement. Reduced price packages, details on request.
Bedrooms: 3 single, 2 twin, 2 family rooms.
Bathrooms: 2 public.
Bed & breakfast: £13-£16 single, £24-£28 double.
Half board: £18-£20 daily, £126-£147 weekly.
Evening meal 6pm (l.o. 4pm).
Parking for 8.

🛏 🖥 👁 👁 📺 🛏 🖥 🛏 ✕ 🖥
DAP

Castle Hotel M
👑👑👑👑 HIGHLY COMMENDED

Castle Green, Taunton, TA1 1NF
☎ (0823) 272671 Telex 46488
CR Prestige
With its own fascinating Norman garden, ideally situated for exploring the West Country. Accent on food and wine.
Bedrooms: 14 single, 21 double.
Bathrooms: 35 private.
Bed & breakfast: £78-£110 single, £110-£180 double.
Half board: from £85 daily.
Lunch available.
Evening meal 7.30pm (l.o. 9pm).
Parking for 40.
Credit: Access, Visa, Diners, Amex.

🛏 🖥 📞 👁 🖥 👁 🖥 ●
🛏 🖥 🛏 ✕ 🛏 ♨ ✕ 📶
🛏 🆃

Falcon Hotel M
👑👑👑 APPROVED

Henlade, Taunton, TA3 5DH
☎ (0823) 442502
Comfortable and well-equipped small hotel, 1 mile from M5, junction 25 on the A358 Yeovil road.

Bedrooms: 3 single, 4 double & 3 twin, 1 family room.
Bathrooms: 11 private.
Bed & breakfast: £19-£45 single, £38-£55 double.
Lunch available.
Evening meal 7pm (l.o. 9.30pm).
Parking for 25.
Credit: Access, Visa.

🛏 🖥 📞 👁 🖥 👁 🖥
🛏 🖥 🛏 ✕ ♨ ✕ 📶 🆃

Forde House
👑👑 COMMENDED

9 Upper High St., Taunton, TA1 3PX
☎ (0823) 279042
Peaceful location in the centre of town, close to all amenities, including public park and golf course. Warm welcome guaranteed.
Bedrooms: 1 single, 2 double & 2 twin.
Bathrooms: 5 private.
Bed & breakfast: £22-£25 single, £44-£46 double.
Parking for 5.

🖥 🛏 👁 🆄 🖥 🛏 🛏 ✕ 🛏

Fursdon Guest House M

88-90 Greenway Rd., Taunton, TA2 6LE
☎ (0823) 331955
A newly refurbished high standard guest house close to town centre and Taunton railway station. Full en-suite facilities available.
Bedrooms: 5 single, 1 double & 6 twin, 2 family rooms.
Bathrooms: 7 private, 1 public; 3 private showers.
Bed & breakfast: £14-£16 single, £28-£36 double.
Parking for 9.

🛏 🖥 🛏 👁 🆄 🖥 ✕ 🛏

Higher Dipford Farm
Dipford, Trull, Taunton, TA3 7NU
☎ Taunton (0823) 275770
120-acre dairy farm. Old Somerset longhouse with inglenook fireplaces. Real farmhouse fare using own produce from the dairy. Fresh salmon a speciality. Friendly atmosphere.
Bedrooms: 2 double & 1 twin, 2 family rooms.
Bathrooms: 5 private.
Bed & breakfast: £30 single, £50 double.
Half board: £39 daily, £244 weekly.
Evening meal 7pm (l.o. 10pm).
Parking for 12.

🛏 🖥 🖥 🛏 👁 📺 👁 🖥
📺 🛏 🖥 🛏 ♨ ✕ ✕ ✕
✕ 🛏 ♨ 🛏

The Jays Nest
⚜⚜
Meare Green, Stoke St.
Gregory, Taunton, TA3 6HZ
☎ Taunton (0823) 490250
*Detached country hotel in
peaceful setting in West
Sedgemoor, ideal for walking
and wildlife, central for coast,
Mendips, Quantocks and
Exmoor.*
Bedrooms: 3 double & 2 twin,
1 family room.
Bathrooms: 2 private,
1 public.
Bed & breakfast: £15-£20
single, £30-£40 double.
Half board: £23.50-£28 daily,
£160-£185 weekly.
Lunch available.
Evening meal 6pm (l.o.
10pm).
Parking for 18.

Meryan House Hotel
⚜⚜⚜⚜ COMMENDED
Bishops Hull, Taunton,
TA1 5EG
☎ (0823) 337445
*Delightful 18th C period
residence set in peaceful
surrounding, with easy access
to Taunton centre. Personal
attention assured at all times.*
Bedrooms: 1 single, 9 double
& 2 twin.
Bathrooms: 12 private.
Bed & breakfast: £30-£35
single, £40-£50 double.
Half board: £37-£45 daily,
£250-£285 weekly.
Lunch available.
Evening meal 7.30pm (l.o.
8pm).
Parking for 17.
Credit: Access, Visa.

The Mount Somerset ♨
⚜⚜⚜⚜⚜ HIGHLY COMMENDED
Lower Henlade, Taunton,
TA3 5NY
☎ (0823) 442500
Fax (0823) 442900
*Elegant country house hotel in
a superb elevated postion with
well-appointed rooms,
restaurant and fine wine list.*
Bedrooms: 6 double & 8 twin.
Bathrooms: 14 private.
Bed & breakfast: £93.50-
£140.25 single, £110-£165
double.
Lunch available.
Evening meal 7pm (l.o.
9.30pm).
Parking for 56.

Credit: Access, Visa, Diners,
Amex.

Old Manor Farmhouse ♨
⚜⚜⚜ COMMENDED
Norton Fitzwarren, Taunton,
TA2 6RZ
☎ (0823) 289801
*Edwardian property in an acre
of orchard and kitchen garden.
Cosy log fire in restaurant,
where fresh produce is served
and vegetarians welcome. Ideal
for walking and touring.*
Bedrooms: 2 single, 2 double
& 3 twin.
Bathrooms: 7 private,
1 public.
Bed & breakfast: £28-£30
single, £38-£42 double.
Evening meal 7pm (l.o. 7pm).
Parking for 12.
Credit: Access, Visa, C.Bl.,
Diners.

Rumwell Manor Hotel ♨
⚜⚜⚜⚜ COMMENDED
Rumwell, Taunton, TA4 1EL
☎ (0823) 461902
*Large Georgian house, 1.5
miles from Taunton on A38.
Stands back from the road in 5
acres of landscaped gardens.
Outdoor pool.*
Bedrooms: 3 single, 8 double
& 7 twin, 2 family rooms.
Bathrooms: 20 private,
1 public.
Bed & breakfast: £42.50-
£52.50 single, £59-£69 double.
Lunch available.
Evening meal 7pm (l.o.
8.30pm).
Parking for 30.
Credit: Access, Visa, Diners,
Amex.

The symbols are
explained on the
flap inside the
back cover.

Map references
apply to the colour
maps towards the
end of this guide.

TEIGNMOUTH
Devon
Map ref 1D2

Set on the north bank of
the beautiful Teign
Estuary, busy fishing and
shipbuilding port handling
timber and locally-
quarried ball-clay. A
bridge crosses to the
pretty town of Shaldon
and there are good views
of the estuary from here.
*Tourist Information
Centre ☎ (0626) 779769*

Cockhaven Manor Hotel
⚜⚜⚜ APPROVED
Cockhaven Rd.,
Bishopsteignton,
Teignmouth, TQ14 9RF
☎ Teignmouth (0626) 775252
*Part 16th C village hotel set in
own grounds, with river estuary
views. Four-posters available.*
Bedrooms: 9 double & 3 twin.
Bathrooms: 12 private,
2 public.
Bed & breakfast: £31 single,
£52 double.
Half board: £37 daily, £222
weekly.
Lunch available.
Evening meal 7pm (l.o.
9.30pm).
Parking for 50.
Credit: Access, Visa.

London Hotel ♨
⚜⚜⚜
Bank St., Teignmouth,
TQ14 8AW
☎ (0626) 776336
*Situated in town centre with
easy access to beaches and
moors. Families catered for.
Full leisure facilities including
swimming pool.*
Bedrooms: 2 single, 14 double
& 8 twin, 6 family rooms.
Bathrooms: 30 private,
2 public.
Half board: £39-£45 daily.
Lunch available.
Evening meal 6pm (l.o.
10.30pm).
Parking for 10.
Credit: Access, Visa, Diners,
Amex.

Rathlin House Hotel
⚜⚜
Upper Hermosa Rd.,
Teignmouth, TQ14 9JW
☎ (0626) 774473
*Friendly family hotel with
homely atmosphere and
tastefully furnished for your
holiday relaxation. Home
cooking.*
Bedrooms: 1 single, 3 double
& 1 twin, 5 family rooms.
Bathrooms: 3 private,
2 public.
Bed & breakfast: £12-£14
single, £24-£28 double.
Half board: £16-£18 daily,
£90-£130 weekly.
Evening meal 6.30pm (l.o.
5.30pm).
Parking for 14.
Open March-October.

TIMSBURY
Avon
Map ref 2B2

3m N. Midsomer Norton

Old Malt House Hotel ♨
⚜⚜⚜
Radford, Timsbury, Bath,
BA3 1QF
☎ (0761) 70106
*Family-run hotel and
restaurant, in lovely
countryside. Tastefully
converted and furnished,
including antiques. Ideal for
touring Bath, Wells and the
Mendip Hills.*
Bedrooms: 2 single, 4 double
& 2 twin, 2 family rooms.
Bathrooms: 10 private.
Bed & breakfast: £29-£30
single, £48-£51 double.
Half board: £35.75-£43.25
daily, £234.50-£287 weekly.
Lunch available.
Evening meal 7pm (l.o.
8.30pm).
Parking for 26.
Credit: Access, Visa, Diners,
Amex.

Individual proprietors have supplied all
details of accommodation. Although we
do check for accuracy, we advise you to
confirm prices and other information at
the time of booking.

TINTAGEL

Cornwall
Map ref 1B2

Coastal village near the legendary home of King Arthur. A lofty headland with the ruin of a Norman castle and traces of a Celtic monastery still visible in the turf.

Atlantic View Hotel ▲
👑👑👑 APPROVED

Treknow, Tintagel, PL34 0EJ
☎ Camelford (0840) 770221
Situated in the tiny hamlet of Treknow this coastal country house offers sea views, cocktail bar and indoor heated pool.
Bedrooms: 7 double & 1 twin, 1 family room.
Bathrooms: 9 private.
Bed & breakfast: £16.50-£22.50 double.
Half board: £28-£34 daily, £180-£223 weekly.
Lunch available.
Evening meal 7.30pm (l.o. 9.15pm).
Parking for 20.
Credit: Access, Visa.
🖙2🎭📺⊙🖃 ☑ ⅋ ⊨
📺 🕮🛋🎋☼🅿️⅌ SP

Bosayne Guest House

Atlantic Rd., Tintagel, PL34 0DE
☎ Camelford (0840) 770514
Spacious, comfortable, family-run guesthouse situated in an historical beauty spot, offering a warm welcome and personal service.
Bedrooms: 2 single, 3 double & 2 twin, 3 family rooms.
Bathrooms: 1 private, 2 public.
Bed & breakfast: £11-£12 single, £22-£26 double.
Half board: £14-£15 daily, £85-£105 weekly.
Evening meal 7pm (l.o. 6pm).
Parking for 8.
🖙🎭☼⛺️ 🖑 ☑ ⊨ 📺🕮
🛋🍴 🅳🅰️🅿️ ⅌

Bossiney House Hotel ▲
👑👑👑 APPROVED

Tintagel, PL34 0AX
☎ Camelford (0840) 770240
Family-run hotel set in 2.5 acres of garden. Close to castle and overlooking the beautiful north Cornwall coast.
Bedrooms: 10 double & 7 twin, 3 family rooms.
Bathrooms: 17 private, 1 public.
Bed & breakfast: £28-£33 single, £46-£52 double.
Half board: £31-£33 daily, £190-£225 weekly.

Evening meal 7pm (l.o. 8pm).
Parking for 30.
Open March-October.
Credit: Access, Visa, Diners, Amex.
🖙🎭☼⛺️ 🖑 ☑ ⊨ 📺🕮 🛋
🍴 🖃🍂⊙☼ 🅳🅰️🅿️ ⅌ SP 🇹

Castle Villa
👑👑 COMMENDED

Molesworth St., Tintagel, PL34 0BZ
☎ Camelford (0840) 770373
Over 150 years old, Castle Villa is within easy walking distance of the 11th C church, post office and King Arthur's castle.
Bedrooms: 1 single, 2 double & 1 twin, 1 family room.
Bathrooms: 2 public.
Bed & breakfast: £10.50-£13.50 single, £21-£27 double.
Half board: £19-£22.50 daily, £119.70-£141.75 weekly.
Evening meal 7pm (l.o. 10am).
Parking for 6.
Credit: Access, Visa.
🖙🖃⊙🖑 🖑 ☑ ⅋ ⊨ 📺
🕮 🛋 🎋 🅳🅰️🅿️ ⅌ SP

Ferny Park
👑👑

Bossiney Hill, Tintagel, PL34 0BB
☎ Camelford (0840) 770523
Comfortable modernised house with pretty garden and stream, on B3263 between Rocky Valley and Bossiney Cove. Ideal for walking, birdwatching and painting. Evening meals available by arrangement.
Bedrooms: 1 double & 1 twin.
Bathrooms: 2 public.
Bed & breakfast: £20-£22 double.
Half board: £15.50-£16.50 daily.
Evening meal 6pm.
Parking for 3.
🖙☼⛿ ☑ ⅋ ⊨ 📺🕮 🛋
☼ 🎋 🇼

The Mill House Inn

Trebarwith, Tintagel, PL34 0HD
☎ Camelford (0840) 770200
Formerly a corn mill situated in Trebarwith Valley with trout stream flowing past. Ten minutes' walk from beach and coastal path.
Bedrooms: 1 single, 6 double & 1 twin, 1 family room.
Bathrooms: 9 private.
Bed & breakfast: £19.50-£25 single, £37-£50 double.
Lunch available.

Evening meal 7pm (l.o. 9pm).
Parking for 60.
Credit: Access, Visa.
🖙10🖃⊙🖵🖑 🟏 ☑ ⊨ 🕮
🛋🕭⊙ 🎋 SP 🇫🇷

Old Malt House

Fore St., Tintagel, PL34 0DA
☎ Camelford (0840) 770461
13th/14th C property with interesting features, situated in village centre very close to the old post office and castle.
Bedrooms: 1 single, 5 double & 1 twin, 1 family room.
Bathrooms: 3 private, 2 public.
Bed & breakfast: £12-£14 single, £24-£28 double.
Half board: £20-£22 daily, £140-£154 weekly.
Lunch available.
Evening meal 5pm (l.o. 9pm).
Parking for 12.
Open March-October.
🖙🖃⊙🖵🖑 🟏 ⊨ 🕮🛋🇫🇷

Penallick Hotel

Treknow, Tintagel, PL34 0EJ
☎ Camelford (0840) 770296
Close to cliff walks and sandy beaches with lovely scenery. Ideal for touring Cornwall. Sea views and beautiful sunsets.
Bedrooms: 1 single, 5 double & 1 twin, 1 family room.
Bathrooms: 5 private, 2 public; 1 private shower.
Bed & breakfast: from £17.50 single, from £35 double.
Half board: from £27 daily, £150-£173 weekly.
Lunch available.
Evening meal 7pm (l.o. 9pm).
Parking for 15.
Open March-December.
Credit: Access, Visa.
🖙🖵🖑⊙⊨📺🛋🕭⊙
⅌ SP

Pengenna Hotel

Fore St., Tintagel, PL34 0DD
☎ Camelford (0840) 770223
Nearest hotel to King Arthur's Castle. Enjoy the Pengenna experience. Teas, luncheons and dinners served in our beautiful gardens. Snug bar and old world restaurant.
Bedrooms: 5 double & 2 twin.
Bathrooms: 2 private, 4 public.
Bed & breakfast: £32-£36 double.
Lunch available.
Evening meal 6pm (l.o. 9.30pm).
Parking for 10.
Open April-November.
Credit: Access, Visa.
🖙🖃⊙🖵🖑 🟏 ☑ ⊨ 📺🇽
SP

Polkerr Guest House
👑👑 COMMENDED

Tintagel, PL34 0BY
☎ Camelford (0840) 770382
Period country house, quality accommodation. Home cooking, close to village. Ideal for touring and bathing.
Bedrooms: 1 single, 4 double & 2 twin, 2 family rooms.
Bathrooms: 5 private, 1 public.
Bed & breakfast: £12-£14 single, £24-£30 double.
Half board: £18-£21 daily.
Evening meal 6.30pm (l.o. 5.30pm).
Parking for 9.
🖙🎭🖵🖑 ⛿ ⊨ 📺🕮 🛋
☼ 🇽 🎋

Trewarmett Lodge Hotel
👑👑

Trewarmett, Tintagel, PL34 0ET
☎ Camelford (0840) 770460
Converted from village pub to family-run hotel and restaurant, providing comfortable, homely accommodation and personal service. Situated in a beautiful area.
Bedrooms: 1 single, 2 double & 1 twin, 2 family rooms.
Bathrooms: 1 private, 2 public.
Bed & breakfast: £16.50-£21 single, £31-£36 double.
Half board: £24.50-£30 daily, £144-£159 weekly.
Lunch available.
Evening meal 6.30pm (l.o. 9.30pm).
Parking for 10.
Credit: Access, Visa.
🖙☼ ☑ ⅋ ⊨ 📺🕮 🛋
🍴☼ 🖃 🅳🅰️🅿️ ⅌ SP 🇫🇷🇹

> ### Classifications
> ### and quality
> ### commendations
> ### were correct at the
> ### time of going to
> ### press but are
> ### subject to change.
> ### Please check at the
> ### time of booking.

> ### Half board prices
> ### shown are per
> ### person but in some
> ### cases may be based
> ### on double/twin
> ### occupancy.

TIVERTON

Devon
Map ref 1D2

Busy market and textile town, settled since the 9th C, at the meeting of 2 rivers below southern Exmoor. Town houses, Tudor almshouses and parts of the fine church were built by wealthy cloth merchants; a medieval castle is incorporated into a private house and the original building of Blundells School is preserved by the National Trust.
Tourist Information Centre ☎ *(0884) 255827*

Bridge Guest House
🏠🏠 COMMENDED
23 Angel Hill, Tiverton, EX16 6PE
☎ (0884) 252804
Attractive Victorian town house on the bank of the River Exe, with pretty riverside tea garden.
Bedrooms: 5 single, 2 double & 1 twin, 2 family rooms.
Bathrooms: 2 private, 2 public.
Bed & breakfast: £15-£15.50 single, £30-£35 double.
Half board: £22.50-£25 daily, £145-£165 weekly.
Evening meal 6.30pm (l.o. 7pm).
Parking for 7.
🛏🖒🕭☐♨🖁 Ⓥ 🗗 TV
🎗🛆🥄🍴 DAP SP 🖽

Tiverton Hotel M
🏠🏠🏠
Blundells Rd., Tiverton, EX16 4DB
☎ (0884) 256120 Telex 42551 EXONIAG
Modern, comfortable hotel on edge of Tiverton town in heart of beautiful River Exe Valley. Ideal base for touring West Country.
Bedrooms: 15 double & 15 twin, 45 family rooms.
Bathrooms: 75 private.
Half board: £33-£38 daily.
Lunch available.
Evening meal 6.30pm (l.o. 9.15pm).
Parking for 130.
Credit: Access, Visa, Diners, Amex.
🛏🖒🕭☐♨🖁 Ⓥ 🗗
🗗Ⓞ🛆🍴🕭🖒🏹 🔌 SP T
🕭 Display advertisement appears on page 460.

TORCROSS

Devon
Map ref 1D3

3m N. Start Point

Torcross Apartment Hotel M
🏠🏠🏠
Torcross, Kingsbridge, TQ7 2TQ
☎ Kingsbridge (0548) 580206
At the water's edge on Slapton Sands, beautifully-appointed apartments, some ground floor. Superb sea views. Waterside restaurant and village inn serving fresh local fish.
Bedrooms: 6 twin.
Bathrooms: 6 private.
Bed & breakfast: £36-£39 double.
Lunch available.
Evening meal 7pm (l.o. 9.30pm).
Parking for 25.
🛏🖒☐♨🖁 🗗 TV 🖿 🛆
🖒 🕭 SP 🖽

TORMARTON

Avon
Map ref 2B2

3m SE. Chipping Sodbury

Compass Inn M
🏠🏠🏠🏠 COMMENDED
Tormarton, Badminton, GL9 1JB
☎ Badminton (045 421) 242 & 577 Fax (045 421) 741
Ⓡ Inter
Traditional Cotswold stone inn with log fires and modern bedrooms. Hot and cold buffet and a la carte restaurant.
Bedrooms: 3 single, 12 double & 11 twin, 6 family rooms.
Bathrooms: 32 private.
Bed & breakfast: £49.95-£59.50 single, £64.90-£74.50 double.
Half board: £45.50-£55.50 daily.
Lunch available.
Evening meal 6.30pm (l.o. 10pm).
Parking for 100.
Credit: Access, Visa, Diners, Amex.
🛏🖒🕭Ⓑ☐♨🖁 Ⓥ 🗗
🗗🖽🛆🍴🕭 SP T

The enquiry coupons at the back will help you when contacting proprietors.

TORQUAY

Devon
Map ref 1D2

Devon's grandest resort, developed from a fishing village. Smart apartments and terraces rise from the seafront and Marine Drive along the headland gives views of beaches and colourful cliffs.
Tourist Information Centre ☎ *(0803) 297428*

Abberley Hotel
🏠🏠🏠
100 Windsor Rd., Babbacombe, Torquay, TQ1 1SU
☎ (0803) 329797
Family-run hotel with home cooking, convenient for beaches and shops. All rooms en-suite, colour TV with satellite, tea facilities.
Bedrooms: 4 double & 1 twin, 2 family rooms.
Bathrooms: 7 private.
Bed & breakfast: £12-£16 single, £24-£32 double.
Half board: £16.50-£21 daily, £105-£140 weekly.
Evening meal 6pm (l.o. 6pm).
🛏🖒Ⓑ☐♨🖁 Ⓥ 🗗
🗗 TV 🖽 🛆 🖒 DAP 🔌 SP T

Abbey Lawn Hotel M
🏠🏠🏠🏠 COMMENDED
Scarborough Rd., Torquay, TQ2 5UQ
☎ (0803) 295791 & 299199 & 291460 Telex 299670
HOLTEL G
Central yet secluded location enjoying sea views; in walking distance of English Riviera Centre, Fleet Walk shopping area and promenade.
Bedrooms: 9 single, 27 double & 29 twin.
Bathrooms: 65 private.
Bed & breakfast: £35-£43 single, £70-£86 double.
Half board: £39-£46 daily, £260-£385 weekly.
Lunch available.
Evening meal 7pm (l.o. 8.30pm).
Parking for 40.
Credit: Access, Visa, Diners, Amex.
🖻🕭Ⓑ☐♨🖁 Ⓥ 🗗🖒
Ⓞ🖿🛆🍴🕭🖒 🔌 SP T
🅿Ⓤ🏹🖿🛆 🔌 SP 🖽 T

Allerdale Hotel M
🏠🏠🏠
Croft Rd., Torquay, TQ2 5UD
☎ (0803) 292667
Standing in own spacious grounds with a private path to seafront and a seaview.

Bedrooms: 4 single, 7 double & 7 twin, 3 family rooms.
Bathrooms: 13 private, 5 public; 8 private showers.
Bed & breakfast: £13.50-£18.50 single, £27-£37 double.
Half board: £18-£24 daily.
Evening meal 6.30pm (l.o. 6.30pm).
Parking for 14.
Open April-October.
Credit: Visa.
🛏🖒🕭Ⓑ☐♨🖁 Ⓥ 🗗
🖽🛆🍴🕭🖒 🔌 SP T

Ambergate Hotel
🏠🏠🏠 COMMENDED
Solsbro Rd., Chelston, Torquay, TQ2 6PF
☎ (0803) 605146
A spacious Victorian house with modern facilities and large gardens in quiet location. Near all amenities and conference/leisure centre.
Bedrooms: 4 single, 4 double & 2 twin.
Bathrooms: 6 private, 1 public.
Bed & breakfast: £17-£21 single, £34-£42 double.
Half board: £22-£27 daily, £154-£182 weekly.
Lunch available.
Evening meal 7pm (l.o. 7.30pm).
Parking for 8.
🖒☐♨🖁 🗗 TV 🖽 🛆 🔨 🏹
🖽 DAP 🔌 SP

The Amberwood Private Hotel
🏠🏠🏠
65 Walnut Rd., Chelston, Torquay, TQ2 6HU
☎ (0803) 605293
Large Victorian house with spacious rooms, within walking distance of the promenade, town and railway station.
Bedrooms: 1 single, 4 double & 1 twin.
Bathrooms: 2 public.
Bed & breakfast: £16 single, £28 double.
Half board: £22 daily, £140 weekly.
Evening meal 6.30pm (l.o. 7pm).
Credit: Access, Visa, Amex.
🖒☐♨Ⓤ🗗 TV 🖽 🛆 🍴
🏹🖽 🔌

Apsley Hotel
🏠🏠🏠
Torwood Gardens Rd., Torquay, TQ1 1EG
☎ (0803) 292058
Family hotel with accommodation on 2 floors. In level position near the harbour, beaches and shops.
Bedrooms: 6 single, 11 double & 12 twin, 2 family rooms.
Bathrooms: 27 private, 1 public.

Continued ▶

TORQUAY
Continued

Bed & breakfast: £18-£25 single, £36-£50 double.
Half board: £23-£30 daily, £135-£177 weekly.
Lunch available.
Evening meal 6.30pm (l.o. 7.30pm).
Parking for 21.
Credit: Amex.

Ashfield Lodge Hotel
Ashfield Rd., Chelston Torquay, TQ2 6HH
☎ (0803) 607248
Detached Victorian hotel, standing in two-thirds of an acre, home cooking, ample free parking, elevated position with magnificent views.
Bedrooms: 1 single, 5 double & 1 twin, 3 family rooms.
Bathrooms: 2 private, 2 public.
Bed & breakfast: £12-£16 single, £24-£32 double.
Half board: £16-£21 daily, £85-£116 weekly.
Evening meal 6pm (l.o. 6pm).
Parking for 14.
Open April-October.

Avarest Guest House
32 Thurlow RD, Torquay, TQ1 3EG
☎ (0803) 324225
Family-run guest house offering varied food and pleasant rooms. Clean with relaxed atmosphere.
Bedrooms: 5 double, 2 family rooms.
Bathrooms: 2 public.
Bed & breakfast: £8.50-£11 single, £16-£22 double.
Half board: £12-£16 daily, £75-£95 weekly.
Evening meal 6pm (l.o. 6.30pm).
Parking for 7.

Bahamas Hotel
17 Avenue Rd., Torquay, TQ2 5LB
☎ (0803) 296005
Family hotel with emphasis on food and service. 5 minutes from the sea and English Riviera centre. All en-suite rooms.
Bedrooms: 1 single, 3 double & 6 twin, 2 family rooms.
Bathrooms: 12 private.
Bed & breakfast: £17-£20 single, £34-£68 double.

Half board: £21-£25 daily, £140-£165 weekly.
Lunch available.
Evening meal 6pm (l.o. 6pm).
Parking for 14.
Credit: Access, Visa.

Hotel Balmoral
Meadfoot Sea Rd., Torquay, TQ1 2LQ
☎ (0803) 293381
Uniquely situated, licensed hotel in own grounds overlooking Meadfoot beach, within easy reach of Torquay harbour and shops.
Bedrooms: 3 single, 10 double & 5 twin, 6 family rooms.
Bathrooms: 24 private.
Bed & breakfast: £19-£26 single, £38-£52 double.
Half board: £26-£32 daily, £153-£185 weekly.
Lunch available.
Evening meal 6.45pm (l.o. 7.45pm).
Parking for 18.
Credit: Access, Visa, Amex.

Barn Hayes Country Hotel
COMMENDED
Brim Hill, Maidencombe, Torquay, TQ1 4TR
☎ (0803) 327980
Country hotel in unique Devon coastal hamlet overlooking Lyme Bay. Family suites in delightful gardens with swimming pool.
Bedrooms: 3 single, 4 double & 1 twin, 5 family rooms.
Bathrooms: 8 private, 2 public.
Bed & breakfast: £14.50-£22 single, £29-£40 double.
Half board: £22-£30 daily, £135-£184 weekly.
Lunch available.
Evening meal 6.30pm (l.o. 7.30pm).
Parking for 15.
Open February-December.
Credit: Access, Visa.

Beau Vista Guest House
14 Ash Hill Rd., Torquay, TQ1 3HZ
☎ (0803) 297202
Centrally situated in quiet road near town centre, entertainment and coach station. Sea views and ample parking.
Bedrooms: 2 single, 2 double, 3 family rooms.
Bathrooms: 2 private, 1 public.

Bed & breakfast: £9-£15 single, £18-£30 double.
Half board: £13-£19 daily.
Evening meal 6pm (l.o. 6pm).
Parking for 4.
Open April-October.

Beauly Guest House
COMMENDED
503 Babbacombe Rd., Torquay, TQ1 1HL
☎ (0803) 296993
Warm hospitality with all en-suite rooms, providing quality and value. 600 yards from harbour and amenities. Short breaks welcome.
Bedrooms: 2 twin, 3 family rooms.
Bathrooms: 5 private.
Bed & breakfast: £15-£20 single, £30-£40 double.
Evening meal 6pm.

Belmont Hotel
66 Belgrave Rd., Torquay, TQ2 5HY
☎ (0803) 295028
Fully refurbished, family-run hotel, central to all amenities, conference and leisure facilities. Our reputation is your guarantee.
Bedrooms: 1 single, 3 double & 4 twin, 4 family rooms.
Bathrooms: 7 private, 2 public.
Bed & breakfast: £11-£15 single, £22-£30 double.
Half board: £17-£22 daily.
Evening meal 6pm (l.o. 5pm).
Parking for 4.
Credit: Access, Visa.

Bishops Court
COMMENDED
Lower Warberry Rd., Torquay, TQ1 1QS
☎ (0803) 294649
Bishops Court includes apartments and en-suite hotel rooms. Standing high in the "Warberries" commanding good views of Torbay. Leisure facilities.
Bedrooms: 15 double & 4 twin, 3 family rooms.
Bathrooms: 22 private.
Bed & breakfast: £33.50-£79.50 single, £39-£85.50 double.
Half board: £31.30-£53.15 daily, £205-£335 weekly.
Lunch available.
Evening meal 7pm (l.o. 9pm).
Parking for 61.
Credit: Access, Visa.

Bowden Close Hotel
Teignmouth Rd., Maidencombe, Torquay, TQ1 4TJ
☎ (0803) 328029
Victorian country house hotel with lovely sea and country views. Family-run, offering varied food in a relaxing atmosphere.
Bedrooms: 2 single, 9 double & 5 twin, 4 family rooms.
Bathrooms: 16 private, 1 public; 1 private shower.
Bed & breakfast: £18.50-£20 single, £37-£40 double.
Half board: £24-£27 daily, £150.50-£178.50 weekly.
Lunch available.
Evening meal 6.30pm (l.o. 8pm).
Parking for 32.
Credit: Access, Visa.

Bute Court Hotel
COMMENDED
Belgrave Rd., Torquay, TQ2 5HQ
☎ (0803) 213055
CB Minotels
Family-run hotel overlooking Torbay and adjoining English Riviera Centre. Large lounges and bar. 5-course choice menu.
Bedrooms: 10 single, 13 double & 13 twin, 10 family rooms.
Bathrooms: 42 private, 4 public.
Bed & breakfast: £16-£28.50 single, £30-£54 double.
Half board: £20-£33 daily, £135-£225 weekly.
Lunch available.
Evening meal 6.30pm (l.o. 8pm).
Parking for 38.
Credit: Access, Visa, C.Bl., Diners, Amex.

Cavendish Hotel
Belgrave Rd., Torquay, TQ2 5HN
☎ (0803) 293682/296793
Approximately 200 yards from new conference centre, within walking distance of town centre and beach.
Bedrooms: 6 single, 24 double & 29 twin.
Bathrooms: 36 private, 8 public.
Bed & breakfast: £21-£27 single, £42-£54 double.
Half board: £25-£34.50 daily, £175-£241.50 weekly.
Lunch available.

Evening meal 6.30pm (l.o. 10pm).
Parking for 30.
Credit: Access, Visa, Diners, Amex.

Chelston Manor Hotel
Old Mill Rd., Torquay, TQ2 6HW
☎ (0803) 605142
Old world bed and breakfast inn. Reputation for pub food. Sun-trap gardens with heated swimming pool.
Bedrooms: 2 single, 9 double & 5 twin, 1 family room.
Bathrooms: 11 private, 2 public; 1 private shower.
Bed & breakfast: £14-£22 single, £28-£44 double.
Evening meal 6pm.
Parking for 30.

Claver Guest House
119 Abbey Rd., Torquay, TQ2 5NP
☎ (0803) 297118
A warm welcome awaits you. Close to beach, harbour and all entertainments. Home-cooked food - you'll never leave the table hungry!
Bedrooms: 2 single, 2 double & 1 twin, 3 family rooms.
Bathrooms: 2 public.
Bed & breakfast: £12-£13.50 single, £24-£27 double.
Half board: £17-£18.50 daily, £99.50-£115 weekly.
Evening meal 6pm (l.o. 6pm).
Parking for 4.

Clovelly Guest House
91 Avenue Rd., Torquay, TQ2 5LH
☎ (0803) 292286
Semi-detached property of Victorian construction, on level main road to beach.
Bedrooms: 2 single, 2 double & 1 twin, 2 family rooms.
Bathrooms: 1 public; 1 private shower.
Bed & breakfast: £9.50-£11 single, £19-£22 double.
Half board: £14.50-£16 daily, £101.50-£112 weekly.
Evening meal 6pm (l.o. 7pm).
Parking for 4.

Corbyn Head Hotel ⚋
👑👑👑👑 COMMENDED
Torbay Rd., Seafront, Torquay, TQ2 6RH
☎ (0803) 213611
Fax (0803) 296152

Situated on the seafront, the hotel combines old world charm and modern facilities.
Bedrooms: 7 single, 31 double & 11 twin, 1 family room.
Bathrooms: 50 private.
Bed & breakfast: £30-£48 single, £60-£96 double.
Half board: £40-£60 daily, £198-£314 weekly.
Evening meal 7pm (l.o. 9pm).
Parking for 40.
Credit: Access, Visa, Diners, Amex.

Craig Court Hotel
👑👑 APPROVED
10 Ash Hill Rd., Torquay, TQ1 3HZ
☎ (0803) 294400
Small hotel situated a short distance from the town centre and the harbour. Quiet location with a lovely garden and choice of menus.
Bedrooms: 2 single, 4 double & 2 twin, 2 family rooms.
Bathrooms: 4 private, 3 public.
Bed & breakfast: £15-£18 single, £30-£36 double.
Half board: £22-£25 daily, £140-£161 weekly.
Evening meal 6pm (l.o. 9am).
Parking for 10.
Open April-October.

Cranmore Guest House ⚋
👑👑 APPROVED
89 Avenue Rd., Torquay, TQ2 5LH
☎ (0803) 298488
Friendly, family-run, small hotel offering home cooking. No restrictions, close to all amenities.
Bedrooms: 2 single, 3 double & 1 twin, 2 family rooms.
Bathrooms: 4 private, 1 public.
Bed & breakfast: £10-£12 single, £20-£28 double.
Half board: £15.50-£19.50 daily, £108.50-£136.50 weekly.
Evening meal 6pm (l.o. 6.30pm).
Parking for 4.
Credit: Access, Visa.

Devonshire Hotel ⚋
👑👑 APPROVED
Parkhill Rd., Torquay, TQ1 2DY
☎ (0803) 291123 Telex 42988 DEVLIR Fax (0803) 291710

Hotel is set in its own delightful gardens which are tranquil, yet sufficiently close to harbour, beaches and shops.
Bedrooms: 8 single, 14 double & 40 twin, 9 family rooms.
Bathrooms: 71 private, 6 public.
Bed & breakfast: £26-£35 single, £58-£72 double.
Half board: £29-£36 daily, £178.50-£231 weekly.
Lunch available.
Evening meal 6.45pm (l.o. 8.45pm).
Parking for 53.
Credit: Access, Visa, C.Bl., Diners, Amex.

El Marino Hotel
Lower Warberry Rd., Torquay, TQ1 1QS
☎ (0803) 28606
Friendly family hotel, catering for people of all ages. Games room and outdoor heated swimming pool. Ample free parking, coaches welcome.
Bedrooms: 2 single, 7 double & 7 twin, 7 family rooms.
Bathrooms: 19 private, 1 public.
Bed & breakfast: £15-£20 single, £30-£40 double.
Half board: £20-£30 daily, £120-£160 weekly.
Evening meal 6pm (l.o. 7.30pm).
Parking for 22.
Open April-October.
Credit: Access.

Ellington Court Hotel
👑👑👑 APPROVED
St. Lukes Rd. South, Torquay, TQ2 5NZ
☎ (0803) 294957
Fax (0803) 201383
Licensed hotel in own grounds with sea views. Centrally situated and convenient for beach, shops, harbour, and leisure centre.
Bedrooms: 11 double & 2 twin, 4 family rooms.
Bathrooms: 11 private, 2 public.
Bed & breakfast: £15-£20 single, £30-£40 double.
Half board: £20-£50 daily, £133-£168 weekly.
Evening meal 6pm (l.o. 7pm).
Parking for 12.
Credit: Access, Visa.

Elmsdale ⚋
70 Avenue Rd., Torquay, TQ2 5LF
☎ (0803) 25929
7-bedroomed centrally heated establishment offering full English breakfast and evening meal optional. Colour TV, tea making in all rooms. Fire certificate.
Bedrooms: 1 single, 3 double & 1 twin, 2 family rooms.
Bathrooms: 1 private, 1 public.
Bed & breakfast: £12-£15 single, £24-£24 double.
Half board: £17-£21 daily, £105-£119 weekly.
Evening meal 6pm.
Parking for 8.
Credit: Access, Visa.

Everglades Hotel
👑👑👑👑 APPROVED
32 St. Marychurch Rd., Torquay, TQ1 3HY
☎ (0803) 295389
Detached hotel with own secluded garden, south facing and within easy reach of beaches and main shopping area.
Bedrooms: 1 single, 6 double & 1 twin, 3 family rooms.
Bathrooms: 11 private.
Bed & breakfast: £17.50-£21 single, £34-£41 double.
Half board: £25-£28.50 daily, £165-£185 weekly.
Lunch available.
Evening meal 6.30pm (l.o. 8.30pm).
Parking for 10.
Credit: Access, Visa.

Exmouth View Hotel
St. Albans Rd., Babbacombe, Torquay, TQ1 3LJ
☎ (0803) 327307/329967
Private family-run hotel 50 yards from seafront offering dancing, entertainment and a friendly atmosphere. Close to all amenities.
Bedrooms: 6 single, 13 double & 5 twin, 8 family rooms.
Bathrooms: 19 private, 2 public.
Bed & breakfast: £9.50-£18 single, £19-£36 double.
Half board: £10.75-£29.85 daily, £75-£165 weekly.
Evening meal 6.30pm.
Parking for 24.
Credit: Access, Visa.

TORQUAY
Continued

Fairmount House Hotel ᛗ

ᵛᵛᵛ **COMMENDED**

Herbert Rd., Chelston,
Torquay, TQ2 6RW
☎ (0803) 605446
*Small hotel offering real home
cooking and high quality
accommodation. Peaceful
setting near Cockington
village. Dogs welcome.*
Bedrooms: 2 single, 3 double
& 1 twin, 2 family rooms.
Bathrooms: 8 private,
2 public.
Bed & breakfast: £20-£24
single, £40-£48 double.
Half board: £29.50-£33.50
daily, £198-£219 weekly.
Lunch available.
Evening meal 6.30pm (l.o.
7.30pm).
Parking for 8.
Open March-October.
Credit: Access, Visa, Amex.

Hotel Fluela ᛗ

ᵛᵛᵛ **APPROVED**

15/17 Hatfield Rd., Torquay,
TQ1 3BW
☎ (0803) 297512
*Detached family-run hotel with
friendly atmosphere and home-
cooked food. Centrally located
with private car park.*
Bedrooms: 9 double & 1 twin,
3 family rooms.
Bathrooms: 13 private,
1 public.
Bed & breakfast: £12-£18
single.
Half board: £110-£165
weekly.
Evening meal 6pm (l.o. 9pm).
Parking for 35.
Credit: Access, Visa.

Gleneagles Hotel ᛗ

Asheldon Rd., Wellswood,
Torquay, TQ1 2QS
☎ (0803) 293637 / 297011
*Modern hotel overlooking
Ansteys Cove. There is a path
through the grounds to the
beach. Pool, jacuzzi, solarium
and entertainment provided.*
Bedrooms: 8 single, 15 double
& 9 twin, 8 family rooms.
Bathrooms: 40 private.
Bed & breakfast: £27-£33.50
single, £54-£67 double.
Half board: £30.50-£40 daily,
£185-£236 weekly.
Evening meal 7pm (l.o.
8.30pm).
Parking for 40.

Credit: Access, Visa, Diners,
Amex.

Hantwell House

Listed

487 Babbacombe Rd.,
Torquay, TQ1 1HL
☎ (0803) 293990
*Bright modern friendly guest
house, 700 yards from harbour.
Adjacent to bus stop and all
amenities. Cleanliness assured.*
Bedrooms: 1 single, 2 double,
4 family rooms.
Bathrooms: 1 public.
Bed & breakfast: £12-£17
single, £24-£34 double.
Half board: £18-£23 daily,
£126-£150 weekly.
Evening meal 6pm (l.o. 6pm).

Highbury House

Tor Vale, Torquay, TQ1 4ED
☎ (0803) 35654/325654
*Elegant Victorian villa with old
fashioned hospitality and
service. All rooms well-
appointed. Free car parking.*
Bedrooms: 1 single, 2 double
& 1 twin, 2 family rooms.
Bathrooms: 1 private,
3 public.
Bed & breakfast: £9-£12
single, £18-£24 double.
Half board: £14-£18 daily,
£95-£120 weekly.
Evening meal 6pm (l.o.
6.30pm).
Parking for 6.

Hind Hotel ᛗ

ᵛᵛᵛ

29 Bampfylde Rd., Torquay,
TQ2 5AY
☎ (0803) 297212 &
(0803) 297708
*Family-run hotel offering a
good standard of food and
accommodation. Most rooms
en-suite, all with colour TV
and tea-making facilities.*
Bedrooms: 2 single, 5 double,
6 family rooms.
Bathrooms: 11 private,
1 public.
Bed & breakfast: £20-£24
single, £40-£44 double.
Half board: £27-£31 daily,
£162-£186 weekly.
Evening meal 6pm (l.o.
7.30pm).
Parking for 15.
Credit: Access, Visa.

Hylton Court Hotel

109 Abbey Rd., Torquay,
TQ2 5NP
☎ (0803) 294464/298643
*Centrally situated, within
walking distance of beach and
shopping centre. Friendly and
informal atmosphere. Ample
parking.*
Bedrooms: 4 single, 11 double
& 7 twin, 2 family rooms.
Bathrooms: 7 private,
5 public.
Bed & breakfast: £12-£14.50
single, £24-£29 double.
Half board: £16-£18 daily,
£112-£126 weekly.
Evening meal 6pm (l.o. 7pm).
Parking for 30.
Credit: Visa.

Jesmond Dene Hotel

ᵛᵛᵛ

85 Abbey Rd., Torquay,
TQ2 5NN
☎ (0803) 293062
*Friendly family hotel with
personal service and no
restrictions. Ideally central for
seafront, shops and
entertainments.*
Bedrooms: 4 single, 4 double,
3 family rooms.
Bathrooms: 2 public.
Bed & breakfast: £11-£14
single, £22-£28 double.
Half board: £15-£18 daily,
£82-£95 weekly.
Evening meal 6pm (l.o. 9am).
Parking for 3.

Kingston Hall Hotel ᛗ

ᵛᵛᵛ **COMMENDED**

17 Manor Rd., Babbacombe,
Torquay, TQ1 3JX
☎ (0803) 326058
*Detached licensed hotel and
restaurant, open to non-
residents. Situated on the level,
close to the beach and shops.
Golf, bowling and tennis
facilities nearby.*
Bedrooms: 8 double & 1 twin,
2 family rooms.
Bathrooms: 11 private.
Bed & breakfast: £18.70-
£23.10 single, £34-£42 double.
Half board: £25-£29 daily,
£150-£180 weekly.
Lunch available.
Evening meal 6.30pm (l.o.
8pm).
Parking for 13.
Credit: Access.

Kingston House

ᵛᵛᵛ

75 Avenue Rd, Torquay,
TQ2 5LL
☎ (0803) 212760
*Victorian elegance and
comfort. Beautifully appointed
full en-suite bathrooms and
shower rooms. Home-cooked
food. Level walk to all
amenities.*
Bedrooms: 1 single, 3 double,
2 family rooms.
Bathrooms: 4 private,
1 public.
Bed & breakfast: £12-£15
single, £21-£35 double.
Half board: £16.50-£23 daily,
£99-£145 weekly.
Evening meal 6pm (l.o.
4.30pm).
Parking for 6.
Open April-October.

Lansdowne Hotel ᛗ

ᵛᵛᵛ

Babbacombe Rd., Torquay,
TQ1 1PW
☎ (0803) 299599
*Friendly, modern, comfortable,
hotel centrally situated for
town and amenities. Family
supervised. Reputation for food
and wines. Entertainment 7
nights, children's hours.*
Bedrooms: 2 single, 16 double
& 3 twin, 6 family rooms.
Bathrooms: 27 private.
Bed & breakfast: £19.50-
£26.50 single, £39-£53 double.
Half board: £25.50-£31.50
daily, £139-£209 weekly.
Lunch available.
Evening meal 7pm (l.o.
8.30pm).
Parking for 30.
Credit: Access.

Lincombe Hall Hotel

Meadfoot Rd., Torquay,
TQ1 2JX
☎ (0803) 213361
Fax (0803) 211485
*A delightful Georgian house
built in 1822, set in over 4
acres of gardens and with all
facilities. Various diets
available including diabetic
and vegetarian.*
Bedrooms: 1 single, 23 double
& 10 twin, 9 family rooms.
Bathrooms: 43 private.
Bed & breakfast: £37.50-
£46.75 single, £75-£93.50
double.
Half board: £43-£52.80 daily,
£214-£295.90 weekly.
Lunch available.

Evening meal 7pm (l.o. 8.30pm).
Parking for 60.
Credit: Access, Visa, Diners, Amex.

Livermead Cliff Hotel M
COMMENDED
Sea Front, Torquay, TQ2 6RQ
☎ (0803) 299666
Fax (0803) 294496
Best Western
Situated at the water's edge in a secluded garden, with magnificent views over Torbay. Family owned and run. 950 yards from English Riviera Centre, 1 mile from town centre and shops.
Bedrooms: 12 single, 8 double & 22 twin, 22 family rooms.
Bathrooms: 64 private, 1 public.
Bed & breakfast: £32-£51 single, £60-£96 double.
Half board: £37.50-£57.50 daily, £252-£374.50 weekly.
Lunch available.
Evening meal 7pm (l.o. 8.30pm).
Parking for 77.
Credit: Access, Visa, Diners, Amex.

Meadfoot Bay Hotel M
Meadford Sea Rd, Torquay, TQ1 2LQ
☎ (0803) 294722
Elegant hotel in own grounds with friendly family atmosphere. Peaceful location close to Meadfoot Beach.
Bedrooms: 1 single, 15 double & 3 twin, 6 family rooms.
Bathrooms: 19 private, 2 public.
Bed & breakfast: £19-£28 single, £34-£42 double.
Half board: £24-£32 daily, £160-£205 weekly.
Evening meal 6.30pm (l.o. 7pm).
Parking for 15.
Open February-November.
Credit: Access, Visa, Amex.

Millbrook House Hotel
COMMENDED
Old Mill Rd., Chelston, Torquay, TQ2 6AP
☎ (0803) 297394

Small, elegant hotel noted for comfort and food. Level walk to seafront, Abbey Gardens. Cellar bar, games room, mini-gym.
Bedrooms: 2 single, 4 double & 3 twin.
Bathrooms: 7 private, 1 public; 1 private shower.
Bed & breakfast: £15-£21 single, £30-£42 double.
Half board: £24-£30 daily, £159-£195 weekly.
Evening meal 7pm (l.o. 8pm).
Parking for 12.
Credit: Access, Visa.

Norcliffe Hotel
Sea Front, Babbacombe Downs, Torquay, TQ1 3LF
☎ (0803) 328456
Traditional family hotel in a seafront corner position, close to beaches, shops and golf-course.
Bedrooms: 3 single, 7 double & 6 twin, 4 family rooms.
Bathrooms: 19 private, 2 public.
Bed & breakfast: £14-£25 single, £28-£50 double.
Half board: £20-£32 daily, £140-£225 weekly.
Lunch available.
Evening meal 6.30pm (l.o. 7.30pm).
Parking for 16.
Credit: Visa.

Palace Hotel M
Babbacombe Rd., Torquay, TQ1 3TG
☎ (0803) 202000 Telex 42606
Gracious former Bishop's Palace situated in 25 acres of beautiful gardens and woodland stretching to the edge of the sea.
Bedrooms: 36 single, 18 double & 77 twin, 10 family rooms.
Bathrooms: 141 private.
Bed & breakfast: £50-£108 single, £100-£216 double.
Half board: £61-£125 daily, £342-£700 weekly.
Lunch available.
Evening meal 7.30pm (l.o. 9.15pm).
Parking for 140.
Credit: Access, Visa, Diners, Amex.

Princes Hotel M
Parkhill Rd., Torquay, TQ1 2DU
☎ (0803) 291123 Telex 42988 DER PRI
Enjoying a regal name and ancestry, the former home of the Earl of Cork and Orrery. Fine panoramic sea views over Torbay.
Bedrooms: 10 single, 12 double & 22 twin, 9 family rooms.
Bathrooms: 46 private, 5 public.
Bed & breakfast: £18.50-£33.50 single, £47-£76 double.
Half board: £23.50-£38 daily, £143.50-£245 weekly.
Lunch available.
Evening meal 6.30pm (l.o. 8.30pm).
Parking for 44.
Open April-October.
Credit: Access, Visa, C.Bl., Diners, Amex.

Red House Hotel M
Rousdown Rd., Torquay, TQ2 6PB
☎ (0803) 607811
Newly-built hotel with free use of keep-fit facilities, heated indoor pool, sauna, spa bath. Self-catering apartments adjoining.
Bedrooms: 1 single, 4 double & 2 twin, 3 family rooms.
Bathrooms: 10 private.
Bed & breakfast: £20-£31.50 single, £36-£55 double.
Half board: £22.50-£32 daily, £140-£206.50 weekly.
Evening meal 6.30pm (l.o. 8pm).
Parking for 12.
Credit: Access, Visa.

Hotel Regina
Victoria Pde., Torquay, TQ1 2BE
☎ (0803) 22904
Pleasant hotel adjacent to Torquay harbour in level position and within walking distance of many of the resort's amenities.
Bedrooms: 12 single, 25 double & 26 twin, 9 family rooms.
Bathrooms: 59 private, 9 public.
Bed & breakfast: £16.50-£22.50 single, £33-£45 double.
Half board: £23-£32 daily, £160-£224 weekly.
Lunch available.
Evening meal 6.30pm (l.o. 8pm).

Parking for 10.
Credit: Access, Visa, Diners, Amex.

Rothesay Hotel M
Scarborough Rd., Torquay, TQ5 5UH
☎ (0803) 293161
Family-run hotel where food and good company still matter. Near conference and leisure centre.
Bedrooms: 6 single, 8 double & 4 twin, 9 family rooms.
Bathrooms: 23 private, 2 public.
Bed & breakfast: £18-£21 single, £36-£44 double.
Half board: £26-£31 daily, £163-£194 weekly.
Evening meal 6pm (l.o. 7pm).
Parking for 30.
Open February-December.
Credit: Access, Visa.

Sandhurst Hotel
8 Manor Rd., Babbacombe, Torquay, TQ1 3XJ
☎ (0803) 329722
Situated close to the sea and within easy reach of all amenities.
Bedrooms: 1 single, 9 double & 3 twin, 3 family rooms.
Bathrooms: 12 private, 4 public.
Bed & breakfast: £15-£18 single, £30-£36 double.
Half board: £19-£22 daily, £119-£133 weekly.
Evening meal 6pm (l.o. 6pm).
Parking for 20.
Open April-October.

Sevens Hotel M
27 Morgan Ave., Torquay, TQ2 5RR
☎ (0803) 293523
On a quiet avenue central to all attractions. Large bar and games room.
Bedrooms: 3 single, 5 double & 2 twin, 3 family rooms.
Bathrooms: 3 private, 3 public.
Bed & breakfast: £11-£14 single, £22-£28 double.
Half board: £15-£18 daily, £101-£126 weekly.
Evening meal 6pm (l.o. 6pm).
Parking for 10.

TORQUAY
Continued

Shedden Hall Hotel M
♨♕♕
Shedden Hill, Torquay,
TQ2 5TY
☎ (0803) 292964
Family-run hotel with magnificent views of Torquay and seafront. Town, theatre and leisure centre all within easy walking distance.
Bedrooms: 2 single, 14 double & 8 twin, 5 family rooms.
Bathrooms: 26 private, 2 public.
Bed & breakfast: £23-£25 single, £46-£50 double.
Half board: £30-£32 daily, £202-£216 weekly.
Lunch available.
Evening meal 6.30pm (l.o. 8pm).
Parking for 30.
Credit: Access, Visa, Diners, Amex.
♿ ♨ 📞 ❧ ⊡ 🖵 🖤 ♦ 🆅
🖃 🖩 🅰 ❀ ❦ ✿ ᴅᴀᴘ ❧ SP
ᴛ

Thorn Cottage
Coffinswell, Newton Abbot,
TQ12 4SN
☎ Kingskerswell
(0803) 875227
Attractive 26th C thatched cottage in small beautiful village. Convenient for Torbay and Dartmoor. Friendly personal service.
Bedrooms: 1 family room.
Bathrooms: 1 private.
Bed & breakfast: £12.50-£15 single, £20-£25 double.
Parking for 2.
♿ ⊡ 📞 ❧ ᵁᴸ ⬭ 🆅 🖤 🅰
🖤 🖃

Treander Guest House
Listed APPROVED
10 Morgan Av., Torquay,
TQ2 5RS
☎ (0803) 296906
Ideally situated for all amenities. Open all year. Free car park. Tea making facilities in all bedrooms. Colour TV. Comfort given high priority.
Bedrooms: 1 single, 1 double & 1 twin, 3 family rooms.
Bathrooms: 2 public.
Bed & breakfast: £10.50-£12.50 single, £21-£25 double.
Half board: £14-£16 daily, £89-£99 weekly.
Evening meal 6pm (l.o. 6.30pm).
Parking for 4.
♿ 📞 ❧ ᵁᴸ 🅰 🆅 🖃 ⊡ 🖤
🖃 ᴅᴀᴘ ❧ SP ᴛ

Tregantle Hotel
♨♕♕ COMMENDED
64 Bampflyde Rd., Torquay,
TQ2 5AY
☎ (0803) 297494
Detached, licensed, delightful family-run hotel with chef/proprietor. On level close to seafront, conference centre, en-suite rooms, private car park.
Bedrooms: 1 single, 5 double & 2 twin, 2 family rooms.
Bathrooms: 10 private.
Bed & breakfast: £18-£23 single, £36-£46 double.
Half board: £24-£29 daily, £165-£188 weekly.
Evening meal 6pm (l.o. 7pm).
Parking for 11.
Open January-November.
Credit: Access, Visa.
♿8 🅰 📞 ❧ 🅰 🖃 🖤 🖃 🅰
🍽 ❀ ᴅᴀᴘ SP ᴛ

Two Trees Guest House
♨♕
216 Newton Rd., Torquay,
TQ2 7JN
☎ (0803) 613393
Small guest house situated on the main A380 into Torquay. Run by Eric Collar who will make you welcome.
Bedrooms: 1 single, 1 double & 1 twin.
Bathrooms: 2 public.
Bed & breakfast: £9-£11.50 single, £19-£22 double.
Parking for 5.
Open April-October.
♿12 ❧ 🅰 🖤 ⊡ 🖤 🖃 ❀ 🖃

Westwood Hotel M
♨♕♕
111 Abbey Rd., Torquay,
TQ2 5NP
☎ (0803) 293818
A lovely detatched licensed hotel, with parking and secluded garden. Situated in town centre with easy access to all amenities.
Bedrooms: 2 single, 10 double & 4 twin, 2 family rooms.
Bathrooms: 15 private, 3 public.
Bed & breakfast: £13-£16 single, £26-£32 double.
Half board: £19-£22 daily, £125-£155 weekly.
Evening meal 6pm (l.o. 7.30pm).
Parking for 10.
Credit: Access.
♿ ♨ 📞 ❧ 🅰 🆅 🖃 ⊡ 🖤
🅰 🖃 ❀ ✿ 🍽 🖃 ᴅᴀᴘ ❧ SP

The symbols are explained on the flap inside the back cover.

TOTNES
Devon
Map ref 1D2

Old market town steeply built near the head of the Dart Estuary. Remains of medieval gateways, a noble church, 16th C Guildhall and medley of period houses recall former wealth from cloth and shipping, continued in rural and water industries.
Tourist Information Centre ☎ *(0803) 863168*

Lyssers
4 Chapel La., Bridgetown,
Totnes
☎ (0803) 866513
Converted barn with a wealth of beams. Central for town. High level of personal service and well known for sea food.
Bedrooms: 1 single, 2 double & 2 twin, 1 family room.
Bathrooms: 6 private.
Bed & breakfast: £28-£31 single, £50-£56 double.
Half board: £42-£45 daily, £201.60-£220.50 weekly.
Evening meal 6.30pm (l.o. 9pm).
Parking for 18.
♿5 🅰 🖤 🆅 🖃 ❦ 🅰 ⊡ 🖤 🖩
🅰 🖃 ✓ 🖃 🅰 ᴅᴀᴘ ❧ SP

The Old Forge at Totnes M
♕♕ COMMENDED
Seymour Place, Totnes,
TQ9 5AY
☎ (0803) 862174
Provides all modern comforts in a delightful 600-year-old stone building, with beautiful walled garden, cobbled driveway and fully operational smithy workshop. Weekly and off-season discount.
Bedrooms: 2 double & 2 twin, 4 family rooms.
Bathrooms: 4 private, 1 public.
Bed & breakfast: £27-£40 single, £35-£45 double.
Parking for 10.
Credit: Access, Visa.
♨ ⊡ 📞 ❧ 🅰 🆅 🖃 🖃 🖤
🖩 🅰 ❀ ✿ 🍽 SP 🖃 ᴛ

Royal Seven Stars Hotel M
♨♕♕
The Plains, Totnes,
TQ9 5DD
☎ (0803) 862125 & 863241
Old coaching inn in the centre of Totnes, near River Dart. Short drive to coast and Dartmoor. Brochures available on request.

Bedrooms: 1 single, 11 double & 3 twin, 3 family rooms.
Bathrooms: 12 private, 4 public.
Bed & breakfast: £34-£44 single, £46-£68 double.
Half board: £35.50-£46.50 daily, £212-£335 weekly.
Lunch available.
Evening meal 7pm (l.o. 9.30pm).
Parking for 25.
Credit: Access, Visa, Diners.
♿ 🅰 📞 ⊡ 📞 🖤 🆅 ❧
🖃 ⊡ 🖩 🅰 🍽 ❧ 🖃 ᴛ

Sea Trout Inn
♨♕♕ COMMENDED
Staverton, Totnes, TQ9 6PA
☎ (080 426) 274
Delightful beamed country inn, in attractive village by the River Dart. Friendly atmosphere. Good base for walking and touring Dartmoor and South Devon.
Bedrooms: 7 double & 3 twin.
Bathrooms: 10 private.
Bed & breakfast: £32-£40 single, £40-£60 double.
Half board: £31-£40 daily, £230-£250 weekly.
Lunch available.
Evening meal 7pm (l.o. 10pm).
Parking for 70.
Credit: Access, Visa.
♿ 📞 📞 🖤 🅰 🆅 🖤 🅰 🖃
🅰 ✿ 🖃 ᴅᴀᴘ ❧ SP 🖃 ᴛ

TREKNOW
Cornwall
Map ref 1B2

4m NW. Camelford

Tregosse Guest House
♨♕
Tregosse, Treknow, Tintagel,
PL34 0EP
☎ Camelford (0840) 770482
House situated on cliff alongside National Trust land, with spectacular views. Private showers. Easy parking. Follow road signs for Treknow.
Bedrooms: 2 double & 1 twin.
Bathrooms: 1 public; 3 private showers.
Bed & breakfast: £12-£14 single, £24-£28 double.
Half board: £20-£22 daily, £130-£144 weekly.
Lunch available.
Evening meal 6.30pm (l.o. 4pm).
Parking for 8.
♿ ❧ ᵁᴸ 🅰 🆅 🖃 ⊡ 🖤 ● 🖩
🅰 🖃 ❧ SP

TREVONE BAY

Cornwall
Map ref 1B2

Trevone Bay Hotel
APPROVED
Trevone Bay, Padstow,
PL28 8QS
☎ Padstow (0841) 520243
Hotel to suit all ages, with panoramic views, coastal walks and a sandy beach nearby. Home cooking, choice of menu, 3 lounges and a bar.
Bedrooms: 3 single, 4 double & 3 twin, 4 family rooms.
Bathrooms: 8 private, 2 public.
Bed & breakfast: £14-£20 single, £28-£40 double.
Half board: £20-£26 daily, £125-£170 weekly.
Lunch available.
Evening meal 7pm (l.o. 7.30pm).
Parking for 12.
Open April-October.
Credit: Access, Visa.

TREYARNON BAY

Cornwall
Map ref 1B2

4m W. Padstow

Waterbeach Hotel M
APPROVED
Treyarnon Bay, Padstow,
PL28 8JW
☎ (0841) 520292
Designed to take advantage of the sunshine and views across the Atlantic. Accommodates 30 people in comfort.
Bedrooms: 4 single, 4 double & 5 twin, 7 family rooms.
Bathrooms: 14 private, 2 public.
Bed & breakfast: £21-£26 single, £42-£62 double.
Half board: £28-£35 daily, £179-£235 weekly.
Evening meal 7.30pm (l.o. 8.15pm).
Parking for 25.
Open March-October.
Credit: Access, Visa, Amex.

> **Half board prices shown are per person but in some cases may be based on double/twin occupancy.**

TROWBRIDGE

Wiltshire
Map ref 2B2

Wiltshire's administrative centre, a handsome market and manufacturing town with a wealth of merchants' houses and other Georgian buildings.
Tourist Information Centre ☎ (0225) 777054

Fieldways Hotel & Health Club
COMMENDED
Hilperton Rd., Trowbridge,
BA14 7JP
☎ Bath (0225) 768336/7
Edwardian mansion set in own grounds in the heart of Wiltshire countryside.
Bedrooms: 3 single, 1 double & 7 twin.
Bathrooms: 11 private.
Bed & breakfast: £50 single, £75 double.
Half board: £50 daily.
Lunch available.
Evening meal 7pm (l.o. 10pm).
Parking for 80.
Credit: Access, Visa, Diners, Amex.

Hilbury Court Hotel
Hilperton Rd., Trowbridge,
BA14 7JW
☎ (0225) 752949
Set in its own grounds, the hotel is conveniently situated for business people and tourists alike.
Bedrooms: 3 single, 2 double & 7 twin, 1 family room.
Bathrooms: 8 private,
1 public; 3 private showers.
Bed & breakfast: £32-£39 single, £44-£52 double.
Half board: £43.50-£50.50 daily, £304.50-£353.50 weekly.
Evening meal 6.30pm (l.o. 6.30pm).
Parking for 20.
Credit: Access, Visa.

Old Manor Hotel M
Trowle, Trowbridge,
BA14 9BL
☎ Trowbridge (0225) 777393
Fax (0225) 765443
Quiet hotel set around old manor house with most rooms on ground floor. Antiques, pine, distinctive beds, en-suite rooms. Licensed residents' restaurant. Parking.

Bedrooms: 1 single, 8 double & 5 twin.
Bathrooms: 14 private.
Bed & breakfast: £38-£40 single, £45-£50 double.
Lunch available.
Evening meal 6.30pm (l.o. 8pm).
Parking for 20.
Credit: Access, Visa, Diners, Amex.

The Westbury Hotel
Market Place, Westbury,
BA13 3DB
☎ (0373) 822500
18th C inn recently completely refurbished to provide attractive en-suite accommodation. Situated in the market place, near the church.
Bedrooms: 5 double & 2 twin.
Bathrooms: 7 private.
Bed & breakfast: from £30 single, from £40 double.
Half board: from £35 daily.
Lunch available.
Evening meal 7pm (l.o. 9pm).
Parking for 13.
Credit: Access, Visa, Amex.

TRURO

Cornwall
Map ref 1B3

Cornwall's administrative centre and cathedral city, set at the head of Truro River on the Fal Estuary. A medieval stannary town, it handled mineral ore from West Cornwall; fine Georgian buildings recall its heyday as a society haunt in the second mining boom.
Tourist Information Centre ☎ (0872) 74555

Marcorrie Hotel M
20 Falmouth Rd., Truro,
TR1 2HX
☎ (0872) 77374
Family-run hotel close to the city centre. For business or holiday; central for touring Cornwall.
Bedrooms: 3 single, 3 double & 2 twin, 4 family rooms.
Bathrooms: 6 private,
1 public; 3 private showers.
Bed & breakfast: £17-£27 single, £32-£37 double.
Half board: from £24 daily, from £160 weekly.

Evening meal 7pm (l.o. 5pm).
Parking for 16.
Credit: Access, Visa.

The Royal Hotel
COMMENDED
Lemon St., Truro, TR1 2QB
☎ (0872) 70345 Fax (0872) 42453
A traditional yet friendly and informal hotel with character in the centre of a charming city. An ideal touring base.
Bedrooms: 16 single, 6 double & 8 twin, 4 family rooms.
Bathrooms: 34 private.
Bed & breakfast: £38.50-£42.50 single, from £50 double.
Lunch available.
Evening meal 7pm (l.o. 9.30pm).
Parking for 36.
Credit: Access, Visa, Amex.

TWO BRIDGES

Devon
Map ref 1C2

8m E. Tavistock
Dartmoor hamlet on the banks of the West Dart River.

Cherrybrook Hotel M
Two Bridges, Yelverton,
PL20 6SP
☎ Tavistock (0822) 88260
Old Dartmoor farmhouse in the middle of National Park, now run as a comfortable licensed hotel.
Bedrooms: 1 single, 3 double & 1 twin, 2 family rooms.
Bathrooms: 7 private,
1 public.
Bed & breakfast: from £21.50 single, from £43 double.
Half board: from £31.75 daily, from £210 weekly.
Evening meal 7.30pm (l.o. 7.15pm).
Parking for 10.
Credit: Access.

Prince Hall Hotel M
COMMENDED
Two Bridges, Yelverton,
PL20 6SW
☎ (082 289) 403 / 404
Small friendly country house hotel set in the heart of Dartmoor with beautiful views. Ideal for walking, riding and fishing.
Bedrooms: 1 single, 2 double & 3 twin, 2 family rooms.

Continued ▶

TWO BRIDGES
Continued

Bathrooms: 8 private.
Bed & breakfast: from £68 double.
Half board: from £45 daily.
Evening meal 7.30pm (l.o. 8.30pm).
Parking for 15.
Credit: Access, Visa, Diners, Amex.

Two Bridges Hotel ⋈
👑👑👑
Two Bridges, Yelverton, PL20 6SW
☎ (082 289) 206 Fax (082 289) 575
18th C posting inn with West Dart River frontage in heart of Dartmoor. Ideal for walking, riding, fishing, golf.
Bedrooms: 10 double & 8 twin, 2 family rooms.
Bathrooms: 16 private, 4 public.
Bed & breakfast: £21-£40 single, £36-£60 double.
Lunch available.
Evening meal 6pm (l.o. 8.30pm).
Parking for 120.
Credit: Access, Visa, Diners, Amex.

WADEBRIDGE
Cornwall
Map ref 1B2

Old market town with Cornwall's finest medieval bridge, spanning the Camel at its highest navigable point. Twice-widened, the bridge is said to have been built on woolpacks sunk in the unstable sands of the river bed.

Hendra Country Guest House ⋈
👑👑👑 COMMENDED
St. Kew Highway, Wadebridge, Bodmin, PL30 3EQ
☎ St. Mabyn (020 884) 343
A quiet secluded guest house in rural tranquillity, situated 2.5 miles north east of Wadebridge and half a mile off A39.
Bedrooms: 1 single, 2 double, 2 family rooms.
Bathrooms: 4 private, 1 public.
Bed & breakfast: £32-£42 double.

Half board: £26-£31 daily, £164-£205 weekly.
Evening meal 7.30pm (l.o. 6pm).
Parking for 6.

WARMINSTER
Wiltshire
Map ref 2B2

Attractive stone-built town high up to the west of Salisbury Plain. A market town, it originally thrived on cloth and wheat. Many prehistoric camps and barrows nearby, along with Longleat House and Safari Park.
Tourist Information Centre ☎ (0985) 218548

Old Bell Hotel ⋈
👑👑👑
Market Pl., Warminster, BA12 9AN
☎ (0985) 216611
14th C inn with comfortable accommodation, close to Longleat, Stonehenge, Bath and Salisbury. Home-made bar snacks, cold table and restaurant.
Bedrooms: 5 single, 13 double & 4 twin, 2 family rooms.
Bathrooms: 15 private, 4 public.
Bed & breakfast: £42-£50 single, £50-£60 double.
Lunch available.
Evening meal 6pm (l.o. 10.30pm).
Parking for 20.
Credit: Access, Visa, Diners, Amex.

WATERGATE BAY
Cornwall
Map ref 1B2

Beautiful long, board-riders' beach backed by tall cliffs north-west of Newquay. A small holiday village nestles in a steep river valley making a cleft in the cliffs.

Tregurrian Hotel ⋈
👑👑👑
Watergate Bay, Newquay, TR8 4AB
☎ St. Mawgan (0637) 860280

Please mention this guide when making a booking.

On coast road between Newquay and Padstow, just 100 yards from golden sandy beach in an area reputed to have some of the finest beaches and coastline in Europe.
Bedrooms: 4 single, 11 double & 4 twin, 8 family rooms.
Bathrooms: 22 private, 2 public.
Bed & breakfast: £14.38-£25 single, £28.76-£47 double.
Half board: £21.85-£30 daily, £115-£200 weekly.
Lunch available.
Evening meal 6.45pm (l.o. 7.30pm).
Parking for 25.
Open April-October.
Credit: Access, Visa.

WELLINGTON
Somerset
Map ref 1D1

Beam Bridge Hotel
👑👑
Sampford Arundel, Wellington, TA21 0HB
☎ Greenham (0823) 672223
Commercial lodge type accommodation, anniversary room with four-poster bed and all en-suite rooms. Bar or restaurant meals available. Function suite.
Bedrooms: 3 double & 4 twin, 1 family room.
Bathrooms: 7 private, 1 public.
Bed & breakfast: £24.50-£34.50 single, £39.50-£59.50 double.
Half board: £34.50-£44.50 daily, £241.50-£311.50 weekly.
Lunch available.
Evening meal 7pm (l.o. 9.30pm).
Parking for 60.
Credit: Access, Visa.

Half board prices shown are per person but in some cases may be based on double/twin occupancy.

WELLS
Somerset
Map ref 2A2

Small city set beneath the southern slopes of the Mendips, dominated by its magnificent cathedral. Built between 1180 and 1424, the cathedral is preserved in much of its original glory and with its ancient precincts forms one of our loveliest and most unified groups of medieval buildings.
Tourist Information Centre ☎ (0749) 72552

Ancient Gate House Hotel & Rugantino Restaurant ⋈
👑👑
20 Sadler St., Wells, BA5 2RR
☎ (0749) 72029
14th C gatehouse overlooking cathedral. Interesting hotel with Italian restaurant, friendly atmosphere. 1 mile from Wells Golf Club.
Bedrooms: 2 single, 5 double & 2 twin, 1 family room.
Bathrooms: 3 private, 2 public.
Bed & breakfast: £25-£37 single, £40-£47 double.
Half board: £29-£34 daily, £200-£235 weekly.
Lunch available.
Evening meal 7pm (l.o. 11.30pm).
Credit: Access, Visa, Diners, Amex.

Bekynton House
👑👑👑 APPROVED
7 St. Thomas St., Wells, BA5 2UU
☎ Wells (0749) 72222
Well-appointed, family-run guesthouse close to cathedral, Bishop's Palace. All bedrooms with colour TV, some en-suite. Non-smoking.
Bedrooms: 1 single, 4 double & 2 twin, 2 family rooms.
Bathrooms: 3 private, 3 public.
Bed & breakfast: £17.50-£21 single, £31-£39 double.
Evening meal 6.30pm (l.o. 9pm).
Parking for 7.
Credit: Access, Visa.

The enquiry coupons at the back will help you when contacting proprietors.

Beryl ⋒

Beryl, Wells, BA5 3JP
☎ (0749) 78738
*Bed and breakfast
accommodation in 13 acres of
parkland. 1 mile from Wells.
Take the Radstock road from
Wells. Turn opposite the
Texaco garage.*
Bedrooms: 2 double & 5 twin.
Bathrooms: 7 private.
Bed & breakfast: £25-£35
single, £50-£70 double.
Half board: £40-£50 daily,
£280-£350 weekly.
Evening meal 8pm.
Parking for 14.

Burcott Mill

APPROVED
Burcott, Wells, BA5 1NJ
☎ (0749) 73118
*Restored working watermill
with attached house and craft
workshops. Friendly
atmosphere in a rural setting,
many animals to see. Opposite
good country pub.*
Bedrooms: 1 single, 1 double
& 1 twin.
Bathrooms: 3 private.
Bed & breakfast: max. £17
single, max. £34 double.
Parking for 10.

Charlton House Hotel ⋒

COMMENDED
Charlton Rd., Shepton Mallet,
BA4 4PR
☎ (0749) 342008
*17th C country house hotel, in
7 acres of gardens with river.*
Bedrooms: 2 single, 12 double
& 3 twin, 2 family rooms.
Bathrooms: 19 private.
Bed & breakfast: £50-£70
single, £75-£90 double.
Half board: £55-£75 daily.
Lunch available.
Evening meal 7pm (l.o.
9.30pm).
Parking for 50.
Credit: Access, Visa, Diners,
Amex.

Fenny Castle House ⋒

COMMENDED
Fenny Castle, Wookey, Wells,
BA5 1NN
☎ (0749) 72265
*Riverside setting overlooking
moat and Bailey Castle.
Country house in 60 acres on
boundary of levels. Restaurant,
delightful accommodation.*
Bedrooms: 1 single, 3 double
& 2 twin.

Bathrooms: 6 private.
Bed & breakfast: from £25
single, from £45 double.
Half board: from £35 daily,
from £210 weekly.
Lunch available.
Evening meal 6pm (l.o. 9pm).
Parking for 60.
Credit: Access, Visa.

Swan Hotel ⋒

APPROVED
Sadler St., Wells, BA5 2RX
☎ (0749) 78877 Telex 449658
Ⓑ Best Western
*Privately-owned 15th C hotel
with views of the cathedral's
west front. Restaurant, saddle
bar, log fires, four-poster beds
available.*
Bedrooms: 8 single, 12 double
& 10 twin, 2 family rooms.
Bathrooms: 32 private.
Bed & breakfast: from £55
single, from £75 double.
Half board: from £52 daily.
Lunch available.
Evening meal 7pm (l.o.
9.30pm).
Parking for 30.
Credit: Access, Visa, Diners,
Amex.

Tor Guest House

20 Tor St., Wells, BA5 2US
☎ (0749) 72322
*Historic 17th C building in
delightful grounds overlooking
the cathedral. Attractive,
comfortable, centrally-heated
bedrooms. 3 minutes' walk to
town centre. Car park.*
Bedrooms: 1 single, 2 double
& 2 twin, 2 family rooms.
Bathrooms: 2 private,
2 public.
Bed & breakfast: £16-£20
single, £32-£42 double.
Half board: £26-£31 daily,
£164-£196 weekly.
Lunch available.
Evening meal 6.30pm (l.o.
10am).
Parking for 11.

WEST BAY

Dorset
Map ref 2B3

2m S. Bridport

Durbeyfield Guest House

West Bay, Bridport,
DT6 4EL
☎ (0308) 23307

---

*Family-run guesthouse,
situated amidst charming hills
and coastal scenery. 2 minutes
from beach, harbour and golf-
course. Home cooking.*
Bedrooms: 2 single, 3 double
& 2 twin, 2 family rooms.
Bathrooms: 2 public.
Bed & breakfast: £12-£17.50
single, £24-£35 double.
Half board: £20.50-£26 daily.
Evening meal 6.30pm (l.o.
midday).
Parking for 10.

WEST BEXINGTON

Dorset
Map ref 2A3

3m NW. Abbotsbury

Manor Hotel ⋒

COMMENDED
West Bexington, Dorchester,
DT2 9DF
☎ Burton Bradstock
(0308) 897616 & (0308) 897785
*16th C manor house, 500 yards
from Chesil Beach. Panoramic
views from most bedrooms. 3
real ales and character cellar
bar.*
Bedrooms: 1 single, 6 double
& 2 twin, 1 family room.
Bathrooms: 10 private.
Bed & breakfast: £33.95-
£37.95 single, £56-£63 double.
Half board: £43.95-£48.95
daily, £260-£295 weekly.
Lunch available.
Evening meal 7pm (l.o. 10pm).
Parking for 20.
Credit: Access, Visa, Amex.

WEST CHARLETON

Devon
Map ref 1C3

2m SE. Kingsbridge

West Charleton Grange

Church La., West Charleton,
Kingsbridge, TQ7 2AD
☎ Frogmore (054 85) 31779
*Secluded 16th C family-owned
country house, 5 minutes from
Kingsbridge. Central for
beaches, country walks and
bird-watching. Indoor heated
swimming pool.*
Bedrooms: 1 double & 2 twin.
Bathrooms: 2 private;
1 private shower.
Bed & breakfast: from £35
double.
Parking for 16.
Open January-October.

WEST DOWN

Devon
Map ref 1C1

4m NW. Braunton

The Long House

West Down, Ilfracombe,
EX34 8NF
☎ (0271) 863242
*A country cottage hotel in a
tiny north Devon village. 4
enchanting en-suite bedrooms.
Inspired home cooking and
intriguing wines.*
Bedrooms: 3 double & 1 twin.
Bathrooms: 4 private.
Bed & breakfast: max. £42
double.
Half board: max. £31 daily,
max. £199.50 weekly.
Lunch available.
Evening meal 7.30pm (l.o.
9pm).
Parking for 6.
Open March-November.
Credit: Access.

WESTON-SUPER-MARE

Avon
Map ref 1D1

Large, friendly resort
developed in the 19th C.
Traditional seaside
attractions include
theatres and a dance hall.
The museum shows a
Victorian seaside gallery
and has Iron Age finds
from a hill fort on
Worlebury Hill in Weston
Woods.
*Tourist Information
Centre ☎ (0934) 626838*

Almond House

42 Clevedon Rd., Weston-
super-Mare, BS23 1DQ
☎ (0934) 625113
*Friendly family-run guesthouse
with a truly relaxed
atmosphere for business and
pleasure. Home-made food.*
Bedrooms: 1 double & 1 twin,
2 family rooms.
Bathrooms: 1 public.
Bed & breakfast: £13-£14
single, £26-£28 double.
Half board: £17-£18 daily,
£115-£120 weekly.
Evening meal 6pm (l.o. 6pm).

> We advise you to
> confirm your
> booking in writing.

WESTON-SUPER-MARE
Continued

Arosfa Hotel
♛♛♛

Lower Church Rd., Weston-super-Mare, BS23 2AG
☎ (0934) 419523
3 lounges, bars, dining room and comfortable bedrooms. Situated on level ground 100 yards from the town centre and seafront.
Bedrooms: 15 single, 12 double & 15 twin, 5 family rooms.
Bathrooms: 45 private, 1 public.
Bed & breakfast: £37.50-£42.50 single, £55-£66 double.
Half board: £200-£230 weekly.
Lunch available.
Evening meal 6.45pm (l.o. 7.45pm).
Parking for 6.
Credit: Access, Visa, Diners, Amex.
ॐ ℄ ⏏ ❑ ❖ ⓘ Ⓥ ⌤ ◬
● ⊞ ▦ ♨ ⏉ ⏘ ✈ ⅅⒶⓅ ⍀
ⓈⓅ Ⓣ

Baymead Hotel
♛♛

19/23 Longton Grove Rd., Weston-super-Mare, BS23 1LS
☎ (0934) 622951
Family-run hotel in a central and quiet location 500 yards from the sea. Entertainment in the evenings.
Bedrooms: 10 single, 6 double & 14 twin, 3 family rooms.
Bathrooms: 30 private, 3 public.
Bed & breakfast: £18-£22.50 single, £35-£40 double.
Half board: £23-£27.50 daily, £110-£160 weekly.
Evening meal 6.15pm (l.o. 6.45pm).
ॐ3 ♨ ⏏ ❑ ❖ ⓘ Ⓥ ⌨ ⏴
⊞ ▦ ♨ ⏉ ⏘ ⅅⒶⓅ ⍀ ⓈⓅ Ⓣ

Berni Royal Hotel
♛♛♛♛

South Pde, Weston-super-Mare, BS23 1JN
☎ (0934) 623601
One of Weston's oldest hotels, built in 1810. Yards from the high street, with views over large lawns and seafront. Well appointed, with an air of Georgian elegance. Ground floor beautifully refurbished recently.
Bedrooms: 11 single, 22 double & 4 twin.
Bathrooms: 37 private.

Bed & breakfast: £48.50-£59.50 single, from £70 double.
Lunch available.
Evening meal 6pm (l.o. 10.30pm).
Parking for 150.
Credit: Access, Visa, Diners, Amex.
ॐ ▦ ℄ ⏏ ❑ ❖ ⓘ Ⓥ ⌨
⏴ ● ⊞ ▦ ♨ ⏉ ✳ ✈ ⓈⓅ
▦

Braeside Guest House Ⓜ
♛♛♛ COMMENDED

2 Victoria Pk., Weston-super-Mare, BS23 2HZ
☎ (0934) 626642
Family-run, friendly hotel, ideally located close to seafront. En-suite rooms, colour TV, tea and coffee making facilities. Open all year.
Bedrooms: 1 single, 5 double & 1 twin, 2 family rooms.
Bathrooms: 9 private.
Bed & breakfast: £18-£20 single, £36-£40 double.
Half board: £24.50-£26.50 daily, £147-£166 weekly.
Lunch available.
Evening meal 6pm (l.o. 6pm).
ॐ ❑ ❖ ⓘ Ⓥ ⌨ ▦ ♨ ⍀
ⓈⓅ

Commodore Hotel Ⓜ
♛♛♛♛ COMMENDED

Sand Bay, Kewstoke, Weston-super-Mare, BS22 9UZ
☎ (0934) 415778 Fax (0934) 636483
Traditional hotel facilities with popular restaurant, lounge bar and buffet services. Situated in unspoilt bay close to major resort amenities.
Bedrooms: 4 single, 14 double, 2 family rooms.
Bathrooms: 16 private, 3 public.
Bed & breakfast: max. £45 single, max. £60 double.
Half board: from £56 daily, from £255.50 weekly.
Lunch available.
Evening meal 6.30pm (l.o. 9.30pm).
Parking for 80.
Credit: Access, Visa, Diners, Amex.
ॐ ♨ ℄ ⏏ ❑ ❖ ⓘ Ⓥ ⌨
⏴ ▦ ♨ ⏉ Ⓤ ✳ ✈ ⅅⒶⓅ
ⓈⓅ ▦ Ⓣ

Daunceys Hotel
♛♛♛♛

11/14 Claremont Cres., Weston-super-Mare, BS23 2EE
☎ (0934) 621144
Family-run hotel, directly overlooking the sea. Garden for guests' enjoyment. Two lifts to all floors. Fully licensed.

Bedrooms: 14 single, 11 double & 19 twin, 6 family rooms.
Bathrooms: 41 private, 4 public.
Bed & breakfast: £24-£26 single, £48-£52 double.
Half board: £30-£32 daily, £166-£194 weekly.
Lunch available.
Evening meal 6.30pm (l.o. 6.45pm).
ॐ ♨ ⏏ ❑ ❖ ⓘ Ⓥ ⌨ ▦ ⊞
▦ ♨ ⏉ ❖ ⍀ ⓈⓅ

Midland Hotel
42 Knightstone Rd., Weston-super-Mare, BS23 2BD
☎ (0934) 21217
English family-run hotel on the seafront within reach of all Weston's amenities.
Bedrooms: 4 single, 9 double & 7 twin, 13 family rooms.
Bathrooms: 18 private, 2 public.
Bed & breakfast: £17.25-£21.85 single, £32.20-£41.40 double.
Half board: £23-£28.75 daily, £120-£140 weekly.
Evening meal 6pm (l.o. 6pm).
Parking for 10.
Open March-December.
Credit: Access, Visa.
ॐ ❑ ❖ ⓘ Ⓥ ⌨ ⊞ ✈
⍀ ⓈⓅ

Moorlands Ⓜ
♛♛♛ APPROVED

Hutton, Weston-super-Mare, BS24 9UH
☎ Bleadon (0934) 812283
Family-run 18th C house in mature landscaped grounds. Caring traditional cooking. Log fires. Pony rides for children.
Bedrooms: 2 single, 2 double, 4 family rooms.
Bathrooms: 4 private, 2 public.
Bed & breakfast: £16 single, £32 double.
Half board: £24 daily, £138 weekly.
Evening meal 6.30pm (l.o. 5pm).
Parking for 8.
ॐ ♨ Ⓥ ⌨ Ⓣⓥ ▦ ⓑ ✳ ▦

Newton House
♛♛♛ COMMENDED

79 Locking Rd., Weston-super-Mare, BS23 3DW
☎ (0934) 629331
Friendly, licensed accommodation. En-suites available, satellite TV and tea facilities in all rooms. Some four-poster beds. Car park.
Bedrooms: 2 single, 2 double, 4 family rooms.
Bathrooms: 5 private, 1 public.

Bed & breakfast: £15-£17.50 single, £30-£35 double.
Half board: £22-£24.50 daily, £144-£161.50 weekly.
Lunch available.
Evening meal 6pm (l.o. 2pm).
Parking for 9.
Credit: Access, Visa, Amex.
ॐ ♨ ● ❑ ❖ ⓘ Ⓥ ⌨ Ⓣⓥ
▦ ♨ ⏉ ⅅⒶⓅ ⓈⓅ

Rozel Hotel Ⓜ
♛♛♛♛

Madeira Cove, Weston-super-Mare, BS23 2BU
☎ (0934) 415268
Fax (0934) 415268
Ⓒⓡ Inter
Elegant Victorian building sympathetically modernised offering well-furnished lounges, fully-equipped bedrooms and a friendly relaxed atmosphere.
Bedrooms: 8 single, 12 double & 10 twin, 14 family rooms.
Bathrooms: 44 private, 2 public.
Bed & breakfast: £38-£45 single, £60-£80 double.
Half board: £45-£55 daily, £220-£250 weekly.
Lunch available.
Evening meal 7pm (l.o. 8.30pm).
Parking for 70.
Credit: Access, Visa, Diners, Amex.
ॐ ♨ ▦ ℄ ⏏ ❑ ❖ ⓘ Ⓥ
▦ ⊞ ▦ ♨ ⏉ ❖ ⍀ ⍀
ⓈⓅ

Saxonia Ⓜ
♛♛♛ APPROVED

95 Locking Rd., Weston-super-Mare, BS23 3EW
☎ (0934) 633856
Friendly family-run licensed guesthouse near beach, 15 minutes from Tropicana Leisure Centre. En-suite rooms. Showers and colour TV in all rooms. Stair-lift.
Bedrooms: 2 single, 2 double & 1 twin, 3 family rooms.
Bathrooms: 5 private; 3 private showers.
Bed & breakfast: £14.50-£17 single, £29-£34 double.
Evening meal 6.30pm (l.o. midday).
Parking for 4.
Credit: Access, Visa.
ॐ ❑ ❖ ⓘ Ⓥ ⌨ Ⓣⓥ ⊞ ▦
▦ ⓑ ✈ ⅅⒶⓅ Ⓥ ⍀ ⓈⓅ

Tralee Hotel Ⓜ
32/34 Birnbeck Rd., Weston-super-Mare, BS23 2BX
☎ (0934) 626707
Detached, licensed, seafront hotel with views across Weston Bay. Lift available. Easy level walk to all main amenities.
Bedrooms: 8 single, 14 double & 12 twin, 3 family rooms.

Bathrooms: 9 private,
5 public.
Bed & breakfast: £13.50-£15
single, £23-£30 double.
Half board: £16-£19.50 daily,
£96-£117 weekly.
Lunch available.
Evening meal 6pm (l.o. 6pm).
Parking for 12.
Open April-October.
⌖5 ⌖ ⌖ | V ⌖ TV ⌖ ⌖ ⌖
⌖ SP T

Small resort, whose name
comes from the title of
Charles Kingsley's
famous novel, on
Barnstaple Bay, close to
the Taw and Torridge
Estuary. There are good
sands and a notable golf-
course - one of the oldest
in Britain.

Buckleigh Lodge
⌖⌖⌖ APPROVED
135 Bay View Rd., Westward
Ho!, Bideford, EX39 1BJ
☎ Bideford (0237) 475988
*Fine, late Victorian house in
own grounds, with magnificent
views over the bay and close to
a large, safe sandy beach.*
Bedrooms: 1 single, 2 double
& 2 twin, 1 family room.
Bathrooms: 2 private,
2 public.
Bed & breakfast: £13-£16
single, £26-£32 double.
Half board: £20-£23 daily.
Evening meal 7pm (l.o. 5pm).
Parking for 7.
⌖⌖⌖⌖ | V ⌖ TV ⌖ ⌖
⌖ ⌖ ⌖ ⌖ ⌖ ⌖ ⌖

Ancient port and one of
the south's earliest
resorts. Curving beside a
long, sandy beach, the
elegant Georgian
esplanade is graced with
a statue of George III and
a cheerful Victorian
Jubilee clock tower.
*Tourist Information
Centre* ☎ *(0305) 772444*

Cumberland Hotel
⌖⌖⌖
95 Esplanade, Weymouth,
DT4 7BA
☎ (0305) 785644
*Centre of Weymouth Bay,
close to all amenities, rail and
bus stations.*

Bedrooms: 6 double & 1 twin,
5 family rooms.
Bathrooms: 12 private.
Bed & breakfast: £25-£28
single, £40-£46 double.
Half board: £27-£29 daily,
£135-£160 weekly.
Evening meal 6pm (l.o.
6.30pm).
Parking for 2.
⌖5 ⌖ ⌖ ⌖ ⌖ | V ⌖ ⌖
⌖ ⌖ ⌖ ⌖ SP

Florian Guest House
⌖
59 Abbotsbury Rd.,
Weymouth, DT4 0AQ
☎ (0305) 773836
*Semi-detached guesthouse on
main road leading to seafront
and town.*
Bedrooms: 1 single, 3 double
& 2 twin.
Bathrooms: 6 private.
Bed & breakfast: £13-£16
single, £26-£32 double.
Half board: £16-£18 daily,
£70-£120 weekly.
Evening meal 5.45pm (l.o.
4.30pm).
Parking for 7.
⌖2 ⌖ ⌖ ⌖ | V ⌖ TV
⌖ ⌖ SP

Hazeldene Guest House
Listed
16 Abbotsbury Rd.,
Weymouth, DT4 0AE
☎ (0305) 782579
*Small comfortable guest house,
catering for 20 people. Short
walk to main amenities of
Weymouth.*
Bedrooms: 1 single, 2 double
& 1 twin, 4 family rooms.
Bathrooms: 3 public.
Bed & breakfast: £11.50-£14
single, £28-£30 double.
Half board: £14-£17 daily.
Evening meal 6pm (l.o. 2pm).
Parking for 8.
⌖5 ⌖ ⌖ | V ⌖ TV ⌖ ⌖
⌖ ⌖ SP

Keithlyn Guest House
4 Carlton Rd. S., Weymouth,
DT4 7PJ
☎ (0305) 784202
*Friendly comfortable
accommodation with
unrestricted access and central
heating. Close to beach.*
Bedrooms: 1 single, 4 double
& 1 twin, 3 family rooms.
Bathrooms: 2 public.
Bed & breakfast: £11-£12
single, £22-£24 double.
Half board: from £15 daily.
Evening meal 6pm (l.o. 6pm).
Parking for 7.
Open April-October.
⌖ ⌖ ⌖ | V ⌖ TV ⌖ ⌖ ⌖

Moonfleet Manor ⌖
⌖⌖⌖⌖
Fleet Rd., Weymouth,
DT3 4ED
☎ (0305) 786948
Fax (0305) 774395
*Family activity holiday hotel in
open countryside overlooking
English Channel. Facilities
usually associated with a
country club, including 4 rink
bowls hall.*
Bedrooms: 3 single, 19 double
& 6 twin, 9 family rooms.
Bathrooms: 37 private.
Bed & breakfast: £38-£42
single, £61-£68 double.
Half board: £40-£50 daily,
£235-£250 weekly.
Lunch available.
Evening meal 7pm (l.o.
9.30pm).
Parking for 200.
Credit: Access, Visa, Diners,
Amex.
⌖ ⌖ ⌖ ⌖ ⌖ ⌖ ⌖ ⌖ | V
⌖ ⌖ ⌖ ⌖ ⌖ ⌖ ⌖ ⌖
⌖ ⌖ ⌖ ⌖ ⌖ ⌖ ⌖ ⌖ SP
⌖ T

Richmoor Hotel
146 The Esplanade,
Weymouth, DT4 7PB
☎ (0305) 773435
*Georgian Grade II listed hotel
on seafront. Close to gardens
and all amenities. Colour TV
in all rooms, most en-suite.*
Bedrooms: 5 single, 8 double
& 5 twin, 7 family rooms.
Bathrooms: 21 private,
2 public.
Bed & breakfast: £17.50-
£19.50 single, £35-£39 double.
Half board: £22.50-£24.50
daily, £125-£155 weekly.
Lunch available.
Evening meal 6pm (l.o.
6.30pm).
Parking for 8.
Credit: Access, Visa.
⌖ ⌖ ⌖ ⌖ ⌖ | V ⌖ TV ⌖
⌖ ⌖ ⌖ ⌖ SP ⌖

Rosslare
⌖⌖
145 Dorchester Rd.,
Weymouth, DT4 7LE
☎ (0305) 785913
*Small, licensed friendly
guesthouse situated on the
main Dorchester road leading
into Weymouth.*
Bedrooms: 1 single, 2 twin,
4 family rooms.
Bathrooms: 4 private,
1 public.
Bed & breakfast: £12-£15
single, £24-£32 double.
Half board: £17-£21 daily,
£90-£116 weekly.

Evening meal 6pm (l.o. 5pm).
Parking for 5.
Credit: Access, Visa.
⌖ ⌖ ⌖ ⌖ | V ⌖ TV ⌖ ⌖
⌖ ⌖ ⌖ ⌖ SP

Streamside Hotel
29 Preston Rd., Weymouth,
DT3 6PX
☎ (0305) 833121
*Full of old world charm in a
picturesque setting, surrounded
by award winning gardens. 200
yards from beach. Games
room.*
Bedrooms: 8 double & 3 twin,
4 family rooms.
Bathrooms: 9 private,
3 public; 2 private showers.
Bed & breakfast: £35-£45
single, £50-£65 double.
Half board: £25-£35 daily,
£175-£245 weekly.
Lunch available.
Evening meal 6.30pm (l.o.
9pm).
Parking for 40.
Credit: Access, Visa, Diners,
Amex.
⌖ ⌖ ⌖ ⌖ ⌖ ⌖ | V ⌖
⌖ ⌖ ⌖ ⌖ ⌖ ⌖ ⌖ SP

Sunningdale Hotel ⌖
⌖⌖⌖
52 Preston Rd., Weymouth,
DT3 6QD
☎ Preston (Dorset)
(0305) 832179
*Country-style family hotel with
a relaxed and comfortable
atmosphere, set in 2 acres of
gardens. 1.5 miles from town
centre.*
Bedrooms: 1 single, 7 double
& 4 twin, 8 family rooms.
Bathrooms: 10 private,
3 public; 3 private showers.
Bed & breakfast: £18-£22.50
single, £36-£45 double.
Half board: £23-£29 daily,
£142-£180 weekly.
Lunch available.
Evening meal 6.30pm (l.o.
7pm).
Open April-October.
⌖ ⌖ ⌖ ⌖ | V ⌖ TV ⌖
⌖ ⌖ ⌖ ⌖ ⌖ SP

*5m SW. Dunster
Crossroads hamlet in the
heart of Exmoor National
Park.*

Exmoor House ⌖
⌖⌖⌖ APPROVED
Wheddon Cross, Minehead,
TA24 7DU
☎ Timberscombe
(0643) 841432

Continued ▶

WHEDDON CROSS
Continued

Spacious, comfortable guest house in Exmoor National Park. Perfect centre for touring and walking. Personal attention guaranteed.
Bedrooms: 4 double & 2 twin, 2 family rooms.
Bathrooms: 6 private, 2 public; 1 private shower.
Bed & breakfast: from £14 single, from £28 double.
Half board: from £21 daily, from £138 weekly.
Evening meal 7pm (l.o. 5.30pm).
Parking for 9.
Open March-November.
⛡ ♿ 🅟 📺 ▦ ♨ ✕
📻 SP

WHIMPLE
Devon
Map ref 1D2

4m NW. Ottery St. Mary

Woodhayes Hotel M
Whimple, Exeter, EX5 2TD
☎ (0404) 822237
Small Georgian country house hotel with the atmosphere of private house. Only fresh and home grown produce used.
Bedrooms: 4 double & 2 twin.
Bathrooms: 6 private.
Bed & breakfast: max. £55 single, max. £75 double.
Half board: max. £49.50 daily.
Lunch available.
Evening meal 7.30pm (l.o. 8pm).
Parking for 22.
Credit: Access, Visa, Diners, Amex.
⛡12 📞 🅟 🍴 ▦
♨ ☂ ✿ ✕ 📻 SP 📻
T

WIDECOMBE-IN-THE-MOOR
Devon
Map ref 1C2

Old village in pastoral country under the high tors of East Dartmoor. The 'Cathedral of the Moor' stands near a tiny square, once used for archery practice, which has a 16th C Church House among other old buildings.

Sheena Tower
♨♨
Widecombe-in-the-Moor, Newton Abbot, TQ13 7TE
☎ (036 42) 308

Comfortable moorland guesthouse overlooking Widecombe village, offering a relaxed holiday in picturesque surroundings. Well placed for discovering Dartmoor.
Bedrooms: 1 single, 2 double & 1 twin, 2 family rooms.
Bathrooms: 1 private, 2 public.
Bed & breakfast: £11-£13 single, £22-£26 double.
Half board: £17-£19 daily, £116-£130 weekly.
Evening meal 7pm (l.o. midday).
Parking for 10.
Open February-October.
⛡ ♿ ♨ 🅟 📺 ▦ ♨
✿ 📻

WINCANTON
Somerset
Map ref 2B3

Thriving market town, rising from the rich pastures of Blackmoor Vale near the Dorset border, with many attractive 18th C stone buildings. Steeplechase racecourse.
Tourist Information Centre ☎ (0963) 34063

Holbrook House Hotel M
Holbrook, Wincanton, BA9 8BS
☎ (0963) 32377
Elegant country house in 15 acres of peaceful countryside, 2 hours from London. Ideal base for touring Somerset and Dorset. Reliable, friendly service. Same family ownership since 1946.
Bedrooms: 5 single, 6 double & 5 twin, 3 family rooms.
Bathrooms: 16 private, 4 public.
Bed & breakfast: £38-£45 single, £68-£72 double.
Half board: £82-£85 daily, from £324 weekly.
Lunch available.
Evening meal 7.30pm (l.o. 8.30pm).
Parking for 34.
Credit: Access, Visa, Amex.
⛡ 📞 🅟 ♨ 📺 ▦
♨ ☂ ✿ 🍴 ♨ ✕ 📻
SP 📻

Horsington House Hotel M
♨♨♨ APPROVED
Horsington, Templecombe, Wincanton, BA8 0EG
☎ Templecombe
(0963) 70721 Fax
(0963) 70554

Elegant country house hotel, set in 7 acres, overlooking the Blackmore Vale. Ideal base for exploring Somerset, Dorset and Wiltshire.
Bedrooms: 7 single, 6 double & 8 twin, 2 family rooms.
Bathrooms: 23 private.
Bed & breakfast: £41-£48 single, £62-£69 double.
Half board: £43.50-£65.50 daily, £225-£285 weekly.
Lunch available.
Evening meal 7pm (l.o. 9.30pm).
Parking for 50.
Credit: Access, Visa.
⛡ 📞 🅟 ♨ 📺 ♨
♨ ☂ ✿ 🅟 ✿ DAP 📻 SP 📻
T

WINTERBOURNE STOKE
Wiltshire
Map ref 2B3

5m W. Amesbury

Scotland Lodge M
♨♨ APPROVED
Winterbourne Stoke, Salisbury, SP3 4TF
☎ Shrewton (0980) 620943
Intimate, comfortable country house with private bathrooms. Helpful service. Ideal touring base. French and some German spoken. Also self-contained unit.
Bedrooms: 1 single, 1 double & 1 twin, 1 family room.
Bathrooms: 4 private.
Bed & breakfast: £20-£30 single, £30-£45 double.
Parking for 10.
⛡ 🅟 📺 ▦ ✕ ▦ ♨ ✿
✕ 📻

WIVELISCOMBE
Somerset
Map ref 1D1

9m W. Taunton

Watercombe House
♨♨ COMMENDED
Huish Champflower, Wiveliscombe, Taunton, TA4 2EE
☎ Wiveliscombe (0984) 23725
Country home in quiet beauty spot with unique setting and relaxing atmosphere. Home cooking. Fishing and sailing nearby. Ideal touring and walking centre. Sea within easy reach.
Bedrooms: 1 single, 1 double & 1 twin.
Bathrooms: 1 public.

Bed & breakfast: £14-£16 single, £33-£37 double.
Half board: £24.50-£31.50 daily, £166-£215 weekly.
Evening meal 7.30pm.
Parking for 6.
Open April-October.
♨ UL ♨ 📺 ▦ ♨ ✿
📻 ✿ SP 📻

WOODY BAY
Devon
Map ref 1C1

3m W. Lynton
Rocky bay backed by dramatic cliffs thick with oak woods on the western Exmoor coast. To the west over Martinhoe Hill the River Heddon reaches the sea through a steep wooded valley.

Woody Bay Hotel M
Woody Bay, Parracombe, EX31 4QX
☎ Parracombe (059 83) 264
Nestling in the woods with magnificent views over National Trust woodland and the Exmoor coastline. Very quiet.
Bedrooms: 1 single, 8 double & 4 twin, 1 family room.
Bathrooms: 13 private, 1 public.
Bed & breakfast: £24-£34 single, £44-£74 double.
Half board: £32-£49 daily, £224-£308 weekly.
Lunch available.
Evening meal 7.15pm (l.o. 8.30pm).
Parking for 15.
Open February-December.
Credit: Access, Visa.
⛡8 📻 ♨ ♨ 📺 ▦ ▦ ♨
☂ ♨ 📻 SP

WOOKEY HOLE
Somerset
Map ref 2A2

2m NW. Wells
A series of spectacular limestone caverns on the southern slopes of the Mendips, near the source of the River Axe. The river flows through elaborate formations of stalactites and stalagmites.

Glencot House M
♨♨♨ COMMENDED
Glencot La., Wookey Hole, Wells, BA5 1BH
☎ (0749) 77160

Large, comfortable country house in 18 acres, with own river, indoor jet stream pool, snooker room and sauna.
Bedrooms: 1 single, 5 double & 3 twin, 1 family room.
Bathrooms: 10 private, 2 public.
Bed & breakfast: £30-£40 single, £48-£60 double.
Half board: £38-£44 daily, £250-£290 weekly.
Lunch available.
Evening meal 6.30pm (l.o. 8pm).
Parking for 15.
Credit: Access, Visa.

WOOLACOMBE
Devon
Map ref 1C1

Between Morte Point and Baggy Point, Woolacombe and Mortehoe offer 3 miles of the finest sand and surf on this outstanding coastline. Much of the area is owned by the National Trust.

Caertref Hotel
Beach Rd., Woolacombe, EX34 7BT
☎ (0271) 870361
Small, informal hotel where the proprietors aim to please. Plentiful meals. Close to beach and shops.
Bedrooms: 1 single, 7 double & 2 twin, 3 family rooms.
Bathrooms: 7 private, 2 public; 1 private shower.
Bed & breakfast: from £12.50 single, from £25 double.
Half board: from £18.50 daily.
Evening meal 6.30pm (l.o. 6.30pm).
Parking for 13.
Credit: Access, Visa.

Crossways Hotel
The Esplanade, Woolacombe, EX34 7DJ
☎ (0271) 870395
Friendly, family-run hotel in quiet seafront position overlooking Combesgate beach and valley. All rooms recently refurbished.
Bedrooms: 1 single, 3 double, 5 family rooms.
Bathrooms: 5 private, 1 public; 2 private showers.

Bed & breakfast: £14.75-£20.25 single, £29.50-£40.50 double.
Half board: £19.25-£24.75 daily, £135-£170 weekly.
Lunch available.
Evening meal 6.30pm (l.o. 6.30pm).
Parking for 11.
Open March-October.

Devon Beach Hotel M
The Esplanade, Woolacombe, EX34 7DJ
☎ (0271) 870449
Family-run holiday hotel with easy access to 3 beaches and glorious National Trust countryside on 3 sides.
Bedrooms: 10 single, 11 double & 11 twin, 4 family rooms.
Bathrooms: 24 private, 4 public.
Bed & breakfast: £20-£25 single, £46-£60 double.
Half board: £24-£38 daily, £150-£240 weekly.
Lunch available.
Evening meal 7pm (l.o. 8.15pm).
Parking for 32.
Open April-October, December.
Credit: Access, Visa.

Lundy House Hotel M
Chapel Hill, Mortehoe, Woolacombe, EX34 7DZ
☎ Woolacombe (0271) 870372
Magnificently situated on coastal path with spectacular sea views. Traditional home cooking, licensed bar lounge. Pets welcome. Bargain breaks.
Bedrooms: 3 single, 2 double, 5 family rooms.
Bathrooms: 5 private, 1 public.
Bed & breakfast: £15-£18 single, £30-£40 double.
Half board: £22.50-£27.50 daily, £166-£186 weekly.
Lunch available.
Evening meal 7.30pm (l.o. 4pm).
Parking for 10.
Open January-October.

The Old Vicarage
Lee Bay, Ilfracombe, EX34 8LW
☎ (0271) 63195
Large, comfortable Victorian house in Fuschia Valley 400 yards from sheltered rocky cove.

Bedrooms: 6 double & 2 twin, 2 family rooms.
Bathrooms: 1 private, 3 public.
Bed & breakfast: £26-£40 double.
Half board: £25-£32 daily, £175-£224 weekly.
Evening meal 7pm (l.o. 4pm).
Parking for 7.

Pebbles Hotel and Restaurant M
COMMENDED
Combesgate Beach, Mortehoe, Woolacombe, EX34 7EA
☎ Woolacombe (0271) 870426
Hotel with integral restaurants, adjoining National Trust land. Spectacular views of sea and coast. Direct access to beach.
Bedrooms: 1 single, 7 double & 1 twin, 3 family rooms.
Bathrooms: 11 private, 1 public.
Bed & breakfast: £18-£22 single, £36-£44 double.
Half board: £27-£31 daily, £182-£210 weekly.
Lunch available.
Evening meal 7pm (l.o. 9.30pm).
Parking for 31.
Open February-December.
Credit: Access, Visa.

Springside Country House
Mullacott Rd., Woolacombe, EX34 7HF
☎ (0271) 870452
All bedrooms overlook open countryside to the sea. Ideal centre for touring, midway between Woolacombe and Ilfracombe. Home-from-home.
Bedrooms: 1 single, 2 double & 1 twin, 4 family rooms.
Bathrooms: 5 private, 1 public.
Bed & breakfast: £14.50-£18 single, £29-£36 double.
Evening meal 6.30pm (l.o. 5pm).
Parking for 10.
Open April-October.

Waters Fall Hotel M
Beach Rd., Woolacombe, EX34 7AD
☎ (0271) 870365
Always a warm welcome. Cooking by highly qualified chef/proprietor. Beautiful position with sea and country views. Large level car park.
Bedrooms: 2 single, 7 double & 4 twin, 4 family rooms.

Bathrooms: 15 private, 2 public.
Bed & breakfast: £24-£32 single, £48-£64 double.
Half board: £30-£38 daily, £177-£220 weekly.
Evening meal 7pm (l.o. 8pm).
Parking for 17.
Open March-October, December.
Credit: Access, Visa.

Woolacombe Bay Hotel M
Woolacombe, EX34 7BN
☎ Woolacombe, (0271) 870388
Consort
Gracious hotel in 6 acres of gardens leading to the sea. With solarium, spa bath, pitch and putt, in-house video, aerobics, aquarobics and short mat bowling.
Bedrooms: 1 single, 24 double & 10 twin, 24 family rooms.
Bathrooms: 59 private.
Half board: £43-£95 daily, £215-£532 weekly.
Evening meal 7.30pm (l.o. 9.30pm).
Parking for 70.
Open February-December.
Credit: Access, Visa, Diners, Amex.

WOOTTON BASSETT
Wiltshire
Map ref 2B2

6m W. Swindon
Small hillside town with attractive old buildings and a 13th C church. The church and the half-timbered town hall were both restored in the 19th C and the stocks and ducking pool are preserved.

Fairview Guest House
52 Swindon Rd., Wootton Bassett, Swindon, SN4 8EU
☎ Swindon (0793) 852283
Detached guesthouse close to the M4 junction 16 and major tourist resorts. Also motel style annexe with 4 bedrooms.
Bedrooms: 3 single, 2 double & 5 twin, 2 family rooms.
Bathrooms: 4 public; 3 private showers.
Bed & breakfast: £18-£28 single, £34-£38 double.
Half board: £25.50-£27 daily, £178.50-£189 weekly.

Continued ▶

WOOTTON BASSETT

Continued

Evening meal 6.30pm (l.o. 2pm).
Parking for 19.

ら ▲ ⑧ ☐ ⇦ ⓤ ⓘ Ⅴ ⇥
ⓉⅤ Ⅲ ▲ ⓰ ᴰᴬᴾ ⇘ ꜱᴾ

YELVERTON

Devon
Map ref 1C2

Village on the edge of Dartmoor, where ponies wander over the flat common. Buckland Abbey is 2 miles south-west, while Burrator Reservoir is 2 miles to the east.

Blowiscombe Barton M
⚜⚜⚜ COMMENDED

Milton Combe, Yelverton,
PL20 6HR
☎ Yelverton (0822) 854853
Modernised farmhouse surrounded by rolling farmland, yet only 800 yards from village pub and National Park. Heated swimming pool. 8 miles from Plymouth centre.

ら ☐ ⇦ ⓘ Ⅴ ⇥ ⓉⅤ Ⅲ ▲
⓰ ⇘ ꜱᴾ

Bedrooms: 2 double & 1 twin.
Bathrooms: 2 private,
1 public.
Bed & breakfast: £12-£16 single, £24-£32 double.
Half board: £18-£22 daily, £110-£137 weekly.
Evening meal 6.30pm (l.o. 8.30pm).
Parking for 6.

ら ☐ ⓤ Ⅴ ⇥ ⓉⅤ Ⅲ ▲ ⤳
⓾ ▶

Rosemont Hotel
⚜⚜ COMMENDED

Greenbank Ter., Yelverton,
PL20 6DR
☎ (0822) 852175
Small, friendly, family hotel. Quality food. Situated in quiet village on edge of Dartmoor. An ideal spot for touring West Country.
Bedrooms: 2 single, 3 double & 2 twin, 2 family rooms.
Bathrooms: 1 private,
3 public.
Bed & breakfast: £14.50 single, £29 double.
Half board: £22.50 daily.
Lunch available.
Evening meal 6.30pm (l.o. 6.30pm).
Parking for 9.

ら ☐ ⇦ ⓘ Ⅴ ⇥ ⓉⅤ Ⅲ ▲
⓰ ⇘ ꜱᴾ

Waverley Guest House M
⚜⚜ APPROVED

5 Greenbank Ter., Yelverton,
PL20 6DR
☎ (0822) 854617
Family-run guesthouse on edge of Dartmoor, 9 miles from Plymouth and 6 miles from Tavistock. Children and pets welcome.
Bedrooms: 1 single, 1 double & 1 twin, 2 family rooms.
Bathrooms: 1 public;
5 private showers.
Bed & breakfast: from £15 single, from £30 double.
Half board: from £22 daily, from £154 weekly.
Evening meal 6pm (l.o. 9am).
Parking for 3.

ら ▲ ☐ ⇦ ⓤ ⓘ Ⅴ ⇥ ⓉⅤ
Ⅲ ▲ ⓰

Somerset
Map ref 2A3

Lively market town set in dairying country beside the River Yeo, famous for glove making. Interesting parish church. Museum of South Somerset at Hendford Manor.
Tourist Information Centre ☎ *(0935) 71279*

Preston Hotel and Motel

64 Preston Rd., Yeovil,
BA20 2DL
☎ (0935) 74400
Friendly, comfortable 17-bedroomed hotel. Most rooms en-suite with telephone and TV. Restaurant open all day. Facilities for disabled.
Bedrooms: 6 single, 7 double & 4 twin.
Bathrooms: 11 private,
2 public.
Bed & breakfast: £22-£35 single, £47 double.
Half board: £30.95-£43.95 daily.
Lunch available.
Evening meal 6pm (l.o. 9.30pm).
Parking for 20.
Credit: Access, Visa.

ら ▲ ⓵ ☐ ⇦ ⓘ Ⅴ ⇥ Ⅲ
▲ ⓣ & ⓣ

Key to symbols

Information about many of the services and facilities at establishments listed in this guide is given in the form of symbols. The key to these symbols is inside the back cover flap. You may find it helpful to keep the flap open when referring to the entry listings.

Avon Hotel

**Bathwick Street, Bath, Avon BA2 6NX
Telephone reservations (0225) 446176 & 422226
Fax: (0225) 447452**

The **Avon Hotel** is 830 metres level walk* to the Roman Baths, main tourist areas and shopping centre with easy access to the Ring road and M4 Motorway.

Our **large floodlit car park** is freely available to our guests even after checkout time.

All rooms have en-suite facilities, are centrally heated and equipped with colour TV, alarm radio and welcome tray.

There are several large **ground floor** bedrooms some with **four poster beds** and **family suites**.

Our ''Honeymoon Special'', includes four poster ground floor room with fresh flowers and iced Champagne.

We have several rooms specially reserved for *non-smokers*.

Write or phone for brochure and room rates.

*We stress LEVEL because the steep hills of Bath are not for the faint hearted!!!!!

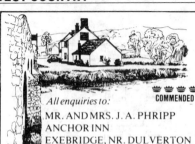

The Castle Rock Hotel

Port Isaac, North Cornwall PL29 3SB.
☎ **(0208) 880300.**

👑👑👑
APPROVED   AA ★★   RAC ★★   Ashley Courtenay

Superbly situated overlooking the Atlantic and Port Isaac Bay, with magnificent panoramic views of the North Cornish Heritage Coastline, to Tintagel and Hartland Point.
19 de-luxe en-suite bedrooms, most with a spectacular sea view. High standard of comfort and cuisine. Spring Autumn, Christmas and New Year breaks.
Brochure with pleasure.

Chymorvah-Tolgarrick Hotel
Marazion, Cornwall TR17 0DQ.

🔲 **RAC ACCLAIMED**   ETB 👑👑👑 COMMENDED 🏴

Wonderful views • Access to beach • Menu choice • Optional evening meal • FREE parking • Colour TV & telephone all bedrooms • Fully en-suite • Babysitting • Open all year • Central heating • Mid-week bookings accepted • Ground floor bedroom available.
B&B from £15.00 per night.

Write or telephone Resident Proprietors Pete and Hazelmary Bull for colour brochure.
☎ Penzance (0736) 710497.

The Dower House Hotel

Rousdon, Nr Lyme Regis, Dorset DT7 3RB
Tel: Seaton (0297) Management 21047
Residents 20240

👑👑👑 Commended   RAC ★★   Ashley Courtenay

Why not join us in our beautiful old world country mansion set in beautiful acres of tree-fringed grounds? Open all year except November. Excellent cuisine, varied and plentiful. All rooms en-suite with colour TV, tea and coffee-making facilities. Central heating and roaring log fires in winter. New indoor heated swimming pool. An ideal place for walking, golf or just lazing around. 6 minutes from Lyme Regis, Dorset and Seaton, Devon.

THE EDGAR HOTEL

64 Great Pulteney Street, Bath BA2 4DN ☎ (0225) 420619

A Grade 1 listed Georgian Town House which has been converted into a comfortable hotel. A short level walk to the town centre, Pump Room and Roman Baths. Each bedroom has private shower/WC. Colour TV. Tea/coffee making facilities. The proprietors offer personal service together with a high standard of accommodation. Full English breakfast. AA, RAC recommended. Winter breaks.

BHRA   L

PRICES ARE PER ROOM, AND INCLUDE ENGLISH BREAKFAST AND VAT			SINGLE	DBLE/TWN	FAMILY
No. of Bedrooms 16 Private Facilities 16					
MIN RATES:	SINGLE £25	DOUBLE £35	2	13	1
MAX RATES:	SINGLE £30	DOUBLE £50	👑👑 APPROVED		

Follow the sign

It leads to over 560 Tourist Information Centres throughout England offering friendly help with accommodation and holiday ideas as well as suggestions of places to visit and things to do.

In your home town there may be a centre which can help you before you set out. Details of the locations of Tourist Information Centres are available from the English Tourist Board, Thames Tower, Black's Road, London W6 9EL, or from England's Regional Tourist Boards.

Use a coupon

When requesting further information from advertisers in this guide, you may find it helpful to use the advertisement enquiry coupons which can be found towards the end of the guide. These should be cut out and mailed direct to the companies in which you are interested. Do remember to include your name and address.

♣ Enjoy the countryside and respect its life and work ♣ Guard against all risk of fire ♣ Fasten all gates ♣ Keep your dogs under close control ♣ Keep to public paths across farmland ♣ Use gates and stiles to cross fences, hedges and walls ♣ Leave livestock, crops and machinery alone ♣ Take your litter home ♣ Help to keep all water clean ♣ Protect wildlife, plants and trees ♣ Take special care on country roads ♣ Make no unnecessary noise

FOLLOW THE COUNTRY CODE

South of England...

the words say it all. The best of Englishness in the warmth of the south. They tell of the Isle of Wight and the mainland above — Hampshire and neighbouring East Dorset to the west. Soft, beautiful scenery in a soft, beautiful climate; coastlines that change from colossal white cliffs to smugglers' coves in the space of a mile or so; forests, downs and rich rolling farmland.

» The Isle of Wight is staggeringly pretty, full of winding lanes, visitor attractions and natural wonders like the Needles. There are family resorts like Shanklin and Sandown, fashionable Cowes, quaint Yarmouth, Ryde with its long pier and six-mile beach, and Ventnor — known as 'the Madeira of England'. A well-nigh irresistible holiday experience...

» ...fully matched by the mainland! Here you can walk the coastal footpaths and slice the azure depths. And enjoy beach-life at Bournemouth, 'Queen' of the resorts, or Swanage with its beautiful bay. Then there's Lulworth Cove, lively Poole and the harbour, Portsmouth's Southsea and, for the perfect water-based family holiday,

The Needles, Isle of Wight

Hayling Island. Throughout the south are beaches awarded the Blue Flag for excellence.

» Inland, take a wagon-train through the 1,000-year-old New Forest, ever enchanting with its sparkling streams and free-roaming ponies and deer. Maybe drink in blue views from

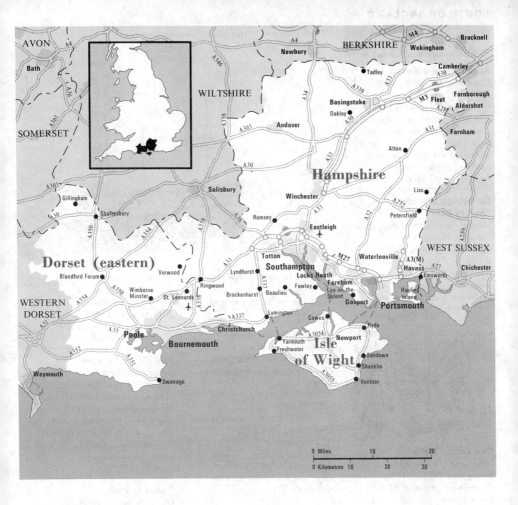

a picnic point, or perhaps potter around Thomas Hardy or Watership Down country. Possibly angle in rivers like the Test, Itchen, Stour and Avon.

▸▸ You might prefer to explore old ships and maritime museums at Gosport, Southampton and Portsmouth; military museums in Aldershot and Andover. Or gaze in awe at Wimborne Minster and Winchester Cathedral, dream at historic houses like Stratfield Saye and Broadlands, visit pretty towns like Shaftesbury and Blandford Forum.

▸▸ By then you'll surely be planning your 1992 return visit to the warm and balmy South!

▸▸ Please refer to the colour maps at the back of this guide for all places with accommodation listings.

463

Where to go, what to see

HMS Victory — the oldest surviving ship in commission with the Royal Navy

Jane Austen's House
Chawton, Alton, Hampshire
GU34 1SD
☎ Alton (0420) 83262
The house in which Jane Austen and her family lived from 1809-1817, containing numerous exhibits from their lifetime. Pleasant garden suitable for picnics.

Sir George Staunton Country Park
Middle Park Way, Leigh Park, Havant, Hampshire
☎ Havant (0705) 453405
Beautiful Victorian landscape created by Sir George Staunton, complete with farm animals, buildings, trees and shrubs.

New Forest Butterfly Farm
Longdown, Ashurst, Hampshire SO4 4UH
☎ Ashurst (0703) 292166
Large indoor tropical garden housing numerous exotic free-flying butterflies and moths from all over the world. Other insects, dragonfly ponds, woodland wagon rides.

Royal Marines Museum
Southsea, Hampshire PO4 9PX
☎ Portsmouth (0705) 819385
History of the Royal Marines from 1664 to present day. Dynamic Falklands audio-visual and chilled Arctic display.

The D Day Museum
Clarence Esplanade, Portsmouth, Hampshire PO5 3PA
☎ Portsmouth (0705) 827261
Displays of D Day action and some of the vehicles that took part. Overlord Embroidery depicting Allied invasion of Normandy.

Beaulieu Palace House
Beaulieu, Hampshire SO42 7ZN
☎ Beaulieu (0590) 612345
Home of Lord Montague since 1538.

HMS Victory
HM Naval Base, Portsmouth, Hampshire PO1 3PZ
☎ Portsmouth (0705) 294901
Laid down in 1759, Nelson's flagship is the oldest surviving ship in commission with the Royal Navy.

Sea Life Centre
Clarence Esplanade, Portsmouth, Hampshire PO5 3PB
☎ Portsmouth (0705) 734461
An exciting display of marine life, in thousands of gallons of water.

Tudor House Museum
St. Michael's Square, Bugle Street, Southampton, Hampshire SO1 0AD
☎ Southampton (0703) 332513
Large half-timbered Tudor house, with exhibitions of Victorian life. Tudor garden.

Broadlands
Romsey, Hampshire SO51 9ZD
☎ Romsey (0794) 516878
Historic Palladian home of Lord Mountbatten and Palmerston. Fine pictures and furniture, Mountbatten exhibition. Landscaping by 'Capability' Brown.

The Hillier Gardens and Arboretum
Jermyns Lane, Ampfield, Romsey, Hampshire SO51 0QA
☎ Braishfield (0794) 68787
The largest collection of trees and shrubs of its kind in the British Isles, planted within an attractive landscape of over 160 acres.

Paultons Park
Ower, Romsey, Hampshire SO51 6AL
☎ Southampton (0703) 814442
140 acres of parkland with exotic birds, gardens, lake, waterwheel, Kids' Kingdom, railway, animated shows, bumper boats, Romany museum and pets' corner.

Museum of Army Flying
Middle Wallop, Stockbridge, Hampshire SO20 8DY
☎ Andover (0264) 62121 Ext 421/428
Purpose-built museum on the edge of airfield tells the story of 100 years of army flying. Exciting and unique collection of aircraft.

Marwell Zoological Park
Colden Common, Winchester,
Hampshire SO21 1JH
☎ Owslebury (096 274) 406
*Large zoo breeding endangered
species. Over 800 animals
including big cats, giraffes, deer,
zebras, monkeys, rhino, hippos
and birds.*

Breamore House
Breamore, Hampshire SP6 2DF
☎ Downton (0725) 22233/
22468
*Elizabethan manor house with
fine collection of works of art.
Furniture, tapestries,
needlework, paintings.*

Osborne House
East Cowes, Isle of Wight
PO32 6JY
☎ Isle of Wight (0983) 200022
*Queen Victoria's royal and state
apartments, Swiss cottage and
museum.*

Isle of Wight Steam Railway
Railway Station, Havenstreet,
Isle of Wight PO33 4DS
☎ Isle of Wight (0983) 882204

*Steam train rides behind
locomotives between 60 and 110
years old, in original Isle of
Wight carriages. Museum of
island railwayana.*

Newport Roman Villa
Cypress Road, Newport, Isle
of Wight PO36 1EY
☎ Isle of Wight (0983) 529720
*Underfloor heated bath system,
tesselated floors displayed in
reconstructed rooms, corn-drying
kiln, small site museum.*

Arreton Manor
Arreton, Isle of Wight PO30 3AA
☎ Isle of Wight (0983) 528134
*17th C manor house and gardens
with period furniture and
panelled rooms. Folk Museum,
National Wireless Museum and
Dolls and Toys Museum.*

Carisbrooke Castle
Newport, Isle of Wight
PO30 1XX
☎ Isle of Wight (0983) 522107
*Splendid Norman castle, where
Charles I was imprisoned. The
Governor's Lodge houses the*

*county museum. Wheelhouse
with wheel operated by donkeys.*

Ventnor Botanic Garden
The Undercliffe Drive, Ventnor,
Isle of Wight PO38 1UL
☎ Isle of Wight (0983) 855397
*22 acres of garden containing
some 10,000 plants. Rare and
exotic trees, shrubs, alpines,
perennials, succulents, conifers,
temperate house.*

Calbourne Watermill
and Rural Museum
Newport, Isle of Wight
PO30 4JN
☎ Calbourne (098 378) 227
*Fine example of an early 17th
C watermill still in working
order. Granary, waterwheel,
water and pea fowl.*

Blackgang Chine
Fantasy Theme Park
Blackgang Chine, Chale,
Ventnor, Isle of Wight
PO38 2HN
☎ Isle of Wight (0983) 730330
*Theme park with water and
clifftop gardens. dinosaur park,
Frontierland, model village,
maze, Nurseryland.*

Winchester Cathedral
The Close, Winchester,
Hampshire SO23 9LS
☎ Winchester (0962) 53137
*Norman architecture with
various additions to 16th C.
Splendid tombs and medieval
wall paintings.*

Kingston Lacy
Wimborne, Dorset BH21 4AE
☎ Wimborne (0202) 883402
*Historic house recently restored
by the National Trust. Fine
collection of paintings. Garden
and park.*

Corfe Castle
Wareham, Dorset
☎ Corfe Castle (0929) 480921
*Ruins of former castle besieged
and 'slighted' in 1646.*

Highclere Castle
Highclere, Nr. Newbury,
Berkshire RG15 9RN
☎ Highclere (0635) 253210 ▶

Peter Watts

*The Museum of Army Flying includes an exciting and unique
collection of aircraft*

Marwell Zoological Park has over 800 animals including big cats, giraffes, deer, monkeys and zebras

▶ *Splendid example of early Victorian architecture, built in 1838-42. Home of the Earl of Carnarvon. Unique display of Egyptian antiquities. Plant centre, gift shop.*

Mary Rose Ship Hall and Exhibition
HM Naval Base, Portsmouth, Hampshire PO1 3PZ
☎ Portsmouth (0705) 812931
Reconstruction and conservation of Henry VIII's warship, viewed from footbridge over dry dock. Exhibition of the ship's treasures.

HMS Warrior
Victory Gate, HM Naval Base, Portsmouth, Hampshire PO1 3QX
☎ Portsmouth (0705) 291379
The world's first iron battleship. Four decks completely restored to show life in the Victorian Navy of 1860. Cabins, wardroom, engine and cannon.

Make a date for...

Bournemouth Forties Festival
Various venues, Bournemouth, Dorset
4 − 17 May

Portsmouth Heavy Horse Parade
Castle Field Arena, Portsmouth, Hampshire
6 May

Bournemouth International Music Festival
Bournemouth, Dorset
22 June − 6 July

Portsmouth and Southsea Show
Southsea Common, Portsmouth, Hampshire
2 − 4 August

Cowes Week
Cowes, Isle of Wight
3 − 11 August

Hampshire County Show
Royal Victoria Country Park, Netley Abbey, Hampshire
9 − 11 August

Southampton Boat Show
Mayflower Park, Southampton, Hampshire
13 − 21 September

Southern Ski Show
Colshot Activities Centre, Fawley, Southampton, Hampshire
28 − 29 September

Find out more

Further information on holidays and attractions in the South of England region is available from:
Southern Tourist Board,
40 Chamberlayne Road, Eastleigh, Hampshire SO5 5JH.
☎ (0703) 620006.

These publications are available free from the Southern Tourist Board (please telephone (0703) 616027):

Southern England Holidays '91 − a guide to the region and its accommodation

Take a Break − value for money breaks

The Isle of Wight Guide

Places to stay

⟫ Accommodation entries in this regional section are listed in alphabetical order of place name, and then in alphabetical order of establishment.

⟫ The map references refer to the colour maps towards the end of the guide. The first figure is the map number; the letter and figure which follow indicate the grid reference on the map.

⟫ The symbols at the end of each accommodation entry give information about services and facilities. A 'key' to these symbols is inside the back cover flap, which can be kept open for easy reference.

ALTON

Hampshire
Map ref 2C2

10m SE. Basingstoke
Pleasant old market town standing on the Pilgrim's Way, with some attractive Georgian buildings. The parish church still bears the scars of bullet marks, evidence of a bitter struggle between the Roundheads and the Royalists.

The Grange Hotel M
17 London Road,
Holybourne, Alton,
GU34 4EG
☎ (0420) 86565 Fax (0420) 541346
A privately-run country house hotel, set in 2 acres, with a restaurant and bar open to non-residents.
Bedrooms: 11 single, 10 double & 11 twin, 2 family rooms.
Bathrooms: 34 private.
Bed & breakfast: £45-£49.50 single, £59.50-£69.50 double.
Half board: £69.45-£79.45 daily, £416.50-£486.50 weekly.
Lunch available.
Evening meal 7pm (l.o. 9pm).
Parking for 60.
Credit: Access, Visa, Diners, Amex.

Half board prices shown are per person but in some cases may be based on double/twin occupancy.

AMPFIELD

Hampshire
Map ref 2C3

3m E. Romsey
Village 3 miles east of Romsey. The Hillier Garden and Arboretum lies three quarters of a mile west off the A31 along Jermyns Lane.

Potters Heron Hotel M
COMMENDED
Ampfield, Nr. Romsey,
SO51 9ZF
☎ Southampton
(0703) 266611 Telex 47459
Lansbury
Thatched building in rural surroundings. Recently completely refurbished. Well placed for Winchester, New Forest and Test Valley.
Bedrooms: 37 double & 23 twin.
Bathrooms: 60 private.
Bed & breakfast: £35-£77 single, £70-£90 double.
Half board: £46-£105 daily.
Lunch available.
Evening meal 7pm (l.o. 10pm).
Parking for 200.
Credit: Access, Visa, Diners, Amex.

ANDOVER

Hampshire
Map ref 2C2

13m NW. Winchester
Town that achieved importance from the wool trade and now has much modern development. A good centre for visiting places of interest.
Tourist Information
Centre ☎ (0264) 24320

Amberley Hotel M
70 Weyhill Road, Andover,
SP10 3NP
☎ (0264) 52224 Telex 477055
Small, comfortably furnished hotel, with attractive restaurant open to non-residents. Private meetings, luncheons and wedding receptions can be booked.
Bedrooms: 6 single, 3 double & 5 twin, 3 family rooms.
Bathrooms: 9 private, 2 public.
Bed & breakfast: £21-£32 single, £34-£42 double.
Half board: from £29 daily, from £196 weekly.
Lunch available.
Evening meal 6.45pm (l.o. 9.15pm).
Parking for 16.
Credit: Access, Visa, Diners, Amex.

Amport Inn M
Amport, Nr. Andover,
SP11 8AE
☎ (0264) 710371

Friendly inn in attractive Hampshire village, with race courses, riding and fishing nearby. Businessmen welcome weekdays. Breakaway weekends available. Jacuzzi, sauna and indoor pool.
Bedrooms: 3 double & 4 twin, 2 family rooms.
Bathrooms: 9 private, 1 public.
Bed & breakfast: £40-£50 single, £50-£60 double.
Lunch available.
Evening meal 7.30pm (l.o. 10pm).
Parking for 54.
Credit: Access, Visa.

Ashley Court Hotel M
COMMENDED
Micheldever Road, Andover,
SP11 6LA
☎ (0264) 57344
Half a mile from town centre, set in nearly 4 acres of grounds. New wing recently opened. All accommodation refurbished to a high standard. Friendly atmosphere. Good conference and recreational facilities.
Bedrooms: 10 single, 12 double & 13 twin.
Bathrooms: 35 private.
Bed & breakfast: £48-£64 single, £60-£80 double.
Half board: £62-£78 daily.
Lunch available.
Evening meal 7pm (l.o. 9.30pm).

Continued ▶

ANDOVER
Continued

Parking for 80.
Credit: Access, Visa, Amex.

BARTON ON SEA
Hampshire
Map ref 2B3

Seaside village with views of the Isle of Wight. Within easy driving distance of the New Forest.

The Old Coastguard Hotel M
👑👑👑 APPROVED

53 Marine Drive East, Barton on Sea, BH25 7DX
☎ New Milton (0425) 612987
Peaceful clifftop hotel close to the New Forest, with English cooking and personal service in a friendly atmosphere. Some ground floor rooms.
Bedrooms: 4 double & 3 twin.
Bathrooms: 5 private, 1 public.
Bed & breakfast: £32-£40 double.
Half board: £24-£28 daily, £155-£185 weekly.
Evening meal 7pm (l.o. 6pm).
Parking for 10.

BASINGSTOKE
Hampshire
Map ref 2C2

Rapidly developing commercial and industrial centre. The town is surrounded by charming villages and places to visit.
Tourist Information Centre ☎ (0256) 817618

Audleys Wood Thistle Hotel M
👑👑👑👑 HIGHLY COMMENDED

Alton Road, Basingstoke, RG25 2JT
☎ (0256) 817555
Telex 858273
Ⓒ Thistle
19th C mansion set in beautiful landscaped grounds. All rooms have marble-tiled bathroom and all modern facilities. Gourmet restaurant. Golf, croquet.
Bedrooms: 41 double & 27 twin, 3 family rooms.
Bathrooms: 71 private.

Bed & breakfast: from £83 single, from £111 double.
Lunch available.
Parking for 100.
Credit: Access, Visa, C.Bl., Diners, Amex.

Fernbank Guest House M
👑👑

4 Fairfields Road, Basingstoke, RG21 3DR
☎ (0256) 21191
Situated in a quiet residential area, close to restaurants and sports facilities. Tastefully decorated to a high standard, this hotel has optional en-suite rooms.
Bedrooms: 11 single, 4 double & 2 twin, 2 family rooms.
Bathrooms: 9 private, 4 public.
Bed & breakfast: £22-£36 single, £33-£44 double.
Parking for 18.
Credit: Access, Visa.

Hilton National Basingstoke M
👑👑👑👑

Aldermaston Roundabout, Ringway North, Basingstoke, RG24 9NV
☎ (0256) 20212 Telex 858223
Ⓒ Hilton
Extensively refurbished modern hotel with comfortable new restaurant, piano bar and eating house. Executive suites with jacuzzis. New leisure centre includes indoor heated pool and gymnasium.
Bedrooms: 30 single, 90 double & 15 twin, 3 family rooms.
Bathrooms: 138 private.
Bed & breakfast: £31-£86.95 single.
Lunch available.
Evening meal 7pm (l.o. 10pm).
Parking for 150.
Credit: Access, Visa, Diners, Amex.

BLANDFORD FORUM
Dorset
Map ref 2B3

Almost completely destroyed by fire in 1731, the town was rebuilt in a handsome Georgian style. The church is large and grand and the town is the hub of a rich farming area.
Tourist Information Centre ☎ (0258) 51989

Anvil Hotel & Restaurant M
👑👑👑👑 COMMENDED

Salisbury Road, Pimperne, Blandford, DT11 8UQ
☎ (0258) 453431 & 480182
16th C thatched hotel and restaurant in the heart of Dorset. Beamed restaurant with log fire and flagstone floor.
Bedrooms: 1 single, 5 double & 2 twin, 1 family room.
Bathrooms: 9 private.
Bed & breakfast: from £37 single, from £55 double.
Lunch available.
Evening meal 7pm (l.o. 9.45pm).
Parking for 25.
Credit: Access, Visa, Diners, Amex.

La Belle Alliance M
👑👑👑👑

Portman Lodge, Whitecliff Mill Street, Blandford Forum, DT11 7BP
☎ (0258) 452842
Comfortable small hotel with emphasis on quality, cuisine and service.
Bedrooms: 3 double & 2 twin, 1 family room.
Bathrooms: 5 private.
Bed & breakfast: £42-£48 single, £55-£65 double.
Half board: £42-£52 daily.
Evening meal 7pm (l.o. 10pm).
Parking for 8.
Open February-December.
Credit: Access, Visa, Amex.

BOURNEMOUTH
Dorset
Map ref 2B3

Seaside town set among the pines with a mild climate, sandy beaches and fine coastal views. The town has wide streets with excellent shops, a pier, a pavilion, museums and conference centre.
Tourist Information Centre ☎ (0202) 291715

Hotel Albercourt M
👑👑

18 Florence Road, Bournemouth, BH5 1HF
☎ (0202) 395213
Character hotel in quiet surroundings with car park. Close to sea, shops and entertainment. English food and choice of menu.
Bedrooms: 4 single, 12 double & 3 twin, 5 family rooms.
Bathrooms: 20 private, 3 public.
Bed & breakfast: £10-£19 single, £20-£38 double.
Half board: £14-£23 daily, £70-£135 weekly.
Evening meal 6pm.
Parking for 18.
Credit: Access, Visa.

Albrightleigh Guest House M
👑👑👑

4 Burnaby Road, Westbourne, Bournemouth, BH4 8JF
☎ (0202) 764054
Comfortable and friendly family-run guesthouse with views across Alum Chine and sea. Within minutes' walk of the beach.
Bedrooms: 1 double & 2 twin, 2 family rooms.
Bathrooms: 3 private, 1 public.
Bed & breakfast: £12-£16 single, £24-£32 double.
Half board: £16-£20 daily, £100-£125 weekly.
Evening meal 6pm (l.o. 6pm).
Parking for 4.

Alum Bay Hotel M
19 Burnaby Road, Alum Chine, Bournemouth, BH4 8JF
☎ (0202) 761034
A family-run hotel which offers every comfort, with home-cooked food, nicely furnished public rooms and cosy bar.

The symbol Ⓒ and the name of a hotel group or consortium after a hotel address means that bookings can be made through a central reservations office. These are listed on pages 559 & 560.

Bedrooms: 1 single, 4 double
& 3 twin, 4 family rooms.
Bathrooms: 7 private,
1 public.
Bed & breakfast: £19-£22.50
single, £34-£41 double.
Half board: £24.50-£30 daily,
£147-£180 weekly.
Evening meal 6pm (l.o. 6pm).
Parking for 10.
Credit: Access, Visa.

Alum Grange Hotel M

1 Burnaby Road, Alum
Chine, Bournemouth,
BH4 8JF
☎ (0202) 761195
*Attractively furnished hotel,
200 yards from beach. All
bedrooms en-suite with ground
floor and non-smoking
bedrooms. Captains bar, menu
choices and a la carte.*
Bedrooms: 2 single, 4 double
& 4 twin, 4 family rooms.
Bathrooms: 12 private,
1 public.
Bed & breakfast: £25 single,
£50 double.
Half board: £33 daily,
£192.50 weekly.
Evening meal 6pm (l.o. 6pm).
Parking for 10.
Credit: Access, Visa.

Arlington Hotel

Exeter Park Road, Lower
Gardens, Bournemouth,
BH2 5BD
☎ (0202) 552879 & 553012
*Family-run hotel overlooking
Bournemouth pine gardens.
100 metres equidistant traffic
free, level walk to square,
beach, shops and Bournemouth
International Centre.*
Bedrooms: 3 single, 11 double
& 8 twin, 6 family rooms.
Bathrooms: 28 private,
1 public.
Bed & breakfast: £24-£29.50
single, £48-£59 double.
Half board: £27.50-£35.50
daily, £159.50-£225 weekly.
Lunch available.
Evening meal 6.30pm (l.o.
8pm).
Parking for 24.
Credit: Access, Visa.

Au-Levant Hotel M

15 Westby Road, Boscombe,
Bournemouth, BH5 1HA
☎ (0202) 394884

*Small family-run hotel near
shops and beach, with home
cooking and friendly
atmosphere. TV and tea
facilities in all rooms. Licensed
restaurant, open all year round.
Children welcome.*
Bedrooms: 3 single, 4 double
& 1 twin, 2 family rooms.
Bathrooms: 2 private,
2 public.
Bed & breakfast: £15-£17.50
single, £35-£40 double.
Half board: £17.50-£20 daily,
£108-£130 weekly.
Evening meal 6pm (l.o. 6pm).
Parking for 3.

Avonwood Hotel M

20 Owls Road, Boscombe,
Bournemouth, BH5 1AF
☎ (0202) 394704
*A friendly, family-run hotel,
with a relaxed atmosphere and
home cooking. 4 minutes' walk
from beaches and shops.*
Bedrooms: 3 single, 9 double
& 3 twin, 5 family rooms.
Bathrooms: 10 private,
4 public.
Bed & breakfast: £14-£19
single, £28-£38 double.
Half board: £19.50-£24.50
daily, £125-£169 weekly.
Evening meal 6pm (l.o. 4pm).
Parking for 16.
Credit: Access, Visa.

Balmoral Hotel M

11-13 Kerley Road, West
Cliff, Bournemouth,
BH2 5DW
☎ (0202) 21186 & 290037
*Traditional family hotel in fine
clifftop position overlooking the
sea.*
Bedrooms: 8 single, 10 double
& 8 twin, 6 family rooms.
Bathrooms: 25 private,
3 public; 4 private showers.
Bed & breakfast: £18.50-£22
single, £37-£44 double.
Half board: £25-£29 daily,
£145-£175 weekly.
Evening meal 6.30pm (l.o.
7.30pm).
Parking for 40.
Credit: Access, Visa, Diners,
Amex.

Bay View Hotel M

Southbourne Overcliff Drive,
Bournemouth, BH6 3QB
☎ (0202) 429315

*Clifftop location on more
relaxing side of Bournemouth,
close to Christchurch. Safe
bathing and walks nearby.
Close to flat and crown green
bowls.*
Bedrooms: 1 single, 10 double
& 3 twin.
Bathrooms: 12 private,
1 public.
Bed & breakfast: £13-£22
single, £25-£44 double.
Half board: £35-£54 daily,
£120-£169 weekly.
Evening meal 6.30pm (l.o.
7.30pm).
Parking for 12.
Open April-October.

Bella Vista Hotel M

Listed APPROVED

5 Studland Road, Alum
Chine, Bournemouth,
BH4 8HZ
☎ (0202) 763591
*Small family hotel, close to sea
and situated in beautiful Alum
Chine. All home cooking by
Gwen and Wallace. Full board
on Sundays.*
Bedrooms: 2 single, 5 double
& 2 twin, 4 family rooms.
Bathrooms: 6 private,
2 public.
Bed & breakfast: £17.25-
£18.50 single, £34.50-£37
double.
Half board: £21.50-£22.75
daily, £155-£162 weekly.
Evening meal 6pm (l.o. 7pm).
Parking for 8.
Open April-October.

Bournemouth
Heathlands Hotel M

COMMENDED APPROVED

Grove Road, East Cliff,
Bournemouth, BH1 3AY
☎ (0202) 553336
Telex 8954665 VBSTLX G
Ref.QUA
*115 bedrooms equipped to high
specification, with suites and
studios available. Fitted with
satellite TV, direct dial
telephones and hair dryers. In
house health and leisure
facilities.*
Bedrooms: 22 single,
22 double & 52 twin,
19 family rooms.
Bathrooms: 115 private.
Bed & breakfast: £48-£52
single, £76-£84 double.
Half board: £288-£310
weekly.
Lunch available.
Evening meal 7pm (l.o.
8.30pm).
Parking for 90.

Credit: Access, Visa, Diners,
Amex.

The Bournemouth
Highcliff M

COMMENDED

St. Michael's Road, West
Cliff, Bournemouth,
BH2 5DU
☎ (0202) 557702 Telex 417153
Best Western
*Cliff top position, close to main
shopping area and car parking.
Bar, brasserie and nightclub
within grounds and children's
playrooms indoors and out.*
Bedrooms: 25 single,
66 double & 66 twin, 3 family
rooms.
Bathrooms: 160 private.
Bed & breakfast: £70-£75
single, £110-£120 double.
Half board: £48 daily.
Lunch available.
Evening meal 7pm (l.o. 9pm).
Parking for 130.
Credit: Access, Visa, Diners,
Amex.

Burlington Hotel

Owls Road, Boscombe,
Bournemouth, BH5 1AD
☎ (0202) 398079
*Imposing Victorian hotel,
overlooking Bournemouth Bay.
Has the benefit of modern
sports facilities and indoor
heated pool. Beach close by.*
Bedrooms: 7 double, 7 family
rooms.
Bathrooms: 14 private.
Bed & breakfast: £24-£29
single, £48-£58 double.
Half board: £33-£38 daily,
£150-£224 weekly.
Lunch available.
Evening meal 6.30pm (l.o.
9.30pm).
Parking for 125.
Credit: Access, Visa, Diners,
Amex.

Carisbrooke Hotel M

42 Tregonwell Road,
Bournemouth, BH2 5NT
☎ (0202) 290432
*Modern family hotel in
excellent central location,
adjacent to Winter Gardens
and near sea and International
Centre.*
Bedrooms: 3 single, 6 double
& 5 twin, 8 family rooms.

Continued ▶

469

BOURNEMOUTH
Continued

Bathrooms: 19 private,
2 public.
Bed & breakfast: £19.50-£25
single, £39-£50 double.
Half board: £24-£28 daily,
£155-£175 weekly.
Evening meal 6.30pm (l.o.
7pm).
Parking for 19.
Open February-December.
Credit: Access, Visa.

Carlton Court Hotel ♠
♛♛♛
Cranbourne Road,
Bournemouth, BH2 5BR
☎ (0202) 27007 Fax (0202)
21160
*New hotel situated 3 minutes
from the town centre and
beach, yet on a quiet, secluded
road.*
Bedrooms: 20 single, 6 double
& 6 twin, 2 family rooms.
Bathrooms: 34 private.
Bed & breakfast: £25-£35
single, £50-£70 double.
Half board: £35-£45 daily,
£215-£285 weekly.
Lunch available.
Evening meal 6.30pm (l.o.
8pm).
Parking for 21.
Credit: Access, Visa, Diners.

Catherington House Hotel ♠
♛♛♛ COMMENDED
38 Parkwood Road,
Southbourne, Bournemouth,
BH5 2BL
☎ (0202) 428521
*A delightful, small private
hotel with attractively
furnished en-suite bedrooms.
Noted for cuisine. Conveniently
situated for sea and shops.*
Bedrooms: 1 single, 1 double
& 1 twin, 1 family room.
Bathrooms: 4 private.
Bed & breakfast: £18.50-£20
single, £37-£40 double.
Half board: £25-£27.50 daily,
£155-£166 weekly.
Evening meal 6.30pm.
Parking for 8.
Credit: Access, Diners,
Amex.

Chequers Hotel ♠
♛♛♛ APPROVED
West Cliff Road, West Cliff,
Bournemouth, BH2 5EX
☎ (0202) 553900

*Well-appointed with fitted
furniture throughout and large
car park. Opposite Durley
Chine, 10 minutes' walk from
conference centre, town and
pier.*
Bedrooms: 2 single, 15 double
& 1 twin, 6 family rooms.
Bathrooms: 20 private,
1 public.
Bed & breakfast: £19-£27
single, £38-£54 double.
Half board: £22-£31 daily,
£125-£205 weekly.
Evening meal 6.30pm (l.o.
10pm).
Parking for 27.
Open February-December.
Credit: Access, Visa.

Chesterwood Hotel ♠
East Overcliff Drive,
Bournemouth, BH1 3AR
☎ (0202) 558057 Fax (0202)
293457
*Situated on the East Cliff
facing the sea. Bournemouth's
main shopping centre is close
by. Good service and personal
attention. Dancing during the
season and some weekends.*
Bedrooms: 8 single, 15 double
& 16 twin, 13 family rooms.
Bathrooms: 50 private,
2 public.
Bed & breakfast: £26-£39.50
single, £42-£74 double.
Half board: £33-£46 daily,
£210-£290.50 weekly.
Lunch available.
Evening meal 7pm (l.o.
8.30pm).
Parking for 38.
Credit: Access, Visa, Diners,
Amex.

Chine Cote Private Hotel
♛♛
25 Studland Road, Alum
Chine, Bournemouth,
BH4 8JA
☎ (0202) 761208
*Small, family-run hotel,
situated in Alum Chine, just a
4 minute stroll through pine-
wooded chine to the sea.*
Bedrooms: 1 single, 4 double,
4 family rooms.
Bathrooms: 4 private,
1 public; 1 private shower.
Bed & breakfast: £15-£21
single, £26-£38 double.
Half board: £16-£22 daily,
£100-£140 weekly.
Evening meal 6pm (l.o. 6pm).
Parking for 5.

Chine Grange Hotel ♠
Listed
25 Durley Chine Road, West
Cliff, Bournemouth,
BH2 5LB
☎ (0202) 553201
*Detached hotel of character,
standing in its own grounds.
Only 500 yards from beach
and within easy walking
distance of shops and
entertainments.*
Bedrooms: 2 single, 6 double
& 3 twin, 2 family rooms.
Bathrooms: 12 private;
1 private shower.
Bed & breakfast: £16.50-£20
single, £33-£40 double.
Half board: £36-£46 daily,
£135-£160 weekly.
Evening meal 6pm (l.o. 6pm).
Parking for 13.
Open March-November.

Chine Hotel ♠
♛♛♛♛ APPROVED
Boscombe Spa Road,
Boscombe, Bournemouth,
BH5 1AX
☎ (0202) 396234 Telex 41338
*Faces due south overlooking
the sea, with panoramic views
of the whole of Poole Bay and
Boscombe Chine gardens.*
Bedrooms: 18 single,
15 double & 55 twin, 9 family
rooms.
Bathrooms: 97 private.
Bed & breakfast: £40-£50
single, £80-£100 double.
Half board: £50-£60 daily,
£300-£360 weekly.
Lunch available.
Evening meal 7pm (l.o.
8.30pm).
Parking for 45.
Credit: Access, Visa, Diners,
Amex.

Chinebeach Hotel ♠
14 Studland Road, Alum
Chine, Bournemouth,
BH4 8JA
☎ (0202) 767015
*Catering for health and price
conscious people of all ages, set
in an attractive location. All
facilities at competitive rates.*
Bedrooms: 3 single, 7 double
& 3 twin, 10 family rooms.
Bathrooms: 17 private,
2 public.
Half board: £80-£180 weekly.
Evening meal 6pm (l.o. 3pm).
Parking for 10.
Credit: Access, Visa.

Chinehead Hotel ♠
♛♛♛
31 Alumhurst Road,
Westbourne, Bournemouth,
BH4 8EN
☎ (0202) 752777
*Family-run hotel within easy
walking distance of beach, with
cosy lounge bar, varied food,
spacious comfortable rooms
and high standard of service.*
Bedrooms: 3 single, 13 double
& 3 twin, 2 family rooms.
Bathrooms: 21 private.
Bed & breakfast: £24-£28
single, £48-£56 double.
Half board: £32.50-£37.50
daily, £175-£192 weekly.
Lunch available.
Evening meal 6.30pm (l.o.
8.30pm).
Parking for 22.
Credit: Access, Visa.

The Chines Private Hotel ♠
♛♛
9 Rosemount Road, Alum
Chine, Bournemouth,
BH4 8HB
☎ (0202) 761256
*Friendly, family-run hotel with
comfortable accommodation
coupled with choice of varied
home cooking. Traffic free
walk to beach.*
Bedrooms: 2 single, 4 double
& 2 twin, 3 family rooms.
Bathrooms: 4 private,
2 public.
Bed & breakfast: £11-£16
single, £22-£32 double.
Half board: £15-£20.50 daily,
£96-£141 weekly.
Evening meal 6.15pm (l.o.
4pm).
Parking for 5.
Credit: Access, Visa.

Clevedon Private Hotel
♛♛
11 Walpole Road, Boscombe,
Bournemouth, BH1 4HA
☎ (0202) 36145
*Well-established hotel near
main shops and all amenities.
Within short walking distance
of the sea. Cosy bar, renowned
for food and friendly
atmosphere.*
Bedrooms: 3 single, 2 double
& 1 twin, 4 family rooms.
Bathrooms: 3 public.
Bed & breakfast: £11.50-
£14.50 single, £23-£29 double.
Half board: £16.50-£20 daily,
£85-£121 weekly.

Evening meal 6pm (l.o. 6.30pm).
Parking for 9.
Open January-November.

Cliffeside Hotel M
⚜⚜⚜
East Overcliff Drive,
Bournemouth, BH1 3AQ
☎ (0202) 555724
Telex 418297 (C.H.)
On East Cliff with views to the Isle of Wight and the Purbeck Hills. Within easy reach of the town centre.
Bedrooms: 10 single,
20 double & 21 twin,
10 family rooms.
Bathrooms: 61 private,
4 public.
Bed & breakfast: £31.75-£46 single, £63.50-£92 double.
Half board: £34.75-£49 daily, £238-£300 weekly.
Lunch available.
Evening meal 6.45pm (l.o. 8.15pm).
Parking for 50.
Credit: Access, Visa.

Hotel Collingwood M
⚜⚜⚜⚜
11 Priory Road, West Cliff,
Bournemouth, BH2 5DF
☎ (0202) 27575
Privately owned, licensed, 54 en-suite bedroomed hotel in central position, with leisure centre, indoor pool, games room, snooker room, dancing, sun terrace, lift and parking.
Bedrooms: 8 single, 24 double & 10 twin, 15 family rooms.
Bathrooms: 54 private,
3 public.
Bed & breakfast: £32-£45 single, £64-£90 double.
Half board: £35-£45 daily, £210-£275 weekly.
Lunch available.
Evening meal 6.30pm (l.o. 8.30pm).
Parking for 30.
Credit: Access, Visa.

The Cottage M
⚜⚜⚜ COMMENDED
12 Southern Road,
Southbourne, Bournemouth,
BH6 3SR
☎ (0202) 422764
Charming, detached character house with tastefully furnished, comfortable rooms. Close to Fishermans Walk gardens, putting/bowling greens and lift to promenade.

Bedrooms: 1 single, 1 double & 2 twin, 3 family rooms.
Bathrooms: 4 private,
2 public.
Bed & breakfast: £12-£14 single, £24-£28 double.
Half board: £17.50-£19.50 daily, £115-£125 weekly.
Evening meal 6pm (l.o. 6pm).
Parking for 8.

Croham Hurst Hotel
9 Durley Road South, West Cliff, Bournemouth, BH2 5JH
☎ (0202) 552353
Modern hotel, set in its own grounds, personally supervised by resident proprietors.
Bedrooms: 4 single, 17 double & 10 twin, 9 family rooms.
Bathrooms: 40 private.
Bed & breakfast: £22.50-£27.50 single, £50-£60 double.
Half board: £25-£30 daily, £154-£200 weekly.
Lunch available.
Evening meal 6.30pm (l.o. 7.15pm).
Parking for 35.
Open February-December.
Credit: Access, Visa.

⚑ Display advertisement appears on page 500.

Crosbie Hall Hotel
⚜⚜
21 Florence Road, Boscombe, Bournemouth, BH5 1HJ
☎ (0202) 34714
Delightful family hotel offering charm, character and comfort, with a relaxed, friendly atmosphere. Very close to beach, gardens, shops and transport.
Bedrooms: 3 single, 5 double & 2 twin, 7 family rooms.
Bathrooms: 12 private,
2 public.
Bed & breakfast: £12-£22 single, £24-£44 double.
Half board: £18-£26 daily, £106-£163 weekly.
Evening meal 6pm (l.o. 6.15pm).
Parking for 14.
Open January-October.

Cumberland Hotel M
⚜⚜⚜⚜
East Overcliff Drive,
Bournemouth, BH1 3AF
☎ (0202) 290722
Telex 418297 CuH
Modern luxury hotel with all rooms en-suite, offering a high standard of personal service, entertainment and amenities for businessmen and holidaymakers alike.

Bedrooms: 12 single,
32 double & 52 twin, 6 family rooms.
Bathrooms: 102 private,
1 public.
Bed & breakfast: £34.50-£44.50 single, £69-£76 double.
Half board: £41.50-£45.50 daily, £240.50-£269 weekly.
Lunch available.
Evening meal 7pm (l.o. 8.30pm).
Parking for 50.
Credit: Access, Visa.

Denby Private Hotel M
⚜⚜
24 Southern Road,
Southbourne, Bournemouth,
BH6 3SR
☎ (0202) 428958
Family-run hotel, ideally situated adjacent to seafront, close to shops and transport.
Bedrooms: 5 single, 2 double & 1 twin, 1 family room.
Bathrooms: 2 public.
Bed & breakfast: £13-£14.50 single, £26-£28 double.
Half board: £18-£19.50 daily, £98-£126 weekly.
Evening meal 6pm (l.o. 6pm).
Parking for 8.

Dorset Rivers Hotel M
⚜⚜ APPROVED
17 Drummond Road,
Boscombe, Bournemouth,
BH1 4DP
☎ (0202) 396550
Small hotel close to Boscombe Gardens. Easy walk to sea and new shopping centre. Chef/proprietor.
Bedrooms: 3 single, 2 double & 1 twin, 2 family rooms.
Bathrooms: 3 private,
1 public; 1 private shower.
Bed & breakfast: £12.50-£17 single, £25-£34 double.
Half board: £17.50-£22 daily, £94.50-£135 weekly.
Evening meal 6pm (l.o. 2pm).
Parking for 3.

Durley Grange Hotel M
⚜⚜⚜
6 Durley Road, West Cliff,
Bournemouth, BH2 5JL
☎ (0202) 554473
Modern, family-run, 50 bedroom hotel. All rooms en-suite, with TV, tea making facilities and direct dial telephone.
Bedrooms: 10 single,
24 double & 10 twin, 6 family rooms.

Bathrooms: 50 private.
Bed & breakfast: £25-£28 single, £50-£56 double.
Half board: £29-£33 daily, £160-£210 weekly.
Evening meal 6.30pm (l.o. 8pm).
Parking for 40.
Open March-December.
Credit: Access, Visa.

Durley Hall Hotel M
⚜⚜⚜
7 Durley Chine Road,
Bournemouth, BH2 5JS
☎ (0202) 766886
ⓒⓡ Consort
Located close to town centre and beach. Additional amenities include hairdresser, beautician, solarium, jacuzzi, steam cabinet, children's indoor pool, 'Trymnasium' and Le Cafe Boulevard, open from 7.15 am.
Bedrooms: 12 single,
31 double & 20 twin,
18 family rooms.
Bathrooms: 81 private.
Bed & breakfast: £53-£58 single, £79-£84 double.
Half board: £67-£72 daily, £276-£285 weekly.
Lunch available.
Evening meal 7pm (l.o. 8.45pm).
Parking for 150.
Credit: Access, Visa, Diners, Amex.

East Anglia Hotel M
⚜⚜⚜ APPROVED
6 Poole Road, Bournemouth,
BH2 5QX
☎ (0202) 765163 Fax (0202) 752949
Ideally situated for town centre, beach and Bournemouth International Centre. Fully modernised hotel offering every comfort plus solarium, free jacuzzi, sauna and mini gym.
Bedrooms: 17 single,
16 double & 22 twin,
18 family rooms.
Bathrooms: 73 private.
Bed & breakfast: £35-£38 single, £64-£76 double.
Half board: £40-£46 daily, £252-£294 weekly.
Lunch available.
Evening meal 6.30pm (l.o. 8.30pm).
Parking for 60.
Credit: Access, Visa, Diners, Amex.

BOURNEMOUTH
Continued

East Cliff Court Hotel M
👑👑👑👑

East Overcliff Drive,
Bournemouth, BH1 3AN
☎ (0202) 24545
Set on the prestigious East Cliff with panoramic views across the bay. Close to town centre.
Bedrooms: 14 single,
22 double & 23 twin, 9 family rooms.
Bathrooms: 68 private.
Bed & breakfast: £37-£60 single, £70-£110 double.
Half board: £42-£65 daily,
£170-£364 weekly.
Lunch available.
Evening meal 7pm (l.o. 8.45pm).
Parking for 100.
Credit: Access, Visa, Amex.
ॐ ♨ ⬚ ╲ © ▯ ♥ ▮ Ⓥ
⧖ ◉ ☰ ⧉ ☎ ⏋ ✦ ♣ ⟋
⦰ SP

Edgewood Guest House
26 Foxholes Road,
Southbourne, Bournemouth,
BH6 3AT
☎ (0202) 429798
Small, friendly guest house in quiet residential road close to sandy beach, with home cooked-food by chef/owner our speciality. Non-smokers only please.
Bedrooms: 1 single, 1 double & 1 twin, 2 family rooms.
Bathrooms: 1 public.
Bed & breakfast: £13-£16 single, £26-£32 double.
Half board: £18-£21 daily,
£120-£140 weekly.
Evening meal 6.30pm (l.o. 6.30pm).
Parking for 4.
ॐ ♥ ▮ Ⓥ ⧖ ⏋ ▦ ✕ ⟋
⦰ SP

Fairmount Hotel M
👑👑👑 COMMENDED

15 Priory Road, West Cliff,
Bournemouth, BH2 5DF
☎ (0202) 551105
A family-run hotel within 3 minutes of beach, conference centre and main shopping centre. Telephone and satellite TV in all rooms, also a baby listening service. New extension and lift for 1991.
Bedrooms: 4 single, 9 double & 1 twin, 7 family rooms.
Bathrooms: 18 private,
2 public.
Bed & breakfast: £18-£24 single, £36-£48 double.
Half board: £24-£30 daily,
£140-£195 weekly.

Evening meal 6.15pm.
Parking for 14.
Credit: Access, Visa.
ॐ 5 ♨ ╲ ▯ ⧖ ⏋ ▦ ✕ ✿
DAP ⦰ SP

Ferndale Private Hotel
👑👑

10 Pembroke Road, Alum
Chine, Bournemouth,
BH4 8HE
☎ (0202) 761320
Comfortable, family-run hotel offering home cooking. Situated in Alum Chine within walking distance of beach and local shops.
Bedrooms: 1 single, 2 double & 1 twin, 1 family room.
Bathrooms: 2 private,
1 public.
Bed & breakfast: £13-£17 single, £25-£32 double.
Half board: £17.50-£21.50 daily, £80-£105 weekly.
Evening meal 6pm (l.o. 9am).
Parking for 5.
Open April-September.
ॐ4 ⧖ ▮ ⏋ ▦ ⬚ ✕ ▦ DAP
SP

Fircroft Hotel M
👑👑 APPROVED

Owls Road, Bournemouth,
BH5 1AE
☎ (0202) 309771
Long established family hotel, close to sea and comprehensive shopping. Free entry to hotel-owned sports and leisure club between 9.00am and 6.00pm.
Bedrooms: 6 single, 16 double & 12 twin, 15 family rooms.
Bathrooms: 49 private.
Bed & breakfast: £22-£26 single, £44-£52 double.
Half board: £27-£35 daily,
£150-£203 weekly.
Lunch available.
Evening meal 6.30pm (l.o. 8pm).
Parking for 50.
Credit: Access, Visa.
ॐ ♨ ╲ © ▯ ⧖ ▮ Ⓥ ⏋
◉ ☰ ⧉ ▦ ⬚ ⏋ ✦ ♣ ▦
⟋ DAP ⦰ SP T

The Five Ways Hotel M
👑👑👑 APPROVED

23 Argyll Road, Boscombe,
Bournemouth, BH5 1EB
☎ (0202) 301509 & 304971
Near beach and shopping parade, especially suitable for family holidays. All rooms en-suite. 5% discount for pensioners, off season.
Bedrooms: 4 single, 5 double & 1 twin, 5 family rooms.
Bathrooms: 15 private.
Bed & breakfast: £16.50-£19.50 single, £33-£39 double.
Half board: £21-£24.50 daily,
£112.50-£147.50 weekly.
Lunch available.

Evening meal 6pm (l.o. 10am).
Parking for 10.
Open February-December.
Credit: Access, Visa.
ॐ ╲ © ▯ ⧖ ▮ Ⓥ ⧖ ⏋
▦ ⬚ ⏋ ✦ DAP ⦰ SP

Gervis Court Hotel
👑👑

38 Gervis Road, East Cliff,
Bournemouth, BH1 3DH
☎ (0202) 556871
Family-run hotel in its own grounds, within walking distance of town centre, conference facilities and beach.
Bedrooms: 3 single, 6 double & 4 twin, 3 family rooms.
Bathrooms: 7 private,
3 public.
Bed & breakfast: £19.50-£21.50 single, £34-£47 double.
Half board: £23-£29.50 daily,
£106-£180 weekly.
Lunch available.
Evening meal 6.30pm (l.o. 7.15pm).
Parking for 15.
Open April-October.
Credit: Access, Visa.
ॐ ♨ ♨ ▮ Ⓥ ⏋ ⧖ T ▮ ⏋
✕ ⬚ DAP SP T

Hartford Court Hotel M
👑👑👑 COMMENDED

48 Christchurch Road,
Bournemouth, BH1 3PE
☎ (0202) 21712 & 293682
Recently extended hotel with additional bedrooms and tastefully refurbished public areas. Large car park. Close to sea and town centre.
Bedrooms: 9 single, 19 double & 4 twin, 4 family rooms.
Bathrooms: 24 private,
1 public.
Bed & breakfast: £20-£24 single, £40-£48 double.
Half board: £26-£30 daily,
£165-£190 weekly.
Evening meal 6pm (l.o. 7pm).
Parking for 36.
Credit: Access, Visa.
ॐ10 ╲ © ▯ ⧖ ▮ Ⓥ ⏋
☰ ⧉ ⬚ ⏋ ✦ ▦ ⦰ SP T

Hawaiian Hotel M
4 Glen Road, Boscombe,
Bournemouth, BH5 1HR
☎ (0202) 393234
Immaculate small, licensed family hotel. Short walk from beach and shops. Fresh home cooking. Rooms en-suite. Open all year. Please send stamped, addressed envelope for brochure.
Bedrooms: 2 single, 6 double & 1 twin, 3 family rooms.
Bathrooms: 7 private,
1 public.
Bed & breakfast: £14-£16 single, £28-£32 double.

Half board: £19-£22 daily,
£114-£138 weekly.
Evening meal 6pm.
Parking for 8.
Open March-October.
ॐ4 ▯ ⧖ ▮ Ⓥ ⏋ TV ▦ ⬚
DAP SP

The Hermitage Hotel M
👑👑👑👑 COMMENDED

Exeter Road, Bournemouth,
BH2 5AH
☎ (0202) 557363
Fax (0202) 559173
Old world charm, with seafront, beach and pleasure gardens bordering hotel grounds. Pier 1 minute's walk.
Bedrooms: 24 single,
43 double, 4 family rooms.
Bathrooms: 71 private.
Bed & breakfast: £36-£46.50 single, £72-£88 double.
Half board: £45.50-£49.50 daily, £276.50-£329 weekly.
Lunch available.
Evening meal 6.45pm (l.o. 8.45pm).
Parking for 60.
Credit: Access, Visa, Diners, Amex.
ॐ ♨ ╲ © ▯ ⧖ ▮ Ⓥ ⧖
⧖ ◉ ☰ ▦ ⬚ ⏋ ✦ ♣ ▶
⟋ SP ▦ T

Highclere Private Hotel M
👑👑👑 APPROVED

15 Burnaby Road, Alum
Chine, Bournemouth,
BH4 8JF
☎ (0202) 761350
Small family hotel with ample parking, garden, playroom, solarium and some bedrooms with sea views. Children very welcome at reduced tariff.
Bedrooms: 3 double & 1 twin, 5 family rooms.
Bathrooms: 9 private.
Bed & breakfast: £15.50-£17.50 single, £31-£35 double.
Half board: £22-£44 daily,
£130-£150 weekly.
Evening meal 6pm (l.o. 5.30pm).
Parking for 7.
Open April-October.
ॐ3 ╲ © ▯ ⧖ ▮ Ⓥ ⏋ TV
▦ ⬚ ✕ DAP SP T

Hilde's Guest House
211 Holdenhurst Road,
Bournemouth, BH8 8DE
☎ (0202) 25171
Comfortable, small guest house with a homely atmosphere, close to coach and railway stations, superb shopping centre and magnificent beaches.
Bedrooms: 2 single, 4 double & 2 twin, 1 family room.
Bathrooms: 2 public.
Bed & breakfast: £13-£16 single, £26-£32 double.

Half board: £19-£24 daily,
£130-£170 weekly.
Evening meal 6pm (l.o.
6.30pm).
Parking for 8.
⌂ ♦ 🖥 ⬜ 👤 ⬛ ⬜ ◄ ✕ ⬚

Hinton Firs ♨
♨♨♨ **COMMENDED**

Manor Road, East Cliff,
Bournemouth, BH1 3HB
☎ (0202) 555409
Fax (0202) 299607
*Friendly family hotel set
among pines in the heart of the
East Cliff, with 4 sunny
lounges facing sheltered garden
and pool.*
Bedrooms: 12 single,
13 double & 11 twin, 16 family
rooms.
Bathrooms: 52 private,
1 public.
Bed & breakfast: £29.50-£48
single, £59-£84 double.
Half board: £34.50-£54 daily,
£241.50-£320 weekly.
Lunch available.
Evening meal 7.15pm (l.o.
8.30pm).
Parking for 40.
Credit: Access, Visa.
⌂ ♨ ☎ ⬚ 🖥 👤 V ⬜
TV ● ⬜ ⬛ ⬛ ⓣ ♣ ♠ ⬚
♣ ✕ ⬚ ⬚ SP
● Display advertisement
appears on page 500.

Holmcroft Hotel ♨
♨♨♨ **COMMENDED**

Earle Road, Alum Chine,
Bournemouth, BH4 8JQ
☎ (0202) 761289
*Quietly situated, south-facing
hotel. Family-run with home
cooking. A short walk from
sandy beach and wooded
chines.*
Bedrooms: 2 single, 8 double
& 6 twin, 3 family rooms.
Bathrooms: 19 private.
Bed & breakfast: £18-£25
single, £36-£50 double.
Half board: £25-£32 daily,
£146-£165 weekly.
Evening meal 6pm (l.o.
6.45pm).
Parking for 17.
Credit: Access, Visa.
⌂ ☎ ⬚ 🖥 👤 V ⬜ TV ⬜
✕ ⬚ ⬚

Kiwi Hotel
♨♨

West Hill Road,
Bournemouth, BH2 5EG
☎ (0202) 555889 & 557137
*Family-run hotel 150 yards
from clifftop and a few minutes
from town centre. Children
welcome and choice of menu at
all meals.*
Bedrooms: 5 single, 27 double
& 1 twin, 14 family rooms.
Bathrooms: 40 private,
4 public; 1 private shower.

Bed & breakfast: £19.50-
£26.50 single, £35-£49 double.
Half board: £25-£32 daily,
£120-£179 weekly.
Evening meal 6pm (l.o. 7pm).
Parking for 27.
Credit: Access, Visa.
⌂ ♨ ☎ ⬚ 🖥 👤 V ⬜ ⬜
⬛ ✕ ⬚ ⬚ DAP ⬚ SP

Kryston House
Listed

29 Pinecliffe Avenue,
Southbourne, Bournemouth,
BH6 3PY
☎ (0202) 423089
*Small, comfortable guest
house. Friendly atmosphere.
Quiet location close to
Southbourne cliffs and
amenities. Bournemouth 3.5
miles, easy reach New Forest.*
Bedrooms: 1 double, 2 family
rooms.
Bathrooms: 1 public;
1 private shower.
Bed & breakfast: £12-£16
single, £24-£26 double.
Half board: £17-£18.50 daily,
£114-£125 weekly.
Evening meal 6pm (l.o.
10am).
Parking for 4.
Credit: Access, Visa.
⌂ ♦ ⬜ ⬚ 🖥 TV ⬜ ⬚ DAP
⬚ SP

Langtry Manor Hotel ♨
♨♨♨ **COMMENDED**

Derby Road, East Cliff,
Bournemouth, BH1 3QB
☎ (0202) 23887
Ⓒⓡ Consort
*Royal "love-nest" built by
Edward VII for Lillie Langtry.
Many antiques; four-poster
beds; magnificent dining hall.
Saturday Edwardian dinner
party.*
Bedrooms: 1 single, 7 double
& 4 twin, 2 family rooms.
Bathrooms: 14 private.
Bed & breakfast: £59.50
single, £85-£142 double.
Evening meal 7pm (l.o. 9pm).
Parking for 30.
Credit: Access, Visa, Diners,
Amex.
⌂ ♨ ⬛ ☎ ● ⬚ ♦ 👤 V
✗ ⬜ ⬜ ⬛ ♣ ⬚ ❄ ⬚ SP
⬛ ⓣ

Lindon Hotel
♨♨

66 R.L. Stevenson Avenue,
Westbourne, Bournemouth,
BH4 8EG
☎ (0202) 766537
*Close to sea, shops and
entertainments, the Lindon
offers a relaxed and friendly
atmosphere, comfort and
personal service.*

Bedrooms: 1 single, 2 double,
4 family rooms.
Bathrooms: 2 public.
Bed & breakfast: £13.50-£16
single, £27-£32 double.
Half board: £18-£19.50 daily,
£99-£115.50 weekly.
Evening meal 6pm (l.o. 6pm).
Parking for 6.
⌂ ♦ 👤 V ⬜ TV ✕ ⬜ DAP
SP

Lynden Lodge ♨
Listed

5 Herbert Road, Westbourne,
Bournemouth, BH4 8HD
☎ (0202) 763094
*Residential natural therapy
centre, with courses on stress
management, reflexology,
astrology and massage.
Rejuvenation breaks for long
weekends to relax and unwind.
Sauna, spa-pool and steam
room facilities available.*
Bedrooms: 8 twin.
Bathrooms: 2 private,
6 public.
Bed & breakfast: £17.25-£23
single, £23-£28.75 double.
Half board: £28.75-£33.35
daily, £201.25-£233.45
weekly.
Lunch available.
Evening meal 6pm.
Parking for 7.
Credit: Access, Visa, Amex.
⬚ ♦ CB 👤 V ✗ ⬜ ⬚
⬛ ♣ ✕ ⬚ SP

Marsham Court
Hotel ♨
♨♨♨♨ **APPROVED**

Russell-Cotes Road, East
Cliff, Bournemouth,
BH1 3AB
☎ (0202) 552111 Fax (0202)
294744 Telex 41420
*Overlooking bay in quiet
central situation with sun
terraces, outdoor swimming
pool. Edwardian bar and
summer entertainment. Free
accommodation for children.
Snooker. Parking.*
Bedrooms: 10 single,
21 double & 44 twin,
11 family rooms.
Bathrooms: 86 private.
Bed & breakfast: £47-£52
single, £84-£94 double.
Half board: £54.50-£59.50
daily, £287-£322 weekly.
Lunch available.
Evening meal 7pm (l.o. 9pm).
Parking for 100.
Credit: Access, Visa, Diners,
Amex.
⌂ ☎ ● ⬚ ♦ 👤 V ⬜ ●
⬛ ⬜ ⬛ ♣ ⬛ ⬚ ♠ ✕ ⬚
❄ ⬚ SP ⬚
ⓣ

Mayfield Private Hotel
♨♨

46 Frances Road,
Bournemouth, BH1 3SA
☎ (0202) 551839
*Overlooking public gardens
with tennis, bowling and
putting greens. Central for sea,
shops and main rail/coach
stations. Some rooms with
shower or toilet/shower.*
Bedrooms: 1 single, 4 double
& 2 twin, 1 family room.
Bathrooms: 3 private,
2 public; 4 private showers.
Bed & breakfast: £10-£13
single, £20-£26 double.
Half board: £14-£17 daily,
£85-£110 weekly.
Evening meal 6pm.
Parking for 5.
Open January-November.
⌂ ♨6 ♦ 👤 V ⬜ TV ⬜ ✕ ⬚ DAP
SP

Melford Hall Hotel ♨
♨♨♨♨

St. Peters Road,
Bournemouth, BH1 2LS
☎ (0202) 551516
Fax (0202) 292533
*Quiet town centre location,
close to all shops and sea front.
New indoor pool and fitness
suite.*
Bedrooms: 8 single, 17 double
& 18 twin, 17 family rooms.
Bathrooms: 55 private,
4 public.
Bed & breakfast: £22-£34
single, £44-£68 double.
Half board: £25-£42 daily,
£150-£285 weekly.
Lunch available.
Evening meal 6.30pm (l.o.
8pm).
Parking for 55.
Credit: Access, Visa, Diners,
Amex.
⌂ ♨ ☎ ● ⬚ ♦ 👤 V ⬜
● ⬛ ⬜ ⬛ ♣ ⬛ ♠ ✕
❄ ⬚ SP ⬚ ⓣ

Hotel Mon Bijou
47 Manor Road, East Cliff,
Bournemouth, BH1 3EU
☎ (0202) 551389
*An enchanting hotel of
character personally
maintained by proprietors.
Exquisitely furnished. Well-
appointed bedrooms, trouser
press, hair-dryer, video. French
cuisine.*
Bedrooms: 5 double & 2 twin.
Bathrooms: 7 private.
Bed & breakfast: £35 single,
£45-£65 double.
Half board: from £48 daily,
from £270 weekly.
Evening meal 7pm (l.o.
9.30pm).

Continued ▶

473

BOURNEMOUTH

Continued

Parking for 8.
Credit: Access, Visa.

🏠12 🏊 ⚓ 📞 🅿 ♦ ⚓
📺 ❄ 🏛 ♨ 🍴 ✗ 🏕 🔌 SP
🎱

Newark Hotel M
COMMENDED

65 St. Michaels Road, West
Cliff, Bournemouth,
BH2 5DP
☎ (0202) 294989
*Privately-run, warm friendly
hotel conveniently situated for
beaches, town centre and
Bournemouth Conference
Centre. Home cooking and
friendly atmosphere assured.*
Bedrooms: 3 single, 4 double
& 2 twin, 2 family rooms.
Bathrooms: 3 public.
Bed & breakfast: £12-£17
single, £24-£34 double.
Half board: £16.50-£21.50
daily, £115-£150 weekly.
Evening meal 6pm (l.o. 6pm).
Parking for 1.
Credit: Access.

🏠4 🏊 ♦ ⚓ ♦ 📺 ❄ 🏛 ♨
✗ 🏕 🔌 SP

Norfolk Royale Hotel M
HIGHLY COMMENDED

Richmond Hill,
Bournemouth, BH2 6EN
☎ (0202) 21521 & Toll Free
Number (0800) 444444
Telex 418474
*Edwardian country home in the
heart of Bournemouth. Dome
covered pool. Gourmet and
brasserie restaurant. 5 minutes
from beach and gardens.*
Bedrooms: 9 single, 46 double
& 32 twin, 8 family rooms.
Bathrooms: 95 private.
Bed & breakfast: £80-£300
double.
Half board: £48-£65 daily.
Lunch available.
Evening meal 7pm (l.o.
11pm).
Parking for 88.
Credit: Access, Visa, C.Bl.,
Diners, Amex.

🏠 📞 🅿 📟 ♦ ⚓ 📺 ❄ ♦
🍷 🅿 🏛 ♨ 🍴 🎱 ⚓ 🔌 ♻
🅿 ❄ ✗ 🔌 🔌 SP 🎱 T

Norland Private Hotel
APPROVED

6 Westby Road, Boscombe,
Bournemouth, BH5 1HD
☎ (0202) 396729
*Comfortable, family hotel with
residential licence, English food
and attentive service at all
times. Children and senior
citizens at reduced rates.*

Bedrooms: 1 single, 5 double,
3 family rooms.
Bathrooms: 3 private,
2 public.
Bed & breakfast: £12-£14
single, £24-£28 double.
Half board: £16-£18 daily,
£92-£112 weekly.
Evening meal 6pm (l.o. 4pm).
Parking for 7.

🏠 📞 ♦ ⚓ ♦ 📺 📺 🏛 ♨
📟 🔌 SP

Overcliff Hotel M
☗☗☗

58 Grand Avenue,
Southbourne, Bournemouth,
BH6 3PA
☎ (0202) 428300
*Family hotel overlooking the
sea, offering comfortable
friendly service with choice of
English food. Dance floor, with
entertainment provided several
nights of the week, including
electric organ in bar.*
Bedrooms: 4 single, 11 double
& 7 twin, 6 family rooms.
Bathrooms: 22 private,
4 public.
Bed & breakfast: £17-£22
single, £34-£44 double.
Half board: £22-£33 daily,
£140-£195 weekly.
Lunch available.
Evening meal 6.30pm (l.o.
7.30pm).
Parking for 21.
Open February-December.
Credit: Access, Visa.

🏠 📞 🅿 ♦ 📺 ❄ 📺 🏛 ♨
🍴 ✗ 🔌 📟 🔌 SP

Hotel Piccadilly M
☗☗☗

Bath Road, Bournemouth,
BH1 2NN
☎ (0202) 552559 & 556420
*Central location with food
served in attractive Fountains
restaurant. Stylish bedrooms
recently refurbished providing
every convenience. Car parking
facilities.*
Bedrooms: 5 single, 24 double
& 14 twin, 2 family rooms.
Bathrooms: 45 private.
Bed & breakfast: £36-£44
single, £52-£68 double.
Half board: £32-£40 daily,
£205-£290 weekly.
Lunch available.
Evening meal 6.30pm (l.o.
9pm).
Parking for 36.
Credit: Access, Visa, Diners,
Amex.

🏠 🏊 ⚓ 📞 🅿 📟 ♦ ⚓ ♦ 📺
❄ 🅿 🏛 ♨ 🍴 ✗ 🔌 📟
T

Pinetops Hotel

4 Earle Road, Alum Chine,
Bournemouth, BH4 8JQ
☎ (0202) 761192

---

*Small, privately owned hotel
with friendly atmosphere. A
few minutes' walk to chine and
beach. Families welcome.*
Bedrooms: 1 single, 3 double
& 1 twin, 3 family rooms.
Bathrooms: 1 private,
1 public.
Bed & breakfast: £12-£16
single, £24-£32 double.
Half board: £16-£20 daily,
£102-£130 weekly.
Evening meal 6pm (l.o. 6pm).
Parking for 7.
Credit: Visa.

🏠 📞 📟 ♦ ⚓ ♦ 📺 ✗ ❄ 📺
🏛 ✗ 🏕 📟 🔌 SP T

Pinewood Guest House

197 Holdenhurst Road,
Bournemouth, BH8 8DG
☎ (0202) 292684
*Friendly guesthouse, close to
rail, coach stations and all
amenities. Satellite TV in all
rooms.*
Bedrooms: 1 single, 2 double
& 1 twin, 4 family rooms.
Bathrooms: 2 public.
Bed & breakfast: £13-£15
single, £26-£30 double.
Parking for 8.

🏠 📞5 ⚓ ♦ ⚓ ♦ 📺 🏛 ♨ ✗

Queen's Hotel M
☗☗☗

Meyrick Road, East Cliff,
Bournemouth, BH1 3DL
☎ (0202) 554415
Telex 418297
*Modern, family-run hotel near
the beach, ideal for family
holidays, with facilities for
business conventions.*
Bedrooms: 9 single, 47 double
& 46 twin, 8 family rooms.
Bathrooms: 110 private.
Bed & breakfast: £34-£42.50
single, £68-£85 double.
Half board: £42.50-£52.50
daily, £250-£300 weekly.
Lunch available.
Evening meal 7pm (l.o. 9pm).
Parking for 80.
Credit: Access, Visa.

🏠 📞 ⚓ 📟 ♦ ♦ 📺 ♦
🅿 🏛 ♨ 🍴 🎱 ♦ 📟 🔌 SP T

Riviera Hotel M
☗☗☗ APPROVED

12-16 Burnaby Road, Alum
Chine, Bournemouth,
BH4 8JF
☎ (0202) 763653 Telex 41363
🅖🅡 Calotels
*Family hotel occupying unique
position overlooking Alum
Chine with uninterrupted views
of the Isle of Wight.*
Bedrooms: 6 single, 24 double
& 15 twin, 32 family rooms.
Bathrooms: 77 private.
Half board: £27-£44 daily,
£209-£300 weekly.
Lunch available.

Evening meal 7pm (l.o.
8.30pm).
Parking for 80.
Credit: Access, Visa.

🏠 🏊 📞 📟 ♦ ♦ ⚓ 📺 ❄
🅿 🏛 ♨ 🍴 🎱 ♦ 🔌 ♻
❄ 📟 🔌 SP T

Hotel Riviera
☗☗☗

Westcliff Gardens,
Bournemouth, BH2 5HL
☎ (0202) 552845
*On the West Cliff of
Bournemouth overlooking the
sea, with a garden which has
direct access to the clifftop.*
Bedrooms: 7 single, 13 double
& 10 twin, 4 family rooms.
Bathrooms: 34 private.
Bed & breakfast: £22-£27
single, £44-£54 double.
Half board: £27-£31 daily,
£160-£190 weekly.
Lunch available.
Evening meal 6.30pm (l.o.
7.15pm).
Parking for 24.
Open April-October.
Credit: Access, Visa, Amex.

🏠 📞 ⚓ 📟 ♦ ⚓ ♦ 📺 🏛 ● ♦
🏛 🎱 ♦ 📟 🔌 SP T

Rivoli Hotel M
☗☗☗

95 St. Michael's Road, West
Cliff, Bournemouth,
BH2 5DS
☎ (0202) 290292
*Detached building situated on
Bournemouth's West Cliff, 150
yards from clifftop walk, with
access to beach and pier
without crossing road.*
Bedrooms: 6 single, 5 double
& 3 twin, 4 family rooms.
Bathrooms: 10 private,
2 public.
Bed & breakfast: £16.50-
£21.50 single, £33-£49.50
double.
Half board: £22.50-£27.50
daily, £132-£185 weekly.
Evening meal 6.30pm (l.o.
7pm).
Parking for 14.
Open February-December.
Credit: Access, Visa.

🏠 📟 ⚓ ♦ ⚓ ♦ 📺 ❄ 📺 🏛
🏛 ✗ 🔌 SP

Rosedale Guest House
Listed APPROVED

46 St. Michael's Road, West
Cliff, Bournemouth,
BH2 5DY
☎ (0202) 555950
*3 minutes' walk to all
activities. Central heating, TV
and tea/coffee facilities in all
rooms. Freshly cooked full
English breakfast. Public car
park and telephone. Our
business is your pleasure.*
Bedrooms: 2 single, 2 double,
2 family rooms.

Bathrooms: 1 public.
Bed & breakfast: £12-£14 single, £24-£26 double.

Roselyn Hotel
55 West Cliff Road, Bournemouth, BH4 8BA
☎ (0202) 761037
Small, family-run hotel with residential licence. Close to sea, shops, buses and chine.
Bedrooms: 1 single, 3 double & 1 twin, 3 family rooms.
Bathrooms: 4 private, 1 public.
Bed & breakfast: £15.50-£18 single, £25-£36 double.
Half board: £18.50-£24 daily, £123.50-£158 weekly.
Parking for 8.

Royal Bath Hotel M
COMMENDED
Bath Road, Bournemouth, BH1 2EW
☎ (0202) 555555 Telex 41375
De Vere
Set in 3 acres overlooking Poole Bay, within a quarter of a mile of Bournemouth town centre. Leisure Pavilion with swimming pool, spa pool, sauna, steam room, multi-gym, beauty and hairdressing salons.
Bedrooms: 21 single, 10 double & 90 twin, 10 family rooms.
Bathrooms: 131 private.
Bed & breakfast: £81-£91.80 single, £124.20-£205.20 double.
Half board: £105-£132.30 daily, £480.60-£891 weekly.
Lunch available.
Evening meal 6.30pm (l.o. 10.30pm).
Parking for 120.
Credit: Access, Visa, Diners, Amex.

Royal Exeter Hotel M
APPROVED
Exeter Road, Bournemouth, BH2 5AG
☎ (0202) 290566 & 290567
Within walking distance of the beach and town centre. The original holiday home of Bournemouth, built 1810.
Bedrooms: 6 single, 17 double & 3 twin, 10 family rooms.
Bathrooms: 36 private.
Bed & breakfast: £46-£52 single, from £61.50 double.
Lunch available.
Evening meal 6pm (l.o. 10pm).
Parking for 65.

Credit: Access, Visa, Diners, Amex.

The Savoy Hotel M
APPROVED
West Hill Road, West Cliff, Bournemouth, BH2 5EJ
☎ (0202) 294241
Telex 418462
Situated on the West Cliff in its own grounds with sea views and close to the town centre.
Bedrooms: 20 single, 31 double & 30 twin, 10 family rooms.
Bathrooms: 91 private.
Bed & breakfast: £39-£55 single, £66.50-£100 double.
Half board: £43-£60 daily, £275-£350 weekly.
Lunch available.
Evening meal 7pm (l.o. 8.30pm).
Parking for 70.
Credit: Access, Visa, Diners, Amex.

Sea Cottage Private Hotel M
Listed
55 Grand Avenue, Southbourne, Bournemouth, BH6 3TA
☎ (0202) 417647
High standard of personal service. Distinctive bedrooms, separate dining tables. Home cooking. 2 minutes from cliff top. Forecourt parking. Non-smoking establishment.
Bedrooms: 2 single, 3 double & 1 twin, 1 family room.
Bathrooms: 1 public.
Bed & breakfast: from £20 single, from £40 double.
Half board: from £29 daily, from £165 weekly.
Evening meal 6pm.
Parking for 5.

Seabreeze Hotel M
32 St. Catherines Road, Southbourne, Bournemouth, BH6 4AB
☎ (0202) 433888
Located opposite beach with easy access to Bournemouth and Christchurch. Peaceful, small hotel with family atmosphere. Generous home cooking. Children half price. Vegetarians welcome.
Bedrooms: 2 single, 1 double & 2 twin, 4 family rooms.
Bathrooms: 6 private, 1 public.
Bed & breakfast: £12-£15 single, £24-£30 double.

Half board: £17-£20 daily, £100-£130 weekly.
Evening meal 6pm (l.o. 4pm).
Parking for 8.

Seagrove Hotel
53 Southern Road, West Southbourne, Bournemouth, BH6 3SS
☎ (0202) 424526
Convenient for beach. 2 minutes' walk to cliff lift and level walk to shops and buses. Sea views from all bedrooms.
Bedrooms: 2 single, 2 double, 6 family rooms.
Bathrooms: 1 public; 3 private showers.
Bed & breakfast: £14-£16 single, £25-£30 double.
Half board: £18-£20 daily, £120-£140 weekly.
Evening meal 6pm (l.o. 6pm).
Parking for 7.

Seaway Wavecrest Lodge
30 St. Catherines Road, Southbourne, Bournemouth, BH6 4AB
☎ (0202) 423636
Delightfully situated overlooking sea, yet within easy reach of Christchurch and Bournemouth.
Bedrooms: 2 single, 2 double & 2 twin, 4 family rooms.
Bathrooms: 5 private, 1 public.
Bed & breakfast: £12.50-£13 single, £23-£27 double.
Half board: £19.50 daily, £115.75 weekly.
Evening meal 6.15pm (l.o. 10am).
Parking for 9.

Shearwater Hotel
61 Grand Avenue, Southbourne, Bournemouth, BH6 3TA
☎ (0202) 423396
Small, centrally heated, family-run hotel, with home-cooked food and choice of menu. 100 yards from clifftop.
Bedrooms: 1 single, 2 double & 2 twin, 3 family rooms.
Bathrooms: 2 private, 2 public.
Bed & breakfast: £11.50-£15.50 single, £23-£31 double.
Half board: £17.50-£21.50 daily, £111-£135 weekly.
Evening meal 6pm (l.o. 10am).

Parking for 5.
Open February-November.
Credit: Access, Visa.

The Squirrels Hotel M
20 Southwood Avenue, Southbourne, Bournemouth, BH6 3QA
☎ (0202) 427415
Small friendly hotel in quiet avenue close to sea and shops, offering personal service for your comfort and relaxation.
Bedrooms: 1 single, 2 double & 2 twin, 2 family rooms.
Bathrooms: 2 private, 1 public.
Half board: £96-£127 weekly.
Evening meal 6pm (l.o. 6pm).
Parking for 5.
Open March-November.

Suncliff Hotel M
East Overcliff Drive, Bournemouth, BH1 3AG
☎ (0202) 291711 Telex 41363
Calotels
Overlooking Bournemouth Bay with uninterrupted views of the Purbeck Hills and Isle of Wight.
Bedrooms: 12 single, 29 double & 25 twin, 29 family rooms.
Bathrooms: 95 private.
Half board: £29-£58 daily, £209-£366 weekly.
Lunch available.
Evening meal 7pm (l.o. 8.30pm).
Parking for 60.
Credit: Access, Visa, Diners, Amex.

Sundorn Private Hotel
31 Burnaby Road, Alum Chine, Westbourne, Bournemouth, BH4 8JF
☎ (0202) 760931
Semi-detached, 3-storey building of mock Tudor appearance with a small car park at front. The interior is warmly decorated with chandeliers and wall lights on ground floor and residents' lounge.
Bedrooms: 1 double & 1 twin, 5 family rooms.
Bathrooms: 1 public.
Bed & breakfast: £25-£31 double.
Half board: £16.50-£19.50 daily, £99-£115 weekly.

Continued ▶

BOURNEMOUTH

Continued

Evening meal 6pm (l.o. 6pm).
Parking for 3.
Credit: Access.

Sunnylees Hotel

231 Holdenhurst Road,
Bournemouth, BH8 8DD
☎ (0202) 395831
*Private hotel with resident
proprietors. Close to a variety
of good eating places, clubs
and local or countrywide travel
facilities.*
Bedrooms: 2 single, 2 double,
4 family rooms.
Bathrooms: 1 public;
3 private showers.
Bed & breakfast: £13-£16
single, £25-£30 double.
Half board: £16-£19 daily.
Evening meal 6pm (l.o. 9pm).
Parking for 12.
Credit: Access, Visa.

Tall Pine Hotel

🎗🎗 **APPROVED**
3 Walpole Road, Boscombe,
Bournemouth, BH1 4EZ
☎ (0202) 37131
*Small, family-run hotel, 8
minutes' stroll from the sea.
Close to shops, entertainments
and bus route, with home
cooking and friendly service.*
Bedrooms: 3 single, 1 double
& 1 twin, 4 family rooms.
Bathrooms: 3 private,
2 public.
Bed & breakfast: £14-£16
single, £28-£37 double.
Evening meal 6pm (l.o. 6pm).
Parking for 9.

Thanet Private Hotel ⋒

🎗🎗🎗 **COMMENDED**
2 Drury Road, Alum Chine,
Bournemouth, BH4 8HA
☎ (0202) 761104
*Small, friendly, licensed hotel
close to Alum Chine, beaches,
shops and main bus routes to
Poole and Bournemouth town
centre.*
Bedrooms: 2 single, 4 double
& 1 twin, 1 family room.
Bathrooms: 3 private,
2 public.
Bed & breakfast: £12-£15
single, £24-£30 double.
Half board: £15-£18 daily,
£95-£125 weekly.
Evening meal 6pm (l.o.
6.15pm).
Parking for 8.

Thorpe Arnold Hotel ⋒

Listed
5 Groveley Road, Alum
Chine, Bournemouth,
BH4 8HF
☎ (0202) 761427
*Friendly private hotel offering
personal service to all our
guests.*
Bedrooms: 2 single, 2 double
& 2 twin, 3 family rooms.
Bathrooms: 2 private,
1 public.
Bed & breakfast: £13.50-
£21.50 single, £27-£45 double.
Half board: £18.50-£25 daily,
£110-£155 weekly.
Evening meal 6pm (l.o. 6pm).
Parking for 6.
Credit: Access, Visa.

Torbryan Private Hotel ⋒

18 Knole Road,
Bournemouth, BH1 4DQ
☎ (0202) 33564
*A private hotel with residential
licence, close to Boscombe
gardens, with access to
pier and beach. Shopping
centres nearby.*
Bedrooms: 4 double & 2 twin,
4 family rooms.
Bathrooms: 5 private,
2 public.
Bed & breakfast: £15-£20
single, £26-£40 double.
Half board: £22-£30 daily,
£110-£130 weekly.
Evening meal 6pm (l.o.
6.30pm).
Parking for 10.

Tralee Hotel ⋒

🎗🎗🎗
West Hill Road, West Cliff,
Bournemouth, BH2 5EQ
☎ (0202) 556246
*Leisure and entertainment
facilities for all the family.
Cliff top position close to town
centre, shops, shows and leisure
centre.*
Bedrooms: 7 single, 28 double
& 5 twin, 52 family rooms.
Bathrooms: 82 private,
2 public.
Bed & breakfast: £29.75-
£39.50 single, £59.50-£79
double.
Half board: £34.75-£44.50
daily, £243.25-£299.50
weekly.
Lunch available.
Evening meal 6.45pm (l.o.
8pm).
Parking for 40.

Credit: Access, Visa, C.Bl.,
Diners, Amex.

Trouville Hotel ⋒

🎗🎗🎗🎗
Priory Road, West Cliff,
Bournemouth, BH2 5DH
☎ (0202) 552262 Fax (0202)
294810
*Centrally situated, recently
refurbished hotel. Within easy
walking distance of the beach
and town centre amenities.*
Bedrooms: 9 single, 27 double
& 29 twin, 14 family rooms.
Bathrooms: 79 private.
Bed & breakfast: £31.50-£45
single, £63-£90 double.
Half board: £36.50-£51 daily,
£73-£102 weekly.
Evening meal 7pm (l.o.
8.30pm).
Parking for 76.
Credit: Access, Visa.

Ullswater Hotel ⋒

🎗🎗🎗
Westcliff Gardens,
Bournemouth, BH2 5HW
☎ (0202) 555181
*On the west cliff, a few minutes
from the town centre and
shops, 150 yards from the
clifftop and path to beach.*
Bedrooms: 8 single, 14 double
& 13 twin, 7 family rooms.
Bathrooms: 42 private.
Bed & breakfast: £19.50-£28
single, £39-£56 double.
Half board: £23.50-£32 daily,
£136.50-£199.50 weekly.
Lunch available.
Evening meal 7pm (l.o. 8pm).
Parking for 10.
Credit: Access, Visa.

Wendover Guest House

Listed
67 Alumhurst Road, Alum
Chine, Bournemouth,
BH4 8HP
☎ (0202) 765924
*Family-run guesthouse with
home-cooked food and relaxed,
friendly atmosphere. Satellite
TV. Access to rooms at all
times.*
Bedrooms: 1 single, 2 double
& 1 twin, 3 family rooms.
Bathrooms: 1 private,
1 public.

Bed & breakfast: £12-£16
single, £24-£32 double.
Parking for 4.
Credit: Visa.

West Cliff Hall Hotel ⋒

🎗🎗🎗
14 Priory Road,
Bournemouth, BH2 5DN
☎ (0202) 299715
*Friendly family-run hotel, close
to sea, shops and
entertainments, and 200 yards
from the Conference Centre.
Generous, varied menu.*
Bedrooms: 9 single, 20 double
& 11 twin, 9 family rooms.
Bathrooms: 49 private,
1 public.
Bed & breakfast: £20-£35
single, £40-£70 double.
Half board: £22-£36 daily,
£132-£210 weekly.
Evening meal 6.30pm (l.o.
8pm).
Parking for 36.
Credit: Access, Visa, Diners,
Amex.
🔟 Display advertisement
appears on page 580.

West Hill Court Hotel ⋒

🎗🎗🎗 **COMMENDED**
121 West Hill Road, West
Cliff, Bournemouth,
BH2 5PH
☎ (0202) 21125
*A family-run hotel with
modern bedrooms, a few
minutes from the sea, town
centre, shops and
entertainments.*
Bedrooms: 1 single, 5 double
& 2 twin, 3 family rooms.
Bathrooms: 5 private,
2 public.
Bed & breakfast: £16-£22
single, £27-£37 double.
Half board: £16.50-£23 daily,
£100-£156 weekly.
Evening meal 6pm (l.o. 4pm).
Open March-November.
Credit: Access, Visa.

Whitehall Hotel

Exeter Park Road,
Bournemouth, BH2 5AX
☎ (0202) 24682
*Adjacent to International
Conference Centre, with private
footpath into central gardens
and traffic-free access to shops
and beach.*
Bedrooms: 13 single,
17 double & 14 twin, 5 family
rooms.
Bathrooms: 44 private,
4 public.

**Map references apply to the colour maps
towards the end of this guide.**

Bed & breakfast: £22-£26 single, £44-£52 double.
Half board: £29-£33 daily, £168-£210 weekly.
Evening meal 6.30pm (l.o. 8pm).
Parking for 25.
Open March-November.
Credit: Access, Visa, Diners, Amex.

ॐ ⪙ ⬩ 🖱 ⌨ ♥ ▯ 🔲 ⮐
📺 ● ⧫ ▥ ♨ ⌷ 🈂 SP

Winter Gardens Hotel ⋔
♚♚♚

32-34 Tregonwell Road, West Cliff, Bournemouth, BH2 5NU
☎ (0202) 555769 Fax (0202) 21330
Quiet but central for all Bournemouth's main theatres, cinemas, shops, leisure and conference centres. Pier and beach within 10 minutes' walk. Indoor leisure centre with 30 ft pool.
Bedrooms: 15 single, 23 double & 14 twin, 29 family rooms.
Bathrooms: 75 private, 10 public.
Bed & breakfast: £15-£28 single, £30-£56 double.
Half board: £19-£38 daily, £120-£230 weekly.
Lunch available.
Evening meal 6.30pm (l.o. 8pm).
Parking for 52.
Credit: Access, Visa, Diners, Amex.

ॐ ⪙ ⬩ 🖱 ⌨ ♥ ▯ ✂ ⮐ 📺 ● ⧫ 🔲 ♨ ⌷ 🈂 ⬩ ♠ 🔲 ❄ ⚓ ♨ SP 🈺 Ⓣ

Winterbourne Hotel ⋔
♚♚♚

Priory Road, Bournemouth, BH2 5DJ
☎ (0202) 296366
Telex 417153 STAR
Enjoying a prime position with magnificent sea view, the hotel is within 500 metres of International Centre, shops, theatres and beach.
Bedrooms: 6 single, 13 double & 10 twin, 12 family rooms.
Bathrooms: 41 private.
Bed & breakfast: £29-£37 single, £48-£66 double.
Half board: £29-£38 daily, £160-£228 weekly.
Lunch available.
Evening meal 6.30pm (l.o. 8pm).
Parking for 34.
Credit: Access, Visa.

ॐ ⪙ ⬩ 🖱 ⌨ ♥ ▯ ⮐ ⧫ 🔲 ♨ 🈂 ♣ ⚓ ⬥ ▶ ❄ ♨ SP Ⓣ

Wood Lodge Hotel ⋔
♚♚♚

10 Manor Road, East Cliff, Bournemouth, BH1 3EY
☎ (0202) 290891
A pleasant and comfortable house of character in delightful surroundings, 300 yards from the East Overcliff Drive. Ideally situated for enjoying Bournemouth's many excellent facilities.
Bedrooms: 2 single, 5 double & 3 twin, 5 family rooms.
Bathrooms: 14 private, 1 public.
Bed & breakfast: £18-£27 single, £36-£54 double.
Half board: £23-£30 daily, £145-£190 weekly.
Evening meal 6.30pm (l.o. 7pm).
Parking for 12.
Open April-October.
Credit: Access, Visa.

ॐ ⪙ 🖱 ⌨ ♥ ▯ ⮐ 📺 🔲 ♨ ❄ ♨

Woodford Court Hotel ⋔
♚♚♚

19-23 Studland Road, Alum Chine, Bournemouth, BH4 8HZ
☎ (0202) 764907
Well-appointed private hotel, delightfully situated facing Alum Chine near sea. Personal service.
Bedrooms: 7 single, 11 double & 5 twin, 12 family rooms.
Bathrooms: 35 private, 2 public.
Bed & breakfast: £16.50-£22 single, £33-£44 double.
Half board: £21-£26 daily, £147-£182 weekly.
Evening meal 6.15pm (l.o. 6.30pm).
Parking for 16.
Open April-October.
Credit: Access, Visa.

ॐ ⪙2 ⪙ 🖱 ⌨ ♥ ▯ ⮐ 📺 🔲 ♨ ❄ ⚓ ⬥ SP Ⓣ

BRAMSHAW
Hampshire
Map ref 2C3

5m NW. Lyndhurst
On the northern fringe of the New Forest, hidden among the trees. At Nomansland, so called as it was originally the squatters who built it, red-brick houses sit back from the village green with its cricket pitch.

Bramble Hill Hotel ⋔
Bramshaw, Nr. Lyndhurst, SO43 7JG
☎ Southampton (0703) 813165

In the quiet part of the New Forest. Own livery stables for guests' horses and 2 golf-courses nearby in Bramshaw.
Bedrooms: 1 single, 8 double & 2 twin, 2 family rooms.
Bathrooms: 9 private, 3 public.
Bed & breakfast: £35-£55 single, £70-£90 double.
Half board: £50-£75 daily, £285-£345 weekly.
Lunch available.
Evening meal 7pm (l.o. 9.30pm).
Parking for 70.
Credit: Access, Visa.

ॐ⪙5 ⪙ 🖱 ⌨ ♥ ▯ ⮐ 📺 🔲 ⬥ ❄ ♨ ⚓ ♨

BROCKENHURST
Hampshire
Map ref 2C3

Attractive village with thatched cottages and a ford in its main street. Well placed for visiting the New Forest.

Careys Manor Hotel ⋔
♚♚♚♚ COMMENDED

Brockenhurst, New Forest, SO42 7RH
☎ Lymington (0590) 23551
Telex 47442
Attractive old manor with most rooms in modern garden wing overlooking lovely gardens. New indoor pool and leisure complex.
Bedrooms: 5 single, 51 double & 24 twin.
Bathrooms: 80 private.
Bed & breakfast: £79-£89 single, £97-£127 double.
Half board: £59-£79 daily.
Lunch available.
Evening meal 7pm (l.o. 10pm).
Parking for 200.
Credit: Access, Visa, Diners, Amex.

ॐ ⪙ 🔲 ⬩ 🖱 ⌨ ♥ ▯ ✂ ⮐ ● 🔲 ♨ ⌷ 🈂 🔲 ❄ ♨ ♨ SP 🈺 Ⓣ

The Cottage Hotel & Restaurant ⋔
♚♚♚ COMMENDED

Sway Road, Brockenhurst, SO42 7SH
☎ Lymington (0590) 22296
Old world cottage with oak beams and log fire in winter. Morning coffee, lunches, cream teas, and dinners by candlelight.
Bedrooms: 1 single, 4 double & 1 twin.
Bathrooms: 6 private.
Bed & breakfast: £38-£40 single, £58-£64 double.
Half board: £41.50-£44.50 daily, £275-£285 weekly.

Lunch available.
Evening meal 7pm (l.o. 9.50pm).
Parking for 10.
Credit: Access, Visa.

ॐ ⪙ ⬩ 🖱 ⌨ ♥ ▯ ⮐ 🔲 ❄ ⬥ ♨ 🔲 SP 🈺

Whitley Ridge Country House Hotel ⋔
♚♚♚♚ COMMENDED

Beaulieu Road, Brockenhurst, SO42 7QL
☎ Lymington (0590) 22354
Beautiful Georgian country house in quiet secluded grounds amidst the forest wildlife. Renowned for food and friendly atmosphere.
Bedrooms: 8 double & 3 twin.
Bathrooms: 11 private.
Bed & breakfast: £52-£60 single, £66-£72 double.
Half board: £49-£52 daily, £259-£269 weekly.
Lunch available.
Evening meal 7pm (l.o. 8.30pm).
Parking for 24.
Credit: Access, Visa, Diners, Amex.

ॐ ⪙ 🔲 ⬩ ♥ ▯ ⮐ 📺 🔲 ♨ ⬥ ♣ ⚓ ♨ ❄ ♨ SP 🈺

BROOK
Hampshire
Map ref 2C3

A hamlet in the New Forest.

The Bell Inn ⋔
♚♚♚

Brook, Nr. Lyndhurst, SO43 7HE
☎ Southampton (0703) 812214
Built in 1782, a listed building, this country inn is located in the New Forest, 1 mile from access point 1 on M27. Other distances - Southampton 12 miles, Salisbury 15 miles, Bournemouth 18 miles. Catering primarily for golfers.
Bedrooms: 3 single, 7 double & 12 twin.
Bathrooms: 22 private.
Bed & breakfast: £51-£65 single, £71-£85 double.
Half board: £65-£75 daily, £450-£500 weekly.
Lunch available.
Evening meal 7.30pm (l.o. 9.30pm).
Parking for 170.
Credit: Access, Visa, Diners, Amex.

ॐ ⪙ ⬩ ⬩ 🖱 ⌨ ♥ ▯ ⮐ 🔲 ⬩ ♣ ▶ ❄ ♨ ⚓ SP 🈺 🔲

BURLEY

Hampshire
Map ref 2B3

5m SE. Ringwood
Attractive centre from
which to explore the
south-west part of the
New Forest. There is an
ancient earthwork on
Castle Hill nearby, which
also offers good views.

Burley Manor Hotel ♨
♛♛♛♛
Burley, Nr.Ringwood,
BH24 4BS
☎ (042 53) 3522 Telex 41565
BURMAN/G
*Beautiful country manor house
hotel set in 54 acres of
parkland in the heart of the
New Forest.*
Bedrooms: 21 double &
8 twin, 1 family room.
Bathrooms: 30 private.
Bed & breakfast: £55-£60
single, £70-£75 double.
Lunch available.
Evening meal 7pm (l.o.
10pm).
Parking for 100.
Credit: Access, Visa, Diners,
Amex.
🛇 🖧 🛲 📞 ⑧ 🖵 ♥ 🛈 Ⅴ
💺 🛏 🎔 ▥ 🛆 🍽 ❣ ☉ ♪ ✷
🐾 🅂🄿 📾 🅃

Rosebay Cottage
Chapel Lane, Burley, Nr.
Ringwood, BH24 4DJ
☎ (042 53) 2471
*Delightful, 100-year-old forest
cottage. Friendly atmosphere.
A few minutes' walk to village
centre. Direct access to forest.*
Bedrooms: 1 double & 1 twin,
1 family room.
Bathrooms: 1 public.
Bed & breakfast: £12 single,
£24 double.
Parking for 4.
Open March-October.
🛇8 ♥ ⑊ ⑂ ▥ 🛋

CORFE CASTLE

Dorset
Map ref 2B3

One of the most
spectacular ruined
castles in Britain. Norman
in origin, the castle was a
Royalist stronghold
during the Civil War and
held out until 1645. The
village had a considerable
marble-carving industry in
the Middle Ages.

Mortons House Hotel ♨
♛♛♛ COMMENDED
East Street, Corfe Castle,
BH20 5EE
☎ (0929) 480988
*Attractive Elizabethan manor
house with castle views.
Walled gardens, coastal and
country pursuits, suites and
four-poster bed. Licensed
gourmet restaurant.*
Bedrooms: 13 double &
3 twin, 1 family room.
Bathrooms: 17 private.
Bed & breakfast: £45-£55
single, £70-£90 double.
Lunch available.
Evening meal 7.30pm (l.o.
10pm).
Parking for 35.
Credit: Access, Visa.
🛇 🖧 🛲 📞 ⑧ 🖵 ♥ 🛈 Ⅴ
💺 🛏 ▥ 🛆 🍽 ☉ ♪ ❣ 🐾
🅂🄿 📾 🅃

CRANBORNE

Dorset
Map ref 2B3

8m N. Wimborne Minster
Village with an interesting
Jacobean manor house.
Lies south-east of
Cranborne Chase,
formerly a forest and
hunting preserve.

The Fleur de Lys ♨
♛♛♛ APPROVED
5 Wimborne Street,
Cranborne, BH21 5PP
☎ (072 54) 282
*Traditional old 16th C inn,
featured in Thomas Hardy's
Tess of the D'Urbervilles and
on the edge of the New Forest.*
Bedrooms: 2 single, 3 double
& 2 twin, 1 family room.
Bathrooms: 7 private;
1 private shower.
Bed & breakfast: £23.50-£30
single, £32-£40 double.
Half board: £35-£47.50 daily,
£220-£297.50 weekly.
Lunch available.

Evening meal 7pm (l.o.
9.45pm).
Parking for 35.
Credit: Access, Visa, Amex.
🛇 🖧 🛲 ♥ 🛈 🛏 ▥ 🛆 🍽 🛋
📾

EASTLEIGH

Hampshire
Map ref 2C3

Town developed around
the railway engineering
works built there in 1889.
The borough stretches
from Southampton Water
to the Test Valley in the
north. Yachting centres at
Hamble and Bursledon.
Tourist Information
Centre ☎ *(0703) 641261*

Homeleigh ♨
184 Southampton Road,
Eastleigh, SO5 5QW
☎ (0703) 616480
*Comfortable guesthouse,
quarter of a mile to airport and
junction 5, M27 to Portsmouth
ferries. 5 minutes' walk
mainline railway station, shops
and restaurants.*
Bedrooms: 3 single, 1 double
& 2 twin.
Bathrooms: 1 public.
Bed & breakfast: £13-£16
single, £26-£32 double.
Half board: £21-£24 daily,
£147-£168 weekly.
🛇 🕭 🖧 🖵 ♥ ⑊ ▥ 🛋 🐾
🄾🄰🄿

Twyford Lodge Guest
House ♨
104-106 Twyford Road,
Eastleigh, SO5 4HN
☎ (0703) 612245
*Friendly, family-run
guesthouse, convenient for
mainline station and airport.
Residents' bar, full fire
certificate.*
Bedrooms: 3 single, 2 double
& 6 twin, 4 family rooms.
Bathrooms: 1 private,
3 public; 1 private shower.
Bed & breakfast: from £14.95
single, from £29.90 double.
Evening meal 6pm (l.o. 7pm).
Parking for 14.
🛇 🖧 🖵 🛈 🛏 ⑪ 🛆 🐾 🛋

EMSWORTH

Hampshire
Map ref 2C3

Old port, now a yachting
centre, set between 2
small creeks on
Chichester Harbour.
Yachtbuilding is the chief
industry. There are some
good Georgian buildings
and 2 tide-mills.

The Brookfield Hotel ♨
♛♛♛ COMMENDED
Havant Road, Emsworth,
PO10 7LF
☎ (0243) 373363
Fax (0243) 376342
*Privately owned and run
country house hotel between
the old fishing village of
Emsworth and Havant on the
A27.*
Bedrooms: 7 single, 22 double
& 12 twin.
Bathrooms: 41 private.
Bed & breakfast: from £52
single, from £65 double.
Half board: from £75 daily.
Lunch available.
Evening meal 7pm (l.o.
9.30pm).
Parking for 80.
Credit: Access, Visa, Diners,
Amex.
🛇 🖧 🛲 📞 ⑧ 🖵 ♥ 🛈 Ⅴ
🛏 ● ▥ 🛆 🍽 ❣ ✕ 🅂🄿

Jingles Hotel ♨
♛♛♛
77 Horndean Road,
Emsworth, PO10 7PU
☎ (0243) 373755
*Fully modernised and
comfortably furnished
Victorian house located
between the South Downs and
Chichester Harbour.*
Bedrooms: 5 single, 5 double
& 2 twin, 1 family room.
Bathrooms: 6 private,
2 public.
Bed & breakfast: from £20
single, from £35 double.
Half board: from £27.50
daily.
Lunch available.
Evening meal 7pm (l.o. 8pm).
Parking for 14.
Credit: Access, Visa.
🛇 🖧 🛲 🖵 ♥ 🛈 Ⅴ 💺 🛏
⑂ ▥ 🛆 🍽 🐾

Merry Hall Hotel ♨
♛♛♛ APPROVED
73 Horndean Road,
Emsworth, PO10 7PU
☎ (0243) 372424
*Well-appointed family-run
hotel offering friendly service,
with spacious lounge
overlooking large attractive
garden. Well situated for
touring southern England.*

Bedrooms: 3 single, 3 double
& 3 twin, 1 family room.
Bathrooms: 7 private;
3 private showers.
Bed & breakfast: £28-£32
single, £48-£52 double.
Lunch available.
Evening meal 6pm (l.o. 9pm).
Parking for 12.
Credit: Access, Visa.

Queensgate Hotel M
APPROVED
80 Havant Road, Emsworth,
PO10 7LH
☎ (0243) 371960 & 377766
*Edwardian house adjacent to
designated area of outstanding
natural beauty. Within easy
reach of Emsworth, Havant,
Chichester and Portsmouth on
the A259.*
Bedrooms: 5 single, 2 double
& 2 twin, 1 family room.
Bathrooms: 2 public;
8 private showers.
Bed & breakfast: from £19.50
single, from £34 double.
Half board: from £28.50
daily.
Evening meal 6.30pm (l.o.
9pm).
Parking for 10.
Credit: Access, Visa, Diners,
Amex.

Strathfield Guest House
Listed
99 Havant Road, Emsworth,
PO10 7LF
☎ (0243) 377351
*Attractive Victorian house, full
of character, set in a beautiful
third of an acre garden. Close
to the South Coast and ports.
Non-smoking.*
Bedrooms: 1 single, 1 double
& 1 twin, 1 family room.
Bathrooms: 4 private.
Bed & breakfast: £34 double.
Evening meal 6.30pm (l.o.
6pm).
Parking for 5.

> **Classifications
> and quality
> commendations
> were correct at the
> time of going to
> press but are
> subject to change.
> Please check at the
> time of booking.**

**Hampshire
Map ref 2C3**

Lies on a quiet backwater
of Portsmouth Harbour.
The High Street is lined
with fine Georgian
buildings.
*Tourist Information
Centre* ☎ *(0329) 221342*

Acton Lodge Hotel M
COMMENDED
225A West Street, Fareham,
PO16 0ET
☎ (0329) 231200
Fax (0329) 822429
*Small commercial hotel and
restaurant, ideally situated on
A27 close to railway station,
main street and shops. Car
park at rear.*
Bedrooms: 3 twin, 2 family
rooms.
Bathrooms: 5 private.
Bed & breakfast: £25-£40
single, £35-£50 double.
Half board: £34.75-£49.75
daily, £250-£300 weekly.
Lunch available.
Evening meal 7pm (l.o.
10.30pm).
Parking for 12.
Credit: Access, Visa, Amex.

Avenue House Hotel M
COMMENDED
22 The Avenue, Fareham,
PO14 1NS
☎ (0329) 232175
*Comfortable, small hotel, with
charm and character, set in
mature gardens. 5 minutes'
walk to town centre, railway
station and restaurants.*
Bedrooms: 2 single, 4 double
& 2 twin, 2 family rooms.
Bathrooms: 10 private.
Bed & breakfast: £29-£40
single, £39-£49 double.
Parking for 12.
Credit: Access, Visa, Amex.

Red Lion Hotel M
COMMENDED
East Street, Fareham,
PO16 0BP
☎ (0329) 822640 Telex 86204
CR Lansbury
*Restored coaching inn, close to
Portsmouth and Southampton.*
Bedrooms: 17 single,
18 double & 7 twin, 2 family
rooms.
Bathrooms: 44 private,
1 public.
Bed & breakfast: £31-£69
single, £62-£82 double.
Half board: £41-£97 daily.
Lunch available.

Evening meal 7pm (l.o.
10pm).
Parking for 136.
Credit: Access, Visa, Diners,
Amex.

The Roundabout Hotel
Wallington Shore Road,
Fareham, PO16 8SB
☎ (0329) 822542
*Family-run hotel with
stimulating and friendly
atmosphere specialising in
traditional home cooking, with
easy access to south coast
towns via M27.*
Bedrooms: 4 single, 8 double
& 3 twin, 2 family rooms.
Bathrooms: 13 private,
2 public.
Bed & breakfast: £25-£40
single, £35-£50 double.
Lunch available.
Evening meal 6pm (l.o.
10pm).
Parking for 42.
Credit: Access, Visa, Diners,
Amex.

Solent Hotel M
Solent Business Park,
Whiteley, Fareham,
PO15 7AJ
☎ (0489) 880000
*A hotel particularly suited to
business and conference
market, with a fine restaurant
and high standard leisure
facilities.*
Bedrooms: 75 twin, 13 family
rooms.
Bathrooms: 88 private.
Bed & breakfast: from £112
single, from £126 double.
Half board: from £126 daily.
Lunch available.
Evening meal 7pm (l.o.
10pm).
Parking for 240.
Credit: Access, Visa, Diners,
Amex.

**Hampshire
Map ref 2C2**

Home of the Royal
Aircraft Establishment
and the site of the
biennial International Air
Show. St. Michael's
Abbey was built by the
Empress Eugenie, wife of
Napoleon III of France
and together with their
son they are buried in the
crypt.
*Tourist Information
Centre* ☎ *(0252) 513838*

Alexandra Hotel M
144 Alexandra Road,
Farnborough, GU14 6RP
☎ (0252) 541050
*Well-appointed, comfortable
hotel, managed by proprietors
and family, with emphasis on
cleanliness and service.*
Bedrooms: 5 single, 1 double
& 5 twin.
Bathrooms: 11 private,
2 public.
Bed & breakfast: from £42
single, from £54 double.
Evening meal 7pm (l.o. 9pm).
Parking for 10.
Credit: Access, Visa, Diners,
Amex.

Falcon Hotel
68 Farnborough Road,
Farnborough, GU14 6TH
☎ (0252) 545378
*Situated on the A325
overlooking Farnborough's
Aerospace Centre, home of the
world-famous air show. Close
to Aldershot garrison town.*
Bedrooms: 8 single, 14 double
& 6 twin, 2 family rooms.
Bathrooms: 30 private.
Bed & breakfast: £55 single,
£65 double.
Half board: £67.50 daily.
Lunch available.
Evening meal 7pm (l.o.
9.30pm).
Parking for 30.
Credit: Access, Visa.

> **The symbols are explained on the flap
> inside the back cover.**

> **The National Crown Scheme is explained
> in full on pages 556 – 558.**

Hampshire
Map ref 2C2

Lismoyne Hotel
Church Road, Fleet,
GU13 8NA
☎ (0252) 628555
*Attractive privately owned
country hotel set in two and a
quarter acres of wooded
seclusion. A la carte and table
d'hote menus.*
Bedrooms: 18 single,
12 double & 12 twin.
Bathrooms: 42 private.
Bed & breakfast: £62-£70
single, £80 double.
Lunch available.
Evening meal 7.30pm (l.o.
9.30pm).
Parking for 80.
Credit: Access, Visa, C.Bl.,
Diners, Amex.

Hampshire
Map ref 2B3

On the north-west of the
New Forest. A medieval
bridge crosses the Avon
at this point and gave the
town its name. A good
centre for walking,
exploring and fishing.

Ashburn Hotel & Restaurant ᴍ
COMMENDED
Station Road, Fordingbridge,
SP6 1JP
☎ (0425) 52060
© Minotels
*Owner-managed country hotel
on the edge of the New Forest.
Good touring centre, ideal for
fishermen. Personal service.*
Bedrooms: 5 single, 9 double
& 7 twin, 2 family rooms.
Bathrooms: 23 private.
Bed & breakfast: £32-£35
single, £60-£70 double.
Half board: £36-£47 daily,
£230-£259 weekly.
Lunch available.
Evening meal 7.30pm (l.o.
9.30pm).
Parking for 60.
Credit: Access, Visa.

The enquiry
coupons at the
back will help you
when contacting
proprietors.

The Old Post Office
Purlieu Lane, Godshill,
Fordingbridge, SP6 2LW
☎ (0425) 53719
*On the edge of the New Forest
and ideal for touring.*
Bedrooms: 1 double & 2 twin.
Bathrooms: 1 public.
Bed & breakfast: £9 single,
£18 double.
Half board: £14 daily, £80
weekly.
Evening meal 6pm (l.o. 9pm).
Parking for 4.

Rakes Restaurant ᴍ
Listed
29-31 High Street,
Fordingbridge, SP1 6AS
☎ (0425) 52006
*300-year-old building, with
beams, open fires and garden
to River Avon. Parking
available opposite.*
Bedrooms: 1 single, 3 double
& 1 twin.
Bathrooms: 1 public.
Bed & breakfast: £17.50-£30
single, £35-£45 double.
Half board: £27.50-£35 daily.
Lunch available.
Evening meal 7.30pm (l.o.
9pm).
Open February-December.
Credit: Access, Visa, Diners,
Amex.

Hampshire
Map ref 2C3

From a tiny fishing
hamlet, Gosport has
grown into an important
centre with many naval
establishments, including
HMS Dolphin, the
submarine base, with the
Naval Submarine
Museum which preserves
HMS Alliance and
Holland I.

Abbey Guest House ᴍ
4 Foster Road, Alverstoke,
Gosport, PO12 2JJ
☎ (0705) 523523
*Newly refurbished guest house,
close to shops, bus routes, the
Solent, HMS Alliance, sailing
and slipway facilities. 1 mile
from Gosport/Portsmouth
ferry.*
Bedrooms: 2 twin, 3 family
rooms.
Bathrooms: 2 public.
Bed & breakfast: £15-£20
single, £25-£30 double.

Half board: £20 daily, £120
weekly.
Parking for 7.

The Kelly Hotel ᴍ
46-48 Bury Road, Gosport,
PO12 3UB
☎ (0705) 586309
*Named after HMS Kelly, the
commander of which was Lord
Mountbatten, and featuring a
museum in the main bar.*
Bedrooms: 6 single, 6 double
& 3 twin.
Bathrooms: 6 private,
2 public.
Bed & breakfast: from £28.50
single, from £44 double.
Half board: £36-£52 daily,
£189-£273 weekly.
Lunch available.
Evening meal 7pm (l.o.
10.30pm).
Parking for 20.
Credit: Access, Visa, Amex.

Rob Roy Guest House
16 Foster Road, Alverstoke,
Gosport, PO12 2JJ
☎ (0705) 583073
*Small, friendly, family guest
house, approximately 1 mile
from sea front.*
Bedrooms: 2 single, 2 double
& 1 twin.
Bathrooms: 1 public.
Bed & breakfast: £10-£12
single, £20-£24 double.

Hampshire
Map ref 2C3

Once a market town
famous for making
parchment. Nearby at
Leigh Park extensive
early 19th C landscape
gardens and parklands
are open to the public.
Right in the centre of the
town stands the
interesting 13th C church
of St. Faith.
*Tourist Information
Centre ☎ (0705) 480024*

Bear Hotel ᴍ
East Street, Havant,
PO9 1AA
☎ (0705) 486501
Telex 869136
© Lansbury
*A Lansbury hotel in a town
centre location, close to shops,
A27/M27, bus and rail station,
Chichester and Portsmouth.*

Bedrooms: 14 single,
15 double & 11 twin, 2 family
rooms.
Bathrooms: 42 private.
Bed & breakfast: £33-£71
single, £66-£85 double.
Half board: £44-£100 daily.
Lunch available.
Evening meal 7pm (l.o.
10pm).
Parking for 150.
Credit: Access, Visa, Diners,
Amex.

Holland Guest House ᴍ
33 Bedhampton Hill, Havant,
PO9 3JN
☎ (0705) 475913
Fax (0705) 470134
*Comfortable, friendly
guesthouse, ideal for touring,
continental ferry port, business
and the sea.*
Bedrooms: 4 single, 1 double,
1 family room.
Bathrooms: 1 public.
Bed & breakfast: £13-£18
single, £25-£30 double.
Evening meal 5pm (l.o.
6.45pm).
Parking for 6.

Hampshire
Map ref 2C3

Small, flat island of
historic interest,
surrounded by natural
harbours and with fine
sandy beaches, linked to
the mainland by a road.
*Tourist Information
Centre ☎ (0705) 467111*

Broad Oak Country Hotel ᴍ
Copse Lane, Hayling Island,
PO11 0QB
☎ (0705) 461188
*Family-run establishment
overlooking Chichester
Harbour, with rural walks
nearby and plenty of parking
at hotel. A must if you want to
relax.*
Bedrooms: 10 double &
10 twin.
Bathrooms: 20 private,
4 public.
Bed & breakfast: £14-£16
single, £26-£30 double.
Half board: £21-£23 daily,
£140-£155 weekly.
Lunch available.

Evening meal 5.50pm (l.o. 6pm).
Parking for 8.

[symbols]

Cockle Warren Cottage Hotel M
[rating symbols]
36 Seafront, Hayling Island, PO11 9HL
☎ (0705) 464961
Seafront hotel set in large garden with heated swimming pool. Attractive four-poster bedroom suite. Candlelit dinners with French and English country cooking. Log fires in winter.
Bedrooms: 4 double & 1 twin.
Bathrooms: 5 private.
Bed & breakfast: £30-£45 single, £48-£68 double.
Half board: £44-£54 daily.
Evening meal 8pm (l.o. 4pm).
Parking for 9.
Credit: Access, Visa.

[symbols]

Newtown House Hotel M
[rating symbols]
Manor Road, Hayling Island, PO11 0QR
☎ (0705) 466131
Fax (0705) 461366
Set in own grounds, a quarter of a mile from seafront. New indoor leisure complex with heated pool, gym and jacuzzi.
Bedrooms: 10 single, 11 double & 4 twin, 3 family rooms.
Bathrooms: 26 private, 2 public.
Bed & breakfast: £30-£42 single.
Half board: £28-£36 daily, £185-£210 weekly.
Lunch available.
Evening meal 7pm (l.o. 9.30pm).
Parking for 45.
Credit: Access, Visa, Diners, Amex.

[symbols]

The Rook Hollow Hotel M
[rating symbols] COMMENDED
84 Church Road, Hayling Island, PO11 0NX
☎ (0705) 467080 & 469620
Very comfortable, pretty hotel. Relax in a friendly atmosphere with Wendy and Pam as your hosts.
Bedrooms: 1 single, 2 double & 4 twin.
Bathrooms: 4 private, 1 public.

Bed & breakfast: £20-£23 single, £36-£48 double.
Half board: £26-£43 daily, £170-£201 weekly.
Lunch available.
Evening meal 6pm (l.o. 9pm).
Parking for 9.
Credit: Access, Visa, Diners, Amex.

[symbols]

HEDGE END
Hampshire
Map ref 2C3

5m E. Southampton
Busy residential and shopping suburb 2 miles west of Botley.

Copper Beeches House Hotel M
Listed
72 Lower Northam Road, Hedge End, Nr. Southampton, SO3 4FT
☎ Botley (0489) 787447
Nicely furnished accommodation with happy atmosphere. In centre of thriving country town, 3 minutes from M27 junction 7 or 8.
Bedrooms: 5 single, 4 double, 1 family room.
Bathrooms: 2 private, 2 public.
Bed & breakfast: £17.50-£24.50 single, £32-£36 double.
Evening meal 6pm (l.o. 9pm).
Parking for 16.

[symbols]

HOOK
Hampshire
Map ref 2C2

Astride the A30 some 6 miles east of Basingstoke.

Raven Hotel M
[rating symbols]
Station Road, Hook, Nr. Basingstoke, RG27 9HS
☎ (0256) 762541
Telex 858901
⊛ Lansbury
In Hook village, convenient for Basingstoke and Hampshire countryside.
Bedrooms: 2 single, 21 double & 15 twin.
Bathrooms: 38 private.
Bed & breakfast: £27-£71 single, £54-£85 double.
Half board: £38-£100 daily.
Lunch available.
Evening meal 7pm (l.o. 10pm).

Parking for 100.
Credit: Access, Visa, Diners, Amex.

[symbols]

HORNDEAN
Hampshire
Map ref 2C3

8m NE. Portsmouth

The Ship & Bell Hotel
[rating symbols]
6 London Road, Horndean, Portsmouth, PO8 0BZ
☎ Portsmouth (0705) 592107
A former 17th C coaching inn with plenty of character, on the A3. Site of the original Gales Brewery.
Bedrooms: 8 double & 5 twin.
Bathrooms: 13 private.
Bed & breakfast: from £35 single, from £45 double.
Half board: £25-£35 daily, £175-£245 weekly.
Lunch available.
Evening meal 7pm (l.o. 9.30pm).
Parking for 20.
Credit: Access, Visa.

[symbols]

HURN
Dorset
Map ref 2B3

Site of the international Bournemouth Airport.

Avon Causeway Hotel & Orient Restaurant M
[rating symbols]
Hurn, Christchurch, BH23 6AS
☎ (0202) 482714 Fax (0202) 708488
Family hotel and public freehouse set in countryside near Bournemouth and Hurn Airport. Formerly a railway station. Bars specialise in serving real ales and there is a train and Pullman carriage, now an Indian restaurant.
Bedrooms: 1 single, 10 double & 2 twin.
Bathrooms: 13 private.
Bed & breakfast: £35-£45 single, £49.95-£89 double.
Half board: £35-£89 daily.
Lunch available.
Evening meal 6.30pm (l.o. 9pm).
Parking for 100.
Credit: Access, Visa, Amex.

[symbols]

Parking for 100.
Credit: Access, Visa, Diners, Amex.

[symbols]

ISLE OF WIGHT-ALVERSTONE
Isle of Wight
Map ref 2C3

The Grange M
[rating symbols] COMMENDED
Alverstone, Nr. Sandown, PO36 0EZ
☎ (0983) 403729
A family-run guesthouse set in the peaceful surroundings of Alverstone, below the downs and yet only 2 miles from sandy beaches.
Bedrooms: 1 single, 2 double & 3 twin, 1 family room.
Bathrooms: 7 private.
Bed & breakfast: £16.50-£18 single, £33-£36 double.
Half board: £27-£30 daily, £144-£167 weekly.
Evening meal 6.30pm (l.o. 7.30pm).
Parking for 6.
Open April-October.

[symbols]

ISLE OF WIGHT-BONCHURCH
Isle of Wight
Map ref 2C3

1m NE. Ventnor
Sheltered suburb at the foot of St. Boniface Down.

The Lake Hotel M
[rating symbols]
Shore Road, Bonchurch, Ventnor, PO38 1RF
☎ (0983) 852613
Charming country house hotel set in 2 acres of beautiful gardens, in secluded situation 400 metres from beach.
Bedrooms: 2 single, 8 double & 4 twin, 7 family rooms.
Bathrooms: 19 private, 5 public.
Bed & breakfast: £15-£17 single, £30-£34 double.
Half board: £20-£26 daily, £136.50-£156.50 weekly.
Evening meal 6.30pm (l.o. 7pm).
Parking for 20.
Open March-October.

[symbols]

> **Half board prices shown are per person but in some cases may be based on double/twin occupancy.**

ISLE OF WIGHT- CALBOURNE

Isle of Wight
Map ref 2C3

Village on the B3401, midway between the north and south coasts.

Swainston Manor Hotel & Restaurant ⋀
≝≝≝≝

Calbourne, PO30 4HX
☎ (0983) 521121 Fax (0983) 521406
11th C manor set in 32 acres of verdant countryside, offering a high standard of accommodation and food.
Bedrooms: 2 single, 4 double & 4 twin, 3 family rooms.
Bathrooms: 13 private.
Bed & breakfast: £45-£56 single, £68-£82 double.
Half board: £48.50-£69.50 daily, £321.20-£471.75 weekly.
Lunch available.
Evening meal 7.30pm (l.o. 10.30pm).
Parking for 200.
Credit: Access, Visa, Diners, Amex.

ISLE OF WIGHT- COLWELL BAY

Isle of Wight
Map ref 2C3

2-mile curving stretch of sand.

Ontario Private Hotel ⋀
≝≝

Colwell Common Road, Colwell Bay, Freshwater, PO39 0DD
☎ (0983) 753237
4 minutes from beach offering accommodation of a high standard with licensed bar, choice of menu. Children and pets welcome.
Bedrooms: 1 single, 2 double & 1 twin, 3 family rooms.
Bathrooms: 3 private, 2 public; 2 private showers.
Bed & breakfast: £15-£17 single, £30-£34 double.
Half board: £21-£23.50 daily, £135-£150 weekly.
Evening meal 6.30pm (l.o. 7pm).
Parking for 9.

ISLE OF WIGHT- COWES

Isle of Wight
Map ref 2C3

Regular ferry and hovercraft services cross the Solent to Cowes. The town is the headquarters of the Royal Yacht Squadron and Cowes Week is held every August.

Crossways House ⋀

Crossways Road, Osborne, Cowes, PO32 6LJ
☎ (0983) 293677
Victorian house set in its own grounds between Osborne House and Barton Manor.
Bedrooms: 1 single, 1 double & 1 twin, 1 family room.
Bathrooms: 2 private, 2 public.
Bed & breakfast: £25 single, £30-£40 double.
Half board: £28-£30 daily, £160-£200 weekly.
Lunch available.
Evening meal 7pm (l.o. 8.30pm).
Parking for 15.

Halcyone Villa ⋀

Grove Road, off Millhill Road, Cowes, PO31 7JP
☎ (0983) 291334
Small, homely Victorian guesthouse with large, comfortable rooms and many English elmwood features.
Bedrooms: 2 single, 2 twin, 1 family room.
Bathrooms: 2 private, 2 public.
Bed & breakfast: £14-£17 single, £25-£27.50 double.
Half board: £18-£30 daily.
Evening meal 7.30pm.

Padmore House Hotel ⋀
≝≝≝≝ APPROVED

Beatrice Avenue, Whippingham, East Cowes, PO32 6LP
☎ (0983) 293210
Beautifully situated in tranquil surroundings overlooking the Medina Valley. 1 mile from Osborne House and close to ferries and hydrofoil.
Bedrooms: 3 single, 3 double & 3 twin.
Bathrooms: 8 private, 1 public; 1 private shower.
Bed & breakfast: £35-£43 single, £65-£70 double.

Half board: £45-£50 daily, £185-£215 weekly.
Lunch available.
Evening meal 7.30pm (l.o. 9.30pm).
Parking for 30.
Credit: Access, Visa, Diners, Amex.

ISLE OF WIGHT- FRESHWATER

Isle of Wight
Map ref 2C3

This part of the island is associated with Tennyson, who lived in the village for 30 years. A monument on Tennyson's Down commemorates the poet.

Denehurst ⋀
APPROVED

Colwell Road, Freshwater, PO40 9SW
☎ (0983) 752571
Small family guest house close to beach and downs. Evening meal and choice of menu. Ample parking.
Bedrooms: 1 single, 4 family rooms.
Bathrooms: 1 public.
Bed & breakfast: £14 single, £28 double.
Half board: £20 daily, max. £140 weekly.
Evening meal 6pm (l.o. midday).
Parking for 6.

Farringford Hotel ⋀
≝≝≝

Bedbury Lane, Freshwater, PO40 9PE
☎ (0983) 752500 & 752700
Telex 417165
Set in 33-acre grounds, offers traditional hotel service and also self-catering suites, the best of both worlds. 9-hole golf-course available.
Bedrooms: 3 single, 29 double & 29 twin, 7 family rooms.
Bathrooms: 68 private.
Bed & breakfast: £25-£40 single, £50-£80 double.
Half board: £35-£50 daily, £210-£300 weekly.
Lunch available.
Evening meal 7.30pm (l.o. 9.30pm).
Parking for 152.
Credit: Access, Visa, Diners, Amex.

Royal Standard Hotel ⋀
≝≝≝

School Green Road, Freshwater, PO40 9AJ
☎ (0983) 753227
Small, family-run hotel, serving comprehensive bar meals. 2 bars, restaurant, function room, freehouse.
Bedrooms: 1 single, 3 double & 1 twin, 2 family rooms.
Bathrooms: 6 private; 1 private shower.
Bed & breakfast: £20-£25 single, £40-£50 double.
Lunch available.
Evening meal 6pm (l.o. 10pm).
Parking for 5.

ISLE OF WIGHT- NEWPORT

Isle of Wight
Map ref 2C3

Commercial capital of the island, lying on the River Medina. Vessels sail into the harbour from Cowes. The town has many historic buildings including the Old Grammar School which was the lodging for Charles II.
Tourist Information Centre ☎ *(0983) 525450*

Martinique

94 Carisbrooke Road, Newport, PO30 1DB
☎ (0983) 522470
Charming Victorian house with gardens and heated pool, 10 minutes' walk from town. 1 en-suite room, colour TV and tea making. American chef.
Bedrooms: 1 double & 1 twin, 1 family room.
Bathrooms: 1 private, 1 public.
Bed & breakfast: £15-£17 single, £28-£34 double.
Half board: £21-£23 daily, £145-£155 weekly.
Lunch available.
Evening meal 6pm (l.o. 7pm).
Parking for 4.

The symbols are explained on the flap inside the back cover.

ISLE OF WIGHT-NITON

Isle of Wight
Map ref 2C3

Part in hollow of the Downs, part along the Undercliff terrace. Once renowned for crabs and for its smuggling activities. Good walking area. St. Catherine's Lighthouse can be visited.

Pine Ridge Country House M
👑👑👑

Niton Undercliff, Ventnor, PO38 2LY
☎ (0983) 730802
Spacious, elegant country house set in 2.5 acres of garden with panoramic views of the sea and surrounding countryside.
Bedrooms: 2 double & 2 twin, 3 family rooms.
Bathrooms: 7 private, 1 public.
Bed & breakfast: from £26 single, from £52 double.
Half board: from £37 daily, from £230 weekly.
Evening meal 7pm (l.o. 8.30pm).
Parking for 12.

ISLE OF WIGHT-RYDE

Isle of Wight
Map ref 2C3

The island's chief entry port, connected to Portsmouth by ferries and hovercraft. 7 miles of sandy beaches with a half-mile pier, esplanade and gardens.

Brantoria Guest House M

44 St. Thomas Street, Ryde, PO33 2DL
☎ (0983) 62724
1 minute from the beach, with car park opposite. Close to ferry and public transport.
Bedrooms: 2 double & 2 twin, 1 family room.
Bathrooms: 1 public.
Bed & breakfast: max. £12 single, max. £24 double.
Half board: max. £18 daily, max. £90 weekly.
Evening meal 6pm.

Dean House Hotel M
👑👑👑

2 Dover Street, Ryde, PO33 2AQ
☎ (0983) 62535
Comfortable, privately-run hotel with excellent restaurant, open all year. Overlooking the Solent, 2 minutes' walk to hovercraft, bus and train terminals, close to town centre. Weekend and Christmas packages available.
Bedrooms: 1 single, 5 double & 3 twin, 5 family rooms.
Bathrooms: 7 private, 2 public.
Bed & breakfast: £20-£28 single, £40-£50 double.
Half board: £28.75-£36.75 daily, £135-£170 weekly.
Lunch available.
Evening meal 6.30pm (l.o. 9.45pm).
Parking for 12.
Credit: Access, Visa, Diners, Amex.

Hotel Ryde Castle M
👑👑👑

Esplanade, Ryde, PO33 1JA
☎ (0983) 63755 Telex 869466 TARAS-G
16th C castle, built by Henry VIII to defend Spithead, overlooking Serpentine. Beautifully furnished, well-appointed en-suite rooms. Renowned for fresh cuisine.
Bedrooms: 6 single, 6 double & 3 twin, 2 family rooms.
Bathrooms: 17 private.
Bed & breakfast: £49.50-£64.90 single, £65.90-£88 double.
Half board: £55-£69.90 daily, £330-£465 weekly.
Lunch available.
Evening meal 7pm (l.o. 10pm).
Parking for 75.
Credit: Access, Visa, Diners, Amex.

Yelf's Hotel M
👑👑👑

Union Street, Ryde, PO33 2LG
☎ (0983) 64602 Fax (0983) 63937
Once an important coaching house, Yelf's has become a popular base for holidaymakers seeking the island's many attractions.
Bedrooms: 5 single, 5 double & 9 twin, 2 family rooms.
Bathrooms: 21 private.
Half board: max. £40 daily, from £245 weekly.
Lunch available.

Evening meal 7pm (l.o. 9pm).
Credit: Access, Visa, Diners, Amex.

ISLE OF WIGHT-SANDOWN

Isle of Wight
Map ref 2C3

The 6-mile sweep of Sandown Bay is one of the island's finest stretches, with excellent sands. The pier has a pavilion and sun terrace; the esplanade has amusements, bars, eating-places and gardens.
Tourist Information Centre ☎ (0983) 403886

Cygnet Hotel M

Carter Street, Sandown, PO36 8DQ
☎ (0983) 402930
Outdoor pool, indoor pool and sauna, jacuzzi, solarium. Licensed bar, tea facilities all rooms, lifts, heated. Open all year.
Bedrooms: 6 single, 21 double & 18 twin, 9 family rooms.
Bathrooms: 32 private, 6 public.
Bed & breakfast: £18-£22 single, £34-£42 double.
Half board: £25-£30.83 daily, £150-£185 weekly.
Evening meal 6.30pm.
Parking for 40.

Denecroft

53 Grove Road, Sandown, PO36 8HH
☎ (0983) 404412
Clean and comfortable, with separate dining tables and resident (City & Guilds) chef. Run personally by owners, Mr. & Mrs. MacDougall.
Bedrooms: 2 double & 1 twin, 3 family rooms.
Bathrooms: 1 private, 1 public.
Bed & breakfast: £16-£17.50 single, £23-£26 double.
Half board: £17.50-£19 daily, £112-£119 weekly.
Evening meal 6pm (l.o. 7pm).
Parking for 5.
Open April-October.

Inglewood M

15 Avenue Road, Sandown, PO36 8BN
☎ (0983) 403485

Family-run, well-situated guesthouse. Close to sea and amenities, including pitch and putt, tennis and sports centre.
Bedrooms: 2 double & 2 twin, 3 family rooms.
Bathrooms: 3 public.
Bed & breakfast: £11-£13 single, £22-£26 double.
Half board: £13.50-£15.50 daily, £84-£99 weekly.
Evening meal 6pm.
Open March-October.

May Dene M
Listed

22 George Street, Sandown, PO36 8JB
☎ (0983) 402650
Homely, family-run guest house, 2 minutes from sea, shops and leisure centre. Lunch provided on request.
Bedrooms: 1 single, 1 double & 1 twin, 2 family rooms.
Bathrooms: 1 public.
Bed & breakfast: £11 single, £22 double.
Half board: £13.50 daily, £92 weekly.
Evening meal 6.15pm (l.o. 6.15pm).
Parking for 2.

Montrene Hotel M
👑👑👑 COMMENDED

Avenue Road, Sandown, PO36 8BN
☎ (0983) 403722
Well situated standing in its own grounds within 100 yards of the beach. Leisure complex with indoor heated pool.
Bedrooms: 5 single, 12 double & 8 twin, 20 family rooms.
Bathrooms: 39 private, 4 public.
Bed & breakfast: £20-£25 single, £40-£50 double.
Half board: £27-£33 daily, £189-£231 weekly.
Lunch available.
Evening meal 6pm (l.o. 7pm).
Parking for 39.
Credit: Access, Visa.

Philomel Private Hotel M

21 Carter Street, Sandown, PO36 8BL
☎ (0983) 402869
12-bedroom, family-run hotel, established 27 years. En-suite rooms, free parking, special offers early and late season.

Continued ▶

ISLE OF WIGHT-
SANDOWN

Continued

Bedrooms: 3 single, 1 double
& 4 twin, 4 family rooms.
Bathrooms: 3 private,
3 public.
Half board: £17-£18.50 daily,
£120-£132 weekly.
Evening meal 6pm (l.o. 6pm).
Parking for 8.
Open April-October.

Rivelin Guest House M

36 Broadway, Sandown,
PO36 9BZ
☎ (0983) 404620
*Family-run guesthouse with
warm and friendly atmosphere,
offering comfortable
accommodation, home cooking,
no fuss and no restrictions.
Children welcome.*
Bedrooms: 1 single, 2 double
& 2 twin, 2 family rooms.
Bathrooms: 2 public.
Bed & breakfast: £10-£12
single, £20-£24 double.
Half board: £14-£16 daily,
£91-£105 weekly.
Evening meal 6pm (l.o.
6.30pm).
Parking for 6.
Open April-October.

Rooftree Hotel M

APPROVED

26 Broadway, Sandown,
PO36 9BY
☎ (0983) 403175
*A small, detached, licensed
hotel with a pleasant garden.
Central for touring the island.
Emphasis placed on a very
tempting menu.*
Bedrooms: 1 single, 4 double
& 1 twin, 4 family rooms.
Bathrooms: 2 private,
2 public.
Bed & breakfast: £14-£16
single, £28-£32 double.
Half board: £16.50-£20 daily,
£110-£130 weekly.
Lunch available.
Evening meal 6.30pm (l.o.
9pm).
Parking for 10.

Sandham Lodge M

30 Nunwell Street, Sandown,
PO36 9DE
☎ (0983) 402714
*Licensed, family hotel in quiet,
secluded area, yet central for
all amenities. Some en-suite
rooms, children welcome, any
day booking and car park.*

Bedrooms: 1 single, 6 double,
5 family rooms.
Bathrooms: 8 private,
2 public.
Bed & breakfast: £16.50-£19
single.
Half board: £19.10-£21.58
daily, £88.70-£140 weekly.
Evening meal 6pm.
Parking for 9.

ISLE OF WIGHT-
SEAVIEW

Isle of Wight
Map ref 2C3

Has a sandy beach and is
very much a family resort.
Good prawn and lobster
fishing.

Northbank Hotel

Circular Road, Seaview,
PO34 5ET
☎ (0983) 612227
*A family hotel by the sea. In a
splendid position on Seaview
waterfront, with magnificent
views of the Solent.*
Bedrooms: 8 single, 6 double
& 4 twin, 2 family rooms.
Bathrooms: 5 public.
Bed & breakfast: £20-£30
single, £40-£60 double.
Half board: £34-£44 daily,
£200-£255 weekly.
Lunch available.
Evening meal 7pm (l.o. 9pm).
Parking for 18.
Open April-October.

Seaview Hotel M

APPROVED

High Street, Seaview,
PO34 5EX
☎ (0983) 612711
*Small, professionally-run,
family hotel next to sea, with
well-known and exceptionally
busy restaurant specialising in
local fish.*
Bedrooms: 4 double &
12 twin.
Bathrooms: 16 private,
2 public.
Bed & breakfast: £40-£63
single, £66-£73 double.
Half board: £42-£70 daily,
£294-£490 weekly.
Lunch available.
Evening meal 7pm (l.o.
10pm).
Parking for 14.
Credit: Access, Visa, Amex.

ISLE OF WIGHT-
SHANKLIN

Isle of Wight
Map ref 2C3

Set on a cliff with gentle
slopes leading down to
the beach, esplanade and
marine gardens. The
picturesque, old thatched
village nestles at the end
of the wooded chine.
*Tourist Information
Centre* ☎ *(0983) 862942*

Alverstone Manor
Hotel M

COMMENDED

32 Luccombe Road, Shanklin,
PO37 6RR
☎ (0983) 862586
*In its own grounds overlooking
Sandown/Shanklin Bay.
Within easy reach of old
village, town and beach. 2
acres of gardens with heated
swimming pool, lawn tennis
court and putting green.*
Bedrooms: 1 single, 3 double
& 1 twin, 7 family rooms.
Bathrooms: 11 private,
3 public.
Bed & breakfast: £22-£25
single, £44-£50 double.
Half board: £27-£31 daily,
£189-£217 weekly.
Evening meal 6.30pm (l.o.
7.30pm).
Parking for 15.
Open March-October.

Avenue Hotel M

COMMENDED

6 Avenue Road, Shanklin,
PO37 7BG
☎ (0983) 862746
*Affordable hotel, ideal for
couples. Featuring a unique
romantic dining room with
heart-shaped tables and
attractive cuisine.*
Bedrooms: 1 single, 5 double
& 2 twin, 2 family rooms.
Bathrooms: 8 private,
2 public.
Bed & breakfast: £16-£18
single, £30-£34 double.
Half board: £22.50-£24.50
daily, £137.50-£157.50 weekly.
Evening meal 6.30pm.
Parking for 7.
Credit: Access, Visa.

Bourne Hall Country
Hotel M

COMMENDED

Luccombe Road, Shanklin,
PO37 6RR
☎ (0983) 862820
CR Minotels
*Country house atmosphere. In
3 acres at the foot of the
downs, close to the sea and Old
Village.*
Bedrooms: 14 double &
7 twin, 7 family rooms.
Bathrooms: 28 private,
1 public.
Bed & breakfast: £30.87-
£41.56 single, £51.75-£73.12
double.
Half board: £36-£43.30 daily,
£238.50-£291.37 weekly.
Evening meal 6.30pm (l.o.
8.30pm).
Parking for 25.
Open February-December.
Credit: Access, Visa, Diners,
Amex.

Brunswick Hotel M

COMMENDED

Queens Road, Shanklin,
PO37 6AN
☎ (0983) 863245
*Well-situated hotel offering all
modern amenities. Fresh local
produce used when available.
Commands a fine position.*
Bedrooms: 2 single, 11 double
& 11 twin, 10 family rooms.
Bathrooms: 34 private,
1 public.
Bed & breakfast: £25-£40
single.
Evening meal 7pm (l.o. 8pm).
Parking for 25.
Open March-November.
Credit: Access, Visa.

The Bungalow Hotel M

COMMENDED

Luccombe Road, Shanklin,
PO37 6RQ
☎ (0983) 862178
*Family-run licensed hotel with
panoramic sea views
overlooking the bay. A few
minutes' walk from Shanklin's
old village.*
Bedrooms: 1 single, 10 double
& 6 twin, 6 family rooms.
Bathrooms: 12 private,
3 public.
Half board: £23-£29 daily,
£154-£196 weekly.
Lunch available.
Evening meal 6.30pm (l.o.
7pm).
Parking for 20.

**Please mention this guide when making
a booking.**

The Carlton Hotel M

☼☼☼

9 Park Road, Shanklin,
PO37 6AY
☎ (0983) 862517
*Small family-run hotel with
beautiful sea views. All rooms
with colour TV and tea/coffee
making facilities. Home
cooking and licensed.*
Bedrooms: 2 single, 6 double
& 3 twin, 2 family rooms.
Bathrooms: 11 private,
2 public.
Bed & breakfast: £20-£24
single, £40-£48 double.
Half board: £24-£28 daily,
£160-£190 weekly.
Lunch available.
Evening meal 6.30pm (l.o.
7pm).
Parking for 10.
Credit: Access, Visa.
🛏 🖚 🗗 ❁ 👗 Ⓥ ㅔ 🆃🆅 ▦
🚪 ❊ 🛠 🛏 OAP 🐾 SP

Culham Lodge M

☼☼☼

31 Landguard Manor Road,
Shanklin, PO37 7HZ
☎ (0983) 862880
*Charming hotel in beautiful
tree-lined road, with heated
swimming pool, solarium,
conservatory, home cooking
and personal service.*
Bedrooms: 1 single, 6 double
& 3 twin.
Bathrooms: 8 private,
2 public.
Bed & breakfast: £13-£14
single, £26-£28 double.
Half board: £18-£19 daily,
£110-£120 weekly.
Evening meal 6pm (l.o. 4pm).
Parking for 8.
Open April-October.
🛏12 🖚 ❁ UL 👗 Ⓥ ㅔ 🆃🆅
▦ 🚪 ❊ 🛠 🛏 OAP SP 🆃

Fernbank Hotel M

☼☼☼☼ COMMENDED

Highfield Road, Shanklin,
PO37 6PP
☎ (0983) 862790
*Fernbank enjoys one of the
most beautiful positions in the
town of Shanklin with
uninterrupted views of country
and downland.*
Bedrooms: 1 single, 18 double
& 1 twin, 9 family rooms.
Bathrooms: 29 private,
1 public.
Half board: £28.80-£31.20
daily, £173-£223 weekly.
Lunch available.
Evening meal 6.30pm (l.o.
8.30pm).
Parking for 22.
Credit: Access, Visa.
🛏7 🖚 🗗 📞 Ⓡ 🗗 ❁ Ⓥ
ㅔ ▦ 🚪 ❊ 🔔 🐾 OAP SP
🆃

Hambledon Hotel M

☼☼☼ COMMENDED •

11 Queens Road, Shanklin,
PO37 6AW
☎ (0983) 862403
*Small, family-run hotel
providing varied food, comfort
and friendly service. All rooms
en-suite, central position. Open
all year.*
Bedrooms: 1 single, 4 double
& 2 twin, 4 family rooms.
Bathrooms: 11 private,
1 public.
Bed & breakfast: £17-£20
single, £17-£40 double.
Half board: £23-£26 daily,
£118-£159 weekly.
Evening meal 6.30pm (l.o.
6.30pm).
Parking for 9.
Credit: Access, Visa.
🛏 🖚 📞 Ⓡ 🗗 ❁ 👗 Ⓥ ㅔ
🆃🆅 ❁ 🛠 🛏 SP 🆃

Hazelwood Hotel M

☼☼☼

14 Clarence Road, Shanklin,
PO37 7BH
☎ (0983) 862824
*Small, friendly, comfortable
hotel, in a quiet, tree-lined road
close to all amenities.*
Bedrooms: 1 single, 3 double
& 2 twin, 4 family rooms.
Bathrooms: 6 private,
2 public.
Bed & breakfast: £13-£14
single, £26-£28 double.
Half board: £17-£18 daily,
£108-£116 weekly.
Evening meal 6pm (l.o. 4pm).
Parking for 3.
Open March-October.
🛏2 🖚 ❁ UL 👗 ㅔ 🆃🆅 ❁
❊ 🛠 OAP 🆃

Holliers Hotel M

☼☼☼

Church Road, Old Village,
Shanklin, PO37 6NU
☎ (0983) 862764
Fax (0983) 867134
*Fully licensed hotel in the
heart of the old village, a short
walk from beach, town and
country.*
Bedrooms: 1 single, 25 double
& 3 twin, 7 family rooms.
Bathrooms: 36 private.
Bed & breakfast: £30-£33
single, £60-£66 double.
Half board: £42-£45 daily,
£245-£280 weekly.
Lunch available.
Evening meal 7pm (l.o.
8.30pm).
Parking for 40.
Credit: Access, Visa, Amex.
🛏 🖚 🗗 📞 Ⓡ 🗗 ❁ 👗 Ⓥ
ㅔ ▦ 🚪 🔔 🐾 🔔 ❊ 🛠
🐾 SP 🆃

Hope View Hotel M

☼☼☼

23 Hope Road, Shanklin,
PO37 6ED
☎ (0983) 863351
*Licensed, family-run hotel, 150
yards from beach, close to
shops. Coaches and children
welcome.*
Bedrooms: 4 single, 4 double
& 2 twin, 11 family rooms.
Bathrooms: 4 private,
3 public.
Half board: £16-£21 daily,
£110-£135 weekly.
Evening meal 6pm (l.o. 6pm).
Parking for 12.
Open March-October.
Credit: Access, Visa, Diners,
Amex.
🛏 🖚 ❁ Ⓥ ㅔ 🆃🆅 ▦ ❊ 🐾
SP

Keats Green Hotel M

☼☼☼

3 Queens Road, Shanklin,
PO37 6AN
☎ (0983) 862742
*Ideally situated on Keats
Green Park overlooking the
sea. 5 minutes' walk to the
beach, town centre and old
village.*
Bedrooms: 4 single, 14 double
& 13 twin, 3 family rooms.
Bathrooms: 33 private,
2 public.
Half board: £125-£195
weekly.
Lunch available.
Evening meal 6.45pm (l.o.
5.15pm).
Parking for 24.
Open March-October.
Credit: Visa.
🛏 Ⓡ 🗗 ❁ 👗 Ⓥ ✂ ㅔ ◐
▦ 🚪 ❊ 🐾 OAP 🐾 SP 🔔

Landguard Manor M

☼☼☼

Shanklin, PO37 7JB
☎ (0983) 864811
Telex 667047
*The manor stands in its own
extensive grounds on the
outskirts of Shanklin, the
record holder for sunshine in
the British Isles.*
Bedrooms: 5 single, 16 twin,
9 family rooms.
Bathrooms: 14 public.
Half board: £23.50-£25 daily,
£163-£177 weekly.
Lunch available.
Evening meal 7pm.
Parking for 20.
Open May-September.
🛏2 🖚 UL 👗 Ⓥ ㅔ 🚪 ❊
🛠 🛏 OAP SP 🆃

Melbourne-Ardenlea Hotel M

☼☼☼

4-6 Queens Road, Shanklin,
PO37 6AP
☎ (0983) 862283
*A family-run hotel, providing
service and courtesy in pleasant
surroundings.*
Bedrooms: 9 single, 12 double
& 19 twin, 12 family rooms.
Bathrooms: 52 private,
2 public.
Bed & breakfast: £18-£30
single, £36-£60 double.
Half board: £23-£36 daily,
£161-£252 weekly.
Lunch available.
Evening meal 6.30pm (l.o.
8pm).
Parking for 30.
Open March-October.
Credit: Access, Visa.
🛏 🖚 🗗 ❁ 👗 Ⓥ ㅔ 🆃🆅 ▦
▦ 🚪 🔔 🐾 ❁ 🐾 ❊ 🛠 SP

Orchardcroft Hotel M

☼☼☼

Victoria Avenue, Shanklin,
PO37 6LT
☎ (0983) 862133
*Set in beautiful secluded
grounds, this elegant hotel
combines well-appointed
facilities with a friendly
atmosphere and personal service.*
Bedrooms: 2 single, 9 double
& 3 twin, 2 family rooms.
Bathrooms: 16 private,
1 public.
Bed & breakfast: £19.50-£24
single, £39-£48 double.
Half board: £26.50-£32 daily,
£176-£215 weekly.
Evening meal 6.45pm (l.o.
7.30pm).
Parking for 14.
Open February-November.
Credit: Access, Visa.
🛏5 🖚 🗗 ❁ 👗 Ⓥ ㅔ
🔔 🛏 🗗 ❁ 🐾 ❊ 🛠 OAP
🐾 SP 🆃

Osborne House Hotel M

☼☼☼ COMMENDED

Esplanade, Shanklin,
PO37 6BN
☎ (0983) 862501
*A tastefully modernised
Victorian residence, 25 yards
from the sea, where bookings
are accepted on a daily basis.
Dining room is non-smoking.*
Bedrooms: 1 single, 9 double
& 2 twin.
Bathrooms: 12 private,
2 public.
Bed & breakfast: from £26
single, from £52 double.
Half board: from £37.50 daily.
Evening meal 6pm (l.o. 8pm).
Open January-October.
Credit: Access, Visa.
🗗 ❁ 👗 ✂ ㅔ ▦ 🚪 🛠 ❁
SP 🆃

The symbols are
explained on the
flap inside the
back cover.

Continued

Queensmead Hotel M
≝≝≝

12 Queens Road, Shanklin,
PO37 6AN
☎ (0983) 862342
*Sea views, spacious public
rooms, heated swimming pool,
solarium, and choice of menu.*
Bedrooms: 2 single, 13 double
& 10 twin, 6 family rooms.
Bathrooms: 29 private,
2 public.
Bed & breakfast: £22-£27
single, £44-£54 double.
Half board: £27-£30 daily,
£175-£199 weekly.
Lunch available.
Evening meal 6.30pm (l.o.
6.30pm).
Parking for 20.
Open March-October,
December.
Credit: Access, Visa.
৯ ৬ ⛷ ◫ ❒ ⓥ ⌇ ⌅ ⓣⱽ
⠿ ▬ ♈ ⸙ ⍾ ⊁ ⸙ SP T

St. Leonards Hotel M
≝≝

22 Queens Road, Shanklin,
PO37 6AW
☎ (0983) 862121
*A 3-storey, family hotel,
pleasantly situated, set back
from road, with flower
bordered lawn and parking
facilities.*
Bedrooms: 2 double, 5 family
rooms.
Bathrooms: 4 private,
2 public.
Bed & breakfast: £13.80-
£15.50 single, £27.60-£31
double.
Half board: £18.80-£20.50
daily, £105.80-£126.50
weekly.
Evening meal 6pm.
Parking for 7.
Credit: Access, Visa.
৯ ❒ ⛷ ◫ ⓥ ⌅ ⓣⱽ ⠿ ▬
⊁ ⸙ ⍾ SP

Scotsgrove Guest House M
≝≝ APPROVED

4 Sandy Lane, Shanklin,
PO37 7DT
☎ (0983) 862565
*Charming, detached guest
house within easy reach of sea,
town, bus and railway station.
Friendly atmosphere.*
Bedrooms: 1 single, 4 double
& 2 twin, 3 family rooms.
Bathrooms: 1 private,
2 public.

Bed & breakfast: £11-£13
single, £22-£26 double.
Half board: £14-£16 daily,
£85-£99 weekly.
Evening meal 6pm (l.o.
6.30pm).
Parking for 10.
Open February-November.
৯ ৬ ⛷ ◫ ❒ ⓣⱽ ⠿ ⸙ ⊁
⸙ DAP SP T

Isle of Wight
Map ref 2C3

On the Freshwater
Peninsula. It is possible
to walk from here around
to Alum Bay.

The Nodes Country Hotel M
≝≝≝

Alum Bay Old Road, Totland
Bay, PO39 0HZ
☎ (0983) 752859
*A country house hotel in
extensive grounds with glorious
countryside and coastal views,
only 10 minutes' walk from
sandy beaches.*
Bedrooms: 1 single, 4 double
& 2 twin, 4 family rooms.
Bathrooms: 8 private,
2 public.
Bed & breakfast: £16-£21
single, £32-£42 double.
Half board: £23-£29.50 daily,
£150-£189 weekly.
Evening meal 6.30pm (l.o.
3pm).
Parking for 15.
৯ ৬ ⑩ ⛷ ◫ ⓥ ⌅ ⓣⱽ ⠿
▬ ♈ ⓤ ⌿ ⸙ ⸙ ⍾ SP

Sandford Lodge Hotel M
≝≝≝ COMMENDED

61 The Avenue, Totland Bay,
PO39 0DN
☎ (0983) 753478
*Delightfully placed for beaches
and downs. Quality home
cooking with an old world
dining room to complement its
taste, and a pretty bedroom to
end your day.*
Bedrooms: 2 single, 2 double
& 1 twin, 1 family room.
Bathrooms: 5 private;
1 private shower.
Bed & breakfast: £14-£19
single, £28-£35 double.
Half board: £20-£26 daily,
£115-£158 weekly.
Evening meal 7pm (l.o. 4pm).
Parking for 7.
৯ ⑩ ⛷ ◫ ⓥ ⌿ ⌅ ⓣⱽ ⠿
▬ ♈ ⊁ ⸙ DAP ⍾ SP

Isle of Wight
Map ref 2C3

Town lies at the bottom of
an 800-ft hill and has a
reputation as a winter
holiday and health resort
due to its mild climate.
There is a pier, small
esplanade and Winter
Gardens.

Bellevue Hotel M
≝≝≝

Bellevue Road, Ventnor,
PO38 1DB
☎ (0983) 855047
*Charming, Victorian building
with lovely views, providing all
desirable modern standards of
food and comfort. Minutes
from beach, town and downs.*
Bedrooms: 1 single, 3 double
& 2 twin, 4 family rooms.
Bathrooms: 6 private,
2 public.
Bed & breakfast: £14-£16
single, £28-£32 double.
Half board: £17.50-£19.50
daily, £120-£130 weekly.
Evening meal 6.30pm (l.o.
7pm).
Parking for 5.
Open April-October.
৯ ⛷ ◫ ⓥ ⌅ ⓣⱽ ⠿ ▬ ⊁
⸙ DAP SP T

Bonchurch Manor M
≝≝≝≝

The Shute, Bonchurch,
Ventnor, PO38 1NU
☎ (0983) 852868
*Delightful country house, set in
gardens overlooking sea in
peaceful village, with varied
choice of menu and indoor
pool.*
Bedrooms: 2 single, 5 double
& 3 twin, 2 family rooms.
Bathrooms: 11 private,
1 public.
Half board: £35-£40 daily,
£225-£260 weekly.
Evening meal 7pm (l.o.
9.30pm).
Parking for 11.
Open February-December.
Credit: Visa.
৯ 7 ⓛ ⓒ ❒ ⛷ ◫ ⓥ ⌅ ⠿
♈ ⌸ ⸙ ⸙ ⍾ SP ⌅ T

Briantree Hotel M
≝

36-38 Albert Street, Ventnor,
PO38 1EZ
☎ (0983) 852446
*Comfortable family-run hotel
on town level between beach
and town centre, providing
home cooking.*
Bedrooms: 1 single, 6 double
& 1 twin, 2 family rooms.

Bathrooms: 1 public;
6 private showers.
Bed & breakfast: £12.50-£13
single, £25-£26 double.
Half board: £16.50-£17 daily,
£100-£110 weekly.
Evening meal 6pm (l.o. 7pm).
৯ ৬ ⛷ ◫ ⌅ ⓣⱽ ⠿ DAP SP

Burlington Hotel M
≝≝≝

Bellevue Road, Ventnor,
PO38 1DB
☎ (0983) 852113
*Friendly family hotel with
heated swimming pool,
commanding wonderful sea
views. Central, yet affords
peace and quiet. All rooms en-
suite.*
Bedrooms: 3 single, 6 double
& 9 twin, 5 family rooms.
Bathrooms: 23 private,
1 public.
Half board: £25-£29 daily,
£175-£203 weekly.
Evening meal 6.30pm (l.o.
8pm).
Parking for 20.
Open March-October.
৯ 3 ৬ ⓛ ⓒ ❒ ⛷ ◫ ⌅
ⓣⱽ ⠿ ▬ ♈ ⊁ ⸙ ⍾ ⊁ ⸙ SP

Cornerways Hotel M
≝≝≝

39 Madeira Road, Ventnor,
PO38 1QS
☎ (0983) 852323
*A detached hotel situated in a
quiet position with all rooms
having views of the sea or
Boniface Downs.*
Bedrooms: 3 single, 2 double
& 2 twin, 5 family rooms.
Bathrooms: 6 private,
2 public.
Bed & breakfast: £14.25-
£15.75 single, £28.50-£31.50
double.
Half board: £19.25-£23 daily,
£134-£160 weekly.
Evening meal 6pm (l.o. 6pm).
Parking for 7.
৯ ৬ ⑩ ⛷ ◫ ⓥ ⌅ ⓣⱽ ⠿
DAP ⍾ SP T

Eversley Hotel M
≝≝≝≝ APPROVED

Park Avenue, Ventnor,
PO38 1LB
☎ (0983) 852244
*A family hotel next to Ventnor
Park offering varied food in
pleasant surroundings.*
Bedrooms: 6 single, 8 double
& 6 twin, 14 family rooms.
Bathrooms: 32 private,
3 public.
Bed & breakfast: £20-£25
single, £18-£22 double.
Half board: £25-£30 daily,
£150-£195 weekly.
Lunch available.
Evening meal 7pm (l.o.
8.30pm).

Parking for 23.
Open April-December.
Credit: Access, Visa.

Hillside Hotel M
😃😃😃 COMMENDED
Mitchell Avenue, Ventnor,
PO38 1DR
☎ (0983) 852271
*Ventnor's only thatched hotel,
built in 1801, in its own 2 acres
of beautifully wooded grounds
overlooking the sea.*
Bedrooms: 1 single, 7 double
& 2 twin, 1 family room.
Bathrooms: 11 private.
Bed & breakfast: £16-£18
single, £32-£36 double.
Half board: £22-£24 daily,
£154-£175 weekly.
Evening meal 6.30pm (l.o.
7pm).
Parking for 15.
Credit: Access, Visa.

The Lawyers Rest Country House Hotel M
😃😃😃 COMMENDED
Undercliff Drive, St.
Lawrence, Ventnor,
PO38 1XF
☎ (0983) 852610
*Early Victorian house in
picturesque coastal village with
superb views across suntrap
terraced gardens to the sea.
Elegant but informal.*
Bedrooms: 1 single, 5 double
& 2 twin.
Bathrooms: 8 private,
1 public.
Bed & breakfast: from £28.75
single, from £66.70 double.
Half board: £225-£235
weekly.
Lunch available.
Evening meal 7pm (l.o.
7.30pm).
Parking for 12.
Credit: Visa, Amex.

St. Maur Hotel M
😃😃😃 COMMENDED
Castle Road, Ventnor,
PO38 1LG
☎ (0983) 852570
*Conveniently situated near
town, beaches, cliff and
downland walks. Set in own
grounds overlooking Ventnor
Park and the sea.*
Bedrooms: 2 single, 4 double
& 4 twin, 4 family rooms.
Bathrooms: 13 private,
2 public.
Bed & breakfast: £14-£18
single, £32-£36 double.

Half board: £22-£24 daily,
£158-£169 weekly.
Evening meal 6.30pm (l.o.
7pm).
Parking for 14.
Open February-December.
Credit: Access, Visa.

The Ventnor Towers Hotel M
😃😃😃 COMMENDED
Madeira Road, Ventnor,
PO38 1QT
☎ (0983) 852277
Telex 8951182 GECOMS
Ⓒ Consort
*Family-run hotel with
extensive leisure facilities in
own grounds overlooking the
sea. Comfortable rooms with
beautiful views. 5-course table
d'hote and a la carte menus.*
Bedrooms: 3 single, 12 double
& 8 twin, 4 family rooms.
Bathrooms: 25 private,
2 public.
Bed & breakfast: £29-£35
single, £58-£70 double.
Half board: £39-£45 daily,
£235-£285 weekly.
Lunch available.
Evening meal 7pm (l.o.
8.30pm).
Parking for 41.
Credit: Access, Visa, Diners,
Amex.

Hampshire
Map ref 2C3

Resort and residential
area with fine views
across the Solent to
Cowes and Calshot.

Belle Vue Hotel M
😃😃😃😃
39 Marine Parade East, Lee
on the Solent, PO13 9BW
☎ (0705) 550258
Fax (0705) 552624
*Modern hotel on the seafront
with uninterrupted views across
the Solent. Lounge bar, fine
restaurant and banqueting
facilities.*
Bedrooms: 3 single, 20 double
& 4 twin.
Bathrooms: 27 private.
Bed & breakfast: from £60
single, from £72 double.
Half board: £48.50-£72.50
daily, £303.75-£423.75
weekly.
Lunch available.

Evening meal 7pm (l.o.
9.45pm).
Parking for 80.
Credit: Access, Visa.

Dorset
Map ref 2B3

5m N. Bournemouth
Astride the A348 Poole to
Ringwood road and on
the north bank of the
River Stour. The river
floods its banks in this
area when the weather is
severe.

Bridge House Hotel M
😃😃😃 COMMENDED
2 Ringwood Road, Longham,
Wimborne, BH22 9AN
☎ Bournemouth
(0202) 578828 Fax (0202)
572620 Telex 48484
*Mediterranean style hotel and
restaurant.*
Bedrooms: 4 single, 23 double
& 10 twin.
Bathrooms: 37 private.
Bed & breakfast: £45-£60
single, £60-£80 double.
Evening meal 7pm (l.o.
10pm).
Parking for 200.
Credit: Access, Visa, Amex.

Hampshire
Map ref 2C3

Small, pleasant town with
bright cottages and
attractive Georgian
houses, lying on the edge
of the New Forest with a
ferry service to the Isle of
Wight. A sheltered
harbour making it a busy
yachting centre.

Albany House M
😃😃😃
Highfield, Lymington,
SO41 9GB
☎ (0590) 671900
*Elegant, Regency house in
Georgian market town, with
charming English walled
garden and views of Isle of
Wight and Solent.*
Bedrooms: 2 single, 1 double
& 1 twin, 1 family room.
Bathrooms: 2 private,
2 public.
Bed & breakfast: £19.50
single, £35-£49 double.

Half board: £27-£34 daily,
£175-£218 weekly.
Evening meal 7pm (l.o. 8pm).
Parking for 7.

Compton Hotel M
😃😃
59 Keyhaven Road, Milford-
on-Sea, Lymington,
SO41 0QX
☎ Lymington (0590) 643117
*Small, private hotel with en-
suite rooms and TV. Outdoor
heated swimming pool. English
and vegetarian cooking.
Licensed.*
Bedrooms: 2 single, 3 double
& 1 twin, 1 family room.
Bathrooms: 4 private,
1 public.
Bed & breakfast: £32-£34
double.
Half board: £145-£150
weekly.
Evening meal 6.30pm (l.o.
6.30pm).
Parking for 8.

Passford House Hotel M
😃😃😃😃 COMMENDED
Mount Pleasant Lane,
Lymington, SO41 8LS
☎ (0590) 682398 Fax
(0590) 683494
*Charming country house on the
edge of the New Forest,
spacious lounges, well-
appointed accommodation and
a recently added leisure centre.*
Bedrooms: 5 single, 18 double
& 27 twin, 4 family rooms.
Bathrooms: 54 private,
2 public.
Bed & breakfast: £66-£80
single, £95-£120 double.
Lunch available.
Evening meal 7pm (l.o. 9pm).
Parking for 84.
Credit: Access, Visa, Amex.

Stanwell House Hotel M
😃😃😃
High Street, Lymington,
SO41 9AA
☎ (0590) 677123
Telex 477463 G
*Georgian-style house with a
walled garden. Set in the heart
of the town within easy reach
of the quay.*
Bedrooms: 6 single, 20 double
& 11 twin.
Bathrooms: 37 private.
Bed & breakfast: from £55
single, from £75 double.
Lunch available.

Continued ▶

LYMINGTON

Continued

Evening meal 7pm (l.o. 10pm).
Credit: Access, Visa.

⟨symbols⟩

LYNDHURST

Hampshire
Map ref 2C3

The 'capital' of the New Forest, surrounded by attractive woodland scenery and delightful villages. The town is dominated by the Victorian Gothic-style church where the original Alice in Wonderland is buried.
Tourist Information Centre ☎ *(0703) 282269*

Crown Hotel ♪
💎💎💎💎 COMMENDED

High Street, Lyndhurst, SO43 7NF
☎ (0703) 282922
Telex 9312110733CHG
⟨CB⟩ Best Western
Mellow elegance in New Forest setting, spotlessly clean. Restaurant, bar, buffet, sitting rooms, sitting rooms, garden, lift, parking. Easy for visits to the National Motor Museum, Beaulieu.
Bedrooms: 6 single, 18 double & 10 twin, 6 family rooms.
Bathrooms: 40 private.
Bed & breakfast: £46-£54 single, £70-£85 double.
Half board: £43-£51 daily, £316-£340 weekly.
Lunch available.
Evening meal 7.30pm (l.o. 9.30pm).
Parking for 60.
Credit: Access, Visa, Diners, Amex.

⟨symbols⟩

Knightwood Lodge ♪
💎💎💎

Southampton Road, Lyndhurst, SO43 7BU
☎ (0703) 282502
Situated on the edge of Lyndhurst overlooking the New Forest. Indoor health centre.
Bedrooms: 2 single, 7 double & 2 twin, 1 family room.
Bathrooms: 12 private.
Bed & breakfast: £26-£32 single, £38-£42 double.
Half board: £25-£38 daily.
Evening meal 6.30pm (l.o. 8.30pm).

Parking for 10.
Credit: Access, Visa, Diners, Amex.

⟨symbols⟩

Lyndhurst Park Hotel ♪
💎💎💎 COMMENDED

High Street, Lyndhurst, SO43 7NL
☎ (0703) 283923
Telex 477802 FODALE G
Elegant Georgian mansion, with comfortable interior, set in own grounds in "capital" of New Forest.
Bedrooms: 5 single, 29 double & 22 twin, 3 family rooms.
Bathrooms: 59 private.
Bed & breakfast: £55-£60.50 single, £70-£77 double.
Lunch available.
Evening meal 7pm (l.o. 10pm).
Parking for 100.
Credit: Access, Visa, Diners, Amex.

⟨symbols⟩

Parkhill Hotel ♪
💎💎💎

Beaulieu Road, Lyndhurst, SO43 7FZ
☎ (0703) 282944 Fax (0703) 283268
Delightful Georgian country house hotel in 12 acres of secluded forest. Offers high standard accommodation in a peaceful and tranquil setting. Ideal for touring the New Forest.
Bedrooms: 1 single, 12 double & 5 twin, 2 family rooms.
Bathrooms: 20 private.
Bed & breakfast: £50-£65 single, £82-£101 double.
Half board: £325-£425 weekly.
Lunch available.
Evening meal 7pm (l.o. 9.30pm).
Parking for 60.
Credit: Access, Visa, Diners, Amex.

⟨symbols⟩

South View Hotel ♪
Listed APPROVED

Gosport Lane, Lyndhurst, SO43 7BL
☎ (0703) 282224
Comfortable rooms close to the town centre, in the heart of the New Forest. Some with private bathrooms.
Bedrooms: 3 double & 3 twin, 1 family room.

Bathrooms: 3 private, 2 public.
Bed & breakfast: £34-£38 double.
Parking for 10.

⟨symbols⟩

Whitemoor House Hotel ♪
💎💎 COMMENDED

Southampton Road, Lyndhurst, SO43 7BU
☎ (0703) 282186
Comfortable hotel with an open outlook to the forest. Within easy reach of Southampton, Beaulieu and the coast.
Bedrooms: 3 double & 1 twin, 1 family room.
Bathrooms: 2 public.
Bed & breakfast: £25-£30 single, £35-£40 double.
Evening meal 6.30pm.
Parking for 10.

⟨symbols⟩

MIDDLE WALLOP

Hampshire
Map ref 2C2

On the main Salisbury to Andover road and between Over Wallop and Nether Wallop. The Army Air Corps (Museum) and Training Centre is 2 miles north-east.

Fifehead Manor ♪
💎💎💎

Middle Wallop, Stockbridge, SO20 8EG
☎ Andover (0264) 781565
Fax (0264) 781400
Comfortable manor house, part of which dates from the 11th C. Located close to the famous River Test.
Bedrooms: 6 single, 6 double & 4 twin.
Bathrooms: 16 private.
Bed & breakfast: £45 single, £75-£95 double.
Half board: £60-£70 daily, £420-£490 weekly.
Lunch available.
Evening meal 7.30pm (l.o. 9.30pm).
Parking for 50.
Credit: Access, Visa, Diners, Amex.

⟨symbols⟩

The enquiry coupons at the back will help you when contacting proprietors.

MILFORD-ON-SEA

Hampshire
Map ref 2C3

Victorian seaside resort with shingle beach and good bathing, set in pleasant countryside and looking out over the Isle of Wight. Nearby is Hurst Castle, built by Henry VIII.

South Lawn Hotel ♪
💎💎💎

Lymington Road, Milford-on-Sea, Lymington, SO41 0RF
☎ Lymington (0590) 643911
Fax (0590) 644820
Attractive country house in peaceful surroundings, where chef/proprietor assures that food, comfort and personal service predominate.
Bedrooms: 6 double & 18 twin.
Bathrooms: 24 private.
Bed & breakfast: from £45 single, from £80 double.
Half board: from £52 daily, from £337 weekly.
Evening meal 7pm (l.o. 8.30pm).
Parking for 50.
Credit: Access, Visa.

⟨symbols⟩

NETLEY ABBEY

Hampshire
Map ref 2C3

4m SE. Southampton
Romantic ruin, set in green lawns against a background of trees on the east bank of Southampton Water. The abbey was built in the 13th C by Cistercian monks from Beaulieu.

La Casa Blanca ♪
💎💎

48 Victoria Road, Netley Abbey, SO3 5DQ
☎ Southampton (0703) 453718
Small, pleasantly situated hotel. Friendly welcome and varied food.
Bedrooms: 4 single, 2 double & 3 twin, 1 family room.
Bathrooms: 1 private, 2 public.
Bed & breakfast: max. £22 single, max. £32 double.
Half board: £22-£28 daily, £154-£196 weekly.
Evening meal 6.30pm (l.o. 9.30pm).
Parking for 3.

⟨symbols⟩

NEW FOREST

See Barton on Sea, Bramshaw, Brockenhurst, Brook, Burley, Fordingbridge, Lymington, Lyndhurst, Milford-on-Sea, New Milton, Ringwood, Sway, Woodlands.

NEW MILTON

Hampshire
Map ref 2B3

New Forest residential town on the mainline railway.

Cliff House Hotel & Restaurant M
COMMENDED

Marine Drive West, Barton on Sea, New Milton, BH25 7QL
☎ New Milton (0425) 619333
Fax (0425) 612462
Fully licensed clifftop hotel with beautiful furnishings and restaurant, bar and lounge, overlooking Christchurch Bay. Chef/proprietor.
Bedrooms: 2 single, 5 double & 2 twin.
Bathrooms: 8 private, 3 public.
Bed & breakfast: £30-£45 single, £66-£80 double.
Half board: £42.50-£67.50 daily, £275-£438 weekly.
Lunch available.
Evening meal 7pm (l.o. 9pm).
Parking for 50.
Credit: Access, Visa, Diners, Amex.

NORTH WALTHAM

Hampshire
Map ref 2C2

Wheatsheaf Hotel M

North Waltham, Nr. Basingstoke, RG25 2BB
☎ Basingstoke (0256) 398282
Telex 859775
Lansbury
Rural hotel, well placed for Basingstoke and the Hampshire countryside.
Bedrooms: 2 single, 25 double, 1 family room.
Bathrooms: 28 private.
Bed & breakfast: £31-£71 single, £62-£85 double.
Half board: £41-£100 daily.
Lunch available.
Evening meal 7pm (l.o. 10.30pm).
Parking for 70.

Credit: Access, Visa, Diners, Amex.

ODIHAM

Hampshire
Map ref 2C2

George Hotel M
COMMENDED

High Street, Odiham, Nr. Basingstoke, RG25 1LP
☎ (0256) 702081 Fax (0256) 704213
15th C coaching inn with many fine beams (especially in bedrooms), oak panelled restaurant with flag stoned floor, fine fireplace said to have come from Basing House and original daub and wattle visible.
Bedrooms: 5 single, 12 double & 1 twin.
Bathrooms: 18 private.
Bed & breakfast: £37.50-£55 single, £55-£75 double.
Lunch available.
Evening meal 7.30pm (l.o. 10pm).
Parking for 30.
Credit: Access, Visa, C.Bl., Diners, Amex.

OWSLEBURY

Hampshire
Map ref 2C3

Small farming village with Marwell Conservation Zoo close by.

Miss E.A. Lightfoot M
Listed COMMENDED

Tayinloan, Owslebury, Nr. Winchester, SO21 1LP
☎ (096 274) 359
Private house with extensive rural views. 4 miles from M3, 11 miles from M27. Easy access to Eastleigh Airport, 9 miles away, and Portsmouth Ferries. Non-smokers only please.
Bedrooms: 1 double & 1 twin, 1 family room.
Bathrooms: 2 private, 1 public.
Bed & breakfast: £14.50-£15 single, £29-£30 double.
Parking for 3.

We advise you to
confirm your
booking in writing.

PETERSFIELD

Hampshire
Map ref 2C3

Grew prosperous from the wool trade and was famous as a coaching centre. Its attractive market square is dominated by a statue of William III. Close by are Petersfield Heath with numerous ancient barrows and Butser Hill with magnificent views.
Tourist Information Centre ☎ (0730) 68829

Langrish House M
COMMENDED

Langrish, Petersfield, GU32 1RN
☎ Petersfield (0730) 66941
Situated on the East Meon road, off the A272 to Winchester, 3 miles from Petersfield.
Bedrooms: 6 single, 6 double & 6 twin.
Bathrooms: 18 private.
Bed & breakfast: £45-£50 single, £55-£65 double.
Half board: £57.50-£65 daily.
Evening meal 7.30pm (l.o. 9.30pm).
Parking for 50.
Credit: Access, Visa, Diners, Amex.

PIMPERNE

Dorset
Map ref 2B3

Village 2 miles north-east of Blandford Forum, on the main Salisbury road.

Fairfield House M

12 Church Road, Pimperne, Blandford Forum, DT11 8UB
☎ Blandford Forum (0258) 456756
Distinctive, Grade II, Georgian house set in a peaceful village. A family home where a warm welcome awaits you. All rooms en-suite. Easy access to the coast/countryside and historical heritage of Dorset. Stable for your horses or riding school lessons and hacks available. Clay shooting and golfing facilities arranged on request. 2 miles north of Blandford Forum.
Bedrooms: 1 single, 1 double & 2 twin, 1 family room.
Bathrooms: 5 private.
Bed & breakfast: £25.50-£32 single, max. £43 double.

POOLE

Dorset
Map ref 2B3

Tremendous natural harbour makes Poole a superb boating centre. The harbour area is crowded with historic buildings including the 15th C Town Cellars housing a maritime museum.
Tourist Information Centre ☎ (0202) 673322

Arndale Court Hotel

62-64 Wimborne Road, Poole, BH15 2BY
☎ (0202) 683746
Small, family-run hotel, close to quay, town, British Rail and ferry terminal.
Bedrooms: 1 single, 6 double & 6 twin, 3 family rooms.
Bathrooms: 12 private, 2 public; 2 private showers.
Bed & breakfast: £22-£35 single, £44-£48 double.
Half board: £32-£45 daily.
Evening meal 7pm (l.o. 9pm).
Parking for 16.
Credit: Access, Visa, Diners, Amex.

Fairlight Hotel M
COMMENDED

1 Golf Links Road, Broadstone, Poole, BH18 8BE
☎ (0202) 694316
Private hotel in own grounds, close to woodland, rivers, golf-course, the coast, Poole and Bournemouth.
Bedrooms: 1 single, 4 double & 5 twin.
Bathrooms: 7 private, 1 public.
Bed & breakfast: £27-£29 single, £42-£46 double.
Half board: £37-£40 daily.
Evening meal 7pm (l.o. 7.30pm).
Parking for 10.
Credit: Access, Visa.

The Golden Sovereigns Hotel M
Listed

97 Alumhurst Road, Alum Chine, Bournemouth, BH4 8HR
☎ (0202) 762088
Continued ▶

POOLE
Continued

Comfortable, interesting small hotel. Beautiful, sandy beaches 4 minutes away. Convenient for both Bournemouth and Poole. A warm welcome awaits you.
Bedrooms: 1 single, 3 double & 3 twin, 2 family rooms.
Bathrooms: 2 private, 2 public.
Bed & breakfast: £13-£17 single, £26-£34 double.
Half board: £18-£22 daily, £105-£140 weekly.
Lunch available.
Evening meal 6pm (l.o. 4.30pm).
Parking for 9.
Credit: Access, Visa.

Harmony Hotel M

19 St. Peter's Road, Parkstone, Poole, BH14 0NZ
☎ (0202) 747510
The hotel offers friendly service in peaceful, residential area close to all local amenities and is ideally placed as a touring centre.
Bedrooms: 4 double & 4 twin, 3 family rooms.
Bathrooms: 8 private, 1 public; 1 private shower.
Bed & breakfast: £21-£27 single, £36-£44 double.
Evening meal 7pm (l.o. 8.30pm).
Parking for 14.
Credit: Access, Visa.

Mansion House Hotel M
COMMENDED

11 Thames Street, Poole, BH15 1JN
☎ (0202) 685666 Telex 41495 SELECT G
Close to quay in the historic part of old town, with well-appointed bedrooms.
Bedrooms: 9 single, 13 double & 6 twin.
Bathrooms: 28 private.
Bed & breakfast: £75-£84 single, £98-£112 double.
Half board: £67-£93 daily.
Lunch available.
Evening meal 7.30pm (l.o. 10pm).
Parking for 40.
Credit: Access, Visa, C.Bl., Diners, Amex.

The Rosemount Hotel

167 Bournemouth Road, Lower Parkstone, Poole, BH14 9HT
☎ (0202) 732138
Small, family-run hotel on main road between Poole and Bournemouth. Offering varied food, cleanliness and friendly service.
Bedrooms: 4 double & 2 twin, 2 family rooms.
Bathrooms: 2 public; 2 private showers.
Bed & breakfast: £14-£16 single, £28-£32 double.
Evening meal 6pm (l.o. 8.30pm).
Parking for 6.

Woodlands Court Guest House

239 Bournemouth Road, Parkstone, Poole, BH14 9HX
☎ (0202) 747656
Friendly, family guest house. Personal attention. Bright, clean accommodation. Home cooking. Ideally situated for Poole, Bournemouth and surrounding area.
Bedrooms: 1 single, 3 double & 1 twin, 1 family room.
Bathrooms: 1 public.
Bed & breakfast: £15-£20 single, £25-£35 double.
Parking for 4.

POOLE-SANDBANKS
Dorset
Map ref 2B3

Lies to the east of Poole. Boats can be hired from here for exploring all the inlets and islands in Poole Harbour, and a car ferry operates to Shell Bay.

Haven Hotel M
COMMENDED

Banks Road, Sandbanks, Poole, BH13 7QL
☎ Bournemouth
(0202) 707333 Telex 41338
Standing on the very edge of the sea overlooking the entrance to Poole Yacht Harbour and Purbeck Hills.
Bedrooms: 18 single, 27 double & 45 twin, 6 family rooms.
Bathrooms: 96 private.
Bed & breakfast: £50-£60 single, £90-£110 double.
Half board: £70-£80 daily, £420-£480 weekly.
Lunch available.
Evening meal 7pm (l.o. 8.30pm).

Parking for 200.
Credit: Access, Visa, Diners, Amex.

Sandbanks Hotel M
COMMENDED

Banks Road, Sandbanks, Poole, BH13 7PS
☎ Bournemouth
(0202) 707377 Telex 41338
On a sand peninsula right on the water's edge with views of the sea and Poole Harbour.
Bedrooms: 16 single, 17 double & 47 twin, 25 family rooms.
Bathrooms: 105 private.
Bed & breakfast: £40-£50 single, £80-£100 double.
Half board: £50-£60 daily, £300-£360 weekly.
Lunch available.
Evening meal 7pm (l.o. 8.30pm).
Parking for 200.
Credit: Access, Visa, Diners, Amex.

PORTSMOUTH & SOUTHSEA
Hampshire
Map ref 2C3

There have been connections with the Navy since early times and the first dock was built in 1194. HMS Victory, Nelson's flagship, is here and Charles Dickens' former home is open to the public. Neighbouring Southsea has a promenade with magnificent views of Spithead.
Tourist Information Centre ☎ (0705) 826722

April House M

7 Malvern Road, Southsea, PO5 2LZ
☎ (0705) 814824
Clean, comfortable guesthouse, close to Rock Gardens, Pyramid centre, beach and all facilities. All rooms have colour TV and electric kettle.
Bedrooms: 2 single, 3 double & 2 twin, 2 family rooms.
Bathrooms: 2 public; 1 private shower.
Bed & breakfast: £12-£16 single, £22-£30 double.
Parking for 4.
Open May-October.

Arcade Hotel M

Winston Churchill Avenue, Portsmouth, PO1 2LX
☎ (0705) 821992
Telex 869429
Newly built, modern city centre hotel within walking distance of shopping centre, main railway station and Guildhall.
Bedrooms: 4 single, 36 double & 77 twin, 27 family rooms.
Bathrooms: 144 private.
Bed & breakfast: £25-£44 single, £35-£52 double.
Lunch available.
Evening meal 6.30pm (l.o. 9.45pm).
Parking for 50.
Credit: Access, Visa, Amex.

Bembell Court Hotel M

69 Festing Road, Southsea, PO4 0NQ
☎ (0705) 735915 & 750497
Family-run, licensed hotel close to sea, shops and ferry port. Comfortable rooms, some with en-suite. Choice of menu.
Bedrooms: 2 single, 4 double & 4 twin, 4 family rooms.
Bathrooms: 5 private, 3 public.
Bed & breakfast: £20-£28 single, £40-£48 double.
Half board: £27-£35 daily, £175-£210 weekly.
Evening meal 6pm (l.o. 4pm).
Parking for 12.
Credit: Access, Visa.

Beverley Guest House

12 Craneswater Avenue, Southsea, PO4 0PB
☎ (0705) 825739
Quiet, friendly guesthouse close to sea, shops and ferry port. Colour TV, central heating and hostess trays in all rooms.
Bedrooms: 1 single, 3 twin, 2 family rooms.
Bathrooms: 1 public.
Bed & breakfast: from £14 single, from £27 double.
Evening meal 6pm.

Briona Lodge

16 Herbert Road, Southsea, PO4 0QA
☎ (0705) 814030
Friendly guesthouse within easy reach of the seafront, ferry port and shops. Licensed bar and evening meals available. Pets welcome.
Bedrooms: 2 single, 3 double, 3 family rooms.
Bathrooms: 1 public.

Bed & breakfast: £11-£13 single, £22-£26 double. **Half board**: £18-£20 daily. Evening meal 6pm (l.o. midday). Parking for 4.

🚲 🕭 ⬚ 📺 🎂 ⓘ ▦ ⚲ 📖

The Dolphins Hotel & Snobbs Cocktail Bar & Restaurant M

⚚⚚⚚

10-11 Western Parade, Southsea, Portsmouth, PO5 3JF
☎ (0705) 823823 & 820833
On the seafront, overlooking the common. Near to Mary Rose, HMS Victory, HMS Warrior and ferry terminals. Attractive bar and restaurant with a la carte and table d'hote menus.
Bedrooms: 10 single, 6 double & 13 twin, 4 family rooms.
Bathrooms: 19 private, 7 public; 2 private showers.
Bed & breakfast: £22-£35 single, £40-£48 double.
Half board: £34.50-£47.50 daily, £230-£320 weekly.
Lunch available.
Evening meal 7.30pm (l.o. 9.45pm).
Credit: Access, Visa, Diners, Amex.

🚲 ⓘ 🕭 📞 🕭 🖂 ⓘ ▦ ⚲
📺 ● ▥ 🎂 ♿ ⏚ 📖 ⚲ 🆂🅿 🆃

Gainsborough House

⚚⚚ COMMENDED

9 Malvern Road, Southsea, PO5 2LZ
☎ (0705) 822604
Long established guesthouse, a few minutes from seafront and wihin easy reach of continental ferry port and local attractions.
Bedrooms: 2 single, 2 double & 2 twin, 1 family room.
Bathrooms: 2 public.
Bed & breakfast: £12.50-£13.50 single, £25-£27 double.

🚲3 ⬚ 🕭 🆄🅻 🖂 📺 ▦ ⚲ 🇽
🖦

Granada House Hotel

29 Granada Road, Southsea, PO4 0RD
☎ (0705) 861575
The hotel offers spacious bedrooms, large car park and English or continental breakfast.
Bedrooms: 1 single, 2 double & 2 twin, 3 family rooms.
Bathrooms: 5 private, 2 public.
Bed & breakfast: from £20 single, from £30 double.

Half board: from £22.50 daily.
Evening meal 6pm (l.o. 8pm).
Parking for 10.

🚲 ⓑ ⬚ 🕭 🆄🅻 ⓘ ▦ 🖂 ▥ ▦
🖦 📖 🆂🅿

Hallam Guest House

8 Auckland Road East, Southsea, PO5 2HD
☎ (0705) 734207
Comfortable, friendly guesthouse situated within minutes of seafront, shops and entertainment. All rooms have colour TV and tea making facilities. Families welcome.
Bedrooms: 3 single, 4 double, 1 family room.
Bathrooms: 2 public.
Bed & breakfast: £12-£14 single, £22-£26 double.
Evening meal 6pm (l.o. 7pm).

🚲 Ⓜ ⬚ 🕭 🆄🅻 🖂 📺 ▦ 🖦
🇽 🖷 📖 🆂🅿

Holiday Inn Portsmouth M

⚚⚚⚚⚚⚚

North Harbour, Portsmouth, PO6 4SH
☎ Cosham (0705) 383151
Telex 86611
Ⓖ Holiday Inn
North of city centre, close to M27 and A3. Children under 19 stay free when sharing parents' room. Indoor pool, squash, gym.
Bedrooms: 94 double, 76 family rooms.
Bathrooms: 170 private.
Bed & breakfast: £50-£94 single, £74-£112 double.
Lunch available.
Evening meal 6.30pm (l.o. 11pm).
Parking for 200.
Credit: Access, Visa, C.Bl., Diners, Amex.

🚲 🕭 🕭 🖂 🕭 ⓘ ▥ 🖂
● ⏚ ▥ 🖦 🖀 ♿ 🇽 🖲
🐦 ⚲ 🆂🅿 🆃

Mayville Hotel

⚚⚚⚚

4 Waverley Road, Southsea, PO5 2PN
☎ (0705) 732461
Well established hotel with plenty of parking, within easy reach of seafront and shops and 10 minutes from ferry terminals and naval heritage museums.
Bedrooms: 8 single, 5 double & 3 twin, 4 family rooms.
Bathrooms: 18 private, 1 public; 2 private showers.
Bed & breakfast: £21-£22 single, £38-£40 double.
Half board: £29-£30 daily, £153-£160 weekly.

Evening meal 6.30pm (l.o. 7pm).
Parking for 21.
Credit: Access, Visa.

🚲 🕭 🕭 🖂 📞 ⬚ ⓘ ▥ 🖂
📺 ▦ 🖦 🆂🅿 🆃

Newleaze Guest House M

Listed

11 St. Edward's Road, Southsea, PO5 3DH
☎ (0705) 832735
Small friendly establishment with home cooking, giving good value for money. Within easy reach of continental ferry port.
Bedrooms: 1 single, 2 double & 2 twin, 1 family room.
Bathrooms: 1 public; 1 private shower.
Bed & breakfast: £12-£14 single, £24-£28 double.
Half board: £16-£19 daily, £100-£120 weekly.
Evening meal 6pm.

🚲 🕭 ⬚ 🕭 🆄🅻 ⓘ ▥ ▦
🖷 📖

Oakleigh Guest House M

48 Festing Grove, Southsea, PO4 9QD
☎ (0705) 812276
Family-run guesthouse, offering personal service, with children and OAP's welcome. Colour TV, hot and cold water, central heating.
Bedrooms: 2 single, 2 double & 1 twin, 2 family rooms.
Bathrooms: 1 public.
Bed & breakfast: from £12 single, from £24 double.
Half board: from £16 daily, from £75 weekly.
Evening meal 6pm (l.o. 4pm).

🚲 ⬚ 🆄🅻 ▥ ▦ 🖦 🇽 🖷
📖

The Old Mill Guest House

Mill Lane, Bedhampton, Havant, PO9 3JH
☎ (0705) 454948
Georgian house in large grounds which contain a lake abundant in wildlife. Modernised, but still a comfortable retreat.
Bedrooms: 2 double & 3 twin.
Bathrooms: 5 private, 1 public.
Bed & breakfast: £23 single, £36 double.
Parking for 10.

🚲 🕭 ⬚ ⓘ ▥ 🖂 📺 ▦ 🖦
🔾 ✿ 🖷 🖦

The Olympic Hotel M

Listed

51-53 Granada Road, Southsea, PO4 0RQ
☎ (0705) 821883

Double fronted, 4-storey Victorian detached house close to seafront and shops.
Bedrooms: 3 single, 4 double & 2 twin, 4 family rooms.
Bathrooms: 3 public.
Bed & breakfast: £15-£20 single, £30-£38 double.
Half board: £21-£26 daily, £120-£140 weekly.
Lunch available.
Evening meal 6pm (l.o. 6.30pm).
Parking for 12.
Credit: Access, Visa.

🚲 🕭 ⬚ 🆄🅻 ⓘ ▥ 🖂 📺
▦ 🖦 📖 🇽

St. David's Guest House M

⚚⚚ COMMENDED

19 St. David's Road, Southsea, PO5 1QH
☎ (0705) 826858
Small, family-run guest house close to shops, restaurants and theatre, convenient for sea front and continental ferry.
Bedrooms: 1 double & 3 twin, 2 family rooms.
Bathrooms: 2 public.
Bed & breakfast: £13-£14 single, £25-£27 double.
Half board: £18-£19 daily, £120-£125 weekly.
Evening meal 6pm.

🚲 ⬚ 🕭 🇽 🆄🅻 ▥ ✕ 🖂 📺 ▦
🖦 🖷 🆃

St. Margarets Hotel M

⚚⚚ COMMENDED

3 Craneswater Gate, Southsea, PO4 0NZ
☎ (0705) 820097
Family-run licensed hotel with 3 ground floor bedrooms. Near to the canoe lake, seafront, Portsmouth maritime heritage and ferryport.
Bedrooms: 3 single, 5 double & 3 twin, 3 family rooms.
Bathrooms: 6 private, 2 public.
Bed & breakfast: £18-£22 single, £34-£40 double.
Half board: £25-£30 daily, £165-£180 weekly.
Evening meal 6pm (l.o. 6pm).
Parking for 4.

🚲 🕭 ⬚ ⓘ ▥ 🖂 📺 ▦ 🖦
♿ 🆂🅿 🆃

Salisbury Hotel M

⚚⚚⚚

59 Festing Road, Southsea, PO4 0NQ
☎ (0705) 823606 & 828147
The hotel is 2 minutes' walk from the sea, in an attractive area of Southsea. The licensed restaurant overlooks a delightful garden, available for residents' use and barbecue parties.

Continued ▶

PORTSMOUTH & SOUTHSEA

Continued

Bedrooms: 7 single, 9 double & 12 twin, 9 family rooms.
Bathrooms: 10 private, 4 public; 8 private showers.
Bed & breakfast: £19-£32 single, £34-£50 double.
Half-board: £26-£42 daily, £150-£210 weekly.
Lunch available.
Evening meal 6.30pm (l.o. 9pm).
Parking for 20.
Credit: Access, Visa, Amex.

The Sandringham Hotel M

Osborne Road/Clarence Parade, Southsea, Portsmouth, PO5 3LR
☎ (0705) 826969 & 822914
Fax (0705) 822330
Impressive 45-roomed hotel with private facilities and sea views from most bedrooms. 100 seat restaurant, function/conference room for 120 complete with bar and dance floor. Large free car park opposite hotel.
Bedrooms: 8 single, 16 double & 14 twin, 7 family rooms.
Bathrooms: 34 private, 4 public; 3 private showers.
Bed & breakfast: £20.50-£28 single, £34-£46 double.
Half board: £29-£36 daily, £130-£180 weekly.
Lunch available.
Evening meal 7pm (l.o. 10pm).
Credit: Access, Visa, Diners, Amex.

The Shropshire Court Guest House M

33 Granada Road, Southsea, PO4 0RD
☎ (0705) 731043
Family-run guesthouse close to sea, ferry port and all amenities. Immaculate accommodation and friendly, informal atmosphere. Early breakfast available.
Bedrooms: 2 single, 2 double & 3 twin, 2 family rooms.
Bathrooms: 3 public.
Bed & breakfast: £14-£15 single, £28-£30 double.
Parking for 7.

Testudo House

19 Whitwell Road, Southsea, PO4 0QP
☎ (0705) 824324
Ideal situation, close to sea, Naval Heritage Centre, all ferry ports and local attractions. Colour TV, tea/making facilities. Lockable car space. Early breakfast served. Reductions for children.
Bedrooms: 1 single, 1 double & 1 twin, 2 family rooms.
Bathrooms: 1 public.
Bed & breakfast: from £13 single, from £25 double.
Parking for 1.

Turret Hotel

Clarence Parade, Southsea, PO5 2HZ
☎ (0705) 291810
On Southsea seafront opposite the new Pyramids Centre and the Lady's Mile. Most unusual building with turret and marvellous views.
Bedrooms: 4 single, 7 double & 2 twin.
Bathrooms: 7 private, 3 public.
Bed & breakfast: £20-£30 single, £40-£50 double.
Credit: Access, Visa.

Waverley Park Lodge Guest House

99 Waverley Road, Southsea, PO5 2PL
☎ (0705) 730402
Comfortable guesthouse with family rooms for overnight accommodation. Easy reach of ferryport, arrangement for early breakfast.
Bedrooms: 1 single, 2 double & 1 twin, 2 family rooms.
Bathrooms: 1 public.
Bed & breakfast: £12-£13 single, £22-£24 double.
Half-board: £18-£19 daily.
Evening meal 6pm (l.o. 6pm).
Credit: Access, Visa.

Please mention this guide when making a booking.

RINGWOOD

Hampshire
Map ref 2B3

Market town by the River Avon comprising old cottages, many of them thatched. Although just outside the New Forest, there is heath and woodland nearby and it is a good centre for horse-riding and walking.

High Corner Inn M

COMMENDED
Linwood, Nr. Ringwood, BH24 3QY
☎ Ringwood (0425) 473973
Fax (0425) 480015
Situated down a drovers' track, in 7 secluded acres in the heart of the New Forest, 4 miles north-east of Ringwood.
Bedrooms: 4 twin, 2 family rooms.
Bathrooms: 6 private.
Bed & breakfast: £55-£65 double.
Half board: £30-£40 daily, £185-£280 weekly.
Lunch available.
Evening meal 7pm (l.o. 10pm).
Parking for 203.
Credit: Access, Visa, Diners, Amex.

⊕ Display advertisement appears on page 501.

Moortown Lodge Hotel & Restaurant M

COMMENDED
244 Christchurch Road, Ringwood, BH24 3AS
☎ (0425) 471404
Elegant Georgian hotel, (circa 1760), and restaurant. Proprietor run. Freshly-cooked food. Situated at edge of New Forest, 1 mile from town centre on B3347.
Bedrooms: 1 single, 2 double & 2 twin, 1 family room.
Bathrooms: 5 private, 1 public.
Bed & breakfast: £28-£35 single, £46-£50 double.
Half board: £31-£47 daily, £217-£329 weekly.
Evening meal 7pm (l.o. 8.30pm).
Parking for 7.
Credit: Access, Visa.

The Struan Hotel M

COMMENDED
Horton Road, Ashley Heath, Ringwood, BH24 2EG
☎ Ringwood (0425) 473553
Fax (0425) 480529
Country inn with a la carte restaurant, on the edge of the New Forest not far from the historic market town of Ringwood.
Bedrooms: 2 single, 6 double & 2 twin.
Bathrooms: 10 private.
Bed & breakfast: £45-£55 single, £60-£75 double.
Half board: £53-£63 daily, from £280 weekly.
Lunch available.
Evening meal 7pm (l.o. 10pm).
Parking for 75.
Credit: Access, Visa, Diners, Amex.

ROMSEY

Hampshire
Map ref 2C3

Town grew up around the important abbey and lies on the banks of the River Test, famous for trout and salmon. Broadlands House, home of the late Lord Mountbatten, is open to the public.

The Abbey Hotel M

APPROVED
Church Street, Romsey, SO51 8BT
☎ (0794) 513360
Small family-run hotel with a relaxed and friendly atmosphere, situated directly opposite Romsey Abbey.
Bedrooms: 2 single, 2 double & 2 twin, 1 family room.
Bathrooms: 7 private.
Bed & breakfast: £43.50-£49.50 single, £54.50-£59.50 double.
Lunch available.
Evening meal 6pm (l.o. 9pm).
Parking for 10.
Credit: Access, Visa.

New Forest Heathlands Hotel at the Vine Inn M

Romsey Road, Ower, Nr. Romsey, Southampton, SO51 6ZJ
☎ Southampton (0703) 814333 Fax (0703) 812123 Telex 8954665 VBSTLX REF QUA

The National Crown Scheme is explained in full on pages 556 – 558.

Traditional hotel, set in 2 acres of gardens, built onto a 16th C inn. Near junction 2 of M27. Open to non residents.
Bedrooms: 2 single, 25 double & 19 twin, 6 family rooms.
Bathrooms: 52 private.
Bed & breakfast: £60-£75 single, £80-£95 double.
Half board: £260-£290 weekly.
Lunch available.
Evening meal 7pm (l.o. 9.30pm).
Parking for 130.
Credit: Access, Visa, Diners, Amex.

The Old Post Office
New Road, Michelmersh, Nr. Romsey, SO51 0NL
☎ Braishfield (0794) 68739
Pretty village location, interesting conversion from old forge, bakery and post office. All ground floor rooms, some beamed. On site parking.
Bedrooms: 3 twin, 1 family room.
Bathrooms: 4 private.
Bed & breakfast: £25 single, £30 double.
Parking for 8.
Credit: Access.

Wessex Guest House
Listed
5 Palmerston Street, Romsey, SO51 8GF
☎ (0794) 512038
200 yards from Broadlands Park, home of the late Lord Mountbatten, now open to the public.
Bedrooms: 1 single, 4 double & 1 twin, 2 family rooms.
Bathrooms: 3 public.
Bed & breakfast: £14-£15 single, £28-£30 double.

St. Leonards Hotel M
Ringwood Road, St. Leonards, Nr. Ringwood, Hampshire BH24 2NP
☎ Ringwood (0425) 471220 Telex 418215
🅒 Lansbury
Rural hotel set in attractive grounds, convenient for New Forest and Bournemouth.
Bedrooms: 15 double & 17 twin, 2 family rooms.
Bathrooms: 34 private.

Bed & breakfast: £33-£65 single, £66-£78 double.
Half board: £44-£93 daily.
Lunch available.
Evening meal 7pm (l.o. 10pm).
Parking for 250.
Credit: Access, Visa, Diners, Amex.

5m NW. Fareham
Village astride the A27.

Dormy Hotel M
APPROVED
21 Barnes Lane, Sarisbury-Warsash, Southampton, S03 6DA
☎ Locks Heath (0489) 572626
Victorian house near Hamble River between Southampton and Portsmouth. Family-run by qualified chef, offering accommodation and food at reasonable cost.
Bedrooms: 2 single, 4 double & 3 twin, 1 family room.
Bathrooms: 6 private, 1 public; 1 private shower.
Bed & breakfast: £20-£32 single, £40-£46 double.
Half board: £27.50-£39.50 daily.
Evening meal 6.30pm (l.o. midday).
Parking for 14.

Hilltop town with a long history. The ancient and cobbled Gold Hill is one of the most attractive in Dorset. There is an excellent small museum containing a collection of buttons for which the town is famous.

Grove House Hotel M
Ludwell, Shaftesbury, SP7 9ND
☎ Donhead (0747) 828365
Small, quiet private hotel in rural area, within easy reach of many places of interest. Varied cuisine and warm hospitality.
Bedrooms: 1 single, 4 double & 5 twin, 1 family room.
Bathrooms: 11 private, 1 public.

Bed & breakfast: £24.50-£27 single, £49-£54 double.
Half board: £38-£42 daily, £222-£245 weekly.
Lunch available.
Evening meal 7pm (l.o. 7.30pm).
Parking for 12.
Open February-November.
Credit: Access, Visa.

Royal Chase Hotel M
Freepost, Dept. ETB, Royal Chase Roundabout, Shaftesbury, SP7 8BR
☎ (0747) 53355 Telex 418414 RCHASE G
🅒 Best Western
Rural country town hotel with new indoor swimming pool/leisure complex. Choice of restaurants and standard or added quality bedrooms.
Bedrooms: 3 single, 7 double & 19 twin, 5 family rooms.
Bathrooms: 34 private.
Bed & breakfast: £43-£63.50 single, £70-£99 double.
Half board: from £264 weekly.
Lunch available.
Evening meal 7pm (l.o. 9.45pm).
Parking for 100.
Credit: Access, Visa, Diners, Amex.

Stock Hill House Hotel & Restaurant M
HIGHLY COMMENDED
Stock Hill, Wyke, Gillingham, SP8 5NR
☎ (0747) 823626
Family-run country house hotel and restaurant in peaceful 10 acres of wildest north Dorset.
Bedrooms: 2 single, 3 double & 3 twin.
Bathrooms: 8 private.
Half board: £70-£80 daily.
Lunch available.
Evening meal 7.30pm (l.o. 8.45pm).
Parking for 40.
Credit: Access, Visa.

The Sunridge Hotel M
Bleke Street, Shaftesbury, SP7 8AW
☎ (0747) 53130
A warm and friendly, family-run hotel with a relaxed atmosphere, offering health and leisure facilities and home-cooked food.

Bedrooms: 4 double & 3 twin, 3 family rooms.
Bathrooms: 10 private.
Bed & breakfast: from £32.50 single, from £45 double.
Half board: from £42.50 daily.
Lunch available.
Evening meal 7pm (l.o. 9pm).
Parking for 12.
Credit: Access, Visa.

Village and site of the Roman town of Calleva.

Romans Hotel & Restaurant M
COMMENDED
Little London Road, Silchester, Nr. Reading, Berkshire RG7 2PN
☎ Reading (0734) 700421 Telex 858122 ATTN ROMANS
🅒 Best Western
Family owned and managed country house hotel, with renowned restaurant catering for the business person and tourist alike.
Bedrooms: 14 single, 5 double & 4 twin, 1 family room.
Bathrooms: 24 private.
Bed & breakfast: £60-£74 single, £70-£90 double.
Lunch available.
Evening meal 7.30pm (l.o. 9pm).
Parking for 42.
Credit: Access, Visa, Diners, Amex.

> The symbol 🅒 and the name of a hotel group or consortium after a hotel address means that bookings can be made through a central reservations office. These are listed on pages 559 & 560.

> We advise you to confirm your booking in writing.

SOUTHAMPTON

Hampshire
Map ref 2C3

One of Britain's leading seaports with a long history, and now developed as a major container port. In the 18th C it became a fashionable resort with the assembly rooms and theatre. The old Guildhall is now a museum and the Wool House a maritime museum. Sections of the medieval wall can still be seen.
Tourist Information Centre ☎ *(0703) 221106*

Addenro House Hotel M
Listed
40-42 Howard Road, Shirley, Southampton, SO1 5BD
☎ (0703) 227144
Family-run small hotel, offering friendly, reliable service at a reasonable cost.
Bedrooms: 8 single, 4 double & 2 twin, 4 family rooms.
Bathrooms: 6 private, 5 public.
Bed & breakfast: £12.50 single, £25 double.
Parking for 18.

Banister House Hotel M
Banister Road, Southampton, SO1 2JJ
☎ (0703) 221279
A friendly welcome in this family-run hotel which is central and in a residential area.
Bedrooms: 11 single, 6 double & 4 twin, 4 family rooms.
Bathrooms: 5 private, 6 public; 9 private showers.
Bed & breakfast: £20.50-£26.50 single, £30.50-£35 double.
Evening meal 6.30pm (l.o. 8pm).
Parking for 14.
Credit: Access, Visa.

Beacon Guest House M
Listed
49 Archers Road, Southampton, SO1 2NF
☎ (0703) 225910
Friendly, comfortable accommodation, commercial and private. Close to city centre, restaurants, docks and county cricket ground, with easy access to the New Forest and Winchester.

Bedrooms: 1 single, 2 double & 1 twin, 2 family rooms.
Bathrooms: 2 public.
Bed & breakfast: £11-£13 single, £21-£24 double.
Parking for 4.

Botleigh Grange Hotel M
Hedge End, Nr. Southampton, SO3 2GA
☎ Botley (0489) 787700
Best Western
Elegant country house hotel with spacious bedrooms overlooking gardens and lakes. Noted for food and service.
Bedrooms: 21 single, 14 double & 8 twin.
Bathrooms: 43 private, 4 public.
Bed & breakfast: £60-£80 single, £73-£100 double.
Lunch available.
Evening meal 7.30pm (l.o. 10pm).
Parking for 306.
Credit: Access, Visa, Diners, Amex.

The Botley Park Hotel & Country Club M
Winchester Road, Boorley Green, Botley, SO3 2UA
☎ (0489) 780888 Fax (0489) 789242
Purpose-designed to cater for the evolving leisure and business demands of the 1990s. Few minutes' drive from M27, 60 minutes from London, less than 50 minutes to Heathrow Airport. Amenities available at the hotel or locally include golf, sauna, solaria, gymnasium, jacuzzi and indoor heated pool. Conference facilities for up to 250.
Bedrooms: 41 double & 56 twin, 3 family rooms.
Bathrooms: 100 private.
Bed & breakfast: £57-£87 single, £67-£105 double.
Lunch available.
Evening meal 7pm (l.o. 10pm).
Parking for 250.
Credit: Access, Visa, Diners, Amex.

The symbols are explained on the flap inside the back cover.

Edgecombe House Hotel M
COMMENDED
188 Regents Park Road, Shirley, Southampton, SO1 3NY
☎ (0703) 773760
Comfortable and friendly, family-run, licensed hotel, within easy reach of the New Forest and Southampton city centre.
Bedrooms: 6 single, 3 double & 3 twin, 1 family room.
Bathrooms: 5 private, 3 public.
Bed & breakfast: £23-£32 single, £40-£46 double.
Evening meal 7pm (l.o. 1pm).
Parking for 12.
Credit: Access, Visa.

The Edwardian Hotel
14 Westwood Road, Portswood, Southampton, SO2 1DN
☎ (0703) 582555
Small, family-run private hotel in quiet residential area. Within easy reach of city centre, station, docks and university.
Bedrooms: 4 single, 2 double & 5 twin, 1 family room.
Bathrooms: 4 private, 3 public.
Bed & breakfast: £19-£30 single, from £45 double.
Evening meal 6.30pm (l.o. 8pm).
Parking for 14.
Credit: Access, Visa.

Elizabeth House Hotel M
43-44 The Avenue, Southampton, SO1 2SX
☎ (0703) 224327
Situated on Southampton's main access route to and from the North. Close to city centre, airport, docks, university, common and motorways. Special weekend rate, £20 per person per night.
Bedrooms: 11 single, 11 double & 2 twin.
Bathrooms: 20 private, 2 public.
Bed & breakfast: £30-£40 single, max. £54 double.
Lunch available.
Evening meal 6pm (l.o. 9pm).
Parking for 20.
Credit: Access, Visa, Diners, Amex.

Fenland Guest House M
Listed APPROVED
79 Hill Lane, Southampton, SO1 5AD
☎ (0703) 220360
Centrally situated, near railway/coach stations and sports facilities.
Bedrooms: 2 single, 2 double & 2 twin, 1 family room.
Bathrooms: 3 private, 1 public.
Bed & breakfast: from £12.50 single, from £25 double.
Parking for 6.

Hill Lodge Hotel M
Listed
126-128 Hill Lane, Shirley, Southampton, SO1 5DD
☎ (0703) 223071
5 minutes from railway and bus station, university, town centre, sports centre. Bedrooms have TV, tea and coffee making facilities.
Bedrooms: 14 single, 1 double & 3 twin, 2 family rooms.
Bathrooms: 5 private, 5 public.
Bed & breakfast: £12.50-£25 single, £25-£38 double.
Half board: £18.50-£31 daily, £129.50-£217 weekly.
Lunch available.
Evening meal 5pm (l.o. 8pm).
Parking for 30.

Hunters Lodge Hotel M
APPROVED
25 Landguard Road, Shirley, Southampton, SO1 5DL
☎ (0703) 227919
Friendly, family hotel, aiming to give a good service to all our guests, 2 minutes' walk from central Southampton.
Bedrooms: 9 single, 4 double & 2 twin, 2 family rooms.
Bathrooms: 7 private, 2 public; 3 private showers.
Bed & breakfast: £23-£32.78 single, £43-£51.18 double.
Half board: £31.63-£51.76 daily, £195.50-£224 weekly.
Evening meal 6.30pm (l.o. 6.30pm).
Parking for 19.
Credit: Access, Visa.

The Lodge
APPROVED
No. 1 Winn Road, The Avenue, Southampton, SO2 1EH
☎ (0703) 557537
Family-run private hotel in quiet surroundings, close to city centre, station and docks. We aim to please.

Bedrooms: 8 single, 1 double
& 4 twin, 1 family room.
Bathrooms: 6 private,
3 public.
Bed & breakfast: £19-£29.50
single, £32-£39.50 double.
Half board: £25-£38.50 daily.
Evening meal 7pm (l.o. 9pm).
Parking for 10.
Credit: Access, Visa.

ॐ ♨ ☎ ⊡ ❑ ╬ 🛎 🗓 V ⌑
📺 ▥ ♨ ♟ 🕸 SP T

Madison House M
♨♨

137 Hill Lane, Southampton,
SO1 5AF
☎ (0703) 333374
*Spacious Victorian house,
offering good standards with
many facilities. All bedrooms
have TV and independent
heating controls. Very friendly
service.*
Bedrooms: 2 single, 3 double
& 2 twin, 2 family rooms.
Bathrooms: 1 private,
2 public.
Bed & breakfast: £14.95-
£17.25 single, £29.90-£34.50
double.
Parking for 6.

ॐ ⊡ ❑ ╬ ⊔ 🗓 ⌑ 📺 ▥
♨ 🕸

The Mayfair Guest House M
♨♨

11 Landguard Road, Shirley,
Southampton, SO1 5DL
☎ (0703) 229861
*A family-run business with the
accent on food and personal
service.*
Bedrooms: 7 single, 1 twin,
2 family rooms.
Bathrooms: 2 public.
Bed & breakfast: £13-£14
single, £26-£28 double.
Half board: £19-£20 daily,
from £133 weekly.
Evening meal 6pm (l.o. 6pm).
Parking for 6.

ॐ ♨ ⊔ 🗓 V ⌑ 📺 ♨
OAP SP

Nirvana Hotel M
Listed APPROVED

386 Winchester Road,
Bassett, Southampton,
SO1 7DH
☎ (0703) 790087 & 790993
*Smaller establishment offering
personal and friendly service.
Comfortably furnished
bedrooms with colour TV, most
with telephones. Cosy Tudor
bar and restaurant open 4 days
per week. Hot bar snacks
available at weekends.*
Bedrooms: 12 single, 4 double
& 2 twin, 2 family rooms.
Bathrooms: 8 private,
3 public.

Bed & breakfast: £24-£40
single, £37-£50 double.
Half board: £36-£52 daily,
£227-£328 weekly.
Lunch available.
Evening meal 7pm (l.o.
8.45pm).
Parking for 21.
Credit: Access.

ॐ ☎ ♈ 🛎 OAP SP T

Novotel Southampton
1 West Quay Road,
Southampton, SO1 0RA
☎ (0703) 330550
Telex 477641
ℂℝ Novotel
*New hotel opened April 1990,
located in the city centre, 5
minutes' walk from railway
station. Easy access from M3,
M27 and docks. Conference
and banqueting facilities for
500. Indoor leisure centre with
a heated indoor swimming
pool, pulse bath, sauna,
exercise area. Ample car park.*
Bedrooms: 121 double.
Bathrooms: 121 private.
Bed & breakfast: £58 single,
£64.50 double.
Lunch available.
Evening meal 6pm (l.o.
11.30pm).
Parking for 100.
Credit: Access, Visa, Diners,
Amex.

ॐ ♨ ☎ ⊡ ❑ ╬ 🛎 V ⌑
● ▥ ♨ ♟ 🐕 🌲 🖎
SP T

Rosida Garden Hotel M
♨♨♨ APPROVED

25-27 Hill Lane,
Southampton, SO1 5AB
☎ (0703) 228501
*Centrally situated with outdoor
heated swimming pool,
changing rooms and sun
terrace with small lake and
wooded area.*
Bedrooms: 14 single, 7 double
& 4 twin, 4 family rooms.
Bathrooms: 29 private.
Bed & breakfast: £45-£48
single, £62-£72 double.
Half board: £55-£59 daily,
£349-£372 weekly.
Evening meal 6.30pm (l.o.
8pm).
Parking for 30.
Credit: Access, Visa, Diners,
Amex.

ॐ ♨ ☎ ⊡ ❑ ╬ 🛎 V ⌑
📺 ▥ ♨ ♟ 🐕 🌲 OAP
SP T

St. John's Guest House
♨

329 Portswood Road,
Southampton, SO2 1LD
☎ (0703) 559790

*Small, traditional, personally-
run establishment, close to
airport, university and railway
station.*
Bedrooms: 1 single, 2 double
& 1 twin, 1 family room.
Bathrooms: 1 public.
Bed & breakfast: £12-£14
single, £22-£24 double.
Parking for 5.

ॐ 7 ♨ ☎ ❑ ╬ ⊔ 📺 ▥ ♨ 🕸

Southampton Moat House M

Highfield Lane, Portswood,
Southampton, SO9 1YQ
☎ (0703) 559555 Telex 47186
ℂℝ Queens Moat Houses
*A modern hotel with high
standard a la carte restaurant,
bar and 4 separate conference
rooms. All public rooms
underwent major refurbishment
during 1987.*
Bedrooms: 15 single,
10 double & 36 twin, 9 family
rooms.
Bathrooms: 70 private.
Bed & breakfast: £55-£65
single, £80 double.
Lunch available.
Evening meal 7pm (l.o.
10pm).
Parking for 100.
Credit: Access, Visa, C.Bl.,
Diners, Amex.

ॐ ♨ ☎ ⊡ ❑ ╬ 🛎 V ⌑
● ▥ ♨ ♟ SP T

Spitfire Hotel M
♨♨

156-158 Hill Lane, Shirley,
Southampton, SO1 5DD
☎ (0703) 638143
*Completely refurbished family-
run hotel. Centrally situated
and an ideal base for touring
Southampton and all
surrounding areas.*
Bedrooms: 10 single, 4 double
& 4 twin, 2 family rooms.
Bathrooms: 7 private,
3 public.
Bed & breakfast: £18.50-£32
single, £32-£46 double.
Half board: £24.50-£38 daily,
£170-£250 weekly.
Evening meal 6.30pm (l.o.
8pm).
Parking for 10.
Credit: Access, Visa.

ॐ ♨ ☎ ⊡ ❑ ╬ 🛎 📺 ▥
♨ ♟ T

┌─────────────────────┐
│ **Half board prices**
│ **shown are per**
│ **person but in some**
│ **cases may be based**
│ **on double/twin**
│ **occupancy.**
└─────────────────────┘

Hampshire
Map ref 2C2

Village in high position on
the downs. Nearby is
Farley Mount Bronze Age
Barrow and Horse
Monument.

Lainston House M
♨♨♨♨

Sparsholt, Winchester,
SO21 2LT
☎ (0962) 863588 Fax (0962)
72672 Telex 477375
ℂℝ Prestige
*Magnificent, Georgian, listed
17th C. country house set in 63
acres of parkland. Recently
completely refurbished and
offering a high standard of
food and service.*
Bedrooms: 7 single, 10 double
& 14 twin, 1 family room.
Bathrooms: 32 private.
Bed & breakfast: from £91
single, £112-£232 double.
Half board: £140-£260 daily.
Lunch available.
Evening meal 7pm (l.o.
10pm).
Parking for 96.
Credit: Access, Visa, C.Bl.,
Diners, Amex.

ॐ ♨ ☎ ⊡ ❑ ⌑ V ⌑ ●
▥ ♨ ♟ 🐕 🌲 J 🌲 🖎 SP
♟ T

Hampshire
Map ref 2C2

Set in the Test Valley
which has some of the
best fishing in England.
The wide main street has
houses of all styles,
mainly Tudor and
Georgian.

Carbery Guest House M
♨♨♨ COMMENDED

Salisbury Hill, Stockbridge,
SO20 6EZ
☎ Andover (0264) 810771
*Fine old Georgian house in 1
acre of landscaped gardens and
lawns, overlooking the River
Test. Games and swimming
facilities, riding and fishing can
be arranged. Ideal for touring
the South Coast and the New
Forest.*
Bedrooms: 4 single, 3 double
& 3 twin, 1 family room.
Bathrooms: 8 private,
1 public.
Bed & breakfast: £17.25-£25
single, £34.50-£40.25 double.

Continued ▶

STOCKBRIDGE

Continued

Half board: £25.87-£33.62 daily, from £180 weekly.
Evening meal 7pm (l.o. 6pm).
Parking for 12.

Grosvenor Hotel M

High Street, Stockbridge,
SO20 6EU
☎ Andover (0264) 810606
Telex 477677
ⓖ Lansbury
Country town hotel in Test Valley, within easy reach of Romsey, Salisbury and Winchester. Enclosed garden.
Bedrooms: 4 single, 14 double & 7 twin.
Bathrooms: 25 private.
Bed & breakfast: £33-£65 single, £66-£78 double.
Half board: £44-£93 daily.
Lunch available.
Evening meal 7.30pm (l.o. 9.45pm).
Parking for 60.
Credit: Access, Visa, Diners, Amex.

The Old Three Cups Hotel

High Street, Stockbridge,
SO20 6HB
☎ (0264) 810527
Old coaching inn with modern comforts and an a la carte restaurant.
Bedrooms: 2 single, 3 double & 1 twin, 2 family rooms.
Bathrooms: 3 private,
1 public.
Bed & breakfast: £22-£32 single, £32-£42 double.
Half board: £30-£40 daily.
Lunch available.
Evening meal 6pm (l.o. 9.30pm).
Parking for 13.
Open February-December.
Credit: Access, Visa.

STUBBINGTON

Hampshire
Map ref 2C3

Crofton Manor Hotel

Titchfield Road,
Stubbington, Fareham
PO14 2EB
☎ (0329) 664216 Fax (0329) 668401
Run as a country house hotel with conference, function and catering facilities.

Bedrooms: 2 single, 3 double & 2 twin.
Bathrooms: 3 private,
2 public.
Bed & breakfast: £20-£35 single, £30-£50 double.
Lunch available.
Evening meal 7pm (l.o. 10pm).
Parking for 200.
Credit: Access, Visa.

STUDLAND

Dorset
Map ref 2B3

On a beautiful stretch of coast and good for walking, with a National Nature Reserve to the north. The Norman church is the finest in the country, with superb rounded arches and vaulting. Brownsea Island, where the first scout camp was held, lies in Poole Harbour but within the parish boundary.

Knoll House Hotel

Studland, Nr. Swanage,
BH19 3AH
☎ (092 944) 251
Independent country hotel in National Trust Reserve. Access to 3-mile beach from 100-acre grounds. Many facilities. Weekly rates are for full board.
Bedrooms: 29 single, 20 twin, 30 family rooms.
Bathrooms: 56 private,
10 public.
Half board: £45-£68 daily, £310-£470 weekly.
Lunch available.
Evening meal 7.30pm (l.o. 8.15pm).
Parking for 100.
Open April-October.

The Manor House M
COMMENDED

Beach Road, Studland, Nr. Swanage, BH19 3AU
☎ (092 944) 288
18th C manor house nestling in secluded gardens overlooking the sea, 3 miles from safe, sandy beaches. Oak-panelled bar and dining room. Tennis courts.
Bedrooms: 6 double & 6 twin, 6 family rooms.
Bathrooms: 18 private,
1 public.
Bed & breakfast: £30-£35 single, £51-£64 double.

Half board: £42.50-£49 daily, £245-£305 weekly.
Lunch available.
Evening meal 7pm (l.o. 8.30pm).
Parking for 40.
Open February-December.
Credit: Access, Visa.

STURMINSTER NEWTON

Dorset
Map ref 2B3

Every Monday this small town holds a livestock market. One of the bridges over the River Stour is a fine medieval example and bears a plaque declaring that anyone 'injuring' it will be deported.

Stourcastle Lodge

Goughs Close, Sturminster Newton, DT10 1BU
☎ (0258) 72320
Small and family-run, ensuring personal service and comfort. Freshly prepared and cooked food with baking a speciality.
Bedrooms: 1 single, 1 double & 1 twin.
Bathrooms: 1 private,
1 public.
Bed & breakfast: £26 single, £39 double.
Half board: £30.50-£36 daily, £199.85-£240 weekly.
Evening meal 7pm (l.o. 10pm).
Parking for 10.

SWANAGE

Dorset
Map ref 2B3

Began life as an Anglo-Saxon port, then a quarrying centre of Purbeck marble. Now the safe, sandy beach set in a sweeping bay and flanked by downs is good walking country, making it an ideal resort.
Tourist Information Centre ☎ *(0929) 422885*

The Haven

Victoria Road, Swanage,
BH19 1LY
☎ (0929) 423088
Attractive, detached hotel in quiet location close to sandy beach and park. Comfortable rooms, mostly en-suite. Ample car parking.
Bedrooms: 1 single, 1 double & 2 twin, 4 family rooms.

Bathrooms: 5 private,
2 public.
Bed & breakfast: £13-£21 single, £26-£42 double.
Parking for 8.
Open March-November.
Credit: Access, Visa.

Havenhurst Hotel
COMMENDED

3 Cranborne Road, Swanage, BH19 1EA
☎ (0929) 424224
Charming, detached, licensed hotel, quietly situated on level. Short walk to beach and shops. Special attention given.
Bedrooms: 3 single, 6 double & 4 twin, 4 family rooms.
Bathrooms: 17 private.
Bed & breakfast: £17-£28.50 single, £34-£47 double.
Half board: £25-£31.50 daily, £150-£186 weekly.
Evening meal 7pm.
Parking for 16.

Ingleside Guest House M

16 Park Road, Swanage,
BH19 2AD
☎ (0929) 423005
Family-run guest house within 2 minutes' walking distance of sea and beach.
Bedrooms: 1 single, 4 double & 1 twin, 1 family room.
Bathrooms: 1 public;
2 private showers.
Bed & breakfast: £13-£16 single, £26-£32 double.
Half board: £19-£22 daily, £119-£132 weekly.
Evening meal 6.30pm (l.o. 4.30pm).

The Limes Hotel M
Listed

48 Park Road, Swanage,
BH19 2AE
☎ (0929) 422664
A small, friendly, family hotel with a host of facilities and a keen price deal for the family holiday.
Bedrooms: 2 single, 1 double, 10 family rooms.
Bathrooms: 10 private,
3 public.
Bed & breakfast: £15-£20 single, £34-£40 double.
Half board: £25-£30 daily, £116-£130 weekly.
Evening meal 6pm (l.o. 4pm).
Parking for 11.

Methodist Guild Holidays, Highcliffe

4 Highcliffe Road, Swanage,
BH19 1LW
☎ (0929) 424806
*Set on clifftop overlooking sea,
Swanage Bay and Ballard
Downs, with private steps to
sandy beach and safe bathing.*
Bedrooms: 6 single, 11 double
& 6 twin, 12 family rooms.
Bathrooms: 11 public.
Half board: from £140
weekly.
Lunch available.
Evening meal 6.30pm.
Parking for 12.

Nethway Hotel

Gilbert Road, Swanage,
BH19 1DU
☎ (0929) 423909
*Conveniently situated very
close to beach, town and all
amenities, on level ground
facing south.*
Bedrooms: 2 single, 4 double
& 3 twin, 3 family rooms.
Bathrooms: 5 private,
3 public.
Bed & breakfast: £17.50-
£18.50 single, £32-£36 double.
Half board: £23-£25 daily,
£135-£145 weekly.
Evening meal 6.30pm (l.o.
6.30pm).
Parking for 10.
Open April-October.

The Oxford Hotel M
COMMENDED

3-5 Park Road, Swanage,
BH19 2AA
☎ (0929) 422247
*100 yards from town centre
and beaches. Basic or en-suite
available. Ideal centre for the
Purbecks. Friendly family
atmosphere. Resident
proprietors.*
Bedrooms: 2 single, 6 double
& 2 twin, 4 family rooms.
Bathrooms: 6 private,
2 public.
Bed & breakfast: £18-£19
single, £36-£38 double.
Half board: £25.50-£26.50
daily, £175-£182 weekly.
Evening meal 6.30pm (l.o.
4pm).
Open March-October.

The Pines Hotel M
APPROVED

Burlington Road, Swanage,
BH19 1LT
☎ (0929) 425211 Fax (0929)
422075 Telex 418297
*Family-run hotel set amid the
Purbeck countryside at quiet
end of Swanage Bay. Own
access to beach.*
Bedrooms: 4 single, 10 double
& 11 twin, 26 family rooms.
Bathrooms: 49 private,
1 public.
Bed & breakfast: £30-£40
single, £60-£80 double.
Half board: £45-£51 daily,
£262-£301 weekly.
Lunch available.
Evening meal 7.30pm (l.o.
9pm).
Parking for 60.
Credit: Access, Visa.

Sandringham Hotel M
COMMENDED

20 Durlston Road, Swanage,
BH19 2HX
☎ (0929) 423076
*In a quiet residential area
overlooking sea, 5 minutes
from town, beach, downs and
country park.*
Bedrooms: 2 single, 3 double
& 1 twin, 5 family rooms.
Bathrooms: 11 private,
1 public.
Bed & breakfast: £19-£22
single, £38-£44 double.
Half board: £27-£30 daily,
£142-£187 weekly.
Evening meal 6.30pm (l.o.
6.30pm).
Parking for 10.
Open March-December.

Vernon Lodge Hotel

87 Kings Road, Swanage,
BH19 1HL
☎ (0929) 422978
*Friendly, private hotel, situated
on level ground within easy
reach of sea and shops.*
Bedrooms: 1 double, 6 family
rooms.
Bathrooms: 2 public.
Bed & breakfast: £12-£14
single, £24-£28 double.
Half board: £17-£19 daily,
£115-£126 weekly.
Evening meal 6pm.
Parking for 4.

White Lodge Hotel M

Grosvenor Road, Swanage,
BH19 2DD
☎ (0929) 422696 & 425510
*Country style residence set in
one-third of an acre garden, 5
minutes from beach, coastal
path and country park. Lovely
views of bay from most rooms.*
Bedrooms: 1 single, 2 double
& 5 twin, 3 family rooms.
Bathrooms: 10 private,
2 public.
Bed & breakfast: £15-£20
single, £30-£35 double.
Half board: £22-£27 daily,
£140-£180 weekly.
Evening meal 6.30pm.
Parking for 10.
Credit: Access, Visa.

SWAY
Hampshire
Map ref 2C3

4m NW. Lymington
Small village on the
south-western edge of
the New Forest. It is
noted for its 220-ft tower,
Peterson's Folly, built in
the 1870s by a retired
Indian judge to
demonstrate the value of
concrete as a building
material.

String of Horses M
COMMENDED

Mead End, Sway, Lymington,
SO41 6EH
☎ Lymington (0590) 682631
*Unique, secluded hotel set in 4
acres, in the New Forest. Well-
appointed bedrooms and
fantasy bathrooms with spa
baths.*
Bedrooms: 6 double.
Bathrooms: 6 private.
Bed & breakfast: £50-£60
single, £60-£85 double.
Lunch available.
Evening meal 7.30pm (l.o.
9pm).
Parking for 12.
Credit: Access, Visa, Amex.

White Rose Hotel M
APPROVED

Village Centre, Sway, Nr.
Lymington, SO41 6BA
☎ Lymington (0590) 682754
*Family-run country house hotel
with 6 acres of grounds, in
small village on edge of New
Forest.*
Bedrooms: 2 single, 5 double
& 2 twin, 2 family rooms.

Bathrooms: 9 private,
2 public.
Bed & breakfast: £33-£40
single, £52-£66 double.
Half board: £36-£50 daily,
£147-£308 weekly.
Lunch available.
Evening meal 7pm (l.o.
8.45pm).
Parking for 50.
Credit: Access, Visa.

WAREHAM
Dorset
Map ref 2B3

This site has been
occupied since pre-
Roman times and has a
turbulent history. In 1762
fire destroyed much of
the town, so the buildings
now are mostly Georgian.

Kemps Country House Hotel M
APPROVED

East Stoke, Wareham,
BH20 6AL
☎ Bindon Abbey
(0929) 462563
*Victorian rectory set in
spacious grounds overlooking
the Purbeck Hills. 2 miles west
of Wareham on the A352.*
Bedrooms: 1 single, 8 double
& 2 twin, 4 family rooms.
Bathrooms: 14 private,
1 public.
Bed & breakfast: £45-£63 ♦
single, £68-£100 double.
Half board: £46-£64 daily,
£239-£395 weekly.
Lunch available.
Evening meal 7pm (l.o.
10pm).
Parking for 36.
Credit: Access, Visa, Diners,
Amex.

WEST LULWORTH
Dorset
Map ref 2B3

Well-known for Lulworth
Cove, the almost
landlocked circular bay of
chalk and limestone cliffs.

Bishop's Cottage Hotel M
APPROVED

West Lulworth, Wareham,
BH20 5RQ
☎ (092 941) 261 & 404
Continued ▶

**Half board prices shown are per person
but in some cases may be based on
double/twin occupancy.**

497

WEST LULWORTH
Continued

Comfortable family hotel close to and overlooking Lulworth Cove. Ideal for seaside and walking.
Bedrooms: 3 single, 12 double & 5 twin, 5 family rooms.
Bathrooms: 17 private, 4 public.
Bed & breakfast: £17.50-£19.50 single, £35-£39 double.
Half board: £27-£29 daily, £175-£190 weekly.
Lunch available.
Evening meal 7pm (l.o. 10pm).
Credit: Access, Visa.

Cromwell House Hotel M
West Lulworth, Wareham, BH20 5RJ
☎ (0929) 41253 Fax (0929) 41566
Family hotel on the Dorset Heritage Coast footpath. Outstanding views over Lulworth Cove. Sea views from secluded garden. Good walking country.
Bedrooms: 1 single, 7 double & 5 twin, 1 family room.
Bathrooms: 14 private.
Bed & breakfast: £20.50-£24.50 single, £43-£51 double.
Half board: £28-£31.50 daily, £182-£206 weekly.
Lunch available.
Evening meal 6.45pm (l.o. 8.30pm).
Parking for 17.
Credit: Access, Visa.

Lulworth Cove Inn
West Lulworth, Nr. Wareham, BH20 5RQ
☎ (092 941) 333
Hotel and pub specialising in home-made food and local seafood. Spectacular views of Lulworth Cove from many bedrooms.
Bedrooms: 10 double & 2 twin, 2 family rooms.
Bathrooms: 14 private, 1 public.
Bed & breakfast: £20-£24 single, £36-£40 double.
Lunch available.
Evening meal 6.30pm (l.o. 9.30pm).
Parking for 11.
Credit: Access, Visa, Diners, Amex.

Shirley Hotel M
COMMENDED
West Lulworth, Wareham, BH20 5RL
☎ (092 941) 358
Homely, modern hotel close to Lulworth Cove and coastal footpath. Ideal for walking or touring. Friendly relaxed atmosphere.
Bedrooms: 5 single, 8 double & 4 twin, 2 family rooms.
Bathrooms: 19 private.
Bed & breakfast: £19.25-£22.25 single, £38.50-£44.50 double.
Half board: £26.10-£30.25 daily, £157.85-£192.15 weekly.
Evening meal 6pm (l.o. 9pm).
Parking for 22.
Open March-October.
Credit: Access, Visa.

WICKHAM
Hampshire
Map ref 2C3

Lying in the Meon Valley, this market town is built around the Square and in Bridge Street can be seen some timber-framed cottages. Still the site of an annual horse fair.

The Old House Hotel
The Square, Wickham, PO17 5JG
☎ (0329) 833049 Fax (0329) 833672
An attractive Georgian house in a historic Georgian village square, skilfully converted in 1969/70 to a hotel with restaurant noted for French regional cooking.
Bedrooms: 3 single, 5 double & 3 twin, 1 family room.
Bathrooms: 12 private.
Bed & breakfast: £70-£80 single, £90-£100 double.
Lunch available.
Evening meal 7.30pm (l.o. 9.30pm).
Parking for 12.
Credit: Access, Visa, Diners, Amex.

We advise you to confirm your booking in writing.

Please check prices and other details at the time of booking.

WIMBORNE MINSTER
Dorset
Map ref 2B3

Market town centred on the twin-towered Minster Church of St. Cuthberga which gave the town the second part of its name. Good touring base for the surrounding countryside, depicted in the writings of Thomas Hardy.
Tourist Information Centre ☎ (0202) 886116

Northill House M
COMMENDED
Horton, Wimborne, BH21 7HL
☎ Witchampton (0258) 840407
A mid-Victorian former farmhouse, modernised to provide comfortable bedrooms. Log fires and cooking using fresh produce.
Bedrooms: 5 double & 3 twin, 1 family room.
Bathrooms: 9 private.
Bed & breakfast: £28 single, £52 double.
Half board: £39 daily, £245.70 weekly.
Evening meal 7.30pm (l.o. 6.30pm).
Parking for 12.
Open February-December.
Credit: Access, Visa.

WINCHESTER
Hampshire
Map ref 2C3

King Alfred the Great made Winchester the capital of Saxon England. A magnificent Norman cathedral, with one of the longest naves in Europe, dominates the city. Home of Winchester College founded in 1382.
Tourist Information Centre ☎ (0962) 867871

Cathedral View
9A Magdalen Hill, Winchester, SO23 8HJ
☎ (0962) 863802
Edwardian guest house with views across historic city and cathedral. 5 minutes' walk from city centre. En-suite facilities, TV, parking.
Bedrooms: 3 double, 2 family rooms.
Bathrooms: 5 private.

Bed & breakfast: £25-£27.50 single, £35-£40 double.
Evening meal (l.o. midday).
Parking for 4.

Chantry Mead Hotel M
Bereweeke Road, Winchester, SO22 6AJ
☎ (0962) 844166 Fax (0962) 852767
Modern, comfortable hotel with plenty of parking, within half a mile of the city centre.
Bedrooms: 5 single, 4 double & 7 twin, 2 family rooms.
Bathrooms: 10 private, 3 public.
Bed & breakfast: £20-£45 single, £35-£60 double.
Half board: £25-£55 daily, £175-£385 weekly.
Lunch available.
Evening meal 7pm (l.o. 9.30pm).
Parking for 22.
Credit: Access, Visa, Amex.

Florum House M
APPROVED
47 St. Cross Road, Winchester, SO23 9PS
☎ (0962) 840427
Elegant Victorian residence in Winchester, with gardens and patio. All bedrooms en-suite, with colour TV, and tea and coffee facilities.
Bedrooms: 2 double & 2 twin, 2 family rooms.
Bathrooms: 6 private.
Bed & breakfast: £30-£34 single, £38-£48 double.
Half board: £31-£36 daily, £217-£252 weekly.
Evening meal 7pm (l.o. 10am).
Parking for 6.

Harestock Lodge Hotel M
Harestock Road, Winchester, SO22 6NX
☎ (0962) 881870
Privately-run country house hotel set in secluded gardens on the edge of historic Winchester.
Bedrooms: 3 single, 7 double & 5 twin, 5 family rooms.
Bathrooms: 9 private, 1 public; 11 private showers.
Bed & breakfast: £33-£39 single, £40-£50 double.
Lunch available.

Evening meal 6.30pm (l.o. 9.30pm).
Parking for 22.
Credit: Access, Visa, Amex.

Portland House Hotel ⋈
☺☺ COMMENDED

63 Tower Street, Winchester, SO23 8TA
☎ (0962) 865195
Quietly situated, family-run establishment, close to city centre and convenient for the station and theatre.
Bedrooms: 3 twin, 2 family rooms.
Bathrooms: 5 private.
Bed & breakfast: £28-£34 single, £38-£45 double.
Parking for 3.

The Royal Hotel ⋈
☺☺☺☺☺ COMMENDED

St. Peter Street, Winchester, SO23 8BS
☎ (0962) 840840
Telex 477071 ROYAL G
ⓒⓡ Best Western
This old traditional hotel retains its original charm and has been refurbished to give its guests 20th C comfort.
Bedrooms: 46 double & 12 twin, 1 family room.
Bathrooms: 59 private.
Bed & breakfast: £83-£85 single, £89.60-£113 double.

Lunch available.
Evening meal 7pm (l.o. 9pm).
Parking for 60.
Credit: Access, Visa, Diners, Amex.

Stratton House ⋈
Listed

Stratton Road, St. Giles Hill, Winchester, SO23 8JQ
☎ (0962) 863919 & 864529
Fax (0962) 842095
A lovely old Victorian house with an acre of grounds, in an elevated position on St. Giles Hill.
Bedrooms: 2 double & 1 twin, 2 family rooms.
Bathrooms: 1 private, 3 public; 2 private showers.
Bed & breakfast: £18-£20 single, £34-£40 double.
Half board: £24-£26 daily, £160-£180 weekly.
Evening meal 6pm (l.o. 4pm).
Parking for 8.

The Winchester Moat House ⋈
☺☺☺☺ COMMENDED

Worthy Lane, Winchester, SO23 7AB
☎ (0962) 868102 Fax (0962) 840862 Telex 47383
ⓒⓡ Queens Moat Houses

New hotel with private leisure facilities, peacefully situated in England's ancient capital. Convenient for touring south coast and New Forest.
Bedrooms: 37 double & 38 twin.
Bathrooms: 75 private.
Bed & breakfast: £46-£80 single, £66-£99 double.
Half board: from £49.50 daily, from £346.50 weekly.
Lunch available.
Evening meal 7pm (l.o. 9.30pm).
Parking for 110.
Credit: Access, Visa, Diners, Amex.

The Wykeham Arms
75 Kingsgate Street, Winchester, SO23 9PE
☎ (0962) 853834
18th C. coaching inn sandwiched between Winchester Cathedral and the college in the quietest and oldest part of Winchester.
Bedrooms: 4 double & 3 twin.
Bathrooms: 7 private, 1 public.
Bed & breakfast: £55 single, £65 double.
Lunch available.
Evening meal 6.30pm (l.o. 8.45pm).
Parking for 12.

Hampshire
Map ref 2C3

Scattered village on the edge of the New Forest west of Southampton.

Busketts Lawn Hotel ⋈
☺☺☺ APPROVED

174 Woodlands Road, Woodlands, Nr. Southampton, SO4 2GL
☎ Ashurst (0703) 292272 & 292077 Fax (0703) 292487
Delightful country house hotel in quiet forest surroundings, 8 miles west of Southampton. Heated swimming pool.
Bedrooms: 4 single, 5 double & 3 twin, 2 family rooms.
Bathrooms: 14 private.
Bed & breakfast: £32.50-£65 single, £65-£95 double.
Half board: £45-£77.50 daily, £245-£296 weekly.
Lunch available.
Evening meal 7pm (l.o. 8.30pm).
Parking for 50.
Credit: Access, Visa, Diners, Amex.

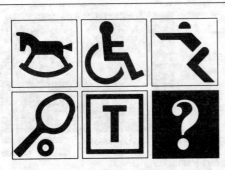

Key to symbols

Information about many of the services and facilities at establishments listed in this guide is given in the form of symbols. The key to these symbols is inside the back cover flap. You may find it helpful to keep the flap open when referring to the entry listings.

High Corner Inn

Linwood, Nr Ringwood, Hants BH24 3QY.
Tel: Ringwood (0425) 473973
Fax: (0425) 480015

COMMENDED   Egon Ronay   Les Routiers

Excellent freehouse and restaurant set deep in the New Forest. Open fires in the winter, large woodland garden for fine days. 7 luxurious bedrooms – all en-suite. Self catering woodland chalet also available.
Squash court and stabling. Beautiful forest walks.

LITTLE UPLANDS COUNTRY MOTEL

Garrison Hill, Droxford, Hampshire SO3 1QL ☎ Droxford (0489) 878507. Fax: 877853

A small family run motel situated in the picturesque Meon Valley in Hampshire. The perfect centre from which to tour the many historic places of Southern England. Ensuite bedrooms with tea & coffee making facilities, telephone, colour TV with satellite channels. Also available tennis, swimming, snooker, pool, sauna, sun-bed, gymnasium and fishing.
Visa, Access, Amex, Diners Card.
RAC Highly Acclaimed

Proprietors: S P Carvosso & A G Willis

𝕾eacourt 𝕳otel

Cliff Path, Sandown, Isle of Wight PO36 8PN.

Set within stone walled secluded gardens SEACOURT stands on the famous Cliff Path where no through traffic passes, spacious car park. Swimming pool, sauna, spa, snooker (full size). Beaches, buses and rail halt are all conveniently close by.

24 hr. DIAL-A-BROCHURE Tel: (0983) 402811 Fax: 407815.
To talk to us about your booking (0983) 403759.

22 EN SUITE ROOMS
Daily Rate Half board £25-£32 B & B £18-£25
Prices per week half board £150-£195
Special Christmas/New Year Programmes

Use a coupon

When requesting further information from advertisers in this guide, you may find it helpful to use the advertisement enquiry coupons which can be found towards the end of the guide. These should be cut out and mailed direct to the companies in which you are interested. Do remember to include your name and address.

South East England

Dazzling white clapboard dwellings, naval ports, the Downs... pictures of South East England. Vineyards, hop fields, chalk cliffs. Let the imagination run riot! Soaring cathedrals, flintstone cottages, oast houses. Bright, sunlit colours. Channel termini, family resorts, endless sands. Reds, blues, greens, yellows. Gardens to addle the eye, rivers to dream by... and so easy to get to — just whoosh to London and step through the door.

•» Wend along Kentish blossom routes, or walk the great white cliffs. Follow in smugglers' footsteps on unspoilt Romney Marsh, or maybe cycle round hills wrapped with orchards. Experience Chaucer again in Canterbury's Pilgrims' Way Centre, walk with Dickens at Rochester and Broadstairs. Shop along Royal Tunbridge Wells' elegant Pantiles, taste the salt of history at Chatham Dockyard and the Medway Heritage Centre.

•» Slide along the lazy Thames in Surrey — or walk the breezy North Downs, taking in charming market towns like Guildford with its castle and modern cathedral, and Dorking, near the famous beauty spot of Box Hill. Lose your tummy on Europe's

Wander past thatched cottages on your way to vineyards, smell the forests.

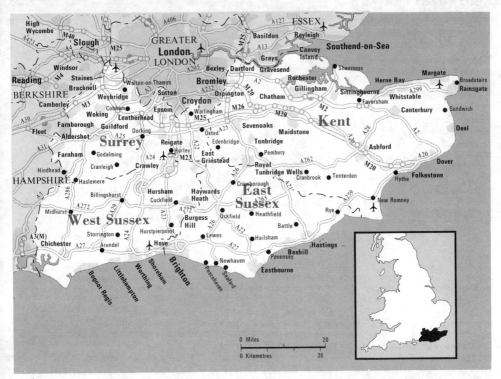

⏵⏵ Please refer to the colour maps at the back of this guide for all places with accommodation listings.

highest log-flume at Thorpe Park, and find romance at houses like the Elizabethan Loseley Park.

⏵⏵ So much pleasure! Wander past thatched cottages on your way to vineyards, smell the forests. Remember 1066 at castles, forts and the battlefield itself. Photograph Chichester Harbour, Arundel Castle and glorious Goodwood. Wander the cobbled streets of old Rye, greet the Seven Sisters, picnic on the South Downs. And enjoy famous resorts like Worthing, Brighton, Eastbourne and Margate, as well as smaller seaside towns. Get buried by the offspring on beaches awarded the coveted Blue Flag for excellence.

⏵⏵ In short, step through the door marked South East England — and find yourself in Wonderland!

Where to go, what to see

The Royal Pavilion in Brighton, now restored to its full glory

Kent and East Sussex Steam Railway
Town Station, Tenterden,
Kent TN30 6HE
☎ Tenterden (058 06) 5155
*Full-size steam railway.
Refurbished Edwardian stations
at Tenterdan and Northiam.
Three engines over 110 years
old, Pullman carriages and
carriages for the physically
handicapped.*

Penshurst Place
Penshurst, Tonbridge, Kent
TN11 8DG
☎ Penshurst (0892) 870307
*Great medieval manor house.
Baron's Hall, state rooms,
portraits, tapestries, furniture.
Home of Sidney family. Park
and lake, toy museum,
adventure playground, gardens.*

Eurotunnel Exhibition Centre
St. Martin's Plain, Cheriton
High Street, Folkestone, Kent
CT19 4QD
☎ Folkestone (0303) 270111
*Model railway layout of tunnels
and terminals, full-size mock-up
section of tunnel train. Network
map of Europe, displays,
models, viewing tower, shop.*

Bartley Mill
Bells Yew Green, Frant,
Tunbridge Wells, Kent TN3 8BH
☎ Lamberhurst (0892) 890372/
890820
*Once part of a thriving hop
farm, now milling organic
wheat. Small museum area,
farm trail, fishing, trout
hatchery, farm shop.*

A Day at the Wells
Corn Exchange, The Pantiles,
Tunbridge Wells, Kent TN2 5QJ
☎ Tunbridge Wells (0892)
546545
*With commentary on personal
stereos, visitors experience the
sights and sounds of 18th C
Tunbridge Wells, escorted by
Beau Nash.*

Port Lympne Zoo Park Mansion and Gardens
Port Lympne, Hythe, Kent
CT21 4PD
☎ Hythe (0303) 264646
*300-acre zoo park breeding rare
animals including deer,
antelope, rhino, tigers,
elephants. Mansion with art
gallery, exhibitions, murals,
gardens.*

Guildford Cathedral
Stag Hill, Guildford, Surrey
GU2 5UP
☎ Guildford (0483) 65287
*New Anglican cathedral,
foundation stone laid in 1936
and consecrated in 1961.
Notable glass engravings,
embroidered kneelers, modern
furnishings. Brass rubbing
centre.*

Guildford Boat House River Trips
River Way, Guildford, Surrey
☎ Guildford (0483) 504494
*Regular trips from Guildford to
St. Catherine's Lock and
Farncombe along the River
Wey. 'Alfred Leroy' cruising
restaurant for teas, and
Edwardian-style electric launch.*

Old Kiln Agricultural Museum
Reeds Road, Tilford,
Farnham, Surrey GU10 2DL
☎ Frensham (025 125) 2300
Museum with farm machines,

*implements, waggons, etc.
Wheelwright's shop, hop press,
working smithy and displays on
past village life.*

Royal Pavilion
Old Steine, Brighton, East
Sussex BN1 1UE
☎ Brighton (0273) 603005
*Eastern-style palace of Prince
Regent, built by Holland and
Nash. Original and
contemporary interiors, Chinese
porcelain. Magnificently
restored music room. Shop.*

Hastings Sea Life Centre
Rock-Nore-Road, Hastings,
East Sussex TN34 3DW
☎ Hastings (0424) 718776
*Display of marine life with
hundreds of sea creatures from
octopus to sharks from
Britains's deeper waters.*

Carr Taylor Vineyards
Yew Tree Farm, Westfield,
Hastings, East Sussex
TN35 4SG
☎ Hastings (0424) 752501
*Mature 21-acre vineyard and
newly planted 16 acres. Winery,
wine-making machinery, cellars.
Wine tasting with tours.*

Michelham Priory
Upper Dicker, Hailsham, East
Sussex BN27 3QS
☎ Hailsham (0323) 844224
13th-16th C priory and

Hastings Sea Life Centre − marine life from British waters

Vala Olafsdóttir

gatehouse with period furniture,
tapestries and picture gallery.
Working watermill, blacksmith's
and wheelwright's museum.

Chichester Cathedral

West Street, Chichester, West
Sussex PO19 1PX
☎ Chichester (0243) 782595
*Mainly Norman cathedral with
detached bell tower, Chagall
window, Sutherland painting,
font by John Skelton, tapestry
by Piper and Ursula Benker-
Schirmer.*

Fishbourne Roman Palace
and Museum

Salthill Road, Fishbourne,
West Sussex PO19 3QR
☎ Chichester (0243) 785859
*Remains of largest Roman
residence in Britain. Large
beautiful mosaics, now under
cover, hypocaust and restored
formal garden. Museum of
finds.*

Weald and Downland
Open Air Museum

Singleton, Chichester, West
Sussex PO18 0EU
☎ Singleton (024 363) 348
*Unusual open-air museum of
restored and re-erected historic
buildings, including medieval
houses, market hall, working
watermill. Woodland walk.*

Leonardslee Gardens

Lower Beeding, Horsham,
West Sussex RH13 6PP
☎ Lower Beeding (0403) 891212

*Large renowned spring-
flowering shrub garden in a
valley. Rhododendrons,
camellias, azaleas, series of
lakes and paths.*

Wakehurst Place Gardens

Ardingly, Haywards Heath,
West Sussex RH17 6TN
☎ Ardingly (0444) 892701
*Large gardens administered by
Royal Botanic Gardens, Kew.
Series of lakes, ponds and
important collection of exotic
trees, plants and shrubs. Heath
garden.*

Make a date for...

Holiday on Ice '91

Brighton Centre, Kings Road,
Brighton, East Sussex
3 − 27 January

World Clowns' Convention

Various venues, Bognor Regis,
West Sussex   *15 − 17 March*

Elaine Sheldrake

Easter Egg Hunt

Leeds Castle, Maidstone, Kent
30 March − 1 April

Pilkington Glass Ladies'
Tennis Championship

Devonshire Park, College
Road, Eastbourne, East
Sussex   *17 − 22 June*

Claremont Landscape
Garden Fête

Claremont, Esher, Surrey
10 − 14 July

Showjumping −
Silk Cut Derby

All England Jumping Course,
Hickstead, West Sussex
1 − 4 August

English Wine Festival
and Regional Food Fair

English Wine Centre,
Drusilla's Roundabout,
Alfriston, East Sussex
7 − 8 September

Lewes Bonfire Celebrations

Town Centre, Lewes, East
Sussex   *5 November*

Find out more

Further information on
holidays and attractions in the
South East England region is
available from:
**South East England Tourist
Board,** The Old Brew House,
Warwick Park, Tunbridge
Wells, Kent TN2 5TU.
☎ (0892) 540766.

These publications are
available free from the South
East England Tourist Board:

South East England '91

Take a Break 1990/91

Diary of Events

Also available are the
following (prices include
postage and packing):

*Hundreds of Places to Visit
in the South East* £1.90

*Leisure Map for South East
England* £3.05

Places to stay

»» Accommodation entries in this regional section are listed in alphabetical order of place name, and then in alphabetical order of establishment.

»» The map references refer to the colour maps towards the end of the guide. The first figure is the map number; the letter and figure which follow indicate the grid reference on the map.

»» The symbols at the end of each accommodation entry give information about services and facilities. A 'key' to these symbols is inside the back cover flap, which can be kept open for easy reference.

ALFRISTON

E. Sussex
Map ref 2D3

4m NE. Newhaven
Ancient town in the Cuckmere Valley and a former smugglers' haunt. The 14th C Clergy House was the first building to be bought by the National Trust. The spaciousness of the 14th C St. Andrew's church has earned it the title of 'Cathedral of the South Downs' and the 13th C Star Inn is one of the oldest in England.

Wingrove Inn
High St., Alfriston,
BN26 5TD
☎ (0323) 870276
Beside Alfriston village green with breathtaking views, Wingrove is one of the most popular country eating places in Sussex with all rooms having en-suite facilities.
Bedrooms: 4 double, 1 family room.
Bathrooms: 5 private.
Bed & breakfast: £40-£50 single, £50-£70 double.
Lunch available.
Parking for 30.
Credit: Access, Visa.
⌂ ☐ ♦ 📞 🛊 Ⓥ ☋ ♣ ❀
ⒹⒶⓅ SP

Map references apply to the colour maps towards the end of this guide.

ARUNDEL

W. Sussex
Map ref 2D3

Pleasant town on the River Arun, dominated by Arundel Castle, home of the Dukes of Norfolk. There are many 18th C houses and the Toy and Military Museum, Wildfowl Trust Reserve and Heritage Centre. *Tourist Information Centre ☎ (0903) 882268*

Arundel Resort Hotel M
♛♛♛♛
16 Chichester Road, Arundel,
BN18 0AD
☎ (0903) 882677 Fax (0903) 884154
Ⓡ Resort
17th C coaching inn with 16 en-suite bedrooms. Recently refurbished. Delightful rural setting, ideal for sightseeing.
Bedrooms: 8 double & 8 twin.
Bathrooms: 16 private.
Bed & breakfast: from £50.50 single, from £67 double.
Evening meal 7.30pm (l.o. 9.30pm).
Parking for 100.
Credit: Access, Visa, Diners, Amex.
⌂ ♨ 📞 ☐ ♦ 🛊 Ⓥ ◖
▥ ☋ 🍴 ▶ ❦ ⦿ SP Ⓣ

Avisford Park Hotel M
♛♛♛♛
Yapton La., Walberton,
Arundel, BN18 0LS
☎ Yapton (0243) 551215
Telex 86137

Georgian manor style house in 62 acres of parkland between Arundel and Chichester. All rooms with views of the grounds.
Bedrooms: 28 single, 44 double & 26 twin, 2 family rooms.
Bathrooms: 100 private.
Bed & breakfast: £70-£85 single, £106-£140 double.
Half board: £76.75-£105 daily.
Lunch available.
Evening meal 7.30pm (l.o. 9.30pm).
Parking for 200.
Credit: Access, Visa, Amex.
⌂ ☋ 📞 Ⓔ ☐ ♦ 🛊 Ⓥ ☋ ◢
◉ ▥ ☋ 🍴 ♫ ⦿ ☍ 🐟 ☌ 🏃 ⋔
🏹 ▶ ❀ 🛩 ☌ SP ⦿ Ⓣ

Bridge House M
♛♛♛
18 Queen St., Arundel,
BN18 9JG
☎ (0903) 882779 & 882142
In the centre of town, with views of castle, river and downs. Ideal centre for exploring beautiful Sussex. 3 double en-suite bedrooms in 16th C cottage annexe.
Bedrooms: 2 single, 4 double & 2 twin, 6 family rooms.
Bathrooms: 7 private, 3 public.
Bed & breakfast: £18-£26 single, £30-£38 double.
Half board: £28-£38 daily, £108.50-£170 weekly.
Parking for 10.
Credit: Access, Visa.
⌂ ♨ ☐ ♦ Ⓤ ⓛ 🛊 Ⓥ ☋ ▥
☌ 🏹 SP ⦿

Burpham Country Hotel M
♛♛♛
Burpham, Nr. Arundel,
BN18 9RJ
☎ (0903) 882160
In one of the most peaceful and unspoilt villages in West Sussex, with superb downland views. Ideal for walking holidays.
Bedrooms: 1 single, 5 double & 4 twin.
Bathrooms: 10 private.
Bed & breakfast: from £40 single, £58-£68 double.
Half board: £42-£47 daily.
Lunch available.
Evening meal 7pm (l.o. 8pm).
Parking for 12.
Credit: Access, Visa.
⌂ ☐ ♦ Ⓥ ⅟ ◢ ☌ 🛊
❀ 🏹 ☌ ☍ SP ⦿

Howards Hotel M
♛♛♛ COMMENDED
Crossbush, Arundel,
BN18 9PQ
☎ (0903) 882655 Fax (0903) 883384
Georgian-style hotel with large bar area, restaurants, traditional carvery and French bistro. Warm and friendly atmosphere.
Bedrooms: 4 double & 5 twin.
Bathrooms: 9 private.
Bed & breakfast: £40-£50 single, £60-£70 double.
Lunch available.
Evening meal 7pm (l.o. 9.45pm).
Parking for 150.
Credit: Access, Visa, Diners, Amex.
⌂ 📞 ☐ ♦ 🛊 Ⓥ ▥ 🍴 ❀
🏹 ☌ SP ⦿

506

Norfolk Arms Hotel M
♛♛♛♛
High St., Arundel, BN18 9AD
☎ (0903) 882101
Telex 878436 NORFOK G
*Charming 18th C Georgian
coaching inn set under the
battlements of Arundel Castle.*
Bedrooms: 3 single, 17 double
& 13 twin, 1 family room.
Bathrooms: 34 private,
2 public.
Bed & breakfast: £44.50-£50
single, £65-£71.50 double.
Half board: £55-£60.50 daily.
Lunch available.
Evening meal 7pm (l.o.
10pm).
Parking for 29.
Credit: Access, Visa, Diners,
Amex.

Swan Hotel M
♛♛♛ APPROVED
High St., Arundel,
BN18 9AG
☎ (0903) 882314
*A small, centrally located,
privately-run hotel. Our
emphasis is on fresh produce,
well cooked and attractively
served in comfortable
surroundings.*
Bedrooms: 2 single, 4 double
& 6 twin, 1 family room.
Bathrooms: 13 private.
Bed & breakfast: max. £47
single, max. £60 double.
Half board: £40-£57 daily.
Lunch available.
Evening meal 7pm (l.o.
9.30pm).
Credit: Access, Visa, Diners,
Amex.

**Individual
proprietors have
supplied all details
of accommodation.
Although we do
check for accuracy,
we advise you to
confirm prices and
other information
at the time of
booking.**

**Please mention this
guide when making
a booking.**

13m SW. Canterbury
Once a market centre for
the farmers of the Weald
of Kent and Romney
Marsh. The town centre
has a number of Tudor
and Georgian houses.
*Tourist Information
Centre* ☎ (0233) 37311
ext 316

Ashford International Hotel M
Simone Weil Avenue,
Ashford, TN24 8UX
☎ (0233) 611444
Ⓒ Queens Moat Houses
*Opened recently and of modern
design, the hotel blends
pleasantly with the surrounding
area. Located at junction 9 of
the M20/A20. Well situated
for both business and pleasure.*
Bedrooms: 45 double &
121 twin, 34 family rooms.
Bathrooms: 200 private.
Bed & breakfast: £86.90-
£126.50 single, £97.90-£165
double.
Lunch available.
Evening meal 7pm (l.o.
10pm).
Parking for 400.
Credit: Access, Visa, Diners,
Amex.

Croft Hotel M
♛♛♛ APPROVED
Canterbury Rd., Kennington,
Ashford, TN25 4DU
☎ (0233) 622140 Fax (0233)
622140
*Old, country-type house
situated in a peaceful, rural
area on the outskirts of the
town.*
Bedrooms: 8 single, 6 double
& 11 twin, 3 family rooms.
Bathrooms: 28 private.
Bed & breakfast: £33-£44
single, £45-£54 double.
Evening meal 6.30pm (l.o.
8pm).
Parking for 32.
Credit: Access, Visa, C.Bl.

Eastwell Manor M
♛♛♛ HIGHLY COMMENDED
Eastwell Park, Ashford,
TN25 4HR
☎ (0233) 35751 Telex 966281
E MANOR
Ⓒ Queens Moat Houses

*Peaceful, secluded hotel set in
62 acres of undulating
parkland in the heart of the
Kentish Downs.*
Bedrooms: 10 double &
13 twin.
Bathrooms: 23 private.
Bed & breakfast: £94-£117
single, £110-£250 double.
Half board: £119-£150 daily.
Lunch available.
Evening meal 7.30pm (l.o.
9.30pm).
Parking for 108.
Credit: Access, Visa, C.Bl.,
Diners, Amex.

Garden Court Holiday Inn
Maidstone Rd., Hothfield,
Ashford, TN26 1AR
☎ Charing (0233) 713333
Ⓒ Holiday Inn
*A new hotel with bar and
bistro-style restaurant, fitness
room and outdoor swimming
pool. Prices are per room,
regardless of number of people,
not including breakfast.*
Bedrooms: 2 single, 60 double
& 44 twin.
Bathrooms: 106 private.
Bed & breakfast: £37.50-
£47.50 single.
Half board: £52.50-£62.50
daily.
Parking for 130.
Credit: Access, Visa, Diners,
Amex.

4m NW. Steyning

Mill House Hotel M
♛♛♛♛
Mill Lane, Ashington,
RH20 3BZ
☎ (0903) 892426 Fax (0903)
892855
*A 1740 period house with some
additions and a pretty garden,
set in a quiet country lane.
Large double lounge with log
fires in winter.*
Bedrooms: 4 single, 5 double
& 1 twin.
Bathrooms: 9 private,
1 public.
Bed & breakfast: £38.50-
£42.50 single, £70-£80 double.
Half board: from £51 daily,
from £294 weekly.
Lunch available.
Evening meal 7pm (l.o.
9.45pm).

Parking for 10.
Credit: Access, Visa, Diners,
Amex.

Built on the site of the
Battle of Hastings, when
William defeated Harold II
and so became the
Conqueror in 1066. This
thriving town contains
many old buildings,
including the impressive
abbey ruins. The museum
deals with history from
the Neolithic age and has
a fine collection relating
to the Sussex iron
industry.
*Tourist Information
Centre* ☎ (04246) 3721

Burnt Wood Hotel and Country Club M
Powdermill La., Battle,
TN33 0SU
☎ Battle (042 46) 5151 Fax
(042 46) 2459
*18-acre smallholding. Country
house hotel 1.5 miles from
centre of Battle, heart of 1066
country. 7 miles from sea.*
Bedrooms: 2 single, 8 double.
Bathrooms: 10 private.
Bed & breakfast: £40-£50
single, £55-£75 double.
Half board: £45-£55 daily,
£265-£300 weekly.
Evening meal 7pm (l.o.
10pm).
Parking for 30.
Credit: Access, Visa, Diners,
Amex.

La Vieille Auberge Hotel and Restaurant M
♛♛♛♛
27 High St., Battle,
TN33 0EA
☎ Battle (042 46) 5171 Fax
(042 46) 4015
*Formerly the Bull Inn, dating
back to 15th C. Rebuilt 1688
using stones from Old Abbey
kitchens. Fine staircase.
Inglenook restaurant, French
cuisine.*
Bedrooms: 2 single, 3 double
& 1 twin, 1 family room.
Bathrooms: 5 private,
1 public.
Bed & breakfast: £35-£45
single, £45-£60 double.
Lunch available.
Continued ▶

BATTLE
Continued

Evening meal 7pm (l.o. 10pm).
Parking for 2.
Credit: Access, Visa, Amex.

Priory House Hotel ⚔

☰☰☰ APPROVED

17 High St., Battle, TN33 0EA
☎ (042 46) 3366
Charming Queen Anne family-run hotel offering value for money and clean accommodation. English food.
Bedrooms: 3 double & 1 twin, 2 family rooms.
Bathrooms: 5 private, 1 public.
Bed & breakfast: £24 single, £38 double.
Half board: £25-£28 daily, £175-£196 weekly.
Lunch available.
Evening meal 7pm (l.o. 9pm).
Credit: Access, Visa.

BEXHILL-ON-SEA
E. Sussex
Map ref 3B4

Popular seaside resort with a gently shelving beach of shingle and firm sand at low tide. A feature is the De la Warr Pavilion, containing a theatre, ballroom, banqueting suite, restaurant and sun terrace. East of the town, at Little Gally Hill, a submerged forest can be seen at low tide, a land bridge which linked Britain to the continent 10,000 years ago.
Tourist Information Centre ☎ (0424) 212023

The Arosa Guest House ⚔

Listed APPROVED

6 Albert Rd., Bexhill-on-Sea TN40 1DG
☎ (0424) 212574
Traditional family guesthouse in Bexhill centre. 2 minutes' walk from seafront, offering value and personal service.
Bedrooms: 3 single, 2 double & 3 twin, 1 family room.
Bathrooms: 2 private, 2 public.
Bed & breakfast: £12-£18 single, £22-£36 double.
Half board: £17-£23 daily, £100-£140 weekly.

Lunch available.
Evening meal 6pm (l.o. midday).

Buenos Aires

Listed

24 Albany Rd., Bexhill-on-Sea, TN40 1BZ
☎ (0424) 212269
Well-established guesthouse adjacent to seafront, theatre and town centre, offering comfortable accommodation and a friendly atmosphere.
Bedrooms: 1 double & 1 twin, 2 family rooms.
Bathrooms: 1 public.
Bed & breakfast: £15 single, £25-£28 double.
Half board: £18.50-£21 daily, £125-£142 weekly.
Evening meal 6pm (l.o. midday).

Cooden Resort Hotel ⚔

☰☰☰

Cooden Beach, Bexhill-on-Sea, TN39 4TT
☎ Cooden (042 43) 2281 Fax (042 43) 6142
⊕ Resort
Beautifully situated on the beach, providing an ideal centre for exploring "1066" country. Golf and other leisure facilities all available, with discounts for guests.
Bedrooms: 11 single, 6 double & 14 twin, 5 family rooms.
Bathrooms: 36 private, 1 public.
Bed & breakfast: £56.50-£61.50 single, £73-£78 double.
Lunch available.
Evening meal 7pm (l.o. 9.30pm).
Parking for 60.
Credit: Access, Visa, Diners, Amex.

The Granville Hotel ⚔

☰☰☰☰ APPROVED

Sea Road, Bexhill-on-Sea, TN40 1EE
☎ Bexhill (0424) 215437
Splendid, modernised, family-owned Victorian hotel, in quiet situation close to town centre and beach.
Bedrooms: 2 single, 14 double & 33 twin, 1 family room.
Bathrooms: 50 private.
Bed & breakfast: £39.50-£49.50 single, £59.50-£69.50 double.
Half board: £40-£55 daily, £225-£275 weekly.
Lunch available.

Evening meal 6pm (l.o. 9pm).
Credit: Access, Visa, Diners, Amex.

Northern Hotel ⚔

☰☰☰ APPROVED

72-82 Sea Rd., Bexhill-on-Sea, TN40 1JN
☎ (0424) 212836
Terrace of 6 large Edwardian town houses in quiet seaside resort. Convenient as touring base for 1066 country.
Bedrooms: 9 single, 4 double & 6 twin, 1 family room.
Bathrooms: 20 private, 3 public.
Bed & breakfast: £32 single, £54 double.
Half board: £35-£45 daily, £222-£253 weekly.
Lunch available.
Evening meal 5.45pm (l.o. 8pm).
Credit: Access, Visa.

Park Lodge Hotel

☰☰☰

16 Egerton Rd., Bexhill-on-Sea, TN39 3HH
☎ (0424) 216547
Family-run hotel. Seafront, park and theatre within 50 yards.
Bedrooms: 1 single, 2 double & 2 twin, 2 family rooms.
Bathrooms: 5 private, 1 public; 1 private shower.
Bed & breakfast: £22-£28 single, £37-£42 double.
Half board: £25-£30 daily, £140-£150 weekly.
Evening meal 6pm (l.o. 7pm).
Credit: Access, Visa.

Victoria Hotel ⚔

☰☰☰

1 Middlesex Rd., Bexhill-on-Sea, TN40 1LP
☎ (0424) 210382
Small family-run hotel offering good sized accommodation and enclosed gardens with a quiet and pleasant outlook. 100 yards from the sea.
Bedrooms: 3 single, 2 double & 2 twin, 3 family rooms.
Bathrooms: 6 private, 2 public.
Bed & breakfast: £17.50-£25 single, £33-£45 double.
Half board: £22-£30 daily, £146.50-£175 weekly.
Lunch available.
Evening meal 6pm (l.o. 6pm).
Parking for 7.

BIDDENDEN
Kent
Map ref 3B4

Perfect village with black and white houses, a tithe barn and a pond. Part of the village is grouped round a green with a village sign depicting the famous Biddenden Maids. It was an important centre of the Flemish weaving industry, hence the beautiful Old Cloth Hall.

Biddenden Place

Tenterden Rd., Biddenden, Ashford, TN27 8BB
☎ (0580) 291419
Elizabethan building set in 2 acres of formal gardens, with a Grecian styled pavilion. Sunday lunch our speciality, coffee, lunch and tea daily.
Bedrooms: 2 single, 2 double, 1 family room.
Bathrooms: 4 private, 1 public.
Bed & breakfast: £13-£18 single, from £44 double.
Lunch available.
Parking for 7.
Credit: Access, Visa.

BIRCHINGTON
Kent
Map ref 3C3

Town on the north coast of Kent with sandy beaches and rock pools. Powell Cotton Museum is in nearby Quex Park.

Crown Inn ⚔

☰☰☰

Sarre, Nr. Birchington, CT7 0LF
☎ Thanet (0843) 47808 Fax (0843) 47914
Beautifully appointed bedrooms with en-suite facilities, TV and telephone. Three bars and an a la carte restaurant.
Bedrooms: 10 double & 2 twin, 1 family room.
Bathrooms: 13 private.
Bed & breakfast: £38.50-£60 single, £55-£60 double.
Half board: £300-£400 weekly.
Lunch available.
Evening meal 7pm (l.o. 9.30pm).
Parking for 27.
Credit: Access, Visa, Diners, Amex.

BOGNOR REGIS

W. Sussex
Map ref 2D3

5 miles of firm, flat sand have made the town a popular family resort. Well supplied with gardens, children's activities in Hotham Park and the Bognor Regis Centre for entertainment.
Tourist Information Centre ☎ (0243) 823140

Beachcroft Hotel M
☲☲

Clyde Rd., Felpham, Bognor Regis, PO22 7AH
☎ (0243) 827142
Family-run hotel in beachside location, with south-facing garden and indoor heated pool. Weekly dancing. Table d'hote and a la carte menus.
Bedrooms: 8 single, 6 double & 16 twin, 5 family rooms.
Bathrooms: 35 private.
Bed & breakfast: £25.25-£28.50 single, £38.50-£54 double.
Half board: £25.75-£33 daily, £174.75-£214 weekly.
Lunch available.
Evening meal 6.30pm (l.o. 9.30pm).
Parking for 40.
Open January-November.
Credit: Access, Visa.

Belle Vue Hotel

The Esplanade, Bognor Regis, PO21 1TA
☎ (0243) 863434
Family hotel overlooking sea and Waterloo square. 2 minutes from town centre. All rooms with TV, central heating, most en-suite. Licensed.
Bedrooms: 2 single, 4 double & 2 twin, 4 family rooms.
Bathrooms: 3 private, 3 public; 4 private showers.
Bed & breakfast: £18.50-£25 single, £30-£38 double.
Half board: £24-£30 daily, £1168-£210 weekly.
Evening meal 6.30pm (l.o. 10.30pm).
Parking for 12.
Credit: Access, Visa, Diners, Amex.

Black Mill House Hotel M
☲☲☲ APPROVED

Princess Ave., Bognor Regis, PO21 2QU
☎ Bognor Regis
(0243) 821945/865596 Fax (0243) 821316

Quiet situation, 300 yards from sea and Marine Gardens. Picnic lunches and afternoon teas. Enclosed garden. Special offers for children.
Bedrooms: 9 single, 5 double & 6 twin, 6 family rooms.
Bathrooms: 18 private, 5 public.
Bed & breakfast: £25-£38.50 single, £42-£68 double.
Half board: £29-£47 daily, £160-£267 weekly.
Lunch available.
Evening meal 7pm (l.o. 8pm).
Parking for 13.
Credit: Access, Visa, Diners, Amex.

Homestead Private Hotel
☲☲

90 Aldwick Rd., Bognor Regis, PO21 2PD
☎ (0243) 823443
Family-run hotel with friendly, relaxed atmosphere, 200 yards from the beach, convenient for shops, entertainment and outdoor recreation.
Bedrooms: 2 single, 2 double & 2 twin, 4 family rooms.
Bathrooms: 1 private, 1 public; 2 private showers.
Bed & breakfast: £10.50-£11 single, £21-£22 double.
Half board: £14.50-£15 daily.
Evening meal 6pm (l.o. 7pm).
Parking for 12.
Credit: Access, Visa.

BOLNEY

W. Sussex
Map ref 2D3

Hickstead Resort Hotel M

Jobs Lane, Bolney, RH17 5PA
☎ Burgess Hill (0444) 248023
Fax (0444) 245280
CR Resort
Just off the A23, midway between Gatwick and Brighton. Fully refurbished bedrooms, bar, restaurants, banqueting/conference facilities and health club.
Bedrooms: 49 double.
Bathrooms: 49 private.
Bed & breakfast: from £61.50 single, from £83 double.
Lunch available.
Evening meal 7pm (l.o. 9.15pm).
Parking for 100.
Credit: Access, Visa, Diners, Amex.

BRENCHLEY

Kent
Map ref 3B4

6m NE. Tunbridge Wells
In the centre of this village is a small green, around which stand half-timbered, tile-hung and weatherboarded houses.

Bull Inn at Brenchley M
☲☲ APPROVED

High Street, Brenchley, TN12 7NQ
☎ (089 272) 2701
Victorian village inn set in the heart of the Weald of Kent. Comfortable accommodation with traditional English ales and home-cooked food.
Bedrooms: 3 double & 1 twin.
Bathrooms: 1 private, 1 public.
Bed & breakfast: £25-£40 single, £32-£45 double.
Half board: £30-£45 daily, £179-£315 weekly.
Lunch available.
Evening meal 6pm (l.o. 9.30pm).
Parking for 10.
Credit: Access, Visa.

Rose and Crown Inn M
☲☲☲ APPROVED

High St., Brenchley, Nr. Tonbridge, TN12 7NQ
☎ (089 272) 2107
Converted 14th C stables and stores opposite palace of Duke of St. Albans, son of Charles II and Nell Gwyn.
Bedrooms: 5 double & 5 twin.
Bathrooms: 10 private.
Bed & breakfast: £30-£35 single, £40-£50 double.
Half board: from £25 daily, from £175 weekly.
Lunch available.
Evening meal 7pm (l.o. 9.30pm).
Parking for 25.
Credit: Access, Visa, Diners, Amex.

Classifications and quality commendations were correct at the time of going to press but are subject to change. Please check at the time of booking.

BRIGHTON & HOVE

E. Sussex
Map ref 2D3

First and largest seaside resort in the south-east. Attractions include the Dome, Royal Pavilion, Theatre Royal, Volks Railway, Aquarium and Dolphinarium, Palace Pier, Stanmer Park, Marina, Conference and Exhibition Centre and 'The Lanes'.
Neighbouring Hove is a resort in its own right with interesting Museum of Art and King Alfred's Leisure Centre.
Tourist Information Centre ☎ (0273) 23755 or (accommodation) 27560; for Hove (0273) 775400 or 720371

Aannabelles Olde English Lodging House M
☲☲

9 Charles Street, Brighton, E.Sussex BN2 1TG
☎ (0273) 605845/677419
Established in 1790 in the heart of Brighton. Still retaining the charm of yesteryear but with all modern facilities available.
Bedrooms: 2 single, 2 double & 1 twin.
Bathrooms: 5 private.
Bed & breakfast: from £24.50 single, £49-£64.50 double.
Parking for 15.
Credit: Access, Visa, C.Bl., Diners, Amex.

Adelaide Hotel M
☲☲ COMMENDED

51 Regency Sq., Brighton, BN1 2FF
☎ (0273) 205286
Telex 877159 BHVTXSG ADELAIDE
Small, quiet and informal hotel. Convenient for all amenities, seafront and conference centre.
Bedrooms: 3 single, 6 double & 2 twin, 1 family room.
Bathrooms: 12 private, 1 public.
Bed & breakfast: £33-£60 single, £52-£70 double.
Half board: £43-£70 daily.
Evening meal 6.30pm (l.o. 8.30pm).
Credit: Access, Visa, Diners, Amex.

BRIGHTON & HOVE

Continued

Albany Hotel
♛♛♛

St. Catherine's Ter.,
Kingsway, Hove, BN3 2RR
☎ (0273) 773807
Situated on Kingsway, Grade II historic building. Sea view from front bedrooms. 1 mile west of Brighton West Pier.
Bedrooms: 1 single, 7 double & 2 twin.
Bathrooms: 10 private.
Bed & breakfast: £19.50-£29.50 single, £29.50-£39.50 double.
Half board: £25.50-£35 daily.
Evening meal 6.30pm (l.o. 5pm).

The Alexandra Hotel ₥
♛♛♛

42 Brunswick Ter., Hove,
BN3 1HA
☎ Brighton (0273) 202722
Telex 877579 ALEXBR G
Grade I Listed Regency hotel on Hove seafront, combining the elegance of a bygone era with modern amenities.
Bedrooms: 22 single, 16 double & 19 twin, 4 family rooms.
Bathrooms: 61 private.
Bed & breakfast: from £65.50 single, from £87.50 double.
Lunch available.
Evening meal 6.30pm (l.o. 9.30pm).
Credit: Access, Visa, Diners, Amex.

Allendale Hotel ₥
3, New Steine, Brighton,
East Sussex BN2 1PB
☎ Brighton
(0273) 675436/672994
Private hotel convenient for town centre and 100 yards from sea front. Panoramic sea views.
Bedrooms: 5 single, 1 double & 2 twin, 5 family rooms.
Bathrooms: 6 private,
2 public; 2 private showers.
Bed & breakfast: £25-£26.50 single, £37.50-£55 double.
Credit: Access, Visa, Amex.

Ambassador Hotel ₥
♛♛♛ APPROVED

22 New Steine, Marine Pde.,
Brighton, BN2 1PD
☎ (0273) 676869

Family-run, licensed hotel overlooking sea, near conference centres. All rooms en-suite. Telephone, radio, tea/coffee facilities and colour TV.
Bedrooms: 3 single, 2 double, 4 family rooms.
Bathrooms: 9 private.
Bed & breakfast: £23-£30 single, £40-£50 double.
Credit: Access, Visa, Diners, Amex.

Amblecliff Hotel
35 Upper Rock Gdns.,
Brighton, BN2 1QF
☎ (0273) 676945/681161
Featured on 2 TV programmes and in the Sunday Times. Close to seafront, all entertainments and conference centre.
Bedrooms: 3 single, 5 double & 3 twin.
Bathrooms: 8 private,
2 public.
Bed & breakfast: £16-£30 single, £32-£48 double.
Half board: £32-£46 daily,
£96-£144 weekly.
Evening meal 6pm (l.o. 6pm).
Parking for 3.
Credit: Access, Visa, Amex.

Arlanda Hotel ₥
♛♛♛ COMMENDED

20 New Steine, Brighton, East Sussex BN2 1PD
☎ Brighton (0273) 699300
Pretty guesthouse in garden square, with sea views. 2 minutes from town centre and 100 metres from sea.
Bedrooms: 4 single, 3 double & 3 twin, 4 family rooms.
Bathrooms: 12 private.
Bed & breakfast: £30 single, £50-£60 double.
Credit: Access, Visa, Diners, Amex.

Ascott House Hotel ₥
♛♛♛

21 New Steine, Marine Pde.,
Brighton, BN2 1PD
☎ (0273) 688085
Central hotel in seafront garden square, close to the Royal Pavilion, Lanes, Palace Pier, aquarium and conference centre.
Bedrooms: 4 single, 4 double, 4 family rooms.
Bathrooms: 9 private,
2 public.

Bed & breakfast: £20-£30 single, £40-£58 double.
Credit: Access, Visa, Diners, Amex.

Beach Hotel
2-4 Regency Sq., Brighton,
BN1 2FG
☎ (0273) 23776 Telex 878149 BRICEN-G
In Regency Square by the seafront, close to conference centre and shops.
Bedrooms: 1 single, 13 double & 16 twin, 2 family rooms.
Bathrooms: 32 private.
Bed & breakfast: £30-£50 single, £40-£60 double.
Evening meal 6.30pm (l.o. 9pm).
Credit: Access, Visa, Diners, Amex.

Hotel Brunswick ₥
♛

69 Brunswick Pl., Hove,
BN3 1NE
☎ (0273) 733326/730785
Telex 877159 BHVTXSG
Elegant Regency hotel with easy access to sea, shops, Brighton centre, golf, tennis and all entertainments. Enjoy our friendly atmosphere.
Bedrooms: 9 single, 4 double & 5 twin, 4 family rooms.
Bathrooms: 2 private,
3 public; 4 private showers.
Bed & breakfast: £19-£23 single, £32-£46 double.
Half board: £28.50-£35.50 daily, £150-£190 weekly.
Evening meal 7pm (l.o. 10pm).
Parking for 6.
Credit: Access, Visa, Diners, Amex.

Cavalaire House
34 Upper Rock Gdns.,
Brighton, BN2 1QF
☎ (0273) 696899
Close to all amenities, offering rooms with or without private facilities.
Bedrooms: 1 single, 3 double & 2 twin, 3 family rooms.
Bathrooms: 2 private,
1 public; 2 private showers.
Bed & breakfast: £14-£18 single, £26-£29 double.

Chatsworth Hotel
9 Salisbury Rd., Hove,
BN3 3AB
☎ (0273) 737360
Long established, well-appointed, comfortable hotel in quiet position close to sea, shops and buses. Accent on food.
Bedrooms: 5 single, 1 twin, 3 family rooms.
Bathrooms: 3 public.
Bed & breakfast: £16-£17 single, £30-£32 double.
Half board: £22-£24 daily,
£112-£119 weekly.
Evening meal 6.30pm (l.o. 7pm).

Cinderella Hotel ₥
♛

48 St. Aubyns, Hove,
BN3 2TE
☎ (0273) 733561/727827
Comfortable hotel near the sea and the King Alfred Sports Centre. Convenient for shops and bus to the Clock Tower. Free road parking. Colour TV in all double bedrooms.
Bedrooms: 2 single, 3 double & 4 twin, 2 family rooms.
Bathrooms: 3 private,
2 public; 3 private showers.
Bed & breakfast: £20-£25 single, £40-£45 double.
Half board: £28-£30 daily,
£140-£175 weekly.
Lunch available.
Evening meal 6.30pm (l.o. 8.30pm).
Parking for 6.
Credit: Access, Visa.

Colson House
17 Upper Rock Gdns.,
Brighton, BN2 1QE
☎ (0273) 694922
Listed Regency hotel with original features throughout. Adjacent to the sea, central for all town's amenities and conference centre.
Bedrooms: 1 single, 3 double & 3 twin.
Bathrooms: 7 private.
Bed & breakfast: from £18 single, £30-£44 double.
Half board: £22.50-£29.50 daily.
Lunch available.
Evening meal 6pm (l.o. 6.30pm).
Credit: Access, Visa.

The symbols are explained on the flap inside the back cover.

Cornerways Hotel
18-20 Caburn Road Hove,
BN3 6EF
☎ (0273) 731882
*An Edwardian house on the
A27 with easy access and
parking. Personal service from
the proprietors and home
cooking. 15 minutes' walk from
seafront.*
Bedrooms: 3 single, 3 double
& 2 twin, 2 family rooms.
Bathrooms: 1 private,
3 public.
Bed & breakfast: from £15
single, from £30 double.
Half board: from £22 daily.
Evening meal 6.30pm (l.o.
2pm).

Cosmopolitan Hotel M
31 New Steine, Marine Pde.,
Brighton, BN2 1PB
☎ (0273) 682461
*A commanding position in a
seafront square, overlooking
the beach and Palace Pier.
Central for shopping,
entertainments and conference
centres.*
Bedrooms: 10 single, 3 double
& 3 twin, 11 family rooms.
Bathrooms: 19 private,
3 public.
Bed & breakfast: £17-£26
single, £34-£50 double.
Credit: Access, Visa, Diners,
Amex.

Cranleigh Guest House
22-23 Terminus Rd.,
Brighton, BN1 3PD
☎ (0273) 27971
*Clean and comfortable with a
friendly atmosphere and the
nearest guest house to Brighton
railway station.*
Bedrooms: 2 single, 2 double
& 3 twin, 2 family rooms.
Bathrooms: 3 public.
Bed & breakfast: £16 single,
£30 double.

Dorset Guest House M
Listed
17 Dorset Gdns., Brighton,
BN2 1RL
☎ (0273) 694646
*This is a typical Brighton
guesthouse restored in period
style. It is in the town centre
with a small park opposite, and
only 100 yards from sea.*
Bedrooms: 2 single, 1 double
& 1 twin, 3 family rooms.
Bathrooms: 2 public;
1 private shower.
Bed & breakfast: £14-£17
single, £28-£34 double.

Half board: £20-£23 daily,
£120-£138 weekly.
Evening meal 6.30pm (l.o.
9pm).
Credit: Diners, Amex.

Four Seasons
3 Upper Rock Gdns.,
Brighton, BN2 1QE
☎ (0273) 681496
*Small, comfortable guesthouse
adjacent to sea, close to
conference centre and all
amenities. Access at all times.*
Bedrooms: 3 double, 3 family
rooms.
Bathrooms: 1 private;
5 private showers.
Bed & breakfast: £30-£40
double.
Credit: Access, Diners,
Amex.

Fredellen Hotel
19 Oriental Pl., Brighton,
BN1 2LL
☎ (0273) 27646
*Situated in central Brighton 50
yards from seafront and main
shopping centre. 500 yards
from Metropole and Brighton
Conference Centre.*
Bedrooms: 4 single, 5 double
& 2 twin, 2 family rooms.
Bathrooms: 5 private,
3 public; 1 private shower.
Bed & breakfast: £14.50-£19
single, £29-£38 double.

Fyfield House
APPROVED
26 New Steine, Brighton,
BN2 1PD
☎ (0273) 602770
*Friendly, family-run hotel, with
a home-from-home atmosphere.
Anna and Peter ensure a nice
stay.*
Bedrooms: 4 single, 3 double
& 1 twin, 1 family room.
Bathrooms: 4 private,
1 public; 1 private shower.
Bed & breakfast: £13-£23
single, £30-£46 double.
Credit: Access, Visa, Diners,
Amex.

Gullivers
10, New Steine, Brighton,
East Sussex BN2 1PB
☎ Brighton (0273) 695415
*Grade II listed Regency bed
and breakfast hotel in seafront
square. Recently opened after
renovation. Sunny, comfortable
rooms. En-suite facilities
available.*

Bedrooms: 2 single, 4 double
& 2 twin, 1 family room.
Bathrooms: 5 private,
1 public; 1 private shower.
Bed & breakfast: £20-£36
single, £46-£52 double.
Credit: Access, Visa.

Hovedene Hotel M
15-17 The Drive, Hove, East
Sussex BN3 3JE
☎ Brighton (0273) 733766
*Family hotel near sea, shops
and cricket ground. Good bus
service to Brighton. Nostalgic
entertainment weekly in bar.*
Bedrooms: 22 single, 3 double
& 1 twin, 2 family rooms.
Bathrooms: 7 private,
4 public.
Bed & breakfast: £20-£25
single, £35-£40 double.
Half board: £27.50-£32.50
daily, £165-£195 weekly.
Lunch available.
Evening meal 6.30pm (l.o.
8pm).
Credit: Access, Visa.

Kempton House Hotel M
33-34 Marine Parade.,
Brighton, BN2 1TR
☎ (0273) 570248
*Recently refurbished seafront
hotel overlooking beach and
Palace Pier. Central to all
amenities. Home-from-home
atmosphere. Licensed bar.*
Bedrooms: 6 double & 2 twin,
4 family rooms.
Bathrooms: 12 private.
Bed & breakfast: £25-£50
single, £40-£54 double.
Half board: from £29 daily.
Evening meal 6pm.
Credit: Access, Visa, Diners,
Amex.

Kimberley Hotel M
APPROVED
17 Atlingworth St., Brighton,
BN2 1PL
☎ (0273) 603504
*Family-run hotel, 2 minutes
from seafront and central for
amusements, shopping, marina
and conference centre.
Licensed residents' bar*
Bedrooms: 3 single, 3 double
& 5 twin, 4 family rooms.
Bathrooms: 1 private,
2 public; 13 private showers.
Bed & breakfast: £20-£24
single, £32-£36 double.

Evening meal 6pm (l.o. 7pm).
Open January-October.
Credit: Access, Visa.

Lanes Hotel M
APPROVED
70 Marine Pde., Brighton,
BN2 1AE
☎ (0273) 674231
*On seafront, close to town
centre and all amenities.
Personally supervised by
resident proprietors. All rooms
with en-suite facilities,
hospitality tray, TV, telephone.
24-hour room service.*
Bedrooms: 3 single, 30 double
& 5 twin, 2 family rooms.
Bathrooms: 36 private,
1 public.
Bed & breakfast: £30-£45
single, £40-£70 double.
Half board: £53.50-£83.50
daily, £350-£450 weekly.
Lunch available.
Evening meal 6.30pm (l.o.
10pm).
Parking for 8.
Credit: Access, Visa, Diners,
Amex.

Lawns Hotel M
Kingsway, Hove, Brighton,
BN3 2GT
☎ (0273) 736277
*Seafront hotel. 10 minutes'
walk from centre. Friendly
atmosphere and good service.
Special group rates.*
Bedrooms: 6 single, 17 double
& 3 twin, 15 family rooms.
Bathrooms: 41 private.
Bed & breakfast: max. £48
single, max. £58 double.
Evening meal 6.30pm (l.o.
8.30pm).
Credit: Access, Visa, Diners,
Amex.

Madeira Hotel M
19-23 Marine Pde., Brighton,
BN2 1TL
☎ (0273) 698331
Telex 878456
*44-bedroom Regency hotel
overlooking the sea, directly
opposite the famous
dolphinarium and aquarium
and next to the Palace Pier.*
Bedrooms: 9 single, 25 double
& 6 twin, 4 family rooms.
Bathrooms: 44 private.
Bed & breakfast: from £48
single, £66 double.
Continued ▶

511

BRIGHTON & HOVE
Continued

Half board: from £57.50 daily.
Lunch available.
Evening meal 7pm (l.o. 9pm).
Parking for 8.
Credit: Access, Visa, Diners, Amex.

Malvern Hotel ⋈
♔♔
33 Regency Sq., Brighton, BN1 2GG
☎ (0273) 24302
Comfortable, modernised Regency building. Full English breakfast with a choice of menu. Convenient for shops and theatre. Friendly, personal service.
Bedrooms: 5 single, 4 double & 4 twin.
Bathrooms: 13 private, 1 public.
Bed & breakfast: from £30 single, from £44 double.
Credit: Access, Visa, Diners, Amex.

Maon Hotel
26 Upper Rock Gdns., Brighton, BN2 1QE
☎ (0273) 694400
Grade II listed building, friendly with a warm welcome. Close to sea and town centre. En-suite rooms available.
Bedrooms: 2 single, 4 double & 2 twin, 1 family room.
Bathrooms: 1 private, 2 public; 5 private showers.
Bed & breakfast: £18-£20 single, £36-£48 double.

Marina House Hotel ⋈
♔♔♔
8 Charlotte St., Marine Parade, Brighton, BN2 1AG
☎ (0273) 605349/679484
Cosy, well-maintained elegant hotel, offering a warm welcome, cleanliness, comfort and hospitality. English breakfast, licensed restaurant. Central for Palace Pier, conference and exhibitions, adjacent to the sea and a few minutes from the marina, Royal Pavilion and all amenities. Flexible breakfast, check-in and check-out times.
Bedrooms: 3 single, 7 double.
Bathrooms: 7 private, 2 public; 3 private showers.
Bed & breakfast: £12.50-£19 single, £24-£37 double.

Half board: £19.50-£26 daily, £121-£151 weekly.
Lunch available.
Evening meal 7pm (l.o. 8pm).
Credit: Access, Visa, Diners, Amex.

● Display advertisement appears on page 546.

Norfolk Resort Hotel ⋈
149 Kings Rd., Brighton, BN1 2PP
☎ (0273) 738201 &
Freephone (0800) 500100
Fax (0273) 821752
⊕ Resort
Regency hotel with 120 en-suite bedrooms, on Brighton's seafront, offering international standard of amenities. Roof-top restaurant and resort club. Conference facilities available. Special short break rates.
Bedrooms: 12 single, 64 double & 41 twin, 3 family rooms.
Bathrooms: 120 private.
Bed & breakfast: from £56.50 single, £83-£93 double.
Lunch available.
Evening meal 7.30pm (l.o. 10pm).
Parking for 57.
Credit: Access, Visa, C.Bl., Diners, Amex.

Paskins Hotel ⋈
♔♔
19 Charlotte St., Brighton, BN2 1AG
☎ (0273) 601203
Small family-run hotel centrally located in town centre. Most rooms with en-suite facilities, some four poster beds. Licensed.
Bedrooms: 6 single, 9 double & 3 twin, 1 family room.
Bathrooms: 16 private, 1 public.
Bed & breakfast: £30-£50 double.
Half board: £23.50-£33.50 daily.
Evening meal 7pm (l.o. 9am).
Credit: Access, Visa, Diners, Amex.

Pier View
♔♔ APPROVED
28 New Steine, Brighton, BN2 1PD
☎ (0273) 605310
Smart, friendly, family-run hotel with a real pier view. Near town centre, shops and many places of interest.
Bedrooms: 2 single, 3 double & 1 twin, 4 family rooms.

Bathrooms: 8 private, 2 public.
Bed & breakfast: £18-£23 single, £40-£50 double.
Credit: Access, Visa, Amex.

Portland House Hotel ⋈
♔♔♔
55-56 Regency Sq., Brighton, BN1 2FF
☎ (0273) 820464
Regency building in seafront square. Minutes away from conference centre, shops and historic Lanes.
Bedrooms: 10 single, 6 double & 6 twin, 2 family rooms.
Bathrooms: 24 private.
Bed & breakfast: £30-£35 single, £50-£85 double.
Half board: £40-£57.50 daily.
Lunch available.
Evening meal 6pm (l.o. 6pm).
Open February-December.
Credit: Access, Visa, Amex.

Preston Resort Hotel ⋈
216 Preston Rd., Brighton, BN1 6UU
☎ (0273) 507853 Fax (0273) 540039
⊕ Resort
34 fully-refurbished bedrooms, newly-built restaurant, bar and health club. On main A23 into Brighton, close to Preston Park.
Bedrooms: 4 single, 18 double & 10 twin, 2 family rooms.
Bathrooms: 34 private.
Bed & breakfast: from £51.50 single, from £68 double.
Lunch available.
Evening meal 7pm (l.o. 9.45pm).
Parking for 60.
Credit: Access, Visa, Diners, Amex.

Prince Regent Hotel
29 Regency Square, Brighton, BN1 2FH
☎ (0273) 29962 & 29963
Fax (0273) 748162
Mid-terrace mansion, whose elegant decor retains all the splendour of the Regency period. Two antique four-poster beds and ground-floor jacuzzi.
Bedrooms: 3 single, 12 double & 4 twin.
Bathrooms: 19 private.
Bed & breakfast: £28-£38 single, £48-£58 double.
Credit: Access, Visa, Diners.

Princes Marine Hotel ⋈
♔♔♔♔ APPROVED
153, Kingsway, Hove, East Sussex BN3 2WE
☎ Brighton (0273) 207660
Recently constructed hotel situated in one of Hove's premier positions. 24 rooms are facing the sea. Bar with real ales. Restaurant, function rooms, conferences and parties. Car park.
Bedrooms: 8 single, 8 double & 29 twin, 3 family rooms.
Bathrooms: 48 private.
Bed & breakfast: £40-£45 single, £55-£60 double.
Half board: £37.50-£42.50 daily, £240-£270 weekly.
Lunch available.
Evening meal 6pm (l.o. 9pm).
Parking for 21.
Credit: Access, Visa, Diners, Amex.

Ryford Hotel ⋈
6-7 New Steine, Brighton, BN2 1PB
☎ (0273) 681576
Family hotel in one of the finest positions on the seafront. Close to Palace Pier, Brighton Centre and main shopping amenities. Brochure on request.
Bedrooms: 7 single, 6 double & 7 twin, 7 family rooms.
Bathrooms: 7 public.
Bed & breakfast: £17-£22 single, £32-£38 double.
Evening meal 6pm.

Sackville Hotel ⋈
♔♔♔♔ COMMENDED
189 Kingsway, Hove, BN3 4GU
☎ (0273) 736292
Telex 877830
Seafront hotel. Some rooms have sea views and balcony. Oak-panelled bar, and restaurant offering comprehensive menus complemented by extensive wine list.
Bedrooms: 12 single, 22 double & 8 twin, 3 family rooms.
Bathrooms: 45 private.
Bed & breakfast: £55-£65 single, £70-£85 double.
Half board: £40-£50 daily.
Lunch available.
Evening meal 7.30pm (l.o. 9.30pm).
Parking for 20.
Credit: Access, Visa, Diners, Amex.

St. Catherines Lodge Hotel ⋈

♛♛♛♛ APPROVED

Kingsway, Hove, BN3 2RZ
☎ Brighton (0273) 778181
Telex 877073
℞ Inter

*Well-established, seafront
hotel. Restaurant specialises in
traditional English dishes.
Four-poster honeymoon rooms.
Attractive cocktail bar, games
rooms, garden, and easy
parking. Situated opposite
King Alfred sports and leisure
centre, water-slides, tenpin
bowling and gym.*
Bedrooms: 11 single,
23 double & 12 twin, 4 family
rooms.
Bathrooms: 40 private,
5 public.
Bed & breakfast: £36-£55
single, £54-£65 double.
Half board: £40-£60 daily,
£190-£240 weekly.
Lunch available.
Evening meal 7pm (l.o. 9pm).
Parking for 4.
Credit: Access, Visa, Diners,
Amex.

Hotel Seafield ⋈

♛♛♛

23 Seafield Rd., Hove,
BN3 2TP
☎ (0273) 735912
*Family-run hotel with home-
cooked food, close to the
seafront and main shopping
centre. Free street parking in
addition to private parking.
Free video film shows every
evening.*
Bedrooms: 1 single, 4 double
& 3 twin, 2 family rooms.
Bathrooms: 10 private,
3 public.
Bed & breakfast: £30-£35
single, £50-£60 double.
Half board: £90-£100 daily.
Evening meal 6pm (l.o. 5pm).
Parking for 7.
Open July-October.

Shalimar Hotel

23 Broad St., Marine Pde.,
Brighton, BN2 1TJ
☎ (0273) 605316 & 694314
*In central Brighton, beautifully
decorated Victorian style house
with cast iron balcony,
overlooking the Palace Pier
and seafront. Most rooms have
private shower, WC and bidet.*
Bedrooms: 1 single, 3 double
& 1 twin, 4 family rooms.
Bathrooms: 5 private,
2 public; 2 private showers.

Bed & breakfast: £32-£40
single, £35-£50 double.
Half board: £35-£40 daily.
Credit: Access, Visa, Diners,
Amex.

Wellington Hotel ⋈

♛♛♛

27 Waterloo Street, Hove,
East Sussex BN3 1AN
☎ Brighton (0273) 23171
*Small, centrally-situated
friendly hotel, individually
decorated bedrooms. Bed,
breakfast and evening dinner
throughout the year.*
Bedrooms: 3 single, 3 double
& 2 twin, 3 family rooms.
Bathrooms: 10 private;
1 private shower.
Bed & breakfast: £17.50-£25
single, £35-£50 double.
Half board: £25.50-£34.50
daily, £150-£185 weekly.
Evening meal 6pm (l.o.
6.30pm).
Credit: Access, Visa.

Whitburn Lodge

12 Montpelier Rd., Brighton,
BN1 2LQ
☎ (0273) 729005
*Small family-run Regency
guesthouse with modern
comforts, 100 yards from the
sea, 5 minutes from the
conference centre and all
amenities.*
Bedrooms: 2 double & 1 twin,
1 family room.
Bathrooms: 2 public.
Bed & breakfast: £28-£34
double.

BROADSTAIRS

Kent
Map ref 3C3

Popular seaside resort
with numerous sandy
bays. Charles Dickens
spent his summers at
Bleak House (now a
museum) where he wrote
parts of David
Copperfield. The Dickens
Festival is held in June,
when many people wear
Dickensian dress.
*Tourist Information
Centre* ☎ *(0843) 68399*

The Admiral Dundonald Hotel

43 Belvedere Rd.,
Broadstairs, CT10 1PF
☎ Thanet (0843) 62236

*Georgian mansion house, a
listed historic building with
cosy bar, restaurant open to the
public, some rooms with private
showers. Personal supervision
of owner.*
Bedrooms: 4 single, 3 double
& 1 twin, 2 family rooms.
Bathrooms: 1 public;
3 private showers.
Bed & breakfast: £15-£34
double.
Credit: Access.

Castlemere Hotel ⋈

♛♛♛ COMMENDED

Western Espl., Broadstairs,
CT10 1TD
☎ Thanet (0843) 61566
*Located at the quiet end of the
western esplanade, in its own
garden, on a cliff overlooking
the English Channel.*
Bedrooms: 17 single, 7 double
& 11 twin, 2 family rooms.
Bathrooms: 30 private,
2 public.
Bed & breakfast: £32-£35.50
single, £60-£73 double.
Half board: £44-£47.50 daily,
£280-£300 weekly.
Lunch available.
Evening meal 7pm (l.o. 8pm).
Parking for 27.
Credit: Access, Visa.

East Horndon Hotel

4 Eastern Esplanade,
Broadstairs, CT10 1DP
☎ Thanet (0843) 68306
*Hotel on seafront. Colour TV
in bedrooms. Baby listening
service. Convenient for shops
and buses. Dickens' "Bleak
House" a few minutes away.
Pets welcome.*
Bedrooms: 2 single, 4 double
& 2 twin, 3 family rooms.
Bathrooms: 2 private,
2 public.
Bed & breakfast: £30-£35
double.
Half board: from £23.50
daily, £125-£146 weekly.
Evening meal (l.o. 6pm).
Open April-October.
Credit: Access, Visa.

Velindre Hotel ⋈

♛♛

10 Western Espl.,
Broadstairs, CT10 1JG
☎ Thanet (0843) 61485
*On top of cliffs, overlooking the
sea with fine panoramic views.
Indoor heated swimming pool
and leisure centre.*
Bedrooms: 4 single, 5 double
& 2 twin, 2 family rooms.

Bathrooms: 1 private,
1 public; 12 private showers.
Bed & breakfast: £18-£24
single, £36-£48 double.
Half board: £24-£35 daily,
£168-£245 weekly.
Evening meal 7pm (l.o. 8pm).
Parking for 6.
Credit: Access, Visa, Diners,
Amex.

Westfield Lodge

Granville Avenue,
Broadstairs, CT10 1PX
☎ Thanet (0843) 62615
*Painting holidays with tuition
from April to end September in
addition to normal holidays.*
Bedrooms: 1 double, 3 family
rooms.
Bathrooms: 1 public.
Bed & breakfast: £11-£12
single, £22-£24 double.
Half board: £15.50-£16.50
daily, £96-£105 weekly.
Evening meal 6pm (l.o. 6pm).

The White House Hotel ⋈

♛♛

59 Kingsgate Ave.,
Kingsgate, Broadstairs,
CT10 3LW
☎ Thanet (0843) 63315
*A small licensed hotel close to
beautiful sandy Botany Bay
and golf-course. Ideal for cliff
walks, fishing and bathing.*
Bedrooms: 3 double & 3 twin,
2 family rooms.
Bathrooms: 3 private,
1 public.
Bed & breakfast: £18-£25.50
single, £32-£42 double.
Half board: £23-£28 daily,
£135-£155.75 weekly.
Evening meal 6.30pm (l.o.
7pm).
Parking for 9.
Credit: Access, Visa.

CAMBER

E. Sussex
Map ref 3B4

Well-known for fine sand
dunes and safe bathing.

Cinque Ports Lodge

♛♛♛ APPROVED

93 Lydd Road, Camber.,
TN31 7RS
☎ Rye (0797) 226017
*Modern, friendly hotel situated
100 yards from sandy beach.
Ancient Rye short ride away.
Health club, swimming pools
adjacent.*

Continued ▶

513

CAMBER

Continued

Bedrooms: 5 double & 2 twin,
1 family room.
Bathrooms: 8 private.
Bed & breakfast: £30-£37.50
single, £40-£55 double.
Half board: £28-£35.50 daily,
£180-£220 weekly.
Lunch available.
Evening meal 6.50pm (l.o.
8.50pm).
Parking for 10.
Credit: Access, Visa.
ॐ ♨ ☎ ⑩ ❑ 🅟 ❙ Ⅴ ⅄ 🚲
⑯ Ⅲ ☎ ♨ Ἶ 🇁 ❧ 🐾 ⚊
ⓢⓟ

CANTERBURY

Kent
Map ref 3B3

Birthplace of English
Christianity and a place of
pilgrimage since the
martyrdom of Thomas
Becket in 1170. Seat of
the Primate of All England
and the site of Canterbury
Cathedral. Not to be
missed are St.
Augustine's Abbey, St.
Martin's (the oldest
church in England), Royal
Museum and Old
Weaver's House and the
exciting new Pilgrim's
Way attraction. At nearby
Bekesbourne is Howletts
Zoo Park.
*Tourist Information
Centre* ☎ *(0227) 766567*

Abba Hotel ₥

⊞⊞

Station Rd West,
Canterbury, CT2 8AN
☎ (0227) 464771 Fax (0233)
720758
*A pleasant Victorian hotel
within easy reach of the city
centre. Quiet location near the
West Gate, close to the railway
station with easy access to
London and the Kent coast.*
Bedrooms: 5 single, 6 double
& 4 twin, 4 family rooms.
Bathrooms: 2 private,
4 public; 1 private shower.
Bed & breakfast: £18-£22
single, £28-£38 double.
Half board: £24-£28 daily,
£170-£200 weekly.
Lunch available.
Evening meal 6.30pm (l.o.
10.30pm).
Parking for 7.
ॐ ♨ ❙ Ⅴ 🅟 ♨ ⑯ Ⅲ ⚊ Ἶ
🐾 ⓣ

Alexandra House ₥

Listed

1 Roper Rd., Canterbury,
CT2 7EH
☎ Canterbury (0227) 767011
*Small family-run guesthouse
close to city centre, cathedral,
university, Canterbury West
station and Marlowe Theatre.
Car parking.*
Bedrooms: 2 single, 2 double
& 2 twin, 3 family rooms.
Bathrooms: 2 public;
4 private showers.
Bed & breakfast: £15-£20
single, £28-£34 double.
Parking for 6.
ॐ ♨ 🅟 ♨ ⓤⓛ Ⅴ 🅟 ⑯ Ⅲ
⚊

Alicante Guest House ₥

4 Roper Rd., Canterbury,
CT2 7EH
☎ (0227) 766277
*Double-fronted Victorian house
close to city centre . Plenty of
parking spaces opposite. Public
telephone in hall for guests
only.*
Bedrooms: 1 single, 1 double
& 1 twin, 3 family rooms.
Bathrooms: 2 public;
1 private shower.
Bed & breakfast: £15-£17
single, £27-£32 double.
Credit: Access, Visa.
ॐ ♨ 🅟 ♨ ⓤⓛ Ⅴ 🅟 Ⅲ 🐾 🅟
ⓢⓟ

Anns House ₥

Listed

63 London Rd., Canterbury,
CT2 8JZ
☎ (0227) 768767
*Comfortable Victorian guest
house close to the city centre
where the family proprietors
offer comfort and friendly
service.*
Bedrooms: 6 double & 9 twin,
4 family rooms.
Bathrooms: 11 private,
2 public; 1 private shower.
Bed & breakfast: £15-£20
single, £30-£40 double.
Parking for 20.
ॐ ♨ 🅿 ♨ ⓤⓛ 🅟 ⑯ ⚊
Ἶ ❉ 🐾 🅟 ⓢⓟ
⑩ Display advertisement
appears on page 545.

Castle Court Guest House ₥

Listed

8 Castle St., Canterbury,
CT1 2QF
☎ (0227) 463441
*Peaceful central position. Close
to cathedral, shops, gardens
and theatre. Car parking
nearby and an easy walk to
station. TV lounge.*
Bedrooms: 4 single, 5 double
& 3 twin.
Bathrooms: 2 public.

Bed & breakfast: £14-£18
single, £28-£32 double.
Parking for 2.
Credit: Access, Visa.
🐾2 ⓤⓛ 🅟 ⑯ Ⅲ ⚊ 🅟 ⓢⓟ 🅟
ⓣ

Cathedral Gate Hotel ₥

36 Burgate, Canterbury,
CT1 2HA
☎ (0227) 464381 Fax (0227)
462800
*Central position at main
entrance to the cathedral. Car
parking nearby. Baby listening
service. Old world charm at
reasonable prices. English
breakfast extra.*
Bedrooms: 6 single, 7 double
& 8 twin, 4 family rooms.
Bathrooms: 12 private,
3 public; 2 private showers.
Bed & breakfast: £19-£40
single, £35-£60 double.
Evening meal 7pm (l.o. 9pm).
Parking for 12.
Credit: Access, Visa, Diners,
Amex.
ॐ ♨ ☎ ⑩ 🅟 ♨ ❙ Ⅴ 🅟
Ⅲ ⚊ 🅟 ⓣ

Clare-Ellen Guest House ₥

⊞⊞ COMMENDED

9 Victoria Rd., Wincheap,
Canterbury, CT1 3SG
☎ (0227) 760205
*Victorian house with large
elegant rooms. 10 minutes'
walk to city centre. 5 minutes
to station. Car park and
garage available.*
Bedrooms: 1 single, 2 double
& 1 twin, 1 family room.
Bathrooms: 3 public.
Bed & breakfast: £14-£17
single, £28-£34 double.
Parking for 8.
ॐ ♨ ⑩ 🅟 ⓤⓛ ❙ Ⅴ Ⅲ ⚊
🐾 🅟 🅟 ⓣ

Ebury Hotel ₥

⊞⊞⊞ COMMENDED

New Dover Rd., Canterbury,
CT1 3DX
☎ (0227) 768433 Fax (0227)
459187
*Family-run, Victorian hotel
just outside city centre.
Licensed restaurant, large
public rooms and bedrooms.
Heated indoor pool and spa.*
Bedrooms: 2 single, 6 double
& 3 twin, 4 family rooms.
Bathrooms: 15 private.
Bed & breakfast: £35-£38.50
single, £50-£58 double.
Half board: £30-£48.50 daily,
£200-£220 weekly.
Evening meal 7pm (l.o.
8.30pm).
Parking for 21.
Credit: Access, Visa, Amex.
ॐ ☎ 🅟 ♨ ❙ Ⅴ 🅟 ⑯
Ⅲ ⚊ 🌊 ❉ 🐾 🅟 🅟 🅟 ⓣ

Ersham Lodge Hotel ₥

12 New Dover Rd.,
Canterbury, CT1 3AP
☎ (0227) 463174 Fax (0227)
455482
*Tudor-style house close to city
centre. Friendly atmosphere.
Elegant public rooms and
patio, comfortable well
furnished bedrooms. Bar.*
Bedrooms: 1 single, 3 double
& 8 twin, 2 family rooms.
Bathrooms: 11 private,
1 public; 2 private showers.
Bed & breakfast: £39-£47.50
single, £47.50-£54 double.
Parking for 12.
Credit: Access, Visa, Amex.
ॐ ♨ ☎ ⑩ 🅟 ❙ 🅟 ⚊
Ἶ 🅟 ⓢⓟ ⓣ

Falstaff Hotel

St. Dunstans St. Canterbury,
CT2 8AF
☎ (0227) 462138 Telex 96394
ⒼⓇ Lansbury
*A former coaching inn dating
back to the 15th C, in the heart
of the town close to Westgate
Towers.*
Bedrooms: 10 single,
11 double & 3 twin, 1 family
room.
Bathrooms: 25 private.
Bed & breakfast: £33-£69
single, £66-£85 double.
Half board: £48-£100 daily.
Lunch available.
Evening meal 7pm (l.o.
9.45pm).
Parking for 50.
Credit: Access, Visa, Diners,
Amex.
ॐ ♨ ☎ ☎ ⑩ 🅟 ❙ Ⅴ
🅟 ⑩ Ⅲ ⚊ Ἶ 🐾 ⓢⓟ 🅟 ⓣ

Guildford Lodge Guest House

42 Nunnery Fields,
Canterbury, CT1 3JT
☎ (0227) 462284
*Small family-run guesthouse
close to city centre, Canterbury
East station and the cricket
ground. Colour TV in all
rooms. Coach parties welcome.*
Bedrooms: 8 single, 4 double
& 6 twin, 3 family rooms.
Bathrooms: 4 private,
3 public.
Bed & breakfast: £10-£15
single, £25-£35 double.
Half board: £15-£20 daily,
£85-£120 weekly.
Lunch available.
Evening meal 6pm (l.o. 5pm).
Parking for 8.
Credit: Amex.
ॐ ♨ 🅟 ♨ ❙ Ⅴ ⅄ 🅟 ⑯
⑩ Ⅲ ⚊ Ἶ 🐾 🅟 ⓢⓟ

Highfield Hotel

Summer Hill, Harbledown,
Canterbury, CT2 8NH
☎ Canterbury (0227) 462772

Victorian house in an acre of garden , 1 mile from city centre off the main London Road into Canterbury.
Bedrooms: 2 single, 3 double & 3 twin.
Bathrooms: 3 private, 2 public.
Bed & breakfast: £22-£24 single, £33-£47 double.
Parking for 12.
Credit: Access, Visa.
⏲5 ♨ 🖰 ▥ ❋ 🗙 🏠

Leura Guest House ♨
Listed **APPROVED**
77 Sturry Rd., Canterbury, CT1 1BU
☎ (0227) 453959
Family-run guesthouse 10 minutes away from the city centre, cathedral and Kings School. Near the stadium, sports centre and swimming pool.
Bedrooms: 1 single, 2 double & 1 twin, 1 family room.
Bathrooms: 2 private, 1 public; 1 private shower.
Bed & breakfast: £13.50-£16 single, £27-£37 double.
Half board: £20-£22.50 daily, from £125 weekly.
Evening meal 6.30pm.
Parking for 4.
⏲ ♨ 🖰 ▤ ▥ ⬚ 🖂 ▥ ⬚ ❋ 🗙

Lindens Guest House
Listed
38b St. Dunstans St., Canterbury, CT2 8BY
☎ (0227) 462339
Victorian house with large sunny rooms, beside the historic St. Dunstan's Church and within walking distance of city centre and cathedral.
Bedrooms: 1 single, 1 double & 1 twin.
Bathrooms: 2 public.
Bed & breakfast: £12-£15 single, £22-£26 double.
Parking for 4.
⏲6 🖰 ▥ ▤ ⬚ ▥

Magnolia House ♨
COMMENDED
36 St. Dunstans Ter., Canterbury, CT2 8AX
☎ (0227) 765121
Georgian house in attractive city street. Close to university, gardens, river and city centre. Very quiet house within a walled garden.
Bedrooms: 2 single, 3 double & 1 twin.
Bathrooms: 3 private, 1 public.
Bed & breakfast: £20-£25 single, £38-£45 double.
Parking for 4.
⏲ ♨ 🖰 ▥ ▤ ⬚ ▥ ⬚ 🖂 ▥
▥ ⬚ 🗙 🏠 ⬚ ⬚ 🏠

The Old Coach House
APPROVED
Dover Road, (A2) Barham, Canterbury, CT4 6SA
☎ (0227) 831218
Situated on A2 midway between Canterbury and Dover. French restaurant, French spoken.
Bedrooms: 2 double & 3 twin.
Bathrooms: 5 private.
Bed & breakfast: £38 single, £47.50 double.
Half board: £50 daily.
Lunch available.
Evening meal 7pm (l.o. 9pm).
Parking for 80.
Credit: Access, Diners.
⏲ 🖰 ▥ ⬚ CB ▥ 🖂 ⬚ ▥ ▤
▥ ♨ ❋ 🗙 🏠

Pointers Hotel ♨
COMMENDED
1 London Rd., Canterbury, CT2 8LR
☎ (0227) 456846
Family-run Georgian hotel close to city centre, cathedral and university.
Bedrooms: 2 single, 8 double & 2 twin, 2 family rooms.
Bathrooms: 8 private, 2 public; 2 private showers.
Bed & breakfast: £28-£35 single, £40-£52 double.
Half board: £32-£47 daily, £168-£224 weekly.
Evening meal 7.30pm (l.o. 8.30pm).
Parking for 10.
Credit: Access, Visa, Diners, Amex.
⏲ ♨ ▥ ⬚ ▥ ⬚ ⬚ ▥ 🖂 ⬚ ▥
▤ ▥ ⬚ 🏠
⑭ Display advertisement appears on page 546.

Raemore House ♨
33 New Dover Road, Canterbury, CT1 3AS
☎ Canterbury (0227) 769740/769432
Family-run guesthouse close to city centre. Four-poster and en-suite rooms, tea/coffee facilities. Private car park.
Bedrooms: 1 single, 5 double & 2 twin, 1 family room.
Bathrooms: 3 private, 2 public.
Bed & breakfast: £15-£18 single, £28-£39 double.
Parking for 9.
⏲ ♨ 🖰 ⬚ ▥ ▤ ▥ ⬚ ▥ 🗙
▥

Slatters Hotel
St. Margaret St., Canterbury, CT1 2TR
☎ (0227) 463271 Fax (0227) 764117 Telex 966227
ⓒⓡ Queens Moat Houses

Comfortable, modern accommodation in ancient building, part Tudor, part Queen Anne with Roman remains. 200 yards from cathedral.
Bedrooms: 8 single, 9 double & 9 twin, 5 family rooms.
Bathrooms: 28 private, 1 public.
Bed & breakfast: £50 single, £60 double.
Half board: £37 daily, £259 weekly.
Lunch available.
Evening meal 6.30pm (l.o. 9.15pm).
Parking for 18.
Credit: Access, Visa, Diners, Amex.
⏲ ⬚ ▥ ▥ ⬚ ▤ 🛡 ▥ ⬚ 🖂
▥ ⬚ 🛡 ▥ ⬚ ▥ 🏠 ⬚ 🏠

Thanington Hotel ♨
COMMENDED
140 Wincheap, Canterbury, CT1 3RY
☎ (0227) 453227
Bed and breakfast in style, 10 bedrooms with all facilities. 5 minutes' walk to city centre. Private car parking. Colour brochure available.
Bedrooms: 5 double & 3 twin, 2 family rooms.
Bathrooms: 10 private.
Bed & breakfast: £40-£47 single, £50-£60 double.
Parking for 12.
Credit: Access, Visa.
⏲ ▥ ⬚ ▥ ▥ ⬚ ▥ ▥ 🖂 ⬚
▥ ▤ 🗙 🏠 ⬚ 🏠

The Three Tuns ♨
24 Watling St., Canterbury, CT1 2UD
☎ (0227) 767371
16th C original listed coaching inn, once patronised by the Prince and Princess of Orange, on an original Roman road. Close links with cathedral.
Bedrooms: 1 single, 4 double & 2 twin.
Bathrooms: 4 private, 2 public.
Bed & breakfast: £33.50-£41 single, £44-£51 double.
Lunch available.
Evening meal 7pm (l.o. 9pm).
Parking for 4.
Credit: Access, Visa, Diners, Amex.
⏲ ♨ ▥ ⬚ ▥ ⬚ 🛡 ▥ 🖂
▥ ▤ 🗙 🏠 ⬚ 🏠

Thruxted Oast
HIGHLY COMMENDED
Mystole, Chartham, Canterbury, CT4 7BX
☎ (0227) 730080

Historic oast house recently converted to high standard accommodation in peaceful surroundings on edge of Canterbury. Picture framing studio and gift shop.
Bedrooms: 3 twin.
Bathrooms: 3 private.
Bed & breakfast: max. £55 single, max. £65 double.
Parking for 5.
Credit: Access, Visa, Diners, Amex.
⏲12 ⬚ ▥ ▤ ⬚ ▥ ▥ 🖂
▥ ▥ ⬚ ❋ 🗙 🏠 🏠 ⬚

Victoria Hotel ♨
APPROVED
59 London Rd., Canterbury, CT2 8JY
☎ (0227) 459333
10 minutes' walk or 3 minutes' drive from the city centre, offering personal service in a friendly, informal atmosphere.
Bedrooms: 10 single, 6 double & 14 twin, 4 family rooms.
Bathrooms: 34 private.
Bed & breakfast: £42-£54 single, from £70 double.
Lunch available.
Evening meal 6pm (l.o. 10.30pm).
Parking for 26.
Credit: Access, Visa, Diners, Amex.
⏲ ♨ ▥ ⬚ ▥ ⬚ 🛡 ▥ 🖂
▥ ⬚ ▤ ▥ ⬚ 🛡 ⬚ ❋ 🗙 ▥
▥ ⬚

The White House ♨
6, St.Peters Lane, Canterbury, CT1 2BP
☎ Canterbury (0227) 761836
Regency house situated within the city walls next to the Marlowe Theatre. Superior family-run accommodation with all rooms en-suite.
Bedrooms: 1 double & 1 twin, 1 family room.
Bathrooms: 3 private.
Bed & breakfast: £25-£30 single, £35-£40 double.
⏲ ♨ ▥ ⬚ ▥ ▥ 🖂 ▥ ⬚ ⬚ ▥
▤ 🗙 🏠 ⬚ ▥ ⬚ ▥ 🏠

Woodpeckers Country Hotel ♨
APPROVED
Womenswold, Nr. Canterbury, CT4 6HB
☎ Canterbury (0227) 831319
Built in 1850, set in 3 acres of gardens. Four-poster and brass bedsteads, bridal rooms. Specialising in home cooking with fresh vegetables. Heated swimming pool.
Bedrooms: 1 single, 2 double & 4 twin, 4 family rooms.
Bathrooms: 6 private, 2 public.

Continued ▶

515

CANTERBURY
Continued

Bed & breakfast: £23-£26 single, £46-£52 double.
Half board: £30-£31 daily, £189-£203 weekly.
Lunch available.
Evening meal 7.30pm (l.o. 8.30pm).
Parking for 42.
Credit: Access, Visa.

Yorke Lodge ⚐
COMMENDED
50 London Rd., Canterbury, CT2 8LF
☎ (0227) 451243 Telex 96118
Spacious, elegant Victorian house, close to city centre. Relax and enjoy a special bed and breakfast. Owners Robin and Lindsay Hall.
Bedrooms: 1 single, 1 double & 1 twin, 3 family rooms.
Bathrooms: 6 private.
Bed & breakfast: £22-£38 single, £38-£40 double.
Parking for 6.

CHARLWOOD
Surrey
Map ref 2D2

5m S. Reigate
Small old village with ancient church, near Gatwick Airport. Close by are Gatwick Zoo and Aviaries.

Stanhill Court Hotel ⚐
Stanhill Rd., Charlwood, Nr. Horley, RH6 0EP
☎ (0293) 862166
Telex 878322 Fax (0293) 862773
Family-run Victorian country house run as hotel/reception centre with country club facilities. 35 acre grounds with clay shooting ground, fishing ponds, native pasture, ancient woodland, open-air theatre, Victorian walled garden. Billiard room. Courtesy transport and term car parking for Gatwick. Four-poster rooms available.
Bedrooms: 2 single, 3 double & 3 twin, 2 family rooms.
Bathrooms: 10 private.
Bed & breakfast: £51.95-£71.95 single, £55-£79 double.
Half board: £39.50-£51.50 daily.
Lunch available.
Evening meal 6.30pm (l.o. 10.30pm).

Parking for 60.
Credit: Access, Visa, Diners, Amex.

CHICHESTER
W. Sussex
Map ref 2C3

The county town of West Sussex with a beautiful Norman cathedral lying beneath the South Downs. Noted for its Georgian architecture but also has modern buildings like the Festival Theatre. Surrounded by places of interest, including Fishbourne Roman Palace and Weald and Downland open-air museum.
Tourist Information Centre ☎ *(0243) 775888*

Bedford Hotel ⚐
Southgate, Chichester, PO19 1DP
☎ (0243) 785766 Fax (0243) 533175
Privately-owned hotel dating back to 1700. Near city centre, train and bus stations.
Bedrooms: 10 single, 6 double & 6 twin, 2 family rooms.
Bathrooms: 12 private, 5 public; 2 private showers.
Bed & breakfast: £33-£43 single, £50-£63 double.
Half board: £43-£53 daily.
Evening meal 7pm (l.o. 9pm).
Parking for 6.
Credit: Access, Visa, Diners, Amex.

Chichester Resort Hotel ⚐
Westhampnett, Chichester, PO19 4UL
☎ (0243) 786351 Fax (0243) 782371
Resort
Modern 70-bedroomed hotel which has just undergone major refurbishment. Ideally located near Chichester. Indoor health and leisure club, conference facilities.
Bedrooms: 20 double & 30 twin, 26 family rooms.
Bathrooms: 76 private.
Bed & breakfast: from £56.50 single, from £73 double.
Lunch available.
Evening meal 7pm (l.o. 9.30pm).
Parking for 108.

Credit: Access, Visa, Diners, Amex.

Hunters Inn ⚐
Midhurst Rd., Lavant, Chichester, PO18 0DA
☎ Chichester (0243) 527329
2 miles north of Chichester on the A286, set in 2 acres of landscaped gardens. Choice of a la carte and bar bistro restaurants.
Bedrooms: 1 single, 1 double & 2 twin, 1 family room.
Bathrooms: 3 private, 1 public.
Bed & breakfast: £15-£25 single, £35-£45 double.
Lunch available.
Evening meal 6.30pm (l.o. 8.30pm).
Parking for 60.
Credit: Access, Visa, Diners, Amex.

The Inglenook ⚐
255 Pagham Rd., Nyetimber, Pagham, PO21 3QB
☎ (024 32) 262495 & 67059
Family-run business, with oak beams and log fires, 1 mile from the sea. Large gardens, pleasant bar, and restaurant with seafood specialities.
Bedrooms: 1 single, 8 double & 7 twin, 2 family rooms.
Bathrooms: 18 private.
Bed & breakfast: from £47 single, from £70 double.
Half board: from £45 daily, from £265 weekly.
Lunch available.
Evening meal 6pm (l.o. 11pm).
Parking for 41.
Credit: Access, Visa, Diners, Amex.

Ship Hotel ⚐
North St., Chichester, PO19 1NH
☎ (0243) 782028 Telex 86276
18th C Georgian hotel in the city centre. Festival Theatre and cathedral 400 yards from hotel. Extensively refurbished in period style.
Bedrooms: 12 single, 12 double & 9 twin, 4 family rooms.
Bathrooms: 37 private.
Bed & breakfast: £32-£60 single, £48-£82 double.
Half board: £34-£70 daily, £212-£420 weekly.
Lunch available.

Evening meal 7.30pm (l.o. 9.30pm).
Parking for 38.
Credit: Access, Visa, Diners, Amex.

Suffolk House Hotel
3 East Row, Chichester, PO19 1PD
☎ (0243) 778899 & 778924
Conveniently situated in the heart of the city, perfect venue for all social and business occasions. Ideal base for visiting a variety of commercial and historical interests.
Bedrooms: 4 single, 5 double & 2 twin.
Bathrooms: 11 private.
Bed & breakfast: £55-£60 single, £75-£85 double.
Lunch available.
Evening meal 6pm (l.o. 10pm).
Parking for 6.
Credit: Access, Visa, Diners.

CLIFTONVILLE
Kent
Map ref 3C3

White Lodge
28 Harold Rd., Cliftonville, Margate, CT9 2HT
☎ Thanet (0843) 223940
A well situated small family hotel within easy reach of beach, shops, Winter Gardens and indoor bowls centre.
Bedrooms: 3 single, 8 double & 2 twin, 1 family room.
Bathrooms: 6 private, 2 public.
Bed & breakfast: £16-£17.50 single, £32-£35 double.
Half board: £21-£22.50 daily, £95-£120 weekly.
Evening meal 6pm (l.o. 6.45pm).
Parking for 3.
Credit: Visa.

COBHAM
Kent
Map ref 3B3

4m SE. Gravesend

Ye Olde Leather Bottle
The Street, Cobham, Nr. Gravesend, DA12 3BZ
☎ Meopham (0474) 814327

Built in 1629, this residential inn is famous for its character and charm, its history and associations with Charles Dickens and, most importantly, its splendid hospitality.
Bedrooms: 2 single, 4 double & 1 twin.
Bathrooms: 2 private; 3 private showers.
Bed & breakfast: £35.50-£41.50 single, from £52 double.
Lunch available.
Evening meal 7pm (l.o. 10pm).
Parking for 52.
Credit: Access, Visa, Diners, Amex.

COBHAM

Surrey
Map ref 2D2

Village in 2 parts, Street Cobham on the A3 Portsmouth Road and Church Cobham with the restored Norman church of St. Andrew and a 19th C mill.

Hilton National Cobham ♨
ⓦⓦⓦⓦⓦ COMMENDED
Seven Hills Rd., Cobham, KT11 1EW
☎ (0932) 64471 Telex 929196
Ⓗ Hilton
Set in 27 acres of gardens and woodland, a choice location for both business and pleasure. On the A3, 1 mile from the M25.
Bedrooms: 88 double & 46 twin, 18 family rooms.
Bathrooms: 152 private.
Bed & breakfast: £97-£125 single, £120-£165 double.
Lunch available.
Evening meal 7pm (l.o. 10pm).
Parking for 200.
Credit: Access, Visa, Diners, Amex.

Classifications and quality commendations were correct at the time of going to press but are subject to change. Please check at the time of booking.

COPTHORNE

W. Sussex
Map ref 2D2

3m NE. Crawley
Residential village on the Surrey/West Sussex border, near Crawley and within easy reach of Gatwick Airport.

Copthorne, Effingham Park ♨
ⓦⓦⓦⓦ
West Park Road, Effingham, Copthorne, Surrey
RH10 3EU
☎ (0342) 714994 Telex 95649
Fax (0342) 716039
Versatile venue for business and pleasure with 9-hole golf-course in grounds. All facilities for conferences, new product launches and banqueting for up to 500 people. All catering by own chefs. Leisure club, swimming pool, 2 restaurants.
Bedrooms: 64 double & 51 twin, 7 family rooms.
Bathrooms: 122 private.
Bed & breakfast: £98-£108 single, £105-£115 double.
Half board: £80-£90 daily.
Lunch available.
Evening meal (l.o. 11pm).
Parking for 300.
Credit: Access, Visa, Diners, Amex.

Copthorne Gatwick Hotel ♨
ⓦⓦⓦⓦ COMMENDED
Copthorne Rd., Copthorne, RH10 3PG
☎ (0342) 714971 Telex 95500
Country house hotel, in over 100 acres of Sussex countryside, within easy reach of Gatwick Airport. Courtesy bus service. Squash club on site.
Bedrooms: 54 single, 100 double & 75 twin, 30 family rooms.
Bathrooms: 259 private.
Bed & breakfast: £98-£108 single, £105-£115 double.
Half board: £75-£85 daily.
Lunch available.
Evening meal 7pm (l.o. 10.30pm).
Parking for 300.
Credit: Access, Visa, C.Bl., Diners, Amex.

CRANBROOK

Kent
Map ref 3B4

An old town, a centre for the weaving industry in the 15th C. The 72-ft-high Union Mill is a 3-storeyed windmill, still in working order.

Hartley Mount Hotel ♨
ⓦⓦⓦⓦ COMMENDED
Hartley Rd., Cranbrook, TN17 3QX
☎ (0580) 712230 & 713099
Fax (0580) 712588
Edwardian country house hotel on the A229 with licensed restaurant. Set in 2-acre garden with glorious views of the Weald. Resident proprietors.
Bedrooms: 1 single, 2 double & 1 twin, 1 family room.
Bathrooms: 5 private.
Bed & breakfast: £45-£48 single, £60-£95 double.
Half board: £57-£60 daily, £342-£360 weekly.
Lunch available.
Evening meal 8pm (l.o. 9.30pm).
Parking for 22.
Credit: Access, Visa.

CRAWLEY

W. Sussex
Map ref 2D2

One of the first New Towns built after World War II, but it also has some old buildings. Set in magnificent wooded countryside.

Cottesmore Golf & Country Club
Buchan Hill, Pease Pottage, Crawley, RH11 9AT
☎ (0293) 28256 & 29196
Country club hotel, all bedrooms with balconies and patios overlooking two 18-hole golf-courses. Squash courts and function facilities provided.
Bedrooms: 11 twin.
Bathrooms: 11 private, 4 public.
Bed & breakfast: £50-£60 single, £70-£80 double.
Half board: £60-£70 daily, £378-£441 weekly.
Lunch available.
Evening meal 6.30pm (l.o. 8.30pm).

Parking for 100.
Credit: Access, Visa, Diners, Amex.

Gatwick Manor Hotel ♨
ⓦⓦⓦⓦ
London Rd., Lowfield Heath (Gatwick), Crawley, RH10 2ST
☎ (0293) 26301 & 35251
Telex 87529
Modern, comfortable accommodation in the old world garden setting of a 13th C manor house which also incorporates a 15th C great hall and a 16th C tithe barn. Situated halfway between London and Brighton, with easy access to Gatwick Airport.
Bedrooms: 7 double & 20 twin, 3 family rooms.
Bathrooms: 30 private.
Bed & breakfast: from £70 single, from £77 double.
Lunch available.
Evening meal 6pm (l.o. 10.30pm).
Parking for 250.
Credit: Access, Visa, Diners, Amex.

Little Foxes Guest House
ⓦⓦ COMMENDED
Ifield Rd., Ifield Wood, Crawley, RH11 0JY
☎ (0293) 552430
Bungalow in 5 acres of grounds. 10 minutes from Gatwick Airport. Free parking and transport included.
Bedrooms: 6 double & 6 twin, 1 family room.
Bathrooms: 13 private.
Bed & breakfast: £34.50-£46 single, £46-£55 double.
Parking for 50.
Credit: Access, Visa, Amex.

CROWBOROUGH

E. Sussex
Map ref 2D2

Pleasant, residential town standing on the highest ridge of the Ashdown Forest.

Winston Manor Hotel
Beacon Rd., Crowborough, TN6 1AD
☎ (0892) 652772 Fax (0892) 665537

Continued ▶

CROWBOROUGH

Continued

Situated on A26 to Brighton, 7 miles from Tunbridge Wells. Ideal for conferences, wedding receptions, private parties. Short or long stay. Leisure complex including indoor pool and coffee shop now open.
Bedrooms: 10 single, 29 double & 8 twin, 3 family rooms.
Bathrooms: 50 private.
Bed & breakfast: max. £88 double.
Lunch available.
Evening meal 7pm (l.o. 9pm).
Parking for 120.
Credit: Access, Visa, Diners, Amex.
🛇 🛏 📞 ⓡ 🖵 💠 ♿ Ⅴ 🚗
🕪 ● 🖹 ▥ ▲ 🍽 🛆 ♿ 🐾 🔾
🐾 SP 🎪

DARTFORD

Kent
Map ref 2D2

Industrial town probably most famous for the Dartford Tunnel. Large Orchard Theatre has a fine variety of entertainment.
Tourist Information Centre ☎ (0322) 343243

Brands Hatch Thistle Hotel Ⓜ

Brands Hatch., Dartford, DA3 8PE
☎ Dartford (0474) 854900
Telex 966449
Ⓖ Thistle
Set at the entrance to the world-famous motor racing circuit, the hotel offers elegance and fine cuisine. Easy access, near M20, M25 and M26.
Bedrooms: 20 single, 56 double & 57 twin, 7 family rooms.
Bathrooms: 140 private.
Bed & breakfast: from £82.75 single, from £102.50 double.
Lunch available.
Evening meal 7.30pm (l.o. 10.30pm).
Parking for 178.
Credit: Access, Visa, C.Bl., Diners, Amex.
🛇 🛆 📞 ⓡ 🖵 💠 ♿ Ⅴ ⅙
🚗 ● ▥ 🍽 ▲ 🍽 🛆 🐾 SP
🔾

Royal Victoria & Bull Hotel

1 High St., Dartford, DA1 1DU
☎ (0322) 223104 & 224415

This 15th C coaching inn in Dartford's town centre is an ideal base for touring south east England.
Bedrooms: 17 single, 2 double & 11 twin.
Bathrooms: 10 private, 6 public; 13 private showers.
Bed & breakfast: £38-£45 single, £50-£56 double.
Half board: from £47 daily.
Evening meal 7pm (l.o. 9.30pm).
Parking for 30.
Credit: Access, Visa, Diners, Amex.
🛇 🛆 📞 ⓡ 🖵 💠 ♿ Ⅴ ▥
🛆 🍽 🎪 🔾

DEAL

Kent
Map ref 3C4

Coastal town and popular holiday resort. Deal Castle was built as a fort and the museum is devoted to finds excavated in the area. Also the Time-ball Tower Museum. Angling available from both beach and pier.
Tourist Information Centre ☎ (0304) 369576

Beachbrow Hotel

Beach St., Deal, CT14 6HY
☎ (0304) 374338 & 373159
Situated directly overlooking pier beach, listed Georgian historic building. Interesting nautical paintings and prints. Ideal for holiday breaks and for golfers.
Bedrooms: 7 single, 9 double & 6 twin, 3 family rooms.
Bathrooms: 6 private, 5 public; 2 private showers.
Bed & breakfast: £17-£22 single, £27-£40 double.
Half board: £25.50-£30.50 daily, £178.50-£213.50 weekly.
Evening meal 7pm (l.o. 9pm).
Credit: Access, Visa, Diners, Amex.
🛇 🖵 🎗 Ⅴ ⅙ 🚗 📺 🍽 ▯ DAP
SP 🎪

Blencathra Country Guest House Ⓜ

☷☷
Kingsdown Hill, Kingsdown, Deal, CT14 8EA
☎ (0304) 373725
Peaceful situation in a private road, with commanding views of the Channel and countryside. Convenient for ferries and hoverport.
Bedrooms: 1 single, 1 double, 3 family rooms.
Bathrooms: 2 private, 2 public; 2 private showers.

Bed & breakfast: £14-£15 single, £28-£30 double.
Parking for 7.
🛇 🖵 💠 Ⅴ 🚗 🖵 📺 ▥ ❄ 🍽
🎪

Finglesham Grange Ⓜ

☷☷☷ **COMMENDED**
Finglesham, Nr. Deal, CT14 0NQ
☎ Sandwich (0304) 611314
Georgian country house in 4.5 acres of secluded grounds situated outside village just 4 miles from both Deal and Sandwich.
Bedrooms: 1 double & 2 twin.
Bathrooms: 3 private.
Bed & breakfast: £20 double.
Half board: from £29 daily, £140 weekly.
Evening meal 7pm (l.o. 5pm).
Parking for 5.
Open March-October.
▥ 🎗 🚗 📺 ▥ 🛆 ❄ 🍽 SP
🎪

Guildford House Hotel Ⓜ

☷☷
49 Beach St., Deal, CT14 6HY
☎ (0304) 375015
Situated on seafront. Family-run hotel with private bar, close to shopping centre and all local historic sights, golf-courses, etc.
Bedrooms: 2 single, 7 twin, 2 family rooms.
Bathrooms: 1 public; 7 private showers.
Bed & breakfast: £17-£19.50 single, £33-£38 double.
Half board: £22.50-£25 daily, £140-£158 weekly.
Lunch available.
Evening meal 7pm (l.o. 9pm).
Credit: Access, Visa.
🛇 🖵 💠 🎗 Ⅴ 🚗 📺 🛆 ▸
🍽 🐾 SP 🎪

Hardicot Guest House

☷☷ **COMMENDED**
Kingsdown Rd., Walmer, Deal, CT14 8AW
☎ (0304) 373867
Large, quiet, detached Victorian house with channel views and secluded garden. Ideal for sea fishing, cliff walks and golfing.
Bedrooms: 1 double & 1 twin, 1 family room.
Bathrooms: 1 public.
Bed & breakfast: £14-£20 single, £28-£40 double.
Parking for 3.
🛇 🖐5 🚗 Ⅶ 🎗 🚗 📺 🛆 ❄
🍽 🎪

Kent House

12 Gilford Rd., Deal
☎ (0304) 367329

Stay as one of the family in a friendly bed and breakfast. Close to the sea and town centre.
Bedrooms: 1 single, 1 double & 2 twin, 1 family room.
Bathrooms: 1 public.
Bed & breakfast: £11-£12.50 single, £22-£25 double.
🛇 🛆 🖵 💠 Ⅶ 🚗 📺 ▥ 🍽
SP

Portland House Hotel

Sondes Rd., Deal, CT14 7BW
☎ Deal (0304) 375050
Licensed hotel beside famous Deal Time-ball tower. Close to coach station. Within reach of golf-courses, adult and children's water fun pool and tennis.
Bedrooms: 5 double & 2 twin, 3 family rooms.
Bathrooms: 3 public.
Bed & breakfast: £27-£30 double.
Half board: £18.50-£20 daily.
Evening meal 7pm (l.o. 10pm).
Credit: Access.
🛇 🛆 ⅙ 🚗 📺 🛆 🎗 🍽

DIAL POST

W. Sussex
Map ref 2D2

8m S. Horsham
Small village on the main road from Horsham to the coast at Worthing.

Swallows Farm

☷☷
Swallows Lane, Dial Post, Horsham, RH13 8NN
☎ Partridge Green (0403) 710385
210-acre mixed farm. Georgian farmhouse in the quiet Sussex countryside half a mile off A24, within easy reach of coast, Downs and many places of historic interest. Gatwick Airport 16 miles.
Bedrooms: 2 double & 2 twin.
Bathrooms: 2 public.
Bed & breakfast: £17-£19 single, £28-£30 double.
Half board: £20-£23 daily.
Evening meal 6.30pm.
Parking for 4.
Open March-October.
🛇 🖐10 🖵 💠 Ⅶ 🚗 📺 ▥ 🛆
❄ 🍽 🍽 🎪

> **Half board prices shown are per person but in some cases may be based on double/twin occupancy.**

DOVER

Kent
Map ref 3C4

Once a Cinque Port, now the busiest passenger port in the world. Still a historic town and seaside resort beside the famous White Cliffs. Numerous buildings trace the town's history from the Roman Painted House and lighthouse, Saxon church, Norman castle to the 13th C Maison Dieu and adjacent Victorian "Old Town Gaol".
Tourist Information Centre ☎ *(0304) 205108*

Amanda Guest House M
Listed
4 Harold St., Dover,
CT16 1SF
☎ (0304) 201711
A large Victorian semi-detached house in a quiet cul-de-sac off the main road. Close to town and ferries.
Bedrooms: 2 double & 2 twin, 2 family rooms.
Bathrooms: 2 public.
Bed & breakfast: £23-£27 double.
Parking for 5.
⌂ ▥ ▮ �📺 ▦ ♋ ≭ ❌ SP ⊞

Ardmore Private Hotel M
👑
18 Castle Hill Rd., Dover,
CT16 1QW
☎ (0304) 205895
Situated in the lee of Dover Castle. Near to sports complex and ruins of Saxon church. Views of harbour and town.
Bedrooms: 2 double & 1 twin, 1 family room.
Bathrooms: 4 private.
Bed & breakfast: £25-£40 double.
Parking for 1.
⌂ ▯ ♨ ▥ �V ≭ ➤ ▦ ❌ ❌ SP ⊞

Conifers Guest House M
👑👑
241 Folkestone Rd., Dover,
CT17 9LL
☎ (0304) 205609
Small family-run guesthouse, 5 minutes from seafront and docks. Reduced rates for children sharing parents' bedroom. Early breakfast available.
Bedrooms: 1 single, 1 twin, 4 family rooms.
Bathrooms: 1 private, 2 public.

Bed & breakfast: £14-£16 single, £24-£30 double.
Half board: £21-£24 daily.
Evening meal 7pm (l.o. 6pm).
Parking for 5.
⌂3 ▯ ♨ ▥ ⓤⓛ ➤ 📺 ▦ ❌ ❌

Dover Moat House M
👑👑👑👑 **COMMENDED**
Townwall St., Dover,
CT16 1SZ
☎ (0304) 203270 Telex 96458
CR Queens Moat Houses
Close to ferry and hovercraft terminals, within easy reach of town centre, seafront and castle.
Bedrooms: 17 single, 30 double & 32 twin.
Bathrooms: 79 private.
Bed & breakfast: £70.25-£78.50 single, £86.50-£97 double.
Lunch available.
Evening meal 7pm (l.o. 9.15pm).
Parking for 8.
Credit: Access, Visa, Diners, Amex.
⌂ ♨ ♦ ▮ ⓒ ▯ ♨ ▮ ▥ ≭ ➤ ♋ 🎲 SP ⊤

Elmo Guest House M
👑👑👑
120 Folkestone Rd., Dover,
CT17 9SP
☎ (0304) 206236
Conveniently situated for ferries and Hoverport terminals and within easy reach of the town centre and railway station; overnight stops our speciality.
Bedrooms: 1 single, 2 double, 3 family rooms.
Bathrooms: 2 public.
Bed & breakfast: £13-£15 single, £22-£25 double.
Half board: £18-£21 daily.
Evening meal 6.30pm (l.o. 9pm).
Parking for 8.
⌂ ♨ ▯ ⓤⓛ ▮ ➤ 📺 ▦ ❌ ⒹⒶⓅ ⊠ SP ⊤

Esther House M
Listed
55 Barton Road, Dover,
CT16 2NF
☎ Dover (0304) 241332
Family Christian guesthouse. Close to town centre and port. Ideal overnight stop to continent or suitable for short breaks.
Bedrooms: 1 single, 1 twin, 1 family room.
Bathrooms: 1 public.
Bed & breakfast: £10-£16 single, £20-£32 double.
⌂ ▨ ▯ ⓤⓛ ▮ ▥ ≭ ▦ ▦ ❌ ⒹⒶⓅ SP

Fleur De Lis Hotel & Restaurant
👑👑👑 **APPROVED**
9-10 Effingham Cres., Dover,
CT17 9RH
☎ (0304) 240224
Small privately owned hotel, in central Dover with French licensed restaurant and cocktail bar set in an old world theme. A la carte menu, open to non-residents. Open all year.
Bedrooms: 4 single, 3 double & 3 twin.
Bathrooms: 5 private, 2 public.
Bed & breakfast: £15-£28 single, £25-£38 double.
Evening meal 7pm (l.o. 10.30pm).
Parking for 1.
Credit: Access, Visa, Diners, Amex.
⌂5 ♨ ▥ ➤ 📺 ▦ ♋ ▮ ❌ ❌

Gateway Hovertel M
👑
Snargate St., Dover,
CT16 9BZ
☎ (0304) 205479
Town motel blended with century-old hotel, close to Hoverport, shops, restaurants, 'take-aways' and both ferry terminals. Stay 2 days and save £10.
Bedrooms: 1 single, 6 double & 13 twin, 7 family rooms.
Bathrooms: 27 private.
Bed & breakfast: £40-£46 double.
Evening meal 6pm (l.o. 7pm).
Parking for 28.
Credit: Access, Visa.
⌂ ♨ ▯ ▮ ▥ ➤ 📺 ● ▦ ♋ ▮ ❌ ⒹⒶⓅ SP ⊤

Longfield Guest House
👑👑
203 Folkestone Rd., Dover,
CT17 9SL
☎ (0304) 204716
Large residential guesthouse close to station and docks. Suitable for ferry travellers.
Bedrooms: 5 single, 1 double & 2 twin, 2 family rooms.
Bathrooms: 2 public.
Bed & breakfast: £13-£15 single, £25-£27 double.
Evening meal 5.30pm (l.o. 7.30pm).
Parking for 9.
Open January-November.
⌂ ♨ ▯ ▮ ▥ ➤ 📺 ▦ ♋ ❌ ❌ ⒹⒶⓅ SP

Mildmay Hotel M
👑👑👑
Folkestone Rd., Dover,
CT17 9SF
☎ (0304) 204278

On the A20 Dover to London road, 2 minutes from the town centre and close to car ferry, hoverport-terminals and Dover Priory railway station.
Bedrooms: 2 single, 6 double & 10 twin, 4 family rooms.
Bathrooms: 22 private.
Bed & breakfast: £36-£40 single, £46-£50 double.
Evening meal 7pm (l.o. 10pm).
Parking for 32.
Open February-December.
Credit: Access, Visa, Diners, Amex.
⌂ ♨ ♦ ⓒ ▯ ▮ ➤ 📺 ▦ ♋ ▮ ❌ 🎲 SP ⊤

The Norman Guest House
Listed
75 Folkestone Rd., Dover,
CT17 9RZ
☎ (0304) 207803
Opposite Dover Priory railway station. Near to shops, ferries, hovercraft ports and all amenities.
Bedrooms: 1 single, 2 double & 2 twin, 3 family rooms.
Bathrooms: 2 public.
Bed & breakfast: £10-£13 single, £20-£24 double.
Half board: £14-£16 daily.
Evening meal 7.30pm (l.o. 8.30pm).
Parking for 6.
⌂ ▯ 📺 ▦ ♋ ❌ ⒹⒶⓅ

Palma Nova Guest House
👑👑👑
126 Folkestone Rd., Dover,
CT17 9SP
☎ (0304) 208109
Victorian town house tastefully modernised and conveniently situated for BR station, hoverport and docks. Specialised services for cross-channel travellers.
Bedrooms: 2 double & 1 twin, 3 family rooms.
Bathrooms: 2 public.
Bed & breakfast: £13-£18 single, £22-£24 double.
Half board: £19-£24 daily, £125-£150 weekly.
Evening meal 6.30pm (l.o. 8.30pm).
Parking for 6.
⌂ ♨ ▯ ⓤⓛ ▮ ▦ ❌ ⒹⒶⓅ SP ⊤

St. Brelades M
👑👑👑
80-82 Buckland Ave., Dover,
CT16 2NW
☎ (0304) 206126
Attractive, friendly guesthouse minutes from docks. Full breakfast service from 7.00am to 9.00 am. Residents' bar and evening meals available.

Continued ▶

DOVER

Continued

Bedrooms: 1 single, 2 double & 1 twin, 4 family rooms.
Bathrooms: 2 public;
2 private showers.
Bed & breakfast: £13-£17 single, £28-£34 double.
Half board: £20-£23 daily.
Evening meal 6pm (l.o. 10pm).
Parking for 7.
Credit: Visa.
❧ ♻ ⌂ 📺 ▥ ➔ ✕ ⌷ ⤢
SP

St. Margaret's Hotel and Country Club
👑👑👑 COMMENDED

Reach Rd., St. Margarets-at-Cliffe, Nr. Dover, CT15 6AE
☎ (0304) 853262
Situated 5 minutes from the A2 off the A249. En-suite bedrooms with telephone. Leisure centre, 2 bars, restaurant and bar food.
Bedrooms: 6 double & 4 twin, 2 family rooms.
Bathrooms: 12 private.
Bed & breakfast: £45-£55 single, £55-£70 double.
Half board: £75-£90 daily.
Lunch available.
Evening meal 7pm (l.o. 9.30pm).
Parking for 100.
Credit: Access, Visa.
❧ ♻ ✆ ⌂ ❑ ▮ ▥ ➔
🍴 🈺 🔒 🅿 ♺ ✸ SP

St. Martins Guest House 🏠
👑👑

17 Castle Hill Rd., Dover, CT16 1QW
☎ (0304) 205938
Situated in the lee of Dover Castle, rear of sports complex and ruins of Saxon church, with views of harbour and town.
Bedrooms: 1 single, 3 double & 3 twin, 2 family rooms.
Bathrooms: 1 public;
7 private showers.
Bed & breakfast: £20-£25 single, £20-£35 double.
Parking for 1.
Credit: Access.
❧ ❑ ♻ ▥ ✂ ⤢ ▥ ➔ ✕
SP 🈺

Sharon Guest House
100-102 Folkestone Rd., Dover, CT17 9SP
☎ (0304) 204373
Christian family-run guesthouse convenient for docks, railway station and town centre. Established 1966.
Bedrooms: 2 single, 3 double & 3 twin, 3 family rooms.
Bathrooms: 2 public.

Bed & breakfast: £10.50-£13 single, £21-£25 double.
Parking for 10.
❧ ♻ ❑ ♻ ⓤⓛ ▥ ➔ ✕ ⌷
SP

Tower Guest House 🏠
👑👑 COMMENDED

98 Priory Hill, Dover, CT17 0AD
☎ (0304) 208212
Converted water tower in quiet surroundings. Most rooms with private bathrooms. 6 minutes' drive to docks. Lock-up garages available.
Bedrooms: 1 double & 2 twin, 2 family rooms.
Bathrooms: 3 private, 1 public.
Bed & breakfast: £26-£33 double.
Parking for 2.
❧ ♻ ❑ ♻ ⓤⓛ ▮ ▥ ➔ 🏰
SP 🈺 ⓣ

Walletts Court Hotel and Restaurant 🏠
👑👑👑 COMMENDED

West-Cliffe, St. Margaret's-at-Cliffe, Dover, CT15 6EW
☎ (0304) 852424
Restored 17th C manor and barn with inglenook fireplaces. Ideal for history enthusiasts, rural setting, 3 miles from Dover. Saturday evening gourmet dinners, non-residents welcome, open as a restaurant Tuesday to Saturday inclusive for dinner only.
Bedrooms: 2 double & 3 twin, 2 family rooms.
Bathrooms: 7 private.
Bed & breakfast: £35-£45 single, £40-£60 double.
Half board: £35-£50 daily, £245-£350 weekly.
Evening meal 6pm (l.o. 9pm).
Parking for 10.
Credit: Access, Visa.
❧ ❑ ♻ ▥ ➔ ▥ ➔ 🍴
✿ 🅿 ✸ ✕ 🎿 SP 🈺

White Cliffs Hotel 🏠
👑👑👑👑

Marine Parade (Sea Front), Dover, CT17 9BP
☎ (0304) 203633 Telex 965422 Fax (0304) 216320
Traditional English hotel on the seafront, close to all departure points for the continent. Pleasant, friendly staff. Special breaks available, terms on request.
Bedrooms: 9 single, 18 double & 23 twin, 5 family rooms.
Bathrooms: 55 private, 4 public.
Bed & breakfast: £45-£60 single, £66-£70 double.
Lunch available.
Evening meal 7pm (l.o. 9.30pm).

Parking for 25.
Credit: Access, Visa, C.Bl., Diners, Amex.
❧ ✆ ❑ ♻ ▥ ▥ ➔ 📺
◐ ▮ ▦ ➔ 🍴 SP 🈺 ⓣ

Whitmore Guest House
261 Folkestone Rd., Dover, CT17 9LL
☎ (0304) 203080
Small well-established family guesthouse, close to railway station, town centre, docks and hoverport. En-suite rooms also available.
Bedrooms: 1 double & 1 twin, 2 family rooms.
Bathrooms: 1 private, 1 public.
Bed & breakfast: £12-£15 single, £24-£28 double.
Half board: £18-£34 daily.
Parking for 4.
❧ ♻ ❑ ♻ ⓤⓛ ▮ ▥ ▥ ⌷
SP 🈺

Winchelsea Hotel 🏠
122-124 Folkestone Rd., Dover, CT17 9SP
☎ (0304) 241572
Small family-run hotel, near the town centre and harbour. Congenial bar and restaurant. Pool table available.
Bedrooms: 2 single, 3 double & 2 twin, 5 family rooms.
Bathrooms: 7 private, 2 public; 5 private showers.
Bed & breakfast: £22-£27 single, £30-£40 double.
Half board: £29-£34 daily, £140-£160 weekly.
Evening meal (l.o. 10.30pm).
Parking for 6.
Credit: Access, Visa, Diners, Amex.
❧ ❑ ▥ ➔ 📺 ▥ ➔ 🍴 ✿
✕ ⌷ SP ⓣ

DYMCHURCH

Kent
Map ref 3B4

4m NE. New Romney
For centuries it was the headquarters for the Lords of the Level, the local government of this area. Probably best known today because of the fame of its fictional parson, the notorious Dr. Syn, who has inspired a regular festival.

Chantry Hotel 🏠
👑👑

Sycamore Gardens, Dymchurch, TN29 0LA
☎ (0303) 873137

Superbly situated secluded Kentish-style hotel. Private access to beach and large green. Comfortable accommodation, variety of food, selection of house wines.
Bedrooms: 1 single, 2 double & 1 twin, 4 family rooms.
Bathrooms: 5 private, 1 public.
Bed & breakfast: £15-£21 single.
Half board: £24.50-£31 daily, £125-£155 weekly.
Lunch available.
Evening meal 6.30pm (l.o. 8pm).
Parking for 15.
❧ ♻ ⌂ ♻ ▮ ▥ ➔ 📺
▥ ➔ 🍴 ⌷ ♺ SP 🈺

Waterside Guest House 🏠
👑👑

15 Hythe Rd., Dymchurch, Romney Marsh, TN29 0LN
☎ (0303) 872253
Friendly and flexible service. 5 minutes to safe sandy beaches, amusements and historic Romney Marshes. Castle, zoo, miniature railway, fun fair and golf nearby.
Bedrooms: 1 single, 2 double & 2 twin, 2 family rooms.
Bathrooms: 2 public; 2 private showers.
Bed & breakfast: £13.50-£15 single, £23-£30 double.
Half board: £30-£37 daily.
Evening meal 7pm (l.o. 7.30pm).
Parking for 7.
❧ ▮ ▥ 📺 ▥ ➔ ✕ 🏰

EAST DEAN

E. Sussex
Map ref 2D3

4m W. Eastbourne
Pretty village on a green near Friston Forest and Birling Gap.

Birling Gap Hotel 🏠
👑👑👑 COMMENDED

East Dean, Eastbourne, BN20 0AB
☎ Eastbourne (0323) 423163 & 423197 Fax (0323) 423030
Magnificent Seven Sisters clifftop position. Views of country, sea, beach, superb downland walks. Old world thatched bar, restaurant and coffee shop, games room, restaurant, function/conference suite.
Bedrooms: 1 single, 4 double & 2 twin, 2 family rooms.
Bathrooms: 9 private, 1 public.
Bed & breakfast: £23-£34.50 single, £34.50-£50 double.

Half board: £24-£41.25 daily,
£142.50-£247.50 weekly.
Lunch available.
Evening meal 6pm (l.o.
9.30pm).
Parking for 100.
Credit: Access, Visa, Diners,
Amex.

EAST GRINSTEAD

W. Sussex
Map ref 2D2

A number of fine old
houses stand in the High
Street, one of which is
Sackville College,
founded in 1609.

Cranfield Lodge Hotel
Maypole Rd., East
Grinstead, RH19 1HW
☎ (0342) 321251/410371/2
*A friendly family hotel in a
pleasant residential area, close
to all amenities. Supervised by
the owners.*
Bedrooms: 6 single, 9 double
& 3 twin, 1 family room.
Bathrooms: 8 private,
3 public; 2 private showers.
Bed & breakfast: £25-£35
single, £42-£48 double.
Evening meal 7pm (l.o. 6pm).
Parking for 10.
Credit: Access, Visa, Amex.

Graveyte Manor ⋔
⚜⚜⚜⚜ **HIGHLY COMMENDED**
Sharpthorne, East Grinstead,
RH19 4LJ
☎ Sharpthorne (0342) 810567
Telex 957239
*Elizabethan manor house set in
William Robinson's famous
English natural garden,
boasting an internationally
famed restaurant and wine list.*
Bedrooms: 2 single, 5 double
& 7 twin.
Bathrooms: 14 private.
Bed & breakfast: £93.15-
£105.80 single, £117.30-
£218.50 double.
Lunch available.
Evening meal 7.30pm (l.o.
9.30pm).
Parking for 30.

**The enquiry
coupons at the
back will help you
when contacting
proprietors.**

EAST HORSLEY

Surrey
Map ref 2D2

*6m SW. Leatherhead
Village on the A246 road
but surrounded by
wooded countryside.
North Downs are nearby
to the south.*

Thatchers Resort Hotel ⋔
Epsom Rd., East Horsley,
KT24 6TB
☎ (048 65) 4291 Fax (048 65)
4222
Resort
*Fine Tudor-style hotel,
refurbished 1984, in delightful
Surrey countryside. Ideal
setting for conferences,
weddings and weekend breaks.*
Bedrooms: 7 single, 28 double
& 11 twin, 13 family rooms.
Bathrooms: 59 private.
Bed & breakfast: £71.50-
£81.50 single, £88-£98 double.
Lunch available.
Evening meal 7.30pm (l.o.
9.30pm).
Parking for 100.
Credit: Access, Visa, Diners,
Amex.

EASTBOURNE

E. Sussex
Map ref 3B4

One of the finest, most
elegant resorts on the
south-east coast and
beautifully situated beside
Beachy Head. Long
promenade, plenty of
gardens, several theatres,
Towner Art Gallery,
Lifeboat Museum and the
Redoubt, housing the
Sussex Combined
Services Museum and
Aquarium.
*Tourist Information
Centre ☎ (0323) 411400*

Bay Lodge Hotel ⋔
⚜⚜⚜
61-62 Royal Pde.,
Eastbourne, BN22 7AQ
☎ (0323) 32515
*Small seafront hotel with most
rooms en-suite. Opposite
Redoubt Gardens, close to
bowling greens, sailing clubs
and entertainments. Large sun-
lounge.*
Bedrooms: 3 single, 5 double
& 4 twin, 1 family room.
Bathrooms: 8 private,
2 public.

Bed & breakfast: £16-£26
single, £25-£45 double.
Half board: £22-£31 daily,
£147-£179 weekly.
Evening meal 6pm (l.o. 6pm).
Open March-October.
Credit: Access, Visa.

Beachy Rise ⋔
⚜⚜⚜
Beachy Head Rd.,
Eastbourne, BN20 7QN
☎ (0323) 639171
*Peaceful Victorian house in
Meads village. Pretty south-
facing garden. Local parking.
English and vegetarian
cooking. Close to South
Downs.*
Bedrooms: 4 double & 1 twin,
1 family room.
Bathrooms: 4 private,
1 public.
Bed & breakfast: £32-£44
double.
Half board: £24-£30 daily,
£160-£200 weekly.
Evening meal 6.30pm (l.o.
10am).
Credit: Access, Visa.

Bracken Guest House
⚜⚜
3 Hampden Ter., Latimer
Rd., Eastbourne, BN22 7BL
☎ (0323) 25779
*Friendly, comfortable family-
run guesthouse, serving
traditional English food. Close
to seafront, town centre and
entertainment.*
Bedrooms: 1 single, 1 double
& 1 twin, 2 family rooms.
Bathrooms: 1 private,
1 public.
Bed & breakfast: £11.50-£16
single, £23-£32 double.
Half board: £15-£19 daily,
£75-£90 weekly.
Evening meal 6pm.
Open May-October,
December.

Camelot Lodge
⚜⚜⚜
35 Lewes Rd., Eastbourne,
BN21 2BU
☎ (0323) 25207
*Licensed hotel in own large car
park within easy reach of all
amenities. Enjoy a relaxed
atmosphere with a high
standard of service.*
Bedrooms: 1 single, 4 double
& 3 twin, 2 family rooms.
Bathrooms: 9 private,
1 public.
Bed & breakfast: £17.50-£20
single, £35-£40 double.

Half board: £24.50-£27 daily,
£128-£163 weekly.
Evening meal 6pm (l.o. 4pm).
Parking for 10.
Credit: Access, Visa.

Cavendish Hotel ⋔
Grand Pde., Eastbourne,
BN21 4DH
☎ (0323) 410222 Fax (0323)
410941 Telex 87579
De Vere
*An elegant hotel enjoying a
prime position overlooking the
sea and close to all amenities.*
Bedrooms: 27 single,
25 double & 55 twin, 4 family
rooms.
Bathrooms: 111 private.
Bed & breakfast: £70-£80
single, £115-£140 double.
Half board: £85-£96 daily,
£405-£460 weekly.
Lunch available.
Evening meal 7pm (l.o.
9.30pm).
Parking for 50.
Credit: Access, Visa, Diners,
Amex.

Chalfont
27 Ceylon Place, Eastbourne,
BN21 3JE
☎ (0323) 23866
*Guesthouse 1 minute from
coach station, within easy
reach of shops, theatres, pier
and gardens. Vegetarians
welcome. Payphone. Colour
TV in all rooms.*
Bedrooms: 1 single, 1 double
& 1 twin, 2 family rooms.
Bathrooms: 1 public.
Bed & breakfast: £12.50-
£14.50 single, £24-£28 double.
Half board: £16.50-£18 daily,
£100-£125 weekly.
Evening meal 6pm (l.o.
6.30pm).

Chalk Farm Hotel ⋔
⚜⚜
Coopers Hill, Willingdon,
Eastbourne, BN20 9JD
☎ (0323) 503800
*A converted 17th C farmhouse
set in 2 acres, on the edge of
the Sussex Downs, only a few
miles from Eastbourne.*
Bedrooms: 1 single, 4 double
& 3 twin, 1 family room.
Bathrooms: 6 private,
2 public.
Bed & breakfast: £25-£28.50
single, £50-£57 double.
Half board: £38-£42.50 daily.
Continued ▶

EASTBOURNE
Continued

Evening meal 7pm (l.o. 9.30pm).
Parking for 20.
Credit: Access, Visa.
🏃♨♿🏷♉🖥📺🔌♨🍴❄
🙌🚬🚭📵
♿ Display advertisement appears on page 545.

Cherry Tree Hotel ♈
15 Silverdale Rd.,
Eastbourne, BN20 7AJ
☎ (0323) 22406
Small hotel and restaurant. All bedrooms en-suite with colour TV, telephone, tea/coffee making. A la carte, table d'hote restaurant.
Bedrooms: 1 single, 4 double & 3 twin, 2 family rooms.
Bathrooms: 10 private.
Bed & breakfast: £20-£25 single, £40-£50 double.
Half board: £28-£33 daily, £157-£180 weekly.
Evening meal 6.30pm (l.o. 9pm).
Credit: Access, Visa.
🏃7♨♿🏷♉🖥♨🖥🔌
🍴🙌🚭📵SP

Congress Hotel ♈
👑👑 APPROVED
31-37 Carlisle Rd.,
Eastbourne, BN21 4JS
☎ Eastbourne
(0323) 32118/20016
Family-run hotel in peaceful location. Close to theatres and seafront.
Bedrooms: 16 single,
15 double & 33 twin, 5 family rooms.
Bathrooms: 44 private,
9 public.
Bed & breakfast: £25.50-£33.50 single, £46-£62 double.
Half board: £28.50-£35.50 daily, £162-£220 weekly.
Lunch available.
Evening meal 6.30pm (l.o. 7.45pm).
Open March-November.
Credit: Visa, Access, Amex.
🏃♏♨♿🏷♉🖥🔌♨🖥
📺♉🖥🖥🔌♨🍴♿♿SP
📵

Downland Hotel ♈
👑👑👑👑
37 Lewes Rd., Eastbourne,
BN21 2BU
☎ (0323) 32689
♏ Minotels
Elegant Edwardian residence beautifully converted to provide every modern comfort. Attentive service, award-winning restaurant. Car park. Temporary membership of nearby sports and leisure complex.

Bedrooms: 2 single, 8 double & 1 twin, 4 family rooms.
Bathrooms: 15 private.
Bed & breakfast: £27.50-£37.50 single, £55-£75 double.
Half board: £187.50-£275 weekly.
Evening meal 7pm (l.o. 9pm).
Parking for 10.
Open February-December.
Credit: Access, Visa, Diners, Amex.
🏃♨♿🖥🔌♨🏷♉🖥
📺🖥🔌♨🍴♉🙌🚬📵SP

Edelweiss Private Hotel ♈
👑👑
10-12 Elms Ave., Eastbourne,
BN21 3DN
☎ Eastbourne (0323) 32071
A fun family-run hotel within easy walking distance of the seafront, pier, shops, theatres, coach and railway stations.
Bedrooms: 3 single, 6 double & 5 twin, 1 family room.
Bathrooms: 3 public.
Bed & breakfast: £12.50-£15 single, £25-£30 double.
Half board: £16-£17.50 daily, £78-£110 weekly.
Evening meal 6pm (l.o. 7pm).
Credit: Access, Visa.
🏃♨♿🖥🔌♨🏷♉🖥📺🖥
♨🍴🙌🚬📵SP

Elms Hotel
👑👑 APPROVED
19/21 Elms Ave., Eastbourne,
BN21 3DN
☎ (0323) 23765
On the sunny side of an elegant avenue, close to all attractions and shops. Lounge patio.
Bedrooms: 3 single, 1 double & 9 twin, 1 family room.
Bathrooms: 4 public;
5 private showers.
Bed & breakfast: from £15 single, £30-£34 double.
Half board: £20-£22 daily, £110-£135 weekly.
Evening meal 6pm (l.o. 11am).
Parking for 4.
🏃5♉🖥🔌♨🖥📺🔌♨🚬♿
📵SP

Far End Private Hotel
👑👑
139 Royal Pde., Eastbourne,
BN22 7LH
☎ (0323) 25666
Family hotel on seafront in a level position close to all amenities, and with car park.
Bedrooms: 2 single, 5 double & 3 twin.
Bathrooms: 4 private,
2 public.
Bed & breakfast: £16-£18 single, £32-£36 double.
Half board: £22-£24 daily, £123-£156 weekly.

Evening meal 6pm (l.o. 6pm).
Parking for 8.
Open April-October.
🖥🔌♨♉🖥📺🖥🔌♨🍴🙌♿
🚬SP

Gladwyn Hotel ♈
16 Blackwater Rd.,
Eastbourne, BN21 4JD
☎ (0323) 33142
Private hotel overlooking Devonshire Park. Close to sea, shops and theatres. Residential licence. TV and tea/coffee making facilites in all bedrooms, most en-suite.
Bedrooms: 2 single, 3 double & 5 twin, 2 family rooms.
Bathrooms: 9 private,
1 public; 1 private shower.
Bed & breakfast: £15.75-£18.75 single, £31.50-£37.50 double.
Half board: £20.75-£23.75 daily, £114.75-£166.25 weekly.
Evening meal 6.30pm.
🏃♨♿🖥🔌♨♉🖥📺🖥♿
🚬SP📵

Grand Hotel ♈
King Edwards Pde.,
Eastbourne, BN21 4EQ
☎ (0323) 412345 Telex 87332
♏ De Vere
Set in its own gardens with heated swimming pool, this internationally famous hotel offers everything for the discerning guest. Indoor leisure club. 2 restaurants.
Bedrooms: 27 single,
36 double & 83 twin,
18 family rooms.
Bathrooms: 164 private.
Bed & breakfast: £75-£100 single, £120-£160 double.
Half board: £65-£90 daily, £450-£630 weekly.
Lunch available.
Evening meal 7pm (l.o. 10.30pm).
Parking for 60.
Credit: Access, Visa, Diners, Amex.
🏃♨♿🖥🔌♨🏷♉🖥♉
🖥🔌♨🍴♿♿♿♉🏹
❄🚬SP🖥📵

Hydro Hotel ♈
👑👑👑
Mount Rd., Eastbourne,
BN20 7HZ
☎ (0323) 20643 Telex 877440
P.Burns.G. Quote HYH
Elegant, 100-bedroomed hotel, in attractive garden setting overlooking the sea, offers facilities for all seasons and all ages.
Bedrooms: 20 single,
22 double & 55 twin, 3 family rooms.
Bathrooms: 80 private,
12 public.

Bed & breakfast: £25-£30 single, from £48 double.
Half board: £30-£45 daily.
Lunch available.
Evening meal 6.45pm (l.o. 8.30pm).
Parking for 50.
Credit: Access, Visa.
🏃♨♿🖥🔌♨♉🖥📺🖥
♉🖥🔌♨🍴♉🏹♿❄
🖥🚬SP📵

Hotel Iverna
32 Marine Pde., Eastbourne,
BN22 7AY
☎ (0323) 30768
Small quiet hotel on seafront close to pier, shops and theatres. Unrestricted views across the channel.
Bedrooms: 2 single, 5 double & 2 twin.
Bathrooms: 3 public.
Bed & breakfast: £16.50-£18.50 single, £33-£37 double.
Half board: £23-£25 daily, £149-£163 weekly.
Evening meal 6pm (l.o. 9.30pm).
Credit: Access, Visa.
🏃8♉🖥🔌♨🏷♉🖥📺🖥♨
🖥🚬SP📵

Lansdowne Hotel ♈
👑👑👑
King Edward's Pde.,
Eastbourne, BN21 4EE
☎ Eastbourne (0323) 25174
Telex 878624
♏ Best Western
Family-run hotel in premier seafront position with bar, spacious lounges and elegant public areas. Theatres, shops and sporting facilities nearby.
Bedrooms: 40 single,
21 double & 63 twin, 6 family rooms.
Bathrooms: 130 private,
4 public.
Bed & breakfast: £43-£55 single, £74-£94 double.
Half board: £41-£62 daily, £259-£434 weekly.
Lunch available.
Evening meal 6.30pm (l.o. 8.30pm).
Parking for 22.
Credit: Access, Visa, Diners, Amex.
🏃♨🔌♨🖥♉🖥♉🔌♨🍴♿♉
🚬SP📵

Loriston Guest House
👑👑 COMMENDED
17 St. Aubyns Rd.,
Eastbourne, BN22 7AS
☎ (0323) 26193
Centrally-heated guesthouse renowned for comfort and food. Access at all times. Unrestricted parking. Close to seafront. Please send stamped, addressed envelope for colour brochure.

Bedrooms: 2 single, 2 double
& 2 twin.
Bathrooms: 1 public.
Bed & breakfast: £12.50-£15
single, £25-£30 double.
Half board: £16-£20 daily,
£75-£100 weekly.
Evening meal 6pm (l.o. 4pm).

Hotel Mandalay M
♛♛♛
16 Trinity Trees, Eastbourne,
BN21 3LE
☎ (0323) 29222
*Town centre position, 2 minutes
from sea front and within easy
walking distance of all
amenities. Ample parking in
hotel grounds.*
Bedrooms: 1 single, 5 double
& 5 twin, 1 family room.
Bathrooms: 12 private.
Bed & breakfast: £24-£27.50
single, £40-£50 double.
Half board: £30-£33 daily,
£160-£195 weekly.
Evening meal 6pm.
Parking for 20.
Credit: Access, Visa.

Mayvere Guest House M
♛♛
12 Cambridge Rd.,
Eastbourne, BN22 7BS
☎ (0323) 29580
*A small family guesthouse,
comfortable and caring, with
emphasis on food. Adjacent to
seafront and a short walk to
the centre. Weekly terms on
application.*
Bedrooms: 1 single, 3 double
& 2 twin, 1 family room.
Bathrooms: 2 public.
Bed & breakfast: £12-£14.50
single, £23-£27 double.
Evening meal 6pm (l.o.
6.30pm).

New Wilmington Hotel
♛♛♛♛
25 Compton St., Eastbourne,
BN21 4DU
☎ (0323) 21219
*Family-run hotel close to
seafront, theatres and shops.
All rooms en-suite and
furnished to a high standard.*
Bedrooms: 5 single, 12 double
& 17 twin, 7 family rooms.
Bathrooms: 41 private.
Bed & breakfast: £29.50-
£34.50 single, £47-£56 double.
Half board: £29-£36 daily,
£197-£260 weekly.
Lunch available.
Evening meal 6.30pm (l.o.
8pm).

Parking for 3.
Open February-December.
Credit: Access, Visa.

Oban Hotel M
♛♛♛
King Edward's Pde.,
Eastbourne, BN21 4DS
☎ (0323) 31581
*Private hotel on seafront with
panoramic views. Pleasant
open sun terrace.*
Bedrooms: 7 single, 5 double
& 19 twin.
Bathrooms: 31 private,
1 public.
Half board: £20-£29 daily,
£140-£250 weekly.
Lunch available.
Evening meal 6.30pm (l.o.
7.30pm).
Open March-October.

One-Two-Three Residency
123 Tideswell Rd.,
Eastbourne, BN21 3RH
☎ (0323) 29571
*Small, friendly guesthouse.
Centrally situated and
convenient for all amenities, 5
minutes from pier. Home
cooking using fresh produce,
varied menu.*
Bedrooms: 1 single, 1 double
& 3 twin.
Bathrooms: 2 public.
Bed & breakfast: £11.50-£13
single, £23-£26 double.
Half board: £15-£16.50 daily,
£89-£97 weekly.
Evening meal 6pm (l.o. 6pm).

Rockville Hotel
20-22 Bourne St., Eastbourne,
BN21 3ER
☎ (0323) 38488
*Comfortable family-run hotel
close to sea and shops with
home cooking, licensed bar, TV
lounge and many facilities.*
Bedrooms: 2 single, 6 double
& 2 twin, 3 family rooms.
Bathrooms: 3 private,
4 public.
Bed & breakfast: £12-£15
single, £24-£30 double.
Half board: £17-£20 daily.
Evening meal 6pm (l.o. 6pm).

**The symbols are
explained on the
flap inside the
back cover.**

Royal Hotel
8-9 Marine Pde., Eastbourne,
BN21 3DX
☎ (0323) 24027
*Seafront hotel near shops,
theatres, restaurants. Majority
of rooms face the sea, many
en-suite, all with TV and tea
making facilities. Central
heating.*
Bedrooms: 2 single, 8 double
& 3 twin.
Bathrooms: 1 private,
2 public; 5 private showers.
Bed & breakfast: £13-£18
single, £26-£34 double.
Evening meal 6pm (l.o.
midday).
Open February-December.

South Cliff House
♛♛♛
19 South Cliff Ave.,
Eastbourne, BN20 7AH
☎ (0323) 21019
*Situated in a picturesque tree-
lined avenue close to the sea.
Conveniently placed for
theatres, bandstand, downlands
and shops.*
Bedrooms: 1 single, 3 double
& 2 twin.
Bathrooms: 2 public.
Bed & breakfast: £15-£16
single, £30-£32 double.
Half board: £18-£19.50 daily,
£110-£120 weekly.
Evening meal 6pm (l.o.
6.30pm).
Open February-November.

Sovereign View Guest House M
♛♛♛
93 Royal Pde., Eastbourne,
BN22 7AE
☎ (0323) 21657
*Comfortable guesthouse on
seafront, close to amenities
with some en-suite room.
Traditional cooking, own keys,
colour TV and unrestricted
parking.*
Bedrooms: 1 single, 5 double
& 2 twin.
Bathrooms: 2 private,
2 public.
Bed & breakfast: £28-£32
double.
Half board: £20-£23 daily,
£115-£125 weekly.
Evening meal 6pm (l.o. 4pm).
Open April-September.

Stratford Hotel and Restaurant
59 Cavendish Pl.,
Eastbourne, BN21 3RL
☎ (0323) 24051

*Ideally situated near
promenade, coaches and
shopping centre. Licensed,
centrally heated throughout.
Ground floor and family rooms
available. Tea making facilities
and colour TV in all rooms.
Most rooms with modern en-
suite.*
Bedrooms: 5 single, 4 double
& 3 twin, 3 family rooms.
Bathrooms: 7 private,
2 public.
Bed & breakfast: £15-£18
single, £30-£36 double.
Half board: £20-£23 daily,
£95-£118 weekly.
Evening meal 6pm (l.o. 6pm).
Credit: Access, Visa, Diners.

Swanley Court Hotel
18-20 Trinity Trees,
Eastbourne, BN21 3LE
☎ (0323) 29298
*Small, friendly licensed hotel
centrally located for shopping
centre and short stroll from
seafront. Lounge bar with
dance floor. TV room.*
Bedrooms: 10 single, 2 double
& 8 twin, 2 family rooms.
Bathrooms: 8 private,
8 public.
Bed & breakfast: £15-£18
single.
Half board: £114-£144
weekly.
Lunch available.
Evening meal 6pm (l.o. 7pm).

The Wish Tower M
King Edward's Pde.,
Eastbourne, BN21 4EB
☎ (0323) 22676
*A spacious hotel on the sea
front, convenient for beach,
shops and conference centre.*
Bedrooms: 25 single,
11 double & 28 twin, 3 family
rooms.
Bathrooms: 59 private,
4 public; 8 private showers.
Bed & breakfast: £55-£65
single, £75-£85 double.
Half board: £246-£294
weekly.
Lunch available.
Evening meal 7pm (l.o.
8.45pm).
Credit: Access, Visa, Diners,
Amex.

York House Hotel M
♛♛♛
14-22 Royal Pde.,
Eastbourne, BN22 7AP
☎ (0323) 412918
Ⓒ Consort

Continued ▶

EASTBOURNE
Continued

90-year-old hotel with many facilities. Elegant lounges, appetising menus in our efficient restaurant, 7-day entertainment programme. Heated indoor swimming pool and games room. Attractive prices for families.
Bedrooms: 26 single, 23 double & 47 twin, 7 family rooms.
Bathrooms: 93 private, 8 public.
Bed & breakfast: £30 single, £60 double.
Half board: £36 daily, £210-£231 weekly.
Lunch available.
Evening meal 6.30pm (l.o. 7.30pm).
Open March-November.
Credit: Access, Visa.

EFFINGHAM
Surrey
Map ref 2D2

4m SW. Leatherhead

Crosslands Guest House
Guildford Road, Effingham, KT24 5PE
☎ Bookham (0372) 53479
Listed building, oldest inhabited house in the village.
Bedrooms: 1 single, 4 twin, 1 family room.
Bathrooms: 2 public.
Bed & breakfast: max. £14 single, max. £28 double.
Half board: max. £19 daily, max. £133 weekly.
Lunch available.
Evening meal 5.30pm (l.o. 9pm).
Parking for 6.

EGHAM
Surrey
Map ref 2D2

In attractive and historic area beside the Thames, near Thorpe Park, Britain's first theme park, with 400 acres of lakes and parkland.

Runnymede Hotel M
Windsor Rd., Egham, TW20 0AG
☎ (0784) 436171
Telex 934900

Delightfully situated overlooking the Thames at Bell-Weir Lock, a modern hotel standing in 10 acres of landscaped gardens. On A308, off the M25 junction 13.
Bedrooms: 48 single, 21 double & 24 twin, 32 family rooms.
Bathrooms: 125 private.
Bed & breakfast: £88.25-£103.25 single, £111.50-£126.50 double.
Lunch available.
Evening meal 7pm (l.o. 9.45pm).
Parking for 250.
Credit: Access, Visa, Diners, Amex.

EPSOM
Surrey
Map ref 2D2

Horse races have been held on the slopes of Epsom Downs for centuries. The racecourse is the home of the world-famous Derby. Many famous old homes are here, among them the 17th C Waterloo House.

Angleside Guest House
`Listed`
27 Ashley Rd., Epsom, KT18 5BD
☎ (037 27) 24303
Owner-run establishment halfway between Gatwick and Heathrow Airports, close to High Street, downs and racecourse.
Bedrooms: 1 single, 2 double & 3 twin, 2 family rooms.
Bathrooms: 1 public; 3 private showers.
Bed & breakfast: £18-£23 single, £35-£40 double.
Parking for 8.

Heathside Hotel M
A217-Brighton Rd., Burgh Heath, Tadworth, KT20 6BW
☎ Burgh Heath (0737) 353355 Telex 929908
Modern, new extension with conference/leisure facilities, conservatory, and restaurant open for breakfast, lunch and dinner. Close to M25, Gatwick, Dover, Epsom Downs racing.
Bedrooms: 2 single, 18 double & 21 twin, 32 family rooms.
Bathrooms: 73 private.
Bed & breakfast: £60-£68 single, £80-£90 double.
Lunch available.

Evening meal 6pm (l.o. 10pm).
Parking for 160.
Credit: Access, Visa, Diners, Amex.

ESHER
Surrey
Map ref 2D2

Residential town beside the River Mole. Claremont, a mansion built for Clive of India in 1772, lies to the south. It is set in fine gardens laid out by Capability Brown and administered separately by the National Trust.

Haven Hotel M
Portsmouth Rd., Esher, KT10 9AR
☎ 081-398 0023
Inter
Licensed hotel and restaurant half a mile from Esher station, 20 minutes to Waterloo. Wooded setting with easy access to M3/4/25.
Bedrooms: 6 single, 6 double & 4 twin, 4 family rooms.
Bathrooms: 20 private.
Bed & breakfast: £55-£62 single, £65-£72 double.
Half board: £41.50-£71 daily.
Lunch available.
Evening meal 7pm (l.o. 8.30pm).
Parking for 20.
Credit: Access, Visa, Diners, Amex.

FARNHAM
Surrey
Map ref 2C2

Town noted for its Georgian houses. Willmer House (now a museum) has a facade of cut and moulded brick with fine carving and panelling in the interior. The 12th C castle has been occupied by Bishops of both Winchester and Guildford.
Tourist Information Centre ☎ (0483) 861111

The Bishop's Table Hotel M
27 West St., Farnham, GU9 7DR
☎ (0252) 715545 & 710222
Fax (0252) 733494
Telex 94016743 BISH G

Best Western
An 18th C inn, once used as a training school for clergy, well situated for exploring Surrey and Hampshire.
Bedrooms: 8 single, 8 double & 1 twin, 1 family room.
Bathrooms: 16 private, 1 public.
Bed & breakfast: from £65 single, £79-£82 double.
Half board: £80-£90 daily.
Lunch available.
Evening meal 7pm (l.o. 9.45pm).
Credit: Access, Visa, Diners, Amex.

The Mariners Hotel M
Millbridge, Frensham, GU10 3DJ
☎ (025 125) 2050 & 4745 Fax (025 125) 2649
On the A287 between Farnham and Hindhead. A traditional country inn with a spacious new function room for conferences, receptions, etc. Comfortable bedrooms. A friendly atmosphere. Real ales and a reasonably-priced menu.
Bedrooms: 9 single, 3 double & 8 twin, 1 family room.
Bathrooms: 21 private.
Bed & breakfast: from £46 single, from £56 double.
Half board: from £58 daily, from £350 weekly.
Lunch available.
Evening meal 6pm (l.o. 10pm).
Parking for 100.
Credit: Access, Visa, Diners, Amex.

Trevena House Hotel M
Alton Rd., Farnham, GU10 5ER
☎ (0252) 716908
Telex 94013011 TREVG
Country house in beautiful setting with relaxed atmosphere, varied and interesting menu. Suitable for short, recuperative breaks.
Bedrooms: 6 single, 8 double & 3 twin, 2 family rooms.
Bathrooms: 19 private.
Bed & breakfast: £25-£50 single, £40-£60 double.
Evening meal 7pm (l.o. 9.30pm).
Parking for 40.
Credit: Access, Visa, Diners, Amex.

FAVERSHAM
Kent
Map ref 3B3

Historic town, once a port, dating back to prehistoric times. Abbey Street has more than 50 listed buildings. Roman and Anglo-Saxon finds and other exhibits can be seen in a museum in the Maison Dieu at Ospringe. Fleur de Lis Heritage Centre.
Tourist Information Centre ☎ (0795) 534542

Syndale Park Motel
London Rd., Ospringe, Faversham, ME13 0RH
☎ (0795) 532595
A country house set in 3 acres of Kent parkland. 1.5 miles from exit 6 on M2 motorway. Dover 24 miles, London 50 miles, Canterbury 9 miles.
Bedrooms: 4 double & 6 twin, 2 family rooms.
Bathrooms: 12 private.
Bed & breakfast: £25-£35 single, £35-£45 double.
Half board: £30-£45 daily, £210-£315 weekly.
Evening meal 7.30pm (l.o. 9pm).
Parking for 50.
Credit: Access, Visa, Diners, Amex.

FAWKHAM
Kent
Map ref 2D2

10m NE. Sevenoaks
Village with small, pretty church set amongst trees. Nearby is the famous motor-racing circuit of Brands Hatch.

Brandshatch Place M
COMMENDED
Fawkham Green, Nr. Sevenoaks, DA3 8NQ
☎ Ash Green (0474) 872239
Redbrick Georgian country house built by Duke of Norfolk in 1806, surrounded by 12 acres of parkland and garden. Elegant decor.
Bedrooms: 3 single, 16 double & 10 twin.
Bathrooms: 29 private.
Bed & breakfast: £75-£85 single, £95-£105 double.
Lunch available.
Evening meal 7pm (l.o. 9.45pm).
Parking for 60.

Credit: Access, Visa, Diners, Amex.

FERRING
W. Sussex
Map ref 2D3

Greystoke Manor Hotel
Greystoke Road, Ferring, BN12 5HW
☎ Worthing (0903) 42077
Quiet, family-run residential 17th C hotel, converted from a manor house.
Bedrooms: 6 single, 5 double & 2 twin, 2 family rooms.
Bathrooms: 7 private, 3 public.
Bed & breakfast: £19.40-£20.40 single, £39.10-£41.40 double.
Half board: £26.45-£27.60 daily, £185.18-£193.20 weekly.
Lunch available.
Evening meal 7pm (l.o. 9.45pm).
Parking for 30.
Credit: Access, Visa.

FOLKESTONE
Kent
Map ref 3C4

Popular resort and important cross-channel port. The town has a fine promenade, the Leas, from where orchestral concerts and other entertainments are presented. Horse-racing at Westenhanger.
Tourist Information Centre ☎ (0303) 58594

Abbey House Hotel M
5-6 Westbourne Gdns., Folkestone, CT20 2JA
☎ (0303) 55514
Friendly Edwardian hotel, fully licensed, close to sea, promenade and bandstand. All rooms with TV, tea making and some en-suite. Unrestricted street parking.
Bedrooms: 3 single, 2 double & 5 twin, 4 family rooms.
Bathrooms: 2 private, 2 public.
Bed & breakfast: £14.50-£16.75 single, £28-£38 double.
Half board: £22-£27 daily, £138.60-£170 weekly.
Lunch available.

Evening meal 6.30pm (l.o. 9.30pm).
Credit: Access.

Augusta Hotel M
4 Augusta Gdns., Folkestone, CT20 2RR
☎ (0303) 850952
Private family-run hotel, central, close to sea, Leas, harbour and ferry terminal. All rooms have hair-dryers and mini-bar with safe. Trouser-press available.
Bedrooms: 3 single, 1 double & 1 twin, 3 family rooms.
Bathrooms: 8 private, 1 public.
Bed & breakfast: £21-£25 single, £42-£46 double.
Lunch available.
Evening meal 6pm (l.o. 7.45pm).
Credit: Access, Visa, Diners, Amex.

Banque Hotel M
COMMENDED
4 Castle Hill Ave., Folkestone, CT20 2QT
☎ (0303) 53797
Small hotel near seafront and shops. All rooms en-suite with colour TV, telephone, radio, tea/coffee facilities and room service. Car park.
Bedrooms: 3 single, 2 double & 5 twin, 2 family rooms.
Bathrooms: 12 private.
Bed & breakfast: £20-£22 single, £40-£84 double.
Evening meal 6pm (l.o. 9pm).
Parking for 4.
Credit: Access, Visa, Diners, Amex.

Folkeleas Guest House M
38 Cheriton Rd., Folkestone, CT20 1BZ
☎ (0303) 51441
Centrally situated for the town, Leas, beaches and ferry. We are proud of our reputation for food. Special reduced rates for children.
Bedrooms: 2 double & 3 twin, 2 family rooms.
Bathrooms: 2 public.
Bed & breakfast: £13-£15 single, £26-£30 double.
Half board: £18-£20 daily, £115-£140 weekly.
Evening meal 6pm (l.o. 5pm).

Harbourside M
14, Wear Bay Road, Folkestone, CT19 6AT
☎ Folkestone (0303) 56528
Well-appointed en-suite accommodation. Spectacular views, warm hospitality and value for money. Licensed and fully geared for your comfort.
Bedrooms: 3 double & 1 twin.
Bathrooms: 3 private.
Bed & breakfast: £35-£45 single, £40-£50 double.
Half board: £35-£44 daily, £200-£280 weekly.

Langhorne Garden Hotel M
10-12 Langhorne Gdns., Folkestone, CT20 2EA
☎ (0303) 57233
Situated in a quiet residential part of the town, close to the Leas and sea, a few minutes by car from the station and ferry terminal.
Bedrooms: 3 single, 5 double & 20 twin, 2 family rooms.
Bathrooms: 23 private, 2 public.
Bed & breakfast: £20-£22 single, £30-£42 double.
Half board: £27.50-£29.50 daily, £130-£160 weekly.
Lunch available.
Evening meal 6.30pm (l.o. 7.30pm).
Credit: Access, Visa, Diners, Amex.

Lismore Hotel
5-7 Trinity Cres., Folkestone, CT20 2ES
☎ (0303) 52717
Situated close to the sea and town centre. Entertainment includes cabaret, dancing and bingo. An a la carte restaurant, La Galleria, below the hotel.
Bedrooms: 5 single, 8 double & 15 twin, 6 family rooms.
Bathrooms: 15 private, 6 public.
Bed & breakfast: £18.85-£21.75 single, £35.25-£41.05 double.
Half board: £24.30-£27.70 daily, £135.35-£151.50 weekly.
Lunch available.
Evening meal 7.30pm (l.o. 10.45pm).
Credit: Access, Visa, C.Bl., Diners, Amex.

FOLKESTONE
Continued

Normandie Guest House
39 Cheriton Rd., Folkestone,
CT20 1DD
☎ (0303) 56233
*Central, near all local
amenities, with parking nearby.
Early breakfast served.
Convenient for the harbour and
trips to the continent.*
Bedrooms: 1 single, 1 double
& 2 twin, 2 family rooms.
Bathrooms: 1 public.
Bed & breakfast: £12-£13.50
single, £24-£27 double.

Royal Norfolk Hotel
♛♛♛
7 Sandgate High St.,
Sandgate, Nr. Folkestone,
CT20 3BD
☎ (0303) 48262
*A tastefully modernised hotel
specialising in functions. 1 mile
from Folkestone on the A259
next to Sandgate Castle.*
Bedrooms: 2 single, 4 double
& 2 twin, 2 family rooms.
Bathrooms: 10 private.
Bed & breakfast: £35.75-
£36.75 single, £43.50-£45.50
double.
Half board: £46.70-£48.65
daily, £280.70-£294.35
weekly.
Lunch available.
Evening meal 4pm (l.o. 9pm).
Parking for 10.
Credit: Access, Visa.

Wards Hotel & Restaurant M
39 Earls Avenue, Folkestone,
CT20 2HB
☎ Folkestone (0303) 45166
*Elegantly appointed hotel close
to channel ports and M20.
Ideal for business executives
and short breaks. Attractive
restaurant.*
Bedrooms: 5 double & 5 twin.
Bathrooms: 10 private.
Bed & breakfast: £39.50-
£59.50 single, £55-£85 double.
Half board: £52-£72 daily.
Lunch available.
Evening meal 7.30pm (l.o.
10pm).
Parking for 18.
Credit: Access, Visa, Diners,
Amex.

Wearbay Hotel M
♛♛♛
23-25 Wear Bay Cres.,
Folkestone, CT19 6AX
☎ (0303) 52586

*In a residential area close to
the seafront, the hotel has some
rooms with sea views. East
Cliff Pavilion is nearby.*
Bedrooms: 2 single, 2 double
& 5 twin, 1 family room.
Bathrooms: 10 private.
Bed & breakfast: from £20
single, from £38 double.
Half board: £27.50-£28.50
daily, £185.85-£192.50
weekly.
Lunch available.
Evening meal 6pm (l.o.
11pm).
Parking for 2.
Credit: Access, Visa, Diners,
Amex.

FOREST ROW
E. Sussex
Map ref 2D2

*3m SE. East Grinstead
On a hillside overlooking
the River Medway, this
village is a good centre
from which to explore
Ashdown Forest.*

Brambletye Hotel M
♛♛♛
The Square, Forest Row,
RH18 5EZ
☎ (034 282) 4144 & 4145 Fax
(034 282) 4833
*Comfortable accommodation
with lunch-time carvery,
evening restaurant and bar
food. Excellent centre for
many places of interest in the
beautiful surrounding
countryside.*
Bedrooms: 4 single, 5 double
& 11 twin, 2 family rooms.
Bathrooms: 22 private.
Bed & breakfast: £48-£52
single, £55-£70 double.
Half board: £35-£60 daily.
Lunch available.
Evening meal 7pm (l.o.
9.30pm).
Parking for 40.
Credit: Access, Visa, Diners,
Amex.

GATWICK AIRPORT

*See also Charlwood,
Copthorne, Crawley, East
Grinstead, Horley,
Redhill, Reigate.*

Gatwick Sterling Hotel M
Gatwick Airport, Crawley,
West Sussex RH6 0PH
☎ (0293) 567070 Telex 87202
STELGW

*Opened autumn 1990,
connected by covered walkway
to North Terminal. Impressive
atrium with 3 restaurants.
Leisure club with pool.*
Bedrooms: 2 single,
267 double & 205 twin.
Bathrooms: 474 private.
Bed & breakfast: £104-£124
single, £123-£143 double.
Lunch available.
Evening meal 6pm (l.o.
11pm).
Parking for 110.
Credit: Access, Visa, C.Bl.,
Diners, Amex.

GILLINGHAM
Kent
Map ref 3B3

The largest Medway
Town, it merges into its
neighbour Chatham.
*Tourist Information
Centre ☎ (Farthing
Corner) (0634) 360323*

Rank Motor Lodge M
Farthing Corner Services,
M2 Motorway, Nr.
Gillingham, ME8 8PW
☎ Medway (0634) 377337
*58 well-equipped new
bedrooms. Close to all South
East tourist and business
destinations. Self-service
restaurant open 24 hours.*
Bedrooms: 42 twin, 16 family
rooms.
Bathrooms: 58 private.
Bed & breakfast: from £27.50
single, from £31.50 double.
Lunch available.
Evening meal (l.o. 10pm).
Parking for 50.
Credit: Access, Visa, Diners,
Amex.

GODALMING
Surrey
Map ref 2D2

Several old coaching inns
are reminders that the
town was once a staging
point. The old Town Hall
is now the local history
museum. Charterhouse
School moved here in
1872 and is dominated by
the 150-ft Founder's
Tower.

Squirrel Inn
Hurtmore Road, Hurtmore,
Nr Godalming, GU7 2RN
☎ Guildford (0483) 860223

*Well-appointed en-suite rooms
converted from 17th C
cottages. Meals are in adjacent
restaurant/bar open 7 days a
week.*
Bedrooms: 2 single, 4 double,
1 family room.
Bathrooms: 7 private.
Bed & breakfast: £35-£45
single, £50-£60 double.
Half board: £35-£50 daily,
£235-£330 weekly.
Lunch available.
Evening meal 6.30pm (l.o.
10.30pm).
Parking for 75.
Credit: Access, Visa.

GOODWOOD
W. Sussex
Map ref 2C3

Goodwood House, an
18th C mansion standing
in lovely parkland, houses
an impressive art
collection. The
racecourse lies high on
the Downs. Nearby is an
excellent 18-hole golf-
course.

Goodwood Park Hotel, Golf and Country Club M
♛♛♛♛ HIGHLY COMMENDED
Goodwood, Nr. Chichester,
PO18 0QB
☎ Chichester (0243) 775537
Telex 869173
Best Western
*Adjacent to Goodwood House,
the hotel has been tastefully
developed and retains the
original character of its 1786
forebear. Swimming pool and
golf course.*
Bedrooms: 1 single, 45 double
& 40 twin, 3 family rooms.
Bathrooms: 89 private.
Bed & breakfast: from £55
single, from £70 double.
Half board: from £55 daily,
from £350 weekly.
Lunch available.
Evening meal 7pm (l.o.
9.30pm).
Parking for 200.
Credit: Access, Visa, Diners,
Amex.

The enquiry
coupons at the
back will help you
when contacting
proprietors.

GOUDHURST

Kent
Map ref 3B4

4m NW. Cranbrook
Village on a hill
surmounted by a square-
towered church with fine
views of orchards and
hopfields. Achieved
prosperity through
weaving in the Middle
Ages. Finchcocks houses
a museum of historic
keyboard instruments.

Star & Eagle
ᗣᗣᗣᗣ

High St., Goudhurst,
TN17 1AL
☎ (0580) 211512
*Picturesque half-timbered inn
with monastic origins, enjoying
panoramic views of the Weald
of Kent. Buffet meals also
available.*
Bedrooms: 1 single, 5 double
& 5 twin.
Bathrooms: 9 private,
1 public.
Bed & breakfast: from £50
single, from £66 double.
Lunch available.
Evening meal 7pm (l.o.
9.30pm).
Parking for 25.
Credit: Access, Visa, Amex.
⛭🏠📞💻🗂🕯🛈 Ⓥ 🛏
🏢 ▲ 🍴 🕐 🖐 ✗ 💈 SP
🏥

GRAVESEND

Kent
Map ref 3B3

Industrial riverside town
where the Thames pilots
are based. The statue of
the Red Indian princess,
Pocahontas, stands by
St. George's church.
*Tourist Information
Centre* ☎ *(0474) 337600*

The Clarendon Royal
Hotel ♏
ᗣᗣᗣ

Royal Pier Rd., Gravesend,
DA12 2BE
☎ (0474) 363151
*A Lord Clarendon once owned
this hotel. It was built in the
days of James II, who is said
to have stayed here. The hotel
overlooks the river and is
1 mile from the town centre.*
Bedrooms: 5 single, 5 double
& 10 twin, 4 family rooms.
Bathrooms: 14 private,
3 public.
Bed & breakfast: £42-£59
single, £54-£65 double.
Lunch available.

Evening meal 6pm (l.o.
10.30pm).
Parking for 140.
Credit: Access, Visa, Diners,
Amex.
⛭🏠📞💻🗂🕯🛈 Ⓥ ✂
🌓 🏢 ▲ 🌼 ✗ 💈 SP 🏥

The Inn on the Lake
Hotel ♏

A2, Shorne, Gravesend,
DA12 3HB
☎ (047 482) 3333
Telex 966356
*The hotel has direct access
from the A2 London to Dover
road. Set in peaceful woodland
with 2 delightful lakes.*
Bedrooms: 35 double &
41 twin, 2 family rooms.
Bathrooms: 78 private.
Bed & breakfast: £65-£75
single, £80-£90 double.
Lunch available.
Evening meal 7.30pm (l.o.
9.45pm).
Parking for 250.
Credit: Access, Visa, Diners,
Amex.
⛭📞💻🗂🕯🛈 Ⓥ 🛏
🌓 🍴 🌼 ✗ 💈

Tollgate Motel

Watling St., Tollgate,
Gravesend, DA13 9RA
☎ (0474) 357655
Telex 966227
*Sited at the A227 junction of
the A2 London/Dover road,
with the M20/M25 motorway
links only 7 miles away.
London 33 miles. Dover 50
miles and the Dartford Tunnel
7 miles. Ideally situated to suit
the needs of both tourist and
businessman.*
Bedrooms: 2 single, 58 double
& 54 twin.
Bathrooms: 114 private.
Bed & breakfast: £46.20-£65
single, £56.10-£75 double.
Lunch available.
Evening meal 6pm (l.o.
10.30pm).
Parking for 200.
Credit: Access, Visa, Diners,
Amex.
⛭🏠📞💻🗂🕯🛈 Ⓥ ●
🌓 ▲ 🍴 🕐 🖐 🌼 🏥 💈

**Classifications
and quality
commendations
were correct at the
time of going to
press but are
subject to change.
Please check at the
time of booking.**

GUILDFORD

Surrey
Map ref 2D2

Bustling town with many
historic monuments, one
of which is the Guildhall
clock jutting out over the
old High Street. The
modern cathedral
occupies a commanding
position on Stag Hill.
*Tourist Information
Centre* ☎ *(0483) 444007*

Badenweiler ♏
🛈

35 Poplar Road, Shalford,
Guildford GU4 8DH
☎ (0483) 506037
*South of Guildford on A281.
Continental cooking. Ample
parking. Children under 10
half price. Non-smokers only
please.*
Bedrooms: 1 single, 1 double
& 1 twin, 1 family room.
Bathrooms: 2 public;
1 private shower.
Bed & breakfast: £15-£17
single, £28-£30 double.
Half board: from £18 daily,
from £91 weekly.
Evening meal 7pm (l.o.
9.30pm).
Parking for 6.
⛭🏠🗃 ▲ 🕯🛈 ✤ UL 🛈 Ⓥ
✂ 🗂 TV 🌓 ▲ 🍴 🌼 ⓞ OAP
SP 🏥

Blanes Court Hotel
ᗣᗣ

Albury Rd., Guildford,
GU1 2BT
☎ (0483) 573171
*Bed and breakfast
accommodation, mostly en-
suite rooms, all with colour TV,
tea/coffee facilities. Garden
lounge, cosy bar serving
snacks. In a quiet area within
easy walking distance of town
and country.*
Bedrooms: 7 single, 6 double
& 4 twin, 1 family room.
Bathrooms: 13 private,
2 public.
Bed & breakfast: £25-£45
single, £50-£55 double.
Parking for 20.
Credit: Access, Visa, Amex.
⛭🏠💻🗂🕯🛈 TV 🌓 ▲
🌼 SP

The Bramley Grange
Hotel ♏

Horsham Rd., Bramley,
Guildford, GU5 0BL
☎ (0483) 893434/898703
Telex 859948 BRAMGH
ⒷⓌ Best Western
*Victorian hotel set in 7 acres of
grounds, just 5 minutes' drive
from Guildford.*

Bedrooms: 5 single, 35 double
& 5 twin, 2 family rooms.
Bathrooms: 47 private.
Bed & breakfast: £65-£120
single, £90-£125 double.
Lunch available.
Evening meal 7.30pm (l.o.
10pm).
Parking for 65.
Credit: Access, Visa, Amex.
⛭🏠📞💻🗂🕯🛈 Ⓥ ✂
🛏 🌓 ▲ 🍴 ⓒ 🅟 🌼 ✗
SP 🕐

Carlton Hotel
ᗣᗣ

London Rd., Guildford,
GU1 2AF
☎ (0483) 576539 & 575158
*Within 3 minutes' walk of
London Road station on the
London to Guildford line via
Cobham. 2 minutes' walk from
the high street and main
thoroughfare.*
Bedrooms: 13 single, 6 double
& 7 twin, 10 family rooms.
Bathrooms: 13 private,
7 public; 6 private showers.
Bed & breakfast: £26-£36
single, £40-£46 double.
Half board: £31-£41 daily,
£217-£287 weekly.
Evening meal 6.30pm (l.o.
8.30pm).
Parking for 50.
Credit: Access, Visa, Amex.
⛭🛏💻🗂🕯🛈 Ⓥ 🛏 TV
● 🏢 ▲ 🌼 ✗

Dene Croft ♏

1, Denmark Road,
Guildford, GU1 4DA
☎ (0483) 506938
*Bright, well decorated and
newly furnished with large
bedrooms.Each bedroom
supplied with colour TV,
tea/coffee/chocolate facilities.*
Bedrooms: 1 single, 4 double,
3 family rooms.
Bathrooms: 1 public.
Bed & breakfast: £20-£25
single, £35-£40 double.
Parking for 5.
⛭🛏💻🗂 UL CB 🛏 TV ●
▲ ✗ 🏥 🕐

Newmans Guest House
(Brian & Jenny's)

24 Waterden Rd., Guildford,
GU1 2AY
☎ (0483) 60558
*Large Victorian family house
situated in a pleasant area of
Guildford, a short distance
from the shops and railway
station. All rooms with Sky
TV.*
Bedrooms: 1 single, 1 double
& 2 twin, 7 family rooms.
Bathrooms: 3 public.
Bed & breakfast: £16-£18
single, £32-£36 double.
Parking for 2.
⛭🗂 UL Ⓥ 🌓 ▲ ✗

GUILDFORD
Continued

Worplesdon Place Hotel & Beefeater Steakhouse
Perry Hill, Worplesdon,
Guildford, GU3 3RY
☎ Worplesdon (0483) 232407
& 232408 & (0483) 235466
Fax (0483) 236427
*19th C country hotel and
Beefeater restaurant set in
picturesque grounds with a
large lake. Situated on A322
Bagshot Road. Worplesdon
village is 3.5 miles north of
Guildford. Half price rate
Friday/Saturday and Sunday.*
Bedrooms: 2 single,
17 double, 3 family rooms.
Bathrooms: 22 private.
Bed & breakfast: £25-£50
single, £30-£60 double.
Lunch available.
Evening meal 6pm (l.o.
10.30pm).
Parking for 120.
Credit: Access, Visa, Diners,
Amex.

HAILSHAM
E. Sussex
Map ref 2D3

An important market town
since Norman times and
still one of the largest
markets in Sussex. 2
miles west, at Upper
Dicker, is Michelham
Priory, an Augustinian
house founded in 1229.
*Tourist Information
Centre* ☎ *(0323) 840604*

Boship Farm Hotel ♨
Lower Dicker, Hailsham,
BN27 4AT
☎ (0323) 844826
Telex 878400 BOSFAR G
*17th C oak-beamed farmhouse,
sympathetically converted into
a comfortable hotel with the
addition of bedroom wings,
conference suite and leisure
facilities.*
Bedrooms: 35 double &
9 twin, 2 family rooms.
Bathrooms: 46 private.
Bed & breakfast: £55-£60.50
single, £65-£71.50 double.
Lunch available.
Evening meal 7pm (l.o.
10pm).
Parking for 100.
Credit: Access, Visa, Diners,
Amex.

Sandy Bank ♨
☐ COMMENDED
Old Road, Magham Down,
Nr. Hailsham, BN27 1PW
☎ Hailsham (0323) 842488
*An attractive garden setting.
Well-appointed rooms in a new
development adjacent to the
house. Friendly atmosphere.
Ideal base for touring Sussex.*
Bedrooms: 2 twin.
Bathrooms: 2 private.
Bed & breakfast: from £18.50
single, from £32 double.
Evening meal 7pm (l.o.
8.30pm).
Parking for 2.

HALLAND
E. Sussex
Map ref 2D3

Village between Uckfield
and Hailsham. Nearby is
the Bentley Wildfowl and
Motor Museum.

Halland Forge Hotel & Restaurant ♨
☐ COMMENDED
Halland, Nr. Lewes,
BN8 6PW
☎ (082 584) 456 Fax
(082 584) 773
Ⓒ Inter
*Attractive hotel with fully
licensed restaurant and coffee
shop. Facilities for meetings
and functions. Garden and
woodland walks. Ideal touring
centre.*
Bedrooms: 11 double &
7 twin, 2 family rooms.
Bathrooms: 20 private.
Bed & breakfast: £45.45-
£55.45 single, £62.40 double.
Half board: from £226.50
weekly.
Lunch available.
Evening meal 7pm (l.o.
9.30pm).
Parking for 70.
Credit: Access, Visa, Diners,
Amex.

HARTFIELD
E. Sussex
Map ref 2D2

Pleasant village in
Ashdown Forest.

Bolebroke Watermill ♨
Edenbridge Rd., Hartfield,
TN7 4JP
☎ Hartfield (0892) 770425
*6.5-acre smallholding.
Watermill and granary (1086)
in romantic, secluded*

woodland. Accommodation of
great character set around
millstones and wheels. Regret
stairs unsuitable for small
children, the elderly and the
disabled.*
Bedrooms: 4 double.
Bathrooms: 4 private.
Bed & breakfast: from £35
single, from £40 double.
Half board: from £50 daily.
Evening meal 7.30pm (l.o.
10am).
Parking for 16.
Open March-October.

HASTINGS
E. Sussex
Map ref 3B4

Ancient town which
became famous as the
base from which William
the Conqueror set out to
fight the Battle of
Hastings. Later became
one of the Cinque Ports,
now a leading resort.
Fishermen's museum and
Hastings Embroidery
inspired by the Bayeux
Tapestry and the new
Sealife Centre.
*Tourist Information
Centre* ☎ *(0424) 718888*

Ashburnham Lodge
☐ APPROVED
62, London Road, St.
Leonards-on-Sea, Hastings,
East Sussex TN37 6AS
☎ Hastings
(0424) 438575/716891
*The hotel provides a high
standard of service at a price
that most people can afford.
Also caters for the disabled.*
Bedrooms: 4 single,
17 double.
Bathrooms: 21 private.
Bed & breakfast: £29.50-£32
single, £42-£52 double.
Half board: max. £29.50
daily, £259.40-£374.85
weekly.
Lunch available.
Evening meal 7pm (l.o. 9pm).
Parking for 7.
Credit: Access, Visa, Amex.
⊕ Display advertisement
appears on page 545.

Beauport Park Hotel ♨
☐ COMMENDED
Battle Rd., Hastings,
TN38 8EA
☎ (0424) 851222
Telex 957126
Ⓒ Best Western

Country house hotel in 33 acres
of woodland and landscaped
gardens.
Bedrooms: 4 single, 10 double
& 7 twin, 2 family rooms.
Bathrooms: 23 private.
Bed & breakfast: £50 single,
£68-£78 double.
Half board: £42-£64 daily,
£260-£274 weekly.
Lunch available.
Evening meal 7pm (l.o.
9.30pm).
Parking for 64.
Credit: Access, Visa, Diners,
Amex.

Beechwood Hotel
59 Baldslow Rd., Hastings,
TN34 2EY
☎ (0424) 420078
*Late Victorian building with
panoramic views of sea, castle
and park, in quiet residential
area. 1 mile from station and
beach.*
Bedrooms: 5 single, 2 double
& 3 twin.
Bathrooms: 3 private,
1 public.
Bed & breakfast: £12-£23
single, £22-£35 double.
Half board: £19-£30 daily,
£120-£180 weekly.
Lunch available.
Evening meal 6pm (l.o.
10pm).
Parking for 6.

Burlington Hotel
2 Robertson Ter., Hastings,
TN34 1JE
☎ (0424) 722303
*Prime seafront position. All
amenities easily accessible. Tea
and coffee making facilities
and colour TV in all rooms.
Home cooking. Relaxing
atmosphere.*
Bedrooms: 2 single, 11 double
& 1 twin, 2 family rooms.
Bathrooms: 10 private,
2 public.
Bed & breakfast: £16-£22.50
single, £32-£45 double.
Half board: £24.50-£30.50
daily, £154.35-£195.30
weekly.
Evening meal 6.30pm (l.o.
9pm).
Credit: Access, Visa, Diners,
Amex.

Churchills Hotel
3 St. Helens Cres., Hastings,
TN34 2EN
☎ (0424) 439359

Comfortable, small, licensed hotel with car park, patio and garden, 2 minutes from Alexander Park and 5 minutes' drive from the shops and sea.
Bedrooms: 2 single, 2 double & 1 twin, 3 family rooms.
Bathrooms: 3 private, 2 public.
Bed & breakfast: £20-£25 single, £34-£38 double.
Half board: from £27.50 daily, £110-£220 weekly.
Lunch available.
Evening meal 6pm (l.o. midday).
Parking for 16.
Credit: Visa.

Clevedon Hotel
常常

51 Warrior Square.,
St.Leonards-on-Sea,
Hastings. TN37 6BG
☎ (0424) 423377
2 minutes from the Marina Pavillion, railway station, beach and seafront. High street shopping and White Rock theatre nearby. Castle, Old Town, Alexandra Park and Pier also nearby.
Bedrooms: 12 single, 6 double & 12 twin, 7 family rooms.
Bathrooms: 9 public.
Bed & breakfast: max. £14.50 single, max. £29 double.
Half board: max. £19 daily, £85-£95 weekly.
Lunch available.
Evening meal 6pm (l.o. 6pm).
Parking for 3.

Eagle House Hotel ₥
常常常

12 Pevensey Rd., St.
Leonards-on-Sea, Hastings,
TN38 0JZ
☎ (0424) 430535 & 441273
Large Victorian residence in its own grounds. Well placed for most local amenities as well as for visiting "1066" country.
Bedrooms: 18 double & 4 twin.
Bathrooms: 19 private, 2 public.
Bed & breakfast: £27-£31 single, £38-£45 double.
Half board: £33.95-£37.45 daily, £237.65-£262.15 weekly.
Lunch available.
Evening meal 6.30pm (l.o. 5.30pm).
Parking for 14.
Credit: Access, Visa, Diners, Amex.

Fairlight Cove Hotel ₥
Waites Lane, Fairlight Nr.
Hastings TN35 4AX
☎ Hastings (0424) 812209
Peaceful, secluded, comfortable country hotel in own grounds near sea and cliffs. All rooms on ground floor, courteous staff, chef prepared farm produce.
Bedrooms: 5 double & 2 twin, 3 family rooms.
Bathrooms: 10 private.
Bed & breakfast: £16.50-£19.50 double.
Half board: £20.50-£28.50 daily, £140-£190.50 weekly.
Lunch available.
Evening meal 6.30pm (l.o. 7.30pm).
Parking for 70.
Credit: Access, Visa.

High Beech Hotel ₥
常常常常 COMMENDED
Battle Rd., St. Leonards-on-Sea, Hastings, TN37 7BS
☎ (0424) 851383
Quality accommodation beautifully situated between the historic towns of Hastings and Battle. 500 yards off A2100.
Bedrooms: 8 double & 2 twin.
Bathrooms: 10 private.
Bed & breakfast: £40-£50 single, £60-£70 double.
Half board: £44-£54 daily.
Lunch available.
Evening meal 7pm (l.o. 9.30pm).
Parking for 100.
Credit: Access, Visa, Diners, Amex.

New Chatsworth Hotel
Carlisle Pde., Hastings,
TN34 1JG
☎ Hastings (0424) 720188
Telex 27656
In the central part of Hastings on the seafront, close to all the town's major amenities. Recently refurbished.
Bedrooms: 15 single, 11 double & 25 twin, 1 family room.
Bathrooms: 52 private.
Bed & breakfast: £30-£50 single, £60-£70 double.
Half board: £38-£48 daily, £240-£280 weekly.
Lunch available.
Evening meal 6pm (l.o. 10pm).
Credit: Access, Visa, Diners, Amex.

Royal Victoria Hotel ₥
Marina, St.Leonards-on-Sea,
Hastings, TN38 OBD
☎ Hastings (0424) 445544
Telex 95529 HOMETEL G
Surrounded by Victorian elegance. Local seafood cuisine a speciality.
Bedrooms: 1 single, 37 double & 12 twin, 2 family rooms.
Bathrooms: 52 private.
Bed & breakfast: £60-£85 single, £85-£110 double.
Lunch available.
Evening meal 7pm (l.o. 10pm).
Parking for 20.
Credit: Access, Visa, Diners, Amex.

The Tamar Guest House
7 Devonshire Rd., Hastings,
TN34 1NE
☎ (0424) 434076
Overlooks Hastings cricket ground and has fine views of the castle. Few minutes' walk from railway stations, main shops and seafront.
Bedrooms: 2 double & 1 twin, 2 family rooms.
Bathrooms: 2 public.
Bed & breakfast: £12-£15 single, £22-£26 double.

Tower House
常常 COMMENDED
28 Tower Road West, St.
Leonards-on-Sea, Hastings,
TN38 0RG
☎ (0424) 427217
An elegant Victorian house situated half a mile from seafront. Pleasant gardens. Separate licensed bar which leads to garden patio. Freshly cooked meals. Ample parking.
Bedrooms: 1 single, 5 double & 6 twin, 1 family room.
Bathrooms: 6 private, 2 public; 1 private shower.
Bed & breakfast: £16-£22 single, £32-£44 double.
Half board: £23-£30 daily, £145-£181 weekly.
Evening meal 6pm (l.o. 7pm).

Tudor
常 COMMENDED
191 Bexhill Rd., St. Leonards-on-Sea, Hastings, TN38 8BG
☎ (0424) 424485

Small, high standard guesthouse offering personal service. All rooms have colour TV. Parking on premises.
Bedrooms: 1 double & 1 twin.
Bathrooms: 1 public.
Bed & breakfast: £12-£15 single, £20-£22 double.
Half board: £16-£17 daily, £105-£112 weekly.
Evening meal 6pm (l.o. 4pm).
Parking for 3.

HAWKHURST
Kent
Map ref 3B4

Village in 3 parts: Gill's Green, Highgate and the Moor. There is a colonnaded shopping centre, large village green, church and inn which is associated with the Hawkhurst smuggling gang.

Tudor Court Hotel ₥
常常
Rye Rd., Hawkhurst,
TN18 5DA
☎ (0580) 752312
Telex 957565
Best Western
Picturesque country house hotel superbly located in the Weald of Kent, on A268 Rye road. Ideally placed for visiting Kent and Sussex beauty spots and nearby Camber Sands.
Bedrooms: 5 single, 6 double & 7 twin.
Bathrooms: 18 private.
Bed & breakfast: from £51.50 single, £82-£87 double.
Half board: £53.50-£56 daily, £374-£392 weekly.
Lunch available.
Evening meal 7.30pm (l.o. 9.15pm).
Parking for 53.
Credit: Access, Visa, Diners, Amex.

Woodham Hall Hotel ₥
常常
Rye Rd., Hawkhurst,
TN18 5DA
☎ (0580) 753428
Country house on the edge of the village, in interesting, historical surroundings. Personal, friendly service. Tennis, snooker and putting available. Ideal for holiday or business.
Bedrooms: 1 single, 2 twin, 2 family rooms.

Continued ▶

529

Continued

Bathrooms: 3 private;
2 private showers.
Bed & breakfast: £24-£28
single, £28-£35 double.
Half board: from £32 daily.
Evening meal 7pm (l.o. 7pm).
Parking for 30.
Credit: Access, Visa, Diners,
Amex.

⚐ ▯ ✿ ▮ Ⅴ ⊟ ⍰ ▦ ◢
♜ ♨ ♪ ✿ ⊁ ⊞

HEATHFIELD

E. Sussex
Map ref 2D3

Old Heathfield is a pretty
village which was one of
the major centres of the
Sussex iron industry.

Little London End ♨
Little London, Heathfield,
TN21 0BB
☎ Horam Road
(043 53) 2659
*Edwardian house in 14 acres
plus 8 acres of woodland with
stream, off A267. Eastbourne
13 miles, Tunbridge Wells 14
miles.*
Bedrooms: 2 single, 2 twin.
Bathrooms: 4 private.
Bed & breakfast: £18 single,
£36 double.

♨ ▣ ▯ ✿ ⊔ Ⅴ ⊁ ⊟ ⍰
◩ ◢ ✿ ⊁ ▦ ▨

HENFIELD

W. Sussex
Map ref 2D3

7m N. Shoreham-by-Sea
In flat or gently sloping
countryside with views to
the Downs. Early English
church with a fine
Perpendicular tower.

Tottington Manor Hotel
👑👑👑👑 COMMENDED
Edburton, Nr. Henfield,
BN5 9LJ
☎ Steyning (0903) 815757
*16th C country manor house
with log fires and oak beams,
set in its own grounds at the
foot of the South Downs.*
Bedrooms: 5 double & 1 twin.
Bathrooms: 6 private.
Bed & breakfast: £35-£45
single, £45-£70 double.
Half board: £60-£70 daily,
£420-£490 weekly.
Lunch available.
Evening meal 7pm (l.o.
8.30pm).

Parking for 80.
Credit: Access, Visa.

⚐ ▮ ⓒ ▯ ✿ ▮ Ⅴ ⊁ ⍰
◩ ◢ ♪ ♜ ▶ ✿ ⊁ ▦ ⍰ ◻
▦ ⊞

HERNE BAY

Kent
Map ref 3B3

Seaside resort which has
7 miles of shingle beach
with excellent bathing,
sailing and sea-angling.
*Tourist Information
Centre* ☎ *(0227) 361911*

Carlton Hotel
👑👑👑
40 Central Pde., Herne Bay,
CT6 5HZ
☎ (0227) 374665 Fax (0227)
740888
*Victorian building with large
bright rooms overlooking the
sea. Licensed restaurant open
to the general public. All
bedrooms en-suite.*
Bedrooms: 2 single, 2 double
& 2 twin, 2 family rooms.
Bathrooms: 8 private.
Bed & breakfast: £30-£35
single, £35-£46 double.
Lunch available.
Evening meal 7.30pm (l.o.
10pm).
Parking for 4.
Credit: Access, Visa, C.Bl.,
Diners, Amex.

⚐ ✆ ⓒ ▯ ✿ ▮ Ⅴ ⊁ ⊟
⍰ ● ◩ ◢ ♪ ▶ ▦ ▨ ⊞

Wimpoles Hotel
👑👑
86-88 Central Parade, Herne
Bay, CT6 5JJ
☎ (0227) 372624
*Comfortable friendly
Victorian-style hotel with
relaxed atmosphere in central
seafront position. Close to
amenities and shopping centre.*
Bedrooms: 8 single, 8 double
& 2 twin, 2 family rooms.
Bathrooms: 6 private,
3 public.
Bed & breakfast: £14-£20
single, £30-£34 double.
Half board: £23-£28 daily,
£150-£190 weekly.
Lunch available.
Evening meal 6pm (l.o. 9pm).
Parking for 4.
Credit: Access, Visa.

⚐ ▮ ⓒ ▯ ✿ ▮ Ⅴ ⊟ ⍰
◩ ◢ ♪ ⊞ ⊞

The National Crown
Scheme is explained
in full on pages
556 – 558.

HERSTMONCEUX

E. Sussex
Map ref 3B4

4m E. Hailsham
Pleasant village noted for
its woodcrafts but
dominated by the
beautiful 15th C
Herstmonceux Castle and
gardens. Now home of
the Royal Greenwich
Observatory which is
open to visitors.

Cleavers Lyng ♨
Church Rd., Herstmonceux,
Nr. Hailsham, BN27 1QJ
☎ (0323) 833131
*Picturesque, 16th C country
hotel in 1-acre gardens. Oak
beams and inglenook fireplace.*
Bedrooms: 2 single, 2 double
& 4 twin.
Bathrooms: 4 public.
Bed & breakfast: £15.25-
£17.25 single, £30.50-£34.50
double.
Half board: £23.20-£26.20
daily, £150-£172.50 weekly.
Lunch available.
Evening meal 7pm (l.o.
7.30pm).
Parking for 16.

⚐ ▮ Ⅴ ⊟ ⍰ ◩ ◢ ♪ ∪
✿ ▦ ⊞ ▦

The Horse Shoe Inn ♨
Windmill Hill,
Herstmonceux, BN27 4RU
☎ (0323) 833265 Fax (0323)
832001
ⓒⓡ Resort
*Elizabethan styled half-
timbered hotel, with 15 en-suite
bedrooms, in peaceful setting
close to station. Good
sightseeing. Golf nearby.
Friendly service in
bar/restaurant.*
Bedrooms: 15 double.
Bathrooms: 15 private.
Bed & breakfast: from £44
single, from £59 double.
Lunch available.
Evening meal 7pm (l.o.
10pm).
Parking for 100.
Credit: Access, Visa, Diners,
Amex.

⚐ ✆ ⓒ ▯ ✿ ▮ Ⅴ ◩ ◢
♪ ⊞ ⊞

Please check prices
and other details at
the time of booking.

HINDHEAD

Surrey
Map ref 2C2

One of Surrey's best
known beauty spots and
a splendid place for views
over Sussex and the
Weald. Much of the
woodland and heath
belongs to the National
Trust.

**Devil's Punch Bowl
Hotel ♨**
👑👑👑👑
London Rd., Hindhead,
GU26 6AP
☎ (042 873) 6565
ⓒⓡ Consort
*An attractive 19th C hotel
adjoining 1000 acres of
National Trust walking land,
ideal touring base for Surrey,
Sussex and Hampshire.*
Bedrooms: 5 single, 20 double
& 13 twin, 2 family rooms.
Bathrooms: 40 private.
Bed & breakfast: £61-£65
single, £72-£75 double.
Lunch available.
Evening meal 7pm (l.o.
10pm).
Parking for 66.
Credit: Access, Visa, Diners,
Amex.

⚐ ✆ ⓒ ▯ ✿ ▮ Ⅴ ⊟
● ◩ ◢ ♪ ⚒ ⊞ ▨ ⊞ ▶

HOLLINGBOURNE

Kent
Map ref 3B4

6m E. Maidstone
Pleasant village near
romantic Leeds Castle in
the heart of the orchard
country at the foot of the
North Downs. Some fine
half-timbered houses and
a flint and ragstone
church.

Great Danes Hotel ♨
👑👑👑👑
Ashford Rd., Hollingbourne,
Nr. Maidstone, ME17 1RE
☎ (0622) 30022 Telex 96198
⚑ Embassy
*In 20 acres of parkland, a
short walk from Leeds Castle.
Own fishing lake, extensive
leisure complex. Other sports
can be arranged nearby.*
Bedrooms: 79 double &
43 twin, 4 family rooms.
Bathrooms: 126 private.
Bed & breakfast: max. £85
single, max. £103 double.
Lunch available.
Evening meal 7pm (l.o.
10.45pm).
Parking for 500.

Please mention this
guide when making
a booking.

Credit: Access, Visa, Diners, Amex.

♿ ⚘ ▯ ♨ ⛤ ▮ Ⓥ ⊟ ◖
🖩 🎔 ⚘ 🏆 🐾 ♞ ⚑ ♪ ✦
► ❀ ⚘ SP Ⓣ

HORLEY
Surrey
Map ref 2D2

Town on the London to Brighton road, just north of Gatwick Airport, with an ancient parish church and 15th C inn.

The Chequers Thistle Hotel M
♛♛♛

Brighton Rd., Horley, RH6 8PH
☎ (0293) 786992
Telex 877550
Ⓖ Thistle
Once a Tudor coaching inn, the hotel retains the original charm and style while providing every modern comfort. Gatwick Airport, 2 miles away, can be easily reached by courtesy coach.
Bedrooms: 1 single, 33 double & 44 twin.
Bathrooms: 78 private.
Bed & breakfast: from £79.75 single, from £100.50 double.
Lunch available.
Evening meal 6.15pm (l.o. 10.15am).
Parking for 185.
Credit: Access, Visa, C.Bl., Diners, Amex.
♿ ⚘ ☎ ▯ ♨ ⛤ Ⓥ ✂
⊟ ◖ 🖩 ⚘ 🏆 ♞ SP 🏤
Ⓣ

Felcourt Guest House M
Listed APPROVED

79 Massetts Rd., Horley, RH6 7EB
☎ (0293) 782651/776255
1 mile from Gatwick, ideal for travellers. En-suite rooms available, tea/coffee facilities, central heating. Long term parking available, £10 per week.
Bedrooms: 2 single, 1 double & 1 twin, 2 family rooms.
Bathrooms: 3 private, 1 public.
Bed & breakfast: £22-£30 single, £32-£38 double.
Parking for 12.
♿ ⚘ ▯ ♨ UL CB 🖩 ⚘ ♿
♞ 🏤 ☐AP ⚘ SP 🏤

The Gables Guest House M
Listed APPROVED

50 Bonehurst Rd., Horley, RH6 8QG
☎ (0293) 774553

---

2 miles from Gatwick and the railway station. Long term parking. Transport to the airport available.
Bedrooms: 3 single, 7 double & 9 twin, 3 family rooms.
Bathrooms: 6 private, 4 public.
Bed & breakfast: £22-£24 single, £30-£32 double.
Parking for 25.
♿ ⚘ ▯ ♨ UL CB TV 🖩 ⚘
❀ ♞ Ⓣ

The Lawn Guest House
♛

30 Massetts Rd., Horley, RH6 7DE
☎ (0293) 775751
Ideal for travellers using Gatwick. Pleasantly situated. Few minutes' walk to town centre, pubs and restaurants. Good base for London and the South Coast.
Bedrooms: 2 double & 5 twin.
Bathrooms: 7 private.
Bed & breakfast: max. £39 double.
Parking for 7.
Credit: Access, Visa.
▯ ♨ UL CB ⛤ ⚘ ⊟ ⚘
Ⓣ

Massetts Lodge
♛♛ COMMENDED

28, Massetts Road, Horley, RH6 7DE
☎ (0293) 782738
Victorian guesthouse 5 minutes from Gatwick (away from flightpath). Central heating, long term car parking and English breakfast.
Bedrooms: 1 single, 3 double & 1 twin, 3 family rooms.
Bathrooms: 5 private, 2 public.
Bed & breakfast: £22-£32 single, £32-£40 double.
Half board: £20.50-£36.50 daily.
Evening meal 6pm (l.o. 8pm).
Parking for 9.
Credit: Access, Visa, Amex.
♿ ⚘ ▯ ♨ UL CB ⛤ Ⓥ ✂
🖩 ⚘ 🏆 ♞ ❀ ♞ Ⓣ

Masslink House
70 Massetts Road, Horley RH6 7ED
☎ (0293) 785798
Comfortable, Victorian family house, close to Gatwick Airport, caters for holiday travellers and London visitors. Holiday parking available.
Bedrooms: 1 single, 2 double & 3 twin, 1 family room.
Bathrooms: 1 public.
Bed & breakfast: £22-£26 single, £32-£35 double.
Parking for 13.
♿ ♨ ⛤ ▮ Ⓥ ⊟ ♞ TV 🖩 ⚘
U Ⓣ

Melville Lodge Guest House M
♛♛

15, Brighton Road, Horley, Nr. Gatwick, RH6 7HH
☎ (0293) 784951
Detached Edwardian house built in early 1900. 5 minutes' drive to Gatwick Airport. 10 minutes' walk to town centre and railway station. Full cooked breakfast.
Bedrooms: 1 single, 2 double & 1 twin, 1 family room.
Bathrooms: 2 public.
Bed & breakfast: £20-£25 single, £35-£38 double.
Half board: £200-£250 weekly.
Parking for 8.
Credit: Access.
♿ ⚘ ☐ ♨ UL ✂ ⚘
♞ ☐AP Ⓣ

Mill Lodge Guest House
♛♛

25 Brighton Rd., Salfords, Nr. Horley, RH1 6PP
☎ (0293) 771170
Victorian rectory which has been thoroughly modernised. Ideal for persons travelling via Gatwick Airport on main A23 London to Brighton road.
Bedrooms: 2 single, 5 double & 1 twin, 1 family room.
Bathrooms: 2 private, 2 public.
Bed & breakfast: £25-£36 single, £36-£43 double.
Parking for 33.
♿ ⚘ ▯ ♨ UL CB ◖ 🖩 ♞
♞ Ⓣ

Rosemead Guest House
19 Church Rd., Horley, RH6 7EY
☎ (0293) 784965
Small guesthouse providing cooked breakfast, 5 minutes from Gatwick.
Bedrooms: 2 single, 1 double & 2 twin, 1 family room.
Bathrooms: 2 public.
Bed & breakfast: £18-£21 single, £32-£35 double.
Parking for 8.
♿ ▯ ♨ UL 🖩 ⚘ ♞ Ⓣ

Skylane Hotel
Brighton Rd., Horley, RH6 8QG
☎ (0293) 786971
Telex 878143
Airport hotel with en-suite rooms, attractive prices. Good restaurant. Friendly service, with courtesy coach to/from Gatwick.
Bedrooms: 1 single, 9 double & 44 twin, 5 family rooms.
Bathrooms: 59 private.
Bed & breakfast: £38.50-£41.50 single, £53-£59 double.
Half board: £48-£55 daily.

Lunch available.
Evening meal 7pm (l.o. 9.45pm).
Parking for 150.
Credit: Access, Visa, Diners, Amex.
♿ ⚘ ⛤ ▯ ♨ ⛤ ▮ Ⓥ ✂
♞ ◖ ⚘ 🏆 ⚘ ☐AP SP 🏤
Ⓣ

Springwood Guest House
58 Massetts Road, Horley, RH6 7DS
☎ (0293) 775998
Elegant detached Victorian house in pleasant residential road close to Gatwick Airport. Long-term car parking.
Bedrooms: 2 single, 2 double & 3 twin, 1 family room.
Bathrooms: 2 public.
Bed & breakfast: £19-£22 single, £32-£35 double.
Parking for 10.
♿ ⚘ ▯ ♨ UL CB 🖩 ⚘ ♞
🏤

Vulcan Lodge Guest House M
♛♛

27 Massetts Rd., Horley, Nr. Gatwick, RH6 7DQ
☎ (0293) 771522
Picturesque, comfortable house featuring exposed beams, 5 minutes from Gatwick Airport. Local restaurants, shops, pubs and trains within easy walking distance.
Bedrooms: 1 single, 1 double & 1 twin.
Bathrooms: 3 private, 1 public.
Bed & breakfast: £22-£29.50 single, £38-£42 double.
Parking for 8.
♿ ☐ ▯ ♨ ⛤ ▮ ⚘ ⊟ 🖩 ⚘
♞ 🏤 🏤

Woodlands Guest House M
42 Massetts Rd., Horley, RH6 7DS
☎ (0293) 782994/776358
1 mile from Gatwick airport. All rooms en-suite with colour TV, tea/coffee facilities. Car parking. Courtesy car by arrangement. Non-smoking.
Bedrooms: 1 single, 2 double & 2 twin, 1 family room.
Bathrooms: 5 private, 1 public.
Bed & breakfast: £25-£27 single, £35-£38 double.
Parking for 18.
♿ 5 ▯ ♨ ⛤ ▮ ✂ ⊟ ⚘ ♞
🏤 Ⓣ

Yew Tree
31 Massetts Rd., Horley, RH6 7DQ
☎ (0293) 785855
Continued ▶

HORLEY

Continued

Tudor-style house with half an acre garden. 3 minutes by taxi from Gatwick and 3 minutes' walk from town centre.
Bedrooms: 2 single, 2 double & 1 twin, 1 family room.
Bathrooms: 1 public;
1 private shower.
Bed & breakfast: £20-£24 single, £32-£36 double.
Parking for 10.
Credit: Access.

HORSHAM

W. Sussex
Map ref 2D2

Busy town with much modern development but still retaining its old character. The museum in Causeway House is devoted chiefly to local history and the agricultural life of the country.
Tourist Information Centre ☎ *(0403) 211661*

Cisswood House Restaurant and Hotel M
☂☂☂☂ COMMENDED
Sandy Gate Lane, Lower Beeding, Horsham, RH13 6NF
☎ Lower Beeding (0403) 891216 & Fax (0403) 891621
Country house restaurant with well-appointed bedrooms, family-run by the chef/proprietor and his wife. Convenient for Gatwick Airport, Crawley and Horsham. 3 conference rooms.
Bedrooms: 7 single, 22 double & 5 twin.
Bathrooms: 34 private.
Bed & breakfast: £62.50-£75 single, £80-£95 double.
Lunch available.
Evening meal 7pm (l.o. 9.15pm).
Parking for 65.
Credit: Access, Visa, Diners, Amex.

HOVE

See Brighton & Hove.

LEATHERHEAD

Surrey
Map ref 2D2

Old county town in the Green Belt, with the modern Thorndike Theatre.

Bookham Grange Hotel M
☂☂☂ APPROVED
Little Bookham Common, Bookham, Nr. Leatherhead, KT23 3HS
☎ Bookham (0372) 52742
Quiet family hotel, 5 minutes' walk from Bookham Station, located at the approach to Bookham Common.
Bedrooms: 9 double & 5 twin, 2 family rooms.
Bathrooms: 16 private, 1 public.
Bed & breakfast: £60-£65 single, £70-£75 double.
Half board: from £66 daily, £270-£480 weekly.
Lunch available.
Evening meal 7pm (l.o. 10pm).
Parking for 150.
Credit: Access, Visa, Diners, Amex.

Preston Cross Hotel & Country Club M
☂☂☂☂ COMMENDED
Rectory la., Little Bookham, Leatherhead, KT23 4DY
☎ (0372) 56642 Fax (0372) 57456
Just off the A246 Leatherhead to Guildford road, this comfortable, friendly hotel is set in 4 acres of landscaped gardens. Ideal for visiting London and the South Coast.
Bedrooms: 4 single, 7 double & 11 twin, 1 family room.
Bathrooms: 23 private.
Bed & breakfast: £50-£65 single, £60-£90 double.
Half board: £65-£80 daily.
Lunch available.
Evening meal 7.30pm (l.o. 10pm).
Parking for 200.
Credit: Access, Visa, Diners, Amex.

LENHAM

Kent
Map ref 3B4

9m SE. Maidstone
Shops, inns and houses, many displaying timber-work of the late Middle Ages, surround a square which is the centre of the village. The 14th C parish church has one of the best examples of a Kentish tower.

Dog and Bear Hotel M
☂☂☂ COMMENDED
The Square, Lenham, Nr Maidstone, ME17 2PG
☎ Maidstone (0622) 858219
Fax (0622) 859415
15th C coaching inn retaining its old world character and serving good Kent ale, lagers and fine wines with home cooking. En-suite rooms. Large car park and function room.
Bedrooms: 1 single, 5 double & 13 twin, 2 family rooms.
Bathrooms: 21 private.
Bed & breakfast: £37-£39 single, £50-£55 double.
Half board: £50-£55 daily.
Lunch available.
Evening meal 7pm (l.o. 10pm).
Parking for 30.
Credit: Access, Visa, Amex.

LEWES

E. Sussex
Map ref 2D3

Historic county town with Norman castle. The steep High Street has mainly Georgian buildings. There is a folk museum at Anne of Cleves House and the archaeological museum is in Barbican House.
Tourist Information Centre ☎ *(0273) 483448*

Berkeley House Hotel M
☂☂ COMMENDED
2 Albion Street, Lewes, East Sussex BN7 2ND
☎ Lewes (0273) 476057
Elegant Georgian townhouse. Quiet, conservation area location in town centre. South - facing roof terrace. Licensed, candlelit restaurant. Non-smokers only please.
Bedrooms: 3 single, 2 double & 1 twin.
Bathrooms: 1 private, 3 public.
Bed & breakfast: £24.75 single, £36-£49.50 double.

Half board: £28.50-£35.25 daily, £189.50-£234.50 weekly.
Evening meal 7.30pm (l.o. 8pm).
Credit: Access, Visa.

Ringmer Inn M
☂☂☂
Lewes Road, Ringmer, BN8 5QB
☎ Ringmer (0273) 812348
Vine-covered Victorian freehouse with elegant restaurant. Family-run, relaxing atmosphere.
Bedrooms: 6 double & 1 twin, 1 family room.
Bathrooms: 8 private.
Bed & breakfast: £38-£48 single, £58-£72 double.
Lunch available.
Evening meal 6pm (l.o. 9.50pm).
Parking for 40.
Credit: Access, Visa, Diners, Amex.

White Hart Hotel M
☂☂☂
55 High St., Lewes, BN7 1XE
☎ (0273) 474676 & 473794
Telex 878468
© Best Western
Oak-beamed bedrooms, 2 with four-poster beds, and panelled public rooms. In a central position in beautiful Sussex, with easy access to stately homes and the coast.
Bedrooms: 3 single, 11 double & 23 twin, 3 family rooms.
Bathrooms: 35 private, 1 public.
Bed & breakfast: £40-£55 single, £50-£80 double.
Half board: £55-£100 daily, £315 weekly.
Evening meal 7pm (l.o. 10.15pm).
Parking for 50.
Credit: Access, Visa, Diners, Amex.

Classifications and quality commendations were correct at the time of going to press but are subject to change. Please check at the time of booking.

Half board prices shown are per person but in some cases may be based on double/twin occupancy.

LITTLEHAMPTON

W. Sussex
Map ref 2D3

8m W. Worthing
Ancient port at the mouth of the River Arun, now a popular holiday resort, offering flat, sandy beaches, sailing, fishing and boat trips. The Sussex Downs are a short walk inland.

Arun View Inn
Listed

Wharf Road, Littlehampton, West Sussex BN17 5DD
☎ (0903) 722335
A pleasant riverside pub, offering a good range of home-cooked food and a wide selection of drinks in a friendly atmosphere.
Bedrooms: 2 single, 1 double & 2 twin.
Bathrooms: 2 public.
Bed & breakfast: £15-£20 single, £30-£40 double.
Lunch available.
Evening meal 7pm (l.o. 10pm).
Parking for 40.
Credit: Access, Visa.

Bracken Lodge Guest House M

43, Church Street, Littlehampton, West Sussex BN17 5PU
☎ Littlehampton (0903) 723174
Character guesthouse close to beach, golf course, swimming and sports centre. All rooms en-suite. Warm welcome assured.
Bedrooms: 1 double & 2 twin, 1 family room.
Bathrooms: 4 private.
Bed & breakfast: £25 single, £45 double.
Half board: £36-£40 daily, £252-£255 weekly.
Evening meal 7pm (l.o. 5.30pm).
Parking for 6.
Credit: Access, Visa.

Colbern Hotel M

South Terrace, Seafront, Littlehampton, BN17 5LQ
☎ (0903) 714270
Telex 934999 TXLINK G MBX 219996530.

Friendly family-run hotel with lounge and balcony overlooking The Greens and sea. River, leisure facilities and town are nearby.
Bedrooms: 2 single, 3 double & 3 twin, 1 family room.
Bathrooms: 9 private, 1 public.
Bed & breakfast: £20-£23 single, £40-£46 double.
Half board: £28.50-£31.50 daily, £178.50-£199.50 weekly.
Evening meal 6.30pm (l.o. 8pm).
Credit: Access, Visa, Diners, Amex.

Sharoleen Private Hotel
APPROVED

85 Bayford Rd., Littlehampton, BN17 5HW
☎ (0903) 713464
Close to town, river and beach. Homely atmosphere and personal service. Some en-suite facilities. Special rates for children and pensioners. Ground-floor room available.
Bedrooms: 2 single, 2 double & 2 twin, 1 family room.
Bathrooms: 2 private, 2 public.
Bed & breakfast: £12-£18 single, £24-£40 double.
Half board: £18.50-£24.50 daily, £129.50-£171.50 weekly.
Evening meal 6pm.

LOWER BEEDING

W. Sussex
Map ref 2D3

4m SE. Horsham
Close to St. Leonard's Forest, once a royal hunting ground, the area is also well-known for its hammer ponds, used when iron was smelted here.

South Lodge M

Brighton Rd., Lower Beeding, Nr. Horsham, RH13 6PS
☎ (0403) 891711
Telex 877765
Prestige
A fine Victorian house set in 90 acres of secluded wooded parkland, with views of the South Downs. From Gatwick take the M23/A23 direction Brighton. Turn off at Handcross A279 on to A281.
Bedrooms: 2 single, 26 double & 7 twin, 4 family rooms.

Bathrooms: 39 private.
Bed & breakfast: £79-£110 single, £110-£155 double.
Half board: £80-£110 daily.
Lunch available.
Evening meal 7pm (l.o. 10pm).
Parking for 80.
Credit: Access, Visa, Diners, Amex.

MAIDSTONE

Kent
Map ref 3B3

Busy county town of Kent on the River Medway has many interesting features and is an excellent centre for excursions. Museum of carriages, Chillington Manor House Museum and Art Gallery, Archbishop's Palace, Allington Castle, Mote Park.
Tourist Information Centre ☎ (0622) 673581

Boxley House Hotel M
COMMENDED

The Street, Boxley, Nr. Maidstone, ME14 3DZ
☎ (0622) 692269 Fax (0622) 683536
Comfortable, quiet, Georgian country house hotel set in 17 acres of beautiful parkland, nestling at the foot of the North Downs.
Bedrooms: 5 single, 7 double & 4 twin, 2 family rooms.
Bathrooms: 18 private.
Bed & breakfast: £48-£52 single, £69-£80 double.
Half board: £50-£65 daily.
Lunch available.
Evening meal 7pm (l.o. 9.30pm).
Parking for 150.
Credit: Access, Visa, Diners, Amex.

Grangemoor Hotel M
COMMENDED

St. Michael's Rd., Maidstone, ME16 8BS
☎ (0622) 677623/57222
1 hour from London and the Kent coast in a quiet position on the edge of town. The hotel has rear gardens, restaurant and bar.
Bedrooms: 10 single, 10 double & 12 twin, 4 family rooms.
Bathrooms: 32 private, 3 public.
Bed & breakfast: £30-£48 single, £42-£62 double.

Half board: £41.50-£59.50 daily, £290.50-£416.50 weekly.
Lunch available.
Evening meal 6.30pm (l.o. 10pm).
Parking for 60.
Credit: Access, Visa.

Rock House Hotel
COMMENDED

102 Tonbridge Rd., Maidstone, ME16 8SL
☎ (0622) 751616
Family-run guesthouse close to town centre. Central for London, Gatwick and Channel Ports. French and Spanish spoken.
Bedrooms: 3 single, 4 double & 3 twin, 2 family rooms.
Bathrooms: 2 public; 6 private showers.
Bed & breakfast: £27-£30 single, £38-£45 double.
Parking for 7.
Credit: Access, Visa.

The White Lodge

Loddington Lane, Linton, Maidstone, ME17 4AG
☎ Maidstone (0622) 43129
Regency house overlooking the Weald of Kent, south facing. Charming garden of 2.5 acres with 2 ponds stocked with carp. Tranquil setting.
Bedrooms: 2 single, 1 double & 3 twin.
Bathrooms: 1 private, 2 public.
Bed & breakfast: from £15 single, from £30 double.
Parking for 10.

Willington Court M
APPROVED

Willington St., Maidstone, ME15 8JW
☎ (0622) 38885
16th C Tudor-style house, traditionally furnished. Antiques, four-poster bed. Adjacent to Mote Park and near Leeds Castle.
Bedrooms: 1 single, 1 double & 1 twin, 1 family room.
Bathrooms: 1 private, 1 public.
Bed & breakfast: from £14 single, £28-£38 double.
Parking for 6.

> The symbols are explained on the flap inside the back cover.

MARGATE

Kent
Map ref 3C3

Oldest and most famous resort in Kent. Many Regency and Victorian buildings survive from the town's early days. There are 9 miles of sandy beach. Bembom Brothers is a 20-acre amusement park and the Winter Gardens offers concert hall entertainment.
Tourist Information Centre ☎ *(0843) 220241*

Braemar Private Hotel ₥
Listed
1 Stanley Rd., Cliftonville, Margate, CT9 2DL
☎ Thanet (0843) 224198
Small hotel with a big warm welcome, within easy reach of all amenities.
Bedrooms: 2 single, 3 twin, 6 family rooms.
Bathrooms: 2 public.
Bed & breakfast: £9.50-£10.50 single, £19-£21 double.
Half board: £14-£15 daily, £75-£85 weekly.
Evening meal 6pm.
🛏 👷 ❖ 🏱 📶 V ➷ 📺 ▥ ⤓
DAP 🐾 SP

Bridge Hotel ₥
👑👑👑
13-15 St. Mildreds Road, Westgate, Margate, CT8 8RE
☎ Thanet (0843) 31023
Totally rebuilt and refurbished 100-year-old establishment upgraded to international standards. Hotel and public house complete with coffee shop/restaurant.
Bedrooms: 1 single, 12 double & 1 twin, 4 family rooms.
Bathrooms: 18 private.
Bed & breakfast: £36.80-£40.50 single, £48.30-£53.50 double.
Lunch available.
Evening meal 7pm (l.o. 9.45pm).
Parking for 8.
Credit: Access, Visa.
🛏 🕮 📞 🖽 📭 ❖ 🏱 V ➷
▥ ⤓ 🅯 🍴 🥂 ➤ DAP 🐾 SP T

Brierdene Hotel ₥
Listed
17/21 Warwick Road, Cliftonville, Margate, CT9 2JU
☎ (0843) 220937
Comfortable, 32-bedroomed hotel in prime position between beaches, shops and bowls complexes. Live entertainment, coach tours and lots more!

Bedrooms: 5 single, 10 double & 6 twin, 11 family rooms.
Bathrooms: 6 private, 6 public.
Bed & breakfast: £16-£18.50 single, £32-£37 double.
Half board: £21-£27 daily, £105-£125 weekly.
Lunch available.
Evening meal 6pm (l.o. 6.30pm).
🛏 👷 ❖ 🏱 V ➷ ➡ 📺 ▥ ⤓ 🅯 🍴 🥂 ➤ DAP 🐾 SP

Charrington Hotel
👑👑
98 Grosvenor Place, Margate, CT9 1UY
☎ (0843) 221162
3 minutes from sea and town centre.
Bedrooms: 2 single, 4 double & 1 twin, 2 family rooms.
Bathrooms: 1 public; 3 private showers.
Bed & breakfast: £12-£14 single.
Half board: £72-£84 weekly.
Evening meal 8pm (l.o. 10.30pm).
🛏 👷 ❖ 🏱 ➷ 📺 ▥ ➡ ➤ ⤓ SP

Clintons
👑👑
9, Dalby Square, Cliftonville, CT9 2ER
☎ Thanet (0843) 290598/299550
Set in illuminated garden square, this elegant hotel offers comfortable en-suite bedrooms, spacious lounge, licensed restaurant, saunas, jacuzzi, gymnasium and solarium.
Bedrooms: 5 double & 5 twin, 3 family rooms.
Bathrooms: 13 private, 4 public.
Bed & breakfast: £20-£25 single, £30-£35 double.
Half board: £20-£22.50 daily, £110-£140 weekly.
Evening meal 6pm (l.o. 8pm).
Parking for 6.
Credit: Access, Visa, Diners.
🛏 🏱 ❖ 🅯 V ➷ 📺 ▥ ➡ 🍴 🖽 🥂 ➤ DAP 🐾 SP T

The Greswolde
👑👑
20 Surrey Rd, Margate, CT9 3LA
☎ (0843) 223956
Elegant Victorian hotel retaining much of its original character, 100 yards from promenade and championship bowling greens. Ideal for touring and golf.
Bedrooms: 2 double & 2 twin, 2 family rooms.

Bathrooms: 6 private.
Bed & breakfast: £18 single, £29 double.
Credit: Access, Visa.
🛏 🏱 ❖ 🅯 ➷ ➡ ▥ ➤ 🖼

Ivyside Hotel ₥
25 Sea Rd., Westgate-on-Sea, Margate, CT8 8SB
☎ Thanet (0843) 31082
Seafront hotel offering special weekend and midweek breaks with excellent reductions. Facilities for families and conferences.
Bedrooms: 8 single, 7 double & 15 twin, 35 family rooms.
Bathrooms: 63 private, 3 public.
Bed & breakfast: £30-£36 single, £60-£72 double.
Half board: £36-£42 daily, £196-£238 weekly.
Lunch available.
Evening meal 6.30pm (l.o. 8.30pm).
Parking for 25.
Credit: Access, Visa.
🛏 👷 📞 ❖ 🍴 🅯 V ➷ 📺
🅿 ➡ 🥂 ➤ 🏱 🖽 🍴 ➤ 🔲
🎿 ❄ ➤ 🐾 SP

The Malvern Private Hotel ₥
👑👑👑
29 Eastern Espl., Cliftonville, Margate, CT9 2HL
☎ Thanet (0843) 290192
The hotel overlooks sea, promenade and lawns. Close to all amenities, shopping, indoor/outdoor bowling greens, entertainments and Channel Ports. Parking outside and opposite hotel. TV and tea making facilities.
Bedrooms: 1 single, 5 double & 3 twin, 1 family room.
Bathrooms: 7 private, 1 public.
Bed & breakfast: £16-£25 single, £38-£36 double.
Evening meal 6pm (l.o. 3pm).
Credit: Access, Visa, Diners, Amex.
🛏 👷 🅯 ❖ 🏱 V ➷ ▥ ➡
🐾 🖼 SP

Raymonde Hotel ₥
Listed
1-7 Ethelbert Rd., Cliftonville, Margate, CT9 1SH
☎ Thanet (0843) 223991
Privately-owned family hotel under the supervision of proprietress. We aim to provide a good standard of food, service and hygiene. Family entertainment most evenings.
Bedrooms: 10 single, 9 double & 7 twin, 5 family rooms.
Bathrooms: 8 private, 4 public.
Bed & breakfast: £15-£20 single, £28-£38 double.

Half board: £22-£27 daily, £120-£135 weekly.
Lunch available.
Evening meal 6pm.
🛏 👷 🕮 ❖ 🅯 V ➷ 📺 ⤓
▥ ➡ 🍴 🥂 ❄ DAP 🐾 SP

Riverdale Hotel ₥
👑👑
40-46 Sweyn Rd., Cliftonville, Margate, CT9 2DF
☎ Thanet (0843) 223628
Close to sandy beaches, promenade, shops and traditional seaside amenities. Versatile and imaginative cuisine. In-house entertainment most nights.
Bedrooms: 7 single, 12 double & 8 twin, 7 family rooms.
Bathrooms: 17 private, 5 public.
Bed & breakfast: £17.50-£24.50 single, £35-£40 double.
Half board: £23.50-£30.50 daily, £118-£157 weekly.
Lunch available.
Evening meal 6pm (l.o. 6.30pm).
Open March-December.
Credit: Access, Visa, Diners, Amex.
🛏 👷 🕮 🏱 ❖ 🅯 V ➷ ●
▥ ➡ ➤ DAP 🐾 SP T

Westbrook Bay House ₥
👑👑
12 Royal Esplanade, Westbrook., Margate, CT9 5DW
☎ Thanet (0843) 292700
10-bedroomed family-run guesthouse situated on the seafront.
Bedrooms: 2 single, 3 double & 1 twin, 4 family rooms.
Bathrooms: 3 private, 2 public; 2 private showers.
Bed & breakfast: from £12.50 single, from £25 double.
Half board: from £17 daily, from £95 weekly.
Evening meal 6pm (l.o. 4pm).
🛏 🕮 🏱 ❖ V ➷ 📺 ▥
DAP 🐾 SP

Individual proprietors have supplied all details of accommodation. Although we do check for accuracy, we advise you to confirm prices and other information at the time of booking.

MIDHURST

W. Sussex
Map ref 2C3

On the outskirts of the
town are the remains of
Cowdray Park, a
substantial 16th C
fortified mansion. There is
a museum and the public
can watch the famous
Cowdray Park polo.

Park House Hotel M
🏆🏆🏆🏆 COMMENDED

Bepton, Nr. Midhurst,
GU29 0JB
☎ (073 081) 2880 & 3543
*A beautifully situated country
house hotel, equipped to give
maximum comfort, with the
atmosphere and amenities of
an English country home.*
Bedrooms: 2 single, 2 double
& 7 twin.
Bathrooms: 11 private,
1 public.
Bed & breakfast: from £46
single, from £82 double.
Half board: from £52 daily,
from £362 weekly.
Lunch available.
Evening meal 8pm (l.o. 9pm).
Parking for 22.
Credit: Access, Visa.

Southdown's Hotel and Country Restaurant M
🏆🏆🏆🏆

Trotton, Rogate, Nr.
Peterfield, Hants GU31 5JN
☎ Rogate (073 080) 521/763
Fax (073 080) 790
Telex 86658
*A country hotel set in its own
gardens, ideal for a peaceful
rest away from it all. Trotton
is 3 miles west of Midhurst.*
Bedrooms: 13 double &
7 twin, 2 family rooms.
Bathrooms: 22 private.
Bed & breakfast: £45-£50
single, £65-£80 double.
Half board: £34-£45 daily,
£210-£350 weekly.
Lunch available.
Evening meal 7.30pm (l.o.
10pm).
Parking for 70.
Credit: Access, Visa, Amex.

NEW ROMNEY

Kent
Map ref 3B4

Capital of Romney Marsh.
Now 1 mile from the sea,
it was one of the original
Cinque Ports. Romney,
Hythe and Dymchurch
Railway's main station is
here.
*Tourist Information
Centre* ☎ *(0679) 64044*

Broadacre Hotel
🏆🏆🏆

North St., New Romney,
TN28 8DR
☎ (0679) 62381
*Small 16th C family-run hotel
offering a warm, friendly
welcome and personal
attention. Intimate restaurant,
lounge bar and family garden.*
Bedrooms: 2 single, 4 double
& 2 twin, 1 family room.
Bathrooms: 7 private,
2 public.
Bed & breakfast: £19-£30
single, £36-£50 double.
Half board: £25-£45 daily,
£168 weekly.
Lunch available.
Evening meal 7pm (l.o. 9pm).
Parking for 9.
Credit: Access, Visa, Diners,
Amex.

Romney Bay House
Coast Road, Littlestone, New
Romney, TN28 8QY
☎ New Romney
(0679) 64747
*Family-run establishment
situated on a private road with
spectacular views of English
Channel. Adjacent to
Littlestone golf-course.*
Bedrooms: 3 single, 2 double
& 4 twin, 2 family rooms.
Bathrooms: 11 private.
Bed & breakfast: £22-£28
single, £44-£56 double.
Half board: £34.50-£40.50
daily, £230-£270 weekly.
Evening meal 7pm (l.o.
9.30pm).
Parking for 20.

NEWHAVEN

E. Sussex
Map ref 2D3

Town has the terminal of
a car-ferry service to
Dieppe in France.

The Old Volunteer Guest House
1 South Rd., Newhaven,
BN9 9QL
☎ (0273) 515204
*Guesthouse was formerly a
public house for 100 years.
5 minutes from railway and
cross-channel boat to Dieppe.*
Bedrooms: 4 single, 6 double
& 3 twin, 4 family rooms.
Bathrooms: 3 private,
3 public; 1 private shower.
Bed & breakfast: £16-£34
single, £26-£44 double.
Credit: Access, Visa, Diners,
Amex.

OCKHAM

Surrey
Map ref 2D2

Hautboy Inn
Ockham, Nr. Guildford,
GU23 6NP
☎ (0483) 225355
*19th C hotel built in local
hand-made bricks by William,
first Earl of Lovelace. All
suites are individually
furnished complementing the
style generated throughout the
hotel.*
Bedrooms: 5 twin.
Bathrooms: 5 private.
Bed & breakfast: from £78
single, from £98 double.
Evening meal 7pm (l.o.
10pm).
Parking for 80.
Credit: Access, Visa, Diners,
Amex.

OXTED

Surrey
Map ref 2D2

Pleasant town on the
edge of National Trust
woodland and at the foot
of the North Downs.
Chartwell, the former
home of Sir Winston
Churchill, is close by.

Hoskins Hotel M
🏆🏆🏆

Station Rd. West, Oxted,
RH8 9EE
☎ (0883) 712338 Fax (0883)
716456
ⓒ Inter

Situated on the Kent/Surrey
border, ideal for Croydon,
Gatwick, Heathrow and within
easy reach of London by train
or by car. Chartwell and Hever
Castle are nearby.
Bedrooms: 5 double & 7 twin.
Bathrooms: 12 private,
1 public.
Bed & breakfast: £36-£60.50
single, £49.50-£69 double.
Lunch available.
Evening meal 7pm (l.o. 9pm).
Parking for 24.
Credit: Access, Visa, Diners,
Amex.

PENSHURST

Kent
Map ref 2D2

Village in a hilly wooded
setting with Penshurst
Place, the ancestral home
of the Sidney family since
1552, standing in
delightful grounds with a
formal Tudor garden.

Leicester Arms Hotel
The High St., Penshurst, Nr.
Tonbridge, TN11 8BT
☎ (0892) 870551/2
*17th century Leicester Arms is
situated in the picturesque
village of Penshurst a few miles
from the A26.*
Bedrooms: 1 single, 5 double
& 1 twin.
Bathrooms: 7 private.
Bed & breakfast: £40-£45
single, £50-£70 double.
Lunch available.
Evening meal 7pm (l.o.
9.30pm).
Parking for 40.
Credit: Access, Visa, Diners,
Amex.

Swale Cottage
Listed COMMENDED

Old Swaylands Lane, Off
Poundsbridge Lane,
Penshurst, Nr. Tonbridge,
TN11 8AH
☎ Penshurst (0892) 870738
*Elegantly converted 18th C
Kentish barn with 3
attractively furnished en-suite
rooms. Close to Penhurst
Place, Hever Castle, Chartwell
and Knole. Half an hour from
Gatwick, near the A26 on the
B2176.*
Bedrooms: 2 double & 1 twin.
Bathrooms: 3 private,
1 public.

Continued ▶

The symbol ⓒ and the name of a hotel
group or consortium after a hotel address
means that bookings can be made through
a central reservations office. These are
listed on pages 559 & 560.

PENSHURST
Continued

Bed & breakfast: £24-£26 single, £32-£40 double. Parking for 4.

🕏10 ⊞ Ⓡ ♉ ⛛ Ⓤ ⒧ ☞ ⛟
🎬 🛆 ✳ 🐾 📶 SP 🎏

PEVENSEY BAY
E. Sussex
Map ref 3B4

Small but popular resort, with spacious beach, near the village of Pevensey.

Napier House
The Promenade, Pevensey Bay, BN24 6HD
☎ Eastbourne (0323) 768875
Situated on seafront in delightful seaside holiday village. Garden on the beach with deck chairs provided. Easy parking.
Bedrooms: 1 single, 5 double & 2 twin, 2 family rooms.
Bathrooms: 5 private, 1 public; 3 private showers.
Bed & breakfast: £13-£17 single, £26-£34 double.
Half board: £18.50-£23 daily, £108-£140 weekly.
Lunch available.
Evening meal 6.50pm (l.o. 4pm).
Parking for 7.
Open March-November.

PLUCKLEY
Kent
Map ref 3B4

7m NW. Ashford
Brick cottages, with shops, school and inn form a small square in front of the 13th C church. A feature of this village are the narrow, round arched white brick 'lucky' Dering windows found on nearly every building.

Elvey Farm Country Hotel
Elvey Farm, Pluckley, Nr. Ashford, TN27 0SU
☎ (023 384) 442
75-acre mixed farm. Hotel in lovely old converted farm buildings. All rooms have modern facilities yet retain traditional character. Special feature - dining room with hand made furniture and a collection of tools.
Bedrooms: 1 single, 2 double & 2 twin, 5 family rooms.

Bathrooms: 10 private.
Bed & breakfast: from £49.50 double.
Evening meal 7.30pm (l.o. midday).
Parking for 25.
Credit: Access, Visa.

PULBOROUGH
W. Sussex
Map ref 2D3

Here is Parham, an Elizabethan mansion with unusually tall, mullioned windows and a long gallery measuring 158 ft. The house and the surrounding park and garden can be visited. In the grounds stands the church of St. Peter.

The Arun Cosmopolitan Hotel
87 Lower St., Pulborough, RH20 2BP
☎ (079 82) 2162 Fax (079 82) 2935
Delightful village centre hotel with licensed restaurant and bar. Unsurpassed views over River Arun to the South Downs.
Bedrooms: 2 single, 3 double & 1 twin.
Bathrooms: 6 private, 1 public.
Bed & breakfast: £35-£40 single, £55-£60 double.
Half board: £43-£48 daily, £270-£305 weekly.
Lunch available.
Evening meal 7pm (l.o. 9pm).
Parking for 14.
Credit: Access, Visa, Diners, Amex.

Chequers Hotel
Church Pl., Pulborough, RH20 1AD
☎ (079 82) 2486 Fax (079 82) 2715 Telex 67596 Att: Chequers
Minotels
Queen Anne hotel in picturesque village, overlooking the South Downs. Licensed restaurant. Bedrooms with all facilities, some on ground floor and some four-posters. New garden conservatory.
Bedrooms: 1 single, 6 double & 2 twin, 2 family rooms.
Bathrooms: 11 private.
Bed & breakfast: £39.50-£44.50 single, £53-£63 double.

Half board: £35-£40 daily, from £234 weekly.
Lunch available.
Evening meal 7.30pm (l.o. 8.30pm).
Parking for 14.
Credit: Access, Visa, Diners, Amex.

RAMSGATE
Kent
Map ref 3C3

Popular holiday resort with good sandy beaches. At Pegwell Bay is the replica of a Viking longship. Terminal for car-ferry service to Dunkirk.
Tourist Information Centre ☎ (0843) 591086

Eastwood Guest House
28, Augusta Road, Ramsgate, CT11 8JS
☎ Thanet (0843) 591505
Comfortable homely guesthouse with sea views on east side of Ramsgate harbour.
Bedrooms: 4 double, 3 family rooms.
Bathrooms: 3 public.
Bed & breakfast: £12.50-£15 single, £22-£25 double.
Half board: £16.50-£19.50 daily, £95-£115 weekly.
Evening meal 6.30pm (l.o. 8pm).
Parking for 14.

The Gentle Breeze Guest House
APPROVED
46, Bellevue Road, Ramsgate, CT11 8LA
☎ Thanet (0843) 589940
Small homely guesthouse, 5 minutes from beach and town centre. All rooms with en-suite, shower, TV and tea-making facilities.
Bedrooms: 1 single, 2 double & 1 twin, 1 family room.
Bathrooms: 3 private; 2 private showers.
Bed & breakfast: £13.50-£15 single, £27-£30 double.
Half board: £18.50-£20 daily, £125-£130 weekly.
Evening meal 6pm.

Goodwin View
19 Wellington Cres., Ramsgate, CT11 8JD
☎ Thanet (0843) 591419

Seafront guesthouse in Grade II listed historic building overlooking harbour and beach. Bookings made for ferry-users, the terminal is within walking distance.
Bedrooms: 6 single, 1 double & 2 twin, 4 family rooms.
Bathrooms: 3 private, 3 public.
Bed & breakfast: £19-£25 single, £34-£44.50 double.
Half board: £24-£32 daily, £154-£205 weekly.
Evening meal 6pm.

Marina Resort Hotel
Harbour Parade, Ramsgate, CT11 8LJ
☎ (0843) 588276 Fax (0843) 586866
Resort
Thanet's newest hotel, overlooking attractive marina, offers health club, a la carte menu, all bedrooms with TV and en-suite facilities.
Bedrooms: 4 single, 15 double & 35 twin, 5 family rooms.
Bathrooms: 59 private.
Bed & breakfast: £59.50-£64.50 single, £78-£83 double.
Lunch available.
Evening meal 7pm (l.o. 9.30pm).
Credit: Access, Visa, Diners, Amex.

Pegwell Village Hotel
81 Pegwell Rd., Pegwell Village, Ramsgate, CT11 0NJ
☎ Thanet (0843) 586001
Seafront hotel high on the cliffs with views across Pegwell Bay. Central for all Thanet's leisure spots, Manston Airport and ferry services to France.
Bedrooms: 1 single, 21 double & 8 twin, 10 family rooms.
Bathrooms: 28 private, 6 public.
Bed & breakfast: £20-£35 single, £40-£50 double.
Half board: £48.50-£60.50 daily.
Evening meal 6.30pm (l.o. 10.30pm).
Parking for 200.
Credit: Access, Visa, Amex.

Shirley's Hotel
8 Nelson Cres., Ramsgate, CT11 9JF
☎ Thanet (0843) 584198

Overlooking Ramsgate harbour and Sally Line ferry terminal. 2 minutes from town centre. All rooms have colour TV and some are en-suite.
Bedrooms: 3 single, 2 double & 5 twin, 2 family rooms.
Bathrooms: 3 private, 2 public.
Bed & breakfast: £12.50-£15 single, £25-£30 double.
Credit: Access, Visa.

Spencer Court Hotel
37 Spencer Sq., Ramsgate, CT11 9LD
☎ Thanet (0843) 594582
Grade II listed building in quiet square overlooking tennis courts, 200 yards from seafront, directly above Sally Line ferry terminal.
Bedrooms: 2 single, 1 double & 4 twin, 2 family rooms.
Bathrooms: 2 public.
Bed & breakfast: £14-£16 single, £24-£30 double.
Evening meal 6.30pm (l.o. 10am).

Sunnymede Private Hotel M
Listed
10 Truro Rd., Ramsgate, CT11 8DP
☎ Thanet (0843) 593974
In ideal position on East Cliff, with sea views from most rooms. All rooms have TV, tea/coffee facilities. En-suite rooms available. Bar and games room. Car park. Adjacent to promenade, close to Granville Theatre. Easy distance to shops, amusements and main bus routes. Near Sally Line ferry to Dunkirk.
Bedrooms: 3 single, 8 double & 3 twin, 2 family rooms.
Bathrooms: 3 private, 5 public.
Bed & breakfast: £14-£18 single, £28-£35 double.
Half board: £21-£25 daily, £85-£95 weekly.
Evening meal 6pm (l.o. 6pm).
Parking for 6.

The Tancliff Private Hotel
♕♕♕
20 Wellington Cres., East Cliff, Ramsgate, CT11 8JD
☎ Thanet (0843) 593016
In a clifftop Regency crescent, overlooking sands and harbour and close to town centre and ferry terminal.
Bedrooms: 2 single, 4 double & 1 twin, 3 family rooms.

Bathrooms: 4 private, 1 public; 4 private showers.
Bed & breakfast: £15-£25 single, £30-£40 double.
Half board: £21-£31 daily, £130-£200 weekly.
Evening meal 6pm (l.o. midday).

York House
7, Augusta Road, Eastcliff, Ramsgate, CT11 8JP
☎ Thanet (0843) 596775
Augusta Road terraces were built circa 1830. They consist of 4-storey properties, curved bay windows and iron balconies. Grade II Listed building.
Bedrooms: 1 single, 2 double & 2 twin, 2 family rooms.
Bathrooms: 2 public.
Bed & breakfast: £8.50-£10 single, £17-£20 double.

REDHILL
Surrey
Map ref 2D2

Part of the borough of Reigate and now the commercial centre. Gatwick Airport is 3 miles to the south.

Arun Lodge Guest House M
Listed APPROVED
37, Redstone Hill, Redhill, RH1 4AW
☎ (0737) 761933
Attractively decorated Edwardian guesthouse, offering high standard of accommodation. Ideal location, Gatwick 13 minutes, London 35 minutes. 1.5 miles to M25, situated by A25.
Bedrooms: 1 single, 2 double & 1 twin, 2 family rooms.
Bathrooms: 2 private, 1 public; 3 private showers.
Bed & breakfast: £26 single, £43-£46 double.
Parking for 6.

Lynwood Guest House
50 London Rd., Redhill, RH1 1LN
☎ Redhill (0737) 766894
Conveniently situated close to Redhill town centre and railway station. Under 15 minutes by train or car from Gatwick Airport.
Bedrooms: 1 single, 1 double & 3 twin, 1 family room.
Bathrooms: 1 private, 1 public; 5 private showers.

Bed & breakfast: £20-£25 single, £38-£40 double.
Parking for 8.

Nutfield Priory M
♕♕♕♕ COMMENDED
Nutfield, Redhill, RH1 4EN
☎ (0737) 822066
Built in 1872 for Joshua Fielden MP, set in 40 acres of Surrey countryside with unsurpassed views. Large ornate building of towers, elaborate carvings, stonework cloisters and stained glass windows.
Bedrooms: 3 single, 19 double & 12 twin.
Bathrooms: 34 private.
Bed & breakfast: £70-£90 single, £95-£210 double.
Lunch available.
Evening meal 7pm (l.o. 9.45pm).
Parking for 150.
Credit: Access, Visa, Diners, Amex.

Rookwood House Hotel
13, London Road, Merstham, RH1
☎ (073 74) 3207
Family hotel situated on the main A23, 15 minutes' drive to Gatwick Airport. Good train service to London and Brighton.
Bedrooms: 2 single, 8 double, 2 family rooms.
Bathrooms: 2 private, 3 public; 2 private showers.
Bed & breakfast: £25-£30 single, £35-£40 double.
Lunch available.
Evening meal 7pm (l.o. 9.30pm).
Parking for 20.

REIGATE
Surrey
Map ref 2D2

Old town on the edge of the North Downs with modern developments. Just outside the town on Reigate Heath stands an old windmill, which has been converted into a church.

Beechwood House
39 Hatchlands Rd., Redhill, RH1 6AP
☎ (0737) 761444 & 764277

Victorian house with easy access to all amenities and Gatwick Airport. 10 minutes' walk from mainline station (Victoria 20 minutes).
Bedrooms: 2 single, 1 double & 3 twin, 1 family room.
Bathrooms: 2 public.
Bed & breakfast: max. £22 single, max. £35 double.
Parking for 9.

Bridge House Hotel & Restaurant
Reigate Hill, Reigate, RH2 9RP
☎ (0737) 246801
Telex 268810
Most rooms have own balcony with views over South Downs. 2 minutes from junction 8 on M25. 15 minutes from Gatwick and 35 minutes from Heathrow.
Bedrooms: 8 single, 6 double & 23 twin, 3 family rooms.
Bathrooms: 40 private.
Bed & breakfast: £40-£63 single, £50-£81 double.
Half board: from £60.81 daily, from £430 weekly.
Lunch available.
Evening meal 7.30pm (l.o. 10.30pm).
Parking for 150.
Credit: Access, Visa, Diners, Amex.

Cranleigh Hotel M
♕♕♕ APPROVED
41 West St., Reigate, RH2 9BL
☎ (0737) 223417
Ⓖ Minotels
Close to town centre and railway station, on the main road to the south-west, within a short distance of Gatwick Airport and easy reach of the centre of London. 1 mile from M25.
Bedrooms: 3 single, 5 double & 5 twin, 3 family rooms.
Bathrooms: 8 private, 4 public.
Bed & breakfast: £45-£60 single, £65-£75 double.
Evening meal 7.30pm (l.o. 8pm).
Parking for 6.
Credit: Access, Visa, C.Bl., Diners, Amex.

Map references apply to the colour maps towards the end of this guide.

ROBERTSBRIDGE

E. Sussex
Map ref 3B4

Small town in well-wooded country near the River Rother, with a number of old timber and boarded houses. An important local industry is the making of Gray-Nicolls cricket bats.

Parsonage Farm

Salehurst, Robertsbridge,
TN32 5PJ
☎ (0580) 880446
300-acre mixed and hops farm. 15th C farmhouse with beams and panelling. Relaxed atmosphere. Within easy reach of south coast resorts and many places of historic interest and natural beauty.
Bedrooms: 1 single, 1 twin, 1 family room.
Bathrooms: 1 public.
Bed & breakfast: from £12 single, from £24 double.
Half board: from £18.50 daily, from £124 weekly.
Evening meal 6.30pm.
Parking for 20.
Open January-August, November-December.
➠ 3 ⚒ ✿ 🛏 UL ♦ TV IIII ⌗ 🏕 🏚

ROCHESTER

Kent
Map ref 3B3

Ancient cathedral city on the River Medway. Has many places of interest connected with Charles Dickens (who lived nearby) including the fascinating Dickens Centre. Also massive castle overlooking the river and Guildhall Museum.
Tourist Information Centre ☎ (0634) 843666

Belmont Guest House M

18/19 New Road, Rochester,
ME1 1BG
☎ Medway (0634) 812262
Proprietor is always available and ready to assist in making guests welcome. Excellent views to front and rear of guesthouse, in a nice area. Evening meals by arrangement.
Bedrooms: 10 single, 5 double & 1 twin.
Bathrooms: 4 public.
Bed & breakfast: £13-£15 single, £20-£22 double.
Parking for 6.
➠ 🛏 ⌷ ✿ UL ✕ ⌗ TV 🖿 🏚 🏚

Medway Manor Hotel

16 New Rd., Rochester,
ME1 1BG
☎ Medway (0634) 847985
Family-run hotel in Rochester with historic and scenic views. Close proximity to London and south east coast. Leisure facilities available.
Bedrooms: 5 single, 25 double & 9 twin, 3 family rooms.
Bathrooms: 31 private, 5 public; 2 private showers.
Bed & breakfast: £30-£35 single, £30-£45 double.
Half board: £24-£50 daily, £168-£350 weekly.
Lunch available.
Evening meal 5.30pm (l.o. 10.30pm).
Parking for 50.
Credit: Access, Visa, Diners, Amex.
➠ 🛏 ⌷ ✿ 🛏 V ⌗ TV ◑ IIII 🖿 ⌑ & 🎋 🎋 ♦ DAP ⅍ SP 🏚 T

ROTTINGDEAN

E. Sussex
Map ref 2D3

5m SE. Brighton
The quiet High Street contains a number of fine old buildings and the village pond and green are close by.

Corner House Guest House

Listed **APPROVED**
Steyning Rd., Rottingdean,
BN2 7GA
☎ Brighton (0273) 304533
Victorian type house, tastefully decorated, serves full English breakfast.
Bedrooms: 1 single, 3 double & 1 twin, 1 family room.
Bathrooms: 2 public.
Bed & breakfast: £14-£15 single, £28-£30 double.
➠ 6 ⌷ UL IIII 🏚

Individual proprietors have supplied all details of accommodation. Although we do check for accuracy, we advise you to confirm prices and other information at the time of booking.

RYE

E. Sussex
Map ref 3B4

Cobbled, hilly streets and fine old buildings make Rye, once a Cinque Port, a most picturesque town. Noted for its church with ancient clock, potteries and antique shops, and Ypres Tower Museum.
Tourist Information Centre ☎ (0797) 226696

Aviemore Guest House M

☷☷
28/30 Fishmarket Road, Rye,
TN31 7LP
☎ (0797) 223052
Owner-run, friendly guesthouse offering a warm welcome and hearty breakfast. Overlooking "Town Salts" and the River Rother. 2 minutes from town centre.
Bedrooms: 1 single, 2 double & 3 twin, 2 family rooms.
Bathrooms: 2 public.
Bed & breakfast: £15-£17 single, £28-£30 double.
Half board: £19-£21 daily, £120-£135 weekly.
➠ ✿ ⌷ V 🛏 TV IIII 🖿 ⌑
🏚 DAP ⅍ SP

Broomhill Lodge Hotel M

☷☷☷☷ **COMMENDED**
Rye Foreign, Rye,
TN31 7UN
☎ Iden (079 78) 421
Early 19th C country house hotel set in 2 acres of gardens with superb views over Sussex countryside. 1.5 miles north-west of Rye.
Bedrooms: 2 single, 7 double & 3 twin.
Bathrooms: 12 private.
Bed & breakfast: £37 single, £57-£69 double.
Half board: £40.50-£45.50 daily, £250-£280 weekly.
Evening meal 7.30pm (l.o. 9.30pm).
Parking for 12.
Credit: Access, Visa.
➠ 6 🖾 ⌷ ✆ ⊛ ⌷ ✿ 🛊 V ⌗ 🖿 ⌑ 🎋 ⊛ ∪ ✿ 🎋 🏚 ⅍ SP 🏚

The Country House at Winchelsea M

☷☷☷ **COMMENDED**
Hastings Rd., Winchelsea,
TN36 4AD
☎ Rye (0797) 226669
A Grade II listed former 17th C Sussex farmhouse set in approximately 2 acres. Walled garden with fine open country views. Close to Winchelsea, Rye and Hastings.

Bedrooms: 3 double & 1 twin.
Bathrooms: 4 private.
Bed & breakfast: £23-£26 single, £33-£36 double.
Half board: £53-£56 daily, £301-£322 weekly.
Evening meal 7.30pm (l.o. 7.30pm).
Parking for 8.
➠ 9 ⊛ ⌷ ✿ V ⌗ IIII ✿ 🎋 🏚 SP 🏚

Flackley Ash Hotel & Restaurant M

☷☷☷☷ **APPROVED**
London Rd., Peasmarsh,
Rye, TN31 6YH
☎ Peasmarsh (079 721) 651
Fax (079 721) 510
Telex 957210 RLTG
☼ Best Western
Georgian country house hotel in 5 acres. Swimming pool and leisure centre. Fresh fish, well-stocked cellar.
Bedrooms: 18 double & 10 twin, 2 family rooms.
Bathrooms: 30 private.
Bed & breakfast: £44.50-£56.50 single, £82.50-£94.50 double.
Half board: £42-£55.50 daily, £240-£300 weekly.
Lunch available.
Evening meal 7pm (l.o. 9.30pm).
Parking for 60.
Credit: Access, Visa, Diners, Amex.
➠ 🛏 ⌷ ✆ ⊛ ⌷ 🛊 V ⌗ IIII ⌑ 🎋 🎋 🖾 🎋 ✿ ⅍ SP 🏚 T

Green Hedges M

☷☷
Rye Hill, Rye, East Sussex
TN31 7NH
☎ Rye (0797) 222185
Large Edwardian country house in a private road. 1.5 acres of landscaped gardens with heated swimming pool. Within 10 minutes' walk of town centre. Ample parking.
Bedrooms: 2 double & 1 twin.
Bathrooms: 3 private, 1 public.
Bed & breakfast: £40-£50 double.
➠ 12 ⌷ ✿ UL 🛊 V ✕ IIII ⌑ 🎋 ✿ 🎋 🏚

Holloway House M

High St., Rye, TN31 7JF
☎ Rye (0797) 224748
15th C Cairn stone. Huge fireplaces in bedrooms and dining rooms. Heavily beamed. Traditional beds. Antique furniture. Hearty breakfast.
Bedrooms: 6 double & 1 twin.
Bathrooms: 7 private.
Bed & breakfast: £30-£50 single, £40-£80 double.

Lunch available.
Evening meal 6pm (l.o. 9pm).
Credit: Access, Visa.

⛵ ♿ 🏥 🖥 ✆ 🚱 🅿 Ⓥ ⛌ 📺
🍴 ⚓ ✕ 🏃 🐾 SP 🏛

The Hope Anchor Hotel
Watchbell St., Rye,
TN31 7HA
☎ (0797) 222216
*17th C hotel at the end of
cobbled street with magnificent
views of surrounding
countryside. Restaurant
specialises in fish dishes.*
Bedrooms: 1 single, 7 double
& 5 twin, 1 family room.
Bathrooms: 8 private,
3 public.
Bed & breakfast: £36-£40
single, £53-£63 double.
Half board: £35-£50 daily.
Lunch available.
Evening meal 7pm (l.o. 9pm).
Credit: Access, Visa.

⛵ 🏥 🖥 ✆ 🚱 Ⓥ ⛌ 🍴 ⚓
🍴 🏃 SP 🏛

Jeake's House M
🏆🏆🏆 **COMMENDED**
Mermaid St., Rye, TN31 7ET
☎ (0797) 222828 Fax (0797)
225758
*Recapture the past in this
historic building, in a
cobblestoned street at the heart
of the old town.*
Bedrooms: 1 single, 6 double
& 1 twin, 3 family rooms.
Bathrooms: 9 private,
2 public.
Bed & breakfast: £20 single,
£36-£46 double.

⛵ 🏥 🖥 🚱 ⓤⓛ Ⓥ ⛌ 🍴 ⚓
🏃 SP 🏛

The Old Vicarage
Hotel M
🏆🏆🏆 **COMMENDED**
15 East St., Rye, TN31 7JY
☎ (0797) 225131
*Family-run Georgian hotel and
restaurant in conservation area.
Spacious rooms and elegant
restaurant with panoramic
views over Romney Marsh.*
Bedrooms: 2 double, 2 family
rooms.
Bathrooms: 4 private.
Bed & breakfast: £42-£47
single, £62-£70 double.
Half board: £252-£266
weekly.
Evening meal 7pm (l.o. 9pm).
Credit: Access, Visa, Diners.

⛵ 🏥 ✆ ☎ 🖥 🚱 ✆ Ⓥ 🍴
🍴 ⚓ 🍴 🏃 🐾 SP 🏛

Playden Cottage
Guesthouse M
🏆🏆🏆 **COMMENDED**
Military Rd., Rye, TN31 7NY
☎ (0797) 222234

*Large character cottage, said
to be "Grebe" from
E.F.Benson's Mapp and Lucia
novels. Personal service in a
comfortable family home.
Grade II listed building.*
Bedrooms: 1 double & 2 twin.
Bathrooms: 3 private,
1 public.
Bed & breakfast: £40-£56
double.
Parking for 7.

⛵12 🏥 ⓤⓛ 🚱 Ⓥ ⛌ 📺 🍴
⚓ ♨ 🐾 ✕ 🏃 SP 🏛

Top o' The Hill at
Rye M
Rye Hill, Rye, TN31 7NH
☎ (0797) 223284
*Small friendly inn offering
varied food and
accommodation. Central for
touring Kent and Sussex with
Channel ports nearby.*
Bedrooms: 3 double & 2 twin,
1 family room.
Bathrooms: 6 private.
Bed & breakfast: £14-£16.50
single, £28-£33 double.
Lunch available.
Evening meal 7pm (l.o.
9.30pm).
Parking for 32.
Credit: Access, Visa.

⛵ 🏥 🖥 🚱 ✆ Ⓥ 📺 🍴 ⚓
♿ ♨ 🏃 🐾 SP 🏛

SEAFORD
E. Sussex
Map ref 2D3

The town was a bustling
port until 1579 when the
course of the River Ouse
was diverted. The
downlands around the
town make good walking
country, with fine views of
the Seven Sisters cliffs.
*Tourist Information
Centre* ☎ (0323) 897426

Abbots Lodge Motor
Inn M
🏆🏆🏆
Marine Parade, Seaford,
Newhaven, BN25 2RB
☎ Seaford (0323) 891055
Telex 878859 ABBOTSG
*Touring hotel, offering chalet-
style accommodation and
friendly service. Ideal for
Newhaven and ferry.*
Bedrooms: 27 double &
39 twin, 4 family rooms.
Bathrooms: 70 private.
Bed & breakfast: max. £39
single, max. £56 double.
Lunch available.
Evening meal 7pm (l.o.
9.30pm).

Parking for 100.
Credit: Access, Visa, C.Bl.,
Diners, Amex.

⛵ ♿ ✆ ☎ 🖥 🚱 ✆ Ⓥ ⛌
🍴 ⦿ 🍴 ⚓ 🍴 🏃 SP 📺

SEDLESCOMBE
E. Sussex
Map ref 3B4

3m NE. Battle
Pretty village with a long,
wide green on which
stands a water pump
under a gable-roofed
shelter. Nearby is the
Pestalozzi Children's
Village.

The Brickwall Hotel
🏆🏆🏆🏆
Sedlescombe, Nr. Battle,
TN33 0QA
☎ (0424) 870253
*16th C manor house set amidst
3 acres of gardens, on quiet
village green.*
Bedrooms: 3 single, 7 double
& 12 twin, 2 family rooms.
Bathrooms: 24 private.
Bed & breakfast: £43-£45
single, £56-£60 double.
Half board: £40-£42 daily,
£234-£240 weekly.
Lunch available.
Evening meal 7pm (l.o. 9pm).
Parking for 28.
Credit: Access, Visa, Diners,
Amex.

⛵ 🏥 🖥 ✆ ☎ 🚱 ✆ 🚱 Ⓥ
🍴 🍴 ⚓ 🍴 ✆ 🍴 ▶ ♨ 🍴
🐾 SP 🏛

SEVENOAKS
Kent
Map ref 2D2

Set in pleasant wooded
country, with a distinctive
character and charm.
Nearby is Knole, home of
the Sackville family and
one of the largest houses
in England, set in a vast
deer park.
*Tourist Information
Centre* ☎ (0732) 450305

Donnington Manor
Hotel M
🏆🏆🏆 **COMMENDED**
London Rd., Dunton Green,
Sevenoaks, TN13 2TD
☎ (0732) 462681
*Hotel with restaurant in
delightful countryside of the
Kentish Weald, close to many
places of interest and pretty
local villages.*
Bedrooms: 35 double &
27 twin, 2 family rooms.
Bathrooms: 64 private,
2 public.

Bed & breakfast: £45-£55
single, £55-£65 double.
Half board: £47-£69.50 daily.
Lunch available.
Evening meal 7pm (l.o.
9.30pm).
Parking for 100.
Credit: Access, Visa, Diners,
Amex.

⛵ 🏥 ✆ ☎ 🖥 🚱 ✆ 🚱 Ⓥ ⛌
🍴 ⦿ 🍴 ⚓ 🍴 ✆ ♨ 🍴 ✕ 🍴
♨ ⓊⒶⒻ 🐾 SP 🏛 📺

Moorings Hotel M
🏆🏆🏆
97 Hitchen Hatch Lane,
Sevenoaks, TN13 3BE
☎ (0732) 452589
*Bed and breakfast hotel in
quiet position near station.
London half an hour by train.
Knole House and Chartwell
nearby.*
Bedrooms: 5 single, 3 double
& 12 twin, 2 family rooms.
Bathrooms: 17 private,
2 public; 2 private showers.
Bed & breakfast: £30-£45
single, £40-£60 double.
Parking for 22.
Credit: Access, Visa.

⛵ 🏥 🖥 🚱 ✆ 🍴 📺 ⦿ 🍴
✕ 📺

The Royal Oak Hotel M
🏆🏆🏆
Upper High St., Sevenoaks,
TN14 5PG
☎ Sevenoaks (0732) 451109
*Georgian coaching inn, in an
attractive part of Sevenoaks,
near Knole. The hotel has
recently been fully refurbished.*
Bedrooms: 7 single, 19 double
& 13 twin.
Bathrooms: 39 private.
Bed & breakfast: from £65
single, from £80 double.
Half board: from £82.50
daily.
Lunch available.
Evening meal 7pm (l.o.
10pm).
Parking for 40.
Credit: Access, Visa, Diners,
Amex.

⛵ 🏥 🖥 ✆ ☎ 🖥 🚱 ✆ Ⓥ
🍴 ⦿ 🍴 ⚓ 🍴 ✆ ♨ 🐾 SP 🏛
📺

Sevenoaks Park Hotel
Seal Hollow Rd., Sevenoaks,
TN13 3SH
☎ (0732) 454245 Fax (0732)
457468 Telex 95571
*Family-run hotel, quietly
situated in 3 acres of
Elizabethan gardens, with
heated outdoor swimming pool.*
Bedrooms: 1 single, 7 double
& 17 twin, 1 family room.
Bathrooms: 17 private,
3 public.
Bed & breakfast: £30-£55
single, £45-£70 double.

Continued ▶

SEVENOAKS
Continued

Half board: £42-£67 daily,
£210-£385 weekly.
Lunch available.
Evening meal 7pm (l.o. 9pm).
Parking for 40.
Credit: Access, Visa, Diners,
Amex.

Stone Ridge
168 Maidstone Road,
Borough Green, Sevenoaks,
TN15 8JD
☎ Borough Green
(0732) 882053
*Comfortable Edwardian
country house with friendly
atmosphere in beautiful
surroundings. Convenient for
famous Kentish places,
motorways and London. Non-
smokers preferred.*
Bedrooms: 1 double, 1 family
room.
Bathrooms: 1 private,
2 public.
Bed & breakfast: £18.50-
£24.50 single, £29-£39 double.
Evening meal 6pm (l.o.
midday).
Parking for 4.

SHEERNESS
Kent
Map ref 3B3

Isle of Sheppey
Commercial port, formerly
a naval base and now a
holiday resort with a long
promenade and a sand
and shingle beach.
Terminal for car-ferry
service to Vlissingen in
Holland.
*Tourist Information
Centre ☎ (0795) 665324*

Alexandra Guest House M
Listed
122 Alexandra Rd.,
Sheerness, ME12 2AU
☎ (0795) 666888
*Attractive family house
providing accommodation of a
high standard. Close to Olau
line ferry.*
Bedrooms: 1 single, 1 double
& 1 twin, 1 family room.
Bathrooms: 1 public.
Bed & breakfast: from £14
single, from £25 double.
Half board: £19.50-£21 daily.
Evening meal 6pm.
Parking for 3.

Sheppey Guest House
Listed
214 Queenborough Rd.,
Halfway, Minster, Sneerness,
ME12 3DF
☎ (0795) 665950
*Small family-run hotel,
approximately 1 mile from the
ferry terminal, offering full en-
suite facilities. Semi-rural
location.*
Bedrooms: 2 single, 1 double
& 3 twin, 2 family rooms.
Bathrooms: 8 private.
Bed & breakfast: from £15
single, from £25 double.
Lunch available.
Evening meal 6pm (l.o. 9pm).
Parking for 8.

SHEPPERTON
Surrey
Map ref 2D2

Made famous by its
connections with the
British film industry, this
town by the Thames
retains an air of
detachment from London,
despite being only 10
miles from the centre of
the capital.

Shepperton Moat House
Felix La., Shepperton,
TW17 8NP
☎ Walton-on-Thames
(0932) 241404 Fax (0932)
245231 Telex 928170
Ⓡ Queens Moat Houses
*Modern hotel set in quiet
location close to banks of the
River Thames. Located off the
B375, exit 11 from M25, 8
miles from Heathrow.*
Bedrooms: 6 single, 70 double
& 73 twin, 4 family rooms.
Bathrooms: 153 private.
Bed & breakfast: £61.50-£78
single, £77.50-£92.50 double.
Lunch available.
Evening meal 7pm (l.o.
9.30pm).
Parking for 225.
Credit: Access, Visa, Diners,
Amex.

We advise you to
confirm your
booking in writing.

Please mention this
guide when making
a booking.

SITTINGBOURNE
Kent
Map ref 3B3

The town's position and
its ample supply of water
make it an ideal site for
the paper-making
industry. Delightful
villages and orchards lie
round about.

Hempstead House
♛♛♛
London Road, Bapchild,
Sittingbourne, ME9 9PP
☎ Sittingbourne
(0795) 428020
*Exclusive country house
situated on main A2 between
London and Dover, offering
well-appointed accommodation
and friendly hospitality.*
Bedrooms: 2 double, 2 family
rooms.
Bathrooms: 2 private,
2 public.
Bed & breakfast: £35 single,
£50 double.
Half board: £50 daily, £300
weekly.
Evening meal 7pm (l.o. 9pm).
Parking for 10.

STAINES
Surrey
Map ref 2D2

Ever since Roman days
Staines has been a river
crossing of the Thames
on the route to the West
from London.

Anne Boleyn Hotel M
29, The Hythe, Staines,
Middlesex TW18 3JD
☎ Staines (0784) 455930 Fax
(0784) 460641
*At junction 13 on M25,
2 minutes from Staines town
centre and 15 minutes from
Heathrow Airport. 5 minutes
from Thorpe Park.*
Bedrooms: 10 single,
15 double & 5 twin, 4 family
rooms.
Bathrooms: 10 private,
6 public; 6 private showers.
Bed & breakfast: £29.90-
£36.90 single, £39.90-£59.90
double.
Half board: from £37.75
daily.
Lunch available.
Evening meal 7.30pm (l.o.
10pm).
Parking for 50.
Credit: Access, Visa, Amex.

TENTERDEN
Kent
Map ref 3B4

Most attractive market
town with a broad main
street full of 16th C
houses and shops. The
tower of the 15th C parish
church is the finest in
Kent.

Collina House Hotel
♛♛♛
5 East Hill, Tenterden,
TN30 6RL
☎ (058 06) 4852
*Edwardian house overlooking
orchards and garden, within
walking distance of picturesque
town. Swiss-trained proprietors
offering both English and
continental cooking.*
Bedrooms: 3 single, 4 double
& 2 twin, 2 family rooms.
Bathrooms: 11 private.
Bed & breakfast: £23-£25
single, £32-£36 double.
Half board: £43-£45 daily,
£180-£220 weekly.
Evening meal 7pm (l.o.
9.30pm).
Parking for 16.
Credit: Access, Visa, Diners,
Amex.

Little Silver Country Hotel M
♛♛♛♛ COMMENDED
Ashford Rd., St. Michaels,
Tenterden, TN30 6SP
☎ (023 385) 321
*Quality accommodation in
Tudor-style hotel. Honeymoon
and brass bedded rooms, all
en-suite. Attractive gardens.
Full a la carte menu available.
Personal service, delightful
atmosphere.*
Bedrooms: 3 double & 4 twin,
3 family rooms.
Bathrooms: 10 private.
Bed & breakfast: £48-£64
single, £62-£90 double.
Half board: from £63 daily.
Lunch available.
Evening meal 5pm (l.o. 8pm).
Parking for 30.
Credit: Access, Visa.

Half board prices
shown are per
person but in some
cases may be based
on double/twin
occupancy.

West Cross House Hotel ⋒
COMMENDED
2 West Cross, Tenterden,
TN30 6JL
☎ (058 06) 2224
*Private hotel in fine, spacious
Georgian house on wide tree-
lined main street of attractive
Kent town, convenient for
touring.*
Bedrooms: 1 single, 2 double
& 2 twin, 2 family rooms.
Bathrooms: 2 public.
Bed & breakfast: £14-£15
single, £28-£30 double.
Half board: £22-£23 daily,
£147-£153 weekly.
Evening meal 7pm (l.o.
10am).
Parking for 7.
Open March-October.

The White Lion Hotel ⋒
High St., Tenterden,
TN30 6BD
☎ (058 06) 5077 Fax (058 06)
4157
ⓒⓡ Resort
*Set in the lovely Cinque Port
town of Tenterden and built
around 1549, offering
comfortable accommodation,
some four-posters beds,
imaginative cuisine and a well-
stocked cellar. Cordial and
cosy atmosphere.*
Bedrooms: 10 double, 5 family
rooms.
Bathrooms: 15 private.
Bed & breakfast: from £44
single, from £59 double.
Lunch available.
Evening meal 7pm (l.o.
10pm).
Parking for 40.
Credit: Access, Visa, Diners,
Amex.

TONBRIDGE
Kent
Map ref 2D2

Ancient town, built on the
River Medway, has a long
history of commercial
importance and is still a
thriving town.
*Tourist Information
Centre* ☎ (0732) 770929

The Tonbridge Hotel ⋒
18-20 London Road.,
Tonbridge, TN10 3DA
☎ Tonbridge (0732) 353311
*Friendly family-run
establishment with all modern
facilities. Extensive menus and
well-stocked bar. Area of
historic interest and beauty.*

Bedrooms: 2 double & 5 twin,
1 family room.
Bathrooms: 8 private.
Bed & breakfast: from £42.50
single, from £52 double.
Lunch available.
Evening meal 7pm (l.o.
9.30pm).
Parking for 20.
Credit: Access, Visa, Diners,
Amex.

TUNBRIDGE WELLS
Kent
Map ref 2D2

This 'Royal' town became
famous as a spa in the
17th C and much of its
charm is retained, as in
the Pantiles, a delightful
shaded walk lined with
elegant shops. Also a
brand new heritage
attraction "A Day at the
Wells". Rich in parks and
gardens and a good
centre for walks.
*Tourist Information
Centre* ☎ (0892) 515675

Danehurst ⋒
COMMENDED
41 Lower Green Rd.,
Rusthall, Tunbridge Wells,
TN4 8TW
☎ (0892) 27739
*Be treated as a privileged guest
in our home, where we
concentrate on high standards
and attention to detail.*
Bedrooms: 1 single, 2 double
& 2 twin, 1 family room.
Bathrooms: 4 private,
1 public.
Bed & breakfast: £23-£36
single, £33-£43 double.
Half board: £31.50-£36.50
daily, £192.50-£225.40
weekly.
Evening meal 7.30pm (l.o.
8.30pm).
Parking for 5.
Credit: Access, Visa.

Firwood Hotel ⋒
89 Frant Rd., Tunbridge
Wells, TN2 5LP
☎ (0892) 511624 Fax (0892)
25596
*A late Victorian property set
back with ample parking,
providing comfortable rooms
ideal for both business and
holiday traveller. All rooms en-
suite, colour TV and telephone.*
Bedrooms: 3 single, 2 double
& 2 twin, 1 family room.
Bathrooms: 8 private.

Bed & breakfast: £40-£48
single, £50-£60 double.
Parking for 18.
Credit: Access, Visa, Diners,
Amex.

Four Keys ⋒
Station Rd., Wadhurst,
E. Sussex TN5 6RZ
☎ (089 288) 2252
*Public house with separate
accommodation built on both
sides.*
Bedrooms: 5 single, 5 double
& 2 twin, 2 family rooms.
Bathrooms: 10 private;
4 private showers.
Bed & breakfast: from £16
single, from £32 double.
Lunch available.
Evening meal 7pm (l.o.
10pm).
Parking for 30.
Credit: Access, Visa.

Hotel Kingswood Birches ⋒
Pembury Rd., Tunbridge
Wells, TN27 9BB
☎ (0892) 35736/511269
*Comfortable Tudor-style
country house hotel,
conveniently situated in
secluded grounds on A264.
Near town centre. Large car
park. Licensed.*
Bedrooms: 3 single, 3 double
& 5 twin, 3 family rooms.
Bathrooms: 14 private.
Bed & breakfast: £40-£48
single, £54-£62 double.
Half board: from £52 daily.
Evening meal 7pm (l.o.
8.30pm).
Parking for 18.
Credit: Access, Visa, Diners,
Amex.

Mount Edgcumbe House Hotel ⋒
The Common, Royal
Tunbridge Wells, TN4 1BX
☎ (0892) 26823 & 31123
*Small elegant hotel in 250
acres of common land, with
restaurant and lively wine bar.*
Bedrooms: 2 single, 1 double
& 2 twin, 1 family room.
Bathrooms: 6 private.
Bed & breakfast: £40-£50
single, £70-£90 double.
Half board: £50-£60 daily,
£350-£420 weekly.
Lunch available.
Evening meal 7pm (l.o.
10pm).
Parking for 25.

Credit: Access, Visa, Diners,
Amex.

Royal Wells Inn ⋒
APPROVED
Mount Ephraim, Tunbridge
Wells, TN4 8BE
☎ (0892) 511188 Fax (0892)
511908
*Family hotel, totally
refurbished. All rooms have
private bathroom. New
conservatory restaurant serving
quality food.*
Bedrooms: 5 single, 12 double
& 6 twin.
Bathrooms: 23 private.
Bed & breakfast: £55-£62.50
single, £70-£80 double.
Lunch available.
Evening meal 7.30pm (l.o.
9.30pm).
Parking for 25.
Credit: Access, Visa, Diners,
Amex.

Russell Hotel ⋒
COMMENDED
80 London Rd., Tunbridge
Wells, TN1 1DZ
☎ (0892) 544833 Fax (0892)
515846 Telex 95177
ⓒⓡ Inter
*Large Victorian house facing
common, only minutes from
town centre. Totally
refurbished to highest modern
standards.*
Bedrooms: 2 single, 11 double
& 10 twin, 3 family rooms.
Bathrooms: 26 private.
Bed & breakfast: £56-£86
single, £62-£98 double.
Half board: £44-£100 daily.
Evening meal 7pm (l.o.
9.30pm).
Parking for 20.
Credit: Access, Visa, Diners,
Amex.

The Spa Hotel ⋒
Mount Ephraim, Tunbridge
Wells, TN4 8XJ
☎ Tunbridge Wells
(0892) 20331 Fax (0892)
510575 Telex 957188
*Built in 1766 and opened as a
hotel in 1880. Located on the
A264 East Grinstead road.
Privately owned, with extensive
leisure and sporting facilities.
Weekend breaks available.*
Bedrooms: 33 single,
17 double & 24 twin, 2 family
rooms.
Bathrooms: 76 private.
Continued ▶

TUNBRIDGE WELLS

Continued

Bed & breakfast: £66-£75 single, £86-£108 double.
Lunch available.
Evening meal 7pm (l.o. 9.30pm).
Parking for 120.
Credit: Access, Visa, Diners, Amex.

Vale Royal Hotel ♠

54-57 London Rd., Tunbridge Wells, TN1 1DS
☎ (0892) 25580
Family hotel, overlooking the common, set in beautiful secluded rose garden. All rooms have radio, tea/coffee making facilities and TV.
Bedrooms: 33 single, 4 double & 11 twin, 2 family rooms.
Bathrooms: 18 private, 7 public.
Bed & breakfast: £25-£30 single, £40-£55 double.
Half board: £30-£35 daily, £150-£175 weekly.
Lunch available.
Evening meal 6.45pm (l.o. 7.45pm).
Parking for 10.
Credit: Access, Visa, Diners.

UCKFIELD

E. Sussex
Map ref 2D3

Once a medieval market town and centre of the iron industry, Uckfield is now a busy country town on the edge of the Ashdown Forest.

Buxted Park ♠

HIGHLY COMMENDED
Buxted, Uckfield, TN22 4AY
☎ (082 581) 2711
Fax (082 581) 2770
Country house hotel in 32 acres of parkland. 43 bedrooms and suites with private facilities, health club, cinema, swimming pool and fishing.
Bedrooms: 2 single, 30 double & 11 twin.
Bathrooms: 43 private.
Bed & breakfast: £60-£150 single, £80-£150 double.
Half board: £75-£165 daily.
Lunch available.
Evening meal 7pm (l.o. 9.30pm).
Parking for 60.

Credit: Access, Visa, Diners, Amex.

⚙ Display advertisement appears on page 545.

Hooke Hall ♠

COMMENDED
250 High St., Uckfield, TN22 1EN
☎ (0825) 761578 & Fax (0825) 768025 Telex 95228 DPL
Elegant Queen Anne town house, recently completely refurbished, with individual comfortably designed rooms equipped to a high standard.
Bedrooms: 1 single, 2 double & 3 twin.
Bathrooms: 6 private.
Bed & breakfast: £40-£60 single, £50-£95 double.
Parking for 7.
Credit: Access, Visa.

WATERINGBURY

Kent
Map ref 3B4

5m SW. Maidstone
On the River Medway which provides excellent coarse fishing.

Wateringbury Hotel

Tonbridge Rd.,
Wateringbury, Maidstone,
ME18 5NS
☎ Maidstone (0622) 812632
Telex 96265
⚙ Lansbury
Recently refurbished hotel in village location, overlooking river and farmland.
Bedrooms: 22 double & 5 twin, 1 family room.
Bathrooms: 28 private.
Bed & breakfast: £31-£75 single, £62-£88 double.
Half board: £41-£103 daily.
Lunch available.
Evening meal 7pm (l.o. 10pm).
Parking for 60.
Credit: Access, Visa, Diners, Amex.

WEYBRIDGE

Surrey
Map ref 2D2

Old town on the site where, according to tradition, Julius Caesar crossed the Thames in 55BC. Now a large suburb with luxurious houses and a famous golf club.

Kingston Guest House

15 Heath Rd., Weybridge,
KT13 8TE
☎ (0932) 856191
Edwardian house within easy walking distance of shops and mainline station. Centrally situated for London, Heathrow Airport, Hampton Court and Windsor Castle. Non-smokers only please.
Bedrooms: 2 twin, 1 family room.
Bathrooms: 1 public; 3 private showers.
Bed & breakfast: £25-£35 single, £35-£45 double.
Parking for 2.

Oatlands Park Hotel ♠

COMMENDED
Oatlands Dr., Weybridge,
KT13 9HB
☎ (0932) 847242
Telex 915123
Country house hotel in its own grounds, with easy access from central London, Heathrow, and the M25 orbital motorway. Special weekend rates available on request.
Bedrooms: 28 single, 45 double & 54 twin, 4 family rooms.
Bathrooms: 117 private, 10 public.
Bed & breakfast: £90-£100 single, £120-£135 double.
Half board: £74-£114 daily, £396.50-£588 weekly.
Lunch available.
Evening meal 7pm (l.o. 10pm).
Parking for 100.
Credit: Access, Visa, Diners, Amex.

The Ship Thistle Hotel ♠

Monument Green,
Weybridge, KT13 8BQ
☎ (0932) 848364
Telex 894271
⚙ Thistle
Close to London and just a short drive from Heathrow Airport, this 18th C hotel has been discreetly modernised to make it an excellent base for the business person or holidaymaker.
Bedrooms: 11 single, 7 double & 21 twin.
Bathrooms: 39 private.
Bed & breakfast: from £86.75 single, from £105.50 double.
Lunch available.
Evening meal 7.30pm (l.o. 9.30pm).
Parking for 50.
Credit: Access, Visa, C.Bl., Diners, Amex.

WILMINGTON

E. Sussex
Map ref 2D3

6m NW. Eastbourne
The Long Man of Wilmington, a great figure cut out of the turf of Windover Hill, overlooks the village. Its origin is a mystery. Wilmington Priory houses an interesting agricultural museum.

Crossways Restaurant & Hotel

Wilmington, Nr. Polegate,
BN26 5SG
☎ Polegate (032 12) 2455
Georgian-style hotel and restaurant, run by chef/ proprietor, in 2 acres of grounds. Directly opposite the Long Man of Wilmington and Wilmington Priory.
Bedrooms: 1 single, 4 double & 2 twin.
Bathrooms: 5 private, 2 public.
Bed & breakfast: £25-£33 single, £50-£54 double.
Evening meal 7.30pm (l.o. 9pm).
Parking for 25.
Credit: Access, Visa.

Individual proprietors have supplied all details of accommodation. Although we do check for accuracy, we advise you to confirm prices and other information at the time of booking.

The enquiry coupons at the back will help you when contacting proprietors.

WINCHELSEA

E. Sussex
Map ref 3B4

3m SW. Rye
Edward I laid out the
present town on its hilltop
site in the 13th C to
replace the ancient
Cinque Port which was
eventually engulfed by the
sea.

Strand House ₥
❀❀❀ APPROVED

Winchelsea, Nr. Rye,
TN36 4JT
☎ Rye (0797) 226276
*Fine old 15th C house with oak
beams and inglenook
fireplaces. Located just off
A259. 10% discount on weekly
price except high season.*
Bedrooms: 5 double & 2 twin,
3 family rooms.
Bathrooms: 9 private.
Bed & breakfast: £20-£24
single, £28-£40 double.
Parking for 15.
❀8 ♨ 🅱 ☐ ♦ ▢ ▥ ⬚ ᵃ
❀ 🕮 SP 🏠

WINGHAM

Kent
Map ref 3C3

On the A257 halfway
between Sandwich and
Canterbury. The main
street is notable for its
many half-timbered
buildings.

Moors House
Station Approach, Adisham,
Nr Canterbury, CT3 3JE
☎ Nonington (0304) 840935
*Friendly guesthouse with
licensed bar. Bed and
breakfast and evening meal. 15
minutes to Dover and
Canterbury. Close to golf.*
Bedrooms: 2 single, 2 double
& 2 twin, 1 family room.
Bathrooms: 4 private,
2 public.
Bed & breakfast: from £20
single, from £30 double.
Half board: from £25 daily.
Lunch available.
Evening meal 6pm (l.o.
10pm).
Parking for 30.
Credit: Access.
❀5 ♨ ▥ 🅱 ☐ ⬚ ▣ 🖥 ⬚ ᵃ 🍴
♿ ❀ 🕮 🕮 ᵈ SP 🏠

WOKING

Surrey
Map ref 2D2

One of the largest towns
in Surrey, which
developed with the
coming of the railway in
the 1830s. Old Woking
was a market town in the
17th C and still retains
several interesting
buildings.

The Dutch
Woodham Rd., Woking,
GU21 4EQ
☎ (0483) 724255
*Small peaceful private hotel,
ideally situated for touring
Surrey. 27 minutes from
London.*
Bedrooms: 1 double & 2 twin,
1 family room.
Bathrooms: 4 private.
Bed & breakfast: £48-£50
single, £64-£66 double.
Half board: £57.50-£59.50
daily, £363-£375 weekly.
Evening meal 7pm (l.o. 8pm).
Parking for 6.
❀3 🅱 ☐ ♦ ▣ ▥ ⬚ ᵃ ❀ 🕮
SP 🕮

WORTHING

W. Sussex
Map ref 2D3

Largest town in West
Sussex, a popular
seaside resort with
extensive sand and
shingle beaches.
Seafishing is excellent
here. The museum
contains finds from
Cissbury Ring.
*Tourist Information
Centre* ☎ (0903) 210022

Avalon ₥
Listed

8 Windsor Rd., Worthing,
BN11 2LX
☎ (0903) 33808
*Attractive semi-detached house
in a residential area, 2 minutes
from sea. Rooms tastefully
decorated. Friendly hosts.*
Bedrooms: 3 single, 1 double
& 1 twin, 2 family rooms.
Bathrooms: 2 public.
Bed & breakfast: £13-£14
single, £26-£28 double.
Evening meal 6pm (l.o. 4pm).
Parking for 2.
Credit: Access, Visa.
❀ ♨ ☐ ♦ ▢ ⬚ ✂ 🖥 ▥
🕮 🕮 SP

The Baltimore Guest House
173 Brighton Rd., Worthing,
BN11 2EX
☎ (0903) 38081
*Guesthouse of historic interest,
facing safe open beach.
Adjacent to national bowling
greens and close to all resort
amenities.*
Bedrooms: 3 single, 1 double
& 1 twin, 1 family room.
Bathrooms: 1 public.
Bed & breakfast: £14-£18
single, £26-£33 double.
Evening meal 6pm (l.o. 9pm).
⬚ ☐ ♦ 🖥 ▥ ✂ 🕮 🕮

Beach Hotel ₥
Marine Pde., Worthing,
BN11 3QJ
☎ (0903) 34001 Fax (0903)
34567
*Privately-owned hotel
overlooking sea, away from
town but within easy walking
distance of shops. Many places
of interest nearby.*
Bedrooms: 52 single, 25 twin,
7 family rooms.
Bathrooms: 84 private.
Bed & breakfast: £46-£53
single, £70-£79 double.
Half board: £55-£62 daily.
Lunch available.
Evening meal 7pm (l.o.
8.45pm).
Parking for 50.
Credit: Access, Visa, Diners,
Amex.
❀8 ☎ 🅱 ☐ ♦ 🅱 ▢ 🖥
⊟ ▥ ⬚ 🍴 ✂ 🕮 🕮 SP 🕮

Blair House
11 St. Georges Rd.,
Worthing, BN11 2DS
☎ (0903) 34071
*Under the supervison of the
proprietor. Close to the town
centre and amenities, 2 minutes
from the sea.*
Bedrooms: 1 single, 3 double
& 2 twin, 1 family room.
Bathrooms: 6 private,
1 public; 1 private shower.
Bed & breakfast: £17-£19.50
single, £34-£39 double.
Half board: £23.95-£26.45
daily, £167-£185 weekly.
Evening meal 6.30pm.
Parking for 4.
Credit: Access, Visa.
⬚ ☐ ♦ 🅱 ▢ 🖥 ⬚ ᵃ ✂
🕮 🕮 SP

Bonchurch Hotel ₥
❀❀ COMMENDED

1 Winchester Rd., Worthing,
BN11 4DJ
☎ (0903) 202492
*'Home from home'. Pleasant
house on A259, close to all
amenities, shops, museum and
downs.*

Bedrooms: 3 single, 2 double
& 2 twin.
Bathrooms: 3 private,
1 public.
Bed & breakfast: £13-£16
single, £26-£32 double.
Half board: £20.50-£23.50
daily, £130-£145 weekly.
Evening meal 6.15pm (l.o.
4pm).
Parking for 4.
❀4 ♨ ☐ ♦ 🅱 🖥 ▣ ▥ ▥
✂ 🕮 ᵈ 🕮 SP

Burcott Guest House
6 Windsor Rd., Worthing,
BN11 2LX
☎ (0903) 35163
*Homely guesthouse in quiet
position, 100 yards from sea.
Personal and caring
supervision, renowned for
making guests welcome and
catering for special dietary
needs. Comfortable
accommodation with all
facilities. Lounge, small library
and a relaxing garden. Access
at all times.*
Bedrooms: 3 single, 2 twin,
2 family rooms.
Bathrooms: 1 public;
2 private showers.
Bed & breakfast: £14-£16
single, £28-£32 double.
Half board: £20-£42 daily,
£140-£157 weekly.
Lunch available.
Evening meal 6pm (l.o. 7pm).
Parking for 4.
⬚ ♨ 🅱 ☐ ♦ 🅱 ▢ ✂ 🖥
▥ ▥ ᵃ ♨ ᵈ 🕮 SP

Cavendish Hotel
115-116 Marine Parade,
Worthing, BN11 3QG
☎ Worthing (0903) 36767
*Fully licensed seafront hotel.
Open to non-residents.
Specialising in food and wine.
Most rooms en-suite.*
Bedrooms: 7 single, 6 double
& 4 twin.
Bathrooms: 13 private,
1 public.
Bed & breakfast: £22-£36
single, £55-£60 double.
Half board: £36-£46 daily,
£200-£245 weekly.
Lunch available.
Evening meal 7pm (l.o. 9pm).
Parking for 4.
Credit: C.Bl.
⬚1 🅱 ♨ 🅱 ☐ ♦ 🅱 ▢ 🖥
🕮 ● ▥ ᵃ 🍴 ✂ 🕮 SP 🕮

**Half board prices
shown are per
person but in some
cases may be based
on double/twin
occupancy.**

**The symbols are explained on the flap
inside the back cover.**

WORTHING
Continued

Delgany Guest House
♛♛

153 Heene Rd., Worthing,
BN11 4NY
☎ (0903) 33703
*Family-run guesthouse with
licensed bar and satellite TV.
A few minutes from Worthing
Station, town centre and
seafront.*
Bedrooms: 3 single, 3 double
& 1 twin, 1 family room.
Bathrooms: 2 private,
1 public.
Bed & breakfast: £12.50-£15
single, £24-£30 double.
Half board: £18.50-£21 daily,
£117-£200 weekly.
Lunch available.
Evening meal 5pm (l.o. 8pm).
Parking for 4.
⏚ ♨ 🖵 ⚘ 🛏 V 🔥 ⏱ Ⓣ
▦ 🛆 ⏲ DAP 🐾 SP

Heene House Hotel ♨
♛♛♛

140 Heene Rd., Worthing,
BN11 4PJ
☎ Worthing (0903) 33213 &
210804
*An imposing detached
Edwardian property in a
conservation area, set in pretty
gardens.*
Bedrooms: 2 single, 7 double
& 4 twin, 2 family rooms.
Bathrooms: 11 private,
2 public.
Bed & breakfast: £28-£38
single, £43-£50 double.
Lunch available.
Evening meal 7pm (l.o.
8.30pm).
Parking for 7.
Credit: Access, Visa, Diners,
Amex.
⏚ ♨ ℂ ⓓ 🖵 ⚘ 🖿 V 🔥
▦ 🛆 ⏲ DAP 🐾 SP

Kingsway Hotel ♨
♛♛♛

117 Marine Pde., Worthing,
BN11 3QQ
☎ (0903) 37542 Fax (0903)
204173
*Central seafront hotel near
shops and entertainments.
South facing, double-glazed
with carvery restaurant.
Comfortable bar and lounges.
Lift and car park.*
Bedrooms: 13 single, 7 double
& 9 twin, 1 family room.
Bathrooms: 30 private,
1 public.
Bed & breakfast: £30-£40
single, £52-£66 double.
Half board: £35-£50 daily,
£220-£325 weekly.
Lunch available.
Evening meal 7pm (l.o. 9pm).
Parking for 12.
Credit: Access, Visa, Amex.
⏚ ℂ ⓡ 🖵 ⚘ 🖿 V 🔥 ⏱
◉ 🖰 ℝ 🛆 ⏲ & 🕮 DAP 🐾
SP 🐎 Ⓣ

Moorings Hotel ♨
♛♛♛ COMMENDED

4 Selden Rd., Worthing,
BN11 2LL
☎ (0903) 208882
*Victorian house, tastefully
renovated and retaining many
original features. Close to the
beach, Beach House Park,
Aquarena, children's
playground and town centre.*
Bedrooms: 3 double & 2 twin,
2 family rooms.
Bathrooms: 7 private.
Bed & breakfast: from £19
single, from £35 double.
Half board: from £25 daily,
from £158 weekly.
Evening meal 7pm.
Parking for 5.
Credit: Access, Visa.
⏚ ⓓ 🖵 ⚘ 🖿 V 🔥 ▦ 🛆
⏲ 🕮 🐎 🐾 SP Ⓣ

New Eversley Hotel
♛♛♛

121/123 Brighton Rd.,
Worthing, BN11 2ES
☎ (0903) 39827 & 821929
*Family-run hotel close to sea,
shops and bowling greens.
Especially suitable for partly-
disabled: all rooms, bar and
restaurant accessible by
wheelchair.*
Bedrooms: 4 single, 6 double
& 3 twin.
Bathrooms: 5 private,
2 public; 5 private showers.
Bed & breakfast: £18-£35
single, £36-£50 double.
Half board: £24-£45 daily,
£160-£210 weekly.
Lunch available.
Evening meal 6pm (l.o.
9.30pm).
Parking for 2.
Credit: Access, Visa.
⏚ 🛆 🖵 ⚘ 🖿 V 🔥 ▦ 🛆
⏲ & 🕮 DAP 🐾 SP 🐎

Windsor House Hotel ♨
♛♛♛ COMMENDED

14-20 Windsor Rd., Worthing,
BN11 2LX
☎ (0903) 39655
*Close to amenities, but away
from main road traffic noise.
Open for coffee, lunch, teas.
Carvery restaurant and car
park.*
Bedrooms: 5 single, 10 double
& 10 twin, 9 family rooms.
Bathrooms: 28 private,
2 public.
Bed & breakfast: £23.50-
£44.10 single, £31.50-£45
double.
Half board: £41-£56 daily,
£282-£322 weekly.
Lunch available.
Evening meal 6pm (l.o. 9pm).
Parking for 18.
⏚ ♨ ℂ ⓓ 🖵 ⚘ 🖿 V 🔥
Ⓣ ▦ 🛆 ⏲ 🐎 DAP 🐾 SP Ⓣ

Woodlands Guest House
♛♛♛ COMMENDED

20-22 Warwick Gdns.,
Worthing, BN11 1PF
☎ (0903) 33557
*Family-run guesthouse
providing home-cooked food
and friendly service. All
bedrooms are well-appointed
and comfortably furnished.*
Bedrooms: 3 single, 4 double
& 3 twin, 2 family rooms.
Bathrooms: 4 private,
2 public.
Bed & breakfast: £14-£18
single, £27-£36 double.
Half board: £19-£24 daily,
£114-£155 weekly.
Evening meal 6pm (l.o. 5pm).
Parking for 8.
⏚ ♨ 🖵 ⚘ V 🔥 🖿 ⏱ ▦
🛆 DAP 🐾 SP

WROTHAM
Kent
Map ref 3B3

Below Wrotham Hill close
to the North Downs Way,
the village has an
impressive 14th C church
and several interesting
old buildings, some
dating from Elizabethan
times.

The Bull Hotel ♨
♛♛♛ APPROVED

Bull La., Wrotham, Nr.
Sevenoaks, TN15 7RF
☎ Borough Green
(0732) 883092
*Privately-run 14th C coaching
inn, in secluded historic village
close to M20 and M25. Half
an hour from Gatwick and
London.*
Bedrooms: 1 single, 2 double
& 5 twin, 1 family room.
Bathrooms: 5 private,
1 public.
Bed & breakfast: £36-£50
single, £44-£54 double.
Lunch available.
Evening meal 7pm (l.o.
10pm).
Parking for 50.
Credit: Access, Visa, C.Bl.,
Diners, Amex.
⏚ ♨ ℂ 🖵 ⚘ 🖿 V 🔥 ⏱
▦ 🛆 ⏲ 🐎 🐎

**Individual
proprietors have
supplied all details
of accommodation.
Although we do
check for accuracy,
we advise you to
confirm prices and
other information
at the time of
booking.**

**Classifications and quality commendations
were correct at the time of going to press
but are subject to change. Please check at
the time of booking.**

**Half board prices
shown are per
person but in some
cases may be based
on double/twin
occupancy.**

Ann's House

63 London Road, Canterbury, Kent CT2 8JZ.
☎ **(0227) 768767**

Anne's House – a pretty Victorian house situated close to the centre of Canterbury city, with the convenience of parking for all residents. Family owned and restored with love and care. Rooms have en-suite facilities, TV's, tea and coffee making facilities. Four poster beds in some bedrooms.
Canterbury – only 20 minutes by car from Dover.

Ashburnham Lodge

62 London Road, St. Leonards on Sea, East Sussex TN37 6AS.

Tel: (0424) 438575   Fax: (0424) 426816

🥢 🥢 🥢 APPROVED

An elegant hotel set in its own grounds, yet near the seafront in St. Leonards. Recently refurbished, Ashburnham Lodge offers the best of modern cuisine. The 21 bedrooms have en-suite facilities and some have been discretely adapted to accommodate guests with mobility difficulties or wheelchairs. Enjoy traditional hospitality in Edwardian style with the facilities that you expect in hotels today.

Buxted Park

Buxted, Uckfield, Sussex TN22 4AY.
Tel: 082581-2711/2781   Fax: 082581-2770

Country Hotel superbly situated in 312 acres of Sussex Countryside – 43 bedrooms all en-suite with TV (including Sky), telephone, tea and coffee making facilities. Health and Leisure club with outdoor heated pool, free use for residents' own fishing lakes.

Chalk Farm Hotel

Coopers Hill, Willingdon, Eastbourne, East Sussex BN20 9JD ☎ **(0323) 503800**

• 17th century country house hotel, nestling at the foot of the South Downs in the village of Willingdon • Candlelit restaurant using fresh local produce, much of which is grown in our own 2.5 acre gardens • Colour televisions, telephones, tea & coffee making facilities in all bedrooms • Bargin 3 day breaks and weekly terms available • Own car park • Perfect picturesque setting for escaping from the hustle and bustle • Write or phone for brochure • Fully licenced.

Highly Commended

·» The tourist boards have introduced a system of quality commendations to help you find accommodation that offers even higher standards than those required for a simple Crown classification.

·» The following establishments, listed in this 'Where to Stay' guide, have been found after rigorous inspection to provide facilities and services to an exceptionally high quality standard and have therefore achieved **HIGHLY COMMENDED** status.

Location	Establishment		
Ashford Kent	Eastwell Manor	**Hertford** Hertfordshire	Hall House
Basingstoke Hampshire	Audleys Wood Thistle Hotel	**Kendal** Cumbria	Holmfield
Bath Avon	Audley House	**Keswick** Cumbria	Stakis Lodore Swiss Hotel
	Priory Hotel & Restaurant		Swinside Lodge
Bolton Abbey N. Yorkshire	Devonshire Arms Country House Hotel	**Kidderminster** Worcestershire	Brockencote Hall
		Leominster Herefordshire	Withenfield Private Hotel
Bournemouth Dorset	Norfolk Royale Hotel	**London W1**	London Hilton on Park Lane
Bridgnorth Shropshire	Old Vicarage Hotel	**Nantwich** Cheshire	Rookery Hall
Broadway Worcestershire	The Old Rectory	**Shaftesbury** Dorset	Stock Hill House Hotel & Restaurant
Buckland Gloucestershire	Buckland Manor	**Shrewsbury** Shropshire	Albright Hussey Hotel & Restaurant
Canterbury Kent	Thruxted Oast		
Castle Bytham Lincolnshire	Bank House	**Skipton** N. Yorkshire	Oats Restaurant Hotel
Castle Combe Wiltshire	Manor House	**St. Austell** Cornwall	Boscundle Manor
Chester Cheshire	Chester Grosvenor	**Stow-on-the-Wold** Gloucestershire	Wyck Hill House
	Crabwall Manor Hotel & Restaurant	**Stratford-upon-Avon** Warwickshire	Ettington Park Hotel
Chipping Campden Gloucestershire	Cotswold House Hotel & Restaurant	**Taunton** Somerset	Castle Hotel
Coniston Cumbria	Coniston Lodge Private Hotel		The Mount Somerset
East Grinstead W. Sussex	Gravetye Manor	**Uckfield** E. Sussex	Buxted Park
Goodwood W. Sussex	Goodwood Park Hotel, Golf & Country Club	**Whalley** Lancashire	Easterly Farm
		Windermere Cumbria	Gilpin Lodge Country House Hotel & Restaurant
Haytor Devon	The Bel Alp House Country Hotel	**York** N. Yorkshire	Grange Hotel

·» Commendations apply to all classification bands so that, for example, a 'Listed' or One Crown B&B or guesthouse may be Highly Commended if its facilities and services, although limited in range, are provided to an exceptionally high quality standard. See page 5 for more details.

·» Use the town index on page 597 to find page numbers for the full entries.

Stay National, Stay Hilton

There are a wide selection of Hilton, Hilton National and Associate hotels to choose from in Britain, offering a wide range of services and facilities, from Portsmouth in the south to Edinburgh in Scotland.

▲ **London Kensington Hilton,**
Holland Park Avenue, London, W11.
▲ **London Langham Hilton,**
(Opening Spring 1991).
▲ **London Olympia Hilton,**
Kensington High Street, London W14.
▲ **London Hilton On Park Lane,**
Park Lane, London, W1.
▲ **London Regents Park Hilton,**
Lodge Road, London, NW8.
▲ **London Mews Hilton,**
Stanhope Row, London, W1.
■ **Hilton National Wembley,**
Empire Way, Middlesex.
■ **The Clive Hotel,**
Primrose Hill Road, London, NW3.
■ **Plaza On Hyde Park,**
Lancaster Gate, London, W2.
■ **Sherlock Holmes Hotel,**
Baker Street, London, W1.
▲ **The Royal Berkshire,**
London Road, Ascot.
■ **Hilton National Basingstoke,**
Aldermaston Roundabout, Ringway North, Basingstoke.
■ **Hilton Lodge Basingstoke,**
Old Common Road, Black Dam, Basingstoke.
■ **Hilton National Bath,**
Walcot Street, Bath.
■ **Hilton National Bracknell,**
Bagshot Road, Bracknell.
▲ **Bristol Hilton,**
Redcliffe Way, Bristol.
■ **Hilton National Cobham,**
Seven Hills Road South, Cobham.
■ **Hilton National East Midlands Airport,**
(Opening November 1990).
▲ **London Gatwick Airport Hilton,**
Gatwick Airport, West Sussex.

■ **Hilton National Hornchurch,**
Southend Arterial Road, Hornchurch.
■ **Pennine Hilton National,**
Ainley Top, Huddersfield.
▲ **Leeds Hilton,**
Neville Street, Leeds.
■ **Hilton National Leeds Garforth,**
Garforth, Leeds.
▲ **Manchester Airport Hilton,**
Outwood Lane, Ringway, Manchester.
■ **Hilton National Newbury,**
Pinchington Lane, Newbury.
■ **Hilton National Portsmouth,**
Eastern Road, Farlington, Portsmouth.
■ **Hilton National Southampton,**
Bracken Place, Chilworth, Southampton.
■ **Hilton National Warwick,**
Stratford Road, Warwick.
■ **Hilton National Watford,**
Elton Way, Watford.
● **Balmer Lawn Hotel,**
Lyndhurst Road, Brockenhurst.
● **Linton Lodge Hotel,**
Linton Road, Oxford.

▲ Hilton Hotels
■ Hilton National Hotels
● Associate Hotels

HILTON
INTERNATIONAL

HILTON
NATIONAL

For UK reservations call: 071-734 6000.   Telex: 897618.   National LinkLine: 0345 581595.
Weekend Breaks (0923) 38877. For worldwide reservations call: 081-780 1155.

Information pages

Hector Breeze

General advice and

Making a booking

When enquiring about accommodation, as well as checking prices and other details you will need to state your requirements clearly and precisely — for example:

1. Arrival and departure dates with acceptable alternatives if appropriate.
2. The accommodation you need. For example: double room with twin beds, private bath and WC.
3. The terms you want. For example: room only; bed & breakfast; bed, breakfast and evening meal (half board); bed, breakfast, lunch and evening meal (full board).
4. If you will have children with you give their ages, state whether you would like them to share your room or have an adjacent room and mention any special requirements such as a cot.
5. Tell the management about any particular requirements such as a ground floor room or special diet.

Misunderstandings can occur very easily over the telephone so we recommend that all bookings should be confirmed in writing if time permits.

When first enquiring in writing about a reservation you may find it helpful to use the booking enquiry coupons (pages 561 – 565) which can be cut out and mailed to the establishment(s) of your choice. Remember to include your name and address and please enclose a stamped and addressed envelope or an international reply coupon if writing from outside Britain.

Deposits and advance payments

For reservations made weeks or months ahead a deposit is usually payable and the amount will vary according to the length of booking, time of year, number in party and so on. The deposit will be deducted from the total bill at the end of your stay.

More and more establishments, particularly larger hotels in big towns, now require payment for the room on arrival if a prior reservation has not been made — especially if you arrive late and/or with little luggage. Regrettably this practice has become necessary because of the number of guests who have left without paying their bills.

If you are asked to pay on arrival it may be advisable to see your room first to ensure that it meets your requirements.

Cancellations

When you accept offered accommodation, on the telephone or in writing, you may be entering into a legally binding contract with the proprietor of the establishment. This means that if you cancel a reservation, fail to take up the accommodation or leave prematurely the proprietor may be entitled to compensation if the accommodation cannot be relet for all or a good part of the booked period. If a deposit has been paid it is likely to be forfeited and an additional payment may be demanded.

However, no such claim can be made by the proprietor until after the booked period, during which time every effort should be made to relet the accommodation. Any circumstances which might lead to repudiation of a contract may also need to be taken into account and, in the case of a dispute, legal advice should be sought by both parties.

It is therefore in your own interests to advise the management immediately if you have to change your travel plans, cancel a booking or leave prematurely.

Hector Breeze

Insurance

Travel and holiday insurance protection policies are available quite cheaply and will safeguard you in the event of your having to cancel or curtail your holiday. Your insurance company or travel agent can advise you further on this. Some hotels also offer insurance schemes.

Arriving late

If you will be arriving late in the evening it is advisable to say so at the time of booking; if you are delayed on your way, a telephone call to inform the management that you will be late might help to avoid problems on arrival.

Service charges and tipping

Many establishments now levy a service charge automatically and if so this fact must be stated clearly in the offer of accommodation at the time of booking. If the offer is then accepted by you the service charge becomes part of the contract.

At establishments where a service charge of this kind is

information

made there is no need for you to give tips to the staff unless some particular or exceptional service has been rendered. In the case of meals the usual amount is 10% of the total bill.

Telephone call charges

Some establishments levy an extra service charge on telephone calls made by guests as a way of defraying the overhead expenses of providing this service.

Before making long-distance calls within Britain or overseas calls, you should check the charges made by the establishment.

Security of valuables

Property of value may be deposited for safe-keeping with the proprietor or manager of the establishment who should give you a receipt and who will then generally be liable for the value of the property in the case of loss. For your peace of mind we advise you to adopt this procedure. In establishments which do not accept articles for safe custody, you are advised to keep valuables under your personal supervision.

You may find that proprietors of some establishments disclaim, by notice, liability for property brought on to their premises by a guest; however, if a guest engages overnight accommodation in a hotel the proprietor is only permitted to restrict his liability to the minimum imposed upon him under the Hotel Proprietors Act, 1956. Under this Act, a proprietor of a hotel is liable for the value of the loss or damage to any property (other than a motor car or its contents) of a guest who has engaged overnight accommodation, but if the proprietor has a notice in the form prescribed by that Act, liability is limited to the sum of £50 in respect of one article and a total of £100 in the case of any one guest.

These limits do not apply, however, if you have deposited the property with the proprietor for safe-keeping or if the property is lost through the default, neglect or wilful act of the proprietor or his staff.

To be effective, any notice intended to disclaim or restrict liability must be prominently displayed in the reception area of, or in the main entrance to, the premises.

Code of Conduct

All establishments appearing in this guide have agreed to observe the following Code of Conduct:
1. To ensure high standards of courtesy and cleanliness; catering and service appropriate to the type of establishment.
2. To describe fairly to all visitors and prospective visitors the amenities, facilities and services provided by the establishment, whether by advertisement, brochure, word of mouth or any other means. To allow visitors to see accommodation, if requested, before booking.
3. To make clear to visitors exactly what is included in all prices quoted for accommodation, meals and refreshments, including service charges, taxes and other surcharges. Details of charges, if any, for heating or for additional services or facilities available should also be made clear. If applicable the establishment should comply with the provisions of the Hotel Industry's Voluntary Code of Booking Practice.

4. To adhere to, and not to exceed, prices current at time of occupation for accommodation or other services.
5. To advise visitors at the time of booking, and subsequently of any change, if the accommodation offered is in an unconnected annexe, or similar, or by boarding out, and to indicate the location of such accommodation and any difference in comfort and amenities from accommodation in the main establishment.
6. To give each visitor, on request, details of payments due and a receipt if required.
7. To deal promptly and courteously with all enquiries, requests, reservations, correspondence and complaints from visitors.
8. To allow an English Tourist Board representative reasonable access to the establishment, on request, to confirm that the Tourist Board Code of Conduct is being observed.

Comments and complaints

Accommodation establishments have a number of legal and statutory responsibilities to their customers in areas such as the provision of information on prices, the provision of adequate fire precautions and the safeguarding of valuables. Like other businesses, they must also meet the requirements of the Trade Descriptions Acts 1968 and 1972 when describing and offering accommodation and facilities. All establishments appearing in this guide have declared that they fulfil all applicable statutory obligations.

The establishment descriptions and other details appearing in this guide have been provided by proprietors and they have paid for their entries to appear. ▶

About the guide

▶ The English Tourist Board cannot guarantee the accuracy of the information in this guide and accepts no responsibility for any error or misrepresentation. All liability for loss, disappointment, negligence or other damage caused by reliance on the information contained in this guide, or in the event of bankruptcy or liquidation or cessation of trade of any company, individual or firm mentioned, is hereby excluded. Prices and other details should always be carefully checked at the time of booking.

We naturally hope that you will not have any cause for complaint but problems do inevitably occur from time to time. If you are dissatisfied, make your complaint to the management at the time of the incident. This gives the management an opportunity to take action at once to investigate and to put things right without delay. The longer a complaint is left the more difficult it is to deal with effectively.

In certain circumstances the English Tourist Board may look into complaints. However, the Board has no statutory control over establishments or their methods of operation and cannot become involved in legal or contractual matters.

We find it very helpful to receive comments about establishments in 'Where to Stay' and suggestions on how to improve the guide. We would like to hear from you. Our address is on page 604.

There are three other guides in the 'Where to Stay' series — see the inside back cover for details.

MAP REFERENCE? THAT'S THE TELEPHONE NUMBER!

Hector Breeze

Locations

Establishments are listed in this guide under the name of the place where they are situated or, in the case of isolated spots in the countryside, under the nearest village or town. City, town and village names are listed alphabetically within each regional section together with the county name. For smaller places an indication of their location is also given. For example '5m N. Anytown' means 5 miles North of Anytown.

Map references are given against each place name. These refer to the colour maps, starting on page 581. The first figure is the map number; the letter and figure which follow indicate the grid reference on the map. Some entries were included just before the guide went to press and therefore may not appear on the maps.

Addresses

The county names are not normally repeated in the entries for each establishment but you should ensure that you use the full postal address and post code when writing.

Telephone numbers

The telephone number, exchange name (where this

differs from the name of the town under which the establishment is listed) and STD code (in brackets) are given immediately below the establishment address in the listings pages of this guide. The STD code applies to calls made anywhere in the UK except for local calls.

Prices

The prices appearing in this publication will serve as a general guide, but we strongly advise you to check them at the time of booking. This information was supplied to us by proprietors in the summer of 1990 and changes may have occurred since the guide went to press. Prices are shown in pounds sterling and include Value Added Tax if applicable.

Some, but not all, establishments include a service charge in their standard tariff so this should also be checked at the time of booking.

There are many different ways of quoting prices for accommodation and in order to make this as clear as possible and provide a basis for comparison we have adopted a standardised approach.
For example, we show:
1. Bed and breakfast. Price for overnight accommodation with breakfast — single room and double room.

The double room price is for two people. If a double room is

entries

Hector Breeze

occupied by one person there is normally a reduction in the quoted tariff, but some establishments may charge the full rate.

2. Half board. Price for room, breakfast and evening meal, per person per day and per person per week.

A number of establishments do not quote or offer an inclusive room and breakfast rate in their published tariff. In such cases the minimum charge for breakfast has been added to the room charge to arrive at a combined price.

Some establishments provide a continental breakfast only for the room and breakfast tariff and make an extra charge if a full English breakfast is ordered. Establishments which provide a continental breakfast only are indicated by the symbol CB.

There is a statutory requirement for establishments which have at least four bedrooms, or eight beds, to display overnight accommodation charges in the reception area or at the entrance. This is to ensure that prospective guests can obtain adequate information about prices before taking up accommodation. When you arrive it is in your own interests to check prices and what they include.

A reduced price is often quoted for children, especially when sharing a room with their parents. Some establishments, however, charge the full price when a child occupies a room which might otherwise have been let at the full rate to an adult.

The upper age limit for reductions for children may vary according to the establishment and should therefore be checked at the time of booking.

Prices often vary according

to the time of year and may be substantially lower outside the peak holiday weeks. Many hotels and other establishments offer special 'package' rates (for example, fully inclusive weekend rates) particularly in the autumn, winter and spring.

Further details of bargain packages can be obtained from the establishments themselves or from the English Tourist Board and England's Regional Tourist Boards. Your local travel agent may also have information about these packages and can help you make bookings.

Bathrooms

Each accommodation entry shows the number of private bathrooms available, the number of public bathrooms and the number of private showers. The term 'private bathroom' means a bath and/or shower plus a WC en suite with the bedroom; 'private shower' means a shower en suite with the bedroom but no WC.

Public bathrooms are normally equipped with a bath and sometimes also a shower attachment. Some establishments, however, have showers only. If the availability of a bath is an important factor, this should be checked before booking.

Meals

The starting time for the serving of evening meals and the last order time (l.o.) is shown in each entry. At some smaller establishments you may be asked at breakfast time or midday whether you will require a meal that evening. So, the last order time for an evening meal could be, say, 9.30am or 1.30pm. The abbreviation 24hr. means that a meal of some kind is always available.

Although the accommodation prices shown in each entry are for bed and breakfast and/or half board, many establishments offer luncheon facilities and this is indicated by the words 'Lunch available'.

Opening periods

Except where an opening period is shown (e.g. Open March-October), the establishment should be open throughout the year. As a result of recent legislation in connection with Community Charges, proprietors may decide to vary the opening periods referred to in their accommodation entries.

Symbols

Information about many of the services and facilities available at establishments is given at the end of each entry in the form of symbols. The key to these symbols can be found inside the back cover flap. You may find it helpful to fold out the flap when referring to the entries.

Alcoholic drinks

Alcoholic drinks are available at all types of accommodation listed in this guide unless the symbol UL appears. However, the licence to serve drinks may be restricted, for example to diners only, so you may wish to check this when enquiring about accommodation. ▶

Holidays for phys

Dogs

Many establishments will accept guests with dogs but we advise you to confirm this at the time of booking when you should also enquire about any extra charges and any restrictions on movement within the establishment. Some establishments will not accept dogs in any circumstances and these are marked with the symbol ✗.

Visitors from overseas should not bring pets of any kind into Britain unless they are prepared for the animals to go into lengthy quarantine. Owing to the continuing threat of rabies, penalties for ignoring the regulations are extremely severe.

Credit cards

Indicated immediately above the line of symbols at the end of each accommodation entry are credit/charge cards that are accepted by the establishment. However, you are advised to check this at the time you make a booking if you intend to pay by this method. The abbreviations are:

Access – Access/Eurocard/ Mastercard
Visa – Visa/Barclaycard/ Trustcard
C.Bl – Carte Blanche
Diners – Diners
Amex – American Express

Conferences and groups

Establishments which can cater for conferences of 10 persons or more have been marked with the symbol ♟. Rates are often negotiable and the price may be affected by a number of factors such as the time of year, number of people and any special requirements stipulated by the organiser.

Hector Breeze

Many of the accommodation establishments listed in this guide show the ♿ symbol to indicate that they may be suitable for physically handicapped guests.

The minimum requirements laid down by the Tourist Board for such establishments are as follows:

At least one entrance must have no steps or be equipped with a ramp whose gradient does not exceed 1:12. The entrance door must have a clear opening width of at least 80cm.

Where provided, the following accommodation must either be on the ground floor or accessible by lift (NB where access to a specified area involves step(s), a ramp with a gradient of no more than 1:12 must be provided): – Reception; Restaurant/Dining Room; Lounge; Bar; TV Lounge; public WC; and at least one bedroom served either by a private bath/ shower and WC en suite or by public facilities on the same floor.

A lift giving access to any of the above must have at least 80cm clear gate opening width; the lift must be at least 140cm deep and 110cm wide.

Doors giving access to any of the above areas (including bath/WC facilities) must have at least 75cm clear opening width.

In bedrooms, private or public bathrooms and WCs used by disabled people, there must be a clear space immediately adjacent to the bed, bath or WC with a width of at least 75cm. In bedrooms, there must be a turning space of 120cm × 120cm (in bathrooms and WCs: 110cm × 70cm) clear of the line of the doorswing.

The Holiday Care Service, which gives advice on holidays for people with special needs, is visiting accommodation establishments throughout the country in order to categorise them according to the degree of accessibility for people with mobility problems.

The two main categories are:

Category 1: Good access for a guest who is confined to a wheelchair. While it is hoped that a wheelchair user will be able to manage in a Category 1 establishment without assistance, this cannot realistically be guaranteed. This category is defined by strict dimensional criteria.

Category 2: These establishments do not meet all the strict criteria of Category 1 but they nevertheless have considerable value in terms of accessibility. A wheelchair user may find it easier if accompanied. It may be necessary to negotiate single step(s).

ically handicapped people

The following establishments, listed in this guide, have been inspected and categorised by the Holiday Care Service.

Guests with mobility problems are strongly advised to discuss their access and any other special requirements with the management of the chosen establishment before making a firm booking.

CATEGORY 1

Location	Hotel
Bristol Avon	Holiday Inn Bristol
London W8	London Tara Hotel
Norwich Norfolk	Hotel Nelson
	Hotel Norwich
St. Leonards Dorset	St. Leonards Hotel

CATEGORY 2

Location	Hotel
Ambleside Cumbria	Borrans Park Hotel
	Langdale Hotel
Ashburton Devon	Holne Chase Hotel
Barnard Castle Co. Durham	Rose & Crown Hotel
Beer Devon	Swallows Eaves
Bridport Dorset	Haddon House Hotel
Camber E. Sussex	Cinque Ports Lodge
Cambridge Cambridgeshire	University Arms Hotel
Chediston Suffolk	Saskiavill
Chelmsford Essex	Boswell House Hotel
Chester Cheshire	Chestermill Euro Hotel
	Hoole Hall Hotel
Chulmleigh Devon	Fox & Hounds, Eggesford House Hotel

Crookham Northumberland	The Coach House
East Dean E. Sussex	Birling Gap Hotel
Hastings E. Sussex	Royal Victoria Hotel
Hartlepool Cleveland	The Dalton Lodge
Horrabridge Devon	Overcombe Hotel
Kirkby Lonsdale Cumbria	Pheasant Inn
London NW1	The White House
London W1	Hotel Intercontinental
London (south east)	Holiday Inn London-Croydon
Newcastle upon Tyne Tyne & Wear	Holiday Inn Newcastle
Peterborough Cambridgeshire	Swallow Hotel
Seaford E. Sussex	Abbots Lodge Motor Inn
Sidmouth Devon	Victoria Hotel
Southampton Hampshire	Rosida Garden Hotel
Stockton-on-Tees Cleveland	Parkmore Hotel
Swaffham Norfolk	Corfield House
Swanage Dorset	The Pines Hotel
Titchwell Norfolk	Titchwell Manor Hotel
Torquay Devon	Fairmount House Hotel
	Palace Hotel
Windermere Cumbria	The Burn How Garden House Hotel
	Lakeside Hotel on Windermere

Use the Town Index at the back of this guide to find page numbers for the full entries. London entries are indexed on page 19.

The Holiday Care Service can be contacted direct at: 2 Old Bank Chambers, Station Road, Horley, Surrey RH6 9HW. ☎ Horley (0293) 774535.

Tourism for All

When travelling, look for the new 'Tourism for All — Accessible' stickers. They indicate those places that have been visited by the Holiday Care Service and found to meet the requirements for a Category 1 listing.

National Crown Scheme

The National Crown Scheme was introduced in 1986 and is now the largest accommodation rating scheme in Britain, with over 16,000 hotels, motels, guesthouses, inns, B&Bs and farmhouses offering you the reassurance of a National Crown Classification.

Wherever you see the Crown sign displayed you can be confident that the facilities and services at the establishment have been inspected and found to meet National Tourist Board minimum standards for the classification. And every classified establishment is re-inspected each year to check the facilities and services.

The past year has seen the launch of quality commendations to identify those places which offer even higher quality standards than those required for a simple classification.

Establishments which apply for a quality commendation are subject to a more rigorous inspection, which takes into account such important aspects as warmth of welcome, atmosphere and efficiency of service as well as the quality of furnishings, fitments and equipment.

Establishments which are found by tourist board inspectors to provide such higher standards are distinguished by the use of the terms Approved, Commended or Highly Commended alongside the Crown classification.

The new quality commendations apply to all the classification bands. So, for example, a Listed or One Crown B&B or guesthouse could be Highly Commended if its facilities and services, although relatively limited in range, are provided to an exceptionally high quality standard.

The new combined classifications and commendations began to appear on tourist board signs at establishments throughout the country during 1990 and will be even more widespread from 1991 onwards as more and more establishments are quality assessed.

All you have to remember is that the CLASSIFICATION (from Listed to Five Crown) indicates the range of facilities and services and the COMMENDATION (Approved, Commended, Highly Commended) indicates the quality standards of those facilities and services.

Classifications and quality commendations are subject to change. The classifications and quality commendations that appear in the accommodation entries in this 'Where to Stay' guide were correct at the time of going to press.

Entries which do not bear a classification may have applied for inspection but had not been inspected at the time of going to press. The absence of a quality commendation may be due to the fact that the establishment had not been quality assessed before this guide went to press.

During 1990 additional minimum requirements were introduced for each of the Crown classification bands. As a consequence the Crown rating of some establishments has been reduced by one or more Crowns. This should not be taken to imply any reduction in the facilities or standards previously provided by the establishments affected. Those mainly affected are B&Bs that do not provide an evening meal.

What follows is a guide to the facilities and services you will find at accommodation establishments with classifications from Listed to Five Crown. Further information is available from the English Tourist Board (address on page 604), from one of the 12 Regional Tourist Boards or from any Tourist Information Centre.

Listed

Establishments displaying the LISTED sign meet the National Tourist Board minimum standards. They fulfil their statutory obligations, including the requirements of the Fire Precautions Act 1971 (if applicable), the Price Display Orders 1977 and 1979 (if applicable) and have public liability insurance.

Buildings, fixtures, furnishings, fittings and decor are maintained in sound and clean condition. In addition, you can expect:

Bedrooms to have...
▶ Internal lock, bolt or equivalent on bedroom door.

Hector Breeze

▶ Reasonable free space for movement and for easy access to beds, doors and drawers.

- ▶ Minimum recommended floor areas, excluding private bath or shower areas, of: 60 sq.ft. single bedrooms, 90 sq.ft. double bedrooms, 110 sq.ft. twin bedded rooms. Family rooms: 30 sq.ft. plus 60 sq.ft. for each double bed plus 40 sq.ft. for each adult single bed plus 20 sq.ft. for each cot.
- ▶ Minimum bed sizes (except for children's beds) of 6′ × 2′6″ for single beds and 6′ × 4′ for double beds.
- ▶ Mattresses in sound condition and either spring interior, foam or similar quality.
- ▶ Clean bedding and in sufficient quantity, with bed linen changed for every new guest and at least once a week. Bed linen other than nylon available on request.
- ▶ Beds made daily and the bedrooms cleaned daily.
- ▶ Clean hand towel for every new guest and bath towels available on request. Fresh soap provided for each new letting.
- ▶ Adequate ventilation, at least one external window and opaque curtains or blinds on all windows.
- ▶ Minimum lighting levels of 100 watts in single bedrooms and 150 watts in double bedrooms. Switches for room light by the door and bed or alternatively a separate bedside light. All bulbs, unless decorative, covered or with shades.
- ▶ Carpet or bedside rugs or mats.
- ▶ A wardrobe or clothes hanging space (with four hangers per person).
- ▶ Dressing table or equivalent with mirror adjacent, bedside table or equivalent, adequate drawer space, one chair or equivalent, waste paper container, ashtray (where smoking permitted), one drinking tumbler per guest, a 13 amp socket or adaptor, electric razor point (or adaptor available).

- ▶ Adequate heating available at no extra charge.

Bathrooms to have...
- ▶ Bath or shower, wash handbasin and mirror (if any bedrooms without a wash handbasin), soap.
- ▶ Adequate heating and ventilation.
- ▶ Hot water available at all reasonable times.
- ▶ No extra charge for baths or showers.
- ▶ There will be at least one bathroom available at all reasonable times for every 10 resident guests (or one for every 15 guests if wash handbasin in every bedroom).

LISTED establishments also provide at least one WC, adequately ventilated, for every 10 resident guests and there will be a sanitary disposal bin and toilet paper in each WC.

Additional benefits of a LISTED establishment include...
- ▶ Provision of cooked breakfast (unless continental breakfast only advertised) in a dining/breakfast room (unless meals are served only in bedrooms).
- ▶ Public areas well lit for safety and comfort, adequately heated (according to season) and cleaned daily.
- ▶ Furthermore, you will be informed, when booking, if access to the establishment is restricted during the day.

One Crown

Accommodation displaying the single CROWN will provide all the minimum standard facilities and services of a Listed establishment plus several additional comforts and conveniences.

For instance, you can expect both single and double beds in a ONE CROWN establishment to be larger − and nylon bed linen will not be used.

There will be a washbasin, with hot and cold running water at all reasonable times, either in the bedroom or in a private

bathroom and there will be a mirror with light adjacent to or above the washbasin.

You will enjoy the comfort of at least one chair or equivalent per guest, with a minimum of two in family rooms. You will have access to your bedroom at all times.

At least one bathroom, with bath or shower, will be provided for every 10 resident guests − and at least one bathroom for the sole use of guests. There will be at least one WC for every 8 resident guests. Access to the bathrooms and WCs from bedrooms will not be through such areas as reception and lounge.

You will find a lounge or foyer area with an adequate number of easy chairs and you will have access at all reasonable times. A cooked breakfast will be available.

There will be a reception facility (or bell to call for attention), you will have use of a telephone and tourist information will be available.

Two Crown

With every additional Crown, you can expect additional facilities.

For instance, TWO CROWN establishments meet all the requirements of Listed and One Crown classifications and offer several additional comforts and services.

The dining/breakfast room will be separate from the lounge unless meals are served only in the bedrooms. You can enjoy early morning tea/coffee in your bedroom − served on request unless there are beverage-making facilities in the bedroom. You may order a hot beverage in the evening, again available on request unless there are facilities in the bedroom.

There may be alarm clocks in bedrooms or else you can request an early morning call. If there is no TV in your room, you can be sure there will be ▶

▶ a colour TV in the lounge, always provided that the establishment is in a signal reception area.

Double beds will have bedside lights or a single bedhead light, will have access from both sides and there will be a bedside table or equivalent for each person. Single beds will have a bedside or bedhead light. You will also find an electric razor point near a mirror and light.

You can request assistance with your luggage when you check in and check out.

Three Crown

Are you particular about having your own bath or shower with WC en suite? The chances are you can arrange this at a THREE CROWN establishment because at least 33% of the bedrooms will have these facilities.

You will find an easy chair in your bedroom (there will be an additional chair if you have booked a twin or double room). There will also be a full-length mirror, luggage stand and fixed heating with automatic and individual control.

Tea/coffee-making facilities will be provided in the bedrooms on request (unless 24-hour room service is offered). Resident guests can also obtain a hot evening meal while, for early departures in the morning, a continental breakfast will be provided on request.

Should you need any assistance, you can talk to the staff or proprietor who will be available throughout the day.

You can also request a hairdryer, iron and ironing board and you will find shoe-cleaning facilities provided. A public telephone will be available unless there are direct-dial telephones in all the bedrooms.

You will have access to the establishment and to your bedroom at all times.

Four Crown

If Three Crown facilities are not enough, why not book into a FOUR CROWN establishment and enjoy even more?

For instance, 75% of all bedrooms will have a private bath or shower and WC en suite. You can relax in your room and watch colour TV or listen to the radio — and your room telephone will enable you to make external calls.

If dining in, you will be able to invite non-resident guests (providing they are pre-booked) and you will be offered a selection of wines and a choice of dishes for each course; last orders will be 20.30hrs or later.

You'll be able to call room service for continental breakfast, drinks and light snacks between 07.00 and 23.00hrs while lounge service of drinks and snacks will be available until midnight.

If the establishment has four or more floors, a passenger lift will ease the upward journey.

Writing tables will be available if comparable facilities are not available in bedrooms and additional facilities like laundry service, message-taking, newspapers and toiletries will be available on request.

You will find reception staff on duty during the day and evening while the proprietor and/or staff will be on site and on call 24 hours a day.

Five Crown

If you are checking into an establishment displaying FIVE CROWNS, you can expect the

most of everything. Every facility of establishments up to the Four Crown classification will be there to enjoy — plus a few more.

Every bedroom, for instance, will have private bath, fixed shower attachment and WC en suite. A bathrobe and/or bathsheet and toiletries will be on hand.

There will be a writing table or equivalent with seat and the direct-dial telephone will be capable of being used at both writing table and bed.

If your clothes need pressing, you can summon a valet and also avail yourself of the 24-hour return service for laundry and dry cleaning (except at weekends).

I'VE CHANGED MY MIND

Hector Breeze

Room service of hot meals is assured from breakfast time to midnight while hot and cold snacks and drinks will be available at any time. If you decide to take breakfast in the restaurant, you can be served at the table and will be offered a choice of hot and cold dishes.

You will benefit from an all-night lounge service, there will be a night porter on duty and a shoe-cleaning service.

The restaurant will be open for breakfast, lunch and dinner and it will offer a wide selection of wines and dishes, with last orders for dinner at 21.00hrs or later.

Additionally, according to the nature of the establishment, you may find extra features, such as a cocktail bar, shop, hairdresser's, leisure facilities, business services, etc.

Central reservations offices

Some of the accommodation establishments in this guide are members of hotel groups or consortia which maintain a central reservations office. These entries are identified with the symbol ⓒⓡ, and the name of the group or consortium, appearing after the establishment's address and telephone number. Bookings or enquiries can be made direct to the establishment or to the central reservations office.

THEY SAY WE'LL STAY AT THE BLUE FERRET AT PRILTBOROUGH AND LIKE IT!

Hector Breeze

BEST WESTERN
Best Western Hotels, Vine House, 143 London Road, Kingston upon Thames, Surrey KT2 6NA
☎ 081-541 0033
Telex 8814912
Fax 081-546 1638

BREND
Brend Hotels, 1 Park Villas, Taw Vale, Barnstaple, Devon EX32 8NJ
☎ Barnstaple (0271) 44496
Fax (0271) 78558

CALOTELS
Calotels, 3rd Floor Suite, Hampshire House, Bourne Avenue, Bournemouth, Dorset BH2 6DP
☎ Bournemouth (0202) 297888
Telex 41363 CALTEL-G
Fax (0202) 299182

CHARACTER
Character Hotels, Moss Lane, Altrincham, Cheshire WA15 8HP
☎ 061-941 6848
Telex 635322
Fax 061-927 7669

CONSORT
Consort Hotels, Ryedale Building, Piccadilly, York, YO1 1PN
☎ York (0904) 643151
Telex 57515
Fax (0904) 611320

DE VERE
De Vere Hotels, De Vere House, Chester Road, Daresbury, Warrington, Cheshire WA4 4BN
☎ Warrington (0925) 65050 ext 371/378
Telex 629462
Fax (0925) 601264

EMBASSY
Embassy Hotels, Reservations Centre, P.O. Box 671, London SW7 5JQ
☎ 0345 581811 (calls charged at local rate)
Telex 8813387
Fax 071-589 8193

FRIENDLY
Friendly Hotels, Ryedale Building, Piccadilly, York, YO1 1PN
☎ 0800 591910 (calls are free)
Telex 57515 (Attn Friendly)
Fax (0904) 611320 (Attn Friendly)

HILTON
Hilton UK, Millbuck House, Clarendon Road, Watford, Hertfordshire WD1 1DN
☎ 071-734 6000
Telex 897618
Fax (0923) 815519

HOLIDAY INN
Holiday Inn, 10-12 New College Parade, Finchley Road, London NW3 5EP
☎ 071-722 7755
Telex 27574
Fax 071-722 5483

INTER
Inter Hotels, 35 Hogarth Road, London SW5 0QH
☎ 071-373 3241
Telex 8951994
Fax 071-370 7870

LANSBURY
Lansbury Hotels, Greens Building, Park Street West, Luton, Bedfordshire LU1 3BG
☎ Luton (0582) 400158
Telex 826259
Fax (0582) 400024

MINOTELS
Minotels, 5 King's Road, Cleveleys, Lancashire FY5 1BY
☎ Blackpool (0253) 866266
Telex 67596 MARCON-G
Fax (0253) 866251

NOVOTEL
Resinter Reservations, Novotel Hotel, 1 Shortlands, London W6 8DR
☎ 071-724 1000
Telex 24361
Fax 081-748 9116

▶

PRESTIGE
Prestige Hotels, 21 Blades
Court, Deodar Road, London
SW15 2NU
☎ 0800 282124 (calls are free)
Telex 269264
Fax 081-877 9477

QUEENS MOAT HOUSES
Queens Moat Houses,
9-17 Eastern Road, Romford,
Essex RM1 3NG
☎ 0800 289330 (calls are free)
Telex 929751
Fax (0708) 761033

RANK
Rank Hotels, 1 Thameside
Centre, Kew Bridge Road,
Brentford, Middlesex TW8 0HF
☎ 081-569 7120
Telex 267270
Fax 081-569 7109

RESORT
Resort Hotels, 2 Frederick
Terrace, Frederick Place,
Brighton, East Sussex BN1 1AX
☎ 0800 500100 (calls are free)
Telex 877247
Fax (0273) 823085

STAKIS
Stakis Hotels, West Mains
Road, East Kilbride, Glasgow
G74 1PQ
☎ East Kilbride (035 52) 49235
Telex 778704
Fax (035 52) 45305

SWALLOW
Swallow Hotels, P.O. Box 8,
Seaburn Terrace, Seaburn,
Sunderland, SR6 8BB
☎ 091-529 4666
Telex 53168
Fax 091-529 5062

THISTLE
Mount Charlotte Thistle Hotels,
Reservations Centre, 5 Victoria
Road, London W8 5RA
☎ 071-937 8033
Telex 24616
Fax 071-938 3658

Follow the sign

It leads to over 560 Tourist Information Centres throughout
England offering friendly help with accommodation and holiday
ideas as well as suggestions of places to visit and things to do.

In your home town there may be a centre which can help
you before you set out. Details of the locations of Tourist
Information Centres are available from the English Tourist
Board, Thames Tower, Black's Road, London W6 9EL, or from
England's Regional Tourist Boards.

Booking coupons

✂

▶ Please complete this coupon and mail it direct to the establishment in which you are interested. Do not send it to the English Tourist Board. Remember to enclose a stamped addressed envelope (or international reply coupon).

▶ Tick as appropriate and complete the reverse side if you are interested in making a booking.

▶ ☐ Please send me a brochure or further information, and details of prices charged.

▶ ☐ Please advise me, as soon as possible, if accommodation is available as detailed overleaf.

My name is: _____ (BLOCK CAPITALS)

Address: _____

_____

_____

Telephone number: _____ Date: _____

Where to Stay 1991
Hotels & Guesthouses in England

🌹 English Tourist Board 👑

✂

▶ Please complete this coupon and mail it direct to the establishment in which you are interested. Do not send it to the English Tourist Board. Remember to enclose a stamped addressed envelope (or international reply coupon).

▶ Tick as appropriate and complete the reverse side if you are interested in making a booking.

▶ ☐ Please send me a brochure or further information, and details of prices charged.

▶ ☐ Please advise me, as soon as possible, if accommodation is available as detailed overleaf.

My name is: _____ (BLOCK CAPITALS)

Address: _____

_____

_____

Telephone number: _____ Date: _____

Where to Stay 1991
Hotels & Guesthouses in England

🌹 English Tourist Board 👑

Booking coupons

✂ —

▶ **Please complete this side if you are interested in making a booking.**

I am interested in booking accommodation for:

_____ adults and _____ children (ages: _____)

(Please give the number of people and the ages of any children)

From (date of arrival): _____ To (date of departure): _____

or alternatively from: _____ to: _____

Accommodation required: _____

_____

_____

Meals required: _____

Other/special requirements: _____

▶ **Please enclose a stamped addressed envelope (or international reply coupon).**
▶ **Please read the information on pages 550 – 554 before confirming any booking.**

✂ —

▶ **Please complete this side if you are interested in making a booking.**

I am interested in booking accommodation for:

_____ adults and _____ children (ages: _____)

(Please give the number of people and the ages of any children)

From (date of arrival): _____ To (date of departure): _____

or alternatively from: _____ to: _____

Accommodation required: _____

_____

_____

Meals required: _____

Other/special requirements: _____

▶ **Please enclose a stamped addressed envelope (or international reply coupon).**
▶ **Please read the information on pages 550 – 554 before confirming any booking.**

Booking coupons

✂

▶ Please complete this coupon and mail it direct to the establishment in which you are interested. Do not send it to the English Tourist Board. Remember to enclose a stamped addressed envelope (or international reply coupon).

▶ Tick as appropriate and complete the reverse side if you are interested in making a booking.

▶ ☐ **Please send me a brochure or further information, and details of prices charged.**
▶ ☐ **Please advise me, as soon as possible, if accommodation is available as detailed overleaf.**

My name is: (BLOCK CAPITALS)

Address: _____

_____

_____

Telephone number: _____   Date: _____

Where to Stay 1991
Hotels & Guesthouses in England

🏵 **English Tourist Board** 👑

✂

▶ Please complete this coupon and mail it direct to the establishment in which you are interested. Do not send it to the English Tourist Board. Remember to enclose a stamped addressed envelope (or international reply coupon).

▶ Tick as appropriate and complete the reverse side if you are interested in making a booking.

▶ ☐ **Please send me a brochure or further information, and details of prices charged.**
▶ ☐ **Please advise me, as soon as possible, if accommodation is available as detailed overleaf.**

My name is: (BLOCK CAPITALS)

Address: _____

_____

_____

Telephone number: _____   Date: _____

Where to Stay 1991
Hotels & Guesthouses in England

🏵 **English Tourist Board** 👑

Booking coupons

✂

▶ **Please complete this side if you are interested in making a booking.**

I am interested in booking accommodation for:

_____ adults and _____ children (ages: _____)

<small>(Please give the number of people and the ages of any children)</small>

From (date of arrival): _____ To (date of departure): _____

or alternatively from: _____ to: _____

Accommodation required: _____

_____

_____

Meals required: _____

Other/special requirements: _____

▶ **Please enclose a stamped addressed envelope (or international reply coupon).**
▶ **Please read the information on pages 550 − 554 before confirming any booking.**

✂

▶ **Please complete this side if you are interested in making a booking.**

I am interested in booking accommodation for:

_____ adults and _____ children (ages: _____)

<small>(Please give the number of people and the ages of any children)</small>

From (date of arrival): _____ To (date of departure): _____

or alternatively from: _____ to: _____

Accommodation required: _____

_____

_____

Meals required: _____

Other/special requirements: _____

▶ **Please enclose a stamped addressed envelope (or international reply coupon).**
▶ **Please read the information on pages 550 − 554 before confirming any booking.**

Booking coupons

✂

▶ Please complete this coupon and mail it direct to the establishment in which you are interested. Do not send it to the English Tourist Board. Remember to enclose a stamped addressed envelope (or international reply coupon).

▶ Tick as appropriate and complete the reverse side if you are interested in making a booking.

▶ ☐ Please send me a brochure or further information, and details of prices charged.

▶ ☐ Please advise me, as soon as possible, if accommodation is available as detailed overleaf.

My name is: (BLOCK CAPITALS)

Address:

Telephone number: Date:

Where to Stay 1991
Hotels & Guesthouses in England

English Tourist Board

✂

▶ Please complete this coupon and mail it direct to the establishment in which you are interested. Do not send it to the English Tourist Board. Remember to enclose a stamped addressed envelope (or international reply coupon).

▶ Tick as appropriate and complete the reverse side if you are interested in making a booking.

▶ ☐ Please send me a brochure or further information, and details of prices charged.

▶ ☐ Please advise me, as soon as possible, if accommodation is available as detailed overleaf.

My name is: (BLOCK CAPITALS)

Address:

Telephone number: Date:

Where to Stay 1991
Hotels & Guesthouses in England

English Tourist Board

Booking coupons

✂ ― ― ― ― ― ― ― ― ― ― ― ― ― ― ―

▶ **Please complete this side if you are interested in making a booking.**

I am interested in booking accommodation for:

_____ adults and _____ children (ages: _____)

(Please give the number of people and the ages of any children)

From (date of arrival): _____ To (date of departure): _____

or alternatively from: _____ to: _____

Accommodation required: _____

_____

_____

Meals required: _____

Other/special requirements: _____

▶ **Please enclose a stamped addressed envelope (or international reply coupon).**
▶ **Please read the information on pages 550 – 554 before confirming any booking.**

✂ ― ― ― ― ― ― ― ― ― ― ― ― ― ― ―

▶ **Please complete this side if you are interested in making a booking.**

I am interested in booking accommodation for:

_____ adults and _____ children (ages: _____)

(Please give the number of people and the ages of any children)

From (date of arrival): _____ To (date of departure): _____

or alternatively from: _____ to: _____

Accommodation required: _____

_____

_____

Meals required: _____

Other/special requirements: _____

▶ **Please enclose a stamped addressed envelope (or international reply coupon).**
▶ **Please read the information on pages 550 – 554 before confirming any booking.**

Advertisement coupons

▶ Please complete this coupon and mail it direct to the advertiser from whom you would like to receive further information. Do not send it to the English Tourist Board.

To (advertiser's name): _____

Please send me a brochure or further information on the following, as advertised by you in the English Tourist Board's *Where to Stay 1991* Guide:

_____

_____

My name and address are on the reverse.

▶ Please complete this coupon and mail it direct to the advertiser from whom you would like to receive further information. Do not send it to the English Tourist Board.

To (advertiser's name): _____

Please send me a brochure or further information on the following, as advertised by you in the English Tourist Board's *Where to Stay 1991* Guide:

_____

_____

My name and address are on the reverse.

▶ Please complete this coupon and mail it direct to the advertiser from whom you would like to receive further information. Do not send it to the English Tourist Board.

To (advertiser's name): _____

Please send me a brochure or further information on the following, as advertised by you in the English Tourist Board's *Where to Stay 1991* Guide:

_____

_____

My name and address are on the reverse.

Advertisement coupons

✂

From (name): _____ (BLOCK CAPITALS)

Address: _____

_____

_____

Postcode: _____

Telephone Exchange: _____ STD Code: _____ No: _____

Date: _____

✂

From (name): _____ (BLOCK CAPITALS)

Address: _____

_____

_____

Postcode: _____

Telephone Exchange: _____ STD Code: _____ No: _____

Date: _____

✂

From (name): _____ (BLOCK CAPITALS)

Address: _____

_____

_____

Postcode: _____

Telephone Exchange: _____ STD Code: _____ No: _____

Date: _____

Advertisement coupons

▶ Please complete this coupon and mail it direct to the advertiser from whom you would like to receive further information. Do not send it to the English Tourist Board.

To (advertiser's name): _____

Please send me a brochure or further information on the following, as advertised by you in the English Tourist Board's *Where to Stay 1991* Guide:

_____

_____

My name and address are on the reverse.

▶ Please complete this coupon and mail it direct to the advertiser from whom you would like to receive further information. Do not send it to the English Tourist Board.

To (advertiser's name): _____

Please send me a brochure or further information on the following, as advertised by you in the English Tourist Board's *Where to Stay 1991* Guide:

_____

_____

My name and address are on the reverse.

▶ Please complete this coupon and mail it direct to the advertiser from whom you would like to receive further information. Do not send it to the English Tourist Board.

To (advertiser's name): _____

Please send me a brochure or further information on the following, as advertised by you in the English Tourist Board's *Where to Stay 1991* Guide:

_____

_____

My name and address are on the reverse.

Advertisement coupons

✂ - - - - - - - - - - - - - -

From (name): _____ (BLOCK CAPITALS)

Address: _____

_____

_____

_____

Postcode: _____

Telephone Exchange: _____ STD Code: _____ No: _____

Date: _____

✂ - - - - - - - - - - - - - -

From (name): _____ (BLOCK CAPITALS)

Address: _____

_____

_____

_____

Postcode: _____

Telephone Exchange: _____ STD Code: _____ No: _____

Date: _____

✂ - - - - - - - - - - - - - -

From (name): _____ (BLOCK CAPITALS)

Address: _____

_____

_____

_____

Postcode: _____

Telephone Exchange: _____ STD Code: _____ No: _____

Date: _____

MILEAGE CHART

The distances between towns on the mileage chart are given to the nearest mile, and are measured along the normal AA recommended routes. It should be noted that AA recommended routes do not necessarily follow the shortest distances between places but are based on the quickest travelling time, making maximum use of motorways or dual-carriageway roads.

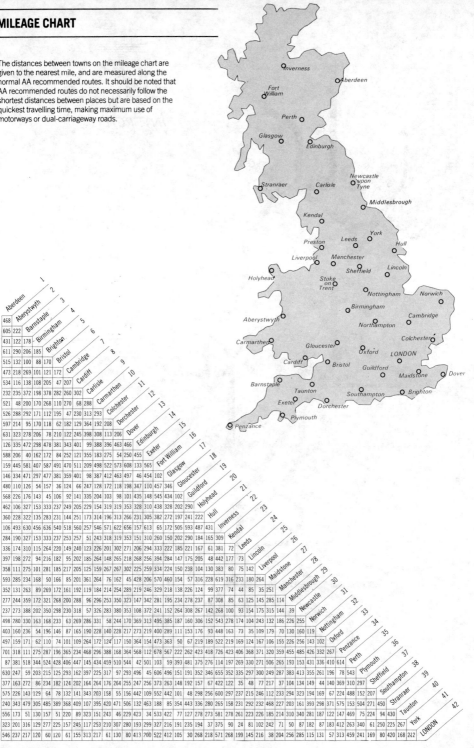

Key to towns (diagonal)

1 Aberdeen · 2 Aberystwyth · 3 Barnstaple · 4 Birmingham · 5 Brighton · 6 Bristol · 7 Cambridge · 8 Cardiff · 9 Carlisle · 10 Carmarthen · 11 Colchester · 12 Dover · 13 Edinburgh · 14 Exeter · 15 Fort William · 16 Glasgow · 17 Gloucester · 18 Guildford · 19 Holyhead · 20 Hull · 21 Inverness · 22 Kendal · 23 Leeds · 24 Lincoln · 25 Liverpool · 26 Maidstone · 27 Manchester · 28 Middlesbrough · 29 Newcastle · 30 Norwich · 31 Nottingham · 32 Oxford · 33 Penzance · 34 Perth · 35 Plymouth · 36 Sheffield · 37 Southampton · 38 Stranraer · 39 Taunton · 40 York · 41 LONDON · 42

Distance table (distances from the town at the start of each row to towns 1 … n−1)

No.	Town	Distances
1	Aberdeen	
2	Aberystwyth	468
3	Barnstaple	605 222
4	Birmingham	431 122 178
5	Brighton	611 290 206 185
6	Bristol	515 132 100 88 170
7	Cambridge	473 218 269 101 121 172
8	Cardiff	534 116 138 108 205 47 207
9	Carlisle	232 235 372 198 378 282 260 302
10	Carmarthen	521 48 200 170 268 110 270 68 288
11	Colchester	526 288 292 171 112 195 47 230 313 293
12	Dover	597 214 95 170 118 62 182 129 364 192 208
13	Edinburgh	631 323 278 206 78 210 122 245 398 308 113 206
14	Exeter	126 335 472 298 478 381 343 401 99 388 396 463 466
15	Fort William	588 206 40 162 172 84 252 121 355 183 275 54 250 455
16	Glasgow	159 445 581 407 587 491 470 511 209 498 522 573 608 133 565
17	Gloucester	146 334 471 297 477 381 359 401 98 387 412 463 497 46 454 102
18	Guildford	480 110 126 54 157 36 124 66 247 128 172 118 198 347 110 457 346
19	Holyhead	568 226 176 143 45 106 92 141 335 204 103 98 101 435 148 545 434 102
20	Hull	462 106 327 153 333 237 249 205 229 154 319 319 353 328 310 438 328 202 290
21	Inverness	360 228 322 135 283 231 144 251 173 314 196 313 266 231 305 382 272 197 241 222
22	Kendal	106 493 630 456 636 540 518 560 257 546 571 622 656 167 613 65 172 505 593 487 431
23	Leeds	284 190 327 153 333 237 253 257 51 243 318 319 353 151 310 260 150 202 290 184 165 309
24	Lincoln	336 174 310 115 264 220 149 240 123 226 201 302 271 206 294 333 222 185 221 167 61 381 72
25	Liverpool	397 198 272 94 216 182 95 202 185 264 148 265 218 268 256 394 284 147 175 205 48 442 177 73
26	Maidstone	358 111 275 101 281 185 217 205 125 159 267 267 302 302 255 259 383 80 75 142 315 309 233 180 264
27	Manchester	593 285 234 168 50 166 85 201 361 264 76 162 45 428 206 570 460 154 57 316 228 619 316 233 180 264
28	Middlesbrough	352 131 263 89 269 172 161 192 119 184 214 254 289 219 246 329 218 138 226 124 99 377 74 44 85 35 251
29	Newcastle	277 244 359 172 321 268 200 288 96 296 253 350 323 147 342 281 195 234 278 237 87 308 85 63 125 145 285 114
30	Norwich	237 273 388 202 350 298 230 318 57 326 283 380 353 108 372 241 152 264 308 267 142 268 100 93 154 175 315 144 39
31	Nottingham	498 280 330 163 168 233 63 269 286 331 58 244 170 369 313 495 385 187 160 306 152 543 278 174 104 243 132 186 226 255
32	Oxford	403 160 236 54 196 146 87 165 190 228 140 228 217 273 219 400 289 111 153 176 93 448 163 73 35 109 179 70 130 160 119
33	Penzance	497 159 171 62 110 74 101 109 264 172 124 117 150 364 154 473 363 50 67 219 189 522 219 169 124 167 106 155 226 256 143 102
34	Perth	701 318 111 275 287 196 365 234 468 296 388 168 367 567 222 678 567 222 423 418 726 423 406 368 371 320 359 455 485 426 332 267
35	Plymouth	87 381 518 344 524 428 406 447 145 434 459 510 544 42 501 103 59 393 481 375 276 114 197 269 330 271 506 265 193 153 431 336 410 614
36	Sheffield	630 247 59 203 215 125 293 162 397 225 317 97 293 496 45 606 496 151 191 352 346 655 352 335 297 300 249 287 383 413 355 261 196 78 543
37	Southampton	377 163 272 86 234 182 124 202 164 264 176 264 255 247 256 373 263 148 192 157 67 422 122 35 48 77 217 37 104 134 149 44 140 369 310 297
38	Stranraer	575 226 143 129 64 78 132 141 343 203 158 55 156 442 109 552 442 101 48 298 256 600 297 237 206 246 112 233 294 323 194 169 67 224 488 152 207
39	Taunton	240 343 479 305 485 389 368 409 107 395 420 471 506 132 463 188 85 354 443 336 280 265 158 231 292 232 468 227 203 161 393 298 371 575 153 504 271 450
40	York	556 173 51 130 157 51 220 89 323 151 243 46 229 423 34 533 422 7 127 278 273 581 278 261 223 226 185 214 310 340 281 187 122 147 469 75 224 94 430
41	LONDON	323 201 316 129 277 225 157 245 117 253 210 307 280 193 299 327 216 191 235 194 37 375 90 24 81 102 242 71 50 87 182 87 183 412 263 340 61 250 225 267
42		546 237 217 120 60 120 61 155 313 61 130 80 413 200 522 142 105 30 268 218 571 268 199 145 216 38 204 256 285 115 131 57 313 459 241 169 80 420 168 242

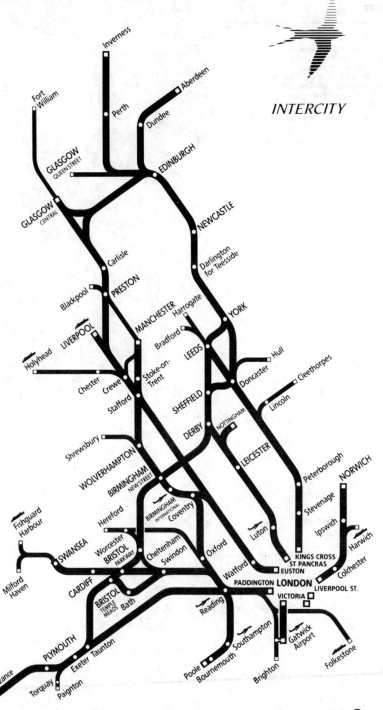

INTERCITY

© British Railways Board 1989/90

A different experience

Consort Hotels offers you a wonderful choice of over 200 very different hotels throughout the British Isles.

Each Consort hotel differs in style, character and location, but all provide value for money and a warm friendly welcome.

Ventnor Towers Hotel, Ventnor

Peebles Hotel Hydro, Peebles

Hall Garth Country House Hotel, Darlington

For reservations and further information contact:

(0904) 643151

or write to: Brian Toplis, Chief Executive, Consort Hotels, Ryedale Building, Piccadilly, York YO1 1PN.

Drink, dine, dream.

Country Lodge inns combine all the atmosphere of the English pub, with traditional country-style food.

And you can enjoy quiet, well-appointed rooms with TV and ensuite bathroom from as little as £27.

So stay on the lookout for the new Country Lodge sign.

For enquiries and a copy of our brochure, call York (0904) 411 856.

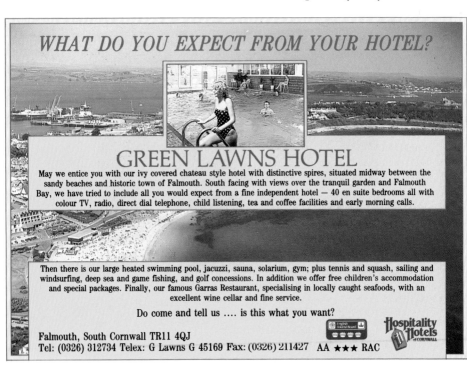

HIDEAWAY HOTEL

This small peaceful hotel attracts a strong following of regulars who appreciate the high standards of comfort and service and enjoy the imaginative and professionally prepared cuisine. (BTA award for excellence in cuisine and service every year since 1978). The hotel is located down a quiet country lane away from the main roads, an important factor when visiting the Lakes, and the bedrooms and public rooms are of a high standard of decor. Ring now for our beautiful brochure; You will be surprised at our reasonable and fair tariff.

Hideaway Hotel, Phoenix Way
Windermere, Cumbria LA23 1DB
Tel: (096 62) 3070

👑👑👑 APPROVED

'*Everything at the Garden is Beautiful*'

Rothay Garden Hotel

Grasmere

Telephone (096 65) 334.

Fax (096 65) 723.

AA ★★ RAC
Merit Awards

ETB 👑👑👑👑

Restaurant and residential licence; 21 bedrooms, all with private bathrooms, children and dogs welcome; car park (30); London 280 miles, Keswick 13, Windermere 9, Ambleside 4.
Our warm-welcoming country house hotel is set in two acres of riverside gardens, and offers quiet, well appointed rooms that really do have views some with four-poster beds and whirlpool baths. A comfortable bar and lounge, and our very elegant restaurant together with our award winning cooking made for your comfort and well being. Wordsworth said of Grasmere "*The loveliest spot that man hath ever known.*" We look forward to meeting you. Chris and Wendy Carss, Proprietors.

Colour maps

» Places with accommodation listed in this guide are shown in black on the maps which follow.

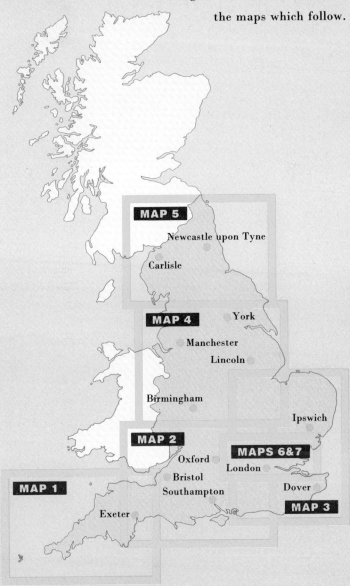

MAP 5

Newcastle upon Tyne

Carlisle

MAP 4

York

Manchester

Lincoln

Birmingham

Ipswich

MAP 2

Oxford

MAPS 6&7

London

Bristol

MAP 1

Southampton

Dover

Exeter

MAP 3

Map 1

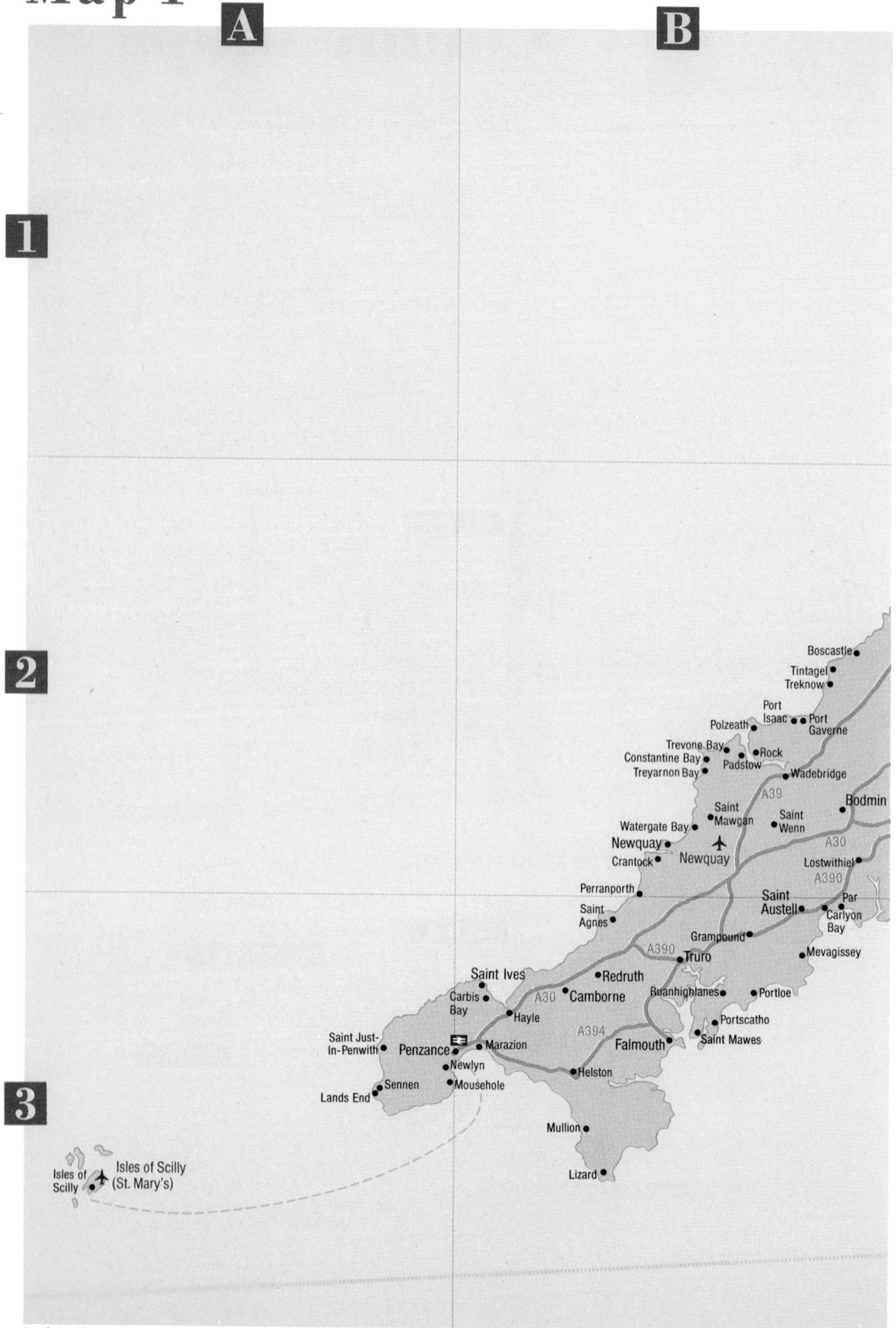

A   B

1

2

Boscastle •
Tintagel •
Treknow •
Port
Polzeath • Isaac • • Port
Gaverne
Trevone Bay • • Rock
Constantine Bay • • Padstow
Treyarnon Bay • • Wadebridge
A39
Saint • Bodmin •
Saint Mawgan • Wenn
Watergate Bay • A30
Newquay • ✈ Lostwithiel •
Crantock • Newquay A390
Perranporth • Saint • Par
Austell • Carlyon
Saint Bay
Agnes • Mevagissey •
Grampound •
Saint Ives • • Redruth A390 Truro •
Carbis A30 Camborne Portloe •
Bay • • Hayle Ruanhighlanes • Portscatho •
Saint Just- A394 Saint Mawes •
In-Penwith • Penzance 🚉 • Marazion Falmouth •
• Newlyn Helston •
Lands End • • Sennen • Mousehole
Mullion •

3

🏝 Isles of Scilly
Isles of (St. Mary's)
Scilly • Lizard •

Produced by COLIN EARL Cartography

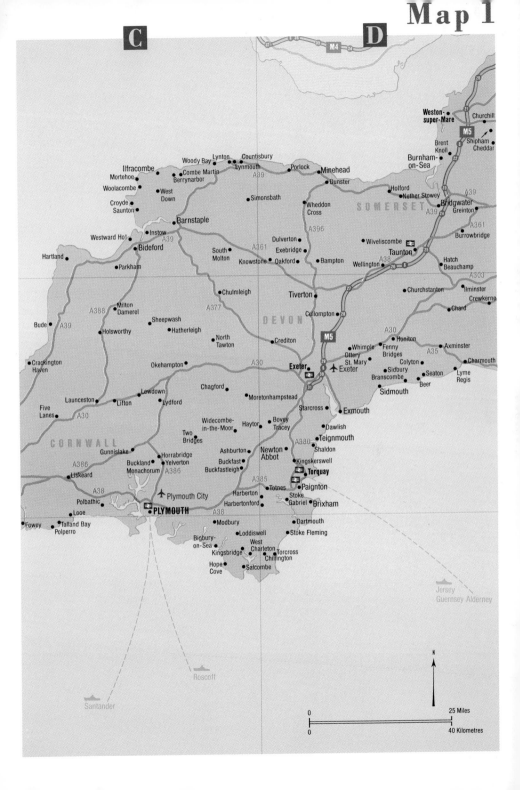

Map 1

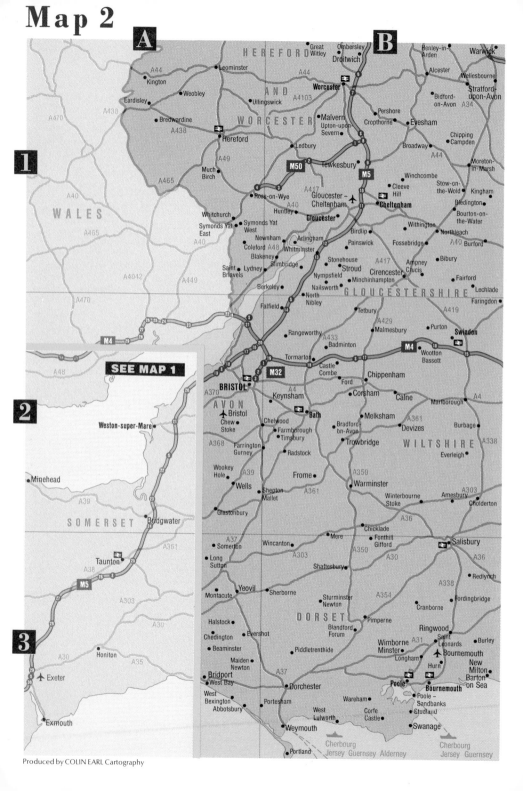

Map 2

A   HEREFORD   B

Great Witley
Ombersley
Droitwich
Henley-in-Arden   Warwick

Leominster   A44   Alcester   Wellesbourne

Kington   Worcester   Bidford-on-Avon   Stratford-upon-Avon

Eardisley   Weobley   Ullingswick   A4103   Pershore   A34

AND

Bredwardine   Cropthorne   Evesham

A438   WORCESTER   Malvern   Chipping Campden

Upton-upon-Severn   Broadway

Hereford   Ledbury   Moreton-in-Marsh

A49   Tewkesbury   Winchcombe

Much Birch   M50   Cleeve Hill   Stow-on-the-Wold   Kingham

A417   Gloucester – Cheltenham   M5   Cheltenham   Bledington

A465   Ross-on-Wye   Bourton-on-the-Water

WALES   Whitchurch   A40   Huntley   Gloucester   Withington   Northleach   Burford

Symonds Yat East   Symonds Yat West   Newnham   Arlingham   Birdlip   Painswick   Fossebridge   A40

Coleford   A48   Whitminster   Stonehouse   Ampney Crucis   Bibury

Blakeney   Slimbridge   Stroud   A417   Fairford

Saint Briavels   Lydney   Nympsfield   Minchinhampton   Cirencester   Lechlade

Berkeley   Nailsworth   GLOUCESTERSHIRE   A419   Faringdon

Falfield   North Nibley   Tetbury   Purton   Swindon

Rangeworthy   A433   Malmesbury   A429   Wootton Bassett   M4

Badminton   M4   A48   Tormarton   Castle Combe   Chippenham

Bristol   M32   Ford   Corsham   Calne   Marlborough   A4

AVON   Keynsham   A4   Melksham   Burbage

Weston-super-Mare   Chelwood   Bath   Bradford-on-Avon   Devizes   WILTSHIRE   A338

Chew Stoke   Farmborough   Timsbury   Trowbridge   Everleigh

A368   Farrington Gurney   Radstock   A350

Minehead   Wookey Hole   A39   Frome   A350   Amesbury   A303

Wells   Warminster   Winterbourne Stoke   Cholderton

A39   Shepton Mallet   A361   A36

SOMERSET   Glastonbury   Chicklade   Salisbury

Bridgwater   A37   Mere   Fonthill Gifford   A30   A36

Somerton   Wincanton   A350

Taunton   Long Sutton   Shaftesbury   A338   Redlynch

A38   M5   A303   Yeovil   Sherborne   A354   Fordingbridge

Montacute   Sturminster Newton   Cranborne

Halstock   DORSET   Pimperne   Ringwood

Chedington   Evershot   Blandford Forum   Wimborne Minster   A31   Saint Leonards   Burley

Beaminster   Piddletrenthide   Longham   Bournemouth   New Milton

Maiden Newton   Hurn   Barton on Sea

A30   Honiton   A35   Bridport   A37   Poole   Bournemouth

Exeter   West Bay   Dorchester   Poole – Sandbanks

West Bexington   Portesham   Wareham   Studland

Abbotsbury   West Lulworth   Corfe Castle   Swanage

Exmouth   Weymouth   Portland   Cherbourg Jersey Guernsey Alderney   Cherbourg Jersey Guernsey

SEE MAP 1

Produced by COLIN EARL Cartography

Map 2

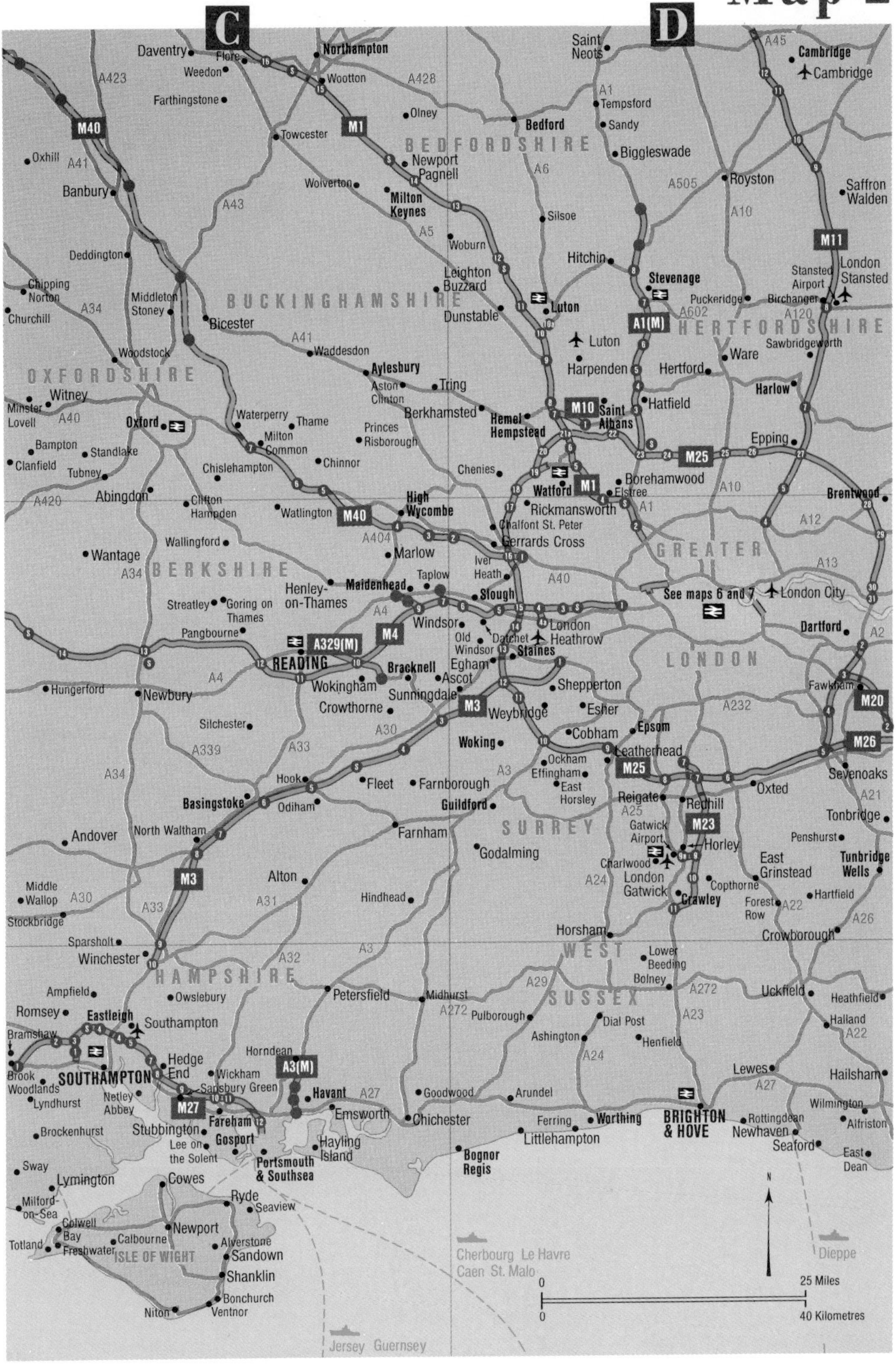
C
D
Daventry
Flore
Weedon
Farthingstone
Northampton
Wootton
A423
A428
Saint Neots
A45
Cambridge
Cambridge
A1
Tempsford
Sandy
Bedford
Olney
M40
M1
Towcester
BEDFORDSHIRE
Oxhill
A41
Newport Pagnell
Biggleswade
A6
Banbury
Wolverton
Milton Keynes
A505
Royston
Saffron Walden
A43
A10
Silsoe
A5
Woburn
M11
Deddington
Hitchin
Stevenage
Stansted Airport
London Stansted
Chipping Norton
Middleton Stoney
BUCKINGHAMSHIRE
Leighton Buzzard
Puckeridge
Birchanger
Churchill
A34
Luton
Dunstable
A602
A1(M)
A120
HERTFORDSHIRE
Bicester
A41
Luton
Waddesdon
Woodstock
Sawbridgeworth
OXFORDSHIRE
Aylesbury
Harpenden
Hertford
Ware
Aston Clinton
Tring
Harlow
Witney
Minster Lovell
A40
M10
Saint Albans
Hatfield
Oxford
Waterperry
Thame
Berkhamsted
Hemel Hempstead
Milton Common
Princes Risborough
Bampton
Standlake
Epping
M25
Clanfield
Chislehampton
Chinnor
Chenies
Tubney
Watford
M1
Borehamwood
Elstree
A10
Abingdon
Clifton Hampden
High Wycombe
Rickmansworth
A1
Brentwood
A420
Watlington
M40
Chalfont St. Peter
A12
Wallingford
A404
Gerrards Cross
GREATER
Wantage
Marlow
A34
BERKSHIRE
Iver Heath
A40
A13
Taplow
Henley-on-Thames
Maidenhead
Slough
See maps 6 and 7
London City
Streatley
Goring on Thames
A4
Pangbourne
Windsor
London Heathrow
Old Windsor
Datchet
Dartford
A2
A329(M)
M4
READING
Staines
Egham
LONDON
A4
Bracknell
Ascot
Hungerford
Newbury
Wokingham
Sunningdale
Shepperton
Fawkham
M20
Esher
Crowthorne
M3
Weybridge
Silchester
A232
A30
Cobham
Epsom
A339
A33
Woking
Leatherhead
M26
A34
M25
Ockham
Effingham
East Horsley
A3
Hook
Fleet
Farnborough
Oxted
Sevenoaks
Basingstoke
Odiham
Guildford
Reigate
Redhill
A25
A21
Tonbridge
Andover
North Waltham
Farnham
SURREY
Gatwick Airport
M23
Horley
Penshurst
Godalming
Charlwood
East Grinstead
Tunbridge Wells
M3
Alton
A24
London Gatwick
Copthorne
Middle Wallop
A30
A31
Hindhead
Crawley
Hartfield
Forest Row
A22
A26
Stockbridge
A33
Sparsholt
Horsham
Crowborough
Winchester
A32
A3
WEST
Lower Beeding
HAMPSHIRE
Bolney
Ampfield
Petersfield
Midhurst
A29
A272
Uckfield
Heathfield
Owslebury
A272
SUSSEX
Romsey
Eastleigh
Southampton
Pulborough
Dial Post
A23
Halland
Bramshaw
Ashington
Henfield
A22
Horndean
A24
Hedge End
Brook
Woodlands
SOUTHAMPTON
Wickham
A3(M)
Lewes
Hailsham
Lyndhurst
Netley Abbey
Swanbury Green
Havant
A27
Goodwood
Arundel
A27
Wilmington
M27
Emsworth
Chichester
Ferring
Worthing
BRIGHTON & HOVE
Rottingdean
Alfriston
Brockenhurst
Fareham
Newhaven
Stubbington
Gosport
Littlehampton
Seaford
Lee on the Solent
Hayling Island
Bognor Regis
East Dean
Sway
Portsmouth & Southsea
Lymington
Cowes
Ryde
N
Milford-on-Sea
Seaview
Colwell Bay
Newport
Totland
Calbourne
Alverstone
Freshwater
ISLE OF WIGHT
Sandown
Cherbourg Le Havre
Caen St. Malo
Dieppe
Shanklin
0
25 Miles
Bonchurch
Niton
Ventnor
0
40 Kilometres
Jersey
Guernsey

Map 3

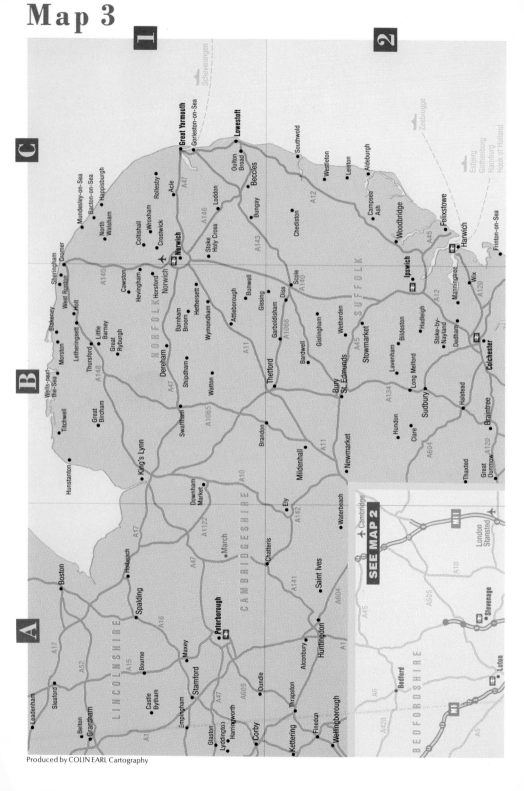

Produced by COLIN EARL Cartography

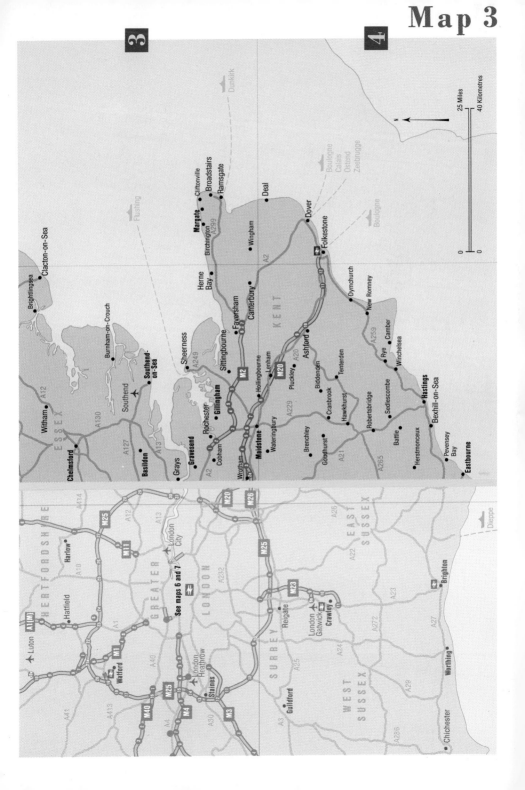

Map 3

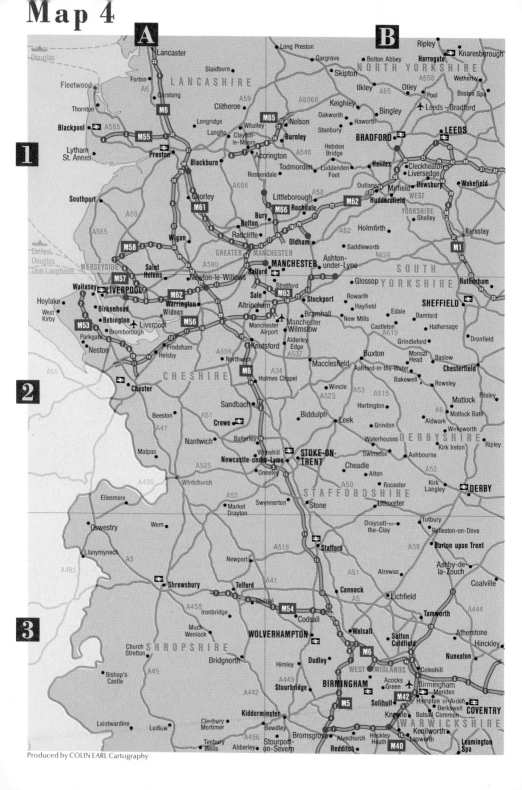

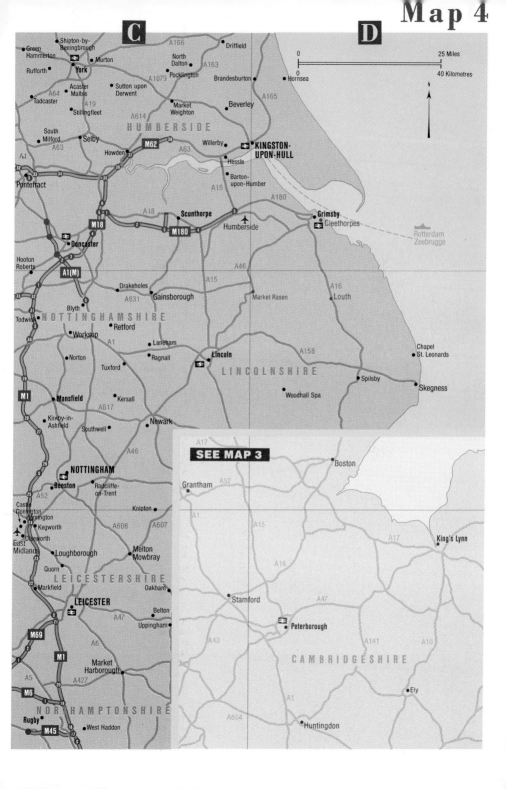

Map 4

Map 5

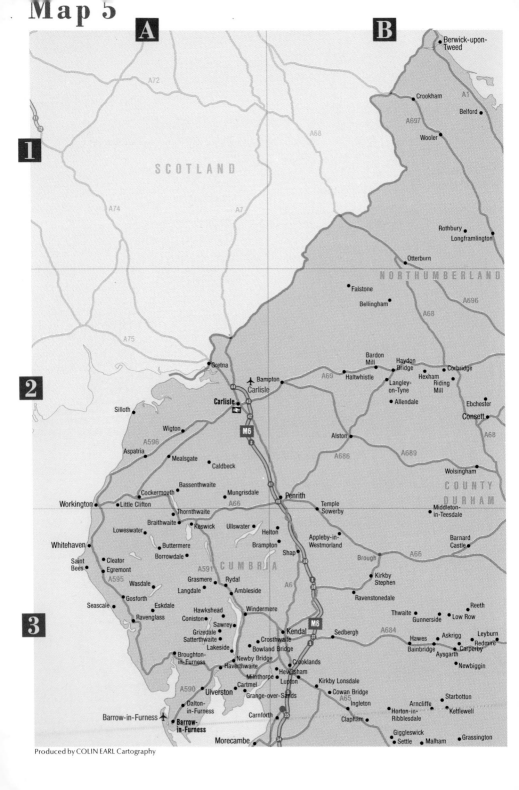

A   B

1

2

3

SCOTLAND

A72

A74

A7

A75

Berwick-upon-Tweed

Crookham

A1

Belford

A697

Wooler

Rothbury

Longframlington

Otterburn

NORTHUMBERLAND

Falstone

Bellingham

A696

A68

Bardon Mill

Haydon Bridge

Corbridge

Haltwhistle

Hexham

Riding Mill

A69

Langley-on-Tyne

Allendale

Ebchester

Consett

Gretna

Bampton

Carlisle

Carlisle

Silloth

Wigton

A596

Aspatria

Mealsgate

Caldbeck

Alston

A686

A689

A68

Wolsingham

Bassenthwaite

Mungrisdale

Cockermouth

A66

Penrith

Temple Sowerby

Middleton-in-Teesdale

COUNTY DURHAM

Workington

Little Clifton

Thornthwaite

Braithwaite

Keswick

Ullswater

Helton

Appleby-in-Westmorland

Barnard Castle

Loweswater

Whitehaven

Buttermere

Borrowdale

Brampton

Shap

Brough

A66

Saint Bees

Cleator

Egremont

A595

Wasdale

A591

CUMBRIA

Grasmere

Rydal

Langdale

Ambleside

A6

Kirkby Stephen

Ravenstonedale

Reeth

Low Row

Seascale

Gosforth

Eskdale

Hawkshead

Coniston

Windermere

Thwaite

Gunnerside

Ravenglass

Sawrey

Kendal

Sedbergh

A684

Hawes

Askrigg

Leyburn

Redmire

Grizedale

Satterthwaite

Lakeside

Crosthwaite

Bowland Bridge

Bainbridge

Aysgarth

Carperby

Broughton-in-Furness

Newby Bridge

Haverthwaite

Crooklands

Heversham

Newbiggin

Minthorpe

Cartmel

Lupton

Kirkby Lonsdale

Ulverston

Grange-over-Sands

Cowan Bridge

Arncliffe

Starbotton

Dalton-in-Furness

Ingleton

Horton-in-Ribblesdale

Kettlewell

Barrow-in-Furness

Carnforth

Clapham

Barrow-in-Furness

Giggleswick

Settle

Malham

Grassington

Morecambe

M6

A590

Produced by COLIN EARL Cartography

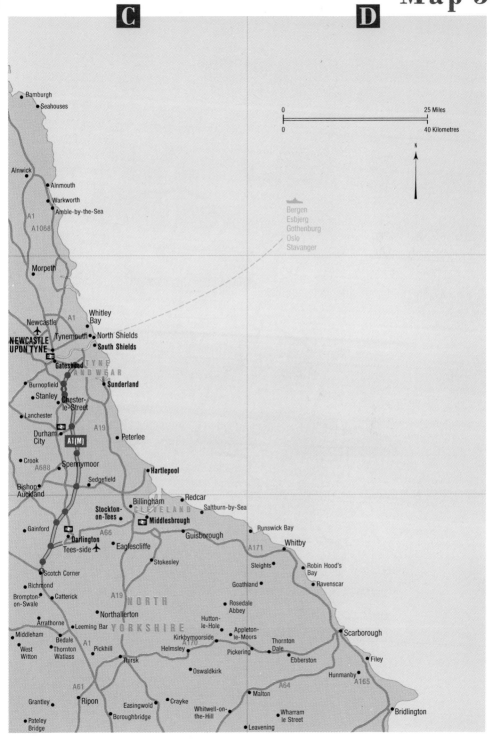

Map 5

C

D

0   25 Miles

0   40 Kilometres

N

Bamburgh

Seahouses

Bergen
Esbjerg
Gothenburg
Oslo
Stavanger

Alnwick

Alnmouth

Warkworth

Amble-by-the-Sea

A1

A1068

Morpeth

Whitley
Bay

Newcastle   A1

Tynemouth • North Shields

NEWCASTLE
UPON TYNE

South Shields

Gateshead

TYNE
AND WEAR

Burnopfield

Stanley

Sunderland

Chester-
le-Street

Lanchester

Durham
City

A19

Peterlee

A1(M)

Crook

A688

Spennymoor

Hartlepool

Sedgefield

Bishop
Auckland

Billingham

Redcar

Stockton-
on-Tees

CLEVELAND

Saltburn-by-Sea

Gainford

Middlesbrough

Runswick Bay

Darlington

A66

Guisborough

Whitby

Tees-side

Eaglescliffe

A171

Stokesley

Sleights

Robin Hood's
Bay

Scotch Corner

Goathland

Ravenscar

Richmond

Brompton-
on-Swale

Catterick

A19

NORTH

Rosedale
Abbey

Arrathorne

Northallerton

YORKSHIRE

Hutton-
le-Hole

Appleton-
le-Moors

Scarborough

Middleham

Bedale

Leeming Bar

Kirkbymoorside

West
Witton

Thornton
Watlass

Pickhill

A1

Helmsley

Thornton
Dale

Pickering

Ebberston

Filey

Thirsk

Oswaldkirk

A170

Hunmanby

A165

A61

Grantley

Ripon

Easingwold

Crayke

Malton

A64

Boroughbridge

Whitwell-on-
the-Hill

Wharram
le Street

Bridlington

Pateley
Bridge

Leavening

Map 6

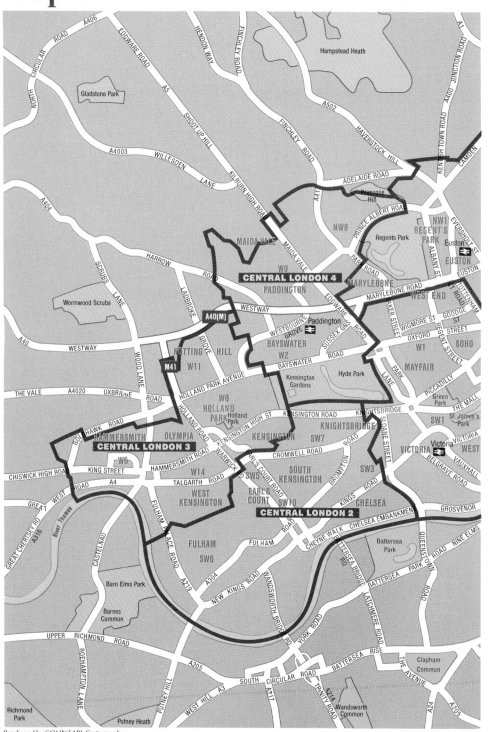

Map 6

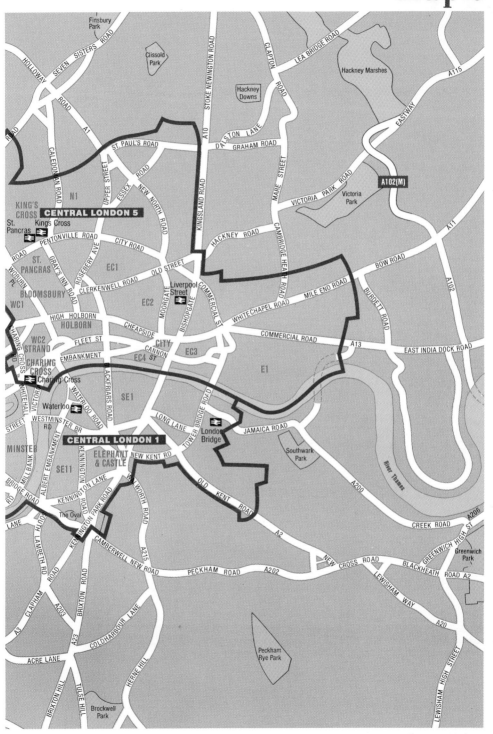

Map 7

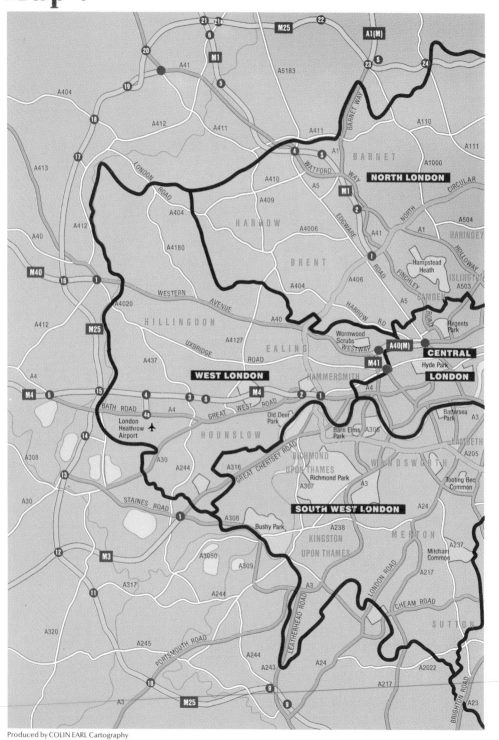

Map 7

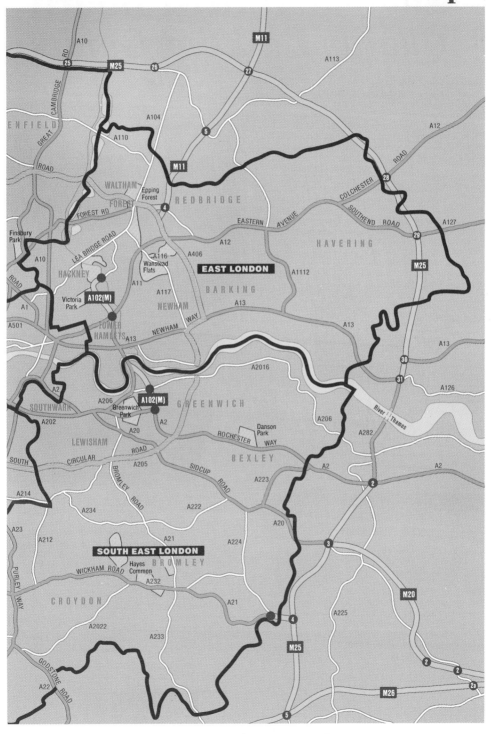

English Tourist Board
Quality Books & Guides

Family Leisure Guides
(In association with Robertson McCarta)
Essential guides for anyone wanting to combine a
favourite sport with a weekend break or short holiday
for all the family. The first two titles in the series are
Horse Racing and Golf. Each is a fully-illustrated guide
to the UK with details of leisure attractions around each
course. (Price £9.95)

Holidays Afloat
Your official guide to boating and watersports around
Britain.(In association with Burlington Publishing and
the British Marine Industries Federation.) Whatever
water-based activity catches your imagination - whether
a relaxing cruise or a course in powerboat handling -
Holidays Afloat contains all the information you need to
plan and enjoy your holiday or short break. Details of
hundreds of holiday companies - complete with
entertaining and informative features. Fully illustrated,
maps, glossaries, etc. (Price £4.95)

Stay On A Farm
(In association with the Farm Holiday Bureau UK and
William Curtis Ltd.) Official guide to nearly 1,000 farms
in membership of the Farm Holiday Bureau. All
inspected and approved by the national tourist boards.
Accommodation includes B&B, half-board, self-catering.
Enjoy the countryside from the unique hospitality of a
working farm. (Price £4.95)

The Countryside Directory
(In association with Sphere and The Royal Agricultural
Society of England.) From farming museums to pick
your own fruit and vegetable farms, agricultural shows to
afternoon teas - whatever you need to know about
countryside activities. (Price £6.99)

Let's Do It!
(In association with William Curtis Ltd.) Hundreds of
ideas for holidays and breaks in England. Discover new
interests or improve existing skills - from action and
sport, study courses, special interests, holidays afloat and
children's holidays. (Price £2.95)

Visit Britain at Work
(In association with Visitor Publications.) A unique
guide to hundreds of fascinating workplaces to visit from
breweries and broadcasting studios to piano workshops
and power stations. (Price £2.95)

Journey Through Britain
(In association with Ravensburger Fisher-Price). Have
fun getting to know Britain with this family game. A race
through Britain's towns and cities answering questions
based on places of interest. Beautifully illustrated.
(Price £12.99 from all good toyshops)

The Tower of London
Cauldron of Britain's Past. (In association with Quiller
Press.) The many roles played by the Tower for nine
centuries are explained and set in the full sweep of
British history. (Hardback, price £14.95)

John Hillaby's Walking in Britain
(In association with Collins). An inspirational and
comprehensive guide to the great walks and walking
country of Britain, with contributions from well-known
enthusiasts such as Hunter Davies, Richard Mabey and
Adam Nicolson. (Hardback, price £14.95, paperback,
price £5.99)

Monopoly London
(In association with Chameleon Publishing.) Make your
way round London with this original guide book based
on the Monopoly board game. A fund of historical and
contemporary anecdote. (Hardback, price £14.95)

For the best choice in books on England, look for the
English Tourist Board logo.

Town index

The following cities, towns and villages all have accommodation listed in this guide. If the place where you wish to stay is not shown, the colour maps (starting on page 581) will help you to find somewhere suitable in the same area.

TOWN INDEX

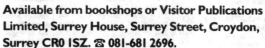

Index to advertisers

⟩⟩ You can obtain further information from any display advertiser in this guide by completing an advertisement enquiry coupon. You will find these coupons on pages 567 – 569.

▶

603

Where to Stay in England

Published by: English Tourist Board, Thames Tower, Black's Road, Hammersmith, London W6 9EL. *Internal Reference Number:* ETB/15/91 AS/1259/45M/90
Managing Editor: Sally Marshall
Assistant Editor: Allyson White
Editorial Assistants: Margaret Polglase, Caroline Medford
Design & Production: Guide Associates, Croydon
Editorial Contributor: John Males
Colour Illustrations: Susie Louis
Colour Photography: Glyn Williams, Peter Titmuss, Syndication International
Cartography: Colin Earl Cartography, Alresford
Typesetting: SB Datagraphics Ltd, Colchester, and Guide Associates, Croydon
Printing & Binding: Bemrose Security Printing, Derby
Advertisement Department: James of Fleet Street Limited, Surrey House, Surrey Street, Croydon, Surrey CR0 1SZ Telephone: 081-686 7155.

The information contained in this guide has been published in good faith on the basis of information submitted to the English Tourist Board by the proprietors of the premises listed, who have paid for their entries to appear. The English Tourist Board cannot guarantee the accuracy of the information in this guide and accepts no responsibility for any error or misrepresentation. All liability for loss, disappointment, negligence or other damage caused by reliance on the information contained in this guide, or in the event of bankruptcy, or liquidation, or cessation of trade of any company, individual or firm mentioned, is hereby excluded.

The English Tourist Board
The Board is a statutory body created by the Development of Tourism Act 1969 to develop and market England's tourism. Its main objectives are to provide a welcome for people visiting England; to encourage people living in England to take their holidays there; and to encourage the provision and improvement of tourist amenities and facilities in England. The Board has a statutory duty to advise the Government on tourism matters relating to England and, with Government approval and support, administers the National Classification & Grading Schemes for tourist accommodation in England.